D1302366

DATE DUE

AUG 1 0 2007			
DEC 1 4 2007			
DEC 2 6 2007			

Demco, Inc. 38-293

MACMILLAN
COMPENDIUM

WORLD
RELIGIONS

**SELECTIONS FROM THE
SIXTEEN-VOLUME**

Macmillan *Encyclopedia of Religion*

MACMILLAN LIBRARY REFERENCE USA

Simon & Schuster Macmillan
New York

Prentice Hall International
London Mexico City New Delhi Singapore Sydney Toronto

Copyright © 1987 by Macmillan Publishing Company. Introductory material ©1998 by Simon & Schuster, Inc.

Produced and Designed by Miller Williams Design Associates, Mundelein, IL USA

Macmillan Library Reference USA
Simon & Schuster Macmillan
1633 Broadway, 5th Floor
New York, NY 10019

Manufactured in the United States of America.

printing number
 2 3 4 5 6 7 8 9 10

Library of Congress Cataloging-in-Publication Data

World Religions.
        p.   cm. — (Macmillan compendium)
Includes index.
ISBN 0-02-864918-4 (alk. paper)
1. Religions—Handbooks, manuals, etc. 2. Religions—Dictionaries. I. Series.
BL82.W67   1997
291—dc21   97-25525
                                                                 CIP

This paper meets the requirements of ANSI/NISO Z39.48-1992 (Permanence of Paper).

WORLD
RELIGIONS

World Religions
Table of Contents

PREFACE 8
ABBREVIATIONS & SYMBOLS 9

A

Abraham 11
Adam 13
Adler, Felix 14
Aegean Religions 15
African Religions 18
Afro-American Religions 34
Afterlife 37
Ainu Religion 44
Akbar 45
Albertus Magnus 46
Alchemy 47
All Fool's Day 55
Altar 56
Amos 57
Anabaptism 59
Analytic Philosophy 60
Ancestors 63
Ancient Near Eastern Religions 68
Angels 68
Anglicanism 70
Anthony of Padua 72
Anthropology, Ethnopology, and Religion 73
Anthropomorphism 76
Anti-Semitism 78
Apocalypse 80
Aramean Religion 85
Archaeology and Religion 87
Architecture 89
Arctic Religions 92
Arhat 95
Aristotle 96
Armenian Religion 97
Ascension 98
Atheism 100
Atonement 103
Augustine of Hippo 105
Australian Religions 107
Aztec Religion 126

B

Baha'is 131
Balinese Religion 134
Baltic Religion 135
Baptism 137
Baptist Churches 139
Barth, Karl 140
Batak Religion 141
Bengali Religions 142
Berber Religion 147
Bhagavadgita 148

Biblical Exegesis 151
Biblical Literature 159
Blasphemy 175
Blessing 177
Blood 181
Bodhidharma 183
Bodhisattva Path 184
Bonhoeffer, Dietrich 186
Boniface 186
Booth, William 187
Bornean Religions 188
Brahma 190
Buber, Martin 190
Buddhism 192
Buddhism, Schools of 208
Bushnell, Horace 218

C

Cain and Abel 221
Calvin, John 221
Canaanite Religion 223
Canon Law 228
Caribbean Religions 230
Catherine of Siena 237
Catholic Orders 238
Celibacy 238
Celtic Religion 239
Central Bantu Religions 245
Chanting 248
Charity 250
Charlemagne 251
Chastity 252
Chinese Religion 253
Chinggis Khan 266
Christian Ethics 267
Christianity 272
Christian Science 285
Christian Social Movements 287
Christmas 290
Chuang-Tzu 291
Church 292
Church and State 294
Cohen, Hermann 297
Community 298
Confession of Sins 301
Confucian Thought 304
Confucius 315
Congregationalism 319
Conscience 320
Conservative Judaism 321
Constantine 323
Conversion 324
Copernicus, Nicolaus 325
Coptic Church 326

Cosmology 328
Councils 331
Covenant 338
Cross 340
Crusades 343
Cuna Religion 346

D

Dalai Lama 349
Dante Alighieri 350
David 350
Dead Sea Scrolls 352
Death 353
Decalogue 356
Deity 356
Demons 359
Dharma 361
Disciples of Christ 365
Divinition 366
Doctrine 368
Dogma 370
Druids 371
Dualism 372

E

East African Religions 375
Easter 378
Eastern Christianity 378
Ecstasy 380
Ecumenical Movement 382
Egyptian Religion 384
Eliade, Mircea 387
Emerson, Ralph Waldo 391
Enlightenment, The 392
Eramus, Desiderius 393
Eremitism 394
Eternity 396
Ethiopian Church 397
Eucharist 399
Evangelical and Fundamental Christianity 400
Evans-Pritchard, E. E. 401
Evil 402
Evolution 403
Excommunication 405
Existentialism 406
Exorcism 407

F

Faith 409
Fall, The 410
Fasting 412
Flood, The 414
Folk Religion 416
Four Noble Truths 417
Francis of Assisi 419
Freemasons 421
Free Will and Predestination 423
Freud, Sigmund 425

G

Galileo Galilei 427

Gandhi, Mohandas 428
Germanic Religion 430
Gnosticism 433
God 438
Goddess Worship 449
Good, The 456
Gospel 457
Grace 459
Greek Orthodox Church 460
Greek Religion 461

H

Hades 467
Halakhah 467
Hanukkah 470
Hasidism 471
Hawaiian Religion 473
Heaven And Hell 475
Hellenistic Religions 476
Heresy 480
Himalayan Religions 482
Hinduism 483
History of Religions 505
Hittite Religion 509
Holocaust, The 511
Humanism 514
Human Sacrifice 518
Hurrian Religion 519

I

Iberian Religion 523
Ibn Rushd 524
Ibn Sina 526
Iconography 527
Idolatry 548
Ignatius Loyola 551
Immortality 553
Inca Religion 559
Incarnation 561
Indian Religions 563
Indo-European Religions 566
Indra 569
Inner Asian Religions 570
Inquisition, The 575
Interlacustrine Bantu Religions 577
International Society for Krishna Consciousness 578
Inuit Religion 580
Iranian Religions 581
Isis 582
Islam 583
Israelite Religion 613

J

Jainism 619
Japanese Religion 622
Javanese Religion 631
Jehovah's Witnesses 633
Jerusalem 635
Jesus 637
Jews and Judaism 641

CONTENTS

Jihad   641
Joan of Arc   642
John The Baptist   643
Joseph   644
Judaism   644
Jung, C. G.   663

K

Ka`bah   667
Kami   668
Karaites   669
Karman   671
Khmer Religion   674
Khoi and San Religion   674
King, Martin Luther, Jr.   675
Kingdom of God   676
Kongo Religion   678
Korean Religion   679
Kushite Religion   682

L

Lao Religion   683
Lao-Tzu   684
Latter-Day Saints   685
Law and Religion   685
Lee, Ann   686
Levites   687
Liturgy   689
Lord's Prayer   690
Lugbara Religion   692
Luther, Martin   693
Lutheranism   694

M

Magi   697
Maimonides, Moses   699
Malcolm X   701
Mandaean Religion   702
Manichaeism   702
Maori Religion   705
Mapuche Religion   706
Mara   708
Marathi Religions   709
Marriage   710
Martyrdom   712
Marxism   714
Mary   716
Maya Religion   717
Meditation   718
Megalithic Religion   720
Mennonites   722
Mesopotamian Religions   724
Messianism   727
Methodist Churches   728
Millenarianism   731
Mimamsa   738
Ministry   739
Miracles   741
Missions   744
Moabite Religion   756
Monasticism   759

Mongol Religions   760
Monotheism   761
Morality and Religion   764
Moravians   767
Mormonism   770
Moses   771
Mosque   773
Muhammad   777
Muslim Brotherhood   780
Mysticism   782

N

Nasir-i Khusraw   787
Nature   788
Neolithic Religion   790
Nestorian Church   793
New Caledonia Religion   795
New Guinea Religions   797
New Religions   799
Nirvana   803
North American Indian Religions   807
North American Religions   847
Nyaya   851

O

Occultism   853
Oceanic Religions   854
Olmec Religion   857
Oracles   858
Oral Tradition   860
Ordination   862
Orthodox Judaism   864
Osiris   867

P

Paleolithic Religion   869
Papacy   871
Paradise   879
Passover   881
Pharisees   883
Philistine Religion   884
Phoenician Religion   886
Pilgrimage   888
Polytheism   894
Prayer   896
Prehistoric Religions   898
Presbyterianism, Reformed   899
Priesthood   899
Prophecy   902
Protestantism   904
Psalms   908
Purification   910
Puritanism   913

Q

Quakers   915
Qur'an   916

R

Rabbinate   921
Redemption   922

Reformation 923
Reform Judaism 926
Reincarnation 928
Religion 929
Repentance 933
Resurrection 935
Retreat 936
Revelation 937
Roman Catholicism 939
Roman Religion 942
Rosenzweig, Franz 947
Russian Orthodox Church 949

S

Saami Religion 951
Sacrament 953
Sacred and the Profane, The 954
Sacrifice 963
Saicho 965
Sainthood 966
Salvation Army 968
Samkhya 970
Samoyed Religion 971
Sanhedrin 973
Santería 974
Sarmatian Religion 976
Satan 977
Schism 978
Science and Religion 981
Scripture 984
Scythian Religion 987
Seventh-Day Adventism 988
Shabbat 989
Shakers 990
Shamanism 991
Shiism 992
Shinto 995
Sikhism 999
Sinhala Religion 1000
Siva 1001
Slavic Religion 1003
Smith, Joseph 1006
Soul 1007
South American Indians 1014
South American Religions 1030
Southeast Asian Religions 1034
Southern African Religions 1039
Spinoza, Barukh 1042
Spiritual Guide 1043
Sufism 1045
Supernatural, The 1048
Superstition 1050
Suzuki, D.T. 1051
Synagogue 1053

T

T`ai-chi 1055
Taiwanese Religions 1056
Talmud 1059
Tamil Religions 1062
Tantrism 1066

Taoism 1072
Tariqah 1080
Temple 1082
Temptation 1089
Ten Commandments 1091
Theology 1092
Theravada 1098
Thérèse of Lisieux 1102
Thomas Aquinas 1103
Thoth 1105
Tibetan Religions 1106
Tikopia Religion 1108
Tillich, Paul 1109
Torah 1113
Tricksters 1118
Trinity 1122
Tunguz Religion 1126
Turkic Religions 1129

U

Ultramontanism 1133
Underworld 1134
Ungarinyin Religion 1136
Uniate Churches 1138
Unification Church 1140
Unitarian Universalist Association 1141

V

Vaisesika 1145
Vatican Councils 1145
Vedanta 1150
Vietnamese Religion 1153
Voodoo 1155

W

Walbiri Religion 1159
West African Religions 1160
Witchcraft 1163
Women's Studies 1166

Y

Yakut Religion 1169
Yeshivah 1171
Yoga 1174
Yoruba Religion 1178
Young, Brigham 1181

Z

Zealots 1183
Zen 1184
Zionism 1186
Zoroastrianism 1188
Zulu Religion 1191

INDEX 1193

Preface

This single-volume is the one reference book on world religions. It is garnered and assembled from the award-winning heritage of the sixteen-volume Macmillan *Encyclopedia of Religion*.

The legacy of the multivolume encyclopedia set goes almost unmatched in honors and awards for its outstanding contribution to religious studies. Foremost among the encyclopedia's accolades is the honor of winning the 1988 Dartmouth Medal for "outstanding quality and significance." Other laurels include the 1987 R. R. Hawkins Award from the Association of American Publishers; a 1987 *Library Journal* Best Reference Book; and a 1987 Outstanding Reference Book as chosen by the American Library Association.

Originally edited by Mircea Eliade, who died in 1986, the text articles in the multivolume encyclopedia, and in these pages, reflect his distinguished professorship at the University of Chicago. Eliade's distinction came from his approach to myth, symbol, and the sacred in religion — an intellectual vanguard that fills many landmark books, including *The Sacred and the Profane*, and the multivolume *History of Religious Ideas*.

Many other noted historians, experts, and professors contributed to the original multivolume *Encyclopedia of Religion*, and selected efforts are presented in this volume. For complete author information, please consult the multivolume set.

From such peerage comes this single-volume encyclopedia of world religions, the *Macmillan Compendium*. It is no simple editorial task to take the 9,112 pages of the multivolume work and publish a 1,200-page version; our editors, therefore, selected the most relevant articles with complete bibliographies and cross-references, and presented them as whole, uncut selections when possible, and as edited versions when content was essential (rather than trying to edit down each of the multivolume's articles into pieces that would fit into 1,200 pages). Thus, this volume is an overview of world religions.

The *Macmillan Compendium: World Religions* is the concise, one source reference for discussion, clarification, definition, research, and elucidation for the reader on world religious history and issues.

— Macmillan Library Reference

Abbreviations and Symbols

abbr. abbreviated;abbreviation
abr. abridged; abridgment
AD *anno Domini,* in the year of the (our) Lord
Afrik. Afrikaans
AH *anno Hegirae,* in the year of the Hijrah
Akk. Akkadian
Ala. Alabama
Alb. Albanian
Am. Amos
AM *ante meridiem,* before noon
amend. amended; amendment
annot. annotated; annotation
Ap. *Apocalypse*
Apn. *Apocryphon*
app. appendix
Arab. Arabic
`Arakh.* *`Arakhin
Aram. Aramaic
Ariz. Arizona
Ark. Arkansas
Arm. Armenian
art. article (pl., arts.)
AS Anglo-Saxon
Asm. Mos. *Assumption of Moses*
Assyr. Assyrian
A.S.S.R. Autonomous Soviet Socialist Republic
Av. Avestan
'A.Z. *'Avodah zarah*
b. born
Bab. Babylonian
Ban. Bantu
1 Bar. *1 Baruch*
2 Bar. *2 Baruch*
3 Bar. *3 Baruch*
4 Bar. *4 Baruch*
B.B. *Bava' batra'*
BBC British Broadcasting Corporation
BC before Christ
BCE before the common era
B.D. Bachelor of Divinity
Beits. *Beitsah*
Bekh. *Bekhorot*
Beng. Bengali
Ber. *Berakhot*
Berb. Berber
Bik. *Bikkurim*
bk. book (pl., bks.)
B.M. *Bava' metsi'a'*
BP before the present

B.Q. *Bava' qamma'*
Brah. Brahmana
Bret. Breton
B.T. Babylonian Talmud
Bulg. Bulgarian
Burm. Burmese
c. *circa,* about, approximately
Calif. California
Can. Canaanite
Catal. Catalan
CE of the common era
Celt. Celtic
cf. *confer,* compare
Chald. Chaldean
chap. chapter (pl., chaps.)
Chin. Chinese
C.H.M. Community of the Holy Myrrhbearers
1 Chr. *1 Chronicles*
2 Chr. *2 Chronicles*
Ch. Slav. Church Slavic
cm centimeters
col. column (pl., cols.)
Col. *Colossians*
Colo. Colorado
comp. compiler (pl., comps.)
Conn. Connecticut
cont. continued
Copt. Coptic
1 Cor. *1 Corinthians*
2 Cor. *2 Corinthians*
corr. corrected
C.S.P. Congregatio Sancti Pauli, Congregation of Saint Paul (Paulisis)
d. died
D Deuteronomic (source of the Pentateuch)
Dan. Danish
D.B. Divinitatis Baccalaureus, Bachelor of Divinity
D.C. District of Columbia
D.D. Divinitatis Doctor, Doctor of Divinity
Del. Delaware
Dem. *Dema'i*
dim. diminutive
diss. dissertation
Dn. *Daniel*
D.Phil. Doctor of Philosophy
Dt. *Deuteronomy*
Du. Dutch
E Elohist (source of the Pentateuch)
Eccl. *Ecclesiastes*
ed. editor (pl., eds.); edition; edited by

'Eduy. *'Eduyyot*
e.g. exempli gratia, for example
Egyp. Egyptian
1 En. *1 Enoch*
2 En. *2 Enoch*
3 En. *3 Enoch*
Eng. English
enl. enlarged
Eph. Ephesians
'Eruv. *'Eruvin*
1 Esd. *1 Esdras*
2 Esd. *2 Esdras*
3 Esd. *3 Esdras*
4 Esd. *4 Esdras*
esp. especially
Est. Estonian
Est. *Esther*
et al. *et alii,* and others
etc. *et cetera,* and so forth
Eth. Ethiopic
EV English version
Ex. *Exodus*
exp. expanded
Ez. *Ezekiel*
Ezr. *Ezra*
2 Ezr. *2 Ezra*
4 Ezr. *4 Ezra*
f. feminine; and following (pl., ff.)
fast. fascicle (pl., fascs.)
fig. figure (pl., figs.)
Finn. Finnish
fl. *floruit,* flourished
Fla. Florida
Fr. French
frag. fragment
ft. feet
Ga. Georgia
Gal. *Galatians*
Gaul. Gaulish
Ger. German
Git. *Gittin*
Gn. *Genesis*
Gr. Greek
Hag. *Hagigah*
Hal. *Hallah*
Hau. Hausa
Hb. *Habakkuk*
Heb. Hebrew
Heb. *Hebrews*
Hg. *Haggai*
Hitt. Hittite
Hor. *Horayot*
Hos. *Hosea*
Hul. *Hullin*
Hung. Hungarian

ibid. *ibidem,* in the same place (as the one immediately preceding)
Icel. Icelandic
i.e. *id est,* that is
IE Indo-European
Ill. Illinois
Ind. Indiana
intro. introduction
Ir. Gael. Irish Gaelic
Iran. Iranian
Is. *Isaiah*
Ital. Italian
J Yahvist (source of the Pentateuch)
Jas. *James*
Jav. Javanese
Jb. *Job*
Jdt. *Judith*
Jer. *Jeremiah*
Jgs. *Judges*
Jl. *Joel*
Jn. *John*
1 Jn. *1 John*
2 Jn. *2 John*
3 Jn. *3 John*
Jon. *Jonah*
Jos. *Joshua*
Jpn. Japanese
JPS Jewish Publication Society translation (1985) of the Hebrew Bible
J.T. Jerusalem Talmud
Jub. *Jubilees*
Kans. Kansas
Kel. *Kelim*
Ker. *Keritot*
Ket. *Ketubbot*
1 Kgs. *1 Kings*
2 Kgs. *2 Kings*
Khois. Khoisan
Kil. *Kil'ayim*
km kilometers
Kor. Korean
Ky. Kentucky
l. line (pl., ll.)
La. Louisiana
Lam. *Lamentations*
Lat. Latin
Latv. Latvian
L. en Th. Licencié en Théologie, Licentiate in Theology
L. ès L. Licencié ès Lettres, Licentiate in Literature
Let. Jer. *Letter of Jeremiah*
lit. literally

Lith. Lithuanian
Lk. Luke
LL Late Latin
LL.D. Legum Doctor, Doctor of Laws
Lv. Leviticus
m meters
m. masculine
M.A. Master of Arts
Ma'as. Ma'aserot
Ma'as. Sh. Ma'aser sheni
Mak. Makkot
Makh. Makhshirin
Mal. Malachi
Mar. Marathi
Mass. Massachusetts
1 Mc. 1 Maccabees
2 Mc. 2 Maccabees
3 Mc. 3 Maccabees
4 Mc. 4 Maccabees
Md. Maryland
M.D. Medicinae Doctor, Doctor of Medicine
ME Middle English
Meg. Megillah
Me'il. Me'ilah
Men. Menahot
MHG Middle High German
mi. miles
Mi. Micah
Mich. Michigan
Mid. Middot
Minn. Minnesota
Miq. Miqva'ot
MIran. Middle Iranian
Miss. Mississippi
Mk. Mark
Mo. Missouri
Mo'ed Q. Mo'ed qatan
Mont. Montana
MPers. Middle Persian
MS. *manuscriptum,* manuscript (pl., MSS)
Mt. Matthew
MT Masoretic text
n. note
Na. Nahum
Nah. Nahuatl
Naz. Nazir
N.B. *nota bene,* take careful note
N.C. North Carolina
n.d. no date
N.Dak. North Dakota
NEB New English Bible
Nebr. Nebraska
Ned. Nedarim
Neg. Nega'im
Neh. Nehemiah
Nev. Nevada
N.H. New Hampshire
Nid. Niddah
N.J. New Jersey
Nm. Numbers

N.Mex. New Mexico
no. number (pl., nos.)
Nor. Norwegian
n.p. no place
n.s. new series
N.Y. New York
Ob. Obadiah
O.Cist. Ordo Cisterciencium, Order of Cîteaux (Cistercians)
OCS Old Church Slavonic
OE Old English
O.F.M. Ordo Fratrum Minorum, Order of Friars Minor (Franciscans)
OFr. Old French
Ohal. Ohalot
OHG Old High German
OIr. Old Irish
OIran. Old Iranian
Okla. Oklahoma
ON Old Norse
O.P. Ordo Praedicatorum, Order of Preachers (Dominicans)
OPers. Old Persian
op. cit. *opere citato,* in the work cited
OPrus. Old Prussian
Oreg. Oregon
'Orl. 'Orlah
O.S.B. Ordo Sancti Benedicti, Order of Saint Benedict (Benedictines)
p. page (pl., pp.)
P Priestly (source of the Pentateuch)
Pa. Pennsylvania
Pahl. Pahlavi
Par. Parah
para. paragraph (pl., paras.)
Pers. Persian
Pes. Pesahim
Ph.D. Philosophiae Doctor, Doctor of Philosophy
Phil. Philippians
Phlm. Philemon
Phoen. Phoenician
pl. plural; plate (pl., pls.)
PM *post meridiem,* after noon
Pol. Polish
pop. population
Port. Portuguese
Prv. Proverbs
Ps. Psalms
Ps. 151 Psalm 151
Ps. Sol. Psalms of Solomon
pt. part (pl., pts.)
1 Pt. 1 Peter
2 Pt. 2 Peter
Pth. Parthian
Q hypothetical source of the synoptic Gospels

Qid. Qiddushin
Qin. Qinnim
r. reigned; ruled
Rab. Rabbah
rev. revised
R. ha-Sh. Ro'sh ha-shanah
R.I. Rhode Island
Rom. Romanian
Rom. Romans
R.S.C.J. Societas Sacratissimi Cordis Jesu, Religious of the Sacred Heart
RSV Revised Standard Version of the Bible
Ru. Ruth
Rus. Russian
Rv. Revelation
Rv. Ezr. Revelation of Ezra
San. Sanhedrin
S.C. South Carolina
Scot. Gael. Scottish Gaelic
S. Dak. South Dakota
sec. section (pl., secs.)
Sem. Semitic
ser. series
sg. singular
Sg. Song of Songs
Sg. of 3 Prayer of Azariah and the Song of the Three Young Men
Shab. Shabbat
Shav. Shavu'ot
Sheq. Sheqalim
Sib. Or. Sibylline Oracles
Sind. Sindhi
Sinh. Sinhala
Sir. Ben Sira
S.J. Societas Jesu, Society of Jesus (Jesuits)
Skt. Sanskrit
1 Sm. 1 Samuel
2 Sm. 2 Samuel
Sogd. Sogdian
Sot Sotah
sp. species (pl., spp.)
Span. Spanish
sq. square
S.S.R. Soviet Socialist Republic
st. stanza (pl., ss.)
S.T.M. Sacrae Theologiae Magister, Master of Sacred Theology
Suk. Sukkah
Sum. Sumerian
supp. supplement; supplementary
Sus. Susanna
s.v. *sub verbo,* under the word (pl., s.v.v.)
Swed. Swedish
Syr. Syriac
Syr. Men. Syriac Menander

Ta'an. Ta'anit
Tam. Tamil
Tam. Tamid
Tb. Tobit
T.D. *Taisho shinshu daizokyo,* edited by Takakusu Junjiro et al. (Tokyo, 1922-1934)
Tem. Temurah
Tenn. Tennessee
Ter. Terumot
Tev. Y. Tevul yom
Tex. Texas
Th.D. Theologicae Doctor, Doctor of Theology
1 Thes. 1 Thessalonians
2 Thes. 2 Thessalonians
Thrac. Thracian
Ti. Titus
Tib. Tibetan
1 Tm. 1 Timothy
2 Tm. 2 Timothy
T. of 12 Testaments of the Twelve Patriarchs
Toh. Tohorot
Tong. Tongan
trans. translator, translators; translated by; translation
Turk. Turkish
Ukr. Ukrainian
Upan. Upanisad
U.S. United States
U.S.S.R. Union of Soviet Socialist Republics
Uqts. Uqtsin
v. verse (pl., vv.)
Va. Virginia
var. variant; variation
Viet. Vietnamese
viz. *videlicet,* namely
vol. volume (pl., vols.)
Vt. Vermont
Wash. Washington
Wel. Welsh
Wis. Wisconsin
Wis. Wisdom of Solomon
W.Va. West Virginia
Wyo. Wyoming
Yad. Yadayim
Yev. Yevamot
Yi. Yiddish
Yor. Yoruba
Zav. Zavim
Zec. Zechariah
Zep. Zephaniah
Zev. Zevahim
* hypothetical
? uncertain; possibly; perhaps
° degrees
+ plus
- minus
= equals; is equivalent to
x by; multiplied by
→ yields

ABRAHAM

ABRAHAM, or, in Hebrew, Avraham; the ancestor of the Hebrews through the line of Isaac and Jacob and of the Arabs through Ishmael.

Religion of Abraham. The traditio-historical approach to the patriarchal stories has led to the view that the tradition reflects a nomadic form of personal religion in which the "god of the fathers" is the patron god of the clan. He is associated with a specific person, such as Abraham, who experiences a theophany and receives the divine promises of land and progeny. Also belonging to this "primitive" level of Israelite religion are the references to sacred trees and stones and the setting up of numerous altars.

The problem with these reconstructions of Israel's early religion is that the emphasis upon Yahveh as the God of Abraham, Isaac, and Jacob are attested only in exilic sources. Furthermore, the themes of the divine promise of land and numerous progeny cannot be shown in a single instance to belong to the oral stage of the tradition's development. One must conclude that the religion of Abraham is the religion of the authors of the present form of the tradition.

The Abraham Tradition in Genesis. A distinctive feature of the Abraham tradition is that it contains a number of short stories that are not linked in a continuous narrative. This has fostered the view that they reflect a stage of oral tradition before their collection into a literary work. Furthermore, a number of stories appear as doublets, carefully composed literary modifications of the earlier stories meant to put forward the author's own point of view and religious concerns.

The twice-told tales. There are two stories about how the patriarch's wife was passed off as his sister in order to protect himself in a foreign land. The first one (*Gn.* 12:10-20) is simply an entertaining folk tale whereby Abraham appears to outsmart the Egyptians and come away with both wealth and wife. The second version (chap. 20) seeks to exonerate the patriarch of any moral wrongdoing. Yet a third version of the story is found in the Isaac tradition (26:1-11), which makes use of elements from both of the earlier stories but with the emphasis here on God's guidance and providence. The account of Hagar's flight (chap. 16) and her later expulsion with Ishmael (21:8-21) are also doublets. The first is an ethnographic etiology on the origin and nature of the

Ishmaelites, while the second transforms this theme into an aspect of the divine promises to Abraham, since Ishmael is also his offspring.

In none of these cases does the later version constitute an independent variant of the tradition. Instead, it is an attempt by a later author to modify the way one understands the earlier story in terms of a later attitude on morals and piety.

Abraham and Lot. The inclusion of Lot in the Abraham tradition affords a contrast between the forefather of the Ammonites and the Moabites and the forefather of the Hebrews. When they go their separate ways (*Gn.* 13), Lot appears to gain the better territory by his choice of the fertile valley in the region of Sodom, while Abraham is left with the land of Canaan.

The story of Sodom and Gomorrah follows a familiar classical theme, as in the story of Baucis and Philemon (Ovid, *Metamorphoses* 8.616ff.), in which the gods send emissaries in the guise of strangers to investigate violence and corruption on earth. The strangers are ill treated by the population, except for an old couple who offer them hospitality and are rewarded while the rest of the population is destroyed. In the

> **The religion of Abraham is the religion of the authors of the present form of the tradition.**

Bible, Abraham's hospitality is rewarded by the promise of Isaac's birth (18:1-15). Lot also entertains the two angels and protects them from the cities' inhabitants, who try to abuse them. This leads to the judgment on Sodom and Gomorrah, but Lot and his family are rescued, except for Lot's wife, who looks back and becomes a pillar of salt.

Covenant of Abraham. The Yahvist who brought together the diverse elements of the Abraham tradition created a sense of unity in the collection by means of the themes of the divine promises of numerous progeny and the gift of the land of Canaan. J begins with God's call to Abraham to leave his homeland for a new land and his promise of nationhood and divine blessing (*Gn.* 12:1-3). As soon as Abraham reaches the land of Canaan, God gives it to him as an inheritance (12:7). The promises are again repeated after Abraham's separation from Lot (13:14-17). The promise theme reaches its climax in chapter 15, in which God assures Abraham again of numerous descendants and makes a covenant with him according to which he gives him the region from the river of Egypt to the Euphrates.

The Priestly writer's treatment of the covenant (chap. 17) builds directly upon J's version but introduces a number of modifications. First, God appears to Abraham as El Shaddai (17:1) instead of as Yahveh (15:7). This change is explained by P in *Exodus* 6:2-3 in the suggestion that the patriarchs knew God only by the name El Shaddai, whereas the name Yahveh was first revealed to Moses. Second, the writer marks the covenant by a change of names from Abram and Sarai to Abraham and Sarah. Third, the covenant with its promises includes the sign of circumcision. Only through this rite may Israelites of a later day be participants in the destiny of the covenant community, an ecclesial conception of identity appropriate to those living in the Diaspora communities.

Abraham in Postbiblical Judaism. One use of the Abraham tradition in postbiblical times can be seen in the anti-Hellenistic work of the Maccabean period known as *Jubilees*, or the *Little Genesis* (chaps. 12-23). There Abraham becomes the model of appropriate Jewish piety. The book tells how Abraham repudiated the idolatry of his native land. After receiving the divine call he went to the land of Canaan. One significant amplification of the biblical tradition of Abraham is the emphasis on Abraham's observance of many of the Mosaic laws and of his giving instruction in these laws to Isaac his son and even to his grandson Jacob. Special emphasis is also given to the covenant of Abraham as the covenant of circumcision and a warning to those Jews who neglect this practice (see 15:9-14, 15:25-34, 16:14). The theme of Abraham's testing by God is more nearly paralleled to that of Job by including in the Abraham story the figure of Mastema (Satan), who becomes responsible for instigating the trials. Abraham endures ten trials, the climax of which is the divine command to sacrifice *Isaac* (17:15-18, 18:1-13; see also *Avot* 5.3, *Judith* 8:25f.).

Josephus Flavius, the Jewish historian of Roman times, presents Abraham as a pious philosopher of great learning (*Jewish Antiquities* 1.7-17). He states that Abraham was the first to reason to a knowledge of God, creator of the universe, by his observations of the heavens. Abraham was, however, forced to leave Babylonia because of religious persecution (see also *Judith* 5:8). He took with him the Babylonian sciences of astronomy and mathematics, which he taught to the Egyptians during his sojourn in their country, and in this way the knowledge of such sciences eventually came to the Greeks. (See also the Hellenistic-Jewish fragments in Eusebius's *Praeparatio evangelica*, 9.17ff., where Abraham teaches the Phoenicians as well.) Josephus places little emphasis upon the distinctively Jewish features of the Abraham tradition.

Abraham in Christianity. The figure of Abraham plays a special role in the New Testament, especially in the thought of the apostle Paul. In *Romans* 4 Paul argues that Abraham was justified by faith in God prior to his being circumcised and therefore prior to any works of the law, so the law is not necessary for justification that is, for being considered righteous before God. Abraham becomes the father of the faithful, and the election of Abraham is thus extended to all who have faith. Nevertheless, Paul is not willing to give up God's special election of the Jews and so argues for their ultimate salvation as well. In *Galatians* 3:6-9 and 3:15-18 Paul uses a somewhat different argument by suggesting that salvation came to the gentiles through Abraham's blessing; this blessing was transmitted through Abraham's "seed," which Paul identifies with Jesus.

The *Letter to the Hebrews* (11:8-12, 11:17-19) uses Abraham as an example of faith, recounting his response to God's call to sojourn in the land of promise, his belief with Sarah in the promise of offspring, and his testing through the sacrifice of Isaac. By contrast, *James* 2:20-24 uses the sacrifice of Isaac as an example of Abraham's being justified by works and not just by faith alone.

Abraham in Islam. Abraham is mentioned more frequently in the Qur'an than is any other biblical figure. He is regarded as the first prophet because he was the first to convert to the true God and to preach against the idolatry of his people (surahs 19:41ff., 21:51ff., 26:69ff., 37:83ff.). He was also the first Muslim because he practiced *islam*—submission to absolute obedience to God—when he was tested by the command to sacrifice his son (2:124ff., 37:102ff.). Abraham, with the aid of his son Ishmael, the father of the Arabs, was responsible for the founding of the Ka`bah in Mecca, the first sanctuary of God (2:125, 2:127). Muhammad viewed himself as the reviver of this ancient faith, which he regarded as older than both Judaism and Christianity (3:65). Following Jewish tradition, he also regarded Abraham as the first recipient of the divine revelation of the book (2:129).

BIBLIOGRAPHY

It is difficult in a brief bibliography to do justice to the broad spectrum of scholarly opinion about the Abraham tradition. On matters of the history of the patriarchal age, John Bright's *A History of Israel*, 3d ed. (Philadelphia, 1981), may be said to represent an American school of thought, while Siegfried Herrmann's *Geschichte Israels in alttestamentlicher Zeit* (Munich, 1973), translated by John Bowden as *A History of Israel in Old Testament Times*, 2d ed. (Philadelphia, 1981), presents an approach favored by many German biblical scholars. A mediating position is that found in Roland de Vaux's *Histoire ancienne d'Israël: Des origines l'installation en Canaan* (Paris, 1971), translated by David Smith as *The Early History of Israel* (Philadelphia, 1978).

On the religion of Abraham, see Albrecht Alt's *Der Gott der Väter: Ein Beitrag zur Vorgeschichte der Israelitischen Religion* (Stuttgart, 1929), translated by R. A. Wilson as "The God of the Fathers," in *Essays on Old Testament History and Religion* (Oxford, 1966), pp. 1-

77; and Frank Moore Cross's *Canaanite Myth and Hebrew Epic: Essays in the History of the Religion of Israel* (Cambridge, Mass., 1973), pp. 3-75.

On the literary development of the tradition, see Hermann Gunkel's *Genesis* (Göttingen, 1901). The introduction to this work was translated and edited by William H. Carruth as *The Legends of Genesis* (Chicago, 1901) and reissued with an introduction by William F. Albright (New York, 1964). See also the commentary in Gerhard von Rad's *Das erste Buch Mose, Genesis*, 3 vols. (Göttingen, 1949-1953), translated by John H. Marks as *Genesis: A Commentary*, 3 vols. (Philadelphia, 1961). A commentary that reflects the American school is the one in Nahum M. Sarna's *Understanding Genesis* (New York, 1966).

Critical reappraisals of the historicity of the Abraham tradition can be found in Thomas L. Thompson's *The Historicity of the Patriarchal Narratives: The Quest for the Historical Abraham* (New York, 1974), and in my *Abraham in History and Tradition* (New Haven, 1975). The latter work also contains a critical discussion of the literary tradition of Abraham.

Recent surveys of the present state of scholarship on Abraham are represented by William G. Denver and W. Malcolm Clark in "The Patriarchal Traditions," chapter 2 of *Israelite and Judaean History*, edited by John H. Hayes and J. Maxwell Miller (Philadelphia, 1977), pp. 70-148; and Claus Westermann's *Genesis*, pt. 2, "Biblischer Kommentar Altes Testament," vol. 1, no. 2 (Neukirchen-Vluyn, 1981). This latter work contains an extensive bibliography.

For a treatment of Abraham in later Jewish sources, see Samuel Sandmel's *Philo's Place in Judaism: A Study of Conceptions of Abraham in Jewish Literature* (Cincinnati, 1955). See also the article "Abraham" in *Theologische Realenzyklopädie*, vol. 1 (New York, 1977).

JOHN VAN SETERS

ADAM

ADAM is the designation and name of the first human creature in the creation narratives found in the Hebrew scriptures (Old Testament). Here the first being is clearly a lone male, since the female was not yet formed from one of his ribs to be his helpmate (*'ezer ke-negdo*; *Gn.* 2:21-23). In the earlier textual account of *Genesis* 1:1-24a, which is generally considered to be a later version than that found in *Genesis* 2:4b-25, God first consults with his divine retinue and then makes an *adam* in his own "form and image": "in the form of God he created him; male and female he created them" (*Gn.* 1:27). If the second clause is not simply a later qualification of a simultaneous creation of a male and a female both known as *adam* (see also *Gn.* 5:1), then we may have a trace of the creation of a primordial androgyne.

Later ancient traditions responded to this version by speculating that the original unity was subsequently separated and that marriage is a social restitution of this polarity. Medieval Jewish Qabbalah, which took the expression "in the image of God" with the utmost seriousness, projected a vision of an *adam qadmon*, or "primordial Adam," as one of the configurations by which the emanation of divine potencies that constituted the simultaneous self-revelation of God and his creation could be imagined. And because Adam is both male and female according to scriptural authority, the qabbalists variously refer to a feminine aspect of the godhead that, like the feminine of the human world, must be reintegrated with its masculine counterpart through religious

> **The dominant rabbinic tradition is that the sin of Adam resulted in mortality for humankind.**

action and contemplation. Such a straight anthropomorphic reading of *Genesis* 1:27 was often rejected by religious philosophers especially (both Jewish and Christian), and the language of scripture was interpreted to indicate that the quality which makes the human similar to the divine is the intellect or will.

According to the first scriptural narrative, this *adam* was the crown of creation. Moreover, this being was commissioned to rule over the nonhuman creations of the earth as a faithful steward (*Gn.* 1:29-2:9). Out of regard for the life under his domain, this being was to be a vegetarian. In the second version (where the specifying designation *ha-adam*, "the Adam," predominates; cf. *Gn.* 2:7-4:1), the creature is put into a divine garden as its caretaker and told not to eat of two trees—the tree of the knowledge of good and evil and the tree of life, that is, the two sources of knowledge and being—under pain of death (*Gn.* 2:15-17). This interdict is subsequently broken, with the result that death, pain of childbirth, and a blemished natural world were decreed for mankind (*Gn.* 3:14-19).

This primordial fault, which furthermore resulted in the banishment of Adam and his companion from the garden (*Gn.* 3:22-24), and the subsequent propagation of the human species as such (*Gn.* 4:1ff.), has been variously treated. The dominant rabbinic tradition is that the sin of Adam resulted in mortality for humankind and did not constitute a qualitative change in the nature of the species. For Christian theology, the innate corruption of human nature that resulted from Adam's fall was restored by the atoning death of a new Adam, Jesus (cf. 1 *Cor.* 15:22). In one Christian tradition, the redemptive blood of Christ flowed onto the grave of Adam, who was buried under Calvary in the Holy Sepulcher. The typologizing of Adam in Jewish tradition often focused on him as the prototype of humankind, and so the episode in Eden was read as exemplary or allegorical of the human condition and the propensity to sin. In this light, various spiritual, moral, or even legal consequences were also drawn, particularly with respect to the unity of the human race deriving from this "one father"—a race formed, according to one legend, from different colored clays found throughout the earth. In addition, mystics, philosophical contemplatives, and gnostics of all times saw in the life of Adam a pattern for their own religious quest of life—as, for example, the idea that the world of the first Adam was one of heavenly luminosity, subsequently diminished; the idea that Adam was originally a spiritual being, subsequently transformed into a being of flesh—his body became his "garments of shame"; or even the idea that Adam in Eden was originally sunk in deep contemplation of the divine essence but that he subsequently became distracted, with the result that he became the prisoner of the phenomenal world. For many of these traditions, the spiritual ideal was to retrieve the lost spiritual or mystical harmony Adam originally had with God and all being.

[*See also* Eve; Fall, The; *and* Paradise.]

BIBLIOGRAPHY

Fishbane, Michael. *Text and Texture*. New York, 1979. See pages 17-23.

Ginzberg, Louis. *The Legends of the Jews* (1909-1938). 7 vols. Translated by Henrietta Szold et al. Reprint, Philadelphia, 1937-1966. See volume 1, pages 49-102; volume 5, pages 63-131; and the index.

Le Bachelet, Xavier. "Adam." *In Dictionnaire de théologie catholique*, vol. 1, cols. 368-386. Paris, 1903.

Sarna, Nahum M. *Understanding Genesis*. New York, 1972. See pages 12-18.

Speiser, E. A. *Genesis*. Anchor Bible, vol. 1. Garden City, N. Y., 1964. See pages 3-28.

MICHAEL FISHBANE

ADLER, FELIX

ADLER, FELIX (1851-1933), social, educational, and religious reformer; founder of the New York Society for Ethical Culture. Born in Alzey, Germany, Alder came to the United States at the age of six when his father, Rabbi Samuel Adler, accepted the country's most prestigious Reform pulpit, at Temple Emanu-El in New York. By example and instruction his parents fostered his passion for social justice, religious sensibilities, and Jewish education. After graduation from Columbia College in 1870, he returned to Germany to study at the Berlin Hochschule für die Wissenschaft des Judentums in order to prepare for a career in the Reform rabbinate. When the school's opening was delayed for almost two years, Adler immersed himself in university studies, first at Berlin and then at Heidelberg, where he received his doctorate in Semitics *summa cum laude* in 1873. His formative German experiences precipitated an intellectual break with Judaism: after his exposure to historicism, evolution, critical studies of the Bible, anthropology, and Neo-Kantianism,

Adler's belief in theism and the spiritual uniqueness of Judaism was undermined. Kant's analysis of ethical imperatives lent authority to Adler's new faith in a moral law independent of a personal deity, and the German industrial order, with its attendant socioeconomic problems for labor and society, along with Friedrich Lange's proposed solutions, brought into focus the major ills of industrial society that Adler came to address in America throughout his life.

Upon his return home, it was expected that he would eventually succeed his father at Emanu-El, but his one sermon on 11 October 1873 alienated some of the established members. Adler's admirers, however, sponsored him as nonresident professor of Hebrew and Oriental literature at Cornell between 1873 and 1876, and they then served as the nucleus of a Sunday lecture movement that he inaugurated on 15 May 1876. The following February this movement was incorporated as the New York Society for Ethical Culture.

Over the years, the society served as Adler's platform not only for philosophical conceptualizations but also for concrete social reforms. In the late 1870s he established the first free kindergarten in New York, the first district nursing program, and a workingman's lyceum; in 1880 he organized a workingman's school (later the Ethical Culture School), and in 1891 he founded the Summer School of Applied Ethics. Adler was also intimately involved in tenement housing reform and good-government clubs and served as chairman of the National Child Labor Committee.

As an intellectual, Adler accumulated impressive scholarly credentials: he founded the *International Journal of Ethics* (1890), was appointed professor of political and social ethics at Columbia (1902), and delivered Oxford's Hibbert Lectures (1923), published as *The Reconstruction of the Spiritual Ideal* (1924). Nevertheless, the fundamental intellectual effort of his last years—the philosophical justification of his ethical ideal of a spiritual universe—had negligible impact. Where this was attempted, as in *An Ethical Philosophy of Life* (1918), it was dismissed as an example of Neo-Kantian religious idealism.

In his day, Adler was publicly lauded as prophet, social visionary, and apostle of moral justice even by the Jewish community he had left. Yet toward the end of his life he was intellectually alienated from his own organization, and today most Ethical Culture members know him only as their movement's founder.

[*See also* Ethical Culture.]

BIBLIOGRAPHY

The fullest biography is Horace L. Friess's *Felix Adler and Ethical Culture* (New York, 1981). Friess (Adler's son-in-law) presents the full scope of Adler's activities combined with personal memories of the man and an insightful analysis of Adler's intellectual evolution and his final ethical position. My own study *From*

Reform Judaism to Ethical Culture: The Religious Evolution of Felix Adler (Cincinnati, 1979) analyzes Adler's religious departure from Judaism, its causes, and its repercussions for both Adler and the American Jewish community. It treats the Jewish reaction to Adler and to the Ethical Culture Society and uses Adler as a model by which to understand new models of Jewish apostasy in modern Jewish history. Robert S. Guttchen's *Felix Adler* (New York, 1974) presents a very useful analysis of Adler's concept of human worth and his educational philosophy. The book is prefaced with a perceptive biographical sketch of Adler by Howard B. Radest. The latter's own book, *Toward Common Ground: The Story of the Ethical Societies in the United States* (New York, 1969), furnishes further information on Adler.

BENNY KRAUT

AEGEAN RELIGIONS

The Aegean world is composed of regions limited in area but geographically and culturally very diverse, whose evolution proceeded in an irregular and more or less independent fashion: whereas the Cyclades, the island microcosm situated between Europe and Asia, flourished as early as the third millennium BCE, Crete reached its apogee in the first half of the second millennium, and the continent, where the Greeks seem to have settled shortly before 2000 BCE, achieved a great civilization at Mycenae only in the second half of the same millennium. Although related, the religions of the Aegean that developed around these three poles preserved an undeniable regional originality.

Cycladic Religion

The Cycladic religion of the Early Bronze Age (third millennium BCE) remains difficult to define even after a century of research. Archaeological data are severely lacking, as no religious architecture has been identified with any certainty.

Especially well known from the Cycladic civilization are the small marble "idols," generally found in a funerary context. The majority are nude female figures, related, despite their slender, elongated forms, to the voluptuous Neolithic fertility figurines of continental Europe. The Cycladic idols do not seem to have served as cult statues. Yet a silver diadem from Syros may represent a religious scene involving two animals and two bird-headed feminine figures with raised arms, separated by stellar motifs. Comparable symbols decorate a type of vase whose function is not well established, the terra-cotta "frying pan." These flat, wide vases with their bifid handles bear on their reverse an incised decoration: a boat against a background of connected spirals and a pubic triangle between stylized plants on an example from Syros, and a stellar motif and pubic triangle on another. The belief in a feminine principle of fertility linked with the celestial and marine worlds and undoubtedly related to Oriental models

appears to be an established fact, even though the forms of worship are unknown to us.

After 2000 BCE the Cyclades seem to have lost their religious autonomy. The site of Akrotiri on the island of Thera, once buried under volcanic ashes, has revealed a series of frescoes that, though inspired by Crete, display a certain originality. While some of the women depicted follow the ritual style of the Minoans, with flounced skirts and bared breasts, a young priestess carrying offerings is clothed in an ample tunic. However, a scene portraying the ritual gathering of crocuses and the presence on the site of stone horns of consecration betray the extent of Minoan influence.

Religious architecture, until then nonexistent, developed at Keos and Melos. A small temple built at Hagia Irini was closer in plan, with its antechamber, interior room, and annexes, to the constructions of the continent than to those of Crete. One of the annexes was crowded with female terracotta statues whose naked, ample breasts and long skirts recall the Cretan prototypes. It has been supposed that they belonged to a cult of Dionysos, whereas at Phylakopi a goddess seems to have been worshiped in the form of a figurine decorated in the ceramic style of Mycenae, thus probably indicating a religious takeover from the continent.

Minoan Religion

Crete remained relatively independent of the neighboring Cyclades during the entire Early Bronze Age. An original Cretan civilization did not reach its height until the beginning of the second millennium BCE, with the building of the palaces attributed to the more or less mythical Minos. Yet no clean break with the preceding period is discernible at that time, especially as far as religion is concerned.

Places of Worship. It is usually maintained that, in contrast to the contemporaneous Near East and Egypt, large constructions of a religious nature were unknown in Minoan Crete. However, without equating the Minoan palace with the Oriental temple, which was at the same time residence of the god, lodging for the priests, and center of many economic activities, one cannot forget that the palace gave a monumental setting to certain religious manifestations.

Still, an important architectural framework was not necessary to the cult, and wherever architecture does appear, it is usually very modest. It is often necessary to turn to figured depictions, the only surviving evidence we have. Thus on a gold ring from Isopata, four female figures can be seen wearing the ritual dress, with exposed breasts and flounced skirts, and dancing in a landscape flowered with clusters of lilies. In other representations, architecture, though present, plays only a secondary role in the form of a small structure out of which grows a tree—clearly, no mere figurative schematization. One may well imagine, therefore, that at least some of the Minoan rites took place in a context of rocks, trees, or landscape unmodified by human intervention.

The same spirit pervades the two great categories of Minoan places of worship: peak sanctuaries and caves. The cave offers a crude natural setting that nature itself has transformed by decorating it with strangely shaped, more or less anthropomorphic or zoomorphic concretions in which, from a very early period, the Minoans saw manifestations of the divinity. Some of these caves are particularly well known: the cave of Kamares in the Ida mountain chain, the cave of Arkalochori, and finally the cave of Psychro, also called the Diktaean Cave. Another cave, at Skotino, has been interpreted as the actual labyrinth of Greek mythology; it may be significant that it is still used each year in July for feasts in honor of Hagia Paraskevi, whose chapel stands on the edge of the chasm.

Undeniably, the peak sanctuaries bring to mind the high places of Canaan. On a sealing from Knossos a feminine form appears on a mountaintop flanked by two lions and holding out a javelin or scepter to a worshiper arching his back in the Cretan attitude of adoration. A fragment from Knossos shows a worshiper in comparable surroundings placing on a rock a basket filled with offerings. Archaeological evidence is less precise: although some installations have been discovered on the mountaintops at Petsofas near Palaikastro, on the Kofinas in the Asteroussia Mountains, and on Mount Juktas near Knossos, no elaborate architecture has been found.

For a long time it was believed that caves and summits were the only public places where rites were celebrated (Nilsson, 1927). It now appears that, in the cities as well as in the country, the Minoans built more or less important religious edifices that functioned independently of other buildings. On the southern coast of the island the settlement of Myrtos, from the prepalatial period, presents a set of four unpretentious rooms in which a low base of stones and clay supported a feminine figurine, evidently an object of collective worship. At Mallia, a group of three rooms dating from the period of the first palaces shows no evidence of architectural progress, but on the floor of the main room there was a rectangular offering table, blackened by fire, to which one could have easy access from the neighboring street.

Outside the towns, the "country villa" of Kannia near Gortyna (if, as its discoverer believes, it has not undergone modification) represents an even more imposing building in which, out of twenty-seven rooms, five appear to have had a religious purpose, making it more akin to a large sanctuary than to a private house. More recently, near Arkhanes on the northern foothills of Mount Juktas, a construction has been discovered with three rooms opening onto a corridor; clay feet, a vase decorated with a bull in relief, and an incised dagger found on a human skeleton endow the site with unquestionable religious significance. As for the sanctuary of Kato Syme near Viannos, it presents features heretofore unique: a building of several rooms situated in a mountain gorge far from any populated area, on the edge of a spring and at the foot of a steep cliff—a site used until Roman times for sacrifices and burnt offerings in honor of a divine couple.

But the religious building *par excellence* in Crete is the palace. Struck by the religious aura that pervaded the edifice he was uncovering at Knossos, Arthur Evans (1901) named it the "palace-sanctuary" and identified it with the labyrinth of Greek legend, the residence of the monstrous Minotaur. The other palaces, at Phaistos, Mallia, and Zakros, while not absolutely identical to that at Knossos, are remarkably similar. To the west (except at Zakros), a wide esplanade is crossed by stone-paved causeways leading to the main entrances and to a "theatral area" (Knossos, Phaistos); at Knossos, two altar bases emphasize the religious function of this courtyard. Inside the edifice, another rectangular court served as a theater for great popular spectacles, as proved by tiers of steps on the sides and, at Mallia, by a hollow altar, or *bothros*, dug in the center. The frescoes covering the walls of the palace at Knossos evoke the rites that took place there: processions, offerings, bullfights.

Cult Ceremonies. We have little information concerning the Minoan priesthood other than a few representations in which the priest is distinguished by his long, Syrian-type dress and fenestrated ax. It is likely that the priests and priestesses usually wore the same attire as both the gods themselves and ordinary worshipers: for the women, flounced skirts leaving the torso nude, and for the men, mere loincloths. Evans (1921) put forward the hypothesis of a "priest-king" with both political and religious functions, who was obliged to have his powers renewed by the divinity every nine years. Although subsequent criticism has demolished Evans's view that the Knossian Priest-King Fresco depicts such a figure, he can undoubtedly be recognized in certain other scenes portraying him as a young man with long hair, wearing bracelets and necklaces and sometimes holding a long stick or spear.

> **The bull was the sacrificial animal *par excellence* in accordance with a tradition deeply rooted in the Near Eastern past. . . .**

As in Near Eastern religions, the first of these rites consisted in the offering of perishable foodstuffs, in baskets or vases. One must distinguish, from the typological and functional points of view, between the altar and the offering table. The altar, which could have been simply an uncut rock, was often made of a more or less cubic block of stone with concave sides. More monumental altars, with or without steps, are also found in the courts of the palaces and in the peak sanctuaries (Mount Juktas). As for the offering table, which appeared in various shapes and dimensions, in stone or clay, with or without legs, it generally included a large hollow for liquid offerings or libations. The rim of one of these, from Phaistos, is incised with a repeated motif of bovines and spirals, illustrating the offering of the blood of sacrificed animals. Another, at Mallia, bears unmistakable traces of fire, which relate it to combustion pits like the one found in the central court of the palace.

Libation ceremonies were performed using jugs and special vases, or rhytons; these, either conical or ovoid in shape, were pierced at the bottom to let the liquid flow out. Several of these stone vases bear decorations in relief that demonstrate an undeniable relationship with the cult; others, in stone or terra-cotta, represent the head of an animal, a lioness or bull, the bull's head probably meant for the blood of that animal.

The sacrifice is a particular form of libation ceremony in which the poured liquid is the blood of the victim. The rest of the animal was burned, as is proved by the bones found in layers of deposit in sanctuaries or sacrificial pits. The bull was the sacrificial animal *par excellence* in accordance with a tradition deeply rooted in the Near Eastern past; at the end of acrobatic bull games it must have been put to death with a double ax, probably in the central court of the palace. As for human sacrifice, in the absence of any incontestable data, one can only observe that the Cretans seem to have practiced it in one form or another, if the legend of Theseus and the Minotaur is to be believed.

Ritual processions ordinarily accompanied the offering of gifts to the divinity. Both on a fragment of a stone vase and on the walls of the Knossian palace, a file of hieratic figures carry cups and rhytons. Processions may also have borne the god's statue or the high priest in the oriental manner in a palanquin, as in the terra-cotta model discovered at Knossos, or the palanquin represented in a fresco painting. In this respect the stone-paved causeways that cross the western esplanades of the palaces seem to mark the requisite approaches to the main entrances and central court: thus at Knossos one of these walks leads to the West Porch, where the Corridor of the Procession begins, named after the paintings that decorate its walls. On a stone rhyton from Hagia Triada called the Harvesters' Vase, peasants carrying pitchforks on their shoulders march joyously to the music of a sistrum, led by a curious figure dressed in a cloak of scales, a prefiguration, in a way, of the Attic komoi of the Dionysian cult.

Mycenaean Religion

Nothing precise can be said about the divinities and cults of the continent before the Mycenaean period. The image of a fertility goddess seems to appear in the numerous representations from the Neolithic period of a naked female figure with hypertrophied forms, but the rites that were practiced are still unknown to us, in the absence of any cult installations.

Data from the Tablets. For a long time no distinction was made between the Mycenaean and Minoan civilizations, especially where religion was concerned. Indeed, in the view of Evans (1921-1936), the Minoans imposed on the Mycenaeans their way of life, their art, their ideas, and their rites. Even though there was mounting opposition to this theory of colonization, Cretan influence was hardly disputed until the deciphering of the Linear B script in 1953, which threw a whole new light on the matter by revealing a pantheon entirely different from that of the Minoans.

The tablets inscribed in Linear B are economic documents and give only indirect indications about the religion, in the form of lists of offerings to a god. Still, it is clear that the supremacy of a great goddess is replaced in the Mycenaean world by that of a male god who bears the name of the great god of the Classical Greeks: Zeus. Around him the pantheon of Olympian divinities was already taking shape: Hera, Athana Potnia (Athena), Enyalios (Ares), Paiawon (Apollo), Poseidaon (Poseidon), perhaps even Hermes and Dionysos; the hierarchies are not identical, however, as Poseidon played a preeminent role at Pylos. Some of these gods seem to mask older divinities whose attributes they took over. At Knossos, Zeus Diktaios ("of Mount Dikte") appears to have had the functions of the goddess of Mount Dikte, Diktynna, while the name *Potnia* ("lady, mistress"), used without other qualification, seems to express the personality of the Great Mother of pre-Hellenic days. As for the "Lady of the Labyrinth," her appellation apparently relates her to the palace of Knossos.

BIBLIOGRAPHY

Our knowledge of the Cycladic religion suffers from a dearth of archaeological and figured data from the Early Bronze Age. The most recent comprehensive study is that of Olof Höckmann, "Cycladic Religion," in *Art and Culture of the Cyclades in the Third Millennium B. C.*, edited by Jürgen Thimme, Pat Getz-Preziosi, and Brinna Otto (Chicago, 1977), an exhibition catalog accompanied by developments concerning the main aspects of the Cycladic culture. The religious significance of the frescoes of Thera is analyzed with new documentation in the work of Nanno Marinatos, *Art and Religion in Thera* (Athens, 1984).

It is because of the wealth of iconographic material that the Minoan religion has been the most explored of the Aegean religions ever since the first discoveries of Arthur Evans in Crete. His first book, *The Mycenaean Tree and Pillar Cult and Its Mediterranean Relations* (London, 1901), brings together a good many scenes of which he proposes a coherent exegesis within the framework of a pillar and vegetation cult. His outstanding publication, *The Palace of Minos*, 4 vols. plus index (London, 1921-1936), remains to this day a fundamental work owing to the abundant material presented and the penetrating character of his analyses, even though they are biased toward a religious interpretation.

Martin P. Nilsson's great work, *The Minoan-Mycenaean Religion and Its Survival in Greek Religion* (1927), 2d ed. rev. (Lund, 1950), gives a systematic account of all the information available at that date and presents a more critical view of religious manifestations in the Aegean in the third and second millennia, but his observations are somewhat weakened by his assimilation of the Minoan with the Mycenaean religion. Another comprehensive review is Charles Picard's *Les religions prhellniques: Crète et Mycènes* (Paris, 1948), which groups material on the question in a convenient fashion but without illustrations. Each of these works must be supplemented by the well-informed synthesis of Emily Townsend Vermeule, *Götterkult*, in volume 3 of "Archeologia Homerica" (Göttingen, 1974); the drafting of the text goes back to 1963 and does not take into account the latest discoveries, in particular those of the frescoes of Thera and the cult center of Mycenae.

The interpretations of Evans, already discussed by Nilsson, have been strongly challenged by new analyses of archaeological data tending toward a more or less complete desacralization of the installations or architectural structures considered by him as sacred. This tendency is particularly noticeable in the article of Luisa Banti, "I culti minoici e greci di Haghia Triada (Creta)," *Annuario della Scuola Archeologica di Atene* 3-5 (1941-1943): 9-74, and in the work of Bogdan Rutkowski, *Cult Places in the Aegean World* (Wroclaw, 1972).

In addition, new iconographic studies of the rich repertoire of Minoan representations with a religious character have been made by Friedrich Matz in his *Göttererscheinung und Kultbild im minoischen Kreta* (Wiesbaden, 1958), and more recently by Rutkowski in his *Frühgriechische Kultdarstellungen* (Berlin, 1981). The relationship between the Aegean and the Greek religions, already studied by Nilsson, was reexamined for Crete by R. F. Willetts in *Cretan Cults and Festivals* (New York, 1963) and, with the addition of Oriental antecedents, by B. C. Dietrich in *The Origins of Greek Religion* (Berlin and New York, 1974).

The great discovery in the field of Aegean religions has been the deciphering of the Linear B script by Michael Ventris and John Chadwick in 1953; its repercussions on our knowledge of the Mycenaean religion are brought to the fore in their joint publication, *Documents in Mycenaean Greek* (Cambridge, 1959). Since that date, commentaries of limited scope have been devoted to the Mycenaean religion in the context of more general works, such as George E. Mylonas's *Mycenae and the Mycenaean Age* (Princeton, 1966), Chadwick's *The Mycenaean World* (Cambridge, 1976), and J. T. Hooker's *Mycenaean Greece* (London, 1976). Following the discoveries made in Mycenae by Lord William Taylour and himself, Mylonas has drawn up a useful review of all the findings on the question as far as architecture is concerned, *Mycenaean Religion: Temples, Altars, and Temenea*, in volume 39 of *Proceedings of the Academy of Athens* (Athens, 1977).

OLIVIER PELON
Translated from French by Anne Marzin

AFRICAN RELIGIONS

[*Further discussion of traditional African religions can be found in* West Africa Religions; East Aftrican Religions; Southern African Religions; *and other entries on the religions of particular peoples. For discussion of traditional religion in* North Africa, *see* Berber Religion.]

An Overview

Prior to the coming of Christianity and Islam to Africa, the peoples south of the Sahara developed their own religious systems, and these formed the basis of much of their social and cultural life. Today, the indigenous religions, modified by colonial and postcolonial experience, continue to exist alongside Christianity and Islam and to play an important role in daily existence.

African traditional religions are closely tied to ethnic groups. Hence it may be said that there are as many different "religions" as there are ethnic language groups, which number over seven hundred south of the Sahara. There are, however, many similarities among the religious ideas and practices of major cultural and linguistic areas (e.g., Guinea Coast, central Bantu, Nilotes), and certain fundamental features are common to almost all African religions. Although these features are not unique to Africa, taken together they constitute a distinctively African pattern of religious thought and action.

Historical Background. Except for the most recent colonial and precolonial past, there is little evidence concerning the early history of African religions. Because of the conditions of climate and habitation, archaeological remains have been discovered at only a few places in eastern, western, and southern Africa, and the cultural contexts of these finds are largely unknown. It was once supposed that the various contemporary hunting-gathering, agricultural, and pastoral societies in Africa developed from a few basic cultural systems, or civilizations, each with its own set of linguistic, racial, religious, economic, and material cultural characteristics. Thus the early cultural and religious history of African societies was seen in terms of the interaction and intermixture of these hypothetical cultural systems, producing the more complex cultural and religious patterns of today. But it is now recognized that elements of language, race, religion, economics, and material culture are not so closely related as was assumed and that the early cultural systems were too speculatively defined. Hence historical reconstruction on these grounds has been abandoned.

Nevertheless, recent research has been able to bring to light important evidence concerning the early phases of religion in certain areas. The rock paintings of southern Africa, which date mostly from the nineteenth century but also from 2000 and 6000 and 26,000 BP, appear to represent a continuous tradition of shamanism practiced by the San hunters and their ancestors. The paintings depict the ritual acts and visionary experiences by which the shamans governed the relationships between human beings, animals, and the spirits of the dead. These relationships lay at the core of San society, and the rock paintings may well record practices that date from the earliest times in southern Africa. [*See* Khoi and San Religion.]

When agriculture began to spread south of the Sahara around 1500 BCE, an important religious development accompanied the gradual change from hunting-gathering to agricultural economies. This was the emergence of territorial cults, organized around local shrines and priests related to the land, crop production, and rain. These autochthonous cults provided political and religious leadership at the local level and also at the clan and tribal level. In central Africa the oral tradition and known history of some territorial cults date back five or six centuries and have been the key to historical reconstruction of religion in this area.

When ironworking penetrated sub-Saharan Africa in 400-500 CE, it gave rise to a number of myths, rites, and symbolic forms. Throughout West Africa ironmaking, hunting, and sometimes warfare formed a sacred complex of rites and symbols under the tutelage of a culture hero or deity.

In northern Nigeria over 150 terra-cotta figures have been found dating from at least 500 BCE to 200 CE, the earliest known terra-cotta sculpture in sub-Saharan Africa. This sculpture, known as Nok sculpture after the site at which it was first found, consists of both human and animal figures. Although it is likely that these pieces had religious significance, either as grave goods or as ritual objects (or both), their meaning at present is entirely unknown.

The famous bronze heads of Ife, Nigeria, date from the twelfth to fifteenth centuries and may be distantly related to Nok sculpture. The sixteen naturalistic Ife heads were found in the ground near the royal palace at Ife. The heads have holes to which beards and crowns were attached. Each head may have represented one of the founders of the sixteen city-states that owed allegiance to Ife, and each may have carried one of the sixteen crowns. Among the Yoruba, the "head" *(ori)* is the bearer of a person's destiny, and the "head" or destiny of a king was to wear the crown. The crown was the symbol of the sacred *ase*, or power of the king, which the crown or the head itself may have contained.

Wherever kingship arose in Africa during the thirteenth to fifteenth centuries, it became a dominant part of the religious system. The rulers, whether sacred or secular, generally attained total or partial control of the preexisting territorial cults above the local level. Most kings were regarded as gods or as the descendants of gods and were spiritually related to the fertility of the land and to the welfare of the people. Even in Buganda in central Uganda, where they did not have such mystical powers, the kings were regarded as sacred personages. It is now recognized that the institution of sacred kingship, which was once thought to be derived from ancient Egypt because of some general similarities with sub-Saharan kingships, was independently invented in various places in the African continent, not only in Egypt.

From the seventeenth to early nineteenth centuries, there is evidence of two types of development: an increase in spirit possession and healing cults, generally known as cults of affliction, and an emphasis upon the concept of the supreme being. The emergence of popular healing cults seems to have been linked to a breakdown in local political institutions and to contact with outside forces and new diseases.

General Characteristics. Common to most African religions is the notion of the imperfect nature of the human condition. Almost every society has a creation myth that tells about the origins of human life and death. According to this myth, the first human beings were immortal; there was no suffering, sickness, or death. This situation came to an end because of an accident or act of disobedience. Whatever the cause, the myth explains why sickness, toil, suffering, and death are fundamental to human existence.

The counterpart to this idea is the notion that the problems of human life may be alleviated through ritual action. They do not promise personal salvation in the afterlife or the salvation of the world at some future time. Through ritual action misfortunes may be overcome, sicknesses removed, and death put off. The assumption is that human beings are largely responsible for their own misfortunes and that they also possess the ritual means to overcome them. The sources of suffering lie in people's misdeeds, or sins, which offend the gods and ancestors, and in the social tensions and conflicts that can cause illness. The remedy involves the consultation of a priest or priestess who discovers the sin or the social problem and prescribes the solution, for example, an offering to appease an offended deity or a ritual to settle social tensions.

At the theological level, African religions contain both monotheistic and polytheistic principles. The concept of a supreme God is widely known in tropical Africa and existed before the coming of Christianity and Islam. The idea of a supreme God expresses the element of ultimacy, fate, and destiny, which is part of most African religions. As the ultimate principle behind things, the supreme God usually has no cult, images, temples, or priesthood.

In contrast, the lesser gods and the ancestor spirits, which often serve as the supreme being's intermediaries, are constantly involved in daily affairs. People regularly attend their shrines to pray, receive advice, and make offerings, usually in the form of animal sacrifice. Thus African religions are both polytheistic and monotheistic, depending upon the context. In matters concerning the ultimate destiny and fate of individuals and groups, the supreme God may be directly involved. In matters concerning everyday affairs, the lesser gods and ancestors are more immediately involved.

From the point of view of African religion, a human being consists of social, moral, spiritual, and physical components united together; the individual is viewed as a composite totality. That is why social conflicts can make people physically ill and why moral misdeeds can cause spiritual misfortunes. Rituals that are aimed at restoring social and spiritual relationships are therefore deemed to affect people's physical health and well-being. A person's life is also seen to pass through several stages. One of the important tasks of traditional religion is to move people successfully through the major stages of life: birth, puberty, marriage, elderhood, death, ancestorhood. Each phase has its duties, and rites of passage make sure that people know their responsibilities. Other rituals divide the year into seasons and give the annual cycle its form and rhythm.

Ritual authorities, such as diviners, prophets, priests, and sacred kings, serve a common religious purpose: the communication between the human world and the sacred world.

Mythology: Creation, Heroes, and Tricksters. African myths deal primarily with the origin of mankind and with the origin of social and ritual institutions. They explain both the structure of the world and the social and moral conditions of human life. Most creation myths posit an original state of cosmic order and unity, and they tell of a separation or division that arose between divinity and humanity, sky and earth, order and disorder, which resulted in human mortality. These myths explain why human beings are mortal by telling how they became mortal. Thus they presuppose that humanity was originally immortal and passed into a state of mortality. The myths usually say that mortality was the result of a deliberate or accidental misdeed committed by a human being, often a woman, or an animal.

Some myths explain the origins and significance of death by showing that it is essentially linked to the agents of human fertility and reproduction: women, food, sexuality, and marriage. The Nuer, who live near the Dinka, say that in the beginning a young girl descended from the sky with her com-

> Whatever his particular form, the trickster image expresses the fundamental ambiguities of human life. He is both fooler and fooled, wily and stupid, maker and unmade.

panions to get food and that she fell in love with a young man whom she met on earth. When she told her companions that she wished to stay on earth, they ascended to the sky and spitefully cut the rope leading to the ground, thus severing the means for immortality. The myth reflects the choice that every Nuer woman must make in marriage when she leaves her childhood home and friends and goes to live with her husband.

Another widely known myth among Bantu-speaking peoples explains the origin of death in terms of a message that failed. In the beginning the creator god gave the message of life to a slow-moving animal (e.g., chameleon, sheep). Later, he grew impatient and gave the message of death to a faster

animal (e.g., lizard, goat). The faster animal arrived first and delivered his message, and death became the lot of mankind. In this myth the natural slowness and quickness of the two animals determine the outcome, making death a natural and inevitable result. Other myths emphasize the similarity between death and sleep and the inability of human beings to avoid either. According to this myth, the creator god told the people to stay awake until he returned. When he came back they had fallen asleep and failed to hear his message of immortality. When they woke up he gave them the message of death.

Hero myths tell how important cultural discoveries, such as agriculture and ironmaking, originated and how major social and ritual institutions, such as marriage, village organization, kingship, priesthood, and cult groups, came into existence. Often the founding deeds of the hero are reenacted in ritual with creative and transforming effect. Many African deities are said to have been heroes who died and returned in spiritual form to serve as guardians and protectors of the people.

Another type of myth is the trickster story. Trickster stories range from fable-like satirical tales to accounts of world creation. The trickster may exist only as a character in stories or as an active deity. Whatever his particular form, the trickster image expresses the fundamental ambiguities of human life. He is both fooler and fooled, wily and stupid, maker and unmade. A seemingly misguided culture hero, the trickster introduces both order and disorder, confusion and wisdom into the world. His comic adventures convey a widely recognized African principle: life achieves its wholeness through the balance of opposites. The trickster's acts of disorder prepare the way for new order; death gives way to birth. In general, African trickster mythology expresses optimism about the paradoxes and anomalies of life, showing that cleverness and humor may prevail in a fundamentally imperfect world. [*See* Tricksters, *article on* African Tricksters.]

Monotheism and Polytheism. African religions combine principles of unity and multiplicity, transcendence and immanence, into a single system; thus they generally contain both monotheistic and polytheistic aspects. Often there is also the concept of an impersonal power, such as the Yoruba concept of *ase* by which all things have their being. In different contexts each of these principles may come to the fore as the primary focus of religious thought and action, although each is part of the larger whole.

As ultimate principles, many supreme Gods are like African sacred kings: they reign but do not rule. They occupy the structural center of the system but are rarely seen or heard, and when they are it is only indirectly. For this reason the supreme Gods belong more to the dimension of myth than to that of ritual. However, the world would cease to exist without them, as would a kingdom without the king. Thus, in many instances the supreme God is the one, omniscient, omnipotent, transcendent, creator, father, and judge. From the time of the first contact with Muslims and Christians, Africans recognized their supreme Gods to be the same as the God of Christianity and Islam.

Divinity and Experience. Unlike the supreme beings, which remain in the background of religious life, the lesser divinities and spirits are bound up with everyday experience. These powers are immanent, and their relation to human beings is reciprocal and interdependent. Hence they require many shrines, temples, priests, cult groups, images, rituals, and offerings to facilitate their constant interactions with people.

Often associated with elements of nature, such as lightning, rain, rivers, wild animals, and forests, they may be understood as images or symbols of collective psychological and social realities that resemble these natural phenomena in their powerful, dangerous, and beneficial aspects. The most common form of encounter between the human and the divine is spirit possession, the temporary presence of a deity or spirit in the consciousness of a person. Spirit possession is an integral part of religion and has a well-defined role within it. In some societies possession is regarded as an affliction, and the aim is to expel the intruding god or spirit so that the suffering person may resume a normal life. Usually the cause is some misdeed or sin that must be redressed through ritual action. In other societies possession is a more desirable phenomenon. People may regularly seek to come closer to their gods, even to identify personally with them, through possession-inducing dances that have beneficial psychological and social effects.

Mediums, Diviners, and Prophets. Sometimes a divinity may wish to form a special relationship with an individual. The god usually makes his desire known through an illness. Indeed, sickness is sometimes seen as a sacred calling that is manifested in the form of a possession. The cure will take the form of apprenticeship and initiation into the service of the deity, and it will place the person in lasting debt to society. Henceforth, the chosen man or woman becomes professionally established at a shrine and becomes the god's medium, devoted to the healing of afflicted people. He or she treats illnesses and social problems through mediumship séances.

In Africa the distinction between mediums, diviners, priests, and prophets is a fluid one, and transition from one to the other is made easily. Generally, diviners and mediums are spiritual consultants, whereas prophets are leaders of men. Prophets may go directly to the people with programs for action and initiate religious and political movements. For this reason prophets are often sources of religious and political change. In circumstances of widespread political unrest, priestly mediums may develop prophetic powers and initiate socio-religious change. This occurred during colonial times in East Africa: traditional prophets became leaders of political resistance in parts of Sudan, Uganda, Tanzania, and Zimbabwe. In Kenya, the Mau Mau resistance movement was also significantly implemented and sustained by traditional ritual procedures.

A more indirect form of spiritual communication involves the use of divination equipment, such as cowrie shells, leather tablets, animals entrails, palm nuts, a winnowing basket, small animal bones, and animal tracks. After careful interrogation of the client, the diviner manipulates and interprets his material in order to reach a diagnosis. Such systems work according to a basic typology of human problems, aspirations, and casual factors. The diviner applies this framework to his client's case by manipulating his divination apparatus.

Diviners and mediums employ methods of treatment that usually involve a mixture of psychological, social, medical, and ritual means. Many illnesses are regarded as uniquely African in nature and hence as untreatable by Western methods. They include cases of infertility, stomach disorders, and a variety of ailments indicative of psychological stress and anxiety. The causes of such illnesses are generally attributed to social, spiritual, or physiological factors, either separately or in some combination.

Ritual: Sacrifice and Rites of Passage. Ritual is the foundation of African religion. The ritual sphere is the sphere in which the everyday world and the spiritual world communicate with each other and blend into one reality. Almost every African ritual is therefore an occasion in which human experience is morally and spiritually transformed. The two most important forms of African ritual are animal sacrifice and rites of passage.

The sacrifice of animals and the offering of vegetable foods accomplish a two-way transaction between the realm of divinity and the realm of humanity. The vegetable offerings and animal victims are the mediating principles. They are given to the gods and spirits in return for their favors. Animal sacrifice is especially prominent because the life of the victim and its blood are potent spiritual forces. By killing the victim, its life is released and offered to the gods for their sustenance in exchange for their blessings, especially in the case of human life that is threatened. Through invocations, prayers, and songs, human desires are made known, sins are confessed, and spiritual powers attracted to the sacrificial scene.

Sacrifices are performed on a variety of occasions in seasonal, curative, life-crisis, divinatory, and other kinds of rituals, and always as isolable ritual sequences. Sacrifices that involve the sharing of the victim's flesh confirm the bond between the people and the spiritual power, to which a portion is given. At the social level, sacrifices and offerings bring together individuals and groups and reinforce common moral bonds. Fundamentally, blood sacrifice is a reciprocal act, bringing gods and people together in a circuit of moral, spiritual, and social unity. In this way sacrifice restores moral and spiritual balance—the healthy equilibrium between person and person, group and group, human beings and spiritual powers—which permits the positive flow of life on earth. As a sacred gift of life to the gods, sacrifice atones for human misdeeds and overcomes the human impediments to the flow of life; thus it is one of the keystones of African religions.

Rites of passage possess a threefold pattern consisting of rites of separation, transition, and reincorporation. The most fundamental rite of passage is that which initiates the young into adulthood. In this way a society not only moves its young into new social roles but also transforms them inwardly by molding their moral and mental disposition toward the world. A Nuer boy simply tells his father that he is ready to receive the marks of *gar*, six horizontal lines cut across the forehead. His socialization is already assumed. In many West African societies the rite is held in the confines of initiation groves where the initiates are given intensified moral and religious instruction. These rites may take place over a period of years and are organized into men's and women's initiation societies, such as the Poro society among the Senufo of the Ivory Coast, Mali, and Upper Volta. By means of stories, proverbs, songs, dances, games, masks, and sacred objects, the children and youths are taught the mysteries of life and the values of the adult world. The rites define the position of the initiates in relation to God, to society, to themselves, and to the world. Some form of bodily marking is usually done, and circumcision and clitoridectomy are widely practiced. Generally, the marks indicate that the transition to adulthood is permanent, personal, and often painful and that society has successfully imprinted itself upon the individual.

Persons, Ancestors, and Ethics. African concepts of the person, or self, share several characteristics. Generally, the self is regarded as composite and dynamic; it consists of several aspects, social, spiritual, and physical, and admits of degrees of vitality. The self is also open to possession by divinity, and its life history may be predestined before birth. After death, the self becomes a ghost, and in the course of several generations it becomes merged with the impersonal ancestors. Each of these aspects and potentialities of the person, sometimes misleadingly described as multiple souls, is important in different contexts and receives special ritual attention.

In West African societies, the success or failure of a person's life is explained by reference to a personal destiny that is given to the individual by the creator god before birth. To realize the full potential of one's destiny, frequent recourse to divination is required to discover what destiny has in store and to ensure the best outcome.

At death, new problems of social and spiritual identity arise. When a family loses one of its members, especially a senior male or female, a significant moral and social gap occurs. The family, together with other kinsmen, must close

this gap through funerary procedures. At the same time the deceased must undergo spiritual adjustment if he or she is to find a secure place in the afterlife and remain in contact with the family left behind. This is accomplished by the construction of an ancestor shrine and sometimes also by the making of an ancestor mask and costume.

The carved images of the ancestors are not intended to be representational or abstract but conceptual and evocative. By means of stylized form and symbolic details the image conveys the characteristics of the ancestor and also helps to make the spiritual reality of the ancestor present among the

> **To realize the full potential of one's destiny, frequent recourse to divination is required. . . .**

people. Thus the carved ancestral icon enables the world of the living and the world of the living dead to come together for the benefit of human life

Superior to living kings and elders, the ancestors define and regulate social and political relations. It is they who own the land and the livestock, and it is they who regulate the prosperity of the lineage groups, villages, and kingdoms. Typically, when misfortune strikes, the ancestors are consulted through divination to discover what misdeeds have aroused their anger. The ancestors are also regularly thanked at ceremonial feasts for their watchful care, upon which the welfare of the community depends.

Not everyone may become an ancestor. Only those who led families and communities in the past as founders, elders, chiefs, or kings may serve in the afterlife as the social and political guides of the future. By contrast, ordinary people become ghosts after death. Such spirits require ritual attention at their graves, but they are finally sent away to "rest in peace," while the more positive influence of the ancestors is invoked generation after generation.

The sufferings and misfortunes brought by the gods and ancestors are punishments aimed at correcting human behavior. By contrast, the sufferings and misfortunes caused by witches and sorcerers are undeserved and socially destructive; they are unequivocally evil. The African concept of evil is that of perverse humanity: the human witch and sorcerer. The African image of the witch and sorcerer is of humanity turned against itself.

For the most part witchcraft accusations in Africa flourished in contexts where social interaction was intense but loosely defined, as between members of the same extended family or lineage group. In such cases witchcraft was sometimes thought to be an inherited power of which the individual might be unaware until accused. In other instances it existed in the form of deliberately practiced sorcery procedures, so-called black magic, which was effective at long range and across lineage groups. [*See* Witchcraft, *article on* African Witchcraft.]

Shrines, Temples, and Religious Art. Shrines and temples serve as channels of communication with the spiritual world, and they may also serve as dwelling places of gods and spirits. Shrines may exist in purely natural forms, such as forest groves, large rocks, rivers, and trees, where gods and spirits dwell. Every African landscape has places of this kind that are the focus of ritual activity. Man-made shrines vary in form. A simple tree branch stuck into the ground is a shrine for a family ghost among the Nuer. A large rectangular building serves as the ancestor stool chapel among the Ashanti. Whatever its form, an African shrine acts as a symbolic crossroads, a place where paths of communication between the human and spiritual worlds intersect. If the shrine serves as a temple, that is, as the dwelling place of a spiritual being, it is built in houselike fashion, like the "palaces" of the royal ancestors in Buganda. Such shrines usually have tow parts: the front section, where the priest and the people gather, and the rear section, where the god or spirit dwells. An altar stands between the two and links them together.

African ritual art, including masks, headdresses, sacred staffs, and ceremonial implements, is fashioned according to definite stylistic forms in order to express religious ideas and major social values. The carved *chi wara* antelope headdress of the Bamana of Mali represents the mythic farming animal, called Chi Wara, that originally showed the people how to cultivate, and the antelope shape of the headdress expresses the qualities of the ideal farmer: strength, industriousness, and graceful form. Male and female headdresses are danced together, while women sing songs to encourage the young men's cultivation groups to compete with each other for high agricultural achievements. The Gelede masks of the Yoruba honor the spiritual power of women, collectively known as "our mothers." This power is both creative (birth) and destructive (witchcraft). The Gelede mask depicts the calm and serene face of a woman and expresses the feminine virtue of patience. The face is often surmounted by elaborately carved scenes of daily activity, for the spiritual power of "the mothers" is involved in every aspect of human life.

BIBLIOGRAPHY

Abimbola, 'Wande. *Ifá: An Exposition of Ifá Literary Corpus*. Ibadan, 1976.

Abrahamsson, Hans. *The Origins of Death*. Uppsala, 1951.

Awolalu, J. Omosade. *Yoruba Beliefs and Sacrificial Rites*. London, 1979.

Beattie, John, and John Middleton, eds. *Spirit Mediumship and Society in Africa*. New York, 1969.

Booth, Newell S., Jr., ed. *African Religions: A Symposium*. New York, 1977.

Dammann, Ernst. *Die Religionen Afrikas*. Stuttgart, 1963. Translated into French as *Les religions de l'Afrique* (Paris, 1964).

Evans-Pritchard, E. E. *Nuer Religion*. Oxford, 1956.

Fortes, Meyer, and Robin Horton. *Oedipus and Job in West African Religion*. Cambridge, 1984.

Griaule, Marcel. *Dieu d'eau*. Paris, 1948. Translated by Robert Redfield as *Conversations with Ogotemmêli* (London, 1965).

Janzen, John M. *Lemba, 1650-1930: A Drum of Affliction in Africa and New World*. New York, 1982.

Karp, Ivan, and Charles S. Bird, eds. *Explorations in African Systems of Thought*. Bloomington, Ind. 1980.

Lewis-Williams, David. *The Rock Art of Southern Africa*. Cambridge, 1983.

Lienhardt, Godfrey. *Divinity and Experience: The Religion of the Dinka*. Oxford, 1961.

Mbiti, John S. *African Religions and Philosophy*. New York, 1969.

Parrinder, Geoffrey. *West African Religion*. 2d ed., rev. London, 1961.

Ranger, T. O., and Isaria N. Kimambo, eds. *The Historical Study of African Religion*. Berkeley, 1972.

Rattray, R. S. *Ashanti*. Oxford, 1923.

Ray, Benjamin C. *African Religions: Symbol, Ritual, and Community*. Englewood Cliffs, N. J., 1976.

Schoffeleers, J. Matthew, ed. *Guardians of the Land: Essays on Central African Territorial Cults*. Gwelo, 1979.

Temples, Placide. *La Philosophie bantoue*. Elizabethville, 1945. Translated by Margaret Mead as *Bantu Philosophy* (Paris, 1959).

Turner, Victor. *The Forest of Symbols: Aspects of Ndembu Ritual*. Ithaca, N. Y., 1967.

Vogel, Susan M., ed. *For Spirits and Kings: African Art from the Paul and Ruth Tishman Collection*. New York, 1981.

Zahan, Dominque. *Religion, spiritualité, et pensée africaines*. Paris, 1970. Translated by Kate E. Martin and Lawrence W. Martin as *The Religion, Spirituality, and Thought of Traditional Africa* (Chicago, 1979).

Zuesse, Evan M. *Ritual Cosmos: The Sanctification of Life in African Religions*. Athens, Ohio, 1979.

BENJAMIN C. RAY

Modern Movements

Over seven thousand new religious movements exist in sub-Saharan Africa. Together they claim more than thirty-two million adherents. These movements have arisen primarily in areas where there has been intensive contact with Christian missionary efforts. However, the groups that are generally referred to as the new religious movements of sub-Saharan Africa are those that have emerged since the early 1930s. Some of these movements actually began earlier but did not gain momentum until that time. Many have persisted in largely the same form that they took fifty years ago. Others have gone underground and resurfaced, often retaining their initial doctrinal and membership requirements.

With reference to doctrinal base, organizational structure, and geographic distribution, three types of new religious movements may be designated: (1) indigenous or independent churches, (2) separatist churches, and (3) neotraditional movements. These groups have taken different forms in central, southern, West and East Africa. They blend elements of African traditional religion with those of the introduced religions, Christianity and Islam. Many of these groups arose in response to the loss of economic, political, and psychological control engendered by colonial domination.

The impetus for the growth of new African religious movements can be traced to five basic factors: (1) The disappointment of local converts with the premises and outcomes of Christianity led to the growth of prophetic, messianic, and millenarian groups. (2) The translation of the Bible into African vernaculars stimulated a reinterpretation of scripture and a spiritual renewal in Christian groups. (3) The perceived divisions in denominational Christianity and its failure to meet local needs influenced the rise of separatist churches and community-based indigenous churches. (4) The weakness of Western medicine in the face of psychological disorders, epidemics, and natural disasters stimulated concern with spiritual healing among new African religious movements. (5) The failure of mission Christianity to break down social and cultural barriers and generate a sense of community led to the strengthening of social ties in small, sectarian groups. In general, the new African churches have tried to create a sense of community and continuity in the new, multiethnic urban environment and in the changing context of the rural village.

Indigenous Churches. Indigenous churches are groups that have been started under the initiative of African leaders outside the immediate context of missions or historic religions. In recent decades, membership was estimated at nearly 15 percent of the Christian population of sub-Saharan Africa. Also called independent churches, these groups have devised unique forms of social and political organization and have developed their own doctrines. These churches were initially a response to the political and religious situation of colonialism. Groups as diverse as the Harrist church in the Ivory Coast, the Aladura church in Nigeria, the Kimbanguist church in Zaire, and the Apostolic movements of Zimbabwe may be classified as indigenous churches. Nevertheless, each of these churches has a distinctive doctrinal thrust and response to government control. These groups also vary on the organizational level depending on the extent of their local appeal and the demographic and cultural composition of their membership. Indigenous churches may be divided into three specific subtypes: prophetic, messianic, and millenarian. All three sub-types evidence doctrinal innovation, efforts at spiritual renewal, and a reaction against the presence of mission churches.

Prophetic indigenous churches. Prophetic groups are tied to the influence of an individual prophet. They generally have a strong central organization and an emphasis on healing. One of the most important prophetic churches in central Africa is the Kimbanguist church, which has more than four million adherents in Zaire. Triggered by Simon Kimbangu's initial healing revival in 1921, this movement grew and increased in intensity after its founder's death in 1951. The

group has transformed from a prophetic protest movement to an established church and is currently one of the four officially recognized religious bodies in Zaire. The Kimbanguist church was admitted to the World Council of Churches in 1969 and resembles many other prophetic movements that have acquired legitimacy in postindependence Africa.

Churches with similar origins and leadership structures that focus on a prophetic figure are found in other regions: for example, Alice Lenshina's Lumpa church in Zambia; the Harrist church in Liberia, the Ivory Coast, and Ghana; and the Zionist churches of South Africa. Common to all these movements is an emphasis on spiritual and physical health.

In 1954, the Lumpa church was begun by Alice Lenshina Mulenga in the Copperbelt of Northern Rhodesia (present-day Zambia). Lenshina claimed at the time that she had died and come back to life with a religious calling. She was viewed as a visionary prophetess and healer. Like Kimbangu, she attracted many former mission catechists and teachers to her movement. Naming her church Lumpa (the "highest" or the "supreme" in Bemba), Lenshina promised health and a new life to those who forsook traditional magic and witchcraft to follow her. Her followers resisted government taxation and political authority; as a result, the cohesiveness of the Lumpa movement was ultimately broken through political struggles and in 1970 its followers were expelled from the country.

Toward the end of 1913 William Wade Harris, a Liberian of Grebo origin claimed that the Angel Gabriel had appeared to him in a vision and instructed him to spread the Christian message as God's prophet. Traveling to the Ivory Coast and the Gold Coast (now Ghana), Harris propagated his message of divine revelation, faith healing, and an improved life for Africans. Although he spent only a short time in the Ivory Coast, the number of his adherents grew rapidly. Within a few

> **Of the approximately three thousand indigenous churches in South Africa, three-quarters . . . emphasize spiritual healing and the charismatic powers of their leaders.**

months of the movement's inception Harris had baptized an estimated 120,000 people. After Harris's death in 1929 the prophet John Ahui and the faith healer Albert Atcho continued to expand the Harrist church in the Ivory Coast. Between 1955 and 1961 especially it grew and attracted many former Roman Catholics. In 1973, the Harrist church celebrated its sixtieth anniversary in the Ivory Coast with governmental support and recognition. Like the Kimbanguists, the Harrists have proceeded successfully from a prophetic movement to an official church with national appeal.

The Aladura movement in Nigeria has often been compared with the Harrist church. It is one of several prophetic movements that developed in western Nigeria in the late 1920s in strong reaction against Anglican mission control. These groups emphasized spiritual healing, divine revelation, prophecy, and self-reliance. The term *aladura* ("people of prayer") refers to several related groups, drawn largely from the Yoruba-speaking population, who share certain spiritual characteristics. The Aladura movement continues to grow and has now established branches outside Africa.

Of the approximately three thousand indigenous churches in South Africa, three-quarters are churches that emphasize spiritual healing and the charismatic powers of their leaders. These churches are classified as Zionist because they trace their origins to John Alexander Dowie's Evangelical Christian Catholic Church, which was established in 1896 in Zion City, Illinois. The concept of Zion represents utopian spiritual liberation. Members of these churches place considerable emphasis on divine healing, spiritual revelations, and testimony. Concentrated heavily among the Zulu and Swazi peoples of South Africa, these Zionist churches have diverse doctrinal and ritual formats but are linked by their focus on the prophetic and healing powers of charismatic leaders. Colorful, almost theatrical, ceremonies are typical of these groups.

Messianic indigenous churches. Resembling the prophetic movements in their origins, messianic churches crystallize around a single figure who is regarded as a new messiah. Messianic groups occasionally experience a crisis and a decline in their appeal after the founder dies or disappears. The prophetic message remains closely tied to the leader and his or her charismatic attraction. Movements of this type include the Mai Chaza church and the Apostolic Church of John Masowe in Zimbabwe and the Isaiah Shembe movement in South Africa.

Mai ("mother") Chaza was initially a member of the Methodist church in Southern Rhodesia (now Zimbabwe). She became seriously ill in 1954 and her followers believed her to have died. Upon recovery, Mai Chaza reported that while she was dead she had communicated with God and had received the gift of healing. She sought out the blind, the crippled, and those possessed by alien spirits. Mai Chaza believed that she was a messenger of God and compared herself to Moses and Jesus. To the members of her movement she was both a savior and a miracle worker.

Mai Chaza died in 1960 leaving no heirs. A Malawian adherent called Mapaulos began to perform extraordinary healings in her name. He assumed the title *vamutenga* ("he who is sent from heaven") and continued the mission of healing at Mai Chaza's center, Guta ra Jehovah, or the City of God. After Mai Chaza's death her followers referred to her as Mai Chaza Jesus, the black messiah and savior of Africa. Like Lenshina, Mai Chaza was seen as a chief and medium.

The extent to which women have been leaders and founders of prophetic and messianic groups—including the Lumpa church, the Aladura movement, and the Mai Chaza group—is particularly noteworthy. The influence of women in these movements may be viewed as a reaction to the ecclesiastical authority of men in the mission churches.

Several other movements in southern Africa have had similar messianic tendencies. In October 1932 an African prophet calling himself John the Baptist, and otherwise known as Shoniwa or Johane Masowe, began to preach among the Shona people in the Hartley district of Southern Rhodesia. Like Mai Chaza, he claimed to have been resurrected from death and consequently endowed with healing and prophetic powers. Masowe moved from village to village baptizing those who accepted his message of healing and a better life.

Masowe's movement combined prophetic, messianic, and millenarian elements. He exhorted his followers to abstain from wage labor for the colonial authorities and to resist colonial religious structures and doctrine. Under political pressure the Apostolic Church of John Masowe, whose members are also known as *vahosanna* (the "hosannas") or as Basketmakers, moved to the Korsten suburb of Port Elizabeth, South Africa, in 1943. In 1960 his church was expelled from South Africa as a political threat. In the meantime many of his followers had already started to move northward, to Northern and Southern Rhodesia. Masowe actually died (according to news accounts) in Ndola, Zambia, in 1973, leaving behind messianic hopes and a millenarian promise of freedom. The group has not chosen a leader to replace him.

Isaiah Shembe (c. 1870-1935) was a self-proclaimed Zulu prophet who founded the amaNazaretha church in South Africa. A man of compelling personality and significant influence, Shembe was widely known as a holy man and divine healer. He is said to have portrayed himself as a messianic figure, a liberator, and a messenger of God. He established a village, Ekuphakameni, to which his followers flocked for festivals, faith healing, and meditation. After his death, the prophet was succeeded by his son, Johannes Galilee Shembe, or Shembe II, who is believed to have inherited his father's charismatic gifts but not his full messianic status.

The messianic movements typified by these three groups center on the personalities and myths of leadership established by their founders. Their doctrinal innovations are rooted in the messages of hope, healing, and possibility offered by their founders. Even after the death of the founders, their messianic traits have been perpetuated as a means of bolstering the faith of the followers and providing a challenge to European missionary efforts.

Many new African religious movements have millenarian tendencies. One of the most widespread millenarian movements in sub-Saharan Africa is the Church of the Watchtower, or Kitawala. Linked to the American Jehovah's

Witnesses, who began missionary activities in Africa at the beginning of the twentieth century, several Watchtower movements arose across central and southern Africa. Among the best known was the Watchtower group formed by Elliot Kamwana of Nyasaland (modern-day Malawi) in 1908. Since 1910 other groups have formed in eastern Zaire, in Zambia, and in South Africa. All these groups believe in the autonomy of religion apart from political control and hope for a coming spiritual golden age.

Separatist Churches. Separatist groups are those that have broken off from established Christian churches or Islamic congregations. In this sense, separatist churches are distinct from indigenous groups that have never been affiliated with a mission body. They may, nevertheless, also be examined in terms of the prophetic, messianic, and millenarian categories that have been used to classify the indigenous churches. Among separatist groups in the Roman Catholic tradition are the Jamaa, the Catholic Church of the Sacred Heart, and the Legio Maria.

The Jamaa movement was started by a Belgian Franciscan, Placide Tempels. Jamaa ("family" in Swahili) emphasizes the importance of the nuclear family, individuality, personhood, fecundity, and love. Officially, certain Jamaa affiliates have remained within the Roman Catholic church. By 1953, however, Jamaa had developed an independent organizational structure. As the group became more established, it was closely scrutinized by the Catholic authorities and was eventually discouraged and repressed in certain areas.

The Legio Maria, or Legion of Mary, began as an offshoot of the Irish Roman Catholic lay organization of the same name. Its origin in Kenya dates from 1963. By the early 1970s the group had over ninety thousand members, primarily drawn from the Luo ethnic group. Among the Bemba of Zambia, a similar group, the Catholic Church of the Sacred Heart, broke away from the established missions in 1955. Each of these separatist movements has emphasized brotherhood, community, and the use of an original form of worship in the local vernacular.

The East African Revival movement, or Balokole ("the Saved Ones"), stands as a primary example of a Protestant separatist church. It began as a charismatic renewal within the Protestant churches of Uganda, Kenya, Tanganyika, and Ruanda-Urundi. Initially part of the activities of the former Rwanda Mission, an evangelical branch of the Anglican Church Missionary Society, the revival had become by 1935 a separatist church with indigenous organizational characteristics and worship practices. It has emphasized conversion, testimony, and aggressive proselytizing.

Neotraditional Movements. Other religious movements have maintained the form of traditional cults. They include the secret societies of West Africa within the Poro-Sande complex; reformative cults, such as the Bwiti in Gabon; and newer groups, such as the Église de Dieu de Nos Ancêtres (Church of the God of Our Ancestors) in southwestern Zaire. In each case the neotraditional cults preserve aspects of traditional religion in a new social and cultural context.

Originally formed as a protective warriors' society, the Poro cult initiates young men into adulthood by instructing them in ritual and social obligations. It continues to be an important form of religious, social, and political organization among the Mande-speaking peoples of Sierra Leone, Liberia, and the Ivory Coast. The counterpart society, the Sande or Bundu, prepares women for their social obligations and shares political authority with the Poro society. The societies themselves remain outside mission control and make no official attempt to incorporate Christian practices.

In contrast, the Bwiti cult, originating at the turn of the century among the Fang of Gabon, attempted to revitalize a traditional ancestral cult by incorporating rituals and beliefs of neighboring people. At a later date elements of Christian theology and symbolism were added. By the 1950s Bwiti cult leaders had adopted the pattern of the messianic prophetic leadership characteristic of some of the indigenous churches. The group was also known as the Église des Banzie (Church of the Initiates) and had nearly ten thousand Fang members by 1965. In recent years the cult has drawn its membership from dissident Roman Catholic catechists and from Protestants, incorporating elements of their beliefs into its new doctrines and religious symbols.

The Église de Dieu de Nos Ancêtres, appearing in the 1950s in the Belgian Congo, has followed a similar pattern. This group combines belief in Luba ancestral spirits and traditional religion with elements of Christianity. Like the Bwiti cult, the Église de Dieu de Nos Ancêtres has moved away from a small cultic organization to the formal model of a church in response to the pressures of urban migration and cultural change experienced by its members.

In all cases these groups have had to confront the increasing pressures of missionary presence and the influence of Christianity or Islam in their areas of operation.

The Future of the New African Religions. A major debate in the field centers on the extent to which new movements may be considered stable over time. It has been argued that the new religions develop through a process of schism and renewal. They break away from the influence of both mission and newly established churches to develop bonds of family and community that are particularly strong at the local level. Utopian ideals and fundamentalist interpretations of scripture reinforce the initial break and the sense of spiritual renewal in these groups.

Although some of the new Christian groups of Africa originate in ethnically homogeneous areas, most emphasize the potential of, and even the necessity for, cultural exchange through overarching symbols and doctrine. These processes of cultural combination and reconstruction allow the members of new religious movements to acquire a reflective stance toward their immediate problems and to preserve past cultural ideas. The neotraditional, millenarian, and revitalistic responses resolve social and cultural clashes through blending old and new interpretations of the sacred.

At the same time a question of stable leadership and its institutionalization arises. As the discussion of prophetic and messianic churches emphasizes, the death or demise of a leader creates an important challenge to the viability of a group. Thus schism continues to threaten the new religious movements even after they have established autonomy from missions or historic churches. This problem has led some scholars to speculate that the new African religions are unstable and highly mutable and that their appearance merely marks one phase of social or religious protest in the emergence of Africa's new nation-states. Nevertheless, historical evidence suggests that these groups have considerable longevity in spite of their shifting leadership structures and new membership. The persistence of such groups as the Bwiti cult and the Kitawala movement—from the turn of the century—follows this trend.

Another important tendency contributing to the eventual stability of the new religious movements is the shift toward ecumenism. Between 1969 and 1981, several well-established indigenous churches affiliated themselves with the World Council of Churches in an attempt to become international in outlook through an association with worldwide ecumenical movements. They include the Church of the Lord Aladura in Nigeria, the Kimbanguist church in Zaire, the African Israel Nineveh Church in Kenya, and the African Church of the Holy Spirit in Kenya.

Local voluntary associations formed by these churches often attempt to retain the doctrinal autonomy of each group while developing joint fund-raising, educational, and cultural

> ## Schism continues to threaten the new religious movements. . . .

efforts. This type of cooperation is evident in the African Independent Churches' Association, formed in 1965 in South Africa, and in similar ecumenical councils and associations that have formed in central and East Africa. Although such associations do not solve the problem of internal group conflict and leadership succession, they do appear to reinforce cooperation and political stability within the independent church movement as a whole.

Cultural and Social Contribution of Africa's New Religions. Many of Africa's new religious movements, from the 1920s to the present, have started as religions of the oppressed and have become movements of protest. Several of these groups, including the early Watchtower movement

inspired by Kamwana in Nyasaland, Kimbanguism in Zaire, and the Harrist church of the Ivory Coast, have also led to or supported movements of political liberation and national independence. The close relationship between political and religious symbols of freedom has contributed to this development.

The social influences of Africa's new religions are not limited to the political sphere. The new images and ideals of community promoted by these groups offer alternative modes of existence to their members and to others who come into contact with the new movements. Through tightly knit communities and internal support structures, Africa's new religions establish claims to loyalty. Culturally they promise a religion that is not alien to the masses. Nevertheless, some of the contemporary groups also emphasize the ultimate attainment of rewards promised in orthodox doctrines. This goal is accomplished through isolation and strict personal adherence to the Bible or the Qur'an. These literal interpretations of sacred writings serve to develop a new fabric of ideas through which individuals attempt to create alternative types of social relationships. In some instances this return to fundamentalist doctrines within the African context has also had the effect of triggering charismatic renewals and new forms of proselytizing within established mission churches.

By means of Africa's new religious movements, conventional cultural and symbolic forms are revived and reinterpreted. Taken from their original source, some of these religious beliefs have been applied to secular life. The ultimate viability of these new religions may, in fact, reside in the capacity of their beliefs and practices to become integrated into the mainstream of modern Africa's social and cultural life. Thus, the greatest impact of these groups may take place through cultural diffusion and sharing rather than through the spread and historical evolution of any particular movement.

BIBLIOGRAPHY

Balandier, George. *The Sociology of Black Africa.* New York, 1970. Historical and sociological account of the colonial situation in sub-Saharan Africa, using the concepts of colonial domination and acculturation as points of departure; useful for understanding the origins of the new African religions.

Barrett, David B. *Schism and Renewal in Africa: An Analysis of Six Thousand Contemporary Religious Movements.* Nairobi, 1968. An analysis of six thousand new African religious movements in thirty-four nations. Contains useful historical and statistical information, provides an excellent general introduction to the new African religions, and examines the causes of, and conditions for, their emergence. Includes extensive bibliographic materials and a comprehensive index of new religious movements and their leaders.

Barrett, David B., ed. *World Christian Encyclopedia: A Comparative Study of Churches and Religions in the Modern World,* A.D. 1900-2000. New York, 1982. A worldwide overview of Christian churches and new religions. Contains an update of the editor's previous statistical estimates for new African religious movements, with some descriptive and photographic materials.

Bellman, Beryl L. *Village of Curers and Assassins: On the Production of Fala Kpelle Cosmological Categories*. The Hague, 1975. An ethnographic account of the Poro and Sande secret societies and various subsidiary societies as they operate in a Fala Kpelle village in northern Liberia; illuminating discussion of the Fala Kpelle belief system as it relates to the secret societies.

Breidenbach, Paul. "The Woman on the Beach and the Man in the Bush: Leadership and Adepthood in the Twelve Apostles Movement of Ghana." In *The New Religions of Africa*, edited by Bennetta Jules-Rosette, pp. 99-115. Norwood, N.J., 1979. A brief account of the history, doctrine, and rituals of the Twelve Apostles movement, an offshoot of the Harrist church in Ghana.

Cheater, Angela P. "The Social Organization of Religious Difference among the Vapostori weMaranke. *Social Analysis* 7 (1981): 24-49. Case study of the Maranke Apostles (Vapo-stori) of Msengeze district, Zimbabwe, with relationship to socioeconomic status, social networks, kinship, and church hierarchy; argues that the group studied is undergoing a process of secularization as evidenced by a decline in organized religious activities.

Daneel, M. L. *Old and New in Southern Shona Independent Churches*, vol. 1, *Background and Rise of the Major Movements*. The Hague, 1971. A detailed historical account of the background and rise of Shona independent churches in Zimbabwe with a discussion of the relationship of these churches to European missions. Spirit-type and Ethiopian churches are distinguished in terms of their history, rituals, and doctrines.

Dillon-Malone, Clive M. *The Korsten Basketmakers: A Study of the Masowe Apostles, an Indigenous African Religious Movement*. Lusaka, 1978. A comprehensive study of the Apostolic Church of John Masowe. Discusses the early history of the church, its development in Zimbabwe, South Africa, and Zambia, and its rituals and doctrine. Compares movement with other Shona indigenous churches.

Fabian, Johannes. *Jamaa: A Charismatic Movement in Katanga*. Evanston, Ill., 1971. An in-depth study of the history and social organization of the Jamaa movement, with a discussion of its beliefs, indoctrination practices, and innovations in worship. The author has compiled reliable firsthand ethnographic data describing the movement.

Fernandez, James. "African Religious Movements: Types and Dynamics." *Journal of Modern African Studies* 2 (1964): 531-549. An analysis of several types of African religious movements in relationship to the processes of syncretism and acculturation; a clear discussion of the organizational and doctrinal changes in different movement types over time.

Fernandez, James W. *Bwiti: An Ethnography of the Religious Imagination in Africa*. Princeton, 1982. Detailed analysis of the history, ritual, and symbolism of the Bwiti cult among the Fang of Gabon; contains in-depth accounts of ceremonies, reproductions of sermon texts, and an extensive glossary.

Haliburton, Gordon Mackay. *The Prophet Harris*. London, 1971. Background of the Grebo prophet William Wade Harris and discussion of the growth of his movement in the Ivory Coast and the Gold Coast from 1913 to 1922; brief analysis of the legacy of Harris's teachings and the more recent converts to the movement.

Jules-Rosette, Bennetta. *African Apostles: Ritual and Conversion in the Church of John Maranke*. Ithaca, N.Y., 1975. A study of the Apostolic Church of John Maranke, an indigenous church with over 300,000 adherents in Zaire, Zambia, and Zimbabwe; a detailed account of the Zairian branch of the church and a discussion of ritual and the conversion process based on firsthand ethnographic data; comprehensive bibliography on the movement.

Köbben, A. J. F. "Prophetic Movements as an Expression of Social Protest." *International Archives of Ethnography* 49, no. 1 (1960): 117-164. Overview of prophetic movements and nativistic cults in Africa, Asia, and the Americas, containing a typology of several movements and a discussion of their causes and doctrines. Extensive bibliography on several movement types.

Lanternari, Vittorio. *The Religions of the Oppressed: A Study of Modern Messianic Cults*. Translated by Lisa Sergio. New York, 1963. An analysis of diverse cults and churches of Africa, Asia, and the Americas as movements of religious protest and responses to colonial domination; comprehensive coverage of diverse twentieth-century movement types.

Martin, Marie-Louise. *Kimbangu: An African Prophet and His Church*. Translated by D. M. Moore. Oxford, 1975. History of the Kimbanguist movement in central Africa from 1918 to 1960, with discussion of responses to colonial authority, doctrine and ritual of the movement, and political attitudes of the followers. Comprehensive bibliography on the Kimbanguist movement.

Peel, J. D. Y. *Aladura: A Religious Movement among the Yoruba*. London, 1968. The best-known survey of Nigeria's Aladura groups, including the Cherubim and Seraphim Society and the Christ Apostolic Church; comprehensive history of the independent church movement in Nigeria.

Perrin Jassy, Marie-France. *Basic Community in the African Churches*. Translated by Sister Jeanne Marie Lyons. Maryknoll, N.Y., 1973. An anthropological examination of daily religious activity among the Luo of Tanzania. Focuses on role of local community in the life of several East African indigenous churches, including the Legio Maria church.

Rotberg, Robert. "The Lenshina Movement of Northern Rhodesia." *Rhodes-Livingstone Journal* 29 (1961): 63-78. A brief account of the early history of Alice Lenshina Mulenga's Lumpa movement in Northern Rhodesia from 1954 through 1956; discussion of early membership, doctrine, and the importance of the movement.

Sundkler, Bengt. *Bantu Prophets in South Africa*. 2d ed. Oxford, 1961. Among the first and best-known historical and sociological surveys of indigenous churches among the Zulu of South Africa; contains detailed accounts of church history, doctrine, and ritual. The second edition adds a chapter on Zulu religious movements between 1948 and 1960.

Sundkler, Bengt. *Zulu Zion and Some Swazi Zionists*. Lund and Oxford, 1976. An update of Sundkler's previous material on Zionist movements among the Zulu with additional information on Swazi independent churches; overlaps with the 1961 volume but addresses more recent debates in the field of new religious studies in South Africa.

Taylor, John V., and Dorothea Lehmann. *Christians of the Copperbelt*. London, 1961. An analysis of several indigenous church movements in northern Zambia, including the Watchtower (Kitawala) movement and the Lumpa church; contains a summary of the worship practices, doctrine, and local impact of these movements.

Turner, Harold W. *Bibliography of New Religious Movements in Primal Societies*, vol. 1, *Black Africa*. Boston, 1977. A comprehensive bibliography designed to update and revise three earlier bibliographic compilations on new African religious movements; cites published materials together with doctoral dissertations, master's theses, and some undergraduate papers.

Walker, Sheila S. "Women in the Harrist Movement." In *The New Religions of Africa*, edited by Bennetta Jules-Rosette, pp. 87-97. Norwood, N.J., 1979. A discussion of the history and social organization of the Deima church of Marie Lalou, an offshoot of the Harrist church in the Ivory Coast, and a general analysis of the role of women in the Harrist movement.

Walker, Sheila S. *The Religious Revolution in the Ivory Coast: The Prophet Harris and the Harrist Church*. Chapel Hill, N.C., 1983. An account of the growth and social organization of the Harrist church in the Ivory Coast from 1913 to 1973, including the early history of the movement, a summary of beliefs and doctrine, and an update on new developments; incorporates and updates Haliburton's material.

West, Martin E. "Independence and Unity: Problems of Co-operation between African Independent Church Leaders in Soweto." *African Studies* 33 (1974): 121-129. A brief discussion of local-level cooperation and ecumenical tendencies in South Africa's independent churches; covers important issues and debates in the field.

West, Martin E. *Bishops and Prophets in a Black City: African Independent Churches in Soweto, Johannesburg.* Cape Town, 1975. A sociological analysis of the interrelationships among indigenous churches in Soweto based on two surveys of the area. Describes the churches in detail and explains the reasons for their rise and appeal in an urban environment.

Wilson, Bryan R. *Magic and the Millennium: A Sociological Study of Religious Movements of Protest among Tribal and Third-World Peoples.* New York, 1973. A comprehensive sociological study of new religious movements in Africa and the Americas. Discusses movement types, causes, and outcomes, emphasizing healing and spirit-type movements. Includes an extensive bibliography on new religious movements in the Third World.

BENNETTA JULES-ROSETTE

History of Study

The classical world had little knowledge of Africa and its peoples, let alone of its religions. With the obvious exceptions of Egypt and, to a limited extent, of the coastal strip facing the Mediterranean, Africa was alleged to be inhabited by fabulous, not wholly human creatures.

Though the Romans ruled the whole of northern Africa for centuries, their interest in the local religions seems to have been as slight as that of the Greeks. In the eleventh century, *al-Bakri* likewise mentions a mountain tribe in southern Morocco that allegedly adored a ram. However, neither he nor the other Arab travelers and geographers of the Middle Ages who visited the Maghrib and the Sudan and described their political organization, trade, and customs tell us much about their religion.

The Portuguese discovery of sub-Saharan Africa's coastal regions in the fifteenth century gave Europeans the first opportunity to observe a number of African societies; however, it took a surprisingly long time before any accurate report of their religions reached Europe. The earliest writings that contain some mention of religious matters are by Duarte Pacheco Pereira (1505-1506) and Valentim Fernandes (1506-1507), which seem to refer to the coastal tribes of what are now the Republic of Guinea and Sierra Leone. The following quotation is given by Yves Person in his essay "The Coastal Peoples," included in volume 4 of UNESCO's *General History of Africa*, edited by D. T. Niane (London, 1984):

The people paid honour to idols carved out of wood; the chief divinity was called Kru; they also practised worship of the dead, who were embalmed before burial. "It is usual to make a memento for all those who die: if he was a notable person, an idol is made resembling him; if he was merely a commoner or a slave, the figure is made of wood and is put in a thatched house. Every year, sacrifices of chickens or goats are made to them."   (Person, in Niane, 1984, p. 307)

In 1483, Portuguese navigator Diogo Cão reached the mouth of the Kongo; by 1491, missionaries had joined the explorers and mariners. These missionaries were devoted far more to converting the people than to understanding the traditional creeds. The most widely read report on central Africa was Filippo Pigafetta's *Relazione del Reame di Congo* (1591; reprint, Milan, 1978), which was based on the notes of Duarte Lopes, a Portuguese merchant who had lived there for many years before he was appointed an envoy to the pope by the converted Kongo king, Alvaro I. According to this report, the natives of Loango "adore whatever they like, holding the greatest god to be the Sun as male, and the Moon as female; for the rest, every person elects his own Idol, which he adores according to his fancy." Of the Kongo proper an even more improbable picture is drawn: "Everyone worshipped whatever he most fancied without rule or measure or reason at all," and when all the religious relics were collected to be destroyed at the summons of the now-baptized king, Afonso I, it is reported that "there was found a huge quantity of Devils of strange and frightful shape," including "Dragons with wings, Serpents of horrible appearance, Tigers and other most monstrous animals... both painted and carved in

> **"Everyone worshipped whatever he most fancied without rule or measure or reason at all."**

wood and stone and other material." This is an unlikely collection, judging from what we know of Kongo sculpture.

In 1586, the Portuguese author Santos wrote of another Bantu-speaking ethnic group, the Yao of Mozambique, in less derogatory terms: "They acknowledge a God who, both in this world and in the next, measures the retribution for the good or evil done in this" (cited by Andrew Lang, *The Making of Religion*, London, 1898). This view, however, again does not tally with what we know today of Yao traditional beliefs.

A century later, Giovanni Antonio Cavazzi's *Istorica descrizione de' tre' regni Congo, Matamba Angola* (Bologna, 1687) marks a slight improvement in accuracy, recording in almost correct form the name for the supreme being of certain central African peoples, Nzambia-mpungu. His reports, however, retain the derogatory view of his predecessors:

Before the light of the Holy Gospel dispelled superstition and idolatry from the minds of the Congolese, these unhappy people were subject to the Devil's tyranny.. . . [Apart from Nzambi] there are other gods, inferior to him, but nevertheless worthy of homage; to these too, therefore, cult and adoration are due.. . . The pagans expose a certain quantity of idols, mostly of wood, roughly sculpted, each one of which has its own name. (my trans.)

An early account of Khoi religion was casually given by the Jesuit priest Gui Tachard in his *Il viaggio di Siam de' padri gesuiti mandati dal re di Francia all'Indie, e alla China* (Milan, 1693). He writes:

These people know nothing of the creation of the world, the redemption of mankind, and the mystery of the Holy Trinity. Nevertheless they adore a god, but the cognition they have of him is very confused. They kill in his honor cows and sheep, of which they offer him meat and milk in sign of gratitude toward this deity that grants them, as they believe, now rain and now fair weather, according to their needs. (my trans.)

Throughout the eighteenth and early nineteenth centuries, information on native African religions continued to stagnate at these poor levels. As a consequence of the slow pace of exploration into the African interior, reports focused on the peoples of the coastal western and central areas and on the eastern and northern countries that were permeated, or at least influenced, by Islam. The observers were mostly navigators, explorers, tradesmen, and naturalists who had no ethnological grounding and only a marginal interest in religious matters. Missionaries, who might have been better qualified to investigate the people's beliefs, were usually biased by a general attitude of contempt or pity for the "heathen" and by a deeply rooted ethnocentrism.

Missionary Reports. In the second half of the nineteenth century, missionaries began to show more care and tolerance in the study of native beliefs. An example of this can be found in the works of the Italian abbot Giovanni Beltrame (*Il Sennaar e lo Sciangallah*, Verona and Padua, 1879; *Il fiume bianco e i Denka*, Verona, 1881), whose attempts to evangelize the tribes of the upper Nile dated back to 1854-1855. Beltrame published, both in the original language and in translation, the splendid chant with which the Dinka celebrate the creative actions of their supreme being known as Dendid, or Dengdit ("great rain"). He also noticed that the Dinka have two verbs, *ciòr* and *lam*, to express the act of praying to God and a separate verb, vtiég, used to indicate "to pray to a man." Moreover, he noted that verbs related to God are always used in the present tense. Hence the Christian expression "God has always been and always will be" is rendered.

Another example of this new attitude can be found in *Among the Primitive Bakongo* (London, 1914) and other works by the English missionary John H. Weeks, who lived for thirty years among the riverine natives of the Kongo and provided a realistic picture of the local religion. He not only recognized the nature of Nzambi as a supreme being but equated this deity with the God of Christianity.

An even more authoritative and sophisticated contribution was given a few years later by another Protestant missionary, Henri A. Junod, who lived among the Thonga of coastal Mozambique from 1907 onward. Whereas Weeks had declared in his preface that he had "no particular leaning towards any school of anthropologists," Junod, by the time he collected his earlier materials for publication in 1927, was fully aware of the theoretical discussions in which anthropologists and historians of religion were engaged and was impressed by the fashionable tenets of evolutionism and the requirements of comparativism. Having found among the Thonga the coexistence of beliefs in a sky god and in ancestral spirits, he attempted to assess the respective antiquity of the two apparently conflicting creeds. To do so, he compared these beliefs with others found among southern Bantu-speaking societies. He followed the assertion of W. Challis and Henry Callaway that the sky was prayed to by the forebears of the Swazi and Zulu before the worship of ancestor spirits was introduced. Though Junod called this change "evolution," he realized that this succession was contrary to the schemes of orthodox evolutionism. In an appendix to the 1936 French edition of *The Life of a South African Tribe* (London, 1912), he states that the two sets of creeds could be parallel among the Bantu speakers. At the same time, however, he conjectures, on the basis of psychological considerations, a chronological sequence—naturism, animism, causalism, euhemerism—that partly accepts Nathan Sderblom's hypotheses as stated in his *Das Werden des Gottesglaubens* (Leipzig, 1916). Junod's ambiguous conclusions reflect the case of an experienced researcher trying to combine personally observed realities with the theoretical speculations of others.

Comparative Syntheses: The Quest for Origins. The decades during which missionaries collected most of our information on African religions coincided with the flourishing of a series of ambitious comparative works that attempted to establish the logical, if not chronological, succession of religious ideas in the world. An early prototype of such attempts was Charles de Brosses's *Du culte des dieux fétiches* (Paris, 1760), which compared black African beliefs and rites with those of ancient Egypt. Several of his data and theses were used in Auguste Comte's six-volume *Cours de philosophie positive* (Paris, 1830-1842). The rise of evolutionist theories in the second half of the nineteenth century—a period that saw the intensive exploration of central Africa—encouraged an increasing use of examples from peoples encountered for the first time in addition to those known through previous literature. These examples were often indiscriminately used to represent instances of the stages of "primitive" religion: fetishism, ancestor worship or euhemerism, animism, totemism, idolatry, polytheism, and so on.

These various evolutionary theories were based only in part on artfully selected African materials in order to support the different authors' theses, and their value has been polemical rather than interpretative. They have served to synthesize previously known facts in attractive combinations and to bring them jointly to the broad public's attention. Examples of such comparative syntheses are John Lubbock's *Origin of Civilisation* (London, 1870), Grant Allen's *The Evolution of the Idea of God* (London, 1897), R. R. Marett's *The Threshold of Religion* (London, 1909), and parts of James G. Frazer's immense work.

One of the earliest comprehensive ethnographic surveys is Theodor Waitz's *Anthropologie der Naturvölker* (Leipzig, 1859-1872). In the second of its six volumes, Waitz discusses African blacks and their kin. Drawing from the investigations of field observers, Waitz writes:

We reach the amazing conclusion that several Negro tribes . . . in the development of their religious conceptions are much further advanced than almost all other savages [*Naturvölker*], so far that, though we do not call them monotheists, we may still think of them as standing on the threshold of monotheism.
(Waitz, 1860, p. 167)

Other eminent evolutionists, such as Lubbock and Herbert Spencer, included some African tribes in the list of backward societies as surviving examples of primitive atheism or as having no religious ideas whatsoever. This categorization was promptly refuted in Gustav Roskoff's *Das Religionswesen der rohesten Naturvölker* (Leipzig, 1880) and in Albert Réville's *Les religions des peuples non-civilisés* (Paris, 1883). This latter work, which was widely read at the time, deals separately with the peoples of different continents. The author's position represents a compromise, as it were, between the derogatory judgments of the early evolutionists and the gradual rehabilitation of African religious ideas. Réville writes:

Naturism, the cult of personified natural features, sky, sun, moon, mountains, rivers, etc., is general of African soil. . . . Animism, the worship of spirits detached from nature and without a necessary link with natural phenomena, has taken a preponderant and so to speak absorbing role. Hence the Negro's fetishism, a fetishism that little by little rises to idolatry. . . . Nevertheless one should not omit, I shall not say a trait, but a certain tendency to monotheism, easily emerging from this confused mass of African religions. Undoubtedly, the African native is not insensitive to the idea of a single all-powerful God.
(Réville, 1883, vol. 1, pp. 188-190)

Such admissions, which clearly contradict the widespread evolutionary theories of the time, were largely ignored in academic circles of the English-speaking world until they were systematically assembled in Andrew Lang's *The Making of Religion* (London, 1898; 3d rev. ed., 1909). Just as Réville had spoken contemptuously of "the incoherence and undisciplined imagination of the Negro," so Lang referred to Africans as belonging to the "low races" and as the "lowest savages." This view did not prevent him, however, from expressing his final opinion of their traditional religion "as probably beginning in a kind of Theism, which is then superseded, in some degree, or even corrupted, by Animism in all its varieties" (Lang, 1909, p. 304).

> **The world's earliest religious ideas are to be found among African Pygmies. . . . representatives of the world's most archaic, or "primeval," culture.**

Lang's assertion of the antiquity of African beliefs in a high god ran parallel to a similar conviction, within a different scientific milieu, in the emerging notion of *Kulturkreiselehre*, or "doctrine of culture circles." One of the founders of this school of thought, Wilhelm Schmidt, published an early introduction to his monumental work, *Der Ursprung der Gottesidee*, at the same time as the publication of the third edition of Lang's *The Making of Religion*; but almost half a century passed before the twelve-volume work appeared (Münster, 1912-1955). Three volumes are dedicated to the peoples of Africa. Schmidt's much debated thesis of a worldwide primeval monotheism that was corrupted by later trends in successive cultural "cycles" cannot be discussed here. It should be noted, however, that according to Schmidt, the remnants of the world's earliest religious ideas are to be found among African Pygmies, considered to be monotheistic and surviving representatives of the world's most archaic, or "primeval," culture.

Independently of the acceptance or rejection of this theory, Schmidt's presentation of the data marks a striking contrast to that of his predecessors. Rather than arbitrarily assembling data from all sources according to a specific topic, he systematically collected and grouped data in reference to specific ethnic groups. Whenever possible, a summary of information on the geographical and anthropological position of a given tribe is followed by data that are arranged in separate sections devoted to beliefs, myths, sacrifices, prayers, conceptions of the soul, eschatology, ancestor worship, and so on. The materials that were assembled by Schmidt remain to this day an invaluable quarry of carefully sifted and well-ordered information. The arduous field investigation of nomadic forest hunter-gatherers such as the Pygmies, in which Schmidt was particularly interested, also should be credited to his influence. He incessantly encouraged, advised, and sponsored fellow missionaries such as O. Henri Trilles, Peter Schumacher, and especially Paul Schebesta, keeping abreast of their ongoing investigations. The final results of this research were synthesized by Schmidt in 1933 (see Schmidt, 1912-1955, vol. 3) and eventually published in Schebesta's masterly *Die Bambuti Pygmäen vom Ituri* (Brussels, 1938-1950), the third volume of which is dedicated entirely to religion, and in Martin Gusinde's *Die Twiden* (Vienna and Stuttgart, 1956), a concise book remarkable for its scientific objectivity and exhaustive bibliography.

Among the relevant works written by this generation of researchers on the general themes of African religion are those devoted to mythology. Alice Werner's *Myths and Legends of the Bantu* appeared in 1933 and was followed, in 1936, by Hermann Baumann's *Schöpfung und Urzeit des Menschen im Mythus der afrikanischen Völker*, a true masterpiece of erudition by a leading German ethnologist.

Raffaele Pettazzoni, a staunch adversary of Schmidt's theory of primeval monotheism, also made a valid contribution to the study of African religious ideas with his four-volume *Miti e leggende* (Turin, 1948-1963). The first volume remains the fullest and most aptly annotated collection of myths from all parts of Africa. In the work that concluded his long career as a historian of religions, *L'onniscienza di Dio* (Turin, 1955), Pettazzoni devotes the first chapter to sub-Saharan Africa. The book closed the century-long controversy among specialists, documenting from a wholly nonconfessional viewpoint the worldwide distribution of beliefs in a supreme being.

Tribal Monographs. With the development of colonialism an important new type of literature appeared and spread rapidly: the tribal monograph. Based on the image of the "closed society," this type of book often ignored both cross-cultural comparison and diachronic developments. It described all aspects of a single tribe or ethnic group, starting with geographical distribution, racial characteristics, and linguistic classification and analyzing all facts of its social structure and culture, including religion. The first decades of the twentieth century produced a particularly rich series of such books, which contributed greatly, though often at a superficial level, to the knowledge of countless African religions. The authors were mostly colonial administrators (or district commissioners) and missionaries but also included scientists, such as linguists and anthropologists. Many of the following have become classics: A. C. Hollis's *The Masai* (Oxford, 1905) and *The Nandi* (Oxford, 1909); Diedrich Westermann's The *Shilluk People* (Berlin, 1912); Günter Tessmann's *Die Pangwe* (Berlin, 1913); Alberto Pollera's *I Baria e i Cunama* (Rome, 1913); Gerhard Lindblom's T*he Akamba in British* East Africa

(2d ed., Uppsala, 1920); Edwin W. Smith and Andrew Dale's two-volume The *Ila-speaking Peoples of Northern Rhodesia* (London, 1920); Heinrich Vedder's two-volume *Die Bergdama* (Hamburg, 1923); John Roscoe's *The Baganda* (London, 1911), The *BaKitara or Banyoro* (Cambridge, 1923), and others; and Louis Tauxier's *Le noir du Soudan* (Paris, 1912) and *Religion, mœurs et coutumes des Agnis de la Côte d'Ivoire* (Paris, 1932). During this period, the Belgians, under the direction of Cyrille van Overbergh, planned and, to a large extent, accomplished the publication of a "Collection de Monographies Ethnographiques" (1907-1913), which was intended to cover the whole range of tribes of the Belgian Congo (present-day Zaire).

The scientific merits of these books vary. On principle, and on the positive side, they respect the scientific requirements summarized in Edwin W. Smith's *African Ideas of God: A Symposium* (London, 1950): "Sociologically speaking, African religion is one aspect of African culture. No one element can be exhaustively studied and understood in isolation from the rest" (p. 14). On the other hand, even before that rule was stated, the progress of studies had clearly shown the religions of preliterate peoples to be far too complex to be adequately condensed in a mere chapter of a general monograph.

Before World War II, researchers had been almost exclusively European. The most significant American contribution was Melville J. Herskovits and Frances S. Herskovits's *An Outline of Dahomean Religious Belief* (Menasha, Wis., 1933). Generally, educated Africans had not yet written about or begun to vindicate their own traditional religions. However, in his well-known *Facing Mount Kenya* (London, 1938), with an appreciative but critical preface by Bronislaw Malinowski, Jomo Kenyatta devoted two chapters to the religion of his Kikuyu; but, here again, his analysis was only a minor part of an all-embracing monograph. The most significant exception was The *Akan Doctrine of God* (London, 1944) by J. B. Danquah, which is devoted entirely to the exposition of the religious creeds of the writer's own nation, Ashanti. A more appropriate title for the book would be *The Ashanti Doctrine* because Danquah, an Ashanti, was concerned with the creeds, epistemology, and ethics of his own powerful tribe and had little regard for the corresponding, but not identical, systems of other branches of the Akan linguistic family (e.g., Anyi, Baule, Brong, Nzema, etc.). Dense with original quotations, subtle though sometimes odd philological arguments and comparisons, and sophisticated speculation, the book struck a decidedly new note in the concert of previous literature on the subject. It left the reader, however, uncertain as to whether it was a true picture of widespread Ashanti beliefs or the outcome of the author's personal philosophical and theological reflections.

Anthologies and New Outlooks. In the postwar years a few scholars devised anthologies that arranged side-by-side, condensed accounts of several religions. Well-known examples are *African Ideas of God: A Symposium* (London, 1950), edited by Edwin W. Smith in collaboration with a team of qualified Protestant missionaries, and *Textes sacrés d'Afrique noire* (Paris, 1965), edited by Germaine Dieterlen, which contains a preface by a leading African intellectual, Amadou Hampaté Ba, and a series of essays by lay ethnologists.

The topics examined in these anthologies include cosmology, epistemology, and a general view of the universe, as is the case in *African Worlds* (London, 1954), edited by Daryll Forde, then director of the International African Institute. Forde assembled a series of essays by anthropological authorities such as Mary Douglas on the Lele of Kasai, Günter Wagner on the Abaluyia of Kavirondo, Jacques J. Maquet on Rwanda, Kenneth Little on the Mende of Sierra Leone, and the Ghanaian scholar and politician K. A. Busia on the Ashanti.

Two of the contributors to *African Worlds*, the French ethnologists Marcel Griaule and Germaine Dieterlen, who jointly wrote the essay on the Dogon, deserve special mention on account of the novelty and sophistication of the cosmological and religious systems they were able to investigate and reveal. The team of Africanists led by Griaule, which included Solange de Ganay and Dieterlen, had been conducting intermittent field research for fifteen years among the Dogon of what is now Mali. One day in 1946, Griaule was unexpectedly summoned by a venerable blind sage called Ogotemmli and, in the course of a month's conversations, obtained from him the revelation of a whole mythological and cosmological system. The complexity of this system far exceeded knowledge of Dogon beliefs that had been previously acquired by the team. The ensuing book, *Dieu d'eau* (Paris, 1948), translated by Robert Redfield as *Conversations with Ogotemmêli* (London, 1965), was received in academic circles with mixed feelings of bewilderment, admiration, and perplexity. Some critics judged that it was inspired by the personal speculations of a single native thinker or, at best, that it was a summary of esoteric teachings that were restricted to a choice minority of the initiated. Griaule had foreseen such doubts and, in the preface to his book, had declared that Ogotemmêli's ontological and cosmological views were understood and shared by most adult Dogon, and that the rites connected with them were celebrated by the whole local population.

Although Dieterlen's *Essai sur la religion bambara* (Paris, 1951) revealed a comparable wealth of symbols, proclivity to abstractions, and original systematization of the universe among the Bambara, these are by no means identical to the Dogon conceptions. This distinction confirms the general fact that even neighboring tribes that share a similar cultural background and, occasionally, belong to the same ethnolinguistic family have developed and maintained independent,

and often markedly different, religious systems. Dieterlen's book is also instructive as an example of a new methodology of investigation that resulted in a striking difference between her account and that published only a generation earlier in Louis Tauxier's *La religion bambara* (Paris, 1927), which was based on field data collected not merely by Tauxier but also by two other experienced Africanists, J. Henry and Charles Monteil. Aware that these discrepancies might cause either the objectivity of the various scholars or the general reliability of native informants to be questioned, Dieterlen benevolently commented on the conscientiousness of her predecessors, if not on the coherence of their reports.

Knowledge of African religions is also drawn from works devoted to myths, proverbs, oral literature, social and political structures, and most aspects of a people's culture. The work that most stimulated a reconsideration of African creeds in the postwar years was *La philosophie bantoue* (Elisabethville, Belgian Congo, 1945), written by a Belgian Franciscan friar, Placide Tempels. This book is not merely a synthesis of religious beliefs and rites; it also discusses criteriology, ontology, "wisdom," metaphysics, psychology, jurisprudence, and ethics. It stresses that in all these realms, the universe is seen as a system of "vital forces," originating in God and radiating to spirits, human beings, animals, plants, and even minerals. These forces can be benign or hostile, strengthened or weakened, as they incessantly influence one another. The idea of the cosmos as a hierarchy of forces was surely not new. What was new was that Tempels seems to have derived this system from his missionary experiences and from conversations with the Luba rather than from sociological or philosophical literature. He quotes no literature throughout the book, with the one exception of Diedrich Westermann's *Der Afrikaner heute und morgen* (Essen, 1934), in which he was surprised to find the fundamental principles of his own theory. Furthermore, Tempels felt sure that these concepts were shared by all Bantu-speaking peoples.

Recent Decades. With the collapse of the colonial system tribal monographs have dwindled and have been replaced tendentially by anthropological monographs and articles that analyze religious beliefs and practices within the broader framework of whole sociocultural systems. In *Theories of Primitive Religion* (Oxford, 1965), Evans-Pritchard writes: "These recent researches in particular societies bring us nearer to the formulation of the problem of what is the part played by religion, and in general by what might be called non-scientific thought, in social life" (p. 113). In cases such as John Middleton's *Lugbara Religion* (London, 1960) and Godfrey Lienhardt's work on the Dinka, *Divinity and Experience* (Oxford, 1961), religion is the central topic; in others, such as Antonio Jorge Dias and Margot Dias's four-volume *Os Macondes de Moçambique* (Lisbon, 1964-1970), it is dealt with only peripherally. In *Una societ* *guineana: Gli Nzema* (Turin, 1977-1978), a two-volume work, Vinigi Grottanelli discusses the Nzema of Ghana, the southernmost branch of the Akan group, who, in spite of nominal conversion to Christianity, have remained staunchly faithful to their traditional "fetishist" beliefs and cults, and I analyze through microbiographical accounts the impact of religion on everyday life.

As the general trend of scientific interests shifted from an abstract theological to a positive social and psychological context, attempts to make worldwide comparisons of religions and to ascertain the relative age of religious conceptions have gradually been abandoned, while detailed studies of specific traits, symbols, and rites are becoming more frequent. One subject, divination, has retained the attention of field anthropologists. Victor Turner's *Ndembu Divination: Its Symbolism and Techniques* (Manchester, 1961) and William R. Bascom's *Ifa Divination* (Bloomington, Ind., 1969), which examines the Yoruba of Nigeria, are the most valuable contributions in this area since Schilde's work. Knowledge has also been acquired concerning the notion of sacrifice, which is the subject of five consecutive issues of the series "Systèmes de pensée en Afrique noire" (1976-1983), published by the École Pratique des Hautes Études, Paris.

By far the most numerous and popular, though not scientifically faultless, sidelights illuminating African religions come from the domain of art history. A growing number of studies on the symbolic meaning and ceremonial use of masks, figurines, and other ritual accessories are shedding an indirect light on vital aspects of African mythology and religious rites, particularly those of West and central Africa. Dominique Zahan's *Antilopes du soleil* (Vienna, 1980), on antelope figures in the sculpture of western Sudanese peoples, is one of the finest among such books. More generally, the fifteen-volume Italian *Enciclopedia universale dell'arte* (Rome, 1958-1967; translated as *Encyclopedia of World Art*, New York, 1959-1983) devotes constant attention to the visual aspects of African religions. [*See* Iconography, *article on* Traditional African Iconography.]

Not only the traditional systems of creeds but also the syncretic, pseudo-Christian, and prophetic movements that continue to attract millions of Africans have been studied with growing attention by both missionaries and anthropologists. An impressive example of these studies is Valeer Neckebrouck's *Le peuple affligé* (Immensee, Switzerland, 1973), which includes a discussion of these movements in Kenya and neighboring countries.

The many books and articles devoted to the religions of single tribes, with their great wealth of details and depth of analysis, have made summaries of the subject a difficult task. The most popular syntheses remain Geoffrey Parrinder's *West African Religion* (London, 1949) and *African Traditional Religion* (London, 1954). In the postwar years, native Africans themselves have written similar surveys, such as E.

Bolaji Idowu's *African Traditional Religion* (London, 1973) and John S. Mbiti's *African Religions and Philosophy* (New York, 1969) and Introduction to African Religion (London, 1975). These contributions are more valuable when restricted to the religion of the writer's own nation, such as The *Religion of the Yorubas* by J. Olumide Lucas (London, 1948). The African scholar Alexis Kagame has pursued the critical reexamination of what Tempels had termed "Bantu philosophy," displaying a wealth of references and a soundness of method that makes his work, *La philosophie bantu comparée* (Paris, 1976), not only far superior to that of his predecessor but also a stimulating encouragement to further studies in this inexhaustible field.

BIBLIOGRAPHY

Reliable guidelines to the large corpus of African studies have been drawn by Charles H. Long in his bibliographic survey entitled "Primitive Religion," in *A Reader's Guide to the Great Religions*, 2d ed., edited by Charles J. Adams (New York, 1977).

VINIGI GROTTANELLI

AFRO-AMERICAN RELIGIONS

An Overview

The Legacy from Africa. Separated from kin, culture, and nation, African slaves of diverse origin could not re-create their religions in North America, but they did retain the fundamental perspectives and worldviews symbolized in their religions, even as they adopted religious traditions from Europeans, Native Americans, and other Africans and combined them in new, "creole" religions. In certain countries (e.g., Haiti, Cuba, and Brazil) the African character of black religious life is still obvious.

In contrast, the influence of Africa upon black religions in North America is more subtle and more difficult to observe. Two major factors help account for this divergence in Afro-American cultures: the differences between Roman Catholic piety and Protestant piety and the differences between patterns of slave distribution in colonial America. In Roman Catholic colonies, like Haiti, Cuba, and Brazil, the cult of the saints provided slaves with a convenient structure to both cover and support their worship of the gods of Africa. In British North America this support was lacking, because Protestants condemned the veneration of saints as idolatry.

The Colonial Period to the Civil War. In British North America during the colonial period, efforts to convert the slaves to Christianity did not begin until the eighteenth century and did not prove effective until the 1740s. During that decade, a series of religious revivals led significant numbers of slaves to accept Christianity. Many more would convert during the revivals at the turn of the century.

Abolition and other social causes. The abolition of slavery was the second great issue with which the Northern black churches and clergy grappled. The most radical attacks against slavery, like those of David Walker (1785-1830) and Henry Highland Garnet (1815-1882), were couched in religious apocalyptic language. In these and other polemics, Afro-Americans began to articulate in print their theological

> ## The abolition of slavery was the second great issue with which the Northern black churches and clergy grappled.

reflections upon their history in North America. Many of the leading black abolitionists were ministers. Besides antislavery movements, they were usually involved in the major social causes of the antebellum period: temperance, moral reform, and women's rights.

Religion under slavery. In the South, Christianity gradually reached more and more slaves during the decades immediately preceding the Civil War. Some slaves attended church with whites, while others, mainly those in urban areas, belonged to separate black churches. Many held their own prayer meetings on the plantations and small farms of the South. Sometimes these prayer meetings were attended by whites; others were held in secret at risk of severe punishment.

Emancipation and Reconstruction. During the Civil War, Northern missionaries, both white and black, journeyed to the South to educate the former slaves and to make them church members. Along with material assistance, the missionaries brought schools, to which the former slaves flocked in large numbers.

Transition: Post-Reconstruction to World War I. The period from the end of Reconstruction in 1877 to World War I was a period of tremendous transition for Afro-Americans. It was a period of the rise of white terrorism, Jim Crow laws, and the beginning of the "great migration" of rural blacks to cities in the South and North. The response of blacks to virulent racism, segregation, and urbanization was largely formulated through the churches, though increasingly voices other than those of the ministers were heard.

Despite the difficulties of the period, few Afro-Americans immigrated to Africa. They did migrate on a large scale within the United States, however—northward, westward, and especially from the country to the city.

Afro-Americans in an Urban Setting. During the twentieth century, urbanization had a tremendous impact upon black culture and religion. From the familiar rural setting, with its social intimacy and traditional values, a basically peasant people was transplanted into the unfamiliar surroundings of anonymous, impersonal, urban America. Crowded into ghettos in a hostile and foreign environment, black migrants sought security in the church.

Under the guidance of socially concerned ministers, some of the larger city churches developed elaborate social programs to help the migrants and other residents of the growing ghettos. The migrants themselves attempted to re-create the closeness of the small rural church by establishing new churches, usually in homes or rented storefronts. The house church and storefront church became familiar sites in urban black communities. In these new church structures, a new religious movement, Holiness-Pentecostalism, took root, though it was in fact a return to the emotionalism and ecstasy of the old-time religion that had waned in many Baptist and Methodist churches.

Urbanization also brought more black people than ever before into contact with Roman Catholicism. Through the mechanism of the parochial school, American blacks came to convert to Roman Catholicism for the first time in large numbers.

The most popular movement, however, was that of Marcus Garvey (1887-1940), a West Indian black whose Universal Negro Improvement Association (founded in 1914) united interest in Africa as a black Zion with the assertion of black racial pride. The association was itself a quasi-religious organization, with its own hymns, sermons, catechism, and baptismal service. At the same time, it enlisted widespread support among black ministers of various denominations.

Civil Rights and Black Power. As the movement for civil rights grew in the 1950s and 1960s, the black churches as the historic centers of social and political organization within the black community assumed leadership. But the involvement of particular congregations or individual ministers did not exhaust the participation of black religion in the movement. For many blacks, the movement itself was a religious movement, and they consciously drew upon the spiritual resonance of hymns, sermons, and biblical imagery to move the conscience of the nation. The classic example of the religious dimension of the civil rights struggle was the leadership of Baptist minister Martin Luther King, Jr. King's career and, in a different way, that of Malcolm X (Malcolm Little, 1925-1965), demonstrated the religious nature of the struggle for equality.

BIBLIOGRAPHY

The best overall view of the black church in the United States remains Carter G. Woodson's *The History of the Negro Church*

(Washington, D. C., 1921). Woodson's book may be supplemented by the more recent and anecdotal treatment of Gayraud S. Wilmore, *Black Religion and Black Radicalism*, 2d ed. (Maryknoll, N. Y., 1983). For the ongoing influence of African perspectives upon Afro-American religions in the Americas, see Robert Farris Thompson's *Flash of the Spirit: African and Afro-American Art and Philosophy* (New York, 1983). Two analyses of the development of slave religion are Lawrence W. Levine's *Black Culture and Black Consciousness: Afro-American Folk Thought from Slavery to Freedom* (Oxford, 1977) and my *Slave Religion: The Invisible Institution in the Antebellum South* (Oxford, 1978). The growth of independent black churches in the North is described in Carol V. R. George's *Segregated Sabbaths: Richard Allen and the Emergence of Independent Black Churches* (New York, 1973). The existence of separate black churches in the South has been well documented in Mechal Sobel's *Trabelin' On: The Slave Journey to an Afro-Baptist Faith* (Westport, Conn., 1979). Two volumes of essays present pioneering scholarship on the history of the black church in the nineteenth and early twentieth centuries: *Black Apostles at Home and Abroad: Afro-Americans and the Christian Mission from the Revolution to Reconstruction*, edited by David W. Wills and Richard Newman (Boston, 1982), and *Black Apostles: Afro-American Clergy Confront the Twentieth Century*, edited by Randall K. Burkett and Richard Newman (Boston, 1978). A sociological description and brief analysis of the urban "new religions" of black America may be found in Arthur Huff Fauset's *Black Gods of the Metropolis* (Philadelphia, 1944). The Garvey movement has been discussed as a black civil religion in Randall K. Burkett's *Garveyism as a Religious Movement: The Institutionalization of a Black Civil Religion* (Metuchen, N. J., 1978). The subject of black Jews, sorely in need of study, has been treated briefly in Howard Brotz's *The Black Jews of Harlem* (New York, 1970). The Nation of Islam has been described in detail in E. U. Essien-Udom's *Black Nationalism: A Search for an Identity in America* (Chicago, 1962). Vinson Synan's *The Holiness-Pentecostal Movement in the United States* (Grand Rapids, Mich., 1971) ably surveys the history of this important religious movement. The religious aspects of the civil rights movement may be seen best through the writings of some of its leaders; see especially Martin Luther King, Jr.'s *Stride toward Freedom: The Montgomery Story* (New York, 1958) and the *Autobiography of Malcolm X* (New York, 1965), written with the assistance of Alex Haley. For the development of black theology, a good collection of primary documents has been assembled by Gayraud S. Wilmore and James H. Cone in *Black Theology: A Documentary History, 1966-1979* (Maryknoll, N. Y., 1979).

ALBERT J. RABOTEAU

Muslim Movements

Moorish Science. In the late nineteenth century, black intellectuals became increasingly critical of white Christians for supporting racial segregation in America and colonialism in Africa. Europeans and Americans, they charged, were in danger of turning Christianity into a "white man's religion." After the turn of the century, Timothy Drew (1886-1929), a black delivery man from North Carolina, began teaching that Christianity was a religion for whites. The true religion of black people, he announced, was Islam. In 1913, the Noble Drew Ali, as his followers called him, founded the first Moorish Science Temple in Newark, New Jersey. Though heretical in the view of orthodox Muslims, the Moorish Science Temple was the first organization to spread awareness of Islam as an alternative to Christianity among black Americans.

Nation of Islam. In 1930, a peddler named Wallace D. Fard (later known as Walli Farrad, Professor Ford, Farrad Mohammed, and numerous other aliases) appeared in the black community of Detroit. Fard claimed that he had come from Mecca to reveal to black Americans their true identity as Muslims of the "lost-found tribe of Shabbazz." Like the Noble Drew Ali, Fard taught that salvation for black people lay in self-knowledge. In 1934, Fard disappeared as mysteriously as he had come. The leadership of the Nation of Islam was taken up by Fard's chief minister, Elijah Poole (1897-1975), a black laborer from Georgia, whom Fard had renamed Elijah Muhammad.

Elijah Muhammad announced to the members of the Nation that Wallace D. Fard was actually the incarnation of Allah and that he, Elijah, was his messenger. For the next forty years, he was regarded as such by his followers, who came to be known as the Black Muslims. According to the teachings of Messenger Muhammad, as he was called, humankind was originally black, until an evil scientist created a race of white people through genetic engineering. The whites he created turned out to be devils.

In the 1950s, Malcolm Little (1925-1965), who had converted to the Nation of Islam in prison, rose to prominence as chief spokesman for Elijah Muhammad. As Malcolm X he became one of the most articulate critics of racial injustice in the country during the civil rights period. Rejecting the nonviolent approach of Martin Luther King, Jr., he argued that separatism and self-determination were necessary if blacks were to achieve full equality. Breaking with Elijah Muhammad, he founded his own organization, the Muslim Mosque, Inc., in New York City. Shortly thereafter, he was assassinated. The life and death of Malcolm X helped to increase interest in Islam among black Americans.

In 1975, Elijah Muhammad died, and his son Warithuddin (Wallace Deen) Muhammad succeeded to the leadership of the Nation of Islam. Under the leadership of Minister Louis Farrakhan, this faction has broken with the American Muslim Mission, returned to the original teachings and ideals of Elijah Muhammad, and readopted the old name, the Nation of Islam.

[*See also the biography of Malcolm X.*]

BIBLIOGRAPHY

Austin, Allan D. *African Muslims in Antebellum America: A Sourcebook.* New York, 1984.
Essien-Udom, E. U. *Black Nationalism: A Search for an Identity in America.* Chicago, 1962.

Fauset, Arthur Huff. *Black Gods of the Metropolis: Negro Religious Cults in the Urban North*. Philadelphia, 1944.

Lincoln, Charles Eric. *The Black Muslims in America*. Boston, 1961.

Malcolm X, with Alex Haley. *The Autobiography of Malcolm X*. New York, 1965.

Waugh, Earle H., Baha Abu-Laban, and Regula B. Qureshi, eds. *The Muslim Community in North America*. Edmonton, 1983.

ALBERT J. RABOTEAU

AFTERLIFE

An Overview

Views of the afterlife, of expectations concerning some form of human survival after death, cannot be isolated from the totality of the understanding of the nature of the divine, the nature of humankind, time and history, and the structure of reality. Not all religious persons have addressed the same kinds of questions, nor have ideas always been formulated in a uniform way by those nurtured within any one of the many religious traditions of the world. Nonetheless, there is a certain commonality in the kinds of basic questions that have been addressed.

The Nature of the Divine

Monotheists have struggled through the ages with questions concerning the corporeality of God, including shape and dimension, and, correspondingly, whether humankind can actually come to gaze in the hereafter on the visage of God. Others have concluded not only that the divine being is not to be conceived in any anthropomorphic form but also that the divine being, in the most absolute sense, is removed from the realm of interaction and rests as the essence of nonmanifestation. Determinations about the nature of the divine have direct ramifications for human understanding of life after death.

The Vision of God. Those religious traditions that have articulated an understanding of the divine in polytheistic form have tended to envision the particular gods in a concrete manner, often with the implication that the dead, or at least some of the dead, will be able to see the gods visually in the afterlife. Pictorial representations from the Middle and New Kingdoms in Egypt portray the dead person being lifted out of the sarcophagus by the jackal Anubis, taken to the Hall of Double Justice and judged, and then brought into the presence of Osiris, to be led by him to the Elysian Fields.

Divine Justice and Judgment. Justice, as an abstract principle of order for many ancient societies, came in monotheistic communities to be translated into a quality of the godhead itself, with the immediate ramification of justice as an ethical imperative for human beings in recognition of the nature and being of God. Thus in Islam there is a clear understanding that because God is just, he requires that a person live justly, and the quality of the individual life is actually the determining factor in the final judgment.

It is, of course, not true that justice need be a less significant factor in the consideration of the afterlife by a society that is professedly polytheistic. What often has been the case is that the concept of ethical responsibility on the part of the individual (with concomitant judgment by the deity in some form) blends with an emphasis on magic and ritual as assurance of a felicitous state in the hereafter. Justice was seen as an extension of a concept of order that characterized the Egyptian worldview and that, as an essential of the eschatological reality, was in direct relationship to the establishment of stability over chaos at the time of creation. Thus it was necessary to rely on ritual and magical formulas, in this way assuring that the dead would always have at their fingertips the necessary knowledge and information to answer any questions that might be posed in the final court of arbitration.

In the development of Old Testament thought, divine justice became a particularly significant issue. If God is truly almighty, his dominion must extend to all parts of the earth and to all portions of time. And if he is truly just, then it is inconsistent that the righteous as well as the wicked should be doomed to the bitter existence of She'ol. It was with regard to God's power and justice that the seeds of an idea of resurrection to an eternal reward began to grow in the Jewish consciousness, laying the ground for the later Christian understanding of the death and resurrection of Jesus.

In Hindu and Buddhist thought, the notion of *karman* presupposes a conception of justice and judgment different from that prevailing in monotheistic traditions. In its simplest form the doctrine of *karman* states that what one is now is a direct result of what one has done and been in past existences, and what one does in this lifetime will, with the accumulation of past karmic debt, be the direct determinant of the state of one's future existence.

Intercession. Issues of justice give rise to questions about the possibility of intercession for the deceased on the part of human or superhuman agency. The forms of intercession are many, from the role played by the living in providing a proper burial and maintaining the mechanical artifices of the tomb to the specific intervention in the judgment process by a figure who can plead for the well-being of the soul whose fate is in the balance. Muslims traditionally have taken great comfort in the thought that the Prophet himself will be on hand to intercede for each individual believer when he comes before the awesome throne of judgment, and through the centuries Christians have relied on the assurance that Jesus Christ sits at the right hand of God to intercede. The Buddhist concept of the *bodhisattva* is, in one sense, an extension of the idea of intercession.

The Nature of Humankind

If it is essential to a vision of the afterlife to have some understanding of the nature of that divine being or reality to whom humankind returns at death, it is no less important to have some conception of what element in the human makeup is considered to do the returning.

The Human Constitution. Conceptions of the constitution of the human being differ not only among different religious traditions but among different schools of thought within the traditions.

The most immediately obvious distinction, and one that has been drawn in most conceptions of the afterlife, is between the physical and the nonphysical aspects of the human person. This can be understood as the body-spirit dichotomy, with a difference sometimes drawn in the latter between spirit and soul. In the Hebrew view, a person was not understood so much as having a body, something essentially different and apart from the nonphysical side of one's being, as being a body, which implies the totality of the individual and the inseparability of the life principle from the fleshly form.

The Relationship of the Human to the Divine. The question of what it is that lives on after death must be seen in relation to the basic issue of whether that which is real or lasting in the human person is identical with the divine reality or is essentially different from it. A position of monism is one end of a spectrum of possible responses. In Advaita Vedanta liberation from successive existences comes only with the realization of the identity of *atman* (the individual soul) and *brahman* (the Absolute).

A very different kind of conceptualization is that characteristic of some traditional societies in which not only is humanity seen to be totally separate from the gods but one exists after death only as a shade or a shadow of one's former self. That which divides the human and the divine in this context is the fact that the gods are immortal and humans are not. In between such alternatives is a range of possibilities suggesting that humans manifest some element of the divine enlivening principle.

Resurrection of the Body. The significance of the body as a continuing entity in the afterlife has been attested to in many traditions. [*See* Resurrection.] The resuscitation of the corpse expected after the elaborate processes of mummification in ancient Egypt implied the hope of permanent physical survival as well as survival of the personality.

In Jewish thought, the soul was first believed to be released from the body at death, but with the development of the idea of resurrection came the belief in the continued importance of the physical body. This belief is carried over to early Christianity: Augustine in the *City of God* says that the resurrected bodies, perfect amalgamations of flesh and spirit, are free to enjoy the satisfactions of food and drink should they so desire.

Continued Existence as Spirit. From the earliest times, characteristic of primitive societies but certainly not exclusive to them, humankind has had a seemingly natural fear of the dead. To some extent this can be explained in terms of one's own apprehension about the meaning of death for one personally. In more extreme cases, this has led to a kind of worship of the dead, in which those who have passed into another existence have sometimes assumed the status of gods. This has been evidenced particularly in China and Japan in the long history of ancestor worship.

Time and History

The way in which time, its passage and its purpose, is understood in different worldviews has a direct bearing on conceptions of the afterlife. Eastern religions and philosophies generally have conceived time as revolving in cycles, within each of which are periods of creation and destruction, with each "final" cataclysm to be followed again by the entire process of generation. At the other pole are those "historical" (usually prophetic) religions that postulate a creation when time is said to have begun and a final eschaton when time as we know it will reach its conclusion. Implicit is the belief that there is a plan to history, although humans may not be able to comprehend it, and that in some sense the end, when all creation will be glorified and time will give way to eternity, is already cast and determined.

Rebirth. Issues of time and history relate directly to the question of how an individual soul (or spirit or body) maintains continuity between this life and that that lies beyond death. Some traditions hold generally to the idea of one life on earth, death, some kind of resurrection or rebirth, and

> **Implicit is the belief that there is a plan to history, although humans may not be able to comprehend it**

then continued existence on another plane. Others believe in reincarnation (metempsychosis or transmigration) with its possibilities of a series of lives on earth or elsewhere.

Eastern mystical thought has articulated the concept of reincarnation with some consistency, although in the Buddhist case the difficult problem arises of identifying what it is that is born in another body if there is nothing that can be called an individual soul. Even those religions that contemplate aeons of potential rebirths, however, do project the hope of a final release from this recurring condition.

Eschatology. For those who adhere to the idea of resurrection, with the implication of some form of life eternal to follow, one of the most pressing questions concerns when that resurrection is going to occur. Millenarian expectations have taken a variety of forms in both Judaism and Christianity, with the chiliastic hope in the latter for Christ's return.

In early Christianity, there was the expectation that the return of Jesus to usher in the new age would be so soon as to come within the lifetime of the community of those who had had fellowship with him.

In the Persian case, Zarathushtra himself apparently had first felt that the kingdom of righteousness would be established on earth and them implied that eternal reward or punishment would instead come after death.

Some variation on the idea of a savior or restorer to appear at a future time is to be found in almost all of the living religious traditions, whatever their concept of the flow and structure of time.

The Structure of Reality

The World in Time and Space. The eternality of the world, and its subsequent relationship to the eternality of heaven or the rehabilitated universe, has been postulated in a variety of ways in the history of religious thought. [*See* Eternity.] The ancient Egyptian expected that the static nature of the world and of society would mean their perpetuation eternally. In the materialistic Zoroastrian construct, the final rehabilitation of the earth implies its purification and its joining, with a purified hell, to the extension of heaven. Judaism presents an example of the constant tension between a hope for this world, renewed, and the kingdom of heaven as an otherworldly and eternal realm.

A classic theme of religious geography has been that the heavens are located somewhere above the earth and the nether regions below, and that these have been identified to a greater or lesser extent with the location of heaven(s) and hell(s) as after-death abodes in whatever form these have been conceived.

Reward and Punishment. It is often in direct relation to the existing understanding of the structure of the universe that the more specific conceptions of heaven and hell arise. These parallel places of reward and punishment were not generally present in ancient thought.

The greatly elaborated heavens and hells, as they came to be developed in Hindu and Buddhist thought, with their graphic descriptions of the tortures of punishment and the raptures of reward, are by nature temporary (or, at least, one's stay in them is temporary). For the Buddhist, one is reborn from these states or conditions into another state or condition, with the understanding that not until one is reborn as a human being will final release be possible.

Quite different is the basic understanding of prophetic religions, which assumes that the eschaton and judgment result in the eternality of the final abode and resting place. The question of whether or not punishment, like reward, is eternal has long perplexed theologians. In the Judeo-Christian tradition, as well as in Islam, God's justice is always understood

as tempered with mercy, and the idea of the eternality of hell has been moderated to whatever extent has seemed consistent with the prevailing theological climate.

[*See also* Soul *and* Immortality; *for more detailed discussion of themes of afterlife, see* Heaven and Hell.]

BIBLIOGRAPHY

Some of the older comparative studies of life after death in different religious traditions, such as Elias H. Sneath's *Religion and the Future Life: The Development of the Belief in Life after Death* (New York, 1922) and Kaufmann Kohler's *Heaven and Hell in Comparative Religion* (New York, 1923), are still useful, although somewhat elementary. More recent and valuable contributions to comparative studies of life after death are *The Judgement of the Dead* by S. G. F. Brandon (london, 1967) and *Religious Encounters with Death*, edited by Frank E. Reynolds and Earle H. Waugh (University Park, Pa., 1977). Christina Grof and Stanislav Grof's *Beyond Death* (New York, 1980) is a more journalistic overview of classical and contemporary afterlife beliefs, with fine color prints. For an understanding of the relationship of theories of time to afterlife concepts, Mircea Eliade's *Cosmos and History: The Myth of the Eternal Return* (New York, 1954) is excellent. A good addition to anthropological studies on attitudes and customs of non-Western cultures toward death and afterlife is *Celebrations of Death: The Anthropology of Mortuary Ritual* (Cambridge, Mass., 1979) by Richard Huntington and Peter Metcalf.

In addition to comparative works, a number of valuable studies deal with the afterlife as envisioned in particular religious traditions. *Death and Eastern Thought*, edited by Frederick H. Holck (Nashville, 1974), deals primarily with Indian beliefs, with brief chapters on China and Japan. Themes of death and resurrection in prophetic traditions are treated in such works as George W. E. Nickelsburg's *Resurrection, Immortality, and Eternal Life in InterTestamental Judaism* (Cambridge, Mass., 1972), John Hick's Death and Eternal Life (London, 1976), and *The Islamic Understanding of Death and Resurrection* (Albany, N. Y., 1981), which I wrote with Yvonne Haddad. Several excellent translations of mortuary texts are available, especially *The Tibetan Book of the Dead*, 2d ed., translated by Lama Kazi Dawasamdup and edited by W. Y. Evans-Wentz (Oxford, 1949); *The Egyptian Book of the Dead*, translated by E. A. Wallis Budge (New York, 1967) and presented as an interlinear translation with hieroglyphics; and *The Islamic Book of the Dead* of Imam `Abd al-Rahman al-Qadi, translated by `A'isha `Abd al-Rahman (Norfolk, England, 1977). A very good series on mythology, including myths of death and afterlife, is published by the Hamlyn Publishing Group Ltd. (1965-); it covers a broad range of literate and nonliterate societies.

A precursor in some ways to contemporary parapsychological studies is the spiritualist movement that began in the nineteenth century in Europe and the United States; it is well documented in J. Arthur Hill's *Spiritualism: Its History, Phenomena and Doctrine* (New York, 1919). Ian Stevenson's continuing research on reincarnation in cross-cultural perspective is presented in *Twenty Cases Suggestive of Reincarnation*, 2d ed. (Charlottesville, Va., 1974). Of the many recent studies of near-death experience and research, two of the best are Michael B. Sabom's *Recollections of Death: A Medical Investigation* (New York, 1981) and Kenneth Ring's *Life at Death: A Scientific Investigation of the Near-Death Experience* (New York, 1980).

JANE I. SMITH

Geographies of Death

Belief in some kind of existence after death is one of the more common elements of religion, as history and anthropology show. While death is everywhere recognized as inevitable, it is seldom accepted as an absolute termination of human existence.

Afterlife in General. The different representations of life after death that we find in different religions are related to their respective conceptions of the structure of the cosmos and of life on earth, and to their different beliefs about the bodily and spiritual constitution of man. The Egyptians, for example, being agriculturalists, looked forward to a future life in the bountiful "Earu fields." In each case the actual economic conditions of life play an important role in determining how one will conceive of the afterlife.

The conception of the soul is also an important factor. A soul that is conceived to be eternal and spiritual leads a different type of afterlife than one that is conceived as the double of the earthly body, or as something that gradually dwindles into nothingness after death, such as we find among certain northern Eurasian religions.

Where the conception of reward or punishment according to ethical principles does occur, it is necessary to divide the abode of the dead into two or more sections that may be localized in different places: heaven(s) and hell(s), and in some instances a place in between where souls are purified before they are allowed to enter heaven: purgatory. In cultures where a belief in reincarnation is accepted, the question of the place of a soul's rebirth is understandably of no great importance and the ideas concerning it often remain vague or contradictory.

Generally the country of the dead is represented more or less as a copy of the world of the living, and life there follows in the main the same lines as life on earth. In these cases it is difficult to speak of a "geography" of death, which would be distinct from the geography of the living.

Geographies of Death. In those cases where there is the elaboration of a distinct geography of death, there appear to be three main possibilities, each with minor variations. The world of the dead may be on earth, under the earth, or in heaven.

In the first case, the world of the dead is situated on earth, but at a lesser or greater distance away from the dwellings of the living.

In the second case, the realm of the dead is situated beneath the earth or under the water. The idea of an underworld as the dwelling place of the departed is probably the commonest of all concepts in this sphere. The idea of an entrance to this region through a deep hole in the ground or a cave is also widespread.

In the final case, the world of the dead may be situated in heavenly spheres. This concept is also a very common one.

We find it, for instance, in Egypt as one of several ideas concerning the location of the hereafter. The belief that this country is to be sought somewhere high in the mountains is only a variation, since in many religions mountaintops symbolize heaven and the dwelling place of the gods, as, for example, Olympus did in Greece.

[*See* Underworld; *and* Heaven and Hell.]

BIBLIOGRAPHY

Cavendish, Richard. *Visions of Heaven and Hell.* London, 1977. A useful book with many illustrations and a selected bibliography.

Champdor, Albert, trans. *Le livre des morts.* Paris, 1963. An up-to-date translation of the Egyptian *Book of Going Forth* by Day. Well illustrated. Further translated by Faubion Bowers as *The Book of the Dead* (New York, 1966).

Clemen, Carl C. *Das Leben nach dem Tode im Glauben der Menschheit.* Leipzig, 1920. Still one of the best short introductions to the theme, albeit dated as regards theory.

Cumont, Franz. *Afterlife in Roman Paganism.* New York, 1959. A standard work.

Evans-Wentz, W. Y., ed. *The Tibetan Book of the Dead.* 2d ed. Translated by Kazi Dawasamdup. London, 1949. Includes a useful introduction.

Faulkner, Raymond O., trans. *The Ancient Egyptian Book of the Dead.* Rev. ed. Edited by Carol Andrews. London, 1985. A fresh translation, lavishly illustrated.

Firth, Raymond. *The Fate of the Soul: An Interpretation of Some Primitive Concepts.* Cambridge, 1955. Short but important.

Jeremias, Alfred. *Hölle und Paradies bei den Babyloniern.* Leipzig, 1900. Short treatment of the Babylonian concepts of the hereafter. Still of value.

Kees, Hermann. *Totenglauben und Jenseitsvorstellungen der alten Ägypter: Grundlagen und Entwicklung bis zum Ende des mittleren Reiches.* 2d ed. Berlin, 1956. The standard work on Egyptian concepts of the hereafter.

Pfannmüller, Gustav, ed. Tod, *Jenseits und Unsterblichkeit in der Religion,* Literatur und Philosophie der Griechen und Romer. Munich, 1953. An anthology with a useful introduction.

TH. P. VAN BAAREN

Jewish Concepts

The Jewish idea of the afterlife has focused upon belief in either corporeal resurrection or the immortality of the soul. While one or the other of these conceptions, and occasionally both together, has been present in every period in the history of Judaism, it can safely be said that these ideas underwent their most significant development during the rabbinic and medieval periods.

The Biblical Period. The notion of the afterlife in the Bible is decidedly vague. After death, the individual is described as going to She'ol, a kind of netherworld, from which he "will not ascend" (*Jb.* 7:9). God, however, is attributed with the power to revive the dead (*Dt.* 32:39, 1 *Sm.* 2:6), and the language of resurrection is several times used in a figurative sense, as in Ezekiel's vision of the dry bones (*Ez.* 37:1-4) and in the apocalypse of Isaiah (*Is.* 26:17-19) to describe the national restoration of the people of Israel.

The Hellenistic Age. The idea of immortality initially appears in Hellenistic Jewish literature in the *Wisdom of Solomon* (3:1-10, 5:15-16) and is more extensively developed in the writings of Philo Judaeus (d. 45-50 CE), who describes how the souls of the righteous return after death to their native home in heaven—or, in the case of rare individuals like the patriarchs, to the intelligible world of the ideas (*Allegorical Interpretation* 1.105-108; *On Sacrifice* 2.5). Although Philo's views were immensely influential in early Christian philosophy, they had no impact upon rabbinic Jewish thought as it developed in the subsequent centuries.

Rabbinic Judaism. Some rabbinic views about the afterlife reflect beliefs commonly held in the ancient world. While the rabbis stated unequivocally that every Israelite has a place in the world to come, they also believed that persons who suffered violent or otherwise untimely deaths might not be permitted to enjoy the afterlife.

In general, the subject of the future world does not appear to have obsessed the rabbis or especially to have exercised their imaginations. While there must have existed among Jews many folk beliefs concerning life after death (some of which can be extrapolated from burial customs), few have been explicitly recorded.

Middle Ages. Between the eighth century and the fifteenth, Jewish views about the afterlife embraced virtually every position on the spectrum of conceivable beliefs, including extreme philosophical interpretations that altogether deny the existence of corporeal resurrection. The Spanish-Jewish philosopher Moses Maimonides (Mosheh ben Maimon, 1135/8-1204), in his *Commentary on the Mishnah*, criticizes several popular views of the world to come, all of which conceive of the eschatological bliss purely in material and sensual terms. It is, however, in the literature of Jewish philosophy and Qabbalah (mysticism) that the most significant developments in Jewish eschatological thinking in the Middle Ages are to be found.

Philosophical approaches. Most medieval Jewish philosophers conceived of the afterlife in terms of the immortality of the soul, which they then defined according to their individual philosophical views. For many of these philosophers, the notion of physical resurrection in the future world is clearly problematic, and they sometimes had to go to extreme lengths to reconcile it with their other ideas about existence in the hereafter.

Probably the most successful in doing this was the early medieval Babylonian philosopher and sage Sa`adyah Gaon (882-942), who, in *The Book of Beliefs and Opinions*, emphasizes the unity of body and soul. Sa`adyah foresees two resurrections, the first for the righteous alone at the beginning of the messianic age (when the wicked would be sufficiently punished by being left unresurrected) and the second for everyone else at the advent of the world to come.

After Sa`adyah, the eschatological doctrines of most Jewish philosophers can be categorized by their orientation as either Neoplatonic or Aristotelian.

Jewish Aristotelian philosophers treated the soul as the acquired intellect and therefore defined the ultimate felicity as a state of "conjunction" between the acquired intellect of the individual philosopher and the universal Active Intellect. Immortality was understood by them mainly as the intellectual contemplation of God. Like their Muslim counterparts, the Jewish Aristotelians disagreed over such issues as whether this state of conjunction can be attained in this world or solely in the next and whether the soul in its immortal state will preserve its individual identity or lose it in the collective unity of the impersonal Active Intellect.

Maimonides, the most celebrated Jewish Aristotelian, appears to adapt conflicting opinions on these questions (*Guide of the Perplexed* 1.74 and 3.54). Although he lists the dogma of resurrection as the thirteenth fundamental of Jewish faith, he also writes that "in the world to come the body and the flesh do not exist but only the souls of the righteous alone" (*Code of Law: Repentance* 3.6).

A very different criticism of the Maimonidean position was put forward in the fourteenth century by the philosopher Hasdai Crescas in *The Light of the Lord*. Crescas criticizes Maimonides' intellectualism and proposes that salvation comes to the soul through love of God (2.6, 3.3). A century later, Yosef Albo (d. 1444) accepted the Maimonidean chronology for the afterlife but also argued with his predecessor's intellectualism, claiming that practice, not just knowledge, of God's service makes the soul immortal (*Book of Principles* 4.29-30).

Qabbalistic views. Unlike medieval Jewish philosophers, Jewish mystics in the Middle Ages had no difficulty with the concept of resurrection or other such aspects of eschatological doctrine.

The Spanish exegete Moses Nahmanides (Mosheh ben Nahman, c. 1194-1270) devotes considerable effort in the *Gate of the Reward* to reconciling a mystical view of the afterlife with Maimonidean eschatology. Nahmanides posits the existence of three distinct worlds that follow this one: (1) a world of souls which the soul enters immediately after death to be rewarded or punished; (2) a future world that is synonymous with the messianic age and will culminate in a final judgment and resurrection; and (3) the world to come, in which "the body will become like the soul and the soul will be cleaving to knowledge of the Most High."

A second stage in the history of qabbalistic eschatology began with the appearance of the *Zohar* (completed in approximately 1300), which describes the afterlife in terms of the separate fates of the three parts of the soul, the *nefesh,* the *ruah*, and the *neshamah*. Since only the first two were considered to be susceptible to sin, they alone were subject to punishment.

Probably the most unusual aspect of qabbalistic eschatology is the belief in *gilgul*, or metempsychosis, the transmigration of souls after death. This belief gained increasing prominence in qabbalistic thought from the thirteenth century onward. Originally considered a unique punishment for extraordinary sins (particularly of a sexual kind), *gilgul* came to be viewed, paradoxically, as an exemplary instance of God's mercy, since the chance to be reborn gave its victims an opportunity to correct their sins and thus restore themselves as spiritual beings.

The Modern Period. With the change in religious temper that occurred during the Enlightenment and has deepened since then, the problem of the afterlife has lost much of its compelling urgency for Jewish theology. Orthodox Judaism, to be sure, maintains the rabbinic dogmatic belief in resurrection as part of its conception of the messianic age, and it similarly preserves the liturgical references in their original form. In general, when the afterlife is considered today, it is usually spoken about in terms of personal immortality, a heritage of the medieval philosophical temper, and as good an indication as any of the gilgulim through which the concept has passed in the course of Jewish history.

[*See also* Messianism, *article on* Jewish Messianism.]

BIBLIOGRAPHY

There exists no single book or study that treats the entire history of Jewish eschatological thought through the ages. On the notion of the afterlife in the Bible and in the apocryphal and pseudipgraphic literature, R. H. Charles's classic *A Critical History of the Doctrine of a Future Life in Israel, in Judaism, and in Christianity* (1899; reprint, New York, 1979) is still informative, but its value has largely been superseded by George W. E. Nichelsburg's *Resurrection, Immortality, and Eternal Life in InterTestamental Judaism* (Cambridge, Mass., 1972).

For early rabbinic eschatology, the clearest and most comprehensive treatment remains George Foot Moore's *Judaism in the First Centuries of the Christian Era, the Age of Annaim*, 3 vols. (Cambridge, Mass., 1927-1930). Volume 2 contains (on pages 279-395) a useful discussion of the methodological problems involved in the study of rabbinic concepts of the afterlife and their historical background as well as translations of most of the relevant sources. An indispensable complement to Moore's summary, particularly for Greco-Roman parallels to the rabbinic concepts, is Saul Lieberman's "Some Aspects of After Life in Early Rabbinic History," in *Harry Austryn Wolfson Jubilee Volume* (English Section), vol. 2 (Jerusalem, 1965). For other special aspects of rabbinic eschatology, see Arthur Marmorstein's two essays on the afterlife in his *Studies in Jewish Theology* (London, 1950) and Martha Himmelfarb's *Tours of Hell: An Apocalyptic Form in Jewish and Christian Literature.* (Philadelphia, 1983).

On medieval philosophical views, the single book to attempt a comprehensive survey is Julius Guttmann's *Philosophies of Judaism: The History of Jewish Philosophy from biblical Times to Franz Rosenzweig*, translated by David W. Silverman (New York, 1964), in which see the index, s.v. *Afterlife*. Moses Maimonides' *Treatise on Resurrection* has now been translated into English by Fred Rosner (New York, 1982), and selected essays dealing with Maimonidean eschatology and its repercussions have been helpfully collected and edited by Jacob Sienstag in *Eschatology in Maimonidean Thought: Messianism, Resurrection, and the World to Come* (New York, 1983), which also contains a bibliography.

On qabbalistic views of the afterlife, the most important discussions are those of Gershom Scholem in *Major Trends in Jewish Mysticism*, 3. ed. (New York, 1961), and *Kabbalah* (New York, 1973). For folk beliefs concerning life after death, see Joshua Trachtenber'g *Jewish Magic and Superstition* (1939; reprint, New York, 1982), pp. 61-68.

DAVID STERN

Chinese Concepts

[*This article is devoted exclusively to pre-Buddhist notions of the afterlife. For a discussion of later developments, see* Chinese Religion, *overview article.*]

The fundamentally this-worldly orientation of ancient Chinese culture placed the world of the dead inside the universein the stars, in distant realms on earth, or under the earth. Death was seen not as the separation of two radically different entities like matter and spirit but as the dispersal of a multiplicity of forces (*ch`i*, "breaths"), forces that were graded but basically formed one continuous spectrum.

Shang Royal Ancestors. The people of the Shang period (late second millennium BCE) were in constant communication with the afterworld, that is, with the deceased members of their royal family, whom they consulted through oracles. No description is given of the realm where the dead existed, but evidence of human sacrifices and the elaborate furnishings found in Shang royal tombs suggest that the dead were thought to exist in a style similar to the living, needing servants and possessions.

Man's Two Souls. Under the reign of the Chou kings (eleventh century-256 BCE) a cult arose dedicated to the deity Heaven (T`ien), an anthropomorphous celestial emperor whose court was composed of the souls of deceased nobles. According to the classical theory that originated in the early Chou, every member of the aristocracy had two souls, which part company at the moment of death. The *hun* "soul," a spiritual and intelligent personality categorized as *yang*, goes to join the court of Heaven; a more physical vital breath, the *p`o* "soul," of *yin* character, follows the body into the grave or descends to Huang Ch`üan (Yellow Springs), a netherworld under the earth.

The Netherworld. Belief in the Yellow Springs, probably a feature of early folk culture, is attested mostly in poetic laments about death, but they are never described in any detail. The Yellow Springs seems to have been a sad realm of the shades, not unlike the Greek Hades.

Identity of Life and Death. Those thinkers who emphasized the universal rhythm of transformation in nature and advocated man's adaptation to this "Way" (tao) saw death as but one phase in the process of change. Lao-tuz and Chuang-tzu both thought that death should be neither feared nor desired, advocating instead a resigned and serene acceptace of death as a part of the ever-changing mechanism of nature.

Prolonging Life in This World. Life was greatly treasured and, in the course of the first millennium BCE, the Chinese came to place more and more emphasis on longevity. This is evidenced by bronze inscriptions from the eighth century BCE onward that speak of *nan-lao* ("retardation of old age"), *pao-shen* ("preservation of the body"), and *wu-ssu* ("deathlessness"). From about 400 BCE onward the belief existed that some men had achieved perpetual life, that their souls had neither gone to the Yellow Springs nor dissipated into the vastness of the universe; instead they were preserved in a perfected spectral body, able to wander on earth and among the stars forever. These were the "immortals" (*hsien*).

The Paradises of the Immortals. The immortals had "transcended the world" (*tu-shih*), "ascended to distant places" (*teng-hsia*), and lived in a world of light, on holy mountains, or in paradises situated at the rim of the world. P'eng-lai, a paradise island, was imagined to be in the East China Sea.

Toward the middle of the Han dynasty (206 BCE–220 CE), new geographical knowledge created a shift of interest to the northwest. Mount K'unl-un on the threshold of Central Asia had long been a mythical nine-layered mountain that led up to the Gate of Heaven. Its deity, the Queen Mother of the West (Hsi Wang Mu), was a timeless creature with the tail of a leopard and the teeth of a tiger, reigning over the land where the sun sets.

Tokens of Immortality in Han Tombs. The recent archaeological discovery of Hsi Wang Mu in fresco paintings, on stone reliefs, and on bronze mirrors in many Han tombs has added a new facet to our knowledge of this deity. Hsi Wang Mu was not only queen of those who had avoided death and achieved immortality, but she seems also to have played a major role in mortuary cults. The rich imagery of the immortality cult is expressed in tomb furnishings, which demonstrate a wish, if not a belief, that the dead too may accede to immortality.

The Netherworld of Mount T'ai. Miracle tales and a fascination with the unique Chinese concept of material immortality must not cloud our view of the ordinary fate of the dead in the centuries preceding the advent of Buddhism in China. Mount T'ai, the Eastern Sacred Peak in Shantung, long since venerated as the origin of all life, in the Han dynasty becomes the seat of the otherworldly administration. It is the tribunal where the records of the living and the dead are kept on jade tablets and whither the *hun* and *p'o* souls are summoned. The deity of Mount T'ai is the "grandson of the Heavenly Emperor"; his realm is a forecourt of Heaven and the earthly branch of a developing stellar bureaucracy of destiny.

The border between this world and the other remains fluid. Messengers from Mount T'ai can be sighted on their errands and unjustly executed men can, in the otherworldly tribunals they reach, have their tormentors condemned to early death. The judge of the dead is the Lord of the Tribunal of Mount T'ai (T'ai-shan Fu-chün). Around the fifth century CE he is dislodged by the Buddhist King Yama, whose scribe he becomes in the Buddhist hells.

The Otherworldly Bureaucracy of Taoism. In the emerging Taoist religion new concepts evolved that helped to shape Chinese Buddhist notions of the afterlife. One's initiation into the Celestial Master sect (T'ien-shih Tao, late second century CE) meant access to the hierarchy of the immortals and salvation from an afterlife existence as a demon in the domain of the subterranean Water Official (Shui-kuan) or in jails inside mountain caverns.

Sinners were criminals, sins were crimes; atonement and advancement followed judiciary procedure. An important concern was the supernatural inspection of man's good and bad deeds, duplicate records of which were kept in stellar offices and in the mountain tribunals. These registers determined the length of man's lifespan, his status in the world beyond the tomb, and sometimes even the destiny of his descendants.

[*See also* Chinese Religion, *article on* Mythic Themes; Soul, *article on* Chinese Concepts; Alchemy, *article on* Chinese Alchemy; *and* Taoism, *overview article and article on* The Taoist Religious Community.]

BIBLIOGRAPHY

The ancestor cult of the Shang is described by Chang Tsung-tung in *Der Kult der Shang-Dynastie im Spiegel der Orakelin-schriften*, edited by Otto Karow (Wiesbaden, 1970), pp. 34-166. A good general presentation of early Chinese ideas about the afterlife, especially the development of immortality beliefs and techniques, may be found in Joseph Needham's *Science and Civilisation in China*, vol. 2 (Cambridge, 1959, pp. 71-126. The quotations from the *Chuang-tzu* are from Burton Watson's *The Complete Works of Chuang Tzu* (New York, 1968). For Han myths and iconography concerning the afterlife, see Michael Loewe's *Ways to Paradise: The Chinese Quest for Immortality* (London 1979), reviewed in Numen 29 (1982): 79-122; and *Chinese Ideas of Life and Death* (London, 1982), pp. 25-37. Sakai Tadao's old but valuable study of the early cult of Mount T'ai, "Taizan shinko no kenkyu," *Shicho* 7 (1937): 70-119, can today be supplemented by much new archaeological data. There is as yet no comprehensive study of the Mount T'ai tribunals or of the bureaucratic netherworld of early Taoism. The *Yüan hun chih* has been translated by Alvin P. Cohen as *Tales of Vengeful Souls, "Varits sinologiques,"* n. s. 68 (Taipei, Paris, and Hong Kong, 1982).

ANNA SEIDEL

AINU RELIGION

The Ainu are a people whose traditional homeland lay in Hokkaido, southern Sakhalin, and the Kurile islands. Scholarly controversies over their cultural, racial, and linguistic identities remain unresolved. Their hunting-gathering way of life was discontinued with the encroachment of the Russians and the Japanese during the latter half of the nineteenth century and the first half of the twentieth century. Generalizations about Ainu culture or religion are dangerous to make, since not only are there a great many intracultural variations among the Ainu of each region, but differences occur within each group as well. Because the following description is aimed, as much as possible, at the common denominators, it may not fit in toto the religion of a particular Ainu group.

An important concept in the Ainu belief system is the soul. Most beings in the Ainu universe have a soul, and its presence is most conspicuous when it leaves the body of the owner. When one dreams, one's soul frees itself from the sleeping body and travels to places where one has never been. Similarly, a deceased person appears in one's dreams, since the soul of the deceased can travel from the world of the dead to visit one. During shamanistic performances the shaman's soul travels to the world of the dead in order to snatch back the soul of a dead person, thereby reviving him or her.

When a soul has been mistreated, it exercises the power to punish. The deities, in contrast, possess the power to punish or reward the Ainu at will. Interpretations among scholars as to the identity of the deities range from those proposing that nature be equated with the deities, to those finding that only certain members of the universe are deified. An important point in regard to the Ainu concept of deities is Chiri Mashio's interpretation that the Ainu consider all the animal deities to be exactly like humans in appearance and to live just like humans in their own country. The animal deities disguise themselves when visiting the Ainu world in order to bring meat and fur as presents to the Ainu, just as Ainu guests always bring gifts. In this view, then, the bear, which is generally considered the supreme deity, is but the mountain deity in disguise.

Evil spirits and demons, called variously *oyasi* or *wenkamuy* ("evil deity"), constitute another group of beings in the universe who are more powerful than humans. They may exercise their destructive power by causing misfortunes such as epidemics. While some of them have always been demons, others are beings that have turned into demons. When a soul is mistreated after the death of its owner, for example, it becomes a demon. The Ainu pay a great deal of attention to evil spirits and demons by observing religious rules and performing exorcism rites.

Of all the rituals of the Ainu, the bear ceremony is by far the most elaborate. It is the only ceremony of the Ainu that occurs in all regions and that formally involves not only all the members of the settlement but those from numerous other settlements as well, thereby facilitating the flow of people and their communication among different settlements. The bear ceremony provides a significant opportunity for male elders to display their wealth, symbolizing their political power, to those from other settlements. Most importantly, from the perspective of the Ainu, the bear ceremony is a funeral ritual for the bear. Its purpose is to send the soul of the bear through a proper ritual so that the soul will be reborn as a bear and will revisit the Ainu with gifts of meat and fur.

The entire process of the bear ceremony takes at least two years and consists of three stages. The hunters capture and raise a bear cub. In the major ceremony, the bear is ritually killed and its soul is sent back to the mountains. Among the Sakhalin Ainu a secondary ceremony follows the major ceremony after several months. A bear cub, captured alive either while still in a den or while ambling with its mother upon emerging from the den, is usually raised by the Ainu for about a year and a half. At times women nurse these newborn cubs. Although the time of the ceremony differs according to the region, it is most often held in the beginning of the cold season; for the Sakhalin Ainu, it takes place just before they move from their coastal settlement to their inland settlement for the cold season.

Although the bear ceremony is distinctly a male ceremony, in that the officiants are male elders and the women must leave the scene when the bear is shot and skinned, shamanism is not an exclusively male vocation. Sakhalin Ainu shamanism differs considerably from that of the Hokkaido

> **Evil spirits and demons . . . exercise their destructive power by causing misfortunes such as epidemics.**

Ainu. Among the former, cultural valuation of shamanism is high; well-regarded members of the society, both men and women, may become shamans. Although shamans sometimes perform rites for divinations of various sorts and for miracle performances, by far the great majority of rites are performed for diagnosis and cure of illnesses. When shamans are possessed by spirits, they enter a trance state, and the spirit speaks through their mouths, providing the client with necessary information, such as the diagnosis and cure of the illness or the location of a missing object. Among the Hokkaido Ainu, whose shamanistic practice is not well recorded, shamans are usually women, who collectively have lower social status than men. The Hokkaido Ainu shaman also enters a possession trance, but she does so only if a male elder induces it in her by offering prayers to the deities. Although she too diagnoses illnesses, her function is confined to diagnosis, after which male elders take over and engage in the healing process. Male elders must, however, consult a shaman before they make important decisions for the community.

While Ainu religion is expressed in rituals as well as in such daily routines as the disposal of fish bones, nowhere is it more articulated than in their highly developed oral tradition, which is both a primary source of knowledge about the deities and a guideline for the Ainu conducts. There are at least twenty-seven native genres of oral tradition, each having a label in Ainu. They may be classified into two types: verses, either epic or lyric, sung or chanted; and prose that is narrated. While the prose in some genres is recited in the third person, the more common genre is first person narrative, in which a protagonist tells his own story through the mouth of the narrator-singer. The mythic and heroic epics are very complex and lengthy; some heroic epics have as many as fifteen thousand verses. While the mythic epics relate the activities of deities, the heroic epics concern the culture hero, sometimes called Aynu Rakkuru, who, with the aid of the deities, fought against demons to save the Ainu, thereby becoming the founder of Ainu people.

BIBLIOGRAPHY

Ainu minzokushi. Tokyo, 1970. Issued by Ainu Bunka Hozon Taisaku *Kyogikai.* See pages 723-770.

Chiri Mashio. "Ainu no shinyo." *Hoppo bunka kenkyu hokoku* (1954): 1-78.

Chiri Mashio. *Bunrui Ainugo jiten,* vol. 3. Tokyo, 1962. See pages 359-361.

Kindaichi Kyosuke. *Ainu bungaku.* Tokyo, 1933.

Kitagawa, Joseph. "Ainu Bear Festival (Iyomante)." *History of Religions* 1 (Summer 1961): 95-151.

Ohnuki-Tierney, Emiko. *The Ainu of the Northwest Coast of Southern Sakhalin* (1974). Reprint, Prospect Heights, Ill., 1984. Pages 90-97 describe the Sakhalin Ainu bear ceremony.

Ohnuki-Tierney, Emiko. "Regional Variations in Ainu Culture." *American Ethnologist* 3 (May 1976): 297-329.

Philippi, Donald L. *Songs of Gods, Songs of Humans.* Princeton and Tokyo, 1979.

EMIKO OHNUKI-TIERNEY

AKBAR

AKBAR (1542-1605), emperor of India in the Timurid, or Mughal, dynasty. He was born on 15 October 1542 in Umarkot, Sind, where his father, Humayun, had fled after being driven from Delhi, his capital, by his Afghan rivals.

Akbar was proclaimed emperor in 1556 under the tutelage of his father's military commander, Bairam Khan, but by 1560 had succeeded in asserting his own power. His reign is one of the most memorable periods of Indian history not only because of his creation of a powerful empire but also because of his apotheosis as the ideal Indian ruler.

Throughout his reign, Akbar was engaged in warfare with neighboring kingdoms. As soon as the central territories around Delhi and Agra were secured, he moved south and east. In 1568, he captured Chitor, a famous stronghold of the Rajput chiefs, champions of Hinduism in North India. In subsequent battles other Rajput princes submitted to him. After defeating the Rajputs, Akbar took them into his service as generals and administrators and took many of their daughters into his royal harem.

After the Rajput conquest, Akbar defeated the wealthy Muslim kingdom of Gujarat in 1573, and in 1575 the Muslim ruler of Bengal submitted. In all areas, frequent uprisings by military leaders against Akbar were a reminder that Mughal power was dependent on continued assertion of central authority.

It was this need for centralized control that led Akbar to reorganize the bureaucratic structure of his empire and to reform the revenue system. He built upon the work of his predecessors, particularly Sher Shah (r. 1538-1545), in carrying out new land assessments and in bringing as much territory as possible under the direct control of imperial authority.

Akbar's religious policies have been the subject of much controversy, leading to his being regarded as an apostate to Islam, a near convert to Christianity, the inventor of a new religion, and a liberal exponent of toleration. The truth seems to be that in his genuine curiosity about religion he encouraged all varieties of religious practitioners, including Hindu yogins and Muslim fakirs as well as European Jesuits who visited his court. Bada'uni, a contemporary historian, while he denounced Akbar as an apostate, says that he spent whole nights in praise of God and would be found "many a morning alone in prayer and meditation in a lonely spot."

Discussions of Akbar's attitude toward orthodox Islam have centered mainly on two incidents. One was his acceptance, in 1579, of a declaration by some major Islamic theologians stating that he, as a just ruler, could, in the case of disputes between *mujtahids* (interpreters of Islamic law), decide which was the correct interpretation. Although orthodox Islamic theologians denounced his action, it was not a denial of Islamic practice, but rather an assertion of his sovereignty and his near equality with the caliph of the Ottoman empire.

The other incident was Akbar's promulgation in 1582 of the *Din-i-ilahi* (The Divine Faith), a syncretic statement that owed much to the *Sufi* tradition of Islam as well as to Hinduism and Zoroastrianism. Emphasizing the union of the soul with the divine, it insisted on such ethical precepts as almsgiving, chastity, vegetarianism, and kindness to all. Elsewhere, Akbar indicated that he believed in the transmigration of souls.

For orthodox Muslims, the *Din-i-ilahi* made clear that Akbar intended to replace Islam with his own heresy, but in fact there is no evidence that it had any followers outside his immediate entourage. It is possible, however, that he dreamed of the "divine faith" becoming the possession of all men, thus ending "the diversity of sects and creeds" that, he once complained, was the source of strife in his kingdom.

Akbar died at Agra on 3 October 1605. The measure of his importance in Indian history is that the cultural achievements of his age along with his administrative structures continued to characterize the Mughal dynasty for over two centuries and remained a model for later rulers.

BIBLIOGRAPHY

The most important sources of information on Akbar's reign are the writings of *Abu al-Fazl `Allami*, especially his *Akbar-nama* and his *A'in-i-Akbari*. The former has been translated by Henry Beveridge in three volumes (1907-1939; reprint, Delhi, 1977); the latter, an account of Akbar's administrative system, was translated by H. Blochmann and H. S. Jarrett in three volumes (1873-1894) and has since been revised by D. C. Phillott and Jadu Nath Sarkar (Calcutta, 1939-1949). S. R. Sharma's *The Religious Policy of the Mughal Emperors* (New York, 1972) has a good section on Akbar, and Vincent A. Smith's *Akbar, the Great Mogul, 1542-1605* (1919; 2d ed., Delhi, 1966) is, although dated, still useful for biographical details.

AINSLIE T. EMBREE

ALBERTUS MAGNUS

ALBERTUS MAGNUS (c. 1200-1280), also known as Albert the Great; German Dominican theologian and philosopher, doctor of the church, patron of natural scientists, and Christian saint. Today he is best known as the teacher of Thomas Aquinas.

Born in Lauingen on the Danube in Bavaria, Albert belonged to a distinguished military family in the service of the Hohenstaufens. While a student at Padua, he entered the mendicant Order of Preachers (Dominicans) in spring 1223, receiving the religious habit from Jordan of Saxony, successor to Dominic. Assigned to Cologne, he completed his early theological studies in 1228, then taught at Cologne, Hildesheim, Freiburg, Regensburg, and Strassburg. Around 1241 he was sent by the master general to the University of Paris for his degree in theology, which he obtained in the summer of 1245, having lectured on the *Sentences* of Peter Lombard and begun writing his *Summa parisiensis* in six parts: the sacraments, the incarnation, the resurrection, the

four coevals, man, and good. In 1248 Albert returned to Cologne with Thomas Aquinas and a group of Dominican students to open a center of studies for Germany.

From 1252 until 1279 Albert was frequently called upon to arbitrate difficult litigations on behalf of the pope or emperor. In June 1254 he was elected prior provincial of the German province of the Dominican order for three years. During Albert's term as provincial he wrote his paraphrases of Aristotle's *On the Soul* (Albert considered this paraphrase one of his most important), *On Natural Phenomena*, and *On Plants*.

Albert was appointed bishop of Regensburg by Pope Alexander IV on 5 January 1260, much against his inclinations. He was at the episcopal castle on the Danube when he wrote his commentary on book 7 of *On Animals*, but in December he set out for the papal curia at Viterbo to submit his resignation. The new pope, Urban IV, accepted his resignation around November 1261. From February 1263 to October 1264 he was the official papal preacher throughout German-speaking lands for a crusade to the Holy Land. With the death of Urban IV, Albert's commission ended, and he retired to Würzburg, where he worked on paraphrases of Aristotle's *Metaphysics* and other works until 1269, when Master General John of Vercelli asked him to reside at the *studium* in Cologne as lector emeritus. From then until his death, Albert lived at Cologne, writing, performing para-episcopal duties, arbitrating difficult cases, and serving as an example of religious piety to all.

Doctrine and Influence. In recent centuries Albert has been presented as a magician or an eclectic encyclopedist with Platonic and mystical tendencies. His writings are said to defy analysis, not only because of their gigantic bulk but also because of their nature in most cases as paraphrases of mainly Aristotle's writings. Although Albert was a bishop who wrote many theological works and biblical commentaries, he was known in his own day principally as a philosopher, and his authority ranked with that of Aristotle, Ibn Sina (Avicenna), and Ibn Rushd (Averroës).

Albert was the only Scholastic to be called "the Great," a title that was used even before his death. His prestige continued to be recognized not only among Albertists in France and Germany in the fifteenth century, but also among philosophers of the Italian Renaissance in the sixteenth century. Among his immediate students, apart from Thomas and Ulrich, were Hugh of Strassburg, John of Freiburg, John of Lichtenburg, and Giles of Lessines. Other German Dominicans, more favorably disposed toward Platonism, developed the mystical elements in Albert's thought. These were transmitted through Theodoric of Freiberg and Berthold of Mossburg to Meister Eckhart, Johannes Tauler, Heinrich Süse, and Jan van Ruusbroec. In the early fifteenth century a distinctive school of Albertists (who opposed the Thomists) developed in Paris under Jean de Maisonneuve and was promoted by Heymerich van den Velde in Paris and Cologne. It quickly spread throughout German, Bohemian, and Polish universities; in Italian universities, however, it was the philosophical opinions of Albert himself that were kept alive.

Numerous miracles were attributed to Albert, and many spurious works—devotional, necromantic, and Scholastic—were ascribed to him. The Protestant Reformation in the early sixteenth century temporarily diverted interest in Albert. He was quietly beatified by Gregory XV in 1622.

His extensive writings, occupying more than forty volumes in the critical edition (Cologne, 1951ff.), touch the whole of theology and scripture, as well as almost every branch of human knowledge in the Middle Ages, such as logic, natural science, mathematics, astronomy, ethics, and metaphysics. Ulrich of Strassburg, a Dominican disciple, described him as "a man so superior in every science that he can fittingly be called the wonder and miracle of our time."

Albert is best known for his belief in (1) the importance of philosophy for theology and (2) the autonomy of each science in its own field by reason of proper principles and method. He paraphrased the whole of Aristotle's philosophy for beginners in theology (1249-1270); he taught and promoted philosophy in his own school of theology (1248-1260); and he chaired the Dominican commission of five masters established to draw up the first program of study in the order that made the study of philosophy mandatory (1259). In philosophy Albert was a moderate realist and fundamentally an Aristotelian, but he did not hesitate to reject certain statements when he thought Aristotle was in error, nor was he averse to incorporating into his Aristotelianism compatible truths expounded by others.

By the decree *In thesauris sapientiae* (15 December 1931), Pius XI declared Albert a saint with the additional title of doctor. By the decree *Ad Deum* (16 December 1941), Pius XII constituted him the heavenly patron of all who cultivate the natural sciences. His body is buried in Cologne, and his feast is observed on 15 November.

BIBLIOGRAPHY

Apart from numerous early printed editions of both authentic and spurious writings ascribed to Albert, two editions of his "complete works" have been published: one in twenty-one folio volumes edited by Pierre Jammy, O.P. (Lyons, 1651), the other in thirty-eight quarto volumes edited by Auguste Borgnet (Paris, 1890-1899). A third, critical edition, under the auspices of the Albertus-Magnus-Institut of Cologne, is now being issued (Münster, 1951-) and is projected at forty volumes. The only authentic work of Albert available in English is his *Book of Minerals*, translated by Dorothy Wyckoff (Oxford, 1967).

Consecutive bibliographies are provided by three complementary works: "Essai de bibliographie albertinienne," by M.-H. Laurent and Yves Congar, *Revue thomiste* 36 (1931): 422-462, covering works published up to 1930; "Bibliographie philosophique de saint Albert le Grand," by M. Schooyans, *Revista da Universidade Catlica de So Paulo* 21 (1961): 36-88, covering the years from 1931 to 1960; and

"Bibliographie," in *Albertus Magnus: Doctor Universalis* 1280/1980, edited by G. Meyer and A. Zimmerman (Mainz, 1980), covering the years from 1960 to 1980.

Among the basic modern studies that should be noted are Paulus von Loë's "De vita et scriptis B. Alberti Magni," *Analecta Bollandiana* 19 (1900), 20 (1901), and 21 (1902); Gilles Meersseman's *Introductio in opera omnia B. Alberti Magni* (Bruges, 1931); Franz Pelster's *Kritische Studien zum Leben und zu den Schriften Alberts des Grossen* (Freiburg, 1920); and H. C. Scheeben's *Albert der Grosse: Zur Chronologie seines Lebens* (Vechta, 1931).

English biographies and studies that can be consulted with profit are Hieronymus Wilms's *Albert the Great, Saint and Doctor of the Church* (London, 1933), Thomas M. Schwertner's *Saint Albert the Great* (New York, 1932), and Lynn Thorndike's *A History of Magic and Experimental Science*, vol. 2 (Baltimore, 1923), pp. 517-592, 692-750. Noteworthy too is *Albertus Magnus and the Sciences: Commemorative Essays*, 1980, a collection of writings edited by me (Toronto, 1980).

JAMES A. WEISHEIPL

ALCHEMY

An Overview

The vocable *alchemia* appears in the West from the twelfth century onward in reference to the medieval quest for a means of transmuting base metals into gold, for a universal cure, and for the "elixir of immortality." In Chinese, Indian, and Greek texts alchemy is referred to as "the Art," or by terms indicating radical and beneficial change, for example, *transmutation*. Until quite recently, historians of science have studied alchemy as a protochemistry, that is, an embryonic science. But the alchemist's quest was not scientific but spiritual.

Esoteric Traditions and the Importance of Secrecy. In every culture where alchemy has flourished, it has always been intimately related to an esoteric or "mystical" tradition: in China to Taoism, in India to Yoga and Tantrism, in Hellenistic Egypt to *gnosis*, in Islamic countries to Hermetic and esoteric mystical schools, in the Western Middle Ages and Renaissance to Hermetism, Christian and sectarian mysticism, and Qabbalah.

For this reason, great emphasis is placed by the alchemist on secrecy, that is, the esoteric transmission of alchemical doctrines and techniques. The oldest Hellenistic text, *Physike kai mystike* (probably written around 200 BCE), relates how this book was discovered hidden in a column of an Egyptian temple.

It is significant that the injunction to secrecy and occultation is not abolished by the successful accomplishment of the alchemical work. According to Ko Hung, the adepts who obtain the elixir and become "immortals" *(hsien)* continue to wander on earth, but they conceal their condition, that is, their immortality, and are recognized as such only by a few fellow alchemists. Likewise, in India there is a vast literature, both in Sanskrit and in the vernaculars, in relation to certain famous *siddhis*, yogin-alchemists who live for centuries but who seldom disclose their identity. One encounters the same belief in central and western Europe.

Origins of Alchemy. The objects of the alchemical quest—namely, health and longevity, transmutation of base metals into gold, production of the elixir of immortality—have a long prehistory in the East as well as in the West. But the central aim of the alchemist was the transformation of ordinary metals into gold. This "noble" metal was imbued with sacrality.

Mining, Metallurgy, and Alchemy. Even if the historical beginnings of alchemy are as yet obscure, parallels between certain alchemical beliefs and rituals and those of early miners and metallurgists are clear. Indeed, all these techniques

> **But the central aim of the alchemist was the transformation of ordinary metals into gold.**

reflect the idea that man can influence the temporal flux. Mineral substances, hidden in the womb of Mother Earth, shared in the sacredness attached to the goddess. Very early we are confronted with the idea that ores "grow" in the belly of the earth after the manner of embryos. Metallurgy thus takes on the character of obstetrics.

With the help of fire, metalworkers transform the ores (the "embryos") into metals (the "adults"). The underlying belief is that, given enough time, the ores would have become "pure" metals in the womb of Mother Earth. Further, the "pure" metals would have become gold if they had been allowed to "grow" undisturbed for a few more thousand years.

The Alchemist Completes the Work of Nature. The transmutation of base metals into gold is tantamount to a miraculously rapid maturation. As Simone da Colonia put it: "This Art teaches us to make a remedy called the Elixir, which, being poured on imperfect metals, perfects them completely, and it is for this reason that it was invented" (quoted in Eliade, 1978, p. 166).

Moreover, the elixir is said to be capable of accelerating the temporal rhythm of all organisms and thus of quickening their growth. It was said to cure all maladies, to restore youth to the old, and to prolong life by several centuries.

Alchemy and Mastery of Time. Thus it seems that the central secret of "the Art" is related to the alchemist's mastery of cosmic and human time. Their elixir was reputed to heal and to rejuvenate men as well, indefinitely prolonging their lives. In the alchemist's eyes, man is *creative:* he redeems nature, masters time; in sum, he perfects God's creation.

BIBLIOGRAPHY

For the earliest relations between the rituals and mythologies of mining, metallurgy, and alchemy, see my book *The Forge and the Crucible: The Origins and Structures of Alchemy,* 2d ed. (Chicago, 1978); critical bibliographies are given therein. For a cultural history of mining, see T. A. Rickard's *Man and Metals: A History of Mining in Relation to the Development of Civilizations,* 2 vols. (New York, 1932). For the history of metallurgy, see R. J. Forbes's *Metallurgy in Antiquity: A Notebook for Archaeologists and Technologists* (Leiden, 1950) and Leslie Aitchison's *A History of Metals,* 2 vols. (London, 1960).

The origin and development of alchemy are presented from different perspectives by several authors: by Edmund von Lippmann in a three-volume work, *Entstehung und Ausbreitung der Alchemie* (Berlin, 1919-1954), of which volume 3 is indispensable; by John Reed in *Through Alchemy to Chemistry* (London, 1957); by Eric John Holmyard in *Alchemy* (Baltimore, 1957); and by Robert P. Multhauf in *The Origins of Chemistry* (London, 1966). On origins and development, see also three articles by Allan G. Debus: "The Significance of the History of Early Chemistry," *Cahiers d'histoire mondiale* 9 (1965): 39-58; "Alchemy and the Historian of Science," *History of Science* 6 (1967): 128-138; and "The Chemical Philosophers: Chemical Medicine from Paracelsus to van Helmont," *History of Science* 12 (1974): 235-259.

The works cited in this article on specific alchemical traditions are Wilhelm Ganzenmller's *Die Alchemie im Mittelalter* (Paderborn, West Germany, 1938), translated into French as *L'alchimie au Moyen-Âge* (Paris, 1940), and Nathan Sivin's *Chinese Alchemy: Preliminary Studies* (Cambridge, Mass., 1968).

MIRCEA ELIADE

Chinese Alchemy

Alchemy began in close alignment with popular religion, especially among educated groups in the Yangtze region. It was considered one of several disciplines that could lead to individual spiritual perfection and immortality. Some Taoist movements took up its practice after about 500 CE; it influenced both Buddhist and Taoist symbolism and liturgy.

Aims and Means. Chinese ideals of individual perfection combined three ideas that would have been incompatible in Egypt or Persia. The desire for immortality, which long preceded formal philosophy or religion, was the first of these ideas. [*See* Immortality.] In popular culture ideals of long life evolved into the notion that life need not end. This was not immortality of the soul in isolation, but immortality of the personality—of all that selfhood implied—within an imperishable physical body.

The potent personal force that may linger on after someone dies was undifferentiated in the thought of the uneducated, but in the conceptions of specialists it was separated into ten "souls" (three *yang hun* and seven *yin p'o*). Their normal postmortem dissipation could be prevented only if the body, their common site, could be made to survive with them. That, as Lu Gweidjen and Joseph Needham have suggested, is why Chinese immortality was bound to be material.

A second implication of immortality was perfection of the spirit. Because there was no dichotomy between the spiritual and the somatic, the refining of the body was not distinct from the activity of spiritual self-cultivation. Immortality was salvation from decrepitude and death. Piety, ritual, morality, and hygiene were equally essential to the prolongation of life.

A third implication of immortality, alongside spiritual and physical perfection, was assumption into a divine hierarchy. In popular thought this hierarchy was bureaucratic, a mirror of the temporal order. In fact, the bureaucratic ideal—of a symmetrical organization in which power and responsibility belonged to the post, and only temporarily to the individual who filled it—evolved more or less simultaneously in politics and religion.

History. Whether alchemy originated earlier in Hellenistic Egypt or China remains uncertain. Cinnabar and similar blood-colored compounds have been connected with ideas of death and immortality since the Neolithic period; that is how most scholars interpret the archaic custom of sprinkling red powders on corpses to be buried. The splendidly preserved corpse of the Lady of Tai (or Dai; died shortly after 168 BCE, excavated 1972) contained high concentrations of mercury and lead. These elements were distributed in a way consistent with ingestion before death. Traces in the intestines include native cinnabar, frequently prescribed by physicians as an immortality drug, rather than an artificial elixir. An edict dated 144 BCE against falsifying gold is sometimes said to show the prevalence of alchemy, but it presents no evidence that anything more was involved than artisans' use of alloys. In 133 BCE the Martial Emperor was told by an occultist that eating from plates of artificial gold would lengthen his life so that he could seek out certain immortals and, with their help, become an immortal himself by performing certain rituals.

Alchemy, Science, and Religion. Alchemy has been studied mainly by historians of chemistry, who have shown that the Chinese art exploited the properties of many chemical substances and even incorporated considerable knowledge of quantitative relations. Scholars of medical history have demonstrated close connections between alchemy and medicine, in the substances and processes on which both drew and in the use of artificial, mainly inorganic "elixirs" by physicians to treat disease and lengthen life. Historians have tended to see alchemy as a fledgling science, a precursor of modern inorganic chemistry and iatrochemistry.

This view overlooks the fact that the goals of alchemy were not cognitive. They were consistently focused on immortality and largely concerned with reenacting cosmic process for purposes of contemplation. It is impossible to say with certainty that alchemists discovered any new chemical interaction or process. Since alchemists were literate and

craftsmen were not, it is only to be expected that innovations by the latter would be first recorded by the former (who were almost the only members of the elite greatly interested in the chemical arts).

The idea that alchemy is Taoist by nature, or was invented by Taoists, has not survived advances since about 1970 in historical studies of Taoism. In the Celestial Master sect and other early Taoist movements drugs (including artificial preparations) were forbidden; only religious exercises could procure health and divine status. Upper-class initiates gradually began to use fashionable immortality drugs in the north. As refugees after the fall of Lo-yang in 311 they encountered elixirs in the Yangtze region, where alchemy had long been established among popular immortality practices. The aristocratic southerners they displaced in positions of temporal power invented new religious structures to assert, by way of compensation, their spiritual superiority. Michel Strickmann (1979) has demonstrated that in doing so they adapted northern Taoist usages to local popular practices, in which immortality and alchemy were central, and in which the religious use of inorganic drugs was usual. T`ao Hung-ching, a man of noble southern antecedents, drew on revelations inherited from fourth-century predecessors when he founded the Supreme Purity (or Mao-shan) Taoist movement under imperial patronage in about 500. T`ao adapted not only old southern techniques but elaborate structures of alchemical and astral imagery. T`ao thus formed a movement that captured upper-class allegiance, supported state power, and was supported in return for more than five centuries. He united alchemy with Taoism—the particular Taoism that he created—for the first time.

BIBLIOGRAPHY

The most detailed modern study of Chinese alchemy is in Joseph Needham's *Science and Civilisation in China* (Cambridge, 1954), vol. 5, pts. 2-5. For a brief summary, see Needham's *The Refiner's Fire: The Enigma of Alchemy in East and West* (London, 1971), the second J. D. Bernal Lecture, or, for cross-cultural comparisons, "Comparative Macrobiotics," in his *Science in Traditional China* (Cambridge, Mass., 1981), pp. 57-84. I discuss the symbolic structures used in alchemy at length in volume 5 of *Science and Civilisation in China*, pt. 4, pp. 210-305, summarized in more final form in "Chinese Alchemy and the Manipulation of Time," *Isis* 67 (1976): 513-526, and reprinted in *Science and Technology in East Asia*, edited by me (New York, 1977). On the religious significance of internal alchemy, see Farzeen Baldrian-Hussein's *Procédés secrets au Joyau magique: Traité d'alchimie taoïste du onzième siècle* (Paris, 1984). Pre-Taoist southern occult traditions, including alchemy, are discussed in Isabelle Robinet's "La revelation du Shangqing dans l'histoire du taoïsme" (Ph. D. diss., University of Paris, 1981). The relation between alchemy and Taoist movements has been trenchantly analyzed in Michel Strickmann's "On the Alchemy of T`ao Hung-ching," in *Facets of Taoism: Essays in Chinese Religion*, edited by Holmes Welch and Anna Seidel (New Haven, 1979), pp. 123-192; see also his *Le taoïsme du Mao-Chan: Chronique d'une révélation*, 2 vols., "Mémoires de l'Institut des Hautes Études Chinoises," no. 17 (Paris, 1981). Guides to methods of research in Chinese alchemy are my *Chinese Alchemy: Preliminary Studies*, "Harvard Monographs in the History of Science," vol. 1 (Cambridge, Mass., 1968), and Ch`en Kuo-fu's *Tao tsang yan liu hs k`ao* (Taipei, 1983).

NATHAN SIVIN

Indian Alchemy

"Gold is immortality." This correspondence from the Brahmanas grounds the worldview of the Indian alchemist. Just as gold neither corrodes nor loses its brilliance with time, so too the human body may realize a perfect and immutable state. In Indian alchemy, this is accomplished through *rasayana*, "the way of *rasa*" (i. e., of essences), which is the Sanskrit term for the alchemist's craft.

There are early references to chemical and metallurgical alchemical processes in the *Arthasastra*, the *Susruta Samhita*, and the so-called Bower manuscript. But the Indian alchemical tradition proper did not begin until these processes were correlated with techniques and goals of perfecting the body. The Indian alchemist's cosmology and metaphysics have their roots in the "emanationism" and microcosm-macrocosm analogues of Samkhya philosophy, of the yogic Upanisads, and of Vedanta. According to these philosophies, everything that exists is an emanation or emission (*vyapana* or *srsti*) from an original source or essence. It is destined for reabsorption (*laya* or *pralaya*) into the same. The emanated universe is hierarchical in structure. At the top of the hierarchy is the Absolute, which is variously conceived as Purusa, Prakrti, *brahman*, or a union of Siva and Sakti. Emanation proceeds down from the Absolute into the manifested world of the five sentient qualities, the senses, and the elements. Here the elements are conceived as stages rather than substances. The process of reintegration conceptually entails the stripping away of sheaths of ultimately illusory form in order to reveal a true and perfect essence.

Because it emphasizes the use of mercury and drugs in transmutation and in the realization of a perfect (*siddha*) and immortal body, Hindu alchemy is also known as mercurial (*dhatuvada*) alchemy, in contrast to Buddhist *rasayana*. The Buddhist yogic and Hindu chemical approaches often overlap, however, and one finds elements of both in the Nath, Siddha, Sahajiya, and Vajrayana Tantric traditions. The flowering of alchemical thought and practice was contemporaneous with that of Tantra, spanning roughly the sixth to the fifteenth centuries CE. Indian alchemists were often characterized as *siddhas* whose metaphysics and techniques at once embraced alchemy, yoga, and Tantra.

The Hindu mercurial alchemist's laboratory is portrayed as a microcosm of the universe. Just as the gross elements of the manifested world ultimately return to the Absolute

according to Vedantic philosophy, here the alchemist attempts to effect an analogous reintegration by using physical substances. He makes use of plant, animal, and mineral substances to remount the hierarchy of metals: lead, tin, copper, silver, and gold. The most essential elements that he employs are mercury (*rasa* or *parada*) and sulphur (*gandhaka*). In Hindu alchemy these elements are conceived as the seed (*bija* or *bindu*) of the male Siva and the sexual essence or blood (*sonita* or *rajas*) of the female Sakti, respectively.

According to Indian alchemy, yoga, and Tantra, every substance and combination of elements in the universe has its sexual valence. In the Hindu Tantric worldview, the manifest world is the emanation of the eternal union of *Siva* and *Sakti*. Their sexual essences, of which mercury and sulphur are hierophanies, are the means for reintegrating and perfecting the world. The alchemical *samskaras* are described in highly evocative language: mercury pierces or penetrates (*vedhana*) sulphur in order that it may be killed (*mrta*) and be "reborn" into a purer, more stable state (*bandha*) where it has a greater capacity for transmuting other elements. In the transmutation process mercury penetrates base metals. They are "killed" and "reborn" into increasingly higher states in the hierarchy of metals until finally perfect alchemical gold emerges from the sloughed-off sheaths of its grosser stages. The language of these samskaras is simultaneously one of initiation (as *diksa*), sexuality, and rebirth. The alchemist's craft is conceived of as a spiritual exercise, a ritual, a sacrifice, an act of devotion, and a participation in the divine play of an expanding or contracting universe. It is in such a context that we may best understand immortality as the ultimate goal of mercurial alchemy. In the alchemical universe, mercury (i. e., *Siva's* seed or *bija*) is capable of purifying and perfecting the human body in the same way that it perfects metallic "bodies."

BIBLIOGRAPHY

The broadest-ranging scientific approach to Indian alchemy remains Prafulla Chandra Ray's *A History of Hindu Chemistry*, 2 vols. (Calcutta, 1904-1909); a revised edition, edited by Priyadaranjan Ray under the title *History of Chemistry in Ancient and Medieval India* (Calcutta, 1956), contains excerpts and partial translations of some alchemical texts. Also highly useful for their compelling syntheses are Mircea Eliade's *The Forge and the Crucible: The Origins and Structures of Alchemy*, 2d ed. (Chicago, 1978), and Sashibhusan Dasgupta's *Obscure Religious Cults*, 3d ed. (Calcutta, 1969). Two excellent recent studies of Indo-Tibetan Buddhist alchemy are Michael Walter's "The Role of Alchemy and Medicine in Indo-Tibetan Tantra" (Ph. D. diss., University of Indiana, Bloomington, 1982) and Edward Todd Fenner's *Rasayana Siddhi: Medicine and Alchemy in the Buddhist Tantras* (Madison, Wis., 1983); the latter contains a translation of the alchemical section of the *Vimala-prabha*, a commentary on the *Kalacakra Tantra*.

Madhava's fourteenth-century work *Sarva-darsana-samgraha*, translated by Edward B. Cowell, 7th ed. (Varanasi, 1978), includes a section on the "Mercurial school" of Indian philosophy, which passes in review the teachings of the major texts of the Hindu alchemical tradition. Most important among these is the Sanskrit *Rasarnavam* (c. tenth century), edited by Indradeo Tripathi, 2d ed. (Varanasi, 1978), which contains references to devotional aspects of alchemy (see 1.37-38, 1.43-52, and 1.109-116) and to the origin myth of sulphur (7.57-66). The *Rasaratnasamucchaya* of Vagbhata (c. fourteenth century), edited by Shridharmananda Sharma, 2d ed. (Delhi, 1962), contains an origin myth of mercury (1.60-66). For discussion of the "historical Nagarjuna" and other alchemists, see K. Satchidananda Murty's *Nagarjuna* (New Delhi, 1971) and Giuseppe Tucci's "Animadversiones Indicae," *Journal of the Asiatic Society of Bengal* 26 (1930): 125-160.

DAVID WHITE

Hellenistic and Medieval Alchemy

By the beginning of the Christian era, a change in secular and religious attitudes can be discerned. The rationalism that had guided the thinking of the elite in previous times waned, and the rise of skepticism and loss of direction led to a philosophical vacuum that stimulated a recourse to mystic intuition and divine mysteries. The area of the Roman empire in which this process became primarily manifest was Egypt, where, after the conquest by Alexander the Great (in 332 BCE), the culture of Hellenism with its fusion of Greek and Eastern features was centered. The fashionable mystery beliefs subsumed under the names of gnosticism and Hermetism exerted a strong attraction for practitioners of the occult sciences (astrology, magic, and medicine) as well as alchemy, the art of making gold: previously, men of science had by thought process and investigations obtained what they now expected to receive through divine revelation or supernatural inspiration. In short, science as revealed knowledge and, for the alchemist, as a means of creating gold-turned into religion.

Such a link between alchemy and gnosticism and Hermetism is most tangibly documented in the occult literature of Hellenistic Egypt from about the second to the fourth century. This emphasizes, first, the fact that alchemy, beyond being a craft devoted to changing matter, has a place also within the history of religions and, second, that in the alchemist's religious beliefs the general gnostic tenets blended with his specific alchemical approach to the world.

Doctrine. The soul is enchained in matter and is to be freed. Science as traditionally expounded in the schools was unable to liberate it. Only gnosis, the knowledge of God, could accomplish the task, and to convey gnosis, alchemy transformed itself into an esoteric religion. The doctrines of alchemy as a religion echoed the principles of alchemy as a science. These were essentially three: primal matter, sympathy, and transmutation.

Primal matter. The *opus alchimicum*, ("the alchemist's labor") centered on matter. Nobody knew, of course, what

matter was, and it remained a secret of alchemy, although many chemical, mythological, and philosophical definitions were ventured in the course of time (Jung, 1953, p. 317). Thus, the *Tabula Smaragdina* (the revelation of secret alchemical teaching, of the ninth century but based on Hermetic sources) identified matter with God, because all created objects come from a single primal matter; and Comarius, an alchemist-philosopher (first century CE?) identified it with Hades, to whom the imperfect souls were chained (Jung, pp. 299, 319). Such perceptions of matter

> The *Tabula Smaragdina . . .* identified matter with God, because all created objects come from a single primal matter.

echo the alchemist's craft: his operation was, in mythical terms, a replica of divine creativity, aiming at the liberation of imprisoned matter.

Transmutation. The third facet of alchemical religiosity was also linked to the alchemist's practice. A basic alchemical tenet stated that all substances could be derived through transmutation from primal matter. The technique of change consisted essentially in "coloring": the Egyptian alchemists did not intend to "make" gold but to color (*baptein*) metals and textiles through tinctures and elixirs so that they would "appear" like gold (or silver or some other metal). A "changed" metal, then, was a "new" metal. The technique of coloring evolved, in the end, into a powerful symbol of alchemical doctrine; for just as the alchemist transformed lead into silver, and silver into gold, so too he posited for matter, in his anthropomorphic view of it, a similar change, from body to spirit to soul. And in the frame of his doctrine, he identified this escalation with the renewal of man, to which he assigned the same chain of transmutations to reach the goal of redemption.

The mystagogues. The myth of transmission added the religious component to alchemical mysticism. The spokesmen invoked the authority of the supreme being, or its prophets, or the sages of old: "Behold [says Isis to her son as alchemist], the mystery has been revealed to you!" (Festugière, 1950, p. 260). Maria Prophetissa claimed that alchemical secrets were revealed to her by God. The Byzantine monk Marianus quoted alchemists saying to Maria: "The divine, hidden, and always splendid, secret is revealed to you."

With Egypt providing the setting of the cult, Egyptian mythical figures and divinities were the prime well-spring of inspiration: chiefly Thoth (hellenized as Hermes Trismegistos), the legendary author of the Hermetica, and Isis, turned into the creators and teachers of alchemy to whom alchemical sayings and doctrines were attributed. Various Greek writings on alchemy that contained traces of Jewish monotheism were ascribed to Moses, probably in a homonymic transfer from the alchemist Moses of Alexandria. Later on, Jewish alchemical tradition evoked Enoch, the Jewish counterpart to Hermes.

Symbols. The alchemist, in the formulation of Wayne Shuhmaker, "did not analyze but analogized," and his own universe, metallurgy, provided the mythical imagery and stimulated new meanings. The alchemical *opus* centered on the change of matter, and transmutation of matter turned into the recurrent theme of the alchemist's cult. To him, the soul imprisoned in matter symbolized the spirit striving to purify itself from the roughage of the flesh. Matter was represented above all by metal and symbolized life and man, its growth comparable to the growth of the fetus.

Many lexical items were drawn into the process: thus, in the Valentinian system of gnosticism (deriving from the second-century Egyptian Valentinus), metallurgical terms such as the following symbolized spiritual concepts. Pneuma signified, first, the product of natural sublimation, then, "divine spirit"; ebullient ("boiling up"), referring to the alchemical process of "separating the pure from the impure," was applied to wisdom; sperma (the "embryonic germ") yielded the "seed" of gnosis; in a similar way, such terms as *refine*, *filter*, and *purify* acquired spiritualized meanings. The transfer, through alchemy, from the literal to the symbolic realm contributed richly to the language of religion and, generally, abstraction. It indicates a conscious effort of the alchemist to frame his views in the terms of his craft.

Antonyms. Hellenistic alchemy tended to emphasize the varied contraries inherent in the craft: hot/cold, moist/dry, earth/air, fire/water. Antonymic structure was symbolically superimposed on matter: Maria Prophetissa distinguished metals as male and female as if they were human, and Zosimos distinguished between the metals' souls and bodies. The same antonymy, but with the focus on man himself, characterizes gnostic dualism with its model of spiritual versus carnal man.

Classical philosophy. The great cognitions of the classical tradition, from the pre-Socratics to Plato, Aristotle, and the Stoics, resurfaced in eclectic Hellenistic philosophy. Numerous doctrines prefigured crucial phases of the alchemical worldview: the concept of a primal matter; the unity of matter (seen in, say, water or fire); cosmic correspondences; the affinity of the similar; the microcosm reflecting the macrocosm; the notion of sympathy; transformation through *pneuma*, the all pervading spirit; genesis, that is, the origin of one element from another, proceding by way of opposites.

Mystery creeds. Hermetism and the alchemical cult overlap in various features. The tie between them is substantiated in the writings of Zosimos, the "divine," the "high-

ly learned," and the outstanding representative of both creeds. The common ground consisted of "mystic reveries" (Festugière): observation and inquiry were rejected, and intuition replaced science; the "sacred craft" was revealed through divine grace; the chosen were few, bound to secrecy; and the goal was the liberation of the soul from the body.

Convergence. These four components of spiritual alchemy can be traced in Hellenistic Egypt. The craft of the goldsmith was flourishing, and metallurgy yielded the imagery while boosting, by its very nature, the identification, ever present in the human mind, of self and matter; Greek philosophy, in a stage of revival then and there, provided the basic concepts of the doctrine; and Hermetism supplied the vital climate of mystery.

Alchemy is described here as a facet of the ancient mystery religions, and this description centers on its style and manifestations in the Hellenistic period. But other cultures, tending in a similar direction, produced other varieties of spiritual alchemy. The relationship (involving the question of polygenesis or monogenesis) between the Chinese, Indian, and Hellenic forms of spiritual alchemy is not very clear. Islamic culture, on the other hand, played a vital role in the transmission of alchemical knowledge; many of the Greek texts were translated into Arabic and through this link, reached the West during the late Middle Ages. Thus, the transmutation of matter continued, with its occult framework, into the Renaissance and beyond.

[*See also* Gnosticism.]

BIBLIOGRAPHY

The literature is large and rapidly growing. A comprehensive bibliography is Alan Pritchard's *Alchemy: A Bibliography of English-Language Writings* (London and Boston, 1980). The previous standard, *Collection des anciens alchimistes grecs*, edited and translated by Marcellin P. E. Berthelot and Charles-Émile Ruelle, 3 vols. (1887-1888; reprint, Osnabrück, 1967), will be superseded by *Les alchimistes grecs*, 12 vols. (1981-), a comprehensive edition of the texts, with French translations.

Good surveys, from varying standpoints and usually with bibliographical information, may be consulted in the standard cyclopedias: Wilhelm Gundel's "Alchemie," in *Reallexikon für Antike und Christentum* (Stuttgart, 1950); Franz Strunz's "Alchemie," in *Die Religion in Geschichte und Gegenwart*, 3d ed., vol. 1 (Tübingen, 1957); René Alleau's "Alchimie," in *Encyclopaedia Universalis*, vol. 1 (Paris, 1968); Bernard Suler's "Alchemy," in *Encyclopaedia Judaica*, vol. 2 (Jerusalem, 1971); Manfred Ullmann's "Al-Kimiya," in *The Encyclopaedia of Islam*, new ed., vol. 5 (Leiden, 1979); and Robert P. Multhauf's "Alchemy," in *Encyclopaedia Britannica*, 15th ed., vol. 1 (Chicago, 1983).

The present overview draws, in particular, on the studies by A.-J. Festugière, *La révélation d'Hermès Trismégiste*, vol. 1 (Paris, 1950), and "Alchymica" (1939), reprinted in *Hermtisme et mystique païenne* (Paris, 1967); Mircea Eliade's *The Forge and the Crucible*, 2d ed. (Chicago, 1978); C. G. Jung's *Psychology and Alchemy*, translated by R. F. C. Hull (Princeton, 1953); and the various articles and reviews by H. J. Sheppard in the journal *Ambix*, listed in the index for volumes I-17.

HENRY and RENÉE KAHANE

Islamic Alchemy

The Arabic term for alchemy is *al-kimiya'*. The word *kimiya'* is alternately derived from the Greek *chumeia* (or *chemeia*), denoting the "art of transmutation," or from *kimiya*, a South Chinese term meaning "gold-making juice."

In the Islamic context, *al-kimiya'* refers to the "art" of transmuting substances, both material and spiritual, to their highest form of perfection. The word *kimiya'* also refers to the agent or catalyst that effects the transmutation and hence is used as a synonym for *al-iksir* ("elixir") and *hajar al-falasifah* ("philosopher's stone"). The search for the ideal elixir has been an ancient quest in many cultures of the world; it was supposed to transform metals to their most perfect form (gold) and minerals to their best potency and, if the correct elixir were to be found, to achieve immortality. All matter of a particular type, metals for example, were supposed to consist of the same elements. The correct *kimiya'* or *iksir* would enable the transposition of the elements into ideal proportions and cause the metal concerned to be changed from a base form to a perfected form, for instance, copper to gold.

Historical Background. In Muslim tradition, alchemy enjoys ancient roots. The cultivation of alchemy is traced back to Adam, followed by most of the major prophets and sages. This chain of transmission is then connected to the "masters" from the ancient world, including Aristotle, Galen, Socrates, Plato, and others. Muslims are considered to have received the art from these masters. In Islamic times, the prophet Muhammad (d. 632 CE), is said to have endorsed the art, lending it grace and power.

The Jabirian corpus. Modern scholarship places the development of Islamic alchemy in the ninth century. Jabir ibn Hayyan is indeed recorded as the first major alchemist, but the writings attributed to him are mainly pseudepigraphical, and many appeared as late as the tenth century. *The Book of Mercy, the Book of the Balances*, the *Book of One Hundred and Twelve*, the *Seventy Books*, and the *Five Hundred Books* are some of the important works in the collection. Movements such as the Ikhwan al-Safa' (Brethren of Purity) probably influenced or even contributed to some of the treatises in the Jabirian corpus, which forms an important source of information on alchemic techniques, equipment, materials, and attitudes.

According to the sulfur-mercury theory of metals introduced in the corpus, all metals were considered to possess these two elements, or the two principles they represent, in varying proportions, the combination of which lends each metal its peculiarities. Sulfur was responsible for the hot/dry features and mercury, the cold/moist ones. (Aristotle considered these four features to be represented by fire, earth, air, and water respectively.) Sulfur and mercury embody the positive and negative aspects of matter, also referred to as male and female properties.

Al-Razi. The physician and philosopher Muhammad ibn Zakariya' al-Razi (d. 925) is the next Muslim alchemist who made a major impact on the art. To the sulfur-mercury theory of the constitution of metals he added the attribute of salinity. The popular conception of alchemy with three elements—sulfur, mercury, and salt—reappeared in Europe and played an important role in Western alchemy. According to al-Razi, bodies were composed of invisible elements (atoms) and of empty space that lay between them. These atoms were eternal and possessed a certain size. This conception seems close to the explanation of the structure of matter in modern physics. Al-Razi's books, *Sirr al asrar* (The Secret of Secrets) and *Madkhal al-ta`limi* (Instructive [or Practical] Introduction), are important sources for understanding the principles and techniques of alchemy as practiced in the tenth-century Muslim world, specifically Iran. In them, he provides a systematic classification of carefully observed and verified facts regarding chemical substances, reactions, and apparatus, described in language that is free of mysticism and ambiguity.

Opposition to the Art. Although widespread, alchemy did not have the approval of all Muslim scholars. Thus Ibn Sina (d. 1035) censured it as a futile activity and contested the assertion that man is able to imitate nature. The great North African historian Ibn Khaldun (d. 1406) also made a critical assessment of Arab-Islamic alchemical activities. He characterized alchemy as the study of the properties, virtues, and temperatures of the elements used for the preparation of and search for an elixir that could transform lesser metals into gold. Ibn Khaldun rejected the alchemists' claims that their transmutations were intended to perfect the work of nature by mechanical and technical procedures.

BIBLIOGRAPHY

For general surveys of Islamic alchemy, the following essays are useful: Salimuzzaman Siddiqi and S. Mahdihassan's "Chemistry," in *A History of Muslim Philosophy*, edited by M. M. Sharif (Wiesbaden, 1966), vol. 2, pp. 1296-1316; Seyyed Hossein Nasr's "Alchemy and Other Occult Sciences," in his *Islamic Science: An Illustrated Study* (Westerham, England, 1976), pp. 193-208; Eric J. Holmyard's "Alchemy in Medieval Islam," *Endeavour* 14 (July 1955): 117-125; Julius Ruska's Turba Philosophorum: Ein Beitrag zur Geschichte der Alchemie (Berlin, 1931); and Manfred Ullmann's "al-Kimiya," in *The Encyclopaedia of Islam*, new ed. (Leiden, 1960-). As yet no comprehensive critical study of the origin, development, and practices of traditional Islamic alchemy is available.

Overviews of Islamic alchemy within the context of global surveys of alchemy or chemistry can be found in Eric J. Holmyard's *Alchemy*

(Baltimore, 1957), chap. 5; George Sarton's *Introduction to the History of Science*, 3 vols. in 5 (Washington, D. C., 1927-1948); Robert P. Multhauf's *The Origins of Chemistry* (London, 1966); *Studien zur Geschichte der Chemie*, edited by Julius Ruska (Berlin, 1927); and Homer H. Dub's "The Beginnings of Alchemy," *Isis* 38 (November 1947): 62-86. Dubs argues that alchemy in Islam originated in China.

Julius Ruska and Karl Garbers discuss the mutual relation of the corpus Jabirian and the writings of al-Razi, large alchemical works written at the end of the ninth and tenth centuries, in "Vorschriften zur Herstellung von scharfen Wässern bei Gabir und Razi," *Islam* 25 (1938): 1-35. Some of the problems surrounding these writings are studied in Ruska's *Chalid ibn Jazid ibn Mu`awija* and *Ga'far al-Sadiq der sechste Imam*, volumes 1 and 2 of *Arabische Alchemisten* (Heidelberg, 1924); in Paul Kraus's "Studien zu Jbir Ibn Hayyân," *Isis* (February 1931): 7-30; and in Gerard Heym's "Al-Razi and Alchemy," *Ambix* 1 (March 1938): 184-191.

A valuable study of the secret names used by Arab alchemists is Julius Ruska and E. Wiedemann's "Alchemistische Decknamen," in *Sitzungsberichte der physikalisch-medicinische Sozietät* (Erlangen, 1924). Their study partially utilizes al-Tugra`i's *Kitab al-Jawhar al-nadir* (Book of the Brilliant Stone).

HABIBEH RAHIM

Renaissance Alchemy

The Renaissance and post-Renaissance period marked both the high point and the turning point of alchemy in the West. During the same years in which Kepler, Galileo, Descartes, Boyle, and Newton wrote their revolutionary scientific works, more alchemical texts were published than ever before. But under the impact first of the Reformation and later of the seventeenth-century scientific revolution, alchemy was profoundly changed and ultimately discredited. The organic, qualitative theories of the alchemists were replaced by an atomistic, mechanical model of change, which eventually undermined the alchemical theory of transmutation. The balance between the spiritual and the physical, which had characterized alchemical thought throughout its long history, was shattered, and alchemy was split into two halves, theosophy and the practical laboratory science of chemistry.

The Practice of Alchemy. For the most part Renaissance alchemists accepted the theories and practices of their ancient and medieval predecessors. By the time the study of alchemy came to Europe, it was already an established discipline with a respected past. The theories upon which it was based were an integral part of ancient philosophy. Western scientists accepted these theories precisely because they provided plausible explanations for the way events were observed to occur in nature and the laboratory.

Alchemy as a Spiritual Discipline. Mystery and religion, which were a part of alchemy from its beginnings, gained in importance from the Renaissance onward. In many cases alchemy moved out of the laboratory altogether and into the monk's cell or philosopher's study. The popularity of alchemy as a spiritual discipline coincided with the breakdown of religious orthodoxy and social organization during the Renaissance and the Reformation.

The interpretation of alchemy as a spiritual discipline offended many churchmen, who viewed the combination of alchemical concepts and Christian dogma in the writings of spiritual alchemists as dangerous heresy. One of the most daring appropriations of Christian symbolism was made by Nicholas Melchior of Hermanstadt, who expounded the alchemical work in the form of a mass.

Alchemists of the sixteenth and seventeenth centuries drew many of their ideas from Renaissance Neoplatonism and Hermetism. In all three systems, the world was seen as a single organism penetrated by spiritual forces that worked at all levels, the vegetable, animal, human, and spiritual. Frances Yates has brillantly described the "magus" mentality that evolved from these ideas and encouraged men to believe they could understand and control their environment. This state of mind is illustrated in the writings of Paracelsus (1493-1541). For Paracelsus, God was the divine alchemist, who created the world by calcinating, congealing, distilling, and sublimating the elements of chaos. Chemistry was the key to the universe, which would disclose the secrets of theology, physics, and medicine. The alchemist had only to read the reactions in his laboratory on a grand scale to fathom the mysteries of creation.

Renaissance Alchemy and Modern Science. No one knows who wrote the Rosicrucian manifestos. They have been attributed to Johann Valentin Andrea (1586-1654), whose acknowledged writings contain a similar blend of utopianism and spiritual alchemy. In his most famous work, *Christianopolis*, Andrea describes an ideal society organized to promote the health, education, and welfare of its citizens. One of the institutions in this society is a "laboratory" dedicated to the investigation of nature and to the application of useful discoveries for the public good.

Francis Bacon (1561-1626) was one of the many philosophers influenced by the Rosicrucian manifestos. Bacon looked forward to what he called a "Great Instauration" of learning that would herald the return of the Golden Age. He described this in his own utopia, *The New Atlantis*.

Neither Andrea nor Bacon said much that was new or significant in terms of science. What was novel in their visions was the idea of a scientific institution whose members worked by a common method toward a common goal. The secrecy and mystery that had been such a basic part of alchemy played no role in the scientific societies each describes, although their visions had been sparked by the utopian schemes of spiritual alchemists. This was one of the most important innovations to emerge in all the utopian literature of the seventeenth century and the one that had the greatest impact on the decline of alchemy. Once alchemists openly communicated their discoveries, the stage was set for the tremendous advances we have come to expect from the natural sciences.

BIBLIOGRAPHY

General accounts of the history of Renaissance alchemy and the emergence of chemistry may be found in my *Alchemy: The Philosopher's Stone* (Boulder, 1980); Allen G. Debus's *The Chemical Philosophy: Paracelsian Science and Medicine in the Sixteenth and Seventeenth Centuries*, 2 vols. (New York, 1977); Eric J. Holmyard's *Alchemy* (Baltimore, 1957); John Read's *Through Alchemy to Chemistry* (London, 1957); and J. R. Partington's *A History of Chemistry*, 4 vols. (London, 196l-1970). *Ambix: The Journal for the Society for the Study of Alchemy and Early Chemistry* (Cambridge, 1937-1979) contains important specialized articles. Maurice P. Crosland's *Historical Studies in the Language of Chemistry* (London, 1962) provides an invaluable guide to the intricacies of alchemical terminology. Betty J. Dobbs's *The Foundations of Newton's Alchemy* (Cambridge, 1975) sheds light on the period of transition from alchemy to chemistry. The best introduction to Paracelsus is Walter Pagel's *Paracelsus* (New York, 1958). Renaissance Neoplatonism, Hermetism, and the Qabbalah are brilliantly described and analyzed in Frances Yates's *Giordano Bruno and the Hermetic Tradition* (London, 1964). She discusses the Rosicrucian manifestos in *The Rosicrucian Enlightenment* (London, 1972). H. J. Sheppard has published important articles on alchemical symbolism in *Ambix*. Jacques van Lennep's *L'art et l'alchimie* (Paris, 1966) is also useful. J. W. Montgomery discusses Luther's views on alchemy in "Cross, Constellation and Crucible: Lutheran Astrology and Alchemy in the Age of Reformation," *Ambix* 11 (1963): 65-86.

There are several collections of Renaissance alchemical texts. Thomas Norton's *Ordinall* and George Ripley's *Twelve Gates* can be found in Elias Ashmole's *Theatrum Chemicum Britannicum* (1652; reprint, New York, 1967). *Theatrum Chemicum* (1659-1661) provides six volumes of alchemical writings. Another collection, the *Musaeum Hermeticum Reformatum* (Frankfurt, 1678) has been translated by Arthur E. Waite as *The Hermetic Museum*, 2 vols. (London, 1893).

ALLISON COUDERT

ALL FOOL'S DAY

The first day of April, known as All Fools' Day or April Fools' Day, is traditionally marked by the custom of playing jokes (usually on friends) and engaging in frivolous activities. It stands as one of the few spring festivals in Christian Europe unaffected by the date of the celebration of Easter. All Fools' Day should not be confused with the Feast of Fools, the medieval mock-religious festival involving status reversals and parodies of the official church by low-level cathedral functionaries and others (held on or about the Feast of the Circumcision, 1 January). April Fools' Day activities, however, are related in spirit to this once-licensed kind of revelry. The actual origins of April Fools' practices and their connection to the first of April are unknown. The day and its tradi-

tions appear to reflect some of the festive characteristics of such non-Christian religious celebrations as the Hilaria of ancient Rome (25 March) and the Holi festival of India (ending 31 March). Traditional celebrations related to the vernal equinox and to the arrival of spring in the Northern Hemisphere, as well as that season's playful and often fickle weather, may also have contributed to the timing and persistence of April Fools' customs.

The development of All Fools' Day has been the subject of much popular speculation. The day has been seen as commemorating the wanderings from place to place of the raven and dove Noah sent from the ark to search for dry land after the biblical flood. It has also been thought to memorialize in an irreverent way the transfer of Jesus from the jurisdiction of one governmental or religious figure to another in the last hours before his crucifixion. In either

> **The day has been seen as commemorating the wanderings from place to place of the raven and dove Noah sent from the ark. . . .**

case, the events in question were believed to have occurred on or near the first of April. An intriguing explanation for April Fools' Day customs in France, on the other hand, concerns confusion over the change in the date for the observance of the New Year. Those who recognized 25 March as the beginning of their year (a number of different dates were used to mark this occasion in medieval Europe) culminated their eight-day celebration of this event on 1 April. When in 1564 Charles IX changed the official date to 1 January, some people either resisted the change or failed to remember when the year was to begin. This confusion led to the practice of exchanging false greetings for the first of the year on the old day of its observance (1 April) and of sending false gifts, as a joke, to those who expected the customary holiday presents on that day. Thus some scholars believe that jests of all sorts soon came to be associated with this date.

BIBLIOGRAPHY

Little worthwhile scholarly work has been done on the subject of All Fools' Day. A valuable English antiquarian source of information on the day's customs is *The Book of Days*, 2 vols., edited by Robert Chambers (1862-1864; Philadelphia, 1914). A more contemporary reflection on April Fools' Day traditions, especially in Great Britain, can be found in Christina Hole's *British Folk Customs* (London, 1976). Hertha Wolf-Beranek's "Zum Aprilscherz in den Sudetenländern," *Zeitscchrift für Volkskunde* 64 (1968): 223-227, provides a short but useful summary of the changes that have taken place, in European usage, in the term describing individuals who are fooled on 1 April. Catherine H. Ainsworth's "April Fools' Day," in volume 1 of her *American Calendar Customs* (Buffalo, N. Y., 1979), inadequately explains the origins of the observance, but her collected accounts of the day as celebrated in the United States are informative.

LEONARD NORMAN PRIMIANO

ALTAR

The English word *altar*, meaning "a raised structure on which sacrifices are offered to a deity," derives from the Latin *altare* ("altar") and may be related to *altus* ("high"). This ancient meaning has been further verified by the corresponding Classical Greek term *bomos* (raised platform, stand, base, altar with a base," i. e., the foundation of the sacrifice). The Latin *altaria* is, in all likelihood, related to the verb *adolere* ("to worship"; originally, "to burn, to cause to go up in smoke or odor"), so that the word has come to signify a "place of fire" or "sacrificial hearth."

The Classical World and Ancient Near East. Greeks and Romans made careful distinctions between different altar forms: the raised altar site where sacrifices to the heavenly gods were performed; the pit (Gr., *bothros*; Lat., *mundus*) that was dug to receive the offerings to the deities of the underworld; and the level ground where gifts to the earth gods were deposited. The altar was a symbol of the unseen presence of the gods and was therefore considered a sacred spot.

Egyptian ritual worship included both portable and stationary altars. Most of the extant stationary altars were used in the sun temples and were surrounded by a low wall indicating the special sacred nature of their place during sun rites that were devoid of imagery.

Hinduism. The nomadic Indo-Aryans who invaded India around 1500 BCE carried with them a portable fire altar drawn on a chariot (*ratha*) and protected by a canopy that marked the holiness of the shrine. This eternally burning fire on a rolling base was eventually replaced by fires kindled for the occasion by rubbing sticks together. In the case of domestic sacrifices, the head of the family made the fire in the home hearth (*ayatana*). For communal offerings, a fire was made on a specially consecrated spot (*sthandila*).

There were no temples during the Vedic period, but a sacrificial hall (*yagasala*) could be erected on holy ground that had first been thoroughly leveled. It consisted of a framework of poles covered with thatching. The sacred area, which like the domestic hearth was called *ayatana*, included subsidiary enclosures and a sacrificial stake (*yupa*) to which the victim was tied. This stake, which represented the cosmic tree, constituted an intermediate station between the divine world and life on earth.

Israelite Religion and Early Judaism. The Hebrew term for altar is *mizbeah* ("a place of sacrificial slaughter"), which is derived from *zabah* ("to slaughter as a sacrifice"). In time, the animal slaughter came to be performed beside, not on, the altar. Other kinds of oblations offered on the altar were grain, wine, and incense. The altar sometimes served a non-sacrificial function as witness (*Jos.* 22:26ff.) or refuge (1 *Kgs.* 1:50f.) for most crimes except murder.

The altars, if not made from natural or rough-hewn rocks, were constructed from unhewn stone, earth, or metal. The tabernacle, or portable desert sanctuary of the Israelites, had a bronze-plated altar for burnt offerings in the court and a gold-plated incense altar used within the tent. Both of these altars were constructed of wood, and each was fitted with four rings and two poles for carrying.

The function of the Israelite altar was essentially the same as in other sanctuaries of the ancient Near East but with some important differences. While sacrifices were still referred to as "the bread of your God" (*Lv.* 22:25) and "a pleasing odor to the Lord" (*Lv.* 1:17), the notion of actually feeding Yahveh was not implied.

Abraham's binding of Isaac on the altar in the land of Moriah is considered the supreme example of self-sacrifice in obedience to God's will, and the symbol of Jewish martyrdom throughout the ages. Abraham himself was, from this point of view, the first person to prepare for martyrdom, and his offering was the last of the ten trials to which he was exposed.

Christianity. Paul contrasted the Christian service with the pagan sacrificial meal by stating that we cannot partake of the Lord's table and the devil's table at the same time (*1 Cor.* 10:21). He thus distinguished between pagan sacrificial altars and the table at which Christ celebrated the Last Supper with his disciples. The New Testament constitutes the dividing point between Judaism and Christianity: Christ has, once and for all, made the full and sufficient sacrifice of himself (*Heb.* 8-10). The terminology of the sacrifice is used figuratively in reference to the dedication of Christian life (*Rom.* 12:1) and to the mission of Paul himself (*Phil.* 2:17).

The Western church eventually settled on the Latin term *altare* ("a raised place") since it corresponded not only to the sacrificial altars of the Temple-centered Israelite religion but also to the various non-Christian cults of the Roman world. The Christians differentiated their altars from pagan ones by using the terms *altare* and *mensa* instead of *ara*, and by referring to their altar in the singular, reserving the plural *altaria* for pagan places of sacrifice.

Following the adoption of the altar by the early Christian churches, its sacred nature became increasingly emphasized. It was the foundation of the elements of the Eucharist, and the special presence of Christ was expressed in the epiclesis of the eucharistic liturgy. A rich symbolism could therefore develop. The altar could be seen as a symbol of the heavenly throne or of Christ himself: the altar is made of stone, just as Christ is the cornerstone (*Mt.* 21:42). It also could be his cross or his grave.

After the Reformation, with its opposition to relic worship and to the conception of the Mass as a sacrifice, it was primarily the Eucharist of the early church that came to be associated with the altar table. The reformers emphasized the importance of the true and pure preaching of the word of God, with the result that the pulpit gained a more prominent position, sometimes at the expense of the altar.

BIBLIOGRAPHY

Behm, Johannes. "Thuo, thusia, thusiasterion." In *Theological Dictionary of the New Testament*, edited by Gerhard Kittel and Gerhard Friedrich, vol. 3. Grand Rapids, Mich., 1966. A standard work; the supplementary bibliography published in 1979 contains only works on sacrifice.

Bonnet, Hans. "Altar." *Reallexikon der ägyptischen Religionsgeschichte*, pp. 14-17. Berlin, 1952.

Eliade, Mircea. *Patterns in Comparative Religion.* New York, 1958.

Eliade, Mircea. *A History of Religious Ideas*, vol. 1, From the Stone Age to the Eleusinian Mysteries. Chicago, 1978.

Fauth, Wolfgang. "Altar." In *Der Kleine Pauly*, vol. 1, cols. 279-281. Stuttgart, 1964. Although brief, refers to the authors of classical antiquity.

Galling, Kurt. "Altar." *In Interpreter's Dictionary of the Bible*, vol. 1, pp. 96-100. A German Old Testament scholar summarizes his important contributions to the discussion of the altar in the ancient Near East.

Gonda, Jan. *Die Religionen Indiens*, vol. 1, *Veda und älterer Hinduismus* (1960). 2d rev. ed. Stuttgart, 1978. By the leading Dutch Indologist.

Gray, Louis H., et al. "Altar." In *Encyclopaedia of Religion and Ethics*, edited by James Hastings, vol. 1. Edinburgh, 1908. Although largely outdated, some sections are still useful (e.g., Christian, Greek).

Hopkins, Thomas J. *The Hindu Religious* Tradition. Belmont, Calif., 1971.

Jacobs, Louis. "Akedah." In *Encyclopaedia Judaica*, vol. 2, cols. 480-487. Jerusalem, 1971.

Kirsch, Johann P., and Theodor Klauser. "Altar: Christlich." In *Reallexikon für Antike und Christentum*, edited by Theodor Klauser, vol. 1, cols. 334-354. Stuttgart, 1950. Well documented, with a lengthy bibliography.

Kohler, Kaufmann, and George A. Barton. "Altar." In *Jewish Encyclopedia*, edited by Isidore Singer, vol. 1, pp. 464-469. New York, 1901. Relates Jewish to Christian material.

Liebert, Gösta. *Iconographic Dictionary of the Indian Religions: Hinduism, Buddhism, Jainism.* Leiden, 1976. Definitions with references to literature.

Maier, Johann. *Die Tempelrolle vom Toten Meer.* Munich, 1978. Translates and comments upon the Hebrew text.

Maurer, Gerd J. *Der Altar aber ist Christus: Zur symbolischen Bedeutung des christlichen Altares in der Geschichte.* Sankt Augustin, West Germany, 1969. A popular but good survey.

Meyer, Jeffrey F. *Peking as a Sacred City.* Taipei, 1976. Cosmic symbolism of various altars.

Milgrom, Jacob, and Bialik M. Lerner. "Altar." In *Encyclopaedia Judaica*, vol. 2, cols. 760-771. Jerusalem, 1971. Stresses Israelite uniqueness.

Reichard, Gladys A. *Navaho Religion: A Study of Symbolism* (1950). 2 vols. Princeton, 1974. A classic.

Staal, Frits, ed. *Agni: The Vedic Ritual of the Fire Altar.* 2 vols. Berkeley, 1983. Collective work of specialists on Indology.

Stuiber, Alfred. "Altar: Alte Kirche." In *Theologische Realenzyklopedie*, edited by Gerhard Krause and Gerhard Muller, vol. 2, pp. 308-318. Berlin, 1978. A fine piece by a well-known patrologist, with an exhaustive bibliography. The preceding section contains a short introduction from the point of view of comparative religion.

Walker, George B. *Hindu World: An Encyclopedic Survey of Hinduism.* 2 vols. New York, 1968. Rather general, without references, and based on a sometimes antiquated literature.

Weltfish, Gene. *The Lost Universe: Pawnee Life and Culture* (1965). Lincoln, Nebr., 1977. Based on many years of fieldwork and linguistic training.

Yavis, Constantine G. *Greek Altars: Origins and Typology.* Saint Louis, 1949.

Ziehen, Ludwig. "Altar: Griechisch-Römisch." In *Reallexikon für Antike und Christentum*, edited by Theodor Klauser, vol. 1, cols. 310-329. Stuttgart, 1950. Well documented, with a lengthy bibliography.

CARL-MARTIN EDSMAN
Translated from Swedish by Kjersti Board

AMOS

AMOS (fl. eighth century BCE) is considered the first classical prophet, the first whose words are preserved in writing, the biblical *Book of Amos.* Whereas other books of the Hebrew Bible such as *Samuel* and *Kings* contain numerous indirect prose reports of earlier prophets' activities, the books of the classical prophets, beginning with Amos, focus on the prophet's words, usually recorded in poetic form.

Historical Context. As the superscription to the *Book of Amos* (1:1) reveals, Amos prophesied during the reign of Jeroboam II (787/6-747/6 BCE). The superscription also states that he was active "two years before the earthquake" (see also *Zec.* 14:5), which, by means of the archaeological evidence at Hazor, has been dated to 760 BCE. Jeroboam's forty-year reign was a period of political stability, military success, and economic prosperity.

Nevertheless, this period of prosperity had apparently created severe social tensions. Although the social elite, who prospered, were content, the people of the land, the small farmers, suffered greatly from the upper classes' pursuit of luxury (for the social structure, see *2 Kings* 24:14). It may be that the sudden increase in the standard of living resulted in greater taxation, which led to further oppression of the poor, who then became even poorer (see *Am.* 1:6-7a, 3:9, 4:1-2, 5:11, 6:4-6, 8:4-6).

Amos's Background and Message. The social inequities and oppression of the time precipitated Amos's protest and call for justice. The prophet's concern, however, was not merely social injustice but religious practice as well. Amos saw the religious practices of the elite as mirroring their perpetuation of social injustice, as indicated in his accusation in 2:7-8, and he labels the religious behavior of the leaders meaningless (4:4ff., 5:4-6, 5:21-27, 8:10).

The question arises: what does Amos's sharp criticism of the cult and its ritual mean? Does he intend to deny the efficacy of cultic worship? Is he opposed to the cult of specific shrines, such as Bethel and Gilgal? Is he calling for another type of worship (cf. 5:16)? In responding to these questions, scholars have intensively investigated Amos's social background. The superscription refers to him as one of the *noqdim*, "shepherds" (sg. *noqed*), and this remark is echoed (though in another term, *boqer*) in 7:14. But in the Bible *noqed* does not refer to a simple shepherd; Mesha, king of Moab, bore the same title (*2 Kgs.* 3:4). Attention has been called to a Ugaritic text in which *nqd* is parallel to *khn* ("priest"), which may suggest that Amos himself was from a priestly family.

Amos definitely does not repudiate the cult, but calls for his audience to approach God. In his vision in 9:1, Amos reports that "I saw my Lord standing by the altar" (JPS). That is, God revealed himself to the prophet in the cultic center that is God's house. Amos's repeated reproach, "yet you did not return to Me" (*Am.* 4:6, 4:8, 4:10, 4:11) and his demand to "seek Me" (5:4, 5:14), which has a cultic connotation (cf. *1 Sm.* 9:9), may be understood as a call for purification of the worship. It can also be argued that Amos felt that the cultic centers of Bethel and Gilgal should cease to function as God's temples because their worshipers had demonstrated their insincerity through their pursuit of luxury and pleasure. Thus, Amos does not call for totally abstract worship and does not oppose the cult in principle. He harshly criticizes, however, the shrines that legitimate social oppression and thus the existence of religious hypocrisy.

Furthermore, the leaders toward whom Amos directs his criticism seem to be devoted worshipers (8:5). We may assume that the political and economic success of the state was taken by the ruling class as a sign of God's protection of Israel. In essence, the cult that assured its worshipers of the stability of their way of life served as religious protection for the social elite. Amos attacks this self-serving belief, pointing out that daily deeds and social justice are inseparable from the cult and, in fact, dominate God's demands of his worshipers.

Amos attacks as well the common belief that God's function is merely to save and protect his people. There was an expectation that there would be a sign, by means of revelation, of God's victories over Israel's enemies. Amos rejects this and argues that "the day of the Lord is darkness, and not light" (*Am.* 5:18-20); the day will be one of punishment, not salvation. Introducing the idea of God's

punishment, he connects it with social crimes and the corruption of ritual.

In his autobiographical account, Amos mentions his occupation as a dresser of sycamore trees (7:14). This is a trade that required travel, especially since Tekoa, Amos's hometown (located about 8 miles [12.9 km] south of Jerusalem), is in an area where the sycamore does not grow (cf. *1 Kgs.* 10:27). Amos's travels may shed light on his broad

> **Amos saw the religious practices of the elite as mirroring their perpetuation of social injustice.**

education and deep knowledge of world affairs (see 1:2-2:16), as well as his contacts with the northern kingdom of Israel. It has also been suggested that Amos's Tekoa was somewhere in the north, which might explain his prophetic activity there; however, no evidence of a northern Tekoa has been found.

Sociologically, we must realize that many prophets (e.g., Amos, Micah, Jeremiah) came from the periphery to preach against urban centers. Villages and small towns preserved a traditional, clear view of the world. Cities, such as Samaria, were centers (especially during Amos's time) of prosperity, new developments, and social change. Social research reveals that it is not unusual for a visitor from a traditional area to be incensed by the breaking of traditional conventions in the city. Thus the changes that defied his traditional views kindled in Amos the fire of criticism and the desire to punish the evildoers.

Literary Style and Structure. An analysis of Amos's style reveals impressive literary variations. He employs the conventional prophetic patterns of speech, such as "Thus says the Lord" (e.g., 1:3, 1:6, 1:9, 1:11, etc.); the prophetic formula for a conclusion, "Says the Lord" (2:3, 2:16); and the prophetic verdict, "Therefore" (3:2). He uses specific conventions of the wisdom literature, for example, the formula 3 x 4 (repeated in chaps. 1-2), comparisons, and rhetorical questions (3:3-8), the latter two reflecting secular language. He also employs ritualistic language, such as the hymn (4:13, 5:8-9, 9:5-6) and the lament (e.g., 5:2; see also 5:16-18, 6:1). Amos reveals himself to be a great poet, a master of language with creative skills who knows how to use various modes of speech effectively. His objective is to appeal to his audience.

The *Book of Amos* is divided into four main parts: (1) the superscription plus the chain of oracles against the nations, including Judah and Israel (1:1-2:16); (2) a series of speeches (chaps. 3-6); (3) the vision accounts (7:1-3, 7:4-6, 7:7-9; 8:1ff., 9:1ff.); and (4) a prophecy of salvation (9:11-15). It has been suggested that the first three visions are Amos's call and should be placed at the beginning of the book.

Nineteenth-century scholarship assigned most of the material in the *Book of Amos* to Amos himself (except, perhaps, the prophecy of comfort at the end of the book). Current scholarship, however, is more skeptical and suggests a lengthy and complex redactional history. It has long been argued that the book's conclusion (9:11-15), a prophecy of comfort focusing on the house of David (and not on the northern kingdom or its rulers), reflects a later period. The prophecy against Judah in 2:4-5, which is foreign in its context, is also considered to be late. Recent scholarship has been attempting to organize the editorial layers in order according to the occurrence of political developments.

These theories of redactional history assume that changed historical conditions led to new theological interpretations. This notion of systematic change and reinterpretation may be challenged, however, in light of Amos's intention to appeal to his audience, which required stylistic and emphatic variety as well as sensitivity to the audience's mood. He may sometimes have called for repentance or perhaps delivered an oracle of salvation based upon his overall religious worldview. Still, this does not mean that Amos was the sole author of the entire book. There may have been specific insertions (e.g., 5:13), which, however, do not imply a systematic editorial process.

BIBLIOGRAPHY

Coote, R. B. *Amos among the Prophets*. Philadelphia, 1981.
Kapelrud, Arvid S. *Central Ideas in Amos*. 2d ed. Oslo, 1961.
Mays, James Luther. *Amos: A Commentary*. Philadelphia, 1969.
Wolff, Hans Walter. *Joel and Amos*. Edited by Dean McBride and translated by Waldemar Janzen. Philadelphia, 1977.

YEHOSHUA GITAY

ANABAPTISM

Anabaptist comes from the Greek word meaning "rebaptizer." It was never used by the Anabaptists, for whom baptism signified the external witness of an inner faith covenant of the believer with God through Jesus Christ. Baptism was always administered in the name of the Trinity, usually by pouring water, but sometimes by sprinkling or immersion.

The Anabaptist movement had multiple origins. An earlier view saw it primarily as an effort on the part of Conrad Grebel (c. 1498-1526), Felix Mantz (c. 1498-1527), and other co-workers of Huldrych Zwingli (1484-1531), the Zurich reformer, to complete the reformation of the church. We are now aware, however, of additional influences in bringing the movement to birth. These include peasant unrest brought on by social and economic injustice; the rhetoric of the fiery German peasant leader Thomas Müntzer (1488?-1525); the writings of Martin Luther (1483-1546) and, especially, Andreas Karlstadt (1480-1541); the influence of late medieval mysticism and asceticism; and the dynamics of reform in specific monasteries. Anabaptism arose as a radical reform movement out of the economic, social, political, and religious situation in early sixteenth-century Europe.

Anabaptism began formally in Zollikon, near Zurich, on 21 January 1525, when Grebel, Mantz, Georg Blaurock (c. 1492-1529), and others baptized each other on confession of faith, thus forming a separatist congregation. This event, however, was preceded by debates with Zwingli and the Zurich city council, beginning in 1523, over the nature of desired reforms. On issues like abolition of the Mass, dietary regulations, the authority of scripture over tradition, and the veneration of relics, these first Anabaptists were in complete agreement with Zwingli. The ultimate break with Zwingli concerned the authority of the city council (the state) over the church, which Zwingli affirmed and his disciples denied. The immediate and final event that precipitated the first baptismal ceremony was a decree issued by the city council demanding the baptism of all infants within eight days, on pain of banishment of the persons involved.

The (Swiss) Brethren, as the new group preferred to be called, found strong support among the people, not so much on the issue of baptism but in the Brethren's anticlericalism, their desire for local congregational autonomy, their rejection of excessive taxation, and practices that met apparent spiritual needs of the people. As a result, the movement grew rapidly, and with its growth there was increasingly severe persecution. Mantz became one of the first martyrs.

In 1530, Melchior Hofmann (c. 1495-1543), a widely traveled Lutheran preacher with chiliastic tendencies, came to Strasbourg, where his contacts must have included not only Swiss Brethren but also spiritualists and other "free spirits." Hofmann left the city the same year, under the duress of the reformers and the city council, because of an inclination to Anabaptism. On arrival in the northern city of Emden he soon attracted a large following, in part at least because of his apocalyptic message of the imminent return of Christ; and in a short time more than three hundred persons had been baptized. Selected leaders were ordained, and they in turn ordained others to help bring in the Kingdom.

Hofmann was pacifistic, but others armed themselves to bring in the Kingdom by force. In May 1530 there was an abortive attempt to take the city of Amsterdam. Other incidents followed. In 1534 the city of Münster in Westphalia was declared to be the New Jerusalem and fell under the control of the Melchiorites, though Hofmann himself had returned to Strasbourg and lay in prison there. In 1535 Münster fell before the onslaught of the regional bishop's troops, and most of its inhabitants were killed. The Münster episode was in large part responsible for the centuries-long designation of Anabaptism as violent and revolutionary. It was also in response to these events that Menno Simons left his nearby Roman Catholic parish and, after going underground for a time of reflection and writing, emerged as the primary leader of peaceful Anabaptism.

Meanwhile, the Swiss and South German Brethren grew in numbers even as persecution increased. As a result, many migrated to other areas, particularly Austria and Moravia. As refugees arrived, a sharing of goods with them seemed both practical and biblical. This practice began in 1529, and by 1533 it had become normative for many in the area under the leadership of Jacob Hutter (d. 1536), who made it a central article of faith. Those who followed this group became known as Hutterian Brethren, or Hutterites. Numerous congregations also emerged in south-central Germany under the leadership of Hans Hut (d. 1527), Hans Denk (c. 1500-1527), Pilgram Marpeck (d. 1556), the more radical Melchior Rink (c. 1494-1545), and others.

The variety of centers from which Anabaptists emerged and the various influences upon them make it difficult to talk about one all-encompassing faith to which all confessed. There was a great deal of pluralism. Nevertheless, there was in all the sixteenth-century Anabaptists a common core of beliefs by which they recognized one another and that in time became normative. The elements of this core came from their statements of faith, the testimony of martyrs, court records, hymns, letters, records of disputations held with authorities and others, and the writings of major leaders.

In September 1524, Grebel and his friends wrote to Luther, Karlstadt, and Müntzer to seek counsel. Only the two letters to Müntzer are extant. In them several emphases are already clear: the primary authority of the scriptures; the Lord's Supper conceived as a memorial and a sign of love among believers; the importance of redemptive church discipline according to *Matthew* 18:15-18; the belief that baptism must follow a personal profession of faith and that it is a sign of such faith rather than a saving sacrament; the belief that children are saved by the redemptive work of the second Adam, Christ; a conviction that weapons of violence have no place among Christians; and the belief that the church is called to be a suffering church.

In 1527 the Anabaptists convened a conference at Schleitheim, on the Swiss-German border. A more separatist-sectarian view emerged. Seven articles constituted the "Brotherly Union," as it was called, a statement summarizing the central issues of faith in which the framers of the statement differed from the "false brethren." Who these brethren were is not clear. In addition, three others were added: a radical church-world dualism that asserted complete separation of believers from all others; the importance of church order and the necessity of pastoral leadership as discerned by the

congregation; and rejection of the oath as an affirmation of truth.

The other documents mentioned above amplify but do not add significant new doctrinal affirmations to the two early statements from Grebel's letter and the Brotherly Union. The primacy of the New Testament over the Old Testament is affirmed, as well as the doctrine of separation that naturally excludes participation in civil or political office. Simons stressed that the church, as the bride of Christ, must be pure; he also stressed the importance of witness and mission, which most Anabaptists took for granted as a part of discipleship. Dirk Philips (1504-1568) affirmed the ordinance of foot washing. In their verbal and written statements, most Anabaptists confirmed their intention of restoring the church to its early New Testament pattern and practice.

BIBLIOGRAPHY

The standard reference work in English is *The Mennonite Encyclopedia*, 4 vols. (Scottdale, Pa., 1955-1959). A helpful bibliographical tool is *A Bibliography of Anabaptism, 1520-1630*, compiled by Hans J. Hillerbrand (Elkhart, Ind., 1962). In the area of historiography, James M. Stayer's "The Anabaptists," in *Reformation Europe: A Guide to Research*, edited by Steven Ozment (Saint Louis, 1982), pp. 135-159, indicates the direction of present research generally. Walter Klaassen has edited a convenient collection of source translations on most Anabaptist theological themes in his *Anabaptism in Outline* (Scottdale, Pa., 1981). For all of this literature, George H. Williams's massive *The Radical Reformation* (Philadelphia, 1962) provides an indispensable contextual framework, as does his edited volume *Spiritual and Anabaptist Writers*, "Library of Christian Classics," vol. 25 (Philadelphia, 1957). In *The Believers' Church: The History and Character of Radical Protestantism* (New York, 1968), Donald F. Durnbaugh places the various movements within Anabaptism into a narrower and more definitive context.

CORNELIUS J. DYCK

ANALYTIC PHILOSOPHY

In a broad sense, the practice of seeking better understanding through the analysis (i. e., the breaking down and restatement) of complex, obscure, or problematic linguistic expressions has been present within philosophy from its pre-Socratic origins to the present. More narrowly considered, analytic philosophy ("linguistic analysis") is a style of philosophizing originating within twentieth-century English-language philosophy and drawing much of its inspiration from the later thought of Ludwig Wittgenstein (1889-1951).

The remote ancestry of analytic philosophy is well illustrated in the dialogues of Plato, where Socrates is shown to be concerned with delineating the meaning of key concepts like "piety," "justice," or "soul." The more immediate origins of analytic philosophy, however, lie in the reaction of British philosophers at the beginning of the twentieth century against the then-dominant Hegelianism of such thinkers as F. H. Bradley (1846-1924), who placed all emphasis on finding meaning in the "whole" rather than any partial expressions and thus placed in jeopardy, it was feared, all finite human understanding. Leaders in the attempt to counter the exaggerated stress on "synthesis" with clarifying analyses of philosophical obscurities were G. E. Moore (1873-1958) and Bertrand Russell (1872-1970). Moore, appealing to "common sense" arguments, provided detailed ordinary language analyses of such important terms as "good" and what it means to have "certain knowledge" of something. Russell, on the other hand, offered more technical translations, using the symbolic logic he had created with Alfred North Whitehead to express, for instance, his "theory of definite descriptions."

To this philosophical context Ludwig Wittgenstein, a former student of Russell's, returned in 1929, to Cambridge from Vienna, fresh from conversations with members of the Vienna Circle, with whom he had helped to develop the logical rule ("the verification principle of meaning") that the meaning of all nontautological statements is to be identified with the method of their sensory verification. Wittgenstein's *Tractatus logico-philosophicus* (completed in 1918 and first published in 1921) had carried to its limit the quest for a powerful and simple formalization of ideal language, rooting all factual meaning in basic propositions naming atomic facts. These ultimate simples had later been identified with sensory observations by the radical empiricists of the Vienna Circle in the creation of logical positivism. Now Wittgenstein began to have misgivings, not only about the empirical interpretation given to his more general theory of language but also about the theory itself. In its simplicity lay its great power, but its application in logical positivism showed also its oversimplicity when compared to the many actual uses of human language for instance, in asking, thanking, cursing, greeting, praying. The assertion of sensorily verifiable fact, Wittgenstein saw, is only one among a vast range of functions of language. Such a function is doubtless of great importance in natural science and in ordinary life, but even such an important function hardly begins to exhaust the richness of speech.

Wittgenstein's subsequent meditations on the limitations of his own *Tractatus* and on the rich complexity of language, published posthumously in 1953 as *Philosophical Investigations* (henceforth abbreviated as *PI*), were enormously influential, particularly after World War II. Philosophically puzzling expressions, Wittgenstein contends, did not need verification so much as analysis of their use. In the use would be found the meaning. "Look at the sentence as an instrument," he advises, "and at its sense as its employment" (*PI*, 421). In this way philosophical confusions can be eliminated by the method of returning a puzzling expression to its origins in ordinary use. "The confusions which occupy us arise when language is like an engine idling, not when it is doing work" (*PI*, 132). This method will not involve the application of a single procrustean technique, like the verification principle, but a generally open attitude toward the various uses that language may be given. Thus philosophical method will be fitted to each occasion. "There is not a philosophical method, though there are indeed methods, like different therapies" (*PI*, 133). Wittgenstein liked and repeated his therapeutic analogy: "The philosopher's treatment of a question is like the treatment of an illness" (*PI*, 255).

For the most part the philosophical climate created by linguistic analysis is not hospitable to eliminative analysis. Such an enterprise would bear too much resemblance to the pugnacious days of logical positivism. Indeed, most attempts to show that a "systematic misuse of language" necessarily infects theological talk, and that people should not talk that way, rest on verificationist assumptions. On the other hand, "illuminative" analysis can be perceived by believers as no less threatening than eliminative analysis if the linguistic functions identified are too meager to accord with the user's own sense of the dignity or importanceor intentof the speechact involved. The logical positivists themselves had granted at least that the utterances of religious people perform the function of expressing or evoking emotion. The shift to linguistic analysis from logical positivism called for penetration. As Wittgenstein himself said: "What am I believing in when I believe that men have souls? What am I believing in, when I believe that this substance contains two carbon rings? In both cases there is a picture in the foreground, but the sense lies far in the background; that is, the application of the picture is not easy to survey" (*PI*, 422).

One answer attempting to penetrate beyond the logical positivist's analysis of religious utterance as merely emotive was offered in 1955 by R. B. Braithwaite (b. 1900) after his conversion to Christianity. Though remaining a philosophical empiricist, and on such grounds finding it impossible to affirm the doctrines of his religion in a traditional sense of belief, Braithwaite suggested that Christian speech can in fact function otherwise, by making and supporting ethical commitments to the "agapeistic" way of life. Images of Christian love (agape) are vividly presented in the sacred writings, all of which, he claimed, refer to or reduce to the love commandment. Uttering words from these writings is not like asserting a matter of factthough the form of the words may suggest thisbut is committing oneself to a way of life authoritatively pictured in these stories.

Braithwaite's analysis, though not widely accepted as adequate to the full functioning of Christian language, showed how a more flexible approach to "how we do things with words" could be applied to the theological context. The highly regarded Oxford philosopher J. L. Austin (1911-1960) further spurred such attempts with his stress on the "performative" significance of language. His influence brought much attention to the fact that sometimes we are not so much describing the world as performing in it when we speak: making promises, uttering commands, taking oaths, naming, bidding at auctions, pronouncing marriage vows, accepting invitations, and the like. In Canada, Donald Evans (b. 1927) offered a detailed account of religious speech, demonstrating the logic of "self-involvement" as performative.

To such analyses were added others aiming to show how the belief-statements of theology might also play an important role, though not, of course, in making simple empirical claims. R. M. Hare (b. 1919), in Oxford, provided an analysis of religious belief-statements as "bliks," or unshakable preconditions for seeing the world in a certain way. Some "bliks" might be insane, as in delusional paranoia, but others might be both sane and essential, as in the conviction that the world is causally bound together in a regular way. John Wisdom (b. 1904), at Cambridge, stressed the way in which certain utterances, though not themselves factual, may direct attention to patterns in the facts that otherwise might be missed. A metaphor of the Taj Mahal, applied to a woman's hat, could change not the facts but the way the facts were seen.

Genuine analysis aims at revealing, not changing, what the user is doing with words.

A linguistic philosophy that is not tied to an *a priori* supposition that certain functions of speech, such as metaphysical ones, are "impossible" will be hospitable to all the various sorts of "work" that are done by religious utterances. These will include, among others, factual claims (e.g., "The Shroud of Turin dates from early in the first millennium AD"), historical claims (e.g., "Ramses III was the pharaoh of the Exodus"), poetic utterances (e.g., "My yoke is easy, and my burden is light"), ethical prescriptions (e.g., "Turn the other cheek"), parables, folk tales, and complex theoretical doctrines. Several functions may be performed by a single type of utterance. Telling the parable of the Prodigal Son under certain circumstances, for example, may involve at the same time the act of self-commitment to a way of life, the receiving of emotional support, the expression of remorse and hope for personal forgiveness, and the affirmation of a doctrine of God's nature. Standing in church and reciting an ancient creed, on the other hand, may sometimes function more as a ritual of group-membership and reverence for continuity with the past than as an assertion. Part of the work of linguistic philosophy as applied to religion is to clarify the subtle differences between these functions and to help the users themselves see more clearly the range of lively possibilities afforded by their speech.

Linguistic analysis is not merely "about language," then, as one unfortunate misconception would have it. The aim of analytic philosophy pursued in the spirit of Wittgenstein is to illuminate the varied functions of speech and the many

meanings of "meaning." Its efforts are spent in allowing whatever is said to be said more effectively and with greater awareness for both speaker and listener. Like all philosophy, it is engaged in the serious exercise of consciousness-raising. This does not entail, of course, that analytic philosophy must somehow "oppose" movements toward conceptual syn-

> **A metaphor of the Taj Mahal, applied to a woman's hat, could change not the facts but the way the facts were seen.**

thesis. All of metaphysics and much of science are engaged in conceptual synthesis. Just as analysis is identifiable from the beginning as a major strand or concern in Western philosophy, so also is the quest for synthesis found in all periods. Mature analytic philosophy recognizes that analysis and synthesis need one another as poles in never-ceasing interaction. Overweening claims on behalf of synthesis helped to stimulate analytic philosophy early in the twentieth century, but similar overweening attitudes, though sometimes unfortunately encountered today, have no proper place among the analysts who themselves have become dominant in English-speaking philosophy during the century.

For theologians, as for simple religious believers, then, there is nothing to fear and much to be gained from analytical philosophy. Properly construed, linguistic analysis claims only at lifting to clarity and self-awareness the complex and powerful human acts of speech. Its prime objective is, in the Socratic mood, the prevention of intellectual confusion due to language and the consequent "corruption of the soul."

BIBLIOGRAPHY

The indispensable book for understanding analytic philosophy is Ludwig Wittgenstein's *Philosophical Investigations*, 2d ed. (Oxford, 1968); it is a posthumously published compilation of Wittgenstein's thoughts from various years after 1929, many of which (part 1) were prepared by him for publication in 1945 but were not actually brought out at that time. For a useful aid to the understanding of Wittgenstein's philosophy and the Investigations, see part 2 of George Pitcher's *The Philosophy of Wittgenstein* (Englewood Cliffs, N. J., 1964). A succinct history of the transition to analytic philosophy can be found in J. O. Urmson`s *Philosophical Analysis: Its Development between the Two World Wars* (Oxford, 1956). Good examples of the analytical style on general topics are represented in J. L. Austin's *How to Do Things with Words*, 2d ed., edited by J. O. Urmson (Cambridge, Mass., 1975), and Gilbert Ryle's *Dilemmas* (1954; reprint, Cambridge, 1966). Specifically directed to cosmological and religious issues, the book *Metaphysical Beliefs* (London, 1957), by Stephen Toulmin, Ronald W. Hepburn, and Alasdair MacIntyre, offers three rather extended treatments, all with a critical stance. Tending to show the use of analysis in defense of religious concerns are the essays in *Faith and Logic: Oxford Essays in*

Philosophical Theology, edited by Basil Mitchell (London, 1957). The application of performative analysis to theological questions is shown in Donald D. Evans's *The Logic of Self-Involvement: A Philosophical Study of Everyday Language with Special Reference to the Christian Use of Language about God as Creator* (London, 1963). A treatment of the emergence of analytic philosophy from logical positivism and the possibilities for constructive theological applications of functional rather than verificational analysis may be found in my *Language, Logic and God* (New York, 1961).

FREDERICK FERRÉ

ANCESTORS

Ancestor Worship

General Characteristics and Research Problems. Ancestor worship has attracted the enduring interest of scholars in many areas of the study of religion. In the late nineteenth century, it was identified as the most basic form of all religion, and subsequent studies of the subject in specific areas have provided a stimulating point of access to related problems of religion, society, and culture.

The worship of ancestors is closely linked to cosmology and worldview, to ideas of the soul and the afterlife, and to a society's regulation of inheritance and succession. In East Asia ancestor worship is found combined with the practice of Buddhism, and ancestral rites compose a major part of the practice of Confucianism. It is generally acknowledged that ancestor worship functions to uphold the authority of elders, to support social control, and to foster conservative and traditionalist attitudes. In addition, ancestor worship is clearly linked to an ethic of filial piety and obedience to elders.

The institution of ancestor worship is properly regarded as a religious practice, not as a religion in itself. It is generally carried out by kinship groups and seldom has a priesthood separable from them. It is limited to the practice of the ethnic group; there is no attempt to proselytize outsiders. Its ethical dimension primarily refers to the proper conduct of family or kinship relations. It does not have formal doctrine as such; where texts exist, these are mainly liturgical manuals. In most cases ancestor worship is not the only religious practice of a society; rather, it exists as part of a more comprehensive religious system.

The meaning of *worship* in *ancestor worship* is problematic. Ancestor worship takes a variety of forms in different areas, and its attitudinal characteristics vary accordingly. The ancestors may be regarded as possessing power equivalent to that of a deity and hence may be accorded cult status and considered able to influence society to the same extent as its deities. Typically, the conception of ancestors is strongly influ-enced by ideas of other supernaturals in the society's religious system. Ancestors may be prayed to as having the power to grant boons or allay misfortune, but their effectiveness is regarded as naturally limited by the bonds of kinship. Thus, a member of a certain lineage prays only to the ancestors of that lineage; it would be regarded as nonsensical to pray to ancestors of any other lineage.

The rites of death, including funerary and mortuary rituals, are regarded as falling within the purview of ancestor worship only when memorial rites beyond the period of death and disposition of the corpse are carried out as a regular function of a kinship group. Thus, the funerary rites and occasional memorials common in Europe and the United States are not regarded as evidence of ancestor worship.

Ancestor Worship in the History of the Study of Religion. In *Principles of Sociology* (1877) Herbert Spencer wrote that "ancestor worship is the root of every religion." According to his view, the cult of heroes originated in the deification of an ancestor, and in fact all deities originate by an analogous process. Spencer's euhemerist theory rested on the idea, familiar in the scholarship of his day, that religion as a whole has a common origin from which its many forms derive. Knowledge of this original form would provide the key to understanding all subsequent developments.

In *Totem and Taboo* (1913), Sigmund Freud postulated that the belief that the living can be harmed by the dead serves to reduce guilt experienced toward the dead. That is, in kinship relations characterized by conscious affection there is inevitably a measure of hostility; however, this hostility conflicts with the conscious ideal of affectionate relations and hence must be repressed. Repressed hostility is then projected onto the dead and takes the form of the belief that the dead are malevolent and can harm the living.

Meyer Fortes considerably refined Freud's hypothesis on the basis of African material. In *Oedipus and Job in West African Religion* (1959), Fortes found that among the Tallensi belief in the continued authority of ancestors, rather than fear of them, is the principle means of alleviating guilt arising from repressed hostility.

Among the Tallensi relations between fathers and sons are affectionate, but, because a son cannot attain full jural authority until his father's death, sons bear a latent resentment of their fathers. However, this resentment does not manifest itself as belief in the malevolence of the dead. Instead, the Tallensi believe that the authority of the father is granted to him by his ancestors, who demand from the son continued subordination. Thus the function of ancestor worship is to reinforce the general, positive valuation of the authority of elders, quite apart from the individual personality of any specific ancestor. A related function is to place a positive value upon subordination of the desires of the individual to the collective authority of tribal elders. This value is useful in ensuring the continued solidarity of the group.

In *Death, Property, and the Ancestors* (1966), Jack Goody studied ancestor worship among the LoDagaa of West Africa. Property to be inherited by descendants is not distributed until the death of the father. Prevented from commanding the full possession of this property, a son experiences a subconscious wish for the father's death. Repression of this guilt takes the form of the belief that the dead have eternal rights to the property they formerly held. In order to enjoy

> **In *Totem and Taboo* (1913), Sigmund Freud postulated that the belief that the living can be harmed by the dead serves to reduce guilt experienced toward the dead.**

those rights, the dead must receive sacrifices from the living. If sacrifices are not forthcoming, the ancestors will afflict their descendants with sickness and misfortune. Thus beliefs concerning ancestral affliction are inextricably linked to social issues of inheritance and succession.

Ancestor Worship in Practice. This section describes the practice of ancestor worship in various cultural areas and in relation to several religious traditions.

Africa. A person without descendants cannot become an ancestor, and in order to achieve ancestorhood, proper burial, with rites appropriate to the person's status, is necessary. After an interval following death, a deceased person who becomes an ancestor is no longer perceived as an individual. Personal characteristics disappear from the awareness of the living, and only the value of the ancestor as a moral exemplar remains. Ancestors are believed to be capable of intervening in human affairs, but only in the defined area of their authority, that is, among their descendants.

In an important study of African ancestor worship, Max Gluckman (1937) established the distinction between ancestor worship and the cult of the dead. Ancestors represent positive moral forces who can cause or prevent misfortune and who require that their descendants observe a moral code. The cult of the dead, on the other hand, is not exclusively directed to deceased kinsmen, but to the spirits of the dead in general. Here spirits are prayed to for the achievement of amoral or antisocial ends, whereas ancestors can be petitioned only for ends that are in accord with basic social principles.

Among the Edo the deceased is believed to progress through the spirit world on a course that parallels the progress of his son and other successors. Events in this world are punctuated by rites and are believed to have a counterpart in the spirit world. Thus it may be twenty years before a spirit is finally merged into the collective dead and

descendants can receive their full complement of authority. In this sense the ancestors continue to exert authority over their descendants long after death. Until that authority ceases, the son must perform rites as prescribed and behave in approved ways.

Among the Ewe of Ghana, ancestor worship is the basis of the entire religious system and a point of reference for the conceptualization of all social relations. The Ewe believe that the human being has two souls. Before birth the being resides in the spirit world; it comes into this world when it finds a mother, and it returns to the spirit world at death. This cycle of movement through the realms is perpetual. The ancestors are invoked with libations on all ceremonial occasions. Rites range from simple, personal libations to complicated rituals involving an entire lineage. During a ritual, the soul of the ancestor returns to be fed through the ceremonial stool that serves as its shrine.

Melanesia. Ancestors are one of many types of spirits recognized by Melanesian tribal peoples. Regarding the role of ancestor worship in tribal life, Roy A. Rappaport's study *Pigs for the Ancestors* (1977) presents an innovative approach not seen in the study of ancestor worship in other areas. Among the highland Tsembaga, ancestral ritual is part of a complex ecological system in which a balanced cycle of abundance and scarcity is regulated. Yam gardens are threatened by the unhindered growth of the pig population, and human beings must supplement their starch-based diet with protein. Propelling this cycle is a belief that pigs must be sacrificed to the ancestors in great numbers. These sacrifices provide the Tsembaga with protein in great quantity. Pigs sacrificed when someone dies or in connection with intertribal warfare supplement the ordinary diet of yams, which is adequate for ordinary activity but not for periods of stress. Thus ancestor worship plays a vital role in the ecological balance of the tribe in its environment.

India. Ancestor worship in India takes a variety of forms, depending upon the area and the ethnic group concerned; however, providing food for the dead is a basic and widespread practice. Orthodox Hindu practice centers on an annual rite between August and September that includes offering sacred rice balls (*pinda*) to the ancestors. *The Laws of Manu* includes specific instructions for ancestral offerings. Descendants provide a feast for the brahmans, and the merit of this act is transferred to the ancestors. The feast itself is called the Sraddha. The form of this rite varies depending on whether it is observed during a funeral or in subsequent, annual observances.

Buddhism. Based on a canonical story, the All Souls Festival, or Avalambana, is observed throughout Southeast and East Asia. The story concerns one of the Buddha's disciples, Maudgalyayana, known for skill in meditation and supranormal powers. The mother of Maudgalyayana appeared to her son in a dream and revealed to him that she was suffering innumerable tortures in the blackest hell because of her *karman*. Through magic Maudgalyayana visited his mother in hell, but his power was of no avail in securing her release. Eventually the Buddha instructed him to convene an assembly of the priesthood which then would recite *sutras* and transfer the merit of those rites to ancestors. In other words, descendants must utilize the mediation of the priesthood in order to benefit ancestors. The result is an annual festival, traditionally observed on the day of the full moon of the eighth lunar month. At this festival special *sutra* recitations and offering rites for the ancestors are held in Buddhist temples, and domestic rites differing in each country are performed. In addition to rites for ancestors, observances for the "hungry ghosts" and for spirits who have died leaving no descendants are performed.

Shamanism. Shamanism in East Asia today consists in large part of mediumistic communications in which the shaman enters a trance and divines the present condition of a client's ancestors. These practices are based on the folk notion that if a person suffers from an unusual or seemingly unwarranted affliction, the ancestors may be the cause. If the ancestors are suffering, if they are displeased with their descendants' conduct, or if they are offered inappropriate or insufficient ritual, they may cause some harm to come to their descendants. However, it is only rarely that this belief is straightforwardly expressed as the proposition that ancestors willfully, malevolently afflict their descendants.

Chinese ancestor worship. An important component at work in the metaphysics of Chinese ancestor cults is indigenous theories of the soul. First of all, since Chou times (c. 1123-221 BCE) the idea of the soul as the pale, ghostly shadow of a man has been a perduring notion found in popular stories. These apparitions are called *kuei*, meaning demons, devils, and ghosts, as opposed to *shen*, the benevolent spirits of ancestors (a word used also to refer to all deities).

Together with this idea of the ghostly soul there developed a conception of the soul in terms of *yin* and *yang*. According to this theory, the *yin* portion of the soul, called *p`o*, may turn into a *kuei* and cause misfortune if descendants do not perform proper ancestral rites. If the *p`o* is satisfactorily placated, however, it will rest peacefully. Meanwhile, the *yang* portion of the soul, called *hun*, associated with *shen*, will bless and protect descendants and their families. [See Afterlife, article Chinese Concepts.] Thus Chinese ancestral rites have been motivated simultaneously by the fear of the vengeful dead and by the hope for ancestral blessings.

Chinese ancestor worship is closely linked to property inheritance; every deceased individual must receive offerings from at least one descendant who will provide him with sustenance in the next life. However, a specific person is only required to worship those ancestors from whom he has received property.

Confucianism. Confucianism lays heavy emphasis upon the correct practice of ancestral ritual. Special attention is given to minute details concerning the content and arrangement of offerings, proper dress, gesture and posture, and the order of precedence in appearing before ancestral altars. According to the *Book of Family Ritual* of the Neo-Confucian scholar Chu Hsi, the *Chu-tzu chia-li*, commemoration of ancestors became primarily a responsibility of eldest sons, and women were excluded from officiating roles in the celebration of rites.

The highest virtue in Confucian doctrine is filial piety, quintessentially expressed in the worship of ancestors. When Buddhism was first introduced to China, one of Confucianism's strongest arguments against it was the assertion that Buddhism was in essence opposed to filial piety and was likely to disrupt the practice of ancestor worship. If sons took the tonsure and failed to perform ancestral rites, then not only would spirits in the other world suffer from lack of ritual attention but social relations in society would also be undermined.

Korea. In Korea women and men hold quite different images of ancestors. A woman marries away from her natal village and enters her husband's household under the authority of his mother and father. The wife's relations with her husband's kin are expected to be characterized by strife and competition. Her membership in the husband's lineage is tenuous and is never fully acknowledged in ritual until her death. Because women's relation to the lineage is strained in these ways, they hold more negative views of the ancestors than do men. Women's negative conceptions are expressed in the idea that ancestors maliciously harm their descendants by afflicting them with disease and misfortune. Men worship ancestors in Confucian rites from which women are excluded, while women perform rites for ancestors in a shamanic mode, utilizing widespread networks of shamans, most of whom are women. This gender-based bifurcation in ancestor worship is a special characteristic of Korean tradition.

Japan. Since the Tokugawa period (1600-1868) Japanese ancestor worship has mainly been carried out in a Buddhist mode, though Shinto rites also exist. As in China, ancestral ritual reflects relations of authority and inheritance, but instead of lineage rites, rites are performed by main and branch households of the traditional family system, the *ie*. Branch families (*bunke*) accept the ritual centrality of the main household (*honke*) by participating in its rites in a subordinate status. The *honke* does not reciprocate. In addition to *honke-bunke* rites, domestic rites performed before a Buddhist altar are a prominent feature of Japanese ancestral worship.

The "new religions" of Japan are a group of several hundred associations that have appeared in the nineteenth and twentieth centuries. Most reserve a special place for ancestor worship in some form. Reiyukai Kyodan (Association of Friends of the Spirits) represents a rare example of a religious group in which worship of ancestors is the main focus of individual and collective rites. Reverence for ancestors in the new religions and in Japanese society in general is closely linked to social and political conservatism and to a traditionalist preference for the social mores of the past.

BIBLIOGRAPHY

Ahern, Emily. *The Cult of the Dead in a Chinese Village*. Stanford, Calif., 1973. A comprehensive study of ancestor worship in Taiwan that clarifies the relation between lineage and domestic observances.

Blacker, Carmen. *The Catalpa Bow*. London, 1975. An evocative study of shamanistic and ancestral practices in Japanese folk religion.

Freedman, Maurice. *Lineage Organization in Southeastern China* (1958). London, 1965. An anthropological study of lineage organization that establishes the distinction between hall and domestic ancestral cults and includes valuable material on geomancy.

Gluckman, Max. "Mortuary Customs and the Belief in Survival after Death among the South-Eastern Bantu." *Bantu Studies* 11 (June 1937): 117-136.

Groot, J. J. M. de. *The Religious System of China* (1892). 6 vols. Taipei, 1967. A comprehensive study of Chinese religions with rich data on ancestor worship, principally from Amoy.

Hardacre, Helen. *Lay Buddhism in Contemporary Japan: Reiyukai Kyodan*. Princeton, 1984. A study of a new religion of Japan with special reference to ancestor worship.

Hsu, Francis L. K. *Under the Ancestors' Shadow*. New York, 1948. A classic study of Chinese ancestor worship.

Janelli, Dawnhee Yim, and Roger L. Janelli. *Ancestor Worship in Korean Society*. Stanford, Calif., 1982. A study of Korean ancestor worship with special reference to gender differences in belief and practice.

Jordan, David K. *Gods, Ghosts, and Ancestors: The Folk Religion of a Taiwanese Village*. Chicago, 1969. A study of ancestor worship and related phenomena, especially spirit marriage, in Taiwan.

Kopytoff, Igor. "Ancestors as Elders in Africa." *Africa* 41 (April 1971): 129-142.

Newell, William H., ed. *Ancestors*. The Hague, 1976. A useful collection of essays on aspects of ancestor worship, especially in Africa and Japan.

Takeda Choshu. *Sosen suhai*. Tokyo, 1971. A study of Japanese ancestor worship with special reference to Buddhism.

Wolf, Arthur P. "Gods, Ghosts, and Ancestors." In his *Religion and Ritual in Chinese Society*, pp. 131-182. Stanford, Calif., 1974.

Yanagita Kunio. *Senzo no hanashi*. Tokyo, 1946. Translated by F. H. Mayer and Ishiwara Yasuyo as *About Our Ancestors* (Tokyo, 1970). A folkloristic view of Japanese ancestor worship and its place in Japanese culture.

HELEN HARDACRE

Mythic Ancestors

Cosmogonic myths are narratives that depict the creation of the world by divine beings. These divine beings and culture heroes form the ancestral lineages of the human race. The situation of the human race is based upon the activities, adventures, discoveries, and disappearance of these first creative ancestors, who appeared in sacred history. [See Cosmogony.]

Primordial Ruptures. In the Mesopotamian myth *Enuma elish*, a tension develops between the first creators and their offspring. This tension leads to a rupture in the initial creation and a struggle between its gods and their offspring. In the ensuing battle, the foundation is established for human existence. In the *Enuma elish*, the god Marduk is the leader of the offspring who fight Tiamat, the mother. In the battle Tiamat is slain, and her body becomes the earth on which human beings live. Certain archetypes for human existence are established as a result of this battle: the cooperation between the offspring gods becomes a model for cooperative enterprise among human beings, which the death of Tiamat affirms.

A Dogon myth from West Africa describes a similar situation. The god Amma began creation by first forming a cosmic egg, in which the embryos of twin deities matured; they were to become perfect beings. One of the twins became impatient and decided to leave the egg before maturation. In so doing it tore out part of the placenta and fell to what is now the earth, creating a place of habitation from the torn placenta of the egg. This was an incomplete creation, however, and Amma, to rectify the situation, sacrificed the other twin. Even with this sacrifice, the creation could not be made perfect. Instead of creating perfect beings who were both androgynous and amphibious, Amma was forced to compromise. Thus, humans are not androgynous but rather composed of two sexes; they are not amphibious but essentially terrestrial; they do not live continuously in a perfect state of illumination (composed of equal parts of dark and light), but in two alternating modes of full light and darkness. In addition to this, the opposing natures of the obedient and the malevolent twin, who are the ancestors of all human beings on earth, define modes of life throughout the universe.

Ancestors not only set forth the general and universal human condition; they are also the founders of clans, families, moieties, and other segments of the human community. N. D. Fustel de Coulanges's classic work *The Ancient City* (1901) describes how ancient Greek and Roman families were founded by ancestors who were heroes or divine beings. The family cult was at once the basis for the order and maintenance of the family and a cult of the ancestor. Similar notions are present among Australian Aborigines, where each totemic group has its own totemic ancestor who controls the food supply and is the basis for authority and marriages among the groups. In almost the same manner, the Tucano Indians of Colombia understand their origins as arising from mythical ancestors, the Desna, who revealed all the forms of nature and modes of being to the human community.

An exemplary expression of the cult of ancestors is found in Chinese religions. It is the duty of Chinese sons to provide for and revere their parents in this life and the life after death; this is a relationship of reciprocity. The household is composed of the living and the dead; the ancestors provide and sustain the foundations of spiritual order upon which the family is based, while the living keep the family in motion. The living are always under the tacit judgment of their ancestors, on

> **Cain in the biblical story is the culture hero who founds the city of Enoch; Romulus is the founder of Rome; Quetzalcoatl, of Tollan.**

account of which they attempt to conduct their lives in an honorable manner.

The Founding of Cities. Not only do divine ancestors and culture heroes form the lineages of families and totemic groups, they are equally present at the beginnings of almost every city foundation in ancient and traditional cultures. Cain in the biblical story is the culture hero who founds the city of Enoch; Romulus is the founder of Rome; Quetzalcoatl, of Tollan. In Southeast Asia, the founding of states and kingship follow the archetypes of the Hindu god Indra.

The founding of a city may be a response to the experience of a hierophany. Hierophanies of space, or ceremonial centers, are revelations of the sacred meaning of space itself. The divine beings or culture heroes who found cities derive their power from such sacred ceremonial centers. In some cases, a sacrifice is necessary to appease the gods of the location; thus, many of the myths involving the founding of cities relate a story of twins, one of whom is killed or sacrificed, as in the case of Cain's slaying of Abel, or Romulus's murder of Remus. In one of the mythological cycles of Quetzalcoatl, for example, a magical combat takes place in which Quetzalcoatl kills his uncle.

The ancestors as founders of a city establish the archetypes for all domesticated space. The normalization of activities in the space of the city, whether in terms of family structures or the public meanings of space, are guaranteed by the founding ancestor. All other establishments or reestablishments of cities will follow the model of the archetypal gestures of the founding ancestor of the city. The ruler of the city represents and symbolizes the presence of the divine ancestor, and elaborate rituals of rulership take place at certain temporal intervals to commemorate and reestablish the founding gestures.

Death. In some myths death enters the world because of an action, inaction, or quarrel among the creator deities. They may have simply forgotten to tell human beings whether they were immortal or not, or the creator deity allows death to enter the world. In a myth from Madagascar two gods create human beings: the earth god forms them from wood and clay,

the god of heaven gives them life. Human beings die so that they may return to the origins of their being.

In most mythic scenarios, however, death is the result of a sacred history that introduces the second meaning of primordiality. Through ignorance, interdiction, or violence, a break is made by the divine offspring from the creator deity, and in this rupture is the origin of death. The origin of the abode of the dead is equally located in this event, for, in the mythic scenarios, the rupture creates divisions in space among which a place of the dead comes into being. For example, in the Dogon myth mentioned above, the placenta of the god Amma is the earth, and at death one returns to the earth which was the original stuff of creation.

Funerary rituals are very important, for they assure that the dead will arrive in the correct manner at the abode of the ancestors. The souls of the dead must be instructed and led on the right path lest they become lost. Funerary rituals prescribe the correct behavior and route to be taken by the dead to the land of the ancestors.

BIBLIOGRAPHY

A general discussion of cosmogonic myths can be found in my *Alpha: The Myths of Creation* (New York, 1963). For Mircea Eliade's discussion of the two types of primordiality, see "Cosmogonic Myth and Sacred History," in his *The Quest* (Chicago, 1969). For ancient Near Eastern myths, see *Ancient Near Eastern Texts relating to the Old Testament*, 3d ed., edited by J. B. Pritchard (Princeton, 1969). N. D. Fustel de Coulanges's *The Ancient City* (1901), 12th ed. (Baltimore, 1980), remains the best general introduction to Greek and Roman religion dealing with the meaning of ancestors. Joseph Rykwert's *The Idea of a Town* (Princeton, 1976) is a brilliant discussion of the myths and rituals of the founding of Rome. Paul Wheatley's *The Pivot of the Four Quarters* (Chicago, 1971) is the best work on the meaning of the ceremonial center as the basis for the founding of cities. Robert Heine-Geldern's "Conceptions of State and Kingship in Southeast Asia," *Far Eastern Quarterly* 2 (November 1942): 15-30, describes state and urban foundaton in Southeast Asia. Davd Carrasco presents the full cycle of the myths, histories, and city foundations of Quetzalcoatl in *Quetzalcoatl and the Irony of Empire* (Chicago, 1982). For the Tucano Indians of Colombia, see Gerardo Reichel-Dolmatoff's *Amazonian Cosmos* (Chicago, 1971). Adolf E. Jensen's *Myth and Cult among Primitive Peoples* (Chicago, 1963), is the best general work on the religious meaning of culture heroes and *dema* deities. For China, see Raymond Dawson's *The Chinese Experience* (London, 1978). Dominique Zahan's *The Religion, Spirituality, and Thought of Traditional Africa* (Chicago, 1979) places the meaning of ancestors within the general structures of African religions. Hans Abrahamsson's *The Origin of Death* (Uppsala, 1951), is still the best study of the myths of death in Africa. For the ancestors of the Dinka, a cattle-raising people in Africa, see Godfrey Lienhardt's *Divinity and Experience: The Religion of the Dinka* (Oxford, 1961). Jack Goody's *Death, Property and the Ancestors* (Stanford, 1962) is a detailed study of death and funerary rituals among the LoDagaa of West Africa. Stanley Wallens's *Feasting with Cannibals* (Princeton, 1981) is a study of the meaning of ancestors among the Kwakiutl.

CHARLES H. LONG

ANCIENT NEAR EASTERN RELIGIONS

[*See articles* Aramean Religion, Canaanite Religion, Egytian Religion, Hittite Religion, Israelite Religion, Mesopotamian Religion, Moabite Religion, Philistine Religion, Phoenician Religion.]

ANGELS

ANGELS belong to the enormous variety of spiritual beings who mediate between the transcendental realm of the sacred and the profane world of man. The term *angel* is specifically used in Western religions to distinguish benevolent from malevolent demons. In most other religions, however, the distinction between good and evil demons is less clear; their behavior depends on the situation and on the conduct of individuals and communities.

Origin and Function. The word *angel* is derived from the Greek *aggelos*, translated from the Hebrew *mal'akh*, meaning "messenger." The literal meaning of the word indicates the primary function of angels as divine messengers. They are sent by God to inform men of their ultimate being, purpose, and destiny.

The role of angels is most fully elaborated in religions based on revelation, such as Zoroastrianism, Judaism, Christianity, and Islam. These religions emphasize the distance between man and God and, consequently, have the greatest need for intermediaries between the two. In polytheistic religions the gap between man and the gods is less pronounced; angelic functions are often performed by the gods themselves in their human incarnations. In monistic religions, angelic intermediaries play a minor part since the gap between man and God is nonexistent. Nevertheless, in both polytheistic and monistic religions, spiritual beings similar to angels do exist to help individuals achieve a proper rapport with the gods and spirits.

Judaism and Zoroastrianism. Angels experienced a similar moral metamorphosis through the centuries. In early biblical stories (e.g., *Ps.* 78:49, 1 *Sm.* 18:10), they can be malevolent and murderous. Later writers stress their benevolence, or at least their righteousness, in contrast to other, malevolent, spirits. The origin of the evil demons and their leader, Satan, was a subject of intense speculation in later Judaism, Christianity, and Islam. The general view was that Satan and his followers were fallen angels, expelled from heaven for envy, pride, or lust.

The development of an elaborate angelology in Judaism was a consequence of the Babylonian exile (sixth century BCE) and the influence of Zoroastrianism. The Zoroastrian myth of the cosmic battle between Ahura Mazda ("benevolent deity") and Angra Mainyu ("hostile deity"), with their attendant armies of angels and devils, profoundly influenced the angelology and demonology of the Hebrew scriptures and the Apocrypha, which, in turn, influenced later Jewish, Christian, and Islamic thought. Like Ahura Mazda, the Old Testament God, Yahveh, is surrounded by an angelic army. He is the "Lord of Hosts," and his warrior angels fight against the forces of evil led by Satan, who gradually assumes the characteristics of the archfiend, Angra Mainyu.

Judaism adopted the Zoroastrian division of the universe into three realms: heaven, earth, and hell. Heaven is the celestial region inhabited by God and his angels; earth, the terrestrial world of man, limited by time, space, cause and effect; hell, the subterranean world of chaos, darkness, and death, the abode of Satan and his demon followers. This tripartite scheme provided the foundation for the religious, metaphysical, and scientific ideas of Jews, Christians, and Muslims until it was undermined by the Copernican revolution in the sixteenth century. In this tripartite cosmos, the earth is an imperfect halfway house inhabited by man, a hybrid creature with conflicting impulses, ignorant of his origin, nature, and destiny. The primary function of the angels is to bridge the cosmic gap separating God and man. In Zoroastrianism, this gap was the result of the primordial battle between the gods that left man stranded in an alien world. In Judaism, Christianity, and Islam, the rift was the result of man's sin and consequent fall. Whatever the reason, humans have become alienated and no longer understand their relationship to their creator or the purpose of their creation. Because angels are able to assume human form, they can bridge the gulf between heaven and earth and reveal the divine plan, will, and law. In emphasizing the revelatory role of angels, Judaism followed Zoroastrianism. Vohu Manah ("good mind"), one of the Amesha Spentas ("holy immortals") in Zoroastrianism, appeared to Zarathushtra (Zoroaster) and revealed the true nature of God and his covenant with man.

In the Hebrew scriptures, angels perform the same functions as in Zoroastrianism: they praise and serve God, reveal divine truth, and act as extensions of the divine will, rewarding the good and punishing the wicked. They help humans understand God and achieve a proper rapport with him, and they conduct the souls of the righteous to heaven.

Angels can be merciless when they enforce the divine law and punish the wicked (*Ez.* 9). In their dealings with the righteous, however, they are models of care and concern. In the apocryphal *Book of Tobit* (second century BCE) the archangel Raphael guides the young hero Tobias on a dangerous journey and reveals the magic formulas that protect him from the demon Asmodeus and restore his father's sight. In his solicitude for Tobias, Raphael behaves like the guardian angels who became so important in the popular piety of later

Judaism and Catholicism. These guardian angels were modeled after Zoroastrian spirits known as *fravashis*, a cross between ancestral spirits, guardian spirits, and the immortal components of individuals.

Two archangels are mentioned in the Hebrew scriptures: Michael ("like God"), the warrior leader of the heavenly hosts, and Gabriel ("man of God"), the heavenly messenger (*Dn.* 8:16). Two other archangels are named in the Apocrypha: Raphael ("God has healed"), who appears in *Tobit*, and Uriel

> **Angels can be merciless when they enforce the divine law and punish the wicked (*Ez. 9*). In their dealings with the righteous, however, they are models of care and concern.**

("God is my light"), who appears in *2 Esdras*. Seven archangels, unnamed, are also mentioned in Tobit. In addition to these archangels, two angelic orders appear in the Hebrew scriptures: the six-winged Seraphim, who surround the divine throne and praise God (*Is.* 6:2ff.), and the Cherubim, described by Ezekiel (1:5ff.)

Angels in Christianity. New Testament angels perform the same functions as their Old Testament counterparts. Christian angelology, however, is more elaborate and reflects the influence of gnostic and popular beliefs. The gnostics, who flourished during the first four centuries of the common era, were a heterogeneous group with Christian, Jewish, and pagan offshoots, but they shared a dualistic view of the universe as a battleground for good and evil. They believed man to be a prisoner within a cosmos created by an evil demiurge. Man's mission lay in returning to the heavens from which he had come. To do this, a soul had to pass through the seven spheres, each of which was controlled by an angel. The angels allowed to pass through only those souls who addressed them with the proper names and recited the appropriate formulas. The knowledge of these names and formulas provided the gnostics with their name, which literally means "the knowing ones."

Many Christians as well as Jews accepted the gnostic belief that angels participated in creation and contributed to the continuance of the cosmos. Clement of Alexandria (AD 150?-215?) believed that angels controlled the movement of the stars and the four elements. The identification of angels with stars explains their enormous number, beauty, and radiance. Some early Christians, probably recruited from among the gnostics, worshiped angels and considered them more powerful mediators than Christ, which explains the polemic against angel worship in the New Testament (*Col.* 2:18, *Heb.* 1:4ff.). The gnostic invocations to angels contributed to the

angelic magic that developed in popular Judaism, Christianity, and Islam.

Like the angels in the Hebrew scriptures, Christian angels are God's messengers and ministers. They announced the birth of Christ and authenticated his mission on earth, as well as the mission of the apostles, saints, and martyrs. Angels are actively involved in the daily lives of Christians. They preside over the sacraments and are therefore present at the most significant moments in a Christian's life. They will announce the Last Judgment and separate the just from the unjust. The archangel Michael weighs the souls of the dead. Angels help Christians achieve salvation in countless ways; no service is beneath them. They carry the prayers of the faithful to God. They strengthen the weak and comfort the oppressed, particularly martyrs. Legend has it that the guardian angels of children occupy a privileged place in heaven, close to God (*Mt.* 18:10).

Angels in Islam. Islamic angelology closely follows Judaic and Christian patterns. According to Islamic tradition, angels revealed the Qur'an to Muhammad. But, mistrusting the source of his revelation and fearing he was possessed by *jinn* or devils, Muhammad was about to throw himself off a mountain when Jibril (Gabriel) appeared and confirmed him as God's prophet. As the angel of revelation, Jibril took Muhammad (mounted on the winged steed Buraq) on a tour of the seven heavens. Other angels are mentioned in the Qur'an. Mikal (Michael) provides men with food and knowledge; `Izra'il is the angel of death; Isafal places souls in bodies and sounds the trumpet signaling the Last Judgment.

According to popular belief, a group of female angelic beings, the *huris*, inhabit the Muslim paradise and have the specific function of providing male Muslims with erotic delight. The *huris* are similar to the enchanting and sexually skilled *apsaras* in the Hindu heavens. The sexuality of both groups is in marked contrast to the asexuality of Christian angels.

Angelic Hierarchies. Angels are usually grouped in four or seven orders. Four orders are described in the *Sibylline Oracles*, Roman sacred books with Jewish and Christian interpolations. The number four represents the four cardinal points and signifies perfection. As the number of known "planets" (five visible planets plus the sun and the moon), seven played an important part in Babylonian astronomy. The influence of Babylonian science on Zoroastrianism is suggested by the significance that the number seven assumed in Zoroastrian cosmology. The seven Holy Immortals are identified with the seven planets and the seven spheres in which the planets were believed to move. Opposed to the Holy Immortals were seven evil spirits, ancestors of the Christian seven deadly sins. Gnostics recognized seven orders of angels and identified them with the seven spheres. Seven angelic orders are enumerated in the New Testament: Thrones, Dominions, Virtues, Powers, Principalities,

Archangels, and Angels. Clement of Alexandria, along with other early Christian theologians, accepted these seven orders.

In the writings of Dionysius the Areopagite (late fifth century), the various strands of Jewish and Christian angelology were united in a systematic whole. To the seven angelic orders mentioned in the New Testament, Dionysius added the two orders mentioned in the Old Testament, the Cherubim and the Seraphim, arranging the total of nine orders into three distinct hierarchies with three choirs apiece. (Thus three, the number of the Trinity, is repeated three times.) The highest of these three new orders, comprising Seraphim, Cherubim, and Thrones, was dedicated to the contemplation of God. The second order, comprising Dominions, Virtues, and Powers, governed the universe, while the third order, comprising Principalities, Archangels, and Angels, executed the orders of their superiors.

Angels in the Modern World. The Copernican revolution undermined the Western tradition of belief in angels. The tripartite division of the universe no longer made sense in a cosmological scheme in which the earth was one planet among others revolving around the sun in a possibly infinite universe. Since there was no longer an up or a down, or a perfect, unchanging heaven, the physical existence of heaven and hell was also questioned.

But whereas the physical sciences undermined belief in the concrete reality of heaven, hell, angels, and devils, the psychological discoveries of the last two centuries have given these entities new plausibility as psychic phenomena. Sigmund Freud located the tripartite cosmos in the structure of the personality itself, with its division into superego, ego, and id. C. G. Jung postulated the existence of a collective unconscious and discussed mythology and religion in terms of the "primordial images," or "archetypes," in the collective unconscious, which every human being inherits. With the insights into psychic conflict provided by modern psychology, the image of angels and devils fighting over individual souls assumes new meaning and relevance.

BIBLIOGRAPHY

For an overall view of the different religious traditions and the place of angels within them, see John B. Noss's *Man's Religions*, 6th ed. (New York, 1980). Zoroastrianism is discussed in Mary Boyce's *A History of Zoroastrianism*, 2 vols. (Leiden, 1975-1982). Robert M. Grant's *Gnosticism and Early Christianity* (New York, 1966) is valuable for understanding the early development of Christian theology. For Christian angelology, see James D. Collin's *The Thomistic Philosophy of Angels* (Washington, D. C., 1947) and Gustav Davidson's *A Dictionary of Angels, Including the Fallen Angels* (New York, 1967). The iconography of angels is discussed in *Anges* by Raymond P. Rgamy, O.P., and Rene Zeller (Paris, 1946).

ALLISON COUDERT

ANGLICANISM

ANGLICANISM, also called the Anglican communion, is a federation of autonomous national and regional churches in full intercommunion through the archbishop of Canterbury of the Church of England. The Anglican churches share a tradition of doctrine, polity, and liturgy stemming from the English Reformation in the sixteenth century. Often classified as "Protestant," they also claim a "Catholic" heritage of faith and order from the ancient, undivided church.

Characteristic of Anglicanism is the endeavor to hold together in a comprehensive middle way (*via media*) the tensions of its Protestant and Catholic elements. This endeavor is a legacy of the English Reformation, which was essentially an act of state and not a popular movement. Without the coercive power of the state, Anglicanism might have died aborning. The long reign of Queen Elizabeth I (r. 1558-1603) ensured its survival. Elizabeth had no intention of submitting England to any papal authority, which her sister, Mary I (r. 1553-1558), had restored. She was equally adamant against agitation for a presbyterian form of church government that would dispense with the royal supremacy, episcopacy, and the liturgy.

Many episcopal sees, including Canterbury, were vacant at Elizabeth's accession. Most of Mary's bishops were deprived of their offices for refusal to accept the new settlement. Careful to maintain the episcopal succession, Elizabeth chose Matthew Parker, a moderate reformer, for her archbishop of Canterbury. He was consecrated on 17 December 1559. Vacant sees were then filled with the queen's supporters.

In 1571, Parliament approved the Thirty-nine Articles, the only official confessional statement of Anglicanism, still printed in most editions of the prayer book. They are not a complete system of doctrine, but point out differences from Roman Catholicism and Anabaptism and indicate nuanced agreement with Lutheran and Reformed positions. The queen added in Article 20 the statement: "The Church hath power to decree Rites and Ceremonies."

Elizabeth's settlement remains the foundation of Anglicanism. It affirms the canonical scriptures to be the final arbiter in all matters of doctrine and to contain all things necessary to salvation.

Today most Anglicans accept as reasonable modern methods of literary and historical criticism of the scriptures and other religious documents. Anglicanism has never had a dominant theologian such as Thomas Aquinas, Luther, or Calvin. The apologetic work of Richard Hooker (1554-1600), *Of the Laws of Ecclesiastical Polity*, is still influential, with its appeal to scripture, church tradition, reason, and experience. Anglican theology tends to be biblical, pastoral, and apologetic rather than dogmatic or confessional.

Anglican polity is episcopal and preserves the ordained orders of bishops, presbyter-priests, and deacons that go back to apostolic times. There is no official doctrine of episcopacy. In all negotiations for unity or intercommunion with other churches, Anglicans insist that an unbroken succession of bishops, together with the other two orders, be maintained.

All Anglican churches are constitutionally governed, each church having its own appropriate canons for executive and legislative authorities. Bishops, clergy, and laity participate in all synodical decision making, but a consensus of these orders, voting separately, is necessary for decisions about major doctrinal, liturgical, or canonical matters. Outside England, bishops are generally elected by a synod of the diocese in which they will serve, subject to confirmation by other bishops and representative clergy and laity from each diocese.

The Church of England is today the only Anglican church that is state-established. The archbishop of Canterbury has a primacy of honor among all Anglican bishops, but he has no jurisdiction outside of his own diocese and province. The Crown, after appropriate consultations, nominates the English bishops, who are then elected by their respective cathedral chapters. Parliament retains final control over doctrine and liturgy, but the Synodical Government Measure of 1969 gave the English church large freedom to order its internal life through a General Synod of bishops, clergy, and laity.

In addition to the episcopate, Anglicanism is bonded by a common liturgy, contained in various recensions of *The Book of Common Prayer*, based either upon the Elizabethan version of 1559 or that of 1549. Use of the prayer book is prescribed in all Anglican churches. With the Bible and a hymnal, it provides everything needed for the churches' rites and ceremonies. The prayer book has been in continuous use since the sixteenth century, except for the years of the English Commonwealth (1645-1660), when it was proscribed in public and private use. It is the only vernacular liturgy of the Reformation period still in use.

The prayer-book formularies, many of them derived from the ancient church, are a principal source of doctrine and a primary basis of the spirituality of both clergy and laity. The daily and Sunday liturgies are set within the framework of the traditional seasons of the Christian year and fixed feasts of Christ and the saints. The sacraments of baptism and the Lord's Supper (also called Holy Communion or Eucharist) are considered generally necessary to salvation.

For almost three centuries the expansion of Anglicanism was hindered by the Church of England's lack of any overall missionary strategy and its concept of a church that must be established by the state and sufficiently endowed. Within the British Isles, the Church in Wales, whose roots go back to the ancient church in Roman Britain, was part of the province of Canterbury from the Norman Conquest until its disestablish-

ment and disendowment in 1920. The English Reformation in Ireland was rejected by 90 percent of the people. Yet not until 1870 was the (Anglican) Church of Ireland disestablished and largely disendowed. Four Anglican dioceses now straddle the border between Northern Ireland and the Republic of Ireland. The Reformation in Scotland was predominantly presbyterian.

Beginning in Virginia in 1607, the English church came to be established in the american colonies. Except in Virginia, Anglicans were outnumbered.

After a brief visit to Maryland, the Reverend Thomas Bray (1658-1730) founded in 1701 the voluntary Society for the Propagation of the Gospel in Foreign Parts, but the American Revolution decimated these accomplishments. With independence, all SPG support was withdrawn. A large proportion of clergy and laity had left for England or Canada. There were no more establishments, and in Virginia disendowment also followed. The remnant of clergy and laity, both patriots and loyalists, began to organize in state conventions. The consecration of Bishop Seabury for Connecticut by Scottish bishops, who were considered schismatic by the Church of England, spurred the English bishops to obtain an act of Parliament in June 1786 enabling them to consecrate American bishops without the customary oaths of obedience to the royal supremacy and the archbishop of Canterbury. Three Americans were so consecrated: for Pennsylvania and New York in 1787 and for Virginia in 1790.

A national church was formed at a general convention in 1789, which adopted a constitution, canons, and a revised prayer book. By the General Convention in 1835, the Episcopal church was strong enough to begin concerted missionary strategy and it organized the Domestic and Foreign Missionary Society, which to this day includes all its baptized members. A bishop was chosen to organize dioceses on the western frontier; and a bishop was resident in China in 1844 and in Japan in 1874. Liberia received its first bishop in 1851.

The Church of England was slow, however, in providing bishops for its burgeoning missions overseas, and voluntary societies could not legally do so. Canada received its first bishop in 1787, followed by India in 1814, the West Indies in 1824, Australia in 1836, New Zealand in 1841, and South Africa in 1847.

In 1960 the first Anglican executive officer, serving under the archbishop of Canterbury, was chosen. His duties were to visit and assess the problems of the various Anglican churches and to promote communication and common strategy for mission among them. In 1971 the Anglican Consultative Council came into being, and the Anglican executive officer became its secretary general. The council meets every two or three years in various parts of the Anglican world. The archbishop of Canterbury is its president, but the council elects its own chairman; to date three of them have been laypersons. Members consist of representative bishops, clergy, and laity of the several Anglican churches.

Anglicanism is much involved in endeavors for Christian unity. The Episcopal church, under the leadership of Bishop Charles Henry Brent (1862-1929), planned the first World Conference on Faith and Order at Lausanne in 1927, over which Brent presided. Delegates from more than one hundred Protestant and Eastern Orthodox churches attended. This movement became part of the World Council of Churches, constituted in 1948.

At Bonn in 1931 the Anglican communion entered into an agreement with the Old Catholic churches of the Union of Utrecht (1889) for full intercommunion, which stated that this does "not require from either Communion the acceptance of all doctrinal opinion, sacramental devotion, or liturgical practice characteristic of the other, but implies that each believes the other to hold all the essentials of the Christian Faith."

Serious efforts to achieve the future reunion of Anglicanism with the Roman Catholic church began in an official visit of Archbishop Ramsey of Canterbury with Pope Paul VI in March 1966. A joint preparatory commission in 1967-1968 sorted major theological issues for dialogue and made recommendations for areas of cooperation. Between 1970 and 1981 the Anglican-Roman Catholic International Commission published substantial agreements on eucharistic doctrine, ministry, and ordination and two agreements on authority in the church. These were gathered, with some elucidations, in the commission's *Final Report* (1982). When Pope John Paul II visited Britain in 1982, he and Archbishop Runcie signed the "Common Declaration" at Canterbury Cathedral on 29 June for a new commission to study further theological issues, pastoral problems, and practical steps for "the next stage" toward unity.

BIBLIOGRAPHY

There is no comprehensive, up-to-date survey of Anglicanism in its developing structures, ecumenical dialogues, and liturgical revisions. Recent developments are summarized in *The Official Year Book of the General Synod of the Church of England* (London, Church Information Office). For the crucial decade of the 1960s, one should consult the account by Stephen F. Bayne, Jr., the first Anglican executive officer, *An Anglican Turning Point: Documents and Interpretations*, "Church Historical Society, Sources," no. 2 (Austin, 1964). Two comprehensive surveys of the Anglican communion, with copious bibliography, are J. W. C. Wand's *Anglicanism in History and Today* (London, 1961) and Stephen C. Neill's *Anglicanism*, 3d ed. (Baltimore, 1965). See also H. G. G. Herklots's engaging *Frontiers of the Church: The Making of the Anglican Communion* (London, 1961) and the detailed eyewitness account of the Lambeth Conference of 1968 by James B. Simpson and Edward M. Story, *The Long Shadows of Lambeth X* (New York, 1969).

On *The Book of Common Prayer*, its texts and sources (1549-1662), Frank E. Brightman's *The English Rite*, 2d ed., 2 vols. (London, 1921), is indispensable. The most recent account of its history, with valuable documents and copious bibliography, is Geoffrey J. Cuming's *A History of Anglican Liturgy*, 2d ed. (London, 1980). For Anglican worship in ecumenical and artistic perspective, nothing surpasses Horton Davies's *Worship and Theology in England*, 5 vols. (Princeton, 1961-1975). Anglican ecumenical involvement is discussed in *A History of the Ecumenical Movement*, 1517-1948, 2d ed., edited by Ruth Rouse and Stephen C. Neill (London, 1967), and, in its relation to the Roman Catholic church, in Bernard Pawley and Margaret Pawley's *Rome and Canterbury through Four Centuries: A Study of the Relations between the Church of Rome and the Anglican Churches*, 1530-1973, with a large bibliography and an American epilogue by Arthur A. Vogel (New York, 1975).

MASSEY H. SHEPHERD, JR.

ANTHONY OF PADUA

ANTHONY OF PADUA (1195?-1231), born Ferdinand de Bulhoes; Franciscan preacher, miracle worker, and saint. Born in Lisbon, Portugal, Ferdinand de Bulhoes entered the monastery of the Canons Regular of Saint Augustine while still an adolescent. He was ordained a priest at the monastery of his order in Coimbra in 1219. Inspired by the martyrdom of Franciscan missionaries in Morocco, he left the monastery to join the Friars Minor in 1220, taking the religious name of Anthony. After an abortive attempt at mission work in Morocco, Anthony went to Italy, where he participated in the general chapter of the Franciscans at Assisi (1221) and, presumably, met Francis of Assisi. In 1223 Anthony was appointed lector in theology at the Franciscan house of studies in Bologna.

By 1226 Anthony had been appointed the Franciscan minister for the Emilia (a region in northern Italy) and served as a Franciscan delegate to the Vatican. In that same year he received permission from Pope Gregory IX to relinquish all offices in order to devote his life to preaching, for which he had demonstrated great flair. For the rest of his brief life, Anthony traveled through the region around Padua as an incessant preacher of reform and as an obdurate opponent of heresy. In 1231 he died at Padua; Gregory IX canonized him the following year at solemn ceremonies in the Cathedral of Spoleto. In 1946 Pius XII named him a doctor of the church.

The only surviving authentic writings of Anthony are two series of sermons, one for Sundays (*Sermones domenicales*) and one for various feast days of the liturgical year (*Sermones in solemnitatibus sanctorum*). From these writings scholars have attempted to reconstruct the saint's theological vision.

Anthony's theology was shaped both by his use of the sermon and by his stated desire to combat the twin heresies of the Cathari and the dissident evangelical sects like the Waldensians. He emphasized the incarnational themes of theology, the need for interior conversion, and a return to the sacraments, especially the sacrament of penance, as a sign of reconciliation with the church. The framework of his sermons was most typically constructed by harmonizing the scriptural texts of the liturgy celebrated on the day he preached. While the sermons were meant for general consumption they still reflect considerable learning, in both theological and mystical literature.

Anthony's mysticism was influenced heavily by Augustine of Hippo and the twelfth-century exegete Richard of Saint-Victor. His scriptural exegesis, based on the traditional four-

> **After an abortive attempt at mission work in Morocco, Anthony went to Italy, where he participated in the general chapter of the Franciscans at Assisi (1221) and, presumably, met Francis of Assisi.**

fold sense of scripture, leans heavily toward the moral sense of the text, which he uses both to exhort to virtue and to warn against the reigning heresies of the time. His focus, typically Franciscan, on the humanity of Jesus led to an emphasis on the healing virtue of the wounds of Christ. Some have seen in the sermons of Anthony the beginnings of the devotion to the Heart of Jesus, a devotional figura that would blossom fully only in late medieval piety. His series of sermons on the Virgin Mary constitute a brief compendium of Mariology; his name was invoked by Pius XII as one of the doctors who held the doctrine of the bodily assumption of Mary into heaven, a doctrine defined by the pontiff in 1950.

While Anthony's contemporaries praised his deep knowledge of scripture and his power as an apologist and preacher, posterity best remembers the saint as a thaumaturge. Celebrated in art and narrated in legend, his miracles have the simple charm associated with early Franciscan charisma. The center of Anthony's cult is the Basilica of Il Santo in Padua, which incorporates the old Church of Santa Maria Materdomini where Anthony was originally buried. One of Donatello's famous bronze panels at the basilica depicts an unbeliever's donkey, which, to the evident discomfiture of its owner, is venerating the Eucharist held by Anthony. The popular fourteenth-century Italian anthology of Franciscan stories known as the *Fioretti* (Little Flowers) reflects Anthony's importance in the estimation of the early Franciscans by associating him with the stories of Francis and his earliest companions.

In the centuries after his death the cult of Saint Anthony developed with an intensity second only to that of Francis himself. From that popular devotionalism springs both some common beliefs (a prayer to Saint Anthony will retrieve lost articles) and charitable practices, such as the collection of alms for the poor under the rubric of "Saint Anthony's bread."

BIBLIOGRAPHY

The standard, if deficient, edition of the sermons of the saint is *Sermones Sancti Antonii Patavini*, 3 vols. in 1, edited by Antonio M. Locatelli (Padua, 1895-1913). Sophronius Clasen's *Saint Anthony: Doctor of the Gospel* (Chicago, 1961) is a work by a noted Franciscan scholar. The article "Antonio di Padova," in the *Bibliotheca Sanctorum*, vol. 1 (Rome, 1960), pp. 156-188, is a generally reliable, if somewhat pious, study of the saint's life, doctrine, iconography, and place in folklore.

LAWRENCE S. CUNNINGHAM

ANTHROPOLOGY, ETHNOPOLOGY, AND RELIGION

In his classic discussion of "the sick soul" in *The Varieties of Religious Experience* (1902), William James observes that "philosophic theism has always shown a tendency to become pantheistic and monistic, and to consider the world as one unit of absolute fact." In contrast, popular or practical theism has "ever been more or less frankly pluralistic, not to say polytheistic, and shown itself perfectly well satisfied with a universe composed of many original principles." While James ultimately deems the divine principle supreme and the rest subordinate, his immediate sympathies lie with less absolute "practicalities," and he situates analyses of religious experience within the felt tension between theistic monism and the pluralism of actual populations. In many respects the anthropological study of religion has sustained and enlarged upon these sympathies.

Anthropology's traditional concentration on nonliterate societies has shaped its approach to religious practice and belief in general. But ethnological theory has seldom been confined to so-called primitive peoples, tribal groups, or even "marginalized" peoples discredited by a dominant religious establishment. Ethnographers have long addressed religious contexts evolved from what Karl Jaspers called "the Axial Age," marked by world-rejecting beliefs in either a transcendental realm or an abstractly negative realm distinct from the worldly or mundane. Anthropologists encounter the entire range of religious values in ideal and implementation at every scale of civilization and all manner of society, sect, and renunciation. Still, when broaching cultural circumstances of world religions, anthropologists tend to emphasize the practitioners' more immediate transmundane concernsfrom spirit cults to ancestor worshipwhose persistence can qualify those transcendental doctrines or ethical canons (paramount for historians of religion) professed by priests, monks, and scribes.

Methodological Foundations. Rival definitions of religion characterize anthropological efforts. Such scholars as Melford E. Spiro retain a notion of the superhuman and rebuke Durkheim for diluting religion to whatever is ritually "set apart." Others, such as Clifford Geertz, empty religion of superhuman, supernatural, or holy content, defining it generally as a set of powerful symbols conjoined to rhetorics of persuasion that are uniquely realistic to adherents and apparent in their moods, motivation, and conceptions. Some working definitions of religion support Mircea Eliade's sense of a distinctive *homo religiosus*; others pose religion as a basically compensatory reaction to mundane deprivation, suffering, or violence. Regardless, anthropologists explore sacred values across domains of illness and cure, aesthetics, law, politics, economy, philosophy, sexuality, ethics, warfare, play, sport, and the many kinds of classifications and performances that both organize and challenge cultural systems of knowledge and affect.

Few introductory works in anthropology are informed by a coherent view of religion; one exception is James L. Peacock and A. Thomas Kirsch's textbook (1980), which employs Robert N. Bellah's Parsonian framework of evolving differential roles in religious and political institutions. Scholarly consensus in the anthropology of religions remains agonistic at best.

Methodological Critiques. As the anthropology of religion advances, it properly intensifies its retrospection. One can better appreciate current trends by reconsidering the emergence of specialized scholarship on primitive religions.

Fallacies in nineteenth-century quests for the origins of religion, taken as a distinct category of human experience, have been often noted. E. E. Evans-Pritchard's succinct *Theories of Primitive Religion* (1965), for example, enumerates earlier, now-rejected studies on the stages of man's religious impulse, proposed in different combinations and sequences by successive evolutionist scholars. In these studies, besides monotheism we find fetishism, manism, nature-mythism, animism, totemism, dynamism, magism, polytheism, and certain psychological states (p. 104). Although some such complexes may be real enough—one thinks particularly of shamanismn—one demonstrably existed as a distinct stage in a progression either toward religious sagacity or beyond it into "mature" scientific objectivity. Recent correlations between religious types and socioeconomic levels appear less monolithic: for example, the shamans of flexibly structured hunter and gatherer societies versus the priests and prophets of stratified civilizations. But even these schemes underestimate copious evidence of coexisting religious specializations enacted as divination, prophecy, calendrical ceremonies, and many blends of magic, sorcery, and thaumaturgy.

In 1962 Claude Lévi-Strauss published a critique of the history of abstracting "totemism," which he defined broadly as analogies between social divisions and categories of the natural surroundings. Since then anthropologists have continued reexamining many analyses produced in the vain pursuit of origins. Evans-Pritchard, again, captures the flavor of prejudicial dichotomies that usually, but not inevitably, favored Europeans: "We are rational, primitive peoples [are] prelogical, living in a world of dreams and make-believe, of mystery and awe; we are capitalists, they communists; we are monogamous, they promiscuous; we are monotheists, they fetishists, animists, pre-animists or what have you, and so on" (p. 105).

The twentieth century brought vigorous responses to Social Darwinism, eugenics movements, and other theories of qualitative divisions in the human species. Franz Boas and his followers in America, Durkheimians in France, and some diffusionists and functionalists in Britain and elsewhere attacked patently false evolutionist schemes of myth, magic, and religion. Scholars today continue to debunk "awe theories" such as those put forth in A. H. Keane's article "Ethnology" in the *Encyclopaedia of Religion and Ethics* (vol. 5, Edinburgh, 1912). Keane recapitulates notions of psycholatry, nature worship, the priority of magic, and primitive confusion between the unclean and the holycommon subjects of debate ordering the rivalries among many comparative philologists, mythologists, and ethnologists, including F. Max Mller, Andrew Lang, W. Robertson Smith, E. B. Tylor, and James G. Frazer. Keane repeats theories of the concept of independent soul, according to which the soul extends from one's "own person" to one's fellows, then to animals, plants, and finally to the organized world.

Historical Revaluations. Anthropologists today seem willing to assess neglected intricacies of dated works, despite their errors. In the history of the anthropology of religion in particular, the way has been cleared not for revisionism but for serious rereading; we are perhaps verging on a more anthropological attitude toward anthropology's own past. Books by early professional anthropologists and the founding figures of Indology, comparative mythology, and folklore up to 1860 (surveyed in Feldman and Richardson, 1972) were punctuated by false explanations; but many of them also manage to involve readers in the unfamiliar, the inexplicable, even the forbidden. Narrative and documentary strategies and rhetorical and discursive devices of bygone scholarship are currently being scrutinized. Even "progressive" historians, such as Evans-Pritchard, resist simply dismissing convoluted studies by R. R. Marett and A. E. Crawley, or Lucien Lvy-Bruhl's controversial ideas of prelogical mentality. There is evident dissatisfaction with a "use and abuse" self-legitimating history of the discipline. Old stereotypes of scientific progress are being shaken, sometimes gently, sometimes violently.

Standardized histories of the discipline have distorted chronologies of development; some new-sounding themes were found not to be so new after all; old paradigms could be discarded before they were exhausted; and figures marginal to eventually dominant schools were sometimes worthier than subsequently portrayed. Durkheim's circle, for example, closed ranks to exclude scholars less committed to the group's view of "socio-logic." Durkheimians were in turn neglected after their hybrid expertise in ethnology, sociology, history, and comparative philology (particularly Sanskrit) was overshadowed by the fieldwork imperative, particularly in the United States and among British functionalists. Certain British scholars as well were consequently "marginalized."

Approaches to Future Study. Several recourses are available for students, laymen, and professionals who might understandably feel frustrated by the plethora of descriptions, theories, methods, and reevaluations of the discipline's findings and its legitimacy. One might, for example, concentrate on a particular topic, such as death rites, lately restored to prominence by both anthropologists and social historians. The study of funerary practices allows scholars to circumvent certain difficulties encountered in defining religion in the abstract. What cultures do to and with their bodies before and after death clarifies religious processes of continuity and schism when relations among the living are thus articulated or redefined with reference to the dead (Bloch and Parry, 1982; Huntington and Metcalf, 1979). Another recourse would be to review the history of documenting the religion or religions of a particular society or region. Finally, one might inspect particular bodies of scholarship in order to appreciate the contributions made by particular anthropologists.

The anthropology of religion, increasingly diverse and boundless, remains devoted to the understanding of religious differences. The discipline has passed beyond the phase of aspiring to confine in a monograph any culture's belief. Fieldwork results cannot be insulated from general issues in phenomenological, existential, hermeneutic, pragmatist, structuralist, or politicized study of religious practice and commentary. Nor can bold ideas in the comparative history of religions remain oblivious to actual contradictions—what Edmund Leach has called the dialectics of practical religion—lived out in religious hinterlands, beyond the margins of rival orthodoxies, and in religious centers as well. In the anthropology of religion, as in many interpretative pursuits of our postmodern age, there is nowhere left to hide. As William James foresaw in his postscript to *The Varieties of Religious Experience*, a sort of polytheism has, in truth, returned upon us.

BIBLIOGRAPHY

Bauman, Richard. *Let Your Words Be Few: Symbolism of Speaking and Silence among Seventeenth Century Quakers.* Cambridge, 1983. An imaginative study of Quaker ritual and restraint that, like the works of Roger Abrahams and others, consolidates approaches from folklore, sociolinguistics, and social interaction.

Bloch, Maurice, and Jonathan Parry, eds. *Death and the Regeneration of Life.* Cambridge, 1982. An important, wide-ranging collection on death and afterlife and after-death practices and beliefs; the study develops and challenges suggestions by such anthropologists as Jack Goody, Edmund Leach, Mary Douglas, and many others.

Boon, James A. *Other Tribes, Other Scribes: Symbolic Anthropology in the Comparative Study of Cultures, Histories, Religions, and Texts.* Cambridge, 1982. An effort to interrelate several arenas of symbolic analysis, including the anthropology of religion, semiotics and structuralism, literary theory, and intellectual history; discusses theorists and institutions.

Dumont, Louis. *Homo Hierarchicus: An Essay on the Caste System.* Rev. ed. Translated by Mark Sainsbury. Chicago, 1980. The indispensable study of Indian society and religion. The revised edition responds to Dumont's numerous critics and clarifies his other studies on individualism and reciprocity.

Dumont, Louis. "A Modified View of Our Origins: The Christian Beginnings of Modern Individualism." *Religion* 12 (January 1982): 1-27.

Eliade, Mircea. *The Forge and the Crucible.* 2d ed. Chicago, 1978. A masterly survey of alchemical and Hermetic constructions in every civilization and many heterodoxies at different periods; contains appendices on Jung, Frances A. Yates's works on Renaissance magi, and much more.

Evans-Pritchard, E. E. *Theories of Primitive Religion.* Oxford, 1965. A standard history of the discipline with some keen insights and assured opinions.

Fabian, Johannes. "Six Theses regarding the Anthropology of African Religious Movements." *Religion* 11 (April 1981): 109-126. A provocative challenge to orthodox anthropological assumptions about the confines of religion. Studies by Fabian, T. O. Beidelman, Ivan Karp, and many others have enlivened recent research on African religion and systems of thought.

Feldman, Burton, and Robert D. Richardson. *The Rise of Modern Mythology,* 1680-1860. Bloomington, Ind., 1972.

Fernandez, James W. *Bwiti: An Ethnography of the Religious Imagination in Africa.* Princeton, 1982. A sweeping, sensitive portrait of an emergent religious culture.

Geertz, Clifford. "Religion: Anthropological Study." In *International Encyclopedia of the Social Sciences*, edited by David Sills, vol. 13. New York, 1968.

Geertz, Clifford. "Religion as a Cultural System." In his *The Interpretation of Cultures.* New York, 1973. Perhaps the most influential essay on religion by an anthropologist in the postwar period.

Huntington, Richard, and Peter Metcalf. *Celebrations of Death.* Cambridge, 1979. A lively, accessible study of death rites and their religious backdrop; it reviews influential theories of Robert Hertz, Arnold van Gennep, Victor Turner, Clifford Geertz, and others, with case studies from Indonesia, Madagascar, European history, modern America, and elsewhere.

Hyde, Lewis. *The Gift: Imagination and the Erotic Life of Property.* New York, 1983. A brilliant consolidation of Marcel Mauss's theories of magic and social exchange with a poetics of personal creativity. An exemplary, nondoctrinaire, interdisciplinary study.

Izard, Michel, and Pierre Smith, eds. *Between Belief and Transgression*. Chicago, 1982. An excellent, representative collection on religion and ritual categories and practice; the authors relate the anthropology of religion to Claude Lévi-Strauss's studies of mythology and kinship and to recent critical work on Classical Greek rites and society by Jean-Pierre Vernant, Marcel Detienne, and others.

Kakar, Sudhir. *Shamans, Mystics, and Doctors: A Psychological Inquiry into India and Its Healing Traditions*. New York, 1982.

Keyes, Charles F., and E. Valentine Daniel. *Karma: An Anthropological Inquiry*. Berkeley, 1983. The articles coordinate issues in the anthropology of religion, the history of religions, and philology, an essential task promoted by many scholars such as Milton Singer, Stanley J. Tambiah, Arjun Appanadurai, and Wendy Doniger O'Flaherty.

La Barre, Weston. Review of *Soma: Divine Mushroom of Immortality* by R. Gordon Wasson. *American Anthropologist* 72 (1970): 368-373.

Lessa, William A., and Evon Z. Vogt, eds. *Reader in Comparative Religion: An Anthropological Approach*. 4th ed. New York, 1979. An indispensable sample and overview of the anthropology of religion; it contains many entries on North American Indian societies and a range of both nonliterate and literate traditions, plus a list of important monographs and background sources.

Lévi-Strauss, Claude. *Totemism*. Translated by Rodney Needham. Boston, 1963. An impeccable rethinking of totemism; this companion study to Lévi-Strauss's *The Savage Mind* (London, 1966) can initiate readers in both the social structural and the mythological side of his complex structuralism.

Littleton, C. Scott. *The New Comparative Mythology: An Anthropological Assessment of the Theories of Georges Dumézil*. 3d ed. Berkeley, 1980.

Needham, Rodney. *Belief, Language, and Experience*. Chicago, 1972.

Obeyesekere, Gananath. *The Cult of the Goddess Pattini*. Chicago, 1984. A challenging ethnographic and historical study informed by fundamental issues in the sociology and psychology of religion.

O'Keefe, Daniel Lawrence. *Stolen Lightning: The Social Theory of Magic*. New York, 1982. An exhaustive survey, studiously positivistic, of every conceivable hypothesis purporting to explain magic, religion, and the occult; it merges scholarly and popular concerns in a most responsible way.

Peacock, James L., and A. Thomas Kirsch. *The Human Direction*. Rev. ed. Englewood Cliffs, N. J., 1980.

Spiro, Melford E. "Religion: Problems of Definition and Explanation." In *Anthropological Approaches to the Study of Religion*, edited by Michael P. Banton, pp. 85-125. New York, 1966.

Turner, Victor. *Dramas, Fields, and Metaphors*. Ithaca, N. Y., 1974. A pivotal collection in Turner's corpus that can steer readers back to his Ndembu ethnography and onward to the dramatically comparative works, grounded in performance metaphors, of his last years.

Wittgenstein, Ludwig. *Remarks on Frazer's Golden Bough*. Edited and revised by Rush Rhees and translated by A. C. Miles. Retford, England, 1979.

JAMES A. BOON

ANTHROPOMORPHISM

Definitions and Distinctions. In a general sense, anthropomorphism can be defined as the description of nonmaterial, "spiritual" entities in physical, and specifically human, form. The idea of human form is an essential part of the definition, since otherwise one would have to deal with representations and manifestations of the divine in all possible material forms. Of course, sharp distinctions are often arbitrary and even misleading, especially since in many religious cultures, the gods often assume, both in mythology and in iconography, animal form (theriomorphism); mixed, hybrid, semianimal-semihuman form (therianthropism); or "unrealistic," wildly imaginative, or even grotesque forms. Deities may be conceived as wholly or partly animal, or they may have animal *avataras*, as does Visnu, who appears as fish, tortoise, manlion, and boar. Gods and goddesses may have multiple heads or arms; goddesses may be many-breasted; or they may be represented with ferociously "demonic" forms of face or figure and with nonnatural combinations of body parts. Indian and ancient Egyptian religions, among others, provide a plethora of examples. Resorting once more to Otto's terminology, one could argue that it is precisely the nonhuman quality of theriomorphic or therianthropic representations that enables them to function as symbols of the numinous as the "wholly other."

While the phenomenon of anthropomorphism proper has been a central problem in the history of religions, theology, and religious philosophy, the transition from theriomorphism to anthropomorphism (according to the evolutionary view current until some decades ago) has often been viewed as marking a definite progress.

A distinction is frequently made between physical anthropomorphism (anthropomorphism proper) and mental or psychological anthropomorphism, also called anthropopathism (i. e., not human form or shape but human feelings: love, hate, desire, anger, etc.). Thus, while there are only faint traces of anthropomorphism proper in the Hebrew scriptures (Old Testament), God is described as loving, taking pity, forgiving, being angry and wroth (at sinners and evildoers), and avenging himself upon his enemies. Even when theological thinking progressively divests the deity of the "cruder" forms of physical and mental anthropomorphism, some irreducible elements remain. For example, certain types of theology of history *(Heilsgeschichte)* imply that God "has a plan" for his creation or for mankind. In fact, religion is often expressed in terms of man's duty to serve the achievement of this divine plan and purpose. The ultimate residual anthropomorphism, however, is the theistic notion of God as personal, in contrast to an impersonal conception of the divine. Also, verbal imagery, no matter how metaphorical it is supposed to be, preserves this basic anthropomorphism: God is father, mother, lover, king, shepherd, judge.

Anthropomorphism and the Criticism of Religion. The expression "criticism of religion" has to be understood on several levels. It merely signifies that religious representations and statements (whether primitive, popular, traditional, or otherwise normative) are criticized because of their allegedly crude and, at times, immoral character. This criticism can come from the outsidefrom philosophy, for exampleor from insidethat is, when religious consciousness becomes more sophisticated, refined, and self-critical (often under the impact of philosophy from outside). Among the earliest and best-known examples of this tendency is the Greek author Xenophanes (fifth century BCE), of whose writings only fragments have been preserved. He ironically notes that Ethiopians represent the gods as black, Thracians depict them as blue-eyed and red-haired, and "if oxen and horses . . . had hands and could paint," their images of gods would depict oxen and horses.

Plato, too, objects to the all too human conception of the gods. For this reason he would also ban traditional Homeric mythology from his ideal republic, "no matter whether [these stories have] a hidden sense or not" (*Republic* 377-378).

When the sixteenth-century French essayist Montaigne wrote that "we may use words like Power, Truth, Justice, but we cannot conceive the thing itself. . . . None of our qualities can be attributed to the Divine Being without tainting it with our imperfection" (*Essais* 2.12), he merely summed up what Muslim, Jewish, and Christian philosophers had already discussed in the Middle Ages. Their problem, like Montaigne's, was not the objectionable character of physical and of certain moral attributes, but the admissibility of attributes as such. The great twelfth-century Jewish philosopher Moses Maimonides (Mosheh ben Maimon), like the Muslim philosophers who had preceded him, taught with uncompromising radicalism that no positive attributes whatever can be predicated of God. It should come as no surprise that most of the efforts of Maimonides, who besides being a great philosopher was also a leading rabbinic authority, should be devoted to explaining away the many anthropomorphisms in the Bible. Once one embarks on this radical road, the next question becomes inevitable: is not "being" or "existence" also a human concept, and is not the definition of God as pure or absolute being also an anthropromorphism, although perhaps a very rarefied one?

Mysticism. The most radical method that religious consciousness can adopt to purge itself of anthropomorphism is the assertion that no adequate statements about the divine are possible in human language.

The challenge of anthropomorphism, or to be more precise, the critical reflection as to how to meet this challenge, thus turns out to be an important factor in the development of mysticism. But this radical mystical "purging" of language ulti-

mately links up with agnostic and even nonreligious criticism. The central text in this respect is David Hume's *Dialogues concerning Natural Religion* (1779), written in the form of a conversation between three interlocutors: a skeptic, a Christian close to the mystical tradition, and a theist. The Christian mystic asserts that the divine essence, attributes, and manner of existence are a mystery to us. The skeptic agrees, but admits the legitimacy of anthropological attributes (wisdom, thought, intention), because human beings simply do not have at their disposal any other form of expression. He merely warns against the mistake of assuming any similarity between our words and the divine qualities. In other words, the mystical and the skeptical, even agnostic, criticisms of anthropomorphism tend to converge. The theist

> A spiritual being of which nothing can be predicated is, in actual fact, no spirit at all.

speaker is not slow to seize on this point. His theism is of a more sophisticated kind; it has absorbed and integrated the anti-anthropomorphic critique. But if all our ideas about the divine are by definition totally incorrect and misleading, then religion and theology necessarily and automatically cease to be of any interest whatever. A spiritual being of which nothing can be predicated is, in actual fact, no spirit at all. Hume's argument that mysticism (including pantheism) and atheism ultimately converge has had far-reaching influence. Nineteenth-century philosophical atheism took up Hume's argument and used the critique of anthropomorphism as well as the dead end to which it leads as leverage for the shift from theology to anthropology: the essence of God is, in fact, nothing but our projection, on a celestial screen, of the essence of man.

BIBLIOGRAPHY

Jevons, Frank B. "Anthropomorphism." In *Encyclopaedia of Religion and Ethics*, edited by James Hastings, vol. 1. Edinburgh, 1908.

Jevons, Frank B. "Anthropomorphismus." In *Reallexikon für Antike und Christentum*, vol. 1. Stuttgart, 1950.

Leeuw, Gerardus van der. *Religion in Essence and Manifestation* (1938). 2 vols. Gloucester, Mass., 1967. See the index, s. v. Anthropomorphism.

Zimmer, Heinrich. *Myths and Symbols in Indian Art and Civilization.* Edited by Joseph Campbell. New York, 1946.

For articles related to anthropomorphism in Islam, see "Tashbih" and "Mu`tazila" in *The Encyclopaedia of Islam* (Leiden, 1913-1938) and "Hashwiyya," "Karramiyya," "Ibn Hazm," and "Ibn Tamiyya" in *The Encyclopaedia of Islam*, new ed. (Leiden, 1960-).

R. J. ZWI WERBLOWSKY

ANTI-SEMITISM

The term *anti-Semitism* was coined in 1879 by the German agitator Wilhelm Marr, author of the anti-Jewish *Der Sieg des Judenthums über das Germanthum*, a work with a gloomy view of the Germanic future. Marr himself was antireligious as well as anti-Jewish, and his term arose out of the pseudoscience of the modern era that regarded race rather than religion as the decisive factor separating Jews from Germans. For this reason, racist anti-Semitism is usually distinguished from medieval Christian anti-Semitism and its antecedents in the patristic and New Testament periods, in which the religious element was paramount.

While anti-Jewish hostility existed in pre-Christian times, notably in ancient Alexandria where local tensions led to the propagation of many anti-Jewish slanders, anti-Judaism was never part of pagan religion as such. It was, rather, a concomitant of ancient ethnocentrism with its proud conviction of Greek (and later Roman) superiority. Judaism was seen as tribalistic, and Jews who resisted the benefits of enlightenment were considered to be filled with enmity toward the human race.

Anti-Judaism in the New Testament. Today, even Christian scholars generally concede that the Gospels and other sections of the New Testament are colored in some measure by hostility toward the Jewish antagonists of the apostolic church in the troubled milieu of the first and second centuries, although the exact nature of this hostility is still under investigation. The *Gospel of Mark*, a work addressed to a Roman gentile audience, reveals an apparent apologetic shift from Roman to Jewish responsibility for the execution of Jesus, possibly because the redactor did not wish to present Jesus as a Jewish insurrectionist at a time when Jews were highly unpopular in Rome as a result of the Judean War (66–

> ... Paul, under gnostic influence, conceived of the Torah as a means of demonic rulership over the fleshly man of the dying age. ...

70 CE). Thus, a reluctant Pilate allows a Jewish council and a Jewish rabble to force his hand. The *Gospel of Matthew* embroiders this theme, portraying the death of Jesus as largely a Jewish deed for which the instigators acknowledge their guilt with a self-inflicted curse: "His blood be on us, and on our children!" (*Mt.* 27:25).

As a postwar composition, the *Gospel of Matthew* seems to reflect the harsh atmosphere of judgment and recrimination characteristic of such eras. Given the redactor's hostile

stance, it is not surprising that the Matthaean Jesus is made to hurl angry denunciations at his Pharisaic opponents. From this diatribe (*Mt.* 23) emerges the composite image, so deeply encased in the Christian imagination, of the hypocritical, legalistic, impious, blind, fanatical, and murderous Pharisee, an image that has played havoc with Jewish-Christian relations ever since. It is, of course, a caricature, but even in milder form, the image remains a problem.

Luke and *Acts*, two works of gentile authorship, reinforce the view that the Jewish populace was responsible for the death of Jesus and that the later destruction of Jerusalem was a consequence of God's wrath. However, although these anti-Jewish themes are present in *Luke* and *Acts*, their impact is softened by other passages, perhaps because Luke hoped for missionary success among Diaspora Jews (Hare, in Davies, 1979).

The *Gospel of John*, a complex and highly stylized composition, casts the Jews in a profoundly hostile light as symbols of a "fallen universe of darkness" who oppose Jesus at every turn in the great drama of the Messiah's "hour" when the Messiah manifests his glory. So negative and intense is the Johannine image that John has sometimes been regarded as the "father of anti-Semitism." Because of its deceptively simple character and the great religious power of its language, this gospel has long been the favorite text of Christian piety, conditioning Christians to think almost instinctively in anti-Jewish terms.

The religious roots of anti-Semitism can also be traced to Paul, sometimes seen as a fanatical convert whose polemic against the Law (*Gal., Rom.*), coupled with his charge that a veil has descended over Jewish minds (*2 Cor.*), has made him seem an archenemy of Judaism. Ruether (1974) argues that Paul, under gnostic influence, conceived of the Torah as a means of demonic rulership over the fleshly man of the dying age, whereas freedom from the Torah signifies freedom from the evil powers for the spiritual man of the coming age. Thus Judaism, or the Israel of flesh, is superseded by Christianity, the Israel of spirit. Although Paul speaks warmly of the Jews, whose covenant remains intact, and of the Torah as "holy, just and good" (*Rom.* 7:12), he nevertheless focuses, in chapters 9–11, on the fact of Jewish disbelief.

Developments during the Middle Ages and the Reformation. Frequent attention has been drawn to the gradual demonization of the Jews in art and folklore, notably in the late Middle Ages. The myths of Jewish crimes such as ritual murder, desecration of the Host, and conspiracy against Christendom intensified the imagined association of Jews with the Prince of Darkness. This process became pronounced in northern Europe as it sank into a state of social crisis colored by religious anxiety after the thirteenth century, when preoccupation with the supernatural was strong. As Norman Cohn reminds us in *The Pursuit of the Millennium: Europe's Inner Demons* (New York, 1970), Catholics and heretics demonized not only each other but also the real or fictional secret societies (e.g., Templars, witches, and Jews) on whom the ills of the time might be blamed. To many Christian sectarians, anticipating a violent climax to history, the Antichrist would prove to be a Jew. Not only sectarians, however, but—if Jeremy Cohen (1982) is correct—also the great religious orders founded in the thirteenth century, the Dominicans and the Franciscans, contributed to the demonization of the Jews by attacking the Talmud as a blasphemous and evil writing that stood between the Jews and their conversion. In addition, the peculiar economic roles forced on the Jewish community by feudal society placed its members under a new stigma. As hucksters and usurers, the latter were not only Cain, who murdered Abel (Christ), but also Judas, who sold Christ for thirty pieces of silver. From this fusion of economic and religious symbols arose the deadly image of the ruthless and rapacious Jew, still an intrinsic part of *antisemitica* today.

The religious and folkloric anti-Judaism of the late Middle Ages came to a boil in the intemperate writings of the old Martin Luther, especially his 1543 tract *On the Jews and Their Lies*. His belief that Christ had been insulted, together with his conviction that Judaism was an evil religion, and further his abhorrence of religious legalism and his disappointment at the Jewish failure to convert to the reformed faith, drove Luther into an anti-Jewish fury so unrestrained that he has since been compared to Hitler. However, unlike Hitler, Luther was no racist, and his anger at the Jews, as Heiko Oberman (1984) has emphasized, was intimately connected with his anger at both the Roman papacy and the Turks, whom the reformer also saw as the devil's storm troops in a final assault on the church during the end time. Moreover, Luther's savage recommendationsthe burning of synagogues and the suppression of Jewish worship and teachingseem to have been motivated by his belief that Jewish "blasphemy" was an active menace in Christian society. The rediscovery of his anti-Jewish works during the renaissance of Luther studies in 1918 coincided with a rebirth of German nationalism, and this fact assisted his transformation into a Germanic hero and greatly distorted his true character. Significantly, Luther's Protestant contemporaries held a poor opinion of his tract; Bucer commented that it sounded like the composition of a swineherd rather than that of a "renowned shepherd of the soul." Yet it cannot be denied that such abuse of the Jews cast a dark shadow over European Christianity, making matters easy for the anti-Semites of the twentieth century.

Modern Anti-Semitism. Although Christian belief was slowly eroded by the rise of secularism and modernity, negative images of Jews were too deeply embedded in the cultural substratum to disappear easily from the European consciousness. Rather, they persisted even among the Enlightenment critics of religion, as the case of Voltaire clearly shows. Within the churches, moreover, neither post-

Tridentine Catholicism nor post-Reformation Protestantism was disposed to reconsider traditional ideas about Jews and Judaism until the ravages of modern totalitarianism made this morally urgent. A new liberal mood in Protestant thought at the end of the eighteenth century softened orthodox doctrine: Friedrich Schleiermacher, for example, in *The Christian Faith* (1821), recognized Judaism as an authentic religion, even if inferior to Christianity because of its "lingering affinity" with fetishism. But classical prejudice remained. As early as J. G. Fichte (1762-1814), a refusal to believe that Jesus was a Jew because of the supposedly materialistic character of Talmudic Judaism was becoming evident. Even the ex-Catholic Ernest Renan in his *Life of Jesus* (Paris, 1863) could only make sense of his hero by describing him as too great to be possessed by an inferior Semitic spirit. In this fashion, the old malevolence survived in new forms, finally with infamous results.

Anti-Judaism in Islam. Anti-Semitism in the Muslim world appears in considerable measure to have stemmed from the infiltration of Christian and Western influences, since the religious basis for anti-Judaism in Islam is smaller than in Christianity, which has the deicide motif. Even the hostile Qur'anic passages echo Christian opinions. Earlier, in pre-Islamic Arabia, such doctrines as Israel's rejection and punishment by God had been propagated by local Christian communities (Poliakov, 1955-1961); not surprisingly, similar sentiments found their way into the Qur'an: "Because of their iniquity, we forbade the Jews good things which were formerly allowed them . . . because they practice usury . . . and cheat others of their possessions" (surah 4:160-161). Abraham is not regarded as a Jew but as the first Muslim: "Surely the men who are nearest to Abraham are those who follow him, this Prophet, and the true believers. . . . Some of the People of the Book wish to mislead you; but they mislead none but themselves, though they may not perceive it" (surah 3:67-68). Furthermore, the Jews on occasion are portrayed in Christian fashion as blind and deaf to the truth, and even murderous toward its messengers (including Muhammad himself): "We made a covenant with the Israelites and sent forth apostles among them. But whenever an apostle came to them with a message that did not suit their fancies they either rejected him or slew him. They thought no harm would come to them: they were blind and deaf. God turned to them in mercy, but many of them again became blind and deaf" (surah 5:70-71). Because of these evil deeds and their disbelief, the Jews have suffered and continue to suffer chastisement on earth as the objects of God's anger: "Ignominy shall attend them wherever they are found, unless they make a covenant with God or with man.

Only in recent times, when the shadow of Western anti-Semitism has descended on a Middle East unsettled by the Arab-Israeli conflict, has a fundamentalist tendency to demonize Jews and Judaism crept into Islam. The contemporary

crisis of modernity in Muslim society has not been salutary for Western-Muslim relations, and Western (Christian?) support for the presence of a Jewish state on what is regarded as Islamic territory has greatly acerbated this crisis. In this context, some Muslim theologians have exploited the hostile side of their tradition in order to vilify Jews in the most unqualified terms.

BIBLIOGRAPHY

Arendt, Hannah. *Antisemitism* (1951). New York, 1974. Originally published as *Origins of Totalitarianism*, pt. 1. A basic work.

Cohen, Jeremy. *The Friars and the Jews*. Ithaca, N. Y., 1982. A study of the manner in which the missionary zeal of the great medieval religious orders, the Dominicans and the Franciscans, changed Christian attitudes toward the Jews and Judaism for the worse.

Davies, Alan, ed. *Antisemitism and the Foundations of Christianity*. New York, 1979. Eleven Christian theologians and biblical scholars respond to Rosemary Ruether's controversial study *Faith and Fratricide*. The book concludes with a reply by Ruether.

Eckardt, A. Roy. *Elder and Younger Brothers*. New York, 1967. A Christian theologian attempts to reconstruct the Jewish-Christian relationship in a healthy, affirmative manner.

Fleischner, Eva, ed. *Auschwitz: Beginning of a New Era*? New York, 1977. A volume of papers and essays on the Holocaust, including both Christian and Jewish contributors.

Gager, John. *The Origins of Antisemitism*. New York, 1983. A study of anti-Judaism in antiquity, including a response to Ruether and her critics.

Isaac, Jules. *Jesus and Israel* (1951). Translated by Sally Gran and edited by Claire Huchet Bishop. New York, 1971. A great classic by a French Jewish historian who lost his family in the Holocaust.

Oberman, Heiko A. *The Roots of Anti-Semitism*. Translated by James I. Porter. Philadelphia, 1984. A study of anti-Semitism during the Renaissance and the Reformation, including such figures as Reuchlin and Erasmus as well as Martin Luther.

Parkes, James. *The Conflict of the Church and the Synagogue* (1934). Reprint, New York, 1961. Another classic exploration of the religious roots of anti-Semitism in early Christian theology and its social and legal implications.

Pawlikowski, John T. *What Are They Saying about Christian-Jewish Relations?* New York, 1980. A useful overview of the present state of the subject and the variety of opinions now current.

Poliakov, Leon. *The History of Antisemitism* (1955-1961). 2 vols. Translated by Richard Howard (vol. 1) and Natalie Gerardi (vol. 2). New York, 1965-1973. A long, informative survey.

Ruether, Rosemary Radford. *Faith and Fratricide*. New York, 1974. A Catholic theologian explores the theological roots of anti-Semitism in an original and controversial study.

Sandmel, Samuel. *Anti-Semitism in the New Testament?* Philadelphia, 1978. A Jewish scholar probes the sources of Christianity with skill and discrimination.

Trachtenberg, Joshua. *The Devil and the Jews*. New Haven, 1943. An old but still important study of the demonization of the Jews in medieval Christendom.

Van Buren, Paul M. *Discerning the Way*. New York, 1980. A more recent attempt on the part of a Christian theologian to construct a theology of the Jewish-Christian relationship without anti-Semitism.

ALAN DAVIES

APOCALYPSE

An Overview

Apocalypse, as the name of a literary genre, is derived from the *Apocalypse of John*, or *Book of Revelation*, in the New Testament. The word itself means "revelation," but it is reserved for revelations of a particular kind: mysterious revelations that are mediated or explained by a supernatural figure, usually an angel. They disclose a transcendent world of supernatural powers and an eschatological scenario that includes the judgment of the dead.

The *Book of Revelation* (about 90 CE) is the earliest work that calls itself an apocalypse (*Rv.* 1:1), and even there the word may be meant in the general sense of "revelation." The usage as a genre label became common from the second century on, and numerous christian compositions are so titled (e.g., the *Apocalypse of Peter*, the *Apocalypse of Paul*). The Cologne Mani Codex (fifth century) refers to the apocalypses of Adam, Sethel, Enosh, Shem, and Enoch. The title is found in some Jewish apocalypses from the late first century CE (e.g., *2 Baruch* and *3 Baruch*), but may have been added by later scribes. The ancient usage is not entirely reliable. The title was never added to some major apocalypses (e.g., those contained in *1 Enoch*) and is occasionally found in works of a different genre (e.g., the *Apocalypse of Moses*, a variant of the *Life of Adam and Eve*).

The Jewish Apocalypses. The genre is older than the title and is well attested in Judaism from the third century BCE on. The Jewish apocalypses are of two main types. The better known of these might be described as historical apocalypses. They are found in the *Book of Daniel* (the only apocalypse in the Hebrew scriptures), *4 Ezra*, *2 Baruch*, and some sections of *1 Enoch*. In these apocalypses, the revelation is given in allegorical visions, interpreted by an angel. The content is primarily historical and is given in the form of an extended prophecy. History is divided into a set number of periods. The finale may include the national and political restoration of Israel, but the emphasis is on the replacement of the present world order by one that is radically new. In its most extreme form the eschatology of this type of apocalypse envisages the end of the world, as, for example, in *4 Ezra* 7, where the creation is returned to primeval silence for seven days.

The second type of Jewish apocalypse is the other-worldly journey. In the earliest example of this type, the "Book of the Watchers" in *2 Enoch* (third century BCE), Enoch ascends to the presence of God, following which the angels take him on a tour that ranges over the whole earth to the ends of the universe. More characteristic of this type is the ascent of the visionary through a numbered series of heavens. More mystical in orientation, these apocalypses often include a vision of the throne of God. The eschatology of these works is focused more on personal afterlife than on cosmic transformation, but they may also predict a general judgment.

These two types of apocalypse are not wholly discrete. The *Apocalypse of Abraham*, an ascent-type apocalypse from the late first century E, contains a brief overview of history in set periods. The *Similitudes of Enoch*, a Jewish work of the mid-first century CE, combines allegorical visions with an ascent and is largely concerned with political and social abuses. Both types are found in the collection of writings known as *1 Enoch*, which is known in full only in Geez (Ethiopic) translations but is now attested in Aramaic fragments from the Dead Sea Scrolls, which date to the second century BCE.

Origins of the Genre. The origins of this genre remain obscure. Descriptions of journeys to the heavens or the netherworld were fairly common in antiquity. Examples can be found as early as book 11 of Homer's *Odyssey*. A more plausible source for the genre, in both its Greek and Jewish forms, has been sought in Persian religion. Some characteristic features of the historical apocalypses, including the division of history into a set number of periods and the resurrection of the dead, were a part of Persian thought from an early time. A full-blown apocalypse of the historical type is found in the *Bahman Yasht*, a *zand*, or commentary, on a lost hymn of the Avesta. Analogous material is found in the *Oracle of Hystaspes*, a pre-Christian Persian work preserved in Latin by Lactantius. Periodization and the eschatological renewal of the world are integral features of the Bundahishn, the great compendium of Persian theology from the twelfth century CE.

The Jewish apocalypses were, in any case, a largely independent development drawing heavily on the Hebrew scriptures. There was obvious continuity with biblical prophecy, especially in the historical apocalypses such as the *Book of Daniel*. In the *Book of Zechariah*, written at the end of the sixth century BCE, after the Babylonian exile, we find allegorical visions interpreted by an angel that are very similar in form to the apocalypses. Characteristic apocalyptic themes, such as the idea of a new creation, appear in other prophetic texts from the same period (*Is.* 65:17). The apocalyptic idea of cosmic judgment could be viewed as a development of the prophetic "day of the Lord" (*Am.* 5:18). The apocalypses differed from biblical prophecy in their belief in the judgment of the dead and also in their relative lack of the direct exhortations that were the trademark of the prophets. Accordingly, some scholars have suggested that they are akin to wisdom rather than to prophecy.

The Genre in Christianity. The apocalyptic genre declined in Judaism after the first century CE, although heavenly ascents continued to play an important part in the Jewish mystical tradition. By contrast, the genre flourished in Christianity. *The Book of Revelation* in the New Testament

has its closest analogies with the *Book of Daniel* and the historical apocalypses, but it is exceptional in not being pseudonymous. The convention of pseudonymity was quickly adopted, however, and apocalypses of Peter, Paul, and others proliferated into the Middle Ages. The genre was also adapted by the gnostics. The Nag Hammadi collection of codices (found in Egypt in 1945), which dates from about 400 CE, includes apocalypses of Adam, Peter, Paul, and James. The gnostic apocalypses differ from the Jewish and Christian ones in their emphasis on salvation in the present through gnosis, or saving knowledge, and their lack of interest in cosmic transformation, although some gnostic apocalypses include the destruction of this world.

BIBLIOGRAPHY

An overview of apocalyptic writing as a genre in antiquity can be found in *Apocalypse: The Morphology of a Genre*, a special issue of *Semeia* 14 (1979). This volume contains essays on material from various cultures: Jewish (John J. Collins), Christian (Adela Yarbro Collins), gnostic (Francis T. Fallon), Greco-Roman (Harold W. Attridge), rabbinic/later Jewish (Anthony J. Saldarini), and Persian (John J. Collins); it includes extensive bibliographies. Essays on apocalypses and related material from several ancient cultures can be found in *Apocalypticism in the Mediterranean World and the Near East*, edited by David Hellholm (Tübingen, 1983). Recent studies of the ancient apocalypses include Christopher Rowland's *The Open Heaven: A Study of Apocalyptic in Judaism and Early Christianity* (New York, 1982) and John J. Collins's *The Apocalyptic Imagination in Ancient Judaism: An Introduction to the Jewish Matrix of Christianity* (New York, 1984).

The influence of the apocalypses on Jewish mysticism is explored by Ithamar Gruenwald in *Apocalyptic and Merkavah Mysticism* (Leiden, 1980). The later Jewish tradition is discussed in several works by Gershom Scholem; see especially *The Messianic Idea in Judaism and Other Essays on Jewish Spirituality* (New York, 1971) and *Jewish Gnosticism, Merkabah Mysticism and Talmudic Tradition*, 2d. ed. (New York, 1965).

For the later Christian material, see especially Bernard McGinn's studies: *Visions of the End: Apocalyptic Traditions in the Middle Ages* (New York, 1979) and *Apocalyptic Spirituality: Treatises and Letters of Lactantius, Adso of Montieren-Der, Joachim of Fiore, the Franciscan Spirituals, Savonarola* (New York, 1979).

For examples of scholarly application of the notion of apocalypse to a much broader range of religious traditions, see Jonathan Z. Smith's "A Pearl of Great Price and a Cargo of Yams," *History of Religions* 16 (1976): 1-19, which examines the applicability of apocalyptic and gnostic patterns of revelation to the Babylonian Akitu festival and a cargo cult in the Moluccas. See also Bruce Lincoln's article " 'The Earth Becomes Flat': A Study of Apocalyptic Imagery," *Comparative Studies in Society and History* 25 (January 1983): 136-153, which begins with a consideration of Plutarch and the Iranian *Bundahishn* and compares these with Chinese and Japanese materials, as well as with colonial rebellions.

JOHN J. COLLINS

Jewish Apocalypticism to the Rabbinic Period

Although scholars have found it extremely difficult to reach consensus with regard to the question of the point of view that will render a clear and overall definition of the term *apocalypticism*, it is safe to say that the term can be applied to a group of writings that pertain to the revelations (the Greek term *apokalupsis* means "revelation") of divine cosmological and historical secrets. These writings were composed from the end of the era of classical prophecy, that is, from the fourth century BCE onward. The history of apocalypticism can be divided into the following parts: (1) Jewish apocalypticism until the institutionalization of rabbinic Judaism (about 100 CE); (2) Jewish apocalypticism in the Mishnaic and Talmudic period until the Islamic rise and conquest of the Orient (from c. 100 to 600 CE); (3) Christian and gnostic apocalypticism in the early centuries of the common era; (4) medieval Jewish and Christian apocalypticism (from the early days of Islam until the thirteenth century); and (5) apocalypticism from the thirteenth century onward. For the sake of brevity, the focus of discussion here will be on the first type of apocalypticism, where the major features and characteristics of apocalypticism have been shaped.

Since scripture, in its variety of books and views, shaped the Jewish mind and worldview in antiquity, any religious corpus of writings that was created in subsequent generations annexed itself to scripture and sought scripturelike authority. In this manner not only the sense of organic continuity—so vital for establishing a religious tradition—was allowed to prevail, but also the need for adapting old concepts and beliefs to changing and new purposes was well served.

Apocalypticism is gradually shifting from the backstage position it so often used to occupy in scholarship to the front of the stage. Scholars have become increasingly aware of the importance of apocalypticism for a better understanding

> **Apocalypticism is gradually shifting from the backstage position it so often used to occupy in scholarship to the front of the stage.**

of certain concepts and religious positions maintained in the Hebrew scriptures, for a more profound evaluation of certain historical and ideological processes in the so-called intestestamental period; for an assessment of such religious streams as the Essene sect, the Dead Sea sect (which in all likelihood is an offshoot of the Essene sect), and *merkavah* mysticism; and for a deeper comprehension of the rise of Christianity and gnosticism.

The link between apocalypticism and scripture was forged in a number of ways. Most striking of these is the way in which the apocalyptic visionaries are made to bear the names of illustrious people whose works and ideas are known from scripture. Some of the great men of scripture, such as Adam, Enoch, Abraham, Moses, Elijah, Isaiah, Baruch, and Ezra, are taken as lending their names to the apocalyptic visionaries. In fact, all apocalypses are pseudepigraphs, that is, writings that are literally attributed to people who lived at an earlier time than that in which they were actually written. Thus, for instance, Enoch, who lived in antediluvian times, became the hero of several apocalyptic writings composed after the destruction of the First and the Second Temples of Jerusalem (587/6 BCE and 70 CE, respectively).

The "Apocalyptic" Stage in the Jewish Religion. I consider apocalypticism in its postscriptural manifestations to mark an important stage in the development of the Jewish religion in antiquity. There are two highly significant concepts, that of knowledge and that of vision, by which this kind of development can be epitomized. When seen from the point of view of these two concepts, apocalypticism brings about a substantial change in the cognitive functions of the Jewish type of religious experience; consequently, new areas of religious awareness are opened to the believer. If we take religion as such to be a mode of cognition that facilitates man's knowledge about himself and the divinely governed world, then apocalypticism may be interpreted as marking the opening of new horizons, both experiential and conceptual, for those who adopted the proper technique and accepted the message.

The oldest classic apocalypse we know of is the Ethiopic *Apocalypse of Enoch*, parts of which, written in Aramaic, were discovered at Qumran. The book contains at least five parts, all of which are said to be separate compositions. With the exception of chapters 37-71, which are not represented in the Qumran fragments, a great deal of the material goes back to the third and even fourth century BCE. It is not absolutely certain that all of the Ethiopic version of the book was indeed prepared from a Greek translation of the Aramaic. In any event, Greek fragments of the book (not always agreeing with the Ethiopic) are known from at least two different Byzantine sources.

Major Features of Apocalypticism. Although the scope of the apocalyptic writings is not great, it is a highly complex corpus of writings with some rather idiosyncratic features. There are several components that are totally absent from scripture but definitely present in apocalypticism. Focusing on those components is vital for defining the origins of apocalypticism, not so much with regard to questions such as the earliest dating and actual birthplace, but with regard to the spiritual milieu in which the crystallization of the apocalyptic worldview took place.

There are three subjects that most clearly bring out the major features of apocalypticism. These are the two concepts of vision and knowledge and the new modes of dualistic thinking that developed in the framework of apocalypticism. Although one could with equal justice refer to other components in apocalypticism that were operative in singling it out in comparison to scripture—such as apocalyptic angelology and the periodization of history—the three components referred to above seem to be of major importance.

Vision and knowledge. One of the major concepts of the Hebrew scriptures is that "the heavens are the heavens of the Lord, but the earth he has given to the sons of men" (Ps. 115:16). Although the immediate sense of this verse in all likelihood is that man was given "dominion over the works of thy hands" (*Ps.* 8:7) on earth, it may also be understood in the sense of "who has ascended to heaven and come down?" (*Prv.* 30:4), that is, no human being was likely to ascend to heaven and come back safely. As can clearly be seen from the case of Elijah, the event of an ascent to heaven actually meant the termination of a person's life on earth (*2 Kgs.* 2:1ff.). Because all of the information a human being needs in order to worship God properly is accessible in terrestrial domains, there is no need to go up to heaven in order to gain any kind of knowledge, not even concerning the Torah (*Dt.* 30:11-12). Accordingly, there is nothing that compels us to interpret, for example, the vision reported in *Isaiah 6* as taking place anywhere but in the earthly Temple of Jerusalem. The same holds true in the case of Daniel's vision of the godhead (*Dn.* 7:9-10), where the scenery may well have been heavenly, although the visionary himself did not leave his earthly dwelling place.

The kind of knowledge displayed in apocalypticism is a total reversal of the kind of knowledge known from scripture. We shall take our point of departure from *Job* 38, which opens the final act in the drama of Job and in which God appears to Job in the whirlwind and addresses him in a long series of questions, the overall effect of which is to convince Job of his inability to know and understand the various functions of nature. The conclusion that God asks Job to draw for himself as a result of this inability is that since no human being is able to equal God in his knowledge and his understanding of and control over nature, nobody is justified in questioning the morality and justice of his providence. God asks Job questions that relate to a wide range of subjects—what may today be described as the natural sciences, such as physics, astronomy, zoology, and biology. All of these subjects rank in the eyes of the writer as belonging to the realm of divine wisdom and are by definition out of the reach of human knowledge and understanding. When, however, we come to the cycle of visions collected in *1 Enoch*, we find that almost everything that in Job's eyes appears to be an insurmountable intellectual challenge opens up like a book in the case of the "Enoch" visionaries. In *1 Enoch* 17-18, 33-36, 41,

51, and 78, one comes across numerous references to natural phenomena, the secrets of which are revealed to the visionaries in the course of their heavenly journeys. "Enoch" saw the storehouses of all the winds and the foundations of the earth (18:1); the cornerstone of the earth (18:2); the winds that turn heaven and cause the disk of the sun and all the stars to set (18:4); the ends of the earth on which heaven rests and the open gates of heaven (33:2); how the stars come out (33:3); and much secret information about all kinds of natural phenomena.

Apocalypticism is almost by definition preoccupied with the revelation of secret knowledge, meaning any kind of knowledge that was not accessible to people who had previously been dependent for its acquisition on scripture and on the modes of cognition presupposed therein, including prophecy and inspired wisdom. In this respect, the contents of ecstatic, or semiecstatic, experiences were accorded high credibility.

Dualism. Another major aspect of the radical break of apocalypticism with scripture is the apocalyptic concept of dualism. Briefly, good and evil as conceived of in scripture are two ways of life (*Dt.* 30:15). They relate to the moral choice that confronts man in his daily behavior. In scripture, evil as such is no independent metaphysical entity. Even Satan, as he is conceived of in scripture, is not the rebellious, mythical figure he becomes in apocalypticism. Ontologically speaking, the scriptural world is monistic. In apocalypticism, on the other hand, we find a clear dualistic outlook. In fact, there are two types of dualism in apocalypticism. The first is more mythological in nature and we find it, for instance, in the Enoch cycle (and most specifically in the first part of *1 Enoch*), where a rebellious group of angels led by Satan challenges the supremacy of God. Consequently, the rebellious angels are severely punished, but not before they attempt to seduce the daughters of men and impart to mankind a series of teachings and practices that are considered to be the source of all sin and evil.

BIBLIOGRAPHY

The most comprehensive collection in English translation of apocalyptic writings is *The Old Testament Pseudepigrapha*, vol. 1, *Apocalyptic Literature and Testaments*, edited by James H. Charlesworth (New York, 1983). Still useful is R. H. Charles's *The Apocrypha and Pseudepigrapha of the Old Testament*, 2 vols. (Oxford, 1913). This collection also contains extensive introductions to each of the writings included therein as well as notes and comments on the texts themselves. The texts are translated mainly from Greek, Latin, and Ethiopic. A collection of apocalyptic writings preserved in the Armenian church was published in English by Jacques Issaverdens as *The Uncanonical Writings of the Old Testament* (Venice, 1907). A comprehensive list of the various editions and translations of apocalyptic writings can be found in James H. Charlesworth's "A History of Pseudepigrapha Research: The Re-Emerging Importance of the Pseudepigrapha," in *Aufstieg und Niedergang der römischen* Welt, vol. 2.19.1, edited by Wolfgang

Haase (New York, 1979). An English translation of several Christian apocalypses is found in Montague R. James's *The Apocryphal New Testament* (1924; reprint, Oxford, 1963). Gnostic apocalypses are contained in *The Nag Hammadi Library in English*, edited by James M. Robinson (San Francisco, 1977). Hebrew apocalypses of the Persian and Islamic periods are contained in Yehudah Even-Shemu'el's *Midreshei ge'ulah* (Jerusalem, 1954).

Two of the most comprehensive introductions to apocalypticism are D. S. Russell's *The Method and Message of Jewish Apocalyptic, 200 B. C.-A. D. 100* (Philadelphia, 1964), which contains an extensive bibliography, and Emil Schürer's *The Literature of the Jewish People in the Time of Jesus* (1903-1910), edited and with an introduction by Nahum N. Glatzer (New York, 1972). Klaus Koch's *The Rediscovery of Apocalyptic*, translated by Margaret Kohl (London, 1972), and Charles C. Torrey's *The Apocryphal Literature* (Hamden, Conn., 1963) elucidate the major problems in the study of apocalypticism and its literature. H. H. Rowley's *The Relevance of Apocalyptic*, rev. ed. (London, 1963), is "a study of Jewish and Christian Apocalypses from Daniel to Revelation." A number of articles by several authors on the various forms of Jewish, Christian, and gnostic apocalypses make up the issue of *Semeia* (Missoula, Mont.) 14 (1979) entitled "Apocalypse: The Morphology of a Genre," edited by John J. Collins.

Robert H. Pfeiffer's *History of New Testament Times*, with an Introduction to the Apocrypha (New York, 1949) is still one of the best introductions to the apocryphal literature. Paul D. Hanson discusses the historical and sociological roots of Jewish apocalyptic eschatology in light of biblical theology and literature in his *The Dawn of Apocalyptic* (Philadelphia, 1975). In my book *Apocalyptic and Merkavah Mysticism* (Leiden, 1980) I have discussed the mystical aspects of apocalypticism, introducing the apocalyptic-mystical writings of the Talmudic period. Frank Moore Cross views the Qumran writings in an apocalyptic matrix in his *The Ancient Library of Qumran and Modern Biblical Studies*, rev. ed. (Garden City, N. Y., 1961). Though preoccupied with the problem of the early church and the crisis of gnosticism, Pheme Perkins's *The Gnostic Dialogue* (New York, 1980) contains information about the gnostic types of divine and angelic revelation. Norman R. C. Cohn discusses "revolutionary messianism" in medieval and Reformation Europe and its connection to modern totalitarian movements in his *The Pursuit of the Millenium: Revolutionary Millenarians and Mystical Anarchists of the Middle Ages*, 3d ed. (New York, 1970). Cohn refers amply to ancient apocalypticism and quotes widely from apocalyptic writings in the Middle Ages.

For more information see the comprehensive annotated bibliography prepared by James H. Charlesworth in his *The Pseudepigrapha and Modern Research with a Supplement* (Chico, Calif., 1981).

ITHAMAR GRUENWALD

Medieval Jewish Apocalyptic Literature

While the Talmudic and Midrashic literature of late antiquity appropriated various elements of the classical apocalyptic of the intertestamental period, it did so in an unsystematic and fragmentary fashion. Apocalyptic themes competed for attention amidst a wide range of contrasting views on eschatological matters in rabbinic literature. The early decades of the seventh century, however, witnessed the reemergence of a full-fledged apocalyptic literature in Hebrew. Produced pri-

marily between the seventh and tenth centuries in the Land of Israel and the Near East, these generally brief but fascinating treatises exhibit a rather clearly recognizable set of messianic preoccupations and literary themes.

This literature may be illustrated by reference to one of the most important and influential of these works, *Sefer Zerubbavel* (Book of Zerubbabel). Composed in Hebrew in the early part of the seventh century, probably shortly before the rise of Islam, the *Book of Zerubbabel* may have been written within the context of the military victories achieved by the Byzantine emperor Heraclius against the Persians in the year 629. These historical events no doubt incited speculation concerning the conditions under which the final messianic battles would be waged and their ultimate outcome.

As is characteristic of apocalyptic literature, the book is pseudepigraphically ascribed to a biblical figure, in this case to Zerubbabel, the last ruler of Judaea from the House of David, whose name is associated with the attempts to rebuild the Temple in Jerusalem following the Babylonian exile. He is presented as the beneficiary of a series of auditions and visions. The angel Michael (or Metatron as he is also called here) reveals himself to Zerubbabel and leads him to Rome, where he encounters a "bruised and despised man" in the marketplace. The latter turns out to be the Messiah, son of David, named here Menahem ben `Ammi'el. The Messiah informs Zerubbabel that he is waiting in Rome until the time is ripe for his appearance. Michael then proceeds to relate to Zerubbabel the events that will lead up to the End of Days.

Zerubbabel is informed that the forerunner of the Messiah, son of David, the Messiah, son of Joseph, identified as Nehemyah ben Hushi'el, will gather all of the Jews to Jerusalem, where they will dwell for four years and where they will practice the ancient sacrifices. In the fifth year the king of Persia will rise over Israel, but a woman who accompanies Nehemyah, Hephzibah, mother of the Messiah, son of David, will successfully resist the enemy with the help of a "rod of salvation" that she possesses.

The Book of Zerubbabel became extremely popular and widely influential. The characters and events depicted in this work provided the basis for a considerable variety of apocalyptic texts over the next several centuries, including the final section of Midrash Vayosha`, the Secrets of Rabbi Shim`on bar Yohai, the Prayer of Shim`on bar Yoh'ai, apocalyptic poems by El`azar Kallir, and the eighth chapter of Sa`adyah Gaon's important philosophical treatise, the Book of Beliefs and Opinions.

The messianic speculation found in these and other works is characterized by several distinctive features, which, when taken together, provide a shape to Jewish medieval apocalyptic literature. There is, for example, a preoccupation with the political vicissitudes of great empires; historical upheavals are regarded as bearing momentous messianic significance. There is, moreover, a concern for the broad march of history, of which contemporary events are but a part, leading up to the final tribulations and vindication of the people of Israel. In the apocalyptic literature, redemption is not a matter for theoretical speculation but a process that has already begun, whose culmination is relatively imminent and whose timing can be calculated. A related feature of this literature is the sense that historical and messianic events have a life of their own, independent of the behavior of human beings. There is an inevitability to the force of events with little regard for the choices that Israel might make, such as to repent and gain God's favor. Nor do the authors of these texts indulge in theorizing about why events unfold as they do, other than the obvious fact that righteousness is destined to win over evil.

From a literary point of view, the apocalyptic treatises are, like their themes, extravagant. They revel in fantastic descriptions of their heroes and antiheroes, richly narrating the events that they reveal, and often regard their protagonists as symbols for the cosmic forces of good and evil. Another feature of apocalyptic literature is its revelatory character; knowledge of heavenly secrets and mysteries not attainable through ordinary means are revealed, typically by angels who serve as messengers from on high.

BIBLIOGRAPHY

The most important collection of primary sources for medieval Jewish apocalyptic literature is *Midreshei ge'ulah*, in Hebrew, edited by Yehudah Even-Shemu'el (Jerusalem, 1954). This volume also contains excellent bibliographical information. A somewhat dated but still useful overview of this literature in English is Abba Hillel Silver's *A History of Messianic Speculation in Israel from the First through the Seventeenth Centuries* (New York, 1927), especially part I, chapter 2. Concerning the apocalyptic tendencies of the Shabbatean movement, see Gershom Scholem's *Sabbatai Sevi: The Mystical Messiah, 1626-1676* (Princeton, 1973).

LAWRENCE FINE

ARAMEAN RELIGION

When the Arameans first appeared in the ancient Near East is not known. The Arameans are characterized by their names and their dialects, the novelty of which strikes the historian as he compares them with the preexistent Akkadian names and language used in Mesopotamia.

In the second half of the eleventh century the Arameans are known to have gained control of large areas of the Syrian desert and thus of its caravan routes. They succeeded in forming in northern Syria and around Damascus major confederacies in which dialects of Aramaic were spoken and written. The Aramean states spread over the great bend of the Euphrates, on the upper and lower Habor, and in the northern Syrian hinterland at Samal, Arpad, Aleppo, and Hama. The Assyrians could not allow a threat to their hegemony in the Near East, however, so Tiglathpileser III (744-727) reduced Damascus to an Assyrian province.

Yet even defeated, the Arameans maintained the prestige of their language, and the gods they called on in treaties and religious inscriptions became the gods of the whole of Syria and remained so up to the first centuries CE. The massive arrival under the Persians (sixth century BCE) and the Greeks (fourth century) of Arab tribes into southern Palestine, the Hauran, Damascus, the Syrian desert, and even northern Syria did not disrupt the traditional ways of living and praying because the newcomers adopted the culture and the language of the Arameans.

The Cults of Hadad and Sin. A bilingual inscription (in Akkadian and Aramaic) found in 1979 at Tell Fekhariye, on the border between Syria and Turkey, records the gratitude of Hadadyisi, ruler of Sikanu and Guzanu, to Hadad of Sikanu. Both the script and the historical context date the life-size statue of the ruler on which the text is engraved to the first part of the ninth century BCE. This is the earliest, most important text in Aramaic ever found, and the mention of the god Hadad (in Akkadian, Adad) becomes of paramount interest to the history of his cult among the Arameans. Hadad is praised in both languages in a formula that is often used to praise Adad in Akkadian inscriptions from Mesopotamia. Hadad is the one "who provides the gods, his brothers, with quietness and sustenance." He, the great lord of Sikanu, is "a merciful god," a deity whose almighty providence ranks him above other gods and makes him for humans a storm god and a weather god.

A colossal statue of Hadad was found in 1890 in a village to the northeast of Zinjirli (Turkey). According to the inscription carved on the monument, it had been erected by King Panamu of Yady (Samal, in the Zinjirli region) to acknowledge that his royal power derived from Hadad. Although Panamu was not a Semite, he gave his son a Semitic name, Barsur, and extolled Semitic gods in his inscription: besides Hadad the text lists El, the high god adored at Ugarit and in pre-Israelite Canaan; Reshef, the ancient Syrian god of pestilence and the underworld, but also of well-being; and Rakib-El, whose name can be interpreted as "charioteer of El," thus becoming a suitable epithet for the moon god, since the crescent of the moon can easily be imagined as a boat navigating across the skies.

The devotion of the Aramean population to the moon god became a distinctive feature of the religiosity of northern Syria, especially when the area came under Babylonian rule after the destruction of the Assyrian empire. At the end of the seventh century, Nabopolassar (625-605) and Nebuchadrezzar (604-562) settled Babylonians in the various countries they conquered. The cult knew a glorious period under Nabonidus, the last king of Babylon (556-539). In the words of Nabonidus himself and of his mother, the priestess of the god at the sanctuary, Sin was "the king of the gods."

Associations of Gods. The very few inscriptions that provide information about the Aramean religion during the eighth, seventh, and sixth centuries BCE record only the religious feelings of the ruling class. No indication of what the religious life of the commoners might have been is ever found. In the final analysis the study of the ancient Near Eastern religion comes down to a listing of divine names, with occasional glimpses as to what a given deity must have meant in concrete terms to an individual.

Late Aramean Religion. Exposed to Assyro-Babylonian influences and in continuous contact with the Canaanite traditions, the Arameans amalgamated cults and beliefs that were not distinctly their own. The disparateness of the Aramean religion is best observed in the fifth-century-BCE texts from Egypt (Memphis, Elephantine, and Aswan), where, beside Jewish and Aramean mercenaries, an Aramaic-speaking populace of deportees, refugees, and merchants settled with their families during the Persian period. This motley community worshiped a host of deities among whom the inscriptions single out the god Nabu and the goddess Banit from Babylon, and the Aramean deities Bethel, Anat-Bethel, and Malkat-Shemen ("queen of heaven").

In the eclectic society of Egypt under the Persians, when Greeks, Cilicians, Phoenicians, Jews, and Syrians lived together, the religious syncretism cherished by the Asiatics is most manifest in those documents that record oaths sworn by Jews in the name of Egyptian and Aramean gods (in addition to the oaths taken by Yahveh) and in the Aramean per-

> **Female deities were prominent in the Aramean pantheons, but their role in the religious life is not always clear, for their personal features are often blurred in the iconography.**

sonal names that reveal the worship of Bel, Shamash, Nergal, and Atar along with the Egyptian deities. yet nothing is known about the religion of the Arameans living in Egypt. The historian must wait until Greco-Roman times to benefit from the overall picture that Semitic and Greek inscriptions provide for the study of the Syrian religion. In general, religion in the Near East was not subject to the challenge of speculative and critical thought that influenced the daily life in Greece at this time, for the inscriptions do not reflect the impact of new fashions.

Female deities were prominent in the Aramean pantheons, but their role in the religious life is not always clear, for their personal features are often blurred in the iconography. Atargatis was the Aramean goddess *par excellence*. Nowhere did her cult excel more than at Hierapolis (modern-day Membidj). According to Lucian (*De dea Syria* 33.47-49), statues of Hadad and Atargatis were carried in procession to the sea twice a year.

During Greco-Roman times the Arab goddess Allat assumed some of the features of other female deities: in Palmyrene iconography she appears both as a Greek Athena and as the Syrian Atargatis. Her sanctuary at Palmyra, excavated in the 1970s, is located in the neighborhood of the temple of Beelshamen, and this fact lends a special character to the city's western quarter, in which Arab tribes settled during the second century BCE. A Greek inscription recently found in this area equates Allat with Artemis (Teixidor, 1979, pp. 53-62). This multiform presence of Allat underlines the formidable impact of the Arab tribes on the Aramaic-speaking peoples of the Near East. Aramean traditions persisted, however. The region of Edessa (modern-day Urfa), called Osrhoene by the Greeks, was ruled by a dynasty of Arab origin from about 132 BCE, but it remained open to cultural influences from Palmyra, Jerusalem, and Adiabene. Notwithstanding the presence of Macedonian colonists and several centuries of commercial activity with the West and the Far East, traditional cults survived. At the beginning of the modern era, Sumatar Harabesi, about twenty-five miles northeast of Harran, became a religious center primarily devoted to the cult of Sin (Drijvers, 1980, pp. 122-128).

BIBLIOGRAPHY

Abou-Assaf, Ali, Pierre Bordeuil, and Alan R. Millard. *La statue de Tell Fekherye et son inscription bilingue assyro-araméenne.* Recherche sur les civilisations, études assyriologiques, no. 7. Paris, 1982.

Drijvers, Han J. W. *Cults and Beliefs at Edessa.* Études préliminaires aux religions orientales dans l'empire romain, vol. 82. Leiden, 1980.

Dupont-Sommer, André. *Les Araméens.* Paris, 1949.

Gibson, John C. L. *Aramaic Inscriptions,* vol. 2 of *Textbook of Syrian Semitic Inscriptions.* Oxford, 1975.

Greenfield, Jonas C. "The Zakir Inscription and the Danklied." In *Proceedings of the Fifth World Congress of Jewish Studies,* vol. 1. Jerusalem, 1971.

Greenfield, Jonas C. "Aramaic Studies and the Bible." In *Vetus Testamentum Supplement,* vol. 32, *Congress Volume;* Vienna 1980. Leiden, 1981.

Grelot, Pierre. *Documents araméens d'Égypte.* Littératures anciennes du Proche-Orient, vol. 5. Paris, 1972.

Lambert, W. G. "Nabonidus in Arabia." In *Proceedings of the Fifth Seminar for Arabian Studies, Held at the Oriental Institute, Oxford, 22nd and 23rd September 1971.* London, 1972.

Levy, Julius. "The Late Assyro-Babylonian Cult of the Moon and Its Culmination at the Time of Nabonidus." *Hebrew Union College Annual* 19 (1945-1946): 405-489.

Malamat, Abraham. "The Aramaeans." *In Peoples of Old Testament Times*, edited by D. J. Wiseman. Oxford, 1973.

Oppenheim, A. Leo. *Ancient Mesopotamia: Portrait of a Dead Civilization*. Rev. ed. Chicago, 1977.

Porten, Bezalel. *Archives from Elephantine: The Life of an Ancient Jewish Military Colony*. Berkeley, 1968.

Pritchard, J. B., ed. *The Ancient Near East: Supplementary Texts and Pictures relating to the Old Testament*. Princeton, 1969.

Roberts, J. J. M. *The Earliest Semitic Pantheon: A Study of the Semitic Deities Attested in Mesopotamia before Ur III*. Baltimore and London, 1972.

Teixidor, Javier. *The Pagan God: Popular Religion in the Greco-Roman Near East*. Princeton, 1977.

Teixidor, Javiere. *The Pantheon of Palmyra*. Études préliminaires aux religions orientales dans l'empire romain, vol. 79. Leiden, 1979.

JAVIER TEIXIDOR

ARCHAEOLOGY AND RELIGION

Historical Perpective. The beginnings of archaeology included looting for the collection of antiquities, searches for lost biblical tribes, and excavations to verify claims of national, racial, or ethnic superiority. The evolution of archaeology as a scholarly field took distinctly different paths in different world regions, and its relationship with the study of religion varied accordingly.

Pre-Columbian archaeology. In the New World, archaeology and the study of religion also started from a historical base. The Spanish conquest and colonization of Mexico and Peru left a legacy of historical description by the conquistadors, inquisitors, and bureaucrats who administered the conquered empires, kingdoms, and tribes of the American Indians. The descriptions from contact and colonial periods throughout the Americas were rich in their coverage of pre-Columbian religion, since it was of particular concern to the missionaries and bureaucrats who were the primary historians and ethnographers of American cultures.

In the first half of the twentieth century archaeological excavations worked back from the rich ethnohistorical record to uncover the art, iconography, and glyphic texts of earlier pre-Columbian religions. Interpretations relied heavily on later ethnographical and historical records, a methodology referred to as the "direct-historical approach" to archaeology. The earlier form and context of Indian religion was elucidated by extensive excavations at the great prehistoric urban and ceremonial centers of the New World: ancient Maya centers such as Copán in Honduras and Chichén Itzá in the Yucatán, as well as imperial capitals like that of the Aztec at Tenochtitlán (now Mexico City).

Prehistoric archaeology. Because of the combination of historical and archaeological approaches, the high civilizations of the Near East, the Mediterranean, Mesoamerica, and Peru initially provided the most information of the greatest reliability for studies of cross-cultural variation in religious behavior and of the history of religious traditions. Yet it was the archaeology of less politically complex societies in North America and Europe that led to most of the methodological and theoretical insights of this century. These breakthroughs eventually allowed the discipline to transcend its dependence on textual evidence and the direct-historical approach.

Religion and evolutionary theory. The ambitions of contemporary archaeological methodology to decipher ancient belief systems, though still struggling, have led to a renewed interest in the role of religion in the evolution of human culture. For the first half of this century, economic, Marxist, and ecological theory dominated studies of the prehistoric development of civilizations. In retrospect it is now clear that this materialist bias was inevitable, given the methodological limitations of archaeology. However, the new methodological concerns resulted in a resurgence of interest in the role of ideology in prehistoric change. In the 1970s archaeologists from diverse theoretical backgrounds began to call for a new look at religion's impact on the rise and fall of civilizations.

Robert M. Adams, in *Heartland of Cities* (1981), takes a holistic perspective on the origins of the state in Mesopotamia. He sees early city-states and their protourban antecedents as centers of security in all senses: subsistence security because of their role in irrigation, storage of surplus, and trade; defensive security provided by a large nucleated population; and spiritual security and identity in the form of the temple.

Similarly, perspectives on cultural evolution in the New World have begun to reincorporate religion into interpretations of the rise and fall of civilizations. These new perspectives argue that such cults helped to drive the explosive expansion of both the Inca empire of Peru (1438-1532 CE) and the Aztec hegemony in Mexico (1428-1519 CE). Indeed, they contend that due to religious and political institutionalization the cults became irreversible forces that destabilized these pre-Columbian empires and predisposed them to swift disintegration.

So, in both the Old World and the Americas archaeologists have rediscovered the study of religion. Appropriate methodologies for the study of prehistoric religion have been suggested and continue to be explored.

The early Near East. In the Near East, the heartland of many of the world's major religions, the contribution of archaeology to the study of the origins of these traditions extends back to the seventh and eighth millennia BCE.

Archaeological research over the past fifty years has unearthed a wealth of data on the religion of the later high civilization of Mesopotamia, and at early Sumerian centers such as Eridu, Uruk, Ur, and Tepe Gawra. This evidence has permitted detailed characterization and dating of the development of Sumerian temple architecture, art, and iconography, as well as the changing cultural context of religion and ritual. Twentieth-century excavations sponsored by British, French, German, and American institutions at Ur, Uruk, Mari, Babylon, Nineveh, and other Mesopotamian sites have also recovered thousands of tablets.

Perhaps the most important and unexpected discovery of recent years came from excavations by an Italian team at Tell Mardikh, in Syria. In 1975 they found a royal archive of over fifteen thousand tablets, detailing the history and culture of the third-millennium kingdom of Ebla. The ongoing decipherment of the Ebla tablets is revolutionizing our understanding of early Near Eastern history and religion.

Biblical archaeology. One beneficiary of these discoveries of early kingdoms in adjacent regions has been biblical archaeology. At Ras Shamra in Syria, Claude F.-A. Schaeffer has directed continuous excavations since 1929, uncovering the ancient city of Ugarit and thousands of Ugaritic tablets. These texts have had a profound impact on biblical studies, since they detail the nature of second-millennium Canaanite religion and society. Meanwhile, progress in biblical archaeology in Palestine itself has been substantial and steady. Literally hundreds of sites relating to the Old Testament period have been excavated in the past half-century, including such important sites as Jericho, Jerusalem, Megiddo, Tel Dan, Gezer, Shechem (modern-day Nablus), Lachish, and Samaria.

Archaeology has provided a richer context of material evidence to check, refine, and extend the historical record on religion in ancient Egypt, early Islam, and early Christianity. Furthermore, many of the actual historical and religious texts have been recovered by systematic archaeological excavations, including most of the Dead Sea Scrolls and numerous papyrus texts in Egypt. The recent excavations and discoveries at Nag Hammadi in Egypt illustrate the close interplay between religious textual studies and archaeology.

China and India. Modern anthropological archaeology has only just begun in China. Recent archaeological contributions to the study of early Chinese religion also include evidence on belief systems in the Neolithic Yang-shao (4000-2500 BCE) and Lung-shan (2500-1800 BCE) periods. Ho Ping-ti and other Chinese archaeologists have argued that iconography, settlement layouts, and even domestic architecture in these village societies reflect uniquely regional views on cosmology, ancestor worship, and fertility. Such interpretations show the potential of future archaeological research.

The archaeology of the Indus Valley civilization (2400-1800 BCE) of Pakistan and India is another field in which evidence and analogy can be used to project intriguing, but still uncertain, connections with historical religions. Archaeologists and Vedic scholars have also noted many

quite specific shared traits between Indus Valley artifacts, glyphs, or iconography and historical descriptions of Aryan culture in the Vedas, for example, the form of incense burners, the lotus sitting position, and possible prototypes of specific deities.

The Mediterranean and Europe. Archaeological research in Greece and Egypt has always been dominated by textual and historical studies. This contribution of assistance to epigraphic research often has been of great significance. For example, the excavations of the sacred capital at Amarna, in Egypt, have uncovered iconography, architecture, and texts that vastly expand our views on the religion of Egypt and adjacent cultures in the fourteenth century BCE.

Archaeological research has also pushed back the chronological limits of our knowledge of religion in ancient Egypt and Greece. In Egypt our understanding of the antiquity and evolution of religion has been extended by the excavation of Neolithic cemeteries and of late predynastic mastaba tombs, the mudbrick antecedents of the pyramids. In the Aegean and Balkans, recent excavations have established a chronological and cultural context for the study of religion, including ample evidence concerning Mycenaean and Minoan religion and even earlier (third and fourth millennia BCE) shrines, funerary practices, and religious icons.

The study of religion and cultural development in prehistoric Europe has turned to the new approaches and ethnographic perspectives popular in American archaeology. European and American prehistoric studies have entered an exciting period of cross-fertilization in anthropological concepts and archaeological methods.

BIBLIOGRAPHY

A good general history of archaeology in the Old World is Glyn E. Daniel's *A Short History of Archaeology* (London, 1981), and for the New World see Gordon R. Willey and Jeremy A. Sabloff's *A History of American Archaeology*, 2d ed. (London, 1981). An important presentation of the new, anthropological approaches to archaeology is Lewis R. Binford's *An Archaeological Perspective* (New York, 1972). Recent works exemplifying the integration of religion into archaeological approaches to cultural evolution are *Ideology, Power, and Prehistory*, edited by Daniel Miller and Christopher Tilley (Cambridge, 1984), and *Religion and Empire* by Geoffrey W. Conrad and myself (Cambridge, 1984). For innovative syntheses of Paleolithic archaeology and religion, see Peter J. Ucko and Andrée Rosenfeld's *Palaeolithic Cave Art* (New York, 1967); André Leroi-Gourhan's *The Dawn of European Art* (Cambridge, 1982); and Alexander Marshack's *The Roots of Civilization* (New York, 1972). A good regional review of archaeology in the Near East is Charles L. Redman's *The Rise of Civilization* (San Francisco, 1978). For later periods and biblical archaeology see Howard F. Vos's *Archaeology in Bible Lands* (Chicago, 1977). Kwang-chih Chang's *Shang Civilization* (New Haven, 1980) includes consideration of early Chinese religion, while Chang's *The Archaeology of Ancient China*, 3d ed. (New Haven, 1977), is the definitive general synthesis. A review of evidence on the Indus Valley civilization and Vedic parallels is given in the first chapters of Arun Bhattacharjee's *History of*

Ancient India (New Delhi, 1979). *The Goddesses and Gods of Old Europe*, 6500-3500 B. C., by Marija Gimbutas (Berkeley, 1982) is a notable study of archaeological evidence on early European religion and an excellent example of the integration of archaeology, iconographic analysis, and the study of religion. For the Americas, traditional regional syntheses of art, archaeology, and religions can be found in *The Handbook of Middle American Indians*, 16 vols., edited by Robert Wauchope (Austin, 1964-1976), and *The Handbook of South American Indians*, 7 vols., edited by Julian H. Steward (Washington, 1946-1959). For broader structural and conceptual approaches to the nature of pre-Columbian religion, see Miguel León-Portilla's *Time and Reality in the Thought of the Maya* (Boston, 1973); my own *Viracocha* (Cambridge, Mass., 1981); and especially Eva Hunt's T*he Transformation of the Hummingbird* (Ithaca, N. Y., 1977).

ARTHUR ANDREW DEMAREST

ARCHITECTURE

Architecture may be defined as the art of building, and consequently *religious architecture* refers to those buildings planned to serve religious purposes. These structures can be either very simple or highly complex. They can take the form of a circle of upright stones (megaliths) defining a sacred space or they may spread over acres like the sanctuary at Angkor Wat. They can be of any and every material from the mounds of earth reared over royal tombs to the reinforced concrete and glass of twentieth-century houses of worship.

Classification according to Terms Used. The terms used to refer to religious buildings provide a preliminary indication of both their variety and their significance.

Typology according to Character. Granting the unavoidable overlap, four main types may be specified.

Divine dwelling. Taking pride of place, because the majority of terms in use emphasize this particular category, is the structure that is regarded as a divine habitation. Since the chief occupant enjoys divine status, the model is believed to have been provided from above. Various passages in the Hebrew scriptures (Old Testament) indicate that the Tabernacle and the Temple were considered to have transcendent exemplars.

The work of the divine architects is frequently held to include not only god-houses but entire cities. Sennacherib received the design of Nineveh drawn in a heavenly script. The New Jerusalem, in the prophet Ezekiel's vision, is described in the greatest detail, with precise dimensions included. The Indian holy city of Banaras is thought to have been not only planned but actually built by Siva.

Similar ideas are present in Christian thought from the fourth century onward. When large churches came to be built, as distinct from the previous small house-churches, recourse was had to the Old Testament for precedent, since the New Testament provided no guidance. Thus the basilica came to be regarded as an imitation of the Jerusalem Temple.

Divine presence. The presence of the god may be represented in a number of ways, most frequently by statues as, for example, in Egyptian, Greek, and Hindu temples, and alternatively by a bas-relief, as at the Temple of Baal in Palmyra. The building is then appropriately called a shrine. Greek sanctuaries were so conceived, and to this day Hindu temples are not only places but objects of reverence, evoking the divine.

Precisely because this type of building is regarded as the mundane dwelling of a deity, constructed according to a transcendental blueprint, it is also understood as a meeting place of gods and humans. So the ziggurat of Larsa, in lower Babylonia, was called "the house of the bond between heaven and earth." This link may be physically represented by a sacred object

The divine is also associated with mountains that rear up into the sky. This symbolism can be applied to the religious building itself. Their superstructure is known as the "crest" *(sikhara)* of a hill, and the contours and tiered arrangement of the whole building derive from a desire to suggest the visual effect of a mountain.

*Sacred and profane.*To speak of the sacred and the profane is to refer to two antithetical entities. The one is potent, full of power, while the other is powerless.

Underlying all this dualism is the concept of two worlds: a sacred world and a secular world. Two realms of being are envisaged, and this opposition finds its visible expression in holy places. The sacred space, defined by the religious building or precinct, is first of all a means of ensuring the isolation and so the preservation of both the sacred and the profane. The wall that keeps the one out also serves to keep the other in; it is the demarcation line *(temenos, tempus, templum)* between the two worlds. But within the sacred enclosure, the profane world is transcended and hence the existence of the holy place makes it possible for humans to pass from one world to another.

Center of reference. Both individuals and communities require some center of reference for their lives so that amid the vagaries of a changing world there is a pivot that may provide an anchor in the ultimate. Religious buildings can and do constitute such centers to such an extent that the idea of a middle point has been taken quite literally. Every Egyptian temple was considered to be located where creation began and was therefore the navel of the earth. In Jewish thought the selfsame term has been applied to Jerusalem, and the site of the Temple is held to be the place of the original act of creation.

Within the same ambit of ideas is the view that a religious building may be related to cosmic forces and therefore assist in geomancy. Hence, for example, the monumental structures at Teotihuacán in Mexico are arranged within a vast precinct in such a way as to observe the relations of the earth to the sun. The orientation of Christian churches so that their sanctuary is at the east end is another way of affirming this cosmic link, while the concern of Hindu architects for the proportions and measurements of their designs rests upon the conviction that the universe as a whole has a mathematical basis that must be embodied in every temple. In Hinduism too the temple plan functions as a *mandala*—a sacred geometrical diagram of the essential structure of the cosmos.

Monument or memorial. The essentials of a sacred place are location and spatial demarcation rather than buildings, but when there are edifices, they too serve to locate and spatially demarcate. In other words the locations are mainly associated with notable happenings in the life of a religious founder or with the exploits of gods and goddesses, and they stand as memorials (remembrancers) or monuments (reminders). One of the units in the complex erected by Emperor Constantine in fourth-century Jerusalem was known as the Martyrium, the testimony to or evidence and proof of the reality of Christ's death and resurrection, which were believed to have occurred at that very site. Also in Jerusalem is the Muslim Dome of the Rock, which enshrines the spot whence the prophet Muhammad is believed to have ascended to heaven. At Sarnath, near Banaras, a stupa commemorates the Buddha's first sermon delivered.

Many religious buildings that function as memorials enclose space: the pyramids of Giza have within them the burial chambers of pharaohs; the Cenotaph in London, on the other hand, a monument to the dead of two world wars shelters nothing. It corresponds to the second of the four fundamental modes of monumental architecture. First, there is the precinct, which shows the limits of the memorial area and finally develops through a typological series to the stadium. Second is the cairn, which makes the site visible from afar and indicates its importance, the ultimate development of this type is the pyramid. Third is the path that signals a direction and can take the sophisticated form of a colonnaded street, thus dignifying the approach to the main shrine. Fourth, there is the hut that acts as a sacred shelter, with the cathedral as one of its most developed types.

Typology According to Function. It is consequently both possible and necessary to specify a second typology according to function, which stems from but also complements the previous typology according to character.

Service of the deities. At home, resident within their temples, the gods require their devotees to perform certain services for them. Perhaps the most striking illustration of need is provided by the toilet ceremonies of ancient Egypt. Each morning the cult image was asperged, censed, anointed, vested, and crowned. At the present day very similar ceremonies are conducted in Hindu temples, where the images are cooled with water in hot weather, anointed, clad in beautiful clothes, and garlanded.

Positive and negative functions. Since the temple is a divine dwelling, to enter its precincts is to come into the presence of the god and so be under his or her protection. As a sacred place, the building is inviolable, and no one can be removed from it by force; to do so would be sacrilege, since a person who is inside the area of holiness has been invested with some of the sacredness inherent in it and thus cannot be touched as long as he or she does not emerge. This is the rationale of sanctuary as it was practiced in the classi-

> **Since the temple is a divine dwelling, to enter its precincts is to come into the presence of the god and so be under his or her protection.**

cal world. The right of fugitives to remain under the protection of their god became legally recognized and in western Europe continued to be so for centuries.

The second example of the gods themselves fulfilling a function on behalf of their followers is the practice of incubation. This is a method of obtaining divine favors by passing a length of time in one of their houses, usually sleeping there. Its primary aspect is medical, to obtain a cure, either immediately or after obeying the divine will disclosed in a vision.

These several functions may all be regarded as positive in character, but a corollary of viewing a religious building as a holy place is the requirement for negative rituals to safeguard it by purifying those who wish to enter. Holy water stoups are to be found just inside the entrance of Roman Catholic churches; baptismal fonts were originally placed either in rooms separate from the main worship area or in entirely distinct buildings. The removal of shoes before entering a Hindu temple, of hats before going into a Christian church—all of these testify to the seriousness of entering a holy place. Many religious buildings have guardians to protect their entrances: the giant figures in the royal complex at Bangkok, the bull Nandin in the temples of Siva.

Determination of form. The interior disposition of those religious buildings conceived to be divine dwellings is very much determined by the forms of the services offered. Where, for example, processions are a habitual feature of the ceremonial, then corridors for circumambulation have to be designed, as in the complex of Horus at Idfu; this also explains the labyrinthine character of many Hindu temples. Where there are sacrifices, altars are needed. Classical Greek temples sheltered statues of the tutelary deities, but the all-important altars were outside; on the Athenian Acropolis, for example, it was in front of the Parthenon.

Conveyance of revelation and teaching. As a center of reference, a religious building may accommodate activities that convey meaning, guidance, and instruction in the faith.

Where a sacred book is central to a religion, provision for its reading and exposition has to be made. In synagogues there has to be a shrine for the Torah and a desk from which to comment on the text. In Christian churches there are lecterns for the Bible and pulpits for the sermon. Islam has its stands for the Qur'an, and its *minbar* is the equivalent of the Christian pulpit.

Congregational worship. The basic understanding of *cult* is evident from its etymology. It derives from *colere*, which means "to till the ground." Next it signifies "to honor" and finally "to worship." The cultus is therefore a cultivating of the gods, a cherishing of them, seeing to their needs; it is the bestowal of labor upon them and the manifestation of regard toward them.

Worship then is meeting: the religious building is the meeting house. Hence worship is a memorial celebration of the saving deeds of the gods, and by it the people are created and renewed again and again. So, in Christian terms, the Body of Christ (the Christian community) progressively becomes what it is by feeding upon the sacramental body of Christ. Worship fosters community identity, and hence in the chapels of Christian monasteries the seating frequently faces inward, thus promoting a family atmosphere.

The precise interior disposition of a building will also depend upon the particular understanding or form of the communal rite. Religions which center on a book of revelation, such as Judaism, Islam, and Sikhism, require auditoria. Protestantism, concentrating upon the word of God, similarly tends to arrange its congregations in rows suitable for an audience (*audientes*, a group of "hearers"). Roman Catholicism, with its greater emphasis on the Mass, stresses the visual dominance of the altar, which is now no longer outside the building, as with Roman and Greek exemplars, but inside.

Symbolization. On whatever basis a typology of religious buildings may be constructed and whatever purposes they may serve, there is one overall function that must be considered: symbolization. Each building proclaims certain beliefs about the deities to whom it is dedicated. One has only to contrast a Gothic cathedral with a Quaker meeting house to appreciate this.

Sometimes the symbolism is intellectually apprehended before it is given visible form, and then it needs interpretation. Baptism, for example, is a sacrament of dying and rising with Christ. A detached baptistery may be hexagonal or octagonal: in the former case it refers to the sixth day of the week, Friday, on which Jesus died and in the latter, to the eighth day, or the first day of a new week when he rose from the dead. The dome, surmounting many a baptistery, is also a habitual feature of Byzantine churches and Muslim mosques; it is a representation of the transcendental realm, an image of heaven. Different parts of a building can have their own messages: towers declare heavenly aspirations; monumental doorways can impress with regal authority.

Architectural Types. There is yet another typology to be reviewed that applies to all buildings whatever their function, and religious buildings are no exception. This is a dual typology that divides structures into the categories of path and place. For a path to be identifiable, it must have (1) strong edges, (2) continuity, (3) directionality, (4) recognizable landmarks, (5) a sharp terminal, and (6) end-from-end distinction. For a place to be identifiable, it must be (1) concentrated in form with pronounced borders, (2) a readily comprehensible shape, (3) limited in size, (4) a focus for gathering, (5) capable of being experienced as an inside in contrast to a surrounding exterior, and (6) largely nondirectional.

The application of these types to religious buildings can be briefly illustrated by contrasting a basilica and a centralized mosque. A basilica is a path leading toward the altar; every detail of the design confirms this. The nave, framed by aisles, has firm edges; there is continuity provided by floor patterns and advancing rows of columns, which themselves indicate a direction—everything points toward the holy table framed in a triumphal arch and backed by the embracing shape of the apse. For a pilgrim people, for those who have here no abiding city, such a royal road is obviously very appropriate. A centralized mosque, on the other hand such as those designed by Sinan in Istanbul, suggests no movement, it is a place, a point of reference and gathering, it is concentrated. Once within, there is no incentive to leave and every enticement to stay. Embodying perfect equipoise, it promotes contemplation; it is indeed embracing architecture. Its spaciousness expresses not the specificity of the Christian doctrine of the incarnation but the omnipresence of the divine; it manifests *tawhid*, which is the metaphysical doctrine of the divine unity as the source and culmination of all diversity.

The difference then between basilica and mosque is not stylistic; they are distinct architectural types, which in these two instances correspond to each religion's self-understanding.

[*For further discussion of individual building types, see* Synagogue and Temple.]

BIBLIOGRAPHY

Arnheim, Rudolf. *The Dynamics of Architectural Form.* Berkeley, 1977.

Davies, J. G. *The Secular Use of Church Buildings.* London, 1968.

Davies, J. G. *Temples, Churches and Mosques: A Guide to the Appreciation of Religious Architecture.* New York, 1982.

Eliade, Mircea. *The Sacred and the Profane.* New York, 1959.

Grabar, André. *Martyrium: Recherches sur le culte des reliques et l'art chrétien antique* (1946). 2 vols. Reprint, London, 1972.

Smith, Baldwin. *The Dome: A Study in the History of Ideas* (1950). Reprint, Princeton, 1978.

Turner, Harold W. *From Temple to Meeting House: The Phenomenology and Theology of Places of Worship*. The Hague, 1979.

J. G. DAVIES

ARCTIC RELIGIONS

An Overview

Arctic religions may be treated together, as constituting a more or less unified entity, for two reasons. First, these religions are practiced by peoples situated in the polar North, who mostly live on the tundra (permanently frozen ground) and partly in the taiga (the northern coniferous forest belt that stretches around the world); like their cultures in general, the religions of these peoples reflect to no little extent the impact of the severe natural environment. Second, the whole Arctic zone constitutes a marginal area and an archaic residue of the old hunting culture and hunting religion; whereas in the south the waves of Neolithic agriculture and animal husbandry inundated the originally Paleolithic hunting culture, the latter was preserved in the high north, where no cultivation of the ground was possible.

Ethnic and Cultural Survey. The tribes and peoples of the Arctic culture area belong to several linguistic families. All of them, with the exceptions of some Paleosiberian peoples and the Inuit, are also represented in cultures south of the high Arctic zone. In the following survey, names of peoples will be given as they are authorized today by their respective governments and by the peoples themselves.

1. *The Uralic language family*. In Scandinavia, in Finland, and on the Kola Peninsula, the Arctic tundra and coast and the northern interior woodland are inhabited by the Saami (Lapps). Most of them are fishing people, but in the mountain regions and in parts of the woodland areas reindeer breeding is a common way of life. East of Lake Onega live the Komi (Zyrians) and who are divided into two main groups: the Nentsy (Yuraks), from the Northern Dvina River to the Ural Mountains, and the Nganasani (Tavgi), from the Ob River to Cape Chelyuskin. Along the lower parts of the Ob and Irtysh rivers live two Ugric peoples (related to the Hungarians), the Khanty (Ostiaks) and the Mansi (Voguls), mostly fishermen and hunters.

2. *The Tunguz language family*. The wide areas from west of the Yenisei River to the Anadyr River in the east and from the tundra in the north to the Sayan Mountains in the south are the country of the dispersed Tunguz tribes: the Evenki, west of the Lena River, and the Eveny, east of it. Their typical habitat is the taiga, where they subsist as reindeer breeders on a limited scale.

3. *The Turkic language family*. The numerous Yakuts on the Lena River and farther east combine reindeer breeding with horse breeding. Their language is also spoken by the Dolgans in the Taimyr Peninsula area, a group of earlier Tunguz tribes.

4. *The Yukagir*. Now almost extinct, the Yukagir, a group that may be related to the Finno-Ugric peoples, once covered a large area east of the Lena. They were hunters and fishermen until the seventeenth century, when they turned into reindeer-breeding nomads.

5. *The Paleosiberian language family*. The Chukchi, on the Chukchi Peninsula, and the Koriak and the Itelmen (Kamchadal), on the Kamchatka Peninsula, make up the Paleosiberian language family. The inland Chukchi are reindeer breeders; the coastal Chukchi, the Koriak, and the Itelmen are ocean fishermen.

6. *The Inuit*. The Inuit (Eskimo) ultimately may be related to the Paleosiberian peoples. Their territory stretches from the easternmost tip of Asia over the coasts and tundras of Alaska and Canada to Greenland. The Aleut, inhabitants of the Aleutian Islands who are closely related to the Inuit, should also be mentioned here. The Inuit are sea hunters and fishermen and, in northern Alaska and on the barren plains west of the Hudson Bay, caribou hunters.

Common Religious Elements. It is not surprising that a wide range of religious phenomena are spread out over most of the region, usually as a combined result of ecological and historical factors. The available data bear out Robert H. Lowie's observation that the whole Arctic area constitutes one gigantic entirety from the angle of religious belief. I would here make a certain reservation for the New World Arctic area, however, because both archaeologically and ethnologically the Inuit lack several common circumpolar features, and the same holds for their religion.

The main characteristics of Arctic religions are the special relationships of people to animals and the elaboration of shamanism. It is possible that the strain of the Arctic climate has stimulated strong religious forms of reaction, just as it has provoked the psychic reactions known as Arctic hysteria. No such explanation can be given for the hypertrophic extension of animal ceremonialism. It has its roots, of course, in ancient Eurasian hunting rituals, but its prolific occurrence in the Arctic probably has to do with the necessary dependence on an animal diet in these barren regions.

The spiritual universe. According to the religious beliefs of the Arctic peoples, the whole world is filled with spirits: mountains, trees, and other landmarks have their spirits, and animals have their spirit masters. It is among all these spirits that the shaman finds his supernatural helpers and guardians. However, such man-spirit relationships could also occur among common people, as the evidence shows among the Saami and North American Indians, and there are obvious tendencies in the same direction among the

Chukchi, as their "general shamanizing" testifies. The multifarious world of spirits may have something to do with the fact that the figure of a supreme being is so often diffuse. There is, it seems, a pattern of spiritualism here.

Supreme power. The inclination to conceive the highest supernatural being or beings more as nonpersonal power than personal figure or figures is generally part of Arctic religions and particularly characteristic of the Samoyeds, the Paleosiberian tribes, and the Inuit. The Saami constitute a great exception, but their high-god beliefs have been heavily influenced by Scandinavian and Finnish as well as Christian religious concepts.

Other spirits and divinities. Next to the supreme being, the most important spirits of the upper world are the Sun, the Moon, and the thunder spirits. The Sun is often related to the high god (as among the Tunguz), and the Moon can represent the mistress of the dead or, among some Inuit, the mistress of the sea animals (who is herself, secondarily, a mistress of the dead).

The surface of the earth is the habitat of a large crowd of spirits—some rule the animal species, some are spirits of the woods, lakes, and mountains (among Eurasian Arctic groups), and some are dangerous ogres, giants, and dwarfs.

Throughout the Eurasian Arctic, the mother goddesses have connections with the door of dwellings and are supposed to live under the ground. The Inuit have no particular birth goddess, but Sedna, the mistress of the sea animals, is in her unclean states a prototype of the woman who is ritually unclean, particularly when pregnant or giving birth. The birth goddess is primarily the protectress of women, and in some tribes female spirits are inherited from mother to daughter.

Cultic Practices. Characteristic of the cultic complexes among Arctic peoples is the simple development of ritual forms and the use of cultic objects—such as crude sculptures in wood and peculiarly formed stones—as symbolic receivers of offerings. The relationships between the sacrificers and these objects varies from veneration to coercive magic.

Cultic images. The stone cult is prominent everywhere. Among the Saami, strangely formed stones, called *seite*, are connected with spirits that control the animals in the vicinity or the fish in water where the stone stands. The Samoyeds make offerings to similar stone gods, as do the Khanty, the Mansi, the Tunguz, and the Inuit. In some reports the stones seem, at least momentarily, identical with the spirits, but otherwise the general idea is that the stone represents the spirit or serves as its abode.

The most common custom, however, was to make crude wooden sculptures of the spirits. Such spirit figures occur all the way from Lapland to Alaska. Throughout northern Eurasia they are surprisingly similar—pointed at the top, usually without limbs, and occasionally decorated with cross

marks on the body. The Khanty and the Samoyeds dress up these spirit images.

Wooden figures also occur in Siberian shamanism among the Tunguz and the Dolgans. For these peoples, the figures symbolize the shaman's helping spirits and the world pole or world tree. A line of seven or nine pillars represents the lower sky worlds, where the shaman's soul or guardian spirit rests on the way to heaven.

Animal ceremonialism. Much of the cultic life centers on animal ceremonialism, that is, the rituals accorded the slain game. Several animal species are shown a ceremonial courtesy after hunting; for example, their bones are buried in anatomical order. All over the area, a special complex of rites surrounds the treatment of the dead bear.

Paleosiberian peoples and Alaska Inuit paid similar attention to the whale. The Inuit celebrated the dead whale ritually for five days, a period corresponding to the mourning period for a dead person. The Alaska Inuit also had a bladder festival in December, at which the bladders of the seals that had been slain during the year were restored to the sea.

Shamanism and soul beliefs. It seems that the extreme development of shamanistic ritual farther to the south in Siberia is somewhat attenuated in the northern Arctic. On the other hand, in the Arctic the intensity of the shaman's ecstatic trance is certainly not weaker, but is in fact stronger, than it is in Siberia. North and south are also remarkably different in regard to the conception of the soul basic to shamanism. As always where true shamanism operates, there is a dualism between the free soul that acts during dream and trance and that represents man in an extracorporeal form and the one or several body souls that keep man alive and conscious during his waking hours. It is typically the shaman's free soul that, in a trance, tries to rescue a sick man's soul (of either type), which has left its body and gone to the land of the dead and possibly reached this place. This is indeed the conception of the soul and disease among the Arctic peoples.

Afterlife. Unlike most other hunting peoples, the peoples in the North generally believe that the realm of the dead is situated in the underworld. The Khanty think that the world of shades extends close to the mouth of the Ob River; it is characterized by cold, eternal darkness, hunger, and silence. The Tunguz view of the underworld is more optimistic. The people there live in birchbark tents, hunt, fish, and tend to their reindeer in the woods. The Central and Eastern Inuit realm of the dead is identical with Sedna's place at the bottom of the sea. It is not bright, but endurable. The rule in most places is that only those who have suffered a violent death go to heaven; among the Chukchi and Inuit these fortunate beings make their appearance in the aurora borealis. Often, the underworld is conceived to be contrary to our world in every respect; for instance, while it is night in the underworld it is day on earth.

[*For discussion of specific Arctic traditions, see* Inuit Religion; Saami Religion; *and* Samoyed Religion.]

BIBLIOGRAPHY

The concept of an Arctic cultural area was first used by Artur Byhan in his *Die Polarvölker* (Leipzig, 1909). An archaeological survey of the area can be found in Guterm Gjessing's *Circumpolar Stone Age* (Copenhagen, 1944). The general features of some Arctic cultures are briefly presented in Nelson H. H. Graburn and B. Stephen Strong's *Circumpolar Peoples: An Anthropological Perspective* (Pacific Palisades, Calif., 1973). This work has also excellent bibliographic references. Various questions related to Arctic culture are discussed in *Circumpolar Problems*, edited by Gösta Berg (Oxford, 1973), and in the serial *Arctic Anthropology* (Madison, Wis., 1962-).

The Siberian Arctic peoples and their cultures are described in *The Peoples of Siberia*, edited by M. G. Levin and L. P. Potapov (Chicago, 1964), and in Gustav Ränk's "Völker und Kulturen Nordeurasiens," in *Handbuch der Kulturgeschichte*, edited by Eugen Thurnher (Frankfurt, 1968).

Arctic religions as a separate entity have hitherto only been described in one major article, Ivar Paulson's "Les religions des peuples arctiques," in *Histoire des religions*, vol. 3, edited by Henri-Charles Puech (Paris, 1976). Arctic religions are part of presentations of northern religions in *Mythology of All Races*, vol. 4, *Finno-Ugric, Siberian* (Boston, 1927), by Uno Holmberg (later Harva); in *Die religiösen Vorstellungen der altaischen Völker* (Helsinki, 1938), by the same author; and in *Les religions arctiques et finnoises* (Paris, 1965), by Ivar Paulson, Karl Jettmar, and me. Much material pertaining to Arctic religions is given in Mircea Eliade's *Shamanism: Archaic Techniques of Ecstasy*, rev. & enl. ed. (New York, 1964); *Studies in Siberian Shamanism*, edited by Henry N. Michael (Toronto, 1963); *Popular Beliefs and Folklore Tradition in Siberia*, edited by Vilmos Diószegi (The Hague, 1968); *Shamanism in Siberia*, edited by Vilmos Diószegi and Mihály Hoppál (Budapest, 1978); and *Shamanism in Eurasia*, 2 vols., edited by Mihály Hoppál (Göttingen, 1984). Although somewhat dated, M. A. Czaplicka's classic work, *Aboriginal Siberia* (Oxford, 1914), is still valuable from the religio-historical point of view.

There is an analysis of the diffusion of Arctic religious traits in my "North American Indian Religions in a Circumpolar Perspective," in *North American Indian Studies*, edited by Pieter Hovens (Göttingen, 1981), as well as in an earlier article by Robert H. Lowie, "Religious Ideas and Practices of the Eurasiatic and North American Areas," in *Essays Presented to C. G. Seligman*, edited by E. E. Evans-Pritchard et al. (London, 1934). There are several papers on selected aspects of Arctic religions, such as A. Irving Hallowell's "Bear Ceremonialism in the Northern Hemisphere," *American Anthropologist* 28 (1926): 1-175; Uno Holmberg's "Über die Jagdriten der nördlichen Völker Asiens und Europas," *Journal de la Société Finno-Ougrienne* (Helsinki) 41 (1926): 1-53; Eveline Lot-Falck's *Les rites de chasse chez les peuples sibériens* (Paris, 1953); Balaji Mundkur's "The Bicephalous 'Animal Style' in Northern Eurasian Religious Art and Its Western Hemispheric Analogues," *Current Anthropology* 25 (August-October 1984): 451-482; Gudmund Hatt's *Asiatic Influences in American Folklore* (Copenhagen, 1949); and Gustav Ränk's *Die heilige Hinterecke im Hauskult der Völker Nordosteuropas* und Nordasiens (Helsinki, 1949). This last work deals with the sacred corner in Arctic homes.

ÅKE HULTKRANTZ

History of Study

The Development of Circumpolar Studies. The exploration of Siberian and Canadian Arctic cultures at the turn of the century made scholars aware of their great similarities. Since this was the time when geographic environmentalism swayed high—and the Arctic is known for its extreme climate—Arctic cultures were readily given an environmentalist interpretation.

Most ethnologists and anthropologists have favored a cultural-historical analysis in which all the Arctic cultures belong together, either as a common field of diffusion or as an archaic residue. This approach originated with the American anthropologist Franz Boas, who compared Paleosiberian and Northwest American Indian mythologies. His speculations resulted in the assumption of a direct communication between North America and North Asia. This perspective was expanded by Austrian and Danish diffusionists.

Particular Areal Studies. Most authors have concentrated their efforts on the study of subfields or tribes within the Arctic area. It is possible to distinguish three main Arctic regions of exploration, usually (but not always) treated as separate from each other:

The Saami field. The scientific analyses of Saami religion on the basis of older sources (there were few vestiges left in the nineteenth century besides folkloric materials) began late in the nineteenth century.

The northern Eurasian field. The first accounts of the "primitive" peoples of the Russian empire and their religious customs date from the seventeenth and eighteenth centuries.

During the postrevolutionary era, Soviet scholars have made several tribal ethnographic investigations of considerable importance, although one-sidedly Marxist and evolutionist in outlook.

The Inuit field. The Danes had already secured important information on the Greenland Inuit in the eighteenth century. Danish scholarship in the field started in the nineteenth century when Gustav Holm and H. Rink described, in particular, the East Greenland Inuit religion.

The twentieth century has seen a rich scholarship on Inuit religion, most of it directed from Copenhagen. Knud Rasmussen covered the whole Inuit area with his insightful analyses of Inuit religious thinking, but first of all the Greenland, Central, and Polar Inuit.

BIBLIOGRAPHY

An early environmental interpretation of circumpolar religions will be found in M. A. Czaplicka's "The Influence of Environment upon the Religious Ideas and Practices of the Aborigines of Northern Asia," *Folklore* 25 (March 1914): 34-54. A later collocation based on religio-ecological analysis is my "Type of Religion in the Arctic Hunting Cultures," in *Hunting and Fishing*, edited by Harald Hvarfner (Luleå, 1965).

Methodological approaches to the distribution and history of religious traits in the area have been discussed in articles mentioned in the bibliography of the overview article on Arctic religions. In addition, there are short comprehensive surveys like Waldemar Bogoraz's "Elements of the Culture of the Circumpolar Zone," *American Anthropologist* 31 (October-December 1929): 579-601, and Gudmund Hatt's "North American and Eurasian Culture Connections," in *Proceedings of the Fifth Pacific Science Congress* (Toronto, 1934). See also I. S. Gurvich's study, cited below.

Studies of religious change have been presented by, for instance, Wilhelm Schmidt, *Der Ursprung der Gottesidee*, vols. 3 and 6 (Münster, 1931 and 1935), and Karl Meuli, "Griechische Opferbräuche," in *Phyllobolia für Peter von der Mühll zum 60. Geburtstage*, by Olof Gigon and others (Basel, 1946). On the development of the bear ceremony, see Hans-Joachim Paproth's *Studien über das Bärenzeremoniell*, vol. 1 (Uppsala, 1976).

Summary reports of the scholarly publications on Saami religion and folklore up to 1950 were issued in the *Journal of the Royal Anthropological Institute* in the 1950s: Knut Bergsland and Reidar Christiansen's "Norwegian Research on the Language and Folklore of the Lapps" (vol. 80, 1950), and my "Swedish Research on the Religion and Folklore of the Lapps" (vol. 85, 1955). Later books and articles on the subject are annotated in Louise Bäckman's and my *Studies in Lapp Shamanism* (Stockholm, 1978).

There is no similar survey of scholarly contributions in tsarist and Soviet Russia, except the studies of shamanism. Some points of view on Soviet studies are presented in I. S. Gurvich's "An Ethnographic Study of Cultural Parallels among the Aboriginal Populations of Northern Asia and Northern North America," *Arctic Anthropology* 16 (1979): 32-38. The comprehensive areal works by Uno Holmberg Harva and Ivar Paulson contain some introductory remarks, but no more. The student has to go to the separate books and articles, most of them published in Russian, but some in western European languages: this applies, of course, first of all to the works of scholars residing in western Europe and America. No collocation of all this scholarship has ever been done.

The same applies to the split publications on Inuit religion. The total research contribution has not yet been evaluated. See, however, the short introduction to the subject by Ivar Paulson, Karl Jettmar, and me in *Les religions arctiques et finnoises* (Paris, 1965), pp. 346f.

ÅKE HULTKRANTZ

ARHAT

History and Development of the Term. In Vedic and non-Vedic contexts, the noun *arhat* and the verb *arhati* applied generally to persons or gods whose particular status earned for them the characterization of "worthy" or "deserving of merit." The terms also denoted "being able to do," or "being capable of doing."

In the Jain *sutras* the term is often used in a sense closer to that found in Buddhist writings. Here the *arhat* is described as one who is free from desire, hatred, and delusion, who knows everything, and who is endowed with miraculous powers. While these characterizations are consistent with the Buddhist use of the term, it should be noted that the Jains applied the word exclusively to the *tirthamkaras* or revealers of religion, whereas in Buddhism arhatship is an ideal to be attained by all serious religious strivers.

Place in Buddhist Soteriology. In its most typical usage in *Theravada* Buddhism, however, the term *arahant* signifies persons who have reached the goal of enlightenment or *nibbana* (Skt., nirvana). In the Pali canon the arahant emerges not simply as the revealer of the religion or the person worthy of receiving gifts but as one who has attained freedom of mind and heart, has overcome desire and passion, has come to true knowledge and insight, has crossed over the flood (of *samsara*) and gone beyond (*paragata*), has destroyed the *asavas* (deadly attachments to the world), is versed in the threefold knowledge (*tevijja*) of past, present, and future, has achieved the thirty-seven factors of enlightenment, and who has attained *nibbana*.

In the Vinaya, the concept of the *arahant* appears to be connected with the concept of *uttarimanussa* ("further being, superhuman being"). Here, the *arahant* is said to possess one or more of the four trance states (*jhana*), one or more of the four stages of sanctification, mastery of the threefold knowledge and the sixfold knowledge (*chalabhiñña*), which includes knowledge of previous rebirths, and to have achieved the destruction of the *asavas*, or "cankers." Indeed, it may be that the notion of *uttarimanussa* constitutes the earliest beginning of a more elaborated and refined concept designated by the term *arahant*.

Arhatship figures prominently into the Theravada notion that the salvific journey is a gradual path (*magga*) in which one moves from the condition of ordinary worldly attachments governed by ignorant sense desires to a state of liberation characterized by utter equanimity and the knowledge of things as they are. As Buddhagosa put it in his *Visuddhimagga* (Path of Purification), the classic synopsis of Theravada doctrine, the arahant has completed all of the purities derived through the observance of the moral precepts, (*sila*), meditational practice (*jhana*), and the purity of knowledge (*pañña-visuddhi*). The *sine qua non* of this path is meditation, which leads to extraordinary cognitive states and stages of consciousness (*jhana*) and, allegedly, to the acquisition of various supernormal "powers" (*iddhi*). These attainments became fundamental to the cult of saints, an important aspect of popular Theravada Buddhist practice. This popular aspect of arhatship has not always been easy to reconcile with the classical notion, which emphasizes the acquisition of what Buddhagosa refers to as the "analytical knowledges," for example, the analysis of reality in terms of its conditioned and co-arising nature (*paticca-samuppada*; Skt., *pratitya-samutpada*).

The Arhat as Cult Figure. In popular Buddhism the arhat has become a figure endowed with magical and apotropaic powers. In Burma, the arahant Shin Thiwali (Pali, Sivali), declared by the Buddha to be the foremost recipient of gifts among his disciples, is believed to bring prosperity and good fortune to those who petition him. The arahant Upagupta, who tamed Mara and converted him to Buddhism, is thought to have the power to prevent storms and floods as well as other kinds of physical violence and unwanted chaos.

The *arhat*, as one who has realized the *summum bonum* of the spiritual path, is worshiped on the popular level as a field of merit *(puny aksetra)* and source of magical, protective power. Claims of arhatship are continuously being made on behalf of holy monks in countries like Sri Lanka, Burma, and Thailand.

In short, the *arhat* embodies one of the fundamental tensions in the Buddhist tradition between the ideal of enlightenment and equanimity and the extraordinary magical power concomitant with this attainment.

BIBLIOGRAPHY

The classic study of the arahant in the Theravada tradition is I. B. Horner's The *Early Buddhist Theory of Man Perfected* (London, 1936). In recent years both historians of religion and anthropologists have studied the Buddhist saint. Nathan Katz has compared the arahant concept in the Sutta Pitaka to the concepts of the bodhisattva and mahasiddha in the Mahayana and Tantrayana traditions in his book, *Buddhist Images of Human Perfection* (New Delhi, 1982). George D. Bond's "The Problems of 'Sainthood' in the Theravada Buddhist Tradition," in *Sainthood in World Religions*, edited by George Bond and Richard Kieckhefer (Berkeley, 1984), provides a general analysis of the Theravada *arahant* while Michael Carrithers's *The Forest Monks of Sri Lanka* (New York, 1983), and Stanley J. Tambiah's *The Buddhist Saints of the Forest and the Cult of Amulets* (Cambridge, 1984) offer anthropological analyses of the Theravada saint in the contexts of modern Sri Lanka and Thailand, respectively. John S. Strong reminds us that the *arhat* receives approbation in the Mahayana as well as the Theravada tradition in "The Legend of the Lion-Roarers: A Study of the Buddhist Arhat Pindola Bharadvaja," *Numen* 26 (June 1979): 50-87.

DONALD K. SWEARER

ARISTOTLE

ARISTOTLE (384-322 BCE), Greek philosopher, who so dominated philosophical thought for almost ten centuries that he was frequently referred to simply as "the Philosopher." According to Dante, Aristotle was "the master of all who know." Writing on almost every known subject of intellectual inquiry, from astronomy through zoology, and inventing entirely new fields, such as logic, Aristotle produced a literary corpus whose influence remains with us even in our everyday language, where we still use such Aristotelian expressions as "substance," "quality," "accident," and "potentiality."

Unlike his two great Greek predecessors, Socrates and Plato, Aristotle was not an Athenian but a northern Greek. He was born in Chalcidice in 384 BCE to a father who was a physician in the Macedonian court, and the son was to inherit the father's interest in the biological sciences. At the age of eighteen, Aristotle went to Athens to study in Plato's Academy, where he stayed for about twenty years, until Plato's death in 347. In 342 he was invited to Macedonia to become the tutor of the young Alexander; a few years later he returned to Athens, where he established a school of his own. For reasons we do not know—perhaps political— Aristotle left Athens in 323, and he died a year later. His school, however, continued for several centuries.

One of Aristotle's main concerns was science, both the special sciences, such as biology and physics, and general methodological questions about scientific goals and procedures. From his various scientific pursuits there emerged a general worldview that proved to have an immense impact upon subsequent philosophical and religious thought. Nature, for Aristotle, is a unified physical system embodying both law and purpose and ultimately explicable in terms of the transcendent supranatural substance, God. As the first, efficient, and final cause of the world's motion and activity, God is responsible for its order and development, as all other living things strive to imitate God's perfection. God is described by Aristotle as one, the object of all desire, pure mind, immutable, eternal, and simple. All of these divine attributes were discussed by later theologians and used in their attempts to "aristotelianize" biblical thought.

One of the more important treatises written by Aristotle is *On the Soul*, which is primarily devoted to a discussion of the various activities of living things, such as sensation, imagi-

> **Man is neither a brute nor a god; hence, he needs to live among others.**

nation, thinking, and feeling. Contrary to Plato, Aristotle generally believed the soul to be inseparable from the body, since it is the form of the living organism. The typical behavior of the organism constitutes its form, or soul. The human soul is the set of all the typical modes of human behavior, for instance, sensing, thinking, feeling, and so on. Of course, each human being will have his or her own soul, individuated by a particular mode of sensing, thinking, and feeling.

Aristotle's psychology provided him with a suitable basis for his moral philosophy. It is Aristotle's general thesis that the truly human life is a life in which the unique characteristics of man are developed to their utmost. Unlike most, if not all, animals, man is both a rational and social being, and as such he ought to perfect his rational and social capacities and live a life wherein these potentialities are most efficiently expressed.

Man is neither a brute nor a god; hence, he needs to live among others. Political groupings are therefore not artificial impositions but natural outgrowths of man's essential being. Nevertheless, man is not just a social animal, he is also endowed with reason. And so Aristotle ultimately insists upon the supremacy of the intellectual virtues, the life of contemplation.

BIBLIOGRAPHY

Works by Aristotle
The Basic Works of Aristotle. Edited by Richard McKeon. New York, 1941. The best one-volume edition.
The Complete Works of Aristotle: The Revised Oxford Translation. 2 vols. Edited by Jonathan Barnes. Princeton, 1984.

General Surveys
Ackrill, J. L. *Aristotle the Philosopher.* Oxford, 1981. The best general monograph on Aristotle in English.
Jaeger, Werner. *Aristotle: Fundamentals of the History of His Development.* Oxford, 1934. The pioneering work in the study of Aristotle's intellectual biography.
Lloyd, G. E. R. *Aristotle: The Growth and Structure of His Thought.* London, 1968. Comprehensive and analytical, especially good on Aristotle's scientific interests.
Ross, W. D. *Aristotle.* London, 1923. Comprehensive and judicious.

Studies and Commentaries
Ackrill, J. L., ed. *"Clarendon Aristotle Series."* Oxford. Especially notable among these translations and commentaries are those on *Categories* and *On Interpretation* (1963), Physics (1970-1983), and Metaphysics (1973).
Barnes, Jonathan, Malcolm Schofield, and Richard Sorabji, eds. *Articles on Aristotle.* 4 vols. London, 1975-1979. Contemporary studies on Aristotle's philosophical and scientific interests.
Moravcsik, J. M. E., ed. *Aristotle: A Collection of Critical Essays.* Garden City, N. Y., 1967. Short but valuable collection of modern studies.
Rorty, Amélie Oksenberg, ed. *Essays on Aristotle's Ethics.* Berkeley, 1980. Essays on Aristotle's moral philosophy by Anglo-American philosophers.
Sorabji, Richard. *Necessity, Cause and Blame: Perspectives on Aristotle's Theory.* Ithaca, N. Y., 1980. A fine study of Aristotle's views on several central problems in metaphysics, the philosophy of nature, and ethics.
Waterlow, Sarah. *Passage and Possibility: A Study of Aristotle's Modal Concepts.* Oxford, 1982. An important study of Aristotle's natural philosophy and its logic.

SEYMOUR FELDMAN

ARMENIAN RELIGION

The Armenians' remotest ancestors immigrated to Anatolia in the mid-second millennium BCE. Related to speakers of the Thraco-Phrygian languages of the Indo-European family, they probably brought with them a religion akin to that of the proto-Greeks, adopting also elements of the cultures of Asianic peoples such as the Hittites, from whose name the Armenian word *hay* ("Armenian") may be derived.

The Armenians were at first concentrated in the area of Van (Urartean Biaina), a city on the southeastern shore of Lake Van, in eastern Anatolia, and in the Sasun region, a mountainous district to the west of the lake. The Armenian god Vahagn (Av., Verethraghna; cf. Sogdian *Vashaghn*), whose cult centered in the area of present-day *Mus*, appears to have assimilated the dragon-slaying exploits of the Urartean Teisheba, a weather god. An Urartean "gate of God" in the rock of Van was consecrated to Mher (Av., Mithra) and is still known in the living epic of Sasun as *Mheri durn* ("gate of Mher"), preserving the Urartean usage.

Although Herodotus in the fifth century BCE still recalled the Armenians as Phrygian colonists of Phrygian-like speech, they had been conquered twice—first by the Medes about 583 BCE, then by the Persians under Cyrus II the Great—and had assimilated elements of the conquering cultures. After the conquest of Cyrus, the faith of the Iranian prophet Zarathushtra (Zoroaster) was to exercise the primary influence upon the Armenian religion; indeed, Zoroaster was believed by Clement of Alexandria and other classical writers to have been identical with Er, the son of Armenios of the *Republic* of Plato. Strabo (*Geography* 11.13.9, 11.14.6) declared that the Armenians and the Medes performed the same religious rites, those "of the Persians," the Medes having been also the source of the way of life (*ethe*) of the Persians themselves. Like the Armenian language, which retains its ancient and distinct character while preserving a preponderance of Northwestern Iranian loanwords of the pre-Sasanid period, the ancient religion of the Armenians apparently retained distinct local features, although the great majority of its religious terms and practices belong to the Zoroastrianism of Arsacid Iran and earlier periods.

Armenian and pre-Sasanid Iranian temples often contained cult statues—such shrines were called in Armenian *bagins* ("places of the god")—but it seems that, with or without images, all Armenian temples had fire altars, called *atrushans* (like *bagin*, a Middle Iranian loanword), so that the major Zoroastrian rites might be consecrated there. A place for fire, and its light, was a focal point of worship and cultic life.

The chief shrine of Vahagn stood at Ashtishat ("rich in *yashts*" ["acts of worship"]), the place later consecrated to Saint John the Baptist by Gregory the Illuminator as the earliest see of the Armenian church. Vahagn is described in a fragment of a hymn preserved by Khorenats`i (1.31) as "sun-eyed" and "fiery-haired," attributes found in the Avesta and later applied in Christian Armenia to Mary and to seraphs. From various sources it appears that Vahagn was regarded as a sun god, perhaps acquiring this feature from Mihr (Mithra), who is closely associated with the sun in

Zoroastrianism. There is oblique evidence of a conflict between devotees of the two gods in Armenia. Nonetheless, the Armenian word for a pagan temple, mehean, containing the name of Mithra, indicates the god's great importance.

Among the other gods, the Armenians worshiped Tir (MIran., Tir), chief of the scribal art and keeper of celestial records, including, some believed, those of human destiny. He survives in modern Armenian folklore as the Grogh ("writer"). Spandaramet (MIran., Spandarmad; Av., Spenta Armaiti), goddess of the earth, was also venerated. (Her name is rendered as "Dionysos" in the fifth-century Armenian translation of the biblical books of the Maccabees.) Tork` of Anggh (Ingila), treated by Khorenats`i as a legendary and fearsome hero, is an Asianic divinity equated with Nergal in the Armenian translation of the Bible. There was an Armenian royal necropolis at Anggh, so it seems that Tork` was regarded as a divinity of the underworld.

Ancient Armenians celebrated the Iranian New Year, Nawasard (OPers., *Navasarda), which was consecrated to Aramazd. A midwinter feast of fire, Ahekan (OPers., *Athrakana), still survives with its rituals intact in Christianity as Tearnendaraj, the Feast of the Presentation of the Lord to the Temple. The old month-name of Mehekan preserves the memory of Mihragan, the feast of Mithra, and Anahit seems to have received special reverence on Vardavar, a feast of roses and of the waters. At year's end, Hrotits` (from Avestan *Fravashayo*) commemorated the holy spirits of the departed, leading Agathangelos (para. 16) to accuse the Armenians of being uruapashtk` ("worshipers of souls").

Gregory the Illuminator, son of an Armenian Arsacid *nakharar* named Suren Pahlav, converted King Tiridates to Christianity in the second decade of the fourth century. The *k`rmapets*, or high priests, resisted with main force this military imposition of a new creed, and many Armenian *nakharars* joined the fifth-century Sasanid king Yazdegerd II in his campaign to reconvert the Armenians to Zoroastrianism. But the iconoclastic state church of southwestern Iran differed too greatly from the old faith to appeal to many Armenians, and the translation of scripture into Armenian with the newly invented alphabet of Mesrop Mashtots` made the patriarchs and the saints "Armenian-speaking" (*hayerenakhaws*), as Koriwn wrote. Christianity triumphed over all but a small sect, the Arewordik` ("children of the sun"), who were said by medieval writers to follow the teachings of "the magus Zoroaster," worshiping the sun and exposing rather than burying the dead.

BIBLIOGRAPHY

Abeghian, Manuk. *Der armenische Volksglaube*. Leipzig, 1899. Reprinted with an Armenian translation in his Erker, vol. 7 (Yerevan, 1975).
Alishan, Lerond. *Hin hawatk` kam het`anosakan kronk` Hayots`*. Venice, 1910.
Ananikian, Mardiros H. "Armenian Mythology." In *The Mythology of All Races*, vol. 7, edited by J. A. MacCulloch, pp. 5-100. Boston, 1925.
Gelzer, Heinrich. "Zur armenischen Götterlehre." *Berichte der königlichen sächsischen Gesellschaft der Wissenschaften* (Leipzig) 48 (1896): 99-148. Translated into Armenian by Y. T`orosean (Venice, 1897).
Russell, J. R. *Zoroastrianism in Armenia*. Cambridge, Mass., forthcoming.

J. R. RUSSELL

ASCENSION

In many religious traditions, the sky is the home of the gods, and a heavenly ascent is a journey into the divine realms from which the soul—living or dead—reaps many rewards. Not only is a transcendent vision (or spiritual knowledge) the result of this upward journey, but even the possibility of divinization, becoming like one of the gods.

Myths from many cultures tell of numerous ways by which the journey can be made. A mountain path, a ladder, a tree, a rope, or even a cobweb will suffice. There is the further possibility of magical flight, if the soul has wings or the person a psychopomp. Rituals of ascent involve the living person who makes the heavenly journey in order to become sanctified as a priest who mediates between his people and their gods, to become initiated into a new, sacred status, or for purposes of healing.

Ecstatic Techniques. In demonstrating that there are a number of parallel beliefs and rituals in all great religions of the world, Mircea Eliade cites shamanism as an example of an objective ecstatic performance. Everything in the behavior and paraphernalia of the shaman is oriented toward one principal goal: the journey to heaven or the netherworld.

These ecstatic techniques, both "objectified" and "interiorized," have played an outstanding role in religious experience from archaic times to the present. Yet ecstasy, whether in the form of wild Dionysiac frenzy or in the form of the shaman's "objective" journey to the netherworld, has repelled the practical Western mind.

Western Culture. In the history of Western culture from Archaic Greece to the Renaissance, it appears that two religious trends have been particularly important. One of them started in Babylonia, was taken over by the Jews, and from there influenced Christian apocalypses and Muslim legends of Muhammad's ascent. The other originated in Archaic Greece, influenced Plato, was dominant during the Hellenistic period and late antiquity, and reached the late Middle Ages through the bias of scholasticism and the Italian Renaissance through the rediscovery of Platonism.

Greek religions. In Greece, belief and practice concerning catalepsy (state of trance) and the flight of the separable soul, either in space or into another dimension, exists apart from the belief in Dionysos, the ecstatic divinity *par excellence*. Rather, Greek medicine men, known in scholarly literature as *iatromanteis* (from *iatros*, "healer," and *mantis*, "seer"), are connected with Apollo, a divinity dwelling in Hyperborea, the mysterious land of the north.

Abaris, Aristeas, Epimenides, and Hermotimos are reported either to fly or to free their souls and leave their bodies in a state of catalepsy. Specifically, the soul of Aristeas, taking

> **Rituals of ascent involve the living person who makes the heavenly journey in order to become sanctified. . . .**

the form of a raven, was said to travel as far as Hyperborea; the soul of Epimenides, to converse with the gods; and the soul of Hermotimos, to visit faraway places and to record local events of which he could give an accurate description once it came back to its sheath (*vagina*, i. e., the body).

Hellenistic religions. By the end of the first century CE when Plutarch wrote his eschatological myths, the idea of an underground Hades was no longer fashionable. Plutarch's ambition was to give a "modern" version of the great myths of Plato. Accordingly, Plato's eschatology was transformed to meet the intellectual exigencies of the time.

Very interesting details about catalepsy and incubation are given by Plutarch in his dialogue *On Socrates' Daemon*, based on traditions concerning the famous oracular cave of Trophonius at Lebadea, ten miles from Chaeronea. The hero of this apocalypse is Timarch of Chaeronea, whose soul leaves his body through the *sutura frontalis* and visits the heavenly Hades, remaining below the sphere of the moon, which is only the first among the seven planetary spheres. In this dialogue, as well as in the dialogue *On the Face in the Moon*, the moon is the receptacle of the souls that are freed of their bodies, apart from those souls that fall again into the circle of transmigration (*metensomatosis*). The earth is viewed here as the lowest and meanest point of the universe; accordingly, the underground Hades and Tartarus of the Platonic myths are no longer needed.

Judaism. The heavenly journey belongs to the constant pattern of Jewish and Jewish-Christian apocalypses, beginning with *1 Enoch*, the oldest parts of which were completed at the end of the third century BCE. The voyage through seven or three heavens became a commonplace of Jewish apocalyptic literature with the *Testaments of the Twelve Patriarchs* (second century BCE.) Seven (heavens or palaces) is the number that prevails in the Jewish tradition of mysticism

related to the merkavah, the chariot carrying God's throne in the vision of Ezekiel (*Ez.* 1).

Iranian religions. Ecstatic experiences induced by hallucinogens seem to be attested to in pre-Zoroastrian Iran. Among the drugs used, two have been identified as being extracted from henbane *(Hyoscyamus niger)* and hemp *(Cannabis indica)*, both called in Middle Persian *bang* (Av., *banha*; cf. Skt. *bhang*). Zoroastrian reform was directed against wild ecstasy, but the Younger Avestan priests reintroduced the use of *bang*, *mang*, and *hom* (Av., *haoma*; cf. Skt. *soma*); these were sometimes mixed with wine.

Islam. The Mi`raj, or ascent of the prophet Muhammad, is extant in three principal groups of Arabic testimonies from the eighth and ninth centuries CE.

Accompanied by the archangel Gabriel, the Prophet is transported to the first heaven either on Buraq (a sort of winged horse) or in a tree growing with vertiginous speed up to the sky. They stop ten to fifteen times, but only the first seven or eight halts represent the "heavens." According to Jewish tradition, these heavens are never associated with the seven "planets" and therefore should not be called "astronomical heavens," as is done now and then in scholarly literature.

Medieval Christianity. Late Hellenistic Christian apocalypses continued to play an important role during the Middle Ages. Very influential was the Latin Vision of Esdra, known in a tenth-century manuscript. The *Vision of Alberic* (1127), written by a monk of Montecassino, contains an episode in which the soul of Alberic, then a boy of ten, is carried by a dove through the planetary heavens up to the throne of God. The order of the heavens is strange (Moon, Mars, Mercury, Sun, Jupiter, Venus, Saturn) and seems to reflect a failed attempt to integrate two traditions: the Jewish-Christian-Muslim on the one hand and the Hellenistic-Hermetic-Neoplatonic on the other. Attempts at such integration did not meet with full success until Dante's Commedia in the early fourteenth century.

BIBLIOGRAPHY

The best single book on shamanism and related phenomena in different religious contexts remains Mircea Eliade's *Shamanism: Archaic Techniques of Ecstasy*, rev. & enl. ed. (New York, 1964). The best book on yoga techniques viewed in a broad historico-religious scope is still Mircea Eliade's *Yoga: Immortality and Freedom*, 2d ed. (Princeton, 1969).

An up-to-date bibliographic survey of the problem of heavenly ascension from Archaic Greece to the medieval apocalypses is included in my work *Psychanodia I: A Survey of the Evidence Concerning the Ascension of the Soul and Its Relevance* (Leiden, 1983). The texts receive an elaborated comment in my *Expériences de l'extase* (Paris, 1984).

Several materials related to ascension in gnosticism and late antiquity are to be found in *The Origins of Gnosticism*, edited by Ugo Bianchi (1967; reprint, Leiden, 1970); *Studies in Gnosticism and Hellenistic Religions*, edited by R. Van den Broek and Maarten J.

Vermaseren (Leiden, 1981); and *La soteriologia dei culti orientali nell'Impero Romano*, edited by Ugo Bianchi and Maarten J. Vermaseren (Leiden, 1982). On the mysteries of Mithra and heavenly ascension, the most fascinating book remains Robert Turcan's *Mithras platonicus: Recherches sur l'hellénisation philosophique de Mithra* (Leiden, 1975). Unfortunately, Turcan's theory does not seem to stand up to the challenge of recent research. On Macrobius and the passage of the soul through the spheres, a good survey is Jacques Flamant's *Macrobe et le néo-platonisme latin, à la fin du quatrième siècle* (Leiden, 1977).

A good survey of the Jewish mysticism of the *merkavah* is Ithamar Gruenwald's *Apocalyptic and Merkavah Mysticism* (Leiden, 1980). A good bibliography concerning heavenly ascent in Iran is given in Gherardo Gnoli's *Zoroaster's Time and Homeland* (Naples, 1980).

There is no up-to-date work on the Mi`raj. Those interested in the topic must still rely on D. Miguel Asín Palacios's *La escatologia musulmana en la Divina comedia, seguida de la historia y crítica de una polémica*, 2d ed. (Madrid, 1943), translated by Harold Sunderland as *Islam and the Divine Comedy* (London, 1926), and Enrico Cerulli's Il *"Libro della Scala": La questione delle fonti arabo-spagnole della Divina Commedia* (Vatican City, 1949) and *Nuove ricerche sul "Libro della Scala" e la conoscenza dell'Islam in Occidente* (Vatican City, 1972).

A good survey of the most important medieval visions and apocalypses is given in Jacques Le Goff's *La naissance du Purgatoire* (Paris, 1981).

On the Renaissance theory of the spiritual vehicle of the soul from Ficino to Campanella, the best book remains Daniel P. Walker's *Spiritual and Demonic Magic: From Ficino to Campanella* (London, 1958). It should be supplemented by my article "Magia spirituale e magia demonica nel Rinascimento," *Biblioteca della Rivista di storia e letteratura religiosa* 17 (1981): 360-408.

IOAN PETRU CULIANU

ATHEISM

The term *atheism* is employed in a variety of ways. For the purpose of the present survey atheism is the doctrine that God does not exist, that belief in the existence of God is a false belief. The word God here refers to a divine being regarded as the independent creator of the world, a being superlatively powerful, wise, and good.

Classical Forms in Eastern Religious Thought. Skepticism about the existence of a god, even the king of gods, and the emergence of impersonal conceptions of the ultimate ground of the universe is not yet atheism, as defined above. Such conceptions have yet to advance arguments that belief in God is a false belief. Such arguments begin to appear where emerging theistic conceptions of God and impersonal conceptions of the absolute source and rule of the world confront one another as philosophical options over an extended period of time.

Heterodox Indian thought. Of the heterodox Indian schools, the Carvaka represents the most radical departure from the tenor of religious thought in the Upanisads. It holds that the Vedas are the work of knaves and fools, and it rejects all sources of knowledge other than the senses. With this, it rejects the principles of inference upon which the Nyaya-Vaisesika school depends to demonstrate the existence of God. The Carvaka holds that the visible world alone exists. The exponents of the Carvaka reject the doctrine of the soul and with it the ideas of *karman* and rebirth. They reject all forms of religious asceticism and hold that religious rites are incapable of any effect.

By contrast, the Jains endorse an intensely ascetic path to the release of the soul *(jiva)* from an otherwise endless cycle of rebirth. According to the Jains, the soul, by nature, is eternal, perfectly blissful, and omniscient. Yet in consequence of accumulated *karman*, conceived as a subtle material substance, all but liberated souls are ensnared in a limiting material body.

The Jains depict the cosmos as uncreated and eternal. They therefore require no doctrine of God in order to explain its existence. Their points against theistic ideas are expressed in differing versions of arguments developed over centuries of dispute.

Unlike the Jains, who accept the reality of the material world, the Buddhists hold that all that can be said to have being is but part of a succession of impermanent phenomena, call *dharmas*. To this way of thinking, the idea of a changeless God is clearly out of place.

Atheism and Religious Thought in Western Philosophy. Religious forms of atheism in India appeared in a context in which differing conceptions of deity and of the ultimate source and order of the universe were each capable of supporting an integrated system of religious thought and action. Early periods of Western thought manifested similarly differing conceptions of deity and of the ultimate ground of all that exists. But just as Chinese intellectual history came to be dominated by the impersonal conception of the natural order of the world, so the personal conception of deity gradually achieved ascendency in the West.

Ancient Greece. The religion of ancient Greece depicted in the poetry of Homer (eighth century BCE) revolved around a pantheon of gods presided over by the sky god Zeus, who was seen not as a creator but as the upholder of moral order. The gods, here associated with various aspects of the universe, are represented as superhuman immortal beings endowed with human passions, frequently behaving in undignified and amoral ways. Nevertheless, the worship of these gods in temples and other holy places, especially by means of sacrifice, constituted the state religion of Greece throughout the Classical period.

Early Christianity. Contemporary research on Christian origins suggests that early Christianity did not unanimously appropriate the view of God set forth in the Hebrew scriptures. A pervading theme of the gnostic literature that circulated widely in early Christian communities is that the world is an untoward environment. It is not the work of an omnipotent and benevolent being but the result of a divine fault. Its creator is unworthy of the religious devotion of man and an obstacle to the religious goal of liberation from the present evil world. The ultimate reality, on the other hand, is not to be thought of as a God at all. It is referred to as the unknown One, the unfathomable, the incomprehensible. Occasionally, this reality is spoken of paradoxically as the One that exists in nonbeing existence. Although, by the fourth century, gnosticism was condemned as unorthodox by a majority of Christian churches, it is undeniable that it represented for its adherents a religious way of life.

The attack upon theism. Since the seventeenth century this conception of God and the arguments that claimed to demonstrate his existence have been subject to persistent attack. In the first place, because Thomas took the physics of Aristotle as the basis for his understanding of cause and motion, his arguments were less capable of supporting theistic belief once Aristotle's views on these matters were supplanted by those of Isaac Newton (1642-1727). For Aristotle, an explanation is required both for the initiation and for the continuance of change. The first mover of Thomas, since it is taken as both initiating and continuing change, supports the view of God both as creator and governor of the universe. Newton's first law of motion, on the other hand, holds that a body will remain at rest or in continuous motion in the same direction unless it is subject to a contravening force. When the idea was developed by Pierre-Simon de Laplace (1749-1827) that the world is a regular and perfectly determinate system, the idea of God as the source of its movement was rendered superfluous. Moreover, once the idea of the universe as a perfect system was established, eternal existence could be attributed to the material world, as in the work of Paul-Henri d'Holbach (1723-1789). Theistic arguments were further eroded by the view articulated by David Hume (1711-1776) that cause itself is but an immanent habit of thought and not a necessary relation between substances or events. With this the possibility of inferring the existence of God from any classical form of a causal argument was undermined.

Influenced by Hume and others, Immanuel Kant (1724-1804), in his famous *Critique of Pure Reason* (1781), gathered the substance of various arguments for the existence of God into three. (1) The ontological argument proceeds from the idea of God to the existence of God. It holds that this idea is such that the nonexistence of God would not be possible. (2) The cosmological argument proceeds from the fact of the existence of the world to the existence of God as the sufficient reason or the ultimate cause of its being. (3) The physico-theological argument proceeds from the evident order, adaptation, or purposefulness of the world to the existence of an intelligent being who made it.

None of these arguments, in the view of Kant, is adequate to prove the existence of God. The ontological argument treats existence as though it could be the property of an idea. The cosmological argument posits the first cause only to avoid an infinite chain of causal relations. And it presupposes the validity of the ontological argument in its use of the category of a necessary being as the first cause. The physico-theological argument presupposes the validity of the first two, but even if accepted could prove only the existence of a designer or architect of the universe and not a creator.

Kant denies, however, that this analysis should lead us to the conclusion that God does not exist. In his *Critique of Practical Reason* (1778), he argues that it is in the domain of moral action that religious ideas have their real significance, and it is here that belief in God can be justified on rational grounds. The substance of his argument is that it is necessary to postulate freedom, immortality, and God in order to live reasonably according to the "moral law within."

It was precisely the transposition of religious ideas from the realm of metaphysics to the realm of practical reason, the idea of belief in God as the support for moral action, that attracted the most violent assault upon theistic ideas in the following generation. Its significance for the nineteenth century is indicated in the view of Ludwig Feuerbach (1804-1872), who argues (1) that religion is the "dream of man," in which he projects his own infinite nature as a being beyond himself and then perceives himself as the object of this projected being; (2) that such a being, as "a contradiction to reason and morality," is quite inadequate to support a genuine human community; and (3) that a new philosophy based upon the being of man must unmask the essential nature of religion, which is to alienate man from himself, and replace theology with the humanistic underpinning for an ethically legitimate order.

Karl Marx (1818-1883) concurred in the judgment that religion is a symptom of alienation. But he argued that a merely intellectual liberation from religion would be unable to bring about the kind of human community that Feuerbach had envisioned. Religion, he argued, is an instrument of economic control. By its construction of an illusory happiness religion presents an obstacle to the liberation of the alienated worker from economic exploitation in the real, that is the material, world. Later in the century Friedrich Nietzsche (1844-1900) articulated a view of the moral significance of theistic faith very different from that of Marx. Yet it is no less hostile to theistic belief. The God of the Judeo-Christian tradition, he held, is the support of a slave morality. God was the instrument of the weak in inflicting a bad conscience upon the powerful and healthy and thus undermining their vitality and love of life.

The twentieth century. To the attack upon theism since the seventeenth century, theologians have responded in a variety of ways. Those of the present century can be discussed as two opposing types: (1) those who continue to affirm the existence of God as the superlatively wise, powerful, and benevolent creator of the world and (2) those who do not affirm the existence of such a God or who even openly deny it. It is within this latter group that the most recent forms of religious atheism are found. The first type includes the revival of scholasticism in Roman Catholic and Anglican theological circles, which was accorded official ecclesiastical support during the First Vatican Council (1870). Among the most influential of these theists were Reginald Marie Garrigou-Lagrange (1877-1964), Jacques Maritain (1882-1973), and Étienne Gilson (1884-1978). Central to this response was a reaffirmation of metaphysics and of the importance of natural theology, at least in the sense of a rational structuring of the truths received through revelation and a clarification of these truths in terms of ordinary experience.

A second movement that belongs to this type, neoorthodoxy, dominated Protestant thought during the first half of the century, especially after World War I. Rejecting the prevalent themes of nineteenth-century Protestant thought, neoorthodoxy rediscovered the personal God of the Bible and the Protestant reformers. It repudiated efforts to find God through human effort, and instead affirmed that he is to be known through his revelation attested in sacred scripture and by means of the obedience of faith. The God of Karl Barth (1886-1968), the most influential exponent of this movement, is a God who exists, who lives, and who has made himself known through mighty acts in history of which the Bible is witness.

A reply to the attack upon theism very different from all of these was developed in the thought of Paul Tillich (1886-1965). It centers upon his view of faith as a state of "being concerned ultimately." This view of faith, according to Tillich, transcends the three fundamental kinds of theism that have been the object of secular attack. (1) "Empty theism" is the affirmation of God employed by politicians and dictators to

> **The experience of divine forgiveness is subject to psychological explanation, and the idea of sin appears relative at best and meaningless at worst.**

produce the impression that they are moral and worthy of trust. (2) Theism as "divine-human encounter" found in the Bible and among the reformers is the immediate certainty of divine forgiveness that is independent of moral, intellectual, or religious preconditions. The experience of divine forgiveness is subject to psychological explanation, and the idea of sin appears relative at best and meaningless at worst. (3) "Theological theism" tries by means of the various proofs for the existence of God to transform the divine-human

encounter into a doctrine about two different beings that have existence independent of one another. Under the gaze of such a being of infinite knowledge and power the alienated human being is deprived of freedom and creativity. Against this kind of theism, says Tillich, the atheism of the nineteenth century was a justified response.

What Tillich calls "absolute faith," on the other hand, accepts and affirms despair and in so doing finds meaning within the disintegration of meaning itself. In "absolute faith" the depth and power of being is revealed in which the negation of being is embraced. Its object is the "God beyond God," the God who appears when the God of theism has disappeared in the anxiety of meaninglessness and doubt. This God is not a being but the ground of Being itself.

The "death of God" theology was a heterogeneous movement encompassing a variety of issues upon which its members often disagreed. Besides the question of God, it was concerned with a variety of forms of alienation within the Christian community, with the significance of the secular world and its intellectual norms, and with the significance for theology of the person and work of Jesus. The movement received its name from the title of a work published in 1961 by Gabriel Vahanian that announced the death of God as a cultural fact, the fact acknowledged by Bonhoeffer and Robinson that modern man functions intellectually and socially without God as a working hypothesis. This cultural fact, for Vahanian, implies a loss of the sense of transcendence and the substitution of a radically immanentist perspective in dealing with questions of human existence. That the death of God has occurred as a cultural fact in no way implies for him, however, that God himself has ceased to exist. God is, and remains, infinite and wholly other, still calling humanity to existential and cultural conversion. Vahanian's concern is for a transfiguration of culture in which the living God is freed from the false images that have reified him.

Vahanian's view of the reality of God sets him clearly apart from other persons associated with the death of God. For Paul M. Van Buren, writing in 1965, the issue for theology is how the modern Christian, who is in fact a secular being, can understand faith in a secular way. Taking his method from the philosophical tradition known as language analysis, he argues that not only the God of theism but also any other conception of God has been rendered meaningless to the modern mind. He concludes that when the language of Christian faith is sorted out, the gospel can be interpreted as the expression of a historical perspective concerning Jesus that has wide-ranging empirical consequences for the ethical existence of the Christian.

For William Hamilton, writing at about the same time, the death of God means the loss of the God of theism and the loss of "real transcendence." His response is a new understanding of Protestantism that liberates it from religion—

from, that is, any system of thought or action in which God is seen as fulfilling any sort of need or as solving any human problem, even the problem of the loss of God. Hamilton's Protestant is a person without God, without faith in God, but also a person in protest against release or escape from the world by means of the sacred. He is a person led into the affairs of the world and into solidarity with his neighbor, in whom he encounters Jesus and where alone he can become Jesus to the world.

In the thought of Vahanian, Van Buren, and Hamilton, the death of God is a metaphor. In the work of Thomas J. J. Altizer, on the other hand, the death of God is to be taken literally. In a work published in 1967 he seems to be saying both that God did once exist and that he really did cease to exist. He believes that the death of God is decisive for theology because in it God has reconciled himself with the world. God, the sovereign and transcendent Lord of the Christian tradition, has taken the form of a servant and entered the world through Christ. With this, the realm of the transcendent and supernatural has become empty and God has died. With the death of God, we are liberated from fears and inhibitions imposed upon us by an awesome mystery beyond.

BIBLIOGRAPHY

The idea that civilization begins at a stage at which the concept of God is absent is developed by David Hume in *The Natural History of Religion* (1757), edited by H. E. Root (Stanford, Calif., 1957). A similar view is developed by John Lubbock in *The Origin of Civilisation and the Primitive Condition of Man* (1870), edited by Peter Rivière (Chicago, 1978). An excellent contemporary study of the significance of God in traditional African religion is John S. Mbiti's *Concepts of God in Africa* (New York, 1970). See also Åke Hultkrantz's *Belief and Worship in Native North America* (Syracuse, N. Y., 1981). Both of these works contain excellent bibliographies. The question whether native peoples are without a concept of God has received new interest in light of John Nance's *The Gentle Tasaday* (New York, 1975).

The most thorough work on the classical philosophies of India remains Surendranath Dasgupta's *A History of Indian Philosophy*, 5 vols. (Cambridge, 1922-1955). Nikunja Vihari Banerjee's *The Spirit of Indian Philosophy* (New Delhi, 1974) is a thoroughly readable introduction containing a useful discussion of arguments for and against the existence of God in Indian thought. Ninian Smart's *Doctrine and Argument in Indian Philosophy* (London, 1964) presents the substance of Indian metaphysics in language accessible to the Western reader. It contains also a useful glossary and bibliography. More specialized studies include Kewal Krishnan Mittal's *Materialism in Indian Thought* (Delhi, 1974); Dale Riepe's *The Naturalistic Tradition in Indian Thought* (Seattle, 1961); and Helmuth von Glasenapp's *Buddhism: A Non-Theistic Religion* (New York, 1966). A useful selection of relevant original texts is presented in translation in *A Source Book in Indian Philosophy*, edited by Sarvepalli Radhakrishnan and Charles A. Moore (Princeton, 1957). A concise introduction to Chinese thought is presented in Fung Yu-lan's *A Short History of Chinese Philosophy* (New York, 1948), which offers a short bibliography.

Relevant works on ancient Greek material include Roy K. Hack's *God in Greek Philosophy* (Princeton, 1931), which contains a selected bibliography, and Anders B. Drachmann's *Atheism in Pagan Antiquity* (1922; Chicago, 1977), which provides extensive notes. For a scholarly treatment of the concept of God in ancient Israel, see William F. Albright's *Yahweh and the Gods of Canaan* (London, 1968) and Harold H. Rowley's *The Faith of Israel: Aspects of Old Testament Thought* (London, 1956). Elaine H. Pagels's *The Gnostic Gospels* (New York, 1979) is an introduction to gnostic Christian literature based on the recent discoveries at Nag Hammadi, Egypt. The development of theism, from Augustine to its criticism through the nineteenth century, is thoroughly discussed in Frederick C. Copleston's *A History of Philosophy*, 8 vols. (New York, 1946-1966). A concise introduction to the development of the Christian idea of God is found in the article "God" in *The Oxford Dictionary of the Christian Church*, 2d ed., edited by Frank Leslie Cross and Elizabeth A. Livingston (London, 1974), which contains a useful bibliography. For a thorough discussion of contemporary developments in theology, including the theology of the "death of God," see Langdon Gilkey's *Naming the Whirlwind: The Renewal of God-language* (Indianapolis, 1969).

Finally, a useful reference work is *The Encyclopedia of Unbelief*, 2 vols., edited by Gordon Stein (New York, 1985). Although clearly focused on the West, it includes a broad range of articles on various forms of unbelief in most parts of the world.

GEORGE ALFRED JAMES

ATONEMENT

Jewish Concepts

Jewish conceptions of atonement consist of various strands reflecting the plurality of connotations of the Hebrew term *kipper* ("to make atonement").

Confession is specifically mandated by the Torah in conjunction with the expiatory rites performed by the high priest on the Day of Atonement as well as with the sacrifice called the *asham* (guilt offering). Rabbinic Judaism construes this latter requirement as paradigmatic for all types of sacrifices offered with the intent to secure forgiveness, expiation, or atonement for sins. Unless preceded by confession, any *hat'at* (sin offering) or *asham* would be stigmatized as "a sacrifice of the wicked which is an abomination" (B. T., *Shav.* 12b).

Repentance. For all the emphasis upon *teshuvah*—the psychological transformation of the self wrought by human effort—one essential component of the traditional view is the notion that divine mercy is necessary to heal or redeem man from the dire aftereffects of sin. Because any transgression of a divine commandment through sins of omission or commission constitutes an offense against God and damages a person's relationship with the Creator, divine grace is required to achieve full atonement. It is for this reason that prayers for atonement are an integral part of the *teshuvah* process.

Expiation and Grace. The rabbinic tenet that "the dead require atonement" (*Sifrei Shoftim* 210) is further evidence that atonement is not merely a function of repentance. Repentance is only feasible for the living, yet Judaism encourages practices such as offering of charity, prayer, or Torah study in behalf of the deceased.

Proper atonement calls for human initiative in returning to God, who will respond by completing the process of purification, ultimately leading to the reintegration of the fragmented human self and resulting in the restoration of a wholesome relationship between man and God.

BIBLIOGRAPHY

Studies in Sin and Atonement in the Rabbinic Literature of the First Century by Adolf Büchler (Oxford, 1928) is a pioneering but somewhat dated exposition of rabbinic conceptions of atonement. A thorough analysis of biblical conceptions in the light of recent research may be found in Herbert Chanan Brichto's "On Slaughter and Sacrifice, Blood and Atonement," *Hebrew Union College Annual* 47 (1976): 19-55. Two pieces by Jacob Milgrom, "Kipper" and "Repentance," in the *Encyclopaedia Judaica* (Jerusalem, 1971), are very useful as introductions to biblical and postbiblical conceptions of atonement. A phenomenological study of Jewish conceptions of atonement and repentance by preeminent philosopher and authority on Jewish law is Joseph Ber Soloveitchik's `Al ha-teshuvah*, edited by Pinchas H. Peli (Jerusalem, 1974). This work has been recently translated into English by Pinchas H. Peli as *Soloveitchik: On Repentance* (Ramsey, N. J., 1984).

WALTER S. WURZBURGER

Christian Concepts

The Gospels and Jesus' Teaching. By parable and by direct discourse Jesus taught forgiveness of sins, relating God's forgiveness to forgivingness between people. Controversy swirled around Jesus' authoritative absolutions, a situation that perhaps more than any other raised for his Jewish hearers the question of his divine status or blasphemy. He regarded his death as likely not simply because many prophets had been martyred for the unpopularity of their message but because he saw it as controlled in some way by a divine must, as a decisive part of his mission to inaugurate the kingdom of God: "For the Son of man also came not to be served but to serve, and to give his life as a ransom (*lutron*) for many" (*Mk.* 10:45).

There is no single New Testament doctrine of the Atonement—there is simply a collection of images and metaphors with some preliminary analysis and reflection from which subsequent tradition built its systematic doctrines and theories. The New Testament asserts that God was in Christ reconciling the world to himself in such a way that the act resembled a military victory, a king establishing his power, a judge and prisoner in a law court, a great ritual sacrifice before priest and altar, the payment of ransom for war prisoners or the payment of a redemption for a slave's freedom, the admission to responsible sonship within a family, and more.

A Typology of Atonement Theories. Gustaf Aulén in his classic *Christus Victor* (1930) suggested three basic types of atonement theory: the classical type, the Latin type, and the subjective type.

Classical theories of atonement. Aulén looked behind the dramatic mythology of the Greek fathers to find the theme of Christus Victor, a view that he claimed integrates ideas of the Incarnation, Atonement, and Resurrection into a unified concept of salvation. One version of the theory had the devil unjustly in possession of humanity; another affirmed the justice of the devil's hold; still another claimed that although the devil had no rights, God graciously withheld from forcibly stripping him of his gains. Special strategies against the devil were the mousetrap (the humanity of Christ as bait to hide his divinity) and Augustine's fishhook play.

Anselmian theories of atonement. *Cur deus homo* (Why the God-man?), written by Anselm, archbishop of Canterbury, in about 1097, is the single most influential book on the Atonement. Anselm criticized all ransom-to-the-devil theories by turning them upside down and asserting that the ransom, which Anselm called "satisfaction," must be paid to God.

Reformation theories of atonement. The Reformation opted for Anselm's unused alternative of punishment. John Calvin in the sixteenth century emphasized Christ's vicarious and substitutionary endurance of God's punishment on behalf of humankind or of the elect. The dominance of Anselmian analysis in Reformation orthodoxy and the Counter-Reformation can be demonstrated by showing that for the Roman Catholic the Atonement continued to be the basis for the ecclesiastical apparatus that mediated salvation while for the Protestant, looking at the Atonement through the doctrine of justification by faith, it became the reason for rejecting that whole apparatus as unnecessary.

Moral-influence theories. Theories of moral influence describe the Atonement as something accomplished in the hearts and minds of those who respond to Jesus' message and example of love. The strength of this view lies in its primary emphasis upon the love of God rather than on God's wrath or justice. The intrinsic weakness of such theories lies in the widespread perception that such declarations by themselves have little power to free the sinner when they alone are seen as constituting the sum total of atonement rather than part of a total atoning activity initiated and carried through by Christ's action.

Few doctrines of Christian faith have produced more theories than the doctrine of atonement, a fact that testifies to the witness of scripture, in which Christ's death is given decisive reconciling power and meaning, but no one theory or family of theories is presented as alone authoritative. The doctrine of atonement is the Christian answer to the human questions about ignorance, suffering, death, and sin, but always the alienation caused by sin is considered more basic than the three other evils.

BIBLIOGRAPHY

Anselm. *Why God Became Man and The Virgin Conception and Original Sin.* Translated with introduction and notes by Joseph M. Colleran. Albany, N.Y., 1969. An accessible and surprisingly readable edition of the most influential book on the Atonement.

Aulén, Gustaf. *Christus Victor: An Historical Study of the Three Main Types of the Idea of the Atonement.* Translated by A. G. Herbert. 1931; reprint, London, 1945. Already a classic in its own right, Aulén's work, which appeared originally in 1930 in Swedish, presents the classic view of the Atonement articulately and with the conviction that the Latin and subjective types are destined to become its satellites.

Barth, Karl. *Church Dogmatics IV: The Doctrine of Reconciliation.* 3 vols. in 4. Translated by G. W. Bromiley. Edinburgh, 1956-1962. Within the larger Barthian corpus these writings on reconciliation and atonement constitute a summa of some 2,600 pages, with impressive interpretations of scripture and footnotes on the history of doctrine.

Dillistone, Frederick W. *The Christian Understanding of Atonement.* Philadelphia, 1968. A comprehensive book analyzing alienation as a problem in human life, with contemporary illustrations from literature, history, psychology, anthropology, and philosophy.

Franks, Robert S. *The Work of Christ: A Historical Study of Christian Doctrine.* New York, 1962. This is a later edition, in one volume, of Franks's earlier definitive work *A History of the Doctrine of the Work of Christ,* 2 vols. (London, 1918).

Leivestad, Ragnar. *Christ the Conqueror: Ideas of Conflict and Victory in the New Testament.* London, 1954. An impressive documentation of the New Testament origins of Aulén's earlier thesis about the classic theory of the Atonement.

Masure, Eugene. *The Christian Sacrifice: The Sacrifice of Christ Our Head.* London, 1944. A point of transition in Roman Catholic writing on the Atonement from the older Anselmian rationale for sacrifice to the new theology on sacrifice that is drawn from scriptural, patristic, and liturgical renewal prior to Vatican II.

Sölle, Dorothee. *Christ the Representative.* London, 1967. A sustained analysis of the kind of representative office that Christ performs, much influenced by Dietrich Bonhoeffer's thought and the christological title "the man for us."

Taylor, Vincent. *Jesus and His Sacrifice* (1937). Reprint, London, 1951. A helpful study of the passion sayings in the Gospels in the light of the Old Testament and from the perspective of form-criticism. Together with Taylor's later works *The Atonement in New Testament Teaching,* 2d ed. (London, 1946), and *Forgiveness and Reconciliation,* 2d ed. (London, 1952), this book constitutes part of an important trilogy, with an emphasis on a sacrificial understanding of the Atonement.

Wolf, William J. *No Cross, No Crown: A Study of the Atonement.* New York, 1957. A historical survey of the chief theories of atonement and their problems, followed by chapters on deliverance from guilt, justification, sanctification, the atoning God, and the atoning life; an attempt to reformulate an understanding of the Atonement.

WILLIAM J. WOLF

AUGUSTINE OF HIPPO

AUGUSTINE OF HIPPO (354-430), Christian theologian and bishop. A creative genius of mystical piety and great philosophical acumen, Augustine wrought a theological-ecclesiological system in which biblical tradition and classical philosophy coalesced. Not only was his thought seminal for the development of Western Christianity, his moral values and personal piety remained norms for medieval and Reformation Europe.

Augustine's life spanned a crucial epoch in state and church. The late Roman empire was disintegrating, and its collapse would devastate the public sense of political stability and continuity. The Christian church, having weathered persecution, moved into a period of doctrinal and ecclesiastical formation. Punic Africa had no small part in these political and religious affairs, and Augustine's self-proclaimed identity as "an African, writing for Africans . . . . living in Africa" (*Letters* 17.2) must not be overlooked. Indeed, the manner in which Augustine united, in his works and in his person, the various currents of his time has definitely marked Western culture.

Early Life. Augustine, known also as Aurelius Augustinus, was born in Tagaste (present-day Souk-Ahras, Algeria) to a pagan father and a Christian mother, whose influence on Augustine was tremendous. He was convinced that her prayers, piety, and relentless pursuit of his conversion were instrumental in bringing about his life-altering encounter with God.

In his native Africa, Augustine established a lay retreat, a monastery, for philosophical contemplation, based at his small estate at Tagaste. He and his friends aimed to be servants of God. Here he composed *De vera religione* (On True Religion), which takes the Trinity as the foundation for true religion, a theme central to the majority of his works, and sees in Christianity the consummation of Plato's teaching.

Two years after becoming a bishop in 396, Augustine, now forty-three, began his *Confessiones,* a treatise expressing gratitude to God in which he employed intimate autobiographical recollections. He wrote with complete candor, revealing to the world his agonizing struggle with himself, his sexual nature, his self-will, and his pride. His aim was to give God the glory for his redemption, to create a paean of praise and thanksgiving, rejoicing in the grace of a God who had stooped so low to save so fallen a sinner.

Simultaneously, the *Confessions* was a theological work in which Augustine presented his positions on the Incarnation and the Trinity. In the three concluding books he proffered a study on memory, time, and Genesis, weaving the work of the Holy Spirit into the act of creation. He developed in the Confessions the theological direction in which he continued to move, emphasizing divine predestination, personal religious experience through conscious conversion, and the direct relationship of the believer to God. Augustine's opus stands as a masterpiece in the world's devotional literature.

Augustine's advocacy of consistent teachings in the church is exemplified by his contributions to ecclesiology. He defined the status and role of the bishop not only as administrator but as teacher, interpreter, and defender of pure doctrine. A bishop was responsible for determining orthodoxy, through use of the pronouncements of councils as well as scripture, and for eradicating heresy.

In his early work *De libero arbitrio* (On Free Will), written 388-396, Augustine endeavored to explain the apparent contradiction of the existence of evil in the world with the goodness of an omnipotent deity. Evil, Augustine assayed, was the result of Adam's free will. God would not permit man to be completely free without giving him the potentiality of doing wrong or right. From Adam's sin all later humanity inherited the inclination toward evil, thus, all humans since Adam have been sinners. Only God's grace could overcome that propensity.

"Know," said Augustine in *Contra Julianum*, "that good will, that good works, without the grace of God . . . can be granted to no one." Salvation is God's doing. In gratitude the believer lives. The mind as God's creation is endowed with a natural capacity for remembering, understanding, and willing. When these powers are rightly directed, the self will recognize the true order of being, its relation to God in whose image it is. In man's fallen condition, sin holds this natural capacity in abeyance but can never completely destroy it. Grace awakens the dormant power in man to see God's image in himself.

The sacraments. Attendant to Augustine's view of grace is his concept of the church: the earthen vessel for sacramental grace. Sacraments are the work of God, and only in the catholic church do the sacraments attain their appropriate function; there alone can that attesting love be found.

Augustine's list of sacraments holds baptism and the Lord's Supper as preeminent; others are ordination, marriage, exorcism, and the giving of salt to the catechumen. Without the sacraments there is no salvation. "The churches of Christ maintain it to be an inherent principle, that without baptism and partaking of the Supper of the Lord it is impossible for any man to attain either to the kingdom of God or to salvation and everlasting life" (*De peccatorum meritis et remissione*; On the Wages and Remission of Sins 1.34).

Trinity and Christology. Recognized even during his lifetime as a doctor of the Latin church, Augustine clarified numerous points of doctrine.

In his view of the Trinity, Augustine emphasized that there are not three Gods but one. These form a "divine unity of one and the same substance in an indivisible equality." In this Trinity "what is said of each is also said of all, on account of

the indivisible working of the one and same substance" (*Trinity* 1.4.7, 1.12.25). He established a metaphysical ground for the Christian's threefold experience of God. In the Father, the believer knows God as source of being; in Christ, the redeemer; and in the Holy Spirit, the sanctifier.

Augustine declared that the whole of doctrine might be summed up as service to God through faith, hope, and love.

Morality and Ethics. Scrupulous observance of the ethical code was required of Augustine's people, especially his clergy. On one occasion, certain members of Augustine's monastery had not complied with the vow of poverty and at death willed large estates to their families. Augustine reacted swiftly and sternly, requiring that all draw up statements of their holdings prior to being admitted to the order. In his monastery, Augustine established a way of life that was to become the prototype for the cenobite. It is claimed that his own widowed sister, abbess of the convent he established in Hippo, was never permitted to converse with her brother save in the presence of a third party. Augustine's moralism must be seen in the context of his ideal of blessedness. It was said of him, "Everyone who lives with him, lives the life described in the *Acts of the Apostles*" (sermon 356).

Final Years. May of 429 saw the army of Genseric's Vandals cross from Spain and march through Mauretania, spreading havoc and desolation. Roman rule in Africa collapsed. Augustine spent these concluding years comforting and reassuring his people.

As Vandals were besieging Hippo, Augustine was dying, insisting—perhaps for the first time—that he be alone; he read, in these final hours, the penitential psalms hung on the walls of his room. On 28 August 430, while prayers were being offered in the churches of Hippo, Augustine died. It was designated his day in the lexicon of Roman Catholic saints.

Augustine's place in Western history is not to be contested. He was a man of science (in spite of his deprecation of scientific knowledge) whose power to scrutinize nature was remarkable. He engaged in an unrelenting quest for knowledge that rendered him a keen observer of human nature, and he probed the deep recesses of the human soul. Augustine set the compass for much of the Western Christian culture that followed.

BIBLIOGRAPHY

Listing all the worthy studies of Augustine would be difficult, if not impossible. The student of Augustine is apt to be overcome by the sheer enormity of the material available. Only a small selection follows.

Works by Augustine. For the serious student, the Latin works are indispensable. A complete collection appears in *Patrologia Latina*, edited by J.-P. Migne, vols. 32-47 (Paris, 1841-1842). In spite of errors and omissions, Migne's edition remains an essential source, but it should be studied along with Palémon Glorieux's *Pour revaloriser Migne: Tables rectificatives* (Lille, 1952). Augustine's collected works can also be found in *Corpus Scriptorum Ecclesiasticorum*

Latinorum, vols. 12, 25, 28, 33-34, 36, 40-44, 51-53, 57-58, 60, 63, 74, 77, and 84-85 (Vienna, 1866-1876), which is the product of good critical scholarship.

Splendid translations into modern English, reflecting superior contemporary scholarship, can be found in "The Library of Christian Classics," edited by John Baillie and others, vols. 6-8 (Philadelphia, 1953-1958); "The Fathers of the Church," edited by Roy Joseph Deferrari, vols. 1-15, 17-18, and 35 (New York, 1947-1963); and "Ancient Christian Writers," edited by Johannes Quasten and Walter J. Burghardt, vols. 2, 9, 15, 22, and 35 (Westminster, Md., 1960-). The several texts are strengthened in their overall usefulness by an impressive amount of supportive background data, copious explanatory notes, full bibliographies, and indexes.

Works about Augustine. Classic works by eminent scholars such as Prosper Alfaric, Adolf von Harnack, and Otto Scheel continue to be mandatory reading for the thoughtful student. Among the most recent publications, Karl Adam's *Die geistige Entwicklung des heiligen Augustinus* (Augsburg, 1931) is a superb work with bibliographical references that are especially helpful. *A Companion to the Study of St. Augustine*, edited by Roy W. Battenhouse (New York, 1955), presents a series of scholarly essays, especially helpful as broad, introductory works. Gerald Bonner's *St. Augustine of Hippo: Life and Controversies* (London, 1963) provides a survey of the enormous literary output of Augustine.

Possidius's fifth-century *Sancti Augustini vita scripta a Possidio episcopo* (Kiel, 1832) is the original biography by one who stood in awe of his subject. Filled with human interest stories, it nonetheless should not be missed. Peter Brown's *Augustine of Hippo* (London, 1967) is unquestionably the best biography available. His *Religion and Society in the Age of Saint Augustine* (London, 1972) is of equally fine scholarship and is indispensable for an understanding of the period. My own *Augustine: His Life and Thought* (Atlanta, 1980) is a lively biography, portraying Augustine against the backdrop of the tumultuous age in which he lived. Frederik van der Meer's *Augustine the Bishop* (London, 1961) is an interpretation of Augustine's episcopate and the cultural milieu.

Étienne Gilson's *The Christian Philosophy of Saint Augustine* (New York, 1960) is an outstanding study of the overall thought of Augustine. A wide range of scholarly articles can be found in *Augustine: A Collection of Critical Essays*, edited by Robert A. Markus (Garden City, N. Y., 1972). Ragnar Holte's *Béatitudes et sagesse: S. Augustin et le problème de la fin de l'homme dans la philosophie ancienne* (Paris, 1962) concentrates on Augustine as philosopher. John Burnaby's *Amor Dei: A Study of the Religion of St. Augustine* (London, 1938) is outstanding, especially in interpreting Augustine's theological understanding of love. Pierre Courcelle's *Recherches sur les Confessiones de S. Augustin* (Paris, 1950) provides one of the best interpretations of the Confessions.

Henri Irénée Marrou's *St. Augustine and His Influence through the Ages* (New York, 1957), Karl Jaspers's *Plato and Augustine* (New York, 1962), and Eugene TeSelle's *Augustine the Theologian* (New York, 1970) are excellent studies of various aspects of Augustine's philosophy and theology. Robert Meagher's *An Introduction to Augustine* (New York, 1978) provides new translations of important passages that are clues to fresh interpretations of Augustine's spiritual life.

Finally, Tarsicius J. van Bavel's *Répertoire bibliographique de Saint Augustin, 1950-1960* (Steenbrugis, Netherlands, 1963) is a useful survey of recent critical studies.

WARREN THOMAS SMITH

AUSTRALIAN RELIGIONS

An Overview

A Living Traditional Religion. Throughout Aboriginal Australia, we could speak of one religion with many differing sociocultural manifestations: basic religious concepts are the same, but there is also considerable variation. Several factors contributed to this seeming diversity. There were regional differences not only in language and in social organization but also in terrain and in climatic conditions. Religious responses to environmental factors are probably just as significant as the ways in which different people structure their relations within and between social groups, categorizing persons they regard as kin and defining those who are responsible for arranging and performing religious rites. Within the range of possible religious content, local aesthetic styles emphasize or select some elements rather than others, so that distinctive patterns emerge.

Aboriginal religion was closely and sensitively linked with local group territories and with the particular physiographic features within them. Nevertheless some religious cults, in terms of their ritual and mythic sponsorship, are spatially widespread and mobile. The Kunapipi (Gunabibi), for example, covers some thousands of kilometers, from Arnhem Land to the Western Desert and beyond, assuming different guises but retaining key symbolic representations. More generally, many mythic beings (or deities) in the creative era of the Dreaming traveled over large stretches of country, through several language or dialectal groups. The mythic fact that they were travelers does not negate or diminish their local relevance to particular areas and sites. However, the high level of mythic and ritual mobility may have had a bearing on the development of key religious similarities.

Source of the sacred. Throughout the continent, Aborigines generally believed that the natural world was originally, and essentially, formless. It was there, as a "given," waiting to be activated. Human time began with the emergence and appearance of mythic beings or gods, in human or other forms. They moved across the country, meeting other characters, changing the contours and shapes of the land and imbuing it with specific meanings. Everywhere they went, whatever they left behind them contained something of their own mythic or sacred essence. Some of them were responsible for creating the first people, the far-distant forebears of contemporary Aborigines. They put such people at places that were to be their "estates," or local group territories, noting the customs they were to follow, the languages they were to speak, and the rites they would have to perform. When those deities "died" physically, or disappeared beyond the sociocultural confines of a particular social unit, or were transformed into something else, they left evidence of their presence on earth in the shape of hills, rocks, paintings, and so on.

These characters themselves, and all that is associated with them, belong to the Dreaming—a time everlasting, eternal. Their spiritual essence lives on at particular sites, within the concept of the Dreaming *and* within the mundane world. However, the idea of a world everlasting depended on them and on the ability of human beings to gain access to the power, the concentrated spiritual quality, that they were believed to possess. This power is, partly, the major concern of the dimension of the sacred: partly, because everything that is either directly or indirectly related to the Dreaming is sacred. And the most sacred of all are the deities themselves. At their sites they remain enshrined in their aura of sacredness, their special power, an ever-present spiritual resource and inspiration for all living things, including human beings.

To understand the idea of the sacred in Aboriginal religion, it is necessary to identify the nature of the power inherent in the deities. Two points are especially relevant to this. First, deities in a spiritual sense are represented in the tangible world by particular creatures or elements. Many of them, not all, were shape-changing, which, in the Dreaming, exemplifies their affinity with nature. They may be simultaneously both human and in the form of an animal or other natural phenomenon. This means that such creatures share the same life force as the deity with which they are associated. Second, in a different sense, human beings also have a direct spiritual relationship with particular deities. Traditional Aborigines believe that no child can be conceived or born without its fetus being first animated through some action relating to a particular mythic character that also involves the child's parents and/or other consanguineous relatives.

For instance, in the central desert area, an unusual event, or one that is interpreted in those terms, must be experienced in order for animation or conception to occur. A man may spear a kangaroo which behaves in a "strange" manner. Later he gives some of the meat to his wife, who vomits after eating it. She may know immediately, or after he has identified the cause in a dream, that a mythic being has either transferred part of his or her sacred essence, via the medium of an intermediary, to the fetus within her or has stimulated or activated the conception. In northeastern Arnhem Land, spirit-landings fulfill this function. Spirit children (or child spirits) are associated with particular water holes or sites and with the relevant mythic beings connected with them. They take the shape of some creature that, when caught, escapes from the hunter or otherwise behaves unusually. Then the spirit child appears to him (or to one of his close sisters or father's sisters) in a dream asking where its mother is. In all such cases, the particular area in which such an incident takes place is of significance in the social and ritual life of the child who is eventually born,

and the area concerned is preferably related to the father's country.

The deities are also responsible for the maintenance of all natural growth, the coming and the going of the seasons, the renewal of the land's fertility, and the replenishment of the species within it. The sites at which the mythic beings reside are reservoirs of this precious force, considered to be an indestructible power that remains unimpaired and active from the beginning of time. However, the power is accessible only in particular circumstances and can be released only by persons who are specifically linked spiritually to the deity concerned. Every region contains a large number of resource centers, each associated with one or more deities or mythic beings. Each of these beings is responsible for particular species—in some cases, for several species. In order to generate seasonal renewal, a fairly wide patterning of ritual cooperation is necessary. This usually involves persons variously associated with differing mythic beings and their representations. The whole country is a living thing: the sites of the deities are latent repositories of life, of particular forms of life, awaiting activation through the intervention of human beings.

While the spiritual animation of a child's fetus might appear to be fortuitous, from an Aboriginal viewpoint it is an essentially predictable occurrence. Two factors need to be taken into account. In the first place, any woman in the appropriate condition is vulnerable when passing near a site where a particular life essence is located. The expectation is that, provided the deity in question is also relevant to her potential child, some event is likely to take place which triggers off the act of animation—or can be interpreted as doing so. The second factor is the actual event itself, an event (that is, consisting of some sign) that must occur before the life essence can be transferred. Thus the life force controlled by a deity is not released automatically: human intervention is necessary, and ritual is the key to that.

Social structuring of religion. Most traditional Aboriginal societies have words that can be translated as "sacred" or "set apart." These imply a special quality which may prove dangerous to persons who do not have the appropriate knowledge and skill and right to handle it. Such words as *mareiin*, *daal*, or *duyu* (in northeastern Arnhem Land), *daragu* or *maia* (in the southeastern Kimberley), *djugurba* or *dumar* (in the Western Desert) or *tjurunga* (in central Australia), and so on refer to particular rituals, emblems, locations or places, songs, objects, or persons who are separated in some way from ordinary everyday affairs. The deities are sacred, as are all things associated with them. The condition of being "set apart" involves particular rules of access and exclusion on the basis of age, sex, and ritual status. However, while such Aboriginal vernacular terms do imply some measure of secrecy, Aborigines do not suggest that their religion is confined solely to that dimension. Religion has a much wider connotation, as does the idea of sacredness. In relation to any one Aboriginal society, all adult members, men and women, have a reasonably good grasp of the main tenets of their religion and what it is intended to achieve. Moreover, although much of the early literature has emphasized men's secret-sacred rituals, there is now recognition of a similar sphere having the same connotation of secrecy in relation to the ritual activities of women (Kaberry, 1939; C. H. Berndt, 1965). What is involved here is a division of labor between the sexes, with each sex being concerned with different but complementary aspects of the same religious system of belief. Each division involves the gradual movement of novices and participants from one level of understanding to the next, and each provides processes that ensure that religious information (*their* information: both general and specific) is handed on from one generation to the next.

With a very few exceptions, the structure of religion in most Aboriginal areas makes it obligatory for men and women to separate on particular occasions as far as their own secret-sacred matters are concerned. Since religion constitutes a celebration in community terms, most large mythic and ritual sequences provide opportunities, and indeed stipulate necessary occasions, for men and women to come together in the performance of ritual and song. Such collective manifestations may take place in a general camping area where a cleared space has been prepared, and they are an integral part of the proceedings. Virtually all of the most important ritual cycles have "inside" and "outside" sections. The efficacy of dramatic performances associated with a ritual sequence would be impaired if, for some reason, they did not incorporate both inside and outside sections.

It is useful to think of Aboriginal religion as including both secret-sacred and open-sacred components. Within the context of the open-sacred dimension, all members of a community participate—men and women, the uninitiated, and children. It is generally agreed, however, that the most spectacular rituals, with the use of a wide range of emblems, are carried out on a corporate basis by fully initiated men on their own secret-sacred ground, which is usually situated away from the main domestic camping areas. Less obtrusive, but no less significant religiously, are the rituals that women in certain regions organize and perform on their own secret-sacred ground. Both concern the same religious mythology, but in partly differing interpretative frames. Each draws on the life-giving properties inherent in such ritual sequences and pays special attention to relationships with particular land.

Two further, mutually exclusive, points should be noted about the secret-sacred grounds of men and women. First, it would be unthinkable in a traditional context for a man to enter or even go near the ground that is set aside for women-only affairs or for a woman to encroach on a men-only domain. Should that occur, even inadvertently, insofar as a

woman is concerned it would have once meant her death by spearing or through sorcery. In any case, the sacred grounds of men and women are mostly regarded as being dangerous to members of the opposite sex. Not all adults of the relevant sex can freely enter the men's or women's secret-sacred ground; entry rests on invitation from those persons who are authorized to give it. The right to enter is dependent, for

> It is useful to think of Aboriginal religion as including both secret-sacred and open-sacred components.

instance, on a person's position in the religious hierarchy or on the degree of familiarity he or she has with the ritual and songs. Only religious leaders and fully initiated men (or women, in their sphere) could go freely to their own ground.

The second point is that most of the large ritual sequences, which traditionally continued over a period of several weeks, usually contained both secret- and open-sacred components. This called for a great deal of preparation. Emblems had to be made or refurbished, the secret-sacred ground had to be attended to, and invitations had to be sent to people in surrounding areas. Not least, food had to be collected and prepared, usually by women. However, specified men would be sent out fairly regularly in order to supplement the diet with meat. Men of ritual importance—who by reason of their spiritual linkage with a particular mythic being are "owners" of the appropriate territorial and myth and ritual combination—act in a directive role. Chronological age is not crucial in this respect. Other things being equal, religious authority devolves upon a man who has considerable religious experience and knowledge as well as influence in his community. Such men are usually middle-aged or a little older. The efficacy of a ritual depends on them. They are the directors, supervising the actual performances that are carried out by the so-called workers, but in a different ritual sequence, controlled by other owners, their roles will be reversed. Any large ritual enterprise is a cooperative undertaking by members of the home camp as well as by visitors from adjacent areas.

Formal exposure to religion. An initiation sequence would normally attract quite a large number of visitors who are specially invited to attend and to participate. A person's initiation really commences with the events surrrounding his or her conception. Those events are ritualized to the extent that they constitute a personal experience with minimal social involvement. Nevertheless, this represents an essential stage in the progression of life because it transfers to the potential social being a sacred quality that is also a hallmark of humanity. Where physical birth is concerned, no such ritual dramatization takes place: it is simply regarded as a natural ritual in itself. In other words, in this respect the importance of the physical act of birth has been transferred to a "man-made" ritual context and is consequently generalized to serve as a basic model that can relate to life renewal. Around that basic concept has been woven a symbolic patterning that is relevant to all initiation rituals and to many of the great ritual epics.

Thus the crises in the life of all males are clustered around prebirth, the onset and completion of formal initiation, subsequent ritual involvement, and eventual physical (not spiritual) death. The process is somewhat different and less formalized for females. Whatever importance may be placed socially and personally on betrothal and marriage, these features have little part to play in religion—except that in a number of examples a man who is responsible for initiating a boy or

> . . . a major task of religious leaders and fully initiated men is to pass on their knowledge selectively. . . .

youth (for example, in relation to circumcision) is usually one of his potential affines and obliged to arrange that he receive a wife. There is, however, no direct religious underpinning in regard to marital arrangements.

Initiation flows, as it were, from and into something else of a religious nature. For example, in northeastern Arnhem Land there are two forms of initiation. One is relevant to novices of the Dua moiety; the other to novices of the complementary moiety, Yiridja. (In that society patrilineal moieties are important social indicators in religious mythology and ritual.) Each is associated with distinctive initiatory ritual. Dua novices between the ages of about six to nine years are introduced to the Djunggawon, the first of three ritual sequences that concern differing aspects of the great Wawalag mythology.

There is, or was, agreement among Aborigines that particular rituals are most appropriate for novices to be exposed to for preliminary religious purposes. Such events are usually marked by a physical operation (or its equivalent) that symbolizes the passing of boys or youths through one stage and indicates their preparedness to go further; the pressures to continue are just as strong as they are for the first initiation rites. The important aspect, however, is that any initation rite, although focused on particular novices, is also a teaching and learning experience that concerns older youths and men as well. Learning is correlated with active participation and occurs in a gradual progression through a series of mythic and ritual revelations. Whatever religious ritual is being carried out, there are always present some persons who are

being taught. Thus a major task of religious leaders and fully initiated men is to pass on their knowledge selectively, to those persons who are entitled or have been prepared to receive it. This is a process that traditionally continues throughout life. Associated with it is the application or utilization of sacred knowledge in order to achieve the aims that are stipulated in regard to specific rites.

Where female initiation is concerned, the focus is on puberty and the time is usually the onset of first mentruation. Generally speaking, female initiation rites are not as spectacular, nor do they extend over such long periods, as those of boys. Moreover, they need not involve the whole community or visitors from other areas.

Women are more heavily involved than men in the domestic round of activities, particularly in regard to nurturing children. Additionally, in the traditional Aboriginal scene, women were usually the main "breadwinners," responsible for supplying the greater part of the food supply for themselves, their menfolk, and their children. On the whole, the men's contribution to the food supply mainly concerned meat or large sea creatures, the supply of which was much less predictable.

There is an additional issue that has a bearing on this division of labor between the sexes. Much of men's ritual, especially when it concerns access to the life force controlled by either male or female deities or both, has to do with species and seasonal renewal. In such circumstances, the physiological attributes of females are emphasized, either directly or in symbolic terms. Where this point was specifically articulated by men, they asserted that women possessed such things naturally, while men needed to simulate them in order to accomplish what was required. There is another factor here. In many areas of Aboriginal Australia, mythic statements claim that women originally had complete control of the realm of the sacred and of all its ritual, verbal, spatial, and material components.

The final life crisis is physical death. The rites associated with death have much in common with the initiation of boys and girls. Initiation is usually treated as symbolic death, followed by ritual and social rebirth—more conspicuously so for boys. In actual physical death, the ritual is designed to ensure the spiritual survival of the deceased and his or her potential rebirth. In both cases, people have claimed that the life power derived from the deities makes such a transition possible. Mortuary rites vary considerably throughout the continent. In all cases they are concerned with re-creating or rechanneling life out of death, releasing the spiritual component of a human being from its physical receptacle and preparing it for its journey to a land of the dead—which in some instances is synonymous with the home of the immortals—there to await reincarnation. The cycle of life, therefore, continues after death, from the physical to the wholly spiritual, returning in due course to the physical dimension. That cycle is also relevant to all natural species. This view recognizes the equal importance of the physical and the spiritual and emphasizes that human beings are spiritually indestructible because they possess that germ of life that was theirs at conception and that came from the mythic beings of the Dreaming.

Ritual activation. Myth and ritual are interdependent and mutually supporting. From the viewpoint of Aborigines, myths portray real events that belong to the realm of the Dreaming. It is true that they are said to have happened in the past. But the mythic characters who participated in them remain in the land, metamorphosed but spiritually alive, still possessing their life-giving power. In many parts of Aboriginal Australia, special words are used to express the idea of this power. In order to gain access to it and to activate it, ritual must be carried out in a particular way and under particular conditions. First, it must be planned and organized by religious leaders and others who are directly related to the mythic being or beings concerned. Second, it must re-create symbolically the original mythological events and circumstances associated with the deity or deities in the same way as they first experienced them. Third, a symbol or image of the deity (or deities), or an emblemic representation, must be present on the ritual ground. The deity (deities) must be attracted to it (them) and temporarily occupy the appropriate vehicle(s). A wide variety of such vehicles is used: for example, the Aranda *tjurunga*; the *rangga* (ritually charged) posts of northeastern Arnhem Land and various other pole and brush structures decorated in ocher designs and hung with feathered pendants; and ground paintings, carved and ornamented posts, bull-roarers, and so on. Fourth, there must be ritual performances in which the actors portray the deities in either their human or other forms. Such performances must replicate in all essential details the events in the myth associated with the deities; they are accompanied by stipulated songs that also recount the mythic deeds.

Regional Religious Systems. Some specific ritual examples, drawn from a cross section of regional religious systems, provide a range of apparently different interpretations.

Mobile adaptive systems. The great Kunapipi (Gunabibi), under different names, has spread across the continent from Arnhem Land to the central-western Northern Territory and as far as the southeastern Kimberley. In all these areas, local people regard it as a "cult in movement," that is, as having been brought from one place to another. It has reached, indirectly, a number of other areas as well. It does not submerge or replace what was already present in terms of local religious ritual. The outcome is rather a matter of coexistence, although in some areas it is also a matter of coordination and adaptation. In Arnhem Land, the culturally defined indigenous systems remained more or less intact. The Kunapipi brought with it both circumcision and subincision. In northeastern Arnhem Land, for instance, there is no

subincision, although novices are circumcized; subincision was not accepted there, although that proved no handicap to the incorporation of basic tenets of that cult. On the other hand, in western Arnhem Land neither circumcision nor subincision was traditionally practiced, but the Kunapipi was accepted.

Northeastern Arnhem Land, as noted, recognizes two patrilineal moiety divisions, and the great mythic and ritual cycle for the Dua moiety is the Djanggawul (Djanggau), sponsored by the mythical two sisters and brother of that name. They shaped the land, gave birth to the first people, and introduced the appropriate Dua moiety *nara* ("nest" or "womb") sacred rituals. Essentially, the myth and songs makes clear the primary intentions in the ritual, which reenacts all the major incidents that took place during the original travels of the Djanggawul, including the natural species they saw.

On the sacred ground, a special hut representing a uterus is erected. Within it are stored secret-sacred *rangga* poles, representing those used by the Djanggawul as well as the unborn children (that is, the first people) within the wombs of the two sisters. In ritual dancing, *rangga* are removed from the hut by one postulant after another, and their actions in manipulating these refer to the revitalization of particular aspects of nature. In the main camp, women and uninitiated youths are covered with *ngainmara* (conical mats) that, again, represent the wombs of the sisters. These are later cast aside and the people emerge, thus reenacting the first mythic scene of birth. Additionally, in the present sense of the ritual, participants reaffirm the continuity of the birth process. Among the ritual sequences is the sacramental eating of cycad palm nut "bread" that has been specially prepared by women. Sacred invocations are called and songs sung over the bread, which is said to be transformed from being ordinarily sacred to achieve the status of a *rangga* emblem possessed of the power inherent in the Djanggawul. On the one hand this bread symbolizes all possible food resources available in the places invoked. On the other, when eaten by Djanggawul ritual participants it is said to enhance their sacred quality and strengthen the bonds between them.

Complementing the Djanggawul cycle is the Laindjung, of the opposite moiety. Laindjung is a mythic being represented as Banaidja, a barramundi fish, who emerged from the sea on the eastern coast of Arnhem Land. A range of mythic characters are associated with him; one, Fire, destroyed a ritual shelter where men were assembled for performances; Crocodile, who was among them, was seriously burned.

Whereas the Djanggawul myth sequences reveal a land resonant with growth and security, the Laindjung-Banaidja provides a view of a potentially dangerous world—where heavy rain and inevitable flooding of the countryside make travel difficult, and where later, when the floodwaters dry up and the grass grows and eventually dries too, fires spread across the land. The supreme danger is expressed in the mythic destruction by fire of the ritual shelter, with the loss of *rangga* and of life.

In the great Wawalag cycle, also a significant mythic and ritual cycle in this region, two sisters in conjunction with Yulunggul, the Great Python, are responsible for the coming of the monsoonal rains. The sisters, however, are not creators; they are only indirectly instrumental in activating a natural phenomenon that, in turn, fertilizes the land. The Djunggawon is an example of a Wawalag ritual which focuses on circumcision. Carved and painted *wangidja* poles, representing the Wawalag, are set up in the main camp. On the secret-sacred ground a triangular cleared space symbolizes the body of Yulunggul. At one end is a hole that is his home and water hole, and there is a special shelter containing a long, decorated drone pipe (*didjeridu*). Novices are painted with ocher designs in the same way as were the mythic Wawalag women, and they are said to represent them. Finally they are taken to the main camp where, screened by a group of men, they are circumcised.

In spite of major sociocultural differences between western and northeastern Arnhem Land, the basic religious themes are similar or complementary. Whereas the Djanggawul came from the east, from the mythical island of Bralgu, their western Arnhem Land counterpart came from the west (from, it is said, the Indonesian islands). Paul Foelsche, prior to 1881, was probably the first person to refer directly to a fertility mother, whom he called Warahmoorungee. Baldwin Spencer (1914, pp. 275-279) called her Imberombera, and since he refers to her in association with the mythic man Wuraka, there is no doubt that he (like Foelsche) was referring to the mother, Waramurungundji, whose husband, Wuragag, was eventually metamorphosed as Tor Rock on the Murganella Plain.

In the Ubar rituals an elongated, triangular secret-sacred ground represents the body of Ngalyod; within it is a shade or hut and the headstone of Ngalyod. The narrow end of the ground is her tail, and at one side is an extension of the dancing ground—her arm(s). Postulants entering the ground are said to be going into the Mother's womb; novices taken for initiation are "swallowed" by her. During the ritual a hollow log (gong, or drum, which is itself the *ubar*) is beaten; this is the Mother, and the sound is her voice informing people that she is spiritually present at the ground. During the final scenes, in the main camp, men and women dance; in pairs, selected women and men climb a *Pandanus* palm or forked stick to call the sacred invocations (see Berndt and Berndt, 1970, pp. 117-120, pp. 128-132).

Such ritual sequences, while focusing on a bountiful mother goddess, are usually associated with a male mythic counterpart. Although conceptually they differ from the Kunapipi, they certainly have much in common with it, both structurally and ideologically. For example, the eastern Arnhem Land manifestation, while utilizing a basic ritual pattern, provides an interpretative system that relates to local Wawalag mythology. The intrusion of the Kunapipi into western Arnhem Land also draws upon local mythology, in this case a father-son pair named Nagugur. They are mythically responsible for performing, as well as introducing, this ritual to different groups as they traveled across the countryside.

A number of examples of the Kunapipi myth (with considerable variations) and associated rites have been recorded. W. E. H. Stanner (1959-1961), for example, discussing his Port Keats (southwest of Darwin) material, writes of "the Mother of All." In that case her name is Mutjingga (an everyday Murinbata word for "old woman"). The relevant ritual concerns the Kalwadi "bull-roarer ceremony" (as Stanner called it; ibid., p. 110). He also discusses the myth of Kunmanggur (the Rainbow Snake; ibid., pp. 234ff.), which has no ritual sequence. This mythic creature is seen as a counterpart of Mutjingga, although mythic interaction between them is minimal. Several parallels can be drawn with Ngalyod in western Arnhem Land.

Segmentary systems. A kind of transitional area demarcates the northern fertility mother cults from those that are more distinctively of the "central" variety. These may be called segmentary because they embrace varying mythic traditions of similar ritual status that are sometimes mythically related but need not be. For example, M. J. Meggitt (1966), in discussing the religious system of the Walbiri, refers to a particular ritual constellation as being the Gadjeri ("old woman," an alternative name for the Kunapipi mother). In the area of which he writes, south of Wave Hill (in the Northern Territory), the Gadjeri rituals are called Big Sunday in English. While they utilize some of the major symbols that are highlighted in the northern versions of the cult, their supporting mythology concerns the two mythic male characters, Mamandabari (either two brothers or a father-son pair). They travel over a large part of Walbiri country, so that no one person would know the whole of the myth. Meggitt points out (ibid., p. 23) a characteristic Western Desert mythology—namely, that by following one myth, one is led to others, which *in toto* form an interconnected pattern. There is separation between myths in terms of content, but multiple ownership of such a constellation is based on the different territories through which the principal characters travel. Meggitt (1966, p. 25) considers that the Gadjeri is an importation, with the Mamandabari providing a rationale that differs considerably from the northern versions.

At Balgo, in southeastern Kimberley, an area contiguous on the southeast and east with the Walbiri and Woneiga, or northern Walbiri, the sociocultural perspective of the Gugadja and Ngadi is typically that of the Western Desert—except that it too has been influenced by the Gadjeri. The religious system is supported by a number of mythic and ritual traditions called Dingari. These are secret-sacred and are associated with various mythic characters, the main ones being the Ganabuda (often equated with the Gadjeri). In these versions, the Ganabuda are a group of women who follow a Dingari ritual group of men who, accompanied by novices, move from one site to another across the country. In their travels they initiate youths and meet other mythic characters who have their own separate traditions.

As preliminaries to the main Dingari ritual, novices, accompanied by their guardians, make a pilgrimage to the main Dingari sites within their own and adjacent territories. While this takes place, cult leaders prepare their secret-sacred *daragu* boards and other emblems. These are incised with designs relating to small sections of the territories over which the Dingari traveled, and they also represent vehicles for the mythic beings to enter during the actual ritual. When the novices return, they are separated from their parents and close kin and sleep in a special camp not too far from the men's secret-sacred ground. This ground contains a *nanggaru* pit (the womb) and a *ganala (kanala)* crescent trench (both similar to those in the northern Gadjeri). Within these a number of dramatic reenactments of the mythology take place. Novices are brought to the ground with their heads covered; the covering is removed only briefly for them to witness a performance. In some of these sequences, when only fully initiated men are present, arm blood is used as an adhesive for feather-down decoration on the bodies of participants or on emblems, and it is sipped to provide strength and oneness among those men present. In the final rites, novices are placed within the *nanggaru* while firebrands are thrown over them, some of the coals falling on them and burning them. (This is equivalent to Mamandabari rituals mentioned by Meggitt, 1966, p. 71.) Later, parents of the novices present gifts to the men who have initiated them, and a feast precedes the showing of sacred objects.

Clearly, preliminary initiation rites cannot be separated from rituals that are also intended to achieve other things beside ensuring that youths are prepared for their adult religious commitments. While novices are experiencing their own initial exposure to ritual, other men are participating in varying ways, depending on their knowledge and ritual status. Moreover, whenever large rituals are held, participants fall within one of two groups: active workers; and the executives or owners whose right it is to direct proceedings. In the case of circumcision ritual, women and children usually enter or come close to the sacred place, where they may dance. At that time novices are regarded as being ritually dead. On leaving the ground, women and children return to the main camp and the actual circumcision takes place. Afterward, novices are given their first bull-roarers *(daragu)* and are anointed with arm blood. Until a youth's subincision, he is traditionally obliged to attend all the rituals (or those sections which are relevant to him at this level). He must learn the songs and the meaning of the ritual performances.

Although the Dingari is known farther south in the Western Desert, its association with the Ganabuda or Gadjeri gradually disappears, and the desert system becomes dominant. While it is useful to separate the western from the eastern side of the desert for particular purposes, mainly because of the complexities of Aranda religion, here both may be regarded as being of desert inspiration.

> ## An important part of this sequence is the throwing of firebrands.

Given mythological variation, the structure of Western Desert initiation ritual remains reasonably constant. While women wail, youths are taken from their domestic camps to a seclusion area: the removal signifies their ritual death. Arm blood from initiated men is collected in a wooden receptacle, which is then passed around for all, including the novices, to sip from; the residue is smeared over the novices' bodies. This symbolically refers not only to their ritual death but also to their spiritual life. At this time, a novice would have his nasal septum pierced, the middle tooth of the top row loosened and knocked out, and a pattern of scars cut on his back. These three operations probably came into the desert areas through early contact with eastern groups. After a lengthy seclusion period, a novice is tossed into the air and then given a waistband and a pearl-shell necklet. An important part of this sequence is the throwing of firebrands. This occurs near the circumcision ground as women perform a special shuffling dance which repeats the mythic actions of the Minmarara or Gunggaranggara women in the Nyirana-Yulana cycle. As the women, making deep grooves in the earth, reach a row of fires that have been placed near the ground, men throw firebrands at and over them and they retreat to the main camp.

A range of postcircumcisional rites takes place over the next couple of years. They include sacred mythic reenactments in which particular emblems are revealed, together with subincision. This rite is regarded as having major religious significance; only after it is performed can a man participate fully in the secret-sacred life. The initial act of subincision is relatively informal, and the main focus is on subsequent rites. During the period of seclusion, blood from the incision is sprinkled over the newly subincised youth or man, and this is accompanied by dance and songs from the Wadi Gudjara and the Nyirana-Yulana mythology (see also Tonkinson, 1978, pp. 76-77). Beyond the explanation that it was originally carried out by a particular mythic character and must, therefore, be followed by human beings, subincision has been said to be primarily therapeutic. In areas farther north, men explicitly state that its purpose is to simulate female menstruation, and the periodic ritual opening and enlarging of the incision seems to support this explanation.

Except for the Aranda and affiliated groups, initiatory themes on the eastern side of the desert do not differ markedly from those in the west. Aranda initiation rites include much variation in detail. Spencer and Gillen (1938, pp. 212-270) reported five basic divisions: tossing of the novice, circumcision, head biting, subincision, and fire ritual. These agree for the most part with information from Strehlow (1947, pp. 96-100). Events commence on the *pulla* secret-sacred ground, where both circumcision and subincision take place. On this ground a novice is introduced to some of the ritual of his group and, after circumcision, receives a bull-roarer. During his subsequent seclusion, he must swing this to warn noninitiated persons of his presence. Generally, during this period he is instructed in the appropriate myths and witnesses relevant rites. In one part of the sequence, men bite the initiand's head so that blood flows, although (as Strehlow points out: ibid., p. 99) the scalp is first opened with a sharp stick. The aim is allegedly to ensure a strong growth of hair. Subincision follows and is accompanied by mythic reenactments. Just prior to the actual subincision, men embrace decorated *tnatantja* poles that represent the mythic Bandicoot. When a youth is seized for the operation, certain women cicatrize themselves in the main camp; the marks are said to represent the incised designs on a *tjurunga*. Women dance as the men return to the main camp, and the undecorated, newly subincised youth is presented to them, then disappears rapidly into the bush. The next morning he is led to a group of dancing women who hold wooden dishes. He holds a shield before his face and the women throw their dishes at this. Then they press their hands on his shoulders and rub their faces on his back, taking the opportunity to cut off locks of his hair, which they later incorporate in the hair-string ornaments they wear.

The desert focus is on particular Dreaming tracks made by the deities during their extensive travels across the land. Members of local descent groups associated with sections of such tracks are in a position to perform the relevant rituals and pass on their knowledge to others. Mythic knowledge is consequently fragmented ritually. In the past, it was not possible or practical to bring together all local sections of one particular myth cycle for a total dramatic performance. This state of affairs has several important implications. It emphasizes the localization of religion in the desert, where within any one region an overview or a total religious perspective could not be achieved through observation—as, broadly speaking, it could be in the big ritual constellations of the northern areas. In the desert, one particular myth is likely to be known, or known about, at the level of intellectual understanding over a very wide region; a large number of persons may recognize its significance even though they may never meet for the actual performances. The wide range of spatial-

ly extensive myths, dispersed among culturally similar people, reveals differing approaches to basic themes—for example, in regard to initiation and species-renewal ritual. One further feature concerns people's mythic and ritual (and personal) identification with specifically noted stretches of country. The deities, although shape-changing, are also virtually manifestations and expressions of local areas. They may be defined partly in relation to those areas.

Despite the issue of segmentation, two aspects draw people together into a religious bond, even though that bond may be a distant one. The first is cooperation within the ritual sphere, where owners of a myth cycle receive direct aid from other persons in the performance of the associated rites. This is a constantly sustaining feature. The other is that secret-sacred boards and relics that are symbolic representations of mythic beings are moved about the desert from one group to another, substantiating the concept of a community of common interests and faith.

Aranda religion is more formalized but still segmented. It too was heavily oriented in terms of particular local groups, each represented by a mythic father-son pair (Strehlow, 1947, pp. 7-8, in relation to the Bandicoot named Karora). Strehlow (1947, p. 25) notes that the northern Aranda, particularly, were a "strongly patrilineal society" in which the people prided themselves on the belief that they and their forefathers had all "come into being from the primal *tnatantja*" (a ritual pole with life-containing properties).

Over and above the large ritual sequences held in particular territories, concentrating on the recreation of the original mythic scenes, special "increase" rites were intended to ensure a plentiful supply of the appropriate species represented by the local guardian deity: for instance, the well-known Witchetty Grub center at Emily Gap (near Alice Springs). The ritual associated with this site is secret-sacred. Such localized rites for species-renewal purposes are common throughout the desert and Aranda areas. Some include the making of elaborate ground designs which represent topographically, in a conventionalized form, the country associated with a particular mythic being; they are obliterated at the conclusion of the ritual.

Mythic sites are, everywhere, a salient focus in Aboriginal religion. In the Western Desert they loom more obviously, and because sections of a particular myth are in the hands of small local groups, they tend, to a greater degree perhaps than in the north, to be more significant ritually. At the same time, such sites are visible manifestations of the "reality" of what took place in the Dreaming, a reality that is transformed into ritual and, in turn, directed toward everyday living and needs.

Focus on deity. Information on eastern and southeastern Australia includes two significant key points. One is the reference to dominant deities of All-Father type or as equivalent to a high god. Their categorization in those terms ignores associated descriptions, but there is no doubt that using such labels for an outstanding mythic being has its own appeal.

Typical of what are usually called Bora rituals was the Guringal (Kuringal) of the Yuin (south of Sydney). The Guringal took place on a specially prepared ground where a number of objects had been assembled: for instance, a spiny anteater made of earth with protruding sticks as quills, a molded brown snake of clay, and a figure of Daramulun (the mythic deity) made of earth and surrounded by implements and weapons. With these were exhibited magical substances. This is the second key point. Aboriginal "doctors" or "clever men" played a major part in the rituals; during the initiation rites, where tooth evulsion was the primary operation, novices witnessed some of their activities. These included disgorging quartz crystals and other substances symbolizing their power. Novices were also taken to see a large figure of Daramulun incised on a tree trunk. Before this image, decorated men danced toward the novices who, one by one, had a couple of teeth loosened with a succession of blows and finally removed by a doctor. Novices were then taken to stand before the figure of Daramulun and told of his power and that he lived beyond the sky and watched what people did. A number of ritual dances followed, among them some related to the mother (or two mothers) of this deity, and there were others that reproduced the behavior of certain natural species. During the final part of the Guringal, a grave was prepared. Within it a Yuin man, said to represent Daramulun, lay covered with branches and leaves and with a small tree, the roots resting on his chest. The novices were then placed alongside the grave. To the accompaniment of songs and the actions of the doctors, the supposedly dead person would rise and perform a magical dance within the grave, holding his magical substances in his mouth. Finally, the grave was covered up.

The contrast between southeastern Bora and rituals of other areas lies mainly in the emphasis on one deity, represented by an image of earth, clay, or as an incised figure on a tree. These were evidently comparable or equivalent to the emblematic poles, posts, wooden boards, and stone *tjurungas* of desert and northern groups and intended as vehicles for the deity to inhabit temporarily. A close inspection of Bora material suggests that other mythic beings were also present (as among the Wuradjeri of western New South Wales), as well as in the Guringal, where performances related to differing natural species. However, the aspect of species renewal is not directly mentioned. A further contrast lies in the presence of clever men and in the magical component of many of these rituals. Wuradjeri evidence suggests that such performances extended over several years, that clever men received their power from Daramulun, and that the "mother of Daramulun" (mentioned in the Guringal) was Emu (categorized as his wife, among the Wuradjeri). In my *Australian Aboriginal Religion* (1974, fasc. 1, p. 29), I note that much of

southeastern ritual was preoccupied with the hereafter and with achieving identification with the deity Daramulun (or Baiame). Moreover, spirits of the dead played an important part. For instance, the grave scene in the Guringal (although it could certainly be interpreted in other terms) was possibly intended to symbolize the common initiation theme of death with subsequent rebirth.

The southeastern sector of Queensland is characterized by rituals that in some respects resemble the Bora, although there are marked differences. For instance, the training of novices in fishing, hunting, and fighting proficiency and the bestowal on novices of power-endowed names were emphasized. It would seem that fighting was a cultural focus (Howitt, 1904, pp. 595-599); fighting is included as part of an initiation sequence. Of course, fighting per se is not excluded from Aboriginal religious mythology, where it appears as a normal aspect of social living.

Transformation of ancestors. The religion of Cape York Peninsula focused on patrilineal clan territories containing auwa sites, or water holes. Near them live particular creatures in spirit form (which have been called "totemic" or, in this case, *pulwaiya*), and it is to these auwa that the spirits of the dead are said to go. As McConnel (1957, p. 171) puts it, the landowners approach the *auwa* of their *pulwaiya* with respect and affection. The rites performed there to ensure the spiritual renewal of the respresentative species differ from one *auwa* to the next; however, it is to spirits of the dead (of the past), identified with the pulwaiya, that invocations are addressed. Also, the *pulwaiya* are associated with a wide range of myths. There are male and female *auwa* with spirit children awaiting rebirth through the performance of the appropriate ritual by a woman who has conceived.

In contrast to ritual connected with *auwa* are the initiation rites discussed by Thomson (1933, pp. 461-489). These concern a culture hero (that is, a mythic being). A secret-sacred

> **Mythic sites are, everywhere, a salient focus in Aboriginal religion.**

area is protected by screens, behind which sacred objects are prepared and stored in readiness for dancing sequences. There are a large number of dances, and in some, actors use masks. Many of the myths associated with these dances are connected with the Torres Strait Islands and the mainland of Papua New Guinea. However, some of the *auwa* dances suggest possible linkages with Arnhem Land.

Variations on a common theme. The Lake Eyre basin (in northeastern South Australia) is best represented by the Dieri, with information derived largely from the early work of Samuel Gason (1874) and Howitt (1904). In many respects the Dieri were culturally close to Western Desert people, especially in their variety of mythic beings, which were referred to as *muramura*. Each deity was associated with a particular ritual sequence. Like their counterparts in other areas, they were metamorphosed into stones or other natural features at specific sites where their spirits remain. Some were regarded as creative. For example, one Dieri myth tells how the *mardu* (a natural species spirit, regarded as a person's own flesh from his or her mother) came into being. They emerged from the earth as natural species (crow, parakeet, emu, etc.), but at that stage they were physically incomplete. They became whole by remaining in the sun, when they stood up as human beings and then scattered over the country. In another myth the Mandra-mankana, a mythic man, swallowed a large number of people. However, some escaped. Helped by the *muramura* Kanta-yulkana ("grass swallower"), they ran off in various directions in the form of natural species (becoming mardu).

The actual localities of these beings were traditionally indicated by wooden guide posts called *toa*. The designs carved or printed on these showed topographic features relevant to particular *muramura* or to their mythic adventures, and in this respect they were similar in intent to the incised tjurunga of the desert.

By far the most important of the postinitiatory rites was the Mindari, which normally followed the Wilyaru. Sponsored by the *muramura* Emu, this was probably the most sacred of all Dieri rituals. A large flattened mound was made and decorated with feathers and red ocher, representing Emu's body. Two women would walk across it to the accompaniment of singing, and as the mound was broken up, invocations were called to persuade emus to breed. Women were also sent as messengers to invite members of neighboring groups to attend the Mindari.

Dieri influences extended farther south, but not along the lower Murray River and the Lakes district, or on the Adelaide plains. There seems to have been more or less equal participation of women and men in ritual life, with a minimal division of labor between them in social activities. Song and dance sequences covered a wide range of subjects: natural species, food collecting and hunting, sickness prevention, and so on, and some songs provided sketches of current events. The major mythic being (deity) was Ngurunderi, who appears only in human form. In a bark canoe, he chased the great Murray Cod down the Murray River, and as it swished its tail from side to side it formed the river's bends and swamps. He was also responsible for setting in train all religious rites; wherever he traveled and camped or wherever some important event took place, part of his sacred essence remained. While these were sacred sites, they were not the subject of ritual or regarded as species-renewal places. However, there are indications that special rites took place, with Ngurunderi as the main focus—especially his going into

the sky to enter the spirit world. The fact that Ngurunderi came from the upper reaches of the Murray suggests that he is associated with the Baiame/Daramulun tradition. In contrast to other areas, Yaraldi (as one language group within the Narrinyeri grouping) men and women possessed spirit familiars or protectors who indirectly referred to mythic beings.

One clue to the religious life of the lower Murray River lies in the concept of *narumba*, a term meaning "sacred" or "taboo." Initiation rites involved depilation of facial hair and observation of a wide range of food taboos; during his period of segregation, a novice was himself *narumba*.

In many respects, the cultures of southwestern Western Australia (now referred to as Nyungar) roughly paralleled those of the lower Murray River in South Australia. Many Nyungar myths told of beings associated with sacred sites. One of the most important was Waugal (a Rainbow Snake), who was responsible for shaping parts of the land and the rivers. Another, Motogen, was said to be a male creative being. There were a number of dance and song sequences, many of which dramatized birds, animals, reptiles, and so on, along with hunting scenes and the feats of clever men.

On the northern side of the continent, Bathurst and Melville islanders culturally resemble, in some respects, the people who lived on the lower Murray River. There is, for instance, no physical operation at initiation except depilation, and they make no major distinctions on the basis of sex in religious matters. The Kulama ritual, first described by Spencer (1914, pp. 91-115), and later by Charles W. M. Hart and Arnold R. Pilling (1960, pp. 93-95), among others, is particularly important. Its mythology involves several beings, among them the White-headed Sea Eagle and the Owl, and its rites are organized by initiated men who enter a state of *pukamani* (which signifies sacredness and taboo). The *kulama* is a dangerous but sacred plant, which produces yams that need to be processed before being eaten. At the appropriate season, the yams are collected and cooked in ovens. Then they are cut up and rubbed on the bodies of men, women, and children; some are mashed up with red ocher and the resultant substance rubbed into men's hair. This is believed to prevent sickness. The yam symbolizes a range of natural phenomena, some of which are explicitly mentioned in the songs and accompanying dances. The power inherent in the Kulama triggers off the monsoonal period and stimulates all growth, but it is also said to control the rain and prevent flooding. In other words, the Kulama, through the special ritual approach to it, safeguards the welfare of the community.

There is some evidence that this particular culture was not restricted to Bathurst and Melville islands but extended on to the mainland, especially into parts of western Arnhem Land where the traditional Mangindjeg ritual (also focusing on an edible root) paralleled the Kulama in certain respects. As we have seen, one important feature which links northern

Australian religion is the fertility mother concept. On Bathurst and Melville islands, traditionally, earth mothers were identified as being responsible for creating human and other natural species. Four of the five phratries that are recognized as social categories there are named after earth mothers who introduced that form of social organization. Among the Laragia (Larrakia) of Darwin, and the Daly River people to the southwest, circular stone structures were built to represent the wombs of their creative mothers.

In contrast to Bathurst and Melville islands and the lower Murray River, where religious life is, or was, relatively open insofar as men and women are concerned, Groote Eylandt culture (on the eastern side of Arnhem Land) traditionally offered a somewhat extreme case of sexual dichotomy in religious affairs. However, that area has been heavily influenced by mainland (northeastern Arnhem Land) religion and emphasizes mortuary ritual designed to transfer a dead person's spirit to the appropriate land of the dead. Subsequently, a lock of the deceased person's hair was ritually put into a small spirit bag and kept for a number of years until it was finally returned to that person's own territory, where it was buried. There were also additional mortuary rites for important persons, which resembled the nara rituals of northeastern Arnhem Land and in which most of the dramatic enactments were secret-sacred and included the use of sacred objects.

Among other localized religious types, the Wandjina are probably the best known. Widely spread in the northwest Kimberley of Western Australia, their graphic representations appear in cave and rock-shelter paintings. The basic rite connected with such paintings, intended to renew species and their environment, calls for retouching the designs and singing. This region has been influenced by the spread of cults from the Northern Territory which have been expanding for a considerable period of time, probably long before the first European settlement. For instance, Gurangara (Kurangara) ritual (a segment of the Kunapipi) is known and performed over much of the northern Kimberley.

Diversified Patterns, Common Aims. One of the problems facing students of Aboriginal religion has been the very real issue of differing cultural patterning, which has often obscured what is considered to be an essential commonality of religious purpose in relation to basic belief and what is intended to be achieved. When comparisons are drawn between regional manifestations, much depends on what criteria are distinguished and how differences and similarities are correlated, as well as delineated.

The patterns that have been presented here are by no means complete; there are others. However, their selection has been made mainly on the basis of contrasts between them, as well as what they have to offer in explanatory terms. For example, what have been called "adaptive mobile systems" have not only a wide spatial relevance; they are also

easily distinguishable in relation to a bountiful (but sometimes dangerous) mother figure who—usually but not always operating with a male counterpart—dominates the ritual scene. The movement of such cults over wide stretches of country is far from unique in Aboriginal Australia. What distinguishes these constellations (for example, the Kunapipi, Gadjeri, and so on) is the ease with which they adapt to localized systems as well as the way they clarify such aspects as the power of a deity and how the life essence is released to ensure the continuance of the status quo for nature as for human beings and for the deities themselves.

The segmentary systems, on the other hand, refer to compartmentalization of extensive mythic and ritual cycles, the details of which are held by members of a number of local descent groups who may or may not live near each other. Each group is traditionally responsible for sustaining part of the total corpus of knowledge relevant to a particular mythic being and his or her travels in the Dreaming. There are major differences in structure between these and the adaptive mobile systems (as they are described here). The Western Desert examples are, of course, mobile but require (except in the Walbiri case) no adaptation. Each segment is a reflection or microcosm of the whole but is not complete in itself. The adaptive mobile systems, on the other hand, always appear to be complete in themselves, no matter what adjustments are made to accommodate local manifestations.

The Bora is distinctive, though not so much because of the attention that has been placed on a lone deity (since in other areas outstanding characters are given prominence). Rather, its uniqueness lies in two directions. One is the pervasive influence of magic in a way which does not occur in other Aboriginal religions. The other feature is the removal of the deity (in spite of the creation of his image and the images of those associated with him in the ritual context) from intimate contact with ritual postulants.

Spirits of the dead had a role to play in the Bora; but turning to the Cape York Peninsula area, we find that role is elaborated in respect of the auwa sites. In both cases, the intention is to transform postulants or newly dead persons into becoming representatives of, or identified with, particular mythic beings, or to merge them into the Dreaming. In comparing the ideologies of these groups with those of others discussed here, we can see that while processes differ, the aims are similar. In a sense, the auwa bring us back to the Dieri system, at least in part. Its religious system has been influenced by external cultures, but it apparently had no difficulty in retaining its distinctive patterning—even though it suggests close similarities to Western Desert religion.

Territorially peripheral, but no less significant, are the systems of the Murray River (South Australia) and Melville and Bathurst islands (with area extensions). While these two cultures are almost as far apart spatially as they could be, there are striking parallels between them in their initiations and highly structured taboo systems. At the same time, they differ radically in regard to the dominance of male or female deities. These two areas also provide examples of equality between males and females in ritual affairs, with virtually no secret-sacred dimension for either sex. At the other extreme, on Groote Eylandt, it would appear that women traditionally had no place in male-dominated religious activities.

Continuing Significance of Aboriginal Religion. Mainstream Aboriginal religion today takes two basic forms. Although modified through non-Aboriginal contact, Aboriginal religion still displays its own traditional orientations. Not all of the religious systems discussed in this contribution are now living realities. The religions of people who originally occupied the southwest of Western Australia, the Lake Eyre basin, the lower Murray River, New South Wales, Victoria, and southwest Queensland have all but disappeared. Two

> ## Two dominant mainstream religions remain, in general terms, in the northern coastal and the central desert regions.

dominant mainstream religions remain, in general terms, in the northern coastal and the central desert regions. In the northern example, the fertility cults have traveled far across the Northern Territory to the edges of the Western Desert and proved sufficiently attractive, at least in border areas, to influence the distinctive desert form. The creative mother, usually present in conjunction with a male deity, is a major focus of mythic and ritual activity, either as a pivotal personage or seen in relation to other characters. Moreover, such cults have been sufficiently resilient to maintain their key identifying symbols through the vicissitudes of cultural differences. They are essentially flexible, adaptive, and responsive to changing circumstances.

In the case of the desert, there is no single coordinating theme; instead, the theme is manifested in a number of similar forms relating to differing mythic occurrences. In the desert, too, male deities predominate, although there is no lack of female mythic representation. Also, an additional contrast can be drawn. In the northern area, the physical aspect of procreation is emphasized, even though the spiritual component is present; in the desert, the spiritual aspects receive more attention. In both examples, the secret-sacred domain of men is similarly stressed. In the northern coastal region women do not usually have their own secret-sacred domain; in the desert, women usually have their own rituals. In both regions men and women come together for the performances of some sections of the major ritual cycles.

Non-Aboriginal influences, including missionary activities, have made some drastic inroads, but where traditional

Aboriginal culture has survived it remains defined in terms of its members' commitment to the indigenous religious form. This was the case in the past, and is so today, particularly insofar as the two mainstream religious constellations are concerned.

Recent decades have seen a religious renaissance, which has taken a number of forms. It is one consequence of an upsurge of interest on the part of Aborigines in their unique identity vis-à-vis the wider Australian society. A contributing factor has been the attempt by governments (both federal and state) to implement more enlightened policies in regard to Aborigines. Not least, there has been a growing interest in the Aboriginal land-rights platform, which basically depends on the linkage of Aboriginal persons and groups to specific land defined in religious terms.

These developments emphasize the resilience of traditional religion, not only in more conspicuous survival zones, but also in many peripheral areas where some of the traditional background has continued to be a part of the background of social life. This is because the traditional religion continues to meet, in some measure, emotional and practical needs *and* political aspirations. Within the two main surviving regional spreads, some innovative religious movements have emerged. These have incorporated alien elements within a traditonal setting and in the presence of continuing traditional religious forms.

This traditional resilience is of particular significance. It is not due solely to the persistence of factors reinforcing or enhancing personal and social identity or to the use of religious knowledge to justify land claims. More particularly, it rests on two features which seem to have characterized all Aboriginal religions. One is their seeming conservatism. The other is their ability to allow room for varying interpretations, provided certain basic values are not impaired. There is a degree of flexibility in Aboriginal religion that permits coordination with changing circumstances.

BIBLIOGRAPHY

Berndt, Catherine H. "Women and the 'Secret Life.' " In *Aboriginal Man in Australia*, edited by Ronald M. Berndt and Catherine H. Berndt, pp. 238-282. Sydney, 1965. Takes up the issue of Aboriginal women's participation in traditional religion as being complementary to men's, and certainly not subordinate or "inferior."

Berndt, Ronald M. *Kunapipi: A Study of an Australian Aboriginal Religious Cult*. Melbourne, 1951. A study of a fertility cult in northern Australia, which includes symbolic representations through ritual and songs.

Berndt, Ronald M. *Australian Aboriginal Religion*. 4 fascs. Leiden, 1974. The first comprehensive overall study of Aboriginal Australian religion; includes bibliographies. It identifies a range of different patterns of belief and practice, recognizing that there are also basic similarities.

Berndt, Ronald M., and Catherine H. Berndt. "A Preliminary Report of Field Work in the Ooldea Region, Western South Australia."

Oceania 12-15 (1942-1945). Reprinted together as an Oceania Bound Offprint (Sydney, 1945). Covers major features of the traditional Great Victoria Desert (southeastern Western Desert) sociocultural scene; much of this has now changed considerably.

Berndt, Ronald M., and Catherine H. Berndt. *Man, Land and Myth in North Australia: The Gunwinggu People.* Sydney, 1970. Through a living Aboriginal community such as the one portrayed in this book, we can appreciate the significance of traditional Aboriginal religion as an integrating force in social affairs.

Curr, Edward M. *The Australian Race.* 4 vols. Melbourne, 1886-1887. Represents the only available material on some traditional southeastern Aboriginal cultures.

Durkheim, Émile. *The Elementary Forms of the Religious Life* (1915). Translated by Joseph Ward Swain. New York, 1965. This classic study is well known to all students of comparative religion. Australian Aboriginal materials were used by Durkheim to explore both the origins and nature of religion in general. However, much new ethnographic data has become available since Durkheim wrote, necessitating revision of some of his assumptions.

Eliade, Mircea. *Australian Religions: An Introduction.* Ithaca, N. Y., 1973. A historian of religions provides a critical and evaluative overview of the literature on Australian Aboriginal religion.

Elkin, A. P. *The Australian Aborigines: How to Understand Them* (1938). 3d ed. Sydney, 1964. A general overview of Aboriginal society and culture, expanded to include further material on religious perspectives (see chapters 7-10). It was on the basis of this study that some of Elkin's students (including, e.g., Ronald M. Berndt, C. H. Berndt, and M. J. Meggitt) developed their own treatments of this topic.

Gason, Samuel. *The Dieyerie Tribe of Australian Aborigines.* Adelaide, 1874. This work also appears in *The Native Tribes of South Australia*, edited by J. D. Woods (Adelaide, 1879), pp. 257-307. One among several other early sources of information on traditional Dieri culture, which is no longer a living reality.

Hart, Charles W. M., and Arnold R. Pilling. *The Tiwi of North Australia.* New York, 1960. A general, quasi-popular book about the Melville and Bathurst Islanders; section 4 treats religious activities.

Howitt, A. W. *The Native Tribes of South-East Australia.* New York, 1904. A classic study and a basic sourcebook for and about Aborigines of southeastern Australia, especially in relation to ritual and mythology.

Kaberry, Phyllis M. *Aboriginal Woman, Sacred and Profane.* London, 1939. The first major study of Aboriginal women. Although it focuses, for example, the place of women in religion, women's secret-sacred rituals, and Durkheim's "sacred-profane" dichotomy.

Lévi-Strauss, Claude. *Le totémisme aujourd'hui.* Paris, 1962. Translated as *Totemism* (Harmondsworth, 1969). In this important study, Lévi-Strauss discusses various theories of totemism, concentrating on Aboriginal Australia and especially, in a critical vein, on Elkin's approach. Chapter 4, on the intellectual significance of totemism, suggests a different way of considering the topic.

Maddock, Kenneth. *The Australian Aborigines: A Portrait of Their Society* (1972). Rev. ed. Ringwood, Australia, 1982. A general study of the Australian Aborigines, including numerous references to Aboriginal religion, especially in chapters 4-7.

McConnel, Ursula. *Myths of the Mungkan.* Melbourne, 1957. Discusses, with specific examples, myths and rituals of the Wik-Mungkan of Cape York; based on field research from the mid-1920s to the early 1930s.

Meggitt, M. J. *Desert People* (1962). Reprint, Sydney, 1974. One of the few available complete ethnographies of an Aboriginal society,

in this case, the Walbiri of the northern Central Desert region. Includes a section on initiation.

Meggitt, M. J. *Gadjari among the Walbiri Aborigines of Central Australia.* Sydney, 1966. A detailed account of the Gadjeri myth-ritual complex among the Walbiri. The Gadjeri, associated with the Kunapipi (see Berndt, 1951), has here been adapted to Desert religion. Of particular importance are Meggitt's comparisons between the Gadjeri and similarly patterned manifestations elsewhere.

Mountford, Charles P. *Ayers Rock.* Sydney, 1965. Various myths associated with this outstanding and sacred place are noted, especially in relation to religious art. The descriptions are accompanied by many illustrations.

Mountford, Charles P. *Winbaraku and the Myth of Jarapiri.* Adelaide, 1968. A companion to the author's *Ayers Rock*, this volume provides a well-illustrated account of one myth, focused on Winbaraku (Blanche Tower, at Mount Liebig). The journey of the main mythic character extends northward to Yuendumu.

Nevermann, Hans, Ernest A. Worms, and Helmut Petri. *Die Religionen der Südsee und Australiens.* Stuttgart, 1968. See pages 125-311. A collection of studies including Australian material by Worms, a Pallotine missionary, and Petri, an anthropologist.

Radcliffe-Brown, A. R. *Structure and Function in Primitive Society.* London, 1952. In this volume of collected essays, chapters 6 and 8 (originally published earlier as separate journal articles) concern Aboriginal religion. They have been critically examined by Lévi-Strauss and Eliade, among others, and continue to be of theoretical interest.

Roth, Walter Edmund. *Ethnological Studies among the North-West-Central Queensland Aborigines.* Brisbane, 1897. One of the major earlier sourcebooks for the ethnography of Aboriginal groups in northwest-central Queensland. Although essential in any attempt to reconstruct the traditional past of that region, much of it is unsystematic and incomplete.

Schmidt, Wilhelm. *Der Ursprung der Gottesidee.* 12 vols. Münster, 1912-1955. Schmidt's monumental work has, unfortunately, not attracted the attention it deserves (especially in relation to the first and third volumes, the latter being on southeastern Australia). The best recent assessment is by Eliade (1973).

Sharp, Lauriston. "Ritual Life and Economics of the Yir-Yoront of Cape York Peninsula." *Oceania* (1934): 19-42. This small contribution, based on field research, supplements the work of McConnel (1957).

Smyth, R. Brough. *The Aborigines of Victoria.* 2 vols. Melbourne, 1878. As an ethnographic source book this is, like Curr's, a valuable source of information on traditional Aboriginal material that has long since disappeared as a living reality.

Spencer, Baldwin. *Native Tribes of the Northern Territory of Australia* (1914). Oosterhout, 1966. Also a valuable sourcebook for and about northern Aboriginal people. It is less detailed than Baldwin's Aranda studies, but provides information on a number of northern cultures that have changed radically in recent years.

Spencer, Baldwin, and F. J. Gillen. *The Native Tribes of Central Australia* (1899). London, 1938. This classic study remains a basic source of information for and about the Aranda and adjacent groups. It contains a great deal of descriptive material on ritual and religious belief, which Durkheim (1915) used in his general study of religion.

Stanner, W. E. H. "On Aboriginal Religion." *Oceania* 30 (1959): 108-127, 245-278; 31 (1960): 100-120, 233-255; 32 (1961): 79-108; 33 (1962): 239-273; 34 (1963): 56-58. Relying heavily on the methodological approaches of Durkheim and Radcliffe-Brown, Stanner used his detailed study of the Port Keats mytho-ritual version of the Old Mother cult to outline a theoretical basis for the examination of Aboriginal religion. It is historically important.

Strehlow, Carl. *Die Aranda-und-Loritja-Stämme in zentral Australien.* 5 vols. in 7. Frankfurt, 1907-1920. A detailed account by this nineteenth-century Lutheran missionary, father of T. G. H. Strehlow, who was able to use and build upon this material in his own later research.

Strehlow, T. G. H. *Aranda Traditions.* Melbourne, 1947. Following on the work of his father, Strehlow concentrated on the Aranda concept of *tjurunga* in relation to a detailed analysis of myth and ritual. There are salient differences between his approach and that of Spencer (1899).

Strehlow, T. G. H. *Songs of Central Australia.* Sydney, 1971. An outstanding contribution to the study of Aranda religious songs, including detailed analysis of the vernacular and translated versions. The attempt to set them in a comparative framework is less significant than the examples and discussion of Aranda material as such.

Taplin, George. *The Narrinyeri.* Adelaide, 1873. This work also appears in *The Native Tribes of South Australia*, edited by J. D. Woods (Adelaide, 1879), pp. 1-156. A missionary's account of Aborigines of the lower Murray River in South Australia. Despite its evident bias against the traditional culture, it is virtually the only early source available on these Aborigines.

Thomson, Donald F. "The Hero Cult: Initiation and Totemism on Cape York." *Journal of the Royal Anthropological Institute* 63 (1933): 453-537. Demonstrates the influence of religious cults of the Torres Strait Islands on the northern Cape York Aboriginal people.

Tonkinson, Robert. *The Mardudjara Aborigines: Living the Dream in Australia's Desert.* New York, 1978. Tonkinson's study complements those of Meggitt (1962) and Berndt (1945) in other parts of the Western Desert and is essential for an overview of that region. Chapters 1, 4, 5, and 6 are directly relevant to the religious dimension of Mardudjara culture.

Warner, Wiliam Lloyd. *A Black Civilization: A Study of an Australian Tribe* (1937). New York, 1958. The first detailed study of one traditional Aboriginal culture. Chapters 8-13 focus on various aspects of magic and religion; the great Wawalag and Djanggawul (Djanggau) mytho-ritual cycles are discussed, analyzed, and interpreted. Heavily influenced by Durkheim, Warner's views about the place of women in Aboriginal religion, including the sacred-profane dichotomy, distorted his ethnographic reporting in this respect and (as he later admitted) require reassessment.

RONALD M. BERNDT

Modern Movements

In the history of conquest and dispossession of Australian Aborigines, well-defined and well-organized religious movements have not been characteristic. Melanesian-type cargo cults have been conspicuous by their absence, although a cargo cult element has been reported in a few instances. Nor has Aboriginal Australia produced any notable prophetic figures or millenarian movements. Initially, Aborigines generally responded to invasion and dispossession of their land with violence, but this resistance eventually proved futile and was followed by a period of quiet adaptation. Only in recent decades has an active political struggle to remedy the injustices of the past arisen. In a theoretical framework of linear evolution, one would have expected an interim period of religious movements whose purpose was to rid the land of intruding aliens or to arrive at a more satisfactory relationship. With a few exceptions, which are described below, such was not the case.

It is true—if not a truism—that the culture of the foraging and seminomadic Aborigines throughout Australia was so vastly different from that of the invaders, and so devastated by superior force, that an effective response to the invasion, aside from short-lived physical resistance in each locale, was unthinkable until a long period of cognitive adjustment had elapsed. Fortunately, sparsely settled areas of the island continent provided circumstances enabling the continuance of Aboriginal traditions during this long period—a continuance which has become the basis of a cultural regeneration adapted to present circumstances. The cataclysmic effect of the invasion on Aboriginal culture does not by itself, however, explain the dearth of well-defined religious movements. It is to the characteristics of Australian Aboriginal religion that attention must be drawn to explain the seeming anomaly.

Traditional Aboriginal Religion. Because of its relative homogeneity throughout the continent, traditional Aboriginal religion can be viewed as a single entity. From place to place and region to region, the complex of mythological figures, specific ritual forms, and ritual emphases vary, but the general outlines of religious ideology and practice remain constant. The Dreaming—a world inhabited by the spiritual ancestors of human and nonhuman life forms alike—is the basis of all Aboriginal religion. It laid down the patterns of the Aboriginal universe for all time. A conservative concept, it is not conducive to rapid adaptation; nevertheless, it is hospitable to changes that fit the elaborate but involuted complex of symbols used by each religious community. The religious duty of all initiated members of the community is to perform faithfully the ceremonies which activate the life-sustaining power of the ancestors. The concept of the Dreaming is decidedly nonmillenarian, nonutopian, and indeed nonhistorical.

Much has been written of the egalitarian nature of Australian Aboriginal society, though some allowances must be made for differences of age and sex. Although Aboriginal women have a religious life of their own in most parts of Australia, in general men maintain a marked attitude of superiority about their secret rites and exclude women from the inner core of their religious life. Over a number of years male novices pass through several ritual grades, or rites of passage, often marked by painful physical ordeals. Ceremonies are controlled by elders who have acquired ritual experience and knowledge after decades of participation.

Aboriginal ceremonies have been categorized as local totemic rites and transcendental rites (Maddock, 1972, pp. 117ff.). Performances of local rites are the prerogative of local clan members and are oriented to the interests of the clan and its territories. Transcendental rites embrace several clans and sometimes several language communities; they are concerned more with rites of passage and with interclan and intertribal interests. Thus transcendental rites often occurred across a whole region and sometimes "traveled" hundreds of miles; these "traveling cults" have been traced and documented in historical times.

The Context of Change. Aboriginal religious structures—developed over millennia on an island continent with little alien contact except along the north coast—were initially incapable of absorbing the onslaught of European culture. Traditions, which were adapted to slow change and in which continuity was valued above all else, either disappeared quickly in regions of intense colonization or persisted, although increasingly dissociated from social realities. Aboriginal cosmology encoded in the concept of the Dreaming was unable to account for cataclysmic changes. Seduced by the material rewards and relative freedom of European employment, young men became estranged from the authority of religious elders. The religious status of men was undermined by their observable inferiority in situations of paternalism at best and outright racism at worst. Parochial concerns of local traditions were of little relevance to the mixture of clans and language communities gathered on reserve lands set aside by governments. In many areas of Australia, Aboriginal religion failed to cope with the changed situation: the young rebelled, others were disillusioned, leaders were demoralized.

> **Only in recent decades has an active political struggle to remedy the injustices of the past arisen.**

In areas of Australia more remote from the gathering momentum of colonization, persisting religious traditions were granted the opportunity to adapt by the historical and geographical circumstances. The bearers of these traditions were subject to similar pressures as their less fortunate coreligionists elsewhere, but the pressures were more extended over time. What appear at this time to be viable adaptations, have been contingent on several factors: non-Aboriginal Australians' improved tolerance of the continuation of Aboriginal culture, a developing Aboriginal consciousness of common identity and interests, and enhanced Aboriginal mobility and communication through the adoption of modern technology.

Syncretic Movements. Christian missionaries followed hard on the heels of settlers and in some cases ventured beyond the frontiers of pastoral settlement. The results were mixed and sometimes unexpected. At the remote Aboriginal community of Jigalong in the Western Desert (Western Australia), rejection of Christianity, at least in the early stages of missionary expansion, was almost complete (Tonkinson, 1974). At Aurukun on Cape York Peninsula in the far northeast, a mixture of local Aboriginal religion and nearby Torres Strait Islands traditions coexist with Christianity in the same ceremonies (as documented in Judith McDougal's film *The House Opening*, 1980). In more densely settled regions, orthodox Christianity filled the vacuum left by the Aboriginal traditions that were totally unable to adapt. In at least two places in Australia, however, creative attempts at syncretism occurred.

Bandjalang-speakers in northeastern New South Wales were missionized by the interdenominational United Aboriginal Mission (UAM). Preaching a fundamentalist version of Christianity, the UAM believed and taught that traditional spirits and mythic figures were not illusory but were evil manifestations of the devil. Traditional beliefs lingered on, despite their incompatibility with social realities: the breakdown of clan organization, the "liberation" of youths, the undermining of the status of male elders, and general anomie. An Aboriginal non-Bandjalang Pentecostal preacher found fertile ground in this demoralized community. Spirit possession, characteristic of Pentecostalism, was individualized in conformity with Aboriginal custom; elements of local Aboriginal myths were incorporated into the Pentecostal belief system and Christian mythology reinterpreted; degrees of initiation (beginning with baptism) were emphasized and elaborated; and various taboos were adopted. The Bandjalang version of Pentecostalism was decidedly anti-European: Europeans were equated with Romans who killed Christ (who was humble and poor like the Bandjalang, who would be rewarded when Christ returned in glory). There was little or no contact with European Pentecostal groups. Bandjalang Pentecostalism provided an outlet for grievances against the Aborigines' oppressors and a means of restoring self-respect as well as satisfying religious experience and belief in keeping with both Aboriginal and Christian pasts (Calley, 1964).

On Elcho Island, off the central-north coast of Australia (northeast Arnhem Land), a syncretic movement developed in the late 1950s (Berndt, 1962). Sacred-secret objects *(rangga)* were publicly displayed, and spiritual ancestors were equated with prophets within the Christian belief system. The Methodist mission on Elcho Island had refrained from denigrating Aboriginal religion, and the leadership of the movement had strong links with both the church and traditional religion. Occupying a remote corner of a large reserve, the Elcho islanders were sheltered from the worst effects of colonization, and the movement, although it was an attempt to stem the drift toward assimilation by offering a compromise, was not overtly anti-European. Its aims were pragmatic: to retain control over Aboriginal affairs, to obtain better educational and employment opportunities, and to unite hitherto parochially oriented Aboriginal groups of eastern Arnhem Land, and perhaps beyond, by publicly sharing religious secrets. The means, however, were based on the false assumption that what eastern Arnhem Landers valued most highly among their possessions, the *rangga*, were also valued highly by Europeans. The movement failed on several counts. Although, as a sign of the new order, women were shown the *rangga* for the first time, they were not told the

> **A more direct threat to traditional religion than the earlier movement, it has set father against son and traditionalists against Christians.**

meanings, which every male novice has revealed to him. Other eastern Arnhem Landers did not follow suit. Worst of all, European government administrators and missionaries were unimpressed.

The fundamentalist movement has spread rapidly across eastern and central Arnhem Land. The features of the movement are not clear at present, but it appears to be another offer of compromise. The religious belief system is more purely Christian, but ritual forms are more akin to Aboriginal than to European traditions. In the context of renewed threats to the inviolability of the Arnhem Land Reserve from government and mining companies, the adherents preach the equality of Aborigines and Europeans, which may convey an appeal—consciously or unconsciously—for Aboriginal control over land and society. Although the movement has had considerable success, adherence to it is by no means universal. A more direct threat to traditional religion than the earlier movement, it has set father against son and traditionalists against Christians.

Western Desert Movements. The cultural block traditionally occupying the huge desert region of eastern Western Australia and western areas of the Northern Territory and South Australia was the area most isolated from Western encroachment. Mainly since the 1930s and particularly since World War II, Aborigines of the Western Desert have moved into government settlements and into the pastoral regions of the southern Kimberley Plateau of northwestern Australia. Here Aborigines have been most successful at adapting their traditional religion to the exigencies of European domination.

On the southern Kimberley Plateau cults here are exchanged across hundreds of miles. An important impetus seems to have been the Pastoral Award in 1969, which granted Aboriginal employees equal pay on cattle properties in the region but was followed by mass expulsion of Aborigines

from land on which they had come to feel secure. The expulsion coincided with a rise in Aboriginal political consciousness and a growing sense of common interests. The cultic movement is intimately linked with demands for Aboriginal title to land.

In the southern Kimberley and in many other places in the Western Desert, a conflict exists between Christians and cultists on the issues of symbolic identity and appropriate role in the wider Australian community. The cultists have adapted traditional religion to meet the demands of youth and women's emancipation, pan-Aboriginal identity, and economic development: initiation ordeals have been considerably reduced, women are admitted into cults on a more equal footing, religious parochialism has been transcended by incorporating ritual elements from various locales, political and religious leadership have separated but remain collaborative, and the ritual calendar is adjusted to the requirements of economic enterprise. Some or all of these elements are accepted in various Western Desert Aboriginal communities, as their members participate in the cult exchanges emanating mainly from the southern Kimberley.

A Community Case Study. Established as a government Aboriginal settlement in about 1950, Lajamanu, formerly Hooker Creek, is a predominantly Walbiri (Warlpiri) community in the central northwest of the Northern Territory. Traditional clan territories of most Lajamanu residents are located to the south in the Tanami Desert, but many clan members have never seen their territory, and few have ever lived there. After the establishment of the settlement, local totemic ceremonies declined in importance. The local Baptist mission gradually acquired converts, and by the mid-1970s, as traditional religion became increasingly anachronistic, the Christian future at Lajamanu looked bright. Local Christians experimented with adaptations of Walbiri ritual forms to Christian content and earned themselves mission-sponsored trips to southern cities to display their minimally syncretic creations.

From about 1976 onward, a new cult from the southern Kimberley was enthusiastically embraced at Lajamanu. The adoption was managed by relatively youthful Aboriginal administrators who were articulate in English, skilled in negotiations with Europeans, politically aware, and in control of the community's telecommunications and motorized transportation facilities. Exchange visits of large contingents were arranged with Aboriginal communities far to the west across the Western Australian border. Far more dramatic and less stylized than Walbiri ritual forms, the ritual forms of the newly arrived cult were well-suited to performance by younger people. Women were admitted to the cult in a seemingly more equal role than in traditional rites, and ritual experience of male elders was set at nought.

The aim of cult leaders at Lajamanu—to replace the old ceremonies with the new—was met with some resistance. To avoid initiation into the new cult, Walbiri Christians gathered in the mission yard, and other people fled to distant places. The European missionary bemoaned the passing of traditional rites. Old men insisted on their sons being initiated traditionally. Youths were more interested in participating in the universal youth culture of rock and roll and in the country-and-western traditions of rural Australia. Whether the new cult succeeds, however, will depend on the extent to which the Lajamanu Walbiri choose to adopt a religious movement which currently seems to offer the best chance of maintaining an Aboriginal identity which is in harmony with the aims of an emerging national Aboriginal polity.

Located directly west of the southern Kimberley corridor of the movment, Lajamanu represents an extension of the movement's axis. If the new cult does take hold and the community enters more fully into cult exchanges with their new allies, these traditional elements may be modified or disappear. Since there are historical precedents for cult exchanges to the north and northeast of Walbiri country, Lajamanu may become a pivot for a more widespread Aboriginal religious movement.

BIBLIOGRAPHY

Berndt, Ronald M. "Influence of European Culture on Australian Aborigines." *Oceania* 21 (March 1951): 229-235.

Berndt, Ronald M. *An Adjustment Movement in Arnhem Land, Northern Territory of Australia*. Paris, 1962.

Calley, Malcom J. C. "Pentecostalism among the Bandjalang." In *Aborigines Now*, edited by Marie Reay, pp. 48-58. Sydney, 1964.

Durkheim, Émile. *The Elementary Forms of the Religious Life*. Translated by Joseph Ward Swain. Reprint, New York, 1965.

Kolig, Erich. "Tradition and Emancipation: An Australian Aboriginal Version of 'Nativism.' " *Newsletter of the Aboriginal Affairs Planning Authority, Western Australia* (Perth) 1, supp. (March 1977).

Lommel, Andreas. "Modern Culture Influences on the Aborigines." *Oceania* 21 (September 1950): 14-24.

Maddock, Kenneth. *The Australian Aborigines: A Portrait of Their Society*. Rev. ed. Ringwood, Australia, 1982.

Meggitt, M. J. *Gadjari among the Walbiri Aborigines of Central Australia*. Sydney, 1966.

Stanner, W. E. H. *On Aboriginal Religion*. Sydney, 1964.

Tonkinson, Robert. *Aboriginal Victors of the Desert Crusade*. Menlo Park, Calif., 1974.

Wild, Stephen A. "The Role of the Katjiri (Gadjari) among the Walpiri in Transition." In *Seminars 1971, Centre for Research in Aboriginal Affairs*, Monash University, pp. 110-135. Clayton, Australia, 1972.

Wild, Stephen A. "Walbiri Music and Dance in Their Social and Cultural Nexus." Ph. D. diss., Indiana University, 1975.

STEPHEN A. WILD

History of Study

The study of Australian Aboriginal religions has been the study of religions without a written record provided by their adherents. We depend on what outsiders to Aboriginal religion have thought worthwhile to commit to writing. Moreover the history of contact in Australia has been a sorry one in the main—Aborigines were dispossessed of land, regarded with contempt, and made socially and politically inferior. The amateur anthropologist A. W. Howitt could observe in 1880 that the frontier was often marked by a line of blood. Indeed, between the late eighteenth century, when European settlement began, and the 1920s, Aboriginal numbers fell so sharply that prophecies of race extinction were neither alarmist by some nor wishful thinking by others. After World War II, in keeping with a new policy of assimilating Aborigines to an ill-defined general Australian standard, there was a great expansion of administrative interference with them. But a more sympathetic attitude toward tradition became prevalent during the 1970s; "self-management" and "self-determination" entered common usage as policy slogans; and a few Aborigines even began to call for sovereignty. In what is now a highly politicized atmosphere, with laws passed or proposed for the grant of land rights, the protection of sacred sites, and the recognition of customary law, it can be an advantage for Aborigines to be—or to appear to be—traditional in outlook and values. It is amid such aftermaths and in such contexts that scholars (mostly anthropologists) have studied Aboriginal religion.

In the course of this strained and unhappy history a remarkable change has occurred in the appreciation of Aboriginal religion. It can best be illustrated by juxtaposing two pairs of quotations. In 1828 Roger Oldfield (pseudonym of the Reverend Ralph Mansfield) wrote that "the religion of the Aborigines, or rather their superstition, is very absurd," and in 1841 another clergyman, Lancelot Edward Threlkeld, described Aborigines as "deluded men" who, "like most ignorant savage tribes, are remarkably superstitious." But by the mid-twentieth century, a number of writers had discussed the status of Aboriginal religion more sympathetically. In 1965, the anthropologist W. E. H. Stanner referred to "the facts that have convinced modern anthropologists that the Aborigines are a deeply religious people."

Such a rise in estimation reflects growing knowledge of and deepening sympathy with Aborigines, but another important cause is the loss of confidence in the validity or usefulness of earlier criteria for distinguishing true religion from false, or religion from superstition and magic. Assertions of Aboriginal religiosity (or spirituality, as it is often called) and studies of aspects of Aboriginal religion have proliferated since the 1950s—coinciding, ironically, with a growing inclusion of Aborigines in the Australian polity and an increasing erosion of the more tangible features of traditional culture. No longer as objectively "other" as they once were, the Aborigines have become subjectively "other" through being credited with a religious dimension largely absent from the secularized society which engulfs them. It would be wrong, however, to imagine that an unbridgeable gulf has opened between earlier and later bodies of opinion. A degree of continuity can be seen even in the writings of Stanner, who worked passionately and to great effect to dispel misperceptions of Aboriginal life and thought.

The Aborigines, he wrote in 1953, have no gods, their afterlife is only a shadowy replica of worldly existence, their ethical insights are dim and coarsely textured, their concept of goodness lacks true scruple, and their many stories about the Dreaming (the far-off creative period when nature and culture were formed) are plainly preposterous, lacking logic, system, and completeness. Does this differ much from Howitt, half a century earlier, who could not see that the Aborigines had any form of religion, and who thought that the supernatural beings in whom they believed showed no trace of a divine nature (being, at most, ideal headmen living in the sky instead of on earth)? Does it differ from Howitt's contemporaries, Baldwin Spencer and F. J. Gillen, in whose monumental works such words as *god*, *religion*, and *divinity* are conspicuous by their absence, though they saw a religious aspect in the Intichiuma, or totemic increase ceremonies, of central Australia? Yet Stanner insisted not only that Aborigines had made the longest and most difficult move toward the formation of a truly religious outlook, but that they had gone far beyond that first step.

Religion's Luxuriant Growth. Stanner suggested in 1965 that one of the best avenues of study of Aboriginal religion was through the surviving regional cults. In fact, anthropological attention has long tended to focus on them, as can be seen by the studies that Howitt and Robert Hamilton Mathews (1841-1918) made of the Bora, or initiation, ceremonies in southeast Australia and that Spencer and Gillen made of the increase and initiation ceremonies of central Australia. This tradition, as it can justly be regarded, has continued until the most recent times. Some of the more notable examples are Ronald M. Berndt's monographs on the Kunapipi and Djanggawul of northern Australia, A. P. Elkin's papers on the Maraian and Yabuduruwa, also of the north, and M. J. Meggitt's monograph on the Gadjari of central Australia, though there has also been valuable work of a more general nature, such as Catherine H. Berndt's and Diane Bell's studies of women's religious beliefs and observances.

The popularity of the cult for study stems from the fact that it is in many ways a natural whole—it seems to be self-bounding. Commonly it has a name (Kunapipi or Kuringal, for example), includes a sequence of ritual episodes—the performance of which may stretch over several weeks—and usually one or more cycles of songs, and has attached to it a body of myths and tangible symbols, such as a musical instrument which may stand for a mythical founder of the cult and be known by the same name as the cult. An outsider who attends a performance may well be reminded of European plays, operas, or ballets, though it would be wrong to think of a cult as necessarily an enactment of a straightforward story. Some episodes do have a narrative quality, but others can be quite cryptic. The performers are not self-chosen or selected at random but occupy roles prescribed according to such criteria as sex, degree of initiatory advancement, moiety (where, as is usual, a dual organization exists), totemic identity, or localized group. All of these criteria, and perhaps others as well, can be relevant in the course of a single cult performance. Another typical aspect of a cult is its anchorage in the landscape: myths and songs refer to numerous places, rites are symbolically or actually performed at such places, and the groups and categories of the social order in terms of which the performers are chosen stand in a variety of jurisprudential relations to those places. A cult, then, is virtually a microcosm of Aboriginal culture.

Throughout much of central and western Australia the maintenance or promotion of fertility in plant and animal nature was aimed at in cult performances. Disposal of the remains of the dead can be an important purpose, as can transformation of spirits of the dead into a state in which they can return to ancestral waters (or other places) and from which they can (in some regions) be reincarnated. Several such purposes can be achieved in a single cult performance. We should not, that is to say, think of there necessarily being a one-to-one correlation of cult and institutionalized purpose. Nor should we think of express purposes as the motives for cult performances. As musical, dramatic, and aesthetic occasions, as mappings-out of landscape and social organization, they can be deeply satisfying for their own sake. This has been brought out especially in the writings of Stanner on the Murinbata of northern Australia, and of T. G. H. Strehlow (1908-1978), the linguist-anthropologist son of Carl Strehlow, on the Aranda.

In spite of seeming to be the natural unit of study, no cult has yet been the subject of a truly comprehensive published work. Howitt and Mathews, for example, concentrated on the sequence of ritual episodes, with the latter also providing detailed descriptions of the shape and dimensions of ceremonial grounds, of the paths between them, and of the objects of art by which they were surrounded. Berndt's Kunapipi monograph runs to 223 pages and his Djanggawul monograph to 320, but both are stronger on myth and song than on ritual description. Elkin on the Maraian, like Meggitt on the Gadjari and Stanner on the cults performed by the Murinbata, neglects the songs (the Yabuduruwa lacks singing). None of these scholars shows, in a really detailed way, how the cults are anchored in landscape and social organization. In short, even at a purely descriptive level, each of our accounts suffers pronounced weaknesses as well as showing characteristic strengths. It is as though the student of a cult is defeated by the sheer abundance of what it offers to eye, ear, and mind. But even if we had a truly comprehensive account of, say, the Kunapipi or Yabuduruwa, we would still be far removed from an adequate grasp of the religious life of the area concerned, for usually several cults coexist.

In southern Arnhem Land, for example, where religious studies have been made by myself, following on earlier work by Elkin, five cults were extant in the 1960s and 1970s, with others still remembered by some older people. The five, in order of degree of secrecy or importance, were Bugabud, Lorgon, Kunapipi and Yabuduruwa (this pair being ranked about equally), and Maraian. All men and women could expect to take part in each of them—they were not the concern, then, of specialized and mutually exclusive groups of votaries. The dual organization, divided into patrilineal moieties named Dua and Yiridja, imposed its pattern on the set of cults: Bugabud, Lorgon, and Maraian existed in two versions, one for each moiety; Kunapipi was classified as Dua and Yabuduruwa as Yiridja. But in each case performers would necessarily be drawn from both moieties by virtue of a prescribed division of labor and responsibilities.

To write an adequate description of such a set of cults would be a mammoth undertaking. But to think of portraying the religious life of southern Arnhem Land by describing discrete cults would be to remain in the condition of theoretical backwardness remarked upon by Kenelm Burridge in 1973. What marks recent advances in the study of religion, he argued, is the transformation of functionalism into some kind of structuralism, by which he meant the abandonment of the concrete institution in favor of the search for the elements of a total semantic field. Institutions would be seen as particular constellations of these elements, and the value of an element would be determined by its position in a constellation. Something like this view is now fairly widely held, and two anthropologists have published substantial approximations of it. Stanner is one, with his perceptive and influential analyses of Murinbata religion. The other is William Lloyd Warner, whose classic study, *A Black Civilization* (New York, 1937), includes a valiant attempt to demonstrate pervasive and recurring themes and symbols in the myths and rites of the Murngin of northern Arnhem Land.

It is clear from the literature that important work can be done in tracing chains of connection between the religious complexes of different areas. Some of the early writers were aware of this possibility—Howitt, for example, in distinguishing eastern and western types of initiation, was recognizing far-flung patterns of similarity and difference—and it has been explored by later writers, including Elkin, Berndt, and Meggitt. The most ambitious effort has come from Worms, who made continent-wide studies of religious vocabulary and

also sought to enumerate the "essentials" of Aboriginal religion and to distinguish them from "accidental accretions."

Main Phases of Study. It may seem artificial to distinguish periods in the study of Aboriginal religion, as distinct from recognizing certain enduring problems posed by the material, yet all but a few of the scholars likely to be taken seriously today belong to one of three main groupings. To a great extent the ways in which they have worked their data have been conditioned, if not determined, by fashions and theories of overseas origin—Stanner, Worms, and the younger Strehlow would be notable exceptions.

A first phase, spanning the late nineteenth and early twentieth centuries, is dominated by the names of Howitt, Spencer and Gillen, Mathews, and the elder Strehlow. Except for Strehlow, who concentrated his researches on the Aranda and their Loritja neighbors, these scholars amassed information over very great areas indeed, although Howitt's work mainly concerned the southeast of the continent and Spencer and Gillen's the Northern Territory. Some of the descriptions of ritual dating from this period, which of course preceded the rise of professional anthropology, are as thorough and detailed as any that have been written since, if not a good deal more so. (It should be noted that the elder Strehlow felt constrained as a missionary not to attend cult performances, so his knowledge of ritual was hearsay, but in studying myths and songs he reaped the benefits of long acquaintance with his informants and of a thorough grasp of their language.) An indication of the quantity of data collected by the workers of this phase is given by Spencer and Gillen's first book, *The Native Tribes of Central Australia* (London, 1899). It has eight chapters, totaling 338 pages, on totems, ceremonies, and the like, with some material in other chapters also being relevant to what we would call religion.

A second phase, beginning in the mid-1920s and flowering especially during the 1930s, the first decade of the journal *Oceania*, owed much to the initial impetus given by A. R. Radcliffe-Brown, Australia's first professor of anthropology. Those years saw the advent of professional anthropology, inspired by functionalist ideas and committed to intensive fieldwork in relatively small areas. Yet the harvest of religious data was meager in comparison with what had been collected in the preceding phase. Before World War II the most substantial portrayal of religious life to emerge from the new wave of scholars was Warner's study of the Murngin, but the chapters of *A Black Civilization* devoted to the subject run to barely two hundred pages (including a good deal of interpretation)—fewer than Berndt would later devote to the Kunapipi alone. The strong point of the writers of this period was their sense of the interconnectedness of the institutions that go to make up a culture, and besides Warner a number of them made useful, albeit somewhat limited, contributions to our religious knowledge. Donald F. Thomson, Ralph Piddington, Ursula H. McConnel, and Phyllis M. Kaberry may particularly be mentioned. Except for Warner they have since been greatly overshadowed by Elkin, Stanner, and the younger Strehlow—scholars who were active in research before World War II, but published their best work on religion long after it, thus overlapping the third phase, which indeed they did much to stimulate.

The third phase really got under way with the expansion of anthropology departments in the universities and the foundation of the Australian Institute of Aboriginal Studies in the 1960s. Intellectually it owes a special debt to papers published by Stanner between 1959 and 1967. Stanner's writings, the product of intensive ratiocination and prolonged reflection, best fit his own prescription for study of, and not merely about, religion. But much that he has to say is difficult, if not positively cryptic, and is best tackled by readers who already enjoy a familiarity with Aboriginal thought and ritual. The store of personally gathered field data on which he relies is far less plentiful than that amassed by Ronald M. Berndt and Catherine H. Berndt or by the younger Strehlow, writers whose work has exerted less influence on their fellows.

The third phase is less clearly distinguishable from the second than the second from the first. The greater degree of continuity is partly due to the shared emphasis on intensive fieldwork by professional anthropologists, as well as to the survival into the 1970s of scholars who had already begun to make their mark forty years earlier and to the appearance of a few students of religion (notably the two Berndts and Meggitt, all trained by Elkin) during the intervening period. Apart from a vast increase in the number of persons doing research, the main differences between the two phases consist in an abandonment of old-style functionalism, a rise of approaches influenced in varying degree by forms of structural or symbolic anthropology, and an intense interest in the significance of the landscape in which Aboriginal lives are set. There is still little sign of philosophers or students of comparative religion challenging the ascendancy of anthropologists.

BIBLIOGRAPHY

The best general exposition of Aboriginal religion is Mircea Eliade's *Australian Religions: An Introduction* (Ithaca, N. Y., 1973), which is based on specialized studies and theoretical arguments published before 1965. Another useful account taking an Australia-wide view is the contribution by Worms, with an updating by Petri, in Hans Nevermann, Ernest A. Worms, and Helmut Petri's *Die Religionen der Südsee und Australiens* (Stuttgart, 1968). A comprehensive selection of readings from anthropologists with field experience among Aborigines is *Religion in Aboriginal Australia*, edited by Max Charlesworth, Howard Morphy, Diane Bell, and me (Saint Lucia, Queensland, 1984). The wealth of detail to be found in particular cults is shown by Ronald M. Berndt in his *Kunapipi* (Melbourne, 1951) and *Djanggawul* (London, 1952) but is most superbly demonstrated in T. G. H. Strehlow, *Songs of Central Australia* (Sydney, 1971), which includes texts and translations of a great many songs. Classic older accounts of Aboriginal religion are in A. W. Howitt's *The Native Tribes of South-East Australia* (New York, 1904), and Baldwin

Spencer and F. J. Gillen's *The Northern Tribes of Central Australia* (London, 1904). Two recent studies on topical themes are Erich Kolig's *The Silent Revolution* (Philadelphia, 1981), a study of change and modernization in Aboriginal religion, and Diane Bell's *Daughters of the Dreaming* (Melbourne, 1983), which is concerned with the religious roles of women. *Australian Aboriginal Mythology*, edited by L. R. Hiatt (Canberra, 1975), is a good example of the approaches of some of the younger workers in the field; see also *The Rainbow Serpent*, edited by Ira R. Buchler and me (The Hague, 1978), which contains studies of one of the most widespread Aboriginal symbols. The classic theoretical analysis remains Émile Durkheim's *The Elementary Forms of the Religious Life* (1915; reprint, New York, 1965), but it relies on nineteenth- and early twentieth-century research and opinion. The most penetrating modern vision and analysis are from W. E. H. Stanner, whose *On Aboriginal Religion* (Sydney, 1964) and *White Man Got No Dreaming: Essays 1938-1973* (Canberra, 1979) are essential.

KENNETH MADDOCK

AZTEC RELIGION

AZTEC RELIGION developed in the capital city of Te-nochtitlán in the Valley of Mexico between the fourteenth and sixteenth centuries CE. The Aztec religious tradition combined and transformed a number of ritual, mythic, and cosmic elements from the heterogeneous cultural groups who inhabited the central plateau of Mesoamerica.

Mexico's central highlands had been the dominant cultural region of central Mesoamerica since the beginning of the common era, when the great imperial capital of Teotihuacán ("abode of the gods") had been established thirty miles north of where Tenochtitlán would later rise. Like Tenochtitlán, Teotihuacán was organized into four great quarters around a massive ceremonial center. Scholars and archaeologists have theorized that the four-quartered city was a massive spatial symbol for the major cosmological conceptions of Aztec religion. In many respects, the cultural and religious patterns of Teotihuacán laid the groundwork for all later developments in and around the Valley of Mexico. The mythologies of successive cultures—the Toltec and the Aztec most prominent among them—looked back to Teotihuacán as their symbolic place of origin and as the source for the legitimacy of their political authority.

Between 1300 and 1521 all roads of central Mesoamerica led into the lake region of the valley from which the magnificent capital of the Aztec arose. When the Aztec's precursors, the Chichimec ("dog lineage"; lit., "dog rope") migrated into the region in the thirteenth century, the valley was held by warring city-states constantly competing for land and tribute. This fragmented world was partly the result of the twelfth-century collapse of the northern Toltec empire centered at the illustrious capital of Tollan ("place of reeds"). The Toltec collapse brought waves of Chichimec and Toltec remnants into the Valley of Mexico, where they interacted with different city-states and religious traditions.

The basic settlement of central Mexico from Teotihuacán times was the *tlatocayotl*, or city-state, which consisted of a capital city surrounded by dependent communities that worked the agricultural lands, paid tribute, and performed services for the elite classes in the capital according to various ritual calendars and cosmological patterns. Around 1325, a Chichimec group who called themselves *México* settled Tenochtitlán and within a hundred years had organized a political unit with the power to dominate an expanding number of cities and towns in the central valley.

One of the major problems in the study of Aztec religion is the fragmentary nature of the pictorial, written, and archaeological sources associated with Tenochtitlán. The Spanish military conquest of Mexico was accompanied by a sustained campaign to eliminate Aztec symbols, images, screenfolds, and ceremonial buildings, as well as members of the military and priestly elites. Surprisingly, a counter attitude developed among certain Spanish officials and priests, who collected indigenous documents and organized their reproduction in order to enhance missionary work and inform Spanish officials about native religion and life. The result is a spectrum of sources including art and architecture; pre-Columbian screenfolds depicting the ritual, divinitory, historical, and genealogical traditions of different cities; post-Conquest codices sometimes accompanied by Spanish commentary; prose sources dependent on indigenous pictorial and oral traditions; histories written by descendants of Aztec royalty; Spanish eyewitness accounts; and large histories and ritual descriptions by Spanish priests who vigorously researched Aztec religion. It is only through a skillful combination of these sources that the complex character of Aztec religion can be discerned.

Cosmogony and Cosmology. The image of the capital city as the foundation of heaven, which the Aztec conceived of as a vertical column of thirteen layers extending above the earth, points to the cosmological conviction underpinning Aztec religion that there existed a profound correspondence between the sacred forces in the universe and the social world of the Aztec empire. This correspondence between the cosmic structure and the political state was anchored in the capital of Tenochtitlán.

In his important summary of religion in pre-Hispanic central Mexico, H. B. Nicholson (1971) outlines the "basic cosmological sequential pattern" of the Aztec cosmogony found in the myths and historical accounts associated with the México. A summary view reveals that Aztec life unfolded in a cosmic setting that was dynamic, unstable, and finally destructive. Even though the cosmic order fluctuated between periods of stability and periods of chaos, the emphasis in many myths and historical accounts is on the destructive forces.

This dynamic universe appears in the sixteenth-century prose accounts *Historia de los Mexicanos por sus pinturas* and the *Leyenda de los soles*. In the former, the universe is arranged in a rapid, orderly fashion after the dual creative divinity, Ometeotl, dwelling in Omeyocan ("place of duality") at the thirteenth level of heaven, generates four children, the Red Tezcatlipoca ("smoking mirror"), the Black Tezcatlipoca, Quetzalcoatl ("plumed serpent"), and Huitzilopochtli ("hummingbird on the left"). They all exist without movement for six hundred years, whereupon the four children assemble "to arrange what was to be done and to establish the law to be followed." Quetzalcoatl and Huitzilopochtli arrange the universe and create fire, half of the sun ("not fully lighted but a little"), the human race, and the calendar. Then, the four brothers create water and its divine beings.

Following this rapid and full arrangement, the sources focus on a series of mythic events that constitute a sacred history. Throughout this sacred history, the dynamic instability of the Aztec universe is revealed. The universe passes through four eras, called "Suns." Each age was presided over by one of the great gods, and each was named for the day (day number and day name) within the calendrical cycle on which the age began (which is also the name of the force that destroys that Sun). The fifth (and last) cosmic age, augured the earthquakes that would inevitably destroy the world.

The creation of this final age, the one in which the Aztec lived, took place around a divine fire in the darkness on the mythical plain of Teotihuacán (to be distinguished from the actual city of that same name). According to the version of this story reported in Fray Bernardino de Sahagún's *Historia general de las cosas de la Nueva España* (compiled 1569-1582; also known as the Florentine Codex), an assembly of gods chose two of their group, Nanahuatzin and Tecuciztecatl, to cast themselves into the fire in order to create the new cosmic age. Following their self-sacrifice, dawn appears in all directions, but the Sun does not rise above the horizon. In confusion, different deities face in various directions in expectation of the sunrise. Quetzalcoatl faces east and from there the Sun blazes forth but sways from side to side without climbing in the sky. In this cosmic crisis, it is decided that all the gods must die at the sacrificial hand of Ecatl, who dispatches them by cutting their throats. Even this massive sacrifice does not move the Sun until the wind god literally blows it into motion. These combined cosmogonic episodes demonstrate the fundamental Aztec conviction that the world is unstable and that it draws its energy from massive sacrifices by the gods. Large-scale sacrifice became a basic pattern in Aztec religion, a ritual means of imposing or maintaining social and cosmological order.

With the creation of the Fifth Sun, the focus of the sacred history shifts from heaven to earth, where agriculture is discovered and human sacrifice is established as the proper ritual response to the requirements of the gods. In one account, Quetzalcoatl, as a black ant, travels to Sustenance Mountain with a red ant where they acquire maize for human beings. Other accounts reveal the divine origins of cotton, sweet potatoes, different types of corn, and the intoxicating drink called pulque. In still others, we learn that warfare was established so that human beings could be captured and sacrificed to nourish the Sun on its heavenly and nocturnal journey. Typically, a god like Mixcoatl creates four hundred human beings to fight among themselves in order for captives to be sacrificed in ceremonial centers to provide the divine food, blood, for the gods who ensure cosmic life.

> **Quetzalcoatl faces east and from there the Sun blazes forth but sways from side to side without climbing in the sky.**

Finally, a number of accounts of the cosmic history culminate with the establishment of the magnificent kingdom of Tollan where Quetzalcoatl the god and Topiltzin Quetzalcoatl the priest-king organize a ceremonial capital divided into five parts with four pyramids and four sacred mountains surrounding the central temple. This city, Tollan, serves as the heart of an empire.

The spatial paradigm of the Aztec cosmos was embodied in the term *cemanahuac*, meaning the "land surrounded by water." At the center of this terrestrial space, called *tlalxico* ("navel of the earth"), stood Te-nochtitlán, from which extended the four quadrants called *nauchampa*, meaning "the four directions of the wind." The waters surrounding the inhabited land were called *ilhuicatl*, the celestial water that extended upward to merge with the lowest levels of the thirteen heavens. Below the earth were nine levels of the underworld, conceived of as "hazard stations" for the souls of the dead, who, aided by magical charms buried with the bodies, were assisted in their quests for eternal peace at the lowest level, called Mictlan, the land of the dead.

The Pantheon. One of the most striking characteristics of the surviving screenfolds, which present ritual and divinatory information, is the incredible array of deities who animated the ancient Mesoamerican world. Likewise, the remaining sculpture and the sixteenth-century prose accounts of Aztec Mexico present us with a pantheon so crowded that H. B. Nicholson's authoritative study of Aztec religion includes a list of more than sixty distinct and interrelated names. Scholarly analysis of these many deities suggests that virtually all aspects of existence were considered inherently sacred and that these deities were expressions of a numinous quality that permeated the "real" world. While it does not appear that the Aztec pantheon or pattern of hierophanies was organized as a whole, it is possible to identify clusters of deities organized around the major cult themes of cosmogonic creativity, fertility and regeneration, and war and sacrificial nourishment of the Sun.

Aztec deities dwelt in the different levels of the thirteen-layered celestial sphere or the nine-layered underworld. The general structuring principle for the pantheon, derived from the cosmic pattern of a center and four quarters, resulted in the quadruple or quintuple ordering of gods. For instance in the Codex Borgia's representation of the Tlaloques (rain gods), the rain god, Tlaloc, inhabits the central region of heaven while four other Tlaloques inhabit the four regions of the sky, each dispensing a different kind of rain. While deities were invisible to the human eye, the Aztec saw them in dreams, visions, and in the "deity impersonators" (*teixiptla*) who appeared at the major ceremonies. These costumed impersonators, sometimes human, sometimes effigies of stone, wood, or dough, were elaborately decorated with identifying insignia such as conch shells, masks, weapons, jewelry, mantas, feathers, and a myriad of other items.

As we have seen, Aztec religion was formed by migrating Chichimec who entered the Valley of Mexico and established important political and cultural centers there. This process of migration and urbanization informed and was informed by their concept of deity. A familiar pattern in the sacred histories of Mesoamerican tribal groups is the erection of a shrine to the patron deity as the first act of settlement in a new region. This act of founding a settlement around the tribal shrine represented the intimate tie between the deity, the *hombre-dios*, and the integrity of the people. In reverse fashion, conquest of a community was achieved when the patron deity's shrine was burned and the *tlaquimilolli* was carried off as a captive.

This pattern of migration, foundation, and conquest associated with the power of a patron diety is clearly exemplified by the case of Huitzilopochtli, patron of the wandering México. According to Aztec tradition, Huitzilopochtli inspired the México *teomama* to guide the tribe into the Valley of Mexico, where he appeared to them as an eagle on a cactus in the lake. There they constructed a shrine to Huitzilopochtli and built their city around the shrine. This shrine became the Aztec Great Temple, the supreme political and symbolic center of the Aztec empire. It was destroyed in 1521 by the Spanish, who blew up the temple with cannons and carried the great image of Huitzilopochtli away.

Creator Gods. The Aztec high god, Ometeotl ("lord of duality") was the celestial, androgynous, primordial creator of the universe, the omnipotent, omniscient, omnipresent foundation of all things. In some sources he/she appears to merge with a number of his/her offspring, a sign of his/her pervasive power. Ometeotl's male aspects (Ometecuhtli and Tonacatecuhtli) and female aspects (Omecihuatl and Tonacacihuatl) in turn merged with a series of lesser deities associated with generative and destructive male and female qualities. The male aspect was associated with fire and the solar and maize gods. The female aspect merged with earth fertility goddesses and especially corn goddesses. Ometeotl inhabited the thirteenth and highest heaven in the cosmos, which was the place from which the souls of infants descended to be born on earth. Ometeotl was more "being" than "action." Most of the creative effort to organize the universe was acomplished by the divine couple's four offspring: Tezcatlipoca, Quetzalcoatl, Xiuhtecuhtli, and Tlaloc.

Tezcatlipoca ("smoking mirror") was the supreme active creative force of the pantheon. He was the arch-sorcerer whose smoking obsidian mirror revealed the powers of ultimate transformation associated with darkness, night, jaguars, and shamanic magic.

Another tremendous creative power was Xiuhtecuhtli, the ancient fire god, who influenced every level of society and cosmology. Xiuhtecuhtli was the generative force at the New Fire ceremony, also called the Binding of the Years, held every fifty-two years on the Hill of the Star outside of Tenochtitlán. At midnight on the day that a fifty-two-year calendar cycle was exhausted, at the moment when the star cluster we call the Pleiades passed through the zenith, a heart sacrifice of a war captive took place.

Fertility and Regeneration. A pervasive theme in Aztec religion was fertility and the regeneration of agriculture. Aztec society depended on a massive agricultural system of *chinampas* ("floating gardens") that constituted large sections of the city's geographical space. Also, surrounding city-states were required to pay sizable amounts of agricultural goods in tribute to the capital. While many female deities inspired the ritual regeneration of agriculture, the most ancient and widespread fertility-rain god was Tlaloc, who dwelt on the prominent mountain peaks, where rain clouds were thought to emerge from caves to fertilize the land through rain, rivers, pools, and storms. The Aztec held Mount Tlaloc to be the original source of the waters and of vegetation. Tlaloc's supreme importance is reflected in the location of his shrine alongside that of Huitzilopochtli in the Templo Mayor. Surprisingly, the great majority of buried offerings excavated at the temple were dedicated to Tlaloc rather than Huitzilopochtli.

Two other major gods intimately associated with Tlaloc were Chalchiuhtlicue, the goddess of water, and Ehécatl, the wind god, an aspect of Quetzalcoatl.

The most powerful group of female fertility deities were the *teteoinnan*, a rich array of earth-mother goddesses, who were representatives of the usually distinct but sometimes combined qualities of terror and beauty, regeneration and destruction. These deities were worshiped in cults concerned with the abundant powers of the earth, women, and fertility. Among the most prominent were Tlazolteotl, Xochiquetzal, and Coatlicue. Tlazolteotl was concerned with sexual powers and passions and the pardoning of sexual transgressions.

Xochiquetzal was the goddess of love and sexual desire and was pictured as a nubile maiden associated with flowers, feasting, and pleasure. A ferocious goddess, Coatlicue ("serpent skirt") represented the cosmic mountain that conceived all stellar beings and devoured all beings into her repulsive, lethal, and fascinating form. Her statue is studded with sacrificed hearts, skulls, hands, ferocious claws, and giant snake heads.

A prominent deity who linked agricultural renewal with warfare was Xipe Totec, whose gladiatorial sacrifice renewed vegetation in the spring and celebrated success on the battlefield. Part of his ceremony, called the Feast of the Flaying of Men, included the flaying of the sacrificial victim and the ceremonial wearing of the skin by the sacred specialist.

Ceremony and Sacrifice. Another important facet of Aztec religious practice was human sacrifice, usually carried out for the purpose of nourishing or renewing the Sun or other deity (or to otherwise appease it), thus ensuring the stability of the universe. The mythic model for mass human sacrifice was the story of the creation of the fifth age, in which the gods themselves were sacrificed in order to empower the Sun. Tonatiuh, the personification of that Sun (whose visage appears in the center of the Calendar Stone), depended on continued nourishment from human hearts.

Cosmology, pantheon, and ritual sacrifice were united and came alive in the exuberant and well-ordered ceremonies carried out in the more than eighty buildings situated in the sacred precinct of the capital and in the hundreds of ceremonial centers throughout the Aztec world. Guided by detailed ritual calendars, Aztec ceremonies varied from town to town but typically involved days of ritual preparation included fasting; offerings of food, flowers, and paper; use of incense and purification techniques; embowering; songs; and processions of deity-impersonators to various temples in ceremonial precincts.

Following these elaborate preparations, blood sacrifices were carried out by priestly orders specially trained to dispatch the victims swiftly. The victims were usually captive warriors or purchased slaves. The typical ritual involved the dramatic heart sacrifice and the placing of the heart in a ceremonial vessel *(cuauhxicalli)* in order to nourish the gods.

All of these ceremonies were carried out in relation to two ritual calendars, the 365-day calendar or *tonalpohualli* ("count of day") consisting of eighteen twenty-day months plus a five-day intercalary period and the 260-day calendar consisting of thirteen twenty-day months. More than one-third of these ceremonies were dedicated to Tlaloc and earth fertility goddesses. Beside ceremonies relating to the two calendars, a third type of ceremony related to the many life cycle stages of the individual. In some cases, the entire community was involved in bloodletting.

Aztec religion, as we have seen, was formed during the rise to empire of a minority population who inherited urban traditions and sociopolitical conflicts of great prestige and intensity. This remarkable tradition came to an abrupt end during the military conquest of Tenochtitlán by the Spanish and the subsequent destruction of ceremonial life. But it is important to note that one of the last images we have of the Templo Mayor of Tenochtitlán before it was blown apart by Spanish cannon is the image of Aztec warriors sacrificing captive Spanish soldiers in front of the shrine to Huitzilopochtli.

BIBLIOGRAPHY

Broda, Johanna. "El tributo en trajes guerreros y la estructura del sistema tributario Mexica." In *Economia, política e ideología en el México prehispanico*. Edited by Pedro Carrasco and Johanna Broda. Mexico City, 1978. A valuable study of the pattern and structure of tributary payments to Tenochtitlán during the height of its dominance.

Brundage, Burr C. *The Fifth Sun: Aztec Gods, Aztec World*. Austin, 1979. The best English-language monograph introduction to Aztec religion which provides an insightful understanding of the Aztec pantheon and human sacrifice.

Carrasco, David. *Quetzalcoatl and the Irony of Empire; Myths and Prophecies in Aztec Tradition*. Chicago, 1982. Utilizing the history of religions approach, the author focuses on the Quetzalcoatl paradigm to study the history of Mesoamerican religions.

López Austin, Alfredo. *Hombre-Dios: Religión y política en el mundo Nahuatl*. Mexico City, 1973. The best Spanish-language account of the interweaving of myth, history, politics, and religious authority in Mesoamerican history.

Matox Moctezuma, Eduardo. *Una visita al Templo Mayor de Tenochtitlán*. Mexico City, 1981. The chief excavator of the Aztec Great Temple describes the fascinating treasures found at the heart of the Aztec empire.

Nicholson, H. B. "Religion in Pre-Hispanic Central Mexico." In *Handbook of Middle American Indians*, edited by Robert Wauchope, vol 10. Austin, 1971. The classic description of Mesoamerican religion in the central plateau of Mexico during the decades prior to the Conquest.

Pasztory, Esther. *Aztec Art*. New York, 1983. The finest single-volume description and interpretation of Aztec art and its religious significance. Excellent prose accompanied by magnificent photographs.

Townsend, Richard. *State and Cosmos in the Art of Tenochtitlán*. Washington, D. C., 1979. A concise, brilliant interpretation of the monumental art of the Aztec capital of Tenochtitlán in the light of a good understanding of religious realities.

DAVID CARRASCO

BAHA'IS

BAHA'IS are the followers of Mirza Husayn `Ali Nuri (1817-1892), known as Baha' Allah ("glory of God"). The new religion arose in the second half of the nineteenth century among those Babis who recognized in Baha' Allah the prophetic figure foretold by their leader, the Bab: "he whom God shall manifest" *(man yuzhiruhu Allah)*.

Historical Development. Mirza Husayn `Ali Nuri was born into a noble Tehran family that had given several ministers to the Persian court. According to Baha'i tradition and his own writings, he never attended school. He was a profoundly religious personality and soon converted to the new Babi teachings, although he never met the Bab personally. From his writings it appears that he never read the Babis' holy book, the *Bayan* (Declaration), but nevertheless knew it by heart.

In the wave of repression against Babis that followed an attempt on the life of Nasir al-Din Shah in 1852, he was thrown into the Tehran prison known as Siyah Chal ("Black Hole"), where he had the mystical experience that Baha'is consider to be the first intimation of his future mission. As he describes this experience in *Lawh-i Ibn Dhi'b* (Epistle of the Son of the Wolf), he heard a voice crying, "Verily we will succor you by means of yourself and your pen. Be not afraid . . . you are in security. And soon God will raise up the treasuries of the heart, namely those men who shall succor you for love of you and your name, by which God will bring to life the hearts of the sages." At other times he felt that a great torrent of water was running from the top of his head to his chest "like a powerful river pouring itself out on the earth from the summit of a lofty mountain."

Upon his release from prison in January 1853, his possessions were confiscated and he was banished with his family to Baghdad. There he exerted increasing spiritual influence on the Babi exiles, while that of his half brother, Mirza Yahya (known as Subh-i Azal, "dawn of eternity") declined. In 1854 Baha' Allah went to Kurdistan, where he lived as a nomadic dervish near Sulaymaniyah. When he returned to Baghdad two years later, his influence upon the Babi exiles and numerous Persian visitors was such that the Persian consul asked the Ottoman authorities to remove him to Istanbul. Shortly before his departure, on 21 April 1863, in the garden of Najib Pasha near Baghdad (called by Baha'is Bagh-i Rizvan, the "garden of paradise"), Baha' Allah declared himself to be "he whom God shall manifest" as promised by the Bab.

After some months in Istanbul, the exiles were sent to Edirne, and there Baha' Allah openly declared his prophetic mission, sending letters (known as *alwah*, "tablets") to various sovereigns, including Pope Pius IX, to invite support for his cause. The majority of the Babis accepted him and came to be known as Baha'is. A minority, followers of Subh-i Azal (hence Azalis), provoked incidents that impelled the Ottomans to banish the Baha'is (with some Azalis) to Palestine and the Azalis (with some Baha'is) to Cyprus. Baha' Allah arrived in Acre with his family in August 1868, and for this reason the Baha'is consider Palestine as the Holy Land.

For nine years Baha' Allah was imprisoned in the fortress at Acre but was then allowed to move to a country house he had rented at Mazra`ah. Between 1877 and 1884 he occupied himself with writing his fundamental work, *Kitab al-aqdas* (The Most Holy Book). About 1880 he was allowed to go to Bahji, near Haifa, where he died twelve years later after a short illness. According to his will *(Kitab `ahdi)*, his eldest

> **The Baha'i faith . . . is practiced in 340 different countries, and its literature has been translated into 700 languages.**

son, `Abbas Effendi (1844-1921), who had faithfully accompanied his father in his travels and his exile, became the infallible interpreter of his father's books and writings and the "center of the covenant" *(markaz-i `ahd)*. He was known thereafter as `Abd al-Baha' ("servant of the glory [of God]"). Baha' Allah's will was contested by his other son, Muhammad `Ali, who set up a rival organization and tried with all his means to compromise his brother in the eyes of the already hostile Ottoman authorities. `Abd al-Baha' was formally released from prison in 1908 under the amnesty granted by the new government of the Young Turks. In 1910 he began his three missionary journeys to the West: to Egypt (1910), to Europe (1911), and to America and Europe (1912-1913); he returned to Palestine in 1913.

The first Baha'i group in America was formed as early as 1894, and in December 1898, the first American pilgrims arrived in Acre. Although one of the objects of `Abd al-Baha's trips was to counter the propaganda of his brother's supporters, he also formed Baha'i groups in the countries he visited. In 1920 he was knighted by the British government; he died the following year and was buried near the Bab in the great shrine on Mount Carmel. In his will he appointed Shoghi Effendi Rabbani (1899-1957), the eldest son of his eldest daughter, as "guardian of the cause of God" *(wali-yi amr Allah)* and infallible interpreter of his writings and those of his father. After studying at Oxford, Shoghi Effendi returned in 1923 to his native Haifa, which became the administrative center of the Baha'i faith. In 1936 he married Mary Maxwell, daughter of the Canadian architect responsible for the shrine of the Bab on Mount Carmel and other Baha'i monuments; she took the name Ruhiyah Khanum. When Shoghi Effendi died without leaving a will, the cause was administered for five years by a Council of the Hands of the Cause residing in Israel; in 1962 the International House of Justice, foretold by Baha' Allah in his *Kitab al-aqdas*, was then selected by an international convention held in Haifa. This body has since been reelected every five years.

The Baha'i faith has spread rapidly all over the world; it is practiced in 340 different countries, and its literature has been translated into 700 languages. The king of independent Samoa is Baha'i, as are entire villages of Indios in Peru and Bolivia. Precise figures for the total number of Baha'is in the world are difficult to supply, since available statistics normally deal only with the number of administrative units, of which there were, in 1985, 143 national spiritual assemblies and 27,887 local assemblies. At that time, the world Baha'i population was estimated at 1.5 to 2 million, with about 300,000 members in Iran constituting that country's largest religious minority. In the late twentieth century the Baha'i faith showed enormous growth in Africa, the Indian subcontinent, and Vietnam, where they were then counted in the hundreds of thousands.

Beliefs and Practices. The core of Baha'i theology can be succinctly expressed as "evolution in time and unity in the present hour." According to Baha'i teachings, "Religious truth is not absolute but relative." The inaccessible essence of God manifests itself through the eternal Logos, but while the Logos is one, its manifestations are many. Their task is to create ever-wider unities in the world. Hence Abraham unified a tribe; Moses, a people; and Muhammad, a nation, while Jesus was to purify the souls of individuals. The task of each manifestation of God has been completely fulfilled: Christianity has not failed, because Christ's task of creating individual sanctity has been achieved. This is not enough, however: collective sanctity of the entire human race is now required. Such was the task of Baha' Allah.

But the manifestation of God through the prophets never ceases. While Muslims hold that Muhammad is the last man-ifestation of the will of God and that no other is needed, the Baha'is insist that people always need a divine manifestation and that even Baha' Allah will not be the last. The Baha'i faith is the only one that foresees its own eventual abolition, although not before "a thousand years," as it is written in the *Kitab al-aqdas*. The Baha'is recognize the divine mission of Muhammad and are willing, in fact, to accept him as the *khatam al-nabiyin* ("seal of the prophets") in the sense that every prophet is the seal of those preceding.

Baha'i psychology is more complex than is often perceived. `Abd al-Baha' distinguished five types of spirit: animal, vegetable, human, that of faith, and the Holy Spirit. The spirit of faith, which is given by God, is the only one that con-

> ## The Baha'i religion has no public ritual nor any sacrament or private rites of a sacred character.

fers "eternal life" on the human spirit (and this tenet explains why some Orientalists have written that the Baha'is do not believe in the immortality of the soul). Faith is essential to Baha'i spiritual life. As the first verse of the *Kitab al-aqdas* proclaims: "The first commandment of God to his servant is knowledge of the dawn of his revelation and the dayspring of his degree [i. e., the prophet, the manifestation of God], who is his appointed representative in the created world. He who has attained this knowledge has attained all good. And he who does not know it is of the world of error even though he performs all good works." Eternity of the soul for the Baha'is means a continuation of the voyage toward the unknowable essence of God. Paradise and hell are symbols, the first standing for the believers' journey toward God and the second for the fruitless path toward annihilation followed by those who knowingly reject the faith and perform evil works.

The Baha'i religion has no public ritual nor any sacrament or private rites of a sacred character. The sole religious duties of a Baha'i are (1) to assemble every nineteen days, on the first day of each Baha'i month, for a celebration called the Feast of the Nineteenth Day; (2) to fast for nineteen days from dawn to sunset, following Muslim usage, for the entire month of `Ala, which concludes with the New Year on 21 March (like the traditional Persian New Year, that of the Baha'is falls on the vernal equinox); (3) to abstain completely from alcoholic beverages; and (4) to pray daily. In contrast to Islamic and Christian practice, the obligatory prayers (Pers., *namaz*; Arab., *salat*) are intended to be performed privately and not, with the exception of a special prayer for the dead, in congregation; likewise, they may be recited in any language rather than in Arabic alone, as is the case with Islam.

Apart from these duties, the *Kitab al-aqdas* lays down precise rules for the division of inheritance (part going to one's teachers), levies a tax of 19 percent on revenues, and prescribes numerous other rules and laws (penal, civil, and religious), which, by the late twentieth century, were followed only by Baha'is living in the East. Men and women are held to be equals, and marriage is monogamous. (Bigamy was permitted in the *Kitab al-aqdas*, but that provision was canceled by `Abd al-Baha'.) A valid marriage requires the consent of the couple's parents; divorce is allowed but discouraged.

Perhaps the most original aspect of Baha'i teaching is the administration of the community, a sort of "democratic theocracy" similar to that of early Islam and considered to be of divine origin. The controlling bodies of the community, pyramidal in structure, are of two types, administrative and instructional. The former include the local and national Spiritual Assemblies and the International House of Justice. Local Spiritual Assemblies, each consisting of nine members elected by universal suffrage, are constituted wherever there are at least that number of Baha'is. Election is considered an act of worship and thus does not imply responsibility on the part of the elected toward the electors, since the latter are considered merely instruments of the will of God. Elections are held yearly during the Rizvan feast (21 April-2 May). When there is a sufficient number of local Assemblies, a convention, elected by universal suffrage, in turn elects a nine-member national Assembly from the Baha'i community at large. Every five years (this period is subject to change), an international convention of all the national Assembly members elects the International House of Justice *(bayt al-`adl-i umumi)*, which functions as the supreme administrative body. It is empowered, when the needs of the time warrant, to abrogate previous laws and to frame new ones not laid down in the *Kitab al-aqdas* or other writings of the founder.

The instructional pyramid includes the Hands of the Cause (first appointed by Baha' Allah, then by Shoghi Effendi), the Continental Board, and the Auxiliary Board, whose members nominate their own assistants. All members of the instructional pyramid obey the administrative bodies in their practical work.

Although the Baha'is have no public worship, the *Kitab al-aqdas* recommends the erection of a temple structure, called Mashriq al-Adhkar (literally "a place where mention of the name of God arises at dawn"), which is a nine-sided building surmounted by a dome of nine sections. It is open to the faithful of every creed. The first such temple, located in `Ishqabad, now Soviet Turkistan, was built in 1920 but later destroyed by an earthquake. In 1910, `Abd al-Baha' laid the first stone of the Mashriq al-Adhkar in Wilmette, Illinois; this building was officially inaugurated in 1953. By the late twentieth century, five others had been completed, in Panama, Australia, Germany, Uganda, and Samoa, and one more was under construction in India. Other significant Baha'i monuments include the tomb of Baha' Allah in Bahji and those of the Bab and `Abd al-Baha' at the World Center of the Faith in Haifa.

The fact that the World Center is located in Israel (formerly Palestine) has caused the Baha'is to be regarded as something of a fifth column in Muslim countries, and they have suffered great persecution as a result. Particularly cruel measures have been taken against the Baha'is in Iran following the proclamation of the Islamic Republic: all religious and testimonial activities were officially banned in August 1983, and more than 170 Baha'is were said to have been executed in the first five years after the Iranian Revolution.

BIBLIOGRAPHY

Baha' Alláh's *Kitab al-aqdas*, written in Arabic, has been edited and translated into Russian by A. G. Tumanski as *Kitab akdes*, in "Zapiski *Imp. Akad. Nauk*," Hist.-Phil. Class, ser. 8, vol. 6 (St. Petersburg, 1899). Among the writings of Baha' Allah that were translated into English by Shoghi Effendi are *Kitab-i-Íqán: The Book of Certitude* (Wilmette, Ill., 1943), *The Hidden Words* (London, 1944), *Prayers and Meditations* (New York, 1938), and *Selected Writings of Bahá'u'lláh* (Wilmette, 1942). Also available in English is *The Seven Valleys and the Four Valleys*, translated by Ali-Kuli Khan assisted by Marzieh Gail, rev. ed. (Wilmette, 1952).

Conversations with `Abd al-Baha' in Acre were collected and translated by Laura Clifford Barney as *Some Answered Questions* (1908; reprint, London, 1961). English translations of `Abd al-Baha's writings include *The Mysterious Forces of Civilization* (Chicago, 1919), *Selected Writings of `Abdu'l Bahá'* (Wilmette, 1942), *Tablets of `Abdu'l Bahá'*, 3 vols. (New York, 1930), and *The Wisdom of `Abdu'l Bahá'* (New York, 1924). Among the published works of Shoghi Effendi are *Baha'i World Faith* (Wilmette, 1943), *Gleanings from the Writings of Baha'ullah* (New York, 1935), and *God Passes By* (Wilmette, 1945).

For the early history of the Baha'is, see Nabil Zarandi's *Ta'rikh-i Nabil*, translated by Shoghi Effendi as *The Dawn-Breakers* (1932; reprint, Wilmette, 1970). *The Bábi and Bahá'i Religions* 1844-1944: *Some Contemporary Western Accounts*, edited by Moojan Momen (Oxford, 1981), offers a documentary history compiled from the writings and records of missionaries, travelers, and government officials. Various aspects of Baha'i activity in the Middle East, North America, and elsewhere are presented in *Studies in Babi and Baha'i History*, vol. 1, edited by Moojan Momen (Los Angeles, 1982), and the second volume, published as *From Iran East and West*, edited by Juan R. Cole and Moojan Momen (Los Angeles, 1984), both of which include extensive bibliographies. For sources in Persian and Arabic, see my entries "Baha' Allah" and "Baha'is" in *The Encyclopaedia of Islam*, new ed. (Leiden, 1960-).

ALESSANDRO BAUSANI

BALINESE RELIGION

Eight degrees south of the equator, toward the middle of the belt of islands that form the southern arc of the Indonesian archipelago, lies the island of Bali, home of the last surviving Hindu-Buddhist civilization of Indonesia. A few kilometers to the west of Bali is the island of Java, where major Hindu-Buddhist kingdoms flourished from the time of Borobudur (eighth century) until the end of the sixteenth century, when the last Javanese Hindu kingdom fell to Islam. Just to the east of Bali is the Wallace Line, a deep ocean channel marking the biogeographical frontier between Asia and the Pacific.

Sources of Balinese Religion. Evidence for the nature of prehistoric Balinese religion comes from three sources: archaeology, historical linguistics, and comparative ethnography. Linguistically, Balinese belongs to the Malayo-Polynesian language family, itself derived from Proto-Austronesian, which is thought to have been spoken by Southeast Asian peoples around six thousand years ago. Proto-Austronesian-speakers on Bali had words for many religious concepts: nature gods, such as a sky god; ancestral spirits (who were probably thought to inhabit mountaintops); a human soul, or perhaps multiple souls; and shamanistic trance.

Sometime in the early first millennium of the common era, Bali came into contact with Indian civilization and thus with the Hindu and Buddhist religions. The nature of this contact

> ## The old Balinese nature gods were perhaps not so much nudged aside as reincorporated into the new Indic pantheon.

and the ensuing process of "indianization" has long been a subject of scholarly debate.

In Bali, the first clear indication of "indianization" is entirely of a religious nature, consisting of several sorts of physical evidence: stone sculptures, clay seals and ritual apparatus, and a series of stone and copperplate inscriptions. The sculptures closely resemble Central Javanese sculptures of the same era (both Hindu and Buddhist), while the clay seals contain Mahayana formulas duplicated in the eighth-century Javanese temple Candi Kalasan.

The first inscriptions appear in the ninth century CE and are the earliest written texts discovered in Bali. They were written by court scribes in two languages, Sanskrit and Old Balinese, using an Indian alphabet. Inscriptions in Sanskrit proclaim the military triumphs of Balinese rulers. The texts specifically mention Tantric and Mahayana Buddhism, the major schools of Saiva Siddhanta and Vaisnava Hinduism, and the cults of Surya and Ganesa. Early sculptures include *dhyani* Buddhas, Padmapani (Avalokitesvara) and Amoghapasa, Visnu on Garuda, Visnu as Narasimha, and Siva in many forms including Ardhanari, quadruplicated as the *catuhkayas*, and accompanied by Durga, Ganesa, and Guru.

In time, the Balinese came to identify their own sacred mountain, Gunung Agung, with the mythical Mount Meru, center of the "Middle World" of Indic cosmology. The old Balinese nature gods were perhaps not so much nudged aside as reincorporated into the new Indic pantheon. The great earth serpent Anantaboga was symbolically buried in the Balinese earth, his head beneath the crater lake of Batur near the island's center, his tail just touching the sea at Keramas. But the old gods were not entirely eclipsed.

Living Traditions. At some time between the fourteenth and nineteenth centuries, the monastic tradition of Bali came to an end, and the various competing sects of Hinduism and Buddhism fused into what is now perceived as a single religion, called Bali Hindu or, more accurately, Agama Tirtha, the Religion of Holy Water. There are, as of 1984, approximately two and a quarter million Balinese, the vast majority of whom adhere to this religion.

The ultimate source of religious knowledge for the Balinese remains ancient Hindu and Buddhist texts, some still written in Sanskrit, the majority in Kawi (Old Javanese) and Balinese. As in India, high priests are invariably brahmans who have studied this literature extensively.

Ritual Life. Religion, for the Balinese, consists in the performance of five related ritual cycles, called *yajña*. Broadly speaking, the five *yajña* are sacrifices, and thus founded on ancient brahmanic theology.

Déwa yajña. Offerings to the gods (*déwa yajña*) are made in temples. The importance of these temples goes far beyond what we usually think of as religion, for temples provide the basic framework of Balinese economic and social organization. For example, consider the "irrigation" or "water temples." Each link in an irrigation system, from the small canal feeding one farmer's fields to the head-waters of a river, has a shrine or temple. The festivals held in these temples determine the schedule of "water openings" (flooding of the fields) for fields downstream. Festivals mark planting, transplanting, appearance of the milky grain (panicle), pest control, and so forth. The rituals of water temples synchronize farming activities for farmers using the same irrigation canals, and perhaps more important, allow higher-level temples to stagger cropping cycles to maximize production and minimize pest damage.

In similar ways, the Balinese version of a Hindu caste system was organized through temple networks—to belong to a caste translated into participating in the festivals of "caste temples," from the family shrine for the ancestors, through regional caste "branch temples," to the "origin temples" for whole castes or subcastes.

Buta yajña. Buta, usually translated into English as "demon," actually is the Balinese version of the Sanskrit word for "element of nature" *(bhuta)*. It is therefore an oversimplification to describe the rituals of *buta yajña* as "demon offerings."

Demons *(buta)* are the raw elements from which the higher realities of consciousness and the world are created. If their energy is not contained, they quickly become destructive.

Manusia yajña. *Manusia yajña* are rites of passage, fitted to the Balinese belief in reincarnation. Twelve days after birth, an infant is given a name, and offerings are made to the four birth spirits *(kanda empat)* who have accompanied him. After three 35-day months, the child and his spirits are given new names, and the child's feet are allowed to touch the earth for the first time, since before this time he is considered still too close to the world of the gods. More offerings are made for the child's 210-day "birthday," at puberty, and finally in the climactic ceremony of tooth filing, which prepares the child for adulthood. The six upper canine teeth and incisors are filed slightly to make them more even, symbolically reducing the six human vices of lust *(kama)*, anger *(krodha)*, greed *(lobha)*, error *(moha)*, intoxication *(mada)*, and jealousy *(matsarya)*. The *ma-nusia yajña* cycle ends with the performance of the marriage ceremony.

Pitr yajña. These rituals are the inverse of *manusia yajña*: they are the rituals of death and return to the world of the gods, performed by children for their parents. The Balinese believe that people are usually reincarnated into their own families—in effect, as their own descendants—after five or more generations. The rituals of preparing the corpse, preliminary burial, cremation, and purification of the soul ensure that the spirits of one's parents are freed from earthly attachments, are able to enter heaven, and eventually are able to seek rebirth.

Rsi yajña. While the other four *yajña* involve everyone, the ceremonies of the consecration of priests *(rsi yajña)* are the exclusive and esoteric provenance of the various priesthoods. In general, each "caste" has its own priests, although "high priests" *(pedanda)* are invariably brahmans. Buddhist traditions are kept alive by a special sect of high priests called *pedanda bodha*. The greatest of the rsi yajña is the ceremony of consecration for a new *pedanda*, during which he must symbolically undergo his own funeral as a human being, to reemerge as a very special kind of being, a Balinese high priest.

[*See also* Southeast Asian Religions, *article on* Insular Cultures.]

BIBLIOGRAPHY

The most influential modern scholar of Balinese religion is Clifford Geertz. Several of his important essays are collected in *The Interpretation of Cultures* (New York, 1973), and his analysis of cosmology and kingship is presented in *Negara: The Theatre State in Nineteenth-Century Bali* (Princeton, 1980). Translations of Balinese texts on religions are provided in the many publications of Christiaan Hooykaas, including *Cosmogony and Creation in Balinese Tradition* (The Hague, 1974) and *Surya-Sevana: The Way to God of a Balinese Siva Priest* (Amsterdam, 1966). Many important essays from the 1930s by scholars such as Margaret Mead and Gregory Bateson are collected in *Traditional Balinese Culture*, edited by Jane Belo (New York, 1970). Belo also provides excellent descriptive accounts in *Bali: Temple Festival* (Locust Valley, N. Y., 1953) and *Trance in Bali* (New York, 1960). Opposing theories on the "indianization" of Bali are presented in J. C. van Leur's *Indonesian Trade and Society: Essays in Asian Social and Economic History* (The Hague, 1955) and in R. C. Majumdar's *Ancient Indian Colonization in South-East Asia* (Calcutta, 1963). Rites of passage are nicely evoked in Katherine Edson Mershon's *Seven Plus Seven: Mysterious Life-Rituals in Bali* (New York, 1971). Many important articles by Dutch scholars of the colonial era have been translated into English in *Bali: Studies in Life, Thought, and Ritual* (The Hague, 1960) and a second volume entitled *Bali: Further Studies in Life, Thought, and Ritual* (The Hague, 1969), both edited by J. L. Swellengrebel.

One of the most delightful books describing the relationship of the performing arts to religion is Beryl de Zoete and Walter Spies's *Dance and Drama in Bali* (1938; reprint, Oxford, 1973). A worthy successor is I. M. Bandem and Frederick De Boer's *Kaja and Kelod: Balinese Dance in Transition* (Oxford, 1981). Urs Ramseyer's survey of *The Art and Culture of Bali* (Oxford, 1977) is a beautifully illustrated encyclopedia of Balinese religious art by a Swiss anthropologist. My *Three Worlds of Bali* (New York, 1983) provides an introduction to the role of religion and art in shaping the evolution of Balinese society.

J. STEPHEN LANSING

BALTIC RELIGION

Latvians, Lithuanians, and Old Prussians constitute the Baltic language and cultural unit. The Baltic peoples have inhabited their present territory from the middle of the second millennium BCE. At that time, however, their territory extended farther east, to Moscow, and southwest, across the banks of the Vistula. Living on the fringe of eastern Europe, they were virtually unknown to the West, and thus were able to remain relatively untouched by the influence of Christianity up to the seventeenth century. As early as the first millennium BCE, these isolated peoples, untouched by foreign developments, had developed from a hunting and fishing culture to an agrarian one. The structure of agrarian society and its routine determined the development of the belief system and the structure of cultic life.

The Baltic peoples came to the attention of European linguists at the end of the eighteenth century. Interest in the languages generated interest in the ethnogenesis of the Baltic peoples. It became apparent that the geographic isolation of these peoples had not only allowed but had furthered an unhindered and uninterrupted development free from external influence. But their rather late appearance in the European arena and their previous isolation have fostered a great deal of guesswork about their linguistic and ethnic origins and kinships.

Any investigation of the Baltic religion must touch upon the central problem of sources, of which there are three types: archaeological evidence, folklore, and historical documents. Despite the dearth of archaeological evidence and historical documentation, the folklore materials of these peoples is one of the richest in all of Europe. Songs (dainas), stories, tales, proverbs, and beliefs have been recorded.

The Sky Gods. Of all the Baltic gods in heaven the most prominent is Dievs. Linguists agree that etymologically the Latvian name Dievs (Lith., Dievas; OPrus., Deivas) is derived from names such as the ancient Indian Dyaus and the Greek Zeus.

The anthropomorphic character of Dievs has been carefully described and compared to that of other divinities. He is clad in a silver overcoat, gray jacket, and hat. He is girded with a decorated belt and wears mittens. In certain situations he also has a sword, but this is probably a later development. His dress resembles that of a prosperous farmer.

Indo-European creator gods are usually so mighty and distant that they retreat to a realm removed from men. This is not the case in the religion of the Balts. Instead, the Baltic gods follow an agricultural way of life that corresponds to that of the Baltic farmer. And this is not only a formal analogy. Dievs, who dwells in heaven, is a neighbor of the farmer on earth. At times of the most important decisions, the farmer meets and consults with Dievs, just as farmers meet and consult among themselves. Dievs rides down on a horse or, more frequently, in his chariot. These visitations coincide with key events in the agricultural calendar.

The cult of Dievs is not so formalized as are the cults of gods of heaven in other religions, but there is no evidence that goods were sacrificed to him in order to ensure his benevolence. That can be concluded only indirectly.

A second important god of heaven is Saule, the personification of the sun. This name is also derived from an Indo-European root (sauel-, and variants). Unlike personifications of the sun in other traditions, Saule is a female deity.

Descriptions of Saule's appearance are incomplete. A white shawl and one or more silver brooches, which secure the shawl, are mentioned in the sources. Occasionally she wears a wreath. Otherwise she appears in peasant dress.

Saule and Dievs are neighbors, and both oversee their farmsteads. Sometimes Saule rides across the sky in her chariot; she also crosses the sea in a boat. The steersman and oarsmen are her servants. She begins her ride in the boat early in the morning, at dawn, and finishes it in the evening, at sundown.

The Balts do not appear to be overly concerned about the composition of the world, or at least no trustworthy record of such speculation has been found. The universe, however, is assigned two levels: the heavens and the earth.

This dualistic worldview is at the base of Baltic religion. The tradition concerning Saule's traveling developed further and is crucial to the Baltic understanding of death. Saule travels by chariot or by boat in the visible world during the day but in the invisible one at night. Similarly, the dead continue to live a life in the invisible world, just as the sun does at night. The land of the dead is located just beyond the horizon, in the place where the sun sets.

In addition to the concepts of the mountain of heaven and the dualistic cosmos there is in the Baltic myths a saules koks ("tree of the sun"). It grows on the mount of heaven and is often referred to as an oak, a linden, or an apple tree. The difference between this tree and common trees on earth is symbolized by its gold or silver color. No mortal has ever seen this tree, although many youths have set out to search for it, only to return unsuccessfully in old age. A magical round object, often compared to a pea or an apple, rolls down its branches. The saules koks on the mount of heaven is one of the oldest elements of Baltic religion. It seems that this tree is the "center of the world," as Mircea Eliade has pointed out, but it also is the "tree of life."

The most significant element of the cult of Saule is the celebration of the summer solstice, in which everyone on the farmstead takes part. After the setting of the sun a fire is lit in a bucket and raised on top of a pole. A feast and dancing around the fire follow, and special songs of praise are sung. The major components of the feast are cheese and newly brewed beer. At this time shepherds become the center of attention.

Meness, the moon god, is also among the gods of heaven. The Latvian word for "moon," meness (Lith., menulis; OPrus., menins), derives from the Indo-European root *me-, meaning "a measure of time." The measure of time was an apt designation for Meness, who periodically disappears from the sky and then reappears in it once again. As a full-standing member of the mount of heaven, he, too, has his own farmstead there, along with his family, sons, servants, and horses. Meness is the god of war, and the stars are his troops, which, like a true general, he counts and leads.

Heavenly nuptials are central to Baltic myths about heaven. Dievs, Meness, or Perkons may be the bridegroom, and Saule is the bride. For linguistic reasons, in some contexts it is hard to determine who participates in the marriage, Saule or her daughter, for Saule is regarded as a maiden and is sometimes referred to as Saules Meita. However, this circumstance does not alter the marriage procedure. A peculiarity of the event is that all the gods take part, each performing his or her specific role.

Gods of Prosperity and Welfare. As one can see from an analysis of the essence and function of the Baltic gods, it is clear that they were an integral part of the daily life cycle. This is especially true of a particular group of gods whose special function was to protect and guarantee the welfare of humans. These gods can be subdivided into two groups: fertility gods and determiners of fate. The most prominent of the second group is Laima, whose name means "fortune." She lives on earth and is involved in the minutest details of everyday life.

The major fertility goddess is Zeme (Lith., Zemyna), a very different type of goddess. Her name means "earth," and she is commonly referred to as Zemes Mate ("earth mother, mother of the earth"). She plays a variety of roles that, over time, have developed into independent hypostases; tradition has it that she has seventy sisters. Some of them have very special functions, indicated by their descriptive names: *Darzu mate* ("mother of the garden"), *Lauku mate* ("mother of the fields"), *Meza mate* ("mother of the forest"), and *Linu mate* ("mother of flax"). These descriptive names point to a specific place or plant that is under each mother's protection.

A special fertility god is Jumis. He has many of the same functions as the fertility gods of other religions, and his rituals resemble theirs.

[*See also* Indo-European Religions, *and, more particularly,* Germanic Religion *and* Slavic Religion.]

BIBLIOGRAPHY

Adamovics, Ludvigs. "Senlatviesu religdija." In *Vestures atzinas un telojumi*, pp. 45-115. Riga, 1937. A concise survey of the main traits of Baltic gods but without an analysis of sources.
Bertuleit, Hans. "Das Religionswesen der alten Preussen mit litauisch-lettischen Parallen." *Prussia* 25 (1924).
Biezais, Haralds. *Die Religionsquellen der baltischen Völker und die Ergebnisse der bisherigen Forschungen*. Uppsala, 1954. An annotated bibliography of sources and studies through 1953.
Biezais, Haralds. *Die Hauptgöttinnen der alten Letten*. Uppsala, 1955.
Biezais, Haralds. *Die Gottesgestalt der lettischen Volksreligion*. Uppsala, 1961.
Biezais, Haralds. "Baltische Religion." In *Germanische und baltische Religion*, edited by Åke Ström and Haralds Biezais, pp. 307-391. Stuttgart, 1965.
Biezais, Haralds. *Die himmlische Götterfamilie der alten Letten*. Uppsala, 1972.
Biezais, Haralds. *Lichtgott der alten Letten*. Uppsala, 1976. My works listed here are the only up-to-date surveys of Baltic religion based on critical analyses of the sources.
Bratins, Ernests. *Latvju dievadziesmas*. 2d ed. Würzburg, 1947. A selected collection of *dainas* (songs) concerning the sky god Dievs.
Clemen, Carl C., ed. *Fontes historiae religionum primitivarum, praeindogermanicum, indogermanicum minus notarum*. Bonn, 1936. A collection of selected Greek and Roman sources.
Gimbutas, Marija. *The Balts*. London, 1963. See pages 179-204 for a short, popular survey of Baltic religion.
Hopkins, Grace. *Indo-European *Deiwos and Related Words*. Philadelphia, 1932. A valuable etymological and semantic study of names of Indo-European sky gods.
Ivinskis, Zenonas. *Senoves lietuviuh religijos bibliografija*. Kaunas, 1938. The best complete bibliography of Baltic religion up to 1938.
Johansons, Andrejs. *Der Schirmherr des Hofes im Volksglauben der Letten*. Stockholm, 1964. Valuable as a collection of material, but the speculative construction of "house god" is false.
Mannhardt, Wilhelm. "Die lettischen Sonnenmythen." *Zeitschrift für Ethnologie* 7 (1875): 73-330. Out of date but still important as a standard study of solar mythology.
Mannhardt, Wilhelm. *Letto-preussische Götterlehre*. Riga, 1936. The best sourcebook on Baltic religion.
Neuland, Lena. *Jumis die Fruchtbarkeitsgottheit der alten Letten*. Stockholm, 1977. A basic study of the fertility cult with extensive analyses of sources and bibliography.
Pisani, Vittore. *Le religioni dei Celti e dei Balto-Slavi nell'Europa precristiana*. Milan, 1950. A brief comparative survey marred by linguistic shortcomings.
Zicans, Eduards. "Die Hochzeit der Sonne und des Mondes in der lettischen Mythologie." *Studia Theologica* 1 (1935): 171-200. Important as a supplement to Wilhelm Mannhardt's solar mythology.

HARALDS BIEZAIS

BAPTISM

The word *baptism* comes from the Greek *baptein*, which means to plunge, to immerse, or to wash; it also signifies, from the Homeric period onward, any rite of immersion in water. The baptismal rite is similar to many other ablution rituals found in a number of religions, but it is the symbolic value of baptism and the psychological intent underlying it that provide the true definition of the rite, a rite usually found associated with a religious initiation.

Pre-Christian Religions. The purifying properties of water have been ritually attested to ever since the rise of civilization in the ancient Near East. In Babylonia, according to the *Tablets of Maklu*, water was important in the cult of Enki, lord of Eridu. In Egypt, the *Book of Going Forth by Day* (17) contains a treatise on the baptism of newborn children, which is performed to purify them of blemishes acquired in the womb.

The property of immortality is also associated with baptism in the Greek world: according to Cretan funeral tablets, it was associated especially with the spring of Mnemosyne (memory). A bath in the sanctuary of Trophonios procured for the initiate a blessed immortality even while in this world (Pausanias, *Description of Greece* 9.39.5).

In Hellenistic philosophy, as in Egyptian speculation, divine water possessed a real power of transformation. Hermetism offered to man the possibility of being transformed into a spiritual being after immersion in the baptismal crater of the *nous*; this baptism conferred knowledge on man and permitted him to participate in the gnosis and, hence, to know the origins of the soul.

In the cult of Cybele, a baptism of blood was practiced in the rite of the *taurobolium*: the initiate went down into a pit and was completely covered with the blood of a bull, whose throat was cut above him. A well-known inscription attests that he who has received baptism of blood is *renatus in aeternum*, that he has received a new birth in eternity (*Corpus inscriptionum Latinarum* 6.510).

The liturgical use of water was common in the Jewish world. Under Persian influence, rites of immersion multiplied after the exile. Some prophets saw in the requirement of physical purity a sign of the necessity of inner and spiritual purification (*Ez.* 36:25-28). The Essenes linked the pouring forth of the divine life in man to purification by baptism in flowing water.

Toward the beginning of the Christian era, the Jews adopted the custom of baptizing proselytes seven days after their circumcision, the rabbis having added the impurity of converted gentiles to the chief impurities enumerated in the Torah. After their baptism, new converts were allowed access to the sacrifices in the Temple.

The ministry of John the Baptist in the Jordanian desert was connected with this baptist movement, which symbolically linked immersion in a river of flowing water to the passage from death to a new and supernatural life. The Mandaeans take their baptismal practice directly from the example of John, whom they consider the perfect gnostic; they administer baptism in the flowing water of a symbolic Jordan.

Christian Baptism. John baptized Jesus, like others who came to him, in the waters of the Jordan. Jesus' baptism inaugurated his public ministry, and he later gave his disciples the mission of baptizing in the name of the trinitarian faith—a mission that they carried out even before their master's death (*Mt.* 28:19, *Jn.* 4:1-2). The apostles continued to practice the baptism of water of the type administered by John; but they emphasized the necessity of an inner conversion preceding the profession of the trinitarian faith, the focus of the new belief.

Every detail of the Christian ritual is intended to symbolize birth to a new life in Jesus Christ. Christian baptismal practice is founded on the commandment of Jesus himself to his disciples (*Mt.* 28:19). Its administration during the first centuries of the church took place at Easter night and Pentecost and was limited to bishops, the heads of the Christian communities. Reception of baptism seems often to have been put off until the moment of death by neophytes who were reluctant to accept the full consequences of inner conversion; and infant baptism, though possible, was probably not practiced in the early period of the church (cf. *Mt.* 19:14, *Acts* 16:33, 1 *Tm.* 2:4).

Because it was the sacrament that indicated entrance into the life of faith and the community of the church, baptism was also considered a means to inner enlightenment. In the Eastern church, those who were initiated into the Christian mysteries by baptism were called the "enlightened," for, as Gregory of Nazianzus explains, the baptismal rite opens the catechumen's eyes to the light that indicates God's symbolic birth in man (Discourse 40: *On Baptism*).

But because it was also the fundamental rite of entry into the church community, baptism was quickly claimed as a prerogative by several rival churches, each of which called itself orthodox and accused the others of heresy and schism. Modifications of baptismal rites by the various sects were inevitable.

From the sixth century on at the latest, the Catholic church permitted the baptism of children, the engagement to follow the faith being taken in their name by adult Christians. The custom of baptizing infants soon after birth became popular in the tenth or eleventh century and was generally accepted by the thirteenth (Thomas Aquinas, *Summa theologiae* 3.68.3). In the fourteenth century, baptismal ritual was simplified, and a rite of spiritual infusion, in which water is poured on the head of a child held above the baptismal font, replaced baptism by immersion. After 1517, the questions posed by the practice of the baptism of small children served as a major foundation for dissident Christian movements stemming from the Reformation.

In 1633, a group of English Baptists immigrated to North America, beginning the development in the New World of a number of Baptist sects and churches, whose members founded their belief on the theological baptism of Paul (cf. *Rom.* 6:4, *Col.* 2:12) and insisted upon a return to strict apostolic practice. These sects and churches have in common the practice of baptism by immersion administered in the name of the Trinity only to adults who believe and confess their faith in Jesus Christ.

[*See also* Purification.]

BIBLIOGRAPHY

Beasley-Murray, G. R. *Baptism in the New Testament*. New York, 1962.

Beirnaert, Louis. "La dimension mythique dans le sacramentalisme chrétien." *Eranos-Jahrbuch* (Zurich) 17 (1949): 255-286.

Drower, Ethel S., trans. *The Canonical Prayerbook of the Mandaeans*. Leiden, 1959.

Gilmore, Alec, ed. *Christian Baptism*. Chicago, 1959.

Lundberg, Per. *La typologie baptismale dans l'ancienne église*. Leipzig, 1942.

Malaise, Michel. *Les conditions de pénétration et de diffusion des cultes égyptiens en Italie*. Leiden, 1972.

Meslin, Michel. "Réalités psychiques et valeurs religieuses dans les cultes orientaux (premier-quatrième siècles)." *Revue historique* 512 (October-December 1974): 289-314.

Payne, Ernest A. *The Fellowship of Believers: Baptist Thought and Practice Yesterday and Today.* 2d ed., enl. London, 1952.

Reitzenstein, Richard. *The Hellenistic Mystery Religions* (1927). Translated by John E. Seeley. Pittsburgh, 1978.

Rudolph, Kurt. *Die Mandäer.* 2 vols. Göttingen, 1960-1961.

Thomas, Jean. *Le mouvement baptiste en Palestine et en Syrie.* Gembloux, 1935.

MICHEL MESLIN
Translated from French by Jeffrey C. Haight and Annie S. Mahler

BAPTIST CHURCHES

As with most denominational names, the name *Baptist* began as a pejorative nickname. It first appeared as *Anabaptist*, or "rebaptizer," since in the sixteenth century, when this group arose in Western Christendom, virtually all persons had already been baptized as infants. These rebaptizers were scandalously denying the validity of that first baptism, setting themselves up as a truer church if not, indeed, the true church. Gradually, as infant baptism became less prevalent and as alternative modes of worship grew more widespread, this still young denomination adopted the shortened form of "Baptist" both as a convenient distinction and a point of honor.

Sharing many of the Puritan concerns about a Church of England still too "papist," still too engrossed with civil enforcement and ecclesiastical preferment, these separating Puritans early distinguished themselves by insisting that the church be a voluntary society. That voluntarism had two critical components: (1) the insistence that members choose their church rather than be born into it; and (2) the conviction that the covenant of believers to work and worship together was a private agreement with which the state had nothing to do, for conscience must be left free. As Thomas Helwys, one of that first generation of English Baptists, wrote, "the King is a mortal man and not God, therefore hath no power over the immortal souls of his subjects, to make laws and ordinances for them, and to set spiritual lords over them."

The leadership of Helwys and two others, John Smyth and John Murton, proved decisive in the first two decades of the seventeenth century as the English "General Baptists" (that is, non-Calvinist, affirming an unrestricted or general atonement for mankind) grew from a scarcely visible knot of believers in 1609 to around twenty thousand members by 1660. Despite this impressive showing, however, the major strength of the modern Baptist churches was to come from a somewhat later development. Under the leadership of John

Spilsbury, in the decade following 1633, a single church became mother to six more. By the time seven such churches existed in and around London, these Calvinist Baptists had also reintroduced the ancient Christian practice of baptism by immersion, this mode being preferred as a more suitable symbol of one's burial with Christ followed by one's new birth or resurrection.

The great growth of Baptists in North America (and by extension in the world) followed the eighteenth century's Great Awakening, that Calvinist explosion of evangelical zeal and intense religious experience. Even though Baptists were not prime leaders in the movement, they were the prime beneficiaries of it. Moreover, the Awakening, even if it did not make an itinerant ministry respectable, did make such traveling evangelism both popular and pervasive.

After the American Revolution, Baptists also made phenomenal advances among the nation's blacks. Using a persuasive preaching style, an accessible theology, an appealing baptismal ritual, and an ecclesiology that granted freedom from white rule, the Baptist message found ready hearers among both enslaved and free blacks. By the end of the nineteenth century, black Baptists had formed their own national organizations, publishing boards, and mission societies. By the mid-twentieth century, approximately two-thirds of America's black Christians were Baptists.

In the bitter conflict over slavery, white Baptists split along geographical lines in 1845, and the Southern Baptist Convention was organized in Augusta, Georgia. (A national organization of Baptists dating back to 1814 enjoyed but a brief life.) The Southern Baptist Convention, with its base initially in the states of the southern Confederacy, moved aggressively to the West, to the North, and to "foreign fields" to become the largest single Baptist entity in the world. By

> In the bitter conflict over slavery, white Baptists split along geographical lines in 1845. . . .

the mid-twentieth century it had also become the largest Protestant denomination in the United States.

In the early 1980s, the northern and southern "halves" had an aggregate membership of around fifteen million, the two oldest black denominations a combined membership of eight to ten million. This leaves uncounted some four or five million Baptists in America who are scattered among a wide variety of other organizations.

Outside the United States, the Baptist churches are unevenly and often sparsely scattered. One may speak most conveniently in terms of continents rather than individual nations in offering estimates of membership: in Africa and Europe, about one million in each area; in Asia, about 1.5

million; and in Central and South America, something less than one million. In Canada, to which New England Baptists began to migrate in the late eighteenth century, there are between one and two hundred thousand Baptists.

BIBLIOGRAPHY

Two books on English Baptists that provide not only good historical background but excellent insight into contemporary life and thought are H. Wheeler Robinson's *The Life and Faith of the Baptists*, rev. ed. (London, 1946), and Ernest A. Payne's *The Fellowship of Believers: Baptist Thought and Practice Yesterday and Today*, rev. ed. (London, 1952). These two works have been reprinted together under the title *British Baptists* (New York, 1980). A world view is provided in Robert G. Torbet's *A History of the Baptists*, 4th ed., rev. (Valley Forge, Pa., 1975), while Torbet and S. S. Hill, Jr., have reviewed the American scene in *Baptists: North and South* (Valley Forge, Pa., 1964). On the Southern Baptist Convention specifically, see Robert A. Baker's *The Southern Baptist Convention and Its People*, 1607-1972 (Nashville, 1974). Two works on Baptist development in early America have made giant historiographical strides over most previous efforts: William G. McLoughlin's *New England Dissent*, 1630-1833, 2 vols. (Cambridge, Mass., 1971), and C. C. Goen's *Revivalism and Separatism in New England*, 1740-1800 (New Haven, 1962). Finally, for an informed view of alter-native ecclesiological styles among Baptists, see *Baptist Concepts of the Church*, edited by Winthrop S. Hudson (Philadelphia and Chicago, 1959).

EDWIN S. GAUSTAD

BARTH, KARL

BARTH, KARL (1886-1968), Swiss Reformed theologian, described by Pope Pius XII as the greatest theologian since Thomas Aquinas, and certainly the most influential of the twentieth century.

Barth was born in Basel on 10 May 1886, the son of Fritz Barth, a professor of church history and New Testament in Bern. He commenced his university studies in Bern, where he began to study the theoretical and practical philosophy of Immanual Kant, whose "Copernican revolution" in the theory of knowledge and ethics awakened Barth to an acute awareness of the question of our knowledge and service of God. At the same time he developed his early and lifelong interest in the theologian Friedrich Schleiermacher, whose analysis of religious experience and desire to commend religion to its "cultured despisers" had dominated German theology from 1834. Like Schleiermacher, Barth was later to interpret Christian dogmatics as the function of the Christian church, scrutinizing scientifically the content of the Christian faith, but unlike Schleiermacher he saw, not religious experience in general, but the revelation of God in Jesus Christ, attested in holy scripture, as the criterion of truth.

In 1907 Barth expressed a desire to study at Marburg with Wilhelm Herrmann (1846-1922). Herrmann defined faith in terms of "inner experience" which has its "ground" in the "inner life of Jesus" and is awakened in man's conscience by the influence of Jesus, the so-called Jesus of history of the nineteenth-century liberal quest. Although influenced by Herrmann, Barth came to feel that his conception conflicted with the New Testament and Reformed understanding of the Christ of faith and with the church's creeds, and that it was more the product of modern individualistic bourgeois liberal idealism and Kantian philosophy than of sound New Testament scholarship. He also felt that the very nature and possibility of a scientific approach to Christian theology was being called into question by the philosophical and historical presuppositions of the "culture-Protestantism" of the day, wherein theology and relativizing historicism, religion, and culture were fused, obscuring the gospel through "reverence before history" and reducing Christian theology to a branch of the general philosophy of religion.

These questions assumed acute importance for Barth once he was ordained to the pastoral ministry. It was during his time as a pastor in Safenwil, Switzerland (1911-1921), that his theological position underwent a drastic change. On the one hand, when World War I broke out, he was deeply disturbed by the "Manifesto of the Intellectuals," when ninety-three scholars and artists, including his own teachers Harnack and Herrmann, supported the war policy of Kaiser Wilhelm II, which seemed to him to question his colleagues' understanding of the Bible, history, and dogmatics. On the other hand, in his industrial parish, he became acutely aware of the issues of social justice, poor wages, factory legislation, and trade union affairs. In 1915 he became a member of the Social Democratic party, but unlike his Christian Socialist friends, he refused to identify socialism with the kingdom of God.

Throughout his life Barth endeavored to interpret the gospel and examine the church's message in the context of society, the state, war, revolution, totalitarianism, and democracy, over against the pretensions of man to solve the problems of his own destiny, without the judgment of the message of the cross and the resurrection of Jesus Christ.

Barth used Paul's letter to the Romans for a critique of philosophical idealism, romanticism, and religious socialism. If his concern was that the church should listen to the divine word of judgment on our political and intellectual towers of Babel, his concern throughout his life was also to assert "that there is joy with God . . . and that the Kingdom on earth begins with joy." Together with his lifelong friend Eduard Thurneysen (1888-1974), he discovered in the Bible "a strange new world, the world of God," which is the kingdom of God, established by God and not man.

There were distinctive stages in Barth's theological development, in each of which he wrestled with the polarities of

God and man. At first, like Herrmann, he identified conscience with the voice of God, but increasingly he argued that the voice of God is heard only in scripture, in encounter with Christ, the living Word.

The chasm between God and man can be bridged by God alone, and not by man. The Word of the cross means that God says no to our human sin and pride and pretensions, while in grace God says yes to his own good creatures in a word of forgiveness. Barth saw that there are elements of negation and affirmation in all human knowledge of God, leading him to see an analogy of "relation," but not of "being," between God and man grounded in grace.

> In 1915 he became a member of the Social Democratic party, but . . . refused to identify socialism with the kingdom of God.

In 1927 Barth began writing *Christian Dogmatics*, intending to expound all the main Christian doctrines, by grounding all he had to say on God's self-revelation in Jesus Christ. The first volume was entitled *Christian Doctrine in Outline, Volume I: The Doctrine of the Word of God, Prolegomena to Christian Dogmatics*. In it he argues that possibility of Christian knowledge of God is grounded on the actuality of the revelation in Jesus, as he makes himself known to faith by the Holy Spirit.

Within this self-revelation of the triune God we can distinguish three forms of the one Word of God: the eternal Word incarnate in Jesus Christ, the written Word in the witness of the Bible to that primary Word, and the Word of God as proclaimed in the church.

The reviewers of this first volume criticized Barth for so casting the gospel into the language of an immediate timeless encounter with God that he was in danger of dehistoricizing the gospel and transposing theology into a new philosophical mold. Barth took this criticism seriously. In 1931 he published *Fide quaerens intellectum* (Faith Seeking Understanding). From Anselm he had learned that the Word of God has its own rational content in God. The polarity of God and man must be interpreted, not so much in the language of an existential encounter between God and man in the crisis of faith, but primarily in terms of the given unity of God and man in Jesus Christ, the incarnate Lord, in whom God has come—not simply *in* a man, but *as* a man—in a once and for all reconciling act in which we are called to participate through the Holy Spirit.

Barth was concerned to unpack the implications of this Christ-centered perspective in every area of life. It proved highly significant in his outspoken opposition to Hitler, to the persecution of the Jews, and to the so-called German Christians who sought to justify National Socialism and its racist policies. Barth felt that this was a betrayal of the Christian understanding of grace by its appeal to sources of revelation other than that given to us in Jesus Christ.

BIBLIOGRAPHY

The best and most authoritative biography is Eberhard Busch's *Karl Barth: His Life from Letters and Autobiographical Texts* (London, 1976). On the early period of the so-called dialectical theology, the most influential work was Barth's *The Epistle to the Romans*, translated by Sir Edwyn C. Hoskyns (Oxford, 1933). The significance of this work is discussed in Thomas F. Torrance's *Karl Barth: An Introduction to His Early Theology, 1910-1931* (London, 1962). Barth's *Protestant Theology in the Nineteenth Century*, translated by Brian Cozens and John Bowden (Valley Forge, 1973), is invaluable for understanding his European theological background. The book that marked his transition to the later period of the *Church Dogmatics* is his *Anselm: Fides Quaerens Intellectum; Anselm's Proof of the Existence of God*, translated by I. W. Robertson (Richmond, 1960). In the Gifford Lectures given in Aberdeen, Barth expounded the 1560 Scots Confession in *The Knowledge of God and the Service of God*, translated by J. L. M. Haire and Ian Henderson (London, 1938). His massive exposition of Christian doctrine is set out in *Church Dogmatics*, 4 vols., edited by Geoffrey W. Bromiley and Thomas F. Torrance (Edinburgh, 1956-1969). Very readable is Barth's short *Evangelical Theology*, translated by Grover Foley (New York, 1963).

JAMES B. TORRANCE

BATAK RELIGION

The Batak societies, located around Lake Toba in North Sumatra, are among the more than three hundred ethnic minorities of Indonesia. Batak religion, like Batak culture as a whole, is ethnically diverse, syncretic, changing, and bound at once to both village social organizational patterns and the monotheistic national culture of Indonesia. Batak myths and rituals focus on the yearly cycle of rice cultivation activities and the local kinship system. Batak religions tie these two realms to a larger cosmological order, which is then represented in various religious art forms (traditional house architecture, village spatial layout, and wood sculpture) and ritual activities (dances, oratory, and gift-giving ceremonies). Batak kinship revolves around marriage alliances that link together lineages of patrilineal clans, called *marga*. Beyond these very localized ethnic patterns, however, Batak religious life extends outward into the world religions: the large majority of homeland Batak and virtually all migrants to cities in Sumatra and Java are Muslim or Christian. In this monotheistic environment, Batak village religion has undeniably lost some of its social and symbolic scope. However, through an inventive reinterpretation of symbols, other sectors of village belief and ritual continue to thrive in new forms.

There are six major Batak societies in the homeland region around Lake Toba. These societies are similar in village social structure and subsistence base (paddy rice farming with some dry field agriculture) but speak different dialects of Batak and have distinct ritual systems. These societies are commonly called the Toba Batak, Karo Batak, Pakpak and Dairi Batak, Simelungun Batak, Angkola and Sipirok Batak, and the Mandailing Batak (although some "Batak" rarely call themselves Batak). Their pre-monotheistic religions are impossible to reconstruct in detail from current evidence because Islam and Christianity have reshaped village ritual and folk memories of the past so thoroughly. It is common, for instance, for committed Muslim and Christian Batak to speak disparagingly of their "pagan" ancestors. In other words, "traditional Batak religion" is in large part a figment of the contemporary Batak imagination.

In all these regions, certain assumptions about the nature of the universe permeated village religion. Binary oppositions between life and death, humans and animals, the village and the forest, metal and cloth, masculinity and femininity, and warfare and farming were recurrent themes in ritual and myth. Both human and agricultural creativity and fertility were thought to come from the temporary, intensely powerful union of such complementary opposites as life and death, masculinity and femininity, and so on.

All Batak religions had extensive soul concepts and generally posited a personal soul that could fragment when startled and escape from a person's head to wander haplessly in the countryside until recalled to his body in special soul-capture ceremonies. *Datu* or *guru* were diviner-sorcerers who performed such religious cures and also served the village chiefs as "village protection experts" in times of warfare, epidemic, or crop failure. Sacrificial rituals were central to the *datu's* protective tasks; in a few areas there may have been occasional ritual cannibalism (a point that is hotly debated among Batak today).

Contact with the monotheistic religions varies considerably from Batak society to society. Karo is an area of fairly recent conversions. Toba is overwhelmingly Protestant; the original, German-sponsored missionary church, the HKBP (Huria Kristen Batak Protestan), has its headquarters in Tarutung. During the Padri Wars in the 1820s Minangkabau Muslims brought their religion to the southern Angkola and Mandailing homelands; today, Mandailing is entirely Muslim while Angkola is about 10 percent Protestant and 90 percent Muslim.

[*See also* Southeast Asian Religions.]

BIBLIOGRAPHY

There is a large literature in Dutch, English, and Indonesian on the Batak societies. Toenggoel P. Siagian's "Bibliography on the Batak Peoples," *Indonesia* 2 (October 1966): 161-184, is a valuable guide to the main research before the mid-sixties, and the bibliographies in *Beyond Samosir: Recent Studies of the Batak Peoples of Sumatra*, edited by Rita Smith Kipp and Richard D. Kipp (Athens, Ohio, 1983), provide references for the last twenty years, a period of much American anthropological fieldwork in the area. Jacob Cornelis Vergouwen's *The Social Organization and Customary Law of the Toba-Batak of Northern Sumatra* (1933), translated by Jeune Scott-Kemball (The Hague, 1964), remains the premier descriptive ethnography of a Batak culture, with much information on non-monotheistic rituals and beliefs. Recent articles and monographs by anthropologists reflect a shift in research toward Batak symbol systems: Rita Smith Kipp's "The Thread of Three Colors: The Ideology of Kinship in Karo Batak Funerals," in *Art, Ritual, and Society in Indonesia*, edited by Judith Becker and Edward M. Bruner (Athens, Ohio, 1979), discusses Karo religion in its marriage alliance context; I discuss religious syncretism and change in *Adat, Islam, and Christianity in a Batak Homeland* (Athens, Ohio, 1981). Two major collections of anthropological essays on similar religious and social systems from other regions of Indonesia provide invaluable comparative material: *The Flow of Life: Essays on Eastern Indonesia*, edited by James Fox (Cambridge, Mass., 1980), and *The Imagination of Reality: Essays in Southeast Asian Coherence Systems*, edited by A. L. Becker and Aram A. Yengoyan (Norwood, N. J., 1979).

SUSAN RODGERS

BENGALI RELIGIONS

The religious profile of the Bengali-speaking region of eastern India (West Bengal) and Bangladesh (formerly East Pakistan) is pluralistic, complex and, like the active delta itself, ever-changing in contour. Two "great traditions," the Islamic and the Brahmanic Hindu, claim the allegiance of the vast majority of Bengalis. Yet in intimate relation to these there persist pockets of scarcely Hinduized tribal peoples, a hardy semi-tribal remnant of a once powerful Buddhist community, a cluster of Christian denominations, small urban settlements of non-Bengali Jains, Sikhs, Parsis, Chinese, and Jews, not to mention legions of Hindus and Muslims whose fundamental commitments or faith would seem to be in Marxist, radical humanist, and other more or less "secular" forms.

The Hindu Setting. The Hindu tradition has been, for perhaps two millennia, the most complex and culturally prolific religious tradition in Bengal (though self-con-sciously Hindu only after sustained contact with Muslims from the thirteenth century onward). It depends heavily upon the Brahmanic great tradition, with its Vedic and Sanskrit sacred texts, but it also draws much from myriad "little traditions" deriving symbolism and practices from indigenous non-Aryan (e.g., Kol-

Munda, Dravidian, Tibeto-Mongolian) peoples. But what is most distinctive of the Hindu tradition in Bengal is the "middle (or regional) tradition," whose oral and written texts are in the vernacular Bengali language. The Hindu tradition provides the sociocultural matrix for Buddhists, Jains, and Sikhs as well as for Hindus in Bengal and constitutes the background from which have come most converts to the small Christian and the massive Muslim communities.

Hindus represent about 75 percent of the population of West Bengal, and about 12 percent of that of Bangladesh. Fewer than 10 percent of Bengali Hindus are considered brahman (Skt., *brahmana*); most of the rest are *sudra*, the latter divided among scores of endogamous groups known as *jatis*, or subcastes.

Bengali Hindus generally share the same sacred Sanskrit texts (Vedas, Dharmasastras, epics, and Puranas), the same pantheon, myths, rituals, and philosophical-theological heritage found throughout India, but with special emphases and exceptions. Vedic solemn *(srauta)* rites are scarcely cultivated, though domestic *(grhya)* rites are maintained. Monumental religious architecture seems not to have flourished in Brahmanic (although it once did in Buddhist) circles, but smaller, gracefully curved temples of bamboo or brick, often embellished with terracotta relief, adorn the Bengali countryside.

Saktism and Tantrism. Goddesses are especially prominent in Bengal. Most lavishly worshiped is the fair, ornately decorated Durga, the multi-armed vanquisher of the buffalo demon. *Puja* for the dark, naked goddess of blood, Kali, supplants Divali, the festival of lights. Other goddesses of eminence in Bengal include Candi/Uma/Parvati (spouse of Siva), Sarasvati (goddess of learning), Sitala (goddess of smallpox and cholera), Sasthi (the protector of children), Manasa (goddess of snakebites), Annada (goddess of grain and food in general), and Radha (idyllic lover of Krsna).

Loosely correlated with the preeminence of goddesses is the prominence of Tantrism in Bengal. The origins (Aryan and

> **Most lavishly worshiped is the fair, ornately decorated Durga, the multi-armed vanquisher of the buffalo demon.**

non-Aryan) of Tantrism are not yet clearly known, but from the mid-first millennium CE Bengal was a leading source of Sanskrit Tantric texts wherein brahman priests and Buddhist monks applied their respective learnings to Tantric principles of ritual and meditation. Hindu Tantra literature in Sanskrit flourished through the Pala period (760-1142 CE), but declined under the Senas in the twelfth century. Not until the revival of sanskritic learning in Navadvip in the sixteenth cen-

tury is there evidence of renewed interest in Tantrism among Bengali brahmans.

However, a simplified variant of Tantrism, called Sahaja or Sahajiya ("natural, born together"), seems to have persisted in Bengal at least from the twelfth century (probably from much earlier) to the present. Sahaja Tantrism is an indigenous kind of yogic discipline specializing in symbolic interpretation and transformation of bodily substances. It selectively adapts from more sophisticated religious systems (Buddhist, Nath, Saiva-Sakta, Vaisnava) elements of imagery, doctrine, and practice so as to forge hybrid systems of spiritual discipline (*sadhana*). A hybrid Vaisnava-Sahajiya flourished in the seventeenth and eighteenth centuries.

Vaisnavism. Vaisnava piety in Bengal, like Saivism and Saktism, may go back to Mauryan times, certainly to Gupta and Pala periods, from which iconographic and other detailed evidence survives. There are statues of Visnu in many forms, of Siva (*lingas* and anthropomorphic forms), of Sakti (as Durga, Candi, Sarvani, and other goddesses), and of Surya, Ganesa, Indra, and Varuna. Images of Krsna and Rama are rare in pre-Islamic Bengal, but there is what appears to be a relief of Krsna and Radha on the Buddhist stupa at Somapura near Paharpur. Devotion (*bhakti*) to Krsna (and to his divine lover Radha) has held a special place in Bengali religious life since the appearance of Krsna-Caitanya (a brahman, born Visvambhara Misra; 1486-1533). To Bengali Vaisnavas he is the divine Krsna or Radha and Krsna combined. Most Vaisnava temples in Bengal are now Krsna temples, and many contain the image of Caitanya as well. The Caitanya (or Gaudiya, i. e., Bengali) Vaisnava movement has bequeathed to Bengali culture a wealth of devotional literature in Sanskrit and Bengali: lyrics (*padavali*), music (*kirtan*), drama, hagiography, and a systematic theology (*bhakti-rasa-sastra*) that combines Sanskrit poetics with Krsnaite philosophy of paradoxical difference and nondifference (*acintyabhedabheda*).

Nineteenth-century renaissance. The nineteenth century brought remarkable religious developments in the midst of profound political, economic, and cultural changes in Bengal. More than half a millennium of Muslim domination had ended. English soon replaced Persian in administration, courts, and higher education, thus opening up new cultural, professional, and business opportunities for those (initially, almost exclusively Hindu *bhadralok*) who would take part.

A floodtide of stimulation and challenge met those who exposed themselves to Western culture, secular and/or religious. Those Bengali *bhadralok* who came to the new colonial metropolis, Calcutta, became de facto the primary mediators between India and the West (until comparable elites emerged in secondary seats of British power). In this heady atmosphere they rapidly explored many avenues pertinent to their anomalous position between two cultures. Such avenues included radical criticism, even rejection, of the

Hindu socio-religious tradition, as by those few of the new elite who became Christian or as by the iconoclastic Young Bengal group inspired by Henry Derozio (1809-1831). Staunchly opposing these and less radical responses to Western religion and culture were diehard conservatives. Between these extremes were varied paths opened by Bengali *bhadralok* reformers who sought to remain within the Hindu tradition, but on terms consonant with their precarious position between two worlds.

Ram Mohan Roy (1774-1833), polyglot, intellectual, and administrator, was the most effective of early nineteenth century *bhadralok* reformers. His appreciation for the oneness of a personal God (gained during youthful studies of Persian and Arabic) and admiration for the ethical teachings of Christ raised unfulfilled hope for his conversion among Christian and Unitarian missionaries, with whom he both cooperated and contended. He argued forcefully, if insensitively, against worship of images and amorous symbolism in myth, ritual, and song, and he campaigned successfully against the self-immolation of widows (*sati*) and other such socioreligious practices.

Succeeding Roy in leadership of the Brahmo Samaj was the austere and meditative Debendranath Tagore (1817-1905), under whose guidance the Samaj gained a richer liturgy and stock of prayers. An enthusiastic younger Brahmo, Keshab Chandra Sen (1838-1884), impatient with Debendranath's cautious socioritual stance, broke away to form the Brahmo Samaj of India. This new group reflected the more radical social ideals of Sen as well as his preference for Vaisnava-style *kirtan* and his effusive devotion to Jesus Christ. A second schism, occasioned by Sen's failure to apply his radical socioritual principles in the marriage of his own daughter, resulted in yet a third Samaj, the Sadharan Brahmo Samaj. Although never attaining a large membership, the Brahmo Samajes provided a crucial rallying place for Bengali *bhadralok* dissatisfied with the Hindu status quo but unwilling to foresake their tradition altogether.

The most venerated nineteenth-century Bengali religious figure was not of the English-trained elite: Ramakrishna (born Gadadhar Chatterji; 1836-1886) was engagingly simple in Bengali conversation and ecstatic in his devotion to the goddess Kali. He sought to experience the divine through Sakta, Vaisnava, Tantric, and Vedantic disciplines as well as through what he considered Christian and Muslim meditations. Ramakrishna and his wife, Sarada Devi, are worshiped jointly by the devout: he as the divine descent *(avatara)*, and she as the consort/power *(sakti)*.

Twentieth-century Hindu nationalism and internationalism. Incipient Hindu nationalism took on a more assertive and chauvinistic political character in the twentieth century, especially during the Bengali *bhadralok's* swadeshi campaign to undo the 1905 partition of Bengal. The campaign succeeded but at the cost of further alienating Muslims. At the violent extreme of the campaign were youthful "Terrorists" who conceived of their acts of violence as sacrificial offerings to the Goddess/motherland.

Sakta imagery of the assertive, potentially violent sort seems to have inspired in a diffuse way nationalist politics in Bengal especially in the "Extremist" form embodied by Netaji Subhas Chandra Bose (1897-1945). Diffusion of the more accommodating and nonviolent Vaisnava ethos into nationalist politics in Bengal was less pronounced, since Bose, rather than Gandhi, had captured the political imagination of Bengali Hindus. However, the mature work of Rabindranath Tagore (1861-1941), Nobel laureate in poetry (for *Gitañjali*), novelist, dramatist, educator, musician, and artist—and very much a formative influence upon literate twentieth-century Bengalis—features certain Vaisnava and Brahmo ideals and attitudes prominently within its vision of global human solidarity. Tagore's "Religion of Man" (as he entitled his Hibbert Lectures), stresses the creative, evolving, aesthetic, and interpersonal qualities of human experience as being at the heart of "religion" at its best.

Traditional Hindu religious institutions flourished in the nineteenth and early twentieth centuries alongside the protean reform movements. Money and talent flowed into building and repairing temples and religious hostels and into evangelization via publishing, preaching, music, and drama. Scholarly editions of Bengali and Sanskrit religious texts were plentiful, and serious research on the Hindu (and also Buddhist) religious past proliferated in this period.

Independence and frustrations. The independence of India and Pakistan in 1947 meant the partition of Bengal, communal violence, and the migration of Hindu and Muslim refugees. West Bengal and Calcutta, suddenly cut off from the greater portion of the once proud Bengal Presidency, were stunted economically and politically and yet bound to assimilate millions of refugees. Starved for resources and

> **Traditional Hindu institutions survive, but in severely depleted condition.**

with little prospect for relief, most institutions in West Bengal—including traditional and reformist religious ones—have languished since 1947, hanging on, but rarely able to mobilize resources for creative or innovative endeavors.

Meanwhile in East Pakistan and (from 1971) Bangladesh the conditions of the Hindu minority have been even less conducive to institutional and, with rare exceptions, individual creativity. Most wealthy and well-educated Hindus left at partition or during disturbances thereafter. Those who remained were preoccupied with day to day survival in an economically deprived and politically unsympathetic milieu. Sporadic harassment culminating in the atrocities and mass exodus in 1971 have been followed by the relative security of independent Bangladesh under the "secular" Awami League and the "Islamic," but not anti-Hindu, military regimes that have followed. Traditional Hindu institutions survive, but in severely depleted condition.

Religious Minorities. A significant number of Bengalis represent non-Hindu and non-Muslim religious traditions. To a certain extent these groups have accommodated to the dominant traditions, but they remain distinct communities nonetheless.

Buddhists. The largest concentration of Buddhists in Bengal is among the Barua/Maghas, Chakmas, and Marammas situated along the eastern periphery of Bangladesh. The Buddhist presence in Bengal goes back probably to Mauryan times and certainly to the early first millennium CE, when Buddhist monks (*bhiksus*, lit., "mendicants") shared royal patronage with brahmans and Jains. Many rulers, especially among the Khadgas (late seventh century) and the Palas, seem to have embraced the Buddhist faith. Under the Palas several major monastic academies were constructed in Bengal and certain of these (e.g., Somapura near Paharpur and Salban near Comilla) were endowed with massive sculptured stupas. Chinese travelers reported many *viharas* (monasteries) with bhiksus of several Buddhist persua-sions: Mahayana, Sthavira, Sarvastivada, Tantrika, and Vajrayana. Buddhist scholarship and art flourished for centuries in ancient Bengal, and during the long Pala period Buddhist Tantra was assiduously cultivated. Subsequent discouragement by the Brahmanical Senas and destruction of remaining viharas by the Turks in the thirteenth century brought about the dispersal of scholar-*bhiksus* and their texts from Bengal. [*See also* Buddhism.]

A hybrid Buddhist Sahaja Tantra, developed by the twelfth century at the latest, may well have survived in Bengal into the postconquest centuries only to have merged gradually with other hybrid forms of rustic piety.

In the middle of the nineteenth century a movement of reform was undertaken by a Theravada monk from Arrakan (but a native of Chittagong), Sangaraj Saramedha. Aided by the Chakma queen, Kalindi, and the ongoing cooperation of the monks Punnacara Dhammodhara and Jnanalamkara Mahasthavir, Saramedha restored proper initiation, removed "offensive" Hindu practices, established educational facilities, and formed the Sangaraj Nikaya, an organization of reformed Buddhists characterized by a close interdependence of bhikkus and laymen.

Sikhs. A substantial Sikh community is concentrated in Calcutta and other centers of business and transportation in West Bengal. Sikh and Vaisnava hagiography both claim that Nanak visited eastern India early in the sixteenth century. Tegh Bahadur visited Sikhs residing in Dhaka in the late seventeenth century and most likely Sikh traders of the Punjabi *khatri* caste had settled in Bengal much earlier. Business opportunities under the British drew Punjabi Sikhs to Calcutta in the nineteenth century, and refugees from West Punjab (West Pakistan) augmented their numbers in 1947. Calcutta Sikhs maintain numerous *gurdwaras* (temples) and educational and welfare institutions. They bring out the noted *Sikh Review*. [See *Sikhism*.]

Parsis. Bengali Parsis are concentrated in Calcutta, where they came for banking and railways in the mid-nineteenth century. Prosperous and well-educated, they have had a fire temple since 1839 and have published a journal, *Navroz*, since 1917.

Christians. The Christians in Bengal are socially, denominationally, and geographically diverse. The largest single denomination has been the Roman Catholic, the major portion of which derives from Portuguese traders of the sixteenth and later centuries and their mixed Portuguese-Bengali descendants. Protestant evangelization began in 1793 with the Baptist Mission, in the Danish enclave, Serampore, where William Carey (1761-1843) and associates pioneered Bengali prose and printing and established Serampore College. Throughout the nineteenth century, Baptists, Lutherans, Anglicans, and Presbyterians were among the missionaries from several countries to establish congregations throughout Bengal.

Christians in Bengal have long been associated with education, nursing, and social welfare. Indeed, the most esteemed saint in late twentieth-century West Bengal is probably the Albanian Catholic nun, Mother Teresa, whose nuns and brothers serve the dying destitutes, lepers, and foundlings with exemplary devotion. In Bangladesh Christians, both Bangladeshi and foreign, have been conspicuous in relief and development work. [*See also* Christianity, *article on* Christianity in Asia.]

Jews. There may be fewer than fifty resident Jews remaining in Calcutta, though their community was once much larger and more influential, as an impressive synagogue and large burial grounds in Calcutta bear witness. [*See also* Judaism.]

The Islamic Majority. Muslims constitute the largest religious community among Bengalis (about 86 percent of Bangladeshis, and about 21 percent of West Bengalis); they are overwhelmingly Sunni of Hanafi orientation, the few Shi`ah deriving mostly from Persian officials of the late Mughal period. The vast majority of Muslims in Bengal are ethnic Bengalis, thanks to massive conversion and natural increase since Muhammad ibn Bakhtyar Khalji's conquest of Bengal (c. 1203 CE). Ethnic and linguistic cleavage between immigrant (e.g., Arab, Turk, Afghan, Pathan, Mughal, and Persian) elite *(ashraf)* and indigenous masses *(atraf, ajlaf)* has affected deeply the character of Bengali Muslim life. The building of a vernacular-based middle tradition, which came so easily to Hindu Bengalis, has occasioned recurrent conflict, confusion, and anxiety for Muslims in Bengal. Indeed, the very use of the Bengali language and the acknowledgement of Bengali ethnicity have been problematic for them.

Conversion: pirs of the "little tradition." The process of conversion of the indigenous population of central and eastern Bengal remains conjectural due to lack of contemporary textual evidence. No doubt, rulers and governors established mosques, *madrasahs* (religious schools and colleges), and other Muslim institutions in those urban centers where immigrant Muslims congregated. But the greatest concentrations of Muslims are found not in such urban centers, but in the rural backcountry where the population would have been overwhelmingly indigenous, a mosaic of unevenly hinduized (with undetermined Buddhist influence) endogamous groups (*jatis*) and tribal peoples. Long after the event Bengali Muslim recollections attribute the massive evangelization to pirs (guides, typically Sufi masters), but the Bengali category of pir is a protean one, embracing elements from legend, folklore, myth, and pre-Muslim rustic theology.

Some historical figures definitely are included among the pirs (e.g., Shah Jalal, who converted many in Sylhet, Zafar Khan Ghazi, the martyred warrior, and Khan Jahan `Ali, the clearer of forests). Many pirs who seem to have a historical foundation are remembered for alleged therapeutic, thaumaturgic, and pragmatic powers rather than for any Sufi spirituality. Human pirs established free hostels (*astanah, khanqah*) in their lifetime and after death their tombs (*mazar, dargah*) became foci of power of the "undying" (*zindah*) pir. Charismatic pioneering pirs were succeeded by sons and/or disciples.

Islamic criticism and reform: Fara'idi and jihad movements. The Bengali Muslim middle and little traditions, though scorned or ignored by the exogenous elite, had for centuries satisfied their respective literate and illiterate constituencies of Bengali-speaking Muslims. But by the early nineteenth century the traumatic loss of power by the Mughals to the British had set in motion processes that would destabilize the longstanding but problematic counterpoise of *ashraf* versus *atraf*, exogenous versus indigenous, and Persian/Urdu-speakers versus Bengali-speakers. There emerged vigorous movements of Muslim self-criticism and reform as responses to the loss of Muslim power.

The Fara'idi movement, led by Hajji Shari`at Allah (1781-1840) and his son Dudu Miyan (1819-1862), sought to restore the fortunes of Islam by rejection of all sorts of indigenous practices, such as veneration of pirs, as un-Islamic, thus calling for—and to a remarkable extent achieving—a thoroughgoing alienation of indigenous rural Muslims from much of Bengali culture.

The Tariqah-i-Muhammadiya, organized by Inayet Ali (1794-1858) and Wilayat Ali (1791-1853) of Patna, along with other *jihad* movements, stirred the enthusiasm of Muslims in Bengal and recruited men to fight in the northwest of India to restore sovereignty to Muslims. The *jihad* movements and the Faraizis helped shatter acceptance of the centuries-old religio-social status quo; they generated passionate concern for Islamic standards that would transcend Bengali particularity, and they motivated the Bengali Muslim masses to confront non-Muslim interests. Yet it was through the Bengali language, however much islamicized, and through the self-commitment of indigenous Bengali Muslims, that these movements had vitality. Forces were stirred that would outlast the movements that stirred them.

Independence: Islamic and secular states. The Muslim League's call for a separate state for Muslims met with overwhelming support in Bengal. Independence in East Pakistan—notwithstanding the agonies of partition and communal violence—began with exuberance, in contrast to the dismay among the Muslim minority left in West Bengal. But the perennial tension between indigenous and exogenous interests soon broke out anew. The attempt to impose Urdu as the sole national language met with resistance and martyrdom. Economic and political dissatisfaction reinforced resentment over language policy. The indigenous-exogenous tension took on the forms of incipient Bangladeshi nationalism *versus* Pakistani national integrity. The exogenous interests once again assumed the mantle of Islam, and the indigenous interests championed Bengali language and culture. The climax came in 1971 with Bangladeshi independence as the Bengali Muslim peasants, rejecting pleas that Islam was in danger, emphatically opted for the Bengali nationalist leadership of Mujibur Rahman (1920-1975).

The short-lived Awami League regime officially endorsed "secularism" (i. e., exclusion of religious parties from politics and religious neutrality by government) and successive military regimes have declared Bangladesh an "Islamic" state. But the former did not mean a rejection of Islam by Bengali Muslims, nor does the latter entail imposition of Islamic law in civil and criminal spheres or suppression of non-Islamic religion. Under both types of regime it has been common knowledge that Islamic religion and Bengali language and culture are fundamental components of Bangladeshi life, whatever the legal or symbolic niceties. However, there has been little constructive dialogue or debate between the `ulama' and the more secular intelligentsia in Bangladesh over how the perennial tension between the imperatives of Islamic faith and the imperatives of Bengali language and culture may be resolved.

[*All of the major religious traditions and many of the deities discussed in this article are the subject of independent entries. For similar overviews of other Indian regions, see* Tamil Religions *and* Marathi Religions. *For further discussion of tribal religions in India, see* Indian Religions.]

BIBLIOGRAPHY

The two-volume *History of Bengal* by R. C. Majumdar (vol. 1, 1943; reprint, Dacca, 1963) and Jadunath Sarkar (vol. 2, Dacca, 1948) remains valuable, as does Majumdar's *History of Medieval Bengal* (Calcutta, 1973). Invaluable for background and religious data is Shashibhusan Dasgupta's *Obscure Religious Cults* (Calcutta, 1962). Especially useful for (not exclusively) Hindu authors is Sukumar Sen's *History of Bengali Literature* (1960; 2d rev. ed., New Delhi, 1971). For detailed treatment of Bengali religious literature, see Sukumar Sen's *Bangla sahityer itihas*, 4 vols. (vol. 1 in 2 parts; Calcutta, varied dates and editions for each volume from 1940) or Asit Kumar Bandyopadhyay's *Bangla Sahityer Itivrtta*, 5 vols. (vol. 3 in 2 parts; Calcutta, dates and editions from 1959 to 1985).

There are two very useful, though not widely distributed, sources for papers and short translations relevant to Bengali religion: annual Bengal Studies Conference volumes, which appear among "Asian Studies Center Occasional Papers, South Asia Series," (Michigan State University, East Lansing), and *Learning Resources in Bengali Studies*, edited by Edward C. Dimock, Jr. (New York, 1974).

For Vaisnava and Sakta piety in Bengal, see David Kinsley's *The Sword and the Flute: Kali and Krsna* (Berkeley, 1975); Alan E. Morinis's *Pilgrimage in the Hindu Tradition: A Case Study of West Bengal* (Delhi, 1984); Sushil Kumar De's *Early History of Vaisnava Faith and Movement in Bengal* (Calcutta, 1961); Edward C. Dimock, Jr.'s *The Place of the Hidden Moon* (Chicago, 1966); and W. L. Smith's *The One-Eyed Goddess: A Study of the Manasa Mangal* (Stockholm, 1980).

Translations of texts important to religious life in Bengal include *Love Song of the Dark Lord: Jayadeva's Gitagovinda*, translated and edited by Barbara Stoler Miller (New York, 1977); *Love Songs of Vidyapati*, translated by Deben Bhattacharya; *Rama Prasada's Devotional Songs: The Cult of Shakti*, translated by Jadunath Sinha (Calcutta, 1966); and *The Gospel of Sri Ramakrishna*, translated by Swami Nikhilananda (New York, 1977).

For contrasting informed perspectives on nineteenth-century developments, see James N. Farquhar's *Modern Religious Movements in India* (New York, 1915) and David Kopf's *The Brahmo Samaj and the Shaping of the Modern Indian Mind* (Princeton, 1979). For introductions to two creative modern Bengali figures, see *A Tagore Reader*, edited by Amiya Chakravarty (Boston, 1966), and *The Essential Aurobindo*, edited by Robert McDermott (New York, 1973).

For Buddhism in Bengal, see Gayatri Sen Majumdar's *Buddhism in Ancient Bengal* (Calcutta, 1983), Per Kvaerne's *An Anthology of Buddhist Tantric Songs: A Study of the Caryagiti* (Oslo, 1977), and Sukomal Chaudhuri's *Contemporary Buddhism in Bangladesh* (Calcutta, 1982). Buddhists are among the tribal peoples treated in an excellent collection of papers edited by Mahmud Shah Qureshi, *Tribal Cultures in Bangladesh* (Rajshahi, 1984).

Accounts of Islam in the Bengal region include Asim Roy's *The Islamic Syncretistic Tradition in Bengal* (Princeton, 1983), Rafiuddin Ahmed's *The Bengal Muslims, 1871-1906: A Quest for Identity* (Delhi, 1981), and Mahmud Shah Qureshi's *Étude sur l'évolution intellectuelle chez les musulmans du Bengale, 1857-1947* (Paris, 1971).

JOSEPH T. O'CONNELL

BERBER RELIGION

It is difficult to refer with any sort of precision to "Berber religion" per se, even as it is difficult to speak about a "Berber people." The term *berber*—originally a derogatory name (cf. Gr. *barbaroi*, Eng. *barbarians*) applied by outsiders—designates the rather heterogeneous, indigenous population of North Africa extending from the Siwa Oasis in the western Egyptian desert to Morocco, Mauretania, and even as far as the great bend of the Niger River. These people, who have been in the region since prehistoric times, exhibit varying physical features, customs, and social organizations. They are united mainly by language.

Ancient Berber Religion. Echoes of prehistoric Berber religiosity may be found in rock paintings and carvings from the Neolithic period. Many of these depictions are difficult to interpret, but some seem to indicate clearly the veneration of certain animals and perhaps even fetishism.

If any deity enjoyed extensive popularity in classical times, it was Saturn. The omnipresence of depictions of this god and his associations with the Punic Baal-Hammon are evidence that he was the real master of the region. One of his iconographic representations, showing him seated on a lion (his animal attribute) and holding a serpent (the symbol of death and fertility), has continued in folk religion down to the present. Rabbi Ephraim Enqawa of Tlemcen, a Jewish saint, who is venerated throughout the Berber regions of southern Morocco, is invariably depicted in the same fashion.

Most of the *dii Mauri* (i. e., Mauretanian gods), for whom some fifty-two names survive, were local spirits. Many of these have recognizably Berber names.

Natural phenomena were the main focuses of Berber veneration, and nature worship has continued to be the core of Berber religiosity into the modern era despite the official overlay of Islam.

Rocks, mountains, caves, and springs were frequently places of sanctity for the ancient Berbers, as they have continued to be for their modern descendants. Few of the spirits inhabiting these holy spots had names; they were impersonal forces, like so many of the *jnun* of later Berber folk belief.

On the basis of archaeological evidence, it seems that the Berbers of antiquity had a well-developed funerary cult. Among the Numidians, charismatic rulers were venerated as gods after their death, a practice that had its parallel in the widespread saint and marabout cults of later Christian and Islamic times.

Berber Religion in Christian Times. During the early centuries of the common era, when Christianity began to spread throughout the Roman empire, many Berbers in the urbanized parts of North Africa adopted the Christian faith. However, Berber particularism frequently imparted to their Christianity an individualistic stamp. The cult of local martyrs was very strong and widely diffused. Many of the practices and votive offerings reflected earlier funerary cults.

Berber Religion in Islamic Times. According to Arab historians, the Berber tribes of North Africa submitted to Muslim rule and accepted Islam at the end of the seventh century, after more than fifty years of fierce resistance. This mass conversion was due more to political interest than to religious conviction.

New Berber religions appeared during the Middle Ages; influenced by Islam, they adopted aspects of its external form but remained native in language, rite, and usage. The earliest of these was the religion of the Barghawatah, who inhabited the Atlantic coastal region of eastern Morocco.

Another new Berber religion influenced by Islam was that of Ha-Mim, who appeared among the Ghumarah tribe in the Rif province of northern Morocco during the tenth century. He too produced a Berber scripture, and had dietary taboos similar to those of the Barghawatah. However, Ha-Mim's religion had only two daily prayers, at sunrise and sunset. An important place was accorded to Ha-Mim's paternal aunt and sister, both of whom were sorceresses. According to al-Bakri and Ibn Khaldun, the Ghumarah sought their aid in times of war, drought, and calamity.

Although Islam had no rivals as the official religion among the Berbers from the thirteenth century onward, many native Berber rites continued to be practiced within the Maghrebi Islamic context.

[*See also* Islam, article on *Islam in North Africa.*]

BIBLIOGRAPHY

There is no single work devoted to the history of Berber religion as a discrete entity, although there is an enormous literature on Maghrebi Islam and on popular beliefs and rituals. Berber religion receives extensive treatment within this broader context.

Though somewhat outdated in part, Alfred Bel's *La religion musulmane en Berbérie*, vol. 1 (the only volume to appear; Paris, 1938), remains the best survey of Berber religious history from antiquity through the later Islamic Middle Ages. An important bibliography precedes each chapter. The chapter on religion in Gabriel Camps's *Berbères: Aux marges de l'histoire* (Paris, 1980), pp. 193-271, goes a long way toward updating and correcting Bel and is especially good for the pre-Islamic periods. Edward A. Westermarck's *Ritual and Belief in Morocco*, 2 vols. (1926; reprint, New Hyde Park, N. Y., 1968), remains a classic source of information on popular religion in Morocco. In addition to a wealth of descriptive detail, the book offers much comparative data. Another valuable survey of popular religious practice is Edmond Doutté's *Magie et religion dans l'Afrique du Nord* (Algiers, 1909).

There are many studies on saint veneration in North Africa. The best dealing with holy men in a Berber society is Ernest Gellner's *Saints of the Atlas* (London, 1969). For a comparison of Muslim and Jewish saints, see my study "Saddiq and Marabout in Morocco," in *The Sepharadi and Oriental Jewish Heritage*, edited by Issachar Ben-Ami (Jerusalem, 1982), pp. 489-500.

NORMAN A. STILLMAN

BHAGAVADGITA

The *Bhagavadgita* is perhaps the most widely read and beloved scripture in all Indian religious literature. Its power to counsel and inspire its readers has remained undiminished in the almost two thousand years since its composition.

The *Bhagavadgita* (Song of the Blessed Lord) is sacred literature, holy scripture—it is a text that has abundant power in its persistence and its presence. The pious Hindu, even if his piety is mild, will inevitably have access to the book or will be able to recite, or at least paraphrase, a few lines from it. The text is intoned during the initiation ceremony wherein one becomes a *samnyasin* (renunciant); teachers and holy men expound upon it; professors translate it and write about it; the more humble listen to the words that, though heard countless times before, remain vibrant. The text is read by all Hindus, esteemed by Saivas as well as by Vaisnavas, venerated by the lower caste as well as by the high, savored by villagers as well as by the more urbane.

One may dispute whether the *Bhagavadgita* teaches the dualistic Samkhya philosophy or the nondualistic Vedanta, whether it is a call to action or renunciation; but what is beyond dispute is that it teaches devotion to god as a means to liberation, whether that liberation is understood as release from the world or freedom in the world: "Hear again My supreme word, the most secret of all: thou are greatly beloved by Me, hence I will speak for thy good. Center thy mind on Me, be devoted to Me, sacrifice to Me, revere Me, and thou shalt come to Me. I promise thee truly, for thou art dear to Me" (18.64-65).

The Text in Context. The *Bhagavadgita* occupies a very small part of the *Mahabharata*—it is but one of the Hundred Minor Books of that enormous epic, that elephantine tale of the great war between the Kauravas and the Pandavas, two descendant branches of the Kurus, the Lunar Race. Yudhisthira, the righteous leader of the Pandavas, having lost his family's portion of the kingdom to the Kauravas in a crooked game of dice, was forced, together with his four brothers, into forest exile for thirteen years. Afterward Yudhisthira asked for the just return of the kingdom, or at least five villages, one for each of the brothers. When this was refused, the great war became inevitable.

Both armies sought allies. Krsna, the princely leader of the Vrsnis, another branch of the Lunar Race, in an attempt to remain neutral and loyal to both families, offered his troops to the Kauravas and his service as charioteer and counselor to his friend Arjuna, one of Yudhisthira's younger brothers.

The battle was ready to begin. Suddenly, seeing his own kinsmen—teachers, fathers, uncles, cousins, and in-laws—arrayed for battle, Arjuna decided that he was unable to fight. Realizing that to kill them would destroy the eternal laws of the family and uncaring as to whether or not he himself would be slain, "Arjuna cast away his bow and arrow and sank down on the seat of his chariot, his spirit overcome by grief" (1.47).

In this dramatic setting the teachings of the *Bhagavadgita* begin. Krsna must show Arjuna why he must fight in this terrible war and, in so doing, he reveals the nature of reality and of himself. Military counsel becomes spiritual instruction; the heroic charioteer discloses his divinity. Krsna-Vasudeva is

> ## The *Bhagavadgita* has attained the functional status of a gospel.

God, the highest reality and eternal self, beyond the world and yet of it as a preserver, creator, and destroyer. In the midst of the theophany Arjuna cries out: "Thou art the imperishable, the highest to be known; Thou art the final resting place of this universe; Thou are the immortal guardian of eternal law; Thou are the primal spirit" (9.18).

By the time the *Bhagavadgita* was incorporated into the story of the great war (probably during the third century BCE), a conception of this world as a dreadful, burning round of death had taken hold and with it renunciatory ideals and impulses for liberation challenged more ancient, hieratic ideals of ritual action and aspirations for heavenly domains. The *Gita* provided a synthesis of conflicting ideals and past and present norms. It harmonized Brahmanic values with a warrior's code, reconciled a traditional pantheism with a seemingly new theistic religiosity, and coalesced a variety of differing and potentially dissentient philosophical trends. This synthetic or syncretic quality of the text invested it with a pan-Indian appeal that it has retained.

The *Bhagavadgita* has attained the functional status of a gospel. Sankara (eighth century), the major proponent of the Advaita Vedanta school of philosophy, quite typically begins his exegesis of the text with the comment that the *Gita* contains the very quintessence of the Veda and that a knowledge of it leads to *moksa*, liberation from the bonds of worldly existence. Ramanuja (eleventh century), who qualified the nondualistic position of Vedanta in order to expound his theology of a supreme and loving god, understood the *Gita* as the actual revelation of the word of that god under the mere pretext of a discourse with Arjuna. And the Bengali saint Ramakrishna (1834-1886), like so many other modern commentators, declared the book to be "the essence of all scriptures" (*The Gospel of Sri Ramakrishna*, New York, 1949, p. 772).

The Philosophy of the Text. The individual human being, according to the *Bhagavadgita*, is at once natural (a product of nature caught up in lawlike relations and filled with desires and longings) and spiritual (an embodiment of the divine).

The individual human being, Krsna tells Arjuna early on in the text, is also immortal. Possessed of an eternal, unchanging spirit, a person can only appear to be an autonomous actor in the natural world. This appearance derives from an ignorance of the true self. Normally identifying himself as an ego self-sufficiently working within the conditions of his psychophysical nature, a person must reidentify himself at a deeper level of integrated selfhood and thereby understand his true role as a social being.

Ideally each person works out his social career according to the dictates of his own nature *(svadharma)* as this is itself a product of past experience. *Dharma, karman* ("action" or "work"), and *samsara* ("rebirth") belong together: action carried over innumerable lives must be informed by a sensitivity to the obligations one has in virtue of one's interdependence with others. Arjuna is a member of the warrior class and must fulfill the duties of this social position—he must fight.

But what is the nature of reality that makes this both possible and imperative? The *Gita's* answer to this is that reality, in its essence, is the presence of a personalized *brahman*, something higher than the impersonal *brahman*, the absolute reality described in the Upanisads. "There are two spirits in this world," Krsna explains, "the perishable and the imperishable." The perishable is all beings and the imperishable is called *kutastha* ("the immovable"). But there is another, the Highest Spirit *(purusottama)*, called the Supreme Self, who, as the imperishable Lord, enters into the three worlds and sustains them. "Since I transcend the perishable and am higher even than the imperishable, I am renowned in the world and in the Veda as the highest Spirit" (15.16-18).

In its analysis of the lower status of the divine, the *Gita* draws heavily upon the Samkhya system of thought. Nature *(prakrti)* is seen as an active organic field constituted by various strands *(gunas)*, which can best be understood as energy systems. Everything in nature, and particularly every individual human being, is constituted by a combination of these forces. *Sattva* represents a state of subtle harmony and equilibrium which is exhibited as clear intelligence, as light. At the other extreme is darkness, *tamas*, the state of lethargy, of heaviness. In between is *rajas*, agitation, restlessness, passion, the motivating force for actions. The *purusa* ("the individual spirit") caught up in *prakrti*, is driven by the *gunas* and is deluded into thinking that, as a given phenomenal fact, it is their master and not their victim. [*See* Samkhya.]

The aim of human life in the Bhagavadgita is to attain a self-realization that "I" am not a separate, autonomous actor but that "I" am at one with a divine reality, and that my ultimate freedom comes from bringing my actions into accord with that reality. The realization of this aim of life is at the heart of the *Bhagavadgita's* teaching, and has been the most controversial among both modern and traditional interpreters of the text.

Following Sañkara, whose commentary is one of the oldest to have survived, many have argued that the central yoga put forward by the *Bhagavadgita* is the way of knowledge, *jñanayoga*: it alone provides the insight into reality that allows for genuine self-realization. Taking the position of Ramanuga, others have argued that *bhaktiyoga*, the discipline of devotion, remains the highest way for the *Gita; bhakti*, in his understanding of the text, provides the basis for a salvific relationship between the individual person and a loving god with absolute power and supremacy over the world. Still others have seen the *Gita* as a gospel of works, teaching most centrally *karmayoga*, the way of action—of acting without attachment to the fruits of one's acts. This multiplicity of interpretations results from the fact that the *Bhagavadgita* does extol each of these ways at various times.

The Persistence of the Text. By the eighth century the *Bhagavadgita* had become a standard text for philosophical and religious exposition. The normative commentary of Sankara generated subcommentaries and inspired responses, new interpretations, new commentaries and more subcommentaries. Ramanuja's theistic exegesis set forth devotional paradigms for understanding the text which were to be elaborated by medieval Vaisnava scholiasts.

Beyond the exegetical tradition, the *Bhagavadgita* became the prototype for a genre of devotional literature in which an Arjuna-like student is urged by a particular sectarian deity to absorb himself in the worship of that deity. So in the *Sivagita* (eighth century), for example, Rama is too disconsolate over his separation from Sita to go into battle with Ravana; Siva counsels and instructs him just as Krsna did Arjuna. In the *Isvaragita* (ninth century) Siva explains the paths to self-realization, the methods of liberation, to ascetics in a hermitage, in more or less the same words as were uttered in the prototype. The form and style of the original *Bhagavadgita* seem to have imbued these later *gitas* with authority and legitimacy. Many of these texts are embedded within the Puranas (e.g., the *Sivagita* in the *Padma Purana*, the *Isvaragita* in the *Kurma Purana*, the *Devi-gita* in the *Devibhagavata Purana*). The later Puranas commonly give quotes from, resumés of, or eulogistic references to, the *Bhagavadgita*; the *Padma Purana* (eighth century) contains a glorification of the book, the *Gitamahatmya*, a paean to the text as the perfect distillation of supreme truth. The text about devotion became itself an object of devotion. It is carried like a talisman by many a wandering holy man.

Throughout Indian history the *Bhagavadgita* has provided social theorists with axioms whereby political issues and problems could be understood in religious and traditional terms. Bal Gangadhar Tilak (1856-1920), one of the most important nationalist leaders of the modern Hindu renaissance, for example, while in prison in Mandalay for sedition, wrote the *Gita rahasya*, an interpretation of the ancient text as a revolutionary manifesto, a call to the Indian people to take up arms against the British. Gandhi, on the other hand, who first became acquainted with the *Bhagavadgita* through British Theosophists in London, asserted, without a trace of self-consciousness, that the *Bhagavadgita* taught nonviolence. He urged his followers to read it assiduously and to live by it. He often referred to the book as Mother *Gita*, and would say, "When I am in difficulty or distress, I seek refuge in her bosom" (*Harijan*, August, 1934).

BIBLIOGRAPHY

The passages from the *Bhagavadgita* cited in this article are from the translation of the text by Eliot Deutsch (New York, 1968). Since Charles Wilkins published his *The Bhagvatgeeta, or, Dialogues of Kreeshna and Arjoon in Eighteen Lectures, with Notes* in 1785 literally hundreds of translations of the text have been made into European languages. Gerald J. Largon has thoughtfully surveyed the stylistic and interpretive trends as exemplified by many of these translations in "The Song Celestial: Two Centuries of the *Bhagavad Gita* in English," *Philosophy East and West* 31 (October 1981): 513-541. Of the readily available translations, Franklin Edgerton's (1925; reprint, Oxford, 1944) is the most literal, so literal in its attempt to preserve the Sanskrit syntax, in fact, that, for the sake of balance, it was originally published together with Sir Edwin Arnold's transformation of the text into Victorian poesy (Cambridge, Mass., 1944). Though Edgerton's always reliable translation is difficult to read, his lengthy commentary is masterful scholarship. The interpretive notes that accompany the translation by W. Douglas P. Hill (London, 1927) remain an important contribution to the literature. Étienne Lamotte's *Notes sur la Bhagavadgita* (Paris, 1929) is a fine example of rigorous exegesis and reflection.

R. C. Zaehner's lucid translation (Oxford, 1969) is a pleasure to read and his analyses are as judicious as they are sensitive; Zaehner introduces the insights of Sankara and Ra-manuja where they are appropriate and he admits his penchant for the theistic interpretation of the latter. For a more detailed understanding of Ramanuja's understanding of the text, see J. A. B. van Buitenen's *Ramanuja on the Bhagavadgita* (The Hague, 1953). Van Buitenen's own translation, *The Bhagavadgita in the Mahabharata* (Chicago, 1981), is heroic scholarship, translation at its best, and his introductory essay is no less insightful. The very important exegesis of Sankara has been translated into English by Alladi Mahadeva Sastri: *The Bhagavad-Gita with the Commentary of Srï Sankarachâryâ*, 5th ed. (Madras, 1961). And the interesting commentary of Abhinavagupta, the *Gitarthasangraha*, has been well translated into English and perceptively introduced by Arvind Sharma (Leiden, 1983).

For significant examples of modern Indian interpretations of the text, see *The Gospel of Selfless Action, or the Gita According to Gandhi*, edited and translated by Mahadev Desai (Ahmadabad, 1948); *Srimad Bhagavadgita Rahasya*, edited by B. G. Ti-lak (Poona, 1936); and Aurobindo Ghose's *Essays on the Gita* (Calcutta, 1926).

ELIOT DEUTSCH and LEE SIEGEL

BIBLICAL EXEGESIS

Jewish Views

The first major figure of medieval biblical exegesis is the Babylonian rabbinic leader Sa`adyah Gaon (d. 942), who, like his successors, engaged in translation into Arabic and commentary written in the same language. Sa`adyah insisted on literal interpretation, but discussed four circumstances in which deviation from the obvious literal meaning of the biblical text is justified: (1) when the literal meaning contradicts reason (e.g., "God is a consuming fire" [*Dt.* 4:24] must be interpreted metaphorically); (2) when the literal meaning contradicts sense-experience (e.g., Eve was not the "mother of all living beings" [*Gn.* 3:21] but rather the mother of human life; (3) when the literal meaning contradicts another biblical passage (e.g., "Thou shalt not test the Lord" seemingly contradicts "Test me and see," thus necessitating reinterpretation); (4) when the literal meaning contradicts the oral tradition (e.g., "Thou shalt not seethe a kid in its mother's milk" [*Ex.* 23:19, 34:26; *Dt.* 14:21] is to be interpreted in conformity with the rabbinic view that this verse refers to all cooking of milk with meat).

The peripatetic Avraham Ibn `Ezra' wrote on almost all of the Bible, often writing multiple commentaries on the same book, not all of which have been published. The quest for exegetical simplicity led Ibn `Ezra' to criticize some earlier approaches to the text. Thus he rejects Ibn Jannah's view that the same Hebrew word can express contradictory meanings, as well as his willingness to transpose words or to substitute words for those in the text. By the same token, he sees no need to employ the rabbinic listing of *tiqqunei soferim* (euphemistic emendations of phrases referring to God). He is troubled neither by variations of phrase, so long as the meaning is conserved (for example, he considers the differences between *Exodus* 20 and *Deuteronomy* 4 insignificant), nor by orthographical inconsistencies.

Ibn `Ezra' has been regarded as a precursor of the Higher Criticism which began with Barukh Spinoza (1632-1677). Several cryptic passages in his commentary (e.g., on *Gn.* 12:7, *Dt.* 1:2) allude to anachronisms in the Torah that have since been interpreted either as signs of a post-Mosaic hand (as first suggested by Yosef Bonfils in the fourteenth century) or as consequences of prophetic familiarity with the future. Attention has also been given his obscure remarks about the postexilic historical setting of *Isaiah* 40-66.

Franco-German Exegesis. The commentary of Rashi (Shelomoh ben Yitshaq, 1040-1105) to the Torah is the most influential work of Jewish exegesis. Combining philological sensitivity with generous quotations from rabbinic literature, it became, at the popular level, almost inseparable from the biblical text itself: until the nineteenth century no text of the Pentateuch was published with any commentary that did not include Rashi's as well. Rashi's popularity, as well as his laconic presentation, inspired hundreds of supercommentaries. The contemporary leader of Lubavitch Hasidism, Menahem Mendel Schneersohn, has devoted the lion's share of his voluminous output to an investigation of Rashi's nuances.

Rashi several times distinguishes the literal meaning *(peshat)* from the homiletical *(derash)*, identifying his own method, despite its heavy use of *aggadah*, with the former (e.g., on *Gn.* 3:8). His interpreters have generally inferred from this that all comments not explicitly labeled as Midrashic (and perhaps even these) are evoked by some peculiarity in the text that Rashi seeks to resolve. Reworking of and deviation from standard rabbinic exegesis occur both in narrative and in legal passages (for the latter, see, for example, *Exodus* 23:2). In his philology, Rashi is limited by his dependence on those grammarians who wrote in Hebrew (Menahem ben Saruq and Dunash ibn Labrat), employing, for example, the doctrine of the two-letter root, later superseded by the idea of a three-letter root. Among Rashi's predecessors, mention must also be made of Menahem ben Helbo.

Among Rashi's contemporaries and successors, Yosef Qara' and Shemu'el ben Meir (Rashbam) are the most influential. The latter, who was Rashi's grandson, reflected on the innovation in the study of *peshat* (see digression at *Genesis* 37:2): earlier generations, in their piety, had been concerned with the legal and moral lessons of scripture, leaving room for the "ever new facets of *peshat* that are every day discovered." Rashbam is more reluctant than Rashi to erect his exegesis

> **Rashi's popularity, as well as his laconic presentation, inspired hundreds of supercommentaries.**

on rabbinic tradition, and he is more prone to seek exegetical alternatives in the legal passages (e.g., his preface to *Exodus* 21). Thus he asserts that day precedes night in *Genesis* 1:5, in contradiction to the halakhic exegetical tradition.

Medieval Philosophical Exegesis. Philosophical concerns play a role in the work of Sa`adyah (who participates in Kalam philosophy) and the Neoplatonist Ibn `Ezra'. Bahye ibn Paquda's ethical treatise *Duties of the Heart* and Yehudah ha-Levi's *Kuzari* also contain remarks pertinent to biblical study. It is, however, with the *Guide of the Perplexed* of Moses Maimonides (Mosheh ben Maimon; 1135/8-1204) that the philosophical approach to scripture becomes central. Maimonides' doctrine of religious language leads him to reinterpret anthropomorphisms and anthropopathisms more rigorously than his predecessors.

The philosophical emphasis in Jewish biblical commentary flourished during the thirteenth to fifteenth centuries. Maimonides' views spread in commentaries on the Prophets and *Psalms* written by both David Kimhi (known as Radak; early thirteenth century) and Menahem Me'iri (late thirteenth century) of Provence. His terminology and concerns deeply affect the work of the antiphilosopher Yitshaq Arama (early fifteenth century) and the more ambivalent exegete and commentator on the *Guide*, Isaac Abravanel. Maimonides is also discussed by Moses Nahmanides (Mosheh ben Nahman, thirteenth-century Spain) and the exegetical tradition stem-

> **Maimonides' doctrine of religious language leads him to reinterpret anthropomorphisms and anthropopathisms more rigorously than his predecessors.**

ming from him. Yosef Albo's *Sefer ha-`iqqarim* (Book of Principles), in which the greatest doctrinal affinity is to Albo's teacher Hasdai Crescas, a trenchant critic of Maimonides, should be cited for several homiletical sections.

Levi ben Gershom (Gersonides; fourteenth-century Provence), a major Jewish philosopher, and more consistent an Aristotelian than Maimonides, is a major biblical commentator as well. Limiting divine providence, he offered rationalistic explanations of the stopping of the sun by Joshua and maintained that it was not Lot's wife but Sodom that became a pillar of salt. Like Maimonides before him, he interprets the *Song of Songs* as an allegory of God and the individual soul, not, as Rashi and Ibn `Ezra' did, as an allegory of God's relationship with the Jewish people. Following Maimonides, he unraveled the speeches of Job and his friends as presentations of philosophical positions on providence. Gersonides affixed to his commentaries a list of *to`aliyyot* ("lessons") to be derived from scripture.

Eclectic Commentaries: Thirteenth-Fifteenth Centuries. David Kimhi combines philological-grammatical perspicuity with liberal quotations from rabbinic literature, discussions of the Targum and its variants, fealty to Maimonides, and references to Rashi, Ibn `Ezra', Yosef Kimhi, who was his father, and his brother Mosheh (author of pseudo-Ibn `Ezra' on *Proverbs* and *Ezra-Nehemiah*).

Nahmanides, like Rashi, is a major Talmudist who devoted himself to a commentary on the Torah; its impact over the centuries is second only to Rashi's. He attends to philology and law and comments on theological issues and psychological factors. Reaching the Land of Israel in his old age, he is occasionally able to draw upon an acquaintance with its

geography and *realia*. A qabbalist, he is the first major commentator in whose work qabbalistic hints are common. Thus, by the fourteenth century, in the aftermath of Maimonides and Nahmanides, we encounter the fourfold division of biblical interpretation—PaRDeS—in which *remez* (hint) and *sod* (esoterica) join the familiar *peshat* and *derash*. Nahmanides frequently quotes and discusses Rashi, particularly in legal sections, less frequently, Ibn `Ezra', toward whom he adopts an attitude of "open rebuke and hidden love." He cites Maimonides, sometimes lauding his views, but on several crucial matters he disagrees sharply, for example, on the meaning of the sacrificial cult (*Lv.* 1:9) and the role of angels in prophecy (*Gn.* 18:1). Nahmanides also employs typological interpretation to explain apparent superfluities in *Genesis*.

Isaac Abravanel (Spain and Italy, d. 1508) represents the last stage of classic medieval commentary. He makes liberal use of the work of his predecessors, ranging over the philological, philosophical, and homiletical approaches. His psychological-political sense is keen; his philosophy, while tending toward fideism, is rooted in an extended and passionate involvement with Maimonides' *Guide*; philological originality, however, is not his strong suit. His prefaces to the biblical books are more elaborate than his predecessors', often devoting detailed attention to the authorship and provenance of the text; here he is willing to challenge rabbinic ascriptions, for example, attributing the *Book of Joshua* to Samuel instead of Joshua.

The Sixteenth-Eighteenth Centuries. The centuries following the expulsion of the Jews from Spain have been erroneously characterized as a stagnant era for Jewish biblical study. M. H. Segal, in his survey, includes only the *Metsuddat David* and *Metsuddat Tsion* (by the Altschuler family, late sev-enteenth-century Germany), a generally unoriginal selection from Rashi, Ibn `Ezra', and Kimhi that became a standard accompaniment to the study of the Prophets and Hagiographa. Jewish exegesis of this period, unlike that of Rashi, Ibn `Ezra', Maimonides, and Kimhi, does not exercise an impact on Christian scholarship. It innovates little of value as regards philology and grammar, beyond the achievements of the medievals.

Pace Segal, however, one cannot gainsay several contributions of the period. `Ovadyah Sforno (sixteenth-century Italy), writing on the Torah and other biblical books, stresses both literal and philosophical interpretation. He follows Nahmanides in regarding the stories of *Genesis* as a typological "blueprint" of history. He is particularly concerned about the placement of legal sections among narrative units (e.g., the laws pertinent to the Land of Israel that follow the story of the spies, *Nm.* 15). Other major figures generally present their comments within a homiletical framework, with a not-infrequent mystical tendency. Efrayim of Luntshits's *Keli yaqar*, the work of a sixteenth-century Polish preacher, and the mystically oriented *Or ha-hayyim* of Hayyim ibn Attar (eighteenth-century Morocco) have become enshrined in many editions of *Miqra'ot gedolot*, the standard rabbinical Bible textbook, as have excerpts from the commentaries of the sixteenth-century Greek preacher Mosheh Alshekh.

It should be noted that this period also marks the heyday of the major supercommentaries on Rashi, which apparently offered an outlet to rabbis interested in extending the medieval methods of study.

Traditional Developments in the Modern Period. Beginning in the late eighteenth century there is a renewal of interest, evident from several Torah commentaries, in the interaction between traditional rabbinic exegesis and extra-traditional exegesis. This renewal may derive from increased availibilty of the full panoply of rabbinic exegesis (i. e., *Sifra'*, *Mekhilta'*, *Sifrei*, the Jerusalem Talmud, and eventually *Mekhilta' de Rabbi Shim`on* and *Sifrei Zuta'*), which drew attention to hermeneutical results other than those preserved in the Babylonian Talmud. Whatever its sources, it is clearly motivated by a desire to defend the authenticity of the oral law against its skeptical ("enlightened" or Reform) detractors by showing the connection between the "text and tradition" (the title of Ya`aqov Mecklenburg's nineteenth-century commentary *Ketav ve-ha-qabbalah*).

One may distinguish between two types of works produced by these authors. The eastern Europeans, such as Eliyyahu ben Shelomoh Zalman, known as the gaon of Vilna (now Vilnius; d. 1796), Naftali Tsevi Berlin (d. 1892), and Me'ir Simhah of Dvinsk (now Daugavpils; d. 1926) often present their own novel interpretations. Those who were most exposed to the aforementioned external challenges, in Germany (Mecklenburg and Samson Raphael Hirsch) or Romania (Malbim), are reluctant to propose legal interpretations contrary to tradition. Eliyyahu ben Shelomoh Zalman's treatment of the Bible is displayed in his commentary to *Proverbs*, to sections of other books, and in notes to others. He seeks an integration of all dimensions of Torah study, from the literal to the mystical. This involves the unification of oral and written laws but also precipitates an awareness of the differences between them.

Berlin, in his *Ha`ameq davar* on Torah as well as his commentaries to halakhic *midrashim* and the *Shei'ltot* of Aha'i Gaon (eighth century), continues to cultivate both the unification and differentiation of *peshat* and *derash*. His work on narrative sections is distinguished by psychological perspicuity that is enhanced rather than diminished by his reliance on the qabbalistic typology that identifies the patriarchs with particular *sefirot*. Me'ir Simhah's *Meshekh hokhmah* is valued both for its insightful homiletical pieces and for its comments on, and alternatives to, classic rabbinic tradition.

Samson Raphael Hirsch, who as rabbi in Frankfort contended with Reform, maintained in his German commentaries to Torah and *Psalms* that the written law was dependent on the oral, as a set of notes is dependent on the lecture. Rabbinic hermeneutic, then, is less a matter of correct philology than of access to a code. In seeking to interpret the text, both narrative and legal, and justify tradition regarding the latter, Hirsch resorted to an idiosyncratic etymological method (occasionally used by Mecklenburg as well), whereby phonetically similar consonants are interchanged in order to locate the "essential" meaning of the word. He offered a system of symbolic interpretation in which, for example, the upper half of the altar represents the higher nature of man, while the lower half symbolizes the lower aspects of human nature. Hirsch's rationales sought to explain not only the general purpose of the laws but their particular features as well, including those that are derived through rabbinic interpretation.

In contrast with Hirsch, Malbim proclaimed rabbinic hermeneutics to be the correct grammar of biblical Hebrew. From his premise about the perfection of biblical Hebrew he concludes that the Bible contains no redundancies of style or language: every seeming redundancy must be explained. Thus, Malbim discovers many fine distinctions among the synonyms in biblical parallelism, rejecting the approach of Kimhi and the *Metsuddot* that "the content is repeated in different words." Malbim's identification of rabbinic exegesis with philology is symbolized in his commentary to biblical law, where his independent commentary becomes, instead, a commentary to the corpus of halakhic *midrashim*, insofar as the latter provides the literal meaning of scripture.

Both Hirsch and Malbim had enough awareness of biblical criticism to address such problems as the doublets in biblical narrative through literary analysis. They are both oblivious, however, to the data provided by comparative Semitics or knowledge of the ancient Near East. David Tsevi Hoffmann (d. 1922), the last great traditional biblical exegete of western Europe, is fully aware of contemporary biblical scholarship and its ancillary disciplines. In his German commentaries to *Leviticus*, *Deuteronomy*, and *Genesis* and in *Die wichtigsten Instanzen gegen die Graf-Wellhausensche Hypothese* he marshaled his arguments against non-Mosaic dating of the Torah. A leading Talmudic authority, he concentrated on biblical law, attempting to establish that the laws ascribed to the P and D sources could best be understood within the context of Israel's desert experience, in the order narrated by the Torah, and that these laws were available in their present form during the First Temple period.

Enlightenment and Its Aftermath. The second half of the eighteenth century also marks the entry of Jewish exegesis into the world of general European culture. The founding father of the Jewish Enlightenment was Moses Mendelssohn (d. 1786), whose elegant German translation of the Torah was the first by Jewish hands; the translation was accompanied by a commentary (the Bi'ur) authored by

Mendelssohn and his associates. This commentary follows in the footsteps of the classical medieval exegetes but is quite conservative in accepting rabbinic tradition regarding the legal sections; it is also concerned with aesthetic features of the text. That the *Bi'ur* was banned in many Orthodox circles had little to do with its content.

BIBLIOGRAPHY

While several modern exegetical works have appeared in Western languages, such as those of Samson Raphael Hirsch and David Hoffmann, which were published in German, most of the primary literature has appeared in Hebrew. However, several primary sources are available in English translation. A mildly bowdlerized translation of Rashi's commentary on the Pentateuch was prepared and annotated by M. Rosenbaum and A. M. Silbermann under the title *Pentateuch with Targum Onkelos, Haphtaroth and Rashi's Commentary*, 5 vols. (New York,1934). C. B. Chavel's *Ramban (Nachmanides): Commentary on the Torah*, 5 vols. (New York, 1971-1976) is a complete and annotated translation of Nahmanides' commentary on the Pentateuch.

Other medieval biblical exegetes whose works have been translated into English include Avraham ibn `Ezra' on *Isaiah (The Commentary of Ibn Ezra on Isaiah*, translated by Michael Friedländer, vol. 1, London, 1873); David Kimhi's commentary on *Isaiah (The Commentary of David Kimhi on Isaiah* (1926), translated by Louis Finkelstein, reprinted, New York, 1966), as well as his work on *Hosea (The Commentary of Rabbi David Kimhi on Hosea* (1929), translated by Harry Cohen, reprinted, New York, 1965), and on *Psalms*, chaps. 120-150 *(The Commentary of Rabbi David Kimhi on Psalms CXX-CL*, translated by Joshua Baker and E. W. Nicholson, Cambridge, 1973); Levi ben Gershom's commentary on *Job (Commentary of Levi ben Gerson on the Book of Job*, translated by A. L. Lassen, New York, 1946).

A complete listing of all editions of exegetical works written prior to 1540 is to be found in M. Kasher and Jacob B. Mandelbaum's *Sarei ha-elef*, 2d ed., 2 vols. (Jerusalem, 1978). Nehama Leibowitz's studies on each book of the Pentateuch have been translated into English and adapted by Aryeh Newman in six volumes (Jerusalem, 1972-1980) and provide an excellent guide to traditional Jewish commentary. Moshe Greenberg's *Understanding Exodus* (New York, 1969) integrates a generous amount of traditional exegesis.

M. H. Segal's *Parshanut ha-miqra'*, 2d ed. (Jerusalem, 1971) is a fine survey of Jewish exegesis. Ezra Zion Melamed's *Mefarshei ha-miqra'*, 2 vols. (Jerusalem, 1975), covers Rashi, Shemu'el ben Me'ir, Ibn `Ezra', Kimhi, Nahmanides, and the exegesis of rabbinic Targum in detail.

Some aspects of exegesis between Sa`adyah and Ibn `Ezra' are dealt with by Uriel Simon in *Arba` gishot le-sefer Tehillim* (Ramat Gan, Israel, 1982). The exegesis of the medieval Franco-German Jewish scholars is described by Samuel Pozananski in his edition of Eli`ezer of Beaugency's *Perush Yehezqe'l ve-Terei `Asar* (Warsaw, 1909).

An extensive bibliography of recent literature can be found in the *Entsiqeloppedyah miqra'it* (Jerusalem, 1982), in the lengthy entry on biblical exegesis that appears in volume 8 (pp. 649-737).

SHALOM CARMY

Christian Views

Writers of the New Testament. The distinction between "letter" and "spirit," as applied to the canon of the Hebrew scriptures, is a dominant factor in the apostle Paul's exegetical approach and became an abiding paradigm. From Paul's perspective of faith, the "letter" incorporated what was superseded by God's action in Jesus Christ. Spirit has to do with understanding the very heart of divine intention and activity.

Similarly, the *Gospel of John* announces: "The Law was given through Moses; grace and truth came through Jesus Christ" (*Jn.* 1:17). As the Word of God (1:1), Jesus obviates the need for further prophecy. He is in his person the exposition of divine purpose.

For Mark, the words and work of Jesus clarify parts of the Old Testament, which in turn provides the outline for the story of Jesus. Matthew explains the Old Testament principally in terms of the function of Jesus as executive of the communities of believers. Luke's two-volume work (i. e., *Luke* and *Acts*) displays more extensive expository use of the Old Testament. In it, he assesses the significance of Jesus Christ is the reciprocity system, especially as reflected in the Greco-Roman understanding of the relation between civic benefactors and recipients of their bounty.

Demonstration of the superiority of Jesus Christ to all cultic media in Israel's previous history dominates *Hebrews*. Exegesis is embodied in a rhythmic succession of passages or data from the Old Testament, coupled with the author's exposition in terms of the controlling theme of superiority.

Typology plays a dominant role in *Revelation*. Much of the numerology and imagery in this book helps the writer's public to understand the current situation in the light of Israel's experience.

Apostolic Fathers. The writings of the apostolic fathers, a term used here in a broad sense, include a wide range of expository comment. *First Clement* uses the Old Testament in an unimaginative manner as a source for moral instruction. Ignatius of Antioch discusses passages from *Matthew, Luke,* and *John* in language to which even gnostics could subscribe. The anonymous author of *Barnabas* takes pride in the possession of special knowledge, or gnosis, but denies any meaningful relevance of the Old Testament to non-Christian Jews.

Marcion and the Gnostics. Marcion, who in 144 broke with the dominant institutionalized Christianity, disavowed allegorical methodology in his exposition of the Old Testament. His lost commentary on Luke and the Pauline letters, excluding 1 and 2 *Timothy* and *Titus*, bore the title *Antitheses*.

Gnostic Christians were apparently the first producers of biblical commentaries. Preeminent are Valentinus; two of his disciples, Heracleon and Ptolemy; and Basilides. Origen's numerous excerpts from Heracleon's commentary on *John*, apparently the first exposition of an entire gospel, reveal its thoroughgoing allegorical approach and denial of validity to the Old Testament. In a letter to an eminent woman named Flora, Ptolemy puts the Pentateuch under criticism in an attempt to show that Old Testament law is the work of an intermediate deity. Basilides, founder of a gnostic school in Alexandria, composed his own version of the Gospels and commented on it in a work entitled *Exegetica*. Of the Nag Hammadi texts, *A Valentinian Exposition* (11.2) discusses the origin of creation and the redemptive process. Another, *The Interpretation of Knowledge* (11.1), is of unknown authorship, with edifying comment based on selected passages from the New Testament.

Toward Consolidation. In the face of extreme elitist views on admittance to Christian privilege, representatives of the so-called orthodox apostolic tradition felt it was incumbent on them to develop exegetical theory that could challenge the expertise of those whom they considered heretics.

Justin Martyr to Didymus. Justin Martyr argued through allegorical interpretation that the entire Old Testament is a prophecy concerning Jesus, and Irenaeus lent support in a work titled *Against Heresies*. About the year 200, Clement of Alexandria defended allegorical method in the manner of Philo but with a Christocentric orientation, arguing that the Old Testament is enigmatic and requires such methodology to convey its meaning.

Origen, the first exponent of scientific biblical exegesis, extended allegorization to the interpretation of the New Testament. He explained his approach in the treatise *On First Principles*, with a practical demonstration in his *Commentary on John*. Origen ranged over the entire Bible, and his exegetical work is incorporated in scholia, homilies, and commentaries.

More than a century later, Origen's methodology attracted Didymus, a nonclerical Alexandrian theologian who had been blind from the age of four or five. Admired by Jerome, Didymus is credited with commentaries on almost every biblical writing, including *Isaiah* 40-66, which he viewed as a complete book.

The Cappadocian fathers. The era of the Cappadocian fathers was a period of revitalization in the Eastern church. Under the influence of Origen and other Alexandrines, Basil of Caesarea, who said that "when he heard the word grass he understood that grass was meant," drew heavily in the fourth century on Greek science for his explanation of the creation account in nine homilies, collected in *On the Hexaemeron*. Gregory of Nyssa recognized the importance of the literal sense as he pursued Basil's interest in the creation account, but his numerous homilies and discussions of various other portions of the Bible convey his mystical absorption in allegorical exposition.

The Latins. Writing in Greek, Hippolytus of Rome produced what is now the oldest extant Christian exegetical treatise, a commentary on *Daniel*. His influence is apparent in the work of Victorinus of Pettau. Tertullian punctuated his own numerous writings with comments on scripture and introduced the West to theological Latin, but Victorinus was the first exegete, in the proper sense of the term, to write in Latin. His paraphrastic technique is displayed in an exposition of selected passages from *Revelation*.

As the Athanasius of the West, Hilary of Poitiers was the first Latin writer to introduce his part of the world to Eastern patristic theology. His discussions of *Matthew* and *Psalms* sound a homiletical tone, as do the works of Ambrose. Also among the enterprising was the Donatist Ticonius, of North Africa, whose *Book of Rules* is the first book relating to exegetical methodology to be written in Latin.

Jerome and Augustine. Origen's influence is evident in the earliest exegetical efforts of Jerome. Owing to Origen's loss of prestige in ecclesiastical circles, and to his own increasing interest in the Hebrew language, Jerome leaned markedly in the direction of the Antiochenes, as attested especially in his exposition of *Jeremiah*.

In *De doctrina Christiana* (On Christian Doctrine), which pays homage to both allegory and to the letter of scripture, Augustine of Hippo summarized his views on the theologian's responsibility to scripture and the exegetical task and gave a masterful demonstration thereof in a commentary on *Psalms*.

The term *catena*, that is, a chain of select citations, became standard after Thomas Aquinas published in 1484 a collection of excerpts, drawn from at least eighty sources, under the title *Catena aurea*. In the thirteenth century, Ibn al-`Ibri, better known as Bar Hebraeus, incorporated the work of Nestorian and Jacobite exegetes in a book titled *Storehouse of Mysteries*.

Other Medieval Exposition. In contrast to that of the Victorines, most of medieval exegetical production from 600 to 1500 had its roots in Alexandrine allegorization and the hermeneutical theory of Origen, who posited the somatic, the psychic, and the pneumatic as the three senses in scripture, corresponding to humanity's threefold nature: flesh, soul, and spirit. Stimulated by the division of letter and spirit, as championed by Augustine and then by Gregory I, medieval theologians developed an intricate system of exposition that predicated a fourfold sense, summarized by Augustine of Dacia in this jingle:

> Through letter comes the history,
> And things of faith by allegory,
> For doing good we have the moral,
> To mount on high the anagogy.

Thomas Aquinas endorsed the traditional fourfold division, but his interest in dogmatic authority led him to celebrate the importance of the literal sense. The Franciscan

Bonaventure augmented the fourfold sense, and Nicholas of Lyra tried to help his generation keep in touch with the original text. But following Nicholas, biblical exegesis displayed no creativity for almost two centuries.

The Renaissance and the Reformation. The Renaissance, under the lead of popes Nicholas V, Sixtus IV, Alexander VI, and Clement VII, encouraged more efficient tools to carry out the functions of exegetical inquiry.

In six books on Latin rhetoric, Lorenzo Valla endeavored to upgrade the rhetorical taste of his time. His *On the False Donation of Constantine* was only incidentally a manifestation of critical inquiry, but it succeeded in demonstrating the vulnerability of institutionalized theology when confronted with careful research. Valla helped focus attention on basic data for exegetical study.

Commentators who were ignorant of Greek and Hebrew had long been able to project profundity through allegory, but more would be expected after Johannes Reuchlin, in the early sixteenth century, published two works on aspects of Hebrew grammar, thereby encouraging more intense cultivation of the literal sense. The Franciscan Konrad Pellikan, who officially adopted the Reformation cause in 1526, went beyond Reuchlin and became the first Christian to publish a Hebrew grammar. His *Commentaria Bibliorum* runs to seven volumes (1532-1539) and is a model of informed philological exposition.

Signs of things to come were evident in the work of James Cajetan, who used the Greek text of Erasmus, the last great representative of Renaissance humanism. Cajetan questioned the authenticity of *Mark* 16:9-20 and *John* 8:1-11 and cast doubt on the authorship of *Hebrews*, *James*, *2 Peter*, *2* and *3 John*, and *Jude*.

At the crest of his humanistic career, John Calvin produced a commentary on Seneca's *On Clemency*, an enduring achievement that exhibits Calvin's vigorous intellect and his ability to express himself in concise and lucid prose. In 1530 he joined Luther's sympathizers in the signing of the Augsburg Confession. Unlike Luther, who intertwined theology and exegesis in his biblical expositions, Calvin followed the lead of late Scholasticism and separated the domains of exegesis and theology, thus in effect heralding the type of philology that would later dominate Western exegesis.

Post-Reformation Period to the Twentieth Century. If the century after the Victorines was exegetically arid, the late sixteenth century and the seventeenth were somewhat cheerless in Protestant and Lutheran sectors.

Steps toward scientific exegesis. In the vanguard of a fresh attempt at liberation of exegesis from thralldom to systematic theology are four scholars who span the years 1583-1754. Hugo Grotius found in the literal sense of the Old Testament guiding principles for the understanding of natural law. Many of his interpretations anticipate modern proposals for resolution of Old Testament problems, such as the dat-

ing of portions of *Zechariah*. His comments on the New Testament likewise exhibit philological-historical discernment. John Lightfoot's rabbinic exposition of the New Testament opened a new frontier. Johann J. Wettstein combined rabbinic and classical lore with textual-critical study in a two-volume work that ever since its publication in 1751-1752 has undergone pillaging, frequently without attribution. Johann Albrecht Bengel's one-volume commentary on the New Testament is far outweighed in kilograms by Calov's massive production, but it enjoys the kind of temporal durability that the centuries have accorded Euclid's geometry. One wonders what other advances might have been made during this period had scholars like Anna Maria van Schurman, the "Star of Utrecht," who composed an Ethiopian grammar and wrote occasional letters in Hebrew, been encouraged to enter the market where males determined the theological wares.

Although Roman Catholics failed to produce any significant expository work in the eighteenth century, two French scholars raised the curtain for glimpses into the future. Richard Simon made a valiant effort, but his work on the Old Testament was not recognized beyond the Oratory at Paris, where he published his *Histoire critique du texte Vieux Testament* (1678). Some cracking of the shell was heard in the work of Jean Astruc, private physician of Louis XV, who concluded that Moses probably used two major sources, one derived from an Elohist source and the other from a Yahvist source, besides ten smaller documents.

The first commentary to incorporate observations concerning use of divine names in the Pentateuch was published by Henning Witter in 1711, but it received no scholarly attention for two centuries. Jean Astruc, on the other hand, had the good fortune to be noticed by Johann Eichhorn, who profited also from Johann Semler's and Johann Herder's contributions to the founding of historical-grammatical study of the Bible on a scientific basis. Eichhorn was the first scholar to apply such methodology to the study of the entire Bible, and together with Robert Lowth, professor of poetry at Oxford from 1741-1750, he is to be credited with the introduction of the concept of myth into biblical studies.

Reason versus dogma. The literal sense was to take on renewed meaning as Christians accepted the challenge to relieve history of the deadening weight of rationalism in both its orthodox and deistic forms. Defenders of the truth were to come from most unexpected quarters and find themselves under fire for what others would consider dubious assistance in time of disaster.

In the lead were Robert Lowth in England and Johann Semler in Germany. Semler's Pietist background provided personal acquaintance with the hazards of overintellectualization as posed by orthodoxy. Practiced in wariness, he moved against the threat of overextended deistic rationalism. Johann Ernesti had thought to withstand post-Reformation rationalism in its scholastic as well as its deistic forms through basic grammatical-historical research, with stress on philology. Semler went further, with an accent on history, and historical-critical methodology moved one step nearer to classification as a discipline.

Immanuel Kant encouraged German scholars to shake the last traces of narrow dogma out of their theology and at the same time endeavored to undergird the moral sense of scripture. He sowed seeds that would bear fruit more than a century later with the emergence of linguistic science, but Friedrich Schleiermacher, a Moravian preacher, offered an interim solution that would atone for lack of justice to the affective dimension of human experience both in Kantian philosophy and in Semler's historical criticism. Schleiermacher emphasized in a variety of publications the role of self-consciousness in calculating human capacity for knowledge of God. Theologians endeavored to find a firm footing for truth, and G. W. F. Hegel thought that in dialectical law he had found the answer to the ultimate aspiration of the human spirit. Hegel's pupil David Friedrich Strauss skillfully exposed an array of inaccuracies and discrepancies in the Gospels, arguing in his two-volume life of Jesus (1835) that basic human ideas had come to expression in the myths of the New Testament. It was not necessary, he concluded, to renounce true Christianity.

Gospel interrelationships: the synoptic problem. The spell of Augustine, that Mark's gospel epitomizes Matthew's, was broken in 1782 by Johann Koppe and in 1786 by Gottlob Storr. A study by Johann Griesbach titled *Inquiritur in fontes* . . . . (1783) echoed findings of Great Britain's Henry Owen (*Observations on the Four Gospels*, 1764) and exhibited the German scholar's preliminary solution to the question of synoptic interrelationships. Griesbach argued that *Mark* was written later than *Luke* and was dependent on *Matthew* and Luke. A thorough examination of Papias's second-century testimony concerning the Petrine influence on *Mark* led Schleiermacher to conclude in 1832 that the so-called sayings (logia) of *Matthew* did not constitute a gospel but were a collection of dominical sayings.

Contenders for the faith now thought they had a firm historical port in which to drop anchors. Also, it was but a short step to the two-document hypothesis—that *Matthew* and *Luke* are dependent on *Mark* and on a source consisting principally of sayings of Jesus that are common to *Matthew* and *Luke*. In 1826 Christian Wilke showed that *Mark* is basic to *Matthew* and *Luke*, and after Karl Lachmann demonstrated that the earliest source, or "Ur-gospel," was best preserved in *Mark*, Christian Weisse was able to water a seed sown by Herbert Marsh of England and argue that *Mark* incorporates more simply and fully an older document that was also used by *Matthew* and *Luke*, who in turn were dependent on a sayings source. The Griesbach hypothesis, in fulfillment of James Moffat's appraisal as an unlucky and prolific dandelion, blossomed midway in the later decades of the twentieth century under the husbandry of William Farmer and John Orchard, but the majority of scholars endeavored to eradicate it through application of the traditional two-source hypothesis.

New Horizons. It had been thought that the establishment of a historical base through appeal to an early form of the Gospels would offer an impregnable fortress against the type of criticism used by Strauss, who found Griesbach's

> **. . . nondogmatists or "liberals" began to sketch psychological portraits of Jesus. . . .**

synoptic solution helpful in demolition of the extreme naturalistic views of Paulus. Confident of having found the historical Jesus, nondogmatists or "liberals" began to sketch psychological portraits of Jesus, with emphasis on his masterful moral instruction. Leading the parade was Ernest Renan (*Life of Jesus*, 1863). Adolf von Harnack, at the turn of the century, canonized the picture in *Das Wesen des Christentums* (What Is Christianity?). But Albert Schweitzer, taking the opening provided by Johannes Weiss, showed in his watershed book on the history of life-of-Jesus research, *Von Reimarus zu Wrede* (1906), translated as *The Quest for the Historical Jesus* (1910), that the liberal portrait lacked eschatological credentials. Reimarus had concluded that the Gospels' depiction of Jesus as Messiah was an *ex post facto* production by the followers of Jesus. And Wilhelm Wrede had called a halt to nineteenth-century psychologizing of Jesus, specifically his messianic self-consciousness, arguing in *Das Messiasgeheimnis* (The Messianic Secret, 1901) that the Christology evident in *Mark* transcends historical and biographical concerns.

Post-World War I. World War I issued the quietus to human potential for ushering in the kingdom of God through intellectual and moral power. Marxism, offspring of a line of thought that found stimulation in Strauss and Hegel, offered an alternative and focused on the productive capacity of human beings in community as the point of realization of human identity. In 1913 Wilhelm Bousset had documented in *Kyrios Christos* the theological creativity of early Christian communities, and in 1919 Karl Schmidt and Martin Dibelius, followed in 1921 by Rudolf Bultmann, registered the tremor of the time and explored the Gospels as products of early Christian community enterprise.

Research in history of religions and history of form was slow to take hold in England and the Americas. Aside from commentaries by Joseph B. Lightfoot on some of the Pauline letters and the publication of an edition of the Greek New Testament featuring the manuscript tradition of two

Alexandrine manuscripts by B. F. Westcott and Fenton Hort, none of the English-speaking countries had produced anything of exceptional exegetical merit during most of the nineteenth century.

Some originality was projected at the beginning of the twentieth century by Francis Burkitt, who in 1906 tackled the problem of the agreements of *Matthew* and *Luke* against *Mark*. And forty years elapsed after the publication of Wrede's *Messianic Secret* before Vincent Taylor undertook a refutation through a modified form-critical approach in his glosses on *Mark* (1952).

Near the end of the nineteenth century, Adolf Jülicher initiated a new era in research on the parables by rejuvenating Maldonatus's view of one controlling idea in each illustrative story told by Jesus. Paul Fiebig went on to compare the canonical parables with those of the rabbis in two publications (1904 and 1912). A. T. Cadoux, of Great Britain, opened another phase in parabolic interpretation, with emphasis in 1930 on the sociological situation of the early church. Following his lead, and in concert with Rudolf Otto's treatment in 1934 of the emergence of the kingdom of God in Jesus' parabolic teaching, Dodd proclaimed "realized eschatology" in *The Parables of the Kingdom* (1935), the importance of which was acknowledged by Joachim Jeremias in a work published in 1947 on the same subject.

Toward Literary Criticism. With the advent of the 1940s, biblical writers appeared to receive even more recognition as masters of literary production. For the Gospels, paths cleared by Reimarus, Strauss, Wrede, and Robert H. Lightfoot converged in 1948 in an article in which Günther Bornkamm, a pupil of Rudolf Bultmann, showed that *Matthew* reinterprets *Mark's* story of the stilling of the storm. In 1954 Hans Conzelmann produced a major study of *Luke's* theology. He was followed, in 1956, by Willi Marxsen, whose *Mark the Evangelist* used for the first time the term *redaction history*, that is, editorial or compositional criticism. Jack D. Kingsbury moved beyond a redaction-critical study of the parables of Jesus to a detailed analysis, in 1975, of *Matthew's* Christology.

On 30 September 1943, seed sown by Jerome and the Roman Catholic scholars Simon, Astruc, and Lagrange brought a harvest of commendation for scientific study of the Bible in Catholic circles. The papal encyclical *Divino afflante Spiritu* opened windows beyond medieval courtyards, and in the second half of the twentieth century apologetic and polemical glosses in major Roman Catholic exegetical works became so rare that the history of exegesis could be written without recourse to the ecclesiastical labeling that had been customary.

For students of the Old Testament, moves away from atomistic philology and across denominational lines were obvious in a number of commentaries published in the latter half of the twentieth century. Especially noteworthy is the work of Gerhard von Rad on *Genesis* (1952-1953), Brevard S. Childs on *Exodus* (1974), and Hans Hertzberg on 1 and 2 *Samuel* (1965) in the Old Testament Library Series; G. Ernest Wright on *Deuteronomy*, Samuel Terrien on *Job*, and Robert Scott on *Psalms* in the Interpreter's Bible; and Edward Campbell on *Ruth* and Delbert Hiller on *Lamentations* in the Anchor Bible, which was begun in 1964.

The deuterocanonical, or apocryphal, books of the Old Testament have received a large share of comment in both ancient and modern times and across denominational lines. Beginning in 1974, with a commentary by Jacob Myers on *1 and 2 Esdras*, the publishers of the Anchor Bible encouraged even broader acquaintance with the contents and thought of these documents.

Besides becoming increasingly massive during the latter half of the twentieth century, many of the commentaries on the New Testament produced during that period reflected the older diachronic philology. The more durable among them took account of noetic and thematic structures. Vincent Taylor acquainted the English-speaking world with a modified version of form criticism in 700 pages of commentary on *Mark* (1952), but Rudolph Pesch took more conscientious account of *Mark's* literary and cognitive features in a two-volume work (1976-1977).

As the history of exegesis attests, biblical scholarship has ordinarily been a late bloomer. This is especially true with respect to awareness of the potential of modern linguistic theory for exegesis. Not until the publication of the first volume of the series Semeia in 1974 did biblical scholars in the United States begin earnestly to emulate work done in the study of other literatures and exhibit emphasis on synchronic rather than diachronic exegesis.

Biblical exegesis will continue in pursuit of status as a scientific discipline. Exegetes may be expected to take more account of the pseudoapostolic writings of the second century. Discoveries of hitherto unknown documents will probably enjoy more rapid publication. Biblical studies will undoubtedly be done in even closer collegiality with students of other sacred literatures. The sayings of Jesus should certainly undergo ever more penetrating scrutiny. And in the spirit's quest for recognition over the dominance of the letter, it is quite probable that a revised genre of catena or florilegium will draw afresh, across ecclesiastical boundaries, from relatively untapped resources of patristic and other venerated writings.

BIBLIOGRAPHY

Helpful information on the personalities that figure in the history of exegesis can be found in the *New Catholic Encyclopedia*, 17 vols. (New York, 1967-1979), and in *Die Religion in Geschichte und Gegenwart*, 3d ed., 7 vols. (Tübingen, 1957-1965). *Semeia* (Philadelphia, 1975-) is an important journal published by the Society of Biblical Literature, which has also issued various informative volumes since the observance of its centennial in 1980. In addition to these basic sources, the following works can be consulted with profit.

Barth, Karl. *Protestant Theology in the Nineteenth Century: Its History and Background* (1947). Valley Forge, Pa., 1973. A discussion of theological and exegetical developments in political and cultural context.

Danker, Frederick W. *Multipurpose Tools for Bible Study.* 3d ed. Saint Louis, 1970. Descriptions and guides for the use of leading exegetical works. Much historical material.

Farrar, Frederic W. *History of Interpretation: Bampton Lectures, 1885* (1886). Reprint, Grand Rapids, Mich., 1961. Polemics intermingles with a wealth of reference to the principal personalities and interpretive approaches in the history of biblical exegesis.

Grant, Robert M. *A Short History of the Interpretation of the Bible.* Rev. ed. New York, 1963. Brief and nontechnical.

Kümmel, Werner Georg. *The New Testament: The History of the Investigation of Its Problems* (1958). Nashville, 1972. Concentrates on New Testament research from Johann S. Semler to Edwin Hoskyns, with summaries of each scholar's position illustrated by excerpts from the scholar's writings.

Neill, Stephen C. *The Interpretation of the New Testament*, 1861-1961. Oxford, 1964. Designed for the "nontheologian." Offers British antidote to overestimation of continental scholarship.

Rowley, Harold H., ed. *The Old Testament and Modern Study.* Oxford, 1951. A discussion of the main trends.

Schweitzer, Albert. *The Quest of the Historical Jesus: A Critical Study of Its Progress from Reimarus to Wrede* (1906). 2d ed. London, 1911. A probe of principal developments in life-of-Jesus research and so devastating that it practically terminated the production of the genre.

Smalley, Beryl. *The Study of the Bible in the Middle Ages.* 2d ed. Oxford, 1952. Principal resource for study of the organization, techniques, and objectives of biblical studies in northwestern Europe from the Carolingian renaissance to about 1300.

Spicq, Ceslaus. *Esquisse d'une histoire de l'exégèse latine au Moyen-Âge.* Paris, 1944. A fundamental resource for study of exegetical production in the Middle Ages.

FREDERICK W. DANKER

BIBLICAL LITERATURE

Hebrew Scriptures

The terms *Hebrew scriptures* and *Hebrew Bible* are synonyms here restricted to that received, definitive corpus of ancient literature, written in Hebrew except for some sections in Aramaic (*Genesis* 31:47, *Jeremiah* 10:11, and parts of *Daniel* and *Ezra*), that has been traditionally accepted by Jews and Christians alike as having been divinely inspired and, as such, authoritative in shaping their respective faiths and practices.

The word *Bible* is ultimately of Greek derivation and passed into many languages of the world through the medium of Latin. It meant simply "the Books."

Among Christians, the Hebrew Bible has traditionally been referred to as the Old Testament (i. e., Covenant), in contradistinction to the New Testament—theological appellations based upon a christological interpretation of *Jeremiah* 31:30-34. In recognition of the partisan nature of this title, and under the impact of the ecumenical movement of recent times, many scholars have increasingly preferred instead to refer to the Hebrew Bible or Hebrew scriptures.

Canon. As generally used in scholarly parlance, the term *canon* relates particularly to the received and definitively closed nature of the sacred corpus.

The completed canon of the Hebrew Bible exerted a profound influence, first upon the Jewish people that produced it, and then upon a large section of the rest of humanity. It was the major factor in the preservation of the unity of the Jews at a time of desperate national crisis after the destruction of their state in the year 70 (or 68) CE and their subsequent wide dispersion.

Contents. The tripartite division of the Hebrew Bible roughly describes its variegated contents, although, admittedly, some of the books of the third part would not be out of place in the second.

The Torah. More fully called the Torah of Moses, the Torah comprises the first five books of the biblical canon, usually known in English as the Pentateuch: *Genesis, Exodus, Leviticus, Numbers,* and *Deuteronomy*.

The Hebrew term *torah* means "instruction, teaching." In the present context, the Pentateuch comprises a continuous narrative from the creation of the world to the death of Moses in which is embedded a considerable amount of legal and ritual prescription. *Genesis's* first eleven chapters deal with universal history up to the birth of Abraham, and the rest of the book is devoted to the ancestors of the people of Israel. *Deuteronomy,* largely summarizes discourses of Moses and is marked by its own characteristic style and theological tendency. The intervening three books deal with two generations of the people of Israel from the period of the Egyptian oppression and the Exodus.

It is not certain how this corpus was materially preserved in early times. For convenience of study, the material was written on five separate scrolls, but it was also written on a single scroll. It is solely in this form that it has played a role in the Jewish synagogal liturgy.

The Nevi'im. The prophetic corpus naturally divides into two parts. The Former Prophets continues the historical narrative of the Torah, closing with the destruction of the First Temple in Jerusalem, the end of the monarchy, and the Babylonian exile of the Judeans up to the year 560 BCE. This material is contained in the books of *Joshua, Judges, Samuel,* and *Kings*.

The second part of the Nevi'im, the Latter Prophets, comprises the works of the literary prophets in Israel and Judah from the eighth to the fifth centuries BCE. These are *Isaiah,*

Jeremiah, and *Ezekiel*, and "the Book of the Twelve," known in English as the Minor Prophets: *Hosea, Joel, Amos, Obadiah, Jonah, Micah, Nahum, Habakkuk, Zephaniah, Haggai, Zechariah,* and *Malachi*.

The Ketuvim. The Writings, often also called Hagiographa in English, are actually a miscellany of sacred writings of several genres of literature, as the nonspecific nature of the name indicates. There is religious poetry *(Psalms* and *Lamentations)*; love poetry *(*the *Song of Songs)*; wisdom or reflective compositions *(Proverbs, Job,* and *Ecclesiastes)*; historical works *(Ruth, Esther, Ezra-Nehemiah,* and *Chronicles)*; and apocalypse *(Daniel)*.

Tripartite canon. It is widely held that the tripartite nature of the canon represents three successive stages of canonization of the separate corpora. Repeated reference to this threefold division comes from the literature of the period of the Second Temple. *Ben Sira* 39:1, probably written around 180 BCE, mentions the "law of the Most High, the wisdom of all the ancients . . . , and . . . prophecies." About fifty years later, Ben Sira's grandson, who translated the work into Greek, writes in his prologue about "the law and the prophets and the others that came after them," which last are also called "the other books of our fathers" and "the rest of the books," while *2 Maccabees* (2:2-3, 2:13) has reference to "the law, the kings and prophets and the writings of David." In Alexandria, Egypt, the Jewish philosopher Philo Judaeus (d. 45-50 CE) mentions, besides "the law," also "the prophets and the psalms and other writings" *(De vita contemplativa* 3.25). The Jewish historian Josephus Flavius (37-c. 100 CE) tells of the Pentateuch of Moses, the "prophets" and "the remaining books" *(Against Apion* 1.39-41). Similarly, in the New Testament, the *Gospel of Luke* speaks of "the law of Moses and the prophets and the psalms" (24:4). This persistent allusion to the threefold division of the Hebrew scriptures, and the lack of any uniform title for the third collection of writings, in addition to the heterogeneous nature of that corpus, all argue in favor of two closed collections—the Torah and the Prophets—with a third being somewhat amorphous and having no uniform name, undoubtedly a sign of its late corporate canonicity.

Of course, the closing of a corpus tells nothing about the canonical history of the individual books within it. Some parts of the Ketuvim, such as the *Psalms,* for instance, would most likely have achieved canonical status before some of those included within the Nevi'im.

Samaritan canon. The religious community centered on Nablus (ancient Shechem) that calls itself Benei Yisra'el ("children of Israel") or Shomrim ("keepers," i. e., of the truth), and that is known by outsiders as Samaritans, claims to be directly descended from the Israelites of the Northern Kingdom who escaped deportation at the hands of the Assyrian kings who destroyed it in 722/1 BCE (*2 Kgs.* 17:5-6, 17:24-34, 17:41). Their canon consists solely of the Pentateuch, excluding the Prophets and the Writings. This fact has not been satisfactorily explained. The older view, that the final breach between the Samaritans and the Jews occurred in the time of Ezra and Nehemiah (fifth century BCE), before the canonization of the rest of the Hebrew Bible, is no longer tenable because both documentary and archaeological evidence leads to the conclusion that the schism was the culmination of a gradual process of increasing estrangement. A major step was the construction of a Samaritan shrine on Mount Gerizim early in the Hellenistic period; the destruction of the temple on that site by John Hyrcanus in 128 BCE completed the rupture.

Canon at Qumran. The discovery of a hoard of more than five hundred manuscripts in the region of the sectarian settlement at Khirbat Qumran, northwest of the Dead Sea, has raised the question of the nature of the biblical canon recognized by that community, which came to an end about 70 CE. The question is legitimate both in light of the variant canon preserved by the Greek Septuagint, as discussed below, and because copies of extrabiblical books, apocryphal and pseudepigraphical works such as *Tobit, Ben Sira,* the *Letter of Jeremiah, 1 Enoch,* and *Jubilees,* not to mention the sect's own productions, were included among the finds.

A variety of factors combine to render a decisive conclusion all but impossible in the absence of a list that would determine contents and sequence. This lack is aggravated by the practice at that time of writing each biblical book on a separate scroll, and by the very fragmentary form of the overwhelming majority of extant scrolls. Furthermore, since the manuscripts had generally been hidden in the caves in great disorder, we cannot be sure whether we are dealing with a living library or a *genizah,* a storeroom of discarded works.

The following items of evidence are pertinent to the discussion: (1) With the exception of *Esther,* fragments of all the books of the Hebrew Bible have turned up; hence the Qumran canon would have included at least almost every book of the Hebrew Bible. (2) The category of Qumran literature known as the *pesharim,* or contemporizing interpretations of prophetic texts, is, so far, exclusively restricted to the books of the standard Hebrew canon. (3) The Manual of Discipline *(Serekh ha-yahad,* 1QS IX:11) expresses the hope for the renewal of prophecy, the same as is found in *1 Maccabees* 4:46. This suggests that the Qumran community recognized a closed corpus of prophetic literature. (4) The great psalms scroll (11QPs[a]), on the other hand, exhibits not only a deviant order of the standard psalms, but also contains other compositions, largely deriving from Hellenistic times. This scroll circulated in more than one copy, and several other Qumran manuscripts of psalms also vary in sequence and contents. At first glance it would seem that this phenomenon proves that the Qumran community could not have had a concept of a closed canon. However, it may be pointed out that the compiler of 11QPs[a] certainly was dependent on a Hebrew book of psalms much the same as that of the Hebrew Bible, and he may simply have been putting together a liturgical collection, not creating or copying a canonical work. Moreover, the caves of Qumran have yielded numerous psalters that contain only known canonical psalms, apparently without any deviation from the standard sequence. (5) As to the presence of noncanonical works, we have no means of knowing whether these had authority for the community equal with that of the standard Hebrew canonical books. (6) In sum, the evidence so far at hand does not justify the assumption that Qumran sectarians had a concept of canon different from that of their Palestinian Jewish brethren, although the opposite too cannot be proven.

Alexandrian canon (Septuagint). To meet the needs of worship and study, the populous hellenized Jewish community of Alexandria produced a Greek translation of the Hebrew Bible known as the Septuagint, begun in the third century BCE and completed before about 132 BCE. As it has come down to us, it differs from the traditional Hebrew Bible both in content and form, and often textually. It includes works that rabbinic Judaism rejected as noncanonical, and in it the books of the Prophets and Writings are not maintained as separate corpora but are distributed and arranged according to subject matter: historical books, poetry and wisdom, and prophetic literature. This situation has given rise to a widely held hypothesis of an Alexandrian or Hellenistic canon; that is to say, the Septuagint is said to represent a variant, independent concept of canon held by Diaspora Jewry. Alternatively, it is suggested that it derives from a rival canon that circulated in Jewish Palestine itself.

Christian canon. The Christian canon of the Jewish scriptures differs in three ways from the Bible of the Jews. First, its text is not that of the received Hebrew, usually called the Masoretic text, but is based on the Greek and Latin versions. Second, although all the books officially recognized as canonical by the Jews were also accepted by the Christian church, many segments of the latter also included within its canon additional Jewish works that date from the days of the Second Temple. These, generally termed "deuterocanonical" by theologians of the Roman Catholic church, are books of historical and didactic content, composed in Hebrew or Aramaic. They were not sectarian in origin, and they circulated widely in both Palestine and the Greek-speaking Jewish Diaspora in their original language and in Greek translation long after the close of the Hebrew canon. The third way in which the Christian canon diverges from the Jewish canon relates to the order of the books. The Hebrew tripartite division, clearly attested in *Luke* 28:44, was disregarded, and the contents were regrouped, as in the manuscripts of the Septuagint, according to literary categories—legal, historical, poetic-didactic, and prophetic. The variant sequence was best suited to express the claim of the church that the New Testament is the fulfillment of the Hebrew scriptures of the Jews.

Number of books. Until the sixth century CE, it was customary among Jews for the scribes to copy each biblical work onto a separate scroll. The number of books in the biblical canon therefore relates to the number of scrolls onto which the completed Hebrew Bible was transcribed, and which were physically kept together as a unit. Josephus (*Against Apion* 1. 39-41, ed. Loeb, p. 179) is emphatic that there were no more than twenty-two such. What is not clear is whether this figure was arrived at by conjoining books, such as *Judges* and *Ruth*, and *Jeremiah* and *Lamentations*, or whether two books were not yet included in his canon, perhaps the *Song of Songs* and *Ecclesiastes*.

A variant tradition counting twenty-four books eventually prevailed among Jews. This is first found in *2 Esdras* 14:45, written circa 100 BCE. The books are listed by name in a text that antedates 200 BCE cited in the Babylonian Talmud (B. B. 14b). Thereafter, this figure is explicitly given, and it becomes standard in rabbinic literature (cf. B. T., *Ta`an.* 5a). Whether the number has any significance is uncertain. It is of interest that the Old Babylonian bilingual lexical series known as Harra-Hubullu is inscribed on twenty-four tablets, the Mesopotamian *Epic of Gilgamesh* on twelve tablets, the Greek *Theogony* of Hesiod comes in twelve parts, and the old Roman law code was eventually codified as the Twelve Tablets (of wood). At any rate, in Jewish tradition, the biblical books become twenty-four by treating all the twelve Minor Prophets as one.

Canonizing Process. The available sources are silent about the nature and identity of the validating authorities, about the criteria of selectivity adopted in respect of the books included and excluded, and about the individual crucial stages in the history of the growth of the Hebrew biblical canon. This deficiency is aggravated by the fact that the literature that has survived represents at least six hundred years of literary creativity, in the course of which Israelite society underwent far-reaching, indeed metamorphic, change, much of it convulsive. Such a state of affairs militates against the likelihood of uniformity in the processes involved or of unbroken consistency in the considerations that swayed decision-making about individual works and collections of works. For these reasons, any reconstruction of the history of the phenomenon of the canonization of biblical literature must of necessity remain hypothetical.

Nonetheless, it should be noted that well before the year 1000 BCE, the libraries of the temples and palaces of Mesopotamia had organized the classical literature into a standardized corpus in some kind of uniform order and with a more or less official text. In similar manner, by order of Peisistratus, tyrant of Athens, the Homeric epics were codified in the sixth century and endowed with canonical authority. The idea of a canon was thus well based in the ancient world. There is every reason to assume that in Israel, too, temples served as the repositories of sacred texts from early times, and that the priests and scribes played an important role in the preservation and organization of literature. Hence, the formation of the biblical canon should not be viewed as a late development in Israel but as an ongoing process that is coextensive with the biblical period itself.

The definition of *canon* should, furthermore, be extended beyond the purely historical, external, formal aspects relating just to the end result of a process, to which it is usually restricted. In Israel, the conviction that the texts record the word of God or were divinely inspired, however these concepts were understood, would have been a decisive factor in their preservation. For the same reason, they would have been periodically read or recited, and the very force of repe-

> ### . . . "this book of the Torah" is placed beside the Ark of the Covenant.

tition would inevitably and powerfully have informed the collective mind and self-consciousness of the community. This, in turn, would have subtly shaped and reshaped both the existing literature and new compositions in a continual process of interaction between the community and its traditions. A text that appears to be directed to a specific situation in time and space acquires a contemporizing validity and relevance that is independent of such restrictive dimensions and develops a life of its own.

The earliest testimony to the canonizing process of the Torah literature comes from *Exodus* 24:1-11, which describes how Moses mediated the divine commands to the entire people assembled, how the people orally bound themselves to obedience, how Moses then put the stipulations into writing, and how a cultic ceremony was held at which the written record of the covenant just made was given a public reading. This was followed by a collective pledge of loyalty to its stipulations.

Another important text is *Deuteronomy*, chapter 31 (verses 9-13, 24-26). Here, too, Moses writes down the Teaching (Torah), this time entrusting the document to the ecclesiastical authorities for safekeeping, with provision for its septennial national public reading in the future. What is then called "this book of the Torah" is placed beside the Ark of the Covenant. In this case, the sanctity of the book is taken for granted, as is its permanent validity and authority, independent of the person of Moses.

The only other record of a preexilic public reading of Torah literature comes from near the end of the period of the monarchy. *2 Kings* 22-23 (cf. *2 Chr.* 34) recounts the chance discovery of "the book of the Torah" in 622 in the course of the renovations being carried out at the Temple in Jerusalem at the initiative of Josiah, then king. The scope of this work cannot be determined from the narrative, but the royal measures taken as a consequence of the find prove beyond cavil that it at least contained *Deuteronomy*. What is of particular significance is that it had long been stored in the Temple, that its antiquity, authenticity, and authority were recognized at once, and that its binding nature was confirmed at a national assembly. The ceremony centered upon a document that had already achieved normative status, but the impact of the event—the thoroughgoing religious reformation that it generated and sustained ideologically—left an indelible imprint on the subsequent literature and religion of Israel and constituted a powerful stimulus to the elevation of the Torah literature as the organizing principle in the life of the people. In this sense, the developments of 622 are an important milestone in the history of canonization. Between this year and 444 the process gathered apace. It is reasonable to assume that it was consummated in the Babylonian exile after 587/6, for it is impossible to explain the extraordinary survival of the small, defeated, fragmented community of Israelites, bereft of the organs of statecraft, deprived of its national territory, living on alien soil amid a victorious, prestigious civilization, other than through the vehicle of the book of the Torah, which preserved the national identity.

In the period of the return to Zion (the Land of Israel) and beyond, after 538 BCE, the convention of attributing the entire Torah to Moses is frequently attested—in *Malachi, Ezra-Nehemiah, Daniel,* and *Chronicles*. It also appears in *Joshua* (8:32, 23:6) and in *1 Kings* (2:3) and *2 Kings* (14:6, 23:25), but many scholars maintain that these references result from a later revision of these works. At any rate, by the year 444 the "Torah of Moses" had received popular acceptance. *Nehemiah* 8-10 records that in that year a public, national assembly took place in Jerusalem at which the people requested that "the scroll of the Torah of Moses with which the Lord had charged Israel" be read to them. This was done by Ezra, who is himself described as "a scribe, expert in the Torah of Moses," "a scholar in matters concerning the commandments of the Lord and his laws to Israel . . . a scholar in the law of the God of heaven" (*Ezr.* 7:6, 7:11-12, 7:21). It is quite evident that the stress is on the teaching, dissemination, interpretation, and reaffirmation of the Torah, long popularly recognized and accepted, not on its promulgation anew. Ezra had been commissioned by the Persian king Artaxerxes I "to regulate Judah and Jerusalem according to the law of God," which was in his care (*Ezr.* 7:14). True, the texts do not define the scope of this literature, but it can be safely assumed that it was little different from the Pentateuch that has come down to us, for the author of *Chronicles* who composed his history about 400 repeatedly refers to the "Torah of Moses," and it can be shown that this phrase in context applies comprehensively to the entire Pentateuch.

The Bible and the Ancient Near East. It is not surprising that there exist numerous, close affinities in subject matter and form between the biblical writings and the literatures of the ancient Near East. This phenomenon is not necessarily to be explained in terms of dependency or borrowing, but more likely as a result of the sharing of a common cultural heritage. Furthermore, correspondences and parallels are not the same as identity. Contrast is as important a dimension as similarity, and it is the former that accords the Israelite productions their claim to singularity. It is apparent that what was drawn upon from the common Near Eastern stock was thoroughly refined and reshaped to bring it into conformity with the national religious ideology.

The primeval history in *Genesis*, chapters 1-11, well exemplifies this situation. The genealogies, for instance, belong to the same type of document as the Sumerian king-list, but they are used both as connectives to bridge the gap between narrative blocks and for theological purposes. Thus, ten generations are delineated to span the period between Adam and Noah, and another ten between Noah and Abraham, the symmetry being intended to convey the idea that history is the unfolding of God's predetermined plan for humankind. The biblical version has a singularly didactic function and is uniquely placed within a spiritual and moral framework.

The law collection in the Pentateuch is another case in point. No less than six law codes have survived from the ancient Near East, the earliest probably deriving from about seven hundred years before Moses. All these, plus innumerable documents of law-court proceedings, leave no doubt of the existence of a common legal culture in the area that found expression in a similarity of content, legal phraseology, and literary form that Israel shared.

The genre that was truly an international phenomenon is that of biblical wisdom literature. It deals with observations on human behavior and the world order, drawn from experience. One such category has the individual as its focus of interest and is essentially pragmatic and utilitarian, containing precepts for success in living. Its artistic forms are mainly the maxim, the proverb, the pithy question, and the riddle. The other is reflective in nature and is more concerned with the human condition, and with the wider issues of divine-human relationships. Here the literary unit is much longer. Both Egypt and Mesopotamia produced an extensive body of literature of this type, and the analogues with *Proverbs*, *Job*, and *Ecclesiastes* are striking. Yet here, again, although these latter are mostly devoid of national or special Israelite content, they are distinctive in their uncompromising monotheism, in the absence of dream interpretation as an attribute of the sage, and in their insistence on the fear of the Lord as being the quintessence of wisdom.

Historical Complexity of the Text. The model for printed editions of the Hebrew Bible was the second "Great Rabbinic Bible" published at Venice by Daniel Bomberg, 1524-1525, and edited by Ya`aqov ben Hayyim ibn Adoniyyah. All printed editions, as well as all extant medieval Hebrew manuscripts of the Bible—the earliest deriving from the ninth century CE—represent a single textual tradition, known as the Masoretic ("received") text (MT). This standard text comprises three distinct elements: the Hebrew consonants, vocalization signs, and accentuation marks.

Greek Translations. The history of the Jewish community in Egypt can be traced back at least to the beginning of the sixth century BCE. There Jews spoke Aramaic and knew Hebrew, but the influx of Greek-speaking settlers had far-reaching effects on their cultural life. With the conquest of Egypt by Alexander the Great, the local Jewish population was swelled by a great wave of immigration attracted there by the opportunities afforded by the Ptolemies. The Jews concentrated mainly in Alexandria, where they formed an autonomous community with its own synagogues and socio-cultural institutions, and where they came to form a significant segment of the population. They soon adopted Greek as their everyday language.

By the third century BCE, both liturgical and educational considerations dictated the need for a Greek translation of the scriptures, at least of the Pentateuch. The version known as the Septuagint was revolutionary in its conception, its execution, and its impact. No lengthy Eastern religious text had previously been translated into Greek, nor had a written translation of the Jewish scriptures been made hitherto. The Septuagint was one of the great literary enterprises of the ancient world, and it served to fashion and shape a distinctively Jewish-Hellenistic culture, which attempted to synthesize Hebraic and Greek thought and values. Eventually, it became a powerful literary medium for the spread of early Christianity throughout the far-flung Greek-speaking world, thereby transforming the culture and religion of a goodly segment of humanity.

The Septuagint ("seventy") received its Latin name from a legend current among the Jews of Alexandria that it was executed by seventy-two scholars in seventy-two days. Originally applicable only to the translation of the Pentateuch, this abbreviated title was gradually extended to the complete Greek rendering of the entire Jewish scriptures. In the course of time, the origins of the Septuagint came to be embroidered in legend and enveloped in an aura of the miraculous. The *Letter of Aristeas*, Philo's Moses (II, v-vii, 25-40) and rabbinic writings (e.g., B. T., *Meg. 9a*; *Avot de Rabbi Natan*, ms. b, 37) are the principal witnesses to this development, whereby the initiative for the translation was said to have come from Ptolemy II Philadelphus (r. 285-246 BCE).

The fullest and most popular version of the legend is that found in the first of the above-mentioned sources. That the *Letter* is a fiction is apparent from internal evidence, and it has been shown to have been composed by a hellenized Jew writing in the second half of the second century BCE, about a hundred years after the publication of the original Septuagint. It is certain that it was the needs of the Alexandrian Jewish community that called forth the translation in the course of the third century BCE. It is not impossible, however, that the project did receive royal approval, given the known interest and activities of the Ptolemies as patrons of culture. Furthermore, it is quite likely that the translators did come from Palestine and worked in Egypt.

The Greek of the Septuagint is essentially the Koine, that form of the language commonly spoken and written from the fourth century BCE until the middle of the sixth century CE by the Greek-speaking populations of the eastern Mediterranean. Hence, the Septuagint stands as a monument of Hellenistic Greek. The Septuagint was generally competently rendered. If its style is not consistent throughout, this is partly due to the multiplicity of translators and partly to the revolutionary nature of the undertaking in that the translators had neither experience nor real precedent to fall back on.

The turning point in the production of Greek Bibles comes in the fourth century CE attendant upon the conversion to Christianity of Constantine (c. 280-337) and the conferring upon that religion of a privileged position in the Roman empire. An order from Constantine in 332 for fifty vellum Bibles for use in the new churches he was erecting in Constantinople afforded an immense stimulus to the creation of the great and handsome Greek Bibles known technically as majuscules or uncials ("inch high") because of the practice of the scribes to employ capital-size letters without ligatures. The three most important codices of this type that have come down to us in a reasonably complete state are the Codex Sinaiticus (usually designated for scholarly purposes by *S* or by the Hebrew letter alef), the Codex Alexandrinus (given the siglum *A*), and the Codex Vaticanus (indicated by

> ## The adoption of the Septuagint instead of the Hebrew as the Bible of the church was itself a source of discomfort. . . .

the initial *B*). The Sinaiticus, executed in the fourth century CE, is not complete and in places has been seriously damaged by the action of the metallic ink eating through the parchment. Despite the often careless orthography, the manuscript is witness to a very early text tradition. The Vaticanus, also produced in the fourth century, is nearly perfect and constitutes the oldest and most excellent extant copy of the Greek Bible, even though it is not of uniform quality throughout. It was used as the basis of the Roman edition of 1587, the commonly printed Septuagint. The Alexandrinus, con-

taining practically the entire Bible, was probably copied in the early fifth century.

The adoption of the Septuagint instead of the Hebrew as the Bible of the church was itself a source of discomfort to Greek-speaking Jews. That the Greek rendering frequently departed from the by then universally recognized Hebrew text constituted additional and decisive cause for its rejection by the synagogue. Doubtless, the conviction on the part of the Jews that christological changes had been introduced into the original Septuagint also played a role.

On the Christian side, the lack of uniformity and consistency within the Greek manuscripts themselves were to be an embarrassing disadvantage to Christian missionaries in their theological polemics with Jews. This situation would be exacerbated by the discrepancies between the translation used by Christian disputants and the Hebrew text, which was the only authoritative form of the scriptures recognized by Palestinian Jews. Exegetical debate could proceed only on the basis of a mutually acknowledged text, which in this case had to be the only Hebrew text tradition accepted by the Jews.

Translations Based on the Septuagint. The great prestige that the Septuagint acquired as the official, authoritative Bible of the church generated a number of secondary translations as Christianity spread to non-Greek-speaking lands and the churches had to accommodate themselves to the native language. Whereas the early translations had been the work of scholars who knew Hebrew, this was now no longer a requirement. The Greek itself served as the base for subsequent translations. Such was the case in respect to the Coptic, Ethiopic, Armenian, Georgian, Gothic, and Old Latin versions, all of which have little bearing on the history of the Hebrew text but are of lesser or greater importance for the study of the Septuagint itself.

The most important of all the secondary renderings of the Bible is the Latin. This language advanced with the expansion of Roman power, first throughout Italy, then into southern Gaul and throughout the Mediterranean coastal regions of Africa. In Rome itself, Greek remained the cultural language of the church until the third century, but in the African communities Latin was very popular, and it is most probable that the earliest translations thereinto emanated from these circles. The needs of the liturgy and the lectionary dictated renditions into the vernacular, which at first remained oral and by way of interlinear glosses. It is not impossible but cannot be proven that the earliest such efforts were made by Jews directly from the Hebrew. At any rate, by the middle of the second century CE, an Old Latin version, in the colloquial form of the language, based on the Septuagint, was current. Whether we are speaking here of a single text or a plurality of translations is a matter of dispute because of the great variety of readings to be found in extant manuscripts and citations. These divide roughly into African and European types, but it must be remembered that the two interacted with each other.

Despite the fact that the Old Latin is a translation of a translation, and for that reason must be used with extreme caution for text-critical studies, it is nevertheless important since it was made from a pre-Hexaplaric Greek text. For example, it has much in common with the Lucianic recension and with the Vatican and Sinaitic codices. In the case of *Job* and *Daniel*, it has renderings that presuppose a Greek reading that has not otherwise been preserved and that, in turn, indicates an original Hebrew text not identical with that received. The psalms, in particular, are significant for the numerous texts available as a consequence of their having been used in the liturgy, although they were frequently reworked.

BIBLIOGRAPHY

The most reliable and comprehensive work on the Bible is *The Cambridge History of the Bible*, 3 vols., edited by Peter R. Ackroyd (Cambridge, 1963-1970). It summarizes the current state of scholarship in nontechnical language and each chapter is written by a specialist in the field. The excellent bibliographies are arranged by topic. For more concise introductions to the issues and approaches involved in the contemporary study of the Hebrew scriptures there are Herbert F. Hahn's *The Old Testament in Modern Research*, 2d exp. ed., with a survey of recent literature by Horace D. Hummel (Philadelphia, 1966), and John H. Hayes's *An Introduction to Old Testament Study* (Nashville, 1979). The latter work notes only items in English in the useful bibliographies that precede each chapter. Two most frequently used comprehensive traditional introductions to the Bible containing extensive bibliographies are Otto Eisfeldt's *The Old Testament: An Introduction*, translated from the third German edition by Peter R. Ackroyd (New York, 1965), and Georg Fohrer's *Introduction to the Old Testament* (Nashville, 1968).

Two classic works on the history of the canon are Frants Buhl's *Canon and Text of the Old Testament*, translated from the German by John Macpherson (Edinburgh, 1892), and H. E. Ryle's *The Canon of the Old Testament: An Essay on the Gradual Growth and Formation of the Hebrew Canon of Scripture*, 2d ed. (London, 1892). Both contain ample references to and quotations from rabbinic and patristic sources. *The Canon and Masorah of the Hebrew Bible*, edited by Sid Z. Leiman (New York, 1974), provides an indispensable collection of thirty-seven essays by as many scholars relating to various aspects of the biblical canon; all but four are in English. The work lacks an index. Leiman's original contribution to the subject is *The Canonization of Hebrew Scripture: The Talmudic and Midrashic Evidence* (Hamden, Conn., 1976). Extensive citations from rabbinic literature are given both in their original form and in translation. The work is enhanced by copious notes, bibliography, and indexes.

The new concept of canon as a process is explicated by James A. Sanders in his *Torah and Canon* (Philadelphia, 1972) and in his essay "Available for Life: The Nature and Function of Canon," in *Magnalia Dei', The Mighty Acts of God: Essays on the Bible and Archaeology in Memory of G. Ernest Wright*, edited by Frank Moore Cross et al. (Garden City, N. Y., 1976), pp. 531-560. *Introduction to the Old Testament as Scripture* by Brevard S. Childs (Philadelphia, 1979) seeks to describe the form and function of each book of the Hebrew Bible in its role as sacred scripture, and to understand the literature in that context. It contains detailed bibliographies.

Contemporary concerns with canonical criticism are examined by James Barr in his *Holy Scripture, Canon, Authority, Criticism* (Philadelphia, 1983).

Ernst Würthwein's *The Text of the Old Testament*, translated from the German by Peter R. Ackroyd (Oxford, 1957), is a useful key to the critical apparatus of the Kittel edition of the Hebrew Bible. The text is illustrated by forty-four plates. The most detailed and readable work is that by Bleddyn J. Roberts, *Old Testament Text and Versions* (Cardiff, 1951). However, some of the data need to be updated in light of research into the Dead Sea Scrolls. The best all-around discussion of these last-mentioned is *The Ancient Library of Qumrân and Modern Biblical Studies*, rev. ed. (Garden City, N. Y., 1961), by Frank Moore Cross. This work is supplemented by a collection of scholarly essays assembled by the same author together with Shemaryahu Talmon in *Qumran and the History of the Biblical Text* (Cambridge, Mass., 1975). Paul E. Kahle's *The Cairo Genizah*, 2d ed. (New York, 1959), examines and evaluates the impact of the hoard of manuscripts found in the bibliocrypt of the synagogue in Old Cairo and in the caves of Qumran on the scholarship relating to the history of the biblical Hebrew text and the ancient translations, as well as on the ancient pronunciation of Hebrew. The history and critical evaluation of the methodology of textual criticism is given by M. H. Goshen-Gottstein in "The Textual Criticism of the Old Testament: Rise, Decline, Rebirth," *Journal of Biblical Literature* 102 (September 1983): 365-399.

A basic introduction to the Greek versions, their history, character, and the problems they present, is provided by the collection of thirty-five essays assembled by Sidney Jellicoe, *Studies into the Septuagint: Origins, Recensions, and Interpretations* (New York, 1974). Another important work for nonspecialists is Bruce M. Metzger's *Manuscripts of the Greek Bible: An Introduction to Greek Palaeography* (Oxford, 1981). Of a more technical and advanced nature is Imanuel Tov's *The Text-Critical Use of the Septuagint in Biblical Research* (Jerusalem, 1981). Henry Barclay Swete's *An Introduction to the Old Testament in Greek*, 2d ed. (Cambridge, 1902), still remains standard. Harry M. Orlinsky's essay "The Septuagint as Holy Writ and the Philosophy of the Translators," *Hebrew Union College Annual* 46 (1975): 89-114, contributes important insights into the nature of this version. *A Classified Bibliography of the Septuagint* by Sebastian P. Brock, Charles T. Fritsch, and Sidney Jellicoe (Leiden, 1973) is an indispensable scholarly tool.

For Targumic studies, there is Bernard Grossfeld's *A Bibliography of Targum Literature*, 2 vols. (Cincinnati, 1972-1977).

The Bible and the Ancient Near East: Essays in Honor of William Foxwell Albright, edited by G. Ernest Wright (Garden City, N. Y., 1961), contains fifteen studies by as many different scholars summarizing the course taken by scholarly research in various areas of Near Eastern studies bearing on the Bible. J. B. Pritchard has edited a superb collection, *Ancient Near Eastern Texts relating to the Old Testament*, 3d ed. (Princeton, 1969), which gives translations of pertinent texts drawn from all genres of literature, together with brief introductory notes and also indexes of names and biblical references. This collection is supplemented by *The Ancient Near East in Pictures relating to the Old Testament*, 2d ed. (Princeton, 1969), by the same author, which is arranged by topics, and is equipped with a descriptive catalogue giving in concise notation the significant details of each picture, and an index. *Near Eastern Religious Texts Relating to the Old Testament*, edited by Walter Beyerlin, translated from the German by John Bowden (London, 1978), is more restricted in scope, but includes several texts available only since 1969. The accompanying notes are fuller than in the preceding work. Another useful collection of this type, though far more limited in scope, and less up to date, is D. Winton Thomas's *Documents from Old Testament Times* (New York, 1961). Theodor H. Gaster's *Myth,*

Legend, and Custom in the Old Testament (New York, 1969) is a comparative study based on James G. Frazer's *Folk-Lore in the Old Testament*, 3 vols. (London, 1919). The copious notes are especially valuable. A concise yet comprehensive introduction to the geographical and historical settings of the Hebrew Bible is provided by Martin Noth in his *The Old Testament World*, translated by Victor I. Gruhn (Philadelphia, 1966). Frederick G. Kenyon's *Our Bible and the Ancient Manuscripts*, revised by A. W. Adams, with an introduction by Godfrey R. Driver (New York, 1965), is particularly useful for a survey of the ancient versions.

NAHUM M. SARNA

Apocrypha and Pseudepigrapha

The Apocrypha and the Pseudepigrapha, written by Jews during the Hellenistic and Roman periods, closely relate to the thirty-nine Old Testament books canonized by Jews and Christians and sometimes relate to the twenty-seven New Testament books canonized by Christians. These documents were very influential and were frequently considered inspired by many Jewish and Christian communities. However, they are usually preserved only in late manuscripts that are translations of lost originals.

The Apocrypha

The Apocrypha has been variously defined, for there is, of course, no set canon of either the Apocrypha or the Pseudepigrapha. The word *apokrypha* is a transliteration of a Greek neuter plural that means "hidden." Jerome (c. 342-420), however, used the term to denote extracanonical documents. This position is the one adopted by Protestants today; Roman Catholics, since the Council of Trent (during session 4 on 8 April 1546), consider these works "deutero-canonical" and inspired, as do most Eastern Christians.

The Apocrypha contains thirteen writings. They have been dated by experts over a wide period, from the fourth century BCE to the late first century CE; most scholars today correctly date all of them from circa 300 BCE to 70 CE, when the Temple was burned by the Romans. Almost all were written in a Semitic language, except the *Wisdom of Solomon* and *2 Maccabees*, which were probably written in Greek.

Legends, Romantic Stories, and Expansions of the Hebrew Scriptures. Nine documents of the Apocrypha can be regarded as forming a group of legends, romantic stories, and expansions of the Hebrew scriptures: the *Letter of Jeremiah*, *Tobit*, *Judith*, *2 Ezra*, the additions to *Esther*, the *Prayer of Azariah and the Song of the Three Young Men*, *Susanna*, *Bel and the Dragon*, and *1 Baruch*.

Letter of Jeremiah. The *Letter of Jeremiah* is the oldest writing in the Apocrypha according to a Greek fragment dating from around 100 BCE, found in Qumran Cave VII (around 300 is most likely). The document is "a letter" *(epistole)* pseu-donymously attributed to Jeremiah, which presents a passionate sermon or plea to fellow Jews not to fear or worship idols.

Tobit. Written in a Semitic language, probably Aramaic, around 180 BCE. It attempts to edify the reader and to illustrate that God is efficacious and helps the righteous.

Judith. The dramatic and didactic story of Judith was written in Hebrew around 150 BCE in Palestine, relating the attack upon the Jews by Holofernes, the general of the Assyrian king Nebuchadrezzar (chaps. 1-7).

2 Ezra (1 Esdras in the Septuagint, 3 Esdras in the Vulgate). Probably written in Hebrew or Aramaic, this work is a reproduction and rewriting of parts of the Hebrew scriptures, especially *2 Chronicles* 35:1-36:23, all of *Ezra*, and *Nehemiah* 7:38-8:12. Although very difficult to date, it may derive from the late second century, or around 150-100 BCE. Although this document is, of all the apocryphal writings, the one most closely connected to the Hebrew scriptures, its purpose is unclear, some characteristics are notable. The author emphasizes the Temple and its cult.

Prayer of Azariah and the Song of the Three Young Men. Three additions to *Daniel* are collected into the Apocrypha. Two of these, the story of Susanna and the story of Bel and the dragon, are separate, self-contained works in the *Daniel* cycle; the third, the *Prayer of Azariah*, like the additions to Esther, should be read as an insertion of sixty-eight verses into the *Book of Daniel*; in the Septuagint these verses are numbered from 3:24 to 3:90 (hence, the addition begins after 3:23).

All three additions were probably written originally in Hebrew; the date of the additions is difficult to discern; in their present form all, of course, must postdate 164/5, the date of the *Book of Daniel*. The three additions are probably from different times. It is possible that all three, or portions of them, originally reflected a setting different from their present place in the Septuagint.

The *Prayer of Azariah*, clearly composed in Hebrew (see Otto Plöger, *Zusätze zu Daniel*, Gütersloh, 1973, p. 68), emphasizes that there is only one God and that he is always just. This addition to *Daniel* shifts the focus from the evil king and his golden idol to three potential martyrs and their faithfulness in prayer.

Susanna. The colorful tale of Susanna, told in only sixty-four verses, may originally have been independent of the Danielic cycle and is perhaps considerably earlier than the *Book of Daniel*. It describes how a beautiful woman, Susanna, is brought to court, because she refuses to submit to two aroused influential men (elders, *presbuteroi*, and judges, *kritai*), who approached her while she was bathing. There her fate is sealed; the people and judges condemn her without hearing her. As she is being led to be stoned, the Lord hears her cry (verse 44) and arouses a youth, Daniel, who asks the judge to cross-examine the accusors. The story illustrates how God hears and helps the faithful and virtuous woman, and it demonstrates the wisdom of God in Daniel.

Bel and the Dragon (Bel and the Snake). This story of forty-two verses contains two separate tales. The first, describes how Daniel, by pointing out footprints in the ashes he had strewn on the floor of a temple, reveals to the king that the priests, their wives, and children had been eating the food offered to Bel, the Babylonian idol. The king becomes enraged and orders their deaths. Daniel is told to destroy the idol and its temple. The second story tells how Daniel destroys an idol, a great dragon (*drakon*, v. 23), and is subsequently thrown into a lions' den. He survives. The king releases Daniel and casts his enemies into the pit.

1 Baruch. Modern scholars have concluded that at least parts of this document were composed in Hebrew, others in Hebrew or perhaps Greek from the second or first centuries BCE. W. O. E. Oesterley (*An Introduction to the Books of the*

> Daniel . . . reveals to the king that the priests . . . had been eating the food offered to Bel, the Babylonian idol.

Apocrypha, New York, 1935, p. 260) and Whitehouse (in Charles, 1913, p. 575) were certainly wrong to have dated *1 Baruch* after 70 CE. The provenience may be Palestinian.

The document contains a confession of sins and a plea for God's compassion after the destruction of Jerusalem.

Wisdom and Philosophical Literature. Two books in the Apocrypha are from the wisdom school of Hellenistic Judaism, but while each is written by a single author, they are very different. *Ben Sira*, written in Hebrew, is by a conservative traditionalist from Palestine, perhaps even Jerusalem. The *Wisdom of Solomon*, written in Greek, is by a liberal thinker, thoroughly open to and influenced by non-Jewish ideas and philosophy—reminiscent to a certain extent of Philo Judaeus of Alexandria and *4 Maccabees*; it comes from Egypt, probably Alexandria.

The Pseudepigrapha

The Pseudepigrapha has been inadvertently defined incorrectly by the *selections* from this corpus published in German under the editorship of Emil Kautzsch in *Die Apokryphen und Pseudepigraphen des Alten Testaments*, 2 vols. (Tübingen, 1900), and in English under the editorship of R. H. Charles in *The Apocrypha and Pseudepigrapha of the Old Testament*, 2 vols. (Oxford, 1913). Charles's edition of the Pseudepigrapha contains all the documents in Kautzsch's collection plus four additional writings: *2 Enoch*, *Ahiqar*, a Zadokite work, and *Pirke Aboth (Pirqei avot)*. The last two works belong, respectively, among the Dead Sea Scrolls and

the rabbinic writings. All the others and many more, to a total of fifty-two writings plus a supplement that contains thirteen lost Jewish works quoted by the ancients, especially Alexander Polyhistor (c. 112-30s BCE), are included in *The Old Testament Pseudepigrapha*, 2 vols., edited by James H. Charlesworth (Garden City, N. Y., 1983-1984).

The fifty-two main documents in *The Old Testament Pseudepigrapha (OTP)*—which is not a canon of sacred writings but a modern collection of Jewish and Christian writings from circa 200 BCE to 200 CE—can be organized in five categories: (1) apocalyptic literature and related works; (2) testaments, which often include apocalyptic sections; (3) expansions of biblical stories and other legends; (4) wisdom and philosophical literature; and (5) prayers, psalms, and odes. To represent the corpus of the Pseudepigrapha within the confines of this relatively short article demands that comments on each category of writings be brief and sharply focused.

Apocalyptic Literature and Related Works. Nineteen pseudepigrapha can be grouped in the category of apocalyptic literature and related works. These nineteen works cover three overlapping chronological periods.

1. Antedating the burning of Jerusalem by the Romans in 70 CE, the great watershed in the history of Early Judaism (250 BCE-200 CE), are *1 Enoch*, some of the *Sibylline Oracles*, the *Apocrypha of Ezekiel*, and perhaps the *Treatise of Shem*.

2. After 70, the great varieties of religious thought in Judaism waned markedly as religious Jews, with great anxiety, lamented the loss of the Temple and pondered the cause of their defeat. *4 Ezra*, *2 Baruch*, *3 Baruch*, and the *Apocalypse of Abraham* are characterized by an intense interest in theodicy. *4 Ezra* is very pessimistic; its author finds it difficult to see any hope in his remorse. 2 Baruch is much more optimistic than *4 Ezra*; the Temple was destroyed by God's angels because of Israel's unfaithfulness (7:1-8:5), not by a superior culture or the might of the enemy.

3. Later works are documents 3, some of 4, 9, 10, 11, 12, 13, 18, and 19, ranging in date from the lost purported Jewish base of (or traditions in) the *Apocalypse of Adam* in the first or second century CE to the *Apocalypse of Daniel* in the ninth. These works are important for an understanding of Early Judaism only because they apparently preserve some edited works and record some early Jewish traditions.

The most important pseudepigraphon in this group is the composite book known as *1 Enoch*. It is preserved in its entire, final form only in Ethiopic, although versions of early portions of it are preserved in other languages; of these the most important are the Greek and Aramaic. The Qumran

Aramaic fragments, because of their paleographic age, prove that portions of *1 Enoch* date from the third, second, and first centuries BCE.

1 Enoch consists of five works that were composed over three centuries. In chronological order they are *Enoch's Astronomical Book* (*1 Enoch* 72-82), from the third century BCE; *Enoch's Journeys* (*1 Enoch* 1-36), from pre-160 BCE; *Enoch's Dream Visions* (*1 Enoch* 83-90), from pre-160 BCE), *Enoch's Epistle* (*1 Enoch* 91-105), from the second or first century BCE; and *Enoch's Parables* (*1 Enoch* 37-71), from pre-70 CE. Addenda (*1 Enoch* 106-108) are of uncertain date.

Some of the chapters that begin and end the divisions in *1 Enoch* were added or edited as the separate works were brought together into one document; this composite work circulated in Palestine before 70. While the precise dates for these sections of *1 Enoch*, or *Books of Enoch*, are debated, it is clear that the ideas they contain, such as the advocation of a solar calendar, were characteristic of some Jews from the third century BCE to the first century CE. *1 Enoch* is one of our major sources for Hellenistic Jewish ideas on cosmology, angelology, astronomy, God, sin, and mankind.

Testaments. Eight testaments, some of which include apocalyptic sections, make up a second group of pseudepigrapha. Of these, only the *Testament of Job* and the *Testament of Moses* clearly predate 70 CE. *The Testament of Adam*, in its present form, may be as late as the fifth century CE. *The Testament of Solomon* is earlier, perhaps from the third century CE. *The Testament of Isaac* and the *Testament of Jacob* were possibly added in the second or third century to the *Testament of Abraham*, which in its earliest form probably dates from the end of the first century or the beginning of the second century CE.

The most important—and most controversial—document in this group is the *Testaments of the Twelve Patriarchs*. This documents consists of twelve testaments, each attributed to a son of Jacob and containing ethical instruction often with apocalyptic visions.

BIBLIOGRAPHY

The Apocrypha. The best bibliographical guide to the Apocrypha is Gerhard Elling's *Bibliographie zur jüdisch-hellenistischen und intertestamentarischen Literatur, 1900-1970,* "Texte und Untersuchungen," no. 106, 2d ed. (Berlin, 1975). An important introduction to parts of the Apocrypha and Pseudepigrapha, with insightful comments regarding their sources and historical setting, is George W. E. Nickelsburg's *Jewish Literature between the Bible and the Mishnah: A Historical and Literary Introduction* (Philadelphia, 1981). See also Robert H. Pfeiffer's *History of New Testament Times with an Introduction to the Apocrypha* (New York, 1984). A careful, well-written, and authoritative introduction (but a little dated now) is Bruce M. Metzger's *An Introduction to the Apocrypha* (New York, 1957). An earlier work is Charles C. Torrey's *The Apocryphal Literature: A Brief Introduction* (1945; reprint, London, 1963). Reliable introductions to the Apocrypha, from Roman Catholics who consider these books deuterocanonical, can be found in *The Jerome Bible Commentary,* edited by Raymond E. Brown, Joseph A. Fitzmyer, and Roland E. Murphy (Englewood Cliffs, N. J., 1968).

Critical Greek editions of the Apocrypha have been appearing in the Cambridge and Göttingen editions of the Septuagint. A handy Greek edition of the Apocrypha is Alfred Rahlfs's *Septuaginta,* 2 vols. (Stuttgart, 1935; reprint of 8th ed., 1965). A classic work on the Apocrypha is volume 1 of *The Apocrypha and Pseudepigrapha of the Old Testament in English: With Introductions and Critical and Explanatory Notes to the Several Books,* edited by R. H. Charles (Oxford, 1913). More recent and excellent translations are those in *The Jerusalem Bible* (Garden City, N. Y., 1966), which is translated by Roman Catholics, and in *The New Oxford Annotated Bible with the Apocrypha: Revised Standard Version,* exp. ed., edited by Herbert G. May and Bruce M. Metzger (New York, 1977).

The best current commentary series is the Anchor Bible. Volumes 41-44 (Garden City, N. Y., 1976-1983) include Jonathan A. Goldstein's *I Maccabees* (vol. 41, 1976) and *II Maccabees* (vol. 41A, 1983), Jacob M. Myers's *I and II Esdras* (vol. 42, 1974), David Winston's *The Wisdom of Solomon* (vol. 43, 1979; reprint, 1981), and Carey A. Moore's *Daniel, Esther, and Jeremiah: The Additions* (vol. 44, 1977). Also valuable, especially because the Greek text is printed opposite the English translation, is *Jewish Apocryphal Literature,* 7 vols., edited by Solomon Zeitlin (Leiden, 1950-1972). The fruit of the best German scholarship on the Apocrypha and Pseudepigrapha has been appearing in fascicles in the series titled "Jüdische Schriften aus hellenistisch-römischer Zeit" (JSHRZ), edited by Werner Georg Kümmel (Gütersloh, 1973-). Valuable tools for those who know Greek are Christian Abraham Wahl's *Clavis librorum veteris testamenti apocryphorum philologica* (1853; reprint, Graz, 1972) and Edwin Hatch and Henry A. Redpath's *A Concordance to the Septuagint and the Other Greek Versions of the Old Testament, including the Apocryphal Books,* 2 vols. (1897-1906; reprint, Graz, 1972). A model computer-produced reference work is now available for the Apocrypha (and part of the Pseudepigrapha): Bruce M. Metzger et al., *A Concordance to the Apocrypha- Deuterocanonical Books of the Revised Standard Version* (Grand Rapids, Mich., 1983).

The Pseudepigrapha

Charlesworth, James H. *The Pseudepigrapha and Modern Research with a Supplement.* Chico, Calif., 1981. This book succinctly introduces the documents in the Pseudepigrapha and provides a bibliography of publications from 1960 until 1979. All publications mentioned in this article are cited with complete bibliographic data.

Charlesworth, James H., ed. *The Old Testament Pseudepigrapha.* 2 vols. Garden City, N. Y., 1983-1985. This massive collection contains introductions to and English translations of fifty-two writings classified as pseudepigrapha and of thirteen other documents included in a supplement. The introductions by the editor clarify the problems in defining "apocalypses," "testaments," "expansions of the 'Old Testament,'" "wisdom and philosophical literature," and "prayers, psalms, and odes."

Denis, Albert-Marie. *Introduction aux pseudépigraphes grecs d'Ancien Testament.* Leiden, 1970.

Nickelsburg, George W. E. *Jewish Literature between the Bible and the Mishnah: A Historical and Literary Introduction.* Philadelphia, 1981.

Sparks, H. F. D., ed. *The Apocryphal Old Testament.* Oxford, 1984. A selection of some documents usually placed in the Pseudepigrapha.

JAMES H. CHARLESWORTH

New Testament

"New Testament" is the name commonly given to a collection of twenty-seven different writings that function as normative scripture within the Christian churches, namely, the gospel according to Matthew, the gospel according to Mark, the gospel according to Luke, the gospel according to John, the *Acts of the Apostles*, the letter of Paul to the Romans, the first and second letters of Paul to the Corinthians, the letter of Paul to the Galatians, the letter of Paul to the Ephesians, the letter of Paul to the Philippians, the letter of Paul to the Colossians, the first and second letters of Paul to the Thessalonians, the first and second letters of Paul to Timothy, the letter of Paul to Titus, the letter of Paul to Philemon, the *Letter to the Hebrews*, the *Letter of James*, the first and second letters of Peter, the first, second, and third letters of John, the *Letter of Jude*, and the *Revelation to John*. These writings were composed by various Christian authors over approximately one century (c. AD 50-150). They represent a significant portion of early Christian literature, but they do not in every instance represent the oldest extant Christian writings.

The collection and identification of this particular group of writings as a distinct and normative entity was the result of a complex development within the Christian churches. The process, known as canonization, took approximately four centuries. The oldest indisputable witness to the New Testament canon is Athanasius, a fourth-century bishop of Alexandria. Paraphrasing the prologue of the gospel according to Luke in an Easter letter addressed to his congregation in the year 367, Athanasius summarily cited the circumstances that led to the development of the canon. He wrote: "Forasmuch as some have taken in hand, to reduce into order for themselves the books termed apocryphal, and to mix them up with the divinely inspired Scriptures . . . it seemed good to me also . . . to set before you the books included in the Canon, and handed down, and accredited as Divine" (Philip Schaff and Henry Wace, eds., *The Nicene and Post-Nicene Fathers*, vol. 4, Grand Rapids, Mich., 1978, pp. 551-552).

Early Formation

There is no evidence in the New Testament that the Christians of the first two or three generations were a literary group. The only indication that Jesus himself wrote anything is in *John* 8:6-8, a dubious reference in light of scholars' common estimation that *John* 7:53-8:11 did not originally belong to the text of John's gospel. According to the gospel evidence, Jesus' command to his disciples was that they should preach (e.g., *Mk.* 3:14, *Mt.* 28:20); nothing is said about a command or exhortation to write. The Lucan overview of early Christianity contained in the *Acts of Apostles* focuses on the preaching of the apostles. It specifically states that at least Peter and John were unlearned (*agrammatoi*, lit. "illiterate," in *Acts* 4:13). Moreover, even though the greater portion of *Acts* is devoted to Paul's activity, *Acts* presents Paul as a preacher and does not once mention his letter-writing. Paul did write letters, of course, and on occasion he referred to letters he has written (*1 Cor.* 5:9, *2 Cor.* 2:3-9; see also *2 Thes.* 2:3). The only New Testament indication of an authoritative command to write concerns the letters to the seven churches in the Book of Revelation (*Rv.* 1:11; see also *Rv.* 2:1, 2:8, 2:12, 2:18, 3:1, 3:7, 3:14). Thus there is no evidence in the New Testament itself that the earliest Christian communities experienced a need to have what later Christian generations would call a New Testament.

Apocalyptic Context. Not only were the first generations of Jesus' disciples largely unlearned, but the message that Jesus preached was couched in apocalyptic terms. He proclaimed, "The time is fulfilled, and the kingdom of God is at

> There is no evidence in the New Testament that the Christians of the first two or three generations were a literary group.

hand" (*Mk.* 1:15). This message, like that of John the Baptizer before Jesus, focused on the imminent coming of the reign of God. The apocalyptic proclamation of the coming of the kingdom of God was derived from the prophetic proclamation of the Day of the Lord.

Within a generation after the death of Jesus, the expectation of the coming of God's kingdom was associated with the expectation that Jesus himself would return as Son of man and Lord. This was the expectation of the Parousia ("presence" or "arrival," frequently identified in later Christian writings as the Second Coming). Although Paul was a Hellenistic Jew, he too expected that Jesus would come as eschatological Lord during Paul's own lifetime (see *1 Thes.* 4:17). This expectation of an imminent Parousia was characteristic of the hope for the future that first-generation Christians held.

The New Testament is consistent in its affirmation that God raised Jesus from the dead. The Christians' belief in the resurrection of Jesus was the basis of their hope for the future. Jesus' resurrection was understood as an act of God and as the initial event in the eschatological drama. More than a half-century after the death of Jesus, the gospel according to Matthew uses apocalyptic imagery (*Mt.* 27:51-54, 28:2-4) to attest that the death and resurrection of Jesus had been understood within Matthew's Jewish-Christian circles as an eschatological event.

The belief of the earliest Christians that God's kingdom was imminent not only gave a sense of urgency to the proclamation of Jesus' message by his disciples but also impeded production of a specifically Christian literature among the first generation of Jesus' disciples. For the most part they were incapable of literary activity; their expectation of an imminent Parousia rendered such activity redundant.

Belief in the Holy Spirit. Another factor tended to forestall the production of literature among the first generation of Christians: the role attributed to the Holy Spirit. This was the Spirit of the end time, that is, the age to come. This eschatological Spirit empowered and impelled Jesus to proclaim the coming of the Kingdom and to effect exorcisms. As the fragment of a traditional creedal formula cited by Paul in Romans 1:4 explicitly attests, that same Holy Spirit continued to be operative in the resurrection of Jesus.

The conviction that the echatological and prophetic Spirit of God was operative in their midst led the first generations of Christians to revere the voice of Spirit-inspired prophets, among whom Jesus was the paradigm. Even Paul, who

> **"I did not suppose that information from books would help me so much as the word of a living and surviving voice."**

avowed that he also had the Spirit of God (*1 Cor.* 7:40), boasted that he was a preacher (see *1 Cor.* 1:17, 2:1-5). He had recourse to writing only because the circumstances of his later preaching prevented him from being personally present to those whom he had previously evangelized and with whom he wished to be in additional communication (see, e.g., *1 Thes.* 2:17-3:10, *1 Cor.* 4:14-21). Paul appears to have valued personal presence and the spoken word over the written word.

Both Papias (AD 60-130) and Justin Martyr (c. 100-163/165) bear witness to the high regard in which oral tradition, as distinct from written documents, was held as late as the middle of the second century. In fact, Eusebius, the fourth-century church historian, writing at a time when there was considerable discussion among the Christian churches about which writings were traditional, and noting that some writings were commonly accepted by the churches and others were not, recalls that Papias had said: "I did not suppose that information from books would help me so much as the word of a living and surviving voice" (*Church History* 3.39.4). Thus, even when the process of canonization was reaching its climax, the foremost church historian of the time continued to recall that earlier generations of Christians had higher regard for the Spirit-inspired oral message than they did for written words.

The general illiteracy of the first Christians, the expectation of an imminent Parousia, and the high regard for Spirit-inspired prophetic utterance together ensured that the first

generations of Christians would be itinerant, charismatic-type prophetic figures rather than scholarly authors of written works. Their social circumstances and their activity mutually served to prevent their producing written works.

Hebrew Scriptures. The early Christians were even less disposed to produce a specifically religious literature. Jesus and the twelve disciples already had their scriptures: the New Testament portrays Jesus and the disciples as being present in the Temple of Jerusalem and in synagogues, where the scriptures were expounded. All four evangelists describe Jesus interpreting the scriptures, both in rabbinic-type disputation and by way of expository comment. While many of these descriptions owe as much to the creativity and theological purposes of the evangelists as they do to historical reminiscence and the conservative force of tradition, there is little doubt that Jesus accepted the scriptures of his people and his own religious tradition. For Jesus the Hebrew scriptures (*hai graphai* in Greek, the language in which the gospels were written) were a normative expression of the word of God

Letters

Because the Hebrew scriptures were the scriptures *par excellence*, and because the first generation(s) of Christians were essentially Jews who acknowledged the risen Jesus as Christ or Lord, it was unlikely that these early Christians would have produced a sacred literature to compete with that of their Jewish tradition. Even so, the high regard accorded the Hebrew scriptures within both Palestinian and Diaspora Judaism, and the apocalyptic perspective evidenced by the preaching of Jesus and the early writings of Paul, did not preclude the writing of letters. Nonetheless the oldest extant Christian literature consists of the letters of Paul. These letters have always been found in the manuscript and printed editions of the New Testament following the four Gospels and the *Acts of the Apostles;* they are the oldest part of the New Testament.

The Hellenistic Model. Although A. J. Malherbe pleaded that *1 Thessalonians* be understood within the category of the paraenetic letter, it is more generally acknowledged that Paul employed the Hellenistic personal letter as a model for his own correspondence. Paul's first letter to the Thessalonians is substantially longer than the average personal letter of Hellenistic correspondents, but it has the essential form of such a letter.

Hellenistic letters typically followed a tripartite schema: the protocol (introduction), the body of the letter (the *homilia*, or basic message), and the eschatocol (conclusion). The protocol normally followed the format of "A to B, greetings and a health wish." Opening with "Paul, Silvanus, and Timothy, to the church of the Thessalonians in God the Father and the Lord Jesus Christ: Grace to you and peace," Paul's first letter to the Thessalonians followed the traditional format, with the exception of the health wish. The health wish is omitted from all the New Testament epistolary literature, with the exception of *3 John* (v. 2). As with all the Pauline letters deemed authentic by critical scholarship (*Romans*, *1-2 Corinthians*, *Galatians*, *Philippians*, *1 Thessalonians, Philemon*), other Christian evangelizers are associated with Paul in the sending of the greetings. The recipients of *1 Thessalonians* are an assembly (*ekklesia*, "church") of believers, rather than a single individual. This too sets a precedent, since Paul's later letters were similarly addressed to churches. The greeting of *1 Thessalonians* clearly represents a modification of the typical Hellenistic greeting, a simple "greetings" (sg., *chaire*; pl., *chairete*). The greeting of *1 Thessalonians* is a literary neologism (*charis*, "grace"), somewhat homonymous with the Hellenistic greeting, expanded by the typical Semitic greeting (*eirene*, "peace," the Greek equivalent of the Hebrew *shalom*, used as a greeting in personal encounters as well as in letters). Paul may well have taken the two-part greeting from the liturgical usage of the bicultural Christians at Antioch in Syria. Although the greeting of *1 Thessalonians* is the relatively simple "grace and peace," the formula was expanded in his later correspondence to become "grace to you and peace from God the Father and the Lord Jesus Christ." In short, Paul seems to have employed the typical Hellenistic introduction but adapted it to his own purposes.

The First Letter to the Thessalonians. From the standpoint of Paul's appropriation of the personal-letter form, some specific features of *1 Thessalonians* are particularly noteworthy. Paul's use of the "recall motif," his constant allusions to being among the Thessalonians, shows that the letter is an occasional writing. Yet the body of the letter focuses upon God's activity among the Thessalonians. Paul gives thanks that the proclamation of the gospel has been effective among them. He represents his presence to the Thessalonians as that of an "apostle of Christ" (*1 Thes.* 2:7) so that there results a significant modification of the *parousia* function of the letter. Since Paul's presence is an apostolic presence, the section of the letter in which Paul specifically writes of his desire to be with the Thessalonians (*1 Thes.* 2:17-3:13) has been styled "the apostolic parousia" (Robert W. Funk). Paul's later letters have a similar feature.

But Paul's apostolic presence is overshadowed by a still greater presence, that of Jesus Christ the Lord. In *1 Thessalonians* Paul uses the technical term *parousia*, a term used elsewhere in the New Testament in this technical sense only in *2 Thessalonians* and *Matthew*, to express the object of Christian hope. Paul's second thanksgiving period concludes with a wish-prayer (*1 Thes.* 3:11-13) that focuses on the Parousia. Questions about the relationship between the Parousia of the Lord Jesus and the resurrection of the dead seem to have been singularly important among the specific concerns that prompted the writing of the first letter to the Thessalonians. However, Paul's concluding the second

thanksgiving period (see also *1 Thes.* 2:12) with reference to the awaited and desired Parousia inaugurated a pattern of eschatological climax to the thanksgiving period that would characterize his later writings.

The eschatocol of the typical Hellenistic letter consisted of a series of greetings, prayers, and wishes. These elements are in the concluding verses of *1 Thessalonians* (5:23-27). Noteworthy is Paul's exhortation that the letter "be read to all the brethren" (v. 27), which shows that Paul intended that the letter be read to the entire assembly of the Thessalonian Christians. This is the first indication that Christian writings were to be read during the (liturgical) assemblies of Christians. The ensuing practice would be of major significance in the development of the New Testament canon in the following decades.

The Gospels

While reliance upon the voice of Christian prophets, the expectation of an imminent Parousia, and traditional respect for the scriptures impeded production of a specifically religious literature among early generations of Christians, these same factors imparted a sense of urgency to the oral proclamation of the gospel. The message that Jesus had preached was not only the simple, prophetic-like dictum "The time is fulfilled, and the kingdom of God is at hand; repent, and believe in the gospel" (*Mk.* 1:15). It also made use of proverbs, beatitudes, and especially parables. Proverbs and parables alike were types of *mashalim*, figures of comparative speech. Many of the sayings attributed to Jesus in the New Testament are similar to sayings attributed to rabbis and other sages in nonbiblical literature. These similarities allow these sayings to be typed and located in certain social settings.

Jesus himself was an apocalyptic preacher. His story was not written down until about forty years after his death, but in the intervening years his disciples believed that the reign of God Jesus had proclaimed had begun with his own death and resurrection. This conviction was a key element in the process whereby the gospel of Jesus came to be the gospel about Jesus. In the classic words of Rudolf Bultmann, the proclaimer became the proclaimed. What was written down in the form of gospel during the last third of the first century was not only what Jesus said but also what he did.

In the more than two generations that intervened between Jesus' death and the writing of the first gospel, the tradition about Jesus was handed down in oral fashion. The oral tradition was essentially the living memory of Jesus' immediate disciples and the first generations of Christians. Because it was memory, the oral tradition was essentially conservative, as a number of Scandinavian exegetes have pointed out; and because it was living, the oral tradition was essentially creative, as the early form-critics (especially Bultmann) have shown. An appreciation of the oral tradition about Jesus can only be had through an examination of the Gospels. The Gospels are the record of the church's proclamation of Jesus (Willi Marxsen). They are more than that, but they are the only available documentary evidence of that proclamation. [*See also* Gospel.]

The Synoptics. Since the late eighteenth century, it has been customary to identify *Matthew*, *Mark*, and *Luke* as the synoptic Gospels in distinction from the *Gospel of John*. Although John's gospel also provides an account of Jesus' activity from the time of his encounter with John the Baptist until the time of Jesus' death and resurrection, it differs in so many respects from the other three gospels that is should be treated apart from the others. The synoptic ("look-alike") Gospels are remarkably similar to one another, not only in structure but also in the choice of the events narrated and in details of the narration. This similarity of content, form, and structure gives rise to the so-called synoptic problem, namely, how to determine the literary relationship among these three remarkably similar documents.

Mark's gospel, written around AD 70, was the first written New Testament gospel. Just after World War I, Karl Ludwig Schmidt clearly demonstrated that the gospel genre was a Marcan literary creation. Mark was the originator of the genre insofar as he created a quasi-biographical framework into which he incorporated independent units of traditional material. Available to him were independent sayings and stories—some of which may have been previously joined together in small collections—handed down by means of the church's missionary, catechetical, and liturgical activity. These three types of activity were the typical settings in which the traditional material about Jesus was both handed down and shaped by the church. The church's activity thus served to stylize the tradition about Jesus, especially as it adapted the tradition to its own needs. In any event, the Gospels do not constitute a bland historical witness to Jesus of Nazareth. They are a witness in faith to the Jesus who has been acknowledged as Lord. The traditions about Jesus were transmitted by the church into its kerygmatic, didactic, and worship activity because of the belief that the Jesus who died on the cross was the Jesus who had been raised from the dead. Faith in Jesus as the Risen One colors the gospel narrative. This is true in all instances, but in some cases postresurrectional accounts have been retrojected into the gospel narrative. Mark's gospel has been described as a "passion narrative with an extended introduction" (Martin Kähler). The passion narrative concludes with a brief resurrection account that features the kerygmatic statement "He has risen; he is not here" (*Mk.* 16:1-8). As such the Marcan text demonstrates that the individual traditions about Jesus were to be understood in the light of Jesus' death and resurrection. The literary format suited to conveying that conviction was the product of Mark's religious and literary genius. Nonetheless, a few scholars (notably Charles H. Talbert) maintain that, as a liter-

ary form, the written gospel is dependent upon the Hellenistic form of the biographical sketch.

The specific circumstances of Mark's composition were not those of the Syrian Christian churches to which Matthew and Luke belonged in the eighties. Matthew's Hellenistic Jewish-Christian community had its own needs, as did Luke's largely gentile-Christian community. Accordingly both Matthew and Luke rewrote the Marcan narrative with the help of traditional material taken from other sources. Their compositions attest to the early church's need for a witness to Jesus that was pertinent to specific situations.

John. The gospel according to John was written in the last decade of the first century for the benefit of a Christian church that can be cryptically described as "the community of the Beloved Disciple" (Raymond E. Brown). That community had its origins in the circle of the disciples of John the Baptist. It had contacts with various forms of esoteric Judaism (many Johannine idioms and thought patterns are remarkably similar to both Qumranite and gnostic expressions and thoughts), and it had received an influx of Samaritan believers. Somehow this community had maintained a Christian existence in relative independence from other Christian communities, even to the point that some scholars believe it best to conceive of the Johannine community as a Christian sect. Only a relatively small number of scholars hold that the gospel produced within this community was literarily dependent upon one or another of the synoptic Gospels. Nonetheless, the literary form created by Mark had sufficient authority among the Christian churches of the late first century to ensure that the Johannine community's faith narrative about Jesus took the form of a gospel.

Foundations of the Canon

While the literary form of the apostolic letter had its origins in the middle of the first century, and the written gospel came into being about a quarter of a century later, forces at work within the Christian churches, forces that continued to be operative after a distinctively Christian literature had been produced, would eventually give rise to a discernible New Testament canon.

Authority. In a fashion similar to that of other first-century Jewish groups, the early Christians interpreted their experience in the light of the scriptures. The Second Isaian servant canticles, Psalms 2 and 100, were the key elements in the "scriptural apologetic" (Barnabas Lindars) of first-century Christianity. They served to place the Jesus experience in a meaningful context. It was especially the death and resurrection of Jesus that were interpreted "according to the scriptures" (*see 1 Cor.* 15:3-4). In the exposition of this message, Paul argued from the Torah (e.g., *Gn.* 17:5 in *Rom.* 4:17), the prophets (*Hb.* 2:4 in *Rom.* 1:17), and the psalms (*Ps.* 51:4 in *Rom.* 3:4). Citations from and allusions to the Hebrew scriptures served to interpret Paul's own experience. There could be no doubt that the scriptures were authority for Jesus and the first generations of his disciples.

The word of the Lord. A real concern was with other Spirit-endowed authorities. Preeminent among these authorities was the word of the Lord Jesus. Barely a generation after Jesus' death, Paul appealed to the word of the Lord (*1 Thes.* 4:15) in an attempt to assuage the grief over the unexpected death of some Christians at Thessalonica. In *1 Corinthians* 7, Paul carefully distinguished the authority of the word of the Lord from his own. Contemporary with Paul's earliest letters was the collection of a number of Jesus' sayings in a florilegium, no longer extant, known to contemporary scholars as the Q source. Application of the criteria of multiple attestation (sayings contained in different texts and/or different literary forms) and dual exclusion (neither attested in contemporary Jewish sources nor serving specific ecclesiastical needs) allows scholars to judge that many of the gospel sayings derive from Jesus' own words. A history-of-tradition study of the *logia* (sayings of Jesus), as well as a comparative, redaction-critical study of a single saying contained in more than one of the Gospels, indicates that the sayings of Jesus were transmitted by the early Christians in such a way as to be applicable to later situations. Thus the sayings of Jesus enjoyed significant and relevant authority in the churches of the first generations. They were remembered from the past, but they were also applied to contemporary circumstances.

The apostles. As witnesses, the apostles possessed considerable authority among the churches. *Acts* offers a stylized account of the authority enjoyed by Peter. Even more indicative is the biographical section of the letter to the Galatians, where Paul vehemently argues for his own authority on the basis that he had received a revelation of Jesus Christ (*Gal.* 1:12) but acknowledges the contacts he had with the Jerusalem apostles (1:18-19, 2:1).

Within the New Testament, the name "apostle" was not restricted to the twelve disciples, named apostles (*Lk.* 6:12-16, *Mk.* 3:13-19, *Mt.* 10:1-4). Paul himself was an apostle in his own right (*Gal.* 1:1), as even Luke acknowledges in *Acts* (14:4, 14:14). Not only did Paul preach in the power of the Holy Spirit, but he also used his Spirit-endowed authority to render authoritative decisions (*see 1 Cor.* 7:10-11, 7:40). Those whom Paul had evangelized appealed to him to resolve disputes and uncertain matters (*see 1 Cor.* 1:11, 7:1). He served as an authority for the churches he had founded, that is, those he had served as an apostle. The authority of the apostles is also attested to in the phenomenon of apostolic pseudepigraphy: works written by authors unknown to us were attributed to apostles so that they would have apostolic authority (*Ephesians, Colossians, 2 Thessalonians, 1-2 Timothy, Titus, James, 1-2 Peter, Jude*).

Tradition. In the first century the tradition about Jesus became stylized and stereotyped in a variety of oral and literary forms. The New Testament evidence shows how important maintaining the tradition about Jesus was. One of the earliest indications of this was the emergence of creedal formulas that articulated the core content of the kerygma. In AD 50 three different creedal formulas were incorporated into the first letter to the Thessalonians (1:10, 4:14, 5:9-10). Paul used the technical language of the rabbinic schools, "receive" (Gr., *paralambanein*; Heb., *qibbel*) and "deliver" (*paradidomi, masar*), to attest that he was handing along the tradition faithfully (*1*

> **As witnesses, the apostles possessed considerable authority among the churches.**

Cor. 15:3-5). The creedal formulas principally articulated faith in the death and resurrection of Jesus, but the scope of tradition was broader. For example, it included the "liturgical" tradition of the Lord's Supper (*see 1 Cor.* 11:23-32).

The later writings of the New Testament offer evidence of the importance placed on transmitting the tradition faithfully. Luke offers an exhortation on the faithful transmission of the gospel within the context of Paul's farewell discourse at Miletus (*Acts* 20:28-31). The Pastoral letters to Timothy and Titus portray the two as having been carefully taught by Paul (e.g., *1 Tm.* 1:2a) and charged with responsibility for conveying that teaching to others (e.g., *1 Tm.* 4:11). "The saying is sure" functions as a refrain, setting a seal of approval on authoritative pieces of tradition (e.g., 1 Tm. 1:15).

Within early Christianity, Spirit-authority-tradition formed a constellation that can be perceived as constitutive of Christianity itself. The individual writings of the New Testament incorporated and bore witness to these elements in specific and concretized fashions. Each New Testament document was composed within a specific church situation and addressed to a specific situation.

Text of the New Testament

The New Testament was written entirely in Greek. Approximately five thousand ancient Greek New Testament manuscripts exist. These are categorized according to the material on which the texts are transcribed, the type of calligraphy, and the use made of the manuscripts. The oldest complete manuscript of the New Testament is the fourth-century Codex Sinaiticus, which originally contained both the Old and the New Testaments. Written on parchment, the New Testament portion of the codex is the only complete extant copy of the Greek New Testament written in uncial script. The codex was discovered by Konstantin von Tischendorf in the Monastery of Saint Catherine on Mount Sinai in 1844. To symbolize its antiquity, it has been designated in scholarship with the Hebrew letter alef.

Papyri. The oldest available manuscripts of the New Testament are papyrus fragments, none of which offers a complete text of any New Testament book. In the technical literature these fragments are indicated by a Gothic P with an Arabic numeral in exponent position indicating the specific papyrus. Eighty-eight New Testament papyri have been identified and cataloged thus far. The most ancient is P;s52, a second-century fragment containing some letters from *John* 18:31-33 on the recto side and some letters from *John* 18:37-48 on the verso side. These letters are in an uncial script and written with no space between the words. The discovery of the fragment was particularly important because it led scholars almost unanimously to place the time of composition of the gospel according to John in the late first century, when the dominant tendency of critical scholarship was to identify that gospel as a second-century work.

The most important papyri that serve as witnesses to the text of the New Testament are those that belong to the Chester Beatty and Bodmer collections. Three third-century papyri were acquired by A. Chester Beatty in 1930-1931. P45 designates 30 leaves (of a 220-leaf codex) with parts of *Matthew*, *Mark*, *Luke*, *John*, and *Acts*; P46, the oldest of the three papyri, consists of 86 leaves (of 104) with parts of *Romans*, *1 Corinthians*, *2 Corinthians*, *Ephesians*, *Galatians*, *Philippians*, *Colossians*, and *1 Thessalonians*. P47 has 10 leaves (of 32) with *Revelation* 9:10-17:2.

Parchment. Most New Testament manuscripts are written on parchment. For purposes of editing the text of the New Testament, the most important manuscripts are the parchment manuscripts written in uncial script, of which 274 are known to exist. These are identified by a system of sigla devised by Johann Jakob Wettstein (1693-1754), who used the letters of the Latin and Greek alphabets to designate the ancient Greek manuscripts. The discovery of additional manuscripts and the recognition that some manuscripts that Wettstein had designated by a single letter were in fact parts of two manuscripts have rendered his system scientifically inadequate, but it is classic and remains in common use. A more exact system of classification was devised by Caspar René Gregory (1846-1917), who used Arabic numerals preceded by a zero (01, 02, 03, etc.) to designate the manuscripts. Thus the Codex Sinaiticus is designated by the Hebrew letter alef or 01. In addition to the Codex Sinaiticus, for purposes of editing the text of the New Testament, the more important uncial manuscripts are the Codex Alexandrinus, the Codex Vaticanus, the Codex Ephraemi Rescriptus, the Codex Bezae Cantabrigensis, the Codex Claromontanus, the Codex Regius, the Codex Washingtoniensis, and the Codex Koridethi.

The Minuscules. The uncial style of transcribing New Testament manuscripts predominated for about five centuries. In the ninth century a minuscule or cursive style of writing was introduced. Most of the New Testament manu-

scripts written in the second millennium of Christianity are written in this minuscule style. Almost three thousand extant minuscule manuscripts of the New Testament exist, dating from the tenth century to the sixteenth century. As a group they are generally considered to bear witness to the Byzantine or ecclesiastical type of text, but a more recent trend identifies them simply as "the majority." In the technical literature they are simply identified by Arabic numerals. Some of the miniscules share such textural particularities with other manuscripts that they can be recognized as having some sort of dependence on one another. Among the groups so identified are the Lake (MSS 1, 18, 131, etc.) and Ferrar (MSS 13, 69, 124, 346, etc.) families, respectively named after Kirsopp Lake and William Hugh Ferrar, who first identified (Lake in 1902, Ferrar in 1868) the textural relationships among the manuscripts of the groups that today bear their names.

The Lectionaries. A final category of Greek manuscripts is the lectionaries. More than two thousand lectionaries have been classified thus far. The oldest fragmentary lectionary dates from the sixth century; the oldest complete lectionary dates from the eighth. The lectionaries contain New Testament texts arranged for liturgical reading. The text of the lectionaries is characterized by the insertion of appropriate introductory phrases and the additional use of proper nouns for clarity.

BIBLIOGRAPHY

Classic among the standard comprehensive works on the New Testament is Werner Georg Kümmel's *Introduction to the New Testament*, rev. ed. (London, 1975). This volume, which contains abundant bibliographic references, gives background material for each of the New Testament books, treats the collection of these books into the canon, and discusses transmission of the texts. Useful but less encyclopedic are Willi Marxsen's *Introduction to the New Testament: An Approach to Its Problems* (Philadelphia, 1968), Günther Bornkamm's *The New Testament: A Guide to Its Writings* (Philadelphia, 1973), and Norman Perrin and Dennis C. Duling's *The New Testament: An Introduction*, 2d ed. (New York, 1982).

An overview of the formation of the New Testament canon is given in chapter 1 of my *Introduction to the New Testament* (Garden City, N. Y., 1983). The classic study of the matter remains Hans von Campenhausen's *The Format of the Christian Bible* (London, 1972), although Charles F. Moule offers valuable insights in *The Birth of the New Testament*, rev. ed. (San Fransisco, 1981). Of particular interest is a study of the Muratorian fragment by Albert C. Sundberg, Jr., "Canon Muratori: A Fourth Century List," *Harvard Theological Review* 66 (1973): 1-41.

Helmut Koester's two-volume *Introduction to the New Testament* (Philadelphia, 1982) provides much information about the historical and religio-cultural conditions within which early Christian literature was written. Volume 1 is entitled *History, Culture, and Religion of the Hellenistic Age*; volume 2, *History and Literature of Early Christianity*. Various illustrative documents are presented by C. K. Barrett in *The New Testament Background: Selected Documents* (New York, 1961), by Howard Clark Kee in *The Origins of Christianity: Sources and Documents* (Englewood Cliffs, N. J., 1973), and by David R. Cartlidge and David L. Dungan in *Documents for the Study of the Gospels* (Cleveland, 1980). Useful historical studies are Floyd V. Filson's *A New Testament History: The Story of the Emerging Church* (Philadelphia, 1964) and Frederick F. Bruce's *New Testament History* (London, 1969). The religious, cultural, and social dimensions of the New Testament's environment are emphasized by Martin Hengel in *Judaism and Hellenism*, 2 vol. (Philadelphia, 1974), by Eduard Lohse in *The New Testament Environment* (London, 1976), by Gerd Theissen in *Sociology of Early Palestinian Christianity* (Philadelphia, 1978), and by Wayne A. Meeks in *The First Urban Christians: The Social World of the Apostle Paul* (New Haven, 1982).

A general study of the significance of letters in early Christianity is William G. Doty's *Letters in Primitive Christianity* (Philadelphia, 1973); more particular is Harry Gamble's "The Redaction of the Pauline Letters and the Formation of the Pauline Corpus," *Journal of Biblical Literature* 94 (1975): 403-418. Paul's use of the Hellenistic personal letter is analyzed in Helmut Koester's "I Thessalonians—Experiment in Christian Writing," in *Continuity and Discontinuity*, edited by F. Forrester Church and Timothy George (Leiden, 1979), pp. 33-44.

The three pioneering works in the form-critical approach to the New Testament, written in German just after the end of World War I, are still the classic studies of the formation of the synoptic Gospels. They are *The History of the Synoptic Tradition*, rev. ed. (New York, 1968), by Rudolf Bultmann; *From Tradition to Gospel* (New York, 1935) by Martin Dibelius; and *Der Rahmen der Geschichte Jesu* (Berlin, 1919) by Karl Ludwig Schmidt.

The works of Bruce M. Metzger are among the most significant English-language publications on the transmission and editions of the text of the New Testament. Among them are *The Text of the New Testament: Its Transmission, Corruption, and Restoration*, 2d ed. (Oxford, 1968), *The Early Versions of the New Testament: Their Origin, Transmission and Limitations* (Oxford, 1977), and *Manuscripts of the Greek Bible* (Oxford, 1981). An overview of problematic aspects of textual transmission is given in chapter 3 of my *Introduction to the New Testament* (Garden City, N. Y., 1983). A useful introduction to the study of the New Testament manuscripts is Jack Finegan's *Encountering New Testament Manuscripts: A Working Introduction to Textual Criticism* (Grand Rapids, Mich., 1974).

The Cambridge History of the Bible, a three-volume work, remains the classic in this field. Volume 1 is *From the Beginnings to Jerome*, edited by P. R. Ackroyd and C. E. Evans (Cambridge, 1970); volume 2, *The West from the Fathers to the Reformation*, edited by G. W. Lampe (Cambridge, 1969); and volume 3, *The West from the Reformation to the Present Day*, edited by S. C. Greenslade (Cambridge, 1963). Two monographs offer useful surveys of the major translations of the New Testament into the English language: Frederick F. Bruce's *History of the Bible in English*, 3d ed. (New York, 1978), and W. Walden's *Guide to Bible Translations: A Handbook of Versions Ancient and Modern* (Duxbury, Mass., 1979).

RAYMOND F. COLLINS

BLASPHEMY

The word *blasphemy* derives from a Greek term meaning "speaking evil," but in the Judeo-Christian religious tradition the word refers to verbal offenses against sacred values or beliefs. The concept of blasphemy has never remained fixed. It has ranged from the ancient Hebrew crime of cursing the ineffable name of God to irreverent statements that outrage the religious sensibilities of others. What is deemed blasphemous varies from society to society and may differ with time and place, but whatever is condemned as blasphemy is always regarded as an abuse of liberty and reveals what a society cannot and will not tolerate.

Yet the Judeo-Christian religious tradition holds no monopoly on the concept of blasphemy. Every society will punish the rejection or mockery of its gods. Because blasphemy is an intolerable verbal violation of the sacred, it affronts the priestly class, the deep-seated beliefs of worshipers, and the basic religious values that a community shares.

Christendom's concept of blasphemy derived from the Mosaic injunction of *Exodus* 22:28, which declares, "You shall not revile God." The Hebrew scriptures distinguished blasphemy from other offenses against religion, in contrast to the Septuagint. Where, for example, Greek usage showed a preference for *blasphemy* and used that term somewhat loosely, the Hebrew scriptures referred more precisely to "idolatry" or "sacrilege," as in *Isaiah* 66:3 and *1 Maccabees* 2:6. The word connotes also "to pierce [the name of God], rail, repudiate, derogate, speak disrespectfully, denounce, insult, and abuse." Only God can be blasphemed in Jewish thought. And nowhere in Old Testament or Greek-Jewish sacred books is *blasphemy* a synonym for heresy. Indeed, no equivalent for the concept of *heresy* exists in the pre-Christian era. Christianity, though greatly influenced by Greek-Jewish texts, would use the two terms *blasphemy* and *heresy* as equivalents and as more than a God-centered offense. Not until Christianity began did the meaning of *blasphemy* change.

As the term *blasphemy* broadened in Christian usage, it narrowed in Jewish usage. Jewish law avenges God's honor but not that of the Jewish religion. Reviling sacred customs, beliefs, and institutions, whether of Judaism itself, the Temple, the sacerdotal hierarchy, particular rituals, or holy dogmas, did not constitute blasphemy. The Talmud focused on *Exodus* 22:28 and narrowed the capital crime. In rabbinic thought, not even cursing God deserved death unless the blasphemer used the name of God to curse God.

The New Testament retained the God-centeredness of the Mosaic code but expanded the concept of the offense to include the rejection of Jesus and the attribution of his miracles to satanic forces. Although only Mark and Matthew depict a formal trial and condemnation of Jesus by the Sanhedrin, all four evangelists employ the motif that the Jewish rejection of Jesus was blasphemy. Readers understand that whenever the Gospels depicted the Jews as describing Jesus as blasphemous for performing some miracle, or healing on the Sabbath, or forgiving sins, none of which constituted the crime of blasphemy in Jewish law, the Jews by their rejection, and not Jesus, were blasphemous. Thus in the climax of the trial scenes before the Sanhedrin, those who found Jesus guilty were blasphemers because they did not recognize him as the Son of God and the Messiah.

For four centuries after the crucifixion, many different interpretations of Christianity competed with each other as the true faith, producing accusations of blasphemy. Jesus, having joined God as a divine majesty in Christian thought, though not in Arianism, became a target of blasphemers or,

> ## Cursing, reproaching, challenging, mocking, rejecting, or denying Jesus Christ became blasphemy.

rather, the basis for leveling the charge of blasphemy against variant professors of Christianity. Cursing, reproaching, challenging, mocking, rejecting, or denying Jesus Christ became blasphemy. Posing as Jesus, claiming to be equal to him, or asserting powers or attributes that belonged to him, became blasphemy.

Any religious view contrary to church policy was blasphemy, a form of heresy, but the doctrine of the Trinity became the focal point in the controversy over blasphemy. The conflict between Arians and Athanasians involved more than a dispute over the right faith; it concerned the right road to salvation for all Christians. The authority of the church, when backed by the coercion of the state, settled the controversy by fixing on the Nicene Creed, which ultimately became the test of orthodoxy. Constantine's decrees against Arians and Arian books eventually led to the Theodosian Code of 438, enthroning Catholic Christianity as the exclusive religion of the empire, and Christians began persecuting each other. Heresy then superseded blasphemy as the great crime against Christianity. Unfreighted with Old Testament origins, heresy was more flexible and spacious a concept than blasphemy and had as many meanings. Both Athanasius and Augustine freely intermixed accusations of blasphemy and heresy, as if the two terms were interchangeable. But heresy became the encompassing term.

During the seventeenth century blasphemy increasingly became a secular crime. The state began to supplant the church as the agency mainly responsible for instigating and conducting prosecutions. The connection between religious dissent and political subversion and the belief that a nation's religious unity augmented its peace and strength accounted in part for the rising dominance of the state in policing serious crimes against religion. Governments intervened more

frequently to suppress nonconforming sectarians and intellectuals.

In England the prosecution of heresy as a capital crime had begun to die out in the reign of Elizabeth. The earliest Protestant codification of ecclesiastical law in England (1553) had the first separate section on blasphemy. Elizabeth burned five or six Arians and Anabaptists whose crimes included the beliefs that Christ was not God and that infant baptism was unnecessary.

In 1648 Parliament had enacted a statute against blasphemy that reached the doctrines of Socinianism but not those of Ranterism, a phenomenon of the disillusioned and defeated political left that turned to religion for expression. Ranters believed that, as God's grace is unbounded, nothing is sinful. Antinomian sentiment run amok into religious anarchy, the Ranters were seditious, obscene, and blasphemous in ways as flagrantly offensive as possible. A 1650 act against blasphemy cataloged Ranter beliefs but punished them lightly compared to Scotland, which carried out the death penalty. The Ranters recanted easily and disappeared. Unlike the Socinians or the Quakers, they did not have the stuff of martyrs.

George Fox, the founding Quaker, who was prosecuted for blasphemy four times, and his followers endured violent persecution. Their belief in the Christ within seemed blasphemous. In 1656 James Nayler, then the greatest Quaker, was convicted by Parliament for blasphemy because he reenacted Jesus' entry into Jerusalem on Palm Sunday as a sign of the imminent Second Coming. Nayler was savagely beaten and imprisoned. The first person imprisoned for blasphemy after the Restoration was William Penn, accused of antitrinitarianism.

A blasphemy act of 1698 targeted antitrinitarians, showing that England still regarded them as execrable atheists. English precepts about blasphemy made the Atlantic crossing. Virginia's first code of laws (1611) specified death for anyone blaspheming the Trinity or Christianity, and most other colonies followed suit.

The number of blasphemy cases peaked in England and the United States in the first half of the nineteenth century. Between 1821 and 1834 English trials produced seventy-three convictions. The defendants, who in the past had professed to be believing Christians, increasingly became agnostics, deists, and secularists who relied on freedom of the press more than freedom of religion, with as little success. In the American cases the courts maintained the legal fiction that the law punished only malice, never mere difference of opinion. The law aimed, that is, not at what was said but the way it was said; the judicial cliché on both sides of the Atlantic rested on the doctrine that manner, not matter, determined criminality.

The view that received no judicial endorsement in the nineteenth century was that espoused in 1825 by two old men, John Adams and Thomas Jefferson, who agreed that blasphemy prosecutions conflicted with the principle of free inquiry; Jefferson also sought to prove that Christianity was not part of the law of the land and that religion or irreligion did not belong to the cognizance of government. In 1883 the Lord Chief Justice of England supposedly liberalized the law by holding that decency of expression would exempt from prosecution even an attack on the fundamentals of Christianity—a fairly subjective test.

BIBLIOGRAPHY

Theodore Albert Schroeder's *Constitutional Free Speech Defined and Defended in an Unfinished Argument in a Case of Blasphemy* (1919; New York, 1970) is, despite its misleading title, a comprehensive history by a passionate, freethinking radical lawyer who opposed any restraints on expression. Not factually accurate, it is nevertheless a still useful pioneering work. Gerald D. Nokes's *A History of the Crime of Blasphemy* (London, 1928) also has a misleading title. It is a brief and narrowly legalistic study of English cases only, but is well executed. Leonard W. Levy's *Treason against God: A History of the Offense of Blasphemy* (New York, 1981) is easily the fullest treatment of the concept from Moses to 1700; covering religious thought as well as legal history, it is oversympathetic to victims of prosecution, according to reviewers. A promised sequel will bring the subject up to date. Levy's *Blasphemy in Massachusetts: Freedom of Conscience and the Abner Kneeland Case* (New York, 1973) reprints the major primary sources on the most important American case. Roland Bainton's *Hunted Heretic: The Life and Death of Michael Servetus* (Boston, 1953) is the best introduction to the most important blasphemy case of the Reformation. Donald Thomas's *A Long Time Burning: The History of Literary Censorship in England* (New York, 1969) is a vivid account that views the subject of blasphemy against a broad canvas. William H. Wickwar's *The Struggle for the Freedom of the Press, 1819-1832* (London, 1928) is a splendid, scholarly book that recounts prosecutions for blasphemy in England at a time when they peaked in number. George Holyoake's *The History of the Last Trial by Jury for Atheism in England* (1851; London, 1972) is a short autobiographical account by a freethinking victim of a prosecution. Hypatia Bradlaugh Bonner's *Penalties upon Opinion: Or Some Records of the Laws of Heresy and Blasphemy* (London, 1912) is a short account by an opponent of all blasphemy prosecutions and the daughter of the victim of one. William Wolkovich's *Bay State "Blue" Laws and Bimba* (Brockton, Mass., n. d.) is a well-documented study of a 1926 prosecution. Alan King-Hamilton's *And Nothing But the Truth* (London, 1982) is a judge's autobiography containing a chapter on a noted blasphemy case in England.

LEONARD W. LEVY

BLESSING

The term *blessing* has two fundamental meanings. In its first meaning, it is a form of prayer; it is man's adoration and praise of God. In its second meaning, blessing is a divine gift that descends upon man, nature, or things; it is a material or spiritual benefit that results from divine favor. In this second meaning, blessing is the transfer of a sacred and beneficent power, a power that emanates from the supernatural world and confers a new quality on the object of the blessing.

Phenomenology of Blessing. Man as *homo religiosus* "believes that there is an absolute reality, the *sacred*, that transcends this world but manifests itself in this world, thereby sanctifying it and making it real" (Mircea Eliade, *The Sacred and the Profane*, New York, 1959, p. 202). A blessing is thus a type of hierophany. It is one of those mysterious acts through which a transcendent power becomes immanent in this world. In every blessing, therefore, a power intervenes to bestow benefits of divine origin upon a being or object.

Considered as an action, every blessing includes three elements: first, the establishment of a relationship with the realm of the Wholly Other, which is the source of the desired beneficial effect; second, the transfer, to a being or object, of an efficacious quality emanating from that realm, through some form of mediation; finally, the enhancement of the existence of the being or object that receives this quality.

Power. At different times and places, man has given names to the transcendent power or reality that is the source of all blessings. One of the best known of these is *mana*. Of Melanesian origin, *mana* denotes a supernatural reality attached to beings or things—a reality full of the power, authority, and strength inherent in life and truth. Indeed, the idea of a real and effective power is found again and again in nonliterate traditions throughout the world, receiving such names as *orenda* (Iroquois), *manitou* (Algonquian), *wakan* (Lakota), and *uxbe* (Pueblo). In the high civilizations of antiquity, it appears as *brahman* (India), *tao* (China), *kami* (Japan), *khvarenah* (ancient Iran), *me* (Sumer), and *melammu* (Mesopotamia).

Transfer. However conceived, this transcendent power is transferred to the human realm through the blessing. The divine will can carry out this transfer *motu proprio*, without the aid of an intermediary. Nevertheless, a blessing commonly makes use of some form of mediation. The intermediary, who uses both ritual and symbols, may be a king or a priest, a saint, a prophet, or the head of a family. By ritual means he animates the mysterious forces that make communication with the transcendent power possible and thereby creates a special relationship with the divinity.

The spoken word occupies a special place in the symbolism of mediation. The mystical power of words is particularly prominent among archaic peoples. In Australia, the voices of the bull-roarers, symbols of the Great Spirit's presence, are heard throughout every initiation ceremony. In Vedism, *vac* is the celestial word, an aspect of the *brahman*; and the syllable *om* is believed to encompass the universe, the *brahman*, the sound that gives fullness to the sacrifice. The word is also the instrument of divine power, which may be invoked by the civilizing word, the prophetic word, or in the evocation of holy names. The presence of theophoric names and all manner of incantations in all ancient civilizations demonstrates man's belief in the power of the word. Indeed, the Akkadian *amatu* and the Hebrew *davar* refer to the word understood as coincidental with reality itself.

Gifts and favors. The third element of a blessing is the actual benefit that a being or object receives through contact with the transcendent power. This power is dynamic. The Sanskrit *ojas*, the Avestan *aojo*, and the Latin *augustus* all have the sense of an enabling power, one that literally empowers its possessor to fulfill the religious function allotted to him. In *Genesis* 9:1, God blesses Noah and his sons directly, saying to them, "Be fruitful and multiply." In *Numbers* 6:22-27, the sacerdotal blessing is intended to assure divine protection, benevolence, and peace to the faithful. Blessings may also produce less spiritual results: fertility, health, and long life in men or animals, bountiful harvests, material prosperity. Whatever the nature of the gifts or favors he receives, man is always conscious of their divine origin, acknowledging the transcendent power that lies behind the effectiveness of blessing.

Typology of Blessing. This section presents a selective survey of the great variety of forms of blessing practiced by *homo religiosus* at different times and places. It will classify types of blessing according to the methods of transfer that they employ, the methods that actually set the blessing in motion. In particular, it will focus on three essential aspects of such methods: language, gesture, and ritual.

Religions of peoples with oral traditions. Among peoples without writing, blessing is intimately linked to myth. Indeed, in the life of these peoples, myth constitutes a sacred history that puts man in contact with the supernatural world, joining present and primordial time and linking present action to the initial acts of creation. This sacred history furnishes archaic man with models for his life. In addition, he grasps the meaning of the celestial archetype through the symbolic language of myth; blessing constitutes one of the archaic ritual forms that he uses in his various efforts to orient himself in reference to that archetype. Within the vast magico-religious context of archaic ritual, word and gesture are inseparably linked.

In a great many religious traditions, the sacred word, the word spoken by God, appears at the first moment of creation. Among the Dogon, for example, the Nommo spoke three times, pronouncing words of light, of dampness, and of music. In archaic belief, man's spoken word, addressed to the Wholly Other, allows him to participate in divine power or, at least, to benefit from it. Such a belief, admirably documented in the stone prayer carvings of Valcamonica, underlies the beginnings of prayer and is expressed in the incantations that are part of every people's patrimony—incantations that seek to constrain divine power through the repetition of spoken words. In sub-Saharan Africa, the word

approaches its fullest power to the extent that it is joined with rhythm and image, its most effective mediators. The hand also carries meaning, and among the Dogon, the Bambara, and the Fali, the thumb is the symbol of power. Word, rhythm, and gesture are fully integrated in the rituals associated with myths of fertility and initiation; indeed, when used in celebrations of myth, they reestablish, through the reactualization of

> **Within the vast magico-religious context of archaic ritual, word and gesture are inseparably linked.**

the archetypal event, the complete harmony believed to have existed at the beginning. Africans have created from myth, word, and ritual an effective symbolic unity used to reestablish the original harmony. Ancestors are also important in these rituals, for they exist in primordial time and have a major role in the transfer of favors to the living. Likewise, the human intermediary has an important role in the ritual of blessing.

Among the ethnically related groups in Burundi and Rwanda in central Africa, all religious life revolves around belief in Imana, the supreme being, omnipotent creator, good and omniscient protector of man and nature. A child is placed under Imana's blessing at birth, and on the eighth day his father gives him a name associated with the god. In fact, theophoric names signify Imana's permanent blessing and guidance of those who bear them. Human intermediaries, especially heads of families, play an important role in obtaining the effects of blessing. During Kurya Umwaka, the New Year festival celebrated in Burundi in May, the father presides over a meal that consists of "eating the old year"; acting as both intermediary of the god and head of the family, he distributes food from Imana and pronounces wishes for happiness in the new year.

Symbols of the right hand. A number of Mediterranean and Eastern religions have particularly emphasized the symbolic role of the right hand. In the Syrian cults of Jupiter Dolichenus, Atargatis, and Hadad, as in the Phrygian cult of the god Satazius, votive hands indicate the divine presence and symbolize God's power. Statuaries from both the East and—especially—the West furnish many examples of gods extending their hand in a gesture of blessing and protection; indeed, Zeus is sometimes called Hyperdexios, the protector with the extended hand. This gesture is also represented on effigies of Asklepios, the god of healing. In all these artifacts invoking the vast symbolic system surrounding blessing, the right hand is both a sign of power and the expression of a benevolent divine will, of the gods' transfer of part of their strength and power.

The symbolism of the hand appears in another form in the *dexiosis*, the handshake—always of right hands—that creates mysterious bonds of union. A number of documents concerning the dexiosis come from the Roman world, where the gesture was associated with the *fides*, an agreement of alliance and voluntary, reciprocal obligation. Representations of the *dexiosis* sometimes show clasped hands together with ears of wheat, symbols of the prosperity that comes from concord, itself the result of the divine blessing of the goddess Fides; here, the *dexiosis* shifts notions of concord and obligation into the religious domain of the blessing. The *dexiosis* is found in the liturgy of the cults of Dionysos, Sabazios, and Isis; in all these cults, the ritual signifies both the celestial apotheosis of the god and the entrance of the devout into the elite group of initiates who have received divine gifts. The *dextrarum iunctio* is a gesture binding the initiate to his god's power; as ancient Latin authors wrote, "Felix dextra, salutis humanae pignus."

Dexiosis and blessing in Mithraism and Manichaeism. The *dexiosis* played a major role in the myth and ritual that are intertwined in Mithraic liturgy. A number of illustrated documents from Rome, Dura-Europos (present-day Salahiyeh, Syria), and the Danubian area represent the *dexiosis* of Mithra and Helios, seated together in the celestial chariot; the scene evokes the apotheosis of the young Mithra, conqueror of evil and darkness, and at the same time presents the mythical archetype to which the ritual dexiosis alludes in the Mithraic initiation. At the conclusion of the initiation ceremony, the *pater*, the *magister sacrorum* ("chief priest") of the Mithraic community, welcomes the initiate by extending his right hand to him; by this gesture, the initiate becomes one of the participants in the rite, who then join in the same gesture and are thereby introduced to the cult's salvation mysteries. This dexiosis seals the agreement between Mithra and the initiate and creates a bond that insures the initiate's salvation. By joining their right hands, the initiates take part in the mystic *dexiosis* of Mithra and Helios and at the same time ensure, through this authentic ritual of blessing, the transfer of the benefits of salvation promised by Mithra to those inducted into his mysteries.

The ritual of the *dexiosis* in Mithraic mysteries of the Roman empire has been clarified by evidence recently discovered at Nimrud-Dagh and at Arsameia Nymphaios in the ancient province of Commagene, where Mithraism was a royal cult during the centuries immediately preceding the Christian era. Several representations show the gods Mithra, Herakles, Zeus, and Apollo extending their right hands to King Antiochus I, son of the cult's founder, Mithradates I Kallinikos.

The pattern uniting myth, ritual, and *dexiosis* is found again in Manichaeism in Mani's great myth of the struggle between Light and Darkness. The Living Spirit, second messenger of the Father of Greatness, walks toward the boundary of the Realm of Darkness to save Primordial Man, prisoner of Darkness; he lets out a great cry, "Tochme," heard by Primordial Man, who replies, "Sotme." The Living Spirit then extends his right hand; grasping it, Primordial Man, the savior saved, regains the Paradise of Light. Used similarly in the Manichaean community, the saving gesture of the *dexiosis* became the gnostic gesture *par excellence* since it both symbolized and realized the communication of the dualistic mysteries, the sources of salvation.

Power of the word. The energy of the word is central to Indian religious thought; indeed, the word is considered a power in itself. Sanskrit includes a number of words that are close in meaning to "blessing" or "to bless" or that suggest the result of a blessing: *asis* ("wish, blessing"), *asirvada* ("benediction"), *kusala* ("prosperous"), *dhanya* ("that which brings good fortune"), *kalyana* ("excellent"). The word *brahman* means "sacred word"; originally, it signified "the word that causes growth."

Brahmanaspati, or Brhaspati, is chaplain of the gods, charged with reciting the sacred formulas. As *purohita*, or chief priest of the gods, he is charged with reciting the sacred formulas; they become beneficent in his mouth. Indeed, to be effective, the formulas must be pronounced, but once pronounced they are real, beneficent, and effective by themselves, not through the chaplain's mediation. The Vedic priest, the *brahmana*, sometimes asks for the help of Brahmanaspati, who can suggest effective words to him. "I put a splendid word in your mouth," the *purohita* says to the *brahmana* (Rgveda 10.98.2). Words of blessing are also spoken by the father at the birth of a son: "Be imperishable gold. Truly you are the One called son. Live a hundred autumns."

Blessing in the Hebrew scriptures. The Semitic root *brk*, "bless," was the common property of all peoples of the ancient Near East. In its plural form, *brk* is used to indicate the act of blessing, which may be carried out by God, angels, or men.

In the typology of blessing found in the Hebrew scriptures a first major tendency is exemplified by God's dispensation of benefits among people or among created things generally. After the creation, he blesses the beings he has just made (*Gn.* 1:22-28); after the Flood, he blesses Noah and his children (*Gn.* 9:1). Likewise, he blesses the patriarchs Abraham, Isaac, and Jacob, and finally, all the children of Israel (*Gn.* 12:2-3, 27:16, 35:9; *Dt.* 1:11), all of whom become *barukh*, beneficiaries of divine blessing. This blessing can also apply to nonliving things that assist in the execution of the divine plan: the Sabbath (*Gn.* 2:3), bread and water (*Ex.* 23:25), the home of the righteous (*Prv.* 3:33). Faith in the value of God's blessing underlies the many wishes for good fortune found in the Hebrew scriptures: "Blessed be Abram by God Most High" (*Gn.* 14:19).

In addition, blessing appears in the Old Testament in a truly original way, one that goes well beyond the conventional Semitic meaning of *brk*. To the ancient Hebrews, blessing was also the expression of the divine favor stemming from God's choice of a particular people whom he surrounds with his solicitude. This spiritual and universal idea of divine blessing finds its fullest development in the Covenant and the teachings of the prophets, where the blessing conferred on Abraham becomes a program of salvation upon which God insists (*Gn.* 18:18-19, 22:16-18, 26:4-5, 28:13-15). Israel's mission, which is the Covenant, and the prophetic movement are rooted in God's blessing of Abraham; hence, this blessing is part of the history of salvation.

The second important tendency in the Old Testament typology of blessing involves the blessing conferred by God through an intermediary—family head, king, or priest—charged with a mission. Among the Phoenicians and the

> ## To the ancient Hebrews, blessing was also the expression of the divine favor stemming from God's choice of a particular people. . . .

Arameans, the father of the family was the intermediary, addressing the gods on behalf of his wife and children; among the nomadic clans of Syria and Canaan, the ancestral cult and the chiefs' hereditary authority strongly influenced life in the clan and were, in fact, as important in malediction as in blessing. Nevertheless, while this Semitic heritage is present in certain customs of the chosen people, the Hebrew scriptures are marked chiefly by the presence of God in the midst of the people whom he has chosen for himself and whom he leads through selected intermediaries. Words of blessing pronounced by the king, or in his favor, are rooted in God's choice of David and of his dynasty (*2 Sm.* 7:29, *1 Chr.* 17:27). The father of the family gives his blessing by both the spoken word and the laying on of hands, a practice that seems to be a specific mark of the chosen people. An archetypal rite that goes back to the patriarchal period, the laying on of hands is described at length in Genesis 48:1-20 and appears throughout both the Old and the New Testaments.

Barakah among the Arabs and in Islam. In the pre-Islamic Arab world, *baraka* came to mean "having many descendants"; it also suggested the transfer of strength and fertility from father to children. Additionally, *baraka* meant "to prosper, to enjoy large herds, abundant grasses, and rich harvests"; it denoted a quality in beings and things that brought them prosperity and success. In the Arab mind, the idea seems to have developed of transferring this quality; *barakah* (noun; pl., *barakat*) could be transferred to such acts as kissing a hand or touching a holy object. In popular Islam,

traces of this nomadic notion of *barakah* remain in attitudes toward localities, historical personalities, and sacred objects.

In the uncompromising monotheism of Islam, the omnipotence and omnipresence of God stand at the center of the life of the faithful and the community. God is the source of all that is sacred; the sacred refers only to the will of Allah, the holy God, Al-Quddus, a term that implies the power, strength, and mastery that God alone can possess. In the Qur'an, *barakat* are sent to people by God; *barakah* is God's blessing, the gift that he makes to mortals of the power to dispense his benefits, all of which proceed from him. Linked to the holiness of God, barakah is an influence that proceeds from all that touches God closely: the Qur'an, the Prophet, the Five Pillars of Islam, the mosques, and the saints. Yet because Islam has neither clergy nor ministry, *barakah* finds no human intermediary: all blessing comes from God.

Christian blessing. The Septuagint translates *berekh* with the word *eulogein*, which in the Vulgate is *benedicere*. *Berakhah* is rendered by *eulogia*, a word that can denote either the praise creatures lift up to God or the gifts God makes to his creatures. *Eulogia* results from an act of blessing; it is the blessing itself, the gift given to a being. Eulogesis denotes the act through which the blessing is conferred, the action of the church's minister, who gives the blessing.

The Gospels report a number of Jesus' blessings of persons and things. He blesses little children (*Mk.* 10:16) and the bread that he will multiply (*Mt.* 14:19); immediately before his ascension, he blesses his disciples (*Lk.* 24:50). The editors of *Luke* and *Mark* also recorded Jesus' gestures. He blessed the children by laying his hands on them, while to the disciples he raised his hands in blessing. Such gestures of blessing were already familiar to the Jews. According to the Talmud, the priests gave the blessing in the temple daily, during the morning sacrifice; they remained standing, their arms upraised, during the ceremony.

The expression "Pax vobis," used by Jesus when speaking with his disciples, is an authentic formula of blessing (*Lk.* 24:36, *Jn.* 20:19, 20:21). Christ charges those whom he sends forth to pronounce this blessing in their apostolic work (*Mt.* 10:12, *Lk.* 10:5, *Jn.* 20:21); Paul uses it repeatedly in his letters (*Rom.* 1:7, *Phil.* 4:7, *Col.* 3:15); John of Patmos places it at the beginning of the *Revelation* (*Rv.* 1:4). As the epistles of Ignatius of Antioch attest, the church quickly took up this formula, thus establishing what will become a long ecclesiastical tradition. The "Pax vobis" is by no means intended merely as a polite greeting. It is, rather, a blessing that brings to its recipients the messianic peace, with all that that implies. The apostles' use of the words *charis* ("grace") and *eirene* ("peace") should be understood in the context of this blessing (*Rom.* 1:7, *1 Cor.* 1:7, *1 Pt.* 1:2).

Jesus' words and gestures of blessing passed into the various Christian communities. From the *Clementine Homilies* and the *Acts of Thomas*, it is clear that the ritual of blessing was customary in Christian circles. At a very early date, blessing appears in liturgical regulations such as the *Apostolic Tradition*. In the eyes of the church, the sacerdotal blessing is effective because it comes from God through his priests, who are also his ministers. Hence, the Council of Laodicea (c. 363) prohibited receiving blessings from the hands of heretics, and theologians later defined blessing as a sacred ritual through which the church brings divine favors—primarily spiritual favors—upon people and things.

Ancient documents dealing with rites of blessing are plentiful. Catacomb paintings and references in literature show that in the second century the usual gesture of Christian blessing was the laying on of hands; during the third century, this gesture was gradually replaced by the *sphragis tou Christou* ("the sign of the cross"). Indeed, it is evident from the *Sibylline Oracles*, from writings of Tertullian and Cyril of Jerusalem, and from mural paintings and the first Christian sarcophagi that the sign of the cross pervaded Christian customs from the third century onward. The shift from the laying on of hands to the sign of the cross as the characteristic gesture of blessing, combined with the increased use of prayer formulas, shows that Christians were aware of the transcendence of the ritual of blessing and hence were indifferent about actual physical contact with the hand or hands, and about the hands' position, in the ritual itself. Over the centuries, blessings multiplied and took different forms in different countries; until the Middle Ages, they were grouped with other rites of the church under the general name of sacraments. In the twelfth century, however, from the influence of Hugh of Saint-Victor (d. 1142), Abelard (d. 1142), and Alger of Liège (d. 1131), the denomination of sacred rite was given to blessing, and emphasis in the rite was placed more upon its formula than upon gestures. This emphasis was accentuated by Luther's Reformation. To the reformers, God's presence and action are known and carried out through the word; in the word, therefore, is found the whole effectiveness of blessing.

BIBLIOGRAPHY

Bianchi, Ugo, ed. *Mysteria Mithrae: Proceedings of the International Seminar on the Religio-Historical Character of Roman Mithraism, with Particular Reference to Roman and Ostian Sources, Rome and Ostia, 28-31 March 1978*. Leiden, 1979. Includes numerous documents; a veritable compendium on Mithraism.

Chelhod, Joseph. "La baraka chez les Arabes." *Revue de l'histoire des religions* 148 (July-September 1955): 68-88.

Coppens, Joseph. *L'imposition des mains et les rites connexes dans le Nouveau Testament et dans l'église ancienne*. Paris, 1925.

Eliade, Mircea. *Patterns in Comparative Religion*. New York, 1958.

Junker, Hubert. "Segen als heilsgeschichtliches Motivwort im Alten Testament." In *Sacra Pagina*, edited by Joseph Coppens et al., vol. 1, pp. 548-558. Paris, 1959.

Keller, C. A., and G. Wehmeier. "*Brk*, segnen." In *Theologisches Handwörterbuch zum Alten Testament*, vol. 1, pp. 359-376. Munich, 1971.

Leeuw, Gerardus van der. *Religion in Essence and Manifestation*. 2d ed. 2 vols. New York, 1963.

Leglay, Marcel. "La dexiôsis dans les mystères de Mithra." In *Études mithriaques*, edited by Jacques Duchesne-Guillemin, pp. 279-303. Tehran, 1978. A thorough study of the *dexiosis* in Hellenistic and Roman religions.

Scharbert, Josef. *Solidarität in Segen und Fluch im Alten Testament und in seiner Umwelt*. Bonn, 1958.

Thomas, Louis-Vincent, and René Luneau. *La terre africaine et ses religions*. Paris, 1974.

Walmann, Helmut. *Die kommagenischen Kultreformen unter König Mithradates I: Kallinikos und seinem Sohne Antiochos I*. Leiden, 1973. A precise study of archaeological evidence and Mithraic inscriptions from Commagene.

Westermann, Claus. *Blessing: In the Bible and the Life of the Church*. Philadelphia, 1978.

JULIEN RIES
Translated from French by Jeffrey C. Haight
and Annie S. Mahler

BLOOD

Among the religions of the world one finds many ambivalent or contradictory attitudes toward blood. Blood is perceived as being simultaneously pure and impure, attractive and repulsive, sacred and profane; it is at once a life-giving substance and a symbol of death. Rites involving blood require the intervention of individual specialists (warriors, sacrificers, circumcisers, butchers, or executioners) and always the participation of the group or community.

In many primitive societies, blood is identified as a soul substance: of men, of animals, and even of plants. The Romans said that in it is the *sedes animae* ("seat of life"). In pre-Islamic times, Arabs considered it the vegetative, liquid soul that remains in the body after death, feeding on libations. For the Hebrews, "the life of the flesh is in the blood" (*Lv.* 17:4).

The spilling of blood is often forbidden. This ban applies to certain categories of humans and animals: sacrificial victims, royalty, game, and so on. The Iroquois, the Scythians (Herodotus, 4.60-61), and the old Turco-Mongols, as well as the rulers of the Ottoman empire, forbade shedding the blood of persons of royal lineage. There is reason to believe that the Indian Hindu religions that have abolished sacrifices, and the feasting that goes with sacrifice, have done so more to avoid the shedding of blood than to comply with the dogmas of nonviolence and reincarnation. According to *Genesis* 9:4, the eating of raw meat is forbidden. The Islamic tradition has similar restrictions.

Attitudes toward blood can be divided into two general categories: toward the blood of strangers, foreigners, or enemies and toward the blood of members of one's own community.

The blood of enemies usually is not protected by any taboo. The killing of enemies is sometimes mandatory. Among the Turkic peoples in ancient times and again during the Islamic period in the sixteenth century, an adolescent did not acquire his adulthood, his name, and thus his soul until he committed his first murder.

Within the community, however, attitudes toward blood and killing are different. Members of the community are connected by consanguinity, and they share collective responsibility for one another; the blood of each is the blood of all. The group's totemic animals may be included in this community, which is connected to the animals by adoption or alliance. A stranger can enter the group through marriage of "blood brotherhood," a custom practiced among the Fon of West Africa and among Central Asian peoples.

Murder within the community is forbidden. To kill one's relative is tantamount to shedding one's own blood; it is a crime that draws a curse that lasts for generations. When Cain murdered Abel, Abel's "blood cried out for vengeance," and Cain's descendants suffered as a result. When Oedipus unknowingly killed his father, he gouged out his own eyes to confess his blindness, but his punishment fell upon his children. According to Matthew, after the sentencing of Jesus to be crucified the Jews cried: "Let his blood be upon us and upon our children" (27:25).

A murder between families or between clans is a grave wrong that must be avenged by killing the guilty party. The latter, who in turn becomes the victim, will have his own avenger from among his relatives. Thus develops the cycle of vendetta killing, which can be broken only by "paying the blood price." Vendetta killing is found in ancient Greece, pre-Islamic Arabia, modern Corsica, and among the Nuer of the Sudan.

Under certain circumstances killing is perceived as a creative act, especially in the realm of the gods, where suicide or parricide sometimes leads to birth or new life. Mesopotamian and Babylonian cosmogonies feature gods who were slain in order to give life. The Greek Kronos severed the testicles of his father Ouranos (Sky) with a billhook while the latter lay in a tight embrace with Gaia (Earth). The blood of Ouranos's genital organs gave birth to new beings and, according to some traditions, to Aphrodite herself. This kind of suicide—relinquishing a part to preserve the whole—was sometimes magnified into a supreme act of love or redemption: Odin gave up one eye for the sake of supernatural "vision"; Attis emasculated himself; Abraham was prepared to slit the throat of his only son; Jesus accepted death voluntarily.

Some kinds of sacrifice are centered around blood. [*See* Sacrifice.] Blood is the drink of the gods or the drink shared by mortals with the gods.

In the Christian concept of sacrifice, the slitting of an animal's throat is abolished, and the animal is replaced by the "Lamb of God," Jesus on the cross. Crucifixion and asphyxiation, although not bloody in themselves, are perceived as fundamentally bloody. The sacrifice (at least, as it is understood outside Protestantism) is renewed daily; it is both expiatory and redemptory. The sacrifice is accompanied by a communal meal (Eucharist) where the believer is invited to eat bread, symbolizing the body of Christ, and to drink wine, symbolizing his blood. Charles Guignebert has noted that the bread has been of less interest than the wine; the wine "is the symbolism of blood that dominates in the Eucharist . . . and affirms its doctrinal richness" (Guignebert, 1935, p. 546). Christ, who offers the cup to his disciples, says, "This is the blood of the new testament that is shed for many for the remission of sins."

Judaism had already established that the covenant between God and his people was one of blood, of circumcision and sacrifice. Moses sprinkled the people with the blood of sacrificed bulls, saying, "Behold the blood of the covenant which the Lord hath made with you" (*Ex.* 24:8).

The idea of establishing a covenant through blood is found in many cultures. Some peoples in Central Asia, in Siberia, and on the steppes of eastern Europe cut a dog or other animal in two to seal a treaty or to take a solemn oath, thus guaranteeing their loyalty. The protective force of blood is illustrated in the covenant between God and Israel in *Exodus* 13:7-13; the Israelites, remaining in their homes, which were marked with blood, were spared from the death that struck the Egyptians. A similar idea is expressed in Indonesia when the doors and pillars of houses are smeared with blood during sacrifices of domestic dedication.

Blood can eliminate flaws and weaknesses. In Australia, a young man would spread his blood on an old man in order to rejuvenate him. Some Romans, in honor of Attis, emasculated themselves and celebrated the *dendrophoria* by beating their backs, hoping thus to escape the disease of death and to wash themselves of its stain. Similarly, Shi`i flagellants relive the martyrdom of Husayn ibn `Ali, grandson of the prophet Muhammad.

The most common type of self-inflicted wound is circumcision. In the female the incision of the clitoris sometimes corresponds with this rite. Male circumcision is required in Hebrew tradition, where it is the sign of a covenant with God. It is common also in Islam. Many explanations have been given for this almost universal rite. It is seen primarily as a manifestation of the desire to eliminate any traces of femininity in the male. If the sexual act is considered a defilement, the removal of the foreskin could, in effect, rid the sexual organ of impurity transmitted from the mother. Yet there are some societies where the circumcised male is considered to be as impure as the menstruating female.

BIBLIOGRAPHY

Nearly all works on the history of religions mention blood, but there are no valuable monographs on the subject other than G. J. M. Desse's *Le sang dans le rite* (Bordeaux, 1933). The reader is referred also to Lucien Lévy-Bruhl's *The "Soul" of the Primitive* (New York, 1928) and to Mircea Eliade's *Rites and Symbols of Initiation* (New York, 1958). Numerous facts on the topic are found in Bronislaw Malinowski's *Sex and Repression in Savage Society* (London, 1927) and *Crime and Custom in Savage Society* (New York, 1926). W. Robertson Smith's *Lectures on the Religion of the Semites*, 3d ed. (London, 1927), is still fundamental in the study of sacrifice. Charles Guignebert discusses the symbolism of blood as found in the Christian Eucharist in *Jesus* (London, 1935). On circumcision, see B. J. F. Laubscher's *Sex, Custom and Psychopathology* (London, 1937). On blood brotherhood, see Georges Davy's *La foi jurée* (Paris, 1922). Bruno Bettelheim's *Symbolic Wounds: Puberty Rites and the Envious Male* (Glencoe, Ill., 1954) and Paul Hazoumé's *Le pacte de sang au Dahomey* (Paris, 1937) are also worth consulting.

JEAN-PAUL ROUX
Translated from French by Sherri L. Granka

BODHIDHARMA

BODHIDHARMA (fl. c. 480–520), known in China as Ta-mo and in Japan as Daruma; traditionally considered the twenty-eighth patriarch of Indian Buddhism and the founder of the Ch`an (Jpn., Zen) school of Chinese Buddhism.

The "Historical" Bodhidharma. Accounts of Bodhidharma's life have been based until recently on largely hagiographical materials. However, the discovery of new documents among the Tun-huang manuscripts found in Central Asia at the turn of this century has led scholars to question the authenticity of these accounts. The oldest text in which Bodhidharma's name is mentioned is the *Lo-yang ch`ieh-lan chi*, a description of Buddhist monasteries in Lo-yang written in 547 by Yang Hsüan-chih. In this work, a monk called Bodhidharma from "Po-ssu in the western regions" (possibly Persia) is said to have visited and admired the Yung-ning Monastery. Consequently, Bodhidharma's visit must have taken place around 520. But no other biographical details can be inferred from this, and the aged western monk (he was purportedly one hundred and fifty years old at the time) bears no resemblance to the legendary founder of Chinese Ch`an.

The most important source for Bodhidharma's life is the *Hsü kao-seng chuan*, a work written by Tao-hsüan in 645 and revised before his death in 667. It states that Bodhidharma was a brahman from southern India. After studying the Buddhist tradition of the Greater Vehicle (Mahayana), Bodhidharma decided to travel to China in order to spread Mahayana doctrine. In Lo-yang, he attempted to win converts, apparently without great success. Nonetheless, he eventually acquired two worthy disciples, Hui-k`o (487–593) and Tao-yü (dates unknown), who studied with him for several years. He is said to have transmitted the *Lankavatara Sutra*, the scripture he deemed best fitted for Chinese practitioners, to Hui-k`o. Bodhidharma seems also to have met with some hostility and slander. Tao-hsüan stresses that Bodhidharma's teaching, known as "wall-gazing" (*pi-kuan*),

> That Bodhidharma's teachings evoked hostility in China is evident from the fact that after his death, his disciple Hui-k`o felt it necessary to hide for a period.

or as the "two entrances" (via "principle," *li-ju*, and via "practice," *hsing-ju*), was difficult to understand compared to the more traditional and popular teachings of Seng-ch`ou (480–560). Tao-hsüan states that Bodhidharma died on the banks of the Lo River. That Bodhidharma's teachings evoked hostility in China is evident from the fact that after his death, his disciple Hui-k`o felt it necessary to hide for a period. Since the locale mentioned is known to have been an execution ground, it is possible that Bodhidharma was executed during the late Wei rebellions.

Although Tao-hsüan's account is straightforward, succinct, and apparently fairly authentic, it presents some problems. Most important, it presents two different, almost contradictory, images of Bodhidharma—as a practicer of "wall-gazing," intent on not relying on the written word, and as a partisan of the *Lankavatara Sutra*. Primarily, he draws on the preface to the so-called *Erh-ju ssu-hsing lun* (Treatise on the Two Entrances and Four Practices), written around 600 by Bodhidharma's (or Hui-k`o's) disciple T`an-lin (dates unknown) and on information concerning the reputed transmission of the *Lankavatara Sutra*. This latter had probably been given to Tao-hsüan by Fa-ch`ung (587?–665), an heir of the tradition. In any case, at the time of Tao-hsüan's writing, Bodhidharma was not yet considered the twenty-eighth patriarch of Indian Buddhism.

**The Legend of Bodhidharma within the Ch`an Sect.** According to the *Ch`uan fa-pao chi*, Bodhidharma practiced wall-gazing at Sung-shan monastery for several years. He thus became known as the "wall-gazing brahman," the monk who remained without moving for nine years in meditation in a cave on Sung-shan (eventually losing his legs, as the popular iconography depicts him). There he also met Hui-k`o, who, to show his earnestness in searching for the Way, cut off his own arm. (The *Ch`uan fa-pao chi* severely criticizes Tao-hsüan for claiming that Hui-k`o had his arm cut off by bandits.) This tradition, fusing with the martial tradition that developed at Sung-shan, resulted in Bodhidharma becoming the "founder" of the martial art known as Shao-lin boxing (Jpn., Shorinji kempo).

Bodhidharma's legend continued to develop with the *Li-tai fa-pao chi* (c. 774), the *Pao-lin chuan* (801), and the *Tsu-t`ang chi* (Kor., *Chodangjip*, 952), and reached its classical stage in 1004 with the *Ching-te chuan-teng lu*. In the process, it borrowed features from other popular Buddhist or Taoist figures such as Pao-chih or Fu Hsi (alias Fu Ta-shih, "Fu the Mahasattva," 497-569, considered an incarnation of Maitreya). But its main aspects were already fixed at the beginning of the eighth century.

It is also noteworthy that many early Ch`an works formerly attributed to Bodhidharma have recently been proved to have been written by later Ch`an masters such as Niu-t`ou Fa-jung (594-657) or Shen-hsiu (606-706). That so many works were erroneously attributed to Bodhidharma may be due simply to the fact that the Ch`an school was at the time known as the Bodhidharma school, and that all works of the school could thus be considered expressive of Bodhidharma's thought. Whatever the case, these works have greatly contributed to the development of Bodhidharma's image, especially in the Japanese Zen tradition. Further confusing the issue is the "discovery," throughout the eighth century, of epitaphs supposedly written shortly after his death. In fact, these epitaphs were products of the struggle for hegemony among various factions of Ch`an.

Bodhidharma in Popular Religion. The *Genkoshaku-sho*, a well-known account of Japanese Buddhism written by a Zen monk named Kokan Shiren (1278-1346), opens with the story of Bodhidharma crossing over to Japan to spread his teachings (a development of the iconographic tradition representing him crossing the Yangtze River). In Japan, Bodhidharma's legend seems to have developed first within the Tendai (Chin., T`ien-t`ai) tradition brought from China at the beginning of the Heian period (794-1191). Kojo (779-858), a Japanese monk, was instrumental in linking the Bodhidharma legend to the Tendai tradition and to the legend of the regent Shotoku (Shotoku Taishi, 574-622), who was considered a reincarnation of Nan-yüeh Hui-ssu (515-577), one of the founders of the T`ien-t`ai school. In his *Denjutsu isshin kaimon*, a work presented to the emperor, Kojo mentions the encounter that took place near Kataoka Hill (Nara Prefecture) between Shotoku and a strange, starving beggar—considered a Taoist immortal in the version of the story given by the *Kojiki*. Kojo, arguing from a former legendary encounter between Hui-ssu and Bodhidharma on Mount T`ien-t`ai in China, and from Bodhidharma's prediction that both would be reborn in Japan, has no difficulty establishing that the beggar was none other than Bodhidharma himself.

This amalgam proved very successful and reached far beyond the Tendai school. Toward the end of the Heian period a Zen school emerged from the Tendai tradition, and its leader, Dainichi Nonin (dates unknown), labeled it the

"Japanese school of Bodhidharma" (Nihon Darumashu). This movement was a forerunner of the Japanese Zen sect.

But it is in popular religion that Bodhidharma's figure developed most flamboyantly. Early in China, Bodhidharma not only borrowed features from Taoist immortals but became completely assimilated by the Taoist tradition; there are several Taoist works extant concerning Bodhidharma. In Japan, Bodhidharma's legend developed in tandem with that of Shotoku Taishi; a temple dedicated to Daruma is still to be found on the top of Kataoka Hill.

BIBLIOGRAPHY

Demiéville, Paul. "Appendice sur 'Damoduolo' (Dharmatra[ta])." In *Peintures monochromes de Dunhuang* (Dunhuang baihua), edited by Jao Tsong-yi, Pierre Ryckmans, and Paul Demiéville. Paris, 1978. A valuable study of the Sino-Tibetan tradition that merged Bodhidharma and the Indian translator Dharmatrata into a single figure, which was subsequently incorporated into the list of the eighteen legendary disciples of the Buddha.

Dumoulin, Heinrich. "Bodhidharma und die Anfänge des Ch`an-Buddhismus." *Monumenta Nipponica* (Tokyo) 7, no. 1 (1951): 67-83. A good summary of the first Sino-Japanese re-examinations of the early Ch`an tradition.

Sekiguchi Shindai. *Daruma no kenkyu*. Tokyo, 1967. An important work, with an abstract in English, on the Chinese hagiographical tradition concerning Bodhidharma.

Yanagida Seizan. *Daruma*. Tokyo, 1981. The most recent and authoritative work on Bodhidharma. It examines the historical evidence and the development of the legend in Ch`an (Zen) and in Japanese popular religion and also provides a convenient translation in modern Japanese of Bodhidharma's thought as recorded in the *Erh-ju ssu-hsing lun*.

BERNARD FAURE

BODHISATTVA PATH

Etymologically, *bodhisattva* is a term compounded out of *bodhi*, meaning here "enlightenment [of the Buddha]," and *sattva*, denoting "living being." Thus, *bodhisattva* refers either to a person who is seeking *bodhi* or a "*bodhi* being," that is, a being destined to attain Buddhahood.

In early Buddhism and in conservative schools such as the Theravada, the term *bodhisattva* designates a Buddha-to-be. It refers in this context merely to one of a very limited number of beings in various states of existence prior to their having attained enlightenment. Its principal use was thus confined to the previous lives of the Buddha Sakyamuni; however, the existence of other *bodhisattvas* in aeons past was acknowledged, as was the bodhisattvahood of the future Buddha, Maitreya.

History and Development of the Term. Early Buddhism maintained that there was only one Buddha in any one epoch within our world system. The career of the being destined to become the Buddha Gautama was held to have begun with a vow *(pranidhana)* to attain enlightenment taken before another Buddha (Dipamkara) ages ago. This vow was confirmed by a prophecy *(vyakarana)* by Dipamkara that at such-and-such a time and such-and-such a place the being who had taken this vow would become the Buddha for our particular world age. During countless subsequent births the future Buddha labored to perfect himself in a variety of virtues *(paramitas,* "perfections"), principal among which were wisdom *(prajña)* and selfless giving *(dana).* This mythic structure was also held to obtain for Buddhas in other epochs, all of whom had uttered a vow, undertaken religious practices *(bhavana),* and perfected themselves in various ways prior to their enlightenment. This religious path, then, was conceived as the exclusive domain of a very small number of beings (eight or twenty-five by the most common reckonings), whose appearance in the world as Buddhas was deemed metaphorically "as rare as the appearance of the udumbara blossom."

Often, the *bodhisattva* path is held to be one of three vehicles to liberation: the path of the *bodhisattva,* the path of the *arhat,* and a path that culminates in a Buddhahood attained by one who has never heard the Dharma preached, but who by his own efforts naturally comes to an understanding of *pratitya-samutpada* (the doctrine of causality).

Bodhisattva Practice. The career of the *bodhisattva* is traditionally held to begin when the devotee first conceives the aspiration for enlightenment *(bodhicitta)* and formulates a vow to become a Buddha and work for the weal of all beings. The uttering of this vow has profound axiological consequences for the *bodhisattva*: henceforth, it will be the vow that will be the ultimate controlling factor in one's karmic destiny, inaugurating one on a path of spiritual perfection that will take aeons to complete. The specific contents of this vow vary from case to case: all *bodhisattvas* take certain vows in common, among which, of course, are the resolve to postpone one's own enlightenment indefinitely while endeavoring to save others, to freely transfer merit to others, and so forth; but the *sutras* also record vows specific to the great figures of the Buddhist pantheon. Amitabha, for instance, while the *bodhisattva* Dharmakara, is said to have formulated a series of vows in which he resolves to create a "Pure Land" where beings can be reborn to hear the Dharma preached by a Buddha. The *Dasabhumika Sutra* enumerates ten "great aspirations" *(mahapranidhana)* of the *bodhisattva,* among which are the resolve to provide for the worship of all Buddhas, to maintain the Buddha's Dharma, to bring all beings to spiritual maturity, and to practice the *paramitas.*

Ultimately, the *bodhisattva path* calls for the practitioner to perfect a series of six or ten virtues called *paramitas,* "perfections." The enumeration of six virtues, found in such texts

as the Prajñaparamita Sutras or the Lotus, consists of *dana* ("giving"), *sila* ("morality, the precepts"), *ksanti* ("patience, forbearance"), *virya* ("effort"), *dhyana* ("contemplation"), and *prajña* ("transcendental insight"). Later texts such as the *Dasabhumika Sutra* add *upaya* ("skill in means"), *pranidhana* ("resolution," i. e., the *bodhisattva* vow), *bala* ("strength"), and *jñana* ("knowledge").

Another enumeration of *bodhisattva* practices is afforded by the thirty-seven so-called *bodhipaksya dharmas,* or "principles conducive to enlightenment." These comprehend four *smrtyupasthanani,* or "states of mind fulness"; four *prahanani,* or "abandonments"; four *rddhipadah,* or "elements of supernatural power"; the five *indriyani,* or "moral faculties"; five *balani,* or "moral powers"; seven *bodhyangani,* or "components of perception"; and the Noble Eightfold Path.

Bodhisattva Disciplines. The disciplines of the *bodhisattva* are set forth in the *Bodhisattvabhumi,* traditionally ascribed to Maitreyanatha. Here are described the so-called Threefold Pure Precepts of the *bodhisattva: samvarasila,* or adherence to the Pratimoksa, aims at suppressing all evil acts on the part of the practitioner; *kusaladharma samgrahakam silam,* "practicing all virtuous deeds," aims at cultivating the roots of virtuous acts *(karman)* of body, speech, and mind; *sattvartha-kriya silam,* "granting mercy to all beings," aims at inculcating in others the practice of compassion and mercy toward all beings. The latter two practices comprise the specifically Mahayana component of the *bodhisattva* discipline, emphasizing as they do not merely the suppression of unwholesome acts but the positive injunction to do good on behalf of others. Another text, the *Brahmajala Sutra* (Sutra of Brahma's Net), was widely esteemed in East Asia as a source of precepts for *bodhisattvas.* Although in China monks continue to be ordained according to the Vinaya of the Dharmaguptaka school, in Japan, the *Brahmajala Sutra* provided a set of Mahayana precepts (Jpn., *bonmokai)* observed by Tendai ordinands in lieu of the Vinaya altogether. Other Mahayana precepts appear in the *Bodhisattvapratimoksa Sutra* (identical with the *Vinayaviniscaya-upalipariprccha)* and the *Srimaladevi Sutra.* The vows of Queen Srimala in this latter work constitute a discipline all their own, prohibiting transgressions against morality, thoughts of anger, covetousness, jealousy, and disrespect toward others, and enjoining liberality, sympathy, help to those in need, and faith and confidence in the Dharma.

BIBLIOGRAPHY

Dayal, Har. *The Bodhisattva Doctrine in Buddhist Sanskrit Literature* (1932). Reprint, Delhi, 1970.

Kajiyama Yuichi. "On the Meaning of the Words Bodhisattva and Mahasattva." In *Indological and Buddhist Studies: Articles in Honor of Professor J. W. de Jong,* edited by L. A. Hercus et al., pp. 253-270. Canberra, 1982.

Nakamura Hajime. *Indian Buddhism: A Survey with Bibliographical Notes*. Osaka, 1980.

NAKAMURA HAJIME

Bonhoeffer, Dietrich

BONHOEFFER, DIETRICH (1906-1945), Lutheran pastor, theologian, and martyr. A student of Adolf von Harnack, Bonhoeffer was deeply influenced by the writings of the young Karl Barth. From 1930 to 1931, he studied at Union Theological Seminary in New York with Reinhold Niebuhr. He then returned to Berlin, teaching theology and becoming student chaplain and youth secretary in the ecumenical movement.

As early as 1933 Bonhoeffer was struggling against the nazification of the churches and against the persecution of the Jews. Disappointed by the churches' nonaction against Nazism, he accepted a pastorate for Germans in London. However, when the Confessing church (i. e., Christians who resisted Nazi domination) founded its own seminaries, he returned to Germany to prepare candidates for ordination, a task he considered the most fulfilling of his life. As a result of this work, he was forbidden to teach at the University of Berlin. In 1939, after conflicts with the Gestapo, he accepted an invitation to the United States, again to Union Theological Seminary. After four weeks, however, he returned to Germany, convinced he would be ineffectual in the eventual renewal of his nation were he to live elsewhere during its most fateful crisis. He then became an active member of the conspiracy against Hitler. On 5 April 1943 he was imprisoned on suspicion. After the plot to assassinate Hitler failed, Bonhoeffer was hanged (April 1945), along with five thousand others (including three other members of his family).

Bonhoeffer's writings have been widely translated. His early work reflects his search for a concrete theology of revelation. His first dissertation, "Sanctorum Communio," published in Germany in 1930, relates the revelational character of the church to its sociological features. An original statement at the time, it remains evocative. His second dissertation, "Act and Being," was written in 1931 against a background of such opposing philosophies as Kantian transcendentalism and Heideggerian ontology.

Turning to the actual life of the church and to criticism of it, Bonhoeffer, in 1937, published his controversial *The Cost of Discipleship* (New York, 1963). Asserting that "cheap grace is the deadly enemy of our Church," this work, which is based on the Sermon on the Mount, critiques a Reformation heritage that breaks faith and obedience asunder. In *Life Together* (New York, 1976), Bonhoeffer's most widely read

book, the author considers experiments to renew a kind of monastic life for serving the world.

The most influential of Bonhoeffer's posthumous publications has become *Letters and Papers from Prison* (New York, 1972). Among his daily observations was a vision of a future Christianity ready for "messianic suffering" with Christ in a "nonreligious world." To Bonhoeffer "religion" was a province separated from the whole of life—providing cheap escapism for the individual—and a tool in the hands of the powers that be for continuing domination of dependent subjects. Bonhoeffer was critical of Western Christianity because of its complicity with the Holocaust; his letters reveal his conviction that a life with Christ means "to exist for others." It was his belief in a "religionless Christianity"—that is, a praying church that responds to Christ out of the modern (not sinless) strength of human beings and their decisions—that enabled Bonhoeffer to begin to write a revised theology of "Jesus, the man for others," and to participate in the conspiratorial counteraction against the deadly forces of Hitler.

Bonhoeffer's thought emerged from his cultural heritage of German liberalism. He suffered when he experienced its weakness in the face of Nazism. He rethought this heritage within a Christocentric theology, thus becoming a radical critic of his contemporary church and of contemporary theology because they seemed to him to touch only the insignificant corners of life.

BIBLIOGRAPHY

For a comprehensive listing of primary and secondary literature, see Clifford J. Green's "Bonhoeffer Bibliography: English Language Sources," *Union Seminary Quarterly Review* (New York) 31 (Summer 1976): 227-260. This admirable work is continually revised and amended in *The News Letter* of the English Language Section of the International Bonhoeffer Society for Archival Research.

In addition to the works by Bonhoeffer mentioned in the article, see three collections of letters, lectures, and notes titled *No Rusty Swords* (New York, 1965), *The Way to Freedom* (New York, 1966), and *True Patriotism* (New York, 1973). For works about Bonhoeffer, see my *Dietrich Bonhoeffer: Theologian, Christian, Contemporary*, 3d abr. ed. (New York, 1970); André Dumas's *Dietrich Bonhoeffer: Theologian of Reality* (New York, 1971); Clifford J. Green's *The Sociality of Christ and Humanity: Dietrich Bonhoeffer's Early Theology, 1927-1933* (Missoula, Mont., 1972); and Keith W. Clements's *A Patriotism for Today: Dialogue with Dietrich Bonhoeffer* (Bristol, 1984).

EBERHARD BETHGE

Boniface

BONIFACE (673-754), the most distinguished in the group of English missionaries who, in the eighth and succeeding centuries, felt impelled to cross the seas and to preach the gospel to the peoples of the continent of Europe who were still non-Christians. Winfrith, to whom the pope, as tradition has it, gave the name Boniface in 722, was a missionary, founder of monasteries, diffuser of culture, and church organizer. Born in Devonshire, he was introduced to monastic life at an early age. Here he grew up in an atmosphere of strict observance of the Benedictine rule and acceptance of the vivid culture which was spreading abroad from Northumbria. His many gifts would have assured him of a distinguished career in the growing English church but he felt within himself an intense inner call to carry the gospel to the as yet non-Christian world.

In 719, Winfrith made the journey to Rome and received a commission from the pope as missionary to the Frankish lands. This commission was later strengthened by his consecration as bishop.

The first period of Boniface's work was marked by notable successes in Hesse and Thuringia. At Geismar he dared to fell the sacred oak of Thor. This episode was understood by the people of the time as a conflict between two gods. When Boniface felled the oak and suffered no vengeance from the resident Germanic god, it was clear that the God whom he preached was the true God who alone is to be worshipped and adored.

Boniface was successful in securing the confidence and support, first of the all-powerful Frankish ruler, Charles Martel, and, after Charles's death in 741, of Martel's sons Carloman and Pépin. This helped Boniface greatly in his work of restoring or creating order in the churches in the dominions of the Franks, the goal of his second period of the work. He was successful in creating four bishoprics in Bavaria, where churches existed but without settled order. He also called into being four dioceses in the territories to the east of the Rhine. During this period he brought in many colleagues, both men and women, and founded a number of religious houses.

Until 747 Boniface had been a primate and archbishop without a diocese. In 747 he was appointed archbishop of Mainz. In the meantime his influence had extended westward, until it was felt in many parts of what is now France. In 742 he was able to hold a synod of the French churches, commonly known as the German Council, and in 744 an even more important meeting at Soissons. It is to be noted that the decrees of the earlier council were issued in the name of Carloman and became the law of the church as well as of the state.

Two special features of the work of Boniface are to be noted. Boniface was too busy to become an accomplished scholar but was deeply concerned for the spread of culture and used his monasteries as centers for the diffusion of knowledge. He himself wrote Latin clearly and elegantly, coming between the over-elaborate style of Aldhelm (d. 709) and the rather flat scholastic Latin of the Middle Ages.

In 752, Boniface, feeling that his work was done, and perhaps wearied by the increasing opposition of the Frankish churchmen to the English dominance, resigned all his offices and returned as a simple missionary to Friesland, where he had begun his missionary career. Great success marked the first year of this enterprise. But on 4 June 754 Boniface and his companions found themselves surrounded by a band of

> **Boniface . . . used his monasteries as centers for the diffusion of knowledge.**

pagans, determined to put a stop to the progress of the gospel. Boniface forbade armed resistance, and he and fifty-three of his followers met their death with the quiet fortitude of Christian martyrs.

BIBLIOGRAPHY

The primary authority is the large collection of the letters of Boniface, to be found in Latin, *Bonifacius: Die Briefe des heiligen Bonifacius and Lullus*, vol. 1 (Berlin, 1916), admirably edited by Michael Tangl. A good many of these letters are available in English in *The Anglo-Saxon Missionaries in Germany*, edited and translated by Charles H. Talbot (New York, 1954). For those who read German the outstanding modern work is Theodor Schieffer's *Winfrid Bonifatius und die christliche Grundlegung Europas* (Darmstadt, 1972). In English the pioneer work is William Levison's *England and the Continent in the Eighth Century* (Oxford, 1946). Among more popular works, Eleanor S. Duckett's *Anglo-Saxon Saints and Scholars* (New York, 1947), pages 339-455, can be specially recommended as both scholarly and readable.

STEPHEN C. NEILL

BOOTH, WILLIAM

BOOTH, WILLIAM (1829-1912), English evangelist, founder of the Salvation Army. William Booth was born on 10 April 1829 in Nottingham, England, to Samuel and Mary Moss Booth. The elder Booth, an unsuccessful building contractor, and his wife were no more than conventionally religious, but William, intelligent, ambitious, zealous, and introspective, was earnest about Christianity from an early age. He was converted at the age of fifteen and two years later gave himself entirely to the service of God as the result of the preaching of James Caughey, a visiting American Methodist revivalist. From the age of thirteen until he was twenty-two Booth worked as a pawnbroker's assistant, first in Nottingham, then London. His zeal and compassion for the poor drove him to preach in the streets and, in 1852, to become a licensed

Methodist minister. Although Booth had been forced by his father's financial ruin to withdraw from a good grammar school at age thirteen, he read avidly, sought instruction from older ministers, and developed an effective style in speech and writing. In 1855 he married Catherine Mumford, a woman of original and independent intelligence and great moral courage, who had a strong influence on him. They had eight children.

In 1861 Booth began to travel as an independent and successful evangelist, sometimes appearing with Catherine, who publicly advocated an equal role for women in the pulpit. In 1865 the couple established a permanent preaching mission among the poor in the East End of London. This new endeavor, which soon included small-scale charitable activities for the poor, was known for several years as the Christian Mission. In 1878 the mission was renamed the Salvation Army.

The military structure suggested by the new name appealed to the Booths and to the co-workers they had attracted to their work. Booth remained an orthodox Methodist in doctrine, preaching the necessity of repentance and the promise of holiness—a voluntary submission to God that opened to the believer a life of love for God and for humankind. A premillennialist as well, he was convinced that the fastest way to complete the work of soul winning that would herald the return of Christ was to establish flying squads of enthusiasts who would spread out over the country at his command. The General, as Booth was called, saw evangelism as warfare against Satan over the souls of men; the militant tone of scripture and hymn were not figurative to Booth and his officers, but literal reality. The autocracy of military command was well suited to Booth's decisive and uncompromising personality; and it appealed both to his close associates, who were devoted to him and who sought his counsel on every matter, and to his "soldiers," recently saved from sin, most of them uneducated, new to religion, and eager to fit themselves into the great scheme.

William and Catherine were convinced from the beginning of their work in London that it was their destiny to carry the gospel to those untouched by existing religious efforts; to them this meant the urban poor. Their sympathy for these people led them to supplement their evangelism by immediate and practical relief. They launched campaigns to awaken the public to the worst aspects of the life of the poor. Soup kitchens, men's hostels, and "rescue homes" for converted prostitutes and unwed mothers became essential parts of the Army's program.

In 1890 William Booth published *In Darkest England and the Way Out*, which contained a full-fledged program to uplift and regenerate the "submerged tenth" of urban society. The heart of the scheme was a sequence of "city colonies" (urban missions for the unemployed), "land colonies" (where rest would be combined with retraining in agricultural skills), and "overseas colonies" (assisted emigration to America or one of Britain's colonies). The book also explained existing programs like the rescue homes and promised many new schemes in addition to the colonies: the "poor man's lawyer," the "poor man's bank," clinics, industrial schools for poor children, missing-persons inquiries, a "matrimonial bureau," and a poor-man's seaside resort, "Whitechapel-by-the-Sea." *The Darkest England* scheme was widely endorsed.

Booth would not have claimed to be a saint in any conventional sense. Always overworked and chronically unwell, he often had strained relationships with his close associates, especially after the death of Catherine in 1890. Many of his statements about the Army overlooked the fact that much of its program was not original. He offered no criticism of the basic social and political structure that surrounded him, and his confidence in the desirability of transferring the urban unemployed to the more healthful and "natural" environment of the country was romantic and impractical. Yet the fact remains that Booth combined old and new techniques of evangelism and social relief in an immensely effective and appealing program.

Guileless and unsentimental, Booth showed a rare and genuine single-mindedness in the cause of evangelism. His last public message, delivered three months before his death on 20 August 1912, is still cherished by the Army that is his most fitting memorial. The concluding words of the message were these: "While there yet remains one dark soul without the light of God, I'll fight—I'll fight to the very end!"

[*See also* Salvation Army.]

BIBLIOGRAPHY

William Booth has received surprisingly little attention from serious scholarship. Incomparably the best published biography remains St. John Ervine's *God's Soldier: General William Booth*, 2 vols. (New York, 1935). Harold Begbie's *The Life of General William Booth, the Founder of the Salvation Army*, 2 vols. (New York, 1920) is still valuable. William Booth's *In Darkest England and the Way Out* (1890; reprint, London, 1970) is indispensable to an understanding of Booth and his work. The best biography of Catherine Booth remains that of her son-in-law, Commissioner Frederick de Latour Booth-Tucker, *The Life of Catherine Booth, the Mother of the Salvation Army*, 2 vols. (London, 1892).

EDWARD H. MCKINLEY

BORNEAN RELIGIONS

From earliest times, the coasts of Borneo have been visited by travelers going between ancient centers of civilization in Asia. Since the sixteenth century Islam has slowly spread from coastal trading centers, such as Brunei in the north and Banjarmasin in the south. Immigrant Chinese have brought the practices of their homeland, and in the last century Christian missionaries have been increasingly successful in the interior, prompting syncretic revivalist cults. Of the indigenous religions of the great island many of these have passed out of existence or are imminently about to do so without being studied in depth.

Ethnic Diversity. All the indigenous peoples of Borneo speak Austronesian languages, but they exhibit bewildering ethnic diversity. There is still no generally agreed upon taxonomy, and many of the most familiar ethnic terms are vague.

The General Concept of Religion. Many of the cultures of interior Borneo lack the concept of a separate domain of religion. Instead, ritual observance is incorporated into a spectrum of prescribed behaviors that includes legal forms, marriage practices, etiquette, and much else. All of these are matters of collective representations shared by autonomous communities.

The religions of interior Borneo are rich in both ritual and cosmology. In perhaps the best known account, Schärer (1963) describes the subtle notions of the godhead found among the Ngaju, replete with dualistic aspects of upper world and underworld, multilayered heavens, and complex animal and color symbolism. Other peoples have comparably extensive spirit worlds. Because of the archaeologically attested antiquity of contact with India, some authors have discerned elements of Hindu belief. Schärer (1963, p. 13) attributes one of the names of the Ngaju supreme deity to an epoch of Indian influence. In the north there are features of the religion—for instance, in number symbolism—that may indicate influence from China, but there is no overall similarity to Indian or Chinese religions.

The Prominence of Mortuary Ritual. One element of ancient Southeast Asian provenance is a central feature of many Bornean religions: a focus on death and, in particular, on secondary treatment of the dead. This mortuary complex has been associated with Borneo at least since the publication of Robert Hertz's classic essay (1907). By no means did all interior peoples practice secondary disposal in recent times. The custom is found across much of the southern third of the island but has only a scattered distribution further north. Stöhr (1959) surveys the variety of death rites across the island. Where secondary treatment occurs, it is part of an extended ritual sequence, often the most elaborate of that religion (Metcalf, 1982).

Agricultural Rites. Major calendrical rituals are usually coordinated with the agricultural cycle. This is especially true among the Iban, who speak of the soul of the rice in anthropomorphic terms, and focus rites upon it at every stage of cultivation (Jensen, 1974, pp. 151-195).

Head-hunting Rites. Head-hunting is another practice commonly associated with Borneo. Formerly prevalent, it usually occurred in the context of warfare or as an adjunct to mortuary rites. Frequently heads were required in order to terminate the mourning period for community leaders. In contrast to other parts of Southeast Asia, heads were the focus of much ritual.

Ritual Specialists. Even in societies with little technological and political specialization, ritual specialists are important. But there is great variation in the particular combinations of roles played by priest, shaman, and augur. Women often play a major part. Among the Dusun of northern Borneo, for example, priestesses officiate at all major rituals (Evans, 1953, p. 42). Often in association with death rites there are psychopomps to conduct the deceased to the land of the dead. Often the major function of priests and priestesses is to recite long chants that deal with mythical events. Ritual is often accompanied by the sacrifice of chickens, pigs, or buffalo.

Shamanism is found everywhere and typically involves the recovery of errant souls through séances.

Ritual and Social Differentiation. Some societies of interior Borneo are hierarchically stratified, while others are egalitarian. But even in the latter, major public rituals are closely bound up with the forms of leadership and social control. There is a dearth of rites of prestation, in which wealth passes between similar collectivities. This may in part be a result of social organization that is predominantly cognatic.

BIBLIOGRAPHY

Evans, Ivor H. N. *The Religion of the Tempasuk Dusuns of North Borneo.* Cambridge, 1953. Describes in list format the beliefs and ceremonies of a subgroup of the extensive but culturally varied Dusun people of Sabah. The major emphasis is on folklore and mythology.

Hertz, Robert. "A Contribution to the Study of the Collective Representation of Death" (1907). In *Death and the Right Hand*, two of Hertz's essays translated from the French by Rodney Needham and Claudia Needham. New York, 1960. A brilliant essay by a prominent student of Émile Durkheim concerning the significance of mortuary rites, particularly secondary treatment of the dead. Hertz utilized published sources, and much of his data came from the Ngaju of southern Borneo.

Hose, Charles, and William McDougall. *The Pagan Tribes of Borneo.* 2 vols. London, 1912. Despite the title, these volumes mostly concern the people of central northern Borneo, particularly the Kayan. Based on Hose's years of experience as a government officer. Contains much useful information; most of that on religion is in volume 2.

Jensen, Erik. *The Iban and Their Religion.* Oxford, 1974. A readable ethnographic account based on Jensen's seven years among the Iban as an Anglican missionary and community development officer. Emphasizes world view, cosmology, and longhouse festivals.

Metcalf, Peter. *A Borneo Journey into Death: Berawan Eschatology from Its Rituals.* Philadelphia, 1982. Describes in detail the elaborate mortuary ritual sequence, involving secondary treatment of the dead, in a small ethnic group of central northern Borneo. Shows how these rites reflect Berawan concepts of the soul in life and death.

Schärer, Hans. *Ngaju Religion: The Conception of God among a South Borneo People* (1946). Translated from the German by Rodney Needham. The Hague, 1963. Schärer was a missionary with the Baseler Mission in southern Borneo for seven years and later studied under J. P. B. de Josselin de Jong at Leiden. His account of Ngaju cosmology is impressive, but he unfortunately gives little idea of the social or ritual context.

Stöhr, Waldemar. *Das Totenritual der Dajak*. Ethnologica, n. s. vol. 1. Cologne, 1959. A compendium of sources on death practices from the entire island. Contains no analysis but is useful as a guide to bibliography.

PETER METCALF

BRAHMA

BRAHMA is the creator in Hindu mythology; sometimes he is said to form a trinity with Visnu as preserver and Siva as destroyer. Yet Brahma does not have the importance that creator gods usually have in mythology, nor is his status equal to that of Siva or Visnu. Though Brahma appears in more myths than almost any other Hindu god, he was seldom worshiped in India; at least one important version of the myth in which Siva appears before Brahma and Visnu in the form of a flaming phallus explicitly states that Brahma will never again be worshiped in India (to punish him for having wrongly sworn that he saw the tip of the infinite pillar). Brahma's ability to create is little more than an expertise or a technical skill that he employs at the behest of the greater gods.

Brahma's mythology is derived largely from that of the god Prajapati in the Brahmanas. Unlike Brahma, Prajapati is regarded as the supreme deity, and he creates in a variety of ways: he casts his seed into the fire in place of the usual liquid oblation; he separates a female from his androgynous form and creates with her through incestuous intercourse; or he practices asceticism in order to generate heat, from which his children are born. In this way he creates first fire, wind, sun, moon; then all the gods and demons; then men and animals; and then all the rest of creation. In the epics and Puranas, when Brahma takes over the task of creation he still uses these methods from time to time, but his usual method is to create mentally: he thinks of something and it comes into existence. While he is under the influence of the element of darkness *(tamas)* he creates the demons; under the influence of goodness *(sattva)* he creates the gods. Or he may dismember himself, like the Rgvedic cosmic man (Purusa), and create sheep from his breast, cows from his stomach, horses from his feet, and grasses from his hairs.

Brahma's name is clearly related both to *brahman*, the neuter term for the godhead (or, in earlier texts, for the principle of religious reality), and to the word for the priest, the *brahmana*. In later Hinduism Brahma is committed to the strand of Hinduism associated with *pravrtti* ("active creation,

worldly involvement") and indifferent, or even opposed, to *nivrtti* ("withdrawal from the world, renunciation"). He therefore comes into frequent conflict with Siva when Siva is in his ascetic phase, and competes with Siva when Siva is in his phallic phase. Brahma's unilateral attachment to *pravrtti* may also explain why he alone among the gods is able to grant the boon of immortality, often to demon ascetics: he deals only in life, never in death. This habit unfortunately causes the gods serious problems in dealing with demons, who are usually overcome somehow by Siva or Visnu. Immortality (or release from death) is what Brahma bestows in place of the moksa (release from rebirth and redeath) that Siva and Visnu may grant, for these two gods, unlike Brahma, are involved in both *pravrtti* and *nivrtti*. This one-sidedness of Brahma may, finally, explain why he failed to capture the imagination of the Hindu worshiper: the god who is to take responsibility for one's whole life must, in the Hindu view, acknowledge not only the desire to create but the desire to renounce creation.

BIBLIOGRAPHY

The best study of Brahma is Greg Bailey's *The Mythology of Brahma* (Oxford, 1983), which also contains an extensive bibliography of the secondary literature. Many of the relevant texts are translated in my *Hindu Myths* (Baltimore, 1975), pp. 25-55, and interpreted in my *Siva: The Erotic Ascetic* (Oxford, 1981), pp. 68-77 and 111-140.

WENDY DONIGER O'FLAHERTY

BUBER, MARTIN

BUBER, MARTIN (1878-1965), Jewish philosopher and educator. Born in Vienna, Buber studied at universities in Vienna, Leipzig, Zurich, and Berlin, and received his Ph. D. from Vienna in 1904 after completing a dissertation on Nicholas of Cusa and Jakob Boehme. Buber was married to Paula Winkler, a well-known German writer, and they had two children, Raphael and Eva (Strauss). Alienated from traditional Judaism, Buber returned to the Jewish community through the newly formed Zionist movement, whose official journal *(Die Welt)* he edited from 1901 to 1904.

Buber advocated a renewal of Jewish spiritual nationalism and wrote extensively on Judaism and Jewish nationalism. A five-year intensive study of Hasidism produced two volumes in German: *Tales of Rabbi Nachman* (1906) and *The Legends of the Baal Shem* (1908), followed by volumes of essays and translations including *For the Sake of Heaven* (1945), *Tales of the Hasidim* (1947), and *The Origin and Meaning of Hasidism* (1960), which first appeared in Hebrew, and *Hasidism and Modern Man* (1954). Other early writings include studies in mysticism: *Ekstatische Konfessionen*

(1909) and *Reden und Gleichnisse des Tschuang-Tse* (1910).

Widely regarded by Jewish youth as a spiritual leader, Buber taught at the University of Frankfurt from 1923 to 1933. He was also active in Jewish cultural life and lectured at the Frankfurt Judische Lehrhaus directed by Franz Rosenzweig. His lectures and writings were a source of spiritual inspiration for the besieged Jewish community in Nazi Germany. After emigrating to Palestine in 1938, he became professor of social philosophy at the Hebrew University in Jerusalem and was active in adult education. Buber was a founder and active participant in Berit Shalom and Ihud, movements for Arab-Jewish rapprochement. In this function he endorsed, until 1948, a binational state.

Philosophy of Judaism. Inspired by the emphasis placed in Hasidism on the hallowing of mundane, physical acts, Buber detached the teachings of that eighteenth-century pietist movement from their traditional rabbinic framework and revised them to create a unique, existential interpretation of Judaism. Rejecting orthodoxy, he espoused creative, spontaneous, individual "religiosity" over static, institutionalized "religion."

In such works of biblical interpretation as *Kingship of God* (1932), *Moses* (1946), *Prophetic Faith* (1949), and *On The Bible* (1968), Buber combined existential insight and scholarly method as he attempted to recover the living situations from which the biblical text emerged.

Philosophy of Relation and Dialogue. Under the influence of mystics (Boehme, Eckhart), existentialists (Kierkegaard, Nietzsche), and German social theorists (Tönnies, Simmel, Weber), Buber held that modern life and thought estrange the individual from his authentic self, other persons, nature, and God. Following World War I, however, he shifted from an individualistic philosophy to one rooted in social experience.

Buber eschewed systematic philosophy. Like Kierkegaard and Nietzsche, he endeavored to change the way in which people understand their relation to other human beings, the world, and God. His philosophy centered around two basic modes of relation, "I-You" and "I-It." In the "I-It" mode, which is characterized by a goal-oriented, instrumentalist attitude, we relate to others in terms of their use and value. However, whereas such an approach is appropriate to technology and practical activities, the intrusion of the I-It mode into the realm of interhuman relationships leads to widespread alienation. Rather than relate to others as unique beings, we reduce them to the status of objects or tools.

An alternative is the I-You mode. Through direct, nonpurposive relations one relates to another as an end (You), rather than a means (It), confirming and nurturing that person's uniqueness. The moments of I-You relating provide us with a basic sense of meaning and purpose; the absence of such experiences has a dehumanizing effect.

Religious Faith and the Eternal You. Buber developed a relational conception of religion, elaborated in *Two Types of Faith* (1951), *Eclipse of God* (1952), and *Good and Evil* (1953). Although he admitted the possibility of direct divine-human encounters, he emphasized the "interhuman" as the locus of genuine religious life. We live religiously by hallowing those human and other living beings whom we encounter. By confirming their unique qualities and potential, we nurture the divine spark in each of them, thereby actualizing God in the world.

Genuine relation both presupposes and fosters genuine community, rooted in authentic relations between members and between members and leader. To Buber, Israel's unique vocation is to actualize true community in its daily life. Like his mentor, the romantic socialist and anarchist Gustav Landauer (1870-1919), Buber advocated a community based on "utopian socialism," that is, mutual ownership and mutual aid.

Judaism and Genuine Community. Buber's conception of Jewish existence is characterized by a simultaneous commitment to humanity and the Jewish people. The Jews are a people united by common kinship, fate and memory, who, from its beginnings, accepted responsibility for actualizing genuine dialogue and genuine community in its daily life. Israel fulfills its responsibility as a nation by actualizing in its social life genuine, non-exploitative, confirming relations between people. In the Israeli *kibbuts*, Buber saw one of history's most successful examples of genuine community based upon mutual responsibility.

To live as a Jew means to dedicate oneself to actualizing genuine relation in all spheres of life. Rejecting all prepackaged recipes, norms, and principles, Buber emphasized Israel's continuing responsibility to draw anew the "line of demarcation" separating just from unjust action. For Buber, the Arab-Jewish conflict is the greatest test of the Jewish people's ability to actualize its vocation.

Buber was a major spokesman for a small group of Jews espousing Arab-Jewish rapprochement. Advocating a binational state in which Jews and Arabs would live as two culturally autonomous people with absolute political equality, he reluctantly accepted the state of Israel as necessitated by historical circumstances. Nevertheless, he continually criticized Israel's political leadership for shifting the context of the Arab-Jewish debate from the realm of human relationships to the realm of power politics.

For Buber, Israel was a microcosm of general humanity. Criticizing the existential mistrust that permeates modern society and the centralized power of the nation state, he envisioned a network of decentralized communities based upon mutual production and direct relations.

BIBLIOGRAPHY

A comprehensive bibliography of Buber's writings is *Martin Buber: A Bibliography of His Writings, 1897-1978* by Margot Cohn and Rafhael Buber (Jerusalem and New York, 1980). Available works by Buber not mentioned in the body of the article include *Israel and The World: Essays in a Time of Crisis*, 2d ed. (New York, 1963), which includes important essays on Judaism, the Bible, and Zionism; *A Believing Humanism: My Testament, 1902-1965*, translated and with an introduction and explanatory comment by Maurice S. Friedman (New York, 1967); and *Pointing the Way*, translated, edited, and with an introduction by Maurice S. Friedman (New York, 1957). A valuable collection of writings on the Arab question is *A Land of Two Peoples: Martin Buber on Jews and Arabs*, edited with an incisive introductory essay and notes by Paul R. Mendes-Flohr (Oxford, 1983). *The Writings of Martin Buber*, selected, edited, and introduced by Will Herberg (New York, 1956), is a useful collection, but includes none of Buber's writings on Hasidism.

The specifics of Buber's life, previously available only to the reader of German in Hans Kohn's fine study *Martin Buber: Sein Werk und seine Zeit* (Cologne, 1961), can now be found in Maurice S. Friedman's three-volume biography, *Martin Buber's Life and Work* (New York, 1981-1984). Friedman's *Martin Buber: The Life of Dialogue*, 3d ed. (Chicago, 1976), still remains the most comprehensive introduction to his thought in English. Grete Shaeder's *The Hebrew Humanism of Martin Buber*, translated by Noah J. Jacobs (Detroit, 1973), emphasizes the aesthetic and humanistic dimension of Buber's writings, traced biographically. Important criticisms with Buber's response are found in *The Philosophy of Martin Buber*, edited by Paul A. Schilpp and Maurice S. Friedman (Lasalle, Ill., 1967), and *Philosophical Interrogations*, edited by Sydney Rome and Beatrice Rome (New York, 1964), pp. 15-117.

For recent discussions of Buber's philosophy, see the proceedings (translated into English) of the Buber Centenary Conference held in 1978 at Ben Gurion University in Israel in *Martin Buber: A Centenary Volume*, edited by Haim Gordon and Jochanan Bloch (New York, 1984). Valuable critical insights into Buber's life and thought in the context of modern Jewish culture are provided in several articles by Ernst Simon: "Martin Buber and German Jewry," *Yearbook of The Leo Baeck Institute* 3 (1958): 3-39; "The Builder of Bridges," *Judaism* 27 (Spring, 1978): 148-160; and "From Dialogue to Peace," *Conservative Judaism* 19 (Summer, 1965): 28-31. These and other articles by Simon on Buber appear in his *Ye`adim, zematim, netivim: Haguto shel Mordekhai Martin Buber* (Tel Aviv, 1985). A brief discussion of Buber's early writings up to *I and Thou* is found in my article "Martin Buber: The Social Paradigm in Modern Jewish Thought," *Journal of the American Academy of Religion* 49 (June, 1981): 211-229.

LAURENCE J. SILBERSTEIN

BUDDHISM

An Overview

Buddhism began around the fifth or fourth century BCE as a small community that developed at a certain distance, both self-perceived and real, from other contemporary religious communities, as well as from the society, civilization, and culture with which it coexisted.

Despite the importance of this early phase of Buddhist history our knowledge about it remains sketchy and uncertain. Three topics can suggest what we do know: the source of authority that the new Buddhist community recognized, the pattern of development in its teaching and ecclesiastical structures, and the attitude it took toward matters of political and social order.

One primary factor that both accounts for and expresses Buddhism's emergence as a new sectarian religion rather than simply a new Hindu movement is the community's recognition of the ascetic Gautama as the Buddha ("enlightened one") and of the words that he had reportedly uttered as a new and ultimate source of sacred authority.

Some scholars have maintained that early Buddhism was a movement of philosophically oriented renouncers practicing a discipline of salvation that subsequently degenerated into a popular religion. A second group has contended that Buddhism was originally a popular religious movement that took form around the Buddha and his religiously inspiring message, a movement that was subsequently co-opted by a monastic elite that transformed it into a rather lifeless clerical scholasticism. A third group has argued that as far back as there is evidence, early Buddhist teaching combined philosophical and popular elements, and that during the earliest period that we can penetrate, the Buddhist community included both a significant monastic and a significant lay component. This argument, which is most convincing, has included the suggestion that the philosophical/popular and monastic/lay dichotomies should actually be seen as complements rather than oppositions, even though the understandings of the relative importance of these elements and their interrelationships have varied from the beginning of the Buddhist movement.

Buddhism as Civilizational Religion

Buddhism has never lost the imprint of the sectarian pattern that characterized its earliest history, largely because the sectarian pattern has been reasserted at various points. But Buddhism did not remain a purely sectarian religion. With the reign of King Asoka, Buddhism entered a new phase of its history in which it became what we have chosen to call a "civilizational religion," that is, a religion that was associated with a sophisticated high culture and that transcended the boundaries of local regions and politics.

History and Legend of the Asokan Impact. Asoka (r. circa 270-232 BCE) was the third ruler in a line of Mauryan emperors who established the first pan-Indian empire through military conquest. In one of the many inscriptions that provide the best evidence regarding his attitudes and actual policies, Asoka renounced further violent conquest and made a commitment to the practice and propagation of

Dharma. He also sent special representatives to ensure that the Dharma was appropriately practiced and taught by the various religious communities within his realm.

It would seem from Asoka's inscriptions that the Dharma that he officially affirmed and propagated was not identical to the Buddhist Dharma, although it was associated with it, especially insofar as Buddhist teaching impinged on the behavior of the laity. However, the inscriptions give clear evidence that if Asoka was not personally a Buddhist when he made his first commitment to the Dharma, he became so soon thereafter.

During the Asokan and immediately post-Asokan era there are at least three specific developments that sustained the transformation of Buddhism into a civilizational religion. The first, a realignment in the structure of the religious community, involved an innovation in the relationship and balance between the monastic order and its lay supporters. In addition, this realignment in the structure of the Buddhist community fostered the emergence of an important crosscutting distinction between monks and laypersons who were participants in the imperial-civilizational elite on the one hand, and ordinary monks and laypersons on the other.

The transformation of Buddhism into a civilizational religion also involved doctrinal and scholastic factors. During the Asokan and post-Asokan periods, factions within the monastic community began to formulate aspects of the teachings more precisely, and to develop those teachings into philosophies that attempted to explain all of reality in a coherent and logically defensible manner.

Developments in the areas of symbolism, architecture, and ritual were also significant components in the transformation of Buddhism into a civilizational religion. Some changes were related to the support Buddhism received from its royal and elite supporters. Royal and elite patronage seems to have been crucial to the emergence of large monastic establishments throughout India.

Imperial Buddhism Reasserted and Transcended. Despite the importance of Asoka to the history of Buddhism, the imperial order that he established persisted only a short time after his death. Within fifty years of his death (i. e., by the year 186 BCE), the Buddhist-oriented Mauryan dynasty collapsed and was replaced by the Sunga dynasty, more supportive of Brahmanic Hindu traditions. Buddhism emerged as a dominant religion in areas outside northeastern India where the Sungas were unable to maintain the authority and prestige that their Mauryan predecessors had enjoyed.

From the second century BCE through the first century CE Buddhism became a powerful religious force in virtually all of India. A major aspect of the transformation of Buddhism into a fully civilizational religion was the differentiation that occurred between Buddhism as a civilizational religion and Buddhism as an imperial religion. During late Mauryan times the civilizational and imperial dimensions had not been

clearly differentiated. However, by the beginning of the common era Buddhism had become a civilizational religion that transcended the various expressions of imperial Buddhism in particular geographical areas. As a direct correlate of this development, an important distinction was generated within the elite of the Buddhist community. By this period this elite had come to include both a truly civilizational component that maintained close international contacts and traveled freely from one Buddhist empire to another and beyond, as well as overlapping but distinguishable imperial components that operated within the framework of each particular empire.

Closely associated developments were taking place at the level of cosmology and its application to religious practice. In the Hinayana context the most important development was probably the rich portrayal of a set of six cosmological *gatis*, or "destinies" (of gods, humans, animals, *asuras* or titans, hungry ghosts, and beings who are consigned to hell), which depicted, in vivid fashion, the workings of *karman* (moral action and its effects). These texts, which were probably used as the basis for sermons, strongly encouraged Buddhist morality and Buddhist merit-making activities.

Buddhism as Pan-Asian Civilization. The geographical expansion of Buddhism was both a cause and an effect of its civilizational character. But Buddhism's role as a pan-Asian civilization involved much more than a pan-Asian presence. Buddhist monasteries, often state supported and located near capitals of the various Buddhist kingdoms, functioned in ways analogous to modern universities. There was a constant circulation of Buddhist monks, texts, and artistic forms across increasingly vast geographical areas. Indian and Central Asian missionaries traveled to China and with the help of Chinese Buddhists translated whole libraries of books into Chinese, which became a third major Buddhist sacred language alongside Pali and Sanskrit. In the fifth century Buddhist nuns carried their ordination lineage from Sri Lanka to China. Between 400 and 700 a stream of Chinese pilgrims traveled to India via Central Asia and Southeast Asia in order to visit sacred sites and monasteries and to collect addition-

> There was a constant circulation of Buddhist monks, texts, and artistic forms across increasingly vast geographical areas.

al scriptures and commentaries. In the sixth century Buddhism was formally introduced into Japan; in the following century Buddhists from Central Asia, India, and China made their way into Tibet. Beginning in the eighth and ninth centuries monks from Japan visited China in order to receive Buddhist training and acquire Buddhist texts. These are only a few illustrations of the kind of travel and interaction that characterized this period.

Within the Mahayana tradition this period of Buddhist efflorescence as a civilizational religion was characterized by a high level of creativity and by a variety of efforts toward systematization. In the earlier centuries the Mahayanists produced a rich and extensive collection of new *sutras*, including the *Saddharmapundarika Sutra* (Lotus of the True Law), the *Mahaparinirvana Sutra*, the *Lankavatara Sutra*, and the *Avatamsaka Sutra*. With the passage of time, voluminous commentaries were written on many of these *sutras* in India, Central Asia, and China.

By the second half of the first millennium CE a new strand of Buddhist tradition, the Vajrayana, or Esoteric Vehicle, began to come into the foreground in India. This new vehicle accepted the basic orientation of the Mahayana, but supplemented Mahayana insights with new and dramatic forms of practice, many of them esoteric in character. The appearance of this new Buddhist vehicle was closely associated with the composition of new texts, including new *sutras* (e.g., the *Mahavairocana Sutra*), and the new ritual manuals known as tantras. By the eighth and ninth centuries this new vehicle had spread through virtually the entire Buddhist world and was preserved especially in Japan and in Tibet.

During the period of its hegenomy as a pan-Asian civilization, Buddhism retained a considerable degree of unity across both the regional and text-oriented boundaries that delimited particular Buddhist traditions.

Buddhism as Cultural Religion

For more than a thousand years, from the time of King Asoka to about the ninth century, Buddhism exhibited a civilizational form that began as pan-Indian and ultimately became pan-Asian in character. Like the sectarian pattern that preceded it, this civilizational pattern left an indelible mark on all subsequent Buddhist developments.

The Period of Transition. The increasing importance of Tantra in late Indian Buddhism and the success of the Pure Land (Ching-t`u) and Ch`an (Zen) schools in China during the Sui and T`ang period (598-907) are further indications that the Buddhist tradition was becoming more local in self-definition. Chinese Buddhism had a new independent spirit in contrast to the earlier India-centered Buddhism. Moreover, the new movements that emerged at that time seem to be the result of a long development that took place apart from the major cosmopolitan centers. Far more than in the past, expressions of Buddhism were being made at all levels of particular societies, and there was a new concern for the interrelation of those levels within each society.

During the last centuries of the first millennium CE, Buddhist civilization developed a new, somewhat independent center in China that reached its peak during the Sui and T`ang dynasties. Thus, when Buddhist texts and images were introduced into Japan during the sixth century they were presented and appropriated as part and parcel of Chinese culture.

The processes of acculturation that had first become evident in the sixth century in India and China repeated themselves beginning in the tenth century in Japan, Korea, Tibet, Sri Lanka, and Southeast Asia. In each of these areas distinct cultural forms of Buddhism evolved. There was a reorganization of the Buddhist community with an increased emphasis on the bonds between elite and ordinary Buddhists in each particular area. There was a renewed interest in efficacious forms of Buddhist practice and the Buddhist schools that preserved and encouraged such practice. Within each area there was a development of Buddhist symbols and rituals that became representative of distinct Buddhist cultures, particularly at the popular level.

> **As a result of persecutions in the ninth century, Buddhism lost its distinctively civilizational role.**

Buddhism had some limited success in India during the last centuries of the first millennium. It benefited from extensive royal and popular support in northeastern India under the Pala dynasty from the eighth to the twelfth century, but Hindu philosophy and theistic *(bhakti)* movements were aggressive critics of Buddhism. Hardly any distinct Buddhist presence continued in India after the last of the great monasteries were destroyed by the Muslims. In China there was more success, although the Confucian and Taoist traditions were powerful rivals. As a result of persecutions in the ninth century, Buddhism lost its distinctively civilizational role, but it continued as a major component of Chinese religion, becoming increasingly synthesized with other native traditions.

Monastic Order, Royal Order, and Popular Buddhism. The transformation of Buddhism from a civilizational religion to a cultural religion depended on a fundamental realignment in the structure of the Buddhist community. As a civilizational religion, Buddhist community life had come to include a largely monastic elite that traveled extensively, was multilingual, and operated at the civilizational level; an imperial elite made up of monks and laypersons associated more closely with royal courts and related aristocracies; and a less exalted company of ordinary monks and laypersons living not only in urban areas but in the countryside as well. In Buddhism's zenith as a civilizational religion the central organizing relationship was that between the largely monastic civilizational elite and the imperial elites. With the transformation of Buddhism into a cultural religion, however, this situation was drastically altered.

One aspect of this transformation was major changes that took place at three different levels: monastic, imperial, and popular. The demise of the monastic network through which the civilizational aspect of Buddhism had been supported and maintained was decisive. To be sure, there were elements of the monastic community that never lost their international vision, and travel and exchanges between specific cultural areas was never totally absent, but it would be difficult to speak of a pan-Asian Buddhist elite after the ninth or tenth century.

The pattern at the imperial level was altered by the loss of monastic power and influence coupled with increased state control in monastic affairs. In China and Japan, and to a lesser extent in Korea and Vietnam, state control became thoroughly bureaucratized. In Sri Lanka and the Theravada areas of Southeast Asia, state control was implemented more indirectly and with considerably less efficiency by royal "purifications" of the *sangha*.

The demise of the international Buddhist elite and the weakening of the large and powerful establishments were counterbalanced by a strengthening of Buddhist life at the grass-roots level. Smaller, local institutions that for a long time had coexisted with the great monasteries took on new importance as focal points in Buddhist community life.

The Preeminence of Practice. The era of comprehensive Buddhist philosophizing and the formulation of original systems of thought came to an end, for the most part, with the demise of Buddhism as a civilizational religion. There continued to be philosophical innovations, and some of the great systems that were already formulated were adjusted to meet new circumstances. However, the real creativity of Buddhism as a cultural religion came to the fore in schools and movements that emphasized efficacious modes of Buddhist practice.

A major component in the development of various Buddhist cultures is the ascendancy of schools or movements that combined a strong emphasis on the importance of discipline (particularly although not exclusively the monastic discipline) with an accompanying emphasis on meditation. [*See* Meditation.] In China and Japan, Ch`an and Zen, with their emphasis on firm discipline and meditative practices, are representative of this kind of Buddhist tradition. [*See* Zen.]

Esoteric or Tantric modes of religion also were a significant part of cultural Buddhism in East Asia. In China the Esoteric elements were closely related to influences from the Vajrayana tradition in Tibet as well as interactions with forms of indigenous Taoism. In Japan more sophisticated Esoteric elements persisted in the Tendai (Chin., T`ien-t`ai) and Shingon schools, while more rustic and indigenous elements were prominent in groups that were integrated into these schools, for example, the Shugendo community that was made up of mountain ascetics known as *yamabushi*.

In Sri Lanka in the twelfth and thirteenth centuries devotional religion also seems to have been influential in the Buddhist community, generating new genres of Buddhist literature that were written primarily in Sinhala rather than Pali. Although no specifically devotional "schools" were formed, a whole new devotional component was incorporated into the Theravada tradition and subsequently diffused to the Theravada cultures in Southeast Asia. Similarly, there were, as far as we know, no "schools" that were specifically Esoteric or Tantric in character. However, there is some evidence that indicates that Esoteric elements played a very significant role in each of the premodern Theravada cultures. This kind of influence seems to have been particularly strong in northern Burma, northern Thailand, Laos, and Cambodia.

Another important component of Buddhism as a cultural religion was the mitigation, in some circles at least, of traditional distinctions between monks and laity. This trend was least evident in the more discipline-oriented contexts, but even here there was some movement in this direction. For example, in the Ch`an and Zen monasteries, monks, rather than being prohibited from engaging in productive work as the Vinaya had stipulated, were actually required to work. In the Pure Land schools in Japan, and in some of the Esoteric schools in Japan and Tibet, it became permissible and common for clergy to marry and have families.

The Pervasiveness of Ritual. Alongside the particular schools and movements that characterized Buddhism as a cultural religion there were also modes of Buddhist practice that, although influenced by those schools and movements, were more pervasively involved in Buddhist cultures as such. Pilgrimage was in the forefront of these practices.

Virtually every instance of Buddhism as a cultural religion had its own particular patterns of Buddhist pilgrimage. [*See* Pilgrimage.] In many cases these pilgrimage patterns were a major factor in maintaining the specificity of particular, often overlapping, religious and cultural complexes. Many of the sites that were the goals of major Buddhist pilgrimages were mountain peaks or other places that had been sacred from before the introduction of Buddhism and continued to have sacred associations in other traditions that coexisted with Buddhism.

Wherever Buddhism developed as a cultural religion it penetrated not only the sacred topography of the area but also the cycle of calendric rites. In China, for example, the annual cycle of Buddhist ritual activities included festivals honoring various Buddhas and *bodhisattvas*, festivals dedicated to significant figures from Chinese Buddhist history, a great vegetarian feast, and a very important "All Soul's" festival in which the Chinese virtue of filial piety was expressed through offerings intended to aid one's ancestors. While these rituals themselves involved much that was distinctively Chinese, they were interspersed with other festivals, both Confucian and Taoist, and were supplemented by other, lesser rituals associated with daily life that involved an even greater integration with non-Buddhist elements.

Buddhism in its various cultural expressions also became associated with life cycle rites, especially those of the male initiation into adulthood and those associated with death. The Buddhist involvement in male initiation rites was limited primarily to Southeast Asia. In many Buddhist countries children and young men were educated in the monasteries, but only in Southeast Asia did temporary initiation into the order, either as a novice (as in Burma) or at a later age as a full-fledged monk (as in central Thailand), become a culturally accepted necessity for the attainment of male adulthood. Buddhist involvement in funerary rituals was, on the other hand, a phenomenon that appeared again and again all across Asia. Once Buddhism became established as a cultural religion, it was these rituals that enabled it to maintain its position and influence, and to do so century after century on into the modern era.

Buddhism in the Modern World

The modern encounter of cultures and civilizations has not been monolithic. Three stages can be identified in Buddhist Asia. The first was the arrival of missionaries with traders in various parts of Asia. This onslaught was sometimes physically violent, as in the Portuguese destruction of Buddhist temples and relics in Sri Lanka, but for the most part it was an ideological assault. A second stage was more strictly colonial, as some European powers gained control over many different areas of the Buddhist world. Some Buddhist countries, such as Sri Lanka, Burma, and the Indochinese states, were fully colonized while others, such as Thailand, China, and Japan, were subjected to strong colonial influences. In virtually every situation (Tibet was a notable exception), the symbiotic relationship between the political order and the monastic order was disrupted, with adverse effects for Buddhist institutions.

The twentieth-century acceptance of Western political and economic ideologies, whether democratic capitalism or communism, represents a third stage. Buddhists in China, Mongolia, Tibet, and parts of Korea and Southeast Asia now live in communist societies, and the future of Buddhist communities in these areas looks bleak. Capitalism has been dominant in Japan, South Korea, Sri Lanka, and parts of Southeast Asia (Thailand being the prime example), and greater possibilities for the Buddhist tradition are presumed to exist in these areas.

Conclusion

Buddhism as a whole has not yet developed a distinctive character in the modern period. On the contrary, there is a great deal of continuity between the historical development of Buddhism and the current responses and innovations. Thus the sectarian, civilizational, and cultural patterns continue to exert a predominant influence in the evolution of Buddhist tradition.

At the same time, we can see that Buddhism, like other world religions, participates in a modern religious situation that is, in many respects, radically new. Buddhism has thus come to share certain modern elements with other contemporary religions. We can see such elements in the search for new modes of religious symbolism, as is found in the writings of the Thai monk Buddhadasa and the Japanese Kyoto school of Buddhist philosophy. We can also see these common elements in the preoccupation with the human world and this-worldly soteriology that is emerging in many Buddhist contexts.

[*For further discussion of the doctrinal and practical stance(s) of the tradition, see* Nirvana. *For an overview of some of the means by which Buddhism and local cultures become syncretized, see* Folk Religion. *Various regional surveys treat Buddhism as a component of local and regional cultures. See in particular* Indian Religions, Southeast Asian Religions, Tibetan Religion, Chinese Religion, Mongol Religions, Korean Religions, *and* Japanese Religion.]

BIBLIOGRAPHY

"A Brief History of Buddhist Studies in Europe and America" is provided by J. W. de Jong in two successive issues of *Eastern Buddhist*, n. s. 7 (May and October 1974): 55-106 and 49-82, which he has brought up to date in his "Recent Buddhist Studies in Europe and America 1973-1983," which appeared in the same journal, vol. 17 (Spring 1984): 79-107. One of the few books that treats a significant theme within this fascinating scholarly tradition is G. R. Welbon's *The Buddhist Nirvana and its Western Interpreters* (Chicago, 1968).

Among the book-length introductory surveys of Buddhism, the second edition of Richard H. Robinson and Willard L. Johnson's *The Buddhist Religion* (Encino, Calif., 1977) is, overall, the most satisfactory. The only modern attempt to present a full-scale historical survey by a single author is to be found in the Buddhism sections of Charles Eliot's three-volume work *Hinduism and Buddhism*, 3d ed. (London, 1957), taken together with his *Japanese Buddhism* (1935; reprint, New York, 1959). Although these books are seriously dated (they were first published in 1921 and 1935, respectively), they still provide a valuable resource. Five other important works that attempt cross-cultural presentations of a particular aspect of Buddhism are Junjiro Takakusu's *The Essentials of Buddhist Philosophy*, 3d ed., edited by Wing-tsit Chan and Charles A. Moore (Honolulu, 1956); Paul Mus's wide-ranging *Barabudur: Esquisse d'une histoire du bouddhisme fondée sur la critique archéologique des textes*, 2 vols. (Hanoi, 1935); Robert Bleichsteiner's *Die gelbe Kirche* (Vienna, 1937), which was translated into French and published as *L'église jaune* (Paris, 1937); W. Randolph Kloetzli's *Buddhist Cosmology* (Delhi, 1983); and David L. Snellgrove's edited collection *The Image of the Buddha* (London, 1978).

Many of the most important studies of the early, sectarian phase of Buddhism in India extend their discussions to the later phases of Indian Buddhism as well. This is true, for example, of Sukumar Dutt's *Buddhist Monks and Monasteries of India* (London, 1962) and of Edward Conze's *Buddhist Thought in India* (Ann Arbor, 1967). For those interested in Buddhist doctrines, Conze's book may be supplemented by David J. Kalupahana's *Causality: The Central*

Philosophy of Buddhism (Honolulu, 1975), which focuses on sectarian Buddhism, and Fredrick J. Streng's *Emptiness: A Study in Religious Meaning* (New York, 1967), which examines the work of the famous early Mahayana philosopher Nagarjuna.

A historical account that is focused more exclusively on the sectarian period and the transition to civilizational Buddhism is provided by Étienne Lamotte in his authoritative *Histoire du bouddhisme indien: Des origines á l'ère Saka* (Louvain, 1958). A somewhat different perspective on the same process of development is accessible in three closely related works that can profitably be read in series: Frank E. Reynolds's title essay in *The Two Wheels of Dhamma*, edited by Frank E. Reynolds and Bardwell L. Smith, "AAR Studies in Religion," no. 3 (Chambersburg, Pa., 1972); John C. Holt's *Discipline: The Canonical Buddhism of the Vinayapitaka* (Delhi, 1981); and John Strong's *The Legend of King Asoka: A Study and Translation of the Asokavadana* (Princeton, 1983).

Good books that treat Buddhism as an international civilization are hard to come by. Three that provide some assistance to those interested in the topic are Trevor O. Ling's *The Buddha: Buddhist Civilization in India and Ceylon* (London, 1973); Erik Zürcher's *The Buddhist Conquest of China: The Spread and Adaptation of Buddhism in Early Medieval China*, 2 vols. (Leiden; 1959); and René Grousset's *In the Footsteps of the Buddha*, translated by J. A. Underwood (New York, 1971). Works that focus on the process of acculturation of Buddhism in various contexts include Hajime Nakamura's *Ways of Thinking of Eastern Peoples*, the revised English translation of which was edited by Philip P. Wiener (Honolulu, 1964); Alicia Matsunaga's *The Buddhist Philosophy of Assimilation* (Tokyo and Rutland, Vt., 1969); and Kenneth Ch`en's *The Chinese Transformation of Buddhism* (Princeton, 1973).

Studies of particular Buddhist cultures are legion. Some valuable studies focus on Buddhism in the context of the whole range of religions that were present in a particular area. Good examples are Giuseppe Tucci's *The Religions of Tibet*, translated by Geoffrey Samuel (Berkeley, 1980), and Joseph M. Kitagawa's *Religion in Japanese History* (New York, 1966). Other treatments of particular Buddhist cultures trace the Buddhist tradition in question from its introduction into the area through the period of acculturation and, in some cases, on into modern times. Two examples are *Religion and Legitimation of Power in Sri Lanka*, edited by Bardwell L. Smith (Chambersburg, Pa., 1978), and Kenneth Ch`en's comprehensive *Buddhism in China* (Princeton, 1964). Finally, some interpretations of particular Buddhist cultures focus more narrowly on a specific period or theme. See, for example, Lal Mani Joshi's *Studies in the Buddhistic Culture of India* (Delhi, 1967), which deals primarily with Buddhist culture in Northeast India during the seventh and eighth centuries; Daniel Overmyer's *Folk Buddhist Religion: Dissenting Sects in Late Traditional China* (Cambridge, Mass., 1976); and William R. La Fleur's *The Karma of Words: Buddhism and the Literary Arts in Medieval Japan* (Berkeley, 1983).

There is also a myriad of books and articles that consider the development of Buddhism in the modern period. The most adequate overview of developments through the early 1970s is provided in *Buddhism in the Modern World*, edited by Heinrich Dumoulin and John Maraldo (New York, 1976). In addition, there are two excellent trilogies on particular traditions. The first, by Holmes Welch, includes *The Practice of Chinese Buddhism, 1900-1950* (1967), *The Buddhist Revival in China* (1968), and *Buddhism under Mao* (1972), all published by the Harvard University Press. The second, by Stanley J. Tambiah, includes *Buddhism and the Spirit Cults in North-East Thailand* (1970), *World Conqueror and World Renouncer: A Study of Buddhism and Polity in Thailand against a Historical Background* (1976), and *The Buddhist Saints of the Forest and the Cult of Amulets* (1984), all published by the Cambridge University Press.

For those interested in pursuing the study of Buddhism in a cross-cultural, thematic manner, Frank E. Reynolds's *Guide to the Buddhist Religion* (Boston, 1981), done with the assistance of John Holt and John Strong, is a useful resource. It provides 350 pages of annotated bibliography of English, French, and German materials (plus a preface and 65 pages of index) organized in terms of eleven themes, including "Historical Development," "Religious Thought," "Authoritative Texts," "Popular Beliefs and Literature," "Social, Political and Economic Aspects," "The Arts," "Religious Practices and Rituals," and "Soteriological Experience and Processes: Path and Goal."

FRANK E. REYNOLDS and CHARLES HALLISEY

Buddhism in India

Buddha. Scholars generally tend to accept the years 563 to 483 BCE as the most plausible dating for the life of Gautama Buddha. Assuming, moreover, that the legend is reliable in some of its details, we can say that the history of the religion begins when he was thirty-five (therefore, in about 528), with his first sermon at Sarnath (northeast of the city of Varanasi).

His first sermon was followed by forty-five years of wandering through the Ganges River valley, spreading his teachings. Although tradition preserves many narratives of isolated episodes of this half century of teaching, no one has been able to piece together a convincing account of this period.

At the age of eighty (c. 483), Siddhartha Gautama, the Buddha Sakyamuni, died near the city of Kusinagara. To his immediate disciples perhaps this fading away of the Master confirmed his teachings on impermanence, but the Buddha's death would soon come to be regarded as a symbol of his perfect peace and renunciation: with death he had reached his *parinirvana*, that point in his career after which he would be reborn no more.

Dharma. His first preaching, known as the "First Turning of the Wheel of Dharma" symbolizes the appearance in history of the Buddhist teaching, whereas Sakyamuni's enlightenment experience, or "Great Awakening" *(mahabodhi)*, which occurred in the same year, represents the human experience around which the religion would develop its practices and ideals. This was the experience whereby Sakyamuni became an "Awakened One" *(buddha)*. His disciples came to believe that all aspects of Buddhist doctrine and practice flow from this experience of awakening *(bodhi)* and from the resultant state of freedom from passion, suffering, and rebirth called *nirvana*. The teachings found in the Buddha's sermons can be interpreted as definitions of these two experiences, the spiritual practices that lead to or flow from them, and the institutions that arose inspired by the experience and the human beings who laid claim to it. [*See* Nirvana.]

It is difficult to determine to what extent early Buddhism had an accompanying metaphysics. Some of the earliest strata of Buddhist literature suggest that the early community may have emphasized the joys of renunciation and the peace of abstention from conflict—political, social, and religious—more than a philosophical doctrine of liberation. Such are the ascetic ideals of one of the earliest texts of the tradition, the *Atthakavagga (Suttanipata)*. There is in this text a rejection of doctrine, rule, and rite that is a critique of the exaggerated claims of those who believed they could become pure and free through ritual, knowledge, or religious status.

If such statements represent some of the earliest moments in the development of the doctrine, then the next stage must have brought a growing awareness of the need for ritual and creed if the community was to survive. This awareness would have been followed in a short time by the formation of a metaphysic, a theory of liberation, and a conscious system of meditation. In the next strata of early Buddhist literature these themes are only surpassed in importance by discussions of ascetic morality. The ascetic ideals of the early community were then expanded and defined by doctrine—as confession of faith, as ideology, and as a plan for religious and moral practice. The earliest formulations of this type are perhaps those of the Eightfold Path, with its triple division into wisdom, moral practice, and mental concentration. The theoretical or metaphysical underpinnings are contained in the Four Noble Truths and in the Three Marks (impermanence, sorrow, and no-self), both traditionally regarded as the subject matter of the Buddha's first sermons.

Buddhist Remnants and Revivals in the Subcontinent

After the last days of the great monastic institutions (twelfth and thirteenth centuries) Indian Buddhism lingered on in isolated pockets in the subcontinent. During the period of Muslim and British conquest (thirteenth to nineteenth century) it was almost completely absorbed by Hinduism and Islam, and gave no sign of creative life until modern attempts at restoration (nineteenth and twentieth centuries).

Attempted Revival: The Mahabodhi Society. Attempts to revive Buddhism in the land of its origin began with the Theosophical Society, popularized in Sri Lanka in the early 1880s by the American Henry S. Olcott. Although the society eventually became the vehicle for broader and less defined speculative goals, it inspired new pride in Buddhists after years of colonial oppression. The Sinhala monk Anagarika Dharmapala (1864-1933; born David Hewavitarane) set out to modernize Buddhist education. He also worked untiringly to restore the main pilgrimage sites of India. To this end he founded in 1891 the Mahabodhi Society, still a major presence in Indian Buddhism.

Ambedkar and "Neo-Buddhism." The most significant Buddhist mass revival of the new age was led by Dr. Bhimrao Ramji Ambedkar (1891-1956). He saw Buddhism as the gospel for India's oppressed and read in the Buddhist scriptures ideals of equality and justice. After many years of spiritual search, he became convinced that Buddhism was the only ideology that could effect the eventual liberation of Indian outcastes. On 14 October 1956 he performed a mass "consecration" of Buddhists in Nagpur, Maharashtra.

Other Aspects of Modern Buddhism. The most fruitful and persistent effort in the rediscovery of Indian Buddhism has been in the West, primarily among Western scholars. The combined effort of Indian, North American and European historians, archaeologists, and art historians has placed Indian Buddhism in a historical and social context, which, though still only understood in its rough outlines, allows us to see Buddhism in its historical evolution.

Another interesting phenomenon of the contemporary world is the appearance of "neo-Buddhists" in Europe and North America. Although most of these groups have adopted extra-Indian forms of Buddhism, their interest in the scriptural traditions of India has created an audience and a demand for research into India's Buddhist past. The Buddhist Society, founded in London in 1926, and the Amis du Bouddhisme, founded in Paris in 1928, both supported scholarship and encouraged the Buddhist revival in India.

In spite of the revived interest in India of the last century, the prospects of an effective Buddhist revival in the land of Sakyamuni seem remote. It is difficult to imagine a successful living Buddhism in India today or in the near future. The possibility of the religion coming back to life may depend on the reimportation of the Dharma into India from another land. It remains to be seen if Ambedkar and Anagarika Dharmapala had good reasons for hope in a Buddhist revival.

[*See also* Indian Religions.]

BIBLIOGRAPHY

Bareau, André. "Le bouddhisme indien." In *Les religions de l'Inde*, vol. 3, pp. 1-246. Paris, 1966. In addition to this useful survey, see Bareau's "Le bouddhisme indien," in *Histoire des religions*, edited by Henri-Charles Puech vol. 1, (Paris, 1970), pp. 1146-1215. Bareau has written the classical work on the question of the dating of the Buddha's life, "La date du Nirvana," *Journal asiatique* 241 (1953): 27-62. He surveys and interprets classical documents on the Hinayana schools in "Les sectes bouddhiques du Petit Véhicule et leurs Abhi-dharmapitaka." *Bulletin de l'École Française d'Extrême-Orient* 50 (1952): 1-11; "Trois traités sur les sectes bouddhiques dus à Vasumitra, Bhavya et Vinitadeva," *Journal asiatique* 242-244 (1954-1956); *Les premiers conciles bouddhiques* (Paris, 1955); *Les sectes bouddhiques de Petit Véhicule* (Saigon, 1955); "Les controverses rélatives à la nature de l'arhant dans le bouddhisme ancien," *Indo-Iranian Journal* 1 (1957): 241-250. Bareau has also worked extensively on the "biography" of the Buddha: *Recherches sur la biographie du Bouddha,*

3 vols. (Paris, 1970-1983); "Le parinirvana du Bouddha et la naissance de la religion bouddhique," *Bulletin de l'École Française d'Extrême-Orient* 61 (1974): 275-300; and, on a more popular but still scholarly bent, *Le Bouddha* (Paris, 1962).

Basham, A. L. *The Wonder That Was India*. London, 1954. This is the most accessible and readable cultural history of pre-Muslim India. A more technical study on the religious movements at the time of the Buddha is Basham's *History and Doctrine of the Ajivikas* (London, 1951).

Beal, Samuel. *Travels of Fa-hian and Sung-Yun, Buddhist Pilgrims from China to India (400 A. D. and 518 A. D.)*. London, 1869. The travel records of two early pilgrims. See also Beal's *Si-yu-ki: Buddhist Records of the Western World*, 2 vols. (London, 1884). Translation of Hsüan-tsang's accounts of his travels to India.

Bechert, Heinz. "Zur Frühgeschichte des Mahayana-Buddhismus." *Zeitschrift der Deutschen Morgenländischen Gesellschaft* 113 (1963): 530-535. Summary discussion of the Hinayana roots of Mahayana. On the same topic, see also "Notes on the Formation of Buddhist Sects and the Origins of Mahayana," in *German Scholars on India*, vol. 1 (Varanasi, 1973), pp. 6-18; "The Date of the Buddha Reconsidered," *Indologica Taurinensia* 10 (1982): 29-36; "The Importance of Asoka's So-called Schism Edict," in *Indological and Buddhist Studies in Honour of Proj. J. W. de Jong* (Canberra, 1982), pp. 61-68; and "The Beginnings of Buddhist Historiography," in *Religion and Legitimation of Power in Sri Lanka*, edited by Bardwell L. Smith (Chambersburg, Pa., 1978), pp. 1-12. Be-chert is also the editor of the most recent contribution to the question of the language of Buddha and early Buddhism, *Die Sprache der ältesten buddhistischen Überlieferung / The Language of the Earliest Buddhist Tradition* (Göttingen, 1980).

Bechert, Heinz, and Georg von Simson, eds. *Einführung in die Indologie: Stand, Methoden, Aufgaben*. Darmstadt, 1979. A general introduction to indology, containing abundant materials on Indian history and religion, including Buddhism.

Bechert, Heinz, and Richard Gombrich, eds. *The World of Buddhism*. London, 1984. This is by far the most scholarly and comprehensive survey of Buddhism for the general reader. Indian Buddhism is treated on pages 15-132 and 277-278.

Demiéville, Paul. "L'origine des sectes bouddhiques d'après Paramartha." In *Mélanges chinois et bouddhiques*, vol. 1, pp. 14-64. Brussels, 1931-1932.

Demiéville, Paul. "A propos du Concile de Vaisali." *T'oung pao* 40 (1951): 239-296.

Dutt, Nalinaksha. *Aspects of Mahayana Buddhism and Its Relation to Hinayana*. London, 1930. Although Dutt's work on the development of the Buddhist sects is now largely superseded, there are no comprehensive expositions to replace his surveys. His *Mahayana Buddhism* (Calcutta, 1973) is sometimes presented as a revision of Aspects, but the earlier work is quite different and far superior. Most of Dutt's earlier work on the sects, found hidden in various journals, was compiled in *Buddhist Sects in India* (Calcutta, 1970). See also his *Early Monastic Buddhism*, rev. ed. (Calcutta, 1960).

Dutt, Sukumar. *The Buddha and Five After-Centuries*. London, 1957. Other useful, although dated, surveys include *Early Buddhist Monachism* (1924; new ed., Delhi, 1960) and *Buddhist Monks and Monasteries in India* (London, 1962).

Fick, R. *The Social Organization in Northeast India in the Buddha's Time*. Calcutta, 1920.

Frauwallner, Erich. "Die buddhistische Konzile." *Zeitschrift der Deutschen Morgenländischen Gesellschaft* 102 (1952): 240-261.

Frauwallner, Erich. *The Earliest Vinaya and the Beginnings of Buddhist Literature*. Rome, 1956.

Frauwallner, Erich. "The Historical Data We Possess on the Person and Doctrine of the Buddha." *East and West* 7 (1956): 309-312.

Fujita Kotatsu. *Genshi jödoshiso no kenkyu*. Tokyo, 1970. The standard book on early Sukhavati beliefs.

Glasenapp, Helmuth von. "Zur Geschichte der buddhistischen Dharma Theorie." *Zeitschrift der Deutschen Morgenländischen Gesellschaft* 92 (1938): 383-420.

Glasenapp, Helmuth von. "Der Ursprung der buddhistischen Dharma-Theorie." *Wiener Zeitschrift für die Kunde des Morgenlandes* 46 (1939): 242-266.

Glasenapp, Helmuth von. *Buddhistische Mysterien*. Stuttgart, 1940. Discusses most of the theories on early Brahmanic influence on Buddhist doctrine.

Glasenapp, Helmuth von. *Buddhismus und Gottesidee*. Mainz, 1954.

Gokhale, Balkrishna Govind. *Buddhism and Asoka*. Baroda, 1948. Other of this author's extensive writings on the social and political contexts of early Buddhism include "The Early Buddhist Elite," *Journal of Indian History* 43 (1965): 391-402; "Early Buddhist View of the State," *Journal of the American Oriental Society* 89 (1969): 731-738; "Theravada Buddhism in Western India," *Journal of the American Oriental Society* 92 (1972): 230-236; and "Early Buddhism and the Brahmanas," in *Studies in History of Buddhism*, edited by A. K. Narain (Delhi, 1980).

Gómez, Luis O. "Proto-Mädhyamika in the Pali Canon." *Philosophy East and West* 26 (1976): 137-165. This paper argues that the older portions of *Suttanipata* preserve a stratum of the tradition that differs radically from the dominant themes expressed in the rest of the Pali canon, especially in its Theravada interpretation. The question of dedication of merit in the Mahayana is discussed in "Paradigm Shift and Paradigm Translation: The Case of Merit and Grace in Buddhism," in *Buddhist-Christian Dialogue* (Honolulu, forthcoming). On Mahayana doctrine and myth, see also my "Buddhism as a Religion of Hope: Polarities in the Myth of Dharmakara," *Journal of the Institute for Integral Shin Studies* (Kyoto, in press).

Grousset, René. *The Civilizations of the East*, vol. 2, *India*. London, 1931. One of the best surveys of Indian history. See also his *Sur les traces du Bouddha* (Paris, 1957) for a modern expansion and retelling of Hsüan-tsang's travels.

Hirakawa Akira. *Indo bukkyoshi*. 2 vols. Tokyo, 1974-1979. A valuable survey of Indian Buddhism from the perspective of Japanese scholarship (English translation forthcoming from the University Press of Hawaii). The development of the earliest Vinaya is discussed in *Ritsuzo no kenkyu* (Tokyo, 1960) and in *Shoki daijo bukkyo no kenkyu* (Tokyo, 1969). The author's "The Rise of Mahayana Buddhism and Its Relationship to the Worship of Stupas," *Memoirs of the Research Department of the Toyo Bunko* 22 (1963): 57-106, is better known in the West and summarizes some of the conclusions of his Japanese writings.

Horner, I. B. *Early Buddhist Theory of Man Perfected*. London, 1936. A study of the *arhat* ideal in the Pali canon. See also Horner's translation of the dialogues between King Menander and Nagasena, *Milinda's Questions* (London, 1964), and *Women under Primitive Buddhism* (1930; reprint, Delhi, 1975).

Horsch, P. "Der Hinduismus und die Religionen der primitivstämme Indiens." *Asiatische Studien / Études asiatiques* 22 (1968): 115-136.

Horsch, P. "Vorstufen der Indischen Seelenwanderungslehre." *Asiatische Studien / Études asiatiques* 25 (1971): 98-157.

Jayatilleke, K. N. *Early Buddhist Theory of Knowledge*. London, 1963. Discusses the relationship between early Buddhist ideas and sramanic and Upanisadic doctrines.

Jong, J. W. de. "A Brief History of Buddhist Studies in Europe and America." *Eastern Buddhist* 7 (May 1974): 55-106. (October

1974): 49-82. For the most part these bibliographic surveys, along with the author's "Recent Buddhist Studies in Europe and America: 1973-1983," *Eastern Buddhist* 17 (1984): 79-107, treat only the philological study of Indian Buddhism. The author also tends to omit certain major figures who are not in his own school of Buddhology. These articles are nonetheless the most scholarly surveys available on the field, and put forth truly excellent models of scholarly rigor.

Joshi, Lal Mani. *Studies in the Buddhistic Culture of India.* Delhi, 1967. Indian Buddhism during the middle and late Mahayana periods.

Kajiyama Yuichi. "Women in Buddhism." *Eastern Buddhist* 15 (1982): 53-70.

Kajiyama Yuichi. "Stupas, the Mother of Buddhas, and Dharma-body." In *New Paths in Buddhist Research*, edited by A. K. Warder, pp. 9-16. Delhi, 1985.

Kimura Taiken. *Abidammaron no kenkyu.* Tokyo, 1937. A survey of Sarvastivada Abhidharma, especially valuable for its analysis of the *Mahavibhasa.*

Lamotte, Étienne. "Buddhist Controversy over the Five Propositions." *Indian Historical Quarterly* 32 (1956). The material collected in this article is also found, slightly augmented, in Lamotte's *magnum opus, Histoire du bouddhisme indien des origines à l'ère Saka* (Louvain, 1958), pp. 300-319, 542-543, 575-606, 690-695. This erudite work is still the standard reference tool on the history of early Indian Buddhism (to circa 200 CE). Unfortunately, Lamotte did not attempt a history of Indian Buddhism for the middle and late periods. He did, however, write an article on the origins of Mahayana titled "Sur la formation du Mahayana," in *Asiatica: Festschrift Friedrich Weller* (Leipzig, 1954), pp. 381-386; this is the definitive statement on the northern origin of Mahayana. See also *Der Verfasser des Upadesa und seine Quellen* (Göttingen, 1973). On early Buddhism, see "La légende du Buddha," *Revue de l'histoire des religious* 134 (1947-1948): 37-71; *Le bouddhisme de Sakyamuni* (Göttingen, 1983); and *The Spirit of Ancient Buddhism* (Venice, 1961). Lamotte also translated a vast amount of Mahayana literature, including *Le traité de la grande vertu de sagesse*, 5 vols. (Louvain, 1944-1980); *La somme du Grand Véhicule d'Asanga*, 2 vols. (Louvain, 1938); and *L'enseignement de Vimalakirti* (Louvain, 1962), containing a long note on the concept of Buddha field (pp. 395-404).

La Vallée Poussin, Louis de. *Bouddhisme: Etudes et matériaux*, London, 1898. One of the most productive and seminal Western scholars of Buddhism, La Vallée Poussin contributed to historical studies in this and other works, as *Bouddhisme: Opinions sur l'histoire de la dogmatique* (Paris, 1909), *L'Inde aux temps des Mauryas* (Paris, 1930), and *Dynasties et histoire de l'Inde depuis Kanishka jusqu'aux invasions musulmanes* (Paris, 1935). Contributions on doctrine include *The Way to Nirvana* (London, 1917); *Nirvana* (Paris, 1925); "La controverse du temps et du pudgala dans la Vijñanakaya," in *Études asiatiques, publiées à l'occasion du vingt-cinquième anniversaire de l'École Française d'Extrême-Orient*, vol. 1 (Paris, 1925), pp. 358-376; *La morale bouddhique* (Paris, 1927); and *Le dogme et la philosophie du bouddhism* (Paris, 1930). On Abhidharma, see "Documents d'Abhidharma," in *Mélanges chinois et bouddhiques*, vol. 1 (Brussels, 1931-1932), pp. 65-109. The Belgian scholar also translated the most influential work of Abhidharma, *L'Abhidharmakosa de Vasubandhu*, 6 vols. (1923-1931; reprint, Brussels, 1971). His articles in the *Encyclopaedia of Religion and Ethics*, edited by James Hastings, are still of value. Especially useful are "Bodhisattva (In Sanskrit Literature)," vol. 2 (Edinburgh, 1909), pp. 739-753; "Mahayana," vol. 8 (1915), pp. 330-336; and "Councils and Synods (Buddhist)," vol. 7 (1914), pp. 179-185.

Law, B. C. *Historical Gleanings.* Calcutta, 1922. Other of his numerous contributions to the early history of Buddhism include *Some Ksatriya Tribes of Ancient India* (Calcutta, 1924), *Tribes in Ancient India* (Poona, 1943), and *The Magadhas in Ancient India* (London, 1946).

Law, B. C., ed. *Buddhistic Studies.* Calcutta, 1931. A collection of seminal essays on the history and doctrines of Indian Buddhism.

Legge, James. *A Record of Buddhist Kingdoms.* Oxford, 1886. English translation of Fa-hsien's accounts.

Majumdar, R. C., ed. *History and Culture of the Indian People*, vols. 2-5. London, 1951. A major survey of the periods of Indian history when Buddhism flourished.

Masson, Joseph. *La religion populaire dans le canon bouddhique Pali.* Louvain, 1942. The standard study on the interactions of high tradition Buddhism with the substratum, not superseded yet.

Masuda Jiryo. "Origins and Doctrines of Early Indian Buddhist Schools." *Asia Major* 2 (1925): 1-78. English translation of Vasumitra's classical account of the Eighteen Schools.

May, Jacques. "La philosophie bouddhique de la vacuité." *Studia Philosophica* 18 (1958): 123-137. Discusses philosophical issues; for historical survey, see "Chugan," in *Hobogirin*, vol. 5 (Paris and Tokyo, 1979), pp. 470-493, and the article coauthored with Mimaki (below). May's treatment of the Yogacara schools (including the school of Saramati), on the other hand, is both historical and doctrinal; see "La philosophie bouddhique idéaliste," *Asiatische Studien / Études asiatiques* 25 (1971): 265-323.

Mimaki Katsumi and Jacques May. "Chudo." In *Hobogirin*, vol. 5, pp. 456-470. Paris and Tokyo, 1979.

Mitra, Debala. *Buddhist Monuments.* Calcutta, 1971. A handy survey of the Buddhist archaeological sites of India.

Mitra, R. C. *The Decline of Buddhism in India.* Calcutta, 1954.

Nagao Gadjin. "The Architectural Tradition in Buddhist Monasticism." In *Studies in History of Buddhism*, edited by A. K. Narain, pp. 189-208. Delhi, 1980.

Nakamura Hajime. *Indian Buddhism: A Survey with Bibliographical Notes.* Tokyo, 1980. Disorganized and poorly edited, but contains useful information on Japanese scholarship on the development of Indian Buddhism.

Nilakanta Sastri, K. A. *Age of the Nandas and Mauryas.* Vara-nasi, 1952. See also his *A History of South India from Prehistoric Times to the Fall of Vijayanagar* (Madras, 1955) and *Development of Religion in South India* (Bombay, 1963).

Oldenberg, Hermann. *Buddha, sein Leben, seine Lehre, seine Gemeinde* (1881). Revised and edited by Helmuth von Glasenapp. Stuttgart, 1959. The first German edition was translated by W. Hoey as *Buddha, His Life, His Doctrine, His Order* (London, 1882).

Paul, Diana. *The Buddhist Feminine Ideal: Queen Srimala and the Tathagatagarbha.* Missoula, Mont., 1980. See also her *Women in Buddhism* (Berkeley, 1980).

Prebish, Charles S. "A Review of Scholarship on the Buddhist Councils." *Journal of Asian Studies* 33 (February 1974): 239-254. Treats the problem of the early schools and the history and significance of their Vinaya. Other works on this topic include Prebish's "The Pratimoksa Puzzle: Facts Versus Fantasy," *Journal of the American Oriental Society* 94 (April-June 1974): 168-176; and *Buddhist Monastic Discipline: The Sanskrit Pratimoksa Sutras of the Mahasanghikas and the Mulasarvastivadins* (University Park, Pa., 1975).

Prebish, Charles S., and Janice J. Nattier. "Mahasanghika Origins: The Beginning of Buddhist Sectarianism." *History of Religions* 16 (1977): 237-272. An original and convincing argument against the conception of the Mahasamghika as "liberals."

Rhys Davids, T. W. *Buddhist India*. London, 1903. A classic, although its methodology is questionable. Also of some use, in spite of its date, is his "Sects (Buddhist)," in the *Encyclopaedia of Religion and Ethics*, edited by James Hastings, vol. 11 (Edinburgh, 1920), pp. 307-309.

Robinson, Richard H. "Classical Indian Philosophy." In *Chapters in Indian Civilization*, edited by Joseph Elder, vol. 1, pp. 127-227. Dubuque, 1970. A bit idiosyncratic, but valuable in its attempt to understand Buddhist philosophy as part of general Indian currents and patterns of speculative thought. Robinson's "The Religion of the Householder Bodhisattva," *Bharati* (1966): 31-55, challenges the notion of Mahayana as a lay movement.

Robinson, Richard H., and Willard L. Johnson. *The Buddhist Religion: A Historical Introduction*. 3d rev. ed. Belmont, Calif., 1982. A great improvement over earlier editions, this book is now a useful manual, with a good bibliography for the English reader.

Ruegg, David S. *The Study of Indian and Tibetan Thought*. Leiden, 1967. The most valuable survey of the main issues of modern scholarship on Indian Buddhism, especially on the early period. The author has also written the definitive study of the Tathagata-garbha doctrines in *La théorie du tathaga-tagarbha et du gotra* (Paris, 1969). See also on the Madhya-mika school his "Towards a Chronology of the Madhyamaka School," in *Indological and Buddhist Studies in Honour of J. W. de Jong* (Canberra, 1982), pp. 505-530, and *The Literature of the Madhyamaka School of Philosophy in India* (Wiesbaden, 1981).

Schayer, Stanislaus. "Precanonical Buddhism." *Acta Orientalia* 7 (1935): 121-132. Posits an early Buddhism not found explicitly in the canon; attempts to reconstruct the doctrines of Buddhism antedating the canon.

Schopen, Gregory. "The Phrase *'sa prthivipradesas caityabhuto bhavet'* in the *Vajracchedika*: Notes on the Cult of the Book in Mahayana." *Indo-Iranian Journal* 17 (1975): 147-181. Schopen's work has opened new perspectives on the early history of Mahayana, emphasizing its religious rather than philosophical character and revealing generalized beliefs and practices rather than the speculations of the elite. See also "Sukhavati as a Generalized Religious Goal in Sanskrit Mahayana Sutra Literature," *Indo-Iranian Journal* 19 (1977): 177-210; "Mahayana in Indian Inscriptions," *Indo-Iranian Journal* 21 (1979): 1-19; and "Two Problems in the History of Indian Buddhism: The Layman/Monk Distinction and the Doctrines of the Transference of Merit," *Studien zur Indologie und Iranistik* 10 (1985): 9-47.

Schlingloff, Dieter. *Die Religion des Buddhismus*. 2 vols. Berlin, 1963. An insightful exposition of Buddhism, mostly from the perspective of canonical Indian documents.

Snellgrove, David L., ed. *Buddhist Himalaya*. Oxford, 1957. Although the context of this study is modern Himalayan Buddhism, it contains useful information on Buddhist Tantra in general. Snellgrove's two-volume *The Hevajra Tantra: A Critical Study* (London, 1959) includes an English translation and study of this major Tantric work. In *The Image of the Buddha* (Tokyo and London, 1978) Snellgrove, in collaboration with other scholars, surveys the history of the iconography of the Buddha image.

Stcherbatsky, Theodore. *The Central Conception of Buddhism and the Meaning of the Word "Dharma"* (1923). Reprint, Delhi, 1970. A classic introduction to Sarvastivadin doctrine. On the Madhyamika, Stcherbatsky wrote *The Conception of Buddhist Nirvana* (Leningrad, 1927). On early Buddhism, see his "The Doctrine of the Buddha," *Bulletin of the School of Oriental Studies* 6 (1932): 867-896, and "The 'Dharmas' of the Buddhists and the 'Gunas' of the Samkhyas," *Indian Historical Quarterly* 10 (1934): 737-760. Stcherbatsky categorized the history of Buddhist thought

in "Die drei Richtungen in der Philosophie des Buddhismus," *Rocznik Orjentalistyczny* 10 (1934): 1-37.

Takasaki Jikido. *Nyoraizo shiso no keisei—Indo daijo bukkyo shiso kenkyu*. Tokyo, 1974. A major study of Tathagata-garbha thought in India.

Thapar, Romila. *Asoka and the Decline of the Mauryas*. London, 1961. Controversial study of Asoka's reign. Her conclusions are summarized in her *History of India*, vol. 1 (Baltimore, 1965). Also relevant for the study of Indian Buddhism are her *Ancient Indian Social History: Some Interpretations* (New Delhi, 1978), *Dissent in the Early Indian Tradition* (Dehradun, 1979), and *From Lineage of State* (Bombay, 1984).

Thomas, Edward J. *The Life of the Buddha as Legend and History* (1927). New York, 1960. Still the only book-length, critical study of the life of Buddha. Less current, but still useful, is the author's 1933 work *The History of Buddhist Thought* (New York, 1975).

Varma, V. P. *Early Buddhism and Its Origins*. New Delhi, 1973.

Vetter, Tilmann. "The Most Ancient Form of Buddhism." In his *Buddhism and Its Relation to Other Religions*. Kyoto, 1985.

Warder, A. K. *Indian Buddhism*. 2d rev. ed. Delhi, 1980. One of the few modern surveys of the field, this work includes a bibliography of classical sources (pp. 523-574). Unfortunately, the author does not make use of materials available in Chinese and Tibetan translation.

Watanabe Fumimaro. *Philosophy and Its Development in the Nikayas and Abhidhamma*. Delhi, 1983. The beginnings of Buddhist scholasticism, especially as seen in the transition from Sutra to Abhidharma literature.

Watters, Thomas. *On Yuan Chwang's Travels in India*. 2 vols. London, 1904-1905. Extensive study of Hsüan-tsang's travels.

Wayman, Alex. *The Buddhist Tantras: Light on Indo-Tibetan Esotericism*. New York, 1973. Not a survery or introduction to the study of Indian Tantra, but a collection of essays on specific issues and problems. Chapter 1.2 deals with the problem of the early history of Tantra. See also Wayman's *Yoga of the Guhyasamajatantra: The Arcane Lore of Forty Verses; A Buddhist Tantra Commentary* (Delhi, 1977). In his "The Mahasanghika and the Tathagatagarbha (Buddhist Doctrinal History, Study 1)," *Journal of the International Association of Buddhist Studies* 1 (1978): 35-50, Wayman discusses possible connections between the Mahasamghika subsects of Andhra and the development of Mahayana. His "Meditation in Theravada and Mahisasaka," *Studia Missionalia* 25 (1976): 1-28, is a study of the doctrine of meditation in two of the leading schools of Hinayana.

Winternitz, Moriz. *Geschichte der indischen Literatur*, vol. 2. Leipzig, 1920. Translated as *A History of Indian Literature* (Delhi, 1983). Largely dated but not superseded.

Zelliot, Eleanor. *Dr. Ambedkar and the Mahar Movement*. Philadelphia, 1969.

LUIZ O. GÓMEZ

Buddhism in Southeast Asia

Southeast Asian Buddhism in the Modern Period. The classical Southeast Asian religio-cultural synthesis, of which Theravada Buddhism has been a major component, has given the cultures of Burma, Thailand, Cambodia, Laos, and Vietnam a unique sense of identity and has sustained them to the present. Faced with Western imperialistic expansion from the seventeenth century onward and the challenge of modernity, the classical religious worldview, institutional structures, and cultural ethos have been changed, modified, and reasserted in a variety of ways.

Modernization and reform. The eve of the assertion of colonial power in the Buddhist countries of Southeast Asia found them in differing states and conditions. The Burmese destruction of Ayutthaya in 1767 provided the Thai (the designation applied to Tai living in the modern nation-state) the opportunity to establish a new capital on the lower Chaophraya River at present-day Bangkok. Because of its accessibility to international commerce the new site was much better situated for the new era about to dawn; the new dynastic line was better able to cope with the increasing impact of Western influence and was also committed to building a new sense of national unity.

The classical Thai Buddhist worldview had been set forth in the *Traibhumikatha* of King Lü Thai of Sukhothai. In one sense this text must be seen as part of Lü Thai's program to reconstruct an administrative and political framework and to salvage the alliance structure that had collapsed under the policies of his predecessor. In laying out the traditional Buddhist stages of the deterioration of history, Lü Thai meant to affirm the meaningfulness of a karmically calculated human life within a given multitiered universe. As a Buddhist sermon it urges its listeners to lead a moral life and by so doing to reap the appropriate heavenly rewards.

Modernization of the Thai Buddhist worldview was accompanied by a reform of the Buddhist *sangha*. Before his coronation in 1851 King Mongkut had been a monk for twenty-five years. During that time his study of the Pali scriptures and his association with Mon monks of a stricter discipline convinced him that Thai Buddhism had departed from the authentic Buddhist tradition. He advocated a more serious study of Pali and Buddhist scripture as well as the attainment of proficiency in meditation. His efforts at religious reform resulted in an upgrading of monastic discipline in an effort to make it more orthodox. The group of monks who gathered around Mongkut at Wat Bovornives called themselves the Thammayut ("those adhering to the doctrine") and formed the nucleus of a new, stricter sect of Thai Buddhism.

The development of a reformist Buddhist tradition that embodied Mongkut's ideals brought about further changes in the monastic order, especially as the *sangha* became part of the policies and programs of Mongkut's son Chulalongkorn. At the same time that he implemented reforms designed to politically integrate outlying areas into the emergent nation-state of Thailand, Chulalongkorn also initiated policies aimed at the incorporation of all Buddhists within the kingdom into a single national organization. As a consequence, monastic discipline, as well as the quality of monastic education, improved throughout the country. A standard monastic curriculum, which included three levels of

study in Buddhist history, doctrine, and liturgy, and nine levels of Pali study, was established throughout the country. In addition, two Buddhist academies for higher studies were established in Bangkok.

Buddhism and the modern nation-state. Buddhism proved to be a crucial factor during the end of the colonial and the postcolonial periods, as Burma, Thailand, Cambodia, Laos, and Vietnam became modern nation-states. On the one hand, Buddhism contributed decisively to the development of the new nationhood; on the other, it resisted in various ways to changes forced upon traditional Buddhist thought and practice.

Historically, Buddhism played an important role in the definition of the classical Southeast Asian states. It was

> **Historically, Buddhism played an important role in the definition of the classical Southeast Asian states.**

inevitable, therefore, that it would be a crucial factor in the redefinition of these states. In those cases, for example, in which a country was dominated by a colonial power, nationalist movements grew out of, or were identified with, a religious base or context. Take Burma as a case in point. Buddhism provided the impetus for the independence movement that arose there during the first decades of the twentieth century. The YMBAs (Young Men's Buddhist Association) of Rangoon and elsewhere in Burma quickly assumed a political role.

When U Nu became prime minister in January 1948, following Aung San's assassination, he put Buddhism at the heart of his political program. He created a Buddhist Sasana Council in 1950 to propagate Buddhism and to supervise monks, appointed a minister of religious affairs, and ordered government departments to dismiss civil servants thirty minutes early if they wished to meditate. In 1960 U Nu committed himself and his party to making Buddhism the state religion of Burma, an unpopular move with such minorities as the Christian Karens. This attempt was one of the reasons given for General Ne Win's coup in March 1962, which deposed U Nu as prime minister.

Buddhism figured prominently in other Southeast Asian countries, both as a basis of protest against ruling regimes and as an important symbolic component of political leadership. In the 1960s politically active Vietnamese monks contributed to the downfall of the Diem regime, and afterward the United Buddhist Association, under the leadership of Thich Tri Quang and Thich Thien Minh, remained politically active. In Cambodia, Prince Sihanouk espoused a political philosophy based on Buddhist socialism and was the last

Cambodian ruler to represent, although in an attenuated way, the tradition of classical Southeast Asian Buddhist rule.

In Thailand the centralization of the Thai *sangha* under King Chulalongkorn and his able *sangharaja*, Vaji-rañana, not only improved monastic discipline and education but also integrated the monastic order more fully into the nation-state. Chulalongkorn's successor, Vajiravudh (1910-1925), made loyalty to the nation synonymous with loyalty to Buddhism; in effect, he utilized Buddhism as an instrument to promote a spirit of nationalism.

Buddhism has continued to be an important tool in the government's policy to promote national unity. In 1962 the Buddhist Sangha Act further centralized the organization of the monastic order under the power of the secular state. In the same year the government organized the Dhammadhuta program, and in 1965 the Dhammacarika program. The former supported Buddhist monks abroad and those working in sensitive border areas, especially the northeastern region of the country, while the latter has focused on Buddhist missions among northern hill tribes.

Other, more radical Buddhist responses to the emerging nation-state developed in various parts of Southeast Asia and usually centered on a charismatic leader who was sometimes identified as an incarnation of the *bodhisattva* Maitreya. In Burma several rebellions in the early twentieth century aimed to overthrow British rule and to restore the fortunes of both Burmese kingship and Burmese Buddhism. One of these was led by Saya San, who had been a monk in the Tharrawaddy district in lower Burma but disrobed to work in a more directly political way to overthrow the British. Saya San's movement had a strongly traditional religious and royal aura, and much of his support came from political monks associated with nationalistic associations *(wunthanu athins)* that had formed in the 1920s. Saya San was "crowned" as "king" in a thoroughly traditional Burmese manner in a jungle capital on 28 October 1930. An armed group was trained and the rebellion launched toward the end of December. As the conflict spread throughout lower Burma and into the Shan States, the British army was called in to help the police forces repress the rebellion. Only after eight months of fighting did the warfare end.

Recent trends. The modern period has seen increased lay leadership at various levels of religious life. The YMBAs of Burma and the Buddhist "Sunday schools" that have arisen in Thailand have obviously been influenced by Western Christian models. Lay associations have developed for various purposes. For example, prior to the revolution Cambodia had the Buddhist Association of the Republic of Cambodia (1952), the Association of Friends of the Buddhist Lycée (1949), the Association of Friends of Religious Welfare Aid Centers, the Association of Religious Students of the Republic of Cambodia (1970), the Association of the Buddhist Youth of Cambodia (1971), and so on. Buddhist laity

have also been actively involved in the worldwide Buddhist movement. Most notable of the laity groups are the World Fellowship of Buddhists, which has headquarters in Bangkok, and the World Council of Churches, which holds interreligious dialogue consultations.

While meditation has become a lay as well as monastic practice in contemporary Southeast Asian Buddhism, this development has not precluded a movement to formulate a strong, activist social ethic. The Vietnamese Zen monk Thich Nhat Hahn attempted to work out a Buddhist solution to the military conflict in his country during the 1960s, and there has been a widespread interest in formulating a Buddhist theory of economic development that is critical of Western capitalism but not necessarily indebted to Marxism. Buddhists have also acted to solve particular social problems, such as drug addiction, and have spoken out strongly against the proliferation of nuclear arms. Southeast Asian Buddhists have also joined with members of other religious groups, both within their own countries as well as in international organizations, to work for such causes as world peace and basic civil rights for all peoples. Buddhist interpreters, such as the Thai monk Bhikkhu Buddhadasa, have referred to Buddhism as a practical system of personal and social morality.

[*An examination of the relationship between the samgha and the larger societies of which it is a part can be found in* Southeast Asian Religions. *See also* Pilgrimage, Burmese Religion, Khmer Religion, Lao Religion, Thai Religion, *and* Vietnamese Religion.]

BIBLIOGRAPHY

Works on Buddhism in Southeast Asia include text translations and doctrinal studies, histories of the development of Buddhism in various Southeast Asian countries, anthropological treatments of popular, village Buddhism, and studies of Buddhism and political change. Georges Coedès's studies, *The Indianized States of Southeast Asia*, edited by Walter F. Vella and translated by Susan Brown Cowing (Canberra, 1968), and *The Making of South-East Asia*, translated by H. M. Wright (Berkeley, 1966), are standard treatments of the region, as is Reginald Le May's *The Culture of South-East Asia* (London, 1954). The classic study of Southeast Asian religion and kingship is Robert Heine-Geldern's *Conceptions of State and Kingship in Southeast Asia* (Ithaca, N. Y., 1956). A readable, general study of the history of Theravada Buddhism in Southeast Asia and its present teachings and practices is Robert C. Lester's *Theravada Buddhism in Southeast Asia* (Ann Arbor, 1973). My *Buddhism and Society in Southeast Asia* (Chambersburg, Pa., 1981) is an analysis of Theravada Buddhism in terms of the themes of syncretism, political legitimation, and modernization. The theme of Buddhism and political legitimation is discussed in several seminal articles in *Buddhism and Legitimation of Power in Thailand, Laos, and Burma*, edited by Bardwell L. Smith (Chambersburg, Pa., 1978).

The monumental work on the early Pagan period is Gordon H. Luce's *Old Burma—Early Pagán*, 3 vols. (Locust Valley, N. Y., 1969-1970). Two of the important Burmese chronicles have been translated: *Hmannan maha yazawintawkyi: The Glass Palace Chronicle of* the Kings of Burma, translated by Pe Maung Tin and G. H. Luce (London, 1923); and Pannasami's The History of the Buddha's Religion (Sasanavamsa), translated by B. C. Law (London, 1952). Standard treatments of both Pali and Sanskritic Buddhism in Burma are Nihar-Ranjan Ray's An Introduction to the Study of Theravada Buddhism in Burma (Calcutta, 1946), and his Sanskrit Buddhism in Burma (Calcutta, 1936). A more recent study is Winston L. King's A Thousand Lives Away (Cambridge, Mass., 1964). Two standard anthropological studies are Melford E. Spiro's Buddhism and Society: A Great Tradition and its Burmese Vicissitudes, 2d. ed. (Berkeley, 1982), and Manning Nash's The Golden Road to Modernity (New York, 1965). Nash was also the general editor of Anthropological Studies in Theravada Buddhism (New Haven, 1966), which contains valuable articles on Burmese and Thai Buddhism by Nash, David E. Pfanner, and Jasper Ingersoll. E. Michael Mendelson's Sangha and State in Burma, edited by John P. Ferguson (Ithaca, N. Y., 1965), although difficult going is a mine of information. Buddhism and the early nationalist period are studied in Emanuel Sarkisyanz's Buddhist Backgrounds of the Burmese Revolution (The Hague, 1965), and Donald E. Smith's Religion and Politics in Burma (Princeton, 1965).

The standard Thai history with much information about Thai Buddhism is David K. Wyatt's Thailand: A Short History (New Haven, 1984); Kenneth E. Wells's Thai Buddhism: Its Rites and Activities (Bangkok, 1939), while somewhat dated and rather dry is still very useful. One of the major northern Thai chronicles, Ratanapanya's Jinakalamalipakaranam, has been translated by N. A. Jayawickrama as The Sheaf of Garlands of the Epochs of the Conqueror (London, 1968). Frank E. Reynolds and Mani B. Reynolds have translated the major Thai cosmological treatise, Trai Phumi Phra Ruang, as Three Worlds according to King Ruang (Berkeley, 1982). Prince Dhani-Nivat's A History of Buddhism in Siam, 2d ed. (Bangkok, 1965), provides a brief historical overview of the development of Buddhism in Thailand. Much recent, significant work on Thai Buddhism has been done by anthropologists; see especially Stanley J. Tambiah's World Conqueror and World Renouncer (Cambridge, 1976) and several articles by Charles F. Keyes, for example, "Buddhism and National Integration in Thailand," Journal of Asian Studies 30 (May 1971): 551-567. Historians of religion have also contributed to our knowledge of Thai Buddhism. Frank E. Reynolds has written several articles including, "The Holy Emerald Jewel: Some Aspects of Buddhist Symbolism and Political Legitimation in Thailand and Laos," in Religion and Legitimation of Power in Thailand, Laos, and Burma, edited by Bardwell L. Smith (Chambersburg, Pa., 1978), pp. 175-193. I have analyzed a major northern Thai monastery in Wat Haripuñjaya: A Study of the Royal Temple of the Buddha's Relic, Lamphun, Thailand (Missoula, Mont., 1976).

French scholars have made the major contribution to the study of Buddhism in Laos, Cambodia, and Vietnam. Louis Finot's "Research sur la littérature laotienne," Bulletin de l'École Française d'Extrême-Orient 17 (1917) is an indispensable tool in the study of Lao Buddhist literature. Marcel Zago's Rites et cérémonies en milieu bouddhiste lao (Rome, 1972) provides a comprehensive treatment of Lao religion, although Charles Archaimbault's "Religious Structures in Laos," Journal of the Siam Society 52 (1964): 57-74, while more limited in scope is very useful. Lawrence Palmer Brigg's "The Syncretism of Religions in Southeast Asia, especially in the Khmer Empire," Journal of the American Oriental Society 71 (October-December 1951): 230-249, provides a survey of the development of religion in Cambodia. Adhémard Leclère's classic study, Le bouddhisme au Cambodge (Paris, 1899) remains the standard work. The classic study of Vietnamese religion is Leopold Michel Cadière's Croyances et pratiques religieuses des Viêtnamiens, 3 vols. (Saigon, 1955-1958), but more accessible is the brief sketch in the trilingual volume by Chanh-tri Mai-tho-Truyen, Le bouddhisme au Vietnam, Buddhism in Vietnam, Phat-giao Viet-nam (Saigon, 1962). Thich Thien-An's Buddhism and Zen in Vietnam in Relation to the Development of Buddhism in Asia, edited by Carol Smith (Los Angeles, 1975), studies the development of Buddhist schools from the sixth to the seventeenth century. Thich Nhat-Hanh's Vietnam: Lotus in a Sea of Fire (New York, 1967) puts the Buddhist situation in the 1960s into historical perspective.

Interested readers may also wish to consult the following works: Heinz Bechert's three-volume study, Buddhismus, Staat und Gesellschaft in den Ländern Theravada-Buddhismus (Frankfurt, 1966-1973); Religion in South Asia, edited by Edward B. Harper (Seattle, 1964), especially the articles by Michael Ames and Nur Yalman; and Religion and Progress in Modern Asia, edited by Robert N. Bellah (New York, 1965).

DONALD K. SWEARER

Buddhism in Tibet

The Modern Era. Among the intellectual giants of the eighteenth century, Ka'-thog Rig-'dzin Tshe-dban-nor-bu (1698-1755) must be mentioned. He was not content with merely repeating what secondary sources claimed to be authoritative, but attempted to go back to the original sources, often reaching startling conclusions. His main interests were history and geography. No less important is 'Jigs-med-glin-pa (1730-1798) whose major contributions are the Klon chen sñin thig practices, which he developed after having had a vision of Klonchen Rab-'byams-pa. Despite his wide interests, profoundness of thought, and remarkable scholarship, 'Jigs-med-glin-pa never attained the brilliant organization and beauty of style that mark the writings of his model, Klonchen Rab-'byams-pa. Another important figure of this period was Gzan-phan-mtha'-yas (b. 1740), who stressed the importance of monastic rules (which he considered indispensable for education) and held that monks had an obligation to society. In this sense he was the first social reformer in Tibet.

The Ris-med movement in the nineteenth century counted among its members such illustrious persons as `Jammgon Kon-sprul Blo-gros-mtha'-yas (1813-1899), a competent physician and the author of the encyclopedia Ses bya kun khyab and a unique nonsectarian collection of texts pertaining to spiritual training, the Gdams nag mdzod; 'Jam-dbyans Mkhyen-brtse'i-dban-po (1820-1892), a master of Buddhist poetry; and, last but not least, 'Ju Mi-pham 'Jam-dbyans-rnam-rgyal-rgya-mtsho (1841-1912), who wrote on every imaginable topic. There were, and still are, other figures of significance.

When the Chinese occupied Tibet in 1959, a move that probably was a preemptive strike against other aspirants, the initial policy was one of destruction. This policy has changed from time to time, however, and reports coming from Tibet are conflicting. What may be stated with assurance is that the political power that the monasteries once wielded is a matter of the past. In those monasteries where the lamas are permitted to continue to perform religious ceremonies, no other activities are allowed, which means that no intellectual support is forthcoming.

[*The interactions between Buddhism and indigenous Tibetan religions are discussed in* Himalayan Religions.]

BIBLIOGRAPHY

The best readily available book on Buddhism in Tibet is Giuseppe Tucci's *The Religions of Tibet* (Berkeley, 1980), translated from the German and Italian by Geoffrey Samuel. This book also contains an exhaustive bibliography, although the Tibetan titles listed may be difficult to locate. Valuable material is also found in R. A. Stein's *Tibetan Civilization* (Stanford, Calif. 1972), translated by J. E. Stapleton Driver. In this book the Tibetan source material has been listed so as to be identifiable. Stein has also used Chinese sources. David Snellgrove and Hugh Richardson's *A Cultural History of Tibet* (New York, 1968) is very readable but is sketchy and politically oriented.

HERBERT GUENTHER

Buddhism in China

Buddhism in modern and contemporary China. The late nineteenth century witnessed the first attempts, undertaken by some cultured laymen, to revive Buddhism. It was part of a general tendency to overcome China's backwardness in the face of Western and Japanese dominance, and also, more specifically, a reaction to the impact of the Christian missions in China. After the revolution and the establishment of the republic (1912), various attempts were made to organize the Buddhist clergy on a national scale, to raise its cultural level through the founding of Buddhist seminars, and to establish contacts with Japan, India, and the Buddhist countries in South and Southeast Asia.

Following the establishment in 1949 of the People's Republic, official Chinese policy toward the Buddhist clergy oscillated between political supervision (exercised through a completely politicized Buddhist Association) and violent suppression, notably during mass campaigns such as the Cultural Revolution (1966-1969). Where Buddhism is tolerated, it is clearly a truncated Buddhism, limited to devotional activities and divested of all the social and economic functions that the monasteries once had. The clergy itself, on which no reliable quantitative data are available, has no doubt been decimated by laicization and the lack of new ordinations. In general, prospects for Buddhism on the Chinese mainland are gloomy.

[*See also* Chinese Religion.]

BIBLIOGRAPHY

The best and most up-to-date monographic works dealing with the history of Chinese Buddhism as a whole are Kenneth Ch`en's *Buddhism in China* (Princeton, 1964) and *The Chinese Transformation of Buddhism* (Princeton, 1973). The best short presentation of the subject is to be found in Paul Demiéville's masterly survey *Le bouddhisme chinois* (Paris, 1970). A. F. Wright's *Buddhism in Chinese History* (1959; reprint, Stanford, Calif., 1965) is readable but somewhat superficial. The history of Indo-Chinese relations as illustrated by Chinese Buddhism is treated by Probodh C. Bagchi in *India and China: A Thousand Years of Cultural Relations*, 2d ed. (Bombay, 1950). The early period (until the early fifth century CE) is extensively covered in my book *The Buddhist Conquest of China*, 2 vols. (1959; reprint, Leiden, 1979). The social and economic aspects of the Buddhist clergy in the medieval period (fifth to ninth centuries) have been excellently treated by Jacques Gernet in *Les aspects économiques du bouddhisme* (Saigon, 1956). There is a voluminous Western-language literature on Ch`an (Zen) Buddhism, most of which is of mediocre quality. Positive exceptions are *The Secrets of Chinese Meditation* (London, 1964) by Charles Luk (K`uan Yü Lu) and *The Platform Sutra of the Sixth Patriarch*, edited and translated by Philip B. Yampolsky (New York, 1967). On the tensions between state and church in premodern China the only overall study still is the now outmoded and rather partisan *Sectarianism and Religious Persecution in China*, 2 vols. (Amsterdam, 1903-1904), by J. J. M. de Groot. The best surveys of Chinese Buddhism in modern times can be found in the relevant parts of Wing-tsit Chan's *Religious Trends in Modern China* (New York, 1953) and of Yang Ch`ing-k`un's *Religion in Chinese Society* (Berkeley, 1961); for a more detailed treatment of Chinese Buddhism in the twentieth century, see Holmes Welch's *The Practice of Chinese Buddhism, 1900-1950* (Cambridge, Mass., 1967) and *The Buddhist Revival in China* (Cambridge, Mass., 1968). Welch has also described the fate of Buddhism in the People's Republic of China up to the late 1960s in *Buddhism under Mao* (Cambridge, Mass., 1972).

ERIK ZURCHER

Buddhism in Korea

Buddhism during the Modern Era. After the annexation of Korea in 1910, some Korean monks felt that the fortunes of the religion were dependent upon arranging a merger with a major Japanese sect. Yi Hoe-gwang went so far as to negotiate a combination of the Korean church with the Japanese Soto sect, but most Korean Son monks regarded the gradualistic teachings of the Soto sect as anathema to the subitist orientation of their own tradition, and managed to block the merger. Another movement threatened to further divide the Buddhist church. As early as 1913, Han Yong-un (1879-1944), the only Buddhist signatory to the 1919 Korean independence declaration and a major literary figure, had shocked his contemporaries by advocating that monks be allowed to marry, a move he felt was necessary if Buddhism were to maintain any viable role in modern secular society. While this position was diametrically opposed to the traditional celibate orientation of the Korean ecclesia, the

Japanese colonial government ultimately sustained it in 1926 with its promulgation of new monastic regulations that legalized matrimony for monks. Within a decade, virtually all temple abbots were married, thereby producing a dramatic change in the traditional moral discipline of the Korean church.

After independence in 1945, Korean Buddhism was badly split between two irreconcilable sects. The T'aego-chong, a liberal sect of married monks, had flourished under Japanese patronage and was based principally in the cities where it catered to the lay Buddhist population. The Chogye-chong was a smaller, religiously conservative faction of monks who had managed to maintain their celibacy during the long years of Japanese occupation; their concern was to restore the meditative, scholastic, and disciplinary orientations of traditional Korean Buddhism. Only after years of intense conflict did the Chogye-chong finally win government support for its position in 1954.

BIBLIOGRAPHY

It remains difficult for the nonspecialist to find reliable books on Korean Buddhism in Western languages. Some summaries of research by Korean and Japanese scholars have appeared in *Buddhist Culture in Korea*, "Korean Culture Series," vol. 3, edited by Chun Shin-yong (Seoul, 1974). J. H. Kamstra's *Encounter or Syncretism: The Initial Growth of Japanese Buddhism* (Leiden, 1967), part 3, includes a useful survey of Three Kingdoms Buddhism and its influence on early Japan. The biographies of several prominent monks of the early Three Kingdoms period are translated in Peter H. Lee's *Lives of Eminent Korean Monks: The Haedong Kosung Chon* (Cambridge, Mass., 1969). A liberal rendering of a major Korean hagiographical and doxographical collection dealing with Three Kingdoms Buddhism appears in *Samguk Yusa: Legends and History of the Three Kingdoms of Ancient Korea*, translated by Tae-hung Ha and Grafton K. Mintz (Seoul, 1972). The travelogue of a Korean monk's pilgrimage to India and central Asia has been newly translated by Han Sung Yang, Yün-hua Jan, and Shotaro Iida in *The Hye Ch'o Diary* (Berkeley, 1984). Korean Hwaom thought receives some coverage in Steve Odin's *Process Metaphysics and Hua-yen Buddhism: A Critical Study of Cumulative Penetration vs. Interpenetration* (Albany, N.Y., 1982); the appendix includes a translation of Uisang's outline of Hwaom philosophy. Ch'egwan's survey of Ch'ont'ae philosophy has been translated in David W. Chappell and Masao Ichishima's *T'ien-t'ai Buddhism: An Outline of the Fourfold Teachings* (Honolulu, 1984).

Korean Son Buddhism is covered in my own book *The Korean Approach to Zen: The Collected Works of Chinul* (Honolulu, 1983). My introduction there includes a rather extensive survey of the early history of Korean Buddhism, and particularly the Son tradition, in order to trace the contexts of Chinul's life and thought; specialists may also consult the bibliography of works in Asian languages on Korean Buddhism that appears there. Chinul's contributions to Korean Buddhism have also been examined in Hee-sung Keel's *Chinul: Founder of the Korean Son Tradition* (Berkeley, 1984). A provocative exposition of Korean Son practice appears in Sung Bae Park's *Buddhist Faith and Sudden Enlightenment* (Albany, N. Y., 1983). The principal works of Won Buddhism are translated in Chon Pal-khn's *The Canonical Textbook of Won Buddhism* (Seoul, 1971).

A number of seminal literary compositions by Korean Buddhists from all periods are translated in Peter H. Lee's *Anthology of Korean Literature: From Early Times to the Nineteenth Century* (Honolulu, 1981). A representative selection of philosophical and hagiographical writings by Korean Buddhist authors will appear in *Sources of Korean Tradition*, edited by Peter H. Lee (New York, forthcoming). The few Western-language works on Korean Buddhism written up to 1979 are listed in *Studies on Korea: A Scholar's Guide*, edited by Han-Kyo Kim (Honolulu, 1980); see chapter 4, "Philosophy and Religion."

ROBERT EVANS BUSWELL, JR.

Buddhism in Japan

Buddhism in Modern Japan. The modern period in Japanese history began with the Meiji restoration in 1868 and brought a series of radical changes in all spheres of life, including religion. Buddhism was deeply affected both in a positive and negative sense by the rapid process of modernization. One of the most pronounced changes took place on the institutional level, particularly in the relation of Buddhism to the state. In its attempt to mobilize the nation under the authority of the emperor, the Meiji government gave a definite priority to Shinto and thereby put an end to the age-old Shinto-Buddhist syncretism. Certainly, in the beliefs and practices of the common people the two traditions are still regarded as harmoniously united. Even today, many Japanese pay homage to Shinto shrines at the same time that they are associated with Buddhist temples.

These changes in the social milieu, combined with the influences from the Christian West that began to enter the country beginning in the latter half of the nineteenth century, elicited a number of responses from traditional Buddhist organizations on different levels and in various forms. One was a new and active engagement in educational and social work projects. Parallel to this trend, one can also observe a renewal of missionary efforts, which in some cases even led to the establishment of overseas missions.

Side by side with these reforms, many Buddhist leaders felt the need to cope with the challenge of modernity. Thus, new academic studies of Buddhism, both philosophical and philological in nature, were initiated.

Finally, a number of new movements appeared on the fringes of or outside the established groups. Insofar as they do not conform to the traditional clerical framework, they may be loosely characterized as lay Buddhist movements. Some of them remain rather small, consisting of only a handful of people dedicated to spiritual quest and the study of Buddhist ideas.

[*For an overview of the role of Buddhism in Japanese culture, see* Japanese Religion. *For Buddhist cultic life, see* Pilgrimage.]

BIBLIOGRAPHY

Works in English. The number of Western-language materials dealing with this subject belies its importance. Among the few works now available, some treat Buddhism within the larger context of Japanese religion. A standard reference of this category remains Masaharu Anesaki's *History of Japanese Religion with Special Reference to the Social and Moral Life of the Nation* (1930; reprint, Rutland, Vt., and Tokyo, 1963), although some of its data and interpretations are naturally outdated. Fortunately we have an excellent successor to it in Joseph M. Kitagawa's *Religion in Japanese History* (New York, 1966). Intending to treat Japanese religion as a whole, the book traces the intricate relationship between various religious systems of Japan roughly from the third century to the post-World War II period. It also contains an extensive bibliography and glossary.

For the study of the position and role of Buddhism in Japan, the pertinent sections of H. Byron Earhart's *Japanese Religion: Unity and Diversity*, 3d rev. ed. (Belmont, Calif., 1982) as well as of *Japanese Religion* (Tokyo and Palo Alto, Calif., 1972), issued by the Agency for Cultural Affairs of the Japanese Government, may be consulted with profit. As for books addressing themselves specifically to Buddhism in Japan, Charles Eliot's *Japanese Buddhism* (1935; reprint, New York, 1959) deserves attention. While not exhaustive, it nevertheless gives important insights into some aspects of Buddhism in Japan. Very useful is Daigan Matsunaga and Alicia Matsunaga's *Foundation of Japanese Buddhism*, 2 vols. (Los Angeles and Tokyo, 1974-1976). These volumes contain detailed information about the historical transmission and the basic tenets of major schools together with a brief description of the social background, but their coverage is limited roughly to the end of the medieval period.

Generally, Buddhism after the medieval period is a subject that has so far been relatively neglected and publications in this area are scarce even in Japanese. In this sense, *Japanese Religion in the Meiji Era*, compiled and edited by Hideo Kishimoto and translated by John F. Howes (Tokyo, 1956), is noteworthy as it gives a succinct account of the situation of Buddhism from the Tokugawa through the Meiji era.

Specialized studies. In addition to works of a more general nature, there are materials dealing either with a particular period, a particular school, or personalities, of which the following represents only a tentative selection. About the ancient period, we have Marinus Willem de Visser's *Ancient Buddhism in Japan*, 2 vols. (Paris, 1928-1935). There have been relatively few titles on Esoteric Buddhism despite its popularity. Minoru Kiyota's *Shingon Buddhism: Theory and Practice* (Los Angeles, 1978) is one of the recent books to fill in this gap, together with E. Dale Saunders's *Mudra: A Study of Symbolic Gestures in Japanese Buddhist Sculpture* (New York, 1960). Of the works on the life and thought of Honen, the founder of the Jodoshu, Harper Coates and Ryugaku Ishizuka's *Honen, the Buddhist Saint*, 5 vols. (1925; reprint, Kyoto, 1949) is most basic, being the translation of the authorized biography with a careful introduction. Nichiren, the founder of another influential school, is vividly portrayed in Masaharu Anesaki's *Nichiren the Buddhist Prophet* (1916; reprint, Gloucester, Mass., 1966). Heinrich Dumoulin's *A History of Zen Buddhism*, translated by Paul Peachey (New York, 1963), gives a good survey both of the historical background and of the development of Zen in Japan. The influence of Zen on Japanese culture is a topic that has enjoyed some popularity, for which D. T. Suzuki's *Zen and Japanese Culture*, 2d ed., rev. & enl. (1959; reprint, Princeton, 1970), may be regarded as classic, although the author tends to stress somewhat one-sidedly the impact of Zen. As for the new religious movements derived from Buddhism, basic information can be found in Clark B. Offner and Henry van Straelen's *Modern Japanese Religions* (Leiden, 1963) as well as in Harry Thomsen's *The New Religions of Japan* (Tokyo and Rutland, Vt., 1963).

Further references. Because of the nature of the subject, the bulk of source materials as well as of research results are published in Japanese. In order to supplement the perhaps uneven selection listed above, a few descriptive bibliographies in English on Japanese publications may be cited. These are *A Bibliography on Japanese Buddhism*, edited by Shojun Bando, Shoyu Hanayama, Ryojun Sato, Shinko Sayeki, and Keiryu Shima (Tokyo, 1958), and *K. B. S. Bibliography of Standard Reference Books for Japanese Studies, with Descriptive Notes*, vol. 4, Religion, edited by the Kokusai Bunka Shinkokai (Tokyo, 1963). The former has about 1,660 entries and the latter, under the heading of Buddhism, 92 basic works. A successor to the latter is *An Introductory Bibliography for Japanese Studies* (Tokyo, 1975-), published by the Japan Foundation in two- to three-year intervals. It gives a brief report on the research works done in the area of Japanese Buddhism during the years under review.

Works in Japanese. Each of the major schools of Japanese Buddhism has collected its own textual corpus. See *Tendaishu zensho*, 25 vols., edited by the Tendai Shuten Kankokai (Tokyo, 1935-1937); *Shingonshu zensho*, 42 vols., edited by the Shingonshu Zensho Kankokai (Wakayama, 1933-1939); *Jodoshu zensho*, 21 vols., edited by the Jodoshu Shuten Kankokai (Tokyo, 1929-1931), and its sequel, *Zoku Jodoshu zensho*, 20 vols., edited by the Shusho Hozonkai (Tokyo, 1940-1942); *Shinshu zensho*, 74 vols., edited by Tsumaki Naoyoshi (Tokyo, 1913-1916); *Kokuyaku Zengaku taisei*, 25 vols., edited by Miyauchi Sotai and Sato Koyo (Tokyo, 1930-1931); and *Nichirenshu zensho*, 30 vols., edited by the Nichirenshu Zensho Shuppankai (Tokyo, 1910-1916). These sources provide fuller documentation for the sectarian traditions than is available in such standard canonical collections as the *Taisho shinshu daizokyo*, 100 vols. (Tokyo, 1924-1932) or the *Dainihon zokuzokyo*, 150 boxes (Kyoto, 1905-1912).

While Buddhist studies in the premodern period had been pursued mostly in the form of dogmatic exegesis, historical scholarship has flourished in this century. Among its many achievements, by far the most basic reference is Tsuji Zennosuke's *Nihon bukkyoshi*, 11 vols. (Tokyo, 1944-1953). Covering the whole of Buddhist history from its inception down to the dawn of the Meiji era, it gives a vivid picture of Buddhism in the context of the social, political, and intellectual situation of each period. While not as voluminous, Tamamuro Taijo's *Nihon bukkyoshi gaisetsu* (Tokyo, 1940) is very instructive. Written from the perspective of socioeconomic history, it successfully clarifies the position of Buddhist organizations throughout Japanese history. Representative of a different, intellectual history, approach are Ienaga Saburo's *Jodai bukkyo shisoshi kenkyu* (Tokyo, 1948) and *Chusei bukkyo shisoshi kenkyu* (Kyoto, 1947). In many essays collected in these two books, Ienaga tries to decipher the peculiarity of the Buddhist outlook and its impact on the Japanese mentality. On the history of Buddhism in modern Japan, a hitherto unexplored field, Yoshida Kyuichi's *Nihon kindai bukkyoshi kenkyu* (Tokyo, 1959) gives a succinct overview. Finally, *Bukkyogaku kankei zasshi rombun bunrui mokuroku*, 2 vols., edited by the Ryukoku Daigaku Toshokan (Kyoto, 1931-1961), serves as a useful guide to the research works undertaken from the beginning of the Meiji era to the late 1950s.

TAMARU NORIYOSHI

BUDDHISM, SCHOOLS OF

An Overview

Like all world religions, Buddhism presents a picture of bewildering variety: doctrinal, liturgical, linguistic, and organizational. This diversity was largely the combined result of geographical diffusion and cultural adaptation. Wherever it was introduced, over an area ranging from Afghanistan to Indonesia and Japan, Buddhism became an integral part of different cultures, partly coexisting with local beliefs and cults, and partly absorbing them into its own system. But diversity was also stimulated by certain features within Buddhism itself: the absence of a central doctrinal authority; social stratification within the clergy; the relation of the Buddhist order with the temporal powers; royal patronage; the influence of the laity; and, in some cases, competition between large monastic centers. However, in spite of all this diversity we must not lose sight of the basic and always recognizable identity of Buddhism: a doctrine of salvation, aimed at the acquisition of liberating insight and at the complete extinction of attachment, and, consequently, of continued rebirth in the world of suffering. In most cases, the way to achieve that goal is indissolubly connected with the monastic life (with a few exceptions, such as the Japanese Jodo Shinshu with its married preachers, or Chinese lay Buddhism in Indonesia); the Buddhist order of monks, or *samgha*, has remained the very heart of religious life and the most important unifying element throughout the Buddhist world.

Movements, Monastic Traditions, Schools, and Sects. A clarification of terms is needed, for much confusion has been created by the indiscriminative use of these words.

Movements. In the course of its long history, Buddhism has seen the development of three huge complexes of religious doctrine and practice, each of which represents a well-defined "way leading to release"; these are characteristically called *yana* ("vehicles"). We shall refer to them as "movements." They represent three basic orientations within Buddhism, each with its own doctrinal ideas, cultic practices, sacred scriptures, and iconographic traditions.

The first movement comprises the whole complex of ancient Buddhism, of which one type is still alive in Sri Lanka and most of continental Southeast Asia. Since the name *Hinayana*, the "Lesser Vehicle," sounds pejorative, its adherents now prefer their type of Buddhism to be called Theravada, "the Doctrine of the Elders" (originally the name of one school). Theravada Buddhism has, among other things, always been characterized by an extreme emphasis on monastic life; by the ideal of becoming an *arhat*, who has reached individual saintliness and is assured of his total extinction at the end of his life, and a conception of the Buddha as a sublime yet mortal teacher who, after having reached his final *nirvana*, has ceased to be at whatever level of existence.

Since the beginning of the common era, Hinayana was challenged by a new movement that called itself the "Great Vehicle" (Mahayana). It claimed to be a more comprehensive and universal way toward liberation, with a more ambitious religious ideal (Buddhahood instead of arhatship); the belief in *bodhisattvas* as superhuman guides and saviors; the idea of a transcendental, all-pervading and eternal Buddha or "Buddha nature"; a philosophical reinterpretation (in many variations) of the most basic ontological concepts of ancient Buddhism, and a much higher estimate of the status of lay believers as potential "candidates for release."

In the sixth century, possibly even somewhat earlier, a third orientation emerged, the movement called the "Diamond Vehicle" (Vajrayana), commonly referred to as Tantric or Esoteric Buddhism in the West. It was characterized by its use of spells, symbols, and very complicated rituals, and the acquisition of magic powers as a way toward enlightenment; by the development of psychophysical "techniques" (partly of a sexual nature); and by a system of esoteric transmission from master to disciple.

It is clear that in these three cases we cannot speak of "schools," let alone "sects." They were by no means localized: both Mahayana and Vajrayana spread like waves throughout the Buddhist world. Above all, they were not mutually exclusive. In the Mahayana vision, the whole complex of Theravada teachings is not rejected but incorporated as a kind of "simple revelation," intended by the Buddha to raise the minds of his "hearers" *(sravaka)* to a certain level of preliminary insight. In the same way, Tantric Buddhism claims to incorporate (and, of course, to transcend) the two previous Vehicles, without denying their limited applicability. In fact, Mahayana doctrinal literature freely quotes from Theravada scriptures as teachings of the Buddha that are, at that level, both authentic and authoritative.

Monastic traditions. What we call monastic traditions are basically different from such large and many-sided movements. Their origin is closely related to the paramount role of the disciplinary code (Vinaya), and notably of the detailed set of rules governing the monk's daily life that had to be recited at every fortnightly Pratimoksa confessional by all monks resident in a single self-governing "parish" or begging circuit *(sima)*. The early dissemination of Buddhism over the Indian subcontinent was a continuous process of expansion of contact: since any local center of population could only support a certain number of mendicants, the clerical surplus had to move out to establish new parishes elsewhere. The process was further stimulated by the itinerant life led by many monks outside the rainy season, and by the missionary ideal that has been characteristic of Buddhism from the very beginning. Thus, Buddhism spread in ever-widening circles, but without any central authority that could impose doctrinal and ritual uniformity. The only binding element was the Vinaya, and the frequent Pratimoksa recitation in fact functioned as the only instrument to preserve the homogeneity of the Buddhist order.

However, as the territory covered by Buddhism widened, local variations in the disciplinary code started to develop, partly owing to lack of communication and probably also caused by the necessity to adapt the rules to local circumstances. If the Buddhist tradition speaks of the emergence of eighteen of such monastic traditions in the first two centuries after the Buddha's decease, we must realize that the difference that divided them mainly concerned details of discipline rather than doctrinal matters. No less than five different Vinayas of various early schools have been preserved in the Chinese Buddhist canon: extensive works that differ among themselves as to number of rules, prescriptions governing minute details of daily behavior, and the degree of elaboration of stories justifying each particular rule, but that as far as doctrine is concerned show very little variation.

Schools. Of quite another nature are the schools found in Theravada and (to a much larger extent) in Mahayana Buddhism. Here the accent is on the interpretation of certain basic elements of the doctrine of release, issues such as the nature of the *arhat*, the nonexistence of a permanent self, the process of causation, and so forth. In Mahayana Buddhism we find a proliferation of such schools, ranging from the earliest propagation of the doctrine of universal "emptiness" *(sunyavada)* in India to Chinese and Japanese Ch`an (Zen) Buddhism, with its iconoclastic message of "no words" and "no mind."

In spite of their endless variety, such schools share some common features. In the first place, their field of activity is not discipline but scholastics: the various Abhidharma of Theravada Buddhism and the many systematizing treatises of Mahayana scholars. A second feature shared by most schools is the prominent role of famous "masters of the Law," both as founding fathers and as transmitters of the teachings of a particular school: Katyayaniputra, Vasumitra, and other "patriarchs" of the Sarvastivada tradition that flourished in northwestern India and Kashmir; Nagarjuna and Aryadeva, who systematized the doctrines of the School of Emptiness; Asanga and Vasubandhu, who, probably in the fifth century CE, founded the Yogacara school, and, in East Asia, the great masters who founded and developed the major schools of Chinese Buddhism: the vast and complicated system of the T`ien-t`ai school founded by Chih-i (538-597), the Hua-yen doctrine of all-pervading totality of Fa-tsang (643-712); the Pure Land (Ching-t`u) devotionalism of T`an-luan (476-542) and Tao-ch`o (562-645), and the many "patriarchs" and branch founders of Ch`an (Zen) in China, Korea, and Japan.

Third, although such schools recognize the validity of all Buddhist scriptures (even if in some schools texts favored by other schools are considered "provisional teachings," as we

have seen), many of them tend to be focused on one particular scripture or group of scriptures that are supposed to contain the final and supreme revelation of truth. Thus, the School of Emptiness largely relied on the class of Mahayana scriptures known as the Prajñaparamita ("perfection of wisdom") literature, just as the Yogacara school appealed to the authority of the *Lankavatara Sutra.* For the founder of the T`ien-t`ai school, the highest revelation was to be found in the message of universal salvation as expounded in the *Saddharmapundarika Sutra* (Scripture of the Lotus of the Good Law), whereas Fa-tsang found the expression of ultimate truth in the vast *Avatamsaka Sutra* (Chin., *Hua-yen*; Flower Garland Scripture). And even Ch`an, in spite of its rejection of written texts, in its first stage largely relied on the *Lankavatara Sutra.* The scholastic and "learned" nature of all such schools also appears from the fact that they essentially remained a clerical phenomenon: the creation and exclusive domain of an elite of scholar-monks, in which the laity took no part. Their bastions were the large and richly endowed monasteries that all over the Buddhist world functioned as centers of Buddhist learning and doctrinal disputes. However, one of their most remarkable features is that they were by no means exclusive communities with a well-defined "membership." Monks would travel from one monastery to another irrespective of the school that dominated in each center; in many cases several scholastic interpretations could be studied successively or even simultaneously, and both eclecticism and syncretism flourished without any stigma of "unorthodoxy."

Sects. This, then, may be the dividing line between schools and sects, the latter being characterized by a high degree of exclusivity, a clear concept of "membership," and, in general, a very important role played by the laity. As a rule, sectarian movements are centered around a charismatic leader who in his own person exemplifies the religious message of the sect: in many cases he claims to be the incarnation or the manifestation of a Buddha (notably the future Buddha Maitreya) or a powerful *bodhisattva.* In contrast to the schools that are not confined to one area (the Representation-Only doctrine reached from India to Japan, and Ch`an/Zen was found all over East Asia), most sects are localized, and deeply rooted in local circumstances. As I shall show, sects generally belong to strata lower, both socially and intellectually, than the schools mentioned above; the latter may be said to represent the "great tradition" of Buddhism at its highest level of expression.

Parameters of Diversification. In the diffusion of Buddhism we can recognize a number of factors that contributed to the process of ongoing diversification. Only the most important ones can be treated within the limits of this article.

Distance from the center. As noted above, the spread of Buddhism over the Indian subcontinent mainly took the form of gradual expansion of contact, a process that offers the best chances for maintaining a fairly high degree of homogeneity. However, once outside its country of origin, the propagation of Buddhism assumed the character of long-distance diffusion in various directions: from northwestern India through the empty heart of the continent to China; along the sea routes from the east coast of India to continental Southeast Asia, Sumatra, and Java; from the Ganges Basin crossing the Himalayas into Tibet. In all those outlying regions, far from the center of expansion, Buddhism developed independently. As a result, both China and Tibet eventually became secondary centers of diffusion: Korean and Japanese Buddhists were inspired by Chinese examples and had hardly any contact with India; in all of East Asia, classical Chinese became the Buddhist scriptural language. In the same way, Tibetan Buddhism, especially in its lamaist form, developed into a unique system far removed from any Indian prototype. In the sixteenth century Tibet also became a secondary center of expansion, from which Lamaism was spread to Mongolia.

In Southeast Asia, Buddhism at first was introduced not independently but as one element in a general process of cultural borrowing; from the second to the fifth centuries, the spread of Indian culture in the whole area from Burma to Sumatra led to the formation of a whole series of more or less indianized states in which Buddhism (mainly in its Mahayana and Tantric forms) coexisted with Hinduism. This independent development of Buddhism in peripheral areas was naturally reinforced by its disappearance in India itself after the twelfth century. It may not be fortuitous that around that time Sri Lanka, where the Theravada *sangha* had been restored and reorganized under the powerful king Parakkamabahu II (1236-1271), became a strong center of diffusion. It was owing to Sinhala missionary efforts that Theravada Buddhism became the state religion in Burma, Thailand, Laos, and Cambodia between the twelfth and fourteenth centuries.

Confrontation with local cultures. Wherever it arrived, Buddhism was in varying degrees influenced by local beliefs and practices, the incorporation of which led to further differentiation. In some areas, like the oasis kingdoms along the Silk Road and Southeast Asia, the cultural resistance against Buddhism appears to have been slight; there the Indian religion was taken over as an instrument of higher civilization, often together with other elements of Indian culture like statecraft, astronomy, representational arts, and the script. Elsewhere, notably in China, Buddhism had to compete with strong preexisting philosophical and social traditions that on many points were opposed to Buddhist ideals and practices. In China, it had to grow up in the shadow of the dominant Confucian ideology, and much that is characteristic in Chinese Buddhism is the result of "adaptation under pressure." However, everywhere, and especially at a popular

level, Buddhism merged with and incorporated non-Buddhist traditions: Taoist eubiotics and Confucian morality in China; Shinto in Japan; elements borrowed from the indigenous Bon religion in Tibet; and from shamanism in Mongolia.

> **Buddhism had to compete with strong preexisting philosophical and social traditions that on many points were opposed to Buddhist ideals and practices.**

Social stratification. Since the earliest times, monastic Buddhism was for its very existence dependent on the patronage of the ruling elite; the close ties between the *samgha* and the temporal powers form a constant feature in the history of all countries where Buddhism penetrated. This cooperation (and in some areas, such as Sri Lanka, even complete interdependence) has produced both positive and negative results: on the one hand, corruption and abuse of power; on the other hand, the formation of a clerical elite within the *samgha*, associated with the largest monastic centers, to whom we owe the most sophisticated products of Buddhist thought, literature, and art. This articulate group only constituted a tiny minority—the thin top layer of the Buddhist establishment. In all Buddhist countries, we find a vertical differentiation between the cultured clerical elite residing in the major monasteries and the vast majority of "priests among the people," who perform their humble services in countless small temples and local shrines, at the grass-roots level, where they often are the only people who can boast of a modicum of literary training. If the world of court priests, learned doctors, and scholastic philosophy constitutes the "great tradition" of Buddhism, it is everywhere counterbalanced by an endless variety of popular Buddhist beliefs and cults that represent its "little traditions." It is at that level that we mostly find the traces of (generally not well documented) sectarian movements of the type mentioned above. In general, their message is extremely simple, centering around one or two basic ideas derived from the Buddhist scriptural tradition: the theme of the dark "final age" in which the doctrine will disappear and the world will be steeped in chaos and corruption, and the belief in the imminent appearance of the Buddha Maitreya, who will come to create a world of piety and justice. [*See also* Folk Religion.]

Movements espousing such ideas have often been persecuted as "subversive," both by the temporal powers and by the representatives of the clerical establishment. These movements sometimes assumed a violent character. Examples of such sectarian activities can be found in many parts of the Buddhist world: the millenarian movements that have time and again appeared in continental Southeast Asia in times of crisis; the militant and protonationalist sect founded by the Japanese reformer Nichiren (1222-1282), who combined socio-religious activism and opposition against the established clergy with an extremely simple way to salvation, and, in China, the equally militant activities of the complex of Buddhist-inspired secret societies collectively known as the White Lotus, which harassed Chinese political authorities from the fourteenth century until modern times. But such violent activism and social protest have always been the exception rather than the rule—the vast majority of Buddhist religious life at the grass roots level presents the familiar and peaceful picture of local societies, fraternities, and associations devoted to mutual help, charitable activities, and collective ceremonies. [*See also* Millenarianism.]

Linguistic differentiation. Unlike the Brahmanic tradition, which is based on Sanskrit as a scriptural medium, Buddhism never has known the concept of a "sacred language." Buddhist scriptures have for many centuries been translated in a great variety of regional languages, and even Pali, the written medium of Theravada Buddhism, certainly does not represent the language of the original Buddhist sermons. However, in the course of time the diffusion of Buddhism from secondary centers led to the use of some languages, in petrified forms, as what we may call "clerical literary idioms": classical Chinese in Japan and Korea; Pali in continental Southeast Asia; and literary Tibetan. But here again, social stratification was at work, for in all these areas, popular tracts and other types of simplified religious literature (both written and oral) generally made use of the living language—in fact, Chinese vernacular literature owes its origin to simple Buddhist stories written in the metropolitan dialect and destined to be recited to a largely illiterate public of lay devotees. Thus, the linguistic aspect combines the two main features that we have observed in the spread of Buddhism as a whole: geographic diffusion coupled with ongoing regional differentiation, and internal stratification producing a great diversity of expression at various social levels, both within the Buddhist clergy and among the lay population.

[*For a review of the geographic dispersion of the tradition, see* Missions, *article on* Buddhist Missions.]

BIBLIOGRAPHY

The following works contain information on the main themes treated in this article: the diversity of Buddhism (monastic traditions, schools, sects), social stratification (elite versus popular Buddhism), and adaptation to cultural environments.

Anesaki Masaharu. *Nichiren: The Buddhist Prophet* (1916). Reprint, Gloucester, Mass., 1966.
Bareau, André. *Les sectes bouddhiques du petit véhicule.* Saigon, 1955.
Bechert, Heinz. *Buddhismus, Staat und Gesellschaft in den Ländern des Theravada-Buddhismus.* 3 vols. Frankfurt, 1966-1973.
Bechert, Heinz, ed. *Buddhism in Ceylon and Studies in Religious Syncretism in Buddhist Countries.* Göttingen, 1978.
Chan, Wing-tsit. *Religious Trends in Modern China.* New York, 1953.
Ch`en, Kenneth. *Buddhism in China: A Historical Survey.* Princeton, 1964.
Dutt, Nalinaksha. *Early History of the Spread of Buddhism and the Buddhist Schools* (1925). Reprint, New Delhi, 1980.
Dutt, Nalinaksha. *Buddhist Sects in India.* Calcutta, 1970.
Groot, J. J. M. de. *Sectarianism and Religious Persecution in China.* 2 vols. Amsterdam, 1903-1904.
Hackmann, Heinrich Friedrich. *Laien-Buddhismus in China.* Stuttgart, 1924.
Hanayama Shinsho. *A History of Japanese Buddhism.* Tokyo, 1960.
Hoffmann, Helmut. *The Religions of Tibet.* Translated by Edward Fitzgerald. New York, 1961.
Lester, Robert C. *Theravada Buddhism in Southeast Asia.* Ann Arbor, 1973.
Malalgoda, Kitsiri. *Buddhism in Sinhalese Society, 1750-1900.* Berkeley, 1976.
Matsunaga, Alicia. *The Buddhist Philosophy of Assimilation.* Tokyo, 1969.
Miller, Robert J. *Monasteries and Culture Change in Inner Mongolia.* Wiesbaden, 1959.
Thomsen, Harry. *The New Religions of Japan.* Rutland, Vt., 1963.

ERIK ZURCHER

Hinayana Buddhism

The term *Hinayana* refers to the group of Buddhist schools or sects that appeared before the beginning of the common era and those directly derived from them. The word *Hinayana*, which means "small vehicle," was applied disdainfully to these early forms of Buddhism by the followers of the great reformist movement that arose just at the beginning of the common era. The Mahayana charged those of the Hinayana with selfishly pursuing only their own personal salvation, whereas they themselves claimed an interest in the liberation of all beings and vowed to postpone their own deliverance until the end of time.

Although it is directly descended from the earliest Buddhism—that originally preached by the Buddha himself—this early Buddhism is distinguished from it by the continual additions and reformulations of its adherents and teachers in their desire to deepen and perfect the interpretation of the ancient teaching.

The Indic word, both Sanskrit and Pali, that we translate here as "school" or "sect" is *nikaya*, meaning, properly, "group." In our context, it refers to a group of initiates, most likely monks *(bhiksus)* rather than laymen, who sincerely profess to be faithful disciples of the Buddha but are distinguishable from other similar groups in that they base their beliefs on a body of canonic texts that differs from others to a greater or lesser extent. These differences between canonic texts involve not only their wording or written form but also a certain number of doctrinal elements and rules of monastic discipline. Schisms did occur within many of them, leading to the formation of new schools, but to judge from the documents we have—though these are unfortunately very scarce—it seems that relations among these various groups were generally good. Their disputes remained at the level of more or less lively discussion.

> **For at least five centuries, the Buddha's teaching was actually preserved by oral transmission alone. . . .**

Several factors account for these divisions and for the formation of these sects or schools. First of all, the Buddhist monastic community (samgha) never knew a supreme authority.

For at least five centuries, the Buddha's teaching was actually preserved by oral transmission alone, very probably in different, though related, dialects. This, and the absence of an authoritative ecclesiastical hierarchy in the samgha, constitute two obvious sources of progressive distortion and alteration of the message left by the Blessed One to his immediate disciples. Furthermore, this message was not entirely clear or convincing to everyone it addressed. Thus, monks and lay disciples, as well as people outside Buddhism but curious and interested in its doctrine—brahman opponents, Jains, and others—easily found numerous flaws, errors, and contradictions in the teaching. Although the Buddhist preachers who improvised answers to these varied questions and objections were guided by what they knew and understood of the Buddha's teaching, their attempts expanded upon the original teaching and at the same time inevitably created new causes for differences and disputes within the heart of the community itself.

All the documents from which we can draw information about the origin of the early Buddhist groups were written after the beginning of the common era and are therefore unreliable. Nevertheless, since the oldest of these texts generally agree on the main points, we can attempt to restore with a certain amount of confidence the common tradition from which they derive.

The first division of the community probably occurred toward the middle of the fourth century BCE. The schism was probably caused by a number of disagreements on the nature of the arhats, who, according to some authorities, retained imperfections even though they had attained nirvana in this world. Because they were more numerous, the supporters of these ideas formed a group called the Mahasamghikas, "those of the larger community." Their opponents, who claimed to remain faithful to the teaching of the Buddha's first disciples and denied that the arhat could retain

any imperfections, took the name Sthaviravadins, "those who speak as the elders."

Each of these two groups were then, in turn, divided progressively into several sects or schools.

Among the groups that developed from the Mahasamghika were the Ekavyavaharika, then the Gokulika, and finally the Caitika schools. The Ekavyavaharikas probably gave rise, in turn, to the Lokottaravadins, but it may be that the Lokottaravadins were simply a form taken by the Ekavyavaharikas at a particular time because of the evolution of their doctrine. From the Gokulikas came the Bahusrutiyas and the Prajñaptivadins. At least a part of the Caitika school settled in southern India, on the lower Krishna River, shortly before the beginning of the common era. From them two important sects soon arose: the Purvasailas and the Aparasailas, then a little later the Rajagirikas and the Siddharthikas. Together, the four sects formed Andhraka group, which took its name from the area (Andhra) where they thrived during the first few centuries CE.

The Sthaviravada group seems to have remained united until about the beginning of the third century BCE, when the Vatsiputriyas, who maintained the existence of a quasi-autonomous "person" (pudgala), split off. A half century later, probably during the reign of Asoka (consecrated c. 268 BCE), the Sarvastivadins also separated from the non-Vatsiputriya Sthaviravadins and settled in northwest India. This time the dispute was over the Sarvastivadin notion that "everything exists" (sarvam asti). In the beginning of the second century, the remaining Sthaviravadins, who appear to have taken at this time the name Vibhajyavadins, "those who teach discrimination," to distinguish themselves from the Sarvastivadins, found themselves divided once again. Out of this dispute were born the Mahisasakas and the Dharmaguptakas, who opposed each other over whether the Buddha, properly speaking, belonged to the monastic community and over the relative value of offerings made to the Blessed One and those made to the community. At an unknown date about the beginning of the common era four new groups sprang from the Vatsiputriyas: the Dharmottariyas, the Bhadrayaniyas, the Sannagarikas, and the Sammatiyas. The Sammatiyas, who were very important in Indian Buddhism, later gave rise to the Avantaka and the Kurukulla schools. One group broke from the Sarvastivadins: the Sautrantikas, who can be identified with the Darstantikas and the Samkrantivadins.

Some of the Vibhajyavadins settled in southern India and Lanka in the mid-third century BCE and seem to have maintained fairly close relations for some time with the Mahisasakas, whose presence is attested in the same area. Adopting Pali as a canonical language and energetically claiming their teaching to be the strict orthodoxy, they took the name Theravadins, a Pali form of the Sanskrit Sthaviravadins. Like the Sthaviravadins, they suffered from internal squabbles and divisions: some years before the common era, the Abhayagirivasins split from the Mahaviharas, founded at the time of the arrival of Buddhism in Lanka; later, in the fourth century, the Jetavaniyas appeared.

Except for a few of the more important of these sects and schools—such as the Theravadins, who left us the treasure of their celebrated Sinhala chronicles—we know nothing of the history of these different groups. Their existence is nevertheless assured, thanks to the testimony of a fair number of inscriptions and other substantial documents.

BIBLIOGRAPHY

Aung, Schwe Zan, and C. A. F. Rhys Davids, trans. *Points of Controversy* (1915). London, 1969. A translation of the Pali *Kathavatthu*, a text treating the doctrinal controversies between the various Hinayana sects from the Theravada point of view.

Bareau, André. *Les sectes bouddhiques du Petit Véhicule.* Publications de l'École Français d'Extrême-Orient, vol. 38. Saigon, 1955. An exhaustive survey based on all available documents.

Bechert, Heinz, and Richard Gombrich. *The World of Buddhism.* London, 1984. This excellent work includes a discussion of schisms on page 82.

Ch`en, Kenneth. *Buddhism in China; a Historical Survey.* Princeton, 1964. See pages 129-131 and 301-303 for information on the Hinayana-derived Chinese sects.

Demiéville, Paul. "L'origine des sectes bouddhiques d'après Paramartha." In *Mélanges chinois et bouddhiques*, vol. 1, pp. 15-64. Brussels, 1932. A masterfully annotated French translation of one of the principal documents on the subject.

Dube, S. N. *Cross Currents in Early Buddhism.* New Delhi, 1980. Interesting study of doctrinal disputes among early sects, but based primarily on the Kathavatthu.

Dutt, Nalinaksha. *Buddhist Sects in India.* 2d ed. Calcutta, 1978. Good general description of the history and, especially, the doctrines of the Hinayana sects.

Fujishima Ryauon. *Les bouddhisme japonais: Doctrines et histoire de douze sectes bouddhiques du Japon* (1889). Reprint, Paris, 1983. This old book is the most complete description in a Western language of Japanese Buddhist sects, particularly the three derived from the Hinayana.

Hajime, Nakamura. *Indian Buddhism: A Survey with Bibliographical Notes.* Hirakata, 1980. This large work brings into focus our knowledge of the whole of Indian Buddhism and contains an extremely rich and up-to-date bibliography. A long chapter concerns the Hinayana sects (pp. 90-140).

Lamotte, Étienne. *Histoire du bouddhisme indien: Des origines à l'ère Saka.* Louvain, 1958. A large part (pp. 571-705) of this excellent work discusses early sects, their origins and distribution, Buddhist languages, and the sects' doctrinal evolution.

La Vallée Poussin, Louis de, trans. *L'Abhidharmakosa de Vasubandhu* (1923-1931). 6 vols. Reprint, Brussels, 1971. This French translation of the famous treatise includes copious notes and a very long introduction by the great Belgian scholar. It is rich in information on the doctrinal controversies that concerned the Sarvastivadins.

Law, Bimala Churn. *A History of Pali Literature.* London, 1933. Complete, very detailed description of Theravada literature.

Masuda Jiryo. "Origins and Doctrines of Early Indian Buddhist Schools." *Asia Major* 2 (1925); 1-78. English translation, with notes, of the *Samayabhedoparacanacakra*, an account of the Hinayana sects and their main tenets.

Renou, Louis, and Jean Filliozat. *L'Inde classique.* Paris, 1953. Volume 2, pages 315-608, deals especially with the Hinayana sects, their literature, and doctrines. The collaboration of the Sinologist Paul Demiéville and the Tibetologist Marcelle Lalou is invaluable.

Shizutani Masao. *Shojo bukkyoshi no kenkyu; Buha bukkyo no seiritsu to hensen.* Kyoto, 1978. The most recent work on the origin and evolution of the Hinayana sects. Detailed and complete study of literary and epigraphic sources.

Takakusu Junjiro, trans. *A Record of the Buddhist Religion as Practiced in India and the Malay Archipelago (A. D. 671-695)* (1896). Reprint, Dehli, 1966. English translation of I-ching's account of his pilgrimage to South and Southeast Asia.

Warder, A. K. *Indian Buddhism.* 2d rev. ed. Dehli, 1980. Treats Hinayana sects at length, offering interesting solutions to the problems they pose.

Watters, Thomas, trans. *On Yuan Chwang's Travels in India, 629-645 A. D.* 2 vols. London, 1904-1905. English translation of numerous extracts from the accounts of Hsüan-tsang's journey, with excellent commentary correcting most of the many errors of earlier translations (those of Stanislas Julien, Samuel Beal, etc.), which are today unusable.

ANDRÉ BAREAU
Translated from French by David M. Weeks

Mahayana Buddhism

The Sanskrit term *mahayana* literally means "the great vehicle [to enlightenment]." It refers to a form of Buddhism that developed in northern India and Central Asia from about the first century before the advent of the common era, and that is prevalent today in Nepal, Sikkhim, Tibet, China, Mongolia, Vietnam, Korea, and Japan. Mahayana Buddhism was also transmitted to Sri Lanka and the Indo-Chinese peninsula, but it eventually vanished from South Asia.

Mahayana Buddhism is characterized by a variety of doctrines, practices, and orientations that at once distinguish it from the Hinayana tradition.

Worship of Multiple Buddhas and Bodhisattvas. In early Buddhism the term *bodhisattva* referred to the Buddha (or, later, to *a* Buddha) prior to the time of his enlightenment, including all previous existences during which he had aspired to become a Buddha. In keeping with the soteriology and cosmology of these early teachings, it was assumed that there was only one *bodhisattva* in any one world cycle. Later, this idea was elaborated and integrated into the Jataka stories, tales of Sakyamuni Buddha's previous lives. A few Conservative Buddhists embraced the belief that there were many Buddhas at any one time, but this belief was most highly developed in Mahayana, where myriads of Buddhas are said to inhabit myriads of world systems simultaneously.

Some Mahayana *sutras* enjoin adoration of all Buddhas in an equal manner (e.g., *The Sutra Enumerating Buddha's*

Names) and some twenty-one sutras extol recitation of the names of many Buddhas. Repeated utterance of the names of Buddhas and *bodhisattvas* is also encouraged in the *Namasamgiti*.

But it is not simply in their profusion that the Buddhas of the Mahayana differ from their Hinayana counterparts. Mahayana Buddhas enjoy many more superhuman and divine traits than does the single Buddha of the Conservative tradition. Nonetheless, they retain many of the same physical and spiritual characteristics. Glorification of and speculation on the nature of Buddhas led Mahayana practitioners to develop the theory of the "triple body" (*trikaya*) of the Buddha, in which the Buddha is conceived as having three aspects or "bodies": a cosmic body (*dharmakaya*), the ineffable Absolute itself; an "enjoyment" body (*sambhogakaya*), a body of magical transformation that the Buddha "enjoys" as the fruit of the merit generated through aeons of religious practice (often conceived as surrounded by a supernal region, a Pure Land, similarly generated); and the body that appears in living form to save people from suffering (*nirmanakaya*). Sakyamuni, of course, is such a Buddha (i. e., *nirmanakaya*) for our age.

The *bodhisattva* Mañjusri plays an important role in many sutras. One sutra (T. D. no. 463) describes the efficacy of worship of Mañjusri at the moment of death. In another (T. D. no. 464), Mañjusri explains enlightenment; and elsewhere (T. D. no. 843) he demonstrates *animitta* ("formlessness") through magical power.

As in Hinayana Buddhism, the *bodhisattva* Maitreya was worshiped as a Buddha of the future, one who, at some time to come, will leave his present abode in the Tusita Heaven and be born on earth for the benefit of sentient beings. Devotees of Maitreya thus focused their aspirations on rebirth in Tusita and eventual descent to earth in his company.

But the *bodhisattva* most adored throughout Asia is Avalokitesvara, the "Lord Who Looks Down [with infinite pity on all beings]." The best-known scripture concerning his virtues is the twenty-fourth chapter of the *Saddharma-pundarika* (Lotus Sutra), which emphasizes the rewards in this world that he grants to believers and the virtue of help-fulness to others that he represents. In the *Gandavyuha*, his homeland is called Potalaka. In Pure Land Buddhism, he is Amitabha's companion and attendant.

But if there is one feature of the Mahayana *bodhisattva* doctrine that truly separates it from that of other forms of Buddhism, it is the Mahayana insistence that the goal of all religious practice is Buddhahood itself, making all those whose conceive of the aspiration to be liberated *bodhisattvas*, or future Buddhas. The Mahayana *bodhisattva* is committed to work ceaselessly for the benefit of other beings and to transmit to them the merit generated by his or her own religious practice.

Disciplines. There is no unanimously agreed upon code of discipline in Mahayana, reflecting the fact that it is institutionally less coherent than is Conservative Buddhism. But Mahayana distinguishes two ways of practice: the *sravaka-marga* ("way of the disciples") for those who follow the Hinayana practices and the *bodhisattvamarga* ("way of *bodhisattvas*") for those who adhere to Mahayana values, particularly the intention to save other suffering beings. Those who practice the latter way are deemed worthy of worship and are relied upon because they have refrained from entering Buddhahood, preferring instead to dwell among the living in order to save them from their sufferings.

> **Repentance is the theme and object of several Mahayana *sutras*.**

Mahayana ethics were most explicitly set forth in the "Discipline Sutras," the essence of which is altruism. Among the sutras that provided the theoretical basis for the Mahayana orders is the *Sarvadharmapravrttinirdesa*, which was highly esteemed by the Japanese monk Saicho (767-822). Others that explicated Mahayana discipline are the "Buddha Treasure Sutra" (T. D. no. 653), the "Enlightenment-mind Sutra" (T. D. no. 837), and the *Dharmavinayasamadhi Sutra*. Some texts reflect the Mahayana idea that discipline is to be practiced by both clergy and laity; one, the *Bodhisattvapratimoksa Sutra*, sets forth the "Vinaya" of *bodhisattvas*, here referring to both clerics and lay practitioners. The precepts in the *Srimaladevi Sutra* were well known in China and Japan.

The most famous and controversial of these texts is the *Brahmajala Sutra*. Greatly esteemed in China, it became the fundamental discipline text for Japanese monks. Scholars now believe that this text was produced in China, where there is evidence that it was in use in some form as early as the year 350.

Repentance is the theme and object of several Mahayana *sutras*. One of these *sutras* (T. D. no. 1493) shows that repentance leads to delight in the deeds of others, moral admonition, and transference of merit. Another text teaches that a reaffirmation of the insight that all things are originally pure can dissolve the obstacles created by *karman* (T. D. no. 1491). Bondage in *karman* (*karmavarana*) can be destroyed by repentance, meditation, or by repeated application of magical formulas.

Lay Buddhism. The position of the layman was recognized and exalted by most Mahayana texts, although a few display a tendency to place the ascetic life of the monk above the lay life. However, the notion of emptiness (*sunyata*) that is the foundation of most Mahayana thought provides for the identity of liberation and mundane existence, *nirvana* and *samsara*, thus providing a rationale for the sanctity of lay life.

To be sure, many Mahayana practitioners were *bhiksus*, and some were termed *bodhisattva bhiksus* (in the *Mahayanasutralamkara*, the *Siksasamuccaya*, etc.). But the tendency toward lay Buddhism remained conspicuous. The *Ugradattapariprccha*, an early Discipline Sutra composed before Nagarjuna (fl. 150-250), prescribes five conditions for the lay practice of the Mahayana. Later, codes of discipline intended specifically for laymen were composed. Among the disciplines required of laymen was observance of the regulations for *uposadha* days (when the fortnightly confessions were made).

The presence of the notion of filial piety, another lay ideal, in Buddhism represents an accommodation and syncretization of values that occurred under the stimulus of Chinese culture. Filial piety was the most important virtue in Confucian ethics, which required one-sided obedience from children toward their parents. A Buddhist concept of filial piety also took shape in the Ullambana Sutra, which extols a rite that centers on offerings to one's dead parents.

BIBLIOGRAPHY

Burtt, Edwin Arthur. *The Teachings of the Compassionate Buddha.* New York, 1955.

Conze, Edward. *Buddhist Thought in India: Three Phases of Buddhist Philosophy* (1962). Reprint, Ann Arbor, 1970.

Conze, Edward, ed. and trans. *Buddhist Scriptures.* Harmondsworth, 1959.

Conze, Edward, et al., eds. *Buddhist Texts through the Ages.* New York, 1954. A comprehensive collection of Indian Mahayana texts.

Cowell, E. B., et al., eds. *Buddhist Mahayana Texts.* Sacred Books of the East, edited by F. Max Müller, vol. 49. Oxford, 1894; reprint, New York, 1969.

Dayal, Har. *The Bodhisattva Doctrine in Buddhist Sanskrit Literature* (1932). Reprint, Delhi, 1975.

Dutt, Nalinaksha. *Aspects of Mahayana Buddhism and Its Relation to Hinayana.* London, 1930.

Frauwallner, Erich. *Die Philosophie des Buddhismus.* 3d rev. ed. Berlin, 1969.

Glasenapp, Helmuth von. *Der Buddhismus in Indien und im Fernen Osten.* Berlin, 1936.

Hamilton, Clarence H., ed. *Buddhism: A Religion of Infinite Compassion; Selections from Buddhist Literature.* New York, 1952.

Hirakawa Akira. "The Rise of Mahayana Buddhism and Its Relationship to the Worship of Stupas." *Memoirs of the Research Department of the Toyo Bunko* 22 (1963): 57-106. A well-documented analysis of a crucial topic in the history of Buddhism.

Hirakawa Akira. *Indo bukkyoshi.* 2 vols. Tokyo, 1974-1979. This comprehensive survey of Indian Buddhism contains extensive bibliographies of Japanese secondary sources.

Lamotte, Étienne. *Histoire du bouddhisme indien des origines à l'ère Saka.* Louvain, 1958. Extensive footnotes and a comprehensive index make this work an invaluable reference tool.

Lamotte, Étienne, trans. *Le traité de la grande vertu de sagesse.* 5 vols. Louvain, 1944-1980. A translation from Kumarajiva's Chinese translation *(Ta chih-tu lun)* of the Sanskrit *Mahaprajñaparamita*

Sastra, a commentary on the *Pañcavimsatisahasrika-prajña-paramita.* the original Sanskrit commentary, sometimes attributed to Nagarjuna, is no longer extant.

La Vallée Poussin, Louis de. *Bouddhisme.* Paris, 1909.

McGovern, William Mongomery. *An Introduction to Mahayana Buddhism.* New York, 1922.

Radhakrishnan, Sarvepalli. *Indian Philosophy,* vol. 1. 2d ed. London, 1927. A lucid introduction for the beginning student.

Schayer, Stanislaw. *Vorbereiten zur Geschichte der Mahayanistischen Erlösungslehren.* Munich, 1921. Translated by R. T. Knight as *Mahayana Doctrines of Salvation* (London, 1921).

Stcherbatsky, Theodore. *Buddhist Logic* (1930-1932). 2 vols. Reprint, New York, 1962.

Suzuki, Beatrice Lane. *Mahayana Buddhism* (1938). 3d ed. New York, 1959.

Suzuki, D. T. *Outlines of Mahayana Buddhism* (1907). Reprint, New York, 1963.

Thomas, Edward J. *The History of Buddhist Thought.* 2d ed. New York, 1951.

Thomas, Edward J., trans. *The Quest of Enlightenment: A Selection of the Buddhist Scriptures.* London, 1950. A brief anthology of Mahayana texts in translation with particular reference to the career of the *bodhisattva.*

Wassiljew, W. *Der Buddhismus.* Saint Petersburg, 1860.

The Way of the Buddha. Delhi, 1957. Published by the Publications Division of the Ministry of Information and Broadcasting, Government of India.

Wayman, Alex. *The Buddhist Tantras: Light on Indo-Tibetan Esotericism.* New York, 1973.

Wayman, Alex, trans. *Calming the Mind and Discerning the Real: Buddhist Meditation and the Middle View, from the Lam rim chen mo of Tson-kha-pa.* New York, 1978.

Winternitz, Moriz. *Der Mahayana-Buddhismus, nach Sanskrit und Prakrittexten.* 2 vols. Tübingen, 1930.

Winternitz, Moriz. *A History of Indian Literature,* vol. 2, *Buddhist Literature and Jaina Literature* (1933). Reprint, New York, 1971. Even now, this work remains probably the best introduction to the subject.

NAKAMURA HAJIME

Esoteric Buddhism

Buddhist esotericism is an Indian movement obscure in its beginnings. Combining yoga and ritual, it calls itself the Diamond Vehicle (Vajrayana)—where *diamond* means "the unsplittable"—or the Mantra Vehicle (Mantrayana)—where *mantra* means "magical speech." The revealed texts of the tradition are called *tantra*, in contrast to *sutra* (the generic name of the non-Tantric Buddhist scriptures), but both these words have the implication "thread" or "continuous line." In the case of the Tantras, the "continuous line" can be understood in various ways: the lineage of master-disciple, the continuity of vows and pledges in the practitioner's stream of consciousness, or the continuity of practice leading to a religious goal.

Much of Tantric literature is ritualistic in nature, manifesting Brahmanic influence by the use of incantations *(mantra)* and the burnt offering *(homa)*, both of which were employed for magical purposes. Many of the hand gestures and foot stances of Buddhist Tantric practice are also found in Indian dance. However, as specifically Buddhist Tantras, such texts are colored both by Buddhist theories and practices and by the typical terminology of Mahayana Buddhism. These texts regularly employ such ancient Buddhist formulations as the triad body, speech, and mind, and draw upon such common Mahayana notions as the pair "means" *(upaya)* and "insight" *(prajña)*. The Tantras accept the old Buddhist ontology of three worlds filled with deities and demons, and contribute the premise that one can relate to these forces by ritualistic manipulation of one's nature (body, speech, and mind), thereby attaining "success" *(siddhi)* in such mundane forms as appeasing the deities, or the supermundane success of winning complete enlightenment (Buddhahood), possibly in a single lifetime. The old Buddhist terminology "son or daughter of the family," here the Buddhist family, was extended to refer to Buddha families. Initially, the texts propose a triad of three Buddhas or Tathagatas: Vairocana, Amitabha, and Aksobhya. Later, Ratnasambhava and Amoghasiddhi are added to make up a family of five, and Vajrasattva to make a family of six. A supreme Buddha, referred to variously as Maha-Vajradhara, Heruka, or Adibuddha ("Primordial Buddha"), is also mentioned. But the texts do not use the term "Dhyani Buddhas" that is sometimes found in Western books on the subject.

BIBLIOGRAPHY

Bhattacharyya, Benoytosh. *The Indian Buddhist Iconography.* 2d ed., rev. & enl. Calcutta, 1958.
Chou, Yi-liang. "Tantrism in China." *Harvard Journal of Asiatic Studies* 8 (March 1945): 241-332.
Eliade, Mircea. "Yoga and Tantrism." In his *Yoga: Immortality and Freedom*, pp. 200-273. New York, 1958.
Evans-Wentz, W. Y. *Tibetan Yoga and Secret Doctrines.* 2d ed. London, 1967.
First Panchen Lama. *The Great Seal of Voidness.* Prepared by the Translation Bureau of the Library of Tibetan Works and Archives. Dharamsala, 1976.
George, Christopher S., ed. and trans. *The Candamaharosana Tantra, Chapters 1-8.* American Oriental Series, vol. 56. New Haven, 1974. In English and Sanskrit.
Guenther, Herbert V., ed. and trans. *The Life and Teachings of Naropa.* Oxford, 1963.
Guenther, Herbert V., ed. and trans. *Yuganaddha: The Tantric View of Life.* Chowkhamba Sanskrit Studies, vol. 3. 2d rev. ed. Varanasi, 1969.
Hakeda, Yoshito S., ed. and trans. *Kukai: Major Works.* New York, 1972. With an account of his life and study of his thought.
Kvaerne, Per. "On the Concepts of Sahaja in Indian Buddhist Tantric Literature." *Temenos* (Helsinki) 11 (1975): 88-135.
Kvaerne, Per. *An Anthology of Buddhist Tantric Songs.* New York, 1977.
Lessing, Ferdinand D. *Yung-ho-kung: An Iconography of the Lamaist Cathedral in Peking.* Stockholm, 1942.
Lessing, Ferdinand D. and Alex Wayman, eds. and trans. *Fundamentals of the Buddhist Tantras.* Indo-Iranian Monographs, vol. 8. The Hague, 1968. A translation of Mkhas-grub-rje's *Rgyud sde spyi'i rnam par bzag pa rgyas par bsad pa*.
Snellgrove, David L., ed. and trans. *The Hevajra Tantra: A Critical Study.* 2 vols. London Oriental Series, vol. 6. London, 1959.
Tajima, Ryujun. *Étude sur le Mahavairocana-sutra.* Paris, 1936.
Tajima, Ryujun. *Les deux grands mandalas et la doctrine de l'esoterisme Shingon.* Paris, 1959.
Tsuda, Shin'ichi. *The Samvarodaya-tantra: Selected Chapters.* Tokyo, 1974.
Tsuda, Shin'ichi. "A Critical Tantrism." *Memoirs of the Research Department of the Toyo Bunko* 36 (1978): 167-231.
Tucci, Giuseppe. "The Religious Ideas: Vajrayana." In *Tibetan Painted Scrolls*, vol. 1, pp. 209-249. Translated by Virginia Vacca. Rome, 1949.
Wayman, Alex. *The Buddhist Tantras: Light on Indo-Tibetan Esotericism.* New York, 1973.
Wayman, Alex. "The Ritual in Tantric Buddhism of the Disciple's Entrance into the Mandala." *Studia Missionalia* 23 (1974): 41-57.
Wayman, Alex. *Yoga of the Guhyasamajatantra: The Arcane Lore of Forty Verses.* Delhi, 1977.
Wayman, Alex. "Reflections on the Theory of Barabudur as a Mandala." In *Barabudur: History and Significance of a Buddhist Monument*, edited by Hiram W. Woodward, pp. 139-172. Berkeley, 1981.
Wayman, Alex. "The Title and Textual Affiliation of the Guhyagarbhatantra." In *Daijo Bukkyo kara Mikkyo e* [From Mahayana Buddhism to Tantra: Honorary Volume for Dr. Katsumata Shunkyo], pp. 1320-1334 (Japanese order), pp. 1-15 (English order). Tokyo, 1981.
Wayman, Alex, ed. and trans. *Chanting the Names of Mañjusri: The Mañjusri-nama-samgiti (Sanskrit and Tibetan Texts).* Boston, 1985.

ALEX WAYMAN

Chinese Buddhism

In any discussion of the schools of Chinese Buddhism it is important to bear in mind that the widely used English term *school* is simply the conventional translation of the Chinese word *tsung*. The practice of equating school and tsung has resulted in some persistent misconceptions about what actually constitutes a school in Chinese Buddhism. In Buddhist texts, it is used primarily in three different senses: (1) it may indicate a specific doctrine or thesis, or a particular interpretation of a doctrine; (2) it may refer to the underlying theme, message, or teaching of a text; and (3) it may signify a religious or philosophical school.

Tsung as Doctrine. Tsung in the sense of doctrine or thesis is frequently encountered in fifth-century texts in such phrases as *k`ai-tsung*, "to explain the [basic] thesis," or *hsü-tsung*, "the doctrine of emptiness." Especially common was the use of the term *tsung* to categorize doctrinal interpretations of theses enumerated in a series.

The term *tsung* was also used to designate the major categories of Buddhist doctrines. Although there were classifications that reduced the Buddhist teachings to two, three, four, five, six, and ten types of doctrine *(tsung)*, the most influential were the four-doctrine classification devised by Hui-kuang (468-537) and the ten-doctrine classification established by Fa-tsang (643-712). Hui-kuang divided the Buddhist teachings into four essential doctrines *(tsung)*, none of which refers to an institutionalized Buddhist school: (1) the doctrine that phenomena arise in accordance with preexisting causes and conditions *(yin-yüan tsung)*, the basic teaching of the Abhidharma, advanced in refutation of the non-Buddhist view of spontaneous production; (2) the doctrine of the *Ch'eng-shih lun* that phenomena were no more than empirical names *(chia-ming tsung)* insofar as they could not exist independently of the causes and conditions that produced them; (3) the doctrine proclaimed in the *Po-jo ching* and the *San-lun* (Three Treatises) that even empirical names are deceptive *(k'uang-hsiang tsung)* insofar as there are no real or substantial phenomena underlying them; and (4) the doctrine taught in the *Nieh-p'an ching* (Mahaparinirvana Sutra), *Hua-yen ching* (Avatamsaka Sutra; Flower Garland Sutra), and other such *sutras* that the Buddha nature is ever abiding *(ch'ang tsung)* and constitutes the ultimate reality.

BIBLIOGRAPHY

The single most important study of the concept of school in Chinese Buddhism is T'ang Yung-t'ung's "Lun Chung-kuo fochiao wu shih tsung," *Hsien-tai fo-hsüeh* 4 (1962): 15-23. Also of value, although in some ways superseded by the preceding study, is the same scholar's *Sui T'ang fochiao shih kao* (Peking), which was written in the late 1920s but not published until 1962. The treatment of the schools in post-T'ang Buddhist literature is surveyed in detail in Yamanouchi Shinkei's *Shina bukkyoshi no kenkyu* (Kyoto, 1921). For a comparative study of the rise of schools in India, China, and Japan, see Mano Shojun's *Bukkyo ni okeru shu kannen no seiritsu* (Tokyo, 1964). Hirai Shun'ei's *Chugoku hannya shisoshi kenkyu* (Tokyo, 1976) is primarily a study of the San-lun tradition, but it also contains a valuable discussion of the definition of school in Chinese Buddhism (pp. 25-57). A traditional account in English of the doctrines of the various schools is given in Takakusu Junjiro's *The Essentials of Buddhist Philosophy*, edited by Wing-tsit Chan and Charles A. Moore (Honolulu, 1947). The most reliable account of the role of schools in twentieth-century China is found in Holmes Welch's *The Practice of Chinese Buddhism*, 1990-1950 (Cambridge, Mass. 1967).

STANLEY WEINSTEIN

Japanese Buddhism

Prior to its official introduction into the court in 552 CE, Buddhism had been brought to Japan by Chinese and Korean immigrants and was presumably practiced widely among their descendants.

Although Japanese understanding of Buddhism was superficial and fragmented in the early stages of assimilation, it gained religious depth through the course of history. The rise of Japanese Buddhism and the growth of schools or sects were closely related to and influenced by the structure of the state bureaucracy, which was itself in the initial stages of development. Yomei (r. 585-587) was the first emperor officially to accept Buddhism, but it was his son, the prince regent Shotoku (574-622), who was responsible for creating Japan's first great age of Buddhism. In addition to building many Buddhist temples and sending students and monks to study in China, he wrote commentaries on three texts—the *Saddharmapundarika* (Lotus) Sutra, the *Vimalakirti Sutra*, and the Srimala *Sutra*—and is supposed to have promulgated the famous "Seventeen-Article Constitution" based on Buddhist and Confucian ideas. Later, Shotoku was worshiped as the incarnation of the *bodhisattva* Avalokitesvara. His promotion of Buddhism fell strictly within the bounds of the existing religio-political framework of Japanese sacral kingship: he upheld the imperial throne as the central authority and envisioned a "multireligious system" in which Shinto, Confucianism, and Buddhism would maintain a proper balance under the divine authority of the emperor as the "son of Heaven." Shotoku's religious policies, his indifference to the doctrinal and ecclesiastical divisions of Buddhism, his dependence on the universalistic soteriology of the *Lotus Sutra*, and his emphasis on the path of the lay devotee significantly influenced the later development of Japanese Buddhism.

BIBLIOGRAPHY

Anesaki Masaharu. *History of Japanese Religion* (1935). Reprint, Tokyo and Rutland, Vt., 1963.
Ienaga Saburo, Akamatsu Toshihide, and Tamamura Taijo, eds. *Nihon bukkyoshi.* Kyoto, 1972.
Kitagawa, Joseph M. *Religion in Japanese History.* New York, 1966.
Saunders, E. Dale. *Buddhism in Japan.* Philadelphia, 1964.
Takakusu Junjiro. *The Essentials of Buddhist Philosophy.* Edited by Wing-tsit Chan and Charles A. Moore. Honolulu, 1947.
Tsuji Zennosuke. *Nihon bukkyoshi.* 10 vols. Tokyo, 1944-1955.

ARAKI MICHIO

Tibetan Buddhism

The various sects or schools of Buddhism in Tibet are probably best referred to as "religious orders" in that most of them are in many ways analogous to Christian monastic orders in the West, namely Benedictines, Dominicans, and so forth. Thus, not only do they accept as fundamental the same

Tibetan Buddhist canon, but many of them were founded by outstanding men of religion, just as the various Christian orders were established. So far as doctrine and religious practice is concerned there are no considerable differences between them. Conversely, the various sects or schools of Indian Buddhism were clearly distinguishable at two levels: first, they began to separate according to their various diverging versions of the traditional "monastic rule" (Vinaya), attributed by all of them to Sakyamuni Buddha himself; second, ever greater divergences developed from the early centuries CE onward as some communities adopted philosophical views and religious cults typical of the Mahayana, while other communities held to the earlier traditions.

Distinctions of these kinds do not exist in Tibetan Buddhism, since all Tibetan religious orders have accepted unquestioningly the monastic rule of one particular Indian Buddhist order, namely that of the Mulasarvastivadins, who happened to be particularly strong in Central Asia and in northern India, and it was in these circles that the Tibetans found their first Indian teachers. Moreover, the form of Buddhism which became established in Tibet represents Indian Buddhism in its late Mahayana and Vajrayana form, with the result that the earlier sects, known collectively as Hinayana, have left no impression on Tibetan Buddhism and are known in Tibet only in a historical and doctrinal context. These considerations inevitably lent an overall unity to Tibetan Buddhism that was lacking in India.

The idea of a religious lineage, that is to say, of a particular religious tradition, usually involving special kinds of religious practice, which is passed in succession from master to pupil, is absolutely fundamental in Tibetan thought, and it is precisely this idea which gives coherence to their various religious orders and explains the many links which may exist between them. As distinct from a "lineage," which is bound up with the personal relationships of those involved in the various lines of transmission, who may often belong to different religious orders, we may define a "religious order" (or sect) as one which is to outward appearances a separate corporate body distinguished by its own hierarchy and administrative machinery, by the existence of its various monastic houses, and by its recognized membership. It is precisely in these respects, as well as in the manner of its foundation, that some Tibetan orders may be said to resemble Christian ones. However, religious lineage remains so important in Tibetan Buddhism that some supposed religious orders exist rather as a group of lineages than as an order in any understandable Western sense.

BIBLIOGRAPHY

Kapstein, Matthew. "The Shangs-pa bKa'-brgyud: An Unknown Tradition of Tibetan Buddhism." In *Tibetan Studies in Honour of Hugh Richardson*, edited by Michael Aris and Aung San Suu Kyi, pp. 136-143. Warminster, 1979.

Kvaerne, Per. "The Canon of the Bonpos." *Indo-Iranian Journal* 16 (1974): 18-56, 96-144.
Kvaerne, Per. "Who are the Bonpos?" *Tibetan Review* 11 (September 1976): 30-33.
Li An-che. "Rñin-ma-pa: The Early Form of Lamaism." *Journal of the Royal Asiatic Society* (1948): 142-163.
Li An-che. "The bKa'-brgyud-pa Sect of Lamaism." *Journal of the American Oriental Society* 69 (1949): 51-59.
Petech, Luciano. "The 'Bri-gun-pa Sect in Western Tibet and Ladakh." In *Proceedings of the Csoma de Kofrös Memorial Symposium*, edited by Louis Ligeti. Budapest, 1978, pp. 313-325.
Richardson, Hugh E. "The Karma-pa Sect: A Historical Note." *Journal of the Royal Asiatic Society* (1958): 139-165 and (1959): 1-18.
Richardson, Hugh E. "The Rva-sgreng Conspiracy of 1947." In *Tibetan Studies in Honour of Hugh Richardson*, edited by Michael Aris and Aung San Suu Kyi. Warminster, 1979.
Ruegg, David S. "The Jo-nan-pas: A School of Buddhist Ontologists According to the *Grub-mtha' sel-gyi-me-lon*." *Journal of the American Oriental Society* 83 (1963): 73-91.
Sperling, Elliot. "The Fifth Karma-pa and Some Aspects of the Relationship between Tibet and the Early Ming." In *Tibetan Studies in Honour of Hugh Richardson*, edited by Michael Aris and Aung San Suu Kyi, pp. 280-287. Warminster, 1979.
Snellgrove, David L., and Hugh E. Richardson. *A Cultural History of Tibet* (1968). Reprint, Boulder, 1980.
Tarthang Tulku. *A History of the Buddhist Dharma*. Crystal Mirror, no. 5. Berkeley, 1977.
Tucci, Giuseppe. *The Religions of Tibet*. Translated by Geoffrey Samuel. Berkeley, 1980.

DAVID L. SNELLGROVE

BUSHNELL, HORACE

BUSHNELL, HORACE (1802-1876), Congregational minister and theologian. Born in Bantam, Connecticut, Bushnell attended Yale College and the Law School in New Haven. Stirred by a revival that swept the college in 1831, he decided to enter Yale Divinity School. In 1833 he was ordained pastor of the North Church of Hartford. He experienced an extraordinary spiritual illumination in 1848, a year in which he was also invited to lecture at Harvard, Andover, and Yale. The books resulting from these lectures and from Bushnell's attempts to clarify and refine their content in the face of criticism (*God in Christ*, 1849, and *Christ in Theology*, 1851) stirred up a hornet's nest of controversy and brought charges of heresy from conservative churchmen. In 1858 Bushnell's *Nature and the Supernatural* was published, and *Christian Nurture*, probably his best-known work, appeared in 1861 (an earlier version had come out in 1847). Persistent health problems forced him to resign his North Church pastorate in April 1861, but he continued to be active during the last fifteen years of his life, preaching, lecturing, and producing such additional books as *Work and Play* (1864), *Christ and His Salvation* (1864), *The Vicarious Sacrifice* (1866), *Moral*

Uses of Dark Things (1868), *Forgiveness and Law* (1874), and *Building Eras in Religion* (published posthumously in 1881).

Four traits of Bushnell's theological thought suggest something of the distinctive contribution he made to his times. The first is its high degree of originality. Bushnell did not prize originality for its own sake; he saw it as necessary for penetrating to the enduring heart of Christian teaching and rediscovering its relevance to the needs and concerns of human beings in a time of rapid change. Second, his theology was intended to be a mediating theology, one seeking grounds of consensus that could allay the spirit of divisiveness and contumely that marked so much of the theological debate of his day. Third, Bushnell held that the decisive test of any doctrine is an experiential one, that is, the contributions it can make to the transformation of life and character. Fourth, Bushnell tried to put theological discourse and method on a new footing by arguing that the language of religion, including that of the Bible, is the language of analogy, metaphor, and symbol, and that its function is to suggest and evoke truths and modes of awareness that cannot be literally expressed.

BIBLIOGRAPHY

Cherry, Conrad. *Nature and Religious Imagination: From Edwards to Bushnell*. Philadelphia, 1980. Explores Jonathan Edwards's symbolic vision of nature and its religious meanings, shows how this vision suffered sharp decline among religious thinkers in New England after Edwards's death, and then exhibits the resurgence of a similar vision in the thought of Bushnell.

Crosby, Donald A. *Horace Bushnell's Theory of Language*. The Hague, 1975. Investigates Bushnell's theory of language and religious language in the context of other philosophies of language in nineteenth-century America, discussing its implications for theological content and method. Examines and evaluates reactions to Bushnell's language theory from his theological peers.

Cross, Barbara M. *Horace Bushnell: Minister to a Changing America*. Chicago, 1958. Occasionally misinterprets Bushnell's thought but is a very useful placing of his ideas and the events of his life in the context of his time.

Smith, David L. *Symbolism and Growth: The Religious Thought of Horace Bushnell*. Chico, Calif., 1981. Argues that the principal focus of Bushnell's thought is his theory of how human beings influence each other through their social and linguistic interactions. Seeks to show how Bushnell used this theory to explain God's communications of himself for the purpose of nurturing and redeeming human character.

Smith, H. Shelton, ed. *Horace Bushnell*. New York, 1965. Valuable collection of some of Bushnell's most important writings, with informative general introduction and introductions to each selection. Includes an extensive bibliography of works by and about Bushnell.

DONALD A. CROSBY

CAIN AND ABEL

CAIN AND ABEL, the first two sons of Adam and Eve, the progenitors of the race according to the Bible, after their banishment from the garden of Eden (*Gn.* 4). Cain (Heb., Qayin), the elder, was a farmer; Abel (Heb., Hevel) was a shepherd. Both made (apparently votary) offerings to the Lord: Cain presented a meal offering of his fruits and grains, while Abel offered up the firstlings of his sheep. The offering of Cain was rejected by the Lord, and that of Abel was accepted. Cain's despondency led to a divine caution to resist the temptation to sin (*Gn.* 4:6-7); presumably this refers to the jealous urges and hostile resentments Cain felt. But the elder brother was overwrought and killed his brother in the field. This led to the punishment of Cain: like his father, he would not farm a fertile earth; and he would be banished "eastward of Eden." Fearing further retribution, Cain was given a protective "sign," whose aspect delighted the fancy in later legends and art.

The murder of Abel by Cain in *Genesis* 4:1-17 is the first social crime recorded in the Bible, and it complements on the external level the inner temptation and misuse of will depicted in similar language in *Genesis* 3. The tradition of Cain's act of murder and his subsequent punishment is followed by a genealogical list that presents him as the progenitor of several culture heroes. His son, Enoch, founded the first city

> **The murder of Abel by Cain in *Genesis* 4:1-17 is the first social crime recorded in the Bible. . . .**

(*Gn.* 4:18); and two other descendants, Jubal and Tubal-cain, were respectively named the cultural ancestors of "all who play the lyre and the pipe" (*Gn.* 4:21) and those "who forged all implements of copper and iron" (*Gn.* 4:22). Early rabbinic interpretation drew forth various elements of the story for moral and theological emphasis.

BIBLIOGRAPHY

Aptowitzer, Vigdor. *Kain und Abel in der Agada den Apokryphen, der hellenistischen, christlichen und muhammedanischen Literatur.* Vienna, 1922.

Fishbane, Michael. *Text and Texture.* New York, 1979. See pages 23-27.

Ginzberg, Louis. *The Legends of the Jews* (1909-1938). 7 vols. Translated by Henrietta Szold et al. Reprint, Philadelphia, 1937-1966. See volume 1, pages 55-59.

Réau, Louis. *Iconographie de l'art chrétien,* vol. 2. Paris, 1956. See pages 93-100.

Speiser, E. A. *Genesis.* Anchor Bible, vol. 1. Garden City, N. Y., 1964. See pages 29-38.

MICHAEL FISHBANE

CALVIN, JOHN

CALVIN, JOHN (1509-1564), primary Protestant reformer, biblical scholar, church organizer, and theologian. Also a humanist and linguist, Calvin helped to shape and standardize French language and literary style.

Calvin was reclusive and reticent; hence the only Calvin we know is the public figure. He spent his first thirteen years in Noyon, benefiting from the rich traditions of this historic episcopal city where his father served as attorney for the cathedral and secretary to the bishop, Charles de Hangest.

Intimately associated as a youth with the de Hangest household, Calvin developed aristocratic tastes and demeanor. Church benefices permitted him to further his education at the University of Paris; he spent nearly eleven years in Paris, participating in the intellectual life both of the university and the large circle of humanist scholars at the court of the king, Francis I.

At the university, preparing for a career in theology, Calvin had completed the master of arts degree when his father had a falling-out with the bishop. The father ordered his son to change to a career in law. Obediently Calvin moved to Orléans, where the best law faculty in France, under the leadership of Pierre de l'Étoile, was located. Though more interested in humanist studies, he completely immersed himself in the law (at Orléans, Bourges, and Paris) and took his doctorate and his licentiate in three years.

In 1532 Calvin published his first book, a commentary on Seneca's *On Clemency.* Though distinguished for its learning, the book did not win him any acclaim. His days of humanist study in Paris were cut short when, in 1533, his close friend Nicholas Cop, rector of the University of Paris, delivered an address that incorporated ideas of the Lutheran Reformation. Reaction by the theologians at the Sorbonne was strong, and because Calvin had a hand in the composition of the address, he, along with Cop, was forced to flee for his life. Although scholarly opinion differs, it appears that shortly thereafter he underwent the "sudden conversion" he speaks about later. A marked man in France, Calvin spent the rest of his life in exile.

Having turned his considerable talents to the support of the Reformation, in early 1536 Calvin published at Basel the first edition of his epochal *Institutes of the Christian Religion.* Intended as a defense of the French Protestants to the king of France, it marked Calvin as the foremost mind of Protestantism. The desired life of solitude and study that permitted its composition could never again be Calvin's. In late July of 1536, he happened to stop in the small city of Geneva; there God "thrust him into the fray," as he was to say. Geneva had recently declared for the Protestant faith under the urging of the fiery evangelist Guillaume Farel, one of Calvin's colleagues from his Paris days. Farel, learning of Calvin's presence in the city, sought him out and urged him to join in the work of reform at Geneva. When Calvin refused, Farel thundered that God would punish him for turning his back on that work. The shaken Calvin agreed to stay. He was henceforth associated with the city and republic of Geneva in a stormy ministry designed to bring the city into conformity with the biblical model as he understood it.

Calvin's ideal for Geneva was that church and state work hand in hand to create and govern a utopian society in which the biblical worldview was enforced. But the Genevan state was determined to keep the church under its control. A man of courage and indomitable will, Calvin took up the battle. Armed only with the power of the pulpit and of the church institutions, through persistence, adherence to biblical principles, organizational talents, and moral conviction, he managed to overcome massive resistance and to see most of his ideals realized. Geneva was transformed from a city of ill repute to one in which a strict moral code regulated the lives of all.

Unquestionably, Calvin was first and foremost a man of ideas, although he effectively blended thought and action. True to his Renaissance humanist orientation, he was interested only in what was useful. As a theologian he intended only to set forth scriptural teaching.

For Calvin, the word of God in scripture is generated by the Holy Spirit and, therefore, properly interpreted only by the Holy Spirit. It is, thus, a spiritual message. Hence Calvin should not be viewed as an academic theologian, or as a the-

ologian writing for intellectual purposes. He wrote for the church, for believers; his purpose was to edify, to form the pious mind that would emerge in reverential, grateful worship and adoration of God. He constantly warned his readers not to indulge in idle speculation, not to seek to know anything except what is revealed in the scripture, not to forget that theology is more of the heart than of the head.

> # Human beings are in bondage to sinful nature. . . .

The principal source for Calvin's thought is, of course, the *Institutes.* This book is best understood as a manual on spirituality. And, although the corpus of his writings is great, Calvin's ideas, whether found in sermons, biblical commentaries, or polemical literature, are consistent with what is presented in the *Institutes.*

In general Calvin had fully accepted Luther's idea that salvation is by grace alone through faith. The often-discussed doctrines of providence and predestination, for example, are presented by Calvin as the response or affirmation of a man of faith, affirming the control of God in his life, not as an epistemological program. To approach his theology from specific topics such as these has not been fruitful. There are, however, larger, general ideas or themes that point to what is essential in his thought. He understood the redemptive message to be the same in both the Old and the New Testament; hence his theology can be seen as all of a piece, permitting the dominance of the thematic approach rather than the topical.

Calvin's theological program is based on the dictum of Augustine that man is created for communion with God and that he will be unfulfilled until he rests in God. Calvin usually expresses this idea in terms of a union with the Maker and Redeemer, which is presented as essential to man's spiritual life. Thus the relationship between God and man is made the basis of all theological discourse, and this union or communion is established and maintained through what Calvin calls knowledge, a theme or idea that becomes an ordering principle of his theology. Knowledge of God the creator and knowledge of God the redeemer are the two divisions of his thought. He uses the term *knowledge* practically synonymously with the term *faith.* As with all of his theological ideas, two poles or foci must be kept in balance: the knowledge of God and the knowledge of self.

Although he always keeps in mind the perfect condition in which all things were created, because of the cataclysmic event of the Fall, all of Calvin's theology is concerned with redemption. Christ alone is the mediator who both reveals and effects this redemption, or restoration. Human beings are in bondage to sinful nature, so anything relating to this restoration must be initiated by God through Christ. Restoration occurs when the person is united to Christ by responding in faith to the provision made through Christ's death and resurrection.

Calvinists were the most vital of the Protestant groups, spreading throughout Europe and the New World. Scholarly opinion is divided over whether this success is due mainly to Calvin's theological teaching, to his training and educational program (the complete revamping of the elementary schools and the creation of the University of Geneva), or to his organizational talent. Probably all of these are contributory factors.

Although its unique blend of theory and practicality meant that Calvin's theology could be drawn upon by a variety of different interests, it can also be shown that his theology was revised almost beyond recognition very shortly after his death and that the *Institutes* were not widely read in the late sixteenth and early seventeenth centuries.

BIBLIOGRAPHY

Primary Sources. The numerous works of Calvin are available, in the original texts, in the fifty-nine volumes of the magisterial *Ioannis Calvini opera quae supersunt omnia,* edited by J. W. Baum and others (Braunschweig, 1863-1900), and in its continuation, the *Supplementa Calviniana,* a collection of subsequently discovered sermons edited by Erwin Mülhaupt and others (Neukirchen, 1961-), seven volumes to date with more to come. In English, the best edition of the *Institutes of the Christian Religion* is that of J. T. McNeill, translated by Ford Lewis Battles (Philadelphia, 1960) in two volumes. Many other works are available in English translation, including the important edition of *The New Testament Commentaries* edited by Thomas F. Torrance and David W. Torrance (Edinburgh, 1959-).

Secondary Sources. An excellent guide to the secondary literature is J. T. McNeill's "Fifty Years of Calvin Study: 1918-1968," which is prefaced to Williston Walker's *John Calvin, the Organiser of Reformed Protestantism, 1509-1564* (reprint, New York, 1969). T. H. L. Parker's *John Calvin* (Philadelphia, 1975), is fully informed and reliable, but the fullest and best biography, in spite of its hagiographic character, is Émile Doumergue's seven-volume *Jean Calvin, les hommes et les choses de son temps* (Lausanne, 1899-1927).

On Calvin's thought and influence, current scholarly opinion can be found in the proceedings of the International Congress on Calvin Research edited by W. H. Neuser in three volumes (vols. 1-2, Kampen, Netherlands, 1975, 1979; vol. 3, Bern, 1983). Benoît Giradin's *Rhétorique et théologique . . .* (Paris, 1979) is indispensable for the explication of the nature and structure of his thought, and E. A. Dowey's *The Knowledge of God in Calvin's Theology* (New York, 1952) is one of the better introductions. Richard Stauffer's *Dieu, la création et al providence dans la prédication de Calvin* (Bern, 1978) is an excellent corrective to the exclusively Christocentric interpretation of many recent scholars. On Calvin's influence, Robert M. Kingdom's Geneva and the Coming of the *Wars of Religion in France,* 1555-1563 (Geneva, 1956) and *Geneva and the Consolidation of the French Protestant Movement,* 1564-1572 (Geneva and Madison, Wis., 1967) are representative and excellent studies.

BRIAN G. ARMSTRONG

CANAANITE RELIGION

An Overview

Before the late nineteenth century, there were only two sources for the study of the Canaanite religion. The first, the Hebrew scriptures, contains numerous references to the Canaanites and their practices, which are generally condemned as abominable (e.g., *Lv.* 18:3, 27-28). It is generally agreed that the biblical witness to Canaanite religion is highly polemical and, therefore, unreliable; biblical evidence must at the least be used with extreme caution, and in conjunction with extrabiblical sources.

The second source for knowledge of Canaanite religion was those classical texts that preserve descriptions of aspects of it. The best known of these are the *Phoenician History of Philo Byblius,* of which portions are preserved in Eusebius's *Praeparatio evangelica,* and *The Syrian Goddess,* attributed (perhaps falsely) to Lucian of Samothrace. At best, Philo's information probably sheds light on the religion of late hellenized Phoenicians, and offers no direct evidence for second-millennium Canaanite religion. The same generalization applies to (Pseudo-) Lucian.

Firsthand evidence for Canaanite culture in the second millennium BCE (or, in archaeological terms, the Middle Bronze and Late Bronze periods) comes from artifactual evidence found at many archaeological sites (more than sixty for the first part of the Middle Bronze period alone—mostly tombs) and from textual evidence stemming mainly from three great discoveries: (1) the eighteenth-century royal archives of "Amorite" Mari; (2) the diplomatic correspondence between several Levantine vassal princes and the pharoahs Amenophis III and IV (first half of the fourteenth century), found at Tell al-'Amarna; and (3) the mainly fourteenth- and thirteenth-century texts found at Ras Shamra (ancient Ugarit) and nearby Ras Ibn Hani, both within the present-day administrative district of Latakia, on the Mediterranean coast of Syria. The artifactual evidence is crucial for understanding material culture, socioeconomic developments, population movements, and the like, and provides considerable data about funerary practices. Most significant for the study of religion are the figurines, thought to represent gods and goddesses, that have been recovered in virtually every archaeological context.

The ancient city of Mari was peripheral to both the Mesopotamian and the Levantine spheres of influence. Culturally and linguistically, it was clearly West Semitic, but to label it "Canaanite" goes beyond the evidence (the designation "Amorite" represents, to some extent, a scholarly compromise). The Mari texts are virtually all concerned with economic, juridical, and administrative matters. One text in particular testifies to the eclecticism and heterogeneity of Mari's religious cult in the eighteenth century, listing the sacrificial sheep distributed among the various gods and temples of Mari. The most striking group of Mari texts is the small collection of so-called prophetic texts. These twenty-odd letters attest to a type of oracular speaking that shows significant affinities with biblical prophecies of a millennium later. Some of this oracular speaking seems to have been done by cultic personnel, and some apparently consisted of messages transmitted by the gods through ordinary people. It may be suggested, on the basis of these Mari texts and related evidence, that the phenomenon broadly termed *"prophecy"* represented a peculiar and peripheral kind of divine intermediation among the West Semites generally.

Most of the Amarna letters report on Levantine military, economic, and political matters to the Egyptian court. The letters were written in Babylonian, the diplomatic language of the period, but they regularly reveal the Canaanite character of their authors.

By far the most significant evidence for Canaanite religion in the second millennium is found at Ugarit. From the beginning of the millennium until the city's destruction at the hands of the Sea Peoples (c. 1180-1175 BCE), Ugarit was a thriving cosmopolitan trading center. In the Middle Bronze period, Ugarit underwent considerable expansion. During this period, two large temples (dedicated to the gods Baal and Dagan respectively) were erected on top of older ruins, forming, in effect, an acropolis in the city. The pottery of the period is predominantly Canaanite, and other material evidence demonstrates that Ugarit was in contact with Egypt, the Aegean, and Mesopotamia. At the same time, Ugarit's population was augmented by an influx of Indo-European-speaking Hurrians from the northeast.

The best-attested period at Ugarit is the last two centuries of its existence (Late Bronze III, c. 1365-1180). The Ugaritic texts date from this period, although some of the religious texts are undoubtedly older, and were merely written down at this time.

In addition to the mythological texts from the high priest's library, the excavations of this and several other archives of Ugarit and Ras Ibn Hani have turned up related mythological material, descriptive ritual texts, lists of sacrificial offerings, god-lists, prayers and liturgies, incantations, divinatory texts, and dedicatory inscriptions.

Deities. The essential information about Ugarit's deities comes from what appears to be a canonical god-list. Two reasons are generally given for the order of the gods in the list: either it reflects their relative importance, or else it gives the order in which their symbols were paraded in a cultic procession. The list begins with two or three Ils (El)—the sources are evenly split on the number. *Il* is the common Semitic word for "god"; it is the proper name of the head of the Ugaritic pantheon in the mythological texts. The first Il in

the god-list is associated with Mount Sapan (Tsafon), the Canaanite Olympus, which was traditionally identified with Jebel al-Aqra, about fifty kilometers north of Ugarit at the mouth of the Orontes River. (The mountain was itself deified, and appears in the god-list.)

The second Il is called *Ilib*. The Akkadian and Hurrian parallels show that this name is a portmanteau composed of the elements *il* ("god") and *ab* ("father"), but the precise significance of the combination is uncertain. Most likely the name denotes an ancestral spirit, the numen manifest in the Ugaritic cult of the dead.

The third Il is presumably to be identified with the head of the pantheon in the mythological texts. His epithets and activities in those, and in the cultic texts, provide a fair picture of

> **Baal represents the divine power that is immanent in the world, activating and effectuating things or phenomena.**

his character. He is the father of the gods, who are called his "family" or "sons," and he is styled "father of humankind" and "builder of built ones." He may have been regarded as the creator of the world, but the Ugaritic evidence is inconclusive on this point. He bears the epithet "bull," a symbol of virility and power (although one mythological text casts some doubt on his sexual prowess).

The next deity on the list is Dagan. The Mari texts attest to his great importance in the Middle Euphrates region (especially Terqa). One of the two temples on the acropolis of Ugarit was evidently consecrated to Dagan. During excavations carried out in 1934, two inscribed stone slabs were found just outside the temple. The inscriptions, the only known examples of Ugaritic carved in stone, commemorate *pgr* sacrifices of a sheep and an ox offered to Dagan.

Following Dagan come seven Baals. The first is the Baal of Mount Sapan, who dwells in the same place as the Baal in the mythological texts (the "heights" or "recesses" of Sapan); the term *sapan* surely refers to the Baal temple of Ugarit as well. The Akkadian rendition of *Baal* is *Adad,* which is the name of the most prominent West Semitic mountain and weather god. The significance of the other six Baals (none qualified by epithets and all identified with Adad) is uncertain, although sevenfold lists of all sorts, including divine heptads, are common throughout the ancient Near East: the number seven evidently denotes completeness or perfection.

The name *Baal* is derived from the common Semitic noun meaning "lord, master, husband." In contrast to the numinous Il, Baal represents the divine power that is immanent in the world, activating and effectuating things or phenomena. Given the paucity of rainfall in most of the Levant, it is not surprising that the lord of the storm is the most prominent god of this type.

Following the seven Baals, the god-list continues with Ars wa-Shamem ("earth and heaven"). Binomial deities are common in Ugaritic; they represent either a hendiadys (as in this case) or a composite of two related gods who have been assimilated to one another. This god's function is unknown; perhaps the domain over which Baal holds sway is deified. There are also two other geographical deities: Sapan (discussed above) and "Mountain and Valley" (significance unknown, unless it defines the domain of Athtar, the god occupying the preceding place on the god-list).

The remaining divine names on the list may be grouped in four categories: individual goddesses and gods who are known or at least mentioned in the mythological texts; collective terms that designate groups of lesser deities; Hurrian deities; and otherwise unknown or poorly attested gods.

The two most prominent goddesses in the mythological texts are Athirat (Asherah) and Anat. Athirat is the consort of Il, and as such she is the highest-ranking goddess in the pantheon. In contrast, Anat is a violent goddess of sexual love and war, "sister" (perhaps consort) of Baal and vanquisher of Baal's enemy Mot. Her principal epithet is "maiden," a tribute to her youth, beauty, and desirability, but pugnacity is her primary trait.

There are three other Canaanite goddesses on the god-list. Shapash is the all-seeing sun (male in Mesopotamia, but female at Ugarit), "luminary of the gods." Pid-ray ("fat"?) and Arsay ("earth," perhaps, on the basis of the Akkadian parallel, having some connection with the netherworld) are two of the daughters of Baal; the third, Talay ("dew"), does not appear on the god-list. Two other non-Canaanite goddesses are on the list, undoubtedly via the Hurrians, although the deities themselves are not necessarily Hurrian in origin: Ushharay (Ishhara), the scorpion goddess, who appears in several cultic texts but never in the myths, and Dadmish, probably a warrior goddess but very poorly attested. The one remaining goddess on the list is Uthht (pronunciation uncertain; the sex of the deity is, in fact, only surmised from the feminine ending); possibly Mesopotamian in origin, and most likely signifying a deified incense burner.

Seven male deities remain on the god-list, all but one of whom are at least mentioned in the mythological texts. Yarikh is the moon god, and he figures prominently in a poem that describes his marriage to the moon goddess, Nikkal. This text is undoubtedly a Hurrian myth in Ugaritic guise. The other clearly astral god is Shalim (the divine element in the name of the city Jeru*salem* and of King *Solom*on), who represents the evening twilight or Venus as evening star.

The god Kothar ("skilled one"; also known as Kothar wa-Hasis, "skilled and wise one") is the divine craftsman. In various sources he is a master builder, weapon maker, seaman,

and magician. It has been suggested that he is the genius of technology.

The god Rashap (the biblical *Reshef,* which means both "pestilence" and "flame") is blamed in the epic of Kirta for the demise of part of the title character's family. But Rashap's real importance at Ugarit and Ras Ibn Hani emerges from the cultic texts, where he is the recipient of numerous offerings.

The remaining god on the list is Kinar, who is perhaps the deified lyre. Nothing is known about him, but he has been identified with the Cypriot hero Kinyras, father of Adonis.

Rituals and Cultic Personnel. Assuming that the biblical and related data are reliable, they evidently refer to local manifestations of first-millennium Phoenician cults (such as that of northern Israel). The simple assumption of continuity between second-millennium Canaan and first-millennium Phoe-nicia is unjustified—as is, more generally, the facile identification of "Canaanites" with "Phoenicians."

As for the myth-and-ritual claim, the seasonal interpretation of the Baal texts is by no means certain. There is no evidence that the Baal texts were ever used in conjunction with cultic activity. In fact, there is only one Ugaritic mythological text containing rubrics for ritual performance; it apparently entails some sort of fertility rite, but one not necessarily connected with the seasonal cycle. Knowledge of the Ugaritic calendar and its fixed festivals is too scanty to permit the claim that Ugaritic religion was organized with respect to the agricultural year.

The Ugaritic ritual texts describe a highly organized sacrificial cult under the patronage of the king. The sacrifices seem to be of the gift or tribute type; that is, they were performed to curry favor with the gods, to secure their aid and protection. It is undeniable that offerings might have been made to deities (particularly chthonic ones) to promote the fertility of the land and the fecundity of the flocks. But the one mass public ritual that has survived, and the one attested prayer to Baal as well, both seem more concerned with protection from Ugarit's potential military opponents. In view of the shifting alliances and political instability that marked Ugarit's last two centuries, this concern seems only natural.

Most of the known Ugaritic rituals were performed by or on behalf of the king. The best-attested type of ritual is found in seven different texts. In it the king of Ugarit performs, at specified times, a ritual lustration to purify himself, and then offers a series of sacrifices to various deities. At sundown, the king "desacralizes" himself in a way that is not clear. The most interesting of these texts is evidently a prescriptive ritual to which is appended a prayer to Baal, perhaps recited by the queen, that seems to specify the occasion on which the rites were to be performed.

A second type of ritual is preserved in three texts that describe the transfer of cult statues from one place to another. The remainder of the text describes essentially the same rituals as those performed for a different collection of gods (on a different occasion?), the poorly attested *gthrm*.

One substantial ritual text is unique in the corpus, and has been the subject of many studies. It is unique in its poetic/hymnic quality and in the acts it describes. It seems to depict a great public assembly in which the entire population of Ugarit, male and female, king and commoner alike, participated. The ritual appears to have been a mass expiation or purgation of sins, or some sort of mass purification rite, designed to protect Ugarit against its threatening neighbors.

> **The ritual appears to have been a mass expiation or purgation of sins, or some sort of mass purification rite. . . .**

A parallel has been drawn between it and the Jewish Yom Kippur, the "day of purgation [of sin]." In the Ugaritic text, the men and women of the community are alternately summoned to offer sacrifices, which they do. While the sacrifices are performed the people sing, praying that their offerings will ascend to "the father of the sons of Il" (that is, to Il himself), to the "family of the sons of Il," to the "assembly of the sons of Il," and to *Thkmn wa-Shnm,* Il's son and attendant (the one who cares for him when he is drunk; in one of his epithets, Il is called "father of *Shnm*").

Only one mythological text, the poem about the birth of Shahr and Shalim (the *ilima naimima,* "gracious gods"), includes rubrics for ritual performance. These rubrics, interspersed throughout the poem, describe the activities of the king and queen, and of cultic functionaries called *aribuma* (some kind of priests?) and *tha-nanuma* (members of the king's guard?). They offer sacrifices, participate in a banquet, and sing responsively to musical accompaniment. It seems almost certain that the poem itself was acted out as a type of ritual drama. It describes the subjugation of Death by some sort of pruning rite, followed by Il's sexual relations with Athirat and Rahmay ("womb" = Anat?). The poem concludes with the birth of Shahr and Shalim, and their youthful activities. The text and its accompanying ritual may commemorate (or attempt to foster) the birth of a royal heir to the reigning king and queen of Ugarit; they bear some relation to Mesopotamian sacred marriage rites and to Hittite rituals designed to protect the life and vigor of the king and queen.

Most difficult to reconstruct, but obviously of great importance, was the Ugaritic cult of the dead. The dead were summoned, by a liturgy accompanied by offerings, to participate in a banquet. The banquet, which was apparently a drunken orgy, was intended to propitiate the dead and to solicit the aid and protection provided by their numinous power. The most important group of the deified dead was comprised of Ugarit's kings (*malikum*). The larger assemblage, variously called "healers" (*rpim*), "healers of the netherworld" (*rpi ars*), "ancient healers" (*rpim qdmyn*), "divine spirits" (*ilnym*), and "assembly of Ditan/Didan" (*qbs dtn/ddn*), included two men who are prominent in the epic texts, Danil and Kirta, as well as several other spirits who are identified by name in a liturgical invocation of the dead.

Another important text invokes the god Rapiu, "king of eternity" (that is, of the netherworld). Rapiu is clearly the patron of the deified dead; at first he is invited to drink, and at the end of the text he is asked to exert his "strength, power, might, rule, and goodness" for the benefit of Ugarit. If Rapiu is indeed to be identified with Il, this text comports well with the mythological fragment that depicts Il getting drunk at a *marzih*.

Alongside the cult of the dead must be placed the texts that apparently describe the ritual offerings to the gods of the netherworld (*ilm ars*). The clearest of these begins with an offering to Rashap and mentions several other chthonic deities. There is also a strange god-list that appears to include a collection of netherworld demons. Finally, an inscribed clay model of a liver may record a sacrifice offered to a person (or deity?) who is "in the tomb."

Popular Religion. As is generally the case in the ancient Near East, little can be said with any certainty about popular religion at Ugarit, since only kings, priests, and members of the elite are represented in the texts. The Ugaritic texts were apparently only a part of the larger cosmopolitan scribal tradition of Ugarit, which was modeled on the Babylonian scribal schools. The same scribes who produced the *Baal* texts were also trained to write in Babylonian cuneiform, and they copied Sumerian and Akkadian texts in almost every genre. Surviving evidence demonstrates that Ugarit's educated elite was conversant with the Mesopotamian Gilgamesh traditions, wisdom and proverbial literature, and legal formulas, although little of this material is reflected in texts in the Ugaritic language.

It is not at all certain, then, how much of the literary tradition might have filtered down to the commoners of Ugarit. Still, speculation about popular religion may be made in four areas: conceptions of gods reflected in personal names; the evidence of votive figurines; evidence for magic and divination; and possible religious, ethical, or "wisdom" teachings derived from the texts.

Popular conceptions of the gods may emerge from a consideration of personal names, since a great number of names are composites of divine names (or surrogates) and nominal or verbal elements. The standard collection of Ugaritic personal names, Frauke Gröndahl's *Die Personennamen der Texte aus Ugarit* (Rome, 1967), lists over fifty divine elements that appear in them. The most popular are Il, Baal, Ammu ("uncle," a surrogate for a divine name), Anat and her "masculine" equivalent Anu, Athtar, Yamm, Kothar, Malik, Pidr (masculine equivalent of Pidray?), Rapiu, Rashap, and Shapash. In some names, a god is described as father, mother, brother, sister, or uncle (e.g., *Rashapabi*). In others, the bearer of the name is the god's son, daughter, servant, or devotee (e.g., *Abdi-Rashap,* "servant of Rashap"). A large class of names describes characteristics of the gods.

The second class of evidence for popular religion comes from metal figurines that are generally thought to represent gods and goddesses. A comprehensive catalog of these figurines, compiled by Ora Negbi (1976), describes over seventeen hundred of them. They are considered to have been miniature copies of now-lost wooden cult statues, and were probably used as votive idols. The fact that so many have been found at cultic sites suggests that they had some ceremonial function. Negbi notes that these idols "may have been used as amulets for magic purposes in domestic and funerary cults as well" (p. 2).

Some textual evidence has been recovered for magic and divination at Ugarit. There are two versions of a long and impressive incantation against the bite of a venomous serpent; several important deities are summoned from their mythical abodes during the course of the incantations.

Finally, one very difficult text reports a divine oracle. It begins: "When the lord of the great/many gods [Il?] approached Ditan, the latter sought an oracle concerning the child." Some individual presumably wishes to inquire of Il about his (sick?) child. (A comparable episode occurs in the Kirta epic.) Il can be reached through an intermediary, Ditan, the eponymous patron of those deified dead known as the "assembly of Ditan." The text continues with a series of instructions (broken and unclear) that will enable the inquirer to obtain the desired oracular response. The text seems to conclude with several instructions, "and afterward there will be no suffering [?]".

Taken together, these texts indicate a lively interest in the mantic arts at Ugarit. There is practically no evidence, however, about the specialists who practiced those arts; perhaps that is because they operated on the periphery of the official cultic institutions.

The most problematic aspect of popular religion is the interpretation of the Ugaritic religious texts. Assuming that they were in some way normative and that they were diffused orally, they would embody the religious "teachings" of Ugarit. There are, however, no surviving interpretations of the texts or expositions of religious doctrine that explain what those teachings might have been or what impact they had on the life of a community of believers. The Ugaritic mythic and epic texts (as opposed to the descriptive ritual texts) can be read as homilies on the nature of the world in which people live. Ancient readers or hearers of these texts would have sought their own place in the "cosmos" they describe. Ugaritic believ-

ers, like modern believers, would presumably have formulated a special application of sacred texts to their own lives.

The *Baal* texts punctualize eternal truths in a symbolic realm that is only superficially remote from human experience. The gods experience joy and mourning, battle and tranquillity, life and death, power and impotence. The mightiest of the gods confronts the world's challenges and surmounts them all, until he encounters Death, the one enemy to whom gods and humans alike succumb. Baal's triumphs and trials, furthermore, illustrate the contiguity and interrelationship of everything in the world: the gods, nature, the political order, and human life are all part of the same order. When Baal is vanquished, political order collapses and the earth turns infertile—not because Baal "symbolizes" order and fertility in some simplistic way, but because the intricate balance of the world has been subverted. The same upset of the natural order occurs when Kirta, a human king, becomes mortally ill.

Overarching the flux of the world, and apparently not subject to it, is the wise and beneficent Il. At critical moments in the *Baal* texts, the gods journey (or send emissaries) to him in order to obtain his favor and advice. After Kirta's family is annihilated by malevolent forces, Il comforts the king in a dream; later on, Il provides the cure for Kirta's terrible illness. And in the Aqhat epic, Baal implores Il to grant a son to the childless Danil. Il consents, and appears to Danil in a dream with the good news. In every case, Il manifests transcendent power that is wielded justly, in response to urgent pleas.

The epic texts (perhaps "historico-mythic" would be a better designation for them) Aqhat and Kirta parallel and supplement the mythic texts. They narrate the existential encounter of humans with the gods. Historical (or pseudo-historical) figures become exemplary or admonitory paradigms of human behavior.

The crises that move the plot of the Aqhat text demonstrate the conjunction and contiguity of the human and divine realms. Danil, who is, like Kirta, a man become god (one of the deified rapium—from the point of view of the reader, that is), is an embodiment of that contiguity. Danil is clearly an ideal type, pious and just; he brings his plea for a son before the gods in humble obeisance, and he is rewarded. The incubation rite performed by Danil at the beginning of the story seems to be a model of personal piety.

The Kirta epic, like that of Aqhat, begins with its hero childless, this time because of catastrophe instead of impotence. Dramatic tension arises from the situation of a king without an heir, which could result in disruption of both the political and the natural order. The story conveys the fragility of power and the delicate relationship between humans and deities.

The texts are all firmly on the side of reward for virtue and piety, and punishment for wickedness, blasphemy, and folly.

Yet even someone who is justly suffering the wrath of the gods may appeal to the gracious Il and be heard.

Survivals. Survivals of Canaanite religion are observable in two first-millennium cultural spheres, the Levant and the Aegean. Phoenician religion, both in the Levant and in its wider Mediterranean sphere of influence, represents, to some extent, a continuation of Canaanite traditions. Northern Israel's official cult was among the Levantine successors of Canaanite religion. It has often been noted that biblical polemics against that cult (for example, in the *Book of Hosea*) are directed against a characteristically Canaanite feature—the idea that the god (in this case Yahveh = Baal) was immanent in nature and subject to its flux. The Israelite god was, on the other hand, comfortably assimilated to the transcendent Il.

In the Aegean area, the nature of Canaanite influence is more controversial. But there is compelling evidence for the existence of direct West Semitic contact with Mycenaean Greece, creating a legacy of Semitic names, literary motifs, and religious practices that became part of the Hellenic cultural heritage.

BIBLIOGRAPHY

There are excellent, comprehensive articles on Amarna, Mari, and Ras Shamra in the *Dictionnaire de la Bible, Supplément,* vol. 1, cols. 207-225 (by Édouard Dhorme); vol. 5, cols. 883-905 (by Charles F. Jean); and vol. 9, cols. 1124-1466, respectively (Paris, 1928-). The Ras Shamra article, by several distinguished experts, is magisterial—the best survey to be found anywhere. In English, the journal *Biblical Archaeologist* has published a number of good survey articles: on Mari by George E. Mendenhall, vol. 11 (February 1948), pp. 1-19, and by Herbert B. Huffmon, vol. 31 (December 1968), pp. 101-124 (on the "prophetic texts"); on Amarna by Edward F. Campbell, vol. 23 (February 1960), pp. 2-22; on Ugarit by H. L. Ginsberg, vol. 8 (May 1945), pp. 41-58, and by Anson F. Rainey, vol. 28 (December 1965), pp. 102-125. All of these articles have been reprinted in The *Biblical Archaeologist Reader,* edited by David Noel Freedman and G. Ernest Wright, vols. 2 and 3 (Garden City, N. Y., 1961-1970). More recently, *Biblical Archaeologist* 47 (June 1984) is a special issue devoted to Mari.

Turning specifically to Ugarit, an excellent popular introduction is Gabriel Saadé's *Ougarit: Métropole cananéenne* (Beirut, 1979). Saadé gives a thorough account of the excavations, with complete bibliographical information and many illustrations. Most of the technical information is derived from articles in the journal *Syria,* beginning with volume 10 (1929), and from the volumes in the series "Mission de Ras-Shamra," 9 vols., edited by Claude F.-A. Schaeffer (Paris, 1936-1968). Two other useful works on the archaeological data are Patty Gerstenblith's *The Levant at the Beginning of the Middle Bronze Age* (Winona Lake, Ind., 1983) and Ora Negbi's *Canaanite Gods in Metal* (Tel Aviv, 1976).

A good detailed account of Ugarit's history is Mario Live-rani's *Storia di Ugarit* (Rome, 1962), and an unsurpassed description of Ugaritic society is Anson F. Rainey's *The Social Structure of Ugarit* (in Hebrew; Jerusalem, 1967). Readers of English can consult Rainey's Ph. D. dissertation, "The Social Stratification of Ugarit" (Brandeis University, 1962).

On the study of Canaanite religion before the discovery of Ugarit, there is a fine survey by M. J. Mulder, "Von Seldon bis Schaeffer: Die Erforschung der kanaanäischen Götterwelt," in the leading scholarly journal devoted to Ugaritic studies, *Ugarit-Forschungen* 11 (1979): 655-671. The best general introduction to Canaanite religion is Hartmut Gese's "Die Religionen Altsyriens," in *Die Religionen Altsyriens, Altarabiens und der Mandäer* (Stuttgart, 1970), pp. 3-181. On the Canaanite gods, the standard work is still Marvin H. Pope and Wolfgang Röllig's "Syrien," in *Wörterbuch der Mythologie,* edited by H. W. Haussig, vol. 1 (Stuttgart, 1965), pp. 219-312. On the rituals and cultic personnel, an excellent presentation of the data is Jean-Michel de Tarragon's *Le culte à Ugarit* (Paris, 1980), which should be consulted alongside Paolo Xella's *I testi rituali di Ugarit* (Rome, 1981). There is an exceptionally interesting theoretical discussion of Canaanite religion by David L. Petersen and Mark Woodward in "Northwest Semitic Religion: A Study of Relational Structures," *Ugarit-Forschungen* 9 (1977): 232-248. The outstanding representative of the myth-and-ritual approach is Theodor H. Gaster's *Thespis,* 2d ed. (1961; New York, 1977).

There is not yet an adequately introduced and annotated English translation of the Ugaritic texts. The best English translations are those of H. L. Ginsberg, in J. B. Pritchard's *Ancient Near Eastern Texts relating to the Old Testament,* 3d ed. (Princeton, 1969), pp. 129-155, and those in J. C. L. Gibson's revision of G. R. Driver's *Canaanite Myths and Legends,* 2d ed. (Edinburgh, 1978). The serious student should consult *Textes ougaritiques,* translated and edited by André Caquot and others (Paris, 1974), and the even more comprehensive Spanish work by Gregorio del Olmo Lete, *Mitos y leyendas de Canaán según la tradición de Ugarit* (Madrid, 1981), complemented by the same author's *Interpretación de la mitología cananea* (Valencia, 1984). A more popular introduction and translation that is both readable and of high quality is Paolo Xella's *Gli antenati di Dio* (Verona, 1982). A comparable but inferior volume in English is Stories from *Ancient Canaan,* edited and translated by Michael D. Coogan (Philadelphia, 1978).

Works on Ugarit and the Bible are legion. The serious student is directed to *Ras Shamra Parallels,* edited by Loren R. Fischer, 2 vols. (Rome, 1972-1975). The contributions are uneven in quality, but the many proposed parallels are presented with full bibliographic information. A convenient survey of comparative studies is Peter C. Craigie's "Ugarit and the Bible," in *Ugarit in Retrospect,* edited by Gordon Douglas Young (Winona Lake, Ind., 1981), pp. 99-111. John Gray's *The Legacy of Canaan,* 2d ed. (Leiden, 1965), has become a standard work in this area; its great learning and originality are marred by eccentricity, especially in the translation of the Ugaritic texts. On the most important classical account of "Canaanite" religion, see the definitive work by Albert I. Baumgarten, *The Phoenician History of Philo of Byblos* (Leiden, 1981). Semitic influence on the Aegean world is one of the main topics of Cyrus H. Gordon's stimulating book *Before the Bible: The Common Background of Greek and Hebrew Civilizations* (London, 1962); a more technical work on the subject is Michael C. Astour's brilliant *Hellenosemitica* (Leiden, 1967).

ALAN M. COOPER

CANON LAW

Canon law refers to the law internal to the church. In the early centuries of Christianity, *canon* was used for internal church norms, to distinguish them from the imperial *nomos* (*leges* in Latin) or laws. Church norms have also been known as sacred or divine, to distinguish them from civil or human laws. At times they are referred to as the "sacred canons" or the "canonical order." The term *ecclesiastical law* is used synonymously with *canon law,* although at times *ecclesiastical law* also refers to the civil law adopted in various nations to regulate church affairs. The term *canon law* is used in the Roman Catholic, Anglican, and Orthodox communions.

Over the centuries three major approaches have characterized the development of canon law. The first corresponds to the more communal structure of Christian churches in the first millennium; the second, a more Western phenomenon, is marked by the *Corpus iuris canonici,* or "body of canon law," developed during the centralization of church authority; the third is the relatively recent development in Roman Catholicism of a code of canon law.

The primitive church adopted practical norms in response to specific needs and followed precedents that were thought to have come from the apostles.

As local, regional, and eventually ecumenical councils were held, the bishops adopted disciplinary norms they called canons. These were frequently repeated by subsequent councils in the same and other areas. Eventually collections were developed in the East containing conciliar legislation (canons), imperial laws dealing with religious questions *(nomos),* and combinations of the two (nomocanons). These form the body of canon law for Eastern Orthodox churches today, with subsequent modifications enacted for specific autocephalous churches by their respective synods. Eastern churches in communion with Rome are also governed by this traditional body of law, modified through subsequent synods and papal enactments.

Around 1140 John Gratian, a monk who had studied at Bologna the rediscovered civil law of the sixth-century Roman emperor Justinian, produced his *Concordia discordantium canonum.* Known popularly as Gratian's Decretum ("decree"), this was the most successful attempt to that time to put some sense of order into canon law. With Gratian begins the second major period of history for canon law. His work became the standard textbook and administrative reference manual for Western church law. It contained decrees of councils, decretals of popes, and Gratian's own comments organizing and explaining the interrelationship of his sources.

In 1500 the *Corpus iuris canonici* was published at Paris. It contained Gratian's Decretum, the three subsequent official collections, and two later private collections of decretals, the *Extravagantes Ioannes XXII* and the *Extravagantes communes,* decretals circulating outside the official collections. This new collection served as the body of canon law for the Roman Catholic church until 1917.

The Council of Trent (1545-1563) issued a number of decrees supplementing the canon law on sacraments, clergy discipline, and related issues.

Pius X (r. 1903-1914) began the effort of codification, entrusting it to Cardinal Pietro Gasparri. The final product was promulgated by Benedict XV (r. 1914-1922) in 1917. The *Codex iuris canonici* (Code of Canon Law) marks a new stage in the history of canon law. Instead of the previous system, which reported both the law and its historical source, the new code contained canons devoid of historical basis, all having the same authority based on the pope as legislator. Later editions did contain historical notes appended by Gasparri, which were intended to aid in understanding the

> **The term *canon law* is used in the Roman Catholic, Anglican, and Orthodox communions.**

canons, but the 1917 code represents an entirely new approach to canon law deliberately patterned on civil models.

Subsequent to the code, canon law became a process of interpreting the text of the canons and observing further instructions issued by Roman offices or local bishops. Conciliar activity to produce new canons was restricted to missionary areas, and only rarely did these go beyond the application of the code to local circumstances.

In 1959, when he announced plans to hold the Second Vatican Council, John XXIII also called for a renewal of the code. The work began in earnest in 1965, when the council concluded. Paul VI (r. 1963-1973) directed that the revision not only clear up ambiguities and questions relating to the 1917 code but also implement the new way of thinking characteristic of the council. His desire was for a canon law based on church considerations rather than on imitation of civil legal systems.

The commission for the Latin code began its work first. Canons for the revised code were circulated in sections (schemata, or drafts) for comments by bishops around the world, revised and reorganized as a new code in 1980, and subjected to further study by an enlarged commission in 1981. The text was then studied by the pope with the aid of six advisers, and a final text of the revised *Codex iuris canonici* was promulgated on 25 January 1983 by John Paul II, twenty-four years after the announcement by John XXIII that the revision would take place. Work on the Eastern code is still in the consulting stage.

Although it continues the system of expressing canons devoid of their historical sources, the new code replaces the organization of the old one with a more theological arrangement of the canons. After an expanded initial book of general norms, there follow three substantive books based on

Vatican II categories. The second book of the code, entitled "The People of God," begins with norms that apply to all the Christian faithful. It contains a first effort to provide a common bill of obligations and rights, followed by a set of canons on the obligations and rights of laity. Clergy are treated in combination with laity before the book turns to the hierarchical structures of the church, both at the level of supreme authority and in particular churches (dioceses) and groupings of churches. The final portion of the book considers religious and secular institutes ("consecrated life") and apostolic societies.

Increased importance is given to the word of God in book 3, on the teaching office of the church, and to the sacraments in book 4, on the church's sanctifying office. Canons on temporal goods are grouped into book 5. A revised and considerably reduced section on sanctions is found in book 6, while procedures are detailed in book 7.

Several issues mark current canon law discussions in the Roman Catholic church, some of which have significance for other churches that use a system of canon law. There is obviously the debate over the opportuneness of promulgating a code so soon after Vatican II, with many issues still under debate. The consensus articulated in the *Corpus iuris canonici* and later in the 1917 *Codex* is not that evident in Roman Catholicism today.

More fundamentally, the relationship of canon law to theology, to civil law, and even to "law" as such has been questioned. Paul VI sought to find the basis for canon law in the church's own self-understanding, and John Paul II points to scripture as the ultimate source for the new code. Some see in this a genuine effort to provide a more theological basis for canon law.

Finally, is canon law really "law"? In light of contemporary understanding of religious liberty and the traditional teaching on the freedom of the act of faith, canon law must be seen more as the norm of a voluntary association than as a binding code for a nation or state. Current practice, which relies on administrative action more than on strictly legislative or canonical procedures, may already be a tacit admission of this fact.

BIBLIOGRAPHY

On the history of canon law, see the detailed synopsis by René Metz in the *New Catholic Encyclopedia* (New York, 1967) and in Amleto Giovanni Cicognani's *Canon Law,* 2d ed. (Philadelphia, 1935). Standard commentaries on the 1917 Code of Canon Law in English are T. Lincoln Bouscaren and Adam C. Ellis's *Canon Law: A Text and Commentary,* 4th ed. (Milwaukee, 1966); John A. Abbo and Jerome D. Hannan's *The Sacred Canons,* 2d ed., 2 vols. (Saint Louis, 1952); and Stanislaus Woywod and Calistus Smith's *A Practical Commentary on the Code of Canon Law,* rev. ed. (New York, 1963). For the 1983 code, see text in *Code of Canon Law, Latin-English Edition* (Washington, D. C., 1983), and the commentary edited by James A. Coriden, Thomas J. Green, and Donald E. Heintschel, *The Code of Canon Law: A Text and Commentary* (New York, 1984). For Anglican canon law, see Eric Kemp's *An Introduction to Canon Law in the Church of England* (London, 1957).

JAMES H. PROVOST

CARIBBEAN RELIGIONS

Pre-Columbian Religions

European explorers noted three major aboriginal groups in the Caribbean at the time of contact (1492 and the years immediately following): Island Arawak, Island Carib, and Ciboney. There is an abundance of information concerning the religious practices of the Island Arawak and Island Carib, but very little is known of Ciboney religion.

This essay will focus on the Island Arawak and the Island Carib. The Island Arawak were concentrated in the Greater Antilles, a group of large, mainly sedimentary islands near Puerto Rico. The Island Carib inhabited the small, mainly volcanic islands of the Lesser Antilles.

Both the Island Arawak and the Island Carib originally migrated from the South American mainland (Rouse, 1964). The Island Arawak settled in the Greater Antilles at about the beginning of the common era and were followed several hundred years later by the Carib, who claimed to have begun their migrations into the Lesser Antilles only a few generations before the arrival of Columbus.

Deities. Both the Island Arawak and the Island Carib possessed a notion of a high god, though, as the chroniclers' reports make clear, their high god differed conceptually from the God of Christianity. We know, too, that aboriginal high gods were thought to exert very little direct influence on the workings of the universe. Many of the early chroniclers, including Fray Ramón Pané, Gonzalo F. de Oviedo, and Raymond Breton, refer to Arawak and Carib high gods as kinds of *deus otiosus;* that is, they are inactive gods far removed from human affairs and concerns. Neither the Island Arawak nor the Island Carib conceived of their high god as creator of the universe, and it is unclear how powerful the high god was thought to be. Chroniclers differ somewhat on this. Pané suggests that the high god was a powerful deity who chooses to be inactive. Other chroniclers stress the inactivity of the high god and the lack of attention accorded him. The bulk of the evidence, including what we know of other American Indian religions (Hultkrantz, 1979), supports the latter interpretation.

Island Arawak. The identification of Island Arawak deities is often a problem. Their high god was known by two names: Iocauna and Guamaonocon (spellings differ from chronicler to chronicler). Peter Martyr reports that the Arawak supreme being was not self-created but was himself brought forth by a mother who has five names or identities. He also reports other appellations for the high god, including Jocakuvaque, Yocahu, Vaque, Maorocon, and Macrocoti. Pané provides an equally complex list of male and female deities, and it is apparent that most deities in the Arawak pantheon were recognized by a number of appellations.

Other prominent Island Arawak deities include: Guabancex, goddess of wind and water, who had two subordinates: Guatauva, her messenger, and Coatrischio, the tempest-raiser; Yobanua-Borna, a rain deity; Baidrama (or Vaybruma), a twinned deity associated with strength and healing; Opigielguoviran, a doglike being said to have plunged into the morass with the coming of the Spanish; and Faraguvaol, a tree trunk able to wander at will.

One of the most important differences between Arawak and Carib religions is that among the Island Arawak nature worship seems to have been closely associated with ancestor worship. The bones of the Island Arawak dead, especially the bones of their leaders and great men, were thought to have power in and of themselves. This notion also existed among the Island Carib, but their ceremonies and representations were not so elaborate.

Island Carib. Like the Island Arawak, the island Carib recognized a multitude of spirit beings as well as a high god whose name varies according to text.

Of the spirits directly involved in human affairs, Icheiri and Mabouia are the most frequently mentioned. Icheiri, whose name comes from the verb *ichéem,* meaning "what I like" (Breton, 1665, p. 287), has been interpreted as a spirit of good, while Mabouia, from the same root as the word *boyé,* or "sorcerer," has been interpreted as a spirit of evil. The Carib informed Breton that it was Mabouia who brought about eclipses of the sun and caused the stars to disappear suddenly.

Another major category in the Island Carib spirit world was that of the *zemiis. Zemi,* too, appears to have been a very general term; the word is of Arawak origin and indicates the strong influence of Island Arawak language and culture on the Island Carib. Among the Carib, to get drunk, *chemerocae,* literally meant "to see *zemiis.*" *Zemiis* were thought to live in a paradise far removed from the world of the living, but every so often, according to La Borde (1704), Coualina, chief of the *zemiis,* would become angry about the wickedness of some *zemiis* and drive them from paradise to earth, where they became animals. This is but one example of the constant transformations from deity to animal in Island Carib mythology.

Afterlife. Both the Island Arawak and the Island Carib had a notion of the afterlife. The Island Arawak conceived of spirits of the dead, called *opias* or *hubias,* who were said to wander about the bush after dark. Occasionally *opias* joined the company of the living and were said to be indistinguishable from the living, except for the spirits' lack of navels. In both Arawak and Carib religions, the activities of the dead were thought to resemble the activities of the living.

Pané reports that the Arawak of Haiti believed in a kingdom of death, Coaibai, which was situated on their own island. Every leader of importance had his own kingdom of death, usually located within his own dominion. In addition, there were uninhabited places where the spirits of evil people were said to roam.

The Island Carib, on the other hand, had a much more diffuse notion of the afterlife. All spirits of the body, *omicou,* went to the seashore or became *mabouias* in the forest. There was no concept of an underworld.

Elaborate burial ceremonies were noted among both the Island Arawak and the Island Carib. Archaeological evidence indicates that the Island Arawak performed several types of burials: (1) direct interment; (2) interment within a raised mound; (3) interment within a grave covered with an arch of branches; and (4) burial in caves.

Burial customs among the Island Carib were not so varied. Breton (1665) noted that the Island Carib dreaded death, and that it was forbidden to utter the name of the deceased. The Island Carib referred to the dead indirectly (e.g., "the husband of so-and-so") because to do otherwise would cause the deceased to come back to earth.

Rites and Ceremonies. The most important ceremonies among the Island Arawak pertained to rain and the growth of crops, but there were also important ceremonies for success in war, burial of the dead, curing of the sick, canoe building, cutting hair, the births of children, marriage, and initiation. In most instances these rites took the form of elaborate dances known as *areitos.* Fewkes (1907) notes that dramatization played a part in all ceremonies. For example, in their war dances the entire war sequence was portrayed: the depar-

> **Tobacco, narcotics, and stimulants played an impotant part in both Island Arawak and Island Carib rites.**

ture of the warriors, surprise of the enemy, combat, celebration of victory, and return of the war party.

The island Carib conducted ceremonies on many of the same occasions as did the Island Arawak. According to La Borde, the Island Carib held rites whenever a council was held concerning their wars, when they returned from their expeditions, when a first male child was born, when they cut their children's hair, when their boys became old enough to go to war, when they cut down trees, and when they launched a vessel.

Island Carib rites met individual as well as societal needs. Each individual had his own personal deity or *zemi*. These personal deities were thought to reveal things to the individual, and it is reported that individuals customarily withdrew from society for six or seven days, without taking any sustenance save tobacco and the juice of herbs. During this period, the individual experienced visions of whatever he or she desired (victory over enemies, wealth, and so on).

Drugs. Tobacco, narcotics, and stimulants played an important part in both Island Arawak and Island Carib rites. Tobacco, called *cohiba,* was used in a number of different forms in all ceremonies. Among the Island Arawak, tobacco smoke was used as an incense to summon the gods. Tobacco was sprinkled on the heads of idols as an offering. Religious leaders among the Island Arawak and Island Carib "stupefied" themselves with tobacco when they consulted their oracles; they also used tobacco in curing rituals.

Throwing *aji* (pepper) onto live coals was part of Island Arawak and Island Carib preparations for warfare. Ricardo E. Alegría (1979) contends that the pepper caused irritation of the mucous membrane, a racking cough, and other discomforts that were thought to induce the proper psychological state for war.

Island Arawak. Major duties of the Arawak *piaie* were to divine the future by consulting their personal *zemiis* and to direct offering to *zemiis* during public ceremonies. In both of these duties, they served as intermediaries between the Island Arawak and their gods (Deive, 1978).

Accounts of Arawak shamanism provide very little detail concerning the *piaie's* role in public ceremonies, and it is unclear whether or not all *piaies* were able to conduct public ritual. It is possible that some *piaies* functioned solely as curers or diviners and could not perform other rites.

Island Carib. The Carib never went to war without first consulting the spirit world to find out if conditions were favorable for victory. Since chiefs were unable to make direct contact with spirits, they required the services of a *boyé* whose predictions had tremendous impact on public opinion. *Boyés* also needed to develop working relationships with chiefs to defray the high costs of apprenticeship. We have no clear notion of the actual length of apprenticeship for shamans among the Island Carib, though in some tribes of the Guianas apprenticeship is said to have lasted from ten to twenty years (Métraux, 1949). This period of training was probably considerably shorter among the Carib.

Boyés were a professional class in Island Carib society. They charged for all services, and I contend that they did not train new shamans without demanding something in return. War chiefs and their families, as wealthier members of their society, were in the best position to take on obligations to senior *boyés* (Glazier, 1980). They were perhaps the wealthiest members of their society. While war chiefs and families had considerable control over the distribution of some resources and war booty, *boyés* had control over the distribution of goods outside kinship obligations.

The *boyés* had great potential for wealth, for there was always demand for their services. In times of trouble, they were called upon to dispel evil spirits; in times of prosperity, they were called upon to insure its continuance; and when there was doubt, they gave assurances for the future.

BIBLIOGRAPHY

Alegría, Ricardo E. "The Use of Noxious Gas in Warfare by the Taino and Carib Indians of the Antilles." *Revista/Review Interamericana* 8 (1979): 409-415.

Alegría, Ricardo E. *Ball Courts and Ceremonial Plazas in the West Indies.* New Haven, 1983.

Alexander, Hartley Burr. "The Antilles." In *The Mythology of All Races,* edited by Louis Herbert Gray, vol. 11, *Latin-American Mythology,* pp. 15-40. Boston, 1920.

Arens, William. *The Man-Eating Myth: Anthropology and Anthropophagy.* Oxford, 1979.

Benzoni, Girolamo. *History of the New World* (1595). Translated by W. H. Smyth. London, 1857.

Breton, Raymond. *Dictionnaire caraïbe-françois.* Auxerre, 1665.

Charlevoix, Pierre-François de. *Histoire de l'Ile Espagnole ou de Saint-Dominique.* 2 vols. Paris, 1930-1931.

Deive, Carlos Esteban. "Fray Ramón Pané y el nacimiento de la etnografía americana." *Boletín del Museo del Hombre Dominicano* 6 (1976): 136-156.

Deive, Carlos Esteban. "El chamanismo taíno." *Boletín del Museo del Hombre Dominicano* 9 (1978): 189-203.

Du Puis, Mathias. *Relation de l'establissement d'une colonie françoise dans la Gardloupe isle de l'Amérique, et des mœurs des sauvages* (1652). Reprint, Basse-Terre, 1972.

Dutertre, Jean-Baptiste. *Histoire générale des Antilles habitées par les François* (1667-1671). 4 vols. Fort-de-France, Martinique, 1958.

Fernández Méndez, Eugenio. *Art y mitologia de los indios Tainos de las Antillas Mayores.* San Juan, Puerto Rico, 1979.

Fewkes, Jesse Walter. *The Aborigines of Porto Rico and Neighboring Islands.* Annual Report of the Bureau of American Ethnology, no. 25. Washington, D. C., 1907. See especially pages 53-72.

Figueredo, Alfredo E., and Stephen D. Glazier. "Spatial Behavior, Social Organization, and Ethnicity in the Prehistory of Trinidad." *Journal de la Société des Américanistes* 68 (1982): 33-40.

García Valdés, Pedro. "The Ethnography of the Ciboney." In *Handbook of South American Indians,* edited by Julian H. Steward, vol. 4, pp. 503-505. Washington, D. C., 1948.

Glazier, Stephen D. "The Boyé in Island-Carib Culture." In *La antropología americanista en la actualidad: Homenaje a Raphael Girard,* vol. 2, pp. 37-46. Mexico City, 1980. Cited in the text as 1980a.

Glazier, Stephen D. "Aboriginal Trinidad and the Guianas: An Historical Reconstruction." *Archaeology and Anthropology: Journal of the Walter Roth Museum* (Georgetown, Guyana) 3 (1980): 119-124. Cited in the text as 1980b.

Gullick, C. J. M. R. *Exiled from St. Vincent.* Valletta, Malta, 1976.

Herrera y Tordesillas, Antonio de. *Historia general de los hechos de los Castellanos en las islas y Terrafirme del Mar Océano.* 17 vols. Madrid, 1934-1957.

Hoffman, Charles A. "The Outpost Concept and the Mesoamerican Connection." In *Proceedings of the Eighth International Congress for the Study of the Pre-Columbian Cultures of the Lesser Antilles,* pp. 307-316. Tempe, Ariz., 1980.

Hultkrantz, Åke. *Religions of the American Indians.* Los Angeles, 1979.

Joyce, Thomas A. *Central American and West Indian Archaeology.* London, 1916.

La Borde, Sieur de. *Voyage qui contient un relation exacte de l'origine, mœurs, coûtumes, réligion, guerres, et voyages des Caraïbes, sauvages des isles Antilles de l'Amérique.* Amsterdam, 1704.

Las Casas, Bartolomé de. *Historia general de las Indias, 1527-61.* 2 vols. Edited by Juan Perez de Tudela and Emilio Lopez Oto. Madrid, 1957.

Layng, Anthony. *The Carib Reserve: Identity and Security in the West Indies.* Lanham, Md., 1983.

Lovén, Sven. *Origins of the Tainan Culture, West Indies.* Göteborg, 1935.

Métraux, Alfred. "Religion and Shamanism." In *Handbook of South American Indians,* edited by Julian H. Steward, vol. 5., pp. 559-599. Washington, D. C., 1949.

Morales Patiño, Osvaldo. "Arqueología Cubana, resumen de actividades, 1946." *Revista de arqueologia y etnografia* (Havana) 1 (1947): 5-32.

Olsen, Fred. *On the Trail of the Arawaks.* Norman, Okla. 1974.

Oviedo y Valdés, Gonzalo Fernández de. *Historia general y natural de las Indias* (1535). 5 vols. Edited by Juan Perez and Tudela Bueso. Madrid, 1959.

Pané, (Fray) Ramón (Father Ramón). *Relación acerca de las antigüedades de los Indios, 1571.* Edited by José Juan Arrom. Mexico City, 1978.

Pérez de Oliva, Fernán. *Historia de la inuención de las Yndias.* Edited by José Juan Arrom. Publicaciones del Instituto Caro y Cuerva, no. 20. Bogotá, 1965.

Pettitjean-Roget, Henri. "De l'origine de la famille humaine ou contribution à l'étude des Pierres à Trois-Pointes des Antilles." In *Proceedings of the Ninth International Congress for the Study of Pre-Columbian Cultures of the Lesser Antilles,* pp. 511-530. Montreal, 1983.

Rochefort, Charles César de. *Histoire naturelle et morale des îles Antilles de l'Amérique.* 2d ed. Rotterdam, 1665.

Rouse, Irving. "The West Indies." In *Handbook of South American Indians,* edited by Julian H. Steward, vol. 4, pp. 49-565. Washington, D. C., 1948.

Rouse, Irving. "Prehistory of the West Indies." *Science* 144 (1964): 499-513.

Rouse, Irving. "On the Meaning of the Term `Arawak.'" In *On the Trail of the Arawaks,* by Fred Olsen, pp. xiii-xvi. Norman, Okla., 1974.

Rouse, Irving, and Louis Allaire. "Caribbean." In *Chronologies in New World Archaeology,* edited by R. E. Taylor and C. W. Meighan, pp. 431-481. New York, 1978.

Taylor, Douglas M. *The Black Carib of British Honduras.* New York, 1951.

Wilbert, Johannes. "Magico-Religious Use of Tobacco among South American Indians." In *Spirits, Shamans and Stars: Perspectives from South America,* edited by David L. Browman and Ronald A. Schwarz, pp. 13-38. The Hague, 1979. This article also appears in *Cannabis and Culture,* edited by Vera D. Rubin (The Hague, 1975), pp. 439-461.

STEPHEN D. GLAZIER

Afro-Caribbean Religions

This essay concentrates on four types of syncretic religious cults found in the Caribbean region, which I shall call the *neo-African cults,* the *ancestral cults,* the *revivalist cults,* and the *religio-political cults.* The experience of Caribbean blacks under the political, economic, and domestic conditions of slavery modified character in a stressful direction, and those who were most sensitive to the stress advanced innovative religious and secular systems to deal with their anxiety. The new religious institutions consisted of elements of African and European beliefs and practices, and, in some cases, parts of American Indian and South Asian religious traditions. A number of new religions arose from the interaction of three major variables: socioeconomic, psychological, and cultural.

Haitian Voodoo. The African dances that were performed in the seventeenth century by slaves in the western part of the island of Hispaniola and the religious beliefs of the Fon, Siniga, Lemba, Yoruba, and other African peoples who had been brought to Hispaniola were combined with certain beliefs of European folk origin about Roman Catholic saints, and, as a result, the neo-African religion of Voodoo developed.

The supernatural phenomena of greatest importance in Voodoo are the *lwa.* Erica Bourguignon (1980) suggests that variety and inconsistency in Haitian Voodoo have developed, and continue to develop, in part through the mechanism of altered states of consciousness, particularly in the forms of possession-trance and dreams. In Haiti, possession-trance is not highly stereotyped and prescribed. During possession-trance, cult leaders and members speak and act in the names of the spirits, behaving in ways that may modify the future performance of the ritual or the adherents' perception of the spirits.

The grand *lwa* comprise both nature spirits and functional spirits that are of African origin. Prominent among the nature spirits are Dambala, the serpent spirit identified with the rainbow and associated with floods; Bade, spirit of the winds; Sogbo, a Fon spirit of thunder; Shango (Yor., *Sango*), the Yoruba spirit of thunder and lightning; and Agwé, spirit of the sea.

The *lwa* are also identified with Catholic saints. For instance, Dambala is identified with Saint Patrick, on whose image serpents are depicted. The *marassa,* spirits of dead twins, are believed to be the twin saints Cosmas and Damian (Price-Mars, 1928; Herskovits, 1937a).

The relationship between Voodoo adherents and the *lwa* is thought to be a contractual one; if one is punctilious about offerings and ceremonies, the *lwa* will be generous with their aid. The lwa must be paid once or twice a year with an impressive ceremony, and small gifts must be presented frequently.

In West Africa, concepts of the "soul" are highly elaborated. In traditional Fon belief, all persons have at least three souls, and adult males have four (Herskovits, 1938). In Haitian Voodoo, every man has two souls.

Adherents fear the power of the dead and observe funerary and postfunerary rites meticulously. A wake is held on the night of death; the funeral itself follows and, if possible, is held in accordance with the rites of the Catholic church. On the ninth night after death is the "last prayer," and on the tenth night a ritual is held in which sacrifices are offered to all the family dead (Métraux, 1959; Herskovits, 1937b).

François Duvalier, the dictatorial president of Haiti from 1957 to 1971, successfully exploited Voodoo for political purposes (Rotberg, 1976). Nevertheless, most observers agree that the cult has been weakened in recent years. An important factor in its decline has been the decay of the large extended family in the rural areas. Many of the large cult centers have split up into minor sects under priests whose training has been inadequate.

Cuban Santería. Most of the non-European elements in the Afro-Cuban syncretic religion known as Santería are derived from Yoruba beliefs and rituals. Animals are sacrificed to Yoruba deities, Yoruba music is played on African-type drums, songs with Yoruba words and music are sung, and dancers are possessed by the orisha (Yor., orisa, "spirit"). Yoruba foods are cooked for the gods and for devotees, beads of the proper color are worn, and leaves with Yoruba names are used in preparing medicines and in washing the stones of the ori-sha and the heads of cult members. In Santería, Elegba (Yor., Esu or Elegba) is identified with Saint Peter, and Shango (Yor., Sango), god of thunder, is identified with Saint Barbara. Shakpana (also Babaluaiye; Yor., Sopona) is equated with Saint Lazarus. Oya (Yor., Oya), one of Shango's wives, is the equivalent of Saint Teresita. Obatala (Yor., Obatala) is Our Lady of Mercy, and Yemaja (Yor., Yemoja) is identified with the Virgin of Regla (a suburb of Havana).

During a Santería ceremony, the blood of animals sacrificed to the gods is allowed to flow onto the sacred stones of the santero (Santería priest). The blood is the food of the deities, and the stones are the objects through which they are fed and in which their power resides (Bascom, 1950). The lucumis (Afro-Cubans of Yoruba extraction) honor each of the gods with choral dances and pantomime in accordance with authentic Yoruba tradition (see Ortiz, 1951, for a detailed and vivid account of lucumi dances; and Simpson, 1978).

The Shango cult in Trinidad. In southwestern Nigeria, each Yoruba deity, including Sango, god of thunder and lightning, has his or her own priests, followers, and cult centers. In the Shango cult in Trinidad, Shango is only one of several dozen "powers," which include twenty or more Yoruba deities (Lewis, 1978). Several non-Yoruba powers—especially Gabriel and Mama Latay—are popular in Trinidad. Ancient

African gods are identified with certain Catholic saints. Each god has his or her favorite colors, foods, and drinks; each is thought to have certain physical traits and to possess certain powers. In Shango, as in Voodoo and Santería, participants can recognize the major spirits who are well known throughout the country, or the principal spirits known in a given locality, by the stylized behavior of devotees possessed by them (Bourguignon, 1980).

Each Shango cult center holds an annual ceremony in honor of the orisha known to its worshipers. The four-day ritual begins with the recitation of original prayers, followed by several repetitions of the Lord's Prayer, Hail Mary, and the Apostle's Creed. The leader then recites in succession prayers such as Saint Francis's prayer, Saint George's prayer, and Blessed Martin's prayer; he recites each prayer line-by-line, and the worshipers repeat each line after him. Next, in an act of dismissal, food for the deity Eshu is placed outside the ceremonial area. Drumming, dancing, singing, and spirit possession continue through the night; the climax comes at dawn with the sacrificing of pigeons, doves, chickens, agoutis, land turtles, goats, and sheep. Similar rites are performed on the following three nights, and often a bull is sacrificed. Aspects of Trinidadian cult life that are closely related to African religious behavior include divination, conjuring, and folk medicine, which are often strikingly similar to West African procedures (Simpson, 1978).

Ancestral Cults. The second type of hybrid religious cult in the Caribbean, the ancestral cult, has fewer African and more European components than does the neo-African-type religion.

Kumina. According to Monica Schuler (1980), Kumina was brought to Jamaica by post-emancipation immigrants from central Africa who chiefly settled in the eastern parish of Saint Thomas. Kumina is primarily a family religion, and each group honors a number of family spirits in addition to other divinities. The three ranks of Kumina spirits (known as zombies) are the sky gods, the earthbound gods, and ancestral zombies. Most Kumina dances are memorial services held to pay respects to the dead ancestors of the participants, but ceremonies are performed on other occasions, such as betrothal, marriage, burial, the naming of a baby, the anniversary of emancipation, and Independence Day (Moore, 1953; Schuler, 1980).

Convince. The Convince ritual practiced in the Jamaican parishes of Saint Thomas and Portland has a number of Christian elements, but its principal powers are the spirits of persons who belonged to the cult during their lifetime. The most powerful bongo ghosts come from Africa, but the spirits of ancient Jamaican slaves and the Maroons (descendants of runaway slaves), who perpetuated the cult until recent times, are also of importance

Each bongo man holds a sacrificial ceremony annually and conducts Convince rites as the need for them arises.

Christian prayers, the reading of Bible passages, and hymn singing precede the main ceremony. Special *bongo* songs, hand clapping, and dances performed by *bongo* men call the spirits to the ceremony. Later, the spirits of the ancestors (that is, devotees possessed by the ghosts) dance.

The Kele cult in Saint Lucia. The Kele ceremony in Saint Lucia resembles, in attenuated form, the Shango ritual in Trinidad. The ritual is performed to ask the ancestors of devotees for health, protection against misfortune in agriculture, and success in important undertakings, as well as to thank the forebears for past favors. The paraphernalia essential for the Kele rite consists mainly of Amerindian polished stone axes (which are called *pièrres tonnerres,* "thunderstones," by devotees, who believe them to have fallen from the sky), drums, and agricultural implements such as machetes, axes, hoes, and forks. Several of the stone axes are placed on the ground to form a cross, with additional axes arranged around the central grouping (Simpson, 1973; Simmons, 1963). A ram is then sacrificed to the ancestors.

Ancestral cult of the Black Carib of Belize. The Black Carib of Belize are descendants of African slaves who escaped from other parts of the West Indies and settled first among the Island Carib in Saint Vincent. At the end of the eighteenth century, they were deported by the English to Roatan, near Honduras, then they spread out along the coast of the mainland. The Black Carib of Belize speak a South American Indian language.

The supernatural beliefs, rites, and practices of the Black Carib are a mixture of African and non-African elements. Singing, drumming, and dancing are intended to placate the ancestors of the family giving the ceremony, and some participants become possessed by the spirits of their deceased ancestors.

> ## The Black Carib of Belize are descendants of African slaves who escaped from other parts of the West Indies. . . .

Revivalist Cults. The third type of Afro-Caribbean religious syncretism, the *revivalist cult,* descends from the Afro-Protestant cults of the late eighteenth century and, in the case of Jamaica, from the Great Revival of 1861-1862.

Revival Zion. A religious movement known as Myalism emerged in the 1760s to protect slaves against European sorcery. This "native" Baptist movement was without serious competition during the forty-year period (1780-1820) when a reinterpretation of Christianity spread across Jamaica. Eventually, a hybrid religion of the Myalists, or Black Baptists, resurfaced. And its vitality has been seen in the multiplication

and flourishing of black revivalist cults (Curtin, 1955; Schuler, 1979).

The Holy Spirit possesses followers during revivalist ceremonies, as do the spirits of Old Testament figures such as Jeremiah, Isaiah, Joshua, Moses, Shadrach, Meshach, and Abednego; New Testament apostles and evangelists such as Matthew, Mark, Luke, John, Peter, and James; the archangels Michael, Gabriel and Raphael; Satan and his chief assistant, Rutibel; beings from Hebrew magical tradition, such as Uriel, Ariel, Seraph, Nathaniel, and Tharsis; Constantine, Melshezdek, and the Royal Angel; and the dead, especially prominent revivalist leaders of the past (Moore and Simpson, 1957; Simpson, 1978).

Weekly services include "spiritual" dancing, stamping feet, hyperventilating, and groaning rhythmically.

Spiritual Baptists (Shouters) of Trinidad. In many ways, the Spiritual Baptist cult (Shouters) in Trinidad is similar to Revival Zion in Jamaica, but there are several noteworthy differences. Among the Shouters, no drums or rattles accompany hymn singing. Spiritual Baptists do not become possessed by the wide variety of spirits that possess Revivalists in Jamaica; as a rule, devotees are possessed only by the Holy Spirit. Certain groups among the Shouters do, however, make ritual offerings to the spirits "of the sea, the land, and the river," and occasionally a Shango "power" may enter a person who is taking part in a ritual.

Spiritual Baptists are often men and women of the lower classes, most of African descent.

The Shakers of Saint Vincent. English rule of the island of Saint Vincent began in 1783, and the first direct religious influence intended for the slave population was brought to the island by a Methodist missionary in 1787. The Shaker cult, which goes back to at least the early part of the twentieth century, has a Methodist base, with an admixture of elements of other Christian denominational traditions. An important feature of this religion is the mild state of dissociation, attributed to possession by the Holy Ghost, that some of its adherents experience.

Religio-Political Cults. The fourth cult type appears when a society is undergoing severe reorganization, as was the case in Jamaica with the unrest that accompanied the Great Depression of the 1930s.

Rastafarianism. An important factor underlying the rise of Rastafarianism is that, since at least the beginning of the twentieth century, Jamaican blacks have identified with Ethiopia on account of its biblical symbolism. The early 1930s saw the founding of a number of associations for black people and the emergence of the Rastafarian movement, named after Ras ("prince") Tafari, who was crowned emperor Haile Selassie of Ethiopia (Abyssinia). Marcus Garvey had formed the Universal Negro Improvement Association in Jamaica in 1914, and his doctrine of racial redemption, together with the coronation of Haile Selassie, furthered interest in the Ethiopian tradition (Hill, 1980).

Since emancipation, persons on the lower rungs of Jamaican society have struggled continuously against exploitation. In the early 1930s, the basic issues for rural Jamaicans were land, rent, and taxation, and their struggles over these questions gave rise to the millenarian visions of the Rastafarian movement, in the face of prejudices.

According to Rastafarian doctrines in 1953, (1) black people were exiled to the West Indies because of their transgressions; (2) the white man is inferior to the black man; (3) the Jamaican situation is hopeless; (4) Ethiopia is heaven; (5) Haile Selassie is the living God; (6) the emperor of Abyssinia will arrange for expatriated persons of African descent to return to the homeland; and (7) black men will soon get their revenge by compelling white men to serve them (Simpson, 1955). These remain the basic beliefs of the movement, but not all adherents subscribe to all of them, nor do they give them equal emphasis. Rastafarians reinterpret the Old Testament in claiming that they are true present-day prophets, the "reincarnated Moseses, Joshuas, Isaiahs, and Jeremiahs." They also believe that they are "destined to free the scattered Ethiopians who are black men" (Nettleford, 1970, pp. 108-109).

Between 1953 and 1960, the Rastafarian movement grew rapidly and became more complex doctrinally. This growth continued through recent decades. Membership came to be drawn from all levels of the society. The militancy of present-day Rastafarianism is seen clearly in its concept of a modern Babylon that includes Britain, the former colonial power; the United States, the present major industrial power; the bourgeois state of Jamaica; and the church. Babylon is said to be the source of Jamaica's misfortunes (Chevannes, 1977). A recent theme of the movement has to do with its concept of nature. In Rastafarian thought nature is nonindustrial society; and this underlies certain aspects of Rastafarian lifestyle—for example, dietary rules, uncombed locks and beards, and the importance of ganja (Chevannes, 1977).

BIBLIOGRAPHY

Barrett, David B., ed. *World Christian Encyclopedia: A Comparative Study of Churches and Religions in the Modern World, A. D. 1900-2000.* Oxford, 1982.

Barrett, Leonard E. *Soul-Force: African Heritage in Afro-American Religion.* New York, 1974.

Barrett, Leonard E. *The Rastafarians: Sounds of Cultural Dissonance.* Boston, 1977.

Bascom, William R. "The Focus of Cuban Santeria." *Southwestern Journal of Anthropology* 6 (Spring 1950): 64-68.

Bascom, William R. "The Yoruba in Cuba." *Nigeria* 37 (1951): 14-20.

Bascom, William R. *Shango in the New World.* Austin, 1972.

Bastide, Roger. *African Civilisations in the New World.* New York, 1971.

Bilby, Kenneth M. "The Kromanti Dance of the Windward Maroons of Jamaica." *Nieuwe West-Indische Gids* (Utrecht) 55 (August 1981): 52-101.

Bourguignon, Erika. "George E. Simpson's Ideas about Ultimate Reality and Meaning in Haitian Vodun." *Ultimate Reality and Meaning* (Toronto) 3 (1980): 233-238.

Chevannes, Barry. "The Literature of Rastafari." *Social and Economic Studies* 26 (June 1977): 239-262.

Courlander, Harold. *Haiti Singing.* Chapel Hill, N. C., 1939.

Courlander, Harold. *The Drum and the Hoe: Life and Lore of the Haitian People.* Berkeley, 1960.

Curtin, Philip D. *Two Jamaicas: The Role of Ideas in a Tropical Colony, 1830-1865.* Cambridge, Mass., 1955.

Davis, E. Wade. "The Ethnobiology of the Haitian Zombie." *Journal of Ethnopharmacology* 9 (1983): 85-104.

Glazier, Stephen D. *Marchin' the Pilgrims Home: Leadership and Decision-Making in an Afro-Caribbean Faith.* Westport, Conn., 1983.

Henney, Jeannette H. "Spirit-Possession Belief and Trance Behavior in Two Fundamentalist Groups in St. Vincent." In *Trance, Healing, and Hallucination: Three Field Studies in Religious Experience*, by Felicitas D. Goodman, Jeannette H. Henney, and Esther Pressel, pp. 6-111. New York, 1974.

Herskovits, Melville J. "African Gods and Catholic Saints in New World Negro Belief." *American Anthropologist* 39 (1937): 635-643. Cited in text as 1937a.

Herskovits, Melville J. *Life in a Haitian Valley.* New York, 1937. Cited in text as 1937b.

Herskovits, Melville J. *Dahomey: An Ancient West African Kingdom.* 2 vols. New York, 1938.

Hill, Robert A. "Dread History: Leonard Howell and Millenarian Visions in Early Rastafari Religions in Jamaica." *Epoche* 9 (1981): 30-71.

Hogg, Donald. "The Convince Cult in Jamaica." *Yale University Publications in Anthropology* 58 (1960): 3-24.

Johnson, Howard. "Introduction." In *Boy in a Landscape: A Jamaican Picture,* by Trevor Fitz-Henley. Gordon Town, Jamaica, 1980.

Laguerre, Michel S. *Voodoo Heritage.* Beverly Hills, Calif., 1980.

Lewis, Maureen Warner. "Yoruba Religion in Trinidad: Transfer and Reinterpretation." *Caribbean Quarterly* 24 (September-December 1978): 18-32.

Leyburn, James G. *The Haitian People.* Rev. ed. New Haven, 1966.

Métraux, Alfred. "The Concept of Soul in Haitian Vodu." *Southwestern Journal of Anthropology* 2 (Spring 1946): 84-92.

Métraux, Alfred. *Voodoo in Haiti.* New York, 1959.

Moore, Joseph G. "Religion of Jamaican Negroes: A Study of Afro-American Acculturation." Ph. D. diss., Northwestern University, 1953.

Moore, Joseph G., and George E. Simpson. "A Comparative Study of Acculturation in Morant Bay and West Kingston, Jamaica." *Zaire* 11 (November-December 1957): 979-1019, and 12 (January 1958): 65-87.

Nettleford, Rex M. *Mirror, Mirror: Identity, Race and Protest in Jamaica.* Kingston, Jamaica, 1970.

Ortiz Fernández, Fernando. *Los bailes y el teatro de los negros en el folklore de Cuba.* Havana, 1951.

Pearse, Andrew C. *The Big Drum Dance of the Carriacou.* Ethnic Folkways Library P 1011.

Pollak-Eltz, Angelina. "The Shango Cult in Grenada, British Westindies." In *Proceedings of the Eighth International Congress of Anthropological and Ethnological Sciences,* vol. 3, pp. 59-60. N. p., 1968.

Price-Mars, Jean. *So Spoke the Uncle.* Washington, D. C., 1983. A translation, with introduction and notes, by Magdeline W. Shannon of Ainsi parla l'oncle (Paris, 1928).

Rigaud, Milo. *La tradicion vaudoo et le vaudoo haitian: Son temple, ses mystères, sa magie.* Paris, 1953.

Rigaud, Odette M. "The Feasting of the Gods in Haitian Vodu." *Primitive Man* 19 (January-April 1946): 1-58.

Rotberg, Robert I. "Vodun and the Politics of Haiti." In *The African Diaspora: Interpretive Essays,* edited by Martin L. Kilson and Robert I. Rotberg, pp. 342-365. Cambridge, Mass., 1976.

Schuler, Monica. "Myalism and the African Religious Tradition in Jamaica." In *Africa and the Caribbean: The Legacies of a Link,* edited by Margaret E. Crahan and Franklin W. Knight, pp. 65-79. Baltimore, 1979.

Schuler, Monica. *"Alas, Alas, Kongo": A Social History of Indentured African Immigration into Jamaica, 1841-1865.* Baltimore, 1980.

Simmons, Harold F. C. "Notes on Folklore in St. Lucia." In *Iouanaloa: Recent Writing from St. Lucia,* edited by Edward Braithwaite, pp. 41-49. Saint Lucia, 1963.

Simpson, George E. "The Vodun Service in Northern Haiti." *American Anthropologist* 42 (April-June 1940): 236-254

Simpson, George E. "The Belief System of Haitian Vodun." *American Anthropologist* 47 (January 1945): 35-59.

Simpson, George E. "Four Vodun Ceremonies." *Journal of American Folklore* 59 (April-June 1946): 154-167.

Simpson, George E. "Political Cultism in West Kingston." *Social and Economic Studies* 4 (June 1955): 133-149.

Simpson, George E. "Jamaican Revivalist Cults." *Social and Economic Studies* 5 (December 1956): 321-442.

Simpson, George E. "The Kele Cult in St. Lucia." *Caribbean Studies* 13 (October 1973): 110-116.

Simpson, George E. *Black Religions in the New World.* New York, 1978.

Simpson, George E. "Ideas about Ultimate Reality and Meaning in Haitian Vodun." *Ultimate Reality and Meaning* (Toronto) 3 (1980): 187-199.

Smith, M. G. "A Note on Truth, Fact, and Tradition in Carriacou." *Caribbean Quarterly* 17 (September-December 1971): 128-138.

Smith, M. G., Roy Augier, and Rex M. Nettleford. *The Ras Tafari Movement in Kingston, Jamaica.* Mona, Jamaica, 1960.

Stone, Doris. *The Black Caribs of Honduras.* Ethnic Folkways Library P 435.

Taylor, Douglas MacRae. *The Black Carib of British Honduras.* New York, 1951.

GEORGE EATON SIMPSON

CATHERINE OF SIENA

CATHERINE OF SIENA (1347-1380), Caterina da Siena; Italian mystic and Christian saint. The particular genius of the spirituality of Catherine of Siena had its earliest beginnings in a visionary experience of Christ when she was six years old, and her subsequent vow of virginity. She persisted in her purpose in spite of family opposition until she was accepted as one of the Mantellate, a Dominican third-order group.

She had learned in her solitude to read, and now she became an enthusiastic conversationalist, feeding insatiably on the theological knowledge of friends she attracted among Dominicans, Augustinians, Franciscans, and Jesuits. She began, too, to draw as disciples people from every walk of life, a circle she would call her *famiglia.*

Catherine turned her energy toward the two issues she considered the root of the dissension: the continuing absence of the popes from Rome and clerical corruption. If the pope would return to Rome, she reasoned, Christians would have no more cause for rebellion, and reform could begin. Catherine can surely be credited with finally moving him. In fact, when dissent deepened after his return to Rome, many including the pope blamed Catherine's advice.

Gregory XI died on 27 March 1378, and within months his successor, Urban VI, was being denounced by a growing number of the cardinals, who in September of that year elected Clement VII as antipope, thus effectively splitting the church. At Urban's invitation Catherine came to Rome to support his cause. Though her health was by this time failing under her fierce asceticism and exertion, she continued to pray and work tirelessly for unity and reform. The weight of this sense of failure surely contributed to her early death on 29 April 1380. She was canonized in 1461 and proclaimed a doctor of the church in 1970; she and Teresa of Ávila were the first women to receive that title.

In 1377 and 1378, in addition to all her other activities, Catherine composed the work since known as *The Dialogue* (because she cast it as an exchange between God and herself). Her intent in writing it was to share with her disciples and others the insights she had gained in prayer and in her own experience. In it she approaches the way of holiness from several vantage points, and develops at length the themes of God's providence, the role of Christ as redeemer and mediator, and the church. Finally, during the last three and a half years of Catherine's life, her secretaries sometimes recorded her prayers when she spoke in ecstasy. Twenty-six such prayers have been preserved.

Her own writing is not speculative or systematic or analytical. Rather, she synthesizes into an integrated whole all of the various aspects of Christian faith on which she dwells. Her purposes are eminently practical, her tone warm and personal. She resorts for clarification not to conceptual argumentation but to literary images, developing the meaning of each as she goes and interweaving them one with another.

BIBLIOGRAPHY

Works by Catherine of Siena. The most complete recent edition of Catherine's letters is *Le lettere di S. Caterina da Siena,* 4 vols., translated and edited by Niccoló Tommaseo, revised by Piero Misciattelli (1860; reprint, Florence, 1940). The first volume of the only truly critical edition was prepared by Eugenio Dupré Theseider, *Epistolario di Santa Caterina da Siena,* vol. 1 (Rome, 1940); the work on this critical edition is being pursued by Antonio Volpato. A complete English translation from the critical edition is in progress under my editorship. I have translated Giuliana Cavallini's critical editions of *Il dialogo* (Rome, 1968) and *Le orazioni* (Rome, 1978) as *The Dialogue* (New York, 1980) and *The Prayers of Catherine of Siena* (New York, 1983), respectively.

Works about Catherine of Siena. A useful primary source for the life of Catherine of Siena is Raymond of Capua's *The Life of Catherine of Siena (1385-1389),* translated by Conleth Kearns (Wilmington, Del., 1980); other biographies in English are *History of St. Catherine of Siena and Her Companions,* by Augusta Theodosia Drane (London, 1899), good for its inclusion of primary source material not otherwise available in English; *Saint Catherine of Siena: A Study in the Religion, Literature and History of the Fourteenth Century in Italy,* by Edmund G. Gardner (New York, 1907), complete on historical contexts and well indexed; and Arrigo Levasti's *My Servant, Catherine,* translated by Dorothy M. White (Westminster, Md., 1954), which concentrates on Catherine's psychology and spirituality and also gives an excellent bibliography. Eugenio Dupré Theseider's entry "Catherine da Siena, Santa," in *Dizionario biographico degli Italiani* (Rome, 1979), covers very well Catherine's life and theology, including debated points, and offers a very comprehensive bibliography.

SUZANNE NOFFKE, O.P.

CATHOLIC ORDERS

[*See article* Monasticism.]

CELIBACY

CELIBACY, the deliberate abstinence from sexual activity, derives its religious value from the vital human significance of sex itself. The reasons offered for celibacy consequently range from concerns for personal physical health to a total rejection of the physical body. Religious institutions, moreover, differ both in the ways of life that they prescribe for the celibate and in the image of celibacy.

Traditional Perceptions. The placement of deliberate religious restraints on physical behavior, celibacy is often explained within tradition through physiological as well as metaphysical concepts. Asian esoteric texts, moreover, can be most explicit about the spiritual potentials of reproductive energies. Traditional understandings of celibacy, then, present a continuity that spans ideas about marriage and procreation, spiritual powers, spiritual purity, and chaste marriage to the divine.

Temporary concentration of reproductive energies. The perception that sexual intercourse during pregnancy and lactation will harm an infant is found in many cultures, including some contemporary Western folk traditions. For the Arapesh of New Guinea, the practice of temporary celibacy has a positive religious significance for procreation. After the child is born, the parents are supposed to sleep together with it, devote their energies to it, and give it special attention. If either parent indulges in sexual activity—even with other partners—before the child can walk, they say that it will become weak and perhaps die. Celibacy then appears to represent here a conscious channeling and concentration of the reproductive power of both parents for the good of the child, lineage, and community.

The power of holy persons. Adepts in the esoteric traditions of Asia are often aware of transmuting their reproductive power into spiritual power and channeling it within. Thus, the power of holy persons also depends in good part on their self-control. The word *yoga,* in fact, deriving from a root meaning "to yoke," can often be best understood in a very concrete sense: a willful harnessing of the vital energies, which are considered prone to rage like beasts. So even in traditions like Christianity that do not explicitly posit a direct continuity between sexual and spiritual energies, celibacy still appears as a measure of powerful mastery over the senses. Latin Catholicism gives us stories of triumphant (and faltering) ascetics struggling with spirits bent on seducing them. For the Shakers, the world of sensual experience itself was so overwhelming that a break with it required radical means: absolute abstention. In this instance, perfect celibacy expresses an attempt at total self-mastery.

Exclusive attachment to the divine. Being an eternal child in God can free the celibate from many worldly responsibilities. Luke's reference to chaste persons as "equal to angels" (20:35-36) suggests not only the innocence of celibates, but also their roles as agents of God, in no way beholden to man. Certainly, the ability to devote all of one's efforts to spiritual matters without the burden of family obligations is a very frequently voiced justification for celibacy in the East as well as in the West. In India, the practical implications of celibacy for a life devoted to religious pursuits has explicit expression in the semantic range of the Sanskrit word *brahmacarya,* which occurs very frequently in religious writings. Used most often to refer to sexual abstention, *brahmacarya* literally means "walking with *brahman,*" the primal divine essence; at the same time, *brahmacarya* may be used to refer specifically to the first stage in the traditional Hindu life cycle, which is supposed to be devoted to religious study.

The Place of Celibacy in Society. Like total sexual abandon, moreover, total abstinence is not a generally recommended practice in most traditions, and the social regulation of sexual behavior may entail curbs on celibacy as well as on indulgence. Indeed, traditional cultures often present celibacy and procreation in a complementary relationship, which can be ordered according to the calendrical cycle, the life cycle, or divisions in the society as a whole. At the same time, separate communities of celibates have their own norms of sexual propriety, and the maintenance of these norms is often crucial for the image of the celibate in the eyes of laypersons.

Procreation and abstinence in traditional societies. Clearly, no civilization can survive for long without some provision for procreation, and religious traditions with strong ethnic roots, like Confucianism and Judaism, may have no place at all for the permanent celibate. Although traditional Judaism proscribes sexual relations outside marriage, all Jews are expected to marry and engage regularly in conjugal relations. Indeed, the Sabbath itself is thought of as a bride, and to celebrate its arrival Jewish husbands are enjoined to have intercourse with their wives joyously on Sabbath eve. In Judaism, then, controlled religious pursuits should also embrace sanctified procreation throughout a mature person's life.

Sexual norms in celibate groups. In Theravada Buddhism, the community of monks—the *samgha*—should be supported by the laity, but the proper ordering of the cosmos depends on the *samgha's* purity. Thus, in the Vinaya Pitaka, the monastic disciplinary code, specific rules governed everyday practices that had even the most subtle sexual implications, from propriety in dress to contact with women.

Perhaps more crucial than the rules regulating the contact between members of a celibate community and potential sexual partners outside it are those controlling the relationships among the community members themselves. The Shakers inhibit physical contact among members. Though the *Rule of Saint Benedict,* which stands behind much of Western monastic life, has little explicit to say about celibacy itself, it does include provisions apparently aimed at the prevention of homosexuality.

Yet more often than not, the physical chastity of cloistered monks is rarely tested; the crucial spiritual role of sexual restrictions on celibates is less the prevention of sexual activity than of sexual thoughts. For celibates living outside the cloister, continually interacting with laypersons, temptation and desire can become particularly problematic. Necessary celibacy for diocesan priests has been frequently questioned, both inside and outside the Roman Catholic church. In pre-Reformation Europe, many priests openly took concubines, and the last half of the twentieth century has heard continuing discussion of the value of requiring celibacy for all priests. The tensions facing the modern priest are understandable: living in a sexually open society and as a confessor hearing detailed accounts of the intimate lives of individuals, he is nevertheless expected to exercise the same sexual discipline—both mentally and physically—of the cloistered monk.

BIBLIOGRAPHY

A monograph on celibacy from a cross-cultural perspective has yet to be written, but a number of works offer interesting perspectives on the subject. In *Purity and Danger* (New York, 1966), Mary Douglas gives a valuable anthropological analysis of kinds of sexual abstinence that are derived from ideas of impurity, with a focus on nonliterate cultures. A comparative treatment of Arapesh abstinence at childbirth is found in Margaret Mead's *Sex and Temperament in Three Savage Societies* (London, 1935). In *Taoist Yoga: Alchemy and Immortality* (London, 1970), Charles Luk presents a translation of a turn-of-the-century Chinese text that treats the spiritual transformation of sexual energies. Mircea Eliade's *Yoga: Immortality and Freedom,* 2d ed. (Princeton, 1969), treats this dimension of celibacy along with many others in Hindu religious traditions. Social-scientific insight on the role of celibate monks in Theravada Buddhist culture is presented in Stanley J. Tambiah's *Buddhism and the Spirit Cults in North-east Thailand* (Cambridge, 1970), and a socioreligious perspective on the Shakers is given in Louis J. Kern's *An Ordered Love* (Chapel Hill, N. C., 1981), which presents the Shakers as a radical Protestant community.

Some of the earliest Christian ideas about chastity are available in Sally Rieger Shore's translations of two of John Chrysostom's tracts, published as *On Virginity; Against Remarriage* (Lewiston, N. Y., 1983). The development of a celibate priesthood in Catholicism is traced in Henry C. Lea's *History of Sacerdotal Celibacy in the Christian Church,* 3d rev. ed., 2 vols. (New York, 1907), which presents a full, but negatively biased, account. *Celibacy in the Church,* edited by William Bassett and Peter Huizing (New York, 1972), presents useful articles reflecting the dialogue on priestly celibacy current in the early 1970s. In the context of that dialogue, the noted Dutch churchman Edward Schillebeekx has written *Celibacy,* translated by C. A. L. Jarrott (New York, 1968), a short but insightful theological monograph with some useful historical background.

DANIEL GOLD

CELTIC RELIGION

By about 500 BCE the Celts were already widely dispersed over central and western Europe, including perhaps Gaul and the Iberian Peninsula, and evidence from the fifth century testifies to further territorial expansion. About 400 BCE this process quickened as tribal bands invaded northern Italy and there established settlements which in due course were to become the Roman province of Gallia Cisalpina. Some Celtic bands raided farther south, as far as Rome and Apulia and even Sicily, and about 387 they captured and sacked the city of Rome. To the east, other Celtic tribes penetrated into the Carpathians and the Balkans during the fourth century BCE. In 279 some of them entered Greece and plundered the shrine at Delphi, and in the following year three Celtic tribes, known collectively to the Greeks as Galatae, crossed into Asia Minor and eventually settled in the region which still bears the name Galatia.

Manuscripts. Written literature in Irish dates from the second half of the sixth century CE, when monastic scholars adapted the Latin alphabet, and it gradually increases in volume during the following centuries. In addition to a good deal of typically monastic learning, both religious and secular, the literature comprises a vast amount of varied material recorded or adapted from oral tradition. However, only fragments of this literature survive in contemporary manuscripts, mostly in the form of annals or of notes and glosses accompanying Latin texts; all the vernacular manuscripts written before the end of the eleventh century have perished. Then, around 1100, came *Lebhor na hUidhre* (The Book of the Dun Cow),

> Probably the most important element in the religious symbolism of the Celts is the number three . . . three-headed deities and its triads of mother goddesses.

probably written in the monastery of Clonmacnois and the first of a series of great vellum manuscript compilations which are part of a conscious endeavor, in the face of ominous political and social change, to conserve the monuments of native tradition. It was followed around 1130 by an untitled collection now at the Bodleian Library, Oxford (MS Rawlinson B 502), and around 1150-1200 by *Lebhor na Nuachongbhála* (The Book of Leinster). Over the next couple of centuries appeared a number of major manuscripts of which the most important are the Great Book of Lecan, the Yellow Book of Lecan, the Book of Ballymote, the Book of Lismore, and the Book of Fermoy. These are capacious *bibliothecae* which embrace all the various genres of traditional literature: hero and king tales, mythological tales, origin legends, genealogies and so on. It is important to remember that, though the surviving manuscripts date from a relatively late period, the matter they contain has generally been copied more or less faithfully from earlier manuscripts. Thus the texts are often demonstrably centuries older than the manuscripts.

As well as these manuscript collections there are several specialized compilations, including *Leabhar Ga-bhála Éireann* (The Book of the Taking of Ireland), commonly known as the *Book of Invasions,* an amalgam of myth and pseudohistory which purports to recount the coming of the Gaels to Ireland and the several immigrations which preceded it; the *Cóir Anmann* (Fitness of Names), a catalog of names of "historical" personages with many imaginative etymologies and references to traditional legends; and the *Dinnshenchas* (Lore of Famous Places), which does in a much fuller and

more elaborate fashion for place-names what the *Cóir Anmann* seeks to do for personal names.

Evidence indicates that the early oral literature of Wales was comparable in volume and variety with that of Ireland. Unfortunately, because of a weaker scribal tradition, the Welsh literature is poorly documented for the pre-Norman period.. However, from the ninth or tenth century onward the Taliesin became the focus of poems and stories (extant only in much later versions) which represent him as a wonder child, seer, and prophet; some of these motifs clearly derive from native mythological tradition. Another important source is the *Trioedd Ynys Prydein* (Triads of the Island of Britain), which contains numerous references to mythological as well as historical characters and events; it may have been compiled in the twelfth century.

Artifacts. The plastic art of the Celto-Roman period is so evidently based on that of Rome that it might appear at first glance to have been borrowed whole and unchanged, but on closer scrutiny it reveals many elements which derive from the Celtic rather than from the Roman tradition. There are forms quite foreign to classical art, such as the tricephalous god, the god with stag's antlers, and the god depicted in the Buddha-like cross-legged position. Animal horns are commonly regarded as signs of fertility, and the antlers which the Celtic deity wears on the Gundestrup Caldron and elsewhere are taken to symbolize his power and fecundity. Another frequent emblem of divinity is the ornamented torque, which, according to Pierre Lambrechts, denotes the "powerful god who affords protection against maleficent spirits".

Probably the most important element in the religious symbolism of the Celts is the number three; the mystic significance of the concept of threeness is attested in most parts of the world, but among the Celts there seems to have been a particularly strong and continuous awareness of it. There are three-headed deities (and even a triphallic Mercury) and its triads of mother goddesses; the latter has an endless variety of ternary groups in which the triad is an expressive restatement of an underlying unity: goddesses like the three Brighids and inseparable brothers like the three companions of the tragic heroine Deirdre.

Continental Deities and Insular Equivalents. Given that the bulk of the relevant evidence belongs to the Roman period, it follows that our view of Gaulish religion is for the most part through Roman eyes, which means that it is perceived and presented in terms of Roman religion.

In Gallo-Roman dedications, deities may be assigned a Roman name, a native Gaulish name, or a Roman name accompanied by a native epithet. In the last two cases we clearly have to do with indigenous gods, and even with the first group this may be so. For example, the numerous statues and reliefs of Mercury in the guise of the Greco-Roman god might have been intended to honor that god, but equally they might have been intended to honor a native god by borrowing the classical form together with the classical name. A large proportion of the Gaulish forms attested in dedications are mere epithets or bynames, and even of those which may be taken to be proper names it would be quite erroneous to suppose that each indicates a separate deity.

Although the functional roles of the several deities are not clearly defined and delimited and frequently overlap with one another, this does not imply that they may be reduced to a single, all-purpose divine overlord. It has often been remarked that in polytheistic systems each god tends to move beyond his normal functional field toward a kind of universalism. Yet, despite this tendency toward the assimilation of roles, the insular Celtic gods are far removed from functional indifferentism, and there are some, like Goibhniu, the smith, and Dian Cécht, the leech, whose central responsibilities are defined very precisely.

Mercury or Lugh. Caesar's observation that "Mercury" was the deity with the greatest number of images in Gaul is confirmed by the surviving evidence of inscriptions, stone statues and reliefs, bronze statuettes, and terracotta figures. His image often appears in the mode of the classical Mercury: youthful, naked, and beardless; equipped with caduceus, petasos, and purse; and accompanied by cock, ram, or tortoise. But his image is also found in Gallo-Roman guise: mature, bearded, and dressed in a heavy cloak. Sometimes, as in the east and the north of Gaul, he is tricephalous. Unlike his Roman counterpart, he has a frequent consort named Maia or Rosmerta, the Provider, and includes the art of war in his range of competence.

One cannot assume that Caesar's "Mercury" coincides with a single native deity throughout the Celtic areas, but there is cogent evidence for identifying him substantially with the Irish god Lugh. In Ireland Lugh was the youthful victor over malevolent demonic figures, and his great achievement was to kill the cyclopean Balar with a slingshot. Lughnasadh, his feast, was a harvest festival, and at least two of its principal sites, Carmun and Tailtiu, were the burial places of eponymous goddesses associated with the fertility of the earth (as was, apparently, the Gaulish Mercury's consort Rosmerta). Lugh was the divine exemplar of sacred kingship, and in the tale *Baile in Scáil* (The God's Prophecy) he appears seated in state as king of the otherworld and attended by a woman identified as the sovereign of Ireland, reminiscent of Rosmerta. His usual epithet, *lámhfhada* ("of the long arm"), relates to his divine kingship. In the Christian period Lugh survived in the guise of several saints known by variants of his name—Lughaidh, Molua, and others—and the motif of the arm is reflected in these Christian traditions as well.

Gaulish Apollo. The classical form of Apollo in Romano-Celtic monuments only partly conceals the several native deities who have been assimilated to him. The use of the plural is probably justifiable, since several of the fifteen or more epithets attached to Apollo's name have a wide distribution, which suggests that they were independent gods. Yet some of these epithets may have referred to a single deity. Belenus was especially honored in the old Celtic kingdom of Noricum in the eastern Alps, as well as in northern Italy, southern Gaul, and Britain. He is sometimes accompanied by a goddess named Sirona. Borvo or Bormo, whose name denotes boiling or seething water, is associated with thermal springs, as at Bourbonne-les-Bains and other sites named after him. His consort is Damona ("divine cow") or Bormana.

His Irish equivalent was Mac ind Óg ("young lad or son"), otherwise known as Oenghus, who was believed to dwell in Bruigh na Bóinne, the great Neolithic, and therefore pre-Celtic, passage grave of Newgrange. He was the son of Daghdha, chief god of the Irish, and of Boann, eponym of the sacred river of Irish tradition. As his name and relationship suggest, he is a youthful god, and, perhaps in keeping with this, he is often treated with a certain affection in the literature, particularly in his familiar roles of trickster and lover.

Gaulish Minerva or Irish Brighid. The goddesses of insular Celtic tradition are involved in a wide range of activities, only one of which Caesar ascribes to "Minerva," namely arts and crafts.. Dedications to Minerva are found throughout the Celtic areas of the continent and in Britain. At Bath she was identified with the goddess Sulis, who was worshiped there in connection with the thermal springs.

The nearest equivalent to Minerva in insular tradition is the goddess known in Ireland as Brighid, daughter of the father god, Daghdha. Like Minerva she was concerned with healing and craftsmanship, particularly metalwork, but she was also patron of *filidhecht,* that is, poetry and traditional learning in general. A remarkable continuity stretches from the pagan goddess to her Christian namesake of the early sixth century. The saint Brighid of Kildare, whose monastery of Cell Dara, the "church of the [sacred] oak," was doubtless on the site of a pagan sanctuary.

Celtic Vulcan. Since he functioned as a very specialized deity, there is a strong probability that his native name among the continental Celts made reference to his craft, as it did in Ireland and Wales, where he was known as Goibhniu and Gofannon, both names derived from the word for "smith." He was known for his healing powers and is invoked in an Old Irish charm for the removal of a thorn. Until the nineteenth century, and in some areas even into the twentieth century, the country smith was still believed to retain something of his ancient preternatural faculty, and he was constantly called on for the healing effects of his charms and spells.

Gaulish Hercules or Irish Oghma. Hercules is well represented in Celto-Roman iconography and has a number of regional epithets assigned to him. Doubtless his popularity derives largely from his identification with native Celtic gods who correspond approximately to his classical character. One of these is mentioned in a curious passage by the Greek writer Lucian in the second century CE describing a Gaulish picture of Hercules "whom the Celts call Ogmios." It showed him armed with his familiar club and bow but pictured him uncharacteristically as an old man, bald and gray, with his skin darkened and wrinkled by the sun. He pulled behind him a willing band of men attached by slender chains which linked their ears to the tip of his tongue.

Gaulish Dis Pater or Irish Donn. All the Gauls believed with their druids that they were descended from Dis Pater. The reference is brief but is sufficient to indicate at least an analogy between the Gaulish god of the dead and his Irish counterpart Donn ("brown or dark one"), whose dwelling place was a small rocky island off the southwest coast of

> ## Water . . . had its special deities, generally female in the case of the rivers.

Ireland known as Tech nDuinn ("house of Donn"). Its English name, the Bull, echoes its other name in early Irish, Inis Tarbhnai ("island of Tarbnae"). *Tarbhnae* derives from *tarbh* ("bull"), and thus there are strong grounds for identifying the god Donn with the great bull of Cuailnge which provides the central motivation for the saga *Táin Bó Cuailnge* and which is also called Donn.

Nature associations. Underlying the tradition of *dinnshenchas* is the belief that prominent places and geological features throughout Ireland were the scene of mythic events or the abode, or even the embodiment, of mythic personages. Many of the numerous women who populate this world of onomastic legend are clear reflexes of the multifaceted goddess whose origins are bound up with the physical landscape—figures like Tailtiu and Carmun, whose burial places, named after them, were the sites of great royal assemblies.

Apart from the general cult of the earth goddess there exists an extensive repertory of deity names attached to individual places or topographical features. There was a god of the clearing or cultivated field (Ialonus), of the rock (Alisanos), of the confluence (Condatis), of the ford (Ritena), and of the fortified place (Dunatis). Water, particularly the moving water of rivers and springs, had its special deities, generally female in the case of the rivers. One can perhaps glimpse the lost mythology of such rivers as the Seine (Sequana), the Marne (Matrona), and the Saône (Souconna) through the legends of insular equivalents like the Boyne (Boann). The names of many rivers throughout the Celtic lands, for example, the French Dives or the Welsh Dyfrdwy, are derived from the stem *dev-* and mean simply "the divine one." Sacred springs are deified, as for example Aventia (Avenches), Vesunna (Périgeux), and Divona (Cahors).

In many instances the holy wells of the Christian period stand close to a specific tree which shares their supernatural aura. Obviously, this is one aspect of the widespread cult of sacred trees. In the Pyrenees there are dedications to the beech (Deo Fago) and to the Six Trees (Sexarbori deo, Sexarboribus) and at Angoulême to the oak (Deo Robori). The Romano-Celtic name of the town of Embrun, *Eburodunum,* contains the name of the deified yew tree.

Zoomorphic gods. Celto-Roman iconography contains a rich abundance of animal imagery, frequently presenting the deities in combinations of zoomorphic and anthropomorphic forms. The animal connections of the Celtic gods are extensive and varied. The iconography shows Cernunnos ("the horned one") associated with the stag, the ram-headed serpent, the bull, and, by implication, with the whole animal world. The iconography also includes boars, horses, dogs, and bears, as well as fish and various kinds of birds, all connected more or less closely with certain deities.

The horse, index and instrument of the great Indo-European expansion, has always had a special place in the affections of the Celtic peoples. Sometimes in insular tradition, particularly in folk tales, he is the bearer of the dead to the otherworld, a role probably reflected in some monuments in southern Gaul, such as the frieze of horses' heads on a lintel from the Celto-Ligurian sanctuary of Roquepertuse, Bouches-du-Rhône. Epona (from *epos,* "horse") was an important Celtic deity and was particularly favored as patron of the cavalry of the Roman army. She has insular analogues in the Welsh Rhiannon and in the Irish Édaín Echraidhe (echraidhe, "horse riding") and Macha, who outran the fastest steeds. There was also a Dea Artio (as well as a Mercurius Artaios), whose name connects her with the bear (Ir., *art,* "bear"); a little bronze group from Bern shows her seated before a large bear with a basket of fruit by her side. Dea Arduinna, who appears seated on a wild boar, may be compared with the Irish goddess Flidhais, who ruled over the beasts of the forest and whose cattle were the wild deer.

Gods of Britain. Early Welsh literary tradition, like the medieval Welsh language, seems further evolved from its archaic roots than its Irish counterpart. This is probably due partly to the cultural effects of the Roman colonization of Britain from the first to the fifth century and partly to the late redaction of the extant material, particularly the prose. But whatever the causes, the result is that Welsh mythological narrative, while preserving some remarkably archaic elements, nevertheless lacks the extensive context found in Irish narrative.

Family of Dôn. The main source for Welsh mythological tradition is the collection of tales known as the *Mabinogi* or *Mabinogion,* especially the group known as the Four Branches. These four tales, which were probably redacted toward the end of the eleventh century, take the gods of Britain as their *dramatis personae.* The last of the four, *Math*

Son of Mathonwy, deals in particular with the group of gods sometimes referred to as the family of Dôn. The Math of the title is lord of Gwynedd in north Wales. His peculiarity is that he must keep his feet in a virgin's lap except in time of war. When his virginal footholder is violated by his sister's son, Gilfaethwy son of Dôn, with the connivance of his brother Gwydion son of Dôn, Math turns the two brothers into male and female animals—stags, boars, and wolves—for three years, during which time they give birth to three sons.

Subsequently, Math seeks a new footholder, and Gwydion suggests his sister, Aranrhod daughter of Dôn. Math asks her to step over his magic wand as a test of her virginity, and as she does so, she drops a yellow-haired boy and something else which Gwydion promptly conceals in a chest. The boy is baptized Dylan and immediately makes for the sea and takes on its nature, for which reason he is henceforth called Dylan Eil Don ("Dylan son of wave"). The object concealed by Gwydion turns out to be another male child, who in due course is given the name Lleu Llaw Gyffes ("Lleu of the skillful hand"). The rest of the tale is taken up with Lleu's relations with his mother, Aranrhod, and with his beautiful but treacherous wife, Blodeuwedd ("flower-aspect"), who had been created for him by Gwydion from the flowers of the oak, the broom, and the meadowsweet.

Family of Llyr. The three members of the family of Llyr—Branwen, Bendigeidvran ("Brân the blessed"), and Manawydan—appear in the Second Branch of the Mabinogi, though it is only in the Third Branch that Manawydan assumes an independent role. The tale is dominated by the enormous figure of Bendigeidvran. When his sister Branwen is ill treated in Ireland, where she has gone as the wife of Matholwch, king of Ireland, he goes with an army to exact vengeance. The British gain victory in a fierce battle with the Irish, but only seven of them survive beside Bendigeidvran, who is wounded in the foot by a poisonous spear. He commands his companions to cut off his head and to bury it at the White Mount in London as a safeguard against invasions. They set out for London and on the way enjoy two periods of otherworldly peace and joy in the presence of his uncorrupted head, at Harlech and on the isle of Gwales.

Pwyll, Rhiannon, and Pryderi. In the First Branch of the *Mabinogi,* Pwyll, lord of Dyfed in southwest Wales, comes to the aid of Arawn, king of Annwn, by slaying his otherworld enemy Hafgan in a single combat which is in fact an ordeal by battle of the kind known in early Irish as *fír fer* ("truth of men or heroes"). As a result he is henceforth known as Pwyll the Head of Annwn. The *Mabinogi* represents him here as a mortal, but since his name literally means "wisdom" and since he is designated lord of Annwn, the otherworld, it is probable that he was originally a deity. The latter part of the tale is concerned with the death of the hero Pryderi. Pwyll marries the lady Rhiannon, who first appears to him riding a white horse, and from their union Pryderi is born. But the newborn child is mysteriously abducted, to be discovered later by Teyrnon, lord of Gwent Is-coed, and reared by him and his wife for several years until they realize the child's true origins and restore him to Pwyll and Rhiannon. After Pwyll's death Pryderi succeeds to the lordship of Dyfed. Later, in the Third Branch, Rhiannon becomes the wife of Manawydan.

Goddesses of the Insular Celts. J. M. Synge in his *The Aran Islands* (1907) says of the Aran Islanders of the beginning of the twentieth century that they were interested in fertility rather than eroticism, and on the evidence of the extant monuments and literature, his observation could apply to those people who created the mythology of the Celtic goddesses. The Celts had no goddess of love, and so far as one can judge from insular tradition, the numerous sexual liaisons of the goddesses generally were motivated by ritual or social causes, not by erotic ones. Their sexuality was merely the instrument of their fertility, whether in terms of progeny or of the fruitfulness of the land with which they were so often identified.

As leader of the Connacht armies Medhbh is associated with war as well as with sovereignty, but in general the warlike aspect of the goddess is manifested indirectly: she influences the fortunes of war rather than actually participating. Other goddesses teach the art of fighting; examples include Buanann ("the lasting one"); Scáthach ("the shadowy one"), from whom Cú Chulainn acquired his heroic skills; and the formidable trio of Morríghan ("phantom queen"), Bodhbh ("scald-crow"), and Nemhain ("frenzy") or Macha, who haunt the battlefield to incite the fighters or to hinder them by their magic. These had their equivalents throughout the Celtic world: the name *Bodhbh Chatha* ("crow/raven of battle") is the exact cognate of *Cathubodua,* attested in Haute Savoie,

> **Their sexuality was merely the instrument of their fertility. . . .**

and the trio of war goddesses recurs in Britain in the Benwell inscription "Lamiis tribus" ("to the three Lamiae").

In direct contrast to these ruthless furies are those charming women who inhabit the happy otherworld in such numbers that it came to be called Tír inna mBan, "the land of women." Sometimes they come as emissaries from the land of primeval innocence where the pleasures of love are untainted by guilt and where sickness and disease are unknown. Conla son of Conn is induced to go there by "a young and beautiful woman of noble race whom neither death awaits nor old age," and Bran son of Febhal is similarly persuaded by a woman bearing a silvery branch from the wondrous apple tree which is a characteristic feature of the Celtic otherworld. But the multiforms of the insular Celtic goddesses are endless, and sometimes the named figure changes her role from one context to another.

Kings and Heroes. Virtually all early Irish narrative literature is to some degree heroic, but there are differences of emphasis that distinguish the king tales from the more specifically heroic narratives. Though the king tales involve heroic values, these are not their main preoccupation. Rather, they are concerned with the affirmation of political and social realities: the status and functions of the king, the ritual of inauguration and relations with the goddess of sovereignty, the origins of tribes and dynasties, battles of historical moment, the deeds and judgments of famous rulers, and so on. The sacral kingship was both the pivot and the foundation of the social order, and the king was its personification; if his conduct or even his person were blemished in any way, this blemish would be visited on his kingdom, diminishing its integrity and prosperity. As the instrument of justice, the king must be fair and flawless in his decisions. Thus the great Cormac mac Airt is pictured as a paragon of kingship and as an Irish Solomon: his accession came about when he proposed a just judgment after his predecessor Lughaidh mac Con had been deposed for delivering an unjust one. Conaire Mór is likewise an exemplary king whose reign brings peace and well-being to the land until he tempers justice with excessive mercy in the case of his three marauding foster brothers. Immediately a train of events is set in motion which leads inexorably to his death in a welter of violence.

Every kingdom, however small, had its sacred king and its inauguration site, but the focus of sacral kingship was at Tara, the goal of ambitious kings throughout the early Middle Ages. Situated in the central province, Midhe (lit., "middle"), and surrounded by the other four provinces, Tara is itself the heart of the Irish cosmographic system, and the traditional accounts of the disposition of the court of Tara show that it was conceived as a microcosmic replica of this cosmographic schema. Feis Temhra ("the feast of Tara") was the great festival held in pagan times to confirm a new king and to celebrate his ritual marriage to his kingdom. At Tara stood the Lia Fáil ("stone of Fál"), the "stone penis" which cried out when it came in contact with the man destined to be king.

BIBLIOGRAPHY

Duval, Paul-Marie. *Les dieux de la Gaule*. Rev. ed. Paris, 1976. An excellent compendium of what is known and surmised about the Gaulish gods. Its exposition of the data is clear, and its commentary balanced and judicious.

Gray, Elizabeth A. *Cath Maige Tuired: The Second Battle of Mag Tuired*. London, 1982. An edition of this important mythological text. Gray's "Cath Maige Tuired: Myth and Structure," Eigse 18 (1981): 183-209 and 19 (1982-1983): 1-35, 230-262, is a detailed interpretive analysis of the content of the tale.

Mac Cana, Proinsias. *Celtic Mythology*. Rev. ed. Feltham, Middlesex, 1983. A short survey of the subject with illustrations of sculpture, metalwork, and so on.

MacCulloch, J. A. *The Religion of the Ancient Celts*. Edinburgh, 1911. Reprinted as *Celtic Mythology* (Boston, 1918). Still useful if read in conjunction with more recent accounts.

MacNeill, Máire. *The Festival of Lughnasa*. Oxford, 1962. A comprehensive inventory of all the local festivals in Ireland that can be shown to continue the Celtic feast of Lugh, together with a very helpful commentary and a rich collection of texts, largely from the oral tradition.

Meyer, Kuno, ed. and trans., and Alfred Nutt. *The Voyage of Bran, Son of Febal, to the Land of the Living*. 2 vols. London, 1895-1897. This work includes a long commentary on the Celtic concept of the otherworld and the doctrine of rebirth. Largely superseded by more recent studies, it still contains many useful insights.

Murphy, Gerard, ed. and trans. *The Book of the Lays of Fionn*, vol. 3, *Duanaire Finn*. Dublin, 1953. Includes a long and valuable commentary on the history of the Fionn cycle and on the relationship between medieval manuscript and modern oral versions.

Nagy, Joseph Falaky. *The Wisdom of the Outlaw: The Boyhood Deeds of Finn in Gaelic Narrative Tradition*. Berkeley, 1983. An excellent, comprehensive interpretation of the Irish Fionn Cycle, or Fianaighecht, and the first extended study of the cycle in terms of modern mythological theory. It explores the internal consistency of the cycle as reflected in some of its constituent narratives and brings out the markedly liminal character of Fionn and his followers.

Ó Cathasaigh, Tomás. *The Heroic Biography of Cormac mac Airt*. Dublin, 1977. A perceptive exposition of the status and function of the Irish hero-king as reflected in the legends of Cormac mac Airt.

O'Rahilly, Thomas F. *Early Irish History and Mythology*. Dublin, 1946. Valuable for its coverage of Irish literary resources in all periods, and for its brilliant analyses of medieval texts, but sometimes rather outmoded and idiosyncratic in its treatment of mythological topics by viewing essentially mythological narratives as reflections of historical events.

Rees, Alwyn, and Brinley Rees. *Celtic Heritage*. London, 1961. An important and stimulating work that seeks to structure insular Celtic tradition in terms of a number of ideological concepts and motivations. It is inspired by the Dumézilian system of analysis, applied in a flexible and imaginative fashion.

Ross, Anne. *Pagan Celtic Britain*. London, 1967. Surveys the British repertory of images for the Celtic gods and their attributes. Contains an extensive and detailed discussion of the several main categories of deity which they comprise (horned god, warrior god, divine animals, among others). Valuable also for its rich comparative documentation from insular literary and folklore sources.

Sjoestedt, Marie-Louise. *Dieux et héros des Celtes*. Paris, 1940. Translated by Myles Dillon as *Gods and Heroes of the Celts* (London, 1949). A short but perceptive survey of Celtic, mainly Irish, mythology and hero tales. At the time of its publication it offered fresh insights into the nature of Celtic myth and is still necessary reading.

Vendryes, Joseph. *Les religions des Celtes*. "Mana," Introduction à l'histoire des religions, vol. 1. Paris, 1948. This is largely a *catalogue raisonné* of the varied data, both continental and insular, relating to Celtic religion. More descriptive than theoretical, it is still a useful source of information.

Vries, Jan de. *Keltische Religion*. Stuttgart, 1961. A comprehensive treatment of the whole of Celtic religion. It is well documented and strong on Indo-European and other comparative aspects, less so on the insular tradition, although the latter is still given generous coverage.

PROINSIAS MAC CANA

CENTRAL BANTU RELIGIONS

The term *central Bantu,* as used here, refers to speakers of languages belonging to the Bantu branch of Niger-Congo who live in the Kongo (Zaire) Basin. They are spread over thousands of square miles stretching from the mouth of the Kongo River on the Atlantic to Lake Malawi and the Shire Basin in the east. They occupy much of Zaire, Angola, Zambia, and Malawi, spilling over into the Congo Republic, Tanzania, and Zimbabwe.

In 1980 the central Bantu peoples were estimated to number around ten million, divided among many groups varying in size from half a million to a few hundred. Lele and Ndembu religions, through the writings of Mary Douglas and Victor Turner, have done much to shape current thought on religious symbols and the nature of ritual.

The Luba and Lunda stress patrilineal descent. The Lozi have a bilateral system. The other central Bantu are matrilineal, but residence upon marriage varies: in Zaire, Angola, and south and west Zambia, the rule was that a wife moved to her husband's residence, and her sons returned to her brothers at maturity. In northern Zambia and Malawi, on the other hand, men joined their wives, and the long-lasting links were those between women.

Common Base. A comparison of the myths and ritual symbols of the Kuba, Luba, and Lunda of Zaire and the Bemba of Zambia led Luc de Heusch to the conclusion that the savanna peoples share a common symbolic vocabulary. He attributes this to their common ideological heritage from proto-Bantu ancestors. This common heritage was reinforced with the expansion of centralized states, which tended to imitate each other, and the growth of trading networks, which by the seventeenth century linked much of the region into one great system. Myths, he suggests, moved along the trade routes like merchandise (de Heusch, 1982, pp. 245-247). In fact, given the importance of charms or fetishes, which could be bought or sold, much ritual material was merchandise, encouraging the spread of cultic objects and organizations.

These materials could be accepted more easily because before the period of colonial rule the religious systems of the region shared common values and beliefs about the nature of the cosmos and the role of humans, spirits, and impersonal powers in the cosmic order. All were based on the assumption that a good human life is part of the natural order laid down at creation. The supreme being, or creator, was seen as beneficent but remote. Spirits active in relation to human interests, whether ancestral spirits or spirits of nature, were beneficent in principle. Power also existed throughout the cosmos and was inherent in all phenomena—in plants, animals, rocks, streams, and pools. It lay ready to be tapped

and used by those who learned the correct techniques, and when it was converted into magic or a charm it could then be used to enhance human felicity or to destroy it.

Another common feature of central Bantu religions was the belief that human disorder disturbed the cosmic order. Drought, other natural disorders, infertility, and illness occurred because of human failure or evil. The natural order could be preserved or restored only by controlling the human disorder.

Central Bantu religions were also pragmatic, emphasizing ritual and practice rather than doctrine. Heresy could not exist. Rituals, moreover, were a means to immediate practical ends and were not intended to merge the human with the divine. They were performed to obtain rain, fertility of crops and women, success in hunting, protection from misfortune, recovery from illness, and to regulate the transition of community members from one life phase to another (especially from death to "protecting ancestor" status). What spirits did—not what they were—was important. Spirits were identified by effect, and when in doubt a diviner was consulted. In the area that has become Zaire, Angola, and western Zambia, Bantu-speaking peoples who used images and masks were concerned with symbolic statement about action rather than with a representation of substance. The majority of peoples who lived in the area that is now Zambia and Malawi made no images. They agreed with the Tonga, who said, "We call all spirits wind. Like wind we cannot see them. We only know what they are by what they do."

Social Setting. By the beginning of the twentieth century, most central Bantu were subsistence cultivators, and their religions echoed their concerns. In general the countryside was well watered, but during the long dry season people depended upon springs and pools, especially in the more arid southeast. Rainfall was problematic, again especially in the southeast where droughts are frequent. It is no accident that so much communal ritual was associated with appeals for rains, while spirits linked to territorial cults were thought to dwell in pools and springs or moist caverns.

Cultivators lived in small villages, ranging in size from forty to five hundred inhabitants, a size that left them highly vulnerable to natural disasters and demographic failure. High value was placed on fecundity and protection against accidents or epidemics. Villages moved to new sites every few years as soils became exhausted and game depleted. Since neither permanent buildings nor ownership of land tied people to a single place, communities were fragile, easily disrupted by quarrels or by events that aroused the fear that witches were at work.

Archaeological evidence for agriculture dates back to the early years of the first millennium. Most crops were annuals, although the Kongo had stands of palm oil and kola nut while the Kuba and Lele grew raffia palm. Staple crops were the millets and sorghums first domesticated in Africa, and many agricultural rituals centered on these. By the end of the nineteenth century they were being displaced by maize and cassava.

Cults and Spirits. Secret cults associated with initiation schools and masked performances existed in the area that has become Zaire and Angola and among Luvale, Chokwe, and Ndembu immigrants near the upper reaches of the Zambezi River. Their theme was access to power. The Chewa near Lake Malawi also used masks in the Nyau cult, which mimed the invasion of domestic space by the spirits of the wild and the reign of disorder. Many central Bantu religions lacked such cults, but there were other cults that existed throughout the region. These have been classified into four cult types: domestic or kinship, territorial, professional, and healing.

Ancestral spirits and domestic cults. The Kuba and Lele were unique in having no ancestral cults, but other central African peoples who believed in reincarnation thought of the reincarnated spirits as free to come and go in the homesteads of their kin. These spirits were invoked in domestic rituals and lineages and also in the professional cults of specialists. It was believed that such spirits affected the welfare of their descendants and members of their descent groups. Whatever the system of descent, children owed service to the spirits of their dead parents, grandparents, and siblings. These spirits were installed as guardians of their households, and they protected their dependents against intruding spirits and against charms sent by human malice. Periodically they were given offerings to assure them that they were remembered and cared for.

The common place of offering in domestic cults was the doorway of the dwelling, which was associated with the coming and going of the spirits. Most offerings took place in early morning before spirits and people had dispersed for the day. The dwelling itself was a shrine to domesticity, for those who lived within were continuing the domestic life laid down by the ancestors. The sexual activity of the married couple, which created new life, was therefore made sacred, as was the cooking fire that helped to sustain life.

Lineages, where they existed, were ritual communities focused on common ancestors, led by elders who themselves had known many of those whose spirits they now summoned. The elder's dwelling could serve as a lineage shrine as well as his household shrine, but special shrines also existed. They took the form of a simple post, a tree planted when the homestead was built, a miniature dwelling, or a gateway formed of two posts with a crossbar. Like all central Bantu shrines they were simple, impermanent, and could be built again when need arose.

Individuals who had special skills bestowed upon them by an ancestor dedicated shrines to their spirit sponsor. Here the spirit was invoked before the person embarked on the hunt or other activity, and it was thanked for success in the enterprise. Such shrines also served as reminders that the living followed a way of life created by those now dead and that they could depend upon the knowledge the dead had acquired.

Territorial cults, heroes, and nature spirits. Some territorial cults had no permanent shrines but rather centered on spirit mediums who spoke under possession as the embodiment of nature spirits, of those who had first settled the land, or of ancient heroes or former rulers who had once had some interest in the territory. Other cults used natural shrines that were seen as places where spirits manifested themselves. These were usually deep pools, waterfalls, caves, and high places. Here offerings of black cloth, black beads, beer, domestic stock, meal, and water were made. Hoes and spears, the essential tools of cultivation and the hunt, were also appropriate offerings.

Officiants in the territorial cults were priests, priestesses, and mediums. The former, if representative of first settlement, are usually called "earth priests." They were of particular importance among acephalous peoples, but even in the centralized kingdoms where royal shrines catered to public concerns, earth priests led local communities.

The earth priest was chosen from the lineage associated either with settlement or with some later community leader. He had a ritual wife who represented the first wife, and together they followed the routine believed to have been established with the foundation of the community. They carried out the rites that organized the agricultural year, initiating clearing of fields, planting, weeding, bird scaring, eating of first fruits, and harvest. When the community moved, their house was the first to be built, and it was from their rekindled fire that fire was taken by others. Since they were associated with fertility, their ritual intercourse gave validity to the promise of reward for hard agricultural labor. Seeds placed beneath their bed were imbued with vitality and were distributed for planting.

Priests and priestesses gave continuity, but mediums provided for communication and innovation. At regular offerings, men and women told the spirits what they desired; the spirits, in turn, made their own demands and gave warnings through mediums. Sometimes they announced the arrival of previously unknown spirits or threatened to abandon the community. When rain was at stake, black beads and black cloth were appropriate offerings to the mediums, for black symbolized the rain clouds. White was offered when they were asked to stop overly abundant downpours. When the spirits demanded sacrifices, black animals were provided.

Although some of the most powerful mediums lived separately and could be approached only through their attendants, the majority lived as ordinary men and women except when they were possessed. During possession, people clapped before them as they did before the shrines or in the presence of a ruler.

Just as first settlers continued to watch over their communities, so dead kings and queens continued to oversee their realms. These royal spirits were often associated with regional shrines. Some territorial shrines served only a neighborhood, while others served a large region as places of last appeal. When nearby shrines and mediums failed to give satisfaction, communities sent delegations to distant shrines and mediums, crossing linguistic and political boundaries. This gave witness that in the last analysis all shared the same human interests. Homogenization of belief and rituals was inevitable.

Professional cults. Many types of professional guilds existed in Zaire, each with its own cult. Elsewhere we have good evidence only for hunting cults and sometimes cults of diviners and smiths. Because they dealt with power, guild members were regarded as dangerously close to the temptation of witchcraft. A breaking of the normal rules was attributed to hunters, who in the reckless search for power engaged in incest and sacrificed kin to obtain spirit companions in the hunt. The very presence of the hunter, linked as he was with blood and death as well as with extraordinary power, was dangerous to small children and pregnant women.

Many central Bantu thought that witches, too, had professional guilds. It was a common belief that witches offered human flesh as a feast and delighted in the evil that they had orchestrated.

Cults of suffering. Cults of suffering, or of affliction as Victor Turner has called them, may have been of minor importance prior to the twentieth century. During this century, however, these cults have proliferated. They are based on the belief that various kinds of spirits seize upon or enter human victims, who then must come to terms with them. Treatment requires identification of the spirit and instruction in how to meet its demands. Thereafter the sufferer becomes an adept able to treat new victims.

In Zaire, Angola, and western Zambia, cults of suffering are associated with spirits known as *mahamba,* identified as former members of alien ethnic groups who ask those possessed to speak in their own tongue and don their costume. *Mahamba* cults may also invoke the spirits of the sufferer's own ancestors.

Early cults of affliction were concerned with the incursion of animal spirits and spirits of the bush and may have developed out of hunting cults. More recent ones are linked to the uncertainties of alien modern experiences; cults centered on such things as the airplane, railroad, city life, warfare, angels, and on those people taken away as slaves to Europe and America have appeared in the last few decades. Each spirit is identified with its own drum rhythms, songs, medicines, and sometimes costume.

Although men and women of all ages may be initiated into cults of suffering, the majority of initiates are women. Lewis

(1971) attributes this to the peripheral role women have in the public sphere. In general, central Bantu religions provided women with important ritual and political roles. Women were sometimes political rulers and held offices in both territorial and kinship cults. On death they became ancestral spirits, and living women could make offerings to the ancestors. Women became diviners and herbalists, and some of the most famous mediums were women.

Religious Transformation. De Craemer, Vansina, and Fox (1976) believe the basic elements and symbols of central African religions have been stable over the centuries

> **At the end of the nineteenth century central Africa was carved up among European powers.**

(perhaps for millennia), although specific religious movements have come and gone. Nevertheless the last four centuries have been marked by religious questioning and transformation, paralleling the turmoil and transformation in political and economic regimes. The Kongo on the Atlantic coast first encountered the Portuguese and Christianity at the end of the fifteenth century. Many Kongo people were baptized. In the sixteenth century the Portuguese also began pushing up the Zambezi River from the Indian Ocean. The slave trade brought about the destruction of many of the ancient kingdoms.

The dispersal of fleeing populations and the caravan movements led to a spread of epidemic disease on an unprecedented scale and to a questioning of the efficacy of existing religion. At the end of the nineteenth century central Africa was carved up among European powers, and formerly independent rulers became suspect as ritual leaders when they were transformed into bureaucrats in colonial governments. Between 1950 and 1980, independence movements brought African governments into power, but these were no more willing to accept claims to authority based on religious inspiration or cultic position than were the colonial governments.

In the twentieth century people have come to depend on the cash economy and world trade. Market conditions are now as important as rainfall in determining well-being. New crops and agricultural techniques dominate the scene; consequently, territorial cults associated with agriculture have become less important. Hunting has little importance in recent decades since game has been largely depleted except in a few refuge areas. Hunting cults, not surprisingly, have largely vanished. And as cheap imported goods have spread and undercut local products, rituals associated with other crafts have also faded.

[*For discussion of particular central Bantu religions, see* Bemba Religion; Kongo Religion; Luba Religion; *and* Ndembu Religion.]

BIBLIOGRAPHY

Balandier, Georges. *Daily Life in the Kingdom of the Kongo.* Translated by Helen Weaver. London, 1968.

Beattie, John, and John Middleton, eds. *Spirit Mediumship and Society in Africa.* New York, 1969.

Binsbergen, Wim van. "Explorations in the History and Sociology of Territorial Cults in Zambia." In *Guardians of the Land,* edited by J. Matthew Schoffeleers, pp. 47-88. Gwelo, 1978.

De Craemer, Willy, Jan Vansina, and Renée C. Fox. "Religious Movements in Central Africa: A Theoretical Study." *Comparative Studies in Society and History* 18 (October 1976): 458-475.

Douglas, Mary. *The Lele of the Kasai.* London, 1963.

Fernandez, James W. "African Religious Movements." *Annual Review of Anthropology* 7 (1976): 195-234.

Heusch, Luc de. *The Drunken King, or The Origin of the State.* Translated by Roy G. Willis. Bloomington, Ind., 1982.

Lewis, I. M. *Ecstatic Religion: An Anthropological Study of Spirit Possession and Shamanism.* Harmondsworth, 1971.

MacGaffey, Wyatt. "Comparative Analysis of Central African Religions." *Africa* 42 (1972): 21-31.

MacGaffey, Wyatt. "African Religions: Types and Generalizations." In *Explorations in African Systems of Thought,* edited by Ivan Karp and Charles S. Bird, pp. 301-328. Bloomington, Ind., 1980.

Schoffeleers, J. Matthew. "The Interaction of the M'Bona Cult and Christianity, 1859-1963." In *Themes in the Christian History of Central Africa,* edited by T. O. Ranger and John Weller, pp. 14-29. Berkeley, 1975.

Schoffeleers, J. Matthew, ed. *Guardians of the Land: Essays on Central African Territorial Cults.* Gwelo, 1978.

Turner, Victor. *The Forest of Symbols: Aspects of Ndembu Ritual.* Ithaca, N. Y., 1967.

Turner, Victor. *The Drums of Affliction: A Study of Religious Processes among the Ndembu of Zambia.* London, 1968.

Turner, Victor. *The Ritual Process: Structure and Anti-Structure.* Chicago, 1969.

Werbner, R. P., ed. *Regional Cults.* New York, 1977.

Willis, Roy G. "Instant Millennium: The Sociology of African Witch-Cleansing Cults." In *Witchcraft Confessions and Accusations,* edited by Mary Douglas, pp. 129-140. New York, 1970.

ELIZABETH COLSON

CHANTING

Hebrew Chant. The term *cantillation* applies primarily to the recitation of the Hebrew Bible by Jews and Samaritans. Cantillation of the Bible on special occasions is already attested to in *Deuteronomy* 31:12, *2 Kings* 22:1-13, and *Nehemiah* 8:1-8. But regular biblical readings were established only in the fifth century BCE, when Ezra the Scribe chanted from the Law in the Jerusalem Temple twice a week on market days to all the people assembled there. This is the earliest evidence of regular biblical recitation in public. Since the reader had to amplify his voice in order to be heard, his unconscious chanting established the first biblical cantillation.

Melodic patterns or motifs were indicated by a system of finger and hand movements called cheironomy (from Greek *cheir,* "hand"), a practice depicted by Sumerians and Egyptians on bas-reliefs and in tombs in the fourth and third millennium BCE. These gestures were intended to refresh the memory of those who had previously learned the melodies by ear. Hindus and Jews employ cheironomic signs even today, and various systems have been developed by different groups.

The first cheironomic signs were simple: the rise of the melody was signaled by an upward stroke of the hand (/), the fall by a downward stroke of the hand (\), and the rise and the fall on a single syllable by the junction of the two signs (^). Various combinations of these basic symbols followed. It was musical notation written on the air.

When Hebrew ceased to be a living language, the Masoretes, transmitters of the biblical tradition, devised written symbols to safeguard the proper pronunciation, phrasing, and melodies of biblical Hebrew. The task took five centuries to complete (fifth to tenth century CE). The Masoretes transferred the cheironomic signs from the air to parchment and paper. It must be noted that other cultures employed similar symbols for similar purposes; indeed, scholars disagree as to which culture was the first to transfer hand movements form the air to parchment. Greece, India, the Middle East, and Europe have all been suggested. But the symbols are so elementary that any culture could have invented them independently without outside influence.

The eastern European types of cantillation practiced by Polish, Lithuanian, Hungarian, and Russian Jews are related. These are, however, unrelated to German, Italian, French, or Sefardic (Spanish-Portuguese) cantillations. But, the Hebrew cantillation is instantly recognizable anywhere in the world. The reasons are unvarying text (Hebrew) and the ekphonetic symbols that are prescribed for every word of the sentence and have a syntactical as well as a musical function. They provide a solid structural basis for cantillation.

In addition to biblical cantillation, Jews recognize formalized chanting without ekphonetic symbols, namely that employed in blessings, certain prayers in the synagogue and at home, the study of Mishnah, the study of the *gemara',* and the study of the *Zohar.* In addition, Yemenite Jews recite from the Aramaic translation of the Bible on the Sabbath and on holidays in the synagogue. It is worth nothing that the Yemenite Jews are the only ones to perpetuate this Second Temple tradition and translate every Hebrew sentence into the Aramaic vernacular of the time.

Chanting in all these cases is based on a melody that consists of an opening motif *(initium),* followed by an undifferentiated two-tone motif *(tenor)* and a final cadence *(finalis).* The melody varies in length according to the number of words in the sentence, but the melodic motifs do not vary.

The Samaritans cantillate the Hebrew Bible according to *sidra' miqrata'* (the Aramaic form of the Hebrew *seder ha-miqra'*), nondiastematic ekphonetic symbols. There are ten in number, but only three basic ones are remembered (see

> **Scholars disagree as to which culture was the first to transfer hand movements from the air to parchment.**

Spector, 1965, pp. 146-147): *arkenu-enged* (has the function of a colon), *afsaq* (full stop), and *anau* (pause, with the function of a semicolon).

Of ten extant cantillation styles, two are most prominent. The *logogenic,* or word-bound style, does not permit the inclusion of extraneous syllables or words. It was originally practiced by priests only and forbidden to the laity. It was intervallically stepwise, syllabic, and without ornamentation of the melody. The *pathogenic-melogenic* style, derived from passionate emotion and melody, permits the interpolation of extraneous nonsense syllables into the text if the text is shorter than the melody. It is particularly effective in the public reading of the Decalogue on the Festival of Shavu`ot. In this recitation the melody often overshadows the text.

Byzantium. Scholars apply the term *Byzantine music* to Eastern ecclesiastical chant sung in Greek. In spite of the language it is maintained that this music was not a continuation of ancient Greek music but contained Near Eastern musical elements.

Byzantine ecclesiastical music, like Near Eastern music, was entirely vocal, monophonic, unaccompanied, and devoid of meter. The use of organs and other musical instruments was forbidden inside the churches, similar to the prohibition in synagogues and (later) mosques. The liturgical books intended for chanting of lessons were performed in ekphonetic style, midway between recitation and singing. On solemn occasions actual singing replaced the cantillation. For training Christian congregations in singing, Jewish readers and precentors from synagogues were chosen who had previously converted to Christianity. Especially trained for the office, they made it possible to introduce into Christian worship not only chanting but also antiphonal singing, particularly psalms for solo voice with congregational responses. Performances varied from simple recitation to elaborate cantillation.

Gregorian Chant. Gregorian chant is the traditional music of the Roman Catholic church. Scholars maintain that it is rooted, like the music of the Byzantine church, in the pre-

Christian service of the Jews. It acquired distinctive characteristics in the third and fourth centuries and was fully developed by the seventh century.

Many Gregorian practices were taken from the synagogue. The melodies show stepwise movement. Melodic rises or falls of the intervals of a second and a third are common, but those of a fifth are rare. The melodies can be classified as syllabic (one note to a syllable), neumatic (two to five notes to a syllable), and melismatic (long, highly ornamented phrases). The chant consists of one melodic line with neither harmony nor polyphony to support it.

Armenia. The Armenian *khaz* numbers ten symbols, five prosodic (*thaw, sosk, aibatatz, entamna,* and *storat*) and five musical (*erkar, ssuch, shesht, olorak,* and *buth*). According to Robert Atajan, the prosodic *khaz* relate to the peculiarities of Armenian phonetic pronunciation and have no bearing on the music. Syntactic symbols in the prosodic system, however, are of particular significance in the musical structure of the sentence: *storaket* ("deep point") is a comma, *mitshaket* ("middle point") is a semicolon or colon, and *vertchaket* ("final point") is a period. The musical signs *erkar* and *ssuch* indicate a lengthening or shortening of tone duration. The other three, *shesht, olorak,* and *buth,* represent tone pitches or rather melodic formulas based on Armenian folk tunes.

The Qur'an. The chanting of the Qur'an is regulated not by ekphonetic signs or neumes but by oral tradition, which varies from place to place. The word is paramount, and no ornamentation is permitted. Sudden stops within the Qur'anic sentence are a special feature. The call to prayer varies from country to country. Syllabic, elaborate melismas are often incorporated; both examples are in *maqam* Hijaz, but other maqamat, or modes, are used in different Muslim areas.

India. The Vedas, the sacred texts of the Hindus, were probably composed by Aryan tribes who invaded India from the northwest around 1500 BCE. The sacred texts had been handed down in oral tradition with accents at least since the fourth century BCE, as reported by the grammarian Panini, who presumably knew the living practice. The interpretation of the accents is by no means uniform. Panini wrote: "A vowel pronounced in a high register is called *udatta,* a vowel pronounced in a low register is called *anudatta,* and the connection of both is called *svarita.*" Some modern scholars maintain that *udatta* is a middle tone, higher than *anudatta,* and that *svarita* is higher than *udatta.* Only male members of the priestly brahman caste are eligible to recite the Vedas.

The Vedas were for hundreds of years handed down orally and not committed to writing, unlike the sacred books of the Jews, Christians, and Muslims. The Hindus relied on the spoken word for three thousand years, and even today the Vedas are recited from memory; every precaution is observed to avoid the smallest error, which, it is believed, may produce disaster.

Tibet. Tibetan Buddhist chants are divided into *'don,* recitation chants; *rta,* melodic chants; and *dbyans,* tone contour chants. The general designation for the monastic chant repertoire is *'don cha.* The recitation chants are stylized recitations that employ reiterating pitch and rhythmic patterns according to the words in the sentences.

Rta are melodic chants with distinctly patterned melodies. Unlike *'don,* they are relatively independent of their texts and are considered melodic and musical. However, their performance is called "speaking." They are similar to melodies in Western and non-Tibetan performance traditions.

Dbyans are tone contour chants and are considered the most beautiful chants used in Tibetan music. They are very slow, low-pitched, and most complex. In contradistinction to *'don* and *rta,* which are "spoken," the *dbyans* are "intoned." They include changes in intonation, pitch, loudness, and (most remarkably) overtone mixtures, which are perceived as two or more pitches produced simultaneously by one singer.

Secular Chant. Secular chanting is prominent in the epic poetry of many countries; thus it is used for the most dignified and elaborate form of narrative poetry dealing with heroic, legendary, and historical events as well as with the drama and romance of love. Epics are usually chanted by a single performer, but in some Asian countries contests between two rival performers are customary and may last several days. In ancient times the narrator of epics chanted without instrumental accompaniment, but contemporary performers, however, accompany themselves on a stringed instrument, preferably a violin (Persian, *kemanje;* Turkmen, *ghyjjak*) or a lute (Kirghiz, *kobuz;* Turkmen, *dutar;* Tajik and Uzbek, *dumbura*).

BIBLIOGRAPHY

Apel, Willi. *Gregorian Chant* (1958). Bloomington, Ind., 1970.
Atajan, Robert. "Armenische Chasen." In *Essays on Armenian Music,* edited by Vrej Nersessian, pp. 131-148. London, 1978.
Belayev, Victor M. *Ocherki po istorii muzyki narodov SSSR.* 2 vols. Moscow, 1962-1963.
Ellingson, Ter. " '*Don rta dbyangs gsum:* Tibetan Chant and Melodic Categories." Asian Music 10 (1979): 112-156.
Fleischer, Oskar. *Neumen-Studien.* 2 vols. Leipzig, 1895-1904.
Fox-Strangways, A. H. *The Music of Hindostan* (1914). Oxford, 1967.
Høeg, Carsten. *La notation ekphonétique.* Copenhagen, 1935.
Idelsohn, A. Z. "Parallelen zwischen gregorianischen und hebraeisch-orientalischen Gesangsweisen." *Zeitschrift für Musikwissenschaft* 4 (1921-1922): 515-524.
Idelsohn, A. Z. *Jewish Music in Its Historical Development* (1929). New York, 1967.
Jairazbhoy, N. A. "An Interpretation of the Twenty-two Srutis." *Asian Music* 6 (1975): 38-59.
Lachmann, Robert. *Die Musik des Orients.* Breslau, 1929.
Spector, Johanna. "A Comparative Study of Scriptural Cantillation and Accentuation (Pentateuch)." Ph. D. diss., Hebrew Union College, 1951.
Spector, Johanna. "The Significance of Samaritan Neumes and Contemporary Practice." In *Studia Musicologica,* edited by Zoltan Kodály, vol. 7, pp. 141-153. Budapest, 1965.
Spector, Johanna. "Musical Tradition and Innovation." In *Central Asia: A Century of Russian Rule,* edited by Edward Allworth, pp. 434-484. New York, 1967.
Szabolcsi, Bence. *A History of Melody.* Translated by Cynthia Jolly and Sara Karig. London, 1965.
Wagner, Peter. *Einführung in die gregorianischen Melodien.* 3 vols. Leipzig, 1895-1921. Volume 1 has been translated as *Origin and Development of the Forms of the Liturgical Chant* (London, 1901).
Wellesz, Egon. *A History of Byzantine Music and Hymnography.* 2d ed. Oxford, 1961.
Werner, Eric. "The Doxology in Synagogue and Church, a Liturgico-Musical Study." *Hebrew Union College Annual* 19 (1946): 275-351.

JOHANNA SPECTOR

CHARITY

The word charity derives from the Latin *caritas* and can be traced to the Greek *charis.* As a theoretical conception, charity has meant both possessive and selfless love, as well as favor, grace, mercy, kindness, righteousness, and liberality. In its practical application, charity denotes the distribution of goods to the poor and the establishment and endowment of such social-welfare institutions as hospitals, homes for the aged, orphanages, and reformatory institutions.

As an applied virtue, charity is expected of everyone, for whoever gives charity will be blessed by the Lord (*Dt.* 15:7-10). In medieval Judaism, in Moses Maimonides particularly, the highest form of charity is not to give alms but to help the poor rehabilitate themselves by lending them money, taking them into partnership, or employing them, for in this way the desired end is achieved without any loss of self-respect for the recipient. But notwithstanding occasional references to liberality toward the gentiles, in Jewish tradition "charity begins at home," and for many centuries the object of charity was the fellow Jew—the individual, the family circle, and the community.

Ancient Greek society saw charity as synonymous with love *(agape), philanthropia, eleos,* and *philoxenia,* and it was manifested through benevolent deeds on behalf of those in need. Compassion for the afflicted and loving hospitality were greatly emphasized in Mycenaean and archaic Greek society (1400-700 BCE). The care of strangers and suppliants was an ethical imperative because such people had been placed under the direct aegis of the divinity. Zeus became known as Xenios, "protector of strangers." This imperative is expressed in Homer's *Od-yssey:* "Receive strangers regardless of who they may be"; That man is sacred who welcomes a wayfaring stranger."

The most important characteristic of Greek thought from as early as the Homeric age is ethical in nature. In the classical Greek city-states, whether in Athens, Thebes, or remote Acragas, charity in the sense of selfless love, almsgiving, pity, and concern for the orphan, the widow, and the elderly was widely and generously practiced.

Under the influence of Socrates, Plato, and Aristotle and the Stoics, charity was perceived as a duty toward all "broken and destitute humanity wherever found." It was a moral and religious obligation, a social and economic need, or as Pythagoras stressed: "All human laws are nourished by one, which is divine." There are no political or economic laws, only moral laws.

Charity in Christianity is synonymous with *agape,* or love. Whether it was a new commandment, as Christ had taught (*Jn.* 13:34), is controversial. One thing is certain: Christianity proved more ecumenical and proclaimed that "there is neither Jew nor Greek, there is neither slave nor free, there is neither male nor female . . . but all [are] one in Christ Jesus" (*Gal.* 3:28). God's love requires that men love one another (*1 Jn.* 4:11). There is no better account of the nature and the fruits of Christian charity than the thirteenth chapter of Paul's *First Letter to the Corinthians.* Charity is defined as the love of God expressed through the God-made-man event in Christ and as man's love of neighbor, the solvent of hatred of the enemy.

The Buddha's Four Noble Truths (*catvari-arya-satyani*) inherently include love and compassion toward fellow human beings. Buddhism sees suffering as a universal reality, but a reality with a cause. Suffering may be relieved through the application of three principles: *metta* or *maitri,* loving-kindness actively pursued; *karuna,* compassion, mercy, which does not repay evil with evil; and *mudita,* a feeling of approval of other people's good deeds. These principles find their expression in works of social welfare, including public works projects and the maintenance of hospitals and shelters or hospices.

The meaning of charity in Hinduism depends upon the interpretation of *dharma,* "the primary virtue of the active life of the Hindu." *Dharma* is the inner disposition and the conserving idea, while the action by which it is realized is known as *karman,* which is expressed in physical, verbal, and mental forms. The physical forms consist of good deeds such as hospitality, duties to wife and children, and assistance to those in need. Verbal charity is identified with proper or gentle speech and courteous behavior. Mental charity is synonymous with piety.

If man is a creature good by nature, then man can develop an ethics of benevolence, justice, or righteousness. Jainism, in particular, which stresses self-cultivation more than social involvement, sees self-perfection as the best means of alleviating social misery. The value of charity as an act of benevolence is judged by the degree of personal culti-

vation and sacrifice involved. It is a spontaneous and personal virtue, instinctive rather than acquired.

Charity in Islam depends on the belief in an omnipotent God, master of mankind, which not only receives God's mercy but is always in danger of incurring his wrath. Thus mankind needs to serve God by means of good works, including almsgiving, both voluntary offerings (*sadaqat*) and legally proscribed ones (*zakat*), kindness, and good treatment of parents, orphans, and the elderly. As the author of moral commandments, God commands, and the believer must practice. "The Lord has decreed . . . kindness to parents. . . . Give the kinsman his due, and the needy, and the wayfarer. . . . Come not near the wealth of the orphan. . . ." These and other similar admonitions constitute the outward signs of piety, the means of expiating offenses, and the path to ultimate salvation.

[*See also* Grace.]

BIBLIOGRAPHY

Berry, Thomas, *Buddhism.* New York, 1975.
Berry, Thomas. *Religions of India: Hinduism, Yoga, Buddhism.* New York, 1971.
Chaudhuri, Nirad C. *Hinduism.* London, 1979.
Constantelos, Demetrios J. *Byzantine Philanthropy and Social Welfare.* New Brunswick, N. J., 1968.
Conze, Edward. *Buddhism: Its Essence and Development.* Oxford, 1951.
Hands, A. R. *Charities and Social Aid in Greece and Rome.* Ithaca, N. Y., 1968.
Jeffrey, Arthur, ed. *Islam: Muhammad and His Religion.* New York, 1958.
May, Herbert G., and Bruce M. Metzger, eds. *The New Oxford Annotated Bible with the Apocrypha.* Rev. ed. New York, 1977.
Nikhilananda. *Essence of Hinduism.* Boston, 1948.
Nygren, Anders. *Agape and Eros.* Translated by Philip S. Watson. Rev. ed. Philadelphia, 1953.
Organ, Troy. *The Hindu Quest for the Perfection of Man.* Athens, Ohio, 1970.
Pétré, Hélène. *Caritas: Étude sur le vocabulaire Latin de la cha-rité chrétienne.* Louvain, 1948.
Pickthall, M. M., trans. and ed. *The Meaning of the Glorious Qur'an.* New York, 1930.
Pritchard, James B., ed. *The Ancient Near East.* 2 vols. Princeton, 1973-1975.
Quell, Gottfried, and Ethelbert Stauffer. "Agapao, agape, agapetos." In *Theological Dictionary of the New Testament,* edited by Gerhard Kittel, vol. 1, pp. 21-55. Grand Rapids, Mich., 1964.

DEMETRIOS J. CONSTANTELOS

CHARLEMAGNE

CHARLEMAGNE (c. 742-814), also known as Charles the Great and Carolus Magnus; king of the Franks (768-800) and first emperor of a revived Empire in the West (800-814). For three years after the death in 768 of Pépin III (the Short), the *regnum Francorum* was divided between his two sons, but in 771 the elder, Charlemagne, became sole ruler, although not without opposition. His unusually long reign was of major importance in the history of western Europe and the Christian church and the Latin culture associated with it. In 773-774, responding to papal appeal, Charlemagne invaded the Lombard kingdom, annexed it to his own and then visited Rome, where he was ceremonially received and given an "authoritative" text of church law.

Involuntary conversions and the establishment of an organized church followed Charlemagne's military victories over the Saxons (beginning in 772), but Saxony was for years beset by bloody and destructive rebellions. Nevertheless, the monastery of Fulda, the bishopric of Würzburg, and new settlements such as Paderborn became centers of organized missionary activity. In 785 the leaders of Saxon resistance accepted baptism, although it may be doubted whether many Saxons followed their example until further pressures, including severe punishment for "pagan" practices, had been employed. The conversion of the Frisians was simultaneously being achieved, although with less violence.

Charlemagne inherited a concept of kingship that emphasized the obligation and legitimacy of extending the Christian faith by force of arms while also securing it at home. To these ends came also the utilization of the church hierarchy as well as lay officials as a means of social control; both groups were expected to give effect to the legal rules and pious exhortations expressed in capitularies promulgated in Latin by the assemblies that brought together bishops, abbots, and leading laymen in 779, 789, and frequently in later years. The king's personal devotion to *religio Christiana,* with which he is credited, was essentially expressed in observance of the externals of worship as provided by the court chaplains, with little regard for spirituality or personal morality. Even before 779, however, church authorities were making the king aware that among his responsibilities should be the encouragement of learning *(eruditio)* as a basis for more effective government and the more correct understanding of the texts on which the Christian faith was grounded.

Peter of Pisa, remembered as the person who taught Charlemagne "Latin grammar," and other learned Italians joined the still-itinerant court. Around 780 Charlemagne seems to have invited churches and monasteries to supply copies of books in their possession; this was the beginning of a court library that by 790 included a range of patristic writings as well as a remarkable collection of pre-Christian classical texts.

Charlemagne and his court increasingly remained at Aachen, where an impressive group of palace buildings including an octagonal chapel was built. This was accompanied by speculation on the nature of the Frankish king's authority over an *imperium Christianum.* In 799 Pope Leo III was the victim of a violent attack in Rome; the latter's representatives cleared the pope of unspecified charges leveled against him, but final judgment on his attackers was reserved for the king. In the year 800 Charlemagne journeyed to Rome, where the Roman rebels were dealt with. On 25 December at mass in Saint Peter's the pope crowned Charlemagne, as he prayed and those present acclaimed him, "Augustus, great and powerful emperor of the Romans."

In 806 Charlemagne planned to divide his territorial empire, probably without passing on the title. The death of two of his sons left him with a single heir, Louis, and in 813 he was personally crowned by his father at Aachen. After Charlemagne died (28 January 814), the old courtiers remained and there was continuity of artistic activity at the new emperor's court.

BIBLIOGRAPHY

The major historical, literary, and documentary sources for the reign of Charlemagne have been edited, some of them several times, in the various series of the "Monumenta Germaniae Historica" (1826-). The Council of Europe Exhibition devoted to Charlemagne and his heritage that took place at Aachen in 1965 was the occasion of the publication of the magnificent *Karl der Grosse: Lebenswerk u. Nachleben,* 4 vols. plus index, edited by Wolfgang Braunfels and others (Düsseldorf, 1965-1968), whose 2,400 pages provide authoritative accounts of almost every aspect of the man and the age. The history of the church is dealt with in volume 1 (organization), volume 2 (learning), and volume 3 (art and architecture). A concise semipopular account is my *The Age of Charlemagne,* 2d ed. (New York, 1973), to be read in conjunction with my "'Europae Pater': Charlemagne and His Achievement in the Light of Recent Scholarship," *English Historical Review* 85 (1970): 59-105. The most recent English-language account of the reign is Rosamond McKitterick's *The Frankish Kingdoms under the Carolingians,* 751-987 (New York, 1983), chaps. 3, 4, and 6.

DONALD A. BULLOUGH

CHASTITY

In many religious traditions, the concept of chastity has generally referred to the adoption of ethical and moral norms in order to achieve a higher and purer life. It is believed to entail the purity of words, thoughts, and deeds. Chastity may also involve the practice of celibacy.

Buddhism. In Buddhism, chastity takes on different forms in the lives of monks and lay persons. Members of Buddhist monastic orders practice chastity through celibacy. According to certain Buddhist teachings, keeping the vow of chastity provides tremendous benefits for the monks, who gain insight, vast knowledge, and magical powers, among other miraculous advantages. It has thus been asserted that a chaste monk would be able to rise in the air, to make his body first expand and then shrink, to rain down water and then fire from his body, and even to make two celestial trips around the earth. However, a monk who breaks the vow of chastity after taking it, and the person who causes another to fail in his vow, would be severely punished.

For lay people, on the other hand, chastity involves a more general purity. The maintenance of the respect and dignity of the institution of marriage is of paramount importance. According to the Buddhist Eightfold Path, purity and chastity in life are required in order to gain *nirvana*.

Judaism. The notion of chastity has been a dominant theological theme in Judaism. In the early period of Israel's history, warriors were consecrated and consequently were required to be chaste (through celibacy) until after the war. In everyday life as well, people were required to be chaste in various ways. According to Jewish tradition, it was an essential requirement that the high priest be chaste. He married, but was not allowed to marry a harlot, a profane woman, a *divorcée,* or even a widow.

Chastity and purity formed a vital element of the marriage system. Except in the case of persons especially devoted to celibacy, marriage in Judaism is recognized as a matter of course and canonically as a holy tie between man and woman. The Talmud teaches that it is imperative for a man to have a wife.

Christianity. Most of the early church fathers considered celibacy a superior form of chastity. According to Clement, God will give virgins, together with holy angels, a special place in his kingdom; this is a reward greater than having sons and daughters. It is even a greater reward than the one received by those who have passed a wedded life in sanctity.

To be chaste in the Christian monastic system is not only to be celibate but also to keep oneself away from every fleshly interest. To avoid lust and keep pure thoughts is stressed as a cardinal element of chastity. The purity of thoughts was required not only of the celibate Christian but also of the married person.

Islam. In Islam, chastity in general is regarded as the state of spiritual and physical cleanliness. Celibacy is not regarded as an essential element of chastity. Islam rejects the monastic life, and even in the Sufi order marriage is recommended. Chastity is considered a necessity on the path to God, and it involves purity of thoughts and actions, resulting in a life spent according to God's commands. Chastity in relation to one's actions involves sexual restraints; physical chastity thus implies that people refrain from sexual activities outside the bonds of marriage. Moreover, the principles of chastity demand that Muslim couples abstain at certain times from sexual intercourse, for example, during the fasting days of Ramadan, or during the pilgrimage to Mecca. A chaste woman is required in some groups to wear a veil that covers most of her face as well as a dress that is long enough to conceal all of her body.

BIBLIOGRAPHY

Kirsch, Felix M. *Training in Chastity*. New York, 1930.
Main, John [Elsie Worthington Parson]. *Religious Chastity: An Ethnological Study*. New York, 1913.
Thurian, Max. *Marriage and Celibacy*. London, 1959.
Williams, Harry Abbott. *Poverty, Chastity and Obedience: The True Virtues*. London, 1975.

GABRIEL ABDELSAYED

CHINESE RELIGION

Early Historical Period

The Shang. The formation of the Shang kingdom was due to technological innovation such as bronze casting, and to the development of new forms of social and administrative control. Extant evidence provides information about the religion of the Shang aristocracy, characterized by elaborate graves and ceremonial objects for the dead.

From inscriptions on oracle bones and in bronze sacrificial vessels, we learn that the most common objects of petition and inquiry were the ancestors of aristocratic clans. These deified ancestors were believed to have powers of healing and fertility in their own right, but also could serve as intermediaries between their living descendants and more powerful gods of natural forces and Shang-ti. Ancestors were ranked by title and seniority.

To contact these sacred powers the Shang practiced divination and sacrificial rituals. The subjects of divination include weather, warfare, illness, administrative decisions, harvests, and other practical issues. Sacrificial animals included cattle, dogs, sheep, and human beings.

There is an emphasis on precision in sacrifice; the correct objects offered in the right way were believed to obligate the spirits to respond. Thus, in Shang sacrifice we already see the principle of reciprocity, which has remained a fundamental patten of interaction throughout the history of Chinese religions.

The Chou. The Chou, who were considered to be an important tributary state, were at first culturally and technologically inferior to the Shang, but learned rapidly and by the eleventh century BCE challenged the Shang for political supremacy. The final Chou conquest took place in about 1050 BCE. Remnants of the Shang royal line were allowed to continue their ancestral practices in the small state of Sung.

The religious activities of the early Chou aristocracy were focused on their ancestors, who were believed to reside in a celestial court presided over by T`ien, "Heaven," the Chou high god. These ancestors had power to influence the prosperity of their descendants, their fertility, health, and longevity. In addition, royal ancestors served as intermediaries between their descendants and T`ien.

Ancestral rituals took the form of great feasts in which the deceased was represented by an impersonator, usually a grandson or nephew. In these feasts the sharing of food and drink confirmed vows of mutual fidelity and aid. The most important ancestor worshiped was Hou Chi, who was both legendary founder of the ruling house and the patron of agriculture. As was true for the Shang, Chou rituals were also directed toward symbols of natural power such as mountains and rivers; most significant natural phenomena were deified and reverenced.

Chou-dynasty diviners eventually produced a text to support and codify their work, the *I ching* (Classic of Change), which classifies human situations by means of sixty-four sets of six horizontal lines (hexagrams), broken and unbroken. The broken line sets represent *k`un,* the female force that completes, while those with solid lines represent *ch`ien,* the male force that initiates. The *I ching* is essentially a book of wisdom for personal and administrative guidance, used since at least the seventh century BCE. However, from the sixth century BCE on commentaries were written to amplify the earliest level of the text and by the first century CE there were ten such levels of exposition, some quite philosophical in tone. The *Classic of Change* was believed to reflect the structure of cosmic movement, and hence became an object of reverent contemplation in itself.

A third focus of Chou worship, in addition to ancestors and nature gods, was the *she,* a sacred earth mound located in the capital of each state and in at least some villages. The state *she* represented the sacred powers of the earth available to a particular domain, and so was offered libations upon such important occasions in the life of the state as the birth of a prince, ascension to rule, and military campaigns. Beside the earth mound stood a sacred tree, a symbol of its connection to the powers of the sky.

The early Chou aristocracy carried out sacrificial rituals to mark the seasons of the year and promote the success of farming. These sacrifices, performed in ancestral temples, were offered both to the high god T`ien and to ancestors.

The most distinctive early Chou contribution to the history of Chinese religions was the theory of *t`ien-ming,* the "mandate of Heaven," first employed to justify the Chou conquest of the Shang. According to this theory, Heaven as a high god wills order and peace for human society. This divine order is to be administered by pious kings who care for their subjects on Heaven's behalf. These kings, called *t`ien-tzu,* "son of Heaven," are granted divine authority to rule, but only so long as they rule well. If they become indolent, corrupt, and cruel, the "mandate of Heaven" can be transferred to another line.

The idea of the mandate of Heaven has gripped the Chinese political imagination ever since. It became the basis for the legitimacy of dynasties, the judgment of autocracy, and the moral right of rebellion. This status it owed in part to its support by Confucius and his school, who saw the mandate of Heaven as the foundation of political morality. In sum, early Chou religion was robust and positive in spirit, a spirit

> **According to this theory, Heaven as a high god wills order and peace for human society. This divine order is to be administered by pious kings. . . .**

that foreshadowed the confident reciprocity of Chinese rituals in later periods, as well as the positive view of human moral potential characteristic of the tradition as a whole.

The early Chou political and social synthesis began to deteriorate in the eighth century as competing local states moved toward political, military, and ritual independence. Rulers from clans lost their power, which reverted to competing local families. This breakdown of hereditary authority led to new social mobility. Changes in religion accompanied those in economy and society. Although many older rituals were continued, they became more elaborate and were focused on the ancestors of the rulers of the states rather than on those of the Chou kings.

Confucius. It was in this context that Chinese philosophy was born, in the teachings of Confucius (c. 551-479 BCE). Confucius (the latinate form of K`ung Fu-tzu, or Master K`ung) was the son of an obscure family in the small state of Lu, a state in which the old Chou cultural traditions were buffeted by repeated invasions and by local power struggles. Confucius's goal was the restoration of the ethical standards, just rule, and legitimate government of the early Chou period as he understood them. To this end he sought public office himself and exhorted the rulers of his day. He also gathered a small group of disciples whom he taught to become *chün-tzu* ("superior men"), men of ethical sensitivity and historical wisdom who could administer benevolent government. In the process he initiated a new level of ethical awareness in Chinese culture and a new form of education, education in what he believed were universal principles for mature humanity and civilization. He assumed that the criteria for holding office were intelligence and high moral principles, not hereditary status, and so further undermined the Chou feudal system that was crumbling around him.

Confucius began a long Chinese tradition of ethical reform in the name of apparently reactionary principles. Statements recorded by his disciples show that in crisis situations the master emphasized that he had a mission from Heaven to restore social harmony. His models for such restoration were the founding kings of the Chou dynasty as described in the ancient *Book of Poetry,* kings who ruled with reverence toward their ancestors and kindness toward their people, ever fearful of losing Heaven's approval. These models had mythic force for Confucius, who saw himself as their embodiment in his own age.

All of Confucius's ethical teachings were intended to describe the "way" *(tao)* of the superior man, a way originating in the will of Heaven for its people. At its best, the inner character of such persons was to be formed by *jen* ("perfect co-humanity"), an ultimately transcendental quality that Confucius believed he had never attained. The actions of an ethically aware person were to be carried out in a balanced way in accord with refined social custom *(li).* Confucius's teachings reveal a religious consciousness that was restrained, philosophical, and prophetic; it is thus not surprising to learn that he did not participate in the exorcism and divination common in his day, nor speculate on the nature of lesser deities and spirits, although he did support veneration of ancestors.

By the fourth and third centuries BCE the end result of Confucius's gentle skepticism was a psychological interpretation of religion in his own school and the absence of any theological discussion by the formative thinkers of other traditions such as the individualists and the theorists of administrative laws and methods (Legalists).

Mo-tzu. Mo-tzu was a thorough-going utilitarian who taught that the fundamental criterion of value was practical benefit to all. He was from Confucius's home state of Lu, and educated in the emerging Confucian tradition, but turned against what he perceived to be its elitism and wasteful concern with elaborate rituals. In his ethical teaching Mo-tzu reinterpreted along utilitarian lines earlier principles such as righteousness and filial reverence, centered on the theme of universal love without familial and social distinctions. He also attracted a group of disciples whom he sent out to serve in various states in an attempt to implement his teachings.

The most significant aspect of Mo-tzu's thought is his concern to provide theological sanctions for his views. For Mo-tzu, T`ien, or Heaven, is an active creator god whose will or mandate extends to everyone; what Heaven wills is love, prosperity, and peace for all. Heaven is the ultimate ruler of the whole world; T`ien sees all, rewards the good, and punishes the evil. In this task it is aided by a multitude of lesser spirits who are also intelligent and vital and who serve as messengers between T`ien and human beings. Mo-tzu advocates that since this is the nature of divine reality, religious reverence should be encouraged by the state as a sanction for moral order.

Meng-tzu. Meng-tzu (or Meng K`e) was a teacher and would-be administrator from the small state of Tsou who amplified Confucius's teachings and placed them on a much firmer philosophical and literary base. Meng-tzu was concerned to prepare his disciples for enlightened and compassionate public service, beginning with provision for the physical needs of the people. He believed that only when their material livelihood is secure can the people be guided to higher moral awareness. This hope for moral transformation is grounded in Meng-tzu's conviction that human nature is potentially good. What is needed are rulers who nourish this potential as "fathers and mothers of the people." These teachings Meng-tzu expounded courageously before despotic kings whose inclinations were otherwise.

Hsün-tzu. The third most important Confucian philosopher before the Han dynasty (202 BCE-220 CE) was Hsün-tzu (Hsün Ch`ing, d. 215 BCE), a scholar from the state of Chao who held offices for a time in the larger states of Ch`i and Ch`u. Hsün-tzu's chief contribution was his reinterpretation of *t`ien* as the order of nature, an order that has no consciousness and is not directly related to human concerns. This interpretation is parallel to the views of the *Lao-tzu (Tao-te ching)* and *Chuang-tzu* texts concerning the cosmic "Way" (Tao). Hsün-tzu was concerned to separate the roles of heaven, earth, and man, with human attention directed toward ethics, administration, and culture.

Early Taoist thought. The earliest writings concerned to direct attention toward the mysterious cosmic "Way" that underlies all things are the first seven chapters of the extant *Chuang-tzu,* a text attributed to a philosopher-poet named Chuang Chou of the fourth century BCE. Chuang Chou was convinced that the world in its natural state is peaceful and harmonious, a state exemplified by the growth of plants and the activities of animals. Disorder is due to human aggression and manipulation. The answer to this problem is to understand and affirm the relativity of views, and thus harmonize them all. This the sage does by perceiving the constant rhythms of change within all life and identifying with them. In his view all dichotomies are unified; hence there is no need for struggle and competition. The sage intuits the Tao within and behind all things, and takes its all-embracing perspective as his own.

The other major early book devoted to discussing the Tao behind all things is the early third-century BCE *Tao-te ching* (The Way and Its Inner Power), also known as the *Lao-tzu,* after its eponymous "author," Lao Tan. The *Tao-te ching* discusses the Way in more direct, metaphysical terms than does the *Chuang-tzu,* all the while protesting that such discussion is ultimately futile. Here we are told that the Tao is the source of all things, "the mother of the universe," the ineffable cosmic womb out of which all emerges. The Tao also "works in the world," guiding all things in harmonious development and interaction. As both source and order of the world the Tao serves as a model for enlightened rulers who gain power by staying in the background and letting their people live spontaneously in response to their own needs.

There are several passages in these books that describe the enlightened person as living peacefully and long because he does not waste his vital powers on needless contention and aggression.

The Beginnings of Empire

In the fifth century BCE the disintegration of the Chou feudal and social order quickened under the pressure of incessant civil wars. The larger states formed alliances and maneuvered for power, seeking hegemony over the others, aiming to reunify the area of Chou culture by force alone. In 256 BCE the state of Ch`in, under the influence of a ruthlessly applied ideology of laws and punishments suggested in the fourth century BCE by Shang Yang, one of the founders of the Authoritarian school, eliminated the last Chou king and then finished off its remaining rivals. Finally, in 221 the state of Ch`in became the empire of Ch`in (221-207 BCE), and its ruler took a new title, "First Emperor of Ch`in" (Ch`in Shih-huang-ti). With this step China as a semicontinental state was born. There were many periods of division and strife later, but the new level of unification achieved by the Ch`in was never forgotten, and became the goal of all later dynasties.

**The Ch`in.** The Ch`in was noteworthy both for its suppression of philosophy and its encouragement of religion. For the Authoritarian (Legalist) tradition, dominant in the state of Ch`in, the only proper standard of conduct was the law, applied by officials concerned with nothing else, whose personal views were irrelevant as long as they performed their task. The only sanctions the state needed were power and effective organization. Not long after Ch`in became an empire it attempted to silence all criticism based on the assumption of inner standards of righteousness that were deemed to transcend political power and circumstance. In 213 BCE the court made it a capital offence to discuss Confucian books and principles and ordered that all books in private collections be burned, save those dealing with medicine, divination, and agriculture, as well as texts of the Authoritarian school. In this campaign, several scores of scholars were executed, and a number of philosophical schools were eliminated as coherent traditions.

By contrast, Ch`in policy toward religion, encouraged a variety of practices to support the state. To pay homage to the sacred powers of the realm and to consolidate his control, the First Emperor included worship at local shrines in his extensive tours. Representatives of regional cults, many of them spirit mediums, were brought to the court, there to perform rituals at altars set up for their respective deities. The Ch`in expanded the late Chou tendency to exalt deities of natural forces; over one hundred temples to such nature deities were established in the capital alone. Elaborate sacrifices of horses, rams, bulls, and a variety of foodstuffs were regularly offered at the major sites, presided over by officials with titles such as Grand Sacrificer and Grand Diviner.

The Han. The defeat of Ch`in forces in the civil wars leading up to the founding of the Han dynasty deposed Authoritarian political thought along with the second and last Ch`in emperor. It took several decades for the new Han dynasty to consolidate its power. Since the Authoritarians had developed the most detailed policies for administering an empire, many of these policies were followed in practice in modified form.

Some early Han scholars and emperors attempted to ameliorate royal power with a revival of Confucian concern for the people and Taoist principles of noninterference (wu-wei). A palace counselor named Chia I (200-168 BCE) echoed Meng-tzu in his emphasis that the people are the basis of the state, the purpose of which should be to make them prosperous and happy, so as to gain their approval. A similar point of view is presented in more Taoist form in the Huai-nan-tzu, a book presented to the throne in 139 BCE by a prince of the Liu clan who had convened a variety of scholars in his court. This book discusses the world as a fundamentally harmonious system of resonating roles and influences. The ruler's job is to guide it, as an experienced charioteer guides his team.

However, the oldest and most widely established of the early Han philosophical schools was the Confucian, and the Confucians survived the Ch`in suppression rather well. Numbers of their books escaped the flames of 213 BCE, and those that did not were reconstructed or written anew, with little but the old titles intact. In the third century BCE scholars such as Hsün-tzu had already incorporated the best thought of their day into fundamentally Confucian expositions that advocated a strong centralized state and an ethical teaching enforced by law. This expanded interpretation of Confucius's teachings served his followers well in the early Han. By the second century BCE Confucian scholars such as Tung Chung-shu (c. 179-104 BCE) incorporated into their teaching the theories of Tsou Yen and the "Naturalists," who in the fourth century BCE had taught that the world is an interrelated organic whole that operates according to such cosmic principles as yin and yang. The Huai-nan-tzu had already given this material a Taoist interpretation, stressing the natural resonance between all aspects of the universe. In the hands of Tung Chung-shu this understanding became an elaborate statement of the relationship of society and nature, with an emphasis on natural justification for hierarchical social roles, focused on that of the ruler.

Tung Chung-shu provided a more detailed cosmological basis for Confucian ethical and social teachings and made it clear that only a unified state could serve as a channel for cosmic forces and sanctions. Tung was recognized as the leading scholar of the realm, and became spokesman for the official class. At his urging, in 136 BCE the Confucian classics were made the prescribed texts studied at the imperial academy. As the generations passed, the tablets of the most influential scholars of the age came to be placed in these temples as well, by imperial decree, and so the cult of Confucius became the ritual focus of the scholar-official class.

Han state rituals were based upon those of Ch'in, but were greatly expanded and more elaborate. The first emperor, Kao-tsu, instituted the worship of a star god believed to be associated with Hou Chi, the legendary founder of the Chou royal line. Temples for this deity were built in administrative centers around the realm, where officials were also instructed to worship gods of local mountains and rivers. Kao-tsu brought shamans to the palace and set up shrines for sacrifices to their regional deities.

It should be noted, that the old Chou concept of the "mandate of Heaven" continued to influence Han political thought in a form elaborated and attenuated at the same time. The "mandate of Heaven" in its earlier and starker form was evoked chiefly as justification for rebellion in periods of dynastic decay. Nonetheless, portent theory in the hands of a conscientious official could be used in attempts to check or ameliorate royal despotism, and hence was an aspect of the state religious system that could challenge political power as well as support it.

The Han emperor Wu (140-87 BCE) devoted much effort to attaining immortality, as had his Ch'in predecessor. As before, shamans and specialists in immortality potions were brought to court, and expeditions were sent off to look for the dwelling places of those who had defeated death.

A common expression of hope for some sort of continuity after death may be seen in tombs of Han aristocrats and officials, many of which were built as sturdy brick replicas of houses or offices, complete with wooden and ceramic utensils, attendants, and animals, as well as food, drugs, clothing, jade, bamboo books, and other precious objects.

What came to be called the Former Han dynasty ended in 8 CE when the throne was occupied by a prime minister named Wang Mang (r. 9-23 CE), who established a Hsin ("new") dynasty that was to last for fourteen years. Wang's chief contribution to the history of Chinese religions was his active promotion of prognostication as a way of understanding the intimate relationship between Heaven and the court. In 25 CE Liu Hsiu (r. 25-57), a member of the Han royal line, led a successful attack on Wang Mang and reestablished the (Latter) Han dynasty. Like Wang Mang, he actively supported prognostication at court, despite the criticism of rationalist scholars such as Huan T'an (43 BCE-28 CE), who argued that strange phenomena were a matter of coincidence and natural causes rather than messages from Heaven.

A related development was controversy between two movements within Confucian scholarly circles, the so-called New Text school of the Former Han, and a later rationalistic reaction against it, the Old Text school. The New Text school

developed out of Tung Chung-shu's concern with portents. Its followers wrote new commentaries on the classics that praised Confucius as a supernormal being who predicted the future hundreds of years beyond his time. By the end of the first century BCE this interpretation of the sage in mythological terms was vigorously resisted by an Old Text school that advocated a more restrained and historical approach. These two traditions coexisted throughout the remainder of the Han dynasty, with the New Text scholars receiving the most imperial support through the first century CE.

The Period of Disunion

By the time the first Buddhist monks and texts appeared in China around the first century CE, the Han dynasty was already in decline. At court, rival factions competed for imperial favor, and in the provinces restless governors moved toward independence. Political and military fragmentation was hastened by the campaigns against the Yellow Turban uprising, after which a whole series of adventurers arose to attack each other and take over territory. In the first decade of the third century three major power centers emerged in the north, southeast, and southwest, with that in the north controlling the last Han emperor and ruling in his name. By 222 these three centers each had declared themselves states, and China entered a period of political division that was to last until late in the sixth century.

The Beginnings of Buddhism in China. From about 100 BCE on it would have been relatively easy for Buddhist ideas and practices to come to China with foreign merchants, but the first reliable notice of it in Chinese sources is dated 65 CE. In a royal edict of that year we are told that a prince administering a city in what is now northern Kiangsu Province

> # The movement of Buddhism to China, one of the great cultural interactions of history, was slow and fortuitous. . . .

"recites the subtle words of Huang-Lao, and respectfully performs the gentle sacrifices to the Buddha." He was encouraged to "entertain *upasakas* and *sramanas*," Buddhist lay devotees and initiates. In 148 CE the first of several foreign monks, An Shih-kao, settled in Lo-yang, the capital of the Latter Han. Over the next forty years he and other scholars translated about thirty Buddhist scriptures into Chinese, most of them from pre-Mahayana traditions, emphasizing meditation and moral principles. However, by about 185 three Mahayana Prajñaparamita (Perfect Wisdom) texts were translated as well.

A memorial dated 166, approving Buddhist "purity," "emptiness," nonviolence, and control of sensual desires, further informs us that in that year the emperor performed a joint sacrifice to Lao-tzu and the Buddha. In 193/194 a local warlord in what is now Kiangsu erected a Buddhist temple that could hold more than three thousand people. It contained a bronze Buddha image before which offerings were made and scriptures were read.

The movement of Buddhism to China, one of the great cultural interactions of history, was slow and fortuitous, carried out almost entirely at a private level. The basic reason for its eventual acceptance throughout Chinese society was that it offered several religious and social advantages unavailable to the same extent in China before. These included a full-time religious vocation for both men and women in an organization largely independent of family and state, a clear promise of life after death at various levels, and developed conceptions of paradise and purgatory, connected to life through the results of intentional actions *(karman)*.

In the early fourth century North China was invaded by the Hsiung-nu, who sacked Lo-yang in 311 and Ch`ang-an in 316. Thousands of elite families fled south below the Yangtze River, where a series of short-lived Chinese dynasties held off further invasions. In the North a succession of kingdoms of Inner Asian background rose and fell, most of which supported Buddhism because of its religious appeal and its non-Chinese origins.

It was in the South that Buddhism first became a part of Chinese intellectual history. Buddhist thought was already well developed and complexly differentiated before it reached China. The Chinese knew of it only through scriptures haphazardly collected, in translations of varying accuracy, for very few Chinese learned Sanskrit. Since all the *sutras* claimed to be preached by the Buddha himself, they were accepted as such, with discrepancies among them explained as deriving from the different situations and capacities of listeners prevailing when a particular text was preached. In practice, this meant that the Chinese had to select from a vast range of data those themes that made the most sense in their pre-existing worldview. For example, as the tradition develops we find emphases on simplicity and directness, the universal potential for enlightenment, and the Buddha mind as source of the cosmos, all of them prepared for in indigenous thought and practice. The most important early Chinese Buddhist philosophers, organizers, and translators contributed to the growth of the young church.

The first important school of Buddhist thought developed in China was the T`ien-t`ai, noted for its synthesis of earlier Buddhist traditions into one system, divided into five periods of development according to stages in the Buddha's teaching.

In 581 China was reunified by the Sui dynasty (581-618) after three and a half centuries of political fragmentation. The Sui founder supported Buddhism, particularly the T`ien-t`ai school, as a unifying ideology shared by many of his subjects in both North and South. After four decades of rule the Sui was overthrown in a series of rebellions, to be replaced by the T`ang (618-907). Although the new dynasty tended to give more official support to Confucianism and Taoism, Buddhism continued to grow at every level of society, and reached the high point of its development in China during the next two centuries.

The Rise of Taoist Religion. Taoism is China's own indigenous higher religion, characterized by the fourth century by a literate and self-perpetuating priesthood, a pantheon of celestial deities, complex rituals, and revealed scriptures in classical Chinese. Taoism is fundamentally a religion of *ch`i,* the vital breath out of which nature, gods, and humans evolve. The source and order of this vital substance is the Tao, the ultimate power of life in the universe. The gods are personified manifestations of *ch`i,* symbolizing astral powers of the cosmos and organs of the human body with which they are correlated. Under the conditions of existence *ch`i* becomes stale and worn out, so it must be renewed through ritual processes that restore its primal vitality.

All branches of Taoism eventually traced their origin to a new revelation from the Most High Lord Lao to Chang Tao-ling, the grandfather of Chang Lu, in 142 CE, establishing him as "Celestial Master." He was empowered to perform rituals and write talismans that distributed this new manifestation of the Tao for the salvation of humankind. Salvation was available to those who repented of their sins, believed in the Tao, and pledged allegiance to their Taoist master. The master in turn established an alliance between the gods and the devotee, who then wore at the waist a list (register) of the names of the gods to be called on for protection. The register also served as a passport to heaven at death. Taoist ritual consists essentially of the periodic renewal of these alliances by confession, visualization, petition, and the offering of incense and sacred documents. Taoist texts are concerned throughout for moral discipline and orderly ritual and organization.

When the Celestial Master sect was officially recognized by the state of Wei (220-266) in the early third century its leadership was established in the capital, Lo-yang, north and east of the old sect base area in modern Szechwan. In the North remnants of the Yellow Turbans still survived, and before long the teachings and rituals of these two similar traditions blended together. A tension remained, however, between those who saw secular authority as a manifestation of the Way and those determined to bring in a new era of peace and prosperity by militant activity. Uprisings led by charismatic figures who claimed long life and healing powers occurred in different areas throughout the fourth century and later.

When the northern state of Chin was conquered by the Hsiung-nu in 316, thousands of Chin gentry and officials moved south, bringing the Celestial Master sect with them. The eventual result was a blending of Celestial Master concern for priestly adminstration and collective rituals with a more individualistic and esoteric alchemical traditions growing in the southeast.

Taoism continued to be active in the North as well, in the Northern Wei kingdom (386-534), which established Taoist offices at court in 400. In 415 and 423 a scholar named K`ou Ch`ien-chih (d. 448) claimed to have received direct revelations from Lord Lao while he was living on a sacred mountain. The resulting scriptures directed K`ou to reform the Celestial Master tradition; renounce popular cults, messianic uprisings, and sexual rituals; and support the court as a Taoist kingdom on earth. K`ou was introduced to the Wei ruler and was promptly appointed to the office of "Erudite of Transcendent Beings." The next year he was proclaimed Celestial Master, and his teachings "promulgated throughout the realm." For the next two decades K`ou and Ts`ui cooperated to promote Taoism at the court. As a result, in 440 the king accepted the title Perfect Ruler of Great Peace, and during the period 444 to 446 proscribed Buddhism and local "excessive cults." Although Ts`ui Hao was eventually discredited and Buddhism established as the state religion by a new ruler in 452, the years of official support for Taoism clarified its legitimacy and political potential as an alternative to Confucianism and Buddhism. Although it continued to develop new schools and scriptural traditions, the basic shape of Taoism for the rest of Chinese history was thus established by the fifth century.

The Consolidation of Empire: Seventh to Fourteenth Century

The Chinese religious traditions that were to continue throughout the rest of imperial history all reached maturity during the T`ang (618-907) and Sung (960-1279) periods. These traditions included Buddhism, Taoism, Neo-Confucianism, Islam, and popular religion in both its village and sectarian forms.

Manichaeism and Islam. The area of the T`ang dynasty rivaled that of the Han, with western boundaries extending far into Central Asia. This expansion encouraged a revival of foreign trade and cultural contacts. Among the new foreign influences were not only Buddhist monks and scriptures but also the representatives of other religions. There is evidence for Zoroastrianism in China by the early sixth century, a result of contacts between China and Persia that originated in the second century BCE and were renewed in an exchange of envoys with the Northern Wei court in 455 and around 470. [See Zoroastrianism.]

A foreign tradition with more important influence on the history of Chinese religions was Manichaeism, a dynamic missionary religion teaching ultimate cosmic dualism founded by a Persian named Mani (216-277?). In 755 a Chinese military commander named An Lu-shan led a powerful rebellion that the T`ang court was able to put down only with the

help of foreign support. One of these allies was the Uighur, from a kingdom based in what is now northern Mongolia. In 762 a Uighur army liberated Lo-yang from rebel forces, and there a Uighur kaghan was converted to Manichaeism. The result was new prestige and more temples for the religion in China.

However, in 840 the Uighurs were defeated by the Kirghiz, with the result that the Chinese turned on the religion of their former allies, destroyed its temples, and expelled or executed its priests. Nonetheless, at least one Manichaean leader managed to escape to Ch`üan-chou in Fukien Province on the southeast coast. In Fukien the Manichaeans flourished as a popular sect until the fourteenth century, characterized by their distinctive teachings, communal living, vegetarian diet, and nonviolence. They were called the Ming-chiao ("religion of light"). They disappeared as a coherent tradition as a result of renewed persecutions during the early Ming dynasty (1368-1644). Several Manichaean texts were incorporated into the Taoist and Buddhist canons, and it is likely that Manichaean lay sects provided models for similar organizations that evolved out of Buddhism later. Manichaean dualism and demon exorcism may have reinforced similar themes in Taoism and Buddhism as they were understood at the popular level. [See Manichaeism]

The major influx of Muslim peoples occurred during the Yüan dynasty (1271-1368) and the Mongols brought in large numbers of their non-Chinese subjects to help administer China. It was in this period that Islam spread all over China and established major population bases in the western provinces of Yunnan and Kansu. Here their numbers increased through marriage with Chinese women and adoption of non-Muslim children, all converted to Islam. Although the result was a dilution of Arab physical characteristics, the use of the Chinese language, and the adoption of some Chinese social customs, for most the Islamic core remained.

Muslims in China have always been predominantly Sunni, but in the sixteenth century Sufism reached China through Central Asia. By the late seventeenth century Sufi brotherhoods began a reform movement that advocated increased use of Arabic and a rejection of certain Chinese practices that had infiltrated Islam, such as burning incense at funerals. Sufism also emphasized ecstatic personal experience of Allah, the veneration of saints, and the imminent return of the Mahdi, who would bring a new age, this last theme due to Shi`i influence as well.

These reformist beliefs, coupled with increased Chinese pressure on Islam as a whole, led eventually to a powerful uprising in Yunnan between 1855-1873, an uprising allowed to develop momentum because of old ethnic tensions in the area and the distraction of the Chinese court with the contemporary Taiping Rebellion (1851-1864). The Yunnan rebellion was eventually put down by a combination of Chinese and loyalist Muslim forces, and the Muslims resumed their role as a powerful minority in China, called the Hui people.

**T`ang Buddhism.** The first T`ang emperor, Kao-tsu (r. 618-626) approved of a plan to limit both Taoist and Buddhist temples. His son T`ai-tsung (r. 626-649) agreed with the Taoist contention that the imperial family was descended from Lao-tzu, whose legendary surname was also Li; however, T`ai-tsung also erected Buddhist shrines on battlefields and ordered monks to recite scriptures for the stability of the empire. Buddhist philosophical schools in this period were matters of both belief and imperial adornment, so, to replace

> **Owing to their efforts, Pure Land devotion became the most popular form of Buddhism in China. . . .**

the T`ien-t`ai school, now discredited on account of its association with the Sui dynasty, the T`ang court turned first to the Fa-hsiang, or Idealist school, the Indian teaching of "consciousness-only." Some texts of this tradition had been translated earlier by Paramartha (499-569), but it came to be thoroughly understood in China only after the return of the pilgrim Hsüan-tsang in 645. Hsüan-tsang was welcomed at court and provided with twenty-three scholar-monks from all over China to assist in translating the books he had brought back from India. The emperor wrote a preface for the translation of one major Vijñanavada text, and his policy of imperial support was continued by his son Kao-tsung.(r. 649-683).

However, the complex psychological analysis of the Vijñanavada school, coupled with its emphasis that some beings are doomed by their nature to eternal rebirth, were not in harmony with the Chinese worldview, which had been better represented by T`ien-t`ai. Hence, when imperial support declined at Kao-tsung's death in 683, the fortunes of the Fa-hsiang school declined as well. At the intellectual level it was replaced in popularity by the Hua-yen ("flower garland") school as formulated by the monk Fa-tsang (643-712). This school taught the emptiness and interpenetration of all phenomena in a way consonant with old Chinese assumptions.

It is no accident that the Hua-yen school was first actively supported by Empress Wu Chao (Wu Tse-t`ien, r. 690-705) who took over the throne from her sons to set up her own dynasty, the Chou. Since Confucianism did not allow for female rulers, Empress Wu, being a devout Buddhist, sought for supporting ideologies in that tradition, including not only Hua-yen but also predictions in obscure texts that the Buddha had prophesied that several hundred years after his death a woman would rule over a world empire. Monks in Wu-Tse asserted that she was a manifestation of the future Buddha Maitreya.

When Empress Wu abdicated in 705 her son continued to support the Hua-yen school, continuing the tradition of close relationship between the court and Buddhist philosophical schools. However, during this period Buddhism continued to grow in popularity among all classes of people. Thousands of monasteries and shrines were built, supported by donations of land, grain, cloth, and precious metals, and by convict workers, the poor, and serfs bound to donated lands. Tens of thousands of persons became monks or nuns, elaborate rituals were performed, feasts provided, and sermons preached in both monastery and marketplace.

By the third century CE texts describing various "pure realms" or "Buddha lands" had been translated into Chinese, and some monks began to meditate on the best known of these "lands," the Western Paradise of the Buddha Amitabha. In the fourth century Chih Tun (314-366) made an image of Amitabha and vowed to be reborn in his paradise, as did Hui-yüan in 402. These early efforts concentrated on visualization of Buddha realms in states of meditative trance.

Philosophers of the fifth and sixth centuries such as Seng-chao and Chih-i discussed the Pure Land concept as part of larger systems of thought, but the first monk to devote his life to proclaiming devotion to Amitabha as the chief means of salvation for the whole of society was T`an-luan (476-542), a monk from North China where there had long been an emphasis on the practical implementation of Buddhism. T`an-luan organized devotional associations whose members both contemplated the Buddha and orally recited his name. It was in the fifth and sixth centuries as well that many Chinese Buddhist thinkers became convinced that the final period of Buddhist teaching for this world cycle was about to begin, a period (called in Chinese mo-fa, the Latter Days of the Law) in which the capacity for understanding Buddhism had so declined that only simple and direct means of communication would suffice.

The next important preacher to base his teachings solely on Amitabha and his Pure Land was Tao-ch`o (562-645). It was he and his disciple Shan-tao (613-681) who firmly established the Pure Land movement and came to be looked upon as founding patriarchs of the tradition. Owing to their efforts, Pure Land devotion became the most popular form of Buddhism in China, from whence it was taken to Japan in the ninth century. Pure Land teachings supported the validity of lay piety as no Buddhist school had before, and hence both made possible the spread of Buddhism throughout the population and furthered the development of independent societies and sects outside the monasteries.

The last movement within orthodox Buddhism in China to emerge as an independent tradition was Ch`an (Jpn., Zen), characterized by its concentration on direct means of individual enlightenment, chiefly meditation. Such enlightenment has always been the primary goal of Buddhism, so in a sense Ch`an began as a reform movement seeking to recover the experiential origins of its tradition. Such a reform appeared all the more necessary in the face of the material success of T`ang Buddhism, with its ornate rituals, complex philosophies, and close relationships with the state.

The first references to a "Ch`an school" appeared in the late eighth century. By that time several branches of this emerging tradition were constructing genealogies going back to Sakyamuni himself; these were intended to establish the priority and authority of their teachings. The genealogy that came to be accepted later claimed a lineage of twenty-eight Indian and seven Chinese patriarchs, the latter beginning with Bodhidharma (c. 461-534), a Central Asian meditation master active in the Northern Wei kingdom. Legends concerning these patriarchs were increasingly elaborated as time passed, but the details of most cannot be verified. The first Chinese monk involved whose teachings have survived is Tao-hsin (580-651), who was later claimed to be the fourth patriarch. Tao-hsin specialized in meditation and monastic discipline, and studied for ten years with a disciple of the T`ien-t`ai founder, Chih-i. He is also noted for his concern with image worship and reciting the Buddha's name to calm the mind.

The Ch`an tradition as a whole has always been characterized by disciplined communal living in monasteries, centered on group meditation. Characteristics of early Ch`an monasteries were their independent establishment in remote areas, their rejection of a central hall containing images in favor of "Dharma halls" with meditation platforms along the sides, private consultations with abbots, and frequent group discussions. Frugality and shared responsibility for work were also emphasized in order to reduce dependence on outside donations with the reciprocal obligations they involved.

By the ninth century Ch`an was widely supported in Chinese society; during the Northern Sung dynasty (960-1127) it was the major form of monastic Buddhism and hence a focal point of institutionalization. In this context Ch`an produced a new type of literature, the "recorded discussions" (yü-lu) of patriarchs and abbots with their disciples as they struggled to attain enlightenment. It is these records, codified as "cases" (Chin., kung-an; Jpn., koan), that were meditated upon by novices as they sought to experience reality directly.

Although Buddhism flourished at all levels of Chinese society in the T`ang period, an undercurrent of resentment and hostility toward it by Confucians, Taoists, and the state always remained. This hostility came to a head in the mid-ninth century, strongly reinforced by the fact that Buddhist monasteries had accumulated large amounts of precious metals and tax exempt land. From 843 to 845 Emperor Wu-tsung (r. 840-846), an ardent Taoist, issued decrees that led to the destruction of 4,600 monasteries and 40,000 temples and shrines, and the return of 260,500 monks and nuns to lay life. Although this suppression was ended in 846 by Wu-tsung's successor, monastic Buddhism never fully regained its momentum.

**T`ang Taoism.** Taoism continued to develop during the T`ang period, in part because it received more support from some emperors than it had under the Sui. The most important Taoist order during the T`ang was that based on Mao-shan in Kiangsu, where temples were built and reconstructed, disciples trained, and scriptures edited. Devotees on Mao-shan studied Shang-ch`ing scriptures, meditated, practiced alchemy, and carried out complex rituals of purgation and cosmic renewal, calling down astral spirits and preparing for immortality among the stars. These activities were presided over by a hierarchical priesthood, led by fa-shih, "masters of doctrine," the most prominent of whom came to be considered patriarchs of the school.

Taoism in the Sung and Yüan Periods. The destruction of the old T`ang aristocracy in the turmoil of the ninth and tenth centuries helped prepare the way for a more centralized state in the Sung, administered by bureaucrats who were selected through civil service examinations. This in turn contributed to increased social mobility, enhanced by economic growth and diversification, the spread of printing, and a larger number of schools. These factors, combined with innovations in literature, art, philosophy, and religion, have led historians to describe the Sung period as the beginning of early modern China. It was in this period that the basic patterns of life and thought were established for the remainder of imperial history.

During the tenth through thirteenth centuries Taoism developed new schools and texts and became more closely allied with the state. A century later, during the reign of Emperor Hui-tsung (r. 1101-1126), the most famous imperial patron of Taoism, three new Taoist orders appeared, one with a popular base in southeastern Kiangsi, another a revival of Mao-shan teachings, and the third the Shen-hsiao Fa (Rites of the Divine Empyrean).

In 1126 the Sung capital Kaifeng was captured by the Jurchen, a people from northeastern Manchuria who, with other northern peoples, had long threatened the Sung. As a result the Chinese court moved south across the Yangtze River to establish a new capital in Hang-chou, thus initiating the Southern Sung period (1127-1279). During this period China was once again divided north and south, with the Jurchen ruling the Chin kingdom (1115-1234). It was here in the north that three new Taoist sects appeared, the T`ai-i (Grand Unity), the Ta-tao (Great Way), and the Ch`üan-chen (Total Perfection). The T`ai-i sect gained favor for a time at the Chin court because of its promise of divine healing. Ta-tao disciples worked in the fields, prayed for healing rather than using charms, and did not practice techniques of immortality. Both included Confucian and Buddhist elements in a Taoist framework.

The Ch'üan-chen sect was founded in similar circumstances by a scholar named Wang Che (1113-1170), but continued to exist into the twentieth century. Wang claimed to have received revelations from two superhuman beings, whereupon he gathered disciples and founded five congregations in northern Shantung. After his death seven of his leading disciples continued to proclaim his teachings across North China. One of them was received at the Chin court in 1187, thus beginning a period of imperial support for the sect that continued into the time of Mongol rule, particularly after another of the founding disciples visited Chinggis Khan at his Central Asian court in 1222.

In its early development the Taoist quest for personal immortality employed a combination of positive ritual techniques: visualization of astral gods and ingestion of their essence, internal circulation and refinement of ch'i, massage, eating elixirs of cinnabar and mica, and so forth, all accompanied by taboos and ethical injunctions. By the eleventh century this quest was further internalized, and alchemical potions were reinterpreted as forces within the body, a tendency well expressed in the writings of Chang Po-tuan (983-1082). Under Confucian and Ch'an influence the Ch'üan-chen school "spiritualized" the terminology of these older practices, turning its physiological referents into abstract polarities within the mind, to be unified through meditation. Perhaps in part because of this withdrawal into the mind, Ch'üan-chen was the first Taoist school to base itself in monasteries, although celibacy to maintain and purify one's powers had been practiced by some adepts earlier, and some Taoist monasteries had been established in the sixth century under pressure from the state and the Buddhist example.

The Revival of Confucian Philosophy. Confucianism had remained a powerful tradition of morality, social custom, and hierarchical status since the fall of the Han, but after the third century it no longer generated fresh philosophical perspectives. From the fourth through the tenth century the best philosophical minds in China were devoted to Buddhism. However, in the eleventh century there appeared a series of thinkers determined to revive Confucianism as a philosophical system. In this task they were inevitably influenced by Buddhist theories of mind, enlightenment, and ethics; indeed, most of these men went through Buddhist and Taoist phases in their early years and were converted to Confucianism later. Nonetheless, at a conscious level they rejected Buddhist "emptiness," asceticism, and monastic life in favor of a positive metaphysics, ordered family life, and concern for social reform. With a few exceptions the leaders of this movement, known in the West as Neo-Confucianism, went through the civil service examination system and held civil or military offices.

In retrospect we can see that Neo-Confucianism split into two general tendencies, the rationalistic and the idealistic, the first more concerned with the ordering principles (li) of life and society, the second with awakening the moral consciousness of the mind (hsin).

In the history of Chinese religions, the impact of Neo-Confucianism is evident at different levels. The intellectual and institutional success of this movement among the Chinese elite led many of them away from Buddhism and Taoism, away from any form of sectarian religion, toward a reaffirmation of the values of family, clan, and state. Another long term impact was the confucianization of popular values, supported by schools, examinations, distribution of tracts, and lectures in villages. This meant that from the Sung dynasty on the operative ethical principles in society were a combination of Confucian virtues with Buddhist karman and compassion, a tendency that became more widespread as the centuries passed.

These developments were rooted in the religious dimensions of the Neo-Confucian tradition, which from the beginning was most concerned with the moral transformation of self and society. [See Confucian Thought.]

Sung Buddhism. Sung Buddhist activities were based on the twin foundations of Ch'an and Pure Land, with an increasing emphasis on the compatability of the two. Although the joint practice of meditation and invocation of the Buddha's name had been taught by Chih-i and the Ch'an patriarch Tao-hsin in the sixth and seventh centuries, the first Ch'an master to openly advocate it after Ch'an was well established was Yen-shou (904-975). This emphasis was continued in the Yüan (1271-1368) and Ming (1368-1644) dynasties, so that by the late traditional period meditation and recitation were commonly employed together in monasteries as two means to the same end of emptying the mind of self-centered thought.

During the Sung dynasty Buddhism physically recovered from the suppression of the ninth century, with tens of thousands of monasteries, large amounts of land, and active support throughout society. By the tenth century the Ch'an school was divided into two main branches, both of which had first appeared earlier, the Lin-chi (Jpn., Rinzai), emphasizing dramatic and unexpected breakthroughs to enlightenment in the midst of everyday activities, and the Ts'ao-tung (Jpn., Soto), known for a more gradual approach through seated meditation. There was some recovery of philosophical studies in Ch'an monasteries, but it did not recapture the intellectual vitality of the T'ang period. However, for the larger history of Chinese religions the most important development in Sung Buddhism was the spread of lay societies devoted to good works and recitation of the Buddha's name.

The Period of Mongol Rule. The Mongols under Chinggis Khan (1167-1227) captured the Chin capital of Yen-ching (modern Peking) in 1215 and established the Yüan dynasty (1271-1368). From China they ruled their vast domain, which extended all the way to central Europe. For the next several decades the "Middle Kingdom" was the eastern end of a world empire.

The Mongols were attracted by the exorcistic and healing rituals of Tantric Buddhism in Tibet, the borders of which they also controlled. In 1260 a Tibetan monk, 'Phags-pa (1235-1280), was named chief of Buddhist affairs and Tibetan monks were appointed as leaders of the *samgha* all over China,

By the early fourteenth century another form of popular religion appeared, the voluntary association or sect that could be joined by individuals from different families and villages. The sects were characterized by predominantly lay membership and leadership, hierarachical organization, active proselytism, congregational rituals, possession of their own scriptures in the vernacular, and mutual economic support. Their best known antecedent was the White Lotus school, an independent sect founded by a monk named Mao Tzu-yüan (1086-1166). Mao combined simplified T`ien-t`ai teaching with Pure Land practice, invoking Amitabha's saving power with just five recitations of his name.

Ming and Ch`ing Religion

Mongol rule began to deteriorate in the early fourteenth century. After twenty years of civil war Chu Yüan-chang, from a poor peasant family, defeated all his rivals and reestablished a Chinese imperial house, the Ming dynasty (1368-1644). Chu (Ming T`ai-tsu, r. 1368-1398) was an energetic ruler of strong personal religious beliefs who revised imperial rituals, promulgated strict laws against a variety of popular practices and sects, and recruited Taoist priests to direct court ceremonies. For him the mandate of Heaven was a living force that had established him in a long line of sacred emperors.

Ming Dynasty. Under the Ming, such factors as the diversification of the agricultural base and the monetization of the economy had an impact on religious life. Sectarian scriptures appeared as part of the same movement that produced new vernacular literature of all types, morality books to inculcate Neo-Confucian values, and new forms and audiences for popular operas. More than ever before the late Ming was a time of economic and cultural initiatives from the population at large, as one might expect in a period of increasing competition for recources by small entrepreneurs. These tendencies continued to gain momentum in the Ch`ing period.

Ming Buddhism showed the impact of these economic and cultural factors, particularly in eastern China where during the sixteenth century reforming monks such as Yün-ch`i Chu-hung (1535-1615) organized lay societies, wrote morality books that quantified the merit points for good deeds, and affirmed Confucian values within a Buddhist framework. Chu-hung combined Pure Land and Ch`an practice and preached spiritual progress through sparing animals from slaughter and captivity. The integration of Buddhism into Chinese society was furthered as well by government approval of a class of teaching monks, ordained with official certificates, whose role was to perform rituals for the people.

Taoism was supported by emperors throughout the Ming, with Taoist priests appointed as officials in charge of rituals and composing hymns and messages to the gods. The Ch`üan-chen sect continued to do well, with its monastic base and emphasis on attaining immortality through developing "internal elixirs." Its meditation methods also influenced those of some of Wang Yang-ming's followers, such as Wang Chi (1497-1582). However, it was the Cheng-i sect led by hereditary Celestial Masters that had the most official support during the Ming and hence was able to consolidate its position as the standard of orthodox Taoism. Cheng-i influence is evident in scriptures composed during this period, many of which trace their lineage back to the first Celestial Master and bear imprimaturs from his successors. The forty-third-generation master was given charge of compiling a new Taoist canon in 1406, a task completed between 1444 and 1445. It is this edition that is still in use today.

By the seventeenth century, Confucian philosophy entered a more nationalistic and materialist phase, but the scholar-official class as a whole remained involved in a variety of private religious practices beyond their official ritual responsibilities. These included not only the study of Taoism and Buddhism but the use of spirit- writing séances and prayers to Wen-ch`ang, the god of scholars and literature, for help in passing examinations. Ming T`ai-tsu had proclaimed

> **More than ever before the late Ming was a time of economic and cultural initiatives from the population at large. . . .**

that each of the "three teachings" of Confucianism, Buddhism, and Taoism had an important role to play, which encouraged synthetic tendencies present since the beginnings of Buddhism in China. In the sixteenth century a Confucian scholar named Lin Chao-en (1517-1598) from Fukien took these tendencies a step further by building a middle-class religious sect in which Confucian teachings were explicitly supported by those of Buddhism and Taoism. Lin was known as "Master of the Three Teachings," the patron saint of what became a popular movement with temples still extant in Singapore and Malaysia in the mid-twentieth century. This tendency to incorporate Confucianism into a sectarian religion was echoed by Chang Chi-tsung (d. 1866) who established a fortified community in Shantung, and by K`ang Yu-wei (1858-1927) at the end of imperial history. Confucian oriented spirit-writing cults also flourished in the late nineteenth and early twentieth centuries, supported by middle level military and civil officials. These cults produced tracts and scriptures of their own.

**Ch`ing Dynasty.** The Manchus, a tribal confederation related to the Jurchen, had established their own state in the northeast in 1616 and named it Ch`ing in 1636. As their power grew, they sporadically attacked North China and absorbed much Chinese political and cultural influence. In 1644 a Ch`ing army was invited into China by the Ming court to save Peking from Chinese rebels. The Manchus not only conquered Peking but stayed to rule for the next 268 years. In public policy the Manchus were strong supporters of Confucianism, and relied heavily on the support of Chinese officials. Most religious developments during the Ch`ing were continuations of Ming traditions, with the exception of Protestant Christianity and the Taiping movement it helped stimulate.

Early Ch`ing emperors were interested in Ch`an Buddhism. The Yung-cheng emperor (r. 1723-1735) published a book on Ch`an in 1732 and ordered the reprinting of the Buddhist canon, a task completed in 1738. He also supported the printing of a Tibetan edition of the canon, and his successor, Ch`ien-lung (r. 1736-1795) sponsored the translation of this voluminous body of texts into Manchu. The Pure Land tradition continued to be the form of Buddhism most supported by the people.

The most significant innovation in Ch`ing religion was the teachings of the T`ai-p`ing T`ien-kuo (Celestial Kingdom of Great Peace and Prosperity), which combined motifs from Christianity, shamanism, and popular sectarian beliefs. The Taiping movement was begun by Hung Hsiu-ch`üan (1814-1864), a would-be Confucian scholar who first was given Christian tracts in 1836. After failing civil service examinations several times, Hung claimed to have had a vision in which it was revealed that Hung was the younger brother of Jesus Christ, commissioned to be a new messiah. Hung proclaimed a new kingdom upon earth, to be characterized by theocratic rule, enforcement of the ten commandments, the brotherhood of all, equality of the sexes, and redistribution of land. Hung and other Taiping leaders were effective preachers who wrote books, edicts, and tracts proclaiming their teachings and regulations and providing prayers and hymns for congregational worship.

They forbade ancestor veneration and the worship of Buddhas and Taoist and popular deities. Wherever the Taipings went they destroyed images and temples. They rejected geomancy and divination and established a new calendar free of the old festivals and concerns for inauspicious days. But, in the end, Taiping teachings and practices had no positive effect on the history of Chinese religions after this time, while all the indigenous traditions resumed and rebuilt.

The End of Empire and Postimperial China

The Ch`ing government, in 1911, collapsed from internal decay, foreign pressure, and military uprisings. Some Chinese intellectuals, free to invest their energies in new ideas and political forms, avidly studied and translated Western writings, including those of Marxism. One result of this westernization and secularization was attacks on Confucianism and other Chinese traditions, a situation exacerbated by recurrent civil wars that led to the destruction or occupation of thousands of temples. However, these new ideas were most influential in the larger cities; the majority of Chinese continued popular religious practices as before. Many temples and monasteries survived, and there were attempts to revive Buddhist thought and monastic discipline.

Since 1949 Chinese religions have increasingly prospered in Taiwan, particularly at the popular level. The same can be said for Chinese popular religion in Hong Kong and Singapore. The Taoist priesthood is active in Taiwan, supported by the presence of hereditary Celestial Masters from the mainland who provide ordinations and legitimacy. Buddhist monasteries and publishing houses are also doing well in Taiwan and Hong Kong.

The constitution of the People's Republic establishes the freedom both to support and oppose religion, although in practice religious activities of all types declined there after 1949, particularly during the Cultural Revolution of 1966 to 1969. In general religion has been depicted along Marxist lines as "feudal superstition" that must be rejected by those seeking to build a new China. Nonetheless, many religious activities continued until the Cultural Revolution, even those of the long proscribed popular sects. The Cultural Revolution was a massive attack on old traditions, including not only religion, but education, art, and established bureaucracies. At the same time a new national cult arose, that of Chairman Mao and his thought, involving ecstatic processions, group recitation from Mao's writings, and a variety of quasi-religious ceremonials. These included confessions of sins against the revolution, vows of obedience before portraits of the Chairman, and meals of wild vegetables to recall the bitter days before liberation. Although the frenzy abated, the impetus of the Cultural Revolution continued until Mao's death in 1976, led by a small group, later called "the Gang of Four," centered around his wife. This group was soon deposed.

Since 1980 many churches, monasteries, and mosques have reopened, and religious leaders reinstated, in part to establish better relationships with Buddhist, Christian, and Muslim communities in other countries.

[*For further discussion of the various traditions treated in this article, see* Buddhism, Taoism, *and* Confucian Thought. *For a discussion of the influence of the major monotheistic religions on Chinese religion, see* Islam, Christianity, *and* Judaism. *For the influence of Inner Asian civilizations on*

Chinese thought, see Inner Asian Religions, Mongol Religions, *and* Buddhism.]

BIBLIOGRAPHY

Berling, Judith. *The Syncretic Religion of Lin Chao-en.* New York, 1980. A detailed study of a Confucian religious teacher in the sixteenth century.

Bilsky, Lester James. *The State Religion of Ancient China.* 2 vols. Taipei, 1975. A detailed discussion of official rituals and deities from the Chou through the early Han dynasties.

Bodde, Derk. *Festivals in Classical China. New Year and Other Annual Observances during the Han Dynasty, 206 B. C.-A. D. 220.* Princeton, 1975. The best study in English of annual festivals in their early development.

Boltz, Judith M. "A Survey of Taoist Literature, Tenth to Seventeenth Centuries." Berkeley, 1985. A very helpful discussion of Taoist texts, schools, and writers.

Chan, Wing-tsit, trans. and comp. *A Sourcebook in Chinese Philosophy. Princeton,* 1963. The standard selection of Chinese philosophical texts in translation. Accurate and comprehensive.

Ch`en, Kenneth K. S. *Buddhism in China, A Historical Survey.* Princeton, 1964. Detailed and comprehensive. The best general view of the topic in English. Good bibliography.

Ch`en, Kenneth K. S. *The Chinese Transformation of Buddhism.* Princeton, 1973. An excellent study of how Buddhist values, rituals, and economic activities adapted to the Chinese environment.

Ch`en Kuo-fu. *Tao-tsang yüan-liu k`ao.* 2 vols. Peking, 1983. Still the standard study of the development of the Taoist canon.

Ch`en Yüan. *Nan Sung ch`u Hopei hsin Tao-chiao k`ao.* Peking, 1941. The first detailed study of the topic; includes a discussion of the Ch`üan-chen school.

Dumoulin, Heinrich. *A History of Zen Buddhism.* New York, 1963. The standard history of Ch`an/Zen in English.

Dunne, George H. *Generation of Giants. The Story of the Jesuits in China in the Last Decades of the Ming Dynasty.* Notre Dame, Ind., 1962. The standard treatment of the topic in English, based primarily on European sources.

Elliott, Allan J. A. *Chinese Spirit Medium Cults in Singapore.* London, 1955. Thorough field-work study of spirit medium initiation and rituals.

Fairbank, John K., ed. *The Missionary Enterprise in China and America.* Cambridge, Mass., 1974. One of several books on American Protestant missions in China produced by Professor Fairbank and his students. Treats missionaries in their political and social contexts.

Fukui Kojun. *Dokyo no kisoteki kenkyu.* Tokyo, 1952. Pioneering studies of the beginnings and early development of Taoism, the T`ai-p`ing ching, and relationships with Buddhism.

Fukui Kojun, Yamazaki Hiroshi, Kimura Eiichi, and Sakai Tadao, eds. *Dokyo.* 3 vols. Tokyo, 1983. The most comprehensive discussion of Taoism available. Includes a lavish bibliography.

Fung Yu-lan. *History of Chinese Philosophy.* 2 vols. Translated by Derk Bodde. Princeton, 1952. The most authoritative and comprehensive study of the topic in English.

Groot, J. J. M. de. *The Religious System of China* (1892-1910). 6 vols. Reprint, Taipei, 1964. Massive study, with translations of Chinese texts provided. Particularly good on funeral rituals, *feng-shui,* demonology, and shamanism.

Hsü, Francis L. K. *Under the Ancestors' Shadow: Chinese Culture and Personality.* New York, 1948. A fine study of ancestor cult in its social context.

Israeli, Raphael. *Muslims in China: A Study in Cultural Confrontation.* London, 1978. The only recent book-length study of the topic in English.

Johnson, David. "The City-God Cults of T`ang and Sung China." *Harvard Journal of Asiatic Studies* 45 (December 1985): 363-457. The most thorough and recent study of the topic.

Jordon, David K. *Gods, Ghosts and Ancestors: Folk Religion in a Taiwanese Village* (1972). Reprint, Taipei, 1986. A good anthropological study of village religion. Sensitive and lively discussion.

Jordan, David K. and Daniel L. Overmyer. *The Flying Phoenix: Aspects of Chinese Sectarianism in Taiwan.* Princeton and Taipei, 1986. The first systematic study of modern Chinese popular religious sects.

Kubo Noritada. *Dokyoshi.* Tokyo, 1977. Rich material on Taoist history, rituals, beliefs, and relationships with popular religion.

Latourette, Kenneth Scott. *A History of Christian Missions in China.* London, 1929. Long the standard authority on the topic.

Li Shih-yü. *Pao-chüan tsung-lu.* The most comprehensive bibliography of popular religious texts, with good introductory discussions.

Lieu, Samuel N. C. *The Religion of Light: An Introduction to the History of Manichaeism in China.* Hong Kong, 1979. A short introduction to the topic, with an excellent bibliography.

Lieu, Samuel N. C. *Manichaeism in the Later Roman Empire and Medieval China.* Manchester, 1985. The most complete modern study of the topic.

Makita Tairyo. *Gikyo kenkyu.* Koyto, 1976. The best study of Buddhist texts written in China, most of them found at Tun-huang.

Maspero, Henri. *Taoism and Chinese Religion* (1971). Translated by Frank A. Kierman. Amherst, Mass., 1981. Maspero was the pioneering Western scholar of Taoist religion; this is a collection of his essays. Those on immortality cultivation and popular religion remain particularly valuable.

Needham, Joseph. *Science and Civilisation in China.* Cambridge, Mass., 1956-. One of the great scholarly projects of the twentieth century. Rich bibliographies. See particularly vol. 2 (1956) on the history of Chinese thought and the classical worldview, and vol. 5, parts 2-5 (1974-) on Taoist immortality practices and alchemy. Comparative analysis throughout.

Noguchi Tetsuro. *Min-dai Byakuren kyoshi no kenkyu.* Tokyo, 1986. The most comprehensive study of popular religious sects during the Ming period (1368-1644), in their historical, economic, and political contexts.

Obuchi Ninji. *Dokyoshi no kenkyu.* Okayama, 1964. Authoritative study by a Japanese master of the topic.

Ogasawara Senshu. *Chugoku jodokyoka no kenkyu.* Kyoto, 1951. A study of the early Pure Land masters Hui-yüan, T`an-luan, Tao-ch`o, and Shan-tao.

Ogasawara Senshu. *Chugoku kinsei jodokyoshi no kenkyu.* Kyoto, 1963. Authoritative study of later Pure Land history and beliefs.

Overmyer, Daniel L. *Folk Buddhist Religion: Dissenting Sects in Late Traditional China.* Cambridge, Mass., 1976. A survey of popular religious sects in the Ming and Ch`ing dynasties.

Reischauer, Edwin O. *Ennin's Travels in T`ang China.* New York, 1955. An excellent account of Buddhism and Chinese life during the ninth century, taken from the travel diary of a Japanese monk.

Sakai Tadao. *Chugoku zensho no kenkyu.* Tokyo, 1960. A pioneering discussion of the long tradition of books for moral exhortation, written and distributed by both literati and commoners.

Sawada Mizuho. *Zoho Hokan no kenkyu.* Tokyo, 1975. Along with the work of Li Shih-yü, the major study of Chinese popular religious scriptures *(pao-chüan),* their types and origins.

Schipper, Kristofer. *Le corps taoïste; corps physique—corps social.* Paris, 1982. A fine survey of Taoist history, ritual, and meditation by the first Western scholar to become an initiated Taoist priest and thus gain access to the oral tradition.

Seidel, Anna. "The Image of the Perfect Ruler in Early Taoist Messianism." *History of Religions* 9 (1969-1970): 216-247. An important study of early Taoist eschatology.

Shih, Vincent Y. C. *The Taiping Ideology*. Seattle, 1967. The most detailed study in English of the religious beliefs of this mid-nineteenth century movement.

Sivin, Nathan. *Chinese Alchemy, Preliminary Studies*. Cambridge, Mass., 1968. A now standard study of the topic.

Strickmann, Michel. "The Mao-shan Revelations: Taoism and the Aristocracy." *T'oung pao* 63 (1977): 1-64. Taoist history, fourth and fifth centuries.

Strickmann, Michel. *Le Taoïsme du Mao-Chan. Chronique d'une révélation*. Paris, 1981. A path-breaking study that reshapes our understanding of Taoist history. Good discussion of important texts.

Strickmann, Michel, ed. *Tantric and Taoist Studies in Honour of R. A. Stein*. 2 vols. Brussels, 1983. Volume two contains several excellent and substantive essays on Taoism.

Suzuki Chusei. "Sodai Bukkyo kessha no kenkyu." *Shigaku zasshi* 52 (1941): 65-98, 205-241, 303-333. Important study of the spread of lay Buddhist devotional associations.

T'ang Yung-t'ung. *Han Wei liang Chin Nan-pei-ch'ao fochiao shih.* Shanghai, 1938. Long the standard Chinese study of this topic.

Thompson, Laurence G. *Chinese Religion: An Introduction*. 3d ed. Belmont, Calif., 1979. The best one-volume introduction to the topic. Fourth edition in preparation, 1986.

Thompson, Laurence G. *Chinese Religion in Western Languages, A Comprehensive and Classified Bibliography of Publications in English, French and German through 1980*. Tucson, 1985. The only comprehensive bibliography of the subject, organized by topics.

Thompson, Laurence G. *The Chinese Way in Religion*. Belmont, Calif., 1973. A good source book, combining translations of Chinese primary texts with selections from the best scholarly studies.

Tsukamoto Zenryu. *A History of Early Chinese Buddhism: From its Introduction to the Death of Hui-yüan* (1979). 2 vols. Translated by Leon Hurvitz. Tokyo, 1985. By far the most detailed study (1305 pages) of the history of Chinese Buddhism through the early fifth century. Both author and translator are masters of the field.

Ui Hakuju. *Zenshushi kenkyu*. 3 vols. Tokyo, 1939-1943. The standard Japanese study of the Ch'an school.

Wang Ming. *T'ai-p'ing ching ho-chiao*. Peking, 1960. A work of fundamental importance for the study of the first Taoist scripture produced during the formative period of this tradition in the second century.

Wechsler, Howard J. *Offerings of Jade and Silk: Ritual and Symbol in the Legitimation of the T'ang Dynasty*. New Haven, 1985. The most thorough study in English of medieval Chinese state religion.

Welch, Holmes. *The Practice of Chinese Buddhism, 1900-1950*. Cambridge, Mass., 1967. Thorough study of monastic Buddhism based on interviews with monks.

Welch, Holmes, and Anna Seidel, eds. *Facets of Taoism: Essays in Chinese Religion*. New Haven, 1979. Authoritative essays from the Second International Conference on Taoism, 1972.

Wolf, Arthur P., ed. *Religion and Ritual in Chinese Society*. Stanford, Calif., 1974. An excellent collection of essays by anthropologists, based on fieldwork in Taiwan and Hong Kong on such topics as village temples, shamanism, and the relationship between gods and ghosts. Includes two articles on Taoist ritual.

Yampolsky, Philip B. *The Platform Sutra of the Sixth Patriarch. The Text of the Tun-huang Manuscript, Translated, with Notes*. New York, 1967. The introduction (pp. 1-121) is a reliable guide to modern studies of Ch'an history.

Yanagida Seizan. *Shoki Zenshu shiso no kenkyu*. Kyoto, 1967. Pathbreaking critical study of Ch'an historical legends.

Yang, C. K. *Religion in Chinese Society. A Study of Contemporary Social Functions of Religion and Some of their Historical Factors*. Berkeley, 1961. A classic sociological study, the best and most comprehensive available. Good discussions of relationships between religion and the state, ethical values, diffuse and institutional forms of religious organization.

Yoshioka Yoshitoyo. *Dokyo to bukkyo*. Tokyo, 1959. Seminal essays on Taoist and Buddhist relations and polemical writings from the Han to the present.

Yoon, Hong-key. *Geomantic Relationships Between Culture and Nature in Korea*. Taipei, 1976. The best study of feng-shui in English, based on Chinese texts and fieldwork in Korea.

Zürcher, Erik. *The Buddhist Conquest of China*. 2 vols. Leiden, 1959. Excellent, detailed study of the first Chinese attempts to understand Buddhist philosophy.

Zürcher, Erik. "'Prince Moonlight.' Messianism and Eschatology in Early Medieval Chinese Buddhism." *T'oung pao* 68 (1982): 1-75. A pioneering study of fifth-century eschatology, based on Buddhist scriptures composed in China.

DANIEL L. OVERMYER

CHINGGIS KHAN

CHINGGIS KHAN (1162?-1227), great Mongol leader and founder of a vast empire in Asia, Chinggis Khan is a striking example of an emperor who became a god.

Born in Mongolia, northeast of present-day Ulan Bator, and called Temüjin in his youth, he was the eldest son of a chieftain of the Mongol Borjigit clan. Having succeeded in

> **. . . he adopted the title of Chinggis Khan and set out to conquer the world.**

uniting the Mongol and Turkic tribes of the area, he adopted the title of Chinggis Khan and set out to conquer the world. He subdued the Chin empire in North China, the Hsi-hsia kingdom northeast of Tibet, the Turkic states in Turkistan, and the empire of Khorezm, comprising Transoxiana as well as Afghanistan and Eastern Iran. Mongol units even advanced as far as India and the Crimea. When Chinggis Khan died in 1227 near Ning-hsia, capital of Hsi-hsia, he left the broad foundations of an empire that would extend, under his sons and grandsons, from Korea to the Near East and southern Europe and from southern Siberia to Indochina.

The thirteenth-century *Secret History of the Mongols,* the first work of Mongolian literature, patterns Chinggis Khan's biography after the model of the hero-king, and thus reflects the indispensable qualities of a ruler and the hopes set upon him. Chinggis Khan possesses the mandate of Heaven and Heaven's support to restore law, order, and peace on earth. He is of noble totemistic descent. Born on the holy mountain, the center of the world, Chinggis Khan goes forth to conquer nations and peoples in all directions, and to this same place his dead body returns. He has a good wife, a good horse, and good companions, and he finds himself in a situation favorable for his activities.

After Chinggis Khan's death, his character develops in three ways: Chinggis Khan becomes a means of political identification, a figure of political theology, and a deity. Chinggis Khan is used as a means of political identification by the Mongols as well as by the Chinese. To the Mongols, as the founder of their unified state, he is a symbol of Mongol national independence, or at least autonomy. To the Chinese, he is the glorious first emperor of a Chinese dynasty of Mongol nationality, a symbol of the multinational character of Chinese history.

Three aspects portray the deification of Chinggis Khan. First, he became the ancestral deity of the ruling Borjigit clan, the state, and the whole Mongol people, guarding them against all evil. Second, Chinggis was incorporated into the Lamaist-Buddhist pantheon as a local guardian deity of comparatively low rank. In the practice of folk religion he became fused with the ancestral deity. Third, traits of an initiatory god were imputed to Chinggis Khan; as this deity, he introduced marriage customs, seasonal festivals connected with the nomadic economy, and certain ritual practices of daily life.

[*See also* Inner Asian Religions *and* Mongol Religions.]

BIBLIOGRAPHY

Basic observations on the religious role of Chinggis Khan have been made by Walther Heissig in his *Die Religionen der Mongolei* (Stuttgart, 1970), translated by Geoffrey Samuel as *The Religions of Mongolia* (Berkeley, 1980). The ideological development of Chinggis Khan's character is dealt with by Herbert Franke in his excellent study *From Tribal Chieftain to Universal Emperor and God: The Legitimation of the Yüan Dynasty* (Munich, 1978). Indispensable for everyone interested in Chinggis Khan's biography and thirteenth-century Mongol political and religious thought are the anonymous *Secret History of the Mongols* and two Persian chronicles written by al-Juwayni and Rashid al-Din. The following English translations are available: *The Secret History of the Mongols, for the First Time Done into English out of the Original Tongue and Provided with an Exegetical Commentary*, 2 vols., by Francis Woodman Cleaves (Cambridge, Mass., 1982-); "The Secret History of the Mongols," translated by Igor de Rachewiltz, *Papers on Far Eastern History* 4 (September 1971): 115-163, 5 (March 1972): 149-175, 10 (September 1974): 55-82, 13 (March 1976): 41-75, 16 (September 1977): 27-65, 18 (September 1978): 43-80, 21 (March 1980): 17-57, 23 (March 1981): 111-146, and 26 (September 1982): 39-84 (chaps. 1-10; chaps 11 and 12 are still to be published); *The History of the World-Conqueror, by `Ala-ad-Din `Ata-Malik Juvaini*, translated by John Andrew Boyle in two volumes (Cambridge, Mass., 1958); and *The Successors of Gengis Khan*, translated from the Persian of Rashid al-Din Tabib by John Andrew Boyle (New York, 1971). An excellent biography of Chinggis Khan written by a Western historian is René Grousset's *Le conquérant du monde* (Paris, 1944), translated into English by Denis Sinor and Marian MacKellar as *Conqueror of the World* (Edinburgh, 1967). The most recent study on Chinggis Khan's life and activities is Paul Ratchnevsky's *Cinggis-Khan: Sein Leben und Wirken* (Wiesbaden, 1983).

KLAUS SAGASTER

CHRISTIAN ETHICS

The three primary manifestations of Christianity—Eastern Orthodoxy, Roman Catholicism, and Protestantism—have recognized that Christian faith involves a particular way of life. The good news of salvation in Jesus Christ calls for a life of discipleship. The scriptures point out that Christian believers are to live and act in certain ways. Conversion to Jesus Christ and membership in the Christian community involve moral exigencies.

Christian Ethics in General. The Bible is the book of Christianity, but it does not contain Christian ethics as such. The Bible does include moral teachings and descriptions of the moral life of believers in Yahveh and in Jesus. The distinction between morality and ethics is most significant. Morality refers to the actions, dispositions, attitudes, virtues, and ways of life that should characterize the moral person and society, in this case the Christian person and the Christian community. Christian ethics operates on the level of the theoretical and the scientific and tries to explain the Christian moral life in a thematic, systematic, coherent, and consistent manner. It is possible for one to attempt a biblical ethic that makes such an explanation of biblical morality, but that ethic would be based on the moral teaching found in scripture. Biblical ethics and Christian ethics are not coextensive. The subject matter of Christian ethics is the Christian moral life and teaching, which is much broader than biblical moral life and teaching.

The relationship between Christian ethics and philosophical ethics is most important. The significant differences between the two result from the different sources of ethical wisdom and knowledge employed. Philosophical ethics is based on human reason and human experience and does not accept the role of faith and revelation that is central to Christian ethics. However, Christian ethics poses the same basic questions and has the same formal structure as philosophical ethics. All ethics attempts to respond to the same questions: what is the good? what values and goals should be pursued? what attitudes and dispositions should characterize the person? what acts are right? what acts are wrong? how do the individual and society go about making ethical decisions?

Contemporary ethicists speak about three generally accepted formal approaches to ethics. The classical forms are teleology and deontology. The teleological approach determines what is the end or the good at which one should aim and then determines the morality of means in relationship to the end. The deontological model understands morality primarily in terms of duty, law, or obligation. Such an approach is primarily interested in what is right. Recently some contemporary ethicists (e.g., H. Richard Niebuhr) have proposed a third model: the responsibility model, which is primarily interested in what is "fitting." Within Christian ethics all these different models have been employed.

Sources. What distinguishes Christian ethics from philosophical ethics and other religious ethics are the sources of wisdom and knowledge that contribute to Christian ethics. All Christian ethics recognizes the Christian scriptures, tradition, and church teaching as the revelatory sources of moral wisdom and knowledge. However, there is much discussion as to how these sources relate to one another and to the non-revelatory sources of Christian ethics. The three major expressions of Christianity—Eastern Orthodoxy, Roman Catholicism, and Protestantism—and their corresponding ethical traditions emphasize different sources of Christian ethics. At least in theory, all these traditions give primary emphasis to sacred scripture, but there is no general agreement about how the scriptures should be used in Christian ethics.

Christian ethics has always grappled with the question of whether human nature, human reason, and human experience can be sources of ethical wisdom and knowledge. The Roman Catholic tradition has emphasized natural law based on the ability of human reason to arrive at ethical wisdom and knowledge. This emphasis has often been more primary than the influence of revelatory sources. Eastern Orthodox and Protestant ethics have been more suspicious of human reason and experience, although today many ethicists in these traditions give reason an important though still subordinate role.

The Eastern Orthodox Tradition. Eastern Orthodox theology, in both its Greek and Russian approaches, is distinguished from other Christian ethics by its emphasis on tradition, especially the teachings of the church fathers, as important sources of moral wisdom and knowledge. The most distinctive characteristic of Orthodox ethics is its relationship to spirituality. Pastoral practice has emphasized the role of monks and confessors as spiritual directors who help guide the spiritual life of the faithful. The goal or end of the moral life is to become like God.

Within the Orthodox tradition there is doubt that natural law is a source of ethical wisdom and knowledge. Many affirm such knowledge on the basis of creation and the image of God embodied in human moral capacity, but others strongly deny this knowledge. At times the polemical nature of discussions between the Orthodox and Roman Catholic traditions seems to have influenced the Orthodox denial of natural law.

Orthodox ethics has been accused of lacking a world-transforming aspect and failing to develop an adequate social ethic, but many defenders of the Orthodox tradition deny this charge. In the past, social ethics was colored by recognition of a "symphony" between the church and the state in the single organism of the Christian empire. Today the diverse settings in which the Orthodox church functions have forced it to try to work out a social ethic and the church's relationship to the state.

Historical Development of Eastern Orthodox Ethics. Christian ethics as a separate discipline emerged comparatively late in the Orthodox tradition. After the Great Schism of the ninth century the penitentials continued to be an important genre of moral teaching in the East. Despite some legalistic and ritualistic tendencies, Orthodoxy's emphasis on spirituality and striving for perfection served as a safeguard against a minimalistic legalism.

In Russian Orthodoxy the seventeenth-century Kiev school attempted to refute Roman Catholicism and its ethics by developing a theology strongly influenced by scholasticism. *The Orthodox Confession* of Petr Moghila (d. 1646), which was approved with slight modifications by the Greek patriarch at the Synod of Jerusalem (1672), explains Christian moral teaching on the basis of the nine precepts of the church, the seven sacraments, the Beatitudes, and the Ten Commandments. However, even the Kiev school stressed more distinctly Russian and patristic theology in its ascetical and spiritual works.

The eighteenth and nineteenth centuries in Russian Orthodox ethics again saw both dialogue and polemics with Roman Catholic and Protestant ethics in the West. Feofan Prokopovich (d. 1736) ignored the Orthodox tradition, rejected Catholic scholasticism, and turned to Protestant authors for his ethical principles.

In the twentieth century, Nikolai Berdiaev and Sergei Bulgakov appealed to the Russian Orthodox tradition in developing what can be called a communitarian personalism with emphasis on subjectivity, freedom, love, and the need to transform the objective world.

According to Stanley S. Harakas, Christian ethics as a separate theological discipline in Greek Orthodoxy developed in the modern period and emerged as a separate, distinct, scientific discipline only in the nineteenth century. Three different schools or approaches characterize Greek Orthodox moral theology from that time. The Athenian school, strongly influenced by philosophical idealism, sees no vital differences between Christian ethics and philosophical ethics. The Constantinopolitan school is Christocentric and depends heavily on scripture and the church fathers. The Thessalonian school is apophatic in character, stresses a personalist perspective, and is heavily dependent on the monastic tradition. In his *Toward Transfigured Life,* Harakas tries to bring these three schools together.

The Roman Catholic Tradition. The characteristics of Roman Catholic "moral theology," as Christian ethics has come to be called in the Catholic tradition, are insistence on mediation, acceptance of natural law, and the role of the church. Mediation is perhaps the most characteristic aspect of Roman Catholic theology in general. There is a distinctive Catholic emphasis on conjunctions—of scripture and tradition, faith and reason, faith and works, grace and nature, the divine and human, Jesus and the church and Mary and the saints, love as well as the virtues and the commandments. This approach is an attempt to be universal and to embrace all elements, but it may fall into dichotomy. For example, rather than seeing tradition as a mediation of revelation whose privileged witness is in sacred scripture, scripture and tradition were seen as two separate fonts of revelation. Further, faith and works, properly understood, mean that the gift of salvation is mediated in and through the human response; a perennial danger is to absolutize works. Likewise, mediation insists on the importance of love, but love mediated through all the other virtues and commandments, which, however, must not be emphasized only in themselves.

In the Roman Catholic tradition, natural law can best be understood as human reason directing human beings to their end in accord with their nature. In the classic tradition based on Thomas Aquinas (d. 1274), human nature has a threefold structure: that which is shared with all substances, that which is common to humans and all the animals, and that which is proper to human beings as such.

The third characteristic of Roman Catholic moral theology is its insistence on relationship to the church. Catholic ecclesiology recognizes a special teaching office in matters of faith and morals that is given to, specifically, the pope and the bishops. Catholic ecclesiology in accord with the teaching of Vatican I (1870) recognizes an infallible teaching function that is exercised through ecumenical councils and the *ex cathedra* teaching of the pope as well as definitive teachings by the pope and the bishops. A noninfallible, authoritative teaching office is also exercised by the councils and especially by the pope through encyclicals, allocutions, and the various offices of the Curia Romana. The vast majority of Catholic moral theologians agree that there has never been an infallible papal teaching on a specific moral matter.

Church rites and practice have also influenced Catholic moral theology. Ever since the seventeenth century the primary purpose of moral theology textbooks has been to train confessors for the sacrament of penance, with emphasis on their role as judges. This narrow orientation resulted in an act-centered approach that was casuistic, based primarily on

law, and aimed at determining the existence and gravity of sins.

Historical Development of Roman Catholic Ethics. Roman Catholic moral theology or Christian ethics developed into a scientific discipline earlier than in Eastern Orthodoxy. In the thirteenth century, systematic and scientific theology appeared with the work of the great Scholastic theologians, especially Thomas Aquinas. Moral theology in Thomas's thought is an integrated part of his systematic theology, not a separate discipline. The basic structure of Thomas's moral theology is teleological. The ultimate end of human beings is a happiness attained when the intellect knows perfect truth and the will loves the perfect good. For the Christian, the beatific vision fulfills and perfects human nature. The Franciscan school, represented by Alexander of Hales (d. 1245), Bonaventure (d. 1274), and John Duns Scotus (d. 1308), affirmed the primacy of the will and of charity and emphasized moral theology as wisdom.

The fourteenth century saw a criticism of Thomas from a nominalist perspective that grounded the good not in ontological reality but solely in the will of God and employed a more deontological approach to ethics. After the thirteenth century there appeared the penitentials, very practical handbooks without any philosophical basis or analysis, which often arranged in alphabetical order the problems that the confessor would face in practice.

The three-volume *Institutiones theologiae* moralis appeared in the seventeenth century. These manuals, which became the standard textbooks of Catholic moral theology until the Second Vatican Council, began with a brief description of the ultimate end, which was followed by treatises on human acts, law as the objective norm of morality, and conscience as the subjective norm of morality. The virtues are mentioned, but sin remains the central concern. The sacraments are discussed, but almost exclusively from the viewpoint of moral and legal obligations. In the seventeenth and eighteenth centuries a controversy that arose between rigorists and laxists was finally resolved after papal intervention through the moderate approach of Alfonso Liguori (1696-1787), who was later named the patron of Catholic moral theology and of confessors.

Beginning with Leo XIII's encyclical *Rerum novarum* in 1891, a series of official teachings on the social question appeared. Leo and his immediate successors used a natural-law methodology, understood the state as a natural human society, proposed an anthropology that insisted on both the personal and communitarian aspects of human existence (thus avoiding the extremes of capitalism and socialism), recognized the right of workers to organize, and called for the state to intervene when necessary to protect the rights of workers or any particular class that was suffering. The tradition of official social teaching still exists, but now it stresses some of the newer methodological emphases in Catholic theology and deals with contemporary political and economic problems, especially in a global perspective.

Bernhard Häring's *The Law of Christ* (1954) was the most significant single work in the renewal of Catholic moral theology in the pre-Vatican II period. Häring proposed a biblically inspired, Christocentric approach to moral theology based on the divine call to be perfect even as the gracious God is perfect.

The Second Vatican Council greatly influenced the renewal of moral theology. Now there was greater dialogue with other Christians, non-Christians, and the modern world in general. Contemporary Catholic moral theology, while upholding the goodness of the natural and of the human, has tried to overcome the dichotomy or dualism between the supernatural and the natural. The gospel, grace, Jesus Christ, and the Holy Spirit are related to what happens in daily life in the world. Contemporary moral theology recognizes the need to consider more than acts and lays more emphasis on the person and the virtues and attitudes of the person. No longer is there a monolithic Catholic moral theology based on a Thomistic natural law; instead, many different philosophical approaches are used. In general there has been a shift from classicism to historical consciousness, from the objective to the subjective, from nature to person, from order to freedom. In addition to developments in methodology, there are also widespread debates in contemporary Catholic moral theology about the existence of intrinsically evil actions, absolute norms, and the possibility of dissent from noninfallible church teaching. As a result of these differences, some contemporary Catholic moral theologians are calling into question some official Catholic teachings in such areas as sexual and medical ethics, but the official teaching office has not changed on these issues.

The Protestant Tradition. Protestant Christian ethics has as its distinctive characteristics an emphasis on freedom, an anticasuistic approach, the primacy of scripture, and an emphasis on the theological nature of the discipline. Martin Luther (d. 1546) and the reformers in general stressed the freedom of the Christian, and freedom has characterized much of Protestant life and ethics. In Protestantism there is no central church teaching authority to propose authoritative teaching on specific issues or to insist upon a particular approach, as in Roman Catholicism. Consequently, in Protestant ethics there is a great pluralism and a diversity of approaches.

The emphasis on freedom colors the Protestant understanding of God and how God acts in human history. God is free to act and to intervene in history. Generally Protestant ethics opposes any attempt to claim that God must always act in a particular way. The stress on God's freedom has also influenced a general Protestant unwillingness to base absolute norms on human reason and nature. The freedom

of the believer as well as God is safeguarded in Protestant ethics.

The early reformers objected to the Roman Catholic emphasis on merit. They held that salvation comes from faith, not from human works. Protestantism ultimately rejected the Catholic sacrament of penance and thus never developed the casuistry involved in carrying out the role of the confessor as judge. Protestant ethics has been described as an ethics of inspiration, primarily because it does not usually get into a minute philosophical discussion of the morality of particular acts.

The Reformation insistence on the importance of the scripture characterizes much of Protestant ethics, but scripture has been used in different ways. When God's immanence is stressed, there is a tendency to find in scripture a moral message that can be lived by Christians in this world. When the transcendence of God is stressed, scripture tends to be used more dialectically to include a judging and critical role with regard to every human enterprise. Perhaps the greatest change in Protestantism came to the fore in the nineteenth-century dispute over a critical approach to scripture. Whereas liberal Protestantism and soon most of mainstream Protestantism employed literary and historical criticism to understand the Bible, fundamentalist Protestantism has continued to see the Bible primarily in terms of propositional truths or ethical norms and rules that God has revealed for all time and that Christians are called to obey. Such a deontological approach based on God's absolute laws given in scripture cannot be accepted by Protestants who approach scripture with the hermeneutical tools of biblical scholarship. Many contemporary Protestants see in scripture the description of the mighty acts of God in history to which followers of Jesus must respond, and they consequently adopt a responsibility model of Christian ethics rather than a deontological approach.

Protestantism in general gives more significance to the theological aspects of Christian ethics than did traditional Roman Catholic ethics. Catholic ethics tended to see the moral life of all in this world in the light of natural law, whereas Protestantism has generally understood life in this world in relationship to the Bible and to theological concerns.

For some Protestants the primacy of grace and of Christ rules out any significant role for the human and the natural in Christian ethics. For others the effects of sin are so strong that human reason and human nature cannot be valid sources of ethical wisdom and knowledge. Even those Protestant ethicists who would be more open to the human on theological grounds shy away from the ontology and metaphysics that undergird Roman Catholic natural-law thinking. Protestants have also tended to give more significance to history than to nature, because history is more compatible with biblical categories and with the insistence on the freedom of God and of human beings.

Historical Development of Protestant Ethics. The first systematic, scientific, and independent treatment of Protestant ethics separated from dogmatic theology was produced by Georg Calixtus (d. 1656). Although the early reformers did not write scientific Christian ethics as such, they dealt with significant methodological and substantive issues affecting Christian ethics.

> **Justification by faith active in love stands at the heart of Lutheran theology. . . .**

Justification by faith active in love stands at the heart of Lutheran theology and is opposed to merit, justification by works, and legalism. The emphasis on scripture, even to the point of accepting the axiom "scripture alone," is another characteristic of the Reformation. Luther stressed freedom above all, but the dialectical aspect of his thought is seen in his famous saying "A Christian is a perfectly free lord of all, subject to none. A Christian is a perfectly dutiful servant of all, subject to all."

Lutheran social ethics is based on the two-realm theory, referring to the realm of creation and the realm of redemption. In the realm of creation, which involves the social life of human beings, there are true vocations for Christians, but the content of these vocations and what one does are not affected by Jesus, faith, or grace. Redemption affects only one's motivations. For this reason Lutheran social ethics has often been accused of passivism and acceptance of the status quo.

John Calvin (d. 1564) shared much of Luther's theological presuppositions but gave greater emphasis to the will both in God and in human beings. God is primarily sovereign will. Justification does not involve a pietistic response in trust; it means that the will of God becomes active in believers. Calvin comes closer to a Roman Catholic understanding, and Calvinists (like Catholics) have tended to become legalists. Like Luther, Calvin stresses the secular vocation of Christians but interprets Christian work in the world in a more active and transforming way. Some later Calvinists see in worldly success a sign of God's predestining will for the individual. In the twentieth century, Max Weber proposed the controversial theory that the spirit of capitalism was compatible with and abetted by Calvinist ethics.

The Anabaptist-Mennonite tradition, or the left wing of the Reformation, from its sixteenth-century origins has stressed the radical call of discipleship, believer's baptism, and a committed, inflexible following of the radical ethical demands of the gospel. The believers form a sect that stands in opposition to the existing culture and society and bears witness to the gospel, especially the call to peace and nonviolence.

There has been no dominant figure in Anglican ethics and thus no established pattern of doing Anglican ethics. However, in the Anglican community there have been important ethical thinkers who have served as a bridge between Roman Catholic ethics and Protestant ethics. Methodism developed a moral theory calling for spiritual growth and moral renewal.

The Enlightenment had a great influence on Protestant theology and ethics. Nineteenth-century Protestantism saw the emergence of liberal theology. Friedrich Schleiermacher (d. 1834), the most outstanding theologian in the nineteenth century, stressed experience and has been called the founder and most famous proponent of Protestant liberalism. Schleiermacher proposed an ethical theory dealing with goods, duties, and virtues, and he saw moral concerns as present and influencing all other areas of life, especially political, intellectual, aesthetic, and religious. Late nineteenth- and early twentieth-century liberal theology stressed the immanence of God working in human experience and history, the possibility of Christians living out the ethics of Jesus, and evolutionary human progress, and downplayed divine transcendence and the power of sin. Within the context of liberal Protestant theology, the Social Gospel movement came to the fore in the first two decades of the twentieth century in the United States, especially under the leadership of Walter Rauschenbusch (d. 1918). In response to the problems created by the industrial revolution and in response to the privatism and individualism of past Christian ethics, the Social Gospel stressed that the kingdom of God should be made more present on earth and that the social order can and should be christianized. In England and in Germany many Christian thinkers embraced a moderate Christian socialism.

The harsh realities of World War I and the Depression occasioned the rise of the neoorthodoxy of Karl Barth in Europe and the Christian realism of Reinhold Niebuhr in the United States. The reaction stressed the transcendence of God, the dialectical relationship between the existing world and the kingdom of God, the power of sin, and the fact that the fullness of God's kingdom lies outside history. In respect to the contemporary international scene, the World Council of Churches has addressed many contemporary social issues with strong support for liberation movements and has called for just, participative, and sustainable societies.

BIBLIOGRAPHY

There is no contemporary, satisfactory overview of the history of Christian ethics. The best available work remains Ernst Troeltsch's *The Social Teaching of the Christian Churches,* 2 vols. (1931; Chicago, 1981), which was originally published in 1911 but is still valuable today despite its datedness and somewhat biased perspectives. Troeltsch, like most Westerners writing on the subject, does not discuss Eastern Orthodox ethics. *Christian Ethics: Sources of the Living Tradition,* edited and with introductions by Waldo Beach and H. Richard Niebuhr (New York, 1955), is a textbook comprising selections from the most significant figures in Western Christian ethics. H. Richard Niebuhr's *Christ and Culture* (New York, 1951) is a frequently cited analysis of Western Christian ethics in the light of five possible models for understanding the relationship between Christ and culture.

There are many studies of individual thinkers in the patristic era, but the best history of the period written by a Christian ethicist is George W. Forell's *History of Christian Ethics,* vol. 1, *From the New Testament to Augustine* (Minneapolis, 1979). Forell is planning to write a three-volume history of Christian ethics.

The literature on Eastern Orthodox ethics in modern Western languages is comparatively little. In addition to encyclopedia articles, George A. Maloney's *A History of Orthodox Theology since 1453* (Belmont, Mass., 1976) and *Man: The Divine Icon* (Pecos, N. Mex., 1973) provide both historical details and anthropological considerations for Christian ethics. Georges Florovsky's *Collected Works,* 5 vols. (Belmont, Mass., 1972-1979), and John Meyendorff's *Byzantine Theology,* 2d ed. (New York, 1979), include helpful chapters dealing with Christian ethics. Stanley S. Harakas's *Toward Transfigured Life* (Minneapolis, 1983) provides a systematic Christian ethics from the Greek Orthodox tradition that includes valuable historical data.

For the historical origins of Catholic moral theology, including Thomas Aquinas, see Thomas Deman's *Aux origines de la théologie morale* (Paris, 1951). The most comprehensive study of the Scholastic period is Odon Lottin's *Psychologie et morale aux douxième et treizième siècles,* 6 vols. in 8 (Louvain, 1942-1960). Bernhard Häring's *The Law of Christ,* 3 vols. (Westminster, Md., 1961-1966), contains an often-cited historical survey of moral theology in chapter 1 of volume 1, *General Moral Theology,* and is the most important contribution to moral theology in the twentieth century. Numbers 1-4 of "Readings in Moral Theology," edited by Charles E. Curran and Richard A. McCormick (New York, 1977-1983), indicate the contemporary developments and discussions within moral theology.

Paul Althaus's *The Ethics of Martin Luther* (Philadelphia, 1972) is an authoritative discussion of Luther. For an overview of the historical development of Protestant thought, which includes materials pertinent to Christian ethics, see John Dillenberger and Claude Welch's *Protestant Christianity Interpreted through Its Development* (New York, 1954). James M. Gustafson's *Protestant and Roman Catholic Ethics: Prospects for Rapprochement* (Chicago, 1978) accurately describes the growing ecumenical convergences and differences. Paul Bock's *In Search of a Responsible World Society* (Philadelphia, 1974) summarizes the social teachings of the World Council of Churches, whereas Donal Dorr's *Option for the Poor* (Maryknoll, N. Y., 1983) analyzes from a somewhat liberationist perspective one hundred years of Vatican social teaching.

CHARLES E. CURRAN

Christianity

An Overview

Christianity is defined by one of its leading modern interpreters, Friedrich Schleiermacher (1768-1834), as "a monotheistic faith . . . essentially distinguished from other

such faiths by the fact that in it everything is related to the redemption accomplished by Jesus of Nazareth." While many interpreters of the meaning of Christianity would dispute the content that Schleiermacher gave to each of the crucial terms in that definition, the definition as such would probably stand. It is beyond the scope of this article, or even of this encyclopedia, to present an exhaustive summary of all that Christianity is and has ever been: entire encyclopedias several times the size of this one (some of them listed in the bibliography, below) have been devoted to such a summary, and even they have been far from exhaustive. What this article can do, supported by other articles throughout this work, is to sketch some of the main points in the history of Christianity and then to identify some of the features of Christianity that most students of the movement, whether professing personal allegiance to it or not, would probably recognize as belonging to its "essence." Although both the "history" and the "essence" are, unavoidably, controversial in that not everyone would agree with this (or with any) account of them, such an account as this can claim to represent a majority consensus.

The History of Christianity

Christianity is a historical religion. It locates within the events of human history both the redemption it promises and the revelation to which it lays claim: Jesus was born under Caesar Augustus and "suffered under Pontius Pilate," at particular dates in the chronology of the history of Rome (even though the specific dates of those two events may be impossible to determine with absolute precision). In this respect Christianity shows its continuing affinities with the Judaism out of which it came, for there too the historical process becomes the peculiar arena of divine activity. The primal revelation for Judaism—and for Christianity—is the divine declaration to Moses (*Ex.* 3:6): "I am the God of Abraham, Isaac, and Jacob." To this primal revelation Christianity adds the assertion (*Heb.* 1:1-2) that the God who in past times had spoken through the prophets and acted through the Exodus from Egypt has now spoken definitively and acted decisively in the life, death, and resurrection of Jesus, seen as the "Christ," the anointed and chosen one of God.

Early Christianity. It is, then, with Jesus of Nazareth that the history of Christianity takes its start. [See Jesus.] Almost everything we know of him, however, comes from those who responded, in loyalty and obedience, to the events of his life and the content of his teaching. Therefore the history of the earliest Christian communities, to the extent that we are in a position to reconstruct it, is at the same time the history of Jesus as they remembered him. His own immediate followers were all Jews, and it is within that framework that they interpreted the significance of what they had received and perceived: he was the Christ, or Messiah, who had been promised to the patriarchs of Israel. As the record of those promises, the Hebrew scriptures were sacred for early

Christians no less than for Jews, enabling them to claim a continuity with the history of the people of God since the creation of the world. The apostle Paul both summarized and reinterpreted the message of the first generation of believers. Together with the written deposit of their memories of Jesus in the Gospels, the writings of Paul and several other documents were circulated widely in Christian communities throughout the Mediterranean world, eventually becoming the Christian addendum (or "New Testament") to the Hebrew scriptures (or "Old Testament"). [*See* Biblical Literature; *and* Gospel.]

Paul was also responsible for the transformation of Christianity from a Jewish sect to a gentile movement by the end of the first century of the common era. The importance of this change for Christian history is impossible to exaggerate. Jesus had been born in an obscure corner of the Roman empire, but now his followers took upon themselves the assignment of challenging that empire and eventually of conquering it in his name. The opposition between empire and church during the second and third centuries sometimes took the form of persecution and martyrdom, but all that was replaced in the fourth century by the creation of a Christian Roman empire, when the emperor Constantine (306-337) first made the new faith legal, then made it his own, then made it the official religion of the realm. [*See* Church and State.] As part of their political and philosophical defense against their adversaries, the apologists for Christianity in the second and third centuries had also sought to clarify its relation to Greek and Roman thought, but with its official adoption their successors in the fourth and fifth centuries undertook to interpret Christian theology as the perennial philosophy in which the aspirations of all religions were now corrected and fulfilled. Among these later apologists, Augustine of Hippo (354-430) in his *City of God* articulated the Christian case against those who charged that by undermining the traditional values of Roman religion the church had been responsible for the decline and fall of the Roman empire. On the contrary, he said, Christianity was the support of just rulers and legitimate governments, and by its faith in the God of history, as well as by its moral teachings about work and the family, it promoted the welfare of society; the City of Earth would function best if it acknowledged the transcendent reality of the City of God, which was beyond history but which had made its presence known within this particular history.

The century that began with Constantine and ended with Augustine also saw the stabilization of the internal life and structure of the Christian movement. One by one, alternative ways of thought and belief that were adjudged to be aberrations were sloughed off or excluded as "heresies" or "schisms." Some of these (particularly the various species of apocalyptic or millenarian expectation) were efforts to perpetuate ways of being Christian that no longer suited the needs of the life of the church when the long-expected second coming of Jesus Christ failed to materialize, while others (notably the several gnostic systems) involved the adaptation to the Christian message of schemes of revelation and salvation that were also manifesting themselves in other religions. [*See* Gnosticism.] In opposition to these alternative ways of thought and belief, Christianity, since before the days during which the books of the New Testament were being written, identified the content of orthodox belief and fixed its form in a succession of creedal statements. The earliest of these, including that eventually formulated as the Apostles' Creed, are put into the mouth of one or another or all twelve of the apostles of Jesus, and the most important creedal statement was adopted (under Constantine's patronage) at the Council of Nicaea in 325 (see "The Pattern of Christian Belief," below). [*For further discussion, see* Heresy *and* Councils.]

During those same early centuries, Christianity was also identifying the structures of authority that were thought to guarantee the preservation of "apostolic" faith and order: the Bible and the bishops. As already noted, the Bible of the Christians consisted of two parts (or "testaments"): the books they had inherited from Judaism, and the combination into a "New Testament" of four gospels about the life and teachings of Jesus, epistles attributed to Paul and other apostolic figures, the *Acts of the Apostles*, and (from among the many extant apocalyptic writings) the *Revelation to John.* The bishops through their uninterrupted succession were believed to certify the continuity of the church with its apostolic foundations. As the church that could claim to have been shepherded by all twelve apostles, Jerusalem held a unique place; but as the church that Peter had governed and to which Paul had written (and where both Peter and Paul had been martyred), and as the congregation at the capital of the civilized world, Rome early acquired a special position as "*the* apostolic see," which it would consolidate by the leadership in faith and life that it exercised during the crises of the fourth and fifth centuries. Actually, the criterion of "apostolicity" was a circular one: apostolic foundation of episcopal sees, apostolic authorship of biblical books, and apostolic orthodoxy of creedal belief supported one another, and no one of them was ever sufficient of itself—even in the case of the see of Rome—to serve as such a criterion in isolation from the others. [*See* Apostles.]

Official Establishment of Christianity. Constantine's acceptance of Christianity and the eventual establishment of it as the official faith of the Roman empire is rightly seen as the most portentous event—for good or ill or some combination of the two—in all of Christian history; conversely, "the end of the Constantinian era," which is how many thoughtful observers have characterized the twentieth century, has brought about the reshaping and rethinking of all the structures of faith and life that Christianity evolved in the aftermath of its new status from the fourth century on. Both in the

Roman West, where Constantine prevailed in 312 "by the power of the cross," as he believed, and in the Byzantine East, where Constantine established the new capital of the Christian Roman empire two decades later, Christianity undertook to create a new civilization that would be a continuation of ancient Greece and Rome and yet would be a transformation of those cultures through the infusion of the spiritual power of Christ as Lord.

The Christian culture of Byzantium. That pattern of continuation with transformation took a special form in the Christian culture of the Byzantine empire, whose history persisted for more than a thousand years from the creation of Constantinople as "New Rome" in 330 CE to its fall to the armies of the Turkish sultan Mehmed II (and its change of name to Istanbul) in 1453. Constantine and his successors— and, above all, the emperor Justinian (r. 527-565)—saw themselves in their Roman capacity as the legitimate heirs of the ancient pagan caesars, but at the same time in their Christian capacity as "equal to the apostles" *(isapostolos)*. In the exercise of this special authority, they frequently became involved in the administrative, liturgical, and doctrinal affairs of the church, and often without opposition and with great success. Contemporary historians tell us that it was the emperor Constantine who came up with the formula "one in being [*homoousios*] with the Father," which resolved, at the Council of Nicaea in 325, the dispute over the metaphysical relation between Christ and God. Later historians have coined for this special status of the Byzantine emperor the term *Caesaropapism*, implying that what the pope was in the West, the caesar was in the East. While the reign of Constantine, and even more that of Justinian, may have merited such a designation, the patriarch of Constantinople repeatedly asserted the authority of the church to determine its own destiny, above all in the areas of belief and worship. Most notably, in the iconoclastic controversies of the eighth and ninth centuries, which were brought on by the campaign of a series of emperors to remove images from the worship of the church, the defenders of the church's autonomy, who included especially monks and empresses, eventually carried the day, and the authority of the emperor to legislate unilaterally for the church was significantly curtailed.

One reason for this success in the iconoclastic disputes was the special place of icons in Byzantine (and later in Slavic) Orthodoxy, which one scholar has called its "distinctive identity." As interpreted by its defenders, the cult of the icons was anything but the relapse into idolatrous paganism of which it was accused by the iconoclasts; instead it represented the commitment of Orthodoxy to the reality of the full incarnation of the Son of God in the human figure of Jesus: worship of the image of Jesus Christ was in fact addressed to one who was in his single person completely God and completely man. Thus, to a degree unknown in the West even in the high Middle Ages, Greek Christianity defined itself by

its liturgy and devotion, not only (perhaps not primarily) by its dogma and life. The very term *orthodoxia* in Greek, and its Slavic counterpart *pravoslavie*, meant in the first instance "correct worship," which also included "correct doctrine." Embodied as it was in the curriculum of Byzantine educational institutions at all levels, the continuing hold that a christianized Neoplatonism exercised over its expositors enabled them to make use of its metaphysics and epistemology in the service of the church's message. The Byzantine icons were only one part of a total Christian culture, in which architecture, poetry, and music also contributed their special part. One feature of this culture was a commitment to preserving the indigenous culture of each people to which the Christian message came: while the Western missionaries, in introducing the Mass, taught each nation Latin when they taught it the gospel (and thus, even without intending to do so, gave it at least some access to pre-Christian Roman culture), Eastern missionaries translated not only the Bible but also the liturgy into the language of the people. [*See* Missions, *article on* Christian Missions.] It was, above all, in the Byzantine missions to the Slavs (where the two philosophies about the proper language of the liturgy clashed) that this peculiarity of the Eastern church served to create an integrally Slavic Orthodoxy, through which the Ukraine, Bulgaria, Russia, and Serbia came of age as nations. [*For further discussion, see* Eastern Christianity.]

Christianity in the Middle Ages. In the Latin West, by contrast, the outcome of the Constantinian settlement took a radically divergent form, in which it was not principally the Christian emperor and the Christian empire, but the bishop of Rome and the papacy, that was to set the tone of the historical development of Christianity. [*See* Roman Catholicism *and* Papacy.] With the transfer of the capital to Constantinople, the pope came to symbolize and to embody the continuity with ancient Rome. Within less than a century after that transfer, the bishop of Rome was calling himself "supreme pontiff" *(pontifex maximus),* a title that had belonged to the pagan caesars. When the various Germanic tribes arrived in western Europe, they found the papacy already present as a political and cultural force. Those tribes that chose to ignore that force by clinging too long to Germanic paganism or to forms of Christianity that had been outlawed as heretical also lost the opportunity to shape the future of European history, but the Franks, by allying themselves with the bishop of Rome, were to determine its subsequent course through much of the Middle Ages. The symbolic high point of the alliance came on Christmas Day in the year 800 with the crowning of the Frankish king Charles, known to history as Charlemagne (c. 742-814), as "emperor" at the hands of Pope Leo III in Rome, even though there was still an emperor in Constantinople. With its own emperor— and, above all, its own bishop and supreme pontiff—the West was free to pursue its own destiny. And although the schism between West and East, in a technical and canonical sense, did not take place until several centuries later, and in a spiritual sense may be said to have happened in 1204, the historical intuition that located it as having originated in the ninth century was in many ways sound. [*For further discussion, see* Schism, *article on* Christian Schism.]

Confrontation with Islam. Each in its own way, both Eastern and Western Christendom were compelled, from the seventh century onward, to come to terms with the reality of Islam. During the one hundred years after the death of the prophet Muhammad in 632 CE, the geographical spread of Islam was both more rapid and more effective than that of Christianity had been during its first several centuries. Several of the major centers of the Eastern churches—Antioch, Alexandria, Jerusalem itself—became Muslim in government, although a large Christian population was able to practice its faith under varying degrees of pressure. Eventually, in 1453, Constantinople also became a Muslim city. The Muslim conquest of Palestine was likewise responsible for the most historic confrontation ever between Christianity and another faith, in the Crusades, as successive armies of Western Christians sought to reconquer the "holy places" associated with the life of Jesus—an enterprise that eventually failed. [*See* Crusades.]

> **The Muslim conquest of Palestine was likewise responsible for the most historic confrontation ever between Christianity and another faith. . . .**

The monks. Because its administrative structure and intellectual tradition were so different from those of the Byzantine East, the medieval Christianity of the West expressed its relation to society and culture in a distinctive fashion as well. In even greater measure than in the East, the bearers of its civilizing force were monks. [*See* Monasticism.] The missionaries who brought the gospel to the barbarians—for example, Boniface (680-754), the "apostle of Germany" sent from Rome, and Cyril (c. 826-869) and Methodius (c. 815-c. 884), the "apostles to the Slavs" sent from Constantinople—were monks. So were the scribes who then brought Classical civilization to the same barbarians; thus the Benedictine monk the Venerable Bede (c. 673-735) laid many of the foundations of scholarship in England. Most of the reformers who throughout the Middle Ages recalled the church to its primitive faith and its ancient loyalties came from monasticism, as was evident above all in the work of Bernard of Clairvaux (1090-1153), "the unmitered pope" of the twelfth century, and then in the program of Francis of Assisi (1181/2-1226). The cloisters likewise supplied most of the theologians

who systematized and defended the faith: Anselm of Canterbury (c. 1033-1109) was a Benedictine abbot, Thomas Aquinas (c. 1225-1274) was a Dominican friar, and Bonaventure (c. 1217-1274) and Duns Scotus (c. 1266-1308) were both Franciscans.

Repeatedly, of course, the monastic communities themselves needed to be reformed, and in virtually every century of the Middle Ages there arose movements of renewal dedicated to the purification of the monastic ideal and, through it, renewal of the life of the total church. When the leaders of such movements managed to establish themselves as leaders of the total church, the result was often a great conflict. Thus in the eleventh century the reformer Hildebrand became Pope Gregory VII (in 1073) and set about renewing the administration, the morals, and the faith and life of the church. He sought to enforce the law of clerical celibacy, to root out financial and political corruption, to free bishops and prelates from the dominance of secular princes, and to purge the church of heresy and schism. This brought him into collision both with his own ecclesiastical subordinates and with the empire, but it also gave him the opportunity to formulate for all time the special prerogatives of the church and the bishop of Rome (see "The Community of Christian Worship," below).

Reformation Christianity. Such reform movements, it seemed, could always be counted on to rescue the church in times of crisis—until, through Martin Luther (1483-1546) and the Reformation, a crisis arose in which the primary impetus for reform was to express itself not *through* monasticism or the papacy, but *against* both monasticism and the papacy (although it must be remembered that Luther, too, was originally a monk). Already in various late medieval reformations, such as those of the "Spiritual" Franciscans and the Hussites, there was the sense that (to cite the four standard "marks" of the church enumerated in the Nicene Creed) Christendom could be neither one nor holy nor catholic nor apostolic until it had replaced the secularized and corrupt authority of the bishop of Rome with the authenticity of the word of God, for which some looked to a church council while others put their confidence in the recovery of the message of the Bible. That sense finally found its voice in the program of the Protestant reformers. Beginning with the belief that they were merely the loyal children of Mother Church recalling her to her genuine self, they soon found themselves so alienated from the structures and teachings of the church of their time that they were obliged to look for, and if need be to invent, alternative structures and teachings of their own.

The structures and teachings of the several Protestant groups covered an extremely wide spectrum, such that those at one end of the spectrum (Lutherans and Anglicans) were in many ways closer to Roman Catholicism and even to Eastern Orthodoxy, despite the schisms both of the Middle Ages and of the Reformation, than they were to Socinianism or even to Anabaptism or even perhaps to Calvinism. In their ecclesiastical structures, the churches that came out of the Reformation ranged from a retention of the historic episcopate (e.g., in England and Sweden) to a presbyterian form of church government (e.g., in Scotland and in many, though by no means all, of the Calvinist churches on the European continent) to an insistence on the primacy and autonomy of the local congregation (e.g., in various of the dissenters from Anglicanism in the seventeenth and eighteenth centuries, including the Congregationalists and Baptists, especially in the New World). While the mainstream of Protestantism has in its doctrine maintained a loyalty to the doctrines of the Trinity, of the person of Christ, of original sin, and of salvation through the death of Christ, as these had been developed in the early and medieval church, it has diverged from earlier development (and thus from Roman Catholicism and Eastern Orthodoxy) above all in its understanding of the nature of the church and of the meaning (and hence the number) of the sacraments, with only baptism and the Lord's Supper being regarded as authentic sacraments by most Protestants. (See "The Pattern of Christian Belief," below.) The principal difference, at least as seen both by the Protestant reformers and by their Roman Catholic adversaries, lay in the area of religious authority: not the church or its tradition, not the papacy or a church council, but the Bible alone, was to be the norm that determined what Christians were to believe and how they were to live. [*See* Reformation.]

The Roman Catholic response to the Protestant Reformation is sometimes called the "Counter-Reformation," although that term has come to be regarded by many scholars as excessively negative in its connotations because it seems to ignore the positive reforms that were not merely a reaction to Protestantism. "The Roman Catholic Reformation" is in many ways a preferable designation. First through a series of responses to the theology and program of the reformers, then above all through the canons and decrees of the Council of Trent (1545-1563), the Catholic Reformation took up the issues addressed by Luther and by his most eminent successor, John Calvin (1509-1564), both in the area of church life and morals and in the area of church teaching and authority. Many of the corruptions that had acted as tinder for the Reformation received the careful attention of the council fathers, with the result that Roman Catholicism and the papacy emerged from the crisis of the Reformation diminished in size but chastened and strengthened in spirit. The creation of the Society of Jesus by Ignatius Loyola (c. 1491-1556) in 1534 provided the church with a powerful instrument for carrying out the program of reform and renewal, and many of the tools employed by the reformers (e.g., the printing press and the catechism) lent themselves to that program just as effectively. A deepening mystical devotion gave new life to medieval spirituality, particularly in sixteenth-century Spain, and the theology of Thomas

Aquinas acquired new authority as the defenders of the faith closed ranks against Protestant thought. The historical coincidence of the discovery of the New World and the Protestant Reformation, which both Protestants and Roman Catholics interpreted as providential, enabled Roman Catholic missionaries to recoup in North and South America the losses in prestige and membership caused by the Reformation. It was above all in Latin America that this recovery became a decisive religious and cultural force. Although divided (by the papal Line of Demarcation of 1493) between Spain and Portugal, Latin America was "united" in the sense that it was colonized and converted by Roman Catholic Christianity; the process of the christianization of native populations was a gradual one, and many beliefs and practices of their pre-Christian history were carried over into their new faith. The effect of these and other missionary campaigns in the sixteenth and seventeenth centuries was to make the term *catholic* in *Roman Catholic* begin to mean in fact what it had always meant in principle: present throughout the known world.

The Christian East. Throughout the Middle Ages and the Reformation there were sporadic efforts in the West to establish (or reestablish) contact with the East; these ranged from the dispatch of various legations, to the translation of various classic works in one direction or the other, to marriages between Western monarchs and Byzantine or Russian princesses. The Crusades, which the East sometimes invited and sometimes dreaded, did at least reacquaint many members of the two traditions with one another, although the most unforgettable instance of such reacquaintance was the catastrophe of the sack of Christian Constantinople by the armies of the Fourth Crusade in 1204. Followed as it was two and a half centuries later by the Muslim capture of Constantinople and the end of the Byzantine empire, the tragedy of 1204 is probably better entitled than any other event to the dubious distinction of being the point at which the Eastern and Western churches came into schism—a schism that, except for repeated but short-lived attempts at reunion (the most notable of which was probably the Union of Florence in 1439), has persisted ever since. Although the loss of Constantinople to the Turks drastically reduced its sphere of influence, the ecumenical patriarchate of Constantinople continued to enjoy a preeminence of honor within Eastern Orthodoxy, as it does to this day. Numerically as well as politically, however, it was Slavic Orthodoxy, above all in Russia, that became the "heir apparent," uniting itself with Russian culture as it had with medieval Greek culture. Plagued though it was by internal schisms, and caught in the political and cultural upheavals of the tsarist empire, the church in Russia went on producing saints and scholars, and through the icons and the liturgy it suffused the faith and life of the common people with the meaning of the Christian faith: the icon painter Andrei Rublev (c. 1360-c. 1430) and, in more modern times, the novelist and spiritual thinker Fedor Dostoevskii (1821-1881) were among the products of this tradition best known in the West. The nineteenth and twentieth centuries witnessed an upsurge of interest in Eastern Orthodoxy throughout Western Christianity, as a consequence partly of the ecumenical movement and partly of the Russian Revolution, as both Protestants and Roman Catholics looked to Orthodoxy for the correction of what had come to be seen as Western deficiencies and overemphases in the aftermath of the Reformation.

Post-Reformation Christianity. The ecclesiastical map of the West after the Reformation shows a Europe divided between an almost solidly Roman Catholic south and a predominantly Protestant north, with the latter in turn divided between Anglican, Lutheran, and Reformed or Calvinist forms of Christianity. [*See* Protestantism.] The same competition was exported into Christian missions in Africa and Asia and into the Americas. Among the most influential developments of the centuries following the Reformation was the effort, which took a distinct form in each denomination but nevertheless manifested a similarity of spirit, to encourage a deeper seriousness about the claims of the Christian gospel upon personal faith and life: Jansenism within French (and then North American) Roman Catholicism, Puritanism (and later on Methodism) within English Protestantism, and Pietism within the Lutheran and Reformed churches of the continent and of the New World. Especially during the eighteenth century, these movements had it as one of their primary goals to combat and counteract the influence, both in the church and in public life, of the rationalism, freethinking, and "infidelity" associated with the Enlightenment. [*See* Enlightenment, The.] Combining as it did the application to Christian history and biblical literature of the methods of historical criticism (particularly in German theological scholarship) with the reexamination or even the rejection of the special claims of Christianity to a privileged place in Western society (particularly in the legislation of the French Revolution), the Enlightenment came to represent the campaign for the secularization of culture. An important feature of that combination of emphases in Enlightenment thought was a fundamental reconsideration of the traditional Christian assertions of finality and uniqueness. As the philosophical and historical basis for such assertions was coming under increasing attack from within such traditionally Christian institutions as the theological faculties of universities, the discovery of other religions both in the historical past and in the distant parts of the present world was bringing such concepts as the uniqueness of the Christian message into serious question. The special privileges that Christianity had enjoyed since the Constantinian era were gradually withdrawn. Separation of church and state, as developed especially in the United States, and the growth of religious toleration and religious liberty were the social and political expressions of the new situation that was beginning to become evident at the end of the eighteenth century.

The nineteenth century. Despite the losses in both influence and numbers that it suffered in the period of the Enlightenment, Christianity entered the nineteenth century with a strong sense of its continuing relevance and special mission. The critical reexamination of the Christian toleration of slavery—long overdue, in the opinion of observers inside and outside the church—came to full realization in the nineteenth century, even though a civil war in the United States was necessary to bring this about. It was likewise in the nineteenth century, surnamed "the great century" in the leading history of Christian missions, that most of the major Christian denominations of the West, Protestant as well as Roman Catholic, set out to evangelize the globe. Although the Christian missionary and the colonialist conqueror often marched arm in arm across that globe, the results for native cultures were quite ambiguous: sometimes a loss of national identity and cultural deracination, but on the other hand no less often a deepening sense of historical particularity and the acquisition of scholarly instruments for understanding it and thus of overcoming both the colonialism and the missions. Significantly, it was from the mission schools founded in the nineteenth century that a disproportionately high number of the revolutionary leaders of the twentieth century in developing nations were to emerge. On the home front, the confrontation between traditional Christian beliefs and the discoveries of modern science engaged the attention of the churches. The most violent such confrontation was brought on by the work of Charles Darwin, whose books *The Origin of Species* (1859) and *The Descent of Man* (1871) called into question the traditional Christian belief in a special creation of the human species in the image of God as based on the biblical accounts of creation in the *Book of Genesis*. [*For broader discussion, see* Evolution.] Yet as the nineteenth century ended, there was a widespread expectation that the next would truly be "the Christian century." *Christianizing the Social Order* by Walter Rauschenbusch (1861-1918), first published in 1912, was a representative statement of that expectation.

The twentieth century. As things turned out, the twentieth century proved to be the age of two world wars, of the coming to power of Marxist regimes throughout most of historic Eastern Christendom, and of moral and intellectual crises (including the Nazi Holocaust and the issues raised by modern technology) that would shake the traditional beliefs and historical confidence of Christians with unprecedented force. The reaction was, if not an overt loss of faith, then a growing indifference in many traditionally Christian groups. The most influential Christian theologian of the twentieth century, Karl Barth (1886-1968), protested the synthesis of the gospel with human culture and called for a reassertion of that gospel in its native power and uniqueness. At the same time, however, the most influential Christian event of the twentieth century, the Second Vatican Council of 1962-1965, undertook a reform of Christian faith and life that reached out to other Christians and to other religious traditions with a new openness. The council was the manifestation within Roman Catholicism of a new ecumenical consciousness that had its

> **The reaction was, if not an overt loss of faith, then a growing indifference in many traditionally Christian groups.**

origins in Protestantism; the divisions that had followed in the wake of the Reformation now came under question in the light of the recognition that what separated Christians from one another was less significant than all the things that still held them together. That ecumenical consciousness throughout the Christian movement found expression in the recovery of historic Christian beliefs, in the creation of contemporary forms of worship, and in the reexamination of patterns of Christian life both individual and corporate. [*For further discussion, see* Ecumenical Movement *and* Vatican Councils, *article on* Vatican II.] It remains to consider these three areas of belief, worship, and life, which, taken together, may be said to constitute the essence of Christianity.

The Essence of Christianity

In these nearly two thousand years of its history, Christianity has manifested an almost infinite variety of expressions as it has spread its presence and influence into all the major cultures of the Western world and into most of those of the East as well. With a billion or more adherents throughout the human race at the end of the twentieth century, it continues to be heterogeneous and pluralistic in its forms of organization and worship, belief, and life—so much so that it appears difficult or foolhardy or impossible to attempt to identify any characteristics as the distinctive genius or continuing essence of Christianity. A well-known criterion was the one proposed by Vincent of Lérins in the fifth century—what has been accepted "everywhere, always, by all" *(ubique, semper, ab omnibus)*—but the welter of detail about the history of Christianity scattered across the hundreds of articles dealing with the subject in the volumes of this encyclopedia should convince even the most casual reader that if there is an "essence of Christianity" it cannot possibly be everything that Christianity has ever been to everyone in every time and every place. Therefore, to quote again from Schleiermacher, "the only pertinent way of discovering the peculiar essence of any particular faith and reducing it as far as possible to a formula is by showing the element which remains constant throughout the most diverse

religious affections within this same communion, while it is absent from analogous affections within other communions."

The search for an essence of Christianity is as old as the primary deposits of Christianity themselves. Already in the Hebrew scriptures, which Christianity took over as its Old Testament, the prophet Micah had declared: "God has told you what is good; and what is it that the Lord asks of you? Only to act justly, to love loyalty, to walk wisely before your God" (NEB *Mi.* 6:8). And an unknown first-century Christian writer, author of what came to be called the letter to the Hebrews in the New Testament, stated that "anyone who comes to God must believe that he exists and that he rewards those who search for him" (*Heb.* 11:6). The most successful formula for the essence of Christianity, however, was that of the apostle Paul: "In a word, there are three things that last for ever: faith, hope, and love; but the greatest of them all is love" (*1 Cor.* 13:13). Already in the second century, Irenaeus (c. 130-c. 200), bishop of Lyons, was invoking this formula as a summary of what "endures unchangeably," and in the fifth century it became the basis and the outline for Augustine's *Enchiridion,* to which Augustine himself usually referred as *On Faith, Hope, and Love.* From Augustine, in turn, the formula went on to provide the table of contents for the early catechisms in the age of Charlemagne and then for the rapid expansion in the number and use of catechisms by all parties in the age of the Reformation. Hence it may serve as a device for organizing this description of the essence of Christianity in its historical sweep, its geographical expansion, and its genius. Considered both in its history and in its contemporary expressions, Christianity has been, and is, a system of faith, of hope, and of love, a pattern of belief (and thought), a community of worship (and culture), and a way of life (and society). Paul's triad of faith, hope, and love may thus be used to correspond to the even more universal schema of the true, the beautiful, and the good. [*For further discussion in broad religious perspective, see* Faith.]

The Pattern of Christian Belief. As a system of faith, Christianity manifests "faith" in all the various meanings that this term has acquired in the history of religion: as loyalty to the divine, based on the prior loyalty of the divine to the world and to humanity; as the confidence that God is trustworthy in truth and love; as dependence on the Father of Jesus Christ, who is the source of all good in this life and in the life to come; as the commitment to direct thought and action in accordance with the divine word and will; and as the affirmation that certain events and declarations, as given by divine revelation, are a reliable index to that will and word. It is the last of those meanings that provides a basis for describing in an epitome what it is that Christianity believes, teaches, and confesses.

"Whoever wishes to be saved must, above all, hold to the catholic faith." These opening words of the so-called Athanasian Creed (not in fact written by Athanasius, but a

Latin and Western creed, compiled perhaps in the fifth century) would not, as they stand, automatically elicit the assent and support of all Christians; nor, for that matter, would all Christians who do accept such a statement be agreed on the precise content and extent of that "catholic faith." Differ though they do on these questions, however, Christians throughout history have affirmed the importance of the act of believing, as well as of the content of what is believed, as a mark of identification by which believers would be known.

The person of Jesus Christ. Christian belief began with the need to specify the significance of the person of Jesus, seen as the "Christ." The initial stages of that process are visible already in the pages of the New Testament. Its titles for him—in addition to Christ, such titles as Son of man, Son of God, Word of God (Logos), and Savior—were an effort to account for that significance, for within the events of Jesus' human life the God of Israel and the creator of the world had been disclosed. Before the theologians had invented ways of defining the content of these titles in any satisfying detail, the devotion and worship of the church were already identifying Jesus with God. This is evident, for example, from the earliest non-Christian account of the church that we possess, the letter of Pliny the Younger (62-113), governor of Bithynia, to the Roman emperor Trajan (r. c. 98-117), which describes Christians as gathering for worship and "addressing a song to Christ as to God" *(Christo ut deo).* But this devotional practice had yet to be squared both with the monotheism that the church inherited from and shared with Israel and with the concrete events of the life of Jesus as these were described in the Gospels. During the second and third centuries the reality of his human life needed to be defended; during the fourth century the divine dimension of his being demanded attention; during the fifth and sixth centuries the relation between the divine and the human in him required clarification. What emerged from the process of debate and definition—especially in the creeds formulated at the councils of Nicaea in 325, Constantinople in 381, and Chalcedon in 451—was a picture of Jesus Christ as having two "natures," divine and human: he was simultaneously "one in being" with God and "one in being" with humanity, and therefore able to mediate between them. The full content of the two natures and of the relation between them has continued to engage the speculative talents of Christian theologians ever since. [*See* God, *articles on* God in the New Testament *and* God in Postbiblical Christianity; Soul, *article on* Christian Concept; Theology; *and* Dogma.]

The Trinity. The final creedal statement of the relation between Christ and God was part of a more complete statement of belief, the Christian doctrine of the Trinity, which many theological exponents of Christianity would regard as the central teaching of the Christian faith. Its fundamental outline is already given in the "great commission"—which, according to the Gospels, Jesus entrusted to his disciples

before withdrawing his visible presence from them (*Mt.* 28:19)—to baptize "in the name of the Father and of the Son and of the Holy Spirit." Threefold though that single "name" was, it was the relation of the Son to the Father that carried the principal weight in the clarification of the formula. Thus the original creed adopted at Nicaea, after enumerating the various "titles of majesty" belonging to Jesus Christ as the Son of God, simply added "And [we believe] in the Holy Spirit," with no similar elaboration of how and why the Third Person was entitled to stand alongside the Father and the Son. But before the fourth century was over, the status of the Holy Spirit, and thus the complete dogma of God as Trinity, had achieved the form it has held in Christian orthodoxy throughout the history of the church. The dogma presents itself as strictly monotheistic. The opening words of the Nicene Creed are "We believe in one God," and everything that follows about Father, Son, and Holy Spirit is set into that framework. The technical philosophical term for the oneness of God was *ousia* in Greek, *substantia* or *essentia* in Latin. But this single divine *ousia* had its being in three *hupostaseis,* or "persons."

The doctrine of the Trinity has from the beginning been one of the most productive—and one of the most problematic—points of contact between Christian theology and speculative philosophy. Both the Greek Neoplatonist Plotinus (c. 205-270) and the German idealist G. W. F. Hegel (1770-1831), with many others between them, taught a philosophical version of the Trinity with which many theologians felt obliged somehow to come to terms. The metaphysical ingenuity of philosophers and theologians—from the first of Latin theologians, Tertullian (160?-225?), and the boldest of Greek theologians, his contemporary Origen (c. 185-c. 254), to philosophical theologians of the twentieth century, such as the Protestant Paul Tillich (1886-1965) and the Roman Catholic Karl Rahner (1904-1984)—has therefore continually experimented with new ways of accounting for (if not of "explaining") the relation between the One and the Three. Perhaps the most creative of such speculations was that of Augustine's *On the Trinity*, which constructed a series of trinitarian analogies in the universe and in the human mind as "images [or footprints] of the divine Trinity." [*For further discussion, see* Trinity.]

Sin and grace. All the councils that formulated these basic doctrines of the Trinity and of the person of Christ were held in the Greek-speaking eastern part of the Christian Roman empire under the patronage of the Christian emperor, who was from the year 330 onward resident at Constantinople, and the creeds, which are in Greek, bear the marks of that origin. Still it is a mistake to ignore the role of the Latin West in the determination of normative Christian teaching: both at Nicaea and at Chalcedon there were decisive interventions from Western theologians and bishops. Nevertheless, the most distinctive and original Western contributions during the first five centuries came not in the doctrines of God and Christ but in the doctrines of sin and grace. With significant anticipations in various Western thinkers, it was once again Augustine who formulated these latter doctrines in the concepts and terms that were to dominate most of subsequent Christian teaching in the West, that of Roman Catholicism but no less the theology of Protestantism. Many early interpreters of Christian belief—for example, Gregory of Nyssa (c. 335-c. 395) in his treatise *On the Creation of Man*—had articulated the biblical teaching (*Gn.* 1:26-27) that, among all creatures on earth, humans alone possessed the special prerogative of having been created "in the image of God," with the promise of immortal life and of a "participation in the divine nature" (*2 Pt.* 1:4). But in so doing they had often spoken more explicitly about human free will than about human sinfulness. Yet this did not imply, Augustine insisted, that every human being faced the same choice between good and evil that Adam and Eve had faced. On the contrary, humanity had since Adam and Eve been under a curse of what Augustine called "the sin of origin" *(peccatum originis)*, which infected every human being except Jesus Christ (and perhaps his mother, the Virgin Mary). Even without committing acts of sin, therefore, each member of the human race was corrupted from birth; the traditional practice of infant baptism (see "The Community of Christian Worship," below) was for Augustine evidence of the universality of this sinful condition. [*See* Grace *and* Free Will and Predestination.]

Redemption. Neither the belief in God as Trinity nor the dogma of Christ as divine and human in nature nor the doctrine of humanity as created in the image of God but fallen into sin is, however, an end in itself for Christian faith. As a religion of redemption, Christianity presents itself as the message of how, through Christ, reconciliation has been achieved between the holiness of God and the sin of a fallen humanity. But while the Trinity, the person of Christ, and (though less universally or explicitly) the doctrine of original sin all have been subjects of a public and ecumenical confession of the church, the manner of this reconciliation has not received such attention. It has been left more to hymnody and preaching than to dogma and metaphysics to supply the metaphors for describing it. One of the most widely distributed such metaphors in early Christian writers, beginning with the sayings of Jesus himself (*Mt.* 20:28), is the description of *redemption* as "ransom" (which is, of course, what redemption means): the death of Christ was paid (to God or to the devil) as the price for setting humanity free. The difficulties that such a notion entailed for the Christian picture of God made a modification of the ransom theory seem imperative: the death of Christ took place in the course of a battle between God-in-Christ and the devil with his allies, a battle in which death triumphed initially by the nailing of Christ to the cross but in which Christ was victorious in the end through his resurrection. It remained once

again for the medieval West to provide the most inventive of these theories. According to Anselm (c. 1033-1109) in his *Why God Became Man*, the reconciliation of the human race with God was fundamentally the reconciliation between the justice of God, which was committed to upholding "the moral order of the universe" *(rectitudo)* and therefore could not ignore human sin or forgive it by a sim-

> **One of the most widely distributed such metaphors in early Christian writers . . . is the description of *redemption* as "ransom."**

ple fiat, and the mercy of God, which was bent on restoring humanity to the condition for which God had intended it by its creation. God became man in Christ, because as man he would be able, by his death, to produce the satisfaction demanded by divine justice, but as God he would render a satisfaction of infinite worth that could thus be applied to the entire human race. With some modifications and refinements, Anselm's theory has established itself both within Roman Catholicism and within most of classical Protestantism. [*For further discussion, see* Atonement, *article on* Christian Concepts.]

Justification. Classical Protestantism differs from Roman Catholicism in the interpretation of redemption not on the way redemption was achieved by God in Christ, but on the way it is appropriated by the Christian. Luther's doctrine of justification by faith—or, more fully and more precisely, justification by grace through faith—directed itself against what he perceived to be the widespread tendency of medieval Christianity to give human works part of the credit for restoring the right relation between God and man. This he attacked as a denial of the purely gratuitous character of salvation. The role of the human will in salvation was purely passive, accepting the forgiveness of sins as a sheer gift and contributing nothing of its own goodness to the transaction with God. Faith, accordingly, was not (or, at any rate, not primarily) an act of the intellect accepting as true what God has revealed but an act of the will entrusting itself unconditionally to the favor of God as conferred in Christ. Such unconditional trust led to the transformation of human life from the self-centered quest for gratification to the God-centered service of others (see "The Christian Way of Life," below). Partly in response to Luther's doctrine, the Council of Trent at its sixth session affirmed that "faith is the beginning of human salvation, the foundation and the root of all justification," but it condemned anyone who "says that the sinner is justified by faith alone, as though nothing else were required to cooperate."

The Community of Christian Worship. As a system of hope, Christianity holds forth the promise of eternal life through Jesus Christ. In the words of what has been called "the gospel in a nutshell" (*Jn.* 3:16), "God loved the world so much that he gave his only Son, that everyone who has faith in him may not die but have eternal life." But that promise and hope of life for those who have faith does not stand in isolation from the full range of Christian hope, the expectation of all the gifts of God for time and for eternity, and the acceptance of those gifts in thankfulness and praise. Hope, consequently, expresses itself chiefly in prayer and worship, both the personal prayer of the individual Christian believer and the corporate worship of the Christian community.

The holy catholic church. One integral component of Christianity both as " a pattern of belief" and as "a community of worship" is expressed in the words of the Apostles' Creed: "I believe in the holy catholic church, the communion of saints." According to the accounts of the New Testament, it was the intention of Jesus to found a church (*Mt.* 16:18): "I will build my church." Whether one accepts the literal historicity of those accounts or not, Jesus did, in fact, gather a community of disciples and establish a table fellowship. The earliest Christianity we are able to uncover is already a churchly Christianity, to which in fact we owe the Gospels and all the other books of the New Testament. For Christians of every persuasion and denomination, the church is at the same time the primary context of worship.

There is, however, far less unanimity about the nature of the church or about its organization and its authority. The tripartite complex of authority that emerged from the conflicts of early Christianity (see "The History of Christianity," above) vested in the office of the monarchical bishop the visible governance of the church and defined the church accordingly. Two formulas of Cyprian (d. 258), bishop of Carthage, summarize this definition: "Where the bishop is, there the church is" (*Ubi episcopus, ibi ecclesia*) and "There is no salvation apart from the church" (*Extra ecclesiam nulla salus*). For Cyprian himself, as became evident in his disputes with Stephen I (bishop of Rome from 254 to 257), each bishop carried the authority of the office on his own and was answerable to the authority of Christ and of his brother bishops, but not to any one bishop as monarch of the entire church. But there were already signs of a developing pyramidal structure of authority, with certain centers having clear jurisdiction over others. Among these, the see of Rome had, and has, preeminence. As noted earlier, this understanding of authority led in the Middle Ages to a definition of the church as a visible monarchy, analogous in some ways to other monarchies, of which the pope was the absolute ruler—"judging all, but being judged by none," as the *Dictatus papae* of Gregory VII said. Orthodoxy, by contrast, has resisted the pyramidal model of church authority, preferring to see the entire company of the church's bishops, particularly when they are in

council assembled, as a corporate and collegial entity, with the bishop of Rome as "first among equals" (*primus inter pares*) but not as monarch. One of the major accents of the Second Vatican Council was a new emphasis on episcopal collegiality but not at the expense of the primacy of the bishop of Rome within the college. That accent was closely joined in the decrees of the council to a recovery of the definition of the church as principally the community of Christian worship. [*See* Church. *For discussion of community as a sacred phenomenon in broad religious perspective, see* Community.]

Protestant views of the church. The Protestant rejection of the authority of the pope is closely joined to a redefinition of the nature of the church. There had always been the recognition in the medieval doctrine of the church, particularly as this had come down from Augustine, that the organizational, empirical church was not coextensive with the church as it exists in the eyes of God: some who participate in, or even preside over, the church as an institution today will ultimately perish, while others who now persecute the church are destined to become members of the body of Christ. That definition of the true church as "the company of the elect," and hence as invisible in its membership and in its essence, appears in one form or another in the thought of most of the Protestant reformers. It did not imply, except in the polemics of a radical few, that there was no visible church. With differing forms of ecclesiastical administration (see "Reformation Christianity," above), the reformers took over or adapted patterns of organization that would suit the church for its function as the community of Christian worship and the center of Christian instruction. A favorite Protestant term for the church, therefore, is the phrase in the Apostles' Creed, "the communion of saints."

The preaching of the word of God. Although they would agree that the church is the community of Christian worship, the several denominations disagree about the structure of that community—and about the content of that worship. It is characteristic of most Protestant groups that in their liturgies and forms of worship they assign centrality to communication of the Christian message through preaching: "Where the word of God is, there the church is" (*Ubi verbum Dei, ibi ecclesia*) is how they have recast Cyprian's formula. As the leader of the worshiping community, the minister is principally (though never exclusively) the proclaimer of the word of God, a word of God that is found in, or identified and even equated with, the Bible. The emphasis on biblical preaching has sometimes led to a didactic understanding of worship, but this has been counterbalanced in Protestantism by the literally tens of thousands of "psalms and hymns and spiritual songs" (Col. 3:16) that the Protestant churches have developed because of their equally great stress on the participation of the congregation and of each individual worshiper in the service. The traditional concern of Protestant Christianity with the authentic faith and experience of the individual—

expressed in Luther's axiom "You must do your own believing as you must do your own dying"— is likewise audible in these hymns, many of which, typically, are cast in the language of the first person singular.

The sacraments. It would, however, be a grave distortion (albeit a distortion to which even sympathetic interpreters of Protestant Christianity have sometimes been subject) to interpret Protestantism as a thoroughgoing individualism in its understanding of worship, for the definition of the church as "the community of Christian worship," in Protestantism as well as in Orthodoxy and in Roman Catholicism, is embodied above all in the celebration of the sacraments. Except for certain details (e.g., whether it is the recitation of the words of institution or the invocation of the Holy Spirit in the epiclesis that effects the transformation of bread and wine into the body and blood of Christ in the Eucharist), Eastern Orthodoxy and Roman Catholicism stand in basic agreement on the nature of sacramental worship and the meaning of the seven sacraments. Among the many definitions of *sacrament* that have appeared in the Christian tradition, two (one from the East and one from the West) may suffice here: "the mystery of faith," since in Christian Greek *musterion* means both "mystery" and "sacrament"; and, in a formula based on Augustine, "sacred sign," which by a visible means represents (or represents) an invisible divine grace. [*See Sacrament.*]

The Eucharist. The primary sacrament and the center of Christian worship is, for both the Eastern and the Western tradition, the Eucharist or Lord's Supper, which is, in one form or another, celebrated by all Christian groups. Although the celebration is also a memorial and an expression of community, what sets the Roman Catholic and Orthodox understanding of the Eucharist apart from that of most other groups is their definition of this sacrament as real presence and as sacrifice. In fulfillment of the words and promise of Jesus, "This is my body" and "This is my blood," the bread and wine presented for the sacrament become the very body and blood of Christ, identical in their substance with the body born of Mary, even though the taste, color, and other attributes or "accidents" of bread and wine remain. The Fourth Lateran Council in 1215 defined this doctrine as "transubstantiation," and it was reaffirmed by the Council of Trent in 1551. As the real presence of the body and blood of the one whose death on the cross and resurrection effected the redemption of the world, the Eucharist is as well a sacrifice— not as though the first sacrifice were inadequate and Christ needed to be sacrificed over and over, but "in union with the sacrifice" of Calvary. The daily offering of that sacrifice for the living and the dead is at the center of Roman Catholic worship, devotion, and doctrine; and although Orthodoxy is, characteristically, less explicit in some of its detailed formulations about the metaphysics of the presence and more content to speak of it as a "mystery," its representatives, when

pressed, will come up with language not far removed from that of the West—especially of the West as in the twentieth century it has, thanks to a repossession of the tradition of the Greek fathers, come to speak about the mystery of the Eucharist.

Whatever differences of emphasis there may be between Roman Catholicism and Eastern Orthodoxy about the Eucharist, they are much smaller than the differences among the several Protestant groups. Luther objected to transubstantiation as an excessively philosophical formula, and above all to the sacrificial understanding of the Eucharist as a diminution of the redemptive work of Christ, but he vigorously defended the real presence against his fellow Protestants. They in turn laid stress on the "true presence" of Christ in his spirit and power rather than on the "real presence" of the actual body and blood. Within Protestantism, consequently, the memorial aspects of the celebration of the Lord's Supper, which Christ according to the Gospels instituted to be eaten in his remembrance, have been prominent and sometimes even central. The other historic accent of Christian eucharistic worship that has found a new emphasis in Protestant practice and devotion is the understanding of the Lord's Supper as a corporate expression of the "communion" of Christian believers with one another. "Body of Christ" in the New Testament refers sometimes to the Eucharist, sometimes to the church, and sometimes (notably in *1 Corinthians*) to both at the same time. Compared with those two themes of memorial and communion, the specification of just how the body and blood of Christ can be present in the sacrament is of lesser significance. [*For further discussion, see* Eucharist.]

Baptism. The other action of the community of Christian worship on whose "sacramental" character all Christians would agree is baptism. Throughout the *Acts of the Apostles*, baptism functions as the means of initiation into the Christian movement and into the reality of Christ himself, and in the epistles of Paul baptism is the way of appropriating the benefits of the death and resurrection of Christ. Although all the explicit references in the New Testament to the practice of baptism mention only adults as its recipients, and that generally only after a profession of their faith, the custom of administering it also to children began quite early; just how early is a matter of controversy, but by the end of the second century infant baptism was sufficiently widespread to have called forth objections from Tertullian. Except for that difference from subsequent tradition, Tertullian formulated in his treatise *On Baptism* what can be regarded as an all but universal consensus about the effects of baptism: remission of sins, deliverance from death, regeneration, and bestowal of the Holy Spirit. Eastern and Western church fathers, all the medieval scholastics, and many of the Protestant reformers would be able to subscribe to that formulation. Because of their misgivings about any view of any of the sacraments that might appear magical, Protestants have tended to avoid describing the conferral of these effects as something automatic. The Anabaptists of the sixteenth century on the continent, and the several bodies of Baptists in England and especially in the United States since the seventeenth century, have carried that position to the conclusion of repudiating the practice of infant baptism and insisting on "believers' baptism" as the only form of administering the sacrament that is consistent both with the original intention of Jesus and with the true nature of the Christian community. [*For further discussion, see* Baptism.]

Other sacraments. Although baptism and the Lord's Supper are for most Protestants the only two ordinances that qualify as sacraments, the medieval development in the West led to a system of seven sacraments, which Eastern Christianity, when obliged to become specific, has likewise affirmed. The sacrament of penance (together with the reception of absolution) developed as a way of coping with sins committed after the reception of forgiveness in baptism. As the contrition of the heart, the confession of the mouth, and the satisfaction of a work restoring what had been taken away by the sin, penance became, in the Latin Middle Ages, one of the principal means by which the imperatives and the promises of the Christian gospel were applied to individuals and communities. With the universal acceptance of infant baptism, the individual's assumption of the responsibilities of Christian discipleship, originally associated with adult baptism, came to be the central content of the sacrament of confirmation. As infant baptism attended the beginning of life with sacramental grace, so at death, or in a crisis or illness that might portend death, the anointing of the sick (or the sacrament of "extreme unction") brought that grace to the end of life as well. The only one of the seven "sacraments" to which the name was applied in the New Testament (*musterion* in Greek, *sacramentum* in Latin) was marriage (*Eph.* 5:32); on that authority, it became part of the sacramental system. And as the ordinance by which all the other sacraments were usually made possible, the ordination of priests itself was defined to be a sacrament. Each of the seven, therefore, combines in a special way what is also the special emphasis of Christian hope and of Christian worship: the sacredness of each person, but in the context of the sacred community.

[*For further discussion of Christian worship, see* Priesthood *and* Ministry. *Related issues are discussed in broad religious perspective in* Confession of Sins; Prayer; Ordination; Marriage; *and* Repentance. *For discussion of Christian expression in the arts, see* Church *and* Iconography.]

The Christian Way of Life. As a system of love—and love is, in the formula of Paul, the "greatest" of the three (*1 Cor.* 13:13)—Christianity presented itself to its hearers as a way of life; especially in *Acts*, "the way" became a standard des-

ignation for Christianity itself. In its symbiosis with the societies and cultures in which it has taken root, the Christian way of life has been characterized by even greater heterogeneity than Christian belief or Christian worship. That heterogeneity makes generalizations about it in such a summary as this even more hazardous, and the specifics of the forms of Christian ethics in society must be left for treatment elsewhere in this encyclopedia. It is nevertheless possible to single out briefly certain leitmotifs that run across the varieties of Christian morality, both individual and social.

The imitation of Christ. Ever since the New Testament, the human life of Jesus Christ has served as an example set forth for imitation; it has usually been more than an example, but never less. "Bend your necks to my yoke, and learn from me, for I am gentle and humble-hearted; and your souls will find relief" the New Testament (*Mt.* 11:29) represents him as commanding. Just what that imitation implies concretely for the Christian in the world has been, however, a continuing issue and problem, for the Christ whom the believer is invited to imitate was not married, did not hold public office, and was not supported chiefly from a trade or profession. The imitation of his example has come to mean, therefore, the application to one's own situation of the love and faithfulness that Christ brought to his. Repeatedly, when the demands of society or, for that matter, the requirements of the church have proved to be too complex or abstract, "the imitation of Christ" has become a way of reducing them to their essence. Thus, in what has probably been, except for the Bible itself, the most widely circulated book in Christian history, *Imitation of Christ* by Thomas à Kempis (1379/80-1471), the summons of the figure in the Gospels rises above the intervening voices with a clarity and directness that has spoken to followers in every century; and in the twentieth century, *The Cost of Discipleship*, by the young Lutheran theologian and martyr under the Nazis, Dietrich Bonhoeffer (1906-1945), has applied that New Testament summons of "Follow me" to a new generation of disciples.

Obedience. The imitation of Christ has also implied obedience to his will, as this was expressed both in his own teachings and in the Mosaic law. In its treatment of that law, the New Testament manifests an ambivalence: Christ is seen as "the end of the law" (*Rom.* 10:4), and yet he himself is represented as warning in the Sermon on the Mount (*Mt.* 5:17), "Do not suppose that I have come to abolish the law and the prophets." The ambivalence manifests itself likewise in the descriptions of the Christian way of life as obedience. The Christian catechisms that have proliferated especially since the sixteenth century (see "Reformation Christianity," above) have usually incorporated an exposition and application of the Mosaic Decalogue as their description of what it means in practical terms to be a Christian. That has been perhaps even more true of Protestant than of Roman Catholic catechisms, despite the polemic of Protestants against "moralism" and "legalism" in Roman Catholic theology and ethics. But both Roman Catholic and Protestant ethicists and teachers have also repeatedly defined Christian obedience as not the strict observance of a legal code, not even of the legal code in the Ten Commandments, but as the spontaneity of the Spirit. "Love God, and do what you will" was Augustine's characteristically epigrammatic way of describing that spontaneity; but that same Augustine is at the same time one of our earliest authorities for the use of the Ten Commandments in Christian pedagogy. Augustine is as well an early source for the adaptation to Christian purposes of the philosophical consideration of the nature and the number of the "virtues": to the classical (or, as they came to be called in Christian parlance, "cardinal") virtues of prudence, temperance, fortitude, and justice, Christian ethical thought added the three "theological" virtues of faith, hope, and love. Obedience to the will of God and the cultivation of these seven virtues were seen as the content of the Christian way of life. [See Ten Commandments and Christian Ethics.]

The transformation of the social order. Each of the "cardinal" and "theological" virtues makes sense only in a social context, and obedience to the will of God has traditionally been seen as pertaining to society as well as to the individual. The petitions of the Lord's Prayer, "Thy kingdom come, thy will be done, on earth as it is in heaven," have been taken to mean that the reign of God and the will of God have as their object here on earth the creation of a social order that conforms as closely as possible to the reign of God in heaven. That is indeed how both the East (see "The Christian Culture of Byzantium," above) and the West (see "Christianity in the Middle Ages," above) have interpreted their mission through most of Christian history, and that was how they carried out their mission within those societies. Calvinism and Puritanism were especially committed to the creation of social and political institutions that lived up to the will of God, and the pacifism of Anabaptist and Quaker groups during the sixteenth and seventeenth centuries was inspired by a similar commitment. During the nineteenth and twentieth centuries, however, such an interpretation of the Christian mission has taken on new urgency—and has occasioned new controversy—in a society where the institutions of Christianity no longer command attention or widespread obedience. The Social Gospel associated with the name of Walter Rauschenbusch (see "The Nineteenth Century," above) was the most ambitious of modern efforts to rethink the fundamentals of the Christian way of life in relation to the situation of an industrial society and to define the very meaning of salvation (as well as of other themes of Christian teaching and devotion) in social terms. Although the Social Gospel has in greater or lesser measure affected the ethical thought of most Protestant groups, Roman Catholicism has, during most of the twentieth century, been the major center for the development of new social and political theory. In a series of "social encyclicals" beginning with the *Rerum novarum* of Pope Leo XIII (1810-1903) of 15 May 1891, the papacy itself has often taken the lead in stimulating such development. But the application of the theory to twentieth-century society—the phenomenon of "worker priests" in France, and especially the creation of "liberation theology" by Roman Catholic theologians in Latin America—has often produced confusion and provoked controversy. Even those whose political or theological conservatism finds such trends dangerous, however, usually speak in the name of a particular definition of the social order that they regard as conforming, at least in some measure, to the same ideals.

Christian universalism. The Christian way of life as love is conventionally seen as finding its ultimate fulfillment in the church as the loving community of believers set apart from the world. But alongside that strain in the Christian tradition there has always stood a concern and a love for the entire world, a Christian universalism no less pronounced than is Christian particularism. It has sometimes expressed itself in a sense of urgency about Christian missions, to "bring the world to Christ." But a less prominent, yet no less persistent, expression of Christian universalism has sought to probe the implications of the unavoidable statements of the New Testament about the entire world as the object of the love of a God "whose will it is that all men should find salvation and come to know the truth" (*1 Tm.* 2:4). Origen in the third century, Gregory of Nys-sa in the fourth century, Nicholas of Cusa in the fif- teenth century—these and other theologians, committed though they were to the church and to its orthodoxy, have taken up the exposition of a universal vision in which the love of God revealed in Christ cannot be completely fulfilled until all God's creation has been reconciled.

Faith, Hope, and Love. The complex, sometimes labyrinthine, interactions of faith, hope, and love with one another throughout Christian history and throughout Christianity as a system suggest the absence of a set of universal principles that could, in the fashion of Euclid's geometry, yield *the* Christian worldview. Christianity is, rather, the product of a continuing and organic history. Its principal institutional expression has been the church in its various organizational forms, but Christianity is more than the church. Although its chief intellectual product has been a theological development that spans twenty centuries, the Christian message is not coextensive with its theology. Its most telling effect on history has been in the faith and life of its celebrated saints and seers, but Christianity has consistently declared that its power and spirit can be found as well among the silent in the land, the meek who shall inherit the earth.

BIBLIOGRAPHY

Christianity is fortunate in having had more works of general reference published about it than any other world religion. Probably the most convenient of these is *The Oxford Dictionary of the Christian Church,* 2d ed., rev. (Oxford, 1983). Also in English, and especially helpful for its bibliographies, is *The New Catholic Encyclopedia,* 17 vols. (New York, 1967-1969). With more articles, a good many of which, however, are relatively brief, the *Lexikon für Theologie und Kirche,* 11 vols., 2d ed., edited by Michael Buchberger (Freiburg, 1957-1967), is a masterpiece of condensation. The succeeding editions of the *Realenzyklopädie für protestantische Theologie und Kirche,* 24 vols., 3d ed. (Leipzig, 1896-1913), whose fourth edition is now in preparation, have contained status reports on research into most of the themes treated in this article. And the *Dictionnaire de théologie catholique,* 15 double vols. (Paris, 1909-1950), presents comprehensive articles, some of them entire monographs, on many of the same themes.

The monographic literature on the history and the theology of Christianity is, quite literally, incomprehensible in its scope and cannot engage our attention here. But among more general works, perhaps the best overall treatment of its history is in *Histoire de l'église depuis les origines jusqu'à nos jours,* edited by Augustin Fliche, Victor Martin, and others (Paris, 1934-1964). *The Pelican History of the Church,* 6 vols., edited by Owen Chadwick (Harmondsworth, 1960-1970), is excellent, except for its omission of a volume on the Christian East, and always readable and often incisive. The more ambitious *Oxford History of the Christian Church,* 2 vols. to date, edited by Henry Chadwick and Owen Chadwick (Oxford, 1977-), may well be a collaborative work destined to match Fliche-Martin in comprehensiveness. *Atlas zur Kirchengeschichte,* edited by Hubert Jedin, Kenneth Scott Latourette, and Jochen Martin (Freiburg, 1970), provides a sense of place for ideas and books that in the theological literature sometimes seem to be suspended in mid- air. The history of those ideas is the concern of my work *The Christian Tradition: A History of the Development of Doctrine,* 5 vols. (Chicago, 1971-), and the books are chronicled with a sureness of touch and with great fairness in Johannes Quasten's *Patrology,* 4 vols. (Utrecht, 1950-1960).

Of the many thousands of attempts at a systematic formulation of Christianity as a religion of faith, hope, and love (and therefore not only of Christian dogmatics, but of the entire Christian message), it may seem presumptuous to select only five: John of Damascus's *On the Orthodox Faith* in the eighth century, which has played a significant part in all three major segments of Christendom, Orthodox, Roman Catholic, and Protestant; Peter Lombard's *Sentences* in the twelfth century, which, with the more than one thousand commentaries that have been written on it, shaped Christian teaching for centuries; Thomas Aquinas's *Summa theologiae* in the thirteenth century, which many students of Christian thought would regard as the climax of its development; John Calvin's *The Institutes of the Christian Religion* in the sixteenth century, which summarized the principal tenets of the Protestant Reformation more masterfully than any other book of theology; and Friedrich Schleiermacher's *The Christian Faith* in the nineteenth century, which, both by its successes and by its failures, is an eloquent statement of the predicament and the promise of the Christian message.

JAROSLAV PELIKAN

CHRISTIAN SCIENCE

CHRISTIAN SCIENCE is a religious movement emphasizing Christian healing as proof of the supremacy of spiritual over physical power. Founded by Mary Baker Eddy, a New Englander of predominantly Calvinistic background, Christian Science emerged as a distinct phenomenon in American religious life during a period of both social and religious crisis.

Mary Baker Eddy from her earliest years showed a deep-seated longing for the divine that was broadly characteristic of the Christian tradition and especially prominent in Puritanism. She found it impossible, however, to reconcile her deepest religious feelings with the theology of a then decadent Calvinism. Yet while other revolts against Calvinism, such as those of Unitarianism and Transcendentalism, led to an attenuation or even an abandonment of Christian convictions, Eddy's Christianity was so deeply ingrained that she found it impossible to think of any ultimate answer to what she called the "problem of being" outside of a theistic, biblical context.

Running parallel to this search, and contributing heuristically to it, was Eddy's own long quest for health. She had exhausted the healing methods of the time, including homeopathy, and although she found useful hints concerning the mental causes of disease, she never found the permanent health for which she was looking. Her growing disenchantment with all curative methods returned her to her spiritual quest, which led to a radically different perception of God and creation. Namely, that reality is, in truth, wholly spiritual.

Eddy identified the advent of this conviction with her "instantaneous" recovery in 1866 from the effects of a severe accident while reading an account of one of Jesus' healings. She described the event as follows: "That short experience included a glimpse of the great fact that I have since tried to make plain to others, namely, Life in and of Spirit; this Life being the sole reality of existence."

There can be no doubt that this moment of recovery marked an important turning point in Eddy's life, impelling the development of the theology and metaphysics to which she gave expression in her major book, *Science and Health with Key to the Scriptures,* first published in 1875. The primary purpose of the book was not to set forth a new systematic theology, but rather to serve as a textbook for religious practice. The focus throughout was on awakening the capacity of its readers to experience the presence of God directly; the "honest seekers for Truth".

A key point of Christian Science is that the understanding of God must include a changed view of reality itself. In effect, *Science and Health* challenged the traditional Christian view of God as the creator of a material world—not on philosophic grounds, even though Eddy's conclusions are partially articulated in philosophic terms—but on the grounds of a radical reinterpretation of the meaning of the gospel. Christian Science takes the works of Jesus, culminating in his resurrection and final ascension above all things material, as pointing to the essential spiritual nature of being. Accordingly, his life exemplifies the possibility of action outside of and contrary to the limits of a finite, material sense of

> **Christian Science does not deify Jesus, a point that its severest critics have sometimes said separates it conclusively from traditional Christianity.**

existence. From the standpoint of traditional Christianity, Jesus' works constituted supernatural interruptions of natural process and law; from the standpoint of Christian Science, they resulted from the operation of divine power comprehended as spiritual law.

Christian Science does not deify Jesus, a point that its severest critics have sometimes said separates it conclusively from traditional Christianity. Jesus' actual role in the achievement of humanity's salvation is as important to its theology as for traditional Christianity. His life of obedience and sacrifice is understood as the means through which the reality of being for humankind has broken through in the midst of ordinary human experience. This true spiritual selfhood is identified as the eternal Christ, as distinct from Jesus, although uniquely and fully incarnated in him. His mission is viewed as opening up the possibility for all men and women to make actual their own spiritual union with God. He did this by proving practically that neither sin nor suffering is part of authentic spiritual selfhood, or Christ.

While Christian Science holds that evil has no God-derived existence and therefore can be regarded ontologically as not real, it strongly emphasizes the need for healing rather than ignoring the manifold manifestations of the carnal mind, and as operating with hypnotic intensity in human experience. Such healing is to be accomplished through yielding to the action of the divine Mind. Salvation, while seen as the effect of divine grace, requires prayer, self-renunciation, and radical, unremitting warfare against the evils of the mortal condition.

Salvation includes obedience to Jesus' command to heal the sick. Sickness is one expression of the fundamental error of the mortal mind that accepts existence as something separate from God. Healing, therefore, must be predicated on the action of the divine Mind or power outside of human thought. Healing is regarded not merely as a bodily change, but as a phase of full salvation from the flesh as well. It is the normalization of bodily function and formation through the

divine government of the human mentality and of the bodily system that that mentality governs.

The emphasis in Christian Science upon healing—primarily of sin, secondarily disease—is based on the concrete issues of everyday lived experience. The healing emphasis differentiates Christian Science from philosophies of idealism with which it is often carelessly identified, including the Emersonian transcendentalism that was part of its immediate cultural background. Indeed, departures from Eddy's teaching within the Christian Science movement itself have tended generally toward metaphysical abstraction, wherein her statements almost completely lose their bearings on daily experience.

In the context of Eddy's writings, however, such statements almost always point to the demand and possibility of demonstrating in actual experience what she understood as spiritual fact. Her abstract statement that "God is All," for instance, taken by itself could imply a pantheistic identification of humankind and the universe with God. Taken in the full context of her teachings, it indicates that God's infinitude and omnipotence rule out the legitimacy, permanence, and substantiality of anything contrary to God's nature as Principle, Mind, Spirit, Soul, Life, Truth, and Love, an assertion that is taken to be demonstrably practical in concrete situations, to some degree at least.

Although Christian Science is explicitly committed to universal salvation, it focuses initially and primarily on the potential for transformation and healing within the individual. This focus, deviant as it has often seemed to conservative Christians, tends to associate it with the traditional Protestant concern over individual salvation, giving it a conservative cast in the eyes of more liberal Christians who wish to transform the social order. The identification of Christian Science with a conservative, well-to-do, middle-class ideology may be as misleading in a sociological sense as it is theologically. In fact, a greater segment of the movement comes from rural or lower-middle-class backgrounds than most outside accounts would suggest.

On the whole, the church does not share the social activism of many mainstream denominations, but its purpose in publishing *The Christian Science Monitor* indicates a substantial commitment to an interest in the public good. Eddy founded the *Monitor* in 1908 as the most appropriate vehicle for the political and social expression of the practical idealism of her teaching. The character of the *Monitor,* to a degree, reflects the educational purpose of the church that publishes it.

It was not part of her original purpose to found a separate denomination; rather, she and a group of her students founded the Church of Christ, Scientist, in 1879, when it became clear that other Christian churches were not disposed to accept her teaching. The overall structure of the church was laid out in a document of skeletal simplicity, the *Manual of*

The Mother Church, which Eddy first published in 1895 and continued to develop until her death.

The central administrative functions of this "mother" church, the First Church of Christ, Scientist, in Boston, are presided over by a five-member, self-perpetuating board of directors. The Mother Church, with its branches, including some 3,000 congregations in fifty countries, constitute the Church of Christ, Scientist; the congregations are self-governing within the framework provided by the *Manual.*

The absence of an ordained clergy, ritualistically observed sacraments, and all but the most spare symbols point to the almost Quaker-like simplicity of the Christian Science concept of worship, in which silent prayer has an important role and the sacraments are conceived of as a process of continuing purification and quiet communion with God.

Christian Science practitioners, listed monthly in *The Christian Science Journal,* are members who devote themselves full time to the ministry of spiritual healing, and a significant body of testimonies of healing— amounting to some 50,000 published accounts—has been amassed in Christian Science periodicals over the years. There is good evidence that this sustained commitment of an entire denomination over more than a century to the practice of spiritual healing has been a significant factor in the reawakening of interest in Christian healing among many denominations in the 1960s and 1970s.

By the 1979 centennial of the founding of the church, the Christian Science movement found itself experiencing greater challenges from the currents of secular materialism than it had encountered since the early days of its founding.

BIBLIOGRAPHY

The basic document of the Christian Science movement is Mary Baker Eddy's *Science and Health with Key to the Scriptures* (1875; reprint, Boston, 1914), which contains the full statement of its teaching. Extensive historical background on Christian Science can be found in Robert Peel's trilogy, *Mary Baker Eddy: The Years of Discovery, The Years of Trial, The Years of Authority* (New York, 1966-1977). Peel's earlier *Christian Science: Its Encounter with American Culture* (New York, 1958) places Christian Science in its New England cultural context, relating it to both transcendentalism and pragmatism, while my own *The Emergence of Christian Science in American Religious Life* (Berkeley, 1973) gives a full account of Christian Science within the context of American religious development. An early, pathbreaking study of the theology of Christian Science is the essay by Karl Holl, "Szientismus," in Gesammelte *Aufsätze zur Kirchengeschichte,* vol. 3 (Tübingen, 1921-1928). A representative though reductionist treatment of Christian Science from a sociological perspective is the section on Christian Science in Bryan R. Wilson's *Sects and Societies: A Sociological Study of the Elim Tabernacle, Christian Science and Christadelphians* (1961; reprint, Westport, Conn., 1978). Charles S. Braden's *Christian Science Today: Power, Policy, Practice* (Dallas, 1958) attempts an overview of organizational developments, drawing largely on dissident sources. One reason for the paucity of adequate academic accounts of Christian Science is suggested in Thomas C. Johnsen's article "Historical Consensus and Christian Science: The Career of a Manuscript Controversy," *New England Quarterly* 53 (March 1980): 3-22. A popular but slapdash history of the early phases of the movement is Norman Beasley's *The Cross and the Crown* (New York, 1952). Basic documentation on Christian Science healing is given in the church-published *A Century of Christian Science Healing* (Boston, 1966).

STEPHEN GOTTSCHALK

CHRISTIAN SOCIAL MOVEMENTS

Christian social movements are distinguished by their increasing ability to assume the right to organize, by their more overt goals of addressing specific social problems or groups, and by a rebirth of historical consciousness that expects human agency, in the service of God, to establish righteousness and overcome social evil by concerted action. Movements sharing these characteristics have evolved in a variety of directions.

Some organizations have been formed specifically to foster social service objectives. Christian hospitals, orphanages, and homes for mentally and physically handicapped persons can today be found in nearly every sizable community in the Western world as well as, increasingly, in developing countries where mission movements have been active. Until the late nineteenth century, most of the colleges and universities of the West were founded by the churches, orders, or sects, or by authorities wanting to foster a specific religious perspective. Other service organizations, such as the Freemasons, developed altogether outside churches or sects.

More radical social action movements are not only found in the Radical Reformation of the sixteenth century, but in subsequent centuries as well. In the course of the Cromwellian Revolution in England, and after the French Revolution, many Christians saw direct political involvement as a duty of faith. Christian political parties were formed in most of the countries of Europe (and, later, in many countries colonized by Europe) in the wake of these democratizing developments. Geared to making the moral and spiritual values of specific Christian groups politically influential, they protected the church groups they represented from domination by other religions or by anti-religious secularization.

Many argue that it was post-Reformation Christianity that was the key stimulus to modern democratic and technological developments. Others argue that political and technical changes brought about new religious developments. Whatever the case, the religiously legitimated democratizing revolutions of the seventeenth and eighteenth centuries, and the technological revolutions of the nineteenth and twentieth, ushered in a series of new paraecclesial efforts, some of which became movements within established churches, some of which produced new sects, and some of which produced new denominations. The Lutheranism of the Prussian Junkers, the Catholicism of much continental peasantry, and the Anglicanism of the British agrarian Tories are some groups that became established.

Further, the experience of pilgrimage to a new land (America) reinforced theories of historical change. Immigration and internal religious developments brought a vast pluralization of religions that even theocratic efforts in such states as Massachusetts could not contain. And the fact that American developments took place in an environment that had no established feudal or imperial traditions that had to be overcome produced a widespread process of social experimentation. These factors interacted to produce a variety of alternative congregations and paraecclesial organizations unique in human history.

By the time that the last state constitutions in the United States were altered so that all churches were disestablished and legally viewed as voluntary associations (i. e., in the 1830s), even those who had fought the trend became enthusiastic proponents of the idea that Christian social witness was to be carried out by voluntary, paraecclesial social movements. The dominant view became one that held that freedom of religion means not only tolerance but the duty of committed people to organize movements for social service and social change outside government and distinct from the worshiping congregation. It was believed that this was precisely what God had intended from the Exodus.

A veritable explosion of social movements took place on these foundations during the nineteenth and twentieth centuries. Nearly all of these claimed to be Christian in root and direction, although they were seldom offically connected to formal church organizations. Mission societies ministering to Native Americans, to the people in the semicivilized Western frontiers, and to the dispossessed inhabitants of the American cities, as well as to the "heathen" abroad, were formed everywhere. Many of the contemporary churches of Asia, Africa, and the Pacific Islands, which today struggle to bring about democratic, pluralistic societies, find their roots in these mission efforts. At home, militant Christian antislavery organizations and antisaloon leagues were soon to arise in the wake of revivalisms.

After the Civil War, which accelerated the American late entry into the industrial revolution, an enormous number of organizations were formed to evangelize and to build schools and hospitals for and with the newly freed black Americans. Black churches proliferated and became the center of worship and community organization over a wide range of issues.

In many rural areas, Christians organized advocacy and cooperative associations. Less self-consciously rooted in theology is the Patrons of Husbandry (The Grange), which drew some patterns of ritual and belief from the Freemasons. The immigrants to the cities from the farms and from the underclasses of Europe were met with City Missionary Societies, an expanding Young Men's Christian Association, the newer but also growing Young Women's Christian Association, settlement houses, and Christian labor unions.

To raise funds to sustain these organizations, the voluntarism of church organization produced a new interpretation of the biblical concept of stewardship, one that called upon church members not only to give sacrificially but to support mission, outreach, cultural activities, social action, and benevolence agencies by paraecclesial institutions that serve the common good. These exhortations have surely not been inconsequential. During the 1970s total giving to the some two million nonprofit, voluntary organizations in the United States roughly paralleled the United States defense budget and employed one out of every six professional workers and one out of eleven service workers, providing one of the most striking contrasts between American society and most other societies of the world.

Many of the funds for Christian social movements in the nineteenth century were raised by women's groups in the churches. Victorian women of means and charitable intent, as well as wives of workers and farmers, organized literary societies, bake sales, quilting bees, and knitting parties "for good Christian causes." The full effect of these organizations has yet to be documented; but the existent literature suggests that these efforts provided the skills, opportunities for sisterhood, and organized channels for developing independent perspectives on political and social issues that were to eventuate in the suffrage movement and in later drives advocating other women's rights. Some contemporary women's organizations have been hostile to the churches, but women's organizations in the churches (such as Church Women United and the Women's Division of the United Methodist Church) have been forceful advocates of change in both church and society.

World War I and the Depression brought other developments that modified the direction of Christian social movements. Some advocates of neoorthodoxy in theology argued that all this energetic American activism in the name of Christ had misunderstood both the depth of sin in human history and the message of the gospel. Second, many of the movements generated out of Christian motivations became little more than interest groups struggling primarily to get as many material rewards for their own constituents as possible. And third, fundamentalism arose as a new kind of independent social and religious movement specifically critical of Darwinist cosmology, anthropology, and social theories.

Two European movements of considerable consequence were also underway. Socialist proletarians of the left engaged in increasingly sharp criticism of any connection between religion and socially progressive movements. Simultaneously, a series of aristocratic conservatives, from John Ruskin in England, to Bishop Wilhem Ketteler in Germany, Comte de Mun in France, and Cardinal Mermillod in Switzerland, also undertook the study of emerging social problems and began a series of protests against democracy, which they saw as the conspiracy of Jewish bankers and Protestant industrialists to reduce the worker and farmer to servitude.

These Anglo-Catholic and Roman Catholic leaders developed their positive proposals on a view of the duties of the "Christian state," the "Christian family," and the "Christian church" as organic, comprehensive communities based on natural law and revealed dogma by which the lives of all persons were to be sustained and guided. One of the great ironies of the period was that the actual programs of the antireligious, socialist left and the "social Catholic," neofeudal right converged to produce legislation promoting the power of workers' guilds, constraining political and religious pluralism, and limiting the development of economic capitalism. When these themes were propagated by Leo XIII, a new course was set for Catholic engagement with modern social issues, one that is having great consequence today with the rise of (essentially Romah Catholic) "political theology" and "liberation theology."

Some Catholics endeavored to form social movements in late nineteenth-century America and adopted motifs from the essentially Protestant Social Gospel. However, when they became too enthusiastic about the virtues of pluralism, democracy, and capitalism as Christian possibilities, their efforts were condemned by Rome as "Americanism" and "modernism." Nevertheless, when Leo XIII's *Rerum novarum* (1891) opened the door to social commentary and action, new patterns of Catholic social thought and activity were stimulated. A new generation of American Catholic scholars and activists fomented social service and social advocacy within a decidedly democratic framework and toward a new form of welfare capitalism. The Bishops' Program of Social Reconstruction (1919) is a landmark of this new direction.

Internationally, the rise of National Socialism in Germany and Stalinism in the Soviet Union, as well as the painful experience of the Great Depression, caused Christian social movements to become increasingly focused on overtly political strategies to overcome both the threats of political tyranny and the chaos of economic anarchy. On the extreme right, paraecclesial organizations, such as the Ku Klux Klan and the White Citizens Councils, expanded and attributed the ills of the nation to blacks, Catholics, Jews, and communists and attempted to use Christian symbols to legitimate their hate. Nearly all church bodies preached against such organiza-

tions and threw their attention instead to a wide variety of theologically based efforts on the other end of the political spectrum such as the Fellowship of Socialist Christians, the Fellowship of Reconciliation, and the Religion and Labor Council. More notable, however, is the successor to the Social Gospel, Christian Realism—a tough-minded theological orientation (often associated with Reinhold Niebuhr) that became the governing form for rearticulation of the Christian

> **The United States involvement in Vietnam also brought about another spate of church and paraecclesial efforts to alter public policy.**

vision during the Depression, World War II, and the cold war. Under this umbrella, many of the social service aspects of previous Christian social movements remained, but government was increasingly pressed to assume responsibility for providing support to those in need.

After World War II, a new generation of leaders arose from the black churches, the most famous of these leaders being Martin Luther King, Jr. He organized a new Christian social movement—the Southern Christian Leadership Conference—to confront the "betrayal of the American dream" and the racist organizations that manipulated discriminatory laws. His efforts were soon emulated by others of many races and creeds.

The United States involvement in Vietnam also brought about another spate of church and paraecclesial efforts to alter public policy. The organization Clergy and Laity Concerned about Vietnam is perhaps the most important nationally, but local organizations seemed to spring from the chaplain's office on nearly every university campus. Many of the people engaged in the antiwar protests were also those who, after the war, became involved in organizing boycotts against lettuce growers who employed migrant workers at below-standard pay rates, clothing manufacturers who resisted unionization, and infant-formula manufacturers who utilized questionable marketing techniques in very poor countries.

These brief references to international issues from the American perspective should not obscure the fact that one of the most important developments in Christian social movements is now very vital in parts of Africa, Latin America, and Asia—generally under the rubric "liberation theology." Roman Catholic church authorities have been critical of this style of political-theological reflection, suspecting that it is too deeply influenced by Marxist social analysis and too independent of ecclesiastical and doctrinal discipline. Further, scholars disagree on whether the perspectives being developed in these regions of the world can be considered "theology" in any classical sense of the word; but even critics acknowledge liberation theology's social importance and its Christian impulses. In Korea, the Philippines, South Africa, and much of Central and South America, these movements may become the most articulate and forceful advocates of human rights, democracy, economic justice, racial equality, and freedom of religion that can be found, or they may become a new form of established folk religiosity legitimating single-party revolutionary governments, as their critics fear.

BIBLIOGRAPHY

Without question, the most important work on Christian social movements written in the twentieth century remains Ernst Troeltsch's *The Social Teaching of Christian Churches,* 2 vols. (1931; reprint, Chicago, 1981). Key subsequent works interpreting the Western and European traditions are *Puritanism and Liberty,* edited by A. S. P. Woodhouse (London, 1938), which focuses on the Cromwellian period; William O. Shanahan's *German Protestants Face the Social Question* (Notre Dame, Ind., 1954), which documents Lutheran struggles with modernization; and James Hastings Nichols's *Democracy and the Churches* (Philadelphia, 1951), which compares Roman Catholic and Reformed political developments.

Both Arend T. van Leeuwen's *Christianity in World History* (New York, 1964) and *The Protestant Ethic and Modernization,* edited by Shmuel N. Eisenstadt (New York, 1968), trace the impact of Western traditions on developing nations; and my *Creeds, Society, and Human Rights: A Study in Three Cultures* (Grand Rapids, Mich., 1984) compares Western social and religious movements to those of eastern Europe and South Asia.

A formative understanding of Christian social movements in America can be found in H. Richard Niebuhr's *The Social Sources of Denominationalism* (New York, 1929), which stresses the influence of social interests on religious teachings and organizations; while major influences of theological traditions on American social directions are collected in *Voluntary Associations: A Study of Groups in Free Societies,* edited by D. B. Robertson (Richmond, Va., 1966). Timothy Smith's Revivalism and *Social Reform in Mid-Nineteenth Century America* (New York, 1957) and George M. Marsden's *Fundamentalism and American Culture* (New York, 1980) trace the rise and influence of evangelical and fundamentalist movements on American society, while Charles Hopkin's *The Rise of the Social Gospel in American Protestantism,* 1865-1915 (New Haven, 1940) and Paul A. Carter's *The Decline and Revival of the Social Gospel* (London, 1956) trace the social teachings and movements of liberal and ecumenical Protestantism. The best new treatment of religious social thought in the United States is A. J. Reichley's *Religion in American Public Life* (Washington, D. C., 1985).

New directions in Roman Catholic social thought, especially as it struggles with pluralistic democracy and the socialism of liberation theology, can be found in David Hollenbach's *Claims in Conflict* (New York, 1979); in the two-volume collection *Human Rights in the Americas,* edited by Alfred Hennelly and John Lagan (Washington, D. C., 1982); and in *Human Rights and Basic Needs in the Americas,* edited by Margaret E. Crahan (Washington, D. C., 1982).

MAX L. STACKHOUSE

CHRISTMAS

CHRISTMAS is the Christian celebration of the birth of Jesus Christ. The name, English in origin, means "Christ's Mass," the mass celebrating the feast of Christ's nativity. Names for Christmas in Romance languages are derived from the Latin *nativitas.*

There is no certain knowledge of the origin of the Christmas feast. By the end of the fourth century the observance on 25 December of the feast of Christ's nativity had spread throughout most of the Christian world. At Antioch, Chrysostom regarded it as the actual date of Christ's birth. In the mid-fifth century the Jerusalem church, too, accepted the 25 December date, which then replaced the older celebration of the nativity there on 6 January.

The Western Christian observance of Christmas was strongly influenced by the celebration of this feast in the city of Rome. Three masses came to be celebrated by the pope on Christmas Day. Since the eighth century the Western Christian celebration of Christmas has been provided with an octave, or eight days of liturgical observance, in imitation of the feasts of Easter and Epiphany.

After the sixteenth century most of the Reformation churches retained the Christmas feast. Martin Luther showed great devotion to Christmas in his preaching. However, the English Puritans tried to do away with the celebration of Christmas altogether in the course of the seventeenth century, but the feast was revived with the restoration of the English monarchy in 1660. Under the Puritan influence in early America, especially in New England, Christmas was a regular workday until the middle of the nineteenth century.

The customs of Christmas in the Northern Hemisphere include, in addition to Christian religious practices and midwinter feasting, various celebrations of the returning light of the sun. To celebrate the victory of life over winter's death and to combat evil spirits, homes are decorated in this darkest period of the year with lights and evergreens of all kinds. Similarly, the Yule log was kindled on Christmas Eve in northern countries and kept burning until Epiphany, and remains of the log were kept to kindle the next year's Yule fire. The Christmas tree itself seems to be of rather recent origin: it may be as late as the sixteenth century that Germans first decorated a fir tree with lights, fruits, and tinsel.

BIBLIOGRAPHY

For a complete bibliography, see Sue Samuelson's *Christmas: An Annotated Bibliography of Analytical Scholarship* (New York, 1982). The most comprehensive treatment of the history of the Christmas celebration is still Hermann Usener's *Das Weihnachtsfest* (Bonn, 1889). For a survey of the liturgical development of the feast, see Ildephonso Schuster's *The Sacramentary* (New York, 1924). A good treatment of the customs associated with Christmas may be found in

Francis X. Weiser's *Handbook of Christian Feasts and Customs* (New York, 1958), as well as in the same author's *The Christmas Book* (New York, 1952). For a treatment of the feast from the perspective of the history of religions, see E. O. James's *Seasonal Feasts and Festivals* (New York, 1961).

JOHN F. BALDOVIN, S.J.

CHUANG-TZU

CHUANG-TZU (369?-286? BCE), the most important exponent of Taoist thought in ancient China. His name was Chuang Chou; *tzu* is a suffix meaning "Master." The brief account of him in chapter 63 of the *Shih chi* or *Records of the Historian* by Ssu-ma Ch'ien (145?-89? BCE) states that he was a native of Meng, served for a time as an official in Ch'i-yüan, and wrote a work in 100,000 words or more that was "mostly in the nature of fable."

Chuang-tzu's thought, like that of Lao-tzu (reputed founder of Taoist philosophy), is strongly mystical in character. He confronts the same essential problem as that faced by the other early Chinese philosophers: how is one to live in a world beset by disorder, strife, and suffering? But whereas other philosophers customarily proposed some program of political, social, or ethical reform by which such evils might be ameliorated, Chuang-tzu approaches the problem in a radically different fashion. Rather than seeking to remake the world, he would free man from suffering by inducing him to shed the system of values that differentiates pleasure from pain, good from evil, and labels one desirable, the other undesirable. In effect, he would have the individual learn to achieve a kind of mystical identification with existence as a whole.

This totality of existence, which Chuang-tzu calls the Tao, or the Way, embraces all forms of being, all life, and is in a constant process of change.

The person who has attained the level of enlightenment that Chuang-tzu envisions will no longer be able to accept the values of ordinary human society. Its promises of pleasure and material gain will seem empty to him, and he will perceive only the perils that attend one who gains too much worldly prominence. His way of life will embody the Taoist ideal of *wu-wei*, or inaction, by which is meant not a forced quietude, but rather the renunciation of any action that is occasioned by conventional concepts of purpose or achievement, or aimed at the realization of conventional goals.

Naturally, it is a vision that can never appeal to more than a small group in society. A society made up entirely of Taoists would very quickly degenerate into chaos. But as a kind of antidote to the overwhelmingly political orientation of the other schools of Chinese philosophy and their emphasis upon conformity, the vision of Chuang-tzu and other Taoists has done much to broaden the Chinese character and nourish in it a respect for individualism and the life of the imagination.

The work known as the *Chuang-tzu* consists of thirty-three sections. It seems to have been condensed from a somewhat larger mass of material by Kuo Hsiang (d. 312 CE), a leader of the Neo-Taoist movement, who edited the text and appended a commentary, the oldest now extant. It is generally agreed that the "inner chapters" are the most brilliant and original in expression and set forth all the important ideas of the work. The remaining chapters, though at times containing passages of almost equal brilliance, are generally less striking in style and content Undoubtedly they are the work of many different hands, and in some cases they may date from as late as the third or fourth century, when Kuo Hsiang edited the text.

Chuang-tzu's thought is highly unconventional in nature, and his method of argumentation is marked by a liberal use of wit, fantasy, and paradox. Seldom does he favor us with a passage of sustained and logical argumentation. Rather, he seems to delight in keeping the reader constantly surprised and off balance, wooing him away from conventional ways of thought by the very strangeness and unpredictability of his discourse.

Because of this disjointed manner of presentation and the combination of whimsy and homey detail that marks the episodes, Chuang-tzu's writings, though of immense literary appeal, are difficult to read, and the difficulties have been greatly compounded by textual corruptions that have crept into the work, presumably as a result of the bafflement of copyists. But, despite these difficulties, the *Chuang-tzu* seems never to have lacked for readers. It enjoyed particular popularity at the time of the Neo-Taoist movement in the third and fourth centuries CE, when Confucianism was temporarily in eclipse, and allusions to the text abound in the poetry of the period. When Buddhism began to attract notice in Chinese intellectual circles at about the same time, apparent similarities between Chuang-tzu's thought and that of the Buddhist philosophers were quickly noted, and Taoist terms were frequently borrowed in an attempt to make Buddhism more readily understandable to Chinese minds.

[*For further discussion of Chuang-tzu's role in the history of Taoist thought, see* Taoism.]

BIBLIOGRAPHY

Fung Yu-lan. *Chuang Tzu: A New Selected Translation* (1933). 2d ed. New York, 1964. A translation of the "inner chapters," with excerpts from the Kuo Hsiang commentary.

Giles, Herbert A., trans. *Chuang Tzu: Mystic, Moralist, and Social Reformer* (1889). 2d rev. ed. London, 1926. A complete translation into Victorian English.

Graham, A. C. *Chuang-tzu: The Seven Inner Chapters and Other Writings from the Book of Chuang-tzu.* London, 1981. Selected translations by an outstanding Chuang-tzu scholar.

Mair, Victor H., ed. *Experimental Essays on Chuang-tzu.* Honolulu, 1983. Essays by various writers on different aspects of the text.

Waley, Arthur. *Three Ways of Thought in Ancient China* (1939). Garden City, N. Y., 1956. Selected translations from the Chuang-tzu with an excellent discussion.

Watson, Burton, trans. *The Complete Works of Chuang Tzu.* New York, 1968. A complete translation into modern colloquial English.

BURTON WATSON

CHURCH

Episcopal Form of Government. The Roman Catholic, Orthodox, and Anglican churches, which considered the historical continuity of ministry from the beginning of Christianity to have the highest priority, retained the episcopacy as the key office in the church. The bishops were viewed as the successors of the twelve apostles. Each of these communions, however, has structured its episcopal commitment in a different way.

Roman Catholic. The Second Vatican Council introduced a new structure known as the Synod of Bishops. Since 1965, this representative body of about two hundred bishops chosen from different regions of the world has met, usually every three years, to aid the pope in promoting faith and morals, in strengthening ecclesiastical discipline, and in directing the church's worldwide activity.

The cardinals of the Roman church, who are appointed for life by a reigning pope, constitute a special college whose chief function is to elect the bishop of Rome. In recent years all areas of the world have been represented in the college of cardinals. The number is not fixed, but since Vatican II it has hovered at about 120. The cardinals also act as a body of advisers when summoned to deal with questions of major importance, and they head some of the offices of the Curia Romana.

The pope usually conducts the business of the universal church through the Curia, which acts in his name and by his authority. Furthermore, the papacy maintains a corps of representatives throughout the world. When these legates are only to the local churches, they are known as apostolic delegates. If they are accredited to states and governments, they are ranked nuncio, pronuncio, or internuncio. (Reciprocally, more than one hundred governments maintain diplomatic relations with the Vatican.) In addition to serving a liaison function, the papal legates, in cooperation with the bishops, clergy, and laity of the country, transmit to Rome lists of potential candidates for the episcopacy.

The Roman Catholic church is made up of particular churches, certain portions of the people of God "in which and from which the one and unique Catholic church exists" (canon 368). A particular church is above all a diocese that is entrusted to a bishop assisted by a presbyterate. As a general rule, a diocese is circumscribed by territorial bounds so as to embrace all the faithful within that area.

It is the prerogative of the pope to appoint bishops to take charge of particular churches or to confirm those who have been legitimately elected. At least every three years the bishops of an ecclesiastical province are to draw up a list of priests suitable for the episcopacy that is then sent to Rome. A diocesan bishop governs the particular church committed to his care with legislative, executive, and judicial power according to the norms of the law. He exercises legislative power personally, executive power either personally or through vicars, and judicial power either personally or through a judicial vicar. He is aided in his government by the presbyterial council (a body of priests) and by his staff. Every five years the bishop is to send to Rome a report on the state of the diocese. Upon reaching the age of seventy-five, he is asked to submit his resignation to the pope.

Of the approximately 784 million Catholics in the world, about 12 million belong to the Eastern churches.

Orthodox and other Eastern churches. The Eastern Orthodox church is not centrally organized but is a federation composed of fourteen autocephalous, or self-governing, churches and seven others, which are known as autonomous. "Autocephaly" connotes the right possessed by a group of eparchies (dioceses) to settle all internal matters on their own authority and to elect their own bishops, including the head of the church. The boundaries of autocephalies are usually coterminous with those of a state or nation. The autonomous churches, while to a large degree self-governing, have not yet achieved full independence:

There is no bishop among the Orthodox churches who holds a position analogous to that of the pope in the Roman church, but the patriarch of Constantinople is recognized as the ecumenical or universal patriarch. He holds a place of honor and precedence, and his authority over the Orthodox world is a moral one, the first among equals. Supreme authority belongs only to a pan-Orthodox council.

The Greek Orthodox Church in North and South America, the largest body of Orthodox in the Western Hemisphere, with two million communicants, enacted a new constitution, which was ratified by the ecumenical patriarch in 1978. The church consists of the Archdiocese of New York, nine dioceses in the United States, and one each in Canada and South America. The archbishop, who resides in New York, is the primate, the highest authority of the church in the Americas; he is the exarch (viceroy) of the ecumenical patriarchate. The archbishop presides over a Holy Synod of bishops, which makes decisions and regulates ecclesiastical life in accord with the canons or laws of the church. [*See* Greek Orthodox Church.]

The second largest Orthodox body in the New World is the Orthodox Church in America, with approximately one million members. It received independent status from the Patriarchate of Moscow in 1970 against the will of the ecumenical patriarch. It too adopted a new statute, in 1971. [*See* Russian Orthodox Church.]

Anglican and Episcopalian churches. The episcopal constitution of the church and apostolic succession are also fundamental to the Anglican communion, which is made up of about twenty-five autonomous and six nonautonomous churches found mainly in English-speaking countries and former colonies of England. Usually every ten years, an assemblage of archbishops and bishops of the entire communion, called the Lambeth Conference, convenes in the Lambeth Palace, London, under the presidency of the archbishop of Canterbury. The conference, which does not publish details of its debates, issues resolutions with only moral binding force.

The parent body, the Church of England, is an established church with the sovereign of the country as its head. Acting upon the advice of the prime minister, the sovereign nominates the archbishops and bishops. The church is divided into the province of Canterbury, whose archbishop is styled "Primate of All England and Metropolitan," and the province of York, whose archbishop is called "Primate of England and Metropolitan." The archbishop oversees all the dioceses with-

> ## The parent body, the Church of England, is an established church with the sovereign of the country as its head.

in the province, confirms the election of every bishop and is his chief consecrator, and hears appeals in his provincial court. The archbishop of Canterbury, with the approval of the crown, may grant licenses and dispensations that are valid throughout the province of York as well.

In the United States the church affiliated with the Anglican communion is the Protestant Episcopal church. It is governed by a bicameral General Convention meeting triennially or at special call. The House of Bishops consists of all bishops. The presiding bishop is entrusted with general executive power over the whole Episcopal church. The House of Deputies comprises not more than four priests and four laypeople elected from each diocese.

To establish a diocese there must be at least six parishes and six voting presbyters. The diocese meets in convention annually with all diocesan clergy and representatives from each parish as members. The convention elects clerical and lay delegates to the provincial synod and to the General Convention. Each diocesan convention also elects a standing committee to advise the bishop between sessions. A bishop must retire at the age of seventy-two.

The diocesan convention is responsible for defining the boundaries of parishes and for establishing new ones. Each parish is governed by a vestry and wardens selected according to diocesan law. The vestry members are the "agents and legal representatives of the parish." The vestry elects the pastor or rector and notifies the bishop of its choice. Though the bishop may try to dissuade the vestry, he has little option but to accept their choice. The appointment is considered to be for life; the rector cannot be removed against his will except with the consent of the bishop.

Methodist churches. The vast majority of the Methodists in the United States recognize the centrality of the episcopacy in their governing structure, although they do not accept it as an order different from the presbyterate. The ordained ministry consists of elders (presbyters) and deacons who are "set apart by the Church for the specialized ministry of Word, Sacrament, and Order" (par. 302, *The Book of Discipline of the United Methodist Church,* 1972).

Presbyterial Form of Government. Presbyterians do not admit as normative a historically validated episcopal succession. They hold that there is no New Testament warrant for a distinct office of bishop; "presbyters" (elders) and "bishops" designate the same leadership body in the church (*Acts* 20:17-28, *1 Tm.* 3:1-13). The polity of presbyterian churches rests on three constitutive principles: (1) "the parity of presbyters" (both clergy and lay); (2) "the right of the people through their representatives or lay elders to take part in the government of the church"; and (3) "the unity of the Church, not simply in faith and order, but in a graduated series of Church Courts [session, presbytery, synod, General Assembly] which express and exercise the common authority of the Church as a divine society" (James Moffatt, *The Presbyterian Churches*, London, 1928).

The presbyteries of a region are grouped into a synod. A synod must have at least three presbyteries. Elected representatives, both clerical and lay, from each of the presbyteries constitute a synod, which meets once a year. It serves as a court of appeal from actions taken by the presbyteries and stands in an intermediary position between the presbyteries and the General Assembly.

Congregational Form of Government. Opposed in principle to any form of control above or outside the local church, a third group of Christian denominations is organized along congregational lines so that each community is independent. The defenders of this ecclesial pattern of government maintain that the New Testament does not recognize any higher structure.

In the United States the Baptists have been the most conspicuous advocates of a democratic polity. Although Baptists do not have an official creed, they generally subscribe to two important confessions of faith, the Philadelphia Confession (1742) and the New Hampshire Confession (1833). Each congregation is self-constituting: the members bind themselves together by covenant, accepting as the sole rule of faith the Bible, which the members interpret according to their own lights. The members choose their own leaders—variously called elders, bishops, pastors—who are set apart for the ministry. The laity retain full control so that all business is determined by majority vote.

Congregationalism is also espoused by the United Church of Christ, which was formed by the merger of four denominations in 1961: the Congregational Church, the Christian Church, the Evangelical Synods, and the Reformed Church. Each of the uniting churches has maintained its own theological position and form of worship. The constitution of the United Church of Christ states explicitly that "the autonomy of the local church is inherent and modifiable only by its own action" (Douglas Horton, *The United Church of Christ*, New York, 1962). The local congregations, however, are joined together for mutual support.

Not all churches fit neatly into one system or another. The Lutheran church, the third largest body of Christians in the world after the Roman Catholics and the Eastern Orthodox, does not hold that any polity is divinely sanctioned.

In the United States the three largest denominations, about 95 percent of the nine million Lutherans in the country, acknowledge varying degrees of local autonomy. Parishes are generally grouped into districts, which in turn are organized into territorial synods. The powers exercised by the synod are specified in a constitution. At all levels, pastors and lay representatives participate in the government. Synodal authority is concerned chiefly with the ordination and discipline of the clergy and ownership of property.

BIBLIOGRAPHY

Campenhausen, Hans von. *Kirchliches Amt und geistliche Vollmacht*. Tübingen, 1953. Translated by J. A. Baker as *Ecclesiastical Authority and Spiritual Power in the Church of the First Three Centuries*. Stanford, Calif., 1969. Treats the relationship between ministerial office and charismatic gifts.

Dulles, Avery. *Models of the Church*. New York, 1974. Discusses five major approaches, types, or models through which the character of the church may be grasped.

Empie, Paul C., and T. Austin Murphy. *Papal Primacy and the Universal Church*. Minneapolis, 1974. Lutherans and Catholics in Dialogue V. Scholars from both churches present a historical and theological view of the papacy.

Huizing, Peter, and Knut Walf, eds. *The Roman Curia and the Communion of Churches*. Concilium Series, no. 127. New York, 1980. Analyzes the central government of the Roman Catholic church in the post-Vatican II era.

Kirk, Kenneth E., ed. *The Apostolic Ministry: Essays on the History and Doctrine of Episcopacy*. London, 1946. A team of writers explores the Christian doctrine of ministry.

Kretschmar, Georg, et al. *The Councils of the Church: History and Analysis*. Edited by Hans J. Margull. Philadelphia, 1966. After a historical treatment of councils, authors from various churches present their respective theologies on the subject.

McNutt, William Roy. *Polity and Practice in Baptist Churches*. Chicago, 1959. An exposition of the congregationalism followed by the Baptist tradition.

Mead, Frank S., ed. *Handbook of Denominations in the United States*. 7th ed. Nashville, 1980. Describes the historical background, main teachings, and governmental organization of more than two hundred and fifty religious bodies.

Meyendorff, John. *The Orthodox Church: Its Past and Its Role in the World Today*. 3d ed. Crestwood, N. Y. 1981. Chapter 8 discusses the autocephalous churches in the post-World War II era.

Neill, Stephen Charles, and Hans-Ruedi Weber, eds. *The Layman in Christian History*. Philadelphia, 1963. Traces the place of laypeople in the church from the beginning up to the present; the Roman Catholic and Protestant traditions are extensively treated.

Niebuhr, H. Richard, and Daniel D. Williams. *The Ministry in Historical Perspectives*. New York, 1956. Nine authors treat the ministry from the primitive church to the twentieth century, with emphasis on Protestantism.

Pelikan, Jaroslav. *Spirit versus Structure: Luther and the Institutions of the Church*. New York, 1968. After sketching Luther's rejection of sacramental ordination, monasticism, and canon law, Pelikan considers the struggles of the reformers to deal with the need for concrete structures.

Portillo, Alvaro del. *Fieles y laicos en la Iglesia*. Pamplona, 1969. Translated by Leo Hickey as *Faithful and Laity in the Church*. Shannon, Ireland, 1972. A Roman Catholic canon lawyer analyzes the rights and duties of the laity that should be recognized in law.

Rudge, Peter F. *Ministry and Management*. London, 1968. An attempt at "managerial theology"; theories of management developed in the lay world of business and public administration are applied to ecclesiastical administration.

Schaver, John Louis. *The Polity of the Churches*. 2 vols. Chicago, 1947. After treating all the Christian churches in the first volume, the author deals in the second volume with the Christian Reformed church.

Stevick, Daniel B. *Canon Law: A Handbook*. New York, 1965. A history of canon law, the constitution of the Protestant Episcopal church in the United States, and the canons of that church. Chapter 3, "Ecclesiastical Polity," provides a good overview of the subject.

JOHN E. LYNCH, C.S.P.

CHURCH AND STATE

Roman Empire. With the conversion of the emperor Constantine in 312 and the establishment of Christianity as the official religion of the Roman empire in 381, the church was brought under the direct support of the imperial authority. Heretics were barred from government and clerical offices. Orthodox clergy were given special military protection, legal privileges, and financial support to spread the faith, to educate the young, to care for the poor, and to build new churches and monasteries.

The church was also brought within the emperor's direct domain. Though he was no longer worshiped as a god, the emperor remained the supreme ruler of both civil and religious affairs.

Neither the Eastern nor the Western emperors, however, ruled the church without restriction. For all their authority, and even sanctity, the emperors were not ordained priests but laymen. During worship they sat in the congregation (though in a place of honor), and they had no authority to administer the sacraments. They had to accept the church's instruction, judgment, and spiritual discipline.

Germanic Kingdoms. The system of imperial or royal rule within the church prevailed in the West until the late eleventh century. Before their conversion to Christianity, the Germanic kings, like the pagan Roman emperors, were considered to be divine and were the cult leaders, as well as the military leaders, of their people. Upon conversion, they too lost their divinity yet continued as sacral rulers of the church within their respective territories. They too found in Christianity an important source of authority in their efforts to extend their rule over the diverse peoples that made up their kingdoms and empires. The clergy not only supported the Germanic Christian kings in the suppression of tribal religions but also looked upon figures such as the Frankish emperor Charlemagne (r. 769-814) and the Anglo-Saxon king Alfred (r.. 871-899) as their spiritual leaders. The kings in turn supported the clergy in the struggle against Christian heresies and gave them military protection.

Papal Revolution. The interrelationship of church and state changed drastically in the century between 1050 and 1150, when a large part of the clergy throughout Western Christendom united under the bishop of Rome to form an independent polity, separate from the secular authority of emperors, kings, and feudal lords. This was the papal revolution, which broke into violence in the Investiture Controversy of 1075-1122. In his famous *Dictates of the Pope* (1075), Gregory VII proclaimed that emperors and kings had no authority over the church; that the bishop of Rome alone had authority to ordain, discipline, depose, and reinstate bishops, to convoke and control councils, and to establish and administer abbeys and bishoprics; that only the pope had authority "to enact new laws according to the needs of the time"; that the papal court was "the court of the whole of Christendom."

In the twelfth century the Roman Catholic church established itself as a unified, hierarchical, autonomous, political-legal entity. The Gelasian injunction was transformed into a "two swords" doctrine, with the papacy wielding the "spiritual" sword and emperors, kings, feudal lords, urban rulers, and other political authorities wielding the "temporal" sword. By the Concordat of Worms (1122) the secular arm lost its right to invest priests and bishops with the symbols of their offices.

The church also asserted its own independent property rights in the vast ecclesiastical holdings that constituted nearly one-third of the land of western Europe.

Conflicts between the ecclesiastical and secular authorities had to be resolved at many different levels. For example, when ecclesiastical courts sought to exercise jurisdiction over disputes involving property in which both clerical and lay interests were involved, or over violent crimes committed by clerics, a secular court might issue a writ of prohibition, which the spiritual arm might resist by threatening to excommunicate the secular judges.

Mostly, however, despite a continual undercurrent of rivalry and tension between them, state and church cooperated with each other.

The dualist character of church-state relationships in the period from Gregory VII to the Protestant Reformation inspired a wide range of theoretical interpretations. In the twelfth and thirteenth centuries the prevailing theory, as set forth by John of Salisbury (c. 1115-1180) and others, taught that Christ as the head of Christendom had appointed the pope as his vicegerent and had vested in him the plenitude of his divine power.

In the fourteenth and fifteenth centuries there were substantial increases in royal power over the church, especially in France, England, Spain, and the various German principalities, and a corresponding decline in papal authority, both in secular affairs and within the church itself.

Despite such shifts in the theory and practice of church-state relationships, a balance was preserved during this period between the universal jurisdiction of the church of Rome (not only over the clergy, but also over various aspects of the life of the laity) and the plural jurisdictions of the various secular polities of Western Christendom.

Reformation Era. With the Protestant Reformation, however, the very concept of a visible, hierarchical, corporate church, exercising a political and legal jurisdiction, came under attack. Martin Luther (1483-1546) replaced the Gregorian "two swords" theory with a theory of two kingdoms, the earthly and the heavenly. The true church, he declared, is the invisible community of faithful believers established by the gospel as part of the heavenly kingdom. In the earthly kingdom, the church, to be sure, assumes a visible form; nevertheless, it retains its divine government in which all are priests, accountable for the spiritual welfare of each other. Therefore, the church needs no clerical hierarchy to mediate between God and the laity, no canon law to define the various paths for salvation, and no ecclesiastical courts to adjudicate laws and convict criminals. [*See* Reformation.] Luther's radical separation of the earthly and heavenly kingdoms left all legal and political authority to the civil ruler, the prince..

Lutheranism became the established religion in most of the principalities of Germany and in Scandinavia. Its implications for church-state relations were spelled out most clearly in the Danish Church Ordinance of 1539, which vested in the Christian monarch supreme authority over the church, entitling him to supervise the preaching of the word, the administration of the sacraments, the Christian upbringing of children, and care of the poor. The ordinance ordered all the monarch's subjects to comply with the Augsburg Confession and Luther's catechism. In passing the ordinance, the king severed all ties with Rome, confiscated land and titles of the Roman Catholic church, closed monasteries and convents, and ordered Catholics to heed his ordinance on pain of banishment.

In Germany, the conflict between the Lutheran and the Roman Catholic parties was resolved in the Peace of Augsburg (1555), which empowered each prince to establish either Catholicism or Lutheranism within his territory. The prince governed the territorial church but had to permit dissenting Christian subjects to emigrate. In the imperial cities, on the other hand, Catholics and Lutherans were to have equal rights. Non-Lutheran Protestants, however, were banned from Germany altogether.

In the English Reformation of the sixteenth century, the Anglican church was established, with the monarch at its head. Through a series of statutes enacted in the 1530s, King Henry VIII severed all ties between the church in England and the pope. The Act of Succession (1534), which annulled Henry's marriage to Catherine of Aragon, denied papal authority over marriage and divorce generally. Succeeding acts effectively divested the Roman church of all its remaining jurisdiction and banned all tithes, annates, and appeals to Rome. [*See* Anglicanism.]

As spiritual and temporal heads of the new Anglican church, Henry and his successors, through their parliaments, established a uniform liturgy, doctrine, and administration of the sacraments and issued *The Book of Common Prayer* in the vernacular.

In sixteenth-century Switzerland, France, and the Netherlands there emerged a number of Calvinist groups. Although affirming many features of Luther's theology, the Calvinists conceived the visible church not as subordinate to the state in any way but as an equal, independent institution. Calvinist churches emphasized their own internal rules of order and discipline, and their officers were called not only to preach the word and administer the sacraments but also to reform the world.

In sixteenth-century Spain, the Habsburg monarchs waged a bloody campaign against Jesuits and other Catholics who opposed their domination of the Roman Catholic church. In the Netherlands the same monarchs persecuted the Calvinists. By the end of the sixteenth century, however, the Spanish monarchy acceded to papal demands for toleration of the Jesuits in Spain and for legal protection of their religious houses and schools, while in the Netherlands it granted Calvinist churches their independence.

Religious Establishment. In the first half of the seventeenth century, Europe experienced bitter wars of religion between and among Roman Catholics and Protestants, which finally ended in the Peace of Westphalia (1648). Confirming the principles of the Peace of Augsburg and the Edict of Nantes, this treaty authorized each ruler to establish either Catholicism, Lutheranism, or Calvinism in his territory.

In France, however, the absolute monarchs gradually abandoned the toleration policy of the Edict of Nantes and the Peace of Westphalia. Supported by the antipapalism of the revived Gallican party and by the theories of absolute monarchy expounded by Jean Bodin and others, the French monarchs organized a national Catholic church, sharply curtailing remaining papal power over church property, ecclesiastical courts, and clerical nomination. Louis XIV passed more than one hundred acts against Huguenots and other dissenters, both Protestant and Catholic, confining their freedoms and imposing crushing taxes upon them. Finally, in the Edict of Fontainebleau (1685), Louis repealed the Edict of

> **Louis XIV passed more than one hundred acts against Huguenots and other dissenters. . . .**

Nantes, ordered all Protestant churches and schools destroyed, proscribed all liturgies and theologies that deviated from officially sanctioned Gallicanism, and banished all dissenting clerics from France.

In England, increased royal repression of the growing number of Protestant sects during the early seventeenth century provoked militant Protestant forces to overthrow the monarchy. In 1649 a Puritan commonwealth was created, which suffered no religious establishment and tolerated both Protestants and Anglicans, though not Roman Catholics. This policy was reaffirmed after the reestablishment of Anglicanism in 1660. In the Bill of Rights and the Toleration Act of 1689, Parliament granted freedom of association and worship to all Protestants. Many of the remaining legal restrictions on the civil and political liberties of Protestants were removed in the following decades.

In the eighteenth century the church in many parts of Europe, whether Roman Catholic or Protestant, was increasingly dominated by civil authorities. The most sweeping controls were imposed by the "benevolent despots" of Prussia (especially Frederick II) and Austria (especially Maria Theresa and Joseph II), who placed church property under state administration, appointed Catholic bishops without papal approval and Protestant clergy without synodal approbation. They freely altered church liturgy, changed diocesan

COHEN, HERMANN

boundaries, taxed convents and religious houses, and closed them if they resisted.

Toleration and Autonomy Philosophers of the Enlightenment, such as Voltaire, who stressed the autonomy of the individual, the freedom to seek one's own happiness, and a person's right to express his own opinion and will, also advocated the religious neutrality of civil government and civil law. These ideas were eventually embodied in the French Revolution of 1789 and came to vivid practical expression in the disestablishment policies adopted by many countries as they fell under the influence of democratic revolutionary changes in the late eighteenth and early nineteenth centuries. No country of Europe, however, enacted such strong guarantees of religious freedom or such severe restrictions on state support of religion as those provided in the United States Constitution of 1791 and in various American state constitutions of that period. [*See* Law and Religion.]

[*See the biographies of Constantine, Charlemagne, and Luther.*]

BIBLIOGRAPHY

Barker, Ernst, ed. and trans. *Social and Political Thought in Byzantium.* Oxford, 1957.

Berman, Harold J. *Law and Revolution: The Formation of the Western Legal Tradition.* Cambridge, Mass., 1983.

Bohatec, Josef. *Calvins Lehre von Staat und Kirche mit besonderer Berücksichtigung des Organismusgedankens* (1937). Reprint, Aalen, 1961.

Carlyle, A. J., and R. W. Carlyle. *A History of Mediaeval Political Theory in the West.* 6 vols. Edinburgh, 1903-1936.

Dawson, Christopher. *Religion and the Modern State.* New York, 1935.

Ehler, Sidney Z, and John B. Morrall, eds. *Church and State through the Centuries: A Collection of Historic Documents with Commentaries.* London, 1954.

Gavin, Frank. *Seven Centuries of the Problem of Church and State.* Oxford, 1938.

Hyma, Albert. *Christianity and Politics: A History of the Principles and Struggles of Church and State.* New York, 1938.

Mueller, William A. *Church and State in Luther and Calvin.* Nashville, 1954.

Southern, Richard W. *Western Society and the Church in the Middle Ages.* Harmondsworth, 1970.

Tellenbach, Gerd. *Church, State and Christian Society at the Time of the Investiture* Conflict. London, 1959.

Tierney, Brian. *The Crisis of Church and State, 1050-1300.* Englewood Cliffs, N. J., 1964.

Tonkin, John. *The Church and the Secular Order in Reformation Thought.* New York, 1971.

Voigt, Karl. *Staat und Kirche von Konstantin dem Grossen bis zum Ende der Karolingerzeit.* Stuttgart, 1936.

Ziegler, Adolf Wilhelm. *Religion, Kirche, und Staat in Geschichte und Gegenwart.* 3 vols. Munich, 1969.

HAROLD J. BERMAN and JOHN WITTE, JR.

COHEN, HERMANN (1842-1918), Jewish philosopher of religion, founder and exponent of Marburg Neo-Kantian philosophy. Born into a cantor's family in the small-town Jewish community of Coswig/Anhalt, Germany, Cohen received intense religious training from his father, in addition to the general education typical of his time and place. The transition from these beginnings to the modern rabbinical seminary of Breslau was natural. Part of the seminary's curriculum was the requirement of university studies. At the University of Breslau, Cohen decided that philosophy, rather than the rabbinate, was his *métier.*

Transferring to the University of Berlin, Cohen first fell under the influence of the "folk-psychological" epistemologists Heymann Steinthal and Moritz Lazarus, but he quickly progressed to a more Kantian and logicistic outlook. His habilitation thesis on Kant's theory of experience was published in 1871, and in the context of the "back to Kant" movement of the day his ideas had a revolutionary impact.

During his long incumbency in Marburg, Cohen not only produced the bulk of his own philosophic oeuvre but also gathered around him a group that came to constitute the Marburg school of Neo-Kantianism. Among the many scholars associated with him were his student and subsequent colleague Paul Natorp and, later, Ernst Cassirer. Cohen attracted many devoted students and disciples, particularly Jews from German-speaking countries, from eastern Europe, and even America. However, his personal, philosophical, and social relations at the university became increasingly strained down through the years, not least because of growing political reaction during that period against the overtly ethical, that is, Kantian, anti-Marxist, and antimaterialist socialism of the Marburg school.

Throughout his life Cohen never ceased to be active in Jewish matters. For example, he published his *The Love of Neighbor in the Talmud: Affidavit before the Royal Court of Marburg* in 1888 (in German) in response to the notorious Rohling/Delagarde anti-Semitic episode in which the old "blood libel" and Jewish xenophobism combined with the then nascent German racism. He wrote voluminously on Jewish subjects; in 1924 his writings were collected in three volumes, edited and introduced by Franz Rosenzweig, author of *The Star of Redemption.*

Cohen's Writings. Cohen's work can be divided into three parts: his exegetical readings of Immanuel Kant, his "system of philosophy," and his specifically Jewish work.

Cohen's radicalized, Neo-Kantian understanding of reality and of ethics that developed directly from his critiques of Kant found expression in his *Logik der reinen Erkentniss* (Logic of Pure Cognition; 1902, 1914), *Ethik des reinen Willens* (Ethics of the Pure Will; 1904-1907), and *Ästhetik* des reinen Gefühls (Aesthetic of Pure Feeling; 1912). Here the universe is determined by the three "interests" of reason (cognition, will, and feeling), which strive for the traditional ideals of truth, goodness, and beauty.

Cohen's specifically Jewish work. His work in this area, intimated in his philosophizing and, increasingly, explicitly identified with it, was systematically elaborated in the final decade of his life and was consummated in the posthumously published *Religion der Vernunft aus den Quellen des Judentums* (Religion of Reason out of the Sources of Judaism; 1919, 1929). Cohen's Jewish philosophical theology (although he did not use this terminology) consists of a translation back into classical Jewish terms of the philosophical position Cohen held from Judaism with the help of the progressive line of thought running from Plato through Maimonides to Kant. Thus God is the idea of the normative, infinite realization of the good in the world. This realization is known in religion as the establishment by means of "the imitation of God" of the messianic kingdom on earth. The Law (*halakhah*) is the historical Jewish specifications of the categorical imperative and the foundation of the universal human moral brotherhood of the "Noachide covenant," which is also the religious, "Prophetic," goal of socialism.

Influence of Cohen's Work. Cohen's philosophical and Jewish influence is scattered in diverse and embattled manifestations. Around the turn of the century a rebellion emerged against what was perceived as the extreme scientific, rationalistic theoreticism of Marburg Neo-Kantianism. In reaction there appeared positions that asserted the ultimate power of "reality" over reason in "life-philosophy," re-hegelianizing historicism, positivism, and nascent existentialist phenomenologism. In German circles the value of historical and even metaphysical "Germanism" *(Deutschtum)* was apostrophized, and in Jewish circles a parallel affirmation of the peoplehood of Israel and the historical or even metaphysical "genius" of the Jewish people was pitted against "bloodless" and "lifeless" assimilationist universalism. The fact that Franz Rosenzweig, a disciple of Friedrich Meinecke and author of important studies on Hegel, became Cohen's last disciple added another complicating element, for Rosenzweig interpreted the "late Cohen" as the precursor of a total break with systematic rationalism in favor of a Schellingian form of metahistoricism.

Politically, religiously, and philosophically very different extrapolations continue to this day to be made from Cohen's fundamental analyses.

BIBLIOGRAPHY

Sponsored by the Hermann-Cohen-Archiv under the direction of Helmut Holzhey, publication of Cohen's *Werke* (Hildesheim and New York, 1978-) is currently under way. Among his works available in English are *Religion and Hope: Selections from the Jewish Writings of Hermann Cohen,* translated by Eva Jospe (New York, 1971), and *Religion of Reason out of the Sources of Judaism,* translated by Simon Kaplan (New York, 1972).

For commentary on Cohen's place in modern Jewish thought, see Julius Guttmann's *Philosophies of Judaism,* translated by David W. Silverman (New York, 1964), pp. 352-367, and Nathan Rotenstreich's *Jewish Philosophy in Modern Times* (New York, 1968), pp. 52-105.

STEVEN S. SCHWARZSCHILD

COMMUNITY

Characteristics of Religious Community. Some form of initiation usually marks entrance into a religious community. Later transition ceremonies often mark the beginning of new status within a group (e.g., ordination or monastic profession). There are also rituals and procedures for leaving a group, by incorporation into a higher status beyond the perimeters of the former group, or by censure and repudiation. Even death, which would seem to end an individual's membership in a community, can be understood as an initiation into a yet higher degree of existence in the group.

Communal ritual activities for other purposes or on other occasions than initiation or ordination are also characteristic marks of religious communities. These rituals may be focused on seasonal change, agricultural processes, famous events of history, and doctrines, usually with all these elements blended together. Gathering as a group for such rites is perhaps the most persistent aspect of religious community, and is arguably its reason for being.

Differentiation of function and of merit or value is often recognized in communal structure. In some cases special functions within the group, especially leadership in ritual activities, are assumed by individuals specially selected and consecrated; in other cases leaders emerge from the group charismatically. That is, some religious traditions are highly sensitive to structural arrangements and carefully delineate lines of command and authority, carefully categorizing all functions and degrees. In other traditions the patterns of authority are quite casual, very much dependent on individual initiative and lacking ritual recognition.

Religious communities often validate, or give religious meaning to, natural or social distinctions. Gender, for example, is often a significant determinant of an individual's role in a religious community. One's role in the family (as mother, son, etc.) or one's lineage (e.g., in a caste system) may also determine religious status, and one's political office or status as a leader in the society at large tends to take on religious significance.

Religious communities are different from other social groups in their concept of the community as a sacred phenomenon. The distinctly religious group sees itself as part of a larger structure, plan, or purpose, one that transcends the immediate or basic needs of humanity.

Where nature and its processes are the focal point of religious attention, the community is conceived and structured with reference to the natural world. The subgroups within a tribe, for example, are linked in the mind with animals, stars, and the like.

Among religious groups for whom nature is not the primary concern, the concept of the community as a sacred entity takes a variety of forms. A special relationship with one or more gods or goddesses may be expressed by seeing the group as the servants, the messengers, or perhaps the co-workers of the divine beings. There is a fine line between metaphors and ontological assertions in theological language, so one often does not know how precisely to take images, such as the church as the "body" of Christ, that seem to give a group a kind of organic participation in the sacred.

A concept of the group as sacred can be linked with the merit or attainments of adepts with various degrees of skill. Those who are most advanced in ascetic practice, meditation, or yoga may constitute a sacred core around or below which those of lesser attainments are ranked. This arrangement leads to a pattern illustrated by Buddhism, according to which the term for the community, *samgha*, may refer to the inner circle of monks *(bhikkhus)* or to the larger group, the laity, who subscribe to the doctrine but practice it less exclusively.

It is possible, of course, for a religious community to be structured along lines that are not particularly religious from the point of view of believer or observer, as is so, for example, in the military model of the Salvation Army and the constitutional administrative arrangement of some American Protestant denominations. In such cases, concepts of the group as a sacred entity might become almost entirely separate from its actual structural appearance. It is odd, for example, to have a monastic pattern that is almost inevitably based on merit and attainment existing within a tradition that doctrinally asserts equality before God or some alternate kind of sacred hierarchy.

To summarize, we can assume that we are observing a religious community, whether it is so labeled or not, when most or all of the following characteristics are evident in reference to the sacred: rituals of initiation and incorporation (as well as those of rejection); other communal rituals; and status levels and functional distinctions.

"Natural" Religious Groups. One of the clearest distinctions to be made among religious communities is that between groups specifically and self-consciously organized around religious beliefs and activities and those societies or "natural" groups wherein whatever is religious is part of the whole social structure.

These broad categories have been labeled in many ways; for example, the terms *differentiated* and *undifferentiated*

have been used, based on the degree to which the religious group is differentiated from the society as a whole. Sometimes it seems better to designate the natural, or undifferentiated, type of religious community as "folk" religion and, by contrast, to see the specific religious community as "universal" in character.

I use the terms *specific* and *natural* in this article to name these groups, even though the latter term presents a problem

> In natural religious groups the religious leaders or functionaries are generally the leaders of the society as a whole.

of multiple meanings. Many presuppositions lie behind any use of *nature,* and most of these are irrelevant to my present use. I do not assume, for example, that natural religious groups are sociobiologically based in a way that specific groups are not.

Even though one is born into such social structures, initiation into "real" participation in the community is one of the signs that the social unit is also a religious community. At birth or puberty, or at both of these life passages, a ceremony such as circumcision or some act of consecration marks the official (or ontological) entrance into society.

In natural religious groups the religious leaders or functionaries are generally the leaders of the society as a whole.

It should also be noted that specific religious organizations may exist within natural religious groups. The primitive secret society is an example of such a group: it has its own dynamics as a voluntary group with special religious functions and rites apart from the society as a whole. Similarly, groups based on family, gender, ethnic background, and related natural factors may be found within or alongside specific religious communities or may even seem to merge with them. Men's fraternities are a common example of a gender-based grouping, and the practical identity (at least in former years) of Spanish background and Roman Catholicism is an example of the apparent merging of the natural with the specific religious community.

We face a special situation in the phenomenon of the nation as a religious community—special in that the basis of community is not necessarily "natural" in the way that it is for gender, family, or lineage. In a nation, unrelated peoples can be joined together, slaves or slave populations may be incorporated into the political unit, and foreigners may have a place in the society as merchants or mercenaries. When the nation is also a religious community, however, it typically develops a set of stories (a mythology) to make the diverse groups appear to be a family.

To the Israelites and other ancient peoples, political and religious functions were indistinguishable. While in modern times we differentiate between religious and civil law, ancient lawgivers recorded both in the same codes and in the same manner. The king was political, military, and religious functionary in one. Society, nature, and the gods were all seen as part of one interrelated organism. This outlook led to such phenomena as blaming crop failure on the weakness or immorality of the king. The king was characteristically seen as a god, the son of a god, or a representative and link from the heavens to earth and society.

This set of concepts is not entirely limited to the past. Some modern nations take on many of these characteristics (for some of their people) and thus become religious communities of a sort. Nations, both ancient and recent, have been known to cultivate epics of their origin, promote their peculiar concepts of the world, claim special connection with a god or gods, and link their success (or failure) to divine purpose. The Shinto tradition of Japan clearly exemplifies this phenomenon.

Specific Religious Communities. Specific religious communities are sometimes called "founded" religions because they have appeared within the scope of recorded history as the result of efforts of a particular person or small group. As noted above, this category could also be termed "universal," "differentiated," or "voluntary."

Sociologists of religion, mainly Westerners interested in Christian groups, have put most of their energies into analyzing specific religious groups. As the examination of the social dimensions of religion became a recognized scholarly discipline, the categories "church" and "sect" were developed to distinguish between religious communities. This terminology applied well to sixteenth-century Europe but was insufficient elsewhere. For America it was necessary to add at least the category "denomination." One widely used typology of religious groups that developed out of the earlier distinctions lists six major types of religious community: cult, sect, established sect (or institutionalized sect), denomination, ecclesia, and universal church. These six types can provide a framework for understanding Christian communities and can be applied with some adjustments to other religions as well.

The kind of group that is least involved in the rest of society is called a "cult." A cult may comprise barely more than the audience for a charismatic leader or healer. It is loosely organized; often it is small and short-lived. Its religious style is personal and emotional.

A "sect" is a religious community that is more clearly organized than a cult, that provides a great amount of religious value to its members (in terms of social relationships, ritual activities, ethical and doctrinal direction, and so forth), but that plays little role in the society at large. Taken to its extreme, a sect can form a completely separate miniature state either mixed into the society geographically or located in its own separate territory.

It is also possible, however, for a sect to move in a different direction and become more stable within the larger society. A sect so changed would be an "established sect," or an "institutionalized sect."

At this point the "denomination" assumes its place in the six-type scheme as another type of Western religious community. It is the kind of group that maintains separate and distinct organization despite its acceptance of the legitimacy of other denominations or communities. It may conceive of itself as the best, but hardly the only, community in which adequate religious practice can be found. It is also relatively more involved with and accepted by the larger society.

The next two categories represent the most established and, culturally and socially, the most prominent kinds of religious community. One has been called the "ecclesia" and consists of the established national churches, for example, the churches of England and of Sweden. The other is termed "universal church." It is as well established as the ecclesia but exists in many nations and cultures; the classic example is the Roman Catholic church of the thirteenth century.

One of the characteristics of the specific religious community as compared with the natural religious community is its voluntary character. Yet this characteristic is almost completely absent in the ecclesia and universal church and is of little importance in the denomination and the established sect. The sect is noted for its emphasis on conversion, a voluntary, adult decision to join the group. The more established churches, however, incorporate the children of members almost automatically into the community, thus operating somewhat like a natural religious group. Furthermore, kings and other political functionaries tend to become semireligious officials in the ecclesia and the universal church categories.

Most of the terminology used here has been derived from studies of Western Christian religious communities, but it can be applied to Eastern Christianity and other religions with some limited success. Sunni Islam can be seen as a universal church; Shi`i Islam in Iran can be seen as an ecclesia; other Shi`i groups can be seen as sects or established sects, and so on.

Communities within Communities. One large distinction that can be made within both natural and specific religious groups is that of "great" and "little" traditions. The professional leadership of a society or a specific religious community promotes a literate, fairly sophisticated, and often transcultural understanding and practice of its religion. The ordinary members of the group, however, may be imperfectly incorporated into this tradition. They may maintain some notions and practices from older religions or participate in the tradition in a way that is based on different media. These two strata do not form clearly separate communities but constitute a pattern in many countries.

On a much smaller scale there are other communal formations that can be found in both natural and specific religious communities. Prominent among these is the master, guru, or teacher with his following. This is the basic format of the cult. Beyond the first generation it must become something like a sect, pursuing a separate identity; it must institutionalize the master-pupil pattern in a more or less monastic structure; or it may do both. The model of the Hindu ashram or of the Muslim Sufi shaykh with his disciples indicates a recognition of this kind of religious community in their respective traditions but without much regularization or institutionalization.

The monastic community is often to be found within larger religious communities. It may be defined as a group of people drawn from a larger religious community who live together for shorter or longer periods of time in order to cultivate religious techniques and disciplines.

Certainly the most common subgroup in any large religious community is the worshiping unit. This can be quite an independent group with little involvement in the larger tradition, or it can be a casual association of people whose primary communal identity is with the larger group. Pilgrimage to a certain shrine can give a very large community the sense of being essentially one worshiping group even when most religious practice actually takes place in various localities.

BIBLIOGRAPHY

The most comprehensive typology of religious communities that attempts to cover all religions and cultures is Joachim Wach's *Sociology of Religion* (1944; reprint, Chicago, 1962). There is a shorter typology in Gerardus van der Leeuw's *Religion in Essence and Manifestation*, 2 vols., translated by J. E. Turner from the 2d German ed. (1938; reprint, Gloucester, Mass., 1967). Werner Stark's *The Sociology of Religion: A Study of Christendom,* 5 vols. (New York, 1966-1972) discusses the forms of community extensively, but it ignores non-Christian examples and structures. The distinction between church and sect was formulated by Ernst Troeltsch in *The Social Teaching of the Christian Churches,* 2 vols., translated by Olive Wyon (1911; reprint, New York, 1931). The form of the denomination was added to Troeltsch's pattern by H. Richard Niebuhr in *The Social Sources of Denominationalism* (New York, 1929). The sixfold typology of religious communities was developed by J. Milton Yinger in *Religion, Society, and the Individual* (New York, 1965) and elaborated by him in *The Scientific Study of Religion* (New York, 1970). A survey of the attempts to develop a typology of religious groups is to be found in Roland Robertson's *The Sociological Interpretation of Religion* (New York, 1970) and in Michael Hill's *A Sociology of Religion* (London, 1973). The dichotomy of the great and little traditions was created by Robert Redfield in *The Primitive World and Its Transformations* (Ithaca, N. Y., 1953) and *The Little Community: Viewpoints for the Study of a Human Whole* (Chicago, 1955). Examples of sects, mostly Christian but from many places around the world, are given in Bryan R. Wilson's *Religious Sects: A Sociological Study* (London, 1970).

GEORGE WECKMAN

CONFESSION OF SINS

The word *confession* has a twofold meaning that can be partially explained by etymology. The Latin *confiteor,* from which *confession* derives, means specifically "to confess a sin or fault," but also, in a more general sense, "to acknowledge or avow." Thus one may speak both of the sinner who confesses his sins and of the martyr who confesses his faith. Since the confession or witness of a martyr normally took place before a tribunal, it did in fact bear a formal resemblance to the confession of sins.

Confession of Sins in Nonliterate Cultures. An interpretation of the confession of sins among nonliterate peoples must consider that there is indeed a tension between theistic conceptions of confession, where the goal is divine forgiveness, and nontheistic conceptions, where the efficacy of confession is intrinsic to the act itself.

One of the most typical, perhaps the most typical subject of confession, is a woman's confession of adultery, particularly when the confession is occasioned by the act of childbirth. The recipient of the confession may be a priest, a sorcerer, the husband, or perhaps another woman. The woman making the confession must either enumerate her partners or identify them by name. This requirement may be intended to allow the offending partner to redress his wrong by offering a sacrifice or paying a fine (as among the Luo of Dyur and the Nuer of East Sudan respectively). Unconfessed adultery possesses an inherently obstructive power that must be removed by means of ritual confession. The Luo, the Nuer, and also the Atcholi of Uganda believe that the destructive

> **Unconfessed adultery possesses an inherently obstructive power that must be removed. . . .**

power of unconfessed adultery may become manifest through the death of the delivered child.

Another typical occasion for making a confession in nonliterate societies is the activity of hunting or fishing. Women must observe particular taboos while their husbands are away hunting in order not to compromise the success of the expedition. The husbands, during the days preceding departure, must abstain from various activities, in particular from cohabitation with their wives. Individual members of the hunting or fishing party must confess their sins prior to departure, since the unacknowledged breaking of a taboo or a persistent condition of impurity and culpability would endanger the success of the entire expedition.

Among the Lotuko of East Sudan, there is a public confession by the warriors at the beginning of the great hunting season. Their confessions are made individually with lowered voice and then repeated by the priest serving the rain god. Probably, the custom is meant symbolically to preserve, to the extent that it is possible, the originally individual character of confession. Other instances of confession on the occasion of annual ceremonies of renewal are found among the Bechuana, the Algonquin, and the Ojibwa.

Confession is also found in association with other rituals. Among the Nandi, a solemn form of confession is associated with circumcision. Among the Sulka (New Britain) and the Maya (Yucatán), confession is associated with initiation, and in Chiapas (Mexico) with marriage. In other words, confession may be an element in rites of passage, both individual and seasonal. Confession is sometimes associated with such ritual and ascetic procedures as fasting, abstinence, and chastity, evidently because of their importance in achieving ritual and/or ethical purity.

Finally, we must note the connection of confession of sins with the ordeal that may be used to test the sincerity of the confessing person. Here two different ritual procedures are intermingled. Evil is not the consequence of a sin that goes unconfessed; it is rather the consequence of a confession that was not sincere. The ethical side of confession becomes paramount; a reference to the elimination of occult sin would be out of place here. This instance makes clear the inadequacy of reducing confession strictly to a material utterance having magic, autonomous effects.

Confession of Sins in Traditional High Cultures and World Religions. We pass now to the significance of confession of sins in traditional high cultures (both past and present), which are mostly polytheistic, and to the world religions.

Mexico and Peru. Confession was practiced in old Mexico in connection with Tlacolteótl, the goddess of impurities. She symbolized the sexual offenses (particularly adultery) that were the main object of confession. The priests of the goddess acted as the recipients of confession, and the confession itself was understood as taking place before the great, omniscient god Tezcatlipoca. The confession was secret and was followed by the imposition of a rather complicated penance, to be performed on the festival day of the goddess.

In modern Mexico, confession is practiced by the Huichol at the time of the annual expedition to collect the hikuli, a sacred plant. This expedition requires a condition of purity in the participants, achieved through confession of sexual offenses. For mnemonic purposes, knots corresponding to

sins are tied in a rope that is then burned at the end, a typical symbolic form of elimination.

Confession was also practiced in Peru, associated with the bath *(upacuna)* and with other eliminatory or symbolic acts, such as blowing away powders. The recipient of confession was the *ichuri,* who was not a priest but belonged, rather, to a low class of diviners. The typical occasion for confession was sickness, whether of oneself or of one's relatives, and the integrity of the confession could be tested by ordeal. Other occasions included bad weather and times of preparation for festivals. The emperor (the *inca*) and the high priest ordinarily confessed their sins directly to the Sun and to the great god Viracocha, respectively.

The site of confession in Peru was the peninsula that provided access to the shrine of the Sun, located on a sacred island in Lake Titicaca. A long and detailed list of sins was employed, and some had to be confessed before the high priest.

Japan and China. The biannual Shinto ceremony of Ohoharahi resembles a rite of confession, but it is only a recitation of a complete list of possible sins or impurities by the *nakatomi,* a high dignitary, or by other priests. In China, eliminatory rituals were related to the grand conception of the Tao, the universal, heavenly order. A disturbance of this order, whether caused by the emperor or by his people, had serious consequences. It was the emperor's duty to redress the wrong, often through the vicarious performance of penance and a written confession of sins. Individual confession was also practiced in China, particularly in the context of the Taoist tradition, especially in the case of sickness.

India. In the Vedas there is an insistence on the purifying properties of fire and water together with faith in Varuna, a heavenly and omniscient god. Varuna punishes sinners by entangling and binding them in his net. He can also liberate the sinner from these bonds. He is connected with ethical laws, especially with the eternal order of *rta,* yet his *modus operandi* is clearly magical, and his jurisdiction extends to involuntary offenses. Nevertheless, the Vedas know nothing of confession proper; they know only of generic declarations of fault.

Jainism. Confession in Jainism (*alocana* and, more generally, *pratikramana*) is mainly a monastic institution, performed twice daily. The laity make confession before their respective gurus. Jainism combines the elimination of sin with the doctrine of the annihilation of *karman,* conceived of as something substantial. Confession before death is considered important, and an insincere confession can perpetuate the cycle of rebirths.

Buddhism. The Patimokkha of the Buddhist monks is a gradated list of possible sins or transgressions, recited bimonthly at the night services called Uposatha. The participant monks must be in a state of purity; sins must be confessed in an individual and reciprocal form. Similar occasion for confession was the *pavarana* ("invitation"), which occurred during the rainy season, when the monks led a sedentary life. Monks would invite from their fellows statements concerning their (i. e., the inviter's) individual conduct.

With Buddhism, the objective conception of sin and purification, found in both Jain and Brahmanic conceptions of *karman,* was abolished. *Karman* was now understood to be produced through the subjective element of volition.

Western Asia and Greece. It is difficult to assimilate the practices described in some of the epigraphic and literary texts of the religions of antiquity to the category of confession of sins. These texts mention the mere acknowledgment and subsequent public declaration of a sin or other offense by an individual. It is scarcely possible to speak of the confession of sins when the regent of Byblos writes to Amenophis IV that he has confessed his fault to the gods, or when the Hittite king Mursilis confesses a sin before the god of heaven. The same applies to the repeated confessional utterances *(homologein, exomologeisthai)* of the "superstitious man" described by Plutarch, a man continually and scrupulously resorting to purificatory rituals in the sanctuary. Nor can the term "confession" be applied to certain texts of Roman poets concerning personal experiences in the context of the cult of Egyptian deities or describing the vicissitudes of mythic or legendary characters.

None of these records mentions the recipient of an oral confession, a necessary element of any penitential structure or institution.

> **Babylonian religion recognized several theistic and magical means for eliminating ethical and ritual offenses.**

Southern Arabia, Babylon, Egypt. Some confessional inscriptions have been discovered in southern Arabia, although their chronology is uncertain. They seem similar to the confessional inscriptions of Phrygia, but with a peculiar emphasis on sexual sins.

Babylonian religion recognized several theistic and magical means for eliminating ethical and ritual offenses. For instance, lists of sins were written on tablets and were then destroyed. Nevertheless, a ritual of confession properly so called is far from clearly attested. The same holds for the Babylonian penitential psalms, despite their ritual background. Herodotus attributed to the people of Babylon the custom of placing the sick in the public square so that they might confess their sins publicly.

More akin to present typology is the negative confession of the king at the beginning of the New Year festival in Babylon, the Akitu festival. True, a negative confession in

which the king declares his innocence of a series of offenses against the city and the people is in a sense the opposite of a confession of sins. Yet both establish an immediate connection between the evocation of sin and the annihilation of it and its consequences. The most famous example of a negative confession is found in the Egyptian *Book of Going Forth by Day* (no. 125) where two complete lists of possible sins are used for the examination and weighing of the soul in the afterlife.

Israelite religion. Strong objections can be raised against the interpretation of many Old Testament texts, including the penitential psalms, as evidence for an institutionalized ritual of the confession of sins within the vast scope of the purification rituals. The same applies to the so-called collective confessions, where the general wording "we have sinned" (corresponding to the "I have sinned" of the former texts) does not properly fit into our typology Although the procedure has an oral, declaratory element, it cannot be assigned to the typology of confession.

Christianity. In the first centuries, the Christian church practiced a canonical penance for sins considered "mortal" or "capital." The penitential act started with the sinner entering the order of the penitents through a confession rendered before the bishop, or at least with the acceptance of the assigned penance. With the gradual introduction of the private form of confession, from the seventh century onward, a new form of the celebration of reconciliation came into practice. The private form of confession necessarily emphasized the "accusation" made by the penitent. The spiritual personality of the priest recipient of private confession was particularly stressed in the tradition of Eastern Christianity.

Zoroastrianism, Mandaean religion, and Manichaeism. From Sasanid times on, Zoroastrianism recognizes a form of the confession of sins, the *patet* ("expiation"), made before a priest or, in his absence, before the sun, the moon, and the divine fire. An annual confession is encouraged, in the month of Mihr (after Mihr, the god Mithra).

There are three main Manichaean texts used in confession. (1) The *Xastvanift,* consists of a list of sins and is intended for the laity (the "hearers"). Also employed were (2) a prayer composed in Chinese and used for communal confession and (3) a form of confession composed in Sogdian and intended for the elite, bearing the title *Manichaean Book of Prayer and Confession.*

The Mandaeans, adherents of a gnostic, ethnic religion that survives still in Iraq, recognize a confession for sins that can be repeated no more than two times before the sinner is excommunicated.

[*See also* Repentance *and, for a more general discussion* Purification.]

BIBLIOGRAPHY

For a discussion of the topic by one of its major interpreters, see Raffaele Pettazzoni's *La confessione dei peccati,* 3 vols. (1929-1936; Bologna, 1968). Pettazzoni's *La confession des péchés,* 2 vols. (Paris, 1931-1932), is the enlarged translation by René Monnot of volume 1 of the work mentioned above. For the Viennese school's criticism, see Leopold Walk's "Pettazzoni, Raffaele's `La Confessione dei peccati,'" *Anthropos* 31 (1936): 969-972, and a series of articles by Michele Schulien, listed in *Etnologia religiosa* (Turin, 1958), p. 286, note 7, by Renato Boccassino. Further studies by Pettazzoni on the theme are found in his *Essays on the History of Religions* (Leiden, 1954): "Confession of Sins and the Classics," pp. 55-67, and "Confession of Sins: An Attempted General Interpretation," pp. 43-54, with further bibliography found on page 54, note 12. P. Wilhelm Schmidt's *Der Ursprung der Gottesidee,* vols. 5, 7, 8 (Münster, 1934, 1940, 1949), discusses the concept among most primitive cultures as well as pastoral cultures (consult the indexes). See Franz Steinleitner's *Die Beicht im Zusammenhange mit der sakralen Rechtspflege in der Antike* (Leipzig, 1913) for the Anatolian confessional inscriptions and related topics. On the confession of sins in other traditions and cultures, see Arthur Darby Nock's *Essays on Religion and the Ancient World,* 2 vols., edited by Zeph Stewart (Cambridge, Mass., 1972), pp. 66 and 427, note 77; Jacques Duchesne-Guillemin's *La religion de l'Iran ancien* (Paris, 1962), pp. 113ff.; and Kurt Rudolph's *Die Mandäer,* vol. 2, *Der Kult* (Göttingen, 1961), pp. 247-254. The last work cited includes an extensive bibliography concerning confession in Zoroastrianism, Manichaeism, and Mandaeism. On doctrine and practice in contemporary Catholicism, see Pope John Paul II's *Reconciliation and Penance* (Washington, D. C., 1984).

UGO BIANCHI

CONFUCIAN THOUGHT

[*This entry consists of four articles:* Foundations of the Tradition, Neo-Confucianism, *and overviews of two specific cultures, namely* Confucianism in Japan *and* Confucianism in Korea.]

Foundations of the Tradition

Confucius and Confucian Thought. Confucius (the latinized form of the Chinese K`ung Fu-tzu, "Master K`ung") could trace this family heritage to nobility, but by the time of his birth the K`ung family was poor. Without benefit of a regular teacher, Confucius nonetheless managed to become a highly learned man, perhaps the most learned of his age, and had by his twenties begun to attract students. According to legend, in his thirties or forties he journeyed to the capital of Chou to consult the Taoist philosopher Lao-tzu (then the custodian of archives) on ceremonies. Upon returning to Lu several months later he encountered a steadily worsening political situation. In order to avoid the outbreak of civil hostilities, he fled to the neighboring state of Ch`i, where he was cordially consulted on government. Later, he returned to Lu and attracted more students. In 501 BCE, when he was fifty-one, he was made a magistrate in Lu. In that same year he also became minister of public works. Subsequently, he served Lu as a minister of justice, whose duties included foreign relations. As a magistrate, Confucius was said to have brought great peace.

Tradition holds that Confucius wrote the *Spring and Autumn Annals (Ch`un-ch`iu)* on the basis of records of his native state from the years 722 to 481 BCE (hence the name of the period), as well as the ten commentaries ("ten wings") of the *Book of Changes (I ching).* He is also credited with having edited the rest of the Six Classics, namely, the *Book of Odes (Shih ching),* the *Book of History (Shu ching),* the *Book of Rites (Li chi),* and the *Book of Music (Yüeh ching).* Modern scholarship has rejected much of this tradition, though recognizing that he was surely familiar with many poems and documents that later entered into these classics. On the other hand, it is likely that he wrote the *Spring and Autumn Annals* and at least one of the "ten wings." He died at the age of seventy-three, disappointed perhaps in public life but regarded by posterity as surely the greatest sage in Chinese history.

For over two thousand years he exercised a tremendous influence on Chinese life and thought. Korea, Japan, and Vietnam, too, periodically benefited from his teachings. Generally speaking, Confucius taught literature, ways of behavior, loyalty, and faithfulness. He often talked about history, poetry, and the performance of ceremonies. In this he started a tradition of liberal and moral education in China that was to eclipse the utilitarian and professionally oriented tradition that had hitherto dominated Chinese education. What is more important, while education had traditionally been reserved for the nobility, for Confucius education was open to all, without any class distinction. Following tradition, he glorified Heaven *(t`ien)* as great and august. He taught his pupils to know Heaven and to stand in awe of it. Significantly, however, Confucius did not regard Heaven as Ti, the Lord or the divine ruler, but as a supreme spiritual presence, the greatest moral power, and the source of everything.

It is clear that the superior man is possessed of many virtues. The greatest virtue that Confucius taught is *jen,* which specifically means benevolence but in a more general sense refers to humanity or what makes man a moral being. This is another new concept advanced by Confucius. Before his time, words like *shan,* meaning "goodness," or *te,* meaning "virtue," were widely employed, but these are terms for specific virtues, not terms for the universal virtue out of which all specific virtues grow. As in the case of *chün-tzu,* pupils asked about *jen* repeatedly. Forty-eight chapters out of 499 in the *Analects* were devoted to reflections on this concept. Confucius never defined it, perhaps because he felt the concept of a universal virtue was incapable of definition. In answer to his pupils' many questions, however, he did say that the man of *jen* loves man. He is a man of earnestness, liberality, truthfulness, diligence, and generosity. He is respectful in private life, serious in handling affairs, and loyal in dealing with others.

Confucius said that there is "one thread" running through his teachings. As his outstanding pupil, Tseng-tzu (505?-436? BCE), understood it, this one thread refers to loyalty in one's moral nature *(chung)* and treating others like oneself *(shu)*. Commentators on the *Analects* are unanimous that *chung* and *shu* are the two sides of *jen*, for they cover the total moral life, that is, both the individual and society. In a word, the man of *jen* is a man of total virtue.

To rule a state and restrain human behavior by insisting on fixed ethical norms, liturgically expressed, was unusual advice to give rulers in an age in which men were accustomed to ruling by force alone. Confucius said, "If a ruler is to govern his kingdom with the compliance proper to the rule of propriety (rites), what difficulty will he have?" When a duke asked Confucius how the ruler should employ his ministers and how the ministers should serve the ruler, he said, "A ruler should employ his ministers according to the rules of propriety, and ministers should serve their ruler with loyalty."

On the surface Confucius's political doctrines seem to center on the ruler, and, to be sure, this perceived emphasis in Confucius's teachings often led to autocracy in later times. However, Confucius gave equal importance to the plight of the ruler's subjects. He said a ruler must be economical in expenditure, love the people, and employ them at the proper seasons; he must enrich the people and educate them. When a pupil asked about government, he replied that there must be sufficiency of food, sufficiency of military equipment, and the confidence of the people; if one or two must be dispensed with, food and military equipment must go first. The ideal state, he declared, is one in which people living inside it are happy and people outside want to come in.

Another ethical doctrine that later became formalized as a philosophical notion is that of the "mean" *(chung)*. When commenting on two pupils, he said one went too far and the other not far enough, and that to go too far is the same as not to go far enough. For Confucius this doctrine means nothing more than moderation, but in the *Doctrine of the Mean* it has become a universal principal of harmony and equilibrium. Confucius himself led a life of moderation. He had no fixed limit for the amount of wine he would drink, but he never became confused or disorderly. In his ideas, he was both a conservative and a radical. To him, "Perfect is the virtue that is according to the Mean."

The Second and Third Generations after Confucius. Very little attention has been paid to Confucius's followers from 500 to 350 BCE, but it is impossible to understand how and why Confucianism came to dominate Chinese history and why it unfolded in the directions it did without under-

standing how Confucius's teachings were developed by his pupils and his pupils' pupils.

Meng-tzu and Hsün-tzu. The two most prominent followers of Confucius, Meng-tzu (372?-289? BCE) and Hsün-tzu (fl. 298-238 BCE), were contemporaries, but although both traveled extensively they never met. They shared an adoration of Confucius, and both believed that all men are capable of becoming the *chün-tzu*. Both held in high regard the Confucian moral values of humanity and righteousness. Both strongly advocated education, the rectification of names, kingly government (in which taxes are light, punishments are slight, and war is avoided), and the necessity of social distinctions such as that between senior and junior.

In their own doctrines, however, they proceeded in opposite directions. Confucius had said merely that people were born alike but that practice made them different. His thesis that all men could become superior men, however, argued by implication for the innate goodness of human nature. Meng-tzu's thought begins at this point by categorically affirming the original goodness of our nature. He maintains that man is born with what he termed the "four beginnings," that is, compassion, which is the beginning of humanity, shame and dislike, which is the beginning of righteousness, the feeling of respect and reverence, which is the beginning of propriety, and the feeling of right and wrong, which is the beginning of wisdom. For Meng-tzu, all people possess innate knowledge of the good and an innate ability to do good. Evil is merely to circumstance and self-neglect. If one should fully develop his nature and recover his "lost mind," he will become a sage. Hsün-tzu attacked Meng-tzu severely, claiming that

> **Meng-tzu insisted that the special relationship between son and father must be the foundation of love.**

man's nature is originally evil. Man is born with desires that cannot be fully satisfied. If followed, these desires, together with envy, which is also inborn, inevitably lead to conflict. Virtue is acquired through man's activities, most notably, education, discipline, and rites.

For Hsün-tzu, however, Heaven is simply nature, devoid of ethical principles, impartial to all men, regular and almost mechanical in its operation.

Both Meng-tzu and Hsün-tzu promoted kingly government, but for Meng-tzu a kingly government must be humane. In fact, Meng-tzu was the first to use the term "humane government" *(jen-cheng)*. To Hsün-tzu, a kingly government was one ruled by the most worthy, powerful, and discriminating. The ideal ruler, a sage-king, keeps order through an organized system of laws, regulations, and taxation. Both subscribed to the Confucian doctrine of love for all, but Meng-tzu insisted that the special relationship between son and father must be the foundation of love. Because of this conviction, he bitterly attacked Mo-tzu (fl. 479-438 BCE), who taught universal (i. e. undifferentiated) love, and Yang Chu (440?-360? BCE), who was primarily concerned with self-preservation and hedonism.

The Supremacy of Confucianism and Tung Chung-shu. Under the leadership of the Legalists, the Ch`in empire replaced the feudal domains with a system of provinces that is still in existence today. The Ch`in also united and somewhat simplified the Chinese written language, finished the Great Wall, and expanded military power beyond existing Chinese boundaries. To forestall critical opinion, books of the ritual schools were burned in 213 BCE, although those in official archives were retained. Confucians were ousted from office. But in fourteen short years rebellions broke out. The successful rebel, Liu Pang, defeated his rivals, overthrew the Ch`in, and founded the Han dynasty in 206 BCE. In spite of the burning of books, many Confucian works had been hidden in walls or committed to memory. Now the Confucian classics once more came into circulation. Since they required glosses and explanations, Confucian scholars gradually acquired importance and began to replace the Legalists in the government.

However, those in control of the government were Taoists, chiefly because both the emperors and empresses were devout followers of the new Taoist religion. As a result of the application of the Taoist philosophy of simple government, the reigns of Wen-ti (r. 179-157 BCE) and Ching-ti (156-141 BCE) were times of peace and adequate supply. Emperor Wu-ti (r. 140-87 BCE) ordered scholars to appear for personal interviews. Among the hundred-odd scholars summoned to court was Tung Chung-shu (176-104 BCE), who convinced the emperor to practice the teachings of Confucius and eliminate whatever trace there was of the harsh rule of Ch`in. The emperor immediately appointed Tung to be chief minister of a princely state. In 136 BCE, at the recommendation of Tung, Emperor Wu officially promoted the classics and established doctoral chairs for them, thus establishing Confucianism as the state ideology. Later, in 125 BCE, again at Tung's advice, he founded a national university to which fifty of the most talented students in the classics were selected. This institution lasted until the twentieth century.

**T`ang Confucianism: Han Yü and Li Ao.** The central Confucian theme of human nature was strongly reasserted in the T`ang period (618-907) by Han Yü (768-829) and Li Ao (fl. 798). In his famous *Yüan-hsing* (An Inquiry on Human Nature), Han Yü offered his own theory of three grades of human nature, the superior, the medium, and the inferior. This theory was meant to refine Meng-tzu's doctrine of original goodness, but inasmuch as the idea of three grades can

be found in the classics and was advanced by several thinkers before Han Yü's time, it represents no real advance in Confucian thought. The theory does reaffirm the fundamental Confucian interest in human nature.

Han Yü's friend and possibly his pupil, Li Ao, advocated a principle that he referred to as "recovering one's nature" *(fu-hsing),* which is highly suggestive of Meng-tzu's injunction to recover one's lost mind. Li Ao's method of having no deliberation or thought may sound Buddhistic, and his recommendation of the fasting of mind *(hsin-chai)* may be derived from Chuang-tzu (369?-286? BCE), but the phrase "having no deliberation or thought" *(wu-ssu wu-lü)* comes from the *Book of Changes* and his "fasting of mind" is essentially the doctrine of "tranquility before the feelings are aroused" as taught in the *Doctrine of the Mean.*

In quoting from the *Doctrine of the Mean* and also the *Great Learning,* Han Yü and Li Ao contributed to the prominence of these two chapters in the *Book of Rites* so that eventually they, along with the *Book of Changes,* became basic texts in Neo-Confucianism. Both Han and Li singled out Meng-tzu as the one who transmitted the true doctrine of Confucius to later generations. All in all, they saved Confucianism from possible eclipse by Buddhism and Taoism, determined the direction of future development of Confucianism in Chinese history, and fixed the line of orthodox transmission from Confucius and Meng-tzu. In these respects, Han and Li were truly precursors of Neo-Confucianism.

BIBLIOGRAPHY

Western Sources

Chai, Ch`u, and Winberg Chai, eds. and trans. *The Humanist Way in Ancient China: Essential Works of Confucianism.* New York, 1965.

Chan, Wing-tsit, trans. and comp. *A Source Book in Chinese Philosophy.* Princeton, 1963. See chapters 2-6, 14, and 27.

Chang, Carsun. *The Development of Neo-Confucian Thought.* New York, 1957. See volume 1, chapters 4 and 5.

Creel, H. G. *Confucius and the Chinese Way.* New York, 1960.

Fu, Charles Wei-hsun. "Fingarette and Munro on Early Confucianism: A Methodological Examination." *Philosophy East and West* 28 (April 1978): 181-198.

Fung Yu-lan. *A History of Chinese Philosophy.* 2d ed. Translated by Derk Bodde. Princeton, 1952. See volume 1, chapters 4, 6, and 12.

Liu, Wu-chi. *A Short History of Confucian Philosophy.* Harmondsworth, 1955.

Liu, Wu-chi. *Confucius: His Life and Time.* New York, 1956.

T`ang Chün-i. "Cosmologies in Ancient Chinese Philosophy." *Chinese Studies in Philosophy* 5 (1973): 4-47.

Waley, Arthur. *Three Ways of Thought in Ancient China.* London, 1939.

Chinese and Japanese Sources

Ch`en Ta-ch`i, et al. *K`ung-hsüeh lun-chi.* 2 vols. Taipei, 1957.

Ch`ien Mu. *Chung-kuo ssu-hsiang shih.* Taipei, 1952. See pages 1-85.

Hou Wai-lu. *Chung-kuo ssu-hsiang t'ung-shih.* Peking, 1957. See chapters 1-6, 11, and 15 in volume 1, and chapters 3, 6, and 9 in volume 2.

Kano Naoki. *Chugoku tetsugakushi.* Tokyo, 1953. See part 1, chapters 1-6; part 3, chapters 2-3; and part 4, chapters 1, 2, and 4.

Liang Ch'i-ch'ao, et al. *Chung-kuo che-hsüeh ssu-hsiang lun-chi: Hsien Ch'in p'ien.* Taipei, 1976. See chapters 1-7, 9-11, and 19.

Lao Ssu-kuang. *Chung-kuo che-hsüeh shih.* Peking, 1981. See volume 1, chapters 1-3 and 6.

Shimizu Nobuyoshi. *Chugoku shiso shi.* Tokyo, 1947. See part 2, chapters 1-4.

T'ang Chün-i. "Meng, Mo, Chuang, Hsün shuo hsin-shen i." *Hsin-ya hsüeh-pao* 1.2 (1956): 29-31.

T'ang Chün-i. "Hsien Ch'in ssu-hsiang chung." *Hsin-ya hsüeh-pao* 2.2 (1957): 1-32.

T'ang Chün-i. *Chung-kuo che-hsüeh yüan-lun: Yüan-hsing p'ien.* Hong Kong, 1968. See chapters 1 and 2.

T'ang Chün-i. *Chung-kuo che hsüeh yüan-lun: Yüan-tao p'ien.* Hong Kong, 1973. See part 1, chapters 1, 2, 5, 6, 13-15, and 21-25.

WING-TSIT CHAN

Neo-Confucianism

The cosmology of Chou Tun-i. Chou Tun-i (given name, Chou Mou-shu; literary name, Chou Lien-hsi) laid the foundation for the Sung dynasty's metaphysical and ethical systems and is generally considered the true founder of Neo-Confucian philosophy. His works include the *T'ung-shu* (Penetrating the *Book of Changes*) in forty "chapters," or short passages, and the *T'ai-chi t'u shuo* (An Explanation of the Diagram of the Great Ultimate). The latter, a short essay of 263 words, has become the most important work in Neo-Confucian literature and invariably heads every Neo-Confucian anthology.

In his explanation of the diagram Chou develops a theory of creation, maintaining that the *wu-chi* ("ultimate of nonbeing"), that is, reality beyond space and time, is also the *t'ai-chi* ("great ultimate"), reality in its totality. Through its movement, the Great Ultimate generates *yang,* the active cosmic force; through tranquility, it generates *yin,* the passive cosmic force. *Yin* and *yang* alternate, each becoming the "root" of the other. This alternation and transformation gives rise to the *wu-hsing* ("five agents"): metal, wood, water, fire, and earth, which in turn produce the myriad things. Of these, man is the most intelligent. When the five moral principles of man's nature (humanity, righteousness, propriety, wisdom, and faithfulness) become active this activity begets good and evil and the various human affairs. The sage, who is in accord with his nature, settles these affairs through the principles of the "mean" *(chung),* correctness, humanity, and righteousness. Chou adds that while the two material forces and the Five Agents operate to produce the myriad things, the many are ultimately one and the one is actually differentiated in the many. This chapter is entitled "Hsing-li-ming," or "Nature, Principle, and Destiny," three terms that became key words in the Neo-Confucian vocabulary.

The numerical cosmology of Shao Yung. Shao Yung, like Chou Tun-i, based much of his thought on the concept of cosmic generation found in the *Book of Changes.* He was most influenced by the passage in the *I ching* that states that the Great Ultimate produces two forces (*yin* and *yang*), which produce four forms (*yin* and *yang* in both major and minor forms), which in turn generate the eight trigrams. These latter ultimately give rise to the myriad things. Reinterpreting this passage, Shao coupled its cosmology to a system of numerology. Underlying universal operations is what he termed "spirit" *(shen),* from which number arises. Number then produces form and form produces concrete objects. Shao's system takes the number four as the basis for the classification of all phenomena. Thus, there are four heavenly bodies (sun, moon, stars, and zodiacal space), four earthly substances (water, fire, earth, and stone), four kinds of creatures (animals, birds, grass, and plants), four sense organs (eye, ear, nose, and mouth), four ways of transforming the world (by truth, virtue, work, and effort), four kinds of rulers, four kinds of the mandate of Heaven, and so forth. To support his theory of numerical evolution and production Shao expanded this systematic, yet arbitrary, scheme of classification to include a mathematical progression from the number 4 to the number 64 (the number of hexagrams in the *Book of Changes*).

Unity and material force in Chang Tsai. Chang Tsai's most important works are the *Cheng-meng* (Correcting Youthful Ignorance), in seventeen chapters, and his short essay, *Hsi-ming* (The Western Inscription). Central to these texts is the concept of material force *(ch'i).* Chang was considered an expert on the *Book of Changes* and was renowned for his public lectures on it. However, unlike Chou Tun-i and Shao Yung, he departed from the normative interpretation of the passage in the *I ching* that speaks of the Great Ultimate generating the two modes, *yin* and *yang.* To Chang, *yin* and *yang* are but two aspects of the Great Ultimate, which is itself identified with material force. In its original reality or substance, material force is formless and as yet unconsolidated. He called this aspect of material force *t'ai-hsü* ("great vacuity"). In its operation or function, it is called *t'ai-ho* ("great harmony"). As *t'ai-ho,* it functions through *yin* and *yang* in their interaction, rise and fall, integration and disintegration, and tranquility and activity, as is borne out by the way in which day and night, life and death, advance and decline in history, and so forth all proceed in natural harmony.

Equally influential is Chang's short essay *The Western Inscription,* which he inscribed on a panel in the western window of his study. He begins by claiming that Heaven and Earth are our parents and all things are our brothers, and that we must therefore devote ourselves to filial piety, education of the young, and care for the elderly in order to complete our lives in peace. Here again, we find evidence of Chang's insistence that man forms one body with the universe.

**The Ch`eng brothers' theory of principle.** The Ch`eng brothers neither spoke of the Great Ultimate nor made material force the focal point of their doctrine. Instead, they were the first in the history of Chinese philosophy to base their thought entirely on the concept of principle *(li)*. They conceived of principle as self-evident, self-sufficient, extending everywhere, and governing all things. Principle cannot be augmented or diminished. It is possessed by everyone and everything and is that by which all things exist and can be understood. By claiming that all specific principles are but one universal principle, they bound man and all things into a unity. Most significant is the fact that they were the first to identify the principle inherent in things with *t`ien-li* (the "principle of Heaven"). This is especially true of Ch`eng Hao, for whom, as for all other Neo-Confucians, the principle of Heaven represents natural law; the principle of Heaven is the universal process of production and reproduction. The Ch`engs further equated principle with the mind and with (human) nature *(hsing)*. Indeed, their declaration that "the nature is principle" has come to characterize the entire Neo-Confucian movement.

The Ch`engs followed Meng-tzu's teaching that human nature is originally good. When Ch`eng Hao said that our nature possesses both good and evil, he meant merely that because our endowment of material force is imbalanced and deviates from the Mean there is bound to be both good and evil. He was quick to stipulate that the imbalance is not due to our original nature. While Ch`eng Hao equated principle with the principle of Heaven and stressed the dynamic and creative aspects of the universe, his younger brother, Ch`eng I, strongly emphasized the unity or universality of principle and the diversity of its manifestations. His dictum "Principle is one but its manifestations are many," reminiscent of Chou Tun-i's idea of the relationship between the one and the many, became a standard formula in Neo-Confucianism.

Metaphysics, the Great Ultimate, and principle. It was Chou Tun-i's *Explanation of the Diagram of the Great Ultimate* that provided the metaphysical basis for Chu Hsi's theory of principle. Chu Hsi interpreted the *chi* of *t`ai-chi* as the "ultimate," that point beyond which one can go no further. He defined *t`ai-chi,* or Great Ultimate, as both the sum total of the principles of all discrete phenomena and the highest principle within each of them. He thus extended Ch`eng I's concept of principle beyond the realm of human affairs to include all affairs within the universe. He posited a theory in which principle transcends time and space: there was principle before the existence of the universe and there will be principle after the collapse of the universe. In Chu Hsi's scheme the whole universe is but one principle, the Great Ultimate, one universal whole with which all individual things are endowed. At the same time, however, he emphasized that each phenomenon is endowed with its own defining principle. Thus, it is by their respective principles that a boat travels on the water and a vehicle travels on the road. The Great Ultimate is also the repository for all actualized and

> **Chu Hsi interpreted the *chi* of *t`ai-chi* as the "ultimate," that point beyond which one can go no further.**

potential principles: as new things appear, their principles also appear. In this way, Chu Hsi was able to explain Ch`eng I's formulaic expression, "Principle is one but its manifestations are many."

Chu Hsi attributed the generative or creative ability to the Great Ultimate rather than to principle or material force. He reaffirmed Chou Tun-i's theory that creation begins with the Great Ultimate, but held that the Great Ultimate transcends such limitations of function and thus cannot be subject to either activity or tranquillity. Rather, the Great Ultimate embodies the principles of activity and tranquility. It is out of these principles that the material forces of *yin* and *yang* naturally ensue. The process of creation is dynamic and ever changing. New principles are always forthcoming and the universe is daily renewed.

The relationship between principle and material force. Chu Hsi's greatest contribution to Neo-Confucian thought was his clarification of the relationship between principle and material force and his concomitant explanation of the actualization of phenomena. Despite the fact that principle and material force are merged in each phenomenon and cannot be separated, they are definitely two different things. Principle is incorporeal, one, eternal, unchanging, and indestructible. It constitutes the essence of things, is the reason for creation, and is always good. Principle represents the metaphysical world. By contrast, material force is necessary to explain physical form and the production and transformation of things. In Ch`eng I's terms, material force constitutes "what exists within form." It is corporeal, many, transitory, individual, changeable, unequal, and destructible. Material force is the vehicle and material for creation and involves both good and evil.

Chu Hsi's ethics and theory of mind. Chu Hsi's metaphysical speculations on the Great Ultimate, principle, and material force provided the basis for his understanding of man's mind and nature and for his development of a system of ethics and a method for moral self-cultivation. He welcomed Ch`eng I's notion that *jen* is the seed from which all other virtues will grow. Reinterpreting the passage in the

Book of Changes that claims "the great virtue of Heaven and Earth is to give life," Ch'eng I had declared that "the mind *(hsin)* of Heaven [the mind of the Tao] and Earth is to produce things." In his treatise on humanity, Chu Hsi brings this interpretation to bear on the nature of man's mind, defining *jen* as the "character of the mind and the principle of love." Thus, he conceives of *jen* as being derived from Heaven:

"Man and things have received this mind of Heaven and Earth as their [own] mind." This aspect of the mind, which Chu calls the "mind of the Tao" *(tao-hsin),* embodies principle in its transcendent form and is associated with man's original nature *(pen-hsing).* It is characterized by humanity and is free from self-interest and selfish desires. The other aspect of the mind, which he called the "human mind" *(jen-hsin),* is determined by man's imbalanced endowment of material force. Because it is the part of the mind that is bound to material force, the human mind is often characterized by selfish desires and causes man to act out of pure self-interest. Chu Hsi taught that in order for man not to be engulfed by selfishness and evil he must cultivate himself in a manner that rectifies the human mind and develops the mind of Heaven.

The school of Mind. Chu Hsi's strongest opponent was Lu Hsiang-shan, who conceived of the mind as morally self-sufficient, endowed with the innate knowledge of good and the innate ability to do good. Going beyond Meng-tzu's statement that all things are complete within the self, Lu proclaimed that "the mind is principle." The universe is one's mind, he held, and one's mind is the universe. Consequently, he advocated complete reliance on the mind, self-sufficiency, self-accomplishment, and self-perfection. Lu criticized Chu's theory of human nature, in which the principle of Heaven, which is always good, is contrasted with human desires, which may or may not be good. Lu also refused to accept Chu Hsi's claim that while there is only one mind, a distinction can be made between the human mind and the mind of the Tao.

The Chekiang school. Early in 1175 Lü Tsu-ch'ien and his friend Chu Hsi collaborated in the compilation of the first Chinese philosophical anthology, the *Chin-ssu lu* (Reflections on Things at Hand). On many issues, however, they differed radically. While Chu Hsi viewed the classics as sacred texts, Lü looked to the dynastic and comprehensive histories for moral and philosophical lessons. He held that history does not simply gather disjointed facts but is a record of growth and transformation.

The Hunan school. In his work *Chih-yen* (Knowing Words) Hu Hung, the founder of the Hunan school, maintained that the mind is the master of all things and that depending on the way the mind uses nature, nature may become good or evil. He challenged the distinction between the principle of Heaven and human desires, claiming instead that in substance they were the same but in function they differed. Chu Hsi was too young to have met Hu Hung, but he strongly criticized *Knowing Words* for philosophically contradicting the traditional Neo-Confucian doctrine of the original goodness of human nature and for equating evil human desires with the principle of Heaven..

Neo-Confucianism in the Yüan Dynasty. With the fall of the Sung dynasty in 1179 and the rise of Mongol hegemony over China the spread of the various Neo-Confucian schools virtually came to an end. The only school to survive was that of Chu Hsi. Its survival was due both to its established domination and to a chance set of circumstances. A Confucian scholar, Chao Fu (c. 1206-1299), was captured by the Mongols in Hupei Province, an area of China under the control of the Chin (1115-1234) and hence little influenced by the Neo-Confucian trend in the south. When Chao was sent to the Mongol capital at Yen-ching (modern-day Peking) he took with him several Neo-Confucian texts, most notably, Chu Hsi's commentaries to the Four Books. In Yen-ching, Chao attracted a large following, including the Chinese scholar Hsü Heng (1209-1281). Later, in his capacity as director of the T'ai-hsüeh (the national university), Hsü was able to influence and in effect dominate the intellectual current of China under the Mongols. Hsü Heng vigorously championed the *Hsiao-hsüeh* (Elementary Education), compiled by Chu Hsi in 1189 for the moral edification of the young in their daily conduct. Hsü also advocated use of the Four Books, which he regarded as sacred, and Chu Hsi's commentaries, which he personally copied. There is no doubt that HsüHeng's adoration of Chu Hsi and his commentaries on the Four Books contributed to the imperial edict of 1313 making the Four Books and the Five Classics the basic required texts for the civil service examinations.

Neo-Confucianism in the Ming Dynasty. By the beginning of the Ming dynasty (1368-1644) the philosophy of the Ch'eng-Chu school was the established orthodoxy. Outstanding philosophers of the period—Ts'ao Tuan (1376-1434), Wu Yü-pi (1391-1469), Hsüeh Hsüan (1392-1464), Hu Chu-jen (1434-1484), and others—were all faithful followers of Chu Hsi. However, these thinkers tended to disregard metaphysical speculation on the Great Ultimate, *yin* and *yang,* and the relation of principle to material force and instead turned their attention toward understanding the mind, nature, self-cultivation, and seriousness *(ching).*

Wang Yang-ming and the school of Mind. The central thesis of Wang Yang-ming's thought is that principle and mind are one. Outside the mind there is no principle and, conversely, all principles are contained within the mind. Related to this is his concept that the mind is master of the body. These concepts brought Wang into direct opposition to the thought of Chu Hsi. Wang took great exception to Chu's redaction of the *Great Learning,* in which he had emended a chapter so as to expound his theory of the investigation of things and had rearranged the order of the text so as to place the chapter on the extension of knowledge before the chapter on the sincerity of the will. In his own *Ta-hsüeh wen* (Inquiry on the *Great Learning*) Wang also criticizes Chu Hsi for establishing a dualism between "making one's virtue clear" *(ming-te)* and "loving the people" *(ch`in-min)*. The essential point of this work is that, for Wang, all things form a unity *(i-t`i)*.

In general, Wang claimed that Chu Hsi divided principle and mind in advocating that one should direct the mind outside to seek principles in external things. Rather than follow Chu's interpretation of *ko-wu* as an investigation *(ko)* of

> **It is man's innate knowledge that gives him his moral sense of right and wrong.**

things, Wang revived the interpretation found in the *Meng-tzu,* where *ko* means "rectification." Thus to Wang, *ko-wu* involved rectifying the mind by eliminating incorrectness and removing evil. Wang also asserted that since it is the will of the mind to realize principle, sincerity of the will must precede the investigation of things. To redress these wrongs, in 1518 Wang published the old text of the *Great Learning* as it is found in the *Li chi* (Book of Rites).

Wang's answer to many of the difficulties raised by Chu's thought was a theory of self-cultivation that combined the concept of innate knowledge *(liang-chih),* derived from the *Meng-tzu,* with the notion of the extension of knowledge *(chih-chih),* derived from the *Great Learning.* Wang equated nature, knowledge, and the original substance of the mind, which is always good and manifests an innate knowledge of the good. It is man's innate knowledge that gives him his moral sense of right and wrong. Thus, man's mind, in its original substance, understands all principles. To cultivate oneself one need not investigate the principles of things external to the mind; rather, one has only to follow the impulses of one's innate knowledge.

To clarify these points, Wang advanced what is regarded as his most original and significant contribution to Neo-Confucianism: a doctrine of the unity of knowledge and action. Knowledge, which in Wang's thought is limited to moral knowledge, must have its logical expression in action and action must be firmly based in knowledge. "Knowledge in its genuine and earnest aspect is action and action in its intelligent and discriminating aspect is knowledge." To illustrate this, Wang refers to the experience of pain, which one cannot know unless one suffers. (This illustration demonstrates the essentially subjective nature of knowledge in Wang's system.) With respect to moral behavior, Wang said that a man who knows the duties of filial piety will fulfill them, but at the same time, can truly understand those duties only through their fulfillment. This doctrine gave Ming Neo-

Confucianism a new dynamic, for it suggests that the extension of innate knowledge is a natural and even irresistible impulse that is true to man's nature. The extension of innate knowlege leads not only to the fulfillment of filial obligations but to love for all beings and the identification of oneself with all things in the universe. This notion is highly reminiscent of Ch`eng Hao's concept that man forms one body with Heaven, earth, and the myriad things.

**Neo-Confucianism in the Ch`ing Dynasty.** Although Wang Yang-ming's doctrine of innate knowledge dominated the philosophy of the fifteenth and sixteenth centuries, it never entirely eclipsed the teachings of the Ch`eng-Chu school. The Manchu rulers, who conquered China in 1644, reaffirmed the philosophy of the Ch`eng-Chu school as the orthodox teaching. The Four Books and Chu Hsi's commentaries on them were upheld as the required school texts and the basis for the civil service examinations. The general tendency of scholars in the late seventeenth century was either to follow the teachings of Chu Hsi or to attempt a compromise between the perceived rationalism of Chu Hsi and the idealism of Wang Yang-ming. There were, however, outstanding Neo-Confucian scholars like Ku Yen-wu (1613-1682) who began to reevaluate their intellectual heritage. Although Ku was strongly influenced by and inclined toward the philosophy of the Ch`eng-Chu school, he attacked the abstract thinking associated with their theories of the Great Ultimate, the mind, and human nature. In their stead he called for practical and objective learning, the pursuit of empirical knowledge, and involvement in practical affairs. Among the thinkers who followed Ku Yen-wu, Yen Yüan (1635-1704) and Tai Chen (1723-1777) took the tendency toward practical learning and objective truth even farther.

Yen Yüan rejected the philosophy of both Chu Hsi and Wang Yang-ming. He believed that all the subjects of Sung and Ming speculation—principle, nature, destiny, and the sincerity of the will—could only be found in such practical arts as music, ceremony, agriculture, and military craft. Yen maintained that there is no principle apart from material force; he insisted that the physical nature endowed with material force is no different from the original nature endowed by Heaven. Because the physical nature is not evil, there is no need to transform it or to repress physical desires. He believed that the investigation of things involved neither the study of principle nor the rectification of the mind, but rather the application of practical experience to the solution of practical problems.

Tai Chen, another critic of Chu Hsi, is generally recognized as the greatest thinker of the Ch`ing dynasty. He was a proponent of the new intellectual movement known as "investigations based on evidence" *(k`ao-cheng)*. He was a specialist in mathematics, astronomy, water-works, and phonetics and was widely respected as an expert in literary criticism. He complained that philosophers like Chu Hsi and

Wang Yang-ming looked upon principle "as though it were a thing." Tai Chen advocated the Han dynasty understanding of principle as an order that is found only in things, by which he meant the daily affairs of men. Principle, he believed, could not be investigated by intellectual speculation, but rather through the objective, critical, and analytical observation of things. He did not follow the Sung Confucians in contrasting the principle of Heaven and human desires as good and evil, respectively. Instead, he held that principle prevails only when feelings are satisfied and that feelings are good as long as they "do not err." In conjunction with this, he postulated the existence of "necessary moral principles," that is, objective and standard principles, that are definite and inherent in concrete things.

The Nineteenth and Early Twentieth Centuries. As China was progressively weakened by both the disintegration of Manchu rule and the onslaught of Western imperialism, Confucianism lost favor as the official state ideology.

During these turbulent times groups of intellectuals continued the effort to reinterpret and reestablish their Confucian heritage. K`ang Yu-wei (1858-1927), an outstanding scholar of the Confucian classics, justified his attempts at institutional reform by recourse to Confucian ideology. Believing that the strength and prosperity of Western nations derived from their having a state religion, K`ang petitioned the emperor to establish Confucianism as the national cult. At the same time, however, other groups of intellectuals called for the final defeat of Confucianism. The intellectual renaissance of 1917 declared Confucianism unsuited to modern life.

For a time it seemed as though Confucianism was doomed. As the revolutionary fervor cooled, however, Chinese intellectuals began to reconsider the role of the tradition in the future of China. Liang Shu-ming (1893-) published a study comparing Chinese and Western civilizations. He championed Confucian moral values and condemned the wholesale adoption of Western institutions as unsuited to the Chinese spirit. During the following twenty years, Fung Yu-lan (1895-) and Hsiung Shih-li (1895-1968) emerged as prominent spokesmen for Confucianism. Fung's *Hsin-li hsüeh* (New Learning of Principle), published in 1939, is a reconstruction of the Ch`eng-Chu school of Neo-Confucianism.

The Status of Confucianism in the Late Twentieth Century. The Communist victory in 1949 and the Cultural Revolution in the 1960s brought a decided end to the attempts to make Confucianism the state ideology and religion. However, scholars never suspended their study of Confucianism; along with members of China's political hierarchy, they have continued to discuss the historical significance and relevancy of Confucianism.

In 1980 a conference was held to study the philosophy of Chu Hsi and Wang Yang-ming. The participants' appraisal of Neo-Confucianism was objective and fair, and their remarks about Chu and Wang at once favorable and unfavorable. The official party position, affirmed at this session, is that Neo-Confucianism played a major role in Chinese history, albeit one that served a feudal society, and thus is worthy of continued study.

BIBLIOGRAPHY

Western Sources
Chan, Wing-tsit, trans. and comp. *A Source Book in Chinese Philosophy*. Princeton, 1963. See chapters 28-35 and 38.
Chan, Wing-tsit. "Chu Hsi's Completion of Neo-Confucianism." *Sung Studies* ser. 2, no. 1 (1973): 59-90.
Chang, Carsun. *The Development of Neo-Confucian Thought*. 2 vols. New York, 1957-1962.
Ching, Julia. *To Acquire Wisdom: The Way of Wang Yang-ming (1492-1529)*. New York, 1976.
Chu Hsi. *Reflections on Things at Hand*. Translated by Wing-tsit Chan. New York, 1967.
de Bary, Wm. Theodore, ed. *Self and Society in Ming Thought*. New York, 1970.
de Bary, Wm. Theodore, ed. *The Unfolding of Neo-Confucianism*. New York, 1975.
Fung Yu-lan. *A History of Chinese Philosophy*. 2d ed. 2 vols. Translated by Derk Bodde. Princeton, 1952-1953. Extensive discussion of Neo-Confucian thought can be found in volume 2.
Graham, A. C. *Two Chinese Philosophers: Ch`êng Ming-tao and Ch`êng Yi-ch`uan*. London, 1958.
Okada Takehiko. "The Chu Hsi and Wang Yang-ming Schools at the end of the Ming and Tokugawa Periods." *Philosophy East and West* 23 (January-April 1973): 139-162.
Tillman, Hoyt C. *Utilitarian Confucianism: Ch`en Liang's Challenge to Chu Hsi*. Cambridge, Mass., 1982.
Wang Shou-jen. *Instructions for Practical Living, and Other Neo-Confucian Writings, by Wang Yang-ming*. Translated and edited by Wing-tsit Chan. New York, 1963.

Chinese and Japanese Sources
Araki Kengo et al., comps. *Yomeigaku taikei*. 12 vols. Tokyo, 1971-1973.
Ch`ien Mu. *Sung Ming li-hsüeh kai-shu*. Taipei, 1953.
Ch`ien Mu. *Chu-tzu hsin hsüeh-an*. 5 vols. Taipei, 1971.
Chung-kuo che-hsüeh shih tzu-liao hsüan-chi. 6 vols. Edited by the Chung-kuo K`o-hsüeh-yuan Che-hsüeh Yen-chiu So. Peking, 1982. See volume 4.
Hou Wai-lu. *Chung-kuo ssu-hsiang t`ung-shih*. Peking, 1959. See volume 4, chapters 10-15 and 20.
Hu Shih. *Tsai Tung-yüan ti che-hsüeh*. Shanghai, 1912.
Huang Tsung-hsi. *Ming-ju hsüeh-an*. Ssu-pu Pei-yao edition.
Huang Tsung-hsi and Ch`üan Tsu-wang. *Sung Yüan hsüeh-an*. Ssu-pu Pei-yao edition.
Jung Chao-tsu. *Ming-tai ssu-hsiang shih*. Shanghai, 1941.
Kusumoto Masatsugu. *So Min jidai jugaku shiso no kenkyu*. Tokyo, 1962.
Liu Shu-hsien. *Chu-tzu che-hsüeh ssu-hsiang ti fa-chan yü wan-ch`eng*. Taipei, 1982.
Lo Kuang. *Chung-kuo che-hsüeh ssu-hsiang shih: Sung-tai p`ien*. Taipei, 1980.
Mo Tsung-san. *Ts`ung Lu Hsiang-shan tao Liu Chi-shan*. Taipei, 1980.
Morohashi Tetsuji, ed. *Shushigaku taikei*. Tokyo, 1974-.
Okada Takehiko. *So Min tetsugaku josetsu*. Tokyo, 1970.

Okada Takehiko. *Chugoku shiso ni okeru rigaku to genjitsu.* Tokyo, 1977.

Tomoeda Ryutaro. *Shushi no shiso keisei.* Rev. ed. Tokyo, 1979.

WING-TSIT CHAN

Confucianism in Japan

The earliest Japanese chronicles tell us that Confucianism was introduced to Japan near the end of the third century CE, when Wani of Paekche (Korea) brought the Confucian *Analects* (Chin., *Lunyü;* Jpn., *Rongo*) to the court of Emperor Ojin. It is also likely that continental emigrants familiar with Confucian teachings arrived in Japan prior to the formal introduction of Confucianism.

Japanese Confucianism to 1600. Both supporting and being supported by the political forces of centralization in the nascent Japanese state, Confucian teachings first achieved prominence in Japan during the time of Shotoku Taishi (573-621), who served as regent to his aunt, the empress Suiko (592-628). In 604, Shotoku Taishi wrote and promulgated the Seventeen-Article Constitution, which was intended to centralize further the administration of Japan by emphasizing administrative efficiency and harmony among contending factions. The constitution reflected the Confucian cosmology that regarded the universe as a triad composed of heaven, earth, and man, with each element having specific and mutual responsibilities. Again under Confucian influence, the cause of centralization and unification was furthered by the Taika Reforms of 645 and 646, which asserted the Confucian imperial principle of unified rule, and by the introduction of a complex legal and administrative system patterned after the codes of the Chinese T`ang dynasty during the eighth century.

The influence of Confucian principles in government administration declined during the ninth and tenth centuries along with the political power of the imperial court. Perhaps disillusioned by this trend, Japanese Confucians of the eleventh and twelfth centuries engaged more in textual analysis and criticism than in original thought or interpretation.

The Neo-Confucian doctrines of Chu Hsi (Jpn., Shuki, more commonly, Shushi; 1130-1200) were introduced to Japan, if the sources are to be believed, soon after Chu Hsi's death. Institutionally, the doctrines were taught in Zen monasteries where such Neo-Confucian practices as "maintaining reverence and sitting quietly" (*jikei seiza*) were regarded as intellectually stimulating variations of what Zen practitioners already knew as "sitting in meditation" (*zazen*). Though Neo-Confucian doctrines were from time to time favorably received at the imperial and shogunal courts, Neo-

Confucianism would remain largely in the shadow of its Zen patrons through the sixteenth century.

Tokugawa Confucianism (1600-1868). Perhaps the only positive result of the abortive Japanese invasions of Korea in the 1590s was the consequent introduction of new texts from the Confucian tradition into Japan. Fujiwara Seika (1561-1619) was made aware of this new tradition during his study in a Zen monastery. He had his first interview with Tokugawa Ieyasu (1542-1616), the future empire builder, in 1593, a decade before Ieyasu would be granted the title of *shogun.* Regarding Neo-Confucianism as a possible basis for stable international relations, Ieyasu invited the philosophically eclectic Fujiwara Seika to join his government, but Seika declined and recommended in his stead a young student of his, Hayashi Razan (1583-1657).

Like his teacher, Hayashi Razan had studied Zen but was soon drawn to the orthodox teachings of Chu Hsi. With his appointment to Ieyasu's government, a degree of official attention was conferred on these teachings, and his descendants would serve as official Confucian advisers to the Tokugawa government throughout the period.

The final important champion of fidelity to the teachings of Chu Hsi in Japan was Yamazaki Ansai (1618-1682). His school, the Kimon, had as its goal the popularization of the ethics of Chu Hsi. Like other Neo-Confucians, this school generally took a dim view of human emotions and feelings, regarding them as potentially disruptive to the delicate balance that must lie at the heart of both man and the cosmos.

During the second half of the seventeenth century, Neo-Confucian assumptions and vocabulary penetrated the new popular culture of Japan, but what has been called the "emotionalism" of the Japanese at this time made the puritanical Neo-Confucian stance on emotions and feelings incompatible with the mainstream of Japanese culture.

In China, the most compelling Confucian alternative to the orthodox teachings of Chu Hsi were the teachings of the fifteenth-century figure Wang Yang-ming (Jap., Oyomei). His teachings, known in Japan as Yomeigaku, were first propagated by Nakae Toju (1608-1648), who emphasized the Wang school's teachings on intuition and action. Kumazawa Banzan (1619-1691), a pupil of Toju, interpreted these activist teachings in terms of their relevance to the samurai class. These teachings would have their greatest impact in Japan during the nineteenth century when such leaders as Sakuma Shozan (1811-1864) and his disciple Yoshida Shoin (1830-1859) became ideological leaders of the Meiji restoration.

In Japan, however, the most intellectually compelling alternative to Neo-Confucian teachings was presented by a succession of schools known collectively as Ancient Learning (Kogaku). Yamaga Soko (1622-1685), the first proponent of Ancient Learning, argued that if the goal of Confucian exegesis was to find the true message of the sages, then that end might better be served by reading the works of Confucius and Mencius (Meng-tzu) directly rather than by reading the commentary on those works by Chu Hsi or others. Yamaga was drawn to the relevance of Confucian teachings in a military age, and he is regarded as the modern founder of the teachings of Bushido, the Way of the Warrior.

The most important Ancient Learning figure, however, was Ogyu Sorai (1666-1728), who located his school, known as the Kobunjigaku (School of Ancient Words and Phrases), in Edo. An ardent Sinophile, Sorai regarded ancient Chinese writings as the repository of intellectual resources for establishing the organization of social institutions, the performance of ancient rituals, and principles of governmental administration. He revolutionized Confucian teachings in East Asia by insisting that the principles of the Confucian way were not a priori principles but were, rather, the products of the sages' own inventive wisdom. Sorai thus insisted that aspiration to sagehood was at the least irrelevant to, and at worst destructive of, the polity.

With the decline of the school of Ogyu Sorai during the mid-eighteenth century, Confucianism as a whole began to decline.

Confucianism in Modern Japan. Confucianism played a relatively passive role through the end of World War I. By this time the originally Confucian notions of loyalty and filial piety had come to be regarded as native Japanese virtues, and in 1937 these virtues were propounded in a work entitled *Kokutai no hongi* (Essentials of the National Polity) as the cardinal principles of Japanese national morality. Confucianism served Japanese imperialist aims in Korea after its annexation in 1910, in Manchuria after 1932, and in the Japanese-controlled portions of North China after 1937. After World War II, Confucian teachings were removed from the Japanese curriculum by the occupation authorities, and Confucianism has not yet recovered from this blow.

BIBLIOGRAPHY

A most valuable source book of materials on Japanese Confucianism is *Sources of Japanese Tradition,* 2 vols., compiled by Ryusaku Tsunoda, Wm. Theodore de Bary, and Donald Keene (New York, 1958). Also useful, although somewhat dated, is Robert C. Armstrong's *Light from the East: Studies in Japanese Confucianism* (Toronto, 1914). Joseph J. Spae's *Ito Jinsai* (New York, 1967) is helpful both for information on the Ancient Learning school and on early Japanese Confucianism. Robert Bellah's *Tokugawa Religion* (New York, 1957) casts the major themes of Japanese Confucianism into a broader perspective. Kate Nakai's "The Nationalization of Confucianism in Tokugawa Japan," *Harvard Journal of Asiatic Studies* 40 (June 1980): 159-199, provides a lucid account of how continental Confucianism was transformed into Japanese Confucianism. From a methodological point of view, the most stimulating volume available in English is Maruyama Masao's *Studies in the Intellectual History of Tokugawa Japan,* translated by Mikiso Hane (Princeton, 1975). It may be the single most important book on this subject. See also the volume that I have edited, *Confucianism and Tokugawa Culture* (Princeton, 1984). Herman Ooms's *Charismatic Bureaucrat: A Political Biography of Matsudaira Sadanobu, 1758-1829* (Chicago, 1975) is a superb account of this important late Tokugawa figure. Finally, the reader is directed to the only available study of the modern fate of Confucian thought in Japan, *Confucianism in Modern Japan,* 2d ed. (Tokyo, 1973), by Warren W. Smith, Jr.

PETER NOSCO

Confucianism in Korea

In the seventh century, the Silla government, at first a tribal federation, turned to Confucianism as a tool of centralization. In 651, the Royal Academy was established, in which officials, drawn from the aristocracy, were exposed to the Confucian classics. Furthermore, Confucian precepts found their way into aristocratic codes of behavior, even becoming incorporated into the rules of conduct for the *hwarang,* a knightly class instrumental in the Silla unification of the Korean Peninsula in 668.

From the inception of the Koryo dynasty (918-1392) an expanded role for Confucian doctrine was envisioned. In the celebrated "Ten Injunctions" addressed to his descendants by the dynastic founder, Wang Kon (r. 918-943), Buddhism was chosen to govern spiritual matters, geomancy was to be used for prophecy and prognostication, and Confucianism was chosen as the guiding principle in the sociopolitical sphere.

In the late tenth century the government was reorganized into a centralized bureaucratic structure. Local officials were appointed by the central government. The Koryo polity transformed into an aristocratic-bureaucratic state in which the power of the ruling elite derived from government position rather than an ancestral seat. This change reflected the Confucian rhetoric of government.

Under this Confucian system, civil officials served in the capital, where the mode of life included the pursuit of scholarly and literary activities.

The military coup of 1170 disrupted this Confucian social order. The Mongols, who invaded Korea in 1231, were instrumental in bringing about the end of military rule in 1259. Koryo kings, married to Mongol princesses and devoid of power, spent a great deal of time prior to their accession and after their retirement in the cosmopolitan Yüan capital. Establishments such as that of the scholar-king Ch'ungson (r. 1289, 1308-1313) served as meeting places for Chinese and Korean scholars, and Korean scholars for the first time had first-hand exposure to Sung dynasty (960-1279) Neo-Confucian scholarship, particularly that of the Ch`eng-Chu school. The result was an impressive array of scholars beginning with An Hyang (1243-1306) and Paek Ijong (fl. 1300), commonly regarded as having introduced Neo-Confucianism to Korea. They succeeded in including the Neo-Confucian texts—the Four Books and Five Classics—in the civil service examination and in the curriculum at the Royal College and in reinstituting the royal lecture, complete with Neo-Confucian texts and teacher-officials who lectured to the king-student.

Founding of the Yi Neo-Confucian Polity. The founding of the Yi dynasty (1392-1910) was, in its sense, not merely a change in political power. Its founders were all confirmed Neo-Confucians and they sought to create a new sociopolitical order based on their moral vision. Chong Tojon (1342-1398), the leader of this group, campaigned to discredit Buddhism. Motivated by the Neo-Confucian belief in the centrality of man, Chong challenged the Buddhist view that this world, the phenomenal world, was illusion, terming such a view invalid and harmful.

Beginning with changes in the political structure, the Yi government launched a massive transformation of Korean society that was not fully realized for several centuries. The most conspicuous changes were the adoption of a new system of education, a restructuring of social organization along patrilineal groups, the adoption of Confucian ritual, and the propagation of Confucian ethics through local associations. In order to disseminate Confucian values more widely to the educated class, the Yi government sought to establish a nationwide public school system. Four schools in the capital and one school in each county supposedly would make primary education widely available, while the Royal College in the capital would provide advanced education for qualified students.

The Development of Confucian Scholarship. By the sixteenth century, Korean scholars turned to the more purely intellectual and speculative aspects of Confucian learning, looking directly to the Ch`eng-Chu school. Despite close ties with Ming dynasty (1368-1644) scholarship, Korean Neo-Confucianism developed independently of contemporary scholarship there. While Korean scholars accepted the authority of the Ch`eng-Chu school, they defined issues in their own way, adding insights and interpretations. The scholars Pak Yong (1471-1540), So Kyongdok (1489-1546), and Yi Onjok (1491-1553) reflect the diversity and independence of the Korean school.

But, it was Yi Hwang (1501-1570), better known as T'oegye, who brought Korean Neo-Confucianism to maturity. Working at a time when Wang Yang-ming's thought seemed to be gaining influence in the Korean scholarly community, he devoted himself to defining orthodoxy, to distinguishing "right learning" from deviant thought. The definition of a Korean orthodoxy within the tradition of the Ch`eng-Chu school, one that excluded the ideas of the Wang Yang-ming school, is often attributed to his efforts. T'oegye accepted Chu Hsi's dual theory of principle and material force and the relation-

ship between them. While Chu Hsi acknowledged that principle and material force cannot exist in isolation, he held that principle is prior and material force posterior. The superiority of principle was a defining feature of his philosophy: principle was identified with the Way *(tao)* and the nature *(hsing)*, which are permanent and unchanging, while material force was identified with physical entities, which constantly change. But Chu Hsi's position proved somewhat ambiguous. One could ask whether the priority of principle was existential or evaluative, that is, did it exist first or did it just have a superior moral value? Further, in what sense did principle exist prior to material force if it could not manifest itself without material force? Much of T'oegye's work was devoted to this question. He concluded that the priority of principle applied in the realm of ethical values, and that principle exerted a positive ethical influence.

Like the Sung Neo-Confucians, Korean scholars including T'oegye were deeply concerned with the problem of human evil. If man's original nature was good, then how can one explain evil? T'oegye again accepted Chu Hsi's concept of human nature based on his dual theory of principle and material force. Principle is immanent in everything in the universe. What individuates one thing from another is material force. Since principle is good, what determines the moral quality of an entity is its material force. Man has an original nature and a physical nature and only when he returns to original nature does he act in accordance with moral principle. What determines the morality of human action is mind. The mind possesses innate knowledge of moral principle and has the cognitive capacity to discern it. Yet, this capacity of mind can be prevented from functioning when it becomes clouded by selfish desire.

Meanwhile, Yi I (1536-1584), known by his pen name, Yulgok, took the formula "obtain truth through one's own effort" as his credo; he regarded adhering too rigidly to previous masters' positions as contrary to the spirit of Neo-Confucian learning.

The intellectual scene in the eighteenth century was somewhat freer and more diverse. This period witnessed the flowering of the Sirhak ("practical learning") school. Centuries of factional struggle and growing competition for office had left many scholars outside the mainstream of political power. Practical Learning scholars were disaffected intellectuals who wrote treatises on social and economic reform. They fall largely into two groups. Yu Hyong-won (1622-1673) and Yi Ik (1681-1763) accepted the Confucian vision of an agrarian society presided over by the rule of virtue and urged social improvement through land reform and moral rule. Pak Chi-won (1737-1805), Hong Taeyong (1731-1783), and Pak Che-ga (b. 1750), on the other hand, searched for alternatives. They addressed themselves to such issues as commerce, trade, and technology. Pak Chi-won's biting satire of the class system, Hong Taeyong's interest in science as it was expressed in his notion of the moving earth, and Pak Che-ga's belief in technology founded on a startling theory of a consumer economy clearly departed from the conventional mode of thinking. Chong Yagyong (1762-1836), often considered the greatest Practical Learning scholar, encompassed both trends in his reform ideas. His attention to the improvement of local government is well known. While these scholars worked within the Confucian political and value system, they are regarded as precursors of modernization for their critique of contemporary society and their innovative proposals for reform.

In the late nineteenth century as Korea came under increasing pressure from the major powers and the Confucian value system itself came under attack, Confucian thinking turned defensive. Confucian scholars committed to preserving the orthodox tradition became conservatives who opposed treaties and modernizing measures. Seeing themselves as the defenders of the only true civilization, they put up real resistance.

The role of Confucianism in the twentieth century, which began with anti-Confusianistic movements, needs yet to be examined in depth.

[See also Buddhism, and Korean Religion.]

BIBLIOGRAPHY

Works in Korean. For an overview of the history of Korean Confucianism, see Youn Sa-soon's *Han'guk yuhak yon'gu* (Seoul, 1980). Works by the major thinkers include: Ch'oe Ikhyon's *Myonamjip* (Seoul, 1906); Chong Tojon's *Sambongjip* (reprint, Seoul, 1961); Chong Yagyong's *Chong Tasan chonso*, 3 vols. (reprint, Seoul, 1960-1961); Hong Taeyong's *Tamhonso*, 2 vols. (reprint, Seoul, 1969); Ki Taesung's *Kobong munjip* (reprint, Seoul, 1976); Pak Chega's *Pukhagui* (Seoul, 1971); Pak Chiwon's *Yonamchip* (1932; reprint, Seoul, 1966); Pak Sedang's *Sabyonnok* (Seoul, 1703); Song Siyol's *Songja taejon*, 7 vols. (1929; reprint, Seoul, 1971); Yi T'oegye's *T'oegye chonso*, 2 vols. (reprint, Seoul, 1958); Yi Yulgok's *Yulgok chonso*, 2 vols. (reprint, Seoul, 1961); Yi Ik's *Songho saesol*, 2 vols. (reprint, Seoul, 1967); Yi Onjok's *Hoejae chonso* (reprint, Seoul, 1973); Yu Hyongwon's *Pan'gye surok* (reprint, Seoul, 1958); and Yun Hyu's *Paekho chonso*, 3 vols. (Taegu, 1974).

Works in English. Articles in English include Martina Deuchler's "The Tradition: Women during the Yi Dynasty," in *Virtues in Conflict*, edited by Sandra Matielli (Seoul, 1977), pp. 1-47; Park Chong-hong's "Historical Review of Korean Confucianism," *Korea Journal* 3 (September 1963): 5-11; and Key P. Yang and Gregory Henderson's "An Outline History of Korean Confucianism," *Journal of Asian Studies* 18 (November 1958 and February 1959): 81-101 and 259-276. *The Rise of Neo-Confucianism in Korea*, edited by Wm. Theodore de Bary and me (New York, 1985), contains a number of important essays. See Julia Ching's "Yi Yulgok on the `Four Beginnings and the Seven Emotions'" (pp. 303-322); Chai-sik Chung's "Chong Tojon: `Architect' of Yi Dynasty Government and Ideology" (pp. 59-88); Martina Deuchler's "Reject the False and Uphold the Straight: Attitudes toward Heterodox Thought in Early Yi Korea" (pp. 375-410); Tomoeda Ryutaro's "Yi T'oegye and Chu Hsi: Differences in Their Theories of Principle and Material Force" (pp. 243-260); and Tu Wei-ming's "Yi T'oegye's Perception of Human Nature: A Preliminary Inquiry into the Four-Seven Debate in Korean Neo-Confucianism" (pp. 261-282).

JAHYUN KIM HABOUSH

CONFUCIUS

CONFUCIUS (552?-479 BCE), known in Chinese as K`ung Ch`iu (also styled Chung-ni); preeminent Chinese philosopher and teacher. The name *Confucius* is the Latin rendering of *K`ung Fu-tzu* ("Master K`ung"). Confucius was born in the small feudal state of Lu, near modern Ch`ü-fu (Shantung Province). Little can be established about his life, forebears, or family, although legends, some of very early origin, are abundant and colorful. The biography in Ssu-ma Ch`ien's *Shih chi* (Historical Annals, second century BCE) is unreliable. The *Lun-yü* (Analects), a record of Confucius's conversations with his disciples, likely compiled in the third century BCE, is probably the best source, although here, too, apocryphal materials have crept in. The *Analects* may be supplemented by the *Tso chuan*, a commentary to the *Ch`un-ch`iu* (Spring and Autumn Annals; also third century BCE), and by the *Meng-tzu* (Mencius; second century BCE).

In all these accounts, fact and legend are difficult to separate. The *Tso chuan* makes Confucius a direct descendant of the royal house of the Shang dynasty (c. 1766-1123 BCE), whose heirs were given the ducal fief of the state of Sung by the succeeding Chou dynasty (1111-256 BCE). According to this account, three to five generations prior to the sage's birth, his forebears moved to the neighboring state of Lu. His father is said to have been a soldier and a man of great strength; his mother, to have been a woman much younger and not the first wife. Some accounts make Confucius the issue of an illegitimate union. Tradition has it that at his birth dragons appeared in his house, and a unicorn *(lin)* in the vil-

> **Tradition has it that at his birth dragons appeared in his house, and a unicorn *(lin)* in the village.**

lage. These may command as much belief as the description of Confucius that endows him with a forehead like that of the sage-king Yao, shoulders like those of the famous statesman Tzu-ch`an, the eyes of Shun, the neck of Yü, the mouth of Kao-yao, the visage of the Yellow Emperor, and the height of T`ang, founder of the Shang dynasty.

Of Confucius's childhood and youth, we hear little even from legends, except for references to the early loss of his father, followed later in his youth by the death of his mother.

His favorite childhood game was reportedly the setting up of sacrificial vessels and the imitation of ritual gestures. He married young; some accounts allege that he later divorced his wife, although that cannot be proved and is unlikely to be true. He is also supposed to have visited the capital of the Chou dynasty (present-day Lo-yang) and to have met Lao-tzu, from whom he sought instruction. But this report as well appears to be unfounded. [*See the biography of Lao-tzu.*]

In the *Analects*, Confucius says that he was of humble status. Perhaps he came from the minor aristocracy, as he received an education—although not from a famous teacher—and also trained in archery and music. He probably belonged to an obscure and impoverished clan. He would say of himself that by age fifteen he had fixed his mind on

Confucius lived in an age of great political disorder.

studying (*Analects* 2.4). As a young man, he held minor offices, first overseeing stores with the task of keeping accounts, and later taking charge of sheep and cattle (*Meng-tzu* 5B.5). Confucius probably served in a junior post at the Lu court, if the *Tso chuan* is correct about his encounter in 525 with the viscount of T`an, a visitor in Lu, of whom he asked instructions regarding the ancient practice of naming offices after birds. At this point Confucius would have been twenty-seven years old.

Confucius lived in an age of great political disorder. The Chou royal house had lost its authority and the many feudal lords were competing for hegemony. He himself was concerned with the problems of restoring order and harmony to society and of keeping alive the ancient virtues of personal integrity and social justice. For him, a good ruler is one who governs by moral persuasion and who loves the people as a father loves his children. Confucius was especially learned in rites and music, finding in them both the inspiration and the means for the achievement of moral rectitude in society. He reflected deeply on the human situation about him in the light of the wisdom of the ancients. By about the age of thirty he felt himself "standing firm" (*Analects* 2.4) on his insights and convictions.

Like others of his time, Confucius viewed service in the government—the opportunity to exert moral suasion on the king—as the proper goal of a gentleman *(chün-tzu).* At about thirty-five, he visited the large neighboring state of Ch`i. He stayed there for about one year and was so enthralled by the *shao* music (attributed to the sage-king Shun) that for three months, he claimed, he did not notice the taste of the meat he ate (*Analects* 7.14). Clearly, he hoped to be of use at the ducal court. The *Analects* (12.11) reports his conversations with Duke Ching of Ch`i about government, and his emphat-

ic belief that a ruler should be a good ruler, the minister a good minister, the father a good father, and the son a good son. The duke decided not to use him (*Analects* 18.3).

In Lu again, Confucius hesitated some time before accepting public office, perhaps because of the complexity of Lu politics. The Chi family, which had usurped power, was itself dominated by its household minister, Yang Hu (or Yang Huo?), and Confucius was reluctant to ingratiate himself with this man (*Analects* 17.1; *Meng-tzu* 3B.7). Perhaps it was at this point that he determined to develop his ideas and to teach disciples. He said of himself that "at forty, I had no more doubts" (*Analects* 2.4). But some time after 502 (*Meng-tzu* 5B.4), at about age fifty, he accepted the office of *ssu-k`ou* (police commissioner?): "At fifty I knew Heaven's decree" (*Analects* 2.4). In 498 he attempted in vain to break the power of the three leading families of Lu and restore power to the duke. Perhaps this failure caused him to leave Lu the following year. The *Analects* (18.4) claims that Confucius left because the head of the Chi family of Lu had been distracted from his duties by dancing girls, while the *Meng-tzu* (6B.6) gives as the reason the fact that the head of Lu had failed to heed his advice. (The *Shih chi* reports that Confucius became prime minister of Lu, but there is reason to question the authenticity of the account.)

After leaving Lu, Confucius traveled for some thirteen years with a small group of disciples. He first visited the state of Wei (*Analects* 13.9). Although Duke Ting of Wei did not have a good reputation, Confucius took office under him, but left his service when the duke asked his advice on military rather than ritual matters (*Analects* 15.1). To avoid assassins sent by an enemy, he had to disguise himself while passing through the state of Sung (*Analects* 7.23; *Meng-tzu* 5A.8). In Ch`en he accepted office under the marquis; but his stay in Ch`en was marred by many difficulties and he was once near starvation (*Analects* 15.2; *Meng-tzu* 7B.18). In 489 he went on to the state of Ts`ai, where he met the governor of She, a visitor from Ch`u. When the governor asked Confucius's disciple Tzu-lu about his master, Confucius offered this description of himself: "[Tell him I am] the kind of man who forgets to eat when trying to solve a problem, who is so full of joy as to forget all worries, and who does not notice the onset of old age" (*Analects* 7.19). He was then about sixty-three years old. He also said of himself: "At sixty, my ears were attuned [to truth]" (*Analects* 2.4).

From Ts`ai, Confucius traveled to Wei via Ch`en and found it in disorder as the deceased duke's son sought to oust the new ruler, his own son, from the ducal throne. Such disputes help us to understand Confucius's insistence on the "rectification of names" *(cheng-ming)*—that fathers should be paternal and sons filial. After extensive travel through states that lay within present-day Shantung and Honan, Confucius returned to Lu around 484. He was given an office, perhaps as a low-ranking counselor (*Analects* 14.21). He also occupied himself with music and poetry, especially the *ya* and the *sung*, which now make up two of the sections of the *Shih ching* (Book of Poetry). During this period he conversed with Duke Ai of Lu and with the head of the Chi family on questions of government and ritual.

It is known that Confucius had at least one son, K`ung Li (Po-yü), and one daughter, whom he married to his disciple Kung-yeh Ch`ang. He also married the daughter of his deceased elder brother to another disciple, Nan Jung (*Analects* 5.1, 11.5). Of his son little is known, except that the father urged him to study poetry and rites (*Analects* 16.13). Although he is popularly portrayed as a severe moralist, the *Analects* show Confucius as fond of classical music and rituals, informal and cheerful at home, affable yet firm, commanding but not forbidding, dignified and yet pleasant, with an ability to laugh at himself. In his old age, he devoted more and more time to his disciples. He also knew that he had reached spiritual maturity: "At seventy I could follow my heart's desires without overstepping the line" (*Analects* 2.4). But his last years were saddened by the successive deaths of his son, his favorite disciple, Yen Hui, and the loyal though flamboyant Tzu-lu.

According to the *Tso chuan*, Confucius died in 479 at the age of seventy-three. While no description exists concerning his last hours, the account of a previous illness shows how Confucius probably faced death. At that time Tzu-lu wanted the disciples to attire themselves like stewards in attendance upon a high dignitary. Confucius rebuked him, saying, "By making this pretence of having stewards when I have none, whom do you think I shall deceive? Shall I deceive Heaven? Besides, is it not better for me to die in the hands of you, my friends, than in the hands of stewards?" (*Analects* 9.12). When Tzu-lu requested permission to pray for him, Confucius replied, "I have already been praying for a long time" (*Analects* 7.35). The word *praying* here has been understood to mean living the life of a just man.

Confucius's political ambitions remained largely unrealized; he is remembered by posterity above all as a teacher, indeed as the greatest moral teacher of East Asia. He is said to have accepted students without regard to their social status or ability to pay. While the *Shih chi* credits him with three thousand disciples, the more conservative number of seventy (or fewer) is more likely. With two known exceptions, most of the disciples were of humble station and modest means. The majority came from Confucius's own state of Lu, although a few were from the neighboring states of Wei, Ch`en, and Ch`i.

The modern scholar Ch`ien Mu divides the disciples into two groups—those who had followed Confucius even before he left Lu for ten years of travel and those who came to him after his return to Lu. The earlier disciples include Tzu-lu, Yen Hui, and Tzu-kung. Tzu-lu was the oldest in age, only some nine years younger than Confucius himself; his valor and

rashness stand out in the *Analects*. Yen Hui, the favorite of Confucius, was about thirty years his junior. His early death at about forty caused much sorrow to Confucius. Tzu-kung, about Yen's age, was an enterprising and eloquent diplomat. Tzu-lu perished—in a manner that had been predicted by Confucius—during a rash effort to rescue his master in the state of Wei (480). Tzu-kung served at the Lu court and was leader of the disciples at the time of Confucius's death. He is reported to have stayed on at his master's grave in Ch`ü-fu for three years longer than the mourning period of twenty-seven months prescribed for the death of one's parents, vivid testimony to the depth of his commitment to his teacher.

The later disciples were mostly much younger, sometimes forty years Confucius's junior. Those mentioned in the *Analects* include Tzu-yu, Tzu-hsia, Tzu-chang, Yu-tzu, and Tseng-tzu, who was only about twenty-seven at the time of his master's death. All five men played important roles in spreading Confucius's teachings, but Tseng-tzu, exemplary for his filial piety, is remembered as the principal spiritual heir through whom Confucius's essential message reached later generations.

Traditionally, Confucius has been credited with the editing of the Five (or Six) Classics: the *Shi ching* (Book of Poetry); the *I ching* (Book of Changes), a divination manual with metaphysical accretions; the *Shu ching* (Book of History), a collection of speeches and documents; the *Li chi* (Book of Rites); the *Ch`un-ch`iu* (Spring and Autumn Annals), historical records of the state of Lu during the years 722 to 481, said to have been compiled by Confucius; and the now lost *Yüeh ching* (Book of Music). Modern scholarship does not support these traditional attributions. Although the *Analects* mentions Confucius's knowledge of the *Poetry, History, and Changes*, there is no evidence that he had a part in editing these texts; nor was it his immediate disciples who, in their study of these texts, started the traditions of transmission for them. Of his relation to antiquity, one can say that Confucius loved the ancients—above all the duke of Chou, to whom the dynasty allegedly owed its rituals and other institutions—and that he read widely in the ancient texts and passed his understanding on to his disciples.

Confucius's place in history derives from his activities as a teacher and from the teachings that he crystallized and transmitted. In an age when only aristocrats had access to formal education he was the first to accept disciples without regard to status. He instructed them—according to each disciple's ability—not only in the rituals, knowledge of which was expected of all gentlemen, but also in the more difficult art of becoming one who is perfectly humane *(jen)*. Although none of his disciples attained high political office, Confucius the teacher wrought a real social change. Because of his teaching, the word *gentlemen* (*chün-tzu*, literally, "ruler's son") came to refer not to social status but to moral character. A new class gradually emerged, that of the *shih* (originally, "officers" or "government counselors"), a class of educated gentry. Those among the shih especially distinguished for scholarship and character were known as the *ju* (originally meaning "weaklings"?). Hence the Confucian school is known in Chinese as "the Ju school."

Confucius had a clear sense of his mission: he considered himself a transmitter of the wisdom of the ancients (*Analects* 7.1), to which he nonetheless gave new meaning. His focus was on the human, not just the human as given, but as endowed with the potential to become "perfect." His central doctrine concerns the virtue *jen*, translated variously as goodness, benevolence, humanity, and human-heartedness. Originally, *jen* denoted a particular virtue, the kindness that distinguished the gentleman in his behavior toward his inferiors. Confucius transformed it into a universal virtue, that which makes the perfect human being, the sage. He defined it as loving others, as personal integrity, and as altruism.

Confucius's teachings give primary emphasis to the ethical meaning of human relationships, finding and grounding what is moral in human nature and revealing its openness to the divine. Although he was largely silent on God and the afterlife, his silence did not bespeak disbelief (*Analects* 11.11). His philosophy was clearly grounded in religion, the inherited religions of Shang-ti ("lord on high") or T`ien ("heaven"), the supreme and personal deities of the Shang and Chou periods, respectively. He made it clear that it was Heaven that protected and inspired him: "Heaven is the author of the virtue that is in me" (*Analects* 7.23). Confucius believed that human beings are accountable to a supreme being, "He who sins against Heaven has no place left where he may pray" (*Analects* 3.13); nevertheless, he showed a certain scepticism regarding ghosts and spirits (*Analects* 6.20). This marked a rationalistic attitude that became characteristic of the Confucian school, which usually sought to resolve problems by active human involvement rather than by hoping or praying for divine intervention.

Confucius himself was devoted to the civilization of the Chou dynasty, although he might have been a descendant from the more ancient Shang royal house. The reason for this may have derived from the fact that Chinese civilization assumed a definitive shape during the Chou dynasty, or from the special relationship Confucius's native state of Lu enjoyed as a custodian of Chou culture. Its rulers were descended from the duke of Chou, the man who established the institutions of the dynasty and who acted as regent after the death of his brother, the dynasty's founder.

Confucius's emphasis on rituals is significant, as it is ritual that governs human relationships. Rituals have a moral and social function as well as a formal and ceremonial one. The Chinese word *li* refers also to propriety, that is, to proper behavior. Confucius teaches also the importance of having the right inner disposition, without which propriety becomes hypocrisy (*Analects* 15.17).

Confucius's philosophy might appear unstructured to those who cast only a cursory glance at the *Analects*, perhaps because the book was compiled several generations after Confucius's death. But the teachings found in the *Analects*, with all their inner dynamism, assume full coherency only when put into practice. Confucius did not attempt to leave behind a purely rationalistic system of thought. He wanted to help others to live, and by so doing, to improve the quality of their society. In defining as his main concern human society, and in offering moral perfection as the human ideal, Confucius has left behind a legacy that is perennial and universal. On the other hand, his teachings also show certain limitations that derive from his culture, the authoritarian character of government, and the superior social status enjoyed by men, for instance. These limitations do not, however, change the validity of his central insights into human nature and its perfectibility.

[*For an account of the rise and development of the tradition that bears Confucius's name, see* Confucian Thought.]

BIBLIOGRAPHY

For information on Confucius in English, a useful reference work is the *Encyclopaedia Britannica* (Macropaedia) (Chicago, 1982). His life is well summarized in Richard Wilhelm's *Confucius and Confucianism*, translated by George H. Danton and Annina Periam Danton (New York, 1931); in H. G. Creel's *Confucius: The Man and the Myth* (New York, 1949), reprinted under the title *Confucius and the Chinese Way* (New York, 1960); in the introduction to James Legge's translation of the Analects (1893; 3d ed., Tokyo, 1913), which is not critical enough of the sources; in the introduction to Arthur Waley's translation, *The Analects of Confucius* (London, 1938), which is definitely better; and in the introduction and appendixes to D. C. Lau's much more recent translation, *Confucius: The Analects* (London, 1979), which is a further improvement. A summary of Confucius's teachings is also given in Liu Wu-chi's *A Short History of Confucian Philosophy* (Harmondsworth, 1955), and in the relevant chapters in Fung Yu-lan's *A History of Chinese Philosophy*, translated by Derk Bodde, vol. 7 (Princeton, 1952). (Volume 2 has excellent chapters on Neo-Confucianism.) My *Confucianism and Christianity* (Tokyo, 1977) is a comparative study from a theological perspective.

Certain Chinese works are indispensable for a study of Confucius's life. Ts`ui Shu's (1740-1816), *Chu-ssu k`ao-hsin lu*, a small work in three chüan (with a three chüan supplement), offers an excellent critical study. Ch`ien Mu's *Hsien Ch`in chu-tzu hsi-nien*, vol. 1 (Hong Kong, 1956), is immensely useful. Ku Chieh-kang's *Ku-shih-pien*, vol. 2 (Shanghai, 1930-1931), should also be consulted.

There are interesting Japanese studies of Confucius's life. Kaizuka Shigeki's *Koshi* (Tokyo, 1951) has been translated into Chinese (Taipei, 1976); Geoffrey Bownas's English translation, *Confucius* (London, 1956), is also recommended. Morohashi Tetsuji's *Nyoze gamon Koshi den* (Tokyo, 1969) reports both facts and legends while distinguishing between them wherever possible.

JULIA CHING

CONGREGATIONALISM

Historical Survey. The roots of the "Congregational way" lay in Elizabethan Separatism, which produced Congregationalism's first three martyrs, Henry Barrow, John Greenwood, and John Penry. Some of the Separatists settled in Holland (and it was from among these that the *Mayflower* group set out for New England in 1620). The Restoration of Charles II was a disaster for their cause, and the Act of Uniformity of 1662 was the first of many efforts to suppress them.

The accession of William and Mary in 1688 made life more tolerable for Congregationalists, and, after a threatened setback in the reign of Queen Anne, they played a significant minor part in eighteenth-century England, where they were particularly active in education.

English Congregationalism shared fully in nineteenth-century ecclesiastical prosperity. As members of the emerging lower middle classes crowded into the churches, they became more politically minded. Voluntarism, opposing state support of denominational education, and the Liberation Society, advocating the disestablishment of the Church of England, were influential.

Congregationalists have also been strong in Wales, where the Welsh-speaking churches, known as the Union of Welsh Independents, retain their identity.

It is in the United States that Congregationalism achieved its greatest public influence and numerical strength. The Separatists of the Plymouth Colony were more radical than the Puritans of Massachusetts Bay, but they had enough in common to form a unified community. Their statement of faith, the Cambridge Platform of 1648, accepted the theology of the English Presbyterian Westminster Confession of 1646 but laid down a Congregational rather than a Presbyterian polity. In this, it was followed by the English Savoy Declaration of 1658.

The original New Englanders were not sectarian; they worked out an intellectually powerful and consistent system of theology and church and civil government that they strove, with considerable success, to exemplify. The very success of the New England settlement made it difficult for succeeding generations to retain the original commitment, and the Half-Way Covenant was devised to find a place for those who were baptized but could not make a strong enough confession of faith. Education was seen as vital from the outset. Harvard College was founded in 1637 to maintain the succession of learned ministers. Yale and others followed, precursors of a long succession of distinguished colleges founded under Congregational auspices across the country.

New life came with the Great Awakening, the revival movement begun in 1734, in which Jonathan Edwards, a minister at Northampton, Massachusetts, and one of the

greatest American theologians, was prominent. Differences emerged at the turn of the century between the two wings of Congregationalism, those who continued to accept the modified Calvinism represented by Edwards and those who were moving toward Unitarianism.

Despite the loss to the Unitarians, who took with them many of the most handsome colonial churches, Congregationalism flourished in the nineteenth century and was active in the westward expansion of the nation. In 1847, Horace Bushnell, a representative theologian, challenged

> **One of the most distinctive Congregational institutions is that of the church meeting. . . .**

the traditional substitutionary view of the atonement; his book *Christian Nurture* questioned the need for the classic conversion experience. The so-called Kansas City Creed of 1913 summed up this liberalism, which represented a break with the Calvinist past. This liberalism continues to prevail, although substantially modified after World War II by the influence of neoorthodoxy.

Beliefs and Practices. The beliefs and practices of most Congregationalists have been broadly similar to those of other mainline evangelical Protestant churches of the more liberal kind. The English historian Bernard Manning described them as "decentralized Calvinists," but this fails to allow for their emphasis on the free movement of the Holy Spirit, which gives them some affinity with the Quakers as well as with Presbyterians.

Preaching is important in Congregationalism because the word in scripture is thought of as constitutive of the church. Baptism and the Lord's Supper are the only recognized sacraments, and infant baptism is customary. Traditionally, public prayer has been *ex tempore,* but in this century set forms have been widely used. Hymns are important.

One of the most distinctive Congregational institutions is that of the church meeting, a regular gathering at which all church members have the right and responsibility to participate in all decisions.

Congregational churches have existed chiefly in English-speaking countries and in communities related to them, and although they have not been among the larger Christian groups, their tradition continues to exercise influence as one element in the life of larger reunited churches in many lands.

BIBLIOGRAPHY

Williston Walker's *Creeds and Platforms of Congregationalism* (New York, 1893) is a classic sourcebook. Douglas Horton's *Congregationalism: A Study in Church Polity* (London, 1952) and *The United Church of Christ* (New York, 1962) are two works by the most representative American Congregationalist of the twentieth century. Geoffrey F. Nuttall's *Visible Saints: The Congregational Way, 1640-1660* (Oxford, 1957) emphasizes the "spiritualizing" element in Congregationalism, and R. Tudur Jones's *Congregationalism in England, 1662-1962* (London, 1962) is a comprehensive tercentenary history. A fresh view of Congregationalism in the light of the ecumenical movement is presented in my book *Congregationalism: A Restatement* (New York and London, 1954), and essays on modern Congregationalism can be found in *Kongregationalismus* (Frankfurt, 1973), edited by Norman Goodall as volume 11 of "Die Kirchen der Welt."

DANIEL JENKINS

CONSCIENCE

Origin of the Notion. Three articulations of human experience appear to be at the basis of the Western notion of conscience: the Hebrew scriptures, the writings of Cicero, and the writings of Paul.

1. In the Hebrew scriptures God is presented as someone who knows and evaluates our entire being.

2. Cicero uses *conscientia* in another sense, to refer to an internal moral authority on important issues. Most of the time conscience is consciousness of something, agreeable consciousness of one or many good deeds (*Orationes Philippicae* 1.9; *Res publica* 6.8) or disagreeable consciousness of a trespass (*Tusculanae disputationes* 4.45, where he speaks metaphorically of the bite of conscience).

3. In the New Testament, Paul uses the notion of conscience (Gr., *suneidesis*) as he finds it in everyday speech and common moral reflections. He puts forward his own unshakable good conscience (*Rom.* 9:1, *2 Cor.* 1:2; see also *Acts* 23:1); he urges respect for the conscience of others, especially when that conscience is weak and judges matters erroneously (*1 Cor.* 8:7, 8:10); he appeals to conscience (*2 Cor.* 4:2); he allows that in evil people conscience is corrupted.

Modern Conflict between Conscience and Consciousness. With the eighteenth century, the sense of a separation between conscience and consciousness became widespread. While moral beings naively went on believing in their stable, good, unerring conscience, literature (the novel especially) increasingly explored the chasm between conscience and the vagaries of consciousness.

Nineteenth-century probings ordinarily shared the conviction that human beings should always be as fully conscious as possible, with actions completely lucid and deliberate.

The nineteenth century is full of denigrations of conscience. The poet William Blake (1757-1827) is sarcastic: "Conscience in those that have it is unequivocal" ("Annotations to Watson"). Goethe (1749-1832) commends an alternative: Faust heals himself, grows by purging himself

of conscience and ever widening his consciousness. Nietzsche (1844-1900) attempts to show that conscience only imitates ready-made values; the hard human task is to embody knowledge in ourselves, to create conscious values; and consciousness is not given gratis.

But the claims of conscience remain tenacious even in the post-Romantic age. Conscience becomes more tragic, more solitary. To Kierkegaard (1813-1855), the inwardness of conscience is demonic: more conscience means more consciousness and deeper despair. Such is also the case in Dostoevskii's *Notes from the Underground* (1864): conscience has become an obsessive inner court; the self is the accuser, the accused, the judge, and the executioner. Self-consciousness merges into compulsive self-humiliation, with no redemption in sight. Conscience is no longer active knowledge immersed in the social flow of life but purely retrospective, solitary self-condemnation, or entirely fearful anticipation.

More balanced statements of this construction are found in the writings of Coleridge (1772-1834) and Conrad (1857-1924). Coleridge stresses that conscience no longer acts "with the ease and uniformity of instinct"; rather, consciousness is the problem. In *Lord Jim,* Conrad shows us his protagonist haunted by a conscience that prevents his awareness of the good new life he has built for himself, while in *Heart of Darkness* we see Kurtz surrendering conscience and letting his consciousness be flooded by instinctual experience.

Application of the Notion to the Study of Religious and Ethical Systems. Hindu and Buddhist philosophies have very articulate and complex theories of consciousness. All religious traditions have notions of moral law and moral

> **Self-consciousness merges into compulsive self-humiliation, with no redemption in sight.**

judgment. All encourage reflectivity and offer conceptual tools and practical techniques for self-evaluation.

Nineteenth-century founders of the science of religion used the idea of evolution of conscience to bridge the gap between themselves, the Western scholars able and desirous to know all mankind, and the people they studied, whose outlook was perceived as regional, if not primitive. So they wrote about the dawn of conscience in the ancient Near East and about the various stages of conscience reached in non-Christian religions. The moral and religious dignity of man was commonly tied to the functioning of this individual organ. The evolutionary view was self-serving and is now discarded, but it had the merit of affirming a commonality among all mankind.

[For discussion of conscience in the Christian tradition, see Christian Ethics. Other related entries are Conversion and Morality and Religion]

BIBLIOGRAPHY

Altizer, Thomas J. J. "Paul and the Birth of Self-Consciousness." *Journal of the American Academy of Religion* 51 (September 1983): 359-370.

Bird, Frederick. "Paradigms and Parameters for the Comparative Study of Religious and Ideological Ethics." *Journal of Religious Ethics* 9 (Fall 1981): 157-185.

Brunschwicg, Léon. *Le progrès de la conscience dans la philosophie occidentale* (1927). 2d ed. 2 vols. Paris, 1953.

Childress, James F. "Appeals to Conscience." *Ethics* 89 (July 1979): 315-335.

Despland, Michel. "Can Conscience Be Hypocritical? The Contrasting Analyses of Kant and Hegel." *Harvard Theological Review* 68 (July-October 1975): 357-370.

Engelberg, Edward. *The Unknown Distance: From Consciousness to Conscience, Goethe to Camus*. Cambridge, Mass., 1972.

Jankélévitch, Vladimir. *La mauvaise conscience* (1933). Paris, 1982.

Jankélévitch, Vladimir. *L'ironie ou la bonne conscience*. 2d ed. Paris, 1950.

Lehmann, Paul L. *Ethics in a Christian Context*. New York, 1963.

Lévinas, Emmanuel. *Difficile liberté*. 2d ed. Paris, 1976.

Little, David L., and Sumner Twiss, Jr. *Comparative Religious Ethics*. New York, 1978.

Neal, J. R. "Conscience in the Reformation Period." Ph. D. diss., Harvard University, 1972.

Nelson, Benjamin. *On the Roads to Modernity*. Totowa, N. J., 1981.

Neusner, Jacob. *Judaism: The Evidence of the Mishnah*. Chicago, 1981.

Smith, Steven G. *The Argument to the Other: Reason beyond Reason in the Thought of Karl Barth and Emmanuel Lévinas*. Chico, Calif., 1983.

Stendahl, Krister. "Paul and the Introspective Conscience of the West." In *Paul among Jews and Gentiles, and Other Essays*. Philadelphia, 1976.

Tillich, Paul. "The Transmoral Conscience." In *The Protestant Era*. Chicago, 1948.

Wallis, R. T. *The Idea of Conscience in Philo of Alexandria*. Berkeley, 1975.

MICHEL DESPLAND

CONSERVATIVE JUDAISM

Background and Institutional History. Conservative Judaism originated in the conviction that the earlier Reform Jewish movement had simply gone too far in its efforts to accommodate modern Judaism to the visible models of Christian church society. In 1845, at the (Reform) Rabbinical Conference in Frankfurt am Main, Zacharias Frankel grew concerned about the increasingly radical tenor of the discussions and finally decided that he could not agree with his Reform colleagues' decision that the Hebrew language was only an "advisable," not a "necessary," feature of Jewish worship. He withdrew from the meeting and issued a widely circularized public denunciation of the extremist departures from tradition that had been countenanced by the participants.

While Frankel did not see fit to launch a new movement, he did insist on periodically expounding his new theological approach to modern Judaism, which he named positive-historical Judaism.

Origins in the United States. In the United States, Conservative Judaism was formally launched in 1886 with the founding of the Jewish Theological Seminary of America. The new seminary was organized in direct reaction to the issuance of the Pittsburgh Platform by a representative group of Reform rabbis in 1885, which set forth their ideological commitment to a Judaism of morality and ethics, but one that was devoid of its national and ritual dimensions and that entertained only a God "idea," not a deep-rooted conviction in a "personal" God. A broad coalition of moderate Reform rabbis, together with several traditionalist rabbis, joined together to establish the new seminary.

The Jewish Theological Seminary began its classes in 1886 in rooms provided by the Shearith Israel congregation in New York. It was largely staffed and funded by its founding volunteers during its early years and was led by its president, Sabato Morais of Philadelphia. Its initial broad constituency, however, did not long endure; the polarization of American Jewry between the German Jews, who inclined toward Reform, and the recent immigrants from eastern Europe, inclined toward Orthodoxy. By the time Sabato Morais died, in 1897, the prospects for the Conservative seminary's survival seemed increasingly dim.

Reorganization of the Jewish Theological Seminary. At that low point, a new and powerful coalition appeared on the seminary's horizon, possessing both the intellectual energy and the material resources necessary to reverse its decline. Organized by Cyrus Adler, librarian of the Smithsonian Institution, this strong cadre of cultured philanthropists included the renowned attorney Louis Marshall, the eminent banker Jacob Schiff, the judge Mayer Sulzberger, and industrialists like Adolph Lewisohn and Daniel and Simon Guggenheim. Adler successfully persuaded them that the Jewish Theological Seminary of America could become a powerful americanizing force for the thousands of Jews who were beginning to arrive from eastern Europe. Through respect for their traditions, it could provide a healthful synthesis of learning and observance, while drawing them into the modernist world of new ideas and open horizons. Above all, it could produce rabbis who would combine the wisdom of the Old World with the disciplines and skills of the New World and facilitate the generational transition from Yiddish-speaking immigrant to upstanding American citizen.

The key to the successful reorganization of the seminary in the minds of these philanthropists and community leaders was the appointment of a world-renowned Jewish scholar and personality to oversee the new institution. The person they sought was Solomon Schechter (1850-1915).

After considerable negotiation, Schechter agreed to undertake the new challenge, and Adler, Schiff, and Marshall proceeded with the reorganization of the Jewish Theological Seminary, appropriating the main administrative positions. Schechter arrived in 1902 to implement the type of academic standards for the seminary to which he had become accustomed..

Growth of the movement. Adler's successor in 1940 as titular head of the Conservative movement (begun in 1913 with the advent of the United Synagogue of America) was Louis Finkelstein, a seminary alumnus who had studied under Schechter and had become a mainstay of the seminary faculty and administration during the Adler era. Finkelstein almost immediately launched a broad-based expansion of the seminary's programs during the wartime and postwar periods, an expansion that was carried forward with vision, energy, effectiveness, and a large measure of success.

The Finkelstein era (1940-1972) was characterized by enormous growth in the number of congregations affiliated with Conservative Judaism, a sharp escalation in the number of programs offered by the institutions of the movement, and greater recognition of the responsibilities that devolved upon the movement in view of its newfound preeminence in American and world Jewish affairs. Having grown from about 200 affiliated congregations in 1940 to some 830 congregations by 1965, the movement had become the largest federation of synagogues in the Diaspora.

The phenomenal growth of Conservative Judaism tapered off in the mid-1960s. By then the movement had established a full network of professional and lay organizations designed to enhance its local, national, and international functioning. Its California branch, the University of Judaism, had become a major force in the growth of West Coast Jewry. The Mesorati ("traditional," i. e., Conservative) movement was launched to establish Conservative congregations in Israel. The Cantors Institute, the Teachers Institute, and the seminary's various graduate schools were seeking to meet the perennial shortage of qualified Jewish professionals. The burgeoning Association for Jewish Studies, serving the academic community, was heavily populated by scholars trained in the Conservative Jewish institutions. Prayer books for the Sabbath, festivals, High Holy Days, and weekday services had been published by the United Synagogue and the Rabbinical Assembly.

In 1972 Finkelstein announced his retirement. His successor, Gerson D. Cohen, also a seminary alumnus, had served with distinction as a professor of Jewish history at Columbia University and at the seminary. He became chancellor of an institution that was now in the forefront of American Jewish institutional life and titular head of the largest of the Jewish religious movements. The agenda for the new administration included resolving some of the lingering ideological issues that had been brushed aside during the rapid expansion period of Conservative Judaism, consolidating the many activities of the movement, and addressing the capital improvement projects that had become increasingly imperative as the movement had grown.

Major Organizations. Over the course of the century, the Conservative movement spread from the Jewish Theological Seminary of America into a web of religious and social institutions which are herewith described.

The United Synagogue of America. Founded by Solomon Schechter in 1913, the United Synagogue is the national association of Conservative congregations, responsible for the coordination of activities and services of the Conservative movement on behalf of its constituent congregations. Divisions of the United Synagogue created for this purpose include some of the most important bodies of the movement. Among these are: The Commission on Jewish Education; The Department of Youth Activities; The National Academy for Adult Jewish Studies; and The Israel Affairs Committee.

The Rabbinical Assembly. The Rabbinical Assembly (RA) is the organization of Conservative rabbis and has a membership of over eleven hundred rabbis. The Rabbinical Assembly has historically served as the religious policy-making body in the Conservative movement; its Committee on Jewish Law and Standards (CJLS) has been recognized as the authoritative forum for the development of Jewish legal precedents for the movement.

The Women's League for Conservative Judaism. More than eight hundred synagogue sisterhoods are affiliated with the Conservative movement through the coordinating body of the Women's League. Founded by Mathilde Schechter in 1918, the Women's League has historically proven to be one of the pioneering organizations in Conservative Judaism in the development of social, educational, and philanthropic programs for the entire movement.

The National Federation of Jewish Men's Clubs. The four hundred men's clubs affiliated with the Conservative movement plan joint ventures for the advancement of Conservative Judaism. The National Federation of Jewish Men's Clubs is particularly active in the areas of social action, youth activities, and Israeli affairs.

The World Council of Synagogues. The international arm of the Conservative movement, the World Council of Synagogues was established in 1959 to assist in bringing the message of Conservative Judaism to the attention of world Jewry outside the borders of North America. It maintains offices in Jerusalem, Buenos Aires, and New York and meets in convention every two years in Jerusalem.

BIBLIOGRAPHY

The standard works on the origins of the Conservative movement are Moshe Davis's *The Emergence of Conservative Judaism* (Philadelphia, 1963), Herbert Parzen's *Architects of Conservative Judaism* (New York, 1964), and my own *Conservative Judaism: A Contemporary History* (New York, 1983). The definitive sociological study of the movement is Marshall Sklare's revised and augmented *Conservative Judaism: An American Religious Movement* (New York, 1972). Conservative views of Jewish tradition can be found in *Tradition and Change* (New York, 1958), an anthology of essays by leading Conservatives edited by Mordecai Waxman, and in a special issue of the magazine *Judaism* 26 (Summer 1977). Conservative approaches to Jewish law are intensively described in Isaac Klein's *A Guide to Jewish Religious Practice* (New York, 1979) and in *Conservative Judaism and Jewish Law,* edited by Seymour Siegel (New York, 1977). Journals published by various arms of the Conservative movement include the following: *Conservative Judaism* (New York, 1945-), published quarterly by the Rabbinical Assembly; *The Outlook* (New York, 1930-), published quarterly by the Women's League for Conservative Judaism: the *Torchlight* (first published as *The Torch* in 1941, renamed in 1977), published quarterly by the National Federation of Jewish Men's Clubs; *The United Synagogue Review* (New York, 1945-), published quarterly by the United Synagogue of America; and *Proceedings of the Rabbinical Assembly* (New York, 1927-), published annually.

Important aspects of Conservative ideology are explored in Simon Greenberg's *A Jewish Philosophy and Pattern of Life* (New York, 1981) and in Elliot N. Dorff's *Conservative Judaism: Our Ancestors to Our Descendants* (New York, 1977). In addition, shorter treatments of Conservative Judaism have been written by Robert Gordis, Simon Greenberg, and Abraham Karp, and there are important chapters on the Conservative movement in large works by Joseph Blau, Arthur Hertzberg, Mordecai Kaplan, Gilbert Rosenthal, and David Rudavsky, among others.

HERBERT ROSENBLUM

CONSTANTINE

CONSTANTINE (272/273-337), known as Constantine the Great, Roman emperor and agent of the christianization of the Roman empire. Born at Naissus, the only son of Helena and Flavius Constantius, Constantine was assured a prominent role in Roman politics when Diocletian, the senior emperor in the Tetrarchy, appointed his father Caesar in 293. He doubtless expected to succeed to his father's position when Diocletian and Maximian abdicated in 305. But Galerius, who may have contrived the abdication and as the new eastern emperor controlled the succession, ignored Constantine and instead nominated as Caesars his own nephew, Severus. Constantine could not challenge this decision immediately, but when his father died at York in July 306,

he reasserted the claim, this time backed by the British and Gallic armies, and requested confirmation from the eastern emperor. Galerius resisted, but to avoid a confrontation offered Constantine the lesser rank of Caesar. For the next seven years civil war disrupted the western half of the empire.

In the end it was Constantine who triumphed. Christian observers who produced accounts of the event a few years later proclaimed this was more than a political triumph. On the eve of the battle, they insisted, Constantine had experienced the vision (or visions) that inspired his conversion to Christianity. Constantine's motives are beyond reconstruction, but it is clear that he believed the victory had been won with divine assistance, Constantine's legislation and activities after 312 attest the evolution of his Christian sympathies.

Whether the "conversion" represented a dramatic break with the pagan past is more problematic. Unlike Galerius, who had vigorously persecuted Christians in the East, Constantine was a tolerant pagan, content with the accumulation of heavenly patrons (Sol Invictus, Apollo). In 312 he may well have considered the God of the Christians simply another heavenly patron, demonstrably more powerful than others but not necessarily incompatible. Though he refused to participate after 312 in distinctly pagan ceremonies, Constantine retained the title *pontifex maximus* and evidently did not find the demands of government and religion irreconcilable. Exclusive commitment and a sense of mission, however, would develop over time. After 324 he did not hesitate to use his office to condemn pagan beliefs and practices and to promote the christianization of the empire.

Politics accounts in large measure for Constantine's transformation from benefactor to advocate. The conversion did not alienate pagans, for religion had not been an issue in the civil war, and nothing indicates that Licinius, whom Galerius had chosen as co-emperor in 308, objected to Constantine's evident Christian sympathies in 312. As political rivalry developed over the next few years, however, the religious policies of the emperors diverged, especially after the inconclusive civil war of 316/7. Politics and religion became so entangled that Constantine, using attacks on Christians in the East as pretext, could declare his campaign against Licinius in 324 a crusade against paganism. His victory at Chrysopolis (18 September) simultaneously removed the last challenge to his authority and legitimized his emerging sense of mission.

Denunciations of pagan practices followed immediately, coupled with lavish grants for the construction of churches and preferential treatment of Christian candidates for administrative posts. Constantine also took the lead in efforts to restore order in an increasingly divided church. The bishops assembled in Nicaea (Bithynia), responding to the counterarguments of Alexander (bishop of Alexandria) and others who did not believe in the divinity of Christ, condemned Arianism and adopted the Nicene Creed that declared the Father and Son to be of the same essence.

BIBLIOGRAPHY

Barnes, Timothy D. *Constantine and Eusebius.* Cambridge, Mass., 1981.

Barnes, Timothy D. *The New Empire of Diocletian and Constantine.* Cambridge, Mass., 1982.

Dörries, Hermann. *Constantine the Great.* Translated by Roland H. Bainton. New York, 1972.

Jones, A. H. M. *Constantine and the Conversion of Europe.* Rev. ed. New York, 1962.

Momigliano, Arnaldo, ed. *The Conflict between Paganism and Christianity in the Fourth Century.* Oxford, 1963.

JOHN W. EADIE

CONVERSION

Definitions of conversion abound. Within Judaism and Christianity, conversion indicates a radical call to reject evil and to embrace a relationship with God through faith. Some scholars in the human sciences limit conversion to sudden, radical alterations in people's beliefs, behaviors, and affiliations.

Tradition, Transformation, and Transcendence. Most studies of conversion tend to focus on one dimension of conversion to the exclusion of other equally important aspects. To appreciate its diversity and complexity, conversion should be understood in three dimensions: tradition, transformation, and transcendence.

Tradition. Tradition encompasses the social and cultural matrix that includes symbols, myths, rituals, worldviews, and institutions. Tradition structures the present circumstances in which people live and ensures connection with the past. Most religious traditions include beliefs and practices that encourage, shape, and evaluate religious change.

Sociologists examine the social and institutional aspects of traditions in which conversion takes place.

Anthropologists delineate the ideological and cultural realms of tradition. They consider culture as a powerful force in the shaping and renewal of individuals, groups, and societies. They study phenomena such as rites of passage, rituals, myths, and symbols, which weave the meaningful fabric of the culture; and they examine a culture's symbols and methods for religious change, the cultural impact of conversion, the ways culture impedes or facilitates religious change, and stages of the development of new religious orientations.

Transformation. The second way to understand conversion is through the dimension of transformation. Transformation may be defined as the process of change

manifested through alteration in people's thoughts, feelings, and actions. Psychology is the discipline that considers transformation, in both objective and subjective aspects, of the self, consciousness, and experience.

Transcendence. Transcendence refers to the domain of the sacred—the encounter with the holy that, according to many religions, constitutes the source and goal of conversion. Religious people affirm that the divine works within the human situation in order to bring people into relationship with the divine and provide a new sense of meaning and purpose. Theologians consider this dimension absolutely essential to the whole process of human transformation; other factors are subordinated to it.

Typology of Conversion. A good theory of conversion requires a heuristic typology that takes into account the diversity and complexity of conversion. The typology proposed in this article seeks to delineate as precisely as possible the range of phenomena that the word conversion designates.

Tradition transition. This refers to the movement of an individual or a group from one major religious tradition to another. Moving from one worldview, ritual system, symbolic universe, and lifestyle to another is a complex process that often takes place in a context of cross-cultural contact and conflict. Christianity and Islam are religions that have initiated and benefited from massive tradition transition. [*See* Missions.]

Institutional transition. This involves the change of an individual or a group from one community to another within a major tradition. An example is conversion from the Baptist to the Presbyterian church in American Protestantism. The process, which sociologists call "denomination switching," can involve affiliation with a church because of convenience (such as geographical proximity) and/or a significant religious change based upon a profound religious experience.

Affiliation. This is the movement of an individual or a group from no commitment or minimal commitment to involvement with an institution or community of faith. Affiliation has recently been viewed as controversial because of the allegation of manipulative and coercive recruitment strategies used by some new religious movements and some fundamentalist groups.

Intensification. This is the revitalized commitment to a faith with which converts have had a previous affiliation, formal or informal. It occurs when nominal members of a religious institution make their belief and commitment a central focus in their lives, or when people deepen and intensify involvement through profound religious experience and/or explosive new insights.

Apostasy/defection. This is the repudiation of a religious tradition or its beliefs by previous members. This change does not involve acceptance of a new religious perspective but often indicates adoption of a nonreligious system of values. Deprogramming, an intensive method sometimes used to get people out of cults, may be seen as a form of forced deconversion or apostasy. Apostasy is included in this typology because the dynamics of leaving a group or of loss of faith constitute an important form of change, both individually and collectively, in the contemporary setting.

BIBLIOGRAPHY

Aviad, Janet O'Dea. *Return to Judaism: Religious Renewal in Israel.* Chicago, 1983. Aviad, combining sophisticated sociological analysis and appreciative empathy for religious aspirations, gives us a fine study of the contemporary ba`alei teshuvah (those who repent and return) movement in Israel. The ba`alei teshuvah, European, American, and Israeli young people who have returned to Judaism through enthusiastic discovery and adoption of Orthodox Judaism, are good examples of conversion as intensification.

Beckford, James A. "Accounting for Conversion." *British Journal of Sociology* 29 (1978): 249-262. Beckford, along with Bryan Taylor (see references below), persuasively argues that learning to give one's personal testimony is an integral part of conversion. The group's ideology becomes the person's story and thus shapes his or her memory and autobiography.

Beidelman, T. O. *Colonial Evangelism.* Bloomington, Ind., 1982. This book is one of the best examples of the importance of giving serious consideration to the converters as well as the converts. Beidelman's analysis provides sophisticated and important perspectives on the nature of religious change.

Conn, Walter E., ed. *Conversion: Perspectives on Personal and Social Transformation.* New York, 1978. Conn's work on conversion is a major contribution. He integrates the thought of Jean Piaget, Lawrence Kohlberg, Erik Erikson, James W. Fowler, Robert Kegan, and Bernard J. F. Lonergan in such a way as to provide a precise, extensive exploration of conversion within the developmental life cycle.

Horton, Robin. "African Conversion." *Africa* 41 (1971): 85-108.

Horton, Robin. "On the Rationality of Conversion: Part 1." *Africa* 45 (1975): 219-235.

Horton, Robin. "On the Rationality of Conversion: Part 2." *Africa* 45 (1975): 373-399. Horton's essays are required reading for anyone interested in conversion and religion in Africa.

James, William. *The Varieties of Religious Experience.* New York, 1902. James's Gifford Lectures of 1901 and 1902 remain seminal in the psychology of conversion. Of enduring significance is his phenomenological approach to the richness and complexity of conversion.

Levtzion, Nehemia, ed. *Conversion to Islam.* New York, 1979. This book contains an excellent collection of original articles on islamization. The bibliography is the most complete listing of works on conversion to Islam available.

Lofland, John, and Norman Skonovd. "Conversion Motifs." *Journal for the Scientific Study of Religion* 20 (1981): 373-385. Lofland and Skonovd argue that a typology of conversion is mandatory in order to bring some clarity to the field of conversion studies. Although very different from the typology proposed in the following article, it is an important contribution to the field.

Lofland, John, and Rodney Stark. "Becoming a World-saver: A Theory of Conversion to a Deviant Perspective." *American Sociological Review* 30 (1965): 862-875. This is perhaps the single most influential article ever written on the sociology of conversion.

MacMullen, Ramsay. *Christianizing the Roman Empire, A. D. 100-400.* New Haven, 1984. MacMullen's vast knowledge of classical antiquity is richly demonstrated in this bold and insightful study of conversion. While fully aware of social, political, economic, and psychological motivations, MacMullen vigorously argues for the importance of religious motivation for conversion. MacMullen's book is one of the few that fully appreciate the complexity and diversity of conversion.

Nock, Arthur Darby. *Conversion: The Old and the New in Religion from Alexander the Great to Augustine of Hippo.* Oxford, 1933. This book continues to be a significant source for understanding conversion during antiquity and the rise of Christianity.

Rambo, Lewis R. "Current Research on Religious Conversion." *Religious Studies Review* 8 (April 1982): 146-159. This bibliographical essay contains more than two hundred items on conversion to many different religious groups and includes material from anthropology, sociology, psychology, history, and theology.

Robertson, Roland. *Meaning and Change.* Oxford, 1978. Excellent sociological analysis of conversion is provided in this splendid book.

Sanneh, Lamin O. *West African Christianity: The Religious Impact.* Maryknoll, N. Y., 1983. This book contains one of the most vigorous arguments for the importance of indigenous creativity and vitality in the conversion process.

Sarbin, Theodore R., and Nathan Adler. "Self-Reconstitution Processes: A Preliminary Report." *Psychoanalytic Review* 57 (1970): 599-616. This is one of the best articles in the psychological literature on conversion. The authors delineate factors that they believe characterize all methods of personality change.

Taylor, Bryan. "Conversion and Cognition." *Social Compass* 23 (1976): 5-22.

Taylor, Bryan. "Recollection and Membership: Convert's Talk and the Ratiocination of Commonality." *Sociology* 12 (1978): 316-324. See the comments on Beckford (1978), above.

Tippett, Alan R. "Conversion as a Dynamic Process in Christian Mission." *Missiology* 5 (1977): 203-221. This article, along with Lofland and Stark (1965), provides the basic structure of the stage model.

Wallace, Anthony F. C. "Revitalization Movements." *American Anthropologist* 58 (1956): 264-281. This is a seminal article for the understanding of cultural and religious change.

LEWIS R. RAMBO

COPERNICUS, NICOLAUS

COPERNICUS, NICOLAUS (1473-1543), Polish cleric and astronomer, known in Polish as Mikolaj Kopernik. Copernicus studied in Italy, receiving doctor's degrees in canon law and medicine while also studying astronomy

Sometime around 1514 Copernicus sketched his heliocentric astronomy in an unpublished manuscript, the *Commentariolus,* which achieved wide circulation. A Lutheran astronomer named Rheticus was attracted by the new system and became Copernicus's chief disciple. Rheticus's *Narratio prima* of 1540 was the first published account of Copernican astronomy. Its favorable reception influenced Copernicus to publish his detailed technical account, *De revolutionibus orbium caelestium* (On the Revolutions of the Heavenly Spheres), in 1543. Reportedly, he was shown the published book just hours before he died. *On the Revolutions* set forth an astronomy based upon a rotating earth that revolved yearly around the sun, the center of the universe. It challenged Ptolemaic astronomy, which assumed a central stationary earth around which all celestial bodies revolved.

As he contemplated astronomical calculations from the perspective of a moving earth, Copernicus discovered something that made astronomy's claim to physical truth unavoidable. The assumption of a moving earth and a central sun provided the reason why the motions of the planets should be of the observed orders, magnitudes, and positions, and not otherwise. Ptolemaic astronomy described these observations as well as Copernican astronomy did.

The Copernican revolution had two great religious consequences. The first concerned the tension between scientific and religious authority. Even before *On the Revolutions* was published, Martin Luther condemned heliocentric astronomy because of scriptural references to a central stationary earth. By 1616 *On the Revolutions* was on the Index of Forbidden Books of the Catholic church, and the new astronomy was labeled atheistic. Up to the condemnation, the church had no formal cosmological position. It even used calculations based on Copernican astronomy from Erasmus Rheinhold's *Prutenic Tables* (1551) to help reform the calendar in 1582.

Second, the problems of Copernican astronomy, which culminated in the laws of Kepler and Newton, led inexorably to the conclusion that the universe was infinite. The perception of man's insignificance in an infinite universe has become one of the decisive experiences of modernity.

BIBLIOGRAPHY

A thorough biography of Copernicus and an excellent annotated bibliography of Copernican scholarship accompany *Three Copernican Treatises: The Commentariolus of Copernicus, the Letter against Werner, the Narratio prima of Rheticus*, 3d ed., rev., edited and translated by Edward Rosen (New York, 1971). A translation of *De revolutionibus* is included in *Ptolemy, Copernicus, Kepler*, "Great Books of the Western World," vol. 16, edited by Robert Maynard Hutchins (Chicago, 1952). At a glance one can compare Ptolemy's and Copernicus's work and see how carefully Copernicus followed Ptolemy in format and content. A very readable discussion of the technical development of Ptolemaic and Copernican astronomy and their cultural consequences is found in Thomas S. Kuhn's *The Copernican Revolution: Planetary Astronomy in the Development of Western Thought*, rev. ed. (New York, 1959). Discussions of religious, scientific, and cultural factors involved with Copernicus can be found in the articles collected in *The Copernican Achievement*, edited by Robert S. Westman (Berkeley, 1975). The religious consequences of the development of science and the complexity of the problem of secularization is discussed in Enrique Dussel's "From Secularization to Secularism: Science from the Renaissance to the Enlightenment," in *Church History: Sacralization and Secularization,* edited by Roger Aubert (New York, 1969).

MICHAEL A. KERZE

COPTIC CHURCH

The Coptic church is the ancient church of Egypt; the name Copt derives from the Greek *Aiguptioi* ("Egyptians"). According to tradition within the church, its founder and first patriarch was Mark the Evangelist, who first preached Christianity in the first century AD. For several centuries the new faith engendered by Mark's preaching and the old pagan culture mingled with the teachings of both Neoplatonism and gnosticism, amid waves of Roman persecutions.

Biblical papyri and parchment codices found in Egypt are testimonies of the penetration of the new faith into Egypt long before the end of the age of persecutions. Such papyri attest to the antiquity of Christianity in Egypt. With the Edict of Milan (313), whereby Constantine made Christianity the official religion of the empire, Alexandria became the seat of Christian theological studies. There, the doctrines of what was an amorphous faith were formulated into a systematic theology.

The Catechetical School of Alexandria. The catechetical school of Alexandria, which began in about 190, was to become a center of Christian scholarship under the leadership of some of the greatest church fathers. It came of age under Origen, perhaps the most prolific author of all time. One of Origen's works, the *Hexapla,* is the first collation of the texts of the Bible in six columns of Greek and Hebrew originals. Origen's exegetical, philosophical, and theological writings had broad influence on the early church. His pupils included the patriarch Heraclas (230-246), who was the first in the annals of Christianity to bear the title of pope, Athanasius, Cyril of Alexandria, and others.

Ecumenical Movement. An ecumenical movement intended to combat heresy was inaugurated by Constantine with the Council of Nicaea (325). At this and subsequent councils, orthodoxy was defined for theological questions concerning divine essence and the divinity and humanity of Christ. At the time of the Second Council of Ephesus (449), a change of emperors drew together Rome and Constantinople, greatly affecting the Alexandrian ecclesiastical hegemony. Cyril's nephew, Dioscorus I, who had dominated that council, was summoned to Chalcedon in 451 by the eastern emperor Marcian and forced to defend his views on Christology (the essence of Christ's divinity and humanity). The council condemned Dioscorus, who was consequently deposed and exiled.

Henceforth, the place of the Coptic church in the Christian world was curtailed. A wave of persecution was begun against the Copts to curb their separatism, with disastrous consequences on the eve of the Arab conquest of Egypt.

Monastic Rule. Though severe social and economic factors must have played a role in accelerating the flight of Copts to the desert, it remains true that monasticism as an institution was initiated principally by Coptic piety. The first or founding stage is associated with Antony (c. 251-356), who fled to the solitude of the eastern desert from his native village of Coma after hearing *Matthew* 19:21. Others followed his example, and a monastic colony arose around his cave in the Red Sea mountains. All practiced a life of austerity and the torture of the flesh to save the soul. Although committed to complete solitude, these men of religion found it spiritually profitable to be within sight of their great mentor for guidance, and physically protective to be within reach of other brothers. These circumstances led to the development of the second stage in monastic evolution, a stage that may be called collective eremiticism.

The third and final stage in the development of cenobitic life must be ascribed to Pachomius (d. 346). Originally a pagan legionary, he was inspired by the goodness of Christian villagers who ministered to the needs of the soldiers and was baptized a Christian. After spiritual training by a hermit, Pachomius developed a community and subsequently an original rule. The rule prescribed communal life in a cenobium and repudiated self-mortification. According to the rule, monks should develop their potential in useful pursuits, both manual and intellectual, while preserving the monastic vow of chastity, poverty, and obedience.

The Copts appear to have introduced Christianity to the British Isles.

Missionary Endeavor. Those who lived in Pachomian monasteries and later took Pachomian monasticism to their homelands may be regarded as unchartered ambassadors of Coptic Christianity, but, further, the Copts themselves were active in extensive missionary enterprise. In North Africa, the Copts concentrated on the easternmost part of Libya, called the Pentapolis. They also penetrated Nubia in the upper reaches of the Nile. The conversion of the kingdom of Ethiopia took place in the fourth century. Coptic activities in Asia lack written evidence, but isolated cases provide instances of missionary work on that continent as well. In Europe, Coptic monks followed in the steps of Roman legionaries to preach the gospel in Gaul, Switzerland, and Britain.

The Swiss mission may be traced to a group of Christian legionaries from Egypt led by Mauritius about the year 285.

The Copts appear to have introduced Christianity to the British Isles. In England, Egyptian monastic rule prevailed until the coming of Augustine of Canterbury in 597, and the powerful Irish Christianity that shaped the civilization of northern Europe may be regarded as the direct descendant of the Coptic church.

From Doctrinal Conflict to Ecumenism. The Council of Chalcedon in 451, with its condemnation of the Coptic patriarch Dioscorus I, and its interpretation of Cyril's formula of the nature and person of Christ contrary to the Coptic profession, led to the cleavage of Christendom into two divergent camps. To this day, Chalcedon is bitterly remembered by the Coptic natives of Egypt, as well as by others (Syrians, Ethiopians, and Armenians). The outcome of Chalcedon was immediately felt in Egypt: the Byzantine emperors who aimed at unity within the church as the sole bearer of cohesion in the empire forcibly imposed that unity on the Egyptian people. Persecution was inaugurated to obliterate all vestiges of separatism. Excessive taxation and horrible torture and humiliation were inflicted upon Egyptians throughout the period from 451 to 641, until the Arab conquest.

The Arabs promised religious freedom to all the "people of the book," that is, to Christians and the Jews. In fact, after the downfall of Alexandria, the conquerors offered the fugitive Coptic patriarch Benjamin I honorable safe-conduct and possession of the vacated Melchite churches. At the time of the conquest, the Arabs referred to Egypt as Dar al-Qibt (Home of the Copts).

Muslim rule created a new barrier between the Christians of the East and those of the West. Internally, the growing Muslim majority generally accorded the Copts a certain status as good neighbors and honest civil servants. In modern times, the Copts were on occasion offered integration with other Christian powers. Peter the Great (1689-1725) offered a merger with the Copts on the condition that they become a Russian protectorate. The Copts, however, systematically chose a life of harmony with their Muslim compatriots.

When the French expedition of 1798-1802 entered Egypt, the Copts began to establish a measure of communication with Western Christendom. Soon after, with the emergence of democracy and the enfranchisement of the Egyptians, the Copts emerged from their closed communities.

Perhaps the most significant demonstration of the rebirth of interaction between East and West is Coptic participation in the World Council of Churches meeting that convened in 1954 in Illinois. Since then, the Copts have been active in the council.

BIBLIOGRAPHY

This bibliography includes a brief selection of general books in English. For further and fuller reference to original sources and to special studies, see Winifred Kammerer's *A Coptic Bibliography* (1950; reprint, New York, 1969) and also the footnotes and bibliography of my *History of Eastern Christianity* (1968; reprint, Millwood, N. Y., 1980).

Burmester, O. H. E. *The Egyptian or Coptic Church.* Cairo, 1967.

Butcher, Edith L. *The Story of the Church of Egypt* (1897). 2 vols. New York, 1975.

Butler, Alfred J. *The Ancient Coptic Churches of Egypt* (1884). 2 vols. Oxford, 1970.

Duchesne, Louis. *Early History of the Christian Church, from Its Foundation to the Fourth Century.* 3 vols. Translated from the fourth French edition. London, 1950-1951.

Fortescue, Adrian. *The Lesser Eastern Churches* (1913). New York, 1972.

Fowler, Montague. *Christian Egypt: Past, Present, and Future.* London, 1901.

Groves, Charles P. *The Planting of Christianity in Africa* (1948-1958). 4 vols. London, 1964.

Hardy, Edward R. *Christian Egypt: Church and People.* Oxford, 1952.

Kidd, Beresford J. *The Churches of Eastern Christendom, from A. D. 451 to the Present Time.* London, 1927.

MacKean, William H. *Christian Monasticism in Egypt to the Close of the Fourth Century.* New York, 1920.

Masri, Iris Habib el. *The Story of the Copts.* Cairo, 1978.

Meinardus, Otto F. A. *Christian Egypt: Ancient and Modern.* Cairo, 1965.

Neale, John Mason. *A History of the Holy Eastern Church: The Patriarchate of Alexandria.* 2 vols. London, 1847.

Waddell, Helen J., trans. *The Desert Fathers.* London, 1936.

Wakin, Edward. *A Lonely Minority: The Modern History of Egypt's Copts; The Challenge of Survival for Four Million Christians.* New York, 1963.

Westerman, William Linn, et al. *Coptic Egypt.* Brooklyn, N. Y., 1944.

Worrell, William H. *A Short Account of the Copts.* Ann Arbor, 1945.

A. S. ATIYA

COSMOLOGY

Images of the World as Subjects for Historians. The history of religions is the only discipline seeking to relate two branches of learning that have been kept apart for a considerable time; the humanities (including history) and the natural sciences.

In most instances, as we shall see, every aspect of a culture or religion seems to presuppose a view of the cosmos. Nevertheless, even this generalization should be made with some caution. It is true that in the case of the modern natural sciences there is no doubt about the pervasiveness of an implicit worldview, even though many of the details of this view may be open to debate. However, in the study of religious images of the world the presupposition of a cosmic view does not necessarily apply. The sacred and the phenomenal world are related, but they are by no means identical. Certainly, notions of "the sacred" vary widely from one tradition to another, yet in every tradition one notion or configuration of "the sacred" is prominent and forms the sine qua non of the religion concerned and constitutes the vantage point for our understanding of it. The same is not true of images of the cosmos, for in certain traditions these are of mere secondary importance (as in Christianity and Buddhism). A hierophany (a manifestation of the sacred) can lead to an image of the cosmos, but images of the cosmos do not necessarily take on a sacred significance.

Classification of Cosmologies. Cosmic worldviews may be examined from two distinct perspectives: in terms of geographical location or in terms of culturally evolved themes.

Geography. A geographic compilation of cosmic views leads to a very natural and necessary first conclusion: man, or humanity, is a central theme in all traditional cosmologies. Whether poetic visions of primordial mountains and oceans or a preoccupation with the risks or failures in human acts prevail, we may indeed say that the world of man is the theme of all traditional mythology.

Cultural themes. Any worldwide survey of cosmological views must consider a crucial factor: the variety of cultural levels on which views of the cosmos have developed. This is not to say that the various livelihoods (hunting-gathering, tilling the soil, livestock raising) are presented as ironclad systems in myths. Yet to quite an extent, views of the cosmos are in harmony with the social order in a tribe or tradition, and as a rule reflect the prevailing mode of production (and may shed light on the legal customs of the society as well).

The generating earth. Even though no unambiguous examples of matriarchy have been found, there are many examples of female cosmic principles and deities. [See Goddess Worship.] In certain very early agricultural societies, as in prehistoric eastern Europe, it seems most likely that supreme goddesses to some extent mirrored the importance of women in society. Evidence of the imageries of a sole maternal figure comes from well-developed early and classical cultures, including those of the Greeks, the Egyptians, the Hittites, and the Japanese. The earth, constituting "the whole place" in which man found himself, evidently was conceived as the center or foundation of the cosmos. A Sanskrit word for earth, *prthivi,* is feminine and literally means "the one who is wide." Taking all evidence together, it is advisable to be cautious in speaking without further qualification of motherhood as the cause of all these imageries.

Divine male fashioner. The great monotheistic systems (those of ancient Israel, Judaism, Christianity, Islam, as well as Zoroastrianism) that also speak of a supreme creator are very different; they brought into existence monotheism properly so called, not the idea of someone who merely creates. Their monotheism is the result of their fight against polytheism of one type or another; it is a matter of a revolution in the development of religion. [*See* Monotheism.] Not by chance are they historically rooted in pastoral traditions and in civilizations far more extensive than those of early hunters and gatherers. Here the father is the undisputed head of the family. The world is governed strictly by the creator; the biblical god, Yahveh, sets the course for the celestial bodies. However, societies of a pronounced patriarchal type with a monotheistic religion are relative latecomers in history, and their diversity is striking.

World parents. Enlarging upon the themes of the earth's generative power and a supreme fashioner is the theme of the world parents. The primordial union out of which all there is was born is often that of sky and earth, that is, the primal pair of parents. We should bear in mind that here also we are not confronted merely with inadequate scientific knowledge and fanciful illusions concerning the structure of the universe but with fundamental issues in a lasting religious quest. In addition to the immediate world of man there exists the sky, at the same time undeniably there and yet unreachable; it is the first image of what in philosophy will come to be called "transcendence." Out of the opposites of earth and sky the world (and one may want to call it more precisely "the human world") is born.

Other motifs. Several other themes that deal with the origin of the world and its structure may be related with certainty to the specific cultural environments in which they are narrated. Nevertheless, they cross cultural boundaries or occur with modifications that can be expected by cultural anthropologists and historians. However, with chthonic creativity and the world parents, it is not necessary here to think in terms of diffusion from one point of the globe to another; on the basis of observation and experience one may conclude that independent origins are not uncommon and in fact are often more likely.

A number of archaic hunters' traditions know of an earth diver, a creature that descends to the bottom of the primordial ocean to pick up the earth from which the dry land is to be fashioned on the surface of the water. (The theme occurs, for example, in North America among the Huron.) In some regions, the motif appears with the addition of a character, often divine, who orders the earth diver to descend and fetch the required particles of earth. Finally, the theme recurs with an earth diver who attempts to keep the earth to himself, or who sets himself up in opposition to the divine creator. There is no doubt that a dualism of Iranian (Zoroastrian) or Manichaean origin is making itself felt here. In the new versions, the earth, in the end, is the product of both the good maker and the "helper," who turns out to be a satanic figure. Thus the existence of evil is acknowledged, but the (good) god is not held responsible for it.

Again, caution is in order in making generalizations, for it goes without saying that the opposition of "good" and "evil" is not alien to any human society, even though in some cases we can infer specific historical influences. Of general importance is the realization, first, that all myths are subject to historical changes, even if we have not yet succeeded in tracing these changes in detail; and second, that a cosmogonic myth of any thematic type is not necessarily wiped out or replaced but can be merely modified when a great religious system is superimposed on a civilization.

Themes that in all probability were created independently in various traditions may be mentioned: the world egg; the cosmic tree; creation *ex nihilo;* creation from chaos; and creation from sacrifice. Each of these usually occurs in conjunction with other themes. The tree of the world and of life occurs in one form or another from the ancient Germanic and Celtic peoples to ancient Babylonia and to classical and modern Java. This symbolism, perhaps even more than the others, allows for interpretations of the cosmos at large (the macrocosm) and the "world" of a person's body and existence (the microcosm).

Common characteristics of religious cosmologies. When symbolism and mythology depict cosmogony and cosmology, the view is confirmed that the cosmos is always the world of man and is not an external object of inquiry. We may add that an ethical concern, which by itself has no evident part in the study of nature or of astronomy, is very much in evidence in religious views of the world. The behavior required of man is often described and always implied in the account of the world's structure.

Even if certain features do not make an obvious ethical impression on most Western readers, they nevertheless may tell us something concerning the rules that govern human behavior. Sacrificial or headhunting techniques are given within the structure of the cosmos. We may also think of the teachings concerning many births and rebirths in Hinduism, Jainism, and Buddhism; they fit in traditions that speak of world cycles, successions of worlds, and multiple worlds. Finally, the intimate relationship of the macrocosm and the microcosm, which is widely attested, is a striking formal link between various views of the cosmos.

Do Science and Religion View the Cosmos Differently? Contrary to popular opinion, it is not often necessary to ponder conflicts between science and religion. It is more to the point to think of differences in questions asked and in subject matter. Pre-Islamic Indian literary sources are almost unanimous with respect to the conception of the continents of the earth. They depict the continents geometrically rather than empirically, and India itself occurs in the center of the world's map. The idea of many long ages and periods with truly astronomical numbers and the concept of many worlds existing both in succession and simultaneously are pan-Indian. As indicated, the center is and remains man and his quest for liberation. This does not at all mean that the large figures of years given in the Puranas are figments of the imagination or betray a disregard for science. Quite the reverse is true, in spite of earlier fashions in scholarship that disparaged India's talent for science (a tradition fostered by some eminent Sanskritists).

On a wider scale a comparable correction has been made with respect to the generally held opinion that prehistoric man and, in his wake, members of every nonliterate tradition were wanting in intellectual power capable of raising scientific questions. This correction has been made through the work of Alexander Marshack, who persuasively interpreted prehistoric data as records of precise astronomic observations. None of this suggests oppositions between religion and science; such oppositions are in fact a very recent phenomenon in history and are restricted to very few sciences and only to specific religious traditions. It is certainly impossible on the basis of the cumulative evidence to regard religious and mythical views of the cosmos merely as precursors to science or as preliminary, inadequate endeavors that are discarded with the development of science. Moreover, not only from the point of view of the historian of religions, but also from that of the historian of science, no single moment in history can ever be established to pinpoint the supposed fundamental change from myth to science. In fact no such moment exists.

The relationship between clearly recognizable religious views and scientific views is complex, but much clarity can be gained by looking critically at the sort of questions that are asked, the nature of the assumptions the questioner makes under the influence of his own culture, or the intellectual habits of his age.

We cannot ignore the modern intellectual problem of creating a dichotomy where our documents show a unity or seem to indicate no more than aspects of the same thing. The contrast between modern science and traditional religious ideas concerning the world and cosmogony has occupied the minds of many Westerners, especially since the eighteenth century. This contrast has blurred the intention of world images given in religious traditions.

The ancient Babylonians thought of the earth as the center of the universe and conceived of it as a mountain, hollow underneath and supported by the ocean, while the vault of heaven kept the waters above from those below; the "waters above" explained the phenomenon of rain. Roughly the same cosmic scheme occurs throughout the entire ancient Near East and returns in the creation account in the Book of Genesis. One may think also of Thales of Miletus (c. 600 BCE), the Ionian "natural philosopher," who is famous for positing water as the primal substance of the universe. If, however, this schematization strikes us as scientifically most primitive, we should remember that such a scheme was in fact never presented in any tradition; it is only the summary that the modern mind, the product of an average education, draws from far more complex mythologies. Although we can choose to study the development of the natural sciences in isolation, the documents of the exact sciences, available from the ancient Babylonians (the period of the Hammurabi dynasty, 1800-1600 BCE) and the ancient Egyptians on, are recorded not only in mathematical signs, as one might expect, but are also surrounded by mythological images. Mythological images simultaneously absorb and appropriate scientific discoveries, calendrical calculations, and estab-

lished views of the world, stars, and planets as their symbols. We have no option but to distinguish the two sciences, yet we must recognize the fact that our documents make no separation and establish no contrast. Various scholars, for example Mircea Eliade and Werner Müller, have stressed the cosmic character of all archaic religious traditions. It is of great importance, however, to add that the history of science points to the interwovenness of science (notably astronomy and physics) and religion.

Epistemological considerations are not separable from socioreligious traditions and cannot be kept for long from the work of a modern scientist. Basic definitions functioning in scientific research are not central in scientific education, yet typically "normal," consensus-bound research ultimately results in revolution. The process of change in religion is quite analogous. As a rule, renowned mystics, prophets, and great reformers have followed their tradition so persistently as to arrive willy-nilly at a change that in some cases amounted to a rebirth or total overhaul of a tradition (e.g., the great reformers in Christianity; Nagarjuna in Buddhism; the great bhakti philosophers, and especially Ramanuja, in Hinduism; al-Ghazali in Islam). Any such great change is reflected in the image of the world.

BIBLIOGRAPHY

For African creation accounts, the most helpful work is Herman Baumann's *Schöpfung und Urzeit des Menschen im Mythus der afrikanischen Völker* (Berlin, 1936). Jean Bayet's *Histoire politique et psychologique de la religion Romaine,* 2d ed. (Paris, 1969), has a special eye for the interwovenness of human orientations and conceptions of the world throughout Roman history. Hendrik Bergema's *De boom des levens in schrift en historie* (Hilversum, Netherlands, 1938) is the most extensive collection of tree symbolisms in religious traditions. A sociological attempt to show that human beings by nature orient themselves toward a more encompassing world than that of their observable social and psychological reality is made by Peter L. Berger and Thomas Luckmann in *The Social Construction of Reality* (Garden City, N. Y., 1966). Edvard Jan Dijksterhuis's *The Mechanization of the World Picture* (Oxford, 1961) is the classic study of philosophies and discussions leading to the birth of science in modern history. Mircea Eliade's *Cosmos and History: The Myth of the Eternal Return* (New York, 1954), *Myth and Reality* (New York, 1963), and *Patterns in Comparative Religion* (New York, 1958) offer the most comprehensive religio-historical studies of cosmic symbolism, especially in archaic societies, with special emphasis on cosmogony as the fundamental myth in any tradition, and on the significance of world renewal. Eliade's *Australian Religions: An Introduction* (Ithaca, N. Y., 1973) elaborates on these and other themes in the particular compass of some culturally most archaic tribal traditions. Adolf E. Jensen's *Myth and Cult among Primitive Peoples* (Chicago, 1963) is especially concerned with the relationship between cosmic views and human behavior. Willibald Kirfel's *Die Kosmographie der Inder* (Bonn, 1920) treats views of the world among Hindus, Buddhists, and Jains.

The most influential works in the history of science to open our eyes to the wider philosophical and religious context of the origins of modern science are by Alexandre Koyré: *Entretiens sur Descartes*

(New York, 1944) and *From the Closed World to the Infinite Universe* (Baltimore, 1957). *Mythologies of the Ancient World,* edited by Samuel Noah Kramer (Garden City, N. Y., 1961), ranges from the ancient Near East to ancient Mexico and to India, China, and Japan, their mythologies, including their cosmic views. The best observations made within the context of Vedic and Brahmanic ritual concerning the cosmos are available in Herta Krick's *Das Ritual der Feuergründung* (Vienna, 1982). W. Brede Kristensen's *Het leven uit de dood* (Haarlem, 1926) is the unsurpassed study on the relation of cosmogonies to the spontaneity of life as a central issue in ancient Egyptian and Greek religion. Including all periods and many civilizations, yet with most relevance to cosmogonies in nonliterate traditions, one of the best collections is Charles H. Long's *Alpha: The Myths of Creation* (New York, 1963).

Alexander Marshack's *The Roots of Civilization* (New York, 1972) was the first work to break down artificial barriers between religion and scientific views of the universe on the basis of prehistoric data. Jacques Merleau-Ponty and Bruno Morando's *The Rebirth of Cosmology* (New York, 1976), is a detailed reflection on the limits of modern astronomy. A collection of studies on cosmos and myth in seventeen different nonliterate traditions, plus one playful attempt at a structural analysis of the *Book of Genesis* as myth by Edmund Leach are collected in *Myth and Cosmos,* edited by John Middleton (Garden City, N. Y., 1967). Marijan Molé's *Culte, mythe et cosmologie dans l'Iran ancien* (Paris, 1963) presents a full discussion of ancient Iranian cosmology, with elaborate textual documentation. Werner Müller's *Die heilige Stadt: Roma quadrata, himlisches Jerusalem und die Mythe vom Weltnabel* (Stuttgart, 1961) discusses the tenacity of cosmic views forming the model of city planning; with lengthy bibliography. Teachings concerning the cosmos and its hierarchy, with special attention to microcosmic views are given in Seyyed Hossein Nasr's *An Introduction to Islamic Cosmological Doctrines* (Cambridge, 1964). Joseph Needham's *Science and Civilisation in China,* vol. 2 (Princeton, 1956), is the best study available on any civilization that illuminates the rise of science, cosmology, views of nature within the course of religious traditions and change. Otto Neugebauer wrote the classic work on *The Exact Sciences in Antiquity,* 2d ed. (New York, 1969). Martin P. Nilsson's *Geschichte der griechischen Religion,* 3d ed., 2 vols. (Munich, 1967-1971), is indispensable for the study of religious complexities within which cosmic views in Greece arose and changed. F. S. C. Northrop's *Man, Nature and God* (New York, 1962) deals with the problem of cosmology, science, and nature within a world that is religiously, culturally, and philosophically diverse, yet has no option but to come to terms with its unity.

The best available text on astronomy from classical India is *The Yavanajataka of Sphujidhvaja,* 2 vols., edited and translated, with commentary, by David Pingree (Cambridge, 1978). For the problem of monotheism and the origin of the cosmos, see Raffaele Pettazzoni's *Essays on the History of Religions* (Leiden, 1954) and *The All-Knowing God* (London, 1956). Don K. Price's "Endless Frontier or Bureaucratic Morass?" and Robert L. Sinsheimer's "The Presumptions of Science," both in *Daedalus* 107 (Spring 1978), present indirect but eloquent arguments for the necessity of a more significant framework for science than science itself can provide. *Ancient Near Eastern Texts relating to the Old Testament,* 3d ed. with supp., edited by James B. Pritchard (Princeton, 1969), is a large collection of myths, laws, and epic texts in which cosmological ideas are embedded. Dualistic views characteristic of Manichaeism are described in Henri-Charles Puech's "Le manichéisme," in *Histoire des religions,* vol. 2, edited by Puech (Paris, 1972). C. F. von Weizsäcker's *The History of Nature* (Chicago, 1949), is a balanced and thoughtful account of the modern natural sciences between philosophy and religion and is of abiding interest. *Studies of A. J.*

Wensinck (New York, 1978) interpret a number of cosmological symbols in Mesopotamian, ancient West Semitic, and Arabic traditions.

KEES W. BOLLE

COUNCILS

Buddhist Councils

Among the final events in the life of Siddhartha Gautama, the historical Buddha, he enjoined the community to appoint no successor in his stead. The Buddha was explicit in arguing that his teaching (Dharma) and disciplinary training (Vinaya) would provide sufficient guidance for the attainment of *nirvana.* He further granted the community authority to abolish all lesser and minor precepts of conduct, although he failed to identify precisely which precepts he deemed minor and lesser. But, with an obvious uncertainty as to which disciplinary rules were to be retained, much confusion could be expected in the days and years following the leader's demise. To combat the anticipated disorientation, it was suggested that a council be convened whose purpose would be to solidify basic Buddhist doctrine and discipline. In this way, the transition from the ministry of the Buddha's charismatic leadership to one of a newly established social identity was softened and advanced. Further, convocation of this first Buddhist council helped to establish a precedent upon which future Buddhist communities could draw for sanction in resolving disputes.

Council Literature. Literature on these various Buddhist councils derives from both primary and secondary sources. Initially, we look to the canonical sources, and this avenue of inquiry yields fruitful results. Appended to the Vinaya Pitaka, or disciplinary portion, of each Buddhist school's canon is a section devoted to a considertion of the Buddha's death and the first two Buddhist councils. Noncanonical sources also unearth a mine of useful material. In this regard, we can consult such texts as the Pali *Dipavamsa,* as well as the *Samayabhedoparacanacakra* of Vasumitra, the *Nikaya-bhedavibhangavyakhyana* of Bhavya, the *Mahaprajña-paramita Sastra,* and others. There is also a wealth of secondary material in Western languages.

Major Indian Councils. Current buddhological research enables us to document no fewer than five Indian Buddhist councils, each of which must be described in order to unearth its import for the history of the tradition.

The First Council: Rajagrha. The first Indian Buddhist council was allegedly held during the rainy season immediately following the Buddha's death in, according to the most popular reckoning, 483 BCE. It was held in the capital city of King Bimbisara, ruler of Magadha and a chief royal patron of the Buddha and the Buddhist community. With food and shelter provided, Rajagrha proved to be an ideal site for the Buddhists' deliberations. As the records recount the story, five hundred monks, all having attained the status of *arhats* (Pali, *arahants;* "enlightened ones"), were selected to participate in the council proceedings. The plan for the enactment of the council was to have the president of the event question first Upali, a disciple known for his mastery of the disciplinary materials, on Vinaya, and then Ananda, allegedly the Buddha's most beloved disciple, on the various sermons of the Buddha. Our sources recount, however, that at the time of his selection Ananda was not yet enlightened. (This fact in and of itself casts some doubt on the accuracy of the account.) In due course, however, Ananda is reported to have attained *nirvana,* thus enabling him to participate in the expected fashion.

During Kasyapa's questioning of Ananda, reference was made to the Buddha's suggestion that the lesser and minor precepts be abolished. With the community in a quandry as to the best course of action, Kasyapa decided to leave all disciplinary rules intact, lest the community fall into disrepute in such matters. After the recitation of the doctrinal and disciplinary materials, other issues of business were entertained and various penalties imposed on individuals who had acted incorrectly. As the convocation prepared to adjourn, a traveling monk, Purana, arrived in Rajagrha and was invited to join the proceedings. He declined, noting that he chose to remember the Dharma and Vinaya precisely as spoken by the Buddha. In so noting, further suspicion is thrown on the authority and impact of the council. Finally, the council concluded, referring to itself as the *vinayasamgiti,* or "chanting of the Vinaya."

The general consensus of scholarship devoted to the first council almost uniformly concludes that the canonical accounts are at best greatly exaggerated and at worst pure fiction. On a small scale, it may be safe to assume that several of the Buddha's intimates gathered after his death to consider their future plight in the Indian religious climate, but the authenticity of the dramatic event presented in the canon is highly questionable.

The Second Council: Vaisali. One hundred years pass before we get any further information on the historical development of the Buddhist community. The occasion for this new look into the ongoing progress of the still-infant Buddhist religion was a council held in the town of Vaisali. The various Vinaya accounts record that a Buddhist monk named Yasas wandered into Vaisali and observed the resident monks, or *bhiksus* (formally identified as the Vrjiputraka *bhiksus*), engaged in ten practices that seemed to conflict with Yasas's understanding of injunctions made explicit in the Vinaya. Yasas, the tale has it, formally protested indulgence in these ten apparently illicit practices, but was rejected by the community of monks and sentenced to a penalty known as the

pratisamharaniya-karma. This punishment required that he beg the pardon of the monks he had offended by his accusation and obtain their forgiveness. When failing to do so, the resident monks banished him from the community.

Undaunted by the formal act of banishment, Yasas journeyed to Kausambi, seeking the support of a learned monk known as Sambhuta Sanavasin. Another well-respected monk, Revata, also decided to come to Yasas's support on

> ## One hundred years pass before we get any further information on the historical development of the Buddhist community.

the issue of the ten practices. All the while, the Vrjiputraka *bhiksus* were gathering supporters to their side as well. The conflict was brought to a conclusion in the convocation of a formal council in Vaisali. Revata was selected to preside over the proceedings. Sarvagamin, an elder monk who had had the Buddha's direct disciple Ananda as his *upadhyaya,* or teacher, was questioned on each of the ten points. One by one, Sarvagamin rejected each point on the basis of various scriptures. With the ten practices condemned and concord renewed, the council concluded, again referring to itself as the "recital of the Vinaya" *(vinayasamgiti)* or as the "recital of the seven hundred," the number of monks who attended the gathering.

Of course it is necessary to consider just what these ten illicit practices were and why this particular event seems to have had so great an impact on the early Buddhist community. The ten points include: (1) preserving salt in a horn; (2) taking food when the shadow is beyond two fingers wide; (3) after finishing one meal, going to another town for another meal; (4) holding several confession ceremonies within the same monastic boundary; (5) confirming a monastic act in an incomplete assembly; (6) carrying out an act improperly and justifying it by its habitual performance in this way; (7) after eating, drinking unchurned milk that is somewhere between the states of milk and curd; (8) drinking unfermented wine; (9) using a mat without a border; and (10) accepting gold and silver. Although there is considerable scholarly disagreement concerning the meaning and implications of these practices, it is abundantly clear that each of the ten points was fully rejected by the Vinaya of each Buddhist nikaya, or school.

Although a reconciliation was effected by the council of Vaisali, the very occasion of the council suggests forcefully that there were significant tensions and disagreements already operative in the Buddhist community.

Pataliputra I: the noncanonical council. By the time of the consecration of King Asoka (c. 270 BCE), the Buddhist sectarian movement was already well advanced. Through the painstaking efforts of Andre Bareau, it has been possible to reconstruct the evidence of a council from which the Buddhist sectarian movement had its birth.

In the study of this new council, only one issue can be found about which all the texts concur: that it was held in Pataliputra. Both the date of the council and the occasion for its convocation are troublesome. Four possible dates appear in the various texts: 100 AN (i. e., after the *nirvana* of the Buddha), 116 AN, 137 AN, and 160 AN. Bareau concludes that the event must have occurred either in 137 AN or 116 AN.

As to the specifics of the council, Bareau tells us that by the reign of Mahapadma the Nandin, the Buddhist community had divided itself into two camps, one lax in discipline and supporting the tenets of Mahadeva, the other rigorous and strongly opposed to him. Unable to resolve their dispute internally, the Buddhists approached King Mahapadma and asked him to mediate the dispute. The king assembled the two groups in his capital of Pataliputra, but being incompetent in religious matters, decided to put the matter to a simple vote. The "laxist" party was apparently in the majority and withdrew, calling itself the Mahasamghikas, or "Great Assembly." The minority party referred to itself as the Sthaviras, or "Elders." Each group then began to develop its own cannon and religious community.

Virtually all the early sources in Buddhist literature conclude that the council described above was a historical event. Further, they consider this initial council of Pataliputra to be the true starting point of the sectarian movement in Buddhism. Recently, however, Bareau's conclusions as to the date and cause of the council have been questioned. Janice J. Nattier and I have suggested that the council took place in 116 AN, under the reign of Kalasoka, and that disciplinary laxity and Mahadeva's theses had nothing at all to do with the schism (1977). Nevertheless, it is clear that the sectarian movement in Buddhism emerged sometime in the century following the Vaisali council; by 200 BCE more than a dozen sects were evident in the Buddhist community.

Pataliputra II: the third canonical council. The *Mahavamsa* (v. 280) indicates that the close of the council was in the seventeenth year of Asoka's reign. The *Dipavamsa* notes the date as 236 AN, or 247 BCE. Apparently, "heretics" had been entering the Buddhist community for some time, undermining the Dharma, and therefore weakening the entire social and religious structure of the *samgha.* In order to remedy the situation, Asoka chose a famous monk, Moggaliputtatissa, to preside over a huge assembly of a thousand monks, who were to determine and restore orthodoxy. Under Tissa's guidance the offending viewpoints were rejected; eventually it was concluded that the Buddha was a *vibhajyavadin,* or "distinctionist." The viewpoints under discussion were recorded in a now well-known Abhidharma text, the *Kathavatthu.*

There is no question that this council was a historical event. It is curious, however, that it is mentioned only in the Pali accounts, lending weight to the supposition that the council may have been only a "party meeting" of the Vibhajyavada sect. It is now well known that this sect was the parent of the Theravada *nikaya.*

The Council of Kaniska. Near the end of the first century CE, Kaniska became the ruling monarch of the great Kushan dynasty. He tried hard to emulate Asoka's example of ruling in accord with the Buddhist Dharma, and championed the Sarvastivadin school of Buddhism. From his capitals of Purusapura and Mathura, he wielded much power in the Buddhist world. Near the end of his reign, about 100 CE, Kaniska sponsored a council, probably in Gandhara (but possibly in Kashmir), to consider the doctrines of the Sarvastivadin school.

Following the suggestion of the Sarvastivadin scholar Parsva, invitations were sent to all the learned Buddhists of the time, from whom 499 were finally chosen to attend the conference. Great debates were held on various aspects of Buddhist doctrine, and expecially on the Abhidharma. The venerable scholar Vasumitra was president of the council, assisted by Asvaghosa. A new Vinaya was committed to writing at the conference, and a great commentary, known as the *Mahavibhasa,* on the Abhidharma text of the *Jñana-prasthana* was compiled. There is no question but that the position this council occupies in the history of the Sarvastivada nikaya is analogous to that of the council convened by Asoka nearly four centuries earlier for the history of the Theravada *nikaya.*

Other Ancient Councils. Recognizing the impact the Indian Buddhist councils have had on the continued growth of the religion in its native land, councils have periodically met in other Buddhist countries as well. Of course Asoka was renowned for exporting Buddhism through a series of missionary endeavors, with Sri Lanka at the forefront of his enterprise. Equally, within several centuries of the close of King Kaniska's reign in India, Buddhism had spread into Central Asia, China, and Tibet. It is no surprise then, that Sri Lanka and Tibet were the sites of other ancient Buddhist councils.

Modern Councils. In the millennium between 800 and 1800 CE little mention was made of Buddhist councils. To be sure, there were numerous proceedings of local import in the various Buddhist countries, but it was not until the latter half of the nineteenth century that another council took place of major impact for the entire Buddhist world.

The fifth Theravadin council. In the Buddhist culture of Southeast Asia it is not at all unusual for royal monarchs to be religious scholars, with prior training from within the Buddhist monastic order. Rama IV of Thailand, for instance, developed extensive scholarship in the Pali texts during his twenty-seven years as a monk. It was in this tradition that

King Mindon Min of Burma (r. 1852-1877) convened the fifth Theravadin council in Mandalay in 1871. The purpose of the council was explicit: to revise the Pali texts. To insure the survival of the new scriptures the king had all the texts entombed in stupas, thus preserving the 729 marble tablets upon which the texts were inscribed.

The sixth Theravadin council. In 1954, nearly one hundred years after the Mandalay council, the sixth Theravadin council was convened in Rangoon, Burma, by the prime minister, U Nu. The fact that the twenty-five hundredth anniversary of the Buddha's death was approaching made the notion of a council even more auspicious. The basic function of this sixth council was to recite and confirm the entire Pali canon. Nearly two years of preparations were made prior to its inauguration on 17 May 1954.

The World Fellowship of Buddhists. In an attempt to carry on the spirit demonstrated by the various Buddhist councils, the World Fellowship of Buddhists was established in 1950 as an expression of true religious ecumenism. The Fellowship has exercised its lofty intention through a series of conferences in various Buddhist countries. These conferences have sometimes expressed political as well as religious concerns, but they nonetheless reflect a spirit of cooperation that is thoroughly consistent with the very first Buddhist conclave, held in the rainy season following the Buddha's death in 483 BCE.

BIBLIOGRAPHY

The best general, comprehensive work on the issue of Indian Buddhist councils is André Bareau's *Les premiers conciles bouddhiques* (Paris, 1955). Much of this material, and the work of other researchers, is summarized in Charles S. Prebish's "A Review of Scholarship on the Buddhist Councils," *Journal of Asian Studies* 33 (February 1974: 239-254. A useful study of the Rajagrha council is presented in Jean Przyluski's *Le concile de Rajagrha* (Paris, 1926-1928). An equally valuable resource for the Vaisali council is Marcel Hofinger's *Étude sur la concile de Vaisali* (Louvain, 1946). The Vaisali council is also discussed in Paul Demiéville's "À propos du concile de Vaisali, *T'oung pao* 40 (1951): 239-296, and Nalinaksha Dutt's "The Second Buddhist Council," *Indian Historical Quarterly* 35 (March 1959: 45-56. For a somewhat dated but still important viewpoint, consult Louis de La Vallée Poussin's "The Buddhist Councils," *Indian Antiquary* 37 (1908): 1-18, 81-106. The most recent and controversial material on Indian Buddhist councils is presented in Janice J. Natier and Charles S. Prebish's "Mahasamghika Origins: The Beginnings of Buddhist Sectarianism," *History of Religions* 16 (February 1977): 237-272. For non-Indian councils, Demiéville's *Le concile de Lhasa* (Paris, 1952) effectively covers the Tibetan materials. Donald Smith's *Religion and Politics in Burma* (Princeton, 1965) is helpful for Theravadin proceedings, and *Buddhism in the Modern World,* edited by Heinrich Dumoulin and John Maraldo (New York, 1976), offers a constructive overview.

CHARLES S. PREBISH

Christian Councils

Early Ecumenical Councils. The first attempt to gather a body of bishops representing the whole Christian world was the council called by the emperor Constantine I at Nicaea, in northwest Asia Minor, in the summer of 325 (18 June-25 August). The Council of Nicaea is still recognized as the first ecumenical Christian council and as the model for later authoritative gatherings. With the style and procedure of the Roman senate likely in mind, Constantine commissioned the 318 bishops who had assembled near his residence in Nicaea, including several representatives from the Latin church of the West, to settle the controversy raised by Arius's denial of the eternity and full divinity of Jesus. In asserting that Jesus, as Son of God, is "begotten, not made" and "of the same substance as the Father," the council's creedal formula laid the groundwork for the classical development of Christian trinitarian theology in the half century that followed. Although the emperor's influence was strongly felt at Nicaea, it was the bishops themselves—under the leadership of Constantine's adviser, Bishop Hosius of Cordova, and of the young Alexandrian priest Athanasius—who formulated common theological and practical decisions. The bishops of the whole Christian world were now publicly recognized as the senate of the church.

After more than fifty years of sharp controversy over the reception and interpretation of the Nicene formula, a period that saw the proliferation of local synods and the production of many new creeds, the emperor Theodosius I convoked a meeting of some 150 Greek-speaking bishops at Constantinople in 381 (May-July) for what later was recognized as the second ecumenical council (Constantinople I). In addition to confirming Nicaea's insistence on the full divinity of Jesus as Son, this council condemned those who denied that the Holy Spirit is a distinct individual within the trinitarian mystery of God. An expanded version of the Nicene Creed, probably professed by the patriarch-elect Nectarius during the council before his installation in the see of Constantinople, was taken by the Council of Chalcedon (451) to be the official creed of the whole gathering and is still used as the standard profession of faith in many Christian liturgies (the "Niceno-Constantinopolitan Creed")..

As a result of a bitter dispute between Nestorius, bishop of Constantinople, and Cyril, bishop of Alexandria, over the proper way of conceiving the relationship of the divine and human aspects of Jesus, the emperor Theodosius II summoned a meeting of bishops at Ephesus on the coast of Asia Minor, in the summer of 431, to resolve the issue, and more particularly to judge the propriety of calling Mary "Mother of God" *(theotokos)*. Representatives of the opposing groups could not agree to meet, and the would-be council ended abortively in mutual excommunication. Later (April 433) Cyril came to an agreement with the more moderate of Nestorius's supporters to excommunicate Nestorius and to accept the title *theotokos* as valid, but also to recognize that in Jesus two distinct natures—the human and the divine—are united without confusion in a single individual. On the basis of this agreement, the meeting of Cyril's party at Ephesus in 431 later came to be regarded as the third ecumenical council.

The fullest articulation of the early church's understanding of the person of Christ was made at a council held at Chalcedon, across the Bosporus from Constantinople, in the fall of 451 (October-November). In response to continuing controversy over whether the humanity of Jesus constituted a distinct and operative reality or "nature" after the incarnation of the Word, the emperor Marcian convoked this meeting of over 350 bishops and forced it to formulate a doctrinal statement on Christ that accommodated a variety of theological traditions. The chief inspiration of the document, however, was the balanced "two-nature" Christology articulated by Leo in his letter to Bishop Flavian of Constantinople in 449. This meaning is regarded as the fourth ecumenical council.

Chalcedon's formulation of the Christian understanding of Christ proved to be only a new beginning for controversy. After more than a century of recriminations, especially in the East, the emperor Justinian I convoked another meeting at Constantinople (Constantinople II) in the year 553 (5 May-2 June) and persuaded the 168 bishops present to reformulate the Christology of Chalcedon in terms that more clearly emphasized the centrality of Jesus' divine identity. The Roman bishop, Vigilius I, was present in Constantinople during the council but refused to attend, suspecting—along with most Western bishops—that it was being forced to weaken the stated faith of Chalcedon in the interests of political unity. In February 554, however, he agreed to accept the decisions of Constantinople II, a step that resulted in decades of controversy in Italy and Africa. This synod has generally been accepted since then as the fifth ecumenical council.

Greek theologians continued to look for ways of reconciling the monophysites, Christians who had broken from the official church after Chalcedon by emphasizing the dynamic unity of the two-natured Christ as a divine person. One such attempt, favored by several seventh-century Byzantine patriarchs and emperors, was the ascription to Christ of a single divine will and "activity," or range of behavior. Led by the exiled Greek monk Maximos the Confessor, a local Roman synod of October 649 rejected this new Christology as a subtle weakening of the integral affirmation of Jesus' humanity. This condemnation was confirmed by a small gathering of mainly Eastern bishops in the rotunda of the imperial palace in Constantinople between 7 November 680 and 16 September 681, a synod subsequently recognized as the sixth ecumenical council (Constantinople III).

Ten years later, the emperor Justinian II summoned another gathering of bishops in the same rotunda to discuss disciplinary issues and formulate practical canons that would supplement the authoritative theological decisions of Constantinople II and III. The membership of this meeting was also entirely Greek, and a number of its canons explicitly rejected Western practices. Although this gathering is not regarded as ecumenical, its legislation became one of the main sources of Orthodox canon law and was also frequently cited by Western medieval canonists.

The main theological controversy in the eighth- and ninth-century Eastern church was related to the legitimacy of using and venerating images in the context of worshiping a transcendent God. In 726, Emperor Leo III began removing and destroying the images in churches (iconoclasm), and his suc-

> In 726, Emperor Leo III began removing and destroying the images in churches. . . .

cessor, Constantine V, convoked a synod of 338 bishops in Constantinople in 754 to ratify this practice, excommunicating those who defended the use of images. In 787 (24 September-7 October), however, the empress Irene convoked another synod at Nicaea (Nicaea II), attended by some 350 Greek bishops and two papal representatives. This synod reversed the decision of the year 754 and affirmed the legitimacy of venerating images and of asking for the intercession of the saints, while insisting also that worship, in the strict sense, is due to God alone. A resurgence of iconoclastic influence in the early ninth century delayed full acceptance of this council's decrees in the East, while the rivalry of the emperor Charlemagne and the poor Latin translation of the acts of Nicaea II that reached his court led to resistance in the West and even to condemnation of the council's decisions at a synod of 350 bishops at Frankfurt in June 794. However, Nicaea II was recognized as the seventh ecumenical council.

Medieval Councils. After the death of Theophilus, the last iconoclastic emperor, in 842, controversy in mid-ninth-century Constantinople over the manner of reinstating the veneration of images led to the forced abdication of the patriarch Ignatius in 858 and to the appointment of the learned civil servant Photios, a layman, as his successor. A local synod of 861 confirmed Photios's elevation and declared that the election of Ignatius had been uncanonical; the pope, however, was persuaded by Ignatius's followers to break communion with Photios two years later. Tension between Rome and Constantinople grew, both over the role of the pope as a source of legitimation and a court of appeal for Eastern bishops and over competing missionary activities of the two churches in Bulgaria. A synod summoned by the Greek emperor Michael in 867 condemned Roman incursions in the East. It asked the Frankish emperor Louis II to depose Pope Nicholas. Another council in Constantinople, summoned by the new Greek emperor, Basil I, in 869-870, deposed Photios in an effort to win the pope's support, but Photios became patriarch again after Ignatius's death in 877 and was recognized by the pope in a council of reunion held in Constantinople in 879-880. This last meeting annulled the decisions of the council of 869-870, but Western canonists in the twelfth century included the earlier gathering among the ecumenical councils, as Constantinople IV, because its twenty-second canon, forbidding the appointment of bishops by laypeople, provided a precedent for their own case against lay investiture.

Eastern and Western bishops ceased to meet for almost four centuries.

It was only in the time of the "Gregorian reform," however, in the eleventh and twelfth centuries, that the popes, as part of their program of strengthening the power and independence of the ordained clergy in ruling the church, thought again of convoking councils with a more than regional representation. Gregory VII, in his canonical summary known as *Dictates of the Pope,* insisted that only the bishop of Rome has the right to convoke an ecumenical council—a principle preserved ever since by Western canon law.

Three twelfth-century Roman synods—the Lateran councils of 1123, 1139, and 1179—demonstrated the concern of the popes of this period to assert the independence of the hierarchy from lay control by enacting a variety of measures that insured the moral and social integrity of the clergy. Far more important, however, was the Fourth Lateran Council,

> ## Eastern and Western bishops ceased to meet for almost four centuries.

convoked in 1215 (11-30 November) by Innocent III. Innocent invited not only all bishops and heads of religious orders from the Western church, but also bishops of the Armenian, Maronite, and Greek churches. Only Latin bishops attended, however, and the council's seventy canons included a strong assertion of papal primacy and a complaint against the Greek church for rebaptizing Latin converts. The meeting—recognized in the West as the twelfth ecumenical council—not only continued the disciplinary reforms of its three predecessors but also issued doctrinal statements on the Trinity and the sacraments.

Continued conflict between the popes and the Hohenstaufen emperors led Innocent IV to convoke a council of some 150 bishops at Lyons in June and July 1245. Besides calling for renewed efforts to reconquer the holy places, this synod excommunicated the German emperor Frederick II, absolving his subjects from the moral duty of

obeying him. Western canonists regard this synod as the thirteenth ecumenical council. Gregory X summoned a second council at Lyons in the summer of 1274 (5 May-17 July), in the hope of restoring communion between the Eastern and Western churches. The Greek emperor, Michael VIII Palaeologus, who had recaptured Constantinople from Latin occupiers in 1261, accepted the invitation to attend, hoping to prevent further Western attacks on his capital. Delegates of the Mongol khan also attended, as did some two hundred bishops and the nonvoting representatives of most Western rulers. The Greek delegation participated in the papal Eucharist on 29 June, the Feast of Saints Peter and Paul, and agreed to a formal reunion of the churches on 6 July. The council is regarded in the West as the fourteenth ecumenical council.

In the face of the increasing attempts of Philip IV ("the Fair") of France to control the church, Clement V—the first pope to reside at Avignon—summoned a council to meet in the independent French town of Vienne in 1311-1312 (16 October-6 May). Eager to acquire the wealth of the Knights Templars, Philip had exerted strong pressure on the pope, even before the council, to suppress the military order on allegations of venality, heresy, and immoral practices. The council found no grounds to support these charges. Western canonists consider it the fifteenth ecumenical council.

In the Greek church a series of local synods in Constantinople (c. 1340) took up the controversy between Gregory Palamas, a monk of Mount Athos, and the Calabrian monk Barlaam about the value of hesychastic prayer (contemplative prayer prepared for by repetition of a mantra) and the possibility of experiencing the presence of God in this life. A synod in July 1351 recognized as orthodox Palamas's doctrine that God's "energies" or activities, if not God's essence, can be experienced in a quasi-visual way by a soul purified through constant prayer, a teaching that has been of central importance for Orthodox monasticism ever since.

In the West, the years of the Avignon papacy (1308-1378) saw continued centralization of papal authority, as well as increasing opposition to papal rule by the German emperors, independent cities, and certain charismatic and millenarian groups within the church. With the beginning of the Great Western Schism in 1378, in which two rival popes claimed the church's obedience, support began to grow among canonists and theologians for a more corporate system of church government. This "conciliarist" theory, first proposed in practical terms by William Durandus of Mende at the time of the Council of Vienne, was seen by a number of prominent theologians in the last decades of the fourteenth century as the only way to end the schism. In 1409, a council at Pisa attempted to put conciliarism into practice by deposing both rival popes and electing a new one (John XXIII). The result, however, was simply that three claimants now vied for the Roman see. In 1414, the emperor Sigismund allied with John

XXIII to convoke another council at Constance to resolve the issue (5 November 1414-22 April 1418). Following the representative system of the medieval universities, the voting members of the council—who included over 325 bishops, 29 cardinals, more than 100 abbots, several princes, and several hundred doctors of theology—decided to divide into four blocks, or "nations," each of which would have one corporate vote in the council's final decisions. These "nations" were the Germans (including eastern Europeans), the French, the English (including the Irish and Scots), and the Italians; from July 1415 the cardinals at the council were allowed to vote as a fifth unit, and a Spanish "nation" was added in October 1416. Debate was conducted within the "nations," and the whole council was managed by a joint steering committee, in which each "nation," as well as the cardinals, was represented. The council's decree, *Sacrosancta,* enacted on 6 April 1415, declared that the gathering was a general council of the church and that it therefore had supreme authority of itself. The council appointed a joint conclave of cardinals and delegates from the "nations," who elected Martin V on 11 November 1417.

Eugenius IV, who succeeded Martin in March 1431, hoped once again to effect a reunion with the Greek church and believed that an Italian setting would be more appropriate for that purpose. As relations with the delegates at Basel grew more strained, Eugenius ordered the council transferred to Ferrara in September 1437, although most of the members refused to go and remained in Basel as a rival assembly until 1448. The Greek delegation arrived in Ferrara in March 1438, and after preliminary discussions the council was moved to Florence in January 1439, where the city had offered to underwrite its costs. Led by Bessarion, metropolitan of Nicaea, the Greek delegation recognized the legitimacy of the Latin doctrines and papal primacy without prejudice to the validity of the Greek tradition. A decree of union between the churches was signed on 6 July 1439. Subsequent decrees of union were signed with the Armenian church (22 November 1439) and with the Copts and Ethiopians (4 February 1442). The date of closure of the council is uncertain. It is regarded by the Western church as the seventeenth ecumenical council. (In Byzantium, however, strong opposition led by Mark Eugenikos, metropolitan of Ephesus, who had also been a delegate to the council, was voiced against the union. A synod in Constantinople in 1484 officially repudiated the Florentine decree in the name of the Greek church.)

Age of Reformation. The wave of institutional and theological reform set in motion by Martin Luther in the 1520s brought new pressure to bear on the popes to convoke a council to deal seriously with "Protestant" issues. Paul III called a council at Mantua in 1537, for which Luther prepared the theses that were later accepted by German Protestants as a kind of manifesto and known as the Smalcaldic Articles.

This meeting was transferred to Vicenza in the same year and then suspended in 1539. After several delays, it was reconvened at the Alpine town of Trent, in imperial territory, on 13 December 1545. Rejecting the conciliar structure agreed on at Constance and Basel, the Council of Trent allowed only cardinals, bishops, and heads of religious orders voice and vote in its full sessions. During its first period (December 1545-March 1547), the council discussed the relation of scripture and tradition, the canon of scriptural books, the doctrines of original sin and justification, and various proposed reforms in church administration. Transferred to Bologna (papal territory) in 1547, to escape the plague, the council continued to discuss the Eucharist and the other sacraments, but Paul III agreed not to let it formulate final decisions until it could return to Trent, where Protestants could participate more freely. A second set of sessions was held in Trent from 1 May 1551 until 28 April 1552, in which documents on these topics were finished. After a ten-year hiatus due largely to continued warfare among the German principalities, Pius IV reconvoked the council on 18 January 1562 for a third and final period, during which documents were issued on the sacrificial character of the Mass, on Holy Orders and the education of the clergy, on the sacramental nature of marriage, and on purgatory, as well as numerous disciplinary decrees. The Council of Trent, recognized by Roman Catholics as a nineteenth ecumenical council, was closed on 4 December 1563. Its decrees laid the foundation for the doctrines and practice of the Roman church for the next four centuries.

The Modern Era. As the spirit of political revolution and scientific positivism swept through European culture in the mid-nineteenth century, however, Catholic interest in a general council that would confront these attacks on religious tradition and give confident expression to the church's teaching again grew. Pius IX appointed a commission to prepare for such a council in 1865 and opened it solemnly—as the First Vatican Council—on 8 December 1869. The 774 bishops who attended from around the world discussed prepared drafts on faith and revelation, authority in the church, reform of the Curia Romana, and other subjects. On 24 April 1870, the constitution *Dei filius* was approved. It affirmed the compatibility of faith and reason and the necessity of supernatural revelation (contained both in scripture and in the church's oral tradition) for a full knowledge of God. A constitution on the church, *Pastor aeternus,* was approved on 18 July, declaring the "immediate, universal jurisdiction" of the pope over all Christians and affirming that when he acts solemnly as spokesman for the universal church in doctrinal matters, the pope "possesses that infallibility with which the divine Redeemer wanted his Church to be endowed in articulating its teaching of faith and morality." [*See* Vatican Councils.]

The Roman Catholic church took a decisive step toward Christian unity in the documents and reforms of the Second

Vatican Council (11 October 1962-8 December 1965), which it recognizes as the twenty-first ecumenical council. [*See* Vatican Councils.*] Conceived by John XXIII in January of 1959 as a way of leading the Catholic church toward spiritual renewal, toward greater cooperation with other Christian churches and other religions, and toward a more open attitude to contemporary culture, the council was attended by between 2,100 and 2,400 bishops and heads of religious orders from within the Roman communion, as well as by invited observers from other Christian churches and religious bodies. Vatican II produced sixteen documents on a wide range of pastoral, institutional, and theological issues.

BIBLIOGRAPHY

A convenient one-volume edition of the decrees of the twenty-one councils recognized as ecumenical by the Roman Catholic church, in their Latin or Greek original, is *Conciliorum oecumenicorum decreta,* 3d ed., edited by Giuseppe Alberigo and others (Bologna, 1972). The most complete collection of Christian synodal and conciliar documents is the *Sacrorum conciliorum nova, et amplissima collectio,* begun in 1759 by the Italian canonist Giovanni Domenico Mansi and continued through Vatican I by Louis Petit and Jean-Baptiste Martin, 57 vols. (1759-1798; reprint in 53 vols., Paris, 1901-1927); the text is often defective, however, and modern critical editions exist of the documents of most major councils.

The most complete history of the Christian councils is still Karl-Joseph von Hefele and Josef Hergenröther's *Concilienge-schichte,* 10 vols. (Freiburg, 1855-1890), especially in its expanded French translation, *Histoire des conciles d'après les documents originaux,* 11 vols., by Henri Leclerq and others (Paris, 1907-1952); the first part of the German original, dealing with the seven ecumenical councils of the early church, has also been translated into English by William R. Clark as *A History of the Christian Councils,* 5 vols. (Edinburgh, 1871-1896). An excellent recent series of monographs on all the councils up to Vatican I, edited by Gervais Dumeige, is "Histoire des conciles oecumeniques" (Paris, 1962-1973). Outstanding studies of individual councils include: on Constantinople I, Adolf Martin Ritter's *Das Konzil von Konstantinopel und sein Symbol* (Göttingen, 1965); on Chalcedon, Robert V. Sellers's *The Council of Chalcedon: A Historical and Doctrinal Survey* (London, 1953); on Constance, Louise R. Loomis, John H. Mundy, and Kennerly M. Woody's *The Council of Constance: The Unification of the Church* (New York, 1961), a translation of the main diaries and documents of the council, with thorough introduction; on Florence, Joseph Gill's *The Council of Florence* (Cambridge, 1959); on Trent, Hubert Jedin's *Geschichte des Konzils von Trient,* 4 vols. (Freiburg, 1949-1975), a monumental work of scholarship, of which the first two volumes have been translated into English by Ernest Graf as *A History of the Council of Trent* (London, 1957-1961), and Remigius Bäumer's *Concilium Tridentinum* (Darmstadt, 1979), a useful collection of historical essays; on Vatican I, Theodor Granderath and Konrad Kirch's *Geschichte des Vatikanischen Konzils,* 3 vols. (Freiburg, 1903-1906); on Vatican II, Giovanni Caprile's *Il Concilio Vaticano II,* 5 vols. (Rome, 1966-1969), the best general history of the council to date, Henri Fesquet's *The Drama of Vatican II* (New York, 1967), a lively diary of the council, *Vatican II: An Interfaith Appraisal,* edited by John H. Miller (Notre Dame, 1966), a useful symposium by representatives of different faiths, and *Commentary on the Documents of Vatican II,* edited by Herbert Vorgrimler, 5 vols. (New York, 1968-1969).

Good brief histories of Christian councils include Edward I. Watkin's *The Church in Council* (London and New York, 1960), Francis Dvornik's *The Ecumenical Councils* (New York, 1961), and Philip Hughes's *The Church in Crisis: A History of the General Councils* (New York, 1961). A useful collection of essays on the history and theology of councils, by Protestant scholars, is Hans-Jochen Margull's *The Councils of the Church* (Philadelphia, 1966). No comprehensive history of local synods exists, but there is a full bibliographical survey of publications on individual meetings: Jakub T. Sawicki's *Bibliographia synodorum particularium* (Vatican City, 1967).

On the history of the theory of councils, the most thorough surveys are those of Hermann-Josef Sieben, *Die Konzilsidee der alten Kirche* (Paderborn, 1979), *Die Konzilsidee des lateinischen Mittelalters* (Paderborn, 1983), and *Traktate und Theorien zum Konzil: Vom Beginn des grossen Schismas bis zum Vorabend der Reformation, 1378-1521* (Frankfurt, 1983). The classic study of the origins of conciliarism is Brian Tierney's *Foundations of Conciliar Theory* (Cambridge, 1955); an excellent recent work on conciliarism in the period before Constance is Giuseppe Alberigo's *Chiesa conciliare: Identità e significato del conciliarismo* (Brescia, 1981).

BRIAN E. DALEY, S.J.

COVENANT

A central idea in the Hebrew scriptures (Old Testament) is that a covenant, a formal sworn agreement, exists between God and certain individuals or the whole chosen people, Israel. Not content with thinking of God as revealed in nature, or under metaphors from family life (as father or mother), Israel sought to capture and express the stability of the deity's relation to men under this figure from political or legal experience. Aspects of ancient Israel's covenant notions were revived by the Essene covenanters, the people of the Dead Sea Scrolls, and, in much revised form, in early Christianity. The idea of a covenant was not, however, prominent in subsequent Christian theology until after the Reformation of the sixteenth century, when Old Testament ideas were deliberately exploited in some varieties of Protestant theology, and eventually had even wider influence.

The Covenant of Grant in the Old Testament. One type of Old Testament covenant is an unconditional divine gift to some man or men. The divine promise to Noah (Gn. 9:8-17) after the Flood is called a covenant, and the rainbow is the "sign of the covenant." Examination of the story shows that the deity alone undertakes obligations; Noah and his descendants are not bound in any way. The significant word *remember* is used of God; God will remember what he has promised.

The Covenant of Obligation in the Old Testament. The other main conception of a covenant pointed in the opposite direction: the deity undertook no specific obligation, but the human partners swore to abide by certain stipulations, the penalty for disobedience being calamitous curses on the community and ultimately its exile. This conception of the religious covenant, which was at times a social and political reality, not just an idea, called for allegiance to a single God and observance of important mutual obligations in the society (respect for life, property, justice, etc.) and thus was a powerful force for national union, an operative principle rather than a theological abstraction.

This and a rich body of other materials have been vigorously exploited in recent scholarly attempts to elucidate the complex of ideas that makes up the Israelite conception of a covenant of obligation, Mendenhall's study of 1954 being the earliest. In his view, the Israelite covenant is similar to these early Near Eastern treaties in major emphases and intent: God gives the covenant—as at Sinai (*Ex.* 20) or Shechem (*Jos.* 24)—based on his past gracious actions, but without himself swearing to any performance. The human partners are bound to specific obligations toward him and one another (the Decalogue), transgression of which will bring awful retribution.

Blending of Old Testament Covenant Ideas in the Priestly Writer. Although two separate and nearly opposite conceptions of the covenant prevailed in ancient Israel, they did not remain apart. The late (sixth-century BCE?) priestly writer provides the most impressive and influential example of an arrangement of contrasting covenants and use of them to structure history. Human history from creation through the time of Moses is divided into eras by the covenants (of grant) with Noah, and then Abraham; finally comes the Sinai covenant (of obligation), for which a separate Hebrew term (`edut*) is used. This discrimination underlies that of Paul (*Gal.* 3) and ultimately much dispensationalism.

Covenant at Qumran and in the New Testament. The nearly contemporary writings of the Qumran community, the people of the Dead Sea Scrolls, and the New Testament reveal contrasting uses of covenant ideas: the former amounts to a repristination of Old Testament practices, with a basic change in orientation, while the latter displays some theological and polemical use of the term but in effect abandons the idea and associated social forms in favor of others.

The Essenes styled themselves "those who entered the new covenant in the land of Damascus" (C D [Damascus Document] VI 19), and the community bound themselves to the Law of Moses by a formal ceremony of oaths involving blessing and cursing, much in the old style. But while the Israelite covenant of obligation was thought of as given by God, at his initiative, the Essene covenant is the result of human determination. Blessing and curse now lie respectively on those within and those outside of the community; they are no longer possibilities confronting those bound to the covenant.

The writer of the letter to the Hebrews uses the term *covenant* rather often, and views Jesus as the "mediator of a new covenant" *(diatheke),* but the covenant concept is not fundamental to his view of the new faith. The reverse is closer to the truth: "covenant" is one Old Testament idea, along with the concepts of priesthood, sanctuary, and so on, whose sense is illumined by Christ.

Paul's employment of *covenant* is rather similar, with a sharp polemical point. The covenant of grace (grant) is older than the Sinai covenant and thus superior in force (*Gal.* 3); the superiority of the new covenant in Christ, which continues the Abrahamic covenant, is argued in *2 Corinthians* 3. Paul uses the Greek *diatheke* for "covenant," following the usage of the ancient Greek translation of the Old Testament (Septuagint). In secular Greek usage, *diatheke* mostly meant "last will" or "testament," a sense never borne by the Hebrew *berit.* Paul exploits the Greek sense to make the point that a covenant (testament), such as that with Abraham, is unchangeable. In so doing he illustrates the extent to which *covenant* has become a word remote from the way the community defines its identity.

Covenant in Christian Theology and Church History. Although the Christian church ultimately retained the Old Testament as sacred scripture and thus assured continued acquaintance with covenant ideas, the interests of its theologians and the forms of its polity led away from any profound concern with the ancient Israelite covenant. This state of affairs endured until the Reformation of the sixteenth century opened the door to a search for new forms of common life and a renewed interest in the Old Testament, especially on the part of Calvin and his followers. The best known, though not the earliest, of the "covenant theologians" was John Koch (Cocceius; 1603-1669), whose teaching of a sequence of divine covenants was especially appealing within Calvinism as grounding human salvation in an arbitrary divine act. The Scottish national covenants of the seventeenth century were an early expression of biblical covenant ideas in the political as well as religious sphere, and influenced the development of English Protestantism. The Puritan movement in England and America drew liberally on biblical covenant ideas.

[*For further discussion of God's covenant with the people of Israel, see* Israelite Religion *and* Judaism.]

BIBLIOGRAPHY

Eichrodt, Walther. *Theology of the Old Testament* (1933-1939). 2 vols. London, 1961-1967. Organizes Old Testament thought around the idea of a covenant.

Hillers, Delbert R. *Covenant: The History of a Biblical Idea.* Baltimore, 1969. A popular survey of the biblical usage of covenant; follows Mendenhall.

McCarthy, Dennis J. *Old Testament Covenant: A Survey of Current Opinions.* Richmond, 1972. A survey drawing on the author's lengthy technical study, *Treaty and Covenant,* 2d ed. (Rome, 1978).

Mendenhall, George. *Law and Covenant in Israel and the Ancient Near East.* Pittsburgh, 1955. Reprinted from "Ancient Oriental and

Biblical Law," *Biblical Archaeologist* 17 (1954): 26-47. The succinct pioneer study that initiated much of the modern discussion of treaty and covenant.

Pritchard, James B. *Ancient Near Eastern Texts*. 3d ed. Princeton, 1969. Contains translations of some important treaty texts.

Weinfeld, Moshe. *Deuteronomy and the Deuteronomic School*. Oxford, 1972. Long portions are devoted to the relation of Deuteronomy to contemporary treaty forms.

DELBERT R. HILLERS

CROSS

The cross is a sign formed by the meeting of two lines intersecting at a center from which four directions depart. The cruciform sign is used in artistic and scientific expression—in mathematics, architecture, geography, and cosmology. It also occupies an important position in culture in a more general sense and, especially, in religion. Sources from remotest antiquity in Egypt, Crete, Mesopotamia, India, and China show that this sign is an important symbol in the life of *homo religiosus.* What are the symbolisms of the cross in Christian and Non-Christian cultures?

Non-Christian Crosses. On statues of Assyrian kings preserved in the British Museum, the cross can be seen hanging from a necklace, whether as jewelry or as a religious sign. In Mesopotamia the cross with four equal arms is the sign for heaven and the god Anu. A cross of four equal branches found in a chapel at Knossos has been considered a symbol of the sovereign divinity of heaven. The cross appears as a decoration on the walls of many Cretan sanctuaries. Thus the cross is present in the ancient cultures of Asia, Europe, North Africa, and America. In sub-Saharan African art, cruciform motifs are numerous in diverse cultures.

Symbolism of non-Christian crosses. The extraordinary dissemination of the cross throughout many different parts of the world prior to Christianity and outside its influence is explained by the multivalence and density of its symbolic signification. In the symbolism of the cross, we will limit ourselves to four essential elements: the tree, the number four, weaving, and navigation.

In the eyes of primordial man, the tree represents a power. It evokes verticality. It achieves communication between the three levels of the cosmos: subterranean space, earth, and sky. It provides one with an access to the invisible, as exemplified by the shaman's stake, Jacob's ladder, the central column of a house or temple, the pole of a Voodoo sanctuary, and the tree symbolizing Mount Meru in India. In many cultures a particular species or a single tree is designated: the oak of the Celts and the Gauls; the oak of Zeus at Dodona, of the Capitoline Jupiter, of Abraham at Sichem and at Hebron; the ash of the Greeks in Hesiod; the date palm of the Mesopotamians; the fig tree in India; the Siberian birch; the Chinese *chien-mu* tree; and the cedar of Lebanon.

Mircea Eliade (1949, pp. 230-231) has classified the principal meanings of the tree into seven groups: (1) the rock-tree-altar microcosm present in the most archaic stages of religious life (Australia, China, India, Phoenicia, the Aegean); (2) the tree as image of the cosmos (Mesopotamia, India, Scandinavia); (3) the tree as cosmic theophany (Mesopotamia, India, the Aegean); (4) the tree as symbol of life in relation to the mother goddess and water (India, the Near East); (5) the tree as center of the world (Altaic peoples, Scandinavians, American Indians); (6) the mystical tree in human life, like the sacrificial stake in India and Jacob's ladder; and (7) the tree as symbol of the renewal of life. Such a wealth of meanings shows a symbolic system encompassing the essential functions of *homo religiosus:* life, ascension toward the invisible, meditation, enlightenment, fertility. The symbolism of the cross draws widely on this multivalence.

In its association with water and the altar, the tree is linked to center symbolism, as in the Australian totemic centers, in India, at Mohenjo-Daro, in Greece, in the Minoan world, and among the Canaanites and the Hebrews. Tree, water, and altar make up a microcosm, a sacred space around the tree representing the *axis mundi.* Associated with water as a sign of life, and with rock, which represents duration, the tree manifests the sacred strength of the cosmos and of life.

Aryan thought in particular has emphasized the symbol of the cosmic tree. India readily represents the cosmos as a giant tree. The *Katha Upanisad* (6.1) shows it as an eternal fig tree with its roots in the air and its branches turned downward to the earth. The same figure of the tree is found in the *Maitri Upanisad* (6.4): brahman is a fig tree with its three roots pointed to the sky and its branches extending toward earth. The *Bhagavadgita* (15.1-3) compares the cosmos to a giant tree, an imperishable *asvattha,* roots skyward and branches turned toward the earth, its leaves being the hymns of the Veda. For the ancient Scandinavians, Yggdrasill, an *askr* (ash, yew, or oak), is the world's axis or support. Its three roots plunge into the realms of gods, giants, and men respectively. It is the beam of Mímir, Odin's adviser. It is also Larad, the tree protecting the family, a sign of fertility. Inhabited by the weaving Norns, it is the tree of destiny. The three springs at its roots make it the tree of all life, knowledge, and destiny. It binds the universe in a coherent whole.

Orientation is a basic need in the life of *homo religiosus.* This need explains the importance of center symbolism. The cosmic tree is a symbol of absolute reality: the tree of earthly paradise, the shaman's tree, the tree against which the Aryan temple is built, the tree of gnosis (knowledge). It is where the divinity lives. The tree Kiskanu of Babylonian cosmology extends toward the ocean, sustaining the world. It is the dwelling place of the fertility goddess Ea. In Vedic India the *yupa*—the sacrificial stake fashioned by the priest after the ritual cutting down of the tree—becomes the road permitting access from the earth to the sky, linking the three cosmic regions. It is by way of the tree, the *axis mundi,* that heaven descends toward man. It is at the foot of a fig tree that the Buddha received enlightenment. Sun and moon descend in the shape of birds, by means of the Siberian larch. In China the chien-mu tree is placed in the center of the world with nine branches and nine roots that touch the nine springs and the nine heavens; by means of it the sovereigns, mediators between heaven and earth, ascend and descend. In Egypt the djed column, representing a tree stripped of branches, plays an essential role in the cult of Osiris and in religious life.

The number four is the number symbolizing the totality of space and time. It is linked to the symbolism of the center that marks the meeting of four directions and the transcen-

> **The number four is the number symbolizing the totality of space and time.**

dence of them. Four is also linked to the symbol of the cosmic tree. The tree and the notion of quaternity are the essential elements in a symbolism of completeness that plays a primordial role in the life of *homo religiosus.*

The number four has various cosmological aspects: four cardinal points, four winds, four lunar phases, four seasons, and the four rivers at the beginning of the world. According to Hartley B. Alexander (1953), the number four is basic to the mind of North American Indians. There are four parts of the terrestrial world and four divisions of time (day, night, moon, year). There are four parts of a plant: root, stem, flower, fruit. To the four celestial beings—sky, sun, moon, stars—correspond four kinds of animals: those that crawl, those that fly, quadrupeds, and bipeds. Among the Dakota, the four masculine virtues of courage, endurance, generosity, and honor correspond to the four feminine virtues of ability, hospitality, fidelity, and fertility. The Indian mystery Wakantanka is fourfold: God the chief, God the spirit, God the creator, God the doer. Alexander observes that the religious philosophy of the Dakota and of all the peoples of the Plains is reminiscent of the Pythagorean tetrad, a numerical symbol of the world order.

Jacques Soustelle has shown that for the ancient Mexicans the cardinal points merged with space and the four directions. There are four quarters of the universe, linked to four time periods (*L'univers des Azteques,* Paris, 1979, pp. 136-140). The fifth direction in space is the center, where the other directions cross and where up meets down. The Codex Borgia designates the center by a multi-colored tree crowned

by a quetzal. The Mexicans distinguish four winds. Four colors characterize the directions of space. The center is the synthesis and meeting place of the four colors, as among the Pueblo. The four primary gods are each designated by one of these colors. (These concepts relating to the cardinal points and colors are identical in China.) The world is built on a cross, on crossroads that lead from east to west and from north to south. In manuscripts, the center and the four cardinal points are shown by stylized trees. Space and time are linked; to be precise, each time connects with a predetermined space. In this cosmological outlook, natural phenomena and human deeds are all immersed in space-time. For the Dogon of Mali, four is the symbol of creation. The Luba of the Kasai River region imagine the world divided into four planes on the branches of a vertical cross oriented from west to east.

The Vedas are divided into four parts. The *Chandogya Upanisad* (4.5) distributes the Brahmanic teachings into quarters, making them correspond to the four realms of the universe: spaces, worlds, lights, senses. In India there are four classes: the three Aryan classes (*brahmana, ksatriya, vaisya*) and the *sudra* class. The three Aryan classes are invited to pass through four *asramas,* stages of life: *brahmacarya* (student), *grhastha* (householder), *vanaprastha* (forest dweller), *samnyasa* (ascetic renunciant).

This idea of wholeness and universality symbolized by the number four is also found in the biblical texts. Out of the Garden of Eden ran a river that divided into four branches (*Gn.* 2:10-15). The twelve tribes of Israel form four camps around the meeting tent. In Ezekiel's vision, there are four animals in the center, each having four faces and four wings (*Ez.* 1:5-6). *Revelation* appropriates this number as characterizing the universe in its totality: four angels, four corners of the earth, and four winds (*Rv.* 7:1). It also speaks of four living beings (*Rv.* 4:6-8).

The Christian Cross. For Christians, the cross is a sign evoking a historical event basic to the history of salvation: the crucifixion and death of Jesus at Calvary.

Christian symbolism of the cross. Against the mysteries of pagan religions, the church fathers set the Christian mystery. In their eyes, the salvation decree proclaimed by God was revealed in the crucifixion of Christ. For Christians, Christ's death on the cross marked the end of Judaism as well as radical separation from pagan cults. They later vigorously opposed the various gnostic theories that refused to see history unfolding within the context of salvation through Christ and his achievement in the world. The Fathers quoted Paul (*Eph.* 1:10) to emphasize that in the crucifixion of Jesus creation was completed and a new world begun. They stressed the reality of the events related by the evangelists: agony, blood, human death, the heart wounded, the cross made of two pieces joined in the center. From the shocking to simplicity of the elements, both Jews and pagans, they developed an understanding of the great mystery of the cross (see *1 Cor.* 1:24-25, 2:8).

Greek thought was familiar to the church fathers in the first centuries. They saw in the cross the cosmic symbolism described by Pythagorean wisdom and developed in the works of Plato (*Timaeus* 36b-c). The two great circles of the world that intersect, forming a prone Greek *chi* around which turns the celestial arch, became for the Christians the cross of heaven. Hanging from the cross, the Logos—creator of the world—contains the cosmos. Thus, in the eyes of Justin Martyr (*1 Apology* 60.1) the celestial chi of Plato symbolizes the cross. For Irenaeus (*Against Heresies* 5.18.3), the sign of the cross is the totality and the visible manifestation of the cosmic future: the four dimensions of the cosmos are reproduced by the cross.

The Latin Christians soon moved in the same direction. At the end of the second century, precisely when pagan mysticism and the solar cults were reaching their apogee, Hippolytus of Rome celebrated the cross by reviving the entire range of ancient symbolic associations (*Paschal Homily* 6). For him, the cross was a tree rising from the earth to the sky, a point of support and repose, a cosmic pole. The mystery of the cross marks all creation: the human body, the flight of birds, agriculture, and the Christian in prayer with arms outstretched.

Christian symbolism of the cross is linked to the mystery of creation as well as to the mystery of redemption. As the church fathers reinterpreted ancient cosmic symbolism, they also reinterpreted images from the Hebrew scriptures (Old Testament). On the day of Christ's crucifixion, the curtain of the Temple was torn revealing in all its fullness the mystery of God hidden within the Ark of the Covenant.

In the writings of the Fathers, each reference to wood in the Old Testament becomes a symbol of the cross. One tree in particular, however, symbolizes the mystery of Golgotha: the Tree of Life planted near the four rivers in the midst of Paradise (*Gn.* 2:9), which is mentioned in *Revelation* (22:14). This tree prefigures the mystery of the cross, for in its place, and in the place of the first Adam, we now have the new Adam whose tree of salvation is erected toward the sky, embracing the cosmos and making the baptismal spring of life flow at its feet. This symbolism of tree and water, taken from *Genesis* and applied to the event at Golgotha, has had extraordinary repercussions. It has inspired the baptismal theology of both the Eastern and Western church fathers.

From the second century on, this symbol system is taken up and developed by Christian thinkers. Justin Martyr devotes all of the fifty-fifth chapter of his first Apology to this symbolism. To show the pagans that the cross is the sign of Christ's strength and power, he asks them to consider a series of objects that come before their eyes: "Could one cut through the sea if that trophy was not raised intact on the ship in the shape of a sail? Is work possible without the cross? Can pioneers or manual laborers work without instruments bearing that shape?" (55.2). He then enumerates several signs that suggest the power of the cross: the human body, its arms outstretched; the banners and trophies that go before armies, and statues of emperors (55.6-7). Justin emphasizes the figure of the trophy shaped by the mast and by the yard on which the sail is hung, because it permits him to elaborate his argument. Just as the mast and the sail are indispensable to the security of sailors and passengers, so only the cross of Christ that they symbolize is capable of granting salvation. Justin similarly perceives the vexilla and tropaia that led the troops into battle in the same way.

BIBLIOGRAPHY

Alexander, Hartley B. *The World's Rim: Great Mysteries of the North American Indians.* Lincoln, Nebr., 1953.

Andresen, Carl, and Günter Klein, eds. *Theologia Crucis, Signum Crucis: Festschrift für Erich Dinkler zum 70.* Geburtstag. Tübingen, 1979.

Armstrong, Gregory T. "The Cross in the Old Testament according to Athanasius, Cyril of Jerusalem and the Cappadocian Fathers." In *Theologia Crucis, Signum Crucis: Fest-schrift für Erich Dinkler zum 70. Geburtstag,* edited by Carl Andresen and Günter Klein, pp. 17-38. Tübingen, 1979.

Blake, Willson W. *The Cross, Ancient and Modern.* New York, 1888.

Bousset, Wilhelm. "Die Seele der Welt bei Plato und das Kreuz Christi." *Zeitschrift für neutestamentliche Wissenschaft* 14 (1913): 273-285.

Casal, Jean-Marie. *La civilisation de l'Indus et ses énigmes: De la Mésopotamie à l'Inde.* Paris, 1969.

Champdor, Albert. *Le livre des morts: Papyrus d'Ani, de Hunefer, d'Anhai du British Museum.* Paris, 1963. Translated by Faubion Bowers as *The Book of the Dead* (New York, 1966).

Champeaux, Gérard de, and Sébastien Sterckx. *Introduction au monde des symboles.* Paris, 1966.

Chevalier, Jean, and Alain Gheerbrant, eds. *Dictionnaire des symboles.* Paris, 1982.

Cramer, Maria. *Das altägyptische Lebenszeichen im christlichen (koptischen) Ägypten.* Wiesbaden, 1955.

Dölger, Franz Joseph. "Beiträge zur Geschichte des Kreuzzeichens." *Jahrbuch für Antike und Christentum* 1 (1958): 5-19, 2 (1959): 15-29, 3 (1960): 5-16, 4 (1961): 5-17, and 5 (1962): 5-22.

Eliade, Mircea. *Traité d'histoire des religions.* Paris, 1949.

Eliade, Mircea. *Images and Symbols: Studies in Religious Symbolism.* New York, 1961.

Erler, Martin. *Das Symbol des Lebens im alten Aegypten.* Munich, 1968.

Goblet d'Alviella, Eugène F. A. "Archéologie de la croix." In *Croyances, rites, institutions,* vol. 1, pp. 63-81. Paris, 1911.

Goblet d'Alviella, Eugène F. A. *La migration des symboles.* Paris, 1891.

Guénon, René. *Le symbolisme de la croix.* Paris, 1957. Translated by Angus Macnab as *Symbolism of the Cross* (London, 1958).

Kennedy, Charles A. "Early Christians and the Anchor." *Biblical Archaeologist* 38 (1975): 115-124.

Korvin-Krasinski, Cyrill von. "Vorchristliche matriarchalische Einflüsse in der Gestaltung ältester koptischer und armenischer Kreuze." *Symbolon: Jahrbuch für Symbolforschung* (Cologne) 3 (1977): 37-73.

Laliberté, Norman, and Edward N. West. *The History of the Cross.* New York, 1960.

Leclercq, Henri. "Croix et crucifis." In *Dictionnaire d'archéologie chrétienne et de liturgie,* edited by Fernand Cabrol, vol. 3, pp. 3045-3144. Paris, 1914. A probing study of the history of the Christian representation of the cross.

Marshall, John, ed. *Mohenjo-Daro and the Indus Civilization.* 3 vols. Delhi, 1973.

Mortillet, Gabriel de. *Le signe de la croix avant le christianisme.* Paris, 1866.

Porter, Arthur K. *The Crosses and Culture of Ireland.* New Haven, 1931.

Rahner, Hugo. *Mythes grecs et mystères chrétien.* Paris, 1954.

Rahner, Hugo. *Symbole der Kirche: Die Ekklesiologie der Väter.* Salzburg, 1964.

Rech, Photina. *Inbild des Kosmos: Eine Symbolik der Schöpfung.* 2 vols. Salzburg, 1966.

Schneider Berrenberg, Rüdiger. *Kreuz, Kruzifix: Eine Bibliographie.* Munich, 1973. Contains more than two thousand headings (iconography, art history, archaeology, theology, philology, and folklore).

Séjourné, Laurette. *La pensée des anciens Mexicains.* Paris, 1982.

Stählin, Wilhelm. "Das Kreuzeszeichen." In *Deine Sprache verrät dich.* Kassel, 1974.

Stierlin, Henri. *L'art des Astèques et ses origines.* Paris, 1982.

Streit, Jakob. *Sonne und Kreuz: Irland zwischen Megalithkultur und frühem Christentum.* Stuttgart, 1977.

Wedemeyer, Inge von. "Das Zeichen des Kreuzes im Alten Peru." *Antaios* (Stuttgart) 12 (1970): 366-379.

JULIEN RIES
Translated from French by Kristine Anderson

CRUSADES

Christian Perspective

Crusades were military expeditions against various enemies of the church; the term refers particularly to the medieval campaigns aimed at liberating the Holy Land from the Muslims. The word *crusade* (Span., *cruzada;* Fr., *croisade*) derives from the Latin *crux* (cross); the Latin term *cruciata* does not occur before the thirteenth century. It recalls the ceremony of "taking the cross" (*Mt.* 10:38), the public act of committing oneself to participate in a crusade. Crusaders wore a red cloth cross sewn to their cloaks as a sign of their status.

Roots and Causes. While the roots of the movement were complex, a major religious impulse came with the fusion of pilgrimage and holy war. The Crusades continued the old tradition of pilgrimage to the Holy Land that was often undertaken in fulfillment of a vow or as a penance. Attractive for pilgrims were not only the holy places themselves but their relics, above all the Holy Sepulcher, to which the emperor Heraclius had restored the True Cross in AD 627.

During the twelfth century armed pilgrimages began to be regarded as just wars fought in defense of the Holy Land against its illegitimate occupation by the Muslim infidel. The notion of a just war as revenge for an injury done to Christ had been invoked in the fight against Muslims in Spain and Sicily and in expeditions against pagans and Saracens. In 878, Pope John VIII offered spiritual incentives to those who would arm themselves against his foes in Italy. Gregory VII (1073-1085) envisaged a militia Christi for the fight against all enemies of God and thought already of sending an army to the East. An additional factor was the expectation of religious benefits. In the popular perception, the Crusade indulgence offered nothing less than full remission of sins and a sure promise of heaven.

Among the political causes of the Crusades, the appeals for help from the Byzantine emperors were prominent. The year 1071 saw the defeat of the Byzantine army at Manzikert in Asia Minor. Jerusalem fell to the Seljuk Turks in 1077. These events caused great alarm and spurred papal offers of assistance. Moreover, in dealing with the fighting spirit of the aristocracy, reform movements such as the Cluniac and the Gregorian were promoting the "Peace of God" (protection of unarmed persons) and the "Truce of God" (*treuga Dei,* suspension of all fighting during specified times). In this situation, participation in holy warfare provided an outlet for the martial vigor of Christian knights.

Campaigns. Any attempt at systematizing the Crusades remains arbitrary. Nevertheless, for clarity's sake, we shall follow the customary numbering of the main expeditions.

First Crusade (1096-1099). Urban II's call for participation in an expedition to the East at the Council of Clermont on 27 November 1095 met with an enthusiastic response. Thousands took the cross, especially French, Norman, and Flemish knights. Several bands of badly armed pilgrims from France and Germany, most of them poor and inexperienced, set out for Constantinople even before the army gathered. Some started by massacring Jews on their way through Germany. Many died in Hungary, and the remnants perished in Anatolia. The main force, under the papal legate Bishop Adhémar of Le Puy and an illustrious baronial leadership (including Godfrey of Bouillon, Baldwin II of Flanders, Raymond IV of Toulouse, Robert II of Normandy, and Bohemond I of Taranto), assembled at Constantinople (December 1096 to May 1097) and set out on a long, arduous march through Asia Minor. After costly victories at Nicaea and Dorylaeum (June-July 1097) and enormous hardships, the Crusaders captured Antioch (3 June 1098) and finally Jerusalem (15 July 1099), consolidating their victory by the defeat of a Fatimid army at Ascalon (12 August 1099). A side expedition under Baldwin had already taken Edessa to the north (6 February 1098). Only Nicaea was returned to the Byzantine emperor, and four Crusader states were organized along the Syro-Palestinian coast. Measured against the original goal, the First Crusade was the only successful one. Its territorial gains, protected by inland ridges and a system of fortresses along the coast, formed the basis that future Crusades sought to defend against mounting Muslim pressure. Constant quarrels among the leaders and rival interests of the major European powers, however, prevented any effective cooperation and success.

> ## Measured against the original goal, the First Crusade was the only successful one.

Second Crusade (1147-1149). The preaching of the Second Crusade had its immediate cause in the loss of Edessa to the Muslims of Syria (1144). Moved by the preaching of Bernard of Clairvaux, Louis VII of France and Conrad III of Germany led separate armies through Asia Minor. The losses suffered by the troops were disheartening. Furthermore, rather than aiming at Edessa, the remnant joined the Palestinian knights in an unsuccessful siege of Damascus (July 1148), which had been at peace with the kingdom of Jerusalem. This diversion worsened the plight of Edessa, Antioch, and Tripoli. The crusade was soon recognized as a disaster.

Third Crusade (1189-1192). At the initiative of the archbishop of Tyre, the Third Crusade responded to the defeat of the Palestinian knights at Hittin in Galilee (4 July 1187) and the resulting loss of Jerusalem to the sultan, Saladin. The leadership included Frederick I Barbarossa, Philip II Augustus of France, and Richard I ("the Lionhearted") of England. But Frederick accidentally drowned during the march, and the crusading effort disintegrated through attrition, quarreling, and lack of cooperation.

Fourth Crusade (1202-1204). Pope Innocent III (1198-1216) made the reorganization of the crusade under papal auspices one of the priorities of his pontificate. At the request of the Venetians, the Crusaders first attacked the Christian city of Zara in Dalmatia (November 1202) and then sailed on to Constantinople, where they hoped to enthrone Alexios, an exiled Byzantine pretender to the crown, and to receive the material assistance they needed. When these plans failed, the Crusaders laid siege to the city and finally stormed it (12 April 1204). Byzantium was looted for its treasure of relics, art, and gold, and was made the residence of a Latin emperor, with Baldwin IX of Flanders as the first incumbent. A Byzantine army recaptured the city almost casually in 1261.

Fifth Crusade (1217-1221). In the Levant, Acre had become the center of Christian activity. From there an expedition under baronial and clerical leadership attempted to strike at the heart of Ayyubid power in Egypt (May 1218). The harbor city of Damietta was forced to surrender (5 November

1219), but further hopes were dashed by the defeat on the way to Cairo (24 July 1221). A stunning novelty was the expedition of Emperor Frederick II of Hohenstaufen (the so-called Sixth Crusade, 1228-1229). Frederick sailed to Cyprus and Acre (June 1228), secretly negotiated a ten-year truce that included the return of Jerusalem, Bethlehem, and Lydda to the Christians, and crowned himself king of Jerusalem (18 March 1229), although he had been excommunicated by Gregory IX for his failure to act on a Crusade vow earlier. The Holy City was retaken by Muslim allies in 1244.

Seventh and Eighth Crusades. Two crusades of the thirteenth century are connected with the name of Louis IX (Saint Louis) of France. In fulfillment of a vow, Louis sailed to Cyprus with a splendid host of fifteen thousand men and attacked Egypt (Seventh Crusade, 1248-1254). Damietta was occupied again (June 1249) but had to be returned together with a huge ransom when the king and his army were routed and taken captive on their slow march south (6 April 1250). Louis took up residence in Acre for four years, attempting to strengthen the Crusader states by, for example, working toward an alliance with the Mongol khan. Another expedition against the sultan of Tunis (Eighth Crusade, 1270-1272) also ended in failure. The king died in North Africa (25 August 1270), and the Muslims succeeded in buying off the Crusaders. In the meantime, all of Palestine as well as Antioch was lost to the Baybars. The last Christian bastion on the Syrian coast, Acre, was stormed by the sultan in 1291.

The fourteenth and fifteenth centuries saw several papal attempts to revive the crusade or support expeditions to the East. In 1365, King Peter I of Cyprus captured Alexandria; this victory was inconsequential. Soon the fight against the Ottoman Turks turned into a defense of Christian lands, especially after Muslim victories over the Serbs, the Hungarians (Nicopolis, 1396), and a last Crusader army under John Hunyadi and Julian Cardinal Cesarini (Varna, 1444). The fall of Constantinople in May 1453 led to a serious initiative on the part of Pius II, who wished to go on the crusade in person. He died on the way to joining the fleet at Ancona (July 1464).

Outcome. The results of the Crusades are difficult to assess. In terms of religion, the failures nourished doubts about God's will, church authority, and the role of the papacy. Religious fervor yielded to apathy, cynicism, and legalism. On the other hand, the Crusades stimulated religious enthusiasm on a large scale and gave Christendom a unifying cause that lasted for centuries. They inspired a great literature of tracts, chronicles, letters, heroic tales, and poetry, not only in Latin but in the vernaculars. Ignorance of Islam was replaced by a measure of knowledge, respect, and occasionally tolerance.

Politically, the Crusades brought few lasting changes. The Crusader states and the Latin empire remained episodes. Their precarious status forced new diplomatic contacts with

Eastern powers but also strengthened the Muslim conviction that holy war *(jihad)* could be carried farther west. In this sense the Crusades led directly to the Turkish wars of later centuries, during which Ottoman expansion threatened even central Europe.

The effect of the Crusades on relations with Byzantium was primarily negative. The Crusades needed Byzantine support as much as Byzantium needed Western armies. But what started as an effort to help Eastern Christians ended in mutual mistrust and enmity.

The Crusades imposed huge burdens on clergy and laity; at times the papacy was unable to support any other cause. Yet they also furthered the growth of a money economy, banking, and new methods of taxation. The widening of the geographic horizon prepared Europe for the age of discovery.

BIBLIOGRAPHY

Many general bibliographies on the Middle Ages feature sections on the Crusades. Two specialized bibliographies provide a thorough introduction to sources and literature: A. S. Atiya's *The Crusade: Historiography and Bibliography* (1962; reprint, Westport, Conn., 1976) and Hans Eberhard Mayer's *Bibliographie zur Geschichte der Kreuzzüge* (Hanover, 1960) with its supplement, *Literaturberichte über Neuerscheinungen zur ausserdeutschen Geschichte und zu den Kreuzzügen,* "Historische Zeitschrift, Sonderheft," vol. 3 (Munich, 1969).

The most comprehensive treatment of the Crusades in English is found in the excellent volumes of *A History of the Crusades,* under the general editorship of Kenneth M. Setton, with Marshall W. Baldwin, Robert Wolff, and especially Harry W. Hazard as editors (vols. 1-2, Philadelphia, 1955-1962; new edition and continuation, vols. 1-5, Madison, Wis., 1969-1984). Steven Runciman's *A History of the Crusades,* 3 vols. (Cambridge, 1951-1954), presents another comprehensive, though somewhat idiosyncratic, approach. The best short introduction is Hans Eberhard Mayer's *The Crusades* (Oxford, 1972).

Carl Erdmann's classic book on the roots of the movement is now available in English: *The Origin of the Idea of Crusade* (Princeton, 1977). Still the most thorough investigation of the religious aspects is Paul Alphandéry's *La Chrétienté et l'idée de croisade,* 2 vols. (Paris, 1954-1959). Benjamin Z. Kedar's *Crusade and Mission: European Approaches toward the Muslims* (Princeton, 1984) stresses the interaction of the two main strategies toward Islam.

Much recent attention has focused on canonical and legal aspects. Major studies are James A. Brundage's *Medieval Canon Law and the Crusader* (Madison, Wis., 1969); Maureen Purcell's *Papal Crusading Policy,* "Studies in the History of Christian Thought," no. 11 (Leiden, 1975); and Joshua Prawer's *Crusader Institutions* (Oxford, 1980). A standard work on critical voices is Palmer A. Throop's *Criticism of the Crusade: A Study of Public Opinion and Crusade Propaganda* (1940; reprint, Philadelphia, 1975).

KARLFRIED FROEHLICH

Muslim Perspective

The Muslims of Syria, who were the first to receive the assault of the Crusaders, thought the invaders were Rum, the Byzantines. Accordingly, they regarded the invasion as still another Byzantine incursion into Islamic territory, and, in fact, one inspired by previous Muslim victories in Byzantine domains. It was only when the Muslims realized that the invaders did not originate in Byzantium that they began referring to them as Franks, never as Crusaders, a term for which there was no Arabic equivalent until modern times. The establishment of Frankish kingdoms in Islamic territory, the periodic reinforcement of troops from Europe, and the recurrence of invasion all contributed to a growing Muslim consciousness of the nature of the Frankish threat in Syria and Palestine.

This consciousness was reflected in the development of propaganda in Arabic designed to support the mobilization of Muslim forces against the infidel troops. The second half of the twelfth century saw the emergence of both a major Muslim leader and a literature to abet his efforts. The leader was Nur al-Din (1118-1174), who succeeded in forging the political unity of the Muslims of northern Syria and upper Mesopotamia, thereby providing the basis of a military force strong enough to confront the Franks. Fatimid Egypt was brought under the control of Nur al-Din's lieutenant, Salah al-Din, known to the West as Saladin (1138-1193). After the death of Nur al-Din, Salah al-Din was able to build on the former's political and military accomplishments and exploit the fervor engendered for a Muslim hero as a means of achieving spectacular success against the Crusaders. Although no single Muslim leader of equal stature emerged under the Ayyubid or Mamluk dynasties that followed, literary support for prosecution of war against the Franks flourished until the very end.

It should be emphasized, however, that with few exceptions active support for a concerted Muslim campaign against the Franks was limited to the areas threatened with occupation, namely Syria, Palestine, and Egypt. Various attempts to enlist the help of the Abbasid caliph of Baghdad were futile, partly, no doubt, because the institution of the caliphate was by this time virtually defunct. Even Salah al-Din, who was assiduous in seeking caliphal sanction for his activities, never received more than symbolic recognition from a reluctant caliph.

It should also be pointed out that war against the Franks was never total, that Muslim rulers often felt no compunctions about allying themselves with Crusader princes in order to gain their own ends. Salah al-Din himself did not hesitate to strengthen Egyptian ties with the Italian commercial cities in order to obtain the materials he needed from Europe for his campaigns.

With the exception of their fortresses and churches, the Franks left few traces in Muslim territory or consciousness.

Although the Muslims looted columns and at least one portal from Crusader structures and incorporated them into their mosques as trophies of victory, Islamic architecture developed independently. Nor is there any evidence of significant influence of Crusader minor arts on Islamic counterparts or, for that matter, of substantial Crusader influence on any aspect of Islamic cultural and intellectual life. There are indications, certainly, in the memoirs of the Syrian knight Usamah ibn Munqidh (1095-1188) and the Spanish traveler Ibn Jubayr (1145-1217) that Muslims observed their Frankish neighbors with interest, interacted with them on occasion, and even approved of some aspects of their behavior—their treatment of peasants, for example. But the Muslims apparently made no effort to imitate the Franks.

BIBLIOGRAPHY

A detailed study of the Muslim response to the Crusades is Emmanuel Sivan's *L'Islam et la croisade: Idéologie et propagande dans les réactions musulmanes aux croisades* (Paris, 1968), which, though it focuses on the ideological reaction, relates it to political and military events as well. For a different perspective on some of the material discussed by Sivan, see Hadia Dajani-Shakeel's "Jihad in Twelfth-Century arabic Poetry: A Moral and Religious Force to Counter the Crusades," *Muslim World* 66 (April 1976): 96-113. See also Amin Maalouf's *The Crusades through Arab Eyes* (London, 1984).

Attitudes of contemporary Arab Muslims toward the Crusades can be studied firsthand in *Arab historians of the Crusades,* edited by Francesco Gabrieli and translated from the Italian by E. J. Costello (Berkeley, 1969), and in Usamah ibn Munqidh's *Memoirs of an Arab-Syrian Gentleman or an Arab Knight in the Crusades,* translated by Philip K. Hitti (1927; reprint, Beirut, 1964). For a comparative study of Muslim and Christian concepts of holy war see Albrecht Noth's *Heiliger Krieg und Heiliger Kampf im Islam und Christentum* (Bonn, 1966).

DONALD P. LITTLE

CUNA RELIGION

There are perhaps forty thousand Cuna Indians today, living mostly in the San Blas Reserve on Panama's Atlantic coast, with small groups along the interior Bayano and Chucanaque rivers and in three villages in Colombia. Having survived the traumatic but ephemeral Spanish conquest of the Darien Isthmus (modern-day Isthmus of Panama) after 1510, the Cuna are one of the few remnants of the flourishing pre-Columbian chieftaincies of the circum-Caribbean. The Cuna maintained their autonomy partly by allying themselves with the buccaneers who harassed the Spaniards.

Cult Organization. Institutionally, Cuna religion is organized in both communal and shamanic cults. The communal cult is maintained by the village chiefs (*sailakana*), who chant from oral mythological texts known as Pap Ikar ("god's way") some three nights a week to the assembled village. Official interpreters (*arkarana*) explain the arcane language of the chants, using homilies on contemporary morality. Female puberty feasts are collective rites sponsored by each village once a year.

The shamanic cult is not conducted communally, save for the rite of village exorcism that occurs during epidemics or other collective dangers. Shamans (*neles*) are credited with clairvoyance, through trance or dreams, into the four layers of the underworld. *Neles,* who may be male or female, are born to their role and are discovered by midwives through signs in their afterbirth. A born *nele* must nurture the gift and be apprenticed to an adult *nele.*

Cosmogony and Mythic Themes. Cuna cosmogony, as disclosed in God's Way, posits an original creation by God, who sends the first man, Wako, to earth. In a primordial paradise, Wako finds the earth to be his mother, and the rivers, the sun, the moon, and the stars to be his brothers. The trees are young women. Wako lives here blissfully until God calls him back. (This image of a primordial paradise resembles the childhood of a male Cuna in a matrilocal household belonging to his mother and composed of his brothers and sisters.)

Through mythic origins, the Cuna define their culture: female puberty ceremonies; bodily cleanliness and, closely associated with it, purity; "correct" (Cuna) kin terms; terms for parts of the body; how to use the magical spirit allies of the shamans and the texts that control them; how to mourn properly; how to build proper houses; how to sleep in hammocks; and, finally, the texts of God's Way. Although the Cuna are a

> ... today heaven also includes skyscrapers, automobiles, and telescopes, which permit souls to gaze upon the living, the underworld, and the United States (located, by implication, somewhere near the underworld).

horticultural people whose staple is the banana in various forms, and whose cash crop is the coconut, neither crop is sacralized or commemorated in any myths yet collected. Cacao, tobacco, balsa wood, and magical stones, all supernatural allies in the struggle against evil, are, however, richly attested in the narratives.

Cosmology. Cuna cosmology, with its four levels above and four below the earth, is continuously revealed by the *neles,* who mystically journey through the cosmos, often forging alliances with evil spirits to learn their secrets. In the underworld are the strongholds of the kings of the spiritual allies. Heaven itself, revealed by the *neles* through a chant that recounts the adventures of a soul brought back from the dead, is a stronghold at the fourth layer above. Its golden buildings not only evoke the ancient chiefly strongholds of nearby Colombia, but today heaven also includes skyscrapers, automobiles, and telescopes, which permit souls to gaze upon the living, the underworld, and the United States (located, by implication, somewhere near the underworld). Souls who arrive at God's golden house do so only after having been physically punished for their earthly sins as they journey through the underworld.

God and Morality. The image of God, called Pap ("father") or Diosaila (from the Spanish *Dios* and the Cuna *saila*, "chief"), is that of a stern and distant paternal figure. He is never directly personified. His morality is consistent with the good and harmonious management of a matrilocal extended household and of a community made up of a number of such households. That morality, preached weekly in the local assemblies, enjoins a man to be hard-working, productive, and cooperative, and a woman to be fertile, clean, industrious, and nurturant. Women must avoid gossip, and men, quarrels. Minor conflicts must be dealt with promptly by wise, paternal chiefs, and punishment meted out swiftly—often in the form of verbal admonishments—after which all is forgiven and forgotten. To do otherwise raises the specter of backsliding into the evil ways of the "animal people."

Mythology and Cultural Survival. Armed with this religion, the Cuna were an insuperable foe to the Spaniards, whom the Cuna associated with the *ponikan,* ("evil ones"), and whom they correctly identified as the source of illnesses. Just as the *ponikan* steal men's souls, so did the Spaniards enslave them. The Cuna borrowed their mythological strategy for dealing with the *ponikan* and applied it to the Spaniards. Just as *neles* ally themselves mystically with friendly spirits, get the *ponikan* drunk magically, and confine them to their proper strongholds, so too did the Cuna form alliances with the Atlantic enemies of Spain, feast the Spaniards, and keep them at arm's length. In 1925, the strategy was played out exactly. The great tribal chief Nele Kantule, who was also a shaman, formed an alliance with an American adventurer and organized an uprising against the Panamanian administration, which took place during Carnival. The plotters fell upon unsuspecting, drunken guardsmen and killed them. The United States imposed on Panama a treaty favorable to the Indians.

BIBLIOGRAPHY

The single most important source for Cuna mythology is Norman MacPherson Chapin's *Pab Igala: Historias de la tradición Cuna* (Panama City, 1970). This comprehensive set of texts is arranged in a sequence that Chapin's chiefly informants agree is correct. The current edition is mimeographed, but a print edition is planned. There has been no such compilation of curing, puberty, or funerary texts. The text for childbirth appears in Nils M. Homer and S. Henry Wassen's *The Complete Mu-Igala in Picture Writing* (Göteberg, 1953). This is the subject of a celebrated essay by Claude Lévi-Strauss, "The Effectiveness of Symbols," in *Structural Anthropology* (New York, 1963). Chapin has corrected Lévi-Strauss's ethnographic errors in "Muu Ikala: Cuna Birth Ceremony," in *Ritual and Symbol in Native Central America,* edited by Phillip Young and James Howe (Eugene, Oreg., 1976). This volume also contains Howe's cogent "Smoking Out the Spirits: A Cuna Exorcism," pp. 69-76. The best study of curing is Chapin's "Curing among the San Blas Cuna" (Ph. D. diss., University of Arizona, 1983).

Unfortunately, recent work has shown the texts of Erland Nordenskiöld's 1920s expedition to the Cuna to be garbled. His *An Historical and Ethnological Survey of the Cuna Indians,* written in collaboration with Ruben Pérez and edited by S. Henry Wassen (Göteberg, 1938), should be read only in connection with other works cited here.

James Howe, Joel Sherzer, and Norman MacPherson Chapin have published *Cantos y oraciones del Congreso Cuna* (Panama City, 1979) in a beautiful edition that presents a number of texts and excellent sociolinguistic and ethnological analyses. Sherzer expounds the different styles used in reciting Cuna sacred texts in "*Namakke, sunmakke, kormakke:* Three Types of Cuna Speech Event," in *Explorations in the Ethnography of Speaking,* edited by Richard Bauman and Joel Sherzer (New York, 1974).

The female puberty ceremony is described, without symbolic analysis and without the major sacred texts, in Arnulfo Prestán Simón's *El uso de la chicha y la sociedad Kuna* (Mexico City, 1975). The continuing open-endedness or *productivité* of Cuna sacred texts is explained in Dina Sherzer and Joel Sherzer's "Literature in San Blas: Discovering the Cuna *Ikala,*" *Semiotica* 6 (1972): 182-199. I have explicated the application of this mystical strategy to practical diplomacy in "Lore and Life: Cuna Indian Pageants, Exorcism, and Diplomacy in the Twentieth Century," *Ethnohistory* 30 (1983): 93-106. My "Basilicas and King Posts: A Proxemic and Symbolic Event Analysis of Competing Public Architecture among the San Blas Cuna," *American Ethnologist* 8 (1981): 259-277, explicates the peculiarly rectangular Cuna house construction both in mythological and symbolic terms. Finally, the single best ethnographic study of the Cuna is James Howe's "Village Political Organization among the San Blas Cuna" (Ph. D. diss., University of Pennsylvania, 1974).

ALEXANDER MOORE

DALAI LAMA

DALAI LAMA, title of the spiritual and formerly political leader of the Tibetan people, is a combination of the Mongolian *dalai* ("ocean"), signifying profound knowledge, and the Tibetan *blama* ("religious teacher"). The title dates from 1578 CE, when it was conferred by Altan Khan of the Mongols upon Bsod-nams-rgya-mtsho (1543-1588), third hierarch of the Dge-lugs-pa school of Tibetan Buddhism, commonly called the Yellow Hat sect. After 1578 the title was given to each of the successive reincarnations of the Dalai Lama. The present Dalai Lama is fourteenth in the lineage.

Incarnation (Tib., *sprul sku*), the manifestation of some aspect of the absolute Buddhahood in human form, is an ancient doctrine and one common to various schools of Mahayana Buddhism, but the concept of the reincarnation *(yan srid)* of a lama is unique to Tibetan Buddhism.

From the inception of the institution, traditional procedures for discovering the rebirth of a Dalai Lama, similar to those used for other reincarnate lamas, were followed. Indicative statements made by the previous Dalai Lama during his lifetime, significant auguries surrounding his death and afterward, and meditative visions by special lamas were recorded and interpreted as guides to finding his rebirth. In time, but no sooner than nine months after the death of the previous Dalai Lama, the people began to expect reports of an exceptional male child born in accordance with various omens. Such a child, usually two or three years old when discovered, was subjected to tests to determine physical fitness, intelligence, and the ability to remember events and objects from his previous existence.

The fifth Dalai Lama was a learned scholar and the author of many texts, including a history of Tibet. During the forty years he was head of state, the Mongols helped to protect his newly established government and to expand its territorial control. In recognition of the important role he played in religio-political history, he is referred to in Tibetan literature as the Great Fifth.

A series of other Dalai Lamas followed over the next several decades without much consequence. Between each successor—until he was found and properly educated—an interim lama sat in their place. Reluctance of successive regents and their supporters to hand over power each time a Dalai Lama reached his majority is blamed, perhaps unjustly, for the fact that the eighth Dalai Lama ruled only for a few years, the ninth and tenth died young without assuming power, and the eleventh and twelth Dalai Lamas ruled only for short periods before their death.

During his long reign as head of state, the thirteenth Dalai Lama was forced to flee to Mongolia to escape invading British troops (1904) and again invading Chinese forces (1910). The Chinese revolution of 1911 that overthrew the Manchu dynasty and established the Republic of China also marked the end of Manchu domination of Tibetan affairs. From 1913 until his death in 1933, the thirteenth Dalai Lama was the head of an independent government. Living in exile in British India motivated the thirteenth Dalai Lama to implement various reforms in Tibet to improve the welfare of his people.

The fourteenth and present Dalai Lama, Bstan-'dzin-rgya-mtsho, was born in 1935 of Tibetan parentage in the Chinghai province of China. During the next decade, half of which was taken up by World War II in Asia, the young Dalai Lama was educated and prepared for the time he would assume his role as religio-political ruler of Tibet.

BIBLIOGRAPHY

The only book dealing with the first thirteen Dalai Lamas in some detail remains Günther Schulemann's *Die Geschichte der Dalailamas*, 2d ed. (Leipzig, 1959). Charles A. Bell's *Portrait of the Dalai Lama* (London, 1946) is a biographical sketch based on the author's personal friendship with the thirteenth Dalai Lama, but part 2 of the book explains what a Dalai Lama is and how he is discovered and educated. A scholarly listing, but with basic dates and data only, of all fourteen Dalai Lamas, as well as the regents who successively served them, can be found in Luciano Petech's "The Dalai-Lamas and Regents of Tibet: A Chronological Study," *T'oung pao* (Leiden) 47 (1959): 368-394.

English translations of three books by the fourteenth Dalai Lama, Tenzin Gyatso, are recommended. His autobiography, *My Land and My People* (New York, 1962), is an interesting narrative of his selection, education, and experiences. *The Opening of the Wisdom-Eye and the History of the Advancement of Buddhadharma in Tibet* (Bangkok, 1968) and *The Buddhism of Tibet and the Key to the Middle Way* (New York, 1975) provide lucid expositions of the fundamental philosophical teachings of Tibetan Buddhism that must be mastered by a Dalai Lama.

Also recommended are David L. Snellgrove and Hugh E. Richardson's *A Cultural History of Tibet* (New York, 1968), Rolf A. Stein's *Tibetan Civilization* (Stanford, Calif., 1972), and Tsepon W. D.

Shakabpa's *Tibet: A Political History* (New Haven, 1967). Each of these works contains an excellent bibliography.

TURRELL V. WYLIE

DANTE ALIGHIERI

DANTE ALIGHIERI (1265-1321), Italian poet, theologian, and philosopher. After producing the *Vita nuova* in 1295, Dante entered the volatile world of Florentine politics, which, however unjustly, subsequently led to his banishment from the city in 1302. In exile for the remainder of his life, he wrote the *Convivio*, the *De vulgari eloquentia*, and the *De monarchia* in the following decade, works that together reveal a commonality of themes: an admiration for the Latin classics, a dedication to the study of philosophy, and a commitment to the revival of the Roman imperial ideal. These concerns are all transfigured in the long and elaborate course of the *Commedia (Inferno, Purgatorio, Paradiso)*, which represents an encyclopedic synthesis of late medieval thought subsumed within an overarching theological vision. The poem is at once profoundly traditional in its religious ordering of human experience and an innovation of substance and form that suggests an utterly new mentality at work. It can be seen both as an attempt to exorcise what would shortly become the spirit of the Renaissance and yet also as a brilliant precursor of it.

In assessing Dante's relation to medieval theology and religious thought it is commonplace to emphasize the formative influence of "the Philosopher" (Aristotle) and the "Angelic Doctor" (Thomas); that is, to stress his strong debt to Scholasticism. It must be remembered, however, that the poet everywhere shows himself to be an independent and eclectic thinker. Thus, while we may well speak of Dante as standing at the crossroads of medieval religious thought, the intersection is one that he personally constructed rather than discovered ready-made. The synthesis of the *Commedia* is idiosyncratically his own.

As a propagator of the Christian religion Dante must, of course, be assessed by the achievement of his great poem, with its account of the state of the soul after death portrayed in the course of a journey undertaken by the poet himself (lasting from Good Friday 1300 to the Wednesday of Easter Week) through the realms of damnation, purgation, and beatitude. In its larger aspect, the poem is itself an invitation to conversion: to the individual reader, to rediscover the Gospels' "true way"; to the church, to recover its spiritual mission; and to the state, to exercise its divinely ordained mandate to foster temporal well-being.

There are other transformations as well. Hell is portrayed not as a place of arbitrary horror, but as the eternal living out of the soul's self-choice, whereby punishments not only fit but express the crimes of sin. Dante also brings Purgatory above ground and into the sun, turning the traditional place of torturous penance into more of a hospital or school than a prison house. But perhaps most significant of all—and most singularly responsible for the *Commedia's* immense and enduring popularity—is Dante's superb representation of the self: ineradicable even in death; more vivid than the theological context in which it is eternally envisioned; more subtly and realistically portrayed than in any other work of medieval literature.

BIBLIOGRAPHY

The quantity of secondary material on Dante written in English alone is staggering. Carole Slade's extensive and somewhat annotated bibliography in *Approaches to Teaching Dante's Divine Comedy* (New York, 1982) gives a fine sense of the whole range. Among those works that deal sensitively with Dante's relation to Christian belief and tradition, one needs to accord special tribute to the critical oeuvre of Charles S. Singleton, who has exerted a powerful influence on American studies of Dante by underscoring the importance of the poem's theological assumptions. In addition to Singleton's translation and commentary (Princeton, 1970-1975), there are his earlier works: *An Essay on the Vita Nuova* (Cambridge, 1949), *Dante Studies 1: Commedia, Elements of Structure*, 2d ed. (Baltimore, 1977), and *Dante Studies 2: Journey to Beatrice*, 2d ed. (Baltimore, 1977). Charles Williams's *The Figure of Beatrice* (London, 1958) gives a coherent theological reading of all of Dante's works, whose point of view informs not only Dorothy Sayers's commentary and notes (Harmondsworth, 1951-1967) but her *Introductory Papers on Dante* (New York, 1954) and *Further Papers on Dante* (New York, 1957). There are also brilliant insights into the religious ethos of the *Commedia* in Erich Auerbach's *Dante: Poet of the Secular World* (Chicago, 1961) as well as in an important chapter of his *Mimesis* (Princeton, 1953). Robert Hollander's *Allegory in Dante's Commedia* (Princeton, 1969) and *Studies in Dante* (Ravenna, 1980) deal masterfully with the poet's claim to write an "allegory of the theologians" (and therefore in the manner of scripture itself). John Freccero's many brilliant essays on the *Commedia*, collected under the title *The Poetry of Conversion* (Cambridge, Mass., 1986), stress the poet's debt to Augustine's *Confessions* and the Christian Neoplatonic tradition. The latter connection is explored in Joseph Anthony Mazzeo's *Structure and Thought in the Paradiso* (Ithaca, N. Y., 1958). Finally, William Anderson's *Dante the Maker* (Boston, 1980) takes seriously the visionary origin of the *Commedia* and therefore forces us to examine again the literal level of the poem and its bid to be believed as a genuine vision of God.

PETER S. HAWKINS

DAVID

DAVID, second king of Israel and Judah (c. 1000-960 BCE), and founder of a dynasty that continued until the end of the

Judean monarchy. David was the youngest son of Jesse from Bethlehem in Judah.

He is regarded by both tradition and modern scholarship as the greatest ruler of the combined states of Israel and Judah. He was able to free them from the control of the Philistines and to gain a measure of domination over some of the neighboring states (Edom, Moab, Ammon) and some of the Aramaean states of Syria; he established treaty relations with Tyre and Hamath; he extended the territories of Judah and Israel to include a number of major Canaanite cities and took Jerusalem by conquest. It became his capital and remained the ruling center of Judah until the end of the monarchy.

The assessment of David's career is based upon sources in *1 Samuel* 16 through *1 Kings* 2. Some of these that mention his military activities reflect annalistic or formal documents. These are now embedded within two literary works often regarded as nearly contemporary with David and an important witness to the events: the story of David's rise to power (*1 Sm.* 16 through *2 Sm.* 2:7, *2 Sm.* 5), and the court history, or succession story (*2 Sm.* 2:8-4:12, 6:16, 6:20-23; *2 Sm.* 9-20; *1 Kgs.* 1-2). It remains less clear how *2 Samuel* 6-8 relates to either of these works or how they all fit into the larger history of the monarchy. The materials in *2 Samuel* 21-24 are supplemental additions that do not belong to the other sources.

David in the Tradition of Israel. David's introduction is directly linked to God's rejection of Saul, so that he immediately appears as the "one after God's own heart" to replace Saul. Shortly after David enters Saul's service as personal armor bearer, musician, and successful military leader, Saul becomes jealous and makes various attempts on his life so that David flees. David establishes a band of followers in Judah and becomes a vassal of the Philistines. Saul, demented, cruel, and forsaken by God, ultimately dies on the battlefield with his sons. David is made king at Hebron, first by Judah and subsequently by Israel. David then captures Jerusalem and wages successful warfare against the Philistines. All of this comes to David because "God is with him." Throughout the entire account, David is viewed as one who can do no wrong.

The dynastic promise. Once the land is at peace, David is able to bring the Ark to Jerusalem (*2 Sm.* 6) and build himself a palace (*2 Sm.* 5:11). He then proposes a plan to Nathan the prophet to build a temple for the Ark. God promises David an eternal dynasty but assigns the task of building the Temple—a permanent abode—to his son Solomon. God will be "a father" to the king, and he will be God's "son." He may be disciplined for disobedience to God's laws, but the dynasty will remain in perpetuity.

David as the "servant of Yahveh" who is completely obedient to God becomes the model for all future kings, especially those of Judah. Not only is his obedience rewarded with an

immediate heir, but it is said to merit the perpetuation of his dynasty even if some future kings are disobedient to God's laws.

This dynastic promise also becomes the basis for the hope of a restoration of the monarchy after the destruction of the state in 587/6 BCE and ultimately leads to messianism—the belief that a son of David will arise and restore the fortunes of Israel and usher in the final reign of God.

Court history. The so-called court history, or succession story, variously regarded as a unique piece of early history writing, a historical novel, and a work of royal propaganda, is a literary masterpiece of realistic narrative.

It was, in fact, a later addition to the history that seeks to counter the idealized view of David by suggesting that he gained the throne from a son of Saul under doubtful circumstances and that the divine promise to David was constantly used by David, Solomon, and others to legitimize very questionable behavior. The "sure house" of David is characterized by endless turmoil, and Solomon finally succeeds David after a palace intrigue. David himself commits adultery and murder.

This pejorative view of David's monarchy and the dynastic promise did not suppress the royal ideology or its evolution into messianism. At most it "humanized" David and gave added appeal to the tradition as a whole.

David in the Books of Chronicles. The historian of *1* and *2 Chronicles* sees in David the real founder of the Jewish state, a state dominated by the Temple and an elaborate priestly hierarchy (*1 Chr.* 10-29). The Chronicler's source for David was the history in *Samuel* and *Kings* modified by his perception of the state, which was based upon his own times

> The "sure house" of David is characterized by endless turmoil, . . . David himself commits adultery and murder.

in the Hellenistic period. He presents David as immediately coming to the throne over all Israel after the death of Saul. David becomes the real founder of the Temple, laying all the plans, providing for all the workmanship and the materials, and even establishing the whole hierarchy of priestly and Temple officials. Of particular importance for later tradition is the association of David with the Temple music, which did much to identify him as the "sweet singer of Israel."

David and the Psalms. David is directly mentioned in only a few psalms (78, 89, and 132), those that make reference to the dynastic promise, all of which are dependent upon *Samuel* and *Kings*. In the Hebrew scriptures the superscriptions, which are all late, and which modern scholarship considers secondary additions, attribute seventy-three psalms to David. But in a number of instances the individual laments (e.g., *Ps.* 51) are associated with particular events in David's life. Thus the psalms that were originally anonymous become increasingly associated with the figure of David.

David in Prophecy. While the royal ideology had at most a minor place in preexilic prophecy, it was only in late prophecy and in exilic and postexilic editing of prophetic books that the dynastic promise to David plays a major role in visions of the future (*Is.* 9:5-6 [Eng. version 6-7], 11:1-10, 61:1-7; *Jer.* 33:14-26; *Ez.* 34:23-24; *Am.* 9:11ff.; *Mi.* 5:1-3 [EV 2-4]; *Zec.* 12:7-9). Hope is expressed for the restoration of the Davidic dynasty and times of prosperity. These prophecies predict an "anointed one" (the Messiah) who would liberate Israel from its enemies, and bring in the reign of Yahveh.

David in Rabbinic Judaism, Christianity, and Islam. Some elements in the Davidic tradition gave the rabbis difficulty, most notably David's sin of adultery with Bathsheba. Some attempted to exonerate him, but those who found him guilty of wrongdoing saw a divine purpose in the events, namely that David was to be an example of contrition and repentance to give hope and encouragement to Israel when it sinned (*Midrash Tehillim* 40.2, 51.1, 51.3). Another problem was the tradition that David was descended from Ruth the Moabite (*Ru.* 4:17), since this would make him ineligible for participation in the congregation of Israel. As a compensation, every attempt was made to enhance David's genealogical line and give him the strongest possible pedigree.

Christianity's emphasis was clearly on the messianic aspects of the tradition. Since Jesus was identified as the Messiah, he received the title "son of David," although he repudiated the political connotation of such a designation. Matthew and Luke, in their birth stories, connect Jesus with Bethlehem, the city of David, and supply genealogies that trace his lineage back to David. David as prophet also bears witness in the psalms to Jesus as the Messiah (*Acts* 2:25-37).

Islam's tradition about David is slight. The Qur'an knows of a few episodes in David's life, such as the victory over Goliath, but this and other stories are confused with those of other biblical figures (2:252).

BIBLIOGRAPHY

Treatments of the historical periods of David's reign may be found in John Bright's *A History of Israel*, 3d ed. (Philadelphia, 1981); the contribution by J. Alberto Soggin, "The Davidic-Solomonic Kingdom," in *Israelite and Judaean History*, edited by John H. Hayes and J. Maxwell Miller (Philadelphia, 1977); and those by Benjamin Mazar and David N. Freedman in *The World History of the Jewish People*, vol. 4, pt. 1, edited by Abraham Malamat (Jerusalem, 1979), pp. 76-125.

The standard treatment on the story of David's rise to power is Jakob H. Grønbaek's *Die Geschichte vom Aufstieg Davids, 1 SAM. 15-2 SAM. 5: Tradition und Komposition*, "Acta Theologica Danica," vol. 10 (Copenhagen, 1971). The classic work on the so-called succession story is Leonhard Rost's *Die Überlieferung von der Thronnachfolge Davids*, "Beiträge zur Wissenschaft vom Alten und Neuen Testament," vol. 3, no. 6 (Stuttgart, 1926), translated by Michael D. Rutter and David M. Gunn as *The Succession to the Throne of David* (Sheffield, 1982). Building upon this study was the important essay by Gerhard von Rad, "Der Anfang der Geschichtsschreibung im Alten Israel," *Archiv für Kulturgeschichte* 32 (Weimar, 1944): 1-42, translated by E. W. Trueman Dicken as "The Beginning of Historical Writing in Ancient Israel," in Gerhard von Rad's *The Problem of the Hexateuch and Other Essays* (Edinburgh, 1966), pp. 166-204. See also the studies by Roger N. Whybray, *The Succession Narrative* (London, 1968), and David M. Gunn, *The Story of King David: Genre and Interpretation* (Sheffield, 1982). A more detailed treatment of my own views may be found in chapter 8 of my *In Search of History: Historiography in the Ancient World and the Origins of Biblical History* (New Haven, 1983).

For a more detailed treatment of the Jewish and Christian traditions with bibliography, see the article "David" in *Theologische Realenzyklopädie*, vol. 8 (New York, 1981).

JOHN VAN SETERS

DEAD SEA SCROLLS

Discovery. In Qumran, in 1947, a young bedouin entered what is now designated Cave I and found a group of pottery jars containing leather scrolls wrapped in linen cloths. Scientific exploration of the cave in 1949 by G. Lankester Harding and Roland de Vaux uncovered additional fragments and many broken jars. From 1951 on, a steady stream of manuscripts has been provided by bedouin and archaeologists.

From the beginning, the dating of the scrolls was a matter of controversy. Some saw the new texts as documents of the medieval Jewish sect of the Karaites. Others believed they dated from the Roman period, and some even thought they were of Christian origin.

Of primary importance for dating the scrolls was the excavation of the building complex immediately below the caves on the plateau. Numismatic evidence has shown that the complex flourished from circa 135 BCE to 68 CE, interrupted only by the earthquake of 31 BCE. Similar conclusions resulted from carbon dating of the cloth wrappings. It is certain, then, that the scrolls once constituted the library of a sect that occupied the Qumran area from after the Maccabean Revolt of 166-164 BCE until the great revolt against Rome of 66-74 CE.

The Scrolls. The scrolls can be divided into three main categories: biblical manuscripts, apocryphal compositions, and sectarian documents.

Fragments of every book of the Hebrew scriptures have been unearthed at Qumran, with the sole exception of the *Book of Esther*. Among the more important biblical scrolls are the two *Isaiah* scrolls (one is complete) and the fragments of

Leviticus and *Samuel* (dated to the third century BCE). William Albright and Frank Moore Cross have detected three recensional traditions among the scrolls at Qumran: Palestinian; Alexandrian; and Babylonian.

By far the most interesting materials are the writings of the sect that inhabited Qumran. Numerous smaller texts throw light on mysticism, prayer, and sectarian law. In recent years, many of these texts have not yet been published or are still awaiting thorough study.

The Sect and Its Beliefs. The Qumran sect saw itself as the sole possessor of the correct interpretation of the Bible. The sect believed that the messianic era was about to dawn and lived a life of purity and holiness on the shore of the Dead Sea.

The sect was organized along rigid lines. There was an elaborate initiation procedure, lasting several years, during which members were progressively received at the ritually pure banquets of the sect. All legal decisions of the sect were made by the sectarian assembly, and its own system of courts dealt with violations and punishments of the sectarian interpretation of Jewish law. New laws were derived by ongoing inspired biblical exegesis.

Dominant scholarly opinion has identified the Dead Sea sect as the Essenes described in the writings of Philo Judaeus and Josephus Flavius of the first century CE. Indeed, there are many similarities between this group and the sect described by the scrolls.

In many details, however, the Dead Sea Scrolls do not agree with these accounts of the Essenes. If, indeed, the Dead Sea community was an Essene sect, perhaps it represented an offshoot of the Essenes who themselves differ in many ways from those described by Philo and Josephus. A further difficulty stems from the fact that the word *essene* never appears in the scrolls and that it is of unknown meaning and etymology.

The contribution of the biblical scrolls to our understanding of the history of the biblical text and versions is profound. We now know of the fluid state of the Hebrew scriptures in the last years of the Second Temple. With the help of the biblical scrolls from Masada and the Bar Kokhba caves, we can now understand the role of local texts, the sources of the different ancient translations of the Bible, and the process of standardization of the scriptures that resulted in the Masoretic text.

In the years spanned by the Dead Sea Scrolls, the text of the Hebrew scriptures was coming into its final form, the background of the New Testament was in evidence, and the great traditions that would constitute rabbinic Judaism were taking shape.

BIBLIOGRAPHY

An excellent introduction is Yigael Yadin's *The Message of the Scrolls* (New York, 1957). The archaeological aspect is discussed thoroughly in Roland de Vaux's Schweich Lectures of 1959, *Archaeology and the Dead Sea Scrolls* (London, 1973). Important scholarly studies are Frank Moore Cross's *The Ancient Library of Qumran and Modern Biblical Studies*, rev. ed. (Garden City, N. Y., 1961), and Géza Vermès's *The Dead Sea Scrolls: Qumran in Perspective* (Philadelphia, 1981). The theology of the Qumran sect is studied in Helmer Ringgren's *The Faith of Qumran*, translated by Emilie T. Sander (Philadelphia, 1963). On the relationship to Christianity, see Matthew Black's *The Scrolls and Christian Origins* (London, 1961) and William S. LaSor's *The Dead Sea Scrolls and the New Testament* (Grand Rapids, Mich., 1972). Two studies of the importance of the scrolls for the history of Jewish law are my books *The Halakhah at Qumran* (Leiden, 1975) and *Sectarian Law in the Dead Sea Scrolls* (Chico, Calif., 1983).

LAWRENCE H. SCHIFFMAN

DEATH

Given the inevitability and definitiveness of death, it is not surprising that in all cultures, so far as our knowledge goes, the idea of dying has captured the thoughts and imagination of human beings. Yet from the point of view of history and anthropology the regarding of death as more important than life is far from common. The majority of religions firmly accent life here and now.

It is true that in a few cultures, the Indian ones among them, both life and death can be relativized. In a great number of cultures there seems to exist a connection, if not direct then, in any case, indirect, between the first coming of death into this world and the origin of both the countless imperfections that are part of the world of man and, more especially, evil.

In any case, death seems to be something whose existence requires explanation. According to the general belief, and practically all cultures conceive it in this manner, the appearance of death is the worst and most basic break in the original normality of human life as it was meant to be in principle.

Although many individuals die in peace, willing resignation in the face of death is rare as a motif in mythology. A myth from the Ivory Coast tells of the time when death was unknown and of its first coming. When Death approached, everyone fled into the bush except one old man who could no longer walk, and he asked his young grandson to make him a mat to lie upon. When Death came the child was still busy working on the mat, and so they both died.

Death as a natural or god-willed designation. A number of religions claim that death is the ordained and god-willed destiny of man. The Lugbara of East Africa, although they believe that practically all matters of importance are in the hands of the ancestors, consider death an act of God. In various parts of Indonesia we find the belief that human beings are somehow identical with the cattle of the gods. Whenever the gods in heaven slaughter an animal, a man on earth dies.

> ## Whenever the gods in heaven slaughter an animal, a man on earth dies.

In Greece we find resignation in the face of death. In a famous passage of the *Iliad* (5.146-149), Homer compares the generations of humans to the leaves on a tree: when the season of winter storms begins, leaves fall from the tree, and, in the same way, one human generation must make way for the next.

The concept of death as resulting from the will and power of a god may lead to religious problems. The tribes of Patagonia (South America), now practically extinct, believed that death was the work of the supreme god Waitaunewa, but they did not accept this belief meekly and passively. On the contrary, when one of their loved ones died they not only wailed but also protested: they accused the god of murder and avenged themselves by killing the animals that belonged to him. In this context it must be mentioned that the problems of death and of all suffering in the world are closely connected with theodicy, as is the problem of the origin of evil.

Death as the result of a divine death. There is a concept that man dies because a god or some other mythical being died first, and in this no question of fault or guilt is ascribed to human beings. The German anthropologist Adolf E. Jensen (1963) has given the name *dema* to a class of mythical beings who, by their deeds in a primeval time, originated human life and culture as we know it now; their deeds, however, ended with their own death. Some myths relate that the *dema* were murdered, but others say that they suffered a voluntary death. The life and death of the dema provide the divine paradigm for human experience, for man follows the pattern set by these mythical originators.

Death as the result of a divine conflict. Human death may also be seen as resulting from a conflict between gods. A myth from the island of Ceram in eastern Indonesia relates an argument between a stone and a banana regarding the way in which man should be created. The stone killed the banana, but on the next day the children of the banana were ready to continue the fight. In the end the stone fell into an abyss and admitted defeat, but with one condition: man would be as the bananas wanted him to be, but he must die just as a banana does.

Another variant of the quarrel between gods is the conflict between the Sun (or some other divinity) and the Moon concerning human life. In these stories Sun and Moon are, of course, mythical beings. A number of these myths can be found in Africa, each one connecting the destiny of man with that of the Moon. This type of myth can also be found all over the world, however, because speculation about the connection of the moon's phases with human life and death is nearly universal.

A myth from the Caroline Islands in the western Pacific states that in the beginning the life and death of man ran parallel to the phases of the moon, but then an evil spirit succeeded somehow in contriving that man should die and never wake up again.

Death as the result of a god's cheating or carelessness. Death sometimes is attributed to divine cheating. Here, of course, the well-known mythical figure of the trickster looms up. According to the myths of the Indian tribes of central California, Sedit, the trickster, personified by the coyote, brings death into the world through his intrigues.

In West Indian Voodoo religion Gèdè is the god of death as well as the trickster. The combination of the trickster and the god of death is apt, for the cruelest joke of the gods is that they have ordered creation in such a way that not only the possibility but even the inevitability of death is built into it, so that every human being must eventually die.

In other cases we find reports that death resulted from the carelessness or stupidity of some mythical being. A myth from the island of New Britain in the western Pacific belongs to a type more frequently found in Melanesia. It ascribes the coming of death to the stupidity of a messenger, rightly called To Purgo ("stupid one"), who is the wise and benevolent god's twin. Without any malice To Purgo confuses his message and pronounces death for man and everlasting life for the snake.

Death as the result of human shortcoming. In another category, death may be seen as having its origins in human nature. That is, it is believed to result from a human shortcoming.

In Africa we find a type of myth that explains the coming of death into the world by saying that during the night God proclaimed to all men the news of life without death, but because they slept on without troubling themselves about this divine revelation they missed the proclamation of their own eternal life. This myth presupposes a certain connection between sleep and death. This connection is, of course, widely recognized and remarked on, but only here and there is it related to the problem of the origin of death.

Death as the outcome of a wrong choice. Death can be viewed as the outcome of a wrong choice made by human beings themselves. The Holoholo, a subtribe of the Luba, say that God gave man the chance to choose between two nuts, one in each of his hands; one symbolized life and the other, death. Man, or, in this case, woman, chose the wrong hand, and so death became the destiny of all mankind, while the snake, which was also present at this scene, received the gift of unrestricted renewal of life.

The Ngala of the upper Kongo region explain the coming of death in a myth that tells how God offered a man working in the forest two bundles, a large one that contained a number of useful and pretty things such as knives and beads, and a small one that contained everlasting life. The man dared not decide on the spot which bundle to take, and so he went to the village to ask advice. In the meantime a few women came along, and God offered them the same choice. They unpacked the large bundle and found mirrors with which they could admire themselves and cloth from which they could make dresses, and so they chose the large bundle. In this way man failed to qualify for eternal life and was subject to death.

Death as the result of human guilt. As can be expected, a great number of myths cite human guilt as the cause of death. The anthropologist Paul Radin must have been mistaken when he wrote that nowhere except in the Bible has man been held responsible for the origin of death. This guilt, it is true, can be conceived of in a variety of ways.

Disobedience. A common motif is the belief that death was caused by man's disobeying God.

The best-known example of the coming of death as a punishment for disobedience is, of course, the biblical myth of Adam and Eve in Paradise as told in the *Book of Genesis.* Some deduce from this story that God had originally intended to give Adam and Eve everlasting life, although this is not expressly mentioned.

Among the Carib of Guyana a myth can be found that tells how the creator-god Pura wanted to give eternal life to man, but because man disobeyed the god's instructions on how to attain this goal, all men became subject to death. Among the Lamba of Zambia is a myth that tells how man received a number of small bundles from God. The messengers to whom the bundles were given were forbidden to inspect them: they had to be handed unopened to the "chief on earth." The messengers, overcome by curiosity, failed to obey and opened the bundles, one of which contained death.

Sexual offense. The guilt that brings about death may be a sexual offense committed by man, but this transgression may also be projected back into the world of the gods. Thus, according to a myth of the Dogon, death came into existence as a result of primordial incest committed by the god Ogo. In Africa we find a myth that tells about God forbidding the first human beings to copulate. When they disobeyed this injunction, death came into existence. A myth from the Baiga of central India connects the beginning of death with the first human copulation. A Baiga man and woman had congress in the forest, a thing unknown before. The earth started to tremble, and they died immediately. Since then, death has formed

part of human life. And the Tucano Indians of Colombia ascribe the first death to lasciviousness.

Killing. The first death is also ascribed to a killing, often considered a murder. In many cases a mythical being is killed in the primeval time related in myth. A myth from the Mentawai Islands, near Sumatra, relates that the first human beings came forth from a bamboo plant and immediately fled into the bush. There they lived a miserable existence until the god Siakau took pity on them and taught and helped them. Later the god changed himself into an iguana, a sacred animal on these islands, and in this shape he was accidentally killed by two of the four original human beings. They had not recognized Siakau in his new shape and had wrongly accused him of destroying their gardens. Their punishment was instant death. The other two persons fled, but death had entered the world forever.

Death as a desire of man. The last category of myth we must consider recounts how man desired death because he did not want to prolong a life that had become burdensome. Abrahamsson (1951) has drawn attention to African myths of this type, according to which man, plagued by disease or suffering from the indignities of old age and, thus, weary of life, wants to die and so calls out for death to come to him. A myth of the Mum of Cameroon relates that God could not understand why so many men became cold and stiff, but Death (here personified) showed him how the old and miserable people cried out for release from this existence. The Ngala tell that man asked for death because there was so much evil and unhappiness in the world. The Nuba of the upper Nile connect the death wish with the fact of overpopulation.

Conclusion. As to the question of the age of the myths on the origin of death, a general answer, in my opinion, cannot be given. We can assume with a modicum of certainty that, given the primary importance of death for all human beings, the search for its origin originated in a very early phase of human culture.

BIBLIOGRAPHY

Abrahamsson, Hans. *The Origin of Death: Studies in African Mythology.* Uppsala, 1951. Authoritative treatment of the African myths on the origin of death.

Baumann, Hermann. *Schöpfung und Urzeit des Menschen im Mythus der afrikanischen Völker.* Berlin, 1936. One chapter treats the origin of death.

Bendann, Effie. *Death Customs* (1930). Reprint, London, 1969. A general introduction.

Boas, Franz. "The Origin of Death." *Journal of American Folk-Lore* 30 (1917): 486-491. First special treatment of the Amerindian myths on the origin of death.

Dangel, R. "Mythen vom Ursprung des Todes bei den Indianern Nordamerikas." *Mitteilungen der anthropologischen Gesellschaft in Wien* 58 (1928): 341-374. Treats the Amerindian myths on the origin of death.

Jensen, Adolf E. *Hainuwele: Volkserzählungen von der Molukken-Insel Ceram.* Frankfurt, 1939. The myth of Hainuwele.

Jensen, Adolf E. *Myth and Cult among Primitive Peoples.* Chicago, 1963. Among other things, contains a thorough treatment of the dema.

Lang, Andrew. *La mythologie.* Paris, 1886. First classification of myths on the origin of death.

Muensterberger, Warner, *Ethnologische Studien an indonesischen Schöpfungsmythen.* The Hague, 1939. Contains material on the origin of death.

O'Flaherty, Wendy Doniger. *The Origins of Evil in Hindu Mythology.* Berkeley, 1976. Also treats the origin of death.

Preuss, Konrad Theodor. *Tod und Unsterblichkeit im Glauben der Naturvölker.* Tübingen, 1930. Still a useful introduction, although dated in regard to theory.

TH. P. VAN BAAREN

DECALOGUE

[*See article* New Testament.]

DEITY

The Polysemy of the Word. *Deity* is a word with a diversity of meanings. It is an ambiguous and often polemical word.

Ambiguity. The word *deity* is ambiguous. It is not a proper name. It is not even a common name, since its possible referents are hardly homogeneous. It is the product of many and heterogeneous abstractions. Most names referring to divine beings or the divine were originally common names singled out in a peculiar way. What was general became specific, concrete, and, like a single being, evocative of emotion. Thus *Allah* probably comes from al-illah, that is, "the God." *Ñinyi* or *Nnui*, the name for God among the Bamum of Cameroon, means "he who is everywhere"—and thus is at once concrete and elusive. *Yahveh* means "he who is" (or "he who shall be"), which becomes being *par excellence* for Christian Scholasticism. *Siva* means "auspicious, benign, kind"—what for the Saivas represents the highest symbol of the deity stripped of any attribute.

At any rate, *deity* is not identical with *god.* One does not believe in deity in the individualized sense in which one may believe in God. Yet one may accept that there is something referred to by the word *deity.* The referent will always retain a certain mystery and show certain features of freedom, infinity, immanence, transcendence, or the like. For others, this mysterious entity becomes the highest example of superstition, primitivism, unevolved consciousness, and a pretense for exploiting others under the menace of an awesome and imaginary power. The ambiguity of the word is great.

Polemical usage. Deity is not only polemical in regard to a personal conception of God. It is polemical also as a sym-

bol of the political use of the divine. We should not forget the wars of religion. Deity has been all too often the cause of strife and war, sometimes under the guise of peace.

Relativity. From the perspective of a sociology of knowledge, the modern use of the word *deity* could be interpreted as the Western effort to open up a broader horizon than that of a monotheistic God but without breaking continuity with tradition.

We may draw two opposing conclusions from the paradoxical fact that this word denotes both the most communicable and the most exclusive aspects of the "divine" reality: everything that is shares a divine character, and nothing—no thing—that is can be said to embody or exhaust the divine, not even the totality of those things that are. In sum: the word says everything, every thing, and nothing, no thing. One legitimate conclusion from this ambiguity may be that one should avoid the word altogether or speak of deities in the plural as special superhuman (divine) entities.

Yet, because of its polysemic nature, this word may become a fundamental category for the study and understanding of religion. The subject matter of religion would then be related to deity, and not just to God or to gods. Polysemy does not need to mean confusion. It means a richness of meanings, a variety of senses. *Deity* could then become a true word, that is, a symbol not yet eroded by habit, rather than a univocal concept.

The Structure of Deity. We must try to make sense of the ideas and experiences humankind has had on the subject. For this we must attempt to understand the context in which the problem has been put. This leads us to distinguish between the methods that can be employed to elucidate the question and the horizons within which the problem of deity is set. The main methods are theological, anthropological, and philosophical. These methods are all interrelated, and distinguishing them is really a question of emphasis. The possible horizons of the problem consist of the presuppositions that we make about what we are looking for when we set about asking about deity and its origins.

Horizons. In order to understand what kind of deity we are talking about, it is essential to reflect on the horizon of the question. Is the deity to be conceived as absolute consciousness? As a supreme being? As the perfect, ideal individual? Or as the creator of the world? In short, where do we situate the divine? Where is the locus of deity? The horizons are, of course, dependent on the culture of any given time or place. Viewed structurally, however, the function of deity always seems to provide an ultimate point of reference. Cosmology, anthropology, and ontology offer us the three main horizons.

Meta-cosmological. Deity is here related to the world. Certainly, it may be identified as immanent to the world, or more probably transcendent to it, but deity is the deity of the world, and the world is the deity's world. What type of function or functions deity is supposed to perform and what kind of relation it has with the world are left to the different cosmologies and traditions. In any case, deity is a kind of pole to the world, a prime mover that sets the world into motion, sustains it, directs it, and even creates it.

Meta-anthropological. Here deity is seen as the symbol for the perfection of the human being. The notion of deity does not come so much as the fruit of reflection on the cosmos or as an experience of its numinous character as it does from anthropological self-awareness. Deity is the fullness of the human heart, the real destiny of man, the leader of the

> **Deity is the fullness of the human heart, the real destiny of man, the leader of the people, the beloved of the mystics, the lord of history, the full realization of what we really are.**

people, the beloved of the mystics, the lord of history, the full realization of what we really are. This deity does not need to be anthropomorphic, although it may present some such traits. Deity is here *atman-brahman*, the fully divinized man, the Christ, the purusa, or even the symbol of justice, peace, and a happy society. Here deity may be considered immanent or transcendent, identified with or distinguishable from man, but its functions are related to the human being. It is a living, loving, or menacing deity, inspiring, caring, punishing, rewarding, and forgiving.

Meta-ontological. Here we encounter the problem of the nothingness of deity, the radical apophatism developed in many traditions. The most salient feature here is immanence and transcendence, the two belonging together. Deity is the immanence and transcendence inserted in the heart of every being.

We should hasten to add that these three horizons are not mutually exclusive. Many a thinker in many a tradition has tried to elaborate a conception of deity embracing all three. Within Hinduism, for instance, *nirguna brahman* would correspond to the third type, *saguna brahman* to the first, and *isvara* might be the personal deity of the devotee. Similarly, the Christian Scholastic tradition would like to combine God, the prime mover (the first type), with the personal God of the believers (the second type), and that of the mystics (the third type). How far all three can be reduced to an intelligible unity is a philosophical and theological problem that different traditions try to solve in different ways.

Methods. We may now turn to the different methods used in the attempt to understand deity. Whatever deity may be, it is neither a sensible nor an intelligible thing, is neither a visible thing nor a mere thought.

So, how do we come to a pre-understanding of deity? We may receive it from tradition. In the case of a direct mystical experience there is not a pre-understanding but an immediate insight that the mystic afterward explicates in terms of the culture in which he or she lives, and so ultimately it comes to the same thing. The mystic needs a post-understanding, as it were, in terms of his or her time and culture, which amounts to an initial pre-understanding for all the others. The pre-understanding of deity is, therefore, a traditional datum. Now, there are three main attitudes toward this datum. If one accepts it as a starting point and proceeds to a critical effort at understanding it, this is the *theological method.* [*See* Theology.] The theologian tries to clarify something from within. If one tries to bracket one's personal beliefs and attempts to decipher the immense variety of opinions throughout the ages regarding the idea of deity, this is the *phenomenological method.* The datum is then the sediment of the history of human consciousness. Finally, if one reflects on one's own experience, enriched as much as possible by the thoughts of others, this is the *philosophical method.*

Theological. The theological method begins with an accepted datum: there exists a world of the gods, the world of deity. We will therefore have to clarify and eventually justify the *raison d'être* of such a world, but we do not necessarily have to prove its existence. In short, the origin of the idea of deity is the deity itself—whatever this deity may be. This forms the core of the so-called ontological argument and of any religious enterprise that wants to clarify the nature of deity. Deity could not be known if it did not exist. The theological problem here consists of determining what kind of existence this is. When Thomas Aquinas, for instance, ends each one of his five proofs for the existence of God by saying "and that is what all call God," he shows his theological method of clarifying the existence of something that we already call God. The deity was already there, certainly, as an idea, but also as a reality that hardly anyone doubted, although its rationality had to be demonstrated and its existence verified as real and not merely apparent.

Phenomenological. The phenomenological method could be described as morphological, or even historical, since it is used in the new science of religions, often called the history of religions.

Use of the phenomenological method uncovers an immense variety of types of deity. We find the so-called animistic conception of deity as an all-pervading and living force animating everything that there is. We find so-called polytheism, the presence of many "gods" as supernatural entities with different powers and functions. We find so-called deism as the belief in a supreme being, probably a creator, who is afterward passive in relation to his creation, a notion that excludes any kind of specially revealed god. We find monotheism of the type of the Abrahamic religions, religions of a living, provident, and creator god. We find the various theisms that modify the exclusiveness of the monotheistic model, and pantheism, the identification of the deity with the universe. We also find all sorts of atheisms, as reactions to theism and especially to monotheism. And of course we find a number of distinctions and qualifications of these broad notions that are intended to respond to the demands of reason or answer difficulties raised by particular or collective experiences.

Philosophical. The philosophical method proceeds differently, although, in ways, not totally disconnected from those of the previous ones. Without entering into the discussion of whether the "living God" is the actus purus or whether one can fall in love with the prime mover, the quintessence of the philosophical method consists in the willingness to question everything.

When this ultimate locus is considered to be being, the question of deity turns out to be what Heidegger calls an "onto-theology," a reflection on the being of beings. Here, the philosophical method meets the historical controversy. Is deity the highest being or is it being as such? In the latter case it cannot be a supreme being. The ontological difference is not the theological one. The history of religions puts the same question by simply asking how the supreme being

> **Deity is visible only in its alleged manifestations—and there is no way to make visible the manifesting power beyond what is manifested.**

is related to the entire reality. This polarity between being and supreme being permeates most of the conceptions about deity. We could phrase it as the polarity between the deity of the intellectuals (being) and the deity of the people (supreme being).

Is deity being *(Sein, sat, esse)* or the supreme being *(höchstes Seiendes, paramatman, ens realissimum)*? One can think about the first, but one cannot worship it. One can adore the second and trust in it, but this God cannot be reasoned about; it is corroded by thinking.

If the philosophical locus of the deity is the ultimate question, we may find as many conceptions of deity as there are ultimate questions. Thus the many and varied answers. The diversity of religions can also be explained from this perspective. Religions give different answers to ultimate questions, and the questions themselves are different. But philosophical reflection may ask still further: what is it that prompts man to ask the ultimate question, whatever this question may be? Why is man an asking being, ever thirsty for questions?

The Texture of Human Consciousness of Deity. In view of the many opinions about deity we have to rely upon the one factor that is common to them all, namely the human consciousness that uses the word *deity* or its homeomorphic equivalents. Deity has this one constitutive feature: it is disclosed to us in an act of consciousness that, in spite of having a transcendent intentionality, has no verifiable referent outside of consciousness. The reference of the word *deity*, in fact, is neither visible nor intelligible, and yet every culture in the world witnesses to the fact that men constantly speak about a "something" that transcends all other parameters. We have then to rely on the cultural documents of the past and the present that witness to this *tertium* we call *deity*.

We rely on the fact that people have meant something when using this word or its equivalents. The analysis of deity is based therefore not on the empirical presence of the object nor on the immediate evidence of thought but on tradition in its precise and etymological meaning, that is, on some cultural good that is being transmitted to us.

Deity is visible only in its alleged manifestations—and there is no way to make visible the manifesting power beyond what is manifested.

Nor is deity intelligible. It would cease to be divine if we could grasp its meaning as something belonging to the human or worldly sphere. The divine is not subject to observation, nor can there be a science of the divine. Thus Meister Eckhart says that we must transcend not only the things of the imagination but even those of the understanding.

Conclusion. Whether the word *deity* means a plurality of divine beings, absolute consciousness, perfect happiness, the supreme being, a divine character of beings, or being as such, thought about deity has no referent. At the same time it seems to be one of the most unvarying and powerful factors in human life throughout ages and across cultures. Words referring to deity or its homeomorphic equivalents are unique. Philosophy avers that the intentionality of human consciousness, while pointing outside itself, cannot show in the realm of the sensible or the intelligible the referent of this intentional act. In a word, there is no object that is deity. Either human consciousness transcends itself, or thought about deity is an illusion, albeit a transcendental illusion of historical reality.

Is the word *deity* broad enough to include all the types of the mystery we have tried to describe? We know that its original field is the cosmological, but we have also noted that we distinguish it from the name *God* precisely to allow it other horizons.

The word *deity* may partially fulfill this role on one essential condition: that it strip itself of all connotations coming from a single group of civilizations. This amounts to saying that it cannot have any specific content, because any attribute, be it being, nonbeing, goodness, creatorship, fatherhood, or whatever, is meaningful only within a given cultural universe (or a group of them). *Deity* becomes then an empty symbol to which different cultures attribute different concrete qualifications, positive or negative. *Deity* would then say something only when translated into a particular language.

BIBLIOGRAPHY

Balthasar, Hans Urs von. *Herrlichkeit*. Einsiedeln, 1961. A treatment of the topic from the perspective of a theology of aesthetics.

Balthasar, Hans Urs von. *Theodramatik*. Einsiedeln, 1978.

Castelli, Enrico, ed. *L'analyse du langage théologique: Le nom de Dieu*. Paris, 1969. Offers a philosophical perspective.

Eliade, Mircea. *A History of Religious Ideas*, vol. I, *From the Stone Age to the Eleusinian Mysteries*. Chicago, 1978.

Gilson, Étienne. *God and Philosophy*. New Haven, 1941.

Heidegger, Martin. *Holzwege*. Frankfurt, 1950. Offers distinctions between concepts of God, deity, the sacred, and salvation.

James, E. O. *The Concept of Deity*. London, 1950. A historical treatment.

Kumarappa, Bharatan. *The Hindu Conception of the Deity as Culminating in Ramanuja*. London, 1934.

Owen, H. P. *Concepts of Deity*. New York, 1971.

Panikkar, Raimundo. *The Unknown Christ of Hinduism*. Rev. & enl. ed. New York, 1981. See pages 97-155.

Panikkar, Raimundo. *Il silenzio di Dio: La risposta del Buddha*. Rome, 1985. An analysis of the Buddhist idea of the emptiness of deity.

Pettazzoni, Raffaele. "The Supreme Being: Phenomenological Structure and Historical Development." In *The History of Religions: Essays in Methodology*, edited by Mircea Eliade and Joseph M. Kitagawa. Chicago, 1959.

Pöll, Wilhelm. *Das religiöse Erlebnis und seine Strukturen*. Munich, 1974. See the chapter entitled "Der göttlich-heilige Pol." A positive analysis of the divine/sacred from a psychological perspective.

Schmidt, Wilhelm. *Der Ursprung der Gottesidee: Eine historisch-kritische und positive Studie*. 12 vols. Munster, 1912-1955. A response to the evolutionary hypothesis concerning the concept of deity.

RAIMUNDO PANIKKAR

DEMONS

An Overview

Demons are spirits or spiritual beings, numinous powers both benevolent and malevolent in nature. In Classical Greek culture, *daimon* may refer to a lesser divinity, a deified hero, a tutelary or protective spirit, an attendant, ministering, or indwelling spirit, or in some cases the genius of a place (e.g., the portal, the hearth, the cattle pen). In Greek mythology, *daimones* are superhuman in that their natures are superior to that of humans, but they are not supernatural because, like humans, their natures are created by God (both evil and good spirits, demons and devils as well as angels).

Tribal Cultures. Among tribal peoples in various geographic locales, it is commonly held that evil spirits or demons are nothing more than the spirits of deceased ancestors who are hostile and malevolent to living humans. In order to neutralize, if not destroy, the vicious powers of such creatures, elaborate rites of ancestor worship and exorcism have been developed in cultures ranging from the simplest primal societies in Australia and Tierra del Fuego at the southernmost tip of South America to the most advanced, including Hinduism, Buddhism, Christianity, and Islam.

Another category of demons in nonliterate cultures assumes a nonanthropomorphic guise—usually that of animals, birds, or sea creatures.

Hinduism. In the Vedas, the most ancient scriptures of Hinduism, the class of demonic beings is divided between the lower deities who, though not fully divine, are largely benevolent to humanity and are localized in the sky (the highest heaven or the high regions of the sky) and the demonic and fiendish hosts who inhabit the earth, caves, and subterranean caverns; these latter demons strike human beings and animals with diseases, poverty, and death and haunt the spirits of mortals even after death.

The pages of the Hindu epics (*Mahabharata* and *Ramayana*) are littered with images of semidivine, angelic, and demonic creatures of a dizzying variety. There are, first of all, the *locii spiritii*, sprites of rivers, mountains, trees, groves, and numerous species of vegetation. Then, there is a diverse array of animal divinities who embody demonic powers (both beneficial and detrimental to humans). In addition, the canvas of Hindu mythology is populated with an impressive variety of other superhuman creatures, among which are *pretas*, ghosts or spirits of deceased ancestors; *pitrs*, the spirits of the fathers; *bhutas*, spirits per se that are generally associated with ghosts, ghouls, and goblins in cremation grounds, with a predominant tendency toward evil; and *raksasas*, *yatudhanas*, and *pisacas*, a triad of spirits, not precisely evil but not sufficiently divine to be regarded as gods.

Buddhism. At the level of popular religion, Buddhism inherited many of the formulaic features as well as the *dramatis personae* of the demonology of Hinduism. In Buddhism, sentient beings are divided into six types: gods, humans, *asuras*, animals, hungry ghosts *(pretas)*, and denizens of hell. In both traditions, beings are subject to rebirth in all of these forms as they undergo the vicissitudes of karmically determined existence.

In Buddhism, the archfiend is Mara, conceived to be either an antigod *(asura)* or a member of the lower order of gods *(deva)*. Mara confronts Gautama on the night preceding his enlightenment with a series of temptations (hedonistic pleasure, power, and wealth, as well as threats of physical destruction) to prevent him from gaining the power of omniscience.

Whereas the worship of evil spirits and demonic forces occupies a minor status in the teachings of the Buddha and the earliest strata of the Buddhist tradition, the fact remains that the masses continued the ancient customs of spirit worship as a necessary and integral part of their religious lives. References to demons in the earliest texts are few in number and quite unsystematic in their treatment. Citations of belief in spirits of all kinds are more numerous in the birth stories (Jatakas) of the Buddha; however the term *yaksa* (Pali, *yakkha*) is used more frequently than *bhuta*, the more customary term in the later literature.

In its simplest form, the Buddha's message is composed of the doctrines of the Four Noble Truths and the Eightfold Path along with a wealth of psychological and ethical instructions for the disciple seeking salvation. Although the Buddha did not deny the existence of good and evil spirits, he viewed them as he did the *devas*—as existent and active throughout the universe but as impotent to affect a person's search for liberation, whether for good or ill. Indeed, it might be argued that the primary objective of the Buddha *dharma* is to free the person from moral and psychological servitude to the kinds of mental states in which one feels either threatened or blessed by invisible beings.

Judaism. In its demonology as in other areas of its theology, Judaism inherited a number of concepts and names of individual demons (e.g., Bel and Leviathan) from its Mesopotamian and Canaanite predecessors. In the earlier books of the Hebrew scriptures, before the Babylonian exile in 587/6 BCE, the belief in demons and evil spirits plays a marginal role in the life of Israel. While these books do not deny the existence of demonic powers, such beings are placed under the suzerainty of the absolute will of Yahveh (*Dt.* 4:35). It was only after the biblical writers came under the influence of foreign ideas, especially the Persian dualistic systems of Zoroastrianism and Zurvanism, that we find a clear separation of powers and personages into good and evil sectors and the solidification of the concept of evil spirits into a distinct company of malicious beings. In rabbinic Judaism, the demons appear prominently only in the *aggadah* (folkloristic rabbinic thought), rarely, if at all, in the *halakhah* (learned tradition).

In the Hebrew scriptures, all spiritual beings, both benign and malevolent, are controlled by the power of God (*2 Sm.* 24:16-17). Even Satan himself is conceived of as a servant or messenger of God, commissioned to test men's loyalty to God (*Jb.* l:6-12, 2:1-7) or to prosecute them for transgressions before the divine tribunal (*Zec.* 3:1-2). However, the imprint of popular Israelite religion upon the biblical literature is attested to by the occurrence of such entities as *shedim* (evil spirits, *Dt.* 32:17), which orthodox writers related to the pagan gods *se'irim* (*Lv.* 17:7) or *lilit* (*Is.* 34:14). These pagan gods traditionally have been depicted as satyrs, as were the *sa'ir* ("hairy ones," *Is.* 13:21).

Christianity. Demonology in the New Testament is a complex amalgamation of historical patterns from other, neighboring traditions that preceded enriched by the emer-

gence of novel concepts unique to Palestine during the first decades of the Christian era.

The general framework for the growth of the Christian concepts of demons was largely inherited from Jewish apocalyptic literature of the second and first centuries BCE. According to *1 Enoch* 6, the angels or offspring of heaven cohabited with the irresistible daughters of men (cf. *Gn.* 6:1-4) and produced a race of giants who in turn gave birth to a

> **. . . it was left to the New Testament writers to synthesize this company of evil spirits into a single satanic figure who served as the leader. . . .**

bevy of evil spirits. Because the primary motive for this illicit congress was the satisfaction of sexual desire, lawlessness and warfare spread throughout the world. At this stage, mention is made of numerous devils, but it was left to the New Testament writers to synthesize this company of evil spirits into a single satanic figure who served as the leader of the demonic troops or fallen angels.

It was also at this same time that Satan came to be identified with the serpent in the Garden of Eden who provoked the fall of mankind through the sins of the first couple and, as a result, was himself expelled from heaven.

Jesus, the gospel writers, and the apostle Paul seem to have adopted wholesale the Jewish understanding of the nature and activities of evil spirits. In keeping with his general theological orientation, Paul represents Satan and the evil powers as operating within a cosmic theater—in the air (*Eph.* 2:2), on the earth, and in the underworld. He also pictures Satan as the personified ruler over the kingdom of evil as well as the force to be embodied in the Antichrist who is expected to precede the second coming of Christ at the end of the world.

The *Book of Revelation* contains a rich and complicated demonology informed by Jewish apocalyptic, Babylonian, and Persian sources. The book dwells primarily upon the final struggle between the forces of good and evil in the Battle of Armageddon and the ultimate triumph of the forces of God.

Islam. From the time of the Qur'an onward, the universe was populated with a diverse array of good and evil spirits exercising direct and formative influence upon the affairs of humanity. One group of such beings, known as *jinn*, possess ethereal or luminescent bodies and are intelligent and invisible. Proud, rebellious creatures in both the human and animal kingdoms, the *jinn* were created from unsmoking fire. They are related in a rather amorphous manner to both the *shaitans* and to the personage Shaiyan (Satan) as well as to a figure addressed as Iblis (a personal name of the devil).

While the *jinn* appear in a majority of orthodox Muslim writings as shadowy, ephemeral creatures who, at most, make life difficult for humans, the shaitans actively assist Iblis in maintaining his position of rebellion against God. They are aggressively involved in leading from God's law those persons who are already inclined to go astray. Orthodox Muslim writers debated questions pertaining to the existence, the nature, and the status of the jinn and formulated an elaborate system for the grading of the various angelic orders. Other writers, such as Ibn Khaldun, flatly denied their existence.

A Modern Assessment. With the spread of scientific and technological values and the propagation throughout the world of the idea of universal education based largely upon modern Western values, belief in heaven and hell and a postmortem existence in a realm apart from this one has receded progressively from the central core of beliefs of many religions throughout the world. On the other hand, belief in the existence of evil forces has far from disappeared altogether. Images of evil powers and the demonic have played a pervasive role in the contemporary arts, though largely in demythologized and depersonalized forms.

C. G. Jung, founder of the school of analytical psychology, offered an unsettling judgment concerning the presence of evil forces that he believed are, even now, at work within the human psyche:

> The daemonism of nature, which man had apparently triumphed over, he has unwittingly swallowed into himself and so become the devil's marionette. . . . When these products [demonic factors in the psyche] were dubbed unreal and illusory, their sources were in no way blocked up or rendered inoperative. On the contrary, after it became impossible for the daemons to inhabit the rocks, woods, mountains, and rivers, they used human beings as much more dangerous dwelling places.
>
> (*Collected Works*, Princeton, 1955, vol. 18, pp. 593-594)

BIBLIOGRAPHY

The entry "Demons and Spirits" in the *Encyclopaedia of Religion and Ethics*, edited by James Hastings, vol. 4 (Edinburgh, 1911), is a series of twenty articles pertaining to demonology in various cultures and is still worth consulting. Also valuable as a general reference is the *Larousse World Mythology*, edited by Pierre Grimal and translated by Patricia Beardsworth (New York, 1965). Gustav Davidson's *Dictionary of Angels*, Including the Fallen Angels (New York, 1967) is a mine of information. In additon to these general references, the following works can be recommended as sources of information on demons in various religious traditions.

Tribal Religions. Ronald M. Berndt and Catherine H. Berndt, The World of the First Australians, 2d ed. (Sydney, 1977). Verrier Elwin, ed. and trans., *Tribal Myths of Orissa* (New York, 1954). E. B. Tylor, *Primitive Culture*, vol. 1, *Religion in Primitive Culture* (1871; reprint, New York, 1970).

Judaism. Edward Langton, *Essentials of Demonology: A Study of Jewish and Christian Doctrines, Its Origin and Development* (London, 1949). "Demonology," in *The Encyclopedia of the Jewish Religion*, edited by R. J. Zwi Werblowsky and Geoffrey Wigoder (New York, 1966).

Christianity. John Hick, *Evil and the Love of God*, 2d ed. (London, 1977). Edward Langton, *Essentials of Demonology* (London, 1949). Eric Maple, *The Dark World of Witches* (London, 1962). Jeffrey B. Russell, *The Devil: Perceptions of Evil from Antiquity to Primitive Christianity* (Ithaca, N. Y., 1977).

Islam. D. Miguel Asín Palacios, *Islam and the Divine Comedy*, translated by Harold Sunderland (London, 1926). Jane I. Smith and Yvonne Haddad, *The Islamic Understanding of Death and Resurrection* (Albany, N. Y., 1981). A. S. Tritton, "Shaitan," in *The Encylopaedia of Islam* (Leiden, 1913-1938). Petrus Voorhoeve, "Djinn," and A. J. Wensinck, "Iblis," in *The Encyclopaedia of Islam*, new ed. (Leiden, 1960-).

Hinduism. W. Norman Brown, "The Rigvedic Equivalent for Hell," *Journal of the American Oriental Society* 61 (June 1941): 76-80. Ananda K. Coomaraswamy, "Angel and Titan: An Essay on Vedic Ontology," *Journal of the American Oriental Society* 55 (1935): 373-419.

Buddhism. James W. Boyd, *Satan and Mara: Christian and Buddhist Symbols of Evil* (Leiden, 1975). Bimala Churn Law, *The Buddhist Conception of Spirits*, 2d ed. (London, 1936). Melford E. Spiro, *Buddhism and Society: A Great Tradition and Its Burmese Vicissitudes*, 2d ed. (Berkeley, 1982). W. G. Weeraratne et al., "Bhuta," in *Encyclopaedia of Buddhism*, edited by G. P. Malalasekera (Colombo, 1971).

J. BRUCE LONG

DHARMA

Hindu Dharma

It is somewhat difficult to find a suitable South Asian word to represent what in English is known as "religion." Perhaps the most suitable would be the Sanskrit *dharma*, which can be translated in a variety of ways, all of which are pertinent to traditional Indian religious ideas and practices.

Types of Dharma. South Asian religious and legal systems have presented a variety of definitions of *dharma* and have seen different modes of its expression in the world and in society. Despite those variations, however, certain notions have remained consistent throughout South Asian history.

Dharma and rta in the Vedic period. The oldest sense of the word—which appears as early as the *Rgveda* (c. 1200 BCE), usually as *dharman*—signifies cosmic ordinance, often in connection with the sense of natural or divine law. As such, it is closely related conceptually to the Vedic notion of *rta*, the universal harmony in which all things in the world have a proper place and function.

In *Rgveda* 5.63.7, for example, the terms *rta* and *dharman* appear together in association with *vrata* ("vow, religious rite"): "You, Mitra and Varuna, through the creative powers of the gods, protect the ceremonial vows [*vrata*] with actions which uphold the world [*dharma*]. Through cosmic order [*rta*] you rule over the whole universe. You placed the sun in the heavens, like a shining chariot."

Varnasramadharma and svadharma. *Varnasrama-dharma* reflects a temporal dimension in orthodox Hindu normative thought. That is, just as a person gains rights and responsibilities while moving in this life from one *asrama* (stage of life) to the next, he claims certain privileges and accepts specific obligations according to his present *varna* (social class), which is determined by his actions in a previous life. Here we see a close ideological assumption connecting *dharma* and *karman*. [*See also* Karman.]

The term *svadharma* (particular responsibilities) in this last passage is not to be understood as referring to one's individual or chosen personal obligations. Rather, *svadharma* describes an impersonal generic ethical category which encapsulates one's duties determined by one's place in society. All farmers therefore have the same *svadharma*, but no farmer has the same *svadharma* as, say, a military officer.

Apaddharma. Some texts note that at times such as severe economic or natural calamity the norms determined by *varna* and *asrama* may be suspended so that society can survive the stress. For example, a priest may assume in those times the duties of a soldier, or a king may take up the responsibilities of a merchant, but they may do so only for the shortest possible time. Such a "duty determined by emergency" is known as *apaddharma*.

Sadharanadharma, samanyadharma, and sanatana-dharma. Most authoritative texts further assert that all people, regardless of their age and occupation, should observe some common moral obligations. Such rules are known as *sadharana* ("pertaining to everybody"), *samanya* ("common"), or *sanatana* ("eternal") in scope.

Sometimes, however, the obligations derived from *svadharma* directly contradict those imperatives of *sadharanadharma*, and a person trying to make an ethical decision must choose between opposing demands. What happens, for instance, when a priest must offer a blood sacrifice or a soldier must fight and kill the enemy? *Sadharanadharma* admonishes them to practice noninjury to all living beings, yet their respective *svadharmas* command them to kill.

Different religious traditions offered various responses to such a quandary. In general, those based most thoroughly in Brahmanic ideology maintained that in order to support cosmic and social harmony one must follow one's *svadharma* at all times. On the other hand, traditions influenced by the Vedanta, Buddhism, and Jainism taught that the demands of *sadharanadharma* always overrule those of *svadharma*.

Authoritative Sources of Dharma. Metaethical quandaries ("how does one know what is right?") appear in legal as well as in theological circles, and therefore questions of

authority arose even in systems revolving around the structures of *varnasramadharma*.

Sruti. According to orthodox thought the primary source for all knowledge, legal and otherwise, lies in the Vedic canon comprised of the Mantra Samhitas (liturgical hymns of the *Rgveda*, *Yajurveda*, *Samaveda*, and *Atharvaveda*), ceremonial instructions (Brahmanas), and philosophical treatises (Aranyakas and Upanisads). Together these texts constitute *sruti*, revealed eternal truths (literally, "that which is heard"). In all orthodox traditions *sruti* was the primary source of normative guidance.

Smrti. Not all questions of *dharma* could be resolved through reference to the timeless *sruti*. Thus, orthodox philosophers and legalists looked also to those more temporal literatures that were passed through the generations. These texts were known as *smrti*, "remembered" truths and injunctions. *Smrti* comprises the six Vedangas ("ancillary texts," collections of aphoristic treatises [*sutras*] that interpret the Veda), the epics *Mahabharata* (including the *Bhagavadgita*) and *Ramayana*, and the Puranas ("stories of old; sacred myths").

Sadacaradharma and sistacaradharma. Most classical texts admit that the example given by the honored members of society serves as a third means by which *dharma* may be discerned. If *sruti* and *smrti* both fail to elucidate a problem, then the community may look for guidance in the actions of people who "practice what is right" *(sadacara)*, or who generally "act according to [Vedic] instruction" *(sistacara)*.

"Conscience." The *Laws of Manu* and other Dharmasastras teach, finally, that when these three sources of *dharma* fail to enlighten an ethically perplexed person, then he or she has recourse to what is described as "that which satisfies the self" (*atmanas tustir; Laws of Manu* 2.6) or "that which pleases the self" (*priyam atmanah; Laws of Manu* 2.12). The vagaries of this category, however, are such that in legal terms personal feelings carry relatively little weight and are always superseded by *sruti*, *smrti*, and *sadacara*.

BIBLIOGRAPHY

Translations of Representative Primary Texts

Bühler, Georg, trans. *The Sacred Laws of the Aryas.* Sacred Books of the East, vol. 2 (Apastambha and Gautama Dharmasutras) and vol. 14 (Baudhayana and Vasistha Dharmasutras), edited by F. Max Müller. Oxford, 1879 and 1882.

Bühler, Georg, trans. *The Laws of Manu* (1886). Sacred Books of the East, vol. 25. Reprint, Delhi, 1964.

Edgerton, Franklin, trans. *Bhagavad-Gita* (1925). Reprint, Oxford, 1944.

Eggeling, Julius, trans. and ed. *The Satapatha-Brahmana.* 5 vols. Sacred Books of the East, vols. 12, 26, 41, 43, 44. Oxford, 1882-1900.

Gharpure, J. R., trans. *Hindu Law Texts: Yajñavalkya Smrti, with Commentaries by Vijñanesvara, Mitra-misra and Sulapani.* 7 vols. Bombay, 1936-1942.

Jolly, Julius, trans. *The Institutes of Visnu* (1880). Sacred Books of the East, vol. 7. Reprint, Delhi, 1962. A translation of the *Visnu Dharmasutra.*

Jolly, Julius, trans. *The Minor Law Books* (1889). Sacred Books of the East, vol. 33. Reprint, Delhi, 1965. A translation of the *Brhaspati and Narada Dharmasastras.*

Kane, P. V., ed. and trans. *Katyayana Dharmasastra.* Poona, 1933.

Keith, Arthur Berriedale, trans. *Rigveda Brahmanas: The Aitareya and Kausitaki Brahmanas of the Rigveda* (1920). Harvard Oriental Series, vol. 25. Reprint, Delhi, 1971.

O'Flaherty, Wendy Doniger, ed. and trans. *The Rig Veda: An Anthology.* Harmondsworth, 1982.

Whitney, William Dwight, trans. *Atharva-Veda Samhita.* 2 vols. (1905). Harvard Oriental Series, vols. 7 and 8. Reprint, Delhi, 1962.

Introductions and Critical Studies

Aiyangar, K. V. Rangaswami. *Some Aspects of the Hindu View of Life according to Dharmasastra.* Baroda, 1952.

Jayaswal, K. P. *Manu and Yajñavalkya: A Comparison and a Contrast; A Treatise on the Basic Hindu Law.* Calcutta, 1930.

Jolly, Julius. *Recht und Sitte.* Strassburg, 1896. Translated by Batakrishna Ghosh as *Hindu Law and Custom* (1928; reprint, Varanasi, 1975).

Kane, P. V. *History of Dharmasastra.* 2d ed. 5 vols. in 7. Poona, 1968-1975.

Lingat, Robert. *Les sources du droit dans le système traditionnel de l'Inde.* Paris, 1967. Translated by J. Duncan M. Derrett as *The Classical Law of India* (Berkeley, 1973).

Mees, Gualtherus H. *Dharma and Society.* The Hague, 1935.

O'Flaherty, Wendy Doniger, and J. Duncan M. Derrett. *The Concept of Duty in South Asia.* New Delhi, 1978.

Sen Gupta, Nares Chandra. *Sources of Law and Society in Ancient India.* Calcutta, 1914.

For a more extensive bibliography, see Ludo Rocher's "Droit hindou ancien," vol. E, part 6 of *Bibliographical Introduction to Legal History and Ethnology,* edited by John Gilissen (Brussels, 1965).

WILLIAM K. MAHONY

Buddhist Dharma and Dharmas

The pan-Indian term *dharma* (from the Sanskrit root *dhr,* "to sustain, to hold"; Pali, *dhamma*; Tib., *chos*) has acquired a variety of meanings and interpretations in the course of many centuries of Indian religious thought. *Dharma* can imply many different meanings in various contexts and with reference to different things.

General Usages. *Dharma* was and still is employed by all the religious denominations that have originated in India to indicate their religious beliefs and practices. In this sense, *dharma* refers broadly to what we would term "religion." *Dharma* also designates the universal order, the natural law or the uniform norm according to which the whole world *(samsara)* runs its course. Within the Buddhist context this universal order is coordinated in the doctrine of dependent origination *(pratitya-samutpada).* This rigorous natural law, which controls the sequence of events and the behavior and acts of beings, has no cause or originator. It is beginningless and functions of its own nature.

The shortest and yet the clearest exposition of *dharma* as the Buddha's word *(buddhavacana)* is epitomized in Sakyamuni's first sermon, when he "set in motion" (i. e., proclaimed) the wheel (lore) of *dharma*: the Four Noble Truths and Eightfold Noble Path. There is suffering and it has a cause that can be eliminated through the knowledge and practice of the path of *dharma* as summarized by the Eightfold Noble Path: right views, right conduct, and so forth. Another presentation of the same path is articulated within the basic trilogy of monastic practice of cultivating wisdom *(prajña)*, morality *(sila)*, and meditation *(dhyana).* Through wisdom one acquires a full vision of *dharma*, through morality one purifies all that obscures the vision of *dharma*, and through meditation one matures *dharma* within oneself and indeed transforms oneself into an epitome of *dharma*.

Technical Usages. Buddhism makes an emphatic and "dogmatic" statement that a "soul" *(atman)* as interpreted by non-Buddhist schools in India does not exist. By denying the existence of a soul as a permanent and unifying factor of a human entity it has removed all grounds for asserting the permanency of the human entity or the existence of any indestructible element therein. Having removed the notion of substance Buddhism has construed an explanation as to how this world functions. According to this explanation, the universe is seen as a flux of *dharmas*, the smallest elements or principles of which it consists, but this flux is not merely a flux of incoherent motion or change. On the contrary, the world evolves according to the strict law of dependent origination *(pratitya-samutpada).*

Dharmas are divided into conditioned *(samskrta)* and unconditioned *(asamskrta).* The conditioned *dharmas* (seventy-two in all) comprise all the elements of phenomenal existence *(samsara).* They are called conditioned because by their nature and in their flow they cooperate in and are subject to the law of causality; they conglomerate or cooperate in the production of life *(prthagjana).* The unconditioned elements (three in all) are those that are not subject to the law that governs phenomenal existence. *Dharmas* are also divided into those that are influenced or permeated by negative tendencies or depravities *(asrava;* in a moral sense, bad *karmas)* and those that are not under the influence of depravities *(anasrava;* morally, good *karmas).* By their nature the unconditioned *dharmas* must be classed among the *dharmas* that are not under the influence of depravities. We should recall here that the chief characteristic of *samsara* is motion or unrest, *duhkha*, and that of *nirvana* is tranquillity, *nirodha.* The *dharmas* can be also divided in relationship to the Four Truths. Here again we have a twofold division. The first two truths (unrest, *duhkha*, and its cause, *samudaya*) refer to the seventy-two *dharmas* that are permeated by depravities or that are conditioned. The two other truths (rest, *nirodha*, and the means to it, *marga*) refer to the three unconditioned *dharmas* that are always at rest *(nirodha)* and to the *dharmas* that are on the way *(marga)* to become extinguished *(nirodha)*.

Having described the general divisions I shall now proceed to list a set of three standard classifications within which individual *dharmas* are distributed. The first classification, which includes the conditioned *dharmas* alone, refers to their grouping as perceived in a sentient life. This classification divides *dharmas* into five aggregates or *skandhas*. Here we have (1) matter or body *(rupaskandha)*: eleven *dharmas*; (2) feelings, sensations, or emotions *(vedanaskandha)*: one

> **Through wisdom one acquires a full vision of *dharma*, through morality one purifies all that obscures the vision of *dharma*.**

dharma; (3) perceptions *(samjñaskandha)*: one *dharma*; (4) impulses or will-forces *(samskaraskandha)*: fifty-eight *dharmas*; (5) consciousness or mind *(vijñanaskandha)*: one *dharma*.

The second classification divides *dharmas* with reference to the process of cognition. Here we have the six sense organs *(indriya)* and the six sense objects *(visaya)* jointy called the "bases" or "foundations" *(ayatana)* of cognition. The six sense organs or internal bases are (1) sense of vision *(caksur-indriyayatana)*; (2) sense of hearing *(srotra-)*; (3) sense of smell *(ghrana-)*; (4) sense of taste *(jihva-)*; (5) sense of touch *(kaya-)*; and (6) consciousness or intellectual faculty *(mana-)*. The six sense objects or external bases are (7) color and form *(rupa-ayatana)*; (8) sound *(sabda-)*; (9) smell *(gandha-)*; (10) taste *(rasa-)*; (11) contact *(sprastavya-)*; and (12) nonsensuous or immaterial objects *(dharma-)*. The first eleven *ayatanas* have one *dharma* each; the immaterial objects comprise sixty-four *dharmas*.

The third classification groups *dharmas* in relationship to the flow *(santana)* of life that evolves within the threefold world *(kama-, rupa-,* and *arupya-dhatu)* as described by Buddhist cosmology. This group is divided into eighteen *dhatus*, or elements. It incorporates the previous division into the twelve bases, to which is added a corresponding set of six kinds of consciousness to the intellectual faculty. Thus we have (13) visual consciousness *(caksur-vijñanadhatu)*; (14) auditory consciousness *(srotra-)*; (15) olfactory consciousness *(ghrana-)*; (16) gustatory consciousness *(jihva-)*; (17) tactile consciousness *(kaya-)*; and (18) nonsensuous con-

sciousness *(mano-)*. Within this group the five sense organs and their five objects contain one *dharma* each (ten *dharmas* in all).

Now I shall list the sixty *dharmas* that are included in all three classifications *(skandha, ayatana,* and *dhatu)*. They are divided into two main groups: one group comprises forty-six associated *dharmas* or mental *dharmas (caittadharma)*, that arise from or in association with pure consciousness or mind *(citta-samprayuk-tasamskara)*; the second group comprises fourteen unassociated *dharmas*, that is to say, *dharmas* that can be associated neither with matter nor with mind *(rupa-citta-viprayukta-samskara)*.

The forty-six associated *dharmas* include ten mental *dharmas* that are present in a sentient life *(citta-mahabhumika)*: (1) feeling, (2) perception, (3) will, (4) contact, (5) desire, (6) comprehension, (7) memory, (8) attention, (9) aspiration, and (10) concentration; ten morally good *(kusala-mahabhumika) dharmas* that are present in favorable conditions: (11) faith, (12) courage, (13) equanimity, (14) modesty, (15) aversion to evil, (16) detachment from love, (17) detachment from hatred, (18) nonviolence, (19) dexterity, and (20) perseverance in good; six obscuring *(klesa-mahabhumika) dharmas* that enter the stream of a sentient life in unfavorable moments: (21) confusion (ignorance), (22) remissness, (23) mental dullness, (24) lack of faith, (25) indolence, and (26) addiction to pleasure; ten additional obscuring *(upaklesa-bhumika) dharmas* that may occur at different times: (27) anger, (28) hypocrisy, (29) maliciousness, (30) envy, (31) ill-motivated rivalry, (32) violence, (33) malice, (34) deceit, (35) treachery, and (36) self-gratification; two universally inauspicious *(akusala-mahabhumika) dharmas*: (37) irreverence, and (38) willful tolerance of offences; and eight *dharmas* that are called undetermined *(aniyata-bhumika)* or undifferentiated in the sense that they can have different moral implications: (39) remorse, (40) deliberation, (41) investigation, (42) determination, (43) passion, (44) hatred, (45) pride, and (46) doubt. All forty-six *dharmas* listed above cannot be associated with (or cofunction with) consciousness at the same time on the general principle that their inner inclinations are variously geared toward either good or evil.

The fourteen unassociated *dharmas* are (47) acquisition *(prapti)*, or the controlling force of an individual flux of life, (48) force *(aprapti)* that suspends some elements, (49) force of homogeneity of existence, (50) force that leads to trance, (51) force produced by effort to enter trance, (52) force that stops consciousness, thus effecting the highest trance, (53) force that projects life's duration, (54) origination, (55) duration, (56) decay, (57) extinction, (58) force that imparts meaning to words, (59) force that imparts meaning to sentences, and (60) force that imparts meaning to sounds.

BIBLIOGRAPHY

The *dharma* theory of the Sarvastivadins is systematically set forth in Vasubandhu's *Abhidharmakosa*, translated by Louis de La Vallée Poussin as *L'Abhidharmakosa de Vasuban-dhu*, 6 vols. (1923-1931; reprint, Brussels, 1971). Theodore Stcherbatsky's *The Central Conception of Buddhism and the Meaning of the Word "Dharma"* (1923; reprint, Delhi, 1970) is a lucid introduction to the topic. For the Theravada view, see especially *A Buddhist Manual of Psychological Ethics: Dhammasangani*, translated by C. A. F. Rhys Davids (London, 1923), a rendering of the first book of the Theravada Abhidharma. Ñyanatiloka's *Guide through the Abhidhamma Pitaka*, 3d ed., revised and enlarged by Ñyanaponika Thera (Colombo, 1957), is the single most useful guide to the study of the Theravada Abhidhamma. The reader will also find useful A. K. Warder's "Dharmas and Data," *Journal of Indian Philosophy* 1 (1971): 272-295.

TADEUSZ SKORUPSKI

DISCIPLES OF CHRIST

The Disciples of Christ is an American-born religious group formed in 1832 by the merger of the Christian movement led by Barton Stone with the "Reforming Baptists," headed by Thomas and Alexander Campbell. Stone was one of the leaders of the Kentucky revival at the turn of the nineteenth century. Distressed by Presbyterian opposition to the revival, in 1804 he and five other ministers left the church, announcing their plan to be "Christians only" in "The Last Will and Testament of the Springfield Presbytery."

Thomas Campbell came to America in 1807, having been a Presbyterian minister in Northern Ireland. Disturbed by the sectarian spirit of the American church, Campbell clashed with the synod, and in 1809 he was suspended from the ministry. Campbell and a few of his supporters almost immediately formed the Christian Association of Washington (Pennsylvania), and Campbell wrote a fifty-six page explanation of his views, called the *Declaration and Address*. Thomas Campbell's son, Alexander, arrived in America shortly after the publication of the *Declaration and Address*. Twenty-one years old at the time, Alexander Campbell immediately embraced his father's independent position.

Preaching similar pleas for Christian union, the Stone and Campbell movements sealed a remarkably successful union in 1832. The new church spread rapidly with the westward migration of population. By 1860, there were 200,000 members.

Two ideas undergird Disciples thought, both of them highly attractive amid the optimism on the American frontier in the 1830s. First was an emphasis on Christian union. Second was an appeal for the "restoration of the ancient order of things" as a means of attaining unity. The battle cry of the movement, stated in 1809 by Thomas Campbell, was "Where the Scriptures speak, we speak; and where the Scriptures are silent, we are silent."

While conceiving of themselves as a protest against sectarian division, the Disciples quickly became a part of the denominational competition in the American Midwest and South. Alexander Campbell's influence among the Baptists was particularly strong, and in some parts of the West, the Disciples devastated Baptist associations.

In spite of the facts that the Disciples were strongest in the border areas and that most of the church's leaders had urged moderation during the slavery controversy, Disciples were seriously divided by the Civil War. In 1863, northern Disciples passed a resolution of loyalty to the Union at the meeting of the American Christian Missionary Society, which had been formed in 1849. Southern Disciples were deeply angered. Although most Disciples argued that the church could not divide because it had no denominational apparatus, in the years after the Civil War northern and southern newspapers and other institutions became increasingly antagonistic. In the census of 1906 the most conservative wing of the movement (which was almost entirely southern) was identified separately and designated the Churches of Christ.

Although the tensions of the nineteenth century had clear sectional and sociological underpinnings, the debate also had a doctrinal focus. As it became ever more apparent that the hoped-for millennium of peace and unity was not imminent, conservative Disciples lost interest in Christian union as a practical goal, and liberal Disciples increasingly discarded legalistic restorationism as a means of attaining union. The most visible issues that divided churches were

> The new church spread rapidly with the westward migration of population. By 1860, there were 200,000 members.

support for the missionary society that had been founded in 1849 and the scripturality of the use of instrumental music in worship. By 1900, hundreds of conservative local congregations had separated from the movement as independent Churches of Christ.

In the early twentieth century the Disciples suffered a second major division and a slowing growth rate. A new generation of Disciples liberals, particularly a group associated with the University of Chicago, pressed for a more ecumenical view of the Disciples mission and a more liberal understanding of the scriptures. Finally, in the 1920s, the conservatives began withdrawing their support from Disciples organizations and in 1927 established the rival North American Christian Convention. These dissentient conservative congregations remained loosely associated in the Undenominational

Fellowship of Christian Churches and Churches of Christ. The more liberal wing of the movement adopted the name Christian Church (Disciples of Christ).

BIBLIOGRAPHY

The best general summary of Disciples history is William E. Tucker and Lester G. McAllister's *Journey in Faith* (Saint Louis, 1975). A sociological interpretation of Disciples history in the nineteenth century can be found in my books *Quest for a Christian America* (Nashville, 1966) and *The Social Source of Division in the Disciples of Christ* (Atlanta, 1973). A survey of the movement written by a leader of the conservative Christian churches is James D. Murch's *Christians Only* (Cincinnati, 1962). A Churches of Christ perspective can be found in Earl I. West's *The Search for the Ancient Order*, 2 vols. (Indianapolis, 1950). Three older works that remain significant are William T. Moore's *A Comprehensive History of the Disciples of Christ* (New York, 1909), and two books by Winfred E. Garrison, *Religion Follows the Frontier* (New York, 1931) and *An American Religious Movement* (Saint Louis, 1945).

DAVID E. HARRELL, JR.

DIVINITION

DIVINATION is the art or practice of discovering the personal, human significance of future or, more commonly, present or past events.

Much of science itself has evolved from forms of divination and may be said to continue certain aspects of it. Astronomy, for example, is deeply indebted to ancient Near Eastern and Hellenistic astrological researches; mathematics and physics were advanced by Indian, Pythagorean, and Arabic divinatory cosmological speculations; and several leading Renaissance scientists were inspired by the divinatory schemes of Qabbalah and Hermitism in their search for the moral harmonies and direction of the universe. Yet it would be incorrect to label divination a mere infantile science or pseudoscientific magic, for modern science and traditional divination are concerned with essentially distinct goals. Divination involves communication with personally binding realities and seeks to discover the "ought" addressed specifically to the personal self or to a group. Science, however, if faithful to its own axioms, cannot enunciate any "oughts" because of its methodological, cognitive, and moral neutrality: it only offers hypotheses about reality and is concerned with general statistical regularities, not with unique persons or events.

Basic Forms. Anything can be used to divine the meaning of events. It is very common to assign spontaneous and arbitrary meaning to signs or omens when one is deeply anxious about the outcome of a personal situation. But the cultural form of divinatory methods and signs is seldom entirely random: each one expresses a specific logic.

A full list of divinatory agents, therefore, would amount to a catalog of both nature and culture. H. J. Rose, in his article "Divination, Introductory and Primitive," in volume 4 of the *Encyclopaedia of Religion and Ethics* (Edinburgh, 1911), classifies the most common means used to obtain insight as follows: dreams (oneiromancy); hunches and presentiments; involuntary body actions (twinges, sneezes, etc.); ordeals; mediumistic possession; consulting the dead (necromancy); observing animal behavior (e.g., ornithomancy, interpreting the flight of birds); noting the form of entrails of sacrificial victims (extaspicy or haruspicy), or the victims' last movements before death; making mechanical manipulations with small objects such as dice, drawing long or short stalks from a bundle, and so on (sortilege); reading tea leaves (tasseography), or using playing cards (cartography), etc.; decoding natural phenomena (as in geomancy, palmistry, phrenology, or astrology); and—of course—"miscellaneous."

It would be more useful to establish what the indigenous theory of divination is, rather than to attempt to assay the states of mind actually experienced by diviners in different cultures and periods. The same conscious experience of heightened awareness can be interpreted in one culture as deep wisdom and in another as spirit possession. Under the influence of such interpretations, in fact, an individual diviner might permit himself to drift into a deeper mediumistic trance, or on the contrary strive toward a more intense lucidity. How a condition is interpreted influences the way it unfolds and realizes itself.

In general, we may distinguish three general types of divination, based on indigenous meanings: those based on the immediate context when interpreted by the spiritual insight of the diviner (intuitive divination); those based on spirit manipulation (possession divination); and those reflecting the operation of impersonal laws within a coherent divine order (wisdom divination).

Intuitive divination. Intuitive divination is perhaps the elementary form out of which, through various interpretations, the other two developed. It is seldom much stressed, although its distribution as hunches and presentiments is universal. The reliability of amateur intuitions is not usually considered very great, yet in many cultures extraordinary spiritual masters are often credited with this type of divinatory insight, which then has more prestige and credence than any other. For example, disciples of a *tsaddiq* or saintly master in Hasidic Judaism frequently claim that their master can look into a person's soul at first meeting and determine not only the past lives but also the future course of that person. Precisely the same claims are made for many Hindu gurus. These insights by the guru are regarded as far more reliable and authoritative than the various forms of wisdom divination common to India, and these in turn are more esteemed than folk mediumistic and possession divination methods.

Possession divination. Full divinatory possession of human beings may be of several theoretical forms: prophetic inspiration, shamanistic ecstasy, mystical illuminations and visions, and mediumistic or oracular trance. They differ according to the degree of ego awareness and lucidity, awareness of the ordinary world, and the theoretical recipient of the divinatory message. The prophets of the Bible seem to

> **For the mystical visionary, the entire ordinary world is eclipsed by the ecstatic revelations, and the mystic is the sole direct recipient of the communications.**

retain a lucid sense of themselves and the world as they exhort their audience, although they are gripped by an overmastering sense of the integral meaning of events as illuminated by God's presence. The recipient of this revelation of temporal meaning is both the prophet and the human community. In shamanistic trance the struggle between ego awareness and the spirits is often portrayed as being so intense that it forces a displacement of the shaman from this world. As recipient of the divinatory communications, the shaman may later report on his conversations to an assembled audience, or may permit the audience to eavesdrop on the actual interviews or even to be directly addressed by the spirits through his mouth, but in any case he remains self-possessed and afterward can recall everything that occurred. For the mystical visionary, on the other hand, the entire ordinary world is eclipsed by the ecstatic revelations, and the mystic is the sole direct recipient of the communications. The oracular medium, however, loses all awareness, it is said, and therefore often remains ignorant of the message that is communicated directly from the spiritual being to the audience.

Wisdom divination. The elaboration of divination systems based on a unified field of impersonal and universal processes that can be studied, harmonized with, and above all internalized by nonecstatic sages, is an important but rare development in the history of religion. It is most often found in complex civilizations that have been defeated by equally powerful cultures and therefore must integrate their own indigenous views with other perspectives. Wisdom divination is a syncretistic movement beyond specific cults, approaching the elemental ground from which all personal spirits and cultic gods as well as cultural groups arise. But the speculative effort must usually begin in court and priestly circles, for it depends on a cumulative effort of generations and a specialized learning of which, in most early civilizations, only centralized priesthoods are capable. Only after literacy and education become general can the sagelike diviner detach

himself from court circles and apply himself to individual and nonpolitical concerns.

Wisdom divination also often works in this way: by freeing the inquirer from customary ways of thought, it frequently reveals fresh insight into problems. Thus the cryptic proverbs or aphorisms (as in the Ifa system or the *I ching*), or the non-binding details and universalizable generalities (as in astrology), open up a cosmic perspective that in itself bestows tranquility and a renewed ability to cope effectively with crises. One learns to see behind appearances and to cultivate a continual attitude of tranquil self-offering. The momentum of wisdom divination, in short, is to internalize the basic attitude operating in all divination; it does this by rendering the structures of the transcendent into a form in which they can be grasped consciously and autonomously. The very vagueness of the answers in most forms of wisdom divination aid in this personal appropriation, making the client participate in shaping meaning out of the session.

BIBLIOGRAPHY

Useful historical surveys of divination and related topics in world cultures include Lynn Thorndike's monumental *A History of Magic and Experimental Science*, 3 vols. (New York, 1923-1958), and Auguste Bouché-Leclerq's still very useful *Histoire de la divination dans l'antiquité*, 4 vols. in 2 (1879-1889; reprint, New York, 1975). Thorndike's history is chiefly oriented to Western culture, but the first two volumes deal with antiquity. Bouché-Leclerq focuses on classical Greco-Roman cultures. A total of seventeen learned articles on divination in particular cultures, and an additional twelve articles on astrology and other religious aspects of heavenly phenomena in world cultures, can be found in the *Encyclopaedia of Religion and Ethics*, 13 vols., edited by James Hastings (Edinburgh, 1908-1926), under "Divination" (vol. 4, 1911) and "Sun, Moon, and Stars" (vol. 12, 1921). More up to date is the excellent survey edited by André Caquot and Marcel Leibovici, *La divination: Études recueillies*, 2 vols., (Paris, 1968), which, in addition to the expected essays on the major ancient Near Eastern, classical, and Asian cultures, contains numerous essays on pre-Christian European cultures; the ancient civilizations of the Americas; native or tribal cultures in Siberia, Africa, and elsewhere; and modern folk and urban Western societies—all with helpful bibliographies. The most recent English symposium is Michael Loewe and Carmen Blacker's *Divination and Oracles* (London, 1981), with nine authoritative essays ranging from Tibetan culture to Islam.

An anthropological symposium on divination that refers to political aspects as well is *Divination et rationalité*, by Jean-Pierre Vernant and others (Paris, 1974). A useful selection of important theoretical anthropological essays on divination is included in *Reader in Comparative Religion: An Anthropological Approach*, 2d ed., edited by William A. Lessa and Evon Z. Vogt (New York, 1965); later editions include some more recent studies but omit much from the second edition. Mediumship has evoked the greatest attention from anthropologists; see, for example, *Spirit Mediumship and Society in Africa*, edited by John Beattie and John Middleton (New York, 1969), in addition to the studies mentioned in the text of the foregoing article.

For an authorative summary of what we know about ancient Mesopotamian divination, see A. Leo Oppenheim's *Ancient Mesopotamia* (Chicago, 1964), pp. 198-227, or W. H. P. Römer's

"Religion of Ancient Mesopotamia," in *Historia Religionum*, edited by C. Jouco Bleeker and Geo Widengren, vol. 1 (Leiden, 1969), especially pp. 172-178. H. W. Parke has summarized his many authoritative studies on Greek mediumship in his brief *Greek Oracles* (London, 1967); he does not ignore social and political implications. Still outstanding is Franz Cumont's *Astrology and Religion among the Greeks and Romans* (1912; reprint, New York, 1960). More recent are Hans Lewy's *Chaldaean Oracles and Theurgy: Mysticism, Magic and Platonism in the Later Roman Empire*, new edition by Michel Tardieu (Paris, 1978), and Frederick Henry Cramer's *Astrology in Roman Law and Politics* (Philadelphia, 1954).

Talmudic views of divination are well discussed by Abraham Cohen in his *Everyman's Talmud*, new ed. (New York, 1949), pp. 274-297; further information is available in the article "Div-ination" by Shmuel Ahituv and others in the *Encyclopaedia Judaica*, 16 vols. (Jerusalem, 1971). A general survey of Muslim divination is available in Toufic Fahd's *La divination arabe* (Leiden, 1966), and in the various symposia mentioned above. On hati geomancy, see the article by Robert Jaulin in the collection by André Caquot and Marcel Leibovici, cited above, and Robert Jaulin's *La géomancie: Analyse formelle* (Paris, 1966). For a penetrating study of the Yoruba Ifa system, see Wande Abimbola's *Ifa: An Exposition of Ifa Literary Corpus* (London, 1976).

Any study of Chinese divination should begin with Joseph Needham's brilliant study *Science and Civilisation in China*, vol. 2 (Cambridge, 1956), pp. 216-395; an excellent bibliography is appended. Among the many perceptive studies of the *I ching* is Hellmut Wilhelm's *Heaven, Earth and Man in the Book of Changes: Seven Eranos Lectures* (Seattle, 1977). A useful survey of other forms of Chinese wisdom divination as well as of allied forms of the *I ching* is Wallace A. Sherrill and Wen Kuan Chu's *An Anthology of I Ching* (London, 1977). Also see Stephan D. R. Feuchtwang's *An Anthropological Analysis of Chinese Geomancy* (Vientiane, Laos, 1974).

EVAN M. ZUESSE

DOCTRINE

Most dictionaries record two related senses of the term *doctrine*: according to the first, it is the affirmation of a truth; according to the second, it is a teaching. The two are not mutually exclusive: to affirm something as true is a way of teaching it, and that which is taught is usually held to be true.

The denotation of the term is thus reasonably clear. However, the connotations (i. e., the feelings and attitudes associated with it), differ according to where the emphasis is placed in a given instance. As the statement of a truth, doctrine has a philosophical cast; as a teaching, it suggests something more practical. The first connotation prevails among the secular sciences. The doctrine of evolution, for example, comprises a body of knowledge that is appropriately characterized as a theory, but not a teaching.

Religious doctrines tend to be characterized by their practical intent. For example, the orientation of Judaism is toward practical obedience to the law of God, not speculative knowl-

edge of his being. [*See* Torah.] The doctrinal element in Judaism thus reveals an intimate connection with the notion of teaching. The most important figure is the rabbi ("teacher"); the most important word is torah ("instruction"), which refers to God's revelation in the Hebrew scriptures and, more specifically, to his law as presented in the five books of the Pentateuch. In a broader sense, *torah* encompasses the oral as well as the written law, together with the continuing tradition of rabbinical interpretations. The Talmud ("study") is an authoritative compilation of expositions of the law and applications of it to particular circumstances. It has been observed that the phrase "to read the Talmud," while grammatically correct, is a violation of the text's religious character, since the only appropriate response to the Talmud is to study it.

A Category of Comparative Religion. Doctrine is not restricted to Christianity. It is significant that each religion makes use of words that, though not exact synonyms for the terms *doctrine* or *teaching*, are very close to them in meaning: torah ("instruction") in Judaism and kalam ("doctrine, theology") in Islam; darsana ("school, viewpoint") in Hinduism; Dharma ("teaching") in Buddhism; chiao ("teaching") in Confucianism and Taoism; Butsudo ("way of the Buddha") in Japanese Buddhism; kami no michi ("way of the Japanese divinities") in Shinto.

> **Doctrine is designed to focus the mind, emotions, and will on the religious goal that the community has accepted as its ultimate concern.**

The prevalence of a doctrinal factor in all of the world's major religions suggests that it ought to be treated as a general category in the academic study of religion. This has, at times, not been recognized with sufficient clarity because of a romantic bias that exalts feeling over thought and deems "doctrine" an alien intrusion into a religious form of existence that is essentially nonrational in character.

However, the notion of a dichotomy between thought and feeling in the religious life is not tenable. Feelings, perceptions, and emotions require form and structure to become the content of human experience. By the same token, mysticism and rationalism reveal an intimate affinity, since most mystics become known to us through the discursive accounts of their ineffable experiences that they produce. Even the symbol systems of nonliterate societies have a doctrinal or rational aspect that gives religious shape to communal life.

Doctrine, then, is a category in the comparative study of religion that belongs with ritual, sacrament, mystical experience, and other factors whose importance has been recognized for some time. Like them, doctrine is designed to focus the mind, emotions, and will on the religious goal that the community has accepted as its ultimate concern.

Theology and Doctrinal Form. At the present time, doctrine is frequently associated with systematic theology. For over a thousand years of church history, theology had diverse meanings, some of which were remote from those of Christian doctrine. Plato used the word *theology* to describe the stories about the gods told by poets; Aristotle used it to describe his doctrine of immutable substance. Augustine distinguished three senses: the theology of the poets, a civic theology based on public ceremonies, and a theology of nature. Sometimes the term was used in a narrow sense by Christian thinkers, who restricted it to the doctrine of God.

Muslim theologians such as al-Ghazali (1058-1111 CE) participated in a golden age of theology devoted to the task of reconciling Greek philosophy with the faith of Islam. During the same period, Maimonides (Mosheh ben Maimon, 1135/8-1204) worked on the reconciliation of Greek thought with Judaism; Thomas Aquinas (1225-1274) undertook a similar task in respect to the Roman Catholic faith. Even more important is the fact that during the twelfth and thirteenth centuries revisions in medieval education were made that, among other things, introduced the notion of doctrinal theology as an academic discipline with a status similar to that of the secular subjects taught in the university curriculum.

Hugh of Saint-Victor (c. 1096-1141) developed an approach to theology that subsumed the two senses of the term *theory* (i. e., both intellectual endeavor and contemplation of God) under the complex notion of "speculation," which had previously been applied, for the most part, to religious meditation. Hugh characterized the method of theology as a kind of thought that is theoretical, both in the rational sense of submission to the norms of logic and in the contemplative sense of religious aspiration and vision. However, the delicate balance that he proposed is the prescription of an ideal and not what most works of systematic theology are, in fact, like.

The fourth book of Augustine's *Christian Doctrine* offers comments about doctrine that are still relevant to the contemporary scene. Augustine suggests that rhetoric is as important as logic in the communication of doctrine. He makes use of the rhetorical tradition derived from Aristotle to explore the capacity of Christian doctrine to teach, delight, and persuade.

BIBLIOGRAPHY

The most up-to-date extended history of doctrine from a Protestant perspective is Jaroslav Pelikan's *The Christian Tradition: A History of the Development of Doctrine*, 4 vols. (Chicago, 1971-1984). A final volume is projected to cover the period since 1700. The work provides many revaluations of conventional historical judgments and includes an extensive bibliographical apparatus of primary and secondary sources. Nineteenth-century studies like Adolf von Harnack's *History of Dogma*, 7 vols. translated by Neil Buchanan (London, 1895-1900), and Reinhold Seeberg's *Text-Book of the History of Doctrines*, 2 vols. translated by Charles E. Hay (Grand Rapids, 1952), among others, remain indispensable in spite of inadequacies of interpretation corrected by later historians. Bernhard Lohse's *A Short History of Christian Doctrine: From the First Century to the Present*, translated by F. Ernest Stoeffer (Philadelphia, 1978) is a brief summary that is also a helpful essay of interpretation; George A. Lindbeck's *The Nature of Doctrine: Religion and Theology in a Postliberal Age* (Philadelphia, 1984) offers an approach to doctrine that makes use of the categories developed by philosophers of language. The *Dictionnaire de theologie catholique*, 15 vols, edited by Jean-Michel-Alfred Vacant et al. (Paris, 1903-1950), is important for an understanding of doctrine from a Catholic perspective. Also useful is the *Encyclopedia of Theology: The Concise Sacramentum Mundi*, edited by Karl Rahner (New York, 1975). "Dogma," an essay by Rahner in this encyclopedia, together with his "Considerations on the Development of Dogma," in his *Theological Investigations*, translated by Kevin Smyth, vol. 4 (Baltimore, 1966), pp. 3-35, offer a sophisticated statement of the standard approach to Catholic doctrine and dogma. An informative account of the emergence of doctrinal theology as an academic discipline is G. R. Evans's *Old Arts and New Technology: The Beginnings of Theology as an Academic Discipline* (Oxford, 1980).

The following works offer useful discussions of rhetorical and literary genres other than systematic theology appropriate for contemporary statements of doctrine: Giles B. Gunn, *The Interpretation of Otherness: Literature, Religion, and the American Imagination* (Oxford, 1979); David Tracy, *The Analogical Imagination: Christian Theology and the Culture of Pluralism* (New York, 1981); Nathan A. Scott, Jr., ed., *The New Orpheus: Essays toward a Christian Poetic* (New York, 1964).

The following are useful studies of the role of doctrine in religions other than Christianity. For Judaism: Judah Goldin, ed. *The Living Talmud* (New York, 1957); Jacob Neusner, *The Way of Torah: An Introduction to Judaism* (Belmont, Calif., 1970); Leo Trepp, *Judaism: Development and Life* (Belmont, Calif., 1982). For Islam: Charles J. Adams, "The Islamic Religious Tradition," in *Religion and Man*, edited by W. Richard Comstock (New York, 1971), pp. 553-617; Fazlur Rahman, Islam, 2d ed. (Chicago, 1979). For the religions of India: Robert Baird, "Indian Religious Traditions," in *Religion and Man* (cited above), pp. 115-250; Ninian Smart, *Doctrine and Argument in Indian Philosophy* (London, 1964). For Buddhism: Edward Conze, *Buddhism: Its Essence and Development* (Oxford, 1951); Melford E. Spiro, *Buddhism and Society: A Great Tradition and Its Burmese Vicissitudes*, 2d ed., exp. (Berkeley, 1982). For the religions of China: Tu Wei-ming, *Humanity and Self-Cultivation: Essays in Confucian Thought* (Berkeley, 1978); C. K. Yang, Religion in Chinese Society (Berkeley, 1961). For the religions of Japan: Alfred Bloom, "Far Eastern Religious Traditions," in *Religion and Man* (cited above), pp. 254-396; H. Byron Earhart, *Japanese Religion: Unity and Diversity*, 3d rev. ed. (Belmont, Calif., 1982). For the religions of preliterate societies: W. Richard Comstock, *The Study of Religion and Primitive Religions* (New York, 1972); Mary Douglas, *Natural Symbols: Explorations in Cosmology* (New York, 1970); Clifford Geertz, "Religion as a Cultural System," in *Anthropological Approaches to the Study of Religion*, edited by Michael Banton (New York, 1966), pp. 1-46.

W. RICHARD COMSTOCK

DOGMA

Dogma, in the strictest sense, whether embodied in the sacred scripture of the Old and New Testaments or in tradition, is understood by the Roman Catholic church to be a truth revealed by God (directly and formally), which is presented by the church for belief, as revealed by God, either through a solemn decision of the extraordinary magisterium (pope or council) or through the ordinary and general magisterium of the church (episcopacy). It is to be accepted by the same faith that is due to the divine word itself *(fides divina)* or to the church's tradition *(fides catholica)*.

The relationship to dogma of the churches and communities produced by the Reformation is defined by the theology of the reformers, which, on the one hand, does not dispute that the church may have to make obligatory statements and that the truth of scripture may only be able to be revealed through a painstaking process. It therefore accepts at least the trinitarian-christological dogma of the old church as an appropriate expression of the matter of the gospel. But, on the other hand, through the principle of *sola scriptura* (over against an association of scripture and tradition), the theology of the reformers takes up a different position, scripture being for them no longer merely the source and norm of all Christian speech, teaching, and preaching, but, rather, the single final authority. All confessions and dogmas are to be measured against it. Negatively, they agree in their rejection of the Roman Catholic understanding of dogma and its function for faith and church as "doctrinal law." Positively, they agree in the conviction that God's word must not only be existentially recognized but also known as objective truth and reproduced in statements and doctrinal teachings, however these may then be interpreted and qualified with regard to their binding character.

In the question of the development of dogma, Roman Catholic theology must proceed from the fact that the church defines statements as revealed by God if they satisfy one of the following conditions: (1) Even if previously stated, they were not always expressly defined or bindingly taught as revealed. (2) They articulate the express contents of statements of the earlier tradition in very different or newly developed conceptual terms. (3) They refer to statements in the tradition that may not be immediately equivalent to them or explicitly capable of being traced back to the apostles or that cannot even be supposed with historical probability to have been once previously available. Thus not only theology but also revelation (to the extent that it is only present in proclamation, acceptance of faith, and practice) has a history, a "development," and a "progress" after Christ, even if this history is essentially different from the development of revelation before Christ.

The first three centuries of Christianity and perhaps the following one and a half centuries, which saw the development and culmination of the first three, present a history of Christian belief and dogma in a confrontational struggle with the simultaneous assimilation of a non-Christian spiritual and cultural (Hellenistic-Roman) environment. However, the second long period after the waning of antiquity, that is, from the early Middle Ages to the Enlightenment, was a time of unfolding and differentiation of the substance of faith from within its own center outward into even more systematized distinctions that, because of their one point of departure from within, could be considered without really major confrontation with external contradictions and as a more or less homogeneous abstraction presupposed by all to be self-evident.

Today (after a long preparation since the Enlightenment, from which time also dates the defensive dialogue with liberalism and modernism) we have doubtless entered upon a new, third phase in the history of faith and thus also in the history of dogma and of theology. Today it is no longer a question of an ever more detailed unfolding of the basic substance of faith within a homogeneous environment that has a common horizon of understanding with the church. It is much more a question of winning a new understanding (naturally preserving the substance of faith which has been handed down) of the one totality of faith in a non-Christian environment, in a new epoch of a global world civilization in which world cultures that were never Christian have appeared.

BIBLIOGRAPHY

A summary introduction to the history of the concept of dogma and the history of the problem of the development of dogma from a Catholic point of view can be found in Georg Söll's "Dogma und Dogmenentwicklung," in *Handbuch der Dogmengeschichte*, vol. 1, fasc. 5 (Freiburg, 1971), which includes an extensive bibliography. From the Protestant perspective the following articles in *Theologische Realenzyklopädie*, vol. 9 (Berlin and New York, 1982), pp. 26-125, should be consulted: "Dogma" by Ulrich Wickert and Carl H. Ratschow, "Dogmatik" by Gerhard Sauter, Anders Jeffner, Alasdair Heron, and Frederick Herzog, and "Dogmengeschichtsschreibung" by Wolf-Dieter Hauschild. See also Karlmann Beyschlag's *Grundriss der Dogmengeschichte*, vol. 1 (Darmstadt, 1982), pp. 1-54.

The relationship between kerygma and dogma (also in conversation with Protestant positions) is analyzed in Karl Rahner and Karl Lehmann's *Kerygma and Dogma* (New York, 1969), Walter Kasper's *Dogma unter dem Wort Gottes* (Mainz, 1965), and Karl Rahner and Joseph Ratzinger's *Offenbarung und Überlieferung* (Freiburg, 1965).

The problem of the development of dogma from a theological-systematic perspective is treated by Karl Rahner and Karl Lehmann in *Das Problem der Vermittlung*, "Mysterium Salutis," vol. 1 (Einsiedeln, 1965), pp. 727-787; by Karl Rahner in "The Development of Dogma," in *Theological Investigations*, vol. 1 (New York, 1961), pp. 39-77; by Karl Rahner in "Considerations on the Development of Dogma," in *Theological Investigations*, vol. 4 (New York, 1966), pp. 3-35; by Joseph Ratzinger in *Das Problem der Dogmengeschichte in der Sicht der katholischen Theologie* (Cologne, 1966); and from an evangelical point of view by Gerhard Ebeling in *Die Geschichtlichkeit der Kirche und ihrer Verkündigung als theologisches Problem* (Tübingen, 1954). An instructive analysis of the more recent Catholic models of the development of dogma can be found in Herbert Hammans's *Die neueren katholischen Erklärungen der Dogmenentwicklung* (Essen, 1965). For the modernist theological-critical approach, the broadly based source study by Émile Poulat, *Histoire, dogme et critique dans la crise moderniste*, 2d ed., rev. (Paris, 1979), should be consulted. It is written, however, from a somewhat sociological perspective.

With regard to the theory and the history of the development of dogma (as well as of the historiography of dogma), the prolegomena of the classic handbooks and manuals of dogmatic history are to be consulted: for example, those by Harnack, Seeberg, Ritschl, Köhler, Schwane, Tixeront, et al. In addition, see, for Catholic theology, *Handbuch der Dogmengeschichte*, edited by Michael Schmaus et al. (Freiburg, 1971-), which is arranged according to treatises; for the Protestant perspective, see Alfred Adam's *Lehrbuch der Dogmengeschichte*, 2 vols. (Gütersloh, 1965-1968), and *Handbuch der Dogmen- und Theologiegeschichte*, 3 vols., edited by Carl Andresen (Göttingen, 1980-1984). Recent positions can also be found in Avery Dulles's *The Survival of Dogma* (New York, 1971) and Gerald O'Collins's *The Case against Dogma* (New York, 1975).

KARL RAHNER and ADOLF DARLAP
Translated from German by Charlotte Prather

DRUIDS

In his brief description of Gaulish society of the first century BCE, Caesar divides his text into three unequal parts dedicated to the druids, the knights, or *equites*, and the plebs (*Gallic Wars* 6.13). His account of the druids is concise and clear:

> In all of Gaul there are two classes of men who count and are honored, for the people are barely more than slaves: they dare do nothing on their own and are consulted on nothing. When most of them become overwhelmed with debt, overburdened by taxes, and are forced to submit to the violence of those more powerful, they put themselves in the service of noblemen who have the same rights over them as masters do over slaves. Of these two classes, one is the druids and the other the knights. The former watch over divine matters, administer public and private sacrifices, and rule all matters of religion. Many young people come to be taught by them and to benefit from their attention. It is they, in fact, who settle disputes, both public and private, and if any crime has been committed, if there has been a murder, or if any dispute arises in regard to an inheritance or boundaries, it is they who decide and assess the damages and fines; if some person or persons do not agree with their decision, that person or those persons are forbidden to participate in the sacrifices. This penalty is the most serious they know. Those who are thus forbidden are considered to be impious and criminal: people stay away from them and shun contact to avoid being stricken with a serious malady. Cases they wish to bring to trial are not admitted, and no honor is accorded them. A sin-

gle leader commands all these druids, and he exercises supreme authority over them. Upon his death, he is succeeded by the preeminent druid; if there are several of equal status, they decide the title by a vote of the druids and sometimes by force of arms. At a certain time of the year, they assemble in a sacred place in the land of the Carnutes, which is thought to be the center of Gaul. To that place come all those with disputes, and they submit to the druids' judgments and decisions. Their doctrine was developed in Britain, and from there, it is thought, it came to Gaul; even today, most of those who wish to learn more about this doctrine go there to learn it. The druids do not customarily go to war and pay taxes, as do the rest of the Gauls; they are exempt from military service and free of all types of obligations. Encouraged by such great privileges, many people of themselves seek instruction by the druids, and others are sent by their parents and relatives. It is said that there they learn a very large number of verses by heart: some of them stay at this school for twenty years. They are of the opinion that religion forbids these verses from being committed to writing, which can be done for public and private reports with the use of the Greek alphabet. It seems to me that they have established this custom for two reasons: because they do not want to spread their doctrine among the people, and because they do not want those who learn by trusting to writing to neglect their memories, since it is usually the case that the aid of texts results in less application to learning by heart and less memory. Above all they try to instill the conviction that souls do not perish, but pass after death from one body to another; this strikes them as being a particularly suitable way to inspire courage by suppressing the fear of death. They also have much to say about the stars and their movements, the greatness of the world and of the earth, the nature of things, and the strength and power of the immortal gods, and they convey these speculations to youth.

Holders of Spiritual Authority. As the holder of spiritual authority, the druid took precedence over temporal power, represented by the king, with whom he formed a couple; the druid was the intermediary between the gods and the king, and the king played the same role between the druid and society. Thus, it was the king who rendered justice, but the druid who made law. The druid was not bound by any obligation, either fiscal or military, but he had the right to bear arms and to make war whenever he wished. The warrior druid is a common personage in Irish epic. Again it was the druid who pronounced the *geasa* ("injunctions, interdicts") that bound all individuals—especially the king—to a closed network of interdicts and obligations of all kinds. One of the most famous interdicts of Ulster was that the Ulates were not to speak before the king and that the king was not to speak before the druid. But the druid—who never courted royalty, save for aberrant and extremely rare cases—was in the service of the king, to whom he owed counsel, information, or prediction that would allow the king to rule his kingdom well.

The alliance between the king and the druid explains why the druid disappeared in Gaul after the Roman conquest: the Gauls' adoption of the Roman political system based on the *municipium* removed the druid's entire *raison d'être*, and it is likely that druidism, despite its initial vitality, declined slowly and became almost clandestine.

BIBLIOGRAPHY

Guyonvarc'h, Christian-J., and Françoise Le Roux. *Textes mythologiques irlandais*, vol. 1. Rennes, 1980.
Le Roux, Françoise, and Christian-J. Guyonvarc'h. *La civilisation celtique.* 4th ed. Rennes, 1983.
Le Roux, Françoise, and Christian-J. Guyonvarc'h. *Les druides.* 3d ed. Rennes, 1982.

FRANCOISE LE ROUX and
CHRISTIAN-J. GUYONVARC'H
Translated from French by Erica Meltzer

DUALISM

As a category within the history and phenomenology of religion, dualism may be defined as a doctrine that posits the existence of two fundamental causal principles underlying the existence of the world. In addition, dualistic doctrines, worldviews, or myths represent the basic components of the world or of man as participating in the ontological opposition and disparity of value that characterize their dual principles. In this specific religio-historical sense, dualism is to be distinguished from the more general philosophical doctrines of transcendence and metaphysical irreducibility, which are opposed to monistic or pantheistic doctrines of immanence. This article will examine dualism only in the former sense, as a religio-historical phenomenon.

In that sense, dualism is more specific than either simple duality or polarity. Not every duality or polarity is dualistic, but only those that involve the duality or polarity of causal principles. Thus not every pair of opposites (such as male and female, right and left) can be labeled as dualistic, even when their opposition is emphasized. They are dualistic only when they are understood as principles or causes of the world and its constitutive elements. In addition, in order for pairs of opposites to be dualistic, it is not necessary that they be mutually irreducible or coeternal. Indeed, one may be the creation of the other, as in the dualistic doctrine of the Bogomils, where Satan, created by God, is in turn the creator of the human body.

Types of Dualism. From the systematic point of view, every form of dualism may be classified by type as either radical or moderate, either dialectical or eschatological, and as either cosmic or anticosmic. I shall examine each of these pairs in turn.

Radical versus moderate. Radical dualism admits two coequal and coeternal principles (in the sense that both of them exist and act from the very beginning, whatever may be their final destiny). Among the Greeks there exists a radical dualism in Orphism, with its conception of the *kuklos tes geneseos* ("the cycle of birth") and the dualistic implications of its metaphysics; in Empedocles' theory of the two opposed principles of Love and Discord; in Heraclitus; and in Plato's doctrines of the two alternating revolutions of the world, mentioned in the *Statesman*, and of the coeternity of the Ideas and the "receptacle" *(chora)*. There are also several forms of radical dualism in India, particularly in the Samkhya system, with its opposed principles of *purusa* and *prakrti*.

Unlike the radical dualism, moderate (or "monarchian") dualism exhibits only one primordial principle, while a second principle somehow derives from the first, often through an incident that took place in a kind of prologue in heaven. This second principle then plays a central role in bringing the world into existence. Many of the gnostic systems provide examples of moderate dualism, in particular the systems of Valentinus, where the very structure of the divine, pneumatic world (the *pleroma*) allows for the possibility of a fall in heaven. The fall of Sophia, the last *aion*, is a result of her location on the periphery of the divine *pleroma*. This dangerous position amounts to a kind of predestination. Although this does not destroy the moderate, or monarchian, character of Valentinianism, it does show that gnostic metaphysics here

> **The distinctive feature of eschatological dualism is the belief that the evil principle will be overcome at the end of history.**

includes a concept of crisis or instability in the divine that is fundamentally dualistic.

Evidence of radical or moderate dualism among nonliterate cultures is ambiguous, and this very fact may be significant for our understanding of the formation process of dualistic ideologies and creeds. Thus while the Algonquin myth of the two brothers Ioskeha and Tawiskaron, born of Ataentsic (a primordial female being) can be traced to a type of radical dualism, since the brothers have, respectively, a positive and negative relation to creation from the very beginning, other American myths of a dualistic character are quite different. They may present a supreme being who in the beginning is unopposed but is later joined by a second figure of unknown origin who begins to interfere in the creation process. The unknown origin of the rival, who is often characterized as a demiurgic trickster, may be intended to indicate that his earlier absence was really an unmanifested presence, and that he is in fact an integral part of a single, all-inclusive scenario.

It would seem, therefore, that the most ancient formulations (or at least the simplest) did not choose between the two possibilities of radical and moderate dualism. Perhaps such an alternative was not recognized.

Dialectical versus eschatological dualism. Dialectical dualism may be distinguished from eschatological dualism by the fact that the two irreducible principles recognized by the former function eternally, whereas in the latter case they do not. In dialectical dualism the two principles are often conceived of as good and evil, respectively, both in the ethical and metaphysical sense. Samples are to be found in Orphic speculation on the one and the many, in Empedocles and Heraclitus, and in Platonism.

The distinctive feature of eschatological dualism is the belief that the evil principle will be overcome at the end of history. Examples of this type of belief can be found in Zoroastrianism, Manichaeism, gnosticism, Bogomilism, and Catharism.

Cosmic versus anticosmic dualism. Cosmic and anticosmic forms of dualism are distinguished by their attitudes towards the world. Cosmic dualism contends that creation is fundamentally good, and evil comes to it from the outside. Zoroastrianism can be named as a typical example. Anticosmic dualism contends to the contrary that evil is intrinsic to the world, present in an essentially negative or delusive principle or substance such as matter, the body, or the inferior soul. The cosmos is created as a providential engine in order to permit the progressive liberation of the souls trapped within it, which are eventually guided to the heavenly paradise.

Dualism in History. The diverse historical forms of dualism can be better explained on the basis of parallel development, provided this approach avoids the presuppositions of evolutionism and physiological development. Given the presence of forms of dualism in the archaic cultures of North America, it is clearly impossible to view all forms of dualism as having a single geographical point of origin, such as Iran. Here it is best to focus only on those connections that can be historically documented.

Such connections can be found between some forms of Manichaean and Zoroastrian dualism. Similar comparative-historical conclusions could be drawn concerning the relationship between the dualistic conceptions found in eastern European folklore and in such western Asian sects as the Yazidis. One could possibly speak of a certain dualistic propensity in the ethnological background of these areas without losing sight of the opposite possibility, namely, the direct influence of the great dualistic religions and the active dualistic sectarian movements such as the Bogomils.

Even in Iran, there have occasionally been peripheral formulations of dualism that cannot be explained on the basis of Zoroastrian ideology alone. The characterization of Ahriman as a kind of demiurge-trickster, for instance, is not unlike the characterization of similar figures in the nonliterate cultures of Asia. Ultimately we are led to question the origins of Zoroastrian dualism itself: to what extent was it influenced or predetermined by the figure of Zarathushtra? To what extent, and in which ways, was Iranian religion characterized by dualistic tendencies prior to Zarathushtra? Which were more important for this, those elements that were paralleled in the Vedic literature of India (such as the parallel figures of Indra-Vrtrahan and Verethraghna), or those that recall Inner Asian folklore?

However these questions are to be answered, one possibility deserves special mention, namely that of "dualistic imperialism." It may be illustrated by considering the historical fate of the so-called earth diver, the mythical theme of a bird or animal that dives into the primordial sea in order to bring up some mud for the creator, who then spreads it on the surface of the waters to create the earth. This motif is quite widespread, being found in Inner Asia, eastern Europe, and North America. What is interesting is that it has dualistic implications only in the Old World, which seems particularly significant in view of the fact that other dualistic myths are far from rare in the New World. It may mean that the originally nondualistic motif of the diver was first given a dualistic interpretation in Asia, some time after versions of it had spread to North America. But once it had taken hold it could have modified the earlier situation and led to the appropriation of themes previously extraneous to dualism. Thus one would have a kind of "dualistic imperialism" whose more peculiar manifestations would have appeared in Iran or at its borders.

BIBLIOGRAPHY

For a vast exposition of the problems concerning the forms and the diffusion of dualism in the nonliterate and literate religions, see my *Il dualismo religioso*, 2d ed. (Rome, 1983). Also see my study *Selected Essays on Gnosticism, Dualism and Mysteriosophy* (Leiden, 1978), which makes reference to dualism in gnosticism and the Iranian traditions. Jacques Duchesne-Guillemin offers a comparative perspective on Iranian dualism in his study *La religion de l'Iran ancien* (Paris, 1962). The role of Zurvanism is somewhat exaggerated in Robert C. Zaehner's *Zurvan: A Zoroastrian Dilemma* (Oxford, 1955). Iranian dualism is also the subject of Mary Boyce's text *A History of Zoroastrianism*, 2 vols. (Leiden, 1975-1982) and my *Zaman i Ohrmazd: Lo zoroastrismo nelle sue origini e nella sua essenze* (Turin, 1958). On dualism in different religions and cultures, consult Mircea Eliade's "Prolegomenon to Religious Dualism," in his study *The Quest: History and Meaning in Religion* (Chicago, 1969), and his *Zalmoxis, the Vanishing God* (Chicago, 1972), especially chapters 2 and 3. Simone Pétrement's *Le dualisme dans l'histoire de la philosophie et des religion* (Paris, 1946) and *Le dualisme chez Platon, les gnostiques et les manichéens* (Paris, 1946) do not distinguish enough between the uses of the term dualism in philosophical-historical and religio-historical studies. The following sources treat particular aspects of dualism: *The Origins of Gnosticism* (1967; Leiden, 1970), which I edited; Hans Jonas's *The Gnostic Religion*, 2d ed., rev. (Boston, 1963); Marcel Griaule and Germaine Dieterlen's *Le renard pâle*, vol. 1 (Paris, 1965); Kurt Rudolph's Gnosis (San Francisco, 1983); and Jacques Duchesne-Guillemin's study *The Western Response to Zoroaster* (Oxford, 1958). Geo Widengren's *"Der Iranische Hintergrund der Gnosis," Zeitschrift für Religions- und Geistesgeschichte* 4 (1952): 97-114, discusses dualism in relation to the Upanisads. Franz Kiichi Numazawa makes a comparative approach to the Chinese Yin-yang ideology in his study *Die Weltanfänge in der japanischen Mythologie* (Fribourg, 1946). Oskar Dähnhardt includes precious information on dualistic folklore through eastern Europe and Asia in his book *Natursagen*, vol. 1 (Leipzig, 1907). Wilhelm Schmidt treats Asian dualistic mythologies in his *Der Ursprung der Gottesidee*, vols. 9-12 (Münster, 1948-1955). For a discussion of "second creation" and "previous sin," which is distinct from "original sin," see my *Selected Essays*, cited above, and the volume that I edited titled *La Doppia creazione dell'uomo* (Rome, 1978). As for dualism in the modern currents of thought and praxis mentioned at the end of the present article, see my *Selected Essays*, pp. 177-186.

UGO BIANCHI

EAST AFRICAN RELIGIONS

An Overview

East African religions do not form a single coherent body of beliefs and practices. They show great diversity in myths and cosmologies and in beliefs about the nature of spiritual powers; in kinds and authority of ritual experts; in the situations when ritual is performed; and in responses to the advent of Islam and Christianity. This diversity is consistent with the ethnic, geographical, and historical diversity of the region. Our knowledge of East African religions is very uneven, and this may also contribute to the seeming diversity.

The total population of East Africa is in the order of some 100 million people. The population comprises some two hundred more or less distinct societies, each defined by its own language and sense of identity, its own traditional territory and political structure, and its own system of family relations, marriage, and religious belief and practice. These groups are distributed very unevenly in areas of high and low population densities.

Divinity and Myth. All East African religions have a belief in a high god, the creator. Perhaps the most accurate term to translate this concept here is Deity. As would be expected, even though there are variations, in all of them the Deity is attributed broadly similar characteristics: omnipotence, everlastingness, ubiquity, and being beyond the comprehension and control of ordinary living people. The variations lie in the idioms and symbols used to express these features and abilities. These general characteristics are found in the high gods representing all the cosmologies of the region: Kwoth (Nuer; the name also means "breath" or "spirit"), Juok (Shilluk), Nhialic (Dinka), Mbori (Azande), Adroa (Lugbara; the name also means "power"), Ngai (Kikuyu), Kyala (Nyakyusa), Mungu (Swahili), and so on. The names are different, but the divine nature is the same. Usually the Deity is considered to be spatially unlocalized, but in some religions it is thought to be associated with mountains and other terrestrial features, as among the Kikuyu, who state that Ngai dwells on Mount Kenya and on lesser mountains of the Rift Valley area.

There is considerable variation in the degree to which it is held that the Deity interferes in the everyday affairs of the living, beyond being responsible for death, and in beliefs held about the relationship between its creation of the world and the later formation of human societies.

These aspects and relations are stated in myth, each society having its own corpus of myth that tells of the creation of the world, the relationship between humankind and the Deity, and the formation of society. A typical example is that of the cosmogony of the Nilotic Shilluk of the upper Nile. Their myths tell of the creation of the world by Juok and of the later formation of the Shilluk kingdom by the culture hero or mediator, Nyikang. The mythical cooperation of creator and hero is a feature of many East African myths, their two activities being distinct in time and usually in place also.

Other than the distinction between the creation of the world and the formation of the particular society, the most widespread mythopoeic feature of the many and varied myths of the region would seem to be the attribution of reverse or inverted characteristics and behavior to the originally created inhabitants. They may be portrayed as incestuous or as being ignorant of kinship; they may be given close identification with animal species, the natural and the social thereby being brought into a single conceptual system; they may be said to have dwelt outside the present homeland in a state of primeval timelessness.

With creation myths are found myths that tell of such matters as the relationships between people and wild and domesticated animals, between men and women, and between peoples of different societies and races; the origins of and reasons for death; the origins of fire and cooking; and the nature and validation of the ties, rights, and obligations of descent, age, sex, and rank. As with myths, most folk tales are concerned with paradoxes and logical contradictions in the experience of the particular culture concerned. Perhaps the great majority of East African folk tales are told about agents who are animals or humans in the guise of animals; their adventures refer essentially and by implication to human behavior.

Lesser Deities and their Relations with the Living. The Deity usually communicates with the living only indirectly, through refractions of its power in the forms of lesser deities, spirits, gods, powers, and ancestors, ghosts, or shades. These mystical entities may "float" freely or they may be attached to social groups (lineages, clans, neighborhoods, and others) by having localized shrines established for them. The relations of communication are complex, but essentially the deities may control or constrain the living by possessing them and making them sick, and the living may contact the deities by sacrifice, prayer, and self-induced trance.

There are many kinds of these deities found in East African religions, but they may conveniently be divided into the categories of spirits and ancestors, each comprising many subtypes. Spirits are considered as different from the transcendent and otiose Deity. They are immanent, more dynamic, and more immediately demanding; they are usually regarded as so numerous as to be beyond counting.

> **As with myths, most folk tales are concerned with paradoxes and logical contradictions in the experience of the particular culture concerned.**

Whereas the Deity is only rarely localized in shrines (as among the Kikuyu, who recognize certain fig trees as shrines for Ngai), many kinds of shrines, temples, and images are built for the spirits where they may be contacted by the living. Since spirits are invisible and unknowable, being of a different order than human beings, they need some locus where the living may contact them.

A spirit may be considered as a representation of some aspect of human experience whose power is thought to be outside the immediate community and beyond the everyday knowledge or control of ordinary people, until it exercises some form of power over a living person by possession or sickness. This experience may be that of nature, as with the smallpox and other disease "gods" of the Ganda or the earthquake and lightning spirits of the Lugbara; it may be experience of outside historical events, as with the "airplane" and "Polish" (refugee) spirits of the Nyoro; or it may be the individual experience of inner psychological states such as guilt and fear, as with the sky divinities of the Dinka.

Another aspect of spirit possession is that the victim is thereby singled out and acquires a new or additional mystical and personal status. In East Africa women appear more usually to be possessed by spirits; it has been suggested that this is so because women suffer from a greater sense of cultural deprivation and ambiguity of role than do men.

The other main category of deity in East African religions is that of the dead, who, unlike spirits, are of the same order of existence as the living and so more easily understood and approached. There are many kinds and levels of ancestral worship, corresponding to the various kinds of ancestors: those of the direct line of descent, those of submerged descent lines, and those of other kin. They may be considered as individual ancestors, remembered by their personal names, or as collectivities of unnamed ancestral kin who are

of less importance in living memory. As they are like the living, they may easily be worshiped by sacrifice.

Sacrifice is made typically to remove sickness or as a response of gratitude for removal of sickness, to avoid sickness and other troubles, and at times on regular occasions of group or individual purification.

In those societies where ancestral cults are important, mortuary rites are likewise important; an example comes from the Lugbara of Uganda, where mortuary rites, especially for senior men, are long, drawn out affairs that involve the participation of kin over great distances.

Initiation rites, more generally for boys than for girls, are most elaborate in those societies in which age-sets and generation-sets provide the basis for political and military action and also regulate marriage. The best-known examples are the Para-Nilotic pastoralist societies such as the Maasai, Samburu, Nandi, Karamojong, and their related neighbors; some southern Ethiopian groups such as the Galla; and others such as the Nyakyusa of southern Tanzania, who also have age systems of political importance and complex initiation rites. These rites, as with all rites of transition, begin with a rite in which the initiates are separated symbolically (and often physically) from their families and is followed by a series of rites that takes place in seclusion or secret from the remainder of society. Finally there are the rites of reaggregation of the "new" person into society with his or her new role as an adult able to have sexual relations, marry, act as a warrior, and so on.

Explanations of and Responses to Evil and Misfortune. All East African religions have a concept of evil. Explanations of evil and responses to it are typically expressed in beliefs in witchcraft and sorcery, which are thus integral parts of any system of religion. The first fully adequate study of witchcraft—one which has not as yet been surpassed—concerns witchcraft beliefs among the Azande people of southwestern Sudan. The Azande distinguish between witchcraft and sorcery. Although this distinction is widespread in East Africa, it is not universal, and many societies refer merely to evildoers who use either or both means of harming others.

Radical social change has occurred in almost all parts of East Africa during and since colonial times. Change leads to increases in disputes and tensions as traditional social roles break down and alter, and this is often expressed in terms of suspicions and fears of witchcraft and sorcery. These evildoers are traitors, coming symboli-cally from the outside of the community, and efforts are made to cleanse whole communities of them by mass purificatory religious movements led by prophets and healers, both Christian and non-Christian.

Religious Change and Prophetic Movements. At times, East African societal change has been rapid and radical. A usual response to the sense of confusion about the present, uncertainty about the future, and in some cases virtual breakdown of the social order has been and is the recourse to prophetic leaders.

Prophets have been a marked feature of the Nuer and Dinka of the Nilotic Sudan. At the end of the nineteenth century the Nuer prophet Ngundeng, claiming inspiration from a Dinka sky divinity and spending much time fasting and living in the wilderness, was able to bring together large, normally autonomous groupings to raid neighboring peoples and to stand together against Arab slavers and, later, British colonial rule.

Among the Lugbara, to the south, a water cult known as Yakan emerged about the turn of the century in response to human and cattle epidemics and to the intrusion of Arabs and Europeans. The disturbance of a traditionally ordered society led the people to seek a famed prophet, Rembe, from the Kakwa people to the north. Rembe dispensed water that was imbued with divine power to his adherents, promising that drinking it would ensure the return of dead livestock and people (and so destroy the traditional ancestral cult), drive away disease and foreign newcomers, and make the drinkers immune to bullets. The cult collapsed at his arrest in 1917, although the spirit Yakan who inspired him is to this day believed to be a wandering spirit.

The communal drinking of divine water was also found in southeastern and central Tanganyika during the Maji Maji rebellion (*maji* is Swahili for "water") against the German colonial government in 1905-1907. It was begun by a diviner or prophet called Kinjikitile, who was possessed by a local spirit as well as by a panethnic deity called Hongo. Those who drank Kinjikitile's water would be immune to bullets and would drive the Germans into the sea. The movement turned beyond his control politically; he was hanged.

East Africa has had many new Christian and Islamic prophetic movements whose leaders promise a new society free of witchcraft, sickness, and poverty; in addition, the Christian message as expressed by missionaries refers, to a large extent, to the problems of physical and moral health and sickness.

Islam has also been a feature of East Africa for many centuries. It has been a part of the religious situation in northern Ethiopia, the Sudan, and the Somali and Swahili coasts since the Middle Ages. If we consider traditional Christian and Muslim prophetic leaders as members of a single category of religious experts, we may see that there are certain clearly defined phases of these movements in East Africa since the latter part of the nineteenth century. The first phase was that of the earlier effects of colonial rule, with which a link was seen with epidemics and other disasters; here the prophets were ultimately unsuccessful as religious or political leaders. The second phase was during the second quarter of this century, when the political aspects were less in evidence and more importance was given to missionization, missionaries being seen as colonial agents and even as betrayers of

the Christian message as it affected Africans. The third and fourth phases have been contemporary. One comprised the movements led by Christian prophets to reform mission churches and to found syncretist or reformed sects and churches; the other has been the rise of more overtly political leaders during the period of gaining political independence from the colonial powers. The acceptance of new faiths, with either the abandonment of the old or a syncretism of the two, does not happen in a historical or social vacuum and cannot be considered in isolation from the traditional religious past. The same people, as individuals, move from traditional to world religions (and often back again): they are not members of separate communities.

[*See also* African Religions. *For further discussion of particular East African religions, see* Interlacustrine Bantu Religions and Lugbara Religion.]

BIBLIOGRAPHY

The basic accounts of East African religions are in the form of monographs on the religious systems of particular societies. Most, although by no means all, are by anthropologists, each of whom has lived among the people in question, has learned their language and ways of life, and can set the beliefs and rites firmly into their social, cultural, and historical contexts. They include two books by E. E. Evans-Pritchard. In *Nuer Religion* (Oxford, 1956), on the Nilotic Nuer of the southern Sudan, he discusses the complex Nuer beliefs of the soul, divinity, sin, sacrifice, and religious symbolism and relates them to the social structure. The other, *Witchcraft, Oracles and Magic among the Azande*, 2d ed. (Oxford, 1950), is essentially on notions of spiritual causation among a "pre-scientific" people of the southwestern Sudan. Both these books are classics in the study of African religions. The Dinka, neighbors of the Nuer and closely related to them, are the subject of Godfrey Lienhardt's *Divinity and Experience: The Religion of the Dinka* (Oxford, 1961), in which the relationships of belief and sacrifice to Dinka efforts to understand and control their experience of the "outside" world are discussed with insight and subtlety. John Middleton's *Lugbara Religion* (London, 1960) deals in a more strictly sociological manner with the use made by the Lugbara of Uganda, who are related to the Azande, of ritual in everyday social and political affairs. The two books on the Nyakyusa, a Bantu-speaking people of southern Tanzania, by Monica Wilson, *Rituals of Kinship among the Nyakyusa* (Oxford, 1957) and *Communal Rituals of the Nyakyusa* (Oxford, 1959), deal in great detail with rituals of many kinds, set in their social context. Bernardo Bernardi's *The Mugwe: A Failing Prophet* (Oxford, 1959) deals with a particular priestly office among the Meru, an offshoot of the Kikuyu of central Kenya. Abdul Hamid M. el-Zein's *The Sacred Meadows* (Evanston, Ill., 1974) is concerned with the elaborate beliefs and rites of the Swahili town of Lamu, on the Kenya coast, which has nominally been Muslim for many centuries. F. B. Welbourn's *East African Rebels* (London, 1961) and F. B. Welbourn and B. A. Ogot's *A Place to Feel at Home* (Oxford, 1966) deal in detail and with sympathy with separatist church movements in southern Uganda and western Kenya respectively.

The other main category of writings on East African religions are surveys of various kinds in which comparisons are made between several local religions. Benjamin C. Ray's *African Religions* (Englewood Cliffs, N. J., 1976) is an excellent introduction to African religions in which those of East Africa feature prominently, in particular the Nuer, Dinka, Shilluk, Ganda, Lugbara, and Kikuyu. *Witchcraft and Sorcery in East Africa,* edited by John Middleton and E. H. Winter (London, 1963), and *Spirit Mediumship and Society in Africa,* edited by John Beattie and John Middleton (New York, 1969), contain essays by various authors on these matters among several different peoples. J. Spencer Trimingham's *Islam in East Africa* (Oxford, 1964) is a useful survey, and John V. Taylor's *The Primal Vision* (London, 1963) is a valuable short introduction to East African religion from a Christian viewpoint.

JOHN MIDDLETON

EASTER

EASTER, the most important of all Christian feasts, celebrates the passion, the death, and especially the resurrection of Jesus Christ. It is the Christian equivalent of the Jewish Passover, a spring feast of both harvest and deliverance from bondage. [*See* Passover.]Fundamentally a nocturnal feast preceded by a fast of at least one day, the celebration took place from Saturday evening until the early morning hours of Sunday.

A number of popular customs mark Easter Sunday and the rest of Easter week. Among the most familiar Easter symbols are the egg and rabbit. The egg symbolizes new life breaking through the apparent death (hardness) of the eggshell. Probably a pre-Christian symbol, it was adapted by Christians to denote Christ's coming forth from the tomb. In many countries the exchange of colored or decorated eggs at Easter has become customary. The Easter Bunny or Rabbit is also most likely of pre-Christian origin. The rabbit was known as an extraordinarily fertile creature, and hence it symbolized the coming of spring. Although adopted in a number of Christian cultures, the Easter Bunny has never received any specific Christian interpretation.

BIBLIOGRAPHY

For a comprehensive survey of the Western liturgical development of Easter, see Ildephonso Schuster's *The Sacramentary* (New York, 1925). Good treatments of Easter and associated popular customs can be found in Francis X. Weiser's *Handbook of Christian Feasts and Customs* (New York, 1958) and in the same author's *The Easter Book* (New York, 1954). For discussion from the point of view of the history of religions, see E. O. James's *Seasonal Feasts and Festivals* (New York, 1961).

JOHN F. BALDOVIN, S.J.

EASTERN CHRISTIANITY

Eastern Christendom is subdivided at present into three main bodies: the Eastern Orthodox church, the "separated" Eastern churches, and the Uniate churches.

Eastern Orthodox Church. The Eastern Orthodox church is the second largest church in the contemporary Christian world, next to—but much smaller than—the Roman Catholic church. It developed from the Greek-speaking church of the eastern Roman or Byzantine empire, but numerically its main strength now lies in the Slavic countries (Russia, Yugoslavia, Bulgaria) and in Romania. It is a fellowship of some fifteen sister churches, all of them agreed in faith, using the same forms of worship, and joined with the others in sacramental communion, but each administratively independent. All acknowledge the honorary primacy of the ecumenical patriarch at Constantinople (Istanbul). The patriarch does not lay claim to a supremacy of universal jurisdiction such as is ascribed to the pope in Roman Catholicism. His position is more similar to that of the archbishop of Canterbury within the worldwide Anglican communion.

The Eastern Orthodox church today comprises various jurisdictions, named here according to the traditional order of precedence. The figures given are at best approximate and indicate numbers of baptized rather than actively practicing members. Of first importance are the four ancient patriarchates: Constantinople (5,000,000 baptized members), Alexandria (350,000), Antioch (600,000), and Jerusalem (80,000). The heads of these four jurisdictions are called patriarchs. The patriarchate of Constantinople consists mainly of Greeks living in Crete or Greeks who emigrated to the United States, Australia, and Western Europe. In the patriarchate of Alexandria, embracing the whole African continent, the episcopate is predominantly Greek, but about half the faithful are Africans in Kenya, Uganda, and Tanzania. The head of this church bears the formal title "Pope and Patriarch." The episcopate and faithful of the patriarchate of Antioch, which has its main centers in Syria and Lebanon, are Arabic-speaking. At Jerusalem the episcopate is Greek, but the flock is almost entirely Arab. The patriarchate of Jerusalem includes within its sphere of influence the semi-independent Church of Sinai.

Second in order of precedence are other patriarchates and the autocephalous (i. e., self-governing) churches of the Eastern Orthodox church: Russia (50,000,000?), Serbia (in Yugoslavia; 8,000,000), Romania (15,000,000), Bulgaria (8,000,000), Cyprus (440,000), Greece (8,000,000), Poland (450,000), Albania (250,000 in 1945), Georgia (500,000?), Czechoslovakia (100,000), and America (1,000,000). The heads of the churches of Russia, Serbia, Romania, and Bulgaria bear the title Patriarch. The head of the Georgian church (the position of which in the order of precedence has not been agreed on) is styled Catholicos-Patriarch. The heads of the other churches are known either as Archbishop (Cyprus, Greece, Albania) or as Metropolitan (Poland, Czechoslovakia, America). The autocephalous status of the last three churches—Georgia, Czechoslovakia, and, more particularly, the Orthodox Church in America—is called into question by some of the other Orthodox churches. Two of the above churches, Cyprus and Greece, are Greek in language and culture; five of them—Russia, Serbia, Bulgaria, Poland, and Czechoslovakia—are Slav, while Romania is predominantly Latin in culture. Georgia (within the Soviet Union) and Albania stand apart, each with its own linguistic and cultural tradition, but many of the Albanian Orthodox are Greek-speaking.

Third in order of precedence are two churches, not as yet fully self-governing, that are termed "autonomous" rather than autocephalous. These are the churches of Finland (66,000) and Japan (25,000).

"Separated" Eastern Churches. One of the "separated" Eastern churches, the East Syrian church (the Nestorian church), developed historically from the bishops and dioceses that refused to accept the Council of Ephesus (431), regarded by other Christians as the third ecumenical council. Theologically the East Syrian church has been influenced above all by the school of Antioch, and especially by Theodore of Mopsuestia (c. 350-428). It does not use the title *theotokos* ("God-bearer" or "Mother of God"), assigned to the Blessed Virgin Mary by the Council of Ephesus, and it rejects the condemnation passed on Nestorius, patriarch of Constantinople, by that council. With its main centers from the fifth century onward inside the Persian empire, the Nestorian church was largely cut off from Christians under Byzantine rule, and still more from Christians in the West. Nestorian missionaries traveled widely, founding communities in Arabia, India, and across eastern Asia as far as China. Now greatly reduced, the Nestorian church numbers no more than 200,000, living in Iraq, Iran, India, and above all the United States. Its head is known as "Catholicos-Patriarch of the East."

Also among the "separated" Eastern churches are the non-Chalcedonian Orthodox churches, which like the Eastern (Chalcedonian) Orthodox church represent a communion of sister churches, although in the case of the non-Chalcedonians there is a wider variety in the forms of liturgical worship. The non-Chalcedonians, also known as the Oriental Orthodox, are so called because they reject the Council of Chalcedon (451), accepted by Eastern Orthodox and Western Christians as the fourth ecumenical council. Thus, whereas Eastern Orthodoxy recognizes seven ecumenical councils, the most recent of them Nicaea II (787), and Roman Catholicism recognizes twenty-one, the most recent Vatican II (1962-1965), the non-Chalcedonians recognize only three: Nicaea I (325), Constantinople I (381), and Ephesus (431). Often called "monophysites" because they ascribe to Christ only one nature *(phusis)* and not two, the non-Chalcedonian churches have been chiefly influenced in their theology by Cyril of Alexandria (375-444). There are five independent non-Chalcedonian churches: the Syrian Orthodox Church of Antioch (200,000), also known as the West Syrian or Jacobite church, headed by a patriarch resident in Damascus, and with members mainly in Syria and Lebanon; the Syrian Orthodox Church of India (1,800,000), closely connected with the Syrian Orthodox Church of Antioch, under the leadership of a patriarch resident in Kottayam, Kerala, South India; the Coptic Orthodox church (4,000,000) in Egypt, headed by a patriarch; the Armenian Orthodox church (2,500,000), with a catholicos resident in Echmiadzin, Soviet Armenia, a second catholicos resident in Antelias, Lebanon, and two patriarchs, at Jerusalem and Constantinople (in the Armenian tradition a patriarch ranks lower than a catholicos); and the Ethiopian Orthodox church (16,000,000), which until 1950 was partially dependent on the Coptic church but since then has been fully self-governing, and whose head is known as the patriarch.

Uniate Churches. While accepting the primacy of the pope and the other doctrines of the Roman Catholic church, the Uniate churches (Eastern Catholics) have retained their own ritual and distinctive practices, such as allowing the clergy to marry. There are Uniate churches parallel to the great majority of the Orthodox churches mentioned above, whether Eastern Orthodox or Oriental. The largest groups among the Uniate churches are the Ruthenians (including the Ukrainians and the Byelorussians, or White Russians), who within the Soviet Union exist only as an underground church but who have over a million members outside the U. S. S. R.; the Malabar Church in India (2,000,000); the Melchites (500,000), mainly in Syria and Lebanon; and the Maronites (1,400,000), also in Lebanon, who alone among the Uniate churches have no parallel within the Eastern Orthodox or Oriental Orthodox churches. In total, outside the Soviet Union and Romania, there were in the early 1980s some 6,500,000 members of the Uniate churches.

The Modern Period. At the end of the twentieth century Orthodox Christianity exists in four different circumstances. (1) As a state church it enjoys official government support; this is the position in Cyprus and to a diminishing extent in Greece. (2) Under communist rule, the government is actively hostile to religion; this is the position of the Orthodox in Eastern Europe and above all in the Soviet Union. Churches in communist lands today comprise nearly 85 percent of the Orthodox communion. (3) Orthodoxy also exists as a minority in predominantly Islamic environments, which is the situation of the ancient patriarchates of Alexandria, Antioch, and Jerusalem. (4) Finally, we also find Orthodoxy as a minority in the Western world, settled in lands traditionally associated with Roman Catholicism or Protestantism.

The great majority of the Orthodox churches, both Eastern and Oriental, participate in the ecumenical movement and are full members of the World Council of Churches. [See Ecumenical Movement.] In addition, most are involved in bilateral dialogues with other Christians. The Eastern Orthodox began official doctrinal discussions, on a worldwide level, with Roman Catholics in 1980, with Old Catholics in 1975, with Anglicans in 1973, and with Lutherans in 1981. During 1964-1971 there were four positive meetings between the Eastern and the non-Chalcedonian Orthodox, at which both parties were able to agree that, despite differences in terminology, there was no essential discrepancy in christological faith, and a promising solution was proposed for the old dispute concerning the number of the natures and wills in Christ. Even though no formal act of union has as yet been effected, there appears to be no fundamental obstacle on the doctrinal level.

BIBLIOGRAPHY

Surveys. Two introductory surveys covering history and doctrine, both by Orthodox authors, are John Meyendorff's *The Orthodox Church: Its Past and Its Role in the World Today*, rev. ed. (New York, 1981), and my *The Orthodox Church*, (1964; reprint, New York, 1983). Neither of these deals with the "separated" Eastern churches; for a general historical introduction to these, see A. S. Atiya's *A History of Eastern Christianity*, (1968; Millwood, N. Y., 1980).

Historical Development. On the evolution of theology in the Byzantine period, the best summary is John Meyendorff's *Byzantine Theology: Historical Trends and Doctrinal Themes*, 2d ed. (New York, 1979); consult also Jaroslav Pelikan's *The Christian Tradition: A History of the Development of Doctrine*, vol. 2, *The Spirit of Eastern Christendom*, 600-1700 (Chicago, 1974). On Christology after 451, see John Meyendorff's *Christ in Eastern Christian Thought* (New York, 1975). Dimitri Obolensky's *The Byzantine Commonwealth: Eastern Europe, 500-1453* (London, 1974) provides a clear and authoritative picture of Byzantine-Slav relations, both cultural and religious.

On the schism between Orthodoxy and Rome, Steven Runciman's *The Eastern Schism: A Study of the Papacy and the Eastern Churches during the Eleventh and Twelfth Centuries* (Oxford, 1955) supplies a well-documented factual narrative. For an Orthodox treatment of the underlying issues, challenging but at times one-sided, see Philip Sherrard's *The Greek East and the Latin West: A Study in the Christian Tradition* (London, 1959). Yves Congar's *After Nine Hundred Years: The Background of the Schism between the Eastern and Western Churches* (New York, 1959) is a perceptive analysis by a sympathetic Roman Catholic. For a full treatment of the hesychastic controversy, see John Meyendorff's *A Study of Gregory Palamas* (London, 1964).

A well-written account of the Turkish period, but one that makes only limited use of Eastern Christian sources, is provided in Steven Runciman's *The Great Church in Captivity: A Study of the Patriarchate of Constantinople from the Eve of the Turkish Conquest to the Greek War of Independence* (Cambridge, 1968). On the Catholic communities, see Charles A. Frazee's *Catholics and Sultans: The Church and the Ottoman Empire, 1453-1923* (Cambridge, 1983).

On the contemporary Orthodox world, consult Peter Hammond's *The Waters of Marah: The Present State of the Greek Church* (New York, 1956), which conveys vividly the atmosphere of Orthodox worship; Mario Rinvolucri's *Anatomy of a Church: Greek Orthodoxy Today* (London, 1966); Christel Lane's *Christian Religion in the Soviet Union: A Sociological Study* (Albany, N. Y., 1978); and Stella Alexander's *Church and State in Yugoslavia since 1945* (Cambridge, 1979).

Doctrine and Worship. The best general treatments of Orthodox theology are by Russians of the emigration; see especially Vladimir Lossky's *The Mystical Theology of the Eastern Church* (London, 1957) and Georges Florovsky's *Collected Works*, 5 vols. to date (Belmont, Mass., 1972-). Sergei Bulgakov's *The Orthodox Church* (London, 1935) deals in detail with the doctrine of the church. For Greek academic theology in the twentieth century, see Frank Gavin's *Some Aspects of Contemporary Greek Orthodox Thought* (Milwaukee, 1923) and Panagiotis N. Trembelas's *Dogmatique de l'église orthodoxe catholique*, 3 vols. (Chevetogne, Belgium, 1966-1968). For a less "scholastic" and more creative approach by younger Greek theologians, see Christos Yannaras's *The Freedom of Morality* (Crestwood, N. Y., 1984), John D. Zizioulas's *Being as Communion: Studies in Personhood and the Church* (Crestwood, N. Y., 1985), and Panayiotis Nellas's *Deification in Christ: Orthodox Perspectives on the Nature of the Human Person.* (Crestwood, N. Y., forthcoming.)

On biblical criticism, consult Veselin Kesich's *The Gospel Image of Christ: The Church and Modern Criticism* (Crestwood, N. Y., 1972). On sacramental theology, see Alexander Schmemann's *Sacraments and Orthodoxy* (New York, 1965) and Paul Evdokimov's *The Sacrament of Love: The Nuptial Mystery in the Light of the Orthodox Tradition* (Crestwood, N. Y., 1985). The services for nine of the twelve Great Feasts are given in *The Festal Menaion* (London, 1969), and the services for Lent in *The Lenten Triodion* (Boston, 1978), both translated by Mother Mary and myself.

Basic texts on the spiritual life, and especially on the Jesus Prayer, can be found in Nikodimos of the Holy Mountain and Makarios of Corinth's *The Philokalia*, translated and edited by G. E. H. Palmer, Philip Sherrard, and myself, 3 vols. to date (London and Boston, 1979-). For a less monastically oriented approach, by a married parish priest, read Alexander El'chaninov's *The Diary of a Russian Priest*, edited by myself (London, 1967). On the early history of the Jesus Prayer, see Iré-née Hausherr's *The Name of Jesus*, "Cistercian Studies," no. 44 (Kalamazoo, Mich., 1978); for its influence in Russia, see the anonymously written *The Way of a Pilgrim, and The Pilgrim Continues His Way*, new ed. (London, 1954). The ministry of spiritual fatherhood is well discussed in Irénée Hausherr's *Direction spirituelle en Orient autrefois*, "Orientalia Christiana Analecta," no. 144 (Rome, 1955). For the different grades in monasticism and the profession rites, consult Nalbro' Frazier Robinson's *Monasticism in the Orthodox Churches* (London and Milwaukee, 1916).

The best interpretation of the icon in its theological and liturgical context is Leonid Ouspensky and Vladimir Lossky's *The Meaning of Icons*, rev. ed. (New York, 1982).

KALLISTOS WARE

ECSTASY

The term *ecstasy* (Gr., *ekstasis*) literally means "to be placed outside," as well as, secondarily, "to be displaced." Both senses are relevant to the study of religion, the first more than the second perhaps, inasmuch as it denotes a state of exaltation in which one stands outside or transcends oneself. Transcendence has often been quintessentially associated with religion. If such an understanding of ecstasy carries the historian of religion into the hinterland of mysticism, the second sense, involving as it does spirit possession and shamanism, carries one to the borderland of anthropology and even psychiatry. The vast range of phenomena covered by the term supports the adoption of an approach toward its understanding that uses a variety of methods, one of which, the philological, has already been engaged. *Ecstasy* can thus mean both the seizure of one's body by a spirit and the seizure of man by divinity. Although seemingly in opposition, the two senses are not mutually exclusive, and between them lies the vast and diverse range of phenomena covered by the umbrella term ecstasy, with the magician standing at one end of the spectrum and the psychiatrist at the other. The historian of religion tries to grasp the significance of the intervening terrain with the help of historical, anthropological, phenomenological, sociological, psychological, and philosophical approaches to the study of religion.

Anthropological Approach. The anthropological approach emphasizes the role of the shaman. Through an ability to achieve a state of ecstatic exaltation, acquired after much rigorous training and careful, often painful initiation, the shaman is able to establish contact with the spirit world. In the course of this exaltation, the shaman may affect the postmortem fate of the deceased, aid or hurt the diseased in this life, as well as encounter the occupants of the spirit world, communicate with them, and then narrate the experiences of ecstatic flight on his or her return from there. [*See* Shamanism.]

Phenomenological Approach. It must be remembered, however, that while all shamans are ecstatics, all ecstatics are not shamans. Taking a broader phenomenological approach, one discovers that a variety of means, such as dancing, drugs, self-mortification, and so on, have been used across cultures, climes, and at various times to induce ecstasy and that these have generated ecstatic states ranging from the shamanistic to the mystical. If the first step of the phenomenological method is to classify, then one may employ Plato's distinction between "two types of mantic or `prophecy', the first the *mantike entheos,* the `inspired madness' of the ecstatic, e.g. that of the Pythia; the second the systematic interpretation of signs, such as the augury of the flight of birds" (van der Leeuw, vol. 1, 1938, p. 225). This last category may be excluded from consideration here as a form of soothsaying.

Sociological Approach. The sociology of ecstasy or ecstatic religion, as explored by I. M. Lewis, provides another useful dimension to the topic. Lewis draws attention to the socially integrative function of the shaman who, at ritual services, instills in the people a sense of solidarity by emphasizing the shunning of adultery, homicide, and other socially disruptive practices, and who often plays an active role in settling disputes. At the same time, however, the study of ecstasy also exposes the limitations of Durkheim's approach in certain contexts: the cultivation of ecstasy, especially in mysticism, may lead to a breach within a religious tradition instead of playing an integrating role in it.

Another issue raised by the sociological approach to the study of religion is the role of ecstasy in societies that are in the process of secularization. Two views seem to prevail. One is to look upon the cultivation of cultic ecstasy as possessing cathartic value in a society undergoing rapid social change. A broader view suggests that the process of secularization does not so much do away with the need for transcendence as it does provide surrogates for it. A convergence exists between the sociology of religion, which maintains that there are religious phenomena that belong to no determined religion, and the Tillichian theological viewpoint, which maintains that, though modern people think they have overcome their need for ultimate concern or transcendence, what has really happened is that they continue to seek it in secular contexts (as, for instance, in ecstatic participation in football matches).

Psychological Approach. The psychoanalytical approach has been applied to ecstasy at two levels, the shamanistic and the mystical. Claude Lévi-Strauss has argued that the cure administered by the shaman—who, unlike the modern analyst listening to the patient's words, speaks out on behalf of the patient—involves "the inversion of all the elements" of psychoanalysis yet retains its analogy with it. J. M. Masson, perhaps being reductionistic, sees in the ecstatic, oceanic feelings of the mystic a reversion to the experience of the fetus in the womb. Such approaches to ecstasy are difficult to assess objectively.

The Cross-Cultural Approach. Following Gershom Scholem's study of Jewish mysticism, we can ask why ecstatic experiences only occur in culture-bound contexts. Why, for instance, did Teresa of Ávila not have ecstatic visions of Kali? The Hindu mystic Rama-krishna is said to have had visions of figures outside Hinduism, but he is known to have been somewhat familiar with the traditions in question. Yet evidence from C. G. Jung's clients shows that certain archetypal ecstatic visions may transcend the bounds of time and space. The role of depth psychology in uncovering the roots of ecstasy, it seems, has yet to be fully explored. The physical symptoms accompanying the states of ecstasy, at the other extreme, also stand in need of exploration. In ecstasies of the shamanistic and prophetic type the hypothalamus has been shown to become inactive so that people in trance become impervious to physical maltreatment or deprivation; they still respond to speech and social communication, however. In ecstasies of the mystical type, signs of life have been known to fade, sometimes to the point of apparent disappearance.

Humanistic psychology has taken some interest in ecstasy in its relation to the concept of peak experience, as explored in the work of Abraham H. Maslow; this interest is even more evident in Ernst Arbman's monumental work, *Ecstasy of Religious Trance* (1963-1970). In this psychological study of ecstasy, Arbman emphasizes the close relation between ecstasy and mystical experience and, within mysticism, between ecstasy and visionary experience. He classifies the latter as assuming three forms, which represents a trichotomy of medieval Christian mysticism traceable to Augustine: corporeal, imaginative, and intellectual. The distinction between these three forms of ecstatic visionary experience is said to lie in the fact that, while the first experience is felt as something actually or objectively perceived, in the second case it is something experienced only inwardly, in a psychic or spiritual sense. Regarding the third type of vision, in which sense of the word *intellectual* seems to correspond more to Platonic than to modern usage, it apprehends its object without any image or form.

BIBLIOGRAPHY

Arberry, A. J. *Sufism: An Account of the Mystics of Islam* (1950). London, 1979.
Arbman, Ernst. *Ecstasy or Religious Trance.* 3 vols. Edited by Åke Hultkrantz. Stockholm, 1963-1970.
Davis, Charles. "Wherein There Is No Ecstasy." *Studies in Religion / Sciences religieuses* 13 (1984): 393-400.
Eliade, Mircea. *Yoga: Immortality and Freedom.* 2d ed. Princeton, 1969.
Eliade, Mircea. *Shamanism: Archaic Techniques of Ecstasy.* Rev. & enl. ed. New York, 1964.
Inge, W. R. "Ecstasy." In *Encyclopaedia of Religion and Ethics*, edited by James Hastings, vol. 5. Edinburgh, 1912.
Leeuw, Gerardus van der. *Religion in Essence and Manifestation*, vol. 1. Translated by J. E. Turner. London, 1938.
Lewis, I. M. *Ecstatic Religion: An Anthropological Study of Spirit Possession and Shamanism.* Harmondsworth, 1971.
Mahadevan, T. M. P. *Outlines of Hinduism.* Bombay, 1956.
Maslow, Abraham. *Religions, Values, and Peak-Experiences.* Columbus, Ohio, 1964.
Nyanatiloka. *Buddhist Dictionary.* Colombo, 1950.
Progoff, Ira, ed. and trans. *The Cloud of Unknowing.* New York, 1957.
Rahula, Walpola. *What the Buddha Taught.* Rev. ed. Bedford, England, 1967.
Tart, Charles T., ed. *Altered States of Consciousness: A Book of Readings.* New York, 1969.
Underhill, Evelyn. *Mysticism* (1911). 12th ed. New York, 1961.
Walker, Benjamin. *The Hindu World*, vol. 2. New York, 1968.
Wavell, Stewart, Audrey Butt, and Nina Epton. *Trances.* London, 1966.
Zaehner, R. C. *Zen, Drugs, and Mysticism.* New York, 1972.

ARVIND SHARMA

ECUMENICAL MOVEMENT

As the early church extended its geographical boundaries, writers begin to refer to the church throughout the *oikoumene* as a way of distinguishing it from local assemblies. And when Christians from different locations began to meet together to discuss aspects of belief and discipline, such gatherings began to be referred to as "ecumenical councils," that is, councils having representation from all parts of the *oikoumene*. Eastern Orthodox churches acknowledge seven ecumenical councils before the Great Schism of AD 1054, while the Roman Catholic church also claims as ecumenical subsequent councils in the West, such as the Council of Trent and the two Vatican councils. The Lutheran Formula of Concord (1577) described the early creeds (Apostles', Nicene, and Athanasian) as "ecumenical creeds" because they had been accepted by all branches of the Christian church. The meaning of the word *ecumenical* was thus extended beyond the theologically neutral notion of "the inhabited world" to include both an understanding of the church in its worldwide sense and expressions of belief that have universal ecclesiastical acceptance. [*See* Councils.]

After a period of relative neglect, the word *ecumenical* reappeared in the twentieth century, with new meanings appropriate to a new situation. Many church bodies, disturbed by their divisions from one another, which were made particularly apparent by the competitive nature of nineteenth-century missionary activities, began to look for ways to overcome their diverse histories. Following a world conference of missionary societies in Edinburgh in 1910, the word *ecumenism* began to be used to signify a concern to reunite the divided Christian family. Alongside this concern for unity was a corresponding concern for mission (from *missio*, "a sending forth") to the *oikoumene*. These twin poles of unity and mission have characterized what has come to be referred to as "the ecumenical movement." However, abroader use of the word *ecumenism* has also emerged to designate an attitude of active goodwill and concern for all peoples. Concerns about world hunger, racism, or political oppression are thus frequently described as "ecumenical concerns" and are often focal points of common action not only among Christians but in conjunction with all people of goodwill.

The World Council of Churches. In 1948 at Amsterdam, the World Council of Churches (WCC) became a reality, fusing the concerns of the Faith and Order and Life and Work commissions. In 1961 the International Missionary Council joined the WCC, thus completing the structural reunification of the three areas of concern originating at Edinburgh. Some 146 churches—Protestant, Anglican, and Orthodox—were the original members of the World Council.

All churches accepting the basic affirmation of "Jesus Christ as God and Savior" have been welcome to apply for membership, and at each world assembly (held every five or six years) new churches have joined, so that after the Vancouver world assembly (1983) there were three hundred member churches representing around four hundred million Christians and including almost all the major Protestant and Orthodox bodies in the world.

At the world assemblies, member churches meet to discuss their common task and to work on problems that have emerged since the previous assembly. The topics of the assemblies give an indication of the central themes of the WCC's ongoing life. From 1948 to 1983, six assemblies were held: "Man's Disorder and God's Design" (Amsterdam, 1948), "Jesus Christ the Hope of the World" (Evanston, 1954), "Jesus Christ the Light of the World" (New Delhi, 1961), "Behold I Make All Things New" (Uppsala, 1968), "Jesus Christ Frees and Unites" (Nairobi, 1975), and "Jesus Christ the Life of the World" (Vancouver, 1983).

> At the world assemblies, member churches meet to discuss their common task and to work on problems that have emerged since the previous assembly.

The Development of Roman Catholic Ecumenism. A major ecumenical turning point occurred when John XXIII invited the major Protestant, Anglican, and Orthodox bodies to send observers to the Second Vatican Council, convened in the fall of 1962. Lasting warm and personal relationships that dissolved the frosty barriers of the centuries were established during the four sessions of the council (1962-1965).

Vatican II enhanced Catholic engagement in ecumenism in a number of ways. For one, the very calling of a council was seen as an instance of *ecclesia semper reformanda* ("the church always being reformed"), a concept Protestants had previously thought was anathema to Rome. Second, the inclusion of the observers demonstrated that Rome did not wish to continue to live in ecclesiastical isolation. Third, the influence of the "missionary bishops" who had often worked with Protestant missionaries brought fresh perspectives to other bishops trained in exclusivist patterns. Fourth, many of the council documents opened new doors of ecumenical understanding.

Of the sixteen promulgated conciliar documents, at least seven had significant ecumenical import. The document on ecumenism opened new doors for dialogue and understanding; the document on the liturgy restored the use of the vernacular and made Catholic worship less foreign to non-Catholics; the document on the church affirmed the "collegiality of the bishops," correcting certain one-sided emphases from Vatican I concerning the primacy of Peter

that had been ecumenically counterproductive; the document on revelation gave scripture a greater prominence and authority in relation to tradition; the document on religious liberty dispelled fears about Catholic ecclesiastical imperialism; the document on the church and non-Christian religions created the possibility of dialogue between Roman Catholics and adherents of other world religions; and the document on the church and the world today indicated areas of concern, such as economics, labor unions, nuclear weapons, and culture, on which Catholics and non-Catholics could work together despite lack of full doctrinal consensus.

Assessments of the long-range impact of Vatican II are diverse. For many Catholics, the council brought the church into the modern world and made new levels of activity and dialogue possible. For other Catholics, the council created so many lines of rapport with modern thought and movements that the distinctiveness of the Catholic faith seemed to be placed in jeopardy. For most Protestants, the council unexpectedly legitimated Catholic attitudes that continue to enrich ecumenical life. [*For further discussion, see* Vatican Councils, *article on* Vatican II.]

Some Unresolved Ecumenical Issues. The real issue in the 1980s and 1990s and beyond may be the degree to which the "older churches" at the "center" can have the grace to be recipients of new understandings of the gospel that will come from the "younger churches" at the "periphery." For the time being, at least, it may be more ecumenically blessed for the older churches to receive than to give. (The World Council of Churches, which at its inception was made up almost entirely of "leaders" from North America and Europe, has responded creatively to the new situation. Increasing numbers of its staff and leadership are drawn from other parts of the world.)

In the area of doctrine there have been a surprising number of theological convergences, even though certain unresolved issues remain central to the question of church reunions. There are increasing degrees of consensus on the meaning of baptism and even on eucharist, though the matter of ministry (i. e., who is properly validated to administer the sacraments) is far from resolved. [*See* Sacraments.]

[*For further discussion of the varieties of Christian experience around the world, see* Christianity. *See also* African Religions, Australian Religions, North American Religions, and Oceanic Religions.]

BIBLIOGRAPHY

For a history of the mission and expansion of Christianity, the movement out of which modern ecumenism grew, the best overall resource is still K. S. Latourette's *Christianity in a Revolutionary Age: A History of Christianity in the Nineteenth and Twentieth Centuries*, 5 vols. (New York, 1958-1962). Documents pertinent to the development of the modern ecumenical movement are conveniently collected in *Documents on Christian Unity*, 4 vols., edited by G. K. A. Bell

(London, 1924-1958), which includes Protestant, Catholic, and Orthodox materials. For a full history of the ecumenical movement, with special attention to the formation of the World Council of Churches, consult *A History of the Ecumenical Movement, 1517-1948*, 2d ed., edited by Ruth Rouse and Stephen C. Neill (London, 1957), and its sequel, *The Ecumenical Advance: A History of the Ecumenical Movement*, vol. 2, *1948-1968,* edited by Harold E. Fey (Philadelphia, 1970). An interpretive account of the Faith and Order movement can be found in *A Documentary History of the Faith and Order Movement, 1927-1963,* edited by Lukas Vi-scher (Saint Louis, 1963), which contains excerpts from all the Faith and Order conferences through the New Delhi assembly (1961). The closest comparable volume tracing the Life and Work movement is Paul Bock's *In Search of a Responsible World Society: The Social Teachings of the World Council of Churches* (Philadelphia, 1974). The reports of all the WCC assemblies contain speeches, reports of the various commissions, and other pertinent information. These are *The First Assembly of the World Council of Churches: The Official Report* (New York, 1949), *The Second Assembly of the World Council of Churches: The Evanston Report* (New York, 1955), *The Third Assembly of the World Council of Churches: The New Delhi Report* (New York, 1962), all edited by W. A. Visser 't Hooft; *The Fourth Assembly of the World Council of Churches: The Uppsala Report,* edited by Norman Goodall (Geneva, 1968); *Breaking Barriers: Nairobi 1975,* edited by David M. Paton (London, 1975); and *Gathered for Life: Official Report, Sixth Assembly of the World Council of Churches,* edited by David Gill (Geneva, 1983). My *The Ecumenical Revolution*, rev. ed. (Garden City, N. Y., 1969), is a history of both Protestant and Catholic ecumenism through the Uppsala assembly in 1968.

For an account of the "ecumenical pioneers" who were active before Roman Catholic ecumenism was widely sanctioned, see Leonard J. Swidler's *The Ecumenical Vanguard* (Pittsburgh, 1966), which gives special attention to the Una Sancta movement. Hans Küng's *Justification: The Doctrine of Karl Barth and a Catholic Reflection* (London, 1964) is a good example of one of the earliest serious attempts to bridge the Protestant-Catholic chasm.

Two accounts of the Second Vatican Council are of special interest: the reports from *Le monde* by the French journalist Henri Fesquet available as *The Drama of Vatican II* (New York, 1967), and Xavier Rynne's *Letters from Vatican City: Vatican Council II* (New York, 1963). The latter is an expansion of a famous series of *New Yorker* accounts, published pseudonymously throughout the council. The most easily available collection of the results of Vatican II is *Documents of Vatican II*, edited by Walter M. Abbott and Joseph Gallagher (New York, 1966). Since Vatican II, a series of volumes known as "Concilium," with more than a hundred titles, has been published by various publishers at regular intervals.

As an example of new theological and ecumenical understanding, Gustavo Gutiérrez's *A Theology of Liberation* (Maryknoll, N. Y., 1973) is the best introduction to post-Vatican II liberation theology, and Paul M. Van Buren's *Discerning the Way* (New York, 1980) and *A Christian Theology of the People Israel* (New York, 1983) represent fresh attempts to reconstitute Christian theology by taking its relationship to Judaism with new seriousness.

The most useful ecumenical periodical is *Journal of Ecumenical Studies* (Pittsburgh, 1974-), published triannually, with articles, extensive reportage on ecumenical activities throughout the world, and book reviews of new ecumenical literature. *The Ecumenical Review* (Geneva, 1948-), a quarterly publication of the World Council of Churches, contains articles, extensive journals of WCC activities, and book reviews covering ecumenical contributions from all over the world. *The Information Service of the Secretariat for Promoting Christian Unity*, published in Rome, gives papers, digests, and summaries of ecumenical activities in which the Secretariat is involved.

ROBERT MCAFEE BROWN

EGYPTIAN RELIGION

An Overview

At the very beginnings of Egyptian history the slate palette of Narmer (c. 3110-3056 BCE) shows this king of Upper Egypt, who is wearing the white crown of the south, smiting a northerner, while on the reverse side of the palette Narmer is shown wearing the red crown of Lower Egypt. Whether Narmer or his son, Aha, was actually the first king (later known as Menes) of the first dynasty is still debatable, but some of the emblematic representations on the palette may have mythological significance. The divinity of the pharaoh and the notion of divine or sacred kingship have recently been challenged because of specific later references indicating that there were clear distinctions between the respect accorded the kings and the worship accorded the greatest gods.

For the first half of the Old Kingdom—the third and fourth dynasties—the great pyramids themselves remain, unfortunately, the principal monuments to the current beliefs. The attention given to these elaborate tombs clearly surpassed any other contemporaneous projects and would seem to show that the power of the king was reflected in the cult of his divine kingship.

Much more significant for our understanding of the religion of this period and of much that had been developing and evolving before it are the Pyramid Texts, first recorded in the interior burial rooms of the pyramid of Unas, the last king of the fifth dynasty. These texts in vertical columns, lacking the illustrations and rubrics of later such mortuary or funerary literature, provided a combination of rituals, hymns, prayers, incantations, and offering lists, all designed to ensure that the king would reach his goal in the afterlife and have the information and provisions that he would need there.

Apart from the central theme of this collection, we learn much more about the religion of Egypt from these texts through the king's relationship to various deities and also through citations or mythological allusions from the texts of the other religions of the Egyptians. Here the king's genealogy is presented clearly by making him the product of the Heliopolitan Ennead. This family of nine gods represents a cosmological or cosmogonical explanation of creation by Atum (the complete one), who by himself created Shu (air) and Tefnut (moisture). From this pair, Geb (earth) and Nut (watery sky) came forth, and in the next generation they produced the two brothers Osiris and Seth and their sisters, Isis and Nephthys. Osiris, the eldest, ruled on earth in place of his father, but he was slain by his stronger brother, Seth. It fell to Osiris' son, Horus, born after his death, to avenge the slaying and assume the rule of this world.

In the fifth dynasty society in general became more open, and many of the highest offices in the land could be attained by people not related to the royal family. At least a few utterances from the Pyramid Texts indicate that they were not written originally for a king, so that the goal of a blessed hereafter was not exclusively a royal prerogative. Further decentralization of power occurs in the sixth dynasty, and local nomarchs are provided with quite respectable tombs. These tombs may have been equipped with religious texts on coffins or papyri that have not survived, but certainly in the First Intermediate Period, with the breakdown of central authority, several claimants to kingship, and actual civil war, the claimants to earthly power also made claim to divinity.

On the inside surface of the bottom of most of the El Bersha coffins was painted an elaborate illustrated plan or map with descriptive texts known today as the Book of Two Ways. (The Book of Two Ways is a collection within the Coffin Texts.) This cosmological plan provided the earliest illustrated guidebook to the beyond and attempted to locate various uncommon demons as well as some commonly known terms for places in the afterlife.

Beginning with Senusret I (1971-1928 BCE) important new claims to kingly divinity surface. In the *Story of Sinuhe* Senusret I is called a god without peer, "no other came to be before him." In order to consolidate his power, Senusret III deposed a number of powerful nomarchs and divided the country into departments that were to be administered from the capital by his appointees. At the same time, in a cycle of songs in his honor and in a loyalist instruction he is called the "unique divine being" and is identified as Re (the sun god) himself. Remarkably, the propaganda literature of this dynasty remained popular for at least 900 years, and the tradition of Senusret's special position among the kings of Egypt also survived through Greek sources to the present.

The Second Intermediate Period was marked both by internal weakness eventually giving way to division and by foreign occupation of at least the major part of the delta. These Hyksos rulers were eventually driven out of their capital at Avaris by a new Theban family, which reunited the land and began the period of greatest imperialistic expansion, the New Kingdom. The new family was devoted to the cult of Amun-Re at Karnak, and also had a special interest in the moon god in several earlier forms, including Iah (the moon itself), Thoth, and Khonsu, who was now the son of Amun-Re and Mut (the mother).

The religious texts with which people were buried in the New Kingdom and later are now known as the *Book of Going Forth by Day* but they actually constituted at least two different collections, again emphasizing in introductions or conclusions either an Osirian or a solar afterlife, often with some elements of both in between. These papyri, illustrated with vignettes, vary greatly in length and include many interesting chapters, such as that with the servant statue or Shawabti spell (chap. 6), the heart spell (chap. 30), a spell to enable the deceased to have all requisite knowledge in one chapter (chap. 162), and the famous negative confession and judgment scene (chap. 125). The negative confession is not confession at all but rather a protestation of innocence between forty-two judges of the underworld. Following the psychosta-

> **Much more significant for our understanding of the religion of this period and of much that had been developing and evolving before it are the Pyramid Texts.**

sia, or weighing of the deceased's heart, in relation to the feather of Maat, or Truth, the deceased inevitably escapes the devourer and is presented to Osiris, but most often goes forth past the gatekeepers and joins Re as well. The New Kingdom copies of the *Book of Going Forth by Day* are commonly called the Theban recension because so many copies come from Theban tombs.

From the beginning of the eighteenth dynasty the principal religious text selected to decorate the walls of the royal burial chambers was the so-called book of Amduat, or *That Which Is in the Netherworld*. This book, which resembles a large-scale papyrus unrolled on the walls, treats of the voyage of the solar bark through the hours of the night sky, but it involves Sokar, the god of the Memphite necropolis (Rosetau), as chief god of the underworld. The nineteenth-dynasty kings, different as they may have been from their eighteenth-dynasty counterparts, were also buried in tombs in the Theban Valley of the Kings, but their tombs were more elaborately decorated, with relief carving and paintings of the Book of Gates and the journey of the sun through the body of the goddess Nut.

Ramses III of the twentieth dynasty was the last great pharaonic ruler of Egypt. His building efforts included a separate small temple at Karnak, as well as a very large mortuary temple for himself at medinet Habu. This latter, which survives in very good condition, contains descriptions of the complete festivals of Min and Sokar in addition to the usual battle scenes, and it also has an elaborate calendar of feasts and offerings.

Throughout the Ramessid period there are indications that all was not what it was supposed to be in this period of religious fervor. Banquet songs stress a *carpe diem* attitude; a workman in the royal necropolis shows no respect for his deceased king, and eventually almost all of the Theban tombs were systematically looted. Some of the robbers were accused and tried, but evidently those chiefly responsible got away with their crimes. The priests reburied the royal mummies, but with none of their original trappings or treasure. The priests apparently did not approve of the reinstatement of Seth by the Ramessid kings, and the god's name was attacked at their capital in the north.

With the Persian conquest of Egypt by Cambyses in 525 BCE, there are indications that the conquering kings had good intentions with regard to maintaining the cultural, legal, and religious traditions of the Egyptians, but with several native rebellions and one last gasp of independence in the thirtieth dynasty, Egypt fell again to the Persians, and in turn welcomed Alexander the Great in 332 BCE as a savior from the Persian oppressors.

Alexander was probably convinced of his own divinity on visiting the oracle of Amun at the Siwa oasis, but this was not enough to guarantee a long life. Under his successor, Philip Arrhidaeus, the sanctuary of the Karnak temple was rebuilt. When Alexander's general, Ptolemy, became king of Egypt, much new construction was begun. Alexandria, with its library, museum, and new government offices, was founded, while other Greek cities in Egypt were enlarged or planned. Under the Ptolemys truly great temples were erected at some ancient cult sites, and countless smaller temples, gates, appendages, and inscriptions were added to other places. All the main structures at the temple of Horus at Edfu are Ptolemaic. The vast main temple and its surrounding walls are covered from top to bottom with scenes and texts dealing with Horus, his myths and rituals. The texts have undergone a complicated encoding with a sixfold increase in the number of hieroglyphic signs used, and a wide range of possible substitutions for many standard signs is also encountered. The language is classical Middle Egyptian, and presumably the texts were from earlier material chosen by Egyptian priests from their own libraries, or perhaps from several sites in Egypt. The inscriptions are quite distinctive but often difficult to translate. They seem intentionally obscure despite their accessibility, and the encoding must have been used to make these texts more esoteric or arcane to their own followers and perhaps to the Greeks as well.

Mythology. Mythology is encountered in almost everything that survives from ancient Egypt. Texts, whether religious, historical, literary, medical, or legal, or merely personal correspondence, all contain mythological allusions. Art of all kinds and on all scales, and artifacts of all types, made use of easily recognizable mythological symbols.

It is not surprising to find that the Egyptians' mythology was not detailed and collected in any one place, but surely the various traditions were handed down by word of mouth and were generally well known. Temple libraries, known in the Late Period as "houses of life," certainly contained medico-magical texts, and also would have had many ritual, historical, and theological texts and treatises. There may have been individual texts relating to the individual cults or sites, such as Papyrus Jumilac. The cosmogonical myths that were excerpted for use in the mortuary literature and that have been briefly summarized above were included in the Pyramid Texts to indicate the power of the king, his genealogy, or his goal, rather than to explain or justify the other gods. The temple texts of individual gods are remarkable for the little mythological information they contain and the vast amount of knowledge they presume.

Some texts, such as the *Story of the Two Brothers* and the *Blinding of Truth by Falsehood,* are in large part mythological without being mythic in purpose. The *Contendings of Horus and Seth* has a totally mythological setting, but it is a burlesque of the real myth, and perhaps a sophisticated attack on the entire pantheon as well. The *Myth of the Destruction of Mankind* is slightly more serious in intent, showing men to be totally at the mercy of the gods if they cross them.

BIBLIOGRAPHY

Allen, Thomas George. *The Book of the Dead or Going Forth by Day.* Chicago, 1974.

Anthes, Rudolf. "Egyptian Theology in the Third Millennium B. C." *Journal of Near Eastern Studies* 18 (1959): 170-212.

Assmann, Jan. *Ägyptische Hymnen und Gebete.* Zurich, 1975.

Bell, H. Idris. *Cults and Creeds of Graeco-Roman Egypt.* Liverpool, 1953.

Bonnet, Hans. *Reallexikon der ägyptischen Religionsgeschichte.* Berlin, 1952.

Breasted, James H. *The Development of Religion and Thought in Ancient Egypt.* New York, 1912.

Cerny, Jaroslav. *Ancient Egyptian Religion.* London, 1952.

Englund, Gertie. *Akh: Une notion religieuse dans l'Égypte pharaonique.* Uppsala, 1978.

Erman, Adolf. *Die Religion der Ägypter: Ihr Werden und ihr Vergehen in vier Jahrtausenden.* Berlin, 1934.

Faulkner, Raymond. *The Ancient Egyptian Pyramid Texts.* Oxford, 1969.

Faulkner, Raymond. *The Ancient Egyptian Coffin Texts.* 3 vols. Oxford, 1973-1978.

Frankfort, Henri. *Kingship and the Gods.* Chicago, 1948.

Frankfort, Henri. *Before Philosophy.* Baltimore, 1954.

Frankfort, Henri. *Ancient Egyptian Religion.* New York, 1961.

Greven, Liselotte. *Der Ka in Theologie und Königskult der Ägypter des Alten Reiches.* Glückstadt, 1952.

Griffiths, J. Gwyn. *The Origins of Osiris and His Cult.* Leiden, 1980.

Hornung, Erik. *Altägyptische Höllenvorstellungen.* Leipzig, 1968.

Hornung, Erik. *Ägyptische Unterweltsbücher.* Zurich, 1972.

Hornung, Erik. *Conceptions of God in Ancient Egypt.* Ithaca, N. Y., 1982.

Junker, Hermann. *Die Götterlehre von Memphis (Schabaka-Inschrift).* Berlin, 1940.

Kees, Hermann. *Das Priestertum in ägyptischen Staat vom Neuen Reich bis zur Spätzeit.* Leiden, 1953.

Kees, Hermann. *Der Götterglaube im alten Ägypten.* 2d ed. Berlin, 1956.

Kees, Hermann. *Totenglauben und Jenseitsvorstellungen der alten Ägypter.* 2d ed. Berlin, 1956.

Lesko, Leonard H. "Some Observations on the Composition of the Book of Two Ways." *Journal of the American Oriental Society 91* (1971): 30-43.

Lesko, Leonard H. "The Field of Hetep in Egyptian Coffin Texts." *Journal of the American Research Center in Egypt 9* (1971-1972): 89-101.

Morenz, Siegfried. *Egyptian Religion.* Ithaca, N. Y., 1973.

Morenz, Siegfried. *Religion und Geschichte des alten Ägypten: Gesammelte Aufsätze.* Weimar, 1975.

Morenz, Siegfried, and Dieter Müller. *Untersuchungen zur Rolle des Schicksals in der ägyptischen Religion.* Berlin, 1960.

Moret, Alexandre. *Le rituel du culte divin journalier en Égypte d'après les papyrus de Berlin et les textes du temple de Séti Premier à Abydos.* Paris, 1902.

Mueller, Dieter. "An Early Egyptian Guide to the Hereafter." *Journal of Egyptian Archaeology 58* (1972): 99-125.

Otto, Eberhard. *Das Ägyptische Mundöffnungsritual.* Wiesbaden, 1960.

Piankoff, Alexandre. *Shrines of Tut-Ankh-Amon.* Princeton, 1955.

Piankoff, Alexandre. *The Wandering of the Soul.* Princeton, 1974.

Posener, Georges. *De la divinité du Pharaon.* Paris, 1960.

Sauneron, Serge. *Les prêtres de l'ancienne Égypte.* Paris, 1957.

Sauneron, Serge. *Les fêtes religieuses d'Esna.* Cairo, 1962.

Schweitzer, Ursula. *Das Wesen des Ka im Diesseits und Jenseits der alten Ägypter.* Glückstadt, 1956.

Sethe, Kurt H. *Dramatische Texte zu den altägyptischen Mysterienspielen.* Leipzig, 1928.

Sethe, Kurt H. *Amun und die acht Urgötter von Hermopolis.* Berlin, 1929.

Sethe, Kurt H. *Urgeschichte und älteste Religion der Ägypter.* Leipzig, 1930.

Spiegel, Joachim. "Das Auferstehungsritual der Unaspyramide." *Annales du Service des Antiquités de l'Égypte 53* (1956): 339-439.

Vandier, Jacques. *La religion égyptienne.* Paris, 1944.

Vandier, Jacques. *Le Papyrus Jumilhac.* Paris, 1961.

Westendorf, Wolfhart, ed. *Aspekte der spätägyptischen Religion.* Wiesbaden, 1979.

Wilson, John A. *The Burden of Egypt.* Chicago, 1951.

Wolf, Walther. *Das schöne Fest von Opet.* Leipzig, 1931.

Zabkar, Louis V. *A Study of the Ba Concept in Ancient Egyptian Texts.* Chicago, 1968.

Zandee, Jan. *Death as an Enemy.* Leiden, 1960.

LEONARD H. LESKO

ELIADE, MIRCEA

ELIADE, MIRCEA (1907-1986), Romanian-born historian of religions, humanist, Orientalist, philosopher, and creative writer. The career of Mircea Eliade, who served as editor in chief of this encyclopedia, was long and multifaceted.

Student Years. Born in Bucharest, the son of an army officer, Eliade witnessed the German occupation of his homeland when he was only nine years old. His lifelong fascination with literature, philosophy, Oriental studies, alchemy, and the history of religions began when he was still at the *lycée.* An early article entitled "The Enemy of the Silkworm" reflects the boy's intense interest in plants, animals, and insects. In fact he had already published his one hundredth article by the time he entered the University of Bucharest in 1925. At the university, he became a devoted disciple of the philosopher Nae Ionescu, who taught him the importance of life experience, commitment, intuition, and the spiritual or psychological reality of mental worlds. At the university Eliade became particularly interested in the philosophy of the Italian Renaissance, especially in Marsilio Ficino's rediscovery of Greek philosophy.

Eliade was blessed with the happy combination of an unusually keen mind, strong intuition, a fertile imagination, and the determination to work hard. Much of the structure of his later thought, and some of the paradoxes of his life, were foreshadowed during his student years. Simultaneously he was both a Romanian patriot and a world citizen. He was proud of Western civilization, although he lamented its provincial character, particularly its will to "universalize" Western ideas and values into the norm for all of humankind. Looking back, he could see that in his country previous generations had had no cause to question their historic mission to consolidate Romania's national identity. His own generation, though, had experienced World War I and seemed to have no ready-made model or mission for themselves. Eliade's plea was that his fellow countrymen should exploit this period of "creative freedom" from tradition and should try to learn from other parts of the world what possibilities for life and thought there were. His ultimate concern was the revitalization of all branches of learning and the arts, and his great hope was to decipher the message of the cosmos, which to him was a great repository of hidden meanings. Judging from his diaries and other writings, it seems that Eliade always had a strong sense of destiny, from his youth until his last day in Chicago, calling him from one phase of life to the next, though he felt he was not always conscious of what lay in store for him along the way.

As though to fulfill Eliade's preordained destiny, the maharaja of Kassimbazar offered him a grant to study Indian philosophy with Surendranath Dasgupta at the University of Calcutta (1928-1932). He also spent six months in the ashram of Rishikesh in the Himalayas. To him, India was more than a place for scholarly research. He felt that a mystery was hidden somewhere in India, and deciphering it would disclose the mystery of his own existence. India indeed revealed to him the profound meaning of the freedom that can be achieved by abolishing the routine conditions of human existence, a meaning indicated in the subtitle of his book on Yoga: *Immortality and Freedom.*

The stay in India also opened his eyes to the existence of common elements in all peasant cultures—for example, in China, Southeast Asia, pre-Aryan aboriginal India, the

Mediterranean world, and the Iberian Peninsula—the elements from which he would later derive the notion of "cosmic religion." In fact, the discovery of pre-Aryan aboriginal Indian spirituality (which has remained an important thread in the fabric of Hinduism to the present) led Eliade to speculate on a comparable synthesis in southeastern Europe, where the ancient culture of the Dacians formed the "autochthonous base" of present-day Romanian culture. (Dacian culture had been reconstructed by a Romanian philosopher-folklorist, B. P. Hasdeu.) Moreover, Eliade came to believe that the substratum of peasant cultures of southeastern Europe has been preserved to this day, underneath the cultural influences of the Greeks, the Romans, the Byzantines, and Christianity, and he went so far as to suggest that the peasant roots of Romanian culture could become the basis of a genuine universalism, transcending nationalism and cultural provincialism. He believed that the oppressed peoples of Asia and elsewhere might take their rightful place in world history through such universalism.

Early Literary and Intellectual Activity. In 1932 Eliade returned to Romania and was appointed to assist Nae Ionescu at the University of Bucharest in the following year. His publication of *Yoga: Essai sur les origines de la mystique indienne* (1936), in which he attempted a new interpretation of the myths and symbolism of archaic and Oriental religions, attracted the attention of such eminent European scholars as Jean Przyluski, Louis de La Vallée Poussin, Heinrich Zimmer, and Giuseppe Tucci. He also plunged feverishly into literary activities. Many people were under the impression then that Eliade thought of himself primarily as a novelist, although he was strongly motivated to engage in scholarly activities as well. Eliade had made his literary debut in 1930 with *Isabel si Apele Divolului* (Isabel and the Devil's Water), which was obviously colored by his Indian experience. According to Matei Calinescu, in his essay " 'The Function of the Unreal': Reflections on Mircea Eliade's Short Fiction" (in Girardot and Ricketts, 1982), most of Eliade's fiction inspired by India was written between 1930 and 1935, and his earlier novels with Indian themes (e.g., *Maitreyi*, 1933) were strongly autobiographical. He also points out that Eliade's later novellas on these themes, such as *Secretul Doctorului Honigberger* (The Secret of Doctor Honigberger) and *Nopti la Serampore* (Night in Serampore), both published in a single volume entitled *Secretul Doctoru-lui Honigberger* (1940), "deal with the major problem of the fully mature Eliade, that of the ambiguities of the sacred and the profane in their characteristical relationship"; Calimescu concludes that "Eliade had discovered the 'ontological' signification of narration" by 1940 (ibid., p. 142).

Eliade once stated that young Romanians had a very short period of creative freedom, and fear that this observation might apply to himself compelled him to work against the clock. Accordingly, he published not only literary works but

also a series of important scholarly studies on alchemy, mythology, Oriental studies, philosophy, symbology, metallurgy, and the history of religions. In 1938 he founded the journal *Zalmoxis: Revue des études religieuses.* (Unfortunately, circulation ceased after 1942.) Eliade was also active in the so-called Criterion group, consisting of male and female intellectuals. This group was a significant collective manifestation of the "young generation" of Romanians, which sponsored public lectures, symposia, and discussion about important contemporary intellectual issues as a new type of Socratic dialogue. "The goal we were pursuing," Eliade said, "was not only to inform people; above all, we were seeking to 'awaken' the audience, to confront them with ideas, and ultimately to modify their mode of being in the world" (*Autobiography*, vol. 1, p. 237).

Meanwhile, Romania could not help but be touched by the political whirlwind that was rising in Europe, manifested in the conflicts and tensions between communism and democracy, fascism and Nazism. Following the assassination of Romanian Prime Minister Duca in December 1933, Eliade's mentor Nae Ionescu was arrested on suspicion that he was an antiroyalist rightist. Also arrested were the leaders of the pro-Nazi Legion of the Archangel Michael, commonly known as the Legionnaires or the Iron Guard, and some of Eliade's friends in the Criterion group. Of course the Criterion experiment ceased to function because it was impossible for Legionnaires, democrats, and communists to share the same platform. Thus, Romania entered a "broken-off era," as Eliade called it with fear and trembling. The tense political atmosphere, the cruelties and excesses of all sorts, find their echoes in Eliade's *Huliganii*, 2 vols. (The Hooligans; 1935), although he explicitly said that the hooligans in the novel were very different from the actual Romanian hooligans of the 1930s—those "groups of young antisemites, ready to break windows or heads, to attack or loot synagogues" (*Autobiography*, vol. 1, p. 301). What concerned Eliade was not only the sad political reality of his homeland. He wrote, "I had had the premonition long before . . . that we would *not have time*. I sensed now not only that time was limited, but that there would come a terrifying time (the time of the 'terror of history')" (ibid., p. 292). In 1938 the royal dictatorship in Romania was proclaimed; then came World War II.

Emigration and Development. In 1940 Eliade was appointed cultural attaché at the Royal Romanian Legation in war-torn London. In the following year he became a cultural counselor in Lisbon, in neutral Portugal. When the war was over in 1945, Eliade went directly to Paris, thus starting the life of self-imposed exile.

In 1946 Eliade was invited to serve as a visiting professor at the École des Hautes Études of the Sorbonne. He then proceeded to publish such famous works as *Techniques du Yoga* (1948), *Traité d'histoire des religions* (1949; revised translation, *Patterns in Comparative Religion*, 1958), *Le mythe de l'eternel retour* (1949; revised translation, *The Myth of the Eternal Return*, 1954), *Le chamanisme et les techniques archaiques de l'extase* (1951; revised and enlarged translation, *Shamanism: Archaic Techniques of Ecstasy*, 1964), and so on. He was also invited by many leading universities in Europe to deliver lectures, and he appeared in a number of seminars and conferences, for example, the annual meetings at Ascona, Switzerland.

In retrospect, it becomes clear that during his stay in Paris (1945-1955) Eliade solidified most of his important concepts and categories, including those of *homo religiosus*, *homo symbolicus*, archetypes, *coincidentia oppositorum*, hierophany, *axis mundi*, the cosmic rope, the nostalgia for Paradise, androgyny, the initiatory scenario, and so on, all of which became integral parts of a coherent outlook or system that aimed at what Eliade later called a total hermeneutics. This may account for the impossibility of isolating, or even criticizing, any part of his system without disturbing the entire framework. Side by side with this development, one notices the shift in his personal orientation. Before World War II, his scholarly and literary activities had focused very much on Romania. In those years, he affirmed that "the orthodox heritage could constitute a total conception of the world and existence, and that this synthesis, if it could be realized,

> **"...we were seeking to 'awaken' the audience, to confront them with ideas, and ultimately to modify their mode of being in the world."**

would be a new phenomenon in the history of modern Romanian culture" (*Autobiography*, vol. 1, p. 132). After the war, he continued to regard himself as a Romanian writer, but something new was added. The sense that his experience suggested the paradigm of the homeless exile as a symbol of religious reality for modern, secularized humankind. In this situation, his literary works, too, took on the "coloring of a *redeeming force (forta recuperatoare)*," to quote Eugene Simon (in Girardot and Ricketts, 1982, p. 136).

Methodology and Imagination. Like many other historians of religions—for example, Raffaele Pettazzoni (1883-1959) and Joachim Wach (1898-1955)—Eliade held that the discipline of the history of religions (*Allgemeine Religionswissenschaft*) consisted of two dimensions, historical and systematic. Characteristically, he worked first on the systematic dimension (using the "morphological" method, inspired by Goethe), as exemplified by his *Traité (Patterns in Comparative Religion)*, which presents an astonishing variety of religious data and their basic "patterns." The book starts with certain "cosmic" hierophanies (i. e., manifestations

of the sacred), such as the sky, waters, earth, and stones. Analyses of these manifestations are based on Eliade's notion of the dialectic of the sacred, in order to show how far those hierophanies constitute autonomous forms. He goes on to discuss the "biological" hierophanies (from the rhythm of the moon to sexuality), "local" hierophanies such as consecrated places, and "myths and symbols." Throughout the book, Eliade examines both the "lower" and "higher" religious forms side by side instead of moving from lower to higher forms, as is done in evolutionary schemes. He takes pain to explain that "religious wholes are not seen in bits and pieces, for each class of hierophanies . . . forms, in its own way, a whole, both morphologically . . . and historically" (*Patterns in Comparative Religion*, New York, 1958, p. xvi).

It is not surprising that Eliade's morphology of religion, which is his version of the systematic aspect of the history of religions, has much in common with the phenomenology of religion of Gerardus van der Leeuw (1890-1950), a Dutch historian of religions, theologian, ethnologist, and phenomenologist. Eliade wrote a very positive review of van der Leeuw's *Religion in Essence and Manifestation* in *Revue d'histoire des religions* 138 (1950): 108-111. Although Eliade is uneasy with van der Leeuw's starting point, he praises the book because it shows that human beings can and do find religious meaning even in the most banal physiological activities such as eating and sexuality, and the book portrays the entire cosmos with its most humble parts serving as grounds for the manifestation of the sacred. It should be noted that religion has two dimensions in van der Leeuw's scheme, namely, "religion as experience," which can be studied phenomenologically, and "religion as revelation," which is basically incomprehensible and thus can be studied only theologically. Furthermore, van der Leeuw never claimed that his phenomenological study is empirical, because to him empirical research is needed only to control what has been understood phenomenologically. Similarly, Eliade never claimed that the history of religions, including its systematic task, is empirical in a narrow scientific sense, even though it certainly has empirical dimensions.

Eliade always felt a need for the alternating modes of the creative spirit—the "diurnal," rational mode of scholarship, which he expressed in his French writings, and the "nocturnal," mythological mode of imagination and fantasy, which he continued to express in Romanian. In 1955, the French translation of his major novel, *Forêt interdite*, appeared. According to Mac Linscott Ricketts, who with M. P. Stevenson translated this novel into English (*The Forbidden Forest*, 1978), Eliade felt it would be more for this work and other fiction that he would be remembered by later generations than for his erudite scholarly works. *The Forbidden Forest* is in a sense a historical novel, dealing with the events and activities of the protagonist and his lovers, friends, and foes during the turbulent twelve years from 1936 to 1948, in Romania, London,

Lisbon, Russia, and Paris. In another sense it is an original novel. Eliade skillfully creates characters, all of whom are caught by "destiny," as people often are in his other stories. All of them try to escape from the network of historical events and from destructive "time," which is the central theme of this novel. To be sure, the novels were not meant to be literary illustrations of Eliade's theories, but he admits there are some structural analogies between the scientific and literary imaginations, such as the structure of sacred and mythical space, and more especially "a considerable number of strange, unfamiliar, and enigmatic worlds of meaning" (*No Souvenirs*, p. ix).

Years in the United States. In 1956 Eliade was invited by the University of Chicago to deliver the Haskell Lectures, which were published under the title *Birth and Rebirth* (1958). In 1957 he joined the University of Chicago faculty and continued to live in that city after his retirement. At the time of his death in 1986, he was the Sewell L. Avery Distinguished Service Professor Emeritus.

Eliade's move to the United States at the age of forty-nine meant a second emigration for him, but he made an excellent adjustment to the new environment. The University of Chicago had traditionally been an important center for the study of the history of religions, and graduates trained by Eliade's predecessor, Joachim Wach, were scattered in many parts of North America and on other continents. Eliade's appointment at Chicago coincided with the sudden mushrooming of departments of religion or religious studies as part of the liberal arts programs of various colleges and universities in North America. Fortunately, his books and articles—mostly the scholarly ones and not his literary works—were beginning to be translated into English, and the reading public devoured them. Eliade made a deep impression on young readers with such works as *Cosmos and History* (1959), *The Sacred and the Profane* (1959), *Myths, Dreams and Mysteries* (1960), *Images and Symbols* (1969), *Myths and Reality* (1963), *Mephistopheles and the Androgyne* (1965), *Zalmoxis* (1972), *The Forge and the Crucible* (1962), *The Quest* (1975), and others. He also exerted a tremendous influence on more advanced students with *Yoga* (1958), *Shamanism* (1964), and *Australian Religions* (1973). The fact that Eliade was willing to use nonphilosophical and nontheological terms in an elegant literary style to discuss religious subjects attracted many secularized youths.

There were three new factors that helped Eliade's cause enormously. The first was the founding in the summer of 1961 of a new international journal for comparative historical studies called *History of Religion*. Wisely, Eliade suggested making it an English-language journal instead of a multilanguage one. For the opening issue, Eliade wrote the famous article entitled "History of Religions and a New Humanism" (*History of Religions* 1, Summer 1961, pp. 1–8). In it, he expressed his sympathy with young scholars who would

have become historians of religions but who, in a world that exalts specialists, had resorted to becoming specialists in one religion or even in a particular period or a single aspect of that religion. Historians of religions, he said, are called to be learned generalists. He recognized the danger of "reductionism" in the history of religions as much as in the interpretation of art and literary works. He insisted that a work of art, for example, reveals its meaning only when it is seen as an autonomous artistic creation and nothing else. In the case of the history of religions he realized that the situation is complex because there is no such thing as a "pure" religious datum, and that a human datum is also a historical datum. But this does not imply that, for historians of religions, a historical datum is in any way reducible to a nonreligious, economic, social, cultural, psychological, or political meaning. And, quoting the words of Raffaele Pettazzoni, he exhorted readers to engage in the twin (systematic and historical) tasks of the history of religions. But to him, ultimately, the history of religions was more than merely an academic pursuit.

Second, Eliade took an active part as a member (and president for a term) of a small group of North American scholars called the American Society for the Study of Religion (ASSR), established in Chicago in 1958. It was through this group that much of Eliade's personal contacts with fellow historians of religions and scholars in related fields in North America were made.

Third, Eliade, who had previously worked either on "systematic" endeavors or on studies of "particular" religious forms (e.g., yoga, shamanism, Romanian folk religion, or

> **Eliade felt it would be for . . . fiction that he would be remembered . . . than for his erudite scholarly works.**

Australian religion) always from the perspective of the history of religions, embarked during his Chicago days on a new genre, namely, a "historical" study of the history of religions. Initially he worked on a "thematic source book" entitled *From Primitive to Zen* (1968) dealing with religious data from nonliterate, ancient, medieval, and modern religions. Then he envisaged the publication of four volumes (though his health prevented his working on the fourth volume himself) entitled *A History of Religious Ideas* (1978–1986). Although the scheme of the series follows manifestations of the sacred and the creative moments of the different traditions more or less in chronological order, readers will recognize that these books reflect faithfully his lifelong conviction about the fundamental unity of all religious phenomena. Thus, in his historical studies as much as in his systematic endeavors, he was true to his hypothesis that "every rite, every myth, every belief or divine figure reflects the experience of the sacred and hence implies the notions of *being*, of *meaning*, and of *truth*" (*A History of Religious Ideas*, vol. 1, Chicago, 1978, p. xiii).

During the latter part of his stay in Chicago, fame and honor came his way from various parts of the world. By that time, many of his books, including his literary works, had been translated into several languages. He had his share of critics. Some people thought that he was not religious enough, while others accused him of being too philosophical and not humanistic enough, historical enough, scientific enough, or empirical enough. But, as hinted earlier, he held a consistent viewpoint that penetrated all aspects of his scholarly and literary works, so that it is difficult to be for or against any part of his writings without having to judge the whole framework.

Eliade's last major undertaking in his life was the *Encyclopedia of Religion*. As he stated himself, what he had in mind was not a dictionary but an encyclopedia—a selection of all the important ideas and beliefs, rituals and myths, symbols and persons, all that played a role in the universal history of the religious experience of humankind from the Paleolithic age to our time. It is to his credit that various scholars from every continent cooperated on the encyclopedia to produce concise, clear descriptions of a number of religious forms within the limits of our present knowledge. As soon as he had completed the major portion of his work as editor in chief of the encyclopedia, he was already thinking of several new projects, among them ones that would develop the themes of cosmos, humankind, and time. Throughout his life, Eliade never claimed that he had the answer to the riddle of life, but he was willing to advance daring hypotheses.

Once Eliade paid a high tribute to his friend and colleague, Paul Tillich, at the latter's memorial service in Chicago, and if the name of Tillich is replaced with that of Eliade, it portrays the latter admirably: "Faithful to his vocation and his destiny [Eliade] did not die at the end of his career, when he had supposedly said everything important that he could say. . . . Thus, his death is even more tragic. But it is also symbolic" (*Criterion* 5, no. 1, 1968, p. 15).

BIBLIOGRAPHY

Both as a scholar and as a writer, Eliade was prolific throughout his life, and his works have been translated into many languages. Thus, it is virtually impossible to list all his books and articles, even the major ones, although efforts were made to include the major titles in the foregoing text. Fortunately, there are some Eliade bibliographies in English that are readily available to readers, such as the one included in *Myths and Symbols: Studies in Honor of Mircea Eliade*, edited by Joseph M. Kitagawa and Charles H. Long (Chicago, 1969), and a more up-to-date one, edited by Douglas Allen and Dennis Doeing, *Mircea Eliade: An Annotated Bibliography*, (New York, 1980). One of the best introductions to Eliade's thought is his *Ordeal by Labyrinth: Conversations with Claude-Henri Rocquet* either in its French original (Paris, 1978) or in its English translation (Chicago, 1982). This book has the virtues of unfolding Eliade's own mature views about himself, and it includes "A Chronology of Mircea Eliade's Life," which calls attention to his major writings. There are also many articles and books in various languages on Eliade's scholarly and literary works, some critical, some sympathetic, and some favorable. The third section of the above-mentioned *Myths and Symbols*, as well as *Imagination and Meaning: The Scholarly and Literary Worlds of Mircea Eliade*, edited by N. J. Girardot and Mac Linscott Ricketts (New York, 1982), and *Waiting for the Dawn: Mircea Eliade in Perspective*, edited by Davíd Carrasco and J. M. Swanberg (Boulder, 1985), make helpful references to his creative writing, although his scholarly side inevitably comes into the picture too.

There are many other works (mentioning only monographs) that readers should find useful. See Douglas Allen's *Structure and Creativity in Religion: Mircea Eliade's Phenomenology and New Directions* (The Hague, 1978); Thomas J. J. Altizer's *Mircea Eliade and the Dialectic of the Sacred* (Philadelphia, 1963); Guilford Dudley's *Religion on Trial: Mircea Eliade and His Critics* (Philadelphia, 1977); Jonathan Z. Smith's *Map Is Not Territory: Studies in the History of Religions* (Leiden, 1978); Ioan Petro Culianu's *Mircea Eliade* (Assisi, 1978); and Antonio B. de Silva's *The Phenomenology of Religion as a Philosophical Problem: An Analysis of the Theoretical Background of the Phenomenology of Religion, in General, and of M. Eliade's Phenomenological Approach, in Particular* (Uppsala, 1982).

JOSEPH M. KITAGAWA

EMERSON, RALPH WALDO

EMERSON, RALPH WALDO (1803-1882), American essayist, poet, and lecturer, a leading figure among the New England Transcendentalists. Born in Boston, Emerson was descended from a long line of Christian ministers. The son of a distinguished Unitarian minister and a deeply religious mother, he was heir to the dual legacy of Boston Unitarianism: liberalism in matters of theology and Puritan piety in matters of personal devotion, morals, and manners.

Emerson himself became a Unitarian minister, and by 1829 he had secured a desirable position as pastor of the Second Church of Boston. This followed an undistinguished four years at Harvard College, from which he graduated in 1817, and a period of study at Harvard Divinity School, during which he also worked, with little satisfaction, as a schoolmaster. With the pastorate of the Second Church, Emerson for the first time felt secure both professionally and financially. During this period he married Ellen Louisa Tucker, a younger woman of a sensitive nature and delicate health. Her death from tuberculosis, less than two years after their marriage, seems to have wrought important changes in Emerson's attitudes and thought. A rebellious strain in his character was perhaps strengthened; incipient attitudes were more strongly voiced. In his solitariness he found his faith in the primacy of the individual's relation to God strengthened, so too an impatience with the theological inheritance of received religion. Emerson eventually gave up the pastorate of the Second Church, taking issue with the congregation's customary administration of the Lord's Supper; by 1838 he stopped preaching altogether.

Though Emerson would certainly always have considered himself a "disciple of Christ," his mature thought, as expressed in his essays and poetry, was not beholden to historical Christianity. He passionately sought for the essential spirit of religion a local habitation—temporally, geographically, and in the life of the individual. In the introduction to *Nature* (1833), which came to be his most widely read essay, he wrote: "The foregoing generations beheld God and nature face to face; we, through their eyes. Why should we not also enjoy an original relation to the universe? Why should we not have . . . a religion of revelation to us and not the history of theirs?"

Emerson was not a systematic thinker, and his ideas resist any ready summation. The essays are homiletic and aphoristic and have a cumulative power not dependent on force of logic. Certain strains can be identified, however, that undermine basic Christian conceptions. Emerson's worldview is essentially nonteleological, his radical assertion being that each individual soul must remake anew an original relation to the world.

The distance between his mature views and his Christian background seems not to have troubled Emerson, perhaps because he did not see the two as incompatible. As prophet to an age "destitute of faith, but terrified of skepticism," as his friend Thomas Carlyle characterized it, Emerson advanced his unorthodox views forthrightly and unapologetically, secure in his advocacy of "truer" religion. There is a consistent strain of optimism in his work that helped win him a wide audience and also has brought him some criticism, namely that he avoided any note of tragedy in his writings, even while his journal reveals that he was well acquainted with tragedy in life.

BIBLIOGRAPHY

The primary resources for the study of Emerson are *The Complete Works of Ralph Waldo Emerson*, 12 vols., edited by Edward W. Emerson and *The Journals and Miscellaneous Notebooks of Ralph Waldo Emerson,* 14 vols. (Cambridge, Mass, 1960-1978). The best recent biography is Gay Wilson Allen's *Waldo Emerson* (New York, 1981). Stephen E. Whicher's *Freedom and Fate: An Inner Life of Ralph Waldo Emerson*, 2d ed. (Philadelphia, 1971), is a watershed study, a point of departure for much later criticism. Jonathan Bishop's *Emerson on the Soul* (Cambridge, Mass., 1964) is another good account of Emerson's intellectual and religious development, as is Joel Porte's *Representative Man: Ralph Waldo Emerson in His Time* (New York, 1979). Two useful collections of criticism are *The Recognition of Ralph Waldo Emerson: Selected Criticism since 1837,* edited by Milton R. Konvitz (Ann Arbor, 1972), and *Critical Essays on Ralph Waldo Emerson,* edited by Robert E. Burkholder and Joel Myerson (Boston, 1983).

DAVID SASSIAN

ENLIGHTENMENT, THE

The eighteenth-century European intellectual movement known as the Enlightenment was affiliated with the rise of the bourgeoisie and the influence of modern science; it promoted the values of intellectual and material progress, toleration, and critical reason as opposed to authority and tradition in matters of politics and religion.

The way was paved for the French Enlightenment (the Enlightenment has always been regarded as predominantly a French movement) by the wide influence of Cartesian philosophy and science in the latter half of the seventeenth century. But it also took stimulus from philosophical and scientific advances elsewhere, particularly in England. Within France, the principal forerunner of the Enlightenment was Pierre Bayle (1647-1706), whose *Historical and Critical Dictionary* (1697) combined sharp wit, copious historical learning, and dialectical skill with a skeptical temper and a deep commitment to the values of intellectual openness and toleration, especially in religious matters. The chief philosophical inspiration for the French Enlightenment was provided by John Locke (1632-1704), whose epistemology, political theory, and conception of the relation of reason to religion became models for French Enlightenment thinkers. [See the biography of Locke.]

The younger generation of French Enlightenment thinkers (or *philosophes*) represents a considerable variety of viewpoints. The leading French philosopher of this generation was Denis Diderot (1713-1784), a versatile and gifted writer, and the principal editor of the massive *Encyclopedia*, unquestionably the greatest scholarly and literary achievement of the French Enlightenment.

The *philosophes* also included some infamous philosophical radicals, particularly Julien Offroy de La Mettrie (1709-1751), Claude-Adrien Helvétius (1715-1771), and Paul-Henri Thiry, baron d'Holbach (1723-1789). La Mettrie expounded an openly materialist theory of the soul in *Man a Machine* (1748) and a blatantly hedonist ethics in *Discourse on Happiness* (1750). Helvétius's *On the Mind* (published posthumously, 1772) presents a thoroughgoing determinist and environmentalist psychology, together with a utilitarian ethical theory. D'Holbach's attack on religion was begun in his *Christianisme dévoilé* (1761; the title is cleverly ambiguous: "revealed Christianity" or "Christianity exposed"); it was continued in his materialistic, deterministic, and atheistic *System of Nature* (1770).

Elsewhere in Europe, the Enlightenment took more moderate forms. In Germany, the alleged religious unorthodoxy of the *Aufklärung's* representatives often made them objects of controversy, sometimes victims of persecution. But in fact there was nothing more radical among them than a rather conservative form of Deism.

The Enlightenment in Britain is represented in theology by the tradition of British Deism (the position of such men as John Toland and Matthew Tindal) and in politics by Whig liberalism. Representative of both trends was the philosopher, scientist, and Presbyterian (and Unitarian) cleric Joseph Priestley (1733-1804). Other Britons displaying the impact of the Enlightenment included the utilitarian Jeremy Bentham (1748-1832), the economist and moral theorist Adam Smith (1723-1790), the historian Edward Gibbon (1737-1794), and the radical political thinker William Godwin (1756-1836).

The founding fathers of the United States included prominent Enlightenment figures: Thomas Paine, Benjamin Franklin, and Thomas Jefferson. The Federalist suspicion of centralized state power and the hostility to clericalism motivating the complete separation of church and state in the new republic both reflect the influence of Enlightenment ideas.

The common twentieth-century view—inherited from nineteenth-century romanticism—is that Enlightenment thinkers were shallow and arrogant, showing an irreverence and contempt for tradition and authority. Of course, any movement that (like the Enlightenment) sets out to deflate the pretensions of pseudo-profundity will naturally be accused of shallowness by those it makes its targets. It is equally natural that people who are outraged by crimes and hypocrisy carried on under the protection of an attitude of reverence for tradition and authority should choose irreverent wit and satire as appropriate vehicles for their criticism. In fact, the Enlightenment attack on religious authority and tradition was motivated by a profound concern for what it conceived to be the most essential values of the human spirit, the foundations of any true religion.

Kant defines "enlightenment" as "the human being's release from self-imposed tutelage"; by "tutelage," he means the inability to use one's understanding without guidance from another, the state of a child whose spiritual life is still held in benevolent bondage by his parents. Tutelage is self-imposed when it results not from immaturity or inability to think for oneself, but rather from a lack of courage to do so. Thus enlightenment is the process by which human individuals receive the courage to think for themselves about morality, religion, and politics, instead of having their opinions dictated to them by political, ecclesiastical, or scriptural authorities.

[*See also* Atheism *and* Faith.]

BIBLIOGRAPHY

The best general study of Enlightenment thought is Ernst Cassirer's *The Philosophy of Enlightenment* (Boston, 1951). Also valuable are Paul Hazard's European *Thought in the Eighteenth Century* (New Haven, 1954) and Frederick C. Copleston's *A History of Philosophy*, vol. 6, *Wolff to Kant* (Westminster, Md., 1963), parts 1 and 2. Carl Becker's *The Heavenly City of the Eighteenth-Century Philosophers* (New Haven, 1932) is a famous and paradoxical defense of the continuity between Enlightenment thinkers and the Christian tradition they criticized. The best known of many replies to it is Peter Gay's *The Enlightenment*, 2 vols. (New York, 1966), especially volume 1, *The Rise of Modern Paganism*.

On the French Enlightenment, see Frank E. Manuel's *The Prophets of Paris* (Cambridge, Mass., 1962); on England, see John Plamenatz's *The English Utilitarians*, 2d ed. (Oxford, 1958). An excellent treatment of the German Enlightenment can be found in chapters 10-17 of Lewis White Beck's *Early German Philosophy: Kant and His Predecessors* (Cambridge, Mass., 1969). Studies emphasizing the religious thought of the four most important Enlightenment thinkers are Norman L. Torrey's *Voltaire and the English Deists* (1930; reprint, Hamden, Conn., 1967); Aram Vartanian's *Diderot and Descartes* (Princeton, 1953); *Hume on Religion* (New York, 1963), edited by Richard Wollheim; and my book *Kant's Moral Religion* (Ithaca, N. Y., 1970).

ALLEN W. WOOD

ERAMUS, DESIDERIUS

ERASMUS, DESIDERIUS (1469?-1536), Dutch scholar, "prince of humanists." Neither the date nor the place of Erasmus's birth is known with certainty; he was probably born in 1469 in Rotterdam (he styled himself Roterodamus).

Life and Works. After his early education, mainly in the school of the Brethren of the Common Life at Deventer (1475-1483), his guardians sent him to the monastery of the Augustinian canons at Steyn. Ordained to the priesthood in 1492, he entered the service of Henry of Bergen, bishop of Cambrai, who gave him leave to study theology at the University of Paris (1495-1498). Later he visited the cradle of the Renaissance, Italy (1506-1509), and made further journeys to England, including Cambridge, before settling in the Netherlands, at Louvain (1517-1521). There, at the height of his fame, he intended to devote himself quietly to the cause of classical and sacred literature.

But from 1518, Erasmus's labors were increasingly overshadowed by the Lutheran Reformation. He could not but welcome the addition of Martin Luther's voice to his own outspoken criticisms of ecclesiastical abuses, yet he distrusted Luther's aggressive manner, which he feared could only harm the cause of learning and piety. His friends and patrons finally induced him to challenge Luther in print. The ostensible theme of his *De libero arbitrio* (On Free Choice; 1524) was the freedom denied by Luther's necessitarianism, but more fundamentally the book was a warning against theological contentiousness.

In 1521, driven from Louvain by the hostility of the Dominicans to the new learning, Erasmus moved to Basel, home of publisher Johann Froben (c. 1460-1527). When Basel turned Protestant, he moved to Freiburg im Breisgau (1529-1535), but it was in Protestant Basel that he died without the ministrations of the old church, which later placed his books on the Index.

Erasmus himself drew up a "catalog" of his numerous writings in nine divisions. The items vary widely in literary form, from letters to treatises, and in readership intended, from schoolboys to princes. But many of them can be distinguished by certain dominant themes. In 1516, Erasmus brought out the first published edition of the Greek New Testament, which he furnished with a new Latin translation, notes, and prefaces, including the famous *Paraclesis* (a prefatory "exhortation" to study the philosophy of Christ). In the succeeding two decades, his series of editions of Greek and Latin fathers appeared, beginning with Jerome (1516) and ending with Origen (1536), his two favorites.

In a third group of writings, Erasmus exposed to mockery the moral failures and religious abuses of the day, notably, in his *Moriae encomium* (Praise of Folly; 1511), some of the *Colloquia familiaria* (Familiar Colloquies; 1st ed., 1518) and, if he did indeed write it, the anonymous pamphlet *Julius exclusus e coelis* (Julius [the warrior pope] Shut Out of Heaven; 1517). Finally, to a fourth group of writings, which present Erasmus's own Christian vision, may be assigned the *Enchiridion militis Christiani* (Handbook [or Weapon] for the Christian Soldier; 1503). The strongly pacifist vein in Erasmus's piety is reflected in his *Institutio principis Christiani* (Instruction for a Christian Prince; 1516) and especially in Querela pacis (The Complaint of Peace; 1517).

The Erasmian Program. A consistent humanistic program, in which learning assumes a moral and religious character, lends unity to Erasmus's many writings. The study of ancient languages and literature is propaedeutic to following the philosophy of Christ, which can be recovered in its purity only if the theologians will leave, or at least moderate, their endless squabbles and turn back to the sources of the faith equipped with the tools of the new learning. The program is not antitheological, but it is antischolastic: moral utility, rather than dialectical subtlety and metaphysical speculation, becomes the test of genuine theology. Erasmus proposed a new ideal of the theologian as more a scholar than a schoolman, an ideal that made a profound impact on many who did not share the Erasmian view of the gospel, including the Protestants.

What Erasmus discovered in the New Testament was, above all, the precepts and example of Christ. To be a Christian is to enlist under Christ's banner.

The work of Erasmus marked an important stage in the course of biblical and patristic scholarship. It is true that his New Testament text rested on inferior manuscripts and had no lasting usefulness, but his biblical studies, even when vitiated by overeagerness to extract an edifying lesson from the text by means of spiritual exegesis, established a new emphasis on the human and historical character of the sacred text. No less historically important is the fact that he arrived, through his study of the Gospels, at a distinctive interpretation of Christianity and of religion generally.

BIBLIOGRAPHY

Erasmus published about one hundred writings, some of which were very popular and went through several editions. Many have been translated into English. An English translation of his voluminous correspondence and all the major writings is being published as *Collected Works of Erasmus*, 40-45 vols. projected (Toronto, 1974-). Erasmus samplers are *The Essential Erasmus*, translated and edited by John P. Dolan (New York, 1964), and *Christian Humanism and the Reformation: Selected Writings of Erasmus with the Life of Erasmus by Beatus Rhenanus*, rev. ed., edited by John C. Olin (New York, 1975). Dolan has the *Enchiridion, Moriae encomium, and Querela pacis;* Olin includes the *Paraclesis,* perhaps the best statement of the Erasmian program. Other translations are *Ten Colloquies of Erasmus* (New York, 1957) and *The Colloquies of Erasmus* (Chicago, 1965), both translated and edited by Craig R. Thompson; *The Education of a Christian Prince,* translated and edited by Lester K. Born (New York, 1936); *The Julius Exclusus of Erasmus,* translated by Paul Pascal, edited by J. Kelley Sowards (Bloomington, Ind., 1968); and *Erasmus-Luther: Discourse on Free Will,* translated and edited by Ernst F. Winter (New York, 1961). An excellent biographical study is Roland H. Bainton's *Erasmus of Christendom* (New York, 1969), and a useful companion to Erasmus's writings is *Essays on the Works of Erasmus,* edited by Richard L. DeMolen (New Haven, 1978).

B. A. GERRISH

EREMITISM

EREMITISM is a form of monastic life characterized by solitariness. (The term derives from the Greek *eremos,* "wilderness, uninhabited regions," whence comes the English *eremite,* "solitary.") In this type of life, the social dimension of human existence is totally or largely sacrificed to the primacy of religious experience. It is thus understandable that Christianity has traditionally regarded eremitism as the purest and most perfect form of a life consecrated to God. While other forms of monasticism or of the religious life have striven to bring religious experience to bear on human relationships (Western Christianity especially emphasizes external service), eremitism has always been purely contemplative in thrust. Hermits live only in order to cultivate their spiritual life in prayer, meditation, reading, silence, asceticism, manual work, and, perhaps, in intellectual pursuits. In eremitism, the celibacy characteristically practiced in monachism extends to the suppression of all social relationships. While Christian monks have always stressed charity in relationships within the monastic group and, in the Middle Ages especially, written treatises on Christian friendship, Buddhist monks have emphasized the necessity for freedom from every affective relationship that might hinder the achievement of enlightenment.

While isolation for a limited period of time is common in many religions, especially as part of a process of initiation or as a special time dedicated to prayer and reflection, eremitism as a permanent vocation or prolonged phase of asceticism is found only in those religions that grant monasticism an established and determinative role. The religions in question are salvation religions, whether in the sense of self-liberation or of redemption. In Buddhism, Jainism, and Christianity religiosity has a personal character as opposed to a merely societal character (religion as a series of beliefs and rites of a tribe, *polis*, or state). Buddhism, Jainism, and Manichaeism are essentially monastic religions, owing to the importance they attach to the pursuit of the self-liberation of the human being. Christian hermits, too, often went into the wilderness in hopes of finding there the answer to the all-absorbing question: "How can I attain salvation?"

Historically, there have been two forms of eremitism. The more common form is that of the anchorite, a term derived from the Greek verb *anachorein,* originally used to designate the act of draft dodging or tax evasion by fleeing to out-of-the-way places. In Hellenistic times, the word came to refer generally to those who moved far away from towns and particularly to sages who withdrew in order to devote themselves to contemplation. The less common type of eremitism is that of the recluse, who often remained in town but enclosed himself in a cell, communicating with the outside world only through a small window. In the Middle East during the early Christian period there were anchorites (male and female) who not only went into the wilderness but also became recluses, in a spirit of penitence. In their different ways both anchorites and recluses profess a life of solitude as a privileged situation for personal growth.

Eremitism in Islam. In Islam, eremitism is regarded as an exceptional type of life. In general, the religious life is lived either in the bosom of the family or in a community made up of a master and a number of disciples. However, a radical form of Sufism is found among itinerant monks, who express their estrangement from the world in a manner somewhat reminiscent of Hindu or Syrian practitioners of pilgrimage. Many Sufis, even if they do not fully profess this type of life, spend a certain number of years traveling throughout the Muslim world in search of a spiritual master. The ideal of the Muslim spiritual masters is "solitude in the midst of the multitude" *(kalwat dar anjuman),* that is, a state of remaining

habitually in the presence of God without being touched by the tumult of one's surroundings. As means for achieving this state spiritual masters recommend detachment, silence, and interior peace. Some Sufi orders insist on both material and spiritual withdrawal or retreat.

Eremitism and Communion. Eremitism in its pure form is beset with a few serious difficulties, because the solitary life projects an image of spirituality exclusively in terms of interiority, an image involving individual prayer or meditation, intense inner struggles, and so on. Understandably, total and sustained isolation soon disappeared in Christianity, and the eremitical life became limited to colonies or lauras, where adherents listened to the word and participated in the sacraments. Today Christian churches would not accept any form of total isolation.

In reality, the difficulties come not only from the communitarian vocation of the believer but also from the basic social

> Christian hermits, too, often went into the wilderness in hopes of finding there the answer to the all-absorbing question: "How can I attain salvation?"

orientation of human beings. We need others, with both their experience and their limitations, in order to grow.

Eremitism and Human Solidarity. The quest for personal salvation, carried out in a type of life withdrawn from society and history, does not seem to leave room for solidarity with the rest of humanity. Today, when human communion and interdependence are so strongly felt, eremitism might seem like little more than a form of solitary egoism, giving rise to serious doubts as to its basic morality. The Buddhist vision of history as pure illusion presents a different perspective. From the Buddhist point of view, no good results from immersing oneself in this illusion, in this flux of sorrows and joys. On the contrary, one would do better to put oneself beyond the contingent and illusory, thus giving others the testimony of one's victory and wisdom.

Christian anchorites, too, often consider themselves alien travelers who cannot afford to be concerned with earthly affairs. But Christian eremitism constantly encounters a serious difficulty. If the transcendent God of the Bible reveals himself in the often tortuous and painful history of the human race, can any Christian turn away from history in order to encounter God?

[*For a discussion of monks living in community, see* Monasticism.]

BIBLIOGRAPHY

General information on eremitism can be found in most encyclopedia articles on monasticism; see, for example, "Mönchtum," in *Die Religion in Geschichte und Gegenwart*, 3d ed., vol. 4 (Tübingen, 1960); "Monachismo," in *Enciclopedia delle religioni,* vol. 4 (Florence, 1972); and "Monasticism," in *Encyclopaedia Britannica,* vol. 12 (Chicago, 1982). On eremitism in Buddhism and Hinduism, see A. S. Geden's "Monasticism, Buddhist" and "Monasticism, Hindu" in the *Encyclopaedia of Religion and Ethics,* edited by James Hastings, vol. 8 (Edinburgh, 1915). For the Hellenic tradition, see A. J. Festugière's *Personal Religion among the Greeks* (Berkeley, 1954). On Christian eremitism, see Clément Lialine and Pierre Doyère's "Eremitisme," in the *Dictionnaire de spiritualité,* vol. 4 (Paris, 1960); Jean Leclercq's "Eremus et eremita," *Collectanae Ordinis Cisterciensium Reformatorum* (Rome) 25 (1963): 8-30; and Louis Bouyer and others' *A History of Christian Spirituality*, 3 vols. (New York, 1963-1969). On Muslim practices, see A. J. Wensink's "Rahbaniya" and "Rahib" in the *Shorter Encyclopaedia of Islam* (Leiden, 1974) and Hermann Landolt's "Khalwa" in *The Encyclopaedia of Islam,* new ed., vol. 4 (Leiden, 1978); see also René Brunel's *Le monachisme errant dans l'Islam* (Paris, 1955) and J. Spencer Trimingham's *The Sufi Orders in Islam* (New York, 1971).

JUAN MANUEL LOZANO

ETERNITY

ETERNITY is the condition or attribute of divine life by which it relates with equal immediacy and potency to all times. The notion emerges at the point of contact of three distinct religious concerns. The oldest of these is the question of the state of life after death, especially in light of the continuing presence of the dead among the living as acknowledged in the various forms of the cult of the dead. A later-developing speculative concern is the question about divine creation, especially when creative power is seen as the production in a divine mind of a world of ideas, a *logos* or paradigm made present in this world as in an image. Finally, there is the concern with contemplative or mystical experience, especially when regarded as a way of partaking of the divine life within the conditions of present existence.

Exempted from all having-been and going-to-be, eternity is familiarly defined as timelessness, in distinction from the everlasting (sometimes also called the sempiternal). The everlasting antecedes and outlasts everything that begins and ends in time, but because it is just as much given over to being partly past, partly future as are things that come to be and perish, it is therefore just as much in time. Eternity, on the other hand, does not transcend finite spans of time extensively, but intensively. It draws the multiplicity of times into a unity no longer mediated by relations of precedence and posteriority and therefore, at least in this specific sense, no longer timelike.

Yet it oversimplifies to call eternity timelessness. Though eternity excludes pastness and futurity, it remains correct to speak of it as presence, which after all is one of the three fundamental determinations of time. In the Platonic tradition, which gave the concept its classical development and passed it on through Muslim and Christian theology to modern European philosophy, the present tense retains its temporal sense in affirmations concerning eternity. In this way the Western notion of eternity differs from some Buddhist accounts of nirvana, into which not just pastness and futurity but presence as well are dissolved. Platonic eternity by contrast is a paradigmatic presence, and the present in time is its partial but authentic image.

The present is called the "now." Latin metaphysics spoke therefore of eternity as *nunc stans*, a "standing now," and of time as *nunc fluens,* a "flowing now." Since the now of time, which is always experienced as having a certain duration, converges under logical analysis toward the limiting concept of the instantaneous, the dimensionless moment of transition, the problem arises whether the eternal Now is itself a kind of frozen instant, a durationless simplicity about which no experiences of life in time are instructive. Remarkably, the single feature most vividly affirmed of eternity by its classic expositors is that it is life, and not just life but divine life, "a god, manifesting himself as he is," as the third-century CE Neoplatonist mystic Plotinus says in one place. How does one incorporate a religious discourse in which eternity is divine life into the stark conceptual analyses of pure metaphysics, which seem to lead to a static, almost mathematical abstraction?

The synthesis of logical, psychological, and theological analyses into a rigorous conception of eternity is proprietary to the Platonic philosophical tradition, and is in many ways the single-handed achievement of Plotinus. There are rather complete analogies to the concept in some of the Upanisads in India, but in Asia one finds in the main only partial parallels; the metaphysical cake that is the complex Western idea is there cut apart in different ways, so to speak. Pending the outcome of more penetrating philosophical study than the Asian texts have so far received from Western translators and historians, the story of eternity remains at present the story of the Plotinian synthesis, its sources and its influences.

Eternity in Non-Western Thought. The Sanskrit *nitya* can be translated "eternity" with some confidence already in Upanisads, especially at the point where "immortality," *amrta,* is pressed beyond the popular image of outliving death, or life after death, to the radical notion of *moksa,* "liberation," deliverance from the cycle of birth and death itself.

Buddhism presents a much more complex situation. The negative assessment of timelike continuity and the rejection of substantiality and causality that are frequent in Buddhist philosophy lead to descriptions of enlightenment that often have a Platonic ring. In Buddhism, the parallels are particularly pronounced in the meditative traditions that emphasize "sudden enlightenment," where the unconditioned and spontaneous quality of transcendental insight (Skt., *prajña*) is stressed. In the Mahayana Pure Land tradition, the paradisical Sukhavati ("land of bliss") of the Buddha Amitabha is sometimes developed in ways reminiscent of the Platonic world of ideal presences, pervaded by divine mentality. If there is an authentic parallel here to the notion of eternity, this will have to be tested by careful analysis of the account of temporal presence itself, for it is this that is ascribed to eternity by Platonism, and in turn made the image of eternity and mark of authentic being for life in time. In those radical portrayals of nirvana as release from all forms of temporal conditioning, not just pastness and futurity, but presence itself sometimes seems to be denied of awakened mind.

BIBLIOGRAPHY

The concept of eternity is still most accessible from primary sources, notably the treatise "On Eternity and Time" of Plotinus, *Enneads* 3.7.45, in *Plotinus,* translated by A. Hilary Armstrong, "Loeb Classical Library," vol. 3 (Cambridge, Mass., 1966), and book 11 of the *Confessions* of Augustine, for which there are many suitable editions. An instructive summary of the concept in the full technical development it received in medieval theology can be found in the article by Adolf Darlap and Joseph de Finance, "Eternity," in *Sacramentum Mundi,* edited by Karl Rahner (New York, 1968), vol. 2. Mircea Eliade's *Cosmos and History: The Myth of Eternal Return* (New York, 1954) remains a standard introduction to the role of a transcending divine time in the religious experience of myth-using cultures. A very helpful account of eternity is incorporated into a sketch of the history of the idea of immortality in the ancient Near East and Christian Europe by John S. Dunne, *The City of the Gods* (Notre Dame, Ind., 1978). The classic exposition of the interior experience of eternity in Western mysticism is Bona-venture's "The Soul's Journey into God," in *Bonaventure,* edited and translated by Ewert Cousins (New York, 1978). For eternity in Indian thought, the edition of *The Principal Upanisads* by Sarvepalli Radhakrishnan (New York, 1953) is especially useful, both for its extensive introduction and its very rich annotations, which include frequent citation of Western parallels.

PETER MANCHESTER

ETHIOPIAN CHURCH

The Ethiopian or Abyssinian church, on the Horn of Africa, is one of the five so-called monophysite churches that reject the Council of Chalcedon (451) and its formula of faith. The church does not call itself monophysite but rather Tawahedo ("Unionite"), a word expressing the union in Christ of the human and divine natures, to distinguish itself from the Eastern Orthodox churches, which accept the formulas accepted at Chalcedon. For the Tawahedo Orthodox Church

of Ethiopia, both Nestorius and Eutyches are heretics. Although formally under the jurisdiction of the Coptic church of Alexandria until 1950, the Ethiopian Orthodox church has managed to retain its indigenous language, literature, art, and music. It expects its faithful to practice circumcision, observe the food prescriptions set forth in the Hebrew scriptures (Old Testament), and honor Saturday as the Sabbath. The church has its own liturgy, including an horologion (initially for each of the twenty-four hours of the day), a missal of over fourteen anaphoras, the Deggwa (an antiphonary for each day of the year), doxologies (various collections of *nags* hymns), and homiliaries in honor of the angels, saints, and martyrs. The most innovative aspect of this church is the provision in the Deggwa for the chanting of *qene* (poetic hymns) in the liturgy.

Until the Ethiopian revolution of 1974, the Ethiopian Orthodox church (which in the mid-1980s had a membership of about twenty million people, or about half of the population) had been a national church defended by the political leader of the country. The monarch's reign had to be legitimized by the church at a religious ceremony where the new king swore allegiance to the church and committed himself to defend the Christian kingdom.

Early History. Historians disagree in assigning a date to the introduction of Christianity into Ethiopia, depending upon which Ethiopian king they think first adopted the faith. However, we do know that Adulis, the famous port of Ethiopia, and Aksum, the capital, were frequented by Christian traders from the Hellenistic world since the early history of Christianity. Some of these settled there, forming Christian communities and attracting to their religion those with whom they interacted daily.

Ethiopia officially joined the Christian world when Frumentius was consecrated its first bishop by Athanasius of Alexandria in about 347.

Medieval Period. The Ethiopian church took many significant steps forward between the fourth and the seventh century. It vigorously translated a great deal of Christian literature from Greek. This included the Old Testament from the Septuagint and the New Testament from the Lucianic recension (the Greek Bible revised by Lucian of Antioch, d. 312) used in the Syrian church. The Ethiopian Bible of eighty-one books includes the *Book of Jubilees* and the *Book of Enoch,* two books which have been preserved in their entirety only in Ethiopic. The *Synodicon* (a collection of canon law), the *Didascalia Apostolorum* (a church order), the *Testament of Our Lord,* and the *Qalementos* (an apocalyptic writing ascribed to Clement of Rome) are also part of the Ethiopian canonical scriptures. The number of churches and monasteries also grew quickly.

It has been suggested that the *Rule of Pachomius* and the theological writings of the Fathers in the *Qerelos* (including writings from Cyril of Alexandria, Epiphanius, et al.) were brought to Ethiopia by the so-called Nine Saints who came from the Hellenistic or Mediterranean world, including Egypt, in the sixth or seventh century.

Unfortunately for the faithful, the young church suffered encroachment and harassment by Islam, starting in the eighth century. Locally, too, a vassal queen of one of the provinces, Gudit, revolted and devastated the Christian civilization, paving the way for another dynasty, the Zagwe (1137-1270).

The Zagwe kings were more interested in religion than in politics. Many of them were priests as well as rulers, and the last four of the dynasty are, in fact, among the saints of the church.

In 1270 the clergy, led by Takla Haymanot, the founder of the Monastery of Dabra Libanos (in Shewa), and Iyyasus

> In the 1950s the Ethiopian church was faced with a most unusual challenge . . . to respond to the need for cultural and racial identity of the oppressed black people.

Mo'a, the founder of the Monastery of Hayq Estifanos (in Amhara), collaborated with Yekunno Amlak to overthrow the Zagwe and to found the Solomonic dynasty. Although the Solomonic kings did not always observe the church's teaching, it was nonetheless during this period that indigenous religious literature flourished, and Christianity spread into the south and west through the efforts of the monks of Dabra Libanos of Shewa.

Religious Controversies. Late in the medieval period and afterward, religious controversies arose because of objections by some to the tradition of undue reverence for the Cross, icons of the Madonna and Child, and the king. The most serious controversy dealt with the concept of the unity and trinity of God. The church taught that each person in the Trinity (three suns with one light) has a form or image, *malke`*, which must look like that of man because man was created in God's image (*Gn.* 1:27). The "heretics," followers of Zamika'el, while admitting that God has an image, refused to define his form, quoting *John* 1:18—"No one has seen God." They also maintained a different theology of the unity and trinity of God (one sun with three attributes—disc, light, and heat).

The Jesuits' Enterprise. The Portuguese came to help the church in her war against Islam with the assumption that "the lost flock," the church of Ethiopia, would come back to the Roman Catholic church. The Ethiopians, however, were never ready to abandon their faith. The pressure of the Jesuits, however, which started with missionaries sent by

Pope Julius III (1487-1555), continued until the seventeenth century, when they succeeded in converting Emperor Suseneyos (r. 1607-1632) to Catholicism. In 1626 a Catholic patriarch, Alphonsus Mendez, came from Rome, and the emperor issued a decree that his subjects should follow his own example. However, the sweeping change that Mendez attempted to introduce into the age-old religious traditions of the nation met with stiff resistance. Led by the monastic leaders, tens of thousands of the faithful were martyred. The Catholic missionaries were finally asked to leave, and the emperor was assassinated, even though he had abdicated the throne to his son Fasiladas (r. 1632-1667). Fasiladas was magnanimous with the Jesuits despite the fact that they had attempted to overthrow him by courting one of his brothers.

Even though the Jesuits left, the controversy stemming from their theology of the two natures of Christ continues to the present, taking a local character and creating schism in the Ethiopian church. Overtly, this controversy is centered on the theological significance of *qeb'at,* "unction" (*Acts* 10:38), and *bakwr,* "first-born" (*Rom.* 8:29), when applied to Christ the Messiah, the only Son of God.

The Church outside Africa. In the 1950s the Ethiopian church was faced with a most unusual challenge. The local church was called upon to respond to the need for cultural and racial identity of the oppressed black people in Africa and the Americas. Churches with the term *Abyssinian* as part of their name started to emerge in these continents. In spite of several problems, the church is gaining strength, especially in the West Indies and the Caribbean (e.g., Jamaica, Guyana, Trinidad, and Tobago).

BIBLIOGRAPHY

For the history of both the church and the country, Jean Doresse's *Ethiopia* (London, 1959) is a good introduction even though it lacks annotation to the sources. Carlo Conti Rossini's *Storia d'Etiopia,* vol. 1, *Dalle origini all' avvento della dinastia Salomonide* (Bergamo, 1928), remains the standard reference for the early history. Unfortunately, however, this book too has neither adequate annotation to sources nor a bibliography. An index for it has been prepared by Edward Ullendorff in *Rassegna di studi etiopici* 18 (1962): 97-141.

The only book that examines many aspects of the Ethiopian Bible is Edward Ullendorff's *Ethiopia and the Bible* (Oxford, 1968). This book also contains an excellent bibliography. See also Roger W. Cowley's *The Traditional Interpretation of the Apocalypse of St. John in the Ethiopian Orthodox Church* (Cambridge, 1983). The introduction to this work offers more than the title suggests. The history of Ge`ez (Ethiopic) literature has been ably surveyed in Enrico Cerulli's *La letteratura etiopica,* 3d ed. (Florence, 1968). Ernst Hammerschmidt's *Studies in the Ethiopic Anaphoras* (Berlin, 1961) summarizes the different studies of the anaphoras in one small volume. For an English version of the anaphoras themselves, see Marcos Daoud and Marsie Hazen's *The Liturgy of the Ethiopian Church* (Cairo, 1959). The most comprehensive study thus far on *qene* hymns is Anton Schall's *Zur äthiopischen Verskunst* (Wiesbaden, 1961).

The period of the Zagwe dynasty and the rock-hewn churches of Lasta are well treated in Georg Gerster's *Churches in Rock* (London, 1970), with many large and impressive photographs and an adequate bibliography. The history of the church from the beginning of the Solomonic dynasty to the Islamic invasion of the sixteenth century has been uniquely treated in Taddesse Tamrat's *Church and State in Ethiopia, 1270-1527* (Oxford, 1972). Francisco Alvarez's *Narrative of the Portuguese Embassy to Abyssinia during the Years 1520-1527*, translated by Lord Stanley of Alderley (London, 1881), is a rare description of church and secular life immediately before the war with the *grañ*. The translation was revised by C. F. Beckingham and G. W. B. Huntingford and published under the title *The Prester John of the Indies,* 2 vols. (Cambridge, 1961).

Some of the sources for the religious controversies of the late medieval period were edited and translated in Enrico Cerulli's *Il libro etiopico dei miracoli di Maria e le sue fonti nelle letterature del medio evo latino* (Rome, 1943) and *Scritti teologici etiopici dei secoli XVI-XVII,* 2 vols., "Studi e testi," no. 198 (Rome, 1958).

The unique source for the destruction of the churches by the forces of the *grañ* in the sixteenth century is *Futuh al-Habashah,* composed by 'Arab Faqih, the chronicler of the imam, edited and translated in René Basset's *Histoire de la conquête de l'Abyssinie (seizième siècle) par Chihab ed-Din Ahmed ben 'Abd el-Qâder surnommé Arab-Faqih,* 2 vols. (Paris, 1898-1901). The Portuguese, too, have left invaluable though sometimes exaggerated and conflicting reports of the campaign. See *The Portuguese Expedition to Abyssinia in 1541-1543, as Narrated by Castanhoso, with Some Letters, the Short Account of Bermudez, and Certain Extracts from Correa* (London, 1902).

The best work on the religious controversies that started in the seventeenth century is Friedrich Heyer's *Die Kirche Äthiopiens: Eine Bestandsaufnahme* (Berlin and New York, 1971). This book is also the best description of the church in its present setting. The history of the religious controversy caused particularly by the Portuguese has been ably and succinctly presented in Germa Beshah and Merid Wolde Aregay's *The Question of the Union of the Churches in Luso-Ethiopian Relations (1500-1632)* (Lisbon, 1964). See also Donald Crummey's *Priests and Politicians: Protestant and Catholic Missions in Orthodox Ethiopia, 1830-1868* (Oxford, 1972). The book has an excellent bibliography with useful comments on some of the works.

Questions about the church that are of interest to Western Christians are answered in *The Teaching of the Abyssinian Church as Set forth by the Doctors of the Same*, translated from Amharic, the vernacular of Ethiopia, by A. F. Matthew (London, 1936). See also Harry Middleton Hyatt's *The Church of Abyssinia* (London, 1928). This work describes in detail the religious practices of the church.

Kirsten Pedersen's *The History of the Ethiopian Community in the Holy Land from the Time of Emperor Tewodros II till 1974* (Jerusalem, 1983) is a result of several years of study of the original and secondary sources on the subject. The minor mistakes pertaining to modern history of Ethiopia do not in any way minimize the usefulness of this work. The major English sources on all aspects of the church are surveyed in Jon Bonk's *An Annotated and Classified Bibliography of English Literature Pertaining to the Ethiopian Orthodox Church* (Metuchen, N. J., 1984).

GETATCHEW HAILE

EUCHARIST

The Eucharist, also known as the Mass, Communion service, Lord's Supper, and Divine Liturgy, among other names, is the central act of Christian worship, practiced by almost all denominations of Christians. Though varying in form from the very austere to the very elaborate, the Eucharist has as its essential elements the breaking and sharing of bread and the pouring and sharing of wine (in some Protestant churches, unfermented grape juice) among the worshipers in commemoration of the actions of Jesus Christ on the eve of his death.

The word *eucharist* is taken from the Greek *eucharistia,* which means "thanksgiving" or "gratitude" and which was used by the early Christians for the Hebrew *berakhah,* meaning "a blessing" such as a table grace. When Christians adopted the word from the Greek into other languages, the meaning was narrowed to the specific designation of the ritual of the bread and wine.

Eucharist is understood by all Christians to commemorate the saving death and resurrection of Jesus, and to mediate communion with God and community among the worshipers. Beyond this basic concept, the theology of the Eucharist varies very widely among the Christian denominations and has often been a cause of bitter dispute between them.

Both Orthodox and Roman Catholic Christians understand the presence of Christ very concretely, taking seriously the so-called words of institution, "This is my body . . . this is my blood." However, the Orthodox insist that while there is an actual change in the bread and wine that justifies these words, the manner of the change is a mystery not to be analyzed or explained rationally.

The meaning and effect of the Eucharist have also been discussed in Catholic theology under the term *real presence.* This emphasizes that the presence of Christ mediated by the bread and wine is prior to the faith of the congregation. Protestant theology has generally rejected the term *real presence* as one liable to superstitious interpretation.

Orthodox and Catholic Christians also agree on an interpretation of the Eucharist in terms of sacrifice; that is, a renewed offering by Christ himself of his immolation in death. Again, there have been determined efforts in the Catholic theological tradition to give intellectually satisfying explanations of this, while Orthodox theology tends to tolerate a variety of explanations at the same time as it insists on fidelity to the words of the liturgy itself.

BIBLIOGRAPHY

The texts of the eucharistic celebrations of the various Western churches are given in *Liturgies of the Western Church,* selected and introduced by Bard Thompson (1961; reprint, Philadelphia, 1980). An account of the Orthodox Divine Liturgy and its theology is given in

Alexander Schmemann's *Introduction to Liturgical Theology* (London, 1966). A description of the early Christians' Eucharist and eucharistic theology, with identification of sources, is presented in *The Eucharist of the Early Christians,* by Willy Rordorf and others (New York, 1978). More specifically concerned with the theology of the Eucharist are Joseph M. Powers's *Eucharistic Theology* (New York, 1967), from a Catholic perspective, and Geoffrey Wainwright's *Eucharist and Eschatology* (1971; reprint, New York, 1981), from a Protestant, particularly a Methodist, perspective. A discussion of the social implications of eucharistic celebration can be found in my own book, *The Eucharist and the Hunger of the World* (New York, 1976).

MONIKA K. HELLWIG

EVANGELICAL AND FUNDAMENTAL CHRISTIANITY

The term *evangelicalism* usually refers to a largely Protestant movement that emphasizes (1) the Bible as authoritative and reliable; (2) eternal salvation as possible only by regeneration (being "born again"), involving personal trust in Christ and in his atoning work; and (3) a spiritually transformed life marked by moral conduct, personal devotion such as Bible reading and prayer, and zeal for evangelism and missions.

"Fundamentalism" is a subspecies of evangelicalism. The term originated in America in 1920 and refers to evangelicals who consider it a chief Christian duty to combat uncompromisingly "modernist" theology and certain secularizing cultural trends. Organized militancy is the feature that most clearly distinguishes fundamentalists from other evangelicals. Fundamentalism is primarily an American phenomenon, although it has British and British empire counterparts, is paralleled by some militant groups in other traditions, and has been exported worldwide through missions.

Both evangelicalism and fundamentalism are complex coalitions reflecting the convergences of a number of traditions.

Although evangelicalism is largely an Anglo-American phenomenon, its origins give it ties with European Protestantism.

In America, evangelicalism was even more influential. Evangelical religion had fewer well-established competitors than in the Old World. The rise of the United States as a new nation and the rise of evangelicalism coincided, so that the religion often assumed a quasi-official status. Evangelical emphasis on voluntary acceptance of Christianity also was well matched to American ideas of individual freedom.

The character of American evangelicalism began to take shape during the Great Awakening of the eighteenth century. This movement, really a series of revivals throughout the middle decades of the century, brought together several movements. These included New England Puritanism, continental pietism, revivalist Presbyterianism, Baptist antiestablishment democratic impulses, the Calvinist revivalism of the Englishman George Whitefield (1714-1770), and Methodism (which surpassed all the others after the Revolutionary era).

In the latter half of the nineteenth century, the vigorous evangelicalism that had grown so successfully in the early industrial era found itself in a new world. The concentrated new industrialism and the massively crowded cities tended to overwhelm the individualistic and voluntaristic evangelical programs. Conceptions of dominating the culture became more difficult to maintain. Evangelicals, accordingly, increasingly stressed those aspects of their message that involved personal commitment to Christ and personal holiness rather than social programs, although aspirations to be a major moral influence on the culture never entirely disappeared.

Some holiness groups, most notably the Salvation Army, founded in England in 1865, combined their evangelism with extensive charitable work among the needy. Others among an emerging number of holiness denominations emphasized more the personal experience of being filled by the Holy Spirit. Such emphases in heightened forms were apparent in the rise in America after 1900 of Pentecostalism, which also brought separate denominations and almost exclusive emphasis on intense personal spiritual experience. By the early twentieth century, evangelicalism was thus subdivided into a variety of camps on questions of personal holiness and the nature of spiritual experience.

Equally important during this same era, from the latter decades of the nineteenth century to World War I, was that evangelicals were finding themselves in a new world intellectually. Darwinism became the focal symbol of a many-faceted revolution in assumptions dominating the culture. A deeper issue, however, was a broader revolution in conceptions of reality and truth. Rather than seeing truth as fixed and absolute, Western people were more and more viewing it as a changing function of human cultural evolution. Religion in such a view was not absolute truth revealed by the deity, but the record of developing human conceptions about God and morality. Such conceptions were devastating when applied to the Bible, which in the higher criticism of the late nineteenth century often was regarded as simply the record of Hebrew religious experience. The widespread evangelical consensus was shaken to its foundations. The absolute authority of the Bible as the source of the doctrine of salvation was widely questioned, even within the churches.

Fundamentalism arose in this context. It combined an organized militant defense of most traditional evangelical doctrines with some of the revivalist evangelical innovations of the nineteenth century. Most important of these innovations, eventually accepted by most fundamentalists, was the elaborate system of biblical interpretation known as dispensationalism. Dispensationalism was a version of the premillennialism popularized among revivalists in the later nineteenth century. Originated in England especially by the Plymouth Brethren leader John Nelson Darby (1800-1882), dispensationalism was developed and promoted in America principally by Bible teacher associates of Dwight L. Moody, such as Reuben A. Torrey (1856-1928), James M. Gray (1851-1935), and C. I. Scofield (1843-1921), editor of the famous dispensationalist *Scofield Reference Bible,* published in 1909. Dispensationalism is a systematic scheme for interpreting all of history on the basis of the Bible, following the principle of "literal where possible"; biblical prophecies, especially, are taken to refer to real historical events. This approach yields a rather detailed account of all human history, which is divided into seven dispensations, or eras of differing relationships between God and humanity.

In America, fundamentalism was only the prominent fighting edge of the larger evangelical movement. During the decades from 1925 to 1945 the public press paid less attention to fundamentalist complaints, but the movement itself was regrouping rather than retreating. During this time fundamentalism developed a firmer institutional base, especially in independent local churches and in some smaller denominations, although considerable numbers of fundamentalists remained in major denominations. The revivalist heritage of the movement was especially apparent in this era, as it turned its strongest efforts toward winning America through evangelization.

Fundamentalist-evangelicals were also founding new sorts of ministries, such as Youth for Christ, begun in 1942, which soon had hundreds of chapters across the country. Bible institutes, such as Moody Bible Institute in Chicago, the Bible Institute of Los Angeles, and many others, remained important centers for the movement, training and sending out evangelists and missionaries, conducting Bible conferences, establishing effective radio ministries, and publishing many books and periodicals.

Following World War II some younger leaders, notably Harold John Ockenga, Carl F. H. Henry, and Edward J. Carnell, organized a "neoevangelical" movement with the explicit purpose of moderating and broadening fundamentalist-evangelicalism. Joined by Charles E. Fuller, they organized the Fuller Theological Seminary in Pasadena, California, in 1947. Their efforts were vastly aided by the emergence of Billy Graham as America's leading evangelist after 1949. This group in 1956 also founded *Christianity Today* to provide a solid periodical base for the movement.

The final break in the fundamentalist-evangelical movement came with Billy Graham's New York crusade in 1957. Graham accepted the cooperation of some prominent liberal church leaders. Separatist fundamentalists such as Bob Jones, Sr. (1883-1968), founder of Bob Jones University; John R. Rice (1895-1980), editor of the influential *Sword of*

the Lord; and Carl McIntire anathematized Graham and the neoevangelicals as traitors from within. Neoevangelicals in turn soon ceased altogether to call themselves fundamentalists, preferring the designation "evangelical."

BIBLIOGRAPHY

Sydney E. Ahlstrom's *A Religious History of the American People* (New Haven, 1972) contains solid introductory surveys of American evangelicalism and fundamentalism. *The Eerd-man's Handbook to the History of Christianity in America,* edited by Mark A. Noll and Nathan O. Hatch (Grand Rapids, Mich., 1983), is a valuable survey by evangelical authors. Of the more specific studies, Ernest R. Sandeen's *The Roots of Fundamentalism: British and American Millenarianism, 1800-1930* (Chicago, 1970) is an outstanding study of the role of dispensational premillennialism in shaping fundamentalism. George M. Marsden's *Fundamentalism and American Culture: The Shaping of Twentieth-Century Evangelicalism 1870-1925* (New York, 1980) looks at the subject in terms of both cultural and religious history. Ferenc M. Szasz's *The Divided Mind of Protestant America, 1880-1930* (University, Ala., 1982) provides additional insights on the same period. A very readable survey of an important aspect of the movement is William G. McLoughlin, Jr.'s *Modern Revivalism: Charles Grandison Finney to Billy Graham* (New York, 1959). Richard Hofstadter's *Anti-intellectualism in American Life* (New York, 1963) draws heavily on McLoughlin but adds some brilliant observations. A valuable biographical treatment of some early twentieth-century fundamentalist leaders is C. Allyn Russell's *Voices of American Fundamentalism* (Philadelphia, 1976). George W. Dollar's *A History of Fundamentalism in America* (Greenville, S. C., 1973) offers a hard-line fundamentalist perspective and some information not found elsewhere. *Aspects of Pentecostal-Charismatic Origins,* edited by Vinson Synan (South Plainfield, N. J., 1975), is valuable on a related movement often confused with fundamentalism. Richard Quebedeaux's *The Worldly Evangelicals* (San Francisco, 1978) provides an impressionistic but informative survey of the American movement in the 1970s. *Varieties of Southern Evangelicalism,* edited by David E. Harrell, Jr. (Macon, Ga., 1981), deals with a major part of American evangelicalism that has not received proportionate scholarly attention. British evangelicalism as a distinct phenomenon has received even less attention. One can gain initial impressions of the dimensions of the movement from surveys such as Owen Chadwick's *The Victorian Church,* 2 vols. (London, 1966-1970), David A. Martin's *A Sociology of English Religion* (London, 1967), and Alan D. Gilbert's *The Making of Post-Christian Britain: A History of the Secularization of Modern Society* (London, 1980). James Barr's *Fundamentalism* (Philadelphia, 1977) is an antifundamentalist polemic with some valuable theological insights, although it confuses fundamentalism with evangelicalism generally.

GEORGE M. MARSDEN

EVANS-PRITCHARD, E. E.

EVANS-PRITCHARD, E. E. (1902-1973), English anthropologist. Edward Evan Evans-Pritchard was the son of a clergyman of the Church of England. He took a degree in history at the University of Oxford and in 1927 a doctorate in anthropology at the University of London, where he was supervised by C. G. Seligman. His thesis was based on field research undertaken from 1926 to 1930 among the Azande of the Sudan. He carried out research among the Nuer, another Sudanese people, intermittently between 1930 and 1935 and also for brief periods among the Anuak, the Luo, and other East African peoples. In 1944 he joined the Roman Catholic church. He taught at the University of London, Fuad I University in Cairo, Cambridge University, and finally Oxford, where in 1946 he succeeded A. R. Radcliffe-Brown as professor of social anthropology. He retired in 1970, was knighted in 1971, and died in Oxford in September 1973.

Evans-Pritchard's work in religion is unique. It is based on brilliant, sensitive, and meticulous field research, on his mastery of languages (he was fluent in Arabic, Zande, and Nuer), and on his deep knowledge and understanding of the work of his predecessors, in particular those sociologists (Durkheim et al.) associated with *L'année sociologique*. Most of his writings on religion fall into one of four main categories: works on the Azande, the Nuer, the Sanusi, and comparative and theoretical topics.

Each piece of Evans-Pritchard's research and writing is based on certain central problems in anthropology, although never limited to them in a narrow sense. His work among the Azande, a cluster of kingdoms of the southwestern Sudan, led to the publication of *Witchcraft, Oracles, and Magic among the Azande* (1937), perhaps the outstanding work of anthropology published in this century.

Evans-Pritchard's *Nuer Religion* (1956) is the final volume of a trilogy on the Nuer of the southern Sudan (the others are *The Nuer,* 1940, and *Kinship and Marriage among the Nuer,* 1951). In this book he presents Nuer religious thought and ritual as a system of theology that has a subtlety and profundity comparable to those of literate cultures. Here he takes up another basic problem raised by Lévy-Bruhl, that of "mystical participation" between men and what in ethnocentric terms are called the supernatural and the natural. Because of Evans-Pritchard's great skill in unfolding the complexity of Nuer religious thought, never since has it been possible for scholars of comparative religion to dismiss a nonliterate religion as "primitive" or as a form of "animism." Throughout this work, as in that on the Azande, Evans-Pritchard stresses what he considered to be the central problem of anthropology, that of translation—not the simple problem of translation of words and phrases in a narrow linguistic sense, but the far more complex question of translation of one culture's experience into the terms of another's.

Evans-Pritchard's other "ethnographic" work on religion is rather different, taking as its basic problem the relationship between prophets (a topic raised earlier in his work on the Nuer) and forms of religious and political authority as exemplified in the history of the Muslim Sanusi order in Cyrenaica

(*The Sanusi of Cyrenaica,* 1951). Here he was able to use written records as well as his own field research, and he produces a model account of religious history and change.

Evans-Pritchard's last achievement in the study of religion is his many critical writings on the history of the anthropology of religion, of which the best known is *Theories of Primitive Religion* (1965). It is a superb and sophisticated study of the relations between thought, ideology, and society.

BIBLIOGRAPHY

The main works of Evans-Pritchard are cited in the article. The most insightful view of his work, in the form of an obituary, is by T. O. Beidelman, "Sir Edward Evan Evans-Pritchard, 1902-1973: An Appreciation," *Anthropos* 69 (1974): 553-567. Beidelman is also the editor of *A Bibliography of the Writings of E. E. Evans-Pritchard* (London, 1974). Mary Douglas's *Edward Evans-Pritchard* (New York, 1980) is a fuller but rather uneven account.

JOHN MIDDLETON

EVIL

If there is one human experience ruled by myth, it is certainly that of evil. One can understand why: the two major forms of this experience—moral evil and physical evil—both contain an enigmatic element in whose shadows the difference between them tends to vanish.

On the one hand, it is only at the conclusion of a thoroughgoing critique of mythical representations that moral evil could be conceived of as the product of a free act involving human responsibility alone. Social blame, interiorized as guilt, is in fact a response to an existential quality that was initially represented as a stain infecting the human heart as if from outside. And even when this quasi-magical representa-

> **Punishment, as suffering, therefore bridges the gap between the evil committed and the evil suffered.**

tion of a contamination by an external or superior power is replaced by the feeling of a sin of which we are the authors, we can feel that we have been seduced by overwhelming powers. Moreover, each of us finds evil already present in the world; no one initiates evil but everyone has the feeling of belonging to a history of evil more ancient than any individual evil act. This strange experience of passivity, which is at the very heart of evildoing, makes us feel ourselves to be the victims in the very act that makes us guilty.

On the other hand, it is also only at the conclusion of a comparable critique of mythical representations that physical evil is recognized as the effect of natural causes of a physical, biological, and even social nature: sickness, which often takes the form of great epidemics ravaging entire populations, simultaneously attacks each person in the very depths of his existence by making him suffer and is spontaneously experienced as an aggression, at once external and internal, coming from maleficent powers that are easily confused with those that seduce the human heart and persuade it to do evil. Moreover, the sort of fate that seems to lead the sick and aging to the threshold of death tends to make mortality the very emblem of the human condition. From this, it is easy to take the next step and consider suffering and death as punishments. Do not guilt and mortality constitute the same enigma?

The persistence of mythical representations of evil can be explained by a third phenomenon, namely the extraordinary way in which guilt and suffering remain intertwined with a stage of development in which the human mind believes it has freed itself from the realm of mythical representations. To declare someone guilty is to declare that person deserving of punishment. And punishment is, in its turn, a suffering, both physical and moral, inflicted by someone other than the guilty party. Punishment, as suffering, therefore bridges the gap between the evil committed and the evil suffered. This same boundary is crossed in the other direction by the fact that a major cause of suffering lies in the violence that human beings exercise on one another. In fact, to do evil is always, directly or indirectly, to make someone else suffer. This mutual overlapping of evil done and evil suffered prevents the two major forms of evil from ever being entirely separate and, in particular, from ever being entirely stripped of their enigmatic character. An essential opaqueness in the human condition is therefore bound up with the experience of evil, which is continually carried back to its darkness, its obscurity, by the exercise of violence, always unjust, and of punishment, even when it is held to be just.

This invincible connection of moral evil and physical evil is expressed on the level of language in the specific "language game" designated by the general term *lamentation.* Lamentation, indeed, is not confined to the moanings rising up from the abyss of suffering, announcing the coming of death. It encompasses the guilty and the victims, for the guilty suffer twice over, first by blame, which states their unworthiness, and then by punishment, which holds them under the reign of violence. With lamentation, the experience of evil becomes heard. The cry becomes a voice, the voice of the undivided enigma of evil. Lamentation forms a bridge between the evil committed or suffered and the myth. And indeed it connects suffering to language only by joining a question to its moaning. "Why evil?" "Why do children die?"

"Why me?" In turning itself into a question, lamentation itself appeals to myth.

BIBLIOGRAPHY

Davis, Stephen T., ed. *Encountering Evil; Live Options in Theodicy.* Edinburgh, 1981.
Ling, T. O. *Buddhism and the Mythology of Evil.* London, 1962.
Murti, T. R. V. *The Central Philosophy of Buddhism.* 2d ed. London, 1955.
O'Flaherty, Wendy Doniger. *The Origins of Evil in Hindu Mythology.* Berkeley, 1976.
Ricoeur, Paul. *The Symbolism of Evil.* Boston, 1967.
Windish, Ernst W. *Mara und Buddha.* Leipzig, 1895.

PAUL RICOEUR

EVOLUTION

Early Religious Responses to Darwin. Even the famous first review of *The Origin of Species,* written by the Anglican bishop of Oxford Samuel Wilberforce for *The Quarterly Review* in 1860, has far more to do with pure science than with matters of faith. Though Wilberforce is remembered as the most notorious of Darwin's clerical foes and as the main antagonist of "Darwin's bulldog" Thomas Huxley, his review is a model of competence and courtesy. It poses only a few modest theological objections toward the end; the bulk of the piece is devoted to studied scientific criticism.

From the viewpoint of well-informed religious thinkers, Darwin's theory was but one more aspect of a challenge that had been under discussion throughout the nineteenth century and with which many had long since made their peace. Together with ancient and biblical archaeology, these critical philological studies had been steadily replacing a naive scriptural literalism with a richer, more rational approach to the Bible. Well before the *Origin* was published, James Hutton's *Theory of the Earth* (1795) and Charles Lyell's *Principles of Geology* (1830-1833) had already made the case that the earth was far older than a literal reading of the Bible would suggest. For those liberal clergy who had come to terms with the new geology and with the findings of scriptural scholarship, it was hardly difficult to accommodate what Darwin had to say about the prehistory of life on the planet. Among the more prominent of these was the Christian Darwinist St. George Jackson Mivart, a biologist who had been born an evangelical and later converted to Catholicism. In his book *On the Genesis of Species* (1871), Mivart sought to demonstrate that the theory of evolution was harmonious with "ancient and most venerable authorities" reaching as far back as Augustine.

Fundamentalism versus Darwinism. It should be emphasized that Darwin (even science as a whole) was only a secondary and indirect target of the fundamentalists. Their primary grievance was moral, and it was addressed to the dominant liberals or "modernists" of the major congregations, whose intellectual pluralism and more compliant ethical standards were viewed as a compromise of traditional Christian teachings. In effect, fundamentalism may be seen as a backlash within the Christian community on the part of those in all the Protestant churches—but mostly the rural, the economically insecure, and meagerly educated—who felt most threatened by the increasing pressures of the surrounding secular civilization. But until well after World War II, the fundamentalists were no more than a beleaguered fringe even within the religious community. In America, fundamentalism, in the form of well-organized and well-financed groups like the Moral Majority, was to find its most potent expression only much later, during the 1970s and 1980s.

Liberal and Left-Wing Responses. The response of the religious center to evolution has been part of a general adaptation by liberal Christians and Jews to the intellectual standards of a scientific and humanistic culture. In making that adaptation, liberal religious thought has tried to draw a significant line of demarcation between itself and science. Its main concession to science has been to withdraw the authority of the scriptures from the areas of history, anthropology, and the physical sciences. As Raymond J. Nogar puts it in *The Wisdom of Evolution,* "The Bible is not a scientific textbook but a book that sets forth religious truths designed to manifest to man the path to eternal salvation" (p. 296). If this represents a retreat by religion, the withdrawal may be viewed as an honorable and orderly one that relinquishes ground improperly occupied or held only by default during the prescientific era. It has also worked to strengthen appreciation of the ethical and existential aspects of the Bible and of theological thought generally. It is surely significant that in the post-Darwinian period, when liberal Christian leaders were busily stripping scripture of its scientific authority, their commitment to the Social Gospel was rapidly expanding. What the Bible was losing as a biological treatise and a historical text, it was gaining as a work of moral wisdom and spiritual counsel.

Religious Contributions to Evolutionary Theory. It is important to emphasize that the various religious responses to evolution dealt with here do not stand on the same footing with respect to science. It continues to insist that the *Book of Genesis* contains a valid account of how the physical universe and life began. It cannot accept the age of the universe as this is now known from numerous empirical sources ranging from astronomical observations to radioactive dating methods; it cannot accept fossil evidence for the history of life on earth.

On the other hand, both religious liberals and metaphysical evolutionists have sought to remain on speaking terms with science and may even have something of value to offer theoretical biology. While scientists may not be able to endorse the more speculative flights of the metaphysical evolutionists, there are at least a few important issues that have emerged from the center-left religious response to Darwin. Two points in particular deserve attention.

1. *Increasing complexity.* Insofar as evolution describes a steady, overall increase in the complexity of living forms (including the complexity of human sentience and human culture), might this not reasonably be identified as the direction in which nature is moving? To that degree, the process is not formless or haphazard but may be said to have a favored tendency. This is not quite the same as teleology; no specific goal need be named, only a net gain in intricacy over time. But this may be enough to serve as a way of finding human meaning in the universe.

2. *Human transcendence.* Insofar as no obvious selective advantage can be adduced for such cultural creations as art, music, higher mathematics, philosophy, or religion, might the human mind not be reasonably regarded as a special element in nature that escapes, perhaps transcends, the forces that determine physical evolution?

BIBLIOGRAPHY

Benz, Ernst. *Evolution and Christian Hope: Man's Concept of the Future from the Early Fathers to Teilhard de Chardin.* Garden City, N. Y., 1966. Includes chapters on evolution in works of Nietzsche, Marx, and Aurobindo Ghose.

Bergson, Henri. *L'évolution créatrice.* Paris, 1907. Translated as *Creative Evolution* (New York, 1911). The basic text for all vitalist theories of evolution.

Bergson, Henri. *Les deux sources de la morale et de la religion.* Paris, 1932. Translated as *The Two Sources of Morality and Religion* (Notre Dame, Ind., 1977). A more extensive discussion of the relationship of evolution to religion.

Deely, John N., and Raymond J. Nogar, eds. *The Problem of Evolution: A Study of the Philosophical Repercussions of Evolutionary Science.* New York, 1973. A valuable collection of essays. See especially Nogar's own contributions.

Eldredge, Niles. *The Monkey Business: A Scientist Looks at Creationism.* New York, 1982. A critique of creationism by a leading American paleontologist.

Gillespie, Neal C. *Charles Darwin and the Problem of Creation.* Chicago, 1979. Reviews doctrine of special creation and pro- and anti-Darwinian theories of evolution.

Himmelfarb, Gertrude. *Darwin and the Darwinian Revolution.* New York, 1968. Gives special attention to religious responses to Darwin, both pro and contra.

Irvine, William. *Apes, Angels, and Victorians: Darwin, Huxley, and Evolution.* New York, 1955. A study of the religious and scientific debates over evolution in Victorian England.

Kitcher, Philip. *Abusing Science: The Case against Creationism.* Cambridge, Mass., 1982. A "manual for self-defense" designed by a philosopher of science to be used by teachers and school administrators under pressure from creationist groups.

Lecomte de Noüy, Pierre. *Human Destiny.* New York, 1947. A theory of metaphysical evolution by a leading vitalist biologist.

Leith, Brian. *The Descent of Darwin.* London, 1982. Reviews scientific criticism of Darwinian evolution to the present day.

Mayr, Ernst. *The Growth of Biological Thought: Diversity, Evolution, and Inheritance.* Cambridge, Mass., 1982. The definitive statement to date of mainstream evolutionary theory. Also deals with issues of teleology and orthogenesis as these relate to metaphysical theories of evolution.

Moore, James R. *The Post-Darwinian Controversies: A Study of the Protestant Struggle to Come to Terms with Darwinism in Great Britain and America, 1870-1900.* London, 1970. A thorough survey.

Morris, Henry M. *The Scientific Case for Creationism.* San Diego, 1977. Christian creationist response to evolution by a leading proponent.

Nogar, Raymond J. *The Wisdom of Evolution.* Garden City, N. Y., 1963. An examination of evolutionary theory by a liberal Roman Catholic theologian.

Ong, Walter J., ed. *Darwin's Vision and Christian Perspectives.* New York, 1960. Essays by liberal Catholics on evolution.

Rogers, Jack B., ed. *Biblical Authority.* Waco, Texas, 1977. Neoevangelical essays revising the doctrine of biblical inerrancy.

Roszak, Theodore. *Unfinished Animal: The Aquarian Frontier and the Evolution of Consciousness.* New York, 1975. Deals with occult and metaphysical evolutionary systems of Blavatsky, Steiner, and Gurdjieff.

Teilhard de Chardin, Pierre. *Le phénomène humain.* Paris, 1955. Translated as *The Phenomenon of Man* (New York, 1959). The major statement of Teilhard's evolutionary theology.

THEODORE ROSZAK

EXCOMMUNICATION

To excommunicate means "to cut off from communion" or "to exclude from fellowship in a community." In a Christian setting, the term *excommunication* also applies to exclusion from Holy Communion, or the Eucharist.

Historically, religious practice admitted some form of putting a person outside the community.In a religious setting this right has often been reinforced by the belief that the sanction affects one's standing before God, inasmuch as it entails being cut off from the community of the saved. In religious traditions in which nonconformity was punishable by death, excommunication was introduced as a mitigation of the death penalty. In medieval Christendom and during the early years of the Reformation, excommunicated persons were turned over to civil authorities, who could inflict the death penalty upon them.

Early Christian practice mixed liturgical excommunications, which were part of the nonrepeatable public penitential practices, with disciplinary ones that could culminate in a person being declared anathema. In the thirteenth century Innocent III specified excommunication as a disciplinary penalty distinct from other punishments, characterizing it as

specifically medicinal, intended to heal the delinquent. The number of crimes for which excommunication could be incurred increased steadily through the eighteenth century, but a marked reduction in their number began with the reforms of Pius IX in 1869 and continued with the promulgation of the Code of Canon Law in 1917.

As a medicinal, or healing, penalty, excommunication under Roman Catholic law may be incurred only if a serious sin has been committed, or if the person is obstinate in a position after being given formal warnings and time to repent. Reflecting medieval and later developments, some excommunications are automatic *(latae sententiae),* incurred by committing a specified act, such as abortion or physically striking the pope. Other excommunications are imposed *(ferendae sententiae)* after an administrative or judicial investigation. Excommunication must always be lifted as soon as the delinquent repents and seeks peace with the church.

An excommunicated person loses basic rights in the church, but not the effects of baptism, which can never be lost. In the revision of the code carried out after Vatican II the effects of excommunication were clarified, and the distinction of *vitandi* and *tolerati* was dropped. Instead, all are treated as *tolerati* so far as the effects are concerned.

Generally, a person who is excommunicated is denied any role in administering the sacraments, especially the Eucharist. He may not receive any of the sacraments or administer sacramentals, such as burials, and he is forbidden to exercise any church offices or functions.

Under the reform of the law, automatic excommunication can be incurred in only six instances, including abortion. It may be imposed for a limited number of other crimes against faith, the Eucharist, or the seal of the confessional in the sacrament of penance. If imposed by a sentence or public declaration, excommunication can be lifted only by a public authority in the church, usually the local diocesan bishop.

BIBLIOGRAPHY

Recommended studies of early Christian practice are Kenneth Helm's *Eucharist and Excommunication: A Study in Early Christian Doctrine and Discipline* (Frankfurt, 1973) and John E. Lynch's "The Limits of *Communio* in the Pre-Constantinian Church," *The Jurist* 36 (1976): 159-190. For historical background and detailed commentary on Roman Catholic canon law through the 1917 Code of Canon Law, see Francis Edward Hyland's *Excommunication: Its Nature, Historical Development and Effects* (Washington, D. C., 1928), and for an overview of efforts to reform Roman Catholic law on this subject, see Thomas J. Green's "Future of Penal Law in the Church," *The Jurist* 35 (1975): 212-275, which includes a bibliography. Both the *Dictionnaire de droit canonique* (Paris, 1953) and the *Lexikon für Theologie und Kirche,* 2d ed. (Freiburg, 1957-1968), offer extensive articles, under the terms *Excommunication* and *Bann,* respectively.

JAMES H. PROVOST

EXISTENTIALISM

EXISTENTIALISM is a type of philosophy difficult to define because it does not have any agreed body of doctrine; it is rather a way of doing philosophy in which life and thought are closely related to each other. Thus, while some existentialists have been theists and others atheists, they have arrived at their different results by rather similar processes of thought. The existentialist who believes in God does so not as a result of intellectual demonstration—he is more likely to say that the attempts to prove God's existence are a waste of time, or even harmful—but on the grounds of passionate inward conviction; likewise the atheistic existentialist rejects God not because he has been persuaded by argument but because the very idea of God poses a threat to the freedom and autonomy of the human being, and so to the integrity of humanity. The existentialists of the twentieth century emerged about the same time as the logical positivists, and both groups shared doubts about the omnicompetence of reason. The existentialist would still claim to be a philosopher, in the sense of a thinker, but, in Kierkegaard's expression, an "existing thinker," that is, a thinker who is always involved in the reality he is thinking about, so that he cannot take up the purely objective attitude of a spectator; also, he is always on his way from one matter to another, so that as long as he exists he never has a complete picture. So existentialism stands opposed to all those grand metaphysical systems that profess to give a comprehensive and objective account of all that is.

The movement belongs essentially to the nineteenth and twentieth centuries. Søren Kierkegaard (1813-1855) is usually regarded as its founder. His philosophy is inextricably entangled with his struggle over what it means to become a Christian. Friedrich Nietzsche (1844-1900) is in many ways at the opposite extreme from Kierkegaard, but his proclamation of the death of God was just as passionate as Kierkegaard's fascination with the God-man paradox. Some Russian thinkers of the same period showed similar existentialist tendencies, notably Fedor Dostoevskii (1821-1881) and Vladimir Solov'ev (1853-1900). The Jewish thinker Martin Buber (1878-1965) had existentialist affinities but criticized the individualism of the typical existentialist.

Some Distinguishing Characteristics. As the name implies, existentialism is a philosophy of existence. It should be noted, however, that the word *existence* is used in a restricted sense. In ordinary speech, we say that stars exist, trees exist, cows exist, men and women exist, and so on of everything that has a place in the spatiotemporal world. The existentialist restricts the term to the human existent.

Although existentialists use the word *existence* in the sense just explained, it retains something of its traditional meaning. In the history of philosophy, existence (referring to the fact *that* something is) has usually been contrasted with essence (referring to *what* something is or the basic properties of that thing). Philosophies of essence (Platonism is the great example) concentrate attention on the universal properties of things. The philosopher of existence, on the other hand, concentrates attention on the concrete, individually existing reality, but this has a particularity and contingency that make it much more resistant to the systematizing tendencies of thought, so that, for such a thinker, reality does not conform to thought, and there are always loose ends that refuse to be accommodated in some tidy intellectual construction.

We should notice too that the existentialist finds room for dimensions of human existence other than thinking. For several centuries, Western philosophy has been deeply influenced by Descartes's famous pronouncement, "I think, therefore I am." The existentialist would claim that this accords too much preeminence to thinking.

It follows from this that existentialism is also a philosophy of the subject. Kierkegaard declared that truth is subjectivity. At first sight, this seems a subversive statement, one which might even imply the abolition of truth. But what Kierkegaard meant was that the most important truths of life are not to be achieved by observation and cannot be set down in textbooks to be looked up when required. They are the kind of truths that can be won only through inward and perhaps painful appropriation.

Implications for Religion. The existentialist recognition of the distinctiveness of human existence as over against the world of nature, together with the claim that the truth of human existence is to be reached by the way of subjectivity, is significant for the philosophy of religion.

The criticism is sometimes made that there is something morbid in the existentialists' preoccupation with anxiety and death, and this criticism also impinges on those Christian theologians who have used these ideas to urge the need for faith and dependence on God. But it should be noted that there is another and more affirmative side to existentialism. Many writers of the school speak also of "transcendence," and by this they do not mean the transcendence of God, as commmonly understood in theology, but the transcendence of the human existent as he moves constantly beyond himself into new situations. Those who stress transcendence believe that the goal of human life is to realize more and more one's authentic possibilities. Whereas the early Heidegger believed that this is to be achieved by human effort, by a steady "resoluteness" in the face of facticity and death, Christian writers such as Gabriel Marcel have thought of human transcendence as a transcendence toward God, and have taught that this is to be achieved not just through human effort but through the assistance of divine grace.

This extremely permissive ethic has seemed to some Christian thinkers to be compatible with Jesus' teaching that love rather than law must guide our conduct, and it is reflected in the various types of "situation ethics" that flourished for a short time.

BIBLIOGRAPHY

An introduction to existentialism is provided in my book *Existentialism* (Baltimore, 1973). Major existentialist texts include Søren Kierkegaard's *Philosophical Fragments,* translated by David F. Swenson (Princeton, 1936); Martin Heidegger's *Being and Time,* translated by me and Edward Robinson (New York, 1962); Jean-Paul Sartre's *Being and Nothingness,* translated by Hazel E. Barnes (New York, 1956); and Fritz Buri's *Theology of Existence,* translated by Harold H. Oliver and Gerhard Onder (Greenwood, S. C., 1965).

JOHN MACQUARRIE

EXORCISM

The Greek root of *exorcism, exorkosis* ("out-oath"), implies the driving out of evil powers or spirits by solemn adjuration or the performance of rituals. Such practices are worldwide, present in archaic as well as modern societies.

Ancient and Modern Japan. Some of the most striking descriptions of exorcisms in past and present times have come from Japan. The thirty-fifth and thirty-sixth chapters of the famous *Tale of Genji,* written by the court lady Murasaki Shikibu in the eleventh century CE, give lengthy accounts of possessions and exorcisms. The *Pillow Book* of Sei Shonagon, written during the same period, presents other vivid pictures of exorcism.

Linking such classical examples to modern times, Carmen Blacker (1975) has given accounts of present-day exorcisms, as revealed by her own research among Nichiren Buddhist priests in Japan. Four kinds of possession are distinguished. The first kind, when only the body is affected by mysterious pains, frequently is attributed to an angry spirit. The second kind consists of hallucinations; the third, of an altered personality which could be blamed on possession by an animal such as a fox. The fourth kind consists of more rare cases when different voices and personalities appear and indicate possession. Blacker notes that the Roman Catholic church now recognizes only cases in the fourth category as true possession.

Any of these afflictions may be treated in Nichiren Buddhist temples. There, exorcisms are based on the teachings of the *Lotus Sutra.* Methods of prayer spells with the help of a medium are used in some temples, but in others, mediums have been generally abandoned "in favour of a direct confrontation between exorcist and patient" (Blacker, 1975, p. 302).

China and North Asia. In China down to modern times exorcisms are held more frequently on behalf of the sick than for any other purpose. J. J. M. De Groot describes a typical healing exorcism. After reciting spells, burning papers of incantations, and offering incense, the shaman began his or her "communication with the medium" (de Groot, 1892-1910, vol. 6, p. 1274). The medium shivered and yawned, but as incantations became louder to the accompaniment of drums and as "eye-opening papers" were burnt in quick succession, he or she began to jump about. Assistants forced the medium to a seat, his limbs shaking, his head and shoulders jerking from side to side, and his eyes staring as if into the invisible world. The consultant (the sufferer or the shaman) put questions to the medium, who replied with incoherent sounds which were interpreted as a divine language and were written down on paper. When the spirit announced its intention to depart, drums were beaten, water and ashes were spurted over the medium, and gold paper money was burned for the spirit. The medium swooned, and when he revived he declared that he had no recollection of the event.

Exorcism was practiced both by Taoist priests and by esoteric Buddhist sects. They performed before altars, surrounded by candles, incense, long scrolls with painted figures, and

> In South India and in Sri Lanka professional exorcisers paint their faces, put on hideous masks . . . and take to dancing in order to impersonate particular demons.

the accompaniment of drums. Reciting texts from the *Shih ching* (Book of Odes) and later writings, they expelled demons by making noise, striking out at the demons with clubs, and spitting water from the mouth in the four cardinal directions.

The shamanistic tradition of the ancient Bon religion of Tibet was preserved almost in its entirety in Buddhist Lamaism. The most famous Tibetan Buddhist monks were said to have performed miracles and exorcisms like other shamans. In one Tibetan legend a notable lama expelled the spirit of sickness in the form of a black pin from a queen, and his fellow worker flew through the air and danced on the roof of a house. However, not a great deal has been done to investigate the shamanistic elements in Bon and Lamaism.

India and South Asia. Parallels to shamanistic techniques and exorcisms are found in Indian classical texts. The *Atharvaveda* (5.15-16) gives spells for exorcising, "speaking away " *(apa-vaktri),* warding off or averting pests and their leaders, as well as rites against demons.

In Indian village religion the activities of professional exorcisers ranged from warding off hailstorms to expelling evil spirits from those possessed by them. L. S. S. O'Malley (1935) describes an exorcism during an epidemic in the sub-Himalayan districts of Uttar Pradesh. The exorcist was simply carried outside the village tied upside down on a bedstead. Driving a wooden peg into the ground, he assured the villagers that the evil spirit had been tied up.

In South India and in Sri Lanka professional exorcisers paint their faces, put on hideous masks, dress in gaudy costumes, arm themselves with symbolic weapons, and take to dancing in order to impersonate particular demons. In this way they induce evil spirits to leave the persons they have possessed. Sinhala exorcism has been described in detail by Paul Wirz (1954).

When a person is ill in Sri Lanka, he sends first for the general medical practitioner, but if the practitioner's remedies do not help the invalid, a soothsayer is called in to determine the cause of the sickness. The soothsayer may suggest an astrologer, who is cheaper, or an exorcist. The exorcist makes his diagnosis by asking where the patient has stayed, whether he has come into contact with harmful spirits, eaten food that attracted them, or lived in a haunted house. He ties a charm on the patient to prevent the sickness from getting worse and to show the demons that a fuller ritual offering will be made.

Other sufferers from evil spirits go to popular shrines, such as the famous center of Kataragama in southeastern Sri Lanka, named after a god who is the second son of the Hindu god Siva. Although primarily a Hindu center for the Tamils, this shrine attracts members of other religions. Enthusiastic devotees have become notorious for walking on fire or hanging in the air by means of skewers through their back muscles. At Kataragama are claimed cures of physical, mental, and spiritual possession. More simply, Buddhists may claim that evil spirits can be exorcised by recitation of the Three Refuges, which causes spirits and ghosts to flee.

In Burma and other countries of Southeast Asia, Buddhist sects practice exorcism for diseases believed to be caused by witchcraft or demonic possession. Combining ancient indigenous beliefs in spirits with faith in the Buddha and his attendants, some monks exorcise evil spirits by enlisting both traditional esoteric skills and the powers of benign Buddhist gods.

Africa and Islamic Lands. In Africa, belief in possession by good or evil spirits flourished in ancient indigenous religions and has survived in modern Islamic and Christian contexts.

In Somalia a victim is said to have been entered or seized by spirits. When this happens, both the spirits and the resulting illness are called *sar* (*zar* in Ethiopia). Somalians believe that these evil spirits are consumed with greed and lust after luxurious food, clothing, jewelry, and perfume. Women, especially married women, are particularly vulnerable to such possession. I. M. Lewis (1971) suggests that this results from women's depressed social status, for divorce and absent husbands are common. Speaking through the lips of the possessed woman, the spirits demand fine clothes, perfumes, and dainties with an authority that the women rarely achieve in ordinary life.

In Tanzania a similar "devil's disease" reveals its presence by hysterical symptoms of craving for food and presents. The exorcism includes not only cathartic dances but also the continuing presence of the exorcist in the house of the possessed woman.

The Islamic world tolerates the belief in witchcraft and possession. Although such beliefs at times are condemned, their prevalence is not questioned. *Sihr* ("glamour, magic") is based upon belief in a world of spirits. Magicians claim that they can control the spirits by obeying Allah and using his name in exorcisms. Illicit magicians are believed to enslave spirits for evil purposes and do so by performing deeds displeasing to God.

BIBLIOGRAPHY

For general studies of exorcism and its practitioners, see Traugott K. Oesterreich's *Possession, Demoniacal and Other* (New York, 1930) and Mircea Eliade's *Shamanism: Archaic Techniques of Ecstasy,* rev. & enl. ed. (New York, 1964). Arthur Waley's translation of *The Tale of Genji* (London, 1925) was long the standard version, but Edward G. Seidensticker's translation under the same title (New York, 1978) is complete and beautifully done. Carmen Blacker's *The Catalpa Bow* (London, 1975)—the title taken from an instrument used by a Japanese exorcist—is an invaluable study of popular religion past and present based on firsthand experience. *The Pillow Book of Sei Shonagon* has been translated and annotated by Ivan I. Morris (Baltimore, 1970). *The Religious System of China,* 6 vols., by J. J. M. de Groot (1892-1910; Taipei, 1967), is full of detail on traditional beliefs and practices, as is L. Austine Waddell's *The Buddhism of Tibet* (1895; Cambridge, 1971). Helmut Hoffmann outlines more modern practices in *The Religions of Tibet* (New York, 1961). *Popular Hinduism* by L. S. S. O'Malley (New York, 1935) provides brief studies. *Exorcism and the Art of Healing in Ceylon* by Paul Wirz (Leiden, 1954) is more detailed and analytical. Stanley J. Tambiah's *Buddhism and the Spirit Cults in North-East Thailand* (Cambridge, 1970) is a more anthropological study. Richard F. Gombrich examines the relationship between "cognitive" and practiced religion in Sri Lanka in *Precept and Practice* (Oxford, 1971). An anthropological study of possession and exorcism with special reference to Africa is found in I. M. Lewis's *Ecstatic Religion* (Harmondsworth, 1971). For a comparative study of beliefs see my *West African Psychology* (London, 1951). On exorcism in popular Islam, see Edward A. Westermarck's *Ritual and Belief in Morocco,* 2 vols. (1926; New Hyde Park, N. Y., 1968).

GEOFFREY PARRINDER

FAITH

FAITH, in probably the best-known definition of it, is "the assurance of things hoped for, the conviction of things not seen." Although this definition itself comes from the Christian scriptures, specifically from the anonymous epistle to the Hebrews in the New Testament, it can, *mutatis mutandis,* be applied across a broad spectrum of religions and religious traditions. More importantly, however, *faith* is used, even in Judaism and Christianity (where it has been the most successfully domesticated), to cover an entire cluster of concepts that are related to one another but are by no means identical.

Faith-as-Faithfulness. In its most fundamental meaning, faith has been defined as faithfulness, and as such, it has been taken as an attribute both of the divine and of believers in the divine. The Latin adjective *pius,* for example, was used in Vergil's *Aeneid* in such a phrase as *pia numina* to characterize the reciprocal fidelity that the gods manifested in their dealings with human beings; something of both senses, presumably, attached to the word when it became a standard part of the official title of the Roman emperor, most familiarly in the case of Antoninus Pius (r. 138-161 CE). The reciprocity implied in the concept of faith when predicated of human social relations, where (as in the notion of "keeping faith" with someone) "faith" has become almost synonymous with "loyalty," has carried over likewise into its use for the divine-human relation. Wherever the gods were said to promise something in that relation, *faith* would seem to be an appropriate term for their keeping or fulfilling the promise.

Faith-as-Obedience. The precise content of such obedience has varied enormously with the content of what was perceived to have been the divine will or law. Obedience, therefore, carried both liturgical and moral connotations. An imperative to reenact, periodically or once in a lifetime, the acts of the divine model required the obedient and meticulous observance of the demands that those acts had placed upon the believer. Initiation into the faith involved learning the specific methods of such ritual observance, with rites of passage frequently serving as the occasion for such learning. Where the divine will was conceived of as having laid down rules not only for ritual actions but for ethics, the obedience of faith meant moral behavior in conformity with divine com-mands; thus in Hinduism, *dharma* as moral law required righteous conduct.

Faith and Works. The definition of faith as obedience, and yet as somehow not reducible to obedience, points to the perennial and unavoidable problem of the relation between faith and works. On the one hand, even the most theocentric versions of faith have found themselves obliged to assert, often in self-defense against the charge that they were severing the moral nerve, that they were in fact reinforcing ethics precisely by their emphasis on its vertical dimension: it has been a universal conviction of believers, across religious boundaries, that "faith without works is dead." On the other hand, those religious systems that have appeared to outsiders, whether critical or friendly, to equate faith and works and to be indifferent to any considerations except the "purely" moral ones prove, upon closer examination, to have been no less sensitive to the dialectic between works and faith. Confucius repeatedly professed ignorance about the mysteries of "Heaven" and avoided discussing the miraculous phenomena in which conventional faith had sought manifestations of supernatural power; even the question of personal immortality did not admit of a clear and definite answer. Rather, he concentrated his attention on works of piety and of service to others, preferring generosity to greed and virtue to success.

Faith-as-Trust. Such a confidence in the providential care of "Heaven" underlies the definition of faith-as-trust. In the classic formulation of Martin Luther, "to 'have a god' is nothing else than to trust and believe him with our whole heart," since "it is the trust and faith of the heart alone that makes both God and an idol" *(Large Catechism).* Many of the conventional metaphors for the divine in various traditions, from "rock" and "mountain" to "mother" or "father," have served as representations of the conviction that "the trust and faith of the heart" could appropriately be vested in such an object, and that the divine object would prove worthy of human trust..

Faith-as-Dependence. If obedience to the divine will was the completion of the circle of faith in the moral realm, dependence on the divine will was the way faith-as-trust affirmed the relation of human weakness to divine power. In those traditions in which the divine has been seen as creator and/or preserver, faith-as-dependence has been, in the first instance, an affirmation of the origin and derivation of humanity and of its world; in those traditions that have tended not to distinguish as sharply between "being" as applied to the divine and as applied to human beings, dependence has been the basis for identifying the locations of both the divine and the human within the "great chain of Being".

Faith-as-Experience. In one way or another, each of these definitions of faith has been derived from faith-as-experience. For even the most transcendent notions of the mystery of the divine will have, by their very act of affirming the mysteriousness of that mystery, laid claim to an experience in which the individual believer or the community tradition has caught a glimpse of just how mysterious the divine could be. Inseparability of faith-as-experience from all the other experiences of life has persuaded some observers of the phenomenon to see it as in fact the sublimation and "supernatural" reinterpretation of an essentially "natural" event.

The Community of Faith. In the sacred literatures of religious faith, faith-as-experience has often been described in highly individualistic terms: how the poet or prophet has come to know the holy in personal experience has dominated how he or she has described that experience for others, so that they in turn, one at a time, might also come to share in such an experience and duplicate it for themselves. Except for passing moments of intense mystical rapture, however, such individualism has been shown to be illusory. And except for occasional glossolalia, the very language in which the individual has spoken about faith-as-experience has been derived from the history of the community, even when that language has been aimed against the present corruption of the community or when it has been directed toward the founding of a new and purer community.

Faith and Worship. The community of faith has always been a community of worship. One of the most important scholarly sources for the new and deeper recognition of faith-as-worship has been the investigation of the interrelation between myth and ritual: myth came to be read as the validation, in the deeds of the ancients or of the gods, of what the ritual now enjoined upon believers; and ritual acquired a new dimension by being understood as not merely outward ceremonial performed *ex opere operato* but as the repetition in the believers' actions of what the myth recited in words about the divine actions that had made the world and founded the community.

Faith-as-Credo. One of the definitions of "faith" is "credo" (which is the Latin for "I believe"). In medieval usage, for example, the Latin word *fides* must commonly be translated as "*the* faith" rather than simply as "faith,". To "have faith," then, meant first of all to "hold *the* faith" as this had been laid down in the apostolic "deposit of faith" and legislated by church fathers, councils, and popes.

Faith and Tradition. "Traditionary religion" has defined itself and its faith on the basis of received tradition. The myth of how holy things have happened; the ritual of how holy acts

were to be performed; the rules of conduct by which the faithful were expected to guide their lives; the structure through which the holy community was founded and governed; the doctrine by which the community gave an account of the myth and ritual—all these expressions of faith have been the subject and the content of the holy tradition.

Faith and Knowledge. Faith has been taken to be a species of knowledge, differing from ordinary knowledge by its superior claims: an arcane character, a transcendent content, privileged channels of communication, or divine certainty (or all of the above). So long as such claims remained publicly uncontested, faith could stand as objectively sure, even when subjectively the individual believer might question or doubt it.

BIBLIOGRAPHY

Eliade, Mircea. *Patterns in Comparative Religion.* New York, 1958.
Feuerbach, Ludwig. *The Essence of Christianity.* Translated by George Eliot. London, 1854.
Freud, Sigmund. *The Future of an Illusion.* London, 1928.
Heiler, Friedrich. *Prayer: A Study in the History and Psychology of Religion.* Oxford, 1932.
Hügel, Friedrich von. *The Mystical Element of Religion.* 2 vols. London, 1961.
James, William. *The Varieties of Religious Experience.* New York, 1902.
Lossky, Vladimir. *In the Image and Likeness of God.* Scarsdale, N. Y., 1974.
Otto, Rudolf. *The Idea of the Holy.* New York, 1928.
Smith, Wilfred Cantwell. *Faith and Belief.* Princeton, 1979.
Söderblom, Nathan. *The Living God: Basal Forms of Personal Religion.* Oxford, 1933.
Wach, Joachim. *Sociology of Religion.* Chicago, 1944.

JAROSLAV PELIKAN

FALL, THE

The concept of the fall appears in myths, traditions, and religions of a great many peoples. In general, the fall is to be thought of as an accident that arose after the creation or genesis of the world bearing consequences for the present human condition; this accident explains a new situation in the world that is recognized as a decline or degradation when contrasted to the original state of man and the cosmos.

The theme of the fall may be considered from the perspective of (1) historical time and its unfolding; (2) theogony; (3) cosmogony; and (4) anthropogony, which encompasses the creation of man and his present condition.

Considered temporally, the fall takes place between *Urzeit* and *Endzeit,* between the beginning and the end of creation. Within historical time, it is very close to the beginnings of time conceived as a golden age in contrast to which the fall and its consequences represent a break or degradation. This temporal and historical conception of the fall can be found in various popular traditions as well as myths of the golden age and paradise lost.

The theogonic aspect of the fall is found in the numerous myths concerning the origin of the gods, of their victory over chaos, or of the victory of the more recent forces of divinity over older ones. Coextensive with the creation, the fall as presented in theogony implies the identification of evil and chaos on the one hand and of salvation and creation on the other. This conception of the fall is found especially in Sumero-Akkadian theogonic myths that recount the victory of order over preexisting chaos; it is found also in the Egyptian myth of the battle between Seth and Horus. Strictly speaking, these theogonic myths are not true myths of the fall, but two of their recurrent themes justify their inclusion in a typology of myths of the fall. First, they emphasize the ritual celebration of the maintenance of the creation and cosmic order, as in the festival of Akitu in Babylon. Second, they present, through a variety of mythologies, the theme of the degradation of divinity that results from the fall of some portion of the divine substance into matter, body, or darkness.

From the perspective of cosmogony, the fall is seen as an accident occurring after the genesis of the world that affects cosmic forces and explains the present condition of earth or the universe. Myths that tell of the progressive degradation of the universe and its destruction and recreation in successive cosmic cycles exemplify this cosmogonic view of the fall. The flood is an important example of this type of fall, and numerous myths of the flood are found among religious traditions of the world.

Anthropogony, however, offers the most important perspective on the fall. From this perspective, the contemporary human condition—a condition of degradation in contrast to that of the golden age of humanity—is explained as the consequence of a fall, a tragic event that bursts into human history. Around this event are clustered those myths and symbols that seek to explain the origins of illness and death and the tragic nature of the human condition after the fall.

From these four perspectives, it is possible to develop a typology through which the myriad myths of the fall in cultures throughout the world become comprehensible.

Myths of the fall clearly show three essential elements: (1) the concept of a golden age in the beginning, (2) the accident that is a break or degradation of original harmony, (3) the explanation of the present human condition. From these three elements, it is possible to trace a historico-phenomenological picture of the traditions dealing with the fall.

World Religions. While the archaic and ancient religions have many traditions relating to the fall, this article has chosen to spotlight each of the world religions—gnosticism and Manichaeism, and the three great monotheisms, Judaism,

Christianity, and Islam—that lend great richness to the concept of the fall.

Gnosticism and Manichaeism. From the second century CE onward, gnosticism, a religious movement composed of a number of different sects, came to maturity throughout the Mediterranean world and in the Near East. The central element of gnostic metaphysical speculation is a dualistic doctrine according to which man possesses a divine spark that, although originating from on high, has fallen into matter, into body, which holds it prisoner in the lower world. The myth of the fall, therefore, is an integral part of gnostic teaching. Each gnostic sect offered salvation through its specific creed and rites of initiation into these dualistic mysteries. These constituted its particular gnosis. Understood only by adherents who were gradually initiated into it, the gnosis brought about an identity of the initiate with the means of his salvation and with divine substance.

Because it claims to possess the most perfect gnosis, Manichaeism holds a special place in the spectrum of gnostic thought. Its founder, Mani (216-277), taught that, as the transmitter of the gnosis, he was the greatest of the prophets

> **Through a choice of his own, man decides his standing before God and at the same time the direction of his destiny.**

and the ultimate revelation, sent by the Holy Spirit, after the trials and failures of his predecessors—most notably Zarathushtra, the Buddha, and Jesus—to establish the church of the end of time, the church of light, and to provide the definitive revelation that would enlighten all men. According to Mani, the soul, a spark detached from divine light and held prisoner by matter, must tear itself away from the darkness of the body in order to return to the realm of light where it had originated.

The symbol of the fall is omnipresent in gnostic texts; indeed, the precosmic fall of a portion of the divine principle is the underlying reason for the genesis of the cosmos and man (Jonas, 1963). In the different metaphysical speculations that explain this fall, it is generally held that the divine principle descended voluntarily, and that guilt came into being as the Aeons turned toward the lower world. Turning toward matter by a burning desire to know it, the soul then sank into it and was swallowed up. Hence, the fall that gave birth to the cosmos also imprisoned the soul in matter.

Judaism. In Hebrew, the word *gan*—*paradeisos* in Greek (related to the Iranian *paridaida*)—designates the place where, according to *Genesis* 2:8, God placed man. [*See* Paradise.]

Adam and Eve enjoy a life of paradise in the garden, living together in harmony. The presence in Eden of the tree of the knowledge of good and evil shows that obedience to God is essential to maintaining this privileged situation. The biblical text emphasizes considerations that are absent in all other myths of the golden age—considerations of freedom, of moral choice in the face of good and evil. Through a choice of his own, man decides his standing before God and at the same time the direction of his destiny.

The editors of chapters 4-11 of *Genesis* saw in the fall of man in Eden not only the loss of paradise and the transformation of the human condition but also the source of a whole series of evils that subsequently beset mankind. Thus, at each stage in the rise of civilization and the institutionalization of the social developments that formed men's lives in antiquity, the biblical text notes humanity's corruption. Since the fall, evil is born in the hearts of men and always remains at the heart of history, an inevitable force in human affairs.

Christianity. It was Paul who was especially interested in the relationship between the fall and sin. In chapters 1-3 of *Romans*, he asserts that no one can escape the domination of sin, and in chapter 7 he gives a lengthy description of the human condition in the earthly paradise, where as yet humans knew neither covetousness nor death, and contrasts this with the actual condition to which they have been reduced by sin and death. He asserts that the actual human condition comes from the first sin, the sin of Adam and Eve in the earthly paradise (*Rom.* 7:13-15); and in *1 Corinthians* 15:21-22, he opposes the first Adam, the author of death, to Christ, the second Adam, the author of life.

Islam. The Qur'an demonstrates the importance Islam attaches to the idea of God the creator, the all-powerful.

God created man and called him *khalifah*, vicar or viceroy (2:28). Adam, *khalifat Allah*, vicar of a God who had placed him at the center of the world, is the preeminent creature, although, made of mud and clay, he owes everything to God (15:26). Many verses of the Qur'an stress the preeminent dignity of man; even the angels must bow down before him (2:32).

God put Adam and his wife in the midst of a garden where they could take fruit from the trees, but he forbade them to approach one tree, under pain of falling among sinners (2:33). But the demon made Adam and his wife sin by eating fruit from that tree and thereby caused their expulsion from the place where God had placed them. The episodes in the Qur'an concerning Adam are reminiscent of *Genesis*: his creation out of earth, his title of vicar, his temptation, fall, and expulsion from paradise. Only the episode of Iblis is not found in the Bible.

[*For further discussion of the fall and its consequences, see* Evil.]

BIBLIOGRAPHY

Baumann, Hermann. *Schöpfung und Urzeit des Menschen im Mythos der afrikanischen Völker.* Berlin, 1936.
Boyce, Mary. *A History of Zoroastrianism,* vol. 1. Leiden, 1975.
Dexinger, Ferdinand. *Sturz der Göttersöhne oder Engel vor der Sintflut.* Vienna, 1966.
Eliade, Mircea. *Patterns in Comparative Religion.* New York, 1958.
Eliade, Mircea. "Nostalgia for Paradise in the Primitive Traditions." In his *Myths, Dreams and Mysteries.* New York, 1960.
Feldmann, Joseph. *Paradies und Sündenfall.* Münster, 1913.
Frazer, James G. *Folk-lore in the Old Testament.* 3 vols. London, 1919.
Jonas, Hans. *The Gnostic Religion.* 2d rev. ed. Boston, 1963.
Kákosy, L. "Ideas about the Fallen State of the World in Egyptian Religion: Decline of the Golden Age." *Acta Orientalia* (Budapest) 17 (1964): 205-216.
Kramer, Samuel Noah. *History Begins at Sumer* (1957). 3d ed. Philadelphia, 1981.
Lambert, W. G., and A. R. Millard. *Atra-Hasis: The Babylonian Story of the Flood.* Oxford, 1968.
Otto, Eberhard. "Das goldene Zeitalter in einem aegyptischen Text." In his *Religions en Egypte hellénistique et romaine.* Paris, 1969.
Ricoeur, Paul. *La symbolique du mal.* 2 vols. Paris, 1960. Translated as *The Symbolism of Evil* (Boston, 1967).
Söderblom, Nathan. *La vie future d'apres le mazdéisme à la lumière des croyances parallèles dans les autres religions.* Paris, 1901.
Thomas, Louis-Vincent. *La mort africaine.* Paris, 1982.
Widengren, Geo. *Les religions de l'Iran.* Paris, 1968.

JULIEN RIES
Translated from French by Jeffrey Haight and
Annie S. Mahler

FASTING

Although the origins of fasting as a moral or religious discipline are obscure, the custom or practice of fasting is attested in many ancient cultures.

Within certain Greco-Roman philosophical schools and religious fellowships (e.g., the Pythagorean), fasting, as one aspect of asceticism, was closely aligned to the belief that humanity had originally experienced a primordial state of perfection that was forfeited by a transgression. Through various ascetic practices such as fasting, poverty, and so forth, the individual could be restored to a state where communication and union with the divine was again made possible. In some religious groups (for example, Judaism, Christianity, and Islam) fasting gradually became a standard way of expressing devotion and worship to a specific divine being.

Although it is difficult to pinpoint a specific rationale or motivation for an individual's or a group's fasting, in most cultures that ascribe to it at least three motivations are easily discernible: (1) preliminary to or preparatory for an important event or time in an individual's or a people's life; (2) as an act of penitence or purification; or (3) as an act of supplication.

Preparatory Fasting. In addition to the basic underlying assumption that fasting is an essential preparation for divine revelation or for some type of communing with the spiritual, many cultures believe that fasting is a prelude to important times in a person's life. It purifies or prepares the person (or group) for greater receptivity in communion with the spiritual. In the Greco-Roman mystery religions, for example, fasting was deemed an aid to enlightenment by a deity, and an initiate into most of these religions had to abstain from all or certain specified foods and drink in order to receive knowledge of the mysteries of the specific religion.

> **Yom Kippur, the Day of Atonement, is such a day of fasting and praying for forgiveness of sins.**

Within some of the mystery cults, fasting was incorporated as part of the ritual preparation for the incubation sleep that, by means of dreams, was to provide answers to specific questions and needs of the person. Dreams and visions were viewed as media through which spiritual or divine revelations were made manifest. Both Greek philosophers (e.g., Pythagoreans and Neoplatonists) and Hebrew prophets believed that fasting could produce trancelike states through which revelations would occur. Plutarch narrates how the priests of ancient Egypt abstained from meat and wine in order to receive and interpret divine revelations (*Isis and Osiris* 5-6), and Iamblichus tells how the prophetess fasted three days prior to giving an oracle (*Egyptian Mysteries* 3.7).

Among the Eastern traditions Hindu and Jain ascetics fasted while on pilgrimage and in preparation for certain festivals. Within classical Chinese religious practice, *chai*, or ritual fasting, preceded the time of sacrifices. By contrast, later Chinese religious thought, particularly Taoism, taught that "fasting of the heart" (*hsin-chai*), rather than bodily fasting, was more beneficial to arriving at "the Way" (*tao*). Confucianism followed the practice of Confucius in approving fasting as preparation for those times set aside for worship of ancestral spirits. Although the Buddha taught moderation rather than excessive fasting, many Buddhist monks and nuns adhered to the custom of eating only one meal per day, in the forenoon, and they were obliged to fast on days of new and full moon.

Within the Judaic tradition only one day of fasting was imposed by Mosaic law, Yom Kippur, the Day of Atonement (*Lv.* 16:29-34), but four additional days were added after the Babylonian exile (*Zec.* 8:19) to commemorate days on which disasters had occurred.

Although formalized fasting was spoken against in the New Testament (*Mt.* 6:16-6:18), it eventually became the favorite ascetic practice of the desert dwellers and monastic men and women who saw it as a necessary measure to free the soul from worldly attachments and desires. Within the Christian tradition there gradually developed seasonal fasts such as the Lenten one of forty days preparatory to Easter; Rogation Days in spring in supplication for good crops; and Ember Days, days of prayer and fasting during each of the four seasons of the year. There were also weekly fasts on Wednesdays and Fridays and fasts prior to solemn occasions celebrating important moments in people's lives (e.g., baptism, ordination to priesthood, admission to knighthood, and reception of the Eucharist).

In the Islamic tradition Muslims continue to observe the ninth month, Ramadan, as one of rigorous fasting (*sawm*), during which days no liquid or food is allowed between dawn and sunset, as stipulated in the Qur'an (2:180ff.). Some of the stricter Muslim groups fast each Monday and Thursday, and the Qur'an recommends fasting as a penance during a pilgrimage, three days going and seven returning (2:193).

Basic to the beliefs of many Native American tribes was the view that fasting was efficacious for receiving guidance from the Great Spirit. In New South Wales, Australia, boys had to fast for two days at their *bora* ceremonies. In the Aztec culture the ritual training required of one who aspired to become a sacrificing priest included fasting as one form of abstinence. While fasting was often viewed as a disciplinary measure that would strengthen the body and character of the individual, prolonged fasting and other austerities were also undergone so that the individual might see or hear the guardian spirit who would remain with him or her for life.

Fasting as Penance or Purification. Ancient Egyptian and Babylonian customs included ritualized fasting as a form of penance that accompanied other expressions of sorrow for wrongdoing. Like people of later times, these nations viewed fasting as meritorious in atoning for faults and sins and thus turning away the wrath of the gods. In the *Book of Jonah,* for example, the Assyrians are depicted as covered with sackcloth, weeping, fasting, and praying to God for forgiveness (*Jon.* 3:5ff.).

For the Jews, fasting was an outward expression of inner penitence, and on various occasions a general fast was proclaimed as a public recognition of the sin of the people (*1 Sm.* 14:24, *1 Kgs.* 21:9, *Jer.* 36:9). Yom Kippur, the Day of Atonement, is such a day of fasting and praying for forgiveness of sins. But fasting is also viewed as a means of orienting the human spirit to something or someone greater. According to Philo Judaeus (25 BCE-50 CE), the Therapeutae, a group of Jewish contemplatives living in community, fasted as a means of purifying the spirit so that it could turn itself to more spiritual activities such as reading and study (*On the Contemplative Life*). The Essenes, a Jewish group who followed their "righteous teacher" into the wilderness at Qumran (c. 135 BCE-70 CE), in their *Manual of Discipline* prescribed fasting as one of the ways of purification, of preparing for the coming of the "end of days."

Although fasting as a means of atonement and purification is evident in other traditions, it was among the Christians that fasting became a predominant feature. With the rapid growth of ascetic movements that incorporated Greek dualism into their thought patterns, fasting became an important means of ridding the body of its attachment to material possessions and pleasures, thus freeing the person for attaining the higher good, the love for and imitation of Christ. The prevailing notion was that whereas food in moderation was a necessary good for maintaining health, abstention from food was particularly effective in controlling the balance between body and spirit.

Modern-day Christian denominations display a considerable diversity of opinion and practice in regard to fasting. For most Protestant denominations, except for some of the more evangelically oriented groups, fasting is left to the discretion of the individual. Although within the Roman Catholic and Greek Orthodox churches prescriptions still govern both individual and corporate practices, rigid fasting practices have been abolished. Roman Catholics still practice partial fasting and abstinence from meat on Ash Wednesday and Good Friday. Within the Greek Orthodox church fasting is usually one of the acts of purification preparing one for participation in the liturgical mysteries.

Although Buddhists generally favor restraint in taking food, and many consider fasting a non-Buddhist practice, it is listed as one of the thirteen Buddhist practices that can serve as an aid to leading a happy life, a means of purification *(dhutanga)*. Therefore, many Buddhist monks have the custom of eating only one meal a day, often eating only from the alms bowl and declining a second helping. For other Buddhists enlightenment was considered more easily attainable by renunciation of wrong ideas and views rather than by fasting. Within Jainism there is the belief that certain ascetic practices, like fasting, are purificatory in that they can remove the accumulation of *karman* that weighs down the life-monad.

Within some of the Native American tribes, the practice of fasting was considered conducive to purifying the body prior to some great feat or challenge. The Cherokee Indians believed that prior to slaying an eagle the individual had to undergo a long period of prayer and fasting that purified the body, strengthening it for the necessary combat. Siouan-speaking Indians believed that before both hunting and war the body had to be purified through fasting for these noble tasks. Among the Incas, fasting from salt, chili peppers, meat, or *chicha* (beer made from maize) was one of the ways of preparing the body for an important event and also for a public form of penance.

Fasting as Supplication. Although it is difficult in many instances to distinguish clearly between fasting as a means of penitence and fasting as a means of supplication, within certain traditions the latter has widespread usage. Within Judaism, for example, fasting was one way of "bending the ear of Yahveh," of asking God to turn to the Jews in mercy and grant them the favor requested. Ahab, for example, fasted to avert the disaster predicted by Elijah (*1 Kgs.* 21:27-29, cf. *Nm.* 1:4, *2 Chr.* 20:3, *Jer.* 36:9). Since penitence and supplication were often dual motivational forces for fasting within Judaism, fasting emerged as both conciliatory and supplicatory. As in the Christian and Islamic traditions, the Jewish notion of fasting reflected an attitude of interior sorrow and conversion of heart. Within the Christian ascetic circles, fasting was viewed as one of the more meritorious acts, which exorcised demons and demonic temptation from the individual's consciousness.

Within other groups fasting was also viewed as meritorious in obtaining rewards from higher powers. In the Intichiuma ceremonies of the tribes in central Australia fasting was practiced to assure an increase in the totem food supply. Young Jain girls fasted as one means of requesting the higher power to give them a good husband and a happy married life. Fasting frequently accompanied or preceded the dance rituals of certain tribes who prayed for a renewal of fertility and a productive harvest from the earth (e.g., the Dakota Sun Dance; the Cheyenne New Life Lodge; the Ponca Sacred Dance, or Mystery Dance).

BIBLIOGRAPHY

Brandon, S. G. F., ed. *A Dictionary of Comparative Religion.* London, 1970.
MacCulloch, J. A., and A. J. Maclean. "Fasting." In *Encyclopaedia of Religion and Ethics,* edited by James Hastings, vol. 5. Edinburgh, 1912.
MacDermot, Violet. *The Cult of the Seer in the Ancient Middle East.* London, 1971.
Rogers, Eric N. *Fasting: The Phenomenon of Self-Denial.* Nashville, 1976.
Ryan, Thomas. *Fasting Rediscovered: A Guide to Health and Wholeness for Your Body-Spirit.* New York, 1981.
Underhill, Ruth M. *Red Man's America: A History of Indians in the United States.* Rev. ed. Chicago, 1971.
Wakefield, Gordon S., ed. *The Westminster Dictionary of Christian Spirituality.* London, 1983.

ROSEMARY RADER

FLOOD, THE

The Antecedents of the Flood; Its Causes. The gods began several times to create humanity on several occasions; floods are one of the means that they used to destroy the unfortunate results of their initial endeavors. After creating the heavens and the earth in darkness, say the Quechua peoples of South America, the god Viracocha made human beings too big; he turned some into statues and destroyed the rest with a flood. In the *Popul Vuh*, the sacred book of the Maya, we see formative or progenitor spirits create the first animated mannequins. These lived and procreated, but "this was only a trial, an attempt at humanity." They disappeared in the course of a complex series of events, in a vast inundation (*Popol Vuh* 3-4). Instead of annihilating an imperfect humanity, sometimes the creator god tries to improve it; he eliminates the defective humans by use of a flood. When everything seemed to be complete, say the Desána of South America, a number of plagues overcame the world, and evil beings ravaged men. Seeing the suffering of those he had created, Sun brought on a flood that drowned all the living, and then a fire that burned everything. There were survivors, however, and the god had them brought up.

The Survivors. In myths where the flood is supposed to destroy the original, defective mankind, sometimes the latter disappears completely. In other cases, there are one or more survivors.

In Hindu myth, Manu is a great *rsi*. A lengthy practice of asceticism raises him above his fellow mortals; he is able to recognize and save the divine being who, in the form of a fish, requests his protection. The biblical Noah by contrast is the only just man in an evil mankind.

The Postdiluvian World. What happens when floods are linked more specifically to the fate of mortals? In some cases, we know that the gods, after completely destroying the original mankind, create another one; in other cases, the survivors themselves must ensure the survival of the human race.

This is not always a matter of course. When only one person escapes death, a miracle is needed to give him offspring. In a Jivaroan myth, we see the solitary man plant a part of his own flesh in the earth; from this a woman is born, with whom he couples. Other South American Indians relate that the woman came from bamboo.

Thus, in the history of mankind, just as it sometimes happens in the history of the cosmos, a destructive flood precedes a sort of new creation. The story of *Genesis* is a good example; Yahveh repeats to Noah's family the words he had spoken to Adam and Eve: "Be fecund, multiply on the earth and rule it" (*Gn.* 9:1ff.; cf. 1:28).

The Position of Postdiluvian Humanity. When the flood is supposed to correct the effects of an initial blunder, it fulfills a positive function and is part of progress. In this case, however, it must be noted that the second race is imperfect; it commits errors and undergoes many vicissitudes. In Quechua myth, the new men ignore Viracocha and do not venerate him. This is why the god causes a fire to fall from the heavens, which burns the earth; only those who beg for mercy are spared.

The flood sometimes appears to be a part of a more general degradation. On the original earth, say the Guaraní of Paraguay, men lived close to the gods. Then incest unleashed a series of events, after which the flood wiped out

> **According to the Guaraní myth, before the flood men lived with the gods on earth; on the second earth, they are alone.**

humanity. A new earth was then created, the land of evil reserved for men. This pessimistic viewpoint is not common. More typically the flood follows a period of degradation and puts an end to it.

In all types of the myth, the new humanity exhibits traits that distinguish it from the old. Not only is it civilized, but many tales associate the flood with the origins of civilization itself. Viracocha teaches the rudiments of civilization to the second Quechua race he has just created, and the *Popul Vuh* relates how Maya civilization developed during the second humanity.

In other narratives, mankind finds itself in a new position vis-à-vis the gods. According to the Guaraní myth, before the flood men lived with the gods on earth; on the second earth, they are alone.

The separation that accompanies the flood is not absolute, however. At the end of the inundation, we see a new sort of relation flourishing between men and gods.

The Forms of the Flood and the Function of the Diluvial Waters. The diluvial waters are not just any water. As we have seen, the water into which the world disappears at the end of its existence coincides with the primordial water. The earth that the Indonesian patriarch unbalanced is an insular earth, located in the original ocean whose waves invade it.

If the flood takes the form of rain, as is often the case, this rain comes from the heavenly waters and can be accompanied by a brutal ascent of underground waters as well. "Nergal tears the beams from the heaven, Ninurta makes it unlock its dams . . . the foundations of the earth are broken like a shattered jar," we read in the *Epic of Gilgamesh*. *Genesis* continues: "All the fountains of the great deep burst forth and the windows of the heavens were opened" (*Gn.* 7:11). The Greek poet Nonnus (early fifth century CE) expresses the same notion. The world is thus submerged by the waters that surround it on all sides. According to some myths, these cosmic waters are the very same primordial waters that were thrown back to the periphery of the universe at the creation.

The diluvial waves thus possess the virtues of water in all their original vigor. It is not only that they can be destructive, but their generative strength is manifested in the marvelous rebirth and proliferation of a purified humanity.

BIBLIOGRAPHY

Eliade, Mircea. "The Waters and Water Symbolism." In his *Patterns in Comparative Religion*, pp. 188-215. New York, 1958.

Gerland, Georg. *Der Mythus der Sintflut*. Bonn, 1912.

Ginzberg, Louis. *The Legends of the Jews*, vol. 1 (1909). Translated by Henrietta Szold et al. Reprint, Philadelphia, 1937. See pages 145-167.

Keeler, Clyde E. *Secrets of the Cuna Earthmother: A Comparative Study of Ancient Religion*. New York, 1960. See pages 59-82.

Lambert, W. G., and A. R. Millard. *Atra-Hasis: The Babylonian Story of the Flood*. Oxford, 1969.

Müller, Werner. "Die altesten amerikanschen Sintfluterzählungen." Ph. D. diss., Rheinische Friedrich-Wilhelms-Universität Bonn, 1930.

Osborne, Harold. *South American Mythology*. Feltham, England, 1968. See pages 100-105.

Pratt, Jane Abbott. *Consciousness and Sacrifice: An Interpretation of Two Episodes in the Indian Myth of Manu*. New York, 1967. See pages 3-33.

Robinson, Roland, et al. *Aboriginal Myths and Legends*. Melbourne, 1966.

Usener, Hermann. *Die Sintflutsagen*. Bonn, 1899.

Villas Boas, Orlando, and Claudio Villas Boas. *Xingu: The Indians, Their Myths*. Edited by Kenneth S. Breecher. New York, 1970.

JEAN RUDHARDT
Translated from French by Erica Meltzer

FOLK RELIGION

Peasant populations (i. e., sedentary agricultural groups forming part of larger, more complex societies) have probably existed since 6000 BCE in southwestern Asia, since 3100 BCE in Egypt, and since 1500 BCE in southeastern Mexico. Unlike agricultural entrepreneurs who are active economic agents or semisubsistence cultivators practicing ritual exchange and barter, peasants are farmers whose surpluses are redistributed to urban centers by more powerful groups.

Because sedentary farming emerged independently at different times and in different parts of the world, taking radically different forms, the search for an original, universal religion based on agriculture seems doomed to wishful speculation. Attempts nevertheless have been made, concentrating on such notions as matriarchy, Earth Mother goddesses, and moon worship.

Yet peasant societies do, by definition, have features in common that set the requirements and limits on the kinds of religion that will serve their members: (1) peasants depend on a particular ecosystem; (2) most live in similar social environments (household-based, on dispersed farms or in small settlements); and (3) they depend on the larger society for which they produce food. Their religion usually provides them with ways to deal with the local natural and social world, as well as the wider social, economic, and political network of which they are a part.

To manage the ecosystem, peasants, like other people, mark the cycles of nature, day and night, the lunar cycle, the solar year, the life cycles of animals and plants—all hold particular importance for cultivators. Many peasant cultures have rituals and routines for transitions relating to equinoxes, planting, germination, and harvest. And because landscape and climate vary widely, peasants tend to establish locally distinct sacred places, times, and divinities. Whether it is at a spring, cave, mountaintop, riverbank, or a special tree, peasants come to pay homage to their divinities according to the calendar, and in times of crisis to seek solutions to such major agricultural threats as drought, hail, and insect plagues.

While peasant religion may be composed of what may appear to be different kinds of elements and survivals from different traditions, in practice these elements usually form an indivisible, functional whole for believers. Where the notion of survivals exists among peasants themselves, it is often the result of church efforts to stigmatize nonapproved behavior as superstitious, or because of the spread of findings of early folklorists bent on unraveling the different strands of peasant religion according to "high" or "low" origin. More recent scholarship has concentrated on seeing how these strands work together as a whole.

A refinement on this method has involved observation of the practical impingement of the institutions of a central religion on the religious life of peasants—the extent to which peasant religion is effectively regulated, updated, and revised from without. For Europe, this has been done through longitudinal studies using field-work, church visitation, and government records.

An alternate approach compares the peasant religion to that of lay nonpeasants in the larger society, as in Clifford Geertz's studies in Java.

Peasant religiosity has been found to share many of the characteristics hitherto considered the domain of the "civilized." For instance, peasant religion is not necessarily homogeneous. Even when there is a single religion practiced, there is likely to be a wide range of doubt, opinion, and speculation, whether in a thirteenth-century French village or a twentieth-century Chinese hamlet. Nor is peasant religion particularly fixed or stable. Throughout history peasants have converted, have been converted, or have attempted to convert from one religion to another. And peasants are not invariably and instinctively religious. There are areas where peasant religious indifference has long been common, and recently entire age and gender groups have been known to abandon religion enthusiastically under militantly atheist governments.

Often peasant religion is mobilized or exploited by nonpeasant leaders. In the nineteenth and twentieth centuries, literary romanticists, folklorists, and nationalists alike have seen in local peasant religion a source of indigenous virtue, the survival of an earlier local culture and identity in the face of foreign domination. In Ireland, Brittany, Poland, the Basque country, Greece, Yugoslavia, Armenia, the Baltic states, as well as in many of Europe's colonial empires worldwide, independence and autonomy movements have fed on an exaltation of peasant religion that on a superficial level involves a kind of ruralization of the urban elite. An extreme but symptomatic example is Mohandas Gandhi's religious transformation from lawyer to peasant.

[*See* Anthropology, Ethnology, and Religion.]

BIBLIOGRAPHY

The search for universal features of the religion of cultivators in keeping with the framework theory of religious evolution, as exemplified by the work of James G. Frazer and Wilhelm Schmidt, is reviewed by Mircea Eliade in his *Patterns in Comparative Religion* (New York, 1958).

A persuasive exposition of general characteristics of peasant life from an anthropological viewpoint is provided in Eric Wolf's *Peasants* (Englewood Cliffs, N. J., 1966), following on Robert Redfield's *Peasant Society and Culture* (Chicago, 1956). A model study by Clifford Geertz, *The Religion of Java* (Glencoe, Ill., 1960), compares the religion of peasants with that of merchants and nobles, all under the wide mantle of Islam. For Buddhism, Stanley J. Tambiah in *Buddhism and the Spirit Cults in North-East Thailand* (Cambridge, 1970) shows how in practice the elements of different religious traditions function as a whole in the religion of a village. For the contemporary religion of European peasantry, I describe Catholicism in northern Spain in its relation to the landscape and social relations in *Person and God in a Spanish Valley* (New York, 1972), and Lucy Rushton admirably relates Greek Orthodox theology to personal life in "Religion and Identity in a Rural Greek Community" (Ph. D. diss., University of Sussex, 1983).

In the last two decades many excellent historical studies of religion as practiced have been published, many of which deal in part with peasants. Much of the early work on popular religion in Europe is discussed in F. Bolgiani's "Religione Popolare," *Augustinianum* 21 (1981): 7-75, with ample bibliographic notes. Richard F. Gombrich in *Precept and Practice: Traditional Buddhism in the Rural Highlands of Ceylon* (Oxford, 1971) argues against the notion of popular religion, as does Jean-Claude Schmitt in " 'Religion populaire' et culture folklorique," *Annales: Économies, sociétés, civilisations* 31 (Sep-tember-October 1976): 941-953. Unusual ethnographic information about peasant religion in the Friuli region of northeast Italy, gathered in the context of diocesan investigations, is provided by Carlo Ginzburg in *I Benandanti: Richerche sulla stregoneria e culti agrari tra Cinquecento e Seicento* (Turin, 1966), translated by John Tedeschi and Anne C. Tedeschi as *The Night Battles: Witchcraft and Agrarian Cults in the Sixteenth and Seventeenth Centuries* (Baltimore, 1983). Emmanuel Le Roy Ladurie's *Montaillou: The Promised Land of Error* (New York, 1978) describes in detail village Catholicism in the Pyranees and the villagers' conversion to Cathar beliefs. Similarly rich in detail, although not about a single community, is Keith Thomas's *Religion and the Decline of Magic: Studies in Popular Beliefs in Sixteenth and Seventeenth Century England* (New York, 1971). Nancy M. Farriss's *Maya Society under Colonial Rule: The Collective Enterprise of Survival* (Princeton, 1984) and Victoria Reifler Bricker's *The Indian Christ, the Indian King: The Historical Substrate of Maya Myth and Ritual* (Austin, 1981) are outstanding historical studies of religious syncretism in the Yucatan, building on a long line of distinguished ethnographies. Peter Brown, in his elegant *The Cult of the Saints: Its Rise and Function in Latin Christianity* (Chicago, 1981), challenges a radical distinction between peasant and nonpeasant religion in the Mediterranean, as I do in *Local Religion in Sixteenth Century Spain* (Princeton, 1981).

Peasant millennial movements are studied in *Millennial Dreams in Action*, edited by Sylvia L. Thrupp (New York, 1970). Charles Tilly's *The Vendée* (Cambridge, Mass., 1964) asks important questions about the social and economic roots of a peasant uprising in the name of religion. And the ways the religions of China have provided the peasantry with a certain defense against the state are discussed by Ann Anagost in her "Hegemony and the Improvisation of Resistance: Political Culture and Popular Practice in Contemporary China" (Ph. D. diss., University of Michigan, 1985).

WILLIAM A. CHRISTIAN, JR.

FOUR NOBLE TRUTHS

All strands of the Buddhist tradition recognize in the Four Noble Truths (Skt., *catvary aryasatyani*; Pali, *cattari ariyasaccani*) one of the earliest formulations of the salvific insight gained by the Buddha on the occasion of his enlightenment. For the Theravada tradition, the discourse on the Four Truths constitutes part of the first sermon of the Buddha, the *Dhammacakkappavattana Sutta*, delivered in the Deer Park near Banaras to his five original disciples. The standard formulaic enumeration of the Four Truths as found in this discourse is as follows:

> This, monks, is the noble truth of *dukkha* ["suffering"]: birth is *dukkha*, old age is *dukkha*, disease is *dukkha*, dying is *dukkha*, association with what is not dear is *dukkha*, separation from what is dear is *dukkha*, not getting that which is wished for is *dukkha*; in brief, the five groups of grasping [i. e., the five *khandhas*; Skt., *skandhas*] are *dukkha*.

> And this, monks, is the noble truth of the uprising [*samudaya*] of *dukkha*: this craving, which is characterized by repeated existence, accompanied by passion for joys, delighting in this and that; that is to say, craving for sensual desires, craving for existence, craving for cessation of existence.

> And this, monks, is the noble truth of the cessation [*nirodha*] of *dukkha*: complete dispassion and cessation of craving, abandonment, rejection, release of it, without attachment to it.

> And this, monks, is the noble truth of the path [*magga*] leading to the cessation of *dukkha*; just this Noble Eightfold

Way; that is to say, proper view, proper intention, proper speech, proper action, proper livelihood, proper effort, proper mindfulness, proper concentration.

(*Samyutta Nikaya* 5.420ff.)

These Four Noble Truths (formulaically, *dukkha, samudaya, nirodha, magga*) constitute a "middle way" between rigorous asceticism and sensual indulgence. The twin foci of truths are craving (Skt., *trsna*; Pali, *tanha*) and ignorance *(avidya)*, craving to hold that which is impermanent, grasping for substantiality where there is no abiding substance, and not knowing that this orientation inevitably yields unsatisfactoriness (Pali, *dukkha*; Skt., *duhkha*). Hence the twin foci draw attention to the fundamental cause *(samudaya)* of *dukkha*, and meditation on *dukkha* leads to a discernment that craving and ignorance are its matrix.

The Eightfold Path, the fourth of the Four Noble Truths, provides a means especially adapted to lead one into salvific insight, a way conforming completely to the Buddha's own

> **The first Truth relates to the basis of craving; the second, to craving itself; the third, to the cessation of craving; and the fourth, to the means to the cessation of craving.**

salvific realization. In this sense, the Eightfold Path is the proper mode of religious living, one that subsumes ethics into soteriology.

Although some uncertainty remains among scholars as to whether the passage quoted above indeed represents the earliest formulation of the Buddha's teaching, in the early phase of the Buddhist tradition in India (the so-called Hinayana phase) the Four Noble Truths played a major role in shaping the fundamental orientation to religious living on the part of Buddhists. Early Buddhist schools in India differed in their interpretations of the Four Noble Truths, but uniformly regarded its underlying thematic structure as one informed by metaphors of healing: symptom-disease, diagnosis-cause, elimination of cause, treatment or remedy. With the rise of the Mahayana tradition the Four Noble Truths became less central as a fundamental statement of the life situation and one's mode of engagement in a soteriological process, but continued to be revered as a fundamental part of the Buddha's early teachings.

Theravada Interpretations. The Theravada Buddhist tradition is prevalent in contemporary Sri Lanka, Burma, and Thailand. For at least two millennia it has regarded the Four Truths as constitutive of its central soteriological doctrine. As a result, considerable effort has been expended in the tradi-

tion on its exegesis. In an extended discussion on the Four Noble Truths, Buddhaghosa, in his fifth century CE classic, *Visuddhimagga* (The Path of Purity), comments at one point on the meaning of the term sacca ("truth"):

> For those who examine [truth] closely with the eye of salvific wisdom [*panna*], it is not distorted, like an illusion, equivocated, like a mirage, and of an undiscoverable inherent nature, like the self among sectarians, but, rather, it is the pasture of noble gnosis [*nana*] by means of its actual, undistorted, authentic condition. Just like [the characteristics of] fire, like the nature of the world, the actual undistorted, authentic condition is to be understood as the meaning of truth.

(*Visuddhimagga* 16.24)

Among the many interpretations offered by Buddhaghosa for the existence of four, and only four, truths is the Buddha's realization that the evolution of suffering, its cause, the devolution of suffering, and its cause are fully comprehensive of an analysis of the human condition and the way to liberation through it. (See *Visuddhimagga* 16.27.) Other analyses of the Four Truths suggest that the first Truth relates to the basis of craving; the second, to craving itself; the third, to the cessation of craving; and the fourth, to the means to the cessation of craving. Similarly, the Truths may be viewed as pertaining, respectively, to the sense of attachment, delight in attachment, removal of attachment, and the means to the removal of attachment. (See *Visuddhimagga* 16.27-28.) According to the *Dhammacakkappavattana Sutta*, the practitioner is to cultivate a fourfold awareness of the Four Truths in which dukkha is to be fully understood; the origin of *dukkha*, abandoned; *nirodha*, realized; and *magga*, cultivated. The Theravada commentarial tradition has maintained that the soteriological moment arises in the simultaneity of this fourfold awareness. (See *Visuddhimagga* 22.92.)

Although the tradition continued to elaborate analyses of the Four Truths arranged according to various numerical configurations (most frequently with the number sixteen), it has held to the conviction that when the Truths are fully penetrated and soteriologically known it is by one knowledge, through a single penetration, and at one instant. This knowledge of the Four Truths, they aver, is in and of itself salvific.

The Theravada has continued to interpret the Eightfold Path as comprising three basic elements deemed integral to religious living at its fullest: *sila* (Skt., *sila*), or moral virtue; *samadhi*, or meditative concentration; and *panna* (Skt., *prajna*), or salvific wisdom. Proper view and intention are classed as salvific wisdom; proper speech, action, and livelihood are classed as expressions of moral virtue; and proper effort, mindfulness, and concentration are classed as forms of meditative concentration.

Finally, the tradition has utilized the notion of "emptiness" (Pali, *suññata*; Skt., *sunyata*) in the analysis of the Four Noble Truths. Buddhaghosa wrote:

In the highest sense, all the truths are to be understood as empty because of the absence of an experiencer, a doer, someone extinguished, and a goer. Hence this is said:

For there is only suffering, no one who suffers,
No doer, only the doing is found,
Extinction there is, no extinguished man,
There is the path, no goer is found.

Or alternatively,

The first pair are empty
Of stableness, beauty, pleasure, self;
Empty of self is the deathless state.
Without stableness, pleasure, self is the path.
Such, regarding them, is emptiness [*suññata*]

(Visuddhimagga 16.90)

Mahayana Interpretations. Although the Theravada tradition applied the notion of "emptiness" in negating permanence, abiding happiness, and substantiality as legitimate descriptions of sentient life, it is within the Mahayana that one finds emptiness as a designation of reality in the highest sense. As part of the general critique of "substantiality" carried out by the Prajñaparamita literature, even the Four Truths are declared void of real existence. In this analysis, suffering, the origin of suffering, the cessation of suffering, and the path to the cessation of suffering are themselves "empty."

In the *Saddharmapundarika Sutra* (Lotus Sutra), the old standard formulas of the epithets of the Buddha and characteristics of *dharma* are repeated for the Tathagata Candrasuryapradipa and his preaching, but the Four Noble Truths are only mentioned by title—there is no elaboration. The *Saddharmapundarika* proclaims that such teaching is taken up and absorbed into the one comprehensive and central soteriological message (i. e., the "single vehicle"; *ekayana*) of the *sutra*.

Although the Four Noble Truths are not featured in their earlier formulation in many Mahayana texts, the basic theme nonetheless persists: life is awry, craving and ignorance are the cause, one's life can be changed, and a way or means that brings this about is available. For example, the verse text of Santideva's *Bodhicaryavatara* does not contain the complete formula of the Four Noble Truths. *Prajñakaramati*, a commentator on this great text, even points to the one verse (chap. 9, verse 41) where he finds a contrast clearly presented between the Four Noble Truths and the "teaching of emptiness." Yet even though a fundamental shift in the under-standing of the path to liberation has taken place in this and other Mahayana texts, the underlying assessment as to the cause of suffering, that is, the basic thematic structure of the Four Truths, remains unchanged.

In the *Madhyamakakarika*, Nagarjuna provides an incisive, penetrating analysis of the Four Noble Truths. He maintains that *duhkha*, which evolves from the interplay of the constituents of individuality and the objects of perception, can no longer be seen as having any fundamental ontological status, even in *samsara*, the fleeting "whirl" of repeated existence. The same is true, for that matter, of *samsara* itself, or even of *nirvana*: all is emptiness *(sunyata)*.

Thus, the older-formulated Eightfold Path, which provided the remedy for the disease *(duhkha)* of undisciplined and uninformed human existence, yielded with this shift in worldview to another formulation of the soteriological process, to another religious orientation that is also to be cultivated—the *bodhisattva* path. Although the ontological interpretation of the Four Noble Truths underwent change in the cumulative development of the Buddhist tradition, as in the case of the great Chinese Buddhist thinker Chih-i (538-597), the fundamental theme that the inadequacy of human life results from craving and ignorance, which can be eradicated by following the path to enlightenment taught by the Buddha, has continued.

BIBLIOGRAPHY

The text of the *Dhammacakkappavattana Sutta* is available in English translation in *Samyutta Nikaya: The Book of Kindred Sayings* (1917-1930), translated by C. A. F. Rhys Davids and F. L. Woodward (London, 1950-1956). For the *Visuddhimagga*, see the reliable translation by Bhikku Ñyanamoli, *The Path of Purification*, 2d ed. (Colombo, 1964). A related text, Upatissa's *Vimuttimagga*, has been translated from the Chinese as *The Path of Freedom* by N. R. M. Ehara, Soma Thera, and *Kheminda Thera* (Kandy, 1977). For an overview and analysis of the Four Truths from a Theravada perspective, see Walpola Rahula's *What the Buddha Taught*, rev. ed. (New York, 1974).

JOHN ROSS CARTER

FRANCIS OF ASSISI

FRANCIS OF ASSISI (Giovanni Francesco Bernardone, 1181/2-1226), Christian saint and founder of the Franciscans. John was Francis's baptismal name, but a fondness for France on the part of his merchant father and an acknowledgment of the national origin of his mother prompted the parents to call him Francis. Endowed with a jovial disposition and the means to pamper it, Francis enjoyed the good life of his times; this life was, however, interrupted when his hometown warred with neighboring Perugia. Inducted, imprisoned, and then released, Francis returned home with his military ambitions dampened. A business career with his father held no attraction.

Francis's conversion was the culmination of a period of prayerful reflection in a local grotto, an encounter with a leper, an invitation from God to repair Assisi's abandoned chapel of San Damiano, and Francis's study of *Matthew* 10, which imparted to him a sense of irreversible dedication to the kingdom of God. Within a few months (by April 1208) others asked to share his life, and thus a brotherhood was born.

In 1209 Francis journeyed to Rome to seek papal approval for the brotherhood. After some hesitation, Innocent III gave verbal assent to the rule authored by Francis, who then returned to Assisi and remained at the chapel of the Portiuncula; from there the brothers, two by two, preached gospel renewal. Intent on extending this preaching, Francis departed for Syria, but bad weather hampered the venture. Later a more successful journey took him to meet the sultan in Damietta. In 1212 Francis offered the religious habit to the young noblewoman Clare, and quickly other young women from Assisi sought to share her way of life at San Damiano, forming the order known as the Poor Clares. In 1215 the Fourth Lateran Council promulgated reforms championed in his preaching.

In 1220 Francis resigned his post as head of the Franciscans. Still, with over five thousand brothers, his involvement continued. After reworking his rule, Francis submitted it to Pope Honorius III in 1223, and it received written approval. That same year Francis presented a living Christmas crèche at Greccio, which encouraged the popularity of that custom in subsequent centuries. At Alverna he received the stigmata (the wounds of Christ crucified), thereby reflecting outwardly that which he interiorly imitated.

Though suffering serious illness in his last years, Francis composed his intensely joyful "Canticle of Brother Sun." The closing strophe addresses "Sister Death," whom he welcomed on 3 October 1226. Within two years Francis was proclaimed a saint. In 1939 he was officially offered to Italy as its patron; in 1979 he was recognized by Pope John Paul II as the patron saint of ecology.

As Francis's brotherhood increased in size, his work encompassed the nurturing of followers including the Poor Clares and the Secular Franciscans (lay men and women who wished to follow Francis). Franciscans were not committed to one particular work but engaged in whatever labors their travel and presence brought them. Francis's work and thought indicate a living, ecclesial faith that seeks to be for and with the poor.

Central to every aspect of his life was Francis's experience of the trinitarian God. He wanted to reveal the Father to all by imitating the Son through the inspiration of the Holy Spirit. Like his Lord, he was eager to make his way back to the Father and to summon all creation to accompany him on that painful but peaceful journey. An adult innocence aided him in transcending the spirit-matter dichotomy, making him a sublime example of both the spirituality of matter and the materialization of spirit.

Francis embraced voluntary poverty because he wanted to imitate his Lord, who had made himself poor (*2 Cor.* 8:9). In this poverty Francis found a freedom that fostered fraterni-

> **The movement founded by Francis . . . combined a contemplative life with an apostolic work that was mobile, diverse, and urban.**

ty. The poor, in their more evident dependence on God, reminded Francis of the mystery of divine sympathy and of each creature's intrinsic poverty. In the spirit of poverty he urged his brothers to renounce their desire to dominate, and though called to minister to all, to favor labor among the lepers and farmhands.

Aware that the Roman Catholic church was capable of taming the gospel, Francis persisted in the belief that Christ was to be found in this institution, especially in the Eucharist. He sought a cardinal protector for the Franciscan order and acknowledged the pontiff to be the final arbiter in spiritual matters. Although Francis's relations with the Curia Romana may have weakened his project, the majority of scholars submit that his relation to the hierarchy was loyal, challenging, and constructive.

Movements for peace and for the marginalized have in Francis a ready patron. He sent his brothers out, not against but among the Saracens, and he required that all his followers (lay included) not bear arms. His pursuit of Lady Poverty inspires those of every age who seek simplicity. His fondness for animals and nature has deepened humanity's understanding of the interrelatedness of all creation grounded in a creator whose richness it reflects.

Francis managed to steer a course that avoided the excesses of feudal authority and of the bourgeois pursuit of money. In his rule he taught his followers to use only that which was needed, to own nothing, and to renounce any desire to dominate; he insisted that authority for the *minores* (those who wished to lead a biblically inspired simple life) meant fraternal service. The church, although initially cautious, soon adopted some of his insights for its own apostolic strategy; between 1218 and 1226 six papal bulls were issued relating to aspects of his vision. The Holy See recognized that the manner of his preaching touched the lives of the people; it also gave the vernacular a new respectability and provided themes for artists such as Cimabue and Giotto. Though no intellectual, Francis's emphasis on humanity inspired the deeply incarnational systems of Bonaventure and of Duns Scotus.

Francis's legacy to the Christian tradition was a revitalized gospel that clearly perceived many forms of brotherhood: with superiors—once, having been denied by a bishop the right to preach in his diocese, Francis exited, paused, reentered, and resubmitted his petition successfully; with strangers—in his rule of 1221 he calls for a simple, non-polemical style of missionary presence; with the underclass—when a brother asked if it were proper to feed some robbers, he responded affirmatively, for in every person he saw a possible thief and in every thief a possible brother or sister; with nature—he urged his brothers when establishing the boundaries of their shelters not to build walls but to plant hedges. The movement founded by Francis offered the church a new form of gospel commitment. It combined a contemplative life with an apostolic work that was mobile, diverse, and urban. Although it was a consecrated life, it was not removed from daily concerns.

[See also Franciscans.]

BIBLIOGRAPHY

Kajetan Esser, the scholar most responsible for the critical texts of Francis's writings, discusses 181 manuscripts in his *Opuscula Sancti Francisci Assisiensis* (Rome, 1978) and his *Rule and Testament of St. Francis* (Chicago, 1977). The excellent *Francis and Clare: The Complete Works* (New York, 1982), edited by Regis J. Armstrong and Ignatius Brady, offers a list for the first time in English of Francis's authentic writings (twenty-eight in all) and inauthentic writings (including the popular "Peace Prayer"). The most practical single volume for primary sources remains *St. Francis of Assisi: Writings and Early Biographies, English Omnibus of the Sources* (Chicago, 1973), edited by Marion A. Habig. It includes lives of Francis by Celano and by Bonaventure, *The Little Flowers of Saint Francis* (a treasure of fourteenth-century popular literature), and an extensive bibliography, though not always reliably translated. Classic biographies include Omer Englebert's astute *Saint Francis of Assisi* (Chicago, 1965), and Father Cuthbert of Brighton's accurate *Life of St. Francis of Assisi* (London, 1912). Paul Sabatier's *Life of St. Francis of Assisi* (London, 1894) is provocative. Of the more than sixty modern biographies, G. K. Chesterton in *St. Francis of Assisi* (London, 1923) captures his heart and Nikos Kazantzakis in *Saint Francis: A Novel* (New York, 1962) presents a poet. A former mayor of Assisi, Arnaldo Fortini, in his *Francis of Assisi* (New York, 1981), offers an invaluable historical appendix. Anglican bishop J. R. H. Moorman presents, in his new edition of *Saint Francis of Assisi* (London, 1976), a precise historical life. Leonardo Boff characterizes Francis, in *Saint Francis* (New York, 1982), as a model for human liberation.

RAYMOND J. BUCHER, O.F.M.

FREEMASONS

A system of moral teachings and a set of fraternal organizations that practice these teachings, Freemasonry cannot properly be called a "secret society," though secrecy is both practiced as a device for instruction during initiation into its rites and used as a symbol. In some instances, the names of members and the existence of the society itself have been withheld from political authorities because of Freemasonry's historical association with political movements in Italy, Spain, and Latin America. As modern fraternal orders, however, Masonic lodges and related organizations have been more open to public scrutiny, and membership is in almost all cases publicly displayed.

History. The history of Freemasonry is shrouded in legend and ambiguity. This historical obscurity stems from the institution's use of legendary history in its rituals and ceremonies, and from the fragmentariness of the records of the early Masonic organizations. Few historians have undertaken a comprehensive study of Freemasonry's history and cultural significance. However, in recent years, both social historians and historians of ideas have sought to understand the significance of Masonic development as an institution and a set of philosophical symbols.

The origin of Freemasonry can be traced to periodic gatherings of operative stonemasons engaged in the building of churches and cathedrals in England. The earliest manuscripts associated with the work and moral symbolism of these stonemasons date from the late fourteenth century. The most noted of these manuscripts is the so-called *Regius Manuscript* (c. 1390). This and similar documents make up the "Gothic Constitutions" that trace the legendary history of the craft of masonry back to the Flood or to the building of the Egyptian pyramids or Solomon's Temple. This collection also contains specific moral responsibilities that are enjoined upon members as apprentices, fellowcraftsmen (or journeymen), and master masons. It is probable that secrecy as a device for teaching and as a symbol dates from this period, when knowledge of the building techniques of individual master masons was restricted to guild members.

The historian of ideas Frances A. Yates claims that during the seventeenth century Freemasonry merged with Elizabethan courtly philosophy and continental, particularly German, Rosicrucianism (*Giordano Bruno and the Hermetic Tradition,* 1964). Elizabethan philosophy was associated with such figures as John Dee, Robert Fludd, Thomas Vaughan, and Giordano Bruno. It was Neoplatonic in character, and evoked the memory of the legendary Hermes Trismegistos, understood in the seventeenth century to be a pre-Christian prophet of Christianity. Rosicrucianism was, according to Yates, a self-conscious reform movement that bore the imprint of classical and Renaissance humanism. The impact of these two movements upon the stonemasons' tradition was twofold: (1) it transformed the working tools of the operatives into a system of symbols for personal morality and transformation through initiation, and (2) it projected the Masonic motif, and subsequently the Masonic institutional organization, into the nonoperative arena of eighteenth-century world affairs. The Masonic initiation in 1646 of the antiquarian Elias Ashmole recommends Yates's interpretation of this period.

Freemasonry as an institution can be dated from the formation of the first national Masonic organization, the "Grand Lodge" of England, which resulted from the combining of four small lodges of nonoperative masons at the Goose and Gridiron alehouse, London, on 24 June 1717. From this time, a general narrative history of Freemasonry can be pieced together from journals, minutes, and newspaper accounts. The order attracted royal patronage, and several members of the Royal Society became members of the Masonic fraternity. Notable among these members was John Theophilus Desaguliers, an Anglican priest of Huguenot ancestry who became the order's third elected Grand Master.

The introduction of the order into France in the early eighteenth century signified the transition of the institution from a largely nonpolitical organization into a body that was closely identified with the Enlightenment concepts of deism and equality. The ritual and symbolism of the craft tradition were soon embellished into a system of *hautes grades,* or high degrees, which altered noticeably the character of the fraternity. The higher degrees were later grouped into two main rites, or systems: the Scottish, which was derived from the French *hautes grades,* and the York, which was the result of a commingling of English and American ceremonials. Several rites of numerous degrees were erected and a new knightly or chivalric motif was added to the earlier craft or stonemason tradition. The rites of the Freemasons in continental Europe incorporated the legends of the Knights Templar, the Teutonic Knights, and Knights Hospitaler of Saint John (or Knights of Malta). These Masonic bodies became avidly anticlerical and advocates of political and social reform.

British Freemasonry, organized into separate Irish, Scottish, and English grand lodges, remained nonpartisan during the political-religious disputes of the eighteenth century, but removed any requirement that its initiates be Christians with the adoption of the *Constitutions of 1723,* revised in 1738 by Scots Presbyterian minister James Anderson. Largely as a result of British imperial expansion, lodges of Freemasons were established in North America, India, and the West Indies.

During the late eighteenth century a schism occurred within English-speaking Freemasonry that signaled the development of a general class distinction among Masons between the "Antients" and the "Moderns." Further, this division led to the addition of the Holy Royal Arch to the basic three-degree system of English Freemasonry, which comprises Entered Apprentices, Fellow Craftsmen, and Master Masons. While not of the highly imaginative character of continental *hautes grades,* the Royal Arch provided Freemasons with a degree that proposed to impart the ineffable name of deity to the degree's recipient. This degree was incorporated into the British Masonic system when the two rival "Antient" and "Modern" grand lodges merged under the grand mastership of Augustus Frederick, Duke of Sussex, son of George III. The Royal Arch, essentially an "Antient" invention, won wide acceptance throughout the Masonic fraternity in the nineteenth century.

Freemasonry in the nineteenth and twentieth centuries continued to develop along the lines established by the differing English and French models. English, Irish, and Scottish Freemasonry shaped the fraternity and its teachings in Canada, the United States, the West Indies, India, and much of Africa. The impact of the French tradition, with its anticlerical, rationalistic, and politicized emphasis, was more deeply felt in Austro-Hungary, Spain, Portugal, Italy, and Latin America. By 1877, communication between these two groups had virtually ceased. This separation was formalized when the Grand Orient of France removed the requirement that its initiates declare a belief in the existence of God as the "Great Architect of the Universe." In English-speaking areas, Freemasonry has in general prospered as a support to constituted government and organized religion. One notable exception is the anti-Masonic episode in the United States. The alleged abduction and murder of William Morgan of Batavia, New York, in 1829 caused a widespread reaction against Freemasonry throughout the country. Other secret societies, including Phi Beta Kappa, were affected, largely as a reaction against the perceived influence of political and social elites. An interesting result of this movement was its precipitating the first American political party convention, that of the Anti-Masonic party in 1832.

Masonic Teachings. Since the origin of Freemasonry as a speculative system, Masonic teachings have remained remarkably consistent. Despite there being no demonstrable, historical tie between Freemasonry in the seventeenth century and the medieval operative stonemasons, the teachings of Freemasonry have been linked to medieval and even to biblical sagas, notably the accounts in *1 Kings and 2 Chronicles* of the building of the Solomonic Temple. Two other strata—the Hermetic-Rosicrucian and the Enlightenment rationalistic-deistic—are superimposed upon the biblical and medieval traditions within the superstructure of Masonic degrees. All Masonic degrees are related to the transformation of the human personality from a state of primitive darkness to a higher level of human consciousness. Mozart's opera *Die Zauberflöte* is in many ways a prototype of Masonic ceremonial.

Because Freemasonry has transposed a system of moral and noetic teaching upon a graded institutional structure, it has frequently been deemed both a threat to confessional and orthodox religion and a religion itself. The basis for such assumptions is the fraternity's use of symbols that describe

> **British Freemasonry, organized into separate Irish, Scottish, and English grand lodges, remained nonpartisan during the political-religious disputes of the eighteenth century.**

the change of personal moral character and human awareness by stages, or degrees. These degrees have been interpreted as a plan for spiritual redemption. A study of the basic ceremonials and teachings, however, suggests that the goal of Masonic initiation is not redemption but rather a shift in the initiate's perception toward the betterment of his personal moral character. The lack of central authority and the multitude of Masonic degrees and ceremonials make it impossible to state unequivocally that Freemasonry is religious in any final or conclusive sense. Since Clement XII's encyclical *In eminenti* in 1738, the Roman Catholic church has proscribed Masonic affiliation. The identification of many major southern European and Latin American revolutionary leaders—such as Benso, Garibaldi, Bolívar, O'Higgins, and Martí y Pérez—with Masonic lodges evoked further condemnation by the nineteenth-century Roman Catholic church. More recently, the Lutheran Church-Missouri Synod, U. S. A., and the General Conference of the Methodist Church in England and Wales have legislated claims that Freemasonry is a system of faith and morals outside of the magisterium of the church.

Protestant opposition to Freemasonry stems from the elements of deism and Hermetic Rosicrucianism in Masonic rituals and is thus more theological in tone. Confessional churches and churches with strong traditions of scholastic orthodoxy, such as Lutheranism, have deemed the humanistic and Neoplatonic elements in Masonic philosophy to be inconsistent with Christian teaching. Churches that have maintained a less exclusive understanding of revelation have been more tolerant of Freemasonry's belief in a universal brotherhood of man under the fatherhood of God.

Freemasonry has a worldwide membership of approximately six million people. It is governed by independent national grand lodges, except in the United States, Canada, and Australia, where grand lodges are organized by state or province. While Freemasonry is racially mixed, there are independent, largely black, grand lodges. The largest of these black lodges is traced to Prince Hall, a freed slave in eighteenth-century Massachusetts. Numerous appendant and collateral bodies, such as the Ancient Arabic Order, Nobles of the Mystic Shrine, and the Order of the Eastern Star are associated with the grand lodges.

BIBLIOGRAPHY

Chailley, Jacques. *The Magic Flute: Masonic Opera.* New York, 1971.
Dumenil, Lynn. *Freemasonry and American Culture, 1880-1930.* Princeton, 1984.
Gould, Robert Freke. *History of Freemasonry.* London, 1886-1887.
Horne, Alex. *Sources of Masonic Symbolism.* Trenton, N. J., 1981.
Jacob, Margaret C. *The Radical Enlightenment: Pantheists, Freemasons and Republicans.* Boston, 1981.
Lipson, Dorothy Ann. *Freemasonry in Federalist Connecticut.* Princeton, 1977.
Pound, Roscoe. *Masonic Addresses and Writings.* New York, 1953.
Stubbs, James W. *The United Grand Lodge of England, 1717-1967.* Oxford, 1967.
Yates, Frances A. *The Rosicrucian Enlightenment.* London, 1972.

WILLIAM H. STEMPER, JR.

FREE WILL AND PREDESTINATION

Free will and predestination constitute a polarity in many of the religions of the world: is salvation determined by a divine choice or is it a matter of personal self-determination? *Free will* in this article does not refer to the general philosophical problem of the will's freedom but to the specific meaning and function of willing and self-determination in the process of salvation. Some religious thinkers have sharply distinguished between the will's freedom in the material and civil affairs of life and its freedom or unfreedom with regard to the spiritual life, and it is with the latter that this article is concerned.

At least two ways of thinking about the freedom of the will in spiritual matters have been common: free will as a freedom of choice, whereby one does freely what one has also had the power to choose to do, and free will as the absence of compulsion, whereby one willingly does what one does without actively choosing what is done. The latter has been described as voluntary necessity. In the first of these meanings of freedom, freedom seems incompatible with divine determination; in the second, it does not, and is opposed not to causality but to constraint.

Predestination is separated from the general consideration of providence, determinism, and fate, and refers only to the voluntary divine choice of certain groups or individuals for salvation. Sometimes predestination is considered as a part of divine providence, namely, that aspect of the divine determination of all things that refers to the supernatural end of souls, as opposed to the determination of persons with regard to all else or of the natural order. But predestination is to be sharply distinguished from some forms of determinism and from fatalism, which do not necessarily involve the theistic concept of a personal deity making conscious choices. *Determinism* may mean any one of a number of systems claiming that all events cannot occur otherwise than they do, sometimes without reference to deity. *Fate* suggests an impersonal determining force that may even transcend the gods.

The terms *election* and *reprobation* have meanings related to predestination. One traditional use of these terms considers predestination the larger divine act, which encompasses the separate decrees of election (predestination to salvation) and reprobation (predestination to damnation). *Reprobation,* however, is seldom used now, and *election* is more commonly simply substituted for *predestination,* because it seems more positive in its connotations. In biblical studies, *election* has been the preferred term for referring to divine choice.

Predestination has been considered not inevitably contradictory to free will. Sometimes both are held together as paradoxical, yet complementary, aspects of truth; but more classically, free will is understood not as freedom of choice but as voluntary necessity. That is, where freedom means the absence of compulsion, necessary acts determined by God nonetheless can be freely done. Almost all predestinarian theologies have therefore maintained that the predestined will acts freely and with consequent responsibility for its actions, even though it lacks the power to choose its actions. In this sense of freedom, even the decree of reprobation has been seen as compatible with responsibility and not as entailing a divine compulsion to do evil. This compatibility of free will and predestination has historically been a commonplace of Augustinian and Calvinistic theology in Christianity, and of Islamic theology through its doctrine of acquisition. Even such a materialistic determinist as Thomas Hobbes thought that necessary acts were entirely voluntary and therefore responsible acts. It is this that sharply distinguishes predestination from fatalism, which may entail compulsion to act in a certain way. Roman Catholic theology refers to any predestinarian doctrine that proceeds without reference to the will's freedom as the error of predestinarianism. Only in rare cases in Christian and Islamic theology has that way of understanding predestination appeared.

While beliefs concerning free will and predestination may be rooted in religious experience, they are also connected to certain intellectual concerns and puzzlements. One motive for such reflection has been the simple observation that some believe while others do not—is this fact the consequence of personal freedom of choice or of divine predetermination?

Reflection on divine omnipotence has led to the inference that the divine choice must be the determining factor in salvation. If some things were excepted from the general principle that all things occur by virtue of a divine causality, then God would seem to lack the efficacy to bring his purposes to fruition. Even the bare acknowledgment of divine foreknowledge seems to entail determinism, for if God knows what will happen from eternity, it must necessarily happen in that way or else his knowledge would be rendered erroneous. And though it may be argued that God foresees actual human choices, nonetheless when the time for those choices arrives, they cannot be other than they are; this is precisely what identifies an event as predetermined. Opponents of this viewpoint have maintained, however, that foresight is not a cause and that therefore a foreseen event need not be a determined one.

Still, the doctrine of predestination has probably been rooted primarily not in this kind of consideration but in the theological need to maintain the gratuitousness of salvation. To connect this with predestination effectively rules out any possibility of human merit.

Theologies that have asserted the will's freedom of choice in salvation have, on the other hand, focused on different theological needs, primarily those of preserving human responsibility in the process of salvation and God's goodness and justice in the governing of his creation. If salvation is entirely God's gift, how can those left out be held responsible? In the modern period, the Augustinian definition of freedom as absence of constraint has not been widely persuasive, in spite of the fact that many elements of contemporary thought, especially in relation to heredity, have provided some basis for considering human freedom in this way.

The problem of theodicy, in Christian thought in particular, seems almost inevitably to rely on the assumption of human freedom of choice in salvation. Even the Puritan poet John Milton, in seeking to "justify the ways of God to man," fell back upon an assertion of such freedom.

BIBLIOGRAPHY

There are several useful introductions to the subject: C. H. Ratschow, Erich Dinkler, E. Kähler, and Wolfhart Pannenberg's "Prädestination," in *Die Religion in Geschichte und Gegenwart,* 3d ed. (Tübingen, 1957-1965), and Henri Rondet and Karl Rahner's "Predestination," in *Sacramentum Mundi: An Encyclopedia of Theology,* edited by Karl Rahner (New York, 1968-1970), both of which give an extensive bibliography in several languages; Giorgio Tourn's *La predestinazione nella Bibbia e nella storia* (Turin, 1978); and Vernon J. Bourke's *Will in Western Thought: An Historico-Critical Survey* (New York, 1964).

Rudolf Otto's *The Idea of the Holy* (1923), 2d ed. (London, 1950), offers a classic phenomenological analysis of the problem. Discussion of the general historical significance of predestination appears in my *Puritans and Predestination* (Chapel Hill, N. C., 1982), pp. 191-196. For the Bible and ancient Judaism, see Harold H. Rowley's *The Biblical Doctrine of Election* (London, 1950), Eugene

H. Merrill's *Qumran and Predestination* (Leiden, 1975), and George Foot Moore's "Fate and Free Will in the Jewish Philosophies according to Josephus," *Harvard Theological Review* 22 (October 1929): 371-389. Two rather traditional Christian theological investigations of the problem, the first Protestant and the second Roman Catholic, are Gaston Deluz's *Prédestination et liberté* (Paris, 1942) and M. John Farrelly's *Predestination, Grace, and Free Will* (Westminster, Md., 1964). For Indian thought, see Sarvepalli Radhakrishnan's *Indian Philosophy*, 2d ed., 2 vols. (London, 1927-1931), pp. 659-721, 731-751, and Rudolf Otto's *Die Gnadenreligion Indiens und das Christentum* (Gotha, 1930), translated by Frank H. Foster as I*ndia's Religion of Grace and Christianity* (New York, 1930). The standard work on this subject for Islam is W. Montgomery Watt's *Free Will and Predestination in Early Islam* (London, 1948).

DEWEY D. WALLACE, JR.

FREUD, SIGMUND

FREUD, SIGMUND (1856-1939), originator of psychoanalysis, a method of treating those mental disorders commonly designated as the neuroses.

Life and Principal Works. As a youth, Freud received an excellent education that emphasized both classics and science. For a while he contemplated a career in law or in politics, but finally decided upon scientific work and attended medical school at the University of Vienna, from which he graduated in 1881.

Partly for financial reasons and partly on account of official anti-Semitism (it was customary for the university to pass over Jewish candidates for research positions), Freud shifted his career goals to the medical practice of psychiatry. He became interested in hysterical patients, and began to collaborate with the eminent Viennese physician Josef Breuer.

Freud and Breuer discovered that the symptoms of hysterical patients diminished as they were encouraged to talk about the intense feelings they held toward those close to them. Freud also noticed that dreams were included in these reports, and he began to evolve his theory that both dreams and hysterical symptoms disguised deeply felt and deeply feared thoughts and feelings. At the end of his period of collaboration with Breuer, Freud began to write his first and most famous book, *The Interpretation of Dreams* (1900). This work contained the essence of all his major ideas about the neuroses, about dreams, and about psychoanalytic treatment—and also the essence of his theory that religious symbols and myths are modeled upon dreams.

In the 1910s and 1920s, Freud's reputation grew. New patients came, and he continued to publish papers and to gather students about him. Many of these men and women underwent psychoanalysis with Freud, and studied his ideas. Among the more eminent were the Swiss psychiatrist Carl Gustav Jung and the socialist Alfred Adler. The most impor-

tant of Freud's many publications during these decades were *Introductory Lectures on Psychoanalysis* (1915), which explained psychoanalytic theory and practice to a lay audience; *Group Psychology and the Analysis of the Ego* (1921), in which Freud analyzed the psychological forces beneath the group behavior of armies and churches; and *The Ego and the Id* (1923), a theoretical treatise on the fundamental psychological structures of the human mind.

The aftermath of World War I, the death of a beloved daughter, and the discovery of a cancerous growth in his jaw, all forced upon him a reflective and resigned attitude, which in turn fueled his most profound studies of culture and religion. Taking up arms in the time-honored conflict between science and religion, Freud asserted (in *The Future of an Illusion,* 1927) that psychoanalysis was but the latest and most compelling scientific argument against the consolations of religion. Three years later, in *Civilization and Its Discontents,* he addressed the oppressive quality of contemporary social life, arguing that society itself carried within it the mechanisms that created neurotic conflict. .

Psychoanalytic Theory. While Freud's psychoanalysis is really a threefold discipline—clinical treatment of neurotic conflict, general theory of personality, and theory of culture and religion—it is important to realize that he generalized from the first to the second and from both to the third. Therefore, all expositions of his thought about religion should begin with the psychoanalytic method and its clinical context, usually referred to as the analytic situation.

Two concepts form the foundation of the analytic situation, the unconscious and childhood. All deliberate, intentional, and conscious life, for the healthy adult and the neurotic alike, is constantly subject to influence by an unconscious dimension of feeling, willing, and intending. Freud often

> **Freud asserted (in *The Future of an Illusion,* 1927) that psychoanalysis was but the latest and most compelling scientific argument against the consolations of religion.**

referred to the unconscious as a portion of mental life split off from, and existing alongside of, the system of conscious mental processes. This separation first occurs during the years of childhood. Because of the prolonged and at times virtually total dependency of the infant upon caretakers, some of the strong feelings of love, hate, envy, and jealousy—in short, portions of all the fundamental wishes and fears of living and being—are forgotten or forced out of awareness. These thoughts and feelings, which Freud described as repressed, live on in the normal activities of the adult, making their appearance symbolically in dreams, slips of the tongue, jokes, and love relationships. The normal adult is capable of introspection and self-analysis when unconscious wishes and thoughts press for attention.

However, under conditions of stress produced by the various tasks and responsibilities of living, even the healthy adult can falter. In such cases, the mental organization of the person returns to earlier patterns of regulation, a process known as regression, and neurotic symptoms (for example, phobias or irrational fears, obsessional ideas, or compulsive acts) serve to defend against the return. Because persons in this condition can no longer control portions of their behavior, psychoanalytic treatment is helpful for them. In the analytic situation the patient allows his or her thoughts and feelings, and especially dreams, to flow freely (in "free association") without moral or intellectual control and in doing so forms an intense, irrational, emotional bond with the doctor. Freud called this bond "transference." Because the transference relation embodies old and forgotten childhood memories, the doctor can interpret the bond in the light of dreams and fantasies, gradually bringing the repressed wishes back under the control of conscious life.

Contribution to the Study of Religion. Because of Freud's appreciation of the power of religious symbols, and despite his skeptical stance toward religion, his theories exercised an important influence upon the religious thought of post–World War II Europe and, especially, America. By this time his ideas had become widely acknowledged, and the leaders of religious communities wanted to use them and to respond to his challenge. In particular, Paul Tillich and Mircea Eliade deserve mention here.

Paul Tillich was convinced that an overly rational society had cut the Christian faith off from its historic depths and from its role as a shaper of culture. He hailed the secular Freud's concept of the unconscious roots of religious reality as an attempt to restore what he called a depth dimension to human reason and cultural life. Even Freud's skeptical side Tillich incorporated into theology, arguing that modern churches had become authoritarian and oppressive to human depth, and that Freud's objections to religion were in this sense well founded.

Like Tillich, Eliade believed that contemporary culture was excessively rational and technological and that a renewal of a religious kind was essential. But unlike Tillich, Eliade turned to primitive religions and to Eastern traditions and myths to renew the life of modern man. Eliade wrote that Freud's view of myth as an unconscious imaginative structure and the links he had built between dreams and myths would enrich the dry, technical tones of modern life, and that both could be used to reinstate a religious view of humanity. In fact, Eliade described the history of religions as a metapsychoanalysis, by which he meant that religion added a dimension to the foundations supplied by Freud.

Yet neither Tillich nor Eliade could tolerate Freud's skepticism, his view that once the unconscious meaning of a religious myth was disclosed, then the consoling sense of specialness that belief conferred would necessarily be given up in the interest of a broader psychological self-understanding.

BIBLIOGRAPHY

Freud's psychological writings have been collected for the English-language reader in *The Standard Edition of the Complete Psychological Writings of Sigmund Freud,* 24 vols., translated from German under the general editorship of James Strachey (London, 1953-1974). Each of Freud's publications in this definitive edition is prefaced by valuable information regarding date of composition and of first publication, relevant biographical details, and a short discussion of its leading ideas in relation to Freud's thought as a whole.

The best single book on Freud's life, social circumstances, and major ideas is Ernest Jones's major study *The Life and Work of Sigmund Freud* edited and abridged by Lionel Trilling and Stephen Marcus (New York, 1961). Philip Rieff's careful, thorough, and clearly written book Freud: *The Mind of the Moralist* (1959; 3d ed., Chicago, 1979) remains the best overall discussion of Freud's social, philosophical, and religious ideas. Rieff also analyzes the impact of psychoanalysis upon both the Western religious heritage and contemporary society. An excellent illustration of the use of Freud's approach to dream symbolism to interpret social and cultural symbols is Bruno Bettelheim's *The Uses of Enchantment: The Meaning and Importance of Fairy Tales* (New York, 1977). The best theological discussion of Freud's theory of religious experience is to be found in Paul Tillich's *The Courage to Be* (New Haven, 1952). The many implications of psychoanalysis for the historical study of religion are clearly stated by Mircea Eliade in *Myths, Dreams and Mysteries* (New York, 1960).

PETER HOMANS

GALILEO GALILEI

GALILEO GALILEI (1564-1642), Italian scientist considered to be the father of modern science. Born at Pisa, Galileo received some of his early schooling there. He then was sent to the ancient Camaldolese monastery at Vallombroso, where, attracted by the quiet and studious life, he joined the order as a novice. His father, however, wished him to study medicine and took him to Florence, where Galileo continued his studies with the Camaldolese monks until he matriculated at the University of Pisa in 1581. During his student years at Pisa, Galileo is said to have made his celebrated observation of the sanctuary lamp swinging like a pendulum from the cathedral ceiling and to have thereby discovered that the time taken for a swing was independent of the size of the arc, a fact that he used later for measuring time in his astronomical studies.

Finding that his talents for mathematics and philosophy were increasingly being recognized, Galileo gave up his medical studies and left the university in 1585, without a degree, to begin lecturing at the Florentine academy. There he published an account of his invention of the hydrostatic balance (1586) and then an essay on the center of gravity in solid bodies (1588), which won him a lectureship at Pisa. In 1592 he was appointed professor of mathematics at the renowned University of Padua, where he remained for eighteen years. There, in 1604, he published his laws of motion of falling bodies in his book *De motu*.

In 1597 Galileo wrote to Johannes Kepler that he had been a Copernican "for several years." Having heard in Venice of the newly invented telescope, Galileo immediately constructed one of his own and in 1610 announced many astronomical discoveries. These included his discovery that the Milky Way is made up of innumerable stars and his observation of the satellites of Jupiter. He also made observations of sunspots and of the phases of Venus. Thus he vastly expanded astronomical knowledge and challenged the established natural philosophy, which was based on Aristotelian ideas that had been reconciled with Christian doctrine by Thomas Aquinas. Shortly after the publication of these discoveries, Galileo was appointed philosopher and mathematician to the grand duke of Tuscany.

In 1613, Galileo's *Letters on Sunspots* was published. Its preface claimed that Galileo had been the first to observe sunspots, an assertion that generated bitter resentment among some Jesuit scholars (who had an arguable claim to priority of observation) and that eventually had serious consequences for Galileo. In this book, he first stated in print his unequivocal acceptance of Copernican astronomy, challenging a basic postulate of the Aristotelian view by insisting that all celestial phenomena should be interpreted in terms of terrestrial analogies. Furthermore, Galileo wished to make science independent of philosophy by his assertions that the essence of things cannot be known and that science should concern itself only with the properties of things and with observed events. It was the philosophers rather than the theologians who were the early opponents of the Copernican system and, insofar as he supported it, of Galileo's work. No doubt they were also put off by Galileo's extremely high opinion of himself, and they exploited personal jealousies and resentments against him and tried to enlist the aid of theologians in condemning both Copernican ideas and Galileo's advocacy of them.

Not until 1616, seventy-three years after the publication of Copernicus's *De revolutionibus orbium coelestium* (On the Revolution of the Heavenly Spheres), did the Theological Consultors of the Holy Office declare it "false and contrary to Holy Scripture" and recommend that Copernicus's book be "suspended until corrected." Cardinal Roberto Bellarmino had earlier written to Galileo warning him to confine himself to the realm of hypothesis until demonstrative proof could be produced. When Galileo went to Rome to defend his position, he was officially cautioned neither to hold nor to defend the Copernican ideas. And Galileo, good Catholic that he was (and remained), agreed.

Throughout, Galileo maintained that the purpose of scripture is not to teach natural philosophy and that issues of faith and issues of science should be kept separate and should be settled on different grounds. He quoted Tertullian approvingly: "We conclude that God is known first through nature, and then again, more particularly, by doctrine; by nature in his works, and by doctrine in his revealed word." He also cited Cardinal Césare Baronio, a contemporary, who had quipped, "The Bible tells us how to go to Heaven, not how the heavens go."

The appearance of the great comets in 1618 stirred up much controversy, which Galileo joined by writing his *Discourse on Comets,* annoying the philosophers still further because of his anti-Aristotelian bias. In 1623, Galileo published *The Assayer,* which he dedicated to Urban VIII, the new pope, who was much more favorably disposed toward intellectuals and their work than his predecessor had been. In 1624, Galileo visited Rome and had six audiences with the pope. In 1632, Galileo published his *Dialogue on the Two Great World Systems.* Having intended this book to be "a most ample confirmation" of the Copernican opinion, Galileo in effect had ignored the spirit of the instructions given him by the church in 1616. Neverthless, during the trial that followed the publication of the *Dialogue,* Galileo maintained that he had obeyed the instructions to the letter.

Galileo's trial in 1633 marked the beginning of what has since become a cliché—namely, the idea that science and religion must inevitably be in conflict. Also, Galileo is often seen as science's first martyr in the perennial battle between the church and the spirit of free inquiry. There is no question that the church took a wrong position (contrary to its own tradition in such matters as established by Augustine and Thomas Aquinas); this much was acknowledged by a statement made by John Paul II in 1979, and it was underscored by the Vatican's publication, in 1984, of all documents from its archives relating to Galileo's trial. However, a considerable amount of blame for Galileo's persecution must also fall on the philosophers. Indeed, the decree of sentence issued by the Holy Office was signed by only seven of the ten cardinal-judges.

Unlike innumerable martyrs who have accepted torture or even death for the sake of their convictions, Galileo chose, most unheroically, to abjure his beliefs. (The myth that he, on leaving the tribunal, stamped his foot and said, "Yet it [i. e., the earth] does move," was invented by Giuseppe Baretti in 1757 and has no basis in fact.) Galileo's sentence was then commuted; there was no formal imprisonment. He was allowed to move back to his country estate near Florence, where he resumed his writing. His *Discourses Concerning Two New Sciences,* regarded by many as his greatest scientific contribution, was published in 1638.

BIBLIOGRAPHY

The best scientific biography of Galileo, tracing the historical development of his thought, is Stillman Drake's *Galileo at Work* (Chicago, 1978). A knowledgeable presentation of Galileo's philosophy is Ludovico Geymonat's *Galileo Galilei: A Biography and Inquiry into His Philosophy of Science* (New York, 1965). For Galileo's theological views and accounts of his trial, the following three books are indispensable: Giorgio de Santillana's *The Crime of Galileo* (New York, 1955), Jerome J. Langford's *Galileo, Science and the Church* (Ann Arbor, 1971), and Stillman Drake's *Galileo* (New York, 1980). The play by Bertolt Brecht, *Galileo* (New York, 1966), is tendentious and historically unreliable. Galileo's own views and remarks con-cerning the relationship between science and religion are scattered throughout his many letters and other writings. Among these the most important are his *Letter to the Grand Duchess Christina* (1615) and *The Assayer* (1623); both of these have been translated by Stillman Drake and are published in his *Discoveries and Opinions of Galileo* (Garden City, N. Y., 1957). The latest, and perhaps the final, effort made by the Roman Catholic church to repair its wrong decision in the case of Galileo is represented by the publication, by the Pontifical Academy of Sciences, of *I documenti del processo di Galileo Galilei* (Rome, 1984), which contains transcriptions of documents relating to Galileo's trial that had been held in the Vatican archives.

RAVI RAVINDRA

GANDHI, MOHANDAS

GANDHI, MOHANDAS (1869-1948), political leader, social reformer, and religious visionary of modern India. Although Gandhi initially achieved public notice as a leader of India's nationalist movement and as a champion of nonviolent techniques for resolving conflicts, he was also a religious innovator who did much to encourage the growth of a reformed, liberal Hinduism in India. In the West, Gandhi is venerated by many who seek an intercultural and socially conscious religion and see him as the representative of a universal faith.

Religious Influences on Gandhi. Mohandas Karamchand Gandhi was born into a *bania* (merchant caste) family in a religiously pluralistic area of western India—the Kathiawar Peninsula in the state of Gujarat. His parents were Vaisnava Hindus who followed the Vallabhacarya tradition of loving devotion to Lord Krsna. His father, Karamchand Uttamchand, the chief administrative officer of a princely state, was not a very religious man, but his mother, Putalibai, became a follower of the region's popular Pranami cult. This group was founded in the eighteenth century by Mehraj Thakore, known as Prananath ("master of the life force"), and was influenced by Islam. Prananath rejected all images of God and, like the famous fifteenth-century Hindu saint Narsinh Mehta, who came from the same region, advocated a direct link with the divine, unmediated by priests and ritual. This Protestant form of Hinduism seems to have been accepted by Gandhi as normative throughout his life.

Other enduring religious influences from Gandhi's childhood came from the Jains and Muslims who frequented the family household. Gandhi's closest childhood friend, Mehtab, was a Muslim, and his spiritual mentor, Raychandbhai, was a Jain. Early contacts with Christian street evangelists in his home town of Porbandar, however, left Gandhi unimpressed.

When Gandhi went to London to study law at the age of nineteen he encountered forms of Christianity of quite a different sort. Respecting vows made to his mother, Gandhi sought meatless fare at a vegetarian restaurant, where his fellow diners were a motly mix of Theosophists, Fabian Socialists, and Christian visionaries who were followers of Tolstoi. These esoteric and socialist forms of Western spirtuality made a deep impression on Gandhi and encouraged him to look for parallels in the Hindu tradition.

When, in 1893, Gandhi settled in South Africa as a lawyer (initially serving in a Muslim firm), he was impressed by a Trappist monastery he visited near Durban. He soon set up a series of ashrams (religious retreat centers) supported by Hermann Kallenbach, a South African architect of Jewish background, whom Gandhi had met through Theosophical circles. Gandhi named one of his communities Tolstoi Farm in honor of the Christian utopian with whom he had developed a lively correspondence. While in South Africa Gandhi first met C. F. Andrews, the Anglican missionary to India who had become an emissary of Indian nationalist leaders and who eventually became Gandhi's lifelong friend and confidant. It was through Andrews that Gandhi met the Indian poet Rabindranath Tagore in 1915, after Gandhi had returned to India to join the growing nationalist movement. Tagore, following the practice of Theosophists in South Africa, designated Gandhi a *mahatma,* or "great soul." *[See the biography of Tagore.]*

Gandhi's Religious Thought. Although the influences on Gandhi's religious thought are varied—from the Sermon on the Mount to the *Bhagavadgita*—his ideas are surprisingly consistent. Gandhi considered them to be Hindu, and in fact, they are all firmly rooted in the Indian religious tradition. His main ideas include the following.

1. *Satya* ("truth"). Gandhi equated truth with God, implying that morality and spirituality are ultimately the same. This concept is the bedrock of Gandhi's approach to conflict, *satyagraha,* which requires a fighter to "hold firmly to truth." While Gandhi did not further define the term, he regarded the rule of *ahimsa* as the litmus test that would determine where truth could be found.

2. *Ahimsa* ("nonviolence"). This ancient Indian concept prohibiting physical violence was broadened by Gandhi to include any form of coercion or denigration. For Gandhi, *ahimsa* was a moral stance involving love for and the affirmation of all life.

3. *Tapasya* ("renunciation"). Gandhi's asceticism was, in Max Weber's terms, "worldly" and not removed from social and political involvements. To Gandhi, *tapasya* meant not only the traditional requirements of simplicity and purity in personal habits but also the willingness of a fighter to shoulder the burden of suffering in a conflict.

4. *Swaraj* ("self-rule"). This term was often used during India's struggle for independence to signify freedom from the British, but Gandhi used it more broadly to refer to an ideal of personal integrity. He regarded *swaraj* as a worthy

goal for the moral strivings of individuals and nations alike, linking it to the notion of finding one's inner self.

In addition to these concepts, Gandhi affirmed the traditional Hindu notions of *karman* and *dharma.* Even though Gandhi never systematized these ideas, when taken together they form a coherent theological position. Gandhi's copious writings are almost entirely in the form of letters and

> **When Gandhi went to London to study law at the age of nineteen he encountered forms of Christianity of quite a different sort.**

short essays in the newspapers and journals he published. These writings and the accounts of Gandhi's life show that he had very little interest in what is sometimes regarded as emblematic of Hinduism: its colorful anthropomorphic deities and its reliance upon the rituals performed by Brahmanic priests.

It is not his rejection of these elements of Hindu culture that makes Gandhi innovative, however, for they are also omitted by the leaders of many other sects and movements in modern India. What is distinctive about Gandhi's Hinduism is his emphasis on social ethics as an integral part of the faith, a shift of emphasis that carries with it many conceptual changes as well. Gandhi's innovations include the use of the concept of truth as a basis for moral and political action, the equation of nonviolence with the Christian notion of selfless love, the broadening of the concept of *karmayoga* to include social service and political action, the redefinition of untouchability and the elevation of untouchables' tasks, and the hope for a more perfect world even in this present age of darkness *(kaliyuga).*

Gandhi's religious practices, like his ideas, combined both social and spiritual elements. In addition to his daily prayers, consisting of a simple service of readings and silent contemplation, he regarded his daily practice of spinning cotton as a form of mediation and his campaigns for social reform as sacrifices more efficacious than those made by priests at the altar. After Gandhi retired from politics in 1933, he took as his central theme the campaign for the uplift of untouchables, whom he called *harijans* ("people of God"). Other concerns included the protection of cows, moral education, and the reconciliation of Hindus and Muslims. The latter was especially important to Gandhi during the turmoil precipitated by India's independence, when the subcontinent was divided along religious lines. It was opposition to Gandhi's cries for religious tolerance that led to his assassination, on 30 January 1948, by a fanatical member of the Hindu right wing.

Gandhi's Legacy. Since Gandhi's death, neither Indian society nor Hindu belief has been restructured along Gandhian lines, but the Gandhian approach has been kept alive in India through the Sarvodaya movement, for which Vinoba Bhave has provided the spiritual leadership, and Jaya Prakash Narayan the political. Gandhi has provided the inspiration for religious and social activists in other parts of the world as well. These include Martin Luther King, Jr., and Joan Baez in the United States, E. M. Schumacher in England, Danilo Dolci in Sicily, Albert Luthuli in South Africa, Lanza del Vasto in France, and A. T. Ariyaratna in Sri Lanka. [*See the biographies of Bhave and King.*]

Over the years, the image of Gandhi has loomed larger than life, and he is popularly portrayed as an international saint. This canonization of Gandhi began in the West with the writings of an American Unitarian pastor, John Haynes Holmes, who in 1921 proclaimed Gandhi "the greatest man in the world today." It continues in an unabated flow of homiletic writings and films, including David Attenborough's *Gandhi,* one of the most widely seen motion pictures in history. At the core of this Gandhian hagiography lies the enduring and appealing image of a man who was able to achieve a significant religious goal: the ability to live simultaneously a life of moral action and spiritual fulfillment. For that reason Gandhi continues to serve as an inspiration for a humane and socially engaged form of religion in India and throughout the world.

[*See also* Ahimsa.]

BIBLIOGRAPHY

Gandhi's own writings are assembled in his *Collected Works,* 89 vols. (Delhi, 1958-1983). Many briefer anthologies are available, however, including *The Gandhi Reader,* edited by Homer Jack (New York, 1961). A reliable biography is to be found in Geoffrey Ashe's *Gandhi* (New York, 1969). The religious ideas of Gandhi are best explored in Margaret Chatterjee's *Gandhi's Religious Thought* (Notre Dame, Ind., 1983) and Raghavan Iyer's *The Moral and Political Thought of Mahatma Gandhi* (New York, 1973). The concept of *satyagraha* is explicated and put into comparative perspective in Joan Bondurant's *Conquest of Violence: The Gandhian Philosophy of Conflict,* rev. ed. (Berkeley, 1965), and my *Fighting with Gandhi* (San Francisco, 1984). Gandhi's saintly politics are described in Lloyd I. Rudolph and Susanne Hoeber Rudolph's *Gandhi: The Traditional Roots of Charisma* (Chicago, 1983), and his image as a universal saint is discussed in my essay "St. Gandhi," in *Saints and Virtues,* edited by John Stratton Hawley (Berkeley, 1986).

MARK JUERGENSMEYER

GERMANIC RELIGION

Germanic Culture. The earliest Germanic culture that archaeologists identify as such is the so-called Jastorf culture, a cultural province of northern Europe in the early Iron Age (c. 600 BCE), covering present-day Holstein, Jutland, northeast Saxony, and western Mecklenburg. From the linguistic point of view, however, the Germanic people constitute an archaic branch of the Indo-European family. At the time they entered into history, their closest neighbors were the Celts in Gaul, as Germanic tribes had spread south toward the Rhine and the wooded hills of southern Germany. To the east their neighbors were the Balts and the Scythians and Sarmatians, Iranian tribes that roamed the plains of Russia. To the north, they were in contact with Lapps and with Finns. Most of the information we have about them from early times comes from classical authors such as Caesar and Tacitus. Although they were primarily pastoralists, they also practiced agriculture. Their cattle were rather puny and could not entirely be depended upon for a livelihood; hunting provided an additional supply of meat. Their social organization was originally geared toward egalitarian communalism, but as contact with the Roman empire changed economic conditions, a more diversified society developed in which wealth and rank tended to prevail, although, nominally, power still rested in the hands of the Ping (Thing), the popular assembly, of all free men able to carry arms.

The Image of the Germanic Mythical World. Man lives in the center of the universe; the major Germanic traditions concur in calling his dwelling place Midgard ("the central abode"; Goth., Midjungards; OHG, Mittilgart; OE, Middangeard; ON, Midgardr). But the center is also the place where the gods built their residence, Ásgardr. It is described as spacious, with numerous dwellings, surrounded by a beautiful green pasture, Idavollr, and by a palisade built by a giant. Outside is Útgardr, the dangerous world of demons, giants (in Jotunheimr), and other frightening creatures.

Germanic myth evinces a real fear of this no-man's-land outside the settlement, and the idea of the frontier is there all the time, with the gods serving to ward off dangers from the wild. The islanders and the people along the shore believe that a universal ocean surrounds the earth, with an unfathomable abyss at the horizon and a huge snake curling at the edge to hold the world together.

For the Germanic people in Norway Útgardr must have been represented by the high mountains and the arctic territories to the north. The road is over land; Skírnir rides to Útgardr on Freyr's horse *(Skírnismál* 10), and Pórr's adventures always take him eastward. There are the realms of Hymir, who lives at the "end of the world"; of Prymr and Hrymr (*Voluspá* 49); and the "iron forest" *(iarnvir),* where the brood of demons is born (*Voluspá* 39).

The sky is the abode of the gods in the later conception of the Germanic people, which transfers Ásgardr to heaven. There, the gods' residences bear names like *Himinbjorg* ("protection of heaven"), for the hall of Heimdallr, the watchman of the gods, located at the rim of the sky (where the celestial outlook Hlidskjálf is also located). Valholl is a typical example of the shift. Originally, it was a subterraneous hall for warriors killed in combat; later connected with Ódinn, it becomes the heavenly residence of his heroic retinue, the *einherjar*. Like the netherworld, the sky is linked with the world by a bridge, this one guarded by Heimdallr; it is called Bilrost ("wavering road," i. e., the rainbow) or Bifrost ("shivering road"). In *Grímnismál* 29, the "bridge of the gods" *(ásbrú)* is "ablaze with flames." Here , the concept may represent a different cosmological view, symbolizing the Milky Way, which the forces of evil from Múspell will walk at the twilight of the world, and which, in many religious systems, is described as the "path of the souls."

The War of the Æsir and the Vanir. The Germanic gods are divided into two groups, the Æsir and the Vanir. The Æsir, appear as ruling gods, while the Vanir appear as gods of fertility.

Though the Vanir live in peace with the Æsir, this was not always the case. At the dawn of time, a bitter war was fought between the two groups, which Snorri Sturluson reports (with varying details) in two distinct works, the *Ynglingasaga* and the *Skáldskaparmál.* According to Snorri, Ódinn leads his army against the Vanir, but they resist vigorously. The two sides are alternately victorious, and they loot each other's territory until they grow tired of fighting and conclude a peace that puts them on equal footing. They exchange hostages: the Vanir Ñordr and his son Freyr are transferred to the world of the Æsir, who, in turn, deliver Mímir and Hœnir to the Vanir. As Mímir is very wise, the Vanir reciprocate by sending "the cleverest among them"—Kvasir—to the

> ## The islanders and the people along the shore believe that a universal ocean surrounds the earth, with an unfathomable abyss at the horizon.

Æsir. In the *Skáldskaparmál,* however, Snorri claims that Kvasir was created from the saliva of the Vanir and the Æsir when they spat into the communal caldron at the conclusion of the peace. Other evidence linking Kvasir's blood to the "mead of poetry" suggests that this second version is closer to the original.

The *Poetic Edda* describes the war between the Æsir and the Vanir in rather allusive terms (*Voluspá* 21-24), but since the theme was well known to any Scandinavian, the poem

did not need to be explicit. The object of the poet is not to teach but to enliven the tale for his listeners.

The Myth of Baldr. The story of Baldr's fate is probably the most moving and most controversial of all the Germanic myths. In this story, best known in Snorri Sturluson's rendition in the *Gylfaginning,* Ódinn's resplendent son Baldr is plagued by evil dreams of impending death. To protect against any danger his mother, Frigg, exacts an oath from everything in the world not to harm him, but neglects the puny mistletoe. Jealous of the attention Baldr receives in the games of the gods, Loki, in the disguise of a woman, wheedles the secret of Baldr's invulnerability out of his mother. He then persuades Baldr's blind brother, Hodr, who has been prevented by his infirmity from any participation in the sportive tossing of objects at Baldr, to throw a dart of mistletoe. Under Loki's guidance the missile hits Baldr and kills him. The gods are dumbfounded, and while preparations for Baldr's ship burial are in progress, they send out Hermódr on Ódinn's horse to the kingdom of Hel to entreat the goddess of the netherworld for the release of the unfortunate god. Meanwhile, Baldr's wife, Nanna, dies of grief and her body is carried onto the ship Hringhorni ("curved prow"), where she joins her husband on the funeral pyre. As for Hermódr, he returns with the message that Baldr will be released only on the condition that "everything in the world, both dead and alive, weeps for him." Immediately the Æsir dispatch messengers all over the universe to request everyone and everything to weep Baldr out of Hel's clutches. Even the stones and the metals participate in the universal grief, but a giantess called Pokk says she has no use for Baldr; as far as she is concerned, Hel can keep him! This is again Loki in disguise, and thus he succeeds in preventing the return of Baldr, who will only come back after Ragnarok.

The Pantheon. The main god is Mercury, whose Latin name, *Mercurius,* is a Roman interpretation of the Germanic name *Wodn[az]*, as also appears from the loan translation of Latin *Mercurii dies* into the Germanic *Wodniz-dag[az]* (Eng., Wednesday; Du., *woensdag*). As Mercury/*Wodan[az]* is the only Germanic god credited by Tacitus with receiving human sacrifice, many scholars assume that the *regnator omnium deus* ("god reigning over all") venerated by the Suevian tribe of the Semnones in their sacred grove and honored as their ethnic ancestor with regular human sacrifices must be the same deity, though perhaps Allan Lund is right in claiming that he must have been worshiped as an eponymous founder under the name *Semno*.

Tacitus also refers to other locally worshiped Germanic deities such as Nerthus, Mother Earth, for whom the Inguaeonic people hold a yearly pageant during which they celebrate the powers of fertility that she incarnates, or the divine twins whom he calls Alcis (Germanic, *Alhiz*) and equates with the Roman twins Castor and Pollux. In both cases he supplies a few details about cult and ritual, specifying, for example, that Nerthus shrouds herself in mystery: she remains hidden in a curtained chariot during her peregrinations among her worshipers; only her priest can approach her, and after the completion of her ceremonial journey she is bathed in a secret lake, but all those who officiate in this lustration rite are drowned afterward to maintain the "sacred ignorance" about her.

In the *Annals,* Tacitus refers to other Germanic deities, such as Tamfana, whose sanctuary was an important center of cultural activities in the territory of the Marsi (between the Lippe and the Ruhr rivers). Her "temple" was allegedly leveled by the Romans during the celebration of an autumnal festival in 4 CE. Its very existence contradicts Tacitus's statement in the *Germania* that the Germanic people "refuse to confine their gods within walls" and the contention that worship generally took place alfresco and in the woods, as with the Frisian goddess, Baduhenna, near whose sacred grove a Roman detachment was massacred.

In the Roman period, inscriptional material provides further data on the deities venerated by the Germanic people (within the boundaries of the empire), such as Nehalennia,

> **The blossoming of Scandinavian literature provides ample information about the pagan gods and the myths and cults of the Germanic North.**

whose sanctuary near Domburg in Sjæland has yielded an abundance of altars and statues. She was worshiped mainly by seamen and traders, mostly natives of the northwestern provinces of the empire, who dedicated the monuments to the goddess in return for the help received from her. Her attributes (cornucopias, specific fruits, dog, etc.) characterize her as a fertility goddess with strong chthonic overtones, but she apparently also shares the patronage of navigation with Isis, whose presence Tacitus mentions "among part of the Suevians" (presumably the Hermunduri, who were in close contact with the Roman province of Noricum where the cult of Isis had been integrated with that of the national goddess Noreia).

Important also are the *matres,* or *matronae,* documented by votive stones with dedicatory inscriptions found mainly in the territory of the Ubii on the left side of the Rhine in the second and third centuries CE. Their worshipers belonged essentially to the lower classes but also included some high officeholders in the Roman administration and army. They were invoked for protection against danger and catastrophes or for the prosperity of the family, and were described as bestowing their blessings generously, as such epithets as *Gabiae* ("givers"), *Friagabis* ("generous donors"), and

Arvagastiae ("hospitable ones") indicate. As they often appear in groups of three and seem to be associated with the fate and welfare of man, they have been compared with the Nornir, especially since one stone carries the inscription "Matrib[us] Parc[is]," referring directly to the *interpretatio Romana* of the three deities of fate.

The blossoming of Scandinavian literature provides ample information about the pagan gods and the myths and cults of the Germanic North. Moreover, in their peregrinations, the Vikings carried with them their religious practices and beliefs, and reports from various sources attest to the prevalence of the worship of Þórr among them.

The pantheon, then, can be sketched as follows in keeping with the Dumézilian trifunctional pattern:

1. Sovereignty is represented in its magical aspect by Óðinn, in its juridical aspect by Tyr.
2. War and physical force are represented by Þórr.
3. Fertility and wealth are presented by Freyr, Freyja, and Ñordr.

Such a presentation, however, oversimplifies the picture of the Scandinavian system, which not only fails to show the characteristic slant toward the second (war) function, as Dumézil himself acknowledges, but ignores such complex figures as Heimdallr and Loki, who hardly fit into this neat matrix. Moreover, some very important functions of the major deities are not covered by the labels in the Dumézilian tripartite ideology. For example, Óðinn is essentially the god of "inspired cerebral activity" and therefore the patron of the poets. Further, though he manifests his sovereign power through potent magical interventions, he is definitely not the only one to wield magical powers.

As for the involvement with war, there is a basic difference between Óðinn's intervention in battles to give victory to whomever he chooses to favor and the direct participation in combat of the divine champion Þórr: the only time Óðinn personally takes to the battlefield is in his deadly encounter with the Fenriswolf at Ragnarok. On the other hand, it seems that the transfer of the Vanic gods as hostages to the realm of the Æsir made them partake of some of the latter's combative spirit, as when the peaceful Freyr, who having readily given up his sword to obtain the favors of a giant maiden he eagerly desired, faces the giant Beli without a weapon and kills him with a hart's horn. And while Óðinn collects half of the heroes who die on the battlefield to serve as his *einherjar* in Valholl, it is certainly striking that Freyja gets the other half.

As for fertility, it is well known that, as thunder god, Þórr was the protector of the peasant class, which depends on the weather for its crops, but he shares control of the atmosphere with Ñordr, who controls the path of the wind and, as sea god, counteracts the effects of the thunderstorms, quieting the sea and smothering the fire.

Heimdallr occupies a marginal position in the pantheon; it is not even clear to which group of gods he should be assigned. Heimdallr was gifted with extraordinary aural perception: "He can hear the grass grow on the earth and the wool on sheep." Therefore, it has been assumed that the Old Norse term *hljóð*—generally translated "horn" in this context (*Voluspá* 27), but usually meaning "silence; listening, hearing," also "music, noise"—must designate one of Heimdallr's ears. On the other hand, as guardian of the gods and watchman of Ásgardr, Heimdallr assumes a military function, which would make him a second-function god in the Dumézilian system.

Similarly, Loki is extremely difficult to classify. Originally a giant, he nevertheless played an important part in the decisions and activities of the gods. Although primarily a mischievous trickster, Loki cannot be described as an "evil demon." He is restless and inventive, but also deceptive and unreliable. Although he frequently got the gods in trouble, he usually redeemed himself by ultimately solving the problem he created.

The minor deities are also problematic: some of them can in some way be integrated into the tripartite functional scheme, for example, Ullr, an archer god living in Ydalir ("yew dales") in Ásgardr, whose importance is made clear by Ódinn's statement in the *Grímnismál* (st. 42) that Ullr especially, among all the gods, will grant his blessing to he who "first quenches the fire." Bragi is another lesser god about whom little is known. His name seems to be related to the Old Norse word *bragr*, which designates "poetic form," and he is described as the "foremost of poets," being in this way in competition with Ódinn as patron of poetry.

Very little information is usually given about the goddesses. Frigg, Ódinn's wife, is the devoted mother of Baldr; she lives in Fensalir ("marshy halls"), attended by her confidant Fulla. Loki claims that she shared her sexual favors with her husband's brothers, Vili and Vé (*Lokasenna* 26).

Jord ("earth"), the mother of Pórr, is also known under the name of *Fjorgyn*, which may mean "goddess of the furrow" (cf. Frisian, *furge*; Germanic, **furho*; Old High German *fur[u]h*, German *Furche*, Old English *furh*, and English *furrow*). Her male counterpart is Fjorgynn, who is either the father or the lover of Frigg, called *Fjorgyns mær* in the *Lokasenna*, (st. 26). The goddess Gefjun is said to have torn away from Sweden a sizable chunk of land, which was dragged to the Danish island of Sjælland; to perform this deed she turned the four sons she had begotton in Jotunheimr into oxen and yoked them to the plow. Though she is mentioned as a separate deity in the *Lokasenna* (st. 20), she seems to be an alter ego of Freyja, who is also known as Gefn ("giver"), a name befitting a fertility goddess.

In many cases it is questionable whether some names of deities quoted by Snorri Sturluson are more than local variants of the names of major gods, used largely to enhance the poetic expressions of the skalds. Thus we have no myths relating to such goddesses as Eir ("the best of physicians," according to the *Gylfaginning*) or to those specializing in bringing people to love, like Siofn, or who, like Lofn ("permission"), bring together those for whom marriage is apparently excluded.

[*For discussion of Germanic religion in a broader context, see* Indo-European Religions.]

BIBLIOGRAPHY

On the Germanic pantheon, see E. O. G. Turville-Petre's general work *Myth and Religion of the North* (London, 1964) and Georges Dumézil's general study *Gods of the Ancient Northmen* (Berkeley, 1973). Other standard works on the topic include Jan de Vries's *Altgermanische Religionsgeschichte,* 2d ed., 2 vols. (Berlin, 1956-1957); R. L. M. Derolez's *Götter und Mythen der Germanen* (1959; Einsiedeln, Switzerland, 1963); and Régis Boyer's *La religion des Anciens Scandinaves* (Paris, 1981). Hilda R. Ellis Davidson's *Gods and Myths of Northern Europe* (Baltimore, 1964) is written for a wider public. A more controversial work is Ake V. Ström's *Germanische Religion,* "Die Religionen der Menschheit," vol. 19 (Stuttgart, 1975). A better summary, strongly influenced by Georges Dumézil, is Werner Betz's "Die altgermanische Religion," in Wolfgang Stammler's *Deutsche Philologie im Aufriss,* vol. 3 (Berlin, 1957). Succinct presentations are found in Lennart Ejerfeldt's contribution to the *Handbuch der Religionsgeschichte,* vol. 1, edited by Jes P. Asmussen and Jørgen Laessøe (Göttingen, 1971), pp. 277-342; and in Eduard Neumann and Helmut Voigt's entry in *Wörterbuch der Mythologie,* vol. 2 of *Das alte Europa,* edited by H. W. Haussig (Stuttgart, 1972).

On Tacitus, compare J. G. C. Anderson's *Cornelii Taciti De origine et situ Germanorum* (Oxford, 1961) and Rudolf Much's *Die Germania des Tacitus erläutert,* edited by Wolfgang Lange and Herbert Jankuhn (Heidelberg, 1967). On the sovereign gods, consult Georges Dumézil's *Les dieux souverains des Indo-Européens* (Paris, 1977). On the divine twins, compare Donald Ward's *The Divine Twins: An Indo-European Myth in Germanic Tradition* (Berkeley, 1968) and Georges Dumézil's *From Myth to Fiction: The Saga of Hadingus* (Chicago, 1973), esp. pp. 109-120.

EDGAR C. POLOMÉ

GNOSTICISM

Origins of Gnosticism

Gnosis ("knowledge") is a Greek word of Indo-Euro-pean origin, related to the English *know* and the Sanskrit *jñana*. The term has long been used in comparative religion to indicate a current of antiquity that stressed awareness of the divine mysteries. This was held to be obtained either by direct experience of a revelation or by initiation into the secret, esoteric tradition of such revelations.

Gnosticism. Ever since the congress on the origins of gnosticism held at Messina, Italy, in 1966, scholars have made a distinction between gnosis and gnosticism. *Gnosticism* is a modern term, not attested in antiquity. Even the substantive *gnostic* (Gr., *gnostikos,* "knower"), found in patristic writings, was never used to indicate a general spiritual movement but was applied only to a single, particular sect. Today gnosticism is defined as a religion in its own right, whose myths state that the Unknown God is not the creator (demiurge, YHVH); that the world is an error, the consequence of a fall and split within the deity; and that man, spiritual man, is alien to the natural world and related to the deity and becomes conscious of his deepest Self when he hears the word of revelation. Not sin or guilt, but unconsciousness, is the cause of evil.

> At present, many scholars are inclined to believe that gnosticism is built upon Hellenistic-Jewish foundations and can be traced to centers like Alexandria.

Until recent times the gnostic religion was almost exclusively known by reports of its opponents, ecclesiastical heresiologists such as Irenaeus (c. 180 CE), Hippolytus (c. 200), and Epiphanius (c. 350). Not until the eighteenth century were two primary sources, the Codex Askewianus (named for the physician A. Askew) and the Codex Brucianus (named after the Scottish explorer James Bruce), discovered in Egypt. These contained several Coptic gnostic writings: (1) *Two Books of Jeû* from the beginning of the third century; (2) book 4 of *Pistis Sophia* from about 225; and (3) *Pistis Sophia,* books 1, 2, and 3, from the second half of the third century. To these can now be added the writings found near Nag Hammadi in Upper Egypt in 1945. The stories told about the discovery are untrustworthy. The only certain fact is that, to date, about thirteen of the codices (books, not scrolls) comprising some fifty-two texts are preserved at the Coptic Museum in Old Cairo.

Origins. The hypothesis once supported by Richard Reitzenstein, Geo Widengren, and Rudolf Bultmann that gnosticism is of Iranian origin has been abandoned; the alleged Iranian mystery of the "saved saviour" has been disproved. At present, many scholars are inclined to believe that gnosticism is built upon Hellenistic-Jewish foundations and can be traced to centers like Alexandria, which had a large Jewish population, much as the city of New York does today. Polemics in the writings of the Jewish philosopher Philo, who himself was an opponent of local heresies, make it clear that he knew Jewish groups that had already formulated certain basic elements of gnosticism, although a consistent system did not yet exist in pre-Christian times.

Jewish Gnosticism. The church father Irenaeus indicates not all those whom modern scholars call "gnostics" but only the adherents of a specific sect. It is misleading to call them Sethians (descendants of Seth, the son of Adam), as some scholars do nowadays. Notwithstanding its name, the *Apocryphon of John* (a disciple of Jesus) contains no Christian elements apart from the foreword and some minor interpolations. It can be summarized as follows: from the Unknown God (who exists beyond thought and name) and his spouse (who is his counterpart and mirror) issued the spiritual world. The last of the spiritual entities, Sophia, became wanton and brought forth a monster, the demiurge. He organized the zodiac and the seven planets. He proclaimed: "I am a jealous god, apart from me there is no other." Then a voice was heard, teaching him that above him existed the Unknown God and his spouse. Next, the "first Man in the form of a man" manifested himself to the lower angels. He is the Glory of *Ezekiel* 1:26. His reflection appears in the waters of chaos (cf. the mirror of the Anthropos in *Poimandres*). Thereupon the lower angels created the body of Adam after the image that they had seen, an imitation of the Man, who clearly serves as an ideal archetype for the human body. For a long time the body of Adam lay unable to move, for the seven planetary angels were unable to raise it up. Then Sophia caused the demiurge to breathe the *pneuma* he had inherited from her into the face of his creature. So begins a long struggle between the redeeming Sophia and the malicious demiurge, the struggle for and against the awakening of human spiritual consciousness.

Written in Alexandria about the beginning of the Christian era, the myth of the *Apocryphon of John*, a pivotal and seminal writing, combines the Anthropos model and the Sophia model. It is very complicated and confusing but had enormous influence in the Near East, where so many remnants of great religions survive today. Their religion features ablutions in streaming water and a funerary mass. When a Mandaean has died, a priest performs a complicated rite in order to return the soul to its heavenly abode, where it will receive a spiritual body. In this way, it is believed, the deceased is integrated into the so-called Secret Adam, the Glory, the divine body of God. This name confirms that, along with the Anthropos of *Poimandres* and the Adam Qadmon of later Jewish mysticism, this divine and heavenly figure is ultimately derived from the vision of the prophet Ezekiel. In Mandaean lore Sophia appears in degraded form as a mean and lewd creature called the Holy Spirit. The creation of the world is attributed to a lower demiurge.

The apostle Paul (or one of his pupils) maintains that Christ, who is for him the second Adam, is "the head of his Church, which is his body" (*Eph.* 1:22-23). The Christian is integrated into this body through baptism. Mandaean speculations about the Secret Adam may elucidate what Paul meant. In defining his view of the church as the mystical body of Christ, the apostle may be reflecting a familiarity with comparable Jewish and Hellenistic speculations about the *kavod* as the body of God. As a matter of fact, it has become clear from the verses of Ezekiel Tragicus that such ideas circulated in Alexandria long before the beginning of our era. They surfaced in Palestine toward the end of the first century CE in strictly Pharisaic circles that transmitted secret, esoteric traditions about the mystical journey of the sage through the seven heavenly places to behold the god Man on the throne of God. The author of the writing *Shi`ur Qoma*, the "measurement of the Body" of God, reports the enormous dimensions of the members of the Glory. The Orphics had taught that the cosmos was actually a divine body. Already early in Hellenistic Egypt similar speculations arose; these were the origin of the remarkable speculations of Palestinian rabbis concerning the mystical body of God. (These speculations ultimately led to the *Zohar*.)

In the ninth century several groups of Islamic gnostics arose in southern Iraq, where several other gnostic sects had found refuge during late antiquity and where the Mandaeans (the Aramaic term for gnostics) continue to live today. [*See* Mandaean Religion.] The best-known Islamic gnostics are the Isma-`iliyah, of which the Aga Khan is the religious leader. Mythological themes central to their religion are (1) the cycles of the seven prophets; (2) the throne and the letters; (3) Kuni, the creative principle, who is feminine (a typical remythologizing of a monotheistic Father religion); (4) the higher Pentad; (5) the infatuation of the lower demiurge; (6) the seven planets and the twelve signs of the zodiac; (7) the divine Adam; and (8) the fall and ascent of the soul.

Since the discovery of the Nag Hammadi codices it has been established that these themes are best explained as transpositions into an Islamic terminology of the gnostic mythemes that are found in the *Apocryphon of John* and kindred documents of Jewish gnosticism.

Christian Gnosis. According to a reliable tradition, Barnabas, a missionary of the Jerusalem congregation, was the first to bring the gospel to Alexandria, a relatively easy journey. Egyptian Christianity is Judaic in origin, not gentile, and the great Egyptian gnostics seem all to have been of Jewish birth. The adherents of Basilides claimed: "We are no longer Jews and not yet Christians." The followers of Valentinus reported: "When we were Hebrews, we were orphans." Basilides and Valentinus both proclaimed a God beyond the Old Testament God, and both were familiar with the myth of the *Apocryphon of John,* which they christianized. The case of Marcion is similar: he was so well-informed about the Hebrew Bible and its flaws that his father, a bishop, may well be presumed to have been Jewish. Through a certain Cerdo, Marcion came to know an already existing gnostic system. Those who reject the god of the Old Testament obviously no longer hold to the Jewish faith, but nevertheless still belong ethnically to the Jewish people. Both

Valentinus and Marcion went to Rome and were excommunicated there between 140 and 150. Basilides, who stayed in Alexandria, remained a respected schoolmaster there until his death. The Christians in Alexandria were divided among several synagogues and could afford to be tolerant, for a monarchic bishop did not yet exist and their faith was pluriform anyhow. Basilides, Valentinus, and Marcion were Christocentric and let themselves be influenced by the *Gospel of John* and the letters of Paul.

Modern gnosis. The gnosis of modern times, launched by the shoemaker Jakob Boehme (c. 1600), was generated spontaneously as a result of direct experience. It differs from ancient gnosticism in that it derives not only the light but also the darkness (not only good but also evil) from the ground of being. Inspired by Boehme is the influential gnosis of the English poet and artist William Blake (1757-1827), the only authentic gnostic of the entire Anglo-Saxon world. It is in the school of Boehme that the scholarly study of gnosticism has its roots, beginning with the *Impartial History of the Churches and Heresies* (1699) by Gottfried Arnold. In this extremely learned work all heretics, including all gnostics, are represented as the true Christians—innocent and slandered lambs.

Ever since, the study of gnosticism has been an accepted academic subject in Germany, but in Germany alone. In his youth Goethe read Arnold's book and conceived his own gnostic system, as reported in his autobiography. Toward the end of his life Goethe recalled the love of his youth when he wrote the finale to *Faust,* the hierophany of "the Eternally Feminine," a version of the gnostic Sophia, the exclusive manifestation of the deity. Johann Lorenz von Mosheim and other great historians also took gnosis quite seriously. The

> **The best-known Islamic gnostics are the Isma-`iliyah, of which the Aga Khan is the religious leader.**

brilliant August Neander, who belonged to the conservative reaction to the Enlightenment called the Great Awakening Revivalism *(Erweckungsbewegung),* wrote his *Genetic Evolution of the Most Important Gnostic Systems* in 1818. Ferdinand Christian Baur, a prominent Hegelian, published his monumental *Christian Gnosis* in 1835, in which he defends the thesis that gnosis was a religious philosophy whose modern counterpart is the idealism of Schelling, Schleiermacher, and Hegel, all based upon the vision of Boehme. According to Baur, even German idealism was a form of gnosis. Yet when "the people of poets and thinkers" became, under Bismarck, a people of merchants and industrial workers, this wonderful empathy, this fantastic feel of gnosis, was almost completely lost.

Adolf von Harnack (1851-1930), the ideologue of Wilhelm's empire, defined gnosticism as the acute, and orthodoxy as the chronic, hellenization (i. e., rationalization) and hence alienation of Christianity. At the time it was difficult to appreciate the experience behind the gnostic symbols. Wilhelm Bousset, in his *Main Problems of Gnosis* (1907), described this religion as a museum of hoary and lifeless Oriental (Indian, Iranian, Babylonian) fossils. The same unimaginative approach led Richard Reitzenstein, Geo Widengren, and Rudolf Bultmann to postulate an Iranian mystery of salvation that never existed but was supposed to explain gnosticism, Manichaeism, and Christianity.

Existentialism and depth psychology were needed to rediscover the abysmal feelings that inspired the movement of gnosis. Hans Jonas (*The Gnostic Religion,* 1958) has depicted these feelings as dread, alienation, and an aversion to all worldly existence, as if the gnostics were followers of Heidegger. In the same vein are the writings of Kurt Rudolph, the expert on Mandaeism.

Under the influence of Carl Gustav Jung, I and other scholars (e.g., Henri-Charles Puech and Károly Kerén-yi) have interpreted the gnostic symbols as a mythical expression (i. e., projection) of self-experience. As a lone wolf, the Roman Catholic convert Erik Peterson suggested that the origins of gnosticism were not Iranian or Greek but Jewish. The gnostic writings from Nag Hammadi have shown Jung and Peterson to be in the right. At last the origins, development, and goal of this perennial philosophy have come to light.

BIBLIOGRAPHY

Jonas, Hans. *The Gnostic Religion: The Message of the Alien God and the Beginnings of Christianity.* 2d ed., rev. & enl. Boston, 1963.
Pagels, Elaine H. *The Gnostic Gospels.* New York, 1979.
Quispel, Gilles. *Gnostic Studies.* 2 vols. Istanbul, 1974-1975.
Robinson, James M., et al. *The Nag Hammadi Library in English.* San Francisco, 1977.
Rudolph, Kurt. *Gnosis.* San Francisco, 1983.

GILLES QUISPEL

Gnosticism as a Christian Heresy

The pluralism of early Christianity in regional faith and praxis, as well as the shifting lines of authority within the first and second centuries, make it difficult to draw the sharp boundaries required to exclude a particular opinion or group as heretical. In *Against Heresies,* Irenaeus says that his predecessors were unable to refute the gnostics because they had inadequate knowledge of gnostic systems and because the gnostics appeared to say the same things as other Christians. Christian gnostics of the second century claimed to have the esoteric, spiritual interpretation of Christian scriptures, beliefs, and sacraments. Their orthodox opponents sought to prove that such persons were not Christians on the grounds that gnostic rites were occasions of immoral behavior, that their myths and doctrines were absurd, and that their intentions were destructive to true worship of God. In short, it appears that gnostics were defined as heretics by their opponents well before they stopped considering themselves to be spiritual members of the larger Christian community.

Three periods characterize the interaction of gnosticism and Christianity: (1) the late first century and early second century, in which the foundations of gnostic traditions were laid at the same time that the New Testament was being written; (2) the mid-second century to the early third century, the period of the great gnostic teachers and systems; and (3) the end of the second century into the fourth century, the period of the heresiological reaction against gnosticism.

The fluid boundaries of Christianity in the first period make it difficult to speak of gnosticism at that time as a heresy. Four types of tradition used in the second-century

> **Irenaeus provided two guidelines for drawing the boundary that would exclude gnostic teachers from the Christian community.**

gnostic systems were developed in this period. First, there was a reinterpretation of *Genesis* that depicts the Jewish God as jealous and enslaving: freedom means escaping from bondage to that God. Second, there arose a tradition of Jesus' sayings as esoteric wisdom. Third, a soteriology of the soul's ascent to union with the divine from the popular forms of Platonism was adopted. And fourth, possibly, there was a mythical story of the descent of a divine being from the heavenly world to reveal that world as the true home of the soul. Each of the last three types of tradition lies behind conflicts or images in the New Testament writings.

Some scholars have argued that the incorporation of the sayings of Jesus into the gospel narrative of his life served to check the proliferation of sayings of the risen Lord uttered by Christian prophets. The soteriology of the soul's divinization through identification with wisdom has been seen behind the conflicts in *1 Corinthians.* Second-century gnostic writings use the same traditions from Philo that scholars invoke as parallel to *1 Corinthians.* The question of a first-century redeemer myth is debated in connection with the Johannine material. While the image of Jesus in the *Gospel of John* could have been developed out of existing metaphorical traditions and the structure of a gospel life of Jesus, the Johannine letters show that Johannine Christians were split over interpretation of the gospel. Both *1 John* and *2 John* condemn other Christians as heretics. Heretics deny the death of Jesus and may have held a docetic Christology.

The second century brought fully developed gnostic systems from teachers who claimed that their systems represented the inner truth revealed by Jesus. During this period, the Greek originals of the Coptic treatises were collected at Nag Hammadi. From the orthodox side, Irenaeus's five books refuting the gnostics marked a decisive turn in Christian self-consciousness. These were followed by the antignostic writings of Hippolytus, Clement of Alexandria, Origen, Tertullian, and Epiphanius. Though Irenaeus may have drawn upon earlier antignostic writings, such as Justin's lost *Suntagma,* his work suggests a turn toward the systematic refutation of gnosticism. Rather than catalog sects and errors, Irenaeus turned to the refutation of gnostic systems using the rhetorical skills and *topoi* of philosophical debate. At the same time, he sought to provide a theoretical explication of orthodox Christian belief that would answer arguments advanced by gnostic teachers.

Irenaeus provided two guidelines for drawing the boundary that would exclude gnostic teachers from the Christian community. The first is reflected in the *regula fidei* of his *Against Heresies* (1.10.3), which gives topics about which legitimate theological speculation is possible and consequently rules out much of the cosmological speculation of the gnostic teachers. The second guideline is Irenaeus's rejection of gnostic allegorization of scripture. He insists that biblical passages must mean what they appear to mean and that they must be interpreted within their contexts. In book five, Irenaeus argues that the gnostics failed to support their claims for a spiritual resurrection in *1 Corinthians* 1:50 because they ignored the eschatological dimensions of the verses that follow.

The heresiologist's concern to draw boundaries between orthodox Christianity and gnostic teachings ran counter to the practice of second-century gnostics. Several of the Nag Hammadi treatises were apparently composed with the opposite aim. Writings such as the *Gospel of Truth* and the *Tripartite Tractate* drew explicit connections between gnostic teaching and both the teaching practice and the sacramental practice of the larger Christian community. Other gnostic writings fell within the developing patterns of ascetic Christianity in Syria and Egypt (e.g., *Gospel of Thomas, Book of Thomas the Contender, Dialogue of the Savior*). The ascetic tradition tended to reject the common Christian assumption that baptism provides a quality of sinlessness adequate to salvation and to insist that only rigorous separation from the body and its passions will lead to salvation.

Other gnostic writings show that the efforts of heresiologists to draw boundaries against gnostics resulted in repressive measures from the orthodox side and increasing separation by gnostics (cf. *Apocalypse of Peter, Second Treatise of the Great Seth*). The *Testimony of Truth,* apparently written in third-century Alexandria, not only contains explicit attacks on the beliefs of orthodox Christians but also attacks other gnostic sects and teachers like Valentinus, Isidore, and Basilides. The author of this gnostic work considers other, nonascetic gnostics as heretics. However, the author still holds to something of the nonpolemical stance that had characterized earlier gnostic teachers, saying that the true teacher avoids disputes and makes himself equal to everyone. Another example of the effectiveness of the orthodox polemic in defining gnostics as heretics is found in what appears to be a gnostic community rule that calls for charity and love among the gnostic brethren as a sign of the truth of their claims over against the disunity of the orthodox in *Interpretation of Knowledge.* This call reverses one of Irenaeus's polemical points that the multiplicity and disunity of gnostic sects condemn their teaching when contrasted with the worldwide unity of the church.

Some scholars think that this third period, in which the gnostics were effectively isolated as "heretic" by orthodox polemic, led to a significant shift within gnostic circles. Gnosticism began to become dechristianized, to identify more with the non-Christian, esoteric, and hermetic elements within its traditions. Gnostics became members of an independent esoteric sect, moved toward the more congenial Mandaean or Manichaean circles, existed on the fringes of Alexandrian Neoplatonism in groups that emphasized thaumaturgy, or joined the monks in the Egyptian desert, where they found a kindred spirit in the combination of asceticism and Origenist mysticism. Those associated with Manichaeism or Origenism would continue to find themselves among the ranks of heretical Christians. The rest were no longer within the Christian sphere of influence.

[*See* Manichaeism.]

BIBLIOGRAPHY

Anyone interested in gnosticism should obtain the English translation of the Nag Hammadi codices edited by James M. Robinson, *The Nag Hammadi Library in English* (San Francisco, 1977). Another book that studies the structure and the apologetics of the gnostic dialogues from the Nag Hammadi collection is my *The Gnostic Dialogue: The Early Church and the Crisis of Gnosticism* (New York, 1980). The only other reliable treatments of the new material and its significance for the interaction of gnosticism and early Christianity are scholarly writings. Three volumes, containing papers by leading scholars in German, French, and English, provide important treatments of the subject: *Gnosis: Festschrift für Hans Jonas*, edited by Barbara Aland (Göttingen, 1978); *The Rediscovery of Gnosticism*, vol. 1, *The School of Valentinus*, and vol. 2, *Sethian Gnosticism*, edited by Bentley Layton (Leiden, 1980-1981). The best study of the gnostic polemic against orthodox Christianity is Klaus Koschorke's *Die Polemik der Gnostiker gegen das kirchliche Christentum* (Leiden, 1978).

PHEME PERKINS

GOD

God in the New Testament

The New Testament enunciates no new God and no new doctrine of God. It proclaims that the God and Father of Jesus Christ is the God of Abraham, Isaac, and Jacob, the God of earlier covenants. What the New Testament announces is that this God has acted anew in inaugurating God's final reign and covenant through the career and fate of Jesus of Nazareth. [*For discussion of Jesus' life and of Christology, see* Jesus.]

The Pre-Easter Jesus. Jesus inherited the Old Testament Jewish faith in Yahveh, which held that God was the creator of the world (*Mk.* 10:6 and parallel) and the one God who elected Israel as his people and gave them his law (*Mk.* 12:29 and parallels). Moreover, God promised the Israelites final salvation (*Is.* 35, 61). At the same time, the sense in the New Testament that God is now realizing ancient promises and is acting anew (cf. *Mt.* 11:4-5, an indubitably authentic saying of Jesus) gives Jesus' image of God a sense of immediacy. God was not merely creator some thousands (or billions) of years ago; he is creator now, feeding the birds and clothing the flowers (*Mt.* 6:26-30, *Lk.* 12:24, and Q, the purported common source of *Matthew* and *Luke*). Not only did God give the law through Moses, but God now demands radical obedience in each concrete situation (cf. the antitheses of the Sermon on the Mount in *Mt.* 5:27-48). Above all, God is now offering in the proclamation and activity of Jesus a foretaste of final salvation. Jesus' announcement of the inbreaking of God's reign (*Mk.* 1:15, *Mt.* 10:7, *Lk.* 9:2, Q) is not an abstract concept detached from Jesus' own word and work. Jesus' word and work are the occasions through which God acts definitively and savingly. The same is true of Jesus' exorcisms: "If I by the Spirit [finger, *Lk.* 11:20] of God cast out demons, then the kingdom [i. e., reign] of God has come upon you" (*Mt.* 12:28, *Lk.* 11:20, Q).

Jesus issues a call, "Follow me" (*Mk.* 1:17, 2:14; cf. *Mt.* 8:22, *Lk.* 9:59, Q?), not because he advances any claim for himself as such, but only because in that call, as in his word and work in the world, God is issuing the call to end-time salvation. To confess Jesus (*Mt.* 10:32, *Lk.* 12:8, Q, *Mk.* 8:38) or to deny him before others is to determine one's ultimate fate on the last day—whether it be judgment or salvation. The verdict of the Son of man on that day will be determined by whether men and women confess Jesus now. Thus, in Jesus' call God is proleptically active as judge and savior. The Fourth Gospel puts it more thematically: God's salvation and judgment are already meted out here and now in the word of Jesus and people's response to it (*Jn.* 3:18, 5:22-27).

Jesus' conduct. Jesus eats with outcasts, and he defends his conduct by telling the parables of the lost (*Lk.*

15). These parables interpret Jesus' action as God's action in seeking and saving the lost and celebrating with them here and now the joy of the reign of God. Ernst Fuchs points out in *Studies of the Historical Jesus* (Naperville, Ill., 1964) that "Jesus . . . dares to affirm the will of God as though he himself stood in God's place" (p. 21).

God as Abba. Jesus' word and work are God's word and work because Jesus has responded to God's call in complete faith and obedience. This is brought out in the baptism, temptation, transfiguration, and Gethsemane narratives of the synoptists (*Mk.* 1:9-11 and parallels, *Mt.* 4:1-11, *Lk.* 4:1-13, Q, *Mk.* 9:2-8 and parallels, *Mk.* 14:32-42 and parallels), and once again it is thematically treated in the discourses of the Fourth Gospel (e.g., *Jn.* 8:28-29). This relation of call and obedience is summarized in Jesus' intimate address to God as Abba ("father"). This is no new doctrine, for the Old Testament and Judaism knew God as Father (e.g., *Is.* 63:16), nor does it imply a claim to metaphysical identity with the being of God or with an aspect of that being, as in later New Testament traditions. Again, Jesus does not pass the Abba appellation on to others as a way of defining God. Rather, he invites those who have responded in faith to his message of God's salvation to call God "Abba" with him. "Abba" is a familial mode of address which presupposes a new relationship with God. Because Jesus first made the response and enables others to make the same response, they too may call God "Abba" (cf. the Lukan version of the Lord's Prayer, *Lk.* 11:2).

Jesus' death. The saving activity in word and deed which fills the whole career of Jesus culminates in his journey to Jerusalem in order to make the last offer of salvation or judgment to his people at the very center of their national life. As a prophet, Jesus is convinced that he will be rejected and put to death and that this death will be the culmination of Israel's constant rejection of God's word as known through the prophets: "It cannot be that a prophet should perish away from Jerusalem" (*Lk.* 13:33; cf. the parable of the vineyard, *Mk.* 12:1-9 and parallels). Since it is the culmination of his obedience, his death, like all his other activity, is seen by Jesus as the saving act of God. The most primitive form of the suffering-Son-of-man sayings, namely, "The Son of man will be delivered into the hands of men" (cf. *Mk.* 9:31), if authentic, expresses this by using the divine passive: God will deliver the Son of man to death. It is God's prerogative to inaugurate covenants. Therefore, at the Last Supper, Jesus speaks of his impending death as a supreme act of service (*Lk.* 22:27; cf. the foot washing in *Jn.* 13:2-15), which inaugurates the final covenant and reign of God (*Lk.* 22:29; cf. *Mk.* 14:24, 25 and parallels). In the references to service, covenant, and kingdom (reign) at the Last Supper lies the historical basis for the post-Easter message of atonement.

Easter. The Easter experiences created in the disciples the faith that, despite the apparent debacle of the crucifixion,

God had vindicated Jesus and taken him into his own eternal presence. The early community expressed this conviction chiefly through testimony about Jesus' resurrection: "God raised Jesus from the dead" (*Rom.* 4:24, 10:9; *1 Thes.* 1:10) or "Christ was raised" (*Rom.* 4:25, 6:9; *1 Cor.* 15:4—a divine passive). After Easter, for the believing community, God is preeminently the God who raised Jesus from the dead. Insofar as there is any specific New Testament definition of God, this is it (e.g., again, *Rom.* 10:9). This results in the ascription of titles of majesty to Jesus. At the resurrection, God made him Lord and Christ (Messiah) (*Acts* 2:36) and even Son of God, originally a royal title (*Rom.* 1:4). Jesus is exalted to a position as close as possible to God, to God's "right hand." That means God continues to act savingly, even after Easter, toward the community and toward the world through the proclamation of Jesus as the Christ. In saving activity, God and Christ become interchangeable subjects: what God does, Christ does at the same time. However, Christ does not replace God. All the titles of majesty declare that Christ is God's agent, not God's surrogate.

The Message of the Post-Easter Church. Like Jesus in his pre-Easter life, the early church did not approach Israel with a new doctrine of God. Its message was that God had decisively inaugurated the fulfillment of his promises in the career and fate of Jesus of Nazareth, and above all in his resurrection. This is the burden of the sermons in the early chapters of the *Acts of the Apostles*: "Jesus of Nazareth, a man attested to you by God with mighty works and signs which God did through him . . . this Jesus, delivered up according to the definite plan and foreknowledge of God . . . God raised him" (*Acts* 2:22-24).

The Hellenistic-Jewish mission. Members of the Greek-speaking Jewish community, initially led by Stephen (*Acts* 6, 7), first found themselves preaching the Christian message to Greek-speaking non-Jews (*Acts* 11:20). In approaching them, it was found necessary to change tactics. Instead of launching straight in with the Christ event as God's act of salvation, they had to start further back, with belief in God. Because these non-Jewish Greeks came from a pagan and often polytheistic environment, it was necessary first to establish belief in the one God before speaking about what this God had done in Christ and was now doing salvifically. In other words, the Hellenistic-Jewish Christians needed an apologetic for monotheism, arguments for the existence of the one God, in their mission to non-Jews. They were able to draw upon the apologetic which had earlier been worked out by Greek-speaking Jews in their approach to the pagan world. One of the earliest references to such an apologetic for monotheism is attested to by Paul when he reminds the Thessalonians of his original preaching to them before their conversion to Christianity: "You turned from idols to serve a living and true God" (*1 Thes.* 1:9). Note how this precedes the second part of the message: "and to wait for this Son from

heaven, whom he raised from the dead" (*1 Thes.* 1:10). A further example of Pauline apologetic for monotheism, and a claim that creation contains a natural revelation of God and his moral demands, occurs in *Romans* 1:18-32 and 2:14-15. Humanity has, however, frequently rejected this revelation and disobeyed God's moral demands, and Paul seeks to recall pagans to such knowledge and obedience. He sees a close connection between idolatry and immorality: "They . . . exchanged the glory of the immortal God for images resembling mortal man or birds or animals or reptiles. . . . Therefore God gave them up in the lust of their hearts to impurity"

> **Jesus speaks of his impending death as a supreme act of service which inaugurates the final covenant and reign of God.**

(*Rom.* 1:23-24). Later examples of an apologetic for monotheism are to be found in *Acts* 14:15-17, addressed to an unsophisticated audience, and in *Acts* 17:24-29, addressed to a cultured one.

Pauline theology. Paul's theology is entirely occasional, that is, it was worked out in response to concrete problems in the Christian communities he knew. The focus of his theology is the death and resurrection of Jesus Christ and its saving consequences. He inherited from the liturgical tradition an understanding of Christ's death as a sacrifice. It was the blood that inaugurated the new covenant (*1 Cor.* 11:25). Christ was the paschal lamb (*1 Cor.* 5:7). But Paul did not develop these sacrificial images in his reflection on Christ's death, perhaps because such language tended to drive a wedge between Jesus and the Father, as though the sacrifice was offered in order to propitiate or appease an angry deity. The language of the (probably pre-Pauline) hymn in *Romans* 3:25-26, especially the word translated in the King James Version as "propitiation" (Gr., *hilasterion*), might be taken in that way. But God is the initiator in the atoning death of Christ ("whom God set forth"), and the word is better translated "expiation," as in the Revised Standard Version. This means that the crucifixion was an act of God dealing with and removing sin, the barrier between God and humanity, rather than an act of Christ directed toward God. It is an act of God's reconciling love, directed toward sinful humanity (*Rom.* 5:8). Through it God justifies the ungodly (*Rom.* 4:5). *Reconciliation*, like *expiation*, is a word denoting God's activity toward us, rather than Christ's activity toward God. Christ does not reconcile the Father to humanity, as traditional theology has often asserted (see, e.g., article 2 of the 1563 Thirty-nine Articles), rather, "God in Christ was [or, was in Christ] reconciling the world to himself" (*2 Cor.* 5:19). Justification and reconciliation (two slightly different images for the same reality) are expressions of the righteousness of God, a central concept in Paul's thinking about God. Righteousness is both an attribute and an activity of God; it is God's action of judging and saving.

A writing on the fringe of the Pauline corpus, not by Paul himself, is the *Letter to the Hebrews*, which interprets the saving act of God in Christ in terms of Christ as the high priest. Once again, this author is careful not to drive a wedge between God and Christ. As high priest, Christ does not offer a sacrifice to God for the purpose of propitiation. Rather, the Son offers his life in perfect obedience to the Father (*Heb.* 10:5-10) in order to make purification for sin. As in Paul, the object of Christ's deed is not God, but sin.

The Incarnation and the Being of Christ. All levels of tradition in the New Testament examined thus far speak of Christ's relation to God in functional terms. He is commissioned, called, and sent as divine agent. God is present with and in him and active through him. These biblical traditions do not raise the question about Jesus' personal identity in relation to God. There is no discussion of Jesus' "divinity" or of his "divine nature" in the earliest sources; these are Greek rather than Hebrew concepts. But given the exalted status of Jesus, which the Christian community believed him to have received at Easter, it was inevitable that the question of Jesus' identity would eventually be raised, especially by the Greek-speaking world. Such reflection initially employed the concept of the divine wisdom to elucidate the revelatory work of Jesus. Historically, Jesus had appeared as a spokesman for the divine wisdom, using the speech forms of the wisdom tradition as these are seen, for example, in *Proverbs*. The

> **Jesus speaks as one fully conscious of personal preincarnate existence within the being of God.**

content of Jesus' wisdom utterances contained an implicit claim that he was wisdom's last and definitive spokesman; this view is drawn out explicitly in the Q material (*Mt.* 11:25-27 and Q parallel). Matthew himself even identifies Jesus with wisdom, although in a functional rather than ontological sense (*Mt.* 11:28-30; cf. *Sir.* 24:25, 51:23-24).

In first-century Judaism, however, the concept of God's wisdom was advancing beyond the stage of poetical personification of an aspect of God's activity, toward a hypostatization (i. e., an attribution of distinct, concrete existence) of an aspect of the being of God. As such, the wisdom of God was an outflow of his being, through which he created the world, became self-revelatory to humanity, called Israel, gave the law, and came to dwell with Israel's notables, such as Abraham, Moses, and the prophets, but this wisdom was constantly rejected by most of the people. In certain hymns in the New Testament (*Phil.* 2:6-11, *1 Cor.* 8:6, *Col.* 1:15-20, *Heb.* 1:1-3) the career and fate of Jesus are linked to this earlier activity of *wisdom* (though the term wisdom itself is not used); a single, continuous subject covers the preincarnate activity of wisdom and the earthly career of Jesus. The result is that Jesus becomes personally identified with the hypostatized wisdom of God. The agent of creation, revelation, and saving activity finally becomes incarnate in Jesus. But this development occurs only in hymnic materials and at this stage is hardly the subject of theological reflection.

Johannine incarnation Christology. The final step toward an incarnation Christology is taken in the Johannine literature, especially in the Fourth Gospel. This gospel is prefaced by the Logos hymn (*Jn.* 1:1-18). *Logos* ("word") was used as a synonym for the divine wisdom in the later wisdom literature. In this hymn *logos* is equated with, yet distinguishable from, the being of God: "In the beginning was the word [*logos*] and the word was with God and the word was God" (*Jn.* 1:1), which we may paraphrase as "God is essentially a self-communicating God. This self-communication was a distinct aspect within God's being, related to him, and partaking in his divine being."

The hymn goes on to speak of the activity of the Logos as the agent of creation, revelation, and redemption and finally states that the Logos became flesh, that is, incarnate (*Jn.* 1:14). There could be no clearer statement of the identity of Jesus of Nazareth with an aspect of the very being of God. In the rest of this gospel, the evangelist sets forth the life of Jesus as the incarnation of the divine wisdom, or Logos. (After *John* 1:14 neither *wisdom* nor *logos* is used in the Fourth Gospel, but imagery from the wisdom/Logos tradition is appropriated, especially in the "I am" sayings.) Jesus speaks as one fully conscious of personal preincarnate existence within the being of God. It is significant, however, that this new "high" christological language does not replace the "lower" Christology, which speaks in terms of call, commission, and the response of obedience. Apparently John understands his "higher" Christology to be an interpretation of the "lower," refraining from abandoning the terms in which the pre-Easter Jesus spoke and acted. Much of later traditional church Christology has ignored the presence of these two levels in *John* and has rewritten the earthly life of Jesus exclusively in terms of the "higher" Christology.

Is Jesus God? Only very cautiously and gradually does the New Testament use the predicate God for Jesus. First, there are possible examples in some Pauline doxologies (e.g., *Rom.* 9:5), although there are problems of text, punctuation, and grammar that make it difficult to decide whether in such passages Paul actually does equate Jesus with God. Then the *Letter to the Hebrews* transfers Old Testament passages which speak of Yahveh-Kurios (Lord) to Christos-Kurios (e.g., *Heb.* 1:10). Only the Johannine writings directly and unquestionably predicate the deity of Christ. First, he is the incarnation of the Logos which was God. Then, according to the now generally accepted reading, he is the "only-begotten God" during his incarnate life (*Jn.* 1:18). Finally, Thomas greets the risen Christ as "my Lord and my God" (*Jn.* 20:28). Then *1 John* sums it up by predicating God as the preexistent, incarnate, and exalted one in a summary formula: ". . . in his Son Jesus Christ. This is the true God and eternal life" (*1 Jn.* 5:20). Thus the New Testament can occasionally speak of Jesus as God, but always in a carefully nuanced way: he is not God-as-God-is-in-himself, but the incarnation of that aspect of the being of God which is God-going-out-of-himself-in-self-communication. [*For discussion of incarnation in various religious traditions, see* Incarnation.]

The Trinity. There is a triadic structure in the Christian experience of God. Through the power of the Holy Spirit, believers know Jesus Christ as the revelation of God the Father. This experience becomes crystallized in triadic formulas (*2 Cor.* 13:14, *Mt.* 28:19) or in unreflected theological statements (*1 Cor.* 12:4-6). But there is no attempt to work out a doctrine of the Trinity, or to integrate the Old Testament Jewish faith in the oneness of God with the Christian three-fold experience. Like the doctrine of the incarnation, this was left to the post-New Testament church. [*For discussion of the development of Christian doctrines concerning God, see* Trinity *and* Theology.]

BIBLIOGRAPHY

Bornkamm, Günther. *Jesus of Nazareth.* New York, 1960. Not a life of Jesus, but a presentation of those dimensions of his message and career that can be critically reconstructed. The chapter entitled "The Will of God" (pp. 96-152) draws out Jesus' teaching on God.

Bultmann, Rudolf. *Theology of the New Testament.* 2 vols. in 1. New York, 1951-1955. The classic work of the leading New Testament scholar of the century. Especially serviceable in reconstructing the monotheistic preaching of the Hellenistic Jewish-Christian community aside from Paul; see vol. 1, pp. 63-92.

Dunn, James D. G. *Christology in the Making: A New Testament Inquiry into the Origins of the Doctrine of the Incarnation.* Philadelphia, 1980. An investigation of all possible lines of development of preexistence-incarnation Christology in the New Testament. Dunn finds this type of Christology exclusively in the Johannine writings. In keeping with the more usual scholarly view I have located such Christology in those earlier christological hymns which indentify Christ as the incarnation of preexistent wisdom.

Hamerton-Kelly, Robert. *God the Father: Theology and Patriarchy in the Teaching of Jesus.* Philadelphia, 1979. Particularly concerned with the viability of the Father image in a postpatriarchal culture.

Lampe, G. W. H. *God as Spirit: The Bampton Lectures of 1976.* Oxford, 1977. The last work of this major British biblical scholar and theologian. Lampe finds the distinctively biblical view of God in the concept of God as Spirit. Jesus is for him the final human bearer of the Spirit but is not ontologically identical with an aspect of the divine being.

Martin, Ralph P., and Peter Toon, eds. *Reconciliation: A Study of Paul's Theology.* Atlanta, 1981. Investigates the leading themes of Paul's doctrine of salvation with special concentration on the passages dealing with reconciliation. Martin stresses that atonement is something done by God in Christ for humanity, not by Christ to God.

REGINALD H. FULLER

God in Postbiblical Judaism

The Rabbinic Approach. Rabbinic thought as contained in the Talmud and the Midrash is unsystematic in presentation. While there is an abundance of references in these sources to the nature of God and his relationship to man and the world, the statements are general responses to particular stimuli, not precise, theological formulations. It is consequently imprecise to speak of the rabbinic doctrine of God, even though the expression is used by some scholars. The Talmud and Midrash are the record of the teachings of many hundreds of individuals, each with his own temperament and disposition, as these individuals reflected on God's dealings with the Jewish people. Nevertheless, on the basic ideas about God there is total agreement. All of the rabbis are committed to the propositions that God is One, creator of heaven and earth; that he wishes all men to pursue justice and righteousness; that he rewards those who obey his will and punishes those who disobey; and that he has chosen the Jewish people from all the nations to give them his most precious gift, the Torah.

From an early period, the tetragrammaton, *YHVH*, was never pronounced by Jews as it is written because it is God's own, special name, too holy to be uttered by human mouth. The name *Adonai* ("my lord") was substituted as a euphemism with regard to which a degree of familiarity was allowed.

The two most frequently found names for God in the Talmud are *Ribbono shel `olam* ("Lord of the universe"), used when addressing God in the second person, and *ha-Qadosh barukh hu'* ("the Holy One, blessed be he"), used when speaking of God in the third person (B. T., *Ber.* 4a, 7a, and very frequently).

It is incorrect, however, to think of these names as implying the transcendence and immanence of God. Abstract terms of this nature are entirely foreign to rabbinic thinking. The description of God as king is ubiquitous in the rabbinic literature with antecedents in the Bible. This metaphor is also founded on the rabbis' experiences of earthly rulers. God is the divine king whose laws must be obeyed. When he is stern to punish evildoers, he is said to be seated on his throne of judgment. When he is gracious to pardon, he is said to be seated on his throne of mercy (B. T., `*A. Z.* 3b).

Especially after the dispersal of many Jews from the Holy Land and the destruction of the Temple in 70 CE, the idea, found only sporadically in the Bible, that God shares human suffering, grieving with the victims of oppression, was deepened by the rabbis. Whenever Israel is in exile, they taught, the Shekhinah is in exile with them (B. T., *Meg.* 29a). The idea that God is affected by human degradation is applied even to a criminal executed for his crimes. The Shekhinah is said to be distressed at such a person's downfall (*San.* 6.5).

Both idolatry and dualism were strongly condemned by the rabbis. The twice-daily reading of the Shema` ("Hear O Israel, the Lord our God, the Lord is One," *Dt.* 6:4), Israel's declaration of faith in God's unity, was introduced at least as early as the first century BCE, probably in order to constantly reject the dualistic ideas prevalent in the Near East. The third-century Palestinian teacher Abbahu, in a polemic evidently directed against both Christian beliefs and dualism, expounded the verse: "I am the first, and I am the last, and beside Me there is no God" (*Is.* 44:6). His interpretation is 'I am the first,' for I have no father; 'and I am the last,' for I have no son; 'and beside me there is no God,' for I have no brother" (*Ex. Rab.* 29.5).

In rabbinic Judaism there is little denial that the legitimate pleasures of the world are God's gift to man, who must give thanks to God when they are enjoyed. In one passage it is even said that a man will have to give an account to God for his rejection of what he is allowed to enjoy (J. T., *Qid.* 4.12, 66d). Yet the emphasis is on spiritual bliss in the hereafter, when man, as a reward for his efforts in this life, will enjoy the nearness of God forever.

The Philosophical Approach. Unlike the Talmudic rabbis, the medieval thinkers presented their ideas on God in a systematic way. Pascal's distinction between the God of Abraham, Isaac, and Jacob and the God of the philosophers generally holds true for the distinction between the rabbinic mode of thinking and that of the medieval theologians. For these theologians, the doctrine that God is One means not only that there is no multiplicity of gods but that God is unique, utterly beyond all human comprehension, and totally different from his creatures, not only in degree but in kind. Moses Maimonides (Mosheh ben Maimon, 1135/8-1204), the most distinguished of the medieval thinkers and the most influential in subsequent Jewish thought, adapts for his purpose the rabbinic saying (B. T., *Ber.* 33b) that to overpraise God is akin to praising a human king for possessing myriads of silver pieces when, in reality, he possesses myriads of gold pieces.

In addition to their discussions regarding God's nature, the medieval thinkers examined God's activity in the finite world, that is, his role as creator and the scope of his providence. That God is the creator of the universe is accepted as axiomatic by all the medieval thinkers, although Gersonides (*Milhamot ha-Shem* 6) is radical here, too, in accepting the

Platonic view of a hylic substance, coeternal with God, upon which God imposes form but does not create. Maimonides (*Guide of the Perplexed* 2.13-15), while at first toying with the Aristotelian idea of the material universe as having the same relation to God as the shadow of a tree to the tree, eventually accepts the traditional Jewish view that God created the world out of nothing. Maimonides' motivation is not only to preserve tradition but to emphasize the otherness of God, whose existence is necessary, whereas that of all created things is contingent.

Like the God of the biblical authors and the rabbis, the God of the medieval thinkers is a caring God whose providence extends over all of his creatures. Both Maimonides (*Guide of the Perplexed* 3.17-18) and Gersonides (*Milhamot ha-Shem* 4) limit, however, God's special providence to humans. For animals there is only a general providence that guarantees the continued existence of animal species, but whether, for instance, this spider catches that fly is not ordained by God but is by pure chance. Yehudah ha-Levi (1075-1141) in his *Kuzari* (3.11) refuses to allow chance to play any role in creation: God's special providence extends to animals as well as to humans.

Sa`adyah Gaon (882-942) anticipated Thomas Aquinas's statement that "nothing that implies a contradiction falls under the scope of God's omnipotence" (*Summa theologiae* 1.25.4). Sa`adyah (*Book of Beliefs and Opinions* 2.13) observes that the soul will not praise God for being able to cause five to be more than ten without adding anything to the former, nor for being able to bring back the day gone by to its original condition.

The Qabbalistic Approach. The qabbalists accepted the arguments of the philosophers in favor of extreme negation of divine attributes. Yet they felt the need, as mystics, to have a relationship with the God of living religion, not with a cold abstraction. In the theosophical scheme worked out by the qabbalists, a distinction is drawn between God as he is in himself and God in manifestation. God as he is in himself is Ein Sof ("no end, i. e., the limitless"), the impersonal ground of being who emerges from concealment in order to become manifest in the universe. From Ein Sof there is an emanation of ten *sefirot* ("spheres"; sg., *sefirah*), the powers of potencies of the godhead in manifestation, conceived of as a dynamic organism. Of Ein Sof nothing whatsoever can be said. More extreme than the philosophers in this respect, the qabbalists refuse to allow even negative attributes to be used of Ein Sof, but God in his aspect of manifestation in the *sefirot* can be thought of in terms of positive attributes. The living God of the Bible and of religion is the godhead as manifested in the sefirot. Ein Sof, on the other hand, is only hinted at in the Bible since complete silence alone is permissible of this aspect of deity. A later qabbalist went further to hold that, strictly speaking, even to use such a negative term as

Ein Sof is improper (see I. S. Ratner, *Le-or ha-Qabbalah*, Tel Aviv, 1961, p. 39, n. 40).

The *sefirot* represent various aspects in the life of the godhead, for instance, wisdom, justice, and mercy. These are combined in a very complex order, and through them the worlds beneath, including the finite, material universe, are controlled, the whole order conceived as a great chain of being from the highest to the lowest reaching back to Ein Sof. There is a male principle in the realm of *sefirot* and a female principle, a highly charged mythological concept that opponents of Qabbalah, medieval and modern, considered to be a foreign, verging on the idolatrous, importation into Judaism (see *responsa* of Yitshaq ben Sheshet Perfet, *Rivash*, edited by I. H. Daiches, New York, 1964, no. 157, and S. Rubin, *Heidenthum und Kabbala,* Vienna, 1893).The sacred marriage between these two means that there is complete harmony on high, and the divine grace can flow through all creation. But the flow of the divine grace depends upon the deeds of man, since he is marvelously fashioned in God's image. Thus in the qabbalistic scheme God has made his purposes depend for their fulfillment on human conduct; in this sense it is not only man who needs God but God who needs man.

> But the flow of the divine grace depends upon the deeds of man, since he is marvelously fashioned in God's image.

The eighteenth-century mystical movement of Hasidism, particularly the more speculative branch of the movement known as Habad, tended toward a panentheistic understanding of the idea of *tsimtsum. Tsimtsum* does not really take place, since the Infinite is incapable of suffering limitation, but *tsimtsum* represents no more than a screening of the divine light so that finite creatures might appear to enjoy separate existence. The only true reality is God. There is a basic difference between this panentheistic ("all is in God") or acosmic view and that of pantheism ("all is God"). In the pantheistic thought of Barukh Spinoza (1632-1676), God is the name given to the totality of things. God is the universe and the universe is God. In Habad thought, without God there could be no universe, but without the universe God would still be the unchanging same; in fact, God is the unchanging same even after the creation of the universe, since from God's point of view there is no universe. The traditionalist rabbis and communal leaders, the *mitnaggedim* ("opponents"), saw the Hasidic view as rank heresy. For them the verse that states that the whole earth is filled with God's glory (*Is.* 6:3) means only that God's providence extends over all and that his glory can be discerned through its manifestation in the world. Speculative Hasidism understands the verse to mean that there is only God's glory as an ultimate.

Modern Approaches. Modern Jewish thinkers have been obliged to face the challenges to traditional theism provided by modern thought. The rise of modern science tended to favor mechanistic philosophies of existence and, in more recent years, both linguistic philosophy and existentialism, in their different ways, cast suspicion on all metaphysics. Although the Jew did not begin to participate fully in Western society and to assimilate Western patterns of thought until the end of the eighteenth century, modern Jewish thinkers have been influenced by all of these trends in Western thought, compelling them to rethink the traditional views concerning God. The result has been an espousal of differing attitudes toward theism, from a reaffirmation of the traditional to a radical transformation in naturalistic terms. In any event, the vocabulary used since, by both the traditionalists and the nonconformists, is that of modern thought, even when it is used to interpret the tradition.

Among twentieth-century Jewish thinkers, Mordecai Kaplan (1881-1983) is the most determined of the naturalists. For Kaplan and his disciples God is not a supernatural, personal being but the power in the universe that makes for righteousness. Kaplan maintains that people really were referring to this power when they spoke of God, even though, in the prescientific age, they expressed their belief in terms of a supreme being, the creator of the world who exercises care over it.

Martin Buber (1878-1965), the best-known of Jewish religious existentialists, stresses, on the contrary, the personal aspect of deity. In Buber's thought, when man has an I-Thou relationship to his fellows and to the world in general, he meets in dialogue the Thou of God. While the medieval thinkers devoted a significant part of their thought to reasoning about God's nature, Buber rejects such speculations as futile, cosmic talk, irrelevant to the life of faith. God cannot be spoken about, but he can be met as a person by persons.

Avraham Yitshaq Kook (1865-1935), the first chief rabbi of Palestine, is completely traditional in his concept of God but accepts the theory of evolution, which, as a qabbalist, he believed to be in full accord with the qabbalistic view. The whole of the universe is on the move, and man is rising to ever greater heights ultimately to meet God.

More than any other event, the Holocaust, in which six million Jews perished, compelled Jewish religious thinkers to examine again the doctrine that God is at work in human history. Efforts of medieval thinkers like Yehudah ha-Levi and Maimonides to account for evil in God's creation were, for many, totally inadequate to explain away the enormity of the catastrophe. Some contemporary thinkers invoke the idea found in the ancient sources that there are times when the face of God is hidden, when God surrenders his universe to chance if not to chaos and conceals himself because

mankind has abandoned him. There is a reluctance, however, to explore such ideas, since they appear to condemn those who were destroyed, laying the blame, to some extent, at the door of the victims. The free-will defense has also been invoked by contemporary thinkers, both Jewish (e.g., Avraham Yitshaq Kook, Milton Steinberg) and non-Jewish (e.g., John Hick). For man to be free and exercise his choice in freedom to meet his God, the world must be a place in which naked evil is possible, even though the price might seem too high.

BIBLIOGRAPHY

There are three works of general Jewish theology in which the Jewish doctrine of God is discussed with full bibliographical references for further study. *Jewish Theology Systematically and Historically Considered* (1918) by Kaufmann Kohler, with new material by Joseph L. Blau (New York, 1968), is a pioneering work but now dated and heavily influenced by Protestant thought of the first decades of the twentieth century. *Jewish Theology: A Historical and Systematic Interpretation of Judaism and Its Foundations* by Samuel S. Cohon (Assen, 1971) and my *A Jewish Theology* (New York, 1973) are more adequate in that they consider more recent trends in theological thought.

On the rabbinic views, *The Old Rabbinic Doctrine of God* by Arthur Marmorstein (1927; reprint, New York, 1968) is a detailed examination of the names of God in rabbinic literature by an expert in this literature. George Foot Moore's *Judaism in the First Centuries of the Christian Era, the Age of Tannaim,* 3 vols. in 2 (1927-1930; reprint, Cambridge, Mass., 1970), contains much information, by a non-Jewish scholar, on early rabbinic discussions of God and his relationship to Israel. *Aspects of Rabbinic Theology* by Solomon Schechter (New York, 1961) is a well-written and scholarly treatment of the subject. There is also a good deal of material in *A Rabbinic Anthology,* edited by C. G. Montefiore and Herbert Loewe (1938; reprint, Philadelphia, 1960), in which a Reform and an Orthodox Jew also debate their differing attitudes to the rabbinic formulations. Occasionally this discussion tends to shade off into apologetics and must be used with a degree of caution.

No work exists devoted specifically to God in medieval Jewish philosophy, but the subject is treated extensively in two histories: *A History of Mediaeval Jewish Philosophy* by Isaac Husik (New York, 1916) and *Philosophies of Judaism: The History of Jewish Philosophy from Biblical Times to Franz Rosenzweig* by Julius Guttmann, translated by David W. Silverman (New York, 1964). For Maimonides' thought on the subject the indispensable work is his *Guide of the Perplexed,* translated with an introduction by Shlomo Pines (Chicago, 1963). On the doctrine of God in qabbalistic literature and in Hasidism the essential work is the classic *Major Trends in Jewish Mysticism* by Gershom Scholem (1941; reprint, New York, 1961).

For useful summaries of modern thinkers on God three works can be recommended. *Anatomy of Faith* by Milton Steinberg, edited by Arthur A. Cohen (New York, 1960), compares modern Jewish thought on God with Christian thought. *Modern Philosophies of Judaism* by Jacob B. Agus (New York, 1941) is an excellent examination of the thought of Buber, Rosenzweig, Kaplan, and other modern Jewish thinkers. My *Jewish Thought Today* (New York, 1970) is an annotated anthology with a section on God.

LOUIS JACOBS

God in Postbiblical Christianity

There was during the early centuries of the Christian era a great divide. On one side were those classical religious thinkers who continued to reflect on God in strictly philosophical ways, trusting their reason to suffice. This tradition reached its apex in Neoplatonism. On the other side were those who accepted the authority of Jewish (supplemented later by Christian or Islamic) scriptures, correlating the ideas found there with the fruits of reason.

Justin Martyr provides an early picture of how Christians understood the relation of their doctrine of God to the wider culture. He reports that he sought knowledge of God from philosophy with little success. A Christian then persuaded him that the human mind lacks the power to grasp the truth of God and that one must begin with what God has revealed. Accordingly, Justin turned to the Hebrew scriptures, read now through Christian eyes, and found there what he wanted.

The matter primarily in dispute was the content of divine activity in relation to humankind, what God had done, was doing, and would do. To be a Christian was to affirm that the God of whom the Hebrew scriptures speak had acted in Jesus for the redemption of the world. This conviction expressed itself in the doctrine of incarnation, and it was this doctrine that most distinguished Christian thought from Jewish and philosophical ideas. While the church insisted that what was incarnate was truly God, it did not simply identify what was incarnate with the one whom Jesus called "Father." Instead, following the prologue in the *Gospel of John,* the Word (or Son) who was with God and who was God was the incarnated one. This required a distinction within the one God. Even so, the church lacked a conceptuality that could show how the Word could both be one with God and become incarnate in Jesus without diminution of Jesus' humanity; and so the assertion, unsupported by intelligible conceptuality, became a "mystery."

Although there was broad consensus that all things derive from God, there were alternative images of the relationship between God and the world. One image emphasized creation as an external act of will. The world is envisaged as coming into being by divine fiat out of nothing. Another image, which envisioned the world as the outworking of the dynamism of the divine life, found its clearest expression in Plotinus's doctrine of emanation. Insofar as this image implied that the world was made of divine substance, it was rejected by the church, but some of its language remained influential. A third image was that of participation, wherein God is seen as perfect being, and creatures are thought to exist as they participate in this being in a creaturely way. A fourth image was that of inclusion, according to which God is the "uncontained, who contains all things" *(Preaching of Peter).*

The Platonic influence on developing Christian beliefs encouraged a correlation between the human intellect and God. A related concept held that the human soul or mind possessed a kinship with God that was lacking to the body. Such ideas encouraged intellectualistic mysticism and bodily asceticism. The Christian struggle to overcome this dualism can be traced from the fourth-century Cappadocians through the fourteenth-century Greek-speaking church. It required both the denial that God is of the order of thought or idea and the rejection of a further development in the thought of Plotinus, which located God as the One beyond thought who could be reached only through thought. At the same time it required the clarification of how human beings could have real communion with God by grace.

The impact of Platonic philosophy in Western thought of God took a different turn chiefly because of Augustine of Hippo. He understood the essence of God to be all that which is common to the persons of the Trinity. God is truth itself, which is at once goodness itself. As the sun is the source of light by which our eyes see the visible world, so God is the source of illumination of the mind by which it sees eternal truths.

The Augustinian tradition argues that knowledge of God's existence is already implicitly given in thought. Thomas Aquinas, on the other hand, seeks to lead the mind by inference from what is known through the senses to the affirmation of God as the supreme cause of the world. The emphasis in Thomas's idea of God shifts, accordingly, from that of the illuminator of the mind to the cause of the existence and motion of all creaturely things.

Thomas subordinated the divine will to the divine wisdom. That is, God wills what is good. In this doctrine, his thought followed that of the church fathers, including Augustine. God remains for Thomas, as for them, the One, the True, and the Good. But there were others for whom this Platonic way of thinking ceased to be convincing, for whom there were no truth and goodness existing in themselves and attracting the human mind and will; they asserted that God is much more the efficient cause of natural motion, that God is free agent, bound to nothing, and, in short, that God is almighty will, determining thereby what is true and good. This voluntaristic emphasis is associated with the rise of medieval nominalism, influenced especially by William of Ockham. Nominalism is the doctrine that universals are names given to certain things. These universals have no existence in themselves. Furthermore, since there is an element of arbitrariness in how we name things, human choice and decision are accented instead of discernment of what is objectively there for the mind to discover. This doctrine entails the theory that God alone chooses what to require of human beings and what to do for them. What God has chosen cannot be learned by human reason; it can only be revealed by God.

During the Renaissance a new wave of Platonic influence gave rise to the Hermetic tradition, which emphasized the mathematical character of the world, the power of movement immanent in things, and the interrelatedness of human thought with these things. The divine was perceived as indwelling power rather than as transcendent will. The voluntaristic tradition had earlier separated revelation from the support of reason and encouraged an authoritarian spirit; the Hermetic tradition, too, separated reason from revelation, but encouraged instead a critique of hierarchical structures in church and society. Together they paved the way for modern philosophy in the seventeenth century, whereupon there ended definitively the unity of theology and philosophy that had dominated Western thought for more than a thousand years.

In the eighteenth century the chief issue was whether God, having established natural laws, ever acted contrary to them. All agreed that God was supernatural. The issue was whether God caused supernatural events in the created world, that is, whether miracles occurred. Orthodox Christians held that the biblical accounts of miracles were true, whereas the Deists held that natural law was perfect and that therefore God did not violate it.

Reflection about God on the European continent in the nineteenth and early twentieth centuries was shaped by the critical philosophy of Immanuel Kant. Kant points out that in addition to the sphere of theoretical reason there is another sphere of practical reason, which deals with how people should act. In this sphere, too, the fundamental moral principle is independent of theology. People should act always according to maxims that they can will to be universal princi-

> **The impact of Platonic philosophy in Western thought of God took a different turn chiefly because of Augustine of Hippo.**

ples. For example, if one cannot will that people in general lie, cheat, or steal whenever it is to their personal advantage to do so, then one ought not to lie, cheat, or steal for one's own advantage. This principle—the "categorical imperative"—holds whether or not God exists.

Although few have followed the exact way in which Kant correlated God with ethics, many have agreed that belief in God belongs with ethics rather than with science. Later in the nineteenth century Albrecht Ritschl was to found a neo-Kantian school, which interpreted theology as statements about values rather than about facts. God is that which is supremely valuable, not a being about whose existence it is suitable to argue.

The most influential theologian of the twentieth century was Karl Barth. He denied, more radically than the Protestant reformers, that God can be known by human reason. We are entirely dependent, Barth maintained, on God's self-revelation, who is Jesus Christ. This revelation is known only in the scriptural witness to him. Central to what is revealed of God is radical, sovereign, dynamic freedom. We can lay no claims on God and make no judgments about how God will act except as we lay hold on the divine promises and the divine self-disclosure.

> **Much of the debate about God is a debate about what we most admire and most desire to emulate.**

The appearance soon after World War II of the writings of Dietrich Bonhoeffer from a Nazi jail struck a responsive chord in those already uncomfortable with Barth's theology. The ideas sketched in these writings indicate a quite different way of thinking of God. "Only a powerless God," Bonhoeffer wrote, "can help." It is the Crucified One rather than the all-determining Lord who can speak to suffering humanity

Although few have followed Bonhoeffer's rhetoric of divine powerlessness, there has been considerable new reflection on the nature of God's power. Alfred North Whitehead held that God's power is persuasive rather than coercive. That this was true with respect to human beings had long been taught—for example, by Augustine. But in Whitehead's view, to exist at all is to have some measure of self-determination. Hence God's relation to all creatures is persuasive. Wolfhart Pannenberg argues that God is to be thought of as the Power of the Future. God is not now extant as one being alongside others making up the given reality, but rather that which will be all in all. Pannenberg argues that all creative realization in the present comes into being from this divine future. Hence God remains all-determinative, but the mode of this determination is quite different from that against which people have protested for the sake of human freedom. Instead it is God's determination of the present that makes us free.

The association of God with the future, building on the eschatological language of the New Testament, has had other supporters. Whereas for Pannenberg it has ontological meaning, for J. B. Metz and Jürgen Moltmann it is associated with a "political theology," which locates salvation primarily in the public historical realm. It is also central to the "liberation theology" of Rubem Alves, Gustavo Gutierrez, Juan Segundo, and other Latin Americans. These German and Latin American theologians argue that God's will is not expressed in the present structures of society or in some romanticized past, but rather in the promise of something quite different. Hence, the overwhelming tendency of religion to justify and even sanctify existing patterns, or to encourage nostalgia for a lost paradise, is opposed by the prophetic challenge in view of the hoped-for future.

Among these theologians, the image of God has been more important than the concept. Indeed, recognition of the difference between image and concept and of the great importance of image has played a large role in recent thought about God. Blacks then need to image God as black to claim their human and religious identity.

Similarly, although theologians have insisted that God is beyond gender, feminists have had no difficulty showing that the Christian image of God is overwhelmingly male: whereas God's whiteness is clearly not biblical and is rightly rejected in the name of the Bible, God's maleness is biblical. Hence the denial of maleness to God requires a radical approach to scripture. Furthermore, the characteristics attributed to God by even those theologians who have rejected anthropomorphism have usually been stereotypically masculine ideals: omnipotence, impassibility, self-sufficiency. Feminists challenge this whole theological tradition. They divide between those, such as Mary Daly, who believe that the Christian God is inherently and necessarily patriarchal, and hence incompatible with women's liberation, and those, such as Rosemary Ruether and Letty Russell, who believe that the Christian deity is a liberator who can free us also from patriarchalism.

The diversity of interests that lead to reflection on God witnesses to the continuing importance of the topic. It also produces great confusion. It is not clear that different statements using the word *God* have, any longer, a common topic. In the Christian context, however, one can almost always understand that, despite all the diversity of concepts and imagery, *God* refers to what Christians worship and trust. Further—with a few exceptions, such as Edgar S. Brightman and William James—God is associated with perfection. Part of the confusion lies in the changing ideal. Whereas for many centuries it seemed self-evident to most Christians that the perfect must be all-determining, affected by nothing external to itself, timeless, and completely self-sufficient, that supposition is no longer so evident today. Much of the debate about God is a debate about what we most admire and most desire to emulate.

[*See also* Theology]

BIBLIOGRAPHY

Collins, James D. *God in Modern Philosophy* (1959). Westport, Conn., 1978.

Gilson, Étienne. *History of Christian Philosophy in the Middle Ages.* New York, 1955.

Grant, Robert M. *The Early Christian Doctrine of God.* Charlottesville, Va., 1966.

Hartshorne, Charles, and William L. Reese. *Philosophers Speak of God.* Chicago, 1953.

Lossky, Vladimir. *The Vision of God.* Clayton, Wis., 1963.

Prestige, George L. *God in Patristic Thought* (1936). London, 1952.

Wolfson, Harry A. *From Philo to Spinoza: Two Studies in Religious Philosophy.* New York, 1977.

Zahrnt, Heinz. *The Question of God.* New York, 1969.

JOHN B. COBB, JR.

God in Traditional Muslim Religious Thought

From a sociophenomenological viewpoint, in every revealed religion the message written down in the book (or books) held to be sacred has a normative value for the religious thought it generates. Faith, by answering man's religious aspirations, cannot avoid the demands for rationality inherent in the human spirit. Indeed, faith provokes and activates this demand and in so doing positions itself in relation to reason. But in this effort of reflection, the first generations of believers always hesitate, if not refuse, to free themselves from the explicit terms (notions and/or terminology) of the message accepted as revealed. Their work nevertheless retains a preferential and normative value for later generations of believers who would periodically attempt a "return to the source."

Historical Outline of the Problem. The God of the Qur'an is al-`Azim, the Inaccessible (e.g., 2:255, 42:4), well beyond the bounds of human understanding, which cannot limit him in any way or compare him to anything. In his knowledge and by his knowledge alone man cannot reach him "whom one does not question" (21:23; see also 21:110). Consequently, it is not surprising that all the schools devoted long preliminary discussions to what human reason can know of God on its own or on the basis of Qur'anic texts.

The Muslim tradition, always active among the community of believers (the *ummah*), has never ceased to confirm, even to protect, the inaccessibility of God, sometimes to the point of jealousy. The doctors of *kalam (mutakallimun),* or Muslim "theologians," were always obliged to contend with the reticence shown by the "pious elders" or their successors, the traditionists, toward any attempt to justify dogma by purely rational means, and the tension was alternately a source of inspiration and controversy. This reticence, transmitted from one generation to the next within the *ummah,* would manifest itself with particular vigor in Hanbali thought, developed by the great and rigid traditionist Ibn Hanbal (ninth century), whose profession of faith was "The Qur'an and the *sunnah* [Muslim tradition]: that is religion." This tendency would continue to oppose the rationalist or modernist trends that were never totally excluded from Islam any more than from Christianity.

The fundamental reaction of the Muslim faith to the inaccessibility of God and the corresponding intellectual attitude is nonetheless not one of narrow-mindedness or intellectual laziness. On the contrary, it rejects a passive and meaningless acceptance of the revealed message and the facile recourse to *taqlid* (acquiescence to accepted opinions), even though the majority of the Hanabilah make *taqlid* the conscious imitation of the Prophet and his companions, who believed without looking for "proofs." It calls instead for a personal effort of enquiry, but one that is always based on the intangible letter of the Qur'an and on the *sunnah.* The ultimate aim of this quest is always to better align the behavior of the believer to the "correct path" that God wishes him to take (e.g., 1:6-7, 37:118). A remarkable example of this attitude is found in the person of the famous Hanbali Ibn Taymiyah (fourteenth century), whose successors the contemporary "orthodox reformers" claim to be.

The concept of divine inaccessibility, uncompromising and absolute as it may be, does not isolate God in an abstract heaven. It is the expression of a separate and separating transcendence in the sense that the intimate life of God remains a guarded mystery. This does not mean, however, that God is distinct from and indifferent to humans. In studying the Qur'anic preaching on God, have we not seen that every affirmation concerning his existence, his perfections, or his means of action toward his creatures was merely a repetition of the unformulated mystery of divine unity-unicity presented in ever renewed expression through the style and rhythm of Qur'anic Arabic? At the same time, each affirmation communicated to man what he needed to know to glorify God on earth and to be worthy of paradise in the hereafter. Thus Muslim faith creates in the souls of true believers an attitude of total and confident surrender *(islam)* to God, whom they know, on his word, to be a reliable, omnipotent, and benevolent guide (as in surah 93).

In Islam the Qur'an is presented and received as the Word revealed by a God who reveals nothing of himself. God imparts no confidence about his mystery. He "stood in

> **God imparts no confidence about his mystery.**

majesty on the highest horizon" when the Prophet "approached him to within two bow-lengths"—woe to him who attempts to go further, to receive from on high the Qur'anic revelation in its literal form (see 53:1-10). The problems of exegesis *(tafsir)* would consequently take on a singular importance for two basic reasons. On the one hand there was a lack of any doctrinal authority to give the guaranteed meaning of what had been supernaturally "dictated." On the other the problems of exegesis exist in their own right.

How can one understand and interpret the revealed words to grasp the thought of "he who spoke"?

The Existence of the Unique God. According to Qur'anic teaching, man has no excuse for not knowing how to affirm the existence of God. On one hand he carries from birth the mark of the *mithaq* like a seal affixed to his heart. This innate predisposition to Islam, traditionally called *fitrah,* appears as a kind of primordial natural religion that finds its fulfillment only in *shahadah.* On the other, "in creation . . . there are truly signs for those who have intelligence" (3:190-191). This does not mean that faith is merely the outcome of a process of metaphysical reasoning using the principle of causality and the analogousness of being to arrive at an Aristotelian "prime mover." Man must learn to recognize the "signs of God" in the "signs of the universe." Faith appears then as a flash of recognition, revitalizing the *mithaq* in the heart of man attracted by the beauties of creation and tempted to go no further in spite of the signs that God has given through them. Man sees the impermanence of the transient world both in and through this dazzling revelation. Muslim thought would always affirm that human reason can and must decipher the "signs of the universe." It would take Abraham's faith as a starting point for a "proof" of God's existence. This was a proof by allusion that, under the influence of Greek thought and logic, would become demonstrative through an argument combining the concept of a beginning in time and that of the contingency of the world (proof *a novitate/a contingentia mundi*).

The Mu'tazili schools taught that, starting from creation, human intelligence can and must rise to the affirmation of God even without the help of a new explicit revelation (the Qur'anic preaching) to make this obligatory. This was to be done by inference, by a dialectic grasp of opposition—an intellectual process that parallels the gift of faith to Abraham but comes about by means of the two-stage reasoning so characteristic of Arab-Muslim thought. The responsibility, or the honor, of giving form to this demonstration of the existence of God *a contingentia mundi* and of giving it a more easily transmitted probative value would fall to the great *falasifah* who had adopted Aristotelian formal logic, such as al-Farabi and Ibn Sina.

The Ash'ari school on the contrary, and al-Ghazali after them, took the position that the (real) capacity of reason can be exercised only if revelation makes this an obligation without which man could not escape the trivialities of the world. For the followers of al-Maturidi reason can in principle exercise this power, but in reality it also requires the authentic signs that the Qur'anic verses constitute: by divine benevolence these correspond to the "signs of the universe" (the same word, *ayat,* designates both "signs"). We can see how such positions, each in its own way, maintain or restore the primacy of Qur'anic teaching over reason (in its approach and its arguments).

The Divine Attributes (Sifat Allah). The appellations and actions ascribed to God by the Qur'anic teaching incited the intelligence of believers to attribute perfections to him. The list of divine attributes was formed even before the birth of the schools of *kalam.* This list would remain effectively unchanged since the *sifat* have, and can have, only one source, the Qur'an. No attribute can be affirmed that is not taught in the Qur'an, either directly or by way of immediate consequence *(tafwid).*

Scholastic disputes would begin with the efforts of the doctors of *kalam* to systematize to some degree the data provided by the Qur'an. These debates would center principally on the meaning of the attributes of God. At the same time they would deal with the reality of the *sifat* and, by extension, the relationship of the latter to the divine essence and/or whether these *sifat* were eternal or not. With time these debates would become increasingly technical and sterile (logic, philology, and so forth) and would lose their appeal even within the Islamic world; consequently I shall allude to them here only in very brief fashion.

1. *Attribute of the essence.* Existence, the attribute consubstantial with the essence, was the positive term expressing the essence without adding any other significance. This was *dhat Allah*, the "self" of God bearing neither comparison with nor analogy to the essence of perishable things. This was his existence *(wujud).*
2. *"Essential" attributes.* These were subdivided into two groups. First came the negative attributes (eternity, everlastingness, dissimilarity from the created, subsistence through himself) that underline divine transcendence and consequently manifest that God has neither equal nor opposite of any sort. Second were the *ma'ani* attributes that "add a concept to the essence." They are not identical to the essence but are not other than it (in a separated or separating way). Some are *'aqliyat,* "rational" (power, will, knowledge, life); the others are *sam'iyat,* "traditional." These latter cannot be grasped by human reason and can only be known by the Qur'anic teaching. Among this group we can mention seeing, hearing, speech, visibility, and perception; their exact meaning has been keenly disputed by the Mu'tazilah and Ash'ariyah.
3. *Attributes of "qualification."* These are the divine names or the *ma'ani* attributes in the verbal form (present participle), such as possessing power, willing, and so forth.
4. *Attributes of action.* These do not intrinsically qualify the essence, but designate what God can do or does not do (creation, command, predetermination, and so on). The schools differed in their view of the relationship of these attributes with knowledge and will; the Ash'ariyah were usually more "voluntarist," the Maturidiyah more "intellectualist."

The "pious elders" had already affirmed several attributes without providing any reasoning, just as they had affirmed the existence of God, both by punctiliously respecting the letter of the Qur'an and by accepting that the divine names were synonyms. However, their fundamentalist attitude with regard to the text of the Qur'an came into conflict with the ambiguities and anthropomorphisms of the *mutashabih* verses. This led them into contradiction, even to the point of being open to the accusation of comparing God to his creatures. Particularly aware of the purity of any affirmation concerning God, the Mu`tazilah, who saw themselves as "the people of justice and *tawhid*," submitted the divine attributes to a severe critique. They rejected by the practice of *tanzih* "distancing" all that evoked the created, supporting themselves by those passages in the Qur'an that invite such an interpretation (e.g., 6:103, 42:9). Finally, this "stripping away" of the attributes *(ta`til)* by a rigorous *via remotionis* tends to weaken the notion of them and to compromise their reality in God. Purified in this way, the attributes exist in God but are identical with the essence. This double affirmation rests on a distinction that can hardly be anything but nominal.

These scholastic disputes can appear tedious, and indeed, they sometimes are. I shall conclude by quoting Louis Massignon's remark at the end of his study on salvation in Islam: "God is not within the reach of man. Man should not be allowed to try to reach God. An abyss separates us from him. Thus emerge the strictness and intransigence of a monotheistic faith among a people to whom prophets have come to remind men that God is separate from them and inaccessible to them. Indeed faith, pure faith, is without doubt the only gift worthy of being offered to him." This is truly what is shown by those pious believers whose submission *(islam)* to the commands of the Law is the basis of a total surrender to God through an act of trust that does not question. [*See also* Free Will and Predestination.]

BIBLIOGRAPHY

Since Qur'anic monotheism lies at the very heart of Islam, it would be most profitable to consult the excellent and comprehensive study of A. J. Wensinck, *The Muslim Creed* (1932; reprint, New York, 1965), or A. S. Tritton's *Muslim Theology* (London, 1947). To deepen Wensinck's synthesis, see my *Dieu et la destinée de l'homme: Les grands problèmes de la théologie musulmane* (Paris, 1967).

On the sources of the Qur'anic faith, see Richard Bell's *Introduction to the Qur'an* (Edinburgh, 1953); and, on the *sunnah*, A. J. Wensinck's *A Handbook of Early Muhammadan Tradition* (1927; reprint, Leiden, 1971). On pre-Islamic monotheism, see the substantial syntheses of W. Montgomery Watt: his article "Hanif" in *The Encyclopaedia of Islam*, new ed., vol. 3 (Leiden, 1971), and his communication "The Qur'an and Belief in a `High God,' " in *Proceedings of the Ninth Congress of the Union Européenne des Arabisants et Islamisants* (Leiden, 1981), edited by Rudolf Peters. On the specific problem of the divine names, see my article "Al-asma' al-husna," in *The Encyclopaedia of Islam*, new ed., vol. 1 (Leiden, 1960); and Jacques Jomier's "Le nom divin *al-Rahman*

dans le Coran," in *Mélanges Louis Massignon*, vol. 2 (Damascus, 1957).

The appearance of the great Muslim theological schools and the elaboration of their problematics are particularly well analyzed by W. Montgomery Watt in *The Formative Period of Islamic Thought* (Edinburgh, 1973), with bibliography. On specific points, see A. J. Wensinck's "Les preuves de l'éxistence de Dieu dans la théologie musulmane," *Mededeelingen der Koninklijke Akademie van Wetenschappen* (Amsterdam) 81 (1936): 41-67; *The Theology of Al-Ash`ari*, edited by Richard J. McCarthy (Beirut, 1953); Henryk S. Nyberg's article "Mu`tazila," in *The Encyclopaedia of Islam* (Leiden, 1934); Richard Walzer's *Greek into Arabic: Essays on Islamic Philosophy* (Cambridge, Mass., 1962), on the *falasifah;* and Joseph van Ess's article "Ibn Kullab," in *The Encyclopaedia of Islam*, supplement to the new edition (Leiden, 1982), a fine example of scholastic debates about divine attributes.

LOUIS GARDET
Translated from French by Richard Scott

GODDESS WORSHIP

An Overview

The scope and antiquity of goddess worship are remarkable. Female sacred images are associated with some of the oldest archaeological evidence for religious expression and they still have efficacy in the contemporary world. Goddess images are depicted in a wide range of forms, from aniconic representations, such as abstract organs of reproduction, to fully elaborated icons decorated with the finery of monarchy. They are linked to all major aspects of life, including birth, initiation, marriage, reproduction, and death. They display the elaborate variegation of religious experiences in different cultural contexts. A historical survey reveals goddess worship to be a continuous phenomenon, despite periodic ebbs and tides during certain critical epochs.

Goddess Worship in the Development of Civilizations.
India. No civilization in the world developed goddess worship so elaborately as did India. Terracotta figurines of mother goddesses have been found in the Indus Valley, dated at 2,500 to 1,500 BCE, along with abstract stone rings representing the yoni and lingam, prototypes for the later god Siva and his female consort. Goddesses rarely functioned separately from male divinities in ancient India. Nor was goddess worship the central theme in the development of Indian civilization except during periodic episodes of florescence. Indeed, the goddess does not appear as a major focus in Indian literature until 600 BCE, in a legend recorded in the *Kena Upanisad*. Not until much later, probably the seventh century CE, did goddess worship emerge as a somewhat separate cult in Hinduism and eventually in Tibetan Buddhism. This Tantric expression of goddess worship was

particularly strong in eastern India where it continues to flourish today, though somewhat less intensely than formerly.

At no point in the development of Indian civilization was goddess worship completely separate from devotion to male deities. The Hindu rajas wielded power through the manipulation of icons of major male deities like Surya, Visnu or Siva. While these gods had female consorts who were worshiped alongside them, goddesses usually played a secondary though by no means unimportant role as images of cultural identity. No doubt at the village level there has been a long, relatively unbroken continuity of goddess worship extending back to Neolithic times. Local village goddesses were besought (as they continue to be today) to increase human fertility, to cause or cure diseases, to bring about good fortune, to enhance the productivity of crops, or to destroy demons. Yet, at the more exalted level of courts and kings, these female deities played a less prominent role. The widely known Hindu goddesses like Sarasvati, Laksmi, and Parvati rarely stand alone. Only Kali and Candi, the more ferocious aspects of female divinity, become focal points for separate worship. Even in these cases the goddess rarely acts as a primary source for establishing the legitimacy of kingship.

The ancient Near East. In the ancient Near East the phenomenon of goddess worship displayed an even more elaborate and subtle set of nuances. Here we encounter several distinct civilizations, some having borrowed heavily from each other. A number of goddesses were prominent in ancient Egypt: Nut, goddess of the sky and consort of the earth god, Geb; the goddess Neith, patroness of victorious weapons and the art of weaving; Isis, goddess of wisdom; and Hathor, another sky goddess who assumed various forms. Some of these goddesses were deeply entwined in the development and continuity of divine kingship. The name *Isis*, for instance, is related linguistically to the term for "chair" or "throne." The throne or "holy seat" of the pharaoh was the "mother of the king." Eventually Isis became universalized as a benevolent goddess of the harvest. Her cult spread from Egypt to Greece and throughout the Roman empire. By 300 BCE the cult of Isis had become a popular mystery religion, with secret initiation rites promising salvation and rebirth.

Another stream in the ancient Near Eastern tradition of goddess worship flows from the Mesopotamian civilization located on the Tigris and Euphrates rivers. In that area the goddess Inanna was worshiped; she was the queen of heaven and earth and the goddess of love, and she was profoundly involved in the rise of Sumerian state-level social organization. Although she was one of many goddesses of ancient Sumer, Inanna outlasted and overshadowed them all. Also known as Ishtar and later worshiped by different Semitic peoples, Inanna had very ancient roots. She was part of an amalgamation of Sumerian and Akkadian religious and political beliefs, extending back to 3000 BCE or possibly

farther, and she is connected to the fertility of crops, the emergence of increasing sedentary patterns of social organization, and the development of the first urban centers.

In the late nineteenth century the world's oldest texts on cuneiform clay tablets were unearthed after having been buried for at least four thousand years. Some of these texts tell the life story of Inanna from adolescence through womanhood and her eventual apotheosis. The texts are extremely rich; they reveal the sexual fears and desires of the goddess, an elaborate history of kinship among various deities in her family tree, her power as queen of Sumer, and her responsibilities for the redistribution of resources and fertility of the earth.

Unlike the female divinities of India and Egypt, the goddess Inanna, who was most likely derived from Neolithic and possibly even earlier Paleolithic roots, played the principal role in the religious tradition of an urban society. She was considered to have equal status with the sky god, An, head of the Sumerian pantheon. In this urban context, Inanna became a focal point for the full emergence of life in city-states, and she assumed the regal responsibility for victory in war and the redistribution of resources among urban peoples. Often these functions have been allotted to male deities in other traditions, as in the case of the Hindu gods Siva and Jagannatha.

Inanna is identified with the Semitic goddess Ishtar and the West Semitic goddess Astarte. These deities, along with the Canaanite goddesses Asherah and Anat (a wrathful warlike deity), were worshiped by the early Hebrew people. We can be certain the early Israelites worshiped the Canaanite

> **In the late nineteenth century the world's oldest texts on cuneiform clay tablets were unearthed after having been buried for at least four thousand years.**

goddess Asherah; even Solomon praised the pillars representing this deity, and his son Rehoboam erected an image of her in the temple at Jerusalem. Probably the female deities of the early monarchic period did not disppear but were changed into different forms, despite repeated efforts to reestablish a strong monotheism in Judaism in the biblical period. Raphael Patai (1967) has argued that various disguises are assumed by the goddess in later Judaism: she appeared in the form of the cherubim (depicted as man and woman in an erotic embrace); in images of Yahveh's wife Astarte; as the one and only God having two aspects, male and female; and in the form of the She-khinah (the personified presence of God on earth). In this latter form, the Shekhinah argues with God in defense of man; she is sometimes manifested as Wisdom and at other times as the Holy Spirit. The feminine element played an important role in qabbalistic thought, especially in the thirteenth-century *Zohar,* which stressed the Shekhinah as female divine entity; she was also referred to there as Matronit ("divine matron"). The Shekhinah was seen as an intermediary between God and the scattered peoples of Israel and was widely accepted in Jewish communities in the fifteenth to eighteenth centuries, when Qabbalah had widely felt influence. According to Patai, the complex concept in Qabbalah that the Shekhinah and God are one, filtered down to the Jewish masses, led to the simplified belief in her as a goddess.

Greece. In Greece, the rebirth theme is found in the Eleusinian mystery cult associated with the earth goddess, Demeter. However, instead of the rebirth of a male deity, a female deity is reborn: Demeter's daughter, Persephone, is resurrected after her abduction by Hades, lord of the underworld. The pre-Olympian goddesses of Greece were usually connected to vegetation rituals. A prime example was Gaia, earth mother and chthonic mother of the gods. This deity was associated with the oracle at Delphi before the oracle became exclusively Apollo's. Her rituals included animal sacrifices, offerings of grain and fruit, and ecstatic possession trance. Many of the later Greek goddesses emerged from pre-Hellenic earth goddesses like Gaia. The famous twelve deities of Olympus included the goddesses Hera, Athena, Aphrodite, Hestia, Artemis, and Demeter. These Olympian goddesses were each given distinct roles to play in accordance with their earlier spheres of influence. The original chthonic aspects of these goddesses were diminished as they became subordinated in the Olympian hierarchy ruled by Zeus. No longer was each goddess an organic link to the generative forces of life and death. Instead, she became highly compartmentalized in her new role in the male-dominated Olympian pantheon. This compartmentalization demarcates a transformation in the role of goddess worship in the development of Greek civilization.

Rome. There was a strong identification of Greek deities with Roman deities. Most Greek goddesses had their Roman counterparts. In 204 BCE Roman aristocrats officially adopted the foreign cult of the Anatolian goddess Cybele, later to be known as the Magna Mater (Great Mother). On 4 April of that year the image of the goddess was carried into the city by Roman matrons, a temple was erected, and she was installed as a national Roman deity. Only self-castrated foreign priests were allowed to serve in the temples dedicated to Cybele, because Roman citizens were forbidden to be priests until the reign of Emperor Claudius (41-54 CE). Driven by Cybele, his angry mother, Attis died of self-castration and then returned to life in response to his mother's intense mourning. This death and rebirth theme was celebrated during a series of holidays at the beginning of spring; the rituals included a procession carrying a pine tree (representing the dead Attis) into the temple of the Magna Mater, violent ritual mourning, a celebration of the rebirth of Attis, and the bathing of Cybele's statue.

China and Japan. The Vajrayana tradition of Tantric Buddhism in Tibet and Mongolia is widely associated with goddess worship. Male and female manifestations of the divine power are depicted as opposite but complementary aspects of each other. This dynamic tension of male and female principles, derived from Tantric Hinduism, has resulted in a large number of goddesses who are intimately related to their male counterparts as consorts. Some goddesses, however, retain a certain degree of autonomy and represent independent deities. This is the case of the goddess Tara, a female *bodhisattva* who became a universal protectress. In Chinese Pure Land Buddhism, Kuan-yin, goddess of mercy, is also considered to be a *bodhisattva.* She is a principal teacher, a savior who can give her devotees assurance of enlightenment and carry believers to the western paradise of O-mi-t`o-fo's Pure Land. This goddess continues to be worshiped throughout China and in Japanese Buddhism.

The tradition of goddess worship is well established in Japan, not only in Buddhism, but also in Japanese Shinto, where many male and female nature deities are propitiated. In Shinto the world was created by a divine creator couple, the god Izanagi and the goddess Izanami. They gave birth to the sun goddess Amaterasu and her brother Susano-o no Mikoto, god of storms, along with other nature deities. Amaterasu eventually became the cult deity of the Japanese royal family, retaining both her Shinto function as sun goddess and a new role as Shining Buddha of Heaven. Until this century the emperor of Japan was considered to be the descendant on earth of Amaterasu. He was charged to keep peace in the world and to support her major pilgrimage shrine, located at Ise.

This survey of archaic goddess worship points to the diversity of the roles goddess worship has played in the development of civilizations. In some parts of the world goddesses were central in the emergence of urbanism and kingship. Elsewhere they were secondary consorts of male divinities or vestiges of mystery cults associated with earlier shamanistic religion. Sometimes they represented a continuity with Neolithic and Paleolithic traditions or were transposed and reconceived as the bearers of complex social organization—waging warfare, presiding over the collection of taxes and controlling the redistribution of resources. The emergence of virtually every major civilization was associated in some way with goddess worship. While there may not be a single "Great Goddess" worshiped universally, the ubiquity of the phenomenon remains unbroken from Paleolithic times.

BIBLIOGRAPHY

Bhardwaj, Surinder Mohan. *Hindu Places of Pilgrimage in India.* Berkeley, 1973. This excellent survey of pilgrimage cycles in North India conducted by a cultural geographer offers many insights into the contrast between pilgrimages to the shrines of male and female deities.

Campbell, Joseph. *The Masks of God*, vol. 1, *Primitive Mythology.* New York, 1959. This work explores the early Upper Paleolithic and Neolithic roots of goddess worship. It represents a Jungian orientation suggesting a universal Great Goddess. Somewhat dated but useful as a secondary source if read critically.

Campbell, Joseph. *The Masks of God*, vol. 2, *Oriental Mythology.* New York, 1962. This work refers frequently to goddess worship in Eastern religious traditions. Much generalization here, but still useful.

Gimbutas, Marija. *The Goddesses and Gods of Old Europe, 7000-3500 B. C.: Myths, Legends, and Cult Images.* London, 1982. An extensive discussion of the art and symbolism of Old Europe for the Neolithic period.

James, E. O. *The Cult of the Mother Goddess.* New York, 1959. A thorough discussion of goddess worship derived from archaeological and documentary evidence for the Middle East, the eastern Mediterranean, and India. An excellent source, although some of the interpretation is dated.

Leach, Edmund. *Virgin Birth.* Cambridge, 1966. The Henry Myers Lecture.

Marshack, Alexander. *The Roots of Civilization.* New York, 1972. An outstanding analysis of Upper Paleolithic data on goddess worship, suggesting that the phenomenon is part of a complex notational system rather than merely an indication of fertility symbolism. While Marshack's thesis may be controversial, the volume is a rich source of information and remains a major scholarly contribution.

Mellaart, James. *Earliest Civilizations of the Near East.* London, 1965. A discussion of archaeological research on the Near East with particular emphasis on the emergence of Neolithic cultures. Mother goddesses are discussed throughout the volume, particularly at the famous site of Çatal Hüyük.

Mellaart, James. *Çatal Hüyük: A Neolithic Town in Anatolia.* New York, 1967. This is the field report of an archaeologist who excavated a major Neolithic town in 1961-1963. The data presented here constitute an important contribution to our understanding of goddess worship in the Neolithic period. At the level of interpretation, the author tends to oversimplify, attributing much of the evidence for goddess worship to a fertility cult.

Obeyesekere, Gananath. *The Cult of the Goddess Pattini.* Chicago, 1984. In this classic study of the goddess cult in Sri Lanka, the author has brought to bear a number of disciplines—anthropology, psychoanalysis, and ethnohistory—to reveal the complex, multifaceted manifestation of goddess worship in Sinhalese religion.

Olson, Carl, ed. *The Book of the Goddess, Past and Present: An Introduction to Her Religion.* New York, 1983. This is one of the most recent volumes dedicated to the study of female deities. The contributions to this book represent a wide variety of studies of goddess worship written by historians of religion and feminists. The articles are uneven in quality; there is no overall synthesis or index.

Patai, Raphael. *The Hebrew Goddess.* New York, 1967. This brilliant essay on goddess worship in Judaism written by an anthropologist represents a major contribution to comparative religions. Its bold thesis, challenging the purity of Jewish monotheism, remains both controversial and stimulating. An important source that deserves special attention.

Preston, James J. *Cult of the Goddess: Social and Religious Change in a Hindu Temple.* New Delhi, 1980. A rare ethnographical work on a Hindu goddess temple located in eastern India. Particularly valuable as a resource for the role of goddesses in the process of cultural change.

Preston, James J., ed. *Mother Worship: Theme and Variations.* Chapel Hill, N. C., 1982. This volume is the most comprehensive and up-to-date collection of data about goddess worship in the field of anthropology. Particularly useful as a source of primary data from firsthand fieldwork on the phenomenon with a comprehensive introduction and conclusion discussing countemporary issues in the study of female sacred images.

Preston, James J. "Goddess Temples in Orissa: An Anthropological Survey." In *Religion in Modern India*, edited by Giri Raj Gupta, pp. 229-247. New Delhi, 1983. An anthropological study of the network of goddess temples in Orissa, eastern India. Particularly valuable as an illustration of how goddess worship reflects religious, political, and social dimensions of human community.

Sangren, P. Steven. "Female Gender in Chinese Religious Symbols: Kuan Yin, Ma Tsu, and the 'Eternal Mother.'" *Signs: Journal of Women in Culture and Society* 9 (1983): 4-25. An excellent anthropological treatment of Chinese goddesses. Particularly valuable here is the author's discussion of how female deities differ from their earthly counterparts.

Turner, Victor, and Edith Turner. *Image and Pilgrimage in Christian Culture.* New York, 1978. An excellent treatment of various Marian shrines within the context of pilgrimage. One of the few anthropological studies of Christianity.

Wolkstein, Diane, and Samuel Noah Kramer. Inanna: *Queen of Heaven and Earth.* New York, 1983. this is the most up-to-date discussion of the ancient Sumerian goddess Inanna. The body of the volume comprises Sumerian texts together with excellent commentaries by several authors on various aspects of Sumerian culture history.

JAMES J. PRESTON

Theoretical Perspectives

Theories about goddess worship have been advanced ever since the emergence of the social sciences disciplines in the nineteenth century. Religion specialists in the fields of anthropology, sociology, folklore, psychology, and comparative mythology have contributed numerous theories to explain the phenomenon of goddess worship. The topic has been revived in recent years, particularly by specialists in the area of women's studies. The following survey of theoretical issues in the study of goddess worship reflects controversies that have raged over broader issues concerning the more general interpretation of religion.

Early Perspectives on Goddess Worship. Nineteenth-century European social scientists and specialists in comparative religion were fascinated by what they conceived to be universal themes of human experience. These writers were concerned with the origins of human institutions such as marriage, law, and religion. Contemporary scholars tend to be more cautious than these early writers about the origins of religion, believing that it is just as dangerous to speculate about the past as it is to develop theories about other cultures without firsthand field observation.

One of the most influential theories in the study of goddess worship was advanced by the nineteenth-century Swiss jurist and historian of Roman law J. J. Bachofen (1815-1887), who linked goddess worship with a more general theory of social development. He asserted that the first human societies were matriarchal and characterized by widespread promiscuity, which was reflected in the worship of female deities. While this theory has been discredited by contemporary anthropologists, early social theorists like Lewis Henry Morgan, Karl Marx, and Friedrich Engels praised it. For Bachofen and his followers, "mother right" marked a fixed and predetermined stage in the evolution of human cultures. This stage in human evolution, according to Bachofen, can be confirmed by myths about goddess worship, which are living expressions "of the stages in a people's development, and for the skillfull observer, a faithful reflection of all the periods in the life of that people" (Bachofen, p. 75). The matriarchal period of human history was one of sublime grandeur, when women inspired chivalry, chastity, and poetry in men. Although men had superior strength, women strove for peace, justice, and religious consecration—guiding the men's "wild, lawless masculinity." This early phase of cultural evolution was displaced, in Bachofen's view, by a later period of conquest and patriarchy.

As early as 1851 proponents of the matriarchy theory were embroiled in a controversy set off by the famous jurist Sir Henry Maine, who insisted that the patriarchal family was the original social unit. This was the same year in which Bachofen was preparing his work *Das Mutterrecht,* asserting exactly the opposite thesis. Over thirty years later, anthropologist and folklorist J. F. McLennan (1886) reasserted the matriarchal theory, citing new anthropological evidence. Again in 1891 the matriarchy concept was discredited by Edward A. Westermarck.

The issue flamed into controversy once again in 1927 with the publication of Robert Briffault's encyclopedic work *The Mothers.* Arguing against Maine and Westermarck, Briffault reasserted the existence of a primitive matriarchy that universally preceded patriarchy. However, unlike Bachofen, who defined matriarchy as a period of mother rule and inheritance through the female line, Briffault conceived matriarchy to be a period when women were socially rather than politically dominant. Briffault speculated that the "male instinct" created the original social herd and that the "female instinct" was responsible for the establishment of the family.

Few psychologists have contributed theories about goddess worship. According to Freud, goddess worship represents universal unconscious fantasies characteristic of a stage in early psychic development in which the mother seems to be all-powerful to the child. C. G. Jung placed the religious impulse in a more central position than did Freud. He postulated a set of innate universal archetypes operative in the human psyche, one of which was the feminine principle. Jung utilized symbolism from primitive, archaic, and contemporary religions to shed light on the operation of these archetypes.

The Jungian perspective has been most fully developed in a classic work by Erich Neumann entitled *The Great Mother* (1955). This massive volume explores the phenomenon of goddess worship from a number of psychological perspec-

> **C. G. Jung . . . postulated a set of innate universal archetypes operative in the human psyche, one of which was the feminine principle.**

tives. Unlike social theorists who traced the development of goddess worship in social time and space, Neumann analyzes the phenomenon purely in terms of inner psychic images. Although he repudiates Bachofen's sociological analysis of matriarchy, he praises him for having made lasting discoveries about the elementary character of the feminine. Neumann's work represents one of the most comprehensive treatments of goddess worship ever assembled by a Western scholar. Not only does he demonstrate the great variety of forms manifested in the phenomenon of goddess worship, he reveals the "transformative" nature of this religious impulse. He sketches out four manifestations of the Great Mother archetype: (1) the Good Mother (associated with childbearing, vegetation mysteries, and rebirth); (2) the Terrible Mother (linked to death, dismemberment, sickness, and extinction); (3) the Positive Transformative Goddess (related to wisdom, vision, ecstasy, and inspiration mysteries); and (4) the Negative Transformative Goddess (connected to rejection, deprivation, madness, and impotence). Any female deity can be classified as one of these four functions of the archetype; some goddesses can be placed in more than one of these categories.

Other than anthropologists and psychologists, some religion scholars have approached goddess worship from a phenomenological perspective. Joseph Campbell for instance, in his monumental four-volume work *The Masks of God* takes a Jungian approach to goddess worship. While he sometimes uses caution in connecting goddess worship with a matriarchal stage in cultural evolution, at other times he perpetuates the nineteenth-century hypotheses of primitive matriarchy. E. O. James (1959) vacillates between a purely historical description of different goddesses in their cultural contexts and generalizations that border on a universal psychic unity approach, much like Erich Neumann's.

Contemporary Issues in the Study of Goddess Worship. After nearly thirty years without a major work on goddess worship, there has been a revival of interest in the topic from three quarters—anthropology, religious studies, and feminist scholarship. Several new books have been published on goddess worship in recent decades. My edited work *Mother Worship: Theme and Variations* (1982) utilizes current data generated by anthropologists to address the topic. Another volume, *The Book of the Goddess: Past and Present* (1983), edited by Carl Olson, is a collection of articles by historians of religion and feminist scholars. Goddess worship is a central theme in the Autumn 1983 issue of *Signs: Journal of Women in Culture and Society,* which is devoted to the study of women and religion.

The matriarchy controversy. The issue of primitive matriarchy, which once plagued the study of goddess worship, has not disappeared. Some modern writers continue to assume there was an early historical phase when females dominated males. They cling to the notion that goddess worship is a remnant of that earlier period. The controversy continues to stir lively debate among popular writers, though many scholars think the issue is a dead one.

Most contemporary historians of religion accept the anthropological view that a stage of matriarchy never existed. However, a few scholars of eminent stature like Joseph Campbell (in Bachofen, 1967, p. lv) continue to support Bachofen's idea of an age of "mother right" that preceded patriarchy. They insist that this has been "confirmed irrefutably" by archaeological evidence. Although most feminist scholars today agree with the anthropological position, there remain a few articulate feminist authors who continue to perpetuate the idea of an original matriarchal stage. An example of this genre is Starhawk's *The Spiral Dance: A Rebirth of the Ancient Religion of the Great Goddess* (1979), in which the author discusses a rediscovery of the ancient "matrifocal civilizations" and the "falsehoods of patriarchal history." According to Sally R. Binford (1981, pp. 150-151) the belief in early matriarchies has taken a religious form for some feminists; mother-goddess worshipers in Los Angeles, for instance, have become organized into a church with a temple and priestesses. They believe that the archaeological data that refute their position reflect a conspiracy against women among professional archaeologists. Binford calls this movement a "New Feminist Fundamentalism."

Even scholars who reject the existence of a historical stage of matriarchy sometimes insist that the symbolism of goddess worship can provide information about the history of female social roles. Some feminists argue, for instance, that the absence of female sacred imagery in Judaism, Christianity, and Islam is due to the repression of women in Western societies. This attempt to draw a parallel between the gender of sacred images and women's roles is misguided. Occasionally the two may parallel each other, but the social role of women may directly contradict or differ significantly from that suggested by a religion's sacred imagery. A study of Hindu goddess worship does not allow us, for instance, to predict with any certainty the relationship of women to men in Indian society.

Today most scholars of comparative religions, including feminists, would agree that primitive matriarchy is a myth. This does not preclude continued research on male and female roles in prehistoric societies. Since fieldwork has not confirmed the existence of even a single matriarchal society, the matriarchy controversy is a quasi-religious issue that has no place in the serious study of goddess worship. Far more important is the contemporary scholarship of feminists who seek to deepen our understanding of the relationship of

> **There remain a few articulate feminist authors who continue to perpetuate the idea of an original matriarchal stage.**

human nature to religion without invoking dubious nineteenth-century issues like primitive matriarchy. In much of this work women are searching for a new focus of identity in the modern world. Goddess worship has been intimately linked to this quest.

The feminist revival of goddess worship. One reason for the increasing popularity of goddess worship as a subject of inquiry is the expanding influence and scholarly development of women's studies. According to Carol Christ (in Olson, 1983, p. 235) feminist writings about the gender of deities reflect two distinct types of argumentation: (1) religions that stress the maleness of the supreme being deify the masculine principle and see it as the only source of legitimate authority; (2) the attribution of male qualities to deities reflects distorted concepts derived from alienated male experience in Western societies. Feminists who use the first argument stress the need to eliminate masculine pronouns and gender-specific titles from Jewish and Christian scriptures and liturgy to restore authority to women. Feminists who assert the second argument oppose this simple solution because in their eyes the distorted male image of divinity in Western religions cannot be removed by merely changing gender-specific language. They argue that the symbolism will remain biased because of the dualistic, conquest-oriented, patriarchal, and hierarchical infrastructure that underlies these male-oriented religions.

Carol Christ (in Olson, 1983, pp. 238-248) presents a schematic view of feminist solutions to the problem of gender in the worship of deities. According to this scholar, there are four approaches advanced by feminist theologians to resolve the problem of male symbolism of God: (1) male symbols of

God can be reinterpreted in nonoppressive ways; (2) language used to refer to God can be made androgynous; (3) female symbolism for the Supreme Being must be introduced in order to create an imagery that reflects dual gender; (4) male symbolism must be deemphasized to provide an opportunity for the Great Goddess, whose existence has been obscured by this symbolism, to reclaim her ascendancy. Western feminists are experimenting with many different ways to introduce female sacred imagery into Judaism and Christianity.

Those feminists who believe sexism to be an integral part of Western religions want no part in saving them from what they see as built-in sexist biases; instead, they advocate a reemergent goddess worship as a focus of religiosity appropriate to complex modern life. These feminists are actively developing extensive experimental liturgies for raising consciousness about goddess worship, both as it existed in antiquity and in religions outside of Western civilization. Thus, goddess worship and imagery are considered to be the focus of a new power for women rooted in the women's liberation movement and grounded in a new symbol system. *The Spiral Dance* by Starhawk is a recipe for the rebirth of an "ancient religion of the Great Goddess." It reflects the conviction among some feminists that goddess worship is a source of strength and creativity for women, and also provides an antidote to the regrettable patriarchal "conquest of nature" theme that characterizes Western thought.

The new comparative religions. A significant new direction is developing in the social sciences after the long siege of behaviorism in psychology and historical particularism in anthropology.Instead of working from a dubious, in fact erroneous, data base, the new comparative religionists are treating these universal themes with the benefit of over fifty years of extensive field-work conducted in various cultures by cautious social scientists. Since the mid-1970s social scientists and religion specialists have been working together more closely. The result is the publication of numerous volumes devoted to the main themes of religion, such as sacrifice, death, rebirth, rites of passage, the evil eye, pilgrimage, and goddess worship. These new works are neither too speculative nor overly cautious about exploring panhuman dimensions of religious experience.

One of the most widely publicized and heavily attended sessions at the American Anthropological Association meetings in San Francisco during 1975 was entitled "Anthropological Inquiries into Mother Worship." This session resulted eventually in an edited volume on the topic (Preston, 1982).

The mid-1970s marked a watershed in the anthropological study of religion. Since that time some anthropologists have been about the business of synthesizing a vast amount of data accumulated over the years on various dimensions of religion. Much of this new information was isolated previously in the contexts of specific ethnographies devoted to the elaboration of particular cultural descriptions. The large numbers of people who attended the session on goddess worship in San Francisco were not attracted by any "star quality" scholars making their usual erudite presentations, but rather the time was ripe for introducing once again a topic that had remained more or less dormant for several decades. An extensive amount of data had been gathered on goddess worship in many different cultural contexts, and no one knew what to do with it. Scholars were seeking a new frame of reference. Historians of religion had been synthesizing the work of anthropologists for years. It was now time for anthropologists to return to their original task of making sense of a topic like goddess worship by placing it in a comparative framework.

The new approach to goddess worship, though cautious, strives to retain a delicate balance between cultural context and the broader panhuman issues that continue to be vital in the comparative study of religion. Despite the early years of ambitious speculation and the later period of overcautious skepticism, many questions about goddess worship remain unanswered.

[*See also* Women's Studies.]

BIBLIOGRAPHY

Bachofen, J. J. *Myth, Religion, and Mother Right.* Translated by Ralph Manheim. Princeton, 1967. A selection of writings translated from Bachofen's *Mutterrecht und Urreligion.* Here Bachofen elaborates on his controversial but dated theory asserting a predetermined universal stage of matriarchy associated with goddess worship.

Binford, Sally R. "Myths and Matriarchies." *Anthropology 81/82* 1 (1981): 150-153. A brief but excellent critique of the current matriarchy controversy. The author is critical of the branch of feminists who cannot accept the fact that there is no evidence for matriarchy. An important source for illustrating the error of predicting sex roles through analysis of sacred images.

Briffault, Robert. *The Mothers* (1927). Abridged by Gordon R. Taylor. New York, 1977. A classic last attempt to argue for the nineteenth century idea linking goddess worship with matriarchy. This voluminous work is outdated. It no longer represents the thinking of contemporary social theorists on the topic.

Campbell, Joseph. *The Masks of God,* vol. 1, *Primitive Mythology.* New York, 1959. This work explores the early Upper Paleolithic and Neolithic roots of goddess worship. It represents the Jungian orientation toward a universal Great Goddess. Somewhat dated but useful as a secondary source if read critically.

Campbell, Joseph. *The Masks of God,* vol. 2, *Oriental Mythology.* New York, 1962. This work is encyclopedic in scope and refers frequently to goddess worship in Eastern religious traditions. Much Jungian generalization here, but still useful.

Fluehr-Lobban, Carolyn. "A Marxist Reappraisal of the Matriarchate." *Current Anthropology* 20 (June 1979): 341-360. An excellent discussion of current anthropological thinking on the matriarchate with implications for goddess worship. Particularly important is the author's attack on the idea that goddess worship represents an epoch of mother-rule in human history.

James, E. O. *The Cult of the Mother Goddess.* New York, 1959. A thorough discussion of goddess worship derived from archaeological and documentary evidence for the Middle East, the eastern Mediterranean, and India. An excellent source although some of the interpretation is dated.

Marshack, Alexander. *The Roots of Civilization.* New York, 1972. An outstanding analysis of Upper Paleolithic data on goddess worship, suggesting the phenomenon is part of a complex notational system rather than merely fertility symbolism. While Marshack's thesis may be controversial, the volume is a rich source of information and remains a major scholarly contribution.

Neumann, Erich. *The Great Mother: An Analysis of the Archetype.* 2d ed. Princeton, 1963. This is one of the most comprehensive discussions of goddess worship ever written. It represents the most thorough treatment of the subject from a Jungian psychological perspective. While some of the interpretation is overly speculative, it is still a valuable resource.

Olson, Carl, ed. *The Book of the Goddess, Past and Present: An Introduction to Her Religion.* New York, 1983. This is one of the most recent volumes dedicated to the study of female deities. The contributions to this book represent a wide variety of studies of goddess worship written by historians of religion and feminists. The articles are uneven; some are excellent, others poor. The editor does not supply an overall synthesis or index.

Preston, James J., ed. *Mother Worship: Theme and Variations.* Chapel Hill, N. C., 1982. This volume is the most comprehensive and up-to-date collection of data about goddess worship in the field of anthropology. Particularly useful as a source of primary data from firsthand fieldwork on the phenomenon with a comprehensive introduction and conclusion discussing contemporary issues in the study of female sacred images.

Starhawk. *The Spiral Dance: A Rebirth of the Ancient Religion of the Great Goddess.* San Francisco, 1979. The author attempts to revitalize goddess worship as a focus of worship for feminists. Though erroneous assumptions are made here, the basic thrust of attempting to develop new forms of religious expression is important.

Turner, Victor, and Edith Turner. *Image and Pilgrimage in Christian Culture.* New York, 1978. An excellent treatment of various Marian shrines within the context of pilgrimage. One of the few anthropological studies of Christianity.

Warner, Marina. *Alone of All Her Sex: The Myth and the Cult of the Virgin Mary.* New York, 1976. An excellent study of Marianism attacking the erroneous idea the female sacred images and women's roles are equivalent.

Wasson, R. Gordon, Carl A. P. Ruck, and Albert Hofmann. *The Road to Eleusis.* New York, 1978. A controversial and provocative discussion of the Greek mystery religion suggesting the possible use of psychotropic drugs.

JAMES J. PRESTON

GOOD, THE

A distinction has to be made between two sets of questions related to the concept of the good. There are ethical problems about how to elaborate reasonable criteria of goodness, where goodness is conceived as a characteristic of human actions and of things or properties that are directly or indirectly relevant to human life. And there are questions concerning the goodness of God or of existence as such, apart from God's benevolence and love for the human race. I shall concentrate upon the latter question.

In archaic and polytheistic religions, gods are not necessarily good either in the sense of caring about human well-being or in the sense of providing us with a model of moral conduct; some are, some are not, and many combine good and evil characteristics in both respects. Yet in the myths of origin, the evil of gods has been connected, as a rule, with destruction and disorder, and goodness with creation and harmony, whether or not any one of the gods was invariably and systematically good or evil. In Iranian dualist mythology good and evil were attributed respectively to one and another mutually hostile divine beings. In all monotheistic religions God is totally good in an absolute and unqualified sense, and his goodness consists not only in that he loves his creatures: it is his intrinsic, nonrelative property; God would be good even if he had not created the universe. So conceived, goodness acquires a metaphysical meaning that probably cannot be further analyzed, cannot be reduced to other concepts, and has an axiomatic character.

Philosophical reflection on this kind of goodness is Plato's legacy; he discovered the idea of the good, which is, of course, desirable and therefore good for us, as well as the source of all goodness; but the good is not good because desirable, but desirable because intrinsically good. This topic was taken up and elaborated by later Platonists, including, in particular, Plotinus; to him the One is good both in terms of our human needs and happiness and good in itself, apart from this relationship. Other Platonists, however, denied that the characteristics of goodness could be meaningfully attributed to the first principle: Speusippus, Plato's successor in the Academy, made the point, and so did the last pagan philosopher, Damascius, to whom the first principle, being utterly ineffable, could not possibly have any properties, whether relative or even absolute; having no name (even the word *principle* is not appropriate) and no relationship with other realities or even with itself, it cannot be called good in any sense.

Christian philosophy, which assimilated many Platonic categories, has always stressed all the meanings of divine goodness: God is good in himself, he is the creator of all goodness, he is benevolent, and he is the source of criteria whereby our acts are called morally good or evil. Whatever else is good is such derivatively and by participation in the goodness of God. And, apart from a few dualistic sects, all creation was, in Christian thinking, attributed to God; since no existence is conceivable apart from God, whatever exists is good by definition. Evil has no positive ontological characteristics and is to be defined as pure negativity, *privatio,* lack of being: evil comes from the ill-will of human or diabolic creatures endowed with freedom of choice and abusing this freedom; yet even the devil, insofar as he exists, is good, even though his will is incurably and totally corrupt. This doctrine has been elaborated in detail by Augustine. In Thomas Aquinas's idiom it is summed up in saying that being and goodness are coextensive (*esse et bonum convertuntur*). Some Christian philosophers and theologians discussed the question (broached already by Plato): are the criteria of good and evil, given us by God, arbitrary or intrinsically

> **Some Christian philosophers and theologians discussed the question: are the criteria of good and evil, given us by God, arbitrary or intrinsically valid?**

valid? In other words, is the good good because God has decreed it to be good (as some nominalists and Descartes believed), or has God told us that it is good because it is good in itself (as Leibniz argued)? If the former, moral rules appear to us as arbitrary and contingent as, say, the rules of traffic; God could have decreed other norms of conduct and said, for instance, that adultery is good and loving one's neighbor wrong—a conclusion that sounds outrageous to common sense; yet, if God orders what is intrinsically good, apart from his decrees, he appears to be bound by laws that do not depend on him, which makes his omnipotence doubtful. The question can be invalidated, however, by saying—in conformity with Thomist metaphysics—that God is what he decrees and that there are no rules of goodness different from his essence, therefore he neither obeys a foreign law nor issues arbitrary decrees of which the content is contingent upon his essence.

If God is good in himself, and not only benevolent to his creatures, it is essential, in Christian terms, that we should love him not only as a benefactor and savior but because he is who he is. The point was strongly stressed by many Christian mystics and other "theocentrically" oriented writers. They argued that God is not only the highest good but the only good proper, therefore we are for God, rather than he for us; we should admire him utterly oblivious of all favors and graces we get from him; indeed our love should be the same even if we knew that he condemned us to hell, and we should be happy to accept his will unconditionally, whatever it means to us; we ought only to want God to be God, whereas to love God in reciprocity for his benevolence is unworthy or perhaps sinful. The standard Christian teaching, while stressing the value of the disinterested love of God, never goes so far as to say that worshiping God in connection with his gifts and graces is a sin or to deny that our salvation is an intrinsic good and not only an instrument whereby God's glory is aug-

mented; indeed, the last two statements sound heretical. The theory of "pure love" was hotly debated in the Catholic church in the seventeenth century.

The idea of divine goodness as a nonrelative property does not seem to be a product of pure philosophical speculation. It is rooted in, and makes explicit, the old tenet of many religions: creation as such is good, and therefore the creator is good as such.

The distinction between autotelic (or intrinsic) and instrumental goods has been almost universally admitted by philosophers since Plato and Aristotle, yet there has never been an agreement about how to draw the line between them and how to define what is good in itself; many philosophers have denied that a collection of properties can be found that would be common to all the things and experiences people have called good. In the conflict between utilitarians and Kantians, and between utilitarians and pragmatists, these problems are among the most often debated.

BIBLIOGRAPHY

A comprehensive listing of bibliographic references to the concept of the good would include works by most Western philosophers, including Plato, Aristotle, the Stoics, Augustine, Thomas Aquinas, Spinoza, Hobbes, Hume, and Kant. The following twentieth-century works can be recommended:

Dewey, John. *Theory of Valuation*. Chicago, 1939.
Ewing, A. C. *The Definition of Good*. New York, 1947.
Hartmann, Nicolai. *Ethics*. 3 vols. Translated by Stanton Colt. London, 1932.
Moore, G. E. *Principia Ethica*. Cambridge, 1903.
Rice, P. B. *On the Knowledge of Good and Evil*. New York, 1955.
Ross, W. D. *The Right and the Good*. Oxford, 1930.
Stevenson, Charles. *Facts and Values*. New Haven, 1963.
Westermarck, Edvard A. *The Origin and Development of the Moral Ideas*. 2d ed. 2 vols. London, 1924.
Wright, Georg H. von. *The Varieties of Goodness*. London, 1963.

LESZEK KOLAKOWSKI

GOSPEL

The Septuagint. In the Septuagint (a Greek translation of the Hebrew scriptures), the verb *euaggelizein*, cognate with *euaggelion*, is commonly used in the profane sense with the meaning "to announce."

The notion of the bearer of the good news of salvation persisted in both Hellenistic and Palestinian Judaism (see the Targum on *Isaiah* 40:9 as well as 1QM 18:14 from among the Dead Sea Scrolls). The mid-first-century *Psalms of Solomon* (11:1-2) uses *euaggelizein* in the eschatological sense, while in postbiblical Judaism bsr and its cognate verb refer not only to concrete historical news but also to prophetic messages of weal and woe, angelic messages, and divine announcements of consolation and blessing.

New Testament. Within the New Testament, *euaggelion* is used far more frequently by Paul than by any other author. His writings are the first literary attestation to the Christian usage of the term. To some authors this suggests that Paul first gave a Christian connotation to the term *euaggelion,* while to others it implies that Paul had taken over an earlier Christian usage. In any event, there is little doubt that the term acquired its Christian significance in a Hellenistic environment.

Paul. In the Pauline letters two passages confirm the thesis that Paul has taken over the absolute use of *euaggelion* from early Christian usage. The passages in question are *1 Corinthians* 15:1-4 and *Romans* 1:1-4. In his first letter to the Corinthians, Paul uses classic language to describe the handing on of traditional teaching and employs *euaggelion* to identify the content of that teaching. Paul explicates the content of the *euaggelion* by citing a creedal formula, probably derived from Palestinian Christian circles, that focuses on the death and resurrection of Jesus. In the opening verses of the letter to the Romans, the content of the gospel is the disclosure of Jesus as the Son of God and our Lord by his resurrection from the dead. Thus, for Paul, the basic content of the gospel is the resurrection by means of which Jesus is constituted as Lord.

Mark. Both in understanding of the term *euaggelion* and in frequency of its usage (seven times), Mark is similar to Paul. Mark, however, uses only *euaggelion*, the noun, and not the related verb. For Mark, *euaggelion* is a technical expression used to denote the kerygmatic announcement of salvation. Jesus is the subject of the gospel insofar as he proclaimed the coming of the kingdom of God (*Mk.* 1:15). When proclamation occurs, that which is proclaimed becomes a reality. Accordingly, the activity of Jesus became the object of the gospel. Mark editorializes on the tradition he has incorporated into his work in order to affirm that the gospel relates to that which has been done in and through Jesus.

Matthew and Luke. Neither Matthew nor Luke employs *euaggelion* so frequently as does Mark, and the Johannine literature does not use the term at all. Matthew uses the term four times but never without further qualification. He writes of "the gospel of the kingdom" (*Mt.* 4:23, 9:35), of "this gospel" (*Mt.* 26:13), and of "this gospel of the kingdom" (*Mt.* 24:14). In all four instances Matthew uses *euaggelion* in relation to a speech complex. For him Jesus is no longer the content of the gospel; instead, he is the communicator of the gospel. The speeches of Jesus are "gospels." Matthew's emphasis is on Jesus' preaching and teaching as providing a paradigm for the Christian way of life.

Luke does not use *euaggelion* at all in the first part of his written work, but it appears twice in *Acts* (15:7, 20:24). Nonetheless, Luke employs the verb *euaggelizomai* ("I bring

the good news") frequently both in his gospel (ten times) and in Acts (fifteen times). By doing so, Luke emphasizes the act of preaching, which is then explained by the direct object that accompanies the verb.

The Written Gospel. Even when *euaggelion* came to be applied to a written text, the word continued to be employed in the singular, and this use of the singular was still widespread in the third century. The usage bespeaks the conviction that the gospel was identical with the teaching of the Lord. This usage is reflected in the formulaic expression "the Lord says in the gospel" (e.g., *2 Clem.* 8:5), but it is also reflected in the titles of the Gospels. The earliest parchment codices of the New Testament, namely, the fourth-century Sinaiticus and Vaticanus codices, entitle the Gospels "according to Matthew," "according to Mark," and so on. This manner of providing each of the written gospels with a title suggests that *euaggelion* applied to the whole collection of the four canonical gospels. Nonetheless, three of the early New Testament papyri have made use of more complete titles: *Gospel According to Matthew* (P[4]) and *Gospel According to John* (P[66], P[75]). Even this is a strange turn of phrase if the sole intention is to designate authorship. These titles seem to suggest that the single gospel was narrated according to the vision of a specific evangelist. There was only one message of final, eschatological salvation, namely, salvation accomplished through the death and resurrection of Jesus, but the message could be conveyed in different ways.

The transference of *euaggelion* from the designation of an oral proclamation to a written text—a usage that most probably derives from the first verse of Mark—attests that these texts had the same content and purpose as the oral proclamation. Both the oral proclamation of the gospel and the written gospel speak of eschatological salvation accomplished in the life and death of Jesus of Nazareth.

BIBLIOGRAPHY

The most comprehensive study of the term *euaggelion* remains the article "Euaggelion" written by Gerhard Friedrich for the *Theological Dictionary of the New Testament*, edited by Gerhard Kittel, vol. 2 (Grand Rapids, Mich., 1964), pp. 721-736. The original German text was first published in 1935. Significant contributions to our knowledge of Paul's understanding of the gospel are Peter Stuhlmacher's *Das paulinischer Evangelium*, in the series "Forschungen zur Religion und Literatur des Alten und Neuen Testament," vol. 95 (Göttingen, 1968), and Ernst Käsemann's *Commentary on Romans* (Grand Rapids, Mich., 1980), pp. 6-10. An analytic study of Mark's understanding of *euaggelion* is Willi Marxsen's *Mark the Evangelist* (Nashville, 1969), pp. 117-150. In this study Marxsen also compares the use of the term by Matthew and Luke with that by Mark. In his *Studies in the Gospel of Mark* (London, 1985) Martin Hengel examines the Marcan use (pp. 53-58) as well as the titles of the Gospels (pp. 64-84). Useful studies of the gospel as a Hellenistic literary genre are G. N. Stanton's *Jesus of Nazareth in New Testament Preaching* (London, 1974), pp. 117-136, and

Charles H. Talbert's *What Is a Gospel? The Genre of the Canonical Gospels* (Philadelphia, 1977). A good introduction to Luther's understanding of the difference between law and gospel has been given by Gerhard Ebeling in chapter 7 of his *Luther: An Introduction to His Thought* (Philadelphia, 1970).

RAYMOND F. COLLINS

GRACE

The religious significance present in the Anglo-French word *grace* is both multifaceted and ambivalent. As a theological term, it may attempt to pinpoint the activity of God here and now, or it may disclose nothing less than the reality underlying all of religion and faith.

This almost transparent term points to the fundamental power and horizon of every revelation, to the ultimate religious question and statement in any religion, for grace stands primarily not for human virtue but for God's presence. Grace is a divine activity in human history and in human lives. The reality signified by *hesed* ("lovingkindness") in the Hebrew scriptures and by *charis* ("grace") in the Greek scriptures can be found in the Tao, in the power of the Hindu triad, and in the radical absence contemplated by Buddhism. Occasionally we can find in these other traditions the same theological discussions about the mediation by grace of the divine in human freedom and suffering.

Christian theologians have filled volumes with definitions and classifications of grace. Since God remains mystery, the ineffable presence of the deity eludes precise definition, and therefore the ultimate meaning of the word remains mysterious. In theology, as distinct from the expression of religion in art (where grace is shown rather than defined), the word *grace* frequently denotes either too much or too little.

Moving back through the Latin *gratia* to the Greek *charis,* with its overtones of graciousness and liberality, the word *grace* assumed a Christian theological importance with Paul. But even for Paul, whose creative interpretation of Christianity began the turbulent odyssey of this term, the word has several meanings. *Charis* can mean a power coming from the spirit of Jesus active in a Christian (the charism of healing or preaching; *1 Cor.* 12), but it can also mean the power of God to help one follow Christ despite the evils and difficulties of human life. And with Paul there is also a more objective meaning of grace. The foundation of all grace and of all graces (charisms) is the generous saving activity of God manifested toward us in the history and destiny of Jesus. God's grace is the gift of persevering, loving, purposeful generosity that becomes visible in a climactic way in the life, teaching, death, and resurrection of Jesus.

Charis means the favor of God, but that favor made active in the advent of Jesus Christ, particularly so in his words and deeds. God's loving generosity in Christ bestows not only forgiveness of sin but a new, death-surviving mode of existence. Jesus Christ is grace objectified, and in and after him the worlds of creation, time, and human personality have been radically (if invisibly) altered. Paul applied Jesus' phrase "the kingdom of God" largely in a concrete manner to Jesus himself, particularly through the triumphant guarantee of newness assured by Jesus risen from the dead.

In a significant phrase, Paul proclaims that while sin inevitably leads to death, the *charisma* of God to us is "eternal life in Christ Jesus" (*Rom.* 6:23). The following chapters of that letter describe this *charisma*: new freedom, familial intimacy with God, the capability to follow the new "law" of love, the indwelling of the Holy Spirit in men and women, and God's advocacy on behalf of needy individuals (*Rom.* 8). Personal entry into this life is begun by baptism conceived as rebirth in Christ's death, burial, and resurrection. The event of Easter has both personal and cosmic results.

A final realization of *charis* for Paul comes from this very baptismal life. The new life of grace is not only a divine favor and an adoption but also a commissioning for action. *Charismata,* charisms, are powers of the Holy Spirit active in mature Christians, empowering them to act on behalf of the reign of God and the life of the church. Christians are not passive. Each Christian has through the baptismal spirit some active gift to aid the church either inwardly or in its mission of service and evangelization. Drawing on his metaphor of the body, Paul faces the difficult challenges of diversity and unity in the young churches and of leadership amid a variety of services. Nonetheless, Paul will not abandon this final realization of the new presence of God where grace continues through time to be present in human life and ministries of service (*Rom.* 12, *1 Cor.* 12).

BIBLIOGRAPHY

For a survey of the history of the theology of grace in Western Christianity, see Johann Auer's *Das Evangelium der Gnade*, vol. 5 of Kleine katholische Dogmatik (Regensburg, 1980). Roger Haight's *The Experience and Language of Grace* (New York, 1979) is a brief survey of the great theologians of grace. Hans Conzelmann's "Charis," in the *Theological Dictionary of the New Testament*, edited by Gerhard Friedrich, vol. 9, (Grand Rapids, Mich., 1969), pp. 310-350, illustrates the Christian origin and initial variety in the meaning of the word *grace*, as does Edward Schillebeeckx's *Christ: The Experience of Jesus as Lord* (New York, 1980). On the great theologians of grace, see Harry J. McSorley's *Luther: Right or Wrong?* (New York, 1969), on Augustine, Thomas Aquinas, and Luther; Karl Barth's *Church Dogmatics,* 13 vols., plus index, edited by Geoffrey W. Bromiley and Thomas F. Torrance (Edinburgh, 1936-1977); Paul Tillich's *Systematic Theology*, 3 vols. (Chicago, 1951-1963), with the study on Tillich's Christian anthropology by Kenan B. Osborne, *New Being: A Study in the Relationship between Conditioned and Unconditioned Being according to Paul Tillich* (The Hague, 1969); Karl Rahner's *Foundations of Christian Faith* (New York, 1978) with the explanatory volume; Leo J. O'Donovan's *A World of Grace* (New

York, 1980); and Leonardo Boff's *Liberating Grace* (New York, 1979), on Latin American liberation theology. For a contemporary ecclesiology of ministry drawn from biblical and systematic theologies of grace, see my *Theology of Ministry* (New York, 1983).

THOMAS F. O'MEARA, O.P.

GREEK ORTHODOX CHURCH

Greek Orthodox Churches Today. In the modern and ethnic sense, Greek Orthodoxy is understood to include those churches whose language, liturgy, and spirit keep Orthodoxy and the Greek ethnic cultural tradition united.

The Church of Greece. Prior to the Greek War of Independence, which began in 1821, Christianity in what is now known as Greece was, for most of its history, part of the ecumenical patriarchate of Constantinople. Even though the church was self-declared autocephalous in 1833, it understands itself to be in direct continuity with the founding of Christianity in Thessalonica, Phillipi, Corinth, Athens, Nicopolis, and other Greek cities by the apostle Paul. Following the early period, when metropolitan sees had been established in the major cities, Greece came under Constantinople, where it stayed—with a few interruptions—until the nineteenth century. Originally, the autocephalous Church of Greece included only the southern part of the modern nation of Greece, since only that area was liberated in 1830. Over the years, as the Greek nation expanded, the church also grew in territorial size and numbers. But this equation of the boundaries of the state and the jurisdiction of the Church of Greece is not absolute. Several areas of the nation of Greece are ecclesiastically under the control of the ecumenical patriarchate: the Dodecanese, Crete, and Mount Athos.

The patriarchate of Constantinople. In 1955, after years of general harassment, government-inspired riots wrought havoc on the Greek community of Istanbul, including churches. Economic and administrative pressures forced a large part of the Greek Orthodox population to leave the last remaining enclave of Greek Orthodoxy in Turkey. Only a few thousand now remain, as the patriarchate clings to its legal rights to remain in its historic city. The patriarchate's numerical strength resides in the numerous Greek Orthodox dioceses, or "eparchies," within its jurisdiction in the diaspora. In addition to four eparchies in Turkey, the Patriarchate of Constantinople exercises jurisdiction over local and national members.

The patriarchate of Alexandria. Egypt was one of the first areas to come under the influence of Islam in the eighth century. Nevertheless, the Greek Orthodox patriarchate of Alexandria continued to exist in Egypt throughout the centuries. Even though the numerical strength of the Greek Orthodox patriarchate in Egypt was broken with the rise of Gamal Abdel Nasser in 1954, the patriarchate continued to serve about 350,000 (1980s figures) Orthodox Christians.

The patriarchate of Jerusalem. In 1517 the area came under the control of the sultan in Constantinople while the church continued to struggle to maintain its rights to the holy places of Jerusalem. Changing political circumstances in the area have required the negotiation of agreements regarding the status of the patriarchate with the British, Jordanians, and Israelis. At the beginning of the 1980s, the patriarchate counted eighty thousand members with sixteen bishops.

The Church of Cyprus. The Church of Cyprus, consisting exclusively of Greek Cypriots, received its independence as an autocephalous church through the eighth canon of the Council of Ephesus (431), but its history goes back to New Testament times (*Acts* 11:19). The Orthodox church is very close to the people of Cyprus, especially since the 1974 Turkish invasion of the island nation when almost half of its members were made refugees in their own land. In 1985, the Church of Cyprus counted more than 440,000 members with six dioceses, seven bishops, and twelve hundred priests.

The Greek Orthodox diaspora. The Greek Orthodox Christians found throughout the world today in traditionally non-Orthodox lands are primarily under the jurisdiction of the Patriarchate of Constantinople.

BIBLIOGRAPHY

Campbell, John, and Philip Sherrard. *Modern Greece.* New York, 1968. A useful chapter on the place of the Orthodox church in modern Greece.

Florovsky, Georges. "Patristics and Modern Theology." In *Procès-verbaux du Premier Congrès de Théologie Orthodoxe à Athènes: 29 novembre-6 décembre 1936,* edited by Hamilcar S. Alivisatos. Athens, 1939. A historic call for a return to the Greek fathers. The final clause, italicized for emphasis, reads "let us be more Greek to be truly catholic, to be truly Orthodox."

Frazee, Charles A. *Orthodox Church in Independent Greece, 1821-1852.* Cambridge, 1969. A detailed account of the establishment of the autocephalous Church of Greece.

Geanakoplos, Deno John. *Byzantine East and Latin West: Two Worlds of Christendom in Middle Ages and Renaissance; Studies in Ecclesiastical and Cultural History.* New York, 1966. An excellent study on the topic, with important insights on the cultural sources of the ecclesiastical conflicts.

Karmiris, Ioannes N. "Nationalism in the Orthodox Church." *Greek Orthodox Theological Review* 26 (Fall 1981): 171-184. An effort to explicate the broad Greek cultural impact upon Orthodox Christianity, while distinguishing the Orthodox faith from modern Greek nationalism, without contrasting it.

Runciman, Steven. *The Great Church in Captivity: A Study of the Patriarchate of Constantinople from the Eve of the Turkish Conquest to the Greek War of Independence.* Cambridge, 1968. The definitive work on this subject.

Vaporis, Nomikos Michael, ed. *Post-Byzantine Ecclesiastical Personalities*. Brookline, Mass., 1978. Biographies of several major Greek figures in the Orthodox church under Ottoman rule.

Vryonis, Speros Jr. *Byzantium and Europe*. New York, 1967. A good, broad cultural introduction to Byzantine history, with a focus on the relationships between East and West. Illustrated.

Ware, Timothy. *Eustratios Argenti: A Study of the Greek Church under Turkish Rule*. Oxford, 1964. Reprint, Willits, Calif., 1974. A fine case study of the practical dimensions of Greek Orthodox Christian life under the Ottomans.

STANLEY SAMUEL HARAKAS

GREEK RELIGION

Mythology and Religion. As adults, the Greeks learned about the world of the gods through the voices of the poets. The rise of a written narrative tradition modified and preserved the very ancient tradition of oral poetry and came to occupy a central place in the social and spiritual life of Greece. Had it not been for all the works of the epic, lyrical, and dramatic poetry, we could speak of Greek cults in the plural instead of a unified Greek religion.

The scholars of the Renaissance, as for the great majority of the scholars of the nineteenth century, agreed that Greek religion was, above all, an abundant treasure of legendary tales transmitted to us by the Greek authors (assisted by the Romans) in which the spirit of paganism remained alive long enough to offer the modern reader in a Christian world the surest path to a clear view of ancient polytheism.

In the fifth century, work was begun that would be systematically pursued in essentially two directions. First, chroniclers undertook the collection and inventory of all the legendary oral traditions peculiar to a city or a sanctuary. Like the atthidographs of Athens, these scholars attempted to set down in writing the history of a city and its people from its earliest beginnings, going back to the fabulous time when the gods mingled with men. Parallel to this effort, which aimed at a systematic summary of the legends common to all Greeks, there became apparent a certain hesitation and uneasiness—already perceptible among the poets—about how much credit should be accorded to the scandalous episodes that seemed incompatible with the eminent dignity of the divine. But it was with the development of history and philosophy that interrogation reached full scale; from then on criticism assailed myth in general. Subjected to the investigations of the historian and the reasonings of the philosopher, the fable, as fable, was deemed incompetent to speak of the divine in a valid and authentic fashion. Yet, from one point of view, no matter if the ancients were carefully collecting myths, if they interpreted or criticized them or even rejected them in the name of another, truer kind of knowledge—it all

came down to recognizing the role generally assigned to myths in the Greek city-state, namely, to function as instruments of information about the otherworld.

During the first half of the twentieth century, however, historians of Greek religion took a new direction. Many refused to consider the legendary traditions as strictly religious documents that could be useful as evidence of the real state of the beliefs and feelings of the faithful. For these scholars, religion lay in the organization of the cult, the calendar of sacred festivals, the liturgies celebrated for each god in his sanctuaries.

Today, the rejection of mythology is based on an anti-intellectualist presumption in religious matters. Scholars of this standpoint believe that behind the diversity of religions—just as beyond the plurality of the gods of polytheism—lies a common element that forms the primitive and universal core of all religious experience. This common element is placed, therefore, outside of intelligence, in the sacred terror that man feels each time he is compelled to recognize, in its irrecusable strangeness, the presence of the supernatural. Such awe would be the basis of the earliest cults, the diverse forms taken by the rites answering, from the same origin, to the multiplicity of circumstances and human needs.

Similarly, it is supposed that behind the variety of names, figures, and functions proper to each divinity, a ritual brought into play the same general experience of the divine, considered a suprahuman power *(kreitton)*. This indeterminate divine being (Gr., *theion*, or *daimonion*), underlying the specific manifestations of particular gods, took diverse forms according to the desires and fears to which the cult had to respond. From this common fabric of the divine, the poets, in turn, cut singular characters; they brought them to life, imagining for each a series of dramatic adventures in what

> **Groups of gods do not conform to a single model that is more important than others; they are organized into a plurality of configurations.**

Festugière does not hesitate to call a "divine novel." On the other hand, for every act of the cult, there is no other god but the one invoked. From the moment he is addressed, "in him is concentrated all divine force; he alone is considered. Most certainly, in theory he is not the only god since there are others and one knows it. But in practice, in the actual state of mind of the worshiper, the god invoked supplants at that moment all the others" (Festugière, 1944, p. 50).

The World of the Gods. Greek religion presents an organization so complex that it excludes recourse to a single reading code for the entire system. To be sure, a Greek god

461

is defined by the set of relationships that unite or put him in opposition to other divinities of the pantheon, but the theological structures thus brought to light are too numerous and, especially, too diverse to be integrated into the same pattern. According to the city, the sanctuary, or the moment, each god enters into a varied network of combinations with the others. Groups of gods do not conform to a single model that is more important than others; they are organized into a plurality of configurations that do not correspond exactly but compose a table with several entries and many axes, the reading of which varies according to the starting point and the perspective adopted.

Take the example of Zeus. His name clearly reveals his origin, based on the same Indo-European root (meaning "to shine") as Latin *dies/deus* and the Vedic *dyeus*. Like the Indian Dyaus Pitr or the Roman Jupiter (Iovpater), Father Zeus (Zeus Pater) is the direct descendant of the great Indo-European sky god. However, the gap between the status of the Zeus of Greece and that of his corresponding manifestations in India and in Rome is so evident, so marked, that even when comparing the most assuredly similar gods one is compelled to recognize that the Indo-European tradition has completely disappeared from the Greek religious system.

Celestial and judicious wielder of supreme power, founder of order, guarantor of justice, governor of marriage, father and ancestor, and patron of the city, the tableau of the sovereignty of Zeus includes still other dimensions. His authority is domestic as well as political. In close connivance with Hestia, Zeus has supreme control not only over each private hearth—that fixed center where the family has its roots—but also over the common household of the state in the heart of the city, the Hestia Koine, where the ruling magistrates keep watch. Zeus Herkeios, the god of the courtyard and the household, circumscribes the domain within which the head of the house has the right to exercise his power; Zeus Klarios, the divider of estates, delineates and sets boundaries, leaving Apollo and Hermes in charge of protecting the gates and controlling the entries.

The different epithets of Zeus, wide as their range may be, are not incompatible. They all belong to one field and emphasize its multiple dimensions. Taken together, they define the contours of divine sovereignty as conceived by the Greeks; they mark its boundaries and delimit its constituent domains; they indicate the various aspects that the power of the king-god may assume and exercise in more or less close alliance (according to circumstances) with the other divinities.

The Civic Religion. Between the eleventh and eighth centuries, technical, economic, and demographic changes led to what the English archaeologist Anthony Snodgrass called the "structural revolution," which gave rise to the city-state *(polis)*. The Greek religious system was profoundly reorganized during this time in response to the new forms of social life introduced by the *polis*. Within the context of a reli-gion that from then on was essentially civic, remodeled beliefs and rites satisfied a dual and complementary obligation. First of all, they fulfilled the specific needs of each group of people, who constituted a city bound to a specific territory. The city was placed under the patronage of its own special gods, who endowed it with a unique religious physiognomy. Every city had its own divinity or divinities, whose functions were to cement the body of citizens into a true community; to

> **The race of heroes formed the legendary past of the Greece of the city-states and the roots of the families, groups, and communities of the Hellenes.**

unite into one whole all the civic space, including the urban center and the *chora*, or rural area; and to look after the integrity of the state—the people and the land—in the presence of other cities. Second, the development of an epic literature cut off from any local roots, the construction of great common sanctuaries, and the institution of pan-Hellenic games and panegyrics established and reinforced, on a religious level, legendary traditions, cycles of festivals, and a pantheon that would be recognized equally throughout all of Hellas.

Without assessing all the religious innovations brought about during the Archaic period, the most important should be mentioned. The first was the emergence of the temple as a construction independent of the human habitat, whether houses or royal palaces. With its walls delimiting a sacred enclosure *(temenos)* and its exterior altar, the temple became an edifice separated from profane ground. The god came to reside there permanently through the intermediacy of his great anthropomorphic cult statue. Unlike domestic altars and private sanctuaries, this house of the god was the common property of all citizens.

Another innovation with partly comparable significance left its mark on the religious system. During the eighth century, it became customary to put into service Mycenaean buildings, usually funerary, that had been abandoned for centuries. Once they were fitted out, they served as cult places where funeral honors were rendered to legendary figures who, although they usually had no relationship to these edifices, were claimed as ancestors by their "progeny," noble families or groups of phratries. Like the epic heroes whose names they carried, these mythical ancestors belonged to a distant past, to a time different from the present, and constituted a category of supernatural powers distinct from both the *theoi*, or gods proper, and the ordinary dead. Even more than the cult of the gods (even the civic gods), the cult of heroes had both civic and territorial value. It was associated with a specific place, a tomb with the subterranean presence of the dead person, whose remains were often brought home from a distant land.

The spread of the cult of the hero did not just comply with the new social needs that arose with the city; the adoration of the heroes had a properly religious significance. Different from the divine cult, which was obligatory for everyone and permanent in character, and also from the funerary rites, which were limited in time as well as to a narrow circle of relatives, the heroic institution affected the general stability of the cult system.

For the Greeks, there was a radical opposition between the gods, who were the beneficiaries of the cult, and men, who were its servants. Strangers to the transience that defines the existence of men, the gods were the *athanatoi* ("the immortals"). Men, on the other hand, were the *brotoi* ("the mortals"), doomed to sickness, old age, and death.

The heroes were quite another matter. To be sure, they belonged to the race of men and thus knew suffering and death. But a whole series of traits distinguished them, even in death, from the throng of ordinary dead. The heroes had lived during the period that constituted the "old days" for the Greeks, a bygone era when men were taller, stronger, more beautiful. Thus the bones of a hero could be recognized by their gigantic size. It was this race of men, later extinct, whose exploits were sung in epic poetry. Celebrated by the bards, the names of the heroes—unlike the names of ordinary men, which faded into the indistinct and forgotten mass of the nameless—remained alive forever, in radiant glory, in the memory of all the Greeks. The race of heroes formed the legendary past of the Greece of the city-states and the roots of the families, groups, and communities of the Hellenes.

Although it did not bridge the immeasurable gulf that separates men from the gods, heroic status seemed to open the prospect of the promotion of a mortal to a rank that, if not divine, was at least close to divinity. However, during the entire Classical period, this possibility remained strictly confined to a narrow sector. It was thwarted, not to say repressed, by the religious system itself. Indeed, piety, like wisdom, enjoined man not to pretend to be the equal of a god; the precepts of Delphi—"know who you are, know thyself"—have no other meaning than that. Man must accept his limits. Therefore, apart from the great legendary figures, such as Achilles, Theseus, Orestes, and Herakles, the status of the hero was restricted to the first founders of the colonies or to persons, such as Lysander of Samos and Timoleon of Syracuse, who had acquired exemplary symbolic worth in the eyes of a city.

The appearance of the hero cult, however, was not without consequences. By its newness it led to an effort to define and categorize more strictly the various supernatural powers. Plutarch noted that Hesiod was the first, in the seventh century, to make a clear distinction between the different classes of divine beings, which he divided into four groups: gods, daemons, heroes, and the dead. Taken up again by the Pythagoreans and by Plato, this nomenclature of the divinities to whom men owed veneration was common enough in the fourth century to appear in the requests that the consultants addressed to the oracle of Dodona. On one of the inscriptions that have been found, a certain Euandros and his wife question the oracle about which "of the gods, or heroes, or daemons" they must sacrifice to and address their prayers to.

The Sacrificial Practices. To find his bearings in the practice of the cult, the believer, therefore, had to take into account the hierarchical order that presided in the society of the beyond. At the top of the hierarchy were the theoi, both great and small, who made up the race of the blessed immortals. These were the Olympians, grouped under the authority of Zeus. As a rule they were celestial divinities, although some of them, such as Poseidon and Demeter, bore chthonic aspects. There was indeed a god of the underworld (Hades), but he was in fact the only one who had neither temple nor cult. The gods were made present in this world in the spaces that belonged to them: first of all, in the temples where they resided but also in the places and the objects that were consecrated to them and that, specified as *hiera* ("sacred"), could be subject to interdiction. These include the sacred groves, springs, and mountain peaks; an area surrounded by walls or boundary markers *(temenos);* crossroads, trees, stones, and obelisks. The temple, the building reserved as the dwelling of the god, did not serve as a place of worship. The faithful assembled to celebrate the rites at the exterior alter *(bomos),* a square block of masonry. Around it and upon it was performed the central rite of the Greek religion, the burnt offering *(thusia),* the analysis of which is essential.

This was normally a blood sacrifice implying the eating of the victim: a domestic animal, crowned and decked with ribbons, was led in procession to the altar to the sound of flutes. If accepted, the victim was immediately carved. The long bones, entirely stripped of flesh, were laid on the altar. Covered with fat, they were consumed with herbs and spices by the flames and, in the form of sweet-smelling smoke, rose toward heaven and the gods.

In the Olympian sacrifice, the orientation toward the heavenly divinities was marked not only by the light of day, the presence of an altar, and the blood gushing upward when the throat of the victim was cut. A fundamental feature of the ritual was that it was inseparably an offering to the gods and a festive meal for the human participants. Although the climax of the event was undoubtedly the moment that, punctuated by the ritual cry *(ololugmos),* life abandoned the animal and passed into the world of the gods, all the parts of the animal, carefully gathered and treated, were meant for the people, who ate them together. The immolation itself took place in an atmosphere of sumptuous and joyful ceremony. The entire staging of the ritual—from the procession in which the untied animal was led freely and in great pomp to the concealment of the knife in the basket to the shudder by which the sprayed animal, sprinkled with an ablution, was supposed to give its assent to the immolation—was designed to efface any traces of violence and murder and to bring to the fore aspects of peaceful solemnity and happy festivity.

As the central moment of the cult, the sacrifice was an indispensable part of communal life (whether family or state) and illustrated the tight interdependence of the religious and the social orders in the Greece of the city-states. The function of the sacrifice was not to wrest the sacrificer or the participants away from their families and civic groups or from their ordinary activities in the human world but, on the contrary, to install them in the requisite positions and patterns, to integrate them into the city and mundane existence in conformity with an order of the world presided over by the gods (i. e., "intraworld" religion, in the sense given by Max Weber, or "political" religion, in the Greek understanding of the term).

> ### Orphism involved neither a specific cult, nor devotion to an individual deity, nor a community of believers organized into a sect.

Without any special preparation, every head of a family was qualified to assume religious functions in his home. Each head of a household was pure as long as he had not committed any misdeed that defiled him. In this sense, purity did not have to be acquired or obtained; it constituted the normal state of the citizen.

Sacrifice established man in his proper state, midway between the savagery of animals that devour one another's raw flesh and the perpetual bliss of the gods, who never know hunger, weariness, or death because they find nourishment in sweet smells and ambrosia. This concern for precise delimitations, for exact apportionment, closely unites the sacrifice, both in ritual and in myth, to cereal agriculture and to marriage, both of which likewise define the particular position of civilized man. Just as, to survive, he must eat the cooked meat of a domestic animal sacrificed according to the rules, so man must feed on *sitos,* the cooked flour of regularly cultivated domestic plants. In order to survive as a race, man must father a son by union with a woman, whom marriage has drawn out of savagery and domesticated by setting her in the conjugal home. By reason of this same exigency of equilibrium in the Greek sacrifice, the sacrificer, the victim, and the god—although associated in the rite—were never confused.

Greek Mysticism. Blood sacrifice and public cult were not the only expressions of Greek piety. Various movements and groups, more or less deviant and marginal, more or less closed and secret, expressed different religious aspirations. Some were entirely or partly integrated into the civic cult; others remained foreign to it. All of them contributed in various ways to paving the way toward a Greek "mysticism" marked by the search for a more direct, more intimate, and more personal contact with the gods. This mysticism was sometimes associated with the quest for immortality, which was either granted after death through the special favor of a divinity or obtained by the observance of the discipline of a pure life reserved for the initiated and giving them the privilege of liberating, even during their earthly existence, the particle of the divine present in each.

In this context, a clear distinction must be made between three kinds of religious phenomena during the Classical period. Certain terms, such as *telete, orgia, mustai,* and *bakchoi,* are used in reference to all three, yet the phenomena they designate cannot in any way be considered identical. Despite some points of contact, they were not religious realities of the same order; nor did they have the same status or the same goals.

First, there were the mysteries. Those of Eleusis, exemplary in their prestige and their widespread influence, constituted in Attica a well-defined group of cults. Officially recognized by the city, they were organized under its control and supervision. They remained, however, on the fringe of the state because of their initiatory and secret nature and their mode of recruiting (they were open to all Greeks and based not on social status but on the personal choice of the individual).

Next there was the Dionysian religion. The cults associated with Dionysos were an integral part of the civic religion, and the festivals in honor of the god had their place like any other in the sacred calendar. But as god of *mania,* or divine madness—because of his way of taking possession of his followers through the collective trance ritually practiced in the *thiasoi* and because of his sudden intrusion here below in epiphanic revelation—Dionysos introduced into the very heart of the religion of which he was a part an experience of the supernatural that was foreign and, in many ways, contrary to the spirit of the official cult.

Finally, there was what is called Orphism. Orphism involved neither a specific cult, nor devotion to an individual deity, nor a community of believers organized into a sect as in Pythagoreanism, whatever links might have existed between the two movements. Orphism was a nebulous phenomenon that included, on the one hand, a tradition of sacred books attributed to Orpheus and Musaios (comprising theogonies, cosmogonies, and heterodox anthropogonies) and, on the other, the appearance of itinerant priests who advocated a style of existence that was contrary to the norm, a vegetarian diet, and who had at their disposal healing techniques and formulas for purification in this life and salvation in the next. In these circles, the central preoccupation and discussion focused on the destiny of the soul after death, a subject to which the Greeks were not accustomed.

What was the relationship of each of these three great religious phenomena to a cult system based on the respect of *nomoi,* the socially recognized rules of the city? Neither in beliefs nor in practices did the mysteries contradict the civic religion. Instead, they completed it by adding a new dimension suited to satisfying needs that the civic religion could not fulfill.

BIBLIOGRAPHY

General Works

Bianchi, Ugo. *La religione greca.* Turin, 1975. For the general reader, this book presents the results of a number of erudite studies on Greek religion (those, for example, of Wilamowitz, Nilsson, Pettazzoni, Guthrie, Kern, Kerényi, et al.) and includes a methodical bibliography and a large number of significant illustrations.

Burkert, Walter. *Griechische Religion der archaischen und klassischen Epoche.* Stuttgart, 1977. Translated as *Greek Religion* (Cambridge, Mass., 1985). This synthesis, supported by an abundant bibliography, covers both the Archaic and Classical periods, examining Minoan and Homeric religion, the ritual, the principal divinities, hero cults, cults of the chthonic deities, the place of religion in the city, the mysteries, and the "religion of the philosophers."

Festugière, A.J. "La Grèce: La religion." In *Histoire générale des religions,* edited by Maxime Gorce and Raoul Mortier, vol. 2, pp. 27-147. Paris, 1944. A general portrayal of ancient Greek religion, organized under four principal headings: origins, the Olympians, the organization of the divine, and the emergence of the individual.

Gernet, Louis, and André Boulanger. *Le génie grec dans la religion.* Paris, 1932. Reprinted in 1969 with a complementary bibliography. Discusses the complex origins of religious concepts in ancient Greece, the rise of civic religion, and the transformation of religious feeling and the decline of the gods of Olympus during the Hellenistic period.

Nilsson, Martin P. *Den grekiska religionens historia.* 2 vols. Stockholm, 1921. Translated by F. J. Fielden as *A History of Greek Religion* (1925); 2d ed., Oxford, 1949), with a preface by James G. Frazer.

Nilsson, Martin P. *Geschichte der griechischen Religion* (1941-1957). 2 vols. 3d rev. ed. Munich, 1967-1974. The basic "manual" for any study of the religion of ancient Greece; a truly comprehensive work, indispensable, especially for its wealth of documentation.

Vian, Francis. "La religion grecque à l'époque archaïque et classique." In *Histoire des religions,* edited by Henri-Charles Puech, vol. 1, pp. 489-577. Paris, 1970. A general study of the formation of Greek religion and its basic components: the nature and agrarian cults, the religion of the family and the city, the federative and pan-Hellenic cults, and the mysteries and ecstatic cults.

Gods and Heroes

Brelich, Angelo. *Gli eroi greci.* Rome, 1958. From the viewpoint of a general history of religions, this book analyzes the role of the Greek heroes in myth and cult and examines their relations with other mythical figures in order to bring out the specific morphology of the Greek hero.

Farnell, Lewis R. Greek *Hero Cults and Ideas of Immortality* (1921). Oxford, 1970. An investigation of the origin of the Greek heroes, proposing a compromise theory between the thesis of Erwin Rohde, who considered the heroes as spirits of the dead, and that of Hermann Usener, who upheld the theory of a divine origin of the heroes.

Guthrie, W. K. C. *The Greeks and Their Gods.* London, 1950. A still useful work on Greek religion, conceived and written for nonspecialists.

Kerényi, Károly. *The Heroes of the Greeks.* Translated by H. J. Rose. London, 1959. Discusses the life, exploits, and deaths of the Greek heroes.

Otto, Walter F. *Die Götter Griechenlands: Das Bild des Göttlichen im Spiegel des griechischen Geistes.* Bonn, 1929. Translated by Moses Hadas as The Homeric Gods: *The Spiritual Significance of Greek Religion* (1954; Boston, 1964). A study of the nature and essence of the gods of Homer, who is treated as a great religious reformer.

Séchan, Louis, and Pierre Lévêque. *Les grandes divinités de la Grèce.* Paris, 1966. A complete scientific file on the principal figures of the Greek pantheon, whose origins, cult manifestations, and figurative representations are analyzed by the authors.

Myth and Ritual

Burkert, Walter. *Structure and History in Greek Mythology and Ritual.* Berkeley, 1979. An analysis of the concepts of myth and ritual from a historical perspective, which seeks to demonstrate the existence of a continuous but constantly transformed tradition from primeval times, through the Paleolithic period, to the Greek and Oriental civilizations.

Detienne, Marcel. *L'invention de la mythologie.* Paris, 1981. Through the study of the status of the "fable" in the eighteenth century, the discourse of the mythologists of the nineteenth century, and the place of myth in ancient Greek society, the author makes an epistemological investigation of mythology, reconsidered as an object of knowledge as well as an object of culture.

Deubner, Ludwig. *Attische Feste* (1932). Hildesheim, 1966. The most complete discussion of the festivals of Attica, indispensable for the wealth of texts cited; places iconographic material in relationship to certain festivals.

Farnell, Lewis R. *The Cults of the Greek States* (1896-1909). 5 vols. New Rochelle, N. Y., 1977. A veritable "encyclopedia" of Greek cults, invaluable for the broad range of materials brought together and analyzed under the name of each divinity of Greece.

Kirk, G. S. *Myth: Its Meaning and Functions in Ancient and Other Cultures.* Berkeley, 1970. Studying the relationship between myth, ritual, and fable, the limits of the structuralist theory of Claude Lévi-Strauss, as well as the specific character of Mesopotamian and Greek myths, the author examines the status of myths as expressions of the subconscious and as universal symbols.

Nilsson, Martin P. *Griechische Feste von religiöser Bedeutung: Mit Ausschluss der Attischen* (1906). Stuttgart, 1957. The best-documented study of the festivals of ancient Greece, with the exception of Attic festivals, classified and analyzed under the name of each divinity.

Parke, H. W. *Festivals of the Athenians.* Ithaca, N. Y., 1977. A description of the festivals of the ancient Athenians, analyzed according to the calendar; accessible to nonspecialists of the Greek world.

Rudhardt, Jean. *Notions fondamentales de la pensée religieuse et actes constitutifs du culte dans la Grèce classique.* Geneva, 1958. A pertinent analysis of the notion of the divine; beliefs concerning the gods, the dead, and the heroes; and the acts of the cult (dances, ritual meals, purifications, religious songs, prayers, sacrifices, etc.).

Vernant, Jean-Pierre. *Mythe et pensée chez les Grecs* (1965). 2 vols. 3d ed. Paris, 1971. Translated as *Myth and Thought among the Greeks* (London, 1983).

Vernant, Jean-Pierre. *Mythe et société en Grèce ancienne.* Paris, 1974. Translated as *Myth and Society in Ancient Greece* (Atlantic Highlands, N. J., 1980). Attempts to determine the intellectual code proper to the Greek myth and to define the logical form that the myth brings into play (a logic of ambiguity, equivocality, and polarity); examines the relationship between the intellectual framework brought out by structural analysis and the sociohistorical context in which myth was produced.

Divination and Oracles

Bouché-Leclercq, Auguste. *Histoire de la divination dans l'antiquité* (1879-1882). 4 vols. Brussels, 1963; New York, 1975. The fundamental book on ancient divination, although outdated on numerous points.

Parke, H. W., and D. E. W. Wormell. *The Delphic Oracle.* 2 vols. Oxford, 1956. The most complete synthesis devoted to the oracle of Delphi, treating all the ancient accounts in the light of archaeological discoveries.

Sacrifice

Burkert, Walter. *Homo Necans: Interpretationen altgriechischer Opferriten und Mythen.* Berlin, 1972. Translated by Peter Bing as *Homo Necans: The Anthropology of Ancient Greek Sacrificial Ritual and Myth* (Berkeley, 1983). Continuing the work of Karl Meuli, the author attempts to articulate a general theory of sacrifice in which the ritual murder of the victim is central to the entire ceremony.

Casabona, Jean. *Recherches sur le vocabulaire des sacrifices en grec, des origines à la fin de l'époque classique.* Aix-en-Provence, 1966. An excellent semantic study of the vocabulary of sacrifice and libations, supported by a meticulous examination of literary texts (from Homer to Xenophon) and epigraphic texts.

Detienne, Marcel, and Jean-Pierre Vernant, eds. *La cuisine du sacrifice en pays grec.* Paris, 1980. An anthropological analysis of the Greek sacrifice as a ritual and civic act situated in the center of the alimentary practices and politico-religious thinking of the city; leads to questioning the pertinence of a Judeo-Christian model pretending to be unitarian and universal. With contributions by Jean-Louis Durand, Stella Georgoudi, François Hartog, and Jesper Svenbro.

Meuli, Karl. "Griechische Opferbräuche." In *Phyllobolia für Peter von der Mühli zum 60. Geburtstage,* edited by Olof Gigon and Karl Meuli, pp. 185-288. Basel, 1946. A comparison between the "Olympian sacrifice" of the Greeks and certain rites of the hunting and herding peoples of northeastern Europe and northern Asia; discerns a sacrificial structure originating in this primitive world and surviving in ancient Greece.

Reverdin, Olivier, ed. *Le sacrifice dans l'antiquité.* Geneva, 1981. Contributors approach questions of method, not in a theoretical and general manner, but through the study of a choice of specific and varied sacrificial rites.

Mysteries, Dionysism, Orphism

Guthrie, W. K. C. *Orpheus and Greek Religion: A Study of the Orphic Movement.* 2d ed., rev. London, 1952. A study of Orpheus and Orphic beliefs, in which the author tries to analyze and assess the influence of Orphism on the life and thought of the Greeks.

Jeanmaire, Henri. *Dionysos: Histoire du culte de Bacchus.* 2 vols. Paris, 1951. A study devoted to the major institutions and the char-acteristic elements of the Dionysian religion as it was constituted especially in the Archaic period; also analyzes the development of the Dionysian myth and mystic speculation in the Hellenistic and Greco-Roman environment.

Kerényi, Károly. *Dionysos: Archetypal Image of the Indestructible Life.* Translated by Ralph Mannheim. Princeton, 1976. Considering the Dionysian element as a chapter of the religious history of Europe, the author retraces the itinerary of the Dionysian religion from "the Minoan period to the Roman empire" with the aid of linguistic, archaeological, philosophical, and psychological research; includes 146 illustrations and a rich bibliography.

Linforth, Ivan M. *The Arts of Orpheus* (1941). New York, 1973. A critical study of texts relating to Orphism and the legend of Orpheus as well as the myth of Dionysos.

Mylonas, George E. *Eleusis and the Eleusinian Mysteries.* Princeton, 1961. An archaeological study of the sanctuary and mysteries of Eleusis, retracing the history of the cult from the first houses of the Bronze Age to the imperial era of Rome.

Otto, Walter F. *Dionysos: Mythos und Kultus.* Frankfurt, 1933. Translated by Robert B. Palmer as *Dionysos: Myth and Cult* (Bloomington, Ind., 1965). Emphasizes the Archaic and pan-Hellenic character of this "god of paradox" and the theme of his "persecution" as well as the typology of his multiple epiphanies.

Sabbatucci, Dario. *Saggio sul misticismo greco.* Rome, 1965. An essay on the Greek concepts of salvation and Orphism, Pythagoreanism, Dionysism, and Eleusinism as alternatives to the politico-religious system of the city.

JEAN-PIERRE VERNANT
Translated from French by Anne Marzin

HADES

Son of Rhea and Kronos, Hades was for the ancient Greeks the lord of the land of the dead, the realm that was granted him in the division of the world with his brothers Zeus and Poseidon following their victory over the Titans (*Iliad* 15.188). In later mythology the abode of departed spirits was itself referred to as Hades.

Situated at the limits of the earth, where night meets day, or in the subterranean regions (*Odyssey* 11 passim; Hesiod, *Theogony* 748ff., 766 ff.), Hades has been conceived of as a musty world clad in darkness, a place odious to mortals and immortals alike. In this country without laughter or sunshine, where all are obliged to make their way sooner or later, the dead, their heads filled with darkness, wander forever among the silent fields of asphodels (daffodils) or atone for their sins in the depths of Erebos or Tartaros. To return to sweet day-

> **Furthermore, as soon as the new arrivals cross the dismal threshold Hades locks the gates, and his agents, who never sleep, prevent any attempt at escape.**

light is impossible, for without memory the dead could not find the way back. Furthermore, as soon as the new arrivals cross the dismal threshold Hades locks the gates, and his agents, who never sleep, prevent any attempt at escape.

Relentless at heart, Hades leaves his abode only to protect the stability of his domain; it is Thanatos (Death) who obtains inhabitants for him. However, Hades became infatuated with Demeter's daughter, Persephone, and carried her off to share with him the honors of the infernal throne. Their union is at once sterile and prosperous: they have no child but enjoy the wealth of the soil, which they dispense to the living as they choose.

If love and abduction suggested the theme of death in ancient Greece, Persephone's return to her mother and the springtime that she brought with her impelled mortals to the Eleusinian mysteries, which opened the path to immortality.

BIBLIOGRAPHY

Kahn-Lyotard, Laurence, and Nicole Loraux. "Mythes de la mort en Grèce." In *Dictionnaire des mythologies,* edited by Yves Bonnefoy, Paris, 1981.
Ramnoux, Clémence. *La nuit et les enfants de la nuit dans la tradition grecque.* Paris, 1959.
Vermeule, Emily. *Aspects of Death in Early Greek Art and Poetry.* Berkeley, 1979.

JEANNIE CARLIER and
SÍLVIA MILANEZI
Translated from French by Alice Otis

HALAKHAH

Structure of Halakhah

Halakhah, in the general sense of the word, is the entire body of Jewish law, from scripture to the latest rabbinical rulings. It is a complete system of law governing every aspect of human life. It has been traditionally viewed as wholly rooted in God's revealed will (B. T., *Hag.* 3b) but subject to the ongoing interpretation of the Jewish jurists (B. T., *B. M.* 59b).

In its more specific sense *halakhah* (pl., *halakhot*) refers to those laws that were traditionally observed by the Jewish people as if they were scriptural commandments *(mitsvot)* even though they were nowhere explicitly found in scripture. The term itself, according to Saul Lieberman in *Hellenism in Jewish Palestine* (New York, 1962), seems to refer to the statement of a juristic norm as opposed to actual case law. The task of much rabbinic exegesis, especially during the tannaitic period (c. 70-200 CE), was to show that through the use of proper hermeneutics the *halakhot* could be derived from the text of scripture, especially the Pentateuch.

Origins. Concerning the origins of *halakhah* there are three main theories.

The first, the traditional, rabbinic approach, is founded on the literal meaning of "a law of Moses from Sinai," namely, that Moses received two sets of teachings at Mount Sinai, one written (the Pentateuch) and the other oral *(torah she-be`al peh),* and that the oral Torah is the authoritative explanation of the written Torah (B. T., *Ber.* 5a).

The second theory is that of Moses Maimonides (Mosheh ben Maimon, 1135/8-1204). Although he too reiterated the literal meaning of the totally Mosaic origin of *halakhah,* in his specific treatment of the constitution of halakhic authority he states that *halakhah* is based on scripture and, equally, on the rulings of the Great Court in Jerusalem (*Mishneh Torah,* Rebels 1.1ff.)

The third theory is that of Zacharias Frankel (1801-1875). Expanding certain medieval comments into a more general theory, Frankel, in *Darkhei ha-Mishnah* (Leipzig, 1859), saw the term "a law of Moses from Sinai" as primarily referring to ancient laws that had become widespread in Jewish practice and whose origins were obscure.

Scriptural Exegesis. Because of the Pharisaic and rabbinic emphasis on the essential unity of the written Torah and the *halakhah,* in contradistinction to the Sadducean, which accepted only the former as authoritative (B. T., *Hor.* 4a), an elaborate hermeneutical system was worked out to derive as many of the halakhot as possible from the words of scripture, which was considered normatively unintelligible without the process of specifically relating it to the *halakhah* (B. T., *Shab.* 31a). This entire process was called *midrash,* literally meaning "inquiry" into scripture.

Rabbinic Law. In the amoraic period (c. 220-c. 500) there emerged a more clear-cut distinction between laws considered scriptural *(de-oraita')* and laws considered rabbinic *(de-rabbanan).* The difference between scriptural law and rabbinic law by this time was that the latter was considered to be evidently rational. As for scriptural law, despite attempts to discover "reasons for the commandments" *(ta`amei ha-mitsvot),* God's will was considered sufficient reason for it.

Rabbinic law, although occasionally justified by indirect scriptural exegesis *(asmakhta'),* was then usually justified as being for the fulfillment of some religious or social need (B. T., *Ber.* 23b). This developed to such an extent that it was claimed that there were only three rabbinic laws for which no reason could be immediately discerned (B. T., *Git.* 14a). Furthermore, the lines between direct and indirect exegesis were considerably blurred (B. T., *Pes.* 39b). Finally, Rava', a fourth-century Babylonian sage who became the most prominent advocate of rational jurisprudence, indicated that the rabbis actually had more legislative power than even scripture (B. T., *Mak.* 22b).

The question of the extent of scriptural law versus rabbinic law was deeply debated among the medieval Jewish jurists. Maimonides, following the Talmudic opinion that scriptural law is limited to 613 Pentateuchal commandments (B. T., *Mak.* 23b), considered any other laws, whether traditional or formulated through exegesis or rabbinical legislation, as having the status of rabbinic laws *(Sefer ha-mitsvot,* intro., sec. 2). Moses Nahmanides (Mosheh ben Nahman, c. 1194-1270), on the other hand, was of the opinion that anything designated by the rabbis as scriptural law, especially those

laws derived hermeneutically in rabbinic literature, has the status of scriptural law. Only those laws specifically designated by the rabbis as rabbinic are to be considered as such. This difference of opinion concerning the very character of *halakhah* is philosophical. Maimonides' prime concern seems to have been with the process of legislation, that is, with the ability of the duly constituted authorities to make new laws and repeal old ones. Nahmanides' prime concern seems to have been with a revival of the whole process of rabbinical exegesis. This distinction can be seen in the fact that Maimonides' chief halakhic contribution was that of a highly innovative codifier, whereas Nahmanides' was that of an exegete. This difference of approach can be seen in the Talmud and throughout the history of the *halakhah,* namely, the apodictic approach (B. T., *Nid.* 73a) as contrasted with the expository approach (B. T., *B. M.* 33a).

Custom. *Minhag* ("custom") is the third constituent element in *halakhah,* after scriptual exegesis and rabbinic law. It basically has three functions.

1. Custom is invoked when the law itself is ambiguous. If there are two reputable opinions as to what a law is, then there are two ways of deciding what is to be done. Either the majority view of the sages is followed (B. T., *Hul.* 11a), or the popular practice of the people is consulted and followed (J. T., *Pe'ah* 8.2, 20c). In the latter situation custom does not establish law but distinguishes between which law is considered normative (*halakhah le-ma`aseh*) and which law is considered only theoretical (*ein morin ken,* J. T., *Yev.* 12.1, 12c).

2. Custom is considered a valid form of law, supplementing scriptural commandments and formal rabbinical legislation. Certain customs are considered universally Jewish. For

> **However, sometimes custom even had the power to abrogate, *de facto,* scriptural law.**

example, the Orthodox objection to the modern practice of men and women sitting together in non-Orthodox synagogues, although some have attempted to find formal halakhic objections to it, is actually based on the fact that theretofore separation of the sexes in the synagogue was undoubtedly universal Jewish custom.

3. Custom sometimes takes precedence over established Jewish practice even when it has no foundation in *halakhah.* Usually this power of custom was used to rescind privileges the *halakhah* had earlier granted (Elon, 1978, pp. 732ff.). However, sometimes custom even had the power to abrogate, *de facto,* scriptural law. For example, the law that certain portions of slaughtered animals be given to descendants of Aaronic priests irrespective of time and place was not considered binding because of customary neglect.

Current Role of Halakhah. Although *halakhah* is a system of law governing every aspect of personal and communal life, there is no Jewish community in the world today where *halakhah* is the sole basis of governance. This inherent paradox—namely, a total system of law forced by historical reality to share legal authority with another system of law, if not to be actually subordinate to it—has led to a number of tensions both in the state of Israel and in the Diaspora.

Halakhah in the state of Israel. In the state of Israel, *halakhah,* as adjudicated by the rabbinical courts, is recognized as the law governing all aspects of public Jewish religious ritual and all areas of marriage and divorce. (The same privilege is extended to the respective systems of law of the various non-Jewish religious communities there.) This political arrangement has led to a number of areas of tension. Thus many secularist Israeli Jews object to having to submit in questions of personal and familial status to the authority of religious courts, whose very religious justification they do not accept. This conflict has manifested itself in the demand by many secularist Israelis for civil marriage and divorce in the state of Israel, something that *halakhah* rejects as unacceptable for Jews. Even more profound is the fact that there is a conflict between *halakhah* and Israeli law on the most basic question of Jewish identity, that is, who is a Jew. According to *halakhah,* anyone born of a Jewish mother or himself or herself converted to Judaism is considered a Jew. According to the Israeli Law of Return (Hoq ha-Shevut), any Jew (with the exception of one convicted of a crime in another country) has the right of Israeli domicile and Israeli citizenship. However, in 1962 in a famous decision the Israeli Supreme Court ruled that Oswald Rufeisen, a Jewish convert to Christianity and a Roman Catholic monk, was not entitled to Israeli citizenship as a Jew because in the popular sense of the term he was not a Jew even though he was one in the technical, halakhic sense. On the other hand, in 1968, in another famous decision, the Israeli Supreme Court ruled that the wife and children of an Israeli Jew, Binyamin Shalit, were not to be considered Jews for purposes of Israeli citizenship because they had not been converted to Judaism, even though they identified themselves as Israeli Jews in the secular sense of the term. In this case, unlike the earlier one, the court accepted a halakhic definition of who is a Jew.

At the present time, furthermore, there is considerable debate in the state of Israel and the Diaspora about what actually constitutes valid conversion to Judaism.

Halakhah in the Diaspora. In the Diaspora, where adherence to *halakhah* is a matter of individual choice in practically every country that Judaism may be freely practiced, there is little ability to enforce the communal authority inherent in the halakhic system itself. This has led to a number of vexing problems. For example, the Talmud empowers a rabbinical court to force a man to divorce his wife for a variety of objective reasons that make normal married life impossible. When Jewish communities enjoyed relative internal autonomy, such enforcement could be carried out regularly. However, today, because of the loss of such communal autonomy, such enforcement is impossible, and many Jewish women, although already civilly divorced and no longer living with their former husbands, are still considered married according to *halakhah* and are unable to remarry because of the refusal of their former husbands to comply with the order of a rabbinical court.

This growing problem in societies where mobility and anonymity are facts of life has led to basically three different approaches. Many in the Orthodox community have attempted to resort to legal measures in the civil courts to force compliance with *halakhah.* In addition to a lack of success heretofore, this has raised, especially in the United States, the constitutional issue of governmental interference in private religious matters. On the other hand, the Conservative movement since 1968 has revived the ancient rabbinical privilege of retroactive annulment (B. T., *Git.* 33a) in cases where it is impossible to obtain a Jewish divorce from the husband. The Reform movement, not being bound by the authority of *halakhah,* accepts a civil divorce as sufficient termination of a Jewish marriage. These three widely divergent approaches to a major halakhic problem are further evidence of the growing divisiveness in the Jewish religious community in both the state of Israel and the Diaspora.

Reconstitution of the Sanhedrin. The only chance for effecting any halakhic unanimity among the Jewish people would be the reconstitution of the Sanhedrin in Jerusalem as the universal Jewish legislature and supreme court. This proposal was actually made by the first minister of religious affairs in the state of Israel, Judah Leib Maimon (1875-1962). However, considering the fact that this reconstitution itself presupposes much of the very unanimity it is to effect, it would seem that it is rather utopian, something the Talmud euphemistically called "messianic *halakhah*" (B. T., *Zev.* 45a).

BIBLIOGRAPHY

Considering the enormous quantity of halakhic literature, it is most unlikely that even a considerable portion of it will ever be translated into English or any other non-Hebrew language. However, some of the classic sources and some excellent secondary sources are available in English translation.

The Mishnah translation most widely used and accepted is that of Herbert Danby (Oxford, 1933). The Babylonian Talmud has been completely translated in the usually adequate Soncino edition (London, 1935-1948). The Palestinian Talmud is now being translated by Jacob Neusner under the title *The Talmud of the Land of Israel* (Chicago, 1982-); several volumes have already appeared. The Tosefta is also being translated by Neusner (New York, 1977-), and a number of volumes have appeared so far. Most of Maimonides' *Mishneh Torah* has been published as *The Code of Maimonides,* 13 vols. (New Haven, 1949-), in a uniformly excellent translation.

The most comprehensive treatment of halakhic institutions in English is *The Principles of Jewish Law,* edited by Menachem Elon

(Jerusalem, 1975), although more detailed questions are dealt with in Elon's Hebrew work, *Ha-mishpat ha-`ivri*, 2d ed. (Jerusalem, 1978). Another helpful work, especially regarding Jewish civil law, is Isaac H. Herzog's *The Main Institutions of Jewish Law*, 2 vols., 2d ed. (New York, 1965). Still the best treatment of the history of halakhah is Louis Ginzberg's "Law, Codification of" in the *Jewish Encyclopedia* (New York, 1905). Ginzberg's "The Significance of the Halachah for Jewish History," translated by Arthur Hertzberg in *On Jewish Law and Lore* (Philadelphia, 1955), is a fascinating but controversial treatment of early *halakhah* from a socioeconomic point of view. Another important general treatment is the article "Halakhah" by Louis Jacobs and Bert De Vries in *Encyclopaedia Judaica* (Jerusalem, 1971).

The number of good monographs on halakhic topics in English is steadily growing. One can read and consult with profit the following finely researched and written works: Boaz Co-hen's *Jewish and Roman Law: A Comparative Study,* 2 vols. (New York, 1966); Louis M. Epstein's *The Jewish Marriage Contract* (1927; reprint, New York, 1973); David M. Feldman's *Birth Control in Jewish Law* (New York, 1968); Solomon B. Freehof's *The Responsa Literature* (Philadelphia, 1955); Aaron Kirschenbaum's *Self-Incrimination in Jewish Law* (New York, 1970); Isaac Klein's *A Guide to Jewish Religious Practice* (New York, 1979); Leo Landman's *Jewish Law in the Diaspora* (Philadelphia, 1968); Samuel Mendelsohn's The Criminal *Jurisprudence of the Ancient Hebrews* (Baltimore, 1891); and my own *The Image of the Non-Jew in Judaism* (New York, 1983).

The articles in *The Jewish Law Annual*, vols. 1-4, edited by Bernard S. Jackson (Leiden, 1978-1981), generally represent some of the best critical scholarship on halakhic topics in English today. A good sampling of the current theological debate over the authority and scope of *halakhah* can be found in a symposium in *Judaism* 29 (Winter 1980).

DAVID NOVAK

HANUKKAH

HANUKKAH ("dedication") is the Jewish winter festival that falls on the twenty-fifth of the month of Kislev and lasts for eight days. It celebrates the victory of the Maccabees over the forces of Antiochus after a three-year battle in the second century BCE. The major sources on the festival's origin are two apocryphal books, *1 Maccabees* and *2 Maccabees.* It is stated there (*2 Mc.* 10:6-8) that the altar was rededicated and the festival of eight days introduced because during the war the Jews were unable to celebrate the eight-day festival of Sukkot. Thus in the earliest period there is no reference to Hanukkah as a feast of lights. That it became such is due to the Talmudic legend (B. T., *Shab.* 21b) that the Maccabees found only one small jar of oil for the kindling of the *menorah* ("candelabrum") in the Temple. This was sealed with the seal of the high priest but contained only sufficient oil to burn for a single night. By a miracle the oil lasted for eight nights. It was consequently ordained that lights be kindled on the eight nights of Hanukkah. However, it is stated in the Talmud (B. T., *Shab.* 21b) that the Shammaites and Hillelites, at the begin-

ning of the present era, debated whether the lights were to be kindled in descending order (eight the first night, seven the second, etc.) or in ascending order (one the first night, two the second, etc.). If this statement is historically correct, it demonstrates either that the legend of the oil was already known at that time or that, at least, there was an association of Hanukkah and light even at this early period. According to some historians, the origin of the festival is to be found in

> **The festival is a time for intensive study of the Torah as well as for almsgiving.**

pagan festivals of light in midwinter. The prayers for Hanukkah refer only to the victory, but in practice the kindling of the lights is the main feature of the festival.

It has long been the custom for each member of the household to kindle the Hanukkah lights in an eight-branched candelabrum frequently called a menorah (though the *menorah* in the Temple had only seven branches) but nowadays also known as a *hanukkiyyah.* The lights are kindled in the synagogue as well as in the home. The older practice was to use only olive oil, and this is still customary among the more pious, but the majority of Jews use candles for the Hanukkah lights. Rabbinical authorities have discussed whether electric lights may be used for this purpose, the consensus being to permit them. One light is kindled on the first night, two on the second night, three on the third night, and so on until all eight are lit. In order to avoid lighting the candles one from the other, an additional candle known as the *shammash* ("retainer") is used to light the others. A declaration is recited:

> We kindle these lights on account of the miracles, the deliverances, and the wonders which thou didst work for our ancestors, by means of thy holy priests. During all the eight days of Hanukkah these lights are sacred, neither is it permitted to make any profane use of them; but we are only to look at them, in order that we may give thanks unto thy name for thy miracles, deliverances, and wonders.

A popular Hanukkah hymn is *Ma`oz tsur* (O Fortress Rock), sung to a familiar melody said to have been originally that of a German drinking song.

Medieval Jewish thinkers understood the Hanukkah lights as representing spiritual illumination. The festival is a time for intensive study of the Torah as well as for almsgiving. Hanukkah is consequently treated as a more "spiritual" festival than the boisterous Purim, so that although fasting is forbidden on Hanukkah, there is no special festive meal. The Torah is read on each day of the festival; the passages chosen are from the account of the gifts brought by the princes at the dedication of the Tabernacle (*Nm.* 7) and the command to kindle the light of the *menorah* (*Nm.* 8:1-7). The Prophetic reading on the Sabbath of Hanukkah is from the vision of the *menorah* seen by Zechariah (*Zec.* 2). An addition to each of the daily prayers thanks God for delivering the strong into the hands of the weak, the many into the hands of the few, the impure into the hands of the pure, and the wicked into the hands of the righteous.

It is nowadays customary for Hanukkah presents to be given to children. This practice is found in none of the early sources and seems certain to have been introduced to offset the giving of Christmas presents at this season of the year.

Children and some adults play a game with a spinning top (dreidel) on each side of which is a different letter representing a move in the game. These letters are the initial letters of the Hebrew words making up the sentence "A great miracle happened there." To the consternation of the more conventional rabbis, cardplaying is often indulged in on Hanukkah.

The Talmudic rabbis stress the need for proclaiming the miracle by kindling the Hanukkah lights outside the door of the home, but eventually this practice was discouraged because it could be misinterpreted by non-Jews as a desire to demonstrate Jewish reluctance to live among their gentile neighbors. The less obtrusive practice of kindling the lights near the door but inside the home became the norm. In modern Israel it is far from unusual to see huge Hanukkah candelabra on top of public buildings and synagogues.

BIBLIOGRAPHY

Lehrman, Simon Maurice. *A Guide to Hanukkah and Purim.* London, 1958.

Shaw, Oliver. *The Origins of the Festival of Hanukkah.* Edinburgh, 1930. A discussion of the history of the festival.

LOUIS JACOBS

HASIDISM

An Overview

Hasidism is the common appellation of a Jewish pietistic movement that developed in eastern Europe in the second half of the eighteenth century, became, before the end of that century, a major force in modern Judaism, and has remained as such into the twentieth century.

History. The history of the early Hasidic movement can be divided into four main periods, each a major step in its development.

1. *The circle of the Besht (c. 1740-1760).* The Besht (Yisra`el ben Eli`ezer) seems to have been in contact with a group of wandering preachers, like himself, who in their homiletics preached a new kind of worship and presented a new conception of the role of the elect in Jewish religion. They were qabbalists, following the main mystical symbols of the Lurianic school but emphasizing the achievements of the individual and his ability to assist his brethren in religious matters. *Devequt* (communion with God) was one of the main subjects they preached, stressing man's ability to attain constant communion with God. It is possible that parallel to the Besht's circle of adherents there were other pietistic groups in some of the major centers of Jewish culture in eastern Europe.

2. *The first Hasidic center in Mezhirich (1760-1772).* After the Besht's death, the leadership of the Hasidic movement was assumed by his disciple, Dov Ber of Mezhirich (now Miedzyrzecz, Poland). He held "court" in his home, where many young Jewish intellectuals as well as common people gathered to listen to his sermons. These were transcribed by his disciples and later published in several versions. In this period begins the history of Hasidism as an organized movement, led by an accepted authority.

3. *The disciples of Dov Ber (1773-1812).* This is the most important period, in which Hasidism became a major force within Judaism. Several of Dov Ber's disciples created "courts" like that of their teacher, and led `edot ("communities"), around which thousands, and then tens of thousands, of adherents gathered, accepting the leadership of that disciple and making their community an alternative social and religious organization of Jews, distinct from the hegemony of the traditional rabbinate. In this period of Hasidic theory of the tsaddiq was developed and began to shape both Hasidic thought and social organization. At this same time the Hasidim became a distinct group, not only because of the internal development of Hasidism, but also because of the growing opposition to it from the school of Eliyyahu ben Shelomoh Zalman, the "Gaon of Vilna," which published several pamphlets against Hasidic ideology and practice, denouncing them as heretics and excommunicating them, even trying to enlist the help of the Russian government against their leaders. This fierce opposition was motivated both by fears that the Hasidim were going to undermine the traditional Jewish social structure.

It was in this period that Hasidic literature was initially published. The first works were those of Ya`aqov Yosef of Polonnoye, the Besht's greatest disciple, whose voluminous collections of sermons include most of the material we have concerning the teachings of the Besht and Dov Ber.By the beginning of the nineteenth century the Hasidic movement had an organized leadership, prolific literature, well-defined communities and areas of influence, and an established standing in the general framework of Jewish life.

4. *The development of Hasidic "houses" or "lines of succession" (shoshalot).* To a very large extent this process has

continued to the present. Many of Dov Ber's disciples served as founders of several Hasidic communities when their disciples scattered and each established his own "house" and community. The custom of passing Hasidic leadership from father to son or, in some cases, son-in-law, became more and more frequent, until it was universally accepted that the new leader had to be from the family of the previous leader. These "houses" usually bore the names of the towns in which they were established, even after the center was moved to another country—Poland, for instance, where many centers were located in Warsaw before the Second World War—or to another continent such as to the United States or Israel, where many of the centers are today. The history of Hasidism has since fragmented into the separate histories of various houses or schools. Only two of the communities have preserved their specific ideological and organizational profile, remaining distinct from all others, throughout this period—Habad Hasidism, founded by Shne'ur Zalman of Lyady, and Bratslav Hasidism, the followers of Nahman of Brat-slav, the Besht's great-grandson. The rift between Hasidim and their opponents has obtained until this day; most Jews of east European descent belong to family lines of either Hasidim or *mitnaggedim* ("opponents").

Spread of the Movement. The persecution by their opponents did not halt the spread of the movement, which gathered momentum and gained new communities and adherents in the end of the eighteenth century and the first half of the nineteenth century. The disciples of Dov Ber and their disciples established the great Hasidic houses. Levi Yitshaq established an important Hasidic community in Berdichev, while Menahem Nahum built the house of Chernobyl, which was continued by his son, Mordechai Twersky, and went on for many generations. Yisra'el of Rizhyn (now Ruzhin, Ukrainian S. S. R.), a descendant of Dov Ber, built the Rizhyn-Sadigora house; his four sons who followed him made it into one of the most important and eminent Hasidic communities in Russia. In Poland and Lithuania Hasidism became a major force through the work of Shelomoh ben Me'ir of Karlin and Hayyim Haiqel of Amdur (Indura). Hasidic communities in the Land of Israel were established in Safad and Tiberias by Menahem Mendel of Vitebsk and Avraham ben Aleksander Kats of Kalisz who migrated to the Land of Israel in 1777. In the beginning of the nineteenth century a group of great leaders gave renewed impetus to the spread of Hasidism, among them Ya'aqov Yitshaq ("the Seer of Lublin"), Ya'aqov Yitshaq ben Asher of Pshischa (now Przysucha, Poland), and Avraham Yehoshu'a Heschel of Apt in Moldavia (now Opatow, Poland). Menahem Morgenstern established the great house of Pshischa-Kozk, and Shalom Rokeah the Belz Hasidim. Mosheh Teitelbaum, a disciple of Ya'aqov Yitshaq of Lublin, created the powerful and influential Satmar Hasidism in Hungary. By the middle of the nineteenth century Hasidism was the dominant force in most Jewish communities in eastern Europe, and most Hasidic houses continued their existence and development until the Holocaust.

Theology and Ethics. It is nearly impossible to describe Hasidic theology and ethics as being distinct from previous Jewish ideologies because Hasidic teachers preached their ideas in the form of sermons, which included all layers of earlier Jewish thought. Almost all the main ideas and trends found in early-eighteenth-century Hebrew homiletical literature also appear in Hasidic thought, and attempts to define specifically Hasidic ideas, or even emphases, usually fail because similar examples can easily be produced from earlier homiletical literature. A second difficulty is that every Hasidic teacher developed his own theology and ethics and his own list of priorities which may distinguish him or his group but never characterize all the hundreds of teachers and writers who created Hasidic literature. It is unfeasible to generalize from one or a group of Hasidic teachers to the movement as a whole. Every definition is therefore a necessarily subjective one. Thus only a few general outlines, qualified by the preceding statements, can be presented concerning Hasidic theology.

Relationship to Lurianic Qabbalah. Hasidic theology, like other qabbalistic schools of the eighteenth century, downplayed the most dramatic mythical symbols of Lurianic mysticism, especially that of *shevirat ha-kelim* ("the breaking of the divine vessels"), the description of the catastrophe within the divine world which is the origin of evil, according to Luria. The idea of *tsimtsum* (divine self-contraction) was elaborated by the Hasidim (especially by Dov Ber), but in a completely different manner than in Luria's original thought. Instead of the original Lurianic idea of a mythological catastrophe, the Hasidim presented a theology in which this process was the result of divine benevolence toward the faithful.

The Hasidim also deemphasized the Lurianic concept of *tiqqun* (restoration), the process by which messianic redemption is enhanced by the collective efforts of the Jewish people as a whole; they preferred instead the concept of *devequt* (communion with God), a process of individual redemption by which a person uplifts his own soul into contact with the divine powers.

Extent of messianism in Hasidism. There is an emphasis in Hasidic literature on personal religious achievement rather than on the general, national, and cosmic impact of religious life. The redemptive element, while still strong in Hasidism, often emphasizes the redemption of the individual's soul rather than that of the nation or of the cosmos as a whole. This is a slight departure from Lurianic Qabbalah.

Hasidic approach to God. In early Hasidic literature there is an emphasis on direct, emotional worship of God and a deemphasis on contact with God through constant study of the Torah and Talmud and diligent observance of the particulars concerning the performance of the *mitsvot.* This does not mean that the Hasidim did not study the Torah or that they disregarded the *mitsvot,* as their opponents often claimed; rather, the Hasidim stressed the importance of mystical contact with God through *devequt,* usually attained while praying but also achieved when a person is working for his livelihood or engaged in any other physical activity.

Good and evil. Hasidic teachers, more than non-Hasidim, contributed to the development of a conception of the way to fight evil within one's soul. Unlike Lurian theology, Dov Ber of Mezhirich and other Hasidic teachers insisted that evil can and should be overcome by absorbing it, uplifting and making it again a part of goodness, believing that the spiritual stature of the "corrected" or "repentant" evil is higher than that of the elements that were always good.

Hasidism as revival of traditional spirituality. The spiritual side of religious life holds a central place in Hasidic teachings, following the traditions of medieval Hebrew ethical and homiletical literature. Great emphasis is placed on the correct qabbalistic intentions in prayers *(kavvanot),* on spiritual repentance, on the love and fear of God, and on social justice and love for fellow men. While very few new ideas on these subjects are to be found in the vast Hasidic literature, the movement undoubtedly represents a revival of these spiritual values within the framework of everyday religious life. In this respect, then, there is no basis to the frequent descriptions of Hasidism as an original phenomenon that changed the face of traditional Judaism; but it can be claimed that the Hasidim collected many spiritualistic ideas and practices from previous Jewish sources and brought them to the foreground of their teachings.

BIBLIOGRAPHY

Several important book-length studies of Hasidism are to be found in English. Simon Dubnow's classic *Geschichte des Chassidismus,* 2 vols. (Berlin, 1931), is still the best factual description of the development of early Hasidism. A brief but profound description of Hasidic mysticism is to be found in "Hasidism: The Last Phase," the last chapter in Gershom Scholem's *Major Trends in Jewish Mysticsm,* 2d ed. (New York, 1954), pp. 325-350; the reader may use previous chapters in this book to study main qabbalistic terminology and symbols. Scholem's studies of Hasidic concepts of communion with God and messianism can be found in his collection of essays, *The Messianic Idea in Judaism and Other Essays on Jewish Spirituality* (New York 1971), pp. 176-250.

The Hasidic idea of the intermediary between God and man is studied in Samuel H. Dresner's book *The Zaddik* (London, 1960), and the biography of one of the creators of this idea, Nahman of Bratslav, is presented in a profound book by Arthur Green, *Tormented Master* (University, Ala., 1980). An anthology of early Hasidic texts in English translation is to be found in my book *The Teachings of Hasidism* (New York, 1983). A selection from the works of an early Hasidic master has been translated and edited by Arthur Green in *Upright Practices: The Light of the Eyes, by Menahem Nahum of Chernobyl* (New York, 1982). The most important collection of Hasidic stories about the Besht is *In Praise of the Baal Shem Tov,* translated and edited by Dan Ben-Amos and Jerome R. Mintz (Bloomington, Ind., 1970).

Many articles about specific problems in Hasidic history and thought were written in English. The most important ones are those of Joseph G. Weiss, especially "Via Passiva in Early Hasidism," *Journal of Jewish Studies* 11 (1960): 137-155, and "The Kavvanoth of Prayer in Early Hasidism," *Journal of Jewish Studies* 9 (1958): 163-192. A recent study of the theory of Hasidic leadership is to be found in Arthur Green's "The Zaddiq as Axis Mundi in Later Judaism," *Journal of the American Academy of Religion* 45 (September 1977): 327-347.

Most of the scholarly work concerning the history and theology of Hasidism was written in Hebrew. Among the most important books are Rivka Schatz Uffenheimer's *Hasidism as Mysticism* (in Hebrew with English summary; Jerusalem, 1968) and her *Maggid devarav le-Ya`aqov* (Jerusalem, 1976), a critical edition of Dov Ber's collection of sermons. A general survey of the works of the main Hasidic teachers is presented in Samuel A. Horodetzky's *He-hasidut veha-hasidim,* 4 vols. in 2 (Tel Aviv, 1951). The history of the controversies around the Hasidic movement, and scholarly edition of the relevant texts, is included in Mordecai Wilensky's *Hasidim ve-mitnaggedim,* 2 vols. (Jerusalem, 1970). The relationship between Hasidism and its sources in earlier Hebrew ethical and homiletical literature is studied in detail in Mendel Piekarz's *Bi-yemei tsemihat he-Ha-sidut* (Jerusalem, 1978). A study of Nahman of Bratslav's life, works and main ideas is to be found in Joseph G. Weiss's Mehqarim be-Hasidut Breslav (Jerusalem, 1970) and Mendel Piekarz's *Hasidut Breslav* (Jerusalem, 1972). A theological discussion of the theology of Habad Hasidism in the second generation is presented in Rachel Elior's *Torat ha-elohut ba-dor ha-sheni shel Hasidut Habad* (Jerusalem, 1982). A detailed study of Hasidic narrative literature is to be found in my book *Ha-sippur he-Hasidi* (Jerusalem, 1975).

A selection of articles on Hasidic history and thought in Hebrew (some with English summaries) is listed below.

Elior, Rachel. "The Controversy over the Leadership of the HaBad Movement." *Tarbiz* 49 (1979-1980): 166-186.

Etkes, Emanuel. "Shitato u-fa`alo shel R. Hayyim mi-Volozhin Ki-teguvat ha-hevah ha-mitnaggdit he-Hasidut." *Proceedings of the American Academy for Jewish Research* 38/39 (1970-1971): 1-45.

Gries, Z. "The Hassidic Conduct *(Hanhagot)* Literature from the Mid-Eighteenth Century to the 1830s." *Zion* 46 (1981): 199-236, 278-305.

Scholem, Gershom G. "New Material on Israel Loebel and His Anti-Hassidic Polemics." *Zion* 20 (1955): 153-162.

Shmeruk, Chone. "Tales about R'Adam Baal Shem in the Versions of *Shivhei ha-Besht.*" *Zion* 28 (1963): 86-105.

Tishby, Isaiah. "The Messianic Idea and Messianic Trends in the Growth of Hassidism." *Zion* 32 (1967): 1-45.

Weiss, Joseph G. "Beginnings of Hassidism." *Zion* 16 (1951): 46-105.

Weiss, Joseph G. "Some Aspects of Rabbi Nahman of Bratzlav's Allegorical Self-Interpretation." *Tarbiz* 27 (1958): 358-371.

JOSEPH DAN

Hawaiian Religion

Priesthoods and Worship Places. The priests, or *kahunas,* who mediated between gods and people, were professional specialists trained, commonly by older kin, in the material techniques and rituals essential for success in their calling. Of the several organized priesthoods, the higher-ranking and stricter order for priests in service to the Ku gods of war and sorcery and the lower and milder order for priests in service to the Lono gods of peace and abundance were given support by the Hawaiian king Kamehameha I (called Kamehameha the Great, 1758?-1819). Each order's high priest, the kahuna-nui, was considered to be its founder's direct descendant and an expert in every branch of religion. The high priest wielded political power by advising the ruler on how to win divine support.

Public worship took place at *heiaus,* or open-air religious centers. Only a king or paramount chief could build the most sacred type of *heiau,* where burned human sacrifices were offered to the highest Ku gods. A chief had a religious duty to build these heiaus in which to pray for divine aid for his chiefdom or to give thanks. Each deity had specific requirements as to size, amount, and color of offerings.

Major Deities

Kanaloa. Called Tangaroa or one of many other cognate names (e.g., Tangaloa, Ta'aroa) elsewhere in Polynesia, Kanaloa was Kane's younger brother. For Hawaiians he was the god of squid and, because of a play on words, also a god of healing (the Hawaiian word *he'e* means both "squid" and "to put to flight").

Kane. Called Tane in southeastern Polynesia, Kane, whose name means "male" or "man," was the most approachable, forgiving, and revered of the four major gods. One worshiper in his prayer would chant, "You and I warm to each other, Kane," and other worshipers would often say, "Life is sacred to Kane." According to more than one myth, Kane, while dwelling on earth with Kanaloa, had plunged his digging stick into the ground to release springs of fresh water to mix with his and Kanaloa's kava (a narcotic drink made from the pounded root of the shrub *Piper methysticum*). The release of fresh water by Kane-of-the-water-of-life, as he was frequently called, was a symbolic sexual act, for the gesture served to fructify the earth.

Lono. The god of two related sources of abundance—peace and seasonal winter storms—Lono (called Rongo or Ro'o in southeastern Polynesia) was also a god of healing. He had numerous *heiaus,* called "houses of Lono," devoted to rainmaking and medical purposes. The Makahiki, the longest ceremonial period, involved everyone in celebrating Lono's annual *(makahiki)* return for four months of the rainy season to preside over rituals for health and ample rain, and over the ritualized collection of taxes, recreation, and release from work. When Captain Cook arrived in 1778, he was greeted as Lono-i-ka-makahiki because he arrived during this period and anchored at the bay called Kealakekua ("the path of the god," i. e., Lono) and because his masted sails resembled the

Lono symbol that led the procession of tax collectors and Lono priests on their coastal circuit of the island.

Ku and Hina. There were many gods in the class called Ku (Tu was the southern Polynesian cognate of the name). Hawaiians regarded the Ku gods either as independent gods or as aspects of a single Ku. Usually an epithet attached to the name suggested the special function or distinctive trait of each particular Ku god. The same principle applies to the class of goddesses called Hina (cognates of the name elsewhere in Polynesia are Hine, Sina, and 'Ina). Some Hinas had more than one name. Hina-of-the-moon is also known as Maimed Lono because, according to myth, her husband tore off her leg as she fled to the moon. Pele's sacred name is Hina-of-the-fire, and Lea's other name is Hina-of-the-ohia-growth. (The ohia is a kind of tree.) Ku and Hina, as well as their varied aspects, function as man and wife in daily rites performed by the populace. With his sister-wife Hina (whose name means "prostrate"), Ku ("upright") united the people into a single stock, for Ku and Hina represented the male and female reproductive principles.

The State Religion and Its Demise. At his death in 1819, Kamehameha the Great, who believed his many gods had made him head of a unified feudal kingdom, left a state religion based on the taboo system that protected the *mana* and authority of the gods and their chiefly descendants from spiritual contamination and consequent weakness. That same year, however, Kamehameha's son Liholiho (1797-1824) took power, adopted the title Kamehameha II, and abolished the official religion without replacing it with another. The Ku priests began destroying heiaus and images, and the excited populace followed suit. Some hid their images and worshiped in secret. Not all customs and beliefs vanished: even today, faith in the aumakuas, for example, lingers on.

BIBLIOGRAPHY

Many of the volumes listed below are classics. Although Malo, Kamakau, Ii, and Kepelino became Christian converts whose adopted religion sometimes colors their views of the indigenous culture, they were personally familiar with the tradition, and they also learned a great deal from their elders. Ii, for example, as a boy had been an attendant of Liholiho (later Kamehameha II) and as an adult had held important positions in the government of the kingdom. The translators and editors have added important explanatory notes. Martha Warren Beckwith's translation and chapters of annotation of the *Kumulipo,* the creation and genealogical chant of King Kalakaua and his sister Queen Lili'uokalani, help make the magnificent but cryptic chant comprehensible. It presents different interpretations by modern Hawaiians and discusses the importance nobility placed on descent. Beckwith's *Hawaiian Mythology* is irreplaceable as a comprehensive reference to the pantheon, including demigods, romantic characters, and others; it has the additional value of containing comparisons with other Pacific traditions, putting the material into cross-cultural perspective. Abraham Fornander, a nineteenth-century judge who married a Hawaiian chief, made an unparalleled collection of myths, traditions, tales, poems, prayers, and descriptions of religion; Thomas G. Thrum's notes shed light on obscure references. E. S. Craighill Handy's *Polynesian Religion* brilliantly discusses the interrelationships of indigenous Polynesian religions, including the Hawaiian, and illustrates the major concepts they share.

June Gutmanis has published a major collection of ancient Hawaiian prayers selected from previously published and unpublished sources. Hawaiian texts are accompanied by English translations (and retranslations) and by commentaries.

Mary Kawena Pukui's book is a popularly written work for social workers and other "members of the helping professions." Pukui, a Hawaiian, draws on her other published writings, her personal experiences, and her wide reading, and with the psychiatrist E. W. Haertig discusses Hawaiian customs, beliefs, and rites as they relate to interpersonal relationships and the life cycle. The book includes modern case histories.

Beckwith, Martha Warren, ed. and trans. *Kepelino's Traditions of Hawaii.* Honolulu, 1932.

Beckwith, Martha Warren. *Hawaiian Mythology* (1940). Reprint, Honolulu, 1970.

Beckwith, Martha Warren, ed. and trans. *The Kumulipo: A Hawaiian Creation Chant* (1951). Reprint, Honolulu, 1972.

Fornander, Abraham, comp. *Fornander Collection of Hawaiian Antiquities and Folklore.* 3 vols. Translated by John Wise and edited by Thomas G. Thrum. Honolulu, 1916-1920.

Gutmanis, June. *Na Pule Kahiko* (Ancient Hawaiian Prayers). Honolulu, 1983.

Handy, E. S. Craighill. *Polynesian Religion.* Honolulu, 1927.

Ii, John Papa. *Fragments of Hawaiian History.* Translated by Mary Kawena Pukui and edited by Dorothy B. Barrere. Honolulu, 1959.

Johnson, Rubellite Kawena. *Kumulipo, the Hawaiian Hymn of Creation.* Honolulu, 1981.

Kamakau, Samuel M. *Ka Po'e Kahiko: The People of Old.* Translated by Mary Kawena Pukui; arranged and edited by Dorothy B. Barrere. Honolulu, 1964.

Malo, David. *Hawaiian Antiquities (Moolelo Hawaii)* (1903). 2d ed. Translated by Nathaniel B. Emerson and edited by W. D. Alexander. Honolulu, 1951.

Pukui, Mary Kawena, E. W. Haertig, and Catherine A. Lee. *Nana i Ke Kumu (Look to the Source).* 2 vols. Honolulu, 1972.

Valeri, Valerio. *Kingship and Sacrifice: Ritual and Society in Ancient Hawaii.* Chicago, 1985.

KATHARINE LUOMALA

HEAVEN AND HELL

As symbolic expressions found in various religious traditions, heaven and hell suggest polar components of a religious vision: a state of bliss and/or an abode of deity or sacred reality on the one hand, and a state of spiritual impoverishment and/or an abode of evil or demonic spirits on the other.

Judaism. The worldview of the ancient Hebrews, as reflected in the Hebrew scriptures, distinguished between the world above, the "heavens" *(shamayin),* as the dwelling place of Yahveh, and the earth, the two comprising the universe of God's creation. Under the earth was She'ol; the ambiguous term *she'ol* was used at times to refer to the grave or tomb itself and at other times to indicate an obscure land of shadows, the realm of the dead. Existence there was understood in largely negative terms, since in She'ol the "spirit" or "breath of life" *(ruah)* through which human beings were endowed by God with life was thought to have departed.

Christianity. Not only is heaven envisioned in early Christianity as the fulfilling state of bliss and reconciled relationship with God of which the followers of Jesus are assured, but it is also the abode of the divine, where Jesus dwelled before his earthly life and to which he proceeded following his death and resurrection.

In Roman Catholic Christianity hell is deemed to be a state of unending punishment for the unrepentant who die without the grace of God.

Protestant Christianity, though generally lacking the teaching on purgatory or intermediate states, has retained the traditional Christian teachings respecting heaven and hell.

Islam. In the Qur'an and the traditions of Islam are manifold descriptions of Heaven and Hell that are expressive of the centrality of judgment as an aspect of Muslim religious anthropology. Perfect justice, one of the attributes of God, will be disclosed at the Last Judgment, followed by the entrance of the believers into Heaven and the relegation of the infidels to Hell.

Traditional Islam adheres to a conviction that the sufferings in Hell will be unending, though there are suggestions of a purgatorial realm from which, after a time, Muslims in need of purificatory restitution to the *ummah* (the Muslim community) will be recovered. Both Heaven and Hell are subdivided into seven regions in Muslim teaching, with an eighth region added to the heavenly realm of the blessed.

Hinduism. By the era of the rise of Hinduism proper (third century BCE), heaven and hell came to be viewed not as a vision of ultimate fulfillment or destiny, but as intermediate states intermittent with a series of earthly existences in a cycle of births and deaths *(samsara).* One's *karman* (Pali, *kamma),* the reservoir of the consequences of thoughts, words, and deeds cumulative over the entire series of one's existences, determines the nature of the soul's passage from one earthly existence to another through one of the several levels of heaven or hell, which are thus intermediate states of varying degrees of suffering or relative bliss. In traditional Hindu cosmology, three realms *(lokas)*—heaven, the earth, and a netherworld (sky)—are supplemented by a vision of fourteen additional realms, seven of which rise above the earth ("heavens") and seven of which (or, in some instances, multiples of seven, such as twenty-one) are below the earth.

Buddhism. Heaven and hell are seen as intermediate and temporary states between one earthly existence and another. Death is thus but a transition from one earthly existence through an intermediate level of one of the heavens or hells to rebirth in yet another earthly existence.

There is no one completely systematic account of the various hells in the Pali canon, the corpus of Theravada texts known as the Tipitaka. The structure of the heavenly realms in Buddhism includes the six heavens of the sensual realm of *kamaloka*, *rupaloka* (the world of form) and *arupaloka* (the formless world, often referred to as the world of mind or consciousness).

Chinese Traditions. The aspiration to achieve harmony in society that has characterized all of Chinese religion and philosophy has given to Chinese understandings of heaven a unique aspect. The focus was placed on human affairs; human beings should begin by seeking harmony in the relationships that immediately address them. Yet the underlying conviction was that if harmony is achieved in human affairs, harmony with Heaven will be assured. Propriety in honoring the ancestors, whose spirits survived death and whose welfare was reciprocally related to that of living persons, became an essential component. Buddhists who presided over masses for the dead and religious Taoists in China subscribed to a cosmology that included levels of heavens above and hells below the earth.

Japanese Traditions. There are, in indigenous traditions of Japan, concepts analogous to those of heaven and hell in other religions. The oldest traditions recorded in the *Nihongi* and the *Kojiki* contained only nascent suggestions concerning the possibility of life beyond death, though this itself was associated with the grave.

[*See also* Paradise *and* Underworld.]

BIBLIOGRAPHY

Asin Palacios, D. Miguel. *Islam and the Divine Comedy.* London, 1936. Comparative analysis of Dante's Commedia and Muhammad's journey and ascension.

Baillie, J. B. *And the Life Everlasting.* London, 1936. An examination of the Christian notion of immortality by a discerning scholar of that tradition.

Blacker, Carmen, and Michael Loese, eds. *Ancient Cosmologies.* London, 1975. Cosmological structures of a variety of traditions, including Jewish, Chinese, Islamic, and Greek.

Brandon, S. G. F. *Man and His Destiny in the Great Religions.* Manchester, 1962. This publication of the Wilde Lectures in Natural and Comparative Religion presents an overview of visions of human destiny in major religious traditions through historical and comparative analysis.

Ch'en, Kenneth. *Buddhism: The Light of Asia.* New York, 1968. A valuable summary interpretation of the Buddhist tradition in interaction with the various cultures of Asia, proceeding country by country.

de Bary, Wm. Theodore, ed. *The Unfolding of Neo-Confucianism.* New York, 1975. A good collection of essays portraying the religious aspects of Neo-Confucianism in distinction from its purely moral and social functions.

Eberhard, Wolfram. *Guilt and Sin in Traditional China.* Berkeley, 1967. Morality as well as concepts of heaven and hell are examined in the context of popular religious movements in China.

Eliade, Mircea. *The Myth of the Eternal Return, or Cosmos and History.* Princeton, 1971. A comparative analysis of cyclical and linear concepts of time in history and their consequence for understanding human meaning and destiny.

Hick, John. *Death and Eternal Life.* London, 1976. An examination of responses to the question of what happens after death, based primarily on Western sources.

Kitagawa, Joseph M. *Religion in Japanese History.* New York, 1966. The most complete and authoritative recent account of the religions of Japan, portraying their development and history.

MacCulloch, J. A., et al. "Blest, Abode of the." In *Encyclopaedia of Religion and Ethics,* edited by James Hastings, vol. 2. Edinburgh, 1909. A still valuable, though dated, collection of essays presenting images of human fulfillment in a comprehensive examination of a variety of traditions, primarily ancient and classical.

Parrinder, Geoffrey. *The Indestructible Soul.* London, 1973. An analysis of the structures of human existence as presented in Indian thought, including focal discussion of life after death.

Reynolds, Frank E., and Earle H. Waugh, eds. *Religious Encounters with Death.* University Park, Pa., 1977. A collection of essays, contributed by a number of specialists, that analyze the import and significance of the myths, ceremonies, and conceptions associated with death in a variety of traditions.

Seltzer, Robert M. *Jewish People, Jewish Thought.* New York, 1980. A general and comprehensive survey of Jewish experience, focusing on intellectual history from ancient to contemporary times.

Smith, Jane I., and Yvonne Haddad. *The Islamic Understanding of Death and Resurrection.* Albany, N. Y., 1981. A descriptive analysis of the basis elements of Muslim understanding of the judgment and destiny of individuals.

Zimmer, Heinrich. *Philosophies of India.* New York, 1956. A comprehensive and illuminating treatment of the classical thought-systems of India.

LINDA M. TOBER and F. STANLEY LUSBY

HELLENISTIC RELIGIONS

Whereas religion is never a mere reflex of political, economic, and social conditions, there are periods in history when these factors exert a palpably strong influence on religious thinking. The Hellenistic age was certainly such a period. Its early phase, which began with the conquests of Alexander the Great in 334 BCE and continued with the rule of his successors, brought military and political upheaval to many peoples. When Roman imperialism later became the dominating power, there was greater apparent political stability, and the consciousness of a unified world, which Alexander's victories had furthered, was enhanced.

Culturally this was a world that gave primacy to the Greek language, and Alexander himself, although a Macedonian, was a fervent disseminator of Greek culture. Alexandria largely replaced Athens as the world's cultural capital and gave a Greek form to its glittering artistic and intellectual achievement. Even before this the Greek world was no narrow enclave, for Greek colonies had long since spread to

Asia Minor and the Black Sea area, to Egypt and North Africa, and to southern Italy, Sicily, Spain, and Gaul. In the wake of the military thrust, Greek settlements and cities were established in many non-Greek areas.

It was not the brute power of military aggression that brought about the change in outlook. Alexander had a dream of unity.

New Trends in State-supported Religion. In spite of the great change in worldview thus effected, the old order was not swept away quickly. The Athenians continued to honor their patron goddess Athena.

A popular feature of the religious life of this age was the great vitality of the associations or clubs formed by adherents of the various cults, with or without the sanction of the state. While these associations were often allowed the use of sacred premises, their main activities were usually convivial and charitable. Naturally the religious element was not ignored, and the name of the patron deity normally appears in records of their proceedings.

A new development that imparted fresh vitality, albeit of dubious sincerity, to the official state worship was the gradual establishment of the cult of the ruler, whether king or emperor. The first clear instance of it in this period was the worship of Alexander the Great as a divine person. In his case it was conspicuously an upshot of religious practices long prevalent in the Eastern countries that he had conquered. In the nations of Mesopotamia the king had regularly been associated with the gods. He had not been defined theologically as a god, but there was an aura of divinity about him.

An aspect of the ruler cult that affected the minds of men was the whole question of divine incarnation. Was it possible to conceive of the divine taking human form? In early Greek thought it is sometimes suggested that the gulf between man and god is not wide and that an affinity exists between them. In the early fifth century BCE Pindar expresses it thus: "Of one stock are men and gods, and from one mother do we draw our breath" (*Nemean Odes* 6.1). Some of the heroes of Greek mythology were deemed to be offspring of mixed unions, the father being divine and the mother moral. Herakles is in this category, for his father was said to be Zeus and his mother the mortal Alkmene, daughter of a king of Mycenae. Zeus was not able to achieve union with her until he disguised himself as a victorious warrior.

Rather different is the process by which historical heroes came to be worshiped after death. Their historicity cannot always be demonstrated, but the likely evolution followed from a lively memory of their deeds. One might rephrase Shakespeare to explain the distinctions enacted: "Some men are born divine, some achieve divinity, and some have divinity thrust upon them." The hero worship that developed among the Greeks outside mythology is akin to the second category; it involved outstanding individuals who by their own

merit and fame came to be especially honored after death. The triumphant commander who "liberated" or "saved" a city naturally qualified for special honors akin to those paid to divinity. An early and successful candidate was the Spartan commander Lysander, whose deeds secured for him this type of apotheosis even during his lifetime. But Alexander decisively outshone heroes of such caliber since his deeds encompassed not only the Greek world but much else as well. When his cult was established in Egypt, followed by that of the Ptolemies, several of the new royal divinities were

> An aspect of the ruler cult that affected the minds of men was the whole question of divine incarnation. Was it possible to conceive of the divine taking human form?

inevitably ill qualified to attract real worship. They might be said to have had divinity thrust upon them automatically.

Magic, Myth, and Miracle. In considering ancient magic, one must avoid any notion of conjuring tricks made possible by sleight of hand or by various illusionary processes. Some charlatans did resort to such stratagems, but the true medium of divine power did not approach his task thus. In the oldest myths of many nations, the creation of the world itself is the result of miraculous divine actions, and the teasing thought of what lay beyond the beginning of things often produced the image of one creator god, who was unbegotten and who had to initiate a process of creation without the help of a spouse.

Removed from the category of gods and heroes was the human purveyor of magic and miracle. At his best he had to be a knowledgeable person. Astrology was often within his professed prowess, and the secrets of astrology were not available to any ignoramus. His attitude to the gods seems to have varied. Respect and devout loyalty characterized him in the role of their chosen instrument. Yet sometimes the magician was expected to compel the gods to act in a certain way, and a number of magical spells are extant in which the gods are fiercely threatened unless they comply. But it was important to use the correct formula and to know the functions and mythology of the deity concerned. In the Hellenistic era magic was especially used for treating disease.

Here the doctrine of demons was often basic. This view regarded all disease as the creation of evil demons. To conquer the disease therefore demanded the defeat and expulsion of the baleful spirit that had taken possession of the victim. The magician was expected to announce the name of the hostile power and to order its expulsion in the name of a superior and beneficent power.

This was not, however, the only technique practiced by magicians and priests. Instead of a frontal attack on the demon, a mollifying approach was sometimes adopted, as when insanity was treated by the playing of soft music. A multitude of medical charms have come down to us, and they combine popular medicine with magical rites.

Magic is customarily divided into the categories of "black" and "white," a division that can certainly be applied to the practice of it by the Greeks. In early prototypes, such as Circe and Medea, the two aspects appear. The Homeric Circe, semidivine in origin, is a powerful magician who uses potions and salves and also teaches Odysseus to summon the spirits of the dead. Medea was the outstanding enchantress of the myths used in Greek tragedy. She enabled the Argonauts to get the golden fleece by putting the dragon of Colchis to sleep; moreover, she possessed the evil eye and could make warriors invulnerable. Orpheus was another master of magic. Son of the muse Calliope, he rendered wild beasts spellbound with his music.

In the context of magic and miracle the most remarkable person in the second sophistic movement was undoubtedly Apollonius of Tyana, who lived in the first century CE and came from Cappadocia in Asia Minor. An account of his life, written about 217 CE by another Sophist, Philostratus, presents him as a wandering scholar whose travels embraced Babylon, India, Egypt, and Ethiopia. In spite of his fame, his life was ascetic and disciplined and modeled on Pythagorean ideals. In addition, however, he frequently performed miracles that included acts of healing, magical disappearances, and even raising the dead, deeds that recall the claims made for Jesus of Nazareth.

Another important divinatory method was by oracle. In the Greek tradition the personal mouthpiece of the god of the oracle was the *prophetes,* who might be a man or a woman. He or she was thought to be possessed by a divine power, a process that Plato compared to poetic inspiration. The medium became *entheos* ("full of the god") and was in a state of *ekstasis* ("standing out of oneself"). In the oracles the power of prophecy was linked to special sites and to particular gods. Here a paradox emerges: the Greeks are famed for their rationalism and are regarded as the pioneers of intellectual enquiry and scientific thinking, yet their belief in oracles belies this approach. To some extent, the inconsistency can be explained through social division: the credulous majority trusted oracles while the educated elite evinced skepticism, the latter trend becoming more pronounced in the Hellenistic era, as Plutarch showed in the first and second centuries CE.

The paradox reveals itself to some degree in the figure of Apollo himself. He is the god of light and reason, yet he is the dominant god at Delphi, seat of the most celebrated oracle. In his *Birth of Tragedy,* the philosopher Nietzsche contrasts Apollo and Dionysos, the one representing the cool temper

of rationalism, the other the passionate surrender to ecstasy. Certainly this antithesis is at the heart of Greek thinking.

Oracles in other countries were also much frequented, such as that of Zeus Amun in Libyan Siwa, where Alexander had a significant personal experience. Sometimes the questions raised were those of individuals, reflecting the private problems of simple people: a man is anxious to know whether his wife will give him a child, a woman wants to be cured of a disease, someone asks a commercial question about the best use of property, or a man wonders whether the child his wife is carrying is his own.

Universalism and Syncretism. Although Alexander the Great did not establish a world state in the world as then known, his empire transcended the national states and induced a sense of cohesion and interdependence. It was in this era that the word *kosmopolites* ("citizen of the world") came into vogue. It was the Stoics, however, who succeeded in giving to this approach a positive and meaningful basis. Initially they were intellectually indebted to the Cynics, but Zeno of Citium in Cyprus (335-263 BCE) went far beyond them and included a religious interpretation in his cosmopolitanism. According to Zeno the whole universe is governed by divine reason, and men should therefore live in conformity with it and with the order of nature established by it.

It was indeed an age when several "utopias" were written. Plato had set an example with his *Republic.* There were a few practical ventures, too, in utopianism. Alexarchus, brother of King Cassander of Macedonia, after being given some land on the Athos peninsula, built a big city that he called Ouranopolis ("city of heaven"), where the citizens were called Ouranidai ("children of heaven"), and the coinage was adorned with figures of the sun, moon, and stars.

In the context of Stoic philosophy the doctrine of world citizenship was elaborated somewhat by Chrysippus (c. 280-207 BCE), who noted that the word *polis* was given two senses: the city in which one lived; the citizens and the state machinery. Similarly, he argued, the universe is a *polis* that embraces gods and men, the former wielding sovereignty while the latter obey; yet gods and men, for all their difference in status, have a means of contact and converse since they both use reason, which is "law by nature." In the last phrase he is overturning a contrast present in previous political thought. A later Stoic, Panaetius (c. 185-109 BCE), was more pragmatic in his approach. A world state seemed no longer within practical reach, but he continued to believe in the general unity of all mankind. At the same time he restored to the city-state a certain secondary role, admitting its usefulness in a realistic sense while denying its claim to decide in any final sense, matters of right and wrong; such decisions were to remain in the domain of reason and nature.

It thus appears that the idea of being a citizen of the world, vague and ill defined as it often was, came to include, under Stoic inspiration, the religious concept of a ruling divine reason. Although the reality of a world state was missing, the idea of mankind as one community had a powerful spiritual effect.

Whatever the variety of the traditions so freely transmitted in the Hellenistic age, in religious matters there was usually a readiness to acknowledge and respect diverging ways of belief, worship, and ritual. A process that went even beyond this was that of syncretism, a term often hailed as the hallmark of the age. In English and other modern languages the noun denotes the attempted union or reconciliation of diverse or opposite tenets or practices, especially in the philosophy of religion. The usage is also often extended to include the equation or identification of diverse deities and the combination or fusion of their cults, the latter practice being a specifically Hellenistic development. Earlier experience was indeed fully conversant with the equation of deities.

In ancient religions the most thorough process of syncretism in this sense is found in the developed phase of Roman religion, when Roman deities were identified with Greek counterparts—Jupiter with Zeus, Juno with Hera, Venus with Aphrodite, Ceres with Demeter, Mars with Ares, and so on. A simple act of comparison could lead to syncretism of this kind: one community compares its own gods with those of another; when similar powers or functions are recognized, the comparison may lead to identification. Of course, this process is valid only with polytheistic communities since monotheism rejects comparisons. Nor does the process arise when there is no contact between communities and therefore no need to make comparisons, except in instances where a plurality of deities within communities of

> The free mingling of many varying divinities suggested to some minds that the world was full of God in some form or another.

the same culture invites an equation of functions. This may lead to assimilation and the use of one divine name instead of several. Thus it appears that among the Greek communities there were several forms of the corn mother, but eventually the name of Demeter, best known, was applied to most of them.

In the fifth century BCE the Greek historian Herodotus indulged freely in the kind of syncretism that meant identifying the gods of different nations. In his second book, which deals with Egypt, he consistently identifies the Egyptian Osiris with the Greek Dionysos and the Egyptian Isis with the Greek Demeter. Probably this was prompted only by recognition of their similar functions, although he does refer to festivals. Later, however, in Hellenistic times, the cults of these

deities influenced one another. Isis, for example, was often depicted with ears of wheat on her headdress in a manner traditionally associated with Demeter, while ivy, the plant of Dionysos, figured in the rites of Osiris.

Increasingly in Hellenistic times, the cults of Oriental deities were introduced to the cities of the Greek world and Italy. Such a procedure had been very difficult, and indeed dangerous, in previous ages, for the orgiastic nature of some of these cults was much feared, and all public cults were rigidly controlled by the state. But a radical change of attitude came in Hellenistic times. State control remained, but often it now actively supported foreign cults, as for instance the cult of Dionysos in Ptolemaic Egypt.

Usually the Greeks raised a temple in honor of one particular deity, as Athena was honored in the Parthenon at Athens, Zeus in the great temple at Olympia, and Apollo in his temples at Delphi and Delos. Yet it was very natural that associated deities, especially those connected in myth, legend, and cult, should be represented and worshiped in the same temple. Thus Artemis was honored with Apollo as his twin sister, just as Hadad was honored with the Syrian goddess Atargatis as her consort.

Popular religious practice and belief are undoubtedly best reflected in inscriptions, whether in temples, on tombstones, or on amulets, and in magical incantations. Often the gods of different countries are named together in dedications and formulaic expressions of thanksgiving. This is also true of inscriptions that are official and public in character. Thus, in an inscription dated between 50 and 35 BCE, Antiochus I of Commagene, a small kingdom north of Syria, presents an exposition of his religion. He begins by calling himself "the God, the righteous God" and "friend of Romans and Greeks," and then declares that he has made his kingdom "the common dwelling place of all the gods." He alludes to the ancient doctrine of Persians and Greeks and refers with reverence to Zeus-Oromasdes, to Apollo-Mithra-Helios-Hermes, and to Artagnes-Herakles-Ares. This showpiece of syncretism contains an element of political expediency: the king is eager to pander to both Romans and Greeks (the Seleucid rulers); his religion is basically Iranian but with Greek embellishments.

One of the results of syncretism in religion was a sense of tolerance and sympathy. People who are ready to borrow from other religions are clearly not about to condemn them. Judaism and Christianity are again the exceptions, and their fervid intolerance was a source of strength in the struggle for survival. Only very rarely does a sense of conflict and hostility appear among the adherents of the pagan religions. Plutarch sometimes inveighs against the primitive cruelties unveiled in facets of mythology; his method is fairly radical in that he is prepared to reject such elements as unworthy of the gods.

In his novel about the ass-man rescued by Isis, Apuleius is appreciative and respectful in his allusions to most other religions. Here there was almost a logical imperative operating since Isis, as he often stresses, combined the attributes of all other goddesses. Yet there are two glaring exceptions to his tolerant attitude. One is the portrait of the baker's wife (9.14), who is described as a retailer of all the vices and as one who "scorned and spurned divine beings and instead of accepting a definite faith . . . falsely and blasphemously professed belief in a god whom she regarded as the one and only god."

In general, syncretism tended to induce a belief in pantheism. The free mingling of many varying divinities suggested to some minds that the world was full of God in some form or another.

BIBLIOGRAPHY

Bell, H. Idris. *Cults and Creeds in Graeco-Roman Egypt* (1953). Reprint, Chicago, 1975. This book deals with religious developments in Egypt that were, in several instances, influential in the Greek world generally.

Borghouts, J. F., trans. *Ancient Egyptian Magical Texts*. Leiden, 1978. Several spells from the Hellenistic period are included.

Farrington, Benjamin. *The Faith of Epicurus*. New York, 1967. A well-written study that shows the debt of Epicurus to Aristotle.

Festugière, A.-J. *Personal Religion among the Greeks*. Berkeley, 1954. A sensitive analysis of the devotional aspects of the cults of Asklepios and Isis.

Festugière, A.-J. *Epicurus and His Gods*. Translated by C. W. Chilton. Cambridge, Mass., 1956. A detailed and warmly sympathetic study that explains the spirit of evangelism in the Epicurean creed and apologetic.

Fraser, P. M. *Ptolemaic Alexandria*. 3 vols. Oxford, 1972. An authoritative work that gives detailed attention to religious themes.

Grant, Frederick C., ed. *Hellenistic Religions: The Age of Syncretism*. New York, 1953. A valuable collection of translated texts.

Griffiths, J. Gwyn, trans. and ed. *Plutarch's De Iside et Osiride*. Cardiff, 1970. An edition with translation and commentary. A representative of Greek culture and religion in the early centuries of imperial Rome, Plutarch presents remarks on the religions of Iran and Greece in addition to his ambitious analysis of the Egyptian cults.

Jones, Christopher P., trans. *Life of Apollonius* (Philostratus). Harmondsworth, 1970. Important for the study of magic and miracle.

Long, A. A. *Hellenistic Philosophy: Stoics, Epicureans, Sceptics*. London, 1974. A learned and lucid study.

Nock, Arthur Darby. *Essays on Religion and the Ancient World*. 2 vols. Cambridge, Mass., 1972. Rigorously academic in style, these collected essays are the work of an outstanding scholar who devoted his attention mainly to the Hellenistic and Roman eras.

Sinclair, Thomas Alan. *A History of Greek Political Thought*. London, 1952. A sound survey with three chapters on Alexander's age and the sequel.

Vermaseren, Maarten J. *Cybele and Attis: The Myth and the Cult*. Translated by A. M. H. Lemmers. London, 1977. A distinguished Dutch scholar traces the impact of these cults of Asia Minor on the Greco-Roman world.

Walbank, F. W. *The Hellenistic World*. Atlantic Highlands, N. J., 1981. Scholarly and readable.

Witt, R. E. *Isis in the Graeco-Roman World*. London, 1971. A comprehensive and well-illustrated study.

J. GWYN GRIFFITHS

HERESY

Scholarly Theories about Heresy. The science of religions borrowed the term *heresy* from Christian usage as fixed in canon law and, as a result, has been very much influenced by the history of the Christian church. The traditional view of "orthodoxy" and "heresy" as equivalent to "true" and "false" was first challenged by Martin Luther in his disputation with Johannes Eck at Leipzig (1517), where he let himself be drawn into saying that even councils (of the church) can err.

In his *Unparteiische Kirchen- und Ketzerhistorie von Anfang des Neuen Testaments bis 1688* (Impartial History of the Church and Heresy from the Beginning of the New Testament to 1688, published in 1699), Gottfried Arnold (1666-1714), a German Pietist theologian, attempted to show that Christian truth is to be found among heretics, schismatics, and sectarians (mystics), and not in the great church itself or in orthodoxy. Among his successors were J. L. von Mosheim *(Ketzergeschichte,* 1746-1748), C. W. F. Walch *(Historie der Ketzereien,* 1762-1785), and Adolf Hilgenfeld *(Die Ketzergeschichte des Urchristentums,* 1884).

Toward the end of the nineteenth century, it became increasingly difficult to make a distinction between heresy and orthodoxy. The multiplicity of competing statements of faith regarding the "saving event" in Jesus Christ and its theological explanation showed ever more clearly that at the beginning of the church's history neither heresy nor orthodoxy was sharply defined or patent; both were concepts developed later. This view of the matter has been presented most notably by Walter Bauer in his well-known book *Rechtgläubigkeit und Ketzerei im ältesten Christentum* (1934; *Orthodoxy and Heresy in Earliest Christianity,* Eng. trans. of 2d ed., 1971).

Religions that give rise to heresy. Religions that have a founder—Judaism, Zoroastrianism, Buddhism, Christianity, Manichaeism, and Islam—lay claim in one way or other to a normative doctrine. This does not from the outset always take the form of a fixed confession of faith, but there is at least a definite conception of faith and doctrine or, better, a central nucleus of doctrine that is used to separate "true" from "false" and that has taken written form in a sacred canon (thus "religions of the Book").

The historian of the "confessional religions" is familiar also with their slow maturation from preliminary stages and their development of a central doctrinal core that then became a distinguishing orthodoxy or orthopraxis. Orthodoxy is in every case an interpretation of the doctrine or message that the founder has left behind and that frequently shows a lack of internal harmony, to say nothing of the fact that it is usually transmitted only in oral form. On the one hand, it is this state of the founder's teaching that leads to a struggle among the groups that subsequently form within the religious community. Local and social differences also play a part. On the other hand, while the preaching of a founder is indeed open to numerous interpretations in matters of detail, the fact is that once the tradition originating with him has been fixed in writing, his teachings as a whole take on a particular shape and

> A tense opposition between "orthodoxy" and "heresy," "church" and "sect," marks the entire history of the founded religions. . . .

form. The result is a certain uniformity among all his followers in regard to the basic norms of doctrine, belief, and behavior.

How heresy develops. In those religions that give rise to the development of heresy, a number of stages mark the process. Even in the lifetime of a founder there may already be disagreements on matters of doctrine or behavior (e.g., between the Buddha and Devadatta on questions of asceticism). The many-sidedness and occasional lack of clarity in the founder's teachings lead, especially after his death, to the formation of groups in the original community (groups that initially had more or less equal standing). In the struggle among these groups, one group emerges—often as the result of a compromise—that interprets and transmits the found-er's heritage in an "orthodox" way. As a result, a point is reached at which there can be heresies or the formation of sects in the strict sense of these terms.

It is difficult at times to determine how one particular movement is able to establish itself as orthodox. In most cases this movement or school preserves the heritage of the founder in a balanced and fully satisfactory way. In some cases only a rough determination of orthodoxy is reached; the result is the continued existence of groups with equal standing.

A tense opposition between "orthodoxy" and "heresy," "church" and "sect," marks the entire history of the founded religions and is also one of their fruitful major themes. Using the history of the Christian church as an example, Ernst Troeltsch has very impressively described this process as one of conflict between the institutional principle and the principle of voluntarism, both of which are contained in the gospel.

[*See also* Schism]

BIBLIOGRAPHY

There is no complete treatment of heresy as a phenomenon in the study of religions. There are, however, countless works on heresy as found in the various traditions. The following list is a selection from these.

General Works

Assmann, Jan. "Die `Häresie' des Echnaton: Aspekte der Amarna Religion." *Saeculum* 23 (1972): 109-126.

Baetke, Walter. "Der Begriff der Unheiligkeit im altnordischen Recht." In his *Kleine Schriften,* edited by Kurt Rudolph and Ernst Walter, pp. 90-128. Weimar, 1973.

Brosch, Joseph. *Das Wesen der Häresie.* Bonn, 1936.

Forkman, Göran. *The Limits of the Religious Community.* Lund, 1972.

Leipoldt, Johannes, and Siegfried Morenz. *Heilige Schriften.* Leipzig, 1953.

Morenz, Siegfried. "Entstehung und Wesen der Buchreligion." *Theologische Literaturzeitung* 75 (1950): 709-715.

Nigg, Walter. *Das Buch der Ketzer.* Zurich, 1949.

Rudolph, Kurt. "Wesen und Struktur der Sekte." *Kairos,* n. s. 21 (1979): 241-254.

Schlier, Heinrich. "Hairesis." In *Theological Dictionary of the New Testament,* edited by Gerhard Kittel, vol. 1. Grand Rapids, Mich., 1964.

Simon, Marcel. "From Greek Hairesis to Christian Heresy." In *Early Christian Literature and the Classical Intellectual Tradition, in Honorem Robert M. Grant,* edited by Wilhelm R. Schoedel and Robert L. Wilken, pp. 101-116. Paris, 1979.

Wach, Joachim. *Sociology of Religion.* Chicago, 1944.

Christianity

Bauer, Walter. *Orthodoxy and Heresy in Earliest Christianity.* Edited by Robert A. Kraft and Gerhard Krodel. Philadelphia, 1971.

Berkouts, Carl T., and Jeffrey Burton Russell. *Medieval Heresies: A Bibliography, 1960-1979.* Toronto, 1981.

Betz, Hans Dieter. "Orthodoxy and Heresy in Primitive Christianity." *Interpretation* 19 (July 1965): 299-311.

Betz, Hans Dieter. "Häresie: Neues Testament." In *Theologische Realenzyklopädie,* vol. 14, pp. 313-318. Berlin, 1984.

Gensichen, Hans-Werner. *Damnamus: Die Verwerfung der Irrlehre bei Luther und im Luthertum des 16. Jahrhunderts.* Göttingen, 1955.

Grundmann, Herbert. *Ketzergeschichte des Mittelalters.* Die Kirche in ihrer Geschichte, no. 3. Göttingen, 1963.

Grundmann, Herbert. *Bibliographie zur Ketzergeschichte des Mittelalters, 1900-1966.* Rome, 1967.

Harrington, Daniel J. "The Reception of Walter Bauer's *Orthodoxy and Heresy in Earliest Christianity* during the 1970s." *Harvard Theological Review* 73 (January-April 1980): 289-298.

Leff, Gordon. *Heresy in the Later Middle Ages.* Manchester, 1967.

Loos, Milan. *Dualist Heresy in the Middle Ages.* Prague, 1974.

Rudolph, Kurt. "Gnosis: Weltreligion oder Sekte." *Kairos,* n. s. 21 (1979): 255-263.

Troeltsch, Ernst. *The Social Teaching of the Christian Churches.* 2 vols. New York, 1931; Chicago, 1981.

Turner, H. E. W. *The Pattern of Christian Truth.* London, 1954.

Judaism

McEleney, Neil J. "Orthodoxy in Judaism of the First Christian Century." *Journal for the Study of Judaism* 4 (1973): 19-42.

Scholem, Gershom. *Major Trends in Jewish Mysticism.* 3d ed., rev. New York, 1954.

Islam

Halm, Heinz. *Die islamische Gnosis.* Zurich, 1982.

Laoust, Henri. *Les schismes dans l'Islam.* Paris, 1965.

Lewis, Bernard. "Some Observations on the Significance of Heresy in Islam." *Studia Islamica* 1 (1953): 43-63.

Zoroastrianism

Boyce, Mary. *Zoroastrians: Their Religious Beliefs and Practices.* London, 1979.

Boyce, Mary. *A History of Zoroastrianism,* vol. 2, *Under the Achaemenians.* Leiden, 1982.

Widengren, Geo. *Die Religionen Irans.* Stuttgart, 1965.

Zaehner, Robert C. *Zurvan: A Zoroastrian Dilemma.* Oxford, 1955.

Hinduism

O'Flaherty, Wendy Doniger. "The Origin of Heresy in Hindu Mythology." *History of Religions* 10 (May 1971): 271-333.

Buddhism

Bareau, André. *Les sectes bouddhiques du petit véhicule.* Saigon, 1955.

Dutt, Nalinaksha. *Buddhist Sects in India.* Calcutta, 1970.

KURT RUDOLPH
Translated from German by Matthew J. O'Connell

HIMALAYAN RELIGIONS

Nepal. In the highlands of Nepal advanced civilizations rich in scriptural traditions have long coexisted with preliterate tribal cultures, and the Kathmandu Valley, the homeland of the ancient Newar people, has seen a succession of sophisticated ideologies and art styles with strong religious overtones.

The earliest documents relating to religious practices in the Kathmandu Valley go back to the period of the Licchavi kings (300-870 CE). In the tolerant ideological climate of that time several faiths flourished side by side. The dominant religions were Hinduism and Buddhism, both of which had absorbed elements of various local cults.

In the thirteenth century, kings of the Malla dynasty established themselves in Nepal; under their rule Hinduism became the dominant religion. At that time both Hindus and Buddhists came under the influence of Tantrism, a religious system that introduced various innovations in devotional practices, including sexual rituals, without, however, developing novel philosophical principles of its own.

In no other part of the Himalayan region are Buddhism and Hinduism as closely entwined as in the Kathmandu Valley. The zone of high altitude along the Tibetan border is almost exclusively inhabited by Tibetan-speaking Buddhist populations, while the southern lowlands are a preserve of Indo-European-speaking Hindus only minimally interspersed with some clusters of tribal people. The large hilly region extending between these two contrasting environmental zones is inhabited by a mixture of Tibeto-Burman-speaking indigenous tribes and some groups of Hindu castes with close cultural affinities to the people of northern India.

The absence of the concepts of merit and sin in their systems of supernatural values is characteristic of most tribal religions of Nepal and other Himalayan countries, a feature that distinguishes these religions fundamentally from Buddhism. Thus the Magar, a tribe widespread over the highlands to the south and southwest of Thak Khola, believe in the existence of a multitude of gods, goddesses, and spirits, and they assume that these invisible beings control health, reproduction, and the fertility of livestock and crops. Although they regard the worship of these beings as conducive to good fortune, the Magar lack the idea that their cult might be instrumental in the acquisition of religious merit. The gods are thought of in anthropomorphic terms and are given offerings of food and drink, including the blood of sacrificial animals, because they are believed to enjoy sensual pleasures such as eating and drinking.

Shamanism is central to the religious practices of the Magar. The shamans play a vital role as mediators between men and supernatural beings, who are believed to dwell in a sphere overlapping with the world of humans. Both men and women can act as shamans and place themselves at will into ecstatic trance.

Spread over the middle ranges of Nepal are several other Tibeto-Burman tribes, the most numerous of whom are the Gurung and the Tamang. In the Annapurna region Gurung dovetail with Bhotia and have absorbed many of the latter's Buddhist beliefs and practices.

The Tamang adhere overtly to Buddhism, and in some of their villages there are temples similar to the gompa of Tibetans and Sherpas; in these temples lamas learned in Tibetan sacred scriptures officiate at Buddhist rituals. Simultaneously, Tamang priests and shamans rooted in traditional tribal religion perform seasonal agricultural rites, propitiate local deities and spirits with prayers and offerings, and conduct the cult of their clan ancestors. In some settlements there is a sacred grove surrounding one or two stone platforms where the village priest worships the earth mother with sacrifices of sheep and fowl. While the functions of lamas and shamans are mutually exclusive, the laity is hardly conscious of the contradictions between the cult of the old Tamang gods and the rites of lamaistic Buddhism.

The Rai and Limbu tribes, which occupy a large territory in the eastern hill regions, have been less influenced by Buddhism and Hinduism than the tribal societies of western Nepal. Their worldview is based on the firm belief that human life is inextricably linked with a multitude of supernatural beings approachable only by shamans, who communicate with them in controlled conditions of ecstasy and possession.

Sikkim. Like Nepal, Sikkim has a heterogeneous population composed of several ethnic groups that settled in the country at different periods of time. The autochthonous inhabitants of the state are represented by the Lepcha, a tribe of Mongoloid race speaking a Tibeto-Burman language. The original religion of the Lepcha is based on the worship of local deities and a variety of nature spirits. By the middle of the twentieth century there were thirty-five monasteries in Sikkim, and Buddhism had spread also among the Lepcha, who gradually adopted the Bhotia language and merged with the Bhotia into a single religious entity.

Bhutan. In Bhutan, the easternmost of the Himalayan kingdoms, Tibetan Buddhism has virtually displaced the older indigenous religions, which contained a number of elements of the Bon cult. Today, large monasteries with hundreds of monks flourish under the patronage of the king's government. Most of them adhere to the Bka'-brgyud-pa sect and have close links with monastic communities of the same sect in Nepal.

Arunachal Pradesh. Where the Indian Union Territory of Arunachal Pradesh borders on Tibet and northeastern Bhutan, tribal populations have come under the influence of Mahayana Buddhism in its lamaistic form. Though remnants of the old Bon religion persist, Buddhist monasteries and nunneries are now the main centers of religious life. The great monastery of Tawang, founded by Tibetan lamas, represents one of the most prominent institutions of the Dge-lugs-pa sect south of the Himalayan main range.

[*See also* Tibetan Religions.]

BIBLIOGRAPHY

The books listed below contain historical information on religious developments in Himalayan countries as well as accounts of present-day religious beliefs and practices prevailing in the region. The works of Bista, Gorer, Hitchcock and Jones, Nebesky-Wojkowitz, Nepali, and myself are of predominantly anthropological character and deal with contemporary populations, whereas the works of Landon, Regmi, Singh, Slusser, and Snellgrove place greater emphasis on historical facts and problems. A comprehensive bibliography of the entire region, including articles in periodicals, is contained in the four volumes of *An Anthropological Bibliography of South Asia* by Elizabeth von Fürer-Haimendorf and Helen Kanitkar (The Hague, 1958-1976).

Bista, Dor Bahadur. *People of Nepal*. Kathmandu, 1967.
Fürer-Haimendorf, Christoph von. *The Apa Tanis and Their Neighbours*. London, 1962.
Fürer-Haimendorf, Christoph von. *The Sherpas of Nepal*. London, 1964.
Fürer-Haimendorf, Christoph von. *Highlanders of Arunachal Pradesh*. New York, 1982.
Gorer, Geoffrey. *Himalayan Village: An Account of the Lepchas of Sikkim*. 2d ed. New York, 1967.
Hitchcock, John T., and Rex L. Jones, eds. *Spirit Possession in the Nepal Himalayas*. Warminister, 1976.
Landon, Perceval. *Nepal*. 2 vols. London, 1928.
Nebesky-Wojkowitz, René de. *Oracles and Demons of Tibet*. The Hague, 1956.
Nepali, Gopal Singh. *The Newars: An Ethno-Sociological Study of a Himalayan Community*. Bombay, 1965.
Regmi, Dilli Raman. *Ancient Nepal*. Calcutta, 1960.
Singh, Nagendra. *Bhutan: A Kingdom in the Himalayas; A Study of the Land, Its People and Their Government*. New Delhi, 1972.
Slusser, Mary Shephard. *Nepal Mandala: A Cultural Study of the Kathmandu Valley*. 2 vols. Princeton, 1982.
Snellgrove, David L. *Buddhist Himalaya: Travels and Studies in Quest of the Origins and Nature of Tibetan Religion*. Oxford, 1957.

CHRISTOPH VON FÜRER-HAIMENDORF

HINDUISM

[*This entry deals exclusively with the Hindu tradition. For a more general survey of the religions of India and their interaction with each other, see* Indian Religions.]

Hinduism is the religion followed by about 70 percent of the roughly seven hundred million people of India. Elsewhere, with the exception of the Indonesian island of Bali, Hindus represent only minority populations. The geographical boundaries of today's India are not, however, adequate to contour a full account of this religion. Over different periods in the last four or five millennia, Hinduism and its antecedents have predominated in the adjacent areas of Pakistan and Bangladesh and have been influential in such other regions as Afghanistan, Sri Lanka, Southeast Asia, and Indonesia. But in these areas Hindu influences have been superseded or overshadowed by the influences of other religions, principally Buddhism and Islam. This account will treat only of Hinduism as it has taken shape historically in the "greater India" of the Indian subcontinent. [*For discussion of Hinduism outside the Indian subcontinent, see* Southeast Asian Religions.]

Indus Valley Religion. There are good reasons to suspect that a largely unknown quantity, the religion of the peoples of the Indus Valley, is an important source for determining the roots of Hinduism.

The Indus Valley civilization arose from Neolithic and Chalcolithic village foundations at about the middle of the third millennium BCE as a late contemporary of Egyptian and Mesopotamian riverine civilizations. It engaged in trade with both, though mostly with Mesopotamia. Reaching its apogee around 2000 BCE, it then suffered a long period of intermittent and multifactored decline culminating in its eclipse around 1600 BCE, apparently *before* the coming of the Aryan peoples and their introduction of the Vedic religious current. At its peak, the Indus Valley civilization extended over most of present-day Pakistan, into India as far eastward as near Delhi, and southward as far as the estuaries of the Narmada River. It was apparently dominated by the two cities of Mohenjo-Daro, on the Indus River in Sind, and Harappa, about 350 miles to the northwest on a former course of the Ravi River, one of the tributaries to the Indus. Despite their distance from each other, the two cities show remarkable uniformity in material and design, and it has been supposed that they formed a pair of religious and administrative centers.

The determination of the nature of Indus Valley religion and of its residual impact upon Hinduism are, however, most problematic. Although archaeological sites have yielded many suggestive material remains, the interpretation of such finds is conjectural and has been thwarted especially by the continued resistance of the Indus Valley script, found on numerous steatite seals, to convincing decipherment. Until it is deciphered, little can be said with assurance. The content of the inscriptions may prove to be minimal, but if the language (most likely Dravidian) can be identified, much can be resolved.

At both Harappa and Mohenjo-Daro, the cities were dominated on the western side by an artificially elevated mound that housed a citadel-type complex of buildings. Though no temples or shrines can be identified, the complex probably served both sacred and administrative functions. A "great bath" within the Mohenjo-Daro citadel, plus elaborate bathing and drainage facilities in residences throughout the cities, suggests a strong concern for personal cleanliness, cultic bathing, and ritual purity such as resurface in later Hinduism. Indeed, the "great bath," a bitumen-lined tank with steps leading into and out of it from either end, suggests not only the temple tanks of later Hinduism but the notion of "crossing" associated with them through their Sanskrit name, *tirtha* ("crossing place, ford").

A granary attached to the citadel may also have involved high officials in ceremonial supervision of harvests and other agricultural rituals. Terracotta female figurines with pedestal waists, found especially at village sites, reveal at least a popular cultic interest in fertility. They are probably linked with worship of a goddess under various aspects, for while some portray the figure in benign nurturing poses, others present pinched and grim features that have been likened to grinning skulls: these are likely foreshadowings of the Hindu Goddess in her benign and destructive aspects.

But most controversial are the depictions on the seals, whose inscriptions remain undeciphered. Most prominently figured are powerful male animals. They are often shown in cultic scenes, as before a sort of "sacred manger," or being led by a priestly ministrant before a figure (probably a deity and possibly a goddess) in a peepul tree, one of the most venerated trees in Hinduism. Male animals also frequently figure in combination with human males in composite animal-human forms. With female figures seemingly linked to the Goddess and males associated with animal power, it has been suggested that the two represent complementary aspects of a fertility cult with attendant sacrificial scenarios such as are found in the animal sacrifice to the Goddess in post-Vedic Hinduism. In such sacrifices the Goddess requires male offerings, and the animal represents the human male sacrificer. Most interesting and controversial in this connection is a figure in a yogic posture who is depicted on three seals and a faience sealing. Though features differ in the four portrayals, the most fully defined one shows him seated on a dais with an erect phallus. He has buffalo horns that enclose a treelike miter headdress, possibly a caricatured buffalo face, wears bangles and necklaces or torques, and is surrounded by four wild animals. Some of these associations (yoga, ithyphallicism, lordship of animals) have suggested an identification with the later Hindu god Siva. Other traits (the buffalo-man composite form, association with wild animals, possible intimations of sacrifice) have suggested a foreshadowing of the buffalo demon Mahisasura, mythic antagonist and sacrificial victim of the later Hindu goddess Durga. Possibly the image crystallizes traits that are later associated with both of these figures.

The notion that features of Indus Valley religion form a stream with later non-Aryan religious currents that percolate into Hinduism has somewhat dismissively been called the substratum theory by opponents who argue in favor of treating the development of Hinduism as derivable from within its own sacred literature. Though this "substratum" cannot be known except in the ways that it has been structured within Hinduism (and no doubt also within Jainism and Buddhism), it is clear that a two-way process was initiated as early as the Vedic period and has continued to the present.

Vedism. The early sacred literature of Hinduism has the retrospective title of Veda ("knowledge") and is also known as *sruti* ("that which is heard"). Altogether it is a prodigious body of literature, originally oral in character (thus "heard"), that evolved into its present form over nine or ten centuries between about 1400 and 400 BCE. In all, four types of texts fall under the Veda-*sruti* heading: Samhitas, Brahmanas, Aranyakas, and Upanisads. At the fount of all later elaborations are the four Samhitas ("collections"): the *Rgveda Samhita* (Veda of Chants, the oldest), the *Samaveda* and *Yajurveda Samhitas* (Vedas of Melodies and Sacrificial Formulas, together known as the "liturgical" Samhitas), and the *Atharvaveda Samhita* (the youngest, named after the sage Atharvan). These constitute the four Vedas, with some early sources referring to the "three Vedas" exclusive of the last. The material of the four was probably complete by 1000 BCE, with younger parts of the older works overlapping older parts of the younger ones chronologically. The Samhitas, or portions of them, were preserved by different priestly schools or "branches" *(sakhas)* through elaborate means of memorization. Many of these schools died out and their branches became lost, but others survived to preserve material for literary compilation and redaction. The subsequent works in the categories of Brahmana, Aran-yaka, and Upanisad are all linked with one or another of the Vedic schools, and thus with a particular Vedic Samhita, so that they represent the further literary output of the Vedic schools and also the interests of the four types of priests who came to be associated differentially with the ritual uses of the four Samhitas. It is from the *Rgveda* that Vedic religion in its earliest sense must be reconstructed.

Although the urban civilization of the Indus Valley had run its course by the time of the arrival of the Aryans in about 1500 BCE, the newcomers met heirs of this civilization in settled agricultural communities. The contrast between cultures was striking to the Aryans, who described the indigenous population as having darker skin, defending themselves from forts, having no gods or religious rituals but nonetheless worshiping the phallus. As small stone phallic objects have been found at Indus Valley sites, this is probably an accurate description of a cult continued from pre-Vedic Indus Valley religion that prefigures the later veneration of the *linga* (phallus) in the worship of Siva. In contrast to this predominantly agricultural population, the invading Aryans were a mobile, warlike people, unattached to cities or specific locations, entering Northwest India in tribal waves probably over a period of several centuries. Moreover, their society inherited an organizing principle from its Indo-European past that was to have great impact on later Indian civilization in the formation of the caste system. The ideal arrangement, which myths and ritual formulas propounded and society was to reflect, called for three social "functions": the priests, the warriors, and the agriculturalist-stockbreeders. Early Vedic hymns already speak of three such interacting social groups, plus a fourth—the indigenous population of *dasa*, or *dasyu* (literally, "slaves," first mythologized as demon foes of the Aryans and their gods). By the time of the late *Rgveda*, these peoples were recognized as a fourth "class" or "caste" in the total society and were known as *sudras*.

Most crucial to the inspiration of the early Vedic religion, however, was the interaction between the first two groups: the priesthood, organized around sacerdotal schools maintained through family and clan lines, and a warrior component, originally led by chieftains of the mobile tribal communities but from the beginning concerned with an ideal of kingship that soon took on more local forms. Whereas the priests served as repositories of sacred lore, poetry, ritual technique, and mystical speculation, the warriors served as patrons of the rites and ceremonies of the priests and as sponsors of their poetry. These two groups, ideally complementary but often having rival interests, crystallized by late Vedic and Brahmanic times into distinct "classes": the *brahmanas* (priests) and the *ksatriyas* (warriors).

Although the *Rgveda* alludes to numerous details of ritual that soon came to be systematized in the religion of the Brahmanas, it brings ritual into relief only secondarily. The primary focus of the 1,028 hymns of the *Rgveda* is on praising the gods and the cosmic order *(rta)*, which they protect.

But insofar as the hymns invoke the gods to attend the sacrifice, there is abundant interest in two deities of essentially ritual character: Agni and Soma. Agni (Fire) is more specifically the god of the sacrificial fire who receives offerings to the gods and conveys them heavenward through the smoke. And Soma is the divinized plant of "nondeath" *(amrta)*, or immortality, whose juices are ritually extracted in the *soma* sacrifice, a central feature of many Vedic and Brahmanic rituals. These two gods, significantly close to mankind, are mediators between men and other gods. But they are especially praised for their capacity to inspire in the poets the spe-

> **Vedic religion is decidedly polytheistic, there being far more than the so-called thirty-three gods, the number to which they are sometimes reduced.**

cial "vision" *(dhi)* that stimulates the composition of the Vedic hymns. Agni, who as a god of fire and light is present in the three Vedic worlds (as fire on earth, lightning in the atmosphere, and the sun in heaven), bestows vision through "illumination" into the analogical connections and equivalences that compose the *rta* (which is itself said to have a luminous nature). *Soma*, the extracted and purified juice of the "plant of immortality," possibly the hallucinogenic fly agaric mushroom, yields a "purified" vision that is described as "enthused" or "intoxicated," tremulous or vibrant, again stimulating the inspiration for poetry. The Vedic poet (*kavi*, *rsi*, or *vipra*) was thus a "see-er," or seer, who translated his vision into speech, thus producing the sacred *mantras*, or verse-prayers, that comprise the Vedic hymns. Vedic utterance, itself hypostatized as the goddess Vac (Speech), is thus the crystallization of this vision.

Vedic religion is decidedly polytheistic, there being far more than the so-called thirty-three gods, the number to which they are sometimes reduced. Though the point is controversial, for the sake of simplification we can say that at the core or "axis" of the pantheon there are certain deities with clear Indo-European or at least Indo-Iranian backgrounds: the liturgical gods Agni and Soma (cf. the Avestan deity Haoma) and the deities who oversee the three "functions" on the cosmic scale: the cosmic sovereign gods Varuna and Mitra, the warrior god Indra, and the Asvins, twin horsemen concerned with pastoralism, among other things. Intersecting this structure is an opposition of Indo-Iranian background between *devas* and *asuras*. In the Rgveda both terms may refer to ranks among the gods, with asura being higher and more primal. But asura also has the Vedic meaning of "demon," which it retains in later Hinduism, so that the deva-asura opposition also takes on dualistic overtones.

Varuna is the *asura par excellence*, whereas Indra is the leader of the *devas*. These two deities are thus sometimes in opposition and sometimes in complementary roles: Varuna being the remote overseer of the cosmic order *(rta)* and punisher of individual human sins that violate it; Indra being the dynamic creator and upholder of that order, leader of the perennial fight against the collective demonic forces, both human and divine, that oppose it. It is particularly his conquest of the *asura* Vrtra ("encloser")—whose name suggests ambiguous etymological connections with Varuna—that creates order or being (*sat*, analogous to *rta*) out of chaos or nonbeing *(asat)* and opens cosmic and earthly space for "freedom of movement" *(varivas)* by gods and men. Considerable attention is also devoted to three solar deities whose freedom of movement, thus secured, is a manifestation of the *rta*, a prominent analogy for which is the solar wheel: Surya and Savitr (the Sun under different aspects) and Usas (charming goddess of the dawn). Other highly significant deities are Yama, god of the dead, and Vayu, god of wind and breath. It is often pointed out that the gods who become most important in later Hinduism—Visnu, Siva (Vedic Rudra), and the Goddess—are statistically rather insignificant in the Veda, for few hymns are devoted to them. But the content rather than the quantity of the references hints at their significance. Visnu's centrality and cosmological ultimacy, Rudra's destructive power and outsiderhood, and the this-worldly dynamic aspects of several goddesses are traits that assume great proportions in later characterizations of these deities.

Although it is thus possible to outline certain structural and historical features that go into the makeup of the Vedic pantheon, it is important to recognize that these are obscured by certain features of the hymns that arise from the type of religious "vision" that inspired them, and that provide the basis for speculative and philosophical trends that emerge in the late Veda and continue into the early Brahmanic tradition. The hymns glorify the god they address in terms generally applicable to other gods (brilliance, power, beneficence, wisdom) and often endow him or her with mythical traits and actions particular to other gods (supporting heaven, preparing the sun's path, slaying Vrtra, and so on). Thus, while homologies and "connections" between the gods are envisioned, essential distinctions between them are implicitly denied. Speculation on what is essential—not only as concerns the gods, but the ritual and the *mantras* that invoke them—is thus initiated in the poetic process of the early hymns and gains in urgency and refinement in late portions of the *Rgveda* and the subsequent "Vedic" speculative-philosophical literature that culminates in the Upanisads. Most important of these speculations historically were those concerning the cosmogonic sacrifices of Purusa in *Rgveda* 10.90 (the *Purusasukta*, accounting for, among other things, the origin of the four castes) and of Prajapati in the

Brahmanas. Each must be discussed further. In addition, speculations on *brahman* as the power inherent in holy speech and on the *atman* ("self") as the irreducible element of personal experience are both traceable to Vedic writings (the latter to the *Atharvaveda* only). We shall observe the convergence of all these lines of speculation in the Upanisads and classical Hinduism.

Religion of the Brahmanas. The elaboration of Vedic religion into the sacrificial religion of the Brahmanas is largely a result of systematization. The first indication of this trend is the compilation of the liturgical Samhitas and the development of the distinctive priestly schools and interests that produced these compendiums. Thus, while the *Rgveda* became the province of the *hotr* priest, the pourer of oblations and invoker of gods through the *mantras* (the term *hotr*, "pourer," figures often in the *Rgveda* and has Indo-Iranian origins), the newer collections developed around the concerns of specialist priests barely alluded to in the *Rgveda* and serving originally in subordinate ritual roles. The *Samaveda* was a collection of verses taken mostly from the *Rgveda*, set to various melodies *(samans)* for use mainly in the *soma* sacrifice, and sung primarily by the *udgatr* priest, who thus came to surpass the *hotr* as a specialist in the sound and articulation of the *mantras*. And the *Yajurveda* was a collection of *yajus*, selected sacrificial *mantras*, again mostly from the *Rgveda*, plus certain complete sentences, to be murmured by the *adhvaryu* priest, who concerned himself not so much with their sound as with their appropriateness in the ritual, in which he became effectively the master of ceremonies, responsible for carrying out all the basic manual operations, even replacing the *hotr* priest as pourer of oblations. A fourth group of priests, the *brahmanas*, then claimed affiliation with the *Atharvaveda* and assumed the responsibility for overseeing the entire ritual performance of the other priests and counteracting any of their mistakes (they were supposed to know the other three Vedas as well as their own) by silent recitation of *mantras* from the *Atharvaveda*. As specialization increased, each priest of these four main classes took on three main assistants.

The Brahmanas—expositions of *brahman*, the sacred power inherent in *mantra* and more specifically now in the ritual—are the outgrowth of the concerns of these distinctive priestly schools and the first articulation of their religion. Each class of priests developed its own Brahmanas, the most important and comprehensive being the *Satapatha Brahmana* of one of the *Yajurveda* schools. The ritual system was also further refined in additional manuals: the Srautasutras, concerned with "solemn" rites, first described in the Brahmanas and thus called *srauta* because of their provenance in these sruti texts, and the Grhyasutras, concerned with domestic rites (from *grha*, "home"), justified by "tradition" *(smrti)* but still having much of Vedic origins. The Srautasutras were compiled over the period, roughly, from the Brahmanas to the Upanisads, and the Grhyasutras were probably compiled during Upanisadic times.

The domestic rites take place at a single offering fire and usually involve offerings of only grain or ghee (clarified butter). Along with the maintenance of the household fire and the performance of the so-called Five Great Sacrifices—to *brahman* (in the form of Vedic recitation), to ancestors, to gods, to other "beings," and to humans (hospitality rites)—the most prominent *grhya* ceremonies are the sacraments or life-cycle rites *(samskaras)*. Of these, the most important are the rites of conception and birth of a male child; the Upanayana, or "introduction," of boys to a *brahmana* preceptor or *guru* for initiation; marriage; and death by cremation (Antyesti, "final offering"). The Upanayana, involving the investiture of boys of the upper three social classes *(varnas)* with a sacred thread, conferred on them the status of "twice-born" *(dvija*, a term first used in the *Atharvaveda)*, and their "second birth" permitted them to hear the Veda and thereby participate in the *srauta* rites that, according to the emerging Brahmanic orthodoxy, would make it possible to obtain immortality.

The *srauta* rites are more elaborate and are representative of the sacrificial system in its full complexity, involving ceremonies that lasted up to two years and enlisted as many as seventeen priests. Through the continued performance of daily, bimonthly, and seasonal *srauta* rites one gains the year, which is itself identified with the sacrificial life-death-regeneration round and its divine personification, Prajapati. In surpassing the year by the Agnicayana, the "piling of the fire altar," one gains immortality and needs no more nourishment in the otherworld (see *Satapatha Brahmana* 10.1.5.4).

Srauta rites required a sacrificial terrain near the home of the sacrificer *(yajamana)*, with three sacred fires (representing, among other things, the three worlds) and an upraised altar, or *vedi*. Nonanimal sacrifices of the first varieties mentioned involved offerings of milk and vegetable substances or even of *mantras*. Animal sacrifices *(pasubandhu)*—which required a more elaborate sacrificial area with a supplemental altar and a sacrificial stake *(yupa)*—entailed primarily the sacrifice of a goat. Five male animals—man, horse, bull, ram, and goat—are declared suitable for sacrifice. It is likely, however, that human sacrifice existed only on the "ideal" plane, where it was personified in the cosmic sacrifices of Purusa and Prajapati. The animal *(pasu)* was to be immolated by strangulation, and its omentum, rich in fat, offered into the fire. *Soma* sacrifices, which would normally incorporate animal sacrifices within them plus a vast number of other subrites, involved the pressing and offering of *soma*. The most basic of these was the annual Agnistoma, "in praise of Agni," a four-day rite culminating in morning, afternoon, and evening *soma* pressings on the final day and including two goat sacrifices. Three of the most ambitious *soma* sacrifices were royal rites: the Asvamedha, the horse sacrifice; the Rajasuya, royal consecration; and the Vajapeya, a *soma* sac-

rifice of the "drink of strength." But the most complex of all was the aforementioned Agnicayana.

A thread that runs through most *srauta* rituals, however, is that they must begin with the "faith" or "confidence" *(sraddha)* of the sacrificer in the efficacy of the rite and the capacity of the officiating priests to perform it correctly. This prepares the sacrificer for the consecration *(diksa)* in which, through acts of asceticism *(tapas)*, he takes on the aspect of an embryo to be reborn through the rite. As *diksita* (one undergoing the *diksa)*, he makes an offering of himself (his *atman)*. This then prepares him to make the sacrificial offering proper (the *yajña*, "sacrifice") as a means to redeem or ransom this self by the substance (animal or otherwise) offered. Then, reversing the concentration of power that he has amassed in the *diksa*, he disperses wealth in the form of *daksinas* (honoraria) to the priests. Finally, the rite is disassembled (the ritual analogue to the repeated death of Prajapati before his reconstitution in another rite), and the sacrificer and his wife bathe to disengage themselves from the sacrifice and reenter the profane world.

In the elaboration of such ceremonies and the speculative explanation of them in the Brahmanas, the earlier Vedic religion seems to have been much altered. In the religion of the Brahmanas, the priests, as "those who know thus" *(evamvids)*, view themselves as more powerful than the gods. Meanwhile, the gods and the demons *(asuras)* are reduced to representing in their endless conflicts the recurrent interplay between agonistic forces in the sacrifice. It is their father, Prajapati, who crystallizes the concerns of Brahmanic thought by representing the sacrifice in all its aspects and processes. Most notable of these is the notion of the assembly or fabrication of an immortal self *(atman)* through ritual action *(karman)*, a self constructed for the sacrificer by which he identifies with the immortal essence of Prajapati as the sacrifice personified. And by the same token, the recurrent death *(punarmrtyu*, "redeath") of Prajapati's transitory nature (the elements of the sacrifice that are assembled and disassembled) figures in the Brahmanas as the object to be avoided for the sacrificer by the correct ritual performance. This Brahmanic concept of Prajapati's redeath, along with speculation on the ancestral *grhya* rites *(sraddhas)* focused on feeding deceased relatives to sustain them in the afterlife, must have been factors in the thinking that gave rise to the Upanisadic concept of reincarnation *(punarjanman*, "rebirth"). The emphasis on the morbid and transitory aspects of Prajapati and the sacrifice, and the insistence that asceticism within the sacrifice is the main means to overcome them, are most vigorously propounded in connection with the Agnicayana.

In the Brahmanas' recasting of the primal once-and-for-all sacrifice of Purusa into the recurrent life-death-regeneration mythology of Prajapati, a different theology was introduced. Though sometimes Purusa was identified with Prajapati, the latter, bound to the round of creation and destruction, became the prototype for the classical god Brahma, personification of the Absolute *(brahman)* as it is oriented toward the world. The concept of a transcendent Purusa, however, was not forgotten in the Brahmanas. *Satapatha Brahmana* 13.6 mentions Purusa-Narayana, a being who seeks to surpass all others through sacrifice and thereby become the universe. In classical Hinduism, *Narayana* and *Purusa* are both names for Visnu as the supreme divinity. This Brahmana passage neither authorizes nor disallows an identification with Visnu, but other Brahmana passages leave no doubt that sacrificial formulations have given Visnu and Rudra-Siva a new status. Whereas the Brahmanas repeatedly assert that "Visnu is the sacrifice"— principally in terms of the organization of sacrificial space that is brought about through Visnu's three steps through the cosmos, and his promotion of the order and prosperity that thus accrue—they portray Rudra as the essential outsider to this sacrificial order, the one who neutralizes the impure forces that threaten it from outside as well as the violence that is inherent within. Biardeau (1976) has been able to show that the later elevation of Visnu and Siva through yoga and *bhakti* is rooted in oppositional complementarities first formulated in the context of the Brahmanic sacrifice.

The Upanisads. Several trends contributed to the emergence of the Upanisadic outlook. Earlier speculations on the irreducible essence of the cosmos, the sacrifice, and individual experience have been mentioned. Pre-Upanisadic texts also refer to various forms of asceticism as performed by types of people who in one way or another rejected or inverted conventional social norms: the Vedic *muni*, *vratya*, and *brahmacarin*, to each of whom is ascribed ecstatic capacities, and, at the very heart of the Brahmanic sacrifice, the *diksita* (the sacrificer who performs *tapas* while undergoing the *diksa*, or consecration). These speculative and ascetic trends all make contributions to a class of texts generally regarded as intermediary between the Brahmanas and Upanisads: the Aranyakas, or "Forest Books." The Aranyakas do not differ markedly from the works that precede and succeed them (the *Brhadaranyaka Upanisad* is both an Aranyaka and an Upanisad), but their transitional character is marked by a shift in the sacrificial setting from domestic surroundings to the forest and a focus not so much on the details of ritual as on its interiorization and universalization. Sacrifice, for instance, is likened to the alternation that takes place between breathing and speaking. Thus correspondences are established between aspects of sacrifice and the life continuum of the meditator.

An *upanisad* is literally a mystical—often "secret"—"connection," interpreted as the teaching of mystical homologies. Or, in a more conventional etymology, it is the "sitting down" of a disciple "near to" (*upa*, "near"; *ni*, "down"; *sad*, "sit") his spiritual master, or *guru*. Each Upanisad reflects the Vedic

orientation of its priestly school. There are also regional orientations, for Upanisadic geography registers the further eastern settlement of the Vedic tradition into areas of the Ganges Basin. But the Upanisads do share certain fundamental points of outlook that are more basic than their differences. Vedic polytheism is demythologized, for all gods are reducible to one. Brahmanic ritualism is reassessed and its understanding of ritual action *(karman)* thoroughly reinterpreted. *Karman* can no longer be regarded as a positive means to the constitution of a permanent self. Rather, it is ultimately negative: "the world that is won by work *(karman)*"

> **The knowledge sought, however, is not that of ritual technique or even of ritual-based homologies, but a graspable, revelatory, and experiential knowledge of the self as one with ultimate reality.**

and "the world that is won by merit *(punya)*" only perish (*Chandogya Upanisad* 8.1.6). The "law of karma" *(karman)* or "law of causality" represents a strict and universal cause-effect continuum that affects any action that is motivated by desire *(kama)*, whether it be desire for good or for ill. Thus even meritorious actions that lead to the Vedic heaven "perish," leaving a momentum that carries the individual to additional births or reincarnations. The result is perpetual bondage to the universal flow-continuum of all *karman*, or *samsara* (from *sam*, "together" and *sr*, "flow"), a term that the Upanisads introduce into the Vedic tradition but that is shared with Jainism and Buddhism. As with these religions, the Upanisads and Hinduism henceforth conceive their soteriological goal as liberation from this cycle of *samsara*: that is, *moksa* or *mukti* ("release").

Moksa cannot be achieved by action alone, since action only leads to further action. Thus, though ritual action is not generally rejected and is often still encouraged in the Upanisads, it can only be subordinated to pursuit of the higher *moksa* ideal. Rather, the new emphasis is on knowledge *(vidya, jñana)* and the overcoming of ignorance *(avidya)*. The knowledge sought, however, is not that of ritual technique or even of ritual-based homologies, but a graspable, revelatory, and experiential knowledge of the self as one with ultimate reality. In the early Upanisads this experience is formulated as the realization of the ultimate "connection," the oneness of *atman-brahman*, a connection knowable only in the context of communication from *guru* to disciple. (Herein can be seen the basis of the parable context and vivid, immediate imagery of many Upanisadic teachings.) The experience thus achieved is variously described as one of unified consciousness, fearlessness, bliss, and tranquillity.

Beyond these common themes, however, and despite the fact that Upanisadic thought is resistant to systematization, certain different strains can be identified. Of the thirteen Upanisads usually counted as *sruti*, the earliest (c. 700-500 BCE) are those in prose, headed by the *Brhadaranyaka* and the *Chandogya*. Generally, it may be said that these Upanisads introduce the formulations that later Hinduism will develop into the *samnyasa* ideal of renunciation (not yet defined in the Upanisads as a fourth stage of life) and the knowledge-path outlook of nondualistic *(advaita)* Vedanta. Even within these early Upanisads, two approaches to realization can be distinguished. One refers to an all-excluding Absolute; the self that is identified with *brahman*, characterized as *neti neti* ("not this, not this"), is reached through a paring away of the psychomental continuum and its links with *karman*. Such an approach dominates the *Brhadaranyaka Upanisad*. *Avidya* here results from regarding the name and form of things as real and forming attachment to them. The other approach involves an all-comprehensive Absolute, *brahman-atman*, which penetrates the world so that all forms are modifications of the one; ignorance results from the failure to experience this immediacy. In the *Chandogya Upanisad* this second approach is epitomized in the persistent formula "Tat tvam asi" ("That thou art").

The later Vedic Upanisads (c. 600-400 BCE) register the first impact of theistic devotional formulations, and of early Samkhya and Yoga. Most important of these historically are two "yogic" Upanisads, the *Svetasvatara* and the *Katha*, the first focused on Rudra-Siva and the second on Visnu. Each incorporates into its terminology for the absolute deity the earlier term *purusa*. As Biardeau has shown in *L'hindouisme* (1981), they thus draw on an alternate term for the Absolute from that made current in the *brahman-atman* equation. The Purusa of *Rgveda* 10.90 (the *Purusasukta*) is sacrificed to create the ordered and integrated sociocosmic world of Vedic man. But only one quarter of this Purusa is "all beings"; three quarters are "the immortal in heaven" (RV 10.90.3). This transcendent aspect of Purusa, and also a certain "personal" dimension, are traits that were retained in the characterization of Purusa-Narayana in the *Satapatha Brahmana* and reinforced in the yogic characterizations of Rudra-Siva and Visnu in the previously mentioned Upanisads. The Upanisadic texts do not restrict the usage of the term *purusa* to mean "soul," as classical Samkhya later does; rather, it is used to refer to both the soul and the supreme divinity. The relation between the soul and the Absolute is thus doubly defined: on the one hand as *atman-brahman*, on the other as *purusa*-Purusa. In the latter case, the *Katha Upanisad* describes a spiritual itinerary of the soul's ascent through yogic states to the supreme Purusa, Visnu. This synthesis of yoga and *bhakti* will be carried forward into the devotional formulations of the epics and the Puranas. But one must note that the two vocabularies are used concurrently and interrelatedly in the Upanisads, as they will be in the later *bhakti* formulations.

The Consolidation of Classical Hinduism. A period of consolidation, sometimes identified as one of "Hindu synthesis," "Brahmanic synthesis," or "orthodox synthesis," takes place between the time of the late Vedic Upanisads (c. 500 BCE) and the period of Gupta imperial ascendancy (c. 320-467 CE). Discussion of this consolidation, however, is initially complicated by a lack of historiographical categories adequate to the task of integrating the diverse textual, inscriptional, and archaeological data of this long formative period. The attempt to cover as much of this span as possible with the name "epic period," because it coincides with the dates that are usually assigned to the formation and completion of the Hindu epics (particularly the *Mahabharata*), is misleading, since so much of what transpires can hardly be labeled "epic." On the other hand, attempts to define the period in terms of heterogeneous forces operating upon Hinduism from within (assimilation of local deities and cults, geographical spread) and without (heterodox and foreign challenges) either have failed to register or have misrepresented the implications of the apparent fact that the epics were "works in progress" during the whole period. The view one takes of the epics is, in fact, crucial for the interpretation of Hinduism during this period. Here, assuming that the epics already incorporated a *bhakti* cosmology and theology from an early point in this formative period, I shall try to place them in relation to other works and formulations that contributed to the consolidation of classical Hinduism.

The overall history can be broken down into four periods characterized by an oscillation from disunity (rival regional kingdoms and tribal confederacies on the Ganges Plain) to unity (Mauryan ascendancy, c. 324-184 BCE, including the imperial patronage of Buddhism by Asoka) to disunity (rival foreign kingdoms in Northwest India and regional kingdoms elsewhere) back to unity (Gupta ascendancy, c. 320-467 CE). The emerging self-definitions of Hinduism were forged in the context of continued interaction with heterodox religions (Buddhists, Jains, Ajivikas) throughout this whole period, and with foreign peoples (Yavanas, or Greeks; Sakas, or Scythians; Pahlavas, or Parthians; and Kusanas, or Kushans) from the third phase on. In this climate the *ideal* of centralized Hindu rule attained no practical realization until the rise of the Guptas. That this ideal preceded its realization is evident in the rituals of royal paramountcy (Asvamedha and Rajasuya) that were set out in the Brahmanas and the Srautasutras, and actually performed by post-Mauryan regional Hindu kings.

When we look to the component facets of the overall consolidation, these four periods must be kept in mind, but with the proviso that datings continue to be problematic: not only datings of texts, but especially of religious movements and processes reflected in them, and in surviving inscriptions.

Most scholars ordinarily assume that when a process is referred to in a text or other document, it has gone on for some time.

Sruti and smrti. Fundamental to the self-definition of Hinduism during this period of its consolidation is the distinction it makes between two classes of its literature: *sruti* and *smrti*. Sruti is "what is heard," and refers to the whole corpus of Vedic literature (also called Veda) from the four Vedas to the Upanisads. *Smrti*, "what is remembered" or "tradition," includes all that falls outside this literature. Exactly when this distinction was made is not certain, but it is noteworthy that the six Vedangas or "limbs of the Veda" (writings on phonetics, metrics, grammar, etymology, astronomy, and ritual) are *smrti* texts that were composed at least in part during the latter half of the Vedic or *sruti* period. The ritual texts (Kalpasutras) are subdivided into three categories: Srautasutras, Grhyasutras, and Dharmasutras. Whereas the first two (discussed above under Brahmanic ritual) pertain to concerns developed in the Vedic period, the Dharmasutras focus on issues of law *(dharma)* that become characteristic of the period now under discussion. [*See* Dharma, *article on* Hindu Dharma.] Dates given for the composition of these texts run from 600 to 300 BCE for the earliest (*Gautama Dharmasutra*) to 400 CE for the more recent works. Both Grhyasutras and Dharmasutras were sometimes called Smartasutras (i. e., *sutras* based on *smrti*), so it seems that their authors regarded them as representative of the prolongation of Vedic orthodoxy (and orthopraxy) that the *smrti* category was designed to achieve. As the term *smrti* was extended in its use, however, it also came to cover numerous other texts composed in the post-Upanisadic period.

This *sruti/smrti* distinction thus marks off the earlier literature as a unique corpus that, once the distinction was made, was retrospectively sanctified. By the time of the *Manava Dharmasastra*, or *Laws of Manu* (c. 200 BCE-100 CE; see Manu 1.23), and probably before this, *sruti* had come to be regarded as "eternal." Its components were thus not works of history. The Vedic *rsis* had "heard" truths that are eternal, and not only in content—the words of the Vedas are stated to have eternal connection with their meanings—but also in form. The works thus bear no stamp of the *rsis'* individuality. Such thinking crystallized in the further doctrine that the Vedas (i. e., *sruti*) are *apauruseya*, not of personal authorship (literally, "not by a *purusa*"). They thus have no human imperfection. Further, it was argued that they are even beyond the authorship of a divine "person" *(Purusa)*. Though myths of the period assert that the Vedas spring from Brahma at the beginning of each creation (as the three Vedas spring from Purusa in the *Purusasukta*), the deity is not their author. Merely reborn with him, they are a self-revelation of the impersonal *brahman*. In contrast to *sruti*, *smrti* texts were seen as historical or "traditional," passed on by "memory" *(smrti)*, and as works of individual authors *(pauruseya)*, even

though mythical authors—both human and divine—often had to be invented for them.

Smrti texts of this period thus proclaim the authority of the Veda in many ways, and nonrejection of the Veda comes to be one of the most important touchstones for defining Hinduism over and against the heterodoxies, which rejected the Veda. In fact, it is quite likely that the doctrines of the eternality and impersonality of the Veda were in part designed to assert the superiority of the Veda over the "authored" and "historical" works of the heterodoxies, whose teachings would thus be on a par with *smrti* rather than *sruti*. But it is also likely that the *apauruseya* doctrine is designed to relativize the "personal" god of *bhakti*. In any case, these doctrines served to place a considerable ideological distance between *sruti* and *smrti*, and to allow *smrti* authors great latitude in interpreting *sruti* and extending Hindu teachings into new areas. *Smrti* thus supposedly functioned to clarify the obscurities of the Veda. But the claim that *smrti* texts need only not contradict the Veda left their authors great freedom in pursuing new formulations.

Varnasramadharma ("caste and life-stage law"). The most representative corpus of *smrti* literature, and the most closely tied to the continued unfolding orthodox interests of the Vedic priestly schools, is that concerned with *dharma* ("law" or "duty"). As a literary corpus, it consists of two kinds of texts: the Dharmasutras (600/300 BCE-400 CE), already mentioned in connection with the *sruti/smrti* distinction, and the Dharmasastras. The most important and earliest of the latter are the *Manava Dharmasastra*, or *Laws of Manu* (c. 200 BCE-100 CE), and the Yajñavalkya Smrti (c. 100-300 CE). But other Dharmasastras were composed late into the first millennium, to be followed by important commentaries on all such texts. The main focus of these two classes of texts is fundamentally identical: the articulation of norms for all forms of social interaction, thus including but going far beyond the earlier Sutras' concern for ritual. Four differences, however, are noteworthy: (1) Whereas the Dharmasutras are in prose, the Dharmasastras are in the same poetic meter as the epics, *Manu* in particular having much material in common with the *Mahabharata*. (2) Whereas the Sutras are still linked with the Vedic schools, the Sastras are not, showing that study and teaching of *dharma* had come to be an independent discipline of its own. (3) The Sastra legislation is more extended and comprehensive. (4) The Sastras are more integrated into a mythic and cosmological vision akin to that in *bhakti* texts, but usually ignoring *bhakti* as such, with references to duties appropriate to different *yugas* (ages), and the identification of north central India as the "middle region" *(madhyadesa)* where the *dharma* is (and is to be kept) the purest.

The theory of *varnasramadharma*, the law of castes and life stages, was worked out in these texts as a model for the whole of Hindu society. There is little doubt that it was stimulated by the alternate lay/monastic social models of the heterodoxies, and no doubt that it was spurred on by the incursions of barbarian peoples—frequently named in these texts as *mlecchas* (those who "jabber")—into the Northwest. The model involves the working out of the correlations between two ideals: first, that society conform to four hierarchical castes, and second, that a person should pass through four life stages *(asramas)*: student *(brahmacarin)*, householder *(grhasthin)*, forest dweller *(vanaprasthin)*, and renunciant *(samnyasin)*. The first ideal is rooted in the *Purusasukta*. The second presupposes the *sruti* corpus, since the four life

> **A further implication is that the life stages can be properly pursued only by male members of the three twice-born *varnas*. . . .**

stages are correlated with the four classes of *sruti* texts. Thus the student learns one of the Vedas, the householder performs domestic and optimally also *srauta* rituals of the Brahmanas, the forest dweller follows the teachings of the Aranyakas, and the *samnyasin* follows a path of renunciation toward the Upanisadic goal of *moksa*. But although all the life stages are either mentioned (as are the first two) or implied in the *sruti* corpus, the theory that they should govern the ideal course of individual life is new to the Dharmasutras. Together, the *varna* and *asrama* ideals take on tremendous complexity, since a person's duties vary according to caste and stage of life, not to mention other factors like sex, family, region, and the quality of the times. Also, whereas a person's development through one life ideally is regulated by the *asrama* ideal, the passage through many reincarnations would involve birth into different castes, the caste of one's birth being the result of previous *karman*. A further implication is that the life stages can be properly pursued only by male members of the three twice-born *varnas*, as they alone can undergo the Upanayana ritual that begins the student stage and allows the performance of the rites pertinent to succeeding stages.

Each of these formulations has persisted more on the ideal plane than the real. In the case of the four *asramas*, most people never went beyond the householder stage, which the Sutras and Sastras actually exalt as the most important of the four, since it is the support of the other three and, in more general terms, the mainstay of the society. The forest-dweller stage may soon have become more legendary than real: in epic stories it was projected onto the Vedic *rsis*. The main tension, however, that persists in orthodox Hinduism is that between the householder and the renunciant, the challenge being for anyone to integrate into one

lifetime these two ideals, which the heterodoxies set out for separate lay and monastic communities.

As to the four *varnas*, the ideal represents society as working to the reciprocal advantage of all the castes, each one having duties necessary to the proper functioning of the whole and the perpetuation of the hierarchical principle that defines the whole. Thus *brahmanas* are at the top, distinguished by three duties that they share with no other caste: teaching the Veda, assisting in sacrifice, and accepting gifts. They are said to have no king but Soma, god of the sacrifice. In actual fact the traditional *srauta* sacrifice counted for less and less in the *brahmana* householder life, and increasing attention was given to the maintenance of *brahmana* purity for the purpose of domestic and eventually temple rituals which, in effect, universalized sacrifice as the *brahmana's dharma*, but a sacrifice that required only the minimum of impure violence. This quest for purity was reinforced by *brahmanas'* adoption into their householder life of aspects of the *samnyasa* ideal of renunciation. This was focused especially on increasing espousal of the doctrine of *ahimsa* (nonviolence, or, more literally, "not desiring to kill") and was applied practically to vegetarianism, which becomes during this period the *brahmana* norm. *Brahmanas* thus retain higher rank than *ksatriyas*, even though the latter wield temporal power *(ksatra)* and have the specific and potentially impure duties of bearing weapons and protecting and punishing with the royal staff *(danda)*. The subordination of king to *brahmana* involves a subordination of power to hierarchy that is duplicated in contemporary rural and regional terms in the practice of ranking *brahmanas* above locally dominant castes whose power lies in their landed wealth and numbers. *Vaisyas* have the duties of stock breeding, agriculture, and commerce (including money lending). Certain duties then distinguished the three twice-born castes as a group from the *sudras*. All three upper *varnas* thus study the Veda, perform sacrifices, and make gifts, whereas *sudras* are permitted only lesser sacrifices *(pakayajñas)* and simplified domestic rituals that do not require Vedic recitation.

Actual conditions, however, were (and still are) much more complex. The four-*varna* model provided the authors of the *dharma* texts with Vedic "categories" within which to assign a basically unlimited variety of heterogeneous social entities including indigenous tribes, barbarian invaders, artisan communities and guilds *(srenis)*, and specialists in various services. Susceptible to further refinement in ranking and regional nomenclature, all such groups were called *jatis*, a term meaning "birth" and in functional terms the proper word to be translated "caste." Thus, although they are frequently called subcastes, the *jatis* are the castes proper that the law books classified into the "categories" of *varna*.

To account for this proliferation of *jatis*, the authors asserted that they arose from cross-breeding of the *varnas*. Two possibilities were thus presented: *anuloma* ("with the grain") unions, in which the husband's *varna* was the same as his wife's or higher (in anthropological terms, hypergamous, in which women are "married up"), and *pratiloma* ("against the grain") unions, in which the wife's *varna* would be higher than the husband's (hypogamous, in which women are "married down"). Endogamous marriage (marriage within one's own *varna*) set the highest standard and was according to some authorities the only true marriage. But of the other two, whereas *anuloma* marriages were permitted, *pratiloma* unions brought disgrace. Thus the *jatis* supposedly born from *anuloma* unions were less disgraced than those born from *pratiloma* unions. Significantly, two of the most problematic *jatis* were said to have been born from the most debased *pratiloma* connections: the Yavanas (Greeks) from *sudra* males and *ksatriya* females (similar origins were ascribed to other "barbarians") and the *candalas* (lowest of the low, mentioned already in the Upanisads, and early Buddhist literature, as a "fifth caste" of untouchables) from the polluting contact of *sudra* males and *brahmana* females. It should be noted that a major implication of the prohibition of *pratiloma* marriage is the limitation for *brahmana* women to marriages with only *brahmana* men. This established at the highest rank an association of caste purity with caste endogamy (and the purity of a caste's women) and thus initiated an endogamous standard that was adopted by all castes—not just *varnas* but *jatis*—by the end of the first millennium.

This accounting of the emergence of *jatis* was integrated with further explanations of how society had departed from its ideal. One is that "mixing of caste"—the great abomination of the *dharma* texts and also of the *Bhagavadgita*—increases with the decline of *dharma* from *yuga* to *yuga*, and is especially pernicious in this Kali age. Another is the doctrine of *apad dharma*, "duties for times of distress" such as permit inversion of caste roles when life is threatened. A third doctrine developed in the Dharmasastras identifies certain duties (*kalivarjyas*) as once allowed but now prohibited in the *kaliyuga* because people are no longer capable of performing them purely. Through all this, however, the ideal persists as one that embraces a whole society despite variations over time and space.

The four purusarthas (goals of man). The theory that the integrated life involves the pursuit of four goals (*arthas*) is first presented in the Dharmasastras and the epics, in the latter cases through repeated narrative illustrations. The development of distinctive technical interpretations of each *artha*, or facets thereof, can also be followed during the period in separate manuals: the *Arthasastra*, a manual on statecraft attributed to Candragupta Maurya's minister Kautilya but probably dating from several centuries later, on *artha* (in the sense now of "material pursuits"); the Kamasutras, most notably that of Vatsyayana (c. 400 CE), on *kama* ("love, desire"); the already discussed Dharmasutras and Dharmasastras on *dharma*; and the Sutras of the "philo-sophical schools" (*darsanas*) insofar as they are concerned with the fourth goal, *moksa*. Early sources often refer to the first three goals as the *trivarga*, the "three categories," but this need not imply that the fourth goal is added later. The Dharmasastra and epic texts that mention the trivarga are focused on the concerns of the householder—and, in the epics, particularly of the royal householder—these being the context for the pursuit of the *trivarga*. The fourth goal, *moksa*, is to be pursued throughout life—indeed, throughout all lives—but is especially the goal of those who have entered the fourth life stage of the *samnyasin*. The *trivarga-moksa* opposition thus replicates the householder-renunciant opposition. But the overall purpose of the *purusartha* formulation is integrative and complementary to the *varnasramadharma* theory. From the angle of the householder, it is *dharma* that integrates the *trivarga* as a basis for *moksa*. But from the angle of the *samnyasin*, it is *kama* that lies at the root of the *trivarga*, representing attachment in all forms, even to *dharma*. Paths to liberation will thus focus on detachment from desire, or its transformation into love of God.

Philosophical "viewpoints" (darsanas) and paths to salvation. As an expression of Hinduism's increasing concern to systematize its teachings, the fourth goal of life (*moksa*) was made the subject of efforts to develop distinctly Hindu philosophical "viewpoints" (*darsanas*, from the root *drs*, "see") on the nature of reality and to recommend paths to its apprehension and the release from bondage to *karman*. Six Hindu *darsanas* were defined, and during the period in

> In terms of mainstream developments within Hinduism, only two schools have ongoing continuity into the present: the Mimamsa and the Vedanta.

question each produced fundamental texts—in most cases *sutras*—that served as the bases for later commentaries.

In terms of mainstream developments within Hinduism, only two schools have ongoing continuity into the present: the Mimamsa and the Vedanta. And of these, only the latter has unfolded in important ways in the postsynthesis period. Nonetheless, all six have made important contributions to later Hinduism. It must thus suffice to discuss them all briefly at this point in terms of their basic features and major impact, and reserve fuller discussion of the Vedanta alone for the period of its later unfolding.

Of the six schools, two—Mimamsa and Vedanta—are rooted primarily in the Vedic *sruti* tradition and are thus sometimes called *smarta* schools in the sense that they develop *smarta* orthodox currents of thought that are based, like smrti, directly on sruti. The other four—Nyaya, Vaisesika,

Samkhya, and Yoga—claim loyalty to the Veda, yet are quite independent of it, their focus instead being on rational or causal explanation. They are thus sometimes called *haituka* schools (from *hetu*, "cause, reason").

Of the *smarta* schools, the Mimamsa is most concerned with ritual traditions rooted in the Vedas and the Brahmanas, whereas the Vedanta is focused on the Upanisads. It is notable that both sustain Vedic orientations that reject (Mimamsa) or subordinate (Vedanta) *bhakti* until the Vedanta is devotionalized in its post-Sankara forms. Beginning with Jaimini's *Mimamsa Sutra* (c. 300-100 BCE), Mimamsa ("reflection, interpretation") provides exegesis of Vedic injunctive speech, in particular as it concerns the relationship between intentions and rewards of sacrifice. Great refinement is brought to bear on issues relating to the authority and eternalness of the Veda and the relationship between its sounds, words, and meanings. Vedic injunctions are taken literally, the many Vedic gods are seen as real although superfluous to salvation (there is an anti-*bhakti* stance here), and it is maintained that the proper use of injunctions is alone enough to secure the attainment of heaven (not a higher release, or *moksa*, as propounded by all the other systems, including *bhakti*). Mimamsa persists in two subschools, but only in small numbers among brahman ritualists.

As to the Vedanta ("end of the Veda," a term also used for the Upanisads), the foundational work is Badara-yana's *Vedanta Sutra*, or *Brahma Sutra* (c. 300-100 BCE), an exegesis of various Upanisadic passages in aphoristic style easily susceptible to divergent interpretations. These it received in the hands of later Vedantic thinkers.

The *haituka* schools are notable for their development, for the first time within Hinduism, of what may be called maps and paths: that is, maps of the constituent features of the cosmos, and paths to deliverance from bondage. Emerging within Hinduism at this period, and particularly in the schools least affiliated with the Vedic tradition, such concerns no doubt represent an effort to counter the proliferation of maps and paths set forth by the heterodoxies (not only Buddhism and Jainism, but the Ajivikas). They allow for a somewhat more open recognition of the deity of *bhakti* (Samkhya excepted) than do the *smarta* schools, though none of the *haituka* schools makes it truly central.

Nyaya and Vaisesika, systems first propounded in Gautama's *Nyaya Sutra* (c. 200 BCE-150 CE) and Kanada's *Vaisesika Sutra* (c. 200 BCE-100 CE), were quickly recognized as a hyphenated pair: Nyaya-Vaisesika. Nyaya ("rule, logic, analysis"), emphasizing logic and methods of argumentation as means to liberation, was viewed as complementary to Vaisesika ("school of distinct characteristics"), which advanced a theory of atomism and posited seven categories to explain such things as atomic aggregation and dualistic distinction between soul and matter. At least by about the fifth century, when the two schools had conjoined, Nyaya logic and Vaisesika cosmology served to provide influential arguments from design for the existence of God as the efficient cause of the creation and destruction of the universe and liberator of the soul from *karman*.

Far more influential, however, were the pair Samkhya ("enumeration") and Yoga. The foundational texts of these schools may be later than those of the others, but they are clearly distillations of long-continuing traditions, datable at least to the middle Upanisads, that had already undergone considerable systematization. Thus Patañjali's *Yoga Sutra* is from either about 200 BCE or 300-500 CE, depending on whether or not one identifies the author with the grammarian who lived at the earlier date. And Isvarakrsna's *Samkhyakarikas* probably date from the fourth century CE. Even though Samkhya's "atheism" and its soteriology of the isolation (*kaivalya*) of the soul (*purusa*) from matter (*prakrti*) have been modified or rejected in other forms of Hinduism (both doctrines may link Samkhya with Jainism), Samkhya's cosmology and basic terminology have become definitive for Hinduism at many levels: not only in the Vedanta, but in *bhakti* and Tantric formulations as well. In fact, given the preclassical forms of theistic Samkhya founded in the Upanisads and the *Mahabharata* and their use in *bhakti* cosmologies, it may well be that the atheism of the classical Samkhya results from a rejection of *bhakti* elements from a fundamentally theistic system. Samkhya thus posits *purusa* without a transcendent, divine Purusa, and its *prakrti* is also abstract and impersonal.

In any case, a number of Samkhya concepts became basic to the Hindu vocabulary, only to be integrated and reinterpreted from different theological and soteriological perspectives by other schools. These include the concepts of the evolution and devolution of *prakrti*, the sexual polarity of *purusa* as male and *prakrti* as female, the enumeration of twenty-three substances that evolve from and devolve back into the *prakrti* "matrix," the concept of matter as a continuum from subtle psychomental "substances" to gross physical ones (in particular the five elements), and the notion of the three "strands" or "qualities" called *gunas* (*sattva*, goodness, lucidity; *rajas*, dynamism; *tamas*, entropy), which are "braided" together through all matter from the subtle to the gross.

Meanwhile, whereas Samkhya provides the map to be "known," Yoga defines the path by which *purusa* can extricate itself from *prakrti*. The "eight limbs" of Yoga (an answer to the Eightfold Path of Buddhism?) represent the most important Hindu formulation of a step-by-step (though also cumulative) path to liberation. The first two "limbs" involve forms of restraint (*yama*) and observance (*niyama*). The next three involve integration of the body and senses: posture (*asana*), breath control (*pranayama*), and withdrawal of the senses from the dominance of sense objects (*pratyahara*). The last three achieve the integration of the mind or the "cessation of the mental turmoil" that is rooted in the effects of *karman*:

"holding" (dharana) to a meditative support, meditative fluency (dhyana), and integrative concentration (samadhi) through which the freedom of purusa can be experienced.

The classical Yoga of Patañjali, known as rajayoga ("royal yoga"), diverges from the Samkhya in acknowledging the existence of God (Isvara). But Isvara is a focus of meditation, not an agent in the process of liberation. The use of the term rajayoga, however, suggests that by Patañjali's time the term yoga had already been used to describe other disciplines or paths, resulting in a situation where the terms yoga ("yoke") and marga ("path") had become interchangeable. One will thus find rajayoga mentioned later along with the more generalized "yogas", or "paths," that become definitive for Hinduism through their exposition in the Bhagavadgita (c. 200 BCE): the paths (or yogas) of karman ("action"), jñana ("knowledge"), and bhakti ("devotion").

Classical bhakti Hinduism. The consolidation of Hinduism takes place under the sign of bhakti. And though Mimamsa ritualism and Vedantic and other "knowledge" trends continue to affiliate with an "orthodox" strain that resists this synthesis, or attempts to improve upon it, classical bhakti emerges as constitutive henceforth of mainstream Hinduism, including forms of devotional sectarianism.

Intimations of bhakti developments are registered as early as the late Vedic Upanisads, and in inscriptions and other records of syncretistic worship of Hindu deities (Visnu and Siva) alongside foreign and heterodox figures in the early centuries of the common era. However, the heterogeneity and scattered nature of the nontextual information available on the emergence of bhakti during this period have allowed for conflicting interpretations of the salient features of the process. But rather than reweave a fragile developmental web from supposedly separate sectarian and popular strands, it is better to look at the texts themselves to see what they attempted and achieved. We should note, however, that to the best of our knowledge it was achieved relatively early in the period of consolidation, for the Bhagavadgita—the text that seals the achievement—seems to be from no later than the first or second century BCE (it is cited by Badarayana in the Vedanta Sutra), and possibly earlier. Of course, continued unfolding occurred after that.

The achievement itself is a universal Hinduism that, following Biardeau's discussion of bhakti in "Études de mythologie hindoue" (1976), we may designate as smarta. It inherits from the Brahmanic sacrificial tradition a conception wherein Visnu and Siva are recognized as complementary in their functions but ontologically identical. The fundamental texts of this devotional smarta vision are the two epics—the Mahabharata (c. 500 BCE-400 CE) and the Ramayana (c. 400-200 BCE)—and the Harivamsa (c. 300-400 CE?). These works integrate much Puranic mythic and cosmological material, which later is spun out at greater length in the classical Puranas ("ancient lore"), of which there are said to be eigh-

teen major and eighteen minor texts. The epics and Puranas are thus necessarily discussed together. But it should be recognized that whereas the smarta vision of the epics and the Harivamsa is fundamentally integrative and universal in intent, the Puranas are frequently dominated by regional and particularistic interests, including in some cases the strong advocacy of the worship of one deity (Siva, Visnu, or the Goddess) over all others. It is thus tempting to think of the period of Purana composition (c. 400-1200 CE?) as one that extends the integrative vision of the fundamental texts but develops it in varied directions. Still, as it is not clear that instances of Puranic theological favoritism are motivated by distinct sects, it is misleading to speak of "sectarian" Puranas.

Taken together, then, the Harivamsa and the Mahabharata (which includes the Bhagavadgita) present the full biography of Krsna, and the Ramayana that of Rama. The Harivamsa (Genealogy of Hari—i. e., Krsna), the more recent of the texts concerning Krsna, presents the stories of his birth and youth, in which he and his brother Balarama take on the "disguise" (vesa) of cowherds. Thus they engage in divine "sport" (lila) with the cowherd women (gopis), until finally they are drawn away to avenge themselves against their demonic uncle Kamsa, who had caused their exile. The Mahabharata (Story of the Great Bharata Dynasty) focuses on Krsna's assistance to the five Pandava brothers in their conflicts with their cousins, the hundred Kauravas, over the "central kingdom" of the lunar dynasty (the Bharata dynasty) at Hastinapura and Indraprastha near modern Delhi. Both texts incorporate telling allusions to the other "cycle," and since both stories must have circulated orally together before reaching their present literary forms, any notions of their separate origins are purely conjectural. The Ramayana (Exploits of Rama) tells the story of Rama, scion of the solar dynasty and embodiment of dharma, who must rescue his wife Sita from the demon (raksasa) Ravana. Though each of these texts has its special flavor and distinctive background, they become in their completed forms effectively a complementary triad. Indeed, in the "conservative" South, popular performances of Hindu mythology in dramas and temple recitations are still dominated by three corresponding specializations: Mahabharata, Ramayana, and Bhagavata Purana, the latter (c. 800-900 CE?) enriching the devotional themes of the Harivamsa in its tenth and eleventh books and in effect replacing it as representing the early life of Krsna.

The smarta universe in these texts is structured around Visnu, and more particularly around his two heroic incarnations, Rama and Krsna. Thus other deities are frequently represented as subordinated to or subsumed by these figures. But there is also recognition of Visnu's complementarity with Siva: some passages that stress mutual acknowledgment of their ontological unity, others that work out the interplay between them through stories about heroic characters who incarnate them, and scenes in which Visnu's incarnations do homage to Siva. It should be clear that efforts to find "tendencies toward monotheism" in such texts involve the reduction of a very complex theology to distinctly Western terms. The same applies to those Puranas that are structured around Siva or the Goddess rather than Visnu but are still framed within the same cosmology and the same principles of theological complementarity and subordination.

This *smarta* vision is not, however, limited to one theological conundrum, for it extends to encompass Siva and Visnu's interaction with other major figures: the god Brahma, masculine form of the impersonal Absolute *(brahman)*, now subordinated to the higher "personal" deities; the Goddess in her many forms; Indra and other *devas* (now "demigods"); their still perennial foes, the demons *(asuras)*; and of course humans, animals, and so on. It also presents an overarching *bhakti* cosmology in which the yogic supreme divinity (Siva or Visnu) encompasses the religious values of *samnyasa*, *tapas*, knowledge, and sacrifice, and introduces the view that taken by themselves, without *bhakti*, these values may be incomplete or even extreme "paths." Further, it incorporates the *smarta* social theory of the Dharmasutras and the Dharmasastras, and works out its implications within the cosmology. The details of this *smarta* vision are best discussed, however, in relation to the Hindu chronometric theory that is presumed and first articulated in these texts and then further developed in the Puranas.

> **These are not human years, however, but divine years, which are 360 times as long as human years.**

Time is structured according to three main rhythms, hierarchically defined, the longer encompassing the lesser. Most down-to-earth is the series of four *yugas* named after four dice throws, which define a theory of the "decline of the *dharma*": first a *krtayuga* ("perfect age"), then a *tretayuga* and a *dvaparayuga*, and finally a degenerate *kaliyuga* ("age of discord"). A *krtayuga* lasts 4,000 years, a *tretayuga* 3,000, a *dvaparayuga* 2,000, and a *kaliyuga* 1,000, each supplemented by a dawn and twilight of one-tenth its total. A full four-*yuga* cycle thus lasts 12,000 years and is called a *mahayuga* ("great yuga"). These are not human years, however, but divine years, which are 360 times as long as human years. Thus a *mahayuga* equals 360 times 12,000, or 4,320,000 human years, and a *kaliyuga* is one-tenth of that total. A thousand *mahayugas* (4,320 million human years) is a *kalpa*, the second major time unit, which is also called a "day of Brahma." Brahma's days are followed by nights of equal duration. Brahma lives a hundred years of 360 such days and

nights, or 311,040 billion human years, all of which are sometimes said to pass in a wink of the eye of Visnu. The period of a life of Brahma, called a *mahakalpa*, is the third major temporal rhythm.

Working backward now, we may observe the *modus operandi* of Visnu and Siva (and of course others) as it is envisioned in the *smarta* Hinduism of our texts.

First, at the highest level, Visnu and Siva are great yogins, interacting with the rhythms of the universe in terms of their own oscillations between activity and yogic concentration *(samadhi)*. At the *mahapralaya* ("great dissolution"), the deity (usually Visnu in these early texts, but just as often Siva or the Goddess in later Puranic ones) oversees the dissolution of the universe into the primal *prakrti* in accord with the cosmological theory of Samkhya-Yoga. This ends the life of Brahma, but it is also to be noted that it marks the restoration to its primordial unity of *prakrti*, which—as feminine—is regarded mythologically as the ultimate form of the Goddess. From a Saiva standpoint, the male (the deity as Purusa) and the female (the Goddess as Prakrti) are reunited at the great dissolution of the universe, a theme that is depicted in representations of the deity as Ardhanarisvara, "the Lord who is half female." Their union is nonprocreative and represents the unitive experience of the bliss of *brahman*. Creation then occurs when the deity (whether Siva or Visnu) emerges from this *samadhi* and instigates the renewed active unfolding of *prakrti*.

The coincidence of the death of Brahma with not only the dissolution of the universe but the reintegration of the Goddess and her reunion with Siva is highly significant. The Goddess is an eternal being, worthy of worship because—like Visnu and Siva—she outlasts the universe and can bestow *moksa*. Brahma, ultimately mortal and bound to temporality, is worshiped not for *moksa* but rather—and mostly by demons—for earthly power and lordship. Stories that portray Siva's severing of Brahma's fifth head and refer to the "head of Brahma" *(brahmasiras)* as the weapon of doomsday, are perhaps mythic echoes of this ultimate cosmological situation wherein the coming together of Purusa and Prakrti coincide with his death.

The primary creation has as its result the constitution of a "cosmic egg," the *brahmanda* ("egg of Brahma"). Further creation, and periodic recreations, will be carried out by Brahma, the personalized form of the Absolute *(brahman)*. Insofar as the *brahman* is personalized and oriented toward the world, it is thus subordinated to the yogin Purusa, the ultimate as defined through *bhakti*. Moreover, the activity of Brahma—heir in his cosmogenic role of the earlier Prajapati—is conceived in terms of sacrificial themes that are further encompassed by *bhakti*.

It is at this level that the three male gods cooperate as the *trimurti*, the "three forms" of the Absolute: Brahma the creator, Siva the destroyer, and Visnu the preserver. Within the *brahmanda*, Brahma thus creates the Vedic triple world of earth, atmosphere, and heaven (or alternatively heaven, earth, and underworld). These three samsaric worlds are surrounded by four ulterior worlds, still within the *brahmanda*, for beings who achieve release from *samsara* but still must await their ultimate liberation. These ulterior worlds are not henceforth created or destroyed in the occasional creations or destructions. As to the triple world, Brahma creates it by becoming the sacrificial boar *(yajñavaraha)* who retrieves the Vedas and the earth from the cosmic ocean. The destruction of the triple world is achieved by Siva. As the "fire of the end of time," he reduces it to ashes, thus effecting a cosmic funerary sacrifice. And Visnu, the god whom the Brahmanas identify as "the sacrifice," maintains the triple world while it is sustained by sacrifices, and also preserves what is left of it after the dissolution when he lies on the serpent Sesa ("remainder") whose name indicates that he is formed of the remnant of the previous cosmos, or more exactly of the "remainder" of the cosmic sacrifice. This form of Visnu, sleeping on Sesa, is called Narayana, a name that the *Satapatha Brahmana* already connects with the Vedic Purusa, the "male" source of all beings. When Visnu-Narayana awakens, Brahma—who in some fashion awakens with him—recreates the universe. Through all these myths the earth is a form of the Goddess, indeed the most concretized form she takes as a result of the evolution of *prakrti* (earth being the last of the evolutes emitted and the first to dissolve).

Thus the greater universe whose rhythms are integrated within the divine yoga of Visnu and Siva encompasses an egg of Brahma, which encloses a triple world whose rhythms form a round sustained by the divine sacrificial acts of the *trimurti*. This pattern is transposed onto the third temporal rhythm, that of the *yugas*. Thus the characteristic religious virtues of the *yugas* are as follows: *dhyana* ("meditation") or *tapas* ("asceticism") in the *krtayuga*; *jñana* ("knowledge") in the *tretayuga*; *yajña* ("sacrifice") in the *dvaparayuga*; and *dana* ("the gift") in the *kaliyuga*. Thus the two *sruti*-based ideals of knowledge and sacrifice are enclosed within a frame-work that begins with yogic meditation as a divine *krtayuga* activity and ends in the *kaliyuga* with the devotional gift. *Bhakti* thus encompasses knowledge and sacrifice.

The distinctive feature of the rhythm of the *yuga* cycle is that it is calibrated by the rise and fall of *dharma* in the triple world. Beings who have achieved release from the triple world oscillate between the four higher worlds, enduring periodic destructions of the triple world and awaiting the great dissolution of the universe that will dissolve the egg of Brahma (coincident with his death) and result in a vast collective ultimate liberation of reabsorption into the supreme Purusa. Needless to say, this is to occur only after an almost incalculable wait. But beings who have attained these ulterior worlds are no more affected by *dharma* than the yogic deity beyond them. The maintenance of *dharma* within the

triple world thus engages the deities in their third level of activity, that of "descent." In classical terms this is the theory of the *avatara*. Though the term is not used in the epics or the *Harivamsa* in its later, specialized sense, these texts are suffused by the concept and its *bhakti* implications, which include narrative situations wherein the divinity looks to all concerned, and sometimes even to himself, as a mere human. The programmatic statement of the *avatara* concept (without mention of the term itself) is thus stated by Krsna in the *Bhagavadgita*: "For whenever the Law [*dharma*] languishes, Bharata, and lawlessness flourishes I create myself. I take on existence from eon to eon [*yuga* to *yuga*], for the rescue of the good and the destruction of evil, in order to establish the Law" (4.7-8; van Buitenen, trans.).

The classical theory of the ten *avataras*—most of whom are mentioned in the epics and the *Harivamsa*, but not in a single list—is worked out in relation to Visnu. One thus has the following "descents" of Visnu in order of appearance: Fish (Matsya), Tortoise (Kurma), Boar (Varaha), Man-Lion (Narasimha), Dwarf (Vamana), Rama with the Ax (Parasurama), Rama of the *Ramayana*, Krsna, the Buddha, and the future *avatara* Kalki, who will rid the earth of barbarian kings and reestablish the *dharma* at the end of the *kaliyuga*. There are various attempts to correlate appearances of the *avataras* with distinct *yugas* and even *kalpas*, but the one feature that is consistently mentioned in these formative texts is that Krsna appeared at the interval between the last *dvaparayuga* and *kaliyuga*, and thus at the beginning of our present age. It is likely that the theory was first formulated around Krsna and Rama along with the Dwarf (the only form to be associated with Visnu in the *sruti* literature) and the apocalyptic Kalki. But in actuality, the *avatara* theory is more complex. In the epics and in living Hinduism, Visnu does not descend alone. In the literature, his incarnations take place alongside those of other deities, including most centrally Vayu, Indra, Surya, the Goddess, and—at least in the *Mahabharata*—Siva. And in localized temple mythologies throughout India, one hears of *avataras* of Siva and the Goddess as well as of Visnu. In devotional terms, the *avatara* is thus a form taken on earth (or, better, in the three worlds) by any one of the three deities we find at the ultimate level of cosmic absorption, where all that remains beside the liberated beings who join them are the eternal yogic deities Visnu and Siva and the primal Goddess.

The classical concept of the *avatara*, structured around Visnu, remains, however, the chief Hindu use of the term. Its formulation in the epics and the *Harivamsa* is thus constitutive for succeeding eras of Hinduism, in which it will only be enriched but not essentially changed by later *bhakti* theologies. Looking at these texts comprehensively, then, with the *Gita* as our main guide, we can outline its main contours. Against the background of the vast, all-embracing *bhakti* cosmology, the involvement of the yogic divinity on earth takes place completely freely, as "sport" or "play" (lila). Still, the god takes birth to uphold the *dharma* and to keep the earth from being unseasonably inundated in the waters of dissolution under the weight of adharmic kings. The *avatara* thus intercedes to uphold the system of *varnasramadharma* and to promote the proper pursuit of the four *purusarthas*. Since he appears in times of crisis, a central concern in the texts is with the resolution of the conflicts between ideals: renunciation versus householdership, *brahmana* versus *ksatriya*, killing versus "not desiring to kill" *(ahimsa)*, *dharma* versus *moksa*, *dharma* versus *kama* and *artha*, and conflicts between different *dharmas* (duties) such as royal duty and filial duty. But though the texts focus primarily on the two upper castes, the full society is represented by singular depictions of figures who evoke the lowest castes and tribal groups. It is also filled in with figures of real and reputed mixed caste.

Confusion of caste is a particularly prominent issue in the *Mahabharata*, where it is raised by Krsna in the *Gita* as the worst of ills. Most significantly, the *Mahabharata* and the *Harivamsa* identify a particularly pernicious form of caste confusion among the barbarian *(mleccha)* peoples of the Northwest (the Punjab), mentioning Yavanas, Sakas, and Pahlavas among others as enemies of the *dharma* and causes for such "mixing." The fact that events of the period from 300 BCE to 300 CE are projected into the distant past indicates that part of the *bhakti* synthesis was the articulation of a mythical theory of historical events. One may thus look at these *smrti* texts as posing a model for the revival of Hinduism in accord with "eternal" Vedic models, with the descent of the *avatara*—and indeed of much of the Vedic pantheon along with him—guaranteeing the periodic adjustment of the sociocosmic world to these eternal norms. Furthermore, the tracing of all Hindu dynastic lines back to the defunct if not mythical "lunar" and "solar" dynasties provided the model for the spatial extension of this ideal beyond the central lands of Aryavarta where the *dharma*, according to both *Manu* and the *Mahabharata*, was the purest.

But the focus of the *avatara* is not solely on the renovation of the *dharma*. He also brings to the triple world the divine grace that makes possible the presence, imagery, and teachings that confer *moksa*. The epics and the *Harivamsa* are full of *bhakti* tableaux: moments that crystallize the realization by one character or another of the liberating vision *(darsana)* of the divine. Most central, however, is the *Bhagavadgita*, which is both a *darsana* and a teaching.

The *Bhagavadgita* (Song of the Lord) takes place as a dialogue between Krsna and Arjuna just before the outbreak of the *Mahabharata* war. Although he is the third oldest of the five Pandavas, Arjuna is their greatest warrior, and Krsna's task in the *Gita* is to persuade him to overcome his reluctance to fight in the battle. Fundamental to the argument is Arjuna's requirement to fulfill his *dharma* as a *ksatriya* rather than adopt the ideal—unsuitable for him in his present life stage—of the renouncer. Thus the *Gita* champions the theory of *varnasramadharma* as upholding the sociocosmic order.

Krsna presents his teaching to Arjuna by revealing a sequence of "royal" and "divine" mysteries that culminate in his granting a vision of his "All-Form" *(Visvarupa-darsana)* as God, creator and destroyer of the universe. In this grand cosmic perspective, Arjuna is told that he will be but the "mere instrument" of the deaths of his foes, their destruction having now come to ripeness through Visnu's own agency in his form as cosmic time, or *kala* (*Bhagavadgita* 11.32-33). Arjuna thus recognizes this omniform deity as Visnu in this climactic scene.

On the way to this revelation, however, Krsna acknowledges the three paths *(yogas)* to salvation: action, knowledge, and devotion. These are presented as instructions by which Arjuna can gain the resolute clarity of insight *(buddhi)* and yogic discipline by which to recognize the distinctions between soul and body, action and inaction, and thus perform actions—including killing—that are unaffected by desire. Ritual action and knowledge are set forth as legitimate and mutually reinforcing paths, but incomplete unless integrated within and subordinated to *bhakti*. Krsna thus presents himself as the ultimate *karmayogin*, acting to benefit the worlds out of no personal desire. He thus bids his devotees *(bhaktas)* to surrender all actions to him as in a sacrifice, but a sacrifice *(karman)* no longer defined in Vedic-Mimamsa terms as a means to fulfill some personal desire. Krsna also presents himself as the object of all religious knowledge, the highest purusa *(uttamapurusa)* and supreme self *(paramatman)*, beyond the perishable and the imperishable, yet pervading and supporting all worlds (15.16-17).

One other facet of the *bhakti* synthesis to which the *Gita* alludes is the transition from traditional Vedic sacrifice *(yajña)* to new forms of offering to the deity *(puja,* literally, "honoring"). This corresponds to the theory that the "gift" is the particularly appropriate religious practice for the *kaliyuga*. Thus Krsna says: "If one disciplined soul proffers to me with love [*bhakti*] a leaf, a flower, fruit, or water, I accept this offering of love from him. Whatever you do, or eat, or offer, or give, or mortify, make it an offering to me, and I shall undo the bonds of *karman*" (9.26-27; van Buitenen, trans.). The passage probably refers to domestic worship of the "deity of one's choice" *(istadevata)*. But it is also likely to allude to temple worship, for it is known from inscriptions and literary sources from the third to first century BCE that sanctuaries existed for Vasudeva and Kesava (presumably as names for Krsna and Visnu), as well as for other deities. By the beginning of the Gupta period, around 320 CE, temple building was in full swing, with inscriptions showing construction of temples for Visnu, Siva, and the Goddess. Temples were built at sites within cities, as well as at remote holy places, and sanctuaries at both such locations became objectives along pilgrimage routes that are first mentioned in the *Mahabharata*. From very early if not from the beginning of such temple worship, the deities were represented by symbols and/or iconic images.

Certain aspects of temple construction and worship draw inspiration from the Vedic sacrifice. The plan of the edifice is designed on the ground as the Vastupurusamandala, a geometric figure of the "Purusa of the Site" *(vastu)*, from whom the universe takes form. The donor, ideally a king, is the *yajamana*. The *sanctum sanctorum*, called the *garbhagrha* ("womb house"), continues the symbolism of the Vedic *diksa* hut: here again the *yajamana* becomes an embryo so as to achieve a new birth, now taking into his own being the higher self of the deity that he installs there in the form of an image. The temple as a whole is thus a Vedic altar comprising the triple world, but also an expanded image of the cosmos through which the deity manifests himself from within, radiating energy to the outer walls where his (or her) activities and interactions with the world are represented. [*See* Temple, *article on* Hindu Temples.]

But the use of the temple for ordinary daily worship involves radically non-Vedic objectives. The Vedic sacrifice is a means for gods and men—basically equals—to fulfill reciprocal desires. *Puja* rites are means for God and man to interact on a level beyond desire: for man to give without expectation of reward, or, more exactly, to get back nothing tangible other than what he has offered but with the paradoxical conviction that the deity "shares" (from the root meaning of *bhakti*) what is given and returns it as an embodiment of his or her grace *(prasada)*. God is thus fully superior, served as a royal guest with rites of hospitality. Basically four moments are involved: offerings, taking sight *(darsana)* of the deity, receiving this *prasada*, and leave-taking by circumambulation of the *garbhagrha* and the image within. The offerings are the *puja* proper and comprise a great variety of devotional acts designed to please the deity, some of which may be worked into a daily round by the temple priests, who offer on behalf of others.

Finally, one last element of the consolidation of Hinduism achieved by early Gupta times is the emergence of the Goddess as a figure whose worship is recognized alongside that of Visnu and Siva and is performed with the same basic rites. Indeed, it is possible that aspects of *puja* ceremonialism are derived from non-Vedic *sudra* and village rites in which female deities no doubt figured highly, as they do in such cults today. The two epics, the *Mahabharata* and the *Ramayana*, reflect themes associated with the Goddess in the portrayals of their chief heroines, Draupadi and Sita, but the *Harivamsa* is probably the first text to acknowledge the Goddess as such. There she takes birth as Krsna and Balarama's "sister" (actually she and Krsna exchange mothers). Some of her future demon enemies are mentioned, and there is also reference to her having numerous places of wor-

ship and a cult that apparently included animal sacrifice. Thus the Goddess is integrated even within the texts of the early *smarta* Hinduism that are centered on Visnu. But the text that registers her full emergence is the *Devimahatmyam* (Glorification of the Goddess). Probably from about 400-600 CE, it was included in the *Markandeya Purana*. Here the Goddess is recognized under all her major aspects, as primal matter embodied in the universe yet beyond it, incarnate in many forms, cause of the joys and miseries of this world and of liberation from it, the power *(sakti)* enabling the roles of the *trimurti*, yet higher than the gods and their last resort in the face of certain demons, most notably the buffalo demon Mahisasura, her most dedicated and persistent foe through cults and myths both ancient and current. This emergence of the Goddess is registered more fully in the development of Tantric Hinduism.

Tantric Hinduism. *Tantra* is literally "what extends." In its Hindu form it may be taken, according to its name, as a movement that sought to extend the Veda (whose pedigree it loosely claimed) and more particularly to extend the universalistic implications of *bhakti* Hinduism. However, although it was quick to integrate *bhakti* elements and to influence *bhakti* in nearly all its forms (late Puranic, popular, and sectarian), its earliest and most enduring forms "extend" Hinduism in ways that were directly opposed to the epic-Puranic *bhakti* synthesis. Nonetheless, it is still formulated within the same cosmology.

> As Tantrism gained currency in succeeding centuries throughout India, the shamanistic and magical features were assimilated to yogic disciplines. . . .

Early Tantrism developed most vigorously, from the fourth to sixth centuries CE, in areas where Brahmanic penetration had been weakest: in the Northwest, in Bengal and Assam in the East, and in the Andhra area of the South. These are areas where one must assume non-Aryan influences in general, and more particularly probably also tribal and folk practices involving shamanism, witchcraft, and sorcery, and, at least in the East and South, a cult of the Goddess. As Tantrism gained currency in succeeding centuries throughout India, the shamanistic and magical features were assimilated to yogic disciplines, while the elevation of the Goddess gave full projection on a pan-Indian scale to roles and images of the Goddess that had been incorporated, but allowed only minimal scope, in the early orthodox *bhakti* and even earlier Vedic sacrificial traditions. The earliest extant Tantric texts are Buddhist, from about the fourth to sixth centuries. [*See* Buddhism, Schools of, *article on* Esoteric Buddhism.] Hindu

Tantric texts include Vaisnava Samhitas, Saivagamas from a slightly later period, and Sakta Tantras (exalting the Goddess as Sakti, or Power) from perhaps the eleventh century on. But from its start Tantrism represented a style and outlook that placed the Goddess at the center of its "extensions" and to a certain extent cut across sectarian and religious distinctions, whether Hindu, Buddhist, or even Jain.

Though Hindu Tantra thus asserts its Vedic legitimacy, its stance is intentionally anti-Brahmanic. It was especially critical of Brahmanic concepts of hierarchy, purity, and sexual status, all of which had been reinforced by the orthodox *bhakti* synthesis and which were in particular bound up with a theology that viewed the supreme divinity as a male (a Purusa, whether Siva or Visnu) whose ultimate form was accessible only beyond the rhythms of the cosmos and its hierarchy of impure and pure, gross and subtle worlds. For Tantrics, dualities were artificial and their experience was the result of delusion. On the analogy of the union between Siva and Sakti, which in Puranic devotional terms is conceivable only at the end of the *mahapralaya*, or great dissolution of the universe, Tantric practice *(sadhana)* addresses itself to experiencing the unity of *purusa* and *prakrti* (purusa being both "soul" and deity, *prakrti* being both "matter" and Goddess), male and female, pure and impure, knowledge and action, and so on. Most important, all this takes place here and now, not only in this world, where *prakrti* and *purusa* on the macrocosmic scale are one, but in the human body, where their microcosmic embodiments can be experienced. The body thus becomes the ultimate vehicle for liberation, the dissolution of opposites taking place within the psychophysical continuum of the experience of the living adept, who realizes beyond duality the oneness of *brahman*.

In terms of practice, Tantra's rejection of Hindu orthopraxy is even more decisive. And practice is clearly exalted above theological or philosophical formulation. Two types of Tantra are mentioned: "left-hand" and "right-hand." The Tantric rejection and indeed inversion of orthopraxy is most pronounced in the former, as the right-hand Tantra interprets the most anti-Brahmanic practices of the left metaphorically, and also includes under its heading a wide variety of ceremonial rituals assimilated into *bhakti* Hinduism that are simply non-Vedic. These include the use of non-Vedic *mantras* as well as *yantras* and *mandalas*, aniconic and non-Vedic geometric devices used for visualization and integration of divine-cosmic forces. Adepts come from all castes, but low-caste and even tribal practitioners and teachers are especially revered. The goal of liberation within the body takes the specific form of seeking magical powers *(siddhis)*, which in orthodox forms of Hinduism are regarded as hindrances to spiritual achievement. Under the tutelage of a guru, who embodies the fulfillment sought and its transmission and who is thus all-important, the *siddhis* are sought through yoga disciplines that show the impact of Tantra through their anatomical analysis

of the "subtle body" *(linga sarira)*. First practiced is hathayoga, the "yoga of exertion or violence," that is, rigorous physical discipline geared to coordinating the body's "ducts" or "channels" *(nadis)* and "energy centers" *(cakras)*. This is followed by *kundaliniyoga*, which awakens the dormant *sakti*, conceived as a coiled-up "serpent power" in the lowest *cakra* between the genitals and the anus, so that it (or she) can pierce and transform all the *cakras* (usually six) and unite with Siva in the "thousand-petaled *cakra*" in the region of the brain.

Beyond these practices, "left-handed" Tantrics pursue in literal fashion the ceremonial of the "five *m*'s" *(pañcamakarapuja)*. That is, they incorporate into their cultic practice five "sacraments" beginning with the syllable *ma*: fish *(matsya)*, meat *(mamsa)*, parched grain *(mudra*, regarded as an aphrodisiac), wine *(madya)*, and finally sexual intercourse *(maithuna)*. It is likely that most if not all of these practices involve the incorporation of elements of the cult and mythology of the Goddess, who already in the *Devimahatmyam* delights in meat and wine and is approached by lustful demons for sexual intercourse. Tantric texts stress that these practices are to be carried out within a circle of adepts and supervised by a male and female pair of "lords of the circle" who insist on strict ritual conventions that guard against an orgiastic interpretation. Classically, the male is to retain his semen at the point of orgasm, this being a sign not only of profound dispassion but an actualization of the nonprocreative union of Siva and Sakti at the dissolution of the universe of dualities.

It is interesting to note that, although their historical validity is debated by scholars, there are strong Indian traditions suggesting that Sankara's philosophical nondualism had practical Tantric repercussions. [*See also* Tantrism.]

Sankara's Advaita Vedanta and Smarta Orthodoxy. The Advaita (nondualist) interpretation of the Vedanta can be traced back at least to Gaudapada (c. 600 CE), but it is Sankara (c. 788–820) who established this viewpoint as the touchstone of a revived *smarta* orthodoxy. Born in a small Kerala village, Sankara spent his alleged thirty-two years as a vigorous champion of the unity of Hinduism over and against intra-Hindu divisions and the inroads of Buddhism and Jainism. He toured India, setting up monasteries *(mathas)* near famous temples or holy places at each of the four compass directions, and appointed a disciple at each center to begin a line of renunciant "pontiffs." And he wrote works of great subtlety and persuasiveness, including commentaries on the Upanisads, the *Brahma Sutra*, and the *Bhagavadgita* that inspired contemporaries, disciples, and authors of later generations to write additional important works from the perspective that he developed.

An essential feature of Sankara's argumentation is that lower views of reality must be rejected as they are contradicted or "sublated" by higher experiences of the real. Finally, all dichotomous formulations must be abandoned upon the nondual experience of the self *(atman)* as *brahman*. The world of appearance is sustained by ignorance *(avidya)*, which "superimposes" limitations on reality. *Maya* ("illusion" or "fabrication"), itself neither real nor unreal, is indescribable in terms of being or nonbeing. It appears real only so long as *brahman* is not experienced. But it is empirically real relative to things that can be shown false from the standpoint of empirical observation. Maya is thus said to be more mysterious and unknowable than brahman, which is experienced as being, consciousness, and bliss *(sat-cit-ananda)*.

As philosophy, Advaita is thus a guide to *moksa*, which is experienced when the ignorance that results from superimposing *maya* on *brahman* is overcome. Liberation arises with knowledge *(jñana)*, but from a perspective that recognizes relative truth in the paths of both action and *bhakti*. Practically, Sankara fostered a rapprochement between Advaita and *smarta* orthodoxy, which by his time had not only continued to defend the *varnasramadharma* theory as defining the path of *karman*, but had developed the practice of *pañcayatana-puja* ("five-shrine worship") as a solution to varied and conflicting devotional practices. Thus one could worship any one of five deities (Visnu, Siva, Durga, Surya, Ganesa) as one's *istadevata* ("deity of choice"). As far as *varnasramadharma* was concerned, Sankara left householder issues largely aside and focused instead on founding ten orders of *samnyasis* (the *dasanami*, "ten names"), each affiliated with one of the four principle *mathas* he founded. But traditional orthodox views of caste were maintained. According to Sankara, as *sudras* are not entitled to hear the Veda, they cannot pursue knowledge of *brahman* as s*amnyasis*; rather they may seek *moksa* through hearing the *Mahabharata* and the Puranas. Four of the ten *samnyasi* orders were thus restricted to *brahmanas*, and it does not seem that any accepted *sudras* until long after Sankara's death. *Bhakti* sectarian reformers were generally more liberal on this point. As to the god (or gods) of *bhakti*, Sankara views the deity (Isvara) as essentially identical with *brahman* and real relative to empirical experience. But by being identified "with qualities" *(saguna)*, God can be no more than an approach to the experience of *brahman* "without qualities" *(nirguna)*. Viewed from the experience of the self as *nirguna brahman*, which "sublates" all other experiences, the deity is but the highest form of *maya*. Clearly, *bhakti* traditions could not rest with this solution. But it should be noted that in opposing Sankara and abandoning the universalist vision of the epic-Puranic devotional synthesis, the sects turned their backs on the main impulses that had attempted to sustain the unity of Hinduism.

Sectarian Hinduism. The elaboration of *bhakti* Hinduism continued to unfold in the later Puranas, linking up with the temple and pilgrimage cultus and with local and regional forms of worship. It thus established itself until the time of

Sankara as the main expression of Brahmanic orthodoxy and the main shaping force of popular Hinduism. But though it proclaimed a universal Hinduism, it gave little weight to the problem of the immediate accessibility of salvation. While caste hierarchy was to remain in effect on earth to assure, among other things, the pure temple worship of the gods by the *brahmanas*, the ultimate release that the Puranas promised was almost infinitely postponed. It is possible that their postponement of a collective liberation was a kind of purification process for liberated souls and thus a prolongation of the concern for *brahmana* purity on earth. In any case, the remoteness of salvation and the defense of caste purity and hierarchy in the Puranic devotionalism of Brahmanic orthodoxy were probably incentives for the development of alternate forms of *bhakti*. These emerged in sectarian traditions, in movements led by saint-singers who inspired vernacular forms of *bhakti* revivalism, and more generally in local and regional forms of Hinduism.

Sectarian traditions. Sectarianism and *bhakti* revivalism are movements of separate origins that converge for the first time in the eleventh and twelfth centuries in the Tamil-speaking area of South India. There the fusion was accomplished

> **Generally speaking, sects followed a reformist impulse, and in most of them one can identify the emergence of the *guru* as a new type of figure.**

in the traditions of the Sri Vaisnavas and the Saiva Siddhanta, sects whose names indicate their distinctive theological preferences for Visnu and Siva. Henceforth, sectarianism and *bhakti* revivalism continued to interact and produce hybrid forms as they spread over all of India.

Generally speaking, sects followed a reformist impulse, and in most of them one can identify the emergence of the *guru* as a new type of figure: not the transmitter of an "impersonal" Vedic teaching, but one who takes inspiration from the personal deity of the sect, with whom he may even be identified. Traditional hierarchy was generally respected, but with the proviso that within the sect divine grace was not limited by caste boundaries. Nonetheless, as groups formed around masters and their teachings, they took on many of the characteristics and functions of castes (endogamy, interior ranking), and certain sects formulated their stands with particularly positive attitudes (the northern school of Sri Vaisnavas) or negative attitudes (Lingayats and Virasaivas) toward *brahmanas*. Sects distinguish themselves over and against each other by many means, and often quite passionately: by bodily markings, forms of yoga discipline, worship, theology, and in particular by their choice of supreme deity, whether Siva,

Visnu, Sakti, or, in the North, Krsna or Rama. Nonetheless, they generally participate in wider Hindu activities such as pilgrimage, festival, and temple worship (the Lingayats are an exception) and draw upon fundamental Hindu belief structures. Thus most sects acknowledge other deities as subordinate to the supreme deity of the sect. In particular, most have worked out ways of encompassing the relation of the God and the Goddess at some fundamental theological level. Persistently the supreme deity is identified both as the ultimate brahman and also as in some way personal. The sects also frequently define various stages of divine descent or interaction with the world, various stages of the soul's ascent, and various types of relation between the soul and God. Thus the sects elaborate upon the epic-Puranic cosmology while modifying and refining the theological and soteriological terms. It is only against this background that their formulations are intelligible.

From the historical vantage point, one may note that the consolidation of the separate strands of sectarianism and *bhakti* revivalism occurs after, and is no doubt in part a response to, the growing success of Sankara's Advaita Vedanta. Prior to Sankara, sectarian groups had centered primarily around distinctive ritual traditions that were increasingly influenced by Tantrism: not only in forms of worship and theological formulation, but also, in some Saiva sects, in actual practice. Thus the Vaisnava Pañcaratras and Vaikhanasas and the Saiva Pasupatas (all mentioned first in the late *Mahabharata*) between the fifth and tenth centuries produced their Samhitas and Agamas to regularize the construction of temples, iconography, and *puja* ceremonialism. Some Pasupatas and Kapalikas (a Tantric Saiva sect) also incorporated forms of abrupt anticonventional behavior modeled on Siva's character as the great yogin ascetic. With the exception of the Pañcaratras, who elaborated an influential doctrine of the emanations *(vyuhas)* of Visnu that paralleled the cosmogonic theory of evolution in the Samkhya system, the theological formulations of these movements were apparently among their secondary concerns.

Saint-singer tradition. Whereas the early sectarian movements were able to spread their impact from north to south using Sanskrit as their medium, the *bhakti* revivalist movement began in the South, drawing on Tamil. Like the sectarian movements, the saint-singers developed their traditions along Vaisnava and Saiva lines. The sixty-three Nayanmar (or Nayanars) promoted the worship of Siva, while the twelve Alvars similarly honored Visnu. Part of the revivalist motivation was provided by the earlier spread of Buddhism and Jainism in the South, both of which lost considerable following as a result of the efforts of the Nayanmar and Alvars, as well as those of their contemporary Sankara.

Some of the most renowned among these two companies of saint-singers have left songs that they composed at the temples of Visnu and Siva, praising the form and presence of the deity therein, the place itself as his manifestation, and the communal attitude of worship generated there through pilgrimage and festival. Though they honor the deities in terms familiar from Puranic myths, the stories are set in the local terrain. The emotional side of *bhakti* thus draws from deep Tamil traditions, including a revival of classical Tamil poetic conventions involving the correlations between different types of landscape, different divinities, and different types of male-female love. In the hands of the saint-singers, erotic love in particular was drawn on as a metaphor for devotional feelings that stressed the feminine character of the soul in relation to the deity and idealized a softening of the mind or heart that could take the forms of "melting" into the divine, ecstatic rapture, divine madness, and possession.

Following the advent of Sankara, most of the sectarian and revivalist movements found common cause in their devotionalist stance against Advaita nondualism and continued to develop for the most part interdependently. Thus, most formatively, the songs of the Alvars were collected in the ninth century for eventual use by the Sri Vaisnavas. And the poems of the Nayanmar—supplemented by the songs of Manikkavacakar, who apparently lived just after the list of sixty-three Nayanmar had been set (ninth century)—were collected to form parts of the canon of the Saiva Siddhanta. However, the revivalist and sectarian strains could also at times follow somewhat independent courses. The saint-singer tradition continued to take Saiva and Vaisnava forms among the Lingayats and the Haridasas of Karnataka, and also to be associated there with sects (the Lingayats themselves and the Brahma Sampradaya or Dvaita Vedanta tradition of Madhva, respectively). But its spread through Maharashtra, the Hindi-speaking areas of North India, and through Bengal was most focused on Visnu, or more accurately on his forms as Rama and Krsna, who in turn, in the Hindi and Bengali areas, became the deities of different sects. In the case of Krsna, erotic devotional poetry opened new dimensions on the theme of Krsna's love-play with his "new" consort, Radha (her name does not appear before the twelfth-century Sanskrit *Gitagovinda* by the Bengali court poet Jayadeva). In Hindi and Bengali poems, not only are the emotions of motherly love for the baby Krsna and erotic love for the youthful Krsna explored, but they are tied in with a classical theory of aesthetic appreciation *(rasa)*.

As to the sects, the impact of Sankara's Advaita is evident at many points. Although Saiva monasticism may predate Sankara by about a century, his establishment of *mathas* around India was highly influential. Certain post-Sankara sects thus adopted institutionalized forms of "monastic" renunciation, either like Sankara setting their *mathas* alongside the temples (Sri Vaisnavas, Dvaita Vedantins, Saiva Siddhantins) or in opposition to the whole temple cultus (Lingayats). Vaisnava sects also assume henceforth the mantle of new "Vedantas" in order to seek Vedic authority for their advocacy of *bhakti* theologies over and against Sankara's nondualism and in their efforts to subordinate the path of knowledge to that of *bhakti*.

Most distinctive and most important theologically among the Vaisnava schools are those of Ramanuja (c. 1017-1137) and Madhva (1238-1317), both of whom attempted to refute Sankara's interpretations of the Upanisads, the *Brahma Sutra*, and the *Bhagavadgita* with their own commentaries on those texts. The more prolific Madhva also wrote commentaries on the *Rgveda* and the epics. Ramanuja, drawing on the ceremonialism and theological formulations of the Pañcaratra sect as well as on the revivalist poetry of the Alvars, developed for the Sri Vaisnavas the first *bhakti* sectarian repudiation of the Advaita. In his "qualified nondualistic Vedanta" *(visistadvaita vedanta)*, he argued that Visnu-Narayana is the ultimate *brahman*, his relation to the world and souls being "qualified" as substance to attribute. World and souls are thus real, as of course is God—all in opposition to Sankara's view that there is no reality other than *brahman*. For Ramanuja the three paths not only culminate in *bhakti* but are crowned by *prapatti*, "surrender" to God or "falling forward" at his feet. Criticizing both Sankara and Ramanuja, Madhva's "dualistic Vedanta" *(dvaita vedanta)* stressed the absolute sovereignty of God and the fivefold set of absolute distinctions between God and souls, God and the world, souls and souls, souls and the world, and matter in its different aspects—all of which are real and not illusory.

On the Saiva side, the most distinctive sect is the Kashmir Saiva, or Trika, school, established in the ninth century, with possibly earlier roots. It is nondualist, but from the standpoint that all is essentially Siva. As pure being and consciousness, Siva is aware of himself through reflection in the universe, which he pervades as the *atman* and in which he is manifest through his *sakti* (power, or female energy, personified as the Goddess). The universe is thus an expression of Siva's aesthetic experience of his creative awareness as self and his delight in unity with his Sakti. "Recognition" of Siva as the *atman*, and experience of the self through *spanda* ("vibration")—an attunement to the blissful throbbing waves of divine consciousness in the heart—are among the means to liberation. One of the foremost systematizers of this school was Abhinavagupta (c. 1000 CE), who developed the view that states of aesthetic appreciation (*rasas*, "tastes") are modes of experiencing the divine Self. Though favoring *santarasa* (the *rasa* of peacefulness), Abhinavagupta's theories influenced the North Indian medieval devotional poetry that explored *bhakti* itself as a state of *rasa*, with such powerfully evocative modes as love of Krsna in the relationships of servant-master, parent-child, and lover-beloved. This type of devotional intensity reached its peak in the person of the Bengali saint Caitanya (1486-1533), founder of the Gaudiya Vaisnava sect, whose ecstatic dancing and singing enabled him to experience the love of Radha and Krsna. Popular tra-

dition regards him as an *avatara* of Krsna, a form assumed by Krsna to experience in one body his union with his Sakti.

Popular Hinduism. The main current of living Hinduism is popular Hinduism. It has been affected by every change the tradition has gone through and may fairly be assumed to have ancient roots, in some aspects traceable to Indus Valley religion, in others to *sudra*, village, and tribal forms of religion that were never more than alluded to—and then negatively—in the ancient and classical sources. *Bhakti* and Tantra are two movements within Hinduism that draw inspiration from this broad current, and popular Hinduism today remains dominated by *bhakti* and Tantric expressions.

It is, however, perilous to look at popular Hinduism from the perspective of what it might have once been: that is, to attempt to isolate or reconstruct its Dravidian, pre-Aryan, or non-Brahmanic components. Although hypotheses about pre-Aryan and non-Aryan forms of popular Hinduism are certainly worth pursuing, they must be informed and restrained by a sound understanding of the comprehensive structures through which both popular and Brahmanic forms of Hinduism are integrated at the popular level. Aspects of popular religion that might look non-Aryan turn out on closer examination to involve Vedic prolongations. Nor are recent constructs like sanskritization, brahmanization, or ksatriyazation—all useful up to a point, but stressing only the adoption by low-caste groups of high-caste models—adequate to account for the multivectored process that must have occurred for a long time as it continues to occur today.

Amid the bewildering variety of popular Hindu rites, customs, and beliefs, two broad structures can be identified that clarify this overall integration. One involves the working out of the implications of *bhakti* in relation to temple worship; the other involves the working out of the implications of the caste system in relation to local forms of worship more generally. As they function, the two structures are intimately related.

Generally speaking, whether one defines a locality in large terms (a region, a former kingdom) or small terms (a city, town, or village), one will find two types of divinities: pure and impure. The pure divinities are forms taken locally—*avataras*—of the great gods Visnu and Siva. Sometimes the Goddess is also purified to this rank, often with a myth explaining her change from violent to peaceful habits (as with the alleged conversion of the goddess Kamaksi at Kanchipuram, Tamil Nadu, by Sankara). And in certain regions Siva's sons Murukan/ Skanda (in Tamil Nadu) and Ganesa (in Maharashtra) also assume this role. In their temples, these gods are offered pure vegetarian food by brahmans. Today, all castes can worship in such temples, thanks to temple entry legislation by the postindependence government; formerly, low castes were excluded. These castes still maintain their own temples where impure gods are served with nonvegetarian offerings, that is, sacrifices of male animals, usually cocks and goats but occasionally water buffalo.

Legislation prohibiting buffalo sacrifices has so far had mixed results.

Whereas worship of pure gods—especially at remote pilgrimage sites—is focused ultimately on renunciation and liberation, that of impure gods is dominated by down-to-earth concerns. One thus finds among the general category of impure gods lineage deities *(kuladevatas)*, caste deities, and village deities *(gramadevatas)*. The first are usually but not always male, and some are deities for brahman as well as low-caste lineages. Caste deities and village deities are usually female, and the category may overlap where the deity of a locally dominant caste becomes also the village deity. Where the village deity (usually a goddess) is the deity of a vegetarian caste or has had her cult purified to bring it into accord with high-caste standards, she frequently has one or

> **Low castes worship the pure gods in their temples. And high castes acknowledge the power of the impure deities.**

more male assistants—impure demons converted to her cause and frequently lineage gods themselves—who handle the animal sacrifice (real or symbolic) for her, often out of her line of sight.

Nonetheless, though opposing principles are each given their play, it is their overlap and interrelation that is most striking. Low castes worship the pure gods in their temples. And high castes acknowledge the power of the impure deities, not only as *kuladevatas*, but through selective (pure) means of participation in festivals sponsored by lower castes. Through the universalization of *bhakti*, the impure gods are sometimes also the prototypes for the demons whose deaths at the hands of the pure deities transform them into their devotees. These local myths have their roots in Puranic mythologies, and the sacrificial practices they evoke involve at least in part prolongations and reinterpretations of the Vedic animal sacrifice.

The second issue—working out of the implications of the caste system in relation to local forms of worship—has thus already been touched upon, but with the focus of issues of purity and impurity as defined by brahman and low-caste involvements. There remains the issue of the role of the *ksatriya*, or more particularly the king, as the ruler of the land. The caste system has traditionally functioned in locally defined territories, "little kingdoms," where the local ruler had certain roles to perform. No matter what his actual caste, whether high or low, pure or impure, he had to function as a *ksatriya*. In his ceremonial status, he performed the role of *jajman*, engaging him at the core of a system of prestations and counterprestations with other castes as a sort of patron

for those who perform services for him. Most significantly, this title derives from the Vedic *yajamana*, "sacrificer," and prolongs not only the yajamana's function as patron of other castes (particularly brahmans, who offer sacrifices for him), but that of "sacrificer" itself. The model of the king as jajman on the regional territorial level has its counterpart in the village in the person(s) of the leader(s) of the locally dominant caste, who assumes the role of *yajamana* at village festivals. When, as was until recently widely the case, the village festival involves the sacrifice of a buffalo, it thus occurs within a continuum that includes the royal buffalo sacrifice traditionally performed in connection with the pan-Hindu festival of Dussera, and the mythology of the goddess Durga and the buffalo demon Mahisasura that is traceable to the *Devimahatmyam* in the *Markandeya Purana*. There are many local and regional transformations of this pattern, but a basic theme is that the Goddess, who personifies victory, acts for the *yajamana* and the kingdom or village in her conquest over demonic forces (impure barbarians, drought, diseases) that threaten the welfare of the local terrain over which she, as goddess, presides.

Hindu Responses to Islam and Westernization. Self-conscious Hindu responses to influences from the West were first worked out in the classical period in the epics, the Dharmasastras, and the Puranas. It seems that military dominance by "barbarian" peoples in that period provided one of the incentives for the articulation of Hindu orthodoxy. Islamic rule and Western rule in India have provided similar incentives, but this often goes unmentioned as historians place their emphasis on what is supposedly new. A full accounting of the impact of almost ten centuries of Islam and five centuries of Western presence in India would have to deal not only with their distinctive new influences but also with the ways in which traditional Hindu models have been revived and applied in new and adaptive ways, often on the folk and popular level. That, however, can only be alluded to here.

Islamic influence on Hinduism has many dimensions, all difficult to assess. From the time of the raids of Mahmud of Ghazni into Northwest India (977-1030) into the period of Mughal dominance, Hindus had to deal periodically with outbreaks of violence and iconoclastic zeal. Regional defense of Hindu traditions against Islam—first by the Rajputs in Rajasthan, then by the Vijayanagar rulers and their successors in South India (1333-eighteenth century), and finally by the Marathas in Maharashtra and the South (late sixteenth century-1761)—clearly fostered the Hindu ideal of the territorial kingdom, big or "little," as a model for the protection of ongoing Hindu values. Under the Muslim rulers, in fact, many Hindu chiefs and petty rajas were left in control of their local realms so long as they paid tribute and supplied military support. In these circumstances, conservative and puritanical tendencies seem to have gained momentum in orthodox Hinduism, particularly in regard to caste and the purity of women. Nonetheless, one finds numerous cases where Muslim themes and figures have been integrated into popular Hindu myth and ritual, but usually in ways that indicate Muslim subordination to a local or regional Hindu deity.

While orthodox, popular, and domestic forms of Hinduism thus drew in on themselves, however, Hindu sectarian traditions multiplied, particularly in the period of the breakup of the Delhi sultanate (1206-1526). Notable at this time were Caitanya in Bengal, and two exemplars of the North Indian *sant* (holy man) tradition: Kabir (c. 1440-1518, from Banaras) and Nanak (1469-1539, from the Punjab). These two latter figures both preached a path of loving devotion to one God that combined aspects of Islamic Sufism and Hindu *bhakti*. They thus formulated probably for the first time in terms partly Hindu an exclusivist monotheism like that found in the Abrahamic traditions of Islam, Christianity, and Judaism. Over and against the direct experience of this one God, all else was mediate and external, whether the practice were Muslim or Hindu. Thus not only caste but idol worship was rejected by these teachers. But though their syncretistic poetry remained highly popular, it did little to change the Hindu practices it criticized. Nanak's work in particular provided the foundation for the Sikh tradition, an increasingly non-Hindu and non-Muslim movement on its own. Nor did the syncretistic interests of the great Mughal emperor Akbar (ruled 1555-1605) do much to encourage theological synthesis, despite the popularity of his, for the most part, religiously tolerant rule. Akbar's successors on the Mughal throne abandoned his policies and pursued expansionist goals that aroused resistance from the heirs of the Vijayanagar and the Rajput kingdoms, and especially from the Sikhs and the new power of the Marathas. The seeds of a nationalist vision of Hinduism may be traced through these movements and back to the imperial ideal of the epics.

Under the British, certain reform tendencies initiated under Muslim rule were carried forward, freshly influenced by Christian missionary activity and Western education. Most notable were the reform movements of the nineteenth century. The Brahmo Samaj was founded in 1828 by Raja Ram Mohan Roy (1772-1833, from Calcutta). In an early treatise Roy wrote an attack on idolatry that showed Muslim influence, but by the time he founded the Samaj he had been more affected by Christianity, and particularly by the Unitarians. Roy thus introduced a kind of deistic monotheism and a form of congregational worship to go along with a rejection of idolatry, caste, sacrifice, transmigration, and *karman*. The Arya Samaj, founded in 1875 by Swami Dayananda Sarasvati (1824-1883, from Kathiawar), denied authenticity to Puranic Hinduism and attempted a return to the Vedas. Showing that the Vedas lent no support to image worship and various social practices, he went further to assert that they were monotheistic. As regards caste, he championed the *varna* theory as an ancient social institution

but denied that it was religious. Both movements split into rival camps.

The Ramakrishna Mission, established on the death of its founder Ramakrishna (1834-1886) and carried forward by his disciples, most notably Vivekananda (1863-1902), is more representative of traditional Hindu values. Strong *bhakti* and Tantric strains converged in the mystical experiences of Ramakrishna and were held in conjunction with an initiation into Advaita Vedanta and experiences of the oneness of all religions through visions not only of Hindu deities but of Jesus and Allah. For many followers, this humble priest of Kali has thus come to be regarded as an *avatara*, in the tradition of Caitanya. Vivekananda, Western-educated and keenly intellectual, attended the World's Parliament of Religions in Chicago in 1893, lectured widely, and established the Vedanta Society of New York. When he returned to India as a recognized champion of Hindu self-pride, he helped to organize the disciples of Ramakrishna into the pan-Indian Ramakrishna Mission. The first such teacher to gain prominence in India by popularity gained abroad, he thus inadvertently set up a pattern that has been followed by many prominent gurus and swamis in the twentieth century. Notable among them are Swami A. C. Bhaktivedanta (1896-1977), founder of the Hare Krishna movement (ISKCON) as an outgrowth of the Bengal Caitanya tradition [*See* International Society for Krishna Consciousness], and Swami Muktananda (1908-1982), exponent of *siddhayoga* teachings that draw on Kashmir Saivism.

An earlier figure, one who attracted a large Western following without ever leaving India, was Sri Aurobindo (1872-1950), whose career spanned nationalist political activism in Bengal (up to 1908), followed by the establishment of an ashram (hermitage) in Pondicherry for the teaching of a type of integral yoga that stressed the "evolutionary" progress of the soul toward the divine. One must also mention Mohandas K. Gandhi (1869-1948), whose reputation upon returning to India in 1915 after twenty-one years in England and Africa was not that of a guru but a champion of Indian causes against social and economic discrimination. As he took on more and more ascetic and saintly aspirations, however, Gandhi sought to combine an ideal of dispassioned and nonviolent service to humanity, modeled on the *Bhagavadgita's* doctrine of *karmayoga*, with work for Indian *svaraj* ("self-rule").

Although sometimes referred to as a Hindu renaissance, the effect of the various reformers since the nineteenth century has been to a certain extent more ideological than religious. Where they founded religious movements, these attracted only small followings. But their religious views—that Hinduism is essentially monotheistic, that caste is not essentially Hindu, that Hindu tolerance does not deny the truths of other religions, that Hinduism is in accord with modern science, and so on—have had major influence on a Western-educated, largely urban elite that, at least for now, controls the media and the educational processes of contemporary India. It remains to be seen how this new vision of unity will square with the traditionally diverse Hinduism of the vast population of the countryside.

BIBLIOGRAPHY

Three introductions to the whole Hindu tradition deserve recommendation: Thomas J. Hopkins's *The Hindu Religious Tradition* (Encino, Calif., 1971) is strongest in the early period (a second edition is expected); Madeleine Biardeau's *L'hindouisme: Anthropologie d'une civilisation* (Paris, 1981) is strongest on the classical period and popular traditions; and J. L. Brockington's *The Sacred Thread: Hinduism in Its Continuity and Diversity* (New York, 1981) is strongest on medieval and modern Hinduism. On Indus Valley religion, a balanced and visually informative presentation is found in Robert E. Mortimer Wheeler's *Civilizations of the Indus Valley and Beyond* (New York, 1966). On pre-Upanisadic Vedic religion as a whole, see Jan Gonda's *Vedic Literature: Samhitas and Brahmanas* (Wiesbaden, 1975), vol. 1, no. 1 of his History of Indian Literature. On Indo-European continuations in early Indian religion, see Georges Dumézil's *The Destiny of the Warrior,* translated by Alf Hiltebeitel (Chicago, 1970). On Rgvedic religion, see Wendy Doniger O'Flaherty's *The Rig Veda: An Anthology* (Harmondsworth, England, 1982) for a selection of important hymns; Jan Gonda's *The Vision of the Vedic Poets* (The Hague, 1963), for an account of the Vedic poetic process; Arthur A. Macdonell's *Vedic Mythology* (1897; reprint, New York, 1974), for the classic account of Vedic myth; and R. Gordon Wasson's *Soma: Divine Mushroom of Immortality* (New York, 1968), for his interpretation of the soma plant. On the Brahmanas and Vedic ritual, see Sylvain Lévi's *La doctrine du sacrifice dans les Brâhmanas,* 2d ed. (Paris, 1966), for a classic study focused on the mythology; Madeleine Biardeau and Charles Malamoud's *Le sacrifice dans l'Inde ancienne* (Paris, 1976), especially the essay by Malamoud on the place of the ritual honoraria *(daksinas)* in the sacrificial round; and Arthur Berriedale Keith's *The Religion and Philosophy of the Veda and Upanishads,* 2d ed. (Westport, Conn., 1971), for a solid overview. On the Upanisads, see Paul Deussen's *The Philosophy of the Upanishads,* 2d ed., translated by A. S. Gelden (New York, 1966), is still the standard comprehensive study. On the classical Hindu period as a whole, Madeleine Biardeau's study in *Le sacrifice* (cited above) and *Cosmogonies puraniques,* (Paris, 1981), vol. 1 of her *Études de mythologie hindoue,* are indispensable for their integrative treatment. On *dharma* literature, see Pandurang Vaman Kane's monumental *A History of Dharmasastra,* 5 vols. (Poona, 1930-1962), which covers far more besides, and Robert Lingat's *The Classical Law of India,* translated by J. D. M. Derrett (Berkeley, Calif., 1973), an invaluable overview. On caste, see Louis Dumont's *Homo Hierarchicus,* translated by Marc Sainsbury, rev. ed. (Chicago, 1970), discussing his own and others' theories. On the six philosophical systems, for the most authoritative overview see Surendranath Dasgupta's *A History of Indian Philosophy,* 5 vols. (Cambridge, 1922-1955). On classical *bhakti* and its mythology in the epics and Puranas, in addition to the works above by Biardeau, see also her important "Études de mythologie hindoue," parts 1 and 2, *Bulletin de l'École Française d'Extrême Orient* 63 (1976): 111-263, and 65 (1978): 87-238. My own *The Ritual of Battle: Krishna in the "Mahabharata"* (Ithaca, N. Y., 1976) and Jacques Scheuer's *Siva dans le Mahabharata* (Paris, 1982) explore complementary roles of the major deities in the *Mahabharata;* see also the classic study of E. Washburn Hopkins, *Epic Mythology* (1915; reprint, New York,

1969). On Puranic materials, see *Classical Hindu Mythology: A Reader in the Sanskrit Puranas,* translated and edited by Cornelia Dimmitt and J. A. B. van Buitenen (Philadelphia, 1978), a representative selection with interpretative introductions; and Wendy Doniger O'Flaherty's *Siva: The Erotic Ascetic* (Oxford, 1973), on major themes in the mythology of Siva, and *Women, Androgynes, and Other Mythical Beasts* (Chicago, 1980), on relations between the sexes and between humans, gods, and animals in the myths. On temple architecture and symbolism, see Stella Kramrisch's *The Hindu Temple,* 2 vols. (Calcutta, 1946). For a sound and highly readable translation of the *Bhagavadgita,* and an important introduction, see *The Bhagavadgita in the Mahabharata* translated and edited by J. A. B. van Buitenen (Chicago, 1981). On Tantra, see Agehananda Bharati's *The Tantric Tradition* (London, 1965) and Sanjukta Gupta, Dirk Jan Hoens, and Teun Goudriaan's *Hindu Tantrism* (Leiden, 1979). For an incisive presentation of Sankara's nondualism, see Eliot Deutsch's *Advaita Vedanta: A Philosophical Reconstruction* (Honolulu, 1969). On Yoga and asceticism, see Mircea Eliade's *Yoga: Immortality and Freedom,* 2d ed. (Princeton, 1969); see also G. S. Ghurye's *Indian Sadhus,* 2d ed. (Bombay, 1964) with discussion of monastic orders. On sectarian Hinduism, see R. G. Bhandarkar's *Vaisnavism, Saivism, and Minor Religious Systems* (1913; reprint, Varanasi, 1965), still a classic overview. On bhakti revivalism, see V. Raghavan's *The Great Integrators: The Saint-Singers of India* (Delhi, 1966). On popular Hinduism, Henry Whitehead's *The Village Gods of South India,* 2d ed., rev. & enl. (Delhi, 1976), is the essential documentary introduction; Marie-Louise Reiniche's *Les dieux et les hommes: Étude des cultes d'un village du Tirunelveli Inde du Sud* (New York, 1979) and Lawrence A. Babb's *The Divine Hierarchy: Popular Hinduism in Central India* (New York, 1975) are important regional studies with significant anthropological insights; David D. Shulman's *Tamil Temple Myths: Sacrifice and Divine Marriage in the South Indian Saiva Tradition* (Princeton, 1980) discusses local temple versions and inversions of the classical *bhakti* myths. On reform movements and modern Hinduism, see John N. Farquhar's *Modern Religious Movements in India* (New York, 1915), on nineteenth-century figures, and Agehananda Bharati's *Hindu Views and Ways and the Hindu-Muslim Interface* (Delhi, 1981), for an interesting inside-outside anthropological view.

ALF HILTEBEITEL

HISTORY OF RELIGIONS

Theoretical Overview

The discipline of the history of religions is characterized by the dialectical relationship that exists between its object of study and its methods of research. It is, of course, the concept of religion that best defines the discipline's object. This concept, however, though a necessary precondition for research, is never allowed to function as an *a priori* category, which would predetermine the direction of the historian's inquiries. Instead, it is held in dialectical tension with the ongoing progress of research. The methods employed in this research are in turn adapted to the deeply historical nature of their subject matter. Such methods are essentially inductive, intended to grasp religion in its concreteness, in its historical creativity, and in its meaningfulness for the cultural, social, and individual lives with which it is interwoven. The dialectic that emerges from this interaction of the concept of religion with specific, ongoing historical investigations may be taken as a distinctive feature of the discipline.

> **While religion is a decidedly historical phenomenon, it must not be reduced to history.**

The nature of this dialectical foundation of the history of religions may be clarified by contrasting it with several alternative approaches to religion. First of all, it must be distinguished from the hermeneutical approach, which fixes upon a single interpretative key to unlock the mysteries of the phenomenon under investigation.

The dialectical character of the history of religions discipline may also be contrasted with the so-called phenomenological method. This method tends to focus only on the synchronic elements of religion, describing and classifying religious forms without reference to particular historical contexts. It aims at capturing the meaning of religious phenomena without committing itself to an analysis of the historical, cultural, social, and psychological settings of those phenomena.

It would be a mistake to conclude from the inadequacies of the phenomenologist's method that the proper alternative lies in historicism. On the contrary, historicism, whether in its idealistic or materialistic form, must also be distinguished from the approach of a historian of religions. While religion is a decidedly historical phenomenon, it must not be reduced to history. Historicism makes religion a mere moment in a dialectic that essentially transcends it.

It is no solution to counter historical reductionism with an appeal to the irreducible character of religion as perceived by the subjective, experiential sensitivity of the phenomenologist. In both cases, that of the phenomenologist as well as that of the historicist, there is an illegitimate appeal to an *a priori,* preconceived conception of religion. It is this *a priori* character of their respective conceptions of religion that is incompatible with the positive, inductive, comparative-historical approach proper to the historian of religions and to the dialectic that the historian must preserve between his tentative interpretative categories and the ongoing progress of his research.

Theory is equally illegitimate in the history of religions when it is applied in an *a priori,* undialectical manner. Nevertheless, it is not to be rejected out of hand. On the contrary, theory is indispensable when it functions as hypothesis open to verification, revision, or rejection on the basis of empirical research.

The Concept of Religion. The appearance of an impasse is created by the way in which the problem is posed. If we assume that a concept of religion is at the same time a prerequisite for and a result of comparison, then we are indeed faced with an insurmountable paradox. But this is not the case if we resort to a dialectic that unites the notion with its employment in such a way as to make them mutually dependent. In this case the concept of religion is inductive in origin, and its clarification goes hand in hand with progress in empirical research.

At this point it is clear that an adequate notion of religion is not to be formed through a mere *a priori* selection of data to which research should be extended. The primary problem is not to extend a conception of religion over the widest possible range of material but rather to discover a conception that is adequate to specific historical contexts. The search for a universally adequate definition of religion can lead quickly to a minimal notion of religion, a kind of lowest common denominator with no practical usefulness. Such a univocal definition, which would seek to rank the different religions as so many species under a single genus, is clearly inadequate for a fundamentally empirical discipline. Such a discipline requires conceptual categories that are continuously being created and are always open to further revision in the light of the development of comparative studies. Far from being a univocal concept, the notion of religion that emerges from the continued comparison of new and varied historical materials is an analogical notion.

If the notion of religion is analogical, the aim of research will not be the progressive extension of a univocal concept but the documentation of sets of partial affinities between different systems of belief and practice, which are the segments of the polychromatic network that constitutes the variegated world of religion. It is clear that this procedure is much more in keeping with the comparative-historical aims proper to the history of religions than any merely phenomenological approach. The approach I am describing is meant to remain constantly in touch with the concreteness of its object; facts and sets of facts (historical contexts and processes) are compared directly, without being submitted to an intermediate process of abstract categorization.

Holistic Approach. In addition to restricting itself to an analogical use of its interpretative categories in creating such a map of the religious universe, the history of religions must also attempt to be holistic in its approach to its materials. It must study religious beliefs and practices within the specific contexts that give them their full meaning. Within these contexts, functional interpretations will often be of positive value. The holisms characteristic of the history of religions must be realized not at the level of univocal theory but at the level of contextualized historical description.

The achievement of such an historical typology of religions will result from modalities of historical comparison that must be further specified. In the first place, comparative-historical research in the history of religions must be distinguished from what we may call "idiographic" research, namely, research concentrated on religion in a particular cultural context. Such specific, noncomparative studies are necessary but not sufficient. Nor can the comparative-historical research envisioned here be identified with a systematic, purely formal typology, nor with a phenomenology that neglects issues of origin, growth, and change. The goal is rather the establishment of specific sets of synchronic and diachronic continuities and discontinuities that apply to more than one religion and perhaps to an entire cultural area. In any given case these patterns may be explained either on the basis of cultural diffusion or as the result of independent but parallel developments. In the latter case, parallelism need not signal a unilinear evolution in the history of religions but may rather point to analogies between specific historical and cultural circumstances.

Historical Typology of Religion

Having dwelt on some methodological issues concerning the history of religions as a comparative-historical discipline, I shall turn now to a brief overview of the subject matter of this discipline, that is, to the presentation of a concise and inevitably selective historical typology of religion.

Religions can be divided into two broad groups, and this divison will provide the general framework for a genuinely historical typology. This initial division is between those religions that are described as ethnic and those that are founded.

Ethnic Religions. Ethnic religions are historical formations that are originally indistinguishable from the formation processes of the cultures and populations to which they belong. Ethnic religions are not restricted to tribal or nonliterate cultures. They may also be found in highly developed literate cultures. Their exact character, which may thus range from unitary to syncretistic, depends upon specific cultural and historical circumstances.

The historical character of ethnic religions, including those of nonliterate cultures, requires that they be studied holistically. Their actual contents and functions in the epochs and contexts for which there is documentary evidence must be closely examined.

Approaches to Comparison. Two main approaches to comparison may be distinguished in the history of religions. The first developed in the nineteenth century, and the other took shape at the end of that century and at the beginning of the twentieth.

The first approach, practiced in the nineteenth century, was inseparably linked to evolutionary thought and to the elaboration of general theories concerning the origins and the growth of religion on a world scale. It was on this basis that notions such as animism and animatism were introduced into what was understood to be scientific research (hence the German name of this field, still with us, of *Religionswissen- schaft*). These notions were intended to apply cross-culturally, indeed universally.

The rise of a descriptive phenomenology of religion contributed to a further refinement of these new patterns. Take, for instance, the case of the notion of shamanism. Once shamanism was differentiated from the generic notion of animism and considered not only as a peculiar element of religious behavior but also as an element of a structure implying a cosmology and a worldview, it could contribute to the transition from an evolutionistic outlook too fond of concepts and representations to a cultural-historical study based on the discovery of cultural wholes and cultural areas. In other words, the elaboration of a more rigorous, multidimensional, and descriptive phenomenology of religion allowed the history of religions *(Religionswissenschaft)* to survive the inevitable crisis of evolutionism and its universal and unilinear stages and to enter a more rewarding phase characterized by a new form of comparison, namely cultural-historical comparison.

Attributions now had to be demonstrated on the basis of cultural-historical inquiry. In this way the study of nonliterate religions entered with full rights into the field of religio-historical research proper. At the same time, the historian of religions was not obliged to renounce his fundamental interest in comparison and (where appropriate) study of historical development, two aspects that had been neglected by the heirs of the older anthropological methods and the practitioners of an exclusively functional social anthropological research.

High Cultures. I have already noted that ethnic religions are found among literate as well as nonliterate cultures. In particular, the high cultures of antiquity produced ethnic religious traditions that make special demands on the historian. Study of them requires a philological competence that clearly excludes any simplistic or superficially phenomenological approach. It remains true, however, that even the historian of religions lacking such specialized knowledge can still contribute to a fuller understanding of these religions on the basis of his typological-historical experience. Take, as an example, the discovery of some of the classical characteristics of the demiurgic trickster in such diverse figures as the Greek Prometheus, the ancient Egyptian Seth, and Yurugu, also named Ogo, of the Dogon of West Africa. This discovery and the accompanying insight into the dualistic cosmology that provides the backdrop for such figures would have been impossible for the classicist or Egyptologist working only within his own speciality. It resulted rather from the comparative method of the historian of religions. This comparative approach can be particularly successful in the comparison of the mythologies of cultures that belong to the same subcontinent but have had different histories.

Another fascinating problem for comparative research concerns the continuities and discontinuities between the nonliterate cultures and religions on the one hand and the high cultures and their religious systems on the other. Given the differences that exist between them as well as the differences that exist within the respective traditions themselves, the question of their mutual interrelationships becomes quite complex

Monotheism and Polytheism. Closely connected to the question of continuities between cultures is the question of the exact nature of monotheism. This question has been the subject of a long debate within the history of religions. Some have claimed to find monotheism in the religions of nonliterate cultures, particularly among hunters and gatherers. Others, in contrast, have viewed it as a late phenomenon in the process of evolution, or even, as Raffaele Pettazzoni put it, as a revolutionary stance against a preceding form of polytheism. Actually these alternatives cannot be formulated so rigidly. The explicit and polemical formulations of monotheism that we find in the Bible and the Qur'an have little in common with the high gods of contemporaneous nonliterate cultures. It must be admitted that not all religious complexes extraneous to polytheism are *ipso facto* monotheistic. The most developed polytheistic systems did not "evolve" in the direction of monotheism, nor did they express a revolutionary movement in that direction. Rather, they tended to become progressively monistic, elaborating the notion of a deity who is "polyonymous" (as is Isis in the aretalogies of the Hellenistic period) or is *pantheos,* a god containing all the gods. In its most mature form, such a deity was conceived as "theopantistic," that is, as identical with the cosmos and at the same time transcending it.

It is important to realize that polytheism, as a historical type of religion, is much more specific than a merely formal notion of a plurality of gods. In fact, polytheism is not found in all types of culture, but is specifically linked to the high cultures of antiquity (and also to some in modern times, particularly in East and South Asia). These cultures characteristically possess an advanced form of cereal agriculture and show a degree of social stratification, with an attendant differentiation of classes, professions (including scribes), a priesthood and nobility, established sanctuaries, and the like. The social and historical specificity of polytheism as a religious type would seem to require that opposition between it and monotheism become acute only in particular historical and religious situations. Such situations include the historical emergence of the Hebrew people and their religion in the Near East, the vogue of the cult of Ahura Mazda in Iran, the rise and diffusion of Christianity in the Mediterranean world, and the preaching of Muhammad against the religion of the pre-Islamic Arabs. Clearly, the problem of polytheism and its relation to monotheism is not to be solved on the basis of a general phenomenological "stratigraphy" of religion and its main forms, any more than it was solved by a unilinear evolutionism. It is not a question of relative anteriority between polytheism and monotheism, homogeneous in themselves, but of specific, noninterchangeable historical formations that can interact with different types of religious and cultural organization. Monotheistic formations may present themselves either as immemorial tradition, as a novelty, or as the message of the one God and his triumph over false deities. Other formations could have evolved into pantheons that inspired and also reflected the complex organization of the high cultures of antiquity.

Scriptural and National Religions. Some ethnic religions are in fact characterized by the existence of sacred scriptures, organized on the basis of a "canon." Acceptance of these is considered an essential aspect of religious affiliation. The outstanding example is the function of the Vedas in Hinduism. Ethnic religions possessing scriptures exist in a situation midway between the nonscriptural religions of tribal societies, where religious affiliation is indistinguishable from the simple fact of social life, and at the other extreme, the universal religions, where the individual as such becomes a convert to the "good news" of a prophetic message written down in a book.

Another important subtype among ethnic religions is that of the national religions, those cults that promote a national and political consciousness. This is the case with state Shinto as practiced in some periods of Japanese history, with some forms of Hinduism, with Zoroastrianism in the Sasanid empire, and with the official cults in ancient Rome, such as the cult of Capitoline Jupiter and the cult of the emperor. It must be added that some of the founded religions may initially embrace a national outlook. Islam, for instance, may have been conceived originally as a prophetic message addressed to the Arab nation, although, to be sure, it is considered to be the final form of the historical revelation of God.

Founded Religions. I shall now look more closely at the founded religions, which include, in addition to Judaism, Christianity, and Islam, the religions of Zarathushtra (Zoroaster) and the Buddha, the religion of the Sikhs, and, with certain qualifications, the plethora of prophetic-nativistic cults and the "new religions." These traditions, which all trace their origin to a specific historical founder.

Among the founded religions the universal religions stand out as a definite subtype. These religions are based on a universal message of salvation, not limited to any particular group, ethnic or otherwise. They are characterized both by eschatological and otherworldly perspectives and by strong this-worldly ethical and social commitments. Their message is addressed to the individual and demands conversion and adherence to a religious community that, in sociological terms, may be described as a church. This community typically undergoes a rapid initial expansion, sometimes suffers persecution, and actively engages in missionary activities aimed at making new converts.

The emphasis on a universal message and personal conversion in response to it, an emphasis that transcends all racial and social barriers, differentiates the universalistic religions from the cults of antiquity that were sometimes their rivals. These cults, such as the mystery religions, would be better described as cosmopolitan rather than universal. Unlike commitment to any of the universal religions, participation in such cults could coexist with whatever other religious commitments an individual might have had, such as to the gods of the tribe, city, or state; the universal religions, however, demanded the individual's total allegiance.

This contrast becomes less clear in the case of the syncretistic tendencies found at the popular levels of the universal religions. Christianity and Islam, for instance, have been influenced, in some of their popular or ethnic manifestations in South America and Africa respectively, by local traditions of animism or "spiritism." The same lack of a clear differentiation between the universal and the local is found in the prophetic-nativistic cults that reinterpret the message of the great universal religions in strictly local terms, although not infrequently these same cults are inimical to preexisting forms of local magic and sorcery.

The case of Buddhism is somewhat unique. Although it displays many of the features that were attributed above to the universal religions, it nevertheless resembles the mystery cults of antiquity in its ability to coexist, in the belief system of a single individual and in a single cultural milieu, with other forms of locally preexistent religious belief and practice. This is especially evident in contemporary Japan, where a single individual may have a double allegiance to Buddhism and Shinto, according to the circumstances. The rather peculiar status of the universalism of Buddhism is linked to the equally peculiar status of Buddhism as a "religion."

Finally, another historical type of religion is comprised of those mysteriosophic (i. e., Orphic) and gnostic movements of antiquity and the Middle Ages that drew heavily on the universal religions of Christianity, Islam, and Zoroastrianism, borrowing many of their basic terms but totally reshaping them to suit their own needs. This procedure is found as well in the scientist theosophy of some contemporary gnostics, whose reinterpretations of the basic tenets of different religions are for the most part superficial.

BIBLIOGRAPHY

For further discussion of the questions raised in this entry, the reader is referred to *Problems and Methods of the History of Religions,* edited by Alessandro Bausani, C. Jouco Bleeker, and myself (Leiden, 1972), to my book *The History of Religions,* (Leiden, 1975), and to *The History of Religions: Retrospect and Prospect,* edited by Joseph M. Kitagawa (New York, 1985). As general references on the history of religions, the following works are also recommended.

Baaren, Th. P. van, and H. J. M. Drijvers, eds. *Religion, Culture and Methodology.* The Hague, 1973.

Baird, Robert D. *Category Formation and the History of Religions.* The Hague, 1971.

Banton, Michael, ed. *Anthropological Approaches to the Study of Religion.* London, 1966.

Bianchi, Ugo. *Probleme der Religionsgeschichte.* Göttingen, 1964.

Eliade, Mircea. *The Quest: History and Meaning in Religion.* Chicago, 1969.

Eliade, Mircea, and Joseph M. Kitagawa, eds. *The History of Religions: Essays in Methodology.* Chicago, 1959.

Evans-Pritchard, E. E. *Theories of Primitive Religion.* Oxford, 1965.

Graebner, Fritz. *Die Methode der Ethnologie* (1911). Reprint, Oosterhout, 1966.

Honko, Lauri, ed. *Science of Religion: Studies in Methodology.* The Hague, 1979.

Kitagawa, Joseph M., ed. *The History of Religions: Essays on the Problem of Understanding.* Chicago, 1967.

Lanczkowski, Günter. *Religionswissenschaft als Problem und Aufgabe.* Tübingen, 1965.

Lanczkowski, Günter, comp. *Selbstverständnis und Wesen der Religionswissenschaft.* Darmstadt, 1974.

Lang, Andrew. *The Making of Religion.* 3d ed. New York, 1909.

Pettazzoni, Raffaele. *L'essere supremo nelle religioni primitive.* Turin, 1957.

Pinard de la Boullaye, Henri. *L'étude comparée des religions.* 4th ed. 3 vols. Paris, 1929-1931.

Puech, Henri-Charles, ed. *Histoire des religions,* vol. 1. Paris, 1970.

Pye, Michael. *Comparative Religion.* New York, 1972.

Rudolph, Kurt. *Die Religionsgeschichte an der Leipziger Universität und die Entwicklung der Religionswissenschaft.* Berlin, 1962.

Rupp, Alfred. *Religion, Phänomen und Geschichte: Prolegomena zur Methodologie der Religionsgeschichte.* Saarbrücken, 1978.

Schlette, Heinz Robert. *Einführung in das Studium der Religionen.* Freiburg, 1971.

Schmidt, Wilhelm. *Der Ursprung der Gottesidee,* vol. 1. 2d ed. Münster, 1926.

Sharpe, Eric J. *Comparative Religion: A History.* London, 1975.

Smart, Ninian. *The Science of Religion and the Sociology of Knowledge: Some Methodological Questions.* Princeton, 1973.

Waardenburg, Jacques. *Classical Approaches to the Study of Religion.* 2 vols. The Hague, 1973-1974.

Widengren, Geo. *Religionsphänomenologie.* Berlin, 1969.

UGO BIANCHI

HITTITE RELIGION

The exact origin of the Hittites, an Indo-European people, is not known. Invading Asia Minor from the east, by the middle of the second millennium BCE they had established an empire covering the greater part of that region. Their empire declined after 1200 BCE, owing to Indo-European invasions and the growing power of Assyria.

Names of Gods. Knowledge about Hittite society, culture, and religion has increased since the deciphering of their cuneiform writing, on clay tablets found early in the twentieth century AD at Bogazköy (in Turkey). Hittite society was ethnically and linguistically diverse, with Hattian, Hurrian, and even some Semitic elements, and this diversity is evident in the divine names.

The earliest identifiable stratum is the Hattian. Because the Hattic language is still very poorly understood, we can only partially understand the meanings of the divine names: *Eshtan* ("sun, day") *Izzishtanu* ("favorable day"), *Kashku* ("moon"), *Kait* ("grain").

The influence of Sumerian and Akkadian religious vocabulary and divine epithets is obvious. Aya, Ishhara, Ellil (Enlil), Anu, and Alalu were originally Mesopotamian deities.

Functions of a Deity. As each mortal had his rank and function in human society, so each deity had his position and role.

General functions. While it is not possible to completely reconstruct the hierarchy of Hittite deities, it is clear that in convocations of gods certain figures naturally assumed leadership. In the Old Hittite vanishing-god myths it is the storm god who presides. But although he presides, he is not always able to enforce his will on the other gods. He must ask advice, plead his case, and seek volunteers for missions. Occasionally he is able to command another figure.

Hierarchical organization is also seen in the New Hittite pantheon. There is a fixed sequence in the god-lists in the state treaties, and there is an order of both gods and goddesses in the processional reliefs at Yazilikaya, near Bogazköy.

In their prayers the Hittites reminded the gods that they required worshipers who would bring regular food-offerings; thus it was in their own interest that they protect and bless the community of faithful worshipers. But aside from this maintenance of the cult, mortal assistance was rarely needed by the gods.

Gods "served" mortals by ensuring material prosperity, protecting them from enemies and natural catastrophes, hearing their prayers, making known to them their sins, and forgiving them (sometimes after a punishment).

Specialized functions. Just as there were storm gods who sent rain and winds to fertilize the crops and make them prosper, so there were deities of grain and vineyards, deities of the rivers who gave water for irrigation, deities of springs, deities of the forest, and deities of wildlife who gave success in hunting. Under the influence of Mesopotamian concepts, the sun god Ishtanu was the all-seeing dispenser of justice to humans and even to animals. There were war gods (the Zababa type) who gave victory to the Hittite armies. There was a god who could confer invisibility on the Hittite troops and enable them to attack the enemy by surprise. There were deities who sent and withdrew plagues, both upon the Hittites

and their enemies. There were deities of human sexual potency. And although one might ask one's personal god for any of these boons, there were divine specialists for many tasks.

Mythology. Mythological texts in the Hittite language may be subdivided into two groups: those of Anatolian origin and those of foreign origin. Myths deriving from Old Hittite originals are all Anatolian. The deities who figure in the Old Hittite Telepinu and Illuyanka myths and the other disappearing-god myths are a mix of what Emmanuel Laroche calls Hattian and Asianic. The myth of the moon falling from heaven occurs in both a Hattic and a Hittite version. There is very little about the Hittite version that linguistically recalls Old Hittite, yet it is surely possible that a long tradition of recopying has removed almost all traces of its original Old Hittite language. All of the Anatolian myths are associated with incantations or rituals. The myths of non-Anatolian origin are all post-Old Hittite. They are generally independent of any incantation or ritual.

Vanishing-god myths. These myths, the best known of which is about the god Telepinu, are paradigms for dealing with natural catastrophes such as drought, blight, and diseases affecting livestock. The god who disappears must be located, appeased, and brought back. Texts recording such oracular inquiry are extremely common in the New Hittite period, but have now been identified in the Old Hittite script, showing that his procedure was probably as common in the earlier period as in the later one. The pacification and return of the god is accomplished by a magic ritual of the type called *mugawar* in Hittite. Directions for such *mugawars* accompany the vanishing-god myths; other *mugawars* are

> These myths . . . are paradigms for dealing with natural catastrophes such as drought, blight, and diseases affecting livestock.

described in ritual texts. It is a characteristic ritual form among the Hittites.

Illuyanka myths. Two stories on the same tablet are about the conflict between the storm god and his antagonist, the great serpent Illuyanka. *Illuyanka* is in fact not a name but a common noun, meaning "serpent" or "snake." But this particular reptile is clearly large and strong enough to have once defeated and disabled the storm god. In both stories the initially defeated storm god secures the help of a mortal who utilizes a trick to help the storm god triumph in his return match with the reptile.

The Hittite Temple. Six Hittite temples have been excavated at Bogazköy. In addition to the cella, where the cult image of the deity was found, each contained a number of rooms that were used to house the permanent personnel and to store temple revenues. Each temple had a central courtyard. Worshipers crossing the courtyard from the temple entrance passed through a portico into the cella, which apparently could accommodate only priests and a small number of worshipers. Some larger temples, such as the principal temple in the lower city at Bogazköy (Temple I), may have contained two or more cellae and therefore housed the cult images of more than one god.

Sin, Death, and the Afterlife. Several Hittite words are translated as "sin," "offense," or "crime." Those occurring in prayers are *washtai-, washtul,* and *shalla-kardatar.* From the Hittite point of view, sins against the gods could be deliberate or accidental. In either case they had to be identified, confessed, and (in most cases) corrected. Identification of sins committed unwittingly was possible only through consulting the god by oracle.

Relatively little is said in the surviving Hittite texts about the fate of man after death. The Old Hittite Kantuzzili prayer rather philosophically observes that if one were to go on living under the present circumstances eternally, that might turn out to be a nightmare, for the ills of this life would become eternal. This would turn out to be a grievance *(kattawatar),* that is, a ground for complaint against the gods. In the description of the lengthy ritual for cremation and interring of the ashes of a dead king we learn that certain farming implements were burned in order to accompany the deceased king to the next life, so that he might cultivate the soil there.

A Hittite religious belief maintained that the spirit of a dead person with a grievance against a living person might continue to haunt the latter until the grievance was resolved. The precise nature of the grievance was determined in the same way as sins against a god: by oracular investigation. When the grievance had been resolved and the spirit had been pacified, he was "set on the road," that is, he was sent on his way to the abode of the dead.

BIBLIOGRAPHY

Bittel, Kurt. *Hattusha: The Capital of the Hittites.* New York, 1970. See pages 91-112.
Bittel, Kurt. "The Great Temple of Hattusha-Bogazköy." *American Journal of Archaeology* 80 (1976): 66-73.
Gurney, O. R. *Some Aspects of Hittite Religion.* London, 1977.
Güterbock, Hans G. "Hittite Religion." in *Forgotten Religions,* edited by Vergilius Ferm, pp. 83-109. New York, 1950.
Güterbock, Hans G. "The Song of UlliKummi." *Journal of Cuneiform Studies* 5 (1951): 135-161 and 6 (1952): 8-42.
Güterbock, Hans G. "Religion und Kultus der Hethiter." In *Neuere Hethiterforschung,* edited by Gerold Walser, pp. 54-73. Wiesbaden, 1964.
Güterbock, Hans G. *Les hieroglyphes de Yazilikaya: À propos d'un travail récent.* Paris, 1982.
Hoffner, Harry A., Jr. "Hittite Mythological Texts: A Survey." In *Unity and Diversity,* edited by Hans Goedicke and J. J. M. Roberts, pp. 136-145. Baltimore, 1975.
Hoffner, Harry A., Jr. "A Prayer of Mursili II about His Stepmother." *Journal of the American Oriental Society* 103 (1983): 187-192.
Kammenhuber, Annelies. "Hethitische Rituale." In *Kindlers Literatur-Lexikon,* edited by Gert Woerner et al., vol. 3. Zurich, 1965-1967.
Masson, Emilia. *Le panthéon de Yazilikaya: Nouvelles lectures.* Paris, 1981.
Moyer, James C. "The Concept of Ritual Purity among the Hittites." Ph. D. diss., Brandeis University, 1969.
Otten, Heinrich. *Hethitische Totenrituale.* Berlin, 1958.
Otten, Heinrich. "The Religion of the Hittites." in *Historia Religionum,* edited by C. Jouco Bleeker and Geo Widengren, vol. 1, *Religions of the Past,* pp. 318-322. Leiden, 1969.
Sturtevant, Edgar H., and George Bechtel. *A Hittite Chrestomathy.* Philadelphia, 1935.
Sürenhagen, Dietrich. "Zwei Gebete Hattusilis und der Puduhepa." *Altorientalische Forschungen* 8 (1981): 83-168.
Ten Cate Houwink, Ph. H. J. "Hittite Royal Prayers." *Numen* 16 (1969): 81-98.

HARRY A. HOFFNER, JR.

HOLOCAUST, THE

Jewish Theological Responses

To grasp the challenge of the Holocaust one must understand the unique racial/Manichaean *Weltanschauung* of Nazism and the role of the Jew in it. For Hitler and his Reich, anti-Semitism and the struggle against world Jewry were not only subjective sentiments of personal will but also actualizations in history of metahistorical antitheses, and as such, necessary and inevitable. Killing Jews, or more precisely eliminating "the Jews," or Judaism itself, was in this modern gnostic myth a sacred obligation. "The Jew," the collective singular, was the generic, supranatural enemy. The *Endlösung,* the "final solution," was not primarily understood by its cruel initiator as a political or socioeconomic force. It was not an expression of class struggle or nationalism in any recognizable sense. It was intended as, and received its enormous power from, the fact that it aimed at nothing less than restructuring the cosmos.

In responding to the catastrophic consequences of this racial fantasy, which claimed six million Jewish lives, Jewish thinkers have explored many theological avenues—some old, some new. As to the old, Jewish history is no stranger to national tragedy and, as a consequence, there is an abundance of traditional explanatory models that could be and have been adapted and reapplied to the Holocaust. From these, six have regularly been looked to by modern thinkers as providing maps for understanding the theological complexities raised by the Holocaust.

**The `Aqedah.** The `Aqedah, or "binding," of Isaac, the biblical narrative recounted in *Genesis* 22:2ff., is often appealed to as a possible paradigm for approaching the Holocaust. (See, for example, Berkovits, 1973, pp. 124-125, and Neher, 1981.) Such a move is rooted in Jewish tradition, especially that of the medieval martyrologies of the Crusader and post-Crusader periods, in which the biblical event became the prism through which the horrific medieval experience became refracted and intelligible. Like Isaac of old, the Jewish children of Europe, and more generally all of slaughtered Israel, are seen as martyrs to God who willingly sacrifice themselves and their loved ones in order to prove beyond all doubt their faithfulness to the Almighty (see Shalom Spiegel, *The Last Trial,* New York, 1967, and the medieval religious poems collected in A. M. Habermann's *Sefer gezerot Ashkenaz ve-Tsarfat,* Jerusalem, 1945).

The appeal of this interpretation lies in its conferring heroic status on the dead because of their sanctity and obedience to the God of Israel. Their death is not due to sin, to any imperfection on their part, or to any violation of the covenant; rather, it is the climactic evidence of their unwavering devotion to the faith of their fathers—not its abandonment.

Job. The biblical *Book of Job,* the best-known treatment of theodicy in the Hebrew Bible, naturally presents itself as a second possible model for understanding the Holocaust. (See, for example, Maybaum, 1965, p. 70, and Greenberg, 1981.) According to such a rendering—which is not unlike that offered by the `Aqedah—*Job* provides an inviting paradigm because again Job's suffering is not caused by his sinfulness but rather by his righteousness, which is perceived by Satan as a cause for jealousy. Moreover, the tale ends on a "happy" note, as Job is rewarded for his faithfulness with God's double blessing. On a deeper level, the resolution of Job's doubts is never really clear; God's reply through the whirlwind is, in important ways, no answer to Job's questions; and Job's first wife and family are still dead through no fault of their own.

The Suffering Servant. One of the richest theological doctrines of biblical theodicy is that of the Suffering Servant. Given its classic presentation in the *Book of Isaiah* (especially chapter 53), the Suffering Servant doctrine is that of vicarious suffering and atonement in which the righteous suffer for the wicked and hence allay, in some mysterious way, God's wrath and judgment, thus making the continuation of humankind possible. According to Jewish tradition, the Suffering Servant is Israel, the people of the covenant, who suffer with and for God in the midst of the evil of creation. By suffering for others, the Jewish people make it possible for creation to endure. In this act of faithfulness the guiltless establish a unique bond with the Almighty. As they suffer for and with him, he shares their suffering and agony and comes to love them in a special way for loving him with such fortitude and depth. (For the rabbinic use of this concept see, in the Babylonian Talmud, *Sanhedrin* 98b, *Berakhot* 5a, and *Sotah* 14a.)

Hester Panim. In wrestling with human suffering, the Hebrew Bible appeals, especially in the Psalms, to the notion of *hester panim*, "the hiding of the face" of God. This concept has two meanings. The first, as in *Deuteronomy* 31:17-18 and later in *Micah* 3:4, is the causal one that links God's absence to human sin. God turns away from the sinner. The second sense, found particularly in certain psalms (e.g., *Ps.* 44, 69, 88 and variants in, e.g., *Ps.* 9, 10, 13; see also *Jb.* 13:24), suggests protest, despair, and confusion over the absence of God for no clear reason, and not as a consequence of sin. Here mankind stands "abandoned" for reasons that appear unknown and unfathomable. Thus the repetitive theme of lament in the Psalms as the psalmists implore God "why" or "how long" he will be absent.

Mippenei Hata'einu. In biblical and later Jewish sources the principal though not unique "explanation" for human suffering was sin, as we have seen. There was a balance in the universal order that was inescapable: good brought forth blessing and sin retribution. Both on the individual and collective level the law of cause and effect, of sin and grief, operated. In our time it is not surprising that some theologians—particularly traditional ones—and certain rabbinical sages have responded to the tragedy of European Jewry with this classical "answer." Harsh as it is, the argument advanced is that Israel sinned grievously and God, after much patience and hope of return, finally "cut off" the generation of the wicked. The reasoning is expressed in the phrase *mippenei hata'einu* ("because of our sins" are we punished). Though the majority of those who have wrestled with the theological implications of the Sho'ah have rejected this line of analysis, an important, if small, segment of the religious community have consistently advanced it.

The Free Will Defense. Among philosophical reflections concerning theodicy, none has an older or more distinguished lineage than that known as the free will defense. According to this argument human evil is the necessary and ever-present possibility entailed by the reality of human freedom. If human beings are to be capable of acts of authentic morality they must be capable of acts of authentic immorality. Applying this consideration to the events of the Nazi epoch, the Sho'ah becomes a case of the extreme misuse of human freedom. At the same time such a position in no way forces a reconsideration of the cosmological structure in which the anthropological drama unfolds, nor does it call into question God's goodness and solicitude, for it is man and not God who perpetrates genocide.

A New Revelation. To this point the first six positions analyzed have all been predicated upon classical Jewish responses to national tragedy. In the last two decades, however, a number of innovative, more radical, responses have been evoked from contemporary post-Holocaust thinkers.

The Covenant Broken: A New Age. A modern thinker who has urged continued belief in the God of Israel, though on new terms, is Irving Greenberg. For Greenberg all the old truths and certainties have been destroyed by the Holocaust. Any simple faith is now impossible. Greenberg explicates this radical notion in this way. There are three major periods in the covenantal history of Israel. The first is the biblical era.

The second, rabbinic phase in the transformation of the convenant idea is marked by the destruction of the Second Temple. Greenberg believes that a "third great cycle in

> For Greenberg all the old truths and certainties have been destroyed by the Holocaust. Any simple faith is now impossible.

Jewish history" has come about as a consequence of the Holocaust. The Sho'ah marks a new era in which the Sinaitic covenantal relationship was shattered and thus an unprecedented form of convenantal relationship, if there is to be any covenantal relationship at all, must come into being to take its place. "In retrospect, it is now clear that the divine assignment to the Jews was untenable. After the Holocaust, it is obvious that this role opened the Jews to a total murderous fury from which there was no escape. . . . Morally speaking, then, God can have no claims on the Jews by dint of the Covenant." What this means, Greenberg argues, is that the covenant

> can no longer be commanded and subject to a serious external enforcement. It cannot be commanded because morally speaking—covenantally speaking—one cannot order another to step forward to die. One can give an order like this to an enemy, but in a moral relationship, I cannot demand giving up one's life. I can ask for it or plead for it—but I cannot order it. (ibid., p. 23)

A Redefinition of God. Arthur A. Cohen, in his *The Tremendum: A Theological Interpretation of the Holocaust* (1981), made a related proposal. Although he draws on the writing of F. W. J. Schelling (1775-1854) and Franz Rosenzweig (1886-1929) and on Qabbalah (Jewish mysticism) as his sources, he is no doubt also familiar with the work of the process theologians. After arguing for the enormity of the Holocaust, its uniqueness, and its transcendence of any meaning, Cohen suggested that the way out of the dilemma posed by classical thought is to rethink whether "national catastrophes are compatible with our traditional notions of a beneficent and providential God" (p. 50). For Cohen the answer is no, at least to the extent that the activity and nature of the providential God must be reconceptual-

ized. Against the traditional view that asks, given its understanding of God's action in history, how it could be that God witnessed the Holocaust and remained silent, Cohen would pose the contrary "dipolar" thesis that "what is taken as God's speech is really always man's hearing, that God is not the strategist of our particularities or of our historical condition, but rather the mystery of our futurity, always our *posse,* never our acts" (p. 97). That is, "if we begin to see God less as an interferer whose insertion is welcome (when it accords with our needs) and more as the immensity whose reality is our prefiguration . . . we shall have won a sense of God whom we may love and honor, but whom we no longer fear and from whom we no longer demand" (ibid.).

God Is Dead. It is natural that many should have responded to the horror of the Holocaust with unbelief. Such skepticism usually takes a nonsystematic, almost intuitive, form: "I can no longer believe." However, one contemporary Jewish theologian, Richard L. Rubenstein, has provided a formally structured "death of God" theology as a response to the Sho'ah.

In Rubenstein's view the only honest response to the death camps is the rejection of God, the statement "God is dead," and the open recognition of the meaninglessness of existence. Our life is neither planned nor purposeful, there is no divine will, and the world does not reflect divine concern. Mankind must now reject its illusions and recognize the existential truth that life is not intrinsically valuable, that the human condition reflects no transcendental purpose, and that history reveals no providence. All theological "rationalizations" of Auschwitz pall before its enormity and, for Rubenstein, the only worthy reaction is the rejection of the entire Jewish theological framework: there is no God and no covenant with Israel. Drawing heavily upon the atheistic existentialists such as Camus, Sartre, and earlier Nietzsche, Rubenstein interprets this to mean that in the face of history's meaninglessness human beings must create and project meaning.

Mystery and Silence. In the face of the Holocaust, recourse to the God of mystery and human silence are not unworthy options. However, there are two kinds of silence, two kinds of employment of the idea of a God of mystery. The first is closer to the attitude of the agnostic: "I cannot know." Hence all profound existential and intellectual wrestling with the enormous problems raised by the Sho'ah and with God after the Sho'ah are avoided. The second is the silence and mystery that Job and many of the prophets manifest, to which the Bible points in its recognition of God's elemental otherness. This is the silence that comes after struggling with and reproaching God, after feeling his closeness or his painful absence. This silence, this mystery, is the silence and mystery of seriousness, of that authenticity that will not diminish the tragedy with a too quick answer, yet that, having forced reason to its limits, recognizes the limits of reason.

Assuredly, there is great difficulty in ascertaining when thought has reached its limit and silence and mystery become proper, but, at the same time, there is the need to know when to speak in silence.

BIBLIOGRAPHY

Berkovits, Eliezer. *Faith after the Holocaust.* New York, 1973.
Berkovits, Eliezer. *Crisis and Faith.* New York, 1976.
Berkovits, Eliezer. *With God in Hell.* New York, 1979.
Biale, David. Review of Emil Fackenheim's *The Jewish Return into History. Association for Jewish Studies Newsletter* (October 1980).
Cain, Seymour. "The Question and the Answers after Auschwitz." *Judaism* 20 (Summer 1971): 263-278.
Cohen, Arthur A., comp. *Arguments and Doctrines: A Reader of Jewish Thinking in the Aftermath of the Holocaust.* New York, 1970.
Cohen, Arthur A. *The Tremendum.* New York, 1981.
Fackenheim, Emil L. *The Religious Dimension in Hegel's Thought.* Bloomington, Ind., 1967.
Fackenheim, Emil L. *Quest for Past and Future.* Bloomington, Ind., 1968.
Fackenheim, Emil L. *God's Presence in History.* New York, 1970.
Fackenheim, Emil L. *Encounters between Judaism and Modern Philosophy.* New York, 1973.
Fackenheim, Emil L. *The Jewish Return into History.* New York, 1978.
Fackenheim, Emil L. *To Mend the World.* New York, 1982.
Greenberg, Irving. "Cloud of Smoke, Pillar of Fire: Judaism, Christianity, and Modernity after the Holocaust." In *Auschwitz: Beginning of a New Era?,* edited by Eva Fleischner, pp. 7-55. New York, 1977.
Greenberg, Irving. "Judaism and History: Historical Events and Religious Change." In *Ancient Roots and Modern Meanings,* edited by Jerry V. Diller, pp. 139-162. New York, 1968.
Greenberg, Irving. "New Revelations and New Patterns in the Relationship of Judaism and Christianity." *Journal of Ecumenical Studies* 16 (Spring 1979): 249-267.
Greenberg, Irving. *The Third Great Cycle in Jewish History.* New York, 1981.
Katz, Steven T. *Post-Holocaust Dialogues: Critical Studies in Modern Jewish Thought.* New York, 1983.
Maybaum, Ignaz. *The Face of God after Auschwitz.* Amsterdam, 1965.
Meyer, Michael A. "Judaism after Auschwitz." *Commentary* 53 (June 1972): 55-62.
Neher, André. *The Exile of the Word: From the Silence of the Bible to the Silence of Auschwitz.* Philadelphia, 1981.
Rubenstein, Richard L. *After Auschwitz.* Indianapolis, 1966.
Rubenstein, Richard L. *The Religious Imagination.* Indianapolis, 1968.
Rubenstein, Richard L. *Morality and Eros.* New York, 1970.
Rubenstein, Richard L. *Power Struggle.* New York, 1974.
Rubenstein, Richard L. *The Cunning of History.* New York, 1975.
Rubenstein, Richard L. *The Age of Triage.* Boston, 1983.
Tiefel, Hans O. "Holocaust Interpretations and Religious Assumptions." *Judaism* 25 (Spring 1976): 135-149.
Wyschogrod, Michael. "Faith and the Holocaust." *Judaism* 20 (Summer 1971): 286-294.

STEVEN T. KATZ

HUMANISM

The Christian humanism of the Renaissance and Reformation period was a complex intellectual movement, primarily literary and philological in nature, but with important historical, philosophical, and religious implications. Humanism was rooted in the love of classical antiquity and the desire for its rebirth, both in terms of form (primarily a search for new aesthetic standards) and of norm (a desire for more enlightened ethical and religious values). The return to original sources is reflected in a parallel way in the reformers' emphasis upon the scripture as norm and New Testament Christianity as the ideal form of church life. Humanism developed in Italy during the fourteenth century and persisted through the Reformation well into the age of the Enlightenment.

The word *humanism* came from the phrase *studia humanitatis* or *humaniora,* the liberal arts or humane studies, a concept derived largely from Cicero. The liberal arts curriculum emphasized grammar, rhetoric, poetry, history, and moral philosophy. While the course of studies owed something to the traditional education of the medieval cathedral schools, it was less concerned with dialectic or logic, natural science, and Scholastic metaphysics. The term *humanist* was originally applied to professional public or private teachers of classical literature who continued the medieval vocation of the dictatores, who taught the skills of letter-writing and proper style in speech and writing. But the word gradually came to assume a more comprehensive meaning, referring to all devotees of classical learning. Humanism came to be cultivated not merely by professional educators but by many men of letters, historians, moral philosophers, statesmen, and churchmen, including regular as well as secular clergy. They set the aurea sapientia, or golden wisdom, of the ancients against the arid dialectic of the Scholastic doctors. Christian humanism tended toward religious syncretism, moralism, and ethical Paulinism, and also toward a Christocentrism that emphasized Christ as an example of good living, rather than a Christology that focused on Christ's sacrifice on the cross as sin-bearer, substitute, and savior.

Italian Renaissance Humanism. It was natural that humanism should emerge most strongly in Italy, given the Roman inheritance and the artistic and architectural reminders of ancient glories. Toward the end of the thirteenth century, a form of protohumanism developed in the north of Italy, in Padua, Verona, and Vicenza, and in Arezzo and Florence in Tuscany. But the "father of humanism" was Francesco Petrarch (1304-1374), who gave to Italian literary humanism its basic character. He is perhaps best remembered for his vernacular lyrics, chiefly love poems to Laura; he was crowned poet laureate on the Capitoline Hill in Rome in 1341. Petrarch stressed the purity of the classical Latin style, revived enthusiasm for ancient Rome, and helped develop a sense of distance from the past and a revulsion toward the medieval "dark ages." He raised important personal and religious questions in such writings as On the Solitary Life, the Secretum, Ascent of Mount Ventoux, and On His Own Ignorance and That of Many Others, in which he wrote as an apologist for the Christian view of man and the humanists' appreciation of the worth of the individual against certain neo-Aristotelians whose natural philosophy subverted those values.

Petrarch's friend Giovanni Boccaccio (1313-1375) gained renown for his Decameron, a collection of a hundred short stories, for books on famous men and women, and for an encyclopedic Genealogy of the Gods, an important handbook of mythology. Petrarchan humanism spread through Italy, largely as a lay, upper-class, and elitist movement. In the search for classical manuscripts, humanists such as Poggio Bracciolini (1380-1459), Francesco Filelfo (1398-1481), Cyriacus of Ancona (c. 1391-1457), and Giovanni Aurispa (1374-1450) excelled, rediscovering key works of Cicero, Quintilian, Vitruvius, Plautus, Pliny the Younger, Tacitus, Thucydides, Euripides, Sophocles, and other ancient authors.

Humanism gained new momentum and direction with the Greek revival. In the final decades of the fourteenth century the Byzantine emperor, threatened by the Ottoman Turks, who were encircling Constantinople, made two expeditions to the West, in 1374 and 1399, to seek help. His efforts were futile, but some Greek scholars, such as Manuel Chrysoloras (c. 1355-1415), John Bessarion (1403-1472), and Gemistus Plethon (c. 1355-1450), remained in the West and introduced Greek literature, patristics, and philosophy. After the fall of Constantinople in 1453, other scholars fled to the West,

> **Humanism gained new momentum and direction with the Greek revival.**

notably John Argyropoulos, Demetrius Calcondylas, and John and Constantine Lascaris, adding new momentum to the Greek revival and broadening the dimensions of philosophical discussion.

Certain humanists placed their rhetorical gifts in the service of the Florentine republic against the threatening tyrants of Milan and Naples. These civic humanists, such as chancellor Coluccio Salutati (1331-1406) and Leonardo Bruni (c. 1370-1444), stirred up the patriotic impulses of the citizenry for the defense of the state. In a broader sense civic humanism was more than an ideology of embattled republicanism, for it stood for a life of action spent for the common good.

Giannozzo Manetti (1396-1459), who wrote On the Dignity and Excellence of Man, once described the whole duty of man as being to understand and to act. Leon Battista Alberti (1404-1472), a truly universal man, the architect of Renaissance churches, palaces, and fountains, wrote treatises that for many decades dominated theory on architecture, painting, and the family.

In order to convey humanist ideals to youth, humanist educators not only wrote influential treatises on education but also established schools to put their theories into practice. Generally optimistic about the educability at least of the upper classes, the humanists cultivated the liberal arts to develop leaders with sound character and lofty vision. Pietro Paolo Vergerio (1370-1444) wrote a treatise on the morals befitting a free man, drawing extensively on Plato, Plutarch, and Cicero. Vittorino Rambaldoni da Feltre (1378-1446) and Guarino da Verona (1370-1460) set up model schools with a humanist curriculum and introduced such innovations as physical education and coeducation.

Among the disciplines emphasized was history, for the humanists valued both ancient and contemporary history. What the humanists learned from classical historians was reflected in their own histories, from the History of Florence of Leonardo Bruni to the History of Florence of Niccoló Machiavelli and the History of Italy in *His Own Times* by Francesco Guicciardini (1483-1540). Flavio Biondo (1389-1463), the founder of modern archaeology, produced massive topographical-historical works on Rome and all of Italy. Lorenzo Valla (1407-1457) anticipated many of the questions raised later by Luther, such as free will and predestination, errors in the Vulgate, and the value of lay piety in contrast to monasticism. In a treatise titled *On the Donation of Constantine,* he proved with philological and historical critical arguments that the *Donation of Constantine* was a forgery purporting to prove that when Constantine moved the capital of the Roman empire to the East, he had given the Lateran Palace and outlying provinces to Pope Sylvester I and his successors, as well as conferring immense privileges upon them.

During the second half of the fifteenth century classical scholarship was more closely integrated with literary composition in the vernacular, printing spread rapidly following the establishment of the first printing press in Italy in 1465, and a new metaphysical emphasis superseded the relatively uncomplicated moral philosophy of the literary and civic humanists with the development of Neoplatonic, neo-Pythagorean, neo-Aristotelian, Hermetic, and qabbalistic philosophies and theodicies. Neoplatonism became the most prominent and characteristic form of Renaissance philosophy. The renewal of interest in patristic writings, aided by scholars such as Ambrogio Traversari (1386-1439), and especially in the Greek fathers, added impetus to the Greek revival. Nicholas of Cusa (1401-1464) was concerned with the search for unity between the infinite One and the infinite multitude of finite things, the *coincidentia oppositorum,* a panentheism that raised the specter of pantheism. Marsilio Ficino (1433-1499), the most eminent Renaissance philosopher, presided over the "Platonic Academy" endowed by Cosimo de' Medici, the de facto ruler of Florence. Ficino did editions of Plato's works and edited the Enneads of Plotinus and works of Greek pagan Neoplatonists such as Proclus and Porphyry, as well as of Dionysius the Areopagite, whose christianized Neoplatonism was so influential throughout the

> **Aristotelianism persisted in the universities, and Neo-Aristotelianism found advocates such as Pietro Pomponazzi. . . .**

medieval period. Among his own influential works were the *Theologia Platonica* and the *De religione Christiana,* in which he used Neoplatonism apologetically as a support for the Christian faith. His understudy, Giovanni Pico della Mirandola (1463-1494), sought to find the religious truth common to Christianity, Platonism, Aristotelianism, Hermetism, Islam, and Qabbalah. He published for public disputation nine hundred theses, the *Conclusiones,* in which he sought to summarize all learning. In his oration *On the Dignity of Man,* sometimes described as the most characteristic Renaissance document, he places man at the center of the "great chain of being," the object of special creation, able to rise upward toward God or to sink downward to the sensate animalistic level, as he chooses. Giordano Bruno (1548-1600), combining Nicholas of Cusa's Neoplatonism and Hermetic ideas with the physical implications of Copernican astronomy, synthesized a philosophy that verged on pantheism. Aristotelianism persisted in the universities, and Neo-Aristotelianism found advocates such as Pietro Pomponazzi (1462-1525), who wrote on the nature of immortality, fate, free will, predestination, and providence.

Northern Humanism. Thanks to close political, commercial, ecclesiastical, and university ties with Italy, the new humanist culture came earlier to Germany than to other countries of northern Europe. The pioneers included wandering poets such as Peter Luder, schoolmaster humanists such as Johannes Murmellius and Rudolf von Langen, half-Scholastic humanists such as Conrad Summenhart and Paul Scriptoris, and moralistic critics of church and society such as Heinrich Bebel, Jacob Wimpfeling, Sebastian Brant, and the preacher Johann Geiler von Kaisersberg. But the man credited with being the father of German humanism was Roelof Huysman (Rodolphus Agricola, 1444-1485), known as the "German Petrarch." After a decade in Italy he returned to "the frozen Northland" and presided over a group of young

humanists in Heidelberg, to whom he expounded his theories of rhetoric. One of his disciples, Conrad Pickel (Conradus Celtis, 1459-1508), the "German arch-humanist," organized young humanists into the Rhenish and Danubian sodalities to promote humanism and to do a topographical-historical work entitled *Germania illustrata,* never completed.

At the universities humanists struggled with Scholastics for positions, and by 1520 humanism had spread to urban centers and to both ecclesiastical and princely courts. The lawyer Conrad Peutinger, the historian Johannes Turmair (Aventinus), the city councilor Willibald Pirckheimer, a friend of Conrad Pickel, and the Nuremberg artist Albrecht Dürer were patrons and advocates of humanism. The clash of humanists and Scholastics came to a head in the celebrated Reuchlin controversy. Johannes Reuchlin (1455-1522) did a Hebrew vocabulary and grammar and wrote two major works, *On the Wonder-Working Word* and *On the Qabbalistic Art,* in which he used the Jewish mystical Qabbalah in support of Christianity. Reuchlin defended some Hebrew books from a vicious book-burner, Johannes Pfefferkorn, a converted Jew, and was in turn attacked by certain Scholastic doctors at Cologne. An Erfurt humanist, Johann Jäger (Crotus Rubianus, c. 1480-1545), and the young knight Ulrich von Hutten (1488-1523) wrote a biting satire, The Letters of Obscure Men, ridiculing the Scholastics and defending Reuch-lin. In Gotha the canon Mutianus Rufus (1471-1526) gathered a circle of young humanists from the University of Erfurt to promote classical learning.

Although there were early ties with Italy during the Avignon papacy and some promise of a flowering early in the fifteenth century, for example in the circle gathered around chancellor Jean de Montreuil (1354-1418), the Hundred Years' War and the struggle between France and Burgundy delayed the full development of humanism in France. The great flowering of humanism came from 1515 to 1547, during the reign of Francis I, a great patron of art and literature. Guillaume Budé (1468-1540) did a commentary on the Pandects (a digest of Justinian's law), a work on numismatics, a commentary on the Greek language, and a major work on Hellenism. Lefèvre d'Étaples (1455-1536) worked on biblical texts, doing a critical edition of Psalms and commentaries on Paul's letters and on the four Gospels; this work was important to Luther and the French reformers. Margaret of Angoulême, Francis I's sister, was not only an author but also a patroness of humanists and young reformers, along with Bishop Guillaume Briçonnet. François Rabelais (c. 1495-1553), author of the witty, gross, and satirical Gargantua and Pantagruel, offered criticism through the story of a giant and his son. Although sometimes called a skeptic, Rabelais is now seen more as an Erasmian Christian humanist interested in reform. The famous essayist Michel de Montaigne (1533-1592) was the greatest French literary figure of the age.

In Spain, Erasmianism, Lutheranism, and mysticism found followers, but nonconformity was effectively suppressed. Cardinal Jiménez de Cisneros (1436-1517) instituted rigorous clerical reforms, founded the University of Alcalá with a trilingual college, and endowed the publication of the Complutensian Polyglot Bible. Antonio de Nebrija (1441-1522), at Salamanca, was an outstanding classicist. The greatest literary figure of Spanish humanism was Miguel de Cervantes (1547-1616), author of Don Quixote.

English humanism developed during the fifteenth century from political and ecclesiastical contacts with Italy. Classical studies were cultivated seriously at Oxford by Thomas Linacre (c. 1460-1524), William Grocyn (c. 1466-1519), and William Latimer (c. 1460-1543). John Colet (1467-1519), dean of Saint Paul's and founder of Saint Paul's School, modeled somewhat after the humanist schools of Italy, corresponded with Ficino and was intrigued by Neoplatonism. But he had a serious theological bent, and in his lectures on Romans he emphasized man's sinfulness and need for God's forgiveness. Thomas More (1478-1535) wrote the most famous work of English humanism, Utopia.

The prince of the northern humanists was Desiderius Erasmus of Rotterdam (1469?-1536), who articulated the loftiest ideals of Christian humanism. A great classicist and patristics scholar, he expressed social and ecclesiastical criticism in The Praise of Folly and the Colloquies, expounded his "philosophy of Christ" in the Enchiridion and in Paraclesis, and did editions, with long introductions, of Latin and Greek classical authors and church fathers. His fame was eclipsed by the advent of the Reformation, and he reluctantly attacked Luther on the question of the freedom of the will. Erasmus inclined toward moralism and spiritualism rather than consequential soteriology, emphasizing Christ the teacher and example rather than the Savior who died on the Cross for the salvation of mankind. [See the biography of Erasmus.]

Humanism and the Reformation. The Reformation owed much to humanism for its success; contributing to an atmosphere favorable to the Reformation were humanism's emphasis on knowledge of the biblical languages and a return to the sources; its criticism of ecclesiastical and social abuses; its negative attitude toward Scholasticism; a concomitant romantic cultural nationalism; the use of the printing press; and the activities of the cadres of young humanists who carried Luther's message to all parts of the Holy Roman Empire in the early years. Luther referred to the Renaissance as akin to John the Baptist heralding the coming of the gospel. The so-called magisterial reformers, Luther, Zwingli, Calvin, Melanchthon, Bucer, Beza, and others, were all university men with some background in classical studies and humanist learning. Led by Luther, they reformed the university curricula in favor of humanist disciplines, reformed old and founded new universities, and established secondary schools, Gymnasiums and lycées, to promote the liberal arts.

They insisted upon compulsory education for boys and girls, thus expanding education beyond the elitist upper-class concerns of the Italian humanists. They stressed teaching as a divine vocation. While Luther loved the classics, rejected Scholasticism, and favored humanism, his colleague Philipp Melanchthon (1497-1560) was the major influence in promoting classicism. In line with Italian humanism, the reformers deemphasized dialectic and stressed the value of rhetoric, poetry, moral philosophy, and history. Along with their concern for pure theology, the proper distinction between law and gospel, and the centrality of sin and grace, the reformers viewed higher culture as a sphere of faith's works and became strong advocates of humanist learning. Learned Protestants such as the polymath Joachim Camerarius (1500-1574), the educator Johannes Sturm (1507-1589), the historian Johannes Philippi (Sleidanus, 1506-1556), the irenic theologian Georg Calixtus (1586-1656), and a host of neo-Latin poets, playwrights, and philosophers carried humanism into the seventeenth century and the beginnings of the Enlightenment. Catholic reformers, too, especially the Jesuits, saw the value of the *humaniora,* or humane studies, and introduced them into their academies, colleges, and universities. The Reformation owed much to humanism and repaid the debt richly by broadening the popular base of education and carrying humanist learning into modern times. [*See* Reformation *and* Enlightenment, The.]

The Reformation brought to an end the role of Renaissance humanism as an independent cultural force, for thereafter it became associated closely with the various Christian confessions. Lutheran, Calvinist, Catholic, and radical humanist learning was cultivated in secondary schools and universities. Where humanism was transmitted in this academic way, it was preserved much longer than where it remained a matter of a few individuals or groups; but humanism took on a more pedantic and less spontaneous character in the universities.

Humanist impulses were not only widespread horizontally on a European scale but reached down vertically through the centuries. Where humanist influence was strong, it nourished tendencies toward universalism, or at least toward latitudinarianism, especially in England and the Netherlands, and fostered an irenic spirit. The humanist way of thinking has remained in evidence into the twentieth century.

BIBLIOGRAPHY

For the historical background of Renaissance humanism, such standard works as *The New Cambridge Modern History,* vol. 1, *The Renaissance, 1493-1520,* edited by G. R. Potter (Cambridge, 1957), and Myron P. Gilmore's *The World of Humanism, 1453-1517 (1952;* reprint, Westport, Conn., 1983) serve as excellent guides. Wallace K. Ferguson's *The Renaissance in Historical Thought: Five Centuries* of Interpretation (Boston, 1948) provides a survey of the changing currents of historiography.

The most excellent work on the thought of the Italian humanists is Charles E. Trinkaus's *In Our Image and Likeness: Humanity and Divinity in Italian Humanist Thought,* 2 vols. (Chicago, 1970), which in a detailed, profound, and comprehensive way shows how the humanists integrated the surging secular activities and achievements of early modern Europe into the beliefs and practices of the Christian inheritance. See also his brilliant essays in *The Scope of Renaissance Humanism* (Ann Arbor, 1983). The Florentine scholar Eugenio Garin, in his *Italian Humanism: Philosophy and Civic Life in the Renaissance* (New York, 1965), offers a succinct analysis of humanism as a reflection of the new urban civic life. The most prolific author and bibliographer of Italian humanism is Paul O. Kristeller, who holds that humanism derived from the *studia humanitatis* in the Italian universities and offered an educational alternative to Scholasticism. Among his many writings one may cite the representative titles *Studies in Renaissance Thought and Letters* (Rome, 1956), *Renaissance Thought: The Classic, Scholastic and Humanistic Strains* (New York, 1961), *Eight Philosophers of the Italian Renaissance* (Stanford, Calif., 1964), and *Renaissance Thought and Its Sources* (New York, 1979). The most discussed book on civic humanism is Hans Baron's *The Crisis of the Early Italian Renaissance: Civic Humanism and Republican Liberty in an Age of Classicism and Tyranny,* rev. ed. (Princeton, 1966), in which Baron argues that the threat to Florence from the Visconti tyrants of Milan led the humanist chancellors of the city to write in defense of the republic.

Significant titles for the study of northern humanism include *Itinerarium Italicum: The Profile of the Italian Renaissance in the Mirror of Its European Transformations,* edited by Heiko A. Oberman and Thomas A. Brady (Leiden, 1975), on the reception of Italian Renaissance culture in France, the Low Countries, England, and Germany; Eckhard Bernstein's *German Humanism* (Boston, 1983); my book *The Religious Renaissance of the German Humanists* (Cambridge, Mass., 1963); James H. Overfield's *Humanism and Scholasticism in Late Medieval Germany* (Princeton, 1984); Franco Simone's *The French Renaissance: Medieval Tradition and Italian Influence in Shaping the Renaissance in France* (London, 1969); and Douglas Bush's *The Renaissance and English Humanism* (Toronto, 1939).

On the Reformation and humanism, see E. Harris Harbison's *The Christian Scholar in the Age of the Reformation* New York, 1956); Marilyn J. Harran's *Luther and Learning* (Selingsgrove, Pa., 1985); Gerhart Hoffmeister's *The Renaissance and Reformation in Germany* (New York, 1977); Manfred Hoffmann's *Martin Luther and the Modern Mind* (New York and Toronto, 1985); and Quirinus Breen's *John Calvin: A Study in French Humanism,* 2d ed. (Hamden, Conn., 1968), underscoring the continuity of humanism in Reformation thought.

LEWIS W. SPITZ

Human Sacrifice

E. B. Tylor (1832-1917) theorized that the origin of religion lay in the primitive tendency to "animate" the entire world with "soul-ghosts." Human sacrifice released these soul-ghosts so that they might join their ancestors and function as a gift to gain particular ends, as homage to a deity, or as a form of renunciation.

Theoretical Perspectives. According to W. Robertson Smith (1846-1894), sacrifice originated in totemism. Sacrifice was a communal meal shared between the people and their god, who was simultaneously their totemic animal and their kinsman. Smith postulated two types of sacrifice. The first, the honorific, was a gift either on a friendly basis of exchange or as a part of homage to a powerful deity. The second, the piacular or expiatory sacrifice, took on a mystical, sacramental flavor when a tribe's own totemic animal was offered as a redemption for a misdeed. The sacrificed animal was reborn by being assimilated into the living bodies of the people who ate it.

James G. Frazer (1854-1941) developed a theory of regeneration of fertility according to which the sacrificial offering possessed tremendous potency. Sacred kings and human vegetative gods were killed to pass on their power to a younger successor, to incorporate their potency into the living who consumed their bodies, and to prevent their decay in old age since decay would endanger the fertility of earthly existence.

In their essay on Vedic and Hebrew sacrifice (1898), Henri Hubert and Marcel Mauss considered sacrifice to be a religious act which, through the consecration of an offering, modified or transformed the condition of the person who accomplished that act by joining the divine and mortal via the sacrifice.

Nine basic purposes of human sacrifice have been commonly cited from these early theorists; (1) humans are sacrificed in order to release souls for the service of the dead ancestors; (2) human sacrifice is a gift that binds deities to people in an exchange or that serves to propitiate the gods ; (3) human sacrifice is a communion meal in which the power of life is assimilated and thus regenerated; (4) the offering of human sacrifice serves as an expiation of past transgressions and has a redemptive character; (5) it brings about atonement, (6) the regeneration of earthly fertility, or (7) immortality; (8) it transforms human conditions; and (9) it unifies the divine and mortal.

Historical Corroboration. The burials at Chan Chan (fourteenth-fifteenth centuries) in Peru are illustrative of the theme of soul-release and kinship with the dead. The themes of expiation, redemption, and communion were central in the sacrificial tradition of the early Christian church. Themes of redemption and abnegation can also be found in the self-sacrifices of the samurai in Japan.

In the Hawaiian Islands, sacrifice stands for transformation, communion, and the capacity to reorder what has been disordered.

The evidence for human sacrifice in Vedic India (c. 1500-600 BCE) is still largely contested. However, by drawing on both textual and archaeological sources, Asko Parpola has suggested that rituals that were precursors of the Agnicayana (Vedic fire sacrifice) included the killing of humans.

The themes of order and disorder play a role in Aztec sacrifice as does the theme of sacrificial exchange.

Human sacrifice may seem remote to civilized sensibilities. Nevertheless, as a human act it must be at least partly intelligible to other humans. On 18 November 1978, in Jonestown, Guyana, 914 members of the People's Temple took their own lives by means of a cyanide-laced fruit drink. Most of them did so willingly. The complex reasons for this massive sacrifice of human lives are both disturbing and challenging to one's capacity to understand. Yet some familiar themes may be recognized. The people of Jonestown, like the Christian martyrs, believed in a utopian world on "the other side." Like the samurai, they chose death as a "revolutionary act" to protest against the racism that they had failed to overcome, and like the Aztecs, they preferred to choose the time and place of their own deaths. As Jim Jones said during that "white night": "I haven't seen anybody yet didn't die. And I like to choose my own kind of death for a change."

BIBLIOGRAPHY

E. B. Tylor's theories of animism and sacrifice as a release of souls is discussed in his *Religion in Primitive Culture* (1871; Gloucester, Mass., 1970), vol. 2, pp. 1-87. The section on sacrifice (pp. 461-496) describes this phenomenon in terms of Tylor's views on its traits, mechanisms, permutations, and survivals. The short article "Sacrifice" in the *Encyclopaedia Britannica*, 9th ed. (Boston, 1886), is W. Robertson Smith's initial and concise explication of his theories of sacrifice in general, including those of human sacrifice. For James G. Frazer's theories of sacrifice, see his twelve-volume work *The Golden Bough: A Study in Magic and Religion,* 3d ed., rev. & enl. (London, 1911-1915). Henri Hubert's and Marcel Mauss's *Sacrifice: Its Nature and Function* (Chicago, 1964) is a short study of the structure and function of Vedic and Hebrew sacrificial rituals and is a classic work that has had widespread influence.

A short article by David N. Keightley, "The Religious Commitment: Shang Theology and the Genesis of Chinese Political Culture," *History of Religions* 17 (February-May 1978): 211-225, gives a concise discussion of the religious perspective that may have provided a basis for, among other things, human sacrifice in the Shang period of early China. Jacquetta Hawkes's *Atlas of Ancient Archeology* (New York, 1974) gives a short description of the Anyang site and includes a bibliography. A comprehensive discussion of martyrdom and its sacrificial theology in the early Christian church can be found in W. H. C. Frend's *Martyrdom and Persecution in the Early Church* (Oxford, 1965). H. Paul Varley's book *The Samurai* (London, 1970), written with Ivan I. Morris and Nobuko Morris, is a popular treatment of the cult of the warrior and its conceptual changes throughout Japanese history from the fourth to the twentieth century. Valerio Valeri's *Kingship and Sacrifice: Ritual and Society in Ancient Hawaii* (Chicago, 1985) is an extensive study of the structure and function of Hawaiian sacrificial rituals, with particular attention to the role of the king. Valeri includes a fine discussion of Hawaiian theology as well.

A lengthy treatment of a contemporary performance of the ancient Vedic fire ritual can be found in Frits Staal's two-volume *Agni: The Vedic Ritual of the Fire Altar* (Berkeley, 1983). This book also includes source material for the historical background of the possibility of human sacrifice in early India. It also includes an article by Asko Parpola, "The Pre-Vedic Indian Background of the Srauta Rituals" (vol. 2, pp. 41-75), which discusses the relationship between the horse sacrifice and human sacrifice.

An extraordinarily rich source of information on the Aztecs was compiled by a sixteenth-century Franciscan father, Bernardino de Sahagun, in his *Historia general de las cosas de la Nueva España,* translated by Arthur J. O. Anderson and Charles E. Dibble as *Florentine Codex: A General History of the Things of New Spain,* 13 vols. (Santa Fe, N. Mex., 1950-1982). Volumes 2, 3, and 7 are particularly good for ritualistic and mythic sources on human sacrifice.

KAY A. READ

HURRIAN RELIGION

A Near Eastern phenomenon dating mainly from the second millennium before the common era, the Hurrian religion is known more from contemporary and later Hittite documents than from native Hurrian sources. The Hurrians were an apparently Armenoid people who moved into northern Syria and northwestern Mesopotamia by at least 2300 BCE. The cities of Nuzi, in the eastern Tigris region, and Alalakh, in northern Syria, were major centers of Hurrian culture by circa 1500 BCE.

The term *Hurrian* is an ethnic designation, and *Subartu* (roughly equivalent to the Hurrian *Aranzakh*) is the Sumero-Akkadian name of the Hurrian-dominated area north and northeast of the Tigris. Mitanni was a Hurrian kingdom of the mid-second millennium in northern Syria and Iraq that had an Indo-Aryan aristocracy, and Urartu (whence Ararat) was a successor kingdom that flourished in southern Armenia circa 800 BCE. The Hurrian language, written in Sumero-Akkadian cuneiform (and, later, in Ugaritic alphabetic cuneiform), remains largely undeciphered. It is neither Semitic nor Indo-European in origin.

Some prominent European scholars would deny that the Horites of the Old Testament are Hurrians (in *Genesis* 14 the Horites are enemies of Abraham; in *Deuteronomy* 2 they are dispossessed by the Edomites; in *1 Chronicles* 1 they are the ancestors of Esau), but most American authors favor the identification. (Similar efforts to identify the Old Testament Hivites with the Hurrians are less convincing.) While admitting the presence of biblical anachronisms, the American scholars cite the extensive evidence that the Hurrians had moved down into the coastal areas and probably into Palestine at least by the Amarna age (mid-first millennium BCE). By the final quarter of the second millennium BCE there was, for example, a large and flourishing Hurrian population farther north at Ugarit, on the Syrian coast. Also notable are the remarkable parallelisms of legal and social customs between Nuzi documents of the fifteenth century BCE and the *Genesis* patriarchal narratives.

Because of the limited natively Hurrian resources, it is difficult to distinguish specifically Hurrian religious and cultic elements from those of their neighbors. The Hurrians borrowed heavily from Mesopotamian religion either by assimilating Assyro-Babylonian divinities into their own pantheon outright or by identifying these divinities with indigenous Hurrian gods. In turn, some of the Hurrian gods and religious practices were adopted by the Hittites. The Hittites also absorbed into their religion pre-Hittite elements and elements from other Anatolian peoples such as the Luwians. Since it is mostly from Hittite mythic and religious texts that scholars have access to the Hurrians, the situation is complicated indeed; many authors have resorted to referring simply to an "Anatolian religion" and have made no substantial effort to separate its strands. The major Hittite sources for Hurrian religion are the archives from Bogazköy (Hattushash), the ancient Hittite capital, and the stone carvings from the shrines at Yazilikaya, about two miles east of Bogazköy.

Hurrian culture is equally notable as a vehicle of exchange of religious concepts and practices, especially from east to west, and as a source of original contributions. The flow of such ideas over almost three millennia was generally from the Mesopotamians to the Hurrians, from the latter to the Hittites and northwestern Semites (Amorites, Canaanites, and Phoenicians), and thence ultimately to Greece and Rome. Recent scholarship suggests that the Hurrians played a far larger role in this process than had previously been detected. Because of the Indic element among their aristocracy, it is also likely that the Hurrians were purveyors of some Indo-Aryan religious motifs to the west.

At the head of the native Hurrian pantheon was the weather god Teshub, the "king of heaven," the later Urartean Tesheba. His genealogy varies somewhat, depending on the way in which the relevant Babylonian material was assimilated. In Hittite texts stemming from the Hurrian myth cycle of Kumarbi (the father of the gods) and in some other texts, there is the following typical sequence of progenitors and offspring: Alalu, (Mesopotamian) Anu, Kumarbi, and Teshub. Early Anatolian iconography uses the symbol of a bull or of lightning bolts in connection with Teshub and other weather gods. The place-name *Tishbe,* designating Elijah's home in Gilead (*1 Kgs.* 17:1), may preserve the name of Teshub, and the same may be true of the name of the Greek city of Thisbe, in Boeotia.

Teshub's consort was Hebat or Hepat, the queen of heaven. Although she is not prominent in the extant mythological texts, worship of her was very widespread, and she was syncretized with other Near Eastern goddesses in later times. In Hittite iconography she is apparently identified with the sun goddess of Arinna, whose name is not known. Hebat has a rather matronly appearance in Anatolian art, and she is frequently depicted standing on the back of a lion.

The son of Teshub and Hebat was Sharruma, whom the Hittites associated with the weather gods of Nerik and Zippalanda. At Yazilikaya the god who is represented by a pair of human legs immediately behind Hebat is doubtless Sharruma. Shaushka (sometimes Shaushga), who in Hittite myths about Kumarbi is called Teshub's sister, is prominent in the extant texts and in works of art, where she is often shown as a winged goddess standing (like Hebat) on the back of a lion. Shaushka's nature is very elusive. The Hittites identified her with the Mesopotamian Inanna-Ishtar, herself a goddess of extraordinarily complex origins and characteristics. Shaushka was said to have had two ladies-in-waiting, Ninatta and Kulitta.

Other Hurrian gods are Sheri ("day") and Hurri, or Khurri ("night") who pull Teshub's wagon and are portrayed as bulls; the moon god Kushukh (the same as the proto-Hattic Kashku) and his consort, the Mesopotamian Ningal; a sun god, Shimigi (the Urartean Shiwini); Shuwaliyatti and his consort, Nabarbi; and Teshub's vizier, Tasmisu. The later Urartean pantheon included Tesheba, Shiwini, and the national god, Haldi (Khaldi). An inscription found at Sargon II names the goddess Bagbarti as Haldi's consort.

Hurrian mythic narratives are known almost exclusively through their Hittite versions, in which the material is considerably intermixed with other Anatolian elements. The most significant myth cycle is that of the god Kumarbi. The two major texts, both in Hittite, are *Kingship in Heaven,* a tale of the struggle for divine kingship strikingly similar to Hesiod's *Theogony,* and the *Song of Ullikummi,* an epic preserved only in disconnected fragments.

In *Kingship in Heaven* Alalu is king of heaven for nine years, and Anu (the Sumerian sky god), "first among the gods," worships at his feet. Anu, however, battles with Alalu and defeats him, reigning in turn for nine years, with Kumarbi now worshiping him. Anu and Kumarbi engage in combat and Anu flees up to the sky. Kumarbi seizes him, drags him down, and bites off his genitals, laughing with glee. Anu cautions: "Do not laugh, for you have a heavy burden: I have impregnated you with the storm god [Teshub], the river Aranzakh [the Tigris], and Tasmisu ." What ensues is not clear, but apparently Teshub captures the kingship from Kumarbi.

In the *Song of Ullikummi,* Kumarbi plots against his upstart son, Teshub. Kumarbi mates with a woman in the form of a stone (or perhaps she is a mountain) and she bears him another son, Ullikummi, made of diorite. Various helper gods place Ullikummi on the shoulders of Ubelluri, an Atlas figure who stands in the midst of the sea, and the young Ullikummi grows rapidly. The sun god notices the mighty figure of Ullikummi rising from the sea and warns Teshub, who weeps bitterly. Teshub appeals to the god Ea, who eventually takes in hand the blade that had originally severed the earth from the heavens and cuts Ullikummi off at the ankles. Presumably—here the story breaks off—Kumarbi and his powerless monster-son are defeated and Teshub's rule is assured.

Other Hurrian myths with religious motifs include the folk tale of Appu of Lulluwa and his wife, prosperous folk who go to bed fully clothed and wonder why they cannot conceive! The gods set them right and they bear two sons, Good and Evil. The myth of Heldammu is a story about a snake demon of the same name whose voracious appetite leads him to devour cities and towns. He is apparently infatuated with Ishtar, who suggests he desist from such dining. The myth of Kessi (or Keshi) is the very fragmentarily preserved story of a stalwart hunter.

Little is known of the actual cultic practices and worship of the Hurrians. From syncretic Hittite texts, mostly from Bogazköy, there is evidence for sympathetic magic, bird sacrifices (also attested in texts from Ugarit), and various forms of divination. As with the Hurrian pantheon, there was clearly much Babylonian influence on the Hurrian cult, and in turn, the Hurrian cult apparently was partially assimilated into that of the Hittites.

BIBLIOGRAPHY

The most extensive treatment of Hurrian material can be found in *Götter und Mythen im Vorderen Orient,* edited by Hans Wilhelm Haussig (Stuttgart, 1965), although this book is difficult to use. Dated, but still the most useful work in English, is O. R. Gurney's *The Hittites,* 2d ed. (Harmondsworth, 1954). Michael C. Astour's *Hellenosemitica* (Leiden, 1967) documents the influence of Anatolian religion on Greek and Roman culture. The Hurrian texts from Ugarit, especially bilinguals, are presented in *Ugaritica V* (Paris, 1968) by Jean Nougayrol and others. For Hurrians and the patriarchal narratives of *Genesis,* see E. A. Speiser's edition of Genesis, volume 1 of the Anchor Bible (Garden City, N. Y., 1964). A good sketch of Hurrians in the Hebrew scriptures can be found under "Hurrians" in John L. McKenzie's *Dictionary of the Bible* (Milwaukee, 1965). The Hittite versions of Hurrian myths have been published in widely scattered specialized journals, but the most important ones are in *Ancient Near Eastern Texts relating to the Old Testament,* 3d ed., edited by James B. Pritchard (Princeton, 1969).

WILLIAM J. FULCO, S. J.

IBERIAN RELIGION

Religion of the Tartessians. The only known Iberian myth concerns the culture hero Habis, who dictated the first laws. He divided his people into seven cities; taught them how to cultivate the land and improve their food supply; and forbade the nobles to work. Like culture heroes in the Greco-Roman world, such as Romulus, Theseus, and Triptolemus, Habis was a king. Other myths of the Tartessian era are Eastern in origin and were brought by the Phoenicians.

The Phoenicians also introduced their gods to the Tartessians, who accepted them. One such goddess is Astarte, whose cult images have been found in El Ca-rambolo (Seville), Castulo (Jaén), Galera (Granada), Berrueco (Salamanca), and Pozo Moro. All of these are modeled on Oriental images of the goddess. The Phoenicians also brought with them the cult of Reshef, of whom various images have been found in Huelva, Medina de las Torres (Badajoz), Carmona (Seville), and Cádiz.

> **The Phoenicians also introduced their gods to the Tartessians, who accepted them.**

Although the Tartessians, and later the Iberians, usually copied the Semitic type of sanctuary, there was a sanctuary, dedicated to Astarte, typical of Archaic Greece on the hillside of El Carambolo. Here cattle were sacrificed and offerings made in clay vessels that probably contained liquid. In Castulo, from the end of the seventh century BCE and going into the sixth, a sanctuary of the type of the Semites of Cyprus and Israel was used.

The Phoenicians introduced the Tartessian peoples to the funeral rites of the East. The most famous necropolises of this time (the seventh and sixth centuries BCE) are those of La Joya (Huelva), Setefilla (Seville), Mede-llín (Cáceres), Castulo, and the grave of La Aliseda. All of these were built by highly semiticized indigenous peoples who followed the Phoenician rituals.

Religion of the Turdetans. From the late sixth century BCE to the arrival of the Romans at the end of the third century BCE, the Turdetan culture—one contemporary to that of the Iberians—flourished in the south of the Iberian Peninsula. The Turdetans continued the Phoenician cult to such goddesses as Astarte (depicted on jewels from Santiago de la Espada, Jaén) and to the Lady of Baza (Granada). Sanctuaries of the Tartessian era continued to be used by the Turdetans and were active until the time of Constantine.

The funeral rites of the Turdetans continued to be the same as those of the Tartessian period, but certain novelties were introduced, such as setting up images of lions or bulls to protect the tombs.

Religion of the Iberians. Iberian religion included a variety of myths and deities, many of which reflect foreign influence. For instance, an Iberian vessel from Los Villares de Caudete de las Fuentes (Valencia, second century BCE) shows that the Iberians had a myth of the battle of the giants that might have been of Greek origin. Similarly, the Phoenician symbolism that had been adopted by the Tartessians and the Turdetans was also employed by the Iberians. More important, however, were the mother goddesses who have been documented among the Iberians (at Serreta de Alcoy, Valencia, and Albufereta, Alicante).

The bust of the Lady of Elche (Alicante), a masterpiece of Iberian art dating from the fifth or fourth century BCE, is probably an image of the cult of the Carthaginian goddess Tanit, who was worshiped by the Iberians with all her Cyprian and Oriental symbolism. A painting on an Elche vessel shows that religious dances were also associated with her cult.

There was a temple in Sagunto dedicated to Artemis, from which a large linen cloth has been preserved. The foundations of another temple have been preserved in Ullastret (Gerona). Mediterranean Spain also had cave sanctuaries, which survived to Roman times and contained small ritual vessel offerings of animal sacrifices and possibly ritual meals.

The Iberians held the bull to be sacred. It is likely that the bull images of Rojales (Alicante) came from a sanctuary associated with a cult of bulls. From a temple dedicated to this animal came the famous bovine heads of Costig (Balearic Islands), from the Hellenistic period.

Religion of the Indo-Europeans in the Iberian Peninsula. Our knowledge of the religion of the Indo-European peoples of the Iberian Peninsula is sketchy. Few Greek or

Latin authors mention it. No priests are mentioned. Only Strabo (154) cites the seers of the Lusitanians, who were identifical in form to the Welsh seers. They seem to have used captives taken in battle for a type of divination. A prisoner was covered with a sack and his stomach was pierced with a sword; divination was based upon the position in which he fell. Strabo (155) also mentions the peoples of the north, who worshiped a warlike god identified with Ares and sacrificed male goats, horses, and prisoners to him. This god is frequently cited in the inscriptions from the northeast. It appears that the sanctuary of Cancho Roano (Badajoz) was dedicated to him; it was probably a blood altar, like those of Greece and central Europe.

The moon was one of the principal deities of the Celt-iberians and their neighbors (Strabo, 164). On nights of the full moon, religious dances were offered to this deity in front of the doors of houses. These dances have survived to our own day.

Few likenesses of gods have been found. Strabo (164) states that the Galicians were atheists, which must be interpreted to mean either that they had no images of their gods or that the gods' names were taboo. On the Numantia pottery there is an image of Cernunnos, the great Welsh god. A sculpture from Candelario (Salamanca) and two reliefs from Riotinto (Huelva) depict a Celtic horned god.

Most of the names of the approximately three hundred and thirty indigenous gods appear only once. These old Indo-European names are found in Latin writings and refer to their respective geographic locations and the name of a tribe or people. One god who seems to have been widely worshiped was Endovellico: there are about eighty inscriptions referring to him. His sanctuary was in San Miguel de Mota (Portugal), and several sculpted heads of him, based on Greek models, have been preserved. He was a god of medicine and cured through sleep.

In the north of Lusitania and in Galicia, the *lares* were highly venerated. Seventeen of their testimonials have been preserved, with such varied names as *Lares Anedici, Ceceaigi, Cerenaeici, Cusicilenses,* and so on. The *matres,* or *matronae* ("mothers"), are also mentioned in inscriptions, principally in the heart of the Iberian Peninsula, where we find several different names: *Matres Aufaniae* (Seville), *Brigaecae* (Burgos), *Galaicae* (Burgos), *Monitucinae* (Burgos), and so on. The goddess Nabia, addressed with various geographic epithets based on the names of peoples or tribes, was also particularly venerated. Her cult reached from the Tagus to the Cantabrico.

Three levels can be discerned in Hispanic religion: on the first level, the sacralization of tribal space is related to personifications of kinship groups; on the second, the original deity is catalyzed into different numinous entities associated with the trifunctional Indo-European sphere; and on the third level, the belief in gods is materialized by the Roman presence in the religion.

BIBLIOGRAPHY

Blázquez, José M. *Diccionario de las religiones preromanas de Hispania.* Madrid, 1975.

Blázquez, José M. *Imagen y mito: Estudios sobre religiones mediterráneas e ibéricas.* Madrid, 1977.

Blázquez, José M. *Primitivas religiones ibéricas,* vol. 2, *Religiones preromanas.* Madrid, 1983.

D'Encarnaçao, José. *Divindades indígenas sob o dominio romano em Portugal.* Lisbon, 1975.

JOSÉ M. BLÁZQUEZ
Translated from Spanish by Erica Meltzer

IBN RUSHD

IBN RUSHD (AH 520-595/1126-1198 CE), more fully Abu al-Walid Muhammad ibn Ahmad ibn Rushd, known in Latin as Averroës; Spanish-Arabic philosopher, jurist, and medical writer. His father and grandfather were distinguished lawyers in Cordova, the leading center of intellectual culture in western Islam, which came under the rule of two successive Moroccan dynasties, the Almoravids (to 1146) and the Almohads (1146-1269). He received an excellent education in the Islamic sciences and Arabic literature, then in the physical sciences, medicine, and philosophy. At a young age he composed several summaries of Aristotle's works, which were all, except for the *Politics,* available in reliable Arabic translations.

These early books drew the attention of Ibn Tufayl, the senior physician to the Almohad emir in Marrakesh, who was interested in Greek philosophy but thought some explanation of Aristotle's texts was needed. After an interview at the palace (c. 1167) Ibn Rushd received a royal commission to continue his summaries and was nominated as a judge in Seville and subsequently as chief justice in Cordova. He held these posts for most of the rest of his life and devoted his free time to writing works of varying lengths on Aristotle's books, known as "summaries," "middle commentaries," and "long commentaries." It was through these works, translated into Latin and Hebrew, that he became known in the new universities of western Europe. He aroused much controversy in Christian circles over doctrines such as the everlasting time span of the physical substance of the universe, unavoidable to a strict Aristotelian, and the single Active Intellect into which all individual human intellects are absorbed after death. Thomas Aquinas (1225-1274) was especially opposed to the latter doctrine, with enormous consequences for the vigor of individualism in Western thought. Averroës was received more favorably by other Latin philosophers and scientists of the thirteenth century, such as Siger of Brabant, Roger Bacon, and a school of "Averroists" at the University of

Padua, where his Aristotelian scholarship stimulated the growth of inductive, empirical sciences.

Ibn Rushd's impact on Islamic philosophy and theology was quite different. While interest in philosophy was growing in the European and British universities in his time, it was declining in the Arab countries and taking mystical forms in Iran. Only a few philosophers, such as Ibn Khaldun, studied the Aristotelian commentaries of Ibn Rushd. But Ibn Rushd also wrote three important works of systematic philosophy that for a while injected new life into the study of Islamic theology.

The first of these was published about 1177 under the title *Fasl al-maqal* (The Decisive Treatise). It is a short work on the legitimacy of philosophy from the standpoint of Islamic law (the *shari`ah*). Citing the authority of the Qur'an to encourage the study of nature in search for signs of divine providence and benevolence, Ibn Rushd pleads that such study must be built on all previous learning in logic and the sciences, especially that of the ancient Greeks, even though they had been pagans.

Some problems then are raised. What if the conclusions of science differ from those of revealed scripture? Since both are sources of truth, a reconciliation must be found, for "truth does not oppose truth, but accords with it and bears witness to it." This stance provides a straightforward denial of the theory of "double truth" wrongly attributed to Ibn Rushd by some European Averroists and long surviving in popular myth. Another persistent misconception has been that Ibn Rushd was concerned with conflicts between philosophy and theology. But theology *(kalam)* in Islam is merely the thought of fallible theologians, with no stamp of official approval by councils or popes. Hence Ibn Rushd felt free to attack it as the work of half-educated philosophers who merely confused people. His concern was to find harmony between philosophy and scripture itself.

These attitudes are fully confirmed by the detailed solutions he offers for three specific problems: (1) the "creation" of the universe means its continuous transformation; (2) God knows the particular facts of the world (denied by Ibn Sina) not as given objects but by his act of creating them; (3) our physical bodies are dissolved at death, but we may receive new celestial ones in a resurrection, and these would hold our reconstituted individual souls. Such conclusions were unlikely to satisfy the powerful conservative clergy. Ibn Rushd hedges his arguments by insisting that they should be taught only to those few who are qualified by their philosophic education to understand them; most people should be left alone with simpler ideas, for fear of undermining their belief in Islam altogether.

Following the *Decisive Treatise,* Ibn Rushd published a longer book with the abbreviated title *Kitab al-kashf* (Programs of Proofs), in which he outlined a system of doctrines for reasonable Muslims who are not philosophers and refuted many erroneous teachings of the theologians. This is an important work that has not yet been sufficiently studied.

In 1184 he brought out his major work of systematic philosophy, in answer to al-Ghazali's attack on the philosophers, *Tahafut al-falasifah* (The Incoherence of the Philosophers), written ninety years earlier but still influential among Muslims. Ibn Rushd's reply, which he entitled *Tahafut Al-tahafut* (The Incoherence of T*he Incoherence*), takes the form of lengthy quotations from al-Ghazali's book, followed by point-by-point refutations of his arguments. These wide-ranging dialogues discuss the creation of the world, the attributes of God, including his will and his knowledge, the nature of causation, and the fate of the soul, among many other topics. Al-Ghazali's aim had been a negative one, to show that the philosophers al-Farabi (873-950) and Ibn Sina (980-1037) had failed to prove twenty theses about God and the world that were irreligious or at least heretical from the viewpoint of Islam. These penetrating criticisms had remained unanswered. Ibn Rushd came to the defense of the original, pure philosophy of Aristotle and often repudiated in the process the arguments of the two Muslim philosophers.

As a result of his open teaching of Aristotelian philosophy and science and, no doubt, his attacks on the traditional theologians, he and a small group of fellow scientists in Cordova were indicted in 1195 on charges of irreligion. He was convicted and sentenced to exile for a few years, until he was taken by the reigning prince to Marrakesh, where he died.

In spite of his Aristotelian writings and the trial in Cordova, Ibn Rushd has generally been regarded as a sincere Muslim, as witnessed by his long career as an Islamic judge *(qadi),* a book he wrote on jurisprudence, and his own conviction about himself. Although he had few disciples or even readers in Muslim countries over the following centuries, he continued to be honored as a learned scholar on Aristotle who had made a heroic but vain effort to reconcile that philosopher with Islam. Only in the last century has interest in him revived in the Muslim world, owing largely to fresh studies by Western scholars and a revival of interest in rationalistic philosophers among an educated Muslim public.

BIBLIOGRAPHY

For translations of writings by Ibn Rushd, see *Teología de Averroës: Estudios y documentos,* translated by Manuel Alonso (Madrid, 1947), *Averroës' Tahafut al-tahafut,* 2 vols., translated by Simon van den Bergh (Oxford, 1954), and *On the Harmony of Religion and Philosophy,* edited and translated by George F. Hourani (London, 1961). Among numerous works about Ibn Rushd, two are particularly recommended: *Ibn Rochd (Averroès),* by Léon Gauthier (Paris, 1948), and *Multiple Averroès: Actes du Colloque International,* edited by Jean Jolivet (Paris, 1978).

GEORGE F. HOURANI

IBN SINA

IBN SINA (AH 370-428/980-1037 CE), more fully Abu `Ali al-Husayn ibn `Abd Allah ibn Sina, known in Latin as Avicenna; Muslim philosopher and physician. Ibn Sina was born in Afshana, a village near Bukhara.

He grew up in a bilingual environment; his native language was Farsi (Persian), but the language of his education was Arabic. The heritage of these two cultures was to lead to the two very different lines of his influence on later thinkers.

The education provided for Ibn Sina by his father was very wide-ranging, encompassing both Muslim religious studies and secular subjects from the Arabic, Greek, and Indian traditions. He began by memorizing the Qur'an and much of the didactic literature known as *adab*, then went on to study Muslim jurisprudence *(fiqh)*. His father and brother were followers of the Isma`ili branch of Shi`i Islam, which encouraged the study of hermetic philosophy, Neoplatonism, and mathematics. When he reached ten years of age, his father hired a tutor to teach him Greek philosophy and science. For the next several years he studied Aristotle's logic, Euclid's geometry, and Ptolemy's astronomy and quickly surpassed his tutor in his knowledge of these subjects.

From age fourteen or fifteen Ibn Sina continued his studies on his own. He completed his education in the following year and a half, reviewing and mastering all the branches of philosophy: logic, mathematics, natural science (or physics), and metaphysics. He was helped in his understanding of metaphysics by the commentary of Abu Nasr al-Farabi (d. 950 CE), whose commentaries on Greek philosophy and original writings had a great influence on Ibn Sina.

Ibn Sina's entry into public life began during this period of study, when he was summoned to treat the Samanid emir in Bukhara and then became part of his court. He was to spend the rest of his life—the next forty years—as a courtier, with all of the vicissitudes of fortune which that position usually entails. He held both medical and political positions in a number of courts in areas that are today part of Iran and Soviet Central Asia.

During the time of this active political involvement, Ibn Sina was also engaged in writing a large and influential corpus of works on medicine and all branches of philosophy. Many of these works have been lost, and many that exist today are unedited, so we cannot speak with certainty about his philosophical development. Most of his major writings have survived, however, with the exception of *Al-insaf* (The Judgment), in which he compared the Eastern and Western views of Aristotle's philosophy. This work was lost during his lifetime; it might have answered some of the questions about his philosophy which exist even today. The two most influential of his works, *Al-qanun fi al-tibb* (The Canon of Medicine) and *Al-shifa'* (The Healing [of the Soul]), were written over a period of years and were intended to be compendia of their subjects, medicine and philosophy. Most of his other major writings that can be dated were composed during the last thirteen years of his life, which he spent in Isfahan or on campaign with its ruler, as his official physician and courtier. During this period he composed some works in Farsi, such as the *Danish-namah-i `Ala'i* (`Ala'i Philosophy), and oversaw the translation of some of his earlier Arabic treatises into Farsi. In all, more than 130 works by Ibn Sina have survived to this day, many of them found only in manuscript form in Middle Eastern libraries.

As can be seen from his major writings, Ibn Sina wished not merely to study all knowledge but to synthesize it as well. Aristotle's philosophy, Neoplatonism, Islamic religious teachings, and quite possibly Zoroastrian concepts were all present in his intellectual background, and traces of all of these traditions can be found in his thought. In his cosmology, for example, he adopts the Neoplatonic theory of emanation from a Necessary Existent through a series of Intelligences to the Active Intelligence, from which emanate the vegetative, animal, and rational souls and the material basis of the sublunary world. This emanation is necessary, since it is implicit in the nature of the Necessary Existent, as is its absolute goodness.

The Necessary Existent is the only exception to Ibn Sina's absolute distinction between essence and existence. For the Necessary Existent, essence and existence are identical; for all other existents they are separate. Even though the Necessary Existent is the Prime Cause of the created universe, the latter is independent of the Necessary Existent, which has no control over the good and (necessary) evil resulting from the process of emanation. Thus he employs Neoplatonic ideas in his attempt to harmonize the theory of Aristotle, which regards matter as coeternal with the Prime Mover, and the belief in creation by God *ex nihilo* held by Muslims.

In his exposition of the relationship between human beings and the Necessary Existent, Ibn Sina likewise advocates a position that draws upon Neoplatonism to synthesize the various positions current in his time. Each human being, he states, is composed of body, soul, and intelligence. The highest aspect of the human being, the intelligence, desires to reach its perfection, to return to the source from which it has emanated. Passing back through the various stages of emanation, which Ibn Sina compares to passing through the stages of the mystical path, the individual intelligence ultimately achieves union with the Necessary Existent. There are similarities between this view and Aristotle's position that the greatest human happiness is found in the godlike activity of contemplation.

In recent years, students of Ibn Sina's religious thought have found traces of Zoroastrian influence, in addition to the influences of Aristotelian, Neoplatonic, and Islamic ideas. His theory of the role of the Intelligences in the universe bears a resemblance to the angelology of Zoroastrianism, and much less to the traditional Islamic view of angels.

BIBLIOGRAPHY

The best account of Ibn Sina's life and works is his brief autobiography and its continuation by his disciple Juzjani, which I have edited and translated as *The Life of Ibn Sina* (Albany, N. Y., 1974). A survey of his writings and their influence on the European and Islamic worlds is found in Soheil M. Afnan's *Avicenna: His Life and Works* (London, 1958); a work emphasizing his influence on Christian and Jewish thought is *Avicenna: Scientist and Philosopher,* edited by G. M. Wickens (London, 1952). The best analysis of his metaphysical theories is Parviz Morewedge's *The Metaphysica of Avicenna (ibn Sina)* (New York, 1973), which is a translation of the *Ilahiyat* (Metaphysics) of the *Danish-namah-i `Ala'i* with an extensive commentary and comparison with Ibn Sina's other works on metaphysics. The negative side of the debate over interpreting his works esoterically is presented by Amélie-Marie Goichon in such works as the introduction and notes in her French translation of the *Isharat: Livre des directives et remarques* (Paris, 1951) and *Le récit de Hayy ibn Yaqzan* (Paris, 1959). The case for an esoteric interpretation is made in Henry Corbin's *Avicenna and the Visionary Recital,* translated by Willard R. Trask (New York, 1960); the connection between Ibn Sina and the Ishraqi school is shown in Seyyed Hossein Nasr's *Three Muslim Sages: Avicenna, Suhrawardi, Ibn `Arabi* (Cambridge, Mass., 1964).

WILLIAM E. GOHLMAN

ICONOGRAPHY

Traditional African Iconography

Only by examining the religious iconography of a variety of cultures can one fully understand how visual images represent distinctive ways of experiencing the world for the peoples of sub-Saharan Africa.

Ancestors and Kings: Two Case Studies. On the granary doors of the Dogon people of Mali, rows of paired ancestor figures called Nommo stand watch over the precious millet stored within. Similar figures, at times androgynous, are placed next to the funeral pottery on ancestral shrines of families and on the shrine in the house of the *hogon,* the religious and temporal leader of a clan. Their elongated, ascetic bodies and proud, dispassionate faces image the Dogon's myths of origin, as well as their perception of themselves when life is filled with spiritual vitality, *nyama.*

Dogon myth, ritual, and iconography express a view of life in which, through a process of differentiation and pairing of related beings, called Nommo, an ordered, fruitful world is to be created. Creation involves human participation through ritual actions that restore life and maintain an ordered world.

Among the materials of the ritual process are village shrines representing a set of twins; shrine sculpture, as well as granary doors with their bas-relief of paired figures, snakes and lizards, zigzag patterns, and female breasts, all symbolically associated with the creation myth; geometric patterns or "signs" on shrine walls, which refer to the basic ontological properties of the world; funerary masquerades and dances through which the deceased is transformed into a venerated ancestor; and secret languages through which the incantations and texts describing the creation of the world and the appearance of death are conveyed from one generation to another.

Among the Edo people along the coastal forest of southeast Nigeria, the iconography of the Benin kingdom reflects a culture with a very different spirituality, one shaped by a monarchical tradition. The magnificently carved ivory tusks projecting from the top of the bronze memorial heads on the royal ancestral shrines (until the British punitive expedition of 1897) symbolized the powers of the king—his political authority and his supernatural gifts. While his authority depended upon statecraft and military conquest, it was by virtue of his descent from *obas* who had become gods and his possession of the coral beads, said to have been taken from the kingdom of Olokun, god of the sea, that the *oba* had *ase,* "the power to bring to pass," the power over life and death.

Over the centuries the royal guild of blacksmiths created more than 146 memorial bronze heads of deceased *obas,* queen mothers, and conquered kings and chiefs; and the royal guild of carvers portrayed on 133 ivory tusks the king, his wives, chiefs, and retainers, as well as leopards and mudfish, emblems of his power over forest and water and of his ability to move across boundaries distinguishing disparate realms.

The Cult of the Hand, *ikegobo,* also known as *ikega,* provides a means for celebrating the ability of the individual to accomplish things and, within limits, to achieve new status. Containers for offerings to the Hand, crafted in bronze for kings and in wood for titled persons, bear images of power such as an *oba* sacrificing leopards, a warrior holding the severed head of an enemy, Portuguese soldiers with guns, or the tools and emblems of office for the blacksmith, carver, or trader. All shrines for the Hand bear the image of the clenched fist, showing the ventral side, with the thumb pointing upward and outward.

Form and Meaning. Notwithstanding the particularity of traditional African iconography, the general observation may be made that it is, in general, essentially conceptual and evocative. It is not representational and illustrative, and it is not abstract.

Presence of power. Among the Igbomina Yoruba of southwestern Nigeria the costumes of the masquerades for the patrilineal ancestors, *egungun paaka,* combine materials of the forest with those of human manufacture, such as layers of richly colored cloths, bits of mirror, and beaded panels. The carved headdress portion will often meld animal and human features. Packets of magical substances will be secreted within the costume. It is the peculiar state of being of the living dead, who cross boundaries and move between two realms, who dwell in heaven yet profoundly affect the well-being of the living, that is materialized, for masquerades are created to reveal a reality not otherwise observable and to evoke an appropriate response, such as awe and dependency, on the part of the observer. Thus, among the Pende of Zaire the concept of *mahamba* signifies an object, such as a mask, or a ritual given by the ancestors to the living for the common good and through which the ancestors periodically manifest themselves and communicate with their descendants.

> Black is said to be woman's color, the color of civilized life. The glistening black surface suggests the lustrous, well-oiled skin with which the initiates will reenter the world.

A similar observation may be made about the reliquary figures of the Kota people of Gabon. Referred to as *mbulungulu,* "image of the dead," the two-dimensional figures consist of a large ovoid head above a simple, diamond-shaped wooden base. On a shrine the sculptured form is seated in a bark container holding the bones of several generations of ancestors. The ovoid face and coiffure are created by applying thin sheets or strips of brass and copper to a wooden form in a variety of interrelated geometric patterns. In every case, it is the power of the eyes that holds and penetrates the beholder, expressing the bond between the living and the deceased and the protective power of the ancestors in and for the life of the extended family.

It is not only the reality of the ancestral presence that Africa's religious art presents. Among the Egba, Egbado, and Ketu Yoruba it is the power of "our mothers" that is celebrated in the spectacle of the Efe/Gelede festival of masquerade, dance, and song at the time of the spring rains. "Our mothers," *awon iya wa,* is a collective term for female power. The total sculpted image is perceived as a visual metaphor, often understood as having multiple levels of significance.

Models of response. Ritual sculpture provides not only images of the powers on which the living depend but models for appropriate response to gods and spirits. The naked male or female, arms at their sides or touching their abdomens, on Lobi shrines in Burkina Faso (see figure 2.4) as well as the figure of a kneeling woman with a thunder ax balanced upon

her head and holding a dance wand for the Yoruba god Sango (see figure 2.2) are images of man and woman as devotees, as inspirited and powerful. They are images through which persons see their spirituality and by which their spirituality is deepened.

Perhaps the most extraordinary images of self and of personal power are carvings that incorporate magical substances (in or on images) to the extent that they alter the human form of the image. They are found for the most part among the Songye and Kongo peoples of the lower Kongo (Zaire) Basin. Some figures have an antelope horn filled with "medicines" projecting from the head, others have nails and small knives pounded into the body or a magic-holding resin box imbedded in the belly. They are visualizations in the extreme of ritual action as manipulative power.

Ritual Activity. There are essentially two types of rituals—those in which a person or group undergoes a change in status, usually referred to as rites of passage, and rituals of world maintenance through which a person or group affirms and seeks to secure in the words and actions of sacrifice a worldview.

Rites of passage. Among many African peoples the masquerade is associated with rites of passage. Among the Mende people of Sierra Leone, Nowo, a female spirit, appears in dance and masquerade to girls being initiated into the Sande (also known as Bundu) ceremonial society. As far as is known, it is the only female mask danced by a woman in Africa. While associated with the Sande society and thought of as the Sande spirit, Nowo appears in other ritual contexts. Her image is carved on the finial of the rhythm pounders used in the boys' initiation rites, on the staff carried by the leader of the men's Poro society, on the carved mace of the Mende king, as well as on divination implements, women's ritual spoon handles, and on weaving-loom pulleys. But it is only to the female initiates into Sande that Nowo appears in the fullness of the masquerade and the movements of the dance.

In the rituals, Nowo is a spiritual presence and images the beauty and power, the nobility, of woman. The head is crowned with an elaborate coiffure into which are woven cowrie shells and seed pods, symbols of wealth and fertility. Black is said to be woman's color, the color of civilized life. The glistening black surface suggests the lustrous, well-oiled skin with which the initiates will reenter the world. Nowo thus provides an image of the physical beauty and the spiritual power of woman.

World maintenance rituals. The role of iconography in Africa's rituals of world maintenance is no less important than in rites of passage. Among the Yoruba, to cite only one example, paired bronze castings of male and female figures joined at the top by a chain, *edan,* are presented to an initiate into the higher ranks of the Osugbo secret society, who worship Onile, "the owner of the house". The house is the cult house, which is a microcosm of the universe. The secret, visualized in the linking of male and female, appears to refer to a vision of life in terms of its completion and transcendence of time.

The seated male and female figures present to the viewer the signs of their power and authority, *ase*. The female holds a pair of *edan,* as she would twin children. The male figure, with clenched fists, makes the sign of greeting to Onile. Four chains with tiny bells are suspended from the sides of each figure's head. The number four, as well as multiples of four, are important in Ifa divination; Orunmila (also called Ifa), the divination god, knows the secret of creation and the sacrifices that will make one's way propitious. Above the spare, ascetic bodies, the heads of the paired figures radiate with their ase. Twelve chains are suspended from the plate below each figure. Twelve is a multiple of three and four, also numbers associated with Osugbo and Ifa ritual symbolism.

BIBLIOGRAPHY

Biebuyck, Daniel. *The Arts of Zaire,* vol. 1, *Southwestern Zaire.* Berkeley, 1985.

Brain, Robert. *Art and Society in Africa.* New York, 1980.

Dark, Philip J. C. *An Introduction to Benin Art and Technology.* Oxford, 1973.

Drewal, Henry John, and Margaret T. Drewal. *Gèlèdé: Art and Female Power among the Yoruba.* Bloomington, Ind., 1983.

Fagg, William B., and John Pemberton III. *Yoruba Sculpture of West Africa.* Edited by Bryce Holcombe. New York, 1982.

Fernandez, James. *Bwiti: An Ethnography of the Religious Imagination in Africa.* Princeton, 1982.

Fischer, Eberhard, and Hans Himmelheber. *Die Kunst der Dan.* Zurich, 1976.

Glaze, Anita J. *Art and Death in a Senufo Village.* Bloomington, Ind., 1981.

Horton, Robin. *Kalabari Sculpture.* Lagos, 1965.

Imperato, Pascal Jaems. *Dogon Cliff Dwellers: The Art of Mali's Mountain People.* New York, 1978.

Lamp, Frederick. *African Art of the West Atlantic Coast: Transition in Form and Content.* New York, 1979.

Laude, Jean. *Les arts de l'Afrique noire.* Paris, 1966. Translated by Jean Decock as *The Arts of Black Africa* (Berkeley, 1971).

Maquet, Jacques. *Civilizations of Black Africa.* Revised and translated by Joan Rayfield. New York, 1972.

McCall, Daniel F., and Edna G. Bay, eds. *African Images: Essays in African Iconology.* New York, 1975.

Meyer, Piet. *Kunst und Religion der Lobi.* Zurich, 1981.

Rattray, R. S. *Religion and Art in Ashanti.* Oxford, 1927.

Siroto, Leon. *African Spirit Images and Identities.* New York, 1976.

Thompson, Robert Farris. *African Art in Motion.* Los Angeles, 1974.

Thompson, Robert Farris. *The Four Movements of the Sun: Kongo Art in Two Worlds.* Washington, D. C., 1981.

Vogel, Susan M., ed. *For Spirits and Kings: African Art from the Paul and Ruth Tishman Collection.* New York, 1981.

Vogel, Susan M. *African Aesthetics: The Carlo Monzino Collection.* New York, 1986.

JOHN PEMBERTON III

Australian Aboriginal Iconography

Art has a central place in Australian Aboriginal religion. The substance of Aboriginal ceremonies and rituals consists of enactments of events from the Dreaming, or ancestral past, events that are conserved in the form of the songs, dances, designs, and sacred objects that belong to a particular clan or totemic cult group. Such forms are referred to collectively by a word that can be translated as "sacred law," and it is as "sacred law" that art mediates between the ancestral past and the world of living human beings.

Designs can be referred to then as "Dreaming," and they are manifestations of the ancestral past in a number of senses. Each originated as a motif painted on an ancestral being's body, as an impression left in the ground by that being, or as a form associated in some other way with ancestral creativity. The meaning of the designs on the objects often refers to the acts of ancestral creativity that gave rise to the shape of the landscape; in this respect, the designs can be said to encode Dreaming events. And finally, the designs can be a source of ancestral power. Paintings on the bodies of initiates are thought to bring the individuals closer to the spiritual domain; sacred objects rubbed against the bodies can have similar effect. In eastern Arnhem Land, upon a person's death, designs painted on his or her chest or on the coffin or bone disposal receptacle help to transfer the soul back to the ancestral world to be reincorporated within the reservoirs of spiritual power associated with a particular place. Art is linked in with the concept of the cycling of spiritual power down the generations from the ancestral past to the present that characterizes Aboriginal religious thought.

Designs in Aboriginal art exist independent of particular media. The same design in Arnhem Land may occur as a body painting, a sand sculpture, an emblem on a hollow log coffin, or an engraving on a sacred object *(rangga).* In central Australia the same design may be incised on a stone disc (tjurunga), painted on the body of a dancer in blood and down, or made into a sand sculpture. Further, it is the design that gives the object its particular ancestral connection: the designs are extensions of ancestral beings and are sometimes referred to as their "shadows." Thus, they can be used in different contexts for different purposes.

Systems of Representation. Meaning in Aboriginal art is encoded in two distinct systems of representation, one iconic and figurative, the other aniconic and geometric. The iconography of Aboriginal religious art arises out of the interplay between these two complementary systems. This distinction extends outside the area of the visual arts to dance and ceremonial action, which involve some components and actions that are essentially mimetic and represent the behavior and characteristics of natural species as well as other components that are abstract and have a conventional and nonrepresentational meaning. The balance between the figurative and the geometric varies from one region to another. The art of central Australia, of groups such as the Walbiri, the Aranda, the Pintubi, and the Pitjantjatjara, is characterized by geometric motifs, whereas western Arnhem Land in contrast is associated with a highly developed figurative tradition.

The forms of Aboriginal art are linked to its various functions in a systematic way. The figurative art presents images of the Dreaming that at one level can be readily interpreted as representations of totemic species and the forms of ancestral beings. The X-ray art of western Arnhem Land, for example, is a figurative tradition that creates images of totemic ancestors associated with particular places, thus linking them directly to the natural world. The figures are in part accurate representations of kangaroos, fish, snakes, and so on. But they are more than that. The X-ray component, representing the heart, lungs, and other internal organs of the animal, adds an element of mystery to the figures and differentiates the representations from those of ordinary animals.

Much of the ceremonial art and most of the secret art of Australia is, however, geometric in form. This property of geometric art enables it to encode the relationship between different phenomena or orders of reality. On one level, a circle in a design may represent a water hole, and the line joining it may represent a creek flowing into the water hole. On another level, the circle may be said to represent a hole dug in the ground and the line, a digging stick. On yet another level, the circle may be interpreted as the vagina of a female ancestral being and the line, the penis of a male ancestor. All three interpretations are related, for digging in the sand is an analogue for sexual intercourse, and the water hole was created through sexual intercourse between two ancestral beings in the Dreaming.

Systems of Interpretation. As people go through life they learn the meanings of designs such as the Wild Honey pattern; they associate it with places created by the ancestral being and with ceremonies that celebrate that being's creative power. For the individual the design is no longer an abstract sign but a manifestation of the ancestral being concerned. Aesthetic aspects of the design reinforce this understanding. In northeastern Arnhem Land, body paintings convey a sense of light and movement through the layering of finely cross-hatched lines across the skin surface. Similar effects are created in central Australian painting through the use of white down and the glistening effect of blood, fat, and red ocher.

Throughout much of Australia, rights to designs and other components of "sacred law" are vested in social groups that exercise some control over their use and have the responsibility to ensure that they continue to be passed down through the generations.

BIBLIOGRAPHY

Berndt, Ronald M., ed. *Australian Aboriginal Art.* New York, 1964. A volume with essays by Ted Strehlow, Charles Mountford, and Adolphus Peter Elkin that provides a broad coverage of Aboriginal art and its religious significance.

Berndt, Ronald M., Catherine H. Berndt, and John E. Stanton. *Australian Aboriginal Art: A Visual Perspective.* Sydney, 1982. A comprehensive general survey of traditional, contemporary, and innovative Aboriginal art, with some detailed descriptions and analysis.

Cooper, Carol, et al. *Aboriginal Australia.* Sydney, 1981. The best general account of Aboriginal art, it contains chapters by Carol Cooper, Howard Morphy, Nicolas Peterson, and John Mulvaney as well as a catalog of 329 illustrated items.

Elkin, A. P., Ronald M. Berndt, and Catherine H. Berndt. *Art in Arnhem Land.* Melbourne, 1950. The pioneering work on Australian Aboriginal art, placing the art of Arnhem Land in its social and mythological context.

Groger-Wurm, Helen M. *Australian Aboriginal Bark Paintings and Their Mythological Interpretation.* Canberra, 1973. The best published account of northeastern Arnhem bark paintings, with detailed interpretations of their meanings.

Morphy, Howard. *Journey to the Crocodile's Nest.* Canberra, 1984. An account of the iconography of a mortuary ceremony in Arnhem Land, detailing the structure of the ceremony and the meaning of the dances and ritual action and their relation to the themes of the ritual.

Mountford, Charles Pearcy. *Art, Myth and Symbolism.* Records of the American-Australian Scientific Expedition to Arnhem Land. Melbourne, 1956. A comprehensive collection of paintings from western and eastern Arnhem Land and Groote Eylandt. The collection is extensively documented with accounts of Aboriginal myths. The documentation is somewhat general and not always accurate, but its coverage is excellent.

Munn, Nancy D. *Walbiri Iconography.* Ithaca, N. Y., 1973. A detailed account of the representational systems of the Walbiri of central Australia and the religious symbolism of the designs. This is the classic work on the geometric art of central Australia.

Ucko, Peter J., ed. *Form in Indigenous Art.* Canberra, 1977. A collection of essays presenting by far the most comprehensive review of Aboriginal art available, covering most parts of the continent. Chapters deal with both the formal properties of Aboriginal art systems and the function of art in ritual contexts.

HOWARD MORPHY

Native American Iconography

Iconography is a living force in North American Indian religious life, past and present. Rooted in mythical imagery, it informs the content of individual dreams and nourishes the themes of contemporary Indian art. A study of the iconography of a people provides a unique opportunity to gain insight into what Werner Müller calls the "pictorial world of the soul" (*Die Religionen der Waldlandindianer Nordamerikas*, Berlin, 1956, p. 57).

Concerning the wide variety of media used, the following general distribution can be observed: in the Far North—ivory, bone, and stone; the Northeast and Southeast Woodlands—wood, bark, skin, quillwork, and beadwork; the Plains—skin, beadwork, pipestone, quillwork, and painting of bodies and horses; the Northwest Coast—cedar, ivory, argillite, blankets, and copper; California—baskets and some stone; the Southwest—sand painting, wood, stone, baskets, pottery, jewelry, and dolls.

The Cosmos. Cosmologies vary from tribe to tribe in both content and imagery. But whereas the mythical image of the universe (its cosmography) may be highly detailed, the iconographical rendering is necessarily restricted. The cosmos is most often graphically limited to those elements that characterize its basic nature and structure, including its non-visual aspects.

The most widespread symbol of the whole cosmos is the ceremonial lodge, house, or tent. The fundamental idea of the ceremonial lodge, such as the Delaware xingwikáon ("big house"), is that all of its parts symbolize, and in ritual contexts actually are, the cosmos. Usually the realms of this cosmos are interconnected with a central post, which is conceived of as extending itself like a world tree up to the heavens. Renewing such a house constitutes the actual renewal of the cosmos.

Representations of the cosmos can refer to the more subtle manifestations of the world, as in the sand paintings of the Luiseño of California, but they can also approach the reality of topographical maps, as in the sand paintings of the neighboring Diegueño. In a completely different approach to the visualization of the cosmos, the well-known Navajo sand painting of Father Sky and Mother Earth illustrates the anthropomorphic representation of the cosmos.

> **The most widespread symbol of the whole cosmos is the ceremonial lodge, house, or tent.**

Supreme Beings. Among the myriad images found in North American Indian iconography are certain divine beings whose representations cut across taxonomic groups; these include supreme beings, tricksters/culture heroes, guardian beings, and other mythical beings. Since the majestic, all-encompassing supreme being is difficult to visualize, its morphology is relatively simple. When not visualized as some object or animal intimately associated with the supreme being, its form tends to be anthropomorphic. For example, the Ojibwa song charts visualize the supreme being, Kitsi Manitu, with a pictograph of a human head, belonging to an initiate in the Mide secret society.

On the other hand, the all-pervasiveness of the supreme being among the Plains Indians can result in the use of symbols of lesser deities to represent it.

Tricksters/Culture Heroes. The most widespread iconographic trickster type is theriomorphic: Raven, Coyote, or Rabbit. The most well-known image is that of Raven among the Northwest Coast tribes, a character who encompasses all of the classical features of the trickster. He is pictured in raven-form on virtually every object throughout the Northwest, usually in the context of a mythical event that somehow affected the ancestor of the house in which the object is found. Even though the trickster is an animal, in mythical thought he can change to human form, and this process is often reflected iconographically, as with the Navajo Coyote and the Delaware and Ojibwa Rabbit.

Guardian Beings. Guardian beings associate themselves most often on a personal level with single individuals, and they function as guardians who bring blessings to their human partners. These guardians can appear in just about any form taken from the natural or the mythological world. Among the Oglala it may be necessary to paint a version of one's vision on the tipi in order to secure its validity, although generally images of the guardian are painted on shields.

In the cultures of the Far North and Arctic areas, the shaman and his guardians are a constant iconographic theme. His guardians are portrayed in several general ways: as diminutive human beings clustered near the shaman or as human faces clustered together, as a human visage under an animal visage such as seen in Alaskan masks, as an animal form reduced in size and resting on the head or shoulders of the shaman, as birdlike shamans or shamans in transformation, as flying spirits being ridden by shamans, as an animal or human being with skeletal markings, or as flying bears or other usually flightless beasts. These images are portrayed in contemporary drawings, ivory sculpture, masks, stone sculpture, bone sculpture, drumsticks, shaman staff, and so on.

Astronomical Beings. The sun, the moon, and the stars are pictured as beings throughout North America. The sun is portrayed most intensely where it is strongest, in southeastern and southwestern North America. The Hopi portray the Sun, Taawa, anthropomorphically but, in keeping with Hopi iconography, he wears a mask that consists of a circular disc fringed with radiating feathers and horsehair. This radial representation of the sun is the most common image known. The moon is usually represented in its quarter phase, although images of the full moon are sometimes found. The stars most often pictured are the Morning Star (Venus), the Pleiades, Orion, Altair, the constellation Ursa Major (which is invariably pictured as a heavenly bear), and the Milky Way.

Meteorological Beings. This group consists of Thunder, Wind, Rain, and Lightning. Thunder is often pictured as the Thunderbird, but other birds can also be used. Wind, on the other hand, is generally associated with the cardinal regions and therefore not visualized directly. Cultures with anthropocentric morphology, however, such as the Navajo and the Ojibwa, picture even this being in human shape.

Rain is usually illustrated as lines falling from cloud symbols or as a being from which rain is falling. Lightning is always shown as zigzag lines regardless of the tribe in question. The lines usually end in arrowheads.

Animal Beings. There are a number of animals which are known and visualized throughout North America, such as the bear, the deer, and the buffalo. However, other animals peculiar to a particular region are the more common iconographical subjects, such as the whales and seals of the northern coasts, or the lizards and snakes of the desert regions. The general rule is that the animal is depicted in its natural form.

The Northwest Coast Indians are the most conspicuous users of totem symbols. These symbols are represented in literally every conceivable medium: poles, house fronts, hats, aprons, spoons, bowls, settees, boat prows, spearheads, fishhooks, dagger handles, facial painting, masks, speaker staffs, paddles, drums, rattles, floats, bracelets, leggings, pipes, and gambling sticks. The question of religious significance may be resolved by the fact that the totem animal is considered either a direct ancestor of the clan or somehow associated with an ancient human ancestor. Thus the symbol at least, if not its use, has religious meaning.

Vegetation Beings. Corn is the plant most commonly visualized. The representation can simply refer to the plant itself, but frequently a maize deity is being invoked. The latter is the case throughout the Southwest, whether among the Pueblo or the Athapascan peoples. The maize deity is usually clearly anthropomorphized. Hallucinogenic plants such as peyote, jimsonweed, or the strong wild tobaccos are more or less realistically pictured; such images refer to the deities of these potent plants.

Human Beings. This category concerns not only human ancestors but also a miscellaneous collection of beings that have human form. The first type are effigies of once-living human beings. These are most commonly figured on Northwest Coast mortuary poles.

Human images can also be material expressions of the ineffable. Human images, such as dolls, can symbolize or are actually considered to be small spritelike creatures who can have an array of functions and duties and who play a part in ceremonial contexts as well. Human representations can also signify the heroes or founders of cults; such is the case with many images on Pueblo altars and other representations on Northwest Coast poles.

Geological Beings. This category of images is based on a type of religious geomorphology. The most prominent geological being envisioned is Mother Earth, although it is seldom that direct representations of it occur. In such anthropocentric iconographies as that of the Navajo, it is no problem to illustrate Mother Earth as a somewhat enlarged female human being. Usually, however, Mother Earth is symbolized by some fertility image, such as an ear of corn, or by a circle. Among the Delaware, the earth is symbolized by the giant tortoise who saved humankind from the flood and upon whose back the new earth was created by Nanabush. Sods of earth can also be used to represent Mother Earth, as in the Cheyenne buffalo-skull altar in the medicine lodge.

Another group of geological beings consists of images of mountains. Except for isolated pockets of flatlands and desert basins, most of North America is covered with mountains, and these are usually believed to be alive or at least filled with life, that is, they are the abodes of the gods. This feature of mountains is highly important and is also recognized iconographically.

[*See also* North American Indians and Shamanism.]

BIBLIOGRAPHY

There is unfortunately no comprehensive work on the religious iconography of the North American Indians. Information about iconography is found in the original ethnographic data on various peoples published in the annual reports and the bulletins of the Bureau of American Ethnology. An ethnographic approach to art in North America, with emphasis on prehistoric art, can be found in Wolfgang Haberland's *The Art of North America,* translated by Wayne Dynes (New York, 1964). General works on the art of American Indians are numerous; the most comprehensive is Norman Feder's *American Indian Art* (New York, 1971). Another useful study is Frederick J. Dockstader's *Indian Art of the Americas* (New York, 1973).

For the Indians of the Far North, see Jean Blodgett's *The Coming and Going of the Shaman: Eskimo Shamanism and Art* (Winnipeg, 1979) and Inge Kleivan and Birgitte Sonne's *Eskimos: Greenland and Canada,* "Iconography of Religions," sec. 8, fasc. 1 (Leiden, 1984). Concerning the Northeast and Southeast Woodlands tribes, see Frank G. Speck's *Montagnais Art in Birch-bark, a Circumpolar Trait,* "Museum of the American Indian, Heye Foundation, Indian Notes and Monographs," vol. 11, no. 2 (New York, 1937), and *Concerning Iconology and the Masking Complex in Eastern North America,* "University Museum Bulletin," vol. 15, no. 1 (Philadelphia, 1950). For the Plains Indians, see Ake Hultkrantz's *Prairie and Plains Indians,* "Iconography of Religions," sec. 10, fasc. 2 (Leiden, 1973), and Peter J. Powell's *Sweet Medicine: The Continuing Role of the Sacred Arrows, the Sun Dance, and the Sacred Buffalo Hat in Northern Cheyenne History,* 2 vols. (Norman, Okla., 1969). For Indians of the Northwest Coast, see Charles Marius Barbeau's *Totem Poles,* 2 vols. (Ottawa, 1950-1951), and Franz Boas's *Primitive Art* (1927; new ed., New York, 1955). Concerning the Pueblo Indians of the Southwest, see my *Hopi Indian Altar Iconography,* "Iconography of Religions," sec. 10, fasc. 4a (Leiden, 1986), and Barton Wright's *Pueblo Cultures,* "Iconography of Religions," sec. 10, fasc. 4 (Leiden, 1985). For the Navajo Indians of the Southwest, see Sam D. Gill's *Songs of Life: An Introduction to Navajo Religious Culture,* "Iconography of Religions," sec. 10, fasc. 3 (Leiden, 1979), and Gladys A. Reichard's *Navajo Medicine Man: Sandpaintings and Legends of Miguelito* (New York, 1939).

ARMIN W. GEERTZ

Mesoamerican Iconography

Each major Mesoamerican culture developed its religious imagery in a distinctive fashion, although all were historically interlinked and drew from the common pool of Mesoamerican stylistic-iconographic tradition.

Olmec. Most archaeologists agree that the earliest sophisticated religious iconographic system in Mesoamerica was that of the Olmec, which flourished between about 1200 and 400 BCE (Middle Preclassic), and was centered in the Gulf Coast region of eastern Veracruz and western Tabasco. [*See also* Olmec Religion.] Olmec style, which conveyed religious concepts imaginatively and effectively, was one of the most striking and original esthetic expressions ever achieved in pre-Hispanic Mesoamerica. Unfortunately, accurately ascertaining the connotations of the intricate Olmec symbol system presents formidable difficulties, and interpretations of prominent students often differ radically.

A major characteristic of Olmec iconography is the blending of anthropomorphic and zoomorphic features. Much of the controversy surrounding the interpretation of Olmec iconography has focused on these fused images, which often exhibit additional overtones of infantilism and dwarfism. The

> **The most popular interpretation has been that they merge feline with human characteristics. . . .**

most popular interpretation has been that they merge feline with human characteristics, and the term *were-jaguar* has become fashionable to refer to them.

Other Olmec composite beings are recognized, but opinions differ concerning the precise zoological identification of their constituent elements. A considerable case has been presented for the importance of a polymorphic, essentially saurian creature with various aspects. Called the Olmec Dragon, it has been postulated as the ancestor of a variegated family of celestial and terrestrial monsters prominent in later Mesoamerican iconography.

Izapa. A series of closely interrelated stylistic and iconographic traditions known as "Izapan," after the major site of Izapa, Chiapas, Mexico, flourished between about 500 BCE and 250 CE. Izapan iconography bears a close relationship to Olmec, from which it partly derives, but its formats are generally somewhat more complex. The style is most typically expressed by low-relief carving, commonly on the perpendicular stone monuments known as stelae, which are sometimes fronted by plain or effigy "altars."

Izapan iconography frequently displays a narrative quality in its compositions, depicting a variety of ritual-mythic scenes, some of considerable complexity. These scenes are often framed by highly stylized celestial and terrestrial registers, interpreted as monster masks. Also prominent on Izapan monuments are downward-flying, winged, anthropomorphic beings, downward-peering celestial faces, combat scenes (humanoid figures versus double-headed serpentine creatures), polymorphic bird monsters, cosmic trees with "dragon-head roots," and diminutive human ritual celebrants accompanied by various ritual paraphernalia.

Classic Lowland Maya. The Izapan tradition led directly into the most sophisticated of all Mesoamerican iconographic and stylistic traditions, that of the Classic Lowland Maya (c. 25-900 CE) [*See also* Maya Religion.] Nearly all of the most common Izapan iconographic themes were retained and often further elaborated. These included the bi- and tricephalous polymorphic celestial-terrestrial creature now frequently conceived as the "ceremonial bar" held by the rulers, the long-lipped dragon in numerous manifestations that eventually evolved into the long-nosed god of rain (Chac), celestial and terrestrial enclosing frames, cosmic trees, and avian composite creatures (serpent birds). Some deities that were clearly prototypical to those represented in the iconography of Postclassic Yucatán can be discerned in Maya religious art of the Classic period. Classic Maya stelae—accurately dated, erected at fixed intervals, and containing long hieroglyphic texts—display profile and frontal portraits of the great Maya dynasts. Their elaborate costumes are replete with religious symbols that invested them with the aura of divinity.

Monte Albán. Another major Mesoamerican cultural tradition, connected in its origins with Olmec and having some Izapan ties, was that of Monte Albán, so named from the huge site near the modern city of Oaxaca. There is general agreement that a numerous pantheon of individualized deities was portrayed, especially in the famous funerary urns, theomorphic ceramic vessels placed in tombs. Many deities are identified by their "calendric names," the day in the 260-day divinatory cycle on which they were believed to have been born. Some can be tentatively connected with deities known to have been propitiated by the Zapotec-speakers who occupied most of the area around Monte Albán at the time of the Conquest, including the basic rain-and-fertility god, Cocijo. The walls of a few tombs at Monte Albán display painted images of deities or deity impersonators, some of them identical to those depicted on the ceramic urns.

Teotihuacán. Dominating the Classic period (c. 100-750 CE) in central Mexico—and spreading its influence throughout Mesoamerica—was the dynamic civilization of Teotihuacán. Symmetry and repetitiveness were hallmarks of Teotihuacán formats, which, particularly in the murals, include processions of ritual celebrants, frontal anthropomorphic and zoomorphic images flanked by profile figures, and complex scenes involving numerous personages engaged in a variety of activities. The dominant theme was clearly the promotion of fertility, featuring what appear to have been at least two major aspects of the preeminent rain-and-fertility deity that was prototypical to the Aztec Tlaloc. Aquatic and vegetational motifs are ubiquitous.

Certain images have also been identified as discrete deities of the Aztec type, and they have often been labeled with Nahuatl names. They include Tlaloc, the rain-and-earth god; a female fertility deity who may be the prototype of various Aztec goddesses (Chalchiuhtlicue, Xochiquetzal, Teteoinnan, and others); an old fire god (Aztec Huehueteotl or Xiuhtecuhtli); the flayed god (Xipe Totec); and Tecciztecatl, the male lunar deity.

Classic Veracruz. During the Early Classic period (c. 100-600 CE), after the fade-out of the Olmec tradition in the Gulf Coast region, a distinct regional stylistic and iconographic tradition emerged, climaxing during the Late Classic and Epiclassic periods (c. 600-900 CE). It was best expressed at the major site of El Tajín, in northwest Veracruz, where a sophisticated style of relief carving, featuring double-outlined, interlocking scroll motifs, decorates a number of structures; these include the famous Pyramid of the Niches, two ball courts with friezes portraying complex sacrificial rituals connected with the ball game, and even more complicated ceremonial scenes on a series of column drums in the Building of the Columns.

The most famous exemplars of Classic Veracruz iconography are the handsomely carved stone objects worn by the ball players or replicas thereof: yokes (ball game belts); *hachas*, thin stone heads; and *palmas*, paddle-shaped stones, the latter two objects attached to the yokes worn by the players. Sculptured on these pieces are various anthropomorphic and zoomorphic beings, especially a monstrous creature probably symbolizing the earth. A major tradition of ceramic sculpture also flouished in this region during the Classic period. Some examples appear to represent deities that were prototypical to those of Postclassic times.

Xochicalco. With its apparent *floruit* during the Epiclassic period (c. 750-900 CE), the extensive hilltop site of Xochicalco flourished in what is now the state of Morelos, Mexico, and gave rise to another distinctive stylistic and iconographic tradition, mainly expressed in relief sculpture. The greatest amount of sculpture decorated one remarkable structure, the Pyramid of the Feathered Serpent. Aside from huge, undulating representations of the feathered serpent, various cross-legged seated personages, reflecting Lowland Maya stylistic influence, are depicted, many identified with their name signs and in some cases, seemingly, place signs as well. Calendric inscriptions are also present, and some scholars have suggested that the carvings may commemorate a major gathering of priests to discuss calendric reform and other ritual-religious matters.

Toltec. At the outset of the Postclassic period a new political and cultural power arose north of the Basin of Mexico, at Tollan, modern Tula, in the state of Hidalgo. Flourishing between about 900 and 1200, Tollan was a major metropolis, capital of an extensive empire. Its stylistic and iconographic tradition was quite eclectic and represented an amalgam of various earlier traditions (Teotihuacán, Xochicalco, El Tajín, and others).

Toltec iconography is known primarily from relief sculpture, decorated ceramics, figurines, and some remarkable cliff paintings at Ixtapantongo, southwest of Tula in the Toluca Basin. The militaristic flavor of Toltec imagery was also expressed by alternating representations of predatory animals and birds: jaguars, pumas, coyotes, eagles, and vultures.

Mixteca-Puebla and Aztec. During the Toltec period a new stylistic and iconographic tradition was apparently emerging to the southeast, centered in southern Puebla, Veracruz, and western Oaxaca (the Mixteca), which has been labeled "Mixteca-Puebla." During the Postclassic period its pervasive influence was felt throughout Mesoamerica, as a kind of final iconographic synthesis of the earlier traditions already described. In contrast to its predecessors, it was characterized by a greater depictive literalness, plus a particular emphasis on symbolic polychromy.

The Aztec sytlistic and iconographic tradition, which flourished in central Mexico during the last century or so before the Conquest, can be considered, from one aspect, a regional variant of Mixteca-Puebla. [*See also* Aztec Religion.] It differs principally in displaying an even greater naturalism in human and animal imagery. It also was expressed much more frequently in monumental three-dimensional stone sculpture, particularly deity images. Virtually all of its principal symbols have been correctly identified as well as the great majority of the numerous deity depictions, which include almost every member of the crowded pantheon mentioned in the primary sources.

BIBLIOGRAPHY

Acosta, Jorge R. "Interpretación de algunos de los datos obtenidos en Tula relativos a la epoca Tolteca." *Revista mexicana de estudios antropológicos* 14, pt. 2 (1956-1957): 75-110. A useful, well-illustrated summary of the archaeological aspect of Toltec culture by the principal excavator of Tula. Includes some discussion of the iconography.

Caso, Alfonso. "Calendario y escritura en Xochicalco." *Revista mexicana de estudios antropológicos* 18 (1962): 49-79. An important study of Xochicalco iconography, focusing on the hieroglyphic writing system and calendric inscriptions.

Caso, Alfonso. "Sculpture and Mural Painting of Oaxaca." In *Handbook of Middle American Indians,* edited by Robert Wauchope and Gordon R. Willey, vol. 3, pp. 849-870. Austin, 1965. Well-illustrated discussion of Monte Albán iconography through sculpture and wall paintings.

Caso, Alfonso. "Dioses y signos teotihuacanos." In *Teotihuacan: Onceava Mesa Redonda, Sociedad Mexicana de Antropología,* pp. 249-279. Mexico City, 1966. A broad survey of Teotihua-cán iconography, extensively illustrated.

Caso, Alfonso, and Ignacio Bernal. *Urnas de Oaxaca.* Memorias del Instituto Nacional de Antropología e Historia, no. 2. Mexico City, 1952. The classic study of the effigy funerary urns of the Monte Albán tradition, illustrated with hundreds of photographs and drawings.

Coe, Michael D. *The Maya Scribe and His World.* New York, 1973. A beautifully illustrated catalog featuring principally Late Classic Lowland Maya painted ceramic vessels, with perceptive analyses of their complex iconographic formats and accompanying hieroglyphic texts.

Joralemon, Peter David. *A Study of Olmec Iconography.* Dumbarton Oaks, Studies in Pre-Columbian Art and Archaeology, no. 7. Washington, D. C., 1971. The most comprehensive study of Olmec iconography, profusely illustrated by line drawings. Includes "A Dictionary of Olmec Motifs and Symbols."

Kampen, Michael Edwin. *The Sculptures of El Tajín, Veracruz, Mexico.* Gainesville, Fla., 1972. An important monograph describing and analyzing the sculptural art of the greatest of the Classic Veracruz sites. Includes a catalog of all known Tajín carvings, illustrated with excellent line drawings.

Kubler, George. *The Iconography of the Art of Teotihaucan.* Dumbarton Oaks Studies in Pre-Columbian Art and Archaeology, no. 4. Washington, D. C., 1967. Significant pioneer discussion and analysis of Teotihuacán iconography, utilizing a linguistic model requiring that "each form be examined for its grammatical function, whether noun, adjective, or verb." Includes a table of approximately one hundred Teotihuacán motifs and themes.

Kubler, George. *Studies in Classic Maya Iconography.* Memoirs of the Connecticut Academy of Arts and Sciences, vol. 18. New Haven, 1969. Preliminary but broad-ranging consideration of Classic Lowland Maya iconography, with special attention to dynastic ceremonies, ritual images, and the "triadic sign."

Nicholson, H. B. "The Mixteca-Puebla Concept in Mesoamerican Archaeology: A Re-Examination." In *Men and Cultures,* edited by Anthony F. C. Wallace, pp. 612-617. Philadelphia, 1960. Discusses and defines the Postclassic Mesoamerican Mixteca-Puebla stylistic and iconographic tradition conceptualized as a "horizon style," with some consideration of its origins and the mechanism of its diffusion.

Nicholson, H. B. "The Iconography of Classic Central Veracruz Ceramic Sculptures." In *Ancient Art of Veracruz: An Exhibit Sponsored by the Ethnic Arts Council of Los Angeles,* pp. 13-17. Los Angeles, 1971. A concise discussion of the iconography of Classic Veracruz ceramic figures, with suggestions that some of them probably represent specific deities.

Nicholson, H. B. "The Late Pre-Hispanic Central Mexican (Aztec) Iconographic System." In *The Iconography of Middle American Sculpture,* pp. 72-97. New York, 1973. Summary discussion of the iconographic system of Late Postclassic central Mexico, with specification of its leading diagnostics.

Parsons, Lee A. "Post-Olmec Stone Sculpture: The Olmec-Izapan Transition of the Southern Pacific Coast and Highlands." In *The Olmec and Their Neighbors,* edited by Elizabeth P. Benson, pp. 257-288. Washington, D. C., 1981. Perceptive, well-illustrated discussion of the Izapan and related stylistic and iconographic traditions as manifested in the Pacific Slope region of Chiapas-Guatemala and adjacent highlands.

Quirarte, Jacinto. *Izapan-Style Art: A Study of Its Form and Meaning.* Dumbarton Oaks Studies in Pre-Columbian Art and Archaeology, no. 10. Washington, D. C., 1973. A significant pioneering attempt to define the leading formal and iconographic features of the Izapan stylistic and iconographic tradition; well illustrated with numerous line drawings.

Robicsek, Francis, and Donald M. Hales. *The Maya Book of the Dead: The Ceramic Codex; The Corpus of Codex Style Ceramics of the Late Classic Period.* Charlottesville, Va., 1981. Extensive album of photographs (including full-surface rollouts and color) of Late Classic Lowland Maya ceramic vessels with scenes and hieroglyphic texts related to the surviving ritual-divinatory paper screenfolds. Includes iconographic analysis and preliminary decipherment of the texts.

H. B. NICHOLSON

Mesopotamian Iconography

Any discussion of the religious iconography of ancient Mesopotamia is hampered by the fact that we have, on the one hand, religious texts for which we possess no visual counterparts and, on the other, representations—sometimes extremely elaborate ones—for which we lack all written documentation. Our best sources for religious iconography are therefore the small objects that are more likely to have survived. Plaques and figurines made of local clay often illustrate a more popular type of religion. At certain periods painted pottery is the vehicle for representations that have religious significance. Decorated votive metal vessels, stone maces, and small bronze figures also occasionally survive.

Early Imagery. Nude female figurines are among the earliest artifacts to which a religious significance can be attached. Among the prehistoric figurines of Mesopotamia are the tall, thin, clay "lizard" figures with elongated heads, coffee-bean eyes, slit mouths, and clay pellets decorating the shoulders. "Lizard" figurines have been found at southern sites in both male and female versions though the latter is dominant. Farther north, at Tell al-Sawwan, female figurines and male sexual organs were carved from alabaster. These figurines also have elongated heads and prominent eyes but are more rounded in shape. In the north, clay figurines often have abbreviated heads, and the emphasis is on a well-rounded, full-breasted body. An opposite trend is attested, however, at Tell Brak, where "spectacle" or "eye idols" were found in a late fourth-millennium temple. Here the eyes are emphasized to the exclusion of everything else, and there has even been debate as to whether they might not, in fact, represent huts.

Animal combats. One motif that seems to have had a special significance throughout Mesopotamian prehistory and history shows a heroic male figure in conflict with wild animals. A pot of the Halaf period (c. 4500 BCE) shows an archer aiming at a bull and a feline. A figure traditionally known as the priest-king appears on a relief and a seal of the Uruk period (late fourth millennium) shooting or spearing lions and bulls, and the same theme reappears in the Assyrian reliefs of the ninth and seventh centuries BCE and forms the subject of the Assyrian royal seal.

At certain periods the theme of animal combat became dominant in the iconographic repertoire. For several centuries during the third millennium, and at various times later on, heroes are shown protecting sheep, goats, and cattle from the attack of lions and other predators.

Early urban imagery. The advent of an organized urban society in the second half of the fourth millennium led to the development of more varied vehicles for the transmission of iconographic concepts. Some examples of monumental sculpture have survived, among them an almost lifesize female head which was probably part of a cult statue. Uruk, where the head was found, was the center of worship of the fertility goddess Inanna, and a tall vase is decorated with a scene where the robed goddess in anthropomorphic form, accompanied by her symbol, the reed bundle, receives offerings from a naked priest and a (damaged) figure who wears a crosshatched skirt.

Other significant motifs are known only from their impression on clay sealings. It seems that certain types of seals were used by particular branches of temple administration: boating scenes used by those connected with fishing and waterways, animal file seals for those dealing with herds.

Later Developments. Banquet scenes were especially popular in Early Dynastic times (mid-third millennium) and are often associated with scenes of war: seals, plaques, and mosaic panels depict these ritual banquets, which are probably to be interpreted as victory feasts in some contexts and as marriage feasts in others. They are to be distinguished from later Neo-Hittite funerary meals, but the preparation of food for the gods is a favorite iconographic motif in the second half of the second and early first millennia BCE.

Deities and their attributes. In Akkadian times (2340-2180 BCE) distinct iconographies were established for the more prominent deities, and their position facing left became fixed, though the detailed representations of myths on seals of this period are generally incomprehensible to us. The role of some deities can be identified by the attributes they hold, others by the sprigs of vegetation, streams of water, rays, or weapons which issue from their shoulders. Often these serve only to establish that the deity is, for instance, a vegetation or a warrior god without being more specific.

In fact, it is only a very few representations which can actually be identified with any degree of certainty. Plows are frequently depicted, especially on Akkadian seals, but this is not always a shorthand for Ninurta (who is, however, depicted in a chariot on the famous Stela of the Vultures). Warrior gods on Old Babylonian seals are probably also to be equated with him in many cases, and he appears on Assyrian reliefs. The temple of Ninhursaga at Al-`Ubaid was decorated with friezes showing dairy scenes. There are clear representations of the water god Enki/Ea in his watery house or with water flowing from his shoulders on Akkadian seals. His Janus-faced attendant, Usmu, is also shown, as is the Zu bird who stole the tablets of destiny.

The moon god Nanna/Sin was a major deity, but there are surprisingly few representations of him. A stela from Ur and one of the wall paintings from the palace of Mari are perhaps the most convincing representations of this god. The iconography of the sun god Utu/Shamash is, however, well attested. He is frequently shown with rays rising from his shoulders, placing his foot on a mountain and holding the saw-toothed knife with which he has just cut his way through the mountains of the east. Often he is accompanied by his animal attribute, the human-headed bull (probably a bison), or by attendants who hold open the gates of dawn. Scorpions likewise can be associated with the sun god, but they are also symbols of fertility and attributes of the goddess of oaths, Ishara.

From Old Babylonian times onward the storm god Adad occurs frequently, often standing on a bull and holding a lightning fork. His consort Shala may appear briefly, on seals and in the form of mass-produced clay figurines of the Old Babylonian period, as a nude goddess, shown frontally. Ishtar (Inanna), the Uruk fertility goddess, appears on Akkadian seals holding a date cluster, calling down rain, and often winged with weapons rising from her shoulders as goddess of war.

BIBLIOGRAPHY

There is no recent study of Mesopotamian religious iconography. An early attempt at bringing order out of chaos is Elizabeth Douglas Van Buren's *Symbols of the Gods in Mesopotamian Art* (Rome, 1945). This is still a useful book but has been superseded to a large extent by Ursula Seidl's detailed study of the Babylonian boundary stones, *Die babylonischen Kudurru-Reliefs* (Berlin, 1968). The symbols which appear on these stones are analyzed, the various possible interpretations and identifications are discussed, and examples from all periods are listed.

Most studies on religious iconography have appeared in catalogs of cylinder seals, beginning with Henri Frankfort's pioneering attempt to relate the seal designs to the texts in his *Cylinder Seals* (London, 1939). Edith Porada's *Corpus of Ancient Near Eastern Seals in North American Collections,* vol. 1, *The Pierpont Morgan Library Collection* (Washington, D. C., 1948), is also a mine of information. The same author has more recently edited *Ancient Art in Seals* (Princeton, 1980), which includes an essay by Pierre Amiet relating the iconography of Akkadian seals to a seasonal cycle. In her introduction Porada summarizes the advances in glyptic studies which have taken place since Frankfort wrote. Many of the objects referred to here are illustrated in André Parrot's *Sumer* (London, 1960) and *Nineveh and Babylon* (New York, 1961) or in J. B. Pritchard's *The Ancient Near East in Pictures relating to the Old Testament* (Princeton, 1969).

DOMINIQUE COLLON

Egyptian Iconography

The principal iconographic sources for ancient Egyptian religion are the representations of scenes, both ritual and mythological, carved in relief or painted on the walls of Egyptian temples and tombs, as well as the numerous images and statues of gods and pharaohs. Additionally, there are many objects of ritual or practical function decorated with carved or painted religious motifs, and finally, numerous hieroglyphic signs belonging to the Egyptian writing system are representations of gods, religious symbols, and ritual objects. These types of sources remain constant throughout the more than three thousand years of ancient Egyptian history from the Old Kingdom to the Roman period (c. 3000 BCE-395 CE).

Scenes carved on the walls of tombs and temples as well as on furniture and ritual objects most frequently show the gods in the company of a king making offerings or performing other ritual acts (such as censing, purifying with water, or embracing the god). All representations of the king facing a divinity illustrate the ongoing relationship of reciprocity between them. In return for the precious object that he presents to the god, the pharaoh receives symbols of life, strength, stability, many years of kingship, and the like.

Statuary. Numerous Egyptian statues made of all possible materials, such as stone, wood, gold, bronze, and faience, represent one, two, or three gods often accompanied by a king. Both gods and king wear crowns and hold characteristic insignia, among which the most frequent are the sign of life (ankh) and various types of scepters. Many elements of the king's dress are identical with those of the gods, thus visualizing the divine aspects of the monarch's nature.

The size of the statues varies according to their function. Small bronze statuettes of votive character were common, especially in the first millennium BCE. Many represent animals sacred to Egyptian gods; sometimes these figures are set on boxes containing mummies of the animals represented. The mummified bodies of larger animals, such as bulls, ibis, crocodiles, and cats, have been found buried within special necropolises near places connected with the cults of various gods.

Large stone statues served as cult objects in Egyptian temples. Pairs of colossal effigies of the seated king usually stood in front of the temple pylons. The sphinx, with its body of a lion and head of the king, was often placed in the front of the temple to symbolize the monarch's identity as solar god. Rows of sphinxes lined both sides of processional ways leading to the principal temple entrances.

Funerary Art. Another important part of our knowledge about ancient Egyptian iconography comes from the decoration of Egyptian tombs and coffins that comprises the great Egyptian religious "books"—literary compositions that combine spells of magical, mythological, and ritual character with pictures illustrating Egyptian visions of the netherworld. The most ancient of these "books" are the Pyramid Texts carved on the walls of some of the rooms inside the royal pyramids (Old Kingdom, c. 3000-2200 BCE).

Temples. As the abode of the gods, Egyptian temples were accessible only to the kings and priests. The king, considered the mediator between the gods and the people, is usually shown in front of the gods in the ritual scenes that decorate the temple walls.

The sanctuary, usually situated at the far end of the temple along its axis, contained the sacred image of the god to whom the temple was dedicated. The statue of Amun-Re, the chief divinity of Thebes and the state divinity since the time of the New Kingdom, stood inside a shrine on a portable bark placed upon a sled.

> The king, considered the mediator between the gods and the people, is usually shown in front of the gods in the ritual scenes that decorate the temple walls.

Narrative cycles. Many temple scenes form standardized sequences of pictures showing summarily, sometimes almost symbolically, successive episodes of mythicized rituals that often refer to important historical events, such as the miraculous birth of the king, his coronation, his victories over enemies, his jubilee, and the founding of the temple. These representations appear in the inner parts of the temple, together with tableaux depicting the daily ritual performed before the statue of the temple's principal deity and scenes showing various offerings being made.

The interior of the walls enclosing the courts are often decorated with episodes of the most important feasts, while the grandiose tableaux found on the exterior of the walls and on the gates (frequently in the form of pylons) commonly illustrate the king's military achievements.

Symbolic motifs. In addition to these scenes referring to particular events, the temple walls are also decorated with numerous motifs of a more symbolic nature, which give visual form to religious, political, or geographical ideas. The so-called geographical processions, for instance, symbolize the provinces of Egypt in the form of hefty divinities personifying the Nile, each bearing offerings in their hands.

Various iconographic patterns invented by the Egyptians give shape to the idea of the unification of Lower and Upper Egypt. The central motif of a great number of them is the heraldic symbol called *sma-tawy*, which is composed of two plants, papyrus (for Lower Egypt) and a kind of bulrush (for Upper Egypt), bound together around the spinal cord and the lungs of an animal. Two divine personifications of the Nile—the motive power of this unification—are often shown holding and binding together the two plants.

The netherworld. The Egyptian realm of the dead lay in the west. The best illustration of ancient Egyptian visual concepts of the netherworld appears in the decoration of New Kingdom royal and noble tombs situated in west Thebes; these iconographic patterns remained a favorite and repeated subject right up to the Roman period. Of the two principal groups of scenes depicted there, the first, usually found in the first room of the tomb, refers to various episodes in the earthly life of the deceased, including such religious ceremonies or feasts as the Beautiful Feast of the Valley, the royal jubilee, the New Year festival, or the harvest feast. Included in all these scenes are processions, offerings (including burnt offerings), incense burning, and performances with playing, singing, and dancing. Of special importance among Egyptian musicians was the harpist, who came to be represented by the squatting figure of a blind man shown in profile.

The other group of scenes, found in the inner room, illustrates various episodes of the funeral rites.

Cult of the dead. Of particular importance in every tomb were the places intended for the cult of the deceased. These featured niches with statues of the dead person (and sometimes of members of his family), stelae often depicting the deceased adoring and making offerings to various gods or royal personages, and lastly, false-door stelae constituting a symbolic passage between the realm of the dead and the world of the living.

Most important in each tomb, however, was the burial chamber, commonly situated underneath the accessible rooms at the bottom of a deep vertical shaft. Here were contained the sarcophagus with the mummy of the deceased and all the funerary offerings, including the four Canopic jars for the viscera of the deceased, the mummiform figures known as *shawabtis (ushabtis),* a copy of the *Book of Going Forth by Day* written on papyrus, and various ritual objects. The sarcophagi and coffins, made of wood or stone, took the form of cubical or body-shaped cases decorated with painted or carved religious motifs. The four Canopic jars were associated with the four sons of the royal deity Horus, with the four cardinal directions, and with the four protective goddesses; they each had distinctive stoppers, often representing the heads of the four sons of Horus or simply anthropomorphic heads.

BIBLIOGRAPHY

The most complete and up-to-date compendium of information concerning the iconography of ancient Egyptian religion is *Egypt* (Leiden, forthcoming), volume 16 in the series "Iconography of Religions," edited by the Institute of Religious Iconography, Groningen. Each of the thirteen fascicles of this volume, arranged in chronological sequence, contains rich photographic materials and a detailed bibliography. Encyclopedic information on particular subjects can be found in Hans Bonnet's *Reallexikon der ägyptischen Religionsgeschichte,* 2d ed. (Munich, 1971), and in *Lexikon der Ägyptologie,* 6 vols., edited by Hans Wolfgang Helck, Eberhard Otto, and Wolfhart Westendorf (Wiesbaden, 1972-). Bonnet's *Ägyptische Religion* (Leipzig, 1924) may be consulted as a valuable complement to these publications. There is an amazing scarcity of scientific literature in English, but see Manfred Lurker's *The Gods and Symbols of Ancient Egypt,* revised by Peter A. Clayton (London, 1980).

KAROL MYSLIWIEC

Greco-Roman Iconography

The religious structures of both Greeks and Romans conform to the typical patterns of divinity and belief found among the Indo-European peoples. Most notable of these is an organized pantheon of deities related by birth or marriage and presided over by a god of the sky who is both ruler and father (e.g., Zeus Pater and Jupiter). Nevertheless, although it is clear that such gods accompanied the movement of the Indo-Europeans into Greece and Italy, it is impossible to state with certainty what iconographic representation, if any, was used to worship them during this earliest period.

Minoan-Mycenaean Iconography (2000-1200 BCE). The study of Cretan (Minoan) religion may be compared to a picture book without a text. The two symbols of Minoan civilization, the double ax and the horns of consecration, clearly had religious significance, perhaps as tools of worship, but their function is not understood. From the archaeological evidence, however, which includes frescoes, seals, and figurines, one may conclude that the representation of the divine was both anthropomorphic and theriomorphic. Found are depictions of female deities encoiled by snakes or with birds perched upon their heads; these figures may explain the prominence of snakes in later Greek religion as well as the association of Greek deities with specific birds. In addition, animal-headed figures reminiscent of contemporaneous Egyptian material have been uncovered. One such type, a bull-headed male, may be the source for the Greek myth of the Minotaur. Also found are representations of demonlike creatures who appear to be performing various ritual acts; these have been cited as evidence of Mesopotamian influence. A number of seals portray the figures both of a huntress, who is called "mistress of the beasts" and whom the Greeks associated with Artemis, and of a male deity, who stands grasping an animal by the throat in each hand. Finally, the seals present strong evidence for the existence of tree cults and pillar cults, the survival of which perhaps may be seen in the Greek myths about dryads, the woodland spirits of nature who inhabit trees.

Archaic and Classical Iconography. There is a great deal of evidence to indicate that, in the conservative ritual of

Greek religion, the older forms of representation of the divine persisted. Aniconic images of the divine, such as the *omphalos* at Delphi, provide proof of its survival. This stone, which in Greek myth was described as the one that Rhea gave to Kronos to swallow when he wished to devour his infant son Zeus, and that the ruler of the Olympians then placed at the center of the world, is clearly a baetyl, a sacred stone that contains the power of the divine. Similarly, the widespread appearance of the herm, a pillar on which was carved an erect phallus and that acted as an agent of fertility and apotropaic magic, points to the survival of earlier conceptions of the divine. Myth also provides a clear illumination of the remnants of a theriomorphic iconography.

The amalgamation of a number of functional deities during the Archaic and Classical periods can be seen in the great variety of epithets by which each god was addressed. Many of the epithets of the Olympians can be considered as proof of older iconographic substrata that reveal functions closely linked to the world of nature: horselike Poseidon, owl-eyed Athena, cow-eyed Hera, cloud-gathering Zeus.

The evolution of the form and content of Greek iconography as a means of expressing spiritual ideals generally parallels that of Greek art, especially in sculpture. The earliest religious sculpture and architecture were executed in wood and have vanished; but in the the seventh century BCE we see the development of monumental stone architecture and sculpture. The most representative forms of sculpture are the *kouros* (male) and the *koure* (female) figures that stand rigidly with stylized features and dress. Perhaps votive offerings, they have been variously identified as divine or human but may represent something in between: an idealized existence shared by gods and mortals alike.

As the institutions of the state evolved, the original gods of nature were made citizens of the polis and given civic functions as protectors and benefactors of the city. Thus, the gold and ivory statue of Athena in the Parthenon portrayed the armed goddess in full regalia as the protector and patron of Athenian civilization, the goddess who had led her people to victory against the Persians. The Parthenon itself is a symbol of the bond between Athena and her city, for the temple frieze depicts the procession of the Panathenaea, a festival held in honor of both the goddess and the powerful city that worshiped her.

Hellenistic and Roman Iconography. The declining political fortunes of the Greek states after the Peloponnesian War paved the way for the rise of Macedon and the magnificent career of Alexander the Great. Religious iconography in the Hellenistic period presents a curious admixture of Eastern and Western values that expressed themselves in the formal magnificence of the tomb of Mausolus at Halicarnassus as well as in the representations of Aphrodite that emphasize her naked human beauty, in sleeping satyrs and playful cupids as well as in the struggling Laocoön

doomed by the gods. The Great Altar of Zeus at Pergamum, with its wide monumental stairway, was encompassed by a frieze that, in depicting the ancient Greek myth of the war between the Olympians and the Giants, displays a remarkable range and intensity of human emotions.

Roman religion seems to have remained rooted in nature to a much greater extent than civic Greek religion had; the early anthropomorphic representations of Mars and Jupiter are exceptions, perhaps occasioned by their clear identification with the political rather than the agricultural life of the Roman people. The conservative values of Roman religion not only inhibited the development of a distinctive iconography but at the same time led to the adoption of those elements in Hellenistic art that seemed best to reflect those values. Although Augustus's attempt to recreate the old Roman religious values through the resurrection of archaic rituals and priesthoods and the rebuilding of ancient temples and shrines was ultimately unsuccessful, his Altar of Augustan Peace (Ara Pacis) illustrates the Roman understanding of the connection between traditional expressions of piety and political success. One of its panels depicts Augustus offering solemn sacrifice; another reveals Mother Earth holding on her lap her fruitful gifts. The peace and prosperity of mortals and gods are attributed to Augustus's piety and devotion.

BIBLIOGRAPHY

Boardman, John. *Greek Art*. Rev. ed. New York, 1973. A useful and thorough survey of the development of Greek art forms from the Mycenaean age through the Hellenistic period.

Dumézil, Georges. *Archaic Roman Religion*. 2 vols. Translated by Philip Krapp. Chicago, 1970. An analysis of early Roman religion that depends primarily on a structural analysis of Indo-European religious institutions and mythologies.

Farnell, Lewis R. *The Cults of the Greek States* (1896-1909). 5 vols. New Rochelle, N. Y., 1977. Although lacking recent archaeological and linguistic evidence, this work remains the standard reference for ancient sources on Greek religion in all its forms.

Guthrie, W. K. C. *The Greeks and Their Gods*. London, 1950. A well-balanced view of the origins of each of the Greek gods, with detailed discussion of the multidimensional roles of the divine in Greek society.

Hauser, Arnold. *The Social History of Art*, vol. 1. New York, 1951. A combination of art criticism and social analysis, Hauser's work attempts to define the cultural forces that determine artistic sensibilities.

Nilsson, Martin P. *A History of Greek Religion* (1925). Translated by F. J. Fielden. 2d ed. Oxford, 1949. Emphasizes the continuity of tradition between Minoan and Mycenaean ritual and practice.

Nilsson, Martin P. *Greek Piety*. Translated by Herbert Jennings Rose. Oxford, 1948. This short work presents a thoughtful study of the various social, historical, and political forces that shaped Greek attitudes about the nature of the divine.

Peters, F. E. *The Harvest of Hellenism*. New York, 1970. A historical, cultural, and religious survey of the Greek and Roman world after Alexander.

TAMARA M. GREEN

Hindu Iconography

Visnu, Siva, and Devi are the basic visual images of Hinduism. Each of these deities is worshiped in a concrete image *(murti)* that can be seen and touched. The image is conceived in anthropomorphic terms but at the same time transcends human appearance. With certain exceptions, Hindu images have more than two arms. Their hands, posed in definite gestures, hold the attributes that connote the deity's power and establish its identity. While the images are concrete in their substantiality, they are but a means of conjuring up the presence of deity: this is their essential function. The image serves as a *yantra,* an "instrument" that allows the beholder to catch a reflection of the deity whose effulgence transcends what the physical eye can see. Visnu, Siva, and Devi (the Goddess) are represented in many types of images, for each of these main deities has multiple forms or aspects.

Siva. The main object of Siva worship is the *linga.* The word *linga* means "sign," here a sign in the shape of a cylinder with a rounded top. The word *linga* also means "phallus" however; some of the earliest Siva *lingas* are explicitly phallus shaped. However, this sign is not worshiped in its mere anthropomorphic reference. It stands for creativity on every level—biological, psychological, and cosmic—as a symbol of the creative seed that will flow into creation or be restrained, transmuted, and absorbed within the body of the yogin and of Siva, the lord of yogins.

The images of Siva visualize the god's two complementary natures: his grace and his terror. Like all Hindu divine images, that of Siva has multiple arms; their basic number, four, implies the four cosmic directions over which extends the power of deity in manifestation. Siva's image of peace and serenity in one of its forms, Daksinamurti, is that of the teacher. Seated at ease under the cosmic tree, he teaches the sages yoga, gnosis, music, and all the sciences. In another image, standing as Pasupati, "lord of animals," Siva protects all the "animals," including the human soul.

The *linga* as both abstract symbol and partly anthropomorphic shape is the main Saiva cult object. In some of the sculptures, a human head adheres to the cylinder of the *linga,* or four heads are positioned in the cardinal directions, implying a fifth head (rarely represented) on top. Five is Siva's sacred number, and the entire Saiva ontology—the five senses, five elements, five directions of space, and further hierarchic pentads—is visualized in the iconic-aniconic, five-faced *linga.*

The facial physiognomy of the image reflects the nature of the particular aspect or manifestation of the god. His calm, inscrutable mien as well as Bhairava's distorted countenance are shown with many nuances of expression that convey the significance of each particular manifestation, defined as it is by specific attributes and cognizances. Siva's crown is his own hair. He is the ascetic god, and his crown shows the long strands of the ascetic's uncut hair piled high on his head in an infinite variety of patterns, adorned by serpents, the crescent moon, and the miniature figure of the celestial river Ganga (Ganges) personified.

An essential cognizance particular to Siva among gods—though not present in every Siva image—is the god's third eye (which also graces deities derived from the Siva concept, such as Devi and Ganesa). Vertically set in the middle of Siva's forehead above sun and moon, his two other eyes, the third eye connotes the fire of the ascetic god.

Visnu. The pervader and maintainer of the universe is represented by his anthropomorphic image in the innermost sanctuary. Invariably the image stands straight like a pillar, and its four arms symmetrically hold the god's main attributes: conch, wheel, mace, and lotus. In addition to the standing image, Visnu may assume two other positions, seated and recumbent. Indeed, no other Hindu god—except a Visnu-derived allegory, Yoganidra—is shown recumbent, and

> **The images of Siva visualize the god's two complementary natures: his grace and his terror.**

together, these three positions render the mode of the god's pervasive presence in the cosmos.

Visnu is also conceived in his five-fold aspect: as ultimate, transcendental reality *(para);* in his emanation *(vyuha);* in his incarnation *(vibhava);* as innermost within man *(antaryamin),* the inner controller; and as *arca* or consecrated image, this fifth instance being an *avatara,* a "descent" into matter.

Devi. The Great Goddess, Devi, represents the creative principle worshiped as female. She is Sakti, the all-pervading energy, the power to be, the power of causation, cognition, will, and experience. She is the power of all the gods; she wields all their weapons in her main manifestations or images.

In certain traditions the buffalo demon while still in human shape adored the goddess. In some of the sculptures of the goddess as slayer of the demon—his body that of a man, his head that of a buffalo—he ecstatically surrenders to her as she slays him. When not depicted in action but standing straight in hieratic stance, the goddess is supported by a lotus or a buffalo head.

The Great Goddess has many forms. Like Siva she has three eyes; like Visnu, in her form as Yoganidra, "yoga slumber," she is represented lying, an embodiment of Visnu's slumber. Yoganidra is most beautiful and has only two arms, whereas the Goddess displays from four to sixteen arms in her other images. Like Siva, the Goddess is seen in divine beauty or in a shape of horror as Kali or Camunda.

Devi is not only represented in her own right as supreme goddess or as the consort of one of the main gods, she is also embodied as a group, particularly that of the "Seven Mothers" *(saptamatrkas)* where, as Mother Goddess, she is shown as the sakti of seven gods, including Brahma, Visnu, and Siva.

Today most of the preserved images are made of stone or metal. The few paintings that have survived over the last four centuries are in watercolor on paper, as a rule small in size, and narrative rather than iconic.

BIBLIOGRAPHY

Banerjea, Jitendra. *The Development of Hindu Iconography.* 2d ed. Calcutta, 1956. A handbook particularly dealing with the beginnings and historical typology of Hindu images.

Coomaraswamy, Ananda K. *The Dance of Shiva* (1918). Rev. ed. New York, 1957. Interpretation of an iconographic theme based on original sources.

Courtright, Paul B. *Ganesa.* New York, 1985. The first comprehensive and insightful presentation of Ganesa.

Eck, Diana L. *Banaras, City of Light.* New York, 1982. A topical study in depth, relating the icon to its setting.

Gopinatha Rao, T. A. *Elements of Hindu Iconography* (1914-1916). 2 vols. in 4. 2d ed. New York, 1968. The standard survey of Hindu iconography.

Kosambi, D. D. *Myth and Reality.* Bombay, 1962. An exposition of the roots of iconic and aniconic traditions.

Kramrisch, Stella. *The Hindu Temple* (1946). Reprint, Delhi, 1976. An exposition of architectural form in relation to the iconography of its images.

O'Flaherty, Wendy Doniger. *The Origins of Evil in Hindu Mythology.* Berkeley, 1976. A study in depth of the interrelation of gods and demons in Hindu mythology.

Shah, Priyabala, ed. *Visnudharmottara Purāna.* 2 vols. Gaekwad's Oriental Studies, vols. 130 and 137. Baroda, 1958 and 1961. The most complete and ancient treatise (c. eighth century CE) of Hindu iconography.

Shulman, David D. *Tamil Temple Myths.* Princeton, 1980. An indispensable background study for South Indian iconography.

Sivaramamurti, Calambur. *The Art of India.* New York, 1977. The best-illustrated and best-documented presentation of Indian sculpture.

Zimmer, Heinrich. *Artistic Form and Yoga in the Sacred Images of India.* Translated and edited by Gerald Chapple and James B. Lawson. Princeton, 1984. A clarification of the function and relation of iconic, sculptural form and abstract, linear diagram.

STELLA KRAMRISCH

Buddhist Iconography

In the course of its development and diffusion, Buddhism has expressed itself through an abundance of visual forms.

Sakyamuni Buddha. Because the Buddha as a personality was deemed to have passed outside of history altogether at his *parinirvana,* or death, his presence was instead symbolized by such motifs as the rich turban of the prince Siddhartha, the throne of the Blessed One, his footprints marked with the Wheel of the Law, the begging bowl *(patra),* or the Bodhi Tree (the Enlightenment). Similarly, the First Sermon among the monks in Banaras is evoked by the *triratna* ("three jewels," a three-pointed motif representing the Buddha, his Law, and his Community) surmounted by the Wheel (symbolizing by its movement the transmission of the dogma) and surrounded by deer. Most important of all, the *parinirvana* of the Buddha is recalled by the stupa, the domical shrine believed to have contained the precious relics of the Master. Together with the image of the Buddha, the stupa, as an actual monument or an iconic representation (and through such transformations as the *dagoba,* or step-pagoda, and the Tibetan *chorchen* remains at the center of the cult and its visual imagery.

The representation of the Buddha that rapidly became universal probably originated in Gandhara or Mathura between the first century BCE and the first century CE; it shows the monk wearing the robe and mantle of the *bhiksu* (mendicant), with his head encircled by a nimbus, probably the result of Hellenistic influences. Among the thirty-two auspicious marks *(laksanas)* that designate a Buddha, the most characteristic ones are the *urna,* the circular tuft of hair on his forehead; the *usnisa,* the bump in his skull that looks like a bun of hair; the distended earlobes; the wrinkles on his neck; his webbed fingers; and his gold skin coloring. His posture, the serenity of his features, and his half-closed eyes suggest the depth of his meditation and detachment from the exterior world.

By the fifth century CE, representations of the Blessed One, standing, seated, or reclining attained colossal dimensions in a variety of media: chiseled in cliffs or modeled in clay, cut into stone or cast in bronze.

The Transcendent Buddha. With the Mahayana, the supernatural vision heralded in the Great Miracle of Sravasti culminates in the myriad Buddhas of the universe, which began to appear in the third and fourth centuries CE and were subsequently painted over and over on sanctuary walls and sculpted or modeled on temples and stupas. This concept of the Buddha's omnipresence is often combined with that of the lotus as cosmic image: each lotus petal constitutes a world, and each torus is occupied by one of the myriad Buddhas, evoking the universe past, present, and future.

These transcendent Buddhas, their bodies covered with images of Mount Meru, the stupa, the sun and moon, aquatic subjects and the lotus, the vajra (thunderbolt), wheel, triratna, and other signs and symbols, are encountered very early along the path of penetration of the Great Vehicle into China.

BIBLIOGRAPHY

Alfred Foucher's *L'art greco-bouddhique du Gandhara,* 3 vols. (Paris, 1905-1923), remains one of the basic sources for the origins of Buddhist iconography. Foucher's *The Beginnings of Buddhist Art and Other Essays on Indian and Central Asian Archeology,* rev. ed. (Paris, 1917), may also be consulted. A different and complementary point of view is expressed in Ananda K. Coomaraswamy's *Elements Of Buddhist Iconography* (Cambridge, Mass., 1935). *The Image of the Buddha,* edited by David L. Snellgrove (Paris, 1978), is a collective work with broad coverage and abundant illustrations.

Étienne Lamotte's *Histoire du bouddhisme indien: Des origines à l'ère Saka* (Louvain, 1958) provides a historical context for the religion. On the cosmology of the stupa from its origins to its most complex forms, see Paul Mus's *Barabudur* (1935), edited by Kees W. Bolle (New York, 1978). A good initiation into the Tantric pantheon is found in Marie-Thérèse Mallmann's *Introduction à l'iconographie du tântrisme bouddhique* (Paris, 1975).

For regional studies, see *Buddhism in Afghanistan and Central Asia,* by Simone Gaulier, Robert Jera-Bezard, and Monique Maillard, 2 vols. (Leiden, 1976), which analyzes the evolution of images along the Silk Route; E. Dale Saunders's *Mudra: A Study of Symbolic Gestures in Japanese Buddhist Sculpture* (New York, 1960), which treats the symbolic language of ritual and iconography; and two museum catalogs: *Bannières et peintures de Touen-houang conservées au Musée Guimet,* 2 vols., compiled by Nicole Vandier-Nicholas et al. (Paris, 1974-1976), and Roderick Whitfield's *The Art of Central Asia: The Stein Collection in the British Museum,* vol. 1, *Paintings from Dunhuang,* 2 vols. (Tokyo, 1982-1983).

SIMONE GAULIER and ROBERT JERA-BEZARD
Translated from French by Ina Baghdiantz

Taoist Iconography

Taoist iconography symbolically expresses ideas concerning (1) the basic Chinese cosmology and mythology, (2) the Founders of the religion, (3) techniques of salvation, (4) those who have attained the goal, (5) immortality as a universal hope, and (6) Taoist concepts of, and relationships with, the numinous dimension and numinous beings.

Iconography and Worldview. The most familiar symbol of the functioning of the Tao by means of its Vital Breaths is the ingenious design of the circle divided into two equal parts by a curving central line, one side of the circle representing the light of *yang* and the other side the darkness of *yin,* but with a bit of *yin* in the *yang* part and a bit of *yang* in the *yin* part. This expressive symbol is found on the liturgical robes of Taoists (a word we use to indicate professional clergy). The most sophisticated summary of the basic cosmology is the Diagram of the Ultimate *(t`ai-chi t`u)* devised by the eleventh-century philosopher Chou Tun-i, but it is not used iconographically.

The Eight Trigrams, each of which is formed from a combination of unbroken *(yang)* and broken *(yin)* lines, constitute another abstract symbol of common occurrence. These were in archaic times already invested with great significance as marks of the combinations and permutations of those forces that produced the world and all beings in it. The classical exposition of the Trigrams appears in the ancient *Chou i* or *I*

ching (Scripture of Change), a seminal source for Taoism as for all traditional thought. The Eight Trigrams are also embroidered on Taoist sacerdotal robes.

Mythological figures in human form include the traditionally accepted heroes of creation, cultural inventions such as cooking, housing, writing, and the calendar, and founders of the earliest polities, but while often encountered in Taoist iconography, they have little specifically Taoist meaning.

Founders. One of these mythological figures has definitely retained his persona as a Taoist, along with his broader identification as a Chinese hero: Huang-ti, the Yellow Emperor. Two millennia later he was followed by the second Founder, Lao-tzu, supposedly a historical person somewhat senior to Master K`ung (Confucius) in the mid-sixth century BCE. The third Founder is again only semihistorical: Chang Ling, or Chang Tao-ling, is presumed to have flourished around the end of the second century CE. All three of the Founders are represented in visual arts. Huang-ti, as an emperor, is depicted wearing a crown topped with a "mortar board" from the front and back of which hang the rows of jade tassels marking his exalted rank. Lao-tzu is most commonly shown as a snowy-bearded old gentleman riding an ox and holding a book, this memorializing the moment he rode off to the West after composing the *Tao-te ching* for the Chinese garrison commander at the frontier pass. Chang Tao-ling rides a tiger, or sits on a tiger throne, symbolizing the great spiritual powers attained during a lifetime of Taoist self-cultivation.

Techniques of Salvation. Salvation in Taoism is attained through various techniques—alchemical, yogic, dietary, sexual—and these are alluded to directly or indirectly in visual imagery. The caldron or mortar in which the elixir of immortality is prepared is a motif evoking the "alchemy of substances" *(wai-tan),* or preparation and ingestion of the elixir; the Chinese see a rabbit pounding the elixir in a mortar rather than a man in the moon. The most common dietary symbol is the *ling-chih* or "efficacious mushroom," a plant whose consumption produces longevity or even immortality.

Those Who Have Attained. As a religion that has kept alive real hopes of immortality—or at least longevity—Taoism naturally has voluminous records of those who have attained the goal. The most common term for such adepts is *hsien,* a word whose graph suggests a person who has retired to the mountains—which was indeed the eremitic life recommended for the alchemist.

Out of the countless immortal transcendents in China's long past a few have naturally captured popular imagination. Outstanding among these is the group called the Eight Immortals, who are constantly depicted in all the arts as well as in literature. Among the eight, Lü Tung-pin, supposedly a historical figure of the eighth century, is foremost, as indicated by the fact that only he has his own temples in modern Taiwan.

Hsien may often be indicated simply by representation of their attributes. Thus, the Eight are denoted by sword, fan, flower basket, lotus, flute, gourd, castanets, and tube drum. The *ru-i* magic wand, the crooked cane, and the fly-whisk (a mark of spiritual attainment and authority taken over from Buddhism) are other common attributes of *hsien.* Perhaps the richest symbol is the gourd, which represents the alchemical caldron or its equivalent, the microcosm of the adept's own body, the universe, ancient notions of cosmogony, the dream of paradisiacal lands, and still other concepts. The paradisiacal lands, or abodes of *hsien,* are depicted very frequently.

Immortality as a Universal Hope. Of course the goal of the Taoists is not their hope alone. Longevity, or even immortality, is one of the most conspicuously prayed-for desires of the Chinese. These desires are given visual form on the roofs of popular temples, where the ridge is lined with images of three star-gods, representing longevity, wealth and elite status, and many sons to carry on the family property and ancestral cult. The star-god of longevity, Shou Hsing, is of course shown as a *hsien.* His happy smile and rosy cheeks bespeak his healthy old age; his stout belly and bulging forehead indicate that he is an adept in cultivating his ch'i, and as he leans on his rough-hewn staff he holds a peach in his hand. The graph of longevity, *shou,* written in a hundred different ways, is a symbol in itself, omnipresent as a decoration on the products of art and craft. *Shou* is also the common euphemism for death, which, it is hoped, leads to immortality.

Taoism and the Numinous Dimension. The numinous realm of Taoism includes both macrocosm (the universe) and microcosm (the human body). Moreover, these two are essentially identical: the interior space corresponds with the exterior and is occupied by the same numinous beings.

Most iconographic representations of spiritual beings fall under the category of popular religion rather than Taoism. It is perhaps the occasion of the rituals of the Chiao, the major liturgical performance of Taoists on behalf of the community, that most commonly shows Taoist concepts in anthropomorphic form. The Chiao serves nicely to set off Taoist icons from popular ones, insofar as during that great service the icons of the popular gods are relegated to a subsidiary, "guest" position within the sacred arena, while the Taoist officiants focus upon the "altar of the Three Pure Ones" (San Ch'ing), who represent different aspects of the Tao. Represented in iconic scrolls as venerable sages, they are the Heaven-Honored One of the Tao and Its Virtues (Tao-te T'ien-tsun), the Heaven-Honored One of the Primal Beginnings (Yüan-shih T'ien-tsun), and the Heaven-Honored One of the Spiritually Efficacious Treasure (Ling-pao T'ien-tsun). As hypostases of the Tao they may also be characterized as the "dharma-bodies" of Lao-tzu. Hung at the same altar, in slightly subordinate positions to "stage left" and "stage right," are

two other iconic portraits. On the left is that of the Supreme Emperor of Jadelike Augustness (Yü-huang Shang-ti), head of both the popular and the Taoist pantheons. The portrait on the right is that of the Lord of the Northern Bushel Constellation (Pei-tou-hsing Chün).

BIBLIOGRAPHY

The problem with most treatments of Chinese symbolism and art is their failure to distinguish clearly between Taoism and popular religion. This limitation should be kept in mind when using a standard handbook such as C. A. S. Williams's *Encyclopedia of Chinese Symbolism and Art Motives* (New York, 1961), a reissue of *Outlines of Chinese Symbolism and Art Motives* (Shanghai, 1932). For the cosmological and religious ideas of Taoism that underlie its iconography, see Kristofer Schipper's *Le corps taoïste* (Paris, 1982). William Charles White's *Chinese Temple Frescoes: A Study of Three Wall-Paintings of the Thirteenth Century* (Toronto, 1940) shows unique examples of Taoist iconography from the Yüan period and gives extensive background and explanations of their meaning. Philip Rawson and Laszlo Legeza's *Tao: The Chinese Philosophy of Time and Change* (London, 1973) is a succinct but penetrating study of the yin and yang concept of Taoism; it is accompanied by many pertinent illustrations of art works that especially point up the sexual expressions of this concept. Legeza is also the author of *Tao Magic: The Chinese Art of the Occult* (New York, 1975), which treats the Taoist talismans *(fu),* their religious symbolism, and their remarkable calligraphy.

LAURENCE G. THOMPSON

Jewish Iconography

Jewish iconography, whether actually represented in works of art or existing only as traditional imagery (and occasionally referred to in literature), was determined from the first by the biblical "prohibition of images." This prohibition, transmitted in the Bible in several versions, could be understood (1) as forbidding, in a religious context, all images, regardless of their subject matter (*Ex.* 20:4, *Dt.* 4:15-18), or (2) specifically forbidding the depiction of God and the ritual use of such a depiction as an idol (*Dt.* 27:15). While the first interpretation of the prohibition did not prevail (the Bible itself provides evidence of this in *1 Kgs.* 6:23-29, *Ez.* 8:5-12), the other was consistently implemented. Possibly the most striking feature of Jewish iconography throughout the ages is the systematic avoidance of any depiction of the figure of God.

Hellenism. The meeting between Judaism and the Greek world—a process that lasted from early Hellenism to late antiquity (roughly, second century BCE to fifth century CE)—resulted in a body of religious images. While the Mishnah and Talmud were being compiled (roughly second to sixth centuries CE) Jewish communities produced a large number of representations, which have been uncovered in Jewish remains (mainly synagogues and burial places) from Tunisia

543

to Italy and eastward to the Euphrates; sites in Israel are particularly rich. Occasionally this imagery includes human figures, either in biblical scenes or in pagan myths (frequently the image of Helios, the Greek sun god).

More often, however, these survivals show objects with definite ritual connotations. Most prominent are the seven-branched *menorah* (candelabrum), Aron ha-Qodesh (the Ark of the Covenant), *lulav* and *etrog* (palm branch and citron), and shofar (ceremonial animal horn). These objects (which reflect the crystallization of Jewish ritual) have no strict hierarchy, but the *menorah,* and the Ark of the Covenant, representing the law itself, are more important than the others. When both are shown together, they always occupy the central place. Besides such explicitly ritual objects, Jewish remains abound in artistic motifs, taken over from Hellenistic art, whose symbolic character is obscure.

Middle Ages. In the European Middle Ages, especially between the thirteenth and fifteenth centuries, Jewish religious imagery developed further. The illumination of manuscripts is the central aesthetic medium of the period; of particular significance are the manuscripts produced in Spain, Italy, and Germany. All these manuscripts are of a ritual nature, the most important groups being the Haggadah for

> ## The illumination of manuscripts is the central aesthetic medium of the period. . . .

Passover and prayer books for the holidays, the *mahzor.* The illuminations (and later, printed illustrations) represent many ritual utensils, but they also include, more often than in Jewish art of other periods and media, human figures, especially in biblical scenes. The iconographic repertoire is enlarged by mythical motifs, attesting to messianic beliefs. Among these motifs are the legendary beasts (such as the *shor ha-bar,* a kind of wild ox), on which the just will feast on the day of redemption; these are particularly prominent in manuscripts produced in Germany. The future Temple that, according to common belief, is to be built after the redemption, is another frequent mythical motif.

Qabbalistic Symbolism. The qabbalistic tradition is a special field of iconographic creation. Qabbalistic literature abounds in visual metaphors, since the authors often tend to express (or to hide) their thoughts and mysteries in visual images and descriptions of supposed optical experiences. The central image of qabbalistic symbolism is the Tree of Sefirot. The godhead is imagined as structured in ten spheres, each of them representing a "divine quality" (Heb., *sefirah*). The shape and place of the spheres, and the spatial relationships between them, are firmly established in the qabbalistic imagination. The overall pattern vaguely resem-

bles a tree (hence the name), but the basic character of the image is abstract rather than figurative.

Qabbalistic literature produced other visual symbols, among them the images of broken vessels, scattered sparks, Adam Qadmon (primordial man) as a figure of God, and so forth.

BIBLIOGRAPHY

For the imagery of the Hebrew Bible (though not necessarily in art only) still useful is Maurice H. Farbridge's *Studies in Biblical and Semitic Symbolism* (1923; reprint, New York, 1970). Erwin R. Goodenough's *Jewish Symbols in the Greco-Roman Period,* 13 vols. (New York, 1953-1968), has a rich collection of photographs; the text is stimulating, albeit sometimes arguable. Mainly for the Middle Ages, see Jacob Leveen's *The Hebrew Bible in Art* (1944; reprint, New York, 1974). For early modern times, see *Beauty in Holiness: Studies in Jewish Customs and Ceremonial Art,* edited by Joseph Gutmann (New York, 1970), a catalog of Jewish artifacts from the Prague Museum shown at the Jewish Museum in New York.

Much can be learned from the discussion of single problems. See, for example, *The Temple of Solomon,* edited by Joseph Gutmann (Missoula, Mont., 1976). Another individual problem is discussed by Zofia Ameisenowa in "The Tree of Life in Jewish Iconography," *Journal of the Warburg and Courtauld Institutes* 2 (1938-1939): 326-345. Qabbalistic imagery is best discussed in Gershom Scholem's *Major Trends in Jewish Mysticism,* 3d rev. ed. (New York, 1954), esp. pp. 205-243. A highly interesting study of a particular subject in qabbalistic symbolism is Scholem's "Farben und ihre Symbolik in der jüdischen Überlieferung und Mystik," *Eranos Yearbook* 41 (1974): 1-49, *The Realms of Colour* (with English and French summaries).

MOSHE BARASCH

Christian Iconography

For the greater part of Christian history, the church's images have been drawn from its liturgical texts, scriptures, and pedagogy and rendered in the styles of the particular age and place the images served. In modern times, the sources for Christian iconography have expanded to include psychological sociopolitical, and nontraditional elements.

Early Christianity. Early Christian art surviving from the first half of the third century reflects the diversity of the Greco-Roman context from which it emerged. The earliest iconographic figures, borrowed directly from late antique conventions, were placed in new compositional and environmental settings on jewelry and other minor arts.

The earliest images of Christ were concerned with his person and role on earth and were borrowed from classical types of teaching figures, miracle workers, and heroes. Conventions for depicting divine attributes were missing, and there was no attempt at historical accuracy. Jesus did not look like an early first-century Jewish man from Palestine, but rather, like a Roman teacher-philosopher or like an Apollo-type mythic hero, such as the Christos-Helios figure in the necropolis of Saint Peter's Basilica in Rome.

Imperial Christianity. Following the adoption of Christianity as the state religion by the Roman emperor Constantine in the early fourth century, the figure of Christ as the imperial reigning Lord emerged. Jesus enthroned as the leader of the church, or in the heavens as an imperial judge, reflected the power the church had gained in that era. Within a hierarchically structured society, Jesus was depicted as a reigning philosopher-emperor who dispensed grace and judgment above all earthly power (see for instance the enthroned Christ in the apse mosaic of Santa Pudenziana in Rome). From the fourth through the sixth century the figure of Jesus, elevated to a ruler over all, came to represent the power of the church over state and society. Christ seated in majesty above the heavens in the apse mosaic of the mausoleum of Santa Constanza in Rome (c. 350) or in the apse mosaic of the Church of San Vitale in Ravenna, Italy (c. 550), reflects christological formulations. Mary appears as an enthroned queen in the mosaics of Santa Maria Maggiore, Rome, after the Council of Ephesus in 431, which declared her *theotokos,* Mother of God. Two types of Christ figures occupy the twenty-six mosaic panels of the Christ cycle in San Apollinare Nuovo in Ravenna (c. 520).

Explicit representation of the crucifixion of Jesus is conspicuously absent from early Christian iconography. Once the crucifixion came to be widely depicted, the preferred type in both East and West through the ninth century was a robed, open-eyed victorious Christ hanging on the cross, such as the ones in the illuminations of the Rabula Gospels from Mesopotamia (dated 586) or on the wall decorations of the Church of Santa Maria Antiqua in Rome.

Byzantine Art. Within the art of the Eastern Orthodox church, the image (as icon) relates to the liturgy in a manner distinguished from that of its Western counterparts. An icon can appear in a variety of media: painting, mosaic, sculpture, or illuminated manuscript. Its subject matter includes biblical figures, lives of the saints, scenes and narrative cycles that relate specifically to the liturgical calendar. To the present day, Byzantine tradition relies heavily on iconography in its worship.

Over the centuries, rules for iconographers in the East were formalized, and copy books determined the style and subject matter of iconography. Paintings of the crucifixion in the Byzantine tradition, for example, often include the figures of Mary and Saint John at the foot of the cross in attitudes of grief, and the corpus traditionally hangs in a limp curve against the rigidity of the cross. This form then became popular in the West, especially in medieval Italy, and influenced painters such as Cimabue (d. 1302?).

Middle Ages. Christian iconography produced in the eighth and ninth centuries became regionally acculturated as its Roman origins disappeared from the face of indigenous expression. Elaborate decorated surfaces enclosed Christian symbols and figures, where, in the service of beautiful patterns, iconography became abstract and emblematic. During the ninth and tenth centuries a shift in emphasis from Christ the victor to Christ the victim took place in the thinking of the church; accordingly, images of the crucifixion with the victorious reigning Lord on the cross were replaced by those of the suffering human victim. The Gero Crucifix in the Cathedral of Cologne, Germany (c. 960), is one of the earliest representations of Christ as a suffering, dying figure.

By the twelfth century the decorative, narrative, and didactic role of the arts gave way to an explicitly sacramental function, one in which the imagery appeared in a context believed to be a model of the Kingdom of Heaven, the church building. Iconography in the church was believed capable of building a bridge that reached from the mundane world to the threshold of the divine spirit. Described in twelfth-century Christian literature as anagogical art, iconography served as an extension of the meaning of the mass.

In the Gothic era a proliferation of Old Testament imagery reflected renewed theological and political interests in manifestations of God working within and through royal hierarchies. During this period the suffering Christ of the Romanesque style became a more benign Savior.

In the late Gothic period, approximately the fourteenth and fifteenth centuries across northern Europe, the iconography of Christianity was populated with aesthetically appealing, elegant figures and decorative surfaces known in modern scholarship as the International Style. Attitudes, dress, and colors emphasized soft, flowing lines, gentle expressions, and rich textures.

Renaissance and Reformation. Christian iconography of the Renaissance in Italy acquired classically human characteristics as interest in Greco-Roman literature and art was revived. Jesus and his followers appeared in a human guise heretofore unknown. Scenes of biblical episodes and historically religious significance were given the illusion of three-dimensional settings that emphasized their reality in the natural world. Fifteenth-century Renaissance art reflected renewed interest in pagan mythology and Christian subject matter alike; therefore pagan iconography competed with traditional Christian iconography. Proportion, perspective, and human experience were new ingredients in the iconography of the Renaissance. For example, between 1495 and 1498 Leonardo da Vinci completed the Last Supper on the wall of the refectory of Santa Maria della Grazie in Milan, Italy.

In northern Europe in the fifteenth and sixteenth centuries exaggerated realism in the treatment of subject matter and pre-Reformation currents of thought shaped Christian iconography. Matthias Grünewald's famous crucifixion panel in the Isenheim Altarpiece (1510-1512) presents Christ as a victim whose physical appearance betrays mutilation and disease and emphasizes divine participation on behalf of human suffering.

The Council of Trent, held in the middle of the sixteenth century, formulated instructions on the uses of iconography on behalf of the church. If the Reformation in some areas limited or forbade the use of images in the church, the Counter-Reformation encouraged a proliferation of them, thereby stimulating the expansion of the Baroque style of art. Eventually the church's use of Baroque forms extended beyond traditional sculptural programs and painted panels to wall surface decor, ceiling plaster, frescoes, elaboration of vestments and liturgical vessels, and extensive programmatic designs for altars and chapels.

Seventeenth and Eighteenth Centuries. Protestant iconography in the seventeenth century emphasized individual experience, and images of Jesus stressed his humanity and participation in the human condition. Rembrandt's portraits of Jesus, for example, show a thirty-year-old Jewish man. Roman Catholic iconography, by contrast, stressed the sacramental presence of a heroic Christ in programmatic sequences such as Peter Paul Rubens's early altarpieces and Nicolas Poussin's two series of paintings entitled *The Seven Sacraments* from the 1640s.

Nineteenth Century. In the nineteenth century, Christian iconography served more private and artistically formal purposes. The recovery of historical styles in nineteenth-century art and architecture carried with it renewed interest in Christian iconographic themes.

Vincent van Gogh (d. 1890), who in his early life had been a Christian missionary, created a personal iconography that eschewed for the most part any specifically Christian subject. Paul Gauguin's paintings of Old Testament subjects, the crucifixion, or religious imagery from life in Tahiti created a recognizable but private iconography that reflected individual interests and goals. The institutional church for the most part disengaged itself from major artists and movements. Under these circumstances, by the late nineteenth century a great part of Christian iconography had become copy work, sentimental and remote from the society at large.

Twentieth Century. A highly individualized Christian iconography has been shaped in the twentieth century by the religious consciousness of individual artists. The German Expressionists, for example, insisted upon interpreting and revealing their individuality. When Wassily Kandinsky (d. 1944) wrote *Concerning the Spiritual in Art,* what was revealed in the art included the feelings of the artist and the expressive properties of color. Emil Nolde's nine-part *Life of Christ* altarpiece (1911-1912) combined Nolde's interest in the impact of color with a traditional Christian format. George Rouault more than any other recognized twentieth-century artist sought to create compelling Christian imagery. His 1926 *Miserere* series compared Christ's suffering with twentieth-century experiences of human sufferings in war. Max Beckmann (d. 1950) equated Adam and Eve in the Fall with the grotesque dimensions of the human condition under fascism. In contrast, the most popular and most often reproduced image of Jesus in the United States in the first half of the twentieth century was W. H. Sallmon's *Head of Christ,* a sentimental figure with widespread influence.

Fantasy painters like Salvador Dali and Marc Chagall used Christian subject matter in a unique manner in order to suggest visions of the mind or vistas of a dream world fashioned out of the subconscious. Paintings such as Dali's *Sacrament of the Last Supper* (1955) and Chagall's *White Crucifixion* (1938) identify a private vision in which traditional Christian iconography is reinterpreted.

The twentieth century has also seen the emergence of Christian iconography in new media, notably film and electronic communications. Biblical stories presented in films with titles like *The Bible, The Ten Commandments, The King of Kings,* and *The Gospel According to St. Matthew* have engaged a public separate from the church. The mass media, which now include home video, have offered traditional Christian subject matter in extended narrative form as dramatic entertainment.

BIBLIOGRAPHY

Bottari, Stefano. *Tesori d'arte cristiana.* 5 vols. Bologna, 1956-1968. Excellent photoessays on major architectural monuments and their contents from early Christian times to the twentieth century. The principles of selection, however, are not clear, and the views printed are sometimes eccentric. Many color illustrations and ground plans.

Cabrol, Fernand, et al., eds. *Dictionnaire d'archéologie chrétienne et de liturgie.* 15 vols. Paris, 1909-1953. Essential material for the history of Christian iconography, architecture, and worship. Illustrations, although small in size and few in number, include good ground plans. A classic research and reference source.

Didron, Adolphe Napoléon. *Christian Iconography: The History of Christian Art in the Middle Ages* (1851-1886). 2 vols. Translated by Ellen J. Millington. New York, 1965. Organized thematically, with each essay treating historical sources in depth. Limited illustrations but valuable for theories concerning iconography.

Ferguson, George. *Signs and Symbols in Christian Art* (1954). New York, 1961. Remains the most reliable single-volume handbook on the subject.

Hall, James. *Dictionary of Subjects and Symbols in Art* (1974). Rev. ed. New York, 1979. Includes Christian subject matter.

Kirschbaum, Englebert, and Wolfgang Braunfels, eds. *Lexikon der christlichen Ikonographie.* 8 vols. Rome, 1968-1976. Volumes 1-4, *Allgemeine Ikonographie,* edited by Kirschbaum, present general articles on Christian iconography, alphabetically arranged; volumes 5-8, *Ikonographie der Heiligen,* edited by Braunfels, present the legends of the saints and their imagery in a separate alphabetical sequence. Both series of volumes include excellent bibliographies and summaries. Illustrations are relatively few in number and small in size.

Réau, Louis. *Iconographie de l'art crétien.* 3 vols. in 6. Paris, 1955-1959. Includes a historical overview (vol. 1), Old and New Testament iconography (vol. 2), and an iconography of the saints with legends and cult status (vol. 3). Very few illustrations.

Schiller, Gertrud. *Ikonographie der christlichen Kunst.* 4 vols. in 5. Gütersloh, 1966-1976. Offers excellent essay introductions to Christian themes in art and their sources, covering presentations of Christ (vols. 1-3), the church (vol. 4, pt. 1), and Mary (vol. 4, pt. 2). An exemplary study with many well-selected and clearly printed illustrations. The first two volumes have been translated by Janet Seligman as *The Iconography of Christian Art,* vol. 1, *The Incarnation and Life of Christ* (Boston, 1971), and vol. 2, *The Passion of Christ* (Boston, 1972).

JOHN W. COOK

Islamic Iconography

Islam is generally considered an iconoclastic religion in which the representation of living things has been prohibited from its very beginning. However, the Qur'an nowhere deals with this problem or explicitly speaks against representation.

Emerging Imagery. The feeling that representation was alien to the original spirit of Islam resulted in the development of abstract ornamental design, both geometric and vegetal, notably the arabesque as the endless continuation of leaves, palmettes, and sometimes animal-like motifs growing out of each other; it also gave calligraphy its central place in Islamic art. However, it would be wrong to claim that early Islam was without any pictures. In secular buildings such as palaces, there was no lack of representations of kings, musicians, dancers, and the like. Decorative painting on ceramics includes not only more or less stylized animal or human figures as individual motifs but also scenes from (often unidentified) tales and romances.

New stylistic features came with the growing Chinese influence during the Mongol occupation of Iran in the late thirteenth century. (Persian literature speaks of China as the "picture house," where Mani, the founder of Manichaeism, acts as the master painter.) Henceforward, illustrative painting developed predominantly in Iran, where the great epic poems (an art form unknown to the Arabs) inspired miniaturists through the centuries to the extent that the iconography of Firdawsi's *Shah-namah* (Book of Kings) and Nizami's *Khamsah* (Quintet) became almost standardized. Early historical works, such as the world history of Rashid al-Din (d. 1317), were rather realistically illustrated.

Islamic painting reached its zenith in Iran and India in the sixteenth and seventeenth centuries, when, partly under the influence of European prints, naturalistic portraiture was developed to perfection. The Mughal emperor Jahangir (r. 1605-1627) inspired the court painters to express his dreams of spiritual world-rule in his portraits by using the motif of the lion and the lamb lying together, or by showing him in the company of Sufis.

The Shape of Spirituality. Portraits of Sufis and dervishes are frequent in the later Middle Ages: many drawings capture the spiritual power or the refinement of a solitary Muslim holy man or illustrate the "sessions of the mystical lovers" *(majalis al-`ushshaq).* Sufis are also shown as teachers or in their whirling dance.

While naturalistic representation of the Prophet and his family was increasingly objected to, other ways of presenting him developed. One might put a *hadith* in superb calligraphy on a single page or write his *hilyah,* an elaboration of the classical Arabic description of his outward and inward beauty, in a special calligraphic style, as was done in Turkey from about 1600. The Prophet's footprints on stone, or representations of them, along with more or less elaborate drawings of his sandals, still belong to the generally accepted items in the religious tradition. One could also produce "pictures" of saintly persons such as `Ali ibn Abi Talib from pious sentences written in minute script (although in Iran quite realistic battle scenes showing the bravery and suffering of Husayn

> While naturalistic representation of the Prophet and his family was increasingly objected to, other ways of presenting him developed.

and other members of the Prophet's family are also found in more recent times).

Calligraphic images have become more and more popular: the letters of the word *bismillah* ("in the name of God") can be shaped into birds and beasts; Qur'anic passages of particular protective importance, such as the "throne verse" (surah 2:256), appear in animal shape; and whenever a calligraphic lion is found, it usually consists of a formula connected with `Ali, who is called the "Lion of God" (Asad Allah, Haydar, Shir, and so forth).

Indeed, the most typical and certainly the most widely used means of conveying the Islamic message was and still is calligraphy. The walls of Persian mosques are covered with radiant tiles on which the names of God, Muhammad, and `Ali in the square Kufic script give witness to the Shi`i form of faith; Turkish mosques are decorated with Qur'anic quotations or with an enormous *Allah.*

Lately, under European influence, a very colorful popular iconography has developed in some parts of the Muslim world. On posters, religious motifs from various traditions are strung together in highly surprising form: Raphael's little angels appear along with the Lourdes Madonna around a deceased Muslim leader in a lush Paradise, or an apotheosis of Ayatollah Khomeini is coupled with the earthbound figure from Andrew Wyeth's *Christina's World.* Such syncretistic pictures are certainly not acceptable to the large majority of pious Muslims. On the other hand, the calligraphic traditions are gaining new importance from Morocco to Indonesia, and some attempts at producing a kind of Qur'anic scriptorial picture (thus Sadiqain and Aslam Kamal in Pakistan) are remarkably successful and deserve the attention of the historian of religion and the art lover.

BIBLIOGRAPHY

Most histories of Islamic art deal with the topic of so-called iconoclasm in Islam. One of the latest publications is Mazhar Sevket Ipsiroglu's *Das Bild im Islam: Ein Verbot und seine* Folgen (Vienna, 1971), which stresses the Sufi influence on Islamic painting but is not completely convincing. The only scholar who has devoted a good number of studies to Islamic iconography is Richard Ettinghausen; out of his many valuable works I shall mention especially "Hilal in Islamic Art," in *The Encyclopaedia of Islam,* new ed. (Leiden, 1960-), with a thorough historical survey; "Persian Ascension Miniatures of the Fourteenth Century," in *Oriente ed occidente nel medio evo* (Rome, 1957), which treats the early pictorial development of the ascension theme; and his religious interpretation of a Mughal painting of Jahangir preferring a Sufi to worldly rulers, "The Emperor's Choice," in *De Artibus Opuscula XL: Essays in Honor of Erwin Panofsky,* edited by Millard Meiss (New York, 1961), vol. 1. See also Ettinghausen's *Islamic Art and Archaeology: Collected Papers,* prepared and edited by Myriam Rosen-Ayalon (Berlin, 1984). The volume dedicated to Ettinghausen, *Studies in Art and Literature of the Near East,* edited by Peter Chelkowski (Salt Lake City, 1974), lists more of his relevant works and contains some articles pertinent to the problem of iconography.

The best pictorial introduction to the *mi`raj* miniatures is *The Miraculous Journey of Mahomet,* edited by Marie-Rose Séguy (London, 1977), based on a Uighur manuscript from the Timurid court at Herat. Popular painting has been dealt with in Malik Aksel's *Türklerde dinï resimler* (Istanbul, 1967), a delightful book with many examples of folk painting and calligraphic pictures from the Bektashi tradition. A very useful introduction into Islamic iconography in Africa (a much neglected topic) is René A. Bravmann's *African Islam* (London, 1983). The calligraphic and iconographic aspects of the Qur'an are lucidly explained in Martin Ling's *The Quranic Art of Calligraphy and Illumination* (London, 1976). A general survey of the calligraphic tradition in connection with the mystical and poetical expressions can be found in my *Calligraphy and Islamic Culture* (New York, 1984).

ANNEMARIE SCHIMMEL

IDOLATRY

The word *idolatry* is formed from two Greek words, *eidolon,* "image," and *latreia,* "adoration." The concept of idolatry originated in a very specific historico-religious context: the monotheism of Israel. Consequently, an authentic approach to the concept must refer to the Hebrew scriptures. In his research on the prophetic reaction to pagan religious concepts, Christopher R. North presents two ideas taken directly from the prophets. First, "Idolatry is the worship of the creature instead of the Creator and, to make matters worse, the creature is made by man, who is himself a creature" (North, 1958, p. 158). He then states: "Idolatry is the worship of what in modern terms we should call process, the 'life-force,' the *élan vital,* or what we will, instead of the Creator who transcends and is in some sort external to creation" (ibid., p. 159).

Idolatry and the Hebrew Scriptures. The formal condemnation of idolatry is found in *Exodus* 20:3-5. The biblical God (whose unvocalized name is YHVH) simultaneously forbids the worship of foreign gods and the making of images that claim to represent him, since it is impossible to represent the God of Israel. A confirmation and amplification of this commandment are found in *Deuteronomy* 4:12-19.

The Mosaic prohibition. The second commandment forbids the making of representations of the divinity (*Ex.* 20:4-6; *Dt.* 4:15-19 and 5:6-9; *Lv.* 26:1). A rigorous tendency took this Mosaic prohibition literally by banishing all ornamentation of religious buildings. This tendency, which became widespread among the Pharisees, insisted on the spiritualization of God and radically opposed the danger of idolatry.

Idolatrous worship of YHVH. Biblical texts refer to this worship on various occasions. The Hebrew tribes underwent the influence of Canaanite culture (*Jgs.* 3:5-6, *Dt.* 7:1-5). Micah of the tribe of Ephraim made a pesel and a *massekhah,* a carved image and idol of cast metal (*Jgs.* 17:1-13), perhaps an image of God. After his victory over Midian, Gideon made use of the gold taken from the enemy to make and set up an *efod* (*Jgs.* 8:22-27). Moreover, we have evidence of the tauriform cult of YHVH in the northern kingdom of Israel after the schism of 935 (*1 Kgs.* 12:26-32, *2 Kgs.* 15:24). In *1 Kings* 12:28, Jeroboam presents God, symbolized by the bull (Hadad and Teshub, fertility gods), as the liberator of Israel at the time of the flight from Egypt. The writer of *2 Kings* 15:24 speaks of the erection of statues of divine bulls. This is the religious tradition of the golden calf. The prophetic argument is simple. It rejects all tangible representation of God as dangerous since the image is distinct from God.

Idolatry as worship of false gods. The most formidable opponents of idolatry were the prophets and their prophecies. At the solemn unveiling of the golden calf at Bethel, a prophet appeared before Jeroboam and announced Yahveh's threat (*1 Kgs.* 13:1-32). Elijah and Elisha fought against the worship of Baal and his priests (*1 Kgs.* 18:22-40). Amos reproached his Judean compatriots for letting themselves be seduced by idols (*Am.* 2:4). Hosea spoke harshly also, because in his eyes the worship of Israel had become idolatry (*Hos.* 4:12-13). Isaiah attacked the idols and announced their fall (*Is.* 2:20, 17:7-8, 30:22).

One of the important themes of the prophetic polemic is the emptiness of false gods. Idols are nothing but stone and wood (*Jer.* 16:20). Hosea does not hesitate to liken idolatry to fetishism, for in his eyes the image is set up in place of

God (*Hos.* 8:4-6). Isaiah writes veritable satires of the Babylonian gods, whom he compares to nothingness (*Is.* 44:14-17).

The *Wisdom of Solomon,* written in Greek on the eve of the Christian era, holds a veritable trial of idolatry, especially in chapters 13-15. The author rejects the worship of nature, idolatry, and zoolatry (worship of animals). However, while remaining completely faithful to the biblical tradition, he reflects his time by paying homage to the beauty of nature and works of art. He attacks the Stoic conception of gods according to which Zeus was the ether, Poseidon the ocean, and Demeter the earth (*Wis.* 13:1-19). He attacks the dynastic cult of the Ptolemies (14:17-20) and the mystery religions (14:23). In his view, the adherents of zoolatry have completely lost their reason (15:18-19). It is in terms of an authentic Yahvism that he judges pagan religions. He considers idolatry a fundamental disorder because it gives the name of God to that which is not God (13:2, 14:15, 14:20).

Idolatry and Christianity. The study of idolatry from the point of view of early Christianity is linked to problems of the birth of Christian art and the question of images, their worship, and the refusal to worship them.

The biblical heritage. Traces of the Old Testament opposition to idols are found in the New Testament, where *eidolon* appears several times in the Pauline epistles. *Galatians* 4:8 takes up the common theme of pagan gods who have no substance. In *1 Corinthians* 10:19, Paul states that when one venerates idols, one is appealing to demons.

The biblical heritage concerning idols also reached Christians by a second route, namely that of Philo Judaeus. In *Allegory of the Law* Philo tries to differentiate the divinity from any human likeness, since "anthropomorphism is an impiety greater than the ocean" (*On the Confusion of Tongues* 27).

The Greek apologists and fathers. In his first *Apology* (9.1-5), Justin Martyr collects the principal themes of second-century polemics against idols: the human form is not suitable to divinity; idols have no soul and are made from a base substance; they are works of depraved artisans and bait for thieves; they bear the names of maleficent demons in whose appearance they are clothed. In his *Apology* Aristides of Athens has no sympathy for the idols of the Greeks. He severely condemns the sin of worshiping created things but is even harsher toward the barbarians, who revere earth, water, the sun, and the moon, and create idols they present as divinities.

Clement of Alexandria wrote his *Protrepticus* in order to convince the worshipers of the gods of what he held to be the stupidity and baseness of pagan myths. He first tries to determine the origin and nature of idols. Blocks of wood and pillars of rock in ancient times, they became human representations thanks to the progress of art, of which the author gives a well-documented survey. Then Clement poses the fundamental question: where did the gods represented by idols come from? The historical response to this question, inspired by euhemerism, is the deification of human beings, of kings who have declared themselves divine, and of kings by their successors. Clement then gives a theological answer, partly inspired by Plato: the pagan gods are demons, shadows, infamous and impure spirits. Consequently, the error and moral corruption of idolatry becomes clear. The error is serious, for it leads the faithful to worship matter and demons as divine.

The Latin apologists. The position taken by the Latin apologists in regard to the pagan gods constitutes a final stage. Here we find the Philonian schema of the *De vita contemplativa* (3-9). Yet, this schema is not a dead weight that condemns the argumentation of the Fathers to die-hard conservatism. Two facts emerge from the study of these documents: on the one hand, we are witnessing a permanent renewal of the antipolytheistic argument; on the other hand, the authors take into account changes in the pagan cults, especially the rise of the mystery cults with their new religiosity. The documents appear at intervals from the late second to the fourth century: *To the Nations, Apology,* and *On Idolatry* by Tertullian; *Octavius* by Minucius Felix; *To Donatus, To Quirinius, To Demetrianus, Quod idola di non sint* by Cyprian; *Divinae institutiones* and *Epitome* by Lactantius Firmianus; and *De errore profanorum religionum* by Firmicus Maternus.

The pagan gods are not idols, states Tertullian: "We stopped worshiping your gods once we realized they do not exist" (*Apology* 10.2). He first substantiates his statement through history, for it is known where these gods were born and where their tombs are. He reproaches the pagans for claiming that their gods became gods after death because of their merits in the service of men. After these considerations inspired by euhemerism, Tertullian tackles the question of *simulacra*. The statues are only inert matter, just like vases, dishes, and furniture. Insensitive to outrage or homage, these statues are given over to commerce if not to destruction. Tertullian treats these questions at greater length in *On Idolatry,* which undertakes to show that idolatry is the gravest sin, encompassing all others.

The Latin apologists also developed the idea that pagan gods are demons. Minucius Felix explains that "the demons hide behind statues and sacred images and, by exhaling their breath," exercise their mysterious effects—spells, dreams, prodigies (*Octavius* 27.1-3).

Augustine. On 24 August 410 the hordes of Alaric entered Rome and subjected the city to pillage. The pagans accused the Christians of having destroyed the worship of the gods and thus chased away the city's protectors. Augustine's answer was the *City of God,* written between 413 and 426, whose twenty-two books constitute the last great apologetic work against ancient paganism. Augustine launches a critique, in turn acerbic and ironic, of the Roman gods, polytheism, and mythology. He knows that idols are not mere beings without substance, invented during the course of history. These idols are also in the hearts of men, for idolatry consists of worshiping creation or a part of it as God. This theme is developed in *On Christian Doctrine* and *On True Religion*, in which Augustine, not content with a critique of the idol, launches a critique of the idol's worshiper, whom he considers a devil worshiper.

Idolatry and Islam. In his work *Kitab al-asnam* (Cairo, 1914), Ibn al-Kalbi described the prosperity of the cult of idols in the pre-Islamic age (Jahiliyah). These idols were *ansab*, or raised stones; *garis*, or stones upon which the blood of sacrifice was poured; sacred trees; and statuettes that were bought and sold at fairs and markets. In Mecca there was an idol in every house. Through this proliferation of idols, the Arab invoked divinity.

Muhammad's opposition to idolatry is a Judeo-Christian inheritance. Abraham becomes the prototype of the monotheistic faith that Muhammad espouses. Abraham is to the prophets what the Arabs are to other Muslim peoples.

> **In Mecca there was an idol in every house. Through this proliferation of idols, the Arab invoked divinity.**

Beginning with Abraham's revelation, Muhammad goes on to see in Islam not only the true monotheism but primordial hanifism (from *hanif*, one who follows the original and true monotheistic religion; a Muslim), which was transmitted by Abraham's son Ishmael, following in his father's footsteps. It is in this original path that we discover the Qur'an's opposition to idolatry.

Throughout the whole Qur'an we find opposition to idols and idolatry. One must turn away from them (15:94) for they bring unhappiness to their worshipers (41:5/6), who are nothing but liars upon whom God will inflict torment after torment (16:88/86-90/88). The idolators' error is a grave one because they have no faith in God (12:106), to whom they compare mere creatures (30:30). A terrible punishment awaits them: they will be treated like their idols (10:29/28), who will abandon them to their sad fate when they stand before the fire (6:23-29). Because of the seriousness of this error, the law of the Qur'an demands that Muslims neither marry a woman idolator nor give their daughters to idolators in marriage (2:220-221).

Idolatry consists of associating a god or gods with God (51:51, 50:25-26). This idea keeps recurring; it is the Qur'an's definition of idolatry, whence the word for associators. Idolatry is an insult to God, since honors reserved for him alone are bestowed on false gods.

Allah is the creator God, judge, dealer of retribution, unique and one in himself, all-powerful, and merciful. He reveals himself through his prophets. He does not show himself, but man recognizes him in the signs of the universe, in the signs of God, *ayat Allah*. He can be known only by his word, his names, his attributes, and his deeds. In any case, he cannot be represented by an image or a representation. Islam is a religion without icons.

Idolatry and Homo Religiosus. The history of religions approaches idolatry in terms of those four fundamental aspects of religious belief and practice that *homo religiosus* has been evolving from prehistoric times down to our own days: the sacred, myth, rite, and symbol. The idol represents a hierophany in which man perceives a manifestation of the sacred that clothes the object in a new dimension. This dimension is obtained by means of rites consecrating the objects of worship, altars, divine statues, and temples: sacral presence and sacred space are indispensable. Through consecration, the image or object now belongs to the divinity and can no longer serve a secular use. The Egyptian rituals for opening the mouth, eyes, nose, and ears of a statue made to represent a divinity attest to a theology of the sacred in which the idol is an incarnation of power and life, a personification; it evokes the greatness of the god. Greek art tried to render this sacral dimension through the whiteness of marble or through protective coatings applied to the idols. Worship reactualizes myths that put the worshiper in contact with primordial time and furnish him models for his life.

This mythical behavior of *homo religiosus* is likewise found in Christian worship, but with an essential difference: the return to a primordial event is not a return to mythical time, but to the historical time of the life of Christ. The Incarnation is effected in a historical time: the Christian who celebrates the mysteries of Christ knows that he is simultaneously attaining the historical time of Jesus and the transhistoric time of the Word of God.

Idolatry is the area in which rites and symbols are multiplied. For man, it is a matter of transcending his human condition through contact with the sacred. His reference point remains the archetype. This is the role of ritual. Religions have left us extraordinary documentation on the rites of celebration, as for instance the sacrificial rites of ancient Greece and Rome, as well as sacred meals with mystical participation of the gods through statues led in procession; rituals of sacrifice with three fires in the Indo-European world; rites of *soma* in India and of *haoma* in Iran; the symbolism of the cults of Cybele and Mithra; the rites of daily worship in Egyptian temples; the power of the rite and of the word in the imitation of the primordial gesture of the god Thoth, creator of the cosmos; funeral rituals of embalming in ancient Egypt, linked to the Osiris myth; and the symbolism of the altar and of gestures in Hindu temples. Incorporated in the life and existence of *homo religiosus*, the symbolism of worship has the function of revelation. In the celebration of worship, such sacred symbolism, myths, and rites help man to penetrate the mystery of salvation, a mystery that is represented for him by the holy history of his religion and culture.

BIBLIOGRAPHY

Barthélémy, Dominique. *God and His Image.* New York, 1966.

Baumer, Iso, Hildegard Christoffels, and Gonsalv Mainberger. *Das Heilige im Licht und Zwielicht.* Einsiedeln, Switzerland, 1966.

Baynes, Norman H. "Idolatry and the Early Church." In *Byzantine Studies and Other Essays,* pp. 116-143. London, 1955.

Bevan, Edwyn Robert. *Holy Images: An Inquiry in Idolatry and Image-Worship in Ancient Paganism and in Christianity.* London, 1940.

Campenhausen, Hans von. "Die Bilderfrage als theologisches Problem der alten Kirche." In *Tradition und Leben,* edited by Campenhausen, pp. 216-252. Tübingen, 1960.

Clerc, Charly. *Les théories relatives au culte des images chez les auteurs grecs du deuxième siècle après J.-C.* Paris, 1915.

Dubarle, A. M. *La manifestation naturelle de Dieu d'après l'écriture.* Paris, 1976.

Duesberg, Hilaire. "Le procès de l'idolâtrie." In *Les scribes inspirés,* vol. 2. Paris, 1939. Second edition (1966) written in collaboration with Frarsen Irénée.

Gelin, Albert. "Idoles, idolâtrie." In *Dictionnaire de la Bible, supplément,* vol. 4. Paris, 1949.

Gilbert, Maurice. *La critique des dieux dans le Livre de la Sagesse.* Rome, 1973.

Goblet d'Alviella, Eugène. "Les origines de l'idolâtrie." In *Croyances, rites, institutions,* vol. 2, pp. 125-147. Paris, 1911.

Goetz, J. "Idolâtrie." In *Catholicisme hier, aujourd'hui, demain,* vol. 5. Paris, 1962.

Mandouze, André. "Saint Augustin et la religion romaine." In *Recherches augustiniennes,* vol. 1, pp. 187-223. Paris, 1958.

Marion, Jean-Luc. *L'idole et la distance: Cinq études.* Paris, 1977.

Michel, A. "Idolâtrie, idole." In *Dictionnaire de théologie catholique,* vol. 7. Paris, 1921.

North, Christopher P. "The Essence of Idolatry." In *Von Ugarit nach Qumran,* edited by Johannes Hempel and Leonhard Rost, pp. 151-160. Berlin, 1958.

Prat, Ferdinand. "Idolâtrie, idole." In *Dictionnaire de la Bible,* vol. 3. Paris, 1912.

Preuss, Horst Dietrich. *Verspottung fremder Religionen im Alten Testament.* Stuttgart, 1971.

Sauser, Ekkart. "Das Gottesbild: Eine Geschichte der Spannung von Vergegenwärtigung und Erinnerung." *Trierer Theologische Zeitschrift* 84 (1975): 164-173.

Schwartz, J. "Philon et l'apologétique chrétienne du second siècle." In *Hommages à André Dupont-Sommer,* edited by André Caquot and M. Philonenko, pp. 497-507. Paris, 1971.

Vermander, Jean-Marie. "La polémique des Apologistes latins contre les Dieux du paganisme." *Recherches augustiniennes* 17 (1982): 3-128.

Will, Robert. *Le culte: Étude d'histoire et de philosophie religieuses.* 3 vols. Paris, 1925-1935.

JULIEN RIES
Translated from French by Kristine Anderson

IGNATIUS LOYOLA

IGNATIUS LOYOLA (c. 1491-1556), author of *Spiritual Exercises,* founder and first superior general of the Jesuits, Christian saint. Iñigo López de Loyola was born to noble, wealthy Basque parents in the castle at Loyola, near Azpeitia, Guipúzcoa province, in northernmost Spain.

Early Life and Education. In the patriarchal family in which Iñigo spent his boyhood, loyalty to Roman Catholic doctrines was unquestioning, and observance of religious practices and moral standards was about average for its social class.

A momentous change in the youngster's life occurred when he was between twelve and sixteen years of age. His father (who died in 1507, long after his wife) accepted the invitation of Juan Velázquez de Cuéllar to receive the boy into his home at Arévalo in Castile, and there raise him as if he were his own son, while preparing him for a career in politics, public administration, and arms. The wealthy and famous Velázquez would act as the boy's patron at the royal court, while utilizing his services as a page.

When Velázquez died in 1517, his page promptly entered the service of the duke of Nájera, viceroy of Navarre, as a courtier, with obligations to military duty if needed. During the revolt of the Comuneros, Iñigo fought in the forefront of the duke's forces in the victorious storming of Nájera (September 1520), but he refused to participate in the customary sack of the town as an act unworthy of a Christian or a gentleman. When the French invaded Navarre in 1521 and attacked Pamplona, its capital, the townsfolk surrendered without a struggle. Almost alone at a council of war, Iñigo advocated resistance to death in the fortress above the city. In the absence of a priest, he prepared for the end by following a medieval custom of confessing his sins nonsacramentally to a comrade-in-arms. During the six-hour bombardment of the citadel on 21 May, a cannon ball struck Iñigo, injuring his left leg and breaking his right one below the knee. This calamity moved the small garrison to surrender; it also effected a metamorphosis in the wounded man's life.

To while away the tedium of convalescence, the sick man turned to reading. Since the meager family library lacked his preferred tales of chivalry, he accepted Spanish versions of Ludolph of Saxony's life of Christ and Jacobus de Voragine's *Golden Legend,* a collection of saints' lives. As he kept rereading and reflecting on these two famous works of edification, Iñigo developed an aversion for his worldly ideals and ways. He resolved to serve and imitate Christ alone and to emulate the deeds of the saints, although in a manner as yet undetermined.

Spiritual Life and Leadership. Early in 1522 Iñigo left home and started on a pilgrimage to the Holy Land. Soon he took a vow of perpetual chastity, dismissed his two servants, and disposed of all his money. At the Benedictine monastery of Montserrat on 22-25 March, he gave away his mule and his fine clothes, donning a coarse pilgrim's garb of sackcloth. Then he made a knightly vigil of arms, praying all night before the altar of Our Lady, where he discarded his sword and dagger. From Montserrat he proceeded to the nearby town of Manresa, where his stay, originally intended to last only a few days, extended to eleven fateful months. At Manresa, the pilgrim, as he now termed himself, refused to divulge his true identity. He led a life of great austerity and underwent bodily penances so severe that they permanently impaired his rugged constitution.

At Manresa Iñigo also composed the substance of *Spiritual Exercises,* although he continued revising and expanding the text until 1541. In its opening paragraph the slender book describes spiritual exercises as "every method of examination of conscience, of vocal and mental prayer, and of other spiritual activities that will be mentioned later . . . to prepare and dispose the soul to rid itself of all inordinate attachments; and after their removal, to seek and find God's will concerning the disposition of one's life for the salvation of the soul." Along with a number of annotations, rules, and notes, the text proposes points for methodical meditations and contemplations on various Christian doctrines and on some key topics original to the author, but mostly on incidents in the life of Christ.

Divided into four stages, the book is a manual of practical directives for a retreat director. Highly compressed and lacking in literary embellishments, the text is not designed for continued pious reading in the usual sense. The book was mainly the product of the author's own experiences within himself and with others. It soon won acclaim as a spiritual masterpiece, original, unified, outstanding for its sound religious psychology and pedagogy, and remarkably well organized. Its contents manifest the essence of Ignatian and Jesuit spirituality, and it has exerted an enormous influence throughout the Catholic world down to the present day. As early as 1548, Paul III's *Pastoralis officii* gave what has been termed the most explicit and honorable papal approval ever accorded a book. A long list of popes have added their own commendations, culminating with Pius XI, who in 1922 officially designated Ignatius as the patron saint of spiritual exercises.

From Manresa the pilgrim traveled by foot and by ship to Jerusalem, arriving on 4 September 1523 by way of Barcelona, Gaeta, and Rome and Venice. Only because he was denied permission to reside permanently in the Holy City, where he had hoped to spend his days visiting the sacred places and evangelizing, did he decide to return to Spain. He set sail for Venice on 3 October 1523 and arrived in Barcelona in February 1524.

Study, motivated by a desire to help souls, preoccupied the next eleven years. He migrated to the University of Paris (1528-1535), where he gained a master of arts degree in philosophy in 1534 and then studied philosophy for a year and a half.

In Paris, new followers were attracted by Iñigo's spiritual exercises. On 15 August 1534, in a chapel on Montmartre, he and six companions vowed to dedicate their lives to the good of their neighbors, while observing strict poverty, and to journey to Jerusalem on pilgrimage or, if this proved impossible (as it did because of war), to place themselves at the disposal of the pope. Three others joined in the renewal of this vow a year later, bringing to ten the original membership of the as yet unforeseen Society of Jesus.

Heading for Jerusalem, Ignatius traveled in December 1535 to Venice, where his nine companions joined him in January 1537. He and six of the nine were ordained priests there the following June. After long deliberations with the whole group, Ignatius resolved to make their association a permanent, structured one, to be called the Society of Jesus. His First Formula of the Institute, a brief draft of a constitution, received solemn confirmation from Paul III on 27 September 1540, canonically establishing it as a religious order. The new order aimed at the salvation and perfection of its members, popularly known as Jesuits, and of all humankind. To this end it incorporated a number of innovations in its organization, manner of life, and scope of ministries.

Because of his rare combination of talents, Ignatius influenced modern religious life as few have done. He was at once a man of prayer, a contemplative, a mystic who reported many visions, a man of action, and a born leader not only in individual spiritual direction but also in practical projects of great magnitude. He was beatified in 1609 and canonized in 1622.

[*See also* Jesuits.]

BIBLIOGRAPHY

For editions of the writings by Ignatius in their original languages and in translations, as well as for the enormous secondary literature about him, see *Bibliographie ignatienne (1894-1957)*, edited by Jean-François Gilmont, s.j., and Paul Daman, s.j. (Paris, 1958), containing 2,872 entries; *Orientaciones bibliográficas sobre San Ignacio de Loyola*, edited by Ignacio Iparraguirre, S.J., vol. 1, 2d ed. (Rome, 1965), with 651 items; and *Orientaciones bibliográficas sobre San Ignacio de Loyola,* edited by Manuel Ruiz Jurado, s.j., vol. 2 (Rome, 1977), adding another 580 items (both volumes contain evaluative comments and references to important book reviews). Complete annual bibliographies appear in *Archivum Historicum Societatis Iesu,* published since 1932 in Rome. An important source, although incomplete, brief, and ending in 1538, is *The Autobiography of St. Ignatius Loyola, with Related Documents,* translated by Joseph F. O'Callaghan and edited with an introduction and notes by John C. Olin (New York, 1974). Ignatius's best-known work is available in several English translations; a particularly good version is *The Spiritual Exercises of St. Ignatius by Louis J. Puhl,* s.j. (Westminster, Md., 1952), reprinted many times. *The Constitutions of the Society of*

Jesus has been translated, with an introduction and commentary by George E. Ganss, S.J. (Saint Louis, Mo., 1970). The best biography available in English is by Paul Dudon, S.J.: *St. Ignatius of Loyola* (Milwaukee, 1949). *Saint Ignatius Loyola: The Pilgrim Years* (London, 1956), by James Brodrick, S.J., covers the years 1491-1538 only and is written by a superior stylist. *The Jesuits, Their Spiritual Doctrine and Practice: A Historical Study* (Chicago, 1964), by Joseph de Guibert, S.J., is an authoritative study.

JOHN F. BRODERICK, S.J.

IMMORTALITY

The concept of immortality can be understood and expanded upon on three levels. In its first sense, immortality is the quality attributed to divine beings, mythical or angelic, who by their very nature are not subject to death. The second sense concerns those heroes who have attained a divine status that they share with the gods. In its third sense, the concept of immortality has to do with the human being who enters upon a new form of eternal and incorruptible existence after death. The present article will deal only with immortality in this third sense, treating the permanence of the human being beyond the phenomenon of death.

Nonliterate Peoples. The study of nonliterate cultures affords insight into a number of the living values of these peoples, their relations with their ancestors, their initiation rites, their sense of time, and their eschatological myths, and in this way we arrive at a better comprehension of the basic patterns of the activity of *homo religiosus.*

Sub-Saharan Africa. For the African there are two kinds of time: mythical time, the time of the eternally valid group and its continuity, and real time, in which the life of the individual and the discontinuity of death take place. Between these two times lies the symbolic mediation of funeral rites, through which the deceased leaves contingent time and

> ## Ancestor worship holds a most important place in African belief and ritual.

passes into mythical time, the time of the pyramid of beings. The funeral rites are the collective response to the death of an individual; they allow the group to endure.

Alongside this vision of the undying ethnos exists the belief in the deathlessness of the personal being, indispensable for the continuity of the group. Among the Bobo of Burkina Faso, real time lies under the sign of Dwo, an unchanging divinity who rules over spirits and genies, the life force *(nyama),* and the ancestors. Also in Burkina Faso, in

the eschatology of the Dagai, a cyclic conception of time is accompanied by the notion of the reincarnation of the deceased—all new births arise from the transformation of the ancestors. After death, the deceased passes first to the land of the spirits, either to become an ancestor or to be reincarnated in the body of a totemic animal.

There are two classes of ancestors, those who are mythical and primordial and those who have entered this state after their life on earth. Ancestor worship holds a most important place in African belief and ritual. The conception of the ancestor is made up of two components: on the one hand, the purity of the social and religious ideal, and on the other, a concern with the continuity and identity of the community. Together the two components form the concept of individual and collective immortality. The ancestor represents the symbolic transposition of the human condition to a numinous plane while continuing to be a part of the world of the living. It is in the role of ancestor that the most important stage of one's destiny after death is realized.

Another aspect of ancestral immortality is found in African beliefs in reincarnation. Reincarnation brings about a reactualization of the deceased that partially interrupts his postmortem fate. Reincarnation implies that the returning ancestor is recognized and present in the memory of the living, and it can only occur in a child of the same lineage and sex.

In all cultures, funeral rituals serve as primary expressions of belief in immortality while at the same time serving as instruments that help to make it real by symbolically absorbing the shock caused by a death. Like the rites of birth and initiation, they effect a passage that is at once a separation and a coming together. In all African communities, funeral rites mark out the successive stages traversed by the deceased.

Australia. The appearance of man in his present form is placed in the Dreaming, a primordial era called *alchera* or *alcheringa* by the Aranda, a central Australian people. The creation myths revolve around the great gods and the civilizing heroes, so that primordiality is fundamental. The cosmogonic and primordial myths play a pivotal role because all the rites of initiation, reproduction, and fertility are reenactments of these myths.

Death is a shock to the tribe and is felt as a disruption of the collective life, hence the cries and wailing, the mourning rituals, the rhythmic chanting, and the search to discover the evil spirit who caused this death. But the Australians believe that death is the final rite of passage that leads one from the profane world to the sacred universe. Man has two souls. The true self, the primordial and preexistent spirit, comes from heaven, the totemic center. At death, the true soul leaves the body and goes back to live forever in the eternal Dreaming, where it was before the individual's birth, while the other soul remains on earth, taking up residence in another person and moving about among the living.

The funeral rites take various forms. Through the rites, the preexisting spirit regains its spiritual domain, sometimes thought of as the primordial totemic center. A whole ritual symbolism punctuates this journey, for example the occasional placing of bones within a totemic coffin. Beliefs in reincarnation, however, are rare and confused. For human beings the life cycle is simple: from the preexisting spirit, birth into a body and entry into the profane world, to the first stage of reintegration into the Dreaming via initiation, and finally the return to the original state through funeral rites.

The Americas. We come now to American Indian beliefs in immortality, as they are found outside the more advanced American civilizations. These are forms of religion that have survived through the post-Columbian era and still exist in some areas of North and South America. The belief in a life beyond the grave seems to have been firmly established in Indian thought in early times, to judge from their conception of the world and of life, from ancestral traditions, and from the testimonies of seers.

Among the American Indian peoples we find a conception of the soul that forms the basis of their beliefs in immortality. In North America the idea of a double soul is extremely widespread. The corporeal soul gives life, consciousness, and the faculty of movement to the body, whereas the dream soul is separate from the body and can move about in space and go to distant places. Death occurs when the separate soul becomes trapped in the realm of the dead. Then the corporeal soul is also detached from the body. The Indians believe that the soul goes to the region of the dead, which is known through myths and tales to be patterned after the world of the living. Thus in North America it is sometimes called the "happy hunting ground."

There are various methods of entombment: inhumation in South America, and in Canada placement of the body on a platform, in a tree, or on the ground. There is also incineration. Among the Iroquois, the Algonquians to the south of the Great Lakes, there are second funerals, involving the burial of the disinterred bones in a common grave or funeral urn. The provision of grave goods—food, drink, weapons, clothing, and jewelry—is widespread in the Andean region.

Inner Asia and the Finno-Ugric peoples. A great similarity in beliefs concerning the soul can be noted on both sides of the Urals. The Khanty (Ostiaks) and Mansi (Voguls), Ugrians from the Ob River region, believe in the existence of a double soul comprising the breath or bodily soul and the shadow or dream soul, which is free and quite incorporeal but is tied to the dead person after death. Thus, after the person's death, the soul that was free and immaterial in life takes on a bodily form because of its ties to the corpse. Corpse and soul together stand for the complete, personal identity of the deceased person. Thus while the body is in the grave, it is also somewhere else thanks to its soul. The Khanty and Mansi believe that the free soul enters a subter-

ranean realm where it represents the deceased and his personality.

Finnic pneumatology is identical to that of the northern Eurasian world. The free soul (image soul, shadow soul) is the extracorporeal manifestation of the person, which can become separated from the body even during life, in dreams, ecstasy, or trance. The corporeal soul, bound to the body, animates physical and psychic life. This dualism has faded under the influence of Christianity, but has left numerous traces in religious practices.

Mesoamerican Religions. The Mesoamerican cultural and religious complex includes three major periods: the Preclassic concludes in the third century CE, and the Classic era extends from that time to the year 1000, followed by the Postclassic era. I shall consider here only the last period, for which we have relatively abundant archaeological and historical records.

The Aztec. The religion of the Aztec—the dominant people in Mexico at the time of the conquest—is a syncretic one in which three principal gods are found: the sun god Huitzilopochtli, the rain god Tlaloc, originally from Teotihuacán, and Quetzalcoatl, the feathered serpent of the Toltec.

After death, people are subject to different fates, according to the choice of the gods. Stillborn children go to the thirteenth heaven, where the "tree of milk" is found that provides them with nourishment for an eternal infancy. Warriors slain on the battlefield and all those who have been sacrificed on an altar, as well as traders who have died on their journeys, become companions of the Sun, who has chosen them to take part in the cosmic salvation.

The second category of the deceased is made up of men and women chosen by Tlaloc, those killed by drowning, lightning, and marsh fevers. These are buried, and go to the eastern abode, to the gardens of the god. All other dying people go to the northern realm, the land of night, until they reach the underworld of the god Mictlan, who will annihilate them.

The Maya. Maya religion is known through the discovery of great cities such as Tikal, Copan, Palenque, and Uxmal. The period of its highest attainment extends from the third to the tenth centuries. In its funeral practices we find again three categories of the dead. The privileged groups are warriors who fall in battle, women dying in childbirth, priests, and suicides by hanging. These are immortal and enjoy eternal gladness in the Maya paradise beneath the sacred ceiba, the tree that crosses all the celestial spheres. This is the "tree of the beginning," Yache, which creates the junction between heaven and earth.

Inca Religion. At a time when various civilizations shared the Andean region (Peru, Bolivia, and Ecuador), new populations came on the scene. Chief among these were the Inca. Various witnesses of the Spanish conquest left accounts of Inca religion, all of which agree that the Inca believed in immortality and imagined the afterlife as a continuation of the present life. The evidence found in Peru attests to funeral customs such as the preservation of the corpse, the giving of a deceased ancestor's name to a newborn child, and the placing of the body in a fetal position in the grave or funeral jar.

Religions of China. China did not produce a hierarchical classification of its beliefs about the fate of the dead. Most of them were destined for the kingdom of the Yellow Springs, while the kings and princes ascended to be near the Lord on High. The lords lived out their afterlives in the temples of the family ancestors, near their graves. This ancient agrarian religion dissolved along with the early social structure once the Han dynasty came to power, beginning in 206 BCE. Taoism then developed spectacularly, reaching its peak under the Six Dynasties, from the fourth to the sixth centuries of our era. As a religion of salvation, it had to offer an afterlife, and as the human being was thought to have many souls, but only one body for them to live in, it was along these lines that thinkers sought immortality. Some envisioned a melting pot of souls, out of which the deceased would receive an undying body, provided that the living were assiduous in practicing the funeral rites. But most tended to the view that the living body was preserved and became an immortal one. To this end they felt one should develop certain organs to be substituted for the corporeal ones. This gave rise to various practices to which the adepts, *tao-shih,* applied themselves in the desire to ensure the immortality of the living (body)—dietary practices to kill demons and maintain bodily vigor, embryonic circular breathing to induce ecstatic experiences, and sexual practices involving a mixing of the semen with the breath in order to stimulate the brain (Henri Maspero, *Taoism and Chinese Religion,* Amherst, 1981). Spiritual techniques such as insight, meditation, and mystical union came to be added to these physical ones. Between the second and sixth centuries, these techniques were supplemented by ceremonies for the dead, rites intended to melt the souls in a fire that would transform them into immortals *(hsien).*

Ancient Egypt. From the time of the Old Kingdom, the Egyptians envisaged a complex spiritual pattern, modeled on the divine life and made up of three elements necessary for life to exist. *Akh* is divine energy. *Ba* is the faculty of movement, human consciousness, and the ability to take various shapes. The divine breath and support of all created beings, *ka,* is the collection of qualities of divine origin that give eternal life; it is the life force connected with Ptah and Re, and it is the divine, living part of man. When the *ka* becomes separated from the body, it disintegrates, and the person must then be recreated through mummification and funeral rites if an afterlife is to be possible.

The *Book of Going Forth by Day* represents a confluence of various doctrines concerning immortality—mummification, psychostasia, or weighing of the *ba,* the judgment of the

dead, the kingdom of the dead, the freedom of the *ba,* and the happy fate of those who have led their lives in accord with Maat. These seemingly contradictory features can be reconciled in terms of the trial of the soul before Osiris and his court. Mummification was intended to bind the *ba* to the body of the deceased and to this world. After vindicating himself before Osiris, the blessed one, *maa kheru,* was free to move about among the gods and spirits of the *tuat.* Meanwhile he also maintained ties with the world of the living, a world of joy in Egyptian eyes. Although Egyptians observed the Osirian funeral, the dependence of immortality on the preservation of the mummy need not be overemphasized. Even if the disintegration of the mummy broke the connection between the *ba* and the world, the deceased who had been consigned to the *tuat* continued to live happily in the Field of Reeds. The

> The *Book of Going Forth by Day* represents a confluence of various doctrines concerning immortality—mummification, psychostasia, or weighing of the *ba.* . . .

happy lot of the just person living in the boat of the Sun was reserved for those who were too poor to secure an Osirian funeral. The vast world of the immortals in the Middle and New Kingdoms was composed of Osirian immortals tied to their preserved mummies, and thus free to move about in the beyond and in this world of the living, Osirian immortals whose mummies had been destroyed but who were still happy in the *tuat* kingdom, where they were constrained to stay, and solarized, blessed immortals in the boat of the Sun. Their happy everlasting life had been prepared for by an ethical life in conformity with Maat ("justice") by the arrangement of the tomb and mummification, and all that went into the construction of the eternal home.

India. In all three of the great directions in Indian religious thought—Vedic, Brahmanic, and *bhakti*—the belief in immortality is clear and constant.

Vedic India. In the Vedic texts, particularly in sacrificial contexts, *amrta* appears together with *soma. Amrta* is the heavenly elixir of immortality, as *soma* is a sacrificial libation offered to the gods by the priests. *Amrta* is the drink of immortality of gods and men; *soma* is the elixir of life that has come from heaven to bestow immortality *(amrtam).* Both words contain the idea of the winning of immortality, conceived as a perpetual renewal of youth and life.

In the *Rgveda* a distinction is made between the body and the invisible principle of the human being, designated by the words *asu,* the life force or breath, and manas, the spirit, the seat of intellect and internal feelings, located in the heart. The nature of the soul can be seen in the Vedic attitude toward death, for the dead are simply the shadows of the living. What survives is the individuality, the essence of the human person, which becomes immortal by being indefinitely prolonged in time, as part of a perfectly ordered cosmos. Immortality is a perpetual remaking in accord with universal law, and consists in being born everlastingly. The Rgvedic hymn 10.129.1-3 speaks of "the One that was before being and nonbeing, before death and non-death." Nondeath is understood in relation to both the birth of organized time and the womb that is synonymous with death and renewal.

Brahmanic India. The symbolism of immortality in the Brahmanas goes beyond the Vedic symbolism. The sacrifice confers long life and immortality, symbolized by the cosmic year; the days and nights are symbols of human lives, of mortal, transient time. The seasons make up the year in its real sense, a limitless rebirth; the year is the symbol of divine life and immortality, and Prajapati is the year. The sacrificial altar is constructed in the course of a year using 10,800 bricks, each one representing an hour. The *garhapatya* fire represents a womb, into which a special *mantra* inspires the breath of life. Through the *ahavaniya* fire the sacrificer rises to heaven, to be born a second time and attain immortality. Thus the sacrifice constitutes the transcendence of death by means of ritual.

Bhakti. *Bhakti* is a loving devotion that gives the believer a greater knowledge of the Lord (Krsna or Isvara) than any meditation or reflection, and it is a divine gift given only to those who have prepared themselves by a loving attitude. Within the wider context of the transmigration of souls, the *bhakti* movement affirms a monotheistic tendency and an emphasis on salvation. *Bhakti* takes the place of the elixir of life, conferring eternal life with Krsna. A number of texts emphasize the destiny of the *bhakta,* who is *siddha* ("perfect"), *amrta* ("immortal"), and *trpta* ("happy").

Buddhism. The Upanisads taught that there exists within every person an *I*, the *atman,* an enduring and eternal entity, an immutable substance underlying the ephemeral world of phenomena. Hence the way to immortality was easily found. The *atman,* they said, becomes immortal not through sacrifice or ritual or ascetic discipline, but by taking possession of the immortal, the *brahman.* For the Upanisads, it is the identification of *atman* and *brahman* that bestows immortality.

The belief in an afterlife and immortality is not ignored by the Buddha. Like the brahman, the yogin, and the mendicant, he seeks "that which endures," "deliverance," and "what is undying."

Celts, Germans, Scandinavians, Thracians, and Getae. A firm belief in an afterlife is attested by the funerary practices of the Celts, Germans, and Scandinavians. Archaeological evidence is abundant, including megalithic tombs, dolmens, and individual burials in coffins marked with solar symbols, and cremation is known from the urnfields as early as 1500 BCE.

The belief in the soul's immortality among the Celts and the Gauls is attested by numerous early witnesses. Caesar (*Gallic Wars* 6.14) says that the druids asserted that souls are immortal, that after death they pass into another body, and that this belief explains the reckless fearlessness of their warriors. For the Germans, the soul is reborn within the *Sippe* (the clan). Celtic traditions give accounts of an aes sídh, or "paradise of the dead," an open world connected by a bridge to the land of the living, sometimes also appearing as an island in the ocean.

The cult of Zalmoxis among the Thracians and the Getae (Herodotus, 4.94-95) also entails the belief in the deathlessness of the soul, obtained through an initiation ritual that belongs among the mystery cults of the Mediterranean world, particularly those having to do with the preparation for a happy existence in the other world.

The Hebrew Scriptures. From remotest times the Hebrews practiced inhumation, placing various objects, weapons, and provisions in the grave for the use of the dead, gestures which seem to constitute at least one facet of a *votum immortalitatis.* The Hebrew Bible sees the human being as a composite of flesh *(basar),* the breath of life, or soul *(nefesh),* and spirit *(ruah).*

After death, people go to She'ol—an immense, underground place, deep, dark, and bolted shut, the abode of shadows—to lead lives that are shadows of their lives on earth, and according to *Job* 7:9-10, this life is one of no return. This idea contrasts with the archaic concept of the "afterlife" of a corpse that makes use of objects and food, and is undoubtedly later. She'ol is not to be confused with the grave, the habitat of the corpse. The shade in She'ol is not the remnant of the mortal being in the grave, it is a "double"; She'ol is an extension of the grave.

The doctrine of She'ol was of popular origin and remained quite vague, but it demonstrates a spiritualistic tendency in the belief in an afterlife found in the Hebrew scriptures. References to an afterlife are found in the Bible. The human being is not destroyed after death, but is reunited with his ancestors. The miracles performed by Elijah and Elisha (*1 Kgs.* 17:17-24, *2 Kgs.* 4:31-37) show that life can be restored to the body. Moreover, the evocation of the dead, characteristic of popular beliefs in an afterlife, shows that the living attempted to get in touch with the deceased.

The *refa'im* of She'ol are the biblical forerunners of immortal souls. Several passages in *Job* and *Psalms* allude to a union with God that death will not destroy. During the persecutions of Antiochus Epiphanes, the fate of the dead is foremost among Israel's preoccupations; the vision of dry bones in *Ezekiel* 37:1-14 serves as the basis of a meditation on resurrection and God's power to bring his believers out of She'ol. In the *Book of Daniel* 7:9, the motif of the "book of life" marks a gradual shift toward individual judgment, and the faith in individual eschatological resurrection is clearly attested in both *Daniel,* which dates from 165 BCE (*Dn.* 11:40-12:13), and in *2 Maccabees* (chaps. 7, 9, 11), written in Greek sometime after 124 BCE.

In the *Wisdom of Solomon,* written in Greek around 50 BCE, the concept of the afterlife is rendered for the first time by *aphtharsia,* "immortality" (1:11-15, 2:23-25), and the immortality of the souls of the righteous is clearly affirmed. They are in the hand of God (3:1-4), and their souls enjoy a never-ending life with God in peace, rest, love, grace, and mercy (3:9, 4:7, 5:15). After the destruction of the Temple in the year 70 CE, a doctrine of resurrection for everyone—not only the righteous but also for nonbelievers—appears within the circle of the tannaim.

The Qumran Texts. The Essenes, as described by Josephus Flavius, believed in the immortality of the soul and its future life freed from bodily ties, hence their renunciation of even the most legitimate of the pleasures of this world. As for the Qumran texts, the *Manual of Discipline* says that those who let themselves be guided and inspired by the spirits of truth and light will be blessed in this world and will enjoy eternal gladness in a world without end. The wicked will be punished in the darkness of an everlasting fire (2.8, 4.7-8).

The Greco-Roman World. The imagination of the ancients endowed the land of Greece with many mouths of the underworld, called the "gates of Hades." For some, these were the paths through which people vanished after death, for others they were the wombs of perpetual rebirth; the Greeks were divided over these two views of the afterlife (André Motte, *Prairies et jardins de la Grèce antique,* Brussels, 1973, p. 239).

Orphism. Monuments to Orpheus are found as early as the sixth century BCE, and allusions to his descent into the underworld appear in the fifth century. Priests who preach salvation in the name of Orpheus and promulgate an initiation that sets people free for their lives in the next world are reported in Classical times. In the Hellenistic period references to Orpheus become more frequent, and Orphism finds fertile ground in Ptolemaic Egypt, where it encounters the cult of Osiris.

Orphism professes the belief in a happy afterlife. The seed of salvation is within man, since his immortal soul is a piece of the divine stuff, and the purpose of life on earth is to come to a permanent choice. The Orphic doctrine of purification allows for the reincarnation of souls. We know from Plato that the Orphians offered rather gloomy descriptions of the torments of the guilty soul and the evils awaiting the damned, plunged into a pool of mud (*Republic* 2.363d).

Early Pythagoreanism. Settling in Magna Graecia in the second half of the sixth century, Pythagoras founded at Croton a brotherhood shrouded in secrecy, which introduced its followers to a new kind of life meant to point the way that led to salvation. In religious matters Pythagoras espoused

Orphic views and brought about, as Eliade (1982) has indicated, a large-scale synthesis of archaic elements (some of them "shamanistic") and bold reevaluations of ascetic and contemplative techniques. The Orphic and Pythagorean doctrines regarding the soul display many features in common: immortality, transmigration, punishment in Hades, and the soul's eventual return to heaven. Pythagoreanism, however, developed its teaching independently, in a closed society. For Pythagoras the human soul is immortal; it is held within the body as if in a prison and can live independently of the body. After death, the soul passes into Hades to be purified, and to the extent that it is not completely cleansed it must return to earth and seek a new body.

Gnostic Religion. The gnostics viewed man as a combination of matter and spirit and saw the body as the prison which holds the soul after its fall. Within this mixture, the soul, an aeon of the same substance as the celestial world, remains intact, for it is incorruptible. The technical term *aphtharsia* ("incorruptibility") is part of the theological vocabulary of all gnostic systems. Incorruptibility is part of the soul's makeup because of its divine origin and is the essence of its immortality, even though by being imprisoned in the body the soul has become steeped in matter.

Salvation consists in the liberation of the soul. A heavenly savior intervenes to stir the captive soul's memory, to remind it of its origin and make it recognize its true "self." This revelation is made through a series of initiatory trials, by the end of which the soul has discovered a luminous vision of its own essence; the vision awakens in it a burning desire to return to its home. Then begins the second stage, that of the return to the "realm of life." The description of this ascension (or *Himmelsreise*) is found in the texts of all the sects; it includes deprivation and release from material bonds, a path passing through many dangers, the presence of a heavenly guide, and a triumphant entry into celestial Paradise for an immortal destiny amid the blessed light. The gathering of all the souls that have been held in bodies reconstitutes the Pleroma.

Manichaeism. In the Manichaean scheme, man is a mixture of light and darkness. His body is the work of the archons, but his soul is a divine spark, a portion of the eternal realm of light that has fallen into the material world and been imprisoned in the body by birth. The saving element in the earthbound soul is the *nous,* while the *psuche* is the part that must be saved; this is the task of Gnosis, a hypostatic divine entity from the realm of light. The gnostic message awakens the *psuche,* makes it aware of its divine origin, and stirs in it the desire to return on high. This awakening of the soul is the beginning of salvation. The gnostic strives to realize the separation of light and darkness within himself. By an unceasing choice he carries out a *katharsis* within himself, a preliminary salvation that will take full effect after death, in a final liberation of the radiant and eternal soul.

Islam. The proclamation of the Day of Judgment comes at the beginning of the Qur'an, and it is seen from the standpoint of the resurrection, *qiyama*. On that day all the race of Adam will be gathered together, each one to receive judgment and everlasting retribution according to his deeds. Fear of the Last Day and of the punishment of Hell is a fundamental feature of the Prophet's teaching. The chosen ones on the right, the believers, will be called to enjoy Paradise, while the unbelieving will be condemned to torture.

Islamic anthropogony. The Islamic view of the nature of man is not particularly clear. The word *ruh* means *pneuma,* "breath"—the subtle breath that comes from the brain, that is, the mind. In some traditions it dies with the body only to be brought back to life with it. This is the spiritual part of the human being. There is also the nafs (Heb., *nefesh*), commonly translated as "soul," the carnal breath that comes "from the viscera."

The spiritualist doctrine of Shiism views the *ruh* as the pure breath of all matter, a spiritual substance that is immortal by nature. In this perspective man is not a body with a soul, but a spirit which temporarily inhabits a body as its instrument. Only on leaving the body does it find its true nature, for it is made to live independently; the soul's pleasure lies in the spiritual world. This tradition sees the spirit as a celestial, radiant substance, imperishable and immortal.

As against the spiritualistic tendency of Shiism, the traditional Sunni theologians held that man is rather a compound of substances, body and soul, and entirely material. The central question is this: what happens at the moment of death? For those who take man to be a material composite of body plus soul, the soul "disappears" at death and is brought back to life on the last day, while those who see in the body only a temporary instrument of the soul believe the human soul to be made for the spiritual life, even after its separation from the body. In the first case the resurrection of the body is indispensable, whereas in the second the afterlife can do without it. As may be seen, the possible viewpoints can differ sharply.

Christianity. In order to understand the Christian doctrine of immortality, the message of the New Testament must be located within its twofold setting in the biblical tradition of Israel on one hand and the context of religious beliefs and philosophical ideas of the Greco-Roman world on the other. At the time of the birth of Christianity, the Platonic doctrines of the human composite of *soma* and *psuche,* the dissolution of this composite by death, and the immortality and afterlife of the *psuche,* were widely held in Mediterranean thought. With this in mind, the central question concerns not the immortality of the soul as such but the originality of Christian revelation concerning the immortality of man, as he is created in the image of God and redeemed by Christ.

The faith in an individual and eschatological resurrection is clearly attested in the *Book of Daniel* and in the *Second Book of the Maccabees,* in the second century BCE. But where did the idea of bodily resurrection fit into the eschatological thought of Jesus? In an early presentation, Jesus affirms that those who enter the kingdom will receive a share in a life of unending peace and happiness, a point of view both communal and personal. The divine gift of eternal life is one of a spiritual nature; whosoever will enter the kingdom easily will be transformed (*1 Cor.* 15:51). This presentation ends by proclaiming the Messiah's passage through death and the reopening of his kingdom after it. This is the idea behind the earthly pilgrimage of the church, through which Jesus shared his own victory over death with his disciples (*1 Cor.* 15:20).

How did apostolic Christianity interpret the resurrection of Christ? After living first in the hope of the Lord's coming (*1 Cor.* 16:22), the apostles focused on the message of resurrection. Jesus is resurrected as the first fruit of the believers who die before his second coming. Later the church gradually accorded more importance to resurrection for all.

[*See also* Soul; Afterlife; *and* Resurrection.]

BIBLIOGRAPHY

Alger, W. R. *A Critical History of the Doctrine of the Future Life.* New York, 1981.

Anati, Emmanuel, ed. *Prehistoric Art and Religion: Valcamonica Symposium* 1979. Milan, 1983.

Beier, Ulli. *The Origin of Life and Death.* London, 1966.

Bianu, Zeno. *Les religions et la mort.* Paris, 1981.

Camps, Gabriel. *La préhistoire: À la recherche du paradis perdu.* Paris, 1982. See pages 371-445 for a remarkable synthesis on prehistoric religious man.

Choisy, Maryse. *La survie après la mort.* Paris, 1967.

Cullman, Oscar. *Immortality of the Soul or Resurrection of the Dead? The Witness of the New Testament.* London, 1958.

Cumont, Franz. *Lux perpetua.* Paris, 1949.

Dumézil, Georges. *Le festin d'immortalité.* Paris, 1924.

Edsman, Carl-Martin. *Ignis divinus: Le feu comme moyen de rajeunissement et d'immortalité; Contes, légendes, mythes et rites.* Lund, 1949.

Eliade, Mircea. *Shamanism: Archaic Techniques of Ecstasy.* Rev. & enl. ed. New York, 1964.

Eliade, Mircea. *Yoga: Immortality and Freedom.* 2d ed. Princeton, 1969.

Eliade, Mircea. *Australian Religions: An Introduction.* Ithaca, N. Y., 1973.

Eliade, Mircea. "The Religions of Ancient China." In his *A History of Religious Ideas,* vol. 2, *From Gautama Buddha to the Triumph of Christianity.* Chicago, 1982.

Fröbe-Kapteyn, Olga. "Gestaltung der Erlösungsidee in Ost und West." In *Eranos Jahrbuch* 1937. Zurich, 1938.

Goossens, W. "L'immortalité corporelle." In *Dictionnaire de la Bible: Supplement,* vol. 4. Paris, 1949.

Guiart, Jean, ed. *Les hommes et la mort: Rituels funéraires.* Paris, 1979.

Guthrie, W. K. C. *Orpheus and Greek Religion.* 2d ed., rev. London, 1952.

Heiler, Friedrich. *Unsterblichkeitsglaube und Jenseitshoffnung in der Geschichte der Religionen.* Basel, 1950.

Heissig, Walther. *The Religions of Mongolia.* Translated by Geoffrey Samuel. Berkeley, 1980.

James, William. *Human Immortality* (1898). 2d ed. New York, 1917.

Klimkeit, Hans J., ed. *Tod und Jenseits im Glauben der Völker.* Wiesbaden, 1978.

La Vallée Poussin, Louis de. *Nirvâna.* Paris, 1925.

Lemaitre, Solange. *Le mystère de la mort dans les religion de l'Asie* (1943). 2d ed. Paris, 1963.

Parrot, André. *Le refrigerium dans l'au-delà.* Paris, 1937.

Pfannmüller, Gustav. *Tod, Jenseits, und Unsterblichkeit.* Munich, 1953.

Preuss, K. T. *Tod und Unsterblichkeit im Glauben der Naturvölker.* Tübingen, 1930.

Ries, Julien, ed. *La mort selon la Bible, dans l'antiquité classique et selon le manichéisme.* Louvain-la-Neuve, 1983.

Silburn, Lilian. *Instant et cause: Le discontinue dans la pensée philosophique de l'Inde.* Paris, 1955.

Söderblom, Nathan. *La vie future d'après le mazdéisme à la lumière des croyances parallèles dans les autres religions.* Paris, 1901.

Stendahl, Krister, ed. *Immortality and Resurrection.* New York, 1965.

Stephenson, Günther. *Leben und Tod in den Religionen.* Darmstadt, 1980.

Théodoridès, A., P. Naster, and Julien Ries, eds. *Vie et survie dans les civilisations orientales.* Louvain-la-Neuve, 1983.

Thomas, Louis-Vincent. *La mort africaine: Idéologie funéraire en Afrique noire.* Paris, 1982.

Tucci, Giuseppe. *The Religions of Tibet.* Translated by Geoffrey Samuel. Berkeley, 1980.

Wenzl, A. *L'immortalité: Sa signification métaphysique et anthropologique.* Paris, 1957.

Zahan, Dominique, ed. *Réincarnation et vie mystique en Afrique noire.* Strasbourg, 1963.

JULIEN RIES
Translated from French by David M. Weeks

INCA RELIGION

The pre-Columbian Andean cultures, of which the Inca empire was the final heir, extended over a geographical area that the Inca believed corresponded to the four quarters *(tahuantinsuyu)* of the world. At the time of the Inca empire's fall to Spanish forces under Francisco Pizarro in 1532, the Inca occupied large portions of present-day Ecuador, Peru, Bolivia, and Chile. The great Andean civilizations flourished in this setting of contrasting ecosystems (coastal desert ribbed with fertile valleys, arable highlands at altitudes of more than four kilometers, Amazonian and montane rain forests) that offered resources for pursuing a variety of means of subsistence, including fishing, hunting and gathering, agriculture, and the herding of llamas, guanacos, and alpacas.

Inca Cosmology. The Inca religious system is usually attributed to either the Inca Tupac Yupanqui or his predecessor, the Inca Pachacuti, and dates to at most one hundred years before the European conquest. The expansion of Cuzco, the Inca capital, was carried out in the name of the superiority of its gods over those of other peoples who, once they were assimilated into the empire, left their principal idol (or its replica) in the Inca capital. The colonization, or federation, was founded on a system of reciprocity overseen by Cuzco. Certain cults and temples were richly endowed by the Inca (the title given the head of the empire); others were suppressed. The great social and religious leaders of the empire went regularly to the capital city, and the Inca brought colonies of collaborators *(mitima)* to the temples of the empire and sometimes had himself named priest of honor. The sanctuaries of the provinces paid tribute in kind to Cuzco, contributing, for example, young children to be sacrificed during the Capacocha ceremony. Rites of communion were held periodically to ensure the political and religious

> At the time of the Inca empire's fall to Spanish forces . . . the Inca occupied large portions of present-day Ecuador, Peru, Bolivia, and Chile.

cohesion of the empire. Generally, these rites took place at the Temple of the Sun, in the center of the tahuantinsuyu, which center was located at the junction of the two rivers of Cuzco.

The inhabitants of the Andean region worshiped a great number of gods, idols, and spirits, which were designated by the generic name *huaca,* a term that was also applied to the shrines. Each family—and, at the higher level, each village and province—claimed to descend from a given *huaca* (a particular man-god, conquering ancestor, founder, or civilizer), who represented a cosmic power and whom they venerated in the form of a mummy, a stone, an animal, or a constellation of stars.

Inca Gods. The kings of Cuzco, reputed to be sons of the Sun, formed a religious, cosmic, and territorial imperial structure in which the Sun reigned over the Andean highlands and the heavens and the god Pachacámac ruled over the lowlands and the underworld.

The Coricancha, the great Temple of the Sun in Cuzco, was flanked by two golden pumas and its walls were covered with gold and silver plaques. The halls contained statues and cosmic representations, and the mummies—or their replicas—of earlier kings and queens. The temple sheltered a large number of priests (the first priest was a close relative of the Inca) and the "virgins of the Sun" *(aclla),* who dedicated themselves to making cloth and corn beer for the cult of the Sun, and who also served as concubines to the Inca.

From the dark bowels of the cosmos, Pachacámac caused earthquakes and sent pestilence. Illapa, who represented thunderbolts, lightning, rain, hail, snow, and frost, was venerated by a large cult in the highlands. The serpent Amaru represented the striking thunderbolt and also the animal or monster who, according to the myths, rose from the lake and moved toward the upper world.

Women were the principal participants in the cult of Quilla, the Moon, who was the sister and wife of the Sun. The Coya ("queen") was believed to be the daughter of the Moon, just as the Inca was believed to be the son of the Sun. The anthropomorphic statues of Quilla were silver, while those of the Sun were gold. A lunar calendar was used along with a solar calendar. Quilla was associated with the earth and the dead. Traditionally, she pursued dead thieves into the underworld at night. One month of the year was especially sacred to her. Men also worshiped her, in Cuzco and elsewhere, particularly in the temple of Nusta, which was located on an island in Lake Titicaca.

When they were not visible, the stars, like the sun and the moon, were believed to go under the earth. The Milky Way—thought of as two rivers—may have inspired the construction of the Coricancha at the junction of the two rivers of Cuzco. Among the constellations, that of the llama, visible during the dry season, was of special importance to cattle raisers. The Pleiades were associated with the rainy season. If they appeared clearly at the end of May, a good harvest was augured.

After death, one of the two souls that were attributed to a man returned to its place of origin, either before or after a journey strewn with obstacles, and dwelt in the land of the souls, which was not unlike the world of the living. The kind of afterlife enjoyed by this soul was conditional on the type of death, social rank, and virtues of the dead. The other soul remained in the body, which had to be preserved intact, and which had the same needs as the living person.

Viracocha was the supreme god of the Inca. He was also a complex deity and was thought of as both one and many, the principle of transformation. Two others of his names were Con-Ticsi-Viracocha and Pachayachachic ("he who gives order to the world") and he had a large family with several sanctuaries. Viracocha was associated with water and the foam of Lake Titicaca, whence he had come, and with the foam of rivers and the surface of the ocean, where, according to some myths, he (in human form) disappeared to the northwest, walking on the waves. These attributes associated him with the rainy season, and others made him the representative of the fire of the heavens and of the triumphant Sun.

Inca Rites. The great religious ceremonies were publicly celebrated in Cuzco. The sacrifices were designed to nourish and placate the gods, and offerings were selected from the great complementary ecosystems of nature (plants, birds, shells, the blood of animals—particularly llamas—and men) and culture (maize, coca, pepper, corn beer,

cloth, statuettes). At the center of the ceremonial place was the *usnu,* a small edifice on which the Inca sat enthroned and that was pierced at its base by underground canals leading to the temples of Viracocha, the Sun, and Illapa. Here the Sun was given "drink," which acted to placate and balance the powers of the lower and upper worlds. The *usnu* may also have served as an astronomical observatory. The golden statues of Viracocha, the Sun, and Illapa, the silver statue of the Moon, and the mummies of dead sovereigns—or their replicas—were set out on ceremonial occasions.

The performance of these ritual duties was also intended to ward off cataclysms (*pachacuti*), especially those caused by excessive heat ("suns of fire") or water (floods). Such cataclysms were believed to result from the dissatisfaction of the cosmic powers of the upper and lower worlds. They were believed to have occurred before, ushering in new cycles, and it was thought that they could happen again. These ideas, which were based on the observation of the movements of the sun and moon and the oppositions of day and night, dry and rainy seasons, and fire and water, were projected through time to construct an explanation of the history of the world. In any case, the important Quechua word *pacha* means both "time" and "space."

BIBLIOGRAPHY

Duviols, Pierre. *La lutte contre les religions autochtones dans le Pérou colonial: "L'extirpation de l'idolâtrie" entre 1532 et 1660.* Lima, 1971. A history of the itinerant Inquisition (called "the extirpation of idolatry") against the Indians, its methods and the reactions of the indigenous peoples.

Duviols, Pierre. "Punchao, ídolo mayor del Coricancha: Historia y tipología." *Antropología andina* 1 (1976): 156-182. Shows the continuity in one of the representations of the Andean solar god.

Duviols, Pierre. *La destrucción de las religiones andinas: Conquista y colonia.* Mexico City, 1977. Studies the means used to suppress the Andean religions and the efforts to replace them with Christianity.

Lumbreras, Luis G. *The Peoples and Cultures of Ancient Peru.* Washington, D. C., 1974.

Mariscotti de Görlitz, Ana María. *Pachamama Santa Tierra.* Berlin, 1978. Monograph on this topic.

Murra, John V. *The Economic Organization of the Inca State.* Greenwich, Conn., 1980. Numerous references to the economics of religion.

Pease, Franklin. *El pensamiento mítico.* Lima, 1982. Anthology of ancient Andean myth, preceded by a study.

Platt, Tristan. "Symétries en miroir: Le concept de *yanantin* chez les Macha de Bolivia." *Annales, economies, sociétés, civilisations* 33 (1978): 1081-1107. Analysis of the concepts of reflection and the double among the Macha of Bolivia.

Rostworowski de Diez Canseco, María. *Estructuras andinas del poder: Ideología religiosa y política.* Lima, 1983. Study of a large number of current works, focusing on the theme of dualism.

Rowe, John Howland. "The Origins of Creator Worship among the Incas." In *Culture in History: Essays in Honor of Paul Radin,* edited by Stanley Diamond, pp. 408-429. New York, 1960.

Taylor, Gerald. "*Camay, Camac,* et *camasca* dans le manuscrit Quechua de Huarochiri." *Journal de la Société des Americanistes* 63 (1974-1976): 231-244. Analyzes an important concept in Andean thought.

Urbano, Henrique. *Wiracocha y Ayar: Héroes y funciones en las sociedades andinas.* Cuzco, Peru, 1981. Anthology of ancient Andean myths, preceded by an attempt at interpretation using the trifunctional model of Georges Dumézil.

Urton, Gary. *At the Crossroads of the Earth and Sky: An Andean Cosmology.* Austin, 1981. Analysis of contemporary Andean astrological beliefs in terms of pre-Columbian Andean astronomy.

Zuidema, R. Tom. *The Ceque System of Cuzco: The Social Organization of the Capital of the Inca.* Leiden, 1962. Analyzes the geometrical and arithmetical organization of the sacred space of Cuzco.

Zuidema, R. Tom. "Mito e historia en el antiguo Perú." *Allpanchis* (Cuzco) 10 (1977): 15-52.

Zuidema, R. Tom. "Hierarchy and Space in Incaic Social Organization." *Ethnohistory* 30 (1983): 49-75.

PIERRE DUVIOLS
Translated from French by Erica Meltzer

INCARNATION

The concept of incarnation (Lat., *incarnatio,* "being in flesh") has been applied in the Christian community to the mystery of union between divinity and humanity in the person of Jesus Christ. More generally, the concept has been extended to take into account a variety of forms of incarnation that the history of religions has described in various lands and among different peoples. The term *incarnation* is broadly defined here as the act or state of assuming a physical body (as a person, an animal, a plant, or even an entire cosmos) by a nonphysical entity such as the soul, the spirit, the self, or the divine being.

The "Primitive" Tradition. The belief in the divine incarnate can be attested as early as the late Paleolithic period, in a considerable number of pictures of human beings in animal forms, often in dancing posture. Among the best known is a figure of the "great sorcerer" in a Trois Frères cave, sporting a deer's head crowned with huge antlers. The same cave has also preserved the portrayal of a dancer disguised as a bison, playing a bow-shaped instrument, possibly a kind of flute. It is certain that the early hunters wore masks and skins of animals for the celebration of their magico-religious ceremonies. These masked figures and many parallel examples were probably believed to be the incarnations of spirits or divine beings akin to the Lord of the Animals.

The belief in the preexistence and incarnation of souls is abundantly documented in the "primitive" world. According to the Caribou Inuit (Eskimo), for example, the immortal soul of a dead person leaves his body, ascending to the supreme being Pinga in heaven who receives it. If the person lived properly according to the rules of life, Pinga lets the soul assume a bodily form, human or animal. Such a belief is also widespread among the North American Indians.

Greece, India, Iran. The ancient Greek doctrine of metempsychosis presupposes the incarnation of preexistent and immortal souls in successive bodies, human and animal, and even in inanimate substances. Pythagoras certainly believed in the transmigration of souls (Xenophanes, frag. 7); according to him, the human soul, despite its immortality, has been imprisoned in the body and condemned to a cycle of reincarnation due to the fall from its original state of bliss.

This Greek mythology of the soul, more or less hostile to the world of matter and the physical body, was incorporated into gnosticism, a set of doctrines characterized by anticosmic dualism. Man, as viewed by the gnostics, is constituted by three components: the self, the soul, and the body. The physical body belongs to the deficient world of nature *(phusis),* but the soul is also part of this evil world. Man's psychic activities arise from and are limited by the continual flux of natural events. It is only the self that transcends the evil world. It is divine in nature, hence not subject to time and change; it is indestructible.

India presents us with a doctrine similar to gnosticism, namely, Samkhya-Yoga, whose central message may be summed up as follows: (1) man's destiny in the world is conditioned by the mysterious interplay between the self *(purusa),* which is indestructible, eternal, and not subject to change, and matter *(prakrti),* which is subject to time and transformation and which constitutes man's psychophysiological complex; (2) the self is essentially a stranger to the world of matter, into which for unknown reasons it has fallen and been enslaved, resulting in the oblivion of its original, true identity; and (3) deliverance *(moksa)* begins when the self remembers its eternal freedom and tries to dissociate itself through the practice of yoga from the world of matter.

The ancient Iranians of the Parthian period had an ardent hope or expectation for Mithra incarnate, who would come at the end of the world as the great universal monarch and savior. This king and savior will descend on the Mount of Victories in the form of a column of light or a shining star to be born in a cave. He will be given birth by a human mother, but in truth he is of heavenly origin; he descends from above with the light, that is, he is the child of light. There were, in fact, magi who lived near the Mount of Victories; every year, at a certain fixed date, they climbed the mountain in which there was a cave, and quietly prayed to the heavenly god for three days, waiting for the appearance of the star.

Kings, Emperors, Imams. The status of kings was often defined in terms of God incarnate. In ancient Egypt, for example, the king was believed to be divine in essence. His coronation, usually celebrated at the beginning of the new year, signified not an apotheosis but an epiphany, a self-manifestation of the god. As long as he ruled, the king was identified with the god Horus; in fact, he was Horus incarnate in his early existence, but upon his death he was mystically assimilated to Osiris, the god of rebirth and immortality.

The Greco-Roman world generally dissociated itself from the notion that the king was the incarnation of a certain god, despite the fact that royal titles such as *The Young Dionysos* and *Epiphanes* were often used by kings in the Hellenistic period. According to Arthur Darby Nock, the only exception was Ptolemy XIII of the mid-first century BCE, who demonstrably considered himself to be Dionysos incarnate, probably under the influence of the pharaonic conception of the king as Horus incarnate.

While the Chinese emperor was generally called Son of Heaven *(t`ien-tzu)* and as such was considered the earthly representative of Heaven or heavenly will, some emperors were regarded as incarnations of the Buddha. For example,

> While the Chinese emperor was generally called Son of Heaven . . . some emperors were regarded as incarnations of the Buddha.

the founder of the Northern Wei dynasty (386-534), T`ai-tzu, was regarded by the eminent monk Fa-kuo as the Tathagata in person, an incarnation of the Buddha. This idea was iconographically represented in the caves of Yün-kang to the west of Ta-t`ung, the capital of the empire until 494. Moreover, toward the end of the seventh century the Empress Wu Chao, who was a strong supporter of Buddhism, was considered to be the incarnation of Maitreya, the future Buddha.

In Islam, more particularly among the Shi`ah, the imam enjoyed a truly exalted and significant status; while among the Sunnis an imam is no more than a leader of congregational prayer at a local mosque, among the Shi`ah the imam was endowed with a power at once political and religious. Like the caliph, he was one who ruled the community in mercy and justice, but unlike the caliph, who had no legal authority, the imam was empowered to interpret the *haqiqah,* or esoteric meanings of the Qur`an and Islamic law. This power was based on the Shi`ah conviction that Muhammad's charisma, or spiritual gift, which he received from God, would be transmitted genealogically only within his household. It was natural that the imam became the central focus of Shi`ah faith to such an extent that he was believed to be the embodiment of the divine light. Some extreme sects of the Isma`ili movement went even further in believing that the imam was the incarnation of the godhead itself.

Buddhism. Buddhism was founded by Siddhartha Gautama of the Sakya clan in India, who left his home in quest of truth, devoted himself to the practice of meditation,

and finally attained enlightenment. Hence he is also called the Buddha, the Enlightened One. As a new trend of the Buddhist movement called the Mahayana developed in the course of the second century BCE, a shift occurred in Buddhology; emphasis was now placed less on the historical Buddha than on the Eternal Buddha. This Eternal Buddha is transcendent, absolute, and infinite, embodying the universal and cosmic truth. Hence he is called the *dharmakaya* ("body of the law"), the essential Buddha who is the ultimate reality as viewed by Mahayana Buddhism. The Eternal Buddha does not wish, however, to hold himself aloof from the phenomenal world; out of his deep compassion for mankind in pain and suffering he has incarnated himself in the person of Siddhartha Gautama, as the *nirmanakaya* ("body of transformation").

Japanese Buddhism, more particularly, the Shingon school of Buddhism, has also unfolded what may be called a cosmotheism, a fascinating conception of the cosmos as the embodiment of the Buddha Mahavairocana. The place of central importance in Shingon Buddhism is occupied no longer by the historical Buddha but rather by the Cosmic Buddha Mahavairocana (Jpn., Dainichi, "great sun"); just as the sun is the source of light, illuminating the whole universe and giving life to all forms of existence, so Mahavairocana is the Great Illuminator of all existence, both animate and inanimate. He is transcendent, absolute, and eternal because he is identified with the *dharmakaya.* However, Mahavairocana is not only transcendent but also immanent in the universe. This Buddha is cosmic in nature because, according to Shingon Buddhism, he embodies himself in the six great elements constituting every form of existence in the universe: earth, water, fire, wind, space, and mind. These six elements are interfused and in a state of eternal harmony.

Christianity. That God was incarnated in the person of Jesus of Nazareth in order to save mankind is a basic tenet of Christianity. One of the earliest confessions of faith pronounced by the primitive church (*Phil.* 2:6-2:11) speaks of the preexistent divine figure Christ Jesus, who condescended to take on human form, won victory in his death over the cosmic forces of evil, and reigns now with God in heaven. In the *Gospel of John,* dating from the end of the first century, Christ Jesus is presented as the incarnate Word (Logos) of God (*Jn.* 1:1-1:14). In sharp contrast to the portrait of the life of Jesus in the synoptic Gospels, John identifies him as the preexistent divine being who, descending from heaven, moves mysteriously through human life, proclaiming heavenly messages and working miracles, and who even foretells his ascension to heaven following his impending suffering and death.

Christian gnostics accepted the belief that Christ was the divine Logos, the chief intermediary between God and man. However, they rejected the idea that the Logos took on human flesh, since to them the flesh was both evil and insubstantial. Characteristically, they denied the reality or historicity of the incarnation: the human life of Christ was spiritual but not material; Christ hovered over mortal life, never really participating in the birth, suffering, and death of the historical Jesus. The Christian church set itself against this docetic view in such affirmation of the Apostles' Creed as "God the Father Almighty, creator of heaven and earth." By implication this was an affirmation of the goodness of all God's creation, material as well as spiritual.

The Christian church attempted to articulate the nature of the person of Jesus Christ as God incarnate at the First Council of Nicaea (325). It adopted a creed that included such phrases to define Christ as "begotten not made," "begotten before all ages," and "of one essence with the Father." Thus Christ was declared to be *homo-ousios,* "consubstantial," with God the Father, a doctrine that was to be formulated later by Augustine as *una substantia tres personae* ("one substance in three persons"); Christ was essentially divine without being a kind of "second God." Once this result was generally accepted, a further question arose: how are the divine and human elements related to each other in the person of the historical Jesus? After apparently endless debates and anathemas, the orthodox view was formulated at the Council of Chalcedon (451): two natures of Christ, divine and human, are perfectly blended in one person; Jesus Christ is *vere Deus vere homo* ("truly God and truly man").

BIBLIOGRAPHY

There is no single book dealing with the problem of incarnation in the general history of religions. On masks and their religious meaning in prehistory, see Johannes Maringer's *Vorgeschichtliche Religion: Religionen im steinzeitlichen Europa* (Einsiedeln, Switzerland, 1956), pp. 184ff., edited and translated by Mary Ilford as *The God of Prehistoric Man* (New York, 1960), pp. 146ff.

Hutton Webster offers us basic information on the periodic return of the ancestral spirits in Polynesia and Melanesia in his *Primitive Secret Societies* (New York, 1980). On the Aranda conception of the immortal soul, there is a fascinating account in Mircea Eliade's *Australian Religions: An Introduction* (Ithaca, N. Y., 1973), pp. 44-59.

The incarnation of the soul in the Greek philosophical tradition has been competently discussed by W. K. C. Guthrie in *The Earlier Presocratics and Pythagoreans* (pp. 306ff.) and *The Presocratic Tradition from Parmenides to Democritus* (pp. 249ff.), volumes 1 and 2 of his *A History of Greek Philosophy* (Cambridge, 1962 and 1965). The best single book on the gnostic view of the destiny of man and his immortal soul in the world remains Hans Jonas's *The Gnostic Religion,* 2d ed., rev. (Boston, 1963). On Samkhya-Yoga, there is a concise account in Robert C. Zaehner's *Hinduism* (London, 1962), pp. 67ff. Focusing his attention on the fate of the immortal self in the world, Mircea Eliade has compared gnosticism with Samkhya-Yoga in his essay "Mythologies of Memory and Forgetting," now included in his *Myth and Reality* (New York, 1963), pp. 114-138. There is a fine comparative study of the avatar beliefs of India and the Christian doctrine of the incarnation in Geoffrey Par-rinder's *Avatar and Incarnation* (New York, 1970).

The eschatological expectation of the birth of the savior Mithra in ancient Iran has been elucidated by Geo Widengren in his *Iranisch-semitische Kulturbegegnung in parthischer Zeit* (Cologne, 1960), pp. 62-86. See also Mircea Eliade's *Méphistophélès et l'androgyne* (Paris, 1962), pp. 60ff., translated by J. M. Cohen as *The Two and the One* (Chicago, 1965), pp. 51-55.

Major problems of Greco-Roman kingship have been discussed authoritatively by Arthur Darby Nock in volume 1 (pp. 134ff.) and volume 2 (pp. 928ff.) of his *Essays on Religion and the Ancient World* (Cambridge, Mass., 1972), with an introduction by Zeph Stewart. On the conception of kingship in ancient Japan, see my article "Sacred Kingship in Early Japan: A Historical Introduction," *History of Religions* 15 (1976): 319-342.

Mahayana Buddhism has attempted to explain the historical Buddha Sakyamuni as an incarnation of the Eternal Buddha. See, in this connection, a brief but illuminating account of the doctrine of the "three bodies" *(trikaya)* of the Buddha by T. R. V. Murti, *The Central Philosophy of Buddhism,* 2d ed. (London, 1970), pp. 284-287. On the conception of the cosmos as the embodiment of the Buddha Mahavairocana, see *Kukai: Major Works,* translated, with an account of Kukai's life and a study of his thought, by Yoshito S. Hakeda (New York, 1972), pp. 76ff.

On the history of the Christian doctrines of the incarnation, there is an admirable account by Jaroslav Pelikan in *The Emergence of the Catholic Tradition, 100-600,* volume 1 of his *The Christian Tradition* (Chicago, 1971).

MANABU WAIDA

INDIAN RELIGIONS

Vedism. Vedic thought was based on the belief in an inextricable coordination of nature, human society, ritual, and the sphere of myth and the divine; it was also founded on the belief that these spheres influence one another continuously and that men have, by means of ritual, an obligatory part to play in the maintenance of universal order and the furtherance of their common interests. In later times also, Indians have constantly sought correspondences between objects and phenomena belonging to distinct spheres of nature and conceptual systems. Many hymns and individual stanzas of the oldest literary corpus (the *Rgveda Samhita,* an anthology drawn from family traditions) were intended for the cult and used in the liturgy of spectacular solemn *(srauta)* ceremonies, which gradually increased in number, length, and complexity. These ceremonies were to ensure the orderly functioning of the world for the benefit of noble or wealthy patrons. The rites were performed in the open on a specially prepared plot—there were no temples or idols—by specialized officiants. Part of this literature was employed, along with texts from the *Atharvaveda Samhita,* in the domestic or magic ritual performed by a householder or single priest to ensure an individual's health, safety, success, prosperity, and longevity. These texts and the ritual formulas of the *Yajurveda,* which invariably fulfill some ritual function, are collectively called *mantras.* They are believed to be revelations of aspects of the divine, the product of the exalted experiences of sages *(rsis)* and hence constitute sacred and inherently powerful verbal formulas for producing a desired result. Some Vedic *mantras* remained in Hinduist rites, which, however, generally require other ones.

Hinduism. Some prehistoric forms of Hinduism—the civilization of the Hindus, consisting of their beliefs, practices, and socioreligious institutions—must have existed at the Vedic period, especially in the unrecorded religion of the lower classes, and probably earlier. Domestic ritual, which is entirely different from the solemn rites, consists of many rites that, though described and systematized by brahman authorities in the Vedic Grhyasutras, are in essence not typically Vedic, or rather constitute Vedic varieties of widespread rites of passage, rites of appeasement, cult of the dead, and so on. Later chapters of this literature show markedly non-Vedic and post-Vedic influences.

Non-Aryan influences. How much influence was exerted by the religions of the non-Aryan inhabitants of India on the formation and development of Hinduism is a matter of dispute. Although aborigines may have contributed some elements, their religion is generally different in many respects (e.g., they do not venerate the cow, and they allow their widows to remarry). The Vedic religion had no demonstrable relation with the great civilizations of Harappa, Mohenjo-Daro, and vast regions to the east of the Indus Valley (c. 2500-1500 BCE). As long as the graphic symbols on seals from these sites are not convincingly deciphered and the language is not identified (that it was Dravidian—the name of non-Aryan languages of southern India—is still unproved conjecture), most of the conclusions drawn from archaeological material and argumentation regarding links with elements or characteristics of older and even contemporary Hinduism remain as speculative as the hypothesis of a predominantly influential Dravidian substratum.

Early history. The history proper of Hinduism begins with the emergence of the great works on *dharma,* the totality of traditional custom and behavior that, agreeing with standards considered to derive their authority from the Vedas, manifests and maintains order and stability. This is also the age of the epics, especially the *Mahabharata* (c. 300 BCE-300 CE), that "encyclopedia of Hinduism" that shows, even then, what appears to be a varied and confused conglomerate of beliefs and practices. However, there are two main currents, soteriologies when viewed from their doctrinal aspect and religions from the viewpoint of their adherents: Vaisnavism and Saivism. Neither current is in itself a unity. Yet all Vaisnavas are essentially monotheistic, believing in Visnu as their immanent high god (Isvara), although in many contexts he appears as one of the divine poly- theistic figures *(devas).* In the Vedas, Visnu represents universal pervasiveness; his beneficent energy, in which all beings abide, reaches the world through the *axis mundi,* the central pillar of the universe. Vaisnavas often worship him through his manifesta-

tions or incarnations *(avataras),* such as Rama or Krsna. Preference for an *avatara* is mainly traditional; in the North, Krsna is more often worshiped; in the South, it is Rama, Visnu himself, or Visnu's consort, Sri. The *Bhagavadgita,* an episode of the *Mahabharata* and the most seminal of all Vaisnava works, founded Vaisnava ethics: fulfilling their duties disinterestedly, men should realize God's presence in themselves, love him and their fellow beings devotedly, and dedicate all their actions to him so as to earn the prospect of final emancipation.

The Hinduist worship, in many different groups and currents, of Siva in his various manifestations results from a complex development to which the often malevolent outsider god Rudra of the Vedas has contributed much. (There may also have been Dravidian influences.) Rudra, primarily representing the untamed aspects of uncultivated nature, was called Siva ("the mild one") when the benevolent and auspicious aspects of his nature were emphasized. Saivism is an unsystematic amalgam of pan-Indian Saiva philosophy, local or folk religion, mythological thought, and popular imagery. Siva's many-sided character, to which accreted features of great gods as well as demoniac powers, is split up into many partial manifestations representing aspects of his ambivalent nature. He is both mild and terrible, a creator and destroyer, an ascetic and a sexualist.

Buddhism and Jainism. The same period saw the spread of two heterodox soteriologies, heterodox because they reject the authority of the Veda and the social prejudices of the brahmans, although they scarcely attack the fundamentals of Hindu belief and practices. The way in which the early Buddhists presented their doctrines has much in common with the oldest Upanisads, which must antedate the spread of the Aryan culture to the south and the activity of Gautama (c. 560-480 BCE). Gautama, the Buddha, first gave an exposition of his basic doctrine in Banaras. He taught that those who wish to be delivered from *samsara* and the automatism of *karman,* which does not rely upon a permanent transmigrating soul (whose existence the Buddha denied), should realize four basic truths: (1) earthly existence is pain; (2) the cause of pain is craving for existence, leading to rebirth; (3) cessation of that craving is cessation of pain; (4) an eightfold path leads to that cessation. Final deliverance is realized only in an ascetic and monastic life by those who, after having successfully observed definite rules of life and reached complete meditation *(samadhi),* experience the undefinable state of *nirvana,* the cessation of all becoming.

As the number of adherents increased, the Buddhist order received large gifts that led to the establishment of monasteries. The multiplying order spread to different parts of India, including the south and Sri Lanka (third century BCE). In the beginning of the fourth century BCE the community began to be split by successive schisms, each of which made its own collection of canonical texts. After about 500 CE, Indian Buddhism began to decline.

The Buddha was not the only illuminated teacher who, after renouncing the world, organized his initiates into a community. In Bihar one of his contemporaries, Vardhamana Mahavira, reformed an existing community and founded the predominantly monastic Jainism, which spread to northern and central India, Gujarat, and the Deccan, and in the last few centuries BCE split into two groups, not on philosophic disagreement but on points of rules for the monks. Jainism is systematic and has never changed in its basic ideology. Its philosophy is dualistic: it posits nonliving entities (including space and time) pervaded by (partly transmigrating, partly emancipated) immaterial and eternal souls; the world, eter-

> ## After about 500 CE, Indian Buddhism began to decline.

nal and changeless, is not governed by a supreme being; the system is characterized by the absence of gods *(devas); karman* is the central power that determines the destiny of unemancipated souls. Man has to perfect his soul and that of his fellow creatures; *ahimsa* and universal tolerance are the main duties and cardinal virtues. Whereas the adherents of Buddhism were from a variety of social classes, Jainism attracted the wealthy and influential.

Saiva Religions and Tantrism. Some religions of India do deviate from common Hinduist traditions and institutions. In contrast to the Saiva Siddhantins of the Tamil-speaking South—who, basing themselves also on the mysticism of the Saiva Tamil saint-poets (Naya-nars), teach that God in the shape of a spiritual guide, or *guru,* graciously permits himself to be realized by the purified soul—the Virasaivas, or Lingayats, in southwestern India (not mentioned before the twelfth century) abandon many traditional elements (e.g., caste, image worship). Doctrinal dissent is always possible. The religio-philosophic idealist and monist Kashmir school of Saivism disagrees in certain important respects with the teaching of Sankara (eighth century), the founder of Advaita monism, derived from the Upanisadic Vedanta as a system of absolute idealism that is mainly followed by the intellectual elite. Sankara, a native of Malabar who resided in Banaras and traveled throughout India, was a superb organizer; he established a monastic order and monasteries *(mathas),* which, like the many hermitages *(asramas)* and the great shrines, became centers of religious activity and contributed to the realization of his ideal of Hindu unity.

From about 500 CE, Tantric ritual and doctrines manifest themselves more or less frequently in Buddhism, Saiva Siddhanta, and Pañcaratra. Tantrism, primarily meant for esoteric circles, yet still an important aspect of Hinduism, is a systematic quest for spiritual excellence or emancipation through realization of the highest principle, the bipolar, bisexual deity, in one's own body. The possibilities of this microcosmos should be activated, sublimated, and made to exert influence on the macrocosmos, with which it is closely connected (physiological processes are thus described with cosmological terminology). Means to this end, partly magical, partly orgiastic, include recitation of *mantras,* contemplation of geometrical cosmic symbols *(mandalas),* leading the performer of the rites to the reintegration of consciousness; appropriate gestures *(mudras),* and meditation. Tantric *puja* is complicated and in many respects differs from conventional ceremonies. Especially in Bengal, Tantrism has tended to merge with the Sakta cult. The term *Tantra* commonly applies to Saiva or Sakta works of the Tantric tradition. Saktism, not always clearly distinguishable from Saivism, is the worship of the Supreme as divine creative energy *(sakti),* a female force that creates, regulates, and destroys the cosmos; when regarded as a person, she usually is Siva's spouse, often the dreadful goddess Durga or Kali.

Vaisnava Religions and Bhakti. Although Vaisnavism, less coherent than Saivism, had, in the sixth century, spread all over India, it reached predominance in Tamil Nadu, which became the cradle of important schools and movements that still have many adherents. The tradition known as the Sri Vaisnavas was inaugurated between about 900 and 1130 by Yamuna, the first apologist of Vaisnava theology, and consolidated by the great philosopher Ramanuja (c. 1050-1137). The Sri Vaisnavas introduced into their temple ceremonies the recitation of Tamil hymns of the Alvars, which evince a passionate belief in and love of God. Considering these poets and their great teachers *(acaryas)* integral parts *(amsas)* of God's nature, they often worship images of them in their temples. According to Ramanuja, *brahman* is as a "person" *(purusa)* the sole cause of his own modifications (emanation, existence, and absorption of the universe), immaterial, perfect, omnipotent, the soul of all being, the ultimate goal of all religious effort, to which God induces the devotee who wishes to please him. The purificatory significance of the ritual, meritorious works, disinterested discharge of duties, and *bhakti* are emphasized.

The influential *Bhagavata Purana* (c. 900?), also composed in Tamil Nadu, teaches that God through his incomprehensible creative ability *(maya)* expands himself into the universe, which is his outward appearance. On the basis of this teaching, Bengal Vaisnavism developed the theory of a relation of inconceivable difference in identity and identity in difference between God and the world, as well as the belief that God's creative activity is his sport *(lila).* As the safest way to God, *bhakti,* a mystical attitude of mind involving an intuitive, immediate apprehension and loving contemplation of God, often overshadows the devotee's aspirations to final emancipation and assumes a character of uncontrollable enthusiasm and ecstasy, marked by tears, hysteria, and fainting.

In northern and central India the *bhakti* movement flourished from the thirteenth to the eighteenth century, producing a vast and varied literature in vernacular languages. Even today these areas feel the influence of a long succession of saint-poets, passionate itinerant preachers (among them Caitanya, in Bengal, 1485-1533), and *gurus*.

Reaction to Foreign Religions. The revival of Hinduism in the south and the spread of the *bhakti* movement also prepared the Indians to withstand the proselytizing of external religions, particularly Islam. From 1000 CE onward, the Muslims conquered the Northwest, made Delhi their capital, and extended their influence to Bengal, the Deccan, and the South, destroying temples and idols and making many converts, particularly among the untouchables. But Islam scarcely affected the Hindu way of life; rather, it provoked a counterreaction in the form of increased adherence to the Hindu *dharma* and the Hindu religions and stricter observance of rites and ceremonies. Nevertheless, the presence of Islam in India involved an age-long conflict between strict monotheism and the various manifestations of Hinduism. In one field, however, Islam and Hinduism could draw near to each other: Muslim and Hindu mystics have in common the idea of an all-embracing unity. To be sure, the Sufis made this idea a channel of islamization, but some Indian spiritual leaders tried to bridge the gulf between Islam and Hinduism.

India's contact with the West, Christianity, and modern life since the early nineteenth century has led to the emergence of many new religious movements and spiritual groups, as diverse in their principles, ideals, and reactions to foreign influences as the personalities of their founders; most distinguish themselves from traditional devotional movements by a more pronounced interest in ethical, social, and national issues. The extent of their influence in India has, however, often been exaggerated in the West, for the beliefs and customs of the Indian masses are still largely traditional.

[*For discussion of specific traditions, see* Hinduism. *For discussion of specific; nonorthodox traditions, see* Buddhism; Jainism and Sikhism. *On the Indo-European components of Vedic religion, see* Indo-European Religions. *For surveys of regional religious traditions in India, see* Bengali Religions; Marathi Religions; Tamil Religions; *and* Sinhala Religion.]

BIBLIOGRAPHY

Carman, John Braisted. *The Theology of Ramanuja: An Essay in Interreligious Understanding.* New Haven, Conn., and London, 1974.

Eliot, Charles. *Hinduism and Buddhism: A Historical Sketch* (1921). 3d ed. 3 vols. London, 1957.

Embree, Ainslie T., ed. *The Hindu Tradition: Readings in Oriental Thought.* New York, 1966.

Gonda, Jan. *Aspects of Early Visnuism* (1954). 2d ed. Delhi, 1969. A third edition is forthcoming.

Gonda, Jan. *Change and Continuity in Indian Religion.* The Hague, 1965. A series of essays and monographs aiming at a fuller appreciation of the many difficulties with which the historian of the Indian religions is confronted.

Gonda, Jan. *Visnuism and Sivaism: A Comparison.* London, 1970. The Jordan Lectures for 1969.

Gonda, Jan. *Medieval Religious Literature in Sanskrit.* Wiesbaden, 1977.

Gonda, Jan. *Die Religionen Indiens.* 2 vols. Vol. 1, *Veda und älterer Hinduismus,* 2d rev. ed. Vol. 2, *Der jüngere Hinduismus.* Stuttgart, 1978, 1963. Comprehensive, detailed, and well-documented histories of all aspects of Vedism and Hinduism. Translated into French as *Les religions de l'Inde,* 2 vols. (Paris, 1962-1965) and into Italian as *Le religioni dell'India,* 2 vols. (Milan, 1981).

Gonda, Jan. *Vedic Ritual: The Non-Solemn Rites.* Leiden and Cologne, 1980.

Gupta, Sanjukta, Dirk Jan Hoens, and Teun Goudriaan. *Hindu Tantrism.* Leiden, 1979.

Keith, Arthur Berriedale. *The Religion and Philosophy of the Veda and Upanishads* (1925). 2 vols. Reprint, Westport, Conn., 1971.

Moore, Charles A., ed. *The Indian Mind: Essentials of Indian Philosophy and Culture.* Honolulu, 1967.

O'Flaherty, Wendy Doniger. *Siva: The Erotic Ascetic.* London, 1981. Reprint of *Asceticism and Eroticism in the Mythology of Siva* (1973). An original discussion of various aspects of Saivism and Indian mythology in general.

Renou, Louis. *Religions of Ancient India.* London, 1953. The Jordan Lectures for 1951.

Renou, Louis, and Jean Filliozat. *L'Inde classique: Manuel des études indiennes.* 2 vols. Paris, 1947-1953.

Zaehner, R. C. *Hinduism.* London, 1962.

JAN GONDA

INDO-EUROPEAN RELIGIONS

Research has confirmed the relations among languages, in the family now known as Indo-European: Germanic, Celtic, Baltic, Slavic, Armenian, Albanian, Anatolian (chiefly Hittite), and Tokharian (an obscure language found in western China and Turkistan).

Based on linguistic and archaeological research, the ancient Indo-European peoples are generally considered to have been semisettled pastoralists, whose wealth consisted of relatively large herds, including domesticated sheep, pigs, goats, and, most important, cattle. Some agriculture seems to have been practiced, although this was much less important and prestigious an activity than herding or war. The pursuit of warfare, especially the raiding of livestock from neighboring peoples, was facilitated not only by use of chariots but also by an elaborate weaponry built on a single metal, probably copper or bronze.

Linguistic data are insufficient to posit the existence of either a homeland or a proto-Indo-European community, and it is possible to view the similarity of the various Indo-European languages as the cumulative result of complex borrowings, influences, and cultural interrelations between multiple social and ethnic groups over many centuries. Some scholars have sought to employ archaeological evidence to demonstrate a specific point of origin for proto-Indo-European society. Of such theories, the most widely accepted is that of Marija Gimbutas, who has delineated what she calls the Kurgan culture, dating to the middle of the fifth millennium BCE and located in the southern Russian steppes, in the area that stretches from the Urals to the land north of the Black Sea, and including such groups as the Jamna culture of the Ural-Volga region north of the Caspian and the Srednii Stog II culture north of the Black Sea.

Mythic Legitimations of Society, Economy, and Polity. It is possible to reconstruct a number of myths that describe the origin, nature, and sometimes problematic interrelationships between the cultures.

Most important of these is the creation myth, a complex, polyphonic story that told how the world was created when the first priest (often bearing the name Man, *Manu) offered his twin brother, the first king (often named Twin, *Yemo), in sacrifice, along with the first ox. From Twin's body, the world was made, in both its material and social components. (The asterisk denotes a reconstructed form unattested in any written source.)

Although we shall return to the cosmic dimensions of this myth, it is its social contents that concern us now. Among these, the following four should be noted:

1. Society consists of vertically stratified classes, with priests or sovereigns in the first position, warriors in the second, and commoners—those entrusted with the bulk of productive labor—in the third. To these, a fourth class of relative outsiders—servants.

2. The characteristic activity of each of these classes is explained and chartered by the part of Twin's body from which they originated. Thus, the intellectuals who direct society by exercise of thought and speech come from his head; those who defend society by their physical prowess come from his chest (heart) and arms; those who produce food, reproduce, and provide material support for the other classes come from the lower body, including belly, loins, legs, and feet.

3. The priest, following the model of Man, has as his prime responsibility the performance of sacrifice, sacrifice being the creative act *par excellence*.

4. The king, following the model of Twin, combines within himself the essence of all social classes and is expected to sacrifice himself for the good of the whole.

Another myth, which has as its central character the first warrior, whose name was Third (*Trito), provided an analysis of the warrior class. Within this story, it was related that cattle originally belonged to Indo-Europeans but were stolen by a monster, a three-headed serpent who was, moreover, specifically identified as a non-Indo-European. Following this theft, it fell to Third to recover the stolen cattle, and he began his quest by invoking the aid of a warrior deity to whom he offered libations of intoxicating drinks. Having won the god's assistance, and himself fortified by the same intoxicant, Third set forth, found the serpent, slew him, and recovered the cattle, which had been imprisoned by the monster.

This myth, which is attested in more reflexes than any other (its traces are still apparent in countless fairy tales), speaks to the eternal themes of wealth and power. It asserts, first, that cattle—the means of production and of exchange in the most ancient Indo-European societies—rightly belong

> ## This myth . . . speaks to the eternal themes of wealth and power.

exclusively to Indo-Europeans, falling into other hands only as the result of theft. Theft is condemned here because of its reliance on stealth and treachery, and it is set in contrast to raiding, which—far from being condemned—is heartily endorsed. Raiding emerges as a heroic action sanctioned by the gods, hedged with ritual, and devoted to regaining what rightfully belongs to the Indo-European warrior or his people. Throughout Indo-European history, Third in his various reflexes has remained the model for warriors, who repeatedly cast themselves in his image—raiding, plundering, and killing their non-Indo-European neighbors, convinced all the while that they were engaged in a sacred and rightful activity.

Cosmology and the Gods. Deities were characterized as radiant celestial beings. In addition to the *deywo-s, however, there was another class of divinities associated with the waters beneath the earth's surface and with darkness. These deities—whose names were regularly formed with the preposition signifying downward motion (*ne-, as in Latin *Neptunus,* Greek *Nereus,* Germanic *Nerthus,* Sanskrit *Nirrti*)—figure in myths that are nothing so much as meditations on the interconnections between "above" and "below," involving immergence into and emersion out of the world ocean.

Speculation on the nature of the cosmos also forms an important part of the creation myth, the social contents of which we touched on above. It must be noted, however, that beyond this social discourse, the myth established a series of homologic relations between parts of the human body and parts of the physical universe—that is to say, an extended parallelism and consubstantiality was posited between the microcosm and the macrocosm. Many texts thus tell of the origin of the sun from the eyes of the first sacrificial victim, stones from his bones, earth from his flesh, wind from his breath, and so forth, while others invert the account.

In these and other texts the elements of the physical universe are converted into the constituent parts of a human body, as cosmogony (a story of the creation of the cosmos) becomes anthropogony (a story of the creation of man). In truth, cosmogony and anthropogony were regarded as separate moments in one continuous process of creation, in which physical matter eternally alternates between microcosmic and macrocosmic modes of existence. Bones thus become stones and stones become bones over and over again, matter and change both being eternal, while the body and the universe are only transient forms, alternate shapes of one another.

Ritual Action. The myths that we have considered were closely correlated with and regularly represented in numerous ritual forms. Thus, the creation myth was inextricably connected to sacrifice, the most important of all Indo-European rites. Insofar as the first priest created the world through the performance of a sacrifice in which a man and an ox were the victims, so each subsequent priest recreated the cosmos by sacrificing men or cattle. This was accomplished through manipulation of the homologies of macrocosm and microcosm, such that when the victim was dismembered, its material substance was transformed into the corresponding parts of the universe.

Other rituals were closely related to the myth of Third. Embarking on cattle raids—which were raised to the status of a sacred act as a result of this mythic charter—Indo-European warriors invoked the assistance of martial deities, poured libations, partook of intoxicating drinks, and aspired to states of ecstatic frenzy. Moreover, each young warrior had to pass through certain initiatory rituals before he attained full status as a member of the warrior class. Regularly his first cattle raid was something of a rite of passage for the young warrior, and other initiations were consciously structured on the myth of Third and the serpent.

While the use of intoxicants was an important part of warrior ritual, these had other applications as well. The oldest Indo-European intoxicating beverage was mead, later followed by beer, wine, and a pressed drink known as *soma* to the Indians and *haoma* to the Iranians; the symbolism and ideology surrounding all of these remained relatively constant. In all instances, the drink appears as a heightener of abilities and activities. When consumed by a priest, it increases his powers of vision and insight. Similarly, it makes a poet more eloquent, a warrior more powerful, a king more generous and just.

A large group of rituals served to forge bonds of community and to cement important social relations. Extremely important in this regard were certain formalized reciprocal obligations, including hospitality and gift exchange, whereby individuals, lineages, and even larger units were brought into repeated contact and friendly interchange. Marriage also must be considered as a prolonged exchange relationship between social groups, given the predominant preference for exogamy.

Verbal rituals—including those of vow, oath, and treaty—played a highly important part in the establishment and preservation of social bonds; accordingly, truth and fidelity were cardinal virtues. Initially, this must be related to the lack of literacy among the most ancient Indo-European peoples, a state of affairs that also contributed to the high development of verbal art (epic poetry, for instance) and mnemonic techniques. But even after the introduction of writing among the scattered Indo-European peoples, a marked preference for the oral transmission of religious lore remained.

Death, Resurrection, and Eschatology. A central issue in Indo-European religions, as in most religions, was what becomes of an individual after death. Although several scholars have devoted attention to certain details of funerary ideology, the full nature of Indo-European thought on this topic remains to be worked out. Among the major contributions thus far are the studies of Hermann Güntert (1919), who showed that there was a goddess *Kolyo ("the coverer") whose physical form incarnated the mixture of fascination and horror evoked by death, for she was seductively beautiful when seen from the front, while hiding a back that was repulsive—moldy and wormeaten—in the extreme. Paul Thieme (1952) has also contributed an important study of the view of death as a reunion with departed ancestors, and Kuno Meyer (1919) has shown that in Ireland as in India it was the first mortal (*Yemo, the twin) who founded the otherworld.

If ideas regarding the fate of the soul are unclear—no reconstructible word approximates the semantic range of the English *soul,* the nearest equivalent being a term for "life-breath"—those on the fate of the body are extremely precise and reveal a remarkable religious content. For death is seen as the last sacrifice that an individual can offer, in which his or her own body is itself the offering. Moreover, that body is transformed into the elements of the physical universe, just as were those of Twin at the time of creation, each death being not only a sacrifice but a representation of the cosmogonic sacrifice.

This is not a final fate, however, for it would seem that nothing within the cosmos was perceived as final. Just as cosmogony was seen to alternate with anthropogony, so also death and resurrection. That matter that assumes its cosmic form when one specific human body dies will once again assume bodily form when that specific cosmos itself dies, as must inevitably happen. Greek, Germanic, and Indo-Iranian evidence permits reconstruction of a temporal scheme involving four world ages, the first of which is most pure and stable, followed by ages in which human virtue and the very order of the cosmos gradually break down. At the end of the fourth world age, there is an apocalyptic collapse, followed by the creation of a new, pure, and regenerated world. One of the cardinal features of the eschatological destruction of the cosmos, however, is the resurrection of the dead, their bodies being formed out of the material substance freed when the cosmos falls apart. The new creation that follows is then in most versions accomplished with an initial act of sacrifice.

BIBLIOGRAPHY

Among the most interesting and important general studies of Indo-European religion are (in chronological order): Joseph Vendryes's "Les correspondances de vocabulaire entre l'indo-iranien et l'italo-celtique," *Mémoires de la Société de Linguistique de Paris* 20 (1918): 265-285; Hermann Güntert's *Der arische Weltkönig und Heiland* (Halle, 1923); Paul Thieme's *Mitra and Aryaman* (New Haven, 1957); Georges Dumézil's *L'idéologie tripartie des Indo-Européens* (Brussels, 1958); Émile Benveniste's *Indo-European Language and Society,* translated by Elizabeth Palmer (Coral Gables, Fla., 1975); Franco Crevatin's *Ricerche d'antichità indeuropee* (Trieste, 1979); and my own *Priests, Warriors, and Cattle: A Study in the Ecology of Religions* (Berkeley, 1981).

Specialized studies of particular merit are Marija Gimbutas's numerous articles on the archaeological record of the Indo-Europeans, most complete of which to date is "An Archaeologist's View of PIE in 1975," *Journal of Indo-European Studies* 2 (Fall 1974): 289-308; Georges Dumézil's three-volume *Mythe et épopée* (Paris, 1968-1973), in which he demonstrates the ways in which many myths were transformed into epic, pseudohistory, and other genres; Stig Wikander's *Der arische Männerbund* (Lund, 1938) and Lily Weiser's *Altgermanische Jünglingsweihen und Männerbunde* (Baden, 1927) on warriors; Wilhelm Koppers's "Pferdeopfer und Pferdekult der Indogermanen," *Wiener Beiträge zur Kulturgeschichte und Linguistik* 4 (1936): 279-411, and Kasten Rönnow's "Zagreus och Dionysos," *Religion och Bibel* 2 (1943): 14-48, on sacrifice (both to be used with caution, however); Daniel Dubuisson's "Le roi indo-européen et la synthèse des trois fonctions," *Annales économies sociétés civilisations* 33 (January-February 1978): 21-34, on kingship; Hermann Güntert's *Kalypso* (Halle, 1919); Kuno Meyer's "Der irische Totengott und die Toteninsel," *Sitzungberichte der preussischen Akademie der Wissenschaften* (1919): 537-546; and Paul Thieme's *Studien zur indogermanischen Wortkunde und Religionsgeschichte* (Berlin, 1952) on death and the otherworld; and my own *Myth, Cosmos, and Society: Indo-European Themes of Creation and Destruction* (Cambridge, Mass., 1986) on the creation myth.

Two papers presented at a panel on Indo-European religion held during the Ninth International Congress of Anthropological and Ethnographic Sciences (Vancouver, 1983) were of considerable importance, and publication is forthcoming in the *Journal of Indo-European Studies* 14 (1986). These are Françoise Bader's "Une mythe indo-européene de l'immersion-émergence" and Cristiano Grottanelli's "Yoked Horses, Twins, and the Powerful Lady: India, Greece, Ireland and Elsewhere."

On the problems and insecurities of research in this area in general, see Ulf Drabin, "Indogermanische Religion und Kultur? Eine Analyse des Begriffes Indogermanisch," *Temenos* 16 (1980): 26-38; Jean-Paul Demoule, "Les Indo-Européens ont-ils existé?" *L'histoire* 28 (1980): 108-120; and Bernfried Schlerath, "Ist ein Raum/Zeit Modell für eine rekonstruierte Sprach möglich?" *Zeitschrift für vergleichende Sprachwissenschaft* 95 (1981): 175-202.

BRUCE LINCOLN

INDRA

In India the worship of the god Indra, king of the gods, warrior of the gods, god of rain, begins properly in the *Rgveda,* circa 1200 BCE, but his broader nature can be traced farther back into the proto-Indo-European world through his connections with Zeus and Wotan. For although the *Rgveda* knows a sky father called Dyaus-pitr, who is literally cognate with Zeus-pater and Jupiter, it is Indra who truly fills the shoes of the Indo-European celestial sovereign: he wields the thunderbolt, drinks the ambrosial *soma* to excess, bestows fertility upon human women (often by sleeping with them himself), and leads his band of Maruts, martial storm gods, to win victory for the conquering Indo-Aryans.

In the *Rgveda,* Indra's family life is troubled in ways that remain unclear. His birth, like that of many great warriors and heroes, is unnatural: kept against his will inside his mother's womb for many years, he bursts forth out of her side and kills his own father (*Rgveda* 4.18). He too is in turn challenged by his own son, whom he apparently overcomes (*Rgveda* 10.28). But the hymns to Indra, who is after all the chief god of the *Rgveda* (over a quarter of the hymns in the collection are addressed to him), emphasize his heroic deeds. He is said to have created the universe by propping apart heaven and earth (as other gods, notably Visnu and Varuna, are also said to have done) and finding the sun, and to have freed the cows that had been penned up in a cave (*Rgveda* 3.31). This last myth, which is perhaps the central myth of the *Rgveda,* has meaning on several levels: it means what it says (that Indra helps the worshiper to obtain cattle, as he is so often implored to do), and also that Indra found the sun and the world of life and light and fertility in general, for all of which cows often serve as a Vedic metaphor.

It was Indra who, in the shape of a falcon or riding on a falcon, brought down the *soma* plant from heaven, where it had been guarded by demons, to earth, where it became accessible to men (*Rgveda* 4.26-27). Indra himself is the *soma* drinker *par excellence;* when he gets drunk, as he is wont to do, he brags (*Rgveda* 10.119), and the worshiper who invites Indra to share his *soma* also shares in the euphoria that *soma* induces in both the human and the divine drinker (*Rgveda* 9.113). But Indra is a jealous god—jealous, that is, of the *soma,* both for lofty reasons (like other great gods, he does not wish to allow mortals to taste the fruit that will make them like unto gods) and for petty reasons (he wants to keep all the *soma* for himself). His attempts to exclude the Asvins from drinking the *soma* fail when they enlist the aid of the priest Dadhyañc, who disguises himself with a horse's head and teaches them the secret of the *soma* (*Rgveda* 1.117.22).

But Indra's principal function is to kill enemies—non-Aryan humans and demons, who are often conflated. As the supreme god of the *ksatriyas* or class of royal warriors, Indra is invoked as a destroyer of cities and destroyer of armies, as the staunch ally of his generous worshipers, to whom Indra is in turn equally generous (Maghavan, "the generous," is one of his most popular epithets). These enemies (of whom the most famous is Vrtra) are often called Dasas or Dasyus, "slaves," and probably represent the indigenous populations of the subcontinent that the Indo-Aryans subjugated (and whose twin cities, Mohenjo Daro and Harappa, in the Indus Valley, may have been the citadels that Indra claims to have devastated). But the Dasas are also frequently identified with the *asuras,* or demonic enemies of the gods themselves. The battles thus take place simultaneously on the human and the divine levels, and are both political and cosmogonic.

Indra's reputation begins to decline in the Brahmanas, about 900 BCE, where his supremacy is preempted by Prajapati, the primordial creator. Indra still drinks the *soma,* but now he becomes badly hung-over and has to be restored to health by the worshiper. Similarly, the killing of Vrtra leaves Indra weakened and in need of purification. In the epics, Indra is mocked for weaknesses associated with the phallic powers that are his great glory in the *Rgveda*. His notorious womanizing leads, on one occasion (when the sage Gautama catches Indra in bed with Ahalya, the sage's wife), to Indra's castration; though his testicles are later replaced by those of a ram (*Ramayana* 1.47-48); in another version of this story, Indra is cursed to be covered with a thousand *yonis* or vaginas, a curse which he turns to a boon by having the *yonis* changed into a thousand eyes. When Indra's excesses weaken him, he becomes vulnerable in battle; often he is overcome by demons and must enlist the aid of the now supreme sectarian gods, Siva and Visnu, to restore his throne. Sometimes he sends one of his voluptuous nymphs, the *apsaras,* to seduce ascetic demons who have amassed sufficient power, through *tapas* ("meditative austerities"), to heat Indra's throne in heaven. And when the demon Nahusa usurps Indra's throne and demands Indra's wife, Saci, the gods have to perform a horse sacrifice to purify and strengthen Indra so that he can win back his throne. Even then Indra must use a combination of seduction and deceit, rather than pure strength, to gain his ends: Saci goads Nahusa into committing an act of hubris that brings him down to a level on which he becomes vulnerable to Indra.

Old Vedic gods never die; they just fade into new Hindu gods. Indra remains a kind of figurehead in Hindu mythology, and the butt of many veiled anti-Hindu jokes in Buddhist mythology. The positive aspects of his person are largely transformed to Siva. Both Indra and Siva are associated with the Maruts or Rudras, storm gods; both are said to have extra eyes (three, or a thousand) that they sprouted in order to get a better look at a beautiful dancing *apsaras;* both are associated with the bull and with the erect phallus; both are castrated; and both come into conflict with their fathers-in-law. In addition to these themes, which are generally characteristic of fertility gods, Indra and Siva share more specific mythological episodes: both of them seduce the wives of brahman sages; both are faced with the problem of distributing (where it will do the least harm) certain excessive and destructive forces that they amass; both are associated with anti-Brahmanic, heterodox acts; and both lose their right to a share in the sacrifice. And just as Indra beheads a brahman demon (Vrtra) whose head pursues him until he is purified of this sin, so Siva, having beheaded Brahma, is plagued by Brahma's skull until he is absolved in Ba-naras. Thus, although Indra comes into conflict with the ascetic aspect of Siva, the erotic aspect of Siva found new uses for the discarded myths of Indra.

[*See also* Siva.]

BIBLIOGRAPHY

For a detailed summary of the mythology of Indra, see pages 249-283 of Sukumari Bhattacharji's rather undigested *The Indian Theogony* (Cambridge, 1970). For a translation of a series of myths about Indra, and a detailed bibliography of secondary literature, see pages 56-96 and 317-321 of my *Hindu Myths* (Harmondsworth, 1975). For the sins of Indra, see Georges Dumézil's *The Destiny of the Warrior* (Chicago, 1970) and *The Destiny of the King* (Chicago, 1973), and my *The Origins of Evil in Hindu Mythology* (Berkeley, 1976). For the relationship between Indra and Siva, see my *Siva: The Erotic Ascetic* (Oxford, 1981), originally published as *Asceticism and Eroticism in the Mythology of Siva* (1973).

WENDY DONIGER O'FLAHERTY

INNER ASIAN RELIGIONS

The History of Inner Asia. The peoples of Inner Asia who lived in the tundra and taiga were widely dispersed in small communities and posed no threat to their neighbors. It was the peoples of the steppes, formed in large tribes with vast herds of sheep, goats, camels, cattle, and horses, who were highly mobile and had the organizational ability to lead military excursions against their sedentary neighbors. When these peoples first appear in historical sources, they come from two great steppe regions: the south Russian (or Pontic) steppe and the Mongolian steppe.

Scythians. The first important Inner Asian people, the Indo-Iranian Scythians, appeared on the south Russian steppe in the eighth century BCE and began to fade out of the historical scene around 175 BCE, although some remnants survived until the third century CE. The Scythians were the first historically known people to use iron, and having defeated the Cimmerians, they assumed full command of the south Russian steppe.

In Persian sources these people were called Saka, and three kinds were enumerated: the Saka beyond the sea, the pointed-hat Saka, and the Saka who revered Hauma. The Scythians of Herodotus lived north of the Black Sea, while the Saka of Persian sources lived beyond the Oxus River (the modern Amu Darya) and south of this area in Iran. The social structure of the Scythians was tripartite: agriculturists,

> **They had cities, centers of metallurgy, and a highly developed, stylized animal art.**

warriors, and priests. They had cities, centers of metallurgy, and a highly developed, stylized animal art.

Animals, particularly horses and cattle, as well as humans were sacrificed as offerings to the gods. Herodotus listed the Scythian gods with what he thought were their Greek equivalents, the supreme deity being Tabiti (Vesta). Images, altars, and temples were used. Scythian soothsayers were called into service when the king was ill; Enarees, womenlike men among the Scythians, practiced divination; elaborate funeral and burial rites, a strong will to protect the tombs of their ancestors, and prescribed ceremonies for oath taking existed. By the late second century BCE, the ethnically and linguistically related nomadic tribes of the Sarmatians began to replace the Scythians, who had reached a degree of civilization perhaps unparalleled by any other Inner Asian empire. [*See also* Scythian Religion.]

Hsiung-nu. On the eastern edge of Inner Asia, the Hsiung-nu were the first clearly identifiable and important steppe people to appear on the borders of China, constantly menacing the frontier with raids that sometimes penetrated deep into Chinese territory. Their center of power was the Mongolian steppe. Appearing in Chinese sources around 230 BCE, an account of the Hsiung-nu was provided by the grand historian of China, Ssu-ma Ch`ien (c. 145-86 BCE). By about 56 BCE internal revolts had begun to rack the Hsiung-nu empire and some tribes moved to the west; in 48 CE the Hsiung-nu finally split into two major groups: the Southern Hsiung-nu and the Northern Hsiung-nu. The former continued to be a serious threat to China and finally faded from the historical scene around 400 CE, while the Northern Hsiung-nu remained on the original homeland of the Mongolian steppe. The Northern Hsiung-nu never regained their former power, however, and about 155 CE they were destroyed by another steppe people, the Hsien-pei.

The military power of the Hsiung-nu, like that of the Scythians, lay in their remarkable skill as highly disciplined mounted archers. In fact, Ssu-ma Ch`ien considered warfare their main occupation. The Chinese set up border markets in an attempt to weaken the Hsiung-nu by supplying them with luxuries and fostering a dependence on Chinese goods. Even though there was a hereditary aristocracy within the Hsiung-nu confederation, internal organization was loose, each tribe having its own pastures.

At set times of the year, sacrifices were offered to ancestors, gods, heaven and earth, while auspicious days were chosen for major events, and the stars and moon were consulted for military maneuvers. Burials were elaborate, particularly for the ruler, with many of his concubines and loyal ministers following him in death. Although condemned by the Chinese for lacking in morals, not understanding court ritual, and not showing respect for the aged, the Hsiung-nu had laws, customs, and manners of their own that contradicted the ethnocentric views of the Chinese.

Yüeh-chih, Wu-sun, and Kushans. The Hsiung-nu greatly affected the history of Inner Asia to the west and south of their domains where, in 160 BCE, they inflicted a terrible defeat on the Yüeh-chih, an Indo-European people located on the Chinese border of modern Kansu Province. This caused the Yüeh-chih to divide; the Lesser Yüeh-chih moved to the south while the Greater Yüeh-chih began moving west. As the latter migrated through the Ili River valley, they abandoned the Mongolian steppe to the complete control of the Hsiung-nu, while they themselves displaced the Sai (or Saka) tribes. The majority of the Yüeh-chih continued to move west into the Greek state of Bactria. At about the same time, the Chinese emperor Wu-ti (r. 140-87 BCE) sent Chang Ch`ien to the Greater Yüeh-chih to form an alliance against the Hsiung-nu. Leaving in 139, Chang Ch`ien had to pass through Hsiung-nu territory, where he was detained and held prisoner for more than ten years. Although his mission to the Yüeh-chih failed, he was sent again in 115 to try to form a different alliance against the Hsiung-nu, this time with the Wu-sun, another people probably of Iranian origin. They also refused to cooperate. It was not until the Hsiung-nu empire was disintegrating that the Wu-sun inflicted serious defeats on them.

The Yüeh-chih tribes that settled in Bactria were later united under one tribe, the Kushans, probably in the first century BCE. Besides Bactria, their kingdom included extensive domains in Central Asia and large portions of Northwest India, where centers of Greco-Buddhist art were established at Gandhara and Mathura. The Kushan period is extremely controversial, and the dates and order of kings are widely disputed. But it was during the reign of Kaniska, a patron of Buddhism, that this Indian religion began to spread into Central Asia and China, heralding a new era for the region. Chinese monks began to travel to India and Sri Lanka to obtain the Buddhist *sutras,* passing through Tun-huang, Khotan, and Turfan on the edge of the Tarim Basin, as well as Ferghana and Sogdiana.

Huns. With the appearance of the Huns toward the end of the fourth century CE, a new movement began on the south Russian steppe. Rumors of invasions spreading fear and panic reached Jerome (c. 311-420) in Palestine, where he wrote that these "wolves of the north"—the Huns—"spared neither religion nor rank nor age." It was with this turmoil on the steppe north of the Sea of Azov that the *Völkerwanderung,* or migration of the peoples, began. Aided by civil wars in Italy that occupied the Roman army, some Hun tribes had established themselves by 409 on the Roman limes and in the Roman province of Pannonia (on the right bank of the Danube). When, in 434, a Hun king named Rua died, he was succeeded by his nephews, Bleda and Attila.

Hun penetration into Europe and the displacing of existing tribes were instrumental in the formation of modern Europe. Aetius, the great fifth-century general and power broker of the Western Roman Empire, provoked some Hun tribes to attack the Burgundians in 437 in order to shatter Germanic power and to strengthen Roman rule in Gaul. The Visigoths, who had been pushed from the east into the Toulouse area, forced the Vandals into Spain and North Africa, an event that caused great consternation to the entire Roman empire. However, Aetius's attempt to use the Huns to defeat the Visigoths failed in 439. Turmoil continued, this time in the Eastern Roman Empire with the Persian decision to attack Byzantium; at the same time, Attila attacked the Byzantines from the north, gaining new treaty concessions. Then in 445 Attila murdered Bleda, thus becoming the sole ruler of the Hun tribes of Pannonia. In the end, a nervous Aetius allied himself with the Visigoths to meet Attila in the Battle of the Catalaunian Plain (451) near Troyes, France, where the Visigoth king Theodoric II lost his life and the Romans withdrew in a battle that left neither Hun nor Roman the victor. With Attila's death in 453, Hun influence on Europe rapidly crumbled.

Hsien-pei and Juan-juan. As already mentioned, the Northern Hsiung-nu state was replaced around 155 CE by that of the Hsien-pei, who probably spoke a Mongol language. Through this victory, the Hsien-pei became the dominant tribal confederacy on the Mongolian steppe. With other nomadic peoples, including the Southern Hsiung-nu and the Wu-huan, they continued attacks on China but were repulsed, particularly by the famous Chinese general Ts`ao Ts`ao. When the Hsien-pei first appeared, during the Wang Mang interregnum (9-23 CE), they had no supreme ruler; unified leadership is not ascribed to them until just before their defeat of the Hsiung-nu: The Hsien-pei failed to create a lasting empire in this fragmented period of steppe history.

From approximately 400 to 550 a new power emerged on the Mongolian steppe: the Juan-juan (or Jou-jan). Their ori-

gins are uncertain but future research may clarify their relation to the Hua and to the Avars who appeared in Europe in the fifth century. According to a widely accepted but yet unproven theory, the Juan-juan in the east are identified with the Avars in the west. Personal names, as given in Chinese, do not appear to be either Turkic or Mongol, but it is with the Juan-juan that the title *kaghan* is first used for the ruler.

Türk. The appearance of the Türk—the first Inner Asian people whose language is known and the first also to use with certainty a Turkic idiom—marks a turning point in the history of the steppe. According to Chinese sources they were metallurgists employed by the Juan-juan, but it is not clear whether the revolt led by Bumin (d. 552) was social in character or a minority uprising. After Bumin's death the empire split, one group, led by his son, establishing itself on the Mongolian steppe, while the other group, under the leadership of his brother Ishtemi, ruled over the more western part of the empire. Because of its commercial interests in the silk trade—represented mainly by Sogdian merchants—the Western Türk empire then found itself embroiled in the conflict between Persia and Byzantium. Persian attempts to stop silk from reaching Byzantium forced the Türk to go directly to Byzantium by a northern route. It was for this reason that embassies were first exchanged between Türk and Byzantium, opening up entire new horizons for Romans as well as for the Chinese. The Western Türk empire disintegrated around 659.

The Eastern Türk empire, in a semipermanent state of war with China and plagued by internal dissension, was finally defeated in 630. Chinese rule then lasted until 682 when the Türk revolted and again seized power, forming a second Türk empire that was overthrown in 743 by the revolt of three Turkic tribes: the Basmil, the Karluk, and the Uighur.

> **Christian and Islamic missionaries had already had some influence among the Khazars, but in 740 the Khazar ruler and his entourage adopted Judaism.**

Avars, Khazars, and Bulgars. The Greek historian Priscus wrote of a migration of peoples taking place from 461 to 465 on the south Russian steppe. An embassy from the Oghur, Onoghur, and Saroghur had arrived in Byzantium, reporting that they had been pushed by the Sabir, who in turn were being displaced by a people in Central Asia called Avar. For almost a century there was no news of them, but in 558 the Avars, now in the Caucasus, sent an embassy to the Byzantine emperor Justinian I (r. 527-565) requesting land in exchange for military protection. Fleeing from the Western Türk, the Avars were given asylum in the Byzantine empire by Justin II, an act that infuriated the Türk, who considered the Avars their own, fugitive subjects. Settled in the Carpathian Basin, the Avars remained there for some two and a half centuries, becoming an effective wedge between the northern and southern Slavs. When they had arrived in the Carpathian Basin, the Avars found two Germanic tribes, the Gepids, whom they destroyed, and the Lombards, who fled and settled in northern Italy. The Avars also menaced the Byzantines and the Franks. In 626 the Avars and the Persians jointly attacked Constantinople and were defeated only when the Byzantine forces destroyed the Persian fleet as it attempted to cross the Bosphorus.

Meanwhile, the south Russian steppe continued to be a place of turmoil. The Turkic-speaking Khazars became increasingly powerful with the weakening of the western Türk, and by the mid-seventh century achieved independence. Christian and Islamic missionaries had already had some influence among the Khazars, but in 740 the Khazar ruler and his entourage adopted Judaism. A Christian Bulgar prince, Kovrat, and his son Asparukh led other Bulgar tribes, mostly Turkic, to the lower Danube region where Asparukh created a Bulgar state between 679 and 681. Some of the Bulgars settled with the Avars in the Carpathian Basin, but the formation of this Bulgar buffer state between the Avars and Byzantium effectively ended Avar-Byzantine relations by 678. As a result, the Avars led a reasonably quiet life for over a century until they were attacked and greatly weakened (although not defeated) in 791, 795-796, and 803 by Charlemagne.

Uighurs. The final blow to the Türk empire was delivered by the Uighurs who, as we have seen, had been a part of the Türk confederacy. Their language was basically the same as that of the Türk, with some of their texts written in runic script and some in a script borrowed from the Sogdians, one that would become a major script used in Inner Asia. Unlike the Türk, whom they overthrew in 743, the Uighurs often allied themselves with China; thus, during the reign of Mou-yü the Uighurs helped China to quell the An Lu-shan rebellion (755-757). When Mou-yü visited Lo-yang in 762-763, he was converted to Manichaeism, which had been propagated in China by the Sogdians. A description of his conversion appears on the trilingual inscription (in Uighur, Sogdian, and Chinese) of Karabalghasun, the Uighur capital city. When Mou-yü returned home he took Manichaean priests with him and made Manichaeism the state religion. Thus, the Uighurs became the first Inner Asian people to adopt an institutionalized, major religion. Many Uighurs disliked the influence gained by Sogdians in Uighur affairs and an anti-Sogdian faction, led by the uncle of Mou-yü, revolted and killed the kaghan and his family. There followed a succession of rulers embroiled in family intrigues, plagued by assassinations and suicide. Even so, Sogdian and Manichaean influence remained in a kingdom dominated by Buddhism.

Not absorbed into the new ruling Kirghiz confederacy, the Uighurs moved. Some went to China, settling in today's Kansu Province, where some of their descendants can still be found; the majority moved to the Tarim Basin and created a new state centered on the city of Kocho (850-1250), where a sophisticated, multi-lingual, and multiethnic civilization developed.

Mongols. The rise of Mongol power and the domination of the Chinggisid states brought unification to Inner Asia in a way that had not existed since prehistoric times.

A mixture of forests rich in game, agricultural land made fertile by abundant rainfall, and pastures suitable for horse and cattle breeding determined the basic economy of Manchuria. The settled way of life also made pig raising an important feature of all Manchurian civilizations. In the fourth century, the Mongol-speaking Kitan began to gain dominance in the region, entering into relations with China in 468, but by the sixth century, they came under Türk domination. A new Kitan rise to power was signalled by their attack and defeat of the Kirghiz ruling over the Mongolian steppe in 924; they then expanded their rule over North China, adopting the Chinese dynastic title of Liao (927-1125). In 1125 Kitan domination was replaced by that of the Jurchen, a Tunguz-speaking Manchurian people who had been Kitan subjects. The Jurchen assumed the Chinese dynastic title of Chin (1125-1234) and maintained their rule over northern China until the Mongol conquest. When the Jurchen moved into North China, some Kitan tribes, with the permission of the Uighurs, moved west across the Tarim Basin through the kingdom of Kocho to Central Asia, where a third Kitan state was founded (after those of Manchuria and China), that of the Karakitai (Black Kitan or Kitai) centered at Bala-sagun in the Chu River valley.

Between Central Asia and Manchuria, two major mongolized Turkic tribes, the Naiman and the Kereit, were vying for power in the eleventh century. Both tribes had been strongly influenced by Nestorianism; the conversion of the Kereit around 1000 was related by the Syriac chronicler Bar Hebraeus (fl. thirteenth century). [*See also* Nestorian Church.] The first united Mongol kingdom ended in the late eleventh century, followed by a period of internecine warfare between Mongol tribes and against the neighboring Tatar tribes. It was not until Chinggis (known as Temüjin before he was elected khan) had defeated all of his rivals that a new and powerful Mongol state emerged.

Chinggis, angered by the Naiman leader Küchlüg, who had defeated the Karakitai in Central Asia, began the great push west, defeating the Naiman in 1218, and then led a punitive campaign against Khorezm aimed at avenging the murder of Mongol envoys. Before Chinggis's death in 1227, Central Asia had been devastated, and the campaigns of the famous Mongol generals Jebe and Sübetei had spilled into Georgia, across the Caucasus, and into Russian territory, where the Russian forces and their Cuman allies were defeated in the Battle of Kalka in the late spring of 1223. The Mongols advanced as far as the city of Bulgar where they were turned back at the very end of the year 1223. With the death of Chinggis, the Mongol empire was to be divided among his four sons. But the eldest son, Jochi, predeceased Chinggis and his appanage of the westernmost Mongols, the so-called Golden Horde, went to his son, Chinggis's grandson, Batu.

Defeating Bulgar in the winter of 1237-1238, the Mongols then swept into eastern and central Europe with a great offensive begun in the winter of 1239-1240. All of Europe now accepted the Mongol threat as real, however, an attitude that opened a period of rapprochement in Mongol-Western relations, begun by Pope Innocent IV (r. 1234-1254) at the Council of Lyons (June 1245). Three groups of papal emissaries were sent to the Mongols: the Dominican Ascelinus, the Dominican Andrew of Longjumeau, and the Franciscan Giovanni da Pian del Carpini, who brought back the first extensive accounts of the Mongols, as did the later Franciscan missionary William of Rubrouck, who journeyed to the Mongols from 1253 to 1255.

With Batu's death in 1256, his brother Berke (r. 1257-1267) became ruler of the Golden Horde. He converted to Islam, thus placing the Golden Horde at odds with the Il-khanids of Persia. The Il-khanids came to power under Hülegü, who sacked Baghdad in 1258 and ended the Abbasid caliphate. The Mamluk sultan Baybars (r. 1259-1277), powerful foe of the Crusaders but also of the Mongols, defeated the Il-khanid forces in the Battle of Ain Jalut (1259), thereby stopping the Mongol conquest of the Arab world. During the reign of the Il-khan Arghun (r. 1284-1291), Buddhism was declared the state religion and close contact was maintained with Europe, particularly with the Vatican and the kings of France and England. Under severe economic pressure, Il-khanid Persia declined and religious tension forced Gazan (r. 1295-1304) to proclaim Islam the official religion. With the death of Abu Sa'id in 1335, Il-khanid Persia fragmented. Meanwhile, the power of the Golden Horde reached its apogee under Özbeg (r. 1313-1341), but attempts to expand its territory brought it into military conflict with ambitious Muscovite princes and the great military leader Timur (Tamarlane; 1336-1405) in Central Asia. Finally, the Golden Horde split into three successor states: the khanates of Kazan, Astrakhan, and the Crimea.

It was Khubilai (r. 1260-1294), the last great Mongol khan, who brought China under Mongol rule (the Yüan dynasty, 1264-1368). With the extended visit of Marco Polo to Khubilai's court (1271-1292) the first reliable information about China came to the West. After the death of Khubilai, Mongol rule in China began to weaken until they were overthrown in 1368 by the Chinese. What remained of Mongol power returned to the steppe where the western Mongols (Oirats, Dzungars, Kalmuks) became a factor in Central Asia, with two successive Oirat states menacing the territory between the western Mongolian steppe and the Caspian Sea from the mid-fifteenth century until their final defeat in 1758 at the hands of the Chinese.

BIBLIOGRAPHY

The classic definition of Inner Asia can be found in Denis Sinor's "Central Eurasia," in *Orientalism and History,* 2d rev. ed., edited by Denis Sinor (Bloomington, Ind., 1970), pp. 93-119, and expanded in textbook form in his *Inner Asia: History, Civilization, Languages; A Syllabus* (Bloomington, Ind., 1969). Sinor's *Introduction à l'étude de l'Eurasie Centrale* (Wiesbaden, 1963) is the basic bibliographic work for the study of Inner Asia and is invaluable for the author's opinion on research in a field dominated by French, German, Russian, and Hungarian scholarship. Other histories of Inner Asia that can be consulted with profit include René Grousset's *The Empire of the Steppes: A History of Central Asia,* translated by Naomi Walford (New Brunswick, N. J., 1970); Wilhelm Barthold's *Turkestan down to the Mongol Invasion,* 3d ed. (London, 1968); and the collection of essays in the *Handbuch der Orientalistik,* vol. 5.5, *Geschichte Mittelasiens,* under the general editorship of Bertold Spuler (Leiden, 1966). *The Cambridge History of Inner Asia*, under preparation by its editor, Denis Sinor, will bring the scholarship on Inner Asia up to date.

For the art of Inner Asia, Karl Jettmar's *The Art of the Steppes,* translated by Ann E. Keep (New York, 1967), provides an excellent introduction plus ample illustrations both in black and white and in color. The best book on the epic in Inner Asia is Nora K. Chadwick and Victor Zhirmunsky's *Oral Epics of Central Asia* (Cambridge, 1969), but it concerns only the Turkic-speaking peoples.

For a discussion of the early Arab penetration into Inner Asia, which opened the region to Islam, H. A. R. Gibb's *The Arab Conquests in Central Asia* (London, 1923) remains a useful account. In a similar vein, Owen Lattimore's *The Inner Asian Frontiers of China* (New York, 1940) and *Studies in Frontier History: Collected Papers* 1928-1958 (Oxford, 1962) are unique in that much of Lattimore's life has been spent in the region.

The most extensive portrayal of the life of the Scythians can be found in Ellis H. Minn's *Scythians and Greeks: A Survey of Ancient History and Archeology on the North Coast of the Euxine from the Danube to the Caucasus* (Cambridge, 1913). The most detailed account of the Huns is J. Otto Maenchen-Helfen's *The World of the Huns: Studies in Their History and Culture,* edited by Max Knight (Berkeley, 1973). Annemarie von Gabain's work on the Uighur kingdom of Kocho, *Das Leben im uigurischen Königreich von Qoco: 850-1250,* in "Veröffentlichungen der Societas Uralo-Altaica," vol. 6 (Wiesbaden, 1973), is unparalleled. There is no good history of the Türk empire, a gap that will be filled by *The Cambridge History of Inner Asia.*

For the Mongols, however, there is an abundance of material. René Grousset's *Conqueror of the World,* translated by Denis Sinor in collaboration with Marian MacKellar (Edinburgh, 1967), is the best book on the life of Chinggis. For the Mongol Il-khans and the Golden Horde, Bertold Spuler's *The Muslim World: A Historical Survey,* vol. 2, *The Mongol Period* (Leiden, 1960); *Die Goldene Horde: Die Mongolen in Russland, 1223-1502,* 2d ed. (Wiesbaden, 1965); and *Die Mongolen in Iran* (Leipzig, 1939) are by far the most useful in this complex period of Mongol history.

RUTH I. MESERVE

INQUISITION, THE

The Early Medieval Inquisition. During the eleventh century, western European society began a metamorphosis that led to great cultural and social achievements during the twelfth and thirteenth centuries. The church found strong leadership in the reformers who had brought institutional and doctrinal innovations to the eleventh-century papacy. Monastic reform, exemplified by Cluny, provided centers of spiritual and liturgical power throughout the West, while the laity discovered a new consciousness of social cohesion through the Peace and Truce of God movements, church-sponsored attempts to control noble and knightly ravages. In the midst of eleventh-century social and economic expansion, a sense of spiritual unity was born: Europe had become Christendom.

However, this new sense of Christian unity was evident in reactions to heretics, who now seemed, to townspeople and rulers alike, to threaten society itself: hence the public burning of a dozen or so heretics at Orleans in 1022, at the command of King Robert and with public approval. In addition, the three-year-old corpse of a heretic was exhumed and ejected from its Christian burial ground. Heretics were burned by popular demand at Milan about 1028, while Henry III of Germany allowed the hanging of purported Cathari at Goslar in 1052.

In the twelfth century, antiheretical activities on the part of church and lay princes accelerated. The dualist Cathari—some of whom may have been victims of eleventh-century popular violence—were expanding into western Europe from eastern Europe, particularly into regions where secular authority was weak or fragmented by competing powers, as in southern France (Languedoc) and northern Italy (Lombardy). Mobs and secular authorities continued to put heretics to death, as at Soissons, Cologne, and Liège, and the king of Aragon officially decreed burning as the penalty for heresy in 1197.

The church dealt with heresy in several twelfth-century councils (Toulouse, 1119; Second Lateran, 1139; Reims, 1157; Tours, 1163), prescribing as punishments excommunication, confiscation of property, and imprisonment. In 1179, at the Third Lateran Council, Pope Alexander III, called attention to the need to quell the Cathari of Languedoc and to confiscate their lands, and again he requested aid from secular lords. The earlier conciliar legislation had had limited effect, however, and in 1184 Pope Lucius III, in association with Emperor Frederick Barbarossa (d. 1190), issued more specific orders. In the bull *Ad abo-lendam,* Lucius regularized the episcopal inquisition, requiring bishops to visit their parishes and ascertain, through witnesses, who was engaged in heretical activity. The accused were to be apprehended and examined.

In 1199 Pope Innocent III (d. 1216), following the lead of earlier canonists, equated heresy with treason, in the bull *Vergentes in senium.* The obstinate were to be handed over, as traitors to God, to the secular powers for (unspecified) punishment, and their lands were confiscated. Roman concepts of lèse-majesté, and appropriate procedures and punishments, were beginning to be absorbed into canonical forms and penances.

The battle against heresy (especially Catharism) during the thirteenth century grew more rigorous and determined under the leadership of powerful popes. Innocent III commissioned Cistercian monks to preach and stir up antiheretical sentiment in Languedoc from 1203 to 1208; he also called upon the French king, Philip II, to mount a crusade against the Cathari in the south. The Albigensian crusade, led by Simon de Montfort, lasted for some twenty years. Many Cathari, and orthodox Christians as well, were killed by the Crusaders, who invaded Languedoc for material as well as spiritual motives.

In the aftermath of the Albigensian crusade, many Cathari returned to Languedoc, but they were far more secretive: they had been driven underground, but not exterminated. Pope Gregory IX was determined to put an end to the heresy and in 1230 he began to enact severe legislation against it. Besides sending out friars as inquisitors, by 1231 he had adopted the canons of the Council of Toulouse (1229) and the punishment of death by fire prescribed by his enemy Emperor Frederick II (in 1224). In 1233 the pope established a tribunal at Toulouse, staffed by legatine-controlled Dominicans, who were to cooperate with the bishop in prosecuting heretics. The popular outcry caused by this inquisition—for its policy of exhuming the corpses of purported heretics, for example—was chronicled by William Pelhisson, one of the Dominican inquisitors assigned to the area. Although Gregory faced difficulties in securing the cooperation of many northern Italian cities, and for political reasons had to suspend the inquisition of Toulouse in 1238 (later reinstated), he had established the Inquisition in its basic outlines. In later decades its powers and procedures were to increase in extent and complexity.

The Cathari of Languedoc suffered a major setback— one from which they never really recovered—when their castle of Montségur was stormed in 1244, following the murder of a party of local inquisitors in 1242. More than two hundred Cathar leaders, known as the *perfecti,* were said to have been burned after the lengthy siege.

In the late 1240s Innocent commissioned the first handbook of inquisitorial procedure, which was drawn up by two inquisitors of Languedoc. Such manuals continued to be compiled until the end of the Middle Ages. More significantly, in the bull *Ad extirpanda* (1252), Innocent ordered that heretics handed over to the secular arm should be executed within five days, and he ordained that torture could be used to elicit information for inquisitorial courts. In doing so, Innocent brought the special tribunal of the Inquisition into line with criminal procedure already followed by thirteenth-century lay governments. Not only the revival of Roman law (with its *inquisitio* and use of torture) but also the abolition of the ordeal and other divine aids encouraged a more rigorous application of human agencies to prove guilt in both secular and inquisitorial courts.

The Later Medieval Inquisition. The heresy of the Cathari, which had helped to bring the Inquisition into being, declined in Languedoc (after a brief revival in the early fourteenth century) and throughout western Europe; by the mid-fourteenth century it had virtually disappeared. At the same time, however, the Inquisition continued to develop in other areas of Europe along procedural lines laid down in the thirteenth century. Under papal leadership it spread into eastern Europe and Germany, though in the latter, local bishops sometimes resisted papal interference. England never accept-

> **. . . Ferdinand and Isabella used the inquisitorial machinery for their own political as well as religious ends.**

ed the institution, whereas by the later fifteenth century, it had been absorbed into the political machinery of Castile and Aragon and would result in the infamous Spanish Inquisition. The Spanish monarchs Ferdinand and Isabella used the inquisitorial machinery for their own political as well as religious ends. Their attempts to expand their authority through persecution of Moriscos and Marranos were guided by the Grand Inquisitor Tomás de Torquemada (1420-1498). In Italy, though Cathari were no longer a problem, the Waldensians continued to interest inquisitors, whose tasks were made more difficult by political rivalries among Italian city-states, and between these states and the papacy. During the sixteenth-century Counter-Reformation, the Inquisition, or Holy Office, underwent reorganization and centralization at Rome.

Political complications are also evident in France, where King Philip IV (d. 1314), in his conflict with the papacy, was sympathetic toward complaints levied against the Inquisition. By 1307, with a compliant pope, the king had turned the Inquisition against the Order of the Knights Templar, which was dissolved at the Council of Vienne (1312). From the mid-fourteenth century, the Parlement and University of Paris tended to exercise inquisitorial powers. Indeed, throughout its history the Inquisition was rivaled by local ecclesiastical and secular jurisdictions. No matter how determined, no pope ever succeeded in establishing complete control of the institution in western Europe: princes, bishops, civil authorities, and kings vacillated between acceptance and resistance.

Historical judgments on the medieval Inquisition have varied from absolute condemnation to qualified approval of at least some of its characteristics. Only a small portion of those who appeared before the Inquisition were sent to their deaths, and in this respect, it was more lenient than violent mobs or contemporary secular criminal courts; yet even in the thirteenth century, some, such as the lawyers who cautioned against the unrestricted use of torture, doubted whether this ecclesiastical tribunal, with its distinctive procedures, served the interests of Christendom.

BIBLIOGRAPHY

A brief, valuable introduction to the Inquisition is Bernard Hamilton's *The Medieval Inquisition* (London, 1982), with a bibliography of recent as well as older, standard works. Walter Ullmann's historical introduction to Henry C. Lea's *The Inquisition of the Middle Ages* (London, 1963) provides a good overview of historiographical changes since the late nineteenth century, when Lea wrote. Elphège Vacandard's *The Inquisition* (London, 1908), though somewhat erratic, is a general survey that also contains extensive excerpts from contemporary documents. The crucial twelfth and thirteenth centuries are well analyzed by Christine Thouzellier in "La répression de l'hérésie et les débuts de l'inquisition" in *Histoire de l'Église,* vol. 10, by Augustin Fliche and others (Paris, 1950). Henri Maisonneuve's *Études sur les origines de l'inquisition,* 2d ed. (Paris, 1960), with full bibliography, is especially interesting in chapters 5 and 6, which set the Inquisition in broad historical context and explore the contrasts between northern and southern European attitudes toward it. A very useful research tool, listing nearly two thousand titles on the late medieval and postmedieval Inquisition, is E. van der Vekene's *Bibliographie der Inquisition: Ein Versuch* (Hildesheim, 1963). See also parts 8 and 9 of Herbert Grundmann's *Bibliographie zur Ketzergeschichte des Mittelalters, 1900-1966* (Rome, 1967), listing twentieth-century works, and Carl T. Berkhout and Jeffrey B. Russell's *Medieval Heresies: A Bibliography, 1960-1979* (Toronto, 1981), particularly part 17, "Repression." Much has been written about the Inquisition in southern France, such as Walter L. Wakefield's *Heresy, Crusade and Inquisition in Southern France, 1100-1250* (Berkeley, 1974), with extensive bibliography, and E. Le Roy Ladurie's *Montaillou: Cathars and Catholics in a French Village, 1294-1324,* translated by B. Bray (London, 1978), which provides an intimate look at how the Inquisition affected peasant life in a specific region. A good idea of contemporary procedure in Languedoc can be gained from Bernard Gui's *Manuel de l'inquisiteur,* 2 vols., translated by G. Mollat (Paris, 1926-1927), a practical guide for heretic hunters. Heretics and the Inquisition in southern France are the subjects of several issues of *Cahiers de Fanjeaux: Collection d'histoire religieuse du Languedoc au treizième et au début du quatorzième siècles* (Toulouse, 1966-). An example of recent historical studies outside this region is *Quellen zur Böhmischen Inquisition im 14 Jahrhundert,* edited by Alexander Patschovsky (Weimar, 1979), with a detailed introduction to over 150 pages of contemporary documents, including notarial registers. Interesting essays on heresy and its repression in general are R. I. Moore's *The Origins of European Dissent* (New York, 1977) and Edward Peters's *The Magician, the Witch and the Law* (Philadelphia, 1978), both containing astute observations on the legal and sociological aspects of repression.

R. C. FINUCANE

INTERLACUSTRINE BANTU RELIGIONS

The term *interlacustrine Bantu,* as used here, encompasses a variety of peoples who live between the Great Lakes of east-central Africa and speak closely related Bantu languages. Their territory includes some of the most densely populated regions of Africa, consisting of all of Uganda south of the Victoria Nile, the states of Rwanda and Burundi, and a substantial portion of northwest Tanzania.

Today most of the people of the region are at least nominally Christians; there is also a substantial minority of Muslims. But the indigenous cults are still widespread and are remarkably similar throughout the area.

The Spirit Powers. All the peoples of the area have the idea of a supreme being, known as Imana in the south, Ruhanga in the Nyoro-speaking north, and Katonda in Uganda; the last two names mean "creator." In some myths the hierarchical class structure mentioned above is ascribed to him, which to a certain degree may have sanctioned its acceptance by the less privileged. But, in a familiar pattern, the creator god, having made the world, was disappointed by it and withdrew from active participation in human affairs. Shrines are not made for him, nor are sacrifices offered as they are to the other gods (though here Buganda seems to have been an exception). In contrast to the lesser spirit powers, no mediumship cult is dedicated to the supreme being. He is, however, thought to be generally well disposed toward humans, and brief prayers and thanks may be offered up to him on a casual basis.

There are many other spirits of nonhuman and sometimes of foreign origin that can be approached through mediumship ritual. These are sometimes known in the northern areas as the "black" *embandwa,* and they include spirits associated with the bush, with certain illnesses, and with some neighboring countries. In the interlacustrine area (as elsewhere in Africa) more recent spirits have come to represent new and formidable forces of all kinds, such as hitherto unknown illnesses, manifestations of Western power such as motorcars, airplanes, and even army tanks, as well as such abstract qualities as "Europeanness."

In addition to the high god and the wide and growing variety of *embandwa* spirits, there are the ghosts of the dead. (Ghost cults are not necessarily ancestor cults. An ancestor cult is concerned with the deceased forebears of a lineage, who are usually conceived as a collectivity and are believed to be directly interested in the well-being of their descendants). But the cult of ghosts is important throughout the region. It is believed that ghosts are left by people after they die; diffused like the wind, such ghosts are sometimes associated with a shadowy underworld, and it is thought that they may bring death, illness, or other calamity on those who have injured or offended them while they were alive. Throughout the interlacustrine area, ghosts are seen as malevolent rather than benevolent, more concerned to punish than to reward.

Cults. Generally people have recourse to the cults as a response to some misfortune, and when things go wrong, the first step is to consult a diviner. He, or possibly she, using one of a wide variety of techniques, is likely to ascribe the client's trouble to an embandwa spirit, an offended ghost, or sorcery.

Séances are dramatic occasions, involving drumming, dancing, and the singing of special songs, and mediums may assume the language and gestures appropriate to their possessing spirits. While possessed, mediums appear to be in a state of trance and may claim afterward that they have no recollection of what happens to them when they are possessed. But evidence from several parts of the area indicates that complete dissociation is seldom, if ever, achieved; generally, the medium is "putting on an act." But this does not mean that they are fraudulent; the play they are performing is a religious one, a "liturgical drama" in Luc de Heusch's phrase. And, in addition to providing a ritual means of influencing powers over which there are no other means of control, the mediumship cults are also a source of dramatic entertainment in their own right.

Admission to the cults requires a complex (and expensive) cycle of initiation ritual, often lasting for several days and culminating in the possession of the novice by the spirit concerned. Threats of the fearful consequences of disclosure confirm the candidate's commitment to secrecy.

Social Context. Important throughout much of the area was the role of the household medium, in the Nyo-ro-speaking region called *omucwezi w'eka* or, if female, *nyakatagara.* One member of the family, usually female and preferably initiated while still a child, links the domestic group with one of the traditional *embandwa* spirits as its medium: this spirit is supposed to have a special concern for the well-being of the family members. Here especially the purity and auspiciousness of the traditional cults are stressed; for only a gentle and well-mannered child is acceptable to the spirits as a household medium.

The relationship between the *embandwa* cults and the traditional kingships was commonly one of implicit or explicit opposition. In several kingdoms, most notably those of Bunyoro and Rwanda, members of the royal clan (including the king himself) were debarred from participation in the mediumship cults. Kings in the interlacustrine region were not priests. Instead, they maintained priests at court—professional mediums who, like everyone else, were subject to the royal authority. Among the larger kingdoms it was only in Buganda, by far the most politically centralized of the interlacustrine states, that the royal line was closely identified with the mediumship cult. The official Ganda cult centered on the ghosts of former kings, whose tombs, carefully maintained, provided the locus for state ritual. But even here it was the *lubale* (i. e., *embandwa*) "priests," and not the king, who were the mediums for the royal ancestors.

In the twentieth century the opposition between religion and state is exemplified in the rise and decline of the Nyabingi cult. This cult focused on a powerful female *embandwa* called Nyabingi and her associates, whose cult has been ascribed to various sources but may have originated in northern Rwanda, whence it spread rapidly into southwest Uganda. It appears to have begun as a reaction both against the traditional Ryangombe cults and against Rwanda's ruling class, the pastoral Tutsi. But with the coming of European colonial power, the cult became a protest movement against all governmental authority. In the 1920s a revolt by Nyabingi adherents against the local administration was crushed by military force, though the cult survived in attenuated form for many years.

It is not surprising that the *embandwa* cults found themselves in opposition to the Christian mission churches, which, with only very limited justification, regarded them as being involved with witchcraft. Since the traditional cults were generally seen as beneficent and as being especially concerned with childbearing, attempts by government officials and missionaries to eradicate them were readily interpreted by the traditionally minded as aimed, in the long term, at the elimination of the indigenous peoples themselves. Mention should also be made here of the revivalist and fundamentalist Balokole ("the Saved Ones") movement within the Anglican church. Although this movement affected only a small minority of Christians, its uncompromising evangelism brought it into conflict not only with the *embandwa* cults— with which it had certain things in common, for example, the notion of being "born again"—but also with the secular authorities.

[*For further discussion of the religions of closely related peoples, see* East African Religions.]

BIBLIOGRAPHY

Three works adopt a comparative approach. In his *Entre le Victoria l'Albert et l'Édouard: Ethnographie de la partie anglaise du Vicariat de l'Uganda* (Rennes, 1920), the missionary P. Julien Gorju gives a good account of the cults and of initiation into them in the Uganda kingdoms. Luc de Heusch's *Le Rwanda et la civilisation interlacustre: Études d'anthropologie historique et structurale* (Brussels, 1966) contains a comprehensive analysis of the Ryangombe cult in Rwanda, taking account also of comparable data from neighboring areas. And Iris Berger's *Religion and Resistance: East African Kingdoms in the Precolonial Period* (Tervuren, Belgium, 1981), although largely concerned with historical reconstruction, includes an up-to-date review and assessment of current information on the cults over the whole area as well as a useful bibliography. Berger notes in particular the important role played in the cults by women.

There are several brief accounts of the religious beliefs and rituals of particular peoples in the area; see, for example, Lucy P. Mair's "Religion and Magic," chapter 9 of her book on the Ganda, *An African People in the Twentieth Century* (1934; New York, 1965); J. J. Maquet's "The Kingdom of Ruanda," in *African Worlds,* edited by Daryll Forde (London, 1954); and John Beattie's "Spirit Mediumship in Bunyoro," in *Spirit Mediumship and Society in Africa,* edited by John Beattie and John Middleton (New York, 1969). A monograph by a Norwegian anthropologist, Svein Bjerke, *Religion and Misfortune: The Bacwezi Complex and the Other Spirit Cults of the Zinza of Northwestern Tanzania* (Oslo, 1981), provides a detailed account, based on field research, of the cults among one of the less well known peoples of the region. Relevant to the study of religion in its political context is Elizabeth Hopkins's "The Nya-bingi Cult of Southwestern Uganda," in *Protest and Power in Black Africa,* edited by Robert I. Rotberg and Ali A. Mazrui (Oxford, 1970), a history of the rise and influence of an anticolonial spirit cult. Finally, for an African academic's view of his own traditional religion, see Abel G. M. Ishumi's "Religion and the Cults," chapter 6 of his *Kiziba: The Cultural Heritage of an Old African Kingdom* (Syracuse, N. Y., 1980)

JOHN BEATTIE

INTERNATIONAL SOCIETY FOR KRISHNA CONSCIOUSNESS

INTERNATIONAL SOCIETY FOR KRISHNA CONSCIOUSNESS (ISKCON) is the missionary form of devotional Hinduism brought to the United States in 1965 by a pious devotee of Krsna who wanted to convert the English-speaking world to "God-consciousness." In less than two decades ISKCON became an international movement with more than two hundred centers worldwide (sixty-one in the United States).

The founding *guru,* A. C. Bhaktivedanta Swami Prabhupada, was born Abhay Charan De in 1896 in Calcutta. Educated in a Viasnava school and later in Scottish Church College, he was a sporadically successful businessman in the pharmaceutical industry. However, after he was initiated in 1922 by Bhaktisiddhanta Sa-rasvati, a Gaudiya (Bengali) Vaisnava in the line of the sixteenth-century saint and reformer Caitanya, he began increasingly to invest time and money in his religious interests. In 1944 Bhaktivedanta established the magazine *Back to Godhead,* and in 1952 he formed the Jhansi League of Devotees. He gave up his life as a householder *(grhasthin)* in 1954 and in 1959 took the formal vows of an ascetic *(samnyasin).*

In September 1965, at the age of sixty-nine, Bhaktivedanta arrived in New York City with a suitcase full of his translations of the *Srimad Bhagavatam* and less than ten dollars in his pocket. He lived with various Indian and American supporters in Manhattan, where he set out daily to chant and sing the praises of Krsna to anyone who would listen. Bhaktivedanta's lectures and devotional services slowly attracted a following, primarily counterculture youths, and preaching centers were eventually established in Los Angeles, Berkeley, Boston, and Montreal. By the late 1960s Los Angeles had become the headquarters of ISKCON and home of its publishing office, which has printed more than fifty different volumes of translations and original works by Bhaktivedanta.

From the earliest years of the movement, Bhaktivedanta's disciples have been known for their public chanting (sankirtan) of the Hare Krsna mantra and their distribution of Back to Godhead as well as Bhaktivedanta's books. Like his Indian predecessors, Bhaktivedanta believed that the recitation of God's name was sufficient for salvation. Further, his guru had

> **Like his Indian predecessors, Bhaktivedanta believed that the recitation of God's name was sufficient for salvation.**

instructed him to make known "Krishna consciousness" to the English-speaking world. Consequently, the "Hare Krishnas" in India and America have been both visible and very missionary-minded.

In July 1970, Bhaktivedanta formed a Governing Body Commission of twelve advanced devotees to administer an ever more widespread and complex ISKCON and to allow him to spend his time preaching and translating. Around the same time, he instituted a series of standardized practices that had the effect of making ISKCON devotees more like their Indian counterparts. Every male devotee who entered the temple had to wear the traditional saffron dress of the monastic novice and shave his head; women wore traditional Indian saris. All temples were to follow a daily regimen of rising at 3:30 A. M. for morning devotional services (puja), chanting sixteen rounds of the Krsna mantra on 108 prayer beads, and attending a lecture on a scriptural passage. A clear distinction was made between brahmacarin or "student" devotees who intended to take the four monastic regulative principles (no meat eating, no intoxicants of any kind, no sexual activity of any kind, and no gambling) and grhasta or "householder" devotees who intended to live in marriage outside the temple and who might also take a modified version of the four vows.

Throughout the 1970s, ISKCON became ever more conscious of its Indian roots at the same time as it was expanding to every continent on the globe. Bhaktivedanta returned frequently to India from 1970 until his death there in Vrndavana in 1977. He received a hearty welcome from most Indians, who jokingly called his devotees "dancing white ele-

phants." He established temples and preaching centers near Bombay, in Vrndavana (the birthplace of Krsna), and in Mayapur (the birthplace of Caitanya). By the early 1980s, the Bombay temple had more than six thousand Indian "lifetime" members and the Vrndavana temple was included in most Krsna pilgrims' circuits.

Bhaktivedanta circled the globe several times in his twelve years of missionary activity and established temples in England and continental Europe. Just before his death, he appointed eleven disciples as initiating gurus to keep the Caitanya chain of disciples unbroken and to missionize the rest of the world. (In 1982 the number was expanded to thirteen.) By the early 1980s his disciples had established forty-five temples or farms in Europe, ten in Africa, thirty-five in Asia, and forty in South America. Whereas the full-time membership of the American temples remained fairly constant after 1977, ISKCON branches grew rapidly overseas, where they often found more tolerant environments.

ISKCON has encountered opposition from anticult groups such as the Citizens Freedom Foundation, but the movement has also experienced challenges from within. In 1970 a group of devotees questioned Bhaktivedanta's disciplic authority, and in 1982 one of his appointed successors left the organization to follow another guru. The movement's practices and techniques of book distribution and proselytizing have most often been at the heart of both external and internal criticism. Yet these practices shaped by the unbounded enthusiasm and organizational inconsistencies of the early years of ISKCON are now, in recent decades, being molded by processes of institutionalization and accommodation that are well under way in ISKCON throughout the world. In the absence of the founding guru, it is the Governing Body Commission and the appointed gurus who will determine the viability of this Indian tradition on foreign soil.

[See also New Religions.]

BIBLIOGRAPHY

J. Stillson Judah's study of California devotees, *Hare Krishna and the Counterculture* (New York, 1974), is now dated, but its emphasis on ISKCON's origin as a religious alternative to and embodiment of countercultural values and attitudes is still instructive. The glossary includes most major terms and names of persons associated with Krsna devotion. An anthropological study that focuses on the Boston, New York, London, and Amsterdam temples is Francine Jeanne Daner's *The American Children of Krsna* (New York, 1976). Daner also places the rise of ISKCON in the context of "counter-culture religions" as well as in the framework of Erik Erikson's identity theory of personality development. My own study, *The Dark Lord* (Philadelphia, 1985), is based on more than one hundred interviews of Krsna devotees from fourteen temples throughout America and presents the various aspects of the American Krsna faith in the framework of anticult criticisms and a history of religions response to those criticisms.

LARRY D. SHINN

INUIT RELIGION

The Inuit (Eskimo) live in the vast Arctic and sub-Arctic area that stretches from the eastern point of Siberia to eastern Greenland. Of the approximately 105,000 Inuit, 43,000 live in Greenland, 25,000 in Arctic Canada, 35,000 (plus 2,000 Aleut) in Alaska, and 1,500 (plus a small number of Aleut) in the Soviet Union.

The word *Eskimo* seems to be of Montagnais origin. The word *Inuit* means "people." Traditionally the Inuit are divided into many geographic groups. The members of each group, or band, were connected through kinship ties, but the band was without formal leadership. The nuclear family was the most important social unit.

Relations between Men and Animals. According to eastern Inuit religious tradition, each animal had its own *inua* (its "man," "owner," or "spirit") and also its own "soul." Since the Inuit believed that the animals they hunted possessed souls, they treated their game with respect. Seals and whales were commonly offered a drink of fresh water after they had been dragged ashore. Having received such a pleasant welcome as guests in the human world, their souls, according to Inuit belief, would return to the sea and soon become ready to be caught again, and they would also let their fellow animals know that they should not object to being caught.

In southern Greenland the head of a slain polar bear was placed in a house facing the direction from which the bears usually came so that the bear's soul could easily find its way home.

During the days before the whaling party set out, the men slept in the festival house and observed sexual and food taboos.

Taboos, Amulets, and Songs. Unlike cultic practices in connection with the deities, which had relatively minor significance, taboos, amulets, and songs were fundamentally important to the Inuit. Most taboos were imposed to separate the game from a person who was tabooed because of birth, menstruation, or death. An infringement of a taboo might result in individual hardship (for example, the loss of good fortune in hunting, sickness, or even death), but often, it was feared, the whole community would suffer. Usually a public confession under the guidance of the shaman was believed sufficient to reduce the effect of the transgression of a taboo.

Amulets, which dispensed their powers only to the first owner, were used primarily to secure success in hunting and good health and, to a lesser degree, to ward off negative influences.

Songs were either inherited or bought. If a song was passed on from one generation to the next, all members of the family were free to use it, but once it was sold it became useless to its former owners.

Rites of Passage. In many localities in Canada and Alaska, women had to give birth alone, isolated in a small hut or tent. The family celebrated particular stages in a child's development, especially in connection with subsistence activities. For example, when a boy killed his first seal, the meat was distributed to all the inhabitants of the settlement, and for each new important species a hunter killed, there was a celebration and ritual distribution.

Death was considered to be a passage to a new existence. There were two lands of the dead: one in the sky and one in the sea (or underground). The Inuit in Greenland considered the land in the sea more attractive because people living there enjoyed perpetual success in whale hunting; those in the sky, on the other hand, led dull existences.

The Bladder Feast, an important calendar feast celebrated in Alaska from Kodiak Island to Point Hope, was held in midwinter. At this feast, the bladders of all the seals that had been caught during the previous year were returned to the sea in order that their souls might come back in new bodies and let themselves be caught again.

Shamans. Prospective shamans often learned from skilled shamans how to acquire spirits and to use techniques such as ecstatic trances. In Greenland and Labrador, the apprentice was initiated by being "devoured" by a polar bear or a big dog while being in trance alone in the wilderness. After having revived, he was ready to become master of various spirits. Shamans in Greenland always used a drum to enter a trance. Masks were also instrumental, especially in Alaska, both in secular and religious connections. The shaman might summon his familiar spirits to the house where a séance was taking place, or he might go on a spiritual flight himself. The Canadian shaman might, for example, go down to the *inua* of the sea, that is, the Sea Woman, to get seals.

Shamans also functioned as doctors. For example, they would suck the sick spot where a foreign object had been introduced or try to retrieve a stolen soul.

The Deities. The Inuit of Canada and Greenland believed that the inua of the sea, the Sea Woman, controlled the sea animals and would withhold them to punish people when they had broken a taboo. The Inuit of eastern Baffin Island ritually killed Sea Woman (*Sedna*) during a feast that was held when the autumn storms came and whose purpose was to make sealing possible again. This ceremony included, *interalia,* a ritual spouse exchange and a tug-of-war, the result of which predicted the weather for the coming winter.

While *Sedna* represented the female principle of the world, the *inua* of the moon, Aningaaq, represented the male principle. An origin myth tells how he was once a man who committed incest with his sister. She became the sun, he the moon.

The air was called Sila, which also means "universe" and "intellect." The *inua* of the air was a rather abstract but feared figure; if it was offended when taboos were broken, it would take revenge by bringing storms and blizzards.

BIBLIOGRAPHY

An excellent survey of Inuit culture from prehistoric to modern times is given in the *Handbook of North American Indians,* vol. 5, edited by David Damas (Washington, D.C., 1984). The best survey of Inuit religion is Margaret Lantis's article "The Religion of the Eskimos," in *Forgotten Religions,* edited by Vergilius Ferm (New York, 1950), pp. 311-339. Lantis is also the author of *Alaskan Eskimo Ceremonialism* (New York, 1947). This well-documented book is based primarily on literary sources, but it also contains Lantis's field notes from Nunivak. A review of the religion of the Inuit in Canada and Greenland has been written by Birgitte Sonne and myself as an introduction to a collection of plates that illustrate the religious life of these people in *Eskimos: Greenland and Canada* (Leiden, 1985), vol. 8, pt. 2, of the series "Iconography of Religions." A strong visual impression of the Bering Sea Inuit culture in the nineteenth century is found in William W. Fitzhugh and Susan A. Kaplan's *Inua: Spirit World of the Bering Sea Eskimo* (Washington, D.C., 1982). This is a fascinating book that examines how the spirit world manifests itself in all areas of the life of these Inuit. A study of the religion of two Inuit groups in Canada is given in J. G. Oosten's *The Theoretical Structure of the Religion of the Netsilik and Iglulik* (Mappel, Netherlands, 1976). Information that has been gathered on rituals in connection with animals is presented in Regitze Soby's article "The Eskimo Animal Cult," *Folk* (Copenhagen) 11/12 (1969-1970): 43-78. The position of the Inuit shaman has been analyzed by Birgitte Sonne in "The Professional Ecstatic in His Social and Ritual Position," in *Religious Ecstasy,* edited by Nils G. Holm (Stockholm, 1982), pp. 128-150, and by Daniel Merkur in his *Becoming Half Hidden: Shamanism and Initiation among the Inuit* (Stockholm, 1985).

Among the many valuable and often quoted books by Knud Rasmussen is *The Netsilik Eskimos: Social Life and Spiritual Culture* (Copenhagen, 1931). This book presents material that Rasmussen collected from various groups of Inuit who had had limited contact with the Euro-American world. Among the many valuable studies on the Alaskan Inuit, two should be mentioned: Robert F. Spencer's *The North Alaskan Eskimo: A Study in Ecology and Society* (Washington, D.C., 1959) and Ann Fienup-Riordan's *The Nelson Island Eskimo: Social Structure and Ritual Distribution* (Anchorage, Alaska, 1983).

An extensive bibliography for Inuit religion is given by John Fisher in his article "Bibliography for the Study of Eskimo Religion," *Anthropologica,* n.s. 15 (1973): 231-271.

INGE KLEIVAN

IRANIAN RELIGIONS

Because of the scarce and fragmented data in our possession, we do not know the religions of ancient Iran, other than Zoroastrianism. It is nonetheless possible to reconstruct a few essential elements of ancient Iranian religions through traces of ideas and beliefs. Such elements pertain mainly to rituals, the pantheon, concepts of death and the afterlife, and cosmology.

Rituals included libations *(zaothra),* offered both to Apas ("water") and to Atar ("fire"). The latter was called Agni by the Indians. The libations offered to water were a blend of three ingredients: milk and the juice or leaves of two plants. Those offered to fire were also a blend of three ingredients: dry fuel, incense, and animal fat.

These offerings were also at the heart of the priestly ritual called the Yasna by the Iranians and Yajña by the Indians, from the root *yaz* ("sacrifice, worship"). Animal sacrifice was certainly practiced in the oldest Yasna and was accompanied by prayers that made it sacred and justified it as a religious act through which the spirits of the household animals being sacrificed became absorbed into a divine entity called Geush Urvan, the "soul of the bull."

> **Both Iranians and Indians believed that the world was divided into seven regions. . . .**

The premises, the instruments, and the ingredients for the ceremony were purified with water in a meticulous and careful way. Purifying and disinfectant properties were also attributed to cattle urine *(gomez),* a substance that played an important role in the Zoroastrian ritual of the Great Purification, Bareshnum, as well as in the initiation of priests and corpse-bearers, in accordance with practices and notions that were certainly Indo-Iranian in origin.

Concerning the pantheon, an Indo-Iranian comparison provides considerable help in reconstructing the pre-Zoroastrian religious environment in Iran. There are many divine entities that derive from a common cultural heritage, although they do, at times, present significant differences. The Iranian pantheon, like the Indian, was subdivided into two main groups of divine beings, *ahuras* and *daivas,* although there exists sufficient evidence to hold that in Iran the latter word at one time indicated the gods in general. This can be inferred from the Avestan expression *daeva/mashya,* analogous to the Vedic *deva/martya,* to which correspond the Greek *theoi/andres* (anthropoi) and the Latin *dii/hominesque,* all of which mean "gods and men." *Daivas,* as gods of an ancient polytheism condemned by Zarathushtra, acquired negative connotations only with the Zoroastrian reform. This happened also with some of the Indo-Iranian gods, such as Indra, Saurva (Sarva in India), and Nanhaithya (Nasatya in India). The term *ahura* ("lord"; *asura* in India), on the other hand, maintained its positive connotations and became part of the name of the supreme god of Zoroastrianism, Ahura Mazda, as well as being attached to the name of some of the ancient gods from the Indo-Iranian pantheon, such as Mithra (Mitra in India) and Apam Napat.

In the cosmogony of pre-Zoroastrian Iran, we find signs of a myth of separation of heaven and earth, in which the figure of Vayu, the god of wind and of the atmosphere, the intermediate zone, must have played an important role. It is likely also that the doctrine of seven consecutive creations, of the sky, of water, earth, vegetation, animal life, man, and fire, which we find in late sources, in fact dates from very ancient times.

Essential elements are also provided by an Indo-Iranian comparison in matters pertaining to cosmology. Both Iranians and Indians believed that the world was divided into seven regions, whose Avestan name was karshvar (Pahl., *keshwar*; Skt., *dvipa*), and that it was surrounded by a mountain range. The central region was called Khvaniratha in Iran and Jambudvipa in India, and at its center was a high mountain called Mount Hara. The views of death and of the afterlife in the most ancient Iranian religions, before the Zoroastrian reform, seem to have included the survival of the soul *(urvan)*. After wandering around the earth for three days, the soul was thought to enter a gray existence in a subterranean world of shadows, ruled by Yima, the first king, or king of the Golden Age, and the first man ever to have died.

Traces of a common concept of initiation can be found in both Iran and India. The idea of the need for an initiation in order to achieve the supreme state of *asha/rta,* held in common by the ancient Indo-Iranian world and by what we may call "Aryan mysticism" (Kuiper, 1964), was also linked to the experience of illumination and of the mystic light. The blessed state of *asha* manifests itself through light (*Yasna* 30.1), and *asha* is to be found in "solar dwellings" (*Yasna* 53.4, 32.2, 43.16). The initiate is, then, first of all a "seer," one who has access to the mysteries of the otherworld and who can contemplate a luminous epiphany.

The Iranian religions other than Zoroastrianism, can, as we have seen, be partially reconstructed, not as organic systems, but rather in some of their particular and characteristic elements.

[*For discussion of Iranian religions in broader context, see* Indo-European Religions.]

BIBLIOGRAPHY

Preeminent among general reference works on Iranian religions is H. S. Nyberg's monumental *Irans forntida religioner* (Stockholm, 1937), translated by Hans H. Schaeder as *Die Religionen des alten Iran* (1938); 2d ed., Osnabrück, 1966. Among other invaluable references are Geo Widengren's *Stand und Aufgaben der iranischen Religionsgeschichte* (Leiden, 1955); Jacques Duchesne-Guillemin's *La religion de l'Iran ancient* (Paris, 1962), translated as *Religion of Ancient Iran* (Bombay, 1973); Geo Widengren's *Die Religionen Irans* (Stuttgart, 1965), translated as *Les religions de l'Iran* (Paris, 1968); and Mary Boyce's *A History of Zoroastrianism,* vol. 1 (Leiden, 1975).

On particular aspects of Iranian religions, the following works are recommended. On ceremonials, see Mary Boyce's *"Atas-Zohr and Ab-Zohr," Journal of the Royal Asiatic Society* (1966): 100-118. For a discussion of the Iranian pantheon and an Indo-Iranian comparison, see Émile Benveniste and Louis Renou's *Vrtra et Vrthragna* (Paris, 1934) and Stig Wikander's *Vayu* (Uppsala, 1941). On epos, see Stig Wikander's "Sur le fonds commun indo-iranien des épopées de la Perse et de l'Inde," *La nouvelle Clio* 1-2 (1949-1950): 310-329;

Marijan Molé's "L'épopée iranienne après Firdosi," *La nouvelle Clio* (1953): 377-393; and Georges Dumézil's *Mythe et épopée,* 3 vols. (Paris, 1968-1973). On the religions of the Hindu Kush, see Karl Jettmar's *Die Religionen des Hindukush* (Stuttgart, 1975) and Giuseppe Tucci's "On Swat: The Dards and Connected Problems," *East and West,* n. s. 27 (1977): 9-103.

For discussion of the common Indo-European background of some concepts of the most ancient cosmography, see G. M. Bongard-Levin and E. A. Grantovskii's *De la Scythie à l'Inde: Énigmes de l'histoire des anciens Aryens,* translated by Philippe Gignoux (Paris, 1981). On the concept of the Iranian *Männerbund,* see Stig Wikander's *Der arische Männerbund* (Lund, 1983) and my "Antico-persiano anusya- e gli immortali di Erodoto," in *Monumentum Georg Morgensterne,* vol. 1, "Acta Iranica," no. 21 (Leiden, 1981), pp. 266-280. For discussion of the concept of *asha* and Aryan mysticism, see F. B. J. Kuiper's "The Bliss of Asa," *Indo-Iranian Journal* 8 (1964): 96-129.

On initiation, see Jacques Duchesne-Guillemin's "L'initiation mazdéenne," in *Initiation: Contributions to the Theme . . .* edited by C. Jouco Bleeker (Leiden, 1965), pp. 112-118, and on the common Indo-Iranian background of initiation through possessing *asha* and the experience of light, see, in particular, my "Asavan: Contributo allo studio del libro di Arda Wiraz," in *Iranica,* edited by me and Adriano V. Rossi (Naples, 1979), pp. 387-452.

For comparison of the Indo-Iranian notions of *ojas/aojah, varcas/varecah,* and so on, see Jan Gonda's *Ancient-Indian 'ojas', Latin '*augos', and the Indo-Iranian Nouns in -es/-os* (Utrecht, 1952), pp. 57-67, and my "Licht-Symbolik in Alt-Iran," *Antaios* 8 (1967): 528-549. On the ancient Iranian tradition of sacred poetry, which was Indo-Iranian (and, more generally, Indo-European) in origin, see the various contributions by J. Wackernagel, Hans H. Schaeder, and Paul Thieme to *In-dogermanische Dichtersprache,* "Wege der Forschung," vol. 165, edited by R. Schmitt (Darmstadt, 1968).

GHERARDO GNOLI
Translated from Italian by Ughetta Fitzgerald Lubin

ISIS

ISIS was one of the principal goddesses in the ancient Egyptian pantheon. She was the daughter of Geb and Nut ("earth" and "sky"), wife of Osiris, and mother of Horus. When Osiris was slain by his brother, Seth, Isis collected the dismembered parts of his body and with the help of Thoth was able to revive him at least partially and temporarily. Most important, she conceived and bore Osiris' son and avenger, Horus. Isis was a support for her husband both in this life and in the afterlife, and in this respect she was the perfect example of a devoted wife. She also shared Osiris' major role in the mortuary cult and became queen of the dead. As the nurturing mother of Horus she was the exemplar of motherhood, the patroness of childbearing, and the protectress of the child. In this connection she was also a role model for the queen of Egypt, who was generally "daughter of the god," "great wife of the king," and "mother of the god." The queen's role in the divine succession was just as important as that of her husband. In the Ramessid period, Isis bore the queenly title of Isis the Great, Lady of Heaven, Mistress of the Two Lands.

The name *Isis* means "seat" or "throne" (of Osiris), and like her sister, Nephthys, who was the spouse of Seth and whose name means "lady of the house," Isis seems to have owed her existence in the Egyptian pantheon primarily to the obvious need for a consort for Osiris. Very little is known of her early origin or of the cult that may have attached to her in the Old Kingdom. She is clearly well established but not adequately described in the Pyramid Texts. In later funerary texts and in *The Contendings of Horus and Seth,* her role is clear, but her position is somewhat ambivalent. She supports Horus, but not to the point of allowing him to destroy her evil brother, Seth. She is regarded as clever, even crafty, yet an enraged Horus can decapitate her for her supposed disloyalty.

Much of the early myth having to do with Isis, Osiris, and Horus was preserved best by Plutarch, and it was in the Ptolemaic and Roman periods that the cult of Isis really developed and spread. She assumed the symbolic emblems, representations, and characteristics both of Hathor, the true early mother goddess and goddess of love, and of Mut ("mother"), who was consort of Amun-Re in the later pharaonic periods. Among the many sites that had temples and shrines dedicated to Isis, certainly the most important was the island of Philae in Upper (southern) Egypt, with its numerous Ptolemaic and Roman buildings.

At the beginning of the Ptolemaic dynasty the cult of Isis, now the highest ranking goddess in Egypt, was already becoming widespread on the Greek mainland, in the Aegean islands, and in the Greek towns of Asia Minor. The cult of Serapis, a later development of Osiris, followed, and the two cults flourished throughout the Roman empire despite several attempts to repress Egyptian cults. These cults owed their appeal partly to their humaneness and partly to their mysteries, but it is also clear that they were no longer, strictly speaking, Egyptian, since the very nature of the gods and their attributes had changed. Isis became an earth goddess and a patroness of sailors. The *Isis-aretalogy* (a first-person account of the virtues and benefactions of the goddess) describes a goddess who was responsible for much of creation, ruled with great power, was patroness of both love and war, and was universally worshiped under different names. This text, preserved only in Greek, must have been largely of Greek origin and presents only a few epithets that can be traced to Egyptian sources.

In Egypt the cult of Isis was the last pagan cult to survive Christianity. Indeed, in part because the Blemmyes of Nubia concluded a peace with the Roman commander in Egypt in 451 AD guaranteeing them access to the temples of Philae, it was not until the sixth century that the temple of Isis was closed by Justinian. Philae was the last of the pagan temples to succumb to Egypt's conversion to Christianity, although it has often been suggested that the cult of Isis was not completely lost, having had considerable influence on the cult of the Virgin Mary.

BIBLIOGRAPHY

Bergman, Jan. *Ich bin Isis.* Acta Universitatis Upsaliensis, Historia Religionum, vol. 3. Uppsala, 1968.

Müller, Dieter. *Ägypten und die griechischen Isis-Aretalogien.* Sächsischen Akademie der Wissenschaften, Abhandlungen, Philologisch-historische Klasse, vol. 53, no. 1. Berlin, 1961.

Münster, Maria. *Untersuchungen zur Göttin Isis vom Alten Reich bis zum Ende des Neuen Reiches.* Münchner ägyptologische Studien, vol. 11. Berlin, 1968.

Witt, R. E. *Isis in the Graeco-Roman World.* London, 1971.

LEONARD H. LESKO

ISLAM

An Overview

The root *slm* in Arabic means "to be in peace, to be an integral whole." From this root comes *islam,* meaning "to surrender to God's law and thus to be an integral whole," and *muslim,* a person who so surrenders. It is important to note that two other key terms used in the Qur'an with high frequency have similar root meanings: *iman* (from *amn*), "to be safe and at peace with oneself," and *taqwa* (from *wqy*), "to protect or save." These definitions give us an insight into the most fundamental religious attitude of Islam: to maintain wholeness and proper order, as the opposite of disintegration, by accepting God's law. It is in this sense that the entire universe and its content are declared by the Qur'an to be *muslim,* that is, endowed with order through obedience to God's law; but whereas nature obeys God's law automatically, humanity ought to obey it by choice. In keeping with this distinction, God's function is to integrate human personality, both individual and corporate: "Be not like those who forgot God, and [eventually] God caused them to forget themselves" (surah 59:19).

Origin and History

Muslims believe that Islam is God's eternal religion, described in the Qur'an as "the primordial nature upon which God created mankind" (30:30). Further, the Qur'an claims that the proper name *Muslim* was given by Abraham (22:78). As a historical phenomenon, however, Islam originated in Arabia in the early seventh century CE. Two broad elements should be distinguished in that immediate religious backdrop: the purely Arab background and the penetration of Judeo-

Christian elements. The Qur'an makes a disapproving reference to star worship (41:37), which is said to have come from the Babylonian star cult. For the most part, however, the bedouin were a secular people with little idea of an afterlife. At the sanctuaries *(harams)* that had been established in some parts, fetishism seems to have developed into idol worship; the most important of these sites was the Ka`bah at Mecca. [*See* Ka`bah.]

The bedouin Arabs believed in a blind fate that inescapably determined birth, sustenance (because of the precarious life conditions in the desert), and death. These Arabs also had a code of honor (called *muruwah*, or "manliness") that may be regarded as their real religious ethics; its main constituent was tribal honor—the crown of all their values—encompassing the honor of women, bravery, hospitality, honoring one's promises and pacts, and last but not least,

> ## The bedouin Arabs believed in a blind fate that inescapably determined birth, sustenance and death.

vengeance *(tha'r)*. They believed that the ghost of a slain person would cry out from the grave until his thirst for the blood of vengeance was quenched. According to the code, it was not necessarily the killer who was slain in retaliation, but a person from among his kin equal in value to the person killed. For reasons of economics or honor, infant girls were often slain, and this practice, terminated by the Qur'an, was regarded as having had religious sanction (6:137).

In southwestern Arabia, a rather highly sophisticated civilization had existed since the Sabian period, with a prosperous economy and agriculture. The Sabian religion was, at the beginning, a trinitarian star cult, which was replaced, in the fourth century CE, by the monotheistic cult of al-Rahman (a term that appears to have traveled north and found a prominent place in the Qur'an, where it means "the merciful"). In the sixth century CE, Jewish and Christian ideas and formulas were adopted, with the term *al-Rahman* applied to the first person of the Trinity.

As for the Judeo-Christian tradition, it was not only present where Jewish and Christian populations existed (Jews in Medina—pre-Islamic Yathrib—in the south and in Khaybar in the north; Christians in the south, in Iraq, in Syria, and in certain tribes), but it had percolated in the air, generally speaking. Indeed, there had been Jewish and Christian attempts at proselytizing the Meccans, but these were unsuccessful because the Meccans wanted a new religion and scripture of their own, "whereby they would be better guided than those earlier communities" (35:42, 6:157). In the process, the Meccans had nevertheless come to know a

good deal about Judeo-Christian ideas (6:92), and several people in Mecca and elsewhere had arrived at the idea of monotheism. Even so, they could not get rid of the "intermediary gods" for whom they had special cults, and there was still no cult for God, whom they called "Allah," or "the God." In addition to these limitations, there was also a great disparity between the rich and the poor and disenfranchised in the thriving commercial community of Mecca. Both of these issues are strongly emphasized from the beginning of the Qur'anic revelation, making it clear that the primary background of Islam is Arab rather than Judeo-Christian, although the latter tradition has strongly influenced Islam. In its genesis, Islam grew out of the problems existing in an Arab Meccan society.

Early Development of the Community. During a twelve-year struggle in Mecca (610-622 CE), the prophet Muhammad had gathered a devoted group of followers, largely among the poor but also among the well-to-do merchants. Yet his movement seemed to reach an impasse because of the unflinching opposition of the mercantile aristocracy, which saw in it a threat to both of their vested interests—their Ka`bah-centered religion, from which they benefited as custodians of the sanctuary and recipients of income from the pilgrimage, and their privileged control of trade. After Muhammad and his followers emigrated from Mecca to Medina in 622 (the beginning of the lunar Islamic calendar, called the *hijri*, or "emigration," calendar), at the invitation of the majority of the Arab inhabitants there, he became the head of both the nascent community and the existing polity. However, while he gave laws, waged peace and war, and created social institutions, he never claimed to be a ruler, a lawgiver, a judge, or a general; he referred to himself always as a messenger of God. As a result, not only were Islamic "religious" doctrine and ritual in the narrower sense regarded as Islamic but so were the state, the law, and social institutions. Islam is thus the name of a total way of life and does not merely regulate the individual's private relationship with God.

In Medina, then, the Prophet was able to institute his social reforms through the exercise of the religious and political power that he had been denied in Mecca. After three battles in which Muslims gained the upper hand over the Meccans and their allies, Islam, now in rapid ascendancy, was able to take Mecca peacefully in AH 8/630 CE along with a large part, if not the whole, of the Arabian Peninsula. In Medina, too, the Muslim community *(ummah muslimah)* was formally launched in 2/624 as the "median community," the only community consciously established by the founder of a religion for a specific purpose, as the Qur'an speaks of those "who, when we give them power on the earth, shall establish prayers and welfare of the poor and shall command good and forbid evil" (22:41). At the same time, the Qur'an (22:40) provided this community with the instrument of *jihad* (utmost exertion in God's cause, including peaceful means but also cold and hot war). [*See* Jihad.] Finally, Mecca was declared to be the goal of annual pilgrimage for the faithful and also the direction *(qiblah)* for prayer instead of Jerusalem. Both the constitution and the anchoring of the community were complete.

After a brief lapse into tribal sovereignty following the Prophet's death, Arab resistance to the acknowledgment of Medina's central authority was broken by force. The tribesmen's energies were turned outward in conquests of neighboring lands under the banner of Islam, which provided the necessary zeal for rapid military and political expansion. Within a century after the Prophet's death, Muslim Arabs were administering an empire stretching from the southern borders of France through North Africa and the Middle East, across Central Asia and into Sind. Muslim rule in the conquered territories was generally tolerant and humane; there was no policy of converting non-Muslims to Islam. The purpose of *jihad* was not conversion but the establishment of Islamic rule. Nonetheless, partly because of certain disabilities imposed by Islamic law on non-Muslim subjects (mainly the *jizyah*, or poll tax—although they were exempt from the *zakat*, or alms tax levied on Muslims, the *jizyah* was the heavier of the two, particularly for the lower strata of the population) and partly because of Islamic egalitarianism, Islam spread quickly after an initial period during which conversions were sometimes even discouraged. This was the first phase of the spread of Islam; later on, as we shall see, Muslim mystics, or the Sufis, were the main vehicles of Islamic expansion in India, Central Asia, and sub-Saharan Africa, although the role of traders in the Indian and Indonesian coastal areas and China must not be minimized. Even in the twentieth century, Turkish soldiers brought Islam to South Korea during the Korean War.

Several major developments in this early period affected the religious texture of the Muslim community as a continuing phenomenon. Less than half a century after the Prophet's death, political dissensions over succession led to civil war. A number of groups called the Kharijis ("those who went out") declared war on the community at large because it tolerated rule by "unrighteous" men; they claimed that a Muslim ceased to be a Muslim by committing a reprehensible act without sincerely repenting, and that other Muslims who did not regard such a person as non-Muslim also became non-Muslim. In reaction to the Kharijis and the ensuing civil strife, the community (both the Sunni mainstream and the Shi`ah, or party of `Ali) generally adopted a religious stand that not only was tolerant of religious and political deviations from strict Islamic norms but was even positively accommodating toward them. The members of the community who took this stand were known as the Murji'ah (from *irja'*, meaning "postponement," in the sense of not judging a person's religious worth, but leaving it to God's judgment on the Last Day). The

net result of this basic development was that excommunication was ruled out so long as a person recognized the community as Muslim and professed that "there is no god but God and Muhammad is his prophet."

This formula created or rationalized accommodation for an amazing range of different religious opinions and practices under one God and Muhammad's prophethood. Oddly enough, the only systematically rigid and illiberal school of doctrine that persecuted its opponents, after it became state creed under the Abbasid caliph al-Ma'mun in the first half of the ninth century, was the liberal rationalist school of the Mu`tazilah. The emergence of this school was largely the result of the impact on the Islamic religion of the wholesale translations of Greek works of science, philosophy, and medicine into Arabic on the orders of al-Ma'mun. The Mu`tazilah tried to create necessary free space by insisting on freedom of human will and God's rational justice, but the Muslim orthodoxy, countering with doctrines of the inefficacy of human will and the absolutism of God's will and divine predeterminism, actually provided more accommodation for varying opinions and human actions and thereby halted the growth of the rationalist school.

With the advent of the Abbasids, there were other political, social, and religious changes as well, among them the improvement of the status of the Iranians, who, under Umayyad rule, were denied an identity of their own as "clients" *(mawali)* of the Arab tribes; and the espousal and implementation of legal measures created by the religious leadership, which had been largely alienated from the Umayyads. All of these developments combined to facilitate the rapid spread of Islam.

Medieval and Later Developments. With the weakening of the central caliphal authority in Baghdad, the tenth century saw not only the virtual fragmentation of the Abbasid empire and the rise of *de facto* independent rulers (sultans and emirs) in the provinces but the almost ubiquitous rise of the Shi`ah. While Baghdad came under the political and fiscal "management" of the orthodox Twelver Shi`ah through the Persian Buyid family, Egypt and North Africa came under the rule of the Isma`ili Fatimids. But if the Buyids were able to influence Islamic practices in some ways—such as the observance of `Ashura', the tenth of Muharram (the first month of the Islamic calendar) as the commemoration of the martyrdom of the Prophet's grandson Husayn at the hands of the Umayyad troops—Fatimid rule, by and large, did not leave much of a trace on later Muslim thought and institutions, despite the fact that the Isma`iliyah had offered a revolutionary ideology claiming to usher in a new world order through the establishment of a universal religion. [*See also* Shiism.]

In purely religious terms, indeed, it was not so much Shiism as the rise and spread of Sufism that constituted the new and greatest challenge to Islamic orthodoxy, in terms of ideas and spiritual orientation, and indeed, it was Shiism that suffered most, in terms of following, as a result of the new movement. From modest beginnings as an expression of refined piety on the part of a spiritual elite in the eighth and ninth centuries, Sufism became a mass religion from the eleventh century onward. In its origins as a deepening of the inner "life of the heart," Sufism was largely complementary to the outer "life of the law," which was the domain of the `ulama', the religious scholars who functioned as custodians of the sha`riah (sacred law) and never claimed to be pastors or custodians of the soul.

In its later development, however, through networks of brotherhoods that spread from the shores of the Atlantic to Southeast Asia, it practically took the place of "official" Islam, particularly in the countryside. Feeding on certain pantheistic ideas of eminent Sufis and generating latitudinarian, indeed protean, tendencies, it served to convert to Islam large populations in the Indian subcontinent, Central Asia, Africa, and Indonesia. A long line of orthodox Sufis, beginning in the eighth and ninth centuries and culminating in the monumental work of al-Ghazali (d. 1111), struggled hard, with a good measure of success, to bring about a synthesis that would ensure a respectable place for Sufi spirituality in the orthodox fold. After the advent of Sufism, and particularly after al-Ghazali's success, the number of converts to Islam expanded dramatically, and the number of Shi`ah shrank equally dramatically, apparently because the demands for an inner life that Shiism had satisfied through its esoteric claims were now satisfied by Sufism. [See also Sufism.]

During the thirteenth and fourteenth centuries, Islam penetrated into the Malay archipelago largely through Arab traders, who went first to the coastal areas of Java and Sumatra and afterward to Malaysia. Shortly after the advent of Islam, however, these lands fell under western European domination. Because the structure of British power in Malaysia differed from Dutch colonialism in Indonesia, in that British overlordship was exercised through regional sultans whereas the Dutch ruled directly, Islam was inhibited in Indonesia: a large percentage of the population of the interior remained abangans, or "nominal Muslims," whose life is still based on ancient custom (`adat) under a thin Islamic veneer. Recently, however, a large-scale thrust of islamization has changed this picture considerably. In Djakarta, for example, a little more than a dozen years ago, there were only a few cathedral mosques for Friday services, but now the number has multiplied spectacularly; indeed, there is a mosque attached to every government department. This process of "consolidation in orthodox Islam," necessitated by the initial compromises made by Sufis with local cultures, has been going on for some decades in the Indian subcontinent as well.

In Africa south of the Sahara, Islam appears to have penetrated through both traders and pilgrims. Although, as noted above, Islam spread there through the influence of Sufi orders, one unique feature of African Islam seems to be the combination of Sufism with militancy, the latter acclaimed as the result of the Islamic teaching on jihad, although it is also congruent with the spirit of local tribalism.

Africa is the only continent where Muslims are in the majority, while in Europe, Islam now constitutes the second largest religion, mainly comprising emigrants from Muslim lands but a few Western converts as well. In North America, Muslims are said to number around two million, most of whom are emigrants from Muslim countries. But there is also in the United States a significant phenomenon of conversion among local blacks, originating in the social protest movement against white ascendancy. The earliest group, known as the Black Muslims, called itself the Nation of Islam during the lifetime of its founder, Elijah Muhammad, and was a heterodox movement. After his death in 1973 it moved closer to the rest of the Muslim community, taking the new name of American Islamic Mission and receiving financial help from oil-rich Arab countries such as Saudi Arabia, Libya, and Kuwait. (The organization was dissolved in 1985.) There are also other numerous, though small, Afro-American Muslim groups scattered throughout the United States. [See Afro-American Religions and the biography of Elijah Muhammad and Malcolm X.]

Arriving at a precise estimate of the Muslim population in China presents a serious problem. According to data collected unofficially by Chinese Muslims in 1939-1940 and extrapolations from these data in terms of population growth, Chinese Muslims might number close to one hundred million in the 1980s. The official Chinese figure given in the early sixties, however, was ten million, a figure revised to between fifteen and twenty million two decades later (religion is a factor not counted in the Chinese census). According to the 1979 United Nations statistics, the world Muslim population is just under one billion.

The Systematic Content of Islam

With the rise of Islamic legal and theological thought in the eighth century CE, a framework had to be articulated within which religious developments were to be set. The most basic sources in this framework were the Qur'an and the sunnah of the Prophet.

The Qur'an. The God of the Qur'an is a transcendent, powerful, and merciful being. His transcendence ensures his uniqueness and infinitude over and against all other creatures, who are necessarily characterized by finitude of being and potentialities. Hence God is all-powerful, and no creature may share in his divinity (belief in such sharing is called shirk and is condemned in the Qur'an as the most heinous and unforgivable sin). This infinite power is expressed, however, through God's equally infinite mercy. The creation of the universe, the fact that there is plenitude of being, rather than emptiness of nothing, is due solely to his mercy. Particularly with reference to humanity, God's creation, sustenance, guidance (in the form of revelations given to the prophets, his messengers), and, finally, judgment, are all manifestations of his power in mercy.

God created nature by his command "Be!" In fact, for whatever God wishes to create, "He says, Be! and there it is" (36:82). But whatever God creates has an orderly nature, and that is why there is a universe rather than chaos. God puts into everything the proper "guidance" or "nature" or laws of behavior to make each part fit into the entire pattern of the universe. "All things are measured" (e.g., 54:49), and only God is the measurer; hence he alone is the commander, and everything else is under his command. This command, which is a fact of automatic obedience in the case of nature (3:83), becomes an "ought" in the case of humans, for whom moral law replaces natural law. Nature is, therefore, a firm, well-knit machine without rupture or dislocations.

Here it is interesting and important to note that while the Qur'an patently accepts miracles of earlier prophets (67:2-3), in response to pressure from Muhammad's opponents for new miracles (e.g., 2:23, 10:38, 11:13), the Qur'an insists that it is itself the Prophet's miracle, and one that cannot be equaled. As for supernatural miracles, they are out of date because they have been ineffective in the past (17:59, 6:33-35). Nature is, therefore, autonomous but not autocratic, since it did not bring itself into being. God, who brought nature into being, can destroy it as well; even so, although the Qur'an, when speaking of the Day of Judgment, often invokes a cataclysm that strongly suggests destruction (see, for example, surah 81), in many verses it speaks instead of a radical transformation and a realignment of the factors of life (e.g., 56:60-63). Finally, the universe has been created for the benefit of human beings, and all its forces have been "subjugated" to them; of all creatures, only they have been created to serve God alone (e.g., 31:20, 22:65).

In its account of the human race, while the Qur'an holds that humans are among the noblest of God's creatures and that Adam had indeed outstripped the angels in a competition for creative knowledge, a fact testifying to his unique intellectual qualities, it nevertheless criticizes them for their persistent moral failures, which are due to their narrowmindedness, lack of vision, weakness, and smallness of self. All their ills are reducible to this basic deficiency, and the remedy is for them to enlarge the self and to transcend pettiness. This pettiness is often represented by the Qur'an in economic terms, such as greed, fraud, and holding back from spending on the poor (as was the case with the Meccan traders): "If you were to possess [all] the treasures of the mercy of my lord, you would still sit on them out of fear of spending [on the needy]" (17:100). It is Satan who whispers into people's ears that they would be impoverished by spending, while God promises prosperity for such investment (2:268). Instead of establishing usurious accounts to exploit the poor, believers should establish "credit with God" (2:245, 57:11, 57:18 et al.).

In its social doctrine and legislation, the Qur'an makes a general effort to ameliorate the condition of the weak and often abused segments of society, such as the poor, orphans, women, and slaves. People are asked to free slaves on freedom-purchasing contracts, "and if they are poor, you give them from the wealth God has bestowed upon you" (24:33). An egalitarian statement concerning males and females is made, but the husband is recognized as "one degree higher" (2:228) because he earns by his strength and expends on his wife. Polygamy is limited to four wives with the provision that "if you fear you cannot do justice [among them], marry only one" (4:3), and the further admonition that

> **Kind and generous treatment of wives is repeatedly emphasized; celibacy is strongly discouraged, although not banned outright.**

such justice is impossible "no matter how much you desire" (4:129). Kind and generous treatment of wives is repeatedly emphasized; celibacy is strongly discouraged, although not banned outright. The basic equality of all people is proclaimed and ethnic differences discounted: "O you people, we have created [all of] you from a male and a female, and we have made you into different nations and tribes [only] for the purpose of identification—otherwise, the noblest of you in the sight of God is the one who is the most righteous" (49:13).

In the economic field, the widespread practice of usury is prohibited. The *zakat* tax is levied on the well-to-do members of the community; it was meant as a welfare tax to be spent on the poor and the needy in general, but surah 9:60, which details the distribution of *zakat*, is so comprehensive in its scope that it covers practically all fields of social and state life. In general, fair play and justice are repeatedly advised. Detailed inheritance laws are given (4:7ff.), the main feature of which is the introduction of shares to daughters, although these shares are set at half of what sons receive. Communal affairs are to be decided through mutual consultation (*shura baynahum*, 42:38), a principle that has never been institutionalized in Islamic history, however.

One noteworthy feature of the moral teaching of the Qur'an is that it describes all wrong done against anyone as "wrong done against oneself" (*zulm al-nafs*, as in 2:231, 11:101, 11:118). In its teaching on the Last Judgment, the Qur'an constantly talks of "weighing the deeds" of all adult and responsible humans (101:6-11, 7:8 et al.). This doctrine of the "weight" of deeds arises out of the consideration that people normally act for the here and now; in this respect, they are like cattle: they do not take a long-range or "ultimate" *(akhirah)* view of things: "Shall we tell you of those who are the greatest losers in terms of their deeds? Those whose whole effort has been lost [in the pursuit of] this life [i. e., the lower values of life], but they think they have performed prodigies" (18:104). The rationale of the Last Judgment is to bring out the real moral meaning, "the weight" of deeds. But whereas the Last Judgment will turn upon individual performance, the Qur'an also speaks about a "judgment in history," which descends upon peoples, nations, and communities on the basis of their total performance and whether that performance is in accord with the teaching of the divine messages brought by their prophets: many nations have perished because of their persistence in all sorts of disobedience and moral wrong, for "God gives inheritance of the earth [only] to good people" (21:105).

The Qur'an, therefore, declares unequivocally that God has sent his messages to *all* peoples throughout history and has left none without guidance (35:24, 13:7). These messages have been essentially the same: to reject *shirk* (associating anyone with God) and to behave according to the law of God. All messages have emanated from a single source, the "Mother of All Books" (13:39) or the "Hidden Book" (56:78) or the "Preserved Tablet" (85:22), and although every prophet has initially come to his people and addressed them "in their tongue" (14:4), the import of all messages is universal; hence it is incumbent on all people to believe in all prophets, without "separating some from the others." For this reason the Qur'an is severely critical of what it sees as proprietary claims upon God's guidance by Jews and Christians and rejects Jewish claims to special status in strong terms (62:6, 2:94-95, 5:18, et al.). Despite the identity of divine messages, moreover, the Qur'an also posits some sort of development in religious consciousness and asserts that on the Last Day every community will be judged by the standards of its own book and under the witness of its own prophet(s) (4:41, 16:84, et al.). The Qur'an protects, consummates, and transcends earlier revelations, and Muhammad is declared to be the "seal of the prophets" (33:40).

Finally, the Qur'an states five basic constituents of faith *(iman)*: belief in God, in angels, in revealed books, in God's messengers, and in the Last Day. Corresponding to these five items of belief, a fivefold practical doctrine was formulated very early on. These "Five Pillars" include (1) bearing witness in public at least once in one's lifetime that "There is no god but God and Muhammad is his prophet"; (2) praying five times a day (before sunrise, early afternoon, late afternoon, immediately after sunset, and before retiring), while facing the Ka'bah at Mecca; (3) paying *zakat*; (4) fasting during Ramadan (the ninth month of the Islamic lunar year), with no eating, drinking, smoking, or sexual intercourse from dawn until sunset, when the daily fast is broken; and (5) performing

the annual pilgrimage to the Ka'bah at least once in one's adult lifetime, provided one can afford the journey and leave enough provisions for one's family. [*See also* Pilgrimage, *article on* Muslim Pilgrimage.]

The pilgrimage is performed during the first ten days of the last month of the Islamic year. One may perform the lesser pilgrimage (*'umrah*) at other times of the year, but it is not a substitute for the great pilgrimage (*al-hajj al-akbar*). The pilgrimage has, through the centuries, played an important role, not only in strengthening general unity in the global Muslim community but also in disseminating religious ideas both orthodox and Sufi, for it provides the occasion for an annual meeting among religious leaders and scholars from different parts of the Muslim world. For the past few decades, it has also served to bring together political leaders and heads of Muslim states. In recent years, too, because of new travel facilities, the number of pilgrims has vastly increased, sometimes exceeding two million each year. [*See also* Qur'an, *articles on* The Text and Its History *and* Its Role in Muslim Piety.]

Sunnah. The word *sunnah* literally means "a well-trodden path," but it was used before Islam in reference to usage or laws of a tribe and certain norms of intertribal conduct accepted by various tribes as binding. After the rise of Islam, it was used to denote the normative behavior of the Muslim community, putatively derived from the Prophet's teaching and conduct, and from the exemplary teaching of his immediate followers, since the latter was seen as an index of the former. In the Qur'an, there is no mention of the term *sunnah* with reference to the Prophet's extra-Qur'anic precepts or example, but the term *uswah hasanah*, meaning a "good model" or "example" to be followed, is used with reference to Muhammad's conduct as well as the conduct of Abraham and his followers (33:31, 60:4, 60:6). The term *uswah* is certainly much less rigid than *sunnah* and does not mean so much a law to be literally implemented as an example to be matched.

Even so, there is clear evidence that the concept of *sunnah* was flexible in the early decades of Islam because, with hardly any written codifications of the *sunnah* (which was used in the sense of an ongoing practice rather than fixed formulas), there was no question of literal imitation. As political, legal, and theological dissensions and disputes multiplied and all kinds of positions sought self-validation, however, the opinions of the first three generations or so were projected back onto the Prophet to obtain the necessary authority, and the phrase *sunnat al-nabi* (the *sunnah* of the Prophet) gradually took the place of the term *sunnah*.

During the second and third centuries AH, the narration and codification of the *sunnah* into hadith was in full swing. A report that claims to convey a *sunnah* (or *sunnahs*) is called a *hadith*. It is reported that while earlier people used to accept a *hadith* as genuine on trust alone, after the civil wars of the late first to early second centuries AH, a *hadith* was accepted only on the basis of some reliable authority. From this situation emerged the convention of the *isnad*, or the chain of guarantors of *hadith*, extending from the present narrator backward to the Prophet. The *isnad* took the following form: "I, So-and-so, heard it from B, who heard it from C, who said that he heard the Prophet say so-and-so or do such-and-such." Then followed the text *(matn)* of the *hadith*. A whole science called "principles of *hadith*" developed in order to lay down meticulous criteria for judging the reliability of the transmitters of *hadith*, and the discipline stimulated in turn a vast literature of comprehensive biographical dictionaries recording thousands of transmitters' names, their lives, character, and whether a transmitter actually met or could have met the person he claims to transmit from. The canons for criticizing transmitters were applied rigorously, and there is hardly a transmitter who has escaped criticism.

The experts on *hadith* also developed canons of "rational critique" alongside the critique of the chains of transmission, but they applied the former with far less rigor than they did the latter. Although the specialists divided *hadith* into several categories according to their "genuineness" and "reliability," to this day it remains the real desideratum of the science to work out and apply what is called historical criticism to the materials of *hadith*. The six authoritative Sunni collections of *hadith* date from the third century AH, while the famous Shi`i collection of al-Kulini, *Al-kafi* (The Sufficient), dates from the early fourth century. In modern times, the authenticity of *hadith* and hence of the recorded *sunnah* of the Prophet (although not so much the biographies of the Prophet and historical works) has come under general attack at the hands of certain Western scholars and also of some Muslim intellectuals—and this is happening increasingly—but the `ulama' have strenuously resisted these attacks because a large majority of Islamic social and political institutions and laws are either based on *hadith* or rationalized through it.

Law. The well-known dictum among Western Islamicists that, just as theology occupies the central place in Christianity, in Islam the central place belongs to law is essentially correct. Law was the earliest discipline to develop in Islam because the Muslims needed it to administer the huge empire they had built with such astonishing rapidity. Recent research has held that the early materials for Islamic law were largely created by administrators on the basis of *ad hoc* decisions and that, in the second stage, systematic efforts were made by jurists to "islamize" these materials and bring them under the aegis of the Qur'an and the *sunnah*. (The content of the latter, in the form of *hadith*, developed alongside this activity of islamization.) This picture is probably too simplistic, however, and it would be more correct to say that the process of subsuming administrative materials and local custom under the Qur'an and the *sunnah* went hand in hand with the reverse process of deriving law from the Qur'an and whatever existed by way of the *sunnah* in the light of new administrative experiences and local custom.

Although clarification of this issue requires further research, it is certain that up to the early third century AH the schools of law were averse to the large-scale use of *hadith* in the formulation of law and that, in fact, some scholars explicitly warned against the rise of "peripheral *hadith*" and advised the acceptance of only that *hadith* that conformed to the Qur'an. However, the need for the anchoring authority of the Prophet had become so great that in the latter half of the second century AH al-Shafi`i (d. 204/819) made a strong and subsequently successful bid for the wholesale acceptance of "reliable" *hadith*—even if narrated by only one person. As a result, *hadith* multiplied at a far greater rate after al-Shafi`i than before him. Nevertheless, the followers of Abu Hanifah (d. 767) continued to reject a single-chain *hadith* in favor of a "sure, rational proof derived from the *shari`ah* principles," just as the followers of Malik (d. 795) continued to give preference to the early "practice of Medina" over *hadith*.

The final framework of Islamic jurisprudence came to recognize four sources of law, two material and two formal. The first source is the text of the Qur'an, which constitutes an absolute "decisive proof"; the second is *hadith* texts, although these can vary from school to school, particularly between the Sunni and the Twelver Shi`i schools. In new cases, for which a "clear text" *(nass)* is not available, a jurist must make the effort *(ijtihad)* to find a correct answer himself. The instrument of ijtihad is analogical reasoning *(qiyas)*, which consists in (1) finding a text relevant to the new case in the Qur'an or the *hadith*, (2) discerning the essential similarity or *ratio legis* (called `illat al-hukm) between the two cases, (3) allowing for differences *(furuq)* and determining that they can be discounted, and (4) extending or interpreting the *ratio legis* to cover the new case. This methodology, although neatly formulated in theory, became very difficult to wield in practice primarily because of the differences of opinion with regard to "relevant texts," particularly in the case of *hadith*.

The fourth source or principle is called *ijma`*, or consensus. Although the concept of consensus in the sense of the informal agreement of the community (for Islam has no churches and no councils to produce formal decisions) has in practice an overriding authority, since even the fact and the authenticity of a Qur'anic revelation are finally guaranteed by it, there is no consensus on the definition of consensus: it varies from the consensus of the `ulama', through that of the `ulama' of a certain age, to that of the entire community. There is also a difference of opinion as to whether a certain consensus can be repealed by a subsequent one or not; the reply of the traditionalists is usually, though not always, in the negative, while that of modern reformers is in the positive.

A special category of punishments called *hudud* (sg., *hadd*) was established by jurists and includes penalties specified in the Qur'an for certain crimes: murder, theft, adultery, and false accusation of adultery, to which was later added drunkenness. The theory is that since God himself has laid down these penalties, they cannot be varied. But in view of the severity of the punishments, the jurists defined these crimes very narrowly (adultery, for example, is defined as the penetration of the male organ into the female) and put such stringent conditions on the requisite evidence that it became practically unattainable (for example, in order to prove adultery, four eyewitnesses to the sexual act itself were required). The legal maxim "Ward off *hadd* punishments by any doubt" was also propounded, and the term *doubt* in classical Islamic law had a far wider range than in any other known system of

> Islamic law does not draw any line between law and morality, and hence much of it is not enforceable in a court, but only at the bar of conscience.

law. In addition, Muslim jurists enunciated two principles to create flexibility in *shari`ah* law and its application: necessity and public interest. The political authority, thanks to these two principles, could promulgate new measures and even suspend the operations of the *shari`ah* law. In later medieval centuries, the Ottoman rulers and others systematically promulgated new laws by invoking these particular principles of the *shari`ah*.

After the concrete and systematic establishment of the schools of law during the fourth and fifth centuries AH, original legal thought in Islam lost vitality; this development is known as "the closure of the door of *ijtihad*." It was not that new thinking was theoretically prohibited but rather that social, intellectual, and political conditions were unfavorable to it. However, a procedure known as *talfiq* (lit., "patchwork") was introduced whereby, if a certain provision in one legal school caused particular hardship, a more liberal provision from another could be borrowed, without necessarily taking over its reasoning. Thus, given the impracticality of the Hanafi school's regulation that a wife whose husband has disappeared must wait more than ninety years before remarrying (according to the reasoning that the wife must wait until her husband can be presumed dead through natural causes), the Maliki school's provision that such a wife may marry after four years of waiting (Malik reasoned that the maximum period of gestation, which he had himself witnessed, was four years) was taken over in practice.

Of the four extant Sunni schools of law, the Hanafi is prevalent in the Indian subcontinent, Central Asia, Turkey, Egypt, Syria, Jordan, and Iraq; the Maliki school in North Africa extends from Libya through Morocco; the Shafi`i, in Southeast Asia, with a considerable following in Egypt; and

the Hanbali school, in Saudi Arabia. Within Shi`i jurisprudence, the Ja`fari (Twelver Shi`i) school prevails in Iran. At one time, the "literalist" (Zahiri) school was represented by some highly prominent jurists, but it has practically no following now, while the Khariji school is represented in Oman, and to a limited extent in East and North Africa.

It must finally be pointed out that when we speak of Islamic law, we mean all of human behavior, including, for example, intentions. This law is therefore very different from other systems of law in the strict sense of the term. Islamic law does not draw any line between law and morality, and hence much of it is not enforceable in a court, but only at the bar of conscience. This has had its advantages in that Islamic law is shot through with moral considerations, which in turn have given a moral temper to Muslim society. But it has also suffered from the disadvantage that general moral propositions have very often not been given due weight and have been selectively construed by jurists as mere "recommendations" rather than commands that must be expressed in terms of concrete legislation: the result has been an overemphasis on the specific dos and don'ts of the Qur'an at the expense of general propositions. For example, the Qur'anic verse 4:3, permitting polygamy up to four wives, was given legal force by classical Muslim jurists, but the rider contained in the same verse, that if a person cannot do justice among co-wives, then he must marry only one, was regarded by them as a recommendation to the husband's conscience that he should do justice.

Theology. At an elementary level, theological speculation in Islam also began very early and was occasioned by the assassination of `Uthman, the third caliph (d. 665), but its rise and development was totally independent of the law, and the first great theological systems were constructed only in the third and fourth centuries AH. The first question to become the focal point of dispute was the definition of a true Muslim. The earliest political and theological schism was represented by the Kharijis (from *khuruj*, meaning "secession"), who contended that a Muslim ceases to be a Muslim by the commission of a single serious sin such as theft or adultery, no matter how many times that person may recite the profession of faith, "There is no god but God and Muhammad is his prophet," unless he or she repents sincerely. They held that `Uthman and `Ali (the fourth caliph) had both become *kafirs* (non-Muslims), since the former was guilty of serious maladministration, including nepotism, and the latter had submitted his claim to rule to human arbitration, even though he had been duly elected caliph. The Kharijis, who were exemplars of piety and utterly egalitarian, and who believed that the only qualification for rule is a person's goodness and piety, without consideration of race, color, or sex, were mostly bedouin, which largely explains both their egalitarianism and their fanaticism. They were "professional rebels" who never united but always fought successive governments in divided groups and were almost entirely crushed out of existence by the middle of the second century AH.

While the Kharijis were not a systematic theological school, a full-fledged school, that of the Mu`tazilah, soon developed from their milieu. These thinkers, who emerged during the second and third centuries AH, held that while grave sinners do not become *kafirs*, neither do they remain Muslims. Their central thesis concerned what they called "God's justice and unity," which they defended to its logical conclusion. God's justice demands that human beings have a free and efficacious will; only then can they be the locus of moral responsibility and deserve praise and blame here and reward and punishment in the hereafter. They carried this belief to the point of holding that just as God, in his justice, cannot punish one who does good, neither can he forgive one who does evil, for otherwise the difference between good and evil would disappear. This position certainly offended religious sensitivities, since the Qur'an repeatedly mentions that God will forgive "whom he will" (2:284, 3:129 et al.).

For the Mu`tazilah, God plays no role in the sphere of human moral acts, except that he gives man moral support provided man does good by himself; God's activity is limited to nature. All anthropomorphic statements in the Qur'an were interpreted by the Mu`tazilah either as metaphors or as Arabic idioms. They rejected *hadith* outright because much of it was anthropomorphic and refused to base law upon it on the ground that *hadith* transmission was unreliable. They further held that good and evil in terms of general principles (but not the positive religious duties) were knowable by human reason without the aid of revelation but that revelation supplied the necessary motivation for the pursuit of goodness. In conformity with this view, they believed that one must rationally ponder the purposes of the Qur'anic ordinances, for in laying these down, God had a positive interest in furthering human well-being *(maslahah)*. This presumably means that law should be rationally grounded; there is, however, no evidence that the Mu`tazilah ever attempted to work out a legal system.

On the issue of God's unity, the Mu`tazilah rejected the separation of God's attributes from his essence, for this would entail belief in a multiplicity of eternal beings, amounting to polytheism. They did not deny that God is "living," "knowing," and "willing," as divine activities, but they denied that God is "life," "knowledge," and "will," as substantives. The development of this particular doctrine was possibly influenced by Christian discussions on the nature of the Trinity, and how and whether three hypostases could be one person, because the terms in which it is formulated are all too foreign to the milieu of pristine Islam. As a consequence of this doctrine, the Mu`tazilah also denied the eternity of the Qur'an, the very speech of God, since they denied the substantiality of all divine attributes. When their credo was made state creed under Caliph al-Ma'mun, they persecuted opposition

religious leaders such as Ibn Hanbal (d. 855), but because of these very doctrines—denial of God's forgiveness and of the eternity of the Qur'an—they became unpopular, and Caliph al-Mutawakkil (d. 861) brought Sunnism back to ascendancy.

What is in fact called Sunnism means nothing more than the majority of the community; it had its content defined in large measure as a reaction to the Kharijis and the Mu`tazilah, for Sunni orthodoxy is but a refined and sophisticated form of that popular reaction that crystalized against these groups. There, no small role was played by popular preachers and popular piety, which had already found its way into *hadith*. In doctrinal form, this reaction can be described as Murji'ism (from *irja'*, "postponement"), the belief that once adults have openly professed that there is no God but Allah and Muhammad is his prophet, if there is no reason to suspect that they are lying, mad, or under constraint, then such people are Muslims, irrespective of whether their deeds are good or whether their beliefs quite conform to orthodoxy, and that final judgment on their status must be "postponed" until the Last Day and left to God.

In conscious opposition to the Kharijis and the Mu`tazilah, the Murji'ah were content with minimal knowledge of Islam and Islamic conduct on the part of a believer. On the question of free will, they leaned heavily toward predestinarianism, and some were outright predestinarians. There is evidence that the Umayyad rulers supported the Murji'ah, apparently for their own political ends, since they were interested in discouraging questions about how they had come to power and set up a dynastic rule that abandoned the first four caliphs' model and high moral and political standards. However, it would have been impossible for these rulers to succeed if popular opinion had not swung toward the Murji'ah, particularly in reaction against the Kharijis.

The chief formulator of the Sunni creed was Abu al-Hasan al-Ash`ari (d. 935), a Mu`tazili who later came under the influence of the traditionists *(ahl al-hadith)* and turned the tables on his erstwhile preceptor and fellows among the Mu`tazilah. For al-Ash`ari, people cannot produce their own actions; rather, God does, and neither man nor nature has any powers or potencies before the actual act. At the time of the act, for example, when fire actually burns, God creates a power for that particular act. Thus God creates an action, while human beings "appropriate" or "acquire" *(kasaba)* it and thereby become responsible for "their" acts. The Ash`ari theologians are, therefore, atomists in terms of both time and space, and they reject causation and the entire idea of movement or process. God is under no obligation to do what human beings call justice; on the contrary, whatever God does is just. Justice involves reference to certain norms under which the agent works; since God has no norms to obey, there is no question of doing justice on his part. He also promised in the Qur'an that he will reward those who do good and punish those who do evil, and this is the proper and only assurance we have of the fate of human beings; if he had chosen to do the reverse, no one could question him. It also follows that good and bad are not natural characteristics of human acts, but that acts become good or bad by God's declaration through the revelation that he has been sending since Adam, the first prophet. It is, therefore, futile to probe rationally into the purposes of divine injunctions, for these are the result of God's will.

On the question of divine attributes, al-Ash`ari taught that these are real, although they are "neither God, nor other than God." God has an eternal attribute of "speech," which al-Ash`ari called "psychic speech," manifested in all divinely revealed books. Although the Qur'an as God's "psychic speech" is eternal, as something recited, written, and heard it is also created: one cannot point to a written copy of the Qur'an or its recital and say "This is eternal."

A contemporary of al-Ash`ari, the Central Asian theologian al-Maturidi (d. 944), also formulated an "official" Sunni creed and theology that in some fundamental ways was nearer to the Mu`tazili stance. He recognized "power-before-the-act" in man and also declared good and bad to be natural and knowable by human reason. Whereas al-Ash`ari belonged to the Shafi`i school of law, which was based principally on *hadith*, al-Maturidi was a member of the Hanafi school, which gave greater scope to reason. Yet, in subsequent centuries, the former's views almost completely eclipsed the latter's, although in the Indian subcontinent such prominent thinkers as Ahmad Sirhindi (d. 1624) and Shah Wali Allah of Delhi (d. 1762) criticized Ash`ari theology. The reason behind this sweeping and enduring success of Ash`ari theology seems to be the overwhelming spread of Sufism (particularly in its pantheistic form), which, in theological terms, was much more akin to Ash`ari thought than to that of Mu`tazilah or even the Maturidiyah, in that it sought to obliterate the human self in the all-embracing and all-effacing self of God, the most important nodal point of this conjunction being al-Ghazali.

In the intellectual field, as we shall see, Sufism grew at the expense of theology and utilized the worldview of the Muslim philosophers. On the moral and spiritual planes, however, the powerful corroboration of theology and Sufism stimulated the vehement reaction of the jurist and theologian Ibn Taymiyah (d. 1328). Struggling all his life against popular Sufi superstitions, against worship of saints and their shrines, and against Ash`ari theology, he tried to resurrect the moral activism of the Qur'an and the *sunnah*. He regarded the Mu`tazili denial of God's role in human actions as an error but considered the Ash`ari denial of human free and effective will as extremely dangerous and, in fact, stated that pantheistic Sufis and the Ash`ari theologians were considerably worse than not only the Mu`tazilah but even the Zoroastrians. He held that the Zoroastrians' postulation of two gods was undoubtedly an error but argued that they had been forced into this belief by

the undeniable distinction between good and evil that both Ash`ari theology and pantheistic Sufism virtually obliterated, leaving no basis for any worthwhile religion. (As we shall see, a similar argument was conducted within Sufism by a later Indian Sufi, Ahmad Sirhindi.) Ibn Taymiyah sought to solve the perennial problem of free will versus divine omnipotence by saying that the actual application of the principle of divine omnipotence occurs only in the past, while the *shariah* imperatives are relevant only to the future. His teaching remained more or less dormant until the eighteenth century, when it inspired the Wahhabi religious revolution in the Arabian Peninsula.

Sufism. The mainspring of Sufism lay in the desire to cultivate the inner life and to attain a deeper, personal understanding of Islam. Among the many proposed etymologies of the word *sufi*, the most credible is the one that derives it from *suf*, meaning "coarse wool," a reference to the kind of garb that many Sufis wore. The first phase of this spiritual movement was definitely moral, and the works of most early Sufis, those of the second and third centuries AH, show a preoccupation with constant self-examination and close scrutiny of one's motivation.

Sufi doctrine. The dialectic of the trappings and self-deception of the soul developed by Hakim al-Tirmidhi (d. 898) in his *Khatm al-awliya'* (The Seal of the Saints) provides one extraordinary example of spiritual insight, but this strongly moral trend continues from Hasan al-Basri (d. 728) through al-Muhasibi (d. 857) to his pupil al-Junayd (d. 910). The essence of their doctrine is moral contrition and detachment of the mind from the "good things" of the world *(zuhd)*. But from its very early times, Sufism also had a strong devotional element, as exemplified by the woman saint Rabi`ah al-`Adawiyah (d. 801). The goal of love of God led to the doctrine of *fana'* or "annihilation" (that is, of the human self in God). There were definitely Hellenistic Christian influences at work here. But the annihilation ideal was soon amended into "survival *(baqa')* after annihilation," or (re)gaining of a new self, and this formula was given different interpretations.

Most Sufis taught that, after the destruction of the human attributes (not the self), mortals acquire divine attributes (not the divine self) and "live in" them. The firm view of the orthodox and influential Sufi al-Junayd was that when a person sheds human attributes and these attributes undergo annihilation, that person comes to think that he or she has become God. But God soon gives that person the consciousness of otherness (not alienation) from God, which is extremely painful and is only somewhat relieved by God's also giving the consolation that this is the highest state attainable by human beings. Yet there were also Sufis who, most probably under the influence of Hellenistic Christianity, believed in human transubstantiation into God. In 922, al-Hallaj, a representative of this school, was charged with having uttered the blasphemous statement "I am God" and was crucified in

Baghdad. Yet, a somewhat earlier mystic, al-Bistami (d. 874), who is said to have committed even graver blasphemies, was never touched by the law. It may be, as some contend, that the real reasons behind al-Hallaj's execution were political, or it may be related to the fact that al-Hallaj was in the capital, Baghdad, whereas al-Bistami lived in an outlying province.

This example of such divergent interpretations of a fundamental doctrine should warn us that with Sufism we are dealing with a truly protean phenomenon: not only do interpretations differ, but experiences themselves must differ as well. However, under pressure from the `ulama'`, who refused to acknowledge any objective validity for the Sufi experience, the Sufis formulated a doctrine of "spiritual stations" (maqamat) that adepts successively attained through their progressive spiritual itinerary (suluk). These stations are as objectifiable as any experience can be. Although the various schools have differed in the lists of these stations, they usually enumerate them as follows: detachment from the world (zuhd), patience (sabr), gratitude (shukr) for whatever God gives, love (hubb), and pleasure (rida) with whatever God desires.

After the violent death of al-Hallaj, another important doctrine of the dialectic of Sufi experience was developed by orthodox Sufis. According to this doctrine, the Sufi alternates between two different types of spiritual states. One type is the experience of unity (where all multiplicity disappears) and of the inner reality. In this state the Sufi is "absent" from the world and is "with God"; this is the state of "intoxication" (sukr). The other state, that of "sobriety" (sahw), occurs when the Sufi "returns" to multiplicity and is "with the world." Whereas many Sufis had earlier contended that "intoxication" is superior to "sobriety" and that, therefore, the saints (awliya') are superior to the prophets (who are "with the world" and legislate for society), the orthodox Sufis now asserted the opposite, for the goodness of saints is limited to themselves, whereas the goodness of prophets is transitive, since they save the society as well as themselves.

On the basis of this doctrine, al-Hallaj's famous statement was rationalized as "one uttered in a state of intoxication" and as such not to be taken at face value. But it was al-Ghazali who effected a meaningful and enduring synthesis of Sufi "innerism" and the orthodox belief system. A follower of al-Ash`ari in theology and of al-Shafi`i in law, al-Ghazali also studied thoroughly the philosophic tradition of Ibn Sina (known in the West as Avicenna, d. 1037), and although he refuted its important theses bearing on religion in the famous work *Tahafut al-falasifah* (The Incoherence of the Philosophers), he was influenced by it in important ways as well. He then adopted Sufism as his "way to God" and composed his *magnum opus*, *Ihya' `ulum al-din* (The Revivification of the Sciences of the Faith). His net accomplishment lies in the fact that he tried to infuse a new spiritual life into law and theology on the one hand and to instill sobriety and responsibility into Sufism on the other, for he

repudiated the Sufi *shatahat* (intoxicated utterances) as meaningless.

Within a century after al-Ghazali's death, however, a Sufi doctrine based on out-and-out monism was being preached by Ibn al-`Arabi (d. 1240). Born in Spain and educated there and in North Africa, Ibn al-`Arabi eventually traveled to the Muslim East; he lived for many years in Mecca, where he wrote his major work, *Al-futuhat al-makkiyah* (The Meccan Discoveries), and finally settled in Damascus, where he died. Ibn al-`Arabi's writings are the high-water mark of theosophic Sufism, which goes beyond the ascetic or ecstatic Sufism of the earlier period, by laying cognitive claims to a unique, intuitive experience (known as *kashf*, "direct discovery," or *dhawq*, "taste") that was immune from error and radically different from and superior to the rational knowledge of the philosophers and the theologians.

Ibn al-`Arabi's doctrine, known as Unity of Being (wahdat al-wujud), teaches that everything is in one sense God and in another sense not-God. He holds that, given God, the transcendent, another factor that in itself is not describable "either as existent or as nonexistent" comes to play a crucial

> **Within a century after al-Ghazali's death . . . a Sufi doctrine based on out-and-out monism was being preached by Ibn al-`Arabi.**

role in the unfolding of reality. This factor is neither God nor the world; it is a "third thing," but it is God with God and world with the world. It is the stuff of which both the attributes of God (for God as transcendent has no names and no attributes) and the content of the world are made. It is eternal with the eternal and temporal with the temporal; it does not exist partially and divided in things: the whole of it is God, and the whole of it is the world, and the whole of it is everything in the world. This "third thing" turns out finally to be the Perfect or Primordial Human Being (who is identified with the eternal, not the temporal, Muhammad), in whose mirror God sees himself and who sees himself in God's mirror. This immanent God and Human Being are not only interdependent but are the obverse and converse of the same coin. There is little doubt that Ibn al-`Arabi represents a radical humanism, a veritable apotheosis of humanity.

This monistic Sufism found certain devoted and distinguished exponents in Ibn al-`Arabi's school, in both prose and poetry, the most illustrious and influential representative of the latter being Jalal al-Din Rumi (d. 1273), whose *Mathnavi* in Persian has been hailed as the "Qur'an in the Persian language." Through poetry, moreover, it has had a profound and literally incalculable influence on the general intellectual culture of Islam, in terms of a liberal humanism, indeed, latitudinarianism, and among the lower strata of Islamic society even antinomianism. A striking feature of this antinomianism, where orthodoxy was unashamedly scoffed at and ridiculed for its rigidity and narrow confines, is that it was tolerated by the orthodox only when it was expressed in poetry, not in prose. Also, because of the latitude and broad range of Sufi spirituality, from roughly the twelfth century to the impact of modernization in the nineteenth century, the more creative Muslim minds drifted from orthodoxy into the Sufi fold, and philosophy itself, although it remained rational in its methods, became mystical in its goals.

I have already noted the severe reaction against Sufi excesses on the part of Ibn Taymiyah in the fourteenth century. It may be mentioned here that for Ibn Taymiyah the ultimate distinction between good and evil is absolutely necessary for any worthwhile religion that seeks to inculcate moral responsibility, and further, that this distinction is totally dependent upon belief in pure monotheism and the equally absolute distinction between man and God. He sets little value on the formal fact that a person belongs to the Muslim community; he evaluates all human beings on the scale of monotheism. Thus, as seen above, he regards pantheistic Sufis (and, to a large extent, because of their predestinarianism, the Ash`ariyah as well), as being equivalent to polytheists; then come the Shi`ah and Christians because both consider a human being to be a divine incarnation; and last come Zoroastrians and the Mu`tazilah, since both posit two ultimate powers.

Later, the Indian shaykh of the Naqshbandi order, Ahmad Sirhindi (d. 1624), undertook a similar reform of Sufism from within. His massive *Maktubat-i Ahmad Sirhindi* (Letters), the main vehicle of his reform, besides the training of disciples, was twice translated into Ottoman Turkish and was influential in Turkey; in the Arab Middle East, his reformist thought was carried and spread in the nineteenth century. Sirhindi, who accepts Ibn al-`Arabi's philosophical scheme at the metaphysical level, introduces a radical moral dualism at the level of God's attributes and, instead of identifying the temporal world with the stuff of divine attributes, as Ibn al-`Arabi does, regards that world as being essentially evil, but evil that has to be transformed into good through the activity of the divine attributes. The basic error of the common Sufis, for him, is that instead of helping to transform this evil into good, as God wants to do through his attributes, they flee from it. The spiritual heights to which they think they are ascending are, therefore, a pure delusion, for the real good is this evil, "this earth," once it has been transformed. But this realization requires a constant struggle with evil, not a flight from it. It is a prophet, then, not a saint, who undertakes the real divine task, and the true test of a person's ascent to real spiritual heights is whether he or she reenters the earth in order to improve and redeem it. Despite the efforts of Ibn Taymiyah,

Sirhindi, and other figures, however, Ibn al-`Arabi's influence has been, until today, very strong in the Muslim world, not just on Sufism but on Islamic poetry as well.

Sufi orders. Up to the twelfth century, Sufism was a matter of limited circles of a spiritual elite that might be aptly described as "schools" with different spiritual techniques and even different spiritual ideologies. From the twelfth century on, however, they developed into networks of orders, involving the masses on a large scale. Systems of Sufi hospices—called variously *zawiyahs* (in Arabic), *tekkes* (in Turkish), and *khanagahs* (in Iran and the Indian subcontinent)—where the Sufi shaykh lived (usually with his family in the interior of the building) and guided his clientele, grew up from Morocco to Southeast Asia. Although in some of the hospices orthodox religious disciplines such as theology and law were taught along with Sufi works, orthodox education was generally carried on in the *madrasahs*, or colleges, while only Sufi works were taught in the Sufi centers.

Sufi orders can be divided into those that are global and those that are regional. The most global is the Qadiri order, named after `Abd al-Qadir al-Jilani (d. 1166), with branches all over the world that are tied only loosely to the center at Baghdad. Somewhat more regional are the Suhrawardi and the Naqshbandi orders. The latter, which originated in Central Asia in the thirteenth century, formulated an explicit ideology early in its career to try to influence the rulers and their courts, with the result that they have often been politically active. One of its branches, the Khalwatiyah, played a prominent role in modernizing reform in Turkey during the eighteenth and nineteenth centuries. Several of the Sufi orders have been associated with guilds and sometimes, particularly in Ottoman Turkey, have been directly involved in social protests and political rebellions against official oppression and injustice.

Another broad and important division is that between urban and "rustic" orders. The former, particularly the Naqshbandi order and its offshoots, were refined and close to the orthodoxy of the `ulama', with the result that an increasingly large number of the `ulama' gradually enrolled themselves in these urban Sufi orders, particularly the orthodox ones. By contrast, many of the rustic orders were without discipline and law *(bi-shar`)*, especially in the Indian subcontinent, where they were often indistinguishable from the Hindu *sadhus* (monks). With the spread of modernization, Sufism and Sufi orders have suffered greatly; in Turkey, they were suppressed by Mustafa Kemal Atatürk in the 1920s, and their endowments were confiscated by the government. It is interesting to note, however, that since the mid-twentieth century some orders have experienced a revival in the industrial urban centers of Muslim lands, probably in reaction to the excessively materialistic outlook generated by modernization, while in Central Asia their underground networks are waging anti-Soviet activities in an organized manner.

Correspondingly, in the West, several intellectuals, such as Frithjof Schuon and Martin Lings, have actively turned to Sufi devotion to escape the spiritual vacuity created by their own overly materialistic culture.

Sects. There are two broad divisions within the Muslim community, the Sunnis and the Shi`ah. The theological views and the legal schools of the Sunnis—the majority of the community—have been dealt with above. The Shi`i schism grew out of the claim of the Shi`ah (a word meaning "partisans," in this context "the partisans of `Ali") that following the Prophet, rule over Muslims belongs rightfully only to `Ali, Muhammad's cousin and son-in-law, and to his descendants. This doctrine, known as "legitimism," was opposed to the Khariji view that rule is open to any good Muslim on a universal basis and to the Sunni view, which was no more than a rationalization of actual facts, that "rulers must come from the Quraysh," the Prophet's tribe, but not necessarily from his clan or house.

The Shi`ah, in early Islam, were primarily sociopolitical dissidents, sheltering under the umbrella of "the house of the Prophet" but actually representing various elements of social protest against Umayyad Arab heavy-handedness and injustices. But it was not long before they began establishing an ideological and theological base for themselves. Until well into the third century AH, Shi`i theology was crude and materialistic: it asserted that God was a corporeal being who sat on an actual throne and created space by physical motion. Hisham ibn al-Hakam (d. 814?), among the best known of the early Shi`i theologians, is reported to have said that God was "a little smaller than Mount Abu Qabis." There were several other early Shi`i theologians who attributed some kind of body, including a physical body, to God, but beginning in the latter half of the ninth century, Shi`i theology was radically transformed, inheriting and asserting with increasing force the Mu`tazili doctrine of human free will against the Sunnis.

In the thirteenth century CE, through the work of the philosopher, theologian, and scientist Nasir al-Din Tusi (d. 1273), philosophy entered Shi`i theology, a process that was further facilitated by Tusi's student, the influential theologian al-Hilli (d. 1325). In his work on the creed, *Tajrid al-`aqa'id* (Concise Statement of the Creeds), which was subsequently commented upon by both Shi`i and Sunni theologians, Tusi describes man as "creator of his own actions." Tusi, however, rejects the philosophical thesis of the eternity of the world. Here it is interesting to compare this Shi`i development with the Sunni position that was articulated about three-quarters of a century earlier at the hands of Fakhr al-Din al-Razi (d. 1209), who expanded the official Sunni theology by incorporating into it a discussion of major philosophical themes. But whereas the Shi`ah accepted many philosophical theses into their theology, al-Razi and other Sunnis after him refuted all the philosophical theses point by point, thus erecting a theology that was an exclusive alternative to philosophy. Against

this background is probably to be understood the fact that while philosophy was exorcized from the curricula in the Arab world from the thirteenth century on and declined sharply in the rest of the Sunni world, it reached its zenith in Shi`i Iran in the seventeenth century and continues unabated until today, although many of the orthodox Shi`ah continue to oppose it.

In law, the Twelver Shi`i school has long been recognized as valid by the Sunnis, despite differences, the most conspicuous being that Shi`i law recognizes a temporary marriage that may be contracted for a fixed period—a year, a month, a week, or even a day. Among the Shi`ah, the nearest school to Sunnism, particularly in law, is that of the Zaydiyah in Yemen, whose founder Zayd ibn `Ali (d. 738), a brother of the fifth imam of the Shi`ah, was a theology student of the first Mu`tazili teacher, Wasil ibn `Ata' (d. 748).

But the most characteristic doctrine of the Shi`ah is their esotericism. This has a practical aspect called *taqiyah*, which means dissimulation of one's real beliefs in a generally hostile atmosphere. This doctrine, apparently adopted in early Islamic times, when the Shi`ah became a subterranean movement, as it were, in the wake of political failure, subsequently became a part of Shi`i dogma. But in its theoretical aspect esotericism is defined by the doctrine that religion, and particularly the Qur'an, has, besides the apparent, "external" meaning, hidden esoteric meanings that can be known only through spiritual contact with the Hidden Imam. In the early centuries of Islam, this principle of esotericism was probably unbridled and fanciful in its application, as is apparent from the ninth- to tenth-century Qur'an commentary of al-Qummi. But as Shiism was progressively permeated by rational thought, esotericism became more systematic, even if it may often seem farfetched (as in certain philosophical interpretations of the Qur'an). As pointed out earlier, the Sufis also patently practiced esotericism in understanding the materials of religion, particularly the Qur'an; the ultimate common source of both Shiism and Sufism lies in gnosticism and other comparable currents of thought, and, indeed, Ibn al-`Arabi's interpretations are often purely the work of his uncontrolled imagination.

Beginning from about the middle of the tenth century, when the Sunni caliph in Baghdad came under the control of the Shi`i Buyid dynasty, there were public commemorations of the martyrdom of Husayn at Karbala on the tenth of Muharram (`Ashura'). These ceremonies caused riots in Baghdad and still do so in some countries such as Pakistan and India today. The commemoration is traditionally marked by public processions in which participants lamenting the death of the Prophet's grandson beat their breasts and backs with heavy iron chains. Scenes of Husayn's death are recreated in passion plays known as *ta`ziyahs*, and he is eulogized in moving sermons and poetry recitals. Fed from childhood with such representational enactments of this event, a

Shi`i Muslim is likely to develop a deep sense of tragedy and injustice resulting in an ideal of martyrdom that is capable of being manipulated into outbursts of frenzied emotionalism, like the spectacular events of the Iranian Revolution.

Shii subsects. In the first and second centuries of the Islamic era, Shiism served as an umbrella for all kinds of ideologies, with a general social protest orientation, and the earliest heresiographers enumerate dozens of Shi`i sects, several with extremely heretical and antinomian views. The main surviving body, the Ithna `Ashariyah, or Twelvers, number probably between fifty and sixty million people. All other sects (except the Zaydiyah of Yemen) are regarded even by the Twelvers themselves as heretical extremists *(ghulat)*. The main one among these, the Isma`iliyah, or Seveners, broke with the Twelvers in a dispute over which son of the sixth imam was to be recognized as the latter's successor: the Twelvers refused to recognize the elder son, Isma`il, because he drank wine, while the Seveners did recognize him (thus the name Isma`ili) and continue to await his return.

> **... the Twelvers refused to recognize the elder son, Isma`il, because he drank wine. . . .**

The Isma`iliyah established a powerful and prosperous empire in North Africa and Egypt from the tenth to the twelfth centuries. Prior to this, the Isma`iliyah had been an underground revolutionary movement, but once they attained political power, they settled down as part of the status quo. Since the late eleventh century, they have been divided into two branches: the Nizariyah, commonly known by the name Assassins, who were active in Syria and Iran, and in recent years have been followers of a hereditary Aga Khan, and the Musta`liyah, who are mainly centered in Bombay. Isma`ili philosophy, which is reflected in the *Rasa'il Ikhwan al-Safa'* (Epistles of the Brethren of Purity), produced by a secret society in the late ninth century, is essentially based on Neoplatonic thought with influences from gnosticism and occult sects.

The Isma`ili sect, which was organized and propagated through a well-knit network of missionaries *(du`ah)*, adheres to a belief in cyclic universes: each cycle comprises seven Speakers, or Messengers, with a revelation and a law; each Speaker is followed in turn by one of the seven Silent Ones, or Imams. The last imam, when he appears, will abrogate all organized religions and their laws and will institute a new era of a universal religion. During the leadership of the third Aga Khan (d. 1957), the Isma`ili community started drawing closer to the mainstream of Islam, a trend that seems to be gaining further strength at present under Karim Aga Khan's leadership: Isma`ili intellectuals now describe their faith as the

"Isma`ili *tariqah* [spiritual order] of Islam." There are other "extremist" subsects within the Shi`ah, including the Druze, Nusayriyah, and `Alawiyun. Of these, the Druze are the most prominent. This sect arose in the eleventh century as a cult of the eccentric Fatimid ruler al-Hakim, who mysteriously disappeared in 1021.

Later sects. In more recent times, there have been two noteworthy sectarian developments, one within Shi`i Islam in mid-nineteenth-century Iran and the other within Sunni Islam in late nineteenth-century India. During an anticlerical movement in Iran, a certain Muhammad `Ali of Shiraz claimed to be the Bab, or "Gate," to God. He was executed by the government under pressure from the `ulama' in 1850. After him, his two disciples, Subh-i Azal and Baha' Allah, went different ways, and the latter subsequently declared his faith to be an independent religion outside Islam. While the origin of the Baha'i religion was marked by strong eschatological overtones, it later developed an ideology of pacifism and internationalism and won a considerable number of converts in North America early in the twentieth century. In Iran itself, Babis and Baha'is are frequent targets of clerical persecution, and many of them have been executed under the Khomeini regime. [*See* Baha'is.]

The Sunni sect called the Ahmadiyah arose in the 1880s when Ghulam Ahmad of Qadiyan (a village in East Punjab) laid claim to prophethood. He claimed to be at once a "manifestation" of the prophet Muhammad, the Second Advent of Jesus, and an avatar of Krsna for the Hindus. It is possible that he wanted to unite various religions under his leadership. After his death, his followers constituted themselves as an independent community with an elected *khalifah* (successor; i. e., caliph). When the first caliph died in 1911, the Ahmadiyah split in two: the main body carried on the founder's claim to prophethood under Ahmad's son, Bashir al-Din, while the other, the Lahore group, claimed that Ghulam Ahmad was not a prophet, nor had he claimed to be one, but rather that he was a reformer or "renovator" *(mujaddid)* of Islam. Both groups have been active with missionary zeal, particularly in Europe and America. In 1974, the National Assembly of Pakistan, where the main body had established its headquarters after the creation of the state, declared both groups to be "non-Muslim minorities."

Modernism. In the eighteenth century, against a background of general stagnation, a puritanical fundamentalist movement erupted in Arabia under Muhammad ibn `Abd al-Wahhab (1703-1792). The movement called for a return to the purist Islam of the Qur'an and the *sunnah* and its unadulterated monotheism, uncompromised by the popular cults of saints and their shrines. Ibn `Abd al-Wahhab married into the family of Sa`ud, a chieftain of Najd, who accepted his teaching and brought all Arabia under his ruling ideology. At the same time, in the Indian subcontinent, Shah Wali Allah of Delhi, a highly sophisticated intellectual (said to have been a fellow student of Ibn `Abd al-Wahhab during his stay in Medina), also advocated a return to pristine Islam although, unlike his Arabian contemporary, he was a Sufi at a high spiritual level.

In the nineteenth century a reformist militant group called the Jihad movement arose out of Wali Allah's school, and three more movements followed in Africa—the Sanusi in Libya, the Fulbe in West Africa, and the Mahdists in the Sudan. Although these three movements emerged from different environments, common to all of them was a reformist thrust in terms of the recovery of the "true pristine Islam" of the Qur'an and the Prophet, particularly emphasizing monotheism; an insistence upon *ijtihad*, that is, rejection of the blind following tradition in both theology and law in favor of an attempt to discover and formulate new solutions to Islamic problems; and finally, resort to militant methods, including the imposition of their reformist ideologies by force. In addition, these movements generally brought to the center of consciousness the necessity of social and moral reforms as such, without recourse to the rewards and punishments of the hereafter. In other words, all three were characterized by a certain positivistic orientation.

While these premodernist reform movements laid great emphasis on *ijtihad*, in practice their *ijtihad* meant that Muslims should be enabled to disengage themselves from their present "degenerate" condition and to recover pristine Islam. Also, it is a general characteristic of all fundamentalist movements that in order to "simplify" religion and make it practical, they debunk the intellectualism of the past and discourage the growth of future intellectualism. In such cases education becomes so simplified that it is virtually sterile, thus leaving little possibility for *ijtihad*. Of the fundamentalist groups I have described above, the progenitors of the Indian and Libyan movements were sophisticated and accomplished scholars, but the leaders of the other three had only a modicum of learning and were primarily activists.

Nonetheless, these movements signaled real stirrings in the soul of Islam and paved the way for the intellectual activity of the Muslim modernists—Muslims who had been exposed to Western ideas and who, by integrating certain key ones among them with the teaching of the Qur'an, produced brilliant solutions to the crucial problems then faced by Islamic society. The influence of premodernist reformism upon the modernists is apparent from the fact that they keep the Qur'an and the tradition of the Prophet as ultimate referents for reform while criticizing or rejecting the medieval heritage. Thus, although their individual views regarding, for example, the relationship between faith and reason differ, all of them insist on the cultivation of positive sciences, appealing to numerous verses of the Qur'an that state that the entire universe has been made subservient to good ends of humankind and that we must study and use it.

In the political sphere, citing Qur'an 42:38, which says that Muslims should decide all their affairs through mutual consultation (*shura*, actually a pre-Islamic Arab institution confirmed by the Qur'an), the modernists contended that whereas the Qur'an teaches democracy, the Muslims had deviated from this norm and acquiesced to autocratic rule. Similarly, on the subject of women, the modernists argued that the Qur'an had granted equal rights to men and women (except in certain areas of economic life where the burden of earning and supporting the family is squarely laid on men), but the medieval practice of the Muslims had clearly departed from the Qur'an and ended by depriving women of their rights. Regarding polygamy, the modernists stated that permission for polygamy (up to four wives) had been given under special conditions, with the proviso that if the husband could not do justice among his co-wives then he must marry only one wife, and that finally the Qur'an itself had declared such justice to be impossible to attain (4:129).

Of the half-dozen most prominent names in Islamic modernism, two were `ulama'-trained along traditional lines: Jamal al-Din al-Afghani (1839-1897), a fiery activist with a magnetic personality, and his disciple, the Egyptian shaykh Muhammad `Abduh (1845-1905). Three were lay intellectuals with modern education: the Turk Namik Kemal (1840-1888) and the two Indians Ameer Ali (d. 1928) and Muhammad Iqbal (1877-1938), while the Indian Sayyid Ahmad Khan (1817-1898), the most radical of them all in theological views, was a premodern lay-educated scholar. Yet, despite their differences and the fact that none of them, except for al-Afghani and `Abduh, ever met any of the others, they shared the basic tenet—à la premodernist reform movements—that medieval Islam had deviated on certain crucial points from the normative Islam of the Qur'an; this argument runs through all the issues that they discuss.

However, while these modernists sought reform within their own societies, they also waged controversies with the West on the latter's understanding of Islam, and some of them, particularly Iqbal, argued about the West's own performance on the stage of history. Iqbal bitterly and relentlessly accused the West of cheating humanity of its basic values with the glittering mirage of its technology, of exploiting the territories it colonized in the name of spreading humanitarian values, which it itself flouted by waging internecine wars born of sheer economic savagery, and of dewomanizing the women and dilapidating the family institution in the name of progress. Iqbal was an equally strong critic of the world Muslim society, which for him represented nothing more than a vast graveyard of Islam. He called the whole world to the "true Islam" of the Qur'an and the Prophet, a living, dynamic Islam that believed in the harnessing of the forces of history for the ethical development of mankind.

Iqbal and others, such as the Egyptian Rashid Rida (d. 1935), proved to belong to a transitional stage from modernism to a new attitude, perhaps best described as neofundamentalism, for unlike the fundamentalism of the premodernist reform movements, the current neofundamentalism is, in large measure, a reaction to modernism, but it has also been importantly influenced by modernism. This influence can best be seen on two major issues: first, the contention that Islam is a total way of life, including all fields of human private and public life, and is not restricted to certain religious rites such as the Five Pillars (to which the Islam of the traditionalist `ulama'` had become practically confined); and, second, that cultivation of scientific knowledge and technology is desirable within Islam.

Besides emphasis on technology (although Iran appears to pay only lip service to science and technology), neofundamentalists have, on the one hand, oversimplified the traditionalist curriculum of Islamic studies, and, on the other, embarked upon a program of "islamization" of Western knowledge. Besides these points, the most basic factor common to the neofundamentalist phenomena is a strong assertion of Islamic identity over and against the West, an assertion that hits equally strongly at most modernist reforms, particularly on the issue of the status and role of women in society. This powerful desire to repudiate the West, therefore, leads the neofundamentalist to emphasize certain points (as a *riposte* to the modernist, who is often seen as a pure and simple westernizer) that would most distinguish Islam from the West. Besides the role of women, which is seen to lie at home, the heaviest emphasis falls on the islamization of economy through the reinstitution of *zakat* and the abolition of bank interest (which is identified with *riba*, or usury, prohibited by the Qur'an). No neofundamentalist government in the Muslim world—including Iran and Pakistan—however, has been successful in implementing either of the two policies, while the Libyan leader Mu`ammar al-Qadhdhafi has declared that the modern banking institution is not covered by the Qur'anic prohibition of *riba*.

Neofundamentalism is by no means a uniform phenomenon. Apart from the fact that there exist, particularly in the Arab Middle East, extremist splinter groups of neofundamentalists that are strikingly reminiscent of the Kharijis of early Islamic times, on most crucial issues, such as democracy or the nature of Islamic legislation, even the mainstream elements are sharply divided. While in Libya, for example, Mu`ammar al-Qadhdhafi has taken a most radical stand on legislation, repudiating the precepts of *hadith* as its source and replacing them with the will of the people, the current rulers of Pakistan and Iran show little confidence in the will of the people. The most interesting attitude in this connection is that of the religious leaders of Iran: while almost all reformers since the mid-nineteenth century—including Shi`i thinkers such as Ameer Ali—have insisted that there can be no theocracy in Islam since Islam has no priesthood, the Iranian religious leaders are asserting precisely the opposite, namely,

that Islam does have a priesthood and that this priestly class must rule, a position expounded even prior to the Islamic Revolution by Ayatollah Khomeini, the chief ruler of Iran, in his work *Vilayat-i faqih* (Rule of the Jurist, 1971). [*See also* Muslim Brotherhood.]

Finally, the phenomenon of international Islamic conferences in modern Islam is also to be noted since, in the absence of political unity in the Muslim world, these help the cause of unity of sentiment, if not uniformity of mind. The beginnings of this phenomenon go back to the 1920s, when conferences were held in Cairo and Mecca to deliberate on the possibility of reinstituting the caliphate after Atatürk abolished it with the secularization of the Turkish state. But from the mid-1940s on, as Muslim countries gained independence from European colonial rule, the sentiment for international Muslim gatherings became progressively stronger. In the mid-1960s all the national and international private Islamic organizations became affiliated with the semiofficial Saudi-sponsored Muslim World League (Rabitat al-`Alam al-Islami), headquartered in Mecca; the league finances Islamic causes both in the Muslim world and in Western countries, where large numbers of Muslim settlers are building mosques and Islamic centers and developing Islamic community life, including programs for education.

At the same time, since the 1969 Muslim Summit Conference held in Rabat, Morocco, an Islamic Secretariat has been set up in Jiddah, Saudi Arabia, as the administrative center for the Organization of Islamic Conferences (OIC) on the state level. Besides holding summit meetings, this organization maintains a developmental economic agenda through which interest-free development banks have been set up, financed principally by oil-rich Arab countries to help poorer Muslim countries (this is in addition to the aid given to non-Muslim countries). All these conferences, whether organized by the OIC or the World Muslim League, discuss political problems affecting the Muslim world and try to formulate a common response to them, through the United Nations and its agencies or through other channels.

Islam's Attitude to Other Religions. According to Qur'anic teaching divine guidance is universal, and God regards all peoples as equal. Every prophet's message, although immediately addressed to a given people, is nevertheless of universal import and must be believed by all humanity. Muhammad himself is made to declare, "I believe in any book God may have revealed" (Qur'an 42:15), and all Muslims are required to do likewise. This is so because God is one; the source of revelation is one, and humankind is also one. The office of prophethood is, in fact, indivisible.

Muslims, however, have, from earliest times, considered Muhammad to be the bearer of the last and consummate revelation. Nevertheless, there is a tension within the Qur'an itself on this issue. In keeping with its fundamental teaching that prophethood is indivisible, the Qur'an, of course, invites

Jews and Christians to Islam; it insists on the unity of religion, deplores the diversity of religions and religious communities, which it insists is based on willful neglect of truth, and denounces both Jews and Christians as "partisans, sectarians," with "each sect rejoicing in what itself has" (30:32).

On the other hand, it states that although religion is essentially one, God himself has given different "institutions and approaches" to different communities so that he might "test them in what he has given them," and that they might compete with each other in goodness (5:48), which implies that these different institutional arrangements have positive value and are somehow meant to be permanent. In fact, the Qur'an categorically states that whether a person is a Muslim or a Jew or a Christian or a Sabian, "whosoever believes in God and the Last Day and does good deeds, they shall have their reward with their Lord, shall have nothing to fear, nor shall they come to grief" (2:62; see also 5:69). This tension is probably to be resolved by saying that it is better, indeed incumbent upon humankind to accept Muhammad's message, but that if they do not, then living up to their own prophetic messages will be regarded as adequate even if it does not fulfill the entire divine command.

The organization of Muslims as a community—which was inherent in the message of the Prophet—set in motion its own political and religious dynamics. The Qur'an itself, while strongly repudiating the claims of Jewish and Christian communities to be proprietors of divine truth and guidance, frankly tells Muslims also (for example, in 47:38) that unless they fulfill the message they cannot take God for granted. Soon after the time of the Prophet, however, the community came to be regarded as infallible, and a *hadith* was put into currency that the Prophet had said "My community shall never agree on an error." This development was necessitated partly by intercommunal rivalry, but largely by the internal development of law, since the doctrine of legal consensus had to be made infallible.

In his last years, the Prophet decided on the policy of forcible conversion of Arab pagans to Islam and gave religious and cultural autonomy to Jews and Christians as "people of the Book" (although Jews were driven out of Medina by Muhammad and later from the rest of the Arabian Peninsula by `Umar I). Muslims had to determine for themselves the status of Zoroastrians, Hindus, and Buddhists when they conquered Iran and parts of Northwest India. It was decided that these populations were also "people of the Book" since they believed in certain scriptures, and consequently they were allowed to keep their religion and culture, like the Jews and Christians, on payment of the poll tax *(jizyah)*. In contrast with their stance toward Jews and Christians however, Muslims were prohibited from having social intercourse or intermarrying with these other groups.

Indeed, when the community became an imperium, further developments took place that had little to do with the Qur'an or the *sunnah* of the Prophet but rather were dictated by the logic of the empire itself. The law of apostasy, for example, which states that a Muslim apostate should be given three chances to repent and in the case of nonrepentance must be executed, has nothing to do with the Qur'an, which speaks of "those who believed and then disbelieved, then once again believed and disbelieved—and then became entrenched in disbelief" (4:137; see also 3:90), thus clearly envisaging repeated conversions and apostasies without invoking any penalty in this world. It is, therefore, important to make these distinctions and to treat historic Islam not as one seamless garment but rather as a mosaic made up of different pieces.

There are numerous other laws that are the product neither of the Qur'an nor of the Prophet's *sunnah*, but of the Islamic imperium, such as the inadmissibility of evidence of a non-Muslim against a Muslim in a criminal case. In this legal genre also falls the juristic doctrine that the world consists of three zones: the Abode of Islam *(dar al-Islam)*, where Muslims rule; the Abode of Peace *(dar al-sulh)*, those countries or powers with whom Muslims have peace pacts; and the Abode of War *(dar al-harb)*, the rest of the world. This doctrine was definitely the result of the early Islamic conquests and the initial Islamic law of war and peace resulting from them. But during the later Abbasid period, the concept of *jihad* was formulated in defensive terms, because the task then was the consolidation of the empire rather than the gaining of further territory through conquest. To this general problem also belongs the consideration advanced by several Western scholars that Islam cannot authentically be a minority religion because the presumption of political power is built into its very texture as a religion. What is true is that Islam requires a state to work out its sociopolitical ideals and programs, but this does not mean that Muslims cannot live as a minority; indeed they have done so throughout history. The Qur'an, in fact, envisages some sort of close cooperation between Judaism, Christianity, and Islam, and it invites Jews and Christians to join Muslims in such a goal: "O People of the Book! Let us come together on a platform that is common between us, that we shall serve naught save God" (3:64).

BIBLIOGRAPHY

General Works. For a general survey of Islam, see *The Cambridge History of Islam,* vol. 2, *The Further Islamic Lands, Islamic Society and Civilization,* edited by P. M. Holt, Ann K. S. Lambton, and Bernard Lewis (Cambridge, 1970), and my own book entitled *Islam,* 2d ed. (Chicago, 1979). Richard C. Martin's *Islam: A Cultural Perspective* (Englewood Cliffs, N. J., 1982) gives a good description of Islamic religious practice. For a developmental view of Islam in a global setting, see Marshall G. S. Hodgson's *The Venture of Islam,* 3 vols. (Chicago, 1974). A collection of essays rarely matched for perspective interpretation of Islamic civilization is H. A. R. Gibb's *Studies on the Civilization of Islam* (Boston, 1962). Two other works of general interest are *The Legacy of Islam,* edited by Thomas W. Arnold and Alfred Guillaume (London, 1931), and *The Legacy of Islam,* 2d ed., rev., edited by C. E. Bosworth and Joseph Schacht (Oxford, 1974).

Topical Studies. For the general reader and the scholar alike, an excellent guide to the Qur'an is *Bell's Introduction to the Qur'an* (Edinburgh, 1970), W. Montgomery Watt's revised and enlarged edition of a work published in 1953 by Richard Bell. My own study, *Major Themes of the Qur'an* (Chicago, 1980), is a systematic presentation of the views of the Qur'an on God, man, society, revelation, and so on. Among translations of the Qur'an, three can be recommended: *The Meaning of the Glorious Koran,* translated and edited by M. M. Pickthall (New York, 1930); *The Koran Interpreted,* translated by A. J. Arberry (New York, 1955); and *The Message of the Qur'an,* translated by Muhammad Asad (Gibraltar, 1980). Both Pickthall's and Arberry's translations have been frequently reprinted and are readily available, but Asad's painstaking and thoughtful translation is well worth seeking out.

Two works on *hadith* that may profitably be consulted are Ignácz Goldziher's *Muslim Studies,* 2 vols., edited by S. M. Stern and C. R. Barber (Chicago, 1966-1973), and Alfred Guillaume's *The Traditions of Islam* (1924; reprint, Beirut, 1966).

Among the many works devoted to the Prophet's biography, none is entirely satisfactory. Alfred Guillaume's *The Life of Muhammad: A Translation of [Ibn] Ishaq's "Sirat Rasul Allah"* (1955; reprint, Lahore, 1967), an English translation of the first extant Arabic biography (second century AH), is the best guide one has at the present. W. Montgomery Watt's *Muhammad at Mecca* (London, 1953) and *Muhammad at Medina* (London, 1956) may be usefully read as secondary sources.

On Islamic theology the following works are recommended: *A Shi'ite Creed: A Translation of "Risalatu'l-I'tiqadat" of Muhammad b. `Ali Ibn Babawayhi al-Qummi,* edited and translated by A. A. Fyzee (London, 1942); D. B. Macdonald's *Development of Muslim Theology, Jurisprudence and Constitutional Theory* (1903; reprint, New York, 1965); W. Montgomery Watt's *The Formative Period of Islamic Thought* (Edinburgh, 1973); and A. J. Wensinck's *The Muslim Creed: Its Genesis and Historical Development* (1932; reprint, New York, 1965).

For information on Islamic law the following works are useful: *Law in the Middle East,* edited by Majid Khadduri and Herbert J. Liebesny (Washington, D. C., 1955); J. N. D. Ander-son's *Islamic Law in the Modern World* (New York, 1959); Noel J. Coulson's *A History of Islamic Law* (Edinburgh, 1971); and Joseph Schacht's *An Introduction to Islamic Law* (Oxford, 1974).

Numerous works on Sufism are readily available. Among them are Reynold A. Nicholson's *The Mystics of Islam* (1914; reprint, Beirut, 1966) and *Studies in Islamic Mysticism* (1921; reprint, Cambridge, 1977); A. J. Arberry's *Sufism: An Account of the Mystics of Islam* (London, 1950); J. Spencer Triming-ham's *The Sufi Orders in Islam* (New York, 1971); and Anne-marie Schimmel's *Mystical Dimensions of Islam* (Chapel Hill, N. C., 1975).

For Islamic political thought and education, the following works are useful: A. S. Tritton's *Materials on Muslim Education in the Middle Ages* (London, 1957); E. I. J. Rosenthal's *Political Thought in Medieval Islam* (Cambridge, 1958); Bayard Dodge's *Muslim Education in Medieval Times* (Washington, D. C., 1962); Ann K. S. Lambton's *State and Government in Medieval Islam,* vol. 1, *The Jurists* (London, 1981); Hamid Enayat's *Modern Islamic Political Thought* (Austin, 1982); and my own *Islam and Modernity: Transformation of an Intellectual Tradition* (Chicago, 1982).

The most important statements on Islamic modernism by Muslim modernists themselves are Syed Ameer Ali's *The Spirit of Islam: A History of the Evolution and Ideals of Islam,* rev. ed. (London, 1974), and Muhammad Iqbal's *Reconstruction of Religious Thought in Islam* (1934; reprint, Lahore, 1960). General writings on and critiques of Islamic modernism by modern Western scholars include H. A. R. Gibb's *Modern Trends in Islam* (Chicago, 1947); G. E. von Grunebaum's *Modern Islam: The Search for Cultural Identity* (Los Angeles, 1962); and Wilfred Cantwell Smith's *Islam in Modern History* (Princeton, 1957).

The following are important regional treatments: Charles C. Adams's *Islam and Modernism in Egypt* (1933; reprint, New York, 1968); Wilfred Cantwell Smith's *Modern Islam in India* (London, 1946); Albert Hourani's *Arabic Thought in the Liberal Age,* 1798-1939, 2d ed. (Cambridge, 1983); Bernard Lewis's *The Emergence of Modern Turkey* (London, 1963); Niyazi Berkes's *The Development of Secularism in Turkey* (Montreal, 1964), a mine of information despite its secularist bias; and J. Boland's *The Struggle of Islam in Modern Indonesia* (The Hague, 1971).

FAZLUR RAHMAN

Islamic law

Shari`ah* is an Arabic term used to designate Islamic law. In the case of Islamic law, the way is one that leads the righteous believer to Paradise in the afterlife. The *shari`ah is not deemed a religious law by virtue of the subject matters is covers, for these range far beyond the sphere of religious concerns strictly speaking and extend to the mundane affairs of everyday life. Rather, its religious character is due to the Muslim belief that it derives from divinely inspired sources and represents God's plan for the proper ordering of all human activities. Although Muslims agree that they are bound by the *shari`ah,* the interpretations of its requirements have differed historically according to sectarian and school divisions and, in modern times, also according to differing views of how the *shari`ah* applies in the changed circumstances of present-day societies.

Origins and Nature. The historical origin of the *shari`ah* lies in the revelation that Muslims believe was given to the prophet Muhammad by God through the vehicle of the archangel Gabriel in the last decades before the Prophet's death in 632 CE. This divine revelation was later recorded in a text known as the Qur'an. Although only a small portion of the Qur'an concerns strictly legal questions, it sets forth a number of general principles regarding how Muslims are to conduct themselves.

The *shari`ah* grew into a vast corpus of law. *Shari`ah* rules were part of the positive law applied by the government of the early Muslim community, which was originally conceived as an entity where political and religious loyalties would be coterminous. At the same time, the *shari`ah* was also understood as a system of moral guidance for the individual believer.

In the Islamic view, governments exist only to ensure that the *shari`ah* is properly administered and enforced. Governments are subordinate to the *shari`ah* and must execute its commands and prohibitions. On the Day of Judgment each Muslim will be held to account for any personal failures to comply with the commands and prohibitions of the *shari`ah.*

Classification of acts. The dual nature of the *shari`ah* as positive law and deontology, serving the combined functions of law and of what in some other religious systems might be moral philosophy, is reflected in the fact that Muslim jurists distinguish between two fundamentally different ways of classifying human acts. One way is to assess the moral character of acts, an assessment that corresponds to the deontological quality of the *shari`ah*. For this task there exists a fivefold scheme of classification, according to which an act may be mandatory, recommended, neutral (that is, entailing no moral consequences), blameworthy, or prohibited. Knowledge of this classification scheme enables pious Muslims to follow a meritorious course of conduct that will ensure their salvation on the Day of Judgment.

The second way of classifying acts reflects the fact that the *shari`ah* is meant to be used as the positive law of Muslim societies. The fundamental distinction made by Muslim jurists in this connection is between acts that are legally binding and valid and those that are of no legal effect or invalid. They also distinguish between licit acts and illicit acts warranting the imposition of penalties or exposing the actor (and potentially persons in privity with the actor) to legal liability.

Principal divisions. The two principal divisions of the *shari`ah* are based on the subject categories of legal rules. The first category is that of the *`ibadat,* or strictly religious obligations. These comprise the believer's duties vis-à-vis the deity. In this category one finds very extensive rules regarding precisely how to carry out the acts of worship and religious observances incumbent on the individual Muslim.

The other main category of *shari`ah* rules is that of the *mu`amalat,* which regulate the conduct of interpersonal relations rather than the relationship of the believer to the deity. There is considerable diversity among the sects and schools regarding the *shari`ah* rules in this category. Today there is also significant controversy about the degree to which these rules, originally formulated by medieval jurists, need to be updated and reformed in the light of modern circumstances.

Historical Development. The question of the historical development of the *shari`ah* cannot be fairly discussed without acknowledging the deep and persistent cleavage between the views set forth in modern Western scholarship and the views of the majority of Muslim scholars. The nature of the differing views and their implications will be explained in what follows.

The relation of the Qur'an to previous law. As already noted, the Qur'an provided the original kernel of *shari`ah* law. Most of the Qur'anic verses dealing with legal questions were transmitted to the Prophet in the decade after the Hijrah, or flight from Mecca to Medina (622 CE).

An unresolved dispute in Islamic jurisprudence stems from the question of whether the rules set forth in the Qur'an should be regarded as a break with the preexisting system of western Arabian customary law or whether the revelations came to modify and reform some aspects of that law while otherwise retaining it. Some Muslim scholars have concluded that the great unevenness in depth of coverage of different topics in Qur'anic legislation should be taken to imply that the resulting gaps were intended to be filled by reference to those pre-Islamic customary laws that were not changed by the Qur'an, while others see in it a fresh starting point for legal development.

The Sunni-Shi`i division. The death of the prophet Muhammad in 632 CE marked the end of the period of Qur'anic revelation to the Muslim community. Until the Umayyad dynasty (661-750) came to power, the community was ruled by four leaders known as the Rashidun, or the "Rightly Guided [Caliphs]." The assumption of leadership by the Umayyads had great consequences for both sectarian and legal developments. Repudiating the Umayyads, the Shi`i and Khariji factions both broke away from the main body of Muslims, who came to be called Sunnis, and their respective legal orientations thenceforth diverged. The Kharijis (also known as the Ibadiyah) believed that the leadership of the Muslim community should be determined by elections and that Muslims had the right to rebel against an unqualified ruler. The Shi`i faction believed that the first three caliphs had usurped the rule of the community, which in their view should have passed to the fourth of the Rashidun, `Ali ibn Abi Talib (d. 661), a cousin and son-in-law of the Prophet.

Not only did the Shi`ah believe that the caliph `Ali had been the rightful successor of the Prophet, but they also

> **The death of the prophet Muhammad in 632 CE marked the end of the period of Qur'anic revelation to the Muslim community.**

believed that leadership of the community rightfully still belonged to Ali's blood descendants after the civil war that resulted in his death and the establishment of a hereditary monarchy by the victorious Umayyads. Those of the caliph `Ali's descendants who inherited his authority were known as imams, and like him they were believed by the Shi`ah to share the same divine inspiration that had enabled the Prophet, while himself not divine, to make authoritative pronouncements on *shari`ah* law. The Shi`i community subsequently split into subsects over questions of who was entitled to succeed to the position of imam. The largest of the subsects, the Twelvers, believes that the last imam, who disappeared in 874, went into a state of occultation from which he is expected eventually to return, while the other subsects follow lines of imams whose descent has continued into the modern era.

The earliest stage of shari`ah law. For Sunnis the possibility of divine revelation and the making of new Islamic law ceased with the death of the Prophet. Subsequent generations of Muslims who were concerned with how to establish a legal system on an Islamic basis were thus faced with a problem of scarce source material. *Ad hoc* measures and a spirit of pragmatism appear to have characterized much of the decision making of the early political leaders, who also served as judges.

The view of Western scholarship is that as the new empire absorbed its early conquests of Syria, Iraq, Egypt, and Iran, it was also exposed to influences from the local civilizations, which included the very highly developed legal cultures of Romano-Byzantine law, Jewish law, Sasanid law, and the law of the Eastern Christian churches. Most Muslim scholars absolutely reject this view and take the position that *shari`ah* law owes no debt whatsoever to any non-Islamic tradition.

Ancient law schools. The jurisprudence of the Sunni branch of *shari`ah* law had its beginnings in what are called the ancient schools of law. Within a century of the Prophet's death there were prominent law schools in various cities in Iraq, Syria, and the Hejaz. It appears that the scholars in these ancient schools felt free to resort to ratiocination to develop legal rules for new situations and that they may also have been influenced in their approach to legal questions by the judicial practice of the tribunals set up by the Umayyad rulers.

The traditionist movement. Meanwhile, a second movement was under way, that of the traditionists, who began to make their influence felt in the course of the second century after the Prophet's death. The traditionists did not accept the authority of the *sunnah* of the ancient schools, nor did they accept the practice of the scholars of those ancient schools who relied on juristic opinion to resolve legal questions. Instead, the traditionists proposed that accounts relating the sayings and doings of the Prophet should be treated as legally binding statements of law. The traditionists collected traditions, known as *hadith* (pl., *ahadith*), which purported to record the Prophet's sayings, and his reactions to the different situations he had confronted.

The genuineness of the *hadith* literature is yet another point on which modern Western scholars tend to find themselves in disagreement with many of their Muslim counterparts. The prevailing view among Western scholars has been that most, if not all, of the *hadith* are pious forgeries put into circulation by traditionists of the first and second Muslim centuries with a view to creating Islamic pedigrees for rules of law that had originally been the products of juristic reasoning or judicial practice, that were inherited from Arabian custom-

ary law, or that were borrowed from other legal cultures. Western scholarship has generally evaluated the traditional science of *hadith* criticism as inadequate for differentiating historically accurate accounts from later fabrications. In the view of most Muslims, including those who have reservations about the genuineness of some of the *hadith* and the adequacy of *hadith* scholarship, these Western criticisms are excessively harsh.

The beginnings of the classical law schools. Despite the initial resistance that it encountered, the traditionists' position steadily gained ground at the expense of the influence of the ancient schools of law in the second century after the death of the Prophet. The ancient schools did not disappear but adapted in differing degrees to the new trends in legal thought. It is in the second century AH (ninth century CE) that the foundations were laid for the development of what were subsequently to become the classical *shari`ah* schools.

The oldest of the classical Sunni schools is the Maliki, which originated in Medina and was named after the prominent legal scholar and traditionist Malik ibn Anas (d. 795). Respect for the *sunnah* of Medina as the place most closely associated with the mission of the Prophet and the first Muslim community persisted in the legal thought of the Maliki school.

The Hanafi school was meanwhile developing in the context of the legal community in Kufa in southern Iraq. Although the school was named after a prominent local jurist, Abu Hanifah (d. 767), its followers actually often showed greater deference to the views of two of his disciples, Abu Yusuf (d. 798) and al-Shaybani (d. 805). The Hanafi school bore many traces of influences from the Iraqi environment in which it developed. Ha-nafi jurists attached great importance to systematic consistency in legal thought and the refinement of legal principles.

Muhammad ibn Idris al-Shafi`i (d. 820), the founder of the school that bears his name, was associated with the city of Medina. He ranks among the foremost figures in the history of Islamic legal thought and was, more than any other person, responsible for the eventual triumph of the traditionist thesis in classical Islamic legal thought. According to al-Shafi`i, the *sunnah* of the Prophet as embodied in the *hadith* totally superseded the *sunnah* of the ancient schools as a normative legal standard. Al-Shafi`i thus elevated the *sunnah* of the Prophet to the status of a source of law coequal with the Qur'an. He articulated the view, which subsequently found widespread acceptance, that the *sunnah* of the Prophet explained the meaning of the Qur'an.

Having established the Qur'an and the much more extensive corpus of *hadith* literature as the material sources of the *shari`ah*, al-Shafi`i rejected the use of juristic opinion or speculative reasoning in formulating legal principles and insisted that jurists be restricted to the use of analogical reasoning *(qiyas),* to extend principles in the sources to cover problems not explicitly addressed in the texts of the Qur'an and *hadith*. In his view, only by insisting that jurists limit themselves to such careful, piecemeal extensions of principles in the texts could one be sure that the jurists were not injecting undue subjective elements into their interpretations of *shari`ah* requirements or distorting the rules set forth in the sources. Al-Shafi`i also refused to accord any weight to juristic consensus and held that the only binding consensus would be one among all members of the Muslim community.

The last of the classical Sunni schools crystalized around Ahmad ibn Hanbal (d. 855), a traditionist from Baghdad who traveled widely among different centers of learning. Subsequent members of the Hanbali school have shared Ibn Hanbal's traditionist orientation and his concern for the consensus of the companions of the Prophet, but individual Hanbali scholars have taken diverging opinions on questions of jurisprudence.

Usul al-fiqh. With the development of the classical schools of Islamic law came the articulation of the principles of *usul al-fiqh,* the roots or sources of jurisprudence. Although the *usul* are often called sources of the *shari`ah,* only the Qur'an and the *sunnah* are material sources. Ultimately, the study of *usul al-fiqh* is concerned with establishing a science of proofs of the Islamic derivation of substantive legal principles, thus enabling the jurist to discern which legal rules are correct statements of *shari`ah* principles. The rules shown by this science to be authentically Islamic are known as the *furu` al-fiqh,* the branches of jurisprudence. The study of *usul* has been one of the major preoccupations of Muslim jurists over the centuries and continues to be so today. As the subsequent history of the development of the *shari`ah* demonstrates, the influence of al-Shafi`i on the fomulation of the classical Sunni theory of *usul al-fiqh*—a formulation that was basically complete by the ninth century—was considerable.

The first root of the *fiqh* is the Qur'an. In the prevailing view, it is to be treated as the eternal and uncreated word of God, part of his essence. Muslim jurists developed an elaborate methodology to interpret the Qur'an. Some differences in the legal principles derived from the Qur'an relate to the sectarian divisions of Islam; perhaps the most striking example lies in the laws of intestate succession among the Sunnis and the Twelver branch of the Shi`ah. In the Sunni view, the Qur'an meant to retain, with only limited modifications, the pre-Islamic Arabian scheme of agnatic succession, in which males inheriting through the male line got a major part of the estate. By contrast, the Twelver Shi`i jurists held that, in designating inheritance shares for females and the children and parents of the deceased, the Qur'an was implicitly repudiating the customary law of pre-Islamic Arabia and setting forth a completely different scheme of succession.

Al-Shafi`i succeeded in persuading subsequent jurists that the *sunnah* of the Prophet should be treated as the sec-

ond root of Islamic jurisprudence and a source co-equal with the Qur'an. It is generally accepted among Muslims not only that the Prophet was a perfect human being and thus worthy of emulation, but also that he enjoyed divine inspiration and thus could make no error in matters of religion or *shari`ah* law. As noted, challenges to the authenticity of the *hadith* literature on which the understanding of the Prophet's *sunnah* rested generated a science of *hadith* criticism to weed out unsound or dubious accounts. In addition, methodologies were worked out to reconcile seeming contradictions and inconsistencies in different *hadith* and between *hadith* and verses of the Qur'an. As in the case of the Qur'an, reading the *hadith* literature without a grasp of how orthodox Islamic scholarship interprets the legal implications of the *hadith* and the relevant jurisprudence can lead to erroneous conclusions.

Qiyas, reasoning by analogy, is a method for expanding the rules in the Qur'an and *sunnah* to cover problems not expressly addressed in the sources. Most Sunnis accept *qiyas* as the third root of *fiqh. Qiyas* involves the application of a legal ruling from a case mentioned in the Qur'an or *sunnah* to a subcase not mentioned in the text but sufficiently related to permit coverage by analogical extension. The extension of rules through *qiyas* ultimately involves human judgment, since it is first necessary to identify the reason underlying the original rule set forth in the text. In practice, jurists have been far from unanimous in their identification of these underlying reasons, with the result that they have extended the rules of the Qur'an and *sunnah* in different ways.

Twelver Shi`i jurists do not accept the Sunni model of *qiyas.* Many of them use forms of juristic reasoning that are not limited to drawing analogies in order to construe the meaning of the Qur'an and *sunnah.* Known as the Usuliyah, Twelver Shi`i jurists who believe that *shari`ah* rules can be extended by human reason have historically been opposed by another faction of jurists, the Akhbariyah, who insist that rules generated by human reason cannot be binding statements of *shari`ah* law and argue that the Qur'an and the *sunnah* of the Prophet and the Shi`i imams alone provide trustworthy guidance.

Ijma`* refers to the retroactive ratification of the correctness of an interpretation of *shari`ah requirements. Most Sunnis treat *ijma`,* which is constituted by the consensus of all the jurists of one generation, as the fourth root of *fiqh.* According to the majority Sunni position, once a legal principle has won such unanimous endorsement, it becomes definitively established and cannot be challenged by subsequent generations. Among the critics of the Sunni view of *ijma`* are the Twelver Shi`ah, who have historically taken a variety of positions on the significance of *ijma`* and how it is constituted.

**Jurists and the development of the shari`ah.** With the foundation of the classical schools of Islamic law and the formulation of the fundamental principles of *usul al-fiqh,* the *shari`ah* became a jurists' law, and exhaustive training in law and ancillary disciplines was essential for interpreting how the shari`ah applied to a given problem. The jurist, or *faqih* (pl., *fuqaha'*), came to enjoy great prestige as a result of his monopoly of expertise regarding the sacred law.

The task of interpreting the requirements of the *shari`ah* is termed *ijtihad,* and the person performing the interpretation is termed a *mujtahid*. The exercise of *ijtihad* by the early jurists defined the basic contours of the *shari`ah* by the start of the tenth century CE. It has been widely believed that at that point in Sunni jurisprudence, the *fuqaha'* were held to be bound by the solutions to legal problems reached by jurists of earlier generations on the grounds that the latter, being closer in time to the prophet Muhammad, were less likely to fall into error than scholars of later generations. This bar to reexamination of previously decided questions of *shari`ah* law has been termed "the closing of the door of *ijtihad*." Never recognized by Twelver Shi`i law, it may have inhibited innovative thought and retarded legal reform in Sunni circles, although not in the Hanbali school, where many jurists denied that they could be bound by the *ijtihad* of their predecessors. However, the common supposition that the corollary doctrine of *taqlid,* or obedience to established legal authority, immutably fixed *shari`ah* doctrines at an early stage and had a stultifying impact on the evolution of *shari`ah* law has never been conclusively established; the necessary scientific examination of the actual historical effect of *taqlid* on the ability of jurists to adjust legal doctrines and respond to the exigencies of the changing environment has not been undertaken.

The Mature Classical Law Schools. From the tenth century until the disruptive impact of European imperialism made itself felt in India in the eighteenth century, and in the other parts of the Muslim world in the nineteenth century, there was no major discontinuity in the development of doctrines of the classical law schools. Instead, one could say that this period was devoted to refining and amplifying the early treatments of Islamic jurisprudence.

As the schools matured, their doctrines became more elaborate—often, as already noted, deviating from the views of their eponymous founders. Although the schools did not require that all members adhere to precisely the same doctrines, within each school there tended to be a core of doctrines that enjoyed widespread acceptance and that embodied a distinctive approach to the resolution of legal problems.

One of the ancillary subjects essential for aspiring *fuqaha'* to master was classical Arabic, the language of God's speech in the Qur'an and the language of the *hadith*. Arabic has continued to be the essential language for the study of the *shari`ah.* No translated versions of the Qur'an or the *hadith* are adequate for use in scholarly investigations. All of the classical *fiqh* works are also in Arabic. Although recently some have become available in translations, these are of very uneven quality and must be used with great caution.

The schools spread far from their original settings. Adherence to one school or another, as well as sectarian allegiances, changed in accordance with the many political

> **One could say that this period was devoted to refining and amplifying the early treatments of Islamic jurisprudence.**

upheavals and vicissitudes suffered by the different parts of the Muslim world over the centuries, and the patterns of school and sect distribution varied significantly at different eras of Islamic history.

It should be recalled that all of the four classical Sunni schools are considered equally orthodox. Although concerns for doctrinal consistency and coherence mandated that a jurist follow the established doctrine of his school, it was not unusual for jurists to study the *fiqh* of other Sunni schools or even to refer extensively to the opinions of other schools in treatises.

Comparisons of the rules of the classical fiqh. In detail the rules of the various Sunni schools are often different enough to affect the outcome of a legal dispute. On the average legal question, the degree of doctrinal difference between a given Sunni school and a Shi`i school is often not much greater. Notwithstanding the different approaches that Sunni and Shi`i *fiqh* purport to have to the sources of law, aside from their differences regarding who should rule the Muslim community, one finds few major divergencies except on some points of religious ritual and worship, certain rules of marriage and divorce, and the laws of inheritance.

Principal figures. The founders of the schools of Sunni law and the imams of the Shi`i sects, who enjoyed the same capacity as the prophet Muhammad to make authoritative pronouncements regarding the requirements of the *shari`ah,* would have to be ranked in the fore-front of the principal figures in the history of Islamic law. Given the vast corpus of writings on the *shari`ah,* it is impossible to present any summary treatment without risking unfair omissions of outstanding figures. The following list must therefore be understood to be only a selection of persons who are representative of some of the important aspects of the Islamic legal heritage and suggestive of its variety and richness.

An early jurist who is notable for a conception of the role of the *shari`ah* different from that of his more orthodox contemporaries was Ibn al-Muqaffa` (d. 756). He unsuccessfully urged the Abbasid caliph al-Mansur to end the confusion and disparities in the *shari`ah* resulting from conflicting interpretations by the jurists of the early law schools by systematizing and codifying the *shari`ah*. He argued that the *shari`ah* should be enacted into uniform legislation that would apply throughout the caliph's domain; his failure to convince others of the correctness of his ideas meant that the *shari`ah* continued to be viewed as a jurist's law independent from and untouchable by political authorities.

Before its extinction, the once-influential Zahiri school enjoyed a flowering in Muslim Spain. The most famous and distinguished Zahiri thinker was Ibn Hazm (d. 1065), a vigorous polemicist who made many enemies in the course of his harsh attacks on the doctrines of other law schools. He challenged the authenticity of much of the *hadith* literature, rejected *qiyas* and the rules it produced, limited *ijma`* to that of the companions of the Prophet, and insisted that, in the absence of explicit commands in the Qur'an and *sunnah*, all conduct should be regarded as outside the concern of religious law.

One of the most eminent figures in Islamic intellectual history, al-Ghazali (d. 1111) examined the teachings of the *shari`ah* in relation to his own theological and philosophical views. Although he is best known for his searching inquiry into the theological fundamentals of Islam, al-Ghazali also wrote a number of important books of Shafi`i *fiqh*. In his greatest work, *Ihya' `ulum al-din* (The Revivification of Religious Sciences), al-Ghazali sought to achieve a synthesis of the teachings of Islam and to define the role of the *shari`ah* in relation to other aspects of religion. His work may constitute the most accomplished statement of what passed for Sunni orthodoxy in medieval Islam.

One of the most original medieval jurists was the Hanbali Ibn Taymiyah (d. 1328), who had an influential disciple in Ibn Qayyim al-Jawziyah (d. 1350). Ibn Taymiyah strongly attacked the doctrine of *taqlid* that bound Muslims to the interpretations of the early jurists. He argued that qualified Muslim thinkers should be free to return to the Qur'an, *sunnah*, and consensus of the companions of the Prophet and interpret them afresh. Muhammad ibn `Abd al-Wahhab (d. 1792), the leader of the puritanical Wahhabi reform movement that won many followers in Arabia and elsewhere, invoked Ibn Taymiyah's ideas in his rejection of the authority of the classical law schools and his insistence on fresh *ijtihad*.

Theories about the need to identify and follow the fundamental policies underlying *shari`ah* provisions and to interpret these provisions in a manner responsive to social needs were developed by the Maliki jurist al-Shatibi (d. 1388). Ibn Nujaym (d. 1562) was a Hanafi jurist who extracted what he saw as the fundamental *shari`ah* principles from the specific instances of applications of rules set forth in the *fiqh*. While not himself a jurist, the Mughal emperor Awrangzib `Alamgir (d. 1707) made his mark on Islamic legal history by ordering the composition of the famous *Fatawa `Alamgiriyah*, a thorough compilation of Hanafi *fiqh*.

Muhammad `Abduh (d. 1905) served as Grand Mufti of Egypt and in that capacity and in his writings on Islamic law

proposed rationalist and liberal reformist interpretations of the *shari`ah*. The influential Salafiyah movement inspired by `Abduh and led by his disciple Rashid Rida advocated a return to a purified version of the *shari`ah* meant to be more authentic than the versions developed in the course of the centuries devoted to the study of medieval *fiqh*. An example of `Abduh's approach may be seen in his famous argument that the *shari`ah* prohibits polygamy. Dismissing traditional support for polygamy among the *fuqaha'*, `Abduh returned to the Qur'an and offered a novel reading of two critical verses, which he claimed were to be taken together, although they had previously been held to apply to different issues. Surah 4:3 of the Qur'an was traditionally interpreted to allow a man to wed up to four women at a time, with a moral injunction to marry only one if he could not treat additional wives justly. Surah 4:129, which says it is not possible for a man to deal equally with his wives, was traditionally interpreted as offering reassurance to the polygamous husband that he was not sinning if he felt stronger attraction to and affection for one of his wives. Treating the injunction to deal equally with wives in the earlier verse as a legally binding precondition for a valid marriage, `Abduh used the later verse as evidence that this precondition could not in practice be met, so that in the *shari`ah*, no polygamous marriage could be valid. `Abduh's practice of interpreting *shari`ah* rules to serve the ends of enlightened social policies had far-reaching intellectual repercussions. His ideas encouraged many Middle Eastern Muslims in the first half of the twentieth century to accommodate liberal political, economic, and social reforms in their interpretations of Islamic law.

Among the principal figures of Twelver Shi`i jurisprudence, Muhammad ibn al-Hasan al-Tusi (d. 1067) wrote a number of works that became treated as classic statements of principles of Shi`i *fiqh*, as were the writings of Muhaqqiq al-Hilli (d. 1277). An important representative of the Akhbari faction of Twelver Shiism was Muhammad Baqir al-Majlisi (d. 1699), who, in addition to producing an encyclopedic statement of *fiqh*, also served as a judge and became the most powerful judicial figure under the Safavids. After the Safavids made Twelver Shiism the state religion of Iran, he, like many major Shi`i jurists, attempted to define the proper political relationship between the Shi`i clergy and the state. Al-Majlisi conceived of a powerful, independent political role for the clergy. A jurist of similar eminence, but representing very different tendencies in Twelver thought, was Murtada Ansari (d. 1864). A member of the Usuli school, which predominated in Iran in the nineteenth century, he wrote a major treatise on the Usuli theory of sources. His writings promoted the view that each layperson was bound to follow the legal interpretations of the most learned of living jurists, the *marja`-i taqlid*, whose *ijtihad* became absolutely binding on his followers. He took the view that public law was not a true concern of the *shari`ah* and stressed instead its ethical dimensions. The single most important Isma`ili jurist is Qadi al-Nu`man (d. 974), who served as the highest judge in the Fatimid empire and also wrote a great treatise of Isma`ili law.

Principal subjects. Classical *fiqh* works have similar, although not always identical, subject divisions. They begin with a section on the very extensive `*ibadat,* the obligations of the individual to God. The remaining subjects belong to the *mu`amalat* category, including (in a representative, though not exhaustive, list) marriage, divorce, manumission of slaves, oaths, criminal penalties, relations between the Muslim community and non-Muslims, treasure troves, missing persons, partnership, religious trusts, sales, guarantee contracts, transfers of debts, rules for judges, evidence, legal claims, acknowledgments of legal obligations, gifts, hire, the purchase of freedom by slaves, the defense of compulsion, incapacity, usurpation and damage of property, preemptive purchases, partition, agency, contracts for cultivation of agricultural land, slaughter of animals (for food), animal sacrifice, hateful practices, cultivation of waste lands, prohibited drinks, hunting and racing competitions, pledge, personal injuries, blood money and fines, intestate succession, and wills.

The Situation in Recent Times. The situation of the *shari`ah* in recent times has two significant dimensions, corresponding to its dual nature as a positive law and a deontology.

Beginning in the nineteenth century, the *shari`ah* was increasingly supplanted as a positive law in the legal systems of Muslim countries by borrowed European law. Historically, substantive *shari`ah* rules survived in the legal systems of modern Muslim countries in rough proportion to the importance traditionally accorded to the subject area involved, but even in those areas where the *shari`ah* was able to maintain itself, it was nonetheless subjected to some reforms. In the twentieth century, *shari`ah* reform became one of the major legal problems faced by Muslim societies and provoked protracted political and intellectual controversies. Despite popular and clerical support for retention of the *shari`ah*, governments have generally moved as quickly as political constraints permit in the direction of westernization. In the 1970s the political influence of forces favoring the retention and/or renewal of the *shari`ah* began to make itself felt, and a process of abrogating westernizing reforms and reinstating *shari`ah* law began in Libya, Iran, Pakistan, Egypt, Sudan, and Kuwait. How far the process of islamization will proceed and what the future role of the *shari`ah* as a positive law will be are at present uncertain.

Also in the twentieth century, Muslim intellectuals concerned with questions of *fiqh* subjected the medieval versions of the *shari`ah* to critical reexamination and brought new interpretive approaches to the *shari`ah* sources. The variety in modern approaches to the *shari`ah* is reminiscent of the situation prevailing in the first centuries after the death

of the Prophet, before the doctrines of the classical schools coalesced. There are still many conservative thinkers who defend the validity of the medieval *fiqh*. Arrayed against them are many who support new interpretations of what the *shari`ah* means. Adding to the fragmentation of legal doctrines is the fact that with the spread of educational opportunities and the increase in literacy, many Muslims who are educated but have not pursued a traditional course of study at a religious institution are contributing interpretations of the *shari`ah*. In other words, laypersons who belong to the modern educated elite do not necessarily feel that they must defer to the specialized knowledge of the *fuqaha'* and are prepared to challenge the monopoly formerly enjoyed by the *fuqaha'* to make authoritative statements on *shari`ah* law. As a result, it has become very difficult to make generalizations about contemporary *shari`ah* doctrines.

The westernization of legal systems in the Muslim world. The westernization of the legal systems of Muslim countries began with the impact of European imperialism on Muslim societies in the eighteenth and nineteenth centuries. The legal systems of Muslim societies subjected to direct colonial rule underwent distinctive transformations in relation to the legal culture of the colonizing power. Thus, there developed in Muslim parts of India under British rule a peculiar blend of common law and elements of the *shari`ah* that became known as Anglo-Muhammadan law. This unique, hybrid law was progressively reformed to eliminate what were regarded as the more archaic features of the shari`ah elements, and it remained influential in the legal systems of India and Pakistan after they achieved independence in 1947. Algeria was part of France from 1830 until independence in 1962, and as a French colony, it also developed a hybrid legal system, known as *le droit musulman algérien*, which incorporated many French features.

Eager to strengthen their relatively backward and weak societies in the face of threatened European domination, most elites in the independent countries of the Muslim world tended to see the *shari`ah* as an obstacle to the achievement of essential modernization. Governments first replaced those parts of the shari`ah that were viewed as impeding economic transformation, such as *shari`ah* commercial law, or those possessing features that seemed particularly archaic by modern standards, as in the cases of *shari`ah* procedural and criminal law.

It was not always the substance of *shari`ah* rules that troubled modernizers. Their arcane formulation and their diffuse mode of presentation in medieval *fiqh* treatises meant that only specialists with a mastery of medieval legal Arabic and an extensive traditional training could find answers to legal questions in a reasonably efficient manner. The cumbersome form of the *fiqh* works could be compared with the streamlined, systematized legal compendia to be found in nineteenth-century continental European codes. Growing impatience with the *fiqh* works encouraged a definite preference for codified law.

At the early stages of this legal reform process, one possibility for saving the *shari`ah* from eclipse by Western law seemed to be that of vastly simplifying and systematizing its presentation. Attempts were made to codify the *shari`ah* in the late nineteenth century, the most notable accomplishment being the promulgation of the Ottoman Majalla in 1877. Starting with some general principles of *shari`ah* law taken from Ibn Nujaym, the Majalla presents a codification of the law of obligations derived from the views of various Hanafi jurists. The Majalla proved its utility, surviving for decades in

> **The westernization of the legal systems of Muslim countries began with the impact of European imperialism on Muslim societies in the eighteenth and nineteenth centuries.**

former Ottoman territories well after they had obtained their independence from the empire. A later code, the Ottoman Family Rights Law of 1917, constituted an original attempt to codify *shari`ah* law on that subject by reference to the doctrines of more than one Sunni law school. This was the first important instance of the application of the technique of *takhayyur*, or picking and choosing the most apt principles from the doctrines of different schools and combining them in an arrangement that had no precedent in the classical *fiqh*. However, the preference for wholesale importation of Western law codes was ultimately so strong that there was soon little incentive to pursue projects for devising further codes on a *shari`ah* basis.

Another factor mandating change from the old *shari`ah*-based system of law was the international political setting. The rulers of Muslim states in the nineteenth and twentieth centuries were obliged to deal with a historical reality that was vastly different from what had been contemplated in early *shari`ah* theory. The *shari`ah* was originally conceived as a law whose application would be coextensive with religious affiliation. The world was to be converted to Islam, and there would result one community of believers with a common political allegiance and a common obligation to follow the *shari`ah*. This conception did not envisage the appearance of obstacles in the way of the realization of this ideal, such as the fragmentation of the Muslim community into separate and mutually hostile political units, the development of national identities and the rise of modern nationalism, the failure of large non-Muslim communities within the Muslim world to convert, and the need to deal with non-Muslim countries possessed of greater economic and military resources.

The continued existence of non-Muslim communities had necessitated one legal adaptation at an early stage of Islamic history, namely, the allowance of separate religious laws and courts for minority communities. Members of the minority religious communities on Muslim territory were permitted to follow their own religious laws in matters of personal status and in transactions between themselves while remaining subject to the *shari`ah* in their interactions with outsiders or in their public activities. This practice was highly developed under the Ottoman empire, where it was known as the *millet* system.

Under outside pressures, this system was further modified by a practice of according a special legal status to non-Muslims from the powerful European states: from the medieval period onward, certain states exacted from Muslim governments agreements, or "capitulations," according extraterritorial status to their nationals. Originally granted only by way of exception, capitulatory privileges were expanded apace with growing European influence. An example of the resulting system of extraterritoriality can be seen in the powerful Mixed Courts of Egypt, set up in 1875, expanded after the British occupation in 1882, and continuing until 1949. Originally established as alternatives to the "native courts" for cases involving foreigners, the Mixed Courts were able to extend their jurisdiction to a wide variety of cases, including those involving Egyptians, in instances where the courts detected some "foreign interest" in the outcome. One reason for the exaction of these concessions, the demands for which became increasingly onerous as Muslim power and wealth declined and that of the West grew, was the Western perception that the substantive provisions of the *shari`ah* were "primitive" and "barbaric" by modern European legal standards, and that the justice meted out by the traditional courts was arbitrary. European powers also objected to the inferior legal status accorded to non-Muslims under the *shari`ah* and exploited this as a pretext for political intervention. In attempts to forestall such intervention, the Ottoman sultan promulgated the Hatt-i Serïf of Gülhane in 1839 and the Hatt-i Humâyûn of 1856, officially establishing the principle that Ottoman citizens regardless of their religion should be equal in terms of their legal rights and obligations.

Retention of *shari`ah* law as the law of the land in these political circumstances thus presented obstacles to setting up a unified national legal system and entailed exposure to risks of compromising the sovereignty and national dignity of the Muslim states. The reluctance of governments to continue to make such sacrifices provided an impetus for law reform that would place legal systems in Muslim countries on a par with the emerging modern international standard.

The formation of modern nation-states in the Muslim world starting in the nineteenth century and the subsequent collapse of the Ottoman empire in World War I prompted Muslims to reassess the relationship between the *shari`ah* law and the new political entities into which the Muslim world had been divided. Although the claims of the Ottoman sultans to be the legitimate successors of the Prophet had been based on tenuous legal and historical arguments, some Sunnis saw in the sultan-caliphs an embodiment of the original *shari`ah* notion that religious allegiance—not nationality—should determine political loyalties. With the ouster of the last of the Ottoman sultan-caliphs in 1924, there ended any real chance in the Sunni world of preserving an Islamic caliphate, a government under which all Muslims would share a common political and religious allegiance.

Iran's *`ulama'* faced a momentous question at the turn of the twentieth century, when a growing movement favored the establishment of a democratic government, and the Constitutional Revolution of 1905-1909, led to the overthrow of the Qajar dynasty. To the *`ulama'*, accepting this revolution meant acknowledging the legitimacy of a government based on the principle of popular sovereignty and the lawmaking authority of the people's representatives. Such changes were seen by some as a challenge to the theoretical primacy of the imamate and the exclusive prerogative of the *`ulama'* to determine and declare the law. Other important jurists, such as Muhammad Na'ini (d. 1936), however, took the position that, pending the return of the Hidden Imam from the state of occultation, it was impossible to have a government that truly accorded with *shari`ah* ideals and that it was therefore permissible for Iran to adopt a constitutional form of government in the interim.

The acceptance of the idea in the Sunni and Shi`i camps that laws should be enacted on a national basis by representatives of the people did not by itself entail a reduction of the role of the *shari`ah*. However, the attendant pressures for systematic uniformity meant that statutes enacted by the state inevitably replaced the old, decentralized system of jurists' law. Thus, the realization that laws would henceforth be made by national governments encouraged the acceptance of the idea that there should be neutral, secular laws that could apply to all persons on the national soil. The typical pattern in Muslim countries in the nineteenth century, and more particularly in the twentieth century, was to abandon the *shari`ah* in favor of imported European law save in matters of personal status and religious trusts, and occasional token provisions in other fields such as the law of contracts.

The timing of the adoptions of Western law was related to the chronology and extent of various countries' exposure to European imperialism. The Ottoman empire was therefore the first Muslim state to adopt Western laws, followed shortly by the semiautonomous province of Egypt. The first French-based codes to be introduced in the Ottoman empire were in the areas of commercial law (1850), penal law (1858), and commercial procedure (1861). The countries that remained most insulated from such influences—Afghanistan, the Yemen, and Saudi Arabia—were the last to undertake westernization of their legal systems. In most countries, legal westernization was largely completed by the 1950s. Alone among Muslim countries, Turkey, under the leadership of Kemal Atatürk after the collapse of the Ottoman empire, abandoned the *shari`ah* in favor of a completely secular legal system. At the opposite extreme, Saudi Arabia has retained the *shari`ah*, or more specifically, Hanbali *fiqh*, as the official norm, which has prevented the government from openly undertaking legislative activity, including the enactment of a constitution.

In contemporary Muslim countries the desire on the part of the governments for legal modernization combined with the need to show respect for the *shari`ah* has resulted in various compromises. In the area of personal status, a number of reforms, by and large modest ones, have been enacted in Muslim countries with a view to improving the status of women in matters of marriage, divorce, support, and child custody. The boldest reforms in this area were enacted in the Tunisian Code of Personal Status of 1956, the Iranian Family Protection Law of 1967 (since abrogated by the revolutionary government), and the South Yemen Family Law of 1974. Only a few very cautious reforms of aspects of the *shari`ah* law of intestate succession have been undertaken.

Even Muslim states with westernized legal systems generally enshrine Islam in the national constitution as the state religion and stipulate that the *shari`ah* is a source of law or even the source of all laws. In some constitutions there are provisions stating that laws must accord with the *shari`ah* or that they may be reviewed and nullified if they are found to violate the *shari`ah*. In the past such provisions often had little more than symbolic significance, but as supporters of the shari`ah gained political strength in the 1970s throughout the Islamic world, there was increasing pressure for reinstatement of *shari`ah* rules and the abrogation of imported laws that conflict with *shari`ah* principles. Thus, the *shari`ah* is tending to be treated more and more as a fundamental law in the legal systems of Muslim countries

BIBLIOGRAPHY

As a general reference with extensive indexes and bibliography, the most reliable and comprehensive scholarly work is Joseph Schacht's *An Introduction to Islamic Law* (Oxford, 1964). Another solid and very detailed reference work is *The Encyclopaedia of Islam,* 4 vols. and supplement (Leiden, 1913-1938), and its condensed version, the *Shorter Encyclopaedia of Islam* (1953; reprint, Leiden, 1974). A new edition of the larger version has been issued alphabetically in fascicles since 1960. To use these works it is necessary to know the Arabic terms for different aspects of Islamic law.

An outstanding bibliography of works in many languages is Erich Pritsch and Otto Spies's "Klassisches Islamisches Recht," in *Orientalisches Recht* (Leiden, 1964), pp. 220-343, suppl. vol. 3 of *Der Nahe und der Mittlere Osten,* first part of *Handbuch der Orientalistik.* An old but still usable general book is Nicolas P. Aghnides's *Muhammadan Theories of Finance* (New York, 1916), with a broader scope than the title suggests. A basic anthology is

Law in the Middle East, vol. 1, Origin and Development of Islamic Law, edited by Majid Khadduri and Herbert J. Liebesny (Washington, D. C., 1955), but not all chapters are of equal quality.

Unparalleled in its depth of analysis and a uniquely valuable contribution to the comparative study of Islamic jurisprudence is Yvon Linant de Bellefonds's Traité de droit musulman comparé, 3 vols. (Paris, 1965-1973), covering aspects of contract and family law. A readable short historical survey of the development of the shari`ah from the beginnings to the modern period is Noel J. Coulson's A History of Islamic Law (1964; reprint, Edinburgh, 1971). A useful general survey work by a modern Muslim scholar—one of the few that have been well translated into English—is S. R. Mahmassani's Falsafat al-Tashri` fi al-Islam: The Philosophy of Jurisprudence in Islam, translated by Farhat J. Ziadeh (Leiden, 1961). A. A. Fyzee's Outlines of Muhammadan Law, 4th ed. (Bombay, 1974), combines a general introduction to the shari`ah with a discussion of features of Anglo-Muhammadan law.

An exceptionally thorough and critical examination of the doctrines of the Maliki school in comparison with the Shafi`i school can be found in David Santillana's Istituzioni del diritto musulmano malichita, 2 vols. (Rome, 1925-1938). It has no equal in Western languages for scope and detail of coverage of the doctrine of a classical Islamic law school. One of the great medieval encyclopedias of fiqh is that of the Hanbali scholar Muwaffaq al-Din ibn Qudamah, Al-mughni, 12 vols., edited by Taha Muhammad al-Zayni (1923-1930; reprint, Cairo, 1968-), notable for its balanced treatment of the doctrines of the different Sunni schools and still a standard reference work.

The most erudite and complete statement of the Western scholarly position on the early development of the shari`ah is Joseph Schacht's The Origins of Muhammadan Jurisprudence (Oxford, 1950). A collection of original and provocative essays of high scholarly merit and importance is Robert Brunschvig's Études d'islamologie, 2 vols. (Paris, 1976). Useful chapters on the interrelationship of theology and law in Islam can be found in the short volume edited by G. E. von Grunebaum, Theology and Law in Islam (Wiesbaden, 1971). An older work on this topic by one of the major European scholars of Islam is Ignácz Goldziher's Introduction to Islamic Theology and Law, published in German in 1910 and now translated by Andras and Ruth Hamori (Princeton, 1981).

A thorough treatment of the legal position of non-Muslims in Muslim society is Antoine Fattal's Le statut légal des non-musulmans en pays d'Islam (Beirut, 1958). A careful comparative study of the doctrines of the different law schools regarding intestate succession is Noel J. Coulson's Succession in the Muslim Family (Cambridge, 1971). The best treatment of the administration of justice in the setting of traditional Islamic civilization is Émile Tyan's Histoire de l'organisation judiciaire en pays d'Islam, 2d ed. (Leiden, 1960). The shari`ah law affecting relations of the Muslim state with the non-Muslim environment is examined in Majid Khadduri's War and Peace in the Law of Islam (Baltimore, 1955).

A number of informative chapters on Twelver Shi`i law are in Le shi`isme imamite: Colloque de Strasbourg, 6-9 mai 1968, edited by Toufic Fahd et al. (Paris, 1970). A very detailed examination of Twelver Shi`i legal doctrines is Harold Löschner's Die dogmatischen Grundlagen des shi`itischen Rechts (Cologne, 1971).

A distinguished assessment of the liberal reformist thought is Malcolm H. Kerr's Islamic Reform: The Political and Legal Theories of Muhammad Abduh and Rashid Rida (Berkeley, 1966). A wide-ranging survey of the current situation of the shari`ah in the legal systems of modern countries of the Muslim world is presented in J. N. D. Anderson's Law Reform in the Muslim World (London, 1976). Surveys of modern law in Egypt, Tunisia, Algeria, Morocco, and Turkey appear in Orientalisches Recht, cited above. An example of a

modern, enlightened approach to interpreting the requirements of Islamic law is Faz-lur Rahman's Islam and Modernity (Chicago, 1982). Chapters on Twelver Shi`i law in the context of political developments since the Islamic revolution in Iran appear in Religion and Politics in Iran, edited by Nikki R. Keddie (New Haven, 1983), and Islamic institutions and the role of the clergy in Iran are examined in detail in Shahrough Akhavi's Religion and Politics in Contemporary Iran (Albany, N. Y., 1980). Both books are useful as illustrations of the connection between questions of shari`ah interpretation and political developments in contemporary Muslim societies.

ANN ELIZABETH MAYER

Islamic Studies

These studies encompass the study of the religion of Islam and of Islamic aspects of Muslim cultures and societies. At the outset we must recognize that the word Islam itself is used in very different senses by faithful Muslims, for whom it is a norm and an ideal, and by scholars (Muslim and non-Muslim Islamicists), who refer to it as a subject of study or a kind of symbol for the focus of their inquiry, as well as by the larger public in the West who are outsiders and give different appreciations of what is felt by them to be "foreign." By extension, a sharp distinction must be made between normative Islam (the prescriptions, norms, and values that are recognized by the community as embodiments of divine guidance) and actual Islam (all those forms and movements, practices and ideas that have in fact existed in the many Muslim communities in different times and places). In other words, Islamic data sought for the sake of scholarly understanding are not the same as the ideals that Muslims as adherents of Islam attach to them, the meaning they attribute to them, or the truth they recognize in them.

The Scope of Islamic Studies

On the basis of these distinctions, it is possible to identify three different enterprises that come under the general rubric of Islamic studies:

1. The normative study of Islamic religion is generally carried out by Muslims in order to acquire knowledge of religious truth. It implies the study of the Islamic religious sciences: Qur'anic exegesis (tafsir), the science of traditions (`ilm al-hadith), jurisprudence (fiqh), and metaphysical theology (kalam). Traditionally pursued in mosques and special religious colleges (madrasahs), it is now usually carried out in faculties of religious law (shari`ah) and of religious sciences (`ulum al-din) at universities or special Islamic institutes in Muslim countries.

2. The nonnormative study of Islamic religion is usually done in universities and covers both what is considered by Muslims to be true Islam (the Islamic religious sciences in

particular) and what is considered to be living Islam (the factual religious expressions of Muslims).

3. *The nonnormative study of Islamic aspects of Muslim cultures and societies* in a broader sense is not directed toward Islam as such. It takes a wider context into consideration, approaching things Islamic from the point of view of history and literature or cultural anthropology and sociology, and not specifically from the perspective of the study of religion.

My focus in this essay is on the two nonnormative forms of study, which we may call Islamic studies in the narrower (2) and the wider (3) sense. In the narrower sense of Islamic studies, the focus is on Islamic religion as an entity in itself; the wider sense of Islamic studies deals with data that are part of given Muslim communities and are culled from the Islamic experience but that may or may not possess a religious (i. e., Islamic) significance for particular Muslim groups.

Islamic Studies as Part of Oriental Studies.
The development of Islamic studies in the nineteenth century was part of the general development of Oriental studies, commonly called "Orientalism." Oriental studies were largely patterned after the classical studies that had arisen in the sixteenth century; they were based on philology in the broad sense of the term, that is, the study of a particular culture through its texts. Islamic studies in this sense lead to nonnormative accounts of Islamic religion as described under (2), above. The field has always been a demanding one, presupposing an intensive study of Arabic and other "Islamic" languages, on the basis of which text editions can be prepared and textual studies, including textual criticism and literary history, can be carried out. Familiarity with the texts, in its turn, is a prerequisite for the further study of history. Supplemented by the study of other Islamic expressions in art and architecture and in present-day religious life, textual, historical, and anthropological research together prepare the way for the study of Islamic culture and religion.

Within the Orientalist tradition, Islamic studies were conceived of as a cultural discipline and exhibited certain assumptions of European civilization of the time, notably the superiority of Western civilization and the excellence of its scholarship. Stress has generally been laid on the differences between Islamic civilization and European culture, with an ethnocentric bias toward the latter. Beyond the interest in its origins, a certain predilection can be discerned for the "classical" period of Islamic civilization, a preference that can also be observed in other branches of Oriental studies. Specialization increasingly led to detailed studies, and the ideal of a comprehensive view of Islam often came down simply to mastering an extraordinary mass of facts.

The Nonnormative Study of Islamic Religion. The history of Islamic religion has been approached in three basic ways. A great number of historians, following the example set by Julius Wellhausen (1844-1918) in his various studies on the early Islamic period, have focused on the external history of Islam.

Another kind of historical research concentrates rather on what may be called the inner developments in Islamic religion and culture. This approach was introduced by one of the major figures in the field, Ignácz Goldziher (1850-1921), who tried to establish the basic framework of an intellectual history of Islam.

Somewhere between the general historians and the historians of religion are cultural historians of the medieval period such as Carl Heinrich Becker (1876-1933), Jörg Kraemer (1917-1961), and Gustav Edmund von Grunebaum (1909-1972), all of whom set religious developments within wider cultural frameworks, which were related in turn to political and military history. The name of Marshall G. S. Hodgson (1921-1968) should also be mentioned here because of his efforts to situate the total history of Islam within a culturally oriented world history.

Muhammad. Various approaches have developed since the mid-nineteenth-century biographies mentioned earlier. In a two-volume biography, *Mohammed* (1892-1895), Hubert Grimme gave an account of the social factors in Muhammad's life and stressed the Prophet's aspect as social reformer; Frants Buhl assembled all historical materials available at the time for a substantial biography of Muhammad in *Das Leben Muhammed* (1930; 2d ed., 1955). Tor Andrae studied later Muslim views of Muhammad as a prophet and paradigmatic figure in his *Die person Muhammeds in lehre und glauben seiner gemeinde* (1918). A breakthrough in establishing the context of Muhammad's life and work is W. Montgomery Watt's two-volume study, *Muhammad at Mecca* (1953) and *Muhammad at Medina* (1956), which focuses attention on the social and economic changes in Arabia (Mecca) that Muhammad tried to address in his prophetic activity. Maxime Rodinson's thought-provoking biography, *Mohammed* (1961; Eng. trans., 1971), interprets historical data from a similar perspective but adds a psychological dimension.

The Qur'an. After the important translation into English by George Sale (1697?-1736), published in 1734 with a famous "preliminary discourse," a great number of translations of the Qur'an have seen the light. I may mention those by Richard Bell (1937), A. J. Arberry (1955), and Marmaduke Pickthall (1930), this last being recognized by Muslims. The classic study of the Qur'anic text remains that of Theodor Nöldeke in its three-volume second edition (1909-1938), enlarged and revised with the help of colleagues. Arthur Jeffery published two important studies, *The Textual History of the Qur'an* (1937) and *The Foreign Vocabulary of the Qur'an* (1938). Rudi Paret's conscientious German translation (1962) was subsequently accompanied by his important commentary (1971). Important is Angelika Neuwirth's *Studien zur Komposition der mekkanischen Suren* (1981). John Wansbrough's *Quranic Studies* (1977) has brought the accepted theory on the early collation of the Qur'anic text into question.

The study of the Qur'an implies that of Muslim commentaries *(tafsirs)* of the Qur'an. See Helmut Gätje's *Koran und Koranexegese* (1971) and compare Mohammed Arkoun's *Lectures du Coran* (1982).

Hadith. Goldziher's critical stand in *Muhammedanische Studien,* vol. 2 (1890; Eng. trans., 1971), with regard to the historical dating of *hadiths* ("traditions") that were ascribed to Muhammad or his companions but were in fact later creations, was carried further by Joseph Schacht (1902-1969) in *The Origins of Muhammadan Jurisprudence* (1950) and led to a debate on their authenticity. Since the *sunnah* (consisting of hadiths) is the second source, after the Qur'an, of religious knowledge and law in Islam, here too Muslims are particularly sensitive to scholarly criticism from outside. See G. H. A. Juynboll's *The Authenticity of the Tradition Literature: Discussions in Modern Egypt* (1969).

Law. The structure of religious law (shari`ah) in Islam, its ideal character, and the rules of juridical reasoning by Muslim jurists were first elucidated by Goldziher and by Christiaan Snouck Hurgronje (1857-1936), who also studied its application, side by side with customary law, in Indonesia. Current trends toward islamicization in Muslim countries are again arousing interest in its juridical aspects. Among the scholars who have worked on changes in the application of the shari`ah in modern Muslim states, the names of J. N. D. Anderson and Noel J. A. Coulson deserve particular mention.

Metaphysical theology. An important study on early Muslim creeds is A. J. Wensinck's *The Muslim Creed* (1933). Georges Anawati and Louis Gardet's *Introduction a la théologie musulmane* (1948) demonstrates the structural similarity of medieval Islamic and Christian theological treatises. Here and in other works these authors stress the apologetic character of Islamic theology. On the other hand, Harry A. Wolfson, in *The Philosophy of the Kalam* (1976) is attentive to parallels between Islamic, Christian, and Jewish theological thought.

Islamic philosophy. It has become clear that there are philosophical traditions of a gnostic nature in Islam, which can be found in Shi`i intellectual circles, both Iranian Twelvers and Isma`ili Seveners. We owe this discovery mainly to the investigations of Henry Corbin (1903-1978), whose works, such as *En islam iranien* (4 vols., 1971-1972), revealed hidden but still living spiritual worlds.

Mysticism. Muslim mystical thought and experience have attracted serious scholarly attention in the West only in the course of the twentieth century, especially through the work of Reynold A. Nicholson (1868-1945) and Louis Massignon (1883-1962). The former concentrated on certain major works and their authors, such as *The Mathnawi* of Jalal al-Din Rumi; the latter focused on the development of mystical terminology and produced a four-volume biography of the tenth-century mystic al-Hallaj (1922; Eng. trans., 1982).

Islamic art and architecture. This field deserves a separate status among the disciplines making up Islamic studies, since it deals with materials other than texts and is linked with art history in general. Among scholars who deserve mention are K. A. C. Creswell (1879-1974), and Richard Ettinghausen (1906-1979), and at present Oleg Grabar and Robert Hillenbrand.

Religious institutions. In recent decades important breakthroughs have been made in the understanding of the relationships between Islamic religious institutions and the societies in which they function. In *La cité musulmane* (1954), Louis Gardet attempted to sketch the outline of the ideal society in terms of orthodox Islam, while H. A. R. Gibb and Harold Bowen addressed the eighteenth-century Muslim "religious structure," especially with regard to processes of modernization in parts 1 and 2 of *Islamic Society and the West* (1950-1957). Considerable attention has been paid to religious authorities (`ulama', Sufi shaykhs) with their different roles in society. Important in this respect is A. C. Eccel's study *Egypt, Islam and Social Change: Al-Azhar in Conflict and Accommodation* (1984).

Modern developments in Islam. It has become clear that recent developments should be described according to the country within which they occur and that although certain patterns can be established as valid for nearly all Muslim countries, in each country various groups, including the government, have their own articulation of Islam. A major contribution to this formulation is *Der Islam in der Gegenwart,* edited by Werner Ende and Udo Steinbach (1984). Events in revolutionary Iran have shown, moreover, that Islamicists in the Orientalist tradition simply have not been adequately equipped to interpret what happens in Muslim countries. On the other hand, *Religion in the Middle East: Three Religions in Concord and Conflict,* edited by A. J. Arberry (2 vols., 1969), may be mentioned here as an example of objective and impartial information about the three major religions that coexist in the Middle East.

Present-Day Islamic Studies in the Wider Sense

As in other scholarly fields and disciplines, new issues have come under discussion in Islamic studies.

Methodological Issues. Intense epistemological debates seem to have been absent from Islamic studies until the 1960s, chiefly because of the inherited pattern established by the scholarly tradition. Yet there have been other currents in Islamic studies too, and with the incorporation of textual research within a larger cultural and even religious perspective, scholars such as Louis Massignon, Gustav E. von Grunebaum, Wilfred Cantwell Smith, and Clifford Geertz have been able to see the Islamic universe in new ways. We shall point here to three matters of paramount importance: (1) the questioning of Islamic identities, (2) the increased assertion of Islamic identities, and (3) Islam as a living religion and faith.

Questioning Islamic identities. Among Western scholars who have reevaluated accepted readings of the Islamic tradition, John Wansbrough has opened up critical research with regard to the text of the Qur'an in the aforementioned *Quranic Studies* and has extended this inquiry to early Islamic history in *The Sectarian Milieu* (1978). In an even more controversial work, *Hagarism: The Making of the Islamic World* (1977), Patricia Crone and Michael Cook have argued that the historical formation of Islamic religion and civilization can be explained in terms of a complex network of Jewish-Arab relations.

Asserting Islamic identities. An intention to assert Islamic identities becomes evident in books such as *Islamic Perspectives: Studies in Honor of Sayyid Abul Ala Mawdudi,* edited by Khurshid Ahmad and Zafar Ishaq Ansari (1979), and *Islam and Contemporary Society,* edited by Salem Azzam (1982). One important contribution of Muslim scholars is that of making Muslim forms of understanding available to other Islamicists; their work should lead, moreover, to discussions within the Muslim community. Noteworthy, for instance, is Mohammed Arkoun's semiotic approach in *Lectures du Coran* (1983) and Fazlur Rahman's studies on the history of Islamic thought, for instance in his *Prophecy in Islam: Philosophy and Orthodoxy* (1979).

Islam as a living religion. Recent methodological and epistemological concerns have been stimulated in large part by a growing interest in Islam as a living religion and faith, which is connected with certain political solidarities and social and economic issues. As a result, the meaning of events and processes in Muslim countries is studied more and more in their contemporary cultural and Islamic framework. Three questions are paramount in these Islamic studies in the wider sense:

1. Which kinds of groups support and transmit various particular interpretations of Islam, and who are the leaders of these groups?
2. How do particular changes occurring in the religious institutions (or in institutions legitimized by religion) relate to changes in society at large, and what are the consequences of such social changes for the institutions concerned (and vice versa)?
3. What general social functions do various Islamic ideas and practices perform within particular Muslim societies, apart from the specifically religious meaning they are meant to have?

Such questions can also be asked about Muslim societies of the past, provided that historical data are available to answer them. Indeed, it is a mark of epistemological progress that subjects excluded from investigation fifty years ago for lack of methodological tools can now come under the purview of Islamic studies.

Tradition in a wider sense. The notion of tradition, too, has attracted new attention in Islamic studies among both historians and anthropologists, who recognize that successive generations of Muslims have interpreted their lives, their world, and history through the religious and cultural framework, or "tradition," of the society into which they have been born. On the one hand, we have the normative "great" tradition with elements ranging from the Qur'an and parts of the *shari`ah* to particular creeds, practices of worship, and paradigmatic figures and episodes in Islamic history. On the other hand, for each region we must add numerous elements of the local "little" tradition, including legendary events in the history of the region, miracles and blessings of particular saints, the meritorious effect of particular practices, and so on, all of which constitute local, popular religion.

New Topics of Research. As a result of these and other methodological issues, new topics of research have come within our horizon, of which the following may be mentioned as examples.

Revitalization of Islam. Different forms of Islamic revitalization have been signaled by both Muslim and non-Muslim observers in a number of countries. While the media have addressed the political and "exotic," even abhorrent dimensions of this revitalization, scholarly investigation is needed to distinguish various sectors of life and society in which such revitalization takes place (as well as its religious from its nonreligious aspects) according to both Islamic criteria and criteria developed by the scientific study of religion. Preceding movements of reform and renewal should be taken into account.

Ideologization of Islam. During the last hundred years a great number of Islamic ideologies have developed; what for centuries was considered a religion based on revelation seems to have evolved in certain quarters into an Islamic system or ideology of a cognitive nature, in which the dimension of faith and religious knowledge seems to have given place to a definite set of convictions and values. This ideologization responds to a need for rationalization and may serve apologetic purposes, against criticism from the West, for instance, or against secularizing trends within society. Often the predicate "Islamic" suggests that a correspondence is sought between the older cultural and religious tradition and the solutions proposed for the problems of the present.

Islam, political action, and social and economic behavior. After a period of Western domination in which a political articulation of Islam was mostly impossible, Islam has again come to play various political roles, in both more conservative and more progressive quarters, usually bypassing the authority of those schooled in religious law (the `ulama`). So the question arises: what are the possibilities and the limits of the political, social, and economic use and abuse of Islam? Islam has permitted very different economic systems (including a form of capitalism) as Maxime Rodinson (1966) has demonstrated. We may go on to ask in what ways Islam can be related positively or negatively to economic development, and to determine what basic values economic development is subordinated to within the Islamic framework. That Islam is articulated basically as a way of life and as social behavior has become evident again, for instance, by the recurrence of the veil and by expressions of solidarity with Muslims in other parts of the world.

Muslim self-interpretations. In the course of the history of Islamic studies, serious hermeneutical mistakes, that is, errors of interpretation, have been made. Western scholars for instance tended to reify Islam, forgetting that "Islam" in itself does not exist, that "Islam" is always Islam *interpreted*, and that Muslims keep this interpretive process going. Much more attention should be paid to what Muslim authors, speakers, groups, and movements actually mean when they express themselves in particular situations, free from interpretations or explanations imposed from outside. Carrying out study in collaboration with Muslim researchers is appropriate here as in many fields.

Interaction and image formation. It is perhaps a sign of renewal of Islamic studies that Islam is no longer studied only as an isolated culture, tradition, and religion that may have assimilated outside influences, but that more attention is given to the spread of Islam, processes of interaction with other communities, and Muslim images of other religions and of the non-Muslim world generally. This direction of inquiry is evidenced first by works of Arab scholars like Albert Hourani, Abdallah Laroui, and others, as well as by publications like Bernard Lewis's T*he Muslim Discovery of Europe* (1982) and *Euro-Arab Dialogue: Relations between the Two Cultures*, edited by Derek Hopwood (1985). This area of study has been opened up as a consequence of the recognition of Islamic religion and culture as an autonomous partner in international religious and cultural relations, which are linked, in turn, to political and other relationships. The recent establishment of considerable Muslim communities living side by side with a non-Muslim majority in a number of Western societies may also have made both North America and Western Europe more sensitive to the plurality of religions and cultures in daily life.

BIBLIOGRAPHY

Full bibliographic data for the literature referred to in the section on the history of Islamic studies, above, can be found in Charles J. Adams's "Islamic Religious Tradition," in *The Study of the Middle East*, edited by Leonard Binder (New York, 1976), pp. 29-96. For further bibliographic data, see *A Reader's Guide to the Great Religions*, 2d ed., edited by Charles J. Adams (New York, 1977), pp. 407-466.

Islamic Studies: A Tradition and Its Problems, edited by Malcolm H. Kerr (Malibu, Calif., 1983), deals admirably with the full scope of Islamic studies. On the history of Islamic studies, see Maxime Rodinson's "The Western Image and Western Studies of Islam," in *The Legacy of Islam*, 2d ed., edited by Joseph Schacht with C. E. Bosworth (Oxford, 1974), pp. 9-62. Rodinson has elaborated his views in his *La fascination d'Islam* (Paris, 1980).

My own study, *L'Islam dans le miroir de l'Occident*, 3d ed. (Paris, 1970), focuses on five prominent Islamicists: Goldziher, Snouck Hurgronje, Becker, Macdonald, and Massignon. This work may be supplemented with my essay "Changes in Perspective in Islamic Studies over the Last Decades," *Humaniora Islamica* 1 (1973): 247-260.

The following works treat the development of Islamic studies in particular European countries. England: A. J. Arberry's *Oriental Essays: Portraits of Seven Scholars* (New York, 1960). France: Claude Cahen and Charles Pellat's "Les études arabes et islamiques," in *Cinquante ans d'orientalisme en France, 1922-1972*, a special issue of *Journal asiatique* 261 (1973): 89-107. Germany: Rudi Paret's *The Study of Arabic and Islam at German Universities: German Orientalists since Theodor Nöldeke* (Wiesbaden, 1968) and Johann Frick's *Die arabischen Studien in Europa* (Leipzig, 1956). Netherlands: J. Brugman and F. Schrödder's *Arabic Studies in the Netherlands* (Leiden, 1979). Spain: James T. Monroe's *Islam and the Arabs in Spanish Scholarship, Sixteenth Century to the Present* (Leiden, 1970).

Islamic studies in the West have not escaped criticism by Muslim Islamicists. See, for instance, A. L. Tibawi's *English-Speaking Orientalists: A Critique of Their Approach to Islam and Arab Nationalism* (Geneva, 1965) and *Second Critique of English-Speaking Orientalists and Their Approach to Islam and the Arabs* (London, 1979). The following works also deserve mention in this connection: Anouar Abdel Malik's "Orientalism in Crisis," *Diogenes* 44 (1963): 103-140; Abdallah Laroui's *The Crisis of the Arab Intellectual* (Berkeley, 1976); Edward Said's *Orientalism* (New York, 1978); and Sadiq al-Azm's "Orientalism and Orientalism in Reverse," *Hamsin* 8 (1981): 5-26.

Finally, I have discussed methodological issues at greater length in "Islam Studied as a Sign and Signification System," *Humaniora Islamica* 2 (1974): 267-285; "Islamforschung aus religionswissenschaftlicher Sicht," in XXI. *Deutscher Orientalistentag, 24-29. März 1980 in Berlin: Ausgewählte Vorträge*, edited by Fritz Steppat (Wiesbaden, 1982), pp. 197-211; and "Assumptions and Presuppositions in Islamic Studies," *Rocznik Orientalistyczny* 43 (1984): 161-170. For an application, see *Islam: Norm, ideaal en werkelykheid*, edited by me (Weesp, Netherlands, and Antwerp, 1984).

JACQUES WAARDENBURG

ISRAELITE RELIGION

General Features

Unique in many ways, Israelite religion is most remarkable for its monotheism. The difference between monotheism and polytheism is not only in number—one god versus a plurality of gods—but in the character and nature of the deity. In contradistinction to the polytheistic system according to which gods are subject to biological rules (the existence of male and female in the divine sphere, which means procreation, struggle for survival, etc.), the God of Israel is transcendent, that is, beyond the sphere of nature and therefore not subject to physical and biological principles.

The transcendence of God explains the absence of mythology in the religion of Israel. The transcendent character of the God of Israel explains, too, the objection of Israelite religion to magic, which was so prominent in polytheistic religions. God's will cannot be revealed unless he himself wishes to do so; his will cannot be revealed through magic, which draws its power from mystic powers not subordinated to the deity.

It is true that the biblical stories as well as the biblical cult contain magical elements. There are many allusions to the

> **Another transcendent feature of Israelite monotheism is the prohibition against representing God by visual symbol or image.**

marvelous transformation of objects: the staffs of Moses and Aaron become serpents (*Ex.* 4:2-4, 7:9-10); Moses divides the sea with his staff (*Ex.* 14:16); Elisha's staff is supposed to revive the Shunammite's son (*2 Kgs.* 4:29); and the three arrows that Joash, the king of Israel, drove into the ground gave him three victories over Aram (*2 Kgs.* 13:14-19). However, all these acts are considered wondrous signs from God. The wonder is seen as "the hand" and power of God and not as originating in the action itself or in the power of the sorcerer, as was the case in pagan religions (cf. *Ex.* 4:1-4, 7:8-10, et al.). Thus, for example, Elisha's staff performs wonders only when accompanied by prayer (contrast *2 Kgs.* 4:29-31 with 4:32-35).

Another transcendent feature of Israelite monotheism is the prohibition against representing God by visual symbol or image: "You shall not make for yourself a sculptured image [pesel] or any likeness" (*Ex.* 20:4, *Dt.* 5:8, et al.). The god which is beyond nature and cosmos cannot be represented by anything earthly and natural.

It is this feature which makes the Israelite religion philosophical, as conceived by the Greeks. For example, it was the observation of Theophrastus (c. 372-287 BCE), a disciple of Aristotle, that "being philosophers by race, [the Jews] converse with each other about 'the Divine' [to theion]" (Menachem Stern, *Greek and Latin Authors on Jews and Judaism,* vol. 1, 1974, p. 10). "The Divine" denotes here the philosophical concept of the one force that governs the world in contrast to the popular belief in various mythical deities.

Historical Development until the Temple Cult

The Religion of the Patriarchs. Tradition considers Abraham the father of Yahvistic monotheism but this has no basis in the Bible itself. On the contrary, the biblical documents show an awareness of a gap between the religion of the patriarchs and the Yahvistic national religion of Israel. The name of God, *Yahveh* (preserved only unvocalized in the texts, i. e., YHVH) is not known before Moses (*Ex.* 3:13f., 6:2ff.), and the nature of the patriarchal creed is completely different from that of Moses and later Israelites. The god of the patriarchs is tied to person and family; the god is called God of Abraham, Isaac, or Jacob or "the God of the father" (*Gn.* 26:24, 28:13, 31:42, 32:10, 46:3, 49:25), as is appropriate to a wandering family.

Historical Circumstances of the Birth of Monotheism. As is well known, the term *Hebrews* (`Ivrim) is associated with the term *Habiru,* which designates the nomadic population in the ancient Near East during the second millennium BCE. The "god of the Hebrews" was worshiped by all sorts of nomads in the area of Sinai and the Negev: the Midianites and Kenites, as well as the Israelites. Most important in this respect is the new, extrabiblical evidence which came to light in the last decades. In the Egyptian topographical lists of King Amenhotep III (1417-1379 BCE) discovered in the temple of Amon at Soleb in Nubia as well as in the list of King Ramses II (1304-1237 BCE) discovered at Amarah West, we find "the land of nomads [of] Yahveh," along with "the land of nomads [of] Seir" (see Raphael Gibeon, *Les bédouins Shosu des documents égyptiens,* Leiden, 1971, nos. 6a, 16a). A land of nomads associated with Yahveh alongside the land of Edom (Seir) reminds us of the old traditions of Israel, according to which Yahveh appeared from Sinai, Edom, Teman, Paran, and Midian (*Dt.* 33:2, *Jgs.* 5:4, *Hb.* 3:3-7). The fact that Yahveh's revelation is associated with places scattered over the whole Sinai Peninsula as well as over the Edomite territory east of Sinai seems to indicate that Yahveh was venerated by many nomads of Sinai and southern Palestine and that "the land of nomads of Yahveh" refers to the whole desert to the east of the delta. To be sure, the god revealed to Moses and adopted by the Israelites reflects a unique phenomenon. Monotheism did come out of Israel and not out of Edom or Midian. However, in the light of the new evidence, one must consider the existence of some kind of proto-Israelite belief in Yahveh in the wilderness region of Sinai and Edom (cf. S. Herrmann, "Der Name Jhw in den Inschriften von Soleb." *Fourth World Congress of Jewish Studies,* vol. 1, Jerusalem, 1967, pp. 213-216; B. Mazar, "Yahveh came out from Sinai," *Temples and High Places in Biblical Times: Proceedings of the Colloquium in Honor of the Centennial of Hebrew Union College-Jewish Institute of Religion, Jerusalem, 14-16 March 1977,* ed. A. Biran, 1981, pp. 5-9).

All this shows that there were close relations between the Israelites and other nomads in the desert, and, as we have indicated above, Yahveh's appellation in *Exodus,* "the god of the Hebrews," seems to support this notion.

Exodus from Egypt. Among the nomadic tribes in the land of Yahveh (that is, the Sinai Peninsula), the Israelites were under Egyptian control, and, as I have indicated, the religion of Israel actually took shape in the course of a struggle with Egyptian religion and culture. The struggle of the Israelite tribes with the Egyptians comes to full expression in the story about the liberation of Israel from "the house of bondage"—that is, the Exodus, which became the hallowed Israelite epic.

Early Cultic Worship. According to Pentateuchal sources, God revealed himself to the people on a specific mountain called Sinai or Horeb. However, ancient poems hail several places in the Sinai Desert as places of theophany. For example, *Deuteronomy* 33 speaks of YHVH coming from Sinai, Seir, and Mount Paran (33:2; cf. *Jgs.* 5:4-8). In *Habakkuk* 3 we read that God comes from Teman and from Mount Paran, and in the continuation of this poem Cushan and Midian are also mentioned. In all of these instances God sets out from his holy abode (on the mountain) to save his people, not to give laws as in the later prosaic sources. Furthermore, in these poems the deity sets out not from a single hallowed place (e.g., Sinai or Horeb) but from various places scattered throughout the Sinai Peninsula and the northwestern Arabian Desert. It seems that there were several holy mountains in this area that served the nomads who venerated YHVH.

Excavational findings suggest that the Sinai Desert was the site of a long tradition of cultic practices; Mount Sinai was only one of many cultic sites. The elaborate biblical descriptions of the cultic practices at Mount Sinai may reveal aspects of worship at such sites throughout the desert. The center of the tribal worship was the Mountain of God, ascent to which was allowed only to the priesthood and the elders (*Ex.* 24:1-2, 24:9, 24:14). Access to the godhead was the privilege of the prophet Moses alone (*Ex.* 3:5, 19:9-13, 19:20-22, 24:15, 33:21-23, 34:2ff.).

Covenant between God and Israel. The covenant of Sinai, which became so central in the religion of Israel, denotes not a bilateral agreement between the deity and the people but rather a commitment by the people to keep the law of YHVH as it is inscribed on tablets and found in the "Book of the Covenant" (*Ex.* 24:3-8). The word *covenant* (Heb., *berit*) means a bond or obligation that is accompanied by a pledge or oath and that is validated by sanctions, dramatized curses, threats, and the like performed in specific cultic rites.

A very old Mosaic cultic rite not repeated in later periods is the blood covenant as described in *Exodus* 24:3-8. After Moses builds an altar at the foot of Mount Sinai and erects twelve stone pillars, he prepares sacrifices and uses the blood of the animal sacrifices for the covenantal ceremonies.

Half of the blood he sprinkles on the altar (and, apparently, on the stone pillars), and the other half he puts into basins in order to sprinkle it over the people. Then he declares: "This is the blood of the covenant that the Lord [YHVH] has cut with you" (*Ex.* 24:8). The fact that the blood ritual is found only in the Sinaitic ceremony may teach us that it belongs to the ancient nomadic reality and therefore reflects a Mosaic background.

Revelation at Sinai. In the description of the Sinaitic cult we find a clear distinction between the place of revelation on Mount Sinai and the place of worship below the mountain. This situation is reflected in the tradition about the tent of meeting (*ohel mo`ed*) at Sinai. According to *Exodus* 33:7-11, Moses pitches the tent of meeting outside the camp, and there it serves as a place of encounter between God and Moses. This contrasts with the later description of the Tabernacle by the Priestly source, which conceives the tent of meeting as the sanctuary in the middle of the camp, where Moses meets God (cf. *Ex.* 29:42-43; 40:34-35). The two phenomena, revelation and cult, which previously existed separately, amalgamated here, a situation which prevailed in later times when prophecy and cult joined hands in the Israelite and Judahite temples.

The place of revelation, be it the top of the mountain or the tent outside the camp, was out of bounds to the people. Indeed, according to the Sinaitic tradition it was Moses alone who received the words of God (the Decalogue), and as mediator, he delivered them afterward to the people.

That the words written on the tablets of the covenant are identical with the commandments of *Exodus* 20 is explicitly said in *Deuteronomy* 5:19, 9:10, and 10:4, and there is no reason to suppose that this was differently understood in former times. A series of cultic commandments in *Exodus* 23:10-19 (paralleled in *Exodus* 34:10-26) has been considered the original Decalogue by some scholars, who see the traditional Decalogue (*Ex.* 20:1-14) as a later ethical decalogue inspired by prophetic circles. But there is no warrant for this supposition. The division of the series of laws in *Exodus* 23:10-19 and 34:10-26 into ten discrete commandments is highly controversial, and the idea that a "cultic decalogue" should be more ancient than an "ethical" one has no basis at all.

The Ten Commandments: Their Essence and Function. From the point of view of content and form there is no difference between the Ten Commandments and other laws. The various law codes of the Bible contain the same injunctions which are attested in the Decalogue in both its versions. The prohibitions against idolatry and swearing falsely, the observance of the Sabbath, the honoring of parents, and the prohibitions against murder, adultery theft, and false witness—all these appear again and again in the various laws of the Pentateuch. The only exception is the injunction against coveting a neighbor's property, and this is indeed indicative of the particular nature of the Decalogue.

Though we do not have clear evidence of when the Decalogue was crystallized and accepted, it seems to be very old. It is referred to by the eighth century BCE prophet Hosea (*Hos.* 4:2) and later by Jeremiah (*Jer.* 7:9) and is cited in two ancient psalms (*Ps.* 50:7, 50:18-19, 81:9-11), and one cannot deny that it might date from the beginning of Israelite history; it may even be traced back to Moses, the founder of Israel's religious polity.

A clear parallel in the ancient world to such a phenomenon as Moses, the prophet who reveals divine commands to the people, is to be found in a Greek document of the Hellenistic period. In a private shrine of the goddess Agdistis in Philadelphia (modern-day Alasehir), in Asia Minor, an oath inscribed in a foundation stone of the sanctuary was found which contains injunctions similar to the ethical part of the Decalogue: not to steal, not to murder, not to commit adultery, and so on. These were revealed in a dream by the goddess Agdistis to the prophet Dionysius, who inscribed them on the stela of the sanctuary (see F. Sokolowski, *Lois sacrées de l'Asie Mineure,* 1955, no. 20, ll. 20ff.). It is also said in the inscription that whoever will violate one of the mentioned commandments will not be allowed to enter the shrine. Although this document is of late origin (first century BCE), it undoubtedly reveals ancient religious practice which is typologically similar to that of the Decalogue: a concise set of commandments revealed by a god to his prophet, who is to transmit them to the believers.

Covenant between God and Israel. The obligation of Israel toward God to keep his law equals the pledge to show loyalty to him. Besides the Mosaic covenant, which is based on the promise to observe the laws, we find in *Joshua* 24 a covenant which stipulates exclusive loyalty to the one God. Joshua's covenant, which took place in Shechem, modern-day Nablus (cf. *Dt.* 27 and *Jos.* 8:30-35), is mainly concerned with the choice of the God of Israel and the observance of strict loyalty toward him: "He is a jealous God. . . . if you forsake the Lord and serve alien gods, . . . he will make an end of you" (*Jos.* 24:19-20). This covenant, which was concerned with loyalty and made at the entrance to the Promised Land, was especially necessary because of the exposure to Canaanite religion and the danger of religious contamination.

In fact, the Shechemite covenant described in *Joshua,* which is associated—as indicated—with the foundation ceremony between mounts Gerizim and Ebal (cf. *Dt.* 27, *Jos.* 8:30-35), is close in its character to the covenant of the plains of Moab, presented in *Deuteronomy.* This covenant takes place before the crossing into the Promised Land and is defined as an act of establishing a relationship between God and Israel (*Dt.* 26:17-19, 27:9-10, 29:12; see expecially *Dt.* 27:9: "This day you have become a people belonging to the Lord your God").

The two covenants presented in the Pentateuch, the one at Sinai (*Ex.* 19-24) and the other at the plains of Moab in *Deuteronomy,* were patterned after the type of covenant prevalent in the ancient Near East between suzerains and vassals.

The notion of exclusive loyalty that is characteristic of the monotheistic belief has been dressed not only in the metaphor of the relationship between suzerain and vassal but also in the metaphor of the relationships between father and son and husband and wife. Just as one can be faithful only to one suzerain, to one father, and to one husband, so one can be faithful only to the God of Israel and not to other gods as well. The prophets elaborated the husband-wife metaphor in describing the relations between God and Israel (*Hos.* 3, *Jer.* 3:1-10, *Ez.* 16, 23).

Centralization of the Cult: The Great Turning Point

Although there had existed in Israel a central shrine since the times of the Judges (cf. the temple at Shiloh, *1 Samuel* 1-2), small chapels and altars were also allowed. We hear about the patriarchs building altars in various places in the land of Canaan (*Gn.* 12:7-8, 13:18, 26:25), and we also find that during the time of the judges altars were built in the fields and on rocks (*Jgs.* 6:24, 13:19; *1 Sam.* 19:35). These other shrines were not prohibited; on the contrary, from Elijah's words at his encounter with God at Horeb (*1 Kgs.* 19:10, 19:14), we learn that the destruction of an altar dedicated to Yahveh is tantamount to killing a prophet of Yahveh. Elijah himself is praised because of his restoration of an altar to Yahveh on Mount Carmel (*1 Kgs.* 18).

The act of Hezekiah was actually the culmination of a process which started in the northern kingdom of Israel in the ninth century. That was the period of the struggle initiated by the prophets against the Tyrian god, Baal (*1 Kgs.* 17-19, *2 Kgs.* 9-10). From this struggle emerged the polemic against the golden calves erected in Dan and in Bethel (*1 Kgs.* 12:28ff.) and, finally, an iconoclastic tendency which affected the high places and altars all over the country, developing further a tendency to purge Israelite religion of pagan elements.

The abolition of the provincial sites created the proper atmosphere for the spiritualization of worship as reflected in *Deuteronomy.* Even the Temple in Jerusalem was now conceived not as the physical house of the Lord but as the house in which God establishes his name (*Dt.* 12:11, 12:21, et al.). Furthermore in the reform movement of Hezekiah and Josiah, which is reflected in *Deuteronomy,* there is a shift from sacrificial ritual to prayer. The author of *Deuteronomy* is not concerned with the cultic activities in the Temple, such as daily offerings, burning incense, kindling the lamp, and so on. On the other hand, he is very interested in worship that involves prayer (*Dt.* 21:7-9, 26:5-10, 26:13-15), because he sees in liturgy the most important form of worship.

The Religion of the Book: Scribes and Wise Men. Hallowed as the "book of the torah" *(sefer ha-torah)* written by Moses (*Dt.* 31:9), *Deuteronomy* became the authoritative, sanctified guidebook for Israel. It was the first book canonized by royal authority and by a covenant between God and the nation, established by the people gathered in Jerusalem in 622 BCE, under the auspices of King Josiah (*2 Kgs.* 23:1-3). Only after other books were appended to *Deuteronomy* did the term Torah refer to the whole Pentateuch.

The sanctification of the holy writ brought with it the need for scribes and scholars who had the ability to deal with written documents. It is in the period of the canonization of *Deuteronomy* that we hear about scribes *(soferim)* and wise men *(hakhamim)* preoccupied with the written Torah (*Jer.* 8:8). After the return to Judah of many Jews from exile in Babylonia, the man who brought with him the book of the Torah and disseminated it in Judah was Ezra the scribe (*Ezr.* 7:6, 7:11). Since the scribes and wise men were preoccupied with education in general, they did not limit themselves to sacred literature but also taught wisdom literature. The latter consists of didactic instructions on the one hand and specu-

> ## Wisdom literature was canonized and turned into an integral part of the holy writ.

lative treatises on justice in the world (e.g., the *Book of Job*) and the meaning of life (e.g., *Ecclesiastes*) on the other. It is true that wisdom literature is cosmopolitan in nature and therefore addresses man as such and does not refer at all to Israel or to other sacred national concepts. However, this did not deter the scribes and wise men in Israel from incorporating this literature into their lore.

Wisdom literature was canonized and turned into an integral part of the holy writ. Furthermore, it was identified with the revealed Torah (cf. *Sir.* 24). *Deuteronomy,* in which the subject of education plays a central role, defines *torah* as wisdom (*Dt.* 4:6), and as has been shown (Weinfeld, 1972, pp. 260ff.), contains a great many precepts borrowed from wisdom tradition. The amalgamation of the divine word of Torah with the rational values of wisdom turned the law of Israel, especially the Deuteronomic law, into a guide of high moral and humane standards.

The Crystallization of Judaism: The Postexilic Period. The period of exile and restoration left its deep marks on the people and changed their spiritual character. Because the exiles were deprived of sacrificial worship as a result of the principle of centralization of worship in Jerusalem, the spiritual, abstract nature of the religion was enhanced. The shift from sacrifice to prayer was facilitated by the very act of centralization, as shown above; however, as long as sacrifice was being practiced in the chosen place in Jerusalem, religion was still tied to the Temple. In the religious vacuum created following the destruction of the First Temple, stress

came to be laid on the spiritual side of religion, and thus the way was paved for the institution of the synagogue, which is based on prayer and the recital of holy scripture. All this leaves no doubt that the synagogue service was already taking shape in the fifth century BCE.

Another important factor which shaped the character of Second-Temple Judaism was the impact of prophecy. The fact that prophets of the First-Temple period had predicted the return to Zion after a period of exile added to the glorification of the prophets and to the trust in their words. People began to believe that the prophecies about Jerusalem as the spiritual center of the world would also be realized and that the nations would recognize the God of Israel and finally abandon their idolatrous vanities.

Observance of the Torah. The exiles took seriously not only the demand for exclusive loyalty to the God of Israel, which meant complete abolition of idolatry and syncretism, but also the positive commands of God embodied in the law of Moses. They felt obliged not only to fulfill the law in a general sense but to do exactly as written in the book.

At this time the Tetrateuch, the first four books of the Pentateuch, was added to the "Book of the Torah," or *Deuteronomy,* which had been sanctified before the exile, with the reform of Josiah in 622 BCE. The Tetrateuch was composed of ancient documents that had already been codified in literary sources, such as the Yahvistic-Elohistic source and the Priestly code. After adding these sources to *Deuteronomy,* the name "Book of the Torah" was extended to the whole of the Pentateuch, namely, the Torah, which was thus also taken as comprising the "Book of Moses."

The Pentateuch, then, comprised various codes representing different schools or traditions and different periods which sometimes contradicted each other. However, all of them were equally obligatory. How then would one fulfill two contradictory laws? According to the Priestly code, for example, one has to set aside a tenth of his crop for the Levites (*Nm.* 18:21f.), while the Deuteronomic code (written after centralization of the cult) commands one to bring the tithe to Jerusalem and consume it in the presence of the Lord (*Dt.* 14:22ff.). These laws reflect different social and historical circumstances, but since both were considered to belong to the law of Moses, both were authoritative.

No less a problem was the exact definition of the ancient law in order to apply it to life circumstances. Thus, for example, the commandment "you shall not do any work on the seventh day" (*Ex.* 20:9) is quite vague. What does work mean? Is drawing water from the well considered work (as in *Jubilees* 50.8)? Interpretation of the law split the people into sects; the most practical were the Pharisees, who fixed thirty-nine chief labors forbidden on the Sabbath (*Shab.* 7.2), and thus tried to adjust the law to life. The Essenes, however, were much more stringent in their understanding of work forbidden on the Sabbath. Before the Maccabean Revolt

(166-164 BCE), making war was forbidden on the Sabbath; in the Maccabean times, when the nation fought for its existence, the people learned that it could not survive without permitting themselves to fight on the Sabbath.

The struggle for the correct interpretation of the Torah was actually the struggle to fulfill the will of the Lord, and in this goal all Jews were united.

BIBLIOGRAPHY

Albright, William F. *Yahweh and the Gods of Canaan.* London, 1968.

Alt, Albrecht. *Der Gott der Väter: Ein Beitrag zur Vorgeschichte der israelitischen Religion.* Stuttgart, 1929.

Cross, Frank Moore. *The Ancient Library of Qumrân and Modern Biblical Studies.* Rev. ed. Garden City, N. Y., 1961.

Cross, Frank Moore. *Canaanite Myth and Hebrew Epic: Essays in the History of the Religion of Israel.* Cambridge, Mass., 1973.

Eissfeldt, Otto. *The Old Testament: An Introduction.* Translated from the third German edition by Peter R. Ackroyd. Oxford, 1965.

Fohrer, Georg. *History of Israelite Religion.* Translated by David E. Green. Nashville, 1972.

Gaster, Theodor H. *Myth, Legend, and Custom in the Old Testament.* New York, 1969.

Kaufmann, Yehezkel. *History of the Religion of Israel* (in Hebrew). 8 vols. in 6. Jerusalem, 1937-1956. Translated by Moshe Greenberg as *The Religion of Israel: From Its Beginnings to the Babylonian Exile.* New York, 1972.

Mowinckel, Sigmund. *The Psalms in Israel's Worship.* 2 vols. Translated by D. R. Thomas. Oxford, 1962.

Noth, Martin. *Gesammelte Schriften zum Alten Testament.* Munich, 1960.

Pedersen, Johannes. *Israel: Its Life and Culture.* 4 pts. Translated by Aslaug Mo/ller and Annie I. Fausbo/ll. Oxford, 1926-1947; reprint, Oxford, 1959.

Rad, Gerhard von. *Gesammelte Studien zum Alten Testament.* Munich, 1958.

Rad, Gerhard von. *Old Testament Theology.* 2 vols. Translated by D. M. G. Stalker. New York, 1962-1965.

Vaux, Roland de. *Les institutions de l'Ancien Testament.* 2d ed. Paris 1961. Translated by John McHugh as *Ancient Israel: Its Life and Institutions.* London, 1965.

Vaux, Roland de. *Histoire ancienne d'Israel* (1971). Translated by David Smith as *The Early History of Israel.* Philadelphia, 1978.

Weinfeld, Moshe. "The Covenant of Grant in the Old Testament and in the Ancient Near East." *Journal of the American Oriental Society* 90 (April-June 1970): 184-203.

Weinfeld, Moshe. *Deuteronomy and the Deuteronomic School.* Oxford, 1972.

Weinfeld, Moshe. "Social and Cultic Institutions in the Priestly Source against Their Ancient Near Eastern Background." In *Proceedings of the Eighth World Congress of Jewish Studies,* pp. 95-129. Jerusalem, 1983.

Wellhausen, Julius. *Prolegomena to the History of Israel.* Translated by J. Sutherland Black. Edinburgh, 1885. Reissued as *Prolegomena to the History of Ancient Israel.* New York, 1957.

Zimmerli, Walther. Gottes Offenbarung: *Gesammelte Aufsätze zum Alten Testament.* Munich, 1963.

MOSHE WEINFELD

JAINISM

History. There remains no objective document concerning the beginnings of Jainism. The date of Maha-vira's death ("entry into *nirvana*"), which is the starting point of the traditional Jain chronology, corresponds to 527/526 BCE, but some scholars believe it occurred about one century later. In any case, the Jain community was probably not "founded" solely by Mahavira. Rather, his adherents merged with the followers of a previous prophet (Parsva); reorganizations and reforms ensued and a fifth commandment was added to the older code, as was the practice of confession and repentance; nakedness came to be recommended to those among the believers who took the religious vows, although apparently it was not imposed on Parsva's disciples.

In 79 CE, the community split into two main churches—the Digambara, "sky-clad" (and thus naked), and the Svetambara, "white-clad." By the time of the separation, however, the doctrine had been fixed for the whole community; this accounts for the fundamental agreement in the main tenets professed by the Svetambaras and the Digambaras. On the other hand, epigraphic and literary records prove that religious "companies" *(gana)* already existed, subdivided into *sakhas* ("branches") and *kulas* ("families" or "schools"). The remarkable organization of Mahavira's church has proved a firm foundation for the welfare and survival of his followers. The community of the monks and nuns is said to have been entrusted by Mahavira to eleven chief disciples, or *ganadha-ras* ("company leaders"). The chief among them was Gautama Indrabhuti, while his colleague Sudharman allegedly taught his own pupil Jambu the words spoken by the Jina. Thus the canon of the Svetambaras goes back to Sudharman through uninterrupted lines of religious masters *(acaryas).*

After Mahavira's time the Jain community spread along the caravan routes from Magadha (Bihar) to the west and south. They claim to have enjoyed the favor of numerous rulers. Notwithstanding possible exaggerations, they probably were supported by a number of princes. By the fifth century (or earlier), the Digambaras were influential in the Deccan, especially in Karnataka. Under the Ganga, Rastrakuta, and other dynasties Jain culture undoubtedly flourished. Numerous sects were founded, among them the

brilliant Yapaniya, now extinct. In the tenth century, however, Vaisnavism and Saivism crushed Jainism in the Tamil area, and in the twelfth century they triumphed over Jainism in Karnataka as well.

As for the Svetambaras, they were especially successful in Gujarat where one of their famous pontifs, Hemacandra (1089-1172), served as minister to the Calukya king Kumarapala (1144-1173) and enforced some Jain rules in the kingdom. Decline was to follow soon after his death, which was hastened by the Muslim invasions. Jain activities did not cease with his demise, however. Elaborate sanctuaries were erected, such as that on Mount Abu, now in Rajasthan. The rise of several reformist sects testifies to the vitality of the Svetambaras, who even succeeded in interesting the Moghul emperor Akbar (r. 1555-1605) in the Jain doctrine.

> **Although the Jain community never regained its former splendor, it did not disappear entirely.**

Although the Jain community never regained its former splendor, it did not disappear entirely; nowadays, the Digambaras are firmly established in Maharashtra and Karnataka and the Svetambaras in Panjab, Rajasthan, and Gujarat.

Literature. From early times the Jains have been engaged in a variety of literary activities. Their works, whether intended for their own adherents or composed with rival groups in view, generally have an edifying, proselytizing, or apologetic purpose. The languages used vary to suit the audience and the epoch.

All of the oldest texts are composed in varieties of Prakrits (i. e., Middle Indo-Aryan), more or less akin to the languages in current use among the people of northern India at the time of the first sermons.

The Jain traditions, while considering that the fourteen Purvas have been lost, contend that part of the material they included was incorporated into later books. The Digambaras boldly assert that some sections are the immediate basis of two of their early treatises (c. first century CE) whereas, according to the Svetambaras, the teachings of the Purvas were embedded in the so-called twelfth Anga of their canon, now considered lost. The earliest extant documents are the canonical scriptures of the Svetambaras and the systematic treatises *(prakaranas)* of the Digambaras.

The Digambaras rely on *prakaranas,* of which the oldest are written in a third variety of Prakrit. Their authors include Vattakera, author of the *Mulacara* (Basic Conduct; approximately 1,250 stanzas) and Kundakunda, a prolific writer and much admired mystic, and author of *Samayasara,* (Essence of the Doctrine).

These books mark the beginning of an important literary genre that was also cultivated by the Svetambaras. One of the fundamental treatises in this category is by Umasvati (c. second century; most likely a Svetambara): with small variants, both churches accept the authority of his *Tattvarthadhigama Sutra* (Sutra for Attaining the Meaning of the Principles), a doctrinal synthesis composed of 350 aphorisms written in Sanskrit. This linguistic selection shows that the Jains were prepared to engage in polemics with other schools of thought and to engage the brahmans with Brahmanic terminology and words of discourse.

Religious Practices. The practices observed among the Jains are dependent on two main factors: specific Jain convictions and the general Indian environment. They reflect, in fact, many parallels with the rules and observances of Brahmanic ascetics and Buddhist monks.

All Jains are members of the four-fold congregation *(samgha),* composed of monks and nuns, laymen and laywomen. They share a common belief in the *triratna* ("three jewels"): *samyagdarsana* ("right faith"), *samyagjñana* ("right knowledge"), and *samyakcaritra* ("right conduct"). Observance of the "three jewels" provides the conditions for the attainment of the goal, that is, liberation from bondage. Deliverance can be attained only by the *nirgrantha,* the Jain monk "free from bonds" both external and internal. The ideal practices therefore are those in force in the (male) religious community.

The monks and nuns take the five "great vows" *(mahavratas).* The life of Mahavira is regarded as an ideal model.

Religious age and hierarchy play a great role: elders look to the material and spiritual welfare of the company; the *upadhyaya* is a specialist in teaching the scriptures; the *acarya* acts as spiritual master. Full ordination takes place after a short novitiate that lasts approximately four months. Admission as a novice is subject to prior examination. At his departure from home, the novice abandons all property and his head is shaved.

Right religious conduct is minutely defined, giving rules for habitation and wandering, begging, study, confession, and penances. During the four months of the rainy season the religious groups remain in one locality; nowadays fixed

places of shelter *(upasrayas)* are prepared for them, often near a temple, where householders visit, ask advice, and listen to teachings.

Called *sravakas* ("listeners") or *upasakas* ("servants"), the lay believers also take five main vows, similar to (but milder than) the *mahavratas,* and hence termed *anuvratas* ("lesser vows"). These include *ahimsa* ("nonviolence") and *satya* ("truthfulness"). They are complemented by three "strengthening vows" and four "vows of spiritual discipline," of which the last, but not the least, is *dana* ("charity").

These practices are evidently relevant in a doctrine that emphasizes individual exertion, and that considers the Jinas to be inaccessible, liberated souls. On the other hand, the Jain church has not been able to ignore the devotional aspirations of the laity, who are also attracted by Hindu ritual. Hence, although temple worship (with the burning and waving of lamps, plucked flowers and fruit, preparation of sandal paste, etc.) implies violence, cultic practices are tolerated, being considered ultimately of help to the worshiper's progress.

Mythology and Cosmology. The Jain representation of the cosmos *(loka)* is akin to (though not identical with) the standard Brahmanical descriptions. [*See* Cosmology.] The cosmos is composed of three main parts: the lower, middle, and upper worlds. It is often represented as a colossal upright human figure, the enormous base of which is formed by seven hells (populated by beings whose past actions were violent and cruel and who consequently suffer terrible torments).

Next is the "middle world". Though small, it has a great importance: there, in a few circumscribed areas, time and the law of retribution prevail, different kinds of men live (among them the civilized *aryas),* and spiritual awakening and perfection can be achieved.

Beginning far above the stars, the upper world appears as a gradually purer and purer counterpart of the lower world. Finally, near the top of the *loka* lies the place, shaped like an inverted umbrella (or the crescent moon) where the *siddhas* ("perfected ones," i. e., liberated souls) are assembled.

Divinities are found in the three worlds, and fall into four main classes. Only mankind, however, can give birth to the Jain prophets, who are called *tirthamkaras,* literally, "ford-makers" across the ocean of rebirths.

Like other Indian systems, Jainism compares the cyclic course of time *(kala)* to the movement of a wheel, and divides it into recurring periods called *kalpas* ("eons").

Doctrine. The tenets of Jainism are well delineated in the Svetambara canon and the Digambara procanonical books, and are systematically presented in the *Tattvarthadhigama Sutra.*

Knowledge *(jñana),* of which the Jains distinguish five kinds, is an essential attribute of the soul *(jiva).* It culminates in *kevala-jñana,* absolute and perfect omniscience.

The Jain system of logic is characterized by the complementary theories of *syadvada* ("[different] possibilities") and of *nayavada* ("[method of] approach"). The first affirms that a statement about an object is valid not absolutely but under one of "several conditions" (hence its other name, *anekantavada);* considering that an object "can be" *(syad)* such, not such, and so forth, seven modes of assertion are distinguished. The *nayavada* defines seven main points of view (generic, specific, etc.) from which to consider an object. The Jains adopt an empirical standpoint.

Jainism is a pluralist substantialism that insists on the reality of change. The world and non-world are basically constituted from five *astikayas* ("masses of being"). Matter furnishes to the souls a body in which to be incorporated and the possibility of corporeal functions. There are five kinds of

> **Like other Indian systems, Jainism compares the cyclic course of time *(kala)* to the movement of a wheel, and divides it into recurring periods called *kalpas* ("eons").**

bodies, each having different functions. All corporeal beings possess at least two of them, the "karmic" and the "fiery" (the latter for digestion).

Bondage occurs because the subtle matter resulting from anterior intentions and volitions is attracted to the soul through the vibration of its "soul-points"; this attraction (called *yoga)* is exercised by means of the material elements of speech, body, and mind. The subtle matter that has been so attracted becomes *karman* when entering the soul. The pious Jain strives to rid the latter of these material extrinsic elements. When life ends, the *jiva,* if it has recovered its essential nature, immediately rejoins the other *siddhas* at the pinnacle of the universe.

Ethics. The essentials of Jain ethics are contained in the sets of vows to be taken by the monks and nuns on the one hand, and by the lay believers on the other. Monks and householders further observe other series of prohibitions and engagements that are meant to favor spiritual progress.

The monks cultivate *samvara,* the spiritual path defined by the cessation of karmic influx, by means of established ethical and behavioral practices. The monk finally sheds the residues of *karman* by means of steadfast and thorough asceticism *(tapas).*

Lists of the virtues required of the householder have received much attention in Jain tradition and literatures. Some lists include as many as thirty-five ethical imperatives incumbent on the nonclerical Jain, but all include five *anuvratas* ("small vows," as opposed to the monks' *mahavratas,*

or "great vows"): *(ahimsa),* truthfulness and honesty in all business affairs *(satya),* that material wealth be gained only through legitimate transactions *(asteya,* lit., "non-stealing"), restraint from all illicit sexual activities *(brahma),* and renunciation of one's attachment to material wealth *(aparigraha).* Moreover, the householder or business person should progress through the higher stages of renunciation involving increasingly complete performance of these vows. Thus, he can come closer and closer to fulfilling the monk's vows as well, and ultimately can attain the purity of the "wise man's death."

The actual path to liberation *(moksa)* is described by Jains as one that includes fourteen "stages of qualification" *(gunasthana).* Leaving the state characterized by "wrong views," the path leads ultimately to the elimination of all passions and culminates in omniscience.

Cultic Structures. It is a specific aspect of the householder's religious life that he is allowed to take part in temple rituals and to worship temple images.

The structure of the Jain temple is on the whole similar to the Hindu temple. [*See* Temple.] The distinctive feature of the Jain shrine is the image of the *tirthamkara* to whom it is dedicated and the idols of the prophets who flank him or occupy the various surrounding niches. Secondary divinities are frequently added (and are very popular); there are also auspicious and symbolic diagrams: the wheel of the Jain law, and the "Five Supreme Ones": *arhats, siddhas, acaryas, upadhyayas,* and *sadhus.* There are also conventional representations of continents, of holy places, and of the great festive congregation *(samavasarana)* in the middle of which the Jina is said to have delivered his sermon for the benefit of all creatures. The offerings placed on the offering plates or planks by the faithful with the rice grains he has brought to the shrine are symbols of the three jewels (three dots), which provide escape from the cycle of bondage (the *svastika)* and lead to *siddhi* (a crescent at the top of the figure).

The example set by great men other than the *tirthamkaras* is also commemorated: homage is paid to the "footprints" *(padukas)* in stone of the great teachers. Above all, Bahubali is a source of inspiration to the Digambaras: "sky-clad" on the crest of the Indragiri hill in Sravana Belgola, his colossal monolithic statue (fifty-seven feet high, erected c. 980) attracts streams of pilgrims, and has been reproduced at several other sites.

Prominent Jain Personalities. Jain achievements are due to the energy and courage of a comparatively united community. Certain brilliant and outstanding individuals, however, have influenced the movement. Recently, Mohandas Gandhi himself paid homage to the Jain jeweller and poet Raychandbhai Mehta (1868-1901). [*See also the biography of Mohandas Gandhi.*] This is the epoch when, after two to three centuries of relative stagnation, a reawakening took place thanks to enlightened monks and householders.

Among those who took part in this renewal, Vijaya Dharma Suri (1868-1922) is one of the best known, both in India and in the West. Among the many others who deserve mention are two Digambara scholars, Hiralal Jain (1898-1973) and A. N. Upadhye (1906-1975), or, on the Svetambara side, those whose collaboration made the foundation of the Lalbhai Dalpatbhai Institute of Indology in Ahmedabad possible: the Muni Punyavijaya (1895-1971), Kasturbhai Lalbhai, and Pandit D. M. Malvania (a pupil of the philosopher Sukhlalji, 1880-1978).

BIBLIOGRAPHY

Interest in Jainism was awakened and placed on a sound basis by the pioneering works of Albrecht Weber and Ernst Leumann, editors of *Indische Studien,* vols. 16-17 (1883; reprint, Hildesheim, 1973), and Hermann Jacobi, editor of *The Kalpasutra of Bhadrabahu (Leipzig,* 1879) and translator of four basic canonical books in the series "Sacred Books of the East," vols. 22, 45 (1884, 1895; reprint, Delhi, 1968), all preceded by very important introductions in English.

Excellent presentations of Jainism are Helmuth von Glase-napp's *Der Jainismus* (1925; reprint, Hildesheim, 1964) and Padmanabh S. Jaini's *The Jaina Path of Purification* (Berkeley, 1979), the latter emphasizing (somewhat unusually) the Digambara point of view. A comprehensive Hindi dictionary of Jainism is Jinendra Jaini's *Jainendra Siddhanta Kosá,* 4 vols. (New Delhi, 1970-1973). A social survey has been presented by Vilas A. Samgave, *Jaina Community,* 2d rev. ed. (Bombay, 1980). The history of Jainism in the different parts of India is the object of numerous monographs; a more general account is given in Jyoti Prasad Jain's *The Jaina Sources of the History of Ancient India, 100 B. C.-A. D. 900* (Delhi, 1964).

Given the considerable literature of the Jains, philological studies are of prime importance. Ludwig Alsdorf has provided a general survey of the scholarly achievements and desiderata in this field in his *Les études jaina: État présent et tâches futures* (Paris, 1965); the same scholar has made many other illuminating contributions.

The doctrine is presented in a masterly book by Walther Schubring, *Die Lehre der Jainas, nach den alten Quellen darge-stellt* (Berlin, 1935), based mostly, but not exclusively, on the Svetambara canon (with an important bibliography up to 1935); it has been translated into English from the revised German edition by Wolfgang Beurlen as *The Doctrine of the Jainas, Described after the Old Sources* (Delhi, 1962), but the above-mentioned bibliography is not included. Schubring has also edited and translated several canonical texts and is the author of basic monographs; see his *Kleine Schriften,* edited by Klaus Bruhn (Wiesbaden, 1977).

The fifth Anga can be regarded as a summary of Jainism: it is very well analyzed in Jozef Deleu's *Viyahapannatti (Bhagavai): The Fifth Anga of the Jaina Canon. Introduction, Critical Analysis, Commentary, and Indexes* (Brugge, 1970). It is impossible to quote all the editions (critical or uncritical) and translations of the original books. A convenient edition of the canon is the two-volume version published in Gurgaon (1954; being by Sthanakvasins, it includes only thirty two texts). Important editorial series have also been created in recent years, the edited texts being often preceded by important introductions, and specialized journals have been published. Excellent English translations of selected Jain texts by A. L. Basham are included in *Sources of Indian Tradition,* compiled by Wm. Theodore de Bary et al. (New York, 1958).

Specialized studies are numerous. Several catalogues of manuscript collections (in India and in Europe) have been published, and contribute to our knowledge of Jain history, literature, and "manuscriptology" (a very important activity of the community); the most recent by Chandrabhal Tripathi, is the *Catalogue of the Jaina Manuscripts at Strasbourg* (Leiden, 1975), scrutinizing the systematic collection assembled there by Ernst Leumann.

Jain polemics against other schools of thought (as well as the commentators' methods) are studied in Willem B. Bollée's *Studien zum Suyagada: Die Jainas und die anderen Weltanschauungen vor der Zeitwende* (Wiesbaden, 1977). Monastic discipline is examined in Shantaram Bhalchandra Deo's *History of Jaina Monachism from Inscriptions and Literature* (Poona, 1956), and by many other scholars. The rules laid down for the laity are well analyzed in R. Williams's *Jaina Yoga* (London, 1963; reprint, Delhi, 1983). Jain cosmology is one of the three main parts of Willibald Kirfel's *Die Kosmographie der Inder* (1920; reprint, Bonn, 1967). See also my *La cosmologie jaïna* (Paris, 1981), which has been translated into English by K. R. Norman as *The Jain Cosmology* (Basel, 1981).

For the history of Jain literature (apart from good contributions in Hindi) reference can be made to Maurice Winternitz's *History of Indian Literature,* vol. 2 (Calcutta, 1933; reprint, Delhi, 1963). Attention has rightly been focused on some of the literary genres cultivated by the Jains; see, for example, Jagdishchandra Jain's *Prakrit Narrative Literature* (in fact, more or less completely Jain; New Delhi, 1981); see also the proceedings of the International Symposium on Jaina Canonical and Narrative Literature (Strasbourg, 1981), an edited version of which can be found in *Indologica Taurinensia* 11 (Turin, 1984).

Many books on Jain art and architecture have been published as a contribution to the celebration of the twenty-five hundredth anniversary of Mahavira's *nirvana.* A comprehensive survey, edited by Amalananda Ghosh, is *Jaina Art and Architecture,* 3 vols. (New Delhi, 1974-1975), and very good monographs are collected in *Jaina Art and Archaeology,* edited by Umakant Premanand Shah and M. A. Dhaky (Ahmedabad, 1975).

Iconography is the subject of Brindavan Chandra Bhattacharyya's *The Jaina Iconography,* 2d rev. ed. (Delhi, 1974), and has inspired numerous important studies by Umakant Premanand Shah, whose *Studies in Jaina Art* (Varanasi,1955) should also be mentioned. Illustrated manuscripts have been studied by W. Norman Brown in *A Descriptive and Illustrated Catalogue of Miniature Paintings of the Jaina Kalpasutra* (Washington, D. C., 1934); on this subject, there exist many books, by Umakant Premanand Shah, for example, *Treasures of Jaina Bhandaras* (Ahmedabad, 1978), as well as Moti Chandra, Sarabhai Manilal Nawab, and others; they include many plates.

COLETTE CAILLAT

JAPANESE RELIGION

An Overview

Like many other ethnic groups throughout the world, the earliest inhabitants of the Japanese archipelago had from time immemorial their own unique way of viewing the world and the meaning of human existence and their own characteristic rituals for celebrating various events and phases of their individual and corporate life. To them the whole of life was permeated by religious symbols and authenticated by myths. From this tradition an indigenous religious form, which came to be designated as Shinto, or "the way of *kami*," developed in the early historic period. Many aspects of the archaic tradition have also been preserved as basic features of an unorganized folk religion. Meanwhile, through contacts with Korea and China, Japan came under the impact of religious and cultural influences from the continent of Asia. Invariably, Japanese religion was greatly enriched as it appropriated the concepts, symbols, rituals, and art forms of Confucianism, Taoism, the Yin-yang school, and Buddhism. Although these religious and semireligious systems kept a measure of their own identity, they are by no means to be considered mutually exclusive; to all intents and purposes they became facets of the nebulous but enduring religious tradition that may be referred to as "Japanese religion."

It is worth noting in this connection that the term *shukyo* ("religion") was not used until the nineteenth century. In Japanese traditions, religious schools are usually referred to as *do*, *to*, or *michi* ("way"), as in Butsudo ("the way of the Buddha") or Shinto ("the way of *kami*"), implying that these are complementary ways or paths within the overarching Japanese religion. Various branches of art were also called *do* or *michi*, as in *chado* (also *sado*, "the way of tea"). This usage reflects the close affinity in Japan between religious and aesthetic traditions.

Early Historical Period. Prior to the introduction of Sino-Korean civilization and Buddhism, Japanese religion was not a well-structured institutional system. The early Japanese took it for granted that the world was the Japanese islands where they lived. They also accepted the notion that the natural world was a "given." Thus, they did not look for another order of meaning behind the natural world. Although the early Japanese did not speculate on the metaphysical meaning of the cosmos, they felt they were an integral part of the cosmos, which to them was a community of living beings, all sharing *kami* (sacred) nature.

Equally central to the early Japanese outlook was the notion of *uji* ("lineage group, clan"), which provided the basic framework for social solidarity. Each *uji* had clansmen *(ujibito),* groups of professional persons *(be)* who were not blood relations of the clansmen, and slaves *(nuhi),* all of whom were ruled by the *uji* chieftain *(uji no kami).* Each *uji* was not only a social, economic, and political unit but also a unit of religious solidarity centering around the *kami.*

Impact of Chinese civilization and Buddhism on Japanese religion. With the gradual penetration of Chinese civilization—or, more strictly, Sino-Korean civilization—and Buddhism during the fifth and sixth centuries, Japanese religion was destined to feel the impact of alien ways of viewing the world and interpreting the meaning of human existence. Sensing the need to create a designation for their hitherto unsystematized religious, cultural, and political tradition, the

Japanese borrowed two Chinese characters—*shen* (Jpn., *shin*) for *kami,* and *tao* (Jpn., *to* or *do*) for "the way." Inevitably, the effort to create almost artificially a religious system out of a nebulous, though all-embracing, way of life left many age-old beliefs and practices out of the new system.

There is little doubt that the introduction of Chinese script and Buddhist images greatly aided the rapid penetration of Chinese civilization and Buddhism. As the Japanese had not developed their own script, the task of adopting the Chinese script, with its highly developed ideographs and phonetic compounds, to Japanese words was a complex one. There were many educated Korean and Chinese immigrants who served as instructors, interpreters, artists, technicians, and scribes for the imperial court and influential *uji* leaders of the growing nation. The Japanese intelligentsia over the course of time learned the use of literary Chinese and for many centuries used it for writing historical and official records.

Through written media the Japanese came to know the mystical tradition of philosophical Taoism, which enriched the Japanese aesthetic tradition. The Japanese also learned of the Yin-yang school's concepts of the two principles (*yin* and *yang*), the five elements (metal, wood, water, fire, and earth), and the orderly rotation of these elements in the formation of nature, seasons, and the human being. The Yin-yang school thus provided cosmological theories to hitherto nonspeculative Japanese religion. It was also through written Chinese works that Japanese society, which had been based on archaic communal rules and the *uji* system, appropriated certain features of Confucian ethical principles, social and political theories, and legal and educational systems.

Prince Shotoku. The regency of Prince Shotoku (573-621), who served under his aunt, Empress Suiko (r. 592-628), marks a new chapter in the history of Japanese religion. To protect Japan's survival in the precarious international scene, Shotoku and his advisers attempted to strengthen the fabric of national community by working out a multireligious policy reconciling the particularistic Japanese religious tradition with the universal principles of Confucianism and Buddhism. Shotoku himself was a pious Buddhist and is reputed to have delivered learned lectures on certain Buddhist scriptures. Moreover, he held the Confucian notion of *li* ("propriety") as the key to right relations among ruler, ministers, and people. [*See* Li.] Shotoku was convinced that his policy was in keeping with the will of the *kami.* In his edict of 607 he states how his imperial ancestors had venerated the heavenly and earthly *kami* and thus "the winter [*yin,* negative cosmic force] and summer [*yang,* positive cosmic force] elements were kept in harmony, and their creative powers blended together," and he urged his ministers to do the same.

Prince Shotoku took the initiative in reestablishing diplomatic contact with China by sending an envoy to the Sui court. He also sent a number of talented young scholars and monks to China to study. Although Shotoku's reform measures remained unfulfilled at his untimely death, the talented youths he sent to China played important roles in the development of Japanese religion and national affairs upon their return.

The Ritsuryo synthesis. Prince Shotoku's death was followed by a series of bloody power struggles, including the coup d'état of 645, which strengthened the position of the throne. During the second half of the seventh century the government, utilizing the talents of those who had studied in China, sponsored the compilation of a written law. Significantly, those penal codes (*ritsu;* Chin., *lü*) and civil statutes (*ryo;* Chin., *ling*), which were modeled after Chinese legal systems, were issued in the name of the emperor as the will of the *kami.* The government structure thus developed during the late seventh century is referred to as the Ritsuryo ("imperial rescript") state. Although the basic principle of the Ritsuryo state was in a sense a logical implementation of Prince Shotoku's vision, which itself was a synthesis of Buddhist, Confucian, and Japanese traditions, it turned out to be in effect a form of "immanental theocracy," in which the universal principles of Tao and Dharma were domesticated to serve the will of the sovereign, who now was elevated to the status of living or manifest *kami.*

Nara Period. During the eighth century Japanese religion reached an important stage of maturity under Chinese and Buddhist inspirations. It was a golden age for the Ritsuryo state and the imperial court. In contrast to earlier periods, when Korean forms of Buddhism influenced Japan, early eighth-century Japan felt the strong impact of Chinese Buddhism. In 710 the first capital, modeled after the Chinese capital of Ch'ang-an, was established in Nara, which was designed to serve as the religious as well as the political center of the nation. During the Nara period the imperial court was eager to promote Buddhism as the religion best suited for the protection of the state. Accordingly, the government established in every province state-sponsored temples (*kokubunji*) and nunneries (*kokubunniji*). In the capital city the national cathedral, Todaiji, was built as the home of the gigantic bronze statue of the Buddha Vairocana. The government sponsored and supported six schools of Chinese Buddhism. Of the six, the Ritsu (Vinaya) school was concerned primarily with monastic disciplines.

Despite such encouragement and support from the government, Buddhism did not have much impact on the populace. More important were three new religious forms that developed out of the fusion between the Japanese religious heritage and Buddhism.

The first new form was the Nature Wisdom school (Jinenchishu), which sought enlightenment by meditation or austere physical discipline in the mountains and forests. Those who followed the path, including some official monks, affirmed the superiority of enlightenment through nature to

the traditional Buddhist disciplines and doctrines. The indigenous Japanese acceptance of the sacrality of nature was thus reaffirmed.

Second is the emergence of a variety of folk religious leaders, variously called private monks (*shidoso*) and unordained monks who appropriated many features of Buddhism and taught simple and syncretistic "folk Buddhism" among the lower strata of society.

A third new form came out of an amalgamation of Buddhism and Shinto called Tyobu Shinto.

Because of the excessive support of religion and culture by the court, which benefited only the aristocracy, the capital of Nara during the second half of the eighth century was doomed by political corruption, ecclesiastical intrigue, and financial bankruptcy. Therefore the capital was moved in 794 from Nara to a remote place and then ten years later to the present Kyoto.

Erosion of the Ritsuryo Ideal. The new capital in Kyoto, Heiankyo ("capital of peace and tranquillity"), was also modeled after the Chinese capital. Freed from ecclesiastical interference, the leaders of the Kyoto regime were eager to restore the integrity of the Ritsuryo system, and they forbade the Nara Buddhist schools to move into the new capital. Instead, the imperial court favored, side by side with Shinto, two new Buddhist schools, Tendai (Chin., T'ien-t'ai) and Shingon (Chin., Chen-yen).

The foundation of the Ritsuryo system was the sacred monarchy. Ironically, during the Heian period the two institutions that were most closely related to the throne, namely, the Fujiwara regency and rule by retired monarchs (*insei*), undercut the structure of the Ritsuryo system. The regency had been exercised before the ninth century only by members of the royal family and only in times when the reigning monarch needed such assistance. But from the late ninth century to the mid-eleventh century the nation was actually ruled by the regency of the powerful Fujiwara family. The institutionalization of the regency implied a significant redefinition of the Ritsuryo system by the aristocracy. The aristocratic families acknowledged the sacrality of the throne, but they expected the emperor to "reign" only as the manifest *kami* and not to interfere with the actual operation of the government.

The Heian period witnessed the phenomenal growth of wealth and political influence of ecclesiastical institutions, both Shinto and Buddhist, equipped with lucrative manors and armed guards.

This period, and the elegant culture it produced, vanished in the late twelfth century in a series of bloody battles involving both courtiers and warriors. Then came a new age dominated by warrior rulers.

Religious Ethos during the Kamakura Period. That the nation was "ruled" by warrior-rulers from the thirteenth to the nineteenth century, even though the emperor continued to "reign" throughout these centuries, is a matter of considerable significance for the development of Japanese religion. There were three such feudal warrior regimes (*bakufu* or shogunates): (1) the Kama-kura regime (1192-1333), (2) the Ashikaga regime (1338-1573), and (3) the Tokugawa regime (1603-1867). Unlike the Ritsuryo state, with its elaborate penal and civil codes, the warrior rule—at least under the first two regimes—was based on a much simpler legal system, which allowed established Shinto and Buddhist institutions more freedom than they had under the cumbersome structure of the Ritsuryo state. It also set the stage for the development of new religious movements, many with roots in the folk tradition.

The warriors for the most part were not sophisticated in cultural and religious matters. Many of them, however, combined simple Buddhist piety with devotion to the pre-Buddhist indigenous tutelary *kami* of warrior families rather than those of the imperial Shinto tradition. At the same time, the peasantry, artisans, and small merchants, whose living standard improved a little under the Kamakura regime, were attracted to new religious movements that promised an easier path to salvation in the dreaded age of degeneration *(mappo).*

New religious leaders became instrumental in the establishment of the three Pure Land (Amida's Western Paradise) traditions. They were Honen (Genku, 1133-1212) of the Jodo (Pure Land) sect, who is often compared with Martin Luther; Shinran (1173-1262) of the Jodo Shin (True Pure Land) sect, a disciple of Honen, who among other things initiated the tradition of a married priesthood; and Ippen (Chishin, 1239-1289) of the Ji (Time) sect, so named because of its practice of reciting hymns to Amida six times a day.

On the other hand, Nichiren (1222-1282), founder of the school bearing his name and a charismatic prophet, developed his own interpretation of the *Hokekyo* (Lotus Sutra), the *Saddharmapundarika Sutra,* as the only path toward salvation for the Japanese nation.

In contrast to the paths of salvation advocated by the Pure Land and Nichiren schools, the experience of enlightenment *(satori)* was stressed by Eisai (Yosai, 1141-1215), who introduced the Rinzai (Chin., Lin-chi) Zen tradition, and Dogen (1200-1253), who established the Soto (Chin., Ts`ao-tung) Zen tradition. Zen was welcomed by Kamakura leaders partly because it could counterbalance the powerful and wealthy established Buddhist institutions and partly because it was accompanied by other features of Sung Chinese culture, including Neo-Confucian learning. The Zen movement was greatly aided by a number of émigré Ch`an monks who settled in Japan. [*See* Zen.]

Despite the growth of new religious movements, old religious establishments, both Shinto and Buddhist, remained powerful during this period; for example, both gave military support to the royalist cause against the Kamakura regime during the abortive Jokyu rebellion in 1221. On the other hand, confronted by a national crisis during the Mongol inva-

sions of 1274 and 1281, both Shinto shrines and Buddhist monasteries solidly supported the Kamakura regime by offering prayers and incantations for the protection of Japan.

Zen, Neo-Confucianism, and Kirishitan during the Ashikaga Period. Unlike the first feudal regime at Kamakura, the Ashikaga regime established its *bakufu* in Kyoto, the seat of the imperial court. Accordingly, religious and cultural development during the Ashikaga period (1338-1573, also referred to as the Muromachi period) blended various features of warrior and courtier traditions, Zen, and Chinese cultural influences. This blending in turn fostered a closer interpenetration of religious and aesthetic values. All these religious and cultural developments took place at a time when social and political order was threatened not only by a series of bloody power struggles within the *bakufu* but also by famines and epidemics that led to peasant uprisings and, further, by the devastating Onin War (1467-1478) that accelerated the erosion of Ashikaga hegemony and the rise of competing daimyo, the so-called *sengoku dai-myo* ("feudal lords of warring states"), in the provinces. In this situation, villages and towns developed something analogous to self-rule. Merchants and artisans formed guilds (*za*) that were usually affiliated with established Buddhist temples and Shinto shrines, whereas adherents of Pure Land and Nichiren sects were willing to defend themselves as armed religious societies. Into this complex religious, cultural, social, and political topography, European missionaries of Roman Catholicism, then known as Kirishitan, brought a new gospel of salvation.

Throughout the Ashikaga period established institutions of older Buddhist schools and Shinto (for example, the Tendai monastery at Mount Hiei, the Shingon monastery at Mount Koya, and the Kasuga shrine at Nara) remained both politically and economically powerful. However, the new religious groups that had begun to attract the lower strata of society during the Kamakura period continued to expand their influence, often competing among themselves.

> **By far the most influential religious sect during the Ashikaga period was Zen. . . .**

Zen and Neo-Confucianism. By far the most influential religious sect during the Ashikaga period was Zen, especially the Rinzai Zen tradition, which became *de facto* the official religion. Many Zen priests served as advisers to administrative offices of the regime. They earned reputations as monk-poets or monk-painters, and Gozan temples became centers of cultural and artistic activities.

Zen priests, including émigré Chinese Ch`an monks, also made contributions as transmitters of Neo-Confucianism, a complex philosophical system incorporating not only classical Confucian thought but also features of Buddhist and Taoist traditions that had developed in China during the Sung (960-1127) and Southern Sung (1127-1279) periods.

The combined inspiration of Japanese and Sung Chinese aesthetics, Zen, and Pure Land traditions, coupled with the enthusiastic patronage of shoguns, made possible the growth of a variety of elegant and sophisticated art: painting, calligraphy, *renga* (dialogical poetry or linked verse), stylized *no* drama, comical *kyogen* plays, flower arrangement, and the cult of tea.

The coming of Kirishitan. When the Onin War ended in 1478 the Ashikaga regime could no longer control the ambitious provincial daimyo who were consolidating their own territories. By the sixteenth century Portugal was expanding its overseas empire in Asia. The chance arrival of shipwrecked Portuguese merchants at Tanegashima Island, south of Kyushu, in 1543 was followed by the arrival in Kyushu in 1549 of the famous Jesuit Francis Xavier. Although Xavier stayed only two years in Japan, he initiated vigorous proselytizing activities during that time.

The cause of Kirishitan (as Roman Catholicism was then called in Japanese) was greatly aided by a strongman, Oda Nobunaga (1534-1582), who succeeded in taking control of the capital in 1568. Angry that established Buddhist institutions were resisting his scheme of national unification, Nobunaga took harsh measures; he burned the Tendai monastery at Mount Hiei, killed thousands of Ikko (True Pure Land) followers, and attacked rebellious priests at Mount Koya in order to destroy their power. At the same time, ostensibly to counteract the residual influence of Buddhism, he encouraged Kirishitan activities. Ironically, this policy was reversed after his death. Nevertheless, by the time Nobunaga was assassinated, 150,000 Japanese Catholics, including several daimyo, were reported to be among the Japanese population.

The initial success of Catholicism in Japan was due to the Jesuits' policy of accommodation. Xavier himself adopted the name *Dainichi* (the Great Sun Buddha, the supreme deity of the Shingon school) as the designation of God; later, however, this was changed to *Deus.* Jesuits also used the Buddhist terms *jodo* ("pure land") for heaven and *so* ("monk") for the title *padre.* Moreover, Kirishitan groups followed the general pattern of tightly knit religious societies practiced by the Nichiren and Pure Land groups. Missionaries also followed the common Japanese approach in securing the favor of the ruling class to expedite their evangelistic and philanthropic activities. Conversely, trade-hungry daimyo eagerly befriended missionaries, knowing that the latter had influence over Portuguese traders. In fact, one Christian daimyo donated the port of Nagasaki to the Society of Jesus in 1580 hoping to attract Portuguese ships to the port, which would in turn benefit him. Inevitably, however, Jesuit-inspired missionary

work aroused strong opposition not only from anti-Kirishitan daimyo and Buddhist clerics but from jealous Franciscans and other Catholic orders as well. Furthermore, the Portuguese traders who supported the Jesuits were now threatened by the arrival of the Spanish in 1592, via Mexico and the Philippines, and of the Dutch in 1600.

Meanwhile, following the death of Oda Nobunaga, one of his generals, Toyotomi Hideyoshi (1536-1598), endeavored to complete the task of national unification. Determined to eliminate the power of Buddhist institutions, he not only attacked rebellious monastic communities, such as those in Negoro and Saiga, but also conducted a thorough sword hunt in various monastic communities. Hideyoshi was interested in foreign trade, but he took a dim view of Catholicism because of its potential danger to the cause of national unification. He was incensed by what he saw in Nagasaki, a port that was then ruled by the Jesuits and the Portuguese. In

> **Determined to eliminate the power of Buddhist institutions, (Toyotomi Hideyoshi) . . . conducted a thorough sword hunt in various monastic communities.**

1587 he issued an edict banishing missionaries, but he did not enforce it until 1596 when he heard a rumor that the Spanish monarch was plotting to subjugate Japan with the help of Japanese Christians. Thus in 1597 he had some twenty-six Franciscans and Japanese converts crucified. The following year Hideyoshi himself died in the midst of his abortive invasion of Korea. [See also Christianity, article on Christianity in Asia.]

The Tokugawa Synthesis. The Tokugawa regime, which was to hold political power until the Meiji restoration in 1867, was more than another feudal regime; it was a comprehensive sixfold order—political, social, legal, philosophical, religious, and moral—with the shogun in its pivotal position.

The religious policy of the Tokugawa regime was firmly established by the first shogun, who held that all religious, philosophical, and ethical systems were to uphold and cooperate with the government's objective, namely, the establishment of a harmonious society. Following the eclectic tradition of Japanese religion, which had appropriated various religious symbols and concepts, the first shogun stated in an edict of 1614: "Japan is called the land of the Buddha and not without reason. . . . *Kami* and the Buddha differ in name, but their meaning is one." Accordingly, he surrounded himself with a variety of advisers, including Buddhist clerics and Confucian scholars, and shared their view that the Kirishitan (Roman Catholicism) religion could not be incorporated into the framework of Japanese religion and would be detrimental to the cause of social and political harmony. Nevertheless, the Tokugawa regime's initial attitude toward Catholicism was restrained; perhaps this was because the regime did not wish to lose foreign trade by overt anti-Kirishitan measures. But in 1614 the edict banning Kirishitan was issued, followed two years later by a stricter edict.

Buddhism and the Tokugawa regime. The Tokugawa regime's anti-Kirishitan measures required every Japanese citizen to become, at least nominally, Buddhist. Accordingly, the number of Buddhist temples suddenly increased from 13,037 (the number of temples during the Kamakura period) to 469,934. Under Tokugawa rule a comprehensive parochial system was created, with Buddhist clerics serving as arms of the ruling regime in charge of thought control. In turn, Buddhist temples were tightly controlled by the regime, which tolerated internal doctrinal disputes but not deviation from official policy. The only new sect that emerged during the Tokugawa period was the Obaku sect of Zen, which was introduced from China in the mid-seventeenth century.

Confucianism and Shinto. Neo-Confucianism was promoted by Zen Buddhists prior to the Tokugawa period. Thus, that Neo-Confucian scholars were also Zen clerics was taken for granted. Fujiwara Seika (1561-1619) first advocated the independence of Neo-Confucianism from Zen. By his recommendation, Hayashi Razan (1583-1657), one of Seika's disciples, became the Confucian adviser to the first shogun. Not surprisingly, Razan and many Neo-Confucians expressed outspoken anti-Buddhist sentiments, and some Confucian scholars became interested in Shinto. Razan, himself an ardent follower of the Shushi (Chu Hsi) tradition, tried to relate the *ri* (Chin., *li*, "reason, principle") of Neo-Confucianism with Shinto. The Shushi school was acknowledged as the official guiding ideology of the regime and was promoted by powerful members of the Tokugawa family.

The second tradition of Neo-Confucianism, Oyomeigaku or Yomeigaku (the school of Wang Yang-ming), held that the individual mind was the manifestation of the universal Mind. Quite different from the traditions of Shushi and Oyomei was the Kogaku ("ancient learning") tradition, which aspired to return to the classical sources of Confucianism.

Throughout the Tokugawa period, Confucian scholars, particularly those of the Shushigaku, Oyomeigaku, and Kogaku schools, exerted lasting influence on the warriors-turned-administrators.

Shinto revival and the decline of the Tokugawa regime. With the encouragement of anti-Buddhist Confucianists, especially those of Suika Shinto, Shinto leaders who were overshadowed by their Buddhist counterparts during the early Tokugawa period began to assert themselves. The nationalistic sentiment generated by the leaders of the Shinto revival, National Learning, and pro-Shinto Confucians began to turn against the already weakening

Tokugawa regime in favor of the emerging royalist cause. The authority of the regime was threatened further by the demands of Western powers to reopen Japan for trade. Inevitably, the loosening of the shogunate's control resulted in political and social disintegration, which in turn precipitated the emergence of messianic cults from the soil of folk religious traditions.

Modern Period. The checkered development of Japanese religion in the modern period reflects a series of political, social, and cultural changes that have taken place within the Japanese nation. These changes include the toppling of the Tokugawa regime (1867), followed by the restoration of imperial rule under the Meiji emperor (r. 1867-1912); the rising influence of Western thought and civilization as well as Christianity; the Sino-Japanese War (1894-1895); the Russo-Japanese War (1904-1905); the annexation of Korea (1910); World War I, followed by a short-lived "Taisho Democracy"; an economic crisis followed by the rise of militarism in the 1930s; the Japanese invasion of Manchuria and China followed by World War II; Japan's surrender to the Allied forces (1945); the Allied occupation of Japan; and postwar adjustment. The particular path of development of Japanese religion was, of course, most directly affected by the government's religious policies.

Meiji era. Although the architects of modern Japan welcomed many features of Western civilization, the Meiji regime was determined to restore the ancient principle of the "unity of religion and government" and the immanental theocratic state. The model was the Ritsuryo system of the seventh and eighth centuries. Accordingly, sacred kingship served as the pivot of national policy (kokutai). Thus, while the constitution nominally guaranteed religious freedom and the historic ban against Christianity was lifted, the government created an overarching new religious form called State Shinto, which was designed to supersede all other religious groups. In order to create such a new official religion out of the ancient Japanese religious heritage an edict separating Shinto and Buddhism (Shin-Butsu hanzen rei) was issued. The government's feeling was that the Shinto-Buddhist amalgam of the preceding ten centuries was contrary to indigenous religious tradition. After the abortive Taikyo Sempu ("dissemination of the great doctrine") movement and the compulsory registration of Shinto parishioners, the government decided to utilize various other means, especially military training and public education, to promote the sacred "legacy of the kami way" (kannagara): hence the promulgation of the Imperial Rescript to Soldiers and Sailors (1882) and the Imperial Rescript on Education (1890). Significantly, from 1882 until the end of World War II Shinto priests were prohibited by law from preaching during Shinto ceremonies, although they were responsible—as arms of the government bureaucracy—for the preservation of State Shinto.

Furthermore, in order to keep State Shinto from becoming involved in overtly sectarian activities, the government created between 1882 and 1908 a new category of Kyoha ("sect") Shinto and recognized thirteen such groups, including Kurozumikyo, Konkokyo, and Tenrikyo, which had emerged in the late Tokugawa period. Like Buddhist sects and Christian denominations, these groups depended on nongovernmental, private initiative for their propagation, organization, and financial support. Actually, Kyoha Shinto groups have very little in common. Some of them consider themselves genuinely Shinto in beliefs and practices, whereas some of them are marked by strong Confucian features. Still others betray characteristic features of folk religious tradition such as the veneration of sacred mountains, cults of mental and physical purification, utopian beliefs, and faith healing.

Buddhism. Understandably Buddhism was destined to undergo many traumatic experiences in the modern period. The Meiji regime's edict separating Shinto and Buddhism precipitated a popular anti-Buddhist movement that reached its climax around 1871. In various districts temples were destroyed, monks and nuns were laicized, and the parochial system, the legacy of the Tokugawa period, eroded. Moreover, the short-lived Taikyo Sempu movement mobilized

> **Understandably Buddhism was destined to undergo many traumatic experiences in the modern period.**

Buddhist monks to propagate Taikyo, or government-concocted "Shinto" doctrines. Naturally, faithful Buddhists resented the Shinto-dominated Taikyo movement, and they advocated the principle of religious freedom. Thus, four branches of the True Pure Land sect managed to secure permission to leave the Taikyo movement, and shortly afterward the ill-fated movement itself was abolished. In the meantime, enlightened Buddhist leaders, determined to meet the challenge of Western thought and scholarship, sent able young monks to Western universities. Exposure to European Buddhological scholarship and contacts with other Buddhist traditions in Asia greatly broadened the vista of previously insulated Japanese Buddhists.

The government's grudging decision to succumb to the pressure of Western powers and lift the ban against Christianity was an emotional blow to Buddhism, which had been charged with the task of carrying out the anti-Kirishitan policy of the Tokugawa regime. Thus, many Buddhists, including those who had advocated religious freedom, allied themselves with Shinto, Confucian, and nationalist leaders in an emotional anti-Christian campaign called *haja kensei* ("refutation of evil religion and the exaltation of righteous reli-

gion"). After the promulgation of the Imperial Rescript on Education in 1890, many Buddhists equated patriotism with nationalism, thus becoming willing defenders and spokesmen of the emperor cult that symbolized the unique national polity *(kokutai)*. Although many Buddhists had no intention of restoring the historic form of the Shinto-Buddhist amalgam, until the end of World War II they accepted completely Buddhism's subordinate role in the nebulous but overarching super-religion of State Shinto.

Confucianism. Confucians, too, were disappointed by the turn of events during the early days of the Meiji era. It is well to recall that Confucians were the influential guardians of the Tokugawa regime's official ideology but that in latter Tokugawa days many of them cooperated with Shinto and nationalist leaders and prepared the ground for the new Japan. Indeed, Confucianism was an intellectual bridge between the premodern and modern periods. And although the new regime depended heavily on Confucian ethical principles in its formulation of imperial ideology and the principles of sacred national polity, sensitive Confucians felt that those Confucian features had been dissolved into a new overarching framework with heavy imprints of Shinto and National Learning (Kokugaku). Confucians also resented the new regime's policy of organizing the educational system on Western models and welcoming Western learning *(yogaku)* at the expense of, so they felt, traditionally important Confucian learning (Jugaku). After a decade of infatuation with things Western, however, a conservative mood returned, much to the comfort of Confucians. With the promulgation of the Imperial Rescript on Education and the adoption of compulsory "moral teaching" *(shushin)* in school systems, Confucian values were domesticated and presented as indigenous moral values. The historic Chinese Confucian notion of wang-tao ("the way of true kingship") was recast into the framework of *kodo* ("the imperial way"), and its ethical universalism was transformed into *nihon-shugi* ("Japanese-ism"). As such, "nonreligious" Confucian ethics supported "super-religious" State Shinto until the end of World War II.

Christianity. The appearance—or reappearance, as far as Roman Catholicism was concerned—of Christianity in Japan was due to the convergence of several factors. These included pressures both external and internal, both from Western powers and from enlightened Buddhist leaders who demanded religious freedom. Initially, the Meiji regime, in its eagerness to restore the ancient indigenous polity, arrested over three thousand "hidden Kirishitan" in Kyushu and sent them into exile in various parts of the country. However, foreign ministers strongly advised the Meiji regime, which was then eager to improve its treaties with Western nations, to change its anti-Christian policy. Feeling these pressures, the government lifted its ban against the "forbidden religion." This opened the door to missionary activity by Protestant as well as Roman Catholic and Russian Orthodox churches. From that time until 1945, Christian movements in Japan walked a tightrope between their own religious affirmation and the demands of the nation's inherent immanental theocratic principle.

The meaning of "religious freedom" was stated by Ito Hirobumi (1841-1909), the chief architect of the Meiji Constitution, as follows:

> No believer in this or that religion has the right to place himself outside the pale of the law of the Empire, on the ground that he is serving his god. . . . Thus, although freedom of religious belief is complete and exempt from all restrictions, so long as manifestations of it are confined to the mind; yet with regard to external matters such as forms of worship and the mode of propagandism, certain necessary restrictions of law or regulations must be provided for, and besides, the general duties of subjects must be observed.

This understanding of religious freedom was interpreted even more narrowly after the promulgation of the Imperial Rescript on Education; spokesmen of anti-Christian groups stressed that the Christian doctrine of universal love was incompatible with the national virtues of loyalty and filial piety taught explicitly in the Rescript. Some Christian leaders responded by stressing the compatibility of their faith and patriotism. Although a small group of Christian socialists and pacifists protested during the Sino-Japanese and Russo-Japanese wars, most Christians passively supported the war effort.

Another burden that the Christian movement has carried from the Meiji era to the present is its "foreignness." The anti-Kirishitan policy and all-embracing, unified meaning-structure of the Tokugawa synthesis that had lasted over two and a half centuries resulted in an exclusivistic mental attitude among the Japanese populace. A new religion thus found it difficult to penetrate from the outside. However, during the time of infatuation with things Western, curious or iconoclastic youths in urban areas were attracted by Christianity because of its foreignness. As a result, Westernized intellectuals, lesser bureaucrats, and technicians became the core of the Christian community. Through them, and through church-related schools and philanthropic activities, the Christian influence made a far greater impact on Japan than many people realize.

Christianity in Japan, however, has also paid a high price for its foreignness. As might be expected, Christian churches in Japan, many of which had close relationships with their respective counterparts in the West, experienced difficult times in the 1930s. Under combined heavy pressure from militarists and Shinto leaders, both the Congregatio de Propanganda Fide in Rome and the National Christian Council of the Protestant Churches in Japan accepted the government's interpretation of State Shinto as "nonreligious." According to their view, obeisance at the State Shinto shrines as a nonreligious, patriotic act could be performed by all Japanese subjects. In 1939 all aspects of religion were placed under strict government control. In 1940 thirty-four Protestant churches were compelled to unite as the "Church of Christ in Japan." This church and the Roman Catholic church remained the only recognized Christian groups during World War II. During the war all religious groups were exploited by the government as ideological weapons. Individual religious leaders who did not cooperate with the government were jailed, intimidated, or tortured. Christians learned the bitter lesson that under the immanental theocratic system created in modern Japan the only religious freedom was, as stated by Ito Hirobumi, "confined to the mind."

Japanese religion today. In the modern world the destiny of any nation is as greatly influenced by external events as by domestic events. As far as modern Japan was concerned, such external events as the Chinese Revolution in 1912, World War I, the Russian Revolution, and the worldwide depression intermingled with events at home and propelled Japan to the world stage. Ironically, although World War I benefited the wealthy elite, the economic imbalance it produced drove desperate masses to rice riots and workers to labor strikes. Marxist student organizations were formed, and some serious college students joined the Communist party. Many people in lower social strata, benefiting little from modern civilization or industrial economy and neglected by institutionalized religions, turned to messianic and healing cults of the folk religious tradition. Thus, in spite of the government's determined effort to control religious groups and to prevent the emergence of new religions, it was reported that the number of quasi religions *(ruiji shukyo)* increased from 98 in 1924 to 414 in 1930 and then to over one thousand in 1935. Many of them experienced harassment, intervention, and persecution by the government, and some of them chose for the sake of survival to affiliate with Buddhist or Kyoha Shinto sects. Important among the quasi-religious groups were Omotokyo, founded by Deguchi Nao (1836-1918); Hito no Michi, founded by Miki Tokuharu (1871-1938); and Reiyukai, founded jointly by Kubo Kakutaro (1890-1944) and Kotani Kimi (1901-1971). After the end of World War II these quasi-religious groups and their spiritual cousins became the so-called new religions *(shinko shukyo)*. [See New Religions.]

The end of World War II and the Allied occupation of Japan brought full-scale religious freedom, with far-reaching consequences. In December 1945 the Occupation force issued the Shinto Directive dismantling the official structure of State Shinto; on New Year's Day 1946 the emperor publicly denied his divinity. Understandably, the loss of the sacral kingship and State Shinto undercut the mytho-historical foundation of Japanese religion that had endured from time immemorial. The new civil code of 1947 effectively abolished the traditional system of interlocking households (ie seido) as a legal institution, so that individuals were no longer bound by the religious affiliation of their households. The erosion of family cohesion greatly weakened the Buddhist parish system (danka) as well as the Shinto parish systems (ujiko).

The abrogation of the ill-famed Religious Organizations Law (enacted in 1939 and enforced in 1940) also radically altered the religious scene. Assured of religious freedom and separation of religion and state by the Religious Corporations Ordinance, all religious groups (Buddhist, Christian, Shinto—now called Shrine Shinto—and others) began energetic activities. This turn of events made it possible for quasi religions and Buddhist or Sect Shinto splinter groups to become independent. Sect Shinto, which comprised 13 groups before the war, developed into 75 groups by 1949. With the emergence of other new religions the total number of religious groups reached 742 by 1950. However, with the enactment of the Religious Juridical Persons Law (Shukyo hojin ho) in 1951, the number was reduced to 379—142 in the Shinto tradition, 169 Buddhist groups, 38 Christian denominations, and 30 miscellaneous groups.

In the immediate postwar period, when many people suffered from uncertainty, poverty, and loss of confidence, many men and women were attracted by what the new religions claimed to offer: mundane happiness, tightly knit religious organizations, healing, and readily accessible earthly deities or divine agents.

It has not been easy for older Buddhist groups to adjust to the changing social situation, especially since many of them lost their traditional financial support in the immediate postwar period. Also, religious freedom unwittingly fostered schisms among some of them. Nevertheless, the strength of the older Buddhist groups lies in their following among the intelligentsia and the rural population. Japanese Buddhological scholarship deservedly enjoys an international reputation. Japanese Buddhist leaders are taking increasingly active roles in pan-Asian and global Buddhist affairs while at the same time attending to such issues as peace and disarmament at home.

BIBLIOGRAPHY

General Introduction

Anesaki, Masaharu. *History of Japanese Religion.* 2d ed. Rutland, Vt., 1963.

Earhart, H. Byron. *Religion in the Japanese Experience: Sources and Interpretations.* Encino, Calif., 1974.

Hori, Ichiro, ed. *Japanese Religion.* Tokyo and Palo Alto, Calif., 1972.

Kitagawa, Joseph M. *Religion in Japanese History.* New York and London, 1966.

Kitagawa, Joseph M. "The Religions of Japan." In *A Reader's Guide to the Great Religions,* 2d ed., edited by Charles J. Adams, pp. 247-282. New York, 1977. This bibliographic essay includes an appendix listing reference works, published bibliographies, and periodicals relevant to the religions of Japan.

Nakamura, Hajime. *Ways of Thinking of Eastern Peoples: India, China, Tibet, Japan.* Honolulu, 1964.

Sansom, George B. *Japan: A Short Cultural History.* New York, 1931.

Sansom, George B. *A History of Japan.* 3 vols. Stanford, Calif., 1958-1963.

Tsunoda, Ryusaku, Wm. Theodore de Bary, and Donald Keene, comps. *Sources of Japanese Tradition.* New York and London, 1958.

Prehistoric Background

Groot, Gerard J. *The Prehistory of Japan.* New York, 1951.

Haguenauer, Charles M. *Origines de la civilisation japonaise,* pt. 1. Paris, 1956.

Kidder, Jonathan Edward, Jr. *Japan before Buddhism.* Rev. ed. New York, 1966.

Kitagawa, Joseph M. "Prehistoric Background of Japanese Religion." *History of Religions* 2 (Winter 1963): 292-328.

Komatsu, Isao. *The Japanese People: Origins of the People and the Language.* Tokyo, 1962.

Oka, Masao. "Kulturschichten in Alt-Japan." Ph. D. diss., Vienna University, 1933.

Early Historical Period. Basic textual sources are two my-tho-historical writings, *Kojiki,* translated by Donald L. Philippi (Princeton and Tokyo, 1969), and *Nihongi: Chronicles of Japan from the Earliest Times to A. D. 697,* translated by William George Aston (Rutland, Vt., and Tokyo, 1972). Other important textual sources available in English are *The Manyoshu: One Thousand Poems,* translated by the Nippon Gakujutsu Shin-kokai (1940; reprint, New York and London, 1965); *Kogoshui: Gleanings from Ancient Stories,* translated by Genchi Kato and Hikoshiro Hoshino, 3d ed. (1926; reprint, New York and London, 1972); and *Izumo Fudoki,* translated by Michiko Y. Aoki (Tokyo, 1971). Regarding the development of the early historic Japanese society and nation, see *Japan in the Chinese Dynastic Histories,* translated and compiled by Ryusaku Tsunoda, and edited by L. Carrington Goodrich (South Pasadena, Calif., 1951); Robert Karl Reischauer's *Early Japanese History, c. 40 B.C.-A.D. 1167,* 2 vols. (Princeton, 1937); Paul Wheatley and Thomas See's *From Court to Capital* (Chicago and London, 1978); Kan'ichi Asakawa's *The Early Institutional Life of Japan: A Study in the Reform of 645 A. D.,* 2d ed. (New York, 1903); and Richard J. Miller's *Ancient Japanese Nobility: The 'Kabane' Ranking System* (Berkeley and London, 1974).

Historical Period. Most of the books available in Western languages on the historical development of Japanese religion focus on particular religious traditions, primarily Shinto and Buddhism.

For translations of primary texts, see *Norito: A New Translation of the Ancient Japanese Ritual Prayers,* translated by Donald L. Philippi (Tokyo, 1959), and *Engi-Shiki: Procedures of the Engi Era,* 2 vols., translated by Felicia Bock (Tokyo, 1970-1972), which give us a glimpse of the Shinto foundation of the Ritsuryo state and its immanental theocracy.

Important studies of Shinto are Karl Florenz's *Die historischen Quellen der Shinto-Religion* (Leipzig, 1919); David Clarence Holtom's *The National Faith of Japan* (1938; reprint, New York, 1965); Genchi Kato's *A Study of Shinto* (Tokyo, 1926); and Tsunetsugu Muraoka's *Studies in Shinto Thought,* translated by Delmer M. Brown and James T. Araki (Tokyo, 1964). Holtom's *The Japanese Enthronement Ceremonies* (1928; reprint, Tokyo, 1972) and Robert S. Ellwood, Jr.'s *The Feast of Kingship* (Tokyo, 1973) portray an important aspect of the "Imperial Household" Shinto.

Works on Japanese Buddhism are numerous, including denominational histories, biographies of important Buddhist figures, and expositions of their writings. Among them, those that deal with Japanese Buddhism as a whole are Masaharu Anesaki's *Buddhist Art in Its Relation to Buddhist Ideals, with Special Reference to Buddhism in Japan* (1915; reprint, New York, 1978); Sir Charles Eliot's *Japanese Buddhism*, 2d ed. (London, 1959); Alicia Matsunaga's *The Buddhist Philosophy of Assimilation: The Historical Development of the 'Honji-Suijaku Theory'* (Tokyo, 1969); E. Dale Saunders's *Buddhism in Japan* (Philadelphia, 1964); Emile Steinilber-Oberlin and Kuni Matsuo's *The Buddhist Sects of Japan,* translated by Marc Logé (London, 1938); Marinus Willem de Visser's *Ancient Buddhism in Japan,* 2 vols. (Leiden and Paris, 1935); and Shoko Watanabe's *Japanese Buddhism: A Critical Appraisal,* rev. ed. (Tokyo, 1968). On the eclectic Mountain Priesthood, see H. Byron Earhart's *A Religious Study of the Mount Haguro Sect of Shugendo* (Tokyo, 1970).

Books in Western languages on Japanese Confucianism are few and mostly dated. However, mention should be made of Robert Cornell Armstrong's *Light from the East: Studies in Japanese Confucianism* (Tokyo, 1914); Kaibara Ekken's *The Way of Contentment,* translated by Ken Hoshino (1904; reprint, New York, 1913); Olaf G. Lidin's translation of Ogyu Sorai's *Distinguishing the Way: Bendo* (Tokyo, 1970); Warren W. Smith, Jr.'s *Confucianism in Modern Japan* (Tokyo, 1959); and Joseph John Spae's *Ito Jinsai* (1948; reprint, New York, 1967). For the nebulous but persistent influence of Taoism and the Yin-yang school on Japanese religion, see Bernard Frank's *Kata-imi et kata-tagae* (Paris, 1958) and Ivan I. Morris's *The World of the Shining Prince: Court Life in Ancient Japan* (1964; reprint, New York, 1979).

The standard work on Japanese folk religion is Hori Ichiro's *Folk Religion in Japan: Continuity and Change,* edited by Joseph M. Kitagawa and Alan L. Miller (Chicago, 1968). Various aspects of folk religion are discussed in Geoffrey Bownas's *Japanese Rainmaking and Other Folk Practices* (London, 1963), U. A. Casal's *The Five Sacred Festivals of Ancient Japan* (Tokyo, 1967), and Cornelis Ouwehand's *Namazu-e and Their Themes* (Leiden, 1964).

Regarding Christianity in Japan, see Otis Cary's *A History of Christianity in Japan,* 2 vols. (1909; reprint, New York, 1971), and Richard Henry Drummond's *A History of Christianity in Japan* (Grand Rapids, Mich., 1971). On the Catholic church in Japan, see Joseph Jennes's *History of the Catholic Church in Japan: From Its Beginnings to the Early Meiji Period, 1549-1873* (Tokyo, 1973). On its development in the sixteenth and seventeenth centuries, see Charles Ralph Boxer's *The Christian Century in Japan, 1549-1650* (1951; reprint, Berkeley, 1967) and George Elison's *Deus Destroyed* (Cambridge, Mass., 1973). For Protestant Christianity in Japan, see Charles W. Iglehart's *A Century of Protestant Christianity in Japan* (Rutland, Vt., and Tokyo, 1959) and Charles H. Germany's *Protestant Theologies in Modern Japan* (Tokyo, 1965).

The most helpful introduction to Japanese religion in the modern period is *Japanese Religion in the Meiji Era,* edited and compiled by Hideo Kishimoto and translated by John F. Howes (Tokyo, 1956). For the guiding ideologies of the prewar Japanese government, see *Kokutai no Hongi,* edited by Robert King Hall and translated by John Owen Gauntlett (Cambridge, 1949), and Hall's *Shushin: The Ethics of a Defeated Nation* (New York, 1949). Charles William Hepner's *The Kurozumi Sect of Shinto* (Tokyo, 1935), Delwin B. Schneider's *Konko kyo: A Japanese Religion* (Tokyo, 1962), and Henry van Straelen's *The Religion of Divine Wisdom* (Tokyo, 1954) discuss the three so-called Sect (Kyoha) Shinto groups. Daniel Clarence Holtom's *Modern Japan and Shinto Nationalism* (Chicago, 1943) deals with the way Shinto was used for political purposes before and during the war.

As to the religious development after World War II, William P. Woodard's *The Allied Occupation of Japan, 1945-1952, and Japanese Religions* (Leiden, 1972) gives us the Occupation army's religious policy and its implications for Japanese religions. Those who want to read of the postwar religious ethos in Japan will find the following works informative: Robert J. Smith's *Ancestor Worship in Contemporary Japan* (Stanford, Calif., 1974), Joseph John Spae's *Japanese Religiosity* (Tokyo, 1971), Fernando M. Basabe, Anzai Shin, and Federico Lanzaco's *Religious Attitudes of Japanese Men* (Tokyo, 1968), and Fernando M. Basabe, Anzai Shin, and Alphonso M. Nebreda's *Japanese Youth Confronts Religion: A Sociological Survey* (Tokyo, 1967). Concerning numerous "new religions" *(shinko shukyo),* which have mushroomed since 1945, consult H. Byron Earhart's *The New Religions of Japan: A Bibliography of Western Language Materials,* 2d ed. (Ann Arbor, 1983).

JOSEPH M. KITAGAWA

JAVANESE RELIGION

The Javanese occupy the central and eastern parts of Java, a moderately sized island over twelve hundred kilometers long and five hundred kilometers wide. The island constitutes only about 7 percent of the total land area of the Indonesian archipelago, which now constitutes the Republic of Indonesia.

Javanese Religious History. Hinduism probably came to Java during the fourth century of the common era through the trade routes from South India, although the earliest traces of a Hindu-Javanese civilization can only be dated to the eighth century. During that period Javanese Buddhism also developed, and the remnants of ancient religious structures such as the Hindu Prambanan and the Buddhist Borobudur seem to indicate that Javanese Hinduism and Javanese Buddhism coexisted peacefully.

Islam also came to Java through the trade routes, via North Sumatra and the Malay Peninsula between the fourteenth and seventeenth centuries. Islam in Java exhibits an emphasis on mystical ideas. Indeed, Islamic mysticism seems to have found fertile ground in Java because of the existing mystical elements in Javanese Hinduism: Muslim literary works written during the early period of Javanese islamization show the importance of mystical Islam, or Sufism (Arab., *tasawwuf*).

As a new religion, Islam initially influenced the port towns and harbor states of Java's north coast, which subsequently became prosperous and powerful and undermined the declining power of the Majapahit empire of East Java. In the following period zealous Muslim missionaries who became holy men, called *wali* (Arab., *wali;* "saint, guardian") in Javanese folklore, spread Islam through the interior regions of East and Central Java.

The court center of the Central Javanese empire, Mataram, traditionally resisted the penetration of Islam from the interior of Java. During the second half of the eighteenth century, however, Islam reached the heartland of the ancient Central Javanese civilization, although not always through peaceful means. The centers of the Hindu-Buddhistic civilization in Central Java merely had to accept the presence of Islam, and thus developed the syncretistic Agami Jawi variant of Javanese Islam.

Agami Jawi. The Agami Jawi belief system includes an extensive range of concepts, views, and values, many of which are Muslim in origin: the belief in God Almighty *(Gusti Allah)*, the belief in the prophet Muhammad *(kanjeng nabi Muhammad)*, and the belief in other prophets *(para ambiya)*. All human actions as well as important decisions are done "in the name of God" *(bismillah)*, a formula pronounced many times a day to inaugurate any small or large endeavor.

Divine beings. God is conceptualized as the totality of nature: he is a tiny divine being, so small that he can enter any human heart, yet in reality as wide as the oceans, as endless as space, and manifested in the colors that make and symbolize everything that exists on earth. In addition to the belief in God and the prophets, the Agami Jawi Javanese also believe in saints. Included among these holy persons are the nine semihistorical "apostles" *(wali sanga)*, or first missionaries of Islam, religious teachers, and certain semihistorical figures who were known to the people through the Babad literature.

Many other elements, such as the belief in a great number of deities *(dewata)*, are of Hindu-Buddhist origin, as one can see from their Sanskritic names. However, the roles and

> **Indigenous Javanese beliefs are primarily concerned with spirits, in particular, ancestral spirits. . . .**

functions of several of the deities are different from those of the original ones. Dewi Sri, for instance, who originated from Sri, the wife of the Hindu god Visnu, is in Javanese culture the goddess of fertility and rice. Bathara Kala was derived from the Hindu concept of time *(kala)*, and this destructive aspect of Siva the creator is in Javanese culture the god of death and calamity.

Indigenous Javanese beliefs are primarily concerned with spirits, in particular, ancestral spirits *(ruh lelu-hur)*, guardian spirits who care for the individual's well-being and are usually conceived of as the soul's twin *(sing ngemong)*. They also believe in a number of ghosts *(lelem-but)*, spooks *(setan)*, and giants *(denawa)*, who are frightening and malevolent creatures *(memedi)*.

The Agami Jawi has a cosmogony *(kang dumadi)*, a cosmology *(bawanagung)*, an eschatology *(akhiring jaman)*, and messianic beliefs *(ratu adil)*. While these are principally of Hindu origin, the Agami Jawi concepts of death and afterlife *(akherat)* have been influenced by Islam.

Cultic life. The Agami Jawi ceremonial and ritual system differs essentially from the dogmatic teachings of Islam. The second pillar *(rukn)* of Islam, the *salat,* or ritual prayer performed five times daily, is considered unimportant and is often ignored. Instead, various kinds of sacred communal meals *(slametan)* are central to its ceremonial system. The family hosting the ceremony usually invites friends, neighbors, and important members of the community. A sacred meal consisting of particular, customary dishes is served after being blessed by a religious official from the mosque who recites of verses *(ayat)* from the Qur'an.

Among the rural peasants, periodic *slametan* are held in connection with the stages of the agricultural cycle, whereas both rural and urban Javanese hold *slametan* meals on religious holidays of the Javanese Muslim calendar. Seasonal, community-sponsored *slametan* ceremonies, the *bersih dhusun,* are meant to purify the community. Intermittant *slametan* ceremonies are held in connection with disturbing events in the individual's life, such as a serious illness, accident, or bad dreams.

An equally important practice of the Agami Jawi is the veneration of the dead and ancestors, through visits to the graves of deceased relatives and ancestors *(nyekar)*. Also indispensable to Agami Jawi observance are the numerous offerings *(sajen)* that appear in nearly all the ceremonies and may be performed independently as well.

Fasting is not only practiced during the Muslim month of the fast, Ramadan, but on many other occasions as well. Other religious practices include deliberately seeking hardship *(tirakat)*, asceticism *(tapabrata)*, and meditation *(samadi)*. Performances of certain *wayang* puppet dramas and religious concerts on sacred *gamelan* sets also accompany religious concepts and activities.

Agami Islam Santri. The Agami Islam Santri belief system of both rural and urban Javanese is composed of puritanical Islamic concepts about God, the prophet Muhammad, creation, personal ethics, death and afterlife, eschatology, the day of resurrection, and so forth. These concepts are all clearly determined by dogmatic creed. In addition to having memorized certain parts of the Qur'an, many have also been exposed to the exegetical literature *(tafsir)*, and prophetic tradition *(hadith)* during their education in more advanced religious schools *(pesantren)*. The Muslim belief system is organized and systematized in the *shari`ah* (Islamic law); the dominant legal school *(madhhab)* in Java, and throughout Indonesia, is that of al-Shafi`i (d. 820).

Most of the Islamic calendrical ceremonial celebrations are observed by the Santri Javanese who also perform rites to celebrate certain events in the life cycle of the individual. However, unlike the Agami Jawi Javanese, who hold numerous *slametan* ceremonies, they prefer to give *sedhekah* sacrifices in accordance with the *shari`ah*. Their funerary ceremonies do not differ significantly from those of the Agami Jawi.

Javanese Spiritual and Religious Movements. There have always been adherents of Agami Jawi for whom recurrent *slametan* rituals, *sajen* offerings at fixed periods, and routine visits to graves represent a superficial, meaningless, and unsatisfactory religious life. Therefore, they search for a deeper understanding of the essence of life and spiritual existence. One response to the demand for a more spiritually meaningful life are the numerous *kebatinan kejawen* spiritual movements, which have emerged and disappeared, but have retained a constant following in the course of Javanese history. The term *kebatinan* refers to the search for truth, *batin* (Arab., *batin*). Since the late 1960s, the number of these movements has increased significantly.

There are also movements with Santri orientation. These are usually based on a particular Islamic religious school (*pesantren*). Unification with God is the central objective of most of those Santri movements.

[*See also* Southeast Asian Religions *and* Islam.]

BIBLIOGRAPHY

Alfian. *Islamic Modernization in Indonesian Politics: The Muhammadijah Movement during the Dutch Colonial Period, 1912-1942.* Madison, Wisc., 1969. An excellent description of the history of the Javanese Muhammadiyah modern reform movement, initiated by K. H. Achmad Dahlan in 1912.

Dhofier, Zamaksyari. *The Pesantren Tradition: A Study of the Role of the Kyai in the Maintenance of the Traditional Ideology of Islam in Java.* Canberra, 1980. A good description of a Javanese Muslim religious school community.

Geertz, Clifford. *The Religion of Java.* Glencoe, Ill., 1960. A description of the two variants of Javanese Islam. The author has ignored the written indigenous religious literature; nevertheless, this book has dominated the literature on Javanese culture and society for more than twenty years.

Hien, Hendrik A. van. *De Javaansche Geestenwereld en de Betrekking, die Tusschen de Geesten en de Zinnelijke Wereld Bestaat: Verduidelijkt door Petangan's of Tellingen bij de Javenen in Gebruik.* 4 vols. Semarang, 1896. An extensive description of the Javanese supernatural world, including lists of over one hundred names with brief annotations of Javanese deities, spirits, and ghosts.

Poensen, Carl. "Bijdragen tot de Kennis van den Godsdien-stigen en Zedelijken Toestand des Javaans." *Mededeelingen Vanwege het Nederlandsche Zendeling Genootschap* 7 (1863): 333-359 and 10 (1866): 23-80. An early description of two variants of Javanese Islam.

Soebardi. "Santri Religious Elements as Reflected in the Book of Tjentini." *Bijdragen tot de Taal-, Land- en Volkenkunde* 127 (1971): 331-349. A historical description of the absorption process of Muslim religious elements in the Hindu-Buddhist-Javanese syncretistic religion of the sixteenth and seventeenth centuries.

Zoetmulder, P. J. *Pantheïsme en monisme in de Javaansche soeloek-litteratuur.* Nijmegen, Netherlands, 1935. An analysis of the ancient Javanese mystical religious literature of the seventeenth and eighteenth centuries.

R. M. KOENTJARANINGRAT

JEHOVAH'S WITNESSES

Along with the Mormons, the Christian Scientists, and perhaps a few other groups, Jehovah's Witnesses is one of the few truly American expressions of religion. Like these others, Jehovah's Witnesses developed from a humble start into a worldwide religious movement. From its inception in 1872 with a handful of believers, it had increased by the 1980s to a membership of more than two million people in about two hundred countries. Powered by distinctive biblical beliefs, made effective by an efficient social organization, and fired by the conviction that the end of the historical era is at hand, the movement has maintained its distinctive appeal.

The organization's name is based on the assumption that the proper name for the Judeo-Christian deity is Jehovah. In their *New World Translation of the Holy Scriptures* (Brooklyn, N. Y., 1961), the Witnesses render as *Jehovah* the more than six thousand references in the Hebrew scriptures to the deity. Employing a variety of scriptural references (such as *Isaiah* 42:8, 43:10-11; *John* 18:37; and *Hebrews* 12:1), the Witnesses also conclude that the proper term for the followers of Jehovah is not *Christians* but *Witnesses*.

History. Jehovah's Witnesses was founded in Allegheny, Pennsylvania (now a suburb of Pittsburgh), by Charles Taze Russell, born in Pittsburgh in 1852 as the second son of Joseph L. and Eliza (Birney) Russell. Brought up as a Presbyterian, Russell came under the influence of the adventist teachings of William Miller (founder of the "Millerites") and others. Russell was prevented from obtaining an extensive education because of responsibilities in his father's chain of clothing stores, but he possessed a keen appreciation of the Bible and an engaging manner, which helped him in forming a small group to study the Bible from the perspective of the second coming of Christ. Russell's group grew, and in time other groups were formed and a publication was organized, *Zion's Watch Tower and Herald of Christ's Presence* (later called simply *The Watchtower*). The watchtower theme, appearing in various forms, has been central to the Witnesses' nomenclature. By 1884 the Zion's Watch Tower Tract Society was formed, later to become the Watch Tower Bible and Tract Society. By 1888 about fifty persons were working full-time to spread Russell's views on the Bible and the anticipated end of the age. Within a few years, groups arose throughout the United States and in a number of other countries. In 1909, finding increased acceptance, the Witnesses moved its headquarters to Brooklyn, New York, from which its international operations have been directed ever since. Russell ably led in the development of the movement despite several setbacks, including the divorce action of his wife Maria Ackley Russell in 1913. He died en route to Kansas on 31 October 1916.

Russell was succeeded by Joseph Franklin Rutherford. Born into a farm family in Morgan County, Missouri, in 1869, Rutherford was admitted to the Missouri bar at twenty-two after having been tutored in the law by a local judge. He joined the Jehovah's Witnesses in 1906 and soon shared public platforms with Russell. At a time when the Witnesses were increasingly involved in litigation, Rutherford's talents became ever more valuable. Two months after Russell's death, Rutherford was elected president of the society. He and other Witnesses believed that the "gentile times" had ended in 1914, ushering in Christ's millennial rule. Since that time, the movement has believed that Satan is the ruler of the nations and that it is therefore proper to assume a neutralist (not pacifist) stance. During World War I, Rutherford and seven other Witnesses were convicted under the Espionage Act and sent to prison, where they organized Bible studies. They were released when wartime emotions subsided.

Rutherford was an able organizer, and he persuaded the movement to use modern methods of advertising and communicating. Under his leadership the Witnesses greatly expanded their membership, the volume of their publications, the number of their full-time workers, and their international scope. In the last twelve years of his life Rutherford grew increasingly aloof from the organization, spending his time in a mansion in San Diego, California, that the society had built to house Abraham and the prophets upon their return to earth. He died at the age of seventy-two in 1942 and was interred in Rossville (Staten Island), New York.

The third president of the society was Nathan Homer Knorr, born in Bethlehem, Pennsylvania, on 23 April 1905. In his youth Knorr attended a Dutch Reformed church, but at sixteen he was attracted to the Witnesses and soon thereafter became a full-time worker. He worked in the printing plant in Brooklyn, was promoted to a higher position in the shipping department, and shortly thereafter became head of all printing operations. In 1935 he became vice-president of the society. Under his leadership, the Jehovah's Witnesses grew even more rapidly. Knorr was an indefatigable worker, an effective preacher, a world traveler for the cause, and an able administrator. He died in June 1977.

Organization and Financing. Although Knorr was succeeded by Frederick W. Franz as president, administrative leadership shifted to the Governing Body, in which no one person enjoys supreme authority. The Governing Body consists of six central committees and the lower administrative units, the branch committees. A new and more bureaucratic

era had arrived. Since 1927 the society's voluminous literature has been produced in an eight-story factory building in Brooklyn, New York. The international headquarters there includes six additional buildings as well as nearby homes to house the workers needed for the printing and other activities of the society. Near Wallkill, New York, a combination farm and factory produces the two principal magazines (*The Watchtower* and *Awake!*) and food for the society's full-time workers. Aside from room and board, these workers receive a small monthly allowance for incidental expenses. The backbone of support for the society in all its activities is the voluntarism of its members.

> **For the Witnesses, God . . . is the one supreme and universal deity.**

Beliefs and Practices. Although the Witnesses' beliefs appear to be based upon the Judeo-Christian Bible and within that context seem to represent an American fundamentalist outlook, they are indeed distinctive. All that they believe is based on the Bible. They "proof text" (that is, supply a biblical citation to support) almost every statement of faith, taking for granted the authority of the Bible, which entirely supplants tradition.

For the Witnesses, God, properly addressed as Jehovah, is the one supreme and universal deity. Jesus is thought to be God's son, but he is held as definitely inferior to Jehovah. Yet Christ holds a special place in Witness theology: he is the first of God's creations; his human life was paid as a ransom for salvation; he died on a stake (not a cross), was raised from the dead as an immortal spirit person, and is present in the world as a spirit. He is the focus of congregational gatherings; the Witnesses pray to Jehovah only through Christ.

Witnesses believe that history has run its course and that the "time of the end" is very close. Until that end, Satan rules the world. For several decades various of the society's publications have used the same title: *Millions Now Living Will Never Die*. The end is that close. Until the end, a Witness must keep apart from the world and must obey only those secular laws and follow only those practices of faith that are in conformity with the society's understanding of the Bible. In this regard, several negative requirements must be upheld. Images must not be used in worship. Spiritualism must be shunned. Witnesses must not participate in interfaith movements. Taking blood into the body, through the mouth or by transfusion, is contrary to Jehovah's laws. A clergy class and distinctive titles are prohibited. No national flag is to be saluted and no pledge of allegiance to a nation is permitted. In maintaining these requirements, the Witnesses in some countries have been prosecuted by civil authorities and at times martyred. Adherence to their beliefs in opposition to the laws of various countries has won admiration from a wide spectrum of civil libertarians, although the society does not aim at extending human freedom, but rather at expressing its own deeply held religious convictions.

Although the Witnesses uphold the doctrine of the virgin birth of Jesus, they refuse to celebrate Christmas, believing that the holiday is of pagan origin. They say that the Bible nowhere teaches that Christ's birth, or indeed, anyone's birthday, should be celebrated. (Actually, the Witnesses believe that Christ was born on 1 October, 2 BC.) They also recognize neither Lent nor Easter. They do, however, have a Lord's Meal ceremony, which takes place once a year.

Witnesses believe that baptism by immersion symbolizes dedication. They deny the obligation of Sunday worship, asserting that the observance of the Sabbath day was pertinent to Old Testament religion only and that this requirement ended with the fulfillment of Mosaic law in Jesus. The Witnesses do, however, conform to social norms in accepting Sunday as a day of rest and worship. They meet in "kingdom halls" for study and worship, as well as in members' homes.

The Witnesses believe that the end of history will begin with a great battle (which the Witnesses call Har-Magedon) between the forces of good and evil. Historical circumstances as heretofore known will be destroyed and a new order created. Satan will be vanquished and wicked human beings eternally destroyed; hell is humankind's common grave. But although human death is a consequence of Adam's sin there is hope of resurrection. Those whom Jehovah approves will receive eternal life. But only a small flock of 144,000 true believers from the whole of history will be born again as spiritual children of God and will go to heaven to rule with Christ.

On earth, however, Christ will establish a new kingdom and will rule in righteousness and peace. Ideal living conditions will be established and the earth will be environmentally restored to perfection, never again to be destroyed or depopulated. In effect, heaven will be established on earth; those who inhabit it will enjoy all good. In the meantime, the Witnesses must give public testimony to the truth of the movement's teachings. This they do through a voluminous publishing program, worldwide efforts at conversion, a variety of weekly meetings and mass celebrations, and—as they have become known to countless non-Witnesses—through door-to-door visitations.

BIBLIOGRAPHY

Of prime importance in understanding Jehovah's Witnesses is the organization's literature, the annual *Yearbook of Jehovah's Witnesses* (Brooklyn, N. Y.), and the many publications of the movement, especially *The Watchtower*, a semimonthly magazine. A number of general accounts have been published, including William Whalen's *Armageddon around the Corner: A Report on the Jehovah's Witnesses* (New York, 1962), a popular overview written in journalistic style, and Chandler W. Ster-ling's *The Witnesses: One God, One Victory* (Chicago, 1975), a generalized report by a retired Episcopalian bishop. An early and comprehensive study is my own work, *The Jehovah's Witnesses* (1945; reprint, New York, 1967). A more recent one is James A. Beckford's *The Trumpet of Prophecy: A Sociological Study of Jehovah's Witnesses* (New York, 1975). Barbara G. Harrison's *Visions of Glory: A History and a Memory of Jehovah's Witnesses* (New York, 1978) is a vivid, personal account by a woman who was a Witness between the ages of nine and twenty-one. George D. McKinney, Jr., offers a critical analysis of the Witnesses' beliefs in *The Theology of the Jehovah's Witnesses* (Grand Rapids, Mich., 1962). Of course, the Witnesses have their critics, and a few of them are in print. William J. Schnell's *Thirty Years a Watch Tower Slave: The Confessions of a Converted Jehovah's Witness* (Grand Rapids, 1956) tells its story in the title. Albert Muller's *Meet Jehovah's Witnesses: Their Confusion, Doubts, and Contradictions* (Pulaski, Wis., 1964) reflects Roman Catholic perspectives.

HERBERT HEWITT STROUP

JERUSALEM

JERUSALEM, an old Canaanite settlement in the uplands of Judaea, enters history when David, king of Israel, decides to make this Jebusite city his capital. He builds an altar there. This spot may have been an earlier Canaanite high place, but it now became the site of a grandiose temple possibly planned by David and certainly built by his son Solomon.

The Temple of Solomon was an enormous structure with interior courtyards of progressively limited access, in the midst of which stood an ornately adorned sanctuary. Outside it stood the great altar of sacrifice, and within, in a curtained inner chamber, the Holy of Holies, was installed the Ark of the Covenant containing the Tablets of the Law and other tokens of the Israelites' deliverance from Egypt.

The Babylonians took Jerusalem in 587/6 BCE, razed the Temple, and carried off many of the Jews into exile. And it is likely that at that time the Ark of the Covenant disappeared as part of the spoils. Sometime after 538 BCE the Persian shah Cyrus II and his Achaemenid successors allowed the exiled Jews to return to Jerusalem. The city was rebuilt by Nehemiah, the Mosaic Law was repromulgated through the efforts of the priestly scribe Ezra, and under the auspices of Zerubbabel a reduced version of Solomon's Temple was constructed on the same site. In the wake of Alexander the Great, Greeks succeeded to Persians in the late fourth century in Palestine, and after 200 BCE the Greco-Macedonian dynasty of the Seleucids ruled over what was a politically modest temple-state at Jerusalem.

The chastening of the Israelites before, during, and immediately after their Babylonian exile produced a new type of religious leader in their midst, the prophet, and in their inspired visions Jerusalem became the symbol of and indeed identical with the Children of Israel and the Land of Israel, now cast down for its idolatry and fornication, now exalted, renewed, and glorified in the new age that would follow the present travails. Thus the historical Jerusalem, which often lay in ruin and misery, was transformed by Isaiah and Ezekiel, among others, into a heavenly and eschatological Jerusalem.

The historical Jerusalem revived under Greek sovereignty, until the king instituted a full-scale attack on Judaism in Judaea and installed a Macedonian garrison and foreign cults in the Temple precinct. The outraged Jews mounted a bold resistance, and under the priestly family called the Maccabees they eventually drove most of the Greeks from Judaea and Jerusalem and in 164 BCE rededicated the Temple there to the cult of the Lord.

The Hasmonean dynasty survived until 37 BCE, when its own weaknesses permitted, and Roman choice dictated, the passage of power to the Idumaean Herod I (r. 37-34 BCE). Jerusalem was still growing;—it now covered the western hill as well as the eastern hill where Solomon's Temple and the City of David had been located. The prodigious building activity of Herod increased the tempo of Greco-Roman urbanization. He extended the street plan, built an immense citadel at the western gate of the city, erected his own palace nearby, and sought to crown his labors by undertaking in 20 BCE a reconstruction of the Temple. This mammoth Herodian temple complex, with its newly extended platform, not only doubled the size of Solomon's installation, it dwarfed every known temple assemblage in the Greco-Roman Near East.

Jewish sovereignty over Jerusalem did not last very long; the Romans by contrast held the city, although they never ruled from it, for six and a half centuries, and different Muslim dynasties, who likewise preferred to put their palaces elsewhere, held sway over Jerusalem from the mid-seventh to the early twentieth century. But however brief the span, Jewish kings ruled over a Jewish state *in* Jerusalem; Roman governors, some pagan, some Christian, ruled *over* Jerusalem; and for a very long time the city was a part, often not a very important part, of some form or other of a Muslim political organization, although never its capital.

Jesus was born under Herodian and died under Roman sovereignty. Although at home in Galilee, he taught, performed miracles, died, and was buried in Herodian Jerusalem. He worshiped in Herod's Temple, with which he identified himself and whose destruction he openly predicted. As he had foreseen, it happened in 70 CE, at the end of a Jewish insurrection against the Romans, but only after Jesus himself had been tried in Jerusalem, crucified outside the western wall of the city, and buried nearby, having said that he would rise again in three days. A century thereafter Jerusalem, too, had its resurrection. In 132 CE the Roman emperor Hadrian published his plans for a new, very Roman Jerusalem. The Jews for their part were banned from the city and its near vicinity.

In 330 CE Constantine, with the urging or the assistance of his mother Helena, set about identifying the chief sites of Jesus' redemptive activity in Palestine. He enshrined them with major basilicas, notably the cave of the nativity in Bethlehem and the places, by then inside Jerusalem's walls, of Jesus' execution, burial, and resurrection. Jesus' tomb was housed under a splendid rotunda, and the site of the execution was enshrined at the corner of an open courtyard; abutting both was an extremely large basilica. The work was capped with both celebrity and authority when in the course of the construction Helena discovered the remains, verified by miracle, of Jesus' own cross.

It was Constantine's initiative that began the conversion of Jerusalem into a Christian holy city, or perhaps better, of Palestine into a Christian holy land. In the wake of Constantine's building program, Christian pilgrims, particularly those from overseas, began to arrive in increasing numbers. What those visitors came to see, and to experience, was not Jerusalem, but the entire network of Palestinian sites connected with Jesus, his apostles, and the early Christian saints.

In the rest of the city, meanwhile, the effect of imperial investment began to manifest itself in the network of churches, shrines, hospices, and even hospitals as marked on the Madeba map. Now, with no claim to either political or commerical eminence—even in the ecclesiastical hierarchy the city lost ground to nearby Caesarea and distant Antioch—Jerusalem was assuming a role it would have until 1967: that of a holy city supported and adorned for its holiness, and for the political benefits accruing from the official recognition of that holiness.

The Jews continued to be prohibited residence there by the Christian as well as by the pagan Roman emperors. But in 638 CE the Muslims came up from the south and took the city from them and their Christian Roman empire in almost perfunctory fashion. Among the Muslims' first acts was to build a mosque on the deserted Temple mount and, within a century, to erect in the middle of that same platform an extraordinary Muslim shrine called the Dome of the Rock.

Although subsequently rebuilt, the mosque on the Temple mount is still called al-Masjid al-Aqsa ("the distant sanctuary," i. e., mosque), as it was from the beginning

The Aqsa, then, was the congregational mosque of Jerusalem, a prayer place that also commemorated that "Distant Sanctuary" mentioned in God's book and visited by the Prophet in the course of his "night journey."

The relationship of Jews, Christians, and Muslims in Jerusalem, where a majority of the population was Christian and the political sovereignty Muslim, was more or less harmonious. In 1009 the assuredly arrogant and possibly envious Fatimid caliph al-Hakim burned down the Christians' Church of the Holy Sepulcher. It was eventually rebuilt, but some deep harm had been done. That harm was chiefly experienced in Christian Europe, which eventually launched a Crusade that took the city back from the Muslims in 1099. [*See* Crusades.]

After the Muslim reoccupation of the city in 1187, Christians continued to come on pilgrimage, still following Jesus' "Way of the Cross" across the city, but now under the most grim of circumstances.

No Christian pope or Muslim caliph—both quite different from a national king to begin with—ever had Jerusalem as his seat. Christian and Muslim governors Jerusalem has had and, during the Crusades, even a number of Christian kings, but that was either sectarian sovereignty or rule by delegated authority.

Jerusalem is more than a city or even a national capital; it is an idea. And it is safe to say that it is a biblical idea. As the Bible unfolds, one can easily follow the progressive identification being drawn between the people of Israel, or the Land of Israel, and Jerusalem and its Temple. People, city, and Temple become one, linked in destiny and God's plan, and then transformed, apotheosized, into the Heavenly Jerusalem.

BIBLIOGRAPHY

On the integration of the Jewish city into both ideology and the popular consciousness, see W. D. Davies's *The Territorial Dimension of Judaism* (Berkeley, 1982); *The Temple of Solomon: Archaeological Fact and Medieval Tradition in Christian, Islamic and Jewish Art,* edited by Joseph Gutmann (Missoula, Mont., 1976); *Zion in Jewish Literature,* edited by Abraham S. Halkin (New York, 1961); and Zev Vilnay's *Legends of Jerusalem,* vol. 1, *The Sacred Land* (Philadelphia, 1973). Vilnay's work includes many of the Muslim legends. On the conversion of Jerusalem to a Christian holy city, see W. D. Davies's *The Gospel and the Land: Early Christianity and Jewish Territorial Doctrine* (Berkeley, 1974); E. D. Hunt's *Holy Land Pilgrimage in the Later Roman Empire, A. D. 312-460* (Oxford, 1982); *Peregrinatio Aetheriae: Egeria's Travels to the Holy Land,* rev. ed., translated by John Wilkinson (London, 1981); and John Wilkinson's *Jerusalem Pilgrims before the Crusades* (Warminster, England, 1977).

On Muslim Jerusalem, the best introduction is the double article in *The Encyclopaedia of Islam,* new ed., vol. 5, fasc. 83-84 (Leiden, 1980), under "al-Kuds"—"Part A: History," by S. D. Goitein, and "Part B: Monuments," by Oleg Grabar. Many of the Muslim historians' and travelers' accounts of the city are collected in *Palestine under the Moslems,* translated by Guy Le Strange (New York, 1890). Sections of this book dealing specifically with Jerusalem have recently been reprinted under the title *Jerusalem under the Moslems* (Jerusalem, n. d.).

For the most revealing travel accounts of the post-Crusader era, consult *Jewish Travellers: A Treasury of Travelogues from Nine Centuries,* 2d ed., edited by Elkan N. Adler (New York, 1966); *The Wanderings of Felix Fabri,* 2 vols., translated by Aubrey Stewart (1892-1893; New York, 1971); and *The Travels of Ibn Battuta, A. D. 1325-1354,* 2 vols., translated and edited by H. A. R. Gibb (Cambridge, 1958-1962).

On the nineteenth- and twentieth-century city, see Meron Benvenisti's *Jerusalem: The Torn City* (Jerusalem, 1976); N. A. Silberman's *Digging for God and Country: Exploration, Archeology and the Secret Struggle for the Holy Land, 1799-1917* (New York, 1982); and Walter Zander's *Israel and the Holy Places of Christendom* (New York, 1971). Finally, for visitors to the Holy City of all the faiths and in all eras, see my *Jerusalem: The Holy City in the Eyes of Chroniclers, Visitors, Pilgrims and Prophets from the Days of Abraham to the Beginnings of Modern Times* (Princeton, 1985).

F. E. PETERS

JESUS

JESUS (c. 7/6 BC–c. AD 30), more fully Jesus of Nazareth, called Christ; founder of Christianity.

Life and Work

The Story. A basic history of Jesus would include at least the following items. He was a Galilean Jew, the son of a woman called Mary who was married to Joseph, a carpenter. Jesus was baptized by John, began to preach and teach, associated in a special way with public sinners and other outcasts, called disciples to follow him, worked miracles, and taught some memorable parables. His challenge to given forms of piety (*Mt.* 6:1-18), his desire to correct certain traditions (*Mk.* 7:1-23), his violation of some Sabbath observances (*Mk.* 2:23-27), his attitude toward the Temple in Jerusalem (*Mk.* 14:58, 15:29 and parallels), and other offenses aroused the antagonism of some Jewish leaders and teachers. In Jerusalem (where he had come for the Passover celebration) he was betrayed, arrested, interrogated by members of the Sanhedrin, condemned by Pontius Pilate, executed on a cross (which bore an inscription giving the charge against Jesus as a messianic pretender), and buried later the same day.

Ministry. Hardly anything is more certain about Jesus' ministry than that through his words and deeds he proclaimed the kingdom, or rule, of God. He understood his activity to be initiating a new, powerful, and final offer of salvation (e.g., *Mt.* 4:23, 9:35: 12:28). Faced with this offer, his audience was called to repent (e.g., *Mk.* 1:15) and accept the divine pardon that Jesus himself communicated in his own person (*Mk.* 2:17 and parallels). Through words of forgiveness (*Mk.* 2:5, *Lk.* 7:48), parables of mercy (e.g., *Lk.* 15:11-32), and table fellowship with outcasts (e.g., *Mt.* 11:19), he aimed to bring sinners back into God's company.

In doing all this, Jesus acted with a striking sense of personal authority (*Mk.* 1:22) that did not hesitate to go beyond the divine law received by Moses (*Mk.* 10:2-9). His call for radical conversion (e.g., *Mt.* 5;1-7:27, *Lk.* 6:20-49) entailed transforming in his own name that law and carrying to the ultimate its inmost spirit (*Mt.* 5:21-48).

How did Jesus assess and describe his own identity? To begin with, he thought of himself as a spiritual physician (*Mk.*

2:17), a shepherd to his people (*Mt.* 15:24), and a divinely authorized prophet (*Lk.* 13:33). Then around seventy times in the synoptic Gospels Jesus calls himself (the) "Son of man," a term that in its Semitic background either was a circumlocution for oneself as speaker (e.g., *Mt.* 8:20) or simply meant "a human being" or "someone." What is not quite certain is whether by the time of Jesus himself "Son of man" was also a clearly defined title associated with a deliverer expected to come in the last times. However, the three contexts in which Jesus designated himself as "Son of man" carried their own distinct meanings. This self-designation was used of Jesus' earthly work and condition (e.g., *Mk.* 2:10, 2:28; *Mt.* 11:19 and parallel); of his suffering, death, and resurrection (*Mk.* 8:31, 9:31, 10:33-34); and of his coming in future glory as a redeemer-judge (e.g., *Mk.* 8:38, 13:26; *Mt.* 24:27 and parallel).

Crucifixion. Jesus' ministry ended in Jerusalem when he was betrayed by Judas, put on trial before members of the Sanhedrin, convicted (for despising the law and blasphemously claiming messianic authority?), handed over to

> ... fidelity to his mission would bring deadly opposition from the public authorities.

Pilate, and executed as a threat to the public order. Did Jesus anticipate and interpret in advance such a violent death?

It was, or at least became, obvious to Jesus—and for that matter to any moderately intelligent observer—that fidelity to his mission would bring deadly opposition from the public authorities (e.g., *Lk.* 11:47, 11:49-50, 13:33-34). Among other things, the fate of John the Baptist suggested such a danger. Then Jesus' demonstrative entry into Jerusalem (*Mk.* 11:1-11) and cleansing of the Temple (*Mk.* 11:15-18) increased the danger from Caiaphas and other leading Sadducees, who under the Roman army retained some power in the capital. This and further evidence (e.g., from the Last Supper and the agony in the garden of Gethsemane) point to the conclusion that Jesus anticipated and accepted his violent end.

Resurrection. As far as the historical evidence goes, the Christian movement began with the simple announcement that the crucified Jesus had been raised to new life and had appeared to some witnesses. At first, individuals who had seen him risen from the dead guaranteed the truth of the resurrection (e.g., *1 Cor.* 15:5, 15:7, 15:8; *Lk.* 24:34). Then the Christian community as such professed this truth (see, for example, the formulations cited in *1 Thessalonians* 4:14, *Romans* 1:3-4, and *Romans* 10:9). The discovery of the empty tomb by Mary Magdalene, accompanied perhaps by other women (*Mk.* 16:1-8; *Jn.* 20:1, 20:11-13; *Lk.* 24:10,

24:23), served as a confirmatory sign. But the New Testament shows a clear awareness that an empty tomb simply by itself did not establish Jesus' resurrection (e.g., *Jn.* 20:2, *Mt.* 28:11-15).

It is not surprising that, together with their claims about Jesus' resurrection, Christians defined God in terms of the risen Christ. Repeatedly Paul cited a formula from the early tradition that identified God as "having raised Jesus from the dead" (e.g., *Gal.* 1:1, *Rom.* 10:9, *1 Cor.* 6:14). Hence, to be wrong about the resurrection would be to "misrepresent" God (*1 Cor.* 15;15). [*See also* Resurrection.]

Christological Developments

Councils of the Church. In the development of Christology, progress often occurred in reaction to views rejected as heterodox. Thus the occasion for the first ecumenical council, the Council of Nicaea (325), came with the teachings of Arius (c. 250-336). To preserve the oneness of God, while at the same time affirming the uniqueness of Jesus Christ, Arius asserted that the Son was a perfect creature, at most a kind of demigod subordinated to the Father. To combat Arius, the council adopted a term that had been used by Origen (c. 185-c. 254) to indicate that Christ shared one common divine being with the Father; *homoousios* ("of one substance"). This teaching on Christ's divinity raised a question: how could believers then maintain Christ's true humanity? One supporter of Nicaea, Apollinaris of Laodicea (c. 310-c. 390), reduced Christ's full humanity by apparently suggesting that at the incarnation the divine Logos (or Word of God) assumed only a body and itself took the place of the human spirit. Against Apollinaris the First Council of Constantinople (381) taught that Christ had a true human soul.

Defenders of the unity between Christ's divinity and humanity went to another extreme. Eutyches of Constantinople (c. 378-454) seemed to maintain that Christ's divinity absorbed his humanity—the so-called mono-physite heresy, according to which the one divine nature *(phusis)* swallowed up Christ's humanity. The Council of Chalcedon (451) reacted by acknowledging in Christ "two natures in one person [*prosopon*] or acting subject [*hupostasis*]." This personal unity left the divine and human natures quite intact and in no way confused or intermingled them with each other.

Chalcedon said nothing about Christ's crucifixion and resurrection. In the centuries that followed, an all-absorbing theology of the incarnation generally monopolized attention. In one important development the Third Council of Constantinople (680) condemned monothelitism, or the view that acknowledged only one will in Christ. The council held for a divine and human will; the duality of Christ's natures entailed a duality of wills.

The Middle Ages. When theology tended to represent Christ largely in terms of his divinity, church art, popular belief, and widespread devotions often defended his truly human existence and experience. Icons, the Christmas crib, carols, the stations of the cross, and later the success of Luther's hymns and Roman Catholic devotion to the Sacred Heart witnessed to the instinctive attachment of ordinary Christians to the real humanity of Jesus.

In his *Cur Deus homo* (1098), Anselm of Canterbury became the first Christian writer to devote a whole work to the redemptive activity of Christ. According to Anselm, sin offended God's honor, and either satisfaction or punishment had to follow that offense. By making satisfaction, Jesus restored the divine honor, and punishment was not involved. Unfortunately, those who drew on *Cur Deus homo*—from Thomas Aquinas, through John Calvin (1509-1564), down to Karl Barth (1886-1968) and others—added punitive elements to Anselm's version of redemption. Nowadays his soteriology, or doctrine of salvation, has fallen on hard times and is often dismissed as legalistic and concerned with the divine honor rather than with God's love. However, John McIntyre, Gispert Greshake, and Walter Kasper have defended Anselm's theology of satisfaction for appreciating the divine fidelity to creation and the moral order.

Modern Times. From the eighteenth century onward Christology began to be deeply affected by the rise of critical methods in historical and biblical research. Scientific history became and in many ways has remained the dominant partner in dialogue with theological thinking about Jesus' person and saving work.

The historical Jesus. In the classical period for the historical study of Jesus' life, writers like David Friedrich Strauss (1808-1874), Ernest Renan (1823-1892), and Adolf von Harnack (1851-1930) attempted to penetrate behind the christological doctrines of Paul and the early church and get back to Jesus of Nazareth as he actually was. They hoped to recover by scientific, unprejudiced use of the earliest sources—in particular Mark's gospel—an authentic picture of the real Jesus.

Despite the work of these scholars, however, no common, scientifically established picture of Jesus emerged. By the time Albert Schweitzer wrote his classic study of this nineteenth-century enterprise, *The Quest of the Historical Jesus* (1906), it had become clear that many had been portraying Jesus largely in the light of their own personal presuppositions and the convictions of their society. Schweitzer protested against all these attempts to modernize Jesus and insisted that the key was to be found in Jesus' eschatology, or views about the end of history.

Contemporary approaches. From Thomas Aquinas in the Middle Ages down to Karl Barth in the twentieth century, classic Christology began its theological interpretation with God. The essential question for this approach was "How did the preexistent Son of God 'come down' and enter this world?" In place of this Christology "from above," much recent thinking has begun "from below," using as its starting point the historical, human situation of Jesus in this world. The key question for such a Christology "from below" is "What does it mean to say that a particular man from Nazareth was both universal savior and 'God among us'?" How could a human being have been such and been recognizable as such?

Wolfhart Pannenberg, who originally championed a Christology "from below" in *Jesus: God and Man* (1964), in the second volume of *Grundfragen systematischer Theologie* (1980) came to question the correctness of setting up sharp alternatives. In *Jesus the Christ* (1974) Walter Kasper sees the two approaches ("from above" and "from below") as complementing each other.

A second major distinction in contemporary Christology concerns its center. For some (e.g., John A. T. Robinson and Pierre Teilhard de Chardin), evolving creation provides the primary focus. Jean Galot, Karl Rahner, and others organize matters around the incarnation. In their varying ways, yet other scholars (e.g., Hans Küng, James Mackey, Edward Schillebeeckx, and Jon Sobrino) have taken the synoptic Gospels' account of the ministry as the center.

Right from the birth of Christianity the convictions embodied in worship supported the centrality of the Easter mystery. Believers expressed liturgically, especially through baptism (Rom. 6:3-5) and the Eucharist (1 Cor. 11:26), the sense that Jesus' crucifixion and resurrection were the heart of the matter. From such a midpoint, Christology can look in one direction (through Jesus' life, the incarnation, and the history of the Israelites) back to creation, and in the other direction (through the coming of the Holy Spirit, the life of the church, and the history of humanity) forward to the future consummation of all things.

Issues

The Resurrection. In the late nineteenth and early twentieth century Wilhelm Bousset, James G. Frazer, and others connected Jesus with myths of dying and rising gods, frequently those of the mystery religions of Greece and the ancient Near East. Belief in the resurrection of the crucified Jesus was taken to be simply another projection of the human need to cope with the changing seasons and common challenges of life.

Subsequently it was maintained that the message of the resurrection was not a statement that claimed to present a fact about Jesus himself but simply functioned to declare a personal commitment of the early Christians to a new way of life (e.g., Paul M. Van Buren in *The Secular Meaning of the Gospel,* 1963).

It has sometimes been argued that the disciples "saw" and announced Jesus risen from the dead simply because they needed his resurrection to cope psychologically and religiously with the horror of his crucifixion. In *The Resurrection of Jesus of Nazareth* (1968), Willi Marxsen takes "resurrection" to have been no more than one possible way of interpreting the experience of "seeing" Jesus and finding faith.

Suffering and Redemption. Moltmann (in *The Crucified God*) and other theologians have developed various kinds of post-Holocaust Christologies that draw partly on the theme of God's pain and sorrow over human sin, which is to be found in the Hebrew scriptures (e.g., *Gen.* 6:6, *Is.* 63:10) and in rab-

> **Belief in the resurrection . . . was taken to be simply another projection of the human need to cope with the changing seasons and common challenges of life.**

binic literature. This approach was anticipated by certain English and Russian kenotic Christologies of the nineteenth and early twentieth centuries, in which the Son of God's self-emptying *(Phil.* 2:7) enabled him to enter into a radical solidarity with the alienated and dehumanized of this world.

The interpretation of the scriptural texts to which these Christologies appeal (e.g., *Mk.* 15:34, *Rom.* 8:32, *Jn.* 3:16) has been widely challenged. The notion of God being open as such to suffering and change through an event of this world (the crucifixion) runs into philosophical and theological difficulties, at least for many schools of thought. The alternative to Moltmann's history of the triune God's suffering is not necessarily a detached God who remains indifferent to human pain and misery. Rather, it can be a belief in a compassionate God whose boundless love freely revealed itself in human history—above all, in the passion and death of Jesus.

Virginal Conception. On the basis of the infancy narratives of Matthew and Luke (*Mt.* 1-2, *Lk.* 1-2), Christian tradition has held that Jesus had no human father but was conceived through the power of the Holy Spirit. Challenges to this tradition have come on a number of grounds. Some rule it out as part of their general rejection of any such miraculous intervention by God. Others maintain that early Christians were under pressure to invent the story of the virginal conception, once Jewish critics began to claim that Jesus was illegitimate. Still others have argued that myths about male gods impregnating earthly women prompted Christians (who already believed in Jesus' divinity) to develop the legend of this virginal conception. Then there are those who think that Christians have misinterpreted the intentions of Matthew and Luke in their infancy narratives.

These challenges to the tradition of the virginal conception are balanced by other arguments. Any adequate discussion of the rejection of divine miraculous intervention would require an enormous parenthesis on the nature and role of miracles. The challenge that the doctrine is a defense against the charge of illegitimacy is weakened by the argument of

Raymond E. Brown in *The Birth of the Messiah* (1977). Brown shows that the charge of illegitimacy, which appeared in the second century, may have emerged only after the composition of the gospels of Matthew and Luke and perhaps even as a reaction to their narratives of the virginal conception. In that case the story of the virginal conception would not have arisen as a Christian response to a charge of illegitimacy that was already in circulation.

With regard to the challenge that Christians have misinterpreted the intentions of Matthew and Luke, Brown argues that while we cannot scientifically trace the way the tradition(s) of the virginal conception originated, were transmitted in the early Christian communities, and reached the evangelists, it seems that "both Matthew and Luke regarded the virginal conception as historical," even if "the modern intensity about historicity was not theirs" (*Birth of the Messiah*, p. 517). The two evangelists refer to the conception of Jesus from different standpoints—Matthew from that of Joseph, Luke from that of Mary—but both agree that the conception came about without human intercourse and through the power of the Holy Spirit.

[*For further discussion of Christian reflection on the life and ministry of Jesus, see* Theology *and* Trinity.]

BIBLIOGRAPHY

The best available studies on the history of Jesus include A. E. Harvey's *Jesus and the Constraints of History* (London, 1982); Joachim Jeremias's *New Testament Theology: The Proclamation of Jesus,* translated by John Bowden (New York, 1971); Howard Clark Kee's *Jesus in History: An Approach to the Study of the Gospels,* 2d ed. (New York, 1977); and Ben F. Meyer's *The Aims of Jesus* (London, 1979). Joseph A. Fitzmyer's *A Christological Catechism: New Testament Answers* (Ramsey, N. J., 1982) accurately sums up the New Testament's presentation of Jesus' story and person. Hans Küng, in *On Being a Christian* (New York, 1977), marshals evidence to show the distinctiveness of the historical Jesus over against other founders of world religions. Pheme Perkins's *Resurrection* (New York, 1984) provides a detailed exegetical study of the New Testament witness to the resurrection of Jesus. The development of doctrines about Jesus in primitive Christianity is covered well by Martin Hengel's *The Son of God* (Philadelphia, 1976) and C. F. D. Moule's *The Origin of Christology* (Cambridge, 1977). Aloys Grillmeier's *Christ in Christian Tradition* (London, 1965) traces the development of Christology from the first century to the Council of Chalcedon. Contemporary Christologies include Walter Kasper's *Jesus the Christ* (New York, 1976); James P. Mackey's *Jesus, the Man and the Myth* (New York, 1979); my *Interpreting Jesus* (Ramsey, N. J., 1983); Wolfhart Pannenberg's *Jesus: God and Man,* 2d ed. (Philadelphia, 1977); Richard P. McBrien's *Catholicism,* vol. 1 (Minneapolis, 1980), pp. 367-563; and Karl Rahner's *Foundations of Christian Faith* (New York, 1978), pp. 176-321. Edward Schillebeeckx, in *Christ: The Experience of Jesus as Lord* (New York, 1980), reconstructs Christian belief in Jesus as Savior within the context of human suffering and the quest for salvation. A notable Jewish study on Jesus is Samuel Sandmel's *We Jews and Jesus* (New York, 1965). Géza Vermès's *Jesus the Jew: A Historian's Reading of the Gospels* (Philadelphia, 1981) presents a Jesus who as prophet, healer, exorcist, and agent of forgiveness belonged to the tradition of charismatic Judaism. M. M. Thomas's *The*

Acknowledged Christ of the Indian Renaissance (London, 1969) surveys ways in which some spiritual leaders in Neo-Hinduism interpret the meaning of Jesus and Christianity for religion and society in modern India. Milan Machovec's *A Marxist Looks at Jesus* (Philadelphia, 1976) is the best study on Jesus by a Marxist. Wismer Don's *The Islamic Jesus: An Annotated Bibliography of Sources in English and French* (New York, 1977) guides the reader to many Muslim studies on Jesus.

GERALD O'COLLINS, S. J.

JEWS AND JUDAISM

[*See article* Judaism.]

JIHAD

JIHAD is the verbal noun of the Arabic verb *jahada,* meaning "to endeavor, to strive, to struggle." It is generally used to denote an effort toward a commendable aim. In religious contexts it can mean the struggle against one's evil inclinations or efforts toward the moral uplift of society or toward the spread of Islam.

Jihad in the Qur'an and the Hadith. In about two-thirds of the instances where the verb *jahada* or its derivatives occur in the Qur'an, it denotes warfare. They are often linked with the phrase "in the way of God" *(fi sabil Allah)* to underscore the religious character of the struggle.

Many later verses on *jihad* order the believers to take part in warfare, promise heavenly reward to those who do, and threaten those who do not with severe punishment in the hereafter. Some verses deal with practical matters such as exemption from military service (9:91, 48:17), fighting during the holy months (2:217) and in the holy territory of Mecca (2:191), the fate of prisoners of war (47:4), safe conduct (9:6), and truce (8:61).

There is an abundant body of *hadith* on *jihad*. The *hadiths* deal with the same topics as the Qur'an but place more emphasis on the excellence of *jihad* as a pious act, on the rewards of martyrdom, and on practical and ethical matters of warfare.

Jihad in Islamic Law. The prescriptions found in the Qur'an and *hadith,* together with the practice of the early caliphs and army commanders, were, from the latter half of the second century AH on, cast in the mold of a legal doctrine to which a separate chapter in the handbooks on Islamic law was devoted. The central part of this doctrine is that the Muslim community as a whole has the duty to expand the territory and rule of Islam. Consequently, *jihad* is a collective duty of all Muslims, which means that if a sufficient number take part in it, the whole community has fulfilled its obligation.

The ultimate aim of *jihad* is "the subjection of the unbelievers" and "the extirpation of unbelief." This is understood, however, in a purely political way as the extension of Islamic rule over the remaining parts of the earth.

The *jihad* chapters in the legal handbooks contain many practical rules. Warfare must start with the summons in which the enemies are asked to embrace Islam or accept the status of non-Muslim subjects. Only if they refuse may they be attacked.

Jihad in History. Throughout Islamic history the doctrine of *jihad* has been invoked to justify wars between Muslim and non-Muslim states and even to legitimate wars between Muslims themselves. Examples of *jihad* movements are the Wahhabiyah in Arabia, founded by Muhammad ibn `Abd al-Wahhab (1703-1787), the Fulbe *jihad* in northern Nigeria led by Usuman dan Fodio (1754-1817), the Sanusiyah in Libya and the Sahara, founded by Muhammad ibn `Ali al-Sanusi, and the Mahdist movement of Muhammad Ahmad in the Sudan (1881-1898). In the twentieth century the *jihad* doctrine lost much of its importance as a mobilizing ideology in the struggle against colonialism.

BIBLIOGRAPHY

The most extensive and reliable survey of the classical doctrine of *jihad* is Majid Khadduri's *War and Peace in the Law of Islam* (Baltimore, 1955). The same author has translated the oldest legal handbook on *jihad,* written by Muhammad al-Shaybani (749-805) and published under the title *The Islamic Law of Nations: Shaybani's Siyar* (Baltimore, 1966). Muhammad Hamidullah's *Muslim Conduct of State,* 6th rev. ed. (Lahore, 1973), is based on an extensive reading of the classical sources but is somewhat marred by the author's apologetic approach. In my *Jihad in Mediaeval and Modern Islam* (Leiden, 1977), I have translated and annotated a classical legal text and a modernist text on *jihad;* also included is a comprehensive bibliography of translations into Western languages of primary sources on *jihad*. Albrecht Noth's *Heiliger Krieg und heiliger Kampf in Islam und Christentum* (Bonn, 1966) and Emmanuel Sivan's *L'Islam et la Croisade: Idéologie et propagande dans les réactions musulmanes aux Croisades* (Paris, 1968) both deal with the *jihad* doctrine in the historical setting of the Crusades. In addition, Noth compares *jihad* with similar notions in Christianity. Hilmar Krüger's study *Fetwa und Siyar: Zur international rechtlichen Gutachtenpraxis der osmanischen Seyh ül-Islâm vom 17. bis 19. Jahrhundert unter besonderer Berücksichtigung des "Behcet ül-Fetâvâ* (Wiesbaden, 1978) examines the role of the *jihad* doctrine in Ottoman international relations from the seventeenth to the nineteenth century. Mohammad Talaat Al Ghunaimi's *The Muslim Conception of International Law and the Western Approach* (The Hague, 1968) attempts to apply the notions of modern international law to the *jihad* doctrine and asserts that islamic law, thus recast, could nowadays be applied in international relations. The political role and the interpretation of the *jihad* doctrine in the nineteenth and twentieth centuries are the main themes of my *Islam and Colonialism: The Doctrine of Jihad in Modern History* (The Hague, 1979). On the Egyptian *jihad* organization see Johannes J. G. Jansen's *The Neglected Duty* (New York, 1986).

RUDOLPH PETERS

JOAN OF ARC

JOAN OF ARC (c. 1412-1431), French visionary; also known as the Maid of Orléans. Joan, who called herself Jeanne La Pucelle, used her claims to mystical experience to influence the course of French history in the fifteenth century. Led by her visions, she inspired the French army to turn the tide of the Hundred Years' War. Born around 1412 in Domrémy-la-Pucelle, a village on the border between Lorraine and France, Joan was a peasant who, in her own words, did not "know A from B." As she grew up she heard the magical lore and local saints' legends of Lorraine and reports of continuing French defeats at the hands of the English.

At age thirteen Joan began to hear a voice from God instructing her to go to the dauphin Charles, the uncrowned Valois king. Believing that she was called to drive the English out of France, Joan privately took a vow of virginity and prepared herself for the role of prophetic adviser to the king, a type of female mystic familiar in the late medieval period. At some point in these troubled years the voice became three voices, whom she later identified as the saints Catherine of Alexandria and Margaret of Antioch, both known for their heroic virginity, and the archangel Michael, protector of the French royal family.

Joan established her authority through her urgent sincerity, by identifying herself with prophecies about a virgin who would save France, and by accurately announcing a French defeat on the day it took place 150 miles away. No longer able to ignore her, the garrison captain at the nearby town of Vaucouleurs refused to endorse her mission to save France until she was exorcised, raising the issue that would haunt her mission henceforth: Did her powers come from God or from the devil? Not fully assured, the captain nonetheless gave her arms and an escort. Cutting her hair short and donning male clothing, Joan and her companions made their way through enemy territory, reaching the dauphin's court at Chinon in late February 1429.

Joan's indomitable belief that only she could save France impressed Charles, his astronomer, and some of the nobles. But they too moved carefully, requiring an examination for heresy by theologians at Poitiers, who declared her a good Christian, and a physical examination by three matrons, who certified that she was indeed a virgin. For a woman about to attempt the "miracle" of defeating the English, virginity added an aura of almost magical power.

Given the desperate nature of Charles's position, he had little to lose in allowing Joan to join the army marching to the relief of Orléans, which had been besieged by the English. Her presence attracted volunteers and raised morale. Charging into the midst of battle, Joan was wounded and became the hero of the day. With Orléans secured, Joan impatiently counseled the army to move on. Town after town

along the Loire fell, others offered their loyalty without battle. By late July, the dauphin could be crowned King Charles VII at Reims with Joan by his side.

But Joan's days of glory were brief. Driven by her voices, she disobeyed the king and continued to fight. Her attack on Paris failed, and several other ventures ended inconclusively. In May 1430, Joan was captured in a skirmish outside Compiègne. Neither Charles nor any of his court made an attempt to rescue or ransom her.

Determined to discredit Joan as a heretic and a witch, the English turned her over to an inquisitional court. Manned by over one hundred French clerics in the pay of the English, Joan's trial in Rouen lasted from 21 February to 28 May 1431. Under inquisitional procedure she could not have counsel or call witnesses. As a layperson she had no religious order to speak for her, nor had she ever enlisted the support of a priest. Yet although she had spent months in military prisons, in chains and guarded constantly by men, Joan began with a strong defense. Reminding her interrogators that she was sent by God, she warned that they would condemn her at great risk. The charges came down to the question of ultimate authority: the judges insisted that she submit to the church's interpretation that her visions were evil, but Joan held to her claim that they came from God. Perhaps without intending it, Joan thus advocated the right of individual experience over the church's authority.

After weeks of unrelenting questioning, Joan began to break. Threatened with death by fire, she finally denied her voices and agreed to wear women's dress. We do not know precisely what happened next, but three days later she was found wearing male clothing again. She claimed that she had repented of betraying her voices; there are indications that her guards may have tried to rape her. Whatever her motivation, her actions sealed her fate. Declared a relapsed heretic on 31 May 1431, Joan was burned at the stake.

In 1450, because he was uneasy that he owed his crown to a convicted heretic, Charles instigated an inquiry into the trial, which led to a thorough papal investigation. Although the verdict of 1431 was revoked in 1456, the main charges against Joan were not cleared. Despite this ambiguity, Joan's memory received continuous attention from the French people through the centuries. It is ironic that in 1920 she was declared a saint, because none of the church's proceedings has acknowledged her right to interpret her divine messages, leaving the main issue for which she was condemned unaddressed.

BIBLIOGRAPHY

The basic materials relative to the trial are found in Jules Quicherat's five-volume *Procès de condamnation et de réhabilitation de Jeanne d'Arc* (Paris, 1841-1849; New York, 1960). For an updated edition of the trial in French and Latin, see *Procès de condamnation de Jeanne d'Arc,* 3 vols., edited by Pierre Tis-set and

Yvonne Lanhers (Paris, 1960-1971), and of the retrial, see *Procès en nullité de la condamnation de Jeanne d'Arc,* 3 vols., edited by Pierre Duparc (Paris, 1979-1983). An abridged English translation of the trial can be found in Wilfred P. Barrett's *The Trial of Jeanne d'Arc* (London, 1932), and of the retrial, in Régine Pernoud's *The Retrial of Joan of Arc,* translated by J. M. Cohen (London, 1955).

Of the vast secondary literature, the following biographies are good places to begin: Frances Gies's *Joan of Arc: The Legend and the Reality* (New York, 1981), Lucien Fabre's *Joan of Arc* (New York, 1954), and Victoria Sackville-West's *St. Joan of Arc* (London, 1936; New York, 1984). See also my study *Joan of Arc: Heretic, Mystic, Shaman* (Lewiston, N. Y., 1985) and Régine Pernoud's *Joan of Arc by Herself and Her Witnesses,* translated by Edward Hyams (London, 1964).

ANNE LLEWELLYN BARSTOW

JOHN THE BAPTIST

Born of a poor priestly family in the hill country of Judea, John renounced the priesthood and entered upon an ascetic existence in the wilderness surrounding the Jordan River. There he inaugurated a baptism rite so unprecedented that he was named for it. His contemporary Jesus unhesitatingly ascribed the impetus for John's baptism to divine revelation (*Mk.* 11:30), and even though priestly lustrations in the Temple, the daily baths at Qumran, or even proselyte baptism (first attested in the second century CE) may provide certain parallels, they are wholly inadequate to account for John's demand that Jews submit to a once-only immersion in anticipation of an imminent divine judgment by fire. Rejecting all claims to salvation by virtue of Jewish blood or the "merits of Abraham," John demanded of each person works that would reflect a personal act of repentance. The examples preserved in *Luke* 3:10-14 indicate that John stood squarely in the line of the prophets, siding with the poor ("He who has two coats, let him share with him who has none; and he who has food, let him do likewise"). He demanded that toll collectors and soldiers desist from extorting unjust exactions from travelers and pilgrims. His dress was the homespun of the nomad, his diet the subsistence rations of the poorest of the poor (locusts and wild honey, *Mk.* 1:6). He even described the eschatological judge, whose near advent he proclaimed, in terms of a peasant or a man of the soil (chopping down trees, separating wheat from chaff).

Through baptism, John provided a means by which common people and other "sinners" (tax collectors and harlots, *Mt.* 21:32) could be regenerated apart from meticulous observance of the Jewish law. His influence on Jesus in this and other respects was profound. Jesus and his disciples were baptized by John. But whereas John demanded that people come out to him in the wilderness, Jesus went to the people in their towns and villages, rejecting an ascetic life

(*Mt.* 11:18-19), and began to regard the future kingdom as an already dawning reality (*Mt.* 11:2-6). Despite these differences, Jesus continued to speak of John in terms of highest respect (*Mt.* 11:7-9, 11a).

John's execution by Herod Antipas was provoked by John's criticism of Herod for divorcing the daughter of the Nabatean king Aretas IV and entering upon an incestuous remarriage with Herodias, his half-brother's wife. John's attacks on Herod took place in Perea, a region controlled by Herod but bordered by Nabatean territory, an area inhabited by Arabs and infiltrated in winter by nomads. Herod's divorce provoked guerrilla warfare, and ultimately Aretas avenged his daughter's shame by a shattering defeat of Herod's army—a defeat that Josephus directly ascribes to divine punishment for Herod's execution of John (*Jewish Antiquities* 18.116-119). John's preaching must also have contributed substantially to popular disaffection from Herod.

Following the publication of the Dead Sea Scrolls, some scholars suggested that John might at one time have been an Essene. It is true that he preached but eight miles from Qumran, that he shared with the Essenes an imminent eschatological hope, and that he lived out (perhaps deliberately) the prophecy of *Isaiah* 40:3 and sought to prepare the way in the wilderness. Both John and the Essenes warned of a coming purgative fire associated with the Holy Spirit and with washing; both issued a radical call to repentance; both employed immersion in water as a religious rite; both believed that only an elect would be saved, and called the rest vipers; both condemned the priesthood and other authorities; both renounced society and abstained from strong drink.

These similarities, however, can in large part be accounted for: both John and the Essenes belonged to the larger phenomenon of Jewish wilderness sectarianism. Their differences, in any case, are more decisive than all their similarities. John was a solitary. He established no settled community, moved around in the Jordan wastes, was inclusive rather that separatist, public rather than reclusive, addressing the whole nation rather than withdrawing into an isolated life. His baptism was granted once and for all, not daily, and for a forgiveness of sins on which eternal salvation hung, not for physical purity. His dress was camel's hair, not white linen. He did not require a long novitiate for his converts, nor did he organize them under rigid requirements. Almost all the other similarities with Qumran can be traced to common dependence on the prophet Isaiah. Indeed, if John had ever been connected with Qumran, his break was so radical that it scarcely seems necessary to posit any original connection at all. When he steps upon the stage of history, his message and mission are altogether his own.

All four evangelists treat John as "the beginning of the gospel." This reflects both the historical fact and the theological conviction that through John, Jesus perceived the nearness of the kingdom of God and his own relation to its coming. The church continued to treat John as the perpetual preparer for the coming of Christ, calling out for people to repent and let the shift of the aeons take place in their own lives, to "make ready the way of the Lord" (*Mk.* 1:2).

BIBLIOGRAPHY

Kraeling, Carl H. *John the Baptist.* New York, 1951. Despite more recent publications, this work remains definitive. Historical sleuthing at its best.
Scobie, Charles H. H. *John the Baptist.* London, 1964. Adds some interesting conjectures on the Samaritans.
Wink, Walter. *John the Baptist in the Gospel Tradition.* Cambridge, 1968. A critical study of the use made of the Baptist traditions by the evangelists.

WALTER WINK

JOSEPH

JOSEPH, or, in Hebrew, Yosef; the firstborn son of Jacob's favorite wife, Rachel. The account of Joseph's life, which the Qur'an calls "the most beautiful of stories" (12:3), is described in a uniquely detailed and sustained biblical narrative.

As Rachel's son, Joseph was treasured by his father. Resentful of Joseph's resulting conceit, his brothers sold him to a group of passing traders, who took him to Egypt where he was purchased by one of Pharaoh's officers. When Joseph, who is described as "attractive and good-looking" (*Gn.* 39:6), rejected the advances of the officer's wife, she accused him of attempted rape and had him imprisoned. In jail, he demonstrated his ability to interpret dreams and was therefore brought to Pharaoh, whose dreams could not be otherwise understood. Joseph recognized them as warning that a period of abundance would be followed by famine. Elevated to high office in order to prepare Egypt for the coming threat, Joseph was given both an Egyptian name (Zaphenath-paneah) and wife (Aseneth).

When difficult times did arrive, Egypt was ready and served as a resource for surrounding peoples. Joseph's brothers came from Canaan to purchase grain; he recognized and tested them before revealing himself and bringing the entire family to settle in the eastern Nile Delta. Joseph died at the age of 110; his bones were brought to Canaan by the Israelites during the Exodus.

Joseph's special status is attested by the ascription to him of two biblical tribes, named after his sons Ephraim and Manasseh. Ephraim was to dominate the northern kingdom of Israel, which therefore is also called the House of Joseph.

Joseph's childhood dreams were thus fulfilled by his descendants as much as during his own lifetime.

The story of Joseph is remarkable for its numerous human touches, which lead to the apparent absence of divine intervention so common elsewhere in *Genesis*. In fact, however, God is very much present, if not always visible, acting through human behavior (*Gn.* 45:5, 50:20). The narrative incorporates many elements found in other biblical tales, most strikingly in the stories of Daniel and Esther, which also describe an Israelite's rise in a foreign court.

The historicity of the Joseph story has been defended on the basis of its incorporation of Egyptian vocabulary, customs, and narrative motifs. Historians since the first-century Josephus Flavius (*Against Apion* 1.103) have linked Joseph with the Hyksos, a West Semitic people who dominated Egypt toward the end of the Middle Bronze Age. Their expulsion in the sixteenth century might then explain the Bible's statement that "there arose a new king over Egypt who did not know of Joseph" (*Ex.* 1:8). Actually, none of these factors is sufficient historical proof. The land of Canaan was long under Egyptian control, and several cases of apparently Semitic figures holding high positions in the Egyptian bureaucracy are attested over a long period of time. Finally, the author's accurate knowledge of Egyptian culture hardly proves the story's historicity; indeed, there are several different periods in which such knowledge could have been acquired.

BIBLIOGRAPHY

An overview of modern scholarship relating to the entire patriarchal period is contained in Nahum M. Sarna's *Understanding Genesis* (New York, 1972). This must now, however, be read in conjunction with the historical information contained in Roland de Vaux's *The Early History of Israel,* translated by David Smith (Philadelphia, 1978). A detailed examination of the Joseph story, including both its literary characteristics and its Egyptian coloration, can be found in Donald B. Redford's *A Study of the Biblical Story of Joseph* (Genesis 37-50) (Leiden, 1970). Louis Ginzberg's *The Legends of the Jews,* 7 vols. (Philadelphia, 1909-1938), contains an exhaustive collection of rabbinic lore relating to biblical stories.

FREDERICK E. GREENSPAHN

JUDAISM

An Overview

Neither of the sacred Jewish classics, the Bible or the Talmud, speaks of "Judaism." Hellenistic Jews created this Greek word to describe their uncommon way of serving God (2 *Mc.* 2:21, 8:1, 14:38; *Gal.* 1:13-14). All such mediating terms, because they utilize alien categories as the means of self-representation, necessarily distort as much as they explain. Thus, while the Jews of the first century CE integrated their ethnicity and their religion, Paul, writing *Galatians* for gentile readers, must sunder faith from folk in order to communicate.

Contemporary Jewish thinkers radically disagree as to the nature of Judaism and even the advisability of employing the term. Interpretations of Judaism today range from steadfast traditionalism to radical universalism. The traditionalists themselves differ strongly on accommodation to modernity.

> ## Zionism and the state of Israel represent the secularization of Judaism at its fullest.

The right-wing Orthodox resist accommodation, while the Modern Orthodox accept any cultural good not forbidden by God's revelation. Debates over the role of mysticism add further diversity. Other contemporary Jews have rejected Orthodoxy because they deem it incompatible with the practice of democracy and the findings of the natural and social sciences, especially critical history.

Among nonreligious Jews, some are humanists who assimilate their Jewishness to contemporary culture, especially ethics. Others identify Judaism with Jewish folk culture. Zionism and the state of Israel represent the secularization of Judaism at its fullest.

Among liberal—that is, non-Orthodox—religious Jews, four differing emphases occur. (1) Jews who have an ethnic attachment to Judaism often find that it acquires a core of universal spirituality that, in turn, revitalizes their attachment. (2) Jews seeking a more disciplined Jewish religiosity direct their ethnic life through Jewish law, dynamically interpreted, as a historically evolving structure. (3) Jews concerned with the demands of rationality assert that Judaism uniquely comprehends the idea of ethical monotheism, a universal truth that is reinforced by their sense of ethnicity. (4) Jews who adopt a personalist approach conceptualize Judaism as a relationship, a covenant mutually created by God and the Jewish people and recreated in every generation. This article describes postbiblical Judaism in terms of the evolving expression of the Jewish people's covenant with God, understood in liberal religious terms.

From the Bible to Rabbinic Judaism

We have little hard data by which to trace the progress from biblical to rabbinic Judaism, despite some help from the biblical *Book of Daniel*. From Ezra and Nehemiah (Hebrew leaders of the mid-fifth century BCE) to the earliest rabbis (the authorities mentioned in the Talmud) in the first half of the first century CE, the sources in Jewish tradition that are considered authoritative provide little reliable historical information. Learned conjectures can fill this gap, but as their validity rests on hermeneutic foundations that often shift, all such speculations are best left to historians.

The rabbis themselves affirmed an unbroken transmission of authoritative tradition, of Torah in the broad sense, from Moses to Joshua to the elders, the prophets, and thence to the immediate predecessors of the rabbis (*Avot* 1.1). By this they meant that along with the written Torah (the first five books of the Bible, also known as the Pentateuch or Law) Moses also delivered the oral Torah, or oral law, which contained substantive teaching (legal and nonlegal) as well as the proper methods for the further development of the Torah tradition. As inheritors and students of the oral (and written) law, the rabbis knew themselves to be the authoritative developers of Judaism.

Modern critical scholarship universally rejects this view. For one thing, the Bible makes no mention of oral law. Then, too, it is reasonable to think of Torah as undergoing historical development. When, over the centuries, Judaism grew and changed, later generations validated this unconscious process by introducing, retroactively, the doctrine of the oral law.

We may see rabbinic Judaism's mix of continuity and creativity more clearly if we briefly note these same features in their late biblical predecessors. Ezra and Nehemiah believe that God and the Jewish people have an ancient pact, and they seek to be faithful to it by their lives. Though they acknowledge that God rules the whole world, they and their fellow Babylonian Jews manifest a deep loyalty to a geographic center returning from an apparently more prosperous land to resettle Jerusalem and restore God's Temple there. They are ethnic separatists, rejecting offers of help from the Samaritans and requiring Jewish males to give up their gentile wives. They carefully restore the Temple cult and insist on observance of the Sabbath. But their Judaism involves sensibility as well as statute. When Nehemiah discovers people collecting debts in a time of hardship, he denounces such hard-heartedness as incompatible with covenant loyalty, and they desist.

Ezra and Nehemiah also evidence a new religious concern: acting in accordance with "the book of God's Torah" (*Neh.* 9:3). In a great public ceremony, the book is read to all the people, men, women, and children, and explained to them in detail. By the mid-fifth century BCE, then, a written tradition has taken the place formerly occupied by divination, prophecy, and priestly teaching. [*See* Israelite Religion.]

Nearly three centuries later, *Daniel* gives us another glimpse of late biblical Judaism. Daniel, the paradigmatic Jew, lives outside the Land of Israel, among idolaters. He perseveres in the prescribed Jewish patterns of eating, drinking, and praying, despite the threat of severe punishment. A heavy eschatological focus distinguishes this book, as do its bizarre visions and their cryptic interpretations. After calamitous persecutions of the holy people, including wars against them by foreign powers, God intervenes, sending one who defeats their foes and establishes their kingdom forever. A time of cosmic judgment follows that dooms the wicked to eternal reprobation while the righteous live on forever. The biblical prophets' expectations of an ideal king, descended from King David, who would one day establish worldwide justice, compassion, and recognition of God have here been radically extended.

The Judaism of the Rabbis

Rabbinic Judaism appears as a mature development in its earliest datable document, the Mishnah, a compilation of Jewish traditions redacted about 200 CE. We can flesh out its sparely written text by consulting the more extensive classic works of rabbinism, the Talmud and the Midrash. The Talmud—essentially a collection of rabbinic discussions on the Mishnah—exists in two forms: the Jerusalem Talmud (*Yerushalmi*), redacted about 400 CE, and the Babylonian Talmud (*Bavli*), redacted about 500 CE and considered the more authoritative of the two. [*See* Talmud.] The Midrash is a body of homiletic and other exegeses of the Bible, of which the earliest compilations date from the third to the sixth centuries CE. The rabbis proceed on the assumption that the Temple, destroyed by the Romans in 70 CE, will be rebuilt only in "the days of the Messiah." They refer to the Temple cult mainly as the stuff of memory and hope and as material for study. Their Judaism centers about the Torah, particularly the oral Torah. To the critical eye, the distinctive features of rabbinic Judaism reflect creative development as much as reverent continuity with the past.

A structural innovation of the rabbis provides a convenient entry into their Judaism. They utilize parallel, mutually reinforcing modes of instruction, *halakhah* ("the way," the law, the required pattern of living) and *aggadah* (all else, including lore, preachment, speculation, and theology). Both are considered Torah, which literally means God's own instruction. In rabbinic texts they are often found organically intertwined, but they carry different degrees of authority. When dealing with *halakhah*, the rabbis, for all their disagreement and debate, seek to attain coherence and to decide what constitutes lawful practice. (The rabbis' courts can inflict severe penalties on transgressors.) By contrast, the realm of the *aggadah* is unregulated. The rabbis appear to delight in finding ingenious ways to amaze their colleagues with their imaginative exegeses and dicta. In all their contradiction and contrariety, these teachings too are part of the oral law.

Way of the Rabbis. For the rabbis, the covenant entails the adoption of a way of life faithful to God more than acquiescence to a specific doctrine. All later varieties of Judaism—including, despite radical differences, the modern ones—have echoed these spiritual priorities. A description of Judaism, therefore, should begin with some highlights of the rabbinic way. What follows represents the norms stated in authoritative rabbinic texts much more than it does the realities of community practice of the rabbinic era, about which we have no direct independent data.

Responsibility of the individual. The bulk of rabbinic literature concentrates on how the ordinary Jewish man ought to conduct himself so as to sanctify his life. Feminists have correctly pointed out that the rabbis take men to be the primary focus of God's instruction, with women essentially considered to be their adjuncts. Thus, men make all the halakhic decisions about women's duties, and though any man might qualify to render such decisions, traditionally no woman can. The rabbis did assign women a comparatively high personal and communal status. Nonetheless, by egalitarian standards, the differentiation of women's duties from those of men, which are viewed as the norm, imposes on women a loss of dignity and worth.

The troubling issue of sexism aside, rabbinic Judaism is remarkably democratic. It calls all Jews to the same attainable virtues: righteousness in deed, piety of heart, and education of the mind. It may derogate the wicked and the ignorant, but it never denies they might change and attain the highest sanctity. The sacred elite, the rabbinate, remains open to any man and recognizes no substantial barriers between rabbis and other Jews.

With the Temple destroyed, rabbinic Judaism made the ordinary Jew a "priest" by transforming many rituals once connected with the Temple cult so that they became a way of sanctifying one's everyday life at home or in the marketplace. Before eating or after excreting, one was to wash one's hands ritually and recite an appropriate blessing. Each morning and afternoon—the times of the Temple sacrifices—men worshiped in a prescribed liturgical structure. (An evening service was added later.) In the morning, men said their prayers wearing head and arm phylacteries (Heb., *tefillin*), small leather boxes that contain biblical citations. (The very pious wore them all day.) The doorpost of a Jewish home bore its own small container, the *mezuzah*, which contained Torah texts. A special fringe on the corner of a man's garment served as a reminder of his responsibility to God.

The Jew's table became an altar. What came to it had to be ritually acceptable, *kasher*. The list of foods proscribed by the Torah was amplified by rabbinic interpretation. Animals had to be slaughtered in a religiously acceptable, humane manner, and their carcasses had to be examined for diseases. Rabbinic law extended the biblical prohibition against boiling a kid in its mother's milk to prohibit mixing any meat with any milk product. It also mandated various blessings to be recited prior to eating bread, fruit, grain, vegetables, and other foods. After a meal, a longer, preferably communal grace was to be said.

The recitation of blessings was a constant part of the Jew's day. Hearing good news or bad news; seeing the sea, or a flowering tree, or an odd-looking person, or a meteor; smelling spices; acquiring something new; passing a place where a miracle had been done—all such occasions, and many more, required brief words of prayer.

The conduct of business also exhibited this intermingling of the commonplace with the transcendent. The rabbis spelled out in detail their religious equivalent of what Western civilization calls civil law. The covenant embraced such issues of justice as the proper treatment by employers of workers and the responsibilities of workers to their employers; the definition of reasonable inducements to customers and of illegitimate restriction of trade; the extent of a fair profit and a seller's responsibility in the face of changing prices; the duty to testify in the rabbinic court and the form in which contracts were to be written. Disputes between Jews on any of these matters were to be taken to the rabbinic court, which had detailed standards for administering justice.

The rabbis made daily study—for its own sake and as a ritual observance—a religious responsibility of the highest significance. The minimum requirement could be satisfied by studying selected biblical verses and rabbinic passages, but even the liturgy included numerous study texts and regular Torah readings. Besides, the acquisition of knowledge was a source of community esteem, a typical example of social custom strengthening rabbinic ideals. The rabbis endowed Jewish religiosity with its bookish cast, and their argumentative, analytic form of study made Jewish life uncommonly verbal and cerebral.

Because much that the rabbis valued could not usefully be made law, they surrounded their precepts with their individual opinions about what constitutes the good person and the ideal community. Like the Bible's authors, they abominate lying, stealing, sexual immorality, violence, and bloodshed. They decry gossip, slander, faithlessness, injustice, hardheartedness, arrogance, and pride. They glorify industry, honesty, compassion, charity, trustworthiness, humility, forgiveness, piety, and the fear of God. Believing in the Jewish community's good sense, they urge individuals to acquire a "good name."

They do not underestimate the difficulties involved in striving to be a good Jew—yet they never doubt that, with God's help, one can be more righteous than wicked. They picture humans as being in perpetual conflict between their *yetser ha-ra`* ("urge to do evil") and their *yetser tov* ("urge to do good"). The former they describe as a relentless, wily, indefatigable foe that seeks to dominate human consciousness and easily infects human sexuality and that can be defeated only momentarily. Realists that they were, the rabbis acknowledge that the evil urge often leads to good. Its driving energy causes people to marry, build homes, engage in useful commerce, and the like. Though one ought never to

underestimate its destructiveness or one's own vulnerability, human beings can harness some of its strength for their own good and to do God's work.

One can best fight off or sublimate the "urge to do evil" by studying, remaining pious, keeping good companions, and above all by observing the Torah. However, nothing guarantees its defeat, and self-righteousness practically invites its victory. Death alone terminates the struggle, and only at the "end of days" will the "urge to do evil" be destroyed. Until then, Jews continually beseech God's help, confident that, as the Bible teaches and the rabbis continually reiterate, God will aid them in their striving for purity.

The rabbis do not expect anyone to remain sinless. (Even Moses, their model, was not sinless.) Having sinned, one should do *teshuvah*, "turning" or "repentance." Elaborating on a biblical theme, the rabbis specify the stages by which sinners right their relationship with God. One begins by becom-

> ## The rabbis consider marriage a cardinal religious obligation. . . .

ing conscious of having sinned and feeling remorse. That should lead to a confession of one's sin before God and thus to confrontation with one's guilt. But morbidity leaves no energy for sanctification. Instead, guilt should motivate one to recompense those one has wronged and ask their forgiveness. Having firmly resolved never to repeat the iniquity, one may then beseech God's mercy with confidence, for God loves this effort of the human will and graciously accepts each sincere initiative, granting atonement.

One need not be Jewish to do *teshuvah*, and the rabbis directed that the *Book of Jonah* be read on the annual Day of Atonement to remind Jews that even the wicked Ninevites had once done so. Even for Jews *teshuvah* involves no special rites or sanctified personnel. Rather, each day's dynamic of striving but often failing to fulfill the Torah involves the individual in practicing *teshuvah*. (On Yom Kippur, the Day of Atonement, the Jewish people, in a unique sequence of four worship services, carries out a corporate *teshuvah*.)]

Family in rabbinic Judaism. The rabbis usually think of individuals not as isolated entities but as organically connected to their families and their people. For the rabbis the Jewish way primarily involves an ethnic group's unique covenant with God and its consequences for the lives of the individuals who constitute the group. The Jewish family replicates in miniature the greater covenant community.

The rabbis consider marriage a cardinal religious obligation, though they tolerate some exceptions. Through marriage one carries out the biblical command to have children. Because marriages were arranged in their era, the rabbis provide much counsel about this important process. They strongly urge that men marry early and that they take a wife from a good family who has a pleasant personality. They favor monogamy but do not require it (it was finally made obligatory by the medieval sages). They subordinate good looks, love, sexual pleasure, and even fecundity—in all of which they delight—to their goal of family well-being, *shalom*, which comes from a couple's mutual dedication to the Torah.

The rabbis hope that a deep love will arise between the spouses, on whom they enjoin sexual fidelity. (Talmudic law defines such fidelity in terms of the wife's behavior; medieval writers tend to apply similar standards to husbands.) They expect male dominance in the household, but counsel the temperate use of power by husbands and fathers. They also display a canny sense of the critical, even decisive, role the wife/mother plays in family affairs.

Despite this exaltation of marriage in their sacred way of living, the rabbis provided for the possibility of divorce. Though they decried the breakup of a family, they did not make divorce administratively impractical. Divorced men and women often remarried.

From biblical times, Jews experienced infertility as grievous suffering. If Jews have no offspring, the covenant expires. Through future generations all prior Jewish devotion hopes to reach completion. Children—particularly sons, in the rabbinic view—therefore come as a great blessing, and if they grow up to be good people, respected in the community, their parents enjoy inestimable fulfillment. Should they be wicked, their parents consider it a major judgment on themselves. Some rabbis identify suffering caused by one's children as the worst of divine visitations.

Only occasionally do the rabbis discuss parents' obligations to their children, perhaps because they believed that natural sentiment, guided by Jewish folkways, would adequately direct them. By contrast, they say much about children's duties toward their parents. The rabbis' amplification of the Fifth Commandment—"Honor your father and mother"—not only reflects their regard for wisdom and experience but testifies to the covenant between the generations that revivifies the covenant between God and Israel. Jewish personal names add to this intimacy, for one is called the "son (or daughter) of so-and-so" and thus carries one's parent in one's personhood all one's life.

These relationships functioned within the Jewish home, the primary scene of ongoing Jewish observance. Particularly since it might also be one's place of business, the home brought the diverse aspects of Jewish life together in mutually strengthening integrity.

Jewish community and Jewish people. In rabbinic times most Jews lived away from the Land of Israel, in the Diaspora, and from about the fifth to the tenth century CE, Babylonian Jewry exercised preeminent religious authority. To carry on their faith, the Jews who were scattered across the Parthian and Roman empires found it helpful to live near other Jews. The experience of anti-Semitism also brought Jews together. As always, the social and the sacred interpenetrated.

The responsibility of the Jewish community to uphold the covenant received its most visible expression in the liturgy of the daily worship services at which communal prayer was offered. (Obligatory individual prayer derives from this corporate duty.) A quorum of at least ten adult males, representing the entire Jewish people, was required to be present. At the morning service on Mondays, Thursdays, Sabbaths, and festivals, and on Sabbath afternoons, the group read a portion of the Torah scroll, often followed by a selection from the prophetic books. If a particularly learned man were in the congregation, he might give a sermon.

Any man with the requisite knowledge could lead the service or read from the scroll. Various religious functionaries enhanced the community's life, but a rabbi was not a requirement. Both a ritual slaughterer (so there could be kosher meat) and a teacher for the children took priority. Devoted volunteers attended and buried the dead and took care of other such communal duties.

Rabbis in the Talmudic period were not employed by the Jewish community but, like other Jews, worked at some ordinary occupation. When the community did have a rabbi, he functioned as both scholar and judge. He exemplified the Jewish duty to study and he answered questions about Jewish law, when necessary convening a rabbinical court *(beit din)*. Decisions of the *beit din* were considered part of the oral law and hence carried divine authority, yet they could be appealed by writing to a greater scholar elsewhere who might, by the authority of his knowledge and piety, indicate that the ruling was faulty.

Corporate life turned about several institutions. One, the synagogue, which may have predated the earliest generations of rabbis, was recognized by them as a surrogate for the destroyed Temple, with prayer as a fully adequate substitute for sacrifice and laymen in the place of priests. The rabbis also made it possible for a synagogue to function anywhere a quorum met, including a private home. A populous settlement might have many congregations. A prosperous community would erect an appropriate building to house synagogue activities.

Another institution was the study house, where those devoted to learning would find a place to study and to meet with other students of Torah. Often this was a room in the synagogue.

The rabbinical court, which was composed of three learned men, did more than hear significant cases. It bore responsibility for the community's spiritual well-being. In special situations, its executive power had few limits, and it could enact decrees that were binding on the community.

The community's rabbinical authorities shared power with its lay leadership. Jewish communities in the Diaspora often possessed considerable legal independence, and their gentile rulers expected the community leaders to collect taxes, regulate the markets, and generally supervise Jewish internal affairs. All these matters were handled by applying the Torah's teaching to the immediate social and political realities.

Community leaders, carrying out a prime Jewish obligation, collected and disbursed charity (the Hebrew term, *tsedaqah*, literally means "justice"). Every Jew had obligations toward every other Jew, particularly those who needed help. Gathering and distributing the funds were among the most honored community tasks. Many communities so esteemed *tsedaqah* that even its recipients gave to others.

Geography and cultural differences produced variations in Jewish practice between the two leading centers of Jewry, one in the Land of Israel (under Roman rule) and the other in Babylonia (under Parthian and, after 226 CE, Sasanid rule). No single agency existed to enforce uniformity in practice or theory. Instead, a relatively loose pattern of authority emerged. From time to time, certain institutions or individuals arose whose scholarship and piety commanded the respect of many Jews. In time, their teachings established precedents for later Jewry.

Despite the open texture of the Judaism of this era, the rabbis exhibited a clear-cut sense of the unity and identity of the Jewish people, who were the sole recipients of God's law and thus bore unique witness to God. They detested the idolatry and immorality they saw all about them. Hence they consciously sought to distinguish and separate Jews from the nations. But most rabbis happily accepted sincere converts. The isolation of the Jews made hospitality to strangers critical: Jews on a journey could always expect to find a welcome in other Jewish communities, which, despite variations in custom, clearly followed the same Torah in the same basic way.

Three rhythms of Jewish time. Jews live in three interrelated dimensions of time: the personal, the annual-historical, and the eschatological. The critical passages of each individual's life are marked by sacred rites. On the eighth day after his birth, a newborn boy receives the physical sign of the covenant in the ceremony of circumcision. At thirteen he assumes personal responsibility for performing the commandments, becoming *bar mitsvah*. Should he complete the study of a classic text, he marks the occasion with a small celebration. Marriage is preceded by formal betrothal. The wedding itself is as elaborate as the family's means and the community's standards will allow. The birth of children, the experience of bereavement and mourning, the dissolution of marriage in divorce are all social acts that involve community participation; many of them are also sanctified by prayer and ritual.

Prayer and ritual similarly mark the great moments of each year. The six workdays climax in the rest, worship, study, and feasting of the Sabbath. On Friday eve (in the Jewish calendar, the day begins at sundown) it is traditional that women light the Sabbath candles and say a blessing over them. Before the special Sabbath meal is eaten, a prayer of sanctification is recited over a cup of wine. When the Sabbath has ended, its "holy time" is demarcated from the "profane time" of the weekday by the recitation of blessings over wine, spices, and a multi-wicked flame in a ritual called Havdalah ("separation").

The year begins in the autumn during the period of the High Holy Days. The solemn synagogal rites of Ro'sh ha-Shanah celebrate God's sovereignty, justice, and mercy. The ensuing ten days of penitence are climaxed by the all-day fast and worship service of Yom Kippur, the Day of Atonement, in which the congregation beseeches God's promised forgiveness. In the course of the year there are three "pilgrimage" festivals, Passover, Shavu`ot (Weeks or Pentecost), and Sukkot (Tabernacles; Feast of Booths). Originally these were agricultural festivals during which all Jews came on pilgrimage to the Temple in Jerusalem, but they were transformed by the rabbis into historical symbols: Passover celebrates the Exodus from slavery in Egypt, Shavu`ot the giving of the Torah, and Sukkot God's providential care of the Israelites in the wilderness. Thus, the undeviating cycle of the year becomes a reminder and renewal of the Jewish people's unique historical experience.

Rabbinic creativity likewise embellished the minor festivals of the year. The rabbis established a ceremony of special psalms, prayers, and a reading from the Torah scroll to greet the beginning of each lunar month. For the fast day of Tish`ah be-Av, commemorating the destruction of the Temple, they enjoined a reading of the *Book of Lamentations*. They memorialized other tragic events with lesser fasts. The salvation of ancient Persian Jewry, recounted in the *Book of Esther*, is remembered on the feast of Purim. The Maccabees' rededication of the Temple in 164 BCE, after its desecration by the Hellenistic ruler of Syria, Antiochus IV, is celebrated as Hanukkah at about the time of the winter solstice with a ritual that includes the kindling of lights in the home over the course of eight nights.

The number of each Jewish year indicates the time since creation, according to rabbinic calculation, even as the rhythm of the year directs attention toward history's promised climax, God's manifest rule on earth. A messianic hopefulness infuses all Jewish observance, for the end might begin at any moment; yet the Jews' heartbreaking experience with premature messiahs—particularly Bar Kokhba in the rebellion against Rome of 132-135 CE—indicated that the Messiah would come only at the "end of days."

We can surmise something of the tone and quality of the rabbis' Judaism from what their traditions tell us about the way they lived. Their teachings show that they can be wildly playful, though they are usually highly serious; exuberant in celebration, yet careful of minutiae; free in opinion, yet obedient to discipline; guilt-stricken at sinning, yet confident of forgiveness; desirous of intention in the performance of *mitsvot* (the commandments), yet content with the deed itself; highly individualistic, yet absorbed in community; concerned with the practical, yet oriented toward the eschatological. They were simultaneously mystic and rationalistic, emotionally demonstrative and devoted to order, foolish sinners and pious martyrs. They were ordinary people who might be one's neighbors, yet they were saintly, endowing their spirituality with intellect and a communal and personal activism. And the communities that were guided by their teachings seem much like them, human and holy at once.

Above all, the rabbis have a passion for this mundane life, despite the finer one to come. They delight in its opportunities to serve God through the routines specified by Torah. Yet they insist that in order to save a life, all the laws of the Torah could—indeed, must—be broken (except the prohibitions against idolatry, murder, and sexual sin). Similarly, when the survival of the Jewish people seems to be at risk, the rabbis find ways to accommodate reality, but not by compromising principle. For they believe, above all, that the world was created for the sanctification of life, and that only through holy Jewish living can it hope to endure and reach completion.

Beliefs of the Rabbis. It is characteristic of the rabbis that their faith is inseparable from their way of life. Their test for heresy was behavioral, not creedal. Their explicit statements of belief are generally more poetic than precise, more fragmentary than general, and they exhibit little interest in systemic coherence.

While acknowledging the notorious elusiveness of what they call rabbinic theology, some modern scholars have yet found it possible to explicate some of its major themes. The rabbis' theological creativity operates mainly in their reshaping of the multitudinous ideas and images of biblical belief. In this process they continue the millennial Jewish experience of reinterpreting the covenant as times change and as their own intellectuality and religious sensitivity demand.

The primacy of continuity in rabbinic belief helps explain what modern readers often consider the rabbis' surprisingly modest response to the Temple's destruction. Though they were deeply traumatized, the rabbis did not see the loss of the Temple as a disaster requiring major theological reconstruction; rather, they found it a confirmation of the Bible's teaching. God had done what God had promised to do and had done once before (in 587/6 BCE). Sin eventually begets punishment, even to the destruction of God's Temple and the exile of God's people. But the punishment has a covenant purpose, to bring the people back to God's service. In due course, the rabbis believed, God would again restore the holy people and their Temple. Continuing the faith of the Bible as they understood it, the rabbis indomitably transcended profane history.

God. Monotheism anchors the rabbis' faith, just as it anchors the later biblical writings. The rabbis abominate idolatry and passionately oppose the notion that there are "two powers" in heaven. That does not prevent their speaking of God's heavenly retinue, the subordinates by whom God's governance of the universe usually proceeds. Similarly, they exhibit no inhibition about using metaphors to describe God. These may be abstract names, such as "the Place," "the Power," "the Holy," or images drawn from human life, such as references to God's phylacteries, or daily schedule, or emotions.

Another typical rabbinic dialectic moves between the utter greatness and the immediate availability of God. The ineffably glorious Sovereign of all universes attends and responds to a human whisper or fleeting meditation.

Rabbinic theology often pivots about God's justice and mercy. The declaration "There is no Judge and no justice" seems to be the rabbinic equivalent of atheism, but the rabbis give elaborate validations of the reliability of God's justice. They believe that the world could not survive if God were absolutely just: human fallibility and willfulness make such stringency impractical. For people freely to come to righteousness, God must also be merciful and compassionate. But if there were mercy without justice, this same rebellious humankind would never become responsible for its own actions. Undaunted by the paradoxes, the rabbis affirm that the one and only God is both just and merciful, demanding and forgiving, the ultimate idealist and realist in one.

Much of what other people might take to be evil the rabbis steadfastly consider the subtle working-out of God's justice. They do not deny that unmerited suffering occurs. Sometimes they explain this as "chastisements of love," torment given to the pious in this world so that rewards will await them in the afterlife. Sometimes they merely ascribe it to God's inexplicable will, God's "harsh decree." (Parallel reasons are offered by the rabbis for the gift of God's unmerited blessing—that is, it comes because of the "merit of the patriarchs," or simply because God loves or chooses to bless the recipient.) Less frequently, the rabbis will picture God, as it were, as somehow unable to prevent a tragedy or as lamenting its occurrence. With reason or without, they hold God to be the ultimate source of evil as well as good and so call for the recitation of a blessing upon hearing evil tidings. They devoutly trust God, whom they know they cannot hope to understand despite all their study and piety.

Perhaps they evince such confidence because they have a strong, full belief in life after death. Several stages of the afterlife may be identified in rabbinic traditions. At death, the soul is taken from the body for preliminary judgment and purification and stays with God until the general bodily resurrection that will take place at the "end of days." Then the soul, rejoined to its purified body, receives judgment. The wicked are utterly destroyed, and the less culpable receive a limited term of expiatory punishment. Finally, the individual enters the "future to come," the blissful but indescribable reward God has promised the righteous.

Humankind and human destiny. The rabbis' conception of humankind stands behind their Jewish self-understanding. Human beings literally constitute a family since God created them from one pair of progenitors. And God made and maintains a covenant with all the descendants of Noah. Under it, God promised that there would be no more annihilatory floods and commanded all people to obey seven laws: six negative—not to blaspheme God, or worship idols, or steal, or murder, or commit sexual offenses, or eat the limb of a living animal—and one positive—to set up courts of justice.

Human nature being so torn between its evil and good urges, people regularly transgress these simple laws. So God brought a special nation into being, the Jews, to serve God devotedly by accepting a covenant of 613 command-

> ## So God brought a special nation into being, the Jews, to serve God. . . .

ments. In the rabbinic sociology of religion, people are either Jews, faithful servants of the only God, or part of "the nations," idolaters and therefore sinners. The Jews' experience of anti-Semitism reinforced this view and strengthened the Jewish commitment to separatism for God's sake.

The customary strife between the nations and the people of Israel will greatly intensify as the "end of days" nears. But God will send the Messiah, a human, Davidic king descended from King David, to lead God's people to victory. Once again, the rabbinic accounts grow hazy and irreconcilable. Some see the nations converting to Judaism; others see them accepting Jewish leadership. There is little elaboration of the biblical poems that prophesy a time of universal justice, peace, contentment, and lack of fear. However, the rabbis anticipate that at the final judgment the nations will be found guilty of wickedness and denied entry to the "future to come." Some rabbis mitigate this attitude by teaching that individuals who are "pious among the nations of the world have a share in the world to come."

Of course, any sinner might become righteous by repenting. The rabbis tell—occasionally with considerable envy—of a number of gentiles and Jews who by a heartfelt act of *teshuvah* immediately gained the life of the world to come.

Most of these matters became part of rabbinic law concerning non-Jews. Hence this doctrine, in general, may be said to be authoritative rabbinic teaching.

Rabbinic theory of Torah. Radical theological creativity appears starkly in the rabbis' doctrine of the oral law. Unlike some of their other distinctive ideas, such as repentance, the

Messiah, and resurrection, the notion of the oral law has no explicit biblical foundation. Since it undergirds all of rabbinic Judaism, it may be said to be the rabbis' most characteristic doctrine. To reiterate what has been said above, the rabbis taught that God gave Moses not only the first five books of the Bible (and, by implication, the rest of it) but also unrecorded verbal instructions, including specific duties and the methods for educing further oral law.

The rabbis also delimit the content of the written law in its broader sense of holy scripture, that is, the Hebrew scriptures. They apparently inherited fixed versions of the five books of the Torah and of the Prophets (including *Joshua, Judges, Samuel,* and *Kings*) and they determined what would be included in the Writings, admitting *Ecclesiastes,* for example, but rejecting *Ben Sira*. With these three divisions (Torah, Prophets, Writings; abbreviated in Hebrew as *Tanakh*) they closed the canon, for they believed that revelation ended with *Haggai, Zechariah,* and *Malachi* and that the books of the Writings had preceded these prophetical books. Though the rabbis occasionally hear a "heavenly echo" concerning matters under discussion, they may disregard it. Effectively, therefore, postbiblical Judaism derives from the rabbis' delimitation of the written law and their continuing explication of the oral law.

God excepted, no aspect of Jewish belief arouses the rabbis' awe as does Torah. They describe it as existing before creation, as God's guide to creation, and as God's most treasured possession, one so precious the angels tried to keep it from being taken to earth. The people of Israel, by virtue of having been given and having accepted the Torah, have become infinitely precious to God and central to human history. The rabbis acknowledge that wisdom may be found among the nations, but for them Torah contains God's fullest truth for humankind, making it the arbiter of all wisdom.

The rabbis do not detail the correct means or institutional structure for amplifying the oral law. Rather, the living practice of the master (*rabbi* means "my master") sets the model for his disciples. From time to time various institutions have emerged that temporarily exercised some general authority, but none lasted or created a form that later generations utilized. We have no way of gauging the extent to which Jews accepted the rabbis' leadership even in their own time. It seems paradoxical to seek control and integrity with such lack of structure and tolerance of diversity, but the arrangement has persisted to the present day.

With God's teaching available in verbal form, learning became a major Jewish religious activity. On a simple level, study motivated Jewish duty and specified its content. On a more advanced level, pondering God's instructions—even those of only theoretical relevance, like the rules for the Temple service—enabled one to have intellectual communion, as it were, with God. Gifted men sought to become rabbis, perhaps even to have their teachings cited by others, but always to set a living example for other Jews. Often reports of a master's deeds themselves became part of the oral law.

This heavy intellectual emphasis should not be divorced from its religious context. The intellectually keenest rabbis are also depicted as deeply pious, passionate in prayer, caring and virtuous in their dealings with people, intimately involved in the ordinary activities of life. Many also were mystics, though we have only hints about their esoteric spirituality.

The rabbinic doctrine of Torah brought fresh dynamism to Judaism. By authorizing new and open forms of authority and practice it enabled the Jewish people to keep the covenant vital, no matter what changes were brought by time and dispersion. With Judaism now centered on the individual and communal practice of Torah rather than on the Temple cult in Jerusalem, one could live as a faithful Jew anywhere. And as life created new problems, one only needed to find or become a learned Jew to determine what God wanted now, God's continuing command, and hence feel God's continuing care and concern. This oversimplifies a highly sophisticated process, but also conveys its providential gist.

The Jews as God's treasured people. The people of Israel uniquely serve the one God of the universe by living by God's teachings. Whatever superiority the people of Israel might claim over the gentiles derives from their faithfulness in living according to the covenant. Having the Torah does not exempt the Jews from God's demand for righteousness; if anything, because they have more commandments to fulfill they bear more responsibility before God. At the same time, God has a special love for the people of the covenant. When the people of Israel sin, God patiently waits for them to repent and helps them do so, sometimes by punishing them to remind them of their responsibilities.

The rabbis directly applied these beliefs to their situation, with the Temple destroyed and Jewish life in the Land of Israel degenerating. They lamented the calamities of their time: their inability to fulfill the commandments regarding God's cult and the material and spiritual distress brought on by dispersion and Roman rule. But their faith did not waver. They held that this people had been justly punished for its sins, though they often pictured God as pained at having had to execute so dire a sentence. To the rabbis, this new exile came because of the covenant and not as its negation; God had fulfilled what the covenant called for in response to egregious iniquity.

The Jews' political and social insignificance in the Roman empire did not negate their faith in their continuing spiritual uniqueness. Rather, the idolatry and immorality of the Romans proved them unworthy of Jewish admiration and God's esteem. To keep their service of God uncontaminated, the Jews set a distance between themselves and the nations. They also lived in the hope that their stubborn loyalty to God would one day be vindicated before all humankind.

The eschatological savior described in the *Book of Daniel* had become an important figure in rabbinic Judaism, the King Messiah. One day—perhaps today—God would send him to restore the holy people to its land, defeat its enemies, reestablish its throne, rebuild its Temple and reconstitute its cult, institute a world order of justice and compassion, and usher in a time when all the promise of creation and the covenant would be fulfilled.

This was a human and historical expectation. As a consequence, some Jews would, from time to time, declare one or another figure of their day to be the anticipated Son of David, in the hope that the Jewish people had so lived up to its covenant responsibilities that God had sent the Messiah. Even if the folk did not merit him, it was understood that God would, in God's own time, send redemption. In either case, the rabbis could only fantasize as to what God would then do to transform and perfect creation. They imagined nature pacified and responsive, the nations admiring of the Torah or even converted to Judaism. Diverse as these conceptions were, all the rabbis agreed that this glorious time will be succeeded by the resurrection of the dead, the final judgment, and the climactic but indescribable "future to come."

The rabbis taught the people of Israel to remain confident of God's rule and favor and to await in history and beyond it God's sure deliverance and blessing—a faith that carried them through history until modern times.

From Talmudic to Modern Times

After the editing of the Talmud, countless variations of the rabbis' way appeared as Jews lived in diverse countries, cultures, social orders, and historical circumstances. Mostly they added observances; some of these became generally accepted, such as the holiday of Simhat Torah (Joy of Torah), which became the ninth day of the festival of Sukkot, and the *yohrtsayt*, the later Ashkenazic practice of memorializing a close relative's day of death. A selective factor also operated, as in the abandonment of the triennial cycle of reading the Torah scroll during worship services in favor of an annual cycle. The range of this cultural creativity was greatly extended by the folk or ethnic nature of the Jews.

Two major cultural streams emerged. The Sefardic tradition (from the medieval Hebrew word *Sefarad* for the Iberian Peninsula) chiefly embraced the Jews of the Mediterranean Basin, many of whom were descended from families exiled from Spain in 1492, as well as those in Arab countries. The Ashkenazic tradition (from the medieval word *Ashkenaz* for northern France and Germany) encompassed the Jews of northern and eastern Europe, from whom most Jews in North America descend. Sefardic rabbis led Jewry throughout the Diaspora from the eleventh through the sixteenth century; meanwhile, the Ashkenazic sages created a halakhic scholarship that eventually brought them to the fore in Jewish life.

Each cultural style encompassed diverse national and local ways of living that changed over the centuries. Sefardic spokesmen have often taken pride in their community's urbanity, its respect for form and decorum, its devotion to liturgy, and its esteem of clear intellectuality. Similarly, Ashkenazic leaders have proudly noted their group's passionate energy, its fierce individuality, its dedication to study, and its love of Talmudic erudition.

Developing the Rabbinic Way. We know little about the actual practices of Jews for much of this period, though we know much about what rabbis said ought to be done. But the quasi-institutional means that evolved to control the development of Jewish life so evidences the spirit of Judaism that it deserves description. In their far-flung Diaspora, Jews recognized no institution or group as universally authoritative. Yet despite the slowness of communication, or lack of it, among the Jewish communities, and the immense diversity in local practice, the Jews remained and recognized one another as one covenant people.

Persecution intensified this sense of identity. With the rise of Islam early in the seventh century, Jews, living mostly in Islamic lands, became a group tolerated, but given second-class social and legal status. Among Christians, the occasional anti-Jewish outbreaks of the early centuries gave way after the First Crusade (1096 CE) to nearly seven centuries of harassment, including economic limitations, forced conversions, pogroms and riots, and communal expulsions, culminating about 1500 CE in the formal creation of the ghetto, the walled-in Jewish quarter of European cities. This pariah status strongly affected Jewish practices and attitudes and helped give rise to an elemental spiritual resistance founded on the certainty of possessing God's revelation and favor. The immediate contrast between their way of life and that of their oppressors empowered Jews to live and die steadfast in their faith.

Jewish communities vested authority in those whose learning and piety evoked it. Early on, the geonim, leaders of the Babylonian academies *(yeshivot)* that produced the Babylonian Talmud, began responding to questions addressed to them by distant Jews. This pattern of questions and answers, *she'elot u-teshuvot*, established itself as a way to get and give authoritative guidance. To this day, *teshuvot*, also known as *responsa*, remain the preeminent device for Jewish legal development. The power of a *teshuvah* derives entirely from the prestige and scholarship of its author. Many *teshuvot* became academic additions to the body of Jewish "case law." Others became widely authoritative, like one of Rav Amram, gaon of the *yeshivah* in Sura, Babylonia, from 856 to 874 CE. His lengthy answer to a question from Spanish Jews about liturgical practice established the prototype for Jewish prayer books.

The geonim and other sages sometimes wrote commentaries to portions of the Talmud or composed treatises on an aspect of the law. Eventually, the growing accretion of law led some teachers to compile codes. Each code became the subject of critical commentaries, some of which are printed alongside the code text in modern editions. The *Shulhan `arukh* of Yosef Karo (1488-1575), a Sefardic master, published in 1565 CE, became generally accepted among Ashkenazic Jews as well after Mosheh Isserles (c. 1525-1572) wrote glosses to it that reflected Ashkenazic practice. To this day, the *Shulhan `arukh* remains the authoritative code of Jewish law, though scholars continue to rework some of its sections.

> **Persecution intensified this sense of identity.**

Only one serious internal challenge to rabbinic Judaism emerged in the medieval period: the Karaite (biblicist) movement, which rejected the authority of the oral law and created a pattern of practice based on the Bible alone. Beginning in the eighth century CE in the Middle East, it reached the peak of its appeal and literary productivity in the eleventh and twelfth centuries. By then rabbinic authorities had declared Karaism heretical and prohibited intermarriage with Karaites. Some few thousand Karaites still exist, largely in the state of Israel. [*See* Karaites.]

In many other fields, as well as law, the range of Jewish study continually expanded. Biblical exegesis, homilies, poetry, mystical accounts, chronicles, polemics, explorations of piety, handbooks for good conduct, philosophy—every period produced its books and the students to ponder them. The invention of printing added further impetus to Jewish learning.

New Ideas and Their Effect on Practice. Four particularly significant, if not always distinguishable, intellectual currents moved through much of the Jewish world during the Middle Ages: pietism, mysticism, philosophy, and polemic. It will help to consider pietism, the most popular, first, though mysticism, an elitist enterprise, predates it.

Medieval pietism. The Talmud and Midrash devote much attention to the virtues a Jew should manifest, but do so only in passing. About the eleventh century, a popular, specifically pietistic literature known as musar began to appear. Well into modern times, large numbers of Jews read and sought to live by the high spiritual standards its authors advocated.

The title of the early, exemplary *musar* book, *Duties of the Heart*, written in Arabic by Bahye ibn Paquda in the late eleventh century, epitomizes the movement's aims. While the Talmud focused on the good Jew's acts, Bahye stressed the inner life as the basis for action. He and other pietists called attention to the need for intimacy between the individual and God, stressing the humility of the one and the greatness of the other. Consciousness of this relationship, they said, should strongly motivate one to cultivate personal holiness, particularly through loving behavior to others—an emphasis so pronounced that the pietists' writings are often called "ethical" books.

Two concerns of *musar* teachers gradually became common in most medieval Jewish writing. First, the pietists strongly contrast the purity of the soul with the grossness of the body. This duality, alluded to in both the Bible and the Talmud, became central and intense in *musar* piety. With corporeality the soul's antagonist, the pietists commend a measure of asceticism and social withdrawal. Yet they do not go so far as to become full-fledged dualists, for they believe that God created the body and ordained social life.

Second, the pietists express great anxiety about sinning and cultivate the fear of incurring guilt. How can anyone who is intensely aware of God's greatness not find the idea of defying God utterly reprehensible? One of the most common *musar* strategies for avoiding or surmounting temptation is to remember the punishment awaiting the wicked in the next world. The *musar* writers therefore urge heartfelt remorse and repentance for every sin, even suggesting compensatory atonements one might undertake. In no small measure, the conflict between the values of modern life and the values of premodern Judaism arose from disagreement over these matters.

Maturation of Jewish mysticism. Whereas pietism reached out to ordinary Jews, mysticism limited itself to select individuals who were initiated into an esoteric doctrine by masters who often concealed as much as they revealed.

The Jewish mystical writings describe and exhibit phenomena that are associated with mysticism in many cultures: stringent spiritual discipline, bizarre language and exalted spiritual expression, techniques for gaining mystical experience, visions of the heavenly realm, physical images of God coupled with assertions of God's utter ineffability, longing for religious consummation and ways of hastening it—all these and more appear refracted in perplexing and fascinating fashion through sensitive temperaments affected by highly diverse situations.

The main tradition of Jewish mysticism is known as Qabbalah. Developed in response to God's revelation of a holy way of life, it has a highly cognitive content that is concerned with cosmogony and theosophy. Its most significant document, the *Zohar* (Book of Splendor), written primarily in Aramaic in late thirteenth-century Spain, is a commentary on the Torah that elaborates a mystical doctrine of God's complex nature. Ultimately, God is Ein Sof, "without limit," hence the one about whom nothing at all can be said. Yet God is also intimately known, contemplated, and related to through interacting loci of divine energy, the *sefirot* (lit., "spheres" or "numbers"; in qabbalistic terminology, emanations from God's inner being). The mystics speak of the *sefirot* with a

freedom of metaphor that is almost limitless, not even excluding sexual anthropomorphisms. Feminine metaphors for God, rare in the Bible and occasional in the Talmud, now come into full use alongside masculine metaphors in explications of God's nature.

The Jewish mystics, for all the immediacy of their relationship with God, believe that Torah—the written and oral law—remains primary to Judaism. They therefore eschew antinomianism—the idea that faith, not law, is sufficient—and cultivate meticulous observance. By ascribing supernal significance to commandments and customs that reason cannot explain, they easily provide absolute justification for them.

Two late developments in Jewish mysticism have had continuing repercussions. The first was the qabbalistic thought of Isaac Luria (1534-1572). According to his cosmogonic explanation of evil, creation began with an act of divine self-contraction that produced an outflow of generative light. God projected this light into the vessels, or material forms, that had been prepared for it. These vessels proved too fragile and shattered, leaving unsanctified shards or husks that contain only sparks of God's creative, transformative light. By observing God's commandments, people can free the heavenly sparks from their husks and mend the broken vessels, thus restoring the world and rescuing it from evil. God appears passive in this process, as it is human action that brings the Messiah—a striking anticipation of modern liberalism.

In the eighteenth century, in southern Poland and the Ukraine, the Hasidic movement transformed qabbalistic tradition through a radical appropriation of God's accessibility (prompting charges by their opponents that the Hasidim were pantheists). To the Hasidim, God's nearness implied that life should be lived with joy and enthusiasm. For cleaving to God, one need not be a spiritual virtuoso but only give God one's heart. This attitude encouraged new practices and fervent observance, though its opponents claimed that its emphasis on spontaneity and inner experience led to laxity in ritual.

Hasidism became a mass movement that carried a dialectical tension. On the one hand, the humblest person could live the mystical life. The Hasidic leaders encouraged this egalitarianism by putting many of their teachings in exoteric form, as tales, stories, and popular preaching, and by promoting a close community life. On the other hand, Hasidism established a religious elite. Each community was led by a *tsaddiq*, or *rebe*. The *tsaddiqim* represent Hasidism's esoteric side, privately practicing an exalted mysticism and serving as the intermediary between their followers and heaven. Their followers believed that the *tsaddiqim* could work wonders and thus beseeched their intercession on every personal problem. Since each community thought its own *tsaddiq* the most powerful, some Hasidic communities isolated themselves even from other Hasidim.

Later, Hasidism became institutionalized around dynasties and antagonistic to modernity. The groups that managed to survive the Holocaust have had a resurgence in the state of Israel and the United States. They have gained recruits from Jews who, disillusioned with secular culture, seek out the intensity of immersion in a separatist Jewish esoteric community.

The encounter with philosophy. The Talmud knows nothing of Philo Judaeus of Alexandria (fl. first century CE) or any other Hellenistic Jewish philosopher. Certain that they possessed God's revelation, the rabbis spurned formal Greek philosophy, which they associated with idolatry. In the ninth century CE, Jews encountered Muslim philosophy, which claimed that it taught the purest monotheism because its doctrine of God had been refined through rational argument. For the next seven centuries—that is, as long as cultural involvement with the Muslims persisted—a tiny Jewish intellectual aristocracy created Jewish philosophy. Their work had little direct impact on Jewish life, though some of their ideas—for example, Moses Maimonides' excoriation of anthropomorphism—became widely influential.

The early philosophical thinkers, such as Sa`adyah Gaon (882-942), adduced proofs for God's creation of the world, from which they deduced God's unity and sovereign power. On this basis they sought to give rational justification to such problems as miracles, providence, evil, and why Judaism was the true revelation. The rational defense of certain inexplicable commands of the Torah evoked considerable philosophic ingenuity.

In the course of time, most medieval Jewish philosophical thought came to employ Aristotelian categories. The occasional Neoplatonic voice found little philosophic resonance, though the mystics found the Neoplatonic concept of emanation congenial to their notion of levels of being. Sometimes, as in the case of Yehudah ha-Levi (c. 1075-1141), a thinker became critical of philosophy and subordinated reason to revelation, rather than making it an equal or senior partner.

Modern thought rejects the medieval concept of causality, and the philosophy based on it remains of interest mainly to academic specialists. However, the contemporary clash between reason and faith seems prefigured in the writings of Moses Maimonides (Mosheh ben Maimon, 1135/8-1204), the preeminent Jewish philosopher. The author of the first great code of Jewish law, the *Mishneh Torah* (lit., "Second Torah"), he gained incomparable stature among Jews. He faced an intellectual crisis: the resolution of the Torah's teachings with the views of Aristotle, who had denied the idea of creation and affirmed the eternity of the universe. Maimonides refused to repudiate the demands either of reason or of faith, and his masterful effort to harmonize Judaism with a scientific view of reality became the model for all later rationalist validations of religious faith. But when, at the end of the fifteenth century, the Jews were expelled from Spain and Portugal, where philosophy was an important part of the

culture, this fruitful intellectual enterprise came largely to an end.

The intellectual defense of Judaism took a more popular form in the polemics against Christianity that circulated from the twelfth century on. The Talmud contains remnants of earlier polemics, but not until major Jewish centers suffered under Christian religious oppression did Jewish books criticizing Christianity appear. (Fewer polemical works were directed against Islam, whose treatment of Jews as inferiors was based on sociopolitical stratification rather than harassment and was often mitigated by pragmatic considerations. Relatively quiescent relations existed between Muslims and Jews after the early centuries of Muslim conquest.)

Jewish teachers could elaborate their faith without reference to Christianity or Islam, though the Bible and Talmud are replete with attacks on idolatry. Besides, the Christian claim that Jesus of Nazareth was the Messiah seemed, to the Jews, self-refuting, as the world remained radically unredeemed. But as the church increasingly attacked Jewish belief, Jewish leaders found it necessary to refute the church's claims and invalidate its doctrines.

Jewish polemics sought to demonstrate Christian misinterpretation of biblical texts by citing the original Hebrew texts and the traditional Jewish understanding of them. Christian converts from Judaism countered these arguments by citing Talmudic and Midrashic passages that were alleged to prove Jesus' messiahship. The Jewish disputants attacked the credibility of the conflicting gospel accounts of Jesus' life and the evangelists' ignorance of Talmudic law (which they assumed to have been operative in Jesus' time). They also caustically exposed the irrationality of such Christian doctrines as the virgin birth, the incarnation, and the Eucharist. By contrast, they contended, Judaism was a religion a rational man could accept. It was a theme that Jews would continue to find persuasive into modern times.

Modernity: Opportunity and Peril

Emancipation, the fitful process by which the segregation and oppression of European Jewry was encouraged to end, began in earnest with the French Revolution. Gradually, as nationality was severed from membership in an official Christian faith, Jews and other minority denominations received equal political rights and social opportunity. As a result, most modern Jews, despite their religious heritage, have avidly supported keeping government and civil society neutral with regard to religion. Because their politics and religion are closely intermixed, the Islamic nations that granted Jews complete equality were among the last states to do so.

After some fifteen hundred years of degradation and centuries of grinding oppression, most European Jews enthusiastically welcomed equality. To those raised in the ghettoes or in the *shtetls* (Yi., "villages") of eastern Europe, every new freedom, no matter how hedged by limitations or by secularized forms of anti-Semitism, came as a near fulfillment of messianic hopes. A politicized, humanistic hope now became the dominant tone of Jewish existence.

But the price of equality was conformity to the larger culture. European society did not allow for much cultural diversity, and although the accepted social conventions were ostensibly secular, they often reflected their Christian origins.

As emancipation proceeded, the consequences for rabbinic Judaism were devastating. One group of Jews rejected modernization altogether, another group rejected the major doctrines of Judaism. Most Jews found these reactions too extreme, preferring a middle way.

A small minority of traditionalists, rather than surrender anything that they felt God asked of them, spurned modernization. Many pious eastern European Jews long refused to immigrate to America with the hundreds of thousands of Jews who began to do so in the last decades of the nineteenth century. This produced a social situation unique in Jewish history. Elsewhere, long established Orthodox institutions formed the basis of community life. The non-Orthodox

> **Practically, emancipation offered Jews a dignity they had known only sporadically for two thousand years.**

movements that arose with the coming of modernity were reactions to them. In the United States, non-Orthodox institutions became well established in the late nineteenth and early twentieth centuries, and only after World War I did Orthodox institutions slowly come to prominence.

Most Jews rejected this strategy of separatism for pragmatic and intuitive reasons. Practically, emancipation offered Jews a dignity they had known only sporadically for two thousand years. Hence their embrace of modernity can be understood as an existentially transformed way of keeping the covenant, arising from the intuition that Western civilization, as evidenced by its movement toward liberation, contained a considerable measure of the universal truth of Judaism.

Some Jews carried this appreciation to the point of urging Jews to assimilate fully and allow their "parochial" faith to die so that they might participate in humankind's emerging universal culture. Again, most Jews demurred. Given their passion for modernity, their insistence on also remaining Jewish has been difficult to explain, especially since no single philosophy of modern Jewish living has ever become widely accepted. Anti-Semitism has kept some Jews Jewish—yet its continuing virulence seems more a reason to defect than to stay. Moreover, even in the absence of overt hatred of Jews, many Jews have refused to assimilate. Modernist believers see this as an act of persistent loyalty to the covenant: Jews

remain personally faithful to their ancient pact even if uncertain about how to live it, while God, in some inexplicable but familiar way, does not let them go.

Postemancipation Jewry has chosen to be both modern and Jewish, thus fixing its continuing agenda: first, establishing a less separatistic, more adaptive way of living; and second, validating the authenticity of that way in Jewish and modern terms.

Sundering the Unity of the Way. Modernity made religion a private affair and defined religious groups in terms derived from Christianity—that is, as communities united by common faith and ritual practice. Nationality was dissociated from religion and subordinated to the nation-state, an arrangement that can still cause social unrest in multinational countries. On both counts, Judaism could not maintain itself as a religio-ethnic entity (the hybrid designation modernity has forced upon students of Judaism). As a result, an unprecedented dichotomy came into Jewish life: one group of Jews defined their Judaism as "religious," while another group defined theirs in secular terms, as an ethnicity.

Religious ways of liberal Jews. Faced with the unacceptable options of either staying Jewish but in an isolated manner—as though still within ghetto walls—or joining modern society by converting to Christianity, some early nineteenth-century German Jewish laymen began experimenting with a Judaism adapted to European modes of religiosity. In that spirit, they reformed synagogue worship. Essentially, they adorned it with a new aesthetic, eliminating liturgical repetitions and poetic embellishments and introducing solemn group decorum, vernacular prayers, sermons, and contemporary musical styles (including the use of a pipe organ and female as well as male singers). They also abolished the halakhic requirement of the separation of the sexes at services, allowing families to sit together in worship.

This early version of Reform Judaism paved the way for subsequent non-Orthodox Jewish movements. The early reformers justified their form of Judaism with the notion, derived from contemporary German culture, that eternal essences take on transient forms. The essence of Judaism, in their view, is ethical monotheism, which its rituals and customs serve to transmit and strengthen. When times change and old forms no longer function well, they should be altered or abandoned and new forms created.

Most modern Jews have accepted moral duty as the core of Jewish obligation. Many believe that the Jewish people have a mission to teach humankind the religious primacy of universal ethics. In any case, modern Jews often reduce the teachings of the Torah to ethics and, though allowing much else in rabbinic Judaism to atrophy, devote themselves to the moral transformation of society. This universalized sense of covenant responsibility accounts for the astonishing record of modern Jewish contributions to the improvement of human welfare.

In the latter part of the nineteenth century, a new movement emerged: Conservative Judaism. Many eastern European immigrants to America found that their sense of Jewish modernity was not satisfied by the adaptive tone and the essentially ethical content of Reform Judaism, which had been brought over by earlier immigrants from Germany. While seeking to be modern, these Russian and Polish Jews also wanted to preserve a considerable measure of particular Jewish practice. Devotion to the Jewish people as the dynamic creator of Jewish law was their counterpoise to the Reform concentration on ethics. Over the decades, smaller movements have also arisen, positioning themselves essentially in relation to these central communal groups. The most significant of these is Reconstructionism, a movement which derives from the theory of Mordecai Kaplan (1881-1983) that the Jewish community, acting in democratic fashion, ought to be authoritative with regard to Jewish practice.

By the 1970s, the denominational lines had become blurred. Most American Jews, regardless of affiliation, now follow one of several patterns of liberal Jewish living. These vary in their loyalty to classic observance and spirituality, but show considerable similarity in the cultural activities they integrate into their Judaism—especially participation in higher education, civic affairs, and the arts, music, and literature. But the interplay between Judaism and modernity can best be illustrated by the devotion of Jews to interpersonal relationships. American Jews today express the longstanding rabbinic commitment to family and community by their disproportionate involvement in the helping professions (such as teaching, social work, and psychotherapy) and their intense concern for family relationships. In these areas they demonstrate a dedication lacking in their observance of the halakhic dietary laws and laws governing sexual relations between spouses. They seem to believe that sanctifying life, their covenant goal, now requires giving these general human activities priority in Jewish duty.

Despite this heavy cultural borrowing, American Jews manifest a significant measure of particular Jewish action. Even at the humanist end of the religious spectrum, the concern with ethics and other universal issues is reinforced by an attachment to the Jewish folk. Such Jews invest energy and self in Jewish charity, organized defense against anti-Semitism, support of the state of Israel, and occasional ritual acts, most notably those associated with life-cycle events, High Holy Day services, and the home Seder, the Passover meal. In this group one sees clearly a problem that continues to bedevil all liberal Jews: the freedom not to be Orthodox is often taken as a license to do and care little about Judaism altogether.

At the other end of the liberal religious spectrum stands a small minority of Jews whose lives are substantially guided by Jewish tradition, interpreted through a modern ethical and cultural sensibility. They exhibit the rabbinic devotion to self, family, people, and God, seeking to live by rabbinic law wherever they can. They constitute the spiritual heart of non-Orthodox Judaism, whose viability depends upon its acceptance of their leadership in combining modernity and tradition.

The outstanding achievements of liberal Judaism derive from its pursuit of a mediating spirituality. It has radically enlarged the horizon of Jewish duty by its dedication to ethics and democracy. It has revolutionized the study of Judaism by its insistence upon the adoption of modern scholarly methods. Above all, it has convinced most of the Jewish community that modernity and Judaism can successfully be integrated. What many in a prior generation passionately feared and fought, most Jews now consider of great benefit to Judaism.

Nothing so well illustrates the continuing promise and problem of liberal Judaism as its response to feminism. Early in the nineteenth century, the German reformers recognized an ethical imperative to break with the Jewish laws and customs that discriminate against women. But it took more than a century for Reform congregations to elect women officers and until 1972 for the first American woman to be ordained a rabbi; women cantors followed quickly. Since then, the Reconstructionist and Conservative movements have accepted both innovations.

Much of the community has welcomed this development, but it is not clear how far it will tolerate alteration of the old patterns—for example, removing the sexist language of the prayer book, or allowing the genuine sharing of power between men and women. If liberal Jewish daring in this matter eventually becomes part of the accepted covenant way, then its experimentation will again have taught Jews a new way of sanctifying Jewish existence. Orthodox critics rejoin that in breaking with the traditional rabbinic understanding of the Torah which defines separate roles for the sexes, the liberals are more likely to dilute Judaism than to win its future.

Religious ways of Orthodox Jews. As a self-conscious movement, Jewish Orthodoxy arose in response to liberal Judaism with the purpose of correctly delineating Jewish authenticity. Traditional Judaism knows only one standard of faithfulness to God: loyalty to God's law as expounded in the Torah, especially the oral law in its continuing development by contemporary sages. The Torah has absolute primacy. Modernity can come into Judaism only as the Torah allows. Hence the lives of believing Orthodox Jews display religious continuity more than religious change. Variations in observance among Orthodox Jews derive from local custom, from the differences between Ashkenazim and Sefardim, Hasidim and other Orthodox Jews, and from the variety of opinion passed down by various sages.

The major forms of Orthodoxy can be distinguished by the degree to which they are open to modernity. They stand united, however, in defense of the Torah against what they consider the faithlessness of most other Jews. Even innovations permissible under Jewish law are often resisted lest they give credence to other Jews' radical departures from tradition.

Orthodox attitudes toward the acceptance of modernity range from antagonistic to embracing. The Hasidic sects visibly project their hostility to modernity and their distance from the gentile world (and other Jews) by their distinctive dress, hair, and body language. Several Orthodox groups also seek to reconstitute the cultural isolation of eastern European Jewry, but in less separatistic ways—a goal more easily accomplished in the state of Israel than elsewhere. The continued use of Yiddish, the Judeo-German vernacular of eastern European Jewry, characterizes this entire wing of Orthodoxy. Its antagonism to modernity does not prevent the pious from utilizing technological advances that enhance observance of the commandments or from having contacts with gentiles when necessary, as in commerce. Some groups have marginal affiliates who live in more modern fashion but maintain their ties to the group by keeping some of its special customs, visiting its communities, and giving financial support.

Another wing, known as Modern Orthodoxy, contends that Jewish law allows, and many sages exemplify, the virtue of embracing any cultural good that enhances human existence as the Torah delineates it. The Modern Orthodox have been most innovative in creating two new instruments for Jewish education, the Jewish university and day school, which feature the sciences and sports, both once considered un-Jewish. They generally speak the vernacular (English in America, Hebrew in Israel), not Yiddish, and their only distinguishing visual sign is the small, often knitted skullcap (Yi., *yarmulke*; Heb., *kippah*) worn by males. But their disciplined loyalty to the Torah appears in such matters as prayer, diet, study, and Sabbath and festival observance.

Orthodoxy has enjoyed a significant resurgence as the twentieth century moves toward its end. Some Jews have lost their once great confidence in Western civilization and have withdrawn from it somewhat by adopting a more distinctive practice of Judaism. A minority have joined the separatistic Jewish sects. Most Orthodox Jews have rejected self-ghettoization, choosing to live a dedicated Jewish life as part of an observant community so as to differentiate themselves from an ofttimes pagan society. Their approach to living the life of Torah has nonetheless carried a modern overlay their Orthodox great-grandparents would probably have opposed; even so, the movement to greater Jewish authenticity has debilitated Modern Orthodoxy's innovative zeal.

The large number of Jews who are only nominally Orthodox testifies to the continuing influence of modernity. Despite their affiliation, these Jews are only sporadically observant and their faith fluctuates or is inconsistent. They often consider their private preferences in Jewish law to be genuine Judaism, a heresy in the eyes of Orthodox sages.

Orthodoxy has notable accomplishments to its credit. Despite dire predictions of its death from the effects of modernity, it has created a cadre of Jews whose personal piety and communal life demonstrate the continuing religious power of rabbinic Judaism. It has kept alive and advanced eastern European Jewry's exalted standards of the study of Jewish law. Particularly in the field of bioethics, but in other areas as well, it has shown the continuing vitality of the oral law.

As with liberal Judaism, the issue of feminism best clarifies the continuing promise and problems of Orthodox Judaism. In refusing to grant women substantial legal equality, contemporary sages have defended the integrity of God's law as they received and understand it. Considering how modernity has shattered family life, they do not deem it to possess a wisdom superior to that of Torah. Rather, every genuine faith demands some sacrifice, and Judaism, abandoned by so many and in such worldwide peril, deserves the obedient dedication of all who wish it to remain true to itself and God.

Many Orthodox authorities have long acknowledged that some laws regarding women create suffering—for example, the woman who, because she cannot meet certain technical criteria, is barred from receiving a Jewish divorce. Liberal Jews perceive the inability of contemporary Orthodox sages to institute legal remedies for this situation as a telling indication that, good will notwithstanding, the laws' inequities are still operative. Feminists cannot believe that, with most Orthodox Jews committed to the general self-fulfillment of women, Orthodox women will long be content with sex-segregated duties and roles. However, Orthodox Judaism has shown no significant loss of membership from its defense of classic Judaism in this matter.

Culture as "Torah" of secular Jews. In late nineteenth-century Europe and mid-twentieth-century America, as Jews became university educated and urban dwelling, they secularized. They believed that modernization meant the acceptance of the idea that there is no God and the end of practices that differentiated Jews from their neighbors. Yet, as they became thoroughly secularized, they generally did not do so to the point of assimilation. Large numbers retained a connection with the Jewish people, if only by discovering that many of the humanitarians they enjoyed associating with were also secularized Jews. Two interrelated major patterns of secular Jewish living arose from this process, one cultural, the other political.

The early foes of emancipation argued that the Jews could not modernize because they had no capacity for high culture. Liberal Jews sought to refute them by aestheticizing Jewish worship. Secular Jews did the same by devoting their lives to literature and the arts, often achieving uncommon success in these areas. Existentially, secular Jews made high culture their "Torah," bringing to it the intense dedication they had once given to faith, for it now validated their existence.

To keep the Jewish people alive, some European Jewish secularists suggested that Jews participate in universal culture through the development of a secular Jewish literature, initially in Hebrew, but later in Yiddish as well. This movement toward Haskalah (Enlightenment) revived the Hebrew language, which had long been used only for traditional scholarship and religious purposes. The long-range hopes of the leaders of Haskalah did not survive the realities of anti-Semitism, acculturation, and migration. Only in the state of Israel, where Jews have created a national culture, has the Hebrew language successfully been used as a means for the modernization of Jewish life. In the Diaspora, few Jews now maintain their Jewishness by utilizing Hebrew or Yiddish to pursue humanism. Yet Diaspora Jews and those of the state of Israel commonly consider a positive attitude to culture an integral part of their Jewishness.

Jewish secularity also directed itself to ethical politics, that is, redeeming the world through the achievement of social justice. Jews became advocates of the rights of labor and the virtues of socialism, seeing in the struggles for civil rights and civil liberties their own cause as it affected other minorities. Prayer and piety no longer seemed effective responses to social injustice. Being politically informed and involved therefore became for Jews the modern equivalent of a commandment.

This movement's effects have been felt both in general society and in the Jewish community. Jewish politicians and Jewish activists have been a significant influence in humanizing modern society. Simultaneously, the notion of pluralistic democracy has reshaped Jewish life in America. The American Jewish community now operates on a fully voluntary basis and features a broad inclusiveness, diverse organizations, and a dynamism undaunted by emergency or changing times. It has raised more money for Jewish charity than any other voluntary philanthropic effort in history. In the midst of secularization, the lineaments of the covenant appear.

Nationalism: Zionism and the State of Israel. The cultural and political drives in Jewish secularization climaxed in Zionism, the movement that reinterpreted Judaism as Jewish nationalism. Organized on a worldwide basis by Theodor Herzl (1860-1904) in 1897, the Zionists began a crusade to liberate Jews on two levels. First, they sought freedom from persecution by acquiring a land where the Jewish masses might find economic opportunity and political security. Second, they wanted to create a genuinely Jewish culture that would express, in an untrammeled way, the Jewish people's spirit.

Many liberal and Orthodox Jews initially opposed Zionism for religious reasons. The former found its secularism Jewishly aberrant and its nationalism a threat to Jewish emancipation in the Diaspora. The latter objected to its notion of a Jewish state independent of the Torah and found its nationalistic activism a usurpation of God's role in bringing the Messiah. Vestiges of these anti-Zionist attitudes still exist, but most religious Jews now ardently support the state of Israel.

Before the founding of the state of Israel in 1948, Zionism generated a new form of Jewish living in the Diaspora, one built on political activity, immigration and the preparation for it, and participation in the renewal of Hebrew culture. The barbarity of Nazi Germany and the callousness of the rest of the world toward the Jews in the 1930s and 1940s gave Zionism an additional concern: acquiring one place in the world to which Jews could immigrate without restriction.

With the birth and growth of Israel, Jews could return to a way of living they had not known for nearly two millennia: as a Jewish community living on the Jewish homeland in Jewish self-determination. Israel is a secular state—though Orthodox Judaism retains special rights in it—and its ethos is

> Outside the state of Israel, Zionism as a total way of life has virtually disappeared.

democratic and welfare-oriented. Its extraordinary effort, amid the most trying political circumstances, to hold itself to ethical standards higher than those pursued by most other nations has won it the admiration and identification of world Jewry. Nothing in postemancipation Jewish life has remotely approached its ability to arouse Jewish devotion and action.

Israeli Jews, the great majority of whom consider themselves nonreligious (that is, non-Orthodox), live by the rhythm of the Jewish calendar and draw their ideals from the Bible, the great national saga. Their everyday language is Hebrew and their culture increasingly reflects the concerns of individuals and a society facing the awesome dilemmas of modern existence. In every human dimension, Jews living in the state of Israel are, even without thinking about it, living Jewishly. And for those who carry on Orthodox Judaism or the tiny minority who are Reform or Conservative Jews, the reconstituted Jewish society provides an incomparable context for religious existence.

Outside the state of Israel, Zionism as a total way of life has virtually disappeared. Most Diaspora Jews do not carry on a Jewish cultural life in Hebrew or plan to immigrate to Israel. They may be deeply emotionally attached to Israel, but it does not provide the essential content of their Jewish lives. Zionism has had an incomparable triumph in the high human and Jewish accomplishment of the state of Israel. Yet Zionism's thorough secularization of the covenant has apparently rendered it incapable of guiding Diaspora Jewish life.

Philosophic Grounds of Modern Jewish Life. Judaism makes its claims upon the Jew in the name of God and the Jewish people's corporate experience—but modernity radically individualizes authority. A modern philosophy of Judaism must mediate between autonomy and tradition and do justice to each of them.

Contemporary Orthodoxy does not wait for each individual to make a decision about what constitutes Jewish duty. Orthodoxy begins with faith and has felt no pressing need for theoretical expositions of its beliefs. It has therefore largely left to liberal Jews the task of constructing systematic Jewish theologies. Five distinctive intellectual statements have gained continuing attention—six, if Zionist ideology can be considered an equivalent system.

Two rationalist interpretations. Rationalism had an irresistible appeal to nineteenth-century Jewish modernizers. It compellingly distinguished between the lastingly valuable essence of Judaism, ethical monotheism, and its transient historical expression in ceremony and ritual. This early liberal criterion of continuity and change first attained sophisticated statement in the work of Hermann Cohen (1842-1918), the famed Marburg Neo-Kantian philosopher.

In rigorous academic works, Cohen delineated the religion a rational person could accept. Cohen sought to demonstrate that rationality requires a philosophical idea of God to integrate its disparate scientific, ethical, and aesthetic modes of thinking. His system was dominated by ethics and he argued that this ethical monotheism appeared for the first time in history in the work of the biblical prophets. As the earliest and purest proponent of ethical monotheism, the Jewish people had a mission to humankind: to teach the universal truth of rational religion. Messianism could no longer be the miraculous advent of God's regent, but became humankind's task of ethically perfecting itself. (This view led Cohen to oppose Zionism as a constriction of the Jewish ethical horizon.) All customs that strengthened Jewish ethical sensitivity or kept Jews faithful to their mission ought to be maintained; those that thwarted them ought to be abandoned. In greatly diluted fashion, Cohen's ethical reworking of Judaism became the accepted ideology of modern Jews.

Leo Baeck (1873-1956), the German thinker who remained closest to Cohen's Judaism of reason, felt the need to supplement reason with the experience of mystery, even though that meant sacrificing Cohen's logical rigor. Baeck pointed to religious consciousness as the deepest foundation of ethical monotheism. He evocatively described the sense human beings have of being creations yet also ethical creators, of being utterly transient yet linked in spirit with that which is eternal.

However, Baeck's rationalism remained sovereign. Fearing the dangers of romanticism, he insisted that religious consciousness should lead to action only as ethics permitted. Thus, while authorizing some nonrational command-

ments, he ruled out anything that smacked of superstition and bigotry. He also conducted a vigorous polemic against Christianity and Buddhism, finding both of them deficient in their ethics and monotheism. He so closely identified Judaism with a universal rational faith that he alone among modern Jewish thinkers urged Jews to seek converts.

Baeck called for a broad horizon of Jewish obligation. He believed the Jewish people to be so historically identified with the idea of ethical monotheism that should Judaism die, ethical monotheism would also die. The Jewish people, therefore, must survive. To keep it alive, the Jewish people continually create group practices that strengthen and protect the people from the perils it encounters in history.

Rational validations for the primacy of peoplehood. Zionist ideologists proclaimed the Jews a nation, not a religion, and looked forward to a renewal of Judaism as the communal life of the Jewish folk resettled on its ancient soil. They demythologized the biblical interpretation of exile—which Jewish mystics had applied metaphorically even to God—and made it a purely sociopolitical concept. Redemption would not come by a Messiah but with geographic relocation, cultural self-expression, and political reconstitution.

One early Zionist debate still roils the community: is modern Jewish nationalism rigorously secular, and thus free of religious and ethnic values, or is it distinctively Jewish? No one raised this issue more penetratingly than the essayist Ahad ha-`Am ("one of the people," pseudonym of Asher Ginzberg, 1856-1927).

Ahad ha-`Am's Zionism drew on the nineteenth-century concepts of folk psychology and cultural nationalism to assert that Jews, like other peoples, had a folk "character" to which they needed to be true. The Jewish national soul exhibited a talent for ethics and high culture with a devotion to absolute justice as the central theme of great literature and other arts, as the Bible indicates. Jewish nationalism, therefore, had to work for the recreation of an ethically and aesthetically elevated Jewish culture. A renascent Jewish state could serve as its worldwide spiritual center, and Diaspora Jewish communities would survive spiritually by participating in its cultural life.

Most Zionist ideologists simply assumed that Zionism mandated humanistic values and rarely sought to explicate them. Besides, crises in Jewish life followed so hard upon one another in the twentieth century that arguing such abstractions seemed frivolous. But various events in the life of the state of Israel have kept the issue alive. Its very persistence testifies to its unusual combination of secularity and religiosity. The Israeli courts, in rulings on the legal definition of Jewishness and other issues, have refused to sever the connectionbetween Jewish nationalism and Jewish religion. Some thinkers therefore insist that, for all its putative secularity, the state of Israel can best be understood as an eccentric development of classic Jewish ethnic religiosity.

An American thinker, Mordecai M. Kaplan (1881-1983), created another distinctive Jewish rationalism in terms of philosophic naturalism. Basing his thinking on ideas derived from the recently developed science of sociology, Kaplan held that for Jewish life today to be meaningful, it must reflect the scientific worldview and democratic commitment of modernity. Kaplan therefore carried on a vigorous polemic against supernaturalism in Judaism. He inverted the central idea of traditional Judaism: that God gave the Torah to the Jewish people (thus giving it its distinctive character). Kaplan now claimed, arguing from the perspective of sociology, that the Jewish people had created Judaism, which he defined as an ethnic civilization, based on a land, a language, a history,

> **Kaplan therefore carried on a vigorous polemic against supernaturalism in Judaism.**

a calendar, heroes, institutions, arts, values, and much else, with religion at its core. Through its concept of God, Jewish civilization expressed its highest values. The Jewish people's health could be restored only by fully reconstructing its folk life; hence Kaplan called his movement Reconstructionism. The involvement of American Jews in Jewish art, music, and other cultural forms owes much to Kaplan. Kaplan also called for the Jewish community to reorganize itself institutionally so that the community, not a given religious movement or synagogue, would be the focus of Jewish affiliation. Though pluralistic, it could then democratically seek to legislate for its members and meet the full range of religious, political, cultural, and social needs of a healthy ethnic group. But no Jewish community has yet so reconstituted itself.

Kaplan proposed a daring definition of God as the power (or process) that makes for "salvation," by which he meant "human fulfillment." Speaking of God in impersonal, naturalistic terms indicates the purely symbolic status of folk anthropomorphisms and the modern rejection of miracles, verbal revelation, and the idea of the chosen people. Equally important, defining God in finite terms—as that aspect of nature that abets human self-development—solves the theological problem of evil. Kaplan's God does not bring evil, only good. We can now maturely see evil as caused by nature and take it as a challenge to our moral creativity.

Kaplan's bold recasting of Judaism won him a small but enthusiastic following. However, his equation of modernity with scientific rationality lost its appeal in the Jewish community as the interest in nonrationalist Jewish thinkers heightened.

Nonrationalist Jewish thinkers. After World War I, Franz Rosenzweig (1886-1929), the youthful German author of a magisterial work on Hegel, pioneered Jewish existentialism with his effort to situate Judaism in selfhood rather than in acts or ideas. Rosenzweig connected being Jewish with acting Jewishly—that is, observing the law insofar as one was existentially able to acknowledge it as possessing the quality of commandment. He thus specified, but never fully clarified, a greatly appealing balance between duty and freedom, bequeathing to later liberal Jewish thought one of its central issues.

Martin Buber (1878-1965), an older contemporary and sometime collaborator of Rosenzweig's, created a more extensive system. He suggested that human existence is dynamically relational, occurring either in an objectifying mode he called I-It, or a value-conferring mode of personal openness and mutuality he called I-Thou, which he carefully differentiated from romanticism and mysticism. Romanticism involves an I-It of emotion or experience; mysticism, a loss of self in the One. Buber had in mind something as subtle yet much more common.

Like all significant personal involvements, an I-Thou relationship with God (the "Eternal Thou") evokes responsive action—it "commands." Transgression of such duty involves guilt and the need to atone. All this has a corporate dimension, for whenever two persons truly meet, God is present as well. Consequently, the I-Thou experience directs us to create true human community, a society of Thou's.

Religions arise when relationships with God take on social forms. In time, this process of institutionalization, instead of expediting living contact with God, obstructs it. Institutionalized faiths may designate one sphere of life as holy, leaving the rest to be profane. But the I-Thou relationship knows no limits, and all life should be lived on its terms. Hence Buber opposed all "religion."

According to Buber, the Hebrew Bible recounts the I-Thou experiences of the Jewish people with God, which, over centuries, created an indissoluble relationship between them—the covenant. No other ethnic group has ever so identified its corporate existence with loyalty to God. Because of its covenant, the Jewish folk undertook the messianic task of creating community among its members and thus, eventually, among humankind. While Jews sometimes lost sight of this task, it could never be completely lost, as indicated by early Hasidism and by Zionism. During Buber's decades of residence in Israel, his public insistence that the state should live up to his ideal of the covenant made him a figure of considerable controversy there.

Another great systembuilder, Abraham Joshua Heschel (1907-1972), integrated much of twentieth-century Jewish experience in his own life. The scion of a Polish Hasidic dynasty, he took a doctorate in Berlin, escaped World War II by going to the United States to teach at the Reform rabbinical school (Hebrew Union College) in Cincinnati. He later taught a near-Orthodox theology at the Conservative seminary in New York.

Heschel faulted the existentialists for defining religion as the movement of people toward God. Modern Jewry's very skepticism, he said, should make it awestruck at the power Someone has given humankind. When such "radical amazement" opens people to the reality of the giver, it becomes apparent, as the Bible indicates, that God pursues humankind, forcing upon it God's self-revelation, and that the biblical prophets accurately transmit God's message.

The meaning of the prophets, Heschel said, is clear: God is a God of pathos, one who suffers when people transgress and who rejoices when they achieve holiness. To argue that God would be more perfect if God had no feelings reflects a Stoic, that is, a Roman point of view, not that of the Bible. Revelation proceeds by "sympathos," by uncommonly gifted individuals coming to feel what God feels. They may verbalize this understanding in different ways, but they do not interpose themselves between God and humankind. The commandments transmitted by Moses and the sages accurately reflect God's injunctions. They are the divinely sanctioned media for meeting God by doing God's will.

Two themes in Heschel's thought mitigate his absolute acceptance of Jewish tradition. First, he emphasized the paucity of revelation compared with the subsequent plethora of interpretation, thereby suggesting the virtue of continuing development. Second, he carefully documented the prophets' intense ethical devotion, implying, perhaps, that human considerations should predominate in interpreting the Torah. He nobly exemplified this in his participation in the civil rights and antiwar struggles of the 1960s. But he never indicated whether he would advocate changes in Jewish law for these or other reasons.

Since the articulation of these six positions, much theological writing and discussion has gone on, but no distinctive new pattern has won substantial acceptance.

The theoretical response to the Holocaust had an ironic outcome.

Confronting the Holocaust. For reasons still debated, not until the mid-1960s did Jewish thinkers confront the theoretical implications of the Nazi murder of six million Jews. With the emergence of the short-lived "death of God" movement, some Jewish philosophers demanded that a Jewish theology be created that would focus on the reality revealed at Auschwitz, the most notorious of the Nazi death camps and the symbol of the Holocaust. Where the revelation at Sinai spoke of God's rule, God's justice, and God's help to the people of Israel, Auschwitz now spoke of God's absence, of the world's injustice, and of the terrible abandonment of the Jewish people. But it was in the creation of the state of Israel that the Jewish people had given its deepest response

to Nazi destructiveness: it was the expression of an intense determination to survive with high human dignity. The Arab-Israeli Six-Day War of 1967 which threatened Israel's (and therefore Jewish) existence catalyzed Jewry worldwide to identify even more intensely with the state of Israel. Israel, therefore, for all its secularity, took on a numinous quality for those who strove to maintain the covenant.

The survival of the Jewish people now became a central preoccupation of Diaspora Jews and a major motive for individuals to assume or extend their Jewish responsibilities. Associated with this was a reassessment of the values of the emancipation. Because of the messianic hope that emancipation had awakened, Jews had surrendered much of their traditional way of life. Now, even as Western civilization began to lose its ultimate confidence in science, technology, education, and culture—in utter human capability—so Jews started to approach their tradition with new receptivity. For some, this partial withdrawal from universal concerns led back to Orthodoxy. Most Jews found that though their social activism could no longer take on redemptive guise, they still could not spurn the ethical lessons of the emancipation, especially with regard to feminism. The critical challenge now facing such chastened liberal Jews is the delineation of their duty and the creation of communities to live it, a concern giving rise to considerable experimentation.

The theoretical response to the Holocaust had an ironic outcome. Experience made substituting Auschwitz for Sinai was unacceptable to most Jews. Despite the mass depravity that continues to plague the twentieth century, the revelation of God's absence and of humanity's depravity in the Holocaust does not constitute the norm of human or Jewish existence. Sanctifying the routine without forgetting the extraordinary remains the Jew's fundamental responsibility, as the revelation at Sinai taught. The primary response to the Holocaust, Jews agree, must be an intensification of human responsibility.

Some Orthodox leaders, like the *rebe* of the Lubavitch Hasidic sect, say, in the tradition of the *Book of Deuteronomy*, that in the Holocaust God grievously punished a sinful generation. Most Jews find it impossible to view the Holocaust as an act of divine justice. Alternatively, rationalist teachers assert that God has only finite power and was incapable of preventing the Holocaust, so humankind must actively help God bring the Messiah. Others have come to a Job-like stance. They remain stunned that God can entrust humans with the freedom to become as heartless as the Nazis did. They admit they do not understand God's ways. Nonetheless, they accept God's sovereignty and seek to build their lives on it.

All these views of evil circulated in the Jewish community well before the Holocaust, leading some to suggest that what truly died in the Holocaust was the Enlightenment's surrogate god, the infinitely competent human spirit. As a result of the loss of absolute faith in humankind, a small minority of modern Jews have sought answers in Jewish mysticism. For others, Orthodoxy has gained fresh appeal. For most Jews, the emancipation has only been qualified, not negated. Mediating between Judaism and modernity continues to be the central spiritual concern of the people who believe themselves to stand in covenant with God, working and waiting for the realization of God's rule on earth.

[*For further discussion of the mainstream movements in contemporary Judaism, see* Hasidism. *Aspects of Judaism that are not rabbinic in origin are discussed in* Folk Religion.]

BIBLIOGRAPHY

The *Encyclopaedia Judaica,* 16 vols. (Jerusalem, 1971), encapsulates contemporary scholarship on Judaism, not altogether replacing the first magisterial survey, *The Jewish Encyclopedia,* 12 vols. (1901-1906; reprint, New York, 1964). Louis Jacobs's *A Jewish Theology* (New York, 1973) provides erudite historical accounts of major Jewish ideas from a believing but nonfundamentalist viewpoint. Robert M. Seltzer's comprehensive survey *Jewish People, Jewish Thought* (New York, 1980) adroitly balances history and religious ideas. The finest recent account of the Jewish religious sensibility of the Bible is Jon D. Levenson's *Sinai and Zion* (New York, 1985).

Reliable, if not altogether comprehensible, English translations of the central rabbinic texts exist: *The Mishnah,* translated by Herbert Danby (Oxford, 1933); *The Babylonian Talmud,* 35 vols. (1935-1948; reprint in 18 vols., London, 1961); and *Midrash Rabbah,* 10 vols., translated by Harry Freedman et al. (London, 1939). An English rendering of the Jerusalem Talmud by Jacob Neusner is under way as *The Talmud of the Land of Israel* (Chicago, 1982-); thirty-five volumes are projected. Current scholarship has raised so many questions about rabbinic Judaism that great care must be exercised in utilizing any single source. A well-rounded overview can be gained from the revised (but not the original) edition of Emil Schürer's *The History of the Jewish People in the Age of Jesus Christ,* 2 vols., edited and revised by Géza Vermès and Fergus Millar and translated by T. A. Burkill et al. (Edinburgh, 1973-1979).

No history of the development of Jewish practice exists. Valuable insights may still be gained from the dated work of Hayyim Schauss, *The Jewish Festivals,* translated by Samuel Jaffe (Cincinnati, 1938), and *The Lifetime of a Jew* (New York, 1950). Menachem Elon treats some central themes of Jewish law in *The Principles of Jewish Law* (Jerusalem, 1975), and an invaluable guide to more specific themes is the presently incomplete *Entsiqlopedeyah Talmudit,* edited by S. Y. Zevin and Meir Bar-Ilan (Jerusalem, 1947-).

The *aggadah,* because of its human appeal, is more readily accessible. Two good anthologies available in English are Louis Ginzberg's *The Legends of the Jews,* 7 vols., translated by Henrietta Szold et al. (Philadelphia, 1909-1938), which follows the organization of the Bible, and C. G. Montefiore and Herbert Loewe's *A Rabbinic Anthology* (1938; reprint, Philadelphia, 1960), which is thematically organized. The most comprehensive anthology, however, is in Hebrew: H. N. Bialik and Y. H. Ravnitzky's *Sefer ha-aggadah,* 3 vols. (Cracow, 1907-1911), often reprinted.

Three valuable, if problematic, introductions to rabbinic thought are Solomon Schechter's *Some Aspects of Rabbinic Theology* (New York, 1909), and George Foot Moore's *Judaism,* 3 vols. in 2 (1927-1930; reprint, Cambridge, Mass., 1970), both of which show apologetic tendencies, and E. E. Urbach's *Hazal* (Jerusalem, 1969), trans-

lated by Israel Abrahams as *The Sages,* 2 vols. (Jerusalem, 1975), which unconvincingly seeks to resolve rabbinic inconsistencies by applying a historical hermeneutic. Jacob Neusner's continuing researches in this literature deserve careful attention. For his demonstration of how ahistorical (by Western academic standards) rabbinic "theology" was, see his *Judaism in Society* (Chicago, 1984).

Most of the great Jewish legal works of the Middle Ages await reliable translation according to the standard set by *The Code of Maimonides,* 15 vols. to date (New Haven, 1949-), the now nearly complete translation of Maimonides' *Mishneh Torah.* The burgeoning scholarship on mysticism builds on the paradigmatic researches of Gershom Scholem, whose synoptic statement is *Major Trends in Jewish Mysticism* (1941; reprint, New York, 1961). Many major works of medieval Jewish philosophy have been translated. The older, still useful survey of the field is Isaac Husik's *A History of Mediaeval Jewish Philosophy* (New York, 1916). Its modern successor is Julius Guttmann's *Philosophies of Judaism,* translated by David W. Silverman (New York, 1964).

The documents of the emancipation and its aftermath are bountifully supplied and valuably annotated in Paul R. Mendes-Flohr and Jehuda Reinharz's *The Jew in the Modern World* (Oxford, 1980). Some sense of the reality of modern Jewish life as it is lived in North America can be gained from the ideals projected in the works of some of its leading guides (respectively, Modern Orthodox, far-right-wing Conservative, tradition-seeking independent, and Reform): Hayim Halevy Donin's *To Be a Jew* (New York, 1972); Isaac Klein's *A Guide to Jewish Religious Practice* (New York, 1979); *The Jewish Catalog,* edited by Richard Siegel, Michael Strassfeld, and Sharon Strassfeld (Philadelphia, 1973); and *Gates of Mitzvah,* edited by Simeon J. Maslin (New York, 1979), and *Gates of the Seasons,* edited by Peter Knobel (New York, 1983).

Developments in Jewish law are difficult to track even for seasoned experts, but since its founding, *The Jewish Law Annual,* edited by Bernard S. Jackson (Leiden, 1978-), has been a most valuable guide. Reliable introductions to current Jewish theologies are William E. Kaufman's *Contemporary Jewish Philosophies* (New York, 1976) and my own *Choices in Modern Jewish Thought* (New York, 1983).

For the Holocaust, the early works of Elie Wiesel, fiction and nonfiction, uniquely limn the paradoxes of trying to live and write about the ineffable. Two focal statements about the Holocaust are Richard L. Rubenstein's *After Auschwitz* (Indianapolis, 1966) and Emil L. Fackenheim's *To Mend the World* (New York, 1982).

Modern Orthodoxy is surveyed in Reuven P. Bulka's *Dimensions of Orthodox Judaism* (New York, 1983), but the ideas of its preeminent theoretician, Joseph B. Soloveitchik, are most available in his early, searching essay *Halakhic Man,* translated by Lawrence Kaplan (Philadelphia, 1983). My book *Liberal Judaism* (New York, 1984) explicates the religious positions of much of American non-Orthodox Judaism.

EUGENE B. BOROWITZ

JUNG, C. G.

JUNG, C. G. (1875-1961), originator of analytical psychology: a theory of individual psychotherapy, of religion, and of Western culture.

Life and Principal Works. Jung was born in the village of Kesswil, Switzerland, the son of a Protestant minister. He earned a medical degree from the University of Basel in 1902. Believing that psychiatry would allow him to combine his scientific and humanistic interests, he joined the staff of the Burghölzli, the psychiatric clinic of the University of Zurich.

Shortly after the beginning of his psychiatric career, Jung's life became active and eventful. In 1900, Sigmund Freud published what came to be his most famous book, *The Interpretation of Dreams,* and began to attract a talented following. Among the most gifted was Carl Jung. The two men became intimate friends and their correspondence became lengthy. Jung concluded that Freud's theories of the unconscious, dreams, childhood conflict, and psychological illnesses (the neuroses) were essentially correct, and he adopted them in his own psychiatric work. He wrote various papers, which he delivered to scientific societies, explaining and advancing Freud's ideas. During this period, Freud considered Jung to be his most promising colleague.

For many reasons, however, this close and spirited collaboration did not last. There were important differences regarding the nature of psychological theory: Freud insisted upon the sexual roots of neurosis, whereas Jung advanced a nonsexual approach. Also significant was the fact that, as both men began to apply psychoanalysis to religion, they evolved different assessments of the psychological significance of religion. Jung believed he could discern a religious dimension in psychoanalysis, whereas Freud insisted upon an entirely scientific understanding of it. As a result, the two broke off their personal correspondence and abandoned all professional collaboration in 1913.

Freud survived his disappointment with Jung by turning his energies to his other followers and to the increased recognition his own ideas were receiving from the world, but Jung had far less upon which to fall back. He found it necessary to isolate himself. Jung entered a period of intense inner psychological stress; he occupied himself with the products of his own mind, analyzing them and devising theories for interpreting them.

In 1918, Jung was able to look back upon this turbulent period and to understand it in retrospect as the most creative time of his entire life. At its close, he wrote what have become his two most important works; they contain all the major ideas of what became, taking its form from these books, analytical psychology. In *Two Essays on Analytical Psychology* (both essays were revised several times during his life), Jung set forth his understanding of the psychological process of individuation, and in *Psychological Types* he created a long and complex set of definitions for the various concepts that were unique to his system of thought. These books established Jung's reputation as the founder of the school of analytical psychology.

For the remainder of his life, Jung practiced his particular approach to psychotherapy, wrote voluminously, and lectured and traveled widely. In addition to psychotherapy, two subjects were of special interest to him, Western religion and the moral failures of modern society. His best-known books on these are *Answer to Job* (1952) and *The Undiscovered Self* (1957). Late in his life Jung dictated an autobiographical memoir, *Memories, Dreams, Reflections* (1963), in which he reviewed and explained his own personal psychological history, his major works, and his philosophical and religious values.

Analytical Psychology of Religion. Although Jung began his professional career as a psychiatrist, he was always deeply interested in religion. His analytical psychology of the mind was therefore also a religious psychology. Furthermore, he in effect situated his psychological theory of psychotherapy and of religion in the flow of Western religious and scientific traditions, creating a sweeping understanding of the modern world.

Jung set forth individuation as the goal of his therapy. By this he meant a process of psychological transformation in which the patient gradually abandoned the stereotyped expectations of conventional society, which Jung called the *persona,* or mask, in order to discover his or her hidden, unique, and true self. Individuation does not proceed by conscious willing and thinking, but by making the unconscious conscious, and this in turn can occur only through the analysis of dream symbols. Dream interpretation integrates the contents of the unconscious into conscious mental life. Jung distinguished between fantasies and dreams deriving from personal development and those that he thought were universal or common to all historical periods and civilizational contexts. He named the latter "archetypes" and linked them to a universally shared unconscious, the collective unconscious. Thus Jung spoke of the archetype of the mother, or of the father, or of the child. So understood, the process of individuation refers not only to the psychology of the immediate psychotherapeutic situation but also to the lifelong process of growth.

Jung's psychology of individuation cannot be completely understood without explicit reference to religion and to the concept of God. Jung discovered that, as his patients neared the end of their treatment, their archetypal imaginings usually portrayed an awesome authority figure who resembled a powerful father, and he named this figure a "god-imago." Once the god-imago or god archetype had been created, projected, experienced consciously, and finally understood or interpreted, the individuation process was well-nigh complete.

A good deal of scholarly discussion of Jung's psychological theories of religion state that he found in Eastern religion a solution or cure for the spiritual ills or meaninglessness of the modern West. Jung proposed that Western culture had developed in three stages—first religious, then scientific, and finally psychological—and that each stage was in effect a different response to the universal reality of the unconscious. He believed that his psychology—and Freud's as well—were sciences; but they were sciences of the unconscious, of the deep psychological forces that had created religion. Therefore analytical psychology brought religion and science into a new synthesis.

Contribution to the Study of Religion. That Jung's psychological theories have exercised more influence on humanistic studies of religion than have Freud's is due at least in part to Jung's own view that religion is an enduring dimension in human life, a view that does not reduce religion to either psychological-developmental or sociological factors. But there are other reasons. Humanistic scholars of religion are principally concerned with figures, symbols, myths, interpretation, and meaning. Jung's psychological theory of unconscious, archetypal dream symbols facilitates the scholar's task of relating the imagination of readers and audiences directly and immediately to the symbols in literary and religious texts. And because archetypes are a kind of universal language of symbols, an analysis of texts can be made without taking into account the historical and sociological contexts in which they were created.

BIBLIOGRAPHY

Jung's writings are available to the English-speaking scholar in *The Collected Works of C. G. Jung,* 20 vols., translated from German by R. F. C. Hull and edited by Gerhard Adler, Michael Fordham, and Herbert Read (Princeton, 1953-1979). Because the range of Jung's works is so wide and because these volumes contain only the briefest editorial information, the general reader is strongly advised to consult Anthony Storr's excellent and thorough selection of Jung's writings: *The Essential Jung* (Princeton, 1983). This includes excerpts from Jung's autobiographical memoir, *Memories, Dreams, Reflections,* edited by Aniela Jaffé and translated from German by Richard Winston and Clara Winston (New York, 1963), which provides the personal circumstances of Jung's intellectual pilgrimage.

A sympathetic and appreciative—though unofficial—intellectual biography by a former patient of Jung, who later became a Jungian analyst, is Barbara Hannah's *Jung: His Life and Work* (New York, 1976). Many of Jung's distinctive clinical-psychological insights are developed in an introductory fashion by John R. Staude in *The Adult Development of C. G. Jung* (London, 1981). Henri F. Ellenberger's comprehensive and somewhat encyclopedic review of the rise of depth psychology, *The Discovery of the Unconscious: The History and Evolution of Dynamic Psychiatry* (New York, 1970), contains informative chapters on Jung's life, thought, and times. Although it has been widely criticized for its lack of historical detail, the best single application of Jung's analytical psychology to the study of world religions remains Joseph Campbell's *The Hero with a Thousand Faces,* rev. ed. (Princeton, 1968).

PETER HOMANS

KA`BAH

The Ka`bah (lit., "cube"), the House of Allah, is located in Mecca. It is the principal Islamic shrine, the *qiblah*, or specific point faced by Muslims when performing the daily ritual prayers *(salat)* anywhere in the world. Located at the center of the great open Haram Mosque, it is the geographical and religious center of the Islamic world, the lifetime goal of Muslims who respond to the Qur'anic obligation to make at least one pilgrimage there. Muslim tradition also locates it directly below the heavenly Ka`bah.

The Ka`bah is constructed of Meccan granite and, as its name indicates, is a cubelike building, measuring more than sixteen meters high, thirteen meters long, and eleven meters wide. Its single door (there are no windows) is located on the northeast side, about two meters above the pavement of the open mosque. On the infrequent occasions when the Ka`bah is opened, mobile stairs give access to its interior. Inside are gold and silver lamps suspended from the ceiling. Three wooden pillars, recently replaced, support the ceiling.

It is, however, the building as a whole, not its contents, that is sacred to Muslims, and the most important object at the Ka`bah is located on the exterior: this is the Black Stone *(al-hajar al-aswad)* embedded in the eastern corner. Actually dark red-brown, and now encased in a massive silver band, the Black Stone is of unknown pre-Islamic origin, possibly meteoric. Myths affirm that it fell from heaven or that it was brought forth by the angels as a white stone to provide the cornerstone for the original Ka`bah; darkened by the touch of humans across the millennia, it serves as a register of human degradation. Muslims commonly refer to it as the "cornerstone of the House" and the "right hand of God on earth," but they are at pains to insist that it is not an idol and not to be worshiped: prayers here are addressed to God, not to the Black Stone. When beginning the rite of circumambulation *(tawaf)* of the Ka`bah, which during the pilgrimage season forms part of the pilgrimage performance, Muslims kiss or touch the Black Stone, as Muhammad is reported to have done. The *tawaf* is performed in the immediate vicinity of the Ka`bah on a broad pavement of polished granite called the mataf, the place of circumambulation.

Between the Black Stone and the raised door is a section of exterior wall known as the *multazam*, where worshipers press their bodies at the conclusion of the circumambulations in order to receive the *barakah* ("blessing, power") associated with the holy house.

The Ka`bah is usually covered by the *kiswah* ("robe"), a thick black and gold embroidered cloth fabricated each year by Meccan artisans. Prior to 1927 it was provided annually by the Egyptians and was brought to Mecca in the pilgrimage caravan from Cairo. The *kiswah* contains wide bands of Arabic calligraphy, mostly verses from the Qur'an.

Near the Ka`bah stands a gilded glass cage (replacing an earlier simple wooden framework) that contains a stone marking the Station of Ibrahim (Abraham). This stone is said to have miraculously preserved the footprint of Ibrahim, who

> **The historical origin of the Ka`bah is uncertain, but it had undoubtedly existed for several centuries before the birth of Muhammad (c. 570 CE).**

stood on it in order to complete the construction of an earlier Ka`bah: it is, as it were, the builder's mark.

Opposite the corner of the Black Stone is a small building housing the sacred well of Zamzam, from which pilgrims drink water at the conclusion of their circumambulations and prayers. Its origin is mythically associated with Hajar (Hagar) and Isma`il (Ishmael), for whom God provided water in this desert place after commanding Ibrahim to abandon mother and child and promising to care for them in his place.

The historical origin of the Ka`bah is uncertain, but it had undoubtedly existed for several centuries before the birth of Muhammad (c. 570 CE). By his time it was the principal religious shrine of central Arabia and, located at the center of a sacred territory *(haram)*, had the characteristics of a Semitic sanctuary. Islam incorporated it as part of its monotheistic cultus, a process begun by Muhammad, who, upon capturing the Ka`bah, cleansed it of the idols (and perhaps icons) it contained.

The Ka`bah has been severely damaged by fire, flood, earthquake, and attack during its long history. The current building dates from the seventeenth century but contains stones from earlier buildings. As recently as 1958 the Saudi government repaired its walls and roof. Two years earlier it began a remodeling and enlargement of the Haram Mosque that added over 6,000 square meters to its area; the mosque now has a total area of 16,326 square meters and can accommodate 300,000 persons.

[*See also* Pilgrimage.]

BIBLIOGRAPHY

Descriptions of the Ka`bah are included in studies and accounts of the *hajj*. The classic studies are Christian Snouck Hurgronje's *Het Mekkaansche Feest* (Leiden, 1880) and Maurice Gaudefroy-Demombynes's *Le pèlerinage à la Mekke* (Paris, 1923). A recent study is David E. Long's *The Hajj Today: A Survey of the Contemporary Makkah Pilgrimage* (Albany, N. Y., 1979). See also Snouck Hurgronje's *Mekka*, 2 vols. (The Hague, 1888-1889), and Eldon Rutter's *The Holy Cities of Arabia*, 2 vols. (London, 1928) for descriptions of the holy places, including the Ka`bah. Accounts of the *hajj* include John L. Burckhardt's *Travels in Arabia* (1829; reprint, London, 1968) and Richard F. Burton's *Personal Narrative of a Pilgrimage to Al-Madinah and Meccah*, 2 vols., edited by Isabel Burton (London, 1893), as well as Saleh Soubhy's *Pèlerinage à la Mecque et à Médine* (Cairo, 1894) and Ahmad Kamal's *The Sacred Journey* (New York, 1961).

HARRY B. PARTIN

KAMI

The Japanese term *kami,* often translated as "gods," or "divine forces," denotes the focus of Shinto worship.

In the *Kojiki* (Records of Ancient Matters), compiled in 712 CE, and the *Nihonshoki* (Chronicles of Japan), compiled in 720 CE, there are two types of *kami*. *Kami* of the first and most important type figure anthropomorphically in the early myths. For example, the first three *kami* were said to have revealed themselves in the High Celestial Plain (according to the *Kojiki*) or among marsh reeds between heaven and earth (according to the *Nihonshoki*). *Kami* of the second type

> **The number of *kami* is infinite, although only a finite number of them are actually enshrined.**

appear as offspring of earlier *kami*. Most "nature" *kami*, stones, mountains, rivers, and trees, and the ancestral *kami* as well, belong to this second category. Entities in nature, including human beings, are individually considered to be *kami*. *Kami,* therefore, can be regarded as the spiritual nature of each individual existence. The number of *kami* is infinite, although only a finite number of them are actually enshrined.

The Japanese emperor, believed to be the direct descendant of both the sun goddess Amaterasu and the "high life-giving *kami*," Takamimusubi, has been especially venerated.

Numerous attempts have been made to establish categories of *kami* from a phenomenological point of view. Some scholars, for instance, speak of nature and ancestral *kami*, while others divide them into family, local, and tutelary *kami*. Most of these categories are not helpful in understanding the nature and function of *kami*, however, as most *kami* do not fit exclusively into a single category. For example, most *kami* of nature are also conceived of as ancestral, family, or tutelary *kami*, and are the object of clan cults. One useful division distinguishes among heavenly *kami*, earthly *kami*, and *kami* of foreign descent, and assigns highest status to the heavenly *kami*.

After Buddhism came to Japan in the sixth century, a gradual change took place in the understanding of *kami*. At first, the Buddha was accepted as a foreign *kami,* but with the support of the imperial household the Buddha attained an independent status politically and socially equal to that of the traditional *kami*. From the ninth century on the syncretization of Buddhism and Shinto was promoted by the Buddhist clergy. Subsequently, *kami* were treated as guardians of the Buddha and were sometimes given the title *bodhisattva*. As a result, Buddhist *sutras* were commonly recited in Shinto shrines for the salvation of *kami*. Moreover, although Shinto originally produced no iconic representations of *kami*, statues of *kami* began to appear during the thirteenth century at some shrines in imitation of Buddhism.

Today, the Association of Shinto Shrines rejects any monotheistic interpretation that could detract from the independent dignity of individual *kami* in the Shinto pantheon. Shinto is a polytheistic religion, permitting worship of many *kami* at the same time, although Amaterasu retains the central and highest position.

[*See also* Shinto.]

BIBLIOGRAPHY

The proceedings of the Second International Conference on Shinto, published by Kokugakuin University as *Jizoku to henka* (Tokyo, 1968) contains much valuable information on the nature and development of the term *kami;* see especially "Kami kannen," pp. 15-38. Other important references include Kono Seizo's "Kami," in *Shinto yogoshu, shukyo hen,* vol. 1 (Tokyo, 1977), pp. 102-112, and my own "Shinto, sonzaironteki rikai e no kokoromi," in *Tozai shii keitai no hikaku kenkyu,* edited by Mineshima Akio (Tokyo, 1977), pp 278-298. For a discussion of the concept of kami in relation to folk belief, see *Kami kannen to minzoku,* vol. 3 of *Nihon no minzoku shukyo,* edited by Miyata Noboru et al. (Tokyo, 1982). *Amaterasu Omikami, kenkyu hen,* vol. 1 (Tokyo, 1982), offers a comprehensive treatment of the figure. Readers of English may want to consult Allan G. Grapard's article "Kami" in the *Encyclopedia of Japan* (Tokyo, 1982).

UEDA KENJI

KARAITES

The Karaites (Heb., Qara'im; Arab., Qara'iyun) are a Jewish sect that recognizes only the Hebrew scriptures as the source of divinely inspired legislation, and denies the authority of the postbiblical Jewish tradition (the oral law) as recorded in the Talmud and in later rabbinic literature. It is the only Jewish sect (excluding the Samaritans) that has survived for more than twelve hundred years, is still in existence, and has produced an extensive scholarly literature, much of which has been preserved.

The Rise of Karaism. Sectarian dissent in Judaism goes back at least as far as the pre-Talmudic period, when it was represented by the Sadducees, the Essenes, the Qumran community (whose literary archives are known as the Dead Sea Scrolls), and possibly other movements, whose literary remains are hopelessly lost or may yet be discovered. The growth and eventual codification of the postbiblical rabbinic tradition in turn gave rise to further dissent, so that Karaism represents not a new phenomenon but another link in the long line of groups insisting that the Hebrew scriptures are the sole genuine depository of God's word, and that no subsequent traditional law may modify or supplement them.

Theological disagreement seems to have been only one of several causes of this new flowering of schisms; others were political, social, and economic.

By the beginning of the tenth century the schism had expanded from its Iranian-Iraqi birthplace into Palestine (Jerusalem), Syria (Damascus), and Egypt (Cairo). So far the relationship between the new sect and the Rabbinite majority seems to have remained, if not amicable, at least indifferent. But about the second quarter of the tenth century a radical change set in. Sa`adyah al-Fayyumi (d. 942), an accomplished and encyclopedic Egyptian Jewish scholar who ultimately became president of the rabbinic academy at Sura, in Iraq, published several polemical works against Karaism, condemning it as outright heresy and branding its adherents as complete seceders from the Mother Synagogue. Sa`adyah's prestige and forceful scholarly argumentation effected a decisive break between the two camps that has never been healed.

At the same time, Sa`adyah's devastating attack and the urgent need to reply to it gave impetus to what became the golden age of Karaite literary activity (tenth-eleventh centuries) in the fields of theology, philosophy, biblical exegesis, and Hebrew philology, with which the Karaites endeavored to meet Sa`adyah's criticisms on an equal level of serious and competent scholarship. A Karaite academy flourished in Jerusalem during the eleventh century and gave advanced training to students from Karaite settlements as far-flung as Muslim Spain.

The onset of the First Crusade in 1099 put a stop to all Jewish activity—Rabbinite and Karaite alike—in Palestine. New Karaite settlements were established in the Balkans (then under Byzantine rule), Cyprus, the Crimea, Lithuania, and Poland. Some Karaite activity continued in the ancient community of Cairo, but on a greatly reduced scale.

Karaite history from the twelfth to the nineteenth century, and indeed down to the middle of the twentieth century, is marked by the characteristic tendency of the Karaites, a small minority of Jewry, to seek safety and strength in withdrawing as far as possible from the world—rabbinic, Christian, or Muslim—that surrounded them. Karaite history from about 1200 to about 1900 is thus almost a blank page.

> The Karaite community in Constantinople, the capital of Byzantium, developed into a substantial scholarly center and continued as such after the Ottoman conquest in 1453.

Karaite history during this long period is thus mainly the record of Karaite scholars and their works.

The Karaite community in Constantinople, the capital of Byzantium, developed into a substantial scholarly center and continued as such after the Ottoman conquest in 1453, when the city was renamed Istanbul. But with the steady decline of Turkish power in the seventeenth and eighteenth centuries, the Karaite communities in the Crimea, Lithuania, and Poland assumed the leading role. Soon thereafter these communities came under Russian rule, and their leadership succeeded in obtaining from the tsarist government full citizenship rights for Karaites; thus they were set even further apart from the Rabbinite majority in Russia, which continued to bear the full weight of the oppressive and discriminatory anti-Jewish laws.

Statistics of the Karaite population in the world at the present time are unreliable, and the usually cited figures of twelve thousand to thirteen thousand are probably far too low.

Karaite Literature and Its Reproduction. If any of the pre-Ananite sectarian leaders did actually commit their teachings to writing, these works are yet to be discovered. The earliest Karaite work available, and then only in fragments, in `Anan's code of law, known under the Hebrew title of *Sefer ha-mitsvot* (Book of Precepts) but written in Aramaic, the language of a large part of the Talmud. `Anan's successors, Binyamin al-Nahawandi and Daniyye'l al-Qumisi, wrote in Hebrew, while later Karaite scholars in the Muslim dominions, up to the fifteenth century, wrote in Arabic. In the Balkans and in Lithuania, Poland, and western Russia,

Karaite scholars wrote in Hebrew. In recent times the Russo-Polish Karaites wrote in part also in the spoken Karaite-Tatar dialect, brought by their ancestors from the Crimea.

The first major scholar of the golden age of Karaite literature was Ya`qub al-Qirqisani (second quarter of the tenth century), whose *magnum opus* is a two-part Arabic commentary on the Pentateuch.

With the transfer of most Karaite literary activity to the Greek-speaking Balkans after the First Crusade, there was a need to translate the Karaite Arabic classics into Hebrew, since the Byzantine (and later on, the Lithuanian-Polish-Russian) Karaites were not fluent in Arabic.

In the Balkans there was a literary revival during the thirteenth to fifteenth centuries. Aharon (the Elder) ben Yosef (fl. late thirteenth century) wrote a philosophical commentary on the Pentateuch, but is best known as the redactor of the official Karaite liturgy. Another Aharon (the Younger), ben Eliyyahu (d. 1369), composed a complete summa of Karaite theology, in three volumes: philosophical (*`Ets hayyim,* Tree of Life), legal (*Gan `Eden,* Garden of Eden), and exegetical (*Keter Torah,* Crown of the Torah). Eliyyahu Bashyatchi (d. 1490) left an unfinished code of law, *Adderet Eliyyahu* (Mantle of Eliyyahu), which was edited by his brother-in-law Kaleb Afendopolo (d. after 1522), a many-sided scholar in both theology and the secular sciences, and became the most esteemed legal manual among most modern Karaites.

As the Ottoman empire progressively declined, the center of Karaite literary activity again shifted northward, to the Crimea, Lithuania, and Poland. The community of Lutsk (in Volhynia, southwest Russia) produced the first Karaite literary historian and bibliographer, Simhah Yitshaq ben Mosheh (d. 1766).

In the nineteenth century the outstanding Karaite man of letters was Avraham Firkovitch (1785-1874), who during his travels in the Crimea, the Caucasus, Syria, Palestine, and Egypt amassed a large collection of Karaite manuscripts, one of the richest on this subject in the world, now in the Leningrad Public Library.

BIBLIOGRAPHY

Modern critical study of Karaism is barely a century and a half old, and scholars who have devoted their full attention to it are few. Much of the early and extremely important Karaite literature is still in manuscript, awaiting scholarly publication and use. Some of it has undoubtedly been lost; some may yet be discovered or recognized. Certain aspects of Karaite history—for example, the role of social and economic factors, at least in medieval and early modern times—have not yet been examined at all. Some basic modern works, while very good as far as they went in their time, are in urgent need of being brought up to date. Even such an important work as the bio-bibliographical dictionary of Karaites left in manuscript by Samuel Poznanski (d. 1921) is still unrevised and unpublished. Moreover, the Firkovitch collection of Karaite manuscripts in Leningrad and similar collections elsewhere in Russia have not yet been properly cata-logued, and access to them by Western scholars is fraught with almost insurmountable difficulties, while Russian scholars seem (whether willingly or unwillingly, one cannot tell) uninterested in this field of study.

It is therefore not surprising that the two general works on Karaism—Julius Fürst's *Geschichte des Karäerthums,* 3 vols. (Leipzig, 1862-1869), and W. H. Rule's *History of the Karaite Jews* (London, 1870)—should be used with great caution. Zvi Cahn's The *Rise of the Karaite Sect* (New York, 1937) is a compilation of minimal value. Simhah Pinsker's *Liqqutei qadmoniyyot* (Vienna, 1860) retains much of its value by virtue of the original documents published in it for the first time. A similar but far more reliable work is Jacob Mann's *Texts and Studies in Jewish History and Literature,* vol. 2, *Karaitica* (Philadelphia, 1935), a veritable treasure trove of original documents and excellent studies, dealing mainly with the modern period after 1500. A thought-provoking but tendentious work is Raphael Mahler's *Karaimer* (Karaites; New York, 1947; in Yiddish), which regards Karaism as a phenomenon of political and socioeconomic liberation rather than as a theological schism, albeit with social and economic overtones. Moritz Steinschneider's *Die arabische Literature der Juden* (Frankfurt, 1902), which also surveys the Arabic literature of the Karaites, was supplemented by Samuel Poznanski in 1904—his additions first appeared in three issues of *Orientalistische Literatur-Zeitung* 7 (July-September 1904) and were later collected in *Zur jüdischearabischen* Literatur (Berlin, 1904)—but a revised and updated edition is one of the major desiderata in this field. Poznanski's *The Karaite Literary Opponents of Saadiah Gaon* (London, 1908) surveys the Karaite polemics against Sa`adyah from the tenth to the nineteenth century. Bernard Revel's *The Karaite Halakah,* pt. 1 (Philadelphia, 1913), surveys Karaite law but is somewhat antiquated. A selection of extracts, in English translation with explanatory notes, from the early (before 1500) Karaite literature, forms my own *Karaite Anthology* (New Haven, 1952). The early Karaite philosophical literature is treated expertly by Isaac Husik in A *History of Mediaeval Jewish Philosophy* (New York, 1916). A useful but imperfect guide to Karaite liturgy is P. S. Goldberg's *Karaite Liturgy and Its Relation to Synagogue Worship* (Manchester, 1957), which should be supplemented by my own "Studies in the History of the Early Karaite Liturgy: The Liturgy of al-Qirqisani," in *Studies in Jewish Bibliography, History and Literature, in Honor of I. Edward Kiev,* edited by Charles Berlin (New York, 1971), pp. 305-332.

See also Salo W. Baron's study *A Social and Religious History of the Jews,* vol 5, *High Middle Ages,* 500-1200, 2d ed., rev. & enl. (New York, 1957), pp. 209-285, 388-416 (for further references to Karaism, see the index to volumes 1-8, New York, 1960); Zvi Ankori's *Karaites in Byzantium: The Formative Years, 970-1100* (New York, 1959); Naphtali Wieder's *The Judean Scrolls and Karaism* (London, 1962); André Paul's *Écrits de Qumran et sectes juives aux premiers siècles de l'Islam: Recherches sur l'origine du Qaraïsme* (Paris, 1969); and Samuel Poz-nanski's "Karäische Drucke und Druckereien," *Zeitschrift für hebraeische Bibliographie* 20, 21, 23 (1917, 1918, 1920).

LEON NEMOY

KARMAN

Hindu and Jain Concepts

As diverse as the culture of India may be, one common assumption undergirds virtually all major systems of South Asian religious thought and practice: a person's behavior leads irrevocably to an appropriate reward or punishment commensurate with that behavior. This, briefly stated, is the law of *karman.*

The importance of the idea of *karman* is not limited to the religions of the subcontinent. It is likely that no other notion from the sacred traditions of India has had more influence on the worldviews assumed by non-Indian cultures than that of *karman,* for in it lie the foundations of a wealth of astute ethical, psychological, metaphysical, and sacerdotal doctrines. Translations of the word (Pali, *kamma; *Tib., *las; *Chin., *yeh* or *yin-kuo; *Jpn., *go* or *inga*) have for centuries been a key part of the religious lexica of the various canonical languages of Asia. Furthermore, the word *karma* (the nominative form of the Sanskrit *karman*) has in the last few generations also entered the vocabulary of European languages, appearing first in technical Indological works and more recently in popular or colloquial use as well.

Originally referring to properly performed ritual activity, the notion was ethicized to include the larger meaning of any correct activity in general. Granting this view, the religious, social, and medical philosophers of India, particularly those intrigued by the doctrines of rebirth and of the origins of suffering (but also of the related problems of the source of personality and the justification of social status), expanded the meaning of the term. Under this new understanding, *karman* came to denote the impersonal and transethical system under which one's current situation in the world is regarded as the fruit of seeds planted by one's behavior and dispositions in the past, and the view that in all of one's present actions lie similar seeds that will have continuing and determinative effect on one's life as they bear fruit in the future.

Possibly originating, therefore, in the agrarian experience of aboriginal India, the notion of an impersonal law of cause and effect subsequently pervaded the (often decidedly unagricultural) ideology of Vedic ritualism, Yoga, the Vedanta, Ayurvedic medicine, and sectarian theism, and it stands as a central theme in the lessons recorded in the scriptures of Jainism and Buddhism.

Early Ritual Notions. The poets who composed the sacred hymns of the Vedic Mantrasamhitas in the twelfth century BCE sang praises to the gods in reverential, supplicatory, and sometimes cajoling tones. Deities were powerful beings who held control over the lives of the people on earth but who nevertheless could be propitiated and pleased with sacrificial gifts and who enjoyed staged battles, chariot racing, gambling, and riddles. The rites were often quite expensive and the rewards not always immediately realized, so the patrons were reassured that their support of the ceremony would benefit them sometime in the future.

Arguments in defense of this notion that the reward for one's present ritual action is reaped in the future laid part of the foundation for later doctrines of rebirth and transmigration.

The Brahmanic notion of *karman* thus centers on the view that a person is born into a world he has made for himself (see *Kausitaki Brahmana* 26.3, for example). This meant that every action in the ritual was important and that every action brought a result of one kind or another, and did so irrevocably.

Karman in Upanisadic thought. The composers of the major Upanisads (eighth to fifth century BCE) generally saw two paths open to the deceased at the time of death. The lower path, one on which the person eventually returns to earth in a subsequent birth, is described as the "way of the fathers" *(pitryana)* and is traveled by those who perform the rituals in hopes of material gain. The higher path, the way of the gods (devayana), is one that does not lead to rebirth on earth and is taken by those who have renounced worldly ends and practice austerities in the forest.

Seeking to understand the Brahmanic notion of the ritual in anthropological rather than sacerdotal terms, the Upanisadic sages taught that all physical and mental activity was an internal reflection of cosmic processes. Accordingly, they held that *every* action, not only those performed in the public ritual, leads to an end.

For the most part the composers of the major Upanisads disdained actions performed for the resulting enjoyment of worldly pleasures, for such material pursuit necessarily leads from one birth to another in an endless cycle characterized by dissatisfaction and, thus, to unhappiness.

The only way to break this turning wheel of life and death *(samsara)* was to free oneself of the structures and processes of *karman.* The composers of the Upanisads understood this liberation to take place through the practice of *yoga* or through the intervention of a personal supreme deity who lived beyond the karmic realm.

Karman in classical Yoga. The practioners and philosophers of classical Yoga agreed with the Upanisadic idea that one's circumstances are determined by one's actions. Like some of those sages they, too, understood *karman* to involve what might be called a substance that leads the soul from one body to another as it moves from birth to birth. A person with a passion for food thus may be reborn as a hog. One eventually gets what one wants, even though it may take more than one lifetime to do so. That's the problem. For in order to get what one wants one needs a body, and in order to have a body one needs to be born. Birth leads to death, death leads to birth. Unless the cycle is broken it never stops.

Without values directed towards the attainment of worldly goals a person will cease to behave according to one's desire, and without that desire no karmic residue, no unmatured seeds, can accumulate.

Ontological or Materialistic Notions. The terms *bija* (seed), *karmasaya* (karmic residue), *vasana* (pychological traces) and others suggest a general South Asian notion that some "thing" is created and left behind by one's actions. At times the Upanisads describe *karman* almost as a substance that not only influences one's subsequent births but can also be passed from one person to another, especially from father to son.

By far the most assertive thinkers concerning the material nature of *karman,* however, are the Jains, who since the sixth century BCE have followed the teachings and traditions surrounding the founder of Jainism, Mahavira Vardhamana. Central to Jain doctrine in general is the notion that the living entity (*jiva,* "life") within a person is by nature blissful and intelligent. Traditional teachings sometimes describe the *jiva* as a pure, colorless, and transparent energy and maintain that all of the infinite creatures in the universe—including animals, plants, and rocks as well as human beings—possess such an ethereal crystalline life within them. But, also according to Jain thought, the spatial world occupied by the *jivas* is permeated with a kind of subtle dust or stained liquid that has existed since time immemorial and that "sticks," as it were, to each *jiva,* soiling and infecting its original nature with a color (*lesya),* the hue and intensity of which corresponds to the amount of desire, hatred, and love with which that being performs any given action.

Thus, Jain tradition demands absolute *ahimsa,* a complete unwillingness to kill or injure any and all living beings. Jains, therefore, are absolute vegetarians, some of whom in their attempts to sustain themselves with food in which no living creature has met a violent death refuse even to pick the living fruit from a tree, waiting instead until it falls of its own (ripened) accord.

A *jiva* finds release from the bonds of rebirth only when it stops accumulating new *karman* and removes that *karman* already there.

A Theistic Notion: Karman in the Bhagavadgita. Some thinkers in ancient India found practical problems in the renunciate attitude towards *karman.* Generally supportive of the value of disciplined meditation (see *Bhagavadgita* 6.10-6.13), those philosophers nevertheless saw the impossibility of complete inaction, for "even the maintenance of your physical body requires activity" (3.8).

For these sages, freedom from the bonds of *karman* comes not when one ceases acting but when one acts without desire, when one renounces the attachment one has for the fruits of one's actions (*Bhagavadgita* 4.19-23).

According to the *Bhagavadgita* and similar devotional texts, this renunciation of desire for specific ends can be obtained only through *bhakti-yoga,* the loving surrender to God's will.

BIBLIOGRAPHY

Bhattacharyya, Haridas. "The Doctrine of Karma," *Visva-Bharati Quarterly* 3 (1925-1926): 257-258.

Bhattacharyya, Haridas. "The Brahmanical Concept of Karma." In *A. R. Wadia; Essays in Philosophy Presented in His Honor,* edited by Sarvepalli Radhakrishnan et al., pp. 29-49. Madras, 1954.

Bhattacharyya, Kalidas. "The Status of the Individual in Indian Metaphysics." In *The Status of the Individual East and West,* edited by Charles A. Moore, pp. 29-49. Honolulu, 1968.

Dilger, D. *Der indischer Seelungswanderungsglaube.* Basel, 1910.

Falke, Robert. *Die Seelenwanderung.* Berlin, 1913.

Farquhar, J. N. "Karma: Its Value as a Doctrine of Life," *Hibbert Journal* 20 (1921-1922): 20-34.

Glasenapp, Helmuth von. *The Doctrine of Karman in Jain Philosophy.* Translated by G. Barry Gifford. Bombay, 1942.

Hall, Rodney. *The Law of Karma.* (Canberra, 1968).

Henseler, Éric de. *L'âme et le dogme de la transmigration dans les livres sacrés de l'Inde ancienne.* Paris, 1928.

Kalghatgi, T. G. *Karma and Rebirth.* Ahmadabad, 1972.

Keyes, Charles F. and E. Valentine Daniel, eds. *Karma: An Anthropological Inquiry.* Berkeley, 1983.

O'Flaherty, Wendy Doniger, ed. *Karma and Rebirth in Classical Indian Traditions.* Berkeley, 1980.

Silburn, Lilian. *Instant et cause: Le discontinu dans la pensée philosophique de l'Inde.* Paris, 1955.

Steiner, Rudolf. *Die Offenbarungen des Karma: Ein Zyklus von elf Vorträgen* Dornach, 1956.

WILLIAM K. MAHONY

Buddhist Concepts

As noted in the previous article, South Asian religious traditions have held a variety of positions regarding the notion that one's behavior and thoughts determine one's destiny. Buddhist texts recorded in Pali in the centuries following the death of the historical Buddha, which occurred about 480 BCE according to the most common dating, imply that Buddhist thinkers of that time were aware of five general and contending philosophical views regarding the cause of a person's fate, pleasant or unpleasant, in this world. The doctrine of no causality (Pali, *adhiccasamuppanna-vada*) held that a person's good or bad fortune has no relation to direct or indirect causes or conditions; all fates, whether fortunate or unfortunate, take place accidentally. This doctrine recommended the appreciation of casual good fortune and the enjoyment of its momentary pleasure, an epicurian position that was advocated by the materialists.

According to early Buddhist thinkers, the more good *karman* a person accumulates, the happier he or she will become and the better the recompense he will receive. Similarly, the more bad *karman* a person accumulates, the unhappier he will be and the worse the influence he will receive.

Varieties of Karman. Buddhist philosophers, especially those teaching in the context of Abhidharma thought, recognized several varieties of *karman.*

The most inclusive category of *karman* is defined in terms of its moral value. Thus, there are said to be ten forms of

> **The most inclusive category of *karman* is defined in terms of its moral value. Thus, there are said to be ten forms of good or meritorious activity.**

good or meritorious activity *(kusala-karman).* These are characterized as (a) refraining from all forms of taking life; (b) refraining from taking what is not given; (c) refraining from sexual misconduct; (d) refraining from lying; (e) refraining from slandering; (f) refraining from abusive language; (g) refraining from gossip; (h) refraining from covetousness; (i) refraining from ill will; and (j) generally maintaining healthy views. The ten bad or abominable forms of activity *(akusala-karman)* are described as the opposite of the ten forms of meritorious actions: taking life; theft; sexual transgression; lying; and so on. Buddhist scholiasts also see a type of action that is neither good nor bad *(av-yakrta-karman).*

Another variety of *karman* is distinguished by the specific mechanism of action. That is, of those actions listed above, the first three pertain to the physical body *(kaya-karman);* the next four, to speech *(vaci-karman);* and the final three, to thought *(mano-karman).*

A third distinction is made in terms of the value of "tainted" *karman (sasrava-karman),* which is acquired in the phenomenal or profane world, and "pure" karman *(anasrava-karman),* sublime or sacred action that extinguishes tainted *karman.*

Buddhist thinkers understood a fourth variety of *karman* in terms of an action's good or bad results.

Buddhist philosophers distinguished a fifth variety of *karman* according to whether its results or fruits will be experienced in this present life *(drstadharma-vedaniya-karman),* in the next life *(upapadya-vedaniya-karman),* in the lives following the next life *(aparya-paryaya-ve-daniya-karman),* or in an undetermined life *(aniyata-ve-daniya-karman).*

A final variety of *karman* relates to the communal scope of action and causation.

Inevitability and Changeability of Karman. The mechanism of *karman* is generally believed to assure inevitable results gained through one's actions and thoughts. Accordingly, Buddhist philosophers hold, for the most part, that a person's present circumstances in life are determined by one's past actions, the fruits of which are inevitably experienced until that person "uses up" all of his acquired *karman* and the law of causation has run its course.

It is believed, however, that a person's *karman* may be altered in three ways. First, by repenting of previous misdeeds and making a habit of leading a good life, one performs good deeds, which themselves become good *karman* and reduce or exterminate the power of bad *karman.* Second, if an individual's close relative, a monk, or a nun chants sacred verses or holds a religious service for him, then such assistance—in addition to his own good deeds—lightens or destroys his own bad *karman.* Third, if a relative or religious specialist chants sacred verses after a person's death, such actions, themselves meritorious, will help alleviate the dead person's accumulated *karman.*

Karman and Transmigration. To some Buddhist philosophers, the theory of *karman* appeared to violate in some way the central Buddhist teaching that there is no immortal soul, that nothing in any realm is stationary or unchanging. According to Buddhist doctrine, all phenomena in the world appear and disappear in a continually changing flux resulting from the ongoing causal chain known as *pratitya-samutpada,* or "dependent co-origination." But does not the doctrine of causal reward and punishment for actions committed in a previous life presume the existence of a soul to which karmic residue accrues?

The general Buddhist response to such criticism is to assert the reality of the *process* of rebirth but to deny that this process is supported by an underlying substance, or "soul."

BIBLIOGRAPHY

Pali sources on karman are conveniently abstracted in Henry Clarke Warren's *Buddhism in Translation* (1896; reprint, New York, 1976) and E. J. Thomas's *The History of Buddhist Thought,* 2d ed. (1933; New York, 1963). For a canonical account, see the various passages in the *Kathavattu,* translated by Shwe Zan Aung and C. A. F. Rhys Davids as *Kathavattu: Points of Controversy* (London, 1915). A more technical introduction to the theories of karman indigenous to other Buddhist schools, including Mahayana traditions, is Étienne Lamotte's "Le traité de l'acte de Vasubandhu: *Karmasiddhiprakarana,*" in *Mélanges chinois et bouddhiques* 4 (1934-1936): 151-288, with a useful summary by this eminent Buddhologist. Recent Japanese studies include two volumes devoted to articles on the topic: *Nihon bukkyogakkai nenpo* 25 (March 1980) and *Go shiso no kenkyu,* a special issue of *Bukkyogaku seminaa* 20 (October 1974).

MIZUNO KOGEN

KHMER RELIGION

The Khmer, who constitute the dominant ethnic population of Cambodia (also known as Kampuchea), have a complex and syncretic religio-cosmological system composed of Theravada Buddhism, indigenous folk traditions, and elements historically derived from other regions such as China and especially India. The prehistoric origin of the Khmer is unclear, but various polities emerged in the general area of what is now Cambodia from about the first century CE, and Khmer civilization reached notable heights of power and magnificence during the Angkor period (802-1431 CE). Some rulers of the ancient kingdoms adopted Mahayana Buddhism or Hinduism (Siva and/or Visnu cults) as the state religion, while others maintained syncretic practices. But when Theravada Buddhism of the Sinhala form entered Cambodia in the thirteenth century, it gradually displaced Hinduism and Mahayana and was adopted by both the ruling elite and the general populace. Theravada remained the state religion throughout Cambodia's succeeding history, including the era of French colonialism and subsequent achievement of independence in 1954, until the communist revolution in the 1970s. Theravada is no longer a state religion, however, and there are fewer monks and temples than in the precommunist period.

Khmer Buddhism is divided into two orders: the Mahanikay, "the great congregation," and the Dham-mayutt (Thommayut), "those who are attached to the doctrine." Monks of both orders are given the highest respect as living embodiments and spiritual teachers of Buddhism; the vatt (wat)—with its temple, meeting hall, shrines, school, and shelters for monks and laypeople—serves as a moral, social, and educational center for its congregants.

There is generally little conflict between Theravada and folk beliefs: shrines for qnak ta are sometimes found on Buddhist temple grounds, and most Khmer combine obeisance both to Buddhism and to the spirit world.

BIBLIOGRAPHY

David P. Chandler's *History of Cambodia* (Boulder, 1983) offers a sophisticated study of Cambodian history from prehistoric to modern times that incorporates recent scholarship, places religion in its sociopolitical context, and provides annotated references to important literature. No detailed study of Cambodian Buddhism exists. A brief but useful account of its nature and organization is François Martini's "Le bonze cambodgien" and "Organisation du clergé bouddhique au Cambodge," *France-Asie* 12 (November-December 1955) 409-425. The major study of Cambodian ceremonialism is Eveline Porée-Maspero's *Étude sur les rites agraires des cambodgiens,* 3 vols. (Paris, 1962-1969). While some points in this work are debatable (including the author's thesis regarding certain cultural influences from early Chinese culture), it is a detailed compendium of Khmer rituals and beliefs going beyond agricultural rites.

Ethnographic accounts of religious beliefs and practices among Khmer villagers are few and are limited primarily to chapters in Gabrielle Martel's *Lovea, village des environs d'Anqkor* (Paris, 1975) and to my own "Svay, a Khmer Village in Cambodia" (Ph. D. diss., Columbia University, 1968) and "Interrelations between Buddhism and Social Systems in Cambodian Peasant Culture," in *Anthropological Studies in Theravada Buddhism,* edited by Manning Nash et al. (New Haven, 1966).

MAY EBIHARA

KHOI AND SAN RELIGION

The Khoi and San are the aboriginal peoples of southern Africa. The appellations formerly applied to them (*Hottentot* and *Bushmen,* respectively) have gone out of use because of their derogatory connotations. Properly, the terms Khoi and San refer to groups of related languages characterized by click consonants and to speakers of these languages, but they are frequently applied in a cultural sense to distinguish between pastoralists (Khoi) and foragers (San). In historical time (essentially, within the past 250 years in this region), these people were found widely distributed below the Cunene, Okavango, and Zambezi river systems, that is, in the modern states of Namibia, Botswana, Zimbabwe, and South Africa. Smaller numbers were, and are, to be found in southern Angola and Zambia. The once large population of

> **Khoi and San agropastoralists have been in the region along with foragers during this entire span of time.**

San in South Africa has been completely eliminated; perhaps 20 percent of contemporary Khoi still live in that country. Accurate censuses of these people are available only for Botswana, where today about half the estimated forty thousand San live. The fifty thousand Khoi (except as noted above) are concentrated in Namibia.

Archaeological and historical evidence document the coexistence in these areas of herding and foraging economies for at least the past fifteen centuries. Bantu-speaking as well as Khoi and San agropastoralists have been in the region along with foragers during this entire span of time. The first ethnographies were compiled by German ethnologists in the last decade of the nineteenth century; a few accounts by missionaries, travelers, and traders are available for the preceding one hundred years.

All of these herders and foragers were seasonally migratory, circulating within group-controlled land tenures in response to seasonal distributions of pastures and plant and animal foods. The basic residential group was an extended family often with close collateral extensions; it seldom exceeded fifty persons in size. Two or more of these units, or segments thereof, came together for social, economic, and ritual reasons at specified times, and contact among adjacent groups was maintained by frequent visiting. Descent among the San is bilateral. Patrilineal clans are attributed to the Khoi. Neither social system contains hierarchical strata at present, although there is evidence for them in the past.

On the surface, Khoisan cosmological concepts are not uniformly coherent. The apparent ad hoc and sometimes ambivalent quality of explanations about natural phenomena has led anthropologists to treat these concepts in a descriptive, folkloristic manner. Yet there is an underlying order of shared symbolic categories that represents an inclusive process of cultural management. In its broad outlines, this system is common to all Khoisan groups, even though there is variation in content and emphasis from one group to another.

The colonial era and its aftermath disrupted the political and economic lives of Khoisan as well as Bantu-speaking peoples; in this process, it is possible but not yet certain that destructive, uncontrollable elements of the cosmological system became emphasized over the constructive forces of creation, and that today the administrator (*//angwa of Zu/-hõasi*) has disproportionate power when compared historically with the role that the creator (*!xo*) has played.

BIBLIOGRAPHY

Biesele, Megan. "Sapience and Scarce Resources." *Social Science Information* 17 (1978): 921-947.

Lee, Richard B. *The !Kung San: Men, Women, and Work in a Foraging Society.* New York, 1979. The first comprehensive view of the San. Although it falls prey to many traditional faults of evolutionary theory in anthropology, it is much more systematic than its predecessors.

Lewis-Williams, David. *Believing and Seeing: Symbolic Meanings in Southern San Rock Paintings.* London, 1981. Excellent integration of prehistoric and historical rock art with contemporary and archival stories. Points the way toward further fruitful research.

Marshall, Lorna. "!Kung Bushman Religious Beliefs." *Africa* 32 (1962): 221-252. Narrative and descriptive account containing useful information but no comprehensive analysis.

Schapera, Isaac. *The Khoisan Peoples of South Africa.* London, 1930. Based on accounts of missionaries and travelers. Valuable information but outdated synthesis.

Silberbauer, George B. *Hunter and Habitat in the Central Kalahari Desert.* Cambridge, Mass., 1981. Primarily an ecological, evolutionary study, but also includes information on the religious system of the G/wi San.

Wilmsen, Edwin N. "Of Paintings and Painters, in Terms of Zu/-hõasi Interpretations." In *Contemporary Studies on Khoisan in Honour of Oswin Köhler on the Occasion of His Seventy-fifth Birthday,* edited by Rainer Vossen and Klaus Keuthmann. Hamburg, 1986. An economic and political analysis of prehistoric and contemporary San paintings.

EDWIN N. WILMSEN

KING, MARTIN LUTHER, JR.

KING, MARTIN LUTHER, JR. (1929-1968), Baptist minister and civil rights leader. The son and grandson of Baptist preachers, Martin Luther King, Jr., was born into a middle-class black family in Atlanta, Georgia. As an adolescent, King grew concerned about racial and economic inequality in American society. Sociology classes at Morehouse College taught him to view racism and poverty as related aspects of social evil, and reading Henry David Thoreau's essay "Civil Disobedience" (1849) convinced him that resistance to an unjust system was a moral duty. At Morehouse, King decided to become a minister, and after graduation he enrolled at Crozier Theological Seminary to study divinity. There he acquired from Walter Rauschenbusch's *Christianity and the Social Crisis* (1907) the conviction that the Christian churches have an obligation to work for social justice. In Mohandas Gandhi's practice of nonviolent resistance he discovered a tactic for transforming Christian love from a merely personal to a social ethic.

King's interest in theology, philosophy, and social ethics led him to enter the graduate program at Boston University School of Theology, where he earned a Ph. D. degree and developed his own philosophical position based upon the tenet that "only personality—finite and infinite—is ultimately real." In Boston, he met and courted Coretta Scott, and in 1953 they were wed. A year later, King accepted a call to be pastor of Dexter Avenue Baptist Church in Montgomery, Alabama. Chosen by E. D. Nixon, president of the Montgomery National Association for the Advancement of Colored People, to lead a boycott of the city's segregated buses, he gained national recognition when the boycott resulted in a Supreme Court decision that declared laws requiring segregated seating on buses unconstitutional.

Following the Montgomery bus boycott, King founded the Southern Christian Leadership Conference (SCLC) to coordinate scattered civil rights activities and local organizations. Operating primarily through the black churches, the SCLC mounted successive attacks against segregation in the early 1960s. For his nonviolent activism, he received the Nobel Peace Prize in 1964.

While organizing a "poor people's campaign" to persuade Congress to take action on poverty, King accepted an invitation to participate in marches for striking sanitation workers in Memphis, Tennessee. There, on 4 April 1968, he was assassinated. Considered a modern prophet by many, King ranks with Gandhi as a major ethical leader of the twentieth century.

BIBLIOGRAPHY

Works by King. The best introduction to King's own version of his goals and values is *Stride toward Freedom: The Montgomery Story* (New York, 1958), which contains a chapter explaining his intellectual development in the midst of an eyewitness description of the bus boycott. *Strength to Love* (New York, 1963) is a collection of sermons. *Why We Can't Wait* (New York, 1964) includes "Letter from Birmingham Jail," one of King's most cogent justifications of his philosophy of nonviolent direct action. *Where Do We Go From Here: Chaos or Community?* (New York, 1967) outlines his detailed program for social justice in the United States.

Works about King. Of the many biographical sketches, the best critical treatment is David L. Lewis's *King: A Biography,* 2d ed. (Urbana, Ill., 1978). Stephen B. Oates's biography, *Let the Trumpet Sound: The Life of Martin Luther King, Jr.* (New York, 1982), is factually more complete but lacks interpretive analysis. *Martin Luther King, Jr.: A Profile,* edited by C. Eric Lincoln (New York, 1970), is a collection of insightful evaluations of King and his role in the civil rights movement. John Ansbro's *Martin Luther King, Jr.: The Making of a Mind* (Maryknoll, N. Y., 1982) is a valuable explication of King's thought.

ALBERT J. RABOTEAU

KINGDOM OF GOD

Among the central concepts of the great religions, that of the kingdom of God may be the most hopeful, for while it recognizes the reality of death and injustice, it affirms that a just and living transcendent reality is entering history and transforming it.

Divine Kingship in the Ancient Near East, Israel, and Greece

Although the notion of divine kingship is defined in human political terms, it is not a mere projection of human kingship onto a divine realm. Rather, the successive phrases in which this notion occurs show that divine kingship was understood as transcending and rejecting human kingship.

"King of the Gods." This phrase implies sovereignty over the created order.

Babylon. The creation epic *Enuma elish,* recited at the spring New Year festival, describes the victory of Marduk over the sea monster Tiamat, from whose body Marduk creates heaven and earth.

Ugarit (modern Ras Shamra, Syria). Although the god El is routinely addressed as king in this literature (Pritchard, pp. 133 and 140), Baal is elevated to kingship after his victory over Yam, "Prince Sea."

Greece. In the Homeric poems, Zeus is called the "father of gods and men" and is once called the "highest and best of the gods" (*Odyssey* 19.303).

Israel. In the face of Israel's ostensible monotheism, a group of other gods, called *benei Elim* (lit., "sons of gods"), is also acknowledged. These gods, however, are not like the one God (who in this context always has the name whose consonants are YHVH, conventionally transcribed "Yahveh."

"Yahveh Is King." This phrase implies sovereignty over the people of Israel. In the historical books of Israel, the kingship of Yahveh is cited solely to refute the claims of human kings (*1 Sm.* 8:7, 12:2; cf. Jgs. 8:23).

In the present, God's kingship is individualized and he becomes "my king" (*Ps.* 5:3ff.); in an indefinite future, Yahveh as king will regather dispersed Israel (*Ez.* 20:33) and reign in Jerusalem (*Is.* 24:23, *Mi.* 4:7; cf. *Is.* 52:7-10).

"Kingship from Heaven." This Babylonian phrase introduces various concepts of the divine sovereignty in the state.

"King of Kings." This phrase indicates first human, then divine, sovereignty over earthly kingships. It was first applied to human rulers annexing vassal kingships.

In Stoicism and the Judeo-Christian tradition, this title is transferred to the God who rules over all human kingship.

"Kingship of Heaven." In the rabbinic tradition this phrase expresses an understanding of the universal sovereignty of God, future and/or eternal.

The Kingdom of God in the Words of Jesus

"The kingdom [*basileia*] of God" is the sole general phrase expressing the object of Jesus' proclamation. (In *Matthew* it mostly appears as "kingdom of heaven," probably as an artificial restoration of the rabbinic usage.) His affirmations about this kingdom are the unifying thread on which all his other sayings are strung.

"The Kingdom of God Is at Hand." Here is implied a preliminary but decisive victory over injustice and death.

The Lord's Prayer. This prayer contains the petitions "Hallowed be thy name, thy kingdom come" (*Lk.* 11:2, *Mt.* 6:9).

Victory over dark powers. In *Luke* 11:20 Jesus proclaims, "But if I by the finger of God cast out demons, then the kingdom of God has come upon you." What is asked for in the Lord's Prayer is here announced as already operative. Jesus instructed his missionaries to "heal those who are sick and say to them, `The kingdom of God has drawn near you'" (*Lk.* 10:9). No less a power, Jesus implies, could do what has already been done through him; hence God's sovereignty has already broken into history.

"To Enter the Kingdom of God." Jesus expresses the condition negatively: "It is easier for a camel to go through the eye of a needle than for a rich man to enter the kingdom of God" (*Mk.* 10:25). He also expresses it positively: "Allow the children to come to me and do not forbid them, for of such is the kingdom of God" (*Mk.* 10:14-15; cf. *Mt.* 18:13-14, *Jn.* 3:3-5). With far-reaching irony he says, "The tax collectors and harlots enter the kingdom of God before you" (*Mt.* 21:31). The kingdom of God is further reserved for the handicapped (*Mk.* 9:47), the persecuted (*Mt.* 5:10), and those in tribulation (*Acts* 14:22). The rabbinic background for these sayings is the concept of "the coming age" *(ha-`olam ha-ba'):* "Master, teach us the paths of life so that through them we may win the life of the coming age" (B. T., *Ber.* 28b).

The link among these groups is a deep structure of Jesus' thought underlying Luke's "Sermon on the Plain." The beatitude "Blessed are you poor, for yours is the kingdom of God" (*Lk.* 6:20) shows that possession of the kingdom is the coming reward for the poor, hungry, and mourning. The saying "Love your enemies . . . and your reward will be great" (*Lk.* 6:35) shows that the characteristic of this ideal poor is love of enemies, that is, nonretaliation to evil.

The Kingdom of God as Object of Search or Struggle. The kingdom is symbolized by the "treasure hidden in a field" and the "pearl of great price" (*Mt.* 13:44-46). But the nature of the "mystery of the kingdom of God" is left unexplained at *Mark* 4:11; and Paul only vaguely suggests with the expression "fellow workers for the kingdom of God" (*Col.* 4:11) the modern idea that the kingdom can be promoted by human energy.

"In the Kingdom of God." This phrase in a fourth group of sayings is always used in connection with a banquet at the end of time. When Jesus affirms, "I shall no more drink of the fruit of the vine until that day when I drink it new in the kingdom of God" (*Mk.* 14:25), he implies that the kingdom can only come in through his suffering.

> **The development of the concept of the kingdom of God occurred primarily in the church of the West.**

The Kingdom of God in Christian Tradition

Luke in his gospel and in the Acts when writing narrative regularly speaks of "preaching the good news of the kingdom of God."

The development of the concept of the kingdom of God occurred primarily in the church of the West. In the thought of the Latin theologians and the official Reformation, it served to legitimate the state through Augustine's doctrine of two cities and Luther's of two kingdoms. The Enlightenment, while discovering the primacy of the kingdom of God in Jesus' thought, tried to accommodate it to rational categories. It was the radical Reformation that most fully recovered Jesus' original understanding, and that transmitted the most vital form of the concept to contemporary Christian believers today.

The visual arts. The church early developed pictorial versions of the human scenes of the Gospels. But an adequate symbol of the kingdom of God first appears in the nineteenth century in the many versions of *The Peaceable Kingdom* painted by the American Quaker primitive Edward Hicks (1780-1849). These paintings illustrate *Isaiah* 11:6-8: against a Delaware River landscape the wolf and lamb, leopard and kid lie down together, the cow and bear feed side by side, and the lion eats straw with the ox, one child leads them, another plays on the serpent's den. In a background vignette William Penn signs his peace treaty with the Indians.

Councils, Catholic and Protestant. Paul had defined the kingdom of God as "righteousness and peace and joy in the Holy Spirit" (*Rom.* 14:17). Those identifications are taken up in the documents of the Second Vatican Council (1963-1965): The Sixth Assembly of the World Council of Churches (Vancouver, 1983) affirms "the identification of the churches with the poor in their witness to God's kingdom"; and in its statement rejecting nuclear weapons says that "as we witness to our genuine desire for peace with specific actions, the Spirit of God can use our feeble efforts for bringing the kingdoms of this world closer to the kingdom of God."

The movement for justice and peace. Dom Helder Câmara of Recife has often said that our world faces twin threats: the actual "M-bomb" of misery and the potential holocaust of the A-bomb. In that situation, the most critical in history, many readers of the New Testament are finding that its apocalyptic images of the end of the world, far from being alien to our mentality, are merely literal. To many Christian believers in the movement for justice and peace the kingdom of God has become the primary name for what is at work in them.

BIBLIOGRAPHY

No comprehensive study of the topic exists. For a well-documented source of texts from the ancient Near East and an extensive bibliography, see Thorkild Jacobsen's *The Treasures of Darkness: A History of Mesopotamian Religion* (New Haven, 1976). The Ugaritic data with relation to Hebrew are clearly presented by Werner H. Schmidt in *Königtum Gottes in Ugarit und Israel: Zur Herkunft der Königsprädikation Jahwes,* 2d ed. (Berlin, 1966). The most reliable surveys for the biblical material as a whole are Rudolf Schnackenburg's *God's Rule and Kingdom* (New York, 1963) and "Basileus" and related entries in the *Theological Dictionary of the New Testament* (Grand Rapids, Mich., 1964). For excellent surveys of Old Testament scholarship on Yahveh's kingship, see Joseph Coppens's contribution to the entry "Règne (ou Royaume) de Dieu," in the *Supplément au Dictionnaire de la Bible,* vol. 10 (Paris, 1981), and the article "Melek" by Helmer Ringgren et al. in the *Theologisches Wörterbuch zum Alten Testament,* vol. 4 (Stuttgart, 1984). Martin Buber's Kingship of God, translated from the third German edition (New York, 1967), is more theological than exegetical in its handling of the topic. John Gray restates the "enthronement-festival theory" uncritically but offers a thorough bibliography in *The Biblical Doctrine of the Reign of God* (Edinburgh, 1979).

The rabbinic sources were first analyzed by Gustaf H. Dalman in *The Words of Jesus Considered in the Light of Post-Biblical Jewish Writings and the Aramaic Language,* rev. Eng. ed. (Edinburgh, 1909); see especially pages 91-102 in volume 1 on the "kingship of heaven." Thousands of rabbinic texts in German translation are included in Hermann L. Strack and Paul Billerbeck's *Kommentar zum neuen Testament aus Talmud und Midrasch,* 6 vols. in 7 (Munich, 1922-1961); see especially the collection on "kingdom of God" in volume 1, pages 172-180. The use of the term *kingdom* in the Targum is analyzed by Bruce D. Chilton in "Regnum Dei Deus Est," *Scottish Journal of Theology* 31 (1978): 261-276.

For an introduction to the teachings of Jesus, see Hans Küng's *On Being a Christian* (Garden City, N. Y., 1976) and Günther Bornkamm's *Jesus of Nazareth* (New York, 1960). The "form-criticism" *(Formgeschichte)* of the gospel materials, important for assessing the historicity of the different sayings on the kingdom, was begun and almost ended with Rudolf Bultmann's *The History of the Synoptic Tradition,* 2d ed. (New York, 1968). On the Aramaic background of the sayings, consult Joachim Jeremias's *New Testament Theology: The Proclamation of Jesus* (New York, 1971). The case for making Jesus a political revolutionary has been restated by S. G. F. Brandon in *Jesus and the Zealots* (Manchester, 1967).

For a bibliography of the research on Jesus' sayings on the kingdom, together with scrupulous exegesis of key ones, see Jacques Schlosser's *Le règne de Dieu dans les dits de Jésus,* 2 vols. (Paris, 1980). Two articles on the subject of Jesus' sayings are especially useful: Hans Windisch's "Die Sprüche vom Eingehen in das Reich Gottes," *Zeitschrift für die neutestamentliche Wissenschaft* 27 (1928): 163-192, and Heinz Kruse's "The Return of the Prodigal: Fortunes of a Parable on Its Way to the Far East," *Orientalia* 47 (1978): 163-214.

Ernst Staehelin offers a very large annotated compilation of texts from the Christian church in *Die Verkündigung des Reiches Gottes in der Kirche Jesu Christi,* 7 vols. (Basel, 1951-1965). The early church fathers' treatment of the concept is indexed in "Basileia," in *A Patristic Greek Lexicon,* edited by G. W. H. Lampe (Oxford, 1961). A reliable guide to Augustine's thought is Étienne Gilson's *The Christian Philosophy of Saint Augustine* (New York, 1960), especially pp. 180-183. For a brief introduction to the thorny controversy surrounding Luther's doctrine, consult Heinrich Bornkamm's *Luther's Doctrine of the Two Kingdoms in the Context of His Theology* (Philadelphia, 1966). Arthur C. Cochrane narrates the struggle within the German church in *The Church's Confession under Hitler* (Philadelphia, 1962).

Read in sequence, three works provide the history of scholarly research into the meaning of the kingdom in Jesus' sayings: Christian Walther's *Typen des Reich-Gottes-Verständnisses: Studien zur Eschatologie und Ethik im 19. Jarhundert* (Munich, 1961) offers the perspective of nineteenth-century thinkers; Albert Schweitzer's *The Quest of the Historical Jesus: A Critical Study of Its Progress from Reimarus to Wrede,* 2d ed. (London, 1911), moves from Reimarus to Schweitzer himself; and Gösta Lundström's *The Kingdom of God in the Teaching of Jesus: A History of Interpretation from the Last Decades of the Nineteenth Century to the Present Day* (Edinburgh, 1963) moves forward to the 1960s. The most extensive contemporary work is the lifetime opus of Norman Perrin: *The Kingdom of God in the Teaching of Jesus* (Philadelphia, 1963),

Rediscovering the Teaching of Jesus (New York, 1967), and *Jesus and the Language of the Kingdom: Symbol and Metaphor in New Testament Interpretation* (Philadelphia, 1976). Werner B. Kümmel's *Promise and Fulfilment: The Eschatological Message of Jesus* (Naperville, Ill., 1957) is also useful.

Numerous texts otherwise barely accessible are cited in H. Richard Niebuhr's *The Kingdom of God in America* (Chicago, 1937); his schematism is to be taken with reserve.

JOHN PAIRMAN BROWN

KONGO RELIGION

The Kikongo-speaking peoples of the Niger-Congo linguistic group represent a rich and diverse cultural heritage associated with the ancient kingdom of Kongo.

There are a number of basic Kongo religious concepts that have persisted amid the profound viscissitudes of Kongo history. Among them is the belief in a supreme being, known as Nzambi Kalunga or Nzambi Mpungu Tulendo, who is thought to be omnipotent. Although Nzambi Kalunga is the creator and the ultimate source of power, lesser spirits and ancestors mediate between humanity and the supreme being. Evil, disorder, and injustice are believed to be the result of such base human motives as greed, envy, or maliciousness. As constant sources of life and well-being, both the land and the matrilineal ancestors buried in it form the basis of the preoccupation in Kongo thought with fertility and the continuity of the community. Patrifilial relations and other alliances formed in the public sphere bring forth in Kongo religion a concern with the nature of power, its sources, applications, and the consequences of beneficent and malevolent uses of it.

Kongo cultic history may be seen as a veritable tradition of renewal, either at the local lineage level, the national level, or in terms of a specific focus. Often the appeal is for restoration of public morality and order; individualized charms are commanded to be destroyed, the ancestors' tombs are restored, cemeteries purified, and group authority is renewed.

Especially important in the context of Kongo religious leaders is the twentieth-century Kongo prophet Simon Kimbangu, whose widely influential teachings eventually gave rise to the largest independent church in Africa.

Mission Christianity, implanted during the Free State and subsequent colonial era by British, Swedish, and American Protestant groups and by Belgian, French, and Portuguese Catholics has given rise to many congregations and conferences, as well as to schools, hospitals, seminaries, and other specialized institutions. Furthermore, it has brought about the far-reaching christianization of the Kongo populace. Many Kongo-speakers in the late twentieth century are nominal Christians. However, paradoxically, most Kongo Christians still subscribe to the fundamental tenets of the Kongo religion and worldview.

Kongo religion is more complex and profound than any single doctrine or congregation represented within it. It is a set of perspectives about life, of symbolic traditions and roles that have formed over centuries of human experience at the mouth of the Kongo River. This experience includes the adversities of the slave trade, massive depopulation, epidemics, colonialism, and droughts, as well as the challenges of christianization and independence. Kongo religion is at the heart of one of the great historic, yet living, human civilizations.

BIBLIOGRAPHY

The English reader may begin a study of Kongo religion with John M. Janzen and Wyatt MacGaffey's *An Anthology of Kongo Religion: Primary Texts from Lower Zaire,* "Publications in Anthropology, University of Kansas," no. 5 (Lawrence, Kans., 1974), an introduction to several facets of the subject as seen in fifty-two translated texts. Wyatt MacGaffey's *Religion and Society in Central Africa: The BaKongo of Lower Zaire* (Chicago, 1986), is a major synthesis of all aspects of historical and current Kongo religion. Kongo religion as reflected in mortuary art is depicted in Robert Farris Thompson's *The Four Moments of the Sun: Kongo Art in Two Worlds* (Washington, D. C., 1981). The *double entendre* of Thompson's title, refering to the dichotomies of visible-invisible and Africa-New World in Kongo belief and ceremonial space, is derived from one of the clearest renderings of Kongo cosmology, A. Fu-kiau kia Bunseki-Lumanisa's *N'kongo ye Nza / Cosmogonie Kongo* (Kinshasa, 1969).

Classics in Kongo culture, including religion, are Jan van Wing's *Études baKongo* (Brussels, 1959), especially part 2 on religion and magic, and Karl Edward Laman's *The Kongo,* 4 vols., "Studia Ethnographica Upsaliensia," nos. 4, 8, 12, and 16 (Uppsala, 1953-1968). Specialized studies include, on Kongo messianism, Effraim Andersson's *Messianic Popular Movements in the Lower Congo* (Uppsala, 1958); on witchcraft and consecrated medicines, Tulu kia Mpansu Buakasa's *L'impensé du discours: "Kinodoki" et "nkisi" en pays kongo du Zaïre* (Kinshasa, 1973); on Christian missions in Kongo, Effraim Andersson's *Churches at the Grass Roots: A Study in Congo-Brazzaville* (London, 1968); and on historic healing cults, John M. Janzen's *Lemba, 1650-1930: A Drum of Affliction in Africa and the New World* (New York, 1981).

JOHN M. JANZEN

KOREAN RELIGION

Confucianism, Taoism, and Buddhism, often said to be Korea's major religions, all came to Korea from or through China. Another faith, indigenous to Korea, has usually been considered superstition rather than religion because it lacks an explicitly formulated, elaborated, and rationalized body of doctrine. Yet this indigenous creed possesses a rich set of supernatural beliefs, a mythology, and a variety of ritual practices. In recent years, therefore, an increasing number of scholars have come to recognize this folk system of beliefs and rites as another of Korea's major religious traditions.

Affiliation with a traditional Korean religion entailed participation at some of its rites or acceptance of at least part of its ideology rather than exclusive membership in a church organization. As a result, participants at rituals usually include already existing social groups—such as family, village, or extended kinship group—rather than a specially constituted church congregation. Another result has been a religious eclecticism constrained not by feelings of commitment to one faith or sense of contradiction between disparate beliefs but by traditional role expectations of men and women. In many Korean families, men perform ancestor rites and consult geomancers whereas women make offerings to household gods and confer with fortune-tellers, but even this gender division of labor is not rigidly observed.

The absence of church congregations not only facilitated eclecticism and adaptation but also allowed significant regional, social, and even interpersonal variations in religious belief and practice. Nowhere is this more evident than in Korea's indigenous folk religion, where the lack of written scripture further encouraged diversity.

Indigenous Folk Religion. The earliest source on the rituals of Korea's folk religion appears in the *Tongguk Yi Sangguk chip,* a collection of poems and essays by Yi Kyubo (1168-1241). One of his poems describes some folk religious practices only briefly, but the description corresponds with the rites presently performed by *mudang* in Kyonggi Province, located in the western-central part of the Korean Peninsula.

Religious specialists. Though different regional terms also exist, the term *mudang* is used throughout Korea to designate the specialists of Korea's folk religion. It is usually translated into English as "shaman," but this translation is problematic because several different definitions have been advanced for the term *shaman.* Moreover, there are two types of mudang—possessed *(kangsin mu)* and hereditary *(sesup mu)*—and only the former fits some of the better-known definitions.

Pantheon. The pantheon of Korea's folk religion is polytheistic. A variety of gods are available to aid supplicants, bring them good fortune, and help them avoid misfortune. Some of these deities are known only in particular regions, but the following are known throughout Korea and are among those that most often receive rites: Mountain God, Earth God, Dragon King God, Smallpox God, Seven-Star God, God of Luck (Chesok), God of the House Site, Kitchen God, and Birth God. These represent only a small fraction of the total pantheon, however.

The deities are not thought to be inherently good or evil; whether they are helpful or harmful depends on the circumstances. If they are treated with regular offerings, they bring good fortune; otherwise, they inflict punishment.

Ancestor Worship. The history of Korean ancestor worship is better documented than the history of Korean folk religion, though it too suffers from a paucity of written records before the end of the Koryo dynasty (918-1392). Some form of rites for the dead probably existed in prehistoric times, and

> **When a bride first enters her husband's family, for example, she bows before the tablets of the ancestors regularly commemorated by his household.**

Buddhism was closely involved with such rites at the time of its importation from China in the fourth century CE. By the end of the Koryo dynasty, both Buddhist and *mudang* rites for the dead evidently existed. Such rites can still be seen today, and traces of Buddhist teachings are still evident in Korean funeral customs.

The establishment of the Choson dynasty (1392-1910) brought the adoption of Neo-Confucianism as Korea's official ideology and government efforts to transform ancestor rites to a Neo-Confucian format. Particularly seminal was the *Chu-tzu chia-li,* a ritual manual attributed to the Chinese philosopher Chu Hsi. By the end of the Choson dynasty, Neo-Confucian ancestor rites, with modifications, became generally accepted throughout most of the population. Even today, many Korean households have etiquette books with instructions for ancestor rites derived in some measure from the *Chu-tzu chia-li.*

Rituals. The kind of ritual activity directed toward an ancestor depends largely on the length of time that has elapsed since his or her death. A funeral usually begins with calling out the name of the deceased while setting forth shoes and rice for the death messenger(s) who come to escort the souls of the deceased along a difficult journey to face judgment in the underworld. The remainder of the funeral, during which visitors make condolence calls and the corpse is prepared for burial, usually lasts three days: the day of death, the following day, and the day of burial.

After the funeral is completed, a spirit shrine is erected at the home of the deceased. There his or her soul is said to reside for the duration of the formal mourning period.

Ritual attention is given to ancestors on yet other occasions. When a bride first enters her husband's family, for example, she bows before the tablets of the ancestors regularly commemorated by his household.

Ideas about the afterlife. Rites for ancestors take place in three different contexts, each implying a different location for the soul: before ancestor tablets, at graves, and at

seances to which ancestors "come" from the otherworld. When pressed, individuals can justify these seemingly disparate practices by reciting the well-known saying that each person has three souls.

In general, the dead are thought to remain in the same condition as they were at the time of death and thus to retain the same need for clothing, shelter, and, especially, food. To meet these needs, sets of clothing are occasionally offered at *mudang* rites, graves are maintained, and food offerings are presented at Neo-Confucian rites.

Divination and Fortune-telling. Most of the divination practiced by professional fortune-tellers falls into two major categories: spirit divination and horoscope reading. The first is used by possessed *mudang* and possessed diviners. Though the latter, unlike *mudang,* do not perform *kut,* their divination techniques are the same. Speaking through the mouth of either a *mudang* or diviner, a supernatural being makes a revelation about the cause of a present misfortune or predicts a future event or condition. Often the fortune-teller mimics the spirit that is providing the revelation, speaking like a child, for example, when possessed by a dead child.

Horoscope reading, the other major form of fortune-telling practiced by professional diviners, is especially prevalent in cities. Based on the theory that the time of a person's birth determines the main course of his or her life, horoscope reading utilizes the system of reckoning time according to the sexegenary cycle. Each year, month, day, and two-hour period is designated by one of sixty pairs of Chinese characters; and combining the four pairs associated with a person's year, month, day, and hour of birth yields eight characters. These are translated into predictions according to a variety of complex methods described in several printed manuals.

Christianity. Korea's first known contact with Christianity came during the late sixteenth century. A Jesuit missionary accompanied the Japanese army that invaded Korea at that time, but there is no evidence to indicate that his visit had any influence on Korean religion.

Christianity first had an influence in Korea during the following century, when Korean envoys to the Chinese court in Peking encountered some of the ideas brought there by Jesuit missionaries. A few of these attracted the interest of some noted Korean intellectuals of the seventeenth and eighteenth centuries. By the last quarter of the eighteenth century, a few Korean literati had formed study groups to examine and discuss Catholicism, and a few individuals even announced their conversion to the new religion.

The Choson dynasty court soon viewed Catholicism as a threat to Korea's established social order, primarily because of Catholic opposition to ancestor rites. Any challenge to filial piety, whether toward living parents or deceased predecessors, had serious political implications. Thus the new religion was officially proscribed by the mid-1780s, and a few executions soon followed. This antipathy toward Catholicism was exacerbated in 1801 by the involvement of some Korean Catholics in an attempt to draw Chinese and Western military forces into Korea in order to ensure freedom for their religion. The incident provoked further persecutions and imprisonment of Catholics. Yet despite bloody, if sporadic, persecutions, Catholicism continued to grow throughout the nineteenth century, largely through the efforts of French missionaries and church officials in Peking.

The growth of Catholicism in Korea was later eclipsed by the successes of Protestant missionaries. Though sustained Protestant missionary efforts began only in the penultimate decade of the nineteenth century, by the mid-1980s Protestants outnumbered Catholics by about four to one in South Korea. Though published statistics vary widely, depending on their sources, Catholics appeared to number about 1.5 million and Protestants about 5.5 million at that time.

New Religions. Like similar movements elsewhere in the world, Korea's new religions have tended to flourish in times of greatest personal distress and social disorder. The final decades of the Choson dynasty and the years following World War II, during which many of these religions emerged and grew, were periods of especially intense social, economic, and political turmoil. In both eras, moreover, threatened or actual foreign military intervention exacerbated Korea's internal difficulties.

Some present-day new religions teach that Korea will eventually become the most important of the world's nations, or they display the South Korean flag prominently during their services.

Though the doctrines of the new religions vary, most are directed toward the resolution of economic or health problems rather than a concern for the afterlife. Many of the new religions offer their followers the promise of utopia on earth. As in Korean folk religion, wealth is not viewed as a hindrance to happiness but rather as a blessing to be actively sought.

BIBLIOGRAPHY

Korean-language scholarship on Korean religion is extensive. A good introduction to the entire field is *Min'gan sinang, chongyo,* "Han'guk minsok taegwan," vol. 3, edited by the Kodae minjok munhwa yon'guso (Seoul, 1983). This work covers the entire spectrum of Korean religion, including both folk religions and established faiths. It also contains footnotes that refer to much of the Korean-language scholarship and has a sixty-page English summary.

For the histories of the various Korean religions, much useful information can be found in Ki-baik Lee's *A New History of Korea,* translated by Edward W. Wagner with Edward J. Shultz (Seoul, 1984). Though some of his interpretations are controversial, Lee's work builds on that of several authors and thereby offers the best English-language survey of scholarship by Korean and other historians. Several chapter subsections, each one or two pages in length, chronicle each of the various faiths in different periods of Korean history.

The most comprehensive bibliography of Western-language works on Korean religion has been compiled by Kah-Kyung Cho and included in chapter 4 of *Studies on Korea: A Scholar's Guide,* edited by Han-Kyo Kim (Honolulu, 1980), pp. 120-133. With few exceptions, Cho's bibliography ends at 1970, but his classified listing of more than two hundred entries, many of them annotated, still provides the easiest entry to most of the Western scholarship.

Many of the best works on traditional Korean religion have appeared since 1970. Youngsook Kim Harvey's *Six Korean Women: The Socialization of Shamans* (Saint Paul, 1979) analyzes recruitment to the role of *kangsin mu* by identifying commonalities in their life histories and personalities. Laurel Kendall's *Shamans, Housewives, and Other Restless Spirits* (Honolulu, 1985) focuses on mudang rites and beliefs, relating these to the roles and social situations common to Korean women. *The Folk Treasury of Korea,* edited by Chang Duk-soon (Seoul, 1970), includes texts of *mudang's* myths as well as a few myths from Korean literary sources compiled during the Koryo dynasty. *Ancestor Worship and Korean Society* (Stanford, Calif., 1982), by Roger L. Janelli and Dawnhee Yim Janelli, presents a description and analysis of rites for ancestors in terms of Korean family, kin group, and class structure. Alexandre Guillemoz's *Les algues, les anciens, les dieux* (Paris, 1983) surveys the diverse religious beliefs and rites of a single Korean village and points to their structural interrelationships.

Korean fortune-telling and geomancy have attracted far less scholarly attention than *mudang* rites and ancestor worship, but here again the best works have appeared within the past few years. For a brief but very informative survey of fortune-telling methods and topics of inquiry in Seoul, see Barbara Young's essay "City Women and Divination: Signs in Seoul," in *Korean Women: View from the Inner Room,* edited by Laurel Kendall and Mark Peterson (New Haven, Conn., 1983). Dawnhee Yim Janelli's "The Strategies of a Korean Fortuneteller," *Korea Journal* 20 (1980): 8-14, provides a brief description of consultation sessions with a horoscope reader in Seoul and identifies some of the techniques she employed to establish and maintain credibility in the eyes of her clients. For an account of Korean almanacs and their use in rural Korea, see M. Griffin Dix's "The Place of the Almanac in Korean Folk Religion," *Journal of Korean Studies* 2 (1980): 47-70. For a description of Korean geomancy, based on an examination of geomantic manuals, legends about geomancy, and interviews with professional geomancers, see Yoon Hong-key's Ph. D. dissertation, *Geomantic Relationships between Culture and Nature in Korea,* available as number 88 of the "Asian Folklore and Social Life Monograph Series" (Taipei, 1976).

Christianity has not enjoyed the same degree of recent growth in scholarly interest as have traditional Korean religions, and earlier books generally remain the most useful. The standard history of Protestantism in Korea is George L. Paik's *The History of Protestant Missions in Korea,* 1832-1910 (1929; 3d ed., Seoul, 1980). For an account of Christianity's growth in terms of its relationships with Korean history and culture, see Spencer J. Palmer's *Korea and Christianity: The Problem of Identification with Tradition,* "Royal Asiatic Society, Korea Branch, Monograph Series," no. 2 (Seoul, 1967).

Among the more recent publications on Korean Christianity, two articles are especially noteworthy. The first is Donald L. Baker's "The Martyrdom of Paul Yun: Western Religion and Eastern Ritual in Eighteenth Century Korea," *Transactions of the Royal Asiatic Society, Korea Branch* 54 (1979): 33-58. Ba-ker's study deals with the introduction of Catholicism into Korea and its perception by both early converts and the central government. The other is Frank Baldwin's "Missionaries and the March First Movement: Can Moral Men Be Neutral?," in *Korea under Japanese Colonial Rule,* edited by Andrew C. Nahm (Kalamazoo, Mich., 1973). Based on an examination of both Japanese and English sources, Baldwin's study depicts the Western missionaries' reluctance to participate in nationalist movements during the Japanese colonial era despite their personal sympathies toward the Korean cause.

Ch'ondogyo and the Unification Church have received far more attention than the other Korean new religions. *The New Religions of Korea,* edited by Spencer J. Palmer and published as volume 43 of the *Transactions of the Royal Asiatic Society,* Korea Branch (Seoul, 1967), is a collection of disparate but informative essays that deal with several of these faiths. It is still the best introduction to these religions.

YIM SUK-JAY, ROGER L. JANELLI, and
DAWNHEE YIM JANELLI

KUSHITE RELIGION

Kush was the name given in ancient times to the area of northeast Africa lying just to the south of Egypt. It is the Aethiopia of Herodotus and other classical writers, and it corresponds in a general way to the Nubia of today.

The northern part of Kush was under direct Egyptian control during the New Kingdom (c. 1580-1000 BCE). Egyptians did not settle in the country in large numbers, but they oversaw the building of temples, towns, and fortresses and the inauguration of the typical pharaonic system of administration and of worship. When the colonial overlords departed, around 1000 BCE, they had laid the basis for an egyptianized successor-state that was to emerge a little later as the empire of Kush. The Kushite rulers assumed all the titles and trappings of the pharaohs, and for a brief period (751-656 BCE) were even accepted as rulers in Egypt itself. Kushite authority in Egypt was ended by an Assyrian invasion, but the empire later expanded southward at least as far as the confluence of the Blue and White Niles, and possibly much farther.

The original capital of Kush was at Napata, near the Fourth Cataract of the Nile, where a great temple of Amun had been erected during the Egyptian colonial regime. The empire of Kush was finally overrun and destroyed by barbarian invaders in the fourth century CE, but some of its traditions persisted until the coming of Christianity two centuries later.

Most of our information is based on the interpretation of reliefs carved on temple and tomb walls and on votive objects.

As in Egypt, the afterlife was a major focus of concern. The Kushite rulers and their families were buried under steep-sided stone pyramids, each of which had attached to it a mortuary chapel like a miniature temple.

BIBLIOGRAPHY

There is no single, detailed work on the religion of Kush, as is to be expected in view of the scanty available evidence. Brief, popular summaries can be found in Peter L. Shinnie's *Meroe: A Civilization of the Sudan* (New York, 1967), pp. 141-152, and in my book *Nubia: Corridor to Africa* (Princeton, 1977), pp. 325-328, 336-338, 374-378. More technical discussions include those of Jean Leclant, "La religion Méroïtique," in *Histoire des religions,* edited by Henri-Charles Puech (Paris, 1970), vol. 1, pp. 141-153, and Nicholas B. Millet, "Meroitic Religion," in *Meroitische Forschungen 1980* (Meroitica 7), edited by Fritz Hintze (Berlin, 1984), pp. 111-121. L. V. Zabkar's *Apedemak, Lion God of Meroe* (Warminster, 1975) discusses at length one particular aspect of Kushite religion.

WILLIAM Y. ADAMS

LAO RELIGION

The Lao people inhabit both banks of the Middle Mekong, from Louang Phrabang in the north to Khong Island in the south. A variety of influences have contributed to the religious contours of the Lao. The dominant cultural vector, however, stems ultimately from the Indian subcontinent. The center and symbol of the rural collectivity, indeed, of all action that is communal in Lao society, remains the *vat* (Pali, *vatthu;* Skt., *vastu*) or Buddhist monastery.

The Phi Cult. The term *phi* is common to all Tai-speaking populations (one finds the term *fi* among certain non-Buddhist Tai in northern Vietnam) and typically designates an ensemble of various entities such as "souls," ancestors, evil spirits, and celestial deities. The performance of *su khwan* ("calling back the souls") is mandated at times of risk: illness, before a voyage or examination, or at the passage to another stage of life.

The Lao have recourse equally to specialist healers *(mo)* and occasionally to female mediums *(nang thiam).* The most powerful among the former is the *mo thevada,* or "master of divinities," a shaman who invokes the aid of his auxiliary spirits, the *phi thevada.*

The cult of the tutelary deity of the village is headed by a master of ritual known as a *caw cam.* His principal task is to organize and execute the annual sacrifice to the tutelary deity, the *liang phi ban,* or "nourishing of the village spirit," in which all households participate.

Buddhist Influences. Buddhism and the *phi* cult are not simply juxtaposed in Lao popular religion; over the course of several centuries they have become syncretized. For example, one utilizes Buddhist formulas for magical purposes and seeks without hesitation the knowledge of a monk before drawing a number in the lottery. One of the great village feasts is the Bun Bang Fai ("rocket festival"). There is no need to overemphasize the sexual symbolism of the giant rockets that are shot against the sky just before the coming of the monsoon with its fecundating rains. That the Buddhist clergy sanctions and effectively participates in this festival is evidenced by the fact that the rockets are placed within the compound of the pagoda under the supervisions of the monks. The festival of the rockets commemorates the Visakha Puja—the triple anniversary of the birth, the enlightenment, and the death of the Buddha.

The Buddhist notion that has most profoundly permeated Lao popular religion seems to be that of *bun* (Pali, *puñña*), "merit." One must acquire merit to enrich one's *kam* (Pali, *kamma;* Skt., *karman*), which permits the attainment of spiritual liberation in the cycles of transmigration.

Another outwardly Buddhist component of Lao society that also serves non-Buddhist functions is the *vat,* or monastery, mentioned above. The monastery rises and grows with the collective it represents. After having cleared a section of the forest and forming a sufficiently autonomous hamlet, a group of farmers may decide to establish a hermitage (*vat pa,* "forest pagoda") for a monk. This small wooden house on stilts becomes the first *kutdi* (Skt., *kuti;* monks' quarters) and grows with the hamlet itself.

The two currents of Buddhist and indigenous folk religious belief intermingle to form Lao religion, but their respective proportions vary with the epochs and regions. As the reigning power reinforces itself and develops the teaching of Buddhism, the *phi* cult's influence tends to diminish. Despite this, Lao farmers do not completely abandon this recourse to nature's forces, which guarantee them the resources necessary for the maintenance and renewal of life.

[*For an overview of Lao culture in the context of mainland Southeast Asia as a whole, see* Southeast Asian Religions.]

BIBLIOGRAPHY

First and foremost, a portion of the many but dispersed publications of Charles Archaimbault has been compiled in one volume, *Structure religieuses lao: Rites et mythes* (Vientiane, 1973). Archaimbault's article "Les ceremonies en l'honneur des phi f'à (phi celestes) et des phi t'ai (phi précieux) à Basak," appears in *Asie du Sud-Est et monde insulindien* 6 (1975): 85-114. Richard Pottier's "Notes sur les chamanes et médiums de quelques groupes thaï," *Asie du Sud-Est et monde insulindien* 4 (1973): 99-103, is supplemented by his very important dissertation, "Le système de santé lao et ses possibilités de développement" (Ph. D. diss., University of Paris, 1979), which he is currently preparing for publication. Another indispensible work on Lao religion is Marcel Zago's *Rites et cérémonies en milieu bouddhiste lao* (Rome, 1972). For more details, I refer the reader to my own essay, "Notes sur le bouddhisme populaire en milieu rural lao," which appeared in consecutive issues of *Archives de sociologie des religions* 13 (1968): 81-110, 111-150. A small section of this essay has been translated into English under the title "*Phiban* Cults in Rural Laos," in *Change and Persistence in*

Thai Society: Essays in Honor of Lauriston Sharp, edited by G. William Skinner and A. Thomas Kirsch (Ithaca, N. Y., 1975), pp. 252-277.

Concerning the Thai-Lao of Phaak Isaan, see Stanley J. Tambiah's *Buddhism and the Spirit Cults in North-East Thailand* (Cambridge, 1970). A useful general bibliographical reference is Frank E. Reynolds's "Tradition and Change in Theravada Buddhism: A Bibliographical Essay Focused on the Modern Period," in *Contributions to Asian Studies,* edited by Bardwell L. Smith, vol. 4 (Leiden, 1973), pp. 94-104.

GEORGES CONDOMINAS
Translated from French by Maria Pilar Luna-Magannon

LAO-TZU

Lao Tan, the Teacher of Confucius. There is no textual evidence that the *Tao-te ching* itself existed prior to about 250 BCE. The source of inspiration for this hypothetical spokesman was a presumably historical figure known only as Lao Tan, "Old Tan." According to the *Li chi* (Book of Rites; c. 100 BCE), Lao Tan's reputation as an expert on mourning rituals was well established. On four occasions, Confucius is reported to have responded to inquiries about ritual procedure by quoting Lao Tan. It was knowledge he had apparently gained firsthand, for Confucius recalls how he had once assisted Lao Tan in a burial service. Lao Tan, on the other hand, is quoted as addressing Confucius by his given name, Ch`iu, a liberty only those with considerable seniority would have taken. Seven episodes supposedly document instances

> **The text Lao-tzu completed was reported to have contained altogether five thousand words filling two folios.**

when Confucius sought advice from Lao Tan on various principles of the Tao. By the first century BCE, the legend that Lao-tzu was the author of the *Tao-te ching* had entered the annals of Chinese history as accepted fact.

Li Erh and the Journey West. Ssu-ma Ch`ien (145-86 BCE) is the first known to have attempted a biography of Lao-tzu. His *Shih chi* (Records of the Historian, c. 90 BCE) gives Lao-tzu's full name as Li Erh or Li Tan. It is said that after living in the domains under Chou rule for a considerable time, Lao-tzu took his leave when he perceived the imminent downfall of the regime. Heading west, he left the central plains of China, but at the Han-ku Pass he was detained by a gatekeeper named Yin Hsi and asked to compose a text on the concepts of *tao* and *te.*

The text Lao-tzu completed was reported to have contained altogether five thousand words filling two folios. That Ssu-ma Ch`ien incorporates this legend on the origins of the *Tao-te ching* into Lao-tzu's biography suggests that the text was fairly well established by his time. The earliest extant versions of a *Te ching* and a *Tao ching* appears to have been made sometime prior to 195 BCE and the other sometime between 180 and 168 BCE, both predating Ssu-ma's *Records* by a century or so. Apocryphal though the attribution to Lao-tzu may be, the *Tao-te ching* became a fundamental text not only for students of pre-Han thought but also for those who came to venerate Lao-tzu as a divine being.

The Divinization of Lao-tzu. An important shrine in the history of the veneration of Lao-tzu lies far to the northeast of Ch`eng-tu, at Lu-i, his putative birthplace. It is at this site, the T`ai-ch`ing Kung (Palace of Grand Clarity), that Emperor Huan (r. 147-167) of the Latter Han dynasty is known to have authorized sacrifices to Lao-tzu in the years 165-166. After a series of cosmic metamorphoses, Lao-tzu is said to have finally achieved an incarnate form and thus to have begun his descent as savior to the mortal realm. He then became a cosmic force capable of multiple reincarnations in the role of preceptor to the ruling elite.

Lao-tzu as Buddha. At the time that Emperor Huan ordered sacrifices at Lu-i, he also presided over an elaborate ritual at court held in honor of both Lao-tzu and the Buddha. An academician named Hsiang K`ai was moved to comment on this service in a memorial that he submitted to the throne in 166. Hsiang alludes in his address to a belief that Lao-tzu transformed himself into the Buddha after having ventured west of his homeland. Thus did the legend of Lao-tzu's disappearance at Han-ku Pass lead to the claim that the Buddha was none other than Lao-tzu, and that his journey was a mission to convert all mortals to the "way of the Tao."

Lao-tzu as a Messiah. The vision of Lao-tzu as a messiah, moving freely between the celestial and mundane realms, inspired a large body of sacred literature. Just as the motives of the authors of these texts varied, so too did their conceptions of what was meant by a deified Lao-tzu. One of the earliest and most enigmatic sources to take up the soteriological theme is the *Lao-tzu pien-hua ching* (Scripture on the Transformations of Lao-tzu).

Lao-tzu is seen as coeval with primordial chaos, circulating in advance of the creation of the universe. He is portrayed as the ultimate manifestation of spontaneity *(tzu-jan),* the source of the Tao itself.

Patterns of Devotion. The importance of the *Tao-te ching* in various scriptural guides to the Taoist way of life cannot be overemphasized. As early as the Han dynasty, the *Tao-te ching* was apparently recited not only for magico-religious purposes, but also as a guide to deportment. From at least the thirteenth century, Lao-tzu was ritually evoked as the primary patriarch of the Ch`üan-chen lineage on the putative date of his birth, the fifteenth day of the second lunar month. It was also customary, according to the Ch`üan-chen tradition established by Wang Che (1112-1170), to call upon Lord Lao to preside over ritual commemorations of immortals sacred to the lineage.

During waves of spiritual innovation, many shrines to Lord Lao arose throughout the countryside, while others were restored or enlarged. Worshipers at these shrines were often rewarded by visions of their Lord, appearing in response to individual pleas for divine intervention. According to one inscription dated 1215, Lord Lao was expressly evoked by Taoist priests in an elaborate ritual to exorcise a victim of possessing spirits.

[*See also* Taoism *and* Millenarianism.]

BIBLIOGRAPHY

Tao Te Ching, rev. ed., translated by D. C. Lau (Hong Kong, 1982), includes a translation of the Wang Pi text of the *Lao-tzu,* together with a rendition based on the Ma-wang-tui man-uscripts. Of special interest in this work are Lau's introductions on Lao-tzu and the Ma-wang-tui texts, and two appendixes on "The Problem of Authorship" and "The Nature of the Work." *Chuang-tzu; The Seven Inner Chapters and Other Writings from the Book Chuang-tzu,* translated by A. C. Graham (London, 1981), includes a thoughtful analysis of the passages that bear on Lao-tzu's encounters with Confucius. Annotated translations of Liu Hsiang's biographies of Lao-tzu and Yin Hsi are found in *Le Liesien tchouan: Biographies légendaires des Immortels taoïstes de l'antiquité,* edited and translated by Max Kaltenmark (Peking, 1953). Anna K. Seidel's *La divinisation de Lao tseu, dans le taoïsme des Han* (Paris, 1969) is an invaluable monograph based on a critical reading of the *Lao-tzu ming* and the *Lao-tzu pien-hua ching.* For a comprehensive study of the *hua-hu* issue from the second to the sixth century, Erik Zür-cher's *The Buddhist Conquest of China,* 2 vols. (1959; Leiden, 1972), remains unsurpassed. Outstanding documentation of the techniques for prolonging life with which Lao-tzu became associated is available in Henri Maspero's *Le taoïsme et les religions chinoises* (Paris, 1971), translated by Frank A. Kierman, Jr., as *Taoism and Chinese Religion* (Amherst, Mass., 1981). Norman J. Girardot's *Myth and Meaning in Early Taoism* (Berkeley, 1983) examines the mythology of Lao-tzu's transformations as it pertains to early cosmogonic theory. His analysis is based in large part on Seidel's work, taken together with Kristofer Schipper's "The Taoist Body," *History of Religions* 17 (1978): 355-386. Schipper offers a more detailed interpretation of Lao-tzu's "cosmogonic body" in *Le corps taoïste* (Paris, 1982). Extensive documentation of the nei-tan tradition is found in Joseph Needham and Lu Gwei-Djen's *Science and Civilisation in China,* vol. 5, pt. 5 (Cambridge, 1983). For a survey of pertinent hagiographies, historical chronologies, and exegeses on the Tao-te ching, see my *A Survey of Taoist Literature, Tenth to Seventeenth Centuries* (Berkeley, 1987).

JUDITH MAGEE BOLTZ

LATTER-DAY SAINTS

[*See article* Mormonism.]

LAW AND RELIGION

If law and religion are viewed narrowly—law as rules of conduct promulgated and enforced by political authorities, and religion as beliefs and practices relating to the supernatural—the two may be treated as largely independent of each other, at least in most cultures. If, however, each is viewed more broadly, they will be seen to be closely interrelated. In virtually all societies the established legal processes of allocating rights and duties, resolving conflicts, and creating channels of cooperation are inevitably connected with the community's sense of, and commitment to, ultimate values and purposes.

> A great deal of Greek and Roman law continued to concern itself with the regulation of religious ceremonies.

The religious dimension of law is apparent in at least four elements found in all legal systems: (1) *ritual,* that is, the ceremonial procedures that symbolize the objectivity of law; (2) *tradition,* that is, the language and practices handed down from the past that symbolize the ongoing character of law; (3) *authority,* that is, reliance on written or spoken sources that are considered to be decisive in themselves and that symbolize the binding power of law; and (4) *universality,* that is, the claim to embody universally valid concepts or insights that symbolize the law's connection with all-embracing morality. All four of these elements connect a society's legal order to its belief in a reality beyond itself.

In some societies law and religion, even in their narrowest sense, are expressly identified with each other. This is true of those rudimentary societies in which persons with religious authority play a dominant role in governing, and where there is no distinct class of lawgivers or judges or lawyers. In many of these societies magical and mechanical legal procedures, such as ordeals and ritual oaths, are used in punishing misconduct and resolving disputes. In an early stage of development of Roman law, the priesthood (pontiffs) played a dominant role and the methods of proof were highly formalistic. In an early stage of the development of law in Greece, judgment, retribution, custom, and apportionment of losses were all hypostatized as Olympian gods whose decrees were divined in the oracles.

A different interconnection between law and religion exists in the Hebrew and Muslim civilizations, where a sophisticated system of law is found in sacred writings, namely the Torah and the Qur'an. There the observance of law is itself a religious act.

In societies where jurisdiction has eventually been transferred from religious to secular authorities, a certain desanctification of legal rules and procedures has inevitably resulted. In Greece and Rome, however, this process was accompanied by the development of a philosophy of natural law in which religious assumptions played a major part. Furthermore, a great deal of Greek and Roman law continued to concern itself with the regulation of religious ceremonies.

Even in cultures where law is most sharply distinguished from religious beliefs, the distinction itself is usually thought to have a religious significance. Thus in traditional China, which considered law *(fa)* to be ad hoc, mechanistic, and based on mere expediency—in contrast to virtue or "principle" *(li)*, which is rooted in nature—*fa* was nevertheless thought to be directed ultimately by the natural (heavenly) world order.

In the West, the interdependence of law and religion took on a different significance in the late Middle Ages with the separation of ecclesiastical and secular polities, each with its own law. Both the canon law of the Roman Catholic church and the various systems of secular law that existed alongside it were supposed to promote the good life. However, the canon law had the still higher purpose of permitting the obedient to be in communion with God. This conception of a spiritual law of the church was rejected by Luther and Calvin and their followers who removed all law to the earthly realm of sin and death. In the original Protestant conception, nevertheless, law remained linked with faith, since faithful Christians—and especially Christian rulers—were called upon to use the law in order that justice be done and the world reformed. Neither Luther nor Calvin shared the antinomian view that the Christian community can live in a state of grace without law. Nor did they or their followers make a contrast, such as some twentieth-century theologians have made, between law and love; they understood both the moral law and the civil law to be directed toward the realization of *caritas* in social relationships.

Undoubtedly there has been a decline, during the twentieth century, of direct religious influences on the legal systems of western Europe and the United States. This has been the result, in part, of the widespread privatization of religion, which has helped produce a tension, and even an antagonism, between religion and law, the two being seen primarily as a matter of personal psychology and social action respectively. This view recognizes that law may ulti-

mately stem from religious beliefs (the usual formula is that law is based on morality, and morality on religion), but considers it important to distinguish between religion and law to the maximum extent possible, partly to maintain both the freedom of religion from legal controls and the freedom of law from religious influences.

The privatization of traditional religions has sometimes been accompanied by the pouring into nontheistic belief systems (ideologies, "isms") of universal theory, apocalyptic vision, and sacrificial passion such as formerly characterized Western Christian movements. In communist countries this has led not only to an extreme separation of church and state (involving virtual withdrawal of public support from the churches, and virtual exclusion of religious believers from participation in political life), but also to an extreme identification of the state with the official belief system. The socialist legal systems of the Soviet Union and other communist countries are intended to directly reflect the belief systems to which those countries are committed. In that broad sense, one might speak of them as (nontheistic) religious legal systems.

BIBLIOGRAPHY

For general surveys of law and religion, see my books *The Interaction of Law and Religion* (Nashville, 1974) and *Law and Revolution: The Formation of the Western Legal Tradition* (Cambridge, Mass., 1983); Karl Bünger's *Religiöse Bindungen in frühen und orientalischen Rechten* (Wiesbaden, 1952); Christopher H. Dawson's *Religion and Culture* (London, 1948); Ze'ev W. Falk's *Law and Religion: The Jewish Experience* (Jerusalem, 1981); Henry Sumner Maine's *Ancient Law: Its Connection with the Early History of Society and Its Relation to Modern Ideas,* 3d ed. (New York, 1879); and *Religion and the Law,* a special issue of *Hastings Law Journal* 29 (July 1978).

On the interrelation of Greek and Roman law and religion, see Werner W. Jaeger's *Paideia: The Ideals of Greek Culture,* 3 vols. (Oxford, 1939-1944); and Pierre Noailles's *Fas et jus: Études de droit romain* (Paris, 1948) and *Du droit sacré au droit civil* (Paris, 1949). On communism as a secular religion and on religious dimensions of Soviet law, see my *Justice in the U. S. S. R.,* rev. ed. (Cambridge, Mass., 1963).

HAROLD J. BERMAN

LEE, ANN

LEE, ANN (1736-1784), English visionary and founder of the American Shakers. Growing up in a poor, working-class family in Manchester, England, Ann Lee was attracted in 1758 to the Shakers, a religious group that engaged in ecstatic dancing and other charismatic activities. Married in 1762, Lee had four children, all of whom died in infancy or early childhood. She interpreted these losses and the pain that she experienced in childbirth as a judgment on her concupiscence. In 1770 a vision convinced her that lust was the original sin in the Garden of Eden and the root of all human evil and misery. Only by giving up sexual intercourse entirely, following the heavenly pattern in which "they neither marry nor are given in marriage," could humankind be reconciled to God.

The Shakers and the celibate message that Ann Lee introduced among them experienced little success in England, where the group was sporadically persecuted but generally ignored. In 1774 Lee and eight of her followers emigrated to America and two years later settled at Niskeyuna (now Watervliet), New York, near Albany. Between 1781 and 1783, during the troubled aftermath of the American Revolution, Lee and the Shakers undertook a major proselytizing effort in New York and New England in the course of which they attracted support primarily from Free Will Baptists. Ensuing persecution, including brutal beatings and harassment, weakened Ann Lee and her brother William, contributing to their premature deaths in 1784.

Although Ann Lee's involvement with the Shakers in America lasted only a decade, her influence at that time was profound and has continued to be so during the groups's subsequent two-hundred year history. Intelligent, dynamic, and loving, she was revered by her followers. They came to believe that in "Mother Ann," as they affectionately called her, God's spirit had been incarnated in female form just as they believed that in Jesus, God's spirit had been incarnated in male form. Whether Lee herself ever claimed such quasi divinity—except in ecstatic utterances subject to symbolic interpretation—is questionable. Yet the conviction that Ann Lee was the second embodiment of Christ's spirit and the inaugurator of the millennium is central to the Shaker faith.

[*See also* Shakers.]

BIBLIOGRAPHY

The most thorough scholarly treatment of Ann Lee is presented in Edward Deming Andrews's *The People Called Shakers*, new enl. ed. (New York, 1963). Anna White and Leila S. Taylor's *Shakerism: Its Meaning and Message* (Columbus, Ohio, 1904) provides a perceptive Shaker assessment of the life and spirit of Ann Lee. The most valuable primary source on Ann Lee's life and beliefs is the rare *Testimonies of the Life, Character, Revelations, and Doctrines of Our Ever Blessed Mother Ann Lee and the Elders with Her* edited by Rufus Bishop and Seth Y. Wells (Hancock, Mass., 1816). An analysis that compares the Shakers under Ann Lee with other radical sectarian movements is Stephen A. Marini's *Radical Sects of Revolutionary New England* (Cambridge, Mass., 1982).

LAWRENCE FOSTER

LEVITES

The "Tribe of Levi." Current scholarship is only able to explain the traditions concerning a tribal origin for the Levites in broad, sociological terms. The biblical record of twelve tribes, into which that set of traditions fits, is questionable historically.

Apart from the genealogical recasting of the early Israelites, so characteristic of Priestly literature, the tradition of a tribe named Levi occurs in two poetic passages. In

> Priests were clearly responsible for maintaining the purity of the Temple and of all cultic utensils, vestments, and such.

Genesis 49, Levi, the eponym of one of Jacob's sons, is the head of a tribe like all the others. Nothing is said about any cultic function associated with Levi.

In *Deuteronomy* 33, the Levites are a tribe, but a tribe of priests. However, later in this same chapter the Levites are not characterized as a tribe, but rather as a group bound by the commitment to a proper Yahvistic cult that superseded their various tribal affiliations.

Priests and Levites. The distinction between priest and Levite, basic to certain Priestly traditions, may have first emerged during the Babylonian exile. In *Ezekiel* 44:9f., the prophet, in his vision of a restored Temple in Jerusalem, favored the priestly line of Zadok exclusively. The Levites who had turned away from Yahveh (when, is not clear) were no longer to officiate at the cult, but were demoted (as it were) to supporting tasks in maintaining the Temple.

This is the first indication outside of the Priestly texts of the Torah of a differentiation between Levitical priests and ordinary Levites, laying the groundwork for the postexilic system wherein priests were considered superior to Levites. Classes of priests, with differentiated functions, were characteristic of Near Eastern temples, and undoubtedly applied to the Temple in Jerusalem at one time or another. Conceivably, a poem of *Genesis* 49 served to explain the demotion of the Levites, which is attributed to some outrageous act.

High-born priestly families, like those recorded in the lists of returning exiles in *Ezra* 2 and *Nehemiah* 7, owned estates outside of Jerusalem and probably derived their income from sources other than mere priestly emoluments. By contrast, the Levites seem a deprived group in the early postexilic period.

Organization. The internal organization of the Israelite priesthood probably changed little over the centuries, from the inception of the monarchies to the destruction of the

Second Temple. A priest was usually in charge of a temple/cult center, and he was referred to simply as *ha-kohen* ("the priest") or as the priest of a particular locality or temple. The Mishnah (*Tam.* 3.1) mentions *ha-memunneh* ("the appointed priest"), who served either as an "officer of the day," or was in charge of a specific bureau or set of rites. In short, the priesthood of the Temples of Jerusalem was organized along royal, administrative lines.

The term *torah,* which has enjoyed wide applications in the Jewish tradition, derives from the priestly context: it is the priest who knows the *torah,* as is indicated in many biblical characterizations of the priesthood (*Jer.* 18:18, *Ez.* 7:26, *Hg.* 2:11). [*See* Torah.]

In addition to their roles as skilled professionals, priests were consecrated persons. The Torah preserves detailed descriptions of the procedures followed in consecration (*Lv.* 8-10, *Ex.* 28-29), including prophylactic rites (involving the use of blood and oil), ablutions, and investiture—all accompanied by purification or expiatory sacrifices. Once consecrated, the priest officiated for the first time and partook of expiatory sacrifice.

Sacrificial and cultic functions. The primary responsibility of the priest was to officiate at sacrificial worship. Apart from actually officiating, priests were undoubtedly responsible for sacrificial *matériel*—mixing spices and incense, preparing flour for grain offerings, and preparing proper oils for various purposes, including lighting of the *menorah* ("candelabra") and the like. According to the later pattern, Levites attended to certain of the preparations, but actual slaughtering of sacrificial animals was a priestly function.

In addition to sacrificial *matériel,* priests were clearly responsible for maintaining the purity of the Temple and of all cultic utensils, vestments, and such. The Torah's priestly laws assign some of these "maintenance" tasks *(mishmeret)* to the Levites, but they usually required priestly supervision.

Oracular functions. Again, some of the earliest biblical references to priests are in connection with oracular activity. Micah and the Danites were served in this way by a young Levite, and the priests who accompanied Saul and David into battle provided similar service. Very likely the laws of *Deuteronomy* 20 are to be understood against the background of oracular inquiry. Before battle the Israelites were addressed by the priest, undoubtedly the high priest, who assured them that God would stand at the side of his people and grant them victory. The priest then stipulated certain deferrals and exemptions from military service.

Oracular inquiry is generally viewed as characteristic of the earlier period of Israelite history, fading out as time went on. Other than the casting of lots, very little is known about the mechanics of oracular inquiry in Israelite Jewish religion. [*See* Prophecy *and* Oracles.]

Instructional and juridical functions. The instructional and juridical functions of the priesthood brought the priesthood into contact with the people. The instructional and juridical roles were, of course, closely interrelated. *Ezekiel* 44:23-24 gives a fairly comprehensive definition of these priestly functions:

> They [the Zadokite priests] shall declare to My people what is sacred and what is profane, and inform them what is pure and what is impure. In lawsuits, too, it is they who shall act as judges: they shall decide therein in accordance with My rules. They shall preserve My teachings and My laws regarding all My fixed occasions, and they shall maintain the sanctity of My Sabbaths.

Administrative and political functions. In addition to conducting the cult of worship, priests were responsible for the overall administration of the Temple and its affairs. In *2 Chronicles* 24, priests and Levites are sent out to collect dues from the people, as well as voluntary contributions for the Temple. As well, temple maintenance meant not only repair but purification, and the priesthood was in charge of these activities.

The political function of the priesthood is more specific during the postexilic period, although it is likely that, as in most societies, leading priests had exercised power and influence under Judahite and northern Israelite kings as well. Whereas such earlier historic books as *Samuel* and *Kings* are primarily concerned with the monarchy, and therefore say little about priestly power, it is the later *Chronicles* that create the myth of deep cooperation between the two establishments—the royal and the sacerdotal—especially during the reign of the "upright" Judahite kings.

In the postexilic period, Levites had specific functions distinct from priests. In *Numbers* 1-4, Levites are assigned the task of guarding the sanctuary, in addition to "bearing" its appurtenances, and other duties. Postexilic traditions also speak of Levites as "teachers, interpreters" (*Ezr.* 8:16, *Neh.* 8:7, 2 *Chr.* 35:3), thereby endorsing the ancient instructional role of priestly and Levitical groups as teachers. Levitical names have turned up at Arad, in the Negev, during the late preexilic period, thus affirming that such families were assigned to royal outposts where there were also temples.

[*See* Israelite Religion.]

BIBLIOGRAPHY

The higher critical point of view regarding the development of Israelite religion and its priestly institutions, according to which these are relatively late phenomena in biblical history, is best presented in Julius Wellhausen's *Prolegomena to the History of Ancient Israel,* translated by J. Sutherland Black (1885; reprint, New York, 1957). In contrast, Yehezkel Kaufmann's *The Religion of Israel,* translated and abridged by Moshe Greenberg (Chicago, 1960), offers a learned argument against the higher position, insisting on the greater antiquity of priestly institutions.

The best, and virtually the only, overall history of the Israelite priesthood is Aelred Cody's *A History of Old Testament-Priesthood* (Rome, 1969). G. B. Gray's *Sacrifice in the Old Testament* (1925), reissued with a prolegomena by myself (New York, 1971), devotes a section to the priesthood (pp. 179-270), analyzing its character primarily on the basis of the biblical textual evidence, and that of post-biblical ancient sources.

Several recent encyclopedia articles summarize and assess scholarly research. They include: Menahem Haran's "Priests and Priesthood," in *Encyclopaedia Judaica* (Jerusalem, 1971); my own "Priests," and Ellis Rivkin's "Aaron, Aaronides," in *Interpreter's Dictionary of the Bible: Supplementary Volume* (Nashville, 1976).

New light is shed on the history of the high priesthood by Frank Moore Cross in his "A Reconstruction of the Judean Restoration," *Journal of Biblical Literature* 94 (1975): 4-18, drawing on the evidence of the Samaria Papyri of the fourth century BCE. The religious and political roles of the postexilic priesthood, in particular, are discussed with considerable insight in Morton Smith's *Palestinian Parties and Politics That Shaped the Old Testament* (New York, 1971). The less explored functions and status of the Levites, as distinct from priests, are investigated, on the basis of biblical terminology, in Jacob Milgrom's *Studies in Levitical Terminology,* 2 vols. (Los Angeles and Berkeley, 1970-1974). All of the above references provide extensive bibliographical information.

The reader will also want to consult ancient sources outside the Bible referred to in this article. The best available English translation of the Mishnah is Herbert Danby's *Mishnah* (Oxford, 1933). The writings of the ancient historian Josephus Flavius, translated by Henry St. J. Thackeray and Ralph Marcus, are available in volumes 1-5 and 7 of the "Loeb Classical Library" (Cambridge, Mass., 1950-1961). *The Apocrypha and Pseudepigrapha of the Old Testament,* 2 vols., edited by R. H. Charles (Oxford, 1913), includes such works as *Ben Sira. Aristeas to Philocrates, or the Letter of Aristeas* has been edited and translated by Moses Hadas (New York, 1951).

The discoveries at Arad, a Negev site principally excavated by the late Yohanan Aharoni, have been carefully summarized in the article by Ze'ev Herzog and others, "The Israelite Fortress at Arad," *Bulletin of the American Schools of Oriental Research* 254 (Spring 1984): 1-34. The inscriptions, originally published with a Hebrew commentary by Aharoni, have been translated by Judith Ben-Or and edited and revised by Anson F. Rainey as *Arad Inscriptions* (Jerusalem, 1981). These inscriptions and the information received from the excavations shed light on the functioning of Levitical priests at such royal outposts as Arad in the late preexilic period.

BARUCH A. LEVINE

LITURGY

Definition. It seems appropriate to use the term *liturgy* to designate any system or set of rituals that is prescribed for public or corporate performance. Thus for phenomenological or comparative purposes we may emphasize both the corporate character of liturgy and its articulation as a set of ritual performances.

Corporate character. Emphasis on the corporate character of liturgy serves to distinguish liturgical rituals from other types: those employed only by and for individuals (as in many forms of magic), the esoteric rituals of cult societies, and the household rituals so important in China and India.

In practice there are a number of transitional examples that may also serve to clarify the specificity of liturgical actions. The Christian Eucharist, for example, has historically been performed not only corporately and publicly but also privately or in solitude. Only in the former case is the sacrament liturgical in the sense here employed. The esoteric rituals of the Antelope and Snake cult societies of the Hopi of the southwestern United States serve also as preparation for the public performance of their dances, which are therefore liturgical in character. In China the household ancestral cult terminates in a public and corporate (i. e., liturgical) performance in celebration of a new year.

> *Liturgy should be understood as referring primarily to the set of corporate rituals that form a coherent structure.*

Systematic character. A striking feature of liturgical rituals is their deployment in a cycle of such rituals, a cycle characterized by both variety and integration. The system may comprise both calendrical rituals governed by solar or lunar cycles and rituals that are occasioned by specific crises or turning points in the life of the community.

Since the cycle of liturgical rituals has a systematic character, the individual rituals that compose the system may be appropriately studied in relation to other component rituals of the cycle as a whole. *Liturgy* should be understood as referring primarily to the set of corporate rituals that form a coherent structure.

Victor Turner has cited a number of illustrations from Africa in which the ritual systems of autochthonous peoples have been assimilated into the ritual structure of conquering groups to produce a new structure. The most familiar illustration, however, is the development of the early Christian liturgical calendar, which was produced through the appropriation of Jewish and Hellenistic ritual practices.

Functions. While a number of different and conflicting theories have been developed to identify the function of ritual in general and of the liturgical system of corporate rituals in particular, it does seem possible to isolate at least four functions:

Temporalization. The tendency for liturgy to acquire an elaborate articulation distributed through time indicates that one of its principal functions or effects is the ordering or structuring of time. While most religious traditions organize their liturgical calendar on an annual cycle, a cycle especially appropriate for agrarian societies, additional forms of periodization, including lunar and diurnal, are used. In some religious traditions this temporalization extends to include, for example, three-year cycles (as in the Christian lectionary). Judaism, at least in theory, calls for a fifty-year cycle (*Lv.* 25). A principal effect of liturgy, then, is to structure time, thereby making it available for conscious experience and intellectual comprehension.

Socialization. In addition to the tendency of liturgy to be distributed through and so regularize temporality, it also has, as we have seen, a decisively corporate character. To be Ndebele or Aztec or Christian or Vaisnava is to participate in the designated corporate actions that both reflect and engender this corporate identity. Indeed, the possibility of experiencing the group or community as such appears to be dependent on participation in its significant corporate action as elaborated through liturgy.

Coordination. A particularly striking feature of liturgical rituals is their tendency to coordinate a variety of dimensions of experience. In the *Rgveda* 10.90 (*Purusasukta*) the fire sacrifice is exhibited as a coordination of phenomena that are bodily (ears, eyes, thighs, feet, etc.), social (the various castes), cosmic (earth, atmosphere, heaven), and natural (spring, summer, fall, equated with butter, firewood, oblation). In the Christian Eucharist, elements of human interaction with nature (bread and wine) and domesticity (eating and drinking) are woven together with the individualized themes of guilt and forgiveness and the historico-apocalyptic themes of the death of Jesus and his expected return.

Liturgical paradigms. The coordination and concentration of disparate regions of experience enables liturgical action to serve as a set of paradigms for actions that occur outside the sphere of liturgy itself and even outside the immediate sphere of religion. The formal and solemn Vedic fire sacrifice serves as a pattern for the less formal domestic, or hearth, rites of the householder. In combination these rites serve to shape the decorum that is appropriate for all acts of welcome and hospitality, acts that also exhibit and reinforce the structuring of society along the lines of caste.

BIBLIOGRAPHY

Helpful information with respect to the history of the term *liturgy* may be found in the appropriate articles of the *Theological Dictionary of the New Testament,* edited by Gerhard Kittel and translated by Geoffrey W. Bromiley (Grand Rapids, Mich., 1964-), and the *Encyclopedia of Theology,* edited by Karl Rahner (New York, 1975).

Standard discussions of liturgy within the Christian context may be found in Dom Gregory Dix's *The Shape of the Liturgy,* 2d ed. (New York, 1982) and Alexander Schmemann's *Introduction to Liturgical Theology,* translated by Asheleigh E. Moorhouse (London, 1966). Discussions of ritual, with particular bearing on the understanding of liturgy, include Mary Douglas's *Natural Symbols* (New York, 1970), Ronald L. Grimes's *Beginnings in Ritual Studies* (Washington, D. C., 1982), Roy A. Rappaport's *Ecology, Meaning and Religion* (Berkeley, 1979), and Victor Turner's *The Ritual Process* (1969; reprint, Ithaca, N. Y., 1977). The collection of materials in *Reader in Comparative Religion,* 4th ed., edited by William A. Lessa and Evon Z. Vogt (New York, 1979), is also helpful. Information on rituals in Hinduism can be found in Thomas J. Hopkins's *The Hindu Religious Tradition* (Encino, Calif., 1971), and Ake Hultkrantz's *Religions of the American Indians,* translated by Monica Setterwall (Los Angeles, 1979), contains useful information on the religious practices of the indigenous peoples of North and South America.

THEODORE W. JENNINGS, JR.

LORD'S PRAYER

When his disciples asked Jesus to teach them to pray, *Luke* 11:2-4 records the Master's reply in words similar to the teaching in the Sermon on the Mount at *Matthew* 6:9-13. In a slightly simplified tabulation, the two versions of the text may be compared as follows, with the Matthean surplus and variations in brackets and two particularly difficult expressions in parentheses:

[Our] Father [who art in heaven],
Hallowed be thy name,
Thy kingdom come,
[Thy will be done,
On earth as it is in heaven].
Give us [this day] our (daily) bread,
And forgive us our sins [Mt.: debts],
For [Mt.: As] we [have] forgive[n] our debtor[s],
And lead us not into (temptation)
[But deliver us from evil].

Use in Christian Worship. The church has taken the Lord's Prayer as indicating both the spirit of Christian prayer and a formula to be employed in worship. The Matthean form is at almost all points the more usual in the liturgy. Liturgical use is the probable source of the concluding doxology, "For thine is the kingdom, the power, and the glory for ever," which is found—though not yet with the addition of the word *kingdom*—in a text that is as early as the first- or second-century church manual the *Didache* (8.2). The Lord's Prayer has been used, formally and informally, in daily worship as well as in the eucharistic liturgy. In the latter case, its place has usually been between the great prayer of thanksgiving and the Communion, whither it was doubtlessly attracted by the bread to be consumed.

Classical Commentaries. The early Fathers taught the prayer's meaning to their catechumens, and it has remained a favorite subject of exposition by spiritual writers. Tertullian and, in his wake, Cyprian both wrote pastoral tracts entitled *On (the Lord's) prayer.* Origen dealt with it in his theological treatise *On Prayer* (chaps. 18-30). Cyril of Jerusalem expounded it to the newly baptized in his *Mystagogical Catechesis* 5.11-18, while Augustine of Hippo preached sermons 56-59 on it to the *competentes* (candidates for baptism) and also treated it as part of his commentary *The Sermon on the Mount* (2.4.15-2.11.39) and elsewhere. John Chrysostom devoted to the Lord's Prayer his *Nineteenth Homily on the Gospel of Matthew.* Gregory of Nyssa discoursed on it in his five *Sermons on the Lord's Prayer.* Conferences on it are ascribed to Thomas Aquinas. Luther explained the prayer in his Large and Small Catechisms and in other writings, such as *A Simple Way to Pray,* written in 1535 for his barber. Calvin presented it in the first edition of his *Institutes of the Christian Religion* (1536; cf. 3.20.34-49 in

> ### The best contemporary exegesis of the Lord's Prayer is that of Raymond E. Brown, who interprets it as an eschatological prayer.

the final edition of 1559) and commented on it in his *Harmony of the Gospels* (1555). Teresa of Ávi-la used the Lord's Prayer to instruct her religious communities in *The Way of Perfection* (chaps. 27-42). John Wesley devoted to the prayer one of his Standard Sermons (numbered variously 21 or 26) and versified it in the hymn "Father of All, Whose Powerful Voice." Karl Barth treated it in his 1947-1949 seminar notes entitled *Prayer* and developed the address and the first two petitions in the unfinished part 4.4 of his *Church Dogmatics.* Simone Weil's thoughts on the subject are contained in her *Waiting on God.*

A Contemporary Exegesis. The best contemporary exegesis of the Lord's Prayer is that of Raymond E. Brown, who interprets it as an eschatological prayer. Jesus announced the coming of the kingdom of God. His followers prayed for the definite establishment of God's eternal rule and intimated their own desire to be part of it. They requested a place at the messianic banquet and asked for forgiveness in the divine judgment as well as for deliverance from the mighty struggle with Satan that still stood between the community and the final realization of its prayer. As hopes for the imminent advent of the final kingdom faded, interpreters adapted the prayer to continuing life in the present age with the assurance that God's kingdom had at least begun its entry into the world through the life, death, and resurrection of Jesus.

Recurrent Themes of Analysis. The Lord's Prayer opens with a bold filial salutation. To address almighty God as "Abba, Father" (*Rom.* 8:14, *Gal.* 4:6) is to share by grace a privilege that Jesus enjoyed by nature (*Mk.* 14:36, cf. *Mt.* 11:25-27). Liturgically, believers do in fact proclaim that they "make bold to say" (*audemus dicere*) this prayer. The heavenly Father is near. Moreover, to address the Father as "*our* Father" is to acknowledge that the Christian faith is a communal matter with brothers and sisters who are, at least potentially, as numerous as the human race. After this opening address six petitions follow, which typically attract the kind of comments next summarized.

1. Hallowed be thy name. God is by definition holy, and strictly speaking, only God can hallow the divine name: he does so in history by vindicating his holiness (*Ez.* 36:22-27, *Jn.* 12:28). But humans join in by not despising the Lord's name (*Ex.* 20:7 and, identically, *Dt.* 5:11), by praising the name of the Lord (*1 Chr.* 29:13 and often in *Psalms*), by calling on the name of the Lord for salvation (*Jl.* 2:32, *Acts* 2:21, *Rom.* 10:13), and by living in accord with the name put upon them in baptism (Augustine, sermon 59; cf. *1 Cor.* 6:11).

2. Thy kingdom come. Instead of "Thy kingdom come" a minor variant reads "May thy Holy Spirit come upon us and purify us." Here outcrops the common view that God's rule may at least begin in the present in human lives. Yet the primary agency in establishing the kingdom remains God's.

3. Thy will be done. In the garden of Gethsemane, Jesus accepted the Father's will (*Mk.* 14:36, *Mt.* 26:39, 26:42; cf. *Jn.* 6:38, *Heb.* 10:7-10). Thereby God's eternal will for salvation was implemented (*Eph.* 1:5, 1:9, 1:11). Humans benefit through faithful and obebient participation. The scope of God's plan is no less than heaven and earth.

4. Give us this day our daily bread. The adjective qualifying bread (Gr., *epiousios*) is otherwise practically unknown. Suggested possibilities for its meaning include: food "suited to our spiritual nature" (Origen); the bread "we need" for our "everyday" lives (Syriac and Old Latin traditions—cf. *Mt.* 6:34); an "excellent" bread surpassing all substances (the Vulgate's *supersubstantialis*). The original eschatological tone of the prayer favors the reading "tomorrow's bread," as in some Egyptian versions and in Jerome's report on the "Gospel of the Hebrews" wherein he employs the Latin word *crastinus* ("for tomorrow"); it is an urgent prayer for the feast of the age to come. Whatever their interpretation of *epiousios,* commentators regularly emphasize the graciousness of the divine provision and the human obligation to share the blessings of God, and most of them make a link with the eucharistic Communion.

5. Forgive us our sins. The parable of the unforgiving servant in *Matthew* 18:23-35 suggests that the final execution of God's will to forgive sinners depends on the sinner's readiness to forgive others (cf. *Mt.* 6:14f., *Lk.* 6:37). While humans cannot compel God's gracious forgiveness, they can be prevented from receiving it by their own unforgiving spirit.

6. Lead us not into temptation. Commentators have stressed the indirect character of God's testing of humans (*Jas.* 1:12-14) and insisted that God "will not let you be tempted beyond your strength" (*1 Cor.* 10:13). Some modern liturgical translations have restored the strictly eschatological character of the petition: "Save us from the time of trial" (cf. *Rv.* 3:10). In the present, the devil still "prowls around like a roaring lion, seeking whom he may devour" (*1 Pt.* 5:8; cf. *Eph.* 6:11-13, 1 *Jn.* 5:19), but his defeat has already been assured by Christ, and the deliverance of believers is certain (*2 Thes.* 3:3, *Jn.* 17:15).

BIBLIOGRAPHY

Studies on the Jewish background to the Lord's Prayer can be found in Jean Carmignac's *Recherches sur le "Notre Père"* (Paris, 1969) and in *The Lord's Prayer and Jewish Liturgy,* edited by Jakob J. Petuchkowski and Michael Brocke (New York, 1978). Raymond E. Brown's "The *Pater Noster* as an Eschatological Prayer" is contained in his *New Testament Essays,* 3d ed. (New York, 1982), while other contemporary exegesis includes Ernst Lohmeyer's *The Lord's Prayer* (New York, 1965), Joachim Jeremias's *The Prayers of Jesus* (London, 1967), and Heinz Schürmann's *Das Gebet des Herrn,* 4th ed. (Leipzig, 1981). The tightly packed lectures of Thomas Aquinas are accessible in a translation by Lawrence Shapcote under the title *The Three Greatest Prayers: Commentaries on the Our Father, the Hail Mary and the Apostles' Creed* by St. Thomas Aquinas (London, 1956). Modern devotional works include William Barclay's *The Plain Man Looks at the Lord's Prayer* (London, 1964), Gerhad Ebeling's *On Prayer: Nine Sermons* (Philadelphia, 1966), and Romano Guardini's *The Lord's Prayer* (New York, 1958).

GEOFFREY WAINWRIGHT

LUGBARA RELIGION

The Lugbara are a Sudanic-speaking people of northwestern Uganda and northeastern Zaire, culturally related to the Azande and Mangbetu to the northwest. Numbering about a quarter of a million, the Lugbara are largely peasant farmers who grow grains and keep some cattle and other livestock.

Myth. The Lugbara have a corpus of myth that tells of the creation of the world and the formation of their society. The myth explains the existence of social groups and settlements, of marriage and the legitimacy of offspring, and of feuds (the traditional basis for the maintenance of social order). Myths explain the form of society, its relationship with the Deity, and the distinction that runs through Lugbara cosmology between the "inside" of home and settlement and the "outside" of the bushland, where spirits and other manifestations of the extrahuman power of the Deity dwell. Lugbara ritual is concerned essentially with the maintenance of the boundary between these two moral spheres.

Sacrifice to the Dead and Spirits. Sacrifice is not made to the Deity. The central cult is that of the dead, who are considered senior members of their lineages and who bridge the main cosmological boundary. Only the heads of lineage segments who leave sons are usually made into ghosts; others join a collectivity of ancestors. The spirit goes to the bushland, where it dwells with the immanent and evil aspect of the Deity (Adro); the *tali* merges with a collectivity of *tali*.

Death is marked by elaborate mortuary rites, which are the only important rites of transition. The corpse is buried and dances are held at which men of lineages related to the deceased dance competitively and aggressively to demonstrate their relative seniority within the total lineage structure.

Ghosts are given individual shrines (in the shape of miniature huts) where they may be offered sacrifices; other patrilineal ancestors have collective shrines; and there are shrines for matrilateral ancestors.

Offerings are also made to many kinds of spirits (*adro*). Spirits are held to be innumerable. At one time or another, some are attached to prophets; others represent expressions of divine power (e.g., lightning, winds). All have as a central attribute the ability to possess a living person and to make the victim tremble or shake, a condition curable only by a diviner.

Divination. The need for the living to know the identity of the dead and the spirits with whom they come into contact requires divination. There are several kinds of oracles and diviners. Their power is thought to come directly from the Deity and is feared as being spiritual and dangerous.

Evil. Evil is represented as the work of harmful human beings assumed to be witches and sorcerers. Using the classic distinction made for the Azande by Evans-Pritchard, witches are believed to harm others by an innate mystical power; among the Lugbara they are older men who bewitch their own kin because of envy or anger. Whereas witchcraft is traditional and, although evil, not particularly morally reprehensible (since the witch merely has the innate power and may not always be able to control it), sorcery is seen as a modern phenomenon and an abomination because it is deliberate and malign in its purpose.

Rainmakers and Prophets. Each subclan has one rainmaker, the senior man of the senior descent line. He is believed to be able to control the rainfall by manipulating rain stones kept in a pot buried in his rain grove. He tells his community the times for planting and harvesting. And he is thought to be able to end epidemics and famines by beseeching the Deity.

Prophets have appeared among the Lugbara on rare occasions, as emissaries of the Deity with a message to reform society in the face of disasters.

BIBLIOGRAPHY

The main source is my *Lugbara Religion: Religion and Authority among an East African People* (London, 1960). I have also given a shorter account in *The Lugbara of Uganda* (New York, 1965).

JOHN MIDDLETON

LUTHER, MARTIN

LUTHER, MARTIN (1483-1546), German theologian and reformer of the Christian church. Luther was born in Eisleben on 10 November. After initial schooling, he matriculated at the University of Erfurt to pursue the customary study of the seven liberal arts. Upon receiving the master's degree in 1505 Luther began the study of law. Less than two months later, however, the experience of a terrifying thunderstorm near Stotterheim prompted his vow to Saint Anne to become a monk. Two years later, on 27 February 1507, Luther was ordained to the priesthood. Completing his doctorate in theology at Wttenberg in October 1512, he assumed the *lectura in Biblia,* the professorship in Bible endowed by the Augustinian order.

In 1515 he became preacher at the parish church in Wittenberg and was appointed district vicar of his order. The latter position entailed the administrative oversight of the Augustinian monasteries in Saxony.

In his later years Luther spoke of having had a profound spiritual experience or insight (dubbed by scholars his "evangelical discovery"), and intensive scholarly preoccupation has sought to identify its exact date and nature. Two basic views regarding the time have emerged. One dates the experience, which Luther himself related to the proper understanding of the concept of the "righteousness of God" (*Rom.* 1:17), as having occurred about 1514, the other in about 1518. The matter remains inconclusive, partly because nowhere do Luther's writings of the time echo the dramatic notions that the reformer in later years associated with his experience. The import of the issue lies both in the precise understanding of what it was that alienated Luther from the Catholic church, and in understanding the theological frame of mind with which Luther entered the indulgences controversy of 1517.

The Ninety-five Theses of 31 October 1517 (the traditional notion that Luther nailed them to the door of the Wittenberg castle church has recently been questioned) catapulted Luther into the limelight. These theses pertained to the ecclesiastical practice of indulgences that had not as yet been dogmatically defined by the church. Luther's exploration of the practice was therefore a probing inquiry.

Almost immediately after the appearance of the Ninety-five Theses, a controversy ensued. Undoubtedly it was fanned by the fact that Luther had focused not merely on a theological topic but had also cited a number of the popular grievances against Rome, thus touching upon a political issue. In addition to sending copies of the theses to several friends, Luther sent a copy to Archbishop Albert of Hohenzollern, whom he held responsible for a vulgar sale of indulgences in the vicinity of Wittenberg, together with a fervent plea to stop the sale. The ensuing debate therefore became a public one, eventually allowing for the formation of a popular movement.

In April 1518 Luther presented a summary of his theological thought, which he called the "theology of the cross," at a meeting of the Augustinian order in Heidelberg. In presenting a caricature of scholastic theology, Luther appropriately emphasized its one-sidedness. Soon afterward he was ordered to appear in Rome in conjunction with the proceedings against him, but the intervention of his territorial ruler, Elector Frederick, caused the interrogation to take place in Augsburg, Germany. With Cardinal Legate Cajetan representing the Curia, the meeting proved unsuccessful, since Luther refused to recant. Luther fled from Augsburg and, upon his return to Wittenberg, he was inadvertently drawn into a disputation held in Leipzig in July 1519. Luther's oppo-

> His own theological formation was essentially complete by 1521; his theological work thereafter consisted in amplification and clarification.

nent, Johann Eck, professor of theology at Ingolstadt, was intent on branding him a heretic.

After the election of Charles V as the new emperor, which had preoccupied the Curia for some time, official proceedings against Luther were resumed.

Luther soon after disappeared from the public scene. A period of self-doubt, it was also an exceedingly creative time, part of which he spent in translating the New Testament from Greek into German. He returned to Wittenberg in March 1522 to calm the restlessness that had surfaced there over the nature of the reform movement. In a series of sermons he enunciated a conservative notion of ecclesiastical reform, and his stance left its imprint on the subsequent course of the Reformation.

His own theological formation was essentially complete by 1521; his theological work thereafter consisted in amplification and clarification.

The year 1525 proved to be a major theological and personal watershed for Luther: he became embroiled in two major controversies—with Erasmus and Thomas Müntzer—that resulted in a marked division in the reform movement. On 13 June of that same year he married Katharina von Bora, a former nun who had left her convent the previous year. Even though the marriage—coming as it did on the heels of the German Peasants' War—was a subject of notoriety among Luther's enemies, it set the tone for a Protestant definition of Christian marriage.

As a political outlaw, he stayed at Coburg (as far south as he was able to travel on Saxon territory), and his close associate Philipp Melanchthon functioned as spokesman for the Lutherans. Several of Luther's most insightful publications appeared during that summer—a tract on translating, an exposition of Psalm 118, and *Exhortation That Children Should Be Sent to School.*

Luther's final years were overshadowed by his growing antagonism toward the papal church. He died on 16 February, 1546.

Not surprisingly, Martin Luther has received considerable scholarly and theological attention throughout the centuries. Assessments of Luther have always been staunchly partisan, with a clear demarcation between Protestant and Catholic evaluations. A key theme in Luther's theology is that of the sole authority of scripture, formulated as the notion of *sola scriptura;* this notion, because it implied the possibility of a divergence of tradition from scripture, raised a startling new question. Late medieval theology had formulated the issue of authority in terms of the possible divergency of pope and council. A related theme in Luther's theology was the relationship of law and gospel, which provided the key to the understanding of scripture. God reveals himself as both a demanding and a giving God, two qualities that Luther loosely assigned to the Old and New Testaments respectively; but in truth, so Luther asserted, grace is found in the Old Testament even as law is found in the New.

The notion of justification by faith is traditionally cited as the heart of Luther's thought. It is, in fact, his major legacy to the Protestant tradition. In contradistinction to the medieval notion of a cooperative effort between man and God, between works and grace, Luther only stressed grace and God. Such grace is appropriated by faith, which affirms the reality of the grace of forgiveness, despite the reality of sin. Luther's "theology of the cross" affirmed that God always works contrary to experience.

[*See also* Reformation.]

BIBLIOGRAPHY

The definitive Weimar edition of Luther's works, *D. Martin Luthers Werke: Kritische Gesammtausgabe,* edited by J. K. F. Knaake and others (Weimar, 1883-1974), in more than a hundred volumes, continues to be the basic tool for Luther research. An exhaustive sampling of Luther in English can be found in his *Works,* 55 vols., edited by Jaroslav Pelikan (Saint Louis, 1955-1976). The *Luther-Jahrbuch* (Munich, 1919-) publishes an annual bibliography, as does, less comprehensively, the *Archiv für Reformationsgeschichte* (Leipzig and Berlin, 1903-). A useful general introduction to facets and problems of Luther scholarship is found in Bernhard Lohse's *Martin Luther: Eine Einführung* (Munich, 1981). Of the numerous Luther biographies, the following deserve to be mentioned: Roland H. Bainton, *Here I Stand* (Nashville, 1955); Heinrich Bornkamm, *Martin Luther in der Mitte seines Lebens* (Göttingen, 1979); H. G. Haile, *Luther* (Garden City, N. Y., 1980); and Eric H. Erikson, *Young Man Luther* (New York, 1958), a controversial psychoanalytic study. Two useful collections of sources are *Martin Luther,* edited by E. G. Rupp and Benjamin Drewery (New York, 1970), and Walther von

Löwenich's *Martin Luther: The Man and His Work* (Minneapolis, 1983).

Important studies on specific aspects of Luther's life and thought are Erwin Iserloh's *The Theses Were Not Posted* (Boston, 1968); Wilhelm Borth's *Die Luthersache (causa Lutheri) 1517-1524* (Lübeck, 1970); and Mark U. Edwards, Jr.'s *Luther and the False Brethren* (Stanford, Calif., 1975) and *Luther's Last Battles* (Ithaca, N. Y., 1983). A creative statement of Luther's theology is Gerhard Ebeling's *Luther* (Philadelphia, 1970).

HANS J. HILLERBRAND

LUTHERANISM

Teaching and Worship. Luther's doctrine of "justification through grace by faith alone, apart from works of law," echoing Paul in his letter to the Romans (3:28), forms the core of Lutheranism. A person is right with God (i. e., "justified") by completely trusting the work of Christ (i. e., "by faith") and not by making any human effort to appease God (i. e., "apart

> **Luther changed little in the liturgy of the Roman Mass, removing only what he called the "sacrifice of the Mass."**

from works of law"). Christ's atonement is communicated both verbally, in preaching and teaching, and visibly, in the celebration of the sacraments. Thus to Luther the doctrine of justification was not one among many doctrines, as medieval theology taught, but was the "chief article of faith" that establishes the norm for Christian faith and life.

In worship, Lutherans have tried to be faithful to the ecumenical tradition of the Mass by regarding its center, the sacrament of Holy Communion, as the means of grace that strengthens and sustains Christians in a world of sin, death, and evil. Luther changed little in the liturgy of the Roman Mass, removing only what he called the "sacrifice of the Mass," namely, the prayers of thanksgiving that surround the act of consecrating bread and wine.

Lutherans recognize only two sacraments, baptism and the Lord's Supper, because Luther could find no clear evidence that Christ instituted any other sacraments.

The core of Luther's reform movement was the proposal that the church return to the Christocentric stance that he had found in scripture and in the early church fathers.

History. The doctrine of baptism proved to be the most revolutionary aspect of Lutheranism, since it allowed Luther to invite territorial princes to become "emergency bishops" of the new churches. Thus German princes interested in liberating themselves from the domination of Rome established Lutheranism in their own territories and encouraged it to spread. Princes, peasants, patricians, priests, and even bishops joined the Lutheran cause, mainly to break from Rome. Danish and Swedish kings declared Lutheranism the religion of their lands.

The Formula of Concord used medieval scholastic terminology and Aristotelian philosophical categories to provide a theological system to protect Lutheranism from both Catholic and Calvinist influences. The result was a systematic, rational interpretation of the doctrines of sin, law, and grace, the cornerstones of a Lutheran theology grounded in the forensic notion that God declared humankind righteous by faith in Christ. The Formula rejected both the Catholic notion of cooperation between human nature and divine grace through free will and Calvin's doctrine of Christ's spiritual (not real or bodily) presence in the Lord's Supper.

Between 1580 and 1680, German Lutherans favored a uniform religion that fused pure doctrine with Christian laws. The resulting alliance between church and state created seventeenth-century Lutheran orthodoxy. Assisted by orthodox theologians, territorial princes dictated what people should believe and how they should behave, and obedience to political authority became the core of Christian ethics. But Lutheran orthodoxy gave rise to a new reform movement, nicknamed "pietist," which stressed a "religion of the heart" rather than the prevalent "religion of the head." Lutheran Pietism emphasized individual conversion, lay ministry, and a morality distinct from worldly ethics. By the nineteenth century, the pietist impulse had created an "inner mission" movement in Germany that established a female diaconate, built hospitals and orphanages, instituted educational programs, cared for the mentally retarded, and advocated prison reform.

In the United States, Henry Melchior Mühlenberg (1711-1787), who had come from Halle to Philadelphia, organized the first American Lutheran synod in Pennsylvania in 1748. Lutheran theological seminaries, colleges, and journals were soon founded in regions where Lutherans predominated. During the Civil War, the United Lutheran Synod of the South was formed. But it was not until after World War I that Lutherans in the United States managed to form larger denominations through mergers.

After World War II, some 184 delegates representing about 80 million Lutherans from 49 churches in 22 countries organized the Lutheran World Federation in 1947. Headquartered in Geneva (which is also the headquarters of the World Council of Churches) the Lutheran World Federation unites Lutheran churches from around the world in common social-action projects and in regular world assemblies but otherwise has no authority over the churches.

BIBLIOGRAPHY

The most comprehensive treatment of Lutheranism, albeit from an American perspective, is offered in E. Clifford Nelson's *The Rise of World Lutheranism: An American Perspective* (Philadelphia, 1982). The same author also has written a readable history, *Lutheranism in North America, 1914-1970* (Minneapolis, 1972). In addition, there is a useful historical survey, stressing European and American Lutheranism, by Conrad Bergendoff, *The Church of the Lutheran Reformation* (Saint Louis, 1967). Normative Lutheran teachings, "the Lutheran confessions," are made available in translation in *The Book of Concord,* edited and translated by Theodore G. Tappert (Philadelphia, 1959). The historical roots and theological significance of the Lutheran confessions are described and analyzed by me and Robert W. Jenson in *Lutheranism: The Theological Movement and Its Confessional Writings* (Philadelphia, 1976). The distinctive features of Lutheranism, especially compared with other traditions in the United States, are sketched in Arthur C. Piepkorn's "Lutheran Churches," in volume 2 of *Profiles of Belief* (San Francisco, 1978). The theological center of Lutheranism has been explored, with an eye on ecumenical implications, in Wilhelm Dantine's *The Justification of the Ungodly,* translated by me and Ruth C. Gritsch (Saint Louis, 1968), and in Gerhard O. Forde's *Justification by Faith: A Matter of Death and Life* (Philadelphia, 1982). Detailed information on Lutheran worship is contained in Luther D. Reed's *The Lutheran Liturgy* (Philadelphia, 1947). Basic information on Lutheranism can be quickly obtained in *The Encyclopedia of the Lutheran Church,* 3 vols., edited by Julius Bodensieck (Minneapolis, 1965).

ERIC W. GRITSCH

MAGI

The Old Persian word *magu,* rendered in Greek by *magos,* is of uncertain etymology. It may originally have meant "member of the tribe," as in the Avestan compound *mogu-tbish* ("hostile to a member of the tribe"). This meaning would have been further restricted, among the Medes, to "member of the priestly tribe" and perhaps to "priest" (Benveniste, 1938; Boyce, 1982). The term is probably of Median origin, given that Herodotus mentions the "Magoi" as one of the six tribes of the Medes.

For a variety of reasons we can consider the Magi to have been members of a priestly tribe of Median origin in western Iran. Among the Persians, they were responsible for liturgical functions, as well as for maintaining their knowledge of the holy and of the occult. Most likely, the supremacy of the Median priesthood in western Iran became established during the time of the Median monarchy that dominated the Persians from the end of the eighth century through the first half of the sixth century BCE until the revolt of Cyrus the Great (550 BCE). The Persians were indebted to the Medes for their political and civil institutions as well. Even if hypotheses have been advanced concerning the existence of Magi of Persian origin in the Achaemenid period (Boyce, 1982), we must still maintain that they were of Median origin. This is demonstrated by the episode of the revolt of Gaumata the Magian, mentioned by Darius I (522-486 BCE) in the inscription at Bisutun (Iran), as well as by Greek sources. Indeed, Herodotus insists on the idea of the usurpatory power of the Medes against the Persians through the conspiracy of the Magi.

The fact that the Magi may have been members of a tribe that handed down the sacerdotal arts in a hereditary fashion naturally did not exclude the possibility that some of them undertook secular professions. This seems to be attested by the Elamite tablets at Persepolis.

There is a thesis, put forth by Giuseppe Messina, that denies that the Magi are members of an ethnic group by suggesting that they are simply members of the priesthood—a priesthood of purely Zoroastrian origin. This thesis is untenable; on the other hand, the hypothesis that their name is related to the Avestan term *magavan,* derived from the Gathic *maga* (Vedic, *magha,* "gift"), is not without foundation (Molé, 1963). The meaning of *maga* can probably be found, in conformity with the Pahlavi tradition, within the context of the concept of purity, or separation of the "mixture" of the two opposed principles of spirit and matter. The *maga,* which has been erroneously interpreted as "chorus," from the root *mangh,* which is said to mean "sing the magic song" (Nyberg, 1966) and has been rendered simply by an expression like *unio mystica,* seems to be an ecstatic condition that opens the mind to spiritual vision. In any case, though there may be a relation between the Old Persian term *magu* and the Avestan terms *magavan* and maga, we must maintain a clear distinction between the Magi and the Avestan priesthood. The Avesta ignores the Median or Old Persian term, despite a recent hypothesis proposed by H. W. Bailey; Old Persian inscriptions ignore the Avestan term for "priest," *athravan*

> **The Magi were the technicians of and experts on worship: it was impossible to offer sacrifices without the presence of a Magus.**

(Vedic, *átharvan*), even if this is perhaps present in an Achaemenid setting in the Elamite tablets of Persepolis (Gershevitch, 1964).

The term *magu* has been present in Zoroastrianism throughout its history; the Pahlavi terms *mogh-mard* and *mobad* represent its continuation. The latter in particular derives from an older form, *magupati* ("head of the Magi"). During the Sasanid period (third to seventh centuries CE), which saw the formation of a hierarchically organized church, the title *mobadan mobad* ("the high priest of high priests") came to be used to designate the summit of the ecclesiastical hierarchy.

The Magi practiced consanguineous marriage, or *khvaetvadatha* (Av.; Pahl., *khwedodah*). They also performed a characteristic funeral rite: the exposure of the corpse to animals and vultures to remove the flesh and thereby cleanse it. The corpse was not supposed to decompose, lest it be contaminated by the demons of putrefaction. This practice later became typical of the entire Zoroastrian community and led to the rise of a complex funeral ritual in Iran and among the Parsis in India. Stone towers, known as *dakhmas,* were built especially for this rite. During the time of Herodotus the practice of exposure of the corpse was in vogue only among the Magi; the Persians generally sprinkled the corpse with wax, then buried it. The practice was widespread, however, among the peoples of Central Asia.

The Magi were the technicians of and experts on worship: it was impossible to offer sacrifices without the presence of a Magus. During the performance of a ritual sacrifice, the Magus sang of the theogony (the Magi were possibly the custodians of a tradition of sacred poetry, but we know nothing about the relationship of this tradition to the various parts of the Avesta) and was called upon to interpret dreams and to divine the future. The Magi were also known for the practice of killing harmful, or "Ahrimanical," animals (khrafstra) such as snakes and ants. They dressed in the Median style, wearing pants, tunics, and coats with sleeves. They wore a characteristic head covering of felt (Gr., tiara) with strips on the sides that could be used to cover the nose and mouth during rituals to avoid contaminating consecrated objects with their breath (Boyce, 1982). The color of these caps, in conformity with a tradition that is probably of Indo-European origin, according to Georges Dumézil, was that of the priesthood: white.

In all likelihood, during the Achaemenid period the Magi were not in possession of a well-defined body of doctrine, and it is probable that they gradually adopted Zoroastrianism; they were most likely a clergy consisting of professional priests who were not tied to a rigid orthodoxy but were naturally inclined to eclecticism and syncretism. Nonetheless, they must have been jealous guardians of the patrimony of Zorastrian traditions. By virtue of this they were the educators of the royal princes. The wisest of them was responsible for teaching the prince the "magic of Zarathushtra, son of Horomazes" and thus the "cult of the gods." Magi who excelled in other virtues were entrusted with the education of the prince so that he would learn to be just, courageous, and master of himself.

During the Achaemenid period the Magi maintained a position of great influence, although they were certainly subordinate to the emperor. Despite several dramatic events such as the massacre they suffered after the death of Gaumata the Magian—in which, according to Herodotus (who calls him Smerdis), the Persians killed a large number of Magi to avenge the usurpation—the Magi nevertheless managed to maintain their influence at court in Media, in Persia, and in the various regions of the empire where they were stationed as a consequence of the Persian civilian and military administration.

No priesthood of antiquity was more famous than that of the Magi. They were renowned as followers of Zarathushtra (Zoroaster); as the teachers of some of the greatest Greek thinkers (Pythagoras, Democritus, Plato); as the wise men who arrived, guided by a star, at the manger of the newborn savior in Bethlehem; and as the propagators of a cult of the sun in India. But they were also known as the Chaldeans, the priesthood of Babylon, known for its occultism; this was perhaps the reason that the term magos had a pejorative sense in Greek, like goes, "expert in the magic arts" (Bidez and Cumont, 1938). Indeed, the Chaldeans were experts in all types of magical arts, especially astrology, and had a reputation for wisdom as well as knowledge.

To understand the reasons for such various and sometimes discordant views, it is necessary to distinguish between the Magi of Iran proper and the so-called western Magi, who were later hellenized. In the Achaemenid period both must have been at least in part Zoroastrian, but the western Magi (those of the Iranian diaspora in Asia Minor, Syria, Mesopotamia, and Armenia), who came in contact with diverse religious traditions, must have, sooner or later and in varying degrees, been influenced by syncretic concepts.

The Greeks were familiar with both kinds of Magi and, depending on their varying concerns, would emphasize one or the other aspect of them. Classical historians and geographers, including Herodotus and Strabo, document their customs, while the philosophers dwell above all on their doctrines: dualism, belief in the hereafter, Magian cosmology and cosmogony, and their theology and eschatology. Those sources most interested in the doctrines of the Magi even speak of Zarathushtra as a Magus. In doing so they are repeating what the Magi themselves said from the Median and Achaemenid periods, when they adopted Zoroastrianism. At that time they embraced Zarathushtra as one of their own and placed themselves under his venerable name.

Zoroastrianism had already undergone several profound transformations in the eastern community by the time of the Achaemenids and was already adapting those elements of the archaic religion that refused to die. It has been said quite often, in an attempt to characterize the precise role of the Magi in the Zoroastrian tradition, that the Vendidad (from vidaevo-data, "the law-abjuring daivas"), part of the Avesta, should be attributed to them. (This collection of texts from various periods is primarily concerned with purificatory rules and practices.) Nonetheless, the hypothesis is hardly plausible, since the first chapter of the Vendidad—a list of sixteen lands created by Ahura Mazda, the supreme god of Zoroastrianism, but contaminated by an attack by Ahriman (Pahl.; Gathic-Avestan, Angra Mainyu), the other supreme god and the ultimate source of all evil and suffering—does not mention western Iran, Persia, or Media (the land of Ragha mentioned in the text cannot be Median Raghiana). Furthermore, it has been noted (Gershevitch, 1964) that if the authors had been Magi the absence of any reference to western Iranian institutions, including their own priesthood, would be very strange.

The Magi were above all the means by which the Zoroastrian tradition and the corpus of the Avesta have been transmitted to us, from the second half of the first millennium BCE on. This has been their principal merit. We can attribute directly to the Magi the new formulation that Iranian dualism assumed, known to us especially from Greek sources and, in part, from the Pahlavi literature of the ninth and tenth centuries CE. According to this formulation, the two poles of the dualism are no longer, as in the *Gathas,* Spenta Mainyu ("beneficent spirit") and Angra Mainyu ("hostile spirit") but Ahura Mazda himself and Angra Mainyu (Gershevitch, 1964). This transformation was of immense consequence for the historical development of Zoroastrianism and was most likely determined by the contact of the Magi with the Mesopotamian religious world. In this new dualism—which was that later known to the Greeks (Aristotle, Eudemus of Rhodes, Theopompus, and others)—we can see the affirmation of a new current of thought within Zoroastrianism, to which we give the name *Zurvanism.*

Thanks to their adherence to Zoroastrianism, the Magi played an enormously important role in the transmission of Zarathushtra's teachings, as well as in the definition of the new forms that these would assume historically. Their natural propensity to eclecticism and syncretism also helped the diffusion of Zoroastrian ideas in the communities of the Iranian diaspora. The Greeks began to study their doctrines and to take an interest in them (Xanthus of Lydia, Hermodorus, Aristotle, Theopompus, Hermippus, Dinon), even writing treatises on the Persian religion, of which only the titles and a few fragments have survived. In the Hellenistic period, the Magi were seen as a secular school of wisdom, and writings on magic, astrology, and alchemy were lent the authority of such prestigious names as Zarathushtra, Ostanes, and Hystaspes, forming an abundant apocryphal literature (Bidez and Cumont, 1938).

Later still, eschatology and apocalyptics were a fertile meeting ground for Iranian and Judeo-Christian religions, as can be seen in the famous *Oracles of Hystaspes,* a work whose Iranian roots are undeniable and which most likely dates from the beginning of the Christian era, probably the second century CE (Widengren, 1968). The Zoroastrian doctrine of the Savior of the Future (Saoshyant) was the basis for the story of the coming of the Magi to Bethlehem in the *Gospel of Matthew* (2:1-12).

The Sasanid period saw the Magi once again play a determining role in the religious history of Iran. Concerned to win back the western Magi (de Menasce, 1956), and eager to consolidate Zoroastrianism as the national religion of Iran, the priests of Iranian sanctuaries in Media and Persia were able to establish a true state church, strongly hierarchical and endowed with an orthodoxy based on the formation of a canon of scriptures. The leading figures in the development of a state religion and of Zoroastrian orthodoxy

were Tosar and Kerder, the persecutor of Mani in the third century.

BIBLIOGRAPHY

Benveniste, Émile. *Les Mages dans l'ancien* Iran. Paris, 1938.

Bickerman, Elias J., and H. Tadmor. "Darius I, Pseudo-Smerdis and the Magi." *Athenaeum* 56 (1978): 239-261

Bidez, Joseph, and Franz Cumont. *Les Mages hellénisés: Zoroastre, Ostanès et Hystaspe d'après la tradition grecque* (1938). 2 vols. New York, 1975.

Boyce, Mary. *A History of Zoroastrianism*, vol. 2. Leiden, 1982.

Gershevitch, Ilya. "Zoroaster's Own Contribution." *Journal of Near Eastern Studies* 23 (1964): 12-38.

Humbach, Helmut. "Mithra in India and the Hinduized Magi." In *Études mithriaques*, edited by Jacques Duchesne-Guillemin, pp. 229-253. Tehran and Liège, 1978.

Menasce, J. de. "La conquête de l'iranisme et la récupération des Mages occidentaux." *Annuaire de l'École Pratique des Hautes Études* 5 (1956): 3-12.

Messina, Giuseppe. *Der Ursprung der Magier und die zarathustrische Religion*. Rome, 1930.

Messina, Giuseppe. *I Magi a Betlemme e una predizione di Zoroastro*. Rome, 1933.

Moulton, J. H. *Early Zoroastrianism*. London, 1913.

Nyberg, H. S. *Irans forntida religioner*. Stockholm 1937. Translated as *Die Religionen des alten Iran* (1938; 2d ed., Osnabrück, 1966).

Widengren, Geo. Die Religionen Irans. Stuttgart, 1965. Translated as *Les religions de l'Iran* (Paris, 1968).

GHERARDO GNOLI
Translated from Italian by Roger DeGaris

MAIMONIDES, MOSES

MAIMONIDES, MOSES (c. 1135/8-1204), hellenized name of Mosheh ben Maimon; also known by the acronym RaMBaM (Rabbi Mosheh ben Maimon); distinguished Talmudist, philosopher, and physician, and one of the most illustrious figures of Jewish history. He had a profound and pervasive impact on Jewish life and thought, and his commanding influence has been widely recognized by non-Jews as well as Jews. His epoch-making works in the central areas of Jewish law *(halakhah)* and religious philosophy are considered to be unique by virtue of their unprecedented comprehensiveness, massive erudition, and remarkable originality and profundity. Their extraordinary conjunction of halakhic authority and philosophic prestige has been widely acknowledged. While the generations before the age of Maimonides produced philosophically trained Talmudists—scholars well versed in both Greek science and rabbinic lore—the extent to which Maimonides thoroughly and creatively amalgamated these disciplines and commitments is most striking.

Early Life and Works. Maimonides was born in Córdoba, Spain; to escape religious persecution, the family fled to Fez for several years. In 1165 Maimonides resumed his wanderings. Stopping for prayer in the holy sites, he settled in Fustat (Old Cairo).

Maimonides emerged as the untitled leader of the Jewish community, combining the duties of rabbi, local judge, appellate judge, administrative chief responsible for appointing and supervising community officials, and overseer of philanthropic foundations. He refused all remuneration for these services, a practice that reflected his religious and philosophical principles: that scholars or religious functionaries should not seek or receive communal support. Some of his most passionate and animated prose (e.g., *Mishneh Torah,* Study of the Torah 3.10, Sanhedrin 23.5; *Commentary on the Mishnah, Avot* 4.7) was elicited by his distaste for this practice and his unyielding opposition to the existence of an institutionalized and salaried rabbinate.

The natural integration of traditional Torah study and philosophy is a pivot of his massive literary achievement and an axiom of his understanding of Judaism. His creativity reflects a strong pedagogic drive. His youthful works (*Millot ha-higgayon,* on logic, and *Ma'amar ha-`ibbur,* on the astronomical principles of the Jewish calendar) were composed in response to specific requests. Throughout his life he wrote hundreds of *responsa (teshuvot)*—decisions concerning the interpretation or application of the law—and letters of advice, comfort, or arbitration to all parts of the world, including Yemen, Baghdad, Aleppo, Damascus, Jerusalem, Alexandria, Marseilles, and Lunel. *Iggeret ha-shemad* (Epistle on Conversion) and *Iggeret Teiman* (Epistle to Yemen) are especially noteworthy. His code of law was intended for "small and great"; indeed, law for him was an educative force leading to ethical and intellectual perfection, and his code was intended to be not only a manual of commands but an instrument of education and instruction.

Maimonides' major works are the *Perush ha-Mishnah* (Commentary on the Mishnah), *Sefer ha-mitsvot* (Book of the Commandments), *Mishneh Torah* (Review of the Torah; also known as *Yad ha-hazaqah*), and *Moreh nevukhim* (Guide of the Perplexed). He also wrote some ten medical treatises that illustrate his vast erudition and the high ethical standards he brought to medicine. They are based to a large extent on Arabic medical literature. One of them deals with Galen and contains a rejoinder to Galen's criticisms of the Mosaic Torah.

Commentary on the Mishnah and Book of the Commandments. The pioneering, comprehensive *Commentary on the Mishnah,* which engaged the attention of Maimonides for about ten years (1158-1168), was intended as both an introduction to and a review of the Talmud. The book includes noteworthy discussions of many problems: prophecy; the reconciliation of physics with the traditional understanding of the biblical account of creation *(ma`aseh bere'shit)* and of metaphysics with traditional interpretations of Ezekiel's vision

of the divine chariot *(ma`aseh merkavah);* the reconciliation of belief in free will with belief in predestination; reward and punishment; the history of religion; magic, medicine, and miracles; immortality and the world to come; and the proper methodological use of allegory.

Maimonides also wrote the *Book of the Commandments,* which provides a complete list of the 613 commandments thereby helping him to guard against forgetfulness and omissions and ensuring the comprehensiveness of the code. A major achievement of this work is the introduction, which defines fourteen guiding principles that determine which laws should be included in the enumeration of the 613. The ninth principle introduces an interesting classification of laws: (1) beliefs and opinions (e.g., to acknowledge the unity of God); (2) actions (e.g., to offer sacrifices); (3) virtues and traits of character (e.g., to love one's neighbor); (4) speech (e.g., to pray).

Mishneh Torah. Completed around the year 1178, the *Mishneh Torah* is a presentation of Jewish law without precedent or sequel in rabbinic literature. It is distinguished by five major characteristics: its codificatory form, its scope, its system of classification, its language and style, and its fusion of *halakhah* and philosophy. This tightly structured work has become a prism through which passes practically all reflection on and analysis of Talmudic study. There is hardly a major literary development in the broad field of rabbinic literature—not only in the field of codification—that does not relate in some way to the *Mishneh Torah,* a work that remains *sui generis,* unprecedented and unrivaled.

Guide of the Perplexed. Maimonides' philosophic testament *par excellence,* his *Guide of the Perplexed,* deals with the basic problems that engaged all medieval religious philosophers: faith and reason, or the relation of philosophy to scripture; the existence, unity, incorporeality, and freedom of God; God's relation to the world in terms of its origin and government; communication between God and man through revelation; and the issues of ethics, free will, and human destiny, including immortality and doctrines of eschatology. The *Guide* was used extensively by Jewish thinkers and also by Christian scholastics, most notably Thomas Aquinas.

Achievement and Legacy. Maimonides' lifework—the fastidious interpretation and thoughtful reformulation of Jewish belief and practice—seems to have been clear in his mind from an early age. There is a conscious unity and progressive continuity in his literary career. It is striking how early his ideas, ideals, and aspirations were formed, how logically they hang together, and how consistently and creatively they were applied. As his work moves from textual explication to independent exposition, and from one level of exposition to another, the reader, moving with it, feels that Maimonides had from the very beginning a master plan to achieve one overarching objective: to bring *halakhah* and philosophy, two apparently incongruous attitudes of mind, into fruitful harmony.

BIBLIOGRAPHY

Altmann, Alexander. "Maimonides' 'Four Perfections.'" *Israel Oriental Studies 2* (1972): 15-24.

Bacher, Wilhelm, Marcus Brann, and David Jacob Simonsen, eds. *Moses ben Maimon.* 2 vols. Leipzig, 1908-1914; reprint, Hildesheim, 1971.

Baron, Salo W., ed. *Essays on Maimonides.* New York, 1941.

Berman, Lawrence. "Maimonides, the Disciple of Alfarabi." *Israel Oriental Studies 4* (1974): 154-178.

Epstein, Isidore, ed. *Moses Maimonides.* London, 1935.

Halkin, Abraham, and David Hartman. *Crisis and Leadership: Epistles of Maimonides.* Philadelphia, 1985.

Hartman, David. *Maimonides: Torah and Philosophic Quest.* Philadelphia, 1976.

Lerner, Ralph. "Maimonides' Letter on Astrology." *History of Religions* 8 (November 1968): 143-158.

Maimonides, Moses. *The Book of Divine Commandments.* Translated and edited by Charles B. Chavel, London, 1940.

Maimonides, Moses. *The Code of Maimonides.* 15 vols. to date. Yale Judaica Series. New Haven, 1949-.

Maimonides, Moses. *Guide of the Perplexed.* Translated by Shlomo Pines with introductory essay by Leo Strauss. Chicago, 1963.

Twersky, Isadore, ed. *A Maimonides Reader.* New York, 1972.

Twersky, Isadore. *Introduction to the Code of Maimonides (Mishneh Torah).* New Haven, 1980.

Wolfson, Harry A. *Studies in the History of Philosophy and Religion,* vol. 2. Cambridge, Mass., 1977.

ISADORE TWERSKY

MALCOLM X

MALCOLM X (1925-1965), American Black Muslim leader, born Malcolm Little on 19 May 1925 in Omaha, Nebraska. His father, the Reverend Earl Little, a follower of Marcus Garvey and a Baptist minister, died when Malcolm was six years old, and his mother, the sole support of nine children, was later committed to an insane asylum. Malcolm attended school in East Lansing, Michigan, dropped out at the eighth grade, and then moved to live with an older sister in the Roxbury section of Boston. There he became involved in petty criminal activities. As an unemployed street hustler and the leader of an interracial gang of thieves in Roxbury, and later in Harlem, he was known as "Detroit Red" for the reddish tinge of his hair. During his prison years (1946-1952), he underwent the first of his two conversion experiences when he converted to the Nation of Islam led by Elijah Muhammad. Following the tradition of the Nation of Islam, he replaced his surname with an *X,* symbolizing what he had been and what he had become: "Ex-smoker. Ex-drinker. Ex-Christian. Ex-slave."

An articulate public speaker, charismatic personality, and indefatigable organizer, Malcolm X expressed the rage and anger of the black masses during the major phase of the civil rights movement from 1956 to 1965. He organized Muslim temples throughout the country and founded the newspaper *Muhammad Speaks* in the basement of his home. He articulated the Nation of Islam's beliefs in racial separation and rose rapidly through the ranks to become minister of Boston Temple No. 11 and was later rewarded with the post of minister of Temple No. 7 in Harlem, the largest and most prestigious temple of the Nation of Islam after the Chicago headquarters. Recognizing Malcolm's talents and abilities, Elijah Muhammad also named him "national representative" of the Nation of Islam, second in rank to Elijah Muhammad himself.

In 1963, after his public comments on President John F. Kennedy's assassination, Malcolm X was ordered by Elijah Muhammad to undergo a period of silence, an order that reflected the deep tensions and disputes among Black Muslim leaders. In March 1964, Malcolm left the Nation of Islam and founded his own Muslim Mosque, Inc. During his pilgrimage to Mecca that same year, he experienced a second conversion, embraced the orthodox universal brotherhood of Sunni Islam, and adopted the Muslim name el-Hajj Malik el-Shabazz. He then renounced the separatist beliefs of the Nation of Islam. In 1965, he founded the Organization for Afro-American Unity as a political vehicle to internationalize the plight of black Americans, to make common cause with Third World nations, and to move from civil rights to human rights. On 21 February 1965, Malcolm X was assassinated while delivering a lecture at the Audubon Ballroom in Harlem. His martyrdom, ideas, and speeches contributed to the development of black nationalist ideology and the black power movement in the late 1960s in the United States.

BIBLIOGRAPHY

Breitman, George, ed. *Malcolm X Speaks.* New York, 1965. A collection of Malcolm X's speeches.

Goldman, Peter. *The Death and Life of Malcolm X.* New York, 1973. Focuses on the last year of Malcolm X's life and on the events, personalities, and controversies surrounding his assassination.

Lincoln, C. Eric. *The Black Muslims in America.* Boston, 1961. Remains the best historical overview of the development of the Nation of Islam under the leadership of Elijah Muhammad and Malcolm X.

Malcolm X and Alex Haley. *The Autobiography of Malcolm X.* Still the best source of insights regarding Malcolm X's life and the development of his views, including his conversion experiences and the reasons for his dispute with other Black Muslim leaders.

Mamiya, Lawrence H. "From Black Muslim to Bilalian: The Evolution of a Movement." *Journal for the Scientific Study of Religion* 21 (June 1982): 138-152. Examines Malcolm X's influence on the leaders of the major schismatic groups in the Black Muslim movement—Warith D. Muhammad and Louis Farrakhan—and their divergent directions.

LAWRENCE H. MAMIYA

MANDAEAN RELIGION

The religion of the Mandaeans (from *manda,* "knowledge") is a self-contained, unique system belonging in the general stratum of the gnosticism of late antiquity. The Mandaeans of today live, as their ancestors did, along the rivers and waterways of southern Iraq and Khuzistan, Iran. Known by their neighbors as Subbi ("baptizers"), they form a gnostic baptist community.

The Mandaean codex and scroll literature is found in the voluminous book *Ginza,* a collection of mythological, revelatory, hortatory, and hymnic material. The Mandaean corpus exceeds anything transmitted from other gnostic traditions, except perhaps that of Manichaeism. Relationships to other forms of gnosticism are difficult to trace.

Mythology. Mandaeism testifies to a basic framework of dualism in which diametrically opposed entities clash but also intertwine and to some extent recognize one another's claims. Good and evil, light and darkness, soul and matter vie for control from the very inception of the world. Mandaean mythological speculations center on the preexistent Lightworld (the upper, "heavenly" realm), on the creation of the earth and of human beings, and on the soul's journey back to its Lightworld origin. The primary Lightworld entity is "the Great Life" (also called by various other names), who resides with his consort, "Treasure of Life," and numerous Lightbeings *(utria).* Manda d-Hiia ("knowledge of life") and his son/brother Hibil are Lightworld envoys, revealers, and saviors, busily shuttling between the Lightworld and the earth. Anosh-Utra, who imitates and competes with Jesus, and Shitil (the biblical Seth) are two less central messengers.

Rituals. Among the Mandaeans, repeated baptism *(masbuta)* takes place on Sundays and special festival days. Two small rites of ablution, *rishama* and *ta-masha,* are performed by the individual Mandaean and, unlike the *masbuta,* require no priest.

The laity undergo baptism as often as they wish. Moreover, baptism is required on specific occasions: at marriage, after childbirth (for a woman), and as close to the moment of death as possible. Water not only cleanses sins and other impurities; it also represents the Lightworld as reflected in the earthly world. *Masbuta* anticipates and in some sense parallels the deathmass, the *masiqta* ("raising up"), a complicated, lengthy, and essentially secret ritual celebrated for the dead and shielded from the view of the laity.

The majority of the symbolic objects in the *masiqta* are foodstuffs that feed the departed and act as creation material. Food links the living to the dead, maintaining the *laufa,* the connection between earth and the Light-world. The priests personify the ascending spirit and soul, act as parents for the new body, and impersonate Lightbeings. The dualism and the relationship between myth and ritual remain among the most urgent issues confronting scholarship on Mandaeism, as do the editing and translating of still-unpublished Mandaean manuscripts. [*See also* Gnosticism.]

BIBLIOGRAPHY

The two main Mandaean collections have been published in German under the editorship of Mark Lidzbarski as *Das Johannesbuch der Mandäer* (1915; reprint, Berlin, 1966) and *Ginza: Der Schatz; oder, Das grosse Buch der Mandäer* (Göttingen, 1925; new edition in preparation by Kurt Rudolph). *The Canonical Prayerbook of the Mandaeans,* translated by Ethel S. Drower (Leiden, 1959), contains a great number of Mandaean hymns and prayers. Representative excerpts from these three main texts (as well as from other Mandaean sources) can be found in *Gnosis: A Selection of Gnostic Texts,* vol. 2, *Coptic and Mandean Sources* (Oxford, 1974), edited by Werner Foerster, which contains an introduction by Kurt Rudolph. The classical eyewitness account of Mandaean religious life remains Ethel S. Drower's *The Mandaeans of Iraq and Iran* (1937; reprint, Leiden, 1962). Kurt Rudolph's *Die Mandäer,* vol. 1, Prolegomena: Das Mandäerproblem, and vol. 2, *Der Kult* (Göttingen, 1960, 1961), is the most comprehensive treatment of Mandaeism to date. The bibliography in this work should be supplemented by that in Rudolf Macuch's *Handbook of Classical and Modern Mandaic* (Berlin, 1965). A list of works on Mandaeism after 1965 appears in *Zur Sprache und Literatur der Mandäer: Studia Mandaica I* (Berlin, 1976), edited by Rudolf Macuch.

JORUNN JACOBSEN BUCKLEY

MANICHAEISM

An Overview

The doctrine professed by Mani and the path to salvation that he revealed constitute a form of gnosis. It originated during the first half of the third century in Mesopotamia, a region of the Parthian empire in which a number of different religious and philosophical schools were actively present, notably Christianity, Judaism, and Zoroastrianism. The sects and communities of the region reflected the influence of one or the other of these cults to varying degrees and were often characterized by an evident gnostic orientation.

The Fundamental Doctrines. Manichaean doctrine places great importance on the concept of dualism, which is deeply rooted in Iranian religious thought.

Dualism. Like Zoroastrian cosmology, which we know through relatively late texts (ninth century CE), Manichaean dualism is based on the doctrine of the two roots, or principles, of light and darkness and the three stages of cosmic history: the golden age before the two principles mixed together; the middle, or mixed, period, Gumezishn (MPers.); the present age, in which the powers of light and darkness battle for ultimate control of the cosmos; and the last age, when the separation of that which had become mixed, and between followers of good and evil, occurs. According to the Zoroastrian doctrine, this is the time of *frashgird* (MPers., "rehabilitation"; Av., *frashokereti*) in which the two poles of good and evil will once again be distinguished.

The two roots are not generated and have nothing in common: they are irreducible opposites in every way. Light is good, equated with God; darkness is evil, equated with matter. Because good and evil are coeval, the problem of the origin of evil (a central dilemma of Christian doctrine) is

> **Manichaeans prided themselves on not asserting any truth without a logical and rational demonstration.**

resolved, in the most radical and extreme way. Its existence cannot be denied; it is everywhere, it is eternal and can only be defeated by knowledge (gnosis), which leads to salvation through the separation of light and darkness.

Knowledge as the path to salvation. An essential and specific characteristic of Manichaeism is its gnosticism, that is, its mixture of religion and science in a sort of theosophy. Manichaeism was attempting to give a universal explanation of the world, and it did not believe that mere faith and dogma were effective instruments in the search for redemption. On the contrary, Manichaean soteriology was based on knowledge: that man could be freed of the authority of faith and tradition and led back to God simply by the strength of reason. Manichaeans, therefore, prided themselves on not asserting any truth without a logical and rational demonstration thereof, and without first opening the doors of knowledge.

Such knowledge was, ultimately, an anamnesis, an awakening; that is, gnosis was an *epignosis,* a recognition, a memory of self, knowledge of one's true ego and, at the same time, knowledge of God, the former being consubstantial with the latter, a particle of light fallen into matter's obfuscating mix. Thus God is a "savior saved," or one to be saved: a transcendental, luminous principle, spirit, or intelligence *(nous).*

The myths. It may appear paradoxical to find that the doctrine of Manichaeism, was expressed in a language of myth. Manichaean myths serve the purpose of illustrating the truth about the drama of existence, both macrocosmic and microcosmic. Manichaean mythology is like a great album of pictures arranged in a sequence aimed at awakening in the adept reminiscences and intuitions that will lead him to knowledge.

Origins. The origins of Manichaeism are still open to question (as are, in fact, those of gnosticism). The most likely interpretation would recognize the dominating imprint of

Iranian dualism since without a doubt the dualistic doctrine is central and pivotal to Mani's thought and to the teachings and practices of his church. We must, however, consider the presence of three different forms of religious doctrine: the Iranian, which is basically Zoroastrian; the Christian or Judeo-Christian; and the Mahayana Buddhist. Of these, the Iranian form held the key to the Manichaean system and provided the essence of the new universalistic religious concept that developed from the main themes and aspirations of gnosticism. If we were to separate the Manichaean system from its Christian and Buddhist elements, it would not suffer irreparably.

The Manichaean Church. At the core of the ecclesiastical structure was a marked distinction among classes of clergy, and above these stood the leader of the faithful, the Manichaean pope.

Different moral codes governed the clergy and the lay population. The liturgy was simple: it recalled episodes of the life of Mani, his martyrdom, and that of the first apostles. The principal festivity was the Bema (Gr.; MPers., *gah;* "pulpit, throne, tribunal"), which, on the vernal equinox, celebrated Mani's passion through gospel worship; the collective confession of sins; the recitation of three hymns to Mani; the reading of the apostle's spiritual testament, the *Letter of the Seal;* chants glorifying the triumphant church; and a sacred banquet offered to the elect by the listeners.

BIBLIOGRAPHY

A work that by now belongs to the prehistory of Manichaean studies is Isaac de Beausobre's *Histoire critique de Manichée et du manichéisme,* 2 vols. (Amsterdam, 1735-1739), which presented Manichaeism as a reformed Christianity. A hundred years later, Manichaean studies reached a turning point with F. C. Baur's *Das manichäische Religionssystem nach den Quellen neu untersucht und entwickelt* (Tübingen, 1831), which gave particular consideration to the Indo-Iranian, Zoroastrian, and Buddhist backgrounds.

In the years following, a number of general studies were published that still remain important—G. Flügel's *Mani, seine Lehre und seine Schriften* (Leipzig, 1862); K. Kessler's Mani: *Forschungen über die manichäische Religion,* vol. 1 (Berlin, 1889); F. C. Burkitt's *The Religion of the Manichees* (Cambridge, 1925); and H. H. Schaeder's *Urform und Fortbildungen des ma-nichäischen Systems* (Leipzig, 1927)—even though more recent studies and discoveries have, by now, gone beyond them. Also useful are A. V. W. *Jackson's Researches on Manichaeism, with Special Reference to the Turfan Fragments* (New York, 1932) and H. J. Polotsky's *Abriss des manichäischen Systems* (Stuttgart, 1934).

A quarter of a century apart, two important status reports concerning the question of Manichaean studies were published: H. S. Nyberg's "Forschungen über den Manichäismus," *Zeitschrift für die neutestamentliche Wissenschaft und die Kunde der älteren Kirche* 34 (1935): 70-91, and Julien Ries's "Introduction aux études manichéennes," *Ephemerides Theologicae Lovanienses* 33 (1957): 453-482 and 35 (1959): 362-409.

General works that remain valuable, although they give a partially different picture of Manichaeism, are Henri-Charles Puech's *Le manichéisme: Son fondateur, sa doctrine* (Paris, 1949) and Geo

Widengren's *Mani and Manichaeism* (London, 1965). We are also indebted to Puech for a very useful collection of essays, *Sur le manichéisme et autres essais* (Paris, 1979), and to Widengren for another, with an important introduction, *Der Manichäismus* (Darmstadt, 1977), pp. ix-xxxii, as well as for a more recent essay, "Manichaeism and Its Iranian Background," in *The Cambridge History of Iran,* vol. 3, edited by Ehsan Yarshater (Cambridge, 1983), pp. 965-990.

The volume *Der Manichäismus* contains some of the most important contributions to Manichaean studies, reprinted entirely or partially (all in German), by H. S. Nyberg, F. C. Bur-kitt, H. H. Schaeder, Richard Reitzenstein, H.-J. Polotsky, Henri-Charles Puech, V. Stegemann, Alexander Böhlig, Mark Lidzbarski, Franz Rosenthal, W. Bang-Kaup, A. Baumstark, Charles R. C. Allberry, Prosper Alfaric, W. Seston, J. A. L. Vergote, W. B. Henning, Georges Vajda, Carsten Colpe, and A. V. W. Jackson. Two noteworthy syntheses of Manichaeism in French are François Decret's *Mani et la tradition manichéenne* (Paris, 1974) and M. Tardieu's *Le manichéisme* (Paris, 1981); the latter is particularly full of original suggestions.

Two works from the 1960s are dedicated more to Mani himself than to Manichaeism, one concerning mainly the social and cultural background from which Manichaeism emerged and the other mainly dedicated to the religious personality of the founder: Otakar Klíma's *Manis Zeit und Leben* (Prague, 1962) and L. J. R. Ort's *Mani: A Religio-Historical Description of His Personality* (Leiden, 1967).

Although the once-classic work on Manichaean literature, Prosper Alfaric's *Les écritures manichéennes,* 2 vols. (Paris, 1918), is now quite dated, there is a wealth of more recent works to which we can turn. A whole inventory of Iranian documents from Central Asia can be found in Mary Boyce's *A Catalogue of the Iranian Manuscripts in Manichaean Script in the German Turfan Collection* (Berlin, 1960). Excellent editions of Iranian and Turkic texts are due to F. W. K. Müller, A. von Le Coq, Ernst Waldschmidt and Wolfgang Lentz, W. Bang, and Annemarie von Gabain, F. C. Andreas, and W. B. Henning, published in the *Abhandlungen* and in the *Sitzungsberichte* of the Prussian Academy of Sciences between 1904 and 1936. W. B. Henning's pupil, Mary Boyce, has also published, in addition to the above-mentioned catalog, two other important contributions to Manichaean studies, The *Manichaean Hymn Cycles in Parthian* (Oxford, 1954) and *A Reader in Manichaean Middle-Persian and Parthian,* "Acta Iranica," no. 9 (Tehran and Liège, 1975). Editions of Iranian texts, as well as a number of extremely careful philological studies, can be found in W. B. Henning's *Selected Papers,* 2 vols., "Acta Iranica," nos. 14-15 (Tehran and Liège, 1977), where are reprinted also Henning's fundamental *Mitteliranische Manichaica aus Chinesisch-Turkestan,* written in collaboration with F. C. Andreas between 1932 and 1934.

W. Sundermann and P. Zieme, two scholars from the Academy of Sciences of the German Democratic Republic, are currently responsible for continuing research in the Iranian and Turkish texts from Turfan, which are preserved in Berlin. We owe to them, among other things, Sundermann's *Mittelpersische und parthische kosmogonische und Parabeltexte der Manichäer* (Berlin, 1973) and Zieme's *Manichäisch-türkische Texte* (Berlin, 1975). On the state of research into Iranian texts, see also Sundermann's "Lo studio dei testi iranici di Turfan," in *Iranian Studies,* edited by me (Rome, 1983), pp. 119-134. Recent research on Sogdian Manichaean texts has been done by N. Sims-Williams (London) and E. Morano (Turin), following the lead of Ilya Gershevitch (Cambridge). Again in the context of Central Asian texts, the handbook for the confession of sins has been carefully edited, after the work of W. Bang and W. B. Henning, and with an ample commentary, by Jes P. Asmussen in *Xastvanift: Studies in Manichaeism* (Copenhagen, 1965); the *Shabuhragan* is the subject of an extremely useful work by D. N. MacKenzie, "Mani's

Sabuhragan," *Bulletin of the School of Oriental and African Studies* 42 (1979): 500-534 and 43 (1980): 288-310.

Concerning the Chinese texts, the following are useful works. On the *Treatise,* see Édouard Chavannes and Paul Pelliot's "Un traité manichéen retrouvé en Chine," *Journal asiatique* (1911): 499-617 and (1913): 99-392. On the *Compendium,* see Chavannes and Pelliot's "Compendium de la religion du Buddha de Lumière, Mani," *Journal asiatique* (1913): 105-116 (Pelliot fragment), and Gustav Haloun and W. B. Henning's "The Compendium of the Doctrines and Styles of the Teaching of Mani, the Buddha of Light," *Asia Major,* n. s. 3 (1952): 184-212 (Stein fragment). On the London Chinese hymn book, see, in addition to the work of Ernst Waldschmidt and Wolfgang Lentz, Tsui Chi's "Mo-ni-chiao hsia-pu tsan," *Bulletin of the School of Oriental and African Studies* 11 (1943): 174-219.

On the Coptic texts of Fayum, a survey of the state of research can be found in Alexander Böhlig's "Die Arbeit an den koptischen Manichaica," in *Mysterion und Wahrheit* (Leiden, 1968), pp. 177-187. Among editions of the texts are *Manichäische Homilien,* by H.-J. Polotsky (Stuttgart, 1934), *Kephalaia,* by C. Schmidt, H.-J. Polotsky, and Alexander Böhlig (Stuttgart, 1935-1940; Berlin, 1966), and Charles R. C. Allberry's *A Manichaean Psalm-Book,* vol. 2 (Stuttgart, 1938). On the Manichaean Codex of Cologne, see Albert Henrichs and Ludwig Koenen's "Ein griechischer Mani-Codex," *Zeitschrift für Papyrologie und Epigraphik* 5 (1970): 97-216, 19 (1975): 1-85, and 32 (1979): 87-200.

Of indirect sources, I shall mention here only the following few. On Augustine, see R. Jolivet and M. Jourion's *Six traités anti-manichéens,* in *Oeuvres de Saint Augustin,* vol. 17 (Paris, 1961); on Theodoros bar Konai, see Franz Cumont's *Recherches sur le manichéisme,* vol. 1 (Brussels, 1908); on Zoroastrian sources, see J.-P. de Menasce's *Une apologétique mazdéenne du neuvième siècle 'Skand-gumanik vicar'* (Fribourg, 1945); and on Islamic sources, see Carsten Colpe's "Der Manichäismus in der arabischen Überlieferung" (Ph. D. diss., University of Göttingen, 1954).

Three valuable anthologies of Manichaean texts are A. Adams's *Texte zum Manichäismus,* 2d ed. (Berlin, 1962), Jes P. Asmussen's *Manichaean Literature* (Delmar, N. Y., 1975), and Alexander Böhlig and Jes P. Asmussen's *Die gnosis,* vol. 3 (Zurich, 1980).

Concerning the spread of Manichaeism in Asia, in North Africa, and in the Roman empire, there are numerous works. The old text by E. de Stoop, *Essai sur la diffusion du manichéisme dans l'Empire romain* (Ghent, 1909), heads the list, followed by Paul Pelliot's "Les traditions manichéennes au Fou-kien," *T'oung pao* 22 (1923): 193-208; M. Guidi's *La lotta tra l'Islam e il manicheismo* (Rome, 1927); Uberto Pestalozza's "Il manicheismo presso i Turchi occidentali ed orientali," *Rendiconti del Reale Istituto Lombardo di Scienze e Lettere,* 2d series, 67 (1934): 417-497; Georges Vajda's "Les Zindiqs en pays d'Islam au debout de la période abbaside," *Revista degli Studi Orientali* 17 (1937): 173-229; Giuseppe Messina's *Cristianesimo, buddhismo, manicheismo nell'Asia antica* (Rome, 1947); H. H. Schaeder's "Der Manichäismus und sein Weg nach Osten," in *Glaube und Geschichte: Festschrift für Friedrich Gogarten* (Giessen, 1948), pp. 236-254; O. Maenchen-Helfen's "Manichaeans in Siberia," in *Semitic and Oriental Studies Presented to William Popper* (Berkeley, 1951), pp. 161-165; Francesco Gabrieli's "La zandaqa au premier siècle abbaside," in *L'élaboration de l'Islam* (Paris, 1961), pp. 23-28; Peter Brown's "The Diffusion of Manichaeism in the Roman Empire," *Journal of Roman Studies* 59 (1969): 92-103; François Decret's *Aspects du manichéisme dans l'Afrique romaine* (Paris, 1970); and S. N. C. Lieu's *The Religion of Light: An Introduction to the History of Manichaeism in China* (Hong Kong, 1979) and *Manichaeism in the Later Roman Empire and Medieval China* (Manchester, 1985).

Among studies devoted to special topics, note should be taken of Charles R. C. Allberry's "Das manichäische Bema-Fest," *Zeitschrift für die neutestamentliche Wissenschaft und die Kunde der älteren Kirche* 37 (1938): 2-10; Geo Widengren's *The Great Vohu Manah and the Apostle of God* (Uppsala, 1945) and *Mesopotamian Elements in Manichaeism* (Uppsala, 1946); Henri-Charles Puech's "Musique et hymnologie manichéennes," in *Encyclopédie des musiques sacrées,* vol. 1 (Paris, 1968), pp. 353-386; and Mircea Eliade's "Spirit, Light, and Seed," *History of Religions* 11 (1971): 1-30. Of my own works, I may mention "Un particolare aspetta del simbolismo della luce nel Mazdeismo e nel Manicheismo," *Annali dell'Istituto Universitario Orientale di Napoli* n.s. 12 (1962): 95-128, and "Universalismo e nazionalismo nell'Iran del III secolo," in *Incontro di religioni in Asia tra il III e il X secolo,* edited by L. Lanciotti (Florence, 1984), pp. 31-54.

In the most exhaustive treatment of Manichaeism to have appeared in an encyclopedic work, Henri-Charles Puech's "Le manichéisme," in *Histoire des religions,* vol. 2, edited by Puech (Paris, 1972), pp. 523-645, we also find a full exposition of the problem concerning the heritage and survival of Manichaeism, with a bibliography to which one should add Raoul Manselli's *L'eresia del male* (Naples, 1963).

Despite the length of the present bibliography, there are some works cited in the text of my article that have not yet been mentioned here. On the relationship between Manichaeism and Zoroastrianism, see Alessandro Bausani's *Persia religiosa* (Milan, 1959); on the Parthian heritage in Manichaeism, see A. D. H. Bivar's "The Political History of Iran under the Arsacids," in *The Cambridge History of Iran,* vol. 3, edited by Ehsan Yarshater (Cambridge, 1983), pp. 21-97; and on the influence of Manichaeism in Tibet, see Giuseppe Tucci's *Die Religionen Tibets* (Stuttgart, 1970), translated as *The Religions of Tibet* (Berkeley, 1980).

GHERARDO GNOLI
Translated from Italian by Ughetta Fitzgerald Lubin

MAORI RELIGION

Gods and Their Influence. In common with other Polynesians, the Maori conceived of reality as divided into two realms: the world of physical existence *(te ao marama,* "the world of light") and the world of supernatural beings (comprising both *rangi,* "the heavens," and *po,* "the underworld"). Communication between the two realms was frequent.

Gods or spirits, termed *atuas,* were frequent visitors to the physical world, where they were extremely active. Indeed, any event for which no physical cause was immediately apparent was attributed to the gods. This included winds, thunder and lightning, the growth of plants, physical or mental illness, menstruation, involuntary twitches in the muscles, the fear that gripped a normally brave warrior before battle, the skill of an artist, even—after the arrival of Europeans—the operation of windmills.

Another critical concept in traditional Maori religion is *tapu* (a term widespread in the Pacific, often rendered in English

as "taboo"). Numerous definitions of the Maori *tapu* have been advanced. Perhaps the most useful view is that of the nineteenth-century magistrate and physician Edward Shortland, who defined *tapu* simply as the state of being under the influence of some *atua.* Because the influencing *atua* might be of any nature, from a protecting and strengthening god to an unwelcome, disease-dealing demon, the condition of a *tapu* person or thing could be anything from sacred to uncommonly powerful or brave; from dangerous to sick, deranged, or dead.

Establishing tapu. One common way of instilling *tapu* (that is, inviting the gods to extend their influence over someone or something) was through ritual incantations called *karakia.*

Another means of attracting *atuas* and disposing them to lend their influence to human affairs was to give them gifts. Many Maori rituals included the preparation of several ovens; the food cooked in one of them was reserved for the gods. When an important new canoe was launched, the heart of a human sacrifice might be offered to the gods for protection of the craft.

The influence of *atuas* was considered to be highly contagious, readily spreading from things that were *tapu* to things that were not. One common pathway was physical contact. Death was highly *tapu,* and anything that came in contact with a corpse—the tree on which it was exposed during decomposition, the people who scraped the bones a year after death, the place where the bones were finally deposited—became *tapu* as well.

The principles of *tapu* contagion were used ritually to introduce godly influence into places or situations where it was desired. One means of doing this was to put rudely carved stone images in sweet potato fields during the growing season. These *taumata atuas* were resting-places that attracted the gods, whose influence would then permeate the field and stimulate the growth of the crop.

Dispelling tapu. *Tapu* was by no means an invariably desirable state. Disease, as I have already noted, was thought to be the work of certain gods or demons noted for their maliciousness. Well-known mischief workers in the Rotorua area were Te Makawe, an *atua* who caused people to be scalded by geysers or hot pools, and the *atua* Tatariki, who rejoiced in swelling people's toes and ankles.

The Maori had a number of means for terminating the *tapu* state. One was simply to leave the area; many *atuas* were limited in their activities to a certain locale.

Water was thought to remove *atua* influence by washing it away. Those who had handled a corpse or who had been involved in the *tapu* activity of teaching or learning sacred lore might immerse themselves in water, preferably the flowing water of a stream.

Women frequently played important roles in *whakanoa* rituals designed to dispel *tapu.* A war party might be released from *tapu* by a rite in which a woman would eat the ear of the first enemy they had killed. Because women were thought to attract *atuas,* the female—specifically her genitalia—represented a passageway between the two realms of existence. When brought in proximity with a woman, an *atua* would be drawn into and through her, and thereby repatriated to the spiritual realm.

The remaining *whakanoa* agent to be discussed is the latrine. Built on the edge of a cliff or brow of a hill, the Maori latrine was made with a low horizontal beam supported by two upright, often carved, posts. The user placed his feet on the beam while squatting, preserving his balance by grasping hand grips planted in the ground in front of the beam. A person could be ritually released from a *tapu* state by biting the latrine's horizontal beam.

The latrine beam marked a sharp line of separation: before it was the village, humming with life; behind it was a silent, shunned area where excrement fell and where people ventured only for murderous purposes, such as to learn witchcraft.

BIBLIOGRAPHY

Among the many fascinating accounts of Maori life written by early visitors to New Zealand, two are George French Angas's *Savage Life and Scenes in Australia and New Zealand,* 2d ed., 2 vols. (London, 1847), and Ernest Dieffenbach's *Travels in New Zealand,* 2 vols. (London, 1843). Two other nineteenth-century works with considerable information on religion are the missionary Richard Taylor's *Te Ika a Maui, or, New Zealand and Its Inhabitants* (London, 1855) and the magistrate Edward Shortland's *Traditions and Superstitions of the New Zealanders,* 2d ed. (London, 1856). An important collection of exclusively Maori myths (despite its title) is George Grey's *Polynesian Mythology* (1855), edited by W. W. Bird (New York, 1970). The anthropologist Elsdon Best has written many works on Maori religion (as on all aspects of Maori culture), among them *Some Aspects of Maori Myth and Religion* (1922; reprint, Wellington, 1954), *Spiritual and Mental Concepts of the Maori* (1922; reprint, Wellington, 1954), *Maori Religion and Mythology* (Wellington, 1924), and *Tuhoe: The Children of the Mist* (Wellington, 1925). Important monographs by the historian of religion J. Prytz Johansen are *The Maori and His Religion in Its Non-Ritualistic Aspects* (Copenhagen, 1954) and *Studies in Maori Rites and Myths* (Copenhagen, 1958). Two recent anthropological studies are Jean Smith's *Tapu Removal in Maori Religion* (Wellington, 1974) and *Counterpoint in Maori Culture* (London, 1983) by F. Allan Hanson and Louise Hanson.

F. ALLAN HANSON

MAPUCHE RELIGION

The Mapuche currently live in Chile and Argentina. In Chile, they have settled between the Bio-Bio River to the north and the Channel of Chacao to the south, a territory that encompasses the provinces of Arauco, Bio-Bio, Malleco, Cautin, Valdivia, Osorno, and Llanquihue (approximately between 37° and 41° south latitude). In Argentina, they are found at similar latitudes in the northern Patagonian province of Neuquén and, to a lesser extent, in the Río Negro and Chubut provinces; to the north there are scattered and isolated groups in the Pampas region. The most optimistic calculations estimate that there are five hundred thousand Mapuche in Chile and fifty thousand in Argentina.

The Mapuche belong to the Araucana-chon linguistic family. Most of the Mapuche live in small settlements in a pattern of scattered encampments. The basic economic activity among the Chilean Mapuche is agriculture; the Argentinians rely on sheep and goat herding, as dictated by varying ecological settings. Patrilineal descent, patrilocal residence, and matrilateral marriage are the most noteworthy traits of contemporary Mapuche society. Patrilineage or, in many cases, a subdivision thereof, as well as the residential family, increasingly constitute the minimal units of the settlement in economic, social, and religious terms.

The structural changes undergone by the Mapuche in the past hundred years—a product of their adaptation to a new natural and social environment—have transformed Mapuche economy and, to a lesser degree, Mapuche society. Nonetheless, despite insistent missionary activity by Roman Catholics and Protestants (particularly fundamentalists), the foundation of their system of religious beliefs and practices remains practically intact in many regions.

To describe their mythico-religious beliefs even briefly, to characterize the numerous major deities, both regional and local, and to elucidate the symbolic content and meanings of each of the many rites of this people are tasks far beyond the scope of this work. I have therefore chosen to summarize them, making use of two cognitive structures common to them all, which will allow me to piece together the complex Mapuche belief system of religious practices and images and to outline their internal logic.

The first structure—apparently the most widespread—is dualism, which orders and defines two polar elements according to their relationships of opposition and complementarity. The second is the tetradic division generated as a result of a first bipartition that brings two opposed couples face to face and a second bipartition of degree that defines in each couple a climax and its attenuation.

The vast Mapuche pantheon is divided into two great antithetical and complementary spheres. The first is made up of beneficent deities, organized into a tetradic family based on a combination of sex and age (old man and old woman, young boy and young girl). These deities are the agents of good, health, and prosperity, and their tetradic nature symbolizes perfection. Cosmologically and vertically, they are found in the celestial sphere, or *wenú mapú,* which is the summit of the positive aspect of the four vertical components of the universe. Horizontally, some of them are ranked, with varying degrees of positivity, with the four regions of the world (the east, south, north, and west cardinal points). Temporally, they are associated with clarity. Given that the tetradic division is also the ordering principle of the day, they have their most exact manifestations in *epewún* ("dawn"), a superlative concretion of *antí* ("clarity"), whose sign is positive, and in *kiriní* ("dusk"), the attenuation of *pún* ("darkness"), whose sign is negative. Finally, they are associated with positive colors—blue (the most important) and white-yellow (denoting attenuation).

The second sphere of this theophanic dualism is made up of the malefic beings, of *wekufí*, who appear isolated, in odd numbers, and of indeterminate age and sex. They are agents

> **... there are five hundred thousand Mapuche in Chile and fifty thousand in Argentina.**

of evil, illness, and chaos, and they symbolize imperfection. Their place in the cosmos is ambiguous; some groups place them in the *anká wenú,* or middle heaven, but generally they are considered to belong to the *pu mapú,* or netherworld—the climax of the negative aspect in the vertical conception of the universe. The temporal acts of the *wekufí* are most evident during *rangín púñ* ("midnight"), the most negative moment, and, to a lesser extent, during *rangíñ ánti* ("midday"), the attenuation of the positive pole. *Wekufí* that are associated with red and black, the malefic hues, play an even greater role in determining the qualities attributed to them.

The implied symbolic network arises from various levels of discourse, such as the *ngetrán* (accounts of mythical or historical events characterized by truthfulness) and the decoding of dreams and signs—present events that anticipate the qualities of future occurrences. The social correlative of this theophanic dualism is incarnated in the figures of the *máchi* ("shaman") and *kalkú* ("witch"), who manipulate the forces of good and evil, respectively. The paraphernalia of the *máchi* include, among other things, the *kultrún* (a kettledrum), which serves as a symbolic microcosm; the *wáda* (a rattle); and the *kaskawílla* (a girdle with small bells). The *máchi* are assisted by benevolent deities and are responsible for staving off illnesses caused by the *kalkú,* who are assisted by the *wekufí* beings.

Shamanic rites include Machiluwún, an initiatory rite carried out after the *máchi* has undergone a period of revelation through illness or dreams and after he has received instruction from an initiated shaman, and the Ngejkurrewén, a postinitiatory rite of power renewal. The Pewutún is a diagnostic ritual. There are two therapeutic rites: the Datwún, for serious illnesses, and the Ulutún, for minor ailments. All these rites and their associated artifacts and actions—including the

réwe, a wood carving representing the cosmic stages; branches from sacred trees; ritual displacements of objects from the right (positive) to the left (negative), facing east and counting in twos, fours, or multiples thereof; songs and dances beseeching the benevolent gods to act; blue and white flags; and the moments (dawn and dusk) when the rites are performed—are symbolic expressions denoting supplication to the forces of good and the restoration of health.

In contrast, the witch directly or indirectly causes *kalkutún* ("harm") by throwing objects with malefic powers around the victim's house or by working magic on the victim's nails, hair, clothing, sweat, or footprints. The witch may poison the victim, or may enlist the help of a *wekufí*—such as a *witranálwe,* the soul of a dead man that has been captured by the *kalkú.* The nocturnal appearance of the *witranálwe* in the form of a great, resplendent, cadaverous horseman causes illness and death.

Community members take part in numerous rituals outside of the specialized orbit of shamanism and witchcraft. The funerary rites, or Awn, are still practiced in the Chilean settlements. Their object is twofold: to ensure that the soul of the dead can cross into the world where the ancestors live (a site that some scholars say is very close to, or is associated with, the domain of the benevolent deities) and to prevent the spirit of the dead person from being captured by a witch and transformed into his aide during his nocturnal ambushes.

The term *ngillatún* alludes to the act of prayer and connotes diverse practices on individual, family, and group levels. Strictly speaking, on the group level it designates a "ritual complex" that varies in several respects according to the traditions of the community performing it. These variations include the number and affiliation of the participants, the extent of group cohesion, the ritual's duration, its association with agrarian or pastoral economic cycles, and its occasional or periodic nature, that is, whether it is carried out to counteract natural phenomena or to observe crucial dates of the annual cycle. Despite this great diversity, what finally defines the *ngillatún* is its strongly propitiatory nature, its characters—varying with the time it is performed—as restorer of the cosmic order, and its enrichment of coherence and meaning within communal life through the ritual congregation.

Within this cultural domain, the symbolic network also impregnates with meaning each of the ritual episodes—for example, the forms of spoken and sung prayer, ritual sprinkling, ritual painting, women's songs, men's dances and mixed dances, sacrifices, libations, and horseback rides. It is this network that determines the temporal bounds of the episodes, the meaning of the displacements, and the colors used, as well as the number of times (twice, four times, or a multiple thereof) that each action must be repeated.

This summary, centered around the ideological principles that serve to organize and define a large part of the symbolic beliefs, rites, and images of the Mapuche, should not lead the reader to suppose that this is a closed system lacking flexibility. The history of the Mapuche people indicates exactly the opposite. They have adapted to new conditions while preserving their traditional knowledge and beliefs, even if these have sometimes been modified or given new meanings.

BIBLIOGRAPHY

Among the classic studies of the subject, the most noteworthy for the Chilean region include Ricardo E. Latcham's *La organización social y las creencias religiosas de los antiguos araucanos* (Santiago, 1924) and Tomas Guevara's *Folklore araucano* (Santiago, 1911) and *Historia de Chile: Chile prehispánico,* 2 vols. in 1 (Santiago, 1925-1927). The North American anthropologist Louis C. Faron, who spent several years living in Chilean settlements, offers an excellent analysis of Mapuche society and its connections with religious practices in *Mapuche Social Structure: Institutional Reintegration in a Patrilineal Society of Central Chile* (Urbana, Ill., 1961); one of his many articles on this ethnic group, "Symbolic Values and the Integration of Society among the Mapuche of Chile," *American Anthropologist* 64 (1962): 1151-1163, deals with the dualism of the Mapuche worldview and offers valuable contributions. Other articles that should be cited, both because of the wealth of their data and the new outlooks they bring to the subject, are Maria E. Grebe's "Mitos, creencias y concepto de enfermedad en la cultura mapuche," *Acta psiquiatrica y psicologica de America Latina* (Buenos Aires) 17 (1971): 180-193, and "Cosmovision mapuche," *Cuadernos de la realidad nacional* (Santiago, Chile) 14 (1972): 46-73.

One of the most extensive monographs on the religion of the Argentinian Mapuche is Rodolfo M. Casamiquela's *Estudio del nillatún y la religión araucana* (Bahía Blanca, 1964). The compilations and observations of Bertha Koessler-Ilg in *Tradiciones araucanas* (La Plata, 1962) are a good addition. Other books worthy of mention are Else Marta Waag's *Tres entidades `wekufü' en la cultura mapuche* (Buenos Aires, 1982), which is outstanding for its wealth of information, and the anthology of essays *Congreso del Area Araucana Argentina* (Buenos Aires, 1963). The theoretical and methodological bases as well as the development and exemplification within different cultural domains of the two cognitive structures summarized in this article can be found in two essays by C. Briones de Lanata and me: "Che Kimí-n: Un aborde a la cosmologica Mapuche," *Runa: Archivo para las ciencias del hombre* (Buenos Aires) 15 (1985) and "Estructuras cognitivas e interacción social: El caso de la brujeria entre los Mapuche argentinos," in *Actas del 45° Congreso Internacional de Americanistas* (Bogotá, 1985).

MIGUEL ANGEL OLIVERA
Translated from Spanish by Erica Meltzer

MARA

MARA ("death-causer") is a god identified in Buddhist legend and cosmology as Lord of the Kamadhatu ("realm of sense-desire") and principal antagonist of the Buddha and his followers. Mara is also called Maccu ("death"), Antaka ("the end"), Papima ("evil one"), and sometimes Kanha ("dark one") or Namuci ("not loosing"). His mount is an elephant; his chief attribute is the snare of worldly thoughts and pleasures that binds his captives to repeated death and suffering.

Mara is best known for his attempts to prevent the Buddha's enlightenment (as described especially in the *Padhana Sutta* of the *Suttanipata* and in the Enlightenment accounts of the *Mahavastu, Lalitavistara, Nidana-katha,* and *Buddhacarita*). As the Buddha-to-be seats himself under the Bodhi Tree and prepares for his final breakthrough, Mara first tries to dissuade him verbally and then attacks, albeit futilely, with the full might of his demonic hosts. In later accounts, this attack culminates with the "earth-touching" incident whose characteristic gesture identified representations of the Enlightenment in Buddhist iconography. Here the Buddha-to-be, with a touch of his finger, summons the earth to witness his claim to preeminence. Several accounts append a return attempt by Mara's daughters, who try to seduce the great being who has conquered their father.

Mara's second most noteworthy deed, described in accounts of the Buddha's last months (for example, *Mahaparinibbana Sutta* 3.1-10), was to ensure the Buddha's final departure from the human realm. When the Master drops broad hints about a Buddha's ability to remain on earth until the end of an aeon, Mara clouds the disciple Ananda's understanding; hence Ananda does not beg his master to linger. Mara himself then urges the Buddha to leave, citing an old promise that the Buddha will depart once his teaching and community are well established. The Buddha then rejects his remaining life span, ensuring that the final *nirvana* will occur three months later.

Mara further harasses both Buddha and disciples in a host of lesser incidents. In the collection of Pali *suttas* called *Marasamyutta* (*Samyutta Nikaya* 1.4), Mara strives to distract or frighten the Buddha, and to tempt him to self-doubt or worldly enjoyment. In the collection called *Bhikkunisamyutta,* he tries unsuccessfully to seduce, confuse, or demoralize ten meditating nuns (*Samyutta Nikaya* 1.5). At times he works within, appearing as an unruly thought or as fear or pain. Or he inspires others to oppose or abuse the monastic community.

Mara's most famous post-Enlightenment target is the monk Upagupta, said to be a contemporary of the emperor Asoka. When Upagupta preaches, Mara distracts his audiences, first by causing a shower of gold and pearls to rain down, and then by staging a competing performance with heavenly musicians and dancers. Upagupta finally traps Mara by garlanding him with corpses, converts him, and persuades the shape-shifter to duplicate for Upagupta the Buddha's own image (retold in a number of sources, especially *Asokavadana*).

Although Mara appears in such legends as a concrete personage, he is also recognized as a figurative summation of the passions, fears, doubts, and delusions that impede a practitioner of the Buddhist path. Thus anger and false views are called his snares; fetters and defilements are his armies; his daughters are craving, discontent, and passion; and his sons are confusion, gaiety, and pride. Mara himself is variously identified with the *klesas* ("impurities"), *asravas* ("depravities"), *avidya* ("ignorance"), and *skandhas* ("personality aggregates") that precipitate craving and hence rebirth and redeath.

BIBLIOGRAPHY

The best sources in English are T. O. Ling's *Buddhism and the Mythology of Evil* (London, 1962) and James W. Boyd's *Satan and Mara: Christian and Buddhist Symbols of Evil* (Leiden, 1975). Ling is based on Pali sources only; Boyd draws on early texts of both the Pali and Sanskrit traditions. See also Ernst W. O. Windisch's *Mara und Buddha* (Leipzig, 1895), the classic study of the textual history of the Mara legend.

NANCY E. AUER FALK

MARATHI RELIGIONS

The Marathi language, which has demarcated the area in western India called Maharashtra for almost a thousand years, is an Indo-European language of North India that includes elements from the Dravidian languages of South India as well.

The Development of Marathi and Maharashtrian Religion. The earliest examples of the Marathi language are found in inscriptions from the eleventh century. By the late thirteenth century, when the Yadava kingdom governed most of the area known as Maharashtra and Marathi literature began to appear, the language was already well developed. Three sorts of writings came into being at about the same time, setting in motion three very different religious movements.

In Vidarbha, a court-supported philosopher, Mukundaraja, wrote the *Vivekasindhu,* a philosophical treatise in the Advaita Vedanta tradition of Sankara. Mukundaraja created no cult or school, but his influence is reflected in later work.

The Des saw the beginnings of two movements, each tracing its origin to a religious thinker of the thirteenth century and continuing today. The Varkari sect, which is the most popular devotional religious movement with an important literature in the area, understands itself to have begun with Jñanesvar, the author of an approximately nine-thousand-verse commentary on the *Bhagavadgita* called the *Jñanesvari.* He is considered the first of a line of poet-saints who composed songs in honor of Vithoba, whom Varkaris take to be a form of Krsna.

The Mahanubhav sect is not so widely popular today as the Varkari sect, but it has an important place in the religious history of Maharashtra. Founded by the thirteenth-century Cakradhar, the Mahanubhav sect produced a large body of prose hagiographies and poetry.

A third sect important in medieval Maharashtra was that of the Naths. The Naths' literature has not survived, but their influence can be discerned in the early history and literature of the Varkaris and Mahanubhavs.

Maharashtrian Deities. Although the two surviving *bhakti* (devotional) sects of Maharashtra are more pronouncedly Vaisnava (Krsnaite) than Saiva, there is evidence of a Saiva background against which they spread. And in the village and pastoral cults of Maharashtra, goddesses and Saiva gods are far more prominent than Visnu or Krsna.

Pilgrimage deities. The most important pilgrimage deity of Maharashtra is Vithoba of Pandharpur, whose primary mythological indentification is with Krsna, but who also has strong connections with Siva and who may have originated in a pastoral hero cult. Besides Vithoba, most other major Maharashtrian pilgrimage deities are goddesses and Saiva gods. Of the many Siva temples in Maharashtra, the two most important to Indian pilgrimage traditions may be Bhimasankar in Pune District and Tryambakesvar in Nasik District. Both temples are basic to the Maharashtrian landscape, since they are at the sources of the important Bhima and Godavari rivers, respectively.

Several other important pilgrimage deities, more or less closely identified with Siva, appear to be deities of pastoralists and warriors, eventually adopted by settled agriculturalists as well. Perhaps the most prominent of these is Khandoba, whose temples at Jejuri, near Pune, and at Malegav (Nanded District) attract large numbers of pilgrims from a wide range of castes.

> The elephant-headed god Ganes or Ganapati is also particularly important in Maharashtra.

Other deities. The figure of Dattatreya illustrates a Maharashtrian reworking of religious influences from both North and South, and the synthesizing of Saiva and Vaisnava motifs as well. A *rsi* ("seer") in Sanskrit epic and Puranic literature, Datta first appears in Marathi literature as one of the five Mahanubhav incarnations of the supreme God, Paramesvara. By the sixteenth century, however, Datta is clearly in the mainstream Hindu tradition, and has begun to be represented as the Brahma-Visnu-Siva triad, in one body with three heads. Shortly before that time, incarnations of the god began to appear on Maharashtrian soil, and many believe that Datta as Sai Baba, as the Svami of Akkalkot, or as some other *avatara* has appeared in modern times. Datta's chief and very popular pilgrimage center is at Gangapur, located to the south of Maharashtra in northern Karnataka state.

The elephant-headed god Ganes or Ganapati is also particularly important in Maharashtra. There is a formal pilgrimage route of eight centers, all fairly near Pune. The god Ram is found in temples throughout Maharashtra.

Rituals. The ritual life of Maharashtrian Hindus includes festivals regulated by the calendar, celebrations of events in the human life cycle, and rituals performed in response to individual or collective crises.

Calendrical rites. Rituals occurring annually include pilgrimage festivals *(jatras)* to particular places at particular times, and festivals celebrated locally or domestically in an annual cycle. The greatest concentration of pilgrimage festivals occurs during the month of Caitra (March-April), the first month of the Hindu calendar.

Life-cycle rites. Besides marriage and funeral rituals, those of the classical Hindu life cycle rites *(samskaras)* most commonly celebrated in Maharashtra today are the ceremony of naming a child (this is performed on or near the twelfth *(barava)* day after the child's birth and is hence called Barsem), and the ceremony, primarily among brahmans, of initiating young boys and investing them with the sacred thread *(muñja)*. In addition, there are several rituals celebrating the early married life and pregnancy of young women. These rituals are generally performed by women and are not included in the classical list of *samskaras*.

Religion in Modern Maharashtra. Modern changes in Maharashtrian religion are many and varied.

The institutional changes of the modern period that do affect life in Maharashtra today include the Gana-pati festival as reorganized by Tilak; the formation of the Rastriya Svayamsevak Sangh, a paramilitary service organization for young men; and, most unusual of all, a mass conversion to Buddhism, chiefly among *mahar* untouchables.

Women have been of consequence in Maharashtrian religion at least from the days of Cakradhar and Jñanesvar. A pattern of prominent women devotees of even more prominent male saints was repeated in the twentieth century as Godavari Mata succeeded Upasani Baba at the important ashram at Sakori in Ahmadnagar District. Here the Kanya Kumari Sthan, a young women's religious training institute, was established.

BIBLIOGRAPHY

The most thorough and prolific writer on the religious traditions of Maharashtra, including folk traditions, is R. C. Dhere, who writes in Marathi. His *Vitthala, Eka Mahasamanvaya* (Poona, 1984) is the most comprehensive work on the Vi-thoba cult to date. The best work on this subject in English is G. A. Deleury's *The Cult of Vithoba* (Poona, 1960). Shankar Gopal Tulpule's *Classical Marathi Literature from the Beginning to AD 1818* in *A History of Indian Literature,* vol. 9, fasc. 4, edited by Jan Gonda (Wiesbaden, 1979), gives a thorough survey of Varkari and Mahanubhav literature, as well as of other premodern religious literature in Marathi; this work includes generous bibliographical footnotes. An earlier work, R. D. Ranade's *Indian Mysticism: The Poet-Saints of Maharashtra* (1933; reprint, Albany, N. Y., 1983) provides extensive summaries of the thought of Ramdas and most of the Varkari poet saints.

Madhukar Shripad Mate's *Temples and Legends of Maharashtra* (Bombay, 1962) describes several of the most important pilgrimage temples of Maharashtra; and thousands of pilgrimage festivals are listed in *Fairs and Festivals in Maharashtra,* vol. 10 of *Census of India,* 1961, part 7B (Bombay, 1969). Günther-Dietz Sontheimer's *Biroba, Mhaskoba und Khandoba: Ursprung, Geschichte und Umwelt von pastoralen Gottheiten in Maharastra* (Wiesbaden, 1976) is a richly detailed study of the religious traditions of Maharashtrian pastoralists, including numerous oral myths in German translation. John M. Stanley analyzes the meaning of a Khandoba festival in "Special Time, Special Power," *Journal of Asian Studies* 37 (1977): 37-48. Two older works containing a wealth of information on Maharashtrian folklore are R. E. Enthoven's *The Folklore of Bombay* (London, 1924) and John Abbott's *The Keys of Power: A Study of Indian Ritual and Belief* (1932; reprint, Secaucus, N. J., 1974).

For the modern period, Matthew Lederle's *Philosophical Trends in Modern Maharastra* (Bombay, 1976) provides a good survey of the major religious-philosophical thinkers. "Tradition and Innovation in Contemporary Indian Buddhism" by Eleanor Zelliot and Joanna R. Macy, in *Studies in the History of Buddhism,* edited by A. K. Narain (Delhi, 1980), pp. 133-153, is a study of the recent movement of conversion to Buddhism.

ELEANOR ZELLIOT and ANNE FELDHAUS

MARRIAGE

Every culture of the world recognizes some form of the institution of marriage. In most cultures and religions neither man nor woman is considered complete, after reaching maturity, without a spouse. Many religions consider marriage as a sacred act that originates from a god or as the union of souls or spirits with the sacred realm.

Purpose of Marriage. The purpose of marriage and the beliefs that surround this institution must be viewed differently for every culture. There are three major categories of belief about the purposes of marriage: marriage may be viewed as existing primarily for the continuation of the family and society through procreation; it may be considered most importantly as an alliance, that is, the means to bring about the integration of society by setting up kinship ties and kinship terminology; and finally, the union of bride and groom may be perceived as a complex system of exchanges between groups and/or individuals.

Continuation of society. The institution of marriage perpetuates society by socially recognizing the union of man and woman and incorporating their offspring into the fabric of social life. There are variants of marriage forms that exist in many cultures to allow for the continuation of the family and of society in the event that one of the marriage partners dies. The two best known forms are the levirate and the sororate. In the levirate, when the husband of a marriage dies, an approved male relative of his may live with the widow and the children. This replacement husband will conceive more children for the deceased as if he were the deceased. In the sororate, the place of a deceased wife is taken by her sister.

While these forms of marriage perpetuate society through those who have died, many societies ensure their continuation into the future by marrying off those individuals not yet born. Among the Tiwi of Australia, a young girl is contracted for her future marriage before her birth, at her mother's wedding ceremony. When the girl enters puberty her wedding ceremony is held. This ceremony is attended by the girl, her father, and her husband, as well as her future sons-in-law. For in the same way that she has been married since her mother's wedding, here at her wedding she also marries her daughters to their future husbands.

Alliance. The importance placed upon marriage in many societies is in its role in integrating society. Marriage is the starting point for the kinship ties that run across and between different and independent kinship or descent groups. A marriage will be used to create an alliance between two lines of descent with very little focus upon the relationship between the bride and groom. In many cases these will be arranged marriages, often making use of go-betweens to reach an agreement between the two families.

System of exchange. In the final category of marriage beliefs, marriage represents the gift or exchange of women between two descent groups. The position of giving or receiving wives sets up a constantly changing mechanism by which status is expressed and validated between the two kinship groups. The ideal exchange is for both descent groups to exchange sisters, thereby maintaining the status of each group as equal. Marrying a woman in compensation for the death of a man is also an exchange recognized as equivalent in many cultures for the settlement of quarrels.

When women are not exchanged equally, then the balance between the two groups remains unequal and must be achieved through other means. This balancing may take the form of payments made on behalf of the husband to the man or the family who has given up the wife. These payments are viewed as equivalent to the reproductive powers of the woman who is being given to another group as well as a return on the labor and usefulness the bride's family will lose upon her marriage. These payments are known as "bride-price" or "bride-wealth."

Forms of Marriage. There are two basic forms of marriage: monogamy, the union of one man with one woman, and polygamy, the union of a man or a woman with multiple marriage partners. Polygamy can also be divided into two types: polyandry, in which a woman has more than one hus-

band, and, conversely, polygyny, in which a man has more than one wife. Polygyny is the most common form of multiple marriage, and the plurality of wives is mainly the privilege of older men and their wealth.

The classic case of polyandry is in Tibet, where a group of brothers may jointly marry a wife. The wedding takes place when the eldest brother has reached the appropriate age, and on formal occasions it is he who will perform the role of father, although all brothers are viewed as the father to the children of the marriage.

Societies regulate not only how many spouses one can have but from what general categories these individuals should be selected. Exogamy, marriage outside a defined kinship group, is primarily concerned with incest prohibitions. Brother-sister and parent-child unions are forbidden in nearly every culture; cousin marriage is forbidden in the third degree of the collateral line among Roman Catholics, while it is recommended among many peoples of Africa.

Creation Myths and the Institution of Marriage. Many origin myths that explain the creation of the world and of humankind also explain marriage. In Samoa the marriage of the creator god Tangaloa with a woman he has created begins the world. The Makasar of Indonesia believe that the son of the sky deity married six female deities and their offspring became the peoples of the world. The union of the Japanese gods Izanagi and Izanami consolidates and fertilizes the moving earth. And, for Jews, Christians, and Muslims alike, the marriage of Adam and Eve, two beings created by God, generates all of humankind.

BIBLIOGRAPHY

One of the first scholars to concern himself with marriage practices was Lewis Henry Morgan in *Ancient Society* (New York, 1877). Following this evolutionary approach, Edward A. Westermarck compiled his classic *The History of Human Marriage* (1891), 3 vols., 5th ed. (1921; reprint, New York, 1971). This three-volume set treats everything believed to be related to marriage in that time, including marriage rites, customs, and kinship organizations. One of the classic studies of the constitution of social groups and their unity was written by W. Robertson Smith following the precedents set by Morgan and Westermarck. Smith's *Kinship and Marriage in Early Arabia,* edited by Stanley A. Cook (1903; Oosterhuit, 1966), goes beyond these first works and is particularly concerned with the laws of marriage and how this institution functioned within the tribal organization in Arabia at the time of Muhammad. The theories of primitive promiscuity and group marriage as the earliest forms of marriage in human history that are put forth by all of these books have never been substantiated, but these works provide valuable insights into human society.

For a contemporary view of love and marriage in the Jewish religion and its place in society, see Maurice Lamm's *The Jewish Way in Love and Marriage* (San Francisco, 1980). This book also includes a thorough description of a contemporary Jewish wedding ceremony. The best review of marriage and kinship beliefs for cultures of Africa is *African Systems of Kinship and Marriage,* edited by A. R. Radcliffe-Brown and Daryll Forde (Oxford, 1962). This book considers marriage in relation to other aspects of culture including economic, political, and religious beliefs. Melford E. Spiro's *Kinship and Marriage in Burma: A Cultural and Psychodynamic Analysis* (Berkeley, 1977) is an excellent presentation of kinship beliefs in Burma and includes a full account of Burmese Buddhist views on marriage. Clifford Geertz's seminal work *The Religion of Java* (Glencoe, Ill., 1960) describes the syncretism of Hindu, Islamic, and folk beliefs that comprise Javanese religion. This book focuses on the five major occupations of the population and their religious beliefs that shape the moral organization of the culture of Java. The mixture of Catholic and Maya Indian beliefs is explored in Evon Z. Vogt's *Zinacantan: A Maya Community in the Highlands of Chiapas* (Cambridge, Mass., 1969). An extensive study of the Tzotzil-speaking Indians of Guatemala, it includes a full account of their religious beliefs and marriage practices, especially the relationships created between families and *compadres,* or ritual godparents. For an excellent view of marriage as a life process, begun before the birth of the bride and occurring in gradual stages as she matures, see Jane C. Goodale's *Tiwi Wives: A Study of the Women of Melville Island, North Australia* (Seattle, 1971).

EDITH TURNER and PAMELA R. FRESE

MARTYRDOM

The badge of martyrdom is awarded by the leadership of a community to men and women who offer their lives voluntarily in solidarity with their group in conflict with another, ideologically contrasting, group. The martyr and his or her slayer are delegates, champions, or defenders of their societies. A few martyrs are suicides, but most are slain by judicial, military, police, religious, or other functionaries. These functionaries execute the martyr as a terrorist, a criminal, or a heretic who threatens fundamental social values or the physical safety of members of the society. The societies of the slayer and the slain struggle to control the meaning of the slaying: is it to be understood by the world as martyrdom or as judicial retribution?

How Martyrdom Fits into Social Life. Martyrdom infuses a mundane event with divine grace. The symbolism parallels that of a sacrificial animal attaining a sacred quality. The martyr, a human sacrifice, attains an indelible sanctity. The sanctity may take the form of a redemptory promise, softening the pain or enabling the martyr to persist despite pain. Early Christians imprisoned and awaiting martyrdom were believed to have the power to forgive sins. Those released might retain this power, perhaps becoming presbyters of the church.

The martyr dies convinced of his or her legitimate authority, an authority challenging that of the executioners. A religious martyr may believe himself or herself to be an incarnation of the Holy Ghost, as did Montanus (Frend, 1972); the Spirit of God, al-Haqq, as did al-Hallaj (Massignon, 1982); or a receiver of the Torah, as did `Aqiva' ben Yosef.

The martyr, deceased, is a sacred symbol of an authority around which the society rallies.

Martyr Types: Political Independence and Action Orientation. The relative political power of the conflicting communities determines the task of martyrdom and the characteristics of the martyrs selected to carry out that task. Crescive, self-determining, and decaying societies all generate a peculiar form of martyrdom.

Martyrdom in crescive societies. A crescive society is one that is politically powerless but beginning to stir, perhaps renascent. The resistance of Jews to hellenization under the Seleucid ruler Antiochus Epiphanes in the second century BCE is an early model. The elderly Eleazar, according to the apocryphal *2 Maccabees,* is the martyr type, choosing to give his life rather than eat pork in an already desecrated Temple in Jerusalem.

The exemplar of Christian martyrdom is the trial and the crucifixion on Golgotha as that event is related in the Gospels. Later martyrs strive to imitate Christ. The sacrificed Lamb of God survives, not in this world, but in the world beyond.

Martyrdom in crescive societies creates authority, escalates the struggle, unifies the minority, and legitimates the new culture by demonstrating its priority over nature. Furthermore, martyrs propel a politically crescive society toward self-determination, toward social and cultural freedom. The death of the martyr makes the ideological choice a matter of life and death. This escalates the struggle, perhaps expediting the resolution in favor of the minority.

Radicalizing and escalating the conflict unifies the two parties internally. The grievous injustice of the slaying of the defenseless martyr and the gruesome inhuman circumstances under which the slaying occurs leave few individuals on the sidelines.

With martyrdom, the culture of the minority, its ideology and law, is sanctified, a covenant established, stamped with blood. It is written in *Mekhilta',* a Jewish interpretative work, that every commandment that the Israelites have not died for is not really established, and every commandment that they have died for will be established among them (Herr, 1967).

The self-determining society: heroic martyrs. The self-determining society has achieved political control of its life. Examples are fourth-century Christians in Asia Minor following the victory of Constantine and Islam of the Umayyad caliphate in eighth-century Damascus. Martyrs in such a society are active, aiding the society in its expansion, openly propagandizing, sending missionaries to the unconverted, and warring against adversaries. In Islam the *jihad* is a religious obligation and the martyr, the *shahid,* one who dies in this sacred battle. The European Christian society that sent an armed pilgrimage to Jerusalem under Pope Gregory VII, in the words of Cohn (1961), raced toward a mass sacrifice, a mass apotheosis in Jerusalem. Defending against external enemies is the major problem; the achievement of internal unity is a minor social problem. Nevertheless, the self-determining society suffers its internal schisms. Islamic historians say little about Muslim martyrs executed by Arab pagans, the early opposition group, beyond the early oppression in Yathrib. The record is clear on Islamic martyrs of internecine conflict, Muslim martyrs killed by Muslims during the crescive and during the self-determining periods are remembered by their sects.

The politically decaying society: victims and anti-martyrs. The politically decaying society is losing its ability to be self-determining. Roman provincial societies were decaying as they were co-opted by a victorious Christianity. The

> **Martyrdom is latent in a decaying society. The adversary claims mere victims who affirm no ideology by their deaths.**

world's smaller societies, such as those of the North American Indian civilization and of the Polynesian islands, were submerged by modern imperial powers.

Martyrdom is latent in a decaying society. The adversary claims mere victims who affirm no ideology by their deaths. Jewish leaders tend to remember the victims of the Holocaust as martyrs for the sanctification of God's name. Breslauer (1981), in a dissent, writes that they were on the whole not sacred witnesses but passive victims, not proud martyrs for a cause but political pawns.

Jewish resistance, independent and in cooperation with local partisans, produced genuine martyrs but was rarely supported by the officials of the *Judenrat,* the Jewish councils of the ghetto. The Warsaw ghetto uprising, authorized by ghetto leaders, was a final suicidal thrust, Samson at the temple of Dagon. Self-immolation requires a residue of moral strength, a will to protect the group's honor. Slaves may commit suicide, like concentration camp inmates throwing their bodies against the electrified wire, in order to relieve their suffering. [*See* Holocaust, The.]

The negotiating victims may become collaborators or even converts. They may even become anti-martyrs. An anti-martyr may be a convert to the dominant ideology, remaining a leader of the minority and seeking to manage the conflict by collaborating with the dominant group. This effort may cost them their own lives. Anti-martyrs may strive to suppress martyrs whom they consider wrong-headed. They are not opportunistic turncoats, moved by personal avarice, but quislings, deeply committed to an enemy ideology, believing it best for their group. If they lose, they die unrelenting.

BIBLIOGRAPHY

Allard, Paul. *La persecution de Dioclétian et le triomphe de l'église.* 3d rev. ed. 2 vols. Rome, 1971.

Ben Sasson, H. H. "Kiddush Hashem: Historical Aspects." In *Encyclopaedia Judaica.* Jerusalem, 1971.

Bickerman, Elias J. *The God of the Maccabees.* Leiden, 1979.

Breslauer, S. Daniel. "Martyrdom and Charisma: Leo Baeck and a New Jewish Theology." *Encounter 42* (Spring 1981): 133-142.

Cohn, Norman R. C. *The Pursuit of the Millenium.* 3d ed. New York, 1970.

Coogan, Tim Pat. *On the Blanket: The H Block Story.* Dublin, 1980.

Frend, W. H. C. *Martyrdom and Persecution in the Early Church.* Oxford, 1965.

Gandhi, M. K. *Satyagraha in South Africa.* Translated by Yalji Govindji Desair. Madras, 1928.

Hazrat, Ahmad. *Ahmadiyyat or the True Islam.* New Delhi, 1980.

Historical Society of Israel. *Milhemet qodesh u-martirologyah.* Jerusalem, 1967.

Jacobs, I. "Eleazar ben Yair's Sanction for Marytrdom." *Journal for the Study of Judaism in the Persian, Hellenistic, and Roman Period* 13 (December 1982): 183-186.

Jacoby, Susan. *Wild Justice: The Evolution of Revenge.* New York, 1983.

Klawitzer, Frederick C. "The Role of Martyrdom and Persecution in Developing the Priestly Authority of Women in Early Christianity: A Case Study of Montanism." *Church History 49* (September 1980): 251-261.

Kogon, Eugen. *The Theory and Practice of Hell.* New York, 1973.

Lamm, Norman. "Kiddush Ha-shem and Hillul Ha-shem." In *Encyclopaedia Judaica.* Jerusalem, 1971.

Maimonides, Moses. *Epistle to Yemen.* New York, 1952.

Maimonides, Moses. *Iggeret ha-shemad.* In *Iggrot ha-Rambam,* pp. 13-68. Jerusalem, 1979.

Massignon, Louis. *The Passion of al-Hallaj: Mystic and Martyr of Islam.* Princeton, 1982.

Mattingly, Garrett. *The Armada.* Boston, 1959.

Peters, Rudolph, trans. *Jihad in Medieval and Modern Islam.* Leiden, 1977.

Poliakov, Leon. *La causalité diabolique: Essai sur l'origine des persécutions.* Paris, 1980.

Rahner, Karl. *On the Theology of Death.* New York, 1961.

Riddle, Donald W. *The Martyrs: A Study in Social Control.* Chicago, 1931.

Rosenberg, Bruce A. *Custer and the Epic of Defeat.* University Park, Pa., 1974.

Rubenstein, Richard L. *The Cunning of History: The Holocaust and the American Future.* New York, 1975.

Sachedina, Abdulaziz Abdulhussein. *Islamic Messianism: The Idea of Mahdi in Twelver Shi'ism.* Albany, N. Y., 1981.

Szaluta, Jacques. "Apotheosis to Ignominy: The Martyrdom of Marshall Petain." *Journal of Psychohistory 7* (Spring 1980): 415-453.

Vööbus, Arthur. *History of Asceticism in the Syrian Orient.* Corpus Scriptorum Christianorum Orientalium, vol. 189. Louvain, 1958.

Warner, Dennis, and Peggy Warner. *The Sacred Warriors: Japan's Suicide Legions.* New York, 1982.

Wensinck, A. J. "The Oriental Doctrine of the Martyrs." In *Semietische Studien uit de Nalatenschap.* Leiden, 1941.

Zerubavel, Yael. "The Last Stand: On the Transformation of Symbols in Modern Israeli Culture." Ph. D. diss., University of Pennsylvania, 1980.

SAMUEL Z. KLAUSNER

MARXISM

Judeo-Christian Influences. Neither Karl Marx (1818-1883) nor Friedrich Engels (1820-1895) had a profound grasp of the Christian faith or the Jewish tradition. Though Marx was the grandson and the nephew of rabbis, his father turned to liberal Protestant Christianity, and Marx was confirmed in the state Church of the Old Prussian Union. Engels was educated in the Reformed piety of Prussian Westphalia but broke with it early in his life. Nevertheless, the Marxism they formulated shared in and interacted with the Judeo-Christian heritage in two fundamental ways: (1) Marxism continually confronted, and drew on, the heritage of radical Christianity, and (2) Marxism was a result of a process, rooted in the Enlightenment and developed by G. W. F. Hegel and the left-wing Hegelians, that transposed the structure of Christian faith and hope into a humanist key.

Marxism's indebtedness to the Enlightenment and to Hegel and the left-wing Hegelians is revealed in three principal stages. The first is the Enlightenment's confidence in the continuity between the human and the divine, between human reason and conscience and divine order, and therefore in the unbounded human capacity for progress. Educated in the Enlightenment tradition, Marx in his youth shared this confidence. The second stage is Hegel's conversion of that continuity into a divine-human dialectical struggle for self-realization in history through alienation (expressed in human oppression and suffering but supremely in the crucifixion of Christ) and reconciliation (the work of the Holy Spirit through human power to establish the supremacy and moral order of a human society). The third stage is embodied in the view of the left-wing Hegelians, given definitive expression in Ludwig Feuerbach's *Essence of Christianity* (1841) that the divine dimension of this struggle is itself alienation, that God

> ## Neither Karl Marx (1818-1883) nor Friedrich Engels (1820-1895) had a profound grasp of the Christian faith or the Jewish tradition.

is essentially a projection of the ideal human essence onto the heavens, and that the whole doctrine and ceremony of the Christian church can be enjoyed as a celebration of the true quality of the human species, realizing itself in love between person and person.

Marx adopted Feuerbach's humanistic inversion of Christianity but radicalized it. Religion is, for him, the projection in fantasy of a humanity that finds no fulfillment in this world. It is "the sigh of the oppressed creature," at once a protest against oppression and an adaptation to it. It is the opium the people take to dull their pain and give them dreams. But it is not enough, he criticizes Feuerbach, to expose this fact; one must go on to analyze the contradictions in human society that produce religious illusions, and one must revolutionize them in practice. In doing this, Marx radicalized left-wing Hegelian humanism into an antitheology that cut all remaining links with spirituality. First, he redefined Feuerbach's concept of "species humanity" not in terms of human relationships, but as "free, conscious activity" of the species expressed in each individual *(Economic Philosophical Manuscripts of 1844,* first published 1927). The human being is a self-creator through labor, the agent who molds nature and history. Second, he rooted Hegel's concept of alienation in the expropriation of the fruits of a person's labor by others who employ or use him. Third, Marx found the savior in this conflict to be the class most completely deprived and exploited, lacking all stake in existing order or power. In the utter negation of proletarian existence the image of true species humanity is formed, in solidarity free from all personal ambition, and in revolutionary determination. Fourth, what for Hegel is the cunning of the Spirit realizing its goals in history through the human struggle becomes for Marx the dialectical operation of the "material" laws of history, expressed in the forces of production overturning the relations of production, by means of the strategy and tactics of the revolutionary struggle. Fifth, communism for Marx, like the kingdom of God for Christians, is genuinely eschatological. Hope in its coming is not dimmed by its delayed arrival. It is always at hand. It will bring a transformation of human nature by new social conditions that, Marx believed, will be prepared in the struggle itself and in transitional socialist societies.

Christian and Marxist Socialism before 1917. Before the death of Marx, the lines of conflict were drawn between the Christian church and Marxist socialism. Karl Kautsky, in *Foundations of Christianity* (1908), recognized Jesus as an early socialist, but was more severe than Engels in his condemnation of the other-worldliness of the Christian religion. Lenin made the propagation of atheism a subordinate but critically important task of the Communist party, before and after it seized power. The Marxist challenge stimulated some churches with a strong precapitalist tradition in ethics to elaborate their own social teachings. In 1891, Leo XIII recognized that in capitalist industrial development, "a small number of very rich men have been able to lay upon the masses of the poor a yoke little better than slavery itself" *(De rerum novarum).* Still rejecting socialism, he set forth the state's responsibility to intervene in the economic order to promote justice, the employers' duty to use wealth and power for the welfare of their workers and the public, and the workers' right to organize Catholic trade unions to assure their rights in the context of seeking harmony between classes. This encyclical laid the foundation of a Roman Catholic social reform movement, redefined forty years later in the *Quadragesimo anno* of Pius XI. A similar response arose among the Protestants with the formation of the Anti-Revolutionary party by Dutch Calvinists, who were led by Abraham Kuyper.

Christian socialists pursued their goals in various relationships to Marxist movements. In Germany Friedrich Naumann organized a Christian socialist group in the 1890s, which, however, had little influence and gradually moved to a left-liberal position. In Switzerland Hermann Kutter and Leonhard Ragaz, inspired in part by Blumhardt, founded a religious socialist movement. In the United States the Society of Christian Socialists was formed in 1889; its publication *The Dawn* published contributions by Marxists but basically promoted socialism as "the application to society of the way of Christ." These movements did not engage Marxism with any depth of analysis.

The Russian Revolution and the Great Depression brought a new depth to Christian social reflection on Marxism and to Christian-Marxist relations. Jacques Maritain in his *Integral Humanism* (1936) contrasted the incarnation of Christ with the "absolute realist immanentism" of Marx. He called for a "secular Christian" pluralist society inspired, but not dominated, by the church toward a practical vision of the common good and composed of a structure of communities gathered around personal (family, neighborhood, cultural affinity) or functional (economic or social) foci, of which the state is the highest and most general.

The most comprehensive Protestant effort to provide an alternative Christian vision, that of the Religious Socialists, was inspired by Paul Tillich. Tillich understood Marxism as "prophecy on the grounds of an autonomous self-contained world" (*The Socialist Decision,* 1933) and saw a structural analogy between Marx's thought and prophetic theology in its view of history, its analysis of human alienation in present society, and its unity of theory and practice in social involvement. According to Tillich, a socialism integrated with religion would enable society to understand its roots in the original powers of creation and its destiny in confrontation with the demand of the unconditioned (God) and could thus lead it from a bourgeois autonomy to a new theonomy that would be open to the grace of God, which informs and transforms human culture.

Soviet Communism from 1917 to 1945. Vladimir Il' ich Lenin (1870-1924) had no personal tolerance for religion in any form. According to Lenin, the state should treat religion as a private matter and separate it totally from education, from influence on public policy, and from participation in public life, while respecting the religious prejudices and practices of people who otherwise behave as good socialist citizens. The party should be an agent, first of the strategy and tactics, second of the dialectical materialist world-

view, of the socialist revolution. To the latter, atheism belongs.

Soviet policy, since the Revolution of 1917, has followed these guidelines. The 1917 laws nationalized property, including that of the church, prohibited religious education in any school, and granted freedom of worship and belief insofar as these did not interfere with public order, civic duty, or

> **The Russian Revolution and the Great Depression brought a new depth to Christian social reflection on Marxism. . . .**

the rights of citizens. In 1929 further restrictions were spelled out; the conduct of worship became the sole legal activity of the church. Religious instruction was allowed only above the age of eighteen, and then only in private. The formula of the Soviet constitution of 1936—"Freedom for religious profession and antireligious propaganda"—has been used to silence all public defense of religion and all public evangelism.

World War II produced a relaxation of restrictions that lasted roughly until the ascendancy of Nikita Khrushchev in 1957.

The present situation is the result of these trends, curbed by new repression under Khrushchev, and somewhat stabilized since then. Churches, synagogues, and mosques do function, though few new ones have been registered and some have been closed in the past generation. They are closely controlled by the Ministry of Religious Affairs, to which the leadership must be acceptable, and they are infiltrated by government agents. Religious leaders have been allowed increasing ecumenical contacts abroad, which are also monitored. Dissenters have been harshly dealt with among Christians and Jews, less harshly among Muslims.

Marxist-Christian Dialogue and Interaction since Stalin. This dialogue began with soul-searching among communists. The discrediting of Stalin and the continuation of so many Stalinist policies led to profound reflection in the East and West about the whole range of Marxist theory and practice, including its relation to the claims of Christian faith and the practice of religion. In Yugoslavia, where an open, flexible philosophical approach to Marxist thought had been established over the previous decade, this dialogue, primarily with the Roman Catholic theologians of Croatia and Slovenia, was especially rich in the variety of its themes and points of view (Mojzes, 1981). In Poland a quiet conversation between Catholic and Marxist intellectuals, which began in 1962, continues to the present. The encounter in Czechoslovakia was especially dramatic and for a time influenced government policy. The high point of this development was the only

Christian-Marxist congress ever to be held in Eastern Europe, in Marianske Lazne, Czechoslovakia, in 1967. But, in August 1968 the Soviet army snuffed out the Czech socialist experiment. Restrictions more severe than before were imposed on churches. The Marxists who had taken part in the dialogue lost their positions and were silenced.

In western Europe and North America, on the other hand, Marxist-Christian dialogue has continued to develop.

BIBLIOGRAPHY

Beeson, Trevor. *Discretion and Valour: Religious Conditions In Russia and Eastern Europe.* Rev. ed. Philadelphia, 1982. This work, by a team of scholars acquainted directly with religious conditions in various eastern European countries, was assembled by the British Council of Churches under Mr. Beeson's direction. It is the most sensitive and informed guide available.

Berdiaev, Nikolai. *The Origin of Russian Communism.* Translated by R. M. French. London, 1937. A classic study of Russia's leading Christian philosopher of the twentieth century.

Fried, Albert, and Ronald Sanders, eds. *Socialist Thought: A Documentary History. Chicago,* 1964. Excerpts and brief expositions of socialist writers from pre-Marxist France to the present, including the social-democratic and communist streams of Marxism.

Gollwitzer, Helmut. *The Christian Faith and the Marxist Criticism of Religion.* Translated by David Cairns. New York, 1970. The most complete study of this subject available in English.

Hopkins, Charles Howard. *The Rise of the Social Gospel in American Protestantism, 1865-1915.* New Haven, 1940. A classic study that traces also Marxist interaction with Christian socialism.

Jones, Peter d'A. *The Christian Socialist Revival, 1877-1914: Religion, Class and Social Conscience in Late-Victorian England.* Princeton, 1968.

Kolarz, Walter. *Religion in the Soviet Union.* New York, 1961. The most thorough study of this field, including the variety of Christian and non-Christian religious communities, up to the time of its publication.

Lenin, V. I. *Religion.* New York, 1933. A Soviet publication containing in a brief pamphlet most of the writings from Lenin on this subject that are usually quoted.

Marx, Karl, and Friedrich Engels. *On Religion.* New York, 1964. A reprint of a compilation by Soviet scholars of the most important statements of the two authors on religion. Includes an introduction by Reinhold Niebuhr.

Mojzes, Paul. *Christian-Marxist Dialogue in Eastern Europe.* Minneapolis, 1981. A complete study of this activity in Communist Europe. Especially informative on Yugoslavia, the author's land of origin, Czechoslovakia, and Poland, but comprehensive both geographically and in subject matter.

Thomas, Madathilparampil M. *The Secular Ideologies of India and the Secular Meaning of Christ.* Bangalore, 1976. Examines Marxism-Leninism in its various expressions, socialist humanism with its Marxist component, liberal rationalism, and several forms of post-Hindu humanism as they relate to Christian and Hindu theology and practice.

Tucker, Robert C., ed. *The Marx-Engels Reader.* 2d ed. New York, 1978. See especially part 1, "The Early Marx." This volume shows the scope of Marx's own humanism.

CHARLES C. WEST

MARY

MARY, the mother of Jesus. The New Testament description of Maria, or Mariam, includes her virginal conception of Jesus. [*See* Jesus.] Preeminent among the saints, the Virgin Mary later became the object of piety and cult and, especially in the Roman Catholic church, of dogmas such as the Immaculate Conception and the Assumption. Protestant treatment of her as a biblical saint varies. She is honored in the Qur'an (surahs 3 and 19).

Mary in the New Testament. The *Gospel of Mark* (written about AD 70) describes Jesus' mother and brothers on the edge of a crowd listening to him teach (*Mk.* 3:31-35). "His own" (3:20), likely "his family" (RSV), have come to take him away because Jesus was, they thought, "beside himself"; they are like the hostile scribes who claim that he is "possessed by Beelzebub" (3:22). The passage in *Mark* 6:1-6a, about the rejection of Jesus in his home synagogue, does nothing to change this picture of Mary and Jesus' brothers as sharing the unbelief of those of the surrounding countryside. Hence the overall picture of Mary in *Mark* is a negative one. (For details, see Brown et al., 1978, pp. 51-72, 286-287.)

In the *Gospel of Matthew* (perhaps before AD 90), a more positive view of Mary results, especially from the first two chapters about the birth and infancy of Jesus, the fruit of meditation upon the Hebrew scriptures within the Matthean community.

Matthew's portrait of Mary during the ministry of Jesus is also ameliorated by other details. In the scene of Jesus' eschatological family (*Mt.* 12:46-50) no reference is made to Jesus' natural family coming to take custody of him. In the synagogue scene at Nazareth (*Mt.* 13:53-58), Matthew drops out the Marcan reference to "his own relatives" in what Jesus says (12:57; cf. *Mk.* 6:4).

The most positive synoptic portrayal of Mary comes in the *Gospel of Luke* plus *Acts* (perhaps after AD 90). In *Acts* 1:14, Mary is a member of the Jerusalem church. In *Luke* 1-2, Mary is described as Joseph's "betrothed" (*Luke* 2:1-20). Accounts show Mary's faith in God (*Lk.* 1:38, 1:45); tell of the virginal conception (*Lk.* 1:31-34, cf. 3:23) and of Mary's status as a "favored one" (*Lk.* 1:28; Vulgate, *gratia plena*), employing the term *hail (ave);* and relate Simeon's prophecy to Mary: "A sword will pierce through your own soul also" (*Luke* 2:35, probably meaning that Mary, too, must transcend the natural bonds of family and come to faith in Jesus).

The *Gospel of John* (c. 90) contains no reference to the virgin birth, in part because the preexistence and incarnation of the Word are emphasized (*Jn.* 1:1-18). The scenes involving "the mother of Jesus" (never "Mary") during Jesus' ministry are totally different from those in the synoptic Gospels. In the story about a wedding feast at Cana (*Jn.* 2:1-11), his mother does not yet seem to have grasped that his "hour" does not parallel the wishes of his natural family. Although she accompanied Jesus to Capernaum (*Jn.* 2:12), perhaps this was because she was seeking to bring him home (cf. *Mk.* 3:20-35). The mother of Jesus appears in one other Johannine scene (*Jn.* 19:25-27), standing at the foot of the cross with the Beloved Disciple. This *stabat mater* reference occurs only in *John,* among all the Gospels.

Marian Piety and Mariology. In the second century, references to Mary are rare, found chiefly in the letters of Ignatius of Antioch about the "mystery" of Jesus' birth (e.g., *Ephesians* 19.1) and in Justin Martyr (*Dialogue with Trypho* 100).

In the christological controversies of the fifth century, Mary took on more and more of the status of her Son. Use of the term *theotokos* also led to emphasis on Mary not simply as *Dei genitrix* ("she who gives birth to God") but also as *mater Dei,* the "mother of God." [*See* Councils.]

Marian festivals generally developed in the East; they rapidly spread elsewhere and multiplied in number. Some had biblical roots, for example, the Annunciation on 25 March (*Lk.* 1:26-38) and the Purification on 2 February (*Lk.* 2:21-39, cf. *Lv.* 12). The Feast of the Immaculate Conception of Mary (8 or 9 December) arose around the theme of her sinlessness from the time of her birth (cf. *Protevangelium of James* 4).

Some of the Protestant reformers grew up with Marian piety of this sort. Luther seems at times to have affirmed Mary's immaculate conception and even her bodily assumption and retained some Marian festivals, but with a christological emphasis. More revealing is Luther's 1521 exposition of the Magnificat (*Works,* Saint Louis, 1956, vol. 21, pp. 297-358), where Mary is "the foremost example" of God's grace and of proper humility. The Lutheran confessions simply assume the virgin birth of Jesus Christ and even use stock phrases like *semper virgo.*

BIBLIOGRAPHY

Walter Delius's *Geschichte der Marienverehrung* (Munich, 1963) provides a standard treatment, supplemented by his *Texte zur Geschichte der Marienverehrung und Marienverkündigung in der alten Kirche,* 2d rev. ed. (Berlin, 1973). Somewhat more popular in tone are Hilda Graef's *Mary: A History of Doctrine and Devotion,* 2 vols. (New York, 1963-1965); Marina Warner's *Alone of All Her Sex: The Myth and Cult of the Virgin Mary* (New York, 1976); and Christa Mulack's *Maria: Die geheime Göttin im Christentum* (Stuttgart, 1985). Sympathetic articles on persons, terms, and themes, with bibliography, will be found in Michael O'Carroll's *Theotokos: A Theological Encyclopedia of the Blessed Virgin Mary,* rev. ed. with supplement (Wilmington, Del., 1983). For biblical materials, see *Mary in the New Testament: A Collaborative Assessment by Protestant and Roman Catholic Scholars,* edited by Raymond E. Brown, Karl P. Donfried, Joseph A. Fitzmyer, and John Reumann (Philadelphia, 1978). *Mary in the Churches,* edited by Hans Küng and Jürgen Moltmann, *Concilium* 168 (New York, 1983), surveys biblical origins and confessional attitudes today as well as trends in feminist and liberation theology and depth psychology and literature. *Mary's Place in Christian Dialogue,* edited by Alberic Stacpoole (Wilton, Conn., 1982), reflects over a decade of work by the Ecumenical Society of the Blessed Virgin Mary. Stephen Benko's *Protestants, Catholics, and Mary* (Valley Forge, Pa., 1978) deals also with Josephology.

JOHN REUMANN

MAYA RELIGION

The religion of Classic Maya civilization (300-900 CE) flourished in the Petén lowlands of northern Guatemala, producing a distinctive cosmology and worldview that still persist. Today, more than three million descendants of the Classic Maya occupy the area stretching from the Yucatán Peninsula in the north to the highlands of Guatemala and Chiapas, Mexico, in the south.

Classic Maya Religion. A concern with the passage of time led the Maya to chart the motion and phases of the sun, moon, Venus, and various constellations. By calculating the duration of different celestial cycles in terms of whole-day units (e.g., 149 lunations = 4,400 days), Classic Maya astronomers were able to compute lunar periods, the length of the solar year, and the revolutions of Venus, all to within minutes of their modern values. These calculations were greatly facilitated by the invention of a system of place-value arithmetic, an achievement that the Maya share only with the ancient Mesopotamians. The coalescence in Maya thought of time, astronomy, mathematics, and writing finds expression in Itzamná, the principal deity of the Classic Maya: he was alternately the creator god, the sun, and the first priest who invented writing and books.

Classic Maya religion, however, involved more than time and astronomy. Figures in Classic inscriptions once thought to depict deities are now known to represent actual Maya rulers, and the dynastic histories of such sites as Yaxchilan, Tikal, and Palenque have been reconstructed. Ancestor worship and the apotheosis of deceased rulers were essential aspects of Classic Maya religion. Some archaeologists further suggest that the impressive temples and pyramids that dominate Maya sites were funerary monuments to these deified rulers. The magnificent tomb of Lord Pacal (603-683 CE) found beneath the Temple of Inscriptions at Palenque clearly supports this theory.

Postclassic Maya Religion. Despite the rapid decline of Classic Maya civilization after 900 CE, Maya religion survived in the Postclassic states of Yucatán and highland Guatemala (900-1530 CE). Old agricultural deities such as the *chacs* (rain gods), the *balams* (guardians of field and hearth), Kauil (the maize god), and Ixchel (the moon goddess and patroness of weaving, medicine, and childbirth) undoubtedly also survived intact. The Spanish conquest of the Maya area (1524-1540 CE) came as only another in a series of foreign incursions that never quite obliterated the distinctiveness of Maya culture and religion.

Contemporary Maya Religion. Contemporary Maya religion has been transformed by Roman Catholicism, but strong continuities with the pre-Hispanic past persist. The motion of the sun still defines Maya cosmology, making the eastern and western horizons the primary cardinal directions. The circular paths of the sun and moon unite the various layers of the cosmos above and below the earth's surface. The preeminence of the sun as "Our Father" or "Our Grandfather" is reflected in its identification with God or, more frequently, Christ. Similarly, the moon is often associated with the Virgin Mary and called "Our Mother" or "Our Grandmother." In quotidian affairs, Catholic saints have become the supernatural guardians of field, hearth, and health, although in Yucatán the old *balams* still persist, and in some highland communities autochthonous ancestral deities remain important.

Human destiny also involves the welfare of the soul. Unlike the eternal Christian soul, Maya souls are largely involved with the here and now, since the soul represents the seat of reason, most concretely expressed in articulate speech and proper social behavior. In their very essence, individuals are enmeshed in their community and the social morality that it presupposes. Individuals can lose all or part of their soul through illness, through experiencing strong emotions such as anger or fright, or through other forms of culturally inappropriate behavior. Saving one's soul requires the constant attention to one's relations with fellow community members rather than merely purity of action and intent.

Individuals serve the saints by joining *cofradías* ("brotherhoods"), where for one year they care for the saint's image and perform the proper rituals, often at considerable personal expense. In return, individuals gain social prestige and access to higher political and religious offices. Outside the *cofradías,* traditional Maya religion recognizes no formal institutions.

BIBLIOGRAPHY

The best general introduction to Maya religion is J. Eric S. Thompson's *Maya History and Religion* (Norman, Okla., 1970), although his views on Classic Maya social structure and the nature of Maya hieroglyphic writing have been challenged. David H. Kelley's *Deciphering the Maya Script* (Austin, 1976) presents a broad view of different approaches to Maya writing, especially in regard to the phonetic nature of the script. The proceedings from four recent conferences concerning Maya epigraphy, religion, and society have been published in six volumes, the latest of which is *Fourth Palenque Round Table 1980* (Austin, 1984), edited by Merle Greene Robertson and Elizabeth Benson. Technical but highly stimulating articles can be found in a volume edited by Norman Hammond and Gordon R. Willey, *Maya Archaeology and Ethnohistory* (Austin, 1979); papers therein by Clemency Coggins, Dennis Puleston, and Gordon Brotherston are extremely valuable. Anthony F. Aveni's *Skywatchers of Ancient Mexico* (Austin, 1980) is an indispensable guide to the "ethnoastronomy" of Mesoamerican civilizations. Of the colonial sources on Maya religion, *Landa's Relación de las cosas de Yucatán* (Cambridge, Mass., 1941), translated and edited by A. M. Tozzer, is the most thoroughly annotated edition of the work of the famous chronicler Diego de Landa, although the pagination in the index and syllabus is occasionally frustratingly faulty. Munro S. Edmonson's translation of *The Book of Counsel: The Popol Vuh of the Quiche Maya of Guatemala* (New Orleans, 1971) was the first to demonstrate the parallel couplet verse form of this epic of Maya mythology and history. Among the many ethnographies of modern Maya religions, Evon Z. Vogt's *Tortillas for the Gods: A Symbolic Analysis of Zinacanteco Rituals* (Cambridge, Mass., 1976) stands out as one of the most extensive and detailed studies to date. Barbara Tedlock's *Time and the Highland Maya* (Albuquerque, 1982) is an excellent study of contemporary Maya divination and calendrics. Finally, Eva Hunt's *The Transformation of the Hummingbird: Cultural Roots of a Zinacantecan Mythical Poem* (Ithaca, N. Y., 1977) provides a masterful structuralist analysis of both contemporary and pre-Hispanic Maya religion.

JOHN M. WATANABE

MEDITATION

Western Traditions

Judaism. Meditation and contemplation in the Jewish tradition acknowledge the centrality and authority of the Hebrew scriptures. Reading and interpreting the Torah require concentration and discursive meditation. This meditation led to the development of commentary, such as the Mishnah and the Talmud, and schools came into being that fostered an experiential approach. Heavily influenced by gnosticism and Hellenism, this movement is referred to as *heikhalot* mysticism. Ascetical practices culminated in a contemplative ascent of the soul through seven heavens to reach its final home in a state of beatitude. The final state is viewed as one in which the mystic stands before the throne of God and sees and hears directly. There is no experience of mystical union, and God remains "wholly other." This tradition remained essentially cataphatic and nonaffective, although the symbolism of the ascent and the attainment of ecstatic consciousness is characteristic of Jewish contemplation.

Christianity. Meditation and contemplation, particularly within monastic circles, reached a high degree of differentiation and sophistication in the Christian tradition. The practices of the early church took form in an atmosphere influenced by Hermetic literature and the philosophy of Neoplatonism. Syncretic in nature, the Hermetic books present the theme of a mystical ascent to the knowledge of God. This important image (found also in Jewish mysticism) becomes central to the mysticism of Christianity. The idea of an ascent from the many to the One is taken over from the thought of the Neoplatonist Plotinus.

For Clement, meditation led to the apprehension of the intelligible realities and then, through *gnosis* as a gift of Christ, to hidden spiritual realities.

Ignatius Loyola (1495-1556), the founder of the Jesuits, wrote a treatise entitled *Spiritual Exercises,* in which he outlines a progression in meditative practice. His methods are of interest insofar as they involve cataphatic visualization techniques that bear some resemblance to Hindu and Buddhist practices. For example, Ignatius's fourth method requires that the practitioner choose a specific image, such as the passion or the resurrection of Jesus, and apply each of the five sens-

> **The object of meditation . . . is to still the mind and the emotions with which the individual usually identifies.**

es to that image. Thus, through seeing, hearing, smelling, tasting, and touching, the image is vivified in the consciousness of the meditator.

Islam. By the eighth century, strict Muslim orthodoxy began to be challenged by Sufism, the generic term for Islamic mysticism. The Sufi movement favored an interiorization and esotericization of the basic institutions of Islam. The orthodox religious attitudes of fear and obedience before the transcendence of God changed in Sufism to an attitude of ecstatic love of God and hope of union with him through a transcendence of the phenomenal self. Meditative and contemplative practices became an important part of this quest, and *dhikr* became a constant practice of the presence of God.

Eastern Traditions

India. A concern for meditative asceticism, which runs through Indian religious history, can be traced as far back as the Indus Valley civilization of the third millennium BCE.

Yoga. The Yoga system is one of the classical *darsanas,* or "viewpoints," of Indian philosophy. The object of meditation and other ascetic practices is to still the mind and the emotions with which the individual usually identifies. When this is accomplished, consciousness can reflect the pure absolute spirit (or *purusa),* which is the principle of consciousness itself. Yoga discipline in a variety of forms becomes an important ingredient in several Indian spiritual traditions and religions, including Jainism, various forms of Hinduism, and Buddhism. [*See* Yoga.]

Hinduism. In the early history of Hinduism, a stage referred to as Brahmanism, there was a movement away from the practice of exoteric ritual and toward meditative inte-

riority and realization. As the tradition developed, Hindus came to be divided into three main sects.

Vaisnavism. The Vaisnavas, worshipers of the god Visnu and his many incarnations, developed a form of active, affective, and cataphatic meditation in which chanting, singing, and dancing were used to induce transic absorption into the deity.

Saivism and Saktism. The devotees of Siva developed their own forms of contemplative worship. One is the growth of a cult dedicated to Sakti, the female consort of Siva. Sakti is the active female energy of the universe in contradistinction to the passive contemplative energy of Siva himself. Saktism became an important part of the Tantric manifestations of Hinduism. Tantric Hinduism developed several techniques of meditation, including the use of the yantra. A yantra is a geometric diagram that represents an abstract form or manifestation of a deity. Deities are essentially formless in their own nature but are thought to manifest themselves in a movement from the subtle to the gross, in the forms of sound, the geometric forms of the *yantra,* a series of triangles, squares, and circles emanating from a central point, which serves to focus the mind of the meditating yogin.

In *kundaliniyoga,* the macrocosmic Sakti is further identified, within the microcosm of the human body, as *kundalini.* *Kundalini* literally means "coiled" and refers to the visualization of Sakti as an energy within the body in the form of a sleeping serpent. This energy is associated with a meditative physiology of the subtle body of man.

Buddhism. Buddhism is a tradition that seeks to penetrate the veil of appearances and social conditioning and, through meditative insight, to achieve a vision of the truth of reality. This vision leads to liberation from the round of karmic cycles and the achievement of ultimate freedom in *nirvana.* *Nirvana* is the goal of Buddhist ascesis subsumed under the term *bhavana,* or meditation. *Bhavana* has two secondary objectives: the first is the achievement of *samatha,* or calm; the second is *vipasyana,* insight or higher vision.

Calming, transic absorption and insight are important features of Buddhist ascesis; they continue to be fundamental in both Hinayana and Mahayana schools. The Tantric form of Buddhist meditation became firmly established in Tibet.

China. Contemplation and meditation have held a position of high importance in Chinese religious traditions.

Taoism. Taoism in its early literary form (here referred to as "classical Taoism") and its later offshoot, which is usually termed "Neo-Taoism," are usually thought of as the primary province of contemplation in the Chinese indigenous tradition. In Taoism there is a contrast between the superficialities of conventional reality and the insight achieved by the Taoist sage. The task of Taoist contemplation is to move from a partial and self-centered view of things to a holistic view of the cosmos and its spontaneously functioning dynamism. The Tao is the primary object of contemplation and meditation in the Taoist tradition. It is the ultimate principle beyond phenomenal manifestations and yet within which all phenomenal manifestations are brought forth and undergo change.

Buddhism. From the time when Buddhism entered China from India and Central Asia around the first century BCE, the Chinese were exposed to a bewildering variety of Buddhist teachings. The major Indian schools were represented, including the Madhyamika (San-lun) and the Yogacara (Fahsiang). Another school that developed in China, the T`ien-t`ai, promulgated an elaborate meditative regime based on a variety of scriptural sources. The Hua-yen school developed a teaching and meditative discipline that led to a vision of the harmony of totality and the mutual interpenetration of all things.

Two schools of Chinese Buddhism, the Ch`an and the Ching-t`u (Pure Land school), developed different understandings of meditation practice. Emphasis is that human beings are not strong enough to bring themselves to *nirvana* through their own meditative practices. Paradoxically, an adherent of this school is advised to call on the name of the saving deity (Amitabha; Chin., O-mi-t`o-fo; Jpn. Amida) with an undivided mind, thus constituting a mantralike form of apophthegmatic practice. Meditation in the "other-power" schools tends toward the affective and cataphatic.

"Self-power" schools, like Ch`an (Jpn., Zen) Buddhism, are more austere and apophatic. The word *ch`an* is a transliteration of the Sanskrit term *dhyana,* which means "meditation" or "contemplation." The Ch`an school emphasized "self-power" and sitting in formless meditation.

[*See also* Mysticism *and* Prayer.]

BIBLIOGRAPHY

Chan, Wing-tsit, trans. and ed. *Instructions for Practical Living, and Other Neo-Confucian Writings by Wang Wang-ming.* New York, 1963.

Chan, Wing-tsit, trans. and comp. *A Source Book in Chinese Philosophy.* Princeton, 1963.

Chang Chung-yüan, trans. and ed. *Original Teachings of Ch`an Buddhism.* New York, 1969.

Conze, Edward. *Buddhist Meditation.* London, 1956.

de Bary, Wm. Theodore, Wing-tsit Chan, and Burton Watson, comps. *Sources of Chinese Tradition.* New York, 1960.

Ernest, John, J. E. L. Oulton, and Henry Chadwick, eds. *Alexandrian Christianity: Selected Translations of Clement and Origen.* London, 1954.

Francis of Sales. *Introduction to the Devout Life.* Rev. ed. Translated and edited by John K. Ryan. New York, 1972.

Kadloubovsky, Eugènie, and G. E. H. Palmer, trans. *Writings from the Philokalia on Prayer of the Heart.* London, 1951.

Naranjo, Claudio, and Robert E. Ornstein. *On the Psychology of Meditation.* New York, 1971.

Needleman, Jacob. *Los Christianity.* New York, 1980.

Radhakrishnan, Sarvepalli, and Charles A. Moore, eds. *A Source Book in Indian Philosophy. Princeton,* 1957.

Schimmel, Annemarie. *Mystical Dimensions of Islam.* Chapel Hill, N. C., 1975.

Scholem, Gershom. *Major Trends in Jewish Mysticism* (1941). New York, 1961.

Suzuki, D. T. *Zen and Japanese Culture.* 2d ed., rev. & enl. Princeton, 1959.

Tart, Charles T. *States of Consciousness.* New York, 1975.

Tsunoda, Ryusaku, Wm. Theodore de Bary, and Donald Keene, comps. *Sources of Japanese Tradition.* 2 vols. New York, 1958.

FREDERIC B. UNDERWOOD

MEGALITHIC RELIGION

The terms *megalithic culture* and *megalithic religion* have been applied to the massive stone monuments found throughout Europe. However, neither a separate megalithic culture nor isolated megalithic religion existed. The culture that produced megalithic monuments was a part of the western European Neolithic and Aeneolithic (a transitional period between the Neolithic and Bronze ages). It consisted of a number of regional culture groups whose religion can be understood in the context of the gynecocentric Old European (i. e., pre-Indo-European) religion inherited from Upper Paleolithic times. [*See* Prehistoric Religions.]

Carbon-14 dating has established that western European megaliths were built over a span of at least three thousand years, from the fifth to the second millennium BCE. They were constructed earlier than the Egyptian pyramids. If there was any diffusion of ideas, it occurred along the seaboard and from the Atlantic coast toward the interior.

Megalithic structures fall into four main categories. The first is the temple, found in the Mediterranean islands of Malta and Gozo. Maltese temples have solid walls of very large stone slabs, and their floor plan has apses that recall the shape of a seated or standing goddess. The second and largest category of megalithic structures is the burial chamber, which is subdivided into dolmens (monuments of two or more upright stones supporting a horizontal slab), passage graves, court tombs, and gallery graves. The third category is the single upright stone, or *menhir* (the word comes from the Welsh *maen*, "a stone," and *hir*, "long"). Some of the menhirs found in Brittany are as high as six meters. The fourth category consists of grouped standing stones, placed either in rows or in elliptical rings.

Archaeologists once assumed that these megalithic monuments had evolved from simple to more complex forms, but the new chronology shows that some very elaborate buildings predate the simple gallery graves.

Temples and tombs were built in the likeness of the Mother of the Dead or Mother Earth's pregnant belly or womb; this is the key to understanding megalithic structures and their floor plans. In western Europe, the body of the goddess is magnificently realized as the megalithic tomb. The so-called cruciform and double-oval tombs, as well as Maltese temples, are unmistakably human in shape.

The earliest form of the grandiose chamber tombs is the passage grave, which consists of a corridor and principal chamber. The natural cave, with its connotations of the goddess's womb (vagina and uterus), was probably the inspiration for the aboveground monumental structures that were erected later. The basic form of the passage grave—a shorter or longer passage and a round, corbel-roofed chamber—dates from the fifth millennium BCE in Portugal, Spain, and Brittany.

The other type of grave is a long barrow whose shape resembles that of a bone, a symbol of death. Like the court tombs, this type of grave has an entrance at the front that leads into an anthropomorphic or uterus-shaped chamber.

Megalithic monuments were built to be seen. Careful excavations and reconstructions have shown that much attention was paid to their outer walls and facades. For example, a reconstruction of a monument at Barnenez, Brittany, dating from the fifth millennium BCE (Giot, 1980), revealed a concentric series of walls with the upper parts of the internal walls visible. Another great structure, dating from the first half of the third millennium BCE, was reconstructed at Silbury, Wiltshire, in southwestern England (Dames, 1976). The exquisite decoration in bas-relief on stones at entrances (as at Newgrange) implies that ceremonies took place in front of the cairns. Settlement debris in Irish court cairns has led some scholars to believe that chambered tombs and long barrows should be considered not burial places but shrines. However, excavations of megalithic chambers over the past two centuries have revealed skeletons.

> **Carbon-14 dating has established that western European megaliths were built over a span of at least three thousand years.**

Long cairns in Britain have yielded so-called mortuary houses, which were constructed of timber or stone and had plank floors.

In megalithic gallery graves of France, Switzerland, and the Funnel-necked Beaker culture in Germany, partition walls sometimes have round holes. Their meaning is apparent if the still-extant veneration of stones with holes is considered. By crawling through the aperture of a stone or tree, a person is symbolically crawling into Mother Earth's womb and giving oneself to her. Strengthened by the goddess's powers, he or she is reborn. The crawling constitutes an initiation rite and is similar to sleeping in a cave, that is, "sleeping with the mother," which means to die and to be resurrected.

The second deity associated with the symbolism of the megalithic monuments is the goddess of death and regeneration in the guise of a bird of prey, usually an owl. Her image is engraved or modeled on statue menhirs, slabs of passage and gallery graves, and on walls of subterranean tombs. She herself, her eyes, or her signs appear also on schist plaques, phalanges (bones of toes or fingers), and stone cylinders laid in graves.

The characteristic features of the owl—round eyes and hooked beak—can be seen on the statue menhirs of southern France and Iberia, as well as in reliefs and charcoal drawings in the hypogea of the Paris Basin. The symbols associated with the owl goddess—wavy lines, hatched or zigzag band, net, labyrinth, meander, honeycomb, tri-line, hook, ax—all seem to be life-source, energy, or life-stimulating signs. Their association with the owl goddess emphasizes regeneration as an essential component of her personality. The agony of death is nowhere perceptible in this symbolism.

The round eyes of the owl goddess stare from bone phalanges and stone cylinders deposited in megalithic tombs in Spain and Portugal. The eyes and brows are incised in the upper part of the bone or stone cylinder and are surrounded by chevrons, triangles, zigzags, and nets. Again, the symbols of death (bones, light-colored stone) are combined with aquatic, life-source symbolism.

Small stone hourglass figurines, sometimes with triangular heads, are frequently found in Iberian megalithic tombs of the Los Millares type, dating from the end of the fourth or early third millennium BCE. Hourglass figures also are painted on Neolithic cave walls in Spain and are engraved on stones of Irish passage graves. The shape may have originated as a doubling of the pubic triangle (vulva) sign, connected at the tip. In Sardinian hypogea, vulva and hourglass signs are interchanged. Engraved triangles and hourglass shapes also appear to be associated on Irish megaliths. Bird feet or claws that appear attached to some hourglass figures on vases of the Cucuteni culture (northeastern Romania and western Ukraine) and of the Sardinian Ozieri culture speak for the association with the bird-of-prey goddess. The hourglass shape itself may symbolize an incipient form of life in which the goddess of death and regeneration emerges from graves or caves.

Many western European tomb-shrines have been constructed so that the entrances align with the winter solstice. The alignment of tomb entrances according to the moon's position at the winter solstice suggests the importance of lunar influences on burial customs and suggests the association with the lunar goddess, who was a cosmic regenerator.

Ceremonial ships are engraved on inner tomb walls in megalithic tombs in Brittany and Ireland. All depictions of ships are highly abstracted; some are just a row of vertical lines connected by a bar at the bottom. However, frequently there is a zoomorphic or spiral head, probably that of a serpent, on the keel. Sometimes an abstracted image of the goddess is shown being pulled by what may be a snake or ship. If the ship and serpent are interchangeable symbols (as they are on Egyptian artifacts and on Scandinavian rocks from the Bronze Age), then many winding serpents engraved on tomb walls are life-renewal symbols.

[*See also* Goddess Worship *and* Prehistoric Religions.]

BIBLIOGRAPHY

Almagro Basch, Martín, and Antonio Arribas. *El poblado y la necrópolis megalíticos de Los Millares.* Madrid, 1963.

d'Anna, A. *Les statues-menhirs et stèles anthropomorphes du midi méditerranéen.* Paris, 1977.

Arnal, Jean. *Les statues-menhirs: Hommes et dieux.* Paris, 1976.

Brennan, Martin. *The Stars and the Stones: Ancient Art and Astronomy in Ireland.* London, 1983.

Burl, Aubrey. *Rites of the Gods.* London, 1981.

Crawford, O. G. S. *The Eye Goddess.* London, 1957.

Dames, Michael. *The Silbury Treasure: The Great Goddess Rediscovered.* London, 1976.

Dames, Michael. *The Avebury Cycle.* London, 1977.

Daniel, Glyn E. *The Megalith Builders of Western Europe.* London, 1958.

Daniel, Glyn E. *The Prehistoric Chamber Tombs of France.* London, 1960.

Daniel, Glyn E., and Poul Kjaerum, eds. *Megalithic Graves and Ritual.* Copenhagen, 1973. A collection of essays, including "Problems of the Megalithic 'Mortuary Houses' in Denmark" by C. J. Becker and "The Relations between Kujavian Barrows in Poland and Megalithic Tombs in Northern Germany, Denmark and Western European Countries" by Konrad Jazdzewski.

De Valera, Ruaidhrí. "The Court Cairns of Ireland." *Proceedings of the Royal Irish Academy* 60, sec. C, 2 (1960): 9-140.

De Valera, Ruaidhrí, and Seán Ó Nualláin. *Survey of the Megalithic Tombs of Ireland,* vol. 3, *Counties.* Dublin, 1972.

Eogan, George. *Excavations at Knowth.* Dublin, 1984.

Giot, P. R. *Barnenez, Carn, Guennoc.* Rennes, 1980.

Giot, P. R., Jean L'Helgouac'h, and Jean-Laurent Monnier. *Préhistoire de la Bretagne.* Rennes, 1979.

Hedges, John W. *Isbister: A Chambered Tomb in Orkney.* Oxford, 1983.

Henshall, Audrey S. *The Chambered Tombs of Scotland.* 2 vols. Edinburgh, 1963-1972.

Herity, Michael. *Irish Passage Graves: Neolithic Tomb-Builders in Ireland and Britain, 2500 B. C.* New York, 1974.

Leisner, Georg, and Vera Leisner. *Die Megalithgräber der iberischen Halbinsel: Der Süden.* Berlin, 1943.

L'Helgouac'h, Jean. *Les sépultures mégalithiques en Armorique: Dolmens à couloir et allées couvertes.* Alençon, 1965.

MacKie, Evan. *The Megalith Builders.* Oxford, 1977.

Madsen, Torsten. "Earthen Long Barrows and Timber Structures: Aspects of the Early Neolithic Mortuary Practice in Denmark." *Proceedings of the Prehistoric Society* 45 (December 1979): 301-320.

Masters, Lionel J. "The Lochhill Long Cairn." *Antiquity* 47 (1973): 96-100.

Müller-Karpe, Hermann. *Handbuch der Vorgeschichte,* vol. 3, *Kupferzeit.* Munich, 1974.

O'Kelly, Michael J. *Newgrange: Archaeology, Art and Legend.* London, 1983.

Renfrew, Colin, ed. *The Megalithic Monuments of Western Europe.* London, 1981. A collection of essays, including "The Megalithic Tombs of Iberia" by Robert W. Chapman, "The Megaliths of France" by P. R. Giot, "Megaliths of the Funnel Beaker Culture in Germany and Scandinavia" by Lili Kaelas, "Chambered Tombs and Non-Megalithic Barrows in Britain" by Lionel J. Masters, "The Megalithic Tombs of Ireland" by Michael J. O'Kelly, and "Megalithic Architecture in Malta" by David Trump.

Thom, A. *Megalithic Remains in Britain and Brittany.* Oxford, 1979.

Twohig, Elizabeth Shee. *The Megalithic Art of Western Europe.* Oxford, 1981.

MARIJA GIMBUTAS

MENNONITES

The Mennonites, a Christian denomination, were first called Menists, or Mennonites, in 1541 by Countess Anna of Friesland after the group's primary leader, Menno Simons (1496-1561). She used this name in order to distinguish the Mennonites, as peaceful settlers whom she welcomed in her lands, from other, revolutionary, groups. Historically and theologically, Mennonites are the direct descendants of sixteenth-century Anabaptists, a radical reform group in Europe. [*See* Anabaptism.]

Early History and Doctrine. One of the most significant influences upon Mennonite history and identity has been the experience of decades of persecution during the sixteenth and seventeenth centuries. Numerous martyrologies, including the classic *Martyrs' Mirror* (1660), testify to this experience. The Mennonites lived in an age that was not ready for religious or social pluralism. In their insistence upon a church constituted of believers only, and in their embodiment of the principles of voluntary church membership and the separation of church and state, they represented a counterculture that society could not tolerate. In their reading of the Bible, however, they found these principles to be self-evident, particularly in the teaching and example of Jesus Christ. In keeping with the vision of their Anabaptist forebears, the Mennonites also shared the vision of a New Testament church restored both in essence and in form.

A church-world dualism was implicit in the Mennonites' theology and social view. It had been given early expression in the "Brotherly Union" of 1527, sometimes called the Schleitheim Confession of Faith, article 4 of which states:

Now there is nothing else in the world and all creation than good or evil, believing and unbelieving, darkness and light, the world and those who are [come] out of the world, God's temple and idols, Christ and Belial, and none will have part with the other.

Toleration came to the Mennonites first in the Netherlands in the 1570s and somewhat later in other parts of Europe, except in Switzerland, where severe restrictions against them remained until the eighteenth century. Increasing freedom in the north led to rapid growth in membership, until by 1700 the Dutch congregations included 160,000 members. The sectarian virtues of frugality and hard work led to considerable affluence and to urbanization. Soon Mennonites became prominent patrons of the arts in the Netherlands. Numerous artists, poets, and writers from among their ranks achieved lasting fame. But the Enlightenment spirit of rationalism and secularism was also a part of these developments, and by 1837 there were only 15,300 members left in the Netherlands. Late-nineteenth- and twentieth-century developments resulted in another increase in membership.

The early pattern of survival through withdrawal from society led to numerous migrations. Records indicate that emigration from the Netherlands eastward to Hamburg and along the coast to Danzig (present-day Gdansk) began as early as 1534. Eventually large settlements developed in the Vistula delta. In 1788, migrations began from there to the Ukraine. By 1835 some 1,600 families had settled on Russian lands. By 1920 this population had grown to 120,000. But migration began again, this time from Russia beginning in the 1870s, primarily to North America.

A similar pattern prevailed among the Swiss and South German Mennonites. Many escaped Swiss persecution by migrating to the Palatinate or to central Germany. Others immigrated to the United States and Canada, beginning in 1663. The first permanent Mennonite settlement in the United States was established at Germantown, six miles north of Philadelphia, in 1683. Yet the total number of western European Mennonites coming to North America did not exceed 8,000, which, along with the approximately 55,000 immigrants from Prussian, Polish, and Russian lands, contributed to a core immigration to North America of no more than 70,000 through the twentieth century. There have also been migrations from North America, primarily from Canada to Mexico, Paraguay, Bolivia, and other Latin American locations. Thus pilgrimage has been central to Mennonite identity.

While Mennonites are noncreedal and affirm the Bible as their final authority for faith and life, they have written numerous confessions throughout their history. Chief among these are the Brotherly Union (1527) and the Dordrecht Confession of Faith (1632). In these the nature of the church as a believing, covenanting, caring, and obedient fellowship is central, as would be in keeping with the vision of restoring the New Testament church. The importance of the new birth and the authority of the Bible are stressed. Peace, including absolute pacifism, is considered an integral part of the gospel and, therefore, part of the discipleship of the believer. This discipleship is possible within the context of an Arminian theology, which acknowledges free will rather than Augustinian determinism. The second Adam, Christ, has undone the damage of the first Adam, making possible a gradual transformation of the disciple's life into the image of Christ himself. Ethics is a part of the Good News. Grace is necessary for discipleship rather than being antithetical to it. The believer who has experienced this grace is ready to receive baptism as a covenanting member of the "Believers' Church," a term commonly used since the 1950s to refer to noninfant baptizers.

Later Developments. Partly through migration and natural increase, but particularly through twentieth-century missionary activities, Mennonites were scattered across the globe by the late twentieth century. In 1984 their total membership was approximately 700,000. The Mennonite World Conference, begun in 1925, meets every five or six years for fellowship and the sharing of ideas, as well as for worship and celebration. It is not a delegate conference, and no decisions binding upon world membership are made.

The extent to which contemporary Mennonites hold to the doctrines of early Anabaptism varies from nation to nation, from group to group, and even from congregation to congregation. Mennonites do form regional and national conferences, but they are basically congregational in polity. The Amish, who split off from Swiss and Alsatian Mennonites in 1693-1697, as well as the Hutterites and some conservative Mennonites, do not form conferences. Historically, pietism, more than other socioreligious movements, has influenced Mennonite theology; fundamentalism has also had an impact in North America. Both movements strengthen the inner, personal, and experiential aspect of faith but weaken social concern, pacifism, and the inherent church-world dualism of the sixteenth century. An enthusiastic recovery of the "Anabaptist vision," led by Harold S. Bender (1897-1962), has modified these influences since the 1940s.

Anabaptists Four Centuries Later (Kauffman and Harder, 1975) provides a profile of late-twentieth-century North American Mennonite religious attitudes and practices. In relation to two doctrinal orthodoxy scales established in the study, 90 percent of the respondents chose the most orthodox response on a liberal-orthodox continuum. About 80 percent of the members could identify a specific conversion experience. The practice of daily personal prayer ranged from a low of 73 percent in one conference to a high of 82 percent in another. More than 80 percent reported regular Sunday school participation, with teenagers having the highest rating. Fewer than 2 percent of the membership had experienced divorce or separation. Some 85 percent considered sexual intercourse before marriage as always wrong. The early emphasis on church-world dualism, pacifism, not taking oaths, and church discipline was affirmed by a range of from 60 to 80 percent, depending upon the conference.

This religious stance is nurtured through worship, attendance at denominational schools, devotional practices, small-group Bible study, and involvement in mission and service projects. Church buildings are generally functional and relatively austere. Worship services are usually sermon-centered. Most congregations enjoy singing, often *a cappella.* The Lord's Supper is celebrated two to four times annually. Some congregations practice the rite of foot washing.

Numerous liberal arts colleges are maintained in North America; they were established originally to train workers for church vocations. Seminaries, Bible schools, secondary schools, and other church institutions are maintained by Mennonites around the world as political and economic conditions permit. Retirement centers, community mental health centers, and medical and disaster aid services are maintained particularly in North America and Europe. The concern for united help for needy people around the world led to organization of the Mennonite Central Committee (MCC) in North America in 1920. A Dutch Mennonite relief agency had been organized two hundred years earlier. In 1983, the MCC had a cash and material aid budget in excess of $25 million, of which over $20 million was spent abroad and the balance on projects in North America. In the same year, a total of 944 workers were involved in fifty-five countries. Approximately one-third of these workers were non-Mennonite.

These activities are a direct extension of the Mennonite conviction that word and deed must be one and that love must be visible. It may, however, also be that these and related activities serve the less altruistic function of legitimizing the social significance and usefulness of a traditionally pacifist and persecuted people. Nevertheless, most Mennonites are deeply concerned about the futility of war and nuclear weapons, as well as about global poverty and the need for peaceful steps toward economic and social justice. These concerns are part of the total global mission to which Mennonites continue to feel committed.

BIBLIOGRAPHY

The standard reference work in English is *The Mennonite Encyclopedia,* 4 vols. plus index, edited by Harold S. Bender and C. Henry Smith (Scottdale, Pa., 1955-1959). Nelson P. Springer and A. J. Klassen have compiled a helpful bibliography, the *Mennonite Bibliography, 1631-1961,* 2 vols. (Scottdale, Pa., 1977). A revised edition of *An Introduction to Mennonite History,* edited by me (Scottdale, Pa., 1981), provides a basic account of the entire Anabaptist and Mennonite movement worldwide from the sixteenth century to the present. J. Howard Kauffman and Leland Harder's *Anabaptists Four Centuries Later* (Scottdale, Pa., 1975) is a statistically rich and well-interpreted study of Mennonite religious attitudes and practices at the time of its publication. A particularly useful volume for a country-by-country study of world Mennonitism is the *Mennonite World Handbook,* edited by Paul N. Kraybill (Lombard, Ill., 1978).

CORNELIUS J. DYCK

MESOPOTAMIAN RELIGIONS

An Overview

Ancient Mesopotamia is the country now called Iraq. Its northern part, down to an imaginary line running east-west slightly north of modern Baghdad, constituted ancient Assyria, with the cities of Ashur (modern Qal'at Shergat), which was the old capital; Calah (Nimrud); and Nineveh (Kouyundjik), which took its place later, at the time of the Assyrian empire in the first millennium BCE. The language spoken in historical times was Assyrian.

The southern part of Mesopotamia, south of the imaginary line mentioned, was ancient Babylonia, with Babylon (Babil) as its capital. The language spoken was the Babylonian dialect of Akkadian.

The designations *Assyria* and *Babylonia* are appropriate only for the second and first millennia BCE, or, more exactly, from about 1700 BCE on, when Ashur and Babylon rose to political prominence. Before that time the later Assyria was known as Subartu, while what was to become Babylonia consisted of two main parts. Dwellers of the region north of an imaginary line running east-west slightly above Nippur (Nuffar) in historical times spoke Akkadian, while those of the region south of it spoke Sumerian

Divine Forms: The Numinous

Basic to all religion, and so also to ancient Mesopotamian religion, is, I believe, a unique experience of confrontation with power not of this world.

Physiomorphism. The original identity of numinous powers with the phenomena they were thought to inform is indicated by divine names such as *An* ("heaven") for the god of heaven, *Hursag* ("foothills") for the goddess of the near ranges, *Nanna* ("moon") for the moon god, *Utu* ("sun") for the sun god, *Ezen* ("grain") for the grain goddess, and so forth. The early selectivity of powers experienced in phenomena of vital economic importance to the settlers shows in the distribution of city gods, who must be considered coeval with their cities, over the various regional economies of the country. The extreme south is marshland with characteristic economies such as fishing, fowling, and hunting. Here was Eridu, the city of Enki, whose other names were *Daradim* ("wild goat fashioner") and *Enuru* ("lord reed-bundle"). Through the marshlands along the Euphrates runs also the country of the ox herdsman and the orchardman. To the ox herdsman's pantheon belonged the bull god Ningublaga and his consort Nineiagara ("lady of the creamery"). Closer to the river itself was the country of the orchardmen, who depended on the river for the irrigation of their plantations. To them belonged Ninazu of Enegir, seemingly a god of waters, and his son Ningishzida ("master of the good tree") of Gishbanda, a deity of tree roots and serpents. At Uruk the country of the orchardmen and the oxherds joins that of the shepherds. Here on the western edge is Uruk with Inanna of the shepherds, goddess of the rains that call up verdure and grazing in the desert.

North and east of the *edin,* finally, lay the plowlands with cities dedicated to cereal and chthonic deities, or deities of the chief agricultural implements, the hoe and plow.

The Pantheon

A pantheon seeking to interrelate and to rank the innumerable deities the ancient Mesopotamians worshiped, or merely recognized, in cities and villages throughout the land evolved gradually through the diligent work of scribes, who produced lists of divine names as part of their general lexical endeavors. The resulting scheme as it is known to us from old Babylonian copies was based primarily on the prominence in the cosmos of the cosmic feature with which the deity in question was associated, secondarily on his or her family and household ties.

An. An (Anum) was god of the sky and father of the gods. The main center of An's cult seems to have been in Uruk. An important aspect of An was his relation to the calendar, the months having their characteristic constellations that announced them. To this aspect belonged monthly and yearly festival rites dedicated to An.

Enlil. God of wind and storms, Enlil was the most prominent member of the divine assembly and executor of its decrees. As leader of the divine assembly and executor of its decrees, he became the power for destruction of temples and cities, the all-obliterating storm with which the assembly overthrew dynasties and their capitals as it shaped history.

Ninurta. In Nippur, the town itself—as distinct from the sacred area around Ekur—had as city god a son of Enlil called Ninurta, whose wife was the goddess Nin-Nibru ("queen of Nippur"). Ninurta's name may be interpreted as containing a cultural loanword, *urta* ("plow"), thus identifying him as god of that implement.

Nusku. To Enlil's household belonged Nusku, in origin a god of lamps. He served as Enlil's trusted vizier and confidant.

Ninhursaga. Ninhursaga ("mistress of the foothills"), earlier simply Hursag ("foothills"), was the power in the fertile near slopes of the eastern mountains, the favorite grazing grounds in the spring. Her cities were Kesh, not yet identified, and Adab, the modern mound Bismaya.

Enki. Enki (Ea) was god of the underground fresh waters that come to the surface in rivers, pools, and marshes. The Sumerians imagined them as a vast subterranean freshwater sea, which they called Abzu or Engur. Enki's city was Eridu (Abu Shahrein), where he resided in the temple called

Eengura ("house of the deep"). The name *Enki* means "productive manager [lord] of the soil."

Asalluhe. Asalluhe ("man-drenching Asar"), city god of Kuar, near Eridu, and god of rain clouds, was Enki's son. He appears predominantly in incantations against all kinds of evil doings.

Marduk. Marduk, or preferably Merodakh, city god of Babylon. His name, abbreviated from *(A)marudak* ("calf of the storm"), characterizes him as a god of thunderstorms visualized as a bellowing young bull. The thundershowers of spring mark the appearance of verdure in the desert and of plowing and sowing; thus Marduk's chief festival, the Akiti (Akitu), or "time of the earth reviving," was further described as "of the seed plowing."

Nanna. Nanna (also Suen or Sin) was the god of the moon. His city was Ur (Muqayyir); his temple there,

> **Nanna . . . was also visualized as a herder driving his herd—the stars—across the pastures of heaven. . . .**

Egishnugal. His wife was Ningal. His own name, *Nanna,* would seem to designate him as the full moon, while *Suen* would be the name of the sickle moon. He was regularly envisioned in a bull shape, an image that hornlike shape of the sickle moon may have encouraged. He was also visualized as a herder driving his herd—the stars—across the pastures of heaven, or as riding in the heavens in a boat, the sickle moon.

Utu. The god of the sun and of justice and fair dealings was Utu (Shamash). His cities were Ararma (Larsa) in the south and Sippar in the north. His temple in both cities was called Ebabbar; his wife was Ninkurra (Aya). As judge, Utu presided each day in various temples at specific places called "the place of Utu."

Ishkur. Ishkur (Adad) was the god of rains and thunderstorms. His original form seems to have been that of a bull.

Inanna. Inanna (Ishtar) was earlier called *Ninana,* which can be understood as either "mistress of the date clusters" or "mistress of heaven." The center of her worship was, in the south, at Uruk, in the temple called Eana, and in the north at Hursagkalamma, near Kish. Characteristic of her is her great complexity and many-sidedness. It is apparent that a variety of originally different deities were syncretized in her and also that the ancients had been able to blend these differences into a fascinating, many-faceted, and convincing character.

Dumuzi. Like Inanna, and perhaps even more so, does her lover and bridegroom, Dumuzi (Tammuz), present a highly complex, syncretized image, one in which it is not always easy to sort out cleanly the various strands woven into it:

1. *Dumuzi as Amaushumgalana,* the power for productivity in the date palm.

2. *Dumuzi the shepherd,* the power causing ewes to produce normal, well-shaped lambs.

3. *Damu the child,* the power for the sap to rise in plants and trees in the spring.

4. *Damu the conscript.* What precise power he represented is not clear; most likely it was one connected with the welfare of cattle herds.

Lugalbanda and Ninsuna. Lugalbanda ("fierce king") and Ninsuna ("mistress of the wild cows") were apparently city god and goddess of Kullab, a city that was early absorbed into Uruk. Both were deities of cattle, but with the absorption of his city Lugalbanda seems to have lost definition, and even his devine status.

Ningirsu. Ningirsu ("master of Girsu") was the city god of Girsu, with the temple Eninnu. His wife was the goddess Baba. Ningirsu was god of the thunderstorms in spring and of the spring flood of the Tigris.

Gatumdug. Gatumdug was goddess of the city of Lagash (Al Hiba), south of Girsu. The meaning of her name is not clear, but other evidence suggests that she was also a goddess of birth giving.

Nanshe. The goddess of fowl and fish was Nanshe. She was city goddess of Nina (Zurghul), with the temple Siratr. She was, according to Gudea, the interpreter of dreams for the gods.

Ninmar. City goddess of Guabba and seemingly a goddess of birds was Ninmar.

Dumuzi-Abzu. Dumuzi-Abzu was city goddess of Kinirsha, and the power for fertility and healthy new life in the marshes.

Nininsina. Nininsina ("mistress of Isin") was city goddess of Isin (Ishan Bahriyat). She seems to have been envisaged in the shape of a dog and was presumably the goddess of dogs.

Ereshkigal. The name of the goddess Ereshkigal (Allatum) meant "queen [of the] greater earth." The ancients believed that there was a "larger heaven" above the visible sky that connected with a "larger earth" below the observable earth. In the larger earth was the realm of the dead, of which Ereshkigal was queen.

Ninazu. The meaning of the name *Ninazu* is not clear, but it apparently has to do with water. Most likely, since he was a netherworld god, his name refers to the waters underground.

Ningishzida. Ningishzida ("master of the well-grown tree") was the god of trees, especially the powers in the root that nourish and sustain the tree. His city was Gishbanda on the lower Euphrates.

Nergal. The other names of Nergal ("lord great city"), originally probably designating different gods, were *Meslamtaea* ("the one issuing from the luxuriant *mesu* tree") and *Irra.*

Meslam or *Emeslam* ("house Meslam") was the name of Nergal's temple at Cutha, in Akkad.

Ashur. Ashur was city god of Ashur (Qal'at Shergat) and chief god of Assyria. No recognizable features characterize him other than those that belong to his role as embodiment of the political aspirations of his city and nation.

The Temple

The earliest Mesopotamian temples may have been in origin storehouses in which nomadic or seminomadic tribes kept their sacred objects and provisions, which were too cumbersome to carry along on their wanderings. Very soon, though, these structures would have been considered, as always later, dwellings of the gods to whom they belonged.

Temples were by preference built on existing high ground. With larger temples it became customary in early dynastic times to surround them with a protective oval wall, called an *ibgal.* Inside the oval, along its sides, were the various storerooms, kitchens, and workshops for the temple personnel, while the house on top of the terraced tower constituted the god's living quarters: bedroom, bath, and so on.

The temple, rising over the houses of the community, was visible and tangible proof of the god's presence and, more, that he was himself a member of the community and had a stake in it, with his house, his servants, his oxen and sheep, and his fields in grain. To have the temple was a privilege.

The Cult

The communal cult of the gods was of two kinds, celebrating the appropriate festivals of the various gods at appropriate times and providing daily services such as would be required by any high human dignitary. The earlier of these are undoubtedly the festivals, most of which are best understood as communal magic rites for prosperity developed into cult dramas performed by community representatives. There is evidence for various types of such dramas: the Sacred Marriage, the Death Drama, the Journey Drama, and the Plowing Drama. Others may have existed.

The Babylonian epic of creation is *Enuma elish,* which tells how Marduk "vanquished Tiamat and assumed kingship." It is generally—and perhaps rightly—assumed to be a cult myth corresponding to a dramatic ritual reenactment of this primordial battle each new year.

The trend toward sociomorphism imposed on the gods the patterns of the human family and household, and this in turn implied service such as was rendered to a human magnate in providing for his bodily comfort and assisting in the running of his estate. All of this became the daily temple cult. A further implication of anthropomorphism and sociomorphism was that since the god had become ruler of the community, it was essential to know what he wanted done. Thus a variety of methods of communication was developed. Some of these left the initiative to the god: he might show signs in the stars or on earth that the initiated could interpret. Others were available when man needed to know the divine will. The earliest of these methods of communication of which we have evidence are dreams sought by incubation in the temple, and inspection of the liver of a sacrificed kid for propitious or nonpropitious shape.

For conveying human wishes and needs to the gods and asking for help, a ritual of seeking audience to present petition and prayers was developed. The petitioner was led in before the deity with his greeting gift, usually a lamb or a kid. Here he libated water or wine in a huge vase with greenery that stood before the deity, and he spoke a formal greeting prayer.

The cult so far described was the communal, public cult. There was, however, a private cult as well. City life and its ever-greater differentiation between the fortunes of families and individuals and those of other families and individuals encouraged feelings that special success was due to a god's personal interest in a man and his family, while, conversely, misfortune would seem to be due to the god's abandonment of his ward for some reason or other. Thus the term for having luck became "to acquire a god." Since no achievement could be had without divine help, that of engendering a child necessarily implied such intervention.

The close connection between the personal god and success could not but raise problems, for experience showed that virtue was not always rewarded; rather, a virtuous man might fall ill or suffer other miseries such as should have happened to evildoers only. The obvious solution, that the virtuous man unwittingly must have offended his god, was accepted in a measure, and prayers often asked for enlightenment as to how a sufferer had sinned, so that he could do penance and mend his ways.

BIBLIOGRAPHY

Bottéro, Jean. *La religion babylonienne.* Paris, 1952.

Dhorme, Édouard. *Les religions de Babylonie et d'Assyrie.* Paris, 1945.

Dijk, V. van. "Sumerische Religion." In *Handbuch der Religionsgeschichte,* vol. 1, edited by Jes Peter Asmussen, Jørgen Laessøe, and Carsten Colpe, pp. 431-496. Göttingen, 1971.

Frankfort, Henri, et al. *Before Philosophy.* Harmondsworth, 1949. First published as *The Intellectual Adventure of Ancient Man* (Chicago, 1946).

Hooke, S. H. Babylonian and Assyrian Religion. New York, 1953.

Jacobsen, Thorkild. *The Treasures of Darkness: A History of Mesopotamian Religion.* New Haven, 1975.

Laessøe, Jørgen. "Babylonische und assyrische Religion." In *Handbuch der Religionsgeschichte,* vol. 1, edited by Jes Peter Asmussen, Jørgen Laessøe, and Carsten Colpe, pp. 497-525. Göttingen, 1971.

Meissner, Bruno. *Babylonien und Assyrien,* vol. 2. Heidelberg, 1925.

Pritchard, J. B., ed. *Ancient Near Eastern Texts relating to the Old Testament.* 3d ed. Princeton, 1969.

Ringgren, Helmer. *Religions of the Ancient Near East.* Translated by John Sturdy. Philadelphia, 1973.

THORKILD JACOBSEN

MESSIANISM

The term *messianism* is derived from *messiah,* a transliteration of the Hebrew *mashiah* ("anointed"), which originally denoted a king whose reign was consecrated by a rite of anointment with oil. In the Hebrew scriptures (Old Testament), *mashiah* is always used in reference to the actual king of Israel. In the intertestamental period, however, the term was applied to the future king, who was expected to restore the kingdom of Israel and save the people from all evil.

Judaism. In the Judaism of the intertestamental period, messianic expectations developed in two directions. One was national and political and is most clearly set out in the pseudepigraphic *Psalms of Solomon* (17 and 18). Here the national Messiah is a descendant of David. He shall rule in wisdom and righteousness; he shall defeat the great powers of the world, liberate his people from foreign rule, and establish a universal kingdom in which the people will live in peace and happiness.

Some apocryphal documents, especially the *Testament of Levi,* speak also of a priestly messiah, one who is to bring peace and knowledge of God to his people and to the world. The Qumran community even expected two anointed ones, a priest and a king, but very little is known about their functions.

The other line of development is found above all in the Ethiopic *Apocalypse of Enoch (1 Enoch)* and in *2 Esdras* (also called *4 Ezra*). It centers around the term *son of man.* This term is used in the Old Testament to refer generally to a human being (*Psalms* 8:5, 80:18 [English version 80:17]).

In the apocalyptic books mentioned, the son of man is a transcendental figure, more or less divine, preexistent, and at present hidden in heaven. At the end of time he will appear to judge the world in connection with the resurrection of the dead.

Christianity. Early Christianity took many of the Jewish ideas about the *Messiah* and applied them to Jesus. *Messiah* was translated into Greek as *Christos,* that is, Christ, thereby identifying Jesus with Jewish messianic expectations. Matthew interpreted *Isaiah* 9:1 (EV 9:2), "The people who walk in darkness shall see a great light," as fulfilled in Jesus (*Mt.* 4:14-18). *Micah* 5:1 (*EV* 5:2) is quoted to prove that the Messiah should be born in Bethlehem (*Mt.* 2:6). *Zechariah* 9:9 is read as a prediction of Jesus' entry into Jerusalem (*Mt.* 21:5), and if the story related by Matthew is authentic, it must mean that Jesus wanted to proclaim himself as the Messiah. Jesus refused to be made king (*Jn.* 6:15); he proclaimed before Pilate: "My kingdom is not of this world" (*Jn.* 18:26). Despite this, he was accused of pretending to be "the king of the Jews" (*Jn.* 19:19).

The New Testament, however, although maintaining that the Messiah is the Son of God, also uses the epithet "Son of man." According to the Gospels, Jesus uses it of himself. In a few cases it could possibly mean simply "a human being"

> **New Testament Christology utilizes a great many traits drawn from Jewish messianism.**

or "this man" (*Mk.* 2:10, *Mt.* 11:8, and parallels; *Mt.* 8:20 and parallels). A number of passages refer to the coming of the Son of man at the end of time (*Mt.* 24:27, 24:37; *Lk.* 18:18, 18:22, 18:69; *Mt.* 10:23; *Mk.* 13:26); these imply the same interpretation of *Daniel* 7:13 as that implied by *1 Enoch* and *2 Esdras* but add a new element in that it is Christ who is to come a second time, returning as the judge of the world. A third group of "Son of man" references allude to the suffering and death of Jesus, sometimes also mentioning his resurrection (*Mk.* 8:31, 9:9, 9:31, 10:33, 14:21, 14:41; *Lk.* 22:48 and others). These introduce the idea of a suffering messiah, which is not entirely unknown in Jewish messianism but is never linked with the Son of man.

New Testament Christology utilizes a great many traits drawn from Jewish messianism. At the same time, it adds a new dimension: the idea that Jesus, though he has already in person fulfilled the messianic expectations, is to return in order to bring them to their final fulfillment.

Islamic Messianism. Ideas comparable to that of the second coming of Christ are found in Islam, probably owing to Christian influence. While the Qur'an envisages God as the judge on the Day of Judgment, later Muslim tradition introduces certain preparatory events before that day. Muhammad is reported to have said that the last day of the world will be prolonged in order that a ruler of the Prophet's family may defeat all enemies of Islam. This ruler is called the Mahdi, "the rightly guided one."

"Nativistic" Movements. As early as the sixteenth century, successive waves of Tupi tribes in Brazil moved to the Bahia coast, impelled by a messianic quest for the "land without evil." Another such migration to find the "land of immortality and perpetual rest" is reported to have inspired the Spaniards' idea of El Dorado.

The Ghost Dance movement in the western United States was initiated in 1869 by a certain Wodziwob, who had visions through which the Great Spirit announced that a major cataclysm would soon shake the entire world and wipe out the white man. The Indians would come back to life, and the Great Spirit would dwell among them in the heavenly era.

In the Kongo region in Africa, Simon Kimbangu, who had been raised in the British Baptist Mission, appeared in 1921 as a prophet to his people. His preaching was a combination of Christian and indigenous elements. He prophesied the imminent ousting of the foreign rulers, a new way of life for the Africans, and the coming of a Golden Age.

In the early twentieth century, Melanesia and New Guinea saw the emergence of the so-called cargo cults. Common to them all is the belief that a Western ship (or even airplane), manned by whites, will come to bring riches to the natives, while at the same time the dead will return to life and an era of happiness will follow.

[*See also* Millenarianism.]

BIBLIOGRAPHY

The standard work for early Jewish messianism is Sigmund Mowinckel's *He That Cometh* (Oxford, 1956). Briefer, but including the Egyptian and Mesopotamian texts referred to in the article, is my book *The Messiah in the Old Testament* (London, 1956). A good introduction to the Son of man question is Carsten Colpe's article "Huios Tou Anthropou," in the *Theological Dictionary of the New Testament,* edited by Gerhard Kittel (Grand Rapids, Mich., 1972). See also Rollin Kearns's *Vorfragen zur Christologie,* 3 vols. (Tübingen, 1978-1982), and Maurice Casey's *Son of Man: The Interpretation and Influence of Daniel 7* (London, 1979). Islamic messianism has been dealt with most recently by Hava Lazarus-Yafeh in her book *Some Religious Aspects of Islam* (Leiden, 1981), pp. 48-57, and by Jan-Olaf Blichfeldt in *Early Mahdism* (Leiden, 1985). On Islam see also my article "Some Religious Aspects of the Caliphate," in The *Sacral Kingship* (Leiden, 1959). Edgar Blochet provides some early observations in *Le messianisme dans l'hétérodoxie musulmane* (Paris, 1903). A comprehensive survey of the millenarian movements is found in Vittorio Lanternari's *The Religions of the Oppressed* (New York, 1965). Lanternari's book includes a good bibliography.

HELMER RINGGREN

METHODIST CHURCHES

Methodism arose from the search of John Wesley and his brother Charles for a deepened religious life within the ordered ways of the Church of England, which John described as "the best constituted national church in the world." He sought no drastic reform in doctrines but rather a greater emphasis upon a personal experience of God's saving and perfecting grace and more opportunity for a spiritual quest within Christian groups, undeterred by denominational barriers. He downplayed the divisive element of his movement, publishing in 1742 an elaboration of Clement of Alexandria's description of a perfect Christian as *The Character of a Methodist* and offering this simple definition in his *Complete English Dictionary* (1753): "A Methodist, one that lives according to the method laid down in the Bible."

John Wesley, both as the living leader and later as the almost legendary "Mr. Wesley" of "the people called Methodists," so greatly influenced the developing thought and churchmanship of Methodism that he demands a far greater proportion of attention than if he had been the mere titular founder of a new denomination.

After his heart was "strangely warmed" on 24 May 1738, Wesley began to preach salvation by faith with the conviction of personal experience, and he gathered around him an organized society in London, the first of many that spread throughout the British Isles. These societies were intended to supplement, not supplant, the worship of the church. In his *Rules* (1743) he argued that a society was simply "a company of men 'having the form, and seeking the power of godliness,' united in order to pray together, to receive the word of exhortation, and to watch over one another in love, that they may help each other to work out their salvation." There was only one condition for membership, "a desire . . . to be saved from [their] sins." To test and reinforce his followers' sincerity, however, the *Rules* insisted that members should avoid evil, do good, and seek holiness, for which illustrative examples were given in all three categories.

In order to proclaim his message and administer his societies Wesley enrolled a steadily increasing number of lay preachers to join the handful of sympathetic clergy who engaged in an itinerant evangelical ministry under his supervision. In 1744 he called these together in London to confer about doctrine and organization. This was the first annual conference of Wesley's Methodism, although the Welsh Calvinistic wing of the movement, who looked to George Whitefield as their chief inspirer, had been holding their "Associations" for several years.

The primary purpose of the Conferences of 1744-1747 was to formulate the major doctrinal emphases of Methodist preaching: salvation by grace through faith, confirmed and exemplified by good works; the witness of the Holy Spirit to a person's salvation from the penalties of past sin and to his power over present temptations to sin; and the theoretical possibility of personal triumph over temptation, under the title of Christian perfection, which Wesley defined as perfect love to God and man, though consistent with human error and with no guarantee of permanence. These doctrines, as taught and illustrated in Wesley's first four volumes of *Sermons* (1744-1760) and his *Explanatory Notes upon the New Testament* (1755), formed the basis of all Methodist preaching.

The early Conferences also consolidated the organization of Methodism into a "connexion," a network of societies served by lay preachers itinerating regularly on a circuit, or round, covering a district such as a county in tours lasting from four to six weeks, but also itinerating between circuits

periodically—at first every three months, then every six, and eventually every year. Each year Wesley's own preaching and administrative journeys took him over most of England. In 1747 Ireland was added to his tour, and in 1751, Scotland. Wesley and his itinerant preachers developed a strong family identity among the societies.

This connexional unity became so strong that in 1749 Wesley published two sets of extracts from the minutes of his conferences, each with the same title—*Minutes of Some Late Conversations between the Revd. Mr. Wesleys and Others*—one summarizing Methodist teaching, the other Methodist organization. In effect they constituted a declaration that Methodism had become an established ecclesiastical body. Inevitably this process of consolidation aroused much criticism of Methodism: the preachers' teaching, so unfamiliar to non-Methodists, was incorrectly described as unorthodox; their vigor, warmth, and ebullience were pejoratively labeled "enthusiasm"; and Wesley's unconventional preaching in the open air and in other men's parishes, and, worse still, his authorizing laymen to preach, were regarded by even sympathetic clergy as a grave breach of ecclesiastical order. Preachers and people were occasionally mobbed, but the somewhat quiescent church authorities took no concerted action.

The chief threat, indeed, came from within the movement. The people's desire to receive the sacraments from their preachers fed the preachers' natural ambitions to improve their status and to transform the society into a church. John Wesley was inclined to let things run their course, but the vehement opposition of his brother Charles led him to tighten the rein on his preachers, most of whom from 1752 onward signed agreements "never to leave the communion of the Church of England without the consent of all whose names are subjoined." Avowed separation from the church was narrowly averted at the Conference of 1755, when all agreed "that (whether it was *lawful* or not) it was no ways *expedient.*" This deferred any open separation for almost thirty years.

Meanwhile British immigrants, especially from Ireland, brought Methodism to America, where it became so firmly rooted that Wesley responded to their plea for help by sending out matched pairs of itinerant preachers in 1769, 1771, 1773, and 1774, of whom by far the best known and most influential was Francis Asbury, who remained throughout the Revolutionary War (1775-1783). With some difficulty Asbury persuaded the American Methodists not to sever their ties with Wesley in their eagerness for religious independence, and thus Wesley himself was able to assist Americans in the birth of the first independent church within Methodism.

The year 1784 was "that grand climacteric year of Methodism." Aided by Dr. Thomas Coke, Wesley prepared a deed poll that legally defined the term *Conference,* and made that body heir to British Methodism after Wesley's death.

Wesley also entrusted to Coke a major part in publishing a revision of *The Book of Common Prayer* for the use of American Methodists, and discussed with him a complementary plan for securing a threefold ministry in American Methodism. Already convinced that in any ecclesiastical emergency the power of ordination resided in presbyters, Wesley ordained two of his preachers, first as deacons and then as elders. With their assistance he then commissioned Coke as "superintendent" of the American flock, with instructions to share his new authority with Asbury upon his arrival in America.

> Within a century after Wesley's death immigrants and missionaries from both sides of the Atlantic had planted Methodism on each continent and in almost every country.

At the "Christmas Conference" in Baltimore (1784-1785) with Wesley's blessing, a new denomination was launched, the Methodist Episcopal Church. In England Methodism still remained a society, governed by a presbyter of the Church of England and at least theoretically within the fold of that church. After Wesley's death in 1791, however, under the terms of his deed poll, the Conference of preachers became the ruling body, with a modified presbyterian system of government rather than the modified episcopalian polity that was being developed in America. Although some of Wesley's Anglican friends had occasionally referred to "the Methodist church" during his lifetime, not until 1893 did the class tickets indicating membership in the Wesleyan Methodist Society carry the word *church*.

When in 1739 Wesley had written, "I look upon *all the world as my parish*," he was defending his disregard of ecclesiastical boundaries in Britain, but in fact he did also cherish a vision of a world renewed in the image of Christ, and was convinced that his liberal, pragmatic approach to theology and to churchmanship should make good missionaries of his people—as indeed it did. He heartily supported Coke's missionary plans, and a month before his death wrote to a native American preacher, "Lose no opportunity of declaring to all men that the Methodists are one people in all the world." Within a century after Wesley's death immigrants and missionaries from both sides of the Atlantic had planted Methodism on each continent and in almost every country.

Methodist missionary expansion during the nineteenth century varied little whether it came from the British or the American type of church polity, because polity was overshadowed by ethos, and the ethos sprang from Wesley. Methodists everywhere remained within a tightly knit "con-

nexion" governed by a conference. They followed Wesley in assigning major responsibilities to laymen, and were progressive in enrolling women as leaders, and even as preachers. They emphasized evangelical preaching and continued to experiment with an adventurous and flexible organization. While making good use of their rich heritage of Charles Wesley's hymns they observed those almost uniquely Methodist forms of worship, the watch-night, the covenant service, and the love-feast, as well as the close fellowship of the class-meeting and the bands, with their cherished tickets of membership. They constantly remembered their early rules, by "avoiding evil of every kind—especially that which is most generally practised," and by "doing good of every possible sort, and as far as is possible to all men."

It is true that the full appreciation of some of these features fell off even during the nineteenth century, and a few were almost forgotten in the twentieth, such as Wesley's constant charge, "Press on to perfection." Human frailty brought about fragmentation into many independent denominations, a process furthered during the twentieth century by the hiving off of national churches from the parent bodies.

The first major division in England, the Methodist New Connexion (1797), was a revolt against the autocracy of the leading Wesleyan preachers, but the Primitive Methodists (1811) and Bible Christians (1819), though also favoring more lay leadership, left because they wished to restore evangelism. The Wesleyan Methodist hierarchy came under increasing attack from 1849 onward in a disruptive pamphlet warfare that led to eventual democratic reforms at the cost of losing many thousands of members. Happily, some of these breaches were progressively healed through the formation of the United Methodist Free Churches in 1857, the United Methodist Church in 1907, and the Methodist Church in 1932.

In America, where membership had almost drawn level with that in the British Isles by Wesley's death, Methodism expanded and divided far more rapidly than in Britain during the nineteenth and twentieth centuries. The controversy over the institution of slavery and other disruptive forces similar to those in England were at work in America. Coke and Asbury had unsuccessfully sought to eradicate slavery from the Methodist Episcopal Church, but even in the abolitionist strongholds of New York and Philadelphia race remained an issue among Methodists. There, blacks forsook their second-class membership to form their own congregations, which eventually became the African Methodist Episcopal Church (1816) and the African Methodist Episcopal Zion Church (1820), each with a community of over a million members. In 1844 the whole Methodist Episcopal Church split into north and south over the issue, though other factors also were at work, including varying views of the episcopacy. In 1870 the Methodist Episcopal Church South blessed the incorporation of their own black members into the Colored (now "Christian") Methodist Episcopal Church. Slavery was also a factor in the formation of the Wesleyan Methodist Connection (1843), which did not name itself a "church" until 1947, and which also sought a return to earlier Wesleyan evangelism and the abolition of the episcopacy. The Free Methodist Church (1860) arose after lengthy preliminaries from a widespread desire to recover Wesley's teaching upon Christian perfection. A similar emphasis within American Methodism upon the need to recover scriptural holiness led to the piecemeal formation of the Church of the Nazarene.

In American Methodism and its missions, as well as in the British Commonwealth, a measure of consolidation took place during the nineteenth and twentieth centuries, notably in the union of the northern and southern churches with the Protestant Methodists in 1939 to form the Methodist Church, which in 1968 united with the Evangelical United Brethren (itself a union of churches with a German-speaking background) to form the United Methodist Church, with a membership of eleven million out of a total world Methodist community of something like fifty million.

These and other unions were consummated largely because of the coming together in Christian fellowship of representatives from dozens of autonomous Methodist churches and missions from all over the world, first decennially from 1881 in the Ecumenical Methodist Conference, then quinquennially from 1951 in the World Methodist Council. Welcome guests at these gatherings are representatives from churches where Methodism has subsumed its identity in an interdenominational union, such as the United Church of Canada (1925), the Churches of North and South India, the Uniting Church in Australia, or other such unions in Belgium, China, Ecuador, Japan, Pakistan, the Philippines, and Zambia. As an important element in the World Council of Churches, Methodism remains true to the spirit of its founder, who gloried in the catholicity of his early societies, open to persons of all creeds, and who firmly maintained, in spite of attacks by his critics, that "orthodoxy, or right opinions, is at best but a very slender part of religion."

BIBLIOGRAPHY

A valuable summary of the history, doctrines, spread, activities, and leaders of Methodism in its many branches through more than two centuries can be found in *The Encyclopedia of World Methodism,* 2 vols., edited by Nolan B. Harmon (Nashville, 1974). The unplanned development of Methodism from a movement into a denomination is described by Frank Baker in *John Wesley and the Church of England* (Nashville, 1970). Fuller details of some British aspects of Methodism, especially in their later stages, are given in *A History of the Methodist Church in Great Britain,* 3 vols. to date, edited by Rupert Davies and Gordon Rupp (London, 1965-1984), and the rise and development of the main stream in the United States is portrayed in *The History of American Methodism,* 3 vols., edited by Emory Stevens Bucke (Nashville, 1964). The latter work should be supplemented by Frank Baker's *From Wesley to Asbury* (Durham, 1976), which traces the transition of British Methodism to the American scene, and by Frederick A. Norwood's *The Story of American Methodism* (Nashville, 1974), which traces later developments in the history of the United Methodists. For the latest statistics about world Methodism, see the World Methodist Council's *Handbook of Information* (Lake Junaluska, N. C., 1982).

FRANK BAKER

MILLENARIANISM

Millenarianism, known also as millennialism, is the belief that the end of this world is at hand and that in its wake will appear a New World, inexhaustibly fertile, harmonious, sanctified, and just. The more exclusive the concern with the End itself, the more such belief shades off toward the catastrophic; the more exclusive the concern with the New World, the nearer it approaches the utopian.

Millenarian Thought. Complexity in millenarian thought derives from questions of sign, sequence, duration, and human agency. What are the marks of the End? At what stage are we now? Exactly how much time do we have? What should we do? Although warranted by cosmology, prophecy, or ancestral myth, the End usually stands in sudden proximity to the immediate era. The trail of events may at last have been tracked to the cliff's edge, or recent insight may have cleared the brier from some ancient oracle.

The root term, *millennium,* refers to a first-century eastern Mediterranean text, the *Apocalypse of John* or *Book of Revelation,* itself a rich source of disputes about the End.

In theory, as a speculative poetic enterprise, millenarianism is properly an adjunct of eschatology, the study of last things. In practice, millenarianism is distinguished by close scrutiny of the present, from which arise urgent issues of human agency. Once the fateful coincidence between history and prophecy has been confirmed, must good people sit tight, or must they gather together, withdraw to a refuge? Should they enter the wilderness to construct a holy city, or should they directly engage the chaos of the End, confront the regiments of evil? Millenarians answer with many voices, rephrasing their positions as they come to terms with an End less imminent or less cataclysmic. Where their image of the New World is that of a golden age, they begin with a restorative ethos, seeking a return to a lost purity. Where their image is that of the land of the happy dead or a distant galaxy of glory, their ethos is initially retributive, seeking to balance an unfortunate past against a fortunate future. Few millenarians remain entirely passive, quietly awaiting a supernatural transformation of the world.

A millenarian's sense of time, consequently, is neither strictly cyclical nor linear. However much the millennium is to be the capstone to time, as in Christian and Islamic traditions, it is also in character and affect the return of that care-free era posited for the start of things. However much the millennium is to be an impost between two of the infinite arches of time, as in Aztec and Mahayana Buddhist traditions, it is for all mortal purposes a release from pain and chaos for many generations.

To the uninitiated, the millenarian mathematics of time may seem mysteriously scaled: how can one account for that arbitrary algebra that assigns the value 3,500 years to the locution "a time, and times, and half a time" (*Rv.* 12:14)? Millenarian thought is figurative in both senses of that word—metaphorical and numerological. Intricate play with numbers of years is founded upon a faith in the impending aesthetic wholeness of the world-historical process. Millenarian searches for laws of historical correspondence between the individually human and the universally human bear a formal similarity to one another, whether the searchers are nineteenth-century social visionaries or twelfth-century monastics. Each discerns a pattern of historical ages that promises both completion and recapitulation.

World religions have known two deep reservoirs of millenarian thought, one noumenal and gnostic, the other phenomenal and nomothetic. When the reservoirs empty into each other—when mathematicians allude to secret knowledge or contemplatives allude to laws of physics (as in fifth-century southern China, seventeenth-century Western Europe, twentieth-century North America)—millenarianism waxes strong.

Among the world religions we can locate two constellations of millenarian thought about an epochal pulsing of time, one Zoroastrian-Jewish-Greek-Christian, the other Hindu-Buddhist-Taoist-Confucian. In the Mediterranean littoral, an epochal aesthetic was elaborated by scribal elites who were resistant first to Greek rule, then Roman rule, and finally to Muslim rule. Feasting upon a cosmopolitan diet of Zoroastrian cosmology, Jewish notions of Sabbath, and Greco-Roman ideas of historical recurrence, these literati stamped the disturbing flux of empires with the template of the divine creative week, which they saw being played out again at length in human history through a reassuringly predictable series of world kingdoms over a period of six or seven thousand years. At the end lay a millennial sabbath, transposed from a time of perpetual rest to a time of truce and earthly reward prior to the final onslaughts of the dragon, tyrant, or false messiah.

Across East Asia, a millenarian aesthetic developed within contexts far less adversarial, and we find no figure antiphonal to the universal perfect ruler (the Hindu *cakravartin,* the Buddhist Rudra Cakin, the Javanese hybrid *Ratu Adil*) or to the future incarnate savior (the Hindu Kalkin, the Maitreya Buddha, a reborn Lao-tzu). Furthermore, the epochal scheme was overwhelmingly degenerative: it fixed all recorded history within the last of the four increasingly chaotic eras *(yugas)* of the aeon *(kalpa).* The problem here was not to expand the prophetic horizon but to foreshorten the 4.3 million-year Indian *kalpa* cycle so that hundreds of thousands of distressing years of the fourth era, the *kaliyuga,* did not still lie ahead.

Each *kalpa* was to end in a cosmic disaster that would, after some blank time, initiate a new cycle whose first *yuga* was always a golden age. Strategic foreshortening brought present catastrophe stern to snout with a renewed world. The foreshortening began in northern India with early Mahayana Buddhist images of *bodhisattvas,* compassionate enlightened beings who chose to work in this world for the benefit of others rather than withdraw into final *nirvana.* Almost simultaneously, Chinese commentators during the Later Han period (25–220 CE) alloyed the Confucian golden age of antiquity, the Ta-t'ung, to the T'ai-p'ing golden age, which according to Taoist sexagenary cycles could be both ancient and imminent, as the Yellow Turban rebels in 184 sincerely hoped. By the sixth century, the colossal four-cycle Indian cosmology had collapsed under the weight of Taoist alchemy, pietist Pure Land Buddhism, and popular Chinese worship of the Eternal Mother (Wu-sheng Lao-mu) and the *bodhisattva* Prince Moonlight (Yüeh-kuang T'ung-tzu).

There were then three accessible ages, associated cosmologically with the Taoist Former, Middle, and Latter Heavens, typologically with the three Buddhas (Lamplighter, Sakyamuni, and Maitreya), and synecdochically with the Buddhas' lotus thrones of azure, red, and white. Each age begins with a new Buddha and then declines, again in triplets: True Doctrine, or Dharma; Counterfeit Doctrine; and Last Days of Doctrine. Since the days of the historical Buddha, Sakyamuni (and, traditionally, of Confucius and Lao-tzu), we have squatted uncomfortably in the dissolute Last Days, awaiting Maitreya or his predecessor, Prince Moonlight, who is due to sweep in at the height of catastrophes one thousand years after Sakyamuni's *parinirvana.*

Common to millenarian aesthetics in all the world religions is this epochal scenario: a calm inaugural and a riotous finale to each act; the circling of two protagonists near the End, one imperial, the other sacramental; and a time at the End that is at once encore, intermezzo, and the throwing open of the doors.

Though flood, plague, famine, or war may summon visions of collective death, millenarians promise more than an accurate prediction of catastrophe. They promise an earth lifted beyond safety to grace. Even at their most catastrophic, millenarians insist that a classical tragedy must be fought through only to reach a genuinely good time.

Typologies of millenarian movements. Altogether, as a system of thought and social movement, millenarianism spins on two axes: golden age or new era; primitive paradise or promised land. This oscillation leads perplexed observers to depict millenarian movements as volatile, metamorphic, undirected, and ephemeral. Journalistic or academic, administrative or missiological, works on the subject abound with images that have shaped policy. Millenarianism is described in five iconic sets:

1. a contagion to be quarantined (as with Mormonism in Utah in the later 1800s);
2. a quicksand to be fenced off (as in the legal actions against the American Shakers in the early 1800s and the present-day anticult campaigns against the Unification Church);
3. a simmering stew to be watched, on the premise that a watched pot never boils (as in police surveillance of the group surrounding Catherine Théot in Paris in 1793 and 1794);
4. a boil to be lanced (as in the English kidnaping of the prophet Birsa from Munda country in northeastern India in 1895 or the Belgian imprisonment of Simon Kimbangu and his first disciples from 1921 to 1957);
5. an explosion to be contained (the German war against the Maji Maji of German East Africa [modern-day Tanzania] in 1905 and 1906 or the Jamaican government's preemption of Rastafarian music and rhetoric in the last two decades).

Millenarianism appears here as an epiphenomenon, a symptom of or a pretext for something more sinister. These images (and policies) have an august history. Church councils in Latin, Byzantine, and Protestant Christianity, legal scholars of Sunni Islam and rabbinic Judaism, the presiding monks of Buddhist *samghas*—all have long regarded millenarianism as a disguised attack on codes of behavior that are meant to govern faith and cult. Rulers and their bureaucracies—Confucian, Islamic, Hindu—have regarded millenarianism as a ritual mask worn by crafty rebels.

Present-day typologists are somewhat more sympathetic. For them, millenarianism is emblematic, a ceremonial flag waved furiously over swamps of injustice. Such an interpretation was codified by the French and German Enlightenments, then refurbished by liberals in the nineteenth century until positivist denials of a religious instinct made religion itself seem epiphenomenal. Latter-day social scientists have made millenarianism doubly emblematic, for they describe it as the sign of transition from a religious to a secular society.

Current typologies work along three scales: temporal focus, soteriology, and sociopolitical engagement. On the first scale, typologists range those movements oriented toward (1) the reconstitution of an earlier social structure (called nativist, traditionalist, conservationist, restorative), (2) the imaginative making of peace with change (called acculturative, adjustive, perpetuative, revitalist, reformative), and (3) the creation of an ideal future society (called messianic or utopian). The second scale runs from those movements concerned exclusively with individual salvation (called redemptive, revivalist, thaumaturgic) to those that demand an overhaul of economy and etiquette (called transformative or revolutionary). The third scale starts at total isolation and finishes with collective assault on the state. This scale especially has been plodded and plowed by rhetoric (reactionary/progressive, passive/active, prepolitical/political, mythological/ideological). Like mule teams, these binary terms are hardworking but perpetually sterile, since millenarians delight in the yoking of opposites.

Dynamic typologies, plotted by such scholars as Mary Douglas (1970), James W. Fernandez, (1964), and Wim M. J. van Binsbergen (1981), are quadrivalent, balancing social pressures against social structures. Douglas uses two vari-

> **Millenarianism appears here as an epiphenomenon, a symptom of or a pretext for something more sinister.**

ables, social cohesion and shared symbolic systems. Fernandez takes acculturation as his ordinate, instrumentality as his abscissa. Van Binsbergen considers both the source of disequilibrium (infrastructural, superstructural) and the nature of the threat ("peasantization," "proletarianization"). Such typologies, more appreciative of the complexity of millenarian movements, still hesitate before the phase shifts through which most movements go.

Motives for the fabrication of typologies may themselves be classified as prophylactic or exploitative. Most typologies mean to be prophylactic. Political scientists, for example, may hope to forestall the rise of charismatic tyranny; anthropologists in colonial settings may want to persuade authorities to handle millenarian movements more reasonably and with less show of force; missionaries may wish to avoid spawning highly independent churches or syncretic cults. Other typologies are exploitative. Marxist and capitalist alike place millenarians on a sociohistorical ladder so as to direct their obvious energies upward, toward national liberation and socialism or toward modern industrialism and oligopoly. Occultists and irenic church people place millenarians on one rung of the ladder of spiritual evolution so as to draw them toward higher consciousness, the Aquarian age, or one broad faith.

Explanations for millenarian movements. Despite the many typologies, there are but two current scholarly explanations for the birth of millenarian movements. The first asserts that millenarianism arises from feelings of relative deprivation in matters of status, wealth, security, or self-esteem. Millenarian movements appear in periods of crisis, when such feelings become most painful. The crisis may be as blatant and acute as the sack of a city or as subtle and

MILLENARIANISM

prolonged as the passage from isolated agrarian community to industrial megalopolis. Whichever it is, the crisis engenders personal fantasies of invulnerability and escape, which are transformed by charismatic individuals who are often members of displaced elites. These prophets shape public expressions of protest at a time when more straightforward political action seems useless. In the necessarily unsuccessful aftermath, millenarians master the cognitive dissonance between expectation and failure by perpetuating millenarian beliefs within a revised chronology and a new missionary plan. The underlying causes for feelings of deprivation will not have been resolved, so a millenarian tradition, halfway between social banditry and the politics of party, burns on.

The second, complementary explanation says that millenarian movements spring from contact between two cultures when one is technologically far superior to the other. Millenarianism spreads within the settled, inferior culture, whose polity is critically threatened. The newcomers, usually white and literate, disrupt traditional systems of kinship, healing, and land rights. Most wrenching are the factorial economics introduced by the newcomers, whose quantitative uses of time and money rasp across the qualitative webs of social reciprocity. The indigenes must redefine their notions of power, status, and law, or they must stave off the well-armed traders, their navies, and their missionaries. Acknowledging the superiority of the newcomers' technology but not that of their ethic of possessive individualism, the indigenes begin to speculate about the true origin of the goods and gods of the stingy, secretive newcomers. The result is the contact cult (also called a "crisis cult" or "cargo cult") devoted to frenzied preparation for the receipt of shiploads of goods (cargo) that will dock unaccompanied by whites or in the company of fair-skinned but unselfish ancestors. Already under intense pressure, the people ceremonially destroy sacred objects and standing crops. They believe that this world is ending and a new one must begin, best with the newcomers gone and themselves masters of the secret of wealth.

Contact is the sociology for which deprivation is the psychology. Contact leads to millenarianism when one group feels unalterably deprived vis-à-vis a new other. The two explanations, compatible with stock images of eruption and contagion, rely on the premise of a closed system. At the millenarian core lies frustration; out of frustration squirms fantasy, and fantasy breeds violence. Early Freudian analyses of hysteria, psychosis, and schizophrenia have been employed here to wire the circuit between individual fireworks and collective explosion.

Deprivation theories prevail despite decades of criticism for their being slackly predictive. Scholars have noted that relative deprivation does not account specifically for millenarianism; it may as easily induce fracas, sabotage, or personal depression. Conversely, millenarian movements have not

"burst out" where relative deprivation has been most apparent: eighteenth-century Ireland, nineteenth-century Ethiopia, the southeastern coast of modern India. Indeed, as critics may add, where across this imperfect world has relative deprivation ever been absent or a crisis lacking?

At this point, theorists invoke a *homo ex machina*, the charismatic prophet who processes the raw stuff of frustration. As a person whose life portends or echoes social crises, the prophet articulates the myth-dream of the people and so becomes invested with the power to direct its expression. Wherever gambols a weak social theory about religious movements, sure to follow is the fleece of charisma. For face-to-face groups, as W. R. Bion showed in his *Experiences in Groups* (New York, 1961), prophetic leaders may embody group fantasies of rebirth. For larger groups—like most millenarian movements—charisma becomes narcotic, a controlled substance rather than a theory of social relations.

Theorists have given particularly short shrift to the remarkable prominence of women as millenarian prophets. In all but Islam and Judaism, women have stridden at the head of millenarian movements, with men as their scribes, publicists, and ideologues. The list is long; a few examples must do: Priscilla and Maximilla of the New Prophecy (the Montanists) in Asia Minor in the late second century; Guglielma of Milan and her women disciples in the late thirteenth century; Dona Béatrice's Antonine movement in the Lower Congo from 1703 to 1706; Joanna Southcott with perhaps twenty thousand followers in England before her death in 1814; Ellen Gould White, chief oracle of the Seventh-day Adventists in the United States, in the late nineteenth century; Jacobina Maurer of the Brazilian Muckers movement from 1872 to 1898; the visionary Gaidaliu in Assam from 1929 to 1930 and 1961 to 1965; Mai Chaza's Guta ra Jehova (City of Jehovah) in Rhodesia from 1954 to 1960; Kitamura Sayo's Dancing Religion (Tensho Kotai Jingukyo) founded in Japan in 1945.

Deprivation theories maintain that women, an injured group, use religion as a means to power otherwise denied them by patriarchies. This makes religion a negative (compensatory) vehicle for women and a positive (creative) vehicle for men, and it fails to explain the power that women gain over men through millenarian movements. There is as yet no sufficient discussion of female charisma. Indeed, where prophetic leadership is male, analysis customarily proceeds from the instrumental, socioeconomic background to doctrine and political tactics; where female, it proceeds from affective, sexual background to ritual and spirit possession. Active men, reactive women: a contact theory of the sexes.

Contact theories are tricky. Amazed by discoveries of previously unknown tribes in the Amazon region and in the Philippines, industrial societies exaggerate the isolation of nonindustrial people. Nonetheless, contact is always a matter of degree: from armies with bulldozers abruptly grading runways in Melanesia to pandemics of smallpox hundreds of miles from (European) vectors. Contact is never so much a shock that some prophecy or other has not already accumulated around a piece of strangeness that years before drifted in on a storm tide or fell from the clouds.

In addition, we have sparse evidence that a number of peoples—the Guaraní of South America, the Karen of Burma, the Lakalai of the island of New Britain, and perhaps the Pacific Northwest Indians—had myths, rituals, and cults whose motifs were millenarian and whose origins were prior to contact with an in-pressing "superior" (Eurasian) culture.

Furthermore, not every uneven contact lights a millenarian "fuse." While the same material imbalance between Europeans and natives faced both Polynesians and Melanesians, millenarian movements have been infrequent among the politically stratified societies of Polynesia. More loosely bunched and socially fluid, Melanesians had inadequate etiquette by which to carry out diplomacy between distinctly separate orders. The customary structure of discourse, not contact itself, seems to have been a key variable in the general absence of cargo cults in Polynesia and their flowering in Melanesia, where consistently powerful Europeans could not be dealt with as easily as could another and analogous order.

At best, deprivation predisposes, contact precipitates. There are six other factors whose presence predisposes to millenarian movements:

1. permeable monastic communities and lay sodalities that extend loyalties beyond the family;
2. tinerant homeopathic healers who carry ritual and rumor across regional borders;
3. a mythopoetic tradition in popular drama and folktale, which makes history prophetic and the people the bearers of prophecy;
4. numerology and astrology, which encourage people habitually to search out relationships between number, event, and time;
5. rituals of inversion, such as carnival or exhaustive mourning, in which endings and beginnings are willfully confused;
6. migration myths that call for the return to an ancestral land or for the return of the dead to a renewed land.

There are negatively prejudicial factors as well. Millenarian movements are least likely at the extremes of the economic spectrum—that is, among those who have complete freedom of mobility and among those absolutely constrained. No millenarian movements occur within groups whose positions are secure, comfortable, and protected by mechanisms of caste (classical North Indian, Japanese, and Roman aristocracies). Nor do millenarian movements occur within groups whose mobility has been severely restricted by

political oppression (prisoners, inmates of concentration camps), economic oppression (slaves), physical illness (hospital patients, the starving), or mental illness (asylum inmates, the autistic).

This verges on tautology: millenarian movements happen where physical movement is possible. But the near tautology is suggestive. Where cultural ideals of physical movement differ, so, correspondingly, may the nature of social movements. For example, to be harshly schematic, Western Europeans have stressed vertical, direct, outbound motion in their sports, their dancing, their tools, and their manners; the head and shoulders lead, with the mass of the body in tow. Sub-Saharan Africans such as the Dogon have a kinesthetic of orchestral, highly oppositional, polyrhythmic motion in which the body twists at the hips. The northern Chinese have in their martial arts, their medicine and calligraphy a kinesthetic of sustained circular motion, an integrated body linked to the flow of universal energy. These differences may be expressed in the European proclivity for a tight echelon of prophets leading an undifferentiated millenarian body, the African tendency toward coextensive and fissiparous leadership, the Chinese history of generational continuity from one guiding millenarian family to the next. Kinesthetic differences may also determine the relative importance of the precipitants of millenarianism: where a society looks for whole-body motion, the triggering instances must affect the entire society; where a society looks for articulated or isolated motions, the triggering instances may be more local.

The following four factors recur cross-culturally as major precipitants of millenarian movements:

1. the evangelism of foreign missionaries whose success requires the reordering of native patterns of marriage, family, diet, and calendar;
2. displacement by refugees or invaders, or as a result of persecution, economic decline, or natural calamity;
3. confusion about landholdings due to shifting settlement, the superposition of a new legal grid, or the advent of new technologies, as foreshadowed most particularly by census taking, geological surveys, rail laying, and road building;
4. generational distortion, where the traditional transfer of loyalties and moral authority is profoundly disturbed by war deaths, schooling, long-distance migrations, or urbanization.

These are, of course, related. Threaded throughout are anxieties about inheritance, boundaries, and language (its intelligibility, its capacity for truth-telling). Set within a matrix of predisposing factors, granted some rumors and good weather, these anxieties should specifically engage the wheels of millenarianism, with its special freight of ages, places, and figures of speech. Expansive millenarianism occurs when believers are imperiled or impressed by forces within their society; astringent millenarianism occurs when the forces seem foreign.

Patterns of millenarian movements in world history. The world's great religions share a larger historical pattern of millenarian activity (although Vedanta Hinduism may be a partial exception). Founded on the fringes of empire or at the fracture line between competing kingdoms, these religions find themselves several centuries later at the center of an empire. Millenarian thought then appears in canonical form, drawing its impetus from those forces of imperial expansion that compel the recalculation of calendars, histories, distances, and sacred geography. The new arithmetic signals a shift in scales of measurement, mediated as much by mystics as by scientists. When an empire seems to have reached its limits, millenarian movements flourish, usually several generations before the dynastic collapse.

When the millennium does not arrive, or when millenarian movements are co-opted by a new dynasty, as in Ming China or Safavid Iran, millenarianism does not fade away. End-of-the-world images linger in the dreams and speech of the people, and end-time ideas are filtered through monasteries, lay brotherhoods, and scientific communities. As these are gradually attracted to the nodes of political power, millenarian movements reappear either as adjuncts of conquest or as resistance to it. Millenarian activity peaks again when the limits of territorial coherence are felt within the empire and along its colonial periphery.

This sequence may obtain for other than the great world religions (e.g., for the Aztec, Iroquois, and Ba-kongo), but materials are lacking that would sustain such an argument for the many preliterate cultures. It is tempting, in the same way that millenarianism itself is tempting, to offer a global explanation—such as climatic cycles—for its rhythms. The quest for global explanations, however, like the quest for a fountain of youth, tells more about the explorers than it does about the territory.

Contemporary Fascination with the End. Why does millenarianism presently seem in such need of some kind of covering law? The answers to this question have to do with the characteristics of the North Atlantic ecumene, which is responsible for most of the law making.

A first answer is that millenarians tend not to fall within the bell of the ecumene's emotional curve. Although sternly depressed about current affairs, millenarians are at the same time exultant about the prospects for a New World. European and North American psychologists interpret ambivalence as a symptom of inner discord; the greater the ambivalence, the more serious the illness. But "sensible" middle-class citizens join UFO cults, buy fifteen million copies of Hal Lindsey's *The Late Great Planet Earth* (Grand Rapids, Mich., 1970), and order bulk goods from End Time Foods, Inc., in Virginia. Why?

A second answer is that millenarians threaten the stability of the ecumene, upsetting the development of outlying colonies. Millenarians seem haphazardly amused by industrial investment and international tariffs. Why do they keep popping up to make a hash of foreign policy, and why do they prefer the "magical" to the "practical"?

A third answer is that the wars of this century have burned the mark of the beast on North Atlantic arts, philosophy, and history. The beast roared through the no-man's-lands of World War I and the gas chambers and radioactive cinders of World War II. Apocalypse has lost its reference to millennium; it has become simply a synonym for disaster.

We can also trace the growth of a catastrophic mood in North Atlantic science over a century of work in astronomy, cosmology, ecology, climatology, and, recently, morphogenetics and mathematics (the last two united by catastro-

> **Although sternly depressed about current affairs, millenarians are at the same time exultant about the prospects for a New World.**

phe theory, which accounts topologically for instant changes of state). The mood has prevailed in popular science from Henry Adams's 1909 essay on the second law of thermodynamics ("The Rule of Phase Applied to History") to the syzygy scare of the so-called Jupiter effect (1974-1982).

A fourth, more upbeat answer is that archaeology, theology, politics, and the Gregorian calendar have conspired to regenerate the utopian side of millenarianism. Although no millenarian movements and exceedingly few prophecies were geared to the year 1000 (few then used such a calendar), the historical myth persists because it seems to many that the year 2000 will be truly millennial. The discovery of the Dead Sea Scrolls since 1947 has underscored the contention, popularized by Albert Schweitzer in 1906, that eschatological hope was vital at the time of apostolic Christianity and should therefore be part of all true Christian belief. Israel's statehood in 1948 and its 1967 reunification of Jerusalem have convinced fundamentalist Christians of the nearness of the Second Coming, for which a principal sign is the Jews' return to Zion. So we see in the ecumene a telephone hot line for news of the latest scriptural prophecies fulfilled, an international conference on end-of-world prophecies (in Jerusalem in 1971), and a new perfume called Millennium: "In the life of every woman's skin there comes a turning point, a time when her face begins to look older. Now there is an alternative."

Outside the ecumene, detached from Christian dates, Hindu and Buddhist revivalists (Hare Krishna, Divine Light

Mission, Soka Gakkai) preach the last era, the kaliyuga or mappo. Shi`is awaiting the Mahdi at century's end (AH 1399/1979-1980 CE) experienced instead the Iranian revolution. Mexican intellectuals of the Movement of the Reappearance of Anauak, following the Aztec calendar, find this a time of cataclysm. Marxists, flipping through an economic almanac, tear off the leaves of late capitalism.

The fifth answer, then, is that from within and without the ecumene, notions of change have taken on a prepotently millenarian cast.

BIBLIOGRAPHY

Millenarian scholarship, chiefly a phenomenon of the North Atlantic ecumene, has followed the same patterns of historical change.

During the sixteenth century, while European merchants redefined time as fortune, millenarians appeared in Roman Catholic histories of heresy and Protestant martyrologies. For Catholics and for the Magisterial Reformers, millenarianism was occasioned by lust (impatience, appetite without love); for radical Protestants, millenarianism came of a desperately loving desire to return to the apostolic model. Then, as today, the bell cows of any overview were the communalistic Taborites in fifteenth-century Bohemia, Thomas Müntzer's rebels in the German Peasants' Revolt of 1524-1525, and the antinomian Anabaptist kingdom at Münster in 1534. In these three episodes the consequences of the millenarian program were so played out that most subsequent commentaries used them to distinguish between legitimate and illegitimate visions of religious and social renewal.

Early seventeenth-century histories, written in a confusing era of religious warfare, tended to describe millenarianism as the confused or gangrenous extension of piety, for which in English was coined the word *enthusiasm,* an outlier of the syndrome of melancholia. Melancholics seemed to resemble the age itself, mixing categories and muddling the practical, the extravagant, and the fantastic.

After the near revolutions of midcentury—the French Fronde with its *illuminés,* the English Civil War with its Levellers and Fifth Monarchists—millenarianism was implicated in political plotting and secret communication. So the medical figure of contagion, used earlier against witchcraft, was resurrected in works about millenarians, who might be possessed or mad or deluded but were likely first to have been infected by conniving knaves. Every one of these explanations was offered for the mass appeal of the great Jewish false messiah, Shabbetai Tsevi, who in 1666, at the height of his career, converted to Islam under penalty of death.

Eighteenth-century accounts, although sometimes pietist and sympathetic to millenarians, moved toward a vaguely biological description: millenarianism was seen as corpuscular, nervous, iatromechanical. In an era of newly accurate clocks and mortality statistics, historical source-criticism and the propaganda of Newtonian science, millenarians seemed to have lost their sense of time and power of memory.

Most modern assumptions about millenarianism were in place soon after the French Revolution. Encyclopedias of religion and dictionaries of sects sank the stakes: millenarianism was a personal reaction to internal chemical imbalance or to feelings of envy or lust; it was a social ploy or a disguise for politicking, money making, or ambition. Later in the century, under the impact of revivalism and labor agitation, millenarianism became part of the sociology of crowds; as a personal disorder it was associated homologically with *dementia praecox* (soon to be called schizophrenia). Anthropologists worked with Europocentric genetic metaphors: if millenarian movements occurred within Western civilization, they were classified as throwbacks to the spiritual childhood of religion; if outside, they were seen as infantile tantrums of primitive societies.

At least three thousand studies of millenarianism have been printed in this century, more and more often with a sympathetic preamble. Even so, because millenarians seem destined to inevitable disappointment, people of all political persuasions have resented the millenarian label, none more so than revolutionaries who want to make it clear that their programs for a New World are neither illusory nor doomed. Since Ernst Bloch's *Thomas Müntzer als Theologe der Revolution* (Munich, 1921), millenarian scholarship has been especially sharpened by political as well as religious polemic.

At midcentury, out tumbled a spate of works insisting on the centrality and continuity of millenarianism: for European culture, Normal R. C. Cohn's *The Pursuit of the Millennium* (1957), 3 ed. (New York, 1970); for peasant culture, Eric J. Hobsbawm's *Primitive Rebels* (New York, 1959); for world culture, *La table ronde's* full issue on "Apocalypse et idée de fin des temps" (no. 110, February 1957); and the human condition, Mircea Eliade's *Cosmos and History: The Myth of the Eternal Return* (New York, 1954). Simultaneously, in *When Prophecy Fails* (1956; reprint, New York, 1964), Leon Festinger, Henry W. Riecken, and Stanley Schachter developed a theory of cognitive dissonance to explain the endurance of millenarian beliefs from the point of view of social psychology. The capstone was a conference in 1960 sponsored by *Comparative Studies in Society and History,* (The Hague, 1958-), the journal that is still the most active in millenarian studies. The event set the agenda for at least a decade of research, prompting scholars to fashion typologies and to formulate distinctions between varieties of millenarian activity. The conference results were published in book form in *Millennial Dreams in Action: Essays in Comparative Study,* edited by Sylvia L. Thrupp (The Hague, 1962).

Although the works discussed above remain the most consistently cited sources in millenarian studies, their popularity is largely a measure of the comfort they have afforded a North Atlantic ecumene that is increasingly upset by liberation movements and cold war apocalypse diplomacy. Millenarianism, they assure us, has a history, a tradition, a phenomenology, a philosophy, and a psychology.

Henri Desroche's *Dieux d'hommes: Dictionnaire des messianismes et millénarismes de l'ère chrétienne* (Paris, 1969), although incomplete and outdated, codified much earlier scholarship. That year also saw a general turn away from theories of social pathology and mental illness to explain millenarian movements. Sophisticated analysis has turned toward the creative and polysemous nature of millenarianism. The following are some of the most thoughtful and evocative works published in English since 1969.

The oxymorons of millenarian thought have been deftly handled by Marjorie E. Reeves in *The Influence of Prophecy in the Later Middle Ages: A Study of Joachimism* (Oxford, 1969) and *Joachim of Fiore and the Prophetic Future* (London, 1976), which should be supplemented by a series of articles by Robert E. Lerner, including "Medieval Prophecy and Religious Dissent," *Past and Present* 72 (1976): 3-24; J. G. A. Pocock's *Politics, Language and Time* (New York, 1971), especially his essay "Time, History and Eschatology in the Thought of Thomas Hobbes," pp. 148-201; and Sacvan Bercovitch's *The Puritan Origins of the American Self* (London, 1975), which is excellently extended in his article "The Typology of America's Mission," *American Quarterly* 30 (Summer 1978): 135-155. Theodore Olson's *Millennialism, Utopianism, and Progress* (Toronto, 1981) moves heroically from the Greeks to the present, slipping and sliding along the way but always serious and sometimes passionate. Joseph Needham's purview is even broader; Needham masterfully draws out the similarities as well as the differences between European and Chinese approaches to time, in "Time and Eastern Man" in his *The Grand Titration: Science and Society in East and West* (Buffalo, N. Y., 1969), pp. 218-298. Like Needham, Charles Webster underlines the philosophical but also the social relations between science and millenarianism in his *The Great Instauration: Science, Medicine and Reform, 1626-1660* (New York, 1976).

Social anthropologists have been at the forefront of theory about millenarian movements. Alluded to in the text were Mary Douglas's *Natural Symbols: Explorations in Cosmology* (New York, 1970); James W. Fernandez's "African Religious Movements," *Annual Review of Anthropology* 7 (1978): 195-234, and "African Religious Movements: Types and Dynamics," *Journal of Modern African Studies* 2 (1964): 531-549; and Wim M. J. van Binsbergen's *Religious Change in Zambia* (Boston, 1981). Highly influential for his sophistication and for his theory of differential access to redemptive media is Kenelm Burridge's *New Heaven, New Earth* (New York, 1969). An interesting and thoroughgoing Marxist approach is presented by Berta I. Sharevskaya in *The Religious Traditions of Tropical Africa in Contemporary Focus* (Budapest, 1973); more accessible may be her article "Toward a Typology of Anticolonial Religious-Political Movements in Tropical Africa," *Soviet Anthropology and Archaeology* 15 (1976): 84-102. Less anthropological but nicely eclectic is Stephen Sharot's *Messianism, Mysticism, and Magic: A Sociological Analysis of Jewish Religious Movements* (Chapel Hill, N. C., 1982).

For particularly well done case studies of millenarian movements, see Mangol Bayat's *Mysticism and Dissent: Socioreligious Thought in Qajar Iran* (Syracuse, N. Y. 1982); Pierre Clastres's *Society against the State,* translated by Robert Harley and Abe Stein (New York, 1977), concerning the Guaraní of South America; Hue-Tam Ho Tai's *Millenarianism and Peasant Politics in Vietnam* (Cambridge, Mass., and London, 1983); Susan Naquin's *Millenarian Rebellion in China: The Eight Trigrams Uprising of 1813* (New Haven and London, 1976) and Shantung *Rebellion: The Wang Lun Uprising of 1774* (New Haven, 1981); my own *The French Prophets: The History of a Millenarian Group in Eighteenth-Century England* (Berkeley, 1980); and Anthony F. C. Wallace's *The Death and Rebirth of the Seneca* (New York, 1972).

Further bibliographies may be found in my "The End of the Beginning: Millenarian Studies, 1969-1975," *Religious Studies Review* 2 (July 1976): 1-15; Harold W. Turner's *Bibliography of New Religious Movements in Primal Societies,* 4 vols. (Boston, 1977-); and Bryan R. Wilson's *Magic and the Millennium* (New York, 1973), pp. 505-531.

HILLEL SCHWARTZ

MIMAMSA

The word *mimamsa* means "investigation" in ordinary Sanskrit. Since the term is applied to an important South Asian philosophical school, it must originally have meant "the investigation of the proper interpretation of the Vedic texts." The Mimamsa school is thus better known as the Purvamimamsa school, which is sometimes called the Dharmamimamsa (inquiry into the nature of *dharma* as laid down by the Vedas, the supreme authority). Uttara-mimamsa is the descriptive name for the Vedanta school, which deals with the nature of *brahman* as laid down in the latter part *(uttara)* of the Vedas, and in the Upanisads, hence also called Brahma-mimamsa (inquiry into the nature of *brahman*). The word *dharma* is of prime importance in this context. It stands here for one's "duty" *(codana)* enjoined by the Vedas, which includes both the religious or sacred duties or actions and the moral duties as well. *Dharma* also denotes the "virtue" attainable by performing such duties or following such courses of actions. Thus *dharma* is the main topic for discussion in the Mimamsa school.

The Vedic scriptures were seriously attacked by the Sramanas (mendicant Brahmanic philosophers) about 500 BCE, and as a result its authority was apparently being devastated by criticisms. Hence the Mimamsa school originated among the Vedic priests who wanted to reestablish this authority by resolving the apparent contradictions and other textual problems found in the Vedic scriptures. The Mimamsa school in this way developed the science of exegesis. A *Mimamsa Sutra* was compiled as early as the first century BCE and it was ascribed to an ancient sage, Jaimini. It is regarded as the key text of the school.

Regarding *dharma*, Mimamsa maintains a form of fundamentalism. It claims that the scriptures are the only means of knowing what is dharma and what is not. Only by following the injunctions of the scriptures can we attain *dharma,* or the "good," that cannot be attained by any other means. Other means of knowledge (perception, inference, reasoning, etc.) are of no help in the realm of *dharma,* for concerns of *dharma* are with transcendental matters, the imperceptibles and the unverifiables, such as the afterlife, heaven, and the moral order. Hence the Mimamsa school defines the essence of the Vedas *(vedata)* as that which informs us about such a transcendental realm. And the authority of the Vedas in such matters is self-evident. The truth of the scriptural statements is self-validating. The Vedas are to be regarded as eternal and uncreated. The scriptures are *revealed* texts, there being no author of them. In short, the truths of the Vedas are transempirical, hence no empirical evidence can conceivably bear on them.

The problem of interpretation has led the Mimamsa school to the study and discussion of topics which are of great philosophical interest. The Mimamsa developed itself into a kind of philosophical discipline, incorporating into it a theory of knowledge, epistemology, logic, a theory of meaning and language, and a realistic metaphysic. With its emphasis on the philosophy of language and linguistics, the Mimamsa has sometimes been called the *vakya-sastra* ("theory of speech"). It also formulated various rules of interpretation in order to resolve and eliminate the apparent inconsistencies of the scriptural texts.

Later on, the Mimamsa school was divided into two subschools (c. 600-700 CE), following the two important exponents of the school, Kumarila Bhatta and Prabhakara. They are called the Bhatta school and the Prabhakara school. Of the many minor differences between the two subschools, only a few of the more notable ones have been noted here.

Kumarila speaks of six *pramanas* ("legitimate ways of knowing")—perception *(pratyaksa),* inference *(anumana),* verbal testimony (*sabda* or *aptavacana*), comparison *(upamana),* presumption *(arthapatti),* and non-apprehension *(anupalabdhi).* Prabhakara accepts the first five only. Since he rejects "absence" *(abhava)* as a separate reality, as a "knowable" entity *(prameya),* he does not need "nonapprehension" to establish such entities. For the Bhattas, a cognition is not a perceptible property, but it is inferred from the "cognizedness" *(jñatata)* of the object cognized: since this pot is cognized by me, a cognition of it must have occurred in me. For the Prabhakaras, a cognition is self-cognized—it perceives itself. But both regard knowledge to be self-validating. Kumarila admits both Vedic and non-Vedic *sabda* (sentences, speech) to be *pramana.* Prabhakara holds that real sabda-pramana is the Vedic *sabda.* Both try to establish the Vedic authority not on God but on such transcendental reality as *dharma* and *moksa.* The Bhattas explicitly hold the *jñana-karma-samuccaya-vada,* that both knowledge and action lead to liberation. The Prabhakara view does not seem to be very different.

The two subschools differ in their views about the correct incentive for man's action (which includes both moral and religious acts). The Prabhakaras say that it is only the sense of duty while the Bhattas argue that both sense of duty and the desire for benefit constitute the correct incentive for action. On another rather technical matter, the two disagree. The Bhattas believe that the sentences get their meanings from their atomistic constituents, the individual word-meanings, while the Prabhakaras believe that the words directly constitute the sentence-meaning as a whole only insofar as they are syntactically connected *(anvita)* with other words in the sentence.

[*See also* Vedanta.]

BIBLIOGRAPHY

Jha, Ganganath. *Prabhakara School of Purva-mimamsa.* Allahabad, 1911.

Ramanujacarya. *Tantra-rahasya* (1923). 2d ed. Edited by Rudrapatha Shamasastry and K. S. Ramaswami Sastri. Gaekwad's Oriental Series, no. 24. Baroda, 1956. Contains an introduction by the editors.

Shastri, Pashupatinath. *Introduction to Purva Mimamsa* (1923). 2d ed. Edited and revised by Gaurinath Sastri. Varanasi, 1980.

BIMAL KRISHNA MATILAL

MINISTRY

The term *ministry* traditionally refers to offices of leadership in the Christian church, but there has been a growing recognition that it also describes the way the mission of the whole church is conducted. Both in terms of specific offices (ministers) and in terms of the work of the church in general, ministry has biblical roots. In Hebrew, *sheret* ("to serve") applies to temple officers and was normally translated *leitourgein* in the Septuagint. This use was carried over into the New Testament, where the various linguistic forms of *leitourgein* are used not only for general acts of service to others (*Rom.* 15:27, *2 Cor.* 9:12, *Phil.* 2:30) but also for worship (*Acts* 13:3) and particularly for priestly and Levitical functions under the Old Covenant (*Lk.* 1:23; *Heb.* 8:2, 8:6, 9:21, 10:11). But the New Testament introduced the words *diakonia* ("service") and *diakonein* ("to serve"), referring to the menial work done by a *diakonos* ("servant") or *doulos* ("slave") to indicate the quality of ministry in the church. These words represent not status but the serving relationship of the minister to the one served: following the example of Christ (and, subsequently, the example of the apostle Paul) is at the heart of the Christian understanding of ministry (*Jn.* 13:1-20; *1 Cor.* 4:16, 11:1; *Phil.* 3:17).

Scholars dispute how far the New Testament reflects a uniform and obligatory pattern of ministerial orders. Roman Catholic scholars generally hold that it does, but most Protestant scholars believe that the New Testament offers several patterns of ministry (*Eph.* 4:11-12; *1 Cor.* 12:27-31; *1 Tm.* 3:1-13, 4:11-16, 5:3-10, 5:17-22). The former view maintains that the orders of ministry are fixed by tradition and that their authority is transmitted by historical succession from the apostles through bishops or the pope as the vicar of Christ (apostolic succession). The latter view regards ministerial orders as essentially functional and focused on faithful transmission of the apostolic testimony.

There is, however, agreement that all ministry traces its authority to Jesus Christ and to the apostles who testified to his saving work and resurrection (*Mt.* 16:13-24, 18:18, 28:18-20; *Jn.* 20:23). Although the apostle Paul could not claim personal connection with the Galilean ministry, he did claim commission from Jesus Christ as the heart of his own call to apostleship (*Gal.* 1:1, 1:11-24, 2:1-21). Churches also generally agree that officers in the church's ministry (i. e., the clergy) have particular responsibility for preaching, for administration of the sacraments (or ordinances), and for the oversight and nurture of their congregations. [*See* Church.]

By the beginning of the second century, three principal orders of ministry—bishop or pastor (*episcopos,* "overseer"), presbyter or priest (*presbuteros,* "elder"), and deacon (*diakonos,* "servant")—had become widely accepted, and although various confessional groups may not agree how far or when these orders became dependent on the Roman pontiff, the primacy of the pope seems to have been widely acknowledged by the time of Leo I (d. 461) and continued in the West until the Reformation. In the Eastern church the break with Rome, the Great Schism, is often given the date 1054, but scholars recognize that this was the end of a process of estrangement over centuries. However, the three-fold ministry remained unchanged in both halves of Christendom through a millennium of Christian history. [*See* Priesthood *and* Papacy.]

Catholic branches of the church claim unbroken succession with this earlier history and believe that these offices are prescribed (i. e., *iure divino*) and guaranteed by apostolic

> . . . the Society of Friends (Quakers) claims that the spirit of the scriptures requires no specially ordained ministers.

succession. Ordination is a sacrament whereby the Holy Spirit is transmitted through the bishop's imposition of hands, which imparts special grace to administer the sacraments and to exercise authority in the church. In the Roman Catholic church these powers derive ultimately from the pope, while among the Orthodox it is exercised by the bishop within the corporate authority of the Orthodox community. Old Catholics and Anglo-Catholics hold a position on apostolic succession close to that of Rome but do not acknowledge the infallible authority of the papacy.

The sixteenth-century Reformation challenged the absolute authority of ecclesiastical tradition and its priesthood. Protestants turned from papal authority to the authority of the Bible, which led to revisions in their understanding of the church and its ministry. In the main, they claimed to restore the New Testament pattern, and in reaction to ecclesiastical legalism they tended to appeal to the Bible as a divine law book. New Testament "restorationism" appears in the early Luther, based on a primary appeal to scripture and on scripture exegeted by "the priesthood of all believers." Luther may be described as advocating a form of "evangelical pragmatism," since he accepted any pattern consistent with scripture that served the effective preaching of the word and the proper administration of the sacraments. Lutheranism has therefore adopted episcopal, consistorial, and congregational forms of churchmanship. [*See* Reformation.]

Attempts to restore a more biblical pattern of church and ministry are to be found in almost every form of Reformation church, and not least the Reformed church. Differences between Ulrich Zwingli (1484-1531) and the Anabaptists

(Swiss Brethren) were not over the primacy of scripture but over its interpretation. John Calvin (1509-1564) systematized the Reformed position, claiming that church and ministry are of divine institution (*Institutes* 4.1, 4.3). Like many in his day, he regarded apostles, prophets, and evangelists as peculiar to the apostolic age, although he recognized that they might be revived "as the need of the times demands." Pastors and teachers, he argued, were indispensable. Pastors exercised general oversight discipline and preached and administered the sacraments; teachers were responsible for doctrine. Calvin also recognized the New Testament office of deacon in care of the poor (within which he included the office of the "widow"). He insisted on both the inward call of a minister and the recognition by the church of that call. In matters of discipline the pastor was to share power with a consistory of elders so that power would not be exclusively in the hands of a single person.

Calvin's fourfold ordering of ministry was taken over by the Reformed church and the Puritans in the British Isles and colonial America in the Presbyterian and Congregational churches. Similar forms of ministry arose out of English Separatism (e.g., Baptist churches) and the Christian Church (Disciples of Christ) movement of the American frontier. Differences between the classic Reformation positions and later restoration movements turned not so much on the appeal to the Bible as on other matters affecting scriptural interpretation: the relationship of the church to civil authorities, insistence on the church's purity, ministerial training, and how far literal appeal to scripture may be modified by the Holy Spirit revealed in scripture. Extreme restorationists reject any deviation from the New Testament pattern; at the other extreme, the Society of Friends (Quakers) claims that the spirit of the scriptures requires no specially ordained ministers.

A different modification of the church's ministry is seen in the Anglican settlement. In the sixteenth century, Henry VIII sought to separate from Rome without changing the shape of the national church, and his daughter, Elizabeth I, followed his lead. She wooed English Catholics by maintaining traditional vestments, liturgy, and forms of church government (episcopal). From the first the Church of England tried to reconcile appeal to scripture and to church tradition. Originally the settlement was based on the authority of the crown (the divine right of kings), but at the turn of the seventeenth century appeals to the divine right of the episcopacy began to appear. Differences concerning the role of the episcopacy are reflected in the so-called high church (Anglo-Catholic), broad church (Latitudinarian), and low church (Evangelical) traditions within Anglicanism. [*See* Anglicanism.]

In the eighteenth century, John Wesley, founder of Methodism, refused to separate from the Church of England. He finally became convinced that priests and bishops were of the same order in the New Testament and that he had the right to ordain ministers for America, but he refused to designate bishops and instead appointed superintendents. The decision to employ the term *bishop* in American Methodism probably arose from the determination to assert independence from Anglicanism. But although Wesley believed that the threefold order of ministry is scriptural, he offered an essentially pragmatic interpretation of these offices. His position was fundamentally the evangelical pragmatism seen in Luther. [*See* Methodist Churches.]

By the mid-1980s there was no acceptance of the ordination of women in the Roman Catholic and Orthodox branches of the church, but a growing acceptance of women into the ordained ministry of Protestant denominations and in some provinces of Anglicanism was evident. Protestant and Anglican practices stem from the theological belief that the call to ministry is open to all God's people. The ecumenical movement has also prompted many churches to reexamine earlier claims and to recognize that they have much to learn from each other. Statements on ministry prepared for the Consultation on Church Union (1984), which reflected the views of ten American Protestant denominations, and by the World Council of Churches (1982) indicate a significant and growing consensus. This consensus reveals an emphasis on the servanthood of ministry as evidenced in the ministry of Jesus; an awareness that the whole church is the proper context in which the ordained ministry should be considered; an awareness that the doctrines of church and ministry cannot be separated; and a recognition that the traditional threefold ordering of ministry should not be lightly discarded. This growing consensus shows that many Christian churches seek to manifest their essential unity and to arrive at a point where their ministries may be mutually recognized.

[*See also* Ecumenical Movement. *For broad discussions of issues related to Christian ministry, see* Ordination.]

BIBLIOGRAPHY

The tendency today is to consider the doctrines of church and ministry holistically, and in any reading list on ministry, books about the doctrine of the church should find a place. Among the older books considering ministry, *The Apostolic Ministry,* edited by Kenneth E. Kirk (London, 1946), and T. W. Manson's *The Church's Ministry* (Philadelphia, 1948) must be mentioned because they illustrate a classic debate on apostolic succession in relation to episcopacy. For a general account of where the churches stand on the issues, *The Nature of the Unity We Seek,* edited by Paul Minear (Saint Louis, 1958), may be consulted, and also the relevant documents in *The Documents of Vatican II,* edited by Walter M. Abbott (New York, 1966), for the Roman Catholic position.

One of the most thorough historical studies to be conducted in the United States is *The Ministry in Historical Perspectives,* edited by H. Richard Niebuhr and Daniel D. Williams (New York, 1956), and H. Richard Niebuhr's theological interpretation of that evidence, *The Purpose of the Church and Its Ministry* (New York, 1956), underscores the recognition that church and ministry cannot be separated. *The Pioneer Ministry,* by Anthony Tyrrell Hanson (London, 1961),

an important biblical study of ministerial leadership in the Pauline churches, responds to assumptions made earlier in Kirk's book, while my own book *Ministry* (Grand Rapids, Mich., 1965) places this Anglo-Saxon debate within its ecumenical context. Ronald E. Osborn's *In Christ's Place: Christian Ministry in Today's World* (Saint Louis, 1967) arrives at similar conclusions on the basis of New Testament evidence.

The most important recent documents on ministry are those coming out of bilateral conversations, such as *The Ministry in the Church* (Geneva, 1982), published by the Roman Catholic/Lutheran Joint Commission; the documents produced by the Consultation on Church Union, such as the *Digest of the Plenary Meetings* (Princeton, 1979-) and *The COCU Consensus: In Quest of a Church of Christ Uniting* (Princeton, 1985); and the documents published by the World Council of Churches, particularly the "Lima Document," in Baptism, *Eucharist and Ministry,* "Faith and Order Paper no. 111" (Geneva, 1982).

ROBERT S. PAUL

MIRACLES

The history of religions has preserved the record of miracles, that is, events, actions, and states taken to be so unusual, extraordinary, and supernatural that the normal level of human consciousness finds them hard to accept rationally. These miracles are usually taken as manifestations of the supernatural power of the divine being fulfilling his purpose in history, but they are also caused to occur "naturally" by charismatic figures who have succeeded in controlling their consciousness through visions, dreams, or the practices of meditation.

Miracles in the Mediterranean World. In archaic Greece, Pythagorasis is especially noteworthy. Pythagoras was a "divine man" *(theios aner),* combining the figure of the popular miracle worker, the portrait of the philosopher, and the idealized image of the practical statesman. His image as miracle worker was enhanced by several recurring motifs: (1) Pythagoras was seen in two cities at the same time; (2) he could recall his previous existences; (3) he was endowed with the ability to stop an eagle in flight; and (4) he could predict events in the future. It is highly probable that, as Neo-Pythagoreanism gained popularity among ordinary people, the image of Pythagoras the thaumaturge was promoted by a circle of followers quite distinct from those who wished to cultivate his reputation as a philosopher and scientist.

Apollonius of Tyana described exorcisms and instances of healing the blind, the lame, and the paralytic in India (see Philostratus, *The Life of Apollonius of Tyana* 3.38-39); more important than that, he performed similar miracles himself. Apollonius reportedly performed even the miracle of raising the dead while he was in Rome (4.45).

The figure of Moses was one of the most important propaganda instruments that Jews of the Hellenistic period used in their competition with non-Jewish schools and cults. In *Deuteronomy* 34:10-12, Moses is described as the greatest prophet in Israel, known for his signs and wonders as well as for his mighty powers and great and terrible deeds.

There are many stories in late Judaism narrating how rabbis worked miracles of healing. The best known, perhaps, is the healing of the son of Yohanan ben Zakk'ai by Hanina' ben Dosa'. Both rabbis lived in Palestine around 70 CE. Hanina' ben Dosa' went to study the Torah with Yohanan ben Zakk'ai, whose son was seriously ill. Yohanan requested: "Hanina', my son, pray for mercy for him that he may live." Hanina' ben Dosa' laid his head between his knees and prayed, and then the boy was cured (B. T., *Ber.* 34).

Throughout late antiquity, Epidaurus was a holy site especially celebrated for the epiphany of Asklepios, the divine healer. According to Strabo, Asklepios was believed to "cure diseases of every kind." His temple was always full of the sick as well as containing the votive tablets on which treatments were recorded (*Geography* 8.6.15).

The Mediterranean world knew Egypt as the home of thaumaturgy, theosophy, and esoteric wisdom. There, the goddess Isis was praised for her miraculous healings; she was credited with bringing the arts of healing to men and, once she had attained immortality, taking pleasure in miraculously healing those who incubated themselves in her temple (Diodorus Siculus, *The Library of History* 1.25.2-5). At her hands the maimed were healed and the blind received their eyesight.

Yogins, Taoist Contemplatives, and Yamabushi. Indian ascetics practicing Yoga are well known for their miraculous powers. [*See* Yoga.]

The yogin acquires the "miraculous powers" *(siddhis)* when he has reached a particular stage of his meditational discipline called *samyama,* referring, more specifically, to the last stages of yogic technique, that is, concentration *(dharana),* meditation *(dhyana),* and samadhi. For example, by practicing *samyama* in regard to the subconscious residues *(samskaras),* the yogin knows his previous existences; this enables him to ideally relive his former existences. Some of the yogin's "miraculous powers" are even more extraordinary: he can make himself invisible by practicing *samyama* concerning the form of the body.

Taoists in ancient China are convinced that man can become an "immortal".

The practice of meditation essential for attaining immortality leads inevitably to the possession of miraculous powers. According to the *Pao-p`u-tzu,* the Taoist immortal Ko Hsüan, one of Ko Hung's paternal uncles, would stay at the bottom of a deep pond for almost a whole day in hot summer weather. This "miracle" was possible because of his mastery of "embryonic respiration": he was able to accumulate his breaths and to breathe like a fetus in its mother's womb.

Mountain ascetics in Japan known as *yamabushi* acquired magico-religious powers through a series of disci-

plines. The *yamabushi* was the master of heat and fire; he walked barefoot on red hot charcoals without injury; he proved his extraordinary power when, with only a white robe on his naked body, he entered a bath of boiling water and came out entirely unscathed; and he surprised his spectators by climbing a ladder of swords, the sharp edge facing upward.

Miracles in Founded Religions. The founders of three major religions of the world—Buddhism, Christianity, and Islam—have each taken a different attitude toward miracle.

Buddhism. The Buddha was well aware that the practice of meditation essential for attaining enlightenment leads eventually to the possession of "miraculous power" (Skt., *siddhi;* Pali, *iddhi*). But he did not encourage his disciples to seek *siddhis.* The true task was not to acquire miraculous powers but to transcend the world of pain and suffering and to attain the state of enlightenment.

According to biographical sources, however, the Buddha was sometimes led to work miracles; for example, when he returned to his native city, Kapilavastu, for the first time after attaining enlightenment, he rose in the air, emitted flames of fire and streams of water from his body, and walked in the sky (see *Mahavastu* 3.115). According to Asvaghosa's *Buddhacarita* (19.12-13), in order to convince his relatives of his spiritual capacities and prepare them for conversion, the Buddha rose in the air, cut his body to pieces, let his head and limbs fall to the ground, and then joined them together again before the amazed eyes of the spectators. Among the eminent disciples of the Buddha, Moggallana (Skt., Maudgalyayana) was well known as the "chief of those endowed with miraculous powers."

Christianity. Jesus Christ performed the miracles of healing and exorcism. In the miracle stories that, together with his sayings and passion narratives, occupy an important place in the synoptic Gospels, Jesus of Nazareth is presented as the supreme thaumaturge, the great miracle worker, the magician.

Typically, the miracle stories of healing and exorcism in the synoptic Gospels all emphasize three motifs: (1) the history of the illness, (2) the actual process or techniques of the healing, and (3) a demonstration of the cure to the satisfaction of spectators.

Particularly interesting are the techniques that Jesus employed for healing and exorcism. There is no question that he considered prayer to be essential for working miracles (*Mk.* 9:29). But, as a thaumaturge, he had to work up his emotions; in healing a leper Jesus was moved with "anger" *(orgistheis),* stretched out his hand, and touched him (*Mk.* 1:40-45). Jesus displayed the emotional frenzy of the thaumaturge (see also *Lk.* 4:39). In the story of the deaf and mute man (*Mk.* 7:32-37), Jesus puts his fingers into his ears, spits and touches his tongue. Looking up to heaven, he sighs and says to him, "Ephphatha" ("Be opened"). In *Mk.* 8:22-26

Jesus heals a blind man by spitting on his eyes and laying his hands on them.

Especially interesting is a cycle of miracle stories in the *Gospel of Mark* (4:35-5:43) that includes the stories of the Gerasene demoniac, the woman with an issue of blood, and the daughter of Jairus. Each of these has all the characteristics of the popular miracle story, and each contributes to the impression that Jesus is a "divine man," tempting New Testament scholars to talk about the development of "divine man Christology" in the *Gospel of Mark.*

> **Particularly interesting are the techniques that Jesus employed for healing and exorcism.**

In the subsequent history of Christianity, charisma or divine gift of "power" was represented on earth by a limited number of exceptional charismatic figures, such as the martyrs of the second and third centuries, the bishops of the late third century, and, finally, the succession of great Christian saints.

Islam. Muhammad, the "seal of the prophets," rejected every request to pose as a miracle worker; in contrast to Moses and other Hebrew prophets, as well as Jesus, who all worked miracles *(mu`jizat),* Muhammad made no attempt to advance his religious authority by performing miracles, although people demanded them.

However, Muhammad is presented in the traditions *(hadiths)* as having worked miracles in public on many occasions. It was especially Sufi saints who performed miracles *(karamat).* Often called the "friends of God" *(awliya', sg. wali),* they worked miracles by divine grace. On the one hand, it is often said by the Sufis that saints must not seek after the gift of miracle working, which might become a serious obstacle in the path to the union with God. On the other hand, the biographies of leading Sufis abound in miracle stories that certainly have been utilized for evangelical purposes: saints traveled a long distance in a short time; walked on water and in the air; talked with such inanimate objects as stones, as well as with animals; miraculously produced food, clothing, and other necessities of life; and made predictions of future events.

[*For a look at some theoretical issues involved in belief in miracles, see* Supernatural, The.]

BIBLIOGRAPHY

There is no comprehensive book dealing with the topic of miracles in the general history of religions. On the problem of interpretation concerning miracles and magico-religious powers in "primitive" societies, see Ernesto de Martino's *Il mondo magico* (Turin, 1948), translated by Paul S. White as *The World of Magic* (New York, 1972). On the miracles and miraculous powers of shamans, there is an admirable account in Mircea Eliade's *Shamanism: Archaic Techniques of Ecstasy,* rev. & enl. ed. (New York, 1964). This book contains an excellent bibliography.

Richard Reitzenstein's *Hellenistische Wundererzählungen* (1906; reprint, Darmstadt, 1963) still remains a classic for the study of the miracle stories in the Hellenistic Mediterranean world. Otto Weinreich has offered a detailed analysis of some of the major motifs appearing in the Greco-Roman stories of healing miracles. See his *Antike Heilungswunder: Untersuchungen zum Wunderglauben der Griechen und Römer* (Giessen, 1909). Valuable information on the miracle stories pertaining to the cult of Asklepios is presented in Emma J. Edelstein and Ludwig Edelstein's *Asclepius: A Collection and Interpretation of the Testimonies,* 2 vols. (Baltimore, 1945). See also Károly Kerényi's important study *Die göttliche Arzt: Studien über Asklepios und seine Kultstätten,* rev. ed. (Darmstadt, 1956), translated by Ralph Manheim as *Asklepios: Archetypal Image of the Physician's Existence* (New York, 1959). Miracle stories in rabbinic Judaism have been collected by Paul Fiebig in his *Jüdische Wundergeschichten des neutestamentlichen Zeitalters* (Tübingen, 1911).

On the miraculous powers of yogins, there is a brilliant account in Mircea Eliade's *Yoga: Immortality and Freedom,* 2d ed. (Princeton, 1969), still the standard work on the theory and practice of Yoga. On Taoist immortals and their miraculous powers, there is a brief but excellent account in Max Kaltenmark's *Lao Tseu et le taoïsme* (Paris, 1965), translated by Roger Greaves as *Lao Tzu and Taoism* (Stanford, Calif., 1969).

On miracles in the life of the Buddha, see a valuable account in Edward J. Thomas's *The Life of Buddha as Legend and History,* 3d rev. ed. (London, 1949).

The modern study of the miracle stories in the synoptic Gospels was initiated shortly after the end of World War I by such brilliant form critics as Martin Dibelius and Rudolf Bultmann. See a fascinating study by Dibelius, *Die Formgeschichte des Evangeliums,* 2d rev. ed. (Tübingen, 1933), translated by Bertram Lee Woolf as *From Tradition to Gospel* (New York, 1935). See also Bultmann's admirable analysis of the miracle stories in his *Die Geschichte der synoptischen Tradition,* 3d ed. (Götting-en, 1958), translated by John Marsh as *The History of the Synoptic Tradition* (New York, 1963). More recently, Gerd Theissen has studied the miracle stories from the perspective of the sociology of literature. See his *Urchristliche Wundergeschichten: Ein Beitrag zur formgeschichtlichen Erforschung der synoptischen Evangelien* (Gutersloh, 1974), translated by Francis McDonagh and edited by John Riches as *The Miracle Stories of the Early Christian Tradition* (Philadelphia, 1983). David L. Tiede, in his very useful study *The Charismatic Figure as Miracle Worker* (Missoula, Mont., 1972), distinguishes between the aretalogy of the sage-philosopher and the aretalogy of the miracle worker. On Christian saints and their miracles, there is an excellent study by Peter Brown, *The Cult of the Saints: Its Rise and Function in Latin Christianity* (Chicago, 1981).

On Muhammad's reinterpretation of the concept ayah ("sign"), there is an admirable account by Toshihiko Izutsu, *God and Man in the Koran: Semantics of the Koranic Weltanschauung* (Tokyo, 1964), pp. 133ff. Reynold A. Nicholson has written on Muslim saints and their miracles in his *The Mystics of Islam: An Introduction to Sufism* (1914; reprint, London, 1963), pp. 120-147. See also a fascinating account by Annemarie Schimmel, *Mystical Dimensions of Islam* (Chapel Hill, N. C., 1975), pp. 204ff.

MANABU WAIDA

MISSIONS

Missionary Activity

Foundations and Motivations. It is possible to venture some generalizations about missionary activity that seem relevant for all the great missionizing religions. The first point is that missionizing religions are religions that, impelled by a unique revelation or a great discovery about the nature of being, or a momentous social transformation and revitalization of purpose sparked by spiritual impulses, have generated a salvific metaphysical-moral vision that they believe to be of universal import for humanity. This vision induces a passion for transcendence that intellectually, morally, and emotionally frees its adherents from local deities and cults, from familial, tribal, clan, caste, or ethnic loyalties, from fixed political-economic conditions, and from traditional "paganisms." The missionary impulse is to become "homeless," for it finds its true home in a transcendent realm that relativizes all that is understood to be "natural." It further evokes a desire to

> **Missionary activity always to some degree alienates its converts from previous belief. . . .**

bring about the universal acceptance and application of the vision, which it holds to be universally true in principle.

Every missionizing religion, thus, is by definition transcultural; where it is not entirely transmundane, it is cosmopolitan. It endows its advocates with a transcendental, ecumenical, cross-cultural, and global perspective, which understands humanity as trapped in chaotic conditions of spiritual and/or physical oppression from which humanity must be delivered by accepting a new foundation of meaning and a new discipline, one that liberates from evil and falsehood and binds to good and truth.

A missionary is one who seizes or is seized by a universalistic vision and who feels a mandate, a commission, a vocation to bring the vision and its benefits to "all." Thus, missionary activity, both domestic and foreign, is most intense in those moments when the metaphysical-moral vision of a religion is engendered or revitalized and held to be pertinent to new conditions. "Home" missions often take the form of new programs for youth, "purification" of religious and cultural practice, proselytism of marginal groups, protest against lax practices among the social elite (including the established clergy), and, often, moral or spiritual attempts to put domestic social, political, and economic policies on a new foundation. "Foreign" missions attempt to take the vision beyond the land of origin and thereby to lay the foundations for a new

spiritual world order by transforming the souls and minds of individuals and the social habits of their society. Missionary activity always to some degree alienates its converts from previous belief and practice, for it introduces a different way of organizing faith and life. Both domestic and foreign missionary activity is marked by intense intellectual activity, for the whole of reality has to be reconsidered from the new perspective.

One or another universalistic vision has provided the foundations and motivations for Buddhism, Christianity, Islam, and that new secular civil religion, communism, to name but four of the most obvious missionizing religions. Certain strands and periods of Judaism, Zoroastrianism, and "syncretistic" religions such as Baha'i, Sikhism, and the Unification Church (Moonies) have a similar dynamic. A universalistic metaphysical-moral vision is less pronounced, however, in the beliefs of the tribal religions and Shinto, and less overt in many strands of Confucianism, Judaism, and Zoroastrianism. However great their spiritual, moral, and intellectual achievements, these latter religions are constitutively tied to specific sociopolitical contexts and, often, to ethnic particularities. These religions may also claim to possess a universalistic message; they may welcome converts, and their metaphysical-moral visions may be espoused by other religions; but they are spread more by the migrations of peoples or by the gradual incorporation of immediate neighbors than by organized missionary activities. Hinduism represents a special and exceedingly complex case, for while it is similar to nonmissionizing traditions in many respects, and while it seems to have spread essentially by a process called sanskritization—the gradual adoption of Vedic practices and brahmanic authority by non-Aryan peoples on the Indian subcontinent (see Srinivas, [1952] 1978)—it has had periods of vigorous missionary activity. Indeed, today, active missions are being carried out by "evangelical" forms of Hinduism such as the Rama-krishna Mission, ISKCON (Hare Krishna), and the Transcendental Meditation movement of Maharishi Mahesh Yogi.

Some Dynamics of Missionary Activity. As a population is missionized, new patterns of educational, familial, cultural, and political-economic conditions are routinized into a transformed "tradition" on new foundations. The tendency to identify the universalistic message with the newly established local or regional patterns of life within particular groups is widespread. The vision "for all" once again becomes "our" vision, "for us," until such time as a new burst of piety and learning renews the awareness of the universalistic vision and revitalizes missionary efforts, demanding a purging of false tendencies to syncretism. Missionary religions are continually or episodically engaged in religious renewal and reformation from within. The great missionizing religions are in part to be contrasted with the occasionally proselytizing, primal, and localistic religions precisely by the enduring and recurring vitality of their universalizing, in contrast to the particularizing and syncretizing tendencies of the localistic religions. It is not surprising that missionary religions are those with an authoritative scripture and "orthodox" doctrine that serve as the standards for periodic renewal.

The great universalistic teachings of the missionizing religions are, however, always treasures borne in "earthen vessels," to paraphrase Paul, the model of all Christian missionaries. And the line between the treasure and the vessel is frequently extremely fine. Early Buddhist missionaries, to cite another example, were sent out presumably armed with nothing but the pure and unadulterated message of Gautama's great discovery of the secret of true enlightenment. Wittingly or not, however, they carried with them both the philosophical presuppositions of Indian religious thought, which were the terms in which and through which the Buddha found his truth, and the political, social, and cultural patterns of Indian society. Theravada Buddhism, as it missionized in Sri Lanka, Burma, and Thailand, brought with it sociopolitical principles that derived from Hindu traditions and which, in part, the Buddha sought to overcome and transcend. (See Smith, 1978.) In Mahayana Buddhism as well, careful scholars can speak of the "Indianization of China." (See Hu, 1937.)

Later, when this stream of Buddhism became wedded to motifs from Confucian and Taoist sources, its movement into Korea and Japan carried powerful elements from these traditions with it. And it is well known that both Christianity and Islam carried Greco-Roman patterns of thought, medicine, and political theory—as well as Hebraic understandings of ethical monotheism—with them as they expanded in the medieval periods. Islam has also always borne a certain Arabic cultural stamp wherever it goes, and communism today bears everywhere the marks of Germanic philosophy, Enlightenment social theory, Western technological hopes from the days of the industrial revolution, and often something of Soviet nationalism. Along with the Gospel, modern Christian missions transmit Western definitions of human rights and scientific methods in the fields of education, technology, management, and agriculture.

Missions and Cultural Imperialism. Two factors differentiate missionary expansion from cultural imperialism. First, the truly religious missionary recognizes a distinction between the message and the accoutrements, the universalistic kernel and the incidental husk. However difficult it is to distinguish the two, the primary concern is with the former. Transformation of the latter is allowed in terms of and for the sake of the former. The imperialist understands the message only in terms of its sociocultural trappings in highly particularist ways. Such imperialism obtains when, for example, Buddhism in Burma becomes identical with the prerogatives of the Burman as opposed to those of the Chin, Kachin, or other Burmese peoples; when Christianity becomes German

in the Nazi period or Afrikaner in South Africa; when Islam in, for instance, Iran, is understood to be coterminous with the fate of the country itself; or when communism is thought to be identical with "socialism in one country" and allied with a personality cult. These domestic forms of cultural imperialism have had their vicious international corollaries wherever particular social traditions, political expansions, or opportunities for economic exploitation are confused with a universalistic religious message and spread by coercive means among colonialized peoples abroad in the name of religion.

Second, missionary activity is rooted in the fundamental assumptions that, once people are exposed to "the truth" that has been proclaimed, they will choose this truth and that they ought to be free to encounter and choose even "foreign" truth. Missions presuppose that a truly universalistic vision is convincing to the mind and compelling to the will. Missions thus require, or provoke, a situation in which some degree of freedom of thought, speech, and religious organization is allowed, where the will and the mind can be exercised in accordance with conscience and conviction. However much missionary activity has been carried out hand in hand with military power, economic opportunism, "brainwashing," and forced conversion, there has been and remains in principle a sharp tension between missionary efforts and imperialistic imposition of religion by force, or "mind-control," a fact increasingly documented by missiologists examining the relative validity of the charge that missions are but the ideological instrument of colonial practice. Those incapable of imagining the transformation of values, attitudes, and habits in conversion to a new truth, however, always attribute the change to nefarious forces.

It is certainly true that every missionizing religion has had periods during which something like the classic Islamic pattern could be documented: H. A. R. Gibb writes of Islam that "while the faith itself was not spread by the sword, it was under the wing of Muslim dominance that its missionaries found most favorable conditions for their activities of conversion. This view of Islam . . . was universally held by its adherents; the theologians found justification for it in the Koran, the jurists made it the basis of their expositions of Muslim law, and the mass of the people accepted it as a self-evident fact" (Gibb, 1932, p. 56; cf. Bulliet, 1979).

Reactions of Missionized People. Every missionary religion must be received as well as proclaimed. Where it is not received, missionary activity dies out, and doubt about the universality of the originating vision sets in. Where it is received under coercion, and not in the heart, mind, or customs of the people, the indigenous religion goes underground, eventually resurfacing as a revitalized indigenous religion and rallying point to overthrow those who hold power or as a heterodox or heretical religion in contention with the one brought by missions. Where the missionary religion is received in the heart and mind, newly converted people soon send out their own missionaries. But it is almost never received as given. It is filtered through the philosophical, sociopolitical, and historical perspectives of the recipients. Thereby, it is inevitably modified by its reception and, over time, at least partially purged of those missionary-borne incidental elements that can be seen as "merely" cultural or sociopolitical.

One of the most fascinating studies of the reception of a religion is the study by Kenneth Ch`en (1973) of the way in which Buddhism was modified, acculturated, and indigenized in China. A message, such as that exported from Indian Buddhism, that called for the breaking of family ties and demanded that kings give honor to monks simply did not make sense in a culture where filial piety and homage to the emperor were absolutely central to both belief and social order. Ch`en demonstrates that, as one speaks of the "indianization of China" with the spread of Buddhism, one must also speak of the "sinicization of Buddhism." In China key Buddhist texts were given fresh interpretation; apologetic literature, new poems, and new laws and regulations were promulgated that modified and, indeed, transformed aspects of the Buddhist message so that it could graft onto, and in some ways revitalize, dimensions of the indigenous folk religions and of the Confucianism and Taoism of that land. Comparable stories can be told of every missionizing religion: the Christianity of Eastern Orthodoxy in Greece is not the same as that of the Kimbanguists of central Africa; the Islam of Tunisia differs from that of Mindanao in significant ways; Communism in Moscow is distinct from that of "Eurocommunism" or that of Marxist-inspired movements in Central America. Today, the degree to which this "contextualization" or indigenization is valid is the subject of heated debate within many of the great world religions.

In this connection, it must be noted that some religions engage in missionary activity precisely as a result of being invited, sought, or adopted with great eagerness. Robin Horton (1975) has shown, for example, that in Africa where traditional systems have been displaced by exploitative cultural contact, war, crop failure, or the failure of a social system to survive its own internal strains, missionary groups bearing universalistic messages are readily embraced, for they offer fresh, symbolic, and cognitive models by which life and its perplexities may be interpreted. Often, the appropriation of a new religion is accompanied by a rational quest for new technological, educational, and sociopolitical frameworks for organizing the common life. Missionaries often agree that such a quest is at the core of their metaphysical-moral vision. Certainly a comparable phenomenon has occurred in quite different locales, as Garrett (1982) has shown in regard to the Pacific Islands, and Downs (1983) has demonstrated concerning the christianization of tribal peoples of Assam in the last century. More ancient examples are the historic reception in the sixth and seventh centuries of

Chinese Buddhism into Japan at the hands of the imperial court (along with Confucian ideals of a well-organized society); the reception in the ninth to eleventh centuries of Eastern Orthodox Christianity into Russia, bringing with it Byzantine art, literature, and political theory; and the reception in the twelfth to fifteenth centuries of Islam (as mediated through India) in the Malay archipelago, accompanied by aspects of mysticism and caste-related political order.

In almost no instance, however, is a new religion received without some resistance. This resistance is sometimes easily overcome. When the indigenous faith is a highly literate and complex religion, however, the resistance is usually prolonged and powerful. The fact that Buddhism originated in India and at one time had nearly swept the subcontinent, but now can scarcely be found there, is one of the dramatic examples of this resistance. Hinduism reasserted itself by a ten-century-long process involving the adoption of some aspects of Buddhism (especially the revitalization of devotional practice in *bhakti*), by the bloody slaughter of Buddhist monks, by extensive philosophical argumentation, and by out-organizing and out-teaching Buddhism among the people. Similarly, Confucianism reasserted itself in China during the "neo-Confucian" period of renewal in the ninth century by a similar process—one that relegated the Buddhists to a somewhat inferior status. Islam encountered intellectual and military resistance when it threatened expansion into Europe from the time of Charlemagne through the Crusades, and the Christianity that expanded into western Asia is now weak and scattered because of Islamic resistance. And most Western Jews and Christians today resist the Hindu, Islamic, and Buddhist missions, as well as the host of hybrid or syncretistic cults rooted in these, or in some heterodox Christian faith, that are to be found in most of the major cities of the West today. (See Needleman and Baker, 1978; Barker, 1981.)

Types of Missionaries. In surveying mission and missionary activity, however, one must not only note the primacy of the metaphysical-moral vision—its relationship to social and cultural patterns, its patterns of reception, and resistances to it—one must also consider certain similarities of institutional form that are characteristic of missionary activity. What groups or classes of people undertake missionary activity, and how do they organize to do so?

Missionaries, merchants, and soldiers. The earliest, unofficial missionaries are, more often than not, traders. One does not have to accept the Marxist interpretation of the relationship between commercial exploitation and religion to observe that, indeed, the spreading of a new religious insight repeatedly follows commercial traffic lanes and that this insight is frequently borne by merchants. Further, it must be noted that both commercial and missionary activities can only be conducted in conditions of relative peace and political stability. Such conditions often obtain, and when they do not, soldiers are frequently brought in to establish them, accompanied by new waves of missionaries. Since traders and soldiers vary widely in their behavior, from the simply marauding to the relatively benevolent, missionary activity has often been conducted within a network of shifting alliances, both economic and military, on the far end of trade routes. It is not possible to make any single generalization about these relationships, however, for missionaries have resisted exploitative trade as often as they have endorsed it and have fought imperial military "pacification" as often as they have embraced it. (See, e.g., Christensen and Hutchison, 1982; cf. Reed, 1983.)

The cross-cultural frequency of missionary activity by merchants, however, invites speculation as to why this general class has played so significant a role in missionizing. Perhaps it is because merchants are people who seek increased opportunity by taking the risk of leaving the settled and accepted patterns of life at home. The very act of engaging in trade on a cross-cultural basis, however crass the individual motivation might be, requires a somewhat more cosmopolitan perspective on the world than is frequently present in those societies where religion and morality run in channels circumscribed by fixed economic roles and duties for people of each specific ethnic, gender, age and class status. In addition, those societies that send merchants farthest and equip caravans or ships the most extensively for trade are usually the more highly developed economically, politically, militarily, and socially. It would not be strange for them to hold the view that their "superiority" in this respect is due in substantial part at least to the "superior" religious, spiritual, and ethical foundations of their faith.

Professional missionaries. New religions are seldom, if ever, however, fully developed in a new location by the sometimes quite unholy alliance of missionaries, merchants, and soldiers, or by general processes of cultural diffusion that accompany them. The introduction of a religion through commercial channels (the character and quality of which influence reception and/or resistance) has everywhere been succeeded by the arrival of professional missionaries. For most religions throughout most of history, the professional missionary has been monastic, that is, organized into ascetic, trained, and disciplined religious orders intentionally "homeless" for the sake of the metaphysical-moral vision held to be universally true.

Missionary monks and nuns attempt to spread their religious convictions by public proclamation and commentary on sacred texts at both popular and learned levels; by teaching hymns, chants, and prayers; by establishing new centers of worship where the truth they know can be celebrated; and by service—that is, by medical, educational, pastoral, and social relief and social advocacy. Needless to say, all missionary religions have relied on "wondrous," magical, or technological demonstrations of "spiritual" power from time to time. The stories well known in the West about saintly missionary monks

such as Patrick, Columba, Boniface, Ramón Lull, and Francis Xavier are paralleled in the lore of Buddhism, in the formation of the *mathas* as a Hindu reaction to the challenge posed by Buddhism, and in the roles played by the "schools" of jurists and even more by the Sufi orders of Islam. (In Eastern Europe, accounts of the "dedicated heroes, martyrs, and organizers" of communist proletarian movements are written for children and young people.)

To carry out their tasks, missionaries have four requirements. First, they must have a dedication, a commitment, a piety, if you will, linked to learning. Missionaries must be able

> The economic ties of a missionary enterprise with its country of origin or with the elites of the host country are the source of enormous distrust of missionary activity.

to articulate the faith and to interpret it in intellectual and cultural terms that are foreign to them. They must be able to understand and put into perspective whatever they encounter in the course of their work. It is no accident that several sciences, including modern comparative linguistics and anthropology, to a large extent have their roots in missionary activity. Everywhere, professional missionaries are given to literary activity; they have published apologetics, propaganda, tracts, commentaries, and they are responsible for the composition and dissemination of poetry, song, and history. (See Kopf, 1969.)

Second, missionary professionals require a reliable institutional foundation, a polity, to sustain them. Missionary orders and societies are surely among the world's first transnational, nonprofit corporations. These polities, however, are ever subject to incorporation into the existing polities of the host countries. Thus, the Buddhist *samgha*, spread under the protectorate of kings, is ever tempted to become simply an instrument of state. Converted Christian communities in India are always in peril of becoming more a subcaste than a church; and the *tariqahs* of Islam tend to become simply trade guilds or sanctified tribal brotherhoods. (See Trimingham, 1971.)

Economic support may derive from state funds, charitable bequests, the establishment of plantations, handicraft manufacturing centers, agricultural communes, and religious taxes. The economic ties of a missionary enterprise with its country of origin or with the elites of the host country are the source of enormous distrust of missionary activity. (See Reed, 1983.)

And fourth, missionaries must have a clear policy, one that coordinates strategies and tactics and prevents divergent teachings from confusing potential converts. These policies must cover such matters as how much of the indigenous culture to allow and what to disallow, how to deal with marriage practices, "pagan" festivals, various "fraternities" that are marginally stamped with traditional religious practices, and the like.

Modern Practices. Modern missionary efforts have been pursued not so much by monastic orders (although these orders continue to missionize around the world) as by nonmonastic missionary "societies." This situation is prompted primarily by the rather unique developments of "free-church" Protestant polities, economic support systems, and policies. While the established churches in Europe had been sending out monastic missionaries for centuries, and the Moravians anticipated later developments, the formation of the London Missionary Society in 1795 inaugurated a new form of paraecclesial organization that continues to this day and is now being emulated by non-Christian missionaries. Missionary societies, of which there are now hundreds, raise funds by free-will contributions and form nonmonastic "voluntary associations" staffed by a combination of nonparochial clergy, lay professionals, and volunteers, not only to save souls from "paganism" but to sweep away superstition and oppression, to offer agricultural, technical, medical, and educational assistance, and to engender a desire for democratic institutions, human dignity, self-sufficiency, and social liberation. Some modern theorists, indeed, suggest that these efforts at social service and social change are the very core of missionizing. (See Dunn, 1980; Yuzon, 1983.)

A notable example of the side effects of this recent pattern can be illustrated by reference to the Young Men's Christian Association. Formed in England in 1844 as a part of a "home mission" voluntary association for youth flocking to the cities to get jobs in factories, and attempting to provide a wholesome place where young men could find physical, mental, social, and spiritual benefit on a biblical foundation, the movement spread to North America and to most of the countries around the world where missions were active. It was often the agent of evangelization and the womb of efforts at social change by young men who came under its influence. Other religions responded by forming counterorganizations on a comparable basis. Today, one can find not only the YMCA but the Young Men's Buddhist Association, the Young Men's Hebrew Association, and the Young Men's Muslim Association, as well as youth hostels for Hindus and for communists, scattered throughout much of Asia; some also are to be found in Africa and South America.

Today, the great Asian religions are not at their peak in terms of missionary activity, although Buddhist and Islamic groups in Southeast Asia have formed a few missionary centers to repropagate the faith in the People's Republic of China, now that the doors of trade and travel are partially open again. Christianity, Islam, and communism are very active, with the latter two having the closest ties to the spread of political control and Christianity again moving along channels established by international commerce. All continue to make major gains in areas where none of the great missionizing religions has established a sustained foothold, with more modest, but significant, gains among "overseas" peoples of Hindu or Confucian background—the Indians of Malaysia and the Chinese of Indonesia, for example.

Increasingly, the great missionizing religions are confronting not only adherents of primal or folk religions but one another. Thus far, missionary efforts to convert adherents of the other great missionary religions have been only marginally successful. This is in part because severe restrictions on missionary activities by other faiths are frequent in Islamic and communist lands.

Although some theorists have argued that these religions are moving toward a great synthesis of world faiths (an essentially Hindu argument), and while others have attempted to find the common moral and symbolic patterns present in all human religions as the clue to their hidden unity (a humanist argument), the way in which these religions will deal with one another in the future is not at all certain. (See Oxtoby, 1983.) None of the great missionary faiths can be satisfied with relativism, the view that what is ultimately true for some is not true for others. The main possibilities are, thus, direct confrontation (with each backed by the political, military, and economic power of the regions where they are predominant), dialogic exchange of perspective in a common quest for transcultural religious truth, and/or openness to redoubled efforts to mutual conversion by allowing free and open debate among the peoples of the world.

BIBLIOGRAPHY

Works on missions and missionary activity within particular traditions are plentiful, but, to my knowledge, no substantive and systematic overview of comparative missiology exists. The works on the following list have been selected to illustrate the range and kinds of materials that would be pertinent to further comparative study in this area.

Barker, Eileen, ed. *Of Gods and Men: New Religious Movements in the West*. Macon, Ga., 1981.

Bulliet, Richard. *Conversion to Islam in the Medieval Period*. Cambridge, Mass., 1979.

Ch`en, Kenneth. *The Chinese Transformation of Buddhism*. Princeton, 1973.

Christensen, Torben, and William R. Hutchison. *Missionary Ideologies in the Imperialist Era*. Århus, Denmark, 1982.

Downs, Frederick S. *Christianity in North East India*. Delhi, 1983.

Dunn, Edmond J. *Missionary Theology: Foundations in Development*. Lanham, Md., 1980.

Forman, Charles W. "A History of Foreign Mission Theory in America." In *American Missions in Bicentennial Perspective*, edited by R. Pierce Beaver, pp. 69-140. Pasadena, Calif., 1977.

Garrett, John. *To Live among the Stars*. Suva, Fiji Islands, 1982.

Gibb, H. A. R. *Whither Islam* (1932). Reprint, London, 1973.

Horton, Robin. "On the Rationality of Conversion." *Africa* 45 (1975): 219-235, 373-399.

Hu Shih. *Independence, Convergence and Borrowing.* Cambridge, Mass., 1937.

Kane, J. Herbert. *A Concise History of the Christian World Mission.* Grand Rapids, Mich., 1978.

Kopf, David. *British Orientalism and the Bengal Renaissance.* Berkeley, 1969.

Latourette, K. S. "Missions." In *Encyclopaedia of the Social Sciences*, edited by E. R. A. Seligman. New York, 1933.

Luzbetak, Louis J. *The Church and Cultures.* Techny, Ill., 1970.

Macy, Joanna. *Dharma and Development.* West Hartford, Conn., 1983.

Needleman, Jacob, and George Baker, eds. *Understanding the New Religions.* New York, 1978.

Oxtoby, Willard G. *The Meaning of Other Faiths.* Philadelphia, 1983.

Rambo, Lewis R. "Current Research on Religious Conversion." *Religious Studies Review* 8 (April 1982): 146-159.

Reed, James. *The Missionary Mind and American East Asia Policy.* Cambridge, Mass., 1983.

Sanneh, Lamin O. *West African Christianity.* Maryknoll, N. Y., 1983.

Sharpe, Eric J. *Comparative Religion: A History.* London, 1975.

Smith, Bardwell, ed. *Religion and Legitimation of Power in Thailand, Laos, and Burma.* Chambersburg, Pa., 1978.

Song, Choan-Seng. *The Compassionate God.* Maryknoll, N. Y., 1982.

Srinivas, M. N. *Religion and Society among the Coorgs of South India* (1952). Reprint, New Delhi, 1978.

Stackhouse, Max L. *Creeds, Societies and Human Rights: A Study in Three Cultures.* Grand Rapids, Mich., 1984.

Trimingham, J. Spencer. *The Sufi Orders in Islam.* London, 1971.

Yuzon, Lourdino A., ed. *Mission in the Context of Endemic Poverty.* Singapore, 1983.

MAX L. STACKHOUSE

Buddhist Missions

According to an ancient tradition, the Buddha himself sent out the first group of disciples to spread the new faith: "Go, monks, preach the noble Doctrine, . . . let not two of you go into the same direction!" This canonical saying illustrates both the missionary ideal that has inspired Buddhism from the earliest times and the way in which it was to be carried out: not by any large-scale planned missionary movement, but rather by the individual efforts of itinerant monks and preachers. And this, in fact, is our general impression of the way in which Buddhism grew from a minor monastic movement in northern India in the fifth century BCE into a world religion covering, at its heyday, a territory that reached from Sri Lanka to Mongolia, and from Iran to Japan. Apart from the missionary ideal and the prescribed inherent mobility of the clergy, its dissemination outside its homeland was no doubt facilitated by three other features of Buddhism. In the first place, the members of the order, "who had gone into the homeless state" and thereby rejected all worldly distinctions, stood outside the caste system. Unlike brahman priests, they were free to associate with people of every description, including foreigners, without fear of ritual pollution. Second, Buddhism, especially Mahayana Buddhism, had a liberal attitude toward all religions. Thus it easily accepted non-Buddhist creeds as preliminary and partial revelations of truth, a tendency toward adaptation and syncretism that also appears in its readiness to incorporate non-Buddhist deities into its pantheon. Third, the scriptural tradition of Buddhism—unlike that of Brahmanism—is not associated with any sacred or canonical language, so that its holy texts could freely be translated into any language. In fact, especially in China, the most prominent foreign missionaries were all active as translators, usually with the help of bilingual collaborators.

The Pattern of Diffusion. The general picture of the spread of Buddhism is one of gradual dissemination at grassroots level, inspired by the Buddha's exhortation and carried out by wandering monks who preached "for the benefit of all beings" (an ideal that became even more explicit in Mahayana Buddhism) and who established monastic centers in the new territories they entered. As the clergy was wholly dependent on the contributions of lay believers, these monastic settlements *(viharas)* tended to be established near the larger cities and to branch out along the major highways that connected them. The spread of Buddhism was also closely related to the development of long-distance trade: it was carried all over Asia by monks who attached themselves to trade caravans and merchant vessels. To some extent, it was also carried by the pilgrims and students who came to India to visit the holy places, to collect texts, and to study under Indian masters.

History of Diffusion from India. This pattern of diffusion accounts for the slow pace of the process, for it took Buddhism some twenty centuries to spread over Asia, from its first propagation in the Ganges basin about 400 BCE to its last major conquest, the conversion of the Mongols in the sixteenth century. By the third century BCE it had spread over India and into Sri Lanka. Under the Kushan rulers in the northwest, in the first and second centuries CE, it reached Parthia (modern-day Iran) and the region of Bukhara and Samarkand. About the same time it was propagated via the oasis kingdoms of Central Asia to China, where it is attested for the first time in 65 CE. The earliest known missionaries and translators (Parthians, Kushans, Sogdians, and Indians) arrived at the Chinese capital Lo-yang in the middle of the second century CE by the transcontinental Silk Road, the main artery of trade between the Chinese Han empire and the Roman orient. Just as Buddhism was carried to China by caravan trade, the development of Indian seaborne trade to the coastal regions of Southeast Asia from the second century CE onward provided the channel through which it started to expand in that direction. From the second to the fifth centuries, commercial contacts and the diffusion of Indian culture led to the rise of several more or less Indianized kingdoms in which Buddhism flourished: the Thaton region in southern Burma; the kingdom of Funan with its center on the lower Mekong; that of Champa in southeastern Vietnam; the Malay Peninsula; and the Indonesian archipelago, where Palembang on Sumatra was already an important Buddhist center by 400 CE.

Secondary Centers of Diffusion: China and Tibet. By 600 CE, when China after centuries of disunity had been reunited under the Sui and T'ang dynasties (589–906 CE), Buddhism in many forms had become a major religion in all parts of China and an important element in the cultural life of all social strata. China had thereby become a secondary center of diffusion, from which Buddhism was spread to Korea, Japan, and northern Vietnam. In all these regions, various types of Chinese Buddhism were introduced as part of a general process of the sinicization of these regions. In the fifth century Buddhism reached Korea and became popular among the ruling elite. The transplantation of Chinese Buddhist sects and schools went on throughout Korean history. From Korea, Buddhism reached Japan about the middle of the sixth century, but the real influx of Chinese-type Buddhism into the emerging island empire began in the early seventh century, when the Japanese court embarked on its remarkable program of massive borrowing of Chinese culture and institutions. Between 625 and 847, all early schools of T'ang Buddhism were transplanted to Japan through the deliberate efforts of prominent scholarly monks, most of whom were sent to China as members of "cultural embassies" from the Japanese court. Much later, in the twelfth century, other Chinese schools—notably the devotional cult of the Buddha Amitabha (Ching-t'u, Pure Land Buddhism, known in Japan as Jodo) and the Ch'an (Jpn., Zen) or Meditation sect—were introduced. To the present day, Japan has remained the stronghold of Buddhism in countless varieties.

The last wave of expansion is associated with the propagation of Buddhism in Tibet and Mongolia, where it eventually developed into the mainly Tantric creed known as Lamaism. Buddhism penetrated the Tibetan kingdom around 650 CE, but became dominant only in the eleventh century. It was from Tibet that Lamaism finally spread to the nomads of the Mongolian steppe in the sixteenth century.

Pilgrimage and Study in India and China. The diffusion of Buddhism from India was for centuries accompanied by a reverse process: the steady flow of pilgrims and scholars to India. Apart from the many inscriptions that they left, the process is documented mainly by the invaluable travelogues of Chinese pilgrims: Fa-hsien, who left China in 399 and spent six years in India; Hui-sheng, who visited northwestern India in 518–522; I-ching, who spent twenty-four years (671–695) in India and Southeast Asia, and above all, the great scholar Hsüan-tsang (c. 596–664), who left a detailed

description of his stupendous journey (621–645) in his *Hsi-yü chi* (Record of the Western Regions). India was the holy land of Buddhism, and the desire to make a pilgrimage certainly played a role in the decision of these travelers to undertake their journeys. It should be stressed, however, that the travelers were at least as much motivated by scholastic as by religious considerations: to collect texts, and to study the Doctrine at Indian centers of learning such as Pataliputra (modern Patna) and Nalanda. They knew what they were looking for, and they came back loaded with canonical and scholastic texts that they later translated.

But as we have seen, in T'ang times China itself became a center of diffusion and there the pattern was repeated by countless Korean and Japanese monks who came to China to collect Chinese Buddhist texts and to study Buddhism in its vastly modified Chinese forms. After their return from China, some of these monks became prominent "Masters of the Doctrine" whose names are linked with the most influential trends in Japanese Buddhism. Saicho introduced the Tendai (Chin., T'ien-t'ai) sect in 804; two years later, Kukai brought Esoteric (Tantric) Buddhism to Japan; and Ennin, apart from his fame as a transmitter of the Doctrine, left an extensive diary of his nine-year stay on the continent (838–849), a diary that presents a fascinating panorama of Buddhist life in T'ang China.

For centuries, India continued to draw pilgrims and students from all over the Buddhist world; the flow came to an end only with the decline of Buddhism in India itself and, finally, with the destruction of the holy places by the Muslim invasions of around 1200. However, Chinese inscriptions found at Bodh Gaya do show that as late as the eleventh century some Chinese pilgrims still followed the examples of Fa-hsien and Hsüan-tsang. For the next seven centuries, Buddhism was nonexistent in its country of origin, to the extent that its holy places became completely forgotten and had to be rediscovered by modern archaeologists. However, as the result of the (still rather modest) revival of Buddhism in India in the twentieth century, pilgrimage has been resumed and is growing steadily.

[*For a fuller account of the dissemination and propagation of Buddhism outside of India, see* Buddhism.]

BIBLIOGRAPHY

Apart from my own book *Buddhism: Its Origin and Spread in Words, Maps and Pictures* (New York, 1962), which presents merely an outline of the diffusion of Buddhism in Asia, there is no monographic study on the subject. Contributions, of very unequal quality, on the introduction and development of Buddhism in various countries can be found in *The Path of the Buddha: Buddhism Interpreted by Buddhists*, edited by Kenneth W. Morgan (New York, 1956). The spread of Buddhism in India and the northwest is extensively treated in Étienne Lamotte's *Histoire du bouddhisme indien: Des origines à l'ère Saka* (Louvain, 1958). For the rest, the reader must be referred to the relevant parts of monographs dealing with

Buddhism in the separate regions. For the diffusion of Indian culture, with Buddhism as one of its essential elements, the best survey is G. Coedès's *Les états hindouïsés d'Indochine et d'Indonésie*, 2d ed. (Paris, 1964); Central Asia is covered in Simone Gaulier, Robert Jera-Bezard, and Monique Maillard's *Buddhism in Afghanistan and Central Asia*, 2 vols. (Leiden, 1976). The introduction and earliest development of Buddhism in China (first to fifth century CE) is extensively treated in my book *The Buddhist Conquest of China*, 2 vols. (1959; reprint, Leiden, 1972); for later periods the best survey is Kenneth Ch`en's *Buddhism in China: A Historical Survey* (1964; reprint, Princeton, 1972). For early Korean Buddhism the reader must still be referred to the somewhat outdated work of Charles A. Clark, *Religions of Old Korea* (New York, 1932). For Japan, the most recent survey is Shinsho Hanayama's *A History of Japanese Buddhism*, translated and edited by Kosho Yamamoto (Tokyo, 1960). For the introduction of Buddhism into Tibet and the formation of Lamaism, see the relevant parts of David L. Snellgrove and Hugh E. Richardson's *A Cultural History of Tibet* (1968; reprint, Boulder, 1980). Apart from one popular work, René Groussert's *Sur les traces du Bouddha* (Paris, 1929), the accounts of the Chinese pilgrims are still accessible only through largely outdated translations. For Fa-hsien, see *The Travels of Fa-hsien 399-414 A. D., or Records of the Buddhist Kingdoms*, rev. ed., translated by Herbert A. Giles (London, 1959); for Hsüan-tsang, *Si-yu-ki, Buddhist Records of the Western World*, 2 vols., translated by Samuel Beal (1884; reprint, Oxford, 1906); additions and corrections in *On Yuan Chwang's Travels in India*, 2 vols., translated by Thomas Watters and edited by T. W. Rhys Davids and S. W. Bushnell (London, 1904-1905); for I-ching, *A Record of the Buddhist Religion as Practiced in India and the Malay Archipelago*, A. D. 671-695, translated by Junjiro Takakusu (1896; reprint, Delhi, 1966). Of Ennin's travelogue there is an excellent translation by Edwin O. Reischauer, *Ennin's Diary: The Record of a Pilgrimage to China in Search of the Law* (New York, 1955), to be used with its companion volume, *Ennin's Travels in T`ang China* (both, New York, 1955).

ERIK ZÜRCHER

Christian Missions

The Early Followers of Jesus. The earliest followers of Jesus seem to have understood the universal dimension of their faith as the fulfillment of Old Testament prophecy (Isaiah, Zechariah), according to which all nations would come up to Jerusalem to receive the law of the Lord in the form of the new covenant in Jesus. Two new factors reversed this original Christian understanding. The first was persecution, which led to many Christians being dispersed from Jerusalem. The second was the adventurous spirit of certain Greek-speaking Jews who crossed over a well-marked boundary and in Antioch began to proclaim the gospel to non-Jews, apparently with considerable success. This new Christian perspective was rationalized by Saul of Tarsus, also called Paul, who, believing that he had received a commission as apostle of the gentiles, worked out a master plan for establishing Christian groups in all the main centers of the Greco-Roman world. He looked to Rome, and beyond

that even to Spain, the western limit of the Mediterranean world.

So great a project was far beyond the strength of one man, but the impulse given by Paul never died. The Christian proclamation was carried out almost entirely anonymously; indeed, the names of the founders of the great churches of the Roman empire remain for the most part unrecorded. Yet this early work had surprisingly rapid success. Within a century of the death of the founder, churches came into existence in many parts of Asia Minor, in Greece, in Italy, in Egypt, almost certainly in France and Spain, and perhaps even as far away as India. To this day, the Thomas Christians in Kerala claim that their church was founded by the apostle Thomas in person.

Whence this rapid success? By around AD 100, many more Jews lived outside Palestine than within its borders. The strict monotheism of the Jewish faith, and the high moral standards inculcated by their law, had attracted many to at least a partial acceptance of the Jewish faith, and this served for some as a preparation for the Christian gospel. In that hard and often cruel world, a fellowship of people who really loved one another and cared for one another's needs clearly had attractive power. The fervent expectations of the Christians, both for the world and for the individual, must have come as a message of hope to those who had none. Jesus became known as the Savior of the world.

Persecution and Stabilization. The persecutions to which the early Christians were periodically exposed seem to have done little to hinder the advance of their faith. Not all Christians were being persecuted all the time, and the number of martyrs was greatly exaggerated in tradition. To be sure, there were signs of hysteria among the faithful, and some failed to stand fast. But persecution often undermined

> **Not all Christians were being persecuted all the time, and the number of martyrs was greatly exaggerated in tradition.**

its own purpose because the courage, dignity, and charity shown by martyrs often won the allegiance and admiration of some who might otherwise have remained indifferent.

The great change in the Christian situation came in 313 when Constantine made Christianity the religion of the empire at a time when its followers cannot have numbered more than about 10 percent of the population. From that time on, the resemblance between Christianity and the other missionary religions has been startlingly close. From the time of Asoka in India (third century BC) to Sri Lanka and Thailand in 1983, Buddhism has always maintained close relations with the ruling powers. In all Muslim countries, and in all those which have come under Marxist domination, the identification of the state with religion or ideology has been undisguised and taken for granted. But since Christians claim to be followers of the Prince of Peace, close connections between interests of state and interests of religion have proved a burden and an embarrassment rather than a help. Justinian, who reigned from 527 to 565, seems to have been the first Roman emperor to accept coercion as a legitimate instrument of conversion to Christianity.

By the year 600, the Mediterranean world was almost entirely Christian, with outliers among the Goths, in the approaches to Inner Asia, in Ethiopia, and in what is now Sudan. At the end of the century, Gregory the Great (540-604) saw the importance of the world which lay north of the Alps and which was yet to be converted. Hence the pope's mission to the Angles in Kent. This was the first mission of the church to be officially organized; it paved the way for the central control over the missions which Rome exercised for many centuries.

A Long Period of Uncertainty. In the year 600, it might have seemed that the gospel was destined to carry all before it. Then suddenly everything went into reverse. In 610 an obscure prophet named Muhammad began to preach a new faith to the tribes of Arabia. By the time of his death he had given to these tribes unity, a simple demanding creed, and a sense of destiny. Only a century later, the Muslim armies were at Tours, in the very heart of France, and were repelled only by the vigor and military skill of Charles Martel (685-741). By that time the Christian churches had almost disappeared in Palestine, Syria, and Egypt, and were gravely threatened in Persia, North Africa, and large parts of Asia Minor. In 1453, the Turks succeeded in capturing Constantinople and destroying the Eastern Empire, which for a thousand years had been the bulwark of the Christian world. Many causes have been adduced for the disappearance of so many churches. Military weakness was no doubt one, but there were others as well: dissensions among Christians, the rise of national feeling in Egypt and elsewhere, and the superficiality of conversion in such areas as North Africa, where the church had failed to express Christian truth in the languages of the local people.

In this period, the wisdom of Gregory was vindicated. During the centuries between 632 and 1232, the Christian faith spread west, north, and east until the conversion of Europe was complete. There was a dark side to this advance. When at the end of the eighth century Charlemagne succeeded in conquering the long-refractory Saxons, he agreed to spare their lives on the condition that they accept baptism. It was only one of many regions in which cross and sword went together. In Scandinavia, conversion proceeded more easily. In many areas the ruler was the first to accept the faith, and this brought about a quiet revolution. Iceland seems to have been unique in accepting the faith (around AD

1000) by genuinely democratic methods. With the conversion of Jagiello (1383), king of the Lithuanians, conversion seems to have reached its natural term.

Monks and nuns played a creative part in the building of churches. In the remote places where they settled they introduced better methods of agriculture and new crops. They laid the foundations of literature in the languages of Europe. They gave to isolated peoples a sense of belonging to one great unity: the catholic church. Out of these beginnings grew the splendid cultures of medieval Europe.

Missionary activity sometimes took on the form of conflict between the old and the new. Such actions as Boniface's felling the oak of Thor at Geismar must not be misinterpreted as mere missionary vandalism. The people of that time believed that the powerful spirit who inhabited the oak would be able to take condign vengeance on any intruder, thus they expected Boniface to fall dead upon the spot. When he survived, they concluded that the god whom he preached was more powerful than their own.

The Eastern church, with its base in Constantinople, beginning with the conversion in 988 of Vladimir, grand duke of Kiev, created the great Slavonic cultures, the Christian origins of which are not disputed even by Marxist opponents of religion. These cultures survived the fall of Constantinople. During the fifteenth century, the faith was received by more remote peoples to the east and north, a process that continued until by the end of the nineteenth century it had reached the shores of the Pacific Ocean.

With the great Franciscan and Dominican movements of the thirteenth century, the missionary enterprise of the Western church looked beyond the limits of Europe; the "friars travelling abroad in the service of Christ" reached strange lands far afield. One of their most remarkable achievements was the creation of an archbishopric in Peking; the first archbishop to fill the post, John of Monte Corvino, lived there from 1294 to 1328, greatly respected by all. But the church's hope of converting the Inner Asian peoples was frustrated by the Muslims' success in winning them to the Islamic faith. The lines of communication with Inner Asia were too tenuous, however, and in the fifteenth century the mission to China faded away. For the moment Christian expansion seemed to be at an end.

The Colonial Period. The last decade of the fifteenth century saw the discovery of America by Columbus in 1492 and the opening up of the sea route to India by Vasco da Gama in 1498. These two events changed the relationships between the nations of the world and in time gravely affected the presentation of the Christian gospel to the non-Christian world.

Roman Catholic monopoly. For two centuries the greater part of the missionary enterprise of the Western church was in the hands of the Portuguese, who, following the precedent of Muslim evangelism in Europe, expected their converts to accept Portuguese names, manners, and customs. There was, however, never total adoption of this principle. By the end of the sixteenth century, the Portuguese had on their hands three considerable blocks of Indian Christianity. In those possessions which they directly controlled, the process of Europeanization was almost complete. The Thomas Christians in Kerala and the Parava converts on the coast of Coromandel, on the other hand, declared and maintained their intention to be and to remain Indian Christians, a stance from which they have not departed in four centuries.

Moreover, in these years two notable attempts were made to adapt Christian thought to the ideas and ways of Asia. The Italian Matteo Ricci in 1601 succeeded in reaching Peking. He and his Jesuit colleagues, by mastering the Chinese language, winning the favor of the emperor and other leaders by their skill in astronomy and other sciences, and by adapting Christian faith to Chinese ideas, were able to maintain their mission, albeit with varying fortunes, through nearly three centuries. In southern India another Italian, Roberto de Nobili, learned Tamil and Sanskrit, and in order to win over the brahmans turned himself into a brahman, and not without success. Unfortunately, in 1744 Rome condemned all such efforts at adaptation, thereby sterilizing the Roman mission for the next two hundred years.

Internationalization of missions. The Lutherans sent their first missionaries to India in 1706. In 1794 the English Baptists, represented by their great pioneer William Carey and his colleagues, set up their work in Bengal. Thus the enormous resources of the English-speaking world, followed by those of the Dutch, the Swiss, and Scandinavians, were let loose throughout the world.

From this time on, relations between the Western governments and Christian missionary forces became unimaginably complicated. On the whole, the British maintained an attitude of lofty neutrality toward missionary activity, modified by the personal interest of a number of Christian government officials. But as government financial aid became available for educational and medical programs and for other forms of service, the Christian missionaries in the forefront of such enterprises profited greatly, perhaps excessively, from the provision of such aid. On the other hand, in British India the Indian rulers prohibited all Christian propaganda in their areas; religious freedom in India was proclaimed not by the British but by the government of independent India after 1947. In northern Nigeria, the British clearly favored Islam at the expense of Christianity.

In German, Dutch, and Belgian colonies, the association of governments with missions was undesirably close. In China, because of Napoleon III's decision that all missionaries, of whatever nationality, must be in possession of French passports, Roman Catholic missions were inevitably stigmatized as dangerous and foreign. By contrast, Hudson Taylor,

the director of the largest Protestant mission, instructed his missionaries that in case of trouble they were to turn not to consular authorities but to the local representatives of the Chinese governments.

A new factor emerged when the Japanese government showed itself as the great colonial power in the East. American missionaries in Korea sympathized deeply with Korean national aspirations and were opposed, though quietly and discreetly, to Japanese colonial enterprise.

Varieties of missionary enterprise. Over two centuries there has been significant diversification of missionary enterprise, including the activities of women missionaries, which indeed have been far more numerous and diverse than those of men. Almost every conceivable means of communication has been employed. Education, on the basis of the Christian conviction that all truth and all knowledge are from God, has been emphasized. Together with this priority has gone the widespread distribution of Christian literature in countless languages. Medical and social services were conceived and have been rendered by Christians, not as propaganda but as manifestations of the universal love of Christ, and they were perceived as such by many who were served. Public lectures to interested non-Christians have in many areas left deep impressions on the minds of the hearers, though debates between the adherents of different religious systems have tended more to exacerbation than to conviction. Preaching in the open air in villages and public places has made many hearers aware of the existence of alternative systems of belief. Quiet study groups, under the guidance of sympathetic Christians, have helped to clarify questions about Christian belief. Where no open propaganda has been permitted, the mere presence of loving Christians as neighbors has proved remarkably effective as witness to the faith.

The nature of conversion. No full and scientific study of the process of conversion in the non-Christian world has as yet been written. Undoubtedly in a number of cases the desire for social advancement and a better manner of life has played a powerful part. But is this a blameworthy motive in the case of those who have been subjected for centuries to ruthless oppression reinforced by religious sanction? For many in the twentieth century, as in the first, the gospel comes with promise of deliverance from the power of evil forces which are believed at all times to threaten and beleaguer the well-being of humans. For some, the gospel represents an immense simplification of religion. It has been stated that in India more people have been converted to Christianity by reading the first three chapters of Genesis than in any other way, for the majestic simplicity of these chapters appeals deeply to those perplexed by the complexity of Hindu mythology. Other converts, oppressed by the burden of sin, are drawn by the promise of forgiveness in Christ, so different from the inexorable law of *karman* in Hinduism. Others, conscious of moral infirmity, have come to believe that Christ can offer the inner rehabilitation which they feel they need. Yet others have been impressed by the intensity of mutual love manifest in the society of Christian believers. Varied as the process may be, in all there is a central unity. Christ himself stands at the center of everything. Only when the risen Christ is seen as friend, example, savior, and lord can genuine Christian conversion be expected to take place. Conversion to Christ is not necessarily identical with acceptance of the church; but in the vast majority of cases this follows, though this second acceptance may prove to be more difficult than the first.

Missionary motives. For more than four centuries the Western powers have exercised a dominating influence on the destinies of the rest of the world. Since so many people, especially in Muslim countries, have identified the West with the Christian West, there has been a natural tendency to regard Christian missionary enterprise as no more than an expression of Western aggression and imperialism. How far is there any adequate basis for this equation?

Many careful studies of missionary motivation have been made. Clearly no human motives are entirely pure. But only

> **The number of missionary martyrs is legion, their sacrifice equaled only by the devotion of their friends. . . .**

in a minority of cases can it be shown that national and imperialistic motives have played a strong part in missionary devotion. More frequently the glory of Christ has been the central and dominant motive. Some missionaries have gone so far in identifying with those they have come to serve as to renounce their own nation and to accept naturalization in the countries they have made their own. All have accepted some measure of acculturation in new surroundings. All who have served long years in alien lands have accepted with equanimity the destiny of becoming strangers in their own homes. The number of missionary martyrs is legion, their sacrifice equaled only by the devotion of their friends in many nations around the world who have also given their lives in the service of Christ.

The Twentieth Century. When in 1910 the first World Missionary Conference was held at Edinburgh, twelve hundred delegates from all over the world (including, however, no Roman Catholic or Orthodox Christians) could look back on a century of almost unimpeded progress. Converts had been won from every form of religion. In almost every country—a notable exception being Tibet—churches had come into existence, and the process by which the foreign mission was being transformed into the independent self-governing church was well advanced.

The years which followed were marked by a number of major setbacks to Christian missionization, such as the Russian revolution and the fading of religion in many Western communities. Yet the *World Christian Encyclopedia*, edited by David B. Barrett (1982) makes it plain that the achievements of the prior seventy years had been greater than those of the preceding century. For the first time in history the possibility of a universal religion appeared a reality. Roughly one-third of the inhabitants of the world had come to call themselves Christians. The progress of Christian missions continues in almost every area of the world. In India, Christians, already the third largest religious community after Hindus and Muslims, are also the most rapidly increasing in number.

Hostile critics of the Christian enterprise have maintained that the gospel has failed to touch deeply the mind and conscience of peoples outside the West, that the Christian churches in these areas are fragile and exotic blooms that came with the colonial powers, have been dependent exclusively on foreign aid and support, and that with the disappearance of the colonial powers these churches will also disappear. The twentieth century has shown that there is no ground at all for these expectations. After the communist takeover in China (1949), it was held even by a number of Christians that "missionary Christianity" in China had no roots and that there was little if any chance of its survival. When relaxation of government control occurred in 1980, however, it was revealed that several million Chinese had remained faithful to the Christian church. Chinese Christians have made known their determination to be fully independent of every kind of foreign control and to work out for themselves a form of Christian faith which will be genuinely Chinese. Elsewhere, if all foreign support has been compulsorily withdrawn, as in Burma, the churches have simply declared their maturity and have planned for a future of self-support and radical independence. Where this has taken place, accessions to the Christian faith have been more numerous than they were in the flourishing colonial days.

Changing world order. As a world phenomenon, the Christian church has not remained unaffected by the violent changes that have taken place in the troubled twentieth century. During the nineteenth century the dominant nations and the churches which were dependent on them assumed that they could plant Christian missions wherever they pleased, sometimes imposing their will by force on unwilling peoples. In the twentieth century all this has changed. A number of nations (e.g., Burma, Guinea, Saudi Arabia) prohibit all religious activity by foreigners which is directed at native citizens. A number of others make it very difficult for missionaries to obtain visas or residence permits. Yet others (e.g., Nepal) admit missionaries with few restrictions, but only on condition that they engage in what the government regards as nation-building activities (such as educational or medical services). Where all access is made impossible, churches in neighboring areas fall back upon the help that can be rendered by prayer alone.

The churches have gladly accepted the claim of these nations to independence and national dignity. No case is on record of a missionary leaving his or her assignment through unwillingness to accept the changed conditions of service. Christian witnesses have desired to stay on and to become in fact what they always wanted to be—servants of those to whom they came to minister. Even in China missionaries stayed on until it became clear that there was no longer any useful service that they could render. From Burma and other areas, foreigners withdrew because they felt that their work was done, since the local churches could carry on without their aid, and that their continued presence might em-bar-rass—and possibly endanger—their Christian friends. Some have been deported, at very short notice, for political reasons.

Anti-Western sentiments and resentments have been strong in many countries of the world since the end of the nineteenth century. Since 1947, decolonization has taken place with quite unexpected rapidity. Yet wounds remain. Some nations have desired to emancipate themselves from Western influences, but this has proved impossible. The more far-sighted leaders have seen it as their task to retain all that is valuable in the Western inheritance and at the same time to assert or to rediscover the integrity of their own national traditions. [See Ecumenical Movement.]

From foreign mission to independent church. The major change in the twentieth century was the process of transfer of power from foreign mission to independent local church, a process almost complete by the end of the century in almost every country in the world. The churches in some emerging nations think that the process has not gone fast enough or far enough; that it is on the way cannot be doubted by any observer of the process of change. Where churches are still wrestling with the problems and the prejudices of the past, they may be unwilling to accept the help of foreigners. Where they have reached maturity, as in India and Korea, and are becoming aware of the immense tasks still before them, they are in many cases glad to accept the help of foreigners, provided that these are prepared to keep their proper place and to accept only such responsibilities for service or leadership as the local church may lay upon them. Nor need it be supposed that all missionaries will be from the Western world; missionary interchange among developing nations is one of the most interesting features of the contemporary situation.

The independence of churches outside Europe and North America is increasingly shown in a number of remarkable ways. One that has attracted considerable attention is the rise of African independent churches, all of which have grown out of the mission-controlled churches of the past. Some of these are unorthodox. But the great majority desire to remain part of the main lines of the Christian tradition and have yet to create for themselves a place in which to feel at home, to think out the gospel for themselves, and to decide for themselves which of the ancient traditions of Africa can be retained within the Christian structure. Many Christians, even in the mainstream churches outside the West, are rethinking their own past in the light of divine providence, expecting to find signs of the working of God no less in their own pre-Christian history than in the special history of which the Old and New Testaments are the record. Some in India, for example, have suggested that the Upanisads are the real "old testament" of the Indian Christian and should take rank at least on the same level as the Hebrew scriptures. The nature of this quest is neatly summed up in the title of a book by Raimundo Panikkar, *The Unknown Christ of Hinduism* (New York, 1981). Genuinely indigenous theology is still in its beginnings, and it has to be confessed that the reapings in this field are still rather scanty; but what there is gives promise of a richer harvest in days to come.

One reason for the Christian quest to discover Christ beyond the historical bounds of Christendom is to be found in the remarkable resuscitation in the twentieth century of the ancient non-Christian faiths. Rediscovering the treasures of their own past, non-Christians feel able to approach Christians with renewed confidence and a sense of security. The Buddhist knows himself to be in contact with the great mystery of nothingness, the Hindu to be in contact with the unchangeable mystery of infinite being, the Muslim with the mystery of the infinite exaltation of God. There need be no Christian doubt about the greatness of these religions. Christian and non-Christian alike have much to teach one another in a manner different from that of the past.

The basis of this approach is a conventional rationale of mutual respect. Through centuries millions of men and women have lived by the teachings that they have received in these various religions, and, therefore, these may not be treated as though they did not matter, even though some of their teachings may be displeasing to the adherents of other religions. So one who engages in dialogue with those of faiths other than his own must come to it in the spirit Chaucer described in the words "gladly would he learn and gladly teach." Confident in the value of what he has experienced through his own faith, the Christian is able to delight in everything that he learns from others of what is true and good and beautiful, and at the same time maintain his hope that those who have seen in their own faith what he must judge to be partial may come to find the full-orbed reality of the true, the good, and the beautiful as he himself has seen it in Jesus Christ. If mission is understood in this sense, some of the asperities of the missionary approach in the past may be mitigated.

A New Understanding of Mission. Almost all Christians who are members of churches outside Europe and North

America are conscious of belonging to a single great world-wide fellowship, regardless of the denominational label they may bear. Several, though not all, are ardent supporters of contemporary ecumenical movements for the unity and renewal of the church. But they too are almost at one in holding that reconsideration of the meaning of the term *mission* is long overdue. Those who have traveled in the lands of older Christian traditions and sensed the decay in Christian allegiance of many in these countries are inclined to think that mission should be labeled as a product intended for universal and international export. In the past, the gospel traveled across continents and oceans almost exclusively in one direction. Has not the time come to establish two-way traffic, to have the gospel travel across continents and oceans in many directions? If this is true, the word *mission* may be in need of new and contemporary definition.

[*For further discussion of Christian missions, see* Christianity.]

BIBLIOGRAPHY

The World Christian Encyclopedia: A Comparative Study of Churches and Religions in the Modern World, A. D. 1900-2000, edited by David B. Barrett (Oxford, 1982), is an astonishing repertory of information about the Christian faith and all other faiths in all the countries of the world. *The Concise Dictionary of the Christian World Mission*, edited by Stephen C. Neill, Gerald H. Anderson, and John Goodwin (Nashville, 1971), gives in much more condensed form information on almost every aspect of the Christian mission. By far the most extensive survey of the whole field is K. S. Latourette's *A History of the Expansion of Christianity*, 7 vols. (New York, 1937-1945), to be supplemented by the same writer's *Christianity in a Revolutionary Age: A History of Christianity in the Nineteenth and Twentieth Centuries*, 5 vols. (New York, 1958-1963). My own *Christian Missions* (Baltimore, 1964) has gathered together information from many parts of the world.

No satisfactory history of Roman Catholic missions exists; the best so far is *Histoire universelle des missions catholiques*, 4 vols., edited by Simon Delacroix (Paris, 1956-1958). No English work on Eastern Orthodox missions can be recommended. Two works in German by Josef Glazik, *Die russisch-orthodoxe Heidenmission seit Peter dem Grossen* (Münster, 1954) and *Die Islammission der russisch-orthodoxe Kirche* (Münster, 1959), are classic.

Special studies of many areas are available. For China, K. S. Latourette's *A History of Christian Missions in China* (New York, 1929), is authoritative up to the date of publication. A reliable survey of what has been happening in China since 1948 remains to be written. My *History of Christianity in India*, 2 vols. (Cambridge, 1984-1985), provides substantial coverage. For Africa, C. P. Groves's *The Planting of Christianity in Africa*, 4 vols. (1948-1958; reprint London, 1964), is a work of patient research but is overweighted on the Protestant side.

Countless lives of Christians, Western, Eastern, and African, have been written, but almost all the older works need to be rewritten in the light of modern knowledge. As a notable example of a biography of a twentieth-century saint, mention may be made of Hugh Tinker's *The Ordeal of Love: C. F. Andrews and India* (New York, 1979). Georg Schurhammer's *Francis Xavier: His Life, His Times*, 4 vols. (Rome, 1973-1982) is a superb example of what

can be achieved by intense industry continued over almost sixty years.

Peter Beyerhaus's *The Responsible Church and the Foreign Mission* (London, 1964) is a pioneer work on the transformation of a foreign mission into an independent local church. The works of Roland Allen, especially *Missionary Methods: St. Paul's or Ours?*, 6th ed. (London, 1968), let loose questionings and discussions which have continued to the present day.

On the Christian confrontation with the non-Christian religions, the World Council of Churches in Geneva has published a whole series of valuable books, under the editorship of Stanley J. Samartha. On contemporary trends in mission thinking and theology, the interconfessional and international series "Mission Trends," edited by Gerald Anderson and Thomas Stransky (Ramsey, N. J., 1974-), will be found full of up-to-date and relevant information on almost all matters related to the Christian mission.

STEPHEN C. NEILL

MOABITE RELIGION

In geographical terms, *Moab* is the name given to that part of the Transjordanian plateau located immediately east of the Dead Sea. The southern boundary of Moabite territory was fixed by the river Zered (modern Wadi al-Hasa), but Moab's northern border was not so stable. In periods of strength, Moabite control extended to the environs of Heshbon (modern Hisbān, Jordan), a line running a few miles north of the Dead Sea's northern shore. In times of weakness, Moabite control was reduced to the region between the Zered and the river Arnon (modern Wadi al-Mawjib). Properly speaking, Moab included only the narrow agricultural strip between the western edge of the plateau and the western fringe of the Syrian desert.

In the present article, the term Moabite refers to the people who inhabited this tiny kingdom from near the end of the Late Bronze Age until the end of the Iron Age (c. 1300-600 BCE). The Moabites undoubtedly inherited some religious elements from their Bronze Age predecessors, whose religion was probably similar to that practiced by the Canaanites. Like their Judean, Ammonite, and Edomite neighbors, the Moabites lost their autonomy during the Babylonian invasion of the early sixth century BCE. The Moabite kingdom never reappeared, and with the arrival of new religions (Nabatean, Greek, and so on), the religion of the Moabites became extinct.

Sources. When compared with the sources available for the investigation of many ancient Near Eastern religions, the sources for the study of Moabite religion are meager. In general, the relevant data come from two kinds of sources, archaeological and textual. Although the archaeological evidence consists of various types of artifacts, most of this evidence is open to a wide range of interpretation. Even some of the written sources are ambiguous. Few texts deal directly with Moabite religion, and much of the information about it must be inferred from texts written by other peoples.

Without question, the two most important sources are the Mesha Inscription (MI)—inscribed on a memorial stela (the so-called Moabite Stone) circa 830 BCE by King Mesha of Moab to celebrate his victories over Israel—and the Hebrew scriptures (Old Testament). While the textual and archaeological sources do not provide enough data for a detailed reconstruction of Moabite religion, a general treatment is possible.

Pantheon. Some scholars assume that the Israelite concept of Yahveh as a national deity was paralleled by the Ammonite, Moabite, and Edomite concepts of Milcom (Molech), Kemosh (Chemosh), and Qaus, respectively. While this comparative approach has merit, each of these ethnic religions is different from the others, and the theology of each religion must be understood in its own terms.

Kemosh. Discussion of the Moabite pantheon must begin with the major god of Moab. Indeed, Kemosh may be viewed as the national god of the Moabites, although it is likely that this people also worshiped other deities throughout their entire history. As important as Kemosh was in Moab, the Moabites were not the only ancient people who honored him.

A god named Kamish appears in tablets listing the deities of Ebla, a Syrian city-state whose royal archives date to circa 2500 BCE. Indeed, Kamish was one of the principal deities at Ebla. Gods with similar names are also known from a tablet found at Ugarit, a North Syrian city that flourished from the fifteenth to thirteenth centuries BCE, and from a Babylonian god-list of the second millennium BCE. The ancient and widespread appearances of these names indicate that Kemosh was part of a broader pantheon with which many Near Eastern peoples were familiar.

Knowledge about the Moabites' understanding of Kemosh's nature and function comes from a variety of sources. The name *Kemosh* appears in the Mesha Inscription twelve times; in most instances, Kemosh is portrayed as the commander of Mesha's war against the Israelites. In the Babylonian god-list mentioned above, Kemosh is associated with Nergal, a Mesopotamian god of war and death. Some scholars emphasize Kemosh's warlike character by associating him with Ares, the Greek god of war. For example, the warrior depicted on a coin found at Areopolis (modern Rabba, Jordan) has been identified as Kemosh; he has also been equated with the javelin-wielding figure on the Shihan Warrior Stela, dating from the ninth or eighth century BCE, which was found near Jebel Shihan in central Moab. Of course, these claims are highly speculative.

No less speculative is the theory that the Balu` Stela, dating from the twelfth or eleventh century BCE, which was also found in central Moab, portrays a worshiper standing before Kemosh and his consort. Some scholars who support this

hypothesis also believe that the presence of a sun disk and crescent moon on the monument may indicate that these two figures represent astral deities. In actuality, there is no artistic portrayal that can be identified with Kemosh with any certainty. That such representations existed is not unlikely, and *Jeremiah* 48:7 may imply the existence of such an image.

Judges 11:24 has been interpreted as equating Kemosh with Milcom, who is usually understood as the chief god of the Ammonites. This interpretation also suggests that *Milcom* was a title for Kemosh ("the king") and that in reality it was

> **A god named Kamish appears in tablets listing the deities of Ebla, a Syrian city-state whose royal archives date to circa 2500 BCE.**

Kemosh who was worshiped by both the Moabites and the Ammonites. Alternatively, it is possible that the Hebrew historian made an error or that the reference to the Ammonites is an interpolation.

However his character was understood, there is no question about Kemosh's elevated status in Moabite life. This fact is seen in the frequency with which his name appears as an element in Moabite names (e.g., *Kemosh-nadab, Kemosh-yehi, Kemosh-tsedeq, Kemosh-yat*).

Ashtar-Kemosh. An important datum for the study of Moabite religion is the Mesha Inscription's reference to a deity with the compound name *Ashtar-Kemosh.* Such compound names are not unusual in ancient Near Eastern religious texts. Although the exact identity of this deity is uncertain, the explanations fall into two basic categories: (1) *Ashtar-Kemosh* is the name of Kemosh's consort, the goddess who was thought of as his female counterpart (e.g., the goddess Ishtar or Astarte); and (2) *Ashtar-Kemosh* is simply a compound name for Kemosh and points to the identification of Kemosh with Athtar (i. e., Ashtar), the Canaanite god of the morning star. Since the Mesha Inscription contains eleven other references to Kemosh, it seems likely that *Ashtar-Kemosh* is another name for the chief Moabite god. The question remains as to whether Athtar and Kemosh were totally equated or were simply associated by reason of their character or cult.

Other Moabite deities. Additional members of the Moabite pantheon might have included the Babylonian god Nabu, whose name may be reflected in the place-name *Nebo,* and the Canaanite god Baal. While it cannot be determined whether the name *Baal* ("lord") refers to the Canaanite god or to his local manifestation (Kemosh?), the name or title survived in the divine name *Baal-peor* (cf. *Nm.* 25:1-9) and in several Moabite place-names: *Bamoth-baal (Beth-bamoth?),*

Beth-baal-meon (cf. Baal-meon), and Beth-baal-peor (cf. Beth-peor).

A number of animal and human figurines dating from the tenth through the eighth century BCE have been found at Moabite sites. Given the cultic use of similar objects in neighboring lands, it is likely that some of these figurines had religious significance, perhaps representing votive offerings, priests or priestesses, and/or gods and goddesses.

Temples and Altars. To give thanks for his victory over Israel, Mesha constructed a high place for Kemosh in Qarhoh (MI, lines 3-4), which was probably a part of Mesha's capital, Dibon (modern Dhiban, Jordan). The last line on a fragmentary inscription found at Dibon can be read *beth Kemosh,* "temple of Kemosh." Taken together, these two references may indicate that there was a temple for Kemosh in Dibon, not just an altar. Indeed, the 1955 excavations at this site revealed the foundations of a building whose size, location, and associated artifacts suggest that it might have been a temple. Among the artifacts recovered near this structure was a fragment of an incense stand. Another inscription dating from the ninth century BCE, found at Kir-hareseth (modern al-Karak, Jordan), implies that there was a sanctuary of Kemosh in Kir-hareseth. (Two additional references to a sanctuary built for Kemosh are found in *1 Kings* 11:7-8 and *2 Kings* 23:13.)

Sacrifices. The Old Testament provides most of the data pertaining to Moabite sacrificial practices. In an effort to rid Moab of the Hebrew intruders, *Numbers* 22:40-23:30 records, King Balak, in the company of the Mesopotamian diviner Balaam, made offerings of oxen, bulls, sheep, and rams; the passage implies that these sacrifices were made to a local manifestation of Baal. Indeed, *Numbers* 25:1-5 describes the sacrifices and orgiastic rites that the Israelites and Moabites performed in honor of Baal of Peor. A more general reference to Moabite sacrificial offerings and the burning of incense is found in *Jeremiah* 48:35.

An extraordinary offering is reported in *2 Kings* 3:27. When besieged in Kir-hareseth by a formidable coalition, King Mesha sacrificed his firstborn son. Believing that Mesha's desperate act would be efficacious, his enemies fled in fear that the local god, probably Kemosh, would support the Moabite cause.

Priests and Prophets. While *Jeremiah* 48:7 refers to the priests of Kemosh, a Moabite priesthood is otherwise unknown. Indeed, the priestly function of offering sacrifices seems to have been performed by the Moabite kings, a practice that was also known among the Canaanites.

The story of Balaam, the foreign seer who was hired by King Balak to pronounce a curse upon the Israelites, indicates that diviners were known and used by the Moabites (cf. *Nm.* 22-24). Indeed, the expression "Kemosh said to me," which appears twice in the Mesha Inscription (lines 14, 32), may point to the presence of oracles or prophets in

Mesha's court. Alternatively, this formula may imply that Mesha's kingship entitled him to direct revelation from Kemosh.

Divine Intervention. The Old Testament refers to the Moabites as the "people of Kemosh" (*Nm.* 21:29, *Jer.* 48:46), a designation that was probably used by the Moabites themselves. Both the Old Testament and the Mesha Inscription maintain that a nation's god gives his people their land; both of these sources also claim that the loss of the deity's goodwill can produce catastrophe in human society. Specifically, the Mesha Inscription (line 5) notes that it was Kemosh's anger with his people that caused the Israelite domination over Moab. Although Kemosh's blessings were probably sought in all aspects of life, his intervention in human affairs became most evident in times of war.

Warfare and herem. As was the practice of many ancient peoples, the vengeful war of Mesha was conducted in the name of religion. The enemies of Mesha were identified with the enemies of Kemosh, and, according to the Mesha Inscription, it was the participation of this god in Mesha's campaigns that brought victory. In both general ideology and specific terminology, the inscription's vivid account of a divinely sanctioned war finds close parallels in the Old Testament (e.g., *Jos.* 8:1, *Jgs.* 4:14-15, 1 *Sm.* 23:4, *2 Kgs.* 3:18).

Neither the Mesha Inscription nor the Old Testament recounts "holy war" in the proper sense, but both of these sources reflect a belief that battles are often fought under the aegis of the sacred. Accordingly, victory over one's opponents should produce thanksgiving. While it was assumed that Mesha's recapture of Moabite towns pleased Kemosh, the victors' gratitude was most clearly demonstrated in the practice of *herem,* or consecration of the defeated populace to destruction. (The same verbal root, *hrm,* meaning "ban" or "destroy utterly," occurs in line 17 of the Mesha Inscription and in numerous Old Testament passages.) As an act of devotion to Ashtar-Kemosh, Mesha took Ataroth and Nebo and slaughtered their Israelite inhabitants (MI, lines 11-12, 14-18). This practice is closely paralleled by accounts in the Old Testament (e.g., *Dt.* 7:2, 20:16-17; *Jos.* 6:17-19, 21; 1 *Sm.* 15:3). Fulfillment of the herem is also found in Mesha's reference to the presentation of Arel before Kemosh (MI, lines 12-13) and in the execution of Agag (1 *Sm.* 15:13).

Afterlife. Though there is no written evidence that relates to a Moabite concept of the afterlife, the Moabites were obviously concerned about proper burial of the dead. This is illustrated in the well-made and elaborately furnished tombs found at Dibon, tombs that date approximately to the time of Mesha. Since Kemosh was sometimes named in association with gods of death and the underworld, it is possible that the Moabites believed that an individual's existence did not end with death and burial.

BIBLIOGRAPHY

Although it is seriously outdated at a number of points, the most comprehensive study on Moabite history and culture remains A. H. van Zyl's *The Moabites* (Leiden, 1960). Van Zyl's chapter on Moabite religion is a convenient point of departure for anyone investigating this subject. More recent and less speculative is J. R. Bartlett's "The Moabites and Edomites," pages 229-258 in *Peoples of Old Testament Times,* edited by D. J. Wiseman (Oxford, 1973). The detailed footnotes and bibliography that follow this excellent synthesis are quite helpful. A classic treatment of Transjordanian history and archaeology is found in Nelson Glueck's *The Other Side of the Jordon,* rev. ed. (Winona Lake, Ind., 1970). Glueck's pioneering study is supplemented by Rudolph Henry Dornemann's *The Archaeology of the Transjordan in the Bronze and Iron Ages* (Milwaukee, 1983), a massive compilation of archaeological data. This book contains excellent discussions on Iron Age figurines, sculpture, and tomb remains, all of which relate to the study of Moabite religion. A standard translation of the Mesha Inscription is William F. Albright's "The Moabite Stone," pages 320-321 in Ancient Near Eastern Texts relating to the Old Testament, 3d ed., edited by James B. Pritchard (Princeton, 1969). Important for its comments on the religious significance of this text is Edward Ullendorff's "The Moabite Stone," pages 195-198 in *Documents from Old Testament Times,* translated and edited by D. Winton Thomas (New York, 1961). A valuable study of the Mesha and al-Karak inscriptions is found in volume 1, *Hebrew and Moabite Inscriptions,* of John C. L. Gibson's *Textbook of Syrian Semitic Inscriptions* (Oxford, 1971). This volume includes Gibson's reconstruction of the original texts, introductory material, and technical notes, as well as translations.

GERALD L. MATTINGLY

MONASTICISM

The Greek word *monos,* from which *monasticism* and all its cognates derive, means "one, alone." According to this etymology, therefore, the basic monastic person may be a hermit, a wandering ascetic, or simply someone who is not married or a member of a household. However, the term *monastic* normally refers to people living in community and thus embraces the cenobitic as well as the eremitic and peripatetic lifestyles. In Western societies, the definition of *monasticism* has often been restricted to its classic manifestations, especially the Benedictine tradition. By this definition clergy who adopt some aspects of monastic life and rule (canons regular or regular clerks), mendicant orders (Franciscan, Dominican, and like associations), and other religious orders are not properly called "monastic." Furthermore, within the classic definition one might be able to include some kinds of non-Christian monasticism—that is, those with goals and life patterns fairly similar to the Benedictines—but not others.

Nevertheless, many religious traditions feature (with varying degrees of formal institutionalization) a recognizable type of social structure for which *monasticism* is an appropriate name. The Buddhist *samgha,* the Christian religious and monastic orders, Jain monasticism, and Hindu *sadhus* or *samnyasins* provide the most obvious examples.

Defining Features. First and most prominent of the essential features of monasticism is the monastic's distinctive social status and pattern of social relationships. The monastic person is identified as one whose self-perception and public role include membership in a special religious category of persons, a status which is deliberate and extraordinary.

The second defining feature of the monastic situation is a specific program or discipline of life. The most obvious examples of formal regulations for the monastic life are the Vinaya of Buddhism and the Benedictine rule, but even less clearly defined categories set up expectations concerning appropriate behavior and activities for monastics. Monastic life, in contrast to the rest of human life, is entirely oriented toward a personal religious goal.

Monastic status is differentiated from other religious roles, offices, and functions in that it is not primarily based on performing some service to others in the religious tradition or to the larger society but on the more private cultivation of a path of transformation. A minister, priest, shaman, or similar expert in sacred procedures exhibits a kind of religious leadership dependent on a community to which sacred values are transmitted. Certainly these roles can be merged: some religious professionals also live like monastics.

Finally, it is important to note the presence of a larger religious tradition and set of institutions within which the monastic phenomenon takes place. Christianity can exist without monasticism because, in the "secular" priesthood and episcopal office, it has a social structure and forms of leadership independent of monastic patterns. Such patterns are even less central in Islam, where much of the tradition disowns monasticism completely. By contrast, monasticism is central to Buddhism and Jainism.

Frequent Characteristics. Even though the most careful definition of *monasticism* could not include communal life as a necessary factor, there can be no doubt that monastic existence is rarely completely solitary. Even wandering or hermit monks assemble periodically.

Sometimes monastic status is lifelong; this would seem to be the normal implication of the initiation into a higher realm. Christian religious orders often have some arrangement whereby lay people can become affiliated with the order without becoming full members. The third order of the Franciscan tradition and the Benedictine oblates are two such orders. In some instances a residential oblate may live just like the other members of the community or order.

Another important aspect of much monasticism, yet one not essential to it, is poverty or simplicity of lifestyle. Accumulation of wealth, as well as other factors that may lead to a change in the character of a monastic community's life over a period of time, have produced successive reforms within long monastic traditions. Benedictine history is a story of reforms: the first notable one took place under the aegis of Benedict of Aniane about three hundred years after Benedict of Nursia founded the order. This was followed by the reform programs of Cluny, the Cistercians, the Trappists, and so on.

Some monastic work involves intellectual activity. Benedict's rule emphasizes reading *(lectio divina)* as a major component of the monastic life along with prayer and work. The path to perfection or religious transformation is often an intellectual path that requires a new understanding of the self and the world. Reading and study in the monastic context is a means of salvation, a technique for the reconstruction of one's worldview. Also, because the rule, religious texts, and other written guides to meditation, prayer, and discipline

> A monastic belonging to an active order may be a teacher, nurse, priest, or support person in some beneficial institution. . . .

must be available to monastics, much of their effort has been put to copying, studying, and teaching these materials.

In some situations charitable acts are held to be more important for the monastic than more individual disciplines. A distinction is made within Christian communities between contemplative orders, where activities like those mentioned above predominate, and active orders, where emphasis is placed on work with beneficial effects for others. A monastic belonging to an active order may be a teacher, nurse, priest, or support person in some beneficial institution, but with an interest or investment in the work that is beyond that of non-monastic colleagues. For the monastic such work is part of a discipline or rule, a means toward a religious goal.

Contemporary Monasticism. In recent decades monastics from various religious traditions have become more aware of each other. Toward the end of his life the famous Trappist monk Thomas Merton wrote and spoke of the many similarities among the world's monastic systems. Roman Catholic monasteries in traditionally non-Christian areas have been interested in this consanguinity and have produced some writing on monasticism as an interreligious phenomenon. Since 1960 an organization known as Aide Inter-Monastères has encouraged dialogue between monastics of various religions. Some Christian monastics and monasteries now practice techniques borrowed from Hinduism and Buddhism.

In the United States many experimental as well as traditional new religious communities have been established. A monastic impulse seems to have been a part of the "counterculture" revolution of the sixties and seventies. Monasticism apparently continues to be a persistent and

beneficial social and religious structure. In the seriousness with which the monastic reexamines life and its goals, in the rigor with which a discipline of life is pursued, the monastic phenomenon offers an alternative way of life and view of the world to the rest of society.

[*See also* Eremitism.]

BIBLIOGRAPHY

Studies of monasticism that take into consideration more than one religious tradition are a fairly recent phenomenon. The best book of this kind is *Blessed Simplicity: The Monk as Universal Archetype* by Raimundo Panikkar and others (New York, 1982). For an informal comparative survey of religious communities, see Charles A. Fracchia's *Living Together Alone: The New American Monasticism* (San Francisco, 1979).

A careful analysis of the theology and practice of Christian monasticism is provided by Louis Bouyer in *The Meaning of the Monastic Life* (London, 1955). The standard teaching and reflection of Christian monks is presented by Claude J. Peifer in *Monastic Spirituality* (New York, 1966). Good books on Christian monasticism and religious orders abound; see especially David Knowles's *The Monastic Order in England*, 2d ed. (Cambridge, 1963), and *The Religious Orders in England*, 3 vols. (Cambridge, 1948-1959). A critical view of medieval monasticism is presented in George G. Coulton's *Five Centuries of Religion*, 4 vols. (Cambridge, 1923-1950). The Benedictine rule, along with indexes and informative articles, is available in *RB 1980: The Rule of St. Benedict in Latin and English, with Notes,* edited by Timothy Fry and others (Collegeville, Minn., 1981).

Hindu monasticism is covered by G. S. Ghurye in *Indian Sadhus*, 2d ed. (Bombay, 1964). Sukumar Dutt's *Buddhist Monks and Monasteries of India* (London, 1962) is the best source on Buddhist monasticism in India. For Chinese Buddhism, see Holmes Welch's *The Practice of Chinese Buddhism, 1900-1950* (Cambridge, Mass., 1967). The Buddhist monastic rule is treated in Charles S. Prebish's *Buddhist Monastic Discipline: The Sanskrit Pratimoksa Sutras of the Mahasamghikas and Mulasarvastivadins* (University Park, Pa., 1975).

On monasticism in Islam, see J. Spencer Trimingham's *The Sufi Orders in Islam* (New York, 1971). An older standard reference is John K. Birge's study of a Sufi order in Turkey, *The Bektashi Order of Dervishes* (1937; New York, 1982). An abridged translation of a Sufi rule is found in Menahem Milson's *A Sufi Rule for Novices* (Cambridge, Mass., 1975).

On *Protestant monasticism,* see François Biot's The Rise of Protestant Monasticism (Baltimore, 1963). Peter F. Anson surveys Anglican communities in his *The Call of the Cloister*, 4th ed., rev. (London, 1964).

GEORGE WECKMAN

MONGOL RELIGIONS

If stereotypical reports from early times are taken into account, the religious forms of the Mongols have been influenced by the religions professed by all ethnic groups who have lived in what later was to become Mongolian territory prior to the emergence of the Mongols. The oldest of these religious forms was shamanism. It remains the perennial dominant religious practice of the Mongols.

Mongol shamanism developed into its current state in various phases. In the original phase, fear of natural powers that were thought to be caused by evil forces led to the worship of the spirits of ancestors. The functions of shamanism, as explained by the shamans themselves, are to invoke the *ongons,* to shamanize with their help, to intercede on behalf of ill persons, to exorcize evil and the powers creating calamities and illness, to expel these into effigies that are then destroyed, and to pronounce charms and prognostications by scapulimancy and other divinatory methods.

In the thirteenth century Mongol shamanism was influenced by administrative measures when the first Mongol emperor in China, Khubilai Khan (r. 1260-1294), established by imperial decree the office of the state shamans. These shamans were responsible for offerings in memory of Chinggis Khan and his house as well as for the worship of fire. According to the *Yüan shih,* the official Chinese history of the Yüan dynasty, these shamans pronounced their prayers and invocations in the Mongolian language. Judged by the evident longevity of the Mongolian oral tradition and its extraordinary reliability, it seems certain that some of the prayers still used today at the so-called Eight White Yurts, the center of worship of the deified Chinggis Khan in the Ordos territory, contain remnants of these early shamanic prayers and supplications.

The ephemeral contacts of Buddhism with the ruling strata of the Mongol nobility during the twelfth and thirteenth centuries and later did not lead to any decisive intrusion of Buddhist notions into the religious conceptions of the bulk of the Mongol populations. Shamanism remained dominant. Only when Buddhist missionary work began among the Mongols in the sixteenth century did shamanism come under heavy attacks. Princes and overlords sustained the missionaries by donating horses and cows to converts while burning the confiscated shamanic idols in iconoclastic purges. Thousands of the idols were destroyed in this period, and the shamans had to renounce their profession and faith. Many fled during the sixteenth century into more remote regions.

Considered by both the Lamaist clergy and most princes to be a meritorious deed that would further the spread of Buddhism, such persecution has been repeated again and again up to the beginning of the twentieth century. Cases of rounding up, mistreating, and burning shamans were reported among the eastern Khalkha Mongols in the nineteenth century and in the remote northwest of Mongolia in 1904. Yet shamanism and related forms of popular religious worship have not been totally subdued. Forced during the periods of worst suppression into some camouflaged forms, it found a

new, more syncretic expression by adding and adapting objects and forms of Buddhist veneration.

In more recent times the healing activities of the shamans have been more and more predominant, the shaman personnel being divided into real shamans *(böge/udaghan)* and non-shamanic healers and singers. The method of healing employed tends toward a kind of group therapeutic treatment of psychic illness *(andai),* which consists of shamans, helpers, and a crowd of laymen singing and arguing with the patient as a means of restoring him to his normal psychic state. In eastern Mongolia this singing therapy has been practiced since at least the mid-nineteenth century.

[*See also* Buddhism, and Shamanism.]

BIBLIOGRAPHY

Banzarov, Dorzi. *"Chernaia vera, ili Shamanstvo u Mongolov" i drugie stat'i.* Edited by G. N. Potanin. Saint Petersburg, 1891. Translated by Jan Nattier and J. R. Krueger as "The Black Faith, or Shamanism among the Mongols," *Mongolian Studies* 7 (1981-1982): 51-91.

Buyanbatu, G. *Mongghol-un böge-yin sasin-u ucir.* Kökekhota, 1985.

Dalai, C. "Mongolyn böögijn mörgölijn tovc tüüh." *Studia Ethnographica* (Ulan Bator) 1 (1959).

Heissig, Walther. "Schamanen und Geisterbeschwörer im Küriye-Banner." *Folklore Studies* (Peking) 3 (1944): 39-72.

Heissig, Walther. "A Mongolian Source to the Lamaist Suppression of Shamanism in the Seventeenth Century." *Anthropos* 48 (1953): 1-29, 493-536.

Heissig, Walther. *The Religions of Mongolia.* Translated by Geoffrey Samuel, Berkeley, 1980.

Hoppál, Mihály. "Shamanism: An archaic and/or Recent System of Beliefs." *Ural-Altaische Jahrbücher* 57 (1985): 121-140.

Nekliudov, Sergei Iu. "Tengri." In *Mify narodov mira,* edited by S. A. Tokarev, vol. 2. Moscow, 1982.

Poppe, Nicholas N. "Zum Feuerkultus bei den Mongolen." *Asia Major* 2 (1925): 130-145.

Sárközi, Alice. "Symbolism in Exorcising the Evil Spirits." Paper delivered at the meeting of the Permanent International Altaistic Conference, 1984.

Sodnam, B. "Mongolyn kharyn böögijn duudlagyn tukhaj." *Studia Mongolica* (Ulan Bator) 4 (1962): 59-112.

Tatár, Magdalena. "Tragic and Stranger Ongons among the Altaic Peoples." In *Altaistic Studies,* edited by Gunnar Jarring and Staffan Rosén, pp. 165-171. Stockholm, 1985.

Zhukovskaia, Nataliia L. *Lamaizm i rannie formy religii.* Moscow, 1977.

WALTHER HEISSIG

MONOTHEISM

Derived from the Greek *mono* ("single") and *theos* ("God"), the term *monotheism* refers to the religious experience and the philosophical perception that emphasize God as one, perfect, immutable, creator of the world from nothing, distinct from the world, all-powerfully involved in the world, personal, and worthy of being worshiped by all creatures. Some forms of monotheism, however, differ about the notions of God as distinct from the world and as personal.

Monotheism in Religious History. Whereas monotheism is most often associated with the Jewish, Christian, and Islamic religions and philosophies, tendencies contributing toward a monotheistic outlook have long been present in human religious history. The streams of the monotheistic vision run dimly through the fertile valleys of archaic agricultural religions with their pluralistic experience of the forces of nature centered on Mother Earth. But a few high gods developed with supreme sovereignty and autonomy, as sources of fecundating power and guarantors of the order and norms of the world and of human society. For example, Zeus and Jupiter were ruling high gods fashioned in accord with the Greek and Roman notions of norm and law. In India, Varuna was sovereign guardian of *rta,* cosmic order, a role taken over later by the great gods Visnu and Siva.

Greek religion. Among Greek thinkers, ideas of a unitary divine reality were expressed as a means of showing the order and reasonableness of the world. Already in pre-Socratic times, it seems, philosophers like Xenophanes depicted the spiritual unity of the whole world in the notion of the All-One. Plato stressed the unity of the Good and identified God with that: God must be perfectly good, changeless, and the maker of the best possible world. Aristotle also made the idea of goodness central to his concept of God, the causal principle of all. In the Hellenistic religions, the sense of God's unicity was expressed by raising one god or goddess to supremacy; for example, Apuleius described Isis as the one Great Mother of all.

Hinduism. There have always been theistic tendencies in Hinduism, but these have been associated with a variety of divine beings. Yet intense concerns of *bhakti* (devotion to a god) have sometimes led Hindus to raise up one god as supreme ruler, or to see the various gods as manifestations of one God. "They call it Indra, Mitra, Varuna, and Agni . . . ; but the real is one, although the sages give different names" (*Rgveda* 1.169). Among Vaisnavas, Visnu tends to become all, and the same is true of Siva among Saivas. Krsna, *avatara* of Visnu, can be put forth as the supreme God behind all names: "Many are the paths people follow, but they all in the end come to me" (*Bhagavadgita* 4.11).

Buddhism. Buddhism, like Hinduism, is essentially a monism which has only an inferior role for those born at the level of gods, trapped as they are like all living beings in the cycles of rebirth. But in Mahayana Buddhism, the idea has arisen that beings who have realized their Buddhahood (that is, Buddhas and *bodhisattvas*) can function similarly to gods in theistic religions. Generally Mahayana Buddhism holds to the multiplicity of these powerful beings, but in certain schools one such Buddha becomes supreme and is wor-

shiped exclusively. Such is the case with Amitabha (Jpn., Amida) Buddha in Pure Land Buddhism, a soteriological monolatry offering the one hope of salvation for this degenerate age.

Egyptian religion. Around 1375 BCE Pharoah Amunhotep IV repudiated the authority of the old gods and their priests and devoted himself exclusively to Aton, the god appearing as the sun disk. He proclaimed himself the son of Aton, taking the name *Akhenaton* ("devoted to Aton"), and he imposed this worship on others. By royal decree Aton became the only God who exists, king not only of Egypt but of the whole world, embodying in his character and essence all the attributes of the other gods. But within twenty-five years Akhenaton was gone, and his successors restored the old cults.

Zoroastrianism. Growing from the ancient Indo-Iranian polytheistic religion, Zoroastrianism unified all divine reality in the high god Ahura Mazda. He creates only good things and gives only blessings to his worshipers. The one God is sovereign over history, working out the plan he has for the world. However, conflict is accounted for as the hostility of two primordial spirits: Spenta Mainyu, the good spirit, and Angra Mainyu (Pahl., Ahriman), the evil spirit. Ahura Mazda apparently fathered these two spirits; the struggle between them has been going on since the beginning of time, when they chose between good and evil. It appears, then, that Ahura Mazda cannot be called omnipotent, for the realm of

> . . . Ahura Mazda cannot be called omnipotent, for the realm of evil is beyond his control. . . .

evil is beyond his control; in that sense it may be said that this is not a complete monotheism. Yet there is no doubt that Zoroastrianism considers the realm of Ahura Mazda to be ultimately victorious.

Judaism, Christianity, and Islam. The three religions that are generally held to be the full expressions of monotheism, Judaism, Christianity, and Islam, also arose against the background of the polytheism of the ancient Near East. These three religions are closely related in that they grew from the Semitic cultural background and the foundations of the religion of ancient Israel.

One might call early Israelite religion henotheistic or monolatrous in the sense that exclusive loyalty was to be given to Yahveh, but Yahveh's power was limited because other nations had their own gods. Some Israelites lived with a polytheistic vision, giving loyalty to Yahveh as the god of the covenant but also worshiping Baal and the other gods of fecundity as they settled in Canaan and became agriculturalists. But the covenant relationship with Yahveh contained the seeds of monotheism; the Israelites experienced Yahveh as personal, showing himself in historical events and demanding exclusive loyalty and ethical behavior according to the covenant law.

Jews, Christians, and Muslims drew on the fundamental monotheistic vision of ancient Israel, each group filling out the picture of God with colorings and shapes drawn from its own particular culture.

Sikhism. Starting with Guru Nanak (1469-1539 CE), an Indian type of monotheism developed that synthesizes the mystical monotheism found in Hinduism and the ethical, personal monotheism brought into India by Islam. In Guru Nanak's teaching, there is only one God, who is immortal, unborn, self-existent, creator of all the universe, omniscient, formless, just, and loving. God is both transcendent as pure potentiality and immanent as world-embodiment.

Monotheism in Contrast to Nonmonotheistic Views. One of the most obvious contexts against which monotheism defines itself is a plurality of divine beings or forces, which is commonly called polytheism. Central to polytheism is the notion of *theoi,* personal divine beings within nature and society. These gods have personal wills, control specific spheres, and interact with one another to make up a functioning organism.

Related to polytheism is what F. Max Müller called henotheism and what others have called monolatry: worshiping one god at a time or raising up one most powerful God as the only one to be worshiped.

A form of thought close to monotheism but still related to polytheism and henotheism is theistic dualism. [*See* Dualism.] Typically, this experience of the divine reality separates out the hurtful or evil elements and associates these with another divine power, thus setting up a divine struggle with echoes in human life. One unified supreme God is posited as the good divine force, and the source of evil can be thought of as many beings or as one evil being.

BIBLIOGRAPHY

The classic study that marshaled much evidence for an *Urmonotheismus* among archaic peoples is Wilhelm Schmidt's *Der Ursprung der Gottesidee: Eine historisch-kritische und positive Studie,* 12 vols. (Münster, 1912-1955); although Schmidt's theory is no longer accepted, much of the material is still useful. More recently, John S. Mbiti has gathered and synthesized concepts about the unity of the high god from all over Africa in *Concepts of God in Africa* (New York, 1970). Greek tendencies to associate unity and goodness with God are discussed by James Adams in *The Religious Teachers of Greece* (Edinburgh, 1908). M. P. Christanand compares Hindu and Sikh monotheistic thought with that of Judaism, Christianity, and Islam in *The Philosophy of Indian Monotheism* (Delhi, 1979). Sikh monotheistic ideas are discussed by Fauja Singh and others in a volume published by Punjabi University: *Sikhism* (Patiala, India, 1969). Donald B. Redford offers a fresh investigation of the Egyptian monotheistic period, including the art associated with it, in

Akhenaten: The Heretic King (Princeton, 1984). A thorough discussion of the development of Zoroastrian religious ideas can be found in *Religion of Ancient Iran* (Bombay, 1973) by Jacques Duchesne-Guillemin.

William F. Albright's *From the Stone Age to Christianity: Monotheism and the Historical Process,* 2d ed. (Garden City, N. Y., 1957), is a well-known study of the development of monotheism in ancient Israel viewed against the background of ancient Near Eastern cultures. The articles in *Monotheismus im alten Israel und seiner Umwelt,* edited by Othmar Keel (Fribourg, 1980), survey the development of monotheism among the Hebrews. The Jewish rabbinic conception of the oneness of God is well presented by Louis Jacobs in *A Jewish Theology* (New York, 1973). A clear and forceful exposition of monotheism in the Jewish view is found in Abraham Heschel's *Man Is Not Alone: A Philosophy of Religion* (New York, 1951). H. P. Owen surveys the various Christian theological and philosophical approaches to God as he defends traditional theism in *Concepts of Deity* (New York, 1971). Paul Tillich presents a monotheistic theology related to his view of God as the "Ground of Being" in his *Systematic Theology,* vol. 1 (Chicago, 1951). In *Radical Monotheism and Western Civilzation* (Lincoln, Neb., 1960), H. Richard Niebuhr has set the standard for discussing the relevance of monotheism for Christian society. The central importance of the unity of God in Islam, as seen through the eyes of a modern thinker, is forcefully presented by Muhammad `Abduh in *The Theology of Unity* (London, 1966). S. A. A. Mawdudi provides a short but compelling statement of the implications of *tawhid,* or unity of God, in *Towards Understanding Islam* (Ann Arbor, Mich., 1980).

A rich sampling of philosophical ideas about God, with an interesting typology of theistic views, is found in Charles Hartshorne and William L. Reese's *Philosophers Speak of God* (Chicago, 1953). A model of current philosophical investigation of monotheism with respect to ethics is found in Lenn E. Goodman's *Monotheism: A Philosophical Inquiry into the Foundations of Theology and Ethics* (Totowa, N. J., 1981). Explications of the current criticism of traditional monotheism can be found in Alain de Benoist's *Comment peut-on être païen?* (Paris, 1981) and in David L. Miller's *The New Polytheism: Rebirth of the Gods and Goddesses* (New York, 1974), where he suggests that monotheism fails to provide religious creativity for the modern age. Material on the feminist critique of concepts of God can be found in Rosemary R. Ruether's *Sexism and God Talk: Toward a Feminist Theology* (Boston, 1983).

Responding to some of these criticisms, Bernard-Henri Lévy in *Le testament de Dieu* (Paris, 1979) attempts to show that monotheism can be a liberating safeguard against all forms of totalitarianism. Jurgën Moltmann counters oppressive monarchical monotheism with a liberating trinitarian model of God in *The Trinity and the Kingdom: The Doctrine of God* (London, 1981). And an issue of Concilium, volume 177, is devoted to the current Christian theological discussion, especially in Europe, of the criticisms of monotheism and the need to rethink and renew this theological concept: Monotheism, edited by Claude Geffré and Jean-Pierre Jossua (Edinburgh, 1985).

THEODORE M. LUDWIG

MORALITY AND RELIGION

In the minds of many people, the terms *morality* and *religion* signal two related but distinct ideas. Morality is thought to pertain to the conduct of human affairs and relations between persons, while religion primarily involves the relationship between human beings and a transcendent reality. In fact, this distinction between religion and morality is a relatively modern one. Although tension between religion and morality is already evident in the writings of Plato and other Greek philosophers, the popular modern conception that religion and morality are separate phenomena is probably traceable to the Enlightenment. At that time, a number of thinkers, reflecting Europe's weariness with centuries of religious strife, sought to elaborate ethical theories based on reason or on widely shared human sentiments. In so doing they established the assumption that the norms governing conduct, morality, and ethics (that is, the effort to reason about or justify these norms) were separable from matters of religious belief.

The Superiority of Moral Norms and Independence of Moral Reasoning. As we look at the variety of religio-ethical traditions, it is striking that a sense of the distinction between religious, ethical, and even legal norms is often not present, and that when it is, it is often a late development. Furthermore, because the very distinctions are lacking, traditions do not always assert the superiority of moral norms over specifically ritual or religious requirements. This does not mean that these ideas are not present; often they are implicit and can be discerned only by a careful examination of how conflicts between norms are handled.

Most historical traditions tend to see the normative structures bearing on human life as an integrated whole, wherein moral requirements are fused with religious, ritual, and legal norms. In this respect it is often strained to speak of Jewish, Hindu, or Islamic "ethics." In Judaism, for example, the sacred norms for human life constitute *halakhah*. Incompletely understood as "law," *halakhah* is more properly thought of as sacred teaching or guidance, although it is also "law" in the sense that many of its specific requirements were upheld by public sanctions and punishments, when Jews were politically able to govern themselves. In all, *halakhah* discusses 613 specific commandments or normative prescriptions identified by commentators in scripture, including the Ten Commandments. While this body of norms does contain many requirements that are recognizably "moral," these are not clearly distinguished from what we would identify as ritual or religious norms.

Commentators on early Christian ethics have noted the striking difference between the tone of early Christian ethical writing and that of the surrounding Greco-Roman world. Whereas Greek and Roman thinkers were concerned with such questions as what constitutes "the good" for man and what patterns of conduct are most conducive to individual and communal well-being, Christian writers commonly established rules for conduct by citing biblical commandments, or by holding up as models for behavior exemplary persons in scripture. Throughout, it is the hope for God's approval (or the avoidance of his wrath) that is pointed to as the principal reason for living a Christian life. As is also true for Judaism and Islam, not human reason but God's will remains the source and sanction for moral conduct.

It is true that in our era each of the biblically based traditions has developed bodies of systematic ethical reflection, and it is also possible today to find treatises on Buddhist, Hindu, or Jain ethics. Yet the separation of moral reasoning from other dimensions of the religious life is largely alien to all these traditions. In Judaism, Christianity, and Islam, the appearance of ethical theorizing initially represents a response to the authority of Greek and Roman philosophy. Thus, some of the earliest thinking about the relationship between religious and rational norms in these traditions—as for instance Sa`adyah Gaon's *Book of Beliefs and Opinions* (933 CE) and Thomas Aquinas's discussion of the forms of the law in his *Summa theologiae* (2.1.90-97)—emerges during the medieval period, when classical philosophy was rediscovered. Similarly, modern efforts to develop statements of Jewish, Christian, or Islamic ethics are very much a response to initiatives in philosophical ethical theory. The authority of Western thought has had a corresponding effect in stimulating thinkers in African and Asian religious traditions to develop systematic approaches to ethics. But in all these cases, writers are usually compelled to begin their discussions with the observation that the moral teachings of their tradition are inseparable from its theological, metaphysical, or ritual dimensions.

Are we to conclude, then, that the separation of ethics from these other aspects of religion is only a Western phenomenon, and one largely traceable to the classical philosophers of Greece and Rome? It is true that systematic, rational thinking about morality—ethics in the modern sense—does emerge primarily in the Greco-Roman world, although one might also speak of ancient Chinese ethics in this sense. Interestingly, in both these cases it was partly the breakdown of an older religious ideal that prompted rational reflection on the human good. But while ethical theorizing per se may be culturally localized, a sense of the independence, special significance, and even superiority of moral norms with respect to other normative requirements is present throughout many of these diverse traditions.

Universality and the Moral Rules. *Universality* has several distinct meanings when used in reference to moral rules. It signifies the fact that at least the basic rules of morality are the same across cultures. It also signifies that these rules are to be regarded as applying across cultural lines presumably to every human being. All who are human are members of the moral community and bear the rights and responsibilities of this status.

Common moral principles. One of the most striking impressions produced by comparative study of religious ethics is the similarity in basic moral codes and teachings. The Ten Commandments of Hebrew faith, the teachings of Jesus in the Sermon on the Mount and of Paul in his epistles, the requirements of *sadharana,* or universal *dharma,* in Hinduism (*Laws of Manu,* 10.63), Buddhism's Five Precepts, and Islam's decalogue in the Qur'an (17:22-39) constitute a very common set of normative requirements. These prohibit killing, injury, deception, or the violation of solemn oaths. C. S. Lewis has called basic moral rules like these "the ultimate platitudes of practical reason," and their presence and givenness in such diverse traditions supports his characterization.

Similar assessments of individual moral worth. Beyond these common moral principles, interesting normative similarities may also be identified with respect to the role played by individual decision and intention in the evaluation of moral worth. Intention is a crucial consideration in estimating the merit or blame of the moral agent. Very often during their earliest periods, traditions evidence an objective assessment of moral culpability: individuals may suffer social or religious penalties for wrongs accidentally committed. Similarly, the earliest strata of some traditions at times display notions of collective guilt whereby all members of a community are regarded as meriting punishment for the wrongdoing of a few.

None of the "daughter traditions"—neither Buddhism, Christianity, nor Islam—defends the idea of corporate punishment, whereas all put much stress on intention in assessing individuals' deeds. Jesus' criticism of religious and moral hypocrisy may not be fair to the Jewish tradition from which he sprang, but it is fully consistent with the spirit of greater interiority in the assessment of worth that marks the development of biblical faith. Much the same might be said of the Buddhist remolding of the doctrine of *karman* to the effect that karmic consequences are seen to derive from the willing of the agent rather than from the outward deed. The importance of intention *(niyah)* in validating religious and moral observance in Islam and of the kindred concept of *kavvanah* in rabbinic Judaism exemplifies this same process of increasing precision in the assessment of individual worth.

Differences between traditions. Despite all these remarkable similarities, there are also important differences among the codes and teachings of these traditions. Thus, the permitted range of sexual conduct differs from tradition to tradition, with the concept of sexual chastity apparently not ruling out polygamy in some cases (ancient Israelite religion,

Islam, Confucianism) but requiring monogamy and even recommending celibacy in others (monastic Christianity and Buddhism). Wrongful killing, too, is variously defined. For Jews and Muslims, killing is permissible if done in self-defense or to punish wrongdoers whose conduct is believed to threaten the community. The New Testament, however, suggests a stance in which even self-defensive killing of other human beings is prohibited. Buddhism and Jainism take this position one step further by discouraging the killing not only of human beings but of all sentient creatures.

Differences of this sort represent an important object of study. Why is it that traditions whose moral attitudes and teachings are in some ways similar tend to differ in other

> **Why is it that traditions whose moral attitudes and teachings are in some ways similar tend to differ in other respects?**

respects? But the significance of these differences for our basic understanding of the relationship between religion and morality should not be exaggerated. For one thing, these differences are manifested against a background of basic similarities in moral teaching. It is sometimes assumed, because religious traditions hold widely different religious beliefs, that their ethics must correspondingly differ; what is remarkable, however, is that these great differences in beliefs apparently do not affect adherence to at least the fundamental moral rules. Furthermore, where moral differences do occur, they do so within the permitted range of moral disagreement.

"Omnipartiality." In making moral choices, we must consider not only the immediate neighbor but all other persons affected by our conduct or choice. Hence the requirements of universality, objectivity, and impartiality in moral reasoning. In fact, the term *impartiality,* though widely used in moral theory today, is inappropriate, because it suggests detachment and distance in reasoning when what is really required is genuine empathetic concern for all those affected by our decisions. In this respect either *omnipartiality* or *omnicompassion* would be a better term.

When we examine the very highest reaches of religious thought, we are struck by the ways in which adoption of this perspective is encouraged. In the Western traditions believers are called upon to imitate God while trying to develop their own moral and religious lives. Modeling their behavior on God's, Jews, Christians, and Muslims are thus called to distance themselves from selfish interests and to adopt an omnipartial point of view. Some Asian religions share this teaching. Adherents of the *bhakti* (devotional) tradition of Hinduism find a model in the god (often embodied in the figure of Krsna) whose love transcends social distinctions of caste, wealth, or gender. In the ancient Chinese and Confucian traditions, Shang-ti ("lord on high") and T'ien ("heaven") represent the standard of impartial justice. Knowing no favorites, Heaven judges by merit alone and casts out the unworthy.

Mystical traditions, which often place less emphasis on obedience to God and more on the adherent's experience of a transcendent reality, arrive at this standpoint in a different way. Characteristically, once a person has joined with or is in contact with transcendent reality (whether as *brahman, nirvana,* or the Tao), the ego assumes reduced importance. No longer clinging to the self, one participates sympathetically in all of reality. In Mahayana Buddhism this experience eventuates in compassion *(karuna)* for all sentient beings and the desire to help extricate them from suffering. The Taoist adept, in achieving mystical insight into the Way, participates in its spontaneity, generosity, and support of all living creatures.

Why Should One Be Moral? Religions are not just bodies of teaching about right and wrong; they are total ways of life. As a result, it is not surprising that they provide answers, whether explicit or implicit, to some of the more urgent "transnormative" questions of morality, among them the questions of why one should be a moral person and how one can attain a morally estimable character.

Retribution. Religious traditions commonly provide answers to the question "Why should I be moral?" by affirming the existence of an order in which moral retribution (reward and punishment) is assured. Those raised in the West are familiar with some of the standard forms of this belief: God is consummately righteous; he is the omniscient judge of human acts and intentions; he upholds the moral law by punishing the wicked and rewarding the righteous; and, in some cases, he metes out reward and punishment directly in the course of a person's life.

Although this retributive scheme prevails in Judaism, Christianity, and Islam, it is not the only one that religions (including these same Western traditions) have elaborated. The idea of eschatological retribution is absent from many nonliterate traditions, and even in biblical faith it is a relatively late development. More common is a perception of death as departure to a state where the discarnate soul suffers neither punishment nor reward. The principal expectation for virtuous conduct, therefore, lies in the hope of worldly prosperity, numerous progeny, good health, and long life, so as to "come in sturdy old age to the grave," as the *Book of Job* (5:26) says.

Neither is the apportionment of reward and punishment always accomplished by a supreme, morally intentioned deity. In many of the nonliterate traditions of Africa and in some Native American religions, lesser supernatural agents such as witches and sorcerers also play a role—indeed, a complex one—in upholding the moral order. These agents are often "negative exemplars," embodying attitudes of selfishness and resentment that are the opposite of the open and generous attitudes expected of a good member of the community. Since witches and sorcerers can themselves expect to be punished for their behavior, the lesson to all is clear: avoid becoming persons of this sort.

Among the traditions of India, moral reward and punishment are also the province of religious thought, but (at least in the post-Vedic period) they are accomplished by means very different from those in the West. In Indian thought the operative mode is the impersonal, natural-moral law of *karman:* the certainty of moral punishment or reward in combination with a belief in metempsychosis or the transmigration of the individual soul. In the world of *karman,* each act and each volition entails consequences for the welfare of the agent. In a sense, it is misleading to label these consequences rewards or punishments, since they do not result from the action of any judge but are part of the natural law of occurrences in the world. As such, these consequences may be experienced within the lifetime of an individual. More commonly they take many successive lifetimes to work their effect as one's *karman* "ripens." When morally caused suffering does occur, it is often suited to the crime. One who habitually lies, for example, may become the victim of slander in some future life; one who drinks to excess may be reborn insane.

Belief in *karman* is so widely shared among the Indian traditions—Jainism, Hinduism, and Buddhism—that it may be called the principal dogma of Indian religious belief. For these traditions, to reject *karman* is to put oneself outside the religious pale.

Redemption. It is important to note that strong affirmation by religious traditions of the existence of a morally retributive order, while it relieves this problem in some ways (by reinforcing confidence in retribution), accentuates it in others. It does so first of all because, in a world assumed to be governed by moral considerations, ordinary forms of suffering (sickness, famine, or premature death) are naturally attributed to moral and religious failures on the part of the individual or community. Not surprisingly, therefore, we find a concern with the expiation of sin present in many nonliterate traditions, and even the earliest documents of the literate traditions (such as the cultic ordinances in *Leviticus,* the *Rgveda,* or the Chinese *Book of Rites*) emphasize these matters. But as traditions develop, a further problem emerges that often leads into the most subtle and paradoxical reaches of religious thought. Moral reasoning, though it may lead to a recognition of the need for some confidence in moral retribution, is nevertheless opposed to basing moral commitment on crass considerations of personal benefit or gain. Indeed, not only are individuals who calculate their commitments in this way morally unreliable (since expediential considerations can easily lead them to be immoral), but they do not attain to the highest standard of moral virtue, in which a spontaneous and pure love of righteousness is the principal motivating ground of conduct.

But since religions inevitably hold out the promise of reward, how are they, at the same time, to lead their adherents into such an elevated level of moral attainment? Or, as the outward behavior of adherents becomes more refined, how are religions to prevent egoism from corrupting the inner core of intention? To answer these questions fully would require an extensive exploration of various traditions' conceptions of sin and redemption. We can, however, identify a very common direction taken by religious thought at this point. Simply stated, in coming to terms with this problem, traditions tend to qualify and soften their own insistence on moral retribution. The world may be a moral order, but ultimate redemption does not necessarily rest on the moral performance or accomplishments of the individual agent. The effect of this teaching is twofold: it relieves the inevitable self-condemnation of the morally conscientious yet knowingly frail person, but at the same time it eliminates any vestiges of cloying self-regard that might corrupt the moral life and make it an instrument of pride and self-assertion.

Traditions effect this qualification of the retributive scheme differently. Judaism, Christianity, and Islam emphasize God's grace and the recurrent possibility of repentance. Pauline Christianity takes this teaching to the extreme conclusion that salvation comes not by works of the moral and religious law, but through God's free, unnecessitated love. Similar conceptions are found in the devotional *(bhakti)* tradition of Hindu thought, but in the Indian-derived traditions the retributive order is more commonly qualified differently: ultimate redemption requires one to attain the consciousness that full liberation *(moksa, nirvana)* is open only to those who transcend attachment to *samsara,* the karmic realm of merit and demerit.

BIBLIOGRAPHY

Among the more important classical discussions of the relationship between religion and morality are Plato's *Euthyphro,* Thomas Aquinas's "Treatise on the Law" *(Summa theologiae,* 2.7.90-97), Immanuel Kant's *Critique of Practical Reason* and *Religion within the Limits of Reason Alone,* Søren Kierkegaard's *Fear and Trembling,* and John Stuart Mill's *Three Essays on Religion.* More recent discussions of the relationship between religion and morality include *Religion and Morality: A Collection of Essays,* edited by John P. Reeder, Jr., and Gene H. Outka (New York, 1973), W. G. Maclagen's *The Theological Frontier of Ethics* (New York, 1961), and W. W. Bartley II's *Morality and Religion* (New York, 1971). Contemporary ethical theory comprises a large domain of views. Good, brief treatments of a number of basic issues can be found in G. J. Warnock's *The Object of Morality* (London, 1971), in William K. Frankena's *Ethics,* 2d ed. (Englewood Cliffs, N. J., 1973), and in Paul W. Taylor's *Principles of Ethics: An Introduction* (Encino, Calif., 1975). Among widely regarded contemporary rationalist approaches to normative ethical theory are Kurt Baier's *The Moral Point of View* (Ithaca, N. Y., 1958), John Rawls's *A Theory of Justice* (Cambridge, Mass., 1971), Bernard Gert's *The Moral Rules* (New York, 1970), and Alan Gewirth's *Reason and Morality* (Chicago, 1978). For treatments of some key moral issues related to religious ethics, see the collections *Ethical Relativism,* edited by John Ladd (Belmont, Calif., 1973), and *Supererogation: Its Status in Ethical Theory,* by David Heyd (New York, 1982).

Much Western thinking about the relationship between religion and morality has focused on the question of whether morality may be based on a divine command. Two recent collections gather together many of the classical and contemporary discussions of this issue: *Divine Command Morality,* edited by Janine Marie Idziak (Lewiston, N. Y., 1980), and *Divine Commands and Morality,* edited by Paul Helms (Oxford, 1981).

Unfortunately, while there are a number of good specific discussions of Christian, Jewish, Hindu, or Buddhist ethics, relatively little work has been done on the comparative analysis of religious traditions in a way comprising not just their specific normative teachings but also their doctrines of retribution and their fundamental ways of relating ethics to other features of the religious life. Two classic discussions in this area are Edward A. Westermarck's *The Origin and Development of the Moral Ideas,* 2 vols., 2d ed. (London, 1924), and his *Christianity and Morals* (1939; reprint, Freeport, N. Y., 1969). These works provide a wealth of information about the moral and religious beliefs of preliterate and literate cultures, though the moral perspective is colored by Westermarck's moral relativism. Even more systematic comparative discussion of specific traditions can be found in Max Weber's pioneering studies of 1915-1919: *Ancient Judaism* (Glencoe, Ill., 1952), *The Religion of India: The Sociology of Hinduism and Buddhism* (Glencoe, Ill., 1958), and *The Religion of China: Confucianism and Taoism* (Glencoe, Ill., 1951), all translated and edited by Hans H. Gerth and Don Martindale. More recent treatments of comparative ethics include my own study *Religious Reason* (Oxford, 1978) and David Little and Sumner B. Twiss, Jr.'s *Comparative Religious Ethics: A New Method* (San Francisco, 1978).

RONALD M. GREEN

MORAVIANS

The Moravian church, as the Unitas Fratrum (Unity of Brethren) is popularly known, is a Protestant denomination with roots in the fifteenth-century Hussite reformation and the eighteenth-century German Pietist movement. By the late nineteenth century, these influences had coalesced to give the denomination its contemporary form and character.

The Unity of Brethren was founded in March 1457 in Kunwald, Bohemia as the Jednota Bratrská ("Society of Brethren"), but the issues behind this event stretch back more than a century. From the mid-fourteenth century there had been growing demands for reform within the Roman Catholic church of Bohemia and neighboring Moravia. The reform movement was centered in the capital city of Prague and the newly established Charles University (1348). Persistent Waldensian influences as well as newer Wyclifite influences from England were evident in this movement.

The calls for reform finally found their most eloquent voice in Jan Hus, priest, university professor, and popular preacher. Although attracted to the doctrines of Wyclif, Hus claimed to advocate independently a return to apostolic simplicity in the church, and he vigorously attacked the lax morality of the clergy. As Hus's popularity increased, so did controversy about his ideas and his difficulties with the hierarchy. He was excommunicated by Pope John XXIII in 1411 but eventually appealed his case to the Council of Constance then in session. After his trial, deemed irregular by later historians, he was burned at the stake on 6 July 1415 as a heretic.

Hus's death served to arouse his followers in Bohemia. His ideas soon became entwined with a developing Bohemian nationalism, and Hus himself became something of a folk hero. When civil war erupted, a series of unsuccessful crusades were launched, with the blessings of the

> **The traditions of the Brethren survived in Bohemia and Moravia through secret meetings and the laxity of government officials in enforcing conformity.**

papacy, in an attempt to subdue the heretics. Among the most ardent Bohemians, highly respected for their military zeal, were a group of radical religious and political reformers headquartered in the town of Tabor. Although they were destroyed as a separate party by the late 1430s, many of their religious ideas lingered on in the population. Bohemia's political situation would remain unstable for a century after Hus's death until 1526, when the crown was acquired by the Habsburg Ferdinand I.

Upheavals occurred also in the religious life of the Bohemians and Moravians as several groups claiming the heritage of Hus emerged alongside the Roman Catholic church. One such group, the Utraquists, represented a conservative attempt at reformation, finally insisting only on the right of all believers to receive the bread and wine at Communion and continuing to hope for a reunion with a purified Roman Catholic church. It was the Utraquist archbishop-elect Jan z Rokycan (c. 1390-1471) whose preaching inspired one of the founders of the Brethren, his nephew Gregory (d. 1474), to pursue more vigorously the goal of reformation. Jan z Rokycan also introduced Gregory to the writings of the radical reformer Petr Chelcicky (c. 1380-c. 1460).

Within ten years of the founding of their society, the Brethren felt the need to establish their own clerical orders to insure the efficaciousness of their ministry. They chose deacons, presbyters, and bishops from among their membership. One of the candidates was a former Roman Catholic

priest, and some Waldensians may have participated in the establishment of the new orders. Modern historians see in these events an attempt by the Brethren to reconstitute the style of ministry of the New Testament church. Any attempt by the Brethren to claim apostolic succession as traditionally understood must be laid to a faulty reading of Waldensian history on their part. The orders established in 1467 have been carried on into the contemporary Moravian church.

The first decades of the Brethren organization were marked by sectarian characteristics including pacifism, rejection of oaths, communal organization, use of the titles "Brother" and "Sister" for all members, suspicion of advanced education, reluctance to admit members of the nobility to membership, and a preference for rural living. This trend was reversed under the leadership of Bishop Luke of Prague (c. 1460-1528), who succeeded in 1494 in having the works of Chelcicky and Gregory reduced to nondogmatic status. The group gave up much of their exclusiveness and moved into the mainstream of society, though not without the defection of a conservative minority. The majority, although retaining a strict church discipline, grew rapidly. It has been estimated that by the 1520s there were from 150,000 to 200,000 members located in 400 congregations in Bohemia and Moravia.

Under the leadership of such bishops as Jan Augusta (1500-1572) and Jan Blahoslav (1523-1571), the Brethren maintained generally friendly contacts with Luther (who wrote favorably about them) and later with leaders of the Reformed churches. Although ecumenical in spirit and experiencing strong influences from first Lutheran and later Reformed theology, the Brethren maintained their own course. They structured their church with dioceses headed by bishops, abandoned clerical celibacy, and eventually accepted a general Reformed understanding of the sacraments of baptism and the Eucharist.

In worship, while ritual was simplified, the church year was retained and lay involvement encouraged through the publication of hymnals and the Czech-language Kralitz Bible (1579-1593) in six volumes with commentary. The church sponsored schools and encouraged the training of clergy in foreign universities.

Since their legal status was often in doubt, the Brethren endured periodic persecutions by the Utraquists and the Roman Catholics. But they continued to maintain their vitality and established congregations in Poland, which later merged with the Reformed church.

The involvement in political affairs of members who were of the nobility helped to bring about disastrous consequences for the Brethren in the opening phase of the Thirty Years' War (1618-1648). With the defeat of the Protestant forces at the Battle of the White Mountain (1620), suppression of Protestantism in Bohemia and Moravia began. The events of this era are highlighted in the career of Bishop Johannes Amos Comenius (1592-1670), the renowned educational theorist. He spent much of his life in exile developing his reforms of education and despite several personal tragedies never lost his belief in the power of the educated mind to serve God's purposes for humanity.

The traditions of the Brethren survived in Bohemia and Moravia through secret meetings and the laxity of government officials in enforcing conformity. Sporadic contacts with Lutherans in border areas also helped to sustain morale.

A group of these secret Brethren were led in 1722 to the German estate of Count Nikolaus Zinzendorf (1700-1760) by the lay evangelist Christian David (1690-1751). There they established the village of Herrnhut. A creative theologian and gifted leader, Zinzendorf became the driving force behind the merger of the Brethren's traditions with the emphases of the Pietist movement.

After initial difficulties, the growing community experienced a series of unifying experiences in the summer of 1727, culminating in a service of Holy Communion on 13 August. The fellowship now developed the unique characteristics that would mark its second phase. The residents were organized into residential groups based on age, sex, and marital status ("the choirs"). The intent was to foster spiritual experience appropriate to one's stage in life and to utilize the resources of a concentrated labor force. From Zinzendorf's Christocentric emphasis flowed a rich liturgical life with stress upon the Advent-Christmas and Holy Week-Easter cycles. The Moravian understanding of the joyous nature of the relationship between the believer and the Savior enabled them to develop education and the arts in his praise, sponsoring schools and producing musicians and artists of note. The Brethren's clerical orders were continued through new ordinations by the two remaining bishops in exile. Since the church developed a conferential form of government, however, the bishops became primarily spiritual leaders.

Worship was characterized by a simplified liturgical ritual that observed the festivals of the Christian calendar with particular attention to the Advent-Christmas and Holy Week-Easter cycles. Unique features included the singing of many hymns, with the minister clad in a surplice for the celebration of the sacraments of baptism and Holy Communion. The Lovefeast, patterned after the agape meals of the early Christians, developed as a significant service. In it participants were served a simple meal as an expression of their fellowship with one another.

Under the leadership of Zinzendorf and his *de facto* successor Bishop Augustus Gottlieb Spangenberg (1703-1792), Herrnhut became the model for some twenty similar communities established in Europe, England, and the eastern United States. These self-sufficient "settlement congregations" were to serve as the home base for two types of outreach developed by the Brethren.

Beginning in 1727 the Moravians sent forth members to serve in their "diaspora" through establishing Pietist renewal societies within existing state churches. This practice is supported by European Moravians today. In 1732, after Zinzendorf's presentation of the plight of the West Indian slaves to the community, the Brethren Leonard Dober (1706-1766) and David Nitschmann (1696-1772) went to Saint Thomas. By 1760 the Moravians had sent out 226 missionaries to the non-European world. This effort introduced into Protestantism the idea that missionary outreach is the responsibility of the whole church, brought the Moravians into significant ecumenical contacts, such as that with John Wesley (1703-1791) in Georgia and England, and helped shape the contemporary Moravian church.

By the mid-nineteenth century, the settlement congregations were given up as no longer viable and the towns opened to all who wished to settle in them. German and Scandinavian immigration to North America in the last century brought new Moravian congregations into being in the eastern and midwestern United States and western Canada. The end of World War II found Herrnhut and the older settlements in East Germany and, through the movement of refugees, a stronger Moravian presence in western Europe. Immigration continues to affect the Moravian church through the recent movements of Surinamese members to the Netherlands and Caribbean-area members to cities in England and North America.

The Moravians have also experienced constitutional changes as they have moved beyond their European origins. The British and American areas of the church gained independence from the German in the mid-nineteenth century, but the foreign missions continued under control of an international board that met in Germany until the end of World War I. Responsibility for the work was then divided among the European, British, and American areas of the church. A major constitutional change in 1957 resulted in the creation of the present seventeen autonomous provinces located in Europe, England, North America, Central America, and Africa, and the undertaking of educational work in India and Israel. The provinces constitute the "Moravian Unity" and send delegates to periodic meetings of the "Unity Synod." The late twentieth century has witnessed the rapid growth of the church in Africa and Central America. In America, the Moravian church did not experience significant growth until after the mid-nineteenth century. Earlier attempts at "diaspora"-style outreach had proved unsuited to America, since there was no religious establishment within which to work. Groups gathered by "diaspora" workers simply became congregations of other denominations. The retention of the exclusive settlement congregations until the 1840s also retarded outreach.

The church has continued to honor many of its traditions of worship and practice. While eschewing a formal dogmatic theological tradition of its own, it affirms the historic creeds of the Christian faith, continues to emphasize the believer's relationship with Christ, and to encourage fellowship among its members. Both men and women are ordained as pastors. The church's historical ecumenical stance is reflected in its participation as a founding member of the World Council of Churches and in the activities of the various provinces in regional councils of churches. Total membership recorded in December 1982 was 457,523.

BIBLIOGRAPHY

The most comprehensive bibliography for the early history of the Moravians is Jarold K. Zeman's *The Hussite Movement and the Reformation in Bohemia, Moravia and Slovakia, 1350-1650: A Bibliographical Study Guide* (Ann Arbor, 1977). Peter Brock discusses *The Political and Social Doctrines of the Unity of Czech Brethren in the Fifteenth and Early Sixteenth Centuries* (The Hague, 1957), while the whole history of the early Moravians is dealt with in Edmund A. De Schweinitz's old but comprehensive *History of the Church Known as the Unitas Fratrum or the Unity of the Brethren*, 2d ed., by Edmund A. De Schweinitz (Bethlehem, Pa., 1901). The later history of the church is found in J. Taylor Hamilton and Kenneth G. Hamilton's *History of the Moravian Church: The Renewed Unitas Fratrum, 1722-1957* (Bethlehem, Pa., 1967). The best recent biographies of central figures in Moravian church history include two works by Matthew Spinka: *John Hus: A Biography* (Princeton, 1968) *and John Amos Comenius: That Incomparable Moravian* (Chicago, 1943). Zinzendorf is the subject of John R. Weinlick's *Count Zinzendorf* (Nashville, 1956) and Arthur J. Lewis's *Zinzendorf: The Ecumenical Pioneer* (Philadelphia, 1962).

DAVID A. SCHATTSCHNEIDER

MORMONISM

The religious movement popularly known as Mormonism encompasses several denominations and sects, the largest of which is the Church of Jesus Christ of Latter-day Saints with headquarters in Salt Lake City, Utah. The second-largest organization, with headquarters in Independence, Missouri, is the Reorganized Church of Jesus Christ of Latter Day Saints.

Mormonism had its beginnings in western New York in the 1820s when a mingling of spiritual and physical developments left many Americans bewildered and confused. Among those passed by in the rush for progress was Joseph Smith. According to a later, official church account, it was in the spring of 1820 that the boy, aged fourteen, retired to a grove on his father's farm, where he prayed for divine guidance. In a vision he beheld God the Father and Jesus Christ and was told to join none of the existing denominations, for they were "all wrong."

As young Joseph matured, he had a number of subsequent visions and revelations. In preparation for this restoration, he was directed by an angel to unearth a set of golden records from a hill near his parents' farm. He then translated these records with divine aid and published them in 1830 as the *Book of Mormon,* a sacred history of three groups of pre-Columbian migrants to America, including the ancestors of the American Indians. According to the *Book of Mormon,* Christ had visited the inhabitants of the Western Hemisphere after his crucifixion, taught the gospel, and instituted a church "to the convincing of the Jew and Gentile that Jesus is the Christ, the Eternal God, manifesting himself to all nations." Although accepted as scripture by believing Mormons and popularly called the Mormon bible by nonbelievers, Smith regarded the *Book of Mormon* as a supplement rather than a substitute for the Bible.

Although the new religion called Church of Jesus Christ of Latter-Day Saints initially met with skepticism and persecution, it succeeded in attracting a substantial following among restorationists who saw in Mormonism the fulfillment of the awaited return of the true church of Christ, led by a divinely ordained priesthood. Perhaps the most prominent and influential of these converts was Sidney Rigdon, who brought virtually his entire Ohio congregation over to the new religion, thus inducing Smith and most of his New York followers to establish a Mormon settlement in 1831 in Kirtland, Ohio. It was there that Smith greatly amplified and broadened his theological and organizational principles in a series of revelations first published in 1833 as the *Book of Commandments* and later enlarged into the canonical *Doctrine and Covenants.* The Saints were enjoined to gather in communities as God's chosen people under an egalitarian economic order called the Law of Consecration and Stewardship and to build a temple that was, literally and symbolically, the sacred center of the community.

These innovations began to arouse the hostility of non-Mormons. The Saints were forced to leave Kirtland in 1838, primarily because of opposition to their kingdom. Internal conflict also intensified as Smith continued to move beyond his early restorationist impulse in favor of a kingdom of God that achieved its fullest expression in Nauvoo. Nauvoo, a settlement founded in 1839 for refugees from Missouri, had become Illinois's largest city, with a population of about eleven thousand by 1844. It was a city under the full religious, social, economic, and political control of the Mormon kingdom.

The success of Nauvoo may well have led Smith to overreach himself. He assumed the leadership of the Mormon militia and announced his candidacy for the presidency of the United States. A group of alarmed anti-Mormons effectively capitalized on internal dissent and formed a mob that killed Smith and his brother Hyrum on 27 June 1844.

History has shown the killers of the Mormon prophet wrong in thinking that they had delivered a mortal blow to Mormonism. As early as 1834, Smith had organized some of his most loyal lieutenants into a council of twelve apostles in restorationist emulation of the primitive church. In 1840, Brigham Young became president of this powerful and prestigious group. It was in this capacity that he was sustained as leader by those Mormons who had unquestioningly accepted Smith's Nauvoo innovations. Most of those devotees followed Young to Great Salt Lake in July 1847 and immediately began to survey a site for a city, with a temple at the center. Aided by a steady stream of immigrants, Young built an inland empire including Utah and parts of Idaho, Wyoming, Arizona, and Nevada that boasted a population of over one hundred thousand by the time of his death in 1877.

When the Saints voted on 6 October 1890 to jettison some of their most distinctive institutions and beliefs—economic communitarianism, plural marriage, and the political kingdom—they followed their erstwhile evangelical adversaries into the pluralistic American cultural mainstream, joining what historian Martin Marty has called "a nation of behavers." In search of new boundaries and symbols of identification, the Mormons, much like the evangelicals, adopted strict codes of behavior: abstinence from alcohol, tobacco, tea and coffee; acceptance of regulated dress norms; adherence to a strict code of sexual morality.

Mormons found these values equally congenial in their own adaptation to a competitive, individualistic social and economic order, and they prepared the rising generation to meet this change. Religious commitment thus became a springboard for social and economic success in the world, which was further facilitated by the Mormons' increasing commitment to education; nearly thirty thousand Latter-day Saints attended Brigham Young University by 1984, and many thousands more were studying at secular universities throughout the United States and the Western world. Mormons serve in prominent positions in the federal government, in the military, in major business corporations, and in major universities.

Mormonism continues to appeal to many socially and culturally disoriented members of society. They are attracted by a lay church that offers active participation to all of its members and provides an instant, socially cohesive group whose authoritarian male leaders set boundaries while providing recognition for behavior that conforms to group standards. Many converts are especially drawn to the Mormon family ideal.

BIBLIOGRAPHY

For more than a century, studies of Mormonism were highly polemical, divided by a simple dichotomy between believers and nonbelievers. The first sophisticated modern study of Mormonism was by Catholic sociologist Thomas F. O'Dea, *The Mormons* (Chicago, 1957). For factual detail, the most comprehensive and reliable scholarly account is that of James B. Allen and Glen M. Leonard, *The Story of the Latter-day Saints* (Salt Lake City, 1976). An interpretive synthesis from a scholarly Mormon perspective is

Leonard J. Arrington and Davis Bitton's *The Mormon Experience: A History of the Latter-day Saints* (New York, 1979). A useful overview of the Reorganized Church is Inez Smith Davis's *The Story of the Church* (Independence, Mo., 1964). This should be supplemented by Alma R. Blair's "Reorganized Church of Jesus Christ of Latter Day Saints: Moderate Mormonism," in *The Restoration Movement: Essays in Mormon History,* edited by F. Mark McKiernan et al. (Lawrence, Kans., 1973), pp. 207-230. Mark P. Leone's *Roots of Modern Mormonism* (Cambridge, Mass., 1979), though offering an insightful and stimulating anthropological perspective, overemphasizes the flexibility of modern Mormonism. My own *Mormonism and the American Experience* (Chicago, 1981) attempts to place Mormonism in the broader context of American culture. Jan Shipps's *Mormonism: The Story of a New Religious Tradition* (Urbana, Ill., 1984) is written from the perspective of a sympathetic non-Mormon scholar; hers is the most successful attempt to transcend the polemical dichotomy.

KLAUS J. HANSEN

MOSES

Literary Tradition. The traditions about Moses are contained in the Peutateuch from *Exodus* to *Deuteronomy,* and all other biblical references to Moses are probably dependent upon these. The view of most critical scholars for the past century has been that the Pentateuch's presentation of Moses is not the result of a single author but the combination of at least four sources, known as the Yahvist (J), the Elohist (E), Deuteronomy (D), and the Priestly writer (P), and composed in that order. A long period of time separates any historical figure from the written presentation of Moses in the Bible. To bridge this gap one is faced with evaluating the diversity of traditions within the Moses legend and with tracing their history of transmission prior to their use by the later authors, as well as with considering the shape and color the authors themselves gave to the Moses tradition as a reflection of their own times and concerns.

Moses as deliverer from Egypt. The general background for the deliverance of the people through Moses is the theme of the oppression and enslavement in Egypt.

Within the tradition of enslavement the JE writer introduces a special theme of attempted genocide (*Ex.* 1:8-22), which provides the context for the story of Moses' birth and his rescue from the Nile by the Egyptian princess (*Ex.* 2:1-10). But once this story is told, the theme of genocide disappears, and the issue becomes again that of enslavement and hard labor. The story of Moses as a threatened child rescued from the basket of reeds and reared under the very nose of Pharaoh to become the deliverer of his people corresponds to a very common folkloric motif of antiquity.

The story of Moses' experience of the burning bush theophany at Sinai/Horeb, in the land of Midian (*Ex.* 3-4), has all the marks of a new beginning. It resembles that of the prophetic-call narratives in which the prophet experiences a theophany and then is given his commission (*Is.* 6, *Ez.* 1-3). The primary concern in the dialogue between Moses and Yahveh is in Moses' role as a spokesman whom the people will believe and who can speak on behalf of the people to the foreign ruler. The author (JE) has drawn upon both the tradition of classical prophecy and the literary history of Gideon and Saul to fashion his rather composite presentation of Moses' call and commission as Israel's deliverer.

The climax of Israel's deliverance is at the Red Sea (*Ex.* 13:17-14:31), and here again Moses' role is to announce judgment on the Egyptians and salvation for Israel. In the JE account Moses and Israel do nothing but witness the divine rescue, while in the P version Moses, at God's command, splits the sea with his rod to create a path for the Israelites and, again at divine command, makes the sea come back upon their pursuers. It is remarkable that except for one late addition to *Deuteronomy* (11:4) there are no references to the Red Sea event in this source even though the Exodus is mentioned many times. This suggests that the Red Sea episode is really secondary to the Exodus tradition.

Moses as leader. Apart from an initial contact with Israel's elders in Egypt, which did not turn out very well (*Ex.* 5), Moses' direct leadership of the people begins only when they depart from Egypt. As their leader he is the one to whom the people complain about their hardships in the wilderness. But it is always God who meets their needs, with manna from heaven, or quails, or water from a rock.

On a few occasions the Israelites are involved in military encounters, but Moses' role in these is very limited. Moses appears to lead the forces in the D account, but in JE he recedes into the background. Moses is not a military hero in these traditions.

Moses as lawgiver. The theme of Moses as lawgiver is more closely associated with the theophany at Sinai/Horeb (*Ex.* 19-20, *Dt.* 4-5), and with the prolonged stay at the mountain of God, during which the Law was given to Israel through Moses. Many scholars have argued that the giving of the Law at Sinai originated as a separate tradition.

Nevertheless Moses has often been viewed as the author of the Ten Commandments. But the two forms, in *Deuteronomy* 5 and *Exodus* 20, are in the sources D and P respectively, and their language is so characteristic of D that there seems little reason to believe that they are any older than the seventh century BCE.

Moses as the Founder of Israelite Religion. Many scholars believe that Moses is the founder of Israel's religion, at least in the form of a worship of Yahveh alone and, ultimately, in the form of monotheism. This position is based upon a number of arguments. The P source explicitly states (*Ex.* 6:2-3) that the name of Yahveh was not known before the time of Moses and that the forefathers worshiped God as El Shaddai. In Genesis there are also frequent references to

forms of El worship among the patriarchs. Yet the JE corpus clearly regards the patriarchs as worshipers of Yahveh and the El epithets as merely titles for Yahveh. This and other aspects of the Moses tradition continue to heat debate about his place in Isrealite Religion.

Rabbinic view of Moses. The rabbinic tradition represents a vast array of sources from the second century to the Middle Ages, containing a wide spectrum of belief and opinion.

In the legal tradition (*halakhah*) Moses represents the great "teacher" by which Israel was instructed in the Torah. This includes not only the laws of the Pentateuch but all the subsequent oral Torah, which was handed down from Moses to Joshua and in succession to the rabbis. All students of the law were really disciples of Moses. The homiletic tradition (*aggadah*) brought to the fore those other aspects of the Moses tradition that were a part of Jewish piety. It continued to embellish the biography of Moses as the "man of God," but more central is his role as the servant of God.

There is also a tradition within the *aggadah* about Moses' heavenly ascent at Sinai that elaborates on his vision of God and his struggles with the angels to acquire the Torah for Israel. There was a certain reticence expressed by some rabbis toward this form of piety and the rather speculative character of its traditions.

Moses in the New Testament. The New Testament accepts Moses as the author of the Pentateuch (*Mt.* 8:4, *Mk.* 7:10, *Jn.* 1:17), but the real significance of the Pentateuch is as a prophecy that discloses the origins of Christianity (*Lk.* 24:25-27). Yet the whole of the institutional and ritual forms of Judaism as well as the Pharisaic-rabbinic tradition is associated with Moses, so that Moses reflects the ambivalent feelings of Christianity's continuity and discontinuity with Judaism.

Moses in Islam. Moses is highly regarded in Islam as the great prophet who foretold the coming of Muhammad, his successor. Details about Moses' life from the *aggadah* are to be found in the Qur'an, but there are additional details with parallels from folklore as well as borrowed from other biblical stories and applied to Moses (see especially surah 28:4-43; also 7:104-158, 20:10-98, 26:11-69).

BIBLIOGRAPHY

The vast literature on the figure of Moses makes any selection difficult. The following list is an attempt to provide a fairly broad range of scholarly opinion on this subject. Some general treatments of the life and work of Moses, based upon a critical appraisal of the biblical traditions, are Elias Auerbach's *Moses* (Amsterdam, 1953), translated from the German and edited by Robert A. Barclay and Israel O. Lehman as *Moses* (Detroit, 1975); Fred V. Winnett's *The Mosaic Tradition* (Toronto, 1949); Martin Buber's *Moses: The Revelation and the Covenant* (Oxford, 1946); and a more technical monograph by Herbert Schmid, *Mose: Überlieferung und Geschichte,* "Bei-hefte zur Zeitschrift für die alttestamentliche Wissenschaft," no. 110 (Berlin,

1968). A classical and still very influential study of the biblical traditions is the one by Hugo Gressmann, *Mose und seine Zeit: Ein Kommentar zu den Mose-sagen* (Göttingen, 1913).

The history of modern research on Moses is treated in Eva Osswald's *Das Bild des Moses in der kritischen alttestamentlichen Wissenschaft seit Julius Wellhausen,* "Theologische Arbeiten," vol. 18 (Berlin, 1962); and R. J. Thompson's *Moses and the Law in a Century of Criticism since Graf,* "Supplements to Vetus Testamentum," vol. 19 (Leiden, 1970).

On the question of Moses' place in history see Roland de Vaux's *Historie ancienne d'Israël* (Paris, 1971), which has been translated by David Smith as *The Early History of Israel* (Philadelphia, 1978); John Bright's *A History of Israel,* 3d ed. (Philadelphia, 1981); and Siegfried Herrmann's *Israels Aufenhalt in Ägypten* (Stuttgart, 1970), translated by Margaret Kohl as *Israel in Egypt* (London, 1973).

Two works that deal with the way in which Moses is used as a paradigm for certain religious and political roles are Gerhard von Rad's *Moses* (New York, 1960) and J. R. Porter's *Moses and Monarchy: A Study in the Biblical Tradition of Moses* (Oxford, 1963). A book that is especially helpful for the treatment of Moses in Judaism, Christianity, and Islam is a collection of essays published under the title *Moïse, l'homme de l'alliance* (Paris, 1955). On the *aggadah,* see especially Louis Ginzberg's *The Legends of the Bible* (New York, 1956), pp. 277-506. This book is an abridgment of the earlier work *The Legends of the Jews,* 7 vols., translated by Henrietta Szold et al. (1909-1938). On Moses in the New Testament and early Judaism, see also Wayne A. Meeks's *The Prophet-King: Moses Traditions and the Johannine Christology* (Leiden, 1967).

JOHN VAN SETERS

MOSQUE

History and Tradition

Name. The word *mosque,* anglicized from the French *mosquée,* comes through the Spanish *mezquita* from the Arabic *masjid,* meaning "a place where one prostrates oneself [in front of God]." The term *masjid* (same in Persian, Urdu, and Turkish) was already found in Aramaic, where it was used in reference to Nabatean and Abyssinian sacred places; it was also a common word in pre-Islamic Arabia.

The *masjid* is frequently mentioned in the Qur'an (principally 2:144, 9:17-18, 9:107-108, 22:40, 62:1, 72:17); there it is applied generally to sanctuaries where God is worshiped but does not refer to a specifically new kind of Muslim building. Whenever a precisely Muslim identification was needed, the term was used in a compound construct, as in *masjid al-haram* in Mecca or *masjid al-aqsa* in Jerusalem. A celebrated *hadith* ("tradition") indicates that a *masjid* exists wherever one prays and thus makes the existence of a Muslim building unnecessary. However, all Muslims are obliged to perform prayers collectively once a week on Fridays at noon, when they also swear allegiance to the Prophet's successor. The great mosque in which the community (*jama`ah*) of wor-

shipers attended the Friday (*jum`ah*) service took the name *masjid al-jama`ah,* or *masjid al-jum`ah,* or *masjid al-jami`* ("place of assembly"), usually called simply *al-jami`.* Subsequently, the word *jami`* has been reserved for large congregational mosques where the Friday *khutbah* ("sermon") is delivered, whereas the word *masjid* refers to small private mosques of daily prayer (with the exception of the mosques of Mecca, Medina, and Jerusalem, which have kept their traditional Qur'anic names of *masjids*). This distinction is still clearly observed in Turkey where the respective terms are correctly used.

Definition. In simple terms, the mosque is a building large enough to contain the community of the believers, laid out with a covered space for prayer and an open space for gatherings, and oriented toward Mecca. The structure, in spite of chronological developments and stylistic and regional variations, has remained unchanged in its essentials. All mosques are built on an axis oriented in the direction of Mecca, the focus of prayer established in the Qur'an (2:139).

> **All mosques are built on an axis oriented in the direction of Mecca, the focus of prayer established in the Qur'an.**

They all have a prayer hall parallel to the wall of the *qiblah* (the direction of Mecca) where Muslim men, on an egalitarian basis, rich or poor, noble or humble, stand in rows to perform their prayers behind the imam. Women, who are expected to say prayers at home, may join in certain mosques but are expected to use a separate place specially screened off for them. Otherwise, Muslim men from all four Sunni legal schools (Shafi`i, Hanafi, Maliki, and Hanbali) go to the same mosque. Shi`i Muslims, on the other hand, pray in mosques of their own.

The building proper has few characteristic symbols that identify it with the requirements of the faith: on the outside, a fountain for ablutions is provided so the Muslims can pray in ritual cleanliness, and a minaret serves to call the believers for prayer, while inside, a small, empty niche (*mihrab*) in the center of the *qiblah* wall indicates the direction of prayer, and in communal Friday mosques (*jami`s*) a pulpit (*minbar*) is placed to the right of the *mihrab* for the prayer leader (*khatib*) to deliver his sermon. Other optional features are an enclosed area for the ruler (*maqsurah*), the respondent's platform (*dikkah*), and a cantor's lectern (*kursi*).

It must be stressed that the mosque is not an exclusively religious space. Rather, like the Greek agora or the Roman forum, the court of the mosque has also been the favored place of public assembly, where the Friday *khutbah* has always addressed issues of politics, war, religion, and so forth, the community has acclaimed caliphs and governors, judges have held court, the treasury has been kept, and teaching has taken place.

Officials. Historically, mosques have been maintained through endowed properties (*waqf*, pl. *awqaf*) administered by a warden *(nazir)* who also oversees the management of the mosque's finances and the appointment of its staff. Since Islam has no clergy and no liturgy, mosque officials are few in number and their functions are simple and clear.

1. The imam, or prayer leader, is the most important appointee. In the early days the ruler himself filled this role; he was leader *(imam)* of the government, of war, and of the common *salat* ("ritual prayer"). Under the Abbasids, when the caliph no longer conducted prayers on a regular basis, a paid imam was appointed. While any prominent or learned Muslim can have the honor of leading prayers, each mosque specifically appoints a man well versed in theological matters to act as its imam. He is in charge of the religious activities of the mosque, and it is his duty to conduct prayers five times a day in front of the *mihrab*. The office is not a profession, for an imam usually has another occupation, such as judge, schoolteacher, or shopkeeper, and the title remains with the job rather than the person.

2. The *khatib*, or preacher of the Friday sermon, is also a religious appointee. The office, like that of the imam, evolved when the Abbasid caliph no longer delivered *khutbahs* on Fridays. A man learned in religious matters was appointed to represent the ruler. *Qadis* ("judges") have been frequently chosen as *khatibs*, and the office is usually hereditary. In large mosques, a number of *khatibs* are appointed to relieve one another, while in smaller mosques the offices of *khatib* and imam can be combined. Besides the *khatib*, the *wa`iz* and the *qass* act as edifying preachers without set forms.

3. The muezzin *(mu'adhdhin)* announces to the faithful the five daily prayers and the Friday noon service. According to tradition, the *adhan* ("announcement") was instituted in the first year of the Muslim era, and Bilal, the Prophet's freed Abyssinian servant (known for his sweet voice), was the first muezzin to convoke the believers to prayer. Originally called out from the top of the mosque, the *adhan* quickly acquired a formal locale in the *ma'dhanah* (minaret). Until the twentieth century, the muezzin climbed to the top of the minaret five times a day to issue the call to prayer, but with the introduction of electrical loudspeakers and recorded *adhans*, the highly developed art of the muezzin is no longer a prerequisite. The muezzins, whose office has sometimes been hereditary, are organized under chiefs *(ru'asa')* who are next to the imam in importance. At times they also perform the role of *muwaqqit*, the astronomer who ascertains the *qiblah*.

Institutions. In early times, mosque construction was viewed as an obligation of the ruler, but with the spread of Islam, governors assumed that role in the provinces and were followed by private individuals. Once the building of

mosques came to be regarded as a religious and social obligation—one *hadith* reported that the Prophet said, "For him who builds a mosque, God will build a home in Paradise"—and as a reflection of prestige, their number increased dramatically. Chronicles and travelers report, for instance, 3,000 mosques for tenth-century Baghdad, 300 for tenth-century Palermo, 241 for twelfth-century Damascus, and 12,000 for fourteenth-century Alexandria.

In addition to its religious and political functions, the mosque had always served as a center of administrative, legal, and educational activity. While the actual work of government was transferred early on from the mosque to a special *diwan* ("office") or *majlis* ("council"), matters of public finance continued to be transacted at the mosque, and the community treasury *(bayt al-mal)* was kept there. Similarly, in the time of the Prophet, legal questions were settled in the mosque; as early as 644/5 the *qadi* of Fustat held his sessions in the mosque, and in tenth-century Damascus the vice-*qadi* occupied a special *riwaq* ("aisle") in the court of the Umayyad mosque. When the judges officially moved to law courts, the mosque remained the center of legal studies. Finally, the mosque has served as the most continuous center of education in Islam, with study circles *(halaqat)* traditionally gathering around the teachers in the courtyard and at the base of columns. Some mosques, such as that of al-Mansur in Baghdad or those in Isfahan, Mashhad, Qom, Damascus, and Cairo, became centers of learning for students from all over the world. Teaching in mosques continued even after the proliferation of *madrasahs* where permanent, state-approved, and state-financed teaching took place. In modern times, the political, administrative, social, and educational functions of the community mosque have been taken over by specialized institutions.

BIBLIOGRAPHY

The classic and most comprehensive study remains Johannes Pedersen's article "Masdjid," in *The Encyclopaedia of Islam* (Leiden, 1913-1936); the basic study of the monument is Jean Sauvaget's *La mosquée omeyyade de Médine* (Paris, 1947); and a brief survey is Lucien Golvin's *La mosquée* (Algiers, 1969). For more recent discussions of the mosque, see the following interesting summaries and explanations: Oleg Grabar's "Islamic Religious Art: The Mosque," in his *The Formation of Islamic Art* (New Haven, 1973), and "The Architecture of the Middle Eastern City from Past to Present: The Case of the Mosque," in *Middle Eastern Cities*, edited by Ira Lapidus (Berkeley, 1979); J. S. Thomine's "La mosquée et la madrasa," *Cahiers de civilisation médiévale* 13 (1970): 97-115; and James Dickie's "Allah and Eternity: Mosques, Madrasahs and Tombs," in *Architecture of the Islamic World*, edited by George Michell (London, 1978).

HAYAT SALAM-LIEBICH

Architectural Aspects

Liturgical Elements. The obligation to perform prayers is of seminal importance for the form of the mosque. The ritualized prayer *(salat)*, a sequence of standing, kneeling, and prostrating postures, is repeated five times daily and performed facing the spiritual center of the Muslim world, the Ka`bah in Mecca. This orientation, the *qiblah*, is the central organizing feature of the mosque. The singular importance of the *qiblah* was evidenced in the practice of Muhammad's armies when out in the field. At the hour of prayer a long line at right angles to the direction of Mecca was drawn in the sand, and ranks of soldiers lined up behind it to pray. As the first row of worshipers enjoyed greater proximity to Mecca, the source of blessing, the tendency was for the line to be broadly drawn. In the mosque likewise, the sanctuary was wide and shallow, in contrast to the narrow and deep configuration of the Christian church. The *qiblah* wall, the broad one turned toward Mecca, marked by an elaborate niche *(mihrab)* in its center, is the architectural culmination and focus of the entire mosque.

Prayer also requires an open, ritually purified floor area. Thus the simplest places of prayer *(musallas)*, used for large outdoor gatherings, are merely open areas with an indicated *qiblah* line or wall. Worshipers bring their own mats or prayer rugs to maintain ritual cleanliness and to define their individual space. For the same reason mosque interiors are generally carpeted and require baring the feet to avoid ritual defilement. To keep interior space open toward the *qiblah* wall, multiple-columned or "hypostyle" halls were the earliest and still prominent solution. Such halls can easily be expanded with additional rows of columns to accommodate a growing population. The hypostyle hall also reflects the equality of supplicants in prayer; lacking a priesthood, the mosques long maintained a communal rather than a hieratic organization. As the diversity of congregations grew, interiors were often elaborated with specially configured rows of pillars or ancillary *mihrab* niches spatially distinguishing areas for the different groups and quarters of the town.

Though prayer is often performed in isolation, the celebration of the *ummah*, or polity, is a concept basic to the mosque. Since Islam does not distinguish between spiritual and temporal power, the congregational or Friday mosque was generally (until the nineteenth century and the institution of colonial civil governments) the center for secular as well as religious practice. At the Friday noon prayer, the main weekly service, the entire adult community assembles at the congregational mosque for the reading of the sermon *(khutbah)*, a compilation of financial and political news. The congregational mosque often forms the core of a major urban center, a complex that can include markets, caravanseries, a government administration center, public baths, saints' shrines, and schools.

The small local or community mosques, simple oratories for daily prayer and without the more complex furnishings of the congregational mosque, are identified with the patrons, prominent families, charitable foundations, or communities. In an urban framework the local mosque establishes the identity of neighborhood quarters. Permission to build such a mosque constitutes official recognition of a community or group. While the congregational mosque and the simpler oratory mosque were originally two discrete types, the distinction is often lost today.

One final requirement for the performance of prayer is sequestration from the profane world. The words of God as spoken in the Qur'an are the subject of prayer and revelation. The mosque concretizes this contemplative arena in a building most often lacking exterior embellishment or elaborate facades. The architectural focus is rather on the secluded realm of the courtyard and the sanctuary. Furthermore, Muslims very early on rejected the depiction of animate objects or human figures in religious environments as degrading to the transcendental state of prayer. The subject of the ornamentation is thus the word itself. Domes, portals, and *mihrabs* are lavishly embellished with Qur'anic passages in stylized calligraphy.

The earliest building used for prayer and an important symbolic and functional precedent for the organization of the mosque was the prophet Muhammad's house in Medina (dating from the Hijrah or Emigration of 622) where his followers gathered for discussion and prayer. A rudimentary courtyard house, enclosed by a high wall with a shaded porch supported by palm trunks along one wall, it became the basis for the early hypostyle mosques of the seventh century. With its square courtyard *(sahn)* and covered sanctuary facing Mecca, the hypostyle plan established two basic features: the division of the mosque into court and sanctuary, and the intersection of the *qiblah* wall with the direction of Mecca. Functionally, it exemplified the dual role of Muhammad's house, and subsequently the mosque, as both an oratory for prayer and a social and political center for the community.

Architectural Elements and Furnishings. With the accession of the Umayyad caliphate (661–750) and the expansion of the empire west into Syria, Palestine, Iraq, North Africa, and Spain, the influence of Hellenism and the development of a formalized liturgy resulted in a more elaborate assembly of parts. Primary among these, the *mihrab*, a niche evoking the symbolic presence of the Prophet, marks the direction of Mecca in the *qiblah* wall and is the symbolic culmination of the mosque. The *mihrab* is typically of an arched apsidal shape, lavishly ornamented and flanked by colonnettes. It may be surmounted by a window to show its directional position or fronted by a dome.

The *minbar*, a stepped pulpit that is as much a symbol of authority as an object for acoustical elevation, is located to the right of the *mihrab*. The top step of the *minbar* is reserved for the Prophet; the imam, or prayer leader, stands on the second step and uses the top one as a seat. After reading the *khutbah*, the imam descends the pulpit to lead the prayer standing before the *mihrab* as member of the assembly, a demonstration of his double role as both lawgiver and religious leader. *Minbars* are usually of wood and encrusted with nacre and ivory, though marble is also used.

The dome is of minor liturgical significance but is, along with the *mihrab*, the object of the most lavish architectural embellishment. Domes are often placed adjacent to the *qiblah* wall, emphasizing it from the exterior and washing it with light inside.

The minaret *(manarah)* evolved from the need for the call to prayer. In contrast to the Jewish use of the shofar (ram's horn) or the Christian use of wooden clappers, in Islam a specially delegated muezzin *(mu'adhdhan)* gives the call to

> ## Tradition requires that the worshiper use running water and wash hands, feet, and face.

prayer *(adhan)*. In Damascus, an early Muslim conquest, the old church tower was adapted to raise the call above the rooftops, a practice subsequently spurring the design of specially built towers. With the addition of a platform or a peripheral balcony the muezzin could broadcast the *adhan* to all corners of the city. Lighter and more slender than church towers encumbered with heavy bells, minarets took a variety of forms, from the square fortresslike towers of North Africa to the slender spires of Ottoman Turkey.

The fountain for ablutions is commonly located in the center of the courtyard. Tradition requires that the worshiper use running water and wash hands, feet, and face. An elevated step or stool may be provided to remove the cleansed supplicant from the impure floor or courtyard pavement. An additional marble jar may be found inside the mosque, a provision for the elderly who cannot be safely exposed to inclement weather. At the entrance to the mosque a low screen demarcates the boundary between ritually pure and impure areas.

The *dikkah*, somewhat analogous to the church choir, is a raised platform holding a group of respondents *(muballighun)* who echo the imam's prayers and postures, transmitting the liturgy to those unable to see or hear the imam himself. In widespread use by the eighth century, the *dikkah* was invented as a means of communicating the prayers among increasingly large congregations. It usually straddles the *qiblah* axis in the middle of the mosque, though it may sit off-axis so the officiant can be seen more readily. With the installation of electronic amplification systems, it has largely fallen into disuse.

A final piece of mosque furniture, the *kursi*, is a lectern for the recitation of the Qur'an. Usually made of wood and placed next to the *dikkah*, the *kursi* is lavishly ornamented and holds a platform for the Qur'an reciter *(qari)* to kneel while facing the *qiblah*. Sometimes it has a V-shaped slot to hold the very large Qur'ans that are often used.

Historical Development. The hypostyle mosque had a pervasive influence over the first six Muslim centuries (seventh to twelfth centuries CE), spreading throughout the Middle East and the southern Mediterranean. The shaded porticoes, interior courtyards, and vast columned or arcuated halls were well suited to the native building practices, climatic conditions, and Hellenistic architectural heritage of the region. To the east a second major mosque tradition arose from indigenous Iranian building and coalesced during the Seljuk dynasty (1038-1194). Like the hypostyle mosque, the *iwan* plan derived from a courtyard house plan, one so culturally predominant in Iran that it was applied interchangeably to house, *madrasah*, and caravansary. The major focus and organizing feature of the plan is the central courtyard, which is faced with four vaulted, open porches *(iwans)*, one in the center of each side, and each encompassed by a giant portal *(pishtaq)*, providing functional, shaded outdoor areas and monumental entryways. Generally, the *iwan* leading to the sanctuary precedes a domed bay directly fronting the *mihrab*. Subsidiary rooms and spaces open off of an arcade surrounding the courtyard. This *iwan* plan yielded a distinctive mosque type featuring large domed spaces, slender round minarets, elaborate decorative brickwork, and polychromed mosaic ornamentation. The *iwan* mosque flourished in Iran, Afghanistan, and Central Asia through the seventeenth century.

Throughout the history of Islam the basic features of the mosque have been repeatedly reinterpreted and adapted to a wide range of geographical, cultural, and historical contexts. Egyptian mosques with richly decorated street facades took on a strong public presence beginning already in the Fatimid era (969-1171). The *iwan* mosque and Seljuk influence penetrated Egypt under the rule of Salah al-Din (Saladin) and his Ayyubid dynasty (1171-1250). Under the patronage of the Mamluk sultans (1250-1517), elaborate mosque complexes with monumental portals and towering domes and minarets delineated in carved and polychrome masonry marked the power, prestige, and material wealth of the rulers and their entourage.

When the Seljuks conquered India in the twelfth century, *iwan* mosques were transformed by a highly sophisticated Hindu building tradition of trabeated stone construction and elaborate inlay and ornamental stone carving into a host of regional developments. In the Indo-Islamic style of the Mughal period (1526-1858), the Hindu influence emerged in a courtyard that was frequently the primary spatial element and a sanctuary reduced to an elaborated pavilion or arcade wall. The giant *iwan* of the sanctuary, the portals, and the arcades were articulated with ogee arches, onion domes, and polychromed masonry bearing the ornamental lineage of both traditions.

In Turkey the Ottomans (1281-1922) made a major contribution with the centralized mosque, dominated both inside and outside by a massive dome. The earlier Seljuk rulers had brought the *iwan* plan to the cold climate of the Anatolian highlands, where the courtyard was soon engulfed by a pillared hall, a skylit dome over the ablution fountain, and a second dome over the *mihrab* bay. Under the Ottomans the *iwan* plan was monumentalized and merged with the Byzantine centralized basilica plan. The courtyard and sanctuary each assumed a square configuration, the courtyard open to the sky and surrounded by domed porches, the sanctuary sheltered beneath a single circular dome buttressed by semidomes. This ascending mountain of domes flanked by two or four needlelike minarets introduced a monumentality into the urban landscape that was alien to the hypostyle mosque.

In sub-Saharan Africa Islam arrived by way of the caravan routes around the year 1000. Along its path a synthesis of Muslim and African architectural concepts evolved. The Sudanic mosques merge indigenous mud architecture with the hypostyle mosque of North Africa in a range of ethnic variations. The Djenné Mosque has been rebuilt repeatedly in its history, most recently in 1909. Engulfing the hypostyle interior the pinnacled and buttressed facade integrates three square, symmetrically ordered minarets reflecting the indigenous monumental design. Projecting wooden dentils serve both as scaffolding for repairs to the adobe surface and as an ornamental motif. Male and female fertility symbols that ornament the towers and buttresses and the twin *mihrabs* and *minbars* are also a reflection of traditional religious beliefs.

The mosques of Southeast Asia and China were largely incorporated into existing building traditions. In China mosque design was influenced by Central Asian precedents but became increasingly sinicized through the centuries. With the first Muslim communities during the T`ang dynasty (618-907), the Central Asian masonry techniques employing domes, vaults, and arches was uniformly adopted. But already by the Laio dynasty (907-1125), the indigenous character of Chinese design asserted itself on both a national and a regional level. In the Niu-chieh Mosque in Peking (962), the prayer hall and ancillary pavilions sit within the confines of a traditional series of axial courtyards and gateways, while the wooden pavilions themselves feature elaborate bracket systems and tiled roofs with the characteristic upward-sloping corners.

In its long history the mosque has been subject to an ever-changing series of contingencies. Like Islam itself, the vitality of the mosque tradition must be seen as tied to its syncretic potential. While its contemplative and liturgical functions have barely altered through time, its specific political and social roles have varied widely according to the historical and cultural context. So, too, have climatic and technical exigencies continuously reshaped and delimited its exterior form. The aesthetic component, coordinating and unifying these diverse elements, has given expression to the particular significance of the mosque in space and time. Today the evolution of the mosque continues as the techniques of modern technology and contemporary society interact with ancient traditions of Islam.

BIBLIOGRAPHY

Creswell, K. A. C. *Early Muslim Architecture* (1932). 2 vols. Rev. ed. Oxford, 1969. A seminal work on the origins of Islamic architecture.

Grabar, Oleg. *The Formation of Islamic Art.* New Haven, 1973. An analytic study including an essay on the mosque that explores how Islamic form both employed and superseded the non-Islamic traditions under its influence.

Hoag, John D. *Islamic Architecture.* New York, 1977. A basic survey of the architectural monuments of Islam, exclusive of China, Southeast Asia, and sub-Saharan Africa.

Michell, George, ed. *Architecture of the Islamic World: Its History and Social Meaning.* New York, 1978. An important collection of essays on various building types, with a valuable appendix catalog covering the major geographic areas and their key monuments.

Papadopoulo, Alexandre. *Islam and Muslim Art.* New York, 1979. A lavishly illustrated compendium of Islamic art and architecture with detailed studies of some key monuments and building components. The book includes several comparative photo essays of particular architectural elements, such as domes and minarets, and a useful lexicon of important religious figures, scholars, and artists.

SUSAN HENDERSON

MUHAMMAD

MUHAMMAD (c. 570-632 CE), the Prophet or (as Muslims usually call him) the Messenger of God, from whose activity the religion of Islam developed.

Life and Career

Muhammad was a political as well as a religious leader, and it is convenient to look first at the external and political aspects of his career before considering the religious aspect in more detail; the latter, of course, cannot be completely excluded at any point.

First Preaching of Islam. It was presumably the frustrations he faced in the years before his marriage that made Muhammad especially sensitive to the community of Mecca. He had skill in handling people and great intellectual gifts, and yet he was unable to use these qualities in trading because of his lack of capital. He is said to have spent a month each year in a cave near Mecca meditating on spiritual matters, including conditions in Mecca itself. About the year 610 he had some strange experiences. As a result of these he became convinced that he had been called to be the "Messenger of God" *(rasul Allah)* who would bear messages or revelations from God to the people of Mecca. He was also convinced that these messages, which he "found in his heart," came from God and were not the product of his own thinking. After his death the messages were collected to form the book still in our hands, the Qur'an.

The messages which were earliest, so far as we can tell, spoke of God's power and his goodness to human beings, called on them to acknowledge their dependence on God and to be generous with their wealth, and warned them that all would appear before God on the Day of Judgment and be assigned to Paradise or Hell according to whether their deeds were good or bad. These messages were clearly relevant to the situation in Mecca. The great merchants thought they could control everything because of their wealth and expertise and that they could flout traditional nomadic moral standards with impunity, especially in such matters as the use of their wealth.

At first Muhammad communicated the messages only to his own household and a few close friends, but gradually an increasing number of people accepted the messages as true. A wealthy young man called al-Arqam offered his house as a meeting place, and the believers gathered there daily. Then, about three years after receiving the call to be Messenger of God, Muhammad began to preach publicly. By this time he had at least fifty followers (whose names have been preserved), and enough was generally known about the content of the messages for bitter opposition to have been aroused among the wealthy merchants.

Rejection at Mecca. Muhammad and his followers deeply resented the treatment they received at the hands of their opponents in Mecca, perhaps chiefly because in the end this made it impossible for Muhammad to continue preaching and gaining disciples there. In themselves many of the measures were not serious, although slaves and those without clan protection could suffer bodily harm. Muhammad himself experienced verbal taunts and petty insults. That Muhammad was able to go on preaching in Mecca as long as he did was due to the fact that his own clan of Hashim continued, as custom and honor required, to protect him, although most of them did not accept what he preached. Attempts were made to persuade the clan either to stop the preaching or to refuse further protection, but Abu Talib, as clan chief, would do neither. In consequence, about 616, most of the clans of Quraysh joined together to boycott Hashim by refusing trade dealings and intermarriage.

When Muhammed learned there was a plot to kill him in Mecca, he and cousin Abu Bakr set out secretly, eluded pur-

suit from Mecca by various ruses, and reached Medina safely on 24 September 622. Medina, about 250 miles north of Mecca, was an oasis in which dates and cereals were grown. The inhabitants included various groups of Jews and Arabs. The groups who were called Jewish had intermarried to a considerable extent with Arabs and had adopted Arab customs, while still following Jewish religious practices. It was probably they who had developed agriculture in the oasis, and for a time they had been politically dominant.

Relationships with Jews and Christians. When Muhammad made the Hijrah to Medina he hoped that the Jews there would accept him as a prophet, since he had been told that the messages or revelations he was receiving were identical in content with those of the biblical prophets. One or two Jews did so accept him and became Muslims, but the majority merely rejected his claim. At the same time Muhammad was coming to rely more on an anti-Jewish party in Medina. Islam was asserted to be the true religion of Abraham, from which Jews and Christians had deviated. It was pointed out that Abraham was neither a Jew nor a Christian (which is true) but a *hanif,* which the Qur'an takes to be one who believes in God without being attached to either Judaism or Christianity.

This ideological "break with the Jews" was followed over the next four years by physical attacks. After this there remained in Medina only a few small groups of Jews, now thoroughly chastened and very dependent on their Arab allies. Finally, soon after the expedition which led to the treaty of al-Hudaybiyah, Muhammad led an attack against the Jews

> One or two Jews did so accept him and became Muslims, but the majority merely rejected his claim.

of Khaybar, who had been trying to bribe Arab nomads to join them in attacking the Muslims.

There were few Christians in either Mecca or Medina. After the welcome given to the Muslims who immigrated to Abyssinia, Christians in general were accounted friends (as is shown by surah 5:82). In the last years of Muhammad's life, however, the Muslims had to fight against hostile Christian tribes along the route to Syria, and attitudes changed. Some of the Qur'anic arguments against Jews were also used against Christians, and there were also arguments against specifically Christian doctrines.

Prophethood

The Call to Be a Prophet. The experiences which led Muhammad to believe that he was called to be a messenger of God or prophet began with two visions which are briefly described in the Qur'an (53:1-18). In the first, he saw a mighty being on the horizon, who then came nearer; in the second, he saw the same being in mysterious circumstances. At first he appears to have thought that this being was God, but later he concluded it must have been the angel Gabriel. The early biographers of Muhammad present accounts of how the angel Gabriel appeared to him and said, "You are the Messenger of God," and then continued, "Recite in the name of your Lord . . ." (the beginning of surah 96, said to be the first revealed). Other accounts make the first revelation "Rise and warn . . ." (74:1-7). Both versions may well be only the conjectures of later scholars.

Many verses imply that Muhammad was a prophet to the Arabs, but there are also suggestions that his mission was universal, such as the title "Mercy to the Worlds" (21:107).

The Nature of Revelation. Traditional Islamic doctrine regards the words of the Qur'an as the actual speech of God, for which Muhammad was only a passive channel of transmission. He himself believed that he could distinguish such revelations from his own thinking, and in this his sincerity must be accepted. The insistence of Muslim scholars that Muhammad's personality contributed nothing to the Qur'an does not entirely rule out the possibility that the messages came somehow or other from Muhammad's unconscious.

The Prophet as Political and Religious Leader. It does not belong to the conception of messenger as such that he should also be political leader of his community. In the earlier passages of the Qur'an Muhammad is spoken of as a "warner" *(nadhir, mudhakkir),* whose function it was to "warn" his fellows that they would all have to appear before God to be judged on the Last Day. When Muhammad went to Medina, it was not part of the formal agreement that he was to be head of state; he was only one clan head out of nine. There was always, however, a readiness among the Arabs, even among his opponents at Mecca, to regard someone capable of receiving messages from God as being the person best able to guide the affairs of his community wisely. Muhammad's political power grew as he came to be respected more by the people of Medina; and the success of most of his expeditions contributed to that growth of respect. In his later years, too, many nomads who came to settle in Medina were attached to the "clan" of Emigrants, so that it became relatively more powerful. If at the end of his life Muhammad was ruling a large part of Arabia, that did not follow automatically from his being a prophet, but was due to his personal qualities. It is also to be noted that it was not his practice to seek revelations in order to solve political problems.

What has not been so clearly recognized is that much of the establishment of Islam as a religion is due to him personally, even in the Islamic view that he contributed nothing to the Qur'an. Although some justification can be found in the Qur'an for the religious institutions of Islam (such as the profession of faith, the five daily prayers, the fast, and the pil-grimage), they are by no means clearly defined there; they derive their precise shape from the practice of Muhammad and the early Muslims, and this was in part recognized by the later use of the *hadith* to justify these institutions.

BIBLIOGRAPHY

The main early source for the life of Muhammad is the *Sirat Rasul Allah* by Ibn Ishaq (d. AH 150?/767? CE) as edited by Ibn Hisham (d. 218?/833?). There is an English translation by Alfred Guillaume, *The Life of Muhammad: A Translation of* [Ibn] Ishaq's *"Sirat Rasul Allah"* (1955; reprint, Lahore, 1967), in which Ibn Hisham's additions are given as an appendix.

The important work of Frants Buhl, first published in Danish in 1903, is best known in the German translation by Heinrich Schaeder, *Das Leben Muhammeds* (1930; reprint, Leipzig, 1955); Buhl also wrote the article "Muhammad `Abd Allah," in the first edition of the *Encyclopaedia of Islam* (Leiden, 1913-1934). The less detailed work of the Swede Tor Andrae, *Mohammed: The Man and His Faith,* translated by Theophil Menzel (1936; reprint, London, 1956), deals mainly with the religious aspects. In *Le problème de Mahomet* (Paris, 1952) Régis Blachère expresses a degree of skepticism about the sources other than the Qur'an. My full studies, *Muhammad at Mecca* (Oxford, 1953) and *Muhammad at Medina* (Oxford, 1956), are based on a qualified acceptance of the main Arabic sources and pay attention to the social, economic, and political aspects as well as the religious; these two works are summarized in my book *Muhammad: Prophet and Statesman* (1961; reprint, London, 1974). Some important discussions of the sources are contained in *La vie du prophète Mahomet* (Paris, 1983), the report of a colloquium held at the Centre d'Études Supérieures Spécialisé d'Histoire des Religions in Strasbourg in 1980.

Tor Andrae also published an impressive study of Muslim beliefs about Muhammad entitled *Die person Muhammeds in lehre und glauben seiner gemeinde* (Uppsala, 1918). Annemarie Schimmel takes up the same topic in *And Muhammad Is His Messenger: The Veneration of the Prophet in Islamic Piety* (Chapel Hill, N. C., 1985), first published as *Und Muhammad ist Sein Prophet* (Düsseldorf, 1981); she has a wealth of examples from poetry, prose, and art.

Biographies of the Prophet by Muslims in the last century or so have been mainly apologetic. Pride of place must be given to the work of Syed Ameer Ali (1849-1928), who in 1873 published a life of the Prophet defending him against views expressed in books he read while a student in London. Throughout his life he kept expanding this work, which became very popular, eventually giving it the title *The Spirit of Islam* (1890), 2d ed. (1922; reprint, London, 1974). In it he attempted to show that Muhammad in particular and Islam in general exemplified all the virtues of nineteenth-century European liberalism. Something similar was attempted by Muhammad Husayn Haykal (1888-1956) in his Arabic life of Muhammad, *Hayat Muhammad* (1935; reprint, Cairo, 1960), but he was primarily a believer in science and reason. The most scholarly work by a Muslim is *Le prophète de l'Islam,* 2 vols. (Paris, 1959), by Muhammad Hamidullah; in this he adopts modern historical methodology, though in a very conservative fashion, and places emphasis on Muhammad as a religious leader. In *Muhammad: His Life Based on the Earliest Sources* (New York, 1983), Martin Lings gives in very readable English a harmonious narrative of the events of the Prophet's life, smoothing over discordances and omitting matters which Muslims find difficult to interpret, such as the incident of the "satanic verses."

W. MONTGOMERY WATT

MUSLIM BROTHERHOOD

Founded in 1928 by Hasan al-Banna' (1906-1949), the Society of Muslim Brothers (al-Ikhwan al-Muslimun) was created to bring Egyptian Muslims back to an awareness of the objectives of religion within a society that had, in the view of al-Banna', been corrupted by alien ideologies and a materialist philosophy imported from the West.

Historical Background. The British occupation of Egypt in 1882 had fueled a nationalist movement seeking independence from British rule; these aspirations culminated in the revolt of 1919 under the leadership of the aging politician Sa`d Zaghlul and the newly formed Wafd ("delegation") party. The decade of the 1920s offered the Egyptians constitutional government and hopes of an impending settlement between Britain and Egypt through a negotiated treaty. When Zaghlul died in 1927, these hopes were eroded, and a number of movements appeared as alternatives to the liberal notions of government that had not been successful, partly through interference on the part of the king and the British authorities in Egypt and partly through ineptness on the part of the parliamentarians. In addition to the fascists and the communists, these movements included the Society of Muslim Brothers, who believed that the path of reforming the country's social and political problems lay in the islamization of institutions.

Hasan al-Banna', a primary school teacher who was the son of a small-town religious teacher, was early attracted to Sufism, which, along with classical Islamic studies, formed his major intellectual foundations and became the linchpins of his group. He described the Muslim Brotherhood as a "Salafiyah movement [espousing return to the early principles of Islam], a Sunni [orthodox] way, a Sufi [mystical] truth, a political organization, an athletic group, a cultural and educational union, an economic company, and a social idea." The movement spread rapidly, representing every segment of society from newly urbanized rural immigrants to high government officials. In its heyday in the 1940s, the Muslim Brotherhood claimed to represent one million members; later estimates are difficult to establish.

The structure of the organization was spelled out in the Fundamental Law of the Organization of the Muslim Brothers, promulgated in 1945 and later amended. Leading the organization was the general guide, who chaired the General Guidance Council (the policy-making body) and the Consultative or General Assembly, both of which were elective bodies. A secretary general was in charge of a secretariat linking the council and the rest of the organization. Two further subdivisions dealt with various committees (press, peasants, students, etc.) and with an administrative body supervising branches outside the capital. A chain of command was thus established over the entire membership.

Spread of the Movement. Weekly lectures, preaching in mosques, and periodic conferences allowed for popular participation, and the establishment of a press soon spread the message of the Society of Muslim Brothers further. Unconcerned with doctrinal differences, the participants concentrated on growth, action, and organization, and by 1939 they were ready for political activity. The war years were to provide them with a forum.

Nationalist agitation against the British continued with labor strikes and student demonstrations until, in 1942, the British threatened King Faruq (Farouk) with deposition and forced him to appoint a Wafd government under Mustafa al-Nahhas. This incident generated further support for the Muslim Brotherhood, by then the only other grouping with a mass base to rival the Wafd. Even among the Wafd leadership there were many who approved of the society as a bulwark against the spread of communism among the working class. For the next few years the society established links with disaffected officers within the army (who were later to carry out the revolution of 1952), and, unknown to even his closest colleagues, al-Banna' stockpiled weapons and created a secret apparatus trained in the use of armed violence for tactical operations.

With the end of the war, agitation for the evacuation of British forces from Egypt started once again, with frequent student demonstrations and acts of violence until the British garrison was finally withdrawn to the Canal Zone. The situation in Palestine and the war against Israel in 1948 provided the Muslim Brotherhood with an opportunity to collect more arms as members volunteered during the war and remained in the forefront of the fighting until their organization was dissolved in December 1948. The immediate cause for the government's action against the society was the death of the Egyptian chief of police, Salim Zaki, who was killed by a bomb thrown at him during student demonstrations protesting the armistice with Israel. Mass arrests followed as the government, fearing the society's growing influence, sought to proscribe it. Three weeks later, the prime minister, Mahmud Fahmi al-Nuqrashi, was assassinated by a Muslim Brother. In February 1949 Hasan al-Banna' was himself assassinated, probably with the complicity, if not the actual participation, of the government of the day.

After the Muslim Brotherhood was proscribed, its property confiscated, and its members put on trial, many of its remaining members fled to other Arab countries, where they founded autonomous branches of the society. In 1951 a Wafd government, seeking a buffer against rising leftist movements, allowed the society to reconvene. A judge with palace connections, Hasan Isma`il al-Hudaybi, was chosen as new leader. That same year the Wafd government unilaterally abrogated the treaty of 1936 with England, and Egyptian youth, including the Muslim Brothers, were encouraged to harass British camps in the Canal Zone. In January 1952

British forces attacked the Ismailia police station, and forty Egyptian policemen were killed. On the following day Cairo was set on fire in a monstrous riot that gutted the heart of the city. The Muslim Brothers were suspected of planning the riot, which they had not, although some of them were among the many participants. From then on the country was virtually without effective government until 23 July 1952, when the Free Officers movement, which included future Egyptian presidents Jamal `Abd al-Nasir (Gamal Abdel Nasser) and Anwar al-Sadat, seized power and three days later sent the king into exile.

> After the Muslim Brotherhood was proscribed, its property confiscated, and its members put on trial, many of its remaining members fled to other Arab countries. . . .

There had been strong links between the Muslim Brotherhood and the Free Officers—Nasser and Sadat had both been members of the society. Once all political parties had been disbanded, the only focus for mass support lay with the society. Nasser knew that it represented the lone challenge to his authority and that its leaders expected to share power with the officers; a power struggle was inevitable. In 1954 a member of the Muslim Brotherhood allegedly attempted to shoot Nasser during a public rally, and once again the society was proscribed and its members arrested.

The society remained underground throughout the Nasser era. When Sadat came to power in 1970 all prisoners were released, including the Muslim Brothers, and, to combat the Nasserite current, Sadat allowed the society to reestablish itself under the leadership of an `alim (religious scholar), Shaykh al-Tilmisani, and to publish its own newspapers. Meanwhile newer associations patterned after the society, the Islamic *jamaat* ("groups"), had appeared. Some of these were extensions of the Muslim Brotherhood; others regarded the society as retrograde and beholden to the government. It was a member of one of the latter, more extremist groups who assassinated Sadat in 1981.

Doctrines and Impact. According to the program of al-Banna', the Society of Muslim Brothers was given a mission to restore the rule of the *shariah* (Islamic law) to Egypt, and to all other Muslim countries where their missionary activities had set up affiliates. Rule of the *shariah* rendered inadmissible the separation of church and state, for the state, they believed, existed in order to serve religion and to facilitate the fulfillment of Islamic religious duties. The Islamic state had the Qur'an as its constitution; its government operated through *shura,* or consultation, and the executive branch, guided by the will of the people, ruled through Islamic principles. The ruler, chosen by the people, was responsible to them and not above the law, with no special privileges. Should he fail in his duties he was to be ousted. Freedom of thought, of worship, and of expression were vital, as was freedom of education. Finally, freedom of possessions was to be maintained within the limits set by Islamic law, which frowns upon the excessive accumulation of wealth and enjoins *zakat* ("alms") as a basic religious duty. Social justice was to be the guiding principle of government.

The significance of the Society of Muslim Brothers and of its modern offshoots, the *jamaat,* is that they represent a protest movement couched in a traditional Islamic idiom that expresses the ethos of a people. The society arose in protest against a foreign occupation that threatened the identity of a people and the dissolution of its culture and religion. It spoke to people in the language they understood and appreciated, that of Islam and its historical past, and it did not posit newfangled notions derived from a Western idiom, although the society did use Western techniques of mass communications and of assembly, even ideas of government, which were garbed in Muslim idiom. As such it was comprehensible to the masses who suffered political discrimination and economic exploitation by a government that was largely indifferent to their welfare, especially during periods of economic recession. Those who were disillusioned with Western ideologies and their ability to solve Egypt's problems, or indeed the problems of any Muslim country, turned to the precepts of the society, or to similar movements that they identified with their roots and cultural authenticity *(asa-lah),* for guidance and spiritual consolation. The same phenomenon was reproduced during the Sadat regime (1970-1981) when the "Open Door" *(infitah)* policy disrupted society and led to rampant consumerism, which, exacerbated by the influx of oil money, raised fears of becoming engulfed by westernization.

Organizations such as the Muslim Brotherhood or the *jamaat* are regarded by some Muslim regimes as dangerous foci of opposition and have thus met with violent repression. In Syria the regime of Hafiz al-Asad has been in conflict with the Muslim Brotherhood since 1976. In 1982 the army shelled the city of Hama, a Muslim Brotherhood stronghold; portions of the city were leveled and casualties were variously estimated at ten thousand to twenty thousand. Similar attacks were repeated in Aleppo, Homs, and Latakia. In Iraq the regime of Sadam Husayn waged a relentless campaign against the Shi`i group al-Da`wah al-Islamiyah. In Saudi Arabia Muslim militants seized the Grand Mosque in Mecca for several days in 1979. In Sudan the Muslim Brotherhood forced the regime of Muhammad Ja`far al-Numayri (Numeiri) to adopt Islamic policies in 1977. Comparable militant groups have spread to most Muslim countries irrespective of their forms of government.

BIBLIOGRAPHY

Enayat, Hamid. *Modern Islamic Political Thought.* Austin, 1982. A thoughtful interpretation of political ideas from major Muslim countries.

Harris, Christina Phelps. *Nationalism and Revolution in Egypt.* The Hague, 1964. An early study of the Muslim Brotherhood, written before much interesting material had been uncovered but useful nonetheless.

Husaini, Ishak Musa. *The Moslem Brethren: The Greatest of Modern Islamic Movements.* Translated by John F. Brown and John Racy. Beirut, 1956. The first account of the society, written by an uncritical admirer but containing many quotes from al-Banna'.

Ibrahim, Saad Eddin. *The New Arab Social Order.* Boulder, 1982. A study of the effect of oil riches on Middle East society, with an excellent discussion of militant movements.

Kotb, Sayed (Qutb, Sayyid). *Social Justice in Islam.* Translated by John B. Hardie. Washington, D. C., 1953. A major work written by a leading Muslim intellectual.

Mitchell, Richard P. *The Society of the Muslim Brothers.* Oxford, 1969. The definitive work on the society. The author died before he could bring his work up to date, but it remains the only critical account of the movement.

Wendell, Charles, trans. and ed. *Five Tracts of Hasan al-Banna (1906-1949).* Berkeley, 1978. Basic source documents with annotations.

AFAF LUTFI AL-SAYYID MARSOT

MYSTICISM

No definition could be both meaningful and sufficiently comprehensive to include all experiences that, at some point or other, have been described as "mystical." In 1899 Dean W. R. Inge listed twenty-five definitions. Since then the study of world religions has considerably expanded, and new, allegedly mystical cults have sprung up everywhere. The etymological lineage of the term provides little assistance in formulating an unambiguous definition.

Mysticism of the Self. Mysticism belongs to the core of all religion. Those religions that had a historical founder all started with a powerful personal experience of immediate contact. But all religions, regardless of their origin, retain their vitality only as long as their members continue to believe in a transcendent reality with which they can in some way communicate by direct experience. The significance of such an experience, though present in all religion, varies in importance. Christianity, especially in its reformed churches, attaches less significance to the element of experience than other faiths do. In Vedantic and Samkhya Hinduism, on the contrary, religion itself coincides with the kind of insight that can come only from mystical experience. Their particular concept of redemption consists in a liberation from change and from the vicissitudes of birth and death. Their craving for a state of changeless permanence aims not at some sort of unending protraction of the present life but rather at the extinction of all desire in this life. Hindu spirituality in all its forms displays an uncommonly strong awareness of the sorrowful quality of the human condition.

The original Vedic religion with its emphasis on sacrifice and rite appears rather remote from what we usually associate with the term *mysticism.* Yet two elements in its development strongly influenced the later, more obviously mystical direction. First, forms of meditation became at some point acceptable substitutes for the performance of the actual sacrifice and were held to yield equally desirable benefits. Though such forms of concentration had little in common with what we understand today by contemplation, they nevertheless initiated an interiorization that Hinduism would pursue further than any other religion (Dasgupta, 1972, p. 19). Second, the term *brahman,* which originally referred to the sacred power present in ritual and sacrifice, gradually came to mean a single, abstractly conceived Absolute.

In the Upanisads (eighth to fifth century BCE) the unifying and the spiritualizing tendencies eventually merged in the idea of an inner soul (atman), the Absolute at the heart of all reality to which only the mind has access. This is not a metaphysical theory, but a mystical path to liberation. It requires ascetical training and mental discipline to overcome the desires, oppositions, and limitations of individual selfhood. "As a man, when in the embrace of a beloved wife, knows nothing within or without, so this person, when in the embrace of the intelligent Soul, knows nothing within or without" (*Brha-daranyaka* 4,3.22). Here lies the origin of the *advaita* (nondualist monism that would become dominant in classical Hinduism).

The Mysticism of Emptiness: Buddhism. It seems difficult to conceive of two religious doctrines more different from one another than Hinduism, especially Samkhya, and Buddhism. In one, we find a quest for an absolute self *(atman, purusa);* in the other, the obliteration of the self (*anatman/anatta*—no soul). Yet upon closer inspection the two appear to have a great deal in common. Both are systems of salvation, rooted in a profoundly pessimistic attitude about the changing world of everyday existence, and they aim at a condition of changelessness that surpasses that existence. The Buddhist description both of the experience and of the path that leads to it is characterized by a spare simplicity as well as by a persistent reluctance to use any but negative predicates. Their development varies from the Hinayana to the Mahayana doctrines. But even in the Theravada tradition, the Eightfold Path of virtue concludes with "right concentration," which, in turn, must be obtained in eight successive forms of mental discipline (the *dhyanas*). Once again we are confronted with a faith that from its origins is headed in a mystical direction. The three negative terms— nonattainment, nonassertion, nonreliance—define a state of utmost emptiness by which Nagarjuna's Madhyamika school (150 CE) described enlightenment.

The ways to emptiness vary. Mental training by the confrontation of paradoxes has been mentioned. Other ways, especially Yogacara Buddhism, emphasize the attainment of "pure thought." This consists not in thinking *about* something but rather in the insight that thought is not in any object but in a subject free of all objects. Yogacara pursues the basic truth of emptiness in a practical rather than a logico-metaphysical way.

Of particular importance here is Ch`an (Jpn., Zen) Buddhism, a doctrine imported into China by the Indian Bodhidharma that later spread to Japan. Most consistent of all in its pursuit of emptiness, it rejected all dependence (nonreliance), including the one based on the Buddha's own words.

Most typical of that final state of emptiness as Zen Buddhists conceive of it is that it results not in a withdrawal from the real but in an enhanced ability to see the real as it is and to act in it unhampered by passion and attachment. Thus emptiness creates a new worldliness.

Mysticism of the Image: Eastern and Early Western Christianity. Unlike some other religions, Christianity has never equated its ideal of holiness with the attainment of mystical states. Nor did it encourage seeking such states for their own sake. Nevertheless, a mystical impulse undeniably propelled it in its origin and determined much of its later development.

The mystical quality of Jesus' life is most clearly stated in the Fourth Gospel. Some of the words attributed to him may have originated in theological reflection rather than in his own expression. But they thereby witness all the more powerfully to the mystical impulse he was able to transmit to his followers.

The first attempt at a systematic theology of the mystical life in Christ was written by Origen. In his *Twenty-seventh Homily on Numbers* Origen compares spiritual life to the Jews' exodus through the desert of Egypt. Having withdrawn from the pagan idols of vice, the soul crosses the Red Sea in a new baptism of conversion. She passes next through the bitter waters of temptation and the distorted visions of utopia until, fully purged and illuminated, she reaches Terah, the place of union with God. In his commentary on the *Song of Songs,* Origen initiated a long tradition of mystical interpretations that see in the erotic biblical poem just such a divine union. His commentary also presents the first developed theology of the image: the soul is an image of God because she houses the primal image of God that is the divine Word. The entire mystical process thus comes to consist in a conversion to the image, that is, to ever greater identity with the indwelling Word. The emphasis on the ontological character of the image of God in man (as opposed to the external copy)

persists throughout the entire Christian tradition and holds the secret of its amazing mystical power.

Augustine (354-430), the towering figure who stands at the beginning of all Western theology (also, and especially, spiritual theology), described the divine image rather in psychological terms. His treatise *On the Trinity* abounds with speculations on the soul's similarity to the Trinity, such as her constituting one mind out of the three faculties of intellect, will, and memory. They would amount to no more than superficial analogies were it not that God's presence in that same inner realm invites the soul to turn inward and convert the static resemblance into an ecstatic union. "Now this Trinity of the mind is God's image, not because the mind resembles, understands and loves itself [the superficial analogy], but because it has the power also to remember, understand and love its Maker" (*On the Trinity* 14.12.15). In actualizing the divine potential of its external resemblance, in allowing it to be directed to its archetype, the soul is gradually united with God.

Johannes Eckhart, possibly the most powerful mystical theologian of the Christian Middle Ages, synthesized the Greek and Augustinian theories of the image with a daring negative theology in one grandiose system.

God is Being, and being in the strict sense is only God. With this bold principle, Eckhart reinterprets a Thomist tradition that "analogously" attributed being to God and finite existence. For Eckhart, the creature *qua* creature does not exist. Whatever being it possesses is not its own, but remains God's property. Both its limited essence (what determines it as this being rather than that) and its contingent existence (that it happens to be) are no more than the negative limits of its capacity to receive God's own being. "Every creature," Eckhart wrote, "radically and positively possesses Being, life and wisdom from and in God, and not in itself."

The soul's being is generated in an eternal now with (indeed, within) the divine Word: "The Father bears his Son in eternity like himself. 'The Word was with God, and God was the Word' (Jn 1:1): the same in the same nature. I say more: He has borne him in my soul. Not only is she with him and he equally with her, but he is in her: the Father in eternity, and no differently" (ibid., p. 135). The mystical process then consists in a person's becoming conscious of his divine being.

Mysticism of Love: Modern Christian Mysticism and Sufism. Some time during the twelfth century, Christian piety underwent a basic change: its approach to God became more human and affective. Love had, of course, always been an essential ingredient. But now it became the whole thing. At first it appeared in conjunction with the newly recovered trinitarian mysticism. The same Cistercians who reintroduced the Greek theology of the image to the West also initiated love mysticism.

The emphasis on love is part of a more general tendency to involve the entire personality in the religious act. The new spiritual humanism (partly influenced by the Spanish Islamic culture) would revive interest in the psychological theory of Augustine and pay an unprecedented spiritual attention to the created world. The first great name to emerge was Bernard of Clairvaux. No Christian mystic has ever surpassed "the mellifluous doctor," as he is called, in the eloquent praise of spiritual love.

The humanization of man's relation to God transforms man's attitude toward a creation in which God now comes to be more intimately present. An interpersonal, and hence more creaturely, relation to God is ready to accept each creature on its own terms and for its own sake. In this respect its attitude differs essentially from the image mysticism that

> **Some time during the twelfth century, Christian piety underwent a basic change: its approach to God became more human and affective.**

holds the creature worthy of spiritual love only in its divine core, where it remains rooted in God. The love mystic also cherishes its finite, imperfect being, which, resulting from a divine act of creation, is endowed with a sacred quality of its own. The mystery of the divine incarnation here attains a more universal level of meaning, as if Christians suddenly understood how much the creation must matter to a God who himself has become flesh.

Sufism. With its stern emphasis on law and orthodoxy, Islam hardly seems to present a fertile soil for intensive personal experience of the love of God. Yet Islam assumes the entire social system, *shari`ah* (the way), into a privileged communal relation with God. Moreover, the Qur'an states that, next to the ordinary believers who serve their creator according to the precepts of the law, there are some to whom God communicates his essential mystery inwardly in peace of the soul and friendship with God (Qur'an 17:27). Here the Prophet allows for the possibility of a realm of personal religion. The possibility was soon actualized and eventually flowered into unparalleled mystical beauty. Even the unique authority of the Qur'an has in an indirect way contributed to Islam's mystical wealth, for precisely because it remains the supreme norm of its interpretation, pious readers may find in it whatever meaning divinely inspired insight *(istinbat)* privately reveals to them. Only when personal interpretation openly clashes with established doctrine (especially its rigorous monotheism) could religious authorities interfere. Thus, paradoxically, Islam, the "religion of the book," allows greater freedom of interpretation than religions that place less

emphasis on the written word. Though early Muslim mysticism stayed in close connection with the Islamic community, conflicts arose. Already at the time of Hasan al-Basri (d. 728), the patriarch of Islamic mysticism, Sunni traditionalists objected to his attempt to go beyond the letter of law and doctrine. Thus began the opposition between "internal" and "external" religion that, from the tenth century on, led to increasingly severe confrontations. Nevertheless, a deep personal piety remained an essential element of the Islam that substantially contributed to rendering it a world religion.

Sufi piety reached a temporary truce with orthodox learning in al-Ghazali (d. 1111), the greatest of the theologians. Bypassing the antinomian trends that had emerged, he returned to a more traditional attempt to emphasize experience over the letter of the law. With Ibn al-`Arabi (d. 1240) the dependence on Neoplatonism (especially the so-called *Theology of Aristotle*) and, with it, the movement toward monism became more pronounced than ever. He provided the link between Western classical culture and Eastern Islamic mysticism that culminated in Jalal al-Din Rumi. Sufi mysticism, however much inclined toward monism, never abandoned the language and imagery of love. Ibn al`Arabi, with al-Ghazali the most philosophical of all Muslim mystics, never ceases to integrate his Neoplatonic vision with the Qur'an's dualistic doctrine of man's relation to God. The Absolute for him is an indistinct One that, overcome by the desire to be known, projects itself through creative imagination into apparent otherness. In this projection the relation of the One to the created world, specifically to man, determines that of the Absolute to the differentiated idea of God, the intellectual pole as opposed to the cosmic pole of finite being. All that the creature is, is divine, yet God always exceeds creation. Through man's mediation the dependent, created world returns to its primordial unity. As the image of God, man imposes that image upon the cosmos and reflects it back to its original.

Eschatological Mysticism: Jewish Mystics. Judaism has produced forms of mysticism so unlike any other and so variant among themselves that no common characteristic marks them all. At most we can say that they "commune" with one another, not that they share an identical spirit. Gershom Scholem wisely embedded this irreducible diversity, reflective of a spiritual Diaspora, in the very title of his authoritative work *Major Trends in Jewish Mysticism* (1941). The closest he comes to a general characteristic is the point at which he draws attention to the persistent presence of eschatological traits in Jewish mysticism: "This eschatological nature of mystical knowledge becomes of paramount importance in the writings of many Jewish mystics, from the anonymous authors of the early He-khaloth tracts to Rabbi Naham of Brazlav" (p. 20). The eschatological element most clearly appears in the earliest trend: the often gnostically influenced mythical speculation on Ezekiel's vision of the throne-chariot, the *merkavah.* Mysticism around this theme began in the first centuries of the common era. It consisted of an attempt to ascend to the divine throne beyond the various intermediate spheres (the *heikhalot*). Except for its biblical starting point (first developed in the Ethiopic *Apocalypse of Enoch*), the impact of gnostic *pleroma* mythology dominates this spiritual "throne world." But also the typically Hellenistic connection of mysticism and magic appears to have been strong. *Merkavah* mysticism declined after the seventh century, but enjoyed a steady revival in Italy in the ninth and tenth centuries, which, in turn, may have influenced medieval German Hasidism.

Hasidic "theology" shows a resemblance to Neoplatonism even in its Greek Christian development. God's glory *(kavod)* is distinct from God's being as a first manifestation of his presence *(shekhinah),* which mediates between this hidden essence and the fully manifest creation. The Hasidim indulged in elaborate speculation about the inner and outer glory of God, and about the kingdom of his created yet hidden presence.

These daring speculations seldom developed into a coherent theology. In that respect they differed from the spiritual movement that, from the fourteenth century on, would largely replace it—Qabbalah. It absorbed the Neoplatonic currents that had swept through the Arabic and Jewish culture of twelfth- and thirteenth-century Spain. Considering the hazardous nature of its thought, its relation to normative tradition and official authority remained, on the whole, remarkably peaceful, if not always amiable. Indeed, the branch that produced the most daring speculation found its expression mostly in traditional rabbinical commentaries on the sacred text. They all aim at assisting the soul to untie the "knots" that bind it to this world of multiplicity and to allow it to return to its original unity (surprisingly named after Aristotle's Agent Intellect). This union may be attained through contemplation of a sufficiently abstract object, such as the letters of the Hebrew alphabet. Any combination of letters results in word figures that in some way refer to the sacred tetragrammaton of the divine name, YHVH.

The theophysical mysticism that resulted in that unsurpassed masterpiece of mystical speculation, is the *Zohar* (Book of Splendor). The writer, familiar with the philosophies of Maimonides and of Neoplatonism, has, above all, undergone the influence of unknown gnostic sources. Synthesizing all qabbalistic writings of the century, he attempts to stem the rationalist trend by giving traditional Judaism a hidden mystical interpretation. Thus this highly esoteric work was, in fact, written for the enlightened Jewish intelligentsia of late-fourteenth-century Spain. Central in the *Zohar* doctrine is the theology of the *sefirot,* the ten "regions" into which the divine emanation extends itself. Importantly, the divine *pleroma* of these *sefirot* does not emanate *from* God: it remains within God as his manifest being, in contrast to the "hidden God."

Jewish mysticism shows an unparalleled variety of forms ranging from deep speculation to purely emotional experience. It consistently appeals to scriptural authority, yet no mystical movement ever strayed further from theological orthodoxy than late messianic Qabbalah.

BIBLIOGRAPHY

A popular edition of many Christian, Muslim, and Jewish mystics with generally good introductions is the series "Classics of Western Spirituality" under the editorship of Richard J. Payne (New York, 1978-). A similar series, "Classics of Eastern Spirituality," is planned by Amity Publishing House.

The best works on mysticism in general remain William James's *The Varieties of Religious Experience* (New York, 1902) and Evelyn Underhill's *Mysticism* (New York, 1911).

Mysticism: Sacred and Profane (Oxford, 1957) by R. C. Zaehner is a biased work, but the author knows the subject well, especially Hindu mysticism. A collection of essays on the mystical experience is *Studies in the Psychology of the Mystics,* edited by Joseph Maréchal (Albany, N. Y., 1964). A sampling of essays on various aspects and schools of mysticism is found in *Understanding Mysticism,* edited by Richard Woods (Garden City, N. Y., 1980).

Two important books on Hindu mysticism are R. C. Zaehner's *Hinduism* (London, 1962) and, older but still valuable, Surendranath Dasgupta's *Hindu Mysticism* (New York, 1927).

A number of good studies on mysticism in Buddhism are available: Edward Conze's *Buddhism: Its Essence and Development* (Oxford, 1951) and D. T. Suzuki's *On Indian Mahayana Buddhism,* translated and edited by Edward Conze (New York, 1968), are two. Frederick J. Streng has published a valuable study of Nagarjuna in his book *Emptiness: A Study in Religious Meaning* (New York, 1967).

For discussions of Christian mysticism, the reader may consult the introductions to many volumes of the "Classics of Western Spirituality" and the three-volume *A History of Christian Spirituality* (New York, 1963-1969) by Louis Bouyer, Jean Leclercq, François Vandenbroucke, and Louis Cognet. An older history is Pierre Pourrat's *Christian Spirituality* (Westminster, Md., 1953-1955), a four-volume work. On French spirituality of the modern age, Henri Brémond's twelve-volume *Histoire litté-raire du sentiment religieux en France,* 2d ed., edited by René Taveneaux (Paris, 1967-1968), remains unsurpassed. On Protestant spirituality, see *The Protestant Mystics,* edited by Anne Fremantle (London, 1964); in addition, volume 3 of the *History of Christian Spirituality* deals with Protestant, Orthodox, and Anglican forms of mysticism. A further discussion of Orthodox mysticism is George P. Fedotov's *A Treasury of Russian Spirituality* (1950; Belmont, Mass., 1975).

For a study of Islamic mysticism, see Annemarie Schimmel's *Mystical Dimensions of Islam* (Chapel Hill, N. C., 1975); Louis Massignon's *Essai sur les origines du lexique technique de la mystique musulmane,* 3d ed. (Paris, 1968); Reynold A. Nicholson's *Legacy of Islam* (London, 1939); and Margaret Smith's *Way of the Mystics: The Early Christian Mystics and the Rise of the Sufis* (London, 1976).

The choice of general works on Jewish mysticism is limited, but the best is a classic by Gershom Scholem, *Major Trends in Jewish Mysticism* (1941; reprint, New York, 1961).

LOUIS DUPRÉ

NASIR-I KHUSRAW

NASIR-I KHUSRAW (AH 394-465 to 470, 1004-1072 to 1077 CE), properly Abu Mu`in ibn Khusraw; distinguished Persian philosopher and poet as well as the most celebrated of Isma`ili thinkers.

Life. Born in the town of Qubadiyan near Balkh, Nasir-i Khusraw hailed from a small family that was either Sunni or Twelver Shi`i but definitely not Isma`ili. Although he came to be considered a descendant of `Ali and was often given the title of `Alawi, many modern scholars doubt this genealogy.

As a young man he was attracted to the study of various sciences and philosophy as well as that of other religions, which remained a major concern for him throughout his life. He entered government service early on and rose to high positions that allowed him to enjoy the life at court, but at the age of forty-two, his life was transformed by a dream admonishing him, ordering him to awake from the life of forgetfulness and journey to Mecca. Following the directives of the dream, he set out immediately for Mecca in December 1045. The transforming experience of this journey was to come, however, in Egypt, where he formally embraced Isma`ili Shiism. Remaining in Cairo for six years, he received the title of *hujjat* ("proof") before leaving as Isma`ili "missionary" *(da`i)* to Khorasan.

In Khorasan he encountered fierce opposition, to the extent that his house was attacked, and he was forced to take refuge in the far-off valley of Yumgan, in the mountains of the Hindu Kush, under the protection of the emir of Badakhshan. In this bleak and isolated valley Nasir-i Khusraw was to spend the rest of his life. To this day his tomb is a center of pilgrimage for Sunni Muslims, who view him as a Sufi pir, and for the Isma`i-liyah of the area, who venerate him as an Isma`ili sage.

Thought and Work. Nasir-i Khusraw's philosophy represents the most complete and mature synthesis of early Isma`ili and Fatimid philosophy and must be considered the final development of the philosophical school that had already produced Abu Hatim Razi (d. 933/4) and Hamid al-Din Kirmani (d. after 1020). Na-sir-i Khusraw was very much concerned with the issues these authors addressed, such as confirmation of the necessity of prophecy as against the views of Muhammad Zakariya' al-Razi (Rhazes; d. 925) and

emphasis upon esoteric hermeneutics *(ta'wil)* as against both legalism and rationalism. Also, like these earlier figures, he had keen interest in religions other than Islam and followed earlier formulations of Isma`ili metaphysics based upon the supraontological principle and the effusion of the intellect, soul, and nature through the process of contemplation.

Many apocryphal works bearing Nasir-i Khusraw's name are known, but only the following eight authentic books remain extant:

1. *The Divan*—The celebrated metaphysical and moral work based, on the one hand, upon Isma`ili philosophical doctrines and, on the other, upon disdain of the world and its pleasures. It also contains some autobiographical material, including the "confessional ode" depicting the dream that transformed his life and beginning with the lines

> O widely read, O globally travelled one,
> still earth-bound, still caught beneath the sky),
> what value would the spheres yet hold for you
> were you to catch a glimpse of hidden knowledge?
> (trans. P. W. Wilson and G. R. Aavani)

2. *Rawshana'i-namah* (The Book of Light)—A poem of some 582 verses dealing with metaphysics and eschatology.
3. *Safar-namah* (Book of Travels)—One of the most famous travel books of the Persian language, which is an important source not only for Nasir-i Khusraw's life but also for the contemporary geography and history of Iran and the Arab East.
4. *Wajh-i din* (The Face of Religion)—A major work of Isma`ili exegesis of both the doctrines and the practices of religion based upon the method of ta'wil.
5. *Gushayish va rahayish* (Release and Deliverance)—Answers to thirty questions dealing at once with metaphysics, physics, and religious law.
6. *Khwan al-ikhwan* (The Feast of the Brethren)—A work written in fairly simple langauge dealing again with both doctrine and practice of religion and using many earlier works, including some of the author's own lost treatises.
7. *Zad al-musafirin* (Provision for Travelers)—An almost purely philosophical work, including extensive quotations from earlier philosophers such as Rhazes.

8. Jami' al-hikmatayn (Harmonization of the Two Wisdoms)—Nasir-i Khusraw's last work, written in Badakhshan in 1070 and perhaps his greatest philosophical masterpiece. It seeks to harmonize the tenets of Greek philosophy, especially the thought of Plato and Aristotle, with the teachings of Islam as expounded in Isma'ili philosophy. The whole book is a response to a well-known philosophical poem by the tenth-century Isma'ili Abu al-Haytham Jurjani.

An additional eight books, including *Bustan al-qulub* (Garden of Hearts) and *Kitab al-miftah wa-al-misbah* (Book of the Key and the Lamp), are mentioned by Nasir-i Khusraw himself but are seemingly lost.

Influence. Nasir-i Khusraw, although greatly neglected in general accounts of Islamic philosophy, must be considered a major philosophical figure in the history of Islamic thought. His influence in this domain is not confined to later Isma'ili thought but extends to later Islamic philosophy in general as it developed in Persia and in certain forms of Sufism. One of the very few Persian poets to be honored with the title of *hakim* ("sage"), he has retained his reputation for centuries. To this day his *divan* remains part and parcel of classical Persian poetry that is read and often memorized from Persia to the borders of China.

BIBLIOGRAPHY

Corbin, Henry. "Nasir-i Khusrau and Iranian Isma'ilism." In The *Cambridge History of Iran*, vol. 4, edited by R. N. Frye, pp. 520-542. Cambridge, 1975.

Corbin, Henry, with Seyyed Hossein Nasr and Osman Yahia. *Histoire de la philosophie islamique*. Paris, 1964.

Ivanow, W. *Nâsir-e Khusrow and Ismailism*. Bombay and Leiden, 1948.

Nasir-i Khusraw. *Kitabe Jami' al-Hikmatain: Le livre réunissant les deux sagesses*. Edited by Henry Corbin and Mohammad Mo'in. Tehran and Paris, 1953.

Nasir-i Khusraw. *Forty Poems from the Divan*. Translated by Peter L. Wilson and Gholam Reza Aavani, with an introduction by Seyyed Hossein Nasr. Tehran, 1977.

Nasir-i Khusraw. *Wajh-i Din (Face of Religion)*. Edited by Gholam Reza Aavani, with an introduction by Seyyed Hossein Nasr. Tehran, 1977.

Nasir-i Khusraw. *Naser-E Khosraw's Book of Travels (Safarnama)*. Translated by Wheeler Thackston, Jr. Albany, N. Y., 1985.

SEYYED HOSSEIN NASR

NATURE

What we ordinarily speak of as "nature"—the physical world, including all living beings beyond the control of human culture—often appears to the religious consciousness as a manifestation of the sacred. Through nature, modes of being quite different from the specifically human reveal themselves to the religious imagination. The sun, the moon, and the earth, for example, can symbolize realities that transcend human experience. Throughout the history of religions, "nature" frequently is perceived as initiating a relationship with humankind, a relationship that is the foundation of human existence and well-being. In large part, this relationship is expressed in forms of adoration, a response of the total personality, or of an entire religious community, to the phenomena of nature.

In the worship of nature, radically different levels of existence are felt to interpenetrate and coexist. The possibilities of the human spirit become coextensive with the sacred capacities of the rest of the physical universe. The worship of nature thus highlights both the freedom of the sacred to appear in any form, and the capacity of the human being to recognize it for what it is in any expression. It also underlines the capacity of profane reality itself to become a transparent symbol of something other than itself, even while remaining what it is. In such a religious perception of the universe, nature transcends its brute physicality. It becomes a cipher, a symbol of something beyond itself.

The sky is often revered as a manifestation of divinity or venerated as the locus of the gods. The Konde of east-central Africa adored Mbamba (also named Kiara or Kyala), a divinity who dwelt with his family in the heights above the sky. The Konde offer prayer and sacrifice to the god who dwells in the sky, especially at times when rain is called for. Many divinities of the sky originally lived on earth or with the first human beings. Eventually, they withdrew on high.

Baiame is the supreme god among tribes of southeastern Australia (Kamilaroi, Euahlayi, and Wiradjuri). He welcomes the souls of the dead into his dwelling place beside the flowing waters of the Milky Way. His voice is thunder; he is omniscient. Although supreme beings of the sky like Baiame reveal important mysteries to the first ancestors before they withdraw on high, and although they play a major part in initiation ceremonies, they do not usually dominate liturgical life.

Objects fallen from the sky come from the sacred locus of the heavens and often become the objects of religious cults. For example, the Numana of the Niger River valley in West Africa, who accord an important place to the divinity of the sky, venerate small pebbles, which they believe have fallen from the sky. They install these sacred pebbles on top of cones of beaten earth some three feet high and offer sacrifices to them. Since the pebbles have fallen from the sky, they are believed to be fragments of the sky god. Actual meteorites are frequently the center of a cult associated with sky gods.

Worship of the sun is widespread, especially at the times of the solstices. The Chukchi of northern Asia, for example, offer sacrifices to the light of the sun. Among the Chagga of Mount Kilimanjaro in Tanzania, Ruwa (Sun) is the supreme being, who receives sacrificial offerings in times of crisis. In societies engaged in intensive agriculture, the sun is worshiped in connection with the fertility of the crops and regenerative life of the cosmos. Such is the case with Inti in the Inca pantheon. Privileged groups of human beings reckon their descent from the sun as did the Inca nobles, the Egyptian pharaoh, and important chiefly families on the island of Timor that reckon they are the "children of the sun."

> ## The earth is sacred in many traditions and is the object of devotion and affection.

In many cultures the sun is believed to traverse the underworld at night. Therefore the sun becomes a sacred guide for the soul's journey through the land of the dead.

The moon is one of the most fascinating and rich religious characters. It has long been an object of worship in many cultures. The moon's shifting shape and changing disposition in the sky at various times of the night, day, and month makes it the focus of a wide range of associations that have led to its veneration. The moon is frequently a lascivious being associated with the wanton powers of fertility. Often the moon is venerated as the source of sexual life and originator of reproductive processes such as menstruation and intercourse. The Canelos Quichua of eastern Ecuador, for example, treat Quilla, the moon, as a central supernatural being. When the new moon is immature, it is called *llullu Quilla*, the "green" or "unripe" moon. During these phases it is a prepubescent girl unable to conceive offspring or fashion pottery or prepare beer. The adult moon, *pucushca Quilla*, however, is a lascivious male whose incestuous exploits with his sister, the bird Jilucu, engendered the stars.

Among the Siriono of eastern Bolivia, Yasi (Moon) is the most important supernatural being. He once lived on earth as a chief, but after creating the first human beings and teaching them the fundamentals of culture, he ascended into heaven. The waxing of the moon occurs as Yasi washes his face clean by degrees after returning from the hunt.

Mountains are an ubiquitous object of cult. In the Kunisaki Peninsula of Japan, for example, a tradition that dates back to the Heian period establishes a systematic, metaphorical relationship between the image of the mountain and the salvific power of the Lotus Sutra (Grapard, 1986, pp. 21-50). The sacred mountain of this peninsula represents the nine regions of the Pure Land and is an important pilgrimage center. Its eight valleys are the eight petals of the lotus blossom that represents the Diamond Mandala and the Womb Mandala. The sacred mountain embodies the six realms (*rokudo*) of existence: that of the gods, human beings, titans, animals, hungry ghosts, and hells. Within these realms, arranged in a vertical hierarchy, all beings and all forms of rebirth have their place.

In South America, offerings are made to the mountains of the Andes throughout the year to sustain and stimulate the life of the community that cultivates food from the body of the mountain. Sacrifices and offerings placed in specific holy sites on the mountain replenish the fat, the power source, of the mountain body (Bastien, 1985, pp. 595-611).

Waters are frequently presented as supernatural beings worthy of worship. Springs, rivers, and irrigation waters are the centers of religious attention throughout the world. They are celebrated not only during the episodes of the agricultural cycle but also at moments of rebirth into initiatory societies and at moments of initiation into culture itself.

In Scandinavian mythology Ægir (the Sea) is the boundless ocean. His wife, Ran, casts her net through the ocean and drags human beings into its depths as sacrificial offerings. The nine daughters of Ægir and Ran represent the various modes and moments of the sea. All of these divine beings dwell in the magnificent castle at the bottom of the ocean where the gods occasionally gather.

Aquatic dragons embody the fertile principles manifest in moisture. The Chinese dragon Yin gathers together all the waters of the world and controls the rain. Images of Yin were fashioned at times of drought and at the onset of the rains (Granet, 1926, vol. 1, pp. 353-356).

The earth is sacred in many traditions and is the object of devotion and affection. As the source of life, Pachamama (Mother Earth) of the Andes is worshiped on various occasions throughout the year. The earth is frequently a partner of the sky or of some other celestial fertilizing divinity. Among the Kumana of southern Africa, for example, the marriage of the sky and the earth makes the cosmos fertile. Liturgical life is directed toward the fruitful accomplishment of this union. Among North American Indian peoples such as the Pawnee, the Lakota, the Huron, the Zuni, and the Hopi, the earth is the fertile partner of the sky and the source of abundant life. The care extended to the earth takes involved forms of worship. Rituals are associated with the earth, such as agricultural orgies.

Plants, trees, and vegetation also have their place in worship. The tree of life or the cosmic tree expresses the sacredness of the entire world. Scandinavian myth offers the example of Yggdrasill, the cosmic tree. Yggdrasill sinks its roots into the earth and into the netherworld where giants dwell. Divinities meet daily near the tree to pass judgment on the world's affairs. The Fountain of Wisdom flows from a spot near the tree as does the Fountain of Memory.

Other kinds of vegetation also manifest sacred powers and divinities. Miraculous trees, flowers, and fruits reveal the presence of divine powers. Rites of spring frequently center on plants, boughs, or trees that are treated as sacred. Around the world, the agricultural cycle is hedged around with religious acts directed toward the furthering of the powers of fertility manifest in various crops. In particular, the moments of sowing and reaping are marked by sacrifices.

Animals have also stimulated the religious imagination in such a way as to warrant devotion. Animals, birds, fish, snakes, and even insects have all become the focus of adoration in one culture or another. Often their bodies represent the transformed expression of supernatural beings that underwent metamorphosis at the beginning of time (Goldman, 1979).

Examples of the worship of nature could be multiplied endlessly. Even the term *nature* carries a range of connotations that obscure the meaning of sacred objects of cult in many cultures. Each generation of scholars in the last century spawned a number of interpretive theories in which the worship of nature figured as a large element in the assessment of religion in general. In fact, the effort to desacralize nature in the Western perception and to identify the perception of nature as sacred with "primitive" peoples played a large role in the foundation of the social sciences and in the self-understanding of the modern West (Cocchiara, 1948). James G. Frazer contended that the worship of nature and the worship of the dead were the two most fundamental forms of natural religion (1926, pp. 16-17). F. Max Müller founded his school of comparative religious studies on the principle that myths spoke about nature. E. B. Tylor also established his influential theory of animism, a still-lingering interpretation of religion on the notion that human beings projected onto nature certain animate qualities of their own character, visible especially in dream and in the rational explanations of death. Claude Lévi-Strauss pushes this intellectualized perception of nature in the formation of religion even further, contending that religion involved the humanization of the laws of nature (Lévi-Strauss, 1966, p. 221).

BIBLIOGRAPHY

General Works. The classic study of the sacral experience that underlies the worship of nature remains Mircea Eliade's *Patterns in Comparative Religion* (New York, 1958), which contains extensive discussions and bibliographies on many of the themes treated briefly above (sun, moon, water, earth, vegetation, et al.). For earlier discussions, see F. Max Müller's *Natural Religion* (London, 1888), E. B. Tylor's *Primitive Culture*, 2 vols. (1871; reprint, New York, 1970), and James G. Frazer's *The Worship of Nature* (London, 1926). Other helpful studies include *The Savage Mind* by Claude Lévi-Strauss (London, 1966) and *Menschenbilder früher Gesellschaften: Ethnologische Studien zum Verhältnis von Mensch und Natur*, edited by Klaus E. Müller (Frankfurt, 1983), which gathers together a number of essays on various aspects of nature (forests, stones, cultivated plants, and pastoral animals) and includes a bibliography.

Specialized Studies
Bastien, Joseph W. "Qollahuaya-Andean Body Concepts: A Topographical-Hydraulic Model of Physiology." *American Anthropologist* 87 (September 1985): 595-711.

Blacker, Carmen. *The Catalpa Bow: A Study of Shamanistic Practices in Japan*. London, 1975.
Cocchiara, Giuseppe. *Il mito del buon selvaggio: Introduzione alla storia delle teorie etnologiche*. Messina, 1948.
Earhart, H. Byron. *A Religious Study of the Mount Haguro Sect of Shugendo*. Tokyo, 1970.
Goldman, Irving. *The Cubeo: Indians of the Northwest Amazon* (1963). Urbana, Ill., 1979.
Granet, Marcel. *Danses et légendes de la Chine ancienne*. 2 vols. Paris, 1926.
Grapard, Allan G. "Lotus in the Mountain, Mountain in the Lotus: *Rokugo kaizan nimmon daibosatsu hongi*." Monumenta Nipponica 41 (Spring 1986): 21-50.
Holmberg, Allan R. *Nomads of the Long Bow: The Siriono of Eastern Bolivia*. Washington, D. C., 1960.
MacCormack, Carol P., and Marilyn Strathern, eds. *Nature, Culture, and Gender*. Cambridge, 1980.
Ortner, Sherry. "Is Female to Male as Nature Is to Culture?" In *Women, Culture, and Society*, edited by Michelle Zimbalist Rosaldo and Louise Lamphere. Stanford, Calif., 1974.
Tambiah, Stanley J. "Animals Are Good to Think and Good to Prohibit." *Ethnology* 8 (October 1969): 423-459.
Taussig, Michael T. *The Devil and Commodity Fetishism in South America*. Chapel Hill, N. C., 1980.
Zolla, Elemire. "Korean Shamanism." *Res* 9 (Spring 1985): 101-113.

LAWRENCE E. SULLIVAN

NEOLITHIC RELIGION

NEOLITHIC RELIGION comprises the religious concepts, cults, and rituals of the early farming communities that sprang up throughout the world in the Early Holocene period (8000-3000 BCE). Unlike the Paleolithic and Mesolithic periods of prehistory, the Neolithic period was characterized by climatic conditions, very similar to those of the present, that directed human activity chiefly to the soil and its fruits.

Because the basic achievements of the Neolithic period were attained neither simultaneously nor in a particular area only, the chronological and territorial boundaries of the Neolithic world are very flexible. Neolithic cultures differed not only in their chronology but, much more important for the study of religion, in their basic content: their methods of production, technological skills, social relations, and achievements in art. The earliest ware was produced in Japan by the Jomon culture during the eighth millennium BCE, long before communities of that region had mastered the cultivation of plants and the domestication of animals.

Archaeological artifacts, which constitute the main sources for the study of Neolithic religions, for the most part still lie buried; those that are known are usually fragmented and ambiguous. The fullest evidence for the study of Neolithic religion comes from Asia Minor and Europe, the two regions that have been best explored.

The Near East. The Neolithic religion of the Near East originated between 8300 and 6500 BCE in the zone of the so-called Fertile Crescent (Palestine, Syria, northern Iraq, and Iran). It flourished between 6500 and 5000 BCE in Anatolia, and disintegrated between 5000 and 3000 BCE in the lowlands of Mesopotamia.

Evidence of a sedentary way of life, a basic trait of the Neolithic period, is clearly discerned in the Natufian culture, which developed in Palestine and Syria between 10,000 and 8300 BCE. Excavations of Natufian settlements have yielded indirect evidence of the use and cultivation of grain (for example, stone mortars, pestles, and sickles). Such evidence, together with the remains of dogs, marks the Natufian as the dawn of Neolithic culture in the Near East (the so-called Proto-Neolithic). Although no objects of an undoubtedly sacred character have been discovered at Natufian sites, it is nevertheless possible to form some idea, on the basis of surviving houses, graves, and art objects, of the religious concepts, cults, and rituals extant in this period.

That all of the figural representations belonging to this culture were carved from pebbles suggests beliefs associated with water and its creative potential. These representations include schematized human heads from Ain Mallaha and Al-Oued and an "erotic" statuette from Ain Sakhri showing an embracing couple, perhaps illustrating the concept of the "holy marriage." Sexual attributes are not marked on any of the figures, and the relationship of the sexes is expressed in an allusive way: the large stone mortars with circular recipients in their middles probably represent the female principle, as the phallus-shaped stone pestles probably represent the male principle.

These mortars were frequently associated with burials and used either as grave markers (Wadi Fallah) or as altars around which graves were arranged in a semicircle (Al-Oued). Frequent burial of the dead in pits used for the storage of grain, and the occasional building of hearths above graves (Ain Mallaha) or in cemeteries (Nahal Oren), emphasizes a close connection between the dead and the processes of providing, keeping, and preparing grain food. Evidence of a cult of ancestors is also found in the complex funeral customs of the Natufians, especially in their burial of detached skulls, sometimes grouped in fives or nines.

Throughout the entire zone of the Fertile Crescent, the period between 8300 and 6500 BCE saw the appearance of villages in which cereals were cultivated and animals domesticated, as is now known through the discovery of remains of barley, wheat, sheep, goats, and pigs at scattered sites. Pottery was very rare, and therefore this period has been termed the Pre-Pottery Neolithic. The number of finds associated with religion is comparatively large, but they were discovered chiefly in Palestine, Syria, and northern Mesopotamia.

Baked or unbaked clay was also used for the making of other cult objects. In the upper Euphrates Valley, in Mureybet and Cayönü, there appear, in addition to the traditional stone statuettes, the earliest figurines made of baked clay. They date from the beginning of the seventh millennium BCE and represent, sometimes realistically but more often in a very schematized way, a standing or seated naked woman. At Munhata in Palestine, only elongated cylindrical figurines, some of them masculine, were made.

Cult centers discovered in Palestine (Jericho and Beida), in the upper Euphrates Valley (Mureybet), and in western Iran (Ganjadareh) provide more detailed evidence for the religion of the Pre-Pottery Neolithic. In Jericho, two rooms and a structure are supposed to have served cult purposes, primarily because of their unusual shapes: a room with a niche in which a block of volcanic rock stood on a stone support was discovered in a house; a pit filled with ashes was found in the middle of another house, which suggests that some ritual was performed in that place; finally, figurines representing oxen, goats, and, perhaps, pigs were found in a large structure with wooden posts placed in an unusual arrangement. In Ganjadareh a room with a niche containing fixed, superimposed rams' skulls was found in the middle of the Neolithic village, and in Mureybet rooms were discovered in which horns of wild oxen, perhaps bucrania (sometimes flanked by the shoulder blades of oxen or asses), were embedded in the walls.

The cults performed in individual households became clearly distinct from those in the care of the broader community. A gap between the sacred and the profane is evidenced by the very limited number of sacred objects, mainly fragmented anthropomorphic and zoomorphic figurines, found in villages from this period, in conjunction with their high concentration in some settlements; this causes us to speak of religious centers.

The best example of such a center is Çatal Hüyük in Anatolia, where fourteen building horizons, dating from 6300 to 5400 BCE, were discovered. Each of these levels consists of dwelling rooms linked with storage spaces and shrines, of varying size, that contain sacred representations (reliefs and frescoes), stone and clay figurines, and graves of privileged members of the community, possibly priests and priestesses. A certain consistency in the arrangement of representations on walls suggests the existence of a coherent religious concept or myth in which the character and mutual relationship of superior powers were clearly defined. We may assume that the reliefs depicted the divine powers, the frescoes described the sacred activities (religious ceremonies, sacrifices, and ritual scenes), and the statuettes represented the chief actors in the myth.

At the beginning of the fifth millennium BCE, Anatolia lost its importance, and the centers of culture and spiritual life were transferred to Mesopotamia, Khuzestan, and the

Transcaspian lowlands. Although a number of distinct and frequently unrelated cultures emerged in the period between 5000 and 3000 BCE, the religion of this period was characterized by three general features: the separation of the world of the living from the world of the dead, as manifested in the increasing practice of burying the dead in special cemeteries outside the settlements; the separation of cult centers from dwellings and the establishment of communal shrines; and the abandonment of figural representations. All these traits already are evidenced clearly in the cultures from the first half of the fifth millennium BCE. In northern Mesopotamia (the Halaf-Hassuna-Samarra cultures), the dead were buried mainly outside the settlements, and only children were interred beneath the floors of houses or shrines.

Southeastern Europe. The Neolithic religion of southeastern Europe was based on local traditions and the religion of the Epi-Paleolithic hunting-gathering communities, the presence of which is attested on numerous sites from Peloponnese to the northern fringe of the Pannonian plain, and from the western shores of the Black Sea to the Alps and the eastern coast of the Adriatic.

The first permanent open-space settlements appeared at the beginning of the eighth millennium BCE, in the central part of the Danu-bian valley, on low river terraces near large whirlpools abounding in fish. The local Epi-Paleolithic culture began to change rapidly and, at the end of the same millennium, evolved into the Proto-Neolithic Lepenski Vir culture. The shrines of this culture were associated not only with the earliest monumental sculptures in Europe but also with the first achievements in the domestication of plants and animals.

A total of 147 dwelling places were discovered at Lepenski Vir, the religious center for the entire central Danubian region between 7000 and 6500 BCE. About 50 of

> **The fifth millennium BCE was the period of the flowering of Neolithic cultures in southeastern Europe. . . .**

them had small shrines, each consisting of a rectangular hearth surrounded by large stone slabs embedded in a floor made of limestone mortar, an altar with a circular or ellipsoid recipient, and anywhere from one to five sculptures made of large boulders. Skeletons of infants (from one to five) were found beneath the floors, and secondary or partial burials (consisting mainly of skulls) were made within the shrines.

In the middle of the seventh millennium BCE, in the period when the cultivation of plants and the keeping of animals were taken out of the ritual context, the Lepenski Vir culture

lost its specific traits and developed into the culture of the earliest Danubian farmers, the so-called Starcevo-Körös-Cris culture. Concurrently or a few centuries later, Early Neolithic cultures appeared, either autonomously or as a result of acculturation, in other regions of southeastern Europe as well.

The sixth millennium was a period of stabilization for Neolithic cultures in southeastern Europe. The most creative regions were Thessaly-Macedonia (the Proto-Sesklo and Sesklo cultures), the Danubian region (the Starcevo culture) and the Maritsa Valley (the Karanovo culture). No shrines have been discovered in any of these regions; the only possible exception is a building in Nea Nikomedeia (Aegean Macedonia), which, because of its large dimensions, was probably a shrine.

Anthropomorphic figurines, mostly representing pregnant women, were common only in Thessaly, Macedonia, and the Danubian region, usually at places where utensils for everyday use were also found. Feminine figurines were the more numerous, but they are not earlier than masculine ones. Zoomorphic figurines (mostly representations of oxen and deer) were produced in great numbers, as were amulets, each in the shape of a stylized bull's head. Types of sacrifices can be deduced on the basis of several finds in Crete and Thessaly, where narrow, deep pits filled with ashes, animal bones, and occasional anthropomorphic figurines have been found.

The fifth millennium BCE was the period of the flowering of Neolithic cultures in southeastern Europe, especially in the inland regions of the Balkan Peninsula and in the Pannonian plain, where the Vinca culture was dominant. Several thousand anthropomorphic figurines and hundreds of ritual vases, amulets, and various cult instruments have been found at Vinca.

The anthropomorphic figurines were very varied and included naked and clothed human figures, figures in flexed, kneeling, or seated positions, two-headed figures, figures of musicians, and masked figures. Some scholars have seen in them representations of particular deities, such as the Great Goddess, the Bird and Snake Goddess, the Pregnant Vegetation Goddess, and the Year God.

The discovery of copper and gold in the Carpathian Mountains at the end of the fifth millennium BCE, and the later inroads of nomads from the southern Russian steppes, caused a crisis in the old values and goals; as a result, traditional shrines lost some of their importance.

At Cascuiareke (Romania), however, a shrine was found that contained evidence of the cult of the sacred pillar and, possibly, of the sun. A group of miniature clay objects (altars, stools, figurines in positions of adoration, and ritual vessels) with painted decoration (concentric circles, triangles, and spirals) representing the sun and other celestial bodies was discovered at Ovcharevo (Bulgaria). Similar ornaments found on painted ware suggest that religious thought was primarily directed to the sky and was concerned with cosmogony.

Other Regions. The separate religious spheres of the Neolithic world were the western Mediterranean with northwestern Europe; the Sahara; the Nile Valley; China; Japan; and Middle America. The hunting-gathering communities of Italy, the Iberian Peninsula, and the adjacent islands became acquainted with the main achievements of the "Neolithic Revolution" at the end of the seventh millennium BCE, but they mostly continued to live in caves and rock shelters and to hold on to ancient customs.

In the fifth millennium BCE, influences from the Aegean began to modify the culture of the Apennine Peninsula, while the Iberian peninsula saw the beginning of processes that in time led to the emergence, throughout western and northwestern Europe, of cultures characterized by megalithic tombs for collective burial (such as dolmens, passage graves, and gallery graves) and by sacred architecture consisting of large stone uprights (menhirs) set in parallel alignments or in circles (cromlechs). These were the basic forms, but some other types of sacred stone structures were built in other regions, for example, shrines with a U-shaped plan in Denmark and temples with niches and a central courtyard in Malta. The dominant cult was that of ancestors.

The religion of the Neolithic populations of Africa was based on quite different concepts and cults. The predominantly pastoral communities of the Sahara left rock paintings and drawings that usually represent oxen or human figures in the position of adoration. Farther east, in Egypt, the first farming communities paid greatest attention to their dead and to the Nile.

The Neolithic religion in the countries of the Far East also had distinct features. The Yang-shao culture of China seems to have fostered the cult of ancestors and fertility. Judging from motifs on painted ware, an important role was also accorded to the cult of evergreen trees (fir and cypress) and, perhaps, mountaintops. A significant role was accorded as well to the dynamic forces of the universe and cosmic radiation, which influence nature and the destiny of man.

BIBLIOGRAPHY

No comprehensive account of Neolithic religion has yet been written. The general surveys of prehistoric religion devote comparatively little space to Neolithic religion and present only the material from the Neolithic sites in Europe and the Near East; see, for example, E. O. James's *Prehistoric Religion* (London, 1957), Johannes Maringer's *The Gods of Prehistoric Man* (New York, 1960), and Étienne Patte's *Les hommes préhistoriques et la religion* (Paris, 1960). Some new and stimulating ideas concerning Neolithic religion have been introduced by Karl J. Narr in the chapter "Kunst und Religion der Steinzeit und Steinkupferzeit," in his *Handbuch der Urgeschichte,* vol. 2 (Bern, 1975), pp. 655-670, and by Mircea Eliade in *A History of Religious Ideas,* vol. 1 (Chicago, 1978), pp. 29-52 and 114-124.

A rich and systematic collection of documents for the study of Neolithic religion is provided by Hermann Müller-Karpe in his *Handbuch der Vorgeschichte,* vol. 2 (Munich, 1968). Several books discuss, in a rather uncritical way, the problem of the meaning of anthropomorphic and zoomorphic figurines in the Neolithic world: Olaf Höckmann's *Die menschengestaltige Figuralplastik der südosteuropäischen Jungsteinzeit und Steinkupferzeit,* 2 vols. (Hildesheim, 1968); Marija Gimbutas's *The Goddesses and Gods of Old Europe,* 6500-3500 B. C., rev. ed. (London, 1982); Elena V. Antonova's *Antropomorfnaia skul'ptura drevnikh zemledel'tsev Perednei i Srednei Azii* (Moscow, 1977); and Nándor Kalicz's *Clay Gods* (Budapest, 1980). A correct methodological approach to these problems is demonstrated by Peter J. Ucko in "The Interpretation of Prehistoric Anthropomorphic Figurines," *Journal of the Royal Anthropological Institute* 92 (January-June 1962): 38-54, and in his *Anthropomorphic Figurines from Egypt and Neolithic Crete with Comparative Material from Prehistoric Near East and Mainland Greece* (London, 1968).

The great spiritual centers of the Neolithic world are outlined in detail in Kathleen M. Kenyon's *Digging Up Jericho* (London, 1957), James Mellaart's *Çatal Hüyük* (London, 1967), Jacques Cauvin's *Religions néolithiques de Syro-Palestine* (Paris, 1972), and my own book *Europe's First Monumental Sculpture: New Discoveries at Lepenski Vir* (London, 1972). A. Rybakov's "Kosmogoniia i mifologiia zemledel'tsev eneolita," *Sovetskaia arkheologiia* 1 (1965): 24-47 and 2 (1965) 13-33, is an important contribution to understanding the semantics of pottery decoration. The Neolithic shrines of southeastern Europe are discussed by Vladimir Dumitrescu in "Édifice destiné au culte découvert dans la couche Boian-Spantov de la station-tell de Casciorele," *Dacia* (Bucharest) 15 (1970): 5-24; by Henrieta Todorova in "Kultszene und Hausmodell aus Ovcarevo," *Thracia* (Sofia) 3 (1974): 39-46; and by Marija Gimbutas in "The Temples of Old Europe," *Archaeology* 33 (November-December 1980): 41-50. Megalithic monuments have been the subject of many recent monographs and papers; however, they discuss the problems of the systematization, distribution, and chronology of these monuments rather than their religious meaning. There are no comprehensive studies of Neolithic religion in eastern and southeastern Asia, although some attention has been devoted to the significance of ornamentation on the pottery of the Yang-shao culture and of figurines from the Jomon period.

DRAGOSLAV SREJOVIC
Translated from Serbo-Croatian by Veselin Kostic

NESTORIAN CHURCH

The proper name of the church that is called Nestorian or Assyrian is the Ancient Church of the East. *Nestorian* is an appellation dating from the fifth century and *Assyrian* from the nineteenth. By *East* is meant those ancient territories lying east of the former Byzantine empire comprising modern-day Iraq, Persia, and the southeastern part of Turkey. According to the *Doctrine of Addai,* Thaddaeus, following the Resurrection and at the behest of Christ, went to Edessa and healed its toparch, Abgar V (d. AD 50). Thaddaeus stayed to preach the gospel, made converts, and ordained his disciple, `Aggai, a bishop. He then journeyed to and preached the gospel in Mesopotamia, southern Turkey, Iraq, and southwestern Persia.

By the second century, Christianity had spread throughout the East. In the third century, Christianity also spread to the Sasanid capital of Seleucia-Ctesiphon, where the bishopric was founded under Phafa. By the latter part of the fifth century, the bishops of Seleucia-Ctesiphon (by that time followers of Nestorius) were claiming that the see had been established by Thaddaeus and his disciple Mari.

The bishop (metropolitan) of Seleucia-Ctesiphon was recognized as being under the jurisdiction of the patriarch of Antioch and was made a catholicos (a church position higher than a metropolitan and lower than a patriarch). He was able to bring under his jurisdiction all the dioceses in the East except the metropolitan see of Riyordashir.

In the first half of the fifth century the Church of the East was rocked by a theological controversy so serious that it resulted in schism. This was the so-called Nestorian controversy. Nestorius, a Syrian by origin, became patriarch of Constantinople in 428. He taught that Jesus Christ had two distinct natures: divine and human. Nestorius was condemned at the Council of Ephesus in 431 but his teaching spread, and by 451 most of the eastern part of the Church of the East had become "Nestorian," rejecting the Council of Ephesus.

After the Arab conquest of Iraq in the beginning of the seventh century, the Nestorians, like other Christians, became *dhimmis* under the protection of the Muslims. Under the Abbasid caliphs (750-1258) the Nestorians enjoyed relative peace, and in 762 their catholicoi moved their see to Baghdad. Although the Nestorians were generally favored, there were times when they, like other Christians, were persecuted or humiliated by the caliphs. The Nestorian catholicoi left Baghdad and settled in northern Iraq (Kurdistan) in the vicinity of Mosul and Alqosh.

The most detrimental effect of the Muslim conquest on the Nestorian church in the countries lying between Persia and China was that its missionary activity, begun among the Mongols, Turks, and Chinese, was cut off. Eventually the early blossom of Christianity in China died.

In the fifteenth century the small Nestorian community on the island of Cyprus joined the church of Rome. Power struggles within the ecclesiastical hierarchy of the mother Nestorian church also caused large segments of it to join Rome.

In the middle of the eighteenth century a Nestorian bishop, Mar Yusuf (Joseph) of Diyarbakir, joined the church of Rome. By then most of the Nestorians of the plains of Mosul had become Roman Catholics. Since then, the Nestorian community has retreated into the mountains of Kurdistan.

For more than a hundred years (1830-1933), the Nestorian community in Kurdistan and Iraq suffered continuous tragedies. Being Christians they were always prey to

Kurdish chieftains, who plundered their villages. The activity and existence of Western missionaries among the Nestorians most probably motivated the Kurds and their patrons, the Ottomans, to agitate against them.

At the outbreak of World War I, about twenty thousand Nestorians struggled to reach the British lines in Iraq to avoid reprisal by Kurds and Ottomans. With fear of reprisal haunting the rest of the Nestorians of Urmia, in the summer of 1918 some hundred thousand of them attempted to reach the Kermanshah-Qazvin region, which was then under British occupation. Less than half made it through.

After the establishment of national rule in Iraq in 1921, the Iraqi government granted autonomy in internal and religious affairs to the Nestorian community (in northern Iraq) led by their catholicos, Mar Ishai Shimon XXI. But Mar Shimon demanded complete independence from Iraq, and was turned down. Finally, in 1933 it notified the Assyrians either to behave as Iraqi citizens or leave.

The Assyrian community, which numbered about 500,000 in 1980, still has many members living in Iraq and Iran, but their greatest concentration is in the United States, especially in Chicago, Illinois. This latter group is mostly composed of immigrants who left Iraq after 1933 and their descendants.

BIBLIOGRAPHY

Perhaps the most important ancient source on the theological teaching and views of Nestorius is the *Bazaar of Heracleides,* translated by Godfrey R. Driver and Leonard Hodgson (Oxford, 1925). Other sources are the "Opera and Literae" of Cyril of Alexandria in *Patrologia Graeca,* edited by J.-P. Migne, vols. 126-127 (Paris, 1859); the *Acts of the Council of Ephesus* in *Sacrorum counciliorum nova et amplissima collectio,* edited by Giovanni Domenico Mansi, vols. 4 and 5 (Florence and Venice, 1758-1798); Giuseppe Simone Assemani's *Bibliotheca Orientalis,* vol. 3, pt. 2 (Rome, 1728); and Friedrich Loofs's *Die Fragmente des Nestorius* (Halle, 1905) and *Nestorius and His Place in the History of Christian Doctrine* (Cambridge, 1914).

The earliest sources on the Nestorian catholicoi are *The Chronicle of Mshiha Zkha,* in *Sources syriaques,* edited by Alphonse Mingana (Leipzig, 1907); *Chronique de Michel le Syrien,* edited by Jean-Baptiste Chabot (Paris, 1890); Bar Hebraeus's *Chronicon ecclesiasticum,* 3 vols., edited by J. B. Abbeloos and T. J. Lamy (Paris, 1872-1877); and *Chronique de Seert, histoire nestorienne* (in Arabic and French), edited by Addai Scher, in *Patrologia Orientalis,* vol. 4 (Paris, 1907).

For the role of the Nestorians in spreading Christianity among the Turks, Mongols, and Chinese, see Alphonse Mingana's "The Early Spread of Christianity in Central Asia and the Far East," *Bulletin of the John Rylands Library* 9 (1925): 297-371; Adolf von Harnack's *The Mission and Expansion of Christianity in the First Three Centuries,* vol. 2, 2d ed. (New York, 1908); and *The Nestorian Monument: An Ancient Record of Christianity in China, with Special Reference to the Expedition of Frits V. Holm,* edited by Paul Carus (Chicago, 1909). For the Nestorians in India, consult John D. Macbride's *The Syrian Church in India* (Oxford, 1856) and William J. Richards's *The Indian Christians of St. Thomas, Otherwise Called the Syrian Christians of Malabor* (London, 1908).

For the general history of the Nestorians, old and modern, see Asahel Grant's *The Nestorians, or The Lost Tribes* (1841; reprint, Amsterdam, 1973) and *History of the Nestorians* (London, 1855); George Percy Badger's *The Nestorians and Their Rituals,* 2 vols. (London, 1852); Henry Holme's *The Oldest Christian Church* (London, 1896); Jerome Labourt's *Le christianisme dans l'empire perse sous la dynastie sassanide, 224-632* (Paris, 1904); William A. Wigram's *An Introduction to the History of the Assyrian Church, or The Study of the Sassanid Empire, 100-640 A.D.* (London, 1910); George David Malech's *History of the Syrian Nation and the Old Evangelical-Apostolic Church of the East* (Minneapolis, 1910); Adrian Fortesque's *The Lesser Eastern Churches* (1913; reprint, New York, 1972); William C. Emhardt and George M. Lamsa's *The Oldest Christian People: A Brief Account of the History and Traditions of the Assyrian People and the Fateful History of the Nestorian Church* (1926; reprint, New York, 1970); Eugène Tisserant's "Nestorienne (L'église)," in *Dictionnaire de théologie catholique,* edited by Alfred Vacant and Eugène Mangenot (Paris, 1931), vol. 2; George Graf's *Geschichte der christlichen arabischen Literatur,* "Bibliotica Apostolica Vaticana," vol. 2 (Rome, 1947); and John Joseph's *The Nestorians and Their Muslim Neighbors: A Study of Western Influence on Their Relations* (Princeton, 1961).

MATTI MOOSA

NEW CALEDONIA RELIGION

NEW CALEDONIA RELIGION is best known from the work of Maurice Leenhardt, a former Protestant missionary (Société des Missions Évangéliques Pratique de Paris), who was Marcel Mauss's successor as professor of comparative religions at the École Pratique des Hautes Études.

Because each local group (*mwaro*) in New Caledonia is linked with an animal or plant or other natural phenomenon, Western observers have described the religion of the island as "totemism." Though this term is now less fashionable than it was in the period from 1880 to 1940, it can still, for convenience' sake, be applied to the New Caledonia religious system. The local groups have divided among themselves all the aspects of nature that either can be utilized or need to be feared, with each group becoming the master of a particular aspect. Within each group, one of the members of the most junior line, referred to as the group's "master," is in charge of performing the ritual that will protect or benefit all the *mwaro.* Thus, the master of the yam ensures a good crop over the whole of the valley. Along the sea one finds masters of the trade winds, the shark, the whale, or the mosquito, while masters of the thunder are to be found nearer the mountain range.

Each master not only ensures prosperity and wards off natural disasters, but also controls the specific sickness thought to be linked with the totemic entity assigned to him.

If someone is ailing, word is sent to a seer, who divines the cause of the sickness. A messenger is then sent to the master in charge of the force responsible for the sickness. The master prays and gives the necessary herbal remedies to the patient; many of these medications are quite effective in treating at least those illnesses that were not brought by Europeans.

The natures of the New Caledonia gods are complex, and Leenhardt spent considerable time attempting to understand them. R. H. Codrington, in *The Melanesians* (1891), distinguished two principal types of gods: those who were once human and those who have never been human. The New Caledonians, however, make no linguistical distinction, both types of gods being referred to either as *bao* or *due.* The two kinds of deities are linked in the figure of Teê Pijopac, a god who has himself never been human but who controls the subterranean or submarine land of the dead, where all must go. According to local belief, the dead reach the entrances to this land by following ridges that lead down to the sea. At one of these entrances, known as Pucangge (near Bourail), the goddess Nyôwau examines all those who wish to enter to make sure that their left earlobe is pierced. She pierces any unpierced lobe with the mussel-shell knife that she also uses to peel yams.

There is constant communication between the living and the dead. The dead can be seen and spoken with when needed. They can be called upon to help in a crisis such as sickness or war, or to favor the results of family labors. Myths speak of the living going to the land of the dead and of the dead acting in the land of the living. There are, for example, various versions of a myth in which a loving husband attempts to bring his young wife back from the land of the dead. He either succeeds in his quest through the help of a bird (a common link for communication with the dead), or he fails. Among the stories about people from the underworld acting among the living there are those that describe an unsuspecting husband who might find, for example, that his new wife snores at night, or that she is double-jointed, both of which are characteristics of people from the underworld. There are also numerous versions of a myth about a goddess, usually Toririhnan, who, after drowning the pregnant wife of a chief, disguises herself as the wife by filling her belly with pots. The true wife, however, is saved by a miracle and taken away to a distant island. Later, this woman returns with her grown sons; their identity is revealed, and the usurper is killed.

Other gods preside over agriculture, such as Kapwangwa Kapwicalo, who protects irrigated taro terraces in the Gomen area, or Toririhnan, who causes it to rain each time she blows her nose at the top of the Hienghène Valley. There are also a great number of gods whose function is the protection of a given clan, protection that is often traced back to the clan's mythical origin. Gods can have sexual relations with humans, an event that either can have terrifying consequences—such as the death of the mortal or the turning backward of his head—or can resemble normal human sexual acts. Myths in which families trace their origins to instances of intercourse between gods and humans record both types of occurrences.

Indeed in Melanesia, as in Polynesia, all genealogies have divine origins, and although the religion of New Caledonia is totemistic in appearance there is no available evidence that any of the kinship groups believe that they are descended from the animal species or natural phenomenon

> **It is important to recognize that the mythical systems of the hundreds of different clans are highly diversified. . . .**

with which they are spiritually associated. These totem entities—called *rhë re* (sg., *rhë e*)—represent the "spiritual belonging" of the group and are passed along through the male line. When a woman marries outside of her totem group, her *rhë e* is sometimes said to follow her. This does not mean, however, that the *rhë e* has left its original abode; because mythical beings are understood to be ubiquitous they are thought to be able to dwell in the two places at once.

There are occasions on which the *rhë re* and the *bao* (who were formerly human) meet. Such a meeting will take place in part of the landscape that is outside of human control, such as the bush, the forest, or the mountain range. The dead, those *bao* who were formerly human, can merge with the *rhë e* that is linked with their clan. Thus, for example, if thunder is associated with a particular group, the rumbling of the thunder is also the voice of the dead of that clan. Also in accordance with this pattern, no ancestor of the octopus group, for example, will appear in the form of a shark, unless they have what early authors referred to as "linked totems," that is, clusters of symbols all of which are linked to a certain *mwaro*. In some cases a group's *rhë e* will manifest itself in various forms depending on the setting: thus, for some chiefly families of the so-called Naacuwe-Cidopwaan group the *rhë e* takes the form of a lizard if seen inland, but becomes a water-snake on the beach, or a shark in the sea, and is also thought of as a masked male dancer said to emerge from the sea.

Missionaries who worked among the New Caledonians attempted to find the natives' idols in order to destroy them; they discovered objects resembling idols that had been carefully preserved by clan leaders over the course of centuries. Pierre Lambert (1900) has published illustrations of some of these items. They are stones of various shapes about which

little is actually known except that they turn up from time to time in yam gardens, are linked with the clan's totem entity, and are in some way connected with success in farming, fishing, weather control, and so forth, as were the thunderstones (meteorites) of the Europeans of old. It has been observed that when these artifacts are used as repositories of the divine presence for sacramental purposes—and not as representations of gods—they can be replaced if lost or confiscated. This provision allows for the indefinite preservation of this type of link with the divine.

It is important to recognize that the mythical systems of the hundreds of different clans are highly diversified, a diversity that appears most clearly in the origin myths of the various groups. Some clans believe their spiritual origin to be the mountain that is called Souma (in the Ajië language) or Caumyë (in the Paici language). The vernacular texts obtained by Leenhardt demonstrated that the mountain had a connection with the creation of mankind and that its importance stems from the gods who live in the various principal mountains. For instance, Ka To Souma, the god associated with Souma, guards one of the possible entrances to the subterranean land of the dead. So great is the respect for, and fear of, this god that his proper name (Gomawe or Kavere) is never uttered. Other clans, usually those living near the watershed, claim a spiritual link with one or another of the forms of thunder. These different forms are grouped in distinctive ways according to the local theology, thereby giving each clan a powerful mythical protector. We can thus classify clans according to their myths; conversely, mythical beings in charge of protecting the various clans may be classified according to the patrilineal marriage moieties with which they are associated in the Paici area or, in the north, according to the political phratries to which they belong.

The nearby Loyalty Islands (Uvéa, Lifou, and Maré) present a different set of problems. Although the inhabitants have been Christians for a century and a half (twice as long as the natives of New Caledonia proper) sacred groves still exist there, the old deities are remembered, and the cult of the dead continues to surface from time to time. However, the distribution of mythical beings among the families of the islands is significantly different from what prevails in New Caledonia. One essential aspect of the religion of the Loyalty Islands is that direct relations with the invisible world are the prerogative of the oldest established clans. These privileged clans, called *ten adro* (on Lifou), *wäi* (on Uvéa), or *èlè-tok* (on Maré), act as hosts to visiting gods. It is this status as host to the gods that provides legitimacy to the chiefly lines of today. The senior clans are also, however, the wardens of the invisible road along which the dead travel, eventually diving into the sea and reaching the island of Heo (Beautemps-Beaupré), where the entrance to the world of the dead is located. At the court of each of the paramount chiefs, a special person (called Atesi on Lifou and, on Maré, Acania) has the role of being the representative of these clans. He acts as their intermediary, for neither they nor their yams can enter a chief's house since their presence would endanger his life. On these islands there is thus a formalized distinction between families having the privilege of communicating with the divine world—each *ten adro* has its own god, to which only it can pray—and those who must be satisfied with praying to their own dead. The latter use diviners to discover whom they must negotiate with in order to ward off any invisible power which is causing injury to the clan.

BIBLIOGRAPHY

The oldest, but still quite illuminating, work on the subject of New Caledonia religion is R. P. Gagnère's *Étude ethnologique sur la religion des Néo-calédoniens* (Saint-Louis, France, 1905). It vividly describes the man and lizard cult relation in the Pouebo area of northeastern New Caledonia. Pierre Lambert's *Moeurs et superstitions des Néo-calédoniens* (Nouméa, New Caledonia, 1900) is interesting, although Lambert is at times less than accurate in his descriptions of the religions of the Belep Islands in the north and the Isle of Pines in the south. The monumental, two-volume *Ethnologie der Neu-Caledonier und Loyalty-Insulaner* (Munich, 1929) by the Swiss ethnographer Fritz Sarasin contains an indispensable atlas. The classic works in the field are Maurice Leenhardt's two volumes: *Notes d'ethnolo-gie néo-calédonienne* (Paris, 1930) and *Documents néo-calédo-niens* (Paris, 1932). Admired for their precision at the time of their publication, Leenhardt's books are full of information, and continue to be valuable research tools. My own contributions to the subject include the following: *Structure de la chefferie en Mélanésie du sud* (Paris, 1963), *Mythologie du masque en Nouvelle-Calédonie* (Paris, 1966), *Des multiples niveaux de signification du mythe* (Paris, 1968), and *Naissance et avortement d'un messianisme* (Paris, 1959). Recent publications in the field include Marie-Joseph Dubois's *Mythes et traditions de Maré, Nouvelle Calédonie: Les Elètok* (Paris, 1975) and Alban Bensa and Jean-Claude Rivière's *Les chemins de l'alliance: L'organisation sociale et ses représentations en Nouvelle-Calédonie* (Paris, 1982).

JEAN GUIART

NEW GUINEA RELIGIONS

The General Structure of the Cosmos. New Guineans' conceived cosmic order has two parts: the empirical— the natural environment, its economic resources (including animals), and its human inhabitants; and the nonempirical— spirit-beings, nonpersonalized occult forces, and, sometimes, totems. Theoretically it has three analytically separate systems: men in relation to the natural environment and its resources, or the economic system; relationships among human beings themselves, or the sociopolitical system; and men in relation to spirit-beings, occult forces, and totems, or religion. In fact, these systems interdepend, so that it is essential to understand how religion impinges on economic and social life and, in so doing, how it contributes to intellectual life and leadership.

The whole of New Guinea (Papua New Guinea and Irian Jaya) has about a thousand distinct language groups, each one virtually a separate society. The economic system is generalized: most of the people are settled agriculturalists with few specialized skills apart from religious ritual, which a limited number of adult males (the leaders) monopolize. Without specialized occupational groups, social structure has to be based on kinship, marriage, and descent, although even within this broad framework there is much variation. Some groups are congeries of relatively large phratries or tribes, while others consist of small clans or even lineages.

In general terms, most New Guineans recognize the following kinds of spirit-beings: autonomous creative or regulative spirit-beings (deities or culture heroes); autonomous noncreative or malevolent spirit-beings (demons, tricksters, and pucks); and spirits of the dead. Many also recognize clan totems and practice sympathetic magic. Variations of belief are most marked with respect to deities and spirits of the dead. Some peoples, such as the Huli and the Kainantu of the Highlands, claim relatively few gods; yet others, such as the Mae Enga of the Highlands and the peoples inland from Madang, believe in many deities.

Yet despite this heterogeneity, New Guineans appear to hold one concept in common, that the cosmos is essentially a finite physical realm with, as hinted, almost no supernatural or transcendental attributes. Gods, ghosts, demons, and totems are superhuman but terrestrial. They are more powerful than humans but still corporeal, taking human or animal form with normal physical attributes.

The Function of Religion. Melanesians believe that they have inherited a generally predictable cosmic order, which is anthropocentric and materialistic. It exists for man's benefit, and its material resources (crops, livestock, and artifacts) are concomitants of his existence. Hence religion has two principal functions. First, myths (regarded as the source of ultimate truth) explain and thereby validate the cosmic order. Second, just as the fulfillment of obligations between human beings maintains the secular social structure, the observance of ritual duties assures men that superhuman beings will guarantee the success of their major undertakings and protect the cosmic order from unforeseeable dangers.

The natural environment and economic resources. Not many New Guinea religions are greatly concerned with the natural environment as a whole. Except for occasional volcanic eruptions and droughts it is never seriously threatened, so that the people do not fear for its continuance. Hence elaborate accounts of its origin and rituals to preserve it are rare.

Mythology and ritual are generally more detailed and complex for the economic system. The performance for economic ends of ritual in honor of the dead is very common in

New Guinea. Specifically, it consists of formal keening at funerals, food offerings, dancing, and the celebration of the male cult. In response, ghosts are said to help their living descendants by protecting gardens from wild pigs and landslides, helping hunters find game, bringing presents, and, especially in dreams, by giving messages about impending events. They regard the recent dead as minatory—interested mainly in punishing transgressors—and expect economic benefits from the remote dead, to whom, with the exception of mortuary ceremonies, they address their rituals. Most seaboard peoples, who do not hold this belief, honor the recent dead, many of whom they remember as living persons. Second, there are different interpretations of the likely responses of the dead to the rituals performed in their honor. Some Highlanders, noted for their general aggressiveness, are said to apply to ghosts the same techniques they apply to the living: bargaining and bribery, in which the aim is to manipulate and curb pugnacious egalitarian rivals. Ghosts are said to respond in kind. Seaboard peoples are less assertive. Their view is that ritual should create strong ties between men and ghosts; as long as men fulfill their obligations, ghosts should automatically reciprocate.

The sociopolitical order. Likewise, total sociopolitical systems receive irregular treatment in religion. Some groups (for example, the Mae Enga, the Kainantu people, and the inhabitants of Wogeo Island) have myths that attribute society's existence and forms to their deities. Others, like the Ngaing, do not. They see no need to validate the social order in its entirety: they are unaware that any other kind of social order exists, and theirs is not threatened by conquest from outside or revolution from within.

The primary function of the male cult is the initiation of boys into manhood. After they are about ten years old, boys in adjacent settlements are assembled, segregated from women, placed under the supervision of adult males (especially leaders) in a cult house, and given special instruction. They are taught the rudiments of myths and ritual. They observe stringent taboos and are subjected to a physical ordeal that may include beating, scarification, penile incision, or forced nose bleeding. Thereafter they are returned to village life. The severity of initiation appears to correlate with society's pattern of male-female relations. In general, men are dominant in both secular and ritual affairs.

The last two important aspects of religion in the context of the sociopolitical order are (1) religion's impingement on moral obligation, and (2) the role of sorcery. Once again, the relationship between religion and moral obligation has no standard pattern: for some groups it is an important issue, but for others it is not. Thus the Huli insist that their primary god Datagaliwabe enjoined moral precepts on them, while the Kai-nantu people have a secondary mythology devoted to the inculcation of ethics, and the Manus of the Admiralty Islands believe themselves to be under the continual sur-

veillance of the dead, who punish the infringement of any rule.

Belief in sorcery is virtually universal. The art has many forms: contagious magic; projection of missiles into a victim; figurative removal and replacement of a victim's head or entrails; and actual immobilization of a victim by inserting slivers of bamboo (or, nowadays, lengths of wire) into vital parts of his body.

Belief in sorcery is motivated by personal anxiety. A person can never be sure where his friends and foes are. Unless he can attribute illness or bad luck to an angry god, ghost, or demon, he will search for a human enemy lurking in his locality.

> **Belief in sorcery is motivated by personal anxiety. A person can never be sure where his friends and foes are.**

Leadership and the intellectual system. Myth and ritual are for many New Guineans the principal means of understanding the cosmic order and maintaining their central position in it. Everyday experience largely endorses their certitude of the truth of religion. Normally crops do mature, livestock and human beings reproduce their kind, and artifacts meet their owners' expectations. The rituals used are obviously effective, so that their acquisition is an essential prerequisite of leadership. Big men are those who "know": they are experts in mythology and, particularly, in harnessing the power of gods and spirits of the dead that will ensure the success of their followers' purely secular activities. Secular skills are "knowledge" but at a low level: they are something anybody can acquire by imitation. It takes a special kind of man, however, to master "true knowledge," the religious secrets that are the core of the instruction given boys during initiation. Thereafter, those who aspire to leadership must undergo a long and exacting apprenticeship under acknowledged experts until they are accepted as qualified practitioners.

BIBLIOGRAPHY

Allen, M. R. *Male Cults and Secret Initiations in Melanesia.* Melbourne and London, 1967. The most detailed general analysis of initiatory ceremonies for males in New Guinea so far published. A standard text.

Baal, Jan van. *Dema.* The Hague, 1966. An important Irian Jaya ethnography, including a detailed account of traditional religion.

Berndt, Ronald M. *Excess and Restraint.* Chicago, 1962. A general ethnography of the Kainantu people of the Papua New Guinea Highlands. Provides background to Berndt's essay in Lawrence and Meggitt (1972).

Burridge, Kenelm. *Tangu Traditions.* Oxford, 1969. A thorough study of a New Guinea people's traditional mythology.

Fortune, Reo F. *Sorcerers of Dobu* (1932). Rev. ed. New York, 1963. An early and classic analysis of religion and sorcery in a traditional Papuan society.

Hogbin, Ian. *The Island of Menstruating Men: Religion in Wogeo, New Guinea.* Scranton, Pa., 1970. Another important account of a traditional religion, written nearly forty years after the field work was done.

Lawrence, Peter. "Statements about Religion: The Problem of Reliability." In *Anthropology in Oceania,* edited by Lester R. Hiatt and Chandra Jayawardena, pp. 140-154. Sydney, 1971. A discussion of the difficulty of assessing the validity of personal belief in and commitment to religion in New Guinea.

Lawrence, Peter. "Religion and Magic." In *The Encyclopaedia of Papua and New Guinea,* edited by Peter Ryan, pp. 1001-1012. Melbourne, 1972. A general introduction to traditional religions in New Guinea. Reprinted in *Anthropology in Papua New Guinea,* edited by Ian Hogbin (Melbourne, 1973), pp. 201-226.

Lawrence, Peter. *The Garia.* Melbourne and Manchester, 1984. An analysis of a traditional cosmic system in New Guinea, with emphasis on religion.

Lawrence, Peter, and M. J. Meggitt, eds. *Gods, Ghosts, and Men in Melanesia* (1965). Oxford, 1972. A symposium of essays on a number of traditional religions in New Guinea and Vanuatu. The best collection available.

McArthur, Margaret. "Men and Spirits in the Kunimaipa Valley." In *Anthropology in Oceania,* edited by Lester R. Hiatt and Chandra Jayawardena, pp. 155-189. Sydney, 1971.

Tuzin, Donald F. *The Voice of the Tambaran: Truth and Illusion in Ilahita Arapesh Religion.* Berkeley, 1980. A detailed and sophisticated analysis of a New Guinea traditional religion. Pays special attention to male initiation rites and the problem of individual belief and commitment.

Williams, Francis E. *Orokaiva Society.* Oxford, 1930. An early monograph that provides much valuable information about traditional religion.

Williams, Francis E. *Drama of Orokolo.* Oxford, 1940. Williams's most mature work; a carefully documented account of an elaborate ceremonial and ritual complex in western Papua. A classic.

PETER LAWRENCE

NEW RELIGIONS

An Overview

The Concept. Terms such as *new religion, new religious movement,* and *cult* are used in widely differing ways, yet their application is not arbitrary: it is conditioned by historical and theological, as well as academic, considerations. While there seems to be agreement that "new religions" are adaptations of such ancient traditions as Shinto, Buddhism, Hinduism, and the primal religions of Africa, the definition of *new religious movement* is much looser. In fact it serves as an umbrella term for a stunning diversity of phenomena ranging from doctrinal deviation within world religions and major churches to passing fads and spiritual enthusiasms of a questionably religious kind. *Cult* also lends itself to different

meanings but is further complicated by pejorative connotations of exoticism and insignificance. In the study of new or "cult" forms of religion, it is important to recognize that disagreement over definitions and concepts is endemic, and that the empirical diversity of these phenomena defies the selection of any single, all-purpose term. Attempts to legislate usage are doomed, but the search for distinctions in usage can help to explain what is taken for granted about the old and the new in different religious traditions.

Meaning. The importance of the study of new religious movements and cults has been established on several grounds. First, it indicates the extent to which established religious organizations are challenged, both for the allegiance of their members and because of the influence that they wield. Second, the conditions in which people are prepared to participate in new movements are revealing in that they display the shifting lines of tension or fracture in social and cultural structures. Third, the controversies which surround many new movements reflect deep-rooted assumptions and prejudices. In short, the main reasons for studying such movements have to do less with what they represent in themselves and more to do with what they indirectly reveal about the state of society, other religious bodies, or structures of meaning.

Systematic studies of new religious movements and cults have helped to scotch several common, but mistaken, assumptions. They show that modern people are not necessarily less religious than their ancestors, that religious innovation is no more likely to be progressive than conservative, that religion is not the exclusive prerogative of church-type organizations, and that the dynamics of new religious movements cannot be separated from social change.

BIBLIOGRAPHY

The most succinct, yet comprehensive, review of social scientific studies of new religious movements in the West in the modern era is Bryan R. Wilson's *Contemporary Transformations of Religion* (Oxford, 1976). *The New Religious Consciousness,* edited by Charles Y. Glock and Robert N. Bellah (Berkeley, 1976), contains introductory descriptions of many new movements in North America, while some contributions to Eileen Barker's collection entitled *New Religious Movements: A Perspective for Understanding Society* (Toronto, 1982) deal with Western Europe as well. *My Cult Controversies* (London, 1985) explores the controversial aspects of Western movements; and Kiyomi Morioka's *Religion in Changing Japanese Society* (Tokyo, 1975) locates innovation in Japanese religion in the context of major social change. The philosophical questions raised by new religious movements in America were examined for the first time in Jacob Needleman's *The New Religions* (Garden City, N. Y., 1970), and only Harvey Cox's *Turning East: The Promise and Peril of the New Orientalism* (New York, 1977) has subsequently reexamined them.

New religious movements in economically less developed parts of the world have been surveyed from a rationalistic point of view in Bryan R. Wilson's *Magic and the Millennium* (New York, 1973) and from a Marxist perspective in Vittorio Lanternari's *Movimenti reli-*

giosi di libertà e di salvezza dei popoli oppressi (Milan, 1960), translated by Lisa Sergio as *The Religions of the Oppressed* (New York, 1963). But the review of types of explanation for millenarian activities made by Kenelm Burridge in his *New Heaven, New Earth* (New York, 1969) remains the best general guide to theoretical problems. For modern African developments, Harold W. Turner's *Religious Innovation in Africa: Collected Essays on New Religious Movements* (Boston, 1979) is indispensable. Christian Lalive d'Epinay's *Haven of the Masses: A Study of the Pentecostal Movement in Chile* (London, 1969), and Felicitas D. Goodman, Jeanette H. Henney, and Esther Pressel's *Trance, Healing and Hallucination* (New York, 1974) illustrates some of the innovative religious movements emerging in the Caribbean and Central and South America. The social aspects of new movements in Indian Buddhism are examined by Trevor O. Ling in *Buddhist Revival in India* (New York, 1980). The resurgence of Islamic fervor in the 1970s has produced a spate of publications, of which Ali E. Hillal Dessouki's collection, *Islamic Resurgence in the Arab World* (New York, 1982), is recommended.

JAMES A. BECKFORD

New Religions and Cults in the United States

Since the 1960s the United States has been experiencing conspicuous spiritual ferment and innovation, which has been compared by some observers to the "Great Awakenings" of the eighteenth and nineteenth centuries. Four principal elements seem to have contributed to the present ferment: (1) a substantial growth of "Eastern" mystical religions (e.g., Hinduism, Buddhism, Sufism); (2) a similiar spread of quasi-religious, therapeutic or "human potential" movements such as Scientology, est (Erhard Seminars Training), Arica, and Silva Mind Control, whose philosophies are often composites of Eastern mysticism and pop psychology; (3) a parallel surge of evangelical, pentecostal, and fundamentalist movements both within established churches and as new independent churches and fellowships; and (4) the growth of a number of controversial authoritarian sects or "cults."

Types of Groups

"Cults." The term *cult* is frequently employed to refer to deviant or marginal religious or therapeutic groups; however, the term really has no precise concensual meaning. Several writers have tried to distinguish between "cults" and "sects" and thereby to assimilate the concept of cult within traditional "church-sect theory" in the sociology of religion. Three partly incompatible conceptions of what constitutes a cult seem to have emerged.

1. Authoritarianism and the related notion of "totalism" appear to be defining properites of "cults" in much popular and journalistic literature.

2. Looseness and diffuseness of organization and an absence of clear "boundaries".

3. Deviancy.

Critical and Normative Typologies. Adaptive movements, we found, promote the assimilation of converts to conventional vocation, educational, and familial roles, and are often associated with other "integrative" outcomes such as drug rehabilitation. In contrast, converts to marginal movements tend to drop out of conventional structures and become encapsulated in self-sufficient and authoritarian communal institutions. Marginal groups are more likely to evoke hostility from the relatives of converts and from other parties.

Well-known marginal groups include the Unification Church, the Children of God, The Way, the Alamo Foundation, ISKCON, and Love Israel. Clearly adaptive groups include followers of Meher Baba, Transcendental Meditation, and est.

Monistic and dualistic systems. Monistic meaning systems employ concepts from Eastern mysticism and affirm the essential "oneness" of reality, the ultimately illusory quality of the phenomenal world, the ideas of reincarnation and karma, and the primacy of inner consciousness and its refinement through enlightenment, although not all essentially monistic groups entail every one of these traits. Generally monistic groups include such "Eastern" groups as the Divine Light Mission, ISKCON, Happy-Healthy-Holy (3HO), the followers of Rajneesh, Meher Baba, and Baba Muktananda, and Tibetan and Zen Buddhist groups as well as such implicitly monistic religiotherapeutic movements as est, Scientology, and Arica.

Implicit in monistic perspectives is a qualified moral relativism and a rejection of absolute polarities in human experience. Dualistic systems, on the other hand, revolve around absolute dualities and the immediate, urgent, and inescapable choices that must be made between right and wrong, God and Satan, and so on. Dualistic religion generally affirms the radical transcendence of the godhead and the ever-present tension between the divine creator and the corrupted human creation. Monism, however, affirms a universal order immanent in the depths of consciousness—a latent universal self—in which all priorities are resolved and transcended.

Univocal vs. multivocal cognitive styles. There is a distinction between one-level and two-level monism related to a broad distinction between univocal and multivocal conceptions of reality. The rationalization of culture has as its linguistic dimension the hegemony of "rational discourse" involving terms that are fixed, precise, and context-free in their meaning and that are clear and specific in their empirical referents. Multivocal symbols give way to univocal signs. Ambiguous metaphysical and supernatural (supraempirical) terms are excluded from rational discourse and rationalized culture. To use Max Weber's term, the world is "disenchanted." However, the symbolic impoverishment of the dominant rationalized culture frustrates human needs for multivocal enchantment and thus engenders spiritual ferment and an alternative culture of multivocal mystiques aimed at reenchanting the world.

A reduction of symbolic conceptions to univocal rationalism can thus transpire simultaneously with a protest against the rationalized "reduction" of religion: that is, the same movements and mystiques can both protest against and embody the cognitive style of univocal rationality. Assuming that reductionism is objectionable and that the recovery of spiritual enchantment is desirable, the distinctions between univocal and multivocal religious conceptions, between monism and dualism, and between technical and charismatic religiosity may lay the foundation for a critical typology of contemporary religious movements (Anthony, Ecker, and Wilber, 1983).

BIBLIOGRAPHY

Anthony, Dick, Bruce Ecker, and Ken Wilber. *Spiritual Standards for New Age Religions and Therapies.* Boulder, 1984. Evaluates spiritual groups and techniques in terms of possible spiritual and psychological hazards.

Anthony, Dick, Jacob Needleman, and Thomas Robbins, eds. *The New Religious Movements: Conversion, Coercion, and Commitment.* New York, 1982. A large collection of papers by outstanding scholars from several disciplines and articulating widely differing viewpoints.

Barker, Eileen, ed. *New Religious Movements: A Perspective for Understanding Society.* Toronto, 1982. An excellent anthology of papers probing the social and cultural underpinnings of the emergence of new movements and the reaction they elicit. See especially Anthony and Robinson, "Contemporary Religious Ferment and Moral Ambiguity."

Beckford, James A. "Politics and the Anti-Cult Movement." *Annual Review of the Social Sciences of Religion* 3 (1979): 169-190. The best short article on controversies over "cults."

Bell, Daniel. "The Return of the Sacred? The Argument on the Future of Religion." *British Journal of Sociology* 28 (December 1977): 419-449. A provocative essay.

Glock, Charles Y., and Robert N. Bellah, eds. *The New Religious Consciousness.* Berkeley, 1976. This well-known collection features separate interpretive essays by the editors: "Consciousness among Contemporary Youth," by Glock, and "The Religious Consciousness and the Crisis in Modernity," by Bellah. It also includes empirical studies collectively delineating the emergence of new religious movements in the San Francisco Bay area as a successor to the fading "hippie" subculture of the late 1960s.

Greeley, Andrew M. *The Denominational Society: A Sociological Approach to Religion in America.* Glenview, Ill., 1972. A general interpretation of modern American religion.

Harris, Marvin. *America Now: The Anthropology of a Changing Culture.* New York, 1981. An interpretation of social change in America since World War II. Chapter 8, "The Cults Are Coming," is a "materialist" analysis that seeks to refute the interpretation offered by Robert Bellah (Glock and Bellah, 1976).

Kaslow, Forence, and Marvin B. Sussman, eds. *Cults and the Family.* New York, 1982. A collection of papers by sociologists, clinicians, parents, and an ex-devotee. Several different perspectives are represented.

Kelley, Dean M. *Why Conservative Churches Are Growing.* Rev. ed. San Francisco, 1977. A classic analysis that is highly relevant to the rise of authoritarian "cults."

Lofland, John, and Norman Skonovd. "Conversion Motifs." *Journal for the Scientific Study of Religion* 20 (December 1982): 373-385. The best short paper on trends in contemporary conversion processes.

Richardson, James T. "The People's Temple and Jonestown: A Corrective, Comparison and Critique." *Journal for the Scientific Study of Religion* 19 (September 1980): 235-255. An important analysis that stresses the substantial differences among relatively authoritarian communal cults.

Richardson, James, and David Bromely, eds. *The Brainwashing-Deprogramming Controversy.* New York, 1983. A large collection of papers by scholars from several disciplines.

Robbins, Thomas, and Dick Anthony. "Cults, Brainwashing, and Counter-Subversion." *Annals of the American Academy of Political and Social Science* 44 (November 1979): 78-90. Compares today's controversies over cults to nineteenth-century attacks on Mormons, Freemasons, and Roman Catholics.

Robbins, Thomas, and Dick Anthony, eds. *In Gods We Trust: New Patterns of Religious Pluralism in America.* New Brunswick, N. J., 1980. A collection of papers on contemporary religious ferment with an emphasis on the sources of new movements and the responses they elicit. See especially Do-ress and Porter, "Kids in Cults"; Horowitz, "The Politics of the New Cults"; and Johnson, "A Sociological Perspective on the New Religion."

Robbins, Thomas, and Dick Anthony. "Brainwashing, Deprogramming and the Medicalization of Deviant Religious Groups." *Social Problems* 29 (February 1982): 283-297.

Robbins, Thomas, Dick Anthony, Thomas Curtis, and Madeline Doucas. "Youth Culture Religious Movements." *Sociological Quarterly* 10 (1975): 48-64.

Robbins, Thomas, Dick Anthony, Madeline Doucas, and Thomas Curtis. "The Last Civil Religion: Reverend Moon and the Unification Church." In *Science, Sin, and Scholarship,* edited by Irving L. Horowitz, pp. 46-73. Cambridge, Mass., 1978. Describes a Unification Church indoctrination workshop and interprets the growth of the movement in terms of its articulation of idealistic concern for the broader community.

Robbins, Thomas, Dick Anthony, and James Richardson. "Research and Theory on Today's 'New Religions.'" *Sociological Analysis* 39 (1978): 95-122.

Robbins, Thomas, William Sheperd, and Jim McBride. *New Religious Movements and the Law.* Chico, Calif., 1984. A collection of papers by legal scholars and social scientists.

Shupe, Anson D., Jr., and David G. Bromley. *The New Vigilantes: Deprogrammers, Anti-Cultists and the New Religions.* Beverly Hills, Calif., 1980. Basic monograph on the "anticult movement."

Stark, Rodney. "Must Religions Be Supernatural?" In *The Social Impact of New Religious Movements,* edited by Bryan R. Wilson, pp. 159-178. New York, 1981. A provocative theory of the persisting appeal of supernaturalism in modern society.

Stone, Donald. "On Knowing How We Know About New Religions." In *Understanding the New Religions,* edited by Jacob Needleman and George Baker, pp. 141-152. New York, 1978. Essay on epistemology and methodology.

Tipton, Steven M. *Getting Saved from the Sixties: Moral Meaning in Conversion and Cultural Change.* Berkeley, 1981. The definitive work on est. Emphasizes the role of new movements in mediating cultural value conflicts.

Wilson, Bryan R., ed. *The Social Impact of New Religious Movements.* New York, 1981. A collection of excellent papers by sociologists at a conference sponsored by the Unification Church.

Wuthnow, Robert. *The Consciousness Reformation.* Berkeley, 1976. Utilizes survey research to probe shifting values in the San Francisco Bay area and their relationship to emerging religious experimentation.

Wuthnow, Robert. *Experimentation in American Religion: The New Mysticisms and Their Implications for the Churches.* Berkeley, 1978. Utilizes survey data to suggest a general interpretation of emerging "religious populism."

THOMAS ROBBINS and DICK ANTHONY

New Religions and Cults in Europe

The new religious movements with which this article is concerned are those which first appeared, or became noticeable, in Europe during the second half of the twentieth century, especially during the late sixties and the seventies. Many, indeed most of them, have their roots in other religions, but they are termed "new" because they arose in a new form, with a new facet to their beliefs, or with a new organization or leadership which renounced more orthodox beliefs and/or ways of life. Some of the movements have been denied, or have themselves rejected the label *religious.* No attempt will be made here to argue what a "real" religion should or should not consist of. The term *new religious movements* is employed merely as a somewhat arbitrary, but usefully general, term by which to refer to a multitude of movements which might be termed cults, sects, spiritual groups, or alternative belief systems by others.

Origins and Classifications. The vast majority of the new movements were not indigenous to Europe. Most can be traced to the United States (frequently California) or Asia (mainly India, but also Japan, Korea, and other parts of Asia). There are also a few groups that have come from Africa, most of these finding their home among the black populations residing in Europe.

In order to try to create some sense of order among the myriad movements, a number of different classificatory systems have been proposed. One of the simplest divisions is based on the origin of the movement.

Those new religions from the mainly Indian tradition of the East include Ananda Marga, Brahma Kumaris, the Divine Light Mission, ISKCON, followers of Meher Baba and of Sathya Sai Baba, the Rajneesh Foundation (Bhagwan Shree Rajneesh), and Transcendental Meditation. Those from Japan include Nichiren Shoshu (Soka Gakkai) and Rissho Koseikai; and from Korea comes the Unification Church. The movements originating in America tend to be either Christian derivatives (or deviations) such as The Way International,

Armstrongism (The World Wide Church of God), Bible Speaks, and The Children of God (The Family of Love), or, alternatively, groups connected with the human potential movement like est (Erhard Seminars Training), Exegesis, Silva Mind Control, P. S. I. (People Searching Inside and the Kundalini Research Institute of Canada), and the Rebirth Society. Occasionally techniques offered primarily for self-improvement are transferred into (and sometimes back from) a movement claiming to be a new religion. Dianetics' transformation into the Church of Scientology (and back into Dianetics) is a case in point. Also from America come innumerable New Age groups and those which deal in the occult, neopaganism, witchcraft, and magic. These are joined by similar, indigenous groups which are most prolific in northern Europe, especially in parts of Scandinavia and Britain. Such groups range from highly secret fellowships practicing ritual "sex magick," to orthodox covens, to the English Gnostic Church (founded in Chicago in 1979), to astrological groups, Druid gatherings, and Aquarian festivals. From Africa come the Aladura churches, and from Jamaica has come the Rastafarian movement, which has gained considerable popularity among the West Indian population in Britain. Among the groups indigenous to Europe there is the Pentecostal Earmark Trust, the Bugbrooke (Christian) Community, Ishvara (an offshoot of the Divine Light Mission), and the Emin, an esoteric group founded by "Leo" (Raymond Armin/Scherlenlieb).

One of the more useful ways in which new religious movements have been classified is by Roy Wallis's threefold distinction between world-rejecting movements, such as the People's Temple, ISKCON, and the Children of God, which see society being in need of and/or about to experience radical change; world-affirming movements, such as Scientology and the human potential groups, which might be called quasi-religious in that, although they pursue transcendental goals by largely metaphysical means, they concentrate on techniques for improvement of their lot within contemporary society, and thus "straddle a vague boundary between religion and psychology"; and, last, world-accommodating movements, such as Neo-Pentecostalism and western branches of Soka Gakkai, which concentrate on providing religion for their followers' personal, interior lives, and which tend to be unconcerned with their followers' social lives.

BIBLIOGRAPHY

There are no books dealing specifically with the new religious movements in Europe as a whole. Much of the American literature is applicable, however, and there are numerous collections of articles that include papers on European movements. Among them are a special issue of *Social Compass* (Louvain, 1983) and books edited by various hands: *New Religions* (Stockholm, 1975), edited by Haralds Beizais; *Salvation and Protest: Studies of Social and*

Religious Movements (New York, 1979), edited by Roy Wallis; Das Entstehen einer neuen Religion: Das Beispiel der Vereinigungskirche (Munich, 1981), edited by Günter Kehrer; Aktuella religiösa rörelser i Finland: Ajankohtaisia uskonnollisia liikkeitä Suomessa (Turku, 1981), edited, with summaries in English, by Nils G. Holm; The Social Impact of New Religious Movements (New York, 1981), edited by Bryan R. Wilson; and New Religious Movements: A Perspective for Understanding Society (New York, 1982) and Of Gods and Men: New Religious Movements in the West (Macon, Ga., 1983), both edited by me. Religious Movements: Genesis, Exodus and Numbers (New York, forthcoming), edited by Rodney Stark, includes his paper discussed in the foregoing article; and Roy Wallis's classification is elaborated in his The Elementary Forms of the New Religious Life (London, 1984). Further information about new religious movements in Britain can be found in Bryan R. Wilson's The Dictionary of Minority Religious Movements (London, forthcoming), and there is a quarterly journal Update (Århus, Denmark), published in English, that provides news, features, and articles about new religious movements.

EILEEN BARKER

New Religions in Japan

The modern era has been a prolific period for new religious movements in Japan. A new religion will have most or all of the following attributes: Common characteristics of the Japanese new religions include the following:

1. Founding by a charismatic figure whose career often recalls the shamanistic model: supernatural calling, initiatory ordeal, wandering, oracular deliverances from the spiritual world.
2. Tendency toward monotheism or a single, monistic source of spiritual power and value. Against the background of the spiritual pluralism of popular Shinto and Buddhism, the new movements set one deity, one founder, and one revelation as definitive.
3. Syncretism, drawing from several strands of religion and culture.
4. A definite, this-worldly eschatology. The new religions usually teach that rapid change is afoot and a divine new age imminent.
5. A sacred center, often an entire sacred city, to which pilgrimage is made, where the faith is headquartered, and which represents a foretaste of the coming paradise.
6. Emphasis on healing.
7. A tendency toward "mentalism," that is, the belief that through the power of affirmative thinking one can heal mind and body and control one's own destiny.
8. A single, simple, sure technique for attaining and employing the special spiritual power offered by the religion. One practice, whether the Daimoku of the Nichirenshu or the jorei of World Messianity, is presented as the key to unlock spiritual power.

9. A simple but definite process of entry, suggesting that the religion is open to all but requires a personal decision and act of commitment.

BIBLIOGRAPHY

Several books accessible to the general reader on the new religions of Japan can be recommended, including H. Neill McFarland's The Rush Hour of the Gods (New York, 1967), a well-researched, sometimes critical overview; Clark B. Offner and Henry van Straelen's Modern Japanese Religions (Leiden, 1963), a careful study emphasizing healing practices; and Harry Thomsen's The New Religions of Japan (Rutland, Vt., 1963), a lively survey. Among accounts of particular religions are Kenneth J. Dale and Akahoshi Susumi's Circle of Harmony (Tokyo, 1975), on the hoza (group counseling) procedures of Rissho Koseikai; James Dator's Soka Gakkai: Builders of the Third Civilization (Seattle, 1969), a substantial sociological study; Robert S. Ellwood's Tenrikyo: A Pilgrimage Faith (Tenri, 1982); Helen Hardacre's Lay Buddhism in Contemporary Japan: Reiyukai Kyodan (Princeton, 1984), representing high-level sociological research; and Delwin B. Schneider's Konko kyo (Tokyo, 1962). For a complete bibliography, see H. Byron Earhart's The New Religions of Japan: A Bibliography of Western Language Materials, 2d ed. (Ann Arbor, 1983).

ROBERT S. ELLWOOD

NIRVANA

About twenty-five centuries ago in northern India, Siddhartha Gautama achieved nirvana. That event ultimately changed the spiritual character of much of Asia and, more recently, some of the West. That something indeed happened is an indisputable fact. Exactly what happened has been an object of speculation, analysis, and debate up to the present day.

Nirvana is both a term and an ideal. As a Sanskrit word (nibbana in Pali), it has been used by various religious groups in India, but it primarily refers to the spiritual goal in the Buddhist way of life. In the broadest sense, the word nirvana is used in much the same way as the now standard English word enlightenment, a generic word literally translating no particular Asian technical term but used to designate any Buddhist notion of the highest spiritual experience.

Nirvana in the Early Buddhist and Abhidharma Traditions. The early Buddhist texts primarily approached nirvana as a practical solution to the existential problem of human anguish. Specifically, they maintained that by undertaking a disciplined praxis the Buddhist practitioner can achieve a nondiscursive awakening (bodhi) to the interdependent nonsubstantiality of reality, especially of the self. With that insight, it was believed, one could be released from the grips of insatiable craving and its resultant suffering.

In most cases nirvana is described in negative terms such as "cessation" (nirodha), "the absence of craving" (*trsnaksaya*), "detachment," "the absence of delusion," and "the unconditioned" (*asamskrta*). Although in the Nikayas and subsequent Abhidharma school commentaries there are scattered positive references to, for instance, "happiness" (*sukha*), "peace," and "bliss." One prominent tendency was to understand *nirvana* as a release from *samsara,* the painful world of birth and death powered by passion, hatred, and ignorance. According to the early texts, the Eightfold Path leading to *nirvana* is the only way to break free of this cycle and to eliminate the insatiable craving at its root.

The Buddhist view of *samsara* developed as the notion of rebirth was taking root in ancient India. So enlightenment came to be understood as the extinction (*nirvana*) of what can be reborn, that is, as the dissolution of any continuing personal identity after death.

Are *samsara* and *nirvana* states of mind or kinds of existence? If *samsara* refers to the psychological worldview conducive to suffering, then the transition from *samsara* to *nirvana* is simply a profound change in attitude, perspective, and motivation. If, on the other hand, *samsara* refers to this pain-stricken world itself, then *nirvana* must be somewhere else. Here the ancient metaphor of *nirvana* as "the farther shore" could assume a metaphysical status. In effect, *nirvana* could be understood as a permanent state of bliss beyond the world of birth, death, and rebirth. The reaction against such an interpretation influenced the Mahayana Buddhist views of enlightenment.

Nirvana in the Indian Mahayana Buddhist Traditions. Indian Mahayana Buddhists minimized the opposition between *nirvana* and *samsara,* renouncing the suggestion that *nirvana* was an escape from the world of suffering. Instead, they thought of enlightenment as a wise and compassionate way of living in that world.

The Perfection of Wisdom and Madhyamika traditions. One Mahayana strategy was to undercut the epistemological and logical bases for the sharp distinction between the concepts of *nirvana* and *samsara.* Madhyamika thought radicalized the Buddha's original silence on this critical issue by trying to demonstrate that any philosophical attempt to characterize reality is limited by the logical interdependence of words or concepts. Assuming an isomorphic relationship between words and nonlinguistic referents, Nagarjuna reasoned that the interdependent character of words precludes their referring to any absolute, nondependent realities. To the very extent we can talk or reason about *nirvana* and *samsara,* therefore, they must depend on each other. Neither can be absolute in itself.

Nirvana in the idealistic and Yogacara traditions. The typical approach of such idealistic texts as the *Lankavatara Sutra* and of its related philosophical school, Yogacara, was to assert that *nirvana* and *samsara* had a common ground, namely, the activity of the mind. The terminology varied from text to text and thinker to thinker, but the thrust of this branch

of Mahayana Buddhism was that the mind was the basis of both delusion (understood as *samsara*) and enlightenment (understood as *nirvana*). For many in this tradition, this implied that there is in each person an inherent core of Buddhahood covered over with a shell of delusional fixations. Sometimes this core was called the *tathagata-garbha* ("Buddha womb, Buddha embryo," or "Buddha matrix"); in other cases it was considered to be part of a store-consciousness (*alaya-vijñana*) containing seeds (*bija*) that could sprout either delusional or enlightened experience. In either case, Buddhist practice was seen as a technique for clarifying or making manifest the Buddha mind or Buddha nature within the individual.

Buddhahood in devotional Mahayana Buddhism. *Nirvana's* ontological or metaphysical nature was also a theme in Mahayana religious practices quite outside the formal considerations of the philosophers. This development was associated with the rise of the notion that the historical Buddha who had died in the fifth century BCE was actually only an earthly manifestation of an eternal Buddha or of Buddhahood itself. This line of thought developed into the construction of a rich pantheon of Buddhas and *bodhisattvas* living in various heavenly realms and interacting with human beings in supportive ways. These heavenly figures became the objects of meditation, emulation, reverence, and supplication.

Nirvana in East Asian Buddhist Traditions. The Mahayana ideal was that of the *bodhisattva,* the enlightened (or, more technically, almost enlightened) being who chooses to be actively involved in alleviating the suffering of others by leading them to enlightenment. In other words, the *bodhisattva* subordinates personal enlightenment to that of others. When Buddhism entered China around the beginning of the common era, Confucianism and Taoism were already well established. Confucianism placed its primary emphasis on the cultivation of virtuous human relationships for the harmonious functioning of society. This emphasis on social responsibility and collective virtue blended well with the Mahayana vision of enlightenment.

Compared to Confucianism, Taoism was relatively ascetic, mystical, and otherworldly. Yet its mysticism was strongly naturalistic in that the Taoist sage sought unity with the Tao by being in harmony with nature. In Taoism, as in Mahayana Buddhism, the absolute principle was completely immanent in this world, accessible to all who attune themselves to it by undertaking the proper form of meditation and self-discipline. [*See also* Taoism.]

Nirvana in the T`ien-t`ai and Hua-yen schools. Eventually there arose new forms of Mahayana Buddhism distinctive to East Asia, schools either unknown or only incipient in India. The term *nirvana,* possibly because it carried connotations of a foreign worldview replete with such ideas as rebirth and the inherent unsatisfactoriness (*duhkha*) of existence, tended to lose its privileged status in favor of such terms as "awakening" (*chüeh*) and "realization" (*wu*).

The Chinese T`ien-t`ai and Hua-yen traditions formulated their own sophisticated philosophical worldviews out of ideas suggested by Indian *sutras*. Both schools emphasized the interpenetration of all things. In T`ien-t`ai terminology as developed by such philosophers as Chih-i (538-597), all the "three thousand worlds" are reflected in a single instant of thought. Reality's underlying, unifying factor was understood to be mind. For T`ien-t`ai followers the fundamental mind is itself always pure and does not contain, as most Indian Yogacarins held, both delusional and enlightened seeds.

Chinese Hua-yen Buddhism also affirmed the interdependence among, and harmony within, all things. Unlike the adherents of T`ien-t`ai, however, the Hua-yen philosophers did not think of mind as the underlying, unifying entity. Fatsang (643-712), for example, preferred to deny any single unifying factor and used the phrase "the nonobstruction between thing and thing" (*shih-shih wu-ai*). In other words, each phenomenon itself was thought to reflect every other phenomenon. Tsung-mi (780-841), on the other hand, favored the phrase "the nonobstruction between absolute principle and thing" (*li-shih wu-ai*). Thus, he regarded principle *(li)* as the fundamental unifying substrate, even the creative source, of reality.

In all these T`ien-t`ai and Hua-yen theories we find a recurrent, distinctively East Asian, interpretation of nirvana. Just as the Confucians sought harmony within the social order and the Taoists harmony within the natural order, the T`ien-t`ai and Hua-yen Buddhists understood enlightenment in terms of harmony.

**Nirvana in the Ch`an (Zen) school.** Ch`an (Kor., Son; Jpn., Zen) is another school with roots in India, but it developed into a full-fledged tradition only in East Asia. It is distinctive in its de-emphasis of the role of formal doctrine and religious texts in favor of a direct "transmission of mind" from master to disciple. Ch`an focused most on the interpersonal aspect of the enlightenment experience. One topic of debate about enlightenment in the Ch`an school concerned the issue of whether enlightenment was "sudden" or "gradual." The Northern school emphasized the inherent purity of the mind and, therefore, advocated a practice intended to remove delusional thoughts covering over that intrinsically undefiled core. Then, it was assumed, the inherent enlightenment of the mind could shine forth ever more brilliantly. The members of the Southern school, on the other hand, accused their Northern school counterparts of reifying enlightenment into an independently existing thing. In other words, enlightenment should be manifest at all times in all one's activities. It is not a separate state or seed to be nurtured or cared for. The goal for the Southern school, therefore, was to make enlightenment manifest while going about one's daily affairs.

Another approach to the sudden/gradual issue was originally taken by the previously mentioned Hua-yen (and Ch`an) master Tsung-mi, and later developed extensively by the great Korean Son master, Chinul (1158-1210). Their view was that the Southern school (which eventually dominated for political as much as religious or philosophical reasons) was correct in maintaining that enlightenment, the awakening to one's own Buddha nature, had to be a sudden realization. Yet Tsung-mi and Chinul also maintained that realization had to be gradually integrated into one's life through a continuously deepening practice of spiritual cultivation.

Nirvana in the Pure Land traditions. All forms of Buddhism discussed up to now have assumed that one can only achieve *nirvana* through years (or even lifetimes) of concentrated practice. The Pure Land tradition, especially as developed by Shinran (1173-1262) in Japan, radically reinterpreted the notion of Buddhist practice, however.

Pure Land Buddhism asserts that human beings today cannot achieve *nirvana* by their "own power" (*jiriki*). Rather than help themselves through the practice of calculated, self-conscious actions (*hakarai*), people should simply resign themselves completely to the "power of another" (*tariki*), that is, the power of Amida's (Buddha's) compassionate vow. Even this act of the "entrusting heart and mind" (*shinjin*) must itself be an expression of Amida's vow and not an effort on one's own part. In this way, Shinran maintained that enlightenment could ultimately only be achieved by first releasing oneself to the spontaneousness "naturalness" (*jinen honi*), the active grace of Amida's compassion as this world itself.

> **Esotericism merged its practices and doctrines with the indigenous shamanistic, archaic religions of . . . Bon and Shinto.**

Nirvana in the Esoteric traditions. The Esoteric, Vajrayana, or Tantric forms of Buddhism can be generally viewed as extensions of Mahayana. In general, however, Esoteric Buddhism was most permanently influential in Tibet (including the Mongolian extensions of Tibetan Buddhism) and in Japan. In both cases, Esotericism merged its practices and doctrines with the indigenous shamanistic, archaic religions of, respectively, Bon and Shinto.

In terms of their understanding of *nirvana* the Esoteric traditions added an important dimension to their otherwise generally Mahayanistic outlook, namely, that enlightenment should be understood as participation in the enlightenment of the Buddha-as-reality (the *dharmakaya*). From this viewpoint, sacred speech (*mantras*), sacred gestures (*mudras*), and sacred envisioning (*mandalas*) constitute a Buddhist ritualistic practice having an almost sacramental character. That is, in performing the rituals outlined in the Tantras, the Esoteric Buddhist believes that one's own speech, action, and thought become the concrete expression of the cosmic Buddha's own enlightenment.

BIBLIOGRAPHY

As the fundamental ideal of Buddhism, *nirvana* is discussed in a wide variety of works: *sutras*, commentaries, and secondary critical works by scholars of various traditions. Any bibliography must be, therefore, incomplete and, at best, highly selective. The following works have been chosen for their particular relevance to the issues discussed in the foregoing article.

Nirvana in the Indian Buddhist Traditions. Of the many references to *nirvana* in the early Indian texts, certain passages have traditionally received the most attention. For example, in the Pali scriptures, the status of the Buddha after death (*parinibbana*) is handled in various ways. Most prominent, undoubtedly, is the traditional account of the Buddha's passing away described in chapter 6 of the *Mahaparinibbana Suttanta.* A translation of this text by T. W. Rhys Davids is readily available as *Buddhist Suttas,* volume 11 of "The Sacred Books of the East," edited by F. Max Müller (1881; reprint, New York, 1969). An interesting feature of this account is its clear distinction between the Buddha's *nirvana* and his meditative capacity to cause the complete cessation (*nirodha*) of perceptions, thoughts, and feelings. This passage is often quoted, therefore, against any claim that the early Buddhist view was simply nihilistic and world-renouncing. Notably absent in this text, however, is any detailed treatment of the classic distinction between *nirvana* with remainder and *nirvana* without remainder. That distinction is more clearly presented in *Itivuttaka,* edited by Ernst Windisch (London, 1889), esp. pp. 38-39. An English translation by F. L. Woodward is in the second volume of *Minor Anthologies of the Pali Canon,* edited by C. A. F. Rhys Davids (London, 1935).

Another commonly analyzed theme is the Buddha's own reticence to describe the status of the enlightened person after death. On this point, there are two particularly provocative textual references. One is the above-mentioned story about Malunkyaputta in *Majjhima-Nikaya,* 4 vols., edited by Vilhelm Trenckner, Robert Chalmers, and C. A. F. Rhys Davids (London, 1887-1925), *suttas* 63-64; the other is in *The Samyutta-nikaya of the Sutta pitaka,* 6 vols., edited by Léon Freer (London, 1884-1904), vol. 3, p. 118. English translations of these two complete collections are, respectively, *The Collection of the Middle Length Sayings,* 3 vols., translated by I. B. Horner (London, 1954-1959), and *The Book of Kindred Sayings,* 5 vols., translated by C. A. F. Rhys Davids and F. L. Woodward (London, 1917-1930).

As already mentioned, descriptions of *nirvana* are for the most part posed in negative terms; the interested reader can find a multitude of examples by consulting, for example, the excellent indexes in the collections of early Pali texts cited above. One particularly striking exception to this rule, however, is found in *The Samyutta-nikaya,* vol. 4, p. 373. This passage gives a rather lengthy string of mostly positive equivalents to *nirvana,* including terms that mean "truth," "the farther shore," "the stable," "peace," "security," "purity," and so forth. Such positive characterizations of *nirvana* are found elsewhere, but never in quite so concentrated a list.

On the issue of the transcendent, mystical, or metaphysical aspect of *nirvana* in the early Buddhist tradition, a pivotal textual reference is in *Udana,* edited by Paul Steinthal (London, 1948). An English translation also occurs in volume 2 of Woodward's *Minor Anthologies,* cited above. On pages 80-81 of *Udana,* we find an indu-bitable reference to a state of mind or a place beyond birth and death, beyond all discrimination and ordinary perceptions. Controversy still continues over the proper interpretation of the passage. In Rune E. A. Johansson's *Psychology of Nirvana* (London, 1969), for example, there is a sustained discussion of the enlightened state of mind as being a mystical, transempirical, nondifferentiated state of consciousness. The passage from *Udana* naturally figures prominently in Johansson's argument. On the other hand, this viewpoint is severely criticized in David J. Kalupahana's *Buddhist Philosophy: A Historical Analysis* (Honolulu, 1976), chap. 7. By interpreting this passage as referring to the state of cessation (*nirodha*) just prior to the Buddha's death but not to ordinary *nirvana* in this world, Kalupahana argues that early Buddhism consistently maintained that the achievement of *nirvana* does not require, or entail, any transempirical form of perception. In this regard, Kalupahana is expanding on the theory that early Buddhism was primarily empirical in outlook, an interpretation first fully developed in Kulitassa Nanda Jayatilleke's *Early Buddhist Theory of Knowledge* (London, 1963).

Another controversial issue among modern scholars is the relationship between early Buddhism and the contemporary form of Hinduism. Whereas Kalupahana's approach sharply distinguishes the early Buddhist view of *nirvana* from the contemporary Hindu ideal of the unity of *atman* with *brahman,* Johansson tends to see a common mystical element in the two. A generally more balanced and convincing position on this point can be found in the thorough discussion of Kashi Nath Upadhyaya's *Early Buddhism and the Bhagavadgita* (Delhi, 1971).

A good introduction to the modern view of nirvana from the standpoint of the only living tradition of Abhidharma, the Theravada, is Walpola Rahula's *What the Buddha Taught,* rev. ed. (Bedford, England, 1967), chap. 4. This small work is highly regarded for its ability to explain the gist of centuries of Abhi-dharmic analysis in a straightforward, accurate, and yet nontechnical manner. On the way *nirvana* actually functions today as an ethical ideal in Theravada daily life, see Winston L. King's *In the Hope of Nibbana: An Essay of Theravada Buddhist Ethics* (La Salle, Ill., 1964). For a more historical and specialized approach to the development of the early Abhidharma views of *nirvana,* see Edward Conze's *Buddhist Thought in India* (1962; reprint, Ann Arbor, 1970), esp. sections 1.5 and 2.3. Although this book is poorly written and organized, it still contains some information not readily available in English elsewhere.

For Nagarjuna and the Madhyamika school, the locus classicus is Nagarjuna's discussion in chapter 25 of his *Mulamadhyamakakarika.* The complete Sanskrit original and English translation of this work with extensive commentary is found in David J. Kalupahana's *Nagarjuna: The Philosophy of the Middle Way* (Albany, 1985). A good discussion of Nagarjuna's basic position with respect to *nirvana* also appears in Frederick J. Streng's *Emptiness: A Study in Religious Meaning* (New York, 1967), pp. 69-81.

For studying the Yogacara and idealist position, the reader may wish to consult *The Lankavatara Sutra,* translated by D. T. Suzuki (1932; reprint, Boulder, 1978). The identifications of *nirvana* with the pure *alaya-vijñana* or the *tathagata-garbha,* as well as with the mind released from delusional discriminations are particularly discussed in sections 18, 38, 63, 74, 77, and 82. For the more systematically philosophical developments of the Yogacara tradition, the reader may refer to the following works. Asanga's *Mahayanasamgraha* has been translated and edited by Étienne Lamotte in *La somme du Grand Véhicule d'Asanga,* vol. 2 (Louvain, 1939). Translations of Vasubandhu's *Vimsatika* and *Trimsika* by Clarence H. Hamilton and Wing-tsit Chan, respectively, can be found in *A Source Book in Indian Philosophy,* edited by Sarvepalli Radhakrishnan and Charles A. Moore (Princeton, 1957). Sylvain Lévi's *Matériaux pour l'étude du système Vijñaptimatra* (Paris, 1932) remains the definitive discussion on Vasubandhu's writings. For an analysis of Dignaga's thought, see Hattori Masaaki's *Dignaga, on Perception* (Cambridge, Mass., 1968).

For a straightforward and detailed discussion of Indian Buddhist theories of *nirvana,* see Nalinaksha Dutt's *Mahayana Buddhism* (rev. ed., Delhi, 1978), chap. 7. Although sometimes biased against the Abhidharma traditions, his account of the differences among the Indian Buddhist schools is very good. For a thorough and fascinating discussion of the attempts of Western scholars to interpret the idea of *nirvana* as found primarily in the Pali texts, see Guy R. Welbon's *The Buddhist Nirvana and its Western Interpreters* (Chicago, 1968). Welbon includes a good bibliography of works in Western languages. His book culminates in the famous debate between Louis de La Vallée Poussin (1869-1938) and Theodore Stcherbatsky (Fedor Shcherbatskii, 1866-1942). Both were noted as first-rate commentators on Mahayana Buddhism, but their own personalities and temperaments led them to take distinctively different views of Buddhism and its intent. Thus, in examining the same early Buddhist texts, the former emphasized the yogic and religious aspects whereas the latter favored the philosophical. Despite their limitations, however, La Vallée Poussin's *Nirvana* (Paris, 1925) and Stcherbatsky's *The Conception of Buddhist Nirvana* (Leningrad, 1927) remain classic works on this subject.

East Asian Traditions. For the reasons given in the essay, the idea of *nirvana* is not discussed as explicitly in the East Asian as the South Asian traditions. When *nirvana* is analyzed by East Asian Buddhists, the sharply etched distinctions among the various Indian Mahayana schools are softened. A clear example of this is D. T. Suzuki's *Outlines of Mahayana Buddhism* (New York, 1963), chap. 13. In this chapter, and indeed throughout the book, Suzuki approaches the ideas of Mahayana Buddhists as coming from discrete traditions but involving an underlying common spirit.

For the view of the T`ien-t`ai school as developed by Chih-i, the most thorough discussion in English is Leon N. Hurvitz's *Chih-i* (538-597); *An Introduction to the Life and Ideas of a Chinese Buddhist Monk* (Brussels, 1962). For the impact of the T`ien-t`ai idea of inherent enlightenment on Japanese Buddhism in the Kamakura period, see the comprehensive study in Tamura Yoshiro's *Kamakura shin-bukkyo shiso no kenkyu* (Tokyo, 1965).

Like T`ien-t`ai, the Hua-yen tradition has not yet been comprehensively studied in Western works. One of the better philosophical overviews of Hua-yen theory in relation to enlightenment is the discussion about Fa-tsang in Fung Yu-lan's *A History of Chinese Philosophy,* translated by Derk Bodde (Princeton, 1953), vol. 2, chap. 8. Fa-tsang is also central to the analysis in Francis D. Cook's *Hua-yen Buddhism: The Jewel Net of Indra* (University Park, Pa., 1977). Essays on the history of Hua-yen practice are included in *Studies in Ch`an and Hua-yen,* edited by Robert M. Gimello and Peter N. Gregory (Honolulu, 1984).

On the theory of the four realms of reality (*fa-chieh*), the culmination of which is the "nonobstruction between thing and things," a key text is Ch`eng-kuan's *Hua-yen fa-chieh hsüan-ching,* a translation of which is found in Thomas Cleary's *Entry into the Inconceivable* (Honolulu, 1983). One noteworthy point about the translation, however, is that it translates *li* as "noumenon" and *shih* as "phenomenon," a rendering popular in earlier English translations, but now usually replaced by terms less speculative and philosophically misleading, such as, respectively, "principle" and "event" (or "principle" and "thing").

On the Ch`an distinction between sudden and gradual enlightenment, the exchange of poems by Shen-hsiu and Hui-neng is recorded in the first ten sections of the *Liu-tsu t`an-ching,* a good translation of which is Philip B. Yampolsky's *The Platform Sutra of the Sixth Patriarch* (New York, 1967). For Tsung-mi's view of sudden enlightenment and gradual cultivation, as well as Chinul's elaboration on this point, see the discussion in *The Korean Approach to Zen,* translated by Robert E. Buswell, Jr. (Honolulu, 1983). For Dogen's view of the oneness of cultivation and enlightenment, see Hee-Jin Kim's *Dogen Kigen: Mystical Realist* (Tucson, 1975), chap. 3, and my *Zen Action/Zen Person* (Honolulu, 1981), chaps. 6-7.

For an overview of the Pure Land tradition and, in particular, Shinran's view that enlightenment is unattainable through any efforts of one's own, see Alfred Bloom's *Shinran's Gospel of Pure Grace* (Tucson, 1965), still the only major objective study of Shinran in English. There are two good translation series of Shinran's works: the "Ryukoku Translation Series" and the "Shin Buddhism Translation Series," both of Kyoto, Japan. Neither series is complete but, between the two, most of Shinran's works have been adequately translated. The quotation in the foregoing essay is from the first volume of the latter series, namely, *The Letters of Shinran: A Translation of Mattosho,* edited and translated by Ueda Yoshifumi (Kyoto, 1978).

For Kukai's view on the distinctiveness of Esoteric Buddhism, a key text is *Benkenmitsu nikyo ron* (On Distinguishing the Two Teachings—Exoteric and Esoteric). On the role of ritual in enlightenment, see his *Sokushin jobutsu gi* (On Achieving Buddhahood with This Very Body) and *Shoji jisso gi* (On Sound-Word-Reality). English translations of these works and others can be conveniently found in Yoshito S. Hakeda's *Kukai: Major Works* (New York, 1972).

THOMAS P. KASULIS

NORTH AMERICAN INDIAN RELIGIONS

Indians of the Far North

The North American sub-Arctic extends from Alaska to Labrador, a vast region comprising several vegetation zones. The tundra covers the area along the Arctic coast, a strip of treeless wilderness between one and four hundred miles wide, which protrudes deep into the interior in northern Alaska and in Canada west of Hudson Bay.

Adaptation to Climate. The inhospitable climate of the region, with its long, severe winters and short summers, shaped the culture of the native inhabitants. Since any form of cultivation was impossible, human existence was dependent on hunting and fishing. And here natural factors proved to be of some assistance. Large deer, such as caribou and moose, sought refuge in the forest zone in the autumn, then wandered back into the northern tundra in spring. This movement back and forth set huge herds of migrating caribou into motion, which facilitated big-game hunting and the accumulation of food reserves. In late winter, however, hunting was limited to stalking of small packs or isolated animals. Extensive river networks that abounded in fish, particularly salmon, provided food in the summer. Hunting and fishing, two seasonally varying activities—the one with lance and arrow, the other with hook and net—formed the basis of the sub-Arctic economy so long as the native population was isolated from outside influences. This alternation in economic life led to nomadism, which often involved a short-term relocation of housing. A round, dome-shaped house covered with bark or straw was erected in the winter; a rectangular, gabled lodge was preferred in the summer. Today these structures have given way to the conical tent, which in turn is beginning to be replaced by the log cabin.

The advancing Europeans encountered tribes belonging to three linguistic families: the Inuit (Eskimo) along the Arctic Ocean, the Athapascan in western Canada, and the Algonquian in eastern Canada. Among the Algonquian we

> **Human existence in the sub-Arctic has always revolved around surviving the winters.**

also include the Abnaki of New Brunswick and Maine (Micmac, Malecite, Passamaquoddy, Penobscot, Abnaki), who have preserved vestiges of their sub-Arctic way of life up to the present. The non-Indian Inuit will not be treated here, as they are the subject of a separate article. [See Inuit Religion.]

The usual division leaves us twenty-four groups or tribes of Athapascan provenance and thirteen of Algonquian provenance. All are unmistakably shaped by the sub-Arctic way of life with its alternation between forest and water, its absence of any cultivation, and its big-game hunting in winter and fishing in summer.

Human existence in the sub-Arctic has always revolved around surviving the winters. January and February witness the worst side of the cold season: the temperature reaches its lowest point, the reserves are exhausted, the short days limit the hunter's range of movement, and the last caribou and moose in the vicinity of the winter camps have already been hunted down. This is a time of extreme hardship. The isolation of families—each has its own hunting grounds—is a hindrance to mutual help and support. The earliest reports tell of famine and starvation and of whole bands fatalistically facing their death.

By way of comparison, the Inuit cultures along the Arctic coast mastered every environmental difficulty: of their inventions one need only think of the igloo, fur clothing, seal hunting at the breathing holes on the ice, and oil lamps—a utilization of natural conditions not to be found among the Athapascan and the Algonquian.

Ages of the World. The mythical chronology falls into three stages (see Rand, 1894; Osgood, 1932; and Pliny Earle Goddard, "The Beaver Indians," *Anthropological*

Papers of the American Museum of Natural History 10, 1916). In the earliest period there were no divisions between living creatures; each could assume any animal's form and discard it again at will. All moving creatures spoke a single language; no barriers stood in the way of understanding. The second period began with the birth of the culture hero, the great teacher and leader of mankind. Material and spiritual knowledge derived from him. The house, tent, snowshoe, sled, bark canoe, bow, arrow, lance, and knife—in short, all man's appurtenances—stem from him, as does knowledge of the land of the dead, the stars and constellations, the sun, the moon, and the calendar months. It was also he who had the muskrat dive into the waters after the Deluge and who then created a new world from the mud that was brought up, thus becoming a second creator (if there had been a first).

The present era is within the third epoch. Although the hero has disappeared, the special position of mankind remains and begins to expand. Only the shamans are able to cross the boundaries between the human and the extrahuman.

Individual tribes expand this universal chronology. The Koyukon, for example, the northwesternmost Athapascan tribe in Alaska, speak of no less than five world periods: (1) the hazy time before there was light on the earth; (2) the epoch when man could change into animals, and animals into men; (3) the time when the culture hero created the present state; (4) the past time of legends; and (5) the present as far back as memory reaches (*Handbook*, vol. 6, p. 595).

Unity of life. The sequence of world epochs is more than a faded memory. It lives on today in traditional beliefs and customs that recall the events or conditions of those epochs—especially the earliest period, with its basic idea of the world family and the unity of all living creatures. Thus the Kutchin, a northern Athapascan tribe that inhabits the territory between the Mackenzie River delta and the upper Yukon, possess a special relationship with the caribou; every man, they believe, carries a small piece of caribou heart within himself, and every caribou a portion of human heart. Hence, each of these partners knows what the other feels and thinks (*Handbook*, vol. 6, p. 526). The Sekani of British Columbia believe that a mystical bond links man and animal (*Handbook*, vol. 6, p. 439); the Koyukon call the bear "Grandfather" and the wolf "Brother" (*Handbook*, vol. 6, p. 593); and the Chipewyan, who live west of Hudson Bay, identify with the wolf (*Handbook*, vol. 6, p. 279).

The names of certain Athapascan tribal groups—Beaver, Dogrib, Hare—point to familial ties with certain animals. In all of these examples we hear an echo of the earliest epoch, when a common language prevailed and all creatures had the ability to transform themselves and thus to overcome every barrier between them.

Also, the game that is killed is treated respectfully. The animal is addressed in familial terms; its death is mourned;

its bones are protected from the dogs. Otherwise, the spirit "master" of the particular type of animal will withhold game from the hunter, subjecting him to hunger. The very concept of a master of the game teaches the Indians to show a religious reverence toward the nonhuman creatures of the world. They know that every animal form has a spirit protector and helper to whom the souls of the killed animals return and, if warranted, make complaints about ill treatment. They know that no game returns to earth without the consent of the master. Finally, they know that this consent is dependent on the keeping of certain religious prescriptions. Thus the activity of the hunter is a religious act: he is constantly aware of being watched by extrahuman beings.

The culture hero. The culture hero remains the most powerful figure within this hierarchy. To the hunter, this heroic figure is an ideal that cannot be equaled. The Ojibwa on the northern side of Lake Superior liken this master to the captain of a steamboat or to the government in Ottawa; he directs all lesser masters (Diamond Jenness, *The Ojibwa Indians of Parry Island,* 1935, p. 30).

The culture hero is responsible, too, for the abundance and richness of sub-Arctic mythology. Around the camp fire or in the tent, the deeds of the hero, teacher, and friend of mankind provide the most important story-telling material. Other mythical figures are patterned after him, so there is a continuous expansion of the cycles of myths. The Koyukon are said to have "a highly developed and sophisticated repertory of myth and legend" (*Handbook*, vol. 6, p. 595); other groups are said to have a "deep respect for and attachment to their mythology" (*Handbook*, vol. 6, p. 195). The oral tradition is not understood merely as entertainment; the mythical stories confer a sacral dimension on it, which is still recognized by the Indians.

The figure of the hero is most clearly developed among the Algonquians of the Atlantic coast. The Micmac of Cape Breton Island, for example, call the teacher of mankind Kuloscap ("liar" or "deceiver") because he always does the opposite of what he says he will do. The stations of his life can still be read in the natural features of the landscape: Cape Breton Island abounds in references to the hero. Every large rock, every river, every waterfall, testifies to his deeds. All the sub-Arctic Indians have a similar mythical geography.

To the west of the Micmac other names for the culture hero appear. Among the Montagnais-Naskapi of Labrador he is called Little Man or Perfect Man; among the Cree on either side of James Bay, the One Set in Flames or the Burning One; among the Chipewyan, Raised by His Grandmother; among the Beaver Indians, He Goes along the Shore.

This last example brings us to the group of names found in northern Athapascan mythologies, which pay particular attention to the hero's unflagging wanderlust. In the regions around the large Canadian lakes, the Kutchin, Koyukon, and Kolchan speak of the Wanderer, Ferryman, Celestial Traveler,

He Paddled the Wrong Way, He Who Went Off Visiting by Canoe, or One Who Is Paddling Around, designations that refer to a particular task of the hero. He is said to labor continuously to combat giants, cannibals, and monsters for the benefit of mankind. The mass of fantasy figures in whose deeds the mythologies abound—such minor heroes as Moon Boy, Moon Dweller, Shrew, Moss Child, Wonder Child, White Horizon, the Hero with the Magic Wand—follow the same path as the tireless figure of the Wanderer.

The Supreme Being. In general, research on religions of sub-Arctic Indians tends to assume the absence of a belief in a supreme being. Lane's statement on the Chilcotin of British Columbia—"There was no belief in a supreme being" (*Handbook*, vol. 6, p. 408)—is supposed to be applicable to all Athapascan and Algonquian groups. Any hints of such a belief that do occur are assumed to be due to Christian influence.

This simplistic assumption might never have arisen had its supporters referred to the dictionary compiled by the French priest Émile Petitot (1876). Under the entry "Dieu" Petitot distinguishes between native terms for the deity and those that came into circulation as a result of missionary activity, some time after 1850. Among the first category are found the following: *The One by Whom One Swears, Vault of the Sky, The One through Whom Earth Exists, Eagle, Sitting in the Zenith, The One Who Sees Forward and Backward, Having Made the Earth, The One through Whom We Become Human.* Alongside these early native names appear the Christian terms *Creator, Father of Mankind, The One Who Dwells in Heaven,* but the first two Christian terms are also found among the early native designations, and Petitot includes them in both categories. He evidently wanted to indicate that the designations *Creator* and *Father of Mankind* existed before the missionaries arrived.

This shifting of basic values, that is, the eradication of the supreme being and the ascendancy of the hero, must have begun long before the first contact with Europeans, for the attempt to degrade the creator can be seen even in the names for the deity. Names that recall Janus figures, like *The One Who Looks Forward and Backward,* are totally unsuitable for a supreme being who has relinquished the function of world-orderer to the culture hero. Likewise, the name *Boatsman* is linked to the wandering hero but not to the regent of the universe.

The contrariness of these two key religious figures is quite evident. The hero is closely identified with man and with man's goals and purposes. The supreme god, however, encompasses the world in its entirety; he is the cosmos itself. "He is in the sun, moon, stars, clouds of heaven, mountains, and even the trees of the earth," according to the Penobscot (Speck, "Penobscot Tales," p. 4). The Naskapi likewise declare, "He is a spirit like the sun, moon, and stars, who created everything including them" (Speck, 1935, p. 29).

Shamanism. The all-encompassing rituals mentioned above form the bulwark of human life in more southerly latitudes. They incorporate everyone into the cosmic unity of life. These universal celebrations provide an indestructible shelter within the world house and prevent isolation of the individual. In the taiga and tundra, however, the individual is dependent on himself. When he needs help, the sub-Arctic Indian turns to the shaman. It is he who provides the only help when bad weather spoils the hunt, when the game withdraws into inaccessible places, when fewer fish swim upstream, when disease announces the loss of the soul, and when continued misfortune bespeaks the attack of a hostile shaman.

Dreams, songs, and journeys. The shaman's important and essential characteristics are attained through dreams. The visions befall selected candidates. The chosen must have a "peculiar aptitude" (*Handbook*, vol. 6, p. 607), but family inheritance can also play a role. The strength of a shaman depends on spirit helpers that are either acquired through dreams or inherited from his father or his maternal uncle. Every hunter has one such helper, acquired in the years of childhood through dream-fasting, but the shaman has at least half a dozen. The spirits manifest themselves in the form of animals, in natural phenomena such as the sun and the moon, or in the souls of deceased shamans (*Handbook*, vol. 6, p. 409).

Every spirit helper has its own song, and when a shaman incants a spirit's song, the spirit addressed hurries to help his master. The activity of the shaman alleviates much more than everyday cares. It is believed that his spirit leaves his body every night, travels on lengthy visits to the sky, and learns there everything he desires to know. When his spirit returns from its flight accompanied by the shaman's helpers, the drum on the wall begins to sound without being touched. His song is heard far and wide, and his body dances six inches above the ground (John Alden Mason, *Notes on the Indians of the Great Slave Lake Area*, 1946, p. 40).

These "journeys" establish the reputation of a shaman. While his body lies rigid and motionless on the floor, his soul hastens through far-off spaces and unknown lands, encounters mythical figures, and receives their instruction. The few reports we have indicate that the images in these dream experiences are the same as those found in the tribal mythologies. The visionary sees in his trance only what he knows. His dream journeys revitalize religious knowledge; without the continual confirmation through dreams, the mythical images would be forgotten. The shaman is thus the most important preserver of tribal traditions.

The shaman's drum. Pictorial representations are mostly to be found on the drum, the most important accessory of the shaman. Physically the drum consists of a skin-covered wooden hoop. The upper side is painted with numerous figures, all illustrations of dream experiences. Animal tendon into which pieces of bone have been twisted is stretched across the drumhead. When the drum is beaten with a wooden stick, the bone fragments begin to vibrate; they "sing."

The drum is used to induce a trance in the drummer; the vibrating and buzzing sound dulls the consciousness and opens the way for the "journey." At the same time the drum beckons the helping spirits.

The shaking tent. In addition to the drum, the eastern Canadian Algonquians use another device to communicate with the spirits: the shaking tent, which is a specially built cylindrical structure with a framework of thick poles. The top of the tent remains open so that the spirits can enter. As soon as the shaman crawls into the tent and begins to sing, the posts, which are dug in deeply, start to shake. The beckoned spirits can be heard rushing by; animal cries arise; the shaman asks questions; and the spirits respond. The séance ends when all the participants are satisfied (*Handbook*, vol. 6, p. 251).

BIBLIOGRAPHY

Our earliest sources on sub-Arctic Indian religions are two myth anthologies compiled by missionaries. Legends of the Micmacs (New York, 1894) is the work of Silas Tertius Rand. Around the middle of the nineteenth century Rand wrote down what the Indians at his mission in New Brunswick related to him. The publication followed several decades later.

Around the same time the monk Émile Petitot was working among the northern Athapascans. His Traditions Indiennes du Canada Nord-Ouest (Paris, 1886) is to this day the most comprehensive collection of texts from the region between the upper Yukon and Mackenzie rivers. Equally indispensable is his comprehensive Dictionnaire de la langue Dènè-Dindjié (Paris, 1876). The author lists the vocabulary in four parallel columns: French, Montagnais, Hare, Loucheux (Kutchin). Individual entries offer deep insight into the religion of the Indians of the time.

The transcribing of the oral tradition was continued in numerous collections. Volume 10 of the Anthropological Papers of the American Museum of Natural History (1917) contains the "Chipewyan Texts" by Pliny Earle Goddard (pp. 1-66) and "Chipewyan Tales" by Robert H. Lowie (pp. 171-200). The Journal of American Folk-Lore 30 (1917) published the "Kaska Tales" by James Teit (pp. 427-473). The "Passamaquoddy Texts" by J. Dyneley Prince appeared in the Publications of the American Ethnological Society 10 (1921): 1-85.

With the rise of modern anthropology a special problem emerged: the widespread inability of the younger generation of researchers to understand and grasp the meaning of the religious heritage of the Indians. A mechanistic worldview reduced religious values to sociological catchwords; fashionable sociological theories blocked the understanding of alien ways of thinking. Frank Gouldsmith Speck's Naskapi: The Savage Hunters of the Labrador Peninsula (1935; reprint, Norman, Okla., 1977) is one exception. Speck was one of the few researchers who recognized that the so-called primitive cultures are steeped in religion and are guided by the spiritual side of life, not by the material.

In comparison to this superb work Cornelius Osgood's otherwise laudable study on the Athapascans appears somewhat pedantic. The author fails to grasp that religion is more than knowledge. He nevertheless takes a positive step by treating religious elements not as material for sociology but as values sui generis. Among his numerous publications are: "The Ethnography of the Great Bear Lake Indians," Bulletin of the National Museum of Canada 70 (1932): 31-97; Contributions to the Ethnography of the Kutchin (New Haven, 1936); and Ingalik Mental Culture (New Haven, 1959).

The same shortcomings mark the Handbook of North American Indians, vol. 6, Subarctic, edited by June Helm (Washington, D. C., 1981). The impression often arises that this collection of short studies is dealing with "religionless" peoples. One exception here is Robin Ridington's article on the Beaver (pp. 350-360).

WERNER MÜLLER
*Translated from German by Anne Heritage
and Paul Kremmel*

Indians of the Northeast Woodlands

The Northeast Woodlands peoples occupy an area within 90º to 70º west longitude and 35º to 47º north latitude. The region can be divided into three smaller geographical areas: (1) the upper Great Lakes and Ohio River Valley region, (2) the lower Great Lakes, and (3) the coastal region.

The most prominent tribes, divided according to language group, are (1) Algonquian-speaking (Southern Ojibwa, Ottawa, Potawatomi, Menomini, Sauk, Fox, Kickapoo, Miami, Illinois, Shawnee, Narraganset, Mohican, Delaware, Nanticoke, and Powhatan), (2) Iroquoian-speaking (Huron, Erie, Neutral, Petun, Seneca, Oneida, Onondaga, Cayuga, Mohawk, and Tuscarora), and (3) Siouan-speaking (Winnebago, Tutelo).

Cosmological Beliefs. The cosmological beliefs of the Northeast Woodlands peoples involve the concept of power as manifested in the land, in the dialectic of the sacred and the profane, and in patterns of space and time. According to the mythic thought of these peoples, power is that transformative presence most clearly seen in the cycles of the day and the seasons, in the fecund earth, and in the visions and deeds of spirits, ancestors, and living people. This numinous power is so manifestly present that no verbal explanation of it is adequate; rather it is itself the explanation of all transformations in life. While generally regarded as neutral, power may be used for good or ill by individuals.

Power. This all-pervasive power is expressed among Algonquian-speaking tribes by the word *manitou* or one of its linguistic variants. *Manitou* is a personal revelatory experience usually manifested in dreams or in visions of a spirit who is capable of transformation into a specific human or animal form. The efficacy of power is symbolized as "medicine," either as a tangible object reverently kept in a bundle or as an intangible "charm" possessed internally.

The belief in *manitou* can be found among the coastal Algonquians from New England to North Carolina. Similarities may be seen in the name for the Great Manitou:

for the Narraganset he was Kautantowwit and for the Penobscot, Ktahandowit. The Delaware worshiped as Great Manitou a spirit called Keetan'to-wit, who had eleven assistants *(manitowuks)*, each having control over one of eleven hierarchically organized "heavens." The most ancient of the *manitou* was Our Grandfather, the great tortoise who carries the earth on his back. The Virginia Algonquians called those *manitou* who were benevolent *quiyoughcosuck*; this was also the name given to their priests. The evil *manitou* were called *tagkanysough*. Southeast Woodlands influences led to the depiction of *manitou* in carvings and statues, usually found in the sacred architecture of the North Carolina and Virginia Algonquians.

The Huron concept of *oki* referred both to a super-abundance of power or ability and to spirit-forces of the cosmos, or guardian spirits. An *oki* could be either benevolent or malevolent. The supreme *oki*, Iouskeha, dwelt in the sky, watched over the seasons and the affairs of humans, witnessed to vows, made crops grow, and owned the animals. He had an evil brother, Tawiskaron.

The Iroquois *orenda*, a magico-religious force, was exercised by spirit-forces called Otkon and Oyaron; it was present in humans, animals, or objects that displayed excessive power, great ability, or large size. The Iroquois had a dualistic system whereby all of the spirit-forces deemed good were associated with the Good Twin and all of those deemed evil with his brother the Evil Twin.

The land. In many of the mythologies of the peoples of the Northeast Woodlands this cosmic power was intimately connected with the land. Both the Algonquian speakers and the Siouan-speaking Winnebago developed cosmologies in which the heavens above and the earth regions below were seen as layered in hierarchies of beneficial and harmful spirits. The highest power was the supreme being called Great Spirit by the Potawatomi, Ottawa, Miami, and Ojibwa; Master of Life by the Menomini, Sauk, and Fox; Finisher by the Shawnee and Kickapoo; and Earthmaker by the Winnebago. This "great mysterious" presence maintained a unique relationship with the last and weakest members of creation, namely, human beings.

Spirit-forces. Power and guidance entered human existence from the cosmic spirit-forces, from the guardian spirits of individuals and medicine societies, and from spirits of charms, bundles, and masks. Dreams, in particular, were a vehicle for contacting power and thus gaining guidance for political and military decisions. New songs, dances, and customs were often received by the dreamer and were used to energize and reorder cultural life; dreams channeled power as consolation and hope during times of crisis, and often initiated contact between visionary power and the shamans. One means of describing the human experience of this cosmic power is through the dialectic of the sacred and the profane.

This dialectic is useful even though the Northeast Woodlands peoples did not draw a sharp distinction between the sacred and profane. The dialectic refers to the inner logic of the manifestation of numinous power through certain symbols. Profane objects, events, or persons might become embodiments of the sacred in moments of hierophany. This manifestation of the sacred in and through the profane frequently became the inspiration for sacred stories and mythologies that narrated the tribal lore. Among the Winnebago and other Northeast Woodlands peoples, narrative stories were distinguished as *worak* ("what is recounted") and *waika* ("what is sacred"). Telling the *worak* stories of heroes, human tragedy, and memorable events was a profane event, whereas narrating the *waika* stories evoked the spirits and was therefore a sacred ritual. Thus the ordinary act of speaking could become the hierophany that manifests power. Not only narrative but also the interweaving of sacred space and time gave real dimensions to cosmic power.

Ceremonial Practices. Some understanding of the rich and complex ritual life of the Northeast Woodlands peoples can be obtained by considering selected ceremonies concerned with subsistence, life cycles, and personal, clan, and society visions.

Subsistence. Through subsistence rituals, tribes contacted power to ensure the success of hunting, fishing, or trapping; gathering of herbs, fruits, or root crops; and agricultural endeavors. Among the Sauk and Me-nomini there were both private and public ceremonials for hunting that focused on sacred objects generically labeled "medicine." The large public medicine-bundles of three types were believed to have been obtained by the trickster-culture hero Manabus from the Grandfathers, or *manitou* spirits. The first hunting bundle, called Misasakiwis, helped to defeat the malicious medicine people who tried to foil the hunter's success. Both the second bundle, Kitagasa Muskiki (made of a fawn's skin), and the third (a bundle with deer, wolf, and owl skins), fostered hunting success. Each bundle might contain a variety of power objects such as animal skins, miniature hunting implements, wooden figures, herbal preparations, and often an actual scent to lure animals. The bundle's owner obtained the right to assemble or purchase such a bundle from a personal vision. Songs, especially, evoked the powers of the bundle; these songs often recalled the agreement between the visionary and the *manitou* as well as the prohibitions and obligations that impinged upon the owner of a bundle. In this way the bundle owner, and the hunters he aided, thwarted the evil ones and contacted the *manitou* masters of the hunted animals. Thus power objects from the environment, the empowered hunters, and the ritually imaged *manitou*-spirits, functioned together to bring sustenance to the people.

Although the growing season varied within the Northeast, most of these peoples practiced some form of agriculture. With the introduction of agriculture new symbol complexes developed, giving meaning and power to this new subsistence activity and integrating it into the larger cosmic order. The northern Iroquois, for example, linked together woman, earth, moon, and the cycles of birth and death.

The domestic ceremony of apology for taking life is found among all these Northeast Woodlands people. This simple ceremony illustrates the moral character of the force that was believed to bind the cosmos together. The ceremony consisted of a spoken apology and a gift of sacred tobacco for the disturbance caused to the web of life by cutting trees, gathering plants, or taking minerals. This ceremony is both a thanksgiving for the blessing of a material boon and an acknowledgment of the environmental morality that binds the human and natural worlds.

Life cycles. Life-cycle rites of passage are illuminating examples of these peoples' recognition that the passage through life's stages required a structured encounter with power. These ceremonies included private actions that invoked power at liminal moments such as menstruation, marriage, and birth. Other life-cycle ceremonials, however, were marked by elaborate ritual activities, such as naming, puberty, and death ceremonies.

Birth and early childhood. Naming ceremonies arise both from the belief that humans are born weak and require power for growth and survival as well as a belief that new life should be introduced into the cosmos. Generally, two types of naming ceremonies have been found. Among the Southeast Woodlands tribes a child was given an ancestral clan name. This situated that child in the clan lineage and empowered the child by directly connecting him or her to the ancestral vision embodied in the clan medicine bundles. Another ceremony associated with the Menomini, Potawatomi, Ojibwa, and Ottawa, but occasionally practiced by the other groups, involved naming by virtue of a dream vision. In this ritual a person was chosen by the parents to undergo a fast or a sweat lodge purification so that they might receive a name for the child from the *manitou*.

Among the Iroquois and Delaware the naming ceremony, which was conducted in the longhouse, was the most significant ritual of early childhood. Delaware parents were attentive to their dreams for a revelation of the name. They would give their child to an elder in the big house who would announce the child's name and offer prayers of blessing for it. A similar ceremony would be conducted for an adult who decided to change his or her name due to a significant deed or because the first name no longer seemed appropriate. The Huron pierced the ears of the child and named it shortly after birth; the child's name then belonged to the clan and could not be used by another member of the tribe. The Iroquois named their children either at the Green Corn ceremony in the summer or before the Midwinter ceremonies. A child who resembled a dead ancestor might be given his or her name since it was believed that the name might have some of the ancestor's personality. The name remained the child's exclusive privilege and the focus of his or her early spiritual formation until the puberty ceremonials.

Puberty. It is uncertain whether the puberty rites of the Algonquians of Virginia and North Carolina involved a vision quest. However, the vision quest was part of the puberty rites of all of the upper Great Lakes peoples with variations according to the tribe. Some southern Ohio River groups such as the Shawnee emphasized less ecstatic experiences such as a boy's first kill. Among the Potawatomi, however, on specially designated mornings the parents or grandparents would offer a youth in his or her early teens a choice of food or charcoal. Encouraged to choose the charcoal and to blacken their faces, the youngsters were taken to an isolated place, often to perch in the limbs of a tree. There, alone, they

> **The vision quest was part of the puberty rites of all of the upper Great Lakes peoples with variations according to the tribe.**

fasted for dream visions. Although boys and girls might undertake vision quests, many tribes in this area had special ceremonies for girls.

The northern Iroquois, the Delaware, and the coastal Algonquians secluded girls in huts during their first menstruation. Among the Delaware the girls observed strict rules regarding food, drink, and bodily care; while in seclusion they wore blankets over their heads, and they were not permitted to leave the huts until their second menstrual period. This rite signified a girl's eligibility for marriage. There is evidence that some northern Iroquoians did not seclude their women during menstruation, although certain taboos had to be observed.

One of the most striking puberty rites was the Huskanawe of the Algonquians of Virginia. This rite was undergone by boys selected to be future chiefs and priests, positions of great importance in a highly stratified society. The ceremony began with the ritual tearing away of the children from their mothers and fathers, who had to accept them thenceforth as "dead." The boys were taken into the forest and were sequestered together in a small hut. For months they were given little to eat and were made to drink intoxicating potions and take emetics. At the end of this period of mental and emotional disorientation, they completely forgot who they were, and they were unable to understand or speak the language they had known. When the initiators were sure that the boys had been deconditioned, they took them back to the village. Under close supervision from their guides, the boys formed a new identity; they relearned how to speak and were

taught what to wear and the intricacies of the new roles now assigned to them. As rulers or priests they had to be free from all attachments to family and friends. Their minds had been cleansed and reshaped so that they might see clearly and act wisely. Their claim to authority and their power to lead others rested on their successful ritual transition to a sacred condition.

Death. The form of death rites varied widely among the Northeast Woodlands peoples. In the tribes of the upper Great Lakes area, bodies were usually disposed of according to the individual's wishes or clan prerogatives for scaffold exposure, ground burial, or cremation. Among the Fox, death was a highly ritualized event announced to the village by a crier. The members of the deceased's clan gathered for a night of mourning. The clan leader addressed the corpse, advising it not to look back with envy on those still alive but to persevere in its journey to the ancestors in the west. After burial there were the rituals of building a grave shed and installing a clan post as a marker. A six-month period of mourning then followed, during which time a tribesperson was ceremoniously adopted to substitute for the deceased person, especially at memorial feasts.

Burial practices differed among the peoples of the lower Great Lakes and coastal region. The Algonquians of Carolina buried common people individually in shallow graves. The Algonquians of Virginia wrapped the bodies of common people in skins and placed them on scaffolds; after the decay of the flesh was complete, the bones were buried. The rulers of both peoples, however, were treated differently. After death their bodies were disemboweled and the flesh was removed, but the sinews were left attached to the bones. The skin was then sewn back on to the skeleton, after being packed with white sand or occasionally ornaments. Oil kept the body's oils from drying. The corpses were placed on a platform at the western end of the temple and attended by priests.

The Nanticoke and other tribes of the southern Maryland and Delaware peninsula area practiced a second ossuary interment, in some cases preceded by an inhumation and in others by scaffold burials. The rulers of most of these tribes were treated like those of the Algonquians of Virginia and North Carolina. Some of the southern Delaware also had a second ossuary burial, but the main tribal group had one inhumation only; no special treatment for chiefs was noted.

These life-cycle ceremonials were an integral part of every tribesperson's passage through life. Indeed, in the Winnebago Medicine rite the image of human aging in four steps is presented as a paradigm of all life. However, such ceremonial rites of passage can be distinguished from certain personal, clan, and group rituals.

Individual, clan, and group. Power objects given by the *manitou*, such as medicine bundles, charms, and face-paintings, became the focus of personal rituals, songs, and dances. An individual evoked his or her spirit and identified with it by means of rhythmic singing, drumming, rattling, or chanting; one would then channel the power brought by the spirit to a specific need such as hunting, the healing of sick people, or, in some cases, toward more selfish ends.

The Huron owned power charms *(aaskouandy)*. Many of these were found in the entrails of game animals, especially those who were difficult to kill. Charms could be small stones, tufts of hair, and so on. One of the abilities of a power charm was to change its own shape, so that a stone, for example, might become a bean or a bird's beak. *Aaskouandy* were of

> **Personal power could overwhelm individuals, causing them to seek only self-aggrandizement.**

two types: (1) those that brought general good luck and (2) those that were good for one particular task. The particular use of a charm would be revealed to its owner in a dream.

An individual or family might collect a number of charms and keep them in a bundle consisting of, for example, tufts of hair, bones or claws of animals, stones, and miniature masks. The owner was periodically obliged to offer a feast to his charms, during which he and his friends would sing to the charms and show them honor. The owner usually established a relationship to the charm spirit, similar to that between an individual and a guardian spirit, although charm spirits were known to be more unpredictable and dangerous than guardian spirits. An individual or family who wished to get rid of a charm had to conduct a ritual and bury it; even then uneasiness surrounded the event.

Among the Huron and Iroquois, there were masks that had to be cared for in addition to a charm or bundle. A person acquired a mask through dreaming of it or having it prescribed by a shaman. A carver would go into the forest and search for a living tree; basswood, cucumber, and willow were the preferred woods. While burning tobacco, he recited prayers to the tree spirit and the False Face spirits. The mask was carved into the tree and then removed in one piece. The finishing touches, including the eye-holes (which were surrounded with metal) and the mouth hole, were added later. If the tree had been found in the morning, the mask would be painted red; if in the afternoon, black. The hair attached to the mask was horsetail.

Personal power could overwhelm individuals, causing them to seek only self-aggrandizement. The Shawnee have myths that relate the origin of witchcraft to that mythic time when a crocodile's heart, which was the embodiment of evil, was cut out and carried home to the village by unwitting tribespeople. While the tribes of the Northeast fostered belief in contact with power, they also condemned the misuse of

such power in sorcery. They tried to control their exceptional personalities by threatening the return of all evil machinations to the perpetrator. Nonetheless, witch societies have been prominent in Menomini history. Even though these destructive medicine practices were at times pervasive among the Northeast Woodlands tribes, their many religious societies never completely abandoned the constructive use of power.

The Miami and Winnebago each had religious societies formed around clan war-bundles. The Kickapoo still have clan societies that hold spring renewals centered on their ancestral bundles. Vision societies also developed among individual Winnebago, Sauk, Fox, Kickapoo, Illinois, Miami, and Shawnee people who had received vision revelations from the same *manitou* spirit. Throughout this region societies also formed around those warriors or braves whose heroic acts in battle were seen as special signs of personal power. So also the Potawatomi Southern Dance temporarily brought together tribespeople who still grieved for deceased relatives. The medicine societies and other groups, such as the Dream Dance (or Drum Dance) and the Native American Church, admitted tribespeople who felt called to these societies and were willing to submit to the societies' ethics.

Religious Personalities. The shaman is the most important religious figure among the upper Great Lakes and Ohio River native peoples. Primarily a healer and diviner, the shaman contacts power by means of a trance and channels that power to specific needs. Shamans are known by a variety of names derived from the calls to their vocation they have received by way of visions, as well as from their particular healing functions. Generally, four shamanic vocations are found among the northeastern Algonquian peoples. There are also a number of shamanic techniques. Both the shamanic vocations and techniques are documented from the seventeenth century.

The manipulation of fire for healing purposes is an ancient shamanic vocation; the Ojibwa call this healer *wabeno*, the Menomini called him *wapanows*, and the Potawatomi, *wapno*. The traditional call to this vocation came from Morning Star, who was imaged as a *manitou* with horns. The *wabeno*, working individually or in a group, healed by using the heat of burning embers to massage and fascinate his patients.

Shamanism among the Huron and the Iroquois of the seventeenth century was primarily an individual enterprise, although a few societies did exist. In subsequent centuries the Iroquois channeled shamanistic powers and skills into the growing number of medicine societies, as described above. The central concern of the Huron shamans was the curing of illness. Illness was caused by either (1) natural events, (2) witchcraft, or (3) desires of the soul. The first could be handled by an herbalist or other practitioner. The second and third required the diagnostic and healing abilities of a shaman *(arendiwane)*, including divining, interpreting dreams, sucking, blowing ashes, and juggling hot coals.

The *ocata* was a shaman skilled in diagnosis. In the case of a hidden desire of the soul whose frustration was causing illness he would seek to have a vision of what was desired. To do this he might gaze into a basin of water until the object appeared or enter into a trancelike state to see the object or lie down in a small dark tent to contact his spiritual allies to assist him.

The spirit-ally *(oki)* was won after a long fast and isolation in the forest; it could take the form of a human, an animal, or a bird such as a raven or eagle. Sometimes the power and skill needed to cure would come through a dream. There were shamanic specialists who handled hot coals or plunged their arms into boiling water without injury; frequently a power song, which allowed the person to accomplish this, was sung. Other shamans cured by blowing hot ashes over a person or by rubbing the person's skin with ashes.

Witchcraft was combatted by the *aretsan*; usually the *aretsan* would suck out the evil spell that the witch had magically injected into his victim. Still other shamans could see things at a distance, cause rain, persuade animal guardian spirits to release game, or give advice on military or political matters.

Outside of these established vocations, certain shamanic techniques were available to all lay people among the tribes of the Northeast. These included tattooing, naming, divining, bloodletting, induced vomiting as a cure, weather control, and herbal healing. However, at times individual shamans or shamanic societies were so strong that they absorbed these and other curing practices as their exclusive prerogative.

Other outstanding religious personalities included the war chiefs, who led war bundle ceremonies and war parties, and the peace chiefs, who did not go to fight but who acted as mediators, working for peace within the tribe as well as between separate tribes. The Menomini chose hereditary war chiefs from the Bear clan and peace chiefs from the Thunderer clan. All Northeast Woodlands tribes used a war and peace chief system, but the clan totems from which these leaders were selected often differed from band to band.

Northeast Woodlands peoples have struggled to maintain their traditions into the present period. Not only have they endured the cultural inroads of a variety of Christian missionaries, but these native traditions have also persisted in the face of tribal fragmentation and degradation. This struggle was reflected in the life of the Seneca leader Handsome Lake; he was able to give focus to his people's plight by drawing on the spiritual power of dreams that came to him during an illness brought on by drunkenness and despair. The traditional sanction of dreams and visions in native Northeast Woodlands religions continues into the present revitalization of the sweat lodge, the vision quest, and medicine-wheel gatherings. The relevance of these traditional ceremonies to contemporary needs is highlighted by the growing participation of non-Indians in these meditative rituals

BIBLIOGRAPHY

Anthropological Papers. New York, 1907-. These volumes, published by the American Museum of Natural History, contain extensive materials on the religious beliefs and practices of Northeast Woodlands peoples as, for example, in Alanson Skinner's *Social Life and Ceremonial Bundles of the Menomini Indians and Folklore of the Menomini Indians*, in volume 13, parts 1 and 3 (New York, 1915).

Beverley, Robert. *The History and Present State of Virginia* (1705). Edited by Louis B. Wright. Chapel Hill, N. C., 1947. A primary document on the Virginia Algonquians drawing on the author's own observations and those of earlier sources, written and verbal. More sensitive than most works of the period regarding both the native peoples and the natural environment.

Blair, Emma, ed. and trans. *The Indian Tribes of the Upper Mississippi Valley and the Region of the Great Lakes* (1911). 2 vols. New York, 1969. A fine collection of primary documents describing the upper Great Lakes and Ohio River native peoples during the seventeenth and eighteenth centuries.

Bureau of American Ethnology. *Annual Reports* and "Bulletins." Washington, D. C., 1888-. These reports and bulletins present materials on native peoples' beliefs and religious practices which, however, often need further interpretation. Special mention can be made here of the following monographs published as "Bulletins of the Bureau of American Ethnology": *The Midewiwin or 'Grand Medicine Society' of the Ojibwa*, no. 7 (1885-1886), and *The Menomini Indians* no. 14, (1892-1893), both by Walter J. Hoffman; *Ethnography of the Fox Indians*, no. 125 (1939), by William Jones; Contributions to Fox Ethnology, 2 vols., nos. 85 (1927) and 95 (1930), and *The Owl Sacred Pack of the Fox Indians*, no. 72 (1921), by Trumen Michelson; and The Winnebago Tribe, no. 37 (1915-1916), by Paul Radin.

Driver, Harold E. *Indians of North America.* 2d ed., rev. Chicago, 1969. Somewhat dated in parts but overall good statistical information on all Native American tribes, including those of the Northeast.

Flannery, Regina. "An Analysis of Coastal Algonquian Culture." Ph. D. diss., Catholic University, 1939. A detailed classification of cultural topics and documentation for all areas of coastal Algonquian life, drawn mostly from sixteenth- and seventeenth-century documents.

Greeman, Emerson F. *The Wolf and Furton Sites.* Occasional Contributions, Museum of Anthropology, University of Michigan, no. 8. Ann Arbor, 1939. Study of a woodland archaeological site of proto-historical period.

Grim, John A. *The Shaman: Patterns of Siberian and Ojibway Healing.* Norman, Okla., 1983. A study of the Ojibwa shaman that, in addition, traces broad patterns of shamanic expression. Includes an extensive bibliography on the religious figure of the shaman.

Hallowell, A. Irving. "Ojibwa Ontology, Behavior, and World View." *In Culture in History: Essays in Honor of Paul Radin*, edited by Stanley Diamond, pp. 19-52. New York, 1960. An important analysis of the categories and orientations of Ojibwa ethnometaphysics that is helpful in interpreting the religious practices of these woodland peoples.

Harrington, Mark R. *Religion and Ceremonies of the Lenape*. New York, 1921. The first and still the best work on the religion of the Delaware in the late nineteenth and early twentieth centuries.

Hewitt, J. N. B., ed. "Iroquois Cosmology," part 1. In *Bureau of American Ethnology Twenty-first Annual Report*, pp. 127-339. Washington, D. C., 1899-1900.

Hewitt, J. N. B., ed. "Iroquoian Cosmology," part 2. In *Bureau of American Ethnology Forty-third Annual Report*, pp. 449-819. Washington, D. C., 1925-1926. The best collection of Iroquois cosmogonic myths available.

Hultkrantz, Åke. *The Religions of the American Indians*. Berkeley, 1979. An overview of phenomenological patterns of religious expression among tribal peoples of North America that is helpful in interpreting the various ethnographies.

Kinietz, W. Vernon. *The Indians of the Western Great Lakes*, 1615-1760. Occasional Contributions, Museum of Anthropology, University of Michigan, no. 10. Ann Arbor, 1940.

Landes, Ruth. *Ojibwa Religion and the Midewiwin*. Madison, 1968.

Landes, Ruth. *The Prairie Potawatomi*. Madison, 1970. Both of Landes's works explore, from an anthropological perspective, selected myths and rituals associated with the presence of religious power.

Radin, Paul, ed. *The Road of Life and Death*. New York, 1945. Contains the text of the Winnebago Medicine rite with some commentary by Radin on the circumstances that prompted Crashing Thunder (Jasper Blowsnake) to narrate this esoteric lore. This book also includes Big Winnebago's autobiography, as edited by Paul Radin.

Speck, Frank G. *A Study of the Delaware Indian Big House Ceremony*. Harrisburg, Pa., 1931. The foremost study of the Big House ceremony among the Delaware of Oklahoma.

Sturtevant, William C., and Bruce Trigger, eds. *Handbook of North American Indians*. Rev. ed. Washington, D. C., 1981. An excellent overview of the specific tribal groups in this area with a brief treatment of religious beliefs and practices.

Thwaites, Reuben Gold, ed. *The Jesuit Relations and Allied Documents . . .*, *1610-1791* (1896-1901). 73 vols. in 39. Reprint, New York, 1959. An indispensable work especially on the tribes of "Huronia" and "Iroquoia" as related by Jesuit missionaries.

Tooker, Elisabeth. *Native North American Spirituality of the Eastern Woodlands*. New York, 1979. Ethnographic selections from the religious rituals of various Northeast Woodlands peoples with some general interpretative sections.

Trigger, Bruce G. *The Children of Aataentsic: A History of the Huron People to 1660*. 2 vols. Montreal, 1976. Excellent reconstruction of the history, culture, and religion of the Hurons, relying on the earliest documents available.

Trowbridge, C. C. *Meearmar Traditions*. Occasional Contributions, Museum of Anthropology, University of Michigan, no. 7. Ann Arbor, 1938. A study of the Miami people.

Trowbridge, C. C., *Shawnese Traditions*. Edited by W. Vernon Kinietz. Occasional Contributions, Museum of Anthropology, University of Michigan, no. 9. Ann Arbor, 1939.

Williams, Roger. *The Complete Writings of Roger Williams* (1643). 7 vols. Edited by Reuben A. Guild et al. New York, 1963. Especially valuable for information on the Narraganset is "The Key into the Language of America" found in volume 1.

JOHN A. GRIM and DONALD P. ST. JOHN

Indians of the Southeast Woodlands

The Indians who were the aboriginal inhabitants of the southeastern United States lived in a region whose boundaries were approximately the same as those of the contemporary South, that is, extending from about 95° west longitude eastward to the Atlantic coast and from about 37° north latitude southward to the Gulf of Mexico. The Indians of the Southeast Woodlands were linguistically diverse. Muskogean was the most important language family, but four additional language families were present: Iroquoian, Siouan, Algonquian, and Caddoan. Both prehistoric and historical forces shaped the cultural and social characteristics of the Southeast Indians.

Various estimates of the Indian population of the Southeast Woodlands have been proposed for the period just prior to European exploration in the sixteenth century. They range from a low of 170,000 to a high of perhaps 1.7 million. But whatever the Indians' aboriginal population, beginning in the sixteenth century they began to suffer from a series of European epidemic diseases that caused very heavy loss of life. By 1755, they may have numbered only about 50,000 to 70,000. It is clear that this demographic collapse caused extensive social and cultural change. The Indians' social structure became less stratified, and their religious and ritual life was simplified. The most detailed information on Southeast Indian religious beliefs and practices was collected in the late nineteenth and early twentieth centuries, although some good information was collected by eighteenth-century observers, and this is complemented by scattered information from the sixteenth and seventeenth centuries. Some threads of continuity can be discerned among beliefs and practices throughout this four-hundred-year period.

The Belief System. The Southeast Indian conception of the cosmos resembled, in its broad outlines, the cosmologies of many other New World peoples. The Southeast Indians believed, for example, that this world—the earth on which they lived—was a circular island that rested upon the waters. The sky above was thought to be a vault of stone, in the form of an inverted bowl. At dawn and at dusk, the bowl rose so that the sun and the moon, two principal deities, could pass beneath it at the beginning and end of their transit through the heavens.

In addition to the earth on which they stood and the world in which they lived, the Indians believed that an upperworld existed above the sky vault and that an underworld existed beneath the earth and the waters. The upperworld was peopled by the sun and the moon, and by large, perfect archetypes of all the creatures that lived on the earth. The underworld was peopled by spirits and monsters living in a chaotic world full of novelty and invention.

For the Southeast Indians, the upperworld was a place of structure, regularity, and perfect order. Its opposite was the underworld, a place of chaos and disorder, as well as fecundity. The Indians appear to have attempted to steer a middle course between the compulsive order of the upperworld and the mad chaos of the underworld. They believed, for example, that in the beginning there were only two worlds, the upperworld and the underworld, and that this world had been created when soft mud was brought up from beneath the waters to form the island earth. Moreover, they believed that the island was suspended rather precariously from the sky

> **The sun, the chief upperworld deity, was represented on earth by sacred fire.**

vault by four cords, one in each of the four cardinal directions. They appear to have believed that man's inability to behave strictly in accordance with moral and religious precepts weakened the cords, and thus they feared that the earth would one day sink beneath the waters.

The Southeast Indians believed that certain kinds of beings were more pure, more sacred, than others. Sacred beings were those that seemed able to resist or to stand above natural, mundane constraints.

The sun, the chief upperworld deity, was represented on earth by sacred fire. The smoke that rose from sacred fire connected this earthly world with the upperworld. The Southeast Indians believed that when they behaved badly in the presence of sacred fire, their behavior was immediately known to the sun. The medium that connected people in this world with the underworld was the water in creeks and rivers, which were thought to be avenues or roads to the underworld. The Cherokee personified rivers and streams, calling them "the long person." Fire and water were considered opposites. As such, fire and water were one of an extensive series of opposed forces and beings in the Southeast Indian belief system.

The Cherokee, and probably other Southeast Indians, classified living beings into large categories, and the relationships among these categories were important structural features of their belief system. The three categories of living beings were people, animals, and plants.

Each of these three categories was further subdivided into smaller categories. People were divided into matrilineal clans. Plants were classified in terms of an elaborate taxonomy. Animals were divided into birds, four-footed animals, and vermin, the latter category including fish, snakes, and other creatures inhabiting the watery realm. Many of these animals were invested with symbolic value. In Southeast Indian thought, each of these three animal categories was epitomized by a particular species. The rattlesnake, the most feared venomous snake in the Southeast, was the epitome of

the vermin category, and the Virginia deer, the region's most important game animal, was the epitome of the four-footed animals. Birds may have been epitomized by two creatures—the bald eagle, the supreme bird of peace, and the peregrine falcon, the supreme bird of war. If frequency of occurrence in late prehistoric art is a reliable measure of symbolic importance, then the peregrine falcon was clearly the more important of the two birds.

In addition to the animals that epitomized the normal categories, the Southeast Indian belief system recognized an extensive series of anomalous beings that did not fit neatly into a single category. In each case, these anomalies were given special symbolic value. For example, the Venus's-fly-trap *(Dionaea muscipula)* and the pitcher plant *(Sarracenia purpurea)*, because they "catch" and "digest" insects, were considered to be plants that behave like animals. The Cherokee believed that the roots of both plants possessed extraordinary magical powers.

The bear was considered anomalous because it is a four-footed animal that possesses certain characteristics reminiscent of people: it is capable of bipedal locomotion; the skeletal structure of its foot closely resembles the human foot; it is as omnivorous in its diet as people are; and its feces resemble human feces. In Cherokee mythology the bear is depicted as a buffoon who attempts to act as humans act, but who fails because of his clumsiness and because he is, after all, an animal.

The most anomalous being in the Southeast Indian belief system was a monster formed of the parts of many creatures. There is evidence that the Indians considered this monster to be an actual being, not a creature whose existence was exclusively spiritual. The Cherokee called this monster the *uktena*. Its body was like that of a rattlesnake, only much larger, the size of a tree trunk. It was believed to live on the margins of the known world, in deep pools of water and near high mountain passes. If a person merely saw an *uktena*, it could cause misfortune, and to smell the breath of an *uktena* brought death.

Witchcraft. The Southeast Indians explained many of the events in their lives as reward and punishment meted out by spiritual beings who acted according to known standards of behavior. For example, young men who were too careless or headstrong to observe certain taboos and rules of behavior could endanger their own safety and the safety of their comrades in warfare. And women were required to segregate themselves during their menses; if they failed to do so, their mere presence was thought to be polluting and could spoil any serious enterprise. Thus the Southeast Indians explained some of the misfortunes in their lives as having emanated from a just principle—bad things happened when people behaved badly.

In Cherokee myths witches are depicted as irredeemably evil people who can take on the appearance of any person, four-footed animal, or bird. Witches are thought particularly likely to assume the appearance of a horned owl or a raven. The Cherokee took pains to stay up all night at the bedside of anyone who was seriously ill because they believed that witches were especially likely to attack such weak and defenseless people. They believed that witches stole the remaining days, months, or years of life of the ill person, extending their own lives by adding this time to their own. For this reason, the Cherokee believed that witches were often old people.

The Cherokee believed that witches' activities could sometimes be discovered through divination. This was especially necessary in the case of people who were ill. The medicine man who was taking care of the afflicted person would rake up a cone-shaped mound of coals in the fireplace and then sprinkle some pulverized tobacco (Nicotiana rustica) on the cone. Using the mound of coals as a kind of compass, the medicine man would recognize the direction of a witch's presence by the place on the cone where the sparks flared. If the particles clung together and flared with a loud burst, the witch was just outside the house. The Cherokee believed that a witch could be killed merely by learning his or her identity. Deceit and deception were at the core of witchcraft, and without these a witch could not exist.

Rituals. The Southeast Indians acted out their beliefs about the world in rituals at both small and large junctures in their lives.

Immersion in water was a ritual that all Southeast Indians were supposed to perform each day, although some practiced it more faithfully than others. One was supposed to go to a moving stream at dawn and immerse oneself in the life-renewing water, even if ice was on the water. This ritual appears to have been kept most strictly by males, and particularly by younger males, upon whose vigor the defense of the society depended.

All important transitions of life were underscored by rites of passage. Mothers generally gave birth in the small houses where women sequestered themselves during menstruation. Before the newborn baby was allowed to suckle, it was taken to a creek or a spring and dipped into the water. Then bear oil was rubbed all over the baby's body. The father of a newborn baby was required to fast for four days.

Marriages were sealed by a series of exchanges. The kinsmen of the groom first collected gifts that were then presented to the kinsmen of the bride. In the marriage ceremony itself, the most essential acts were the killing of a deer or a bear by the groom, symbolizing his role as meat producer, and the cooking of a corn dish by the bride to symbolize her role as corn producer.

The principal concern of young men in the aboriginal Southeast was acquiring war honors, which they earned by meritorious deeds of valor. At each juncture in their military careers, a new name was bestowed upon them at a ceremo-

ny in their honor. The young men to be honored rubbed bear oil over their bodies and wore special clothing. The beloved old men delivered orations on the valor of the young men, and they admonished others to observe sacred precepts.

In curing illness, Southeast Indian priests and medicine men relied upon rituals as much as upon herbal medicines. As has been seen, they believed that many diseases were caused by vengeful spirits of the animals they had slain. If, for example, a medicine man concluded that his patient's disease had been caused by a vengeful fish spirit, he might invoke a kingfisher spirit or heron spirit to fly down and snatch away the offending fish spirit. Or if the illness happened to be rheumatism caused by an angry deer spirit, the medicine man might require the patient to drink a medicine made of several different ferns, and he would then invoke a terrapin spirit to come and loosen the rheumatism from the patient's bones.

Funerals were the rites of passage around which the Southeast Indians organized their most elaborate rituals. In the late prehistoric era, and in some places even in the early historical era, the death of an important person could cause several other people to submit to voluntary death so that they could accompany the dead person to the otherworld. The interment of an important person's body was the occasion of a solemn ceremonial with much mourning. Months later the body was dug up and the bones cleaned and placed in a basket or box that was kept in the temple. Less important people received less elaborate treatment, but even they might be buried with some of their possessions, as well as with containers of food for their journey to the otherworld. In some cases, favorite pets were killed and interred with their masters.

In addition to a multitude of everyday taboos and avoidances, life-crisis rituals, and rites of passage, the Southeast Indians organized periodic ceremonials that were performed on behalf of the entire society. There is evidence that the Southeast Indians in the late prehistoric period performed a series of such rituals throughout the year. But by the eighteenth century only one of these was widely performed—the Green Corn ceremony, was a first-fruits ceremony and a rite of thanksgiving. It was also an important vehicle in the Southeast Indians' never-ending quest for purity. In fact, the Green Corn ceremony was a ritual means of purifying an entire society.

Christian Missions and Modern Religious Movements. The christianization of the Southeast Indians began in the late sixteenth century, when the Spanish built a mission system along the Georgia coast and in northern Florida. An early missionizing attempt by the Jesuits failed, but beginning in 1583 the Franciscans laid the groundwork for a mission system that endured until the late seventeenth and early eighteenth centuries. The Spanish friars taught the mission Indians Roman Catholic dogma, and they taught some of them to speak Spanish; a few Indians even became literate in the language. The missionaries also introduced European grains, vegetables, and fruits. The friars were able to maintain their missions only in the coastal regions; they were never able to missionize effectively in the interior, although a few attempts were made.

The Spanish mission system was rapidly destroyed after the British founded the colony of South Carolina in 1670. In their new colony the British quickly set about building plantations to be worked with slave labor. They armed Indian mercenaries to aid in their attacks on the Spanish missions. They enslaved many of the Indians and put them to work alongside the African slaves. By 1705, the Spanish mission system among the Southeast Indians had been completely destroyed.

Throughout the eighteenth century the Southeast Indians were caught up in the competition among the British, French, and Spanish for supremacy in the Southeast. The French

> ... beginning in the 1830s almost all the Indians of the Southeast Woodlands were forced to migrate to the Indian Territory, now Oklahoma.

sent a few missionaries to the Indians, but they were relatively ineffective. In the British colonies the Anglican Society for the Propagation of the Gospel did some mission work, although never with great enthusiasm. John and Charles Wesley also attempted for a time to missionize the Indians of the Georgia colony, but without success.

The first serious attempt after the Spanish to missionize the Southeast Indians came in the late eighteenth and early nineteenth centuries, when several Protestant groups began working among the Indians. It was also at this time that a nativistic movement swept through one group of Southeast Indians, the Upper Creek, with disastrous results. Partly stimulated by a visit from the Shawnee leader Tecumseh, who attempted to unite the Indians against the Americans, a number of prophets arose among the Upper Creek who believed that they could expel the Americans through combining religious and military action. This led to the Creek War of 1813-1814, which ended in a decisive defeat of the Indians.

At the very time when nineteenth-century Protestant missionaries were trying to "civilize" the Southeast Indians by teaching them not only Christianity but also modern agricultural and mechanical arts, pressure was building among southern planters to "remove" the Indians from their land. Ultimately the planters had their way, and beginning in the 1830s almost all the Indians of the Southeast Woodlands were forced to migrate to the Indian Territory, now Oklahoma.

Although fragments of the old Southeast Indian belief system have lingered on, often in an underground way, such beliefs have become curiosities in the twentieth century. In some places descendants of the Southeast Indians attend "stomp dances," but similar dances are performed by many modern American Indians. In a few places the Green Corn ceremony continues to be performed, although it lacks the powerful and pervasive meaning it once had.

BIBLIOGRAPHY

A definitive book on Southeast Indian religion remains to be written. Introductions to the subject can be found in my books *The Southeastern Indians* (Knoxville, 1976), in which see especially chapters 3 and 6, and *Elements of Southeastern Indian Religion* (Leiden, 1984), which is mainly concerned with iconography. A useful introduction to late prehistoric and early historical iconography and religion is James H. Howard's *The Southeastern Ceremonial Complex and Its Interpretation* (Columbia, Mo., 1968). The best specialized work on late prehistoric iconography is *Pre-Columbian Shell Engravings from the Craig Mound at Spiro*, Oklahoma, vol. 1 (Cambridge, Mass., 1978), by Philip Phillips and others. A useful survey of the Green Corn ceremony is John Witthoft's *Green Corn Ceremonialism in the Eastern Woodlands* (Ann Arbor, 1949), and the Black Drink ceremony is surveyed in a series of papers in *Black Drink* (Athens, Ga., 1979), edited by me.

Information on the religious beliefs and practices of the Cherokee is richer than for any other Southeast Indian group. See especially James Mooney's "Myths of the Cherokee," in the *Nineteenth Annual Report of the Bureau of American Ethnology* (Washington, D. C., 1900), and James Mooney and Frans M. Olbrechts's *The Swimmer Manuscript: Cherokee Sacred Formulas and Medicinal Prescriptions* (Washington, D. C., 1932). See also Raymond D. Fogelson's "An Analysis of Cherokee Sorcery and Witchcraft," in *Four Centuries of Southern Indians* (Athens, Ga., 1975), edited by me; James Mooney's "The Cherokee River Cult," *The Journal of American Folklore* 13 (1900): 1-10; and Frans M. Olbrechts's "Some Cherokee Methods of Divination," in *Proceedings of the Twenty-third International Congress of Americanists* (New York, 1930). Most of the available information on Creek religion is surveyed in John R. Swanton's "Religious Beliefs and Medical Practices of the Creek Indians," in the *Forty-second Annual Report of the Bureau of American Ethnology* (Washington, D. C., 1982). The Spanish mission period is surveyed in John Tate Lanning's *The Spanish Missions of Georgia* (Chapel Hill, N. C., 1935) and in Mark F. Boyd, Hale G. Smith, and John W. Griffin's *Here They Once Stood: The Tragic End of the Apalachee Missions* (Gainesville, Fla., 1951).

CHARLES HUDSON

Indians of the Plains

Plains Indian religion is as varied and complex as the various peoples who inhabit the Plains region, an area delineated by the Rocky Mountains on the west; the Canadian provinces of Alberta, Saskatchewan, and Manitoba on the north; the Mississippi River on the east; and the Gulf of Mexico on the south. The Great Plains measure 1,125,000 square miles, an area roughly equal to one-third the land mass of the United States, and serve as the home for more than thirty American Indian ethnic groups, conventionally known as bands, tribes, nations, and confederacies. The Plains present linguistic as well as ethnic complexity; seven distinct language families are found. In historical times, these language groups have been identified in the following way:

1. *Algonquian,* represented by the Northern Arapaho of Wyoming and the Southern Arapaho of Oklahoma; the Atsina, or Gros Ventre of the Prairies; the Blackfeet Confederacy comprising the Siksika, the Kainah (or Blood), and the Piegan; the Northern Cheyenne of Montana and the Southern Cheyenne of Oklahoma; the Plains Cree; and the Plains Ojibwa (also known as Chippewa, or Bungi).
2. *Athapascan,* represented by the Lipan Apache and the Kiowa Apache of Oklahoma, and the Sarsi of Alberta. The Sarsi are counted with the Blackfeet Confederacy despite the difference in languages.
3. *Caddoan,* represented by the Arikara, or Ree; the Caddo; the Kichai; the Pawnee; and the Wichita. These tribes ranged from Texas to North Dakota but now reside in North Dakota (Arikara) and Oklahoma (all others).
4. *Kiowa-Tanoan,* represented on the Plains by only one tribe, the Kiowa, who now live in Oklahoma.
5. *Siouan,* by far the largest on the Plains, represented by the Assiniboin, also known in Canada as the Stoney; the Crow, or Absoroka, of Montana; a subdivision of the Siouan family known as Deghiha, comprising the Kansa (or Kaw), the Omaha, the Osage, the Ponca, and the Quapaw, all of whom live in Oklahoma; the Hidatsa, or Gros Ventre of the River; the Iowa, Oto, and Missouri, who form a linguistic subdivision called Chiwere and who reside in Oklahoma; the Mandan, who share a reservation with the Arikara and Hidatsa in North Dakota; the Dakota, or Santee; the Lakota, or Teton; and the Nakota, or Yankton. The Mandan, the Arikara, and the Hidatsa are currently referred to as the Three Affiliated Tribes. The Dakota, the Lakota, and the Nakota are conventionally designated as the "Sioux," a term that, despite its pejorative origin, continues to be employed by scholars as the only one available under which to group these three closely related tribes and their numerous subdivisions. [For further discussion, see Lakota Religion.]
6. *Tonkawan,* represented exclusively by the Tonkawa of Oklahoma.
7. *Uto-Aztecan,* represented by one tribe, the Comanche of Oklahoma.

Although population figures are difficult to ascertain, there are currently 225,000 Indians on the Plains, and most authorities believe that, following a dangerous population decline at the turn of the twentieth century, the present-day Indian population equals or surpasses precontact figures.

The Plains culture essentially comprises a potpourri of religious ideas from other parts of the United States and Canada, and it is useful to see the Plains as a point of synthesis of various customs, beliefs, and rituals that amalgamate as a result of emigration and, ultimately, diffusion. Nearly all the basic religious ideas found in other parts of native North America are found on the Plains. If the focus is on the historical period, these basic religious ideas can be seen to fall into three major categories.

The first category may be regarded as tribal religion, idiosyncratic beliefs and rituals that are perceived by their adepts to be unique to their own tribe.

The second category is made up of pantribal religion, beliefs and rituals acknowledged to have been diffused usually from a known single source. Frequently there is a conscious effort made to learn a new religion from a foreign ethnic group.

A third category falls somewhere between the first two and consists mainly of two ubiquitous religious institutions, the vision quest and the Sweat Lodge ceremony, as well as a number of other beliefs and practices that, although present in all Plains tribes, are still considered by their followers to be unique to each.

Vision Quest and Sweat Lodge. The ideas behind the vision quest and the Sweat Lodge ceremony and their associated ritual paraphernalia are essentially the same among all Plains tribes, but there is some variation found within any single tribe. During the vision quest, a person, usually a male, embarks upon an ordeal in which he will isolate himself from the remainder of the tribe. Under the direction of a medicine man, he is led to a hill or other secluded spot, where he stays for an agreed-upon number of days and fasts until he receives a vision that will later be interpreted for him by the medicine man. The vision usually takes the form of a communication between the supplicant and an animal, bird, or inanimate object such as a stone. The supplicant may also envision a ghost, but in all cases, he will receive instructions that will affect his future. He may also be instructed to obtain the skin of an animal or bird or another object that will serve as a personal fetish or good-luck charm. He may learn a song, acquire a name, or even receive a calling to become a medicine man.

Guardians or tutelary spirits sometimes are acquired in the vision quest, at other times obtained in a ritual from a shaman. Guardian spirits may be represented by animals, birds, inanimate objects, or the ghosts of humans. Frequently, the guardian spirit is manifested in the form of a bundle, fetish, or other object that an individual wears or carries during ordeals or dangerous encounters, such as those met on the warpath. Along with the object, a quester may acquire special prayers or songs learned in the vision and may employ these incantations in times of need.

In the Sweat Lodge ceremony, a small number of (usually) males join together with a medicine man in a small dome-shaped lodge constructed of saplings and covered with hides and blankets to make it airtight and dark. In the center of the lodge a hole is dug and stones heated outside are handed in by means of ladles by the fire tender and placed into the center hole. The hides are secured firmly over the lodge and the medicine man sprinkles water over the heated stones, causing a great rush of hot air to fill the lodge. The participants perspire profusely and slap their bodies with switches made from pine boughs or with buffalo tails in order to increase their blood circulation. At the same time they sing and pray together, asking for special favors from the spirits who come into the lodge, and also praying for the general welfare of the people. During the course of the ceremony, the lodge is opened occasionally so that the adepts may breathe fresh air, and at that time the ceremonial pipe is smoked.

Frequently, the Sweat Lodge ceremony is conducted as a prefatory ritual before going on the warpath or before undertaking the vision quest or some other religious ceremony. The Sweat Lodge is regarded as a means of purifying individuals both physically and spiritually.

Ritual Practitioners. The most important figure in Plains religion is the ritual leader, who is known by a variety of names depending on his or her specialization. Normally, a shaman cures people of symbolic illness by ritual means, such as singing, dancing, or praying, while a medicine man or woman is a specialist in herbal curing. In most cases both types of ritual leaders employ the knowledge of the other, and frequently the medicine man or woman relies on supernatural aid in the selection of the proper herb, just as the shaman occasionally uses herbal teas and other concoctions in the course of a shamanic ceremony. Although *shaman* is a preferred term among scholars who study ritual behavior that is highly individualistic and informal, most Plains Indians refer, in English, to both ritual curers and herbalists as "medicine men." In the native languages, however, discrete terms are used.

Each ritual practitioner is well known in a tribal community and achieves high status by performing cures for his patients and by conducting the important ceremonies. He is often a conjurer or magician capable of amazing his adepts with his mystical abilities. The ritual practitioner is usually well paid for his services, previously in horses, buffalo robes, or blankets, now in food and money, although most shamans admit that payment is not required. Part of the popularity of the ritual practitioner is predicated on his success rate with patients and the particular way he conducts the important public ceremonies. Frequently the greatest difference in technique between shamans is stylistic: there are many variants of public and private ceremonies since they are conducted

and performed according to instructions received in visions by individual shamans. In many cases, the popular shaman is simply the one who can put on the most interesting performance, but showmanship is not seen as a detraction from the sincerity of the performances.

Although witchcraft and sorcery are not common on the Plains, several tribes have such beliefs. The Plains Cree and Plains Ojibwa brought from their Great Lakes homeland a number of ceremonies, and although they quickly learned the Sun Dance from the Assiniboin, they continued to bury their dead in the ground and conduct an annual Feast of the Dead. They were particularly frightened of witchcraft and sorcery and had one ceremony, probably related to the ceremonies of the Midewiwin, or Great Medicine society, in the Great Lakes, in which a shaman was bound hand and foot and placed in a lone tipi. It was believed that spirits entered the tipi, untied the shaman, and taught him how to cure the sick and find lost articles. Sometimes to the amazement of the devotees, the tent began to shake while the shaman was being untied and frequently he was found in a ridiculous position, sometimes wedged in between the tipi poles. For this reason, this particular ceremony (called a "shamanic cult institution" in the anthropological literature) is referred to as the Shaking Tent rite. Modified forms of this ceremony are still popular on the northern Plains among the Arapaho, Cheyenne, Lakota, and others. The Lakota call the ritual Yuwipi, a term referring to the act of rolling up into a ball the rope with which the shaman is tied.

The Supernatural. The notions of sacredness and taboo are common to Plains religion. Both designate states, desirable or not, that may be changed through the mediation of prayer, song, dance, or general propitiation of the proper spirits. The idea of the holy is most often expressed by native terms such as the Lakota *wakan*; the Algonquian variants of *manitu*; the Ponca *xube*; and Comanche *puha*. All animate and inanimate objects are capable of serving as a receptacle for this sacred state. The rituals employed to transform persons or objects from a profane state to a sacred one have frequently but erroneously been called in English "medicine," or "making medicine." Frequently the source of a medicine man's personal power is kept in a "medicine bundle." *Medicine* is here a misnomer for *sacred power*.

All Plains people distinguish in their respective languages between power and sacredness. *Great Mystery* and *Great Spirit* are also English terms associated with the Plains belief in a creator god or prime mover, a belief that led to the Christian interpretation that Plains Indians believed in a monotheistic god prior to European contact.

The Plains culture hero or trickster who figures importantly as the mediator between the supernaturals and humankind goes by a number of names—Inktomi ("spider") among the Lakota; Great White Hare among the Algonquian speakers; and Old Man or Coyote among the Crow. In the creation myths this being teaches humans about culture after the establishment of the earth. He also plays another important role in the mythology of the Plains people: he is the principal character in a cycle of morality stories in which positive values of the Indian people are taught through negative examples, that is, the hero always makes mistakes and demonstrates poor judgment. Children are told not to behave as the trickster.

Taboos associated with sexual intercourse, menstruation, and food are as prominent on the Plains as they are elsewhere in American Indian culture, although recent evidence shows that menstrual taboos are positive, in their reinforcement of the female biological role, as well as negative, in their reinforcement of the male fear of "pollution."

The Hereafter. The hereafter was described as a hazy duplicate of the living world. There people dwelled in tipi camps, hunted buffalo, sang, feasted, danced, and were reunited with their kin. Enemies also abounded, and one had to beware of vengeance from the spirit of a slain enemy. It is alleged that the practice of scalping prevented the enemy spirit from going to the spirit camp after death.

The most common forms of burial on the Plains were scaffold and tree burials. The deceased was dressed in fine clothing and wrapped in a buffalo hide. Then the body was placed in the scaffold or tree and secured tightly; it remained there until it decomposed. Most Indians were generally fearful that the spirit of the deceased haunted the place of its burial, so burial grounds were usually avoided. At the time of the burial, however, close relatives of the deceased would come and linger near the corpse. They prepared foods for the spirit's journey to the hereafter and placed new hunting and fighting

> **It is alleged that the practice of scalping prevented the enemy spirit from going to the spirit camp after death.**

implements near the scaffold. Frequently a favorite horse was killed and placed at the foot of the scaffold so that the spirit of the deceased could ride that of the horse in the other world.

It was commonly believed that when a person died, its ghost would attempt to entice a close relative to join it in death. These ghosts heralded their presence in numerous ways and some believed that if they heard a baby crying outside in the night or a wolf howl or a rooster crow, it was some boundless spirit calling someone to die. When this occurred members of the family would fire guns to frighten away the spirit. Shamans would burn incense with an aroma that was displeasing to these angry ghosts. Belief in ghosts was common, and it was accepted that ghosts were capable of advising humans about the welfare of the tribe. Shamans were

believed to commune with ghosts at night. The shamans freely asked the advice of ghosts about how to cure people, and the ghosts predicted certain events in the lives of the living. Ghosts were also capable of finding lost or stolen articles and in some cases were capable of taking another life.

Major Symbols. Perhaps there is no more universal a symbol of Plains Indian religion than the long-stemmed pipe, sometimes called the "peace pipe." The pipe is essentially a medium of prayer, and when people pray with the pipe it is believed that the smoke rising from the pipe will carry the message of the supplicants to the spirits above. Pipe smoking is a necessary prelude to every important religious ceremony. In the past a pipe was also frequently smoked when deliberations had to be made over hunting or warfare. Normally, each man owned his own pipe and carried it in an elaborate bag or bundle.

Several types of Indian tobacco are smoked in the pipe, and it too is considered to have certain sacred powers. It is often wrapped in pouches and hung in trees as offerings to the supernaturals. Prior to the In-dians' confinement to the reservation, there were various types of commercial tobacco traded between traders and Indians, as well as indigenous types cultivated by tribes such as the Crow.

The eagle was regarded by most tribes as the chief of all birds because of its perceived ability to fly higher than any other bird. It was believed that the bird was the paramount messenger of the Great Spirit, and thus its feathers were highly prized for ceremonial purposes and to indicate prestige, as in the famous Plains headdress, the warbonnet.

The Hidatsa are the best known of the Plains tribes for their ability to trap eagles. Eagle trapping was regarded as both a sacred and a dangerous event. Late in the fall the eagle trappers would build a camp a mile or so from the village. High atop hills each trapper dug a pit about three feet deep that he covered with grass and twigs to form a blind. Using a rabbit or small fox for bait, the man climbed into the pit and waited for an eagle to soar overhead and spot the bait. When the eagle landed on top of the pit, the man thrust his hands upward and grabbed the eagle by its legs, pulling it down into the pit, and strangling it. After the feathers were secured there was sometimes a ceremony in which the eagle's body was buried and offerings made to its spirit.

Creation Myths. The sedentary tribes that lived in permanent villages devoted much time to elaborate rituals and accompanying belief systems. The Pawnee seemed to have been great religious innovators, having established one of the most comprehensive philosophies of all the Plains Indians.

The Pawnee elaborated a series of myths that described the creation of the world, the origin of humans, and the power of the gods. The Pawnee believed that Tirawa, the supreme being, was married to the Vault of Heaven, and both reigned somewhere in the heavens in a place beyond the clouds. Yet they were purely spiritual beings and took no earthly shape. Tirawa sent his commands to humans through a number of lesser gods and messengers who manifested themselves to the Pawnee.

Next in importance to Tirawa and his wife was Tcuperika ("evening star"), who was personified as a young maiden. Evening Star was keeper of a garden in the west that was the source of all food. She had four assistants, Wind, Cloud, Lightning, and Thunder. She married Oprikata ("morning star"), and from them was born the first human being on earth. Morning Star was perceived as a strong warrior who drove the rest of the stars before him. In some Pawnee ceremonies, the sacrifice of a young captive girl was offered to him, suggesting some relationship between Pawnee religion and the religions of central Mexico where human sacrifice was also known.

Of lesser status were the gods of the four directions, the northeast, southeast, southwest, and northwest, and next in rank to the four directions were the three gods of the north: North Star, chief of all the stars; North Wind, who gave the buffalo to humans; and Hikus ("breath"), who gave life itself to the people. Next in line came Sun and Moon, who were married and produced an offspring, the second person on earth, whose marriage to the offspring of Morning Star and Evening Star gave rise to the first humans.

Major Corporate Rituals. Not only were the philosophy and mythology of the Pawnee rich, but their ceremonies were many and varied. There were ceremonies to Thunder, to Morning Star and Evening Star, for the planting and harvesting of Mother Corn, as well as lesser ceremonies for the general welfare of the people.

The Hako. One of the best documented rituals of the Plains, the Hako was performed so that the tribe might increase and be strong, and so that the people would enjoy long life, happiness, and peace. The ceremony was conducted by a man called the *kurahus* ("man of years") who was venerated for his knowledge and experience. To him was entrusted the supervision of the songs and prayers, which had to be performed precisely in the same order each time. The Hako was usually performed in the spring when birds were nesting, or in the fall when they were flocking because it was believed that when prayers were offered for life, strength, and growth of the people it must be done when all life was stirring.

Those taking part in the ceremony were divided into two groups, the fathers who sponsored the ceremony and the children who received the intentions, prayers, and gifts from the fathers. The head of the fathers' group, called Father, was responsible for employing the *kurahus*. The head of the children's group, called Son, also played an important part in the ceremony, acting on behalf of the other children.

The most important paraphernalia used in the Hako were the sacred feathered wands resembling pipe stems without the bowls attached. The ceremony took three days and three nights during which time twenty-seven rituals were performed, each ritual and song unveiling Pawnee sacred lore. At the end of the ceremony, the wands were waved over the children, thus sealing the bond between fathers and children.

The Sun Dance. The most characteristic religious ceremony of the Plains was the well-known Sun Dance, usually performed in the early summer in conjunction with the annual communal buffalo hunt. It owes its name to the fact that certain men who had taken vows to participate danced for several days gazing at the sun, or more precisely, in the direction of the sun. It is useful to note that the Sun Dance was held also in cloudy and even rainy weather, and there is some speculation that the progenitor of the dance may actually have been performed at night during the time of a full moon.

There is some agreement that the oldest form of the Sun Dance originated among the Mandan. Unlike the sun dances of other tribes, the Mandan Sun Dance, called Okipa, was held indoors in the tribe's medicine lodge. The ceremony lasted for four days, during which time the dancers were actually suspended by skewers through their chest from the lodge rafters and the bodies spun around by helpers below. The dance was usually done in advance of warriors going out on a war party.

In other tribes, dancers had skewers of wood placed through the fleshy part of their chest; the skewers were attached to rawhide thong ropes that were tied to a center pole. The dancers pulled backward as they bobbed in time with drum beats until they tore the flesh, thus releasing themselves from the thongs. The Lakota philosophized that the only thing that one could offer to the Great Spirit was one's own body since it was the only thing that a human being really owned. The Sun Dance was one form of making such an offering, the skewering of the dancer also being equated with being in a state of ignorance, and the breaking free as symbolic of attaining knowledge.

The Blackfeet form of the Sun Dance was unlike that of other tribes inasmuch as it centered around a woman known for her industry who vowed to lead the dancers and who bore the title "medicine woman." While she did not go through tortures like her male counterparts in other tribes, she did participate in a number of elaborate ceremonies that preceded the actual dance. Two important ceremonies over which she presided were the Buffalo Tongues and the Sweat Lodge ceremonies. Before the Sun Dance, people in the camp were asked to bring buffalo tongues to a certain lodge erected for that purpose. In the lodge the tongues were ceremoniously skinned, cleaned, and boiled and then distributed to the remainder of the people in camp. Later a special sweat lodge was constructed from one hundred willow saplings, which were placed in the ground and tied together at the tops like those of an ordinary sweat lodge. The dancers then fasted and joined in the Sweat Lodge ceremony before dancing.

Sacred Arrow Renewal. In addition to the Sun Dance there were other public ceremonies that Plains tribes participated in. One of the most important for the Cheyenne was the Sacred Arrow Renewal.

The Cheyenne believe that long ago their supreme being, Maiyun, gave four sacred arrows to the mythological hero Sweet Medicine in a cave in what are now called the Black Hills of South Dakota. Sweet Medicine taught them about the ritual of the sacred arrows, the arrows have been kept in a fox-skin bundle, which has been handed down from one gen-

> ### One of the most important [public ceremonies] for the Cheyenne was the Sacred Arrow Renewal.

eration to another and guarded by a person known as the sacred-arrow keeper. In alternate years an individual pledges to sponsor a Sacred Arrow Renewal ceremony and the arrows are unwrapped and displayed to all the male members of the tribe. The man making the pledge does so in order to fulfill a vow, such as is the case with the Sun Dance. The vow was originally made when a warrior was threatened during a fight, or someone became sick and was fearful of dying. Although only one person makes the pledge, the ceremony is given on behalf of all Cheyenne, so that they will be ensured of a long and prosperous life.

The Sacred Arrow Renewal ceremony traditionally took four days to perform. On the second day the sacred arrows were obtained from the keeper and the bundle was opened and examined. If the flight feathers of the arrows were in any way damaged, a man known for his bravery was chosen to replace the feathers. On the third day the arrows were renewed and each of the counting sticks was passed over incense to bless all the families in the tribe. On the last day the arrows were exhibited to the male members of the tribe. The Cheyenne said that it was difficult to look directly at the arrows because they gave off a blinding light.

The Ghost Dance. Although missionaries provided Christianity as a viable option to native Indian religions, Plains Indian traditional religions persist in most parts of the Plains. After missions had been established for only a few years, there was one last attempt to rebel against white domination in a pacifistic movement called the Ghost Dance. It began in the state of Nevada when a Paiute Indian named Wovoka had a vision that the white man would disappear from the face of the earth in a cataclysmic event: the earth would turn over, taking all the white men with it. All the old Indians who had died, as well as the buffalo, now all but

extinct, would return to live the old way of life. Wovoka claimed that in his vision he visited with these spirits of the deceased Indians and they taught him a dance that would bring about the destruction of the whites. Wovoka preached to other tribes that it was useless to fight with the white man anymore, for soon this cataclysm would be upon them and they would disappear.

After the teachings of this Indian messiah, who had been raised by a Bible-reading white family, the Ghost Dance spread rapidly throughout the Plains, spilling over occasionally into bordering culture areas. All but the Comanche, who preferred their own, more individualistic form of religion, participated.

During the dance the dancers performed for long periods of time until they went into trances. When they awoke they sang of great meetings with their dead kin and of how glad they were that the old way of life would soon return.

But the cataclysm did not come. Instead, the federal government, fearing that the Ghost Dance would serve to engender hostilities among the Indians, ordered all dancing stopped. On 29 December 1890 a band of Ghost Dancers under the leadership of Chief Big Foot was halted on Wounded Knee Creek on the present-day location of the Pine Ridge Indian reservation. Shots rang out, and 260 men, women, and children were massacred, thus ending the short-lived movement.

The Native American Church. A pantribal religion that has become popular since the turn of the twentieth century is the Native American Church, better known in the anthropological literature as the peyote cult.

The majority of peyotists are found among the southern Plains tribes, though members of almost all tribes on the Plains as well as other culture areas belong.

Peyotism is strongly influenced by Christianity and individual tribal beliefs; thus there are minor differences in the ceremonies from one tribe to the next. There are two major divisions, analogous to denominations: the Half Moon, by far the most popular, and the Cross Fire. The rituals of the two divisions differ somewhat, the greatest ideological difference being that the Cross Fire uses the Bible in its ceremonies. Peyote ceremonies are likely to vary also from one tribe to the next, or even from one practitioner to the next. If all members attending a meeting are from the same tribe, it is likely that the native language will be used. If members from several tribes congregate, English is used as the religious lingua franca. Despite the many variations of peyotism, however, there are some customs, rituals, and paraphernalia that are common to all.

Peyote meetings are held on Saturday nights, usually from sundown to sunup on Sunday. The ceremony takes place in a traditionally shaped tipi made from canvas. It is especially erected for the occasion and dismantled after the meeting is concluded. The doorway of the tipi faces east, and inside an altar is built containing a fireplace in the center of the lodge behind which is a crescent-shaped earthen altar. On top of the altar is placed a large peyote button called Father, or Chief Peyote. Between the fire and the altar is another crescent made from ashes. Between the fireplace and the doorway of the lodge are placed food and water that later will be ceremonially consumed.

The principal leaders of the meeting are assigned special seats inside the tipi. The peyote chief, also known as the "roadman" or "road chief," sits directly opposite the doorway, in what is for most Plains tribes the traditional seat of honor. On his right sits the drum chief, the keeper of the special drum used in the ceremony. To his left sits the cedar chief. Next to the doorway sits the fire boy. The remainder of the congregation are interspersed between the ritual leaders around the perimeter of the tipi. If a Bible is used it is placed between the earth altar and the peyote chief.

Peyote meetings may be held for special purposes such as curing ceremonies, birthday celebrations, funerals, memorial services, or on occasions when persons leave the Indian community to travel great distances or return from the armed services. Some are simply prayer meetings conducted on a regular schedule similar to Christian services. Persons wishing to participate in the ceremony arrive at the home of the sponsor, who provides all the peyote buttons for consumption during the meeting as well as the food that will be shared by the participants at the conclusion.

As the drum resounds, the peyote chief sings the opening song of the ceremony. This is a rather standardized song at all peyote meetings, no matter what tribe. He sings it four times, the sacred number for most Plains tribes. When he finishes, each member in turn eats some of the peyote buttons and sings four songs. The man on the right of the singer plays the drum while the singer shakes the gourd rattle. In this manner the ritual of eating and singing progresses around the tipi clockwise. The particularly fast drumming on the water drum and the rapid phrasing of the peyote songs may have a great deal to do with creating the hallucinatory effects experienced in peyote meetings.

Concurrent with the visionary experience is the feeling of a closeness with God. Because peyotism is now greatly influenced by Christianity, the members pray to Jesus Christ, equate the consumption of the peyote button with Holy Communion, and espouse the basic tenets of the Christian churches in their prayers and songs.

The praying, eating of peyote, and singing continue until midnight, when there is a special ceremony. The fire boy informs the peyote chief that it is midnight and then leaves the tipi to get a bucket of water. He returns with the water and presents it to the peyote chief, who dips a feather into the bucket and splashes water on the people in the tipi. After smoking and praying, the water is passed around to the members so that each may drink. During this part of the ceremony another standard song is sung. After the water drinking at midnight, the bucket is removed and it is time to resume the peyote eating and singing.

Despite its Christian aspects, peyotism is frowned on by many missionaries. Yet the Native American Church thrives. It has already become increasingly popular among tribes who were once adherents of their native religions or outright Christians. In the early years peyotism was extremely popular with adjacent communities of black Americans, and today many other non-Indians are joining the Native American Church.

BIBLIOGRAPHY

Bowers, Alfred W. *Mandan Social and Ceremonial Organization*. Chicago, 1950. This book, written by a gifted ethnographer, includes a detailed description of the Okipa, the Mandan Sun Dance.

Catlin, George. *O-kee-pa: A Religious Ceremony and Other Customs of the Mandan* (1867). Edited and with preface by John C. Ewers. New Haven, 1967. This edition contains the controversial "Folium Reservatum," not included in the original edition, which discusses sexual symbolism in the ceremony.

Fletcher, Alice C., and Francis LaFlesche. *The Omaha Tribe* (1911). Reprint, Lincoln, Nebr., 1972. Includes important information on Omaha religion by one of the earliest female ethnographers in collaboration with a member of the Omaha tribe.

Grinnell, George Bird. *Blackfoot Lodge Tales* (1892). Reprint, Lincoln, Nebr., 1962. This book is particularly rich in the cosmology of the Blackfeet, written by a pioneer in Plains studies.

Grinnell, George Bird. *The Cheyenne Indians* (1923). 2 vols. Reprint, Lincoln, Nebr., 1972. Volume 2 contains important information on the medicine lodge, Sweet Medicine, and the Massaum ceremony, and is a classic cultural history of the Cheyenne.

Hultkrantz, Åke. *Religions of the American Indians*. Los Angeles, 1979. By a leading historian of comparative religions who specializes in American Indian religion. It contains a great deal of comparative material on Plains Indians.

La Barre, Weston. *The Peyote Cult*. Hamden, Conn., 1964. The best source by the leading expert on the Native American Church.

Lowie, Robert H. "Plains Indian Age-Societies: Historical and Comparative Summary." *Anthropological Papers of the American Museum of Natural History* 11 (1916): 881-984. A summary of research conducted on Plains Indian societies at the turn of the century that includes basic information on ceremonial associations of the Plains Indians.

Lowie, Robert H. *The Crow Indians* (1935). Reprint, New York, 1956. The religious life of the Crow Indians is neatly related to their workaday world in one of the classics of anthropology, by one of the founders of the field in America.

Mooney, James. *The Ghost Dance Religion and the Sioux Outbreak of 1890* (1896). Abridged, with an introduction by Anthony F. C. Wallace. Chicago, 1965. Mooney interviewed participants of the Ghost Dance at the time it was being performed. The book provides comparative materials on the Arapaho, Caddo, Cheyenne, Comanche, Kiowa, Kiowa Apache, Lakota, and some non-Plains tribes.

Powers, William K. *Indians of the Northern Plains*. New York, 1969. A survey of the principal tribes of the northern Plains with a separate chapter on religion.

Powers, William K. *Indians of the Southern Plains*. New York, 1971. A survey of the principal tribes of the southern Plains with separate chapters on traditional religion and on the Native American Church.

Powers, William K. *Oglala Religion.* Lincoln, Nebr., 1977. A structural analysis of the religion of a major subdivision of the Lakota that emphasizes the current persistence of Plains Indian religion despite encounters with Christianity.

Powers, William K. *Yuwipi: Vision and Experience in Oglala Ritual.* Lincoln, Nebr., 1982. A translation of an entire shamanic curing ceremony conducted on the Pine Ridge reservation in 1966, showing the relationship among Yuwipi, the vision quest, and the Sweat Lodge ceremony.

Spier, Leslie. "The Sun Dance of the Plains Indians: Its Development and Diffusion." *Anthropological Papers of the American Museum of Natural History* 16 (1921): 451-527. This is a comparative analysis of the research done on the Sun Dance at the turn of the century by leading anthropologists.

Underhill, Ruth M. *Red Man's Religion.* Chicago, 1965. A classic survey of American Indian religions by the grand dame of ethnology. The language is somewhat dated but there is a wealth of information on the Plains.

Wood, W. Raymond, and Margot Liberty, eds. *Anthropology on the Great Plains.* Lincoln, Nebr., 1980. A state-of-the-art review of anthropological research on the Plains Indians with separate chapters on the Sun Dance, the Ghost Dance, and the Native American Church, compiled by some of the foremost experts on Plains Indian culture.

WILLIAM K. POWERS

Indians of the Northwest Coast

The peoples of the Pacific Northwest Coast of North America lived along a narrow strip of land that extends from the mouth of the Columbia River north to Yakutat Bay in Alaska.

For the sake of convenience, the Northwest Coast culture area has been divided into three subareas: the northern area was inhabited by the Tlingit, Haida, and Tsimshian peoples; the central by the Bella Coola, Nootka, and Kwakiutl groups; and the southern by the Coast Salish and Chinookan tribes of the Washington and Oregon coasts. While the cultures within each sub-area shared some basic traits that distinguished them from one another, the bewildering variety of linguistic, social, political, and ideological variations within each area implied numerous migrations, acculturations, and cultural borrowings that make any retrospective synthesis of Northwest Coast culture a formidable task.

Material Culture. The lives of the Northwest Coast Indians were entirely oriented toward the sea, on whose bounty they depended. The staple food of the area was salmon; varieties of salmon were smoked and stockpiled in immense quantities. However, many other types of fish, sea mammals, large land mammals, water birds, shellfish, and varieties of wild plants were also collected. Though food was plentiful, the rugged topography of the land limited access to food-collecting sites. Access to these sites was also controlled by an oligarchy of hereditary nobles (called "chiefs")

who maintained their power primarily through ritual performances that legitimized their claims.

Northwest Coast technology was based on a complex of wood and animal products. Wood and tree bark, especially from cedars, were the fundamental materials and were used ubiquitously. Humans lived in houses, traveled in canoes, caught fish with hooks, trapped salmon in weirs, stored their belongings and were themselves interred in boxes, and wore clothing and ceremonial costumes all made from wood products. A system of symbolic correspondences between objects underlay the entire ceremonial system. Skins, flesh, and bones from animals were also used and played a critical symbolic role in religious activities.

Social Organization. The basic principles of Northwest Coast social organization have been the object of much theoretical controversy. Traditional tribal appellations may lump together groups with similar languages but very different customs, and vice versa. Essentially the basic unit of social and political organization was the independent extended local family, defined by some degree of lineal descent and by coresidence in a single communal household in a single winter ceremonial village. (Winter was the season in which virtually all ceremonies were held.) Group membership was defined less by kinship than by concerted economic and ceremonial activity, though in the northern subarea suprafamilial kin groups played a role in setting the boundaries of a group. The head of each household was its political and spiritual leader, the inheritor and custodian of the house's aristocratic titles, and its ambassador to both human and supernatural worlds. All aristocratic titles in each area were ranked hierarchically for all ceremonial activities. Whether or not the hierarchical system created a class structure as well as a rank structure is a controversial theoretical question. While there was some social mobility, social position was primarily ascribed and inherited. As one goes north within the area, hierarchical systems seem to increase in importance and are firmly embedded in a religious matrix. The peoples of the southern subarea seemed to put little emphasis on hierarchy and exhibited a social structure and religious ideology with more similarities to peoples of the Plateau and California areas than to the coastal peoples to their north.

Belief and Ritual. There was little synthesis of religious ideas and institutions on the Northwest Coast. Rituals and myths developed into a multiplicity of local traditions that directly integrated local history and geographical features with the more universal elements of creation. Different families and different individuals within families might have conflicting accounts of family history and its mythic events, giving the religion an atomistic quality that permitted a continual restructuring of ceremonies and renegotiating of meanings. However, much of the cognitive conflict that might arise from such discrepancies was mitigated by the fact that although there was an extraordinary amount of public ceremony most rituals were performed in secret and were known only to the rankholder and his heir.

Like the religions of other native North American peoples, the beliefs of the Northwest Coast Indians focused on the critical relationship of hunter to prey and on the set of moral principles that permitted that relationship to continue. Humans were thought to be essentially inferior to the rest of the world's inhabitants and were dependent on other creatures' good will for survival. Humans were important as mediators between different spirit realms because supernatural beings had granted them gifts of knowledge and insight about how the world operates and how they fit into the world. The features unique to Northwest Coast religion centered on the private possession and inherited control of the religious institutions by titled aristocrats. Access to the supernatural beings (called "spirits" by anthropologists because of their essential rather than corporeal nature) and their power was strictly under the control of chiefs, as was access to food.

Spirits. The origin of all power—both the power to control and, more importantly, the power to become aware—was in the spirit world, and the actions of spirit power, which gave form and purpose to everything, were visible everywhere. All objects, ideas, forces, and beings were believed to have inherent power that could be released and directed into human affairs, if correctly integrated into ritual action. The world was seen as filled with spirit power that could be reified in human rituals. Spirits, the personified categories of power, were less characters than ineffable forces. As a salmon could be brought into the human world when caught in a properly constructed net, so could spirit power be brought into the human world when caught in a net of properly constructed ritual action. Humans could never perceive the true nature of spirits, but they could see that the costumes—created as coverings for the spirits—became animated when the spirits covered themselves with them and danced.

The peoples of the Northwest Coast saw their world as one in which myriad personified forces were at work, competing for a limited supply of food and souls. Every human, every group, every species, and every spirit-being had its own needs, its own specialized niche in the food chain. All of their conflicting demands and needs had to be balanced against one another, and this could be achieved only through ritual, which was seen as a method of mediation between the various creatures of the universe. The world was filled with a seemingly endless variety of raptorial creatures who feed on human flesh and souls just as humans feed on salmon flesh. Man-eating birds and other animals, ogres, dwarves, giants, and monsters were believed to prey upon humans as raptorial birds prey upon mice (a frequent image in Northwest Coast myths).

Animals, which were seen as the material representations of spiritual beings, sacrificed themselves for the benefit of human survival because humans had agreed to sacrifice themselves for the benefit of the spirits. The metaphors of Northwest Coast ritual continually repeat the image of the responsibility of humans to support the spirit world. Humans and spirits, living off each other's dead, were intertwined in a reincarnational web. By eating the substance of each other's bodies, they freed the souls and permitted their reincarnation. If any link in the ritual chain was lost, the entire system of reincarnation broke down.

Food. Food was thus a sacramental substance, and meals were inherently ceremonial occasions. Northwest Coast religion placed a heavy emphasis on the control of food-related behavior, on the denial of hunger (which was thought to be a polluting desire), and on the ritual distribution of food and other material substances. The rules, taboos, and rituals associated with food are ubiquitous and enormous in number.

Of all the ceremonies directed toward the propitiation of the animals on which humans feed, those known collectively as the first-salmon ceremonies were the most widespread. These were sets of rituals performed every year in each area over the first part of the salmon catch of each species. Similar ceremonies existed for other species as well. The fish were addressed as if they were chiefs of high rank and were killed, prepared, and served in a ceremonious manner. Their released souls returned to the land of their compatriots to inform them of the proper treatment that they had been accorded. Like most other Northwest Coast rituals, these ceremonies were the property of individual chiefs, who performed them for the benefit of all of the people. All hunting was imbued with ceremony, since success in the hunt was strictly a matter of the proper ritual relationship to the hunted animal. The ceremonies associated with hunting were an important part of a family's inheritance.

Guardian spirits. In theory, a person could obtain a guardian spirit by dedication to a regimen of self-mortification, abstinence, fasting, prayer, and ritual bathing. However, the most powerful contracts with the spirits were obtained in mythic times through the group's ancestors, and these contracts formed the basis of the rank system. Every ranked position was actually an embodiment of a spiritual contract—a covenant between the rankholder and the spirit world. The relationship between the ancestor and the spirit was the primary element of a family's patrimony and was constantly reaffirmed in ritual. As the living representative of the ancestor, the rankholder acted as an intermediary to the spirits on secular occasions and as an impersonator or embodiment of a spirit on sacred occasions.

The relationships between particular aristocrats and particular spirits were manifested in a system of "crests," which were images of spirits that have become allied with individual families. Through the crest, the identity of the aristocrat was connected to that of the spirit being, and through this connection the aristocrat's self expanded to a more cosmic identity. The widespread use of crest objects was graphic proof of the extent to which religious ideas permeated the entire fabric of Northwest Coast culture.

In addition to having shared destinies, humans and spirits were interrelated in that all creatures were considered to be human and to possess human souls. Each lived in its own place in one of the levels of the universe, where it inhabited a house, performed ceremonies, and otherwise acted like a human being. At the proper season, the spirits donned costumes and visited the world of humans, where they appeared in their transformed identity. Similarly, humans who appeared to themselves as humans put on costumes and appeared to the spirits as spirits.

With the exception of Frederica De Laguna's account of Tlingit culture (1972), Northwest Coast Indian ideas of the self, its components, and its relationship to the spirits are not well documented. It is clear that the soul was believed to have several material manifestations as well as several incorporeal components. A person was viewed as a combination of life forces and parts from different planes of existence, and therefore as having spiritual connections in many directions. Whatever their component parts, souls were thought to exist in only limited numbers, to undergo metempsychosis, to be transferred from one species to another, and to be reincarnated alternately in first a human and then either a spirit or animal being. A human death freed a soul for an animal or spirit, and vice versa, linking humans, animals, and spirits in a cycle of mutual dependency. Ideas about the soul and its nature seem to have been better codified among the Northern peoples, though this impression may be an artifact of the high quality of De Laguna's ethnography.

Shamanism. Connections to the spirit world could be made through inheritance or by acquiring, through a vision, the power to cure disease. All illnesses and death were considered a sickness of the spirit that was caused either by the magical intrusion of a foreign substance into the body or by the wandering or the loss of the soul. When methods for reestablishing one's spiritual purity failed to alleviate the symptoms, a curer (or "shaman") was called in. A shaman cured an illness by going into a trance during which his guardian spirits would fight with the soul of the disease or of the witch who had sent the disease. When the shaman came out of his trance, he was able to display a small object that symbolically represented the empty husk of the diseased spirit body. Shamanic paraphernalia, like other ritual objects, were formed and moved so as to direct the spirit power in the proper ways to effect a cure. Shamanic performances were dramatic events, with much stage illusion as well as singing, dancing, and praying.

Shamans acted as intermediaries between humans and the forces of nature and the supernatural, and were thought to be able to foretell the future, control the weather, bring suc-

cess in war or in hunting, communicate with other shamans at a distance, and, most importantly, cure illnesses and restore souls stolen by witches or maleficent spirits. The shaman was believed both to control and to be inspired by the spirits with whom he was connected. Among the Tlingit, shamanic rituals were usually inherited, but among the central tribes they were obtained through visions.

Witches. Northwest Coast Indian beliefs about shamans were complemented by their beliefs about witchcraft. Witches were thought to be motivated by envy and jealousy, either conscious or unconscious, and there was no act, no matter how terrible, of which they were thought incapable. Patterns of witchcraft among the Northwest Coast Indians were parallel to those of other North American groups: it seems likely that few if any people practiced witchcraft, but accusations of witchcraft were an important means of articulating rivalry and competition. Among the central tribes, witches were generally thought to be shamans from enemy tribes; among the northern groups, where fear of witches was more prevalent, witches were thought to belong to the same kin group as their victims. Witches were thought to be under the compulsion of a possessive spirit, from whose influence the witch could be freed by torture.

The causal principle underlying the ideas of the Northwest Coast Indians on the effectiveness of ritual lay in the idea that under the proper analogical conditions, the patterned motions or words of human beings have an inherent ability to coerce the spirits into parallel actions. Thus a human action could be magnified and intensified into a power that alters the state of the world. Human beings were conduits for supernatural power: although they possess no powers themselves, humans could become the vehicles of supernatural power if they observed the proper ritual actions. In creating analogies between themselves and the spirits, humans gained the ability to influence the actions of those more powerful than themselves.

Creation. Supporting the social and ritual systems was an extensive and varied body of myths and tales (which, except in the work of Claude Lévi-Strauss, have been little analyzed). There were few myths about the creation of the world as such, since the world was seen as a place of innumerable eternal forces and essences. Like other North American groups, the Indians of the Northwest Coast were less interested in how the world was created as material substance than in how it was made moral or how the inherent powers of the universe could be controlled for the benefit of its inhabitants. The creation of material phenomena—the sun and moon, human beings, animal species—is always secondary to the moral dilemmas presented in the myths and the resolution (or lack thereof) of those dilemmas. For example, though there are no myths about the sun being created out of nothing, there are many myths about the sun being placed in the sky, in order to fulfill its proper role by enabling people to see—reminding them of the continual motion and flux of the world and of the balance of light and darkness.

Transformers. Although there are few myths about a creator spirit (and those possibly developed after contact with whites), there are cycles of myths about a transformer or trickster figure who through his actions places the forces of the world in balance. The most detailed and integral of these is the Raven cycle found among the Tlingit (though each tribe had some form of trickster or transformer cycle, not always associated with Raven). Raven is a creature of uncontrollable desires and excesses, and in the act of trying to satisfy his desires, he inadvertently creates moral order and constraint. Incidental to each act of moral creation is the creation of some physical attribute of the world—a mountain or other geographical feature, or the color of a mallard's head or an ermine's tail—that serves to remind people of the myth and its moral import. Thus the world is made up of signs and images of mythic significance for those who know the stories behind them.

Myths of origin. Every feature of the geographic, social, and ceremonial world had an origin myth that encapsulated it into the basic structure of power and ideology, and these myths formed the basic material for Northwest Coast religion and ceremony. No public ceremony occurred without the retelling—either in recital or a dance reenactment—of the origin myths of the people involved, which is to say that no ceremony took place without the reenergizing of the connection between humans and spirits. Clan and family myths were integrated individually into the larger corpus of hero mythology, so that every family and person of title was in some specific way linked to the events and forces of the universe. Myth is a depiction of the interaction of universal forces, and the retelling of the myth reactivates and redirects those forces.

Northwest Coast rituals, like myths, developed into a multiplicity of local traditions, resulting in the direct linking of local history to the more cosmic elements of creation. Ceremonies were always changing as new rituals were acquired through war, marriage, new visions, or the emigration of families. There was a constant renegotiation of the meanings and structure of all rituals and stories, as traditions coalesced, melded, or broke apart; conflicting versions of stories were constantly being reworked.

Winter ceremonials. Spirit power was an essential part of the success of any task; thus there was ceremony in all human endeavor. Even so, there was a clear division of the year into secular (summer) and sacred (winter) seasons. Large-scale ceremonial performances were given in the winter. These were most important among the Kwakiutl and Nootka. Among the southern tribes there was a ceremony of spirit-possession and occasional rituals of world renewal similar to those of the peoples of northern California.

The narrative structure of the Kwakiutl winter ceremonials, like that of the family origin myths, was based on a simple set of images that were endlessly elaborated: a hero cuts himself off from the material world of humans, seeks or is kidnapped by spirits who take him to their home, learns the rituals of the spirits, obtains some of the spirits' power, and then brings the rituals back to the human world. These rituals were performed in the most sensationalistic fashion, with elaborate stage effects and illusions, masked performances, complicated props, and stunning displays of strength and athletic agility.

The rituals of the winter ceremonials were under the jurisdiction of groups called "dance societies" or "secret societies." Membership in these groups was inherited and strictly limited. A new member could be invested only upon the retirement of his predecessor, but there were many stages of initiation and many years of preparation before complete initiation. Most of the ceremonies of the dance societies were

> **Of all the winter-ceremonial performances, the most famous and widely discussed is the Hamatsa dance. . . .**

performed away from public scrutiny, to maintain private ownership of the rituals and to prevent the uninitiated from being harmed by the presence of immense spirit power. A small proportion of the ceremonies were performed only for members of the dance society or for a small group of aristocrats, and a very few were performed for the entire village. Yet even this small proportion of rituals went on for hours every day over a period of four or five months. In essence, then, the entire winter period was given over to ceremony—a fact that belies the usual claim by anthropologists that the peoples of the Northwest Coast were primarily interested in status.

Of all the winter-ceremonial performances, the most famous and widely discussed is the Hamatsa dance, which the Kwakiutl considered to be their most powerful ceremony. The Hamatsa dance seems to best encapsulate the ethos of Northwest Coast religious ideology. The *hamatsa* was a human who had been carried away by those supernatural creatures who preyed on the flesh and substance of human beings; while living with these supernatural creatures in their ceremonial house, the *hamatsa* took on their spiritual qualities (especially their affinity with death and killing); and when he returned to the land of human beings, he was possessed with the wild desire to eat human flesh. In a long series of rites, the members of the tribe gradually tamed his wildness through a series of pledges to sacrifice their wealth and (when they eventually died) their souls, to feed the spirits so that the world would remain in equilibrium. The violence and energy with which the *hamatsa* acted was a potent representation of the intensity of the struggle or task that humans had to accept if the world were to be kept moral. The burden of spiritual power demanded not a quiet acceptance but energetic activity, a ferocity for right action.

Conclusion. Although founded on the same basic philosophical principles as that of other native North American religions, Northwest Coast religion developed those ideas into a distinct set of social and religious institutions that were adaptable to the changing fortunes and histories of each village and its individual members. It was a system in which atomistic elements could be separated from their original relationships with each other and reformed in new combinations dealing in a powerful, cohesive, creative, and poetic way with the purposes and dilemmas of human existence.

Unfortunately, much of Northwest Coast culture was irrevocably altered or destroyed in the course of the nineteenth and early twentieth centuries. All Northwest Coast religion was illegal in Canada from 1876 to 1951, though enforcement of applicable laws was uneven, and some ceremonial life persisted. In the last several decades, there has been a new emphasis on the traditional rituals, but how much they retain of their original character and the place they hold in the lives of the people today are questions that remain to be answered. As North American Indians and scholars both reexamine the historical record to determine the significance of the Northwest Coast religion for the present, it can only be hoped that there will be new interpretations and understandings of what is unquestionably one of the most vibrant and fascinating of the world's tribal religions.

BIBLIOGRAPHY

Traditional trait-oriented surveys of Northwest Coast culture can be found in Philip Drucker's *Cultures of the North Pacific Coast* (New York, 1965) and in the excellently illustrated *People of the Totem* by Norman Bancroft-Hunt, with photographs by Werner Forman (New York, 1979). No synthesized scholarly accounts of Northwest Coast religion exist. The best ethnographic accounts of the beliefs of specific tribes are the many volumes by Franz Boas on the Kwakiutl, Philip Drucker's *The Northern and Central Nootkan Tribes* (Washington, D. C., 1951), and Frederica De Laguna's *Under Mount Saint Elias* (Washington, D. C., 1972). Irving Goldman's *The Mouth of Heaven* (New York, 1975) and my *Feasting with Cannibals* (Princeton, 1981) both reanalyze Boas's materials and emphasize the critical role of religious thought in Kwakiutl life. Pamela Amoss's *Coast Salish Spirit Dancing* (Seattle, 1978) is the best account of contemporary Northwest Coast religious activity.

STANLEY WALENS

Indians of California and the Intermountain Region

The Intermountain Region of North America is framed on the east by the Rocky Mountains of Canada and the United States and on the west by the Cascade and the Sierra Nevada ranges. Ethnographers customarily divide this region into two indigenous "culture areas," the Plateau and the Great Basin. The Plateau is bounded on the north by the boreal forests beyond the Fraser Plateau of British Columbia and on the south by the Bitterroot Mountains of Idaho and the arid highlands of southern Oregon and northwestern Montana. It includes the Columbia River's plateau and drainage in Washington, Oregon, and a small portion of northern California. The Great Basin is the area of steppe-desert lying primarily in Nevada and Utah but including parts of southern Idaho, western Wyoming, and western Colorado. It runs south from the Salmon and Snake rivers of Idaho to the Colorado Plateau, is bounded by the Colorado River on the south, and includes the interior deserts of southwestern California.

General Themes

The pervasiveness of religious concerns and behavior in the daily lives of all of these peoples is suggested by the range of religious themes that are common to the three areas, despite the diverse, area-specific expressions given them.

Power. Significant contacts with European influences occurred in the three areas beginning in the eighteenth century and had achieved devastating impact by the mid-nineteenth century. As will be seen, European influence tended to elevate concepts of anthropomorphic creator figures to new eminence. Before contact, however, a widespread perception of a diffuse, generalized, and impersonal cosmic force, often referred to today as "power," was far more significant. This energic field of all potentials is a neutral, amoral, and generative presence that produces all things.

Mythology. In some cases, power was first manifested by a world creator who, through it, brought the world into its present form. Such creators might be culture heroes and transformers, such as Komokums among the Modoc, a people interstitial between California and the Plateau. Komokums and many others like him acted in conjunction with earth divers to form the earth from a bit of soil raised from the depths of a primordial sea. In other cases, especially in north-central California, world creators are likely to be true creator gods, thinking the world into existence or bringing it forth with a word. In southern California we find creation myths of great metaphysical complexity and subtlety, such as those of the Luiseño, for whom creation arose by steps, out of an absolute void. Even here, however, we find a transformer, Wiyot, shaping the present world from an earth that preceded his existence, and this seems the more typical pattern. Such gods and heroes tend to become otiose after their work is accomplished, rather than lingering on as moral overseers.

Unlike the Californians, neither the peoples of the Basin nor those of the Plateau seem to have been much concerned with world origins. Yet they shared with Californians a profound concern for a variety of prehuman spirits—usually animals, but also celestial beings, monsters, and others—who aided in bringing the world to its present shape and in establishing culture. Thus, throughout the region one finds arrays of such prehuman beings, each exercising power for good or ill according to its innate proclivities. The actions of each are recounted in a broad spectrum of myths and stories.

Spirits and Personal Power. Many animal spirits, including tricksters, remained in the world as sources of specialized powers for human beings. Other unique power potentials might reside in celestial and landscape features and in common, manufactured objects. People might encounter such spirits, usually in their anthropomorphic forms, in visions or in dreams. Through such encounters individuals gained spirit-helpers, enhancing the power innate in themselves and gaining particular powers that, through volitional control, brought success in specific endeavors. Vision quests in many different forms are found throughout the three areas.

Seeking increased, specialized power and protection through intentional encounters with spirit-beings was a primary concern of the religions of the Plateau. In the Basin, visions and personal powers tended to come to individuals spontaneously, at the spirits' will, and were not often sought through formal quests. In California, spirit encounters sometimes resulted from stringent austerities and Plateau-style questing, as among the Achomawi and Atsugewi in the northeast. Often they were sought through participation in initiatory "schools" of pubescent boys seeking power collectively under the tutelage of older initiates. Such schools were central to the visionary religions of the south and the elaborate dance and healing societies of northern California.

More generally, both males and females had access to the spirits and, thus, to personal power. In the Plateau, young boys and girls alike often sought visions, although boys did so more frequently than girls. In the Basin, both males and females could receive spirit powers at any time during their lives, although it appears that men were more often so favored. The situation in California was more complex. In each of three major subareas, women were initiated into some groups but not into others and, among these groups, there were often varying, ranked degrees of male and female spirit acquisition and initiation.

Throughout the three culture areas, the specific spirits that one might encounter and the powers that they enabled were varied. Hunting or fishing skill, the ability to cure and to injure, success in courting and in fighting, finesse in crafts and in song making, gambling luck, wealth, wisdom, and many other potentials might be realized.

Although increased and specialized powers could be acquired and maximized through contacts with spirits, they could also be lost by offending those spirits through failure to adhere to taboos imposed in vision or dream; through misuse of songs, rituals, or power objects; through more general breach of custom, or simply through baffling happenstance. Every increase in an individual's power had its price.

Shamans. The shamans were the most powerful of people, the most respected for their spirit contacts, and the most feared. It was they who paid the highest price for their acumen. (*Shaman* here means a healer who obtains and exercises his powers through direct contact with spiritual beings.) In the Plateau, special effort was not usually exerted to obtain the guardian spirits that brought shamanic powers. Here, as in the Basin, both men and women could receive shamanic powers, although male shamans predominated. The same was largely true of Californians, although shamans among Shoshoni, Salinan, and some Yokuts groups were exclusively male, whereas in northwestern California female shamans vastly predominated, those who were the daughters and granddaughters of shamans having the greatest proclivity toward acquiring such powers.

Throughout the three areas, initial encounters with spirits capable of bestowing shamanic powers (sometimes volitionally sought in California and, to a lesser extent, in the Basin) were followed by intensive and often longterm training in the control of the spirit-power and an apprenticeship in its use under a recognized shaman. Such training might include initiation in the secrets of legerdemain, fire handling, and ventriloquism, on which shamanic performances often depended for their dramatic impact. Yet although shamans everywhere were expected to display their powers in such feats, and occasionally to best other shamans in public power contests, their primary function was as curative specialists, and the tricks of the trade were subordinate to success in this important function.

Theories of disease were fairly uniform. Illness came through magical objects projected into the sufferer's body by human sorcery or witchcraft. Again, ghosts or spirits whose rules for conduct had been ignored or whose special places had been defiled might make people ill. The spiritual essence of the patient could be called away by unseen beings or injured by a sorcerer or witch. Finally, one could be poisoned by a witch, either psychically or physically. In the Plateau all such power-related disease was distinguished from natural, physical illness; shamans treated only the former, whereas the latter were treated through exoteric remedies, often by lay specialists. Among the Washo of the Basin, however, all death was attributed to sorcerers.

Shamans in most groups acquired other, noncurative powers and specialties as well. In the Great Basin, in southern California, and north through the central California subarea, rattlesnake handling was practiced by shamans specially related to this powerful creature and capable of curing its bites. Weather shamans who both caused and stopped rains were found in these areas as well. In the Basin, shamans served as hunt leaders, dreaming of quarry such as antelope, leading drives, and charming the game into enclosures. Other specialties abounded. Paiute shamans in the Basin and many in central and northern California became "bear doctors," imitating these animals and using their powers for both benign and malign ends. Others might gain the power to find lost objects, to predict the future, or to conjure, as among the Colville and the Kutenai of the Plateau, whose rites were similar to the shaking tent rites more common far to the east. Virtually everywhere, even among the Plateau and Basin groups whose shamans first obtained their powers without special questing, such practitioners often sought to augment their acumen through gaining additional spirit helpers, often seeking these in special places.

First-Fruits Rites. First-fruits rites, celebrated for a variety of resources throughout the region, were often conducted by shamans. This was true, for example, of the small, local first-salmon rites that were common along many of the rivers and streams of the Plateau, along the northern California coast south to San Francisco Bay, and among the Pyramid Lake Paviosto, the Lemhi Shoshoni, and some other groups in the northern Great Basin. In some cases, however, first-salmon and other first-fruits rites were incorporated into larger-scale renewal ceremonies, as in northwestern California, and were directed by specialized priests—intermediaries between the human and nonhuman worlds who, as holders of inherited and appointed offices, recited codified liturgies.

Girls' Puberty and Menstrual Seclusion. The ritual initiation of females into adulthood at menarche and, often, the public celebration of this event constitute a second wide-

> ## Emphasis on girls' puberty tended to be greater among peoples more dependent on hunting than on gathering.

spread ritual element in the religions of the three culture areas. In general, throughout the region women were isolated at menarche and placed under a variety of restrictions, their conduct during the time being thought to presage their future. Emphasis on girls' puberty tended to be greater among peoples more dependent on hunting than on gathering. Thus, periods of training might be as short as five days, as among the peoples of the western Basin, or extended as long as four years, as among the Carrier Indians of the northern Plateau. In coastal southern California, puberty was a community concern, and all young women reaching menarche during a given year were secluded and instructed together, sometimes being "cooked" in heated pits in a way reminiscent of the training of novice shamans to the north in California. Indeed, it can be argued that puberty rites in many

groups represent a female equivalent of male spirit quests and sodality initiations. Such "cooking" of pubescent girls is found elsewhere, as among the Gosiute of the Basin. Communal rites are paralleled in the Plateau, where the Chilcotin, the Southern Okanogen, the Tenino, and the Nez Perce utilized communal seclusion huts for the initiation of young girls.

The prevalence of concern for female puberty in the three areas is clearly related to a concern for menstruation in general. Menstrual blood was viewed as among the most powerful of substances, highly dangerous if not properly controlled and, although often of positive virtue to the woman herself, inimical to the welfare of others, especially males. The isolation and restriction of girls at menarche was thus widely repeated—although with far less elaboration—at each menses. Communal menstrual shelters were found in some Plateau communities and perhaps in parts of California. Elsewhere, a small hut for the individual menstruant was constructed, as in much of the Basin, or her movements were restricted to the family's dwelling, as among the River Yuman groups. Menstrual seclusion and dietary and other restrictions varied in duration from the time of the flow up to ten or twelve days, as in northwestern California.

Major Religious Systems

In each area, and often in specifiable subareas, the general themes outlined above were manifested within the context of—and were given particular ideological inflections by—area-specific religious systems.

The Great Basin. Basin religion was largely an individual or small-band concern, and shamans provided spiritual leadership sufficient to the needs of most bands. Rituals, such as girls' puberty celebrations, that in other areas served as foci for large gatherings here tended to be small, family affairs. The healing performances of shamans might provide occasions for shared ritual participation, but such gatherings, too, were small, limited to band members, and not held according to a fixed schedule.

Large-scale Big Times did occur with some regularity among the Washo and Paiute of the western Great Basin, several bands gathering together for harvest of the more abundant wild crops (such as piñon nuts) for ritual, and for recreation. The Paiute reciprocated such Big Times with the Mono and Miwok of California. Interband antelope drives, sometimes in conjunction with Big Times, were ritually prepared and imbued with religious significance, as suggested by the many Basin rocks displaying petroglyphs and pictographs that date from the remote past through the nineteenth century.

The Big Times of the western Great Basin and California were supplanted in the eastern portion of the Basin area by other sorts of events. Ute and Shoshoni bands convened several times a year for "round dances." Among the Ute, a more ritually focused Bear Dance, marking the return of bears from hibernation and thus the renewal of the world in spring, was performed annually in late winter.

The Plateau. In the Plateau the common western theme of personal spirit-power was honed to its greatest refinement and served as the basis for an areal religious system keynoted by collective "winter spirit-dances." Although there were a great many variations in the specifics of individual guardian-spirit quests and of winter dances among Plateau tribes, a generalized account may be offered as an introduction.

Among the Sanpoil-Nespelem and most other Salish groups, boys and many young girls began spirit questing at or before puberty, often when they were as young as six or eight. (Sahaptin groups placed less emphasis on spirit quests, and others, such as the Carrier, restricted them to certain males.) The child was sent out to fast, scour himself with rough foliage, bathe in cold pools, and keep vigils in isolated places. In dreams, as among the Carrier, or in visions, the supplicant was visited by an animal spirit or the spirit of an object or place. The spirit instructed the person in a song that often had an associated dance step, and sometimes revealed power objects. In many groups, the supplicant, on returning from a successful quest, "forgot" both encounter and song. (The Kutenai, whose youths sought only a single, immediately effective spirit, present an exception.) Among the Salish, when the individual reached full adulthood, usually about age twenty-five for men, the spirit returned, often causing illness. With the aid of a shaman, the individual "remembered" the song and spirit. Once fully accepted, one's spirit became an intrinsic aspect of one's being, like a soul, a "partner" whose loss was life-threatening. Throughout their lives, people might seek different, additional spirits with associated powers and specialties.

During a two-month period in the winter, anyone who had a guardian spirit—a shaman or a layman—might sponsor a spirit dance. The dances, held in a winter lodge, lasted two or three nights and were scheduled so that people of a given locale might attend several in a winter. Under the supervision of shamans, dancers imitated their own guardian spirits, singing their songs and performing their dance steps. New initiates to whom spirits had recently returned used the occasion to legitimize their relationships with their spirits. Other components of the dances included feasting and the giving of gifts to visitors, the offering of gifts to spirits at a center pole, and shamans' displays and contests. The conduct of the audience was rigidly controlled during the dances, and in some groups their behavior was policed by officiants.

Among the Sanpoil, Colville, Kutenai, Kalispel, Spokan, Coeur d'Alene, and Flathead, a society of men possessing Bluejay as guardian spirit served this policing function. These "Bluejay shamans" identified entirely with Bluejay during the winter dance period, painting their faces black, keeping to themselves, and scavenging food. The Bluejay shamans perched in the rafters of dance houses during performances, swooping down on those who broke the rules of conduct. They also performed services as finders of lost objects and as curers, and were ritually returned to a normal state at the end of the dance period. Although the Bluejay shamans suggest an at least latent sodality structure in the southeastern Plateau, such sodalities were fully developed only in California.

California. There were four major subareal ritual complexes in aboriginal California.

Toloache. From the Yuman tribes of the south, north through the Yokuts and, in diminished forms, to the Miwok, the use of *Datura stramonium*—jimsonweed, or *toloache* (from the Nahuatl and Spanish)—was a common and central feature of religious practice. A psychotropic decoction was made from the root of this highly toxic plant and carefully administered to initiates by shamans or by specialized priests. After a period of unconsciousness the initiates awoke to a trancelike state of long duration during which, guided by adepts, they acquired animal or celestial spirit-helpers. Such collective, drug-induced vision questing was often undertaken by males at puberty and in the context of an extended "school," as among the Luiseño-Juaneño, the Cahuilla, the Ipai-Tipai, the Cupeño, and the Gabrielino. Schooling included severe physical ordeals, instruction in mythic cosmology carried out through dry painting, and in some cases the creation of rock art. In such groups as the Chumash and the Serrano, training was restricted to the sons of an elite. In all cases, the group of initiated men, and—among the Monache and the Yokuts—women, formed a sodality that bore defined religious, economic, and political responsibilities. Among the Chumash, such an organization provided the basis for a highly complex, elite socioreligious guild, *lantap*, led by priest-astronomers. Throughout the subarea, shamans made use of *toloache* in achieving curing trances.

Mourning anniversaries. With their stress on ritual death and rebirth, the *toloache* religions of southern and central California reflected an overriding concern with personal and cosmic death and renewal. A second feature, the "mourning anniversary," accompanied the *toloache* complex. In broad outline, mourning anniversaries were large public gatherings in which effigies of the year's dead, together with large quantities of property, were burned on poles erected in circular brush shelters, the assembled audience mourning its collective losses. The occasion often served as a vehicle for girls' puberty celebrations, for the giving of new names, for honoring chiefs, and for expressing reciprocity between kin groups. Often an Eagle (or Condor) Dance, in which shamans displayed their power by slowly killing a sacrificial bird, formed an important part of the event.

The mourning anniversary, with many local variations, was practiced by the Basin peoples of the southern portion of contemporary California—the Cheme-huevi, the

Panamint, the Kawaiisu, and the Tubatulabal —as well as by virtually all groups in the southern California culture area. The practice extended northward through the *toloache*-using groups and beyond, being performed by the Maidu and Nisenan of northern California in conjunction with another religious complex, the Kuksu cult.

Kuksu. The term Kuksu derives from the Pomo name for a creator-hero who is impersonated by masked dancers in the periodic performances that are the focus of the religious system. A parallel figure, Hesi, was prominent in the performances of groups in the Sacramento Valley and the Sierra Nevada foothills. The Hill Maidu expression of the complex featured a third such figure, Aki, who is found together with Hesi among the Northwestern Maidu. Kuksu and Hesi are sometimes found together among other groups.

Masked and costumed dancers impersonated these and other spirits and mythic figures in elaborate ceremonials performed in dance houses before large audiences during gatherings that lasted several days. Dances at various ceremonial centers were reciprocally supported. As with *toloache* religions, the various Kuksu religions provided collective "schools" for pubescent initiates who were, through cultic indoctrination and participation, conducted into secret, often ranked sodalities. Such sodalities could exercise great political and economic influence, as well as spiritual power. The Kuksu dances themselves returned the world to its pristine, mythic condition and often included first-fruits and curing elements in their scope. Intergroup trading, gambling, shamans' contests, and recreation were features of the Big Times that usually followed Kuksu performances.

Among groups that had both Kuksu and Hesi sodalities, as well as some others, participation was open to young men and also to some young women, as among the Cahto and the Yuki. More commonly, membership in such sodalities was restricted to males. In some groups, membership was further restricted to elite cadres who worked their way up through the sodality's ranked levels, as among the Pomo-speaking groups. In such groups a second sodality, the Ghost society, was open to all young men, as among the Patwin, and sometimes to women as well, as among the Eastern Pomo. These less prestigious sodalities presented masked dances that paralleled those of the Kuksu type and emphasized the honoring of the departed, the curing of ghostdisease, and the continuity of generations. Such themes were present in the mourning anniversaries prevalent to the south. Thus, the Ghost society was not found among groups in the Kuksu subarea (such as the Maidu and the Nisenan) that practiced mourning anniversaries.

World renewal. Mythic reenactment, collective mourning, generational continuity, and world renewal are all motives present in the Kuksu religion that found other expressions in northwestern California, where a fourth areal ritual complex, the World Renewal cult, flourished. This complex featured cyclic ten-day ceremonials within more extended periods of ritual activity performed by specialized officiants. The various dances were given reciprocally at two- to three-year intervals at perhaps thirteen ceremonial centers in Yurok, Karok, and Hupa territories. Close equivalents of these World Renewal dances were held by Tolowa-Tututni, Wiyot, Chilula, and Shasta groups as well. The focal occasions were religious festivals, extended periods of public and private ritual, dancing, feasting, and communality that at times attracted several thousand participants. World Renewal festivals thus replaced both Big Times and mourning anniversaries in the northwestern subarea. However, the primary purpose of these large gatherings was the prevention of world disorder and the reaffirmation of interdependency. The world, potentially imbalanced by the weight of human misconduct, was "fixed" or "balanced" through the Jump Dance, the interdependence and abundance of all life reaffirmed and ensured through the Deerskin Dance. In both, teams of dancers displayed finery and power objects emblematic of the spiritual ascendency of their sponsors, and it was in this sense that such costumes and objects were considered "wealth."

The World Renewal religion was given different inflections by the different participating groups: the Yurok incorporated first-salmon rites and collective fishing as well as the rebuilding of a sacred structure; the Karok included "new fire" (new year) elements, as well as a first-salmon rite; and the Hupa celebrated a first-acorn rite, the rebuilding of a cosmographic structure, and so on. All stressed the reenactment, by priests, of the origins of the dances and their attendant rituals. The recitation of long, codified mythic scenarios was a central feature. School-like organizations of "helpers" were instructed by the priests. These organizations were similar to the initiatory sodalities of south and central California and included both men and women. Neither priests and their assistants nor dancers impersonated spirit beings, however, as was done in Kuksu performances or the spirit dances of the Plateau.

Postcontact Religious Change

The religions of California, the Great Basin, and the Plateau have undergone thousands of years of slow change and development. They were probably changed most suddenly and drastically by the direct and indirect influences of Europeans and Euro-Americans that began in the eighteenth century.

The Roman Catholic missionization of California, beginning in 1769, had largely disastrous effects on the native populations of the area. Voluntary conversions took place, but forced baptism and forced residence in mission communities were more common. Ultimately, the successes of Catholic missionization north to San Francisco Bay were negated by the fearsome toll exacted by the diseases fostered by overcrowded missions and forced labor under the

Spanish *encomienda* system. Success measured in lasting conversions was modest, and negative in terms of human welfare, but the missionaries contributed to native religious revitalization.

Other missionaries, primarily Protestant and Mormon, also made extended efforts in the nineteenth century in California, the Basin, and the Plateau. Yet the effects of later missionization were broadly similar: rather than supplanting native religions, Christianity provided symbolic means through which native religions found new forms to cope with the radically changing circumstances of life.

However, the effects of conquest were not limited to innovations informed by Christian ideology. The introduction of the horse onto the Plains and thence into the Plateau and the northwestern Basin in the early eighteenth century had an important impact on the peoples of these areas. Together with the horse came other Plains influences. Military sodali-

> **In the 1830s, many prophets, not acting in concert, spread the Prophet Dance through the central and southern Plateau.**

ties were integrated into the religions of the Kutenai and the Flathead, as was the Sun Dance. The Sun Dance also spread to the Great Basin, where it was taken up by the Wind River Shoshoni and the Bannock and was introduced to the Utes by the Kiowa as late as 1890.

The preponderant contact phenomena evidenced in the religious life of all three areas, however, were the millenarian crisis cults inspired by a variety of "prophets" whose visions had been shaped by Christian influences. Typically, such visions occurred in deathlike states in which prophets met God or his emissary and received word of the coming millennium and the practices and moral codes that would ensure Indians' survival of it. Perhaps the best known of such crisis cults are the Paiute Ghost Dances of 1870 and 1890.

The first of these, initiated by the prophet Wodziwob in 1870, moved through the Basin and into central California. It was taken up by a number of California groups and moved north to the Shasta. The Ghost Dance doctrine stressed the destruction of the whites by the Creator, the return of the Indian dead, and the restoration of the earth to its pristine, precontact condition. It inspired a number of variants in the years following 1870. Most of these represented fusions of Kuksu-type and Ghost society dances with the new millenarianism. Such cults included the Earth Lodge religion practiced by many central and northern California peoples. Adherents awaited the millennium in large, semisubterranean dance houses. Other cults inspired by the 1870 Ghost Dance included the Big Head and Bole-Maru cults of

the Hill Patwin, the Maidu, and the Pomo-speaking groups, and a succession of other local cults led by various "dreamers."

The 1890 Ghost Dance, initiated in 1889 by the Paiute prophet Wovoka, again spread through the Basin, this time moving east onto the Plains. It directly affected neither California nor the Plateau.

The two Ghost Dances are but the better known of a large number of similar efforts toward religious revitalization that flourished, particularly in the Plateau area, in the nineteenth century. In the 1830s, many prophets, not acting in concert, spread the Prophet Dance through the central and southern Plateau. This round dance, always performed on Sundays and reflecting belief in a high god, showed Christian influence, although some have argued that it had aboriginal precedents as well. The dance took many forms under the guidance of many prophets and dreamers, of whom the best known is perhaps Smohalla, a Sahaptin dreamer who revived the Prophet Dance in the 1870s in a form that spread widely.

In 1881 a Salish Indian from Puget Sound named John Slocum underwent what was by that time the established visionary experience of a prophet. Together with his wife Mary he inaugurated the Indian Shaker church, a Christian church in which the presence of God's power, signified by physical trembling ("the shake"), was used by congregants to cure the sick. This mixture of Christian and native shamanistic elements proved highly appealing, and the Indian Shaker church spread into the Plateau, where it was accepted by Yakima, Umatilla, Wasco-Tenino, Klamath, and, to a lesser extent, Nez Perce Indians. In northwestern California in 1926, churches were built by Yurok, Tolowa, and Hupa congregations. The Shakers' popularity in California began to wane in the 1950s, the result of internal schism, competition with evangelical Christian churches, and increasing stress on "Indianness" and the accompanying return to old ways.

These two apparently conflicting ideologies, based on the salvific powers of Jesus Christ, on the one hand, and on an Indian identity perceived as traditional, on the other, seem to have reached mutual accommodation in peyotism and its institutionalized expression, the Native American Church. The Peyote Way has been accepted by a large number of Basin Indians, spreading among the Ute, Paiute, Gosiute, and Shoshoni in the early twentieth century, its acceptance perhaps facilitated by the collapse of the 1890 Ghost Dance. The Washo received peyote from Ute believers in 1936.

Peyotism spread through the Basin despite the resistance of many traditionalists, becoming itself the basis for a new traditionalism. It was not, however, established in California, although Indians from such cities as San Francisco make frequent trips to take part in peyote meetings sponsored by the Washo and others in Nevada.

Many other postcontact religious systems, including the Sun Dance, continue to be enacted. Chingichngish remains central to religious life on the Rincon and Pauma reservations in southern California; Smohalla's Prophet Dance is still practiced as the basis of the Pom Pom religion of the Yakima and Warm Springs Indians; and Bole-Maru and other post-contact transformations of Kuksu religions are viable among Pomo and other central Californian groups. The Indian Shaker church survives in many communities.

Since the 1960s Indians of all three culture areas have made concerted efforts to reassert religious, as well as political, autonomy; indeed, the two realms continue to be closely intertwined. Traditional religious specialists and, in many cases, collective ritual activities have survived both conquest and christianization. Younger Indians are increasingly turning to elderly specialists and investing themselves in old ritual practices. Annual mourning ceremonies are still prominent in parts of southern California; northwestern Californians continue to dance in World Renewal rituals; and shamanism survives in the Basin, as does spirit questing on the Plateau. A myriad of other native ritual events and private practices continue throughout the region. Such state agencies as California's Native American Heritage Commission, as well as federal legislation such as the 1978 American Indian Religious Freedom Act, support these efforts to a degree. Withal, one can see the durability of the ancient ways, their persistence, and their ability to continue through modern transformations.

BIBLIOGRAPHY

The most valuable sources in the beginning study of the religions of California, the Great Basin, and the Plateau are the pertinent volumes of the *Handbook of North American Indians,* 20 vols. (Washington, D. C., 1978-). Volume 8, *California,* edited by Robert F. Heizer, was issued in 1978, and volumes on the Great Basin and on the Plateau are forthcoming. Heizer's *California* volume to an extent supplants A. L. Kroeber's *Handbook of the Indians of California* (1925; reprint, New York, 1976), although this earlier work remains of interest.

Useful bibliographies can be found in the volumes of the new *Handbook* and in several other important sources: *Ethnographic Bibliography of North America,* 4th ed., 5 vols., edited by George Peter Murdock and Timothy J. O'Leary (New Haven, 1975); Robert F. Heizer, T*he Indians of California: A Critical Bibliography* (Bloomington, Ind., 1976); Joseph P. Jorgensen, *Western Indians* (San Francisco, 1980); and Omer C. Stewart, Indians of the Great Basin (Bloomington, Ind., 1982).

Jorgensen's *Western Indians* is a computer-assisted distributional study with chapters on a number of pertinent topics, placing religious practices in ecological and political context. As such, it is a sophisticated continuation of earlier culture-element distribution surveys. One such study by Harold E. Driver, "Girls' Puberty Rites in Western North America," *University of California Publications in Anthropological Records* 6 (1941/42): 21-90, provides a comprehensive overview of its topic, an important one in all three culture areas under consideration here. Other such Western themes are explored in Willard Z. Park's *Shamanism in Western North America* (1938; reprint, New York, 1975) and in Erna Gunther's two analyses of first-salmon ceremonies in the *American Anthropologist* 28 (1926): 605-

617 and in *Washington University Publications in Anthropology* 2 (1928): 129-173. Park's *Shamanism* contains a detailed account of Northern Paiute (Paviosto) shamanism and thus serves to introduce specific aspects of Great Basin religion, while Verne F. Ray's *Cultural Relations in the Plateau of North America* (Los Angeles, 1939) surveys the complexities of that area's religious life in a way that remains important.

There are various sources on the major religious systems of California. A. L. Kroeber and E. W. Gifford's "World Renewal: A Cult System of Native Northwestern California," *University of California Publications in Anthropological Records* 13 (1949): 1-56, gives good descriptive materials, although its interpretations are rather narrow. Edwin M. Loeb's "The Western Kuksu Cult" and "The Eastern Kuksu Cult," *University of California Publications in American Archaeology and Ethnology* 33 (1932/33): 1-138, 139-232, are comparable, Kroeberian works. More recent studies include *ĺAntap: Californian Indian Political and Economic Organization,* edited by Lowell John Bean and Thomas F. King (Ramona, Calif., 1974), and Raymond C. White's "The Luiseño Theory of 'Knowledge,' " *American Anthropologist* 59 (1957): 1-19. The two, together, provide entrée into the study of southern Californian religions. White's essay is also included in a volume of largely theoretical papers, *Native Californians: A Theoretical Retrospective,* edited by Lowell John Bean and Thomas C. Blackburn (Socorro, N. Mex., 1976), which provides a number of stimulating interpretations of aboriginal California religious systems.

Finally, the *Journal of California and Great Basin Anthropology* (Banning, Calif., 1979-), succeeding the *Journal of California Anthropology* (1974-1979), publishes current explorations in the religions of California and the Great Basin fairly regularly.

THOMAS BUCKLEY

Indians of the Southwest

From the southern end of the Rocky Mountains in Colorado, the Southwest culture area extends southward through the mountains, high sandstone mesas, and deep canyons of northern New Mexico and Arizona, and dips over the Mogollon Rim—the southern edge of the Colorado Plateau—into the arid, flat, and sparsely vegetated, low-lying deserts of southern New Mexico and Arizona and northwestern Mexico, to the warm shores of the Gulf of California. It is interspersed throughout with mountain ranges, some bearing dense forests and large game animals. Major rivers are few: the Colorado, its tributaries, and the Rio Grande are the primary sources of water for large sectors of the southwestern ecosystem.

Given the variegation in topography, vegetation, and climate, it is not surprising that the Southwest should contain an equal cultural variety. Four major language families (Uto-Aztecan, Hokan, Athapascan, Tanoan) are represented by a large number of peoples, and two other languages (Zuni and Keres) comprise language isolates. But it should not be thought that language boundaries are a guide to cultural boundaries. The thirty-one pueblos of New Mexico and Arizona include speakers of six mutually unintelligible languages from four language groups. Yet they share numerous cultural, and specifically religious, features. On the other hand, among the groups speaking Uto-Aztecan languages are found sociocultural forms as disparate as the hunter-gatherer bands of Shoshoneans in the north and the great Aztec state to the south of the Southwest culture area.

Economic Patterns. Edward Spicer (1962) has suggested four major divisions according to distinctive economic types at the time of European contact: rancheria peoples, village peoples, band peoples, and nonagricultural bands. The rancheria peoples all traditionally practiced agriculture based on the North American crop triumvirate of maize, beans, and squash. They lived in scattered settlements with households, or "small ranches," separated by some distance from each other. This general economic pattern was followed by groups as disparate as the Tarahumara and Concho in the Sierra Madre of Chihuahua, the Pima and Papago of southern Arizona, the Yaqui and the Mayo concentrated in the river deltas along the Sonoran coast of the Gulf of California, and the riverine and upland Yuman groups.

The village peoples of Spicer's classification are, by contrast, sedentary communities with tightly integrated populations in permanent villages of stone and adobe construction. These are the Pueblo peoples, who have come to be regarded as the archetypical indigenous agriculturalists of the Southwest. The Tanoan Pueblos include the Tiwa, Tewa, and Towa, whose villages stretch up and down the upper portion of the Rio Grande in New Mexico. Also living for the most part along the Rio Grande or its tributaries are several Keresan Pueblos, with linguistically close Laguna and Acoma a little farther west, on the San Jose River. Moving west across the Continental Divide lies the pueblo of Zuni on a tributary of the Little Colorado River. At the western edge of Pueblo country, on the fingerlike mesas that extend southwestward from Black Mesa of the Colorado Plateau, are the eleven Hopi villages, whose inhabitants speak Hopi, a Uto-Aztecan language. Also located in this vicinity is one Tewa village, Hano, settled by refugees from the Rio Grande valley after the Great Pueblo Revolt of 1680.

The Pueblos are intensive agriculturalists. Among the Eastern Pueblos (those occupying the Rio Grande area) and in Acoma, Laguna, and Zuni (which with the Hopi constitute the Western Pueblos), agriculture is based on a variety of irrigation techniques. Hopi country has no permanent watercourses, and agriculture there is practiced by dry farming. Their sedentariness is a striking feature of the village peoples: Acoma and the Hopi village of Oraibi vie for the status of oldest continuously inhabited community in North America, with ceramic and tree-ring dates suggesting occupation from at least as far back as the twelfth century CE.

Spicer's third subtype is that of the band peoples, all Athapascan speakers. These consist of the Navajo and the several Apache peoples. These Athapascans migrated into the Southwest, probably via the Plains, from northwestern Canada not long before the arrival of Spanish colonists at the turn of the sixteenth century. They variously modified a traditional hunting and gathering economy with the addition of agriculture from the Pueblos (Navajo and Western Apache) and of sheep (Navajo) and horses (all groups) from the Spanish. The means of acquisition of these economic increments—through raiding of the pueblos and Spanish settlements—points up another important feature of Apache economies.

The fourth economic subtype Spicer refers to as non-agricultural bands. The Seri of the northwestern coastline of the Mexican State of Sonora are the primary representatives of this subtype. Traditionally, they hunted small game, fished and caught sea turtles, and gathered wild plant resources along the desert coast of the Gulf of California.

Variations in economy do not, of course, suggest variations in religious structure and orientation *tout court*. Still, modes of environmental adaptation do, within certain bounds, constrain the possibilities of social complexity. Southwest Indian religious patterns frequently do reflect forms of environmental adaptation because of a prevailing notion of social rootedness within a local environmental setting. Since many of the religious concerns of Southwest peoples pertain to man's relationship with environmental forces, the interplay between economic and religious spheres is fundamental.

Religious Patterns. Among the panoply of indigenous Southwestern cultures, two general patterns of religious action are evident: that focusing on the curing of sickness and that celebrating, reaffirming, and sanctifying man's relationship with the cyclical forces of nature. Religious actions of the former type are usually shamanic performances whose participants include an individual patient and an individual ritual specialist (or a small group of specialists). The latter type includes communal rituals involving large groups of participants under the direction of cadres of hereditary priests. These two general forms are present in the Southwest in a variety of combinations and permutations. Among the Yumans, the Tarahumara, and the Apache, shamanistic curing is the prevalent religious form, and little emphasis is placed on communal agricultural rituals. (The Havasupai, who until the turn of the century held masked ceremonial performances at stages of the agricultural cycle—a practice probably borrowed from their near neighbors, the Hopi—provide a partial exception.) Historically the Pima and Papago peoples held communal agricultural rituals as well as shamanic performances, but with sociocultural change the former have passed from existence while the latter, by themselves, have come to represent traditional religion. At the other end of the continuum, the Pueblos devote most religious attention to the calendrical cycle and have even communalized their curing ceremonies by creating medicine societies to fill the role played in less communally oriented societies by the individual shaman. (The Hopi are an exception, in that they still recognize individual medicine men and women.)

Several Caveats to Students of Southwest Religions. A key problem facing the student of Southwest Indian religions is sociocultural change. The Spanish conquest and colonization of the sixteenth and seventeenth centuries affected all Southwest cultures, though individual peoples were treated differently. Our knowledge of indigenous religious beliefs and practices is in some cases (for example, the Seri) severely limited by the wholesale abandonment of indigenous beliefs and their replacement with Christian concepts. Syncretism of traditional and introduced forms is, as among the Yaqui and Mayo, so historically entrenched that it is impossible to isolate the threads of precontact religious life. The traditional Yaqui and Mayo system of three religious sodalities fused in the seventeenth century with Jesuit beliefs and came to embody largely Christian notions, but these peoples' version of Christian ceremonies, such as the rituals recapitulating the Passion of Christ, incorporate traditional figures with clear similarities to the kachinas and clowns of the Pueblos. Since such syncretic processes began long before careful ethnographic records were made of indigenous belief and practice, the "pure forms" are simply irretrievable.

The Pueblos, the Navajo, and the Apache have maintained more of their traditional religious systems intact than other Southwest peoples. Of these groups, the Pueblos have the most complex religious systems, which in many instances preserve indigenous forms intact and distinct from religious elements introduced by Europeans. Hence I shall focus upon the Pueblos in this essay. The persistence of Pueblo religious patterns, despite almost four hundred years of colonial domination, is remarkable. The presence of Puebloan peoples in the Southwest, and of the earlier so-called Basket Makers, with whom there is a clear cultural continuity in the archaeological record, reaches far back into antiquity. The remains found in New Mexico's Chaco Canyon and Colorado's Mesa Verde of the civilization of the Anasazi are simply the better-known evidences of this socially complex and culturally sophisticated people, the direct ancestors of the historical Pueblos. The height of Anasazi culture (twelfth and thirteenth centuries CE) is represented by monumental architecture and elaborately constellated settlement patterns that suggest extensive social networks over large regions. For reasons we can only guess at—perhaps drought, war, disease, population pressure, internal social strife, or all of these in concert—the larger Anasazi pueblos had given way to the smaller pueblos by the time of the earliest historical records (c. 1540).

How much change and persistence have occurred in religion is an unfathomable problem. Nevertheless, the religious conservatism of the modern Pueblos, as well as archaeological indications (such as certain petroglyphs) suggest that more than a few Pueblo religious practices have persisted for a very long time. These two factors—the conservatism and antiquity of Pueblo religious practices—reflect another prominent characteristic: that the more important Pueblo beliefs and ritual practices are deliberately and rigorously preserved by an all-encompassing cloak of secrecy. The Pueblos have been and remain today extremely reluctant to reveal anything beyond the superficial aspects of their religious life. No anthropologists, apart from native Pueblo individuals, have been allowed to conduct extended resident field research by any of the Eastern Pueblos. Questions about religion meet with evasion or a purposive silence. Often information obtained by outsiders has been gathered in unusual ways, such as by interviewing individuals in hotel rooms distant from their pueblos. Only limited aspects of Pueblo religious performances are public; no non-Indian outsider has been permitted to witness a *kachina* performance in any of the Rio Grande pueblos since the seventeenth century.

Secrecy is pervasive not simply to preserve the integrity of traditional religion from the corrupting influences of the outside world, but also to protect the religious practices' integrity within the pueblos themselves. Initiates into religious societies are inculcated with the idea that their disclosure of secret, ritually imparted knowledge will have dire supernatural (their own or their relatives' deaths) and social (their ostracism from the pueblo) consequences. The result is that knowledge of Pueblo religion is fragmentary, flimsy, and in some cases inaccurate. We do know something of the surface contours of Pueblo religion, and these are discussed below. In deference to the Pueblos' rights to maintain their religions as they see fit, perhaps this surface level is as far as we may conscionably prosecute our inquiries.

The Pueblo Cosmos. In Pueblo thought generally, there is no absolute origin of life or of human beings. Although there have been a number of transformations since the earliest times, the earth and the people have always existed. Accordingly, there is less concern with primordial origins than with the process through which human beings were transformed into their present state of being from previous states.

Southwest peoples in general envision a multilayered cosmos whose structure is basically tripartite: "below," "this level," and "above." Each level has subdivisions, but the number and character of the subdivisions vary from culture to culture. All the Pueblos believe themselves to have originated beneath the present earth's surface. The layer below is characterized as a previous world, or as several previous worlds (or "wombs") stacked one atop another. The Zuni and the Keresans conceive of four previous worlds, the Hopi of three, and the Tewa only one. The last world "below" lies under a lake or under the earth's surface. At the beginning of the present age, the people were impelled—by supernatural signs in some versions of the Emergence story, by the need to flee evil in other versions—to seek a new life in the world above. By methods that vary from story to story (in some versions by climbing a tree, in others a giant reed), the people ascended to this level. The earth's condition was soft, and it required hardening. This was accomplished with the supernatural aid of the War Twins, who are found among all the Pueblo groups, or it was done by a human being with special powers—for example by the Winter Chief, who in the Tewa story hardened the ground with cold.

The timing and methods of the creation of natural phenomena vary, but the trajectory of human progress is the same throughout the various Pueblo traditions. After their emergence onto the earth's surface through an opening referred to as an "earth navel," the people migrated over the earth, stopping at locations that are identified by oral tradition with the numerous ruins throughout the Southwest, before reaching their final destination in the present-day villages. Variant migration patterns reflect differing forms of social organization: the matrilineal clans of the Hopi migrated independently and arrived at the present Hopi towns as separate units, whereas the two moieties of the Tewa— Winter and Summer—migrated down opposite banks of the Rio Grande from their Emergence point in the north.

Hence Pueblo origin myths emphasize the process of becoming the Pueblo peoples of the present. Each pueblo is highly independent, and, but for exceptional occasions requiring dire responses (such as in the Pueblo Revolt of 1680 or during severe famines), there is no political unity among pueblos whatsoever. Such independence is reflected in Pueblo worldview: each pueblo regards itself as the center of the bounded universe. Forces radiate both centripetally from the outer limits and centrifugally from a shrine at the pueblo's center, which is represented as the heart of the cosmos. Thus the Zuni are "the people of the middle place," the Hopi of Second Mesa live at the universe center, and each of the various Tewa villages lies about its "earth-mother earth-navel middle place" (Ortiz, 1969, p. 21). The outer limits of the world are marked variously. Among the Eastern Pueblos and the Acoma and Laguna, the world is a rectangular flat surface (although of course broken by topography) bounded by sacred mountains in the cardinal directions. For the Zuni, the surface is circular and is surrounded by oceans that are connected by underworld rivers. The Hopi world is more abstractly bounded, although sacred mountains and rivers act as circumscribing features.

All Pueblo worlds are rigorously aligned by six cardinal directions, four of which correspond to our north, west, south, and east (or, in the Hopi case, sunrise and sunset points on the horizon at the solstices—roughly northwest, southwest, southeast, and northeast) and the zenith and nadir. From the viewpoint of its inhabitants, each pueblo lies at the center

formed by the intersection of the axes of opposed directions. The directions are symbolized by numerous devices: colors, mammals, birds, snakes, trees, shells, sacred lakes, deity houses, and so forth.

The Zuni and the Tewa seem to have elaborated the axial schema to the greatest extent. For the Zuni, the six directions serve as a multipurpose organizational model for society—in terms of matrilineal clan groupings, priesthood sodalities, kiva (ceremonial chamber) groupings—and for nature, in that the taxonomy of species is directionally framed. The fourfold plan (i. e., excluding the vertical axis) of the earth's surface is represented by the Tewa as a series of concentric tetrads, which are marked by four mountains at their extremities and by four flat-topped hills, four directional shrines, and four village plazas as the center is approached. Neither is this a static abstraction in Tewa belief: ritual dancers in the plazas must face the four directions; songs have four parts; and so forth. Each of the physical features marking the corners of the concentric boundaries (the four mountains, hills, shrines, and plazas) is a place of power. Each contains an "earth navel" that connects the three levels of the cosmos and that is presided over by particular supernaturals.

The Pueblo Pantheon. Associated with the levels and sectors of the Pueblo world is a panoply of supernatural beings. Elsie C. Parsons (1939) divides these beings into collective and individualized categories.

Collective supernaturals. The collective category signally includes clouds, the dead, and the *kachinas*. Clouds and the dead have an explicit association: the specific destiny of the deceased person depends upon the role he played during life, but in general the dead become clouds. The cloud beings are classified according to the directions and, accordingly, associated with colors. *Kachina* is a fluid spiritual concept that refers both to supernatural beings and to their masked impersonators at Pueblo ceremonies. *Kachinas* appear in numerous guises and represent many features of the natural and supernatural worlds. They are dramatized in masked impersonation and in stories, where they appear in the forms of animals, plants, birds, the sun, and stars and as spirits such as the War Twins, sky deities, culture heroes, and so on. Some *kachinas* also represent game animals, and *kachinas* associated with the directions are also linked with hunting. *Kachinas* dwell in locations on the edges of the bounded world: in mountains, for instance, or in lakes or other sites associated with the powers of moisture. The three concepts of the dead, the clouds, and the *kachinas* overlap: the dead may become *kachinas*, and *kachinas* may manifest themselves as clouds. The interrelation among clouds, the dead, and *kachinas* points up a significant concern of Pueblo beliefs and ritual practices: the importance of rainfall in this largely arid environment is paramount, and the *kachinas*, as rain spirits, have the power to bring rain to nourish the crops—the central link in the Pueblo chain of being.

Individualized supernaturals. In some respects, individualized supernaturals reflect the arrangement of the cosmos into levels. Thus among the Hopi, Sootukw-nangw ("star-cumulus cloud"), the zenith deity, is associated with lightning and powerful rain; Muyingwu, an earth deity associated with the nadir, is the spirit of maize, germination, and vegetation; and Maasawu is the guardian of this level, the surface of the earth. But each of these figures has multiple aspects and cannot be neatly slotted into an abstract cosmic layer. Through his power to shoot lightning like arrows, Sootukw-nangw is also an important war deity, and Maasawu, especially, has a cluster of characteristics. He is associated with fire, war, death, and the night, and he looks and behaves in a more manlike fashion than do the deities of above and below. Supernaturals associated with cosmic features also embody moral principles (Maasawu represents humility, conservatism, lack of avarice, serious commitment to the duties of life, and the terrifying consequences of excessive individualism) and biological principles (Sootukwnangw's lightning arrows are associated with male fertilization). Further, there is a plethora of other supernaturals who are not arranged hierarchically but who crystallize a number of religious concerns.

> **Prayers to the sun refer to the desire for a long and untroubled path of life for each individual.**

The Pueblo pantheon lacks systematization: supernaturals often overlap in meaning and function, and this is further evident in the pattern of religious organization. Discrete segments of Pueblo society often focus exclusively upon the sets of supernaturals under their control; individuals not in a particular social segment do not have rights of appeal to its set of deities, and they risk severe social repercussions for unauthorized attempts at intercourse with such deities.

The sun, regarded everywhere as male, is a powerful fertilizing force, the father in relation to the earth, who is the mother. Traditionally, every individual was expected to offer cornmeal and to say a prayer to the sun at dawn, when the sun leaves his house (or *kiva*) at the eastern edge of the world and begins his journey to his western house. Prayers to the sun refer to the desire for a long and untroubled path of life for each individual. After a period of seclusion in darkness, the newborn Pueblo infant is taken out and shown to the sun to request a long and happy life and the sun's beneficent attention. As Father, the sun is equated with the care and spiritual nurturance of his children. Songs are addressed to him to ask for his life-giving powers of light and warmth, kept in balance so as not to burn the crops or dry them out.

Sun is also a deity of hunting and war; the Keresans, Tiwa, and Hopi seek his assistance in these endeavors.

Other celestial deities. Less significant by comparison, other celestial deities include, first, the moon, who is variously female (Zuni, where Moonlight-Giving Mother is the sun's wife) and male (Tewa, Towa, Tiwa). Moon is rarely addressed in prayer or song. In association with the sun and some constellations, however, the moon's movements and phases are utilized to plan the calendrical cycle of ceremonies. The antiquity of such practices is suggested by the numerous lunar and solar marking devices found in prehistoric Puebloan sites, such as the well-known Sun-Dagger petroglyphs in Chaco Canyon.

The morning star and the constellations Orion and the Pleiades have associations with war and with the timing of ceremonies. The movement of celestial phenomena is critically linked to the seasonal passage of the year. The ceremonial moiety division of the Tewa into Winter and Summer people, each of which has ritual and political charge of half the year, is an indication of the thoroughgoing nature of seasonal principles. The Hopi and Zuni divide their seasons by the solstices, the Tewa by the equinoxes, but the pattern of opposed dual principles is pervasive.

Dawn is deified in the form of Dawn Youths (Tewa), Dawn Mothers (Zuni), and Dawn Woman (Hopi). At Hopi, Dawn Woman is linked with another female deity, Huruingwuuti ("hard substances woman"), who has a formative role in the cosmogonic process. In the Keresan pueblos, she seems to have a counterpart in Thought Woman, whose every thought became manifest into substance. Thought Woman mythologically precedes Iyatiku, a chthonic being who is the mother of people, *kachinas*, game, and maize and who occupies the most prominent role in the Keresan pantheon. Iyatiku is in some respects parallel to Muyingwu, the Hopi maize and germination deity of the below. The principle of human and animal fertility is represented at Hopi by Tiikuywuuti ("child-water woman"), who is Muyin-gwu's sister.

Other common supernaturals. This group includes the War Twins, who are war gods, culture heroes, and patrons of gamblers; the maternal spirit animating the earth (whose body parts may be represented by vegetation, hills, and canyons); the Feathered and Horned Serpent, who lives in the water forms of the earth—springs, pools, rivers, the oceans—and who is a dangerous, powerful water deity responsible for floods and earthquakes; Spider Grandmother, a cosmogonic creator whom the Hopi consider grandmother of the War Twins; Salt Woman or Salt Man, deities of salt lakes and other salt sources; Fire Old Woman, Ash Man, and Ash Boy, with obvious associations; a giant eagle, or Knife Wing (Zuni), one of several war deities; Poseyemu, generally father of the curing societies, a miracle worker, and a possible syncretic counterpart of Christ; the master spirits of particular animals, such as Bear, Badger,

Mountain Lion, Wolf, and Coyote, who are patrons of specific curing societies; the sun's children, patrons of the clown societies; and many others.

Each of these supernatural entities embodies a different form of power. They are, however, discrete forms and not subsumable under a concept of pervasive supernatural power such as *mana* or *orenda*. They may be harnessed by human beings and used to transform events and states in the world. Access to power is, however, strictly limited in these societies and is based upon initiation into a religious sodality and, especially, a priestly office. There is no vision quest whereby power (at least for males) is democratically accessible.

Religious Organization and Ritual Practice. The basic form of religious organization in the pueblos consists of ritual societies, which serve a variety of purposes. Pueblo religion focuses on a number of issues: agricultural fertility and productivity, human fertility, fertility and productivity of game animals, war, and curing. These major issues are further divisible into aspects. Thus agricultural concerns are trained on the attainment of adequate—but not excessive—moisture, adequate heat and light, and the effective prevention of many crop pests and of excessive wind and cold. Rituals concerning game animals and hunting may be divided according to the species pursued. War society rituals are prophylactic, ensuring strength and success, as well as being celebrations of victory and rituals of purifying and sacralizing scalps taken in battle. Curing societies are organized according to the types of sicknesses they cure. "Bear medicine," "Badger medicine," and so forth are sympathetically and contagiously associated with particular ailments and are used by societies of the same names to produce cures. Typically, societies are composed of small numbers of priests and some lay members, and each society follows an annual cycle of ritual undertakings. In their most spectacular forms, such undertakings climax in dramatic public performances at specified times of the calendrical cycle.

Hopi religious societies. An examination of Hopi religious societies provides insight into the structure of such societies in Pueblo cultures generally. In Hopi thought, the religious societies have different degrees of importance and confer different degrees of power on the initiated. A ranking of the societies into three orders of ascending importance may be constructed as follows (translations are given where Hopi names are translatable): Kachina and Powamuy are third-order societies; Blue Flute, Gray Flute, Snake, Antelope, Lakon, and Owaqöl are second-order societies; and Wuwtsim, One Horn, Two Horn, Singers, Soyalangw, and Maraw are first-order societies.

Each of these societies focuses upon a different set of supernatural beings and a different set of specific concerns. The ranking into three orders parallels the age requirements for initiation into particular societies. All children aged six to ten (male and female) are initiated into either (the choice is their parents') the Kachina or the Powamuy society. After this initiation, they are eligible to join second-order societies, although not all individuals will actually join. (Second-order societies are distinguished by sex: Lakon and Owaqöl are female; the rest male.) At about age sixteen, all males (traditionally) are initiated into one of the four manhood societies (Wuwtsim, One-Horn, Two-Horn, Singers) and females into the Maraw (womanhood) society. Initiation into one of the manhood societies, together with birthright, is prerequisite to participation in the Soyalangw society; since this society carries no formal initiation, it can be regarded as a more exclusive extension of the manhood societies.

The ceremonial cycle. The public dimension of each society's activities is concentrated at particular points in an annual liturgy. The beginning of the year, which is reckoned in lunar months, falls from late October to late November and is marked by the manhood society ceremonies. Following an eight-day retreat in the kivas (semisubterranean ceremonial chambers), which involves private rituals, two of the societies (the Wuwtsim and the Singers) process slowly around the village in two facing columns. (Members of both societies are in each column.) The columns are "guarded" at both ends by some members of the Two-Horn society. The Wuwtsim and Singers sing songs composed for the occasion, some of which poke fun at the sexual proclivities of the Maraw society (the women's counterpart to the Wuwtsim society). The remaining members of the Two-Horn society and all the One-Horns are meanwhile continuing with private rituals in their respective *kivas*. After the final circuit of the Wuwtsim and Singers, all the Two-Horn and One-Horn members, in two separate processions (which are dramatic although unaccompanied by song) visit a series of shrines around the village and deposit offerings. Each manhood society is regarded as complementary to the other three, and each is associated with a particular religious concern: the Wuwtsim and Singers with fertility, the Two-Horns with hunting and game animals, and the One-Horns with the dead and with supernatural protection of the village.

A month later, at the time of the winter solstice, the Soyalangw ceremony occurs. This is one of the most complex Hopi ceremonies and involves the participation of the most important priests in the village. They ritually plan the events of the coming year and perform a variety of ritual activities concerned with reversing the northward movement of the sun and with the regeneration of human, floral (both wild and cultivated), faunal (wild and domestic), and meteorological harmony. Several key themes of Hopi religious concern are sounded in this winter solstice ceremony, which renews and reorients the world and man's position within it. After Soyalangw, game animal dances are held (nowadays particularly Buffalo Dances). These are regarded as "social" dances, as are a group of dances performed in September, which include, among others, Butterfly Dances and "Navajo Dances." The distinction between social dances and sacred performances is not completely clear; songs sung at social dances frequently express desires for beneficial climatic conditions, and in general the social dances evince continuity with the religious concerns of the sacred performances. Clearly, however, the social dances are regarded with less solemnity, and there are only minor religious proscriptions on the performers.

The Soyalangw ceremony opens the *kachina* "season." *Kachinas* are impersonated in repeated public performances from January to July. As has been noted, the *kachina* concept is multiple. The *kachina* costume worn by impersonator-performers includes a mask (there are more than three hundred kinds) and specific garments and body paints. The Hopi regard the masked representations of *kachinas* to be fully efficacious manifestations of the *kachina* spirits; when speaking English, they avoid the term *mask* because of the implication that "masking" is somehow less than real. Many *kachinas* have distinct emblematic calls and stylized body movements. *Kachina* performers represent a great variety of spirits, including those of plant and animal species, deities, and mythological figures of both benign (e.g., the "mudheads") and severe (e.g., the cannibal ogres) countenance. Positive and negative social values are sometimes fused in the same *kachina*. Often a *kachina* represents many elements and practices simultaneously and contains a thick condensation of symbolic devices. Some *kachinas* ("chief *kachinas*") are more important than others and are "owned" by particular clans and regarded as significant clan deities. Usually from January through March *kachinas* appear in groups to dance at night in the *kivas*; for the remainder of the *kachina* season, they appear during the day to dance in the village plaza. During daytime performances, the *kachinas* may be accompanied by a group of unmasked sacred clowns, who conduct a ceremony in parallel to the *kachina* performance. Clowns are given broad license and are social commentators *par excellence*. They expose numerous social aberrancies on the part of village members and poke fun at everything from sacred ceremonial actions to current events.

The two most important *kachina* ceremonies occur in February (Powamuy, "the bean dance") and in July (Niman, "the home dance"). At Powamuy, children may be initiated into either the Kachina or Powamuy society in an evening ceremony inside a *kiva*. During the day a large and multifarious assemblage of *kachinas* proceeds in ceremonial circuits around the village. This facinating and beautiful pageant features a series of minipageants occurring in different parts of the village simultaneously. Powamuy purifies the earth and also prefigures the planting season. Beans are germinated in soil boxes in the *kivas* by the artificial warmth of constant fires. During the day of the public pageant, the bean plants are distributed by *kachinas* to each household, where they

are cooked in a stew. At the same time the kachinas distribute painted wooden *kachina* dolls and basketry plaques to girls and painted bows and arrows to boys, ensuring their futures as fertile mothers and brave warrior-hunters.

The Niman ("homegoing") ceremony, marks the last *kachina* performance of the year. At the close of Niman, the *kachinas* are formally "sent" by several priests back to their mountainous homes in the San Francisco Peaks and elsewhere. They are requested to take the prayers of the people back with them and to present them to the community of *kachina* spirits.

The *kachina* season is followed by the season of "unmasked" ceremonies. In August occur the Snake-Antelope ceremonies or the Flute ceremonies, the performance of which alternates from year to year. In either case, the two societies from which the ceremonies take their names come together at this time to perform complex rituals that last nine days. The Snake-Antelope rites include a public performance in which the Snake men slowly dance in pairs around the plaza while the Antelope men form a horseshoe-shaped line around them and intone chants. The Snake-Antelope and the Flute ceremonies are densely expressive. Both include a magical attempt to bring clouds over the fields to give rain to the crops; both mark the sun's passage; and both dramatize the mythological entrance of particular clans into the village.

Following these ceremonies in the annual liturgy come the ceremonies of the women's societies. The Lakon and Owaqöl, both referred to in English as Basket Dances, feature a circular dance in the plaza. Selected society members run in and out of the circle throwing gifts to the men, who throng the edges of the circle and dispute over the gifts. Both Lakon and Owaqöl women hold basketry plaques in front of them while they sing. The Maraw society's ceremony features a similar circle in which women hold long prayer-sticks. A number of other rites occur during the nine-day Maraw, including burlesques of male ceremonial activities. Maraw rites relate to war and fertility; Lakon and Owaqöl rites stress fertility and the celebration of the harvest.

This bare outline of the Hopi ceremonial cycle reveals some basic concerns of Pueblo religion. The timing of ceremonies is intimately connected with the annual progress of nature. The *kachina* performances are especially related to the life cycle of cultivated plants, and they occur at critical points in this cycle. The first ceremonies of the year prefigure the planting and successful fruition of crops; they are designed to bring snow and rain to saturate the earth with moisture, which will remain there until planting occurs in April. The daytime *kachina* performances likewise seek rainfall to help the crops grow. Niman, the Homegoing, signals the end of the early phases of crop maturation; the kachinas' departure suggests that the spirits of the crops are sufficiently mature no longer to require the *kachinas'* nurturance.

The Snake-Antelope and Flute ceremonies complete the course of metaphysical encouragement and nourishment of the crops. Coming at the hottest, driest time of the year, they invoke powerful forces to bring one last bout of rain to ensure the full maturing of the crops and to prevent the sun's fierce gaze from withering them. The women's society Basket Dances celebrate the success of the harvest by the joyful distribution of basketry plaques and household goods.

Private rituals. All ceremonies include private rituals in *kivas* prior to the public performance. Typically such private rituals include the construction of an altar, which consists of a rectangular sand painting in front of a vertical assemblage of painted and carved wooden pieces that incorporate symbolic designs of birds, animals, and supernaturals. The sand painting also incorporates many symbolic elements. Long songs are incanted over the altar, and tobacco is ceremonially smoked and blown to portray clouds. (Smoking binds together the hearts of the priests as they pass the pipe around a circle and gives them a collective power to express their prayers more forcefully.) The *kiva* itself is a multiplex symbol: it is axially oriented by the directions, and at its center is a hole representing the *sipapu*, the place of emergence from the world below. The *kiva's* four levels, from the underfloor to the roof, are identified with the worlds through which man has ascended; the passage into this world is portrayed by the *sipapu* and the *kiva* ladder that leads to the roof.

Maize Symbolism and Ritual. Maize is the dominant, pervasive symbol of Hopi religious life. Maize is regarded as the mother of people, since it is the primary sustainer of human life. "Corn is life," the Hopi say. Two perfect ears of white maize are given to a newborn child as its "mothers"; when a person dies, ears of blue maize similarly accompany him on his journey beyond life. Maize seeds, ears, tassels, milk, pollen, and meal all serve as sacramental elements in differing contexts. Moreover, other important symbols are related to the maize cycle. Clouds, rains, lightning, feathered serpents, and various species associated with water, such as frogs, ducks, reeds, and so forth, all underline a paramount interest in securing water for maize.

Two devices, above all others, serve as mechanisms for establishing holiness or for communicating with supernatural forces: cornmeal and prayer feathers. Corn-meal is an all-purpose sanctifying substance; it is sprinkled on *kachina* dancers, used to form spiritual paths for *kachinas* and the dead, offered to the sun and to one's own field of growing maize plants, and accompanies all forms of private and public prayer. The act of making a prayer to various supernatural forms with the sprinkled offering of cornmeal may be considered the most fundamental religious act for the Hopi as for all the Pueblos.

Feathers of many different bird species are used in innumerable ways in Hopi ritual; they are worn in the hair and around arms and ankles, and they decorate *kachina* masks, altars, and religious society emblems. Prayer sticks and prayer feathers are the two basic forms of feather offerings. Prayer sticks, carved in human or supernatural forms, are living manifestations of prayer and are simultaneously petitions for aid. Feathers are regarded as particularly effective vehicles for conveying messages to supernaturals: they "carry" the prayers of people with them.

Comparisons. It is evident from the Hopi situation that religious action is multiple. There is no single set of activities we can demarcate as "Hopi religion" as distinct from Hopi agriculture or even Hopi politics, since political activity goes on even within the context of private ceremonial gatherings. Also, the exclusiveness of religious societies above the third order suggests a socially fragmented pattern of religious belief and practice. Religious knowledge is highly valued and tightly guarded, and it serves as the primary means of making status distinctions in Hopi society. Hopi explanations of the diversity of their religious activities point to historical circumstances: each cult is identified with a particular clan that introduced it when the clan negotiated admission to the village in the distant past. Although lay cult members may be from any clan, the chief priests should always be of the clan which "owns" the ceremony. In part, then, ceremonial performances celebrate separate clan identities and mark off particular ritual activities as the exclusive prerogative of particular clans. This pattern of closed ceremonial societies with exclusive rights in certain forms of religious action is a fundamental characteristic of Pueblo religion.

The Zuni cult system. Other Pueblo groups depart significantly from the Hopi scheme yet still exhibit similarities that suggest some common patterns of belief and practice. Ethnologists have identified six major types of cults or societies among the Zuni.

1. *The Sun cult.* Responsibility for the important religiopolitical officer called the *pekwin* (Sun priest) belongs to the Sun cult. Membership is restricted to males, and the sodality conducts its ceremonies at the solstices.

2. *The Uwanami ("rainmakers") cult.* This cult is composed of twelve distinct priesthoods of from two to six members each. Membership is hereditary within certain matrilineal families. Each priesthood holds retreats (but no public ceremonies) during the summer months from July through September.

3. *The Kachina cult.* Unlike the Hopi Kachina society, membership in the Zuni Kachina society is not open to females. The cult has six divisions, which are associated with the six directions and are accordingly headquartered in six *kivas.* Each *kiva* group dances at least three times per year: in summer, in winter following the solstice, and following the Shalako ceremony in late November or early December.

4. *The cult of the kachina priests.* Whereas the Kachina society is primarily concerned with rain and moisture, the cult of the *kachina* priests focuses on fecundity—of human

beings and game animals. The *kachina* priests are responsible for the six Shalako *kachinas*, the ten-foot-tall, birdlike figures whose appearance marks the most spectacular of Zuni religious dramas, and for the *koyemsi* ("mudhead") *kachinas*, who are at once dangerously powerful beings and foolish clowns. Other *kachinas* under the charge of the *kachina* priests appear at solstice ceremonies, at the Shalako ceremonies, and every fourth year at the time when newcomers are initiated into the general Kachina cult.

5. *The War Gods cult.* The Bow priesthood, which is exclusively male, controls the War Gods cult. Traditionally, initiation required the taking of an enemy's scalp. The Bow priests are leaders in war and protectors of the village, and they serve as the executive arm of the religiopolitical hierarchy, in which role they prosecute witches. (The extinct Momtsit society may have been the Hopi counterpart of the Bow priests.)

6. *The Beast Gods cult.* The cult is overseen by twelve curing societies, and membership is open to both men and women. Each society focuses on a particular source of supernatural power, which is embodied in the bear, mountain lion, or another predatory animal. The individual societies practice general medicine, but each also specializes in healing specific afflictions. The collective ceremonies of the societies are held in the fall and winter.

Keresan Pueblo religious practice. Among the Keresan Pueblos—Acoma and Laguna to the west, Santo Domingo, Cochiti, San Felipe, Santa Ana, and Zia to the east on the Rio Grande and its tributaries—the chief religious organizations are referred to as "medicine societies." With variations from pueblo to pueblo, the basic pattern consists of four major medicine societies—Flint, Cikame (an untranslatable Keresan word), Giant, and Fire—and a number of minor societies, including Ant, Bear, Eagle, and Lizard. The medicine societies conduct a communal curing ceremony in the spring, echoing a theme of the Hopi Bean Dance, and they hold performances throughout the year to effect the cure of individual patients. The societies also have rainmaking functions, which they fulfill at private ritual retreats during the summer months. Reportedly, these societies erect altars and construct sand paintings similar to those described for the Hopi and the Zuni. The same major sacramental elements—prayer sticks and cornmeal—are central vehicles for religious action, and extensive songs and prayers designed to make unseen power manifest in the world are a key part of ceremonial content. The medicine societies also have important roles in solstitial ceremonies aimed at reversing the course of the sun.

Other important Keresan societies include a paired group: the Koshare, which is a clown society parallel in many ways to Hopi clown societies, and the Kwirena, which is primarily associated with weather control. A Hunters society, with a permanently installed "hunt chief," and a Warriors society, composed of scalp-takers, are other important societies that traditionally held ceremonies during the winter. A village-wide Kachina society is divided into two ceremonial moieties, Turquoise and Squash, associated with the two kivas in the village. *Kachina* performances by both moieties occur during fall and winter, but especially during the summer immediately following the rainmaking retreats of the medicine societies. These retreats include a supernatural journey to the *sipapu*, from which the *kachinas* are brought back to the village. As among other Pueblo groups, ritual activities among the Keresans are dominated by males; although both sexes may join medicine societies, women serve as secondary assistants, and only men may perform as *kachinas*.

The climatic and ecological situation of the Keresan Pueblos is of much greater reliability than that of the Hopi. The Keresans' religious concern with the agricultural cycle is evident, but, since the Keresans have irrigation and more plentiful precipitation, they put less emphasis on the agricultural and more on the curing functions of religious societies. A primary function of the more important medicine societies is to combat witchcraft by evil-hearted human beings and evil supernaturals, which is believed to be the cause of illness. Witchcraft is, and has been historically, a profound concern of Hopi and Zuni also, although at Hopi the concern receives less concerted attention from the major religious societies.

The theme of dualism, which appears at Hopi and Zuni in the form of the solstitial switching of ritual emphases, is manifested at the Keresan Pueblos with the division of the ceremonial organization into moieties centered in two *kivas*.

Tewa, Tiwa, and Towa religious systems. The theme of dualism in Southwest religion achieves perhaps its maximum expression in the religious life of the six Tewa pueblos: San Juan, Santa Clara, San Ildefonso, Tesuque, Nambe, and Pojoaque. The division of people into Winter and Summer ceremonial moieties is part of a thoroughgoing dual scheme phrased in terms of seasonal opposition. The division of significance among the Tewa is by equinoxes; the seasonal transfer ceremony that is held (roughly) at each equinox places one or the other of the ceremonial moieties in charge of the village for the following season. Hence there are two overarching religious leaders, or caciques, each the head of a moiety. The calendar of religious activities is planned in accordance with the division into summer (agricultural activities) and winter (nonagricultural activities).

Typically, each Tewa pueblo has two *kivas* in which the ceremonial moieties are headquartered. There are eight religious societies in all: the Winter and Summer moiety societies, each headed by a moiety priest; the Bear Medicine society; the Kwirena ("cold clowns") and Kossa ("warm clowns") societies; the Hunt society; the Scalp society; and the Women's society. The most intensive ritual activity occurs between the autumnal and vernal equinoxes. This contrasts with the Hopi model, in which the most active part of the cycle occurs from the winter to the summer solstice (and just thereafter). Parallel elements are otherwise clear: religious-society organization among the Tewa is reminiscent of the nearby Keresans. Religious concerns, too, are similar between the Tewa and Keresan Pueblos, though the Tewa Pueblos place less emphasis on curing. The main sacraments are the same; the *kachina* performance is a fundamental religious practice, though more restricted here than among the Hopi, Zuni, and western Keresans.

The traditional religious practices of the Tiwa pueblos—Taos and Picuris in the north and Sandia and Isleta in the south—are the least well known. Taos, in particular, has been most effective in protecting matters it regards as not appropriate for public consumption. At Taos, each of the six *kivas* (which are divided into three on the "north side" and three on the "south side" of the pueblo) houses a religious society. *Kiva* society initiation involves a set of rituals prolonged over a number of years and is restricted by inheritance to a select group. The *kiva* organization at Taos seems to serve the same purpose as religious societies at other pueblos. At Taos, there is greater ritual emphasis upon game animals and hunting, in line with the pueblo's close cultural ties with Plains peoples, than there is upon the agricultural cycle. Taos may be the only pueblo in which *kachinas* are not represented in masked performances. Picuris seems traditionally to have done so, and it otherwise exhibits more religious similarity with the Tewa pueblos than it does with Taos, its close linguistic neighbor. *Kachinas* do occur, however, in Taos myths.

The southern Tiwa in Isleta pueblo have a system of ceremonial moieties divided into Winter (Black Eyes) and Summer (Red Eyes), each with its "moiety house" (which is equivalent to a *kiva*). In addition, Isleta Pueblo's five Corn groups, associated with directions and colors, seem to parallel *kiva* organizations at Taos. The moieties conduct seasonal transfer ceremonies similar to those at Tewa pueblos, and likewise each moiety controls the ritual activities for the season over which it presides. The ceremonial cycle is attenuated in comparison with that at other pueblos; there is a Land Turtle Dance in the spring and a Water Turtle Dance in the fall. Although unverified, it has been reported that *kachina* performances are conducted by a colony of Laguna Pueblo people who have lived in Isleta since the late nineteenth century.

Jemez, the only modern representative of the Towa Pueblos, exhibits an extraordinarily complex ceremonial organization, with twenty-three religious societies and two *kiva* moieties. Every Jemez male is initiated into either the Eagle society or the Arrow society; other societies are more exclusive. Societies can be classified according to function: curing, rainmaking and weather control, fertility, war and protection, and hunting. The Jemez ceremonial cycle includes a series of retreats by the different religious societies. In the summer, these celebrate agricultural growth; in the fall the ripening of crops; in the winter war, rain, ice, snow, and game animals; and in the spring the renewal of the forces of life. The two ceremonial *kiva* moieties are Turquoise and Squash, the same as among the eastern Keresans, and although the principle of dualism is in evidence it is not so pronounced as among the Tewa.

Life, Death, and Beyond. The Pueblos hold that an individual's life follows a path, or plan, that is present in his fate from birth. A long, good life and a peaceful death in old age are the main requests contained in prayers delivered at the birth of a new person. Through the course of maturation, the person becomes increasingly incorporated, in a ritual sense, into the world. So the Tewa, for example, perform a series of childhood baptismal rites—"name giving," "water giving," "water pouring," and "finishing"—that progressively fix and identify the individual in relation to the forces of society and the cosmos. Religious society initiations and marriage mark further passages in the individual's path of life.

Beliefs about and rituals surrounding death reveal some of the most essential features of Pueblo conceptions of the nature of existence. I have noted above the association between the dead, clouds, and *kachina* spirits. In general,

> **Cloud spirits have myriad conceptual associations, and the dead (or certain of them) may likewise be given special associations.**

Pueblos believe that when a person dies, the spirit, or breath, returns to the place of the Emergence and becomes transformed into cloud. Cloud spirits have myriad conceptual associations, and the dead (or certain of them) may likewise be given special associations. So, although clouds are generally regarded as the spirits of all the ancestral dead, distinctions are also made between different afterlife destinations, which vary according to the status the deceased person held while alive.

All the Pueblos distinguish between two kinds of people: those who hold important religious offices (or who are initiated members of religious societies) and everyone else. The former are regarded as supernaturally and socially powerful, ritually significant people; the latter are commoners. For the Tewa, the distinction is between "made," or "completed," people and "dry food" people; for the Zuni, the distinction is between valuable and ceremonially poor, or unvaluable, people; among the Keresans the term *sishti* ("commoners") denotes those without ceremonial affiliation; and for the Hopi, the distinction is between *pavansinom* ("powerful" or "completed" people) and *sukavungsinom* (common people).

The afterlife fate of these different categories may vary from one Pueblo group to another. Deceased members of the Hopi Two-Horn and One-Horn societies judge the newly dead at the house of the dead. Witches, suffering a different fate from that enjoyed by the righteous, may be transformed into stinkbugs! Zuni rain priests join the *uwanami* spirits who live in the waters, whereas Zuni Bow priests join their spiritual counterparts in the world above as makers of lightning. Other religious society members return to the place of the Emergence, but Zuni commoners go to "*kachina* village," the home of the *kachinas*, which is at a distance of two days' walk to the west of Zuni. In short, the social and religious organization in life is replicated in the organization of the dead,

Syncretism and Change. The Pueblos were first exposed to Christian practices through the Franciscan friars who accompanied Francisco Vasquez de Coronado during his exploration of the Southwest (1540-1542). When the Province of New Mexico was made a colony of Spain in 1598, the Franciscan order was given special jurisdiction over the souls of the Indians. Missions were built in most of the pueblos; tributes were exacted; strenuous discipline was enforced; and extremely brutal punishments were levied for infractions of the total ban on indigenous religious practices. In reaction to this colonial domination, and especially to the religious oppression, all the pueblos united in an uprising in 1680, under the leadership of Popé, a Tewa priest. Many Spanish priests and colonists were killed, and the rest were forced to withdraw from New Mexico. Most of the pueblos immediately dismantled their missions. The Oraibi Hopi record that in the Great Pueblo Revolt the Roman Catholic priests were actually killed by warrior *kachinas*, symbolically demonstrating the spiritual rectitude of the action and the greater power of the indigenous religion.

Removed from the mainstream of Spanish settlements, the Hopi never allowed Spanish missions to be built among them again, and their religious practices remained free of Franciscan influence. The other Pueblos all suffered the reestablishment of missions after the Spanish reconquest of the 1690s. The influence of the missions depended upon the regularity and zeal with which they were staffed. At Zuni, a desultory missionary presence seems to have had little impact on traditional religious forms. The Rio Grande pueblos, on the other hand, came under a great deal of Franciscan influence. These pueblos are all nominally Catholic and observe many ceremonies of the Christian calendar. Each town has a patron saint and holds a large dance—called a Corn Dance or Tablita Dance—to celebrate the saint's day. The dance is thoroughly indigenous in character; however, a Christian shrine honoring the saint stands at one side of the plaza during the dance. At the conclusion of the dance, all the participants enter the church and offer prayers and thanks in a Christian fashion. Thus the two tradi-

tions coexist in a "compartmentalized" fashion. In some areas, such as rites of passage, Christian practices have supplanted indigenous Pueblo forms, especially in those pueblos that have become increasingly acculturated during the twentieth century (Pojoaque, Isleta, Picuris, and Laguna are examples). Many Eastern Pueblos have also taken over Spanish and Mexican religious dramas, such as the Matachine performances, which are also practiced among the Yaqui, Mayo, and Tarahumara.

Protestant churches have been attempting to proselytize the Pueblos since the latter nineteenth century, though in general without much success. Despite sustained longterm efforts by the Mennonites, Baptists, Methodists, Roman Catholics, Mormons, and Jehovah's Witnesses among the Hopi, their rate of conversion to Christianity has remained below 10 percent. On the other hand, major Christian holidays such as Christmas and Easter are popular occasions and may be having some impact on traditional religion. A *kachina* dance is regularly scheduled for Easter weekend nowadays, and among the array of presents they bring the *kachinas* include baskets of colored eggs. Regarding other nontraditional religions, only at Taos has peyotism to some extent been adopted, and even there its practice is evidently kept compartmentalized and apart from both indigenous religious practice and Catholicism.

Conclusion. The religious traditions of other Indians of the Southwest contain their own conceptual and historical complexities. I have chosen to focus upon the Pueblos here because of the richness of their extant religious practices and because of the separate treatment that the Apache and the Navajo receive in this study. This does not imply that Pueblo religions are somehow representative of the religions of other native Southwest peoples, though certain Pueblo themes are echoed in different ways among non-Pueblo peoples. Sodalities and clown societies exist among the Yaqui and Mayo; sand painting is practiced by the Navajo, Pima, and Papago; and masked impersonators of supernatural beings perform rainmaking dances among the Havasupai, Yavapai, Pima, and Papago: but these common threads occur in cloths of quite different weaves. Let me emphasize at the last that the indigenous Southwest is enormously diverse. The sheer complexity of its religious practices belies any attempt to standardize these into a meaningful common pattern.

BIBLIOGRAPHY

On account of their richness and complexity, Southwest Indian religions have proven irresistible to generations of scholars. As the cradle of American anthropology, the indigenous Southwest has produced perhaps a greater volume of ethnographic studies than any other comparably populated area in the world. W. David Laird's *Hopi Bibliography: Comprehensive and Annotated* (Tucson, 1977), for example, contains listings for about three thousand items on this people alone. The contemporary *sine qua non* of Southwest ethnographic material is the *Handbook of North American Indians*, vols. 9 and 10, *The Southwest*, edited by Alfonso Ortiz (Washington, D. C., 1979, 1983). Encyclopedic in scope, these volumes treat Pueblo (vol. 9) and non-Pueblo (vol. 10) cultures; particularly pertinent synthetic articles include Dennis Tedlock's "Zuni Religion and World-View" (vol. 9, pp. 499-508), Arlette Frigout's "Hopi Ceremonial Organization" (vol. 9, pp. 564-576), Louis A. Hieb's "Hopi World View" (vol. 9, pp. 577-580), and Louise Lamphere's "Southwestern Ceremonialism" (vol. 10, pp. 743-763). Complex and detailed statements on specific religious practices may be found in the numerous writings of Jesse Walter Fewkes, H. R. Voth, and A. M. Stephen for the Hopi (see the Laird bibliography mentioned above); Frank H. Cushing for the Zuni; Matilda Coxe Stevenson for the Zuni and Zia; Leslie White for the individual Keresan pueblos; and Elsie C. Parsons for many Pueblo groups (the bibliography in volume 9 of the *Handbook* should be used for specific references).

I recommend a number of works (presented here in order of publication) that either focus specifically on religious practice or devote significant attention to it. H. K. Haeberlin's *The Idea of Fertilization in the Culture of the Pueblo Indians* (Lancaster, Pa., 1916) is an early synthesis that has yet to be superseded. Ruth L. Bunzel's "Introduction to Zuni Ceremonialism," in the *Forty-seventh Annual Report of the Bureau of American Ethnology* (Washington, D. C., 1932), and her other articles in the same volume are excellent windows not only into Zuni religion but into Pueblo religion more generally. The classic, comprehensive (albeit fragmentary) source is Elsie C. Parsons's *Pueblo Indian Religion*, 2 vols. (Chicago, 1939). Mischa Titiev's *Old Oraibi: A Study of the Hopi Indians of the Third Mesa* (Cambridge, Mass., 1944) is perhaps the best single account of the Hopi, although the second volume of R. Maitland Bradfield's *A Natural History of Associations: A Study in the Meaning of Community*, 2 vols. (London, 1973), brings together an enormous amount of earlier material on Hopi religion for a novel synthesis. Alfonso Ortiz's *The Tewa World* (Chicago, 1969) is the most sophisticated and best-written account of any of the Pueblos, and it stands as the single most essential monograph on one Pueblo people. Edward P. Dozier's *The Pueblo Indians of North America* (New York, 1970) is a complete, concise summary concerning all the Pueblos. *New Perspectives on the Pueblos*, edited by Alfonso Ortiz (Albuquerque, 1972), contains several articles on religious practices and beliefs. Although somewhat difficult of access for readers of English, two exceptionally good interpretations of Pueblo ritual and myth have appeared in French: Jean Cazeneuve's *Les dieux dansent à Cibola* (Paris, 1957) and Lucien Sebag's *L'invention du monde chez les Indiens pueblos* (Paris, 1971).

Beyond the Pueblos, and excluding the Navajo and the Apache, little of comparable depth exists. Ruth M. Underhill's *Papago Indian Religion* (New York, 1946) and *Singing for Power* (Berkeley, 1938) are notable exceptions, and her *Ceremonial Patterns in the Greater Southwest* (New York, 1948) is another historic synthesis. For sources on other Southwestern cultures, volume 10 of the *Handbook* is the best guide. Edward H. Spicer's *Cycles of Conquest: The Impact of Spain, Mexico, and the United States on the Indians of the Southwest*, *1533-1960* (Tucson, 1962), cited above, is a thorough historical study of all indigenous Southwestern peoples.

PETER M. WHITELEY

NORTH AMERICAN RELIGIONS

Main Religious Features

North America is a continent with many diverse cultures, and it is therefore meaningless to speak about North American religion as a unified aggregate of beliefs, myths, and rituals. Still, there are several religious traits that are basically common to all the Indians but variously formalized and interpreted among different peoples. Two characteristics are, however, typically Amerindian: the dependence on visions and dreams, which can modify old traditional rituals, and an intricate and time-consuming ceremonialism that sometimes almost conceals the cognitive message of rituals.

Spirit World. To these common elements belongs the idea of another dimension of existence that permeates life and yet is different from normal, everyday existence. Concepts such as the Lakota *wakan* and the Algonquian *manitou* refer to this consciousness of another world, the world of spirits, gods, and wonders.

Supreme being. The supernatural world is primarily expressed through the spiritual powers residing in a host of gods, spirits, and ghosts. In many American tribes prayers are directed to a collectivity of divine or spiritual beings, as in the pipe ceremony. Foremost among these divinities is, in most tribes, a sky god who represents all other supernatural beings or stands as their superior and the ruler of the universe. The Pawnee Indians in Nebraska, for instance, know a hierarchy of star gods and spirits, all of them subservient to the high god in the sky, Tirawa.

The supreme being is closely associated with the axis mundi, or world pillar. The Delaware Indians say that he grasps the pole that holds up the sky and is the center of the world. In ceremonial life the world pole, or world tree, is the central cultic symbol in the great annual rites of peoples of the Eastern Woodlands, the Plains, the Basin, and the Plateau. At this annual celebration the Indians thank the supreme being for the year that has been. In California, a region of frequent earthquakes, similar world renewal rituals have as their main aim the stabilizing of the universe. In the east, the Delaware Big House ceremony is an adaptation of the hunters' annual ceremony to the cultural world of more settled maize-growing peoples: the sacred pillar is here built into a ceremonial house.

The culture hero. The connection of the supreme being with creation is often concealed by the fact that in mythology another supernatural being, the culture hero, is invested with creative powers. His true mission is to deliver cultural institutions, including religious ceremonies, to the first human beings, but he is sometimes an assistant creator as well. In this quality he competes with the Great Spirit and appears as a ludicrous figure, a trickster, or an antagonist of the Great Spirit, an emergent "devil."

Spirits and ghosts. The other beings of the supernatural world—and they are innumerable, vary from tribe to tribe

There are powers such as the dead, who operate in different places in different types of cultures. There is everywhere a belief in ghosts on earth, who are often heard whistling in the night. Independent of these beliefs is a ubiquitous idea of reincarnation or transmigration into animals.

Guardian spirits and vision quests. Other spirits are the guardian spirits acquired in fasting visions by youths of the Plateau and the Northeast Woodlands and by both boys and men of the Plains and the Basin. These spirits are mostly zoomorphic. They may be animal spirits or spirits that show themselves in animal disguise. Everywhere except among the pueblo-dwelling peoples of the Southwest it has been the individual hunter's ambition to acquire one or several of these guardian spirits. They usually appear to the person after a vision quest during which he has spent several days and nights in fasting and isolation at some lonely spot in the wilderness. The spirit endows his client with a particular "medicine," that is, supernatural power (to hunt, to run, to make love, to cure).

Medicine men and medicine societies. The medicine man is a visionary who has succeeded in receiving power to cure people. However, visionaries with other extraordinary powers, such as the capacity to find lost things or divine the future, have also been labeled "medicine men." In cultures with more complicated social organizations, medicine men may join together, exchanging experiences and working out a common, secret ideology. An example of this is the Midewiwin, or Great Medicine society, of the Ojibwa, which is organized like a secret order society and has four or eight hierarchical grades.

Ritual Acts. Harmony or spiritual balance is what North American Indians want to achieve in their relations with the supernatural powers. A harmonious balance can be reached through prayers and offerings or through imitative representation of supernatural events.

Prayers and offerings. Prayers range from a few words at meal offerings to detailed ritual prayers, from casual petitions of blessing to deeply emotional cries for help and sustenance. Indeed, Navajo prayer has been characterized by one researcher as "compulsive words," by another as "creative words."

There are many kinds of offerings. A simple form is throwing tobacco or food into the fire or onto the ground at mealtimes. Another example is the placing of tobacco pouches on the ground at the beginning of dangerous passages, such as crossing a lake or walking over a mountain ridge.

When hunters killed game they usually performed rites over the body. True sacrifices were not common, but did occur in the Northeast Woodlands, where white dogs were sacrificed to the powers. In many places the skins of animals (and, later, pieces of cloth as well) served as offerings. There was religious cannibalism in the East, even endocannibalism (the eating of one's family dead) in ancient times. Mutilations of fingers and other cases of self-mutilation as offerings occurred in the Sun Dance of the Lakota and in the closely related Mandan Okipa ceremony.

Ritual representations. Harmonious relations with the supernatural world could be restored by the dramatic imitation of the creation, often in an annual rite, as, for instance, the Sun Dance. In the enactment of mythical drama, performers assumed the roles of supernatural beings, as in the representation of the *kachina,* cloud and rain spirits, and spirits of the dead in the Pueblo Indian Kachina Dances. In the Pawnee sacrifice to Morning Star, a young captive girl was tied to a frame and shot with arrows; she was supposed to represent Evening Star, a personification of the vegetation whose death promotes the growth of plants. Even today a Navajo patient sits in the middle of a sand painting symbolizing the cosmos and its powers while the practitioner pours colored sand over him.

> **Harmonious relations with the supernatural world could be restored by the dramatic imitation of the creation. . . .**

Historical Survey

Most North American religions express the worldview typical of hunters and gatherers. This is natural, since the first immigrants who arrived perhaps forty to sixty thousands years ago were Paleolithic hunters who came by way of the Bering Strait. This origin in northern Asia explains why so much of American Indian religion bears an Arctic or sub-Arctic stamp, and why so many features even in more temperate areas seem to be derived from northern cultures.

The languages of the North American Indians are enormously diverse, and with the exception of the relatively lately arrived Athapascan groups none seem related to known Old World languages. The common factor joining them all is their polysynthetic structure, whereby many sentence elements are included in a single word by compounding and adding prefixes and suffixes. Paul Radin suggested many years ago that there may be a genetic relationship between most of these languages, except those of the Aleut and Inuit, who differ from the mainstream of American aborigines in race, culture, and religion.

The Paleo-Indians of eastern North America were big-game hunters, concentrating on animals like the mammoth, the giant bison, the three-toed horse, and the camel. In all likelihood the inherited concepts of animal ceremonialism and the master of the animals were applied to these animals. Only one big animal—the bear—survived and continued to be the focus of special rites. The ritual around the slaying of the bear, distributed from the Saami (Lapps) of Scandinavia to the Ainu of northern Japan, and, in North America, from the Inuit and Athapascans in the north and west to the Delaware in the east and the Pueblo Indians in the south, seem to be a leftover from these Paleolithic and Mesolithic days.

The old hunting culture slowly disintegrated into a series of more specialized regional cultures about 7000-5000 BCE, and there are reasons to presume that the religious structures changed accordingly.

An exceptional development took place in the south. In the increasingly arid regions of the Great Basin, the Southwest, and parts of California a so-called desert tradition was established, with heavy dependence on wild plants, seeds, and nuts. The corresponding religious system survived in late Great Basin religions, and part of it was also preserved in many Californian Indian religions. In the Southwest, the Basket Making culture, while an example of the desert tradition, also served as a link to horticultural development.

It seems fairly certain that the cultivation of tobacco spread from Mexico into North America with maize, for maize and tobacco cultivation share the same general distribution within the eastern regions of North America. In the Southwest, however, while maize was cultivated, tobacco was gathered wild.

The introduction of maize into North America occurred in two places, the Southwest and the Southeast. From all appearances it was known earlier in the Southwest, where it is recorded from 3000 to 2000 BCE in the wooded highland valleys of New Mexico. Village agriculture was firmly established about the time of the birth of Christ, and was effective after 500 CE.

The most important evidence of the cultural influence from the south is the architectural planning of the towns: irrigation canals, oval ball courts for ritual games, and platform mounds of earth or adobe serving as substructures for temples with hearths and altars.

The Mexican influence on religion can also be seen in the neighboring Anasazi or Pueblo cultures down to our own time. Mesoamerican symbols appear in the bird designs that decorate Hopi pottery.

The maize complex entered the Southeast slightly later than the Southwest, perhaps sometime after 1000 BCE.

A major change took place with the introduction of the so-called Mississippian tradition about 700 CE. Large rectangular and flat-topped mounds of unprecedented size were arranged around rectangular plazas. The mounds served as foundations of temples, whence the name Temple Mound, also used to designate these cultures. Intensive agriculture belonged to this new tradition, which flourished in the lower and middle Mississippi Valley but was particularly anchored in the Southeast.

The agricultural religions rarely reached such an advanced stage of development in eastern North America, but they spread from the Southeastern hearth in different directions. Mississippian traits mingled with older Woodland traits in the Iroquois culture in the north and, after 1000 CE, with Plains hunting religions in the river valleys to the west.

A Regional Survey

The religions of the indigenous peoples in North America have developed on the foundations that have just been described. However, factors other than historical have contributed to the differentiation in religious profiles that occurs in every region.

As Clark Wissler and others have noted, the geographic regions and the cultural areas correspond closely to each other. Since geographical and ecological factors have influenced religious forms, each region reveals unique features.

Arctic. The barren country around the Arctic coasts is sparsely inhabited by the Inuit and, on the Aleutian Islands, their kinsmen the Aleut. Inuit religion carries all marks of a hunting religion, concentrating on beliefs and rituals related to animals and on shamanism. The hunting rituals are rather intricate, in particular in Alaska where they focus on the whale (whale feasts are also found among the Nootka of the Northwest Coast and the Chukchi and Koriak of Siberia). [*See* Inuit Religion.]

Sub-Arctic. A vast region of the coniferous forests, lakes, and swamps in interior Alaska and Canada, the sub-Arctic is sparsely inhabited by Athapascan-speaking Indians in its western half and Algonquian-speaking Indians in its eastern half. The Athapascans are latecomers from Siberia, arriving perhaps around 9000 BCE; their linguistic affiliations are with the Sino-Tibetan tongues. The Algonquian tribes conserve religious traits that associate them closely with the circumpolar culture.

The region is inhabited by hunting cultures, with inland game, in particular the caribou and the moose, as food resources.

Religion is dominated by hunting ceremonialism and, to a certain extent, by shamanism. Bear ceremonialism is widespread, and hunting taboos are very common. Sweat baths grant their practitioners ritual purity before hunting or important ceremonies. The vision and guardian-spirit quest is fairly common.

Northeast Woodlands. Formerly covered by mixed coniferous and deciduous trees, the Northeast Woodlands held a large population of Algonquian-, Iroquoian-, and Siouan-speaking tribes. In historical and protohistorical times both agriculture and hunting were practiced, particularly by the Iroquoian groups; the Algonquian tribes were hunters with only limited horticulture.

The double economic heritage is to some extent mirrored in the religious pattern. The hunters concentrate on hunting rituals and vision quests, the planters on rituals and beliefs surrounding the crops. The Iroquois, for instance, have a series of calendar rites celebrating the planting, ripening, and harvesting of the "three sisters": maize, squash, and beans.

Southeast Woodlands. In the southern deciduous forests, with their savannas and swamps, the tribes of Muskogean stock, interspersed with Siouan groups and the Iroquoian-speaking Cherokee, kept up a peripheral high culture, the last vestiges of the prehistoric Mississippian culture. The Southeastern Indians were, at least at the beginning of the historical era, predominantly engaged in agriculture, and their sociopolitical organization was adjusted to this fact. Thus, the Creek had a maternal clan system, with clans subordinated to both phratries and moieties. Characteristic of

> ## The main religious ceremony is the maize harvest ceremony, called the Busk.

Creek religion is the emphasis laid on ceremonialism and priestly functions.

The main religious ceremony is the maize harvest ceremony, called the Busk. It is also a New Year ritual, in which old fires are extinguished and a new fire is kindled and people ritually cleanse themselves through washing and the drinking of an emetic.

Prairies and Plains. The tall-grass area between the woodlands in the east and the high Plains in the west is known as the Prairies. The Plains are the short-grass steppe country, too dry for agriculture, that stretches toward the mountains and semideserts in the far West.

The historical cultures were formed during the seventeenth and eighteenth centuries when the acquisition of horses made the wide-open spaces easily accessible to surrounding tribes and white expansion forced woodland Indians to leave their home country for the dry, treeless areas. Algonquian and Siouan tribes immigrated from the east and northeast, Caddoan tribes from the south. Several groups ceased practicing horticulture (the Crow and Cheyenne) and turned into buffalo hunters, but they kept parts of their old social and political organization. In the west, Shoshonean groups held the ground they had traditionally occupied, and groups of Athapascans—for example, the Apache—forced their way to the southern parts of the region.

Whereas the Prairies could be regarded as a periphery of the Eastern Woodlands, the Plains region offers a late cultural and religious complex of its own. The religion is a mixture of derived agricultural ceremonialism and hunters' belief systems. The major New Year ceremony is the Sun Dance,

during which asceticism, dancing, praying, and curing take place. Other forms of ritualism center around tribal and clan bundles, and the sacred ritual known as the Calumet Dance, or Pipe Dance.

Northwest Coast. The broken coastline, high mountains, and deep fjords of the Northwest Coast were the home of the Tlingit, Haida, Tsimshian, and Wakashan tribes and some Coast Salish and Chinookan groups in the south. With their totem poles, their plank houses and canoes, and their headgear reminiscent of East Asian conic hats, these Indians make an un-American impression. The basic substratum seems to be a fishing culture that developed on both sides of the North Pacific and gave rise to both Inuit and Northwest Coast cultures.

The religion is characterized partly by its association with the activities of hunters and fishermen, partly by its secret societies adapted to the complicated social structure. The animal ceremonialism is focused on the sea fauna, and there are many sea spirits in animal forms.

Plateau. The Intermountain area, which includes both the Columbia and the Fraser river drainages, is known as the Plateau; it was inhabited by Salish and Shahaptin tribes that lived on fish and, secondarily, on land animals and roots. In their religion the Plateau Indians stressed the visionary complex and food ceremonies. The vision quests were undertaken at puberty by both sexes. The relation between the guardian spirit and his client was displayed in the Winter Dance, or Spirit Dance, a ceremony, under the supervision of a medicine man, in which the spirit was impersonated.

Great Basin. A dry region of sands and semideserts, the Great Basin was inhabited by Shoshonean (Numic) groups, some of them, like the Gosiute, the most impoverished of North American groups. Seeds, nuts, and rodents provided the principal food. The religious pattern was closely adapted to a lifestyle based on the bare necessities. Hunters had to be blessed by spirits in visions in order to be successful, but there was little elaboration of guardian-spirit beliefs. Medicine men had specialized powers.

California. The central valleys and coastland of California constituted a separate cultural area, known as the California region, densely populated by Penutian, Hokan, and Numic groups. These natives, living in a mild climate, dedicated themselves to collecting, hunting, and fishing. In this diversified culture area religious expressions were most varied. North-central California is known for its lofty concept of a supreme being and for its initiation of youths into religious societies. In the southern part of the area, initiation ceremonies were accompanied by the drinking of drugs prepared from jimsonweed and by various symbolic acts referring to death and rebirth. In some places there were great commemorative ceremonies for the dead.

The Southwest. A magnificent desert country with some oases, particularly along the Rio Grande, the Southwest was populated by hunting and farming groups of Piman and Yuman descent, by former hunters like the Athapascan Apache and Navajo—who did not arrive here until about 1500 CE—and by the Pueblo peoples, intensive agriculturists mostly belonging to the Tanoan and Keresan linguistic families.

Religion penetrates all aspects of Pueblo life. A rich set of ceremonies that mark the divisions of the year are conducted by different religious societies. Their overall aim is to create harmony with the powers of rain and fertility, symbolized by the ancestors, the rain and cloud spirits, and the Sun. Each society has its priesthood, its attendants, its sacred bundles, and its ceremonial cycle. There are also medicine societies for the curing of diseases—the inspired, visionary medicine man has no place in this collectivistic, priestly culture.

BIBLIOGRAPHY

For discussion of sources and research the reader is referred to my work *The Study of American Indian Religions* (Chico, Calif., 1983) and Harold W. Turner's *North America,* vol. 2 of his *Bibliography of New Religious Movements in Primal Societies* (Boston, 1978).

On the topic of North American Indian religions, several surveys and introductions are available. In chronological order there is first Werner Müller's "Die Religionen der Indianervölker Nordamerikas," in *Die Religionen des alten Amerika,* edited by Walter Krickeberg (Stuttgart, 1961), a thoughtful presentation of native religious structures. Ruth M. Underhill's *Red Man's Religion* (Chicago, 1965) describes religious beliefs and practices in their cultural interaction. Two later syntheses are my *The Religions of the American Indians* (Berkeley, 1979), which concentrates on religious ideas in historical perspectives, and Sam D. Gill's *Native American Religions* (Belmont, Calif., 1982), which emphasizes some major features of Indian religious life. A detailed, provocative investigation of the religions east of the Rocky Mountains will be found in Werner Müller's *Die Religionen der Waldlandindianer Nordamerikas* (Berlin, 1956).

A number of scholars in the field have issued collections of their articles on North American native religions. Here could be mentioned Müller's *Neue Sonne—Neues Licht,* edited by Rolf Gehlen and Bernd Wolf (Berlin, 1981), a representative selection of this author's most engaging articles; my *Belief and Worship in Native North America* (Syracuse, N. Y., 1981), which among other things discusses belief patterns, ecology, and religious change; and Joseph Epes Brown's *The Spiritual Legacy of the American Indian* (New York, 1982), a book that beautifully outlines the deeper meaning of Indian philosophy and ceremonialism. An older publication in the same genre is the philosopher Hartley Burr Alexander's posthumous work, *The World's Rim: Great Mysteries of the North American Indians* (Lincoln, Nebr., 1953). Anthologies by several authors are *Seeing with a Native Eye,* edited by Walter Holden Capps (New York, 1976), and *Teachings from the American Earth,* edited by Dennis Tedlock and Barbara Tedlock (New York, 1975). The former contains articles by scholars of religion; the latter, articles by anthropologists.

Among general comparative works, a classic in the field is Ruth Fulton Benedict's *The Concept of the Guardian Spirit in North America* (Menasha, Wis., 1923). Shamanism in North America is the object of a study by Marcelle Bouteiller, *Chamanisme et guérison magique* (Paris, 1950). The patterns of soul and spirit beliefs are analyzed in my work *Conceptions of the Soul among North American Indians* (Stockholm, 1953). The corpus of American Indian myths and legends is carefully annotated in *Tales of the North American Indians,* edited by Stith Thompson (Cambridge, Mass., 1929). My study *The North American Indian Orpheus Tradition* (Stockholm, 1957) is an extensive treatment of the Orpheus myth and its religious prerequisites. One mythological character, the culture hero and trickster, is the subject of Arie van Deursen's detailed research work *Der Heilbringer* (Groningen, 1931). Secret societies and men's societies are penetratingly discussed in Wolfgang Lindig's *Geheimbünde und Männerbünde der Prärie- und der Waldlandindianer Nordamerikas* (Wiesbaden, 1970). Among comparative works on rituals and ritualism three interesting studies are Ruth Underhill's well-known *Ceremonial Patterns in the Greater Southwest* (New York, 1948), John Witthoft's illuminating *Green Corn Ceremonialism in the Eastern Woodlands* (Ann Arbor, 1949), and William N. Fenton's detailed ethnohistorical study *The Iroquois Eagle Dance: An Offshoot of the Calumet Dance* (Washington, D. C., 1953).

An Indian's own view of native American religions in their relations to Christianity and to whites is presented, somewhat polemically, in Vine Deloria, Jr.'s *God Is Red* (New York, 1973).

ÅKE HULTKRANTZ

NYAYA

The Nyaya school of Indian philosophy was founded by Gotama (sixth century BCE?) and has existed without any real discontinuity from pre-Christian times to the present. While the Vaisesika, its sister philosophical school, concentrated more on issues and problems of ontology, philosophers of the Nyaya school took greater interest in questions and themes of epistemology. The Nyaya accepts four distinct sources of knowledge: *pratyaksa* (perception), *anumana* (inference), *upamana* (analogy), and *sabda* (testimony). Perception is knowledge arising from contact between a sense organ and an object and must be certain and non-erroneous. It is of two kinds, relational and nonrelational. From a different point of view perception is classified into two other kinds, perceptions that arise from ordinary contact between a sense organ and an object and those that arise from a nonordinary contact. The latter includes perceptions by a yogin of all things past, present, and future.

Inference is of more than one kind, but the most common kind is typified by the case where the knowledge that the probandum (*sadhya*) belongs to the subject (*paksa*) arises from the knowledge that the connector (*hetu*) belongs to the subject and that the connector is pervaded (*vyapta*) by the probandum. Analogy is identification of the denotation (*vachya*) of a word whose denotation is not already known, based on information received that the thing denoted is similar to another known thing. Testimony is an authoritative statement. Here knowledge (*prama*) is characterized by truth *(yatharthya)* and is a species of ascertainment *(nischaya)*. An ascertainment that something *s* is qualified by something *p* is said to be true if *p* actually belongs to *s*. This account of truth is due to Gangesa (twelfth century CE), reputedly the founder of Navya Nyaya (New Nyaya), who introduced and sharpened a number of concepts and techniques for logical, linguistic, and semantic studies.

Unlike many other schools of Indian philosophy, the Nyaya has accepted and sought to prove the existence of Isvara (God), who is regarded as a soul having eternal knowledge encompassing everything (and also eternal desire and motive). Although Isvara is not a creator of the universe (which is beginningless and includes many other eternal entities besides him), he nevertheless functions as an efficient cause in the production of any effect. Every living being, human or nonhuman, has a soul that is eternal and ubiquitous. The ultimate goal of life is liberation *(moksa)* of the soul from worldly bondage. In keeping with the general Indian tradition, the Nyaya upholds the theory of *karman*, maintaining that one's actions influence later events in one's history and that one must reap the consequences of one's actions, either in the present life or in a subsequent life. Liberation is not regarded as a state of bliss, but is conceived negatively as a state of absolute cessation of all suffering. Knowledge of truth (which is held to be embodied in the Nyaya philosophy) is an indispensable means for attainment of liberation. Such knowledge dispels false beliefs, such as the belief that the soul is identical with the body, and eventually through successive stages this knowledge leads to the arrest of the beginningless cycle of birth and rebirth and thus to the ultimate state of unending freedom from all suffering.

BIBLIOGRAPHY

The best book on Nyaya-Vaisesika philosophy is Gopinath Bhattacharya's edition and translation of the *Tarkasamgraha-dipika* (Calcutta, 1976). For readers who are less technically minded, but still want a comprehensive and precise account, the best book is *Indian Metaphysics and Epistemology: The Tradition of the Nyaya-Vaisesika up to Gangesa*, edited by Karl H. Potter (Princeton, 1977), volume 2 of *The Encyclopedia of Indian Philosophies*. The general reader may profitably consult Mysore Hiriyanna's *Essentials of Indian Philosophy* (London, 1949).

KISOR K. CHAKRABARTI

OCCULTISM

The term *occultism* is properly used to refer to a large number of practices, ranging from astrology and alchemy to occult medicine and magic, that are based in one way or another on the homo-analogical principle, or doctrine of correspondences. According to this principle, things that are similar exert an influence on one another by virtue of the correspondences that unite all visible things to one another and to invisible realities as well. The practices based upon this essentially esoteric principle express a living and dynamic reality, a web of cosmic and divine analogies and homologies that become manifest through the operation of the active imagination.

Occultism, as a group of practices, is to be distinguished from esotericism, which is, roughly speaking, the theory that makes these practices possible. We may therefore accept the following distinction proposed by the sociologist Edward A. Tirya-kian:

> By "occult," I understand intentional practices, techniques, or procedures which (a) draw upon hidden and concealed forces in nature or the cosmos that cannot be measured or recognized by the instruments of modern science, and (b) which have as their desired or intended consequences empirical results, such as obtaining knowledge of the empirical course of events or altering them from what they would have been without this intervention.... By "esoteric" I refer to those religiophilosophic belief systems which underlie occult techniques and practices; that is, it refers to the more comprehensive cognitive mappings of nature and the cosmos, the epistomological and ontological reflections of ultimate reality, which mappings constitute a stock of knowledge that provides the ground for occult procedures. By way of analogy, esoteric knowledge is to occult practices as the corpus of theoretical physics is to engineering applications.
>
> (Tiryakian, 1972, pp. 498-499)

Occultism before Occultism. The first instances of something that can be called occultism appear in the early centuries of the Christian era, combined with esoteric and theosophical teachings. Theurgy can be found in the teachings of the fourth-century *Chaldean Oracles;* in the Alexandrine Hermetism of the *Corpus Hermeticum,* from the second and third centuries; and in the third-century Neoplatonism of Porphyry, that of Iamblichus in the fourth century, and that of Proclus in the fifth. Alchemy flourished at Alexandria until the seventh century. [*See* Alchemy.] Even Stoicism had an occult aspect, insofar as it emphasized the necessity of knowing the concrete universe by harmoniously combining science and technique, and adopted an open attitude toward popular religion, especially toward all kinds of divination.

In the thirteenth century, Albertus Magnus wrote a treatise on minerals and referred to both alchemy and magic. Thomas Aquinas himself believed in alchemy and attributed its efficacy to the occult forces of the heavenly bodies. Roger Bacon, too, took a close interest in the occult, since for him "experimental science" meant a secret and traditional science; that is, a concrete science, but one inseparable from holy scripture.

In the Renaissance, we begin to hear of the "occult sciences," an expression that is common in the works of Blaise de Vigenère. Central to these sciences is the symbolic image of the two books: the "book of nature" and the "book of revelation," or, in other words, the universe and the Bible.

Occultism and Modernity. The industrial revolution naturally gave rise to an increasingly marked interest in the "miracles" of science. It promoted the invasion of daily life by utilitarian and socioeconomic preoccupations of all kinds. Along with smoking factory chimneys came both the literature of the fantastic and the new phenomenon of spiritualism. These two possess a common characteristic: each takes the real world in its most concrete form as its point of departure, and then postulates the existence of another, supernatural world, separated from the first by a more or less impermeable partition. It is interesting that occultism in its modern form—that of the nineteenth century—appeared at the same time as fantastic literature and spiritualism.

The taste for magic in all its forms finds a psychological outlet in fantasy films (Roman Polansky's *Rosemary's Baby* is one example among hundreds). Occultist sects have proliferated as rapidly as the films, offering themselves as a similar sort of spectacle for the world at large. Such cults are in a sense the manifestations of the desire to explore the unknown.

Occultism, like esotericism in general, has been the object of a great number of scholarly works, especially in the last generation or two. Today, historians such as Alain Mercier, Guy Michaud, and Jean Richer are throwing new light on the relationships between occultism, literature, and philosophy. Thus, like the popularization of occultism by the media, current erudition too contributes a new facet to the subject: its sociocultural dimension.

BIBLIOGRAPHY

A comprehensive survey of the history of occultism from antiquity to the seventeenth century is provided by Lynn Thorndike in *A History of Magic and Experimental Science,* 8 vols. (New York, 1923-1958). For the Renaissance and later periods, see the bibliographical notes for "Esotericism" and "Hermetism." See also Will-Erich Peuckert's *Gabalia: Ein Versuch zur Geschichte der Magia naturalis im* 16. bis 18. Jahrhundert (Berlin, 1967). A full account of recent writing on the Renaissance and a valuable summary of the major tendencies is found in Wayne Shuhmaker's study *The Occult Sciences in the Renaissance* (Berkeley, 1972). On modern occultism and literature, see Alain Mercier's *Les sources ésotériques et occultes de la poésie symboliste,* 1870-1914, 2 vols. (Paris, 1969-1974). On esotericism and occultism in general, see Robert Amadou's *L'occultisme: Esquisse d'un monde vivant* (Paris, 1950). An illuminating sociological account is provided by Edward A. Tiryakian in his article "Toward the Sociology of Esoteric Culture," *American Journal of Sociology* 78 (November 1972): 491-512. Valuable, insightful approaches to the study of the occult can be found in *The Occult in America: New Historical Perspectives,* edited by Howard Kerr and Charles L. Crow (Chicago, 1983), and in Mircea Eliade's *Occultism, Witchcraft, and Cultural Fashions: Essays in Comparative Religions* (Chicago, 1976).

ANTOINE FAIVRE
Translated from French by Kristine Anderson

OCEANIC RELIGIONS

An Overview

The Pacific islands are dispersed over the widest expanse of sea in our world. They comprise semicontinents (such as New Guinea), strings of large mountainous islands (along the curve of the Melanesian chain), and groups of more isolated larger and smaller islands further east, with many of those islets or islands arranged as atolls, or, more rarely, organized into whole archipelagoes such as the Tuamotus and the Carolines. The classic view is that one should distinguish between three large cultural areas: Micronesia in the northwest, Melanesia in the south, and Polynesia in the east. The reality is that while Micronesia is somewhat distinct in that its cultures display the influences of constant Asian contacts, Melanesia and Polynesia are artificial concepts created by

Western powers. The Europeans settled and christianized Tahiti and eastern Polynesia, using the peoples of these islands to contact and control islands further west—as soldiers, Christian teachers, and petty civil servants who were accorded a status slightly higher than that of the so-called "cruel" Melanesian savages. In Polynesia the islanders resisted incursion settlement, and land transfers to Europeans were often obtained through marriages with the locals: these practices provided support for the queer conception that the islanders of the east were closer to their colonizers in terms of civilization, while those of the west were uncouth and dangerous.

Hereditary chieftainships exist, and chiefs are often surrounded by such formal behavior and etiquette that Westerners gave the title "king" to all such titular heads of social groups without checking to see if these "kings" in fact had kingdoms.

All things alive (social, biological, or material) are accounted for either by the actions of the dead (who hold, collectively or individually, enormous power), or by those of the so-called culture heroes of the cosmogonic or semicosmogonic myths. Religious concepts are usually a means of justifying the way in which a society and culture function, and thus support institutionalization and not change. Autochthonous Oceanic beliefs are responsible, even now, for stability in the societies of this area. Experience over recent decades has shown that aboriginal religious beliefs and concepts are far from dead in the Pacific islands, although the whole area is nominally Christian. Prayers are still offered to ancestors and to symbolic beings whose invisible presence is still felt.

In the nineteenth century, after research in Vanuatu (formerly New Hebrides) and the Solomon Islands, R. H. Codrington (1891) came to understand that there were two kinds of gods, those who had lived as human beings and those who had never been human. Maurice Leenhardt (1947) later confirmed that most of the so-called gods were believed to have once been human. The transformation from human to god began with their deaths. Their corpses, called *bao* (which is also the word for "human being," and is often translated as "spirit"), were from then on named in prayers.

Death and the Dead. The link between men and women and their dead is one of the keys for the understanding of Pacific islanders' religious behavior. The dead are believed to be living in another form of existence in some faraway place, under the sea or under the earth, where they have arrived after following a set path and after one of that group of gods who have never been human ordains their life in the afterworld. The path that the dead follow can be mapped: it may go from one island to another—so that the dead require, as in Vanuatu, the ghost of a canoe, which transports those from Malekula across to Ambrim—or it may follow, as between Lifou and Uvéa in the Loyalty Islands, some subterranean route where maiden temptresses will try to stop the dead person so as to devour him. When the path follows a known route to the sea or to the underworld, its protection is the responsibility of a given lineage, which will derive prestige and authority from such a privilege.

The geographical location of the dead is not always a precise one. Melanesian groups recognize different openings of the afterworld on each of the coasts of their principal islands, and these places are marked by names such as *Devil's Rock* or *Devil's Point.*

Corpses receive all sorts of ritual treatment. They may be laid in a grave or buried fetuslike in the ground, with the head sticking out; the head might later be removed for use in special mortuary rites. Mortuary techniques vary from place to place, and change according to fashion. For instance, the custom of eating parts of the dead body, particularly the brain, and of rubbing newborn children with the dead person's fat, was introduced into the Fore area of the New Guinea Highlands only four generations ago.

Very generally, a special rite often occurs ten days after death, during which the deceased person is reverentially asked to depart his lifelong place of residence and to go to join the other dead in their abode, where he now belongs.

Some of the dead are unwelcome at all times, since they can only be harmful; these include, for instance, the dead of another group, who should not be allowed to stray out of their own territory, and, especially, the ghosts of those who were left without normal burials, or of women who died in childbirth and who do not have their children—or carved representations of their babies—with them (New Caledonia).

When one looks at the texts of prayers, chants, or invocations *(such as the Maori karakia),* one always finds, directly or indirectly, the mention of the dead and their powers, or of superior beings. These beings often cannot be named because the *tapu* against saying their exact, or secret, name is too high for it to be uttered without great danger. The hints or roundabout ways that vernacular texts have of addressing the dead or superior beings are often incomprehensible even to those Europeans knowledgeable in Oceanic languages.

Status, Power, and Ancestry. Localization is the key to understanding how status and power systems function in the islands. Part of the status, independence, and prestige of each lineage involves its ownership, or mastery, of a portion of the universe. It is the function of each lineage to act in ways prescribed by the tradition so as to make the universe run smoothly and so that each group will benefit from the ritual actions of all of the others and will reciprocate through its own. Such mythical endowment, however, always includes both positive and negative powers.

Belief in a god of creation who is different from the culture heroes is common throughout Oceania. He seems to be a *deus otiosus,* however, who no longer deals with human problems.

Initiation. One of the most imprecise terms used in accounts of Oceanic religions is *initiation.* It is well known that, throughout the Pacific islands, male teenagers are taken away from their mothers and kept in seclusion for a number of weeks. During this time they are given special food (without relish, and roasted instead of boiled). Their mettle is tested through painful experiences such as the incision of the foreskin—rarely complete circumcision—or scarification or tattooing. Older men teach the teenagers the traditional songs. The young men are taught the verse and the prose of their vernacular traditions, and are informed as to what can

> When one looks at the texts of prayers, chants, or invocations one always finds, directly or indirectly, the mention of the dead and their powers, or of superior beings.

and cannot be said in the presence of women and children. They perform plays and dances dealing with the mythical beings associated with their local groups, and they learn to play musical instruments. Some Highland New Guinea youths start at this point to learn the technique of swallowing a rattan vine through the nose as a means of purifying the body of all bad influences. Generally youths are either beaten with stinging nettles or threatened with death if they talk to anybody about what they have been through.

These rites actually represent only a partial initiation, one that highlights the cohesion of allied groups and that teaches what can be told in front of a number of people of different lineages. Another important part of the traditional lore will be taught, over the years, by the mother, the father, the father's sister, the mother's brother, and the grandparents. The key to the lessons of this multiple process of tuition lies in the numerous place names that must be remembered. Each myth, each piece of oral lore is rooted somewhere, belonging not only to a specific social group but also to a specific point in space where—and only where—its story can be told.

Some of the powers and ritual formulas might be kept by the father until his deathbed, because he has waited to transmit them until almost his last breath.

Divination and Witchcraft. Individuals pray directly to their own dead relatives for help, but on occasions when they are in need of greater help—to obtain the favors of a woman, for example, or to discover who has been sending sickness to a next of kin—they go to see a clairvoyant, who may be a man but is often a woman.

Witchcraft is used for retribution when full-scale war is not in order. However, many ideas about witchcraft as a negative institution are entirely wrong. The "sorcerer" is always an ambiguous person. He will heal as well as cause sickness or death, and he protects his own lineage against dangers.

Material Aspects of Religion. In most instances, the contact between man and god was secretive, without any witness. Only in the cases of widely established institutions such as meetings between numerous interlocked lineages do we find large-scale public ceremonies, which had always as much a political as a religious meaning.

One important question regarding the material aspects of Oceanic religions involves the role of monumental stone or wooden carvings, or of the small carved pieces depicting the human figure and popularly called *tiki.* The first missionaries thought that these human carvings represented gods and were cult objects, dismissing them all as "heathen" idols. The only role of the monumental carvings was, however, architectural: they represented a way of conceiving space that took the sky into account. The smaller carved pieces were kept at home, carefully wrapped in rolls of tapa cloth and not taken out much more than once a year. The key to understanding these objects comes from Fiji, where small carvings of human figures, in wood or whale-tooth ivory, circulated in pre-European days.

A single principle is general throughout this area: a carved figure can be the repository of a godly presence, when it must, but the god has no obligation whatsoever to choose this particular abode. Monumental carvings are rarely thought of as possible repositories for godly presences, with the exception of the Hawaiian wickerwork figures covered with parrot feathers that were carried to battle as representations of Ku-ka'ili-moku, the god of war.

BIBLIOGRAPHY

The earliest account of this area was William Ellis's *Polynesian Researches during a Residence of Nearly Eight Years in the Society and the Sandwich Islands,* 4 vols. (London, 1831), which gives us a view of what could be known at the time, translated into European words by an open-minded missionary. R. H. Codrington's *The Melanesians: Studies in Their Anthropology and Folklore* (1891; reprint, New Haven, 1957) provided a much better introduction to the Pacific, as he tried to analyze vernacular concepts. Codrington was followed on the English side by other brother missionaries such as Charles Elliot Fox, with *The Threshold of the Pacific: An Account of the Social Organization, Magic and Religion of the People of San Cristoval in the Solomon Islands* (London, 1924), and on the French side by Maurice Leenhardt, with *Do Kamo,* translated by B. M. Gulati (Chicago, 1979). Leenhardt was the first French author to publish a whole corpus of Oceanic vernacular texts. Following in his footsteps, I have studied Oceanic societies in Vanuatu and New Caledonia: *Un siècle et demi de contacts culturels à Tanna, Nouvelles-Hébrides* (Paris, 1956) shows a ni-Vanuatu society living with and talking to its dead; *Mythologie du masque en Nouvelle-Calédonie* (Paris, 1966) shows the way gods with local associations represented the different names of the lord of the land of the dead and were represented by the mask. Bronislaw Malinowski, in *Magic, Science and Religion* (New York, 1948), tried to express a functionalist, but balanced, view of Oceanic religions, but the best author remains Raymond Firth.

Among Firth's numerous studies of Tikopia (a small Polynesian island far out off the eastern Solomon Islands, which remained entirely traditional until recently), two works are of particular importance: *The Work of the Gods in Tikopia,* 2d ed. (London, 1967), and *History and Traditions of Tikopia* (Wellington, 1961). Adolph Brewster's *The Hill Tribes of Fiji* (London, 1922) did bring to light interesting material, which still needs to be checked against vernacular corpora. Elsdon Best's *Maori Religion and Mythology, Being an Account of the Cosmogony, Anthropogeny, Religious Beliefs and Rites, Magic and Folk Lore of the Maori Folk of New Zealand* (Wellington, 1924) is still our best source on Maori religion. Two rival anthropologists whose fieldwork in New Guinea predates World War II have introduced us to the complex variations of the New Guinea systems, and their work should be cited here, although there are tens of other authors and titles left aside: Reo F. Fortune's *Manus Religion: An Ethnological Study of the Manus Natives of the Admiralty Islands* (1935; reprint, Lincoln, Nebr., 1965) and Gregory Bateson's *Naven: A Survey of the Problems Suggested by a Composite Picture of a New Guinea Tribe,* 2d ed. (Stanford, Calif., 1958). Nevertheless, the best recent book on Oceanic religion has been written by Maori authors and edited by Michael King: *Tihe mauri ora: Aspects of Maori Tanga* (Wellington, 1978) reanalyzes such Maori concepts as *mana, tapu,* and *mauri,* and for the first time puts them in the context of Maori society.

JEAN GUIART

Missionary Movements

While nearly all Pacific islanders today are Christians—except for the natives of inland New Guinea, where Christianity has made only partial inroads—one can still find here and there a village, family, or individual happily clinging to a "heathen" religion. Although Christianity is deeply entrenched in the Pacific, it is lived even now as only one of the several planes on which the islanders simultaneously exist without any sense of contradiction.

The Christianity of the Pacific islanders has a predominantly mythical quality. Even today, many islanders believe the biblical narrative is merely a story and that Jerusalem and other holy places have only a symbolic existence.

History of Christian Missions in the Pacific. Both Protestant and Catholic communities exist on most of the Pacific islands (with adherents of the Protestant churches usually being in the majority). The most recent missions have been those of the Seventh-day Adventists, Jehovah's Witnesses, Latter-Day Saints (Mormons), and Baha'is. Of these only the Seventh-day Adventists and the Mormons have had substantial success. In Hawaii, Tahiti, and the Tuamotus, Mormon missionary activity has even given rise to a breakaway church, the Kanito (or Sanito) movement.

Roman Catholic missions have rarely been the first to arrive in any area of Oceania, which explains why Catholics are in the minority in most places.

The history of christianization shows some regularities inasmuch as all of the missionary bodies, Protestant and

Catholic, have used the same technique: mass conversions were precipitated through the conversion of members of the local aristocracy. Rival chiefs adopted different faiths, and there have been full-fledged Christian religious wars in Samoa, Tonga, Wallis, Fiji, and the Loyalty Islands, especially between Catholic and Protestant converts. The Seventh-day Adventists, to the discomfort of the well-established churches, have thrived by converting groups whose politics do not agree with those of the majority church in any given area. The Assemblies of God, the Jehovah's Witnesses, and to a lesser extent the Mormons, have recently made gains in similar fashions.

Christian missions in the Pacific frequently became involved in local disputes over land and social status. Missionaries were often used by one party to thwart the ambitions of another.

In order to consolidate the effects of sometimes hurried conversions, missionaries established programs to educate native youths as future leaders in the movement to spread the Christian faith.

BIBLIOGRAPHY

An early work, by Methodist missionaries Thomas Williams and James Calvert, is *Fiji and the Fijians, the Islands and Inhabitants: Mission History,* 2 vols., edited by G. S. Rowe (London, 1858). Another, by London Missionary Society missionary Archibald Wright Murray, is *Wonders of the Western Isles, Being a Narrative of the Commencement and Progress of Mission Work in Western Polynesia* (London, 1874). E. S. Armstrong's *The History of the Melanesian Mission* (London, 1900) tells the remarkable story of the Anglican Mission in northern Vanuatu and the Solomon Islands. Alexander Don's *Peter Milne, 1834-1924: Missionary to Nguna, New Hebrides, 1870 to 1924, from the Presbyterian Church of New Zealand* (Dunedin, 1927) describes the life of one of those very opinionated Presbyterian missionaries to Vanuatu. Eric Ramsden's Marsden and the Missions, *Prelude to Waitangi* (Sydney, 1936) describes the situation of the New Zealand missions prior to the British annexation of that country. A description of the French Protestant work in New Caledonia can be found in Maurice Leenhardt's *La grande terre: Mission de Nouvelle-Calédonie,* rev. & enl. ed. (Paris, 1922). James Clifford studied the brilliant figure of Maurice Leenhardt in his *Person and Myth: Maurice Leenhardt in the Melanesian World* (Berkeley, 1982).

The efforts of the Roman Catholic mission are best detailed in two little-known volumes: *Conférence sur la loi naturelle, volume 5 of Comptes-rendus des conférences ecclésiastiques du vicariat apostolique de la Nouvelle-Calédonie* (Saint-Louis, New Caledonia, 1905), and Victor Douceré's *La mission catholique aux Nouvelles-Hébrides* (Lyons, 1934).

A more general analysis of the results of earlier efforts to convert the Pacific islanders to Christianity is given in my essay "The Millenarian Aspect of Conversion to Christianity in the South Pacific," in *Millennial Dreams in Action* (The Hague, 1962), pp. 122-138.

JEAN GUIART

History of Study

Oceania is conventionally defined in terms of the three major cultural divisions of the Pacific islanders: Polynesia, Micronesia, and Melanesia. The best nineteenth-century sources are largely the works of administrators and other longterm residents, such as Abraham Fornander's *An Account of the Polynesian Race* (1878-1885; reprint, Rutland, Vt., 1969) and George Grey's *Polynesian Mythology and Ancient Traditional History of the Maori as Told by Their Priests and Chiefs* (1855; reprint, New York, 1970).

Despite this growing wealth of information about Oceanic cultures, the systematic study of Oceanic religions remained largely undeveloped before the advent of anthropology in the latter part of the nineteenth century.

A major goal of early anthropology was the creation of typological schemes to lay the basis for the reconstruction of evolutionary stages from savagery to civilization. One consequence of this essentially typological orientation was that apparent commonalities tended to be stressed at the expense of the distinctive features of particular religious systems, fostering a spurious sense of uniformity.

Anthropology from the mid-1970s forward witnessed a growing interest in processes of symbolization, and this development, coupled with the impact of previous work, prompted a number of detailed studies placing religion once again at the heart of anthropology in the Pacific.

Two of the most significant recent trends in the study of Oceanic religions are the incorporation of a view that accords to symbols an active role in transforming experience and a concern to come to grips with the dynamism of religious life. These orientations grow out of general anthropological preoccupations and at the same time reflect the necessity of coming to terms with history. Pacific pagans are now few and far between, and the last century has seen the emergence of Christianity as the dominant religious form in Oceania.

DAN W. JORGENSEN

OLMEC RELIGION

The Olmec occupied southern Mexico's tropical lowlands in southeastern Veracruz and western Tabasco between 1200 and 600 BCE. Like other Mesoamerican peoples of the period, they lived in villages, practiced agriculture based on maize cultivation, and produced pottery. However, they differed from their contemporaries in their more complex social and political institutions, in the construction of large centers with temples and other specialized buildings, and in their development of a distinctive style of art expressed in monumental stone sculptures and exquisite small portable objects.

Study of Olmec Religion. Archaeological, historical, and ethnographic information provides the basic data for reconstructing ancient Mesoamerican religions. Archaeological data on prehistoric cultures must be interpreted in light of information about later, better documented cultures or studies of modern groups on approximately similar levels of development. For the Olmec, the archaeological data consist of sculptures, architecture, and artifacts.

Studies of Olmec religion rely heavily on iconographic analyses of the Olmec art style as expressed in over two hundred known stone monuments and hundreds of small portable objects. These studies have particularly emphasized the identification of deities while neglecting ritual and many other topics.

> **For the Olmec, the archaeological data consist of sculptures, architecture, and artifacts.**

Characteristics of Olmec Religion. The fundamental pattern of Olmec belief seems to have centered on the worship of numerous high gods or supernatural forces that controlled the universe and sanctioned the human sociopolitical structure.

The pantheon. The nature of the Olmec pantheon is a topic of some controversy. Some scholars argue that Olmec supernaturals were not gods in the Western sense of recognizably distinct personalities, while others accept the existence of deities but disagree on their identifications. The beings portrayed are frequently "creatures that are biologically impossible," things that "exist in the mind of man, not in the world of nature" (Joralemon, 1976, p. 33).

Religious specialists. Some scholars have called Olmec society a theocracy, but there is no evidence to warrant such a conclusion, although priests were undoubtedly members of the elite. It is not clear whether Olmec shamans were also elite priests, but it does seem likely.

Ritual. One of the least understood aspects of Olmec religion is ritual. We know something about the architectural settings in which rituals were held and about the nonperishable objects that we assume were used in ritual contexts, but Olmec dances, prayers, chants, feasts, and other behaviors are lost forever.

Archaeological excavations have revealed numerous unusual architectural features that were either used in ritual or had some specific sacred meaning. Some authorities have suggested that the numerous colossal heads found at several Olmec sites depict ballplayers wearing helmets, but the most recent consensus is that these remarkable basalt human portraits represent individual Olmec rulers. The ball game played by later Mesoamericans did have secular aspects, but it is generally regarded as a primarily religious observance in which players represented supernaturals.

Museums and private collections contain hundreds of exotic objects to which we can reasonably assign a ritual function even though we do not know their specific uses.

BIBLIOGRAPHY

Anthony F. C. Wallace's *Religion: An Anthropological View* (New York, 1966) provides the framework in which this article has been written. The most recent and thorough synthesis of Olmec culture is Jacques Soustelle's *The Olmecs: The Oldest Civilization in Mexico,* translated by Helen R. Lane (Garden City, N. Y., 1984). Older but still useful books include Michael D. Coe's *America's First Civilization: Discovering the Olmec* (New York, 1968), and Ignacio Bernal's *The Olmec World,* translated by Doris Heyden and Fernando Horcasitas (Berkeley, 1969). Michael D. Coe and my *In the Land of the Olmec,* 2 vols. (Austin, 1980) is the basic source of information on San Lorenzo. The basic data on La Venta are scattered through many works; the two most important are Philip Drucker's *La Venta, Tabasco: A Study of Olmec Ceramics and Art* (Washington, D. C., 1952), and Philip Drucker, Robert F. Heizer, and Robert J. Squier's *Excavations at La Venta, Tabasco, 1955* (Washington, D. C., 1959). Karl W. Luckert's *Olmec Religion: A Key to Middle America and Beyond* (Norman, Okla., 1976) is the only book devoted exclusively to this topic, but its unorthodox methodology and assumptions lead to conclusions not supported by the data. Peter D. Joralemon's *A Study of Olmec Iconography* (Washington, D. C., 1971) contains his initial attempt to delineate the Olmec pantheon. *Origins of Religious Art and Iconography in Preclassic Mesoamerica,* edited by H. B. Nicholson (Los Angeles, 1976) contains Joralemon's definitive study of the Olmec Dragon and the Olmec Bird Monster in addition to many other useful articles. Elizabeth P. Benson's *The Olmecs and Their Neighbors: Essays in Memory of Matthew W. Stirling* (Washington, D. C., 1981) contains articles dealing with many aspects of Olmec culture, and a useful bibliography.

RICHARD A. DIEHL

ORACLES

The word *oracle* is derived from the Latin word *oraculum,* which referred both to a divine pronouncement or response concerning the future or the unknown as well as to the place where such pronouncements were given. (The Latin verb *orare* means "to speak" or "to request.") In English, *oracle* is also used to designate the human medium through whom such prophetic declarations or oracular sayings are given.

Oracles and Prophecy. In Western civilization the connotations of the word *oracle* (variously rendered in European languages) have been largely determined by traditional perceptions of ancient Greek oracles, particularly the oracle of Apollo at Delphi. The term *prophecy,* on the other hand (from the Greek word *propheteia,* meaning "prophecy" or "oracular response"), has been more closely associated with traditions of divine revelation through human mediums in ancient Israel and early Christianity. Since most oracles in the Greek world were given in response to inquiries, oracles are often regarded as verbal responses by a supernatural being, in contrast to prophecy, which is thought of as unsolicited verbal revelations given through human mediums and often directed toward instigating social change. In actuality, question-and-answer revelatory "séances" were common in ancient Israel, and it was only with the appearance in the eighth century BCE of free prophets such as Amos, Isaiah, and Hosea that unsolicited prophecy became common. Further, the preservation of the prophetic speeches of the classical Israelite prophets in the Hebrew scriptures has served to ensure the dominance of this particular image of Israelite prophets and prophecy. Therefore, modern distinctions between "oracles" and "prophecy" are largely based on the discrete conventions of classical and biblical tradition rather than upon a cross-cultural study of the subject, though the terms themselves are often used and interchanged indiscriminately in modern anthropological studies. [*See* Prophecy.]

Oracles and Divination. Oracles are but one of several types of divination, which is the art or science of interpreting symbols understood as messages from the gods. Such symbols often require the interpretive expertise of a trained specialist and are frequently based on phenomena of an unpredictable or even trivial nature. The more common types of divination in the Greco-Roman world included the casting of lots (sortilege), the flight and behavior of birds (ornithomancy), the behavior of sacrificial animals and the condition of their vital organs (e.g., hepatoscopy, or liver divination), various omens or sounds (cledonomancy), and dreams (oneiromancy). Chinese civilization made elaborate use of divination, partly as an expression of the Confucian belief in fate.

Oracles (or prophecies) themselves are messages from the gods in human language concerning the future or the unknown and are usually received in response to specific inquiries, often through the agency of inspired mediums. Oracles have, in other words, a basic linguistic character not found in other forms of divination. This linguistic character is evident in the sometimes elaborately articulated inquiries made of the deities in either spoken or written form. In addition, oracles themselves exhibit a linguistic character ranging from the symbolized "yes" or "no" response, or "auspicious" or "inauspicious" response, of many lot oracles, to the elaborately crafted replies spoken and/or written by mediums while experiencing possession trance or vision trance, or shortly thereafter. This linguistic character of oracles presupposes an anthropomorphic conception of the supernatural beings concerned.

In actuality, oracles are usually so closely associated with other forms of divination that it is difficult to insist on rigid distinctions.

Types of Oracles. Oracles are usually associated either with a sacred place where they are available in the setting of a public religious institution or with a specially endowed person who acts as a paid functionary or a free-lance practitioner.

Oracular places. In the ancient Mediterranean world certain places were thought to enjoy a special sanctity, particularly caves, springs, elevations, and places struck by lightning (especially oak trees). The emphasis on the oracular powers inherent in particular sites is due to the ancient Greek belief that the primal goddess Gaia ("earth") was the source of oracular inspiration. Each of these oracle shrines required supplicants to fulfill a distinctive set of traditional procedures, and each site had a natural feature connected with its oracular potencies.

In the ancient Mediterranean world three distinctive techniques were used at oracular shrines to secure three kinds of oracles:

Lot oracles. The process of random selection that is the basis of all lot oracles is based on the supposition that the result either expresses the will of the gods or occasions insight into the course of events by providing a clue to an aspect of that interrelated chain of events that constitutes the cosmic harmony.

Incubation oracles. Incubation oracles in the ancient Mediterranean world were revelatory dreams sought in tem-

> **Modern distinctions between "oracles" and "prophecy" are largely based on the discrete conventions of classical and biblical tradition.**

ples after completion of preliminary ritual requirements. Most incubation oracles were sought in connection with healing.

Inspired oracles. In the Greco-Roman world many of the local oracles of Apollo employed a cult functionary who acted as an intermediary of the god and responded to questions with oracular responses pronounced in the god's name. Such mediums experience the cross-cultural phenomenon of an altered state of consciousness.

Oracular persons. Professional diviners and intermediaries often have no permanent relationship to temples or shrines. They may practice their divinatory and oracular arts in their homes, in the marketplace, or in various places of employment such as army posts or governmental offices. These specialists often practice either possession trance or vision trance.

Characteristics of Oracles. The linguistic character of oracles does not necessarily render their meaning unambiguous. While lot oracles in a positive or negative mode and oracles dealing with sacrifice and expiation are usually clearly expressed, those dealing with other matters often require the skill of an interpreter. Outside the temple of Apollo at Delphi, free-lance *exegetai* ("expounders") would interpret the meaning of oracles for a fee. Similarly, interpreters are essential in the consultations of the *tang-chi* and in sessions involving automatic writing. In ancient Greek and Roman literature, the ambiguity of oracles that often find unexpected fulfillment became a common motif. Ambiguity also characterizes the prepared oracular responses in certain lot oracles, which must be phrased so as to apply to many situations. A similar ambiguity is found in the verses and commentaries accompanying each of the sixty-four hexagrams in the *I ching* (Book of Changes).

Function of Oracles. Oracles, like other forms of divination, are means of acquiring critical information regarding the future or the unknown that is unavailable through more conventional or rational channels. The very act of consultation requires that what may have been a vague and amorphous concern or anxiety be articulated in a specific, defined, and delimiting manner.

BIBLIOGRAPHY

The only comparative study of oracles and prophecy in the ancient Mediterranean world (including Greco-Roman, Israelite, early Jewish, and early Christian oracular and prophetic traditions) is my *Prophecy in Early Christianity and the Ancient Mediterranean World* (Grand Rapids, Mich., 1983), which has a lengthy, up-to-date bibliography. Two important general cross-cultural studies of possession are Erika Bourguignon's Religion, *Altered States of Consciousness, and Social Change* (Columbus, Ohio, 1973) and I. M. Lewis's *Ecstatic Religion: An Anthropological Study of Spirit Possession and Shamanism* (Harmondsworth, 1971). Still valuable is the older study by Traugott K. Oesterreich, *Possession, Demoniacal and Other* (New York, 1930).

The best book on the oracle of Delphi is Joseph Fontenrose's *The Delphic Oracle: Its Responses and Operations* (Berkeley, 1978), with a catalog of all known Delphic oracles in English translation classified according to grades of authenticity; it includes an extensive bibliography. The earlier standard work on Delphi, with a complete catalog of oracles in Greek, is H. W. Parke and D. E. W. Wormell's *The Delphic Oracle*, 2 vols. (Oxford, 1956); the more recent book by Fontenrose, however, is far superior.

An important introduction to some non-Apollonian oracles, including a collection in English translation of written oracle questions excavated at Dodona, is H. W. Parke's *The Oracles of Zeus: Dodona, Olympia, Ammon* (Oxford, 1967). Two very readable introductions to Greek oracles are H. W. Parke's *Greek Oracles* (London, 1967) and Robert Flacelière's *Greek Oracles* (London, 1965). An important discussion of the function of orcles in ancient Greek city-states is Martin P. Nilsson's *Cults, Myths, Oracles, and Politics in Ancient Greece* (1951; New York, 1972). An older but still useful comparative study of ancient Mediterranean views of revelation is Edwyn Robert Bevan's *Sibyls and Seers: A Survey of Some Ancient Theories of Revelation and Inspiration* (London, 1928). Though now out of date, the most detailed study of Greek divination, useful for putting oracular divination in proper context, is W. R. Halliday's *Greek Divination: A Study of Its Methods and Principles* (1913; reprint, Chicago, 1967). An English translation of the Greek Magical Papyri, including many procedures for securing oracles, is now available in *The Greek Magical Papyri in Translation,* edited by Hans Dieter Betz (Chicago, 1985).

The most important recent study of the sibylline oracles is John J. Collins's *The Sibylline Oracles of Egyptian Judaism* (Missoula, Mont., 1974). A recent translation of the extant fourteen books of sibylline oracles is available in *The Old Testament Pseudepigrapha,* vol. 1, *Apocalyptic Literature and Testaments,* edited by James H. Charlesworth (Garden City, N. Y., 1983), pp. 317-472.

An older work that is still valuable for its consideration of Israelite and Arab traditions with a wide spectrum of prophetic phenomena including "divinatory prophecy," dreams and visions, ecstasy, and magic is Alfred Guillaume's *Prophecy and Divination among the Hebrews and Other Semites* (London, 1938). A book that includes many texts in English translation but that lacks critical discussion is Violet MacDermot's *The Cult of the Seer in the Ancient Middle East* (London, 1971). More recent is a book that considers Old Testament prophecy in the context of comparative studies of possession phenomena: Robert R. Wilson's *Prophecy and Society in Ancient Israel* (Philadelphia, 1980), which includes an extensive bibliography.

The most important work in English on Chinese religion continues to be the magisterial work by J. J. M. de Groot, *The Religious System of China,* 6 vols. (1892-1910; Taipei, 1967); particularly relevant is part 5 in volume 6, "The Priesthood of Animism," pp. 1187ff. A more up-to-date study is Ch'ing-k`un Yang's *Religion in Chinese Society: A Study of Contemporary Social Functions of Religion and Some of Their Historical Factors* (Berkeley, 1961), where aspects of both ancient and modern divination and oracles are considered. Also useful is David Crockett Graham's *Folk Religion in Southwest China* (Washington, D. C., 1961). An excellent anthropological study of modern trance-possession cults among the Chinese of Singapore is Alan J. A. Elliot's *Chinese Spirit-Medium Cults in Singapore* (London, 1955). The most important study of the oracle bones and shells of the Shang period, with an extensive bibliography, is David N. Keightley's *Sources of Shang History: The Oracle-Bone Inscriptions of Bronze Age China* (Berkeley, 1978). Also useful is a book written by one of the excavators, Tung Tso-pin's *Hsü chia ku nien piao* (Tokyo, 1967).

DAVID E. AUNE

ORAL TRADITION

ORAL TRADITION, which operates in all religious institutions, tends to be viewed by literate Western scholars as a defective mechanism for perpetuating tradition. Theologians, secular historians, and sociologists of religion, sharing a dichotomous view of oral and literate intellectual systems, have contrasted the fixity of belief in an immutable truth found in literate religious traditions with the variety and mutability of knowledge typical of oral traditions relying exclusively on memory.

However, recent research on the institutionalization of oral and written communication in different societies tends to undermine the dichotomy between "oral" and "literate" societies. It becomes increasingly clear that in both religious and secular contexts literary and oral methods of learning and teaching coexist and interact. The relative stability of knowledge in a given society depends in large part upon how these different methods are institutionalized as well as upon the educational goals and concepts of knowledge that accompany them.

In general, it seems that knowledge based on memory is not as ephemeral as previously had been thought, nor is written knowledge immutable in the actual conditions of social practice. Thus comparative research into the ways in which written and spoken words are organized and used in different societies at present tends to complicate the picture of what oral tradition is, and of how it is related to the presumed stability of written traditions. Overly simplistic models are giving way to less elegant, but perhaps richer, comparative views, which also offer a more accurate picture of the varieties of religious experience that are embodied in written and spoken words.

The two great questions underlying most of the scholarship on oral tradition in religion are those of historical continuity and communicative effectiveness. Up to the present, these two issues have tended to be addressed by different scholars using different methods. The issue of historical continuity has been prominent in the Western comparative study of religion since the late eighteenth century, when the survival of preliterate belief systems in modern European settings was first recognized.

Literacy is widely regarded by the literate as a facilitator of analytic reasoning and self-conscious intellection. It is believed to enable one to manipulate series of propositions, to reorder them, compare their implications, and identify inconsistencies that would be obscured if one could only consider them in the serial order and social contexts of their immediate presentations.

In the religious context, the writing down of tenets of belief is held to facilitate the development of orthodoxy and of internally consistent bodies of belief, which in turn may contribute to the centralization of religious institutions and religious power.

A comparative approach to the diverse manifestations of such inherited patterns leads to the question of how these patterns are transmitted and institutionalized. A second major approach to the problem of oral tradition has focused directly on the forms and processes of oral transmission.

Stylistic studies that saw in the synoptic Gospels *(Mark, Matthew, and Luke),* for instance, a series of variants of an original oral tradition of the life of Christ, raised once again the questions concerning the historical reliability of these texts.

In the case of Islam, by contrast, the oral substrate of the tradition was directly taken into account by the earliest Muslim theologians. The word qur'an literally means "reading," and the sacred book of the Qur'an was originally received through reading, despite the self-avowed illiteracy of

the prophet Muhammad. The first revelation came to the Prophet in the form of an angelic injunction, "Read!", to which the Prophet replied, "I cannot read." This altercation ended with the celestial voice dictating, "Read: And it is thy Lord the Most Bountiful / Who teacheth by pen, / Teacheth man that which he knew not." The Prophet, waking from a trance,

> It becomes increasingly clear that in both religious and secular contexts literary and oral methods of learning and teaching coexist and interact.

remembered the words "as if inscribed upon his heart." Thus the authoritativeness of written scripture was established by explicit revelation.

Arguments for the oral origin of parts of the Bible, like similar arguments concerning devotional and secular medieval literature, proceed mainly on stylistic grounds, whereas the reconstruction of the actual process of oral composition remains inferential. In societies where literacy is the skill of a minority, verbal compositions intended for a general audience must be organized to facilitate aural comprehension, whether or not they are composed orally. Furthermore, in societies where literacy is new, the indigenous verbal aesthetic is by definition oral, and early literature might be expected to emulate it to some degree.

Much recent research by folklorists and ethnolinguists favors the view that the meaning and power of sacred language emerges from the actual enactment of words by the living, whether the "texts" that serve as the basis for such enactment are written or oral. The dynamism of such oral enactment can often triumph over the professed fixity of a scriptural tradition and become a source of diversity within the tradition. It is in the consciousness and acts (verbal and physical) of living believers that religions manifest their meaning, and in that sense, living tradition is always oral tradition.

[*See also* Folk Religion.]

BIBLIOGRAPHY

The departure point for a great deal of work on continuity and analytic functions in oral and literary traditions is the work of the British anthropologist Jack Goody, particularly his *Literacy in Traditional Societies* (Cambridge, 1968) and *The Domestication of the Savage* Mind (Cambridge, 1977). The best review and critique of the literature on literacy and its effect on knowledge systems is Brian V. Street's *Literacy in Theory and Practice* (Cambridge, 1984). An introduction to the work of Georges Dumézil is C. Scott Littleton's *The New Comparative Mythology,* 3d ed. (Berkeley, 1980), which includes references to Dumézil's writings, including recent translations. Victor Turner's ideas on ritual are developed in *The Forest of*

Symbols (Ithaca, N. Y., 1967) and many other later articles and books. The best starting place for an understanding of Claude Lévi-Strauss's anthropological theories is his Structural Anthropology, 2 vols. (New York, 1963-1976). The key general formulation of the Parry-Lord oral-formulaic theory is Albert B. Lord's The Singer of Tales (Cambridge, Mass., 1960). John Miles Foley's Oral-Formulaic Theory and Research (New York, 1984), which offers a superb annotated bibliography, provides an encyclopedic review of the scholarship pertinent to the theory in both religious and secular traditions. Two excellent collections of essays on, respectively, the relations between oral and written traditions and the relations between oral and written religious language are Spoken and Written Language, edited by Deborah Tannen (Norwood, N. J., 1982), and Language in Religious Practice, edited by William J. Samarin (Rowley, Mass., 1976).

M. M. Pickthall's The Meaning of the Glorious Qur'an (1930; New York, 1980) provides a reliable translation of the Qur'an, together with a historical introduction, from which the quoted traditions about the Prophet's first revelation are taken. Annemarie Schimmel's Mystical Dimensions of Islam (Chapel Hill, N. C., 1975) and As through a Veil: Mystical Poetry in Islam (New York, 1982) contain much information on folk and orthodox Islam and vocal aspects of Sufi mystical practice. Information on ta`awidh is from my own ethnographic experience in Afghanistan. There is a burgeoning literature in folklore, linguistics, and anthropology journals on language in religion, from which the short ethnographic examples at the end of this essay are a sampling. Much relevant work has appeared in the Journal of American Folklore: Steven M. Kane's "Ritual Possession in a Southern Appalachian Religious Sect," vol. 87 (October-December 1974), pp. 293-302; Stanley Brandes's "The Posadas in Tzintzuntzan: Structure and Sentiment in a Mexican Christmas Festival," vol. 96 (July-September, 1983), pp. 259-280; Elaine J. Lawless's "Shouting for the Lord: The Power of Women's Speech in Pentecostal Religious Service," vol. 96 (October-December 1983), pp. 434-459; Terry E. Miller's "Voices from the Past: The Singing at Otter Creek Church," vol. 88 (July-September 1975), pp. 266-282; and William F. Hanks's "Sanctification, Structure and Experience in a Yucatec Ritual Event," vol. 97 (April-June 1984), pp. 131-166. Other studies focusing on particular traditions include Wallace L. Chafe's "Integration and Involvement in Speaking, Writing, and Oral Literature," and Shirley Brice Heath's "Protean Shapes in Literacy Events: Ever-shifting Oral and Literate Traditions," both in Tannen's Spoken and Written Language, cited above. References to Gregory Bateson's ideas are further developed in Tannen's introduction to that volume.

MARGARET A. MILLS

ORDINATION

ORDINATION here refers to the practice in many religions of publicly designating and setting apart certain persons for special religious service and leadership, granting them religious authority and power to be exercised for the welfare of the community. The way each religious community practices ordination depends on that community's worldview and religious beliefs. For example, in traditions that emphasize a direct relationship with the divine being or beings, the ordained person may be thought of primarily as a mediator or priest. Communities that consider human beings to be especially troubled by evil spirits or witchcraft look to shamans or exorcists to counteract the evil influences. In religions that present a goal of inner enlightenment and purified life, the ordained person will be a monk or nun leading the way toward this goal of enlightenment. And religious communities that place much emphasis on living in accordance with the divinely given law set certain persons apart as religious scholars and judges.

Each religion sets up qualifications that candidates must meet before they can be ordained. Sometimes ordination is based on heredity. In many religions the candidate must be male, although some roles are specified for women; other traditions allow both male and female candidates to be ordained. While aptness for the religious role is always a requirement, in some traditions the person must already have demonstrated his suitability for that role before being chosen, while in others it is assumed that the office will be learned through a period of training. Every religion presupposes some kind of divine call or inner motivation on the part of the candidate.

An authority and power not possessed by the ordinary people of the community are conferred on the candidate through ordination. The source of that authority and power may be the divine powers, the consent of the community, or those who have already been ordained. Upon ordination, the person receives a new religious title. The English term priest can be used in many religious traditions to designate those who have been ordained or set apart, but a variety of other terms is sometimes preferred, such as shaman, medicine man, monk or nun, rabbi, bishop, presbyter, deacon, minister, or imam.

Ordination in Ancient and Traditional Societies. Numerous ancient or traditional societies have beliefs and practices according to which they set apart certain persons, endowing them with special authority and power for the performance of essential religious services, such as serving the gods and spirits, sacrificing, communicating with spiritual powers, warding off evil powers, healing, and the like. Among the great diversity of roles dealing with spiritual power, some basic types are priests, shamans, and medicine men.

The term priest generally designates a person ordained with authority to practice the cult of certain divinities or spirits. The priesthood may be hereditary, or priests may be called or chosen by the divinity. After selection or calling, the aspiring priest undergoes a period of purification and training.

Shamans (male and female) are commonly thought to be elected directly by tutelary spirits, who in a visionary experience initiate the future shaman.

Zoroastrian and Hindu Ordination. Among Indo-Europeans the priesthood was an important class, as evidenced in the priesthoods of the ancient Romans, Greeks, Celts, Persians, Aryans, and others. The present-day Zoroastrians (Parsis in India) and the Hindus have continued this emphasis on a class of priests ordained to perform the important purifications, sacrifices, and other ceremonies for the maintenance of a healthy relationship between humans and the eternal divine order of the universe.

The religion of the ancient Persians, as transformed by the prophet Zarathushtra (Zoroaster) into Zoroastrianism, is practiced today in Iran and India.

In Hinduism, brahman priests have always played an important role. In ancient Vedic times they were thought to uphold the whole social order through their mediation, by virtue of their mastery of the sacred rituals, sacrifices, and

> Although traditionally any male Christian could aspire to become a priest or minister, in recent years many Christian denominations have begun to ordain women clergy also.

formulas. Today, especially for people of the high castes, it is important to have a brahman household priest *(purohita)* perform the traditional rituals and chant the Vedic texts properly so that the cosmic order will continue with its health and goodness for each according to his or her place in the total order. Some brahmans prepare to be priests of temple worship, where rituals center on the ceremonial treatment of the images of the gods—although many functions of temple worship can be performed by the people without priestly help.

Ordination among Jains and Buddhists. Two religions that grew up in India along with Hinduism are Jainism and Buddhism, and in these religious traditions spiritual power is understood to reside especially in the monastic communities, that is, among those monks and nuns who have left ordinary secular life to pursue spiritual perfection through ascetic practices. The monks and nuns are primarily devoted to their own spiritual perfection; yet because they possess great power they can perform religious service for the laypeople, such as chanting scripture, performing funeral rites, and teaching.

Ordination of Priests in Taoism and Shinto. Priests in Chinese religious Taoism function as ritual and liturgical specialists, but they also act as exorcists and healers, expelling and pacifying demons. Taoist priests *(tao-shih)* are often designated on the basis of heredity. Since the ritual of Taoism is esoteric, that is, not directly to be understood and witnessed by the laypeople, usually the aspiring priest will join the entourage of a recognized master who knows the important formulas and hidden aspects of ritual Taoism.

The main function of Japanese Shinto priests *(shinshoku)* of all ranks is to worship and serve the *kami,* the spiritual beings associated with the powerful forces of nature and the ancestors. The priests maintain good relations with the *kami* for the divine protection and welfare of the human community.

Priests often come from families with long and strong traditions of Shinto worship. In ancient times a few priestly families supplied most of the priests, although in modern times the priesthood is open to candidates from nonpriestly families also.

Ordination in Judaism. The religion of Judaism after the Babylonian exile and especially after the destruction of the Temple in the Roman period moved away from a sacrificial temple cult and, consequently, the most important religious leaders became those ordained as rabbis. They functioned as judges, scholars, teachers, and expounders of the Torah and Talmud; in modern times, rabbis also function as worship leaders, officiants at marriage and burial ceremonies, and spiritual heads of local communities of Jews.

Some groups have traditional schools *(yeshivot)* that give the traditional *semikhah* ordination with its emphasis on training in the Talmud and Jewish codes. Other groups have seminaries that see preparation for the rabbinate as including not only knowledge of the Talmud and codes but also professional training to function as a synagogue rabbi within modern society.

Ordination in Christianity. Christians hold that Jesus Christ is the great high priest, the real mediator between God and humans, and that all Christians as members of his body participate in his priesthood. While some Christians conclude that there is no need for specially ordained leaders, most Christian groups have recognized the need for ordained priests or ministers to lead the Christian community.

Although traditionally any male Christian could aspire to become a priest or minister, in recent years many Christian denominations have begun to ordain women clergy also, while some denominations, such as the Roman Catholic church, continue to ordain male candidates only. Candidates are given a course of study and training in a theological seminary before being certified and presented to the church denominational authorities for ordination.

Those set apart for special service are given many different titles: priest, minister, pastor, presbyter, bishop, and deacon are the most common among those designating the clergy.

Appointing Spiritual Leaders in Islam. In Islam, every Muslim can perform the religious rites, so there is no class or profession of ordained clergy. Yet there are religious leaders who are recognized for their learning and their ability to lead communities of Muslims in prayer, study, and living according to the teaching of the Qur'an and Muslim law. These religious leaders belong to the learned group of orthodox Muslim scholars and jurists known as the `ulama'` (`alim` in the singular). They have studied at recognized schools of Islamic learning and have secured appointments as mosque functionaries, teachers, jurisconsults, or judges.

The religious leader who is contracted by a local community of Muslims to lead the community in public worship, preach at the Friday mosque prayer, teach, and give advice on religious matters on the local level is called the imam, belonging to the broad group of `ulama'`.

BIBLIOGRAPHY

A classic cross-cultural study of the role of priests in many religions is E. O. James's *The Nature and Function of Priesthood: A Comparative and Anthropological Study* (London, 1955), although he does not single out ordination as a special topic. For practices of setting apart religious leaders in traditional societies, Adolphus P. Elkin's *Aboriginal Men of High Degree,* 2d ed. (New York, 1977), is a thorough study of medicine men among the Aborigines of Australia; and Mircea Eliade's *Shamanism: Archaic Techniques of Ecstasy,* rev. & enl. ed. (New York, 1964), surveys the initiation of shamans in various cultures. The training and initiation of African priests and medicine men and women is discussed in Geoffrey Parrinder's *West African Religion: A Study of the Beliefs and Practices of Akan, Ewe, Yoruba, Ibo, and Kindred Peoples,* 2d ed. (London, 1961), and E. E. Evans-Pritchard's *Witchcraft, Oracles, and Magic among the Azande,* 2d ed. (Oxford, 1950). Melford E. Spiro's *Burmese Supernaturalism,* exp. ed. (Philadelphia, 1978), presents a thorough study of female shamans who become "*nat* wives" in Burmese popular religion.

Rustom Masani's *Zoroastrianism: The Religion of the Good Life* (1938; New York, 1968) includes information about initiation of Parsi priests in his discussion of the religion of the Parsis. The training and social role of household brahman priests in India today is the subject of K. Subramaniam's *Brahmin Priest of Tamil Nadu* (New York, 1974). Along with a presentation of the Jain religion, Padmanabh S. Jaini's *The Jaina Path of Purification* (Berkeley, 1979) provides a close look at the ordination and path of the Jain mendicant. Important studies of the training and role of Theravada Buddhist monks and nuns are found in Melford E. Spiro's *Buddhism and Society: A Great Tradition and Its Burmese Vicissitudes,* 2d ed. (Berkeley, 1982), and Jane Bunnag's *Buddhist Monk, Buddhist Layman: A Study of Urban Monastic Organization in Central Thailand* (Cambridge, 1973). An important study of Mahayana Buddhism in modern China, including information and photographs of monastic ordinations, is Holmes Welch's *The Practice of Chinese Buddhism, 1900-1950* (Cambridge, Mass., 1967). The role of Taoist priests and their ordination rankings is discussed by Michael Saso in his *Taoism and the Rite of Cosmic Renewal* (Seattle, 1972); and much important information on Shinto priests and practices is contained in Jean Herbert's *Shinto: At the Fountainhead of Japan* (London, 1967).

A thorough study of the history of Jewish ordination is Julius Newman's *Semikhah: A Study of Its Origin, History, and Function in Rabbinic Literature* (Manchester, 1950); and several studies on the training of modern American rabbis are included in *The Rabbi and the Synagogue,* vol. 1 of *Understanding American Judaism,* edited by Jacob Neusner (New York, 1975). Of many studies of the Christian ordained ministry, *The Ministry in Historical Perspectives,* edited by Richard Niebuhr and Daniel D. Williams (New York, 1956), provides a good overview. Bernardin Goebel's *Seven Steps to the Altar: Preparation for Priesthood* (New York, 1963) presents a dis-

cussion of what the rites and ceremonies of a Roman Catholic priest's ordination mean to him; and a convenient discussion of Christian ordination together with a sample ordination service is given in *The Ordination of Bishops, Priests, and Deacons,* "Prayer Book Studies," no. 20 (New York, 1970). *Scholars, Saints, and Sufis: Muslim Religious Institutions in the Middle East since 1500,* edited by Nikki R. Keddie (Berkeley, 1972), contains many excellent studies of the religious scholars and saints who form the recognized religious leadership of Islam.

THEODORE M. LUDWIG

ORTHODOX JUDAISM

ORTHODOX JUDAISM is the branch of Judaism that adheres most strictly to the tenets of the religious law *(halakhah)*. Its forebears may be identified in the eighteenth century, by which time the *qehillah,* the Jewish communal organization in each locality, had lost much of its authority in central and western Europe and its prestige in eastern Europe. This, in turn, undermined religious authority, which had heretofore relied not only on the faith of each Jew but also on communal consensus and the formal authority and prestige of communal leaders. The breakdown of the traditional community, coupled with the hope and expectation of political emancipation, encouraged new interpretations of Jewish life and new conceptions of appropriate relationships between Jews and non-Jews. These began to emerge by the end of the eighteenth century in central and western Europe and somewhat later in eastern Europe. Orthodoxy was born as the ideological and organizational response to these new conceptions.

The major tenets of Orthodoxy, like those of traditional Judaism, include the dogma that the Torah was "given from Heaven," that the *halakhah* derives directly or indirectly from an act of revelation, and that Jews are obligated to live in accordance with the *halakhah* as interpreted by rabbinic authority. But unlike traditional Judaism, Orthodoxy is conscious of the spiritual and cultural challenges of the modern world and especially of rival formulations of the meaning and consequences of being Jewish. Orthodoxy, in all its various manifestations and expressions, has never recognized any alternative conception of Judaism as legitimate. But it is aware of itself as a party, generally a minority party, within the Jewish world.

Orthodoxy arose in eastern Europe at the end of the nineteenth century, primarily in response to secular interpretations of Jewish life rather than in opposition to religious reform. The most important centers of Orthodoxy today are in Israel and the United States.

Hungarian Orthodoxy. The ideological and programmatic outlines of Hungarian Orthodoxy were formulated by Rabbi

Mosheh Sofer (1762-1839), better known as the Hatam Sofer, the title of his seven-volume *responsa* to halakhic questions. This earliest variety of Orthodoxy is best described by the term *neotraditionalism* because it rejects any attempt at change and adaptation of the tradition. According to the Hatam Sofer, "all that is new is forbidden by the Torah"; the phrase is a play on the words of an injunction prohibiting consumption of "new" grain from each year's harvest until a portion is offered in the Temple in Jerusalem. Unlike some of his followers, the Hatam Sofer did not oppose all forms of secular education. A knowledge of some secular subjects, for example, is helpful in resolving certain halakhic problems. But in characteristically neotraditional fashion, he legitimated secular education in utilitarian terms, not as an end in itself.

The Hatam Sofer favored immigration to the Land of Israel. Many who favored immigration in those days were reacting to the reformers' rejection of nationalist elements in Judaism. The Hatam Sofer's espousal of an early form of Jewish nationalism and his projection of the importance of the Land of Israel in the Jewish tradition may also have been related to his negative attitude toward political emancipation. He feared its threat to religious authority.

The distinctive instrument of Hungarian Orthodoxy in furthering its neotraditional objectives was the independent communal organization. In 1868 the Hungarian government convened a General Jewish Congress in order to define the basis for the autonomous organization of the Jewish community. The majority of the delegates were sympathetic to religious reform (Neologs), and most of the Orthodox delegates withdrew from the Congress. In 1870 the Hungarian parliament permitted the Orthodox to organize themselves in separate communal frameworks, which might coexist in the same locality with a Neolog community or a Status Quo community (the latter was composed of those who refused to join either the Orthodox or the Neolog community).

Hungarian Orthodoxy included both Hasidic and non-Hasidic elements. Hasidism, which originated in the eighteenth century, was bitterly opposed by the traditional religious elite, who feared that its folkishness, pietism, and ambivalence toward the central importance of Talmudic study undermined the tradition itself. Orthodoxy might have been born in opposition to Hasidism if not for leaders like the Hatam Sofer who sought a *modus vivendi,* recognizing that Hasidic leaders were no less antagonistic to basic changes in tradition than were the traditional religious elite. In fact, by the end of the century, the centers of Hasidic influence in the smaller Jewish communities remained least compromising in their attitude toward modernity.

German Orthodoxy. The year 1850 marks the emergence of German Orthodoxy, with the establishment of the Israelitische Religionsgesellschaft in Frankfurt am Main, a congregation led by Samson Raphael Hirsch from 1851 until his death. But the distinctive ideological formulation of German Orthodoxy (often known as Neo-Orthodoxy) dates, at least in embryo, from the publication of Hirsch's *Nineteen Letters on Judaism* in 1836. The publication a few years later of an Orthodox weekly by Ya`aqov Ettlinger (1798-1871) is also of significance.

Hirsch was the foremost proponent of the idea that Torah-true Judaism (to borrow a popular phrase of German Orthodoxy) was compatible with modern culture and political emancipation. Hirsch envisaged a divine order revealed in nature in which Jews could and should participate. But the divine order was also revealed in the Torah, many of whose commands were specific to Jews. The effect of Hirsch's conception, though not his intent, was the compartmentalization of life for the Orthodox Jew. Modern culture, patriotism, civil law—all become legitimate spheres for Jewish involvement since they were perceived as falling outside the realm proscribed by *halakhah.*

Reform Judaism, as a self-conscious movement in Jewish life, began in Germany with the establishment of the Hamburg temple in 1818. In the first few decades of the century it seemed that Reform conceptions of Judaism would replace those of traditional Judaism in Germany. What Hirsch never forgot was that the attraction of reform was an outgrowth of Jewish desire for emancipation and acceptance, that traditional Judaism appeared to be an obstacle to this goal, and that unless it could be reformulated as compatible with emancipation and modern culture, it had no future in Germany.

Orthodoxy in Eastern Europe. The vast majority of eastern European Jews continued to live in accordance with the religious tradition throughout the nineteenth century,

> Hirsch was the foremost proponent of the idea that Torah-true Judaism was compatible with modern culture and political emancipation.

although the institutions of traditional Judaism were severely undermined. Government law had destroyed many of the traditional privileges and responsibilities of the Jewish community.

Orthodoxy in Israel. Most Orthodox Jews today reside in Israel or the United States. Religiously observant Jews make up 15 to 20 percent of the Jewish population of Israel. The neotraditionalists, once quite marginal to Israeli society, play an increasingly important role. The most colorful and controversial group within their ranks is the successor to the old yishuv, the `Edah Haredit (Community of the Pious), consisting of a few thousand families with thousands of sympathizers located primarily in Jerusalem and Benei Be-raq (on the outskirts of Tel Aviv). These are the most intransigent of the neotraditionalists. They relate to the state of Israel with varying degrees of hostility. They refuse to participate in its elections, the more extreme refuse to bear Israeli identification cards or utilize the state's services (their schools, for example, refuse government support), and the most extreme seek the imposition of Arab rule.

The religious Zionists are in a different category. They make up roughly 10 percent of the Jewish population but are in some sense the symbol of contemporary Israel. Israel's political culture, particularly since the 1970s, focuses on the Jewish people, the Jewish tradition, and the Land of Israel as objects of ultimate value. Symbols of traditional religion, though not traditional theology, pervade Israeli life. Religious Zionists are viewed by many of the nonreligious as most committed to and most comfortable with these values and symbols.

> **The American-born Orthodox Jew, regardless of the home in which he was raised, tends to be punctilious in religious observance.**

The political elite, in particular, has been strongly influenced by the religious Zionist. In no other society do Orthodox Jews, religious Zionists in particular, feel quite so much at home. They are separated from the non-Orthodox population by their distinctive cultural and educational institutions (in the advanced religious Zionist *yeshivot,* students are required to fulfill their military obligations but generally do so in selected units) and their own friendship groups.

But most religious Zionists not only feel that they fully participate as equal members of the society but also sense a wholeness to their lives that they find missing outside of Israel. Nevertheless, they, too, confront the tension between tradition and modernity.

The state of Israel provides basic religious services such as religious schools, supervision over the *kashrut* of foods, religious courts, an established rabbinate with responsibility for marriage and divorce of Jews, ritual baths, and subsidies for synagogue construction and rabbis' salaries. The religious political parties act as intermediaries in the provision of welfare and educational services. Hence, the role of the synagogues proliferate in Israel, there is probably no country in the world where they play a less important role in the life of the Orthodox Jew.

Orthodoxy in the United States. American Orthodoxy bears the mark of two waves of immigrants and a native generation that combines characteristics of each. Many of the eastern European immigrants who came to the United States during the great wave of Jewish immigration between 1881 and 1924 were traditionalists. In the confrontation with American culture and the challenge of finding a livelihood, they abandoned many traditional patterns of religious observance. The dominant Orthodox strategy that emerged in the United States was adaptationism. In fact, in the first few decades of the century it appeared as though the difference between American Orthodox and Conservative Judaism was really the degree or pace of adaptation. The institutions and ideology of American Orthodoxy were severely challenged by neotraditionalist immigrants who arrived just prior to and immediately following World War II. They established their own *yeshivot,* Hasidic *rebeyim* among them reestablished their courts of followers, and they expressed disdain for the modern Orthodox rabbi. He was likely to be a graduate of Yeshiva University, the major institution for the training of Orthodox rabbis in the United States, where rabbinical students are required to have earned a college degree. The neotraditionalists were zealous and very supportive of their own institutions. In addition, they clustered in a few neighborhoods of the largest cities. Their concentration and discipline provided their leaders with political influence, which, in the heydays of the welfare programs of the 1960s and 1970s, was translated into various forms of government assistance.

The neotraditionalist challenge to modern Orthodoxy has had a decided impact on the native generation raised in modern Orthodox homes, and the American environment has left its mark on the generation raised in neotraditionalist homes. The American-born Orthodox Jew, regardless of the home in which he was raised, tends to be punctilious in religious observance, more so than his parents, and hostile to what he considers deviant forms of Judaism (i. e., Conservative or Reform). But he is sympathetic to many aspects of contemporary culture and accepting of secular education, if only for purposes of economic advancement. Finally, there is a general willingness among most American Orthodox Jews to work with the non-Orthodox on behalf of general Jewish interests, those of Israel in particular.

Orthodox Judaism Today. The dominant trend in Orthodoxy throughout the world, since the end of World War II, has been increased religious zealotry, punctiliousness in religious observance, and, with some exceptions, less explicit accommodation to modern values and contemporary culture. This is, at least in part, a result of the direction in which modern values and culture have moved. Increased permissiveness; challenges to authority, order, and tradition in general; and affirmation of self are inimical to all historical religions. But Orthodoxy has become far more skilled, after a century of experience, in developing institutions—such as schools, synagogues, political organizations, a press, and summer camps—to mute the threats of secularism and modernity. In some respects this means that Orthodoxy is more at ease with the world and tolerates certain forms of accommodation (advanced secular education is the outstanding example) that many Orthodox circles denounced in the past. But it also means an increased self-confidence and an absence of fear on the part of Orthodoxy to challenge and reject some of the basic behavioral and ideological assumptions upon which most of modern culture rests.

BIBLIOGRAPHY

Hebrew items are included only where English sources are inadequate and/or the Hebrew source is of major importance.

Hayim Halevy Donin's *To Be a Jew* (New York, 1972) is a practical guide to what it means to be an Orthodox Jew.

There is very little scholarly material in any language on most aspects of the social and religious history of Orthodox Judaism. The best material has been written recently; much is available only in the form of articles or doctoral dissertations.

On the background to Orthodoxy, see the last five chapters in Jacob Katz's *Tradition and Crisis: Jewish Society at the End of the Middle Ages* (New York, 1961) and *Out of the Ghetto: The Social Background of Jewish Emancipation* (Cambridge, Mass., 1973), particularly chapter 9, "Conservatives in a Quandary."

There is no general history of Orthodox Judaism. An outline of the topic is found in two articles by Moshe Samet, "Orthodox Jewry in Modern Times," parts 1 and 2, *Mahalakhim* (in Hebrew), nos. 1 and 3 (March 1969 and March 1970). Much can be learned from the two volumes of uneven biographical chapters edited by Leo Jung entitled *Jewish Leaders,* 1750-1940 (New York, 1953) and *Guardians of Our Heritage,* 1724-1953 (New York, 1958).

The best history of Hungarian Jewry covering the nineteenth and twentieth centuries and devoting considerable attention to Orthodoxy is Nathaniel Katzburg's "History of Hungarian Jewry" (in Hebrew), a lengthy introduction and bibliography to *Pinqas Qehillot Hungariyah* (Jerusalem, 1975). His article "The Jewish Congress of Hungary, 1868-1869," in *Hungarian Jewish Studies,* vol. 2, edited by Randolph Braham (New York, 1969), is the most significant study of a crucial aspect of the topic. The Hatam Sofer is the subject of Jacob Katz's major essay, "Contributions toward a Biography of R. Moses Sofer" (in Hebrew), in *Studies in Mysticism and Religion Presented to Gershom G. Scholem on His Seventieth Birthday, by Pupils, Colleagues and Friends,* edited by E. E. Urbach et al. (Jerusalem, 1967).

The English-language material on German Orthodoxy is more plentiful. Robert Liberles's *Between Community and Separation: The Resurgence of Orthodoxy in Frankfort,* 1838-1877 (Westport, Conn., 1985) treats Hirsch and his community in detail. *Judaism Eternal: Selected Essays from the Writings of Rabbi Samson Raphael Hirsch,* vol. 2, translated from the German by I. Grunfeld (London, 1956), is probably the best place to start in reading Hirsch himself. On understanding some other leaders of German Orthodoxy, see David Ellenson, "The Role of Reform in Selected German-Jewish Orthodox Responsa: A Sociological Analysis," *Hebrew Union College Annual* (Cincinnati, 1982).

For a selection from Isaac Breuer, considered the most profound thinker of twentieth-century German Orthodoxy, see his *Concepts of Judaism,* edited by Jacob S. Levinger (Jerusalem, 1974).

There is no history of eastern European Orthodoxy, Emanuel Etkes's *R. Yisra'el Salanter ve-re'shitah shel tenu`at ha-musar* (Jerusalem, 1982) is an important source for understanding the Musar movement and the world of eastern European yeshivot. Eliyahu E. Dessler's *Strive for Truth* (New York, 1978), edited and translated by Aryeh Carmell, is an excellent example of Musar thought. *The Teachings of Hasidism,* edited by Joseph Dan (New York, 1983), provides some flavor of Hasidic literature.

On Zionism and Orthodox Judaism, see Ben Halpern's *The Idea of the Jewish State,* 2d ed. (Cambridge, Mass., 1969), pp. 65-95. On mainstream religious Zionism, see *Religious Zionism: An Anthology,* edited by Yosef Tirosh (Jerusalem, 1975).

The best study of the old yishuv and its confrontation with modern Zionism is Menachem Friedman's *Society and Religion: The Non-Zionist Orthodox in Eretz-Israel,* 1918-1936 (Jerusalem, 1977; in Hebrew with English summary). An expression of the extreme neo-traditionalist position is I. I. Domb's *The Transformation: The Case of the Neturei Karta* (London, 1958). On Rav Kook, see Avraham Yitshaq Kook's *The Lights of Penitence, The Moral Principles, Lights of Holiness, Essays, Letters, and Poems,* translated by Ben Zion Bokser (New York, 1978).

Charles S. Liebman and Eliezer Don-Yehiya's *Civil Religion in Israel: Judaism and Political Culture in the Jewish State* (Berkeley, Calif., 1983) reviews the role of traditional Judaism in Israel and devotes a chapter to the variety of Orthodox responses to Israel's political culture.

On American Orthodoxy, Charles S. Liebman's "Orthodoxy in American Jewish Life," *American Jewish Year Book* 66 (1965): 21-97, is the most extensive survey. An adaptation of Rabbi Soloveitchik's lectures is Abraham Besdin's *Reflections of the Rav* (Jerusalem, 1979), but Soloveitchik's work "The Lonely Man of Faith," *Tradition* 7 (Summer 1965): 5-67, is a better example of his speculative effort. Norman Lamm's *Faith and Doubt: Studies in Traditional Jewish Thought* (New York, 1971) illustrates the approach of a leading American Orthodox rabbi to problems of contemporary concern.

The halakhic literature remains the heart of the Orthodox enterprise. This literature is virtually closed to the nonspecialist, but the regular feature "Survey of Recent Halakhic Responses," appearing in each issue of *Tradition: A Journal of Orthodox Jewish Thought* (New York, 1958-), provides the nonspecialist with a good sense of that world. At a more academic level, see *The Jewish Law Annual* (Leiden, 1978-).

CHARLES S. LIEBMAN

OSIRIS

OSIRIS, the ancient Egyptian god of the dead, whose myth was one of the best known and whose cult was one of the most widespread in pharaonic Egypt. The mythology of Osiris is not preserved completely from an early date, but allusions to it from the earliest extant religious texts indicate that the essentials of the story are as related by Plutarch in *On Isis and Osiris.*

As the oldest son of Geb ("earth"), Osiris became ruler of the land, but he was tricked and slain by his jealous brother, Seth. According to the Greek version of the story, Typhon (Seth) had a beautiful coffin made to Osiris' exact measurements and, with seventy-two conspirators at a banquet, promised it to the one who would fit it. Each guest tried it for size, and of course Osiris was the one to fit exactly. Immediately Seth and the conspirators nailed the lid shut, sealed the coffin in lead, and threw it into the Nile. The coffin was eventually borne across the sea to Byblos, where Isis, who had been continually searching for her husband, finally located it. After some adventures of her own, she returned the body to Egypt, where Seth discovered it, cut it into pieces, and scattered them throughout the country. Isis, however, found all the pieces (except the penis, which she replicated), reconstituted the body, and, before embalming it to give Osiris eternal life, revivified it, coupled with it, and thus conceived Horus. According to the principal version of the story cited by Plutarch, Isis had already given birth to her son, but according to the Egyptian *Hymn to Osiris,* she conceived him by the revivified corpse of her husband. Although Seth challenged the legitimacy of Isis' son, the gods decided in favor of Horus. The *Contendings of Horus and Seth* is preserved on a late New Kingdom papyrus, which indicates that Re, the chief god, favored Seth, but all the other great gods supported the cause of Horus. In the actual contest, Horus proved himself the more clever god. Horus avenged and succeeded his father without completely destroying Seth, toward whom Isis showed pity.

The popularity of the cult of Osiris is explained in part by the recurring cycle of kingship, with each dead king becoming Osiris and being succeeded by his son, Horus. The cult was also important because of its emphasis on the resurrection of the god and a blessed afterlife.

There were numerous cult centers of Osiris; this is explained mythically either by the burial places of the fourteen (or sixteen) parts of his body or by Isis' attempt to conceal the real burial place from Seth. Busiris was the town of his birth, and Abydos was the necropolis generally believed to have been the place of his burial. It was at Abydos that the greatest number of shrines and stelae were set up in honor of the god and to seek blessings from him. A common scene in the funeral rites depicted on nobles' tombs in the New Kingdom commemorated a pilgrimage with the mummy by boat to Abydos.

BIBLIOGRAPHY

Griffiths, J. Gwyn. *The Origins of Osiris and His Cult.* Rev. & enl. ed. Studies in the History of Religions, vol. 40, Leiden, 1980.

Otto, Eberhard. *Osiris und Amun: Kult und heilige Stätten.* Munich, 1966. Translated by Kate B. Griffiths as *Ancient Egyptian Art: The Cult of Osiris and Amon* (New York, 1967).

LEONARD H. LESKO

PALEOLITHIC RELIGION

The term *Paleolithic* was coined over a hundred years ago to distinguish the simple stone tools discovered in deep gravel pits or caves of the diluvial (or antediluvian) period from the polished stone tools of a later age, the Neolithic. Nowadays the term *Paleolithic* is understood in its strict sense, as the cultural equivalent of the geologic and climatological period known as the Ice Age in which polished stones, pottery, and agriculture were still unknown.

Sources and Their Interpretation. Our knowledge of the Paleolithic period depends mainly on a functional interpretation of material remains, that is, a reconstruction of their use and cultural context in the life of prehistoric human beings. Since the situation in the prehistoric, and especially the Paleolithic, period is to be compared with that of present-day "primitive" societies rather than that of more "developed" ones, we must pay close attention to conditions and modes of behavior examined in the studies of so-called primitive peoples.

Only indirectly and in special circumstances do archaeological finds yield a religious meaning. Although religion is primarily a spiritual phenomenon, it nonetheless uses a wide range of material accessories: artifacts and places that have a cultic and ceremonial significance, images and symbols, sacrificial and votive offerings. In many cases religion makes use of art; to a certain extent inferences about religious conceptions can also be drawn from burial customs.

Our understanding of Paleolithic religion is essentially based on objects whose form and attributes themselves indicate religious or magical use or whose manner of deposition (burial, for example) or other contextual peculiarities suggests such a use, as well as on works of art whose content or situation reflects religious or magical meaning.

The Middle Paleolithic. Neanderthal skeletons often exhibit severe injuries, but for the most part we are not able to say with certainty whether they resulted from fights and battles. Some of the head injuries had healed; others were evidently fatal, and the hipbone of a man from a site on Mount Carmel (Israel) apparently has been pierced by some lancelike object. Evidence of illnesses is also observable in other finds, especially that of an elderly Neanderthal at Shanidar (Iraq) who was probably blind from childhood and

whose right forearm had been amputated. He had survived a number of illnesses and injuries, something possible only if he enjoyed the protection and care of a community. In any case, this instance, as well as others, indicates that Neanderthals were by no means the crude savages they are sometimes made out to be but lived in a kind of community in which not only the law of the jungle and economic utility carried weight.

Burials also provide evidence of the same situation. The dead are typically found with their legs slightly flexed, usually in elongated pits; in some Near Eastern finds, however, the dead are in a tightly crouched position, as though they had been forced down into narrow holes.

Noteworthy, however, is the little cemetery at La Ferrassie (France) where three fine stone artifacts, suited for adults, were found in the grave of three children, including a newborn or stillborn infant. Tools of the same kind were also found with adults, and some sites have yielded pits containing animal bones and artifacts.

We find clear signs that Neanderthals took care of their fellow human beings. The burial gifts really leave no reasonable doubt that the dead were thought to continue to live in some manner. This belief explains why objects were buried along with the dead, to be used in the future; even children were provided with objects that they certainly could not have used during their lifetime. What particular shape these general ideas took we cannot say. We can at least say, however, that the Neanderthals had an understanding of death and had somehow come to grips with it.

In the burial site at Regourdou near Montignac (France), the skull and some other bones of a brown bear were found under a large block of stone. There are also reports of finds, not associated with human burials, of individual skulls of bears, especially of the great cave bear, together with some long bones. Perhaps they represent simple sacrifices of the especially important parts of the prey; perhaps Neanderthal hunters, like those of a later period, buried the bones in order to ensure the survival of the animals and their species.

The Lower Paleolithic. Hominids from the Lower Paleolithic period, who date as far back as over a half million years ago, have skulls with primitive proportions and generally smaller brains than modern man. These characteristics led some researchers to doubt that these hominids were capable of achievements comparable with those of human beings from later periods. But objective findings show that the way of life of these hominids must on the whole have been the same as that of the Neanderthals.

Skulls from the Lower Paleolithic, like those from the Middle Paleolithic, are often found in isolation, as with Java men, for example. Some of these as well as some of the skulls found at the site of Peking man have a basal opening that seems to have been artificially widened. Far more skulls, and especially tops of skulls, were found than other parts of the skeleton, suggesting that the skulls were buried apart from the rest of the body. As no convincing secular explanation of the phenomenon has been offered, we should simply assume that there existed practices in which the skull played a special role that transcended the life of the individual in question.

We have no similar indications for the earliest Paleolithic, which began at least two million years ago, perhaps even earlier. Yet even sites from this time have yielded artificial stone tools that are at least as complex as those of Peking

> **Animals clearly played an extremely important part in the mental world of these hunters, insofar as this world is reflected in their art.**

man, as well as smashed and, in various places, collected bones of animals. Some finds from this period also suggest the presence of huts or shelters from the wind.

The Upper Paleolithic. The people of the Upper Paleolithic are equal to present-day humans in physical appearance, and they are therefore given the same name, *Homo sapiens*. People of this time were still living as hunters and gatherers. Only in the course of the later Upper Paleolithic are more definite signs of specialization, differentiation, and an accumulation of cultural possessions to be seen.

Of special interest is the grave of a powerfully built man found at Brno (Czechoslovakia) and dating from the beginning of the Upper Paleolithic. A great deal of red material was used for the burial; near the skull were over six hundred cut, tubelike fossil mollusks (*Dentalium badense*). In addition, the grave contained two stone rings of a kind previously known from only a very few examples; perhaps all of them were connected with graves.

Our most important sources of information about religion during the Upper Paleolithic are works of art. They primarily depict animals and only rarely, and then most often crudely, represent human beings. In many instances, moreover, the humans are not presented simply as humans but with animal attributes or as hybrid human-animal forms. Only a small

number of the animals are depicted as prey, as indicated by the projectiles being thrown at them. Many anthropomorphic figures with animal attributes are regarded as masked dancers or sorcerers, but a good number are better described as composite figures.

The pictures represent, above all, the essential character of the animal, sometimes in relation to the hunt, sometimes in relation to human beings or to anthropomorphic figures, especially when the latter show a mergence of human and animal forms. Animals clearly played an extremely important part in the mental world of these hunters, insofar as this world is reflected in their art. We may probably assume that to a certain extent the artworks mirror the real role of animals; they probably point even more clearly, however, to the special evaluation of animals and of certain species in particular.

It is probable that we are dealing, at least in principle, with a manifestation similar to one that still characterizes the mental world of numerous more developed hunting cultures. Central to this "animalism" are close relations between animals and humans and a heightened importance of the animal world even outside and above the natural realms. Such zoomorphic higher beings are often group progenitors and culture heroes and appear also as mediators and as hypostases and personifications of a supreme god. In short, animalism is a widely found and dominant manifestation and yet, by its very nature, it should be seen as a lower or marginal sphere of religion, one that is frequently interspersed with other motifs and attitudes, including those of a magical type.

The significance of a painting of a birdlike man in the cave of Lascaux (France) has been much debated. The correct interpretation is probably that the picture depicts a man in a trance. His birdlike head and the bird shown on a pole may represent a shaman and a helping spirit. Anthropomorphic figures with the heads of birds may be interpreted similarly. The figurines of birds that have been found at sites in eastern Europe and Siberia and that were apparently nailed or hung remind us of parts of a shaman's clothing. Other pictures may likewise depict shamans—for example, the drawing of the so-called Sorcerer of Les Trois Frères—but here as in most cases other interpretations are also possible.

Whether small scratch-drawings from the early Upper Paleolithic can be interpreted as pubic triangles or vulvas is uncertain. Only later do the so-called Venus figures make their appearance. These are distinguished for the most part by their ample bodies and large breasts, which perhaps indicate pregnancy in some cases. Frequently, too, care has been taken to represent the style of hair or a head covering, whereas the face is not developed at all. The emphasis is clearly on the areas of the body connected with pregnancy, birth, and nursing. It is reasonable therefore to assume that these little figures are associated with the idea of fertility, but this need not be their only significance. The fact that the figures always appear in dwellings or camps may indicate that they were protectors of dwellings. Even today we frequently find, among peoples of the Northern Hemisphere, the idea of a higher feminine being who is, among other things, a mother or mistress of the animals, a divinity of the underworld.

BIBLIOGRAPHY

General surveys of prehistory, including religion, can be found in my *Urgeschichte der Kultur* (Stuttgart, 1961) and in my *Handbuch der Urgeschichte*, vol. 1, *Ältere und mittlere Steinzeit: Jäger- und Sammlerkulturen* (Bern, 1966).

For early surveys of prehistory that assert the agnosticism of early man, see John Lubbock's *Pre-Historic Times, as Illustrated by Ancient Remains, and the Manners and Customs of Modern Savages* (London, 1865) and Gabriel de Mortillet's *Le préhistorique: Antiquité de l'homme*, 2d ed. (Paris, 1885). Contrasting views regarding the religious thought of early man can be found in Thomas Lucien Mainage's *Les religions de la préhistoire: L'âge paléolithique* (Paris, 1921); Johannes Maringer's *De Godsdienst der Praehistorie* (Roermond en Masseik, 1952), translated by Mary Ilford as *The Gods of Prehistoric Man* (New York, 1960); and my "Approaches to the Religion of Early Paleolithic Man," *History of Religions* 4 (Summer 1964): 1-22. Mainage's book is still the essential work in this area, Maringer's discussion follows the view of the Vienna school, and my essay attempts a general evaluation.

The meaning and content of Paleolithic art are discussed in the following works.

Leroi-Gourhan, André. *Art et religion au paléolithique supérieur*. 2d ed. Paris, 1963.
Leroi-Gourhan, André. *Préhistoire de l'art occidental*. Paris, 1965. Translated by Norbert Guterman as *The Art of Prehistoric Man in Western Europe* (London, 1968). A dualistic interpretation in the sexual sense.
Narr, Karl J. "Bärenzeremoniell und Schamanismus in der Älteren Steinzeit Europas." *Saeculum* 10 (1959): 233-272.
Narr, Karl J. "Weibliche Symbol-Plastik der älteren Steinzeit." *Antaios* 2 (July 1960): 132-157.
Narr, Karl J. "Sentido del arte Paleolitico." *Orbis Catholicus: Revista Iberamericana Internacional* 4 (1961): 197-210.
Narr, Karl J. "Felsbild und Weltbild: Zu Magie und Schamanismus im jungpaläolithischen Jägertum." In *Sehnsucht nach dem Ursprung*, edited by Hans P. Duerr, pp. 118-136. Frankfurt, 1983.
Reinach, Salomon. "L'art et la magie: À propos des peintures et des gravures de l'âge du renne." *L'anthropologie* 14 (1903): 257-266. Starting from totemistic interpretation and asserting magic meaning.
Ucko, Peter J., and Andrée Rosenfeld. *Palaeolithic Cave Art*. New York, 1967. A critical review, neglecting animalism.

KARL J. NARR
Translated from German by Matthew J. O'Connell

PAPACY

The papacy is the central governing institution of the Roman Catholic church under the leadership of the pope, the bishop of Rome. The word *papacy* (Lat., *papatus*) is medieval in origin and derives from the Latin *papa,* an affectionate term for "father."

The Early Period. This era, extending from the biblical origins of Christianity to the fifth century, was marked by the ever-increasing power and prestige of the bishop of Rome within the universal church and the Roman empire.

Scriptural foundation. Traditional Roman Catholic teaching holds that Jesus Christ directly bestowed upon the apostle Peter the fullness of ruling and teaching authority. He made Peter the first holder of supreme power in the universal church, a power passed on to his successors, the bishops of Rome. Peter had a preeminent role in the New Testament, where he is described as the most prominent apostolic witness and missionary among the Twelve. He is the model of the shepherd-pastor, the receiver of a special revelation, and the teacher of the true faith. Gradually Christians, through the providential direction of the Holy Spirit, recognized the papacy, the office of headship in the church, to be the continuation of that ministry given by Christ to Peter.

First three centuries. The early Christian churches were not organized internationally. Yet Rome, almost from the beginning, was accorded a unique position, and understandably so: Rome was the only apostolic see in the West; it was the place where Peter and Paul were martyred; and it was the capital of the empire.

The exact structure of the very early Roman church is not known, but it seems that by the middle of the second century monepiscopacy (the rule of one bishop) was well established. The bishops of Rome in the third century claimed a universal primacy, even though it would be another 150 years before this idea was doctrinally formulated. Rome attracted both orthodox and heterodox teachers—some to have their views heard, others to seek confirmation. More and more, the bishop of Rome, either on his own initiative or by request, settled doctrinal and disciplinary disputes in other churches. Roman influence was felt as far away as Spain, Gaul, North Africa, and Asia Minor. The see of Peter was looked upon as the guarantor of doctrinal purity.

Fourth and fifth centuries. With the Edict of Milan (313) the empire granted toleration of all religions and allowed Christians to worship freely. This policy ended the era of persecution, increased the number of Christians, and shaped the institutional development of the papacy. Once Emperor Constantine decided to move the seat of the empire to Constantinople in 324, the papacy began to play a larger role in the West. By the time Christianity became the official reli-

TABLE 1. The Popes

A Roman numeral in parentheses after a pope's name indicates differences in the historical sources. The names of the antipopes and their dates are given in brackets. The first date for each pope refers to his election; the second date refers to his death, deposition, or resignation. Dates for the first two hundred years are uncertain. Abbreviations: Bl. = Blessed; St. = Saint. [26 Apr. 1164-20 Sept. 1168]

NAMES	DATES	NAMES	DATES
St. Peter	?-64/7	Anastasius II	24 Nov. 496-19 Nov. 498
St. Linus	64/7-79?	St. Symmachus	22 Nov. 498-19 Jul. 514
St. Anacletus (Cletus)	79?-90/2	[Lawrence]	[498; 501-505]
St. Clement I	90/2-99/101	St. Hormisdas	20 Jul. 514-6 Aug. 523
St. Evaristus	99/101-107?	St. John I	13 Aug. 523-18 May 526
St. Alexander I	107?-116?	St. Felix IV (III)	12 Jul. 526-22 Sep. 530
St. Sixtus I	116?-125?	Boniface II	22 Sep. 530-17 Oct. 532
St. Telesphorus	125?-136?	[Dioscorus]	[22 Sep.-14 Oct. 530]
St. Hyginus	136?-140/2	John II	2 Jan. 533-8 May 535
St. Pius I	140/2-154/5	St. Agapitus I	13 May 535-22 Apr. 536
St. Anicetus	154/5-166?	St. Silverius	1 Jun. 536-11 Nov. 537
St. Soter	166?-174?	Vigilius	29 Mar. 537-7 Jun. 555
St. Eleutherius	174?-189?	Pelagius I	16 Apt. 556-4 Mar. 561
St. Victor I	189?-198?	John III	17 Jul. 561-13 Jul. 574
St. Zephyrinus	198?-217?	Benedict I	2 Jun. 575-30 Jul. 579
St. Callistus I	217?-222	Pelagius II	26 Nov. 579-7 Feb. 590
[St. Hippolytus]	[217?-235]	St. Gregory I, the Great	3 Sep. 590-12 Mar. 604
St. Urban I	222-230	Sabinian	13 Sep. 604-22 Feb. 606
St. Pontian	21 Jul. 230-28 Sep. 235	Boniface III	19 Feb.-12 Nov. 607
St. Anterus	21 Nov. 235-3 Jan. 236	St. Boniface IV	25 Aug. 608-8 May 615
St. Fabian	10 Jan. 236-20 Jan. 250	St. Deusdedit (Adeodatus I)	19 Oct. 615-8 Nov. 618
St. Cornelius	Mar. 251-Jun. 253	Boniface V	23 Dec. 619-25 Oct. 625
[Novatian]	[251-258?]	Honorius I	27 Oct. 625-12 Oct. 638
St. Lucius I	25 Jun. 253-5 Mar. 254	Severinus	28 May-7 Aug. 640
St. Stephen I	12 May 254-2 Aug. 257	John IV	24 Dec. 640-12 Oct. 642
St. Sixtus II	30 Aug. 257-6 Aug. 258	Theodore I	24 Nov. 642-14 May 649
St. Dionysius	22 Jul. 259-26 Dec. 268	St. Martin I	July 649-16 Sep. 655
St. Felix I	5 Jan. 269-30 Dec. 274	St. Eugene I	10 Aug. 654-2 Jun. 657
St. Eutychian	4 Jan. 275-7 Dec. 283	St. Vitalian	30 Jul. 657-27 Jan. 672
St. Gaius (Caius)	17 Dec. 283-22 Apr. 296	Adeodatus II	11 Apr. 672-17 Jun. 676
St. Marcellinus	30 Jun. 296-25 Oct. 304	Donus	2 Nov. 676-11 Apr. 678
St. Marcellus I	27 May 308-16 Jan. 309	St. Agatho	27 Jun. 678-10 Jan. 681
St. Eusebius	18 Apr.-17 Aug. 309	St. Leo II	17 Aug. 682-3 Jul. 683
St. Miltiades	2 Jul. 311-11 Jan. 314	St. Benedict II	26 Jun. 684-8 May 685
St. Sylvester I	31 Jan. 314-31 Dec. 335	John V	23 Jul. 685-2 Aug. 686
St. Mark	18 Jan.-7 Oct. 336	Conon	21 Oct. 686-21 Sep. 687
St. Julius I	6 Feb. 337-12 Apr. 352	[Theodore]	[687]
Liberius	17 May 352-24 Sep. 366	[Paschal]	[687]
[Felix II]	[355-22 Nov. 365]	St. Sergius I	15 Dec. 687-8 Sep. 701
St. Damasus I	1 Oct. 366-11 Dec. 384	John VI	30 Oct. 701-11 Jan. 705
[Ursinus]	[366-367]	John VII	1 Mar. 705-18 Oct. 707
St. Siricius	15 Dec. 384-26 Nov. 399	Sisinnius	15 Jan.-4 Feb. 708
St. Anastasius I	27 Nov. 399-19 Dec. 401	Constantine	25 Mar. 708-9 Apr. 715
St. Innocent I	22 Dec. 401-12 Mar. 417	St. Gregory II	19 May 715-11 Feb. 731
St. Zosimus	18 Mar. 417-26 Dec. 418	St. Gregory III	18 Mar. 731-Nov. 741
St. Boniface I	28 Dec. 418-4 Sep. 422	St. Zachary	10 Dec. 741-22 Mar. 752
[Eulalius]	[27 Dec. 418-419]	Stephen (II)	23-25 Mar. 752
St. Celestine I	10 Sep. 422-27 Jul. 432	Stephen II (III)	26 Mar. 752-26 Apt. 757
St. Sixtus III	31 Jul. 432-19 Aug. 440	St. Paul I	29 May 757-28 Jun. 767
St. Leo I, the Great	29 Sep. 440-10 Nov. 461	[Constantine II]	[28 Jun. 767-769]
St. Hilary	19 Nov. 461-29 Feb. 468	[Philip]	[31 Jul. 768]
St. Simplicius	3 Mar. 468-10 Mar. 483	Stephen III (IV)	7 Aug. 768-24 Jan. 772
St. Felix III (II)	13 Mar. 483-1 Mar. 492	Adrian I	1 Feb. 772-25 Dec. 795
St. Gelasius I	1 Mar. 492-21 Nov. 496	St. Leo III	26 Dec. 795-12 Jun. 816

TABLE 1. The Popes

NAMES	DATES	NAMES	DATES
Stephen IV (V)	22 Jun. 816-24 Jan. 817	Benedict IX (second time)	10 Apt.-1 May 1045
St. Paschal I	25 Jan. 817-11 Feb. 824	Gregory VI	5 May 1045-20 Dec. 1046
Eugene II	Feb. 824-Aug. 827	Clement II	24 Dec. 1046-9 Oct. 1047
Valentine	Aug.-Sep. 827	Benedict IX (third time)	8 Nov. 1047-17 Jul. 1048
Gregory IV	827-Jan. 844	Damasus II	17 Jul.-9 Aug. 1048
[John]	[Jan. 844]	St. Leo IX	12 Feb. 1049-19 Apr. 1054
Sergius II	Jan. 844-27 Jan. 847	Victor II	16 Apt. 1055-28 Jul. 1057
St. Leo IV	Jan. 847-17 Jul. 855	Stephen IX (X)	3 Aug. 1057-29 Mar. 1058
Benedict III	Jul. 855-17 Apr. 858	[Benedict X]	[5 Apt. 1058-24 Jan. 1059]
[Anastasius]	[Aug.-Sep. 855]	Nicholas II	24 Jan. 1059-27 Jul. 1061
St. Nicholas I, the Great	24 Apt. 858-13 Nov. 867	Alexander II	1 Oct. 1061-21 Apr. 1073
Adrian II	14 Dec. 867-14 Dec. 872	[Honorius II]	[28 Oct. 1061-1072]
John VIII	14 Dec. 872-16 Dec. 882	St. Gregory VII	22 Apt. 1073-25 May 1085
Marinus I	16 Dec. 882-15 May 884	[Clement III]	[26 Jun. 1080-8 Sep. 1100]
St. Adrian III	17 May 884-Sep. 885	Bl. Victor III	24 May 1086-16 Sep. 1087
Stephen V (VI)	Sep. 885-14 Sep. 891	Bl. Urban II	12 Mar. 1088-29 Jul. 1099
Formosus	6 Oct. 891-4 Apr. 896	Paschal II	13 Aug. 1099-21 Jan. 1118
Boniface VI	Apr. 896	[Theodoric]	[1100]
Stephen VI (VII)	May 896-Aug. 897	[Albert]	[1102]
Romanus	Aug.-Nov. 897	[Sylvester IV]	[18 Nov. 1105-1111]
Theodore II	Dec. 897	Gelasius II	24 Jan. 1118-28 Jan. 1119
John IX	Jan. 898-Jan. 900	[Gregory VIII]	[8 Mar. 1118-1121]
Benedict IV	Jan. 900-Jul. 903	Callistus II	2 Feb. 1119-13 Dec. 1124
Leo V	Jul.-Sep. 903	Honorius II	15 Dec. 1124-13 Feb. 1130
[Christopher]	[Jul. 903-Jan. 904]	[Celestine II]	[Dec. 1124]
Sergius III	29 Jan. 904-14 Apr. 911	Innocent II	14 Feb. 1130-24 Sep. 1143
Anastasius III	Apt. 911-Jun. 913	[Anacletus II]	[14 Feb. 1130-25 Jan. 1138]
Lando	Jul. 913-Feb. 914	[Victor IV]	[Mar.-29 May 1138]
John X	Mar. 914-May 928	Celestine II	26 Sep. 1143-8 Mar. 1144
Leo VI	May-Dec. 928	Lucius II	12 Mar. 1144-15 Feb. 1145
Stephen VII (VIII)	Dec. 928-Feb. 931	Bl. Eugene III	15 Feb. 1145-8 Jul. 1153
John XI	Feb. 931-Dec. 935	Anastasius IV	12 Jul. 1153-3 Dec. 1154
Leo VII	3 Jan. 936-13 Jul. 939	Adrian IV	4 Dec. 1154-1 Sep. 1159
Stephen VIII (IX)	14 Jul. 939-Oct. 942	Alexander III	7 Sep. 1159-30 Aug. 1181
Marinus II	30 Oct. 942-May 946	[Victor IV]	[7 Sep. 1159-20 Apt. 1164]
Agapetus II	10 May 946-Dec. 955	[Paschal III]	[26 Apt. 1164-20 Sep. 1168]
John XII	16 Dec. 955-14 May 964	[Callistus III]	[Sep. 1168-29 Aug. 1178]
Leo VIII	4 Dec. 963-1 Mar. 965	[Innocent III]	[29 Sep. 1179-1180]
Benedict V	22 May-23 Jun. 964	Lucius III	1 Sep. 1181-25 Sep. 1185
John XIII	1 Oct. 965-6 Sep. 972	Urban III	25 Nov. 1185-20 Oct. 1187
Benedict VI	19 Jan. 973-Jun. 974	Gregory VIII	21 Oct.-17 Dec. 1187
[Boniface VII]	[Jun.-Jul. 974; Aug. 984-Jul. 985]	Clement III	19 Dec. 1187-Mar. 1191
		Celestine III	30 Mar. 1191-8 Jan. 1198
Benedict VII	Oct. 974-10 Jul. 983	Innocent III	8 Jan. 1198-16 Jul. 1216
John XIV	Dec. 983-20 Aug.'984	Honorius III	18 Jul. 1216-18 Mar. 1227
John XV	Aug. 985-Mar. 996	Gregory IX	19 Mar. 1227-22 Aug. 1241
Gregory V	3 May 996-18 Feb. 999	Celestine IV	25 Oct.-10 Nov. 1241
[John XVI]	[Apr. 997-Feb. 998]	Innocent IV	25 Jun. 1243-7 Dec. 1254
Sylvester II	2 Apr. 999-12 May 1003	Alexander IV	12 Dec. 1254-25 May 1261
John XVII	Jun.-Dec. 1003	Urban IV	29 Aug. 1261-2 Oct. 1264
John XVIII	Jan. 1004-Jul. 1009	Clement IV	5 Feb. 1265-29 Nov. 1268
Sergius IV	31 Jul. 1009-12 May 1012	Bl. Gregory X	1 Sep. 1271-10 Jan. 1276
Benedict VIII	18 May 1012-9 Apr. 1024	Bl. Innocent V	21 Jan.-22 Jun. 1276
[Gregory]	[1012]	Adrian V	11 Jul.-18 Aug. 1276
John XIX	Apt. 1024-1032	John XXI	8 Sep. 1276-20 May 1277
Benedict IX (first time)	1032-1044	Nicholas III	25 Nov. 1277-22 Aug. 1280
Sylvester III	20 Jan.-10 Feb. 1045	Martin IV	22 Feb. 1281-28 Mar. 1285

TABLE 1. The Popes

NAMES	DATES	NAMES	DATES
Honorius IV	2 Apt. 1285-3 Apt. 1287	Gregory XV	9 Feb. 1621-8 Jul. 1623
Nicholas IV	22 Feb. 1288-4 Apt. 1292	Urban VIII	6 Aug. 1623-29 Jul. 1644
St. Celestine V	5 Jul.-13 Dec. 1294	Innocent X	15 Sep. 1644-7 Jan. 1655
Boniface VIII	24 Dec. 1294-11 Oct. 1303	Alexander VII	7 Apt. 1655-22 May 1667
Bl. Benedict XI	22 Oct. 1303-7 Jul. 1304	Clement IX	20 Jun. 1667-9 Dec. 1669
Clement V	5 Jun. 1305-20 Apr. 1314	Clement X	29 Apt. 1670-22 Jul. 1676
John XXII	7 Aug. 1316-4 Dec. 1334	Bl. Innocent XI	21 Sep. 1676-12 Aug. 1689
[Nicholas V]	[12 May 1328-25 Aug. 1330]	Alexander VIII	6 Oct. 1689-1 Feb. 1691
Benedict XII	20 Dec. 1334-25 Apt. 1342	Innocent XII	12 Jul. 1691-27 Sep. 1700
Clement VI	7 May 1342-6 Dec. 1352	Clement XI	23 Nov. 1700-19 Mar. 1721
Innocent VI	18 Dec. 1352-12 Sep. 1362	Innocent XIII	8 May 1721-7 Mar. 1724
Bl. Urban V	28 Sep. 1362-19 Dec. 1370	Benedict XIII	29 May 1724-21 Feb. 1730
Gregory XI	30 Dec. 1370-26 Mar. 1378	Clement XII	12 Jul. 1730-6 Feb. 1740
Urban VI	8 Apt. 1378-15 Oct. 1389	Benedict XIV	17 Aug. 1740-3 May 1758
Boniface IX	2 Nov. 1389- 1 Oct. 1404	Clement XIII	6 Jul. 1758-2 Feb. 1769
Innocent VII	17 Oct. 1404-6 Nov. 1406	Clement XIV	19 May 1769-22 Sep. 1774
Gregory XII	30 Nov. 1406-4 Jul. 1415	Pius VI	15 Feb. 1775-29 Aug. 1799
[Clement VII, Avignon]	[20 Sep. 1378-16 Sep. 1394]	Pius VII	14 Mar. 1800-20 Aug. 1823
[Benedict XIII, Avignon]	[28 Sep. 1394-23 May 1423]	Leo XII	28 Sep. 1823-10 Feb. 1829
[Clement VIII, Avignon]	[10 Jun. 1423-26 Jul. 1429]	Pius VIII	31 Mar. 1829-30 Nov. 1830
[Benedict XIV, Avignon]	[12 Nov. 1425-1430]	Gregory XVI	2 Feb. 1831-1 Jun. 1846
[Alexander V, Pisa]	[26 Jun. 1409-3 May 1410]	Pius IX	16 Jun. 1846-7 Feb. 1878
[John XXIII, Pisa]	[17 May 1410-29 May 1415]	Leo XIII	20 Feb. 1878-20 Jul. 1903
Martin V	11 Nov. 1417-20 Feb. 1431	St. Pius X	4 Aug. 1903-20 Aug. 1914
Eugene IV	3 Mar. 1431-23 Feb. 1447	Benedict XV	3 Sep. 1914-22 Jan. 1922
[Felix V]	[5 Nov. 1439-7 Apr. 1449]	Pius XI	6 Feb. 1922-10 Feb. 1939
Nicholas V	6 Mar. 1447-24 Mar. 1455	Pius XII	2 Mar. 1939-9 Oct. 1958
Callistus III	8 Apt. 1455-6 Aug. 1458	John XXIII	28 Oct. 1958-3 Jun. 1963
Plus II	19 Aug. 1458-15 Aug. 1464	Paul VI	21 Jun. 1963-6 Aug. 1978
Paul II	30 Aug. 1464-26 Jul. 1471	John Paul I	26 Aug.-28 Sep. 1978
Sixtus IV	9 Aug. 1471-12 Aug. 1484	John Paul II	16 Oct. 1978-
Innocent VIII	29 Aug. 1484-25 Jul. 1492		
Alexander VI	11 Aug. 1492-18 Aug. 1503		
Pius III	22 Sep.-18 Oct. 1503		
Julius II	31 Oct. 1503-21 Feb. 1513		
Leo X	9 Mar. 1513-1 Dec. 1521		
Adrian VI	9 Jan. 1522-14 Sep. 1523		
Clement VII	19 Nov. 1523-25 Sep. 1534		
Paul III	13 Oct. 1534-10 Nov. 1549		
Julius III	7 Feb. 1550-23 Mar. 1555		
Marcellus II	9 Apt.-1 May 1555		
Paul IV	23 May 1555-18 Aug. 1559		
Plus IV	25 Dec. 1559-9 Dec. 1565		
St. Pius V	7 Jan. 1566-1 May 1572		
Gregory XIII	13 May 1572-10 Apr. 1585		
Sixtus V	24 Apr. 1585-27 Aug. 1590		
Urban VII	15 Sep.-27 Sep. 1590		
Gregory XIV	5 Dec. 1590-16 Oct. 1591		
Innocent IX	29 Oct.-30 Dec. 1591		
Clement VIII	30 Jan. 1592-3 Mar. 1605		
Leo XI	1 Apt.-27 Apt. 1605		
Paul V	16 May 1605-28 Jan. 1621		

NOTE

For centuries the popes did not change their names. The first name change occurred when a Roman called Mercury, having been elected pope, chose the more suitable appellation of John II (533-535). From the time of Sergius IV (1009-1012)—his name had been Peter Buccaporca (Peter Pigmouth)—the taking of a new name has continued to the present, with two exceptions: Adrian VI (1522-1523) and Marcellus II (1555). The most popular papal names have been John, Gregory, Benedict, Clement, Innocent, Leo, and Pius. There has never been a Peter II or a John XX. John Paul I was the first pope to select a double name. The legend that a woman pope—Pope Joan—reigned between Leo IV (847-855) and Benedict III (855-858) has long been rejected by historians.

The foregoing list is based generally on the catalog of popes given in the Annuario pontificio, the official Vatican yearbook, with some changes dictated by recent scholarly research. It should be noted that the legitimacy of certain popes—for example, Dioscorus (530), Leo VIII (963-965), Benedict V (964), Gregory VI (1045-1046), and Clement II (1046-1047)—is still controverted. Although Stephen (752) is mentioned in the list, he died three days after his election without being consecrated a bishop.

gion of the empire in 381, several popes were already affirming papal primatial authority. The critical period in the doctrinal systematization of Roman primacy took place in the years between Damasus I (366-384) and Leo I (440-461). In that period, the popes explicitly claimed that the bishop of Rome was the head of the entire church and that his authority derived from Peter.

Damasus I, the first pope to call Rome the apostolic see, made Latin the principal liturgical language in Rome and commissioned Jerome to revise the old Latin version of the New Testament. His successor, Siricius (384-399), whose decretal letters are the earliest extant, promoted Rome's primatial position and imposed his decisions on many bishops outside Italy.

> ## Roman influence was felt as far away as Spain, Gaul, North Africa, and Asia Minor.

It was Leo I, the first of three popes to be called the Great, who laid the theoretical foundation of papal primacy. Leo took the title Pontifex Maximus, which the emperors no longer used, and claimed to possess the fullness of power (*plenitudo potestatis*). Governing the church through a tumultuous period of barbarian invasions and internal disputes, he relentlessly defended the rights of the Roman see. He rejected Canon 28 of the Council of Chalcedon (451), which gave the bishop of New Rome (Constantinople) privileges equal to those of the bishop of Old Rome and a rank second only to that of the pope. Leo believed that Peter's successors have "the care of all the churches" (*Sermons* 3.4), and he exercised his authority over Christian churches in Italy, Africa, and Gaul. The Western Roman empire ended in 476.

The Medieval Papacy. The eventful period from the sixth to the fifteenth century demonstrated the unusual adaptability of the papal office.

The struggle for independence. The popes of the sixth and seventh centuries resisted excessive encroachments but were still subservient to the power of the emperor. The most notable pope at this time was Gregory I, the Great (590-604), a deeply spiritual man who called himself "the servant of the servants of God." A skilled negotiator, he was able to conclude a peace treaty with the Lombards, who threatened Rome; the people of Rome and the adjacent regions considered him their protector. Gregory was respectful of the rights of individual bishops, but he insisted, nevertheless, that all churches, including Constantinople, were subject to the apostolic see of Rome.

The break with the East began when Gregory II (715-731) condemned the iconoclastic decrees of Emperor Leo I, who had prohibited the use of images in liturgical ceremonies.

The gap widened when Stephen II (752-757), the first pope to cross the Alps, met with Pépin, king of the Franks. Pépin agreed to defend the pope against the invading Lombards and apparently promised him sovereignty over large areas in central Italy. The Donation of Pépin was an epoch-making event; it marked the beginning of the Papal States, in existence until 1870. Stephen became the first of a long line of popes to claim temporal rule. Through his alliance with the Frankish kingdom, Stephen was virtually able to free the papacy from the domination of Constantinople. The last step in the division of Rome from the Eastern Empire was when Pope Leo III (795-816) crowned Charlemagne emperor of the West at Saint Peter's Basilica in 800. The primatial prominence of Rome increased when the Muslim conquests destroyed the church in North Africa and ended the strong influence of Rome's great rivals: the patriarchates of Alexandria, Antioch, and Jerusalem.

The tenth century was a bleak one for the papacy. The so-called Ottonian privilege restricted the freedom of papal electors and allowed the emperor the right of ratification. There were some two dozen popes and antipopes during this period, many of low moral caliber.

The reform movement. Advocates of reform found a dedicated leader in Leo IX (1049-1054). He traveled extensively throughout Italy, France, and Germany, presiding over synods that issued strong decrees dealing with clerical marriage, simony, and episcopal elections. Only six months of his entire pontificate were spent in Rome. Further reforms were made under Nicholas II (1059-1061). His decree on papal elections (1059), which made cardinal bishops the sole electors, had a twofold purpose: to safeguard the reformed papacy through free and peaceful elections and to eliminate coercion by the empire or the aristocracy.

The most famous of the reform popes was Gregory VII (1073-1085), surnamed Hildebrand. His ambitious program of reform focused on three areas: to restore prestige to the papacy; to reform clerical corruption; and to reform lay investiture—a practice whereby feudal lords, princes, and emperors bestowed spiritual office through the selection of pastors, abbots, and bishops. Henceforth, the papacy exercised a new style of leadership; the pope emerged not only as the undisputed head of the church but also as the unifying force in medieval western Europe.

The height of papal authority. The papacy reached its zenith in the twelfth and thirteenth centuries. Six general councils between 1123 and 1274 issued many doctrinal and disciplinary decrees aimed at reform and left no doubt that the popes were firmly in control of church policy. During the pontificate of Innocent III (1198-1216), one of the most brilliant of all the popes, the papacy reached the summit of its universal power and supervised the religious, social, and political life of the West. Honorius III (1216-1227) further centralized papal administration and finances and approved the establishment of the Franciscan and Dominican orders. In theory, papal authority extended also to non-Christians. Innocent IV (1243-1254) believed that every creature is subject to the pope—even infidels, Christ's sheep by creation though not members of the church. This idea of a world theocracy under the popes was to be part of the theological and political justification for the Crusades.

> **The church's most wide-ranging answer to the Protestant Reformation was the Council of Trent (1545-1563), convoked by Paul III.**

Two significant changes were made in the procedures for papal elections. At the Third Lateran Council (1179), Alexander III (1159-1181) decreed that all cardinals—not just cardinal bishops—could vote and that a two-thirds majority was required. The Second Council of Lyons (1274), under Gregory X (1271-1276), established the law of the conclave, whereby the cardinal electors had to assemble in the papal palace and remain in a locked room until the election was completed.

Decline of the papacy. Several factors contributed to the decline of the papacy: high taxation, the inappropriate conferral and control of benefices, corruption in the Roman bureaucracy, and, above all, the failure of the popes to foresee the effect of nationalism on church-state relations.

In 1308, Clement V (1305-1314) moved the papal residence to Avignon, which then belonged to the king of Naples, a vassal of the pope. Several factors prompted this decision: the upcoming general council of Vienne (1311-1312); the tension between the pope and the king of France; and the unsafe and chaotic political situation in Rome and Italy. The popes remained in Avignon for seventy years. During their so-called Babylonian Captivity, the popes were French, but the papacy was not a puppet of the French rulers. Centralization and administrative complexity increased, especially under John XXII (1316-1334). The cardinals assumed greater power that at times bordered on oligarchy. They introduced the practice of capitulation—an agreement made by electors of the pope to limit the authority of the person chosen to be pope—and thus tried to restrict papal primacy.

No sooner had Gregory XI (1370-1378) returned to Rome in 1377 than the papacy faced another crisis, the great Western schism. The election of Urban VI (1378-1389) was later disputed by some of the cardinals, who claimed coercion. Five months after Urban's election, they rejected him and elected Clement VII (1378-1394), who went back to Avignon. The two popes had their own cardinals, curial staffs,

and adherents among the faithful. A council was held at Pisa in 1409 to resolve the problem, but instead still another pope was elected, Alexander V, who in less than a year was succeeded by John XXIII (1410-1415). The general council of Constance (1414-1418) confronted the scandal of three would-be popes and pledged to reform the church in head and members. Unity was restored with the election of Martin V (1417-1431).

From the Renaissance to the Enlightenment. Papal authority was severely challenged between the fifteenth and eighteenth centuries.

The Renaissance. Martin V tried to fulfill the provisions of the decree *Frequens* (1417) that emanated from the Council of Constance, which mandated that a general council should be held in five years, another seven years later, and then one regularly every ten years. He convened a council at Siena that later moved to Pavia (1423-1424), but the plague forced its dissolution. Seven years later another council was held, meeting first at Basel and later at Ferrara and Florence (1431-1445), under Eugene IV (1431-1447). Greek and Latin prelates attended, and they were able to agree on several thorny doctrinal issues including the primacy of the pope.

Nicholas V (1447-1455) and his successors made Rome a center of the arts and scholarship. Pius II (1458-1464), one of the most notable examples of papal humanism, in the bull *Exsecrabilis* (1460) prohibited any appeals to future general councils, thus striking at conciliarism. Sixtus IV (1471-1484) concerned himself mostly with the restoration of Rome and the expansion of the Papal States; he is responsible for building the magnificent Sistine Chapel in the Vatican. The most famous of the warrior popes was Julius II (1503-1513), known as Il Terribile. A capable and energetic leader, Julius became the patron of Michelangelo, Raphael, and Bramante; he commissioned the construction of the new basilica of Saint Peter's. Adrian VI (1522-1523) was an exception among the Renaissance popes; in his short pontificate he tried to introduce reform measures, but these met persistent opposition from both civil rulers and highly placed ecclesiastics. In sum, the Renaissance popes were generally more interested in politics, the arts, and the ostentatious display of wealth than in providing genuine religious leadership.

The Reformation and Counter-Reformation. By the beginning of the sixteenth century the papacy was severely weakened by internal decay and a loss of supernatural vision. The faithful throughout Europe were asked to contribute alms to the extravagant building projects in Rome. These factors, coupled with deep-seated religious, social, and economic unrest in Europe, set the stage for the Protestant Reformation. Martin Luther's challenge in 1517 caught the papacy unprepared. Leo X (1513-1521) and his successors badly underestimated the extent and intensity of antipapal sentiment in Europe. The popes neither adequately comprehended the religious intentions of Luther nor understood the appeal that the reformers' ideas had for many who were outraged at both the policies and the conduct of church leaders. What began in the Reformation as a movement to restore genuine apostolic integrity to the church of Rome ended with the creation of a separate church; by the time of Clement VII (1523-1534), millions of Catholics in Germany, Scandinavia, the Low Countries, Switzerland, and Britain had departed from the Roman communion.

The rapid rise of Protestantism had a sobering effect on the papacy: it forced the popes to concentrate on church affairs. Paul III (1534-1549), for example, appointed competent cardinals to administrative posts, authorized the establishment of the Society of Jesus (1540), and reformed the Roman Inquisition (1542). The church's most wide-ranging answer to the Protestant Reformation was the Council of Trent (1545-1563), convoked by Paul III and concluded by Pius IV (1559-1565). In its twenty-five sessions, the council discussed the authority of scripture and of tradition, original sin and justification, the sacraments, and specific reform legislation. It did not, strangely enough, treat explicitly the theology of the church or the papacy.

One of the effects of the Tridentine reform was a reorganization of the church's central administrative system. The Curia Romana, which had existed, at least functionally, since the first century, was plagued by nepotism, greed, and abuse of authority. Sixtus V (1585-1590), who was committed to a reform of the Curia, established fifteen congregations of cardinals to carry out church administration. The popes endeavored to consider moral character and ability in selecting cardinals, whose number was set at seventy in 1588. Under Gregory XIII (1572-1585), papal nuncios to Catholic countries proved most valuable in implementing the ideals of Trent and in supervising the activities of the local bishops. The bishops of dioceses, who now had to submit regular reports to Rome and visit it at specified intervals, became much less independent. The success of the Counter-Reformation resulted from sound papal governance and the extraordinary contributions of the Jesuits and other religious orders.

Seventeenth and eighteenth centuries. Skepticism, rationalism, and secularism became pervasive during the Enlightenment, and many intellectuals were violently opposed to the Catholic church and the papacy.

The Thirty Years War (1618-1648), a series of religious and dynastic wars that involved most of Europe, embroiled the papacy in conflict. Paul V and Gregory XV (1621-1623) had little influence on the conduct of Catholic rulers. Innocent X (1644-1655) protested, albeit futilely, against the Peace of Westphalia (1648), because he felt that Catholics were treated unjustly. This war and its aftermath showed how ineffective the papacy had become in European politics.

During the following decades the popes were active in many areas. In the theological area, Innocent X repudiated five propositions on the theology of grace found in the writings of the Flemish bishop Cornelis Jansen; Alexander VII (1655-1667) rejected laxism as a moral system; and Alexander VIII (1689-1691) acted similarly against rigorism. The most dramatic papal action of the eighteenth century occurred when Clement XIV (1769-1774), bending to pressure from the Bourbon monarchies and fearing possible schism in France and Spain, suppressed the Society of Jesus in 1773.

The Modern Period. Dramatic shifts in the prestige and authority of the papacy have occurred between the era of the French Revolution and the twentieth century.

Revolution and restoration. The French Revolution, which began in 1789, and the subsequent actions of Napoleon created a new political order in Europe that adversely affected the Roman Catholic church. Pius VI (1775-1799), who had little sympathy with the ideals of the revolution, was unable to deal effectively with such vehement defiance of the Holy See and such massive threats to the very existence of religion. At times it seemed as if the papacy itself would be destroyed. The octogenarian and infirm Pius was taken prisoner by Napoleon and died in exile on his way to Paris. Resistance to Napoleonic aggression continued during the pontificate of Pius VII (1800-1823). The Concordat of 1801 with Napoleon, which for over a century regulated the relationship between France and the church, revealed that Pius was willing to make concessions for the sake of peace. Yet in 1809 Napoleon captured Rome, annexed the Papal States, and arrested the pope and held him prisoner until 1814. The Catholic restoration began after the defeat of Napoleon: the Congress of Vienna (1814-1815) returned most of the papal territory to the church, and in 1814 Pius restored the Society of Jesus.

The thirty-two-year pontificate of Pius IX (1846-1878), the longest in history, was significant. Initially hailed as a liberal, he soon showed his advocacy of ultramontanism. He restored the Catholic hierarchies of England (1850) and the Netherlands (1853), began a renewal of Marian devotion by his definition of the Immaculate Conception of Mary (1854), and supported extensive missionary activity. His greatest disappointment was the loss of the Papal States in 1870, which ended a millennium of temporal sovereignty. Pius's greatest triumph was the First Vatican Council (1869-1870), which ended abruptly when Italian troops occupied Rome. It produced two constitutions: *Dei filius*, a reaffirmation of the centrality of revelation, and *Pastor aeternus*, a definition of papal primacy and infallibility.

Vatican I and modernity. The most formal and detailed exposition of papal prerogatives is found in *Pastor aeternus*. In regard to primacy it taught that Jesus conferred upon Peter a primacy of both honor and jurisdiction; that by divine right Peter has perpetual successors in primacy over the universal church; that the Roman pontiff is the successor of Peter and has supreme, ordinary (not delegated), and immediate power and jurisdiction over the church and its members; and that the Roman pontiff is the supreme judge who is not subject to review by anyone. In regard to infallibility, Vatican I taught that by divine assistance the pope is immune from error when he speaks *ex cathedra*—that is, when "by virtue of his supreme apostolic authority he defines a doctrine concerning faith or morals to be held by the universal church." The formidable conception of the papacy at Vatican I was a victory for ultramontanism. Using juridical and monarchical language, it asserted the universal spiritual authority of the pope.

The popes between Vatican I and Vatican II, individuals of superior quality, had much in common. First, they were all committed to the spiritual restoration of Catholicism, using their magisterial and jurisdictional authority to that end. Second, the popes continued to centralize church administration in Rome by increasing the power of the Roman Curia and the diplomatic corps. Third, the papal office actively promoted missionary endeavors. Fourth, the popes, at times reluctantly and unsuccessfully, tried to respond to the demands of a changing world. They sought amicable relations with secular governments, especially through concordats, and worked devotedly for social justice and peace.

The popes of this period continued the ultramontanist policies of the nineteenth century, but with a difference. Leo XIII (1878-1903), for example, was more open to the positive aspects of modernity. His successor, Pius X (1903-1914), desired to renew the interior life of the church, as is shown by his teachings on the Eucharist, the liturgy, and seminary education. During World War I, the complete impartiality of Benedict XV (1914-1922) brought criticism from all sides. In 1917 he promulgated the first Code of Canon Law. The pope of the interwar years was Pius XI (1922-1939), noted for his encyclicals on marriage (*Casti connubii,* 1930) and social thought (*Quadragesimo anno,* 1931). Finally, Pius XII (1939-1958), a trained diplomat with broad interests, addressed almost every aspect of church life, and in a prodigious number of pronouncements applied Catholic doctrine to contemporary problems.

Vatican II and postconciliar developments. John XXIII (1958-1963), elected when he was nearly seventy-seven, began a new era for Roman Catholicism. His open style of papal leadership, enhanced by his appealing personality, was warmly welcomed by Catholics and non-Catholics alike. Although he is well known for his efforts in promoting ecumenism and world peace (*Pacem in terris,* 1963), the pope's greatest accomplishment was the unexpected convocation of the Second Vatican Council (1962-1965). John designed the council to foster reform and reunion, believing that a contemporary reformulation of the Christian tradition would revitalize the Catholic church and ultimately benefit all humankind. Paul VI (1963-1978) skillfully maintained the council's pastoral orientation. To implement its program, he

established the Synod of Bishops, internationalized and increased the number of cardinals, reformed the Curia, and promoted liturgical reform. He made nine trips outside Italy.

Vatican II supplied what was lacking in Vatican I. Its doctrine of collegiality described the relationship between the pope and the bishops. The Constitution on the Church (*Lumen gentium*) stated: "Together with its head, the Roman Pontiff, and never without this head, the episcopal order is the subject of supreme and full power in relation to the universal church. But this power can be exercised only with the consent of the Roman Pontiff" (Article 22). The college of bishops, then, exists only under the leadership of the pope, himself a bishop. The pope is not the executor of the bishops' wishes (Gallicanism), nor are the bishops vicars of the pope (papal absolutism). Both the papacy and the episcopacy have their own legitimate authority, and the purpose of collegiality is to unite the bishops with the pope.

> **John Paul II became the first non-Italian pope in 456 years, the first Polish pope, and the first pope from a Communist country.**

The theory of collegiality has altered the style of papal leadership, making it far less monarchical. The closer relationship between the pope and the bishops is best exemplified by the Synod of Bishops, a consultative body that meets once every three years. Collegiality has made the papacy less objectionable to other Christians since it fosters the idea of authority as service and not domination. This aspect has been noted in the fifth dialogue of the Lutheran-Roman Catholic discussions (1974) and in the Final Report of the Anglican-Roman Catholic International Commission (1982). Both groups recognized the value of a universal Petrine ministry of unity in the Christian church and foresaw the possibility of the bishop of Rome exercising that function for all Christians in the future.

In 1978 two popes died and two were elected. The pontificate of John Paul I, the successor of Paul VI, lasted only thirty-three days. Breaking a tradition that had endured for more than nine hundred years, John Paul I was not installed by a rite of coronation or enthronement. He rejected the obvious symbols of temporal and monarchical authority and was inaugurated at a solemn mass. Instead of the tiara, he was given the pallium, a white woolen stole symbolizing his spiritual and pastoral ministry. His successor, John Paul II, became the first non-Italian pope in 456 years, the first Polish pope, and the first pope from a Communist country. The most-traveled pope in history, John Paul II earned huge popular appeal with his international pastoral visits.

[*For related discussions, see* Councils, Schism, Canon Law, Crusades, Inquisition, Reformation, The, Ultramontanism. Vatican Councils

BIBLIOGRAPHY

Historical Works. Two standard works on papal history are Johannes Haller's *Das Papsttum: Idee und Wirklichkeit,* 5 vols. (1950-1953; reprint, Esslingen am Neckar, 1962), and Franz Xaver Seppelt's *Geschichte der Päpste von den Anfängen bis zur Mitte des zwanzigsten Jahrhunderts,* 5 vols. (Munich, 1954-1959). Dated in some respects but still very useful are two monumental studies: Horace K. Mann's *The Lives of the Popes in the Early Middle Ages,* 18 vols. in 19, 2d ed. (London, 1925-1969), which covers the period from 590 to 1304; and Ludwig von Pastor's *The History of the Popes from the Close of the Middle Ages,* 40 vols. (London, 1891-1953), which concerns the years from 1305 to 1799. Walter Ullmann's *A Short History of the Papacy in the Middle Ages* (London, 1972) and Guillaume Mollat's *The Popes at Avignon, 1305-1378,* translated from the 9th French edition by Janet Love (London, 1963), can be recommended. The papacy in the eighteenth, nineteenth, and twentieth centuries is discussed in Owen Chadwick's *The Popes and European Revolution* (Oxford, 1981); Roger Aubert's *Le pontificat de Pie IX, 1846-1878,* 2d ed. (Paris, 1964); and J. Derek Holmes's *The Papacy in the Modern World, 1914-1978* (New York, 1981). General histories of the church contain much information on the papal office. One of the most comprehensive and reliable is *Histoire de l'Église depuis les origines jusqu'à nos jours,* 21 vols. (Paris, 1934-1964), edited by Augustin Fliche et al. There is valuable material on papal documentation in Carl Mirbt's *Quellen zur Geschichte des Papsttums und des Rö-mischen Katholizismus,* 5th ed. (1895; reprint, Tübingen, 1934), and James T. Shotwell and Louise R. Loomis's *The See of Peter* (New York, 1927).

Theological Works. An analysis of the biblical evidence is found in Raymond E. Brown et al., *Peter in the New Testament* (Minneapolis, 1973). For a detailed study of the theology of the papacy with special emphasis on collegiality see my work, *The Papacy in Transition* (Garden City, N. Y., 1980). Both books contain full bibliographies. Various theological points are discussed in *Papal Primacy in the Church, Concilium,* vol. 64 (New York, 1971), edited by Hans Küng; in Karl Rahner and Joseph Ratzinger's *The Episcopate and the Primacy* (New York, 1962); in Gustave Thils's *La primauté pontificale* (Gembloux, 1972); and in Jean-Marie R. Tillard's *The Bishop of Rome* (Wilmington, Del., 1983). For a discussion of the ecumenical dimension of the papacy, see *Das Papstamt: Dienst oder Hindernis für die Ökumene?* (Regensburg, 1985), by Vasilios von Aristi et al. Excellent articles on the same topic are contained in the following: *Papal Primacy and the Universal Church* (Minneapolis, 1974), edited by Paul C. Empie and T. Austin Murphy; *Teaching Authority and Infallibility in the Church* (Minneapolis, 1980), edited by Paul C. Empie et al.; *The Anglican-Roman Catholic International Commission: The Final Report, Windsor, Sept. 1981* (London, 1982); and John Meyendorff et al., *The Primacy of Peter* (London, 1963).

PATRICK GRANFIELD

PARADISE

The word *paradise* originated from Old Persian *pairidaeza,* which meant "walled enclosure, pleasure park, garden." The earliest known description of a paradisial garden appears on a cuneiform tablet from protoliterate Sumer. It begins with a eulogy of Dilmun, a place that is pure, clean, and bright.

The Garden of Eden. According to the mythical narrative in *Genesis* 2-3, God planted a garden in Eden and therein placed man to till and keep it. God also caused trees to grow in the garden. The Edenic paradise was mainly arboreal, thereby providing food for man. The original human diet seems to have been vegetarian. The garden was the source of the world's sweet waters. A river not only watered the garden but flowed out of it to become four rivers (Pishon, Gihon, Tigris, and Euphrates), apparently to water the four directions or quarters of the world (*Gn.* 2:10-14).

The myth recognizes a deficiency in man's life in Eden: he is alone. This solitariness is soon relieved, for God forms beasts and birds. Still, it is said, man does not have a suitable companion. The account of the creation of woman (Eve) follows. She is said to have been created from the rib (bone) of Adam.

One of the creatures of God, the serpent, approaches Eve and inquires whether God has placed any limits on the trees from which the couple may eat. Earlier in the narrative (2:9), there is reference to the Tree of Life and the Tree of the Knowledge of Good and Evil, and the warning to man that he will die if he eats of the latter (2:17). When Eve reveals the prohibition, the serpent denies that death will result and insists instead that eating the fruit will result in likeness to God in that man will then know good and evil. Both Eve and Adam eat the forbidden fruit. When discovered and questioned, they reveal that they have violated the divine prohibition. Sentence is passed on them as well as the serpent. Henceforth, Eve will experience pain in childbirth and subordination to her husband. Adam is condemned to till the soil under difficult conditions and ultimately to return to the soil or dust from which he originally came, that is, to die.

The concluding verses of the narrative refer to the second of the trees—the Tree of Life—which is earlier said to be in the midst (center?) of the garden. The deity appears concerned that man, if allowed to remain in the garden, will eat also of the Tree of Life and live forever. Adam and Eve are driven from the garden, and an angel and a flaming sword are placed at the entrance to guard the way to the Tree of Life.

The lost paradise of Eden has sometimes been thought actually to have existed somewhere on earth. Since the Bible nowhere indicates its destruction, some people have assumed that the garden, or traces of it, could be discovered. Thus it has been imagined to exist at the headwaters of the Tigris and Euphrates rivers.

Characteristics of the Primordial Paradise. Among the marks or characteristics of the primordial paradise are perfection, purity, plenitude, freedom, spontaneity, peace, pleasure, beatitude, and immortality. Each contrasts with the characteristics of ordinary, postparadisial human life. To this list could appropriately be added harmony and friendship with the animals, including knowledge of their language, and, as well, ease of communication with the gods and the world above.

Human beings and animals live peaceably, sexual tension has not yet appeared, and labor is unnecessary. Paradise is outside ordinary, historical time. Hence there can be no ageing or death.

Nostalgia for Paradise. Although the primordial paradise has been lost, it has not been forgotten. One finds expressions of the desire to recover the essential condition, the condition that would still obtain if all had gone as it should. More significant than wishes, although they may be present, is the nostalgia, the haunting sense of loss and the powerful desire for recovery. The nostalgia for paradise is among the powerful nostalgias that seem to haunt human beings. It may be the most powerful and persistent of all.

Recurring Paradises. Paradises are found in cosmically oriented as well as historically oriented religions. The most impressive example in the history of religion is the Hindu doctrine of the world ages (*yugas*). It is cast in mythical terms by relating the ages of the life of the god Brahma. Briefly, each world cycle is subdivided into four world ages. Hinduism uses the four throws of the Indian game of dice: *krta* (4), *treta* (3), *dvapara* (2), and *kali* (1). Decline and deterioration proceed as age follows age. *Krtayuga* is the perfect age, the age of four (the winning throw in the dice game). The number four is a frequent symbol of totality, plenitude, and perfection in Hinduism. In other words, it is equivalent to the primordial, paradisial age of other religious traditions.

Buddhism adopted essentially the Hindu cyclical view of ages, relating it to the Buddhas and *bodhisattvas.* In the *Maitreyavyakarana,* people will be without blemishes. They will be strong, large, and joyful, and few will be the illnesses among them..

Plato in the *Politicus* (269c ff.) speaks of cyclical return that includes times of regeneration. The time comes when ordinary processes are reversed. Thus human beings begin to grow younger rather than older, returning to infancy and finally ceasing to be. There appears then the age of Kronos in which a new race ("Sons of Earth") is born. Human beings rise out of the earth. Trees provide them with fruits in abundance. They sleep naked (in paradisial nudity) on the soil. The seasons are mild, and all animals are tame and peaceable.

Paradise as the Abode of the Righteous. The biblical conception of paradise is not limited to the primordial Garden of Eden. With the emergence of Jewish belief in the resurrection of the dead, perhaps around 200 BCE, paradise could be taken to refer not only to the original Garden of Eden but also to the eternal abode of the righteous. That is, the righteous dead could expect to have the Garden of Eden, or paradise, as their postresurrection abode (rather than Gehenna, the fiery place of punishment of the wicked). Thus Garden and Gehenna constituted a contrasting pair.

The New Testament contains three specific references to paradise (*2 Cor.* 12:3, *Lk.* 23:43, *Rv.* 2:7). Paradise appears to be thought of as a celestial or heavenly level entered

> **The nostalgia for paradise is among the powerful nostalgias that seem to haunt human beings.**

through ecstasy. The promise is given that one who conquers will be granted to eat of the tree of life in God's paradise.

In the Islamic religion the Arabic word for "garden"—*janna*—is used to refer to the Garden of Eden and, as well, to the heavenly Paradise in which the God-fearing will dwell. In the Qur'an it more commonly refers to the latter.

Representations of Paradise. Paradise is susceptible to a variety of specific representations.

Garden. The garden is the most common representation of paradise. This representation is not limited to religions originating in the Middle East. There is, for example, a Mahayana Buddhist paradise, Sukhavati, the "pure land" of the Buddha Amitabha. In Greek mythology one finds the garden, or orchard, of Hesperides, located in the far west, not far from the Isles of the Blessed.

The association of garden with paradise has been persistent, as shown by Elizabeth Moynihan in *Paradise as a Garden: In Persia and Mughal India* (1979). She demonstrates the continuity of the tradition and symbolic topography of the paradise garden. She points especially to the relationship between water, the central and most essential element in the Persian garden, and trees, symbolizing regeneration or immortality and the possibility of ascension.

It is not difficult to understand why the garden has often provided the setting for the primordial paradise. It seems to constitute another world, different from the ordinary one, a world in which seed, soil, and water combine in evident manifestation of fertility, vitality, and abundance. For humans it provides refreshment as well as nourishment, and signalizes an alluring mode of human existence.

Island. Gardens are not the sole representations of paradise. The Isles of the Blessed in Greek mythology are well known. They are an insular counterpart to Olympus, the mountain of the gods. One finds parallels in Celtic mythology, where isle as well as garden is used as an image of paradise. Moreover, the myth of the submerged world, comparable to Plato's Atlantis, is also found. Here one has the motif of a more or less paradisial world in which something went wrong, resulting in its disappearance beneath the waves.

An island suggests isolation. It can readily symbolize the remoteness and difficulty of access of paradise. Often a river or an ocean has to be traversed. Paradise cannot easily be found, entered, recovered.

Mountain. The mountain is also sometimes associated with paradise, as, for example, in connection with Jerusalem (Mount Zion) in its paradisial dimensions, or with Mount Meru of Hindu mythology. John Milton in book 4 of *Paradise Lost* describes paradise as a mountain. The distinctive characteristic of the mountain is its height. It towers above the earth and therefore can readily symbolize transcendence.

Eschatological Paradises. While paradise is usually thought of as in the past, it also figures in some eschatologies. In the *Book of Revelation* there is envisioned a new heaven and a new earth and, as well, a new Jerusalem, which will come down from God (*Rv.* 21:1ff.). God will then dwell among men, and henceforth mourning, crying, pain, and death will be no more. In Jewish messianism the coming age is frequently described in terms strongly reminiscent of paradisial existence (e.g., *Is.* 11:6-8, *Ez.* 47:1-12). Norman Cohn in *The Pursuit of the Millennium* (1957) found paradisial elements in his study of revolutionary messianism in medieval and Reformation Europe.

In modern times "cargo cults" of Melanesia and Micronesia have been especially generative of paradisial motifs. Briefly, these cults are typically based on myths that prophesy that soon an ancestor-bearing ship will arrive with a wonderful cargo to be received by those who have expected and prepared for its arrival. The return of the ancestors and the arrival of cargo signal profound changes: freedom from laws, traditions, work, poverty, disease, ageing, and death.

[*See also* Heaven and Hell.]

BIBLIOGRAPHY

Armstrong, John H. S. *The Paradise Myth.* London, 1969. Seeks an alternative to the Genesis paradise myth in elements of Sumerian and Greek myths and in themes in Renaissance literature and art.

Baumann, Hermann. *Schöpfung und Urzeit des Menschen im Mythus der afrikanischer Völker.* Berlin, 1936. Myths of beginning and end in Africa.

Cohn, Norman. *The Pursuit of the Millennium.* 3d ed. New York, 1970. Revolutionary messianism in medieval and Reformation Europe and its bearing on modern totalitarian movements.

Lewis, R. W. B. *The American Adam.* Chicago, 1955. The new Adam in American literature of the nineteenth century as an expression of a native American mythology.

Lincoln, Andrew T. *Paradise Now and Not Yet.* Cambridge, 1981. Paradise in Saint Paul's eschatology.

Moynihan, Elizabeth B. *Paradise as a Garden: In Persia and Mughal India.* New York, 1979. The oldest surviving garden tradition. Richly illustrated.

Sanford, Charles L. *The Quest for Paradise.* Urbana, Ill., 1961. Origins and meaning of "the Garden of America" and its broader applications to aspects of American civilization.

Smith, Henry Nash. *Virgin Land.* Cambridge, Mass., 1950. The American West as myth and symbol.

Stevens, Henry Bailey. *The Recovery of Culture.* New York, 1949. Argues that humans once lived in a horticultural paradise before the "fall" into hunting and the subsequent sacrifice-linked agricultural period.

Sylvia Mary, Sr. *Nostalgia for Paradise.* London, 1965. A somewhat comparative study of the longing for paradise done from a Christian religious and theological perspective.

Williams, George H. *Wilderness and Paradise in Christian Thought.* New York, 1962. The ambivalent meanings of wilderness, garden, and desert in the Bible and subsequent appearances of these themes in Christian thought and literature.

HARRY B. PARTIN

PASSOVER

PASSOVER is the joyous Jewish festival of freedom that celebrates the Exodus of the Jews from their bondage in Egypt. Beginning on the fifteenth day of the spring month of Nisan, the festival lasts for seven days (eight days for Jews outside Israel). The Hebrew name for Passover, Pesah, refers to the paschal lamb offered as a family sacrifice in Temple times (*Ex.* 12:1-28, 12:43-49; *Dt.* 16:1-8), and the festival is so called because God "passed over" (*pasah*) the houses of the Israelites when he slew the Egyptian firstborn (*Ex.* 12:23). The annual event is called Hag ha-Pesah, the Feast of the Passover, in the Bible (*Ex.* 34:25). Another biblical name for it is Hag ha-Matsot or the Feast of the Unleavened Bread, after the command to eat unleavened bread and to refrain from eating leaven (*Ex.* 23:15, *Lv.* 23:6, *Dt.* 16:16). The critical view is that the two names are for two originally separate festivals, which were later combined. Hag ha-Pesah was a pastoral festival, whereas Hag ha-Matsot was an agricultural festival. In any event, the paschal lamb ceased to be offered when the Temple was destroyed in 70 CE, and although the name Passover is still used, the holiday is now chiefly marked by the laws concerning leaven and, especially, by the home celebration held on the first night—the Seder ("order, arrangement").

Prohibition on Leavening. On the night before the festival the house is searched thoroughly for leavened bread. Any found is gathered together and removed from the house during the morning of 14 Nisan. This is based on the biblical injunction that not only is it forbidden to eat leaven, but no leaven may remain in the house (*Ex.* 12:15, 12:19). On Passover, observant Jews do not employ utensils used during the rest of the year for food that contains leaven. Either they have special Passover utensils or they remove the leaven in the walls of their regular utensils by firing or boiling them in hot water. Only food products completely free from even the smallest particle of leaven are eaten. In many communities, rabbis supervise the manufacture of packaged Passover foods to verify that they are completely free from leaven, after which they attach their seal of fitness to the product.

The biblical reason given for eating unleavened bread (*matsah*) and refraining from eating leaven (*hamets*) is that during the Exodus the Israelites, having left Egypt in haste, were obliged to eat unleavened bread because their dough had had insufficient time to rise (*Ex.* 12:39). *Matsah* is therefore the symbol of freedom. A later idea is that leaven—bread that has risen and become fermented—represents pride and corruption, whereas unleavened bread represents humility and purity.

Synagogue Service. The synagogue liturgy for Passover contains additional prayers and hymns suffused with the themes of freedom and renewal. On the first day there is a prayer for dew; the rainy season now over, supplication is made for the more gentle dew to assist the growth of the produce in the fields. The scriptural readings are from passages dealing with Passover. On the seventh day, the anniversary of the parting of the sea (*Ex.* 14:17-15:26), the relevant passage is read; some Jews perform a symbolic reenactment to further dramatize the event.

The Seder and the Haggadah. The Seder, celebrated in the home on the first night of Passover (outside Israel, also on the second night), is a festive meal during which various rituals are carried out and the Haggadah is read or chanted. The Haggadah ("telling") is the traditional collection of hymns, stories, and poems recited in obedience to the command for parents to tell their children of God's mighty deeds

> **On Passover, observant Jews do not employ utensils used during the rest of the year for food that contains leaven.**

in delivering the people from Egyptian bondage (*Ex.* 13:8). The main features of the Haggadah are already found in outline in the Mishnah (*Pes.* 10) with some of the material going back to Temple times. It assumed its present form in the Middle Ages, with a few more recent additions. The emphasis in the Haggadah is on God alone as the deliverer from bondage. It is he and no other, neither messenger nor angel, who brings his people out from Egypt. Even Moses is mentioned by name only once in the Haggadah, and then only incidentally, at the end of a verse quoted for other purposes.

A special dish is placed on the Seder table upon which rest the symbolic foods required for the rituals. These are three *matsot,* covered with a cloth; *maror,* bitter herbs that serve as a reminder of the way the Egyptian taskmasters embittered the lives of their slaves (*Ex.* 1:14); *haroset,* a paste made of almonds, apples, and wine, symbolic of the mortar the slaves used as well as of the sweetness of redemption; a bowl of salt water, symbolic of the tears of the oppressed; parsley or other vegetables for a symbolic dipping in the salt water; a roasted bone as a reminder of the paschal lamb; and a roasted egg as a reminder of the animal sacrifice, the *hagigah* offered in Temple times on Passover, Shavu`ot, and Sukkot.

The Seder begins with the Qiddush, the festival benediction over the first cup of wine. The middle *matsah* is then broken in two, one piece being set aside to be eaten as the *afiqoman* ("dessert"), the last thing eaten before the Grace after Meals, so that the taste of the *matsah* of freedom might linger in the mouth. It is customary for the grown-ups to hide the *afiqoman,* rewarding the lucky child who finds it with a present. The parsley is first dipped in the salt water and then eaten. The youngest child present asks the Four Questions, a standard formula beginning with "Why is this night different from all other nights?" The differences are noted in four instances, such as, "On all other nights we eat either leaven or unleaven, whereas on this night we eat only unleaven." The head of the house and the other adults then proceed to reply to the Four Questions by reading the Haggadah, in which the answers are provided in terms of God's deliverances. When they reach the section that tells of the ten plagues, a little wine from the second cup is poured out to denote that it is inappropriate to drink a full cup of joy at the delivery, since in the process the enemy was killed. This section of the Haggadah concludes with a benediction in which God is thanked for his mercies, and the second cup of wine is drunk while reclining.

The celebrants then partake of the meal proper. Grace before Meals is recited over two of the three *matsot* and a benediction is recited: "Blessed art thou, O Lord our God, who has sanctified us with thy commandments and commanded us to eat *matsah.*" The bitter herbs (horseradish is generally used) are then dipped in the *haroset* and eaten. There is a tradition that in Second Temple times the famous sage Hillel would eat *matsah,* bitter herbs, and the paschal lamb together. In honor of Hillel's practice, a sandwich is made of the third *matsah* and the bitter herbs. In many places the first course is a hard-boiled egg in salt water, a further symbol of the tears of the slaves in Egypt and their hard bondage.

Commentators to the Haggadah have read into this theme various mystical ideas about the survival of Israel and the ultimate overcoming of death itself in eternal life. All join in singing these songs, for which there are many traditional melodies. This night is said to be one of God's special protection so that the usual night prayers on retiring to bed, supplicating God for his protection, are not recited since that protection is granted in any event.

BIBLIOGRAPHY

J. B. Segal's *The Hebrew Passover: From the Earliest Times to A. D. 70* (London, 1963), with a comprehensive bibliography, deals with the history and development of the festival through the Temple period and surveys the various critical theories on the origins of the festival. For the later period the best work is Chaim Raphael's *A Feast of History: Passover through the Ages as a Key to Jewish Experience* (New York, 1972). This book also attractively presents one of the very many editions of the Haggadah. Isaac Levy's little book *A Guide to Passover* (London, 1958) provides a useful summary of the traditional laws and customs of the festival. An anthology of teachings with a comprehensive bibliography is Philip Goodman's *The Passover Anthology* (Philadelphia, 1961). For an insightful look at the history of the printed Haggadah one may consult Yosef H. Yerushalmi's *Haggadah and History* (Philadelphia, 1975).

LOUIS JACOBS

PHARISEES

The Pharisees were, along with the Sadducees and the Essenes, one of the three *haereseis* ("schools of thought") that flourished among the Jews from the time of Jonathan the Hasmonean (d. 143/2 BCE) until the destruction of the Second Temple in 70 CE. According to Josephus Flavius, what distinguished them from the other two *haereseis* was their belief that the laws that had been handed down "from the fathers but which were not recorded in the laws of Moses" had to be observed, that there is a delicate interplay between fate and free will, and that every soul is imperishable, with the souls of the good ultimately passing into another body (resurrection) and the souls of the wicked condemned to suffer eternal punishment (cf. *The Jewish War* 2.162-163, 3.374; *Jewish Antiquities* 13.171-173, 18.166).

The name *Pharisees* is derived from the Greek transliteration, with a Greek plural ending, of the Hebrew *perushim*, which means "separatists, deviants, heretics." That the name may have originated as an epithet hurled at these teachers by the Sadducees, who rejected their authority, is indicated by the fact that in the tannaitic literature the term *perushim*, meaning "Pharisees," is used only juxtaposed to *tseduqim* ("Sadducees").

Essential Teachings and Institutions. The essential core of Pharisaism was its affirmation of a triad of faith that sharply distinguished it from the priestly system of Judaism that had flourished uncontested from the time of the promul-

gation of the Pentateuch (c. 397 BCE) until the rise of the Pharisees, probably during the Hasmonean Revolt (166-142 BCE). This triad of faith proclaimed that (1) the one God and Father so loved the individual that (2) he revealed to his people Israel a twofold law, one written down in the five books of Moses, the Pentateuch, and the other transmitted orally from Moses to Joshua to the elders to the prophets to the Pharisees (*Avot* 1.1), so that (3) each individual who internalized this twofold law could look forward to eternal life for his soul and resurrection for his body (cf. *San.* 10.1).

The triad of faith likewise generated novel institutions. The institution launched by the Pharisees that proved to be the most durable was the synagogue. [*See* Synagogue.] The

> As champions of the oral law, they made it a point to formulate their teachings in nonbiblical modes, forms, and language.

individual reaching out for an unmediated relationship with God in his quest for eternal life and resurrection needed a noncultic institution where, in the presence of other co-believers, he could proclaim the Shema` to affirm God's singularity and utter the Tefillah, eighteen blessings that include the statement that God will, with his great mercy, revive the dead.

In addition to novel institutions, the Pharisees developed new notions about God and the peoplehood of Israel. Although God was occasionally conceived of in scripture as a father, it was as the father of his people and not as the father of the individual. The Pharisees, for their part, however, spoke of the father in heaven, who so loves and cares for each individual that he revealed the road by which the individual could reach eternal life and resurrection. The Pharisees further stressed this one-to-one relationship when they coined such new names for God as *Maqom* ("all present, every-place"), *ha-Qaddosh Barukh Hu'* ("the holy one, blessed be he"), and *Shekhinah* ("indwelling presence").

As a class, the Pharisees far more resembled peripatetic teachers, such as the Stoics, than either prophets or priests (cf. Josephus, *The Life* 12). As champions of the oral law, they made it a point to formulate their teachings in nonbiblical modes, forms, and language. Thus they wrote down none of their teachings, framed their laws (*halakhot*) and doctrines (*aggadot*) without regard for historical setting, rejected poetic modes of expression even for the prayers and blessings they formulated, cultivated logical (i. e., deductive) modes of reasoning, and introduced proof texts.

The Pharisees and Jesus. As the authoritative teachers of the twofold law, the Pharisees were troubled by Jesus' refusal to bow to their authority. They therefore challenged his claim to a singular relationship to God. But this was as far as the Pharisees could go, since they were committed to the principle of religious tolerance.

The hostility toward the Pharisees found in the Gospels is thus to be seen as stemming from their authors' anger with these teachers for having rejected Jesus' claims and those of his followers.

Historical Significance. The Pharisees transformed Judaism by elevating themselves to Moses' seat and by proclaiming the twofold law, and not the written law alone, to be normative. The Pharisees' oral law gave birth to the Mishnah, the Palestinian and Babylonian Talmuds, the geonic, medieval, and modern *responsa,* and the various codes of Jewish law—all of which are, for a majority of Jews, still recognized as normative.

Perhaps the most enduring of the achievements of the Pharisees was their focus on the individual and his yearnings for an eternal life for his individual soul and his individual body. By picturing God the Father as so loving every individual that his yearning for immortality might be fulfilled, the Pharisees, and the Christian and Muslim teachers who took up the refrain, enhanced the individual's sense of eternal worth.

BIBLIOGRAPHY

The definition of the Pharisees offered above was first articulated in Solomon Zeitlin's *History of the Second Jewish Commonwealth: Prolegomena* (Philadelphia, 1933), pp. 41-56, and spelled out in detail by him in "Ha-Tseduqim ve-ha-Perushim," *Horeb 3* (1936): 56-89, which appeared in English as "The Sadducees and the Pharisees: A Chapter in the Development of the Halakhah," in Zeitlin's *Studies in the Early History of Judaism,* vol. 2 (New York, 1974), pp. 259-291. It has been further elaborated in my own writings, especially "The Internal City," *Journal of Scientific Study of Religion* 5 (1966): 225-240; "The Pharisaic Revolution," in *Perspectives in Jewish Learning,* vol. 2 (Chicago, 1966), pp. 26-51; "Prolegomenon," in *Judaism and Christianity,* edited by W. O. E. Oesterley (1937-1938; reprint, New York, 1969); "Pharisaism and the Crisis of the Individual in the Graeco-Roman World," *Jewish Quarterly Review* 61 (July 1970): 27-52; "Defining the Pharisees: The Tannaitic Sources," *Hebrew Union College Annual* 40/41 (1969-1970): 205-249; and *A Hidden Revolution: The Pharisees' Search for the Kingdom Within* (Nashville, 1977). Although I am fundamentally in agreement with Zeitlin on the definition of the Pharisees, I diverge radically from him on reconstructing their history; compare Zeitlin's *The Rise and Fall of the Judean State,* vol. 1 (Philadelphia, 1962), pp. 178-187, with my article "Solomon Zeitlin's Contribution to the Historiography of the Inter-Testamental Period," *Judaism* 14 (Summer 1965): 354-367, and my book *A Hidden Revolution,* pp. 211-251.

For the range of scholarly opinion, see especially A. Michel and J. Moyne's comprehensive discussion and extensive bibliography in "Le Pharisiens," in *Dictionnaire de la Bible, supplément,* edited by H. Cazelles and A. Feuillet, fascs. 39-40 (Paris, 1966), and Ralph Marcus's "The Pharisees in the Light of Modern Scholarship," *Journal of Religion* 32 (July 1952): 153-164. Most influential have been the views of Emil Schürer in *A History of the Jewish People in the Time of Jesus Christ,* 2d div., vol. 2, 2d rev. ed. (New York, 1902), pp. 10-28; R. Travers Herford in *The Pharisees* (1924; reprint, Boston, 1962); George Foot Moore in *Judaism in the First Centuries of the Christian Era,* in vol. 1 (Cambridge, Mass., c. 1927), pp. 56-71; Louis Finkelstein in *The Pharisees: The Sociological Background of Their Faith,* 2 vols., 3d ed. (Philadelphia, 1962); and, more recently, Jacob Neusner in *The Rabbinic Traditions about the Pharisees before 70,* 3 vols. (Leiden, 1971), and *From Politics to Piety: The Emergence of Pharisaic Judaism* (Englewood Cliffs, N. J., 1972).

ELLIS RIVKIN

PHILISTINE RELIGION

Although many questions about the Philistines remain unanswered, including questions about Philistine religion, a variety of sources provide a modicum of evidence on this intriguing people. Most important among these are the Old Testament (Hebrew scriptures), the Egyptian texts, and archaeological materials from Palestine.

The Philistines were a warlike people who migrated from somewhere in the Aegean basin to the southern coastal plain of Palestine; the most important and best-documented phase of this migration took place in the early part of the twelfth century BCE. The Philistine invasion of the southeastern Levant is well known from the artistic and literary accounts at Medinet Habu in Egypt, where Ramses III left a record of his military encounter (c. 1190 BCE) with two groups of "Sea Peoples," the Tjekker and the Peleset. The Egyptians repelled the invasion, and some of the Sea Peoples settled in southern Palestine. This region was called Philistia, and the Greek name for the Philistines, *Palastinoi,* later evolved into *Palestine,* the modern name for the land as a whole. The major cities of the Philistines were Gaza, Ashdod, Ashqelon, Gath, and Ekron, the so-called Philistine pentapolis. Because of their expansion into the hinterland of Canaan, the Philistines (Heb., *pelishtim*) were major rivals of the Israelites during the Israelite conquest, settlement, and early monarchy, although the Philistine threat waned after their military defeat by King David (c. 950 BCE).

There is some evidence concerning Philistine origins in the archaeological record and the nonbiblical literature (e.g., the tendency to associate the Philistine migration with the ethnic upheaval at the end of the Greek Bronze Age, around 1200 BCE). But it is the Old Testament that contains the most direct statements concerning the Philistines' ancestral homeland. Several passages linking the Philistines with Caphtor, or Crete (cf. *Dt.* 2:23, *Jer.* 47:4, *Am.* 9:7), are among the many indications pointing to an Aegean background. *Genesis* 10:14 and *1 Chronicles* 1:12 identify Egypt as the

Philistines' place of origin, but this can be understood in light of the Philistine migration route.

Excavations at numerous Palestinian sites, most of which are located in the coastal plain or the Shephelah (the western foothills of the Judean mountains), have yielded significant remains of Philistine material culture; the beautiful and distinctive painted pottery of the Philistines is undoubtedly the best-known aspect of their civilization. Unfortunately—and surprisingly—there is no written text that can be attributed to the Philistines with any degree of certainty. While this dearth of Philistine literature may be eliminated as archaeological research continues, it is obvious that any attempt to describe Philistine religion is severely limited by a lack of primary Philistine texts on the subject. Nevertheless, we are not totally ignorant of the Philistine pantheon and cult, since the Old Testament and the archaeological data can be gleaned for relevant details.

In her important study *The Philistines and Their Material Culture,* Trude Dothan has provided archaeologists with a thorough analysis of the types and groups into which Philistine pottery (found at some thirty Palestinian sites) can be divided. Dothan's summary statement concerning this pottery serves as a general introduction to Philistine religion as well: "Typologically, Philistine pottery reflects the Sea Peoples' Aegean background, plus certain Cypriot, Egyptian, and local Canaanite elements" (p. 94). A careful investigation

> **Excavations at numerous Palestinian sites, most of which are located in the coastal plain or the Shephelah have yielded significant remains.**

of Philistine religion reveals a similar potpourri that points to the eclectic or assimilative nature of Philistine religion. Such assimilation is evident in the Philistines' pantheon, religious practices, temples, and cult objects.

Pantheon. The members of the Philistine pantheon about whom we possess specific information—Dagon (or Dagan), Baalzebub (or Baalzebul), and Ashtoret (or Ashtaroth)—were all deities worshiped for centuries by the pre-Philistine occupants of Canaan. According to the biblical record, Dagon was the supreme god of the Philistine pantheon (*1 Sm.* 5:1-7, *1 Chr.* 10:10). Like many ancient high gods, he was probably understood as a god of war, since we read about the Philistines giving thanks to this deity after victory over two of their archenemies, Samson and Saul (*Jgs.* 16:23-24, *1 Chr.* 10:10). Dagon had temples in Gaza (*Jgs.* 16:21, 23-30), Ashdod (*1 Sm.* 5:1-7; *1 Mc.* 10:83-85, 11:4), and probably in Beth-shan (*1 Chr.* 10:10; cf. *1 Sm.* 31:10). The Ashdod temple housed a statue of Dagon. Interestingly, the biblical

account points to the Philistine acknowledgment of the superiority of Yahveh over Dagon. As noted above, Dagon was an important god in the ancient Semitic pantheon (his name appears in Canaanite toponyms). He is known to have been worshiped at Ugarit, and, in fact, he was honored at ancient Ebla as early as the second half of the third millennium BCE.

Baalzebub, another member of the ancient Semitic pantheon, was closely associated with the Philistine town of Ekron (probably Tel Miqne): *2 Kings* 1:2-16 informs us that Baalzebub was consulted by an oracle and was in some way associated with healing. Baalzebul was a name used at Ugarit for Baal. Texts from the time of Ramses III indicate that the Philistines knew the god Baal when they invaded Egypt.

In addition to these members of the Semitic pantheon, there is evidence that the Philistines worshiped Egyptian deities. The wholesale assimilation apparent in the Philistine pantheon may indicate that the Philistine settlement in Palestine was a more gradual process than has previously been imagined. It should be remembered, however, that such borrowing of divine names and/or epithets was a common practice in ancient Near Eastern religions. Indeed, the Old Testament contains frequent denunciations of the Israelites' attraction toward and participation in religious practices of their neighbors, including the Philistines (*Jgs.* 10:6).

Religious Practices and Functionaries. According to *Judges* 16:23-24, the Philistines and their leaders gathered together for sacrifices and festivals. In fact, the Old Testament records an occasion when the Philistines sent a guilt offering to the God of Israel, since they had learned to respect this other national deity (*1 Sm.* 4:6, 5:1-6:21). Apparently, the Philistines carried or wore portable idols or amulets into battle (*2 Sm.* 5:21; cf. *2 Mc.* 12:40). The advice of priests and diviners was sought (*1 Sm.* 5:5, 6:2-9; cf. *2 Kgs.* 1:2), and the art of soothsaying was developed (*Is.* 2:6). With regard to burial customs, several Philistine sites have yielded whole or fragmentary anthropoid clay coffins, use of which was probably borrowed from the Egyptians.

Clearly, the religious practices of the Philistines were similar to those of their Semitic neighbors; the absence of circumcision seems to be the one exception (*Jgs.* 14:3; *1 Sm.* 17:26, 17:36, 18:25). Indeed, the Philistines' failure to practice this ritual enabled the Israelites to refer to their archenemies as "the uncircumcised" (*Jgs.* 15:18; *1 Sm.* 14:6, 31:4).

Temples and Cult Objects. A large number and wide variety of cult objects have been recovered in the excavations of Philistine strata, especially at Gezer, Ashdod, and Tell Qasile. They include kernos rings and bowls, decorated bowls and vases, zoomorphic and anthropomorphic figurines, ritual stands, rhytons, and so on. Of special interest are the numerous kernos rings and bowls, especially since these Early Iron Age Philistine objects show affinities to objects from the final years of Mycenaean culture. Also important is a series of lion-headed libation cups from

Philistine sites in Palestine, vessels that have similarities with rhytons from the Mycenaean-Minoan tradition.

Without a doubt, the most frequently discussed cult object associated with the Philistines is the stylized female figurine called the Ashdoda (so named after the site where it was found). The Ashdoda looks like a throne or couch into which human body parts—a head, elongated neck, armless torso, and molded breasts—have been merged; the entire figurine is elaborately painted. According to Trude Dothan, this figurine is probably "a schematic representation of a female deity and throne" (p. 234), an object with clear-cut Aegean antecedents. It is part of a group of Ashdodas, now fragmentary, found in strata at Ashdod that date from the twelfth to the eighth century BCE.

The Ashdoda, together with other artifacts and features of Philistine material culture and religion, has prompted many scholars to view Philistine religion in terms of its Aegean background. Here the term *Aegean* is used broadly and includes Crete, Cyprus, and the Greek islands and mainland. Yet it is also clear that the Philistines assimilated much—including a number of religious beliefs and practices—from their Semitic neighbors.

BIBLIOGRAPHY

A classic treatment of the Philistines is R. A. S. Macalister's *The Philistines: Their History and Civilization* (Oxford, 1913). Naturally, much of Macalister's work is dated, but his contribution to our understanding of this important people is noteworthy, especially since his volume was based largely on his own archaeological excavations at Gezer.

The most important and up-to-date source of information on the Philistines is Trude Dothan's magnificent volume, *The Philistines and Their Material Culture* (New Haven, 1982). Dothan's article "What We Know about the Philistines," *Biblical Archaeology Review* 7 (July-August 1984): 20-44, which is well illustrated and written on a more popular level, is an excellent place to begin an investigation of the Philistines. Another reliable source is K. A. Kitchen's essay "The Philistines," in *Peoples of Old Testament Times,* edited by D. J. Wiseman (Oxford, 1973), pp. 53-78. A recent and balanced study of the Philistines is John F. Brug's "A Literary and Archaeological Study of the Philistines" (Ph. D. diss., University of Minnesota, 1984).

For details on Amihai Mazar's excavation of a sequence of Philistine temples at Tell Qasile, see Mazar's two articles "A Philistine Temple at Tell Qasile" and "Additional Philistine Temples at Tell Qasile," *Biblical Archaeologist 36* (1973): 42-48, and 40 (1977): 82-87, and his final reports, *Excavations at Tell Qasile I* (Jerusalem, 1980) and *Excavations at Tell Qasile II* (Jerusalem, 1985).

GERALD L. MATTINGLY

PHOENICIAN RELIGION

The names *Phoenicia* and *Phoenician* come from the Greek *phoinike* and *phoinikias,* respectively. These terms were used by the Greeks to designate the coastal strip on the eastern shores of the Mediterranean and its hinterland, and the Semitic-speaking inhabitants of that territory.

At the beginning of the Iron Age (c. 1200 BCE), the great political and social unrest in the Levant seems to have forced the Phoenicians into some sort of cultural coherence. At the same time, several invading groups (Philistines, Arameans, Hebrews) appeared on the scene, ultimately to establish the nation-states that would occupy the Levant throughout most of the first millennium BCE. The Phoenicians found themselves confined to the coast, in a territory nowhere more than 60 kilometers wide, from Tartus (Antaradus) in the north to `Akko (Acre) in the south.

Since they were generally cut off politically and geographically from the interior, the Phoenicians turned their attention to the sea. Even within their homeland, the Mediterranean provided them with the safest and surest path for transportation and communications. And the Phoenician mastery of navigation led them to establish a series of colonies, trading posts, and settlements across the Mediterranean to the west. These colonies, the most famous of which was Carthage (probably founded by Tyre in the late ninth century), are often called "Punic" (the Latin equivalent of Phoenician), to distinguish them from mainland Phoenicia.

Phoenician political power was at its height in the tenth and ninth centuries BCE, with Tyre emerging as the most important city. The alliance between King Hiram of Tyre and King Solomon of Israel represents the political zenith of both nations. Close relations between Phoenicia and the Israelite kingdoms, including alliance by marriage, lasted into the ninth century.

When the Persians defeated the Babylonians in 539, they made Phoenicia part of their fifth satrapy, and built a royal palace in Sidon. Finally, Alexander conquered Phoenicia in 332, thanks in part to a remarkable feat of military engineering (Diodorus Siculus, *Bibliotheca historica* 17.40-46). Only vestiges of Phoenician autonomy remained in the Seleucid and subsequent Roman periods.

Until the middle of the nineteenth century CE, the Phoenicians were known exclusively from non-Phoenician sources. Two additional factors make a general description of Phoenician religion difficult, if not impossible. First, there seems never to have been a unified national religious consciousness. As a result, the major centers had their own pantheons and idiosyncratic practices. Second, Phoenician religion tended to be adaptive rather than exclusive; in particular, Egyptian, Aramean, and Greek elements are evident.

Deities. The epithet Baal-Shamem ("lord of heaven") denotes the high god of any local Phoenician pantheon. In the eighth-century inscription of King Azitawadda (found at Karatepe, in southern Anatolia), Baal-Shamem takes precedence over the rest of the gods. In the Esarhaddon treaty, he is clearly the lord of the storm, and he is appropriately identified with the old Canaanite Baal of Mount Tsafon, the weather god who was the Baal of Ugarit in the second millennium.

While the high god is the leading deity in the pantheon, he is not the principal object of cultic veneration. Eshmun and Melqart were gods who guaranteed the fertility of the land and the fecundity of the flocks. Eshmun, who is linked with Melqart in the Esarhaddon treaty, was the dying and reviving god venerated at Sidon. At Ugarit, the patron of the deified dead was Rapiu ("healer"), and his name survives in those of the late first-millennium Phoenician deities Shadrafa ("healing spirit") and Baal-Merappe ("healer Baal").

The third important dying and reviving god was Adonis, whose cult was prominent in Byblos, and especially at the spring of Aphaca, near Beirut. The well-known story of the death of Adonis (e.g., Ovid, *Metamorphoses* 10.710-739) is undoubtedly of Semitic origin.

The most prominent deity in the Phoenician and Punic cults was the goddess Astarte. In the Esarhaddon treaty she is invoked as a war goddess, but her personality was more complex; she was also a fertility goddess, a mother goddess, and a goddess of love, having assimilated her many characteristics from various older goddesses such as the Canaanite triad of Athirat, Anat, and Athtart; the Egyptian Hathor; and the Mesopotamian Ishtar. Astarte's character was so diverse, in fact, that she was identified with several Greek goddesses: Aphrodite, goddess of love and fertility; Hera, queen of heaven; and the mother goddess Cybele.

Various other gods comprise the "assembly of the gods," the "holy ones" (so the Yehimilk inscription), or the "whole family of the children of the gods" (Azitawadda). The main feature of the different local pantheons is their diversity. In the Karatepe inscription, for example, King Azitawadda's patron god is the otherwise unknown Baal-*krntrysh* (significance uncertain). The inscription also mentions Rashap (Reshef), one of the most important West Semitic gods from the third millennium onward; but the epithet assigned to Azitawadda's Rashap is unique and problematic. In his curse against anyone who would remove the great portal he has just dedicated, Azitawadda specifically invokes Baal-Shamem, El-Creator-of-the-World, and Eternal Sun. All of these divine titles evoke numerous Near Eastern parallels, but nowhere else do they occur in this form or juxtaposition.

In addition, a number of old gods from different places appear in various cults. In general, though, the old gods belong to a shadowy world of protective geniuses and malevolent demons.

Beliefs and Practices. In Phoenician religion, three kinds of cultic activity predominated: (1) rituals associated with the dying and reviving god, (2) sacrificial rites, and (3) funerary rites. There were three centers of cultic activity: (1) undeveloped natural sites, especially mountains, rivers, and groves of trees, which for one reason or another were considered

sacred (cf. *Is.* 57:3-13); (2) open-air shrines, usually featuring a sacred grove, a small chapel, a sacrificial altar (the biblical "high place"), and one or more conical stone pillars, called betyls, that symbolized divine presence (to be compared with the wooden asherah poles mentioned in the Bible); and (3) fully enclosed temples with large courtyards for public ceremonies, such as Solomon's Phoenician-designed sanctuary.

The cult of the dying and reviving god was associated with sacred natural sites. In an annual celebration of Adonis' death, the people of Byblos would perform mourning rites and lamentations. Then they would offer sacrifices to Adonis "as if to a dead person," following which they would proclaim his revival.

The ultimate source of the festival is clearly the seasonal cycle; the dying and reviving god, whose demise comes with

> **The funerary practices strongly imply Phoenician belief in an afterlife.**

the withering summer heat, personifies that cycle. The return of the god guarantees the return of fertility to the land.

In Phoenicia proper, animal and vegetable offerings were made at the various shrines, especially in conjunction with the seasonal festivals, and in fulfillment of personal vows; human sacrifices were apparently offered in times of crisis. The evidence for the Punic sacrificial cults comes primarily from Carthage, with comparable evidence from other sites in Sardinia, Sicily, and North Africa. Excavations in the area have turned up thousands of urns containing the cremated remains of birds, animals, and small children. The urns have been found in three distinct archeological strata, indicating that the precinct was in continuous use from around 750 BCE until the Romans destroyed the city in 146 BCE. Offering up an innocent child as a vicarious victim was a supreme act of propitiation, probably intended to guarantee the welfare of family and community alike.

Another aspect of the Phoenician attitude toward death shows up in funerary practices. The preferred mode of burial was inhumation, although there were some cremations (aside from sacrificial victims). Wealthier Phoenicians were buried in decorated coffins.

The funerary practices strongly imply Phoenician belief in an afterlife. That impression is confirmed by Phoenician royal tomb inscriptions, which level curses against anyone who would disturb the tombs.

The many Phoenician religious shrines were staffed by various cultic officials, including priests, scribes, musicians, barbers (probably for the ritual shaving mentioned above), and male and female cult prostitutes. The titular head of the cult, in all likelihood, was the king.

BIBLIOGRAPHY

There are two excellent general works on the Phoenicians in English: Donald B. Harden's *The Phoenicians,* 2d ed. (New York, 1980), and Sabatino Moscati's *The World of the Phoenicians,* translated by Alastair Hamilton (New York, 1968). Both are well illustrated and contain extensive bibliographies of older works (which will, therefore, not be listed here). The definitive edition of the Phoenician and Punic inscriptions, still in progress, is the *Corpus Inscriptionum Semiticarum,* part 1 (Paris, 1881-). A thoroughly annotated English translation of Phoenician (but not Punic) texts is John C. L. Gibson's *Textbook of Syrian Semitic Inscriptions,* vol. 3, *Phoenician Inscriptions* (Oxford, 1982). A good selection of both Phoenician and Punic inscriptions with German translations, commentary, and glossary is *Kanaanäische und aramäische Inschriften,* 2d ed., 3 vols., edited by Herbert Donner and Wolfgang Röllig (Wiesbaden, 1966-1969). Of the utmost importance for students of the inscriptions is Javier Teixidor's "Bulletin d'épigraphie sémi-tique," which has appeared more or less regularly in the journal *Syria* since 1967 (vols. 44-). There is also a fine dictionary available in English: Richard S. Tomback's *A Comparative Semitic Lexicon of the Phoenician and Punic Languages* (Missoula, Mont., 1978). The standard survey of the Phoenician gods is Marvin H. Pope and Wolfgang Röllig's "Syrien: Die Mythologie der Ugariter und Phönizier," in *Wörterbuch der Mythologie,* vol. 1, edited by H. W. Haussig (Stuttgart, 1965), pp. 219-312. Phoenician and Punic personal names are collected and analyzed in Frank L. Benz's *Personal Names in the Phoenician and Punic Inscriptions* (Rome, 1972).

The student interested in the state of the art in Phoenician and Punic studies must learn Italian, the primary language of scholarly publication. The most important scholarly journal is the *Rivista di studi fenici* (Rome, 1973-). Fundamental treatments of key issues are Sabatino Moscati's *Problematica della civiltà fenicia* (Rome, 1974) and the essays of Giovanni Garbini collected in *I Fenici, storia e religione* (Naples, 1980). An excellent introduction to the present state of scholarship is the conference volume *La religione fenicia: Matrici orientali e sviluppi occidentali* (Rome, 1981). This volume includes, among a number of important studies, two seminal programmatic statements: Paolo Xella's "Aspetti e problemi dell'indagine storico-religiosa" (pp. 7-25) and Giovanni Garbini's "Continuità e innovazioni nella religione fenicia" (pp. 29-43; also in *I Fenici,* cited above, pp. 151-159).

There are many recommendable studies on special topics. Javier Teixidor's *The Pagan God* (Princeton, 1977) is a brilliant analysis of popular religion in the Greco-Roman Near East, with special attention to Phoenicia, Syria, North Arabia, and Palmyra. Two volumes of essays filled with learning and interest are Robert Du Mesnil du Buisson's *Études sur les dieux phéniciens hérités par l'empire romain* (Leiden, 1970) and *Nouvelles études sur les dieux et les mythes de Canaan* (Leiden, 1973). The two essays that reconstruct the pantheons of Byblos (*Études,* pp. 56-116) and Tyre (*Nouvelles études,* pp. 32-69) are *tours de force.* A characteristically insightful and controversial study of Phoenician religion in relation to the Bible is William F. Albright's *Yahweh and the Gods of Canaan* (London, 1968), pp. 208-264. On the dying and reviving god, two recent studies of extraordinary interest are Édouard Lipinski's "La fête de l'ensevelissement et de la résurrection de Melqart," in *Actes de la Dix-septième Rencontre Assyriologique Internationale,* edited by André Finet (Brussels, 1970), pp. 30-58 (exhaustively annotated), and Noel Robertson's "The Ritual Background of the Dying God in Cyprus and Syro-Palestine," *Harvard Theological Review* 75 (July 1982): 313-359.

A splendid account of the Phoenician colonization of the west is Guy Bunnens's *L'expansion phénicienne en Méditerranée* (Brussels, 1979). A popular account of recent excavations at Carthage that emphasizes the issue of child sacrifice is Lawrence E. Stager and Samuel R. Wolff's "Child Sacrifice at Carthage: Religious Rite or Population Control?," *Biblical Archaeology Review* 10 (January-February 1984): 31-51. The article is generally more sober than the title would suggest, and it is magnificently illustrated. For a powerful argument against the existence of institutionalized child sacrifice, see Moshe Weinfeld's "The Worship of Molech and of the Queen of Heaven and Its Background," *Ugarit-Forschungen* 4 (1972): 133-154.

On Philo Byblius's *Phoenician History,* there is a first-rate translation and commentary by Albert I. Baumgarten, *The Phoenician History of Philo of Byblos* (Leiden, 1981). No similar up-to-date study of *The Syrian Goddess* exists, although there is a readable English translation with brief introduction by Harold W. Attridge and R. A. Oden, Jr., *The Syrian Goddess (De dea Syria)* (Missoula, Mont., 1976). For a fuller commentary, *Lu-kíans Schrift über die syrische Göttin,* edited and translated by Carl Clemen (Leipzig, 1938), is still useful.

Finally, space must be found for Gustave Flaubert's novel of Carthage, *Salammbö,* corr. ed. (Paris, 1879), inspired by his visit to the site in 1858. The chapter entitled "Moloch" includes Flaubert's gruesome account of child sacrifice.

ALAN M. COOPER

PILGRIMAGE

An Overview

A religious believer in any culture may sometimes look beyond the local temple, church, or shrine, feel the call of some distant holy place renowned for miracles and the revivification of faith, and resolve to journey there. The goal of the journey, the sacred site, may be Banaras, India (Hindu); Jerusalem, Israel (Jewish, Christian, Muslim); Mecca, Saudi Arabia (Muslim); Meiron, Israel (Jewish); Ise, Japan (Shinto); Saikoku, Japan (Buddhist); or one of a hundred thousand others.

The Experience of Pilgrimage. Pilgrimage has the classic three-stage form of a rite of passage: (1) separation (the start of the journey), (2) the liminal stage (the journey itself, the sojourn at the shrine, and the encounter with the sacred), and (3) reaggregation (the homecoming). It differs from initiation in that the journey is to a center "out there," not through a threshold that marks a change in the individual's social status (except in the case of the pilgrimage to Mecca). Movement is the pilgrim's element, into which she or he is drawn by the spiritual magnetism of a pilgrimage center.

Spiritual Magnetism of Pilgrimage Centers. A number of factors may be involved in the spiritual magnetism of a pilgrimage center. A sacred image of great age or divine origin may be the magnet. They induce awe and devotion, for they have the power to touch the religious instinct.

Miracles of healing also endow pilgrimage centers with a powerful spiritual magnetism. Such miracles seem to occur when there are both a heightened sense of the supernatural and a profound sense of human fellowship, of shared experience.

Many pilgrimage centers are sites of apparitions, places where supernatural beings have appeared to humans. Or the birthplace, location of life events, or tomb of a holy person may be a pilgrimage magnet.

Historical Classification of Pilgrimages. Pilgrimages have arisen in different periods of history and have taken different paths.

Archaic pilgrimage. Certain pilgrimage traditions have come down from very ancient times, and little or nothing is known of their foundation. Others have been overlaid by the trappings of a later religion, although archaic customs can still be discerned. Such syncretism occurred at Mecca and Jerusalem in the Middle East, at Izamal and Chalma in Mexico, and at Canterbury in England.

Prototypical pilgrimage. As in all new pilgrimage traditions, the foundation is marked by visions and miracles and by the advent of a swarm of fervent pilgrims. They make spontaneous acts of devotion, praying, touching objects at the site, leaving tags on trees, and so on. As the impulse for *communitas* (community fellowship) grows, a strong feedback system develops, further increasing the popularity of the pilgrimage center. A prototypical pilgrimage tradition soon manifests charter narratives and holy books about the founder. A shrine is built and an ecclesiastical structure develops. The Jerusalem and Rome pilgrimages are prototypical for Christianity, Jerusalem for Judaism, Mecca for Islam, Banaras and Mount Kailas for Hinduism, Bodh Gaya and Sarnath, India, for Buddhism, and Ise for Shinto.

Modern pilgrimage. All over the world in the last two centuries a new type of pilgrimage, with a high devotional tone and bands of ardent adherents, has developed. Modern pilgrimage is frankly technological; pilgrims travel by automobile and airplane, and pilgrimage centers publish newspapers and pamphlets. The catchment areas of modern pilgrimage are the great industrial cities. However, the message of the shrine is still traditional, at variance with the values of today. Many Roman Catholic pilgrimages have been triggered by an apparition of the Virgin Mary to some humble visionary with a message of penance and a gift of healing, as at Lourdes, France.

Other centers have arisen from the ashes of some dead pilgrimage shrine. A devotee has a vision of the founder, which heralds new miracles and a virtually new pilgrimage, as at Aylesford, England. Both apparitional and saint-centered pilgrimages in other parts of the modern world abound, as in Japan and at the tomb of the holy rabbi Huri of Beersheva, Israel.

BIBLIOGRAPHY

Aradi, Zsolt. *Shrines to Our Lady around the World.* New York, 1954. A remarkably full listing of world Marian pilgrimages, illustrated, and with short descriptions.

Bhardwaj, Surinder Mohan. *Hindu Places of Pilgrimage in India: A Study in Cultural Geography.* Berkeley, 1973. A much-discussed analysis of levels or rank-order among pilgrimages in India.

Kitagawa, Joseph M. "Three Types of Pilgrimage in Japan." In *Studies in Mysticism and Religion Presented to Gershom G. Scholem,* edited by E. E. Urbach, R. J. Zwi Werblowsky, and Chaim Wirszubski, pp. 155-164. Jerusalem, 1967. Analyzes pilgrimages to sacred mountains, to temples and shrines, and to places hallowed by holy men. A pioneer article.

Kriss-Rittenbeck, Lenz, ed. *Wallfahrt kennt keine Grenzen.* Munich, forthcoming. New aspects of Christian pilgrimage, by international scholars.

Morinis, E. Alan, ed. *Sacred Journeys: The Anthropology of Pilgrimage.* Forthcoming. An essential reference covering many types and aspects of pilgrimage throughout the world, using an advanced theoretical framework.

Palestine Pilgrims Text Society (London). Volumes 1, 3, and 10 (1891-1897) are classic primary sources, constituting the texts of the earliest pilgrims to the Holy Land.

Preston, James J. "Methodological Issues in the Study of Pilgrimage." In *Sacred Journeys,* edited by E. Alan Morinis. Forthcoming. A careful and enlightened essay introducing pilgrimage in all its aspects.

Turner, Victor. "Pilgrimage as Social Process." In his *Dramas, Fields, and Metaphors,* pp. 167-230. Ithaca, N. Y., 1974. The first modern anthropological essay on pilgrimage, introducing the role of pilgrimage in the generation of *communitas,* the sentiment of humankindness; views religious pilgrimage as a moving process, not an arrangement of structures.

Turner, Victor, and Edith Turner. *Image and Pilgrimage in Christian Culture.* New York, 1978. An anthropological study of the cultural, symbolic, and theological aspects of pilgrimage, using important Mexican, Irish, medieval, and Marian examples.

EDITH TURNER

Muslim Pilgrimage

The annual pilgrimage of Muslims to Mecca, in west-central Arabia, is known by the term *hajj.* As a religious duty that is the fifth of the Five Pillars of Islam, the *hajj* is an obligation for all Muslims to perform once in their adult lives, provided they be of sound mind and health and financially able at the time.

Hajj in the Context of Middle Eastern Worldviews. The duty of performing the *hajj* rests on the authority of scripture (Qur'an) and the recorded practice of the prophet Muhammad (*sunnah*), as these are interpreted by the orthodox schools of Islamic law; Shi`i Muslims rely in addition on the teachings of the early imams, leaders descended from the family of the Prophet through the lineage of `Ali.

For Muslims, the shrine in Mecca comprehends several notions: for example, that creation began at Mecca; that the father of the prophets, Ibrahim (Abraham), constructed the first house of worship (Ka`bah, Bayt Allah) at Mecca; that the pagan practices of the Arabs at the Ka`bah were displayed by God's final revelation through Muhammad, his Messenger to the Arabs and to all of humankind. Indeed, the Ka`bah determines the ritual direction, or *qiblah,* the focal point toward which canonical prayers (*salat*) and places of prayer (*masjid,* mosque) are physically oriented, the direction in which the deceased are faced in their graves, and the focus of other ritual gestures as well. The Ka`bah is regarded as the navel of the universe, and it is the place from which the prayers of the faithful are believed to be most effective. [*See also* Ka`bah.]

By the sixth century CE, the bedouin tribes of central Arabia were undergoing political and social changes, reflected especially in the growing commercial importance of settled markets and caravansaries at Mecca. Muhammad's tribe, the Quraysh, dominated caravan trading through the use of force and lucrative arrangements with other tribes. Such trading centers were also pilgrimage sites to which Arabs journeyed annually during sacred months constituting a moratorium of tribal feuding. Although the pilgrimage remained a dangerous undertaking in the face of banditry and unpacified tribal rivalry, the special months and territories provided sanctuary for many of the shared sacred and profane activities of Arab tribal culture. The auspicious times and places of pilgrimage, along with the annual fairs and

> **The pilgrimage to Mecca came to symbolize for Muslim peoples . . . the sacred origins and center of their common confessional heritage.**

markets held at nearby locales along the pilgrims' routes, appear to have played significant roles in stabilizing the segmented polity of Arab tribalism.

Islam did not destroy the pre-Islamic *hajj* rituals, but it infused them with new symbols and meanings. In its own conceptual terms, Islam asserted (or reasserted) monotheism over the polytheism of Jahiliyah. The Qur'an also declared that the sacred months of pilgrimage should be calculated according to a lunar calendar that could not be adjusted every few years. Following the Muslim calendar, the *hajj* and other ceremonials rotate throughout the seasons of the year.

The historic seventh-century shift at Mecca from a polytheistic to a monotheistic cosmology—of which the *hajj* is the supreme ritual expression—is significant for the comparative study of religions and civilizations. Urban geographer Paul Wheatley (*The Pivot of the Four Corners,* 1971) suggests

that cities such as Mecca, by focusing sacredness on cult symbols of cosmic and moral order, were able to organize the previous tribal polities into larger, more efficient economic, social, and political systems. Urban-based great traditions evolved and were perpetuated by literati who canonized the technical requirements and meanings of ritual performance at the shrines. In this way, such traditions provided for the continuity of culture over time and geographic space; they ensured that the cosmic center (*omphalos, axis mundi*) continued to be enshrined and celebrated within the sacred city. The seventh-century shift from local deities and tribal morality to a monotheistic cosmic and moral order in Islam coincided with a period of Arabian hegemony over larger neighboring civilizations. With the islamization of the Arabian *hajj* during this process, therefore, the pilgrimage to Mecca came to symbolize for Muslim peoples and lands across Asia, the Middle East, and North Africa the sacred origins and center of their common confessional heritage.

Requirements and Preparations for the Hajj. Muslim authorities generally agree on the following requirements of eligibility for the *hajj:* (1) one must be a confessing Muslim who (2) has reached the age of puberty, (3) is of rational and sound mind, (4) is a freed man or woman, and (5) has the physical strength and health to undertake the rigors of the journey.

From figures available on *hajj* participation in relation to total Muslim population, it is clear that only a small percentage of Muslims make the pilgrimage in any given year, and that many never undertake the journey at all. Living at great distances from Mecca has tended to make fulfillment of the duty of *hajj* less likely for many Muslims.

Although *hajj* is a duty one owes to God, the decision as to whether and when one should undertake the "journey to the House" belongs ultimately to each individual Muslim.

A pilgrim's separation from familiar social and cultural surroundings constitutes a moment of prayerful anxiety and joyful celebration for all concerned. On the eve of departure, it is traditional for family and friends to gather for prayers, Qur'an recitation, food, and perhaps poetry and singing about the *hajj.* Many pilgrims follow the practice of setting out from home on the right foot, a symbol of good omen and fortune. Similarly, it is auspicious to enter mosques, including the Sacred Mosque in Mecca, on the right foot and depart on the left; the right/left symbolism is associated with several ritual gestures in Islam as well as in other traditions. As on so many occasions during the *hajj,* the actual moment of departure calls for the recitation of a particular verse from the Qur'an, and departing pilgrims recite the words of Noah, uttered to those escaping the deluge: "Board [the Ark]; in God's name be its course and mooring. My Lord is forgiving, merciful" (11:41). Those who complete the *hajj* will be entitled to the epithet *hajj* or *hajji* (*hajjah* or *hajjiyah* if female). This honorific title indicates socially perceived status enhancement in the sense of recognition by one's peers that a sacred duty has been fulfilled, and this is a matter of universal value, if not universal achievement, in Islam.

Ihram, the Condition of Consecration. The *hajj* season lasts from the beginning of the tenth month of the Muslim calendar, Shawwal, until the tenth day of the twelfth month, Dhu al-Hijjah. The rites of preparation and consecration are comprehended by the term *ihram.* Pilgrims assume the condition of ihram before they pass the territorial markers, *al-miqat al-makaniyah,* that are situated several miles outside of Mecca along the ancient routes for caravans from Syria, Medina, Iraq, and the Yemen.

Assuming the condition of *ihram* before passing the territorial markers has several aspects.

1. *Ihram* requires a state of ritual purity, and pilgrims who enter it must perform ablutions much the same as they do for the daily canonical prayers, *salat.* The special condition of *ihram* also requires pilgrims to trim their fingernails and remove underarm and pubic hair, and men must shave off beards and mustaches.

2. *Ihram* is initiated and sustained by prayers of several kinds.

3. In addition to the ablutions and prayers, *ihram* requires each pilgrim to exchange normal clothing for special garments. For males the *ihram* attire consists of two seamless white pieces of cloth, one attached around the waist and reaching to the knees, the other worn over the left shoulder and attached around the torso, leaving the right shoulder and arm free for ritual gesturing. Females wear plain dresses that extend from neckline to ankles and cover the arms.

**`Umrah, the Lesser Pilgrimage.** All accounts of the experience of the final approach to Mecca indicate that it is a moment of high emotions attending the realization of a life-long ambition. The most valued and anticipated task, however, is a visit to the Ka`bah for the rites of `umrah.

From ancient times, the Ka`bah and its environs have been symbols of refuge from violence and pursuit, a sacred space in which wayfaring pilgrims could find sanctuary with the divine. The Ka`bah is now enclosed within the roofless courtyard of the Sacred Mosque of Mecca, al-Masjid al-Haram. Twenty-four gates lead into the mosque courtyard. The Gate of Peace near the northern corner of the Sacred Mosque is the traditional entrance for the performance of `umrah. From there, pilgrims move to a position east of the Ka`bah and face the corner with the Black Stone. The rite of *tawaf,* or circumambulation, begins from this point with a supplication followed by a kiss, touch, or gesture of touching the black stone. The pilgrim turns to the right and begins the seven circumambulations, moving counterclockwise around the Ka`bah. Each circuit has a special significance with recommended prayers that the pilgrim may recite either from *hajj* manuals or by following the words of the *hajj* guide leading the group.

Following the *tawaf,* pilgrims visit shrines adjacent to the Ka`bah. Pilgrims leave through the Gate of Purity on the southeast side. A few yards outside the Gate of Purity is the small hillock of al-Safa. From al-Safa begins the *sa`y,* the rite of trotting seven laps to and from the hillock of al-Marwah, commemorating Hajar's desperate search for water in the Meccan wilderness. This ends the rites of `umrah.

Hajj, the Greater Pilgrimage. The *hajj* proper begins on the eighth of Dhu al-Hijjah, the day of setting out for Arafat, which is located some thirteen miles east of Mecca.

Arafat. Muslim authorities agree that "there is no *hajj* without Arafat," that is, the rite of *wuquf* or "standing" at the Mount

> **On the Day of Standing at Arafat, pilgrims perform an ablution and canonical prayer at a mosque.**

of Mercy. According to legend, Adam and Eve first met and "knew" (`arafu) one another at Arafat after the long separation that followed their expulsion from Paradise. Tradition also teaches that Ibrahim went out to Arafat and performed *wuquf.* The prophet Muhammad addressed a multitude of followers performing *wuquf* during his farewell pilgrimage. On the Day of Standing at Arafat, pilgrims perform an ablution and canonical prayer at a mosque located near the western entrance to the plain. When the sun passes the noon meridian, the Mount of Mercy is covered with pilgrims.

Muzdalifah. At sundown the somber scene of prayer changes abruptly as pilgrims scramble to break camp and begin the "hurrying" to Muzdalifah, a rite of ancient significance. Pilgrims halt for a combined observance of the sunset and evening *salat* prayers. The Qur'an admonishes: "When you hurry from Arafat, remember God at the Sacred Grove (*al-mash`ar al-haram*)," that is, at Muzdalifah (2:198).

Mina. The tenth of Dhu al-Hijjah is the final official day of the *hajj* season. Most of the ritual activities of this day take place in Mina and include (1) the casting of seven small stones at the pillar of Aqaba, (2) the feast of the major sacrifice (`Id al-Adha), (3) the rite of deconsecration from the condition of *ihram,* and (4) the visit to Mecca for the *tawaf,* called *al-ifadah.* It is said that on his return from Arafat, Ibrahim was given the divine command to sacrifice that which was most dear to him, his son Isma`il. Along the way to Mina, Satan whispered to him three times (or to Ibrahim, Isma`il, and Hajar), tempting him (or them) not to obey the heavy command. The legendary response was a hurling of stones to repulse the Tempter. Three brick and mortar pillars stand in the center of Mina as symbols of Satan's temptations, and the pillar called Aqaba is the site where pilgrims gather early on the morning of the tenth of Dhu al-Hijjah to cast seven stones. Following the lapidations, those pilgrims who can afford it offer a blood sacrifice of a lamb or goat (sometimes a camel) to commemorate the divine substitution of a ram for Ibrahim's sacrifice. The meat is consumed by family and friends, with unused portions given to the poor. The festival of the major sacrifice is also celebrated on this day by Muslims around the world in gatherings of family and friends.

Tawaf al-ifadah and tahallul. After the sacrifice and feast, the process of *tahallul,* or deconsecration, is begun with the rite of clipping the hair. Many men follow the tradition of having the head shaved, although for women, and for men if they prefer, the cutting of three hairs meets the ritual requirement. This is followed by a visit to Mecca for another rite of circumambulation known as *tawaf al-ifadah.*

The Ka'bah itself undergoes purification and ritual renewal during the three days of *hajj.* Shortly before the *hajj* begins, the black *kiswah*—weathered and worn by a year of exposure to the open air—is replaced by a white one, suggestive of the *ihram* garb worn by pilgrims. Pilgrims returning for *tawaf al-ifadah* on the tenth of Dhu al-Hijjah are greeted by the sight of a lustrous new black *kiswah.*

When the *tawaf al-ifadah* has been completed, the dissolution of the condition of consecration is made final by doffing the pilgrim garb and wearing normal clothing. All the prohibitions of *ihram* are now lifted, and most pilgrims return to Mina for days of social gathering on the eleventh to the thirteenth of Dhu al-Hijjah. On each of these days it is *sunnah* to cast seven stones at each of the three pillars in Mina. This vast amalgam of pilgrims, dwelling in a river of tents pitched along the narrow valley of Mina, eases into a more relaxed atmosphere of friendly exchanges of religious greetings and visiting with Muslims from around the world.

BIBLIOGRAPHY

A readable modern Muslim *hajj* manual is Ahmad Kamal's *The Sacred Journey* (New York, 1961). A pictorial essay with color photographs and accompanying text has been expertly prepared by Mohamed Amin, *Pilgrimage to Mecca* (Nairobi, 1978). Both the old and new editions of *The Encyclopaedia of Islam* (Leiden, 1913-1938 and 1960-) are valuable sources of information about the *hajj;* see especially the articles "Hadjdj" and "Ka'ba."

Among the works that attempt to analyze and interpret the *hajj* from a history-of-religions and social-science perspective, the most substantial is Maurice Gaudefroy-Demombynes's *Le pèlerinage à la Mekke* (Paris, 1923). On the *hajj* in relation to the study of ritual in the history of religions, see the articles by Frederick M. Denny and William R. Roff in *Islam and the History of Religions,* edited by Richard C. Martin (Berkeley, 1983). David Edwin Long's *The Hajj Today: A Survey of the Contemporary Makkah Pilgrimage* (Albany, N. Y., 1979) analyzes various social and health problems and modern attempts by the Saudi Arabian government to resolve them; it includes a useful bibliography.

Numerous accounts of the *hajj* by travelers and adventurers provide useful historical information about the pilgrimage at specific times in the past. The best known of this genre is Richard F. Burton's *Personal Narrative of a Pilgrimage to al-Madinah and Meccah,* 2 vols. (London, 1893). Eldon Rutter's *The Holy Cities of Arabia,* 2 vols. (London and New York, 1928), is a work written about the 1925 *hajj*—the period of Ibn Saud's incursion into western Arabia—and contains considerable geographical information and descriptions of the major *hajj* sites as well as the numerous points of visitation in and near Mecca. The role of Mecca and the Meccans in relation to the *hajj* was studied in Christiaan Snouck Hurgronje's *Mekka in the Latter Part of the Nineteenth Century* (Leiden, 1931).

RICHARD C. MARTIN

Buddhist Pilgrimage in South and Southeast Asia

In the Buddhist tradition, one undertakes a pilgrimage in order to find the Buddha in the external world; one undertakes meditation to discover the Buddha nature within oneself. The internal pilgrimage brings one closer to the goal of *nirvana* (Pali, *nibbana*) than does the external pilgrimage, but the turning toward the Buddha who is iconically represented in the marks of his presence on earth or in relics constitutes an important preliminary step along the path to enlightenment.

Buddha charged his disciple Ananda to arrange for his cremated remains to be enshrined in stupas. In the *Mahaparinibbana Sutta* it is recorded how, after the death of the Buddha, his body was cremated, and his remains were divided into eight parts, each enshrined in a separate stupa. Two more stupas were also erected; one, built by the brahman who had divided the relics, enshrined the Master's alms bowl, and another, erected by those who had arrived too late to receive a portion of the remains, enshrined the ashes of the funerary pyre.

In addition to bodily relics (Pali, *sariradhatu*), Buddhist tradition also recognizes two other forms of relics that are taken as indicative of the Buddha's presence in the world. In Pali these are termed *paribhogikadhatu* and *uddesikadhatu,* the former referring to objects that the Buddha used (as, for example, his alms bowl) or marks (such as a footprint or shadow) that he left on earth, and the latter referring to votive reminders, such as images and stupas known not to contain actual relics.

From the time of Asoka to the present, Bodh Gaya has remained the most important Buddhist pilgrimage site in India. It is often grouped with three other sites—Lumbini in Nepal, where Siddhartha Gautama, the future Buddha, was born; the Deer Park at Sarnath near Banares, where he "turned the Wheel of the Law," that is, preached his first sermon; and Kusinagara in Uttar Pradesh, where he passed into the state of *nirvana.* None of these other sites, nor any other in India where he was reputed to have performed miracles during his life, however, holds the significance for Buddhists that Bodh Gaya does. Bodh Gaya represents the birth of

Buddhism, the place where the Tathagata realized the fundamental truth that lies at the base of Dharma.

Shrines marking traces left by the Buddha in his supernatural visits to lands that were to become Buddhist as well as shrines enclosing relics that had been transported—naturally or supernaturally—from India to such lands often became pilgrimage centers in their own right. Buddhist pilgrims have long traveled to such important shrines as those housing the Buddha's footprints on Siripada (Adam's Peak) in Sri Lanka and at Saraburi in Thailand and those housing famous Buddhist relics, such as the Temple of the Tooth in Kandy, Sri Lanka; the Shwe Dagon in Rangoon, Burma; the That Luang temple in Vientiane, Laos; and Doi Suthep near Chiang Mai, Thailand. Pilgrims visited these and other holy sites in order to acquire merit or to gain access to the presumed magical power associated with them. While some have made pilgrimages to shrines associated with traces of the Buddha as an end in itself, most have continued, as did Asoka and Fa-hsien, to see pilgrimage as a means for orienting themselves toward the Buddha as a preliminary step along the path to enlightenment.

BIBLIOGRAPHY

The scriptural source for Buddhist pilgrimage is to be found in the *Mahaparinibbana Suttanta,* a text that has been translated by T. W. Rhys Davids in "Sacred Books of the East," vol. 11 (Oxford, 1881), pp. 1-136. A discussion of Asokan pilgrimage, together with translations of the edicts in Asoka, appears in *Asoka* (London, 1928) by Radhakumud Mookerji. The travels of Fa-hsien have been translated by James Legge in *A Record of Buddhistic Kingdoms* (1886; reprint, New York, 1965). The *locus classicus* for an understanding of the cosmological significance of Buddhist stupas is Paul Mus's *Barabadur* (1935; reprint, New York, 1978). Marilyn Stablein has provided an overview of Buddhist pilgrimage among Tibetans in her "Textual and Contextual Patterns of Tibetan Buddhist Pilgrimage in India," *Tibet Society Bulletin* 12 (1978): 7-38. For discussions of Buddhist pilgrimage in Sri Lanka, see Gananath Obeyesekere's "The Buddhist Pantheon in Ceylon and Its Extensions," in *Anthropological Studies in Theravada Buddhism,* edited by Manning Nash et al. (New Haven, 1966), pp. 1-26; Bryan Pfaffenberger's "The Kataragama Pilgrimage: Hindu-Buddhist Interaction and Its Significance in Sri Lanka's Polyethnic Social System," *Journal of Asian Studies* 38 (1979): 253-270; and H. L. Seneviratne's *Rituals of the Kandyan State* (Cambridge, 1978). Buddhist pilgrimage in Thailand has been examined in my article "Buddhist Pilgrimage Centers and the Twelve Year Cycle: Northern Thai Moral Orders in Space and Time," *History of Religions* 15 (1975): 71-89, and in James B. Pruess's "Merit-Seeking in Public: Buddhist Pilgrimage in Northeastern Thailand," *Journal of the Siam Society* 64 (1976): 169-206.

CHARLES F. KEYES

Buddhist Pilgrimage in East Asia

Pilgrimage, especially to sacred mountain sites, has long been a popular religious practice in both China and Japan.

Pilgrimages in China. In mainland China there have been various pilgrimage sites, related to both Buddhism and Taoism. As for the former, there existed the following four major sites: Mount Wu-t`ai, sacred to Mañjusri (Skt.; known in Chinese as Wen-shu); Mount O-mei, sacred to Samantabhadra (Chin., P`u-hsien); Mount P`u-t`o, sacred to Avalokitesvara (Kuan-yin); and Mount Chiu Hua, sacred to Ksitigarbha (Ti-tsang). In the case of Taoist pilgrimages, one of the most famous sites is Mount T`ai.

**Mount Wu-t`ai.** Located in northeastern China, Mount Wu-t`ai has attracted a great number of pilgrims over the centuries. Although it was famous as the sacred site of Mañjusri, it is said to have been originally a sacred place related to the spiritual tradition of Taoism. It was not until the Northern Wei dynasty (386-535) that Buddhist influence became widespread in China, predominating over the indigenous Taoist tradition, and from this time Mount Wu-t`ai became a site holy to Mañjusri. In the T`ang dynasty (618-907), it was so popular as a pilgrimage site that many pilgrims even came to visit the mountain from foreign countries, including Tibet and India.

It is said to have been during the Yüan dynasty (1271-1366), when China was invaded and ruled by the Mongols, that Tibetan Buddhism, which the Mongols preferred to Chinese Buddhism, started to spread its influence at Mount Wu-t`ai. Soon Chinese Buddhism and Tibetan Buddhism came to coexist on this sacred mountain. In other words, the mountain became an important pilgrimage site for two different religious traditions simultaneously. During the Ch`ing dynasty (1644-1912), Tibetan Buddhism gradually came to predominate at Mount Wu-t`ai, partly because the Manchu Ch`ing rulers, who were not ethnically Chinese, began to take a conciliatory policy toward other non-Chinese groups such as the Mongols, who believed in Tibetan Buddhism. As a result, Mount Wu-t`ai became the most holy religious site of the Mongols.

**Mount T`ai.** Long famous as a Taoist pilgrimage site, T`ai-shan has been continually associated with Buddhism in various ways. In Chinese history, this sacred mountain has been well known as one of the so-called Five Peaks, designated as indispensable for the protection of the whole country. From the Sung dynasty (960-1279) up until the modern period, belief was associated with Mount T`ai: that of a goddess. This goddess was worshiped as one who presided over the birth and rearing of children. This special characteristic of the goddess attracted a great number of pilgrims because of its familiarity and closeness with the common people. Accordingly, miniature statues of this particular goddess were enshrined all over China in modern times.

Pilgrimage in modern China. Pilgrimages in China seemed to have disappeared after Communist China was established in 1949. However, in recent years, pilgrimage sites have been rapidly restored and have reopened their doors to pilgrims both from China and from overseas. The majority of the foreign pilgrims are Chinese merchants living abroad. As a result of a rapid growth in the living standards of the Chinese people, there seems to be a tendency for famous pilgrimage sites to become targets of tourism.

Pilgrimages in Japan. In Japanese religious tradition, both Shinto and Buddhism have various pilgrimage sites. In Japan, pilgrimages can be divided into two general types. The first is the type exemplified by the Pilgrimage to the Thirty-three Holy Places of Kannon (Avalokitesvara) in the Western Provinces and by the Pilgrimage to the Eighty-eight Temples of Shikoku, in which one makes a circuit of a series of temples or holy places in a set order. The individual holy places that the pilgrim visits may be separated by great distances, as in the case of the Shikoku pilgrimage, in which eighty-eight temples are scattered along a route of about 1,200 kilometers (746 miles). The order of visitation is an important feature of this type of pilgrimage. The second type is a journey to one particular holy place. Pilgrimage to the Kumano Shrines and Ise Shinto Shrine, as well as to certain holy mountains, belong to this type..

With the increasing popularity of religions involving mountain worship, members of the imperial family, the nobility, and Buddhist monks made pilgrimages to remote holy mountains. Among them, Kumano in the southern part of Wakayama Prefecture is the most famous, having at that early time already developed into a large center for the adherents of mountain worship. Besides Kumano, Hasedera Temple, Shitennoji, Mount Koya, and Mount Kinpu were also popular pilgrimage sites.

In the Edo period (1600-1868) an unprecedented number of people began to visit pilgrimage centers. While the vast majority of pilgrims had previously been member of the upper classes, such as monks, aristocrats, and warriors, in the Edo period the number of pilgrims from the general populace greatly increased. This change was largely owing to the peace established by the Tokugawa feudal regime and to the improvement in the economic condition of both the farming and the merchant classes. Transportation improved, and although government policy restricted travel between provinces, an exception was made for pilgrimages. The number of pilgrims who made journeys to the western provinces, Shikoku, Kotohira Shrine, Zenkoji, Ise, and Mount Fuji increased rapidly, and many new pilgrimage centers developed in various parts of the country.

Travel since the Meiji period (1868-1912) has basically preserved the Edo period pattern of pilgrimage. Even today, many travelers include visits to famous temples and shrines in their itineraries. Even pilgrimage circuits that lack any other attraction, such as the Shikoku pilgrimage, have once again become popular.

BIBLIOGRAPHY

Adachi K. and Shioiri Ryodo, eds. *Nitto guho junrei koki.* 2 vols. Tokyo, 1970-1985. An annotated edition of Ennin's account of his travels in T'ang China.

Kitagawa, Joseph M. "Three Types of Pilgrimage in Japan." In *Studies in Mysticism and Religion Presented to Gershom G. Scholem on His Seventieth Birthday by Pupils, Colleagues and Friends,* edited by E. E. Urbach, R. J. Zwi Werblowsky, and Chaim Wirszubski, pp. 155-164. Jerusalem, 1967.

Maeda Takashi. *Junrei no shakaigaku.* Kyoto, 1971.

Ono Katsutoshi. *Nitto guho junrei gyoki no kenkyu.* 4 vols. Tokyo, 1964-1969. A translation and study of Ennin's account of his travels in T'ang China.

Ono Katsutoshi and Hibino Takeo. *Godaisan.* Tokyo, 1942.

Reischauer, Edwin O., trans. *Ennin's Diary: The Record of a Pilgrimage to China in Search of the Law.* New York, 1955.

Shinjo Tsunezo. *Shaji-sankei no shakai-keizaishiteki kenkyu.* Rev. ed. Tokyo, 1982.

HOSHINO EIKI

POLYTHEISM

The term *polytheism,* derived from the Greek *polus* ("many") and *theos* ("god") and hence denoting "recognition and worship of many gods," is used mainly in contrast with *monotheism,* denoting "belief in one god." Historical (or rather, pseudo-historical) theories concerning the origin of polytheism were closely related to the evolutionist views that characterized early *Religions-wissenschaft.* Primitive humanity was aware of its dependence on a variety of powers that were often conceived as individual nonmaterial ("spiritual") beings—for instance, the spirits of departed humans, especially ancestors—or as supernatural entities.

One is struck by the curious fact that polytheism, while it is one of the major and most widespread phenomena in the history of religions, has attracted less than the attention it deserves. It seems to have fallen, as it were, between the two stools of "primitive religions" and monotheism. Or perhaps we should say three stools, if we also take into account nontheistic religions such as Buddhism. Like all phenomenological ideal types (to borrow Max Weber's term), polytheism does not exist as a pure type. The historical variety is not easily reducible to a common denominator.

Perhaps the most striking fact about polytheism is its appearance in more advanced and literate cultures, such as China, India, the ancient Near East, Greece, and Rome.

In every religion, society attempts to articulate its understanding of the cosmos and of the powers that govern it, and to structure its relationship with these powers in appropriate symbolic systems. In the societies under discussion here, man already faces the cosmos: he is closely linked to it but no longer inextricably interwoven in it. There is a sense of (at least minimal) distance from nature and even more distance from the powers above that now are "gods," that is, beings that are superhuman, different, powerful (though not omnipotent) and hence beneficent or dangerous—at any rate their goodwill should be secured—and to be worshiped by cultic actions such as sacrifices.

One of the most distinctive characteristics of gods, as compared to human beings, is their immortality. Yet, this does not mean that they do not have origins or a history. Unlike the biblical God who makes history but himself has no history, let alone a family history, their history is the subject of mythological tales, including accounts of their family relations, love affairs, offspring, and so on. Hence the mythological genealogies, stories of the gods that preceded the ones ruling at present (e.g., Greek Ouranos-Gaia; followed by

> **Perhaps the best example of a highly developed polytheism with an elaborate ritual system but almost totally lacking a mythology is ancient Rome.**

Kronos, followed by Zeus; or, in later Indian religion, the replacement of originally principal gods like Indra, Varuna, and Mitra by Siva, Visnu, and other deities). These gods are personal (in fact, this personal character is also one of the main features and constitutes one of the main philosophical problems of monotheism), and herein resides their religious significance: they are accessible.

Perhaps the best example of a highly developed polytheism with an elaborate ritual system but almost totally lacking a mythology is ancient Rome. In this respect the contrast with ancient Greece is striking. Yet even when we have a rich body of mythology, its imagery reaches us in comparatively late literary elaborations. Thus the mythology of ancient (pre-Buddhist) Japan is accessible to us only in literary works composed after the absorption of Chinese (i. e., also Buddhist) influences.

Without implying commitment to any simplistic theory about the divine order always and necessarily being a mirror of the human and social order, one cannot deny that the two are correlated. The polytheistic divine world is more differentiated, more structured, and often extremely hierarchized, because the human view of the cosmos is similarly differentiated, structured, and hierarchized. There are many gods because man experiences the world in its variety and manifoldness. Hence there is also specialization among the gods, of a nature that is either local and tribal-ethnic (gods of spe-

cific localities, cities, countries, families) or functional (gods of specific arts, gods of illness, cure, fertility, rains, hunting, fishing, etc.). Each householder had his genius; women had their Junos; children were protected when going in, going out, or performing their natural functions by Educa, Abeone, Potin. In fact, there was a goddess responsible for the toilet and sewage system: Cloacina.

To cite another example of parallel hierarchy, few divine worlds were as hierarchical as the Chinese; in fact, these realms seem to be exact replicas of the administrative bureaucracy of imperial China. Just as the illustrious departed could be deified by imperial decree, so gods too could be promoted to higher rank. (Japan subsequently adopted this Chinese model, as it did so many others.) As late as the nineteenth century, these imperial promotions were announced in the *Peking Gazette*.

An important corollary of polytheism is that, though the major deities can be very powerful, no god can be omnipotent. Only a monotheistic god, being *monos,* can also be all-powerful. With growing moral differentiation, originally ambivalent gods split into positive (good) and negative (bad, evil, or demonic) divinities. Thus the original Indo-Aryan *asuras* (deities) became, in Vedic and post-Vedic India, demonic antigods, in opposition to the *devas.* The multiplicity of gods of necessity produced a hierarchy of major and minor gods and a pantheon, or overall framework in which they were all combined. The more important gods have names and a distinct personality; others form the *plebs deorum,* a body often indistinguishable from the nameless spirits of animism.

Some scholars consider henotheism (the exclusive worship of one god only without denying the existence of other gods) as an intermediary stage between polytheism and monotheism, the latter being defined as the theoretical recognition of the existence of one god only, all the others being (in the language of the Old Testament) sheer "vanity and nothingness." The terminology seems somewhat artificial (both *hen* and *monos* signify "one" in Greek), but it attempts to express a real distinction. Thus it has been claimed that henotheistic vestiges can still be detected even in the monotheistic Old Testament (e.g., *Exodus* 15:11, "Who is like unto thee among the gods, O Yahveh," or *Micah* 4:5, "For all nations will walk each in the name of its god" while Israel walks in the name of Yahveh, their god for evermore).

BIBLIOGRAPHY

There is little, if any, systematic literature on the subject. Discussions of polytheism can be found in articles on monotheism in the older, standard encyclopedias (the *Encyclopaedia of Religion and Ethics,* edited by James Hastings, *Die Religion in Geschichte und Gegenwart,* and so on) as well as in accounts of specific polytheistic religions (for example, Germanic and Celtic; ancient Near Eastern; Greek and Roman; Indian, Chinese, and Japanese; Mesoamerican and South American). Perhaps the first modern discussion of polytheism, in the Western sense, is David Hume's *The Natural History of Religion* (1757), though Hume's account is obviously shaped by eighteenth-century European Enlightenment attitudes. Systematic considerations can be found in Gerardus van der Leeuw's *Religion in Essence and Manifestation*, 2 vols. (1938; Gloucester, Mass., 1967); E. O. James's *The Concept of Deity* (New York, 1950); and Angelo Brelich's "Der Polytheismus," *Numen* 7 (December 1960): 123-136. On the relationship of polytheism to more highly developed political organization (e.g., the Greek polis), see Walter Burkert's "Polis and Polytheism," in his *Greek Religion* (Cambridge, Mass., 1985), pp. 216-275.

R. J. ZWI WERBLOWSKY

PRAYER

PRAYER, understood as the human communication with divine and spiritual entities, has been present in most of the religions in human history. Viewed from most religious perspectives, prayer is a necessity of the human condition.

Prayer as Text. Prayer is thought of most commonly as the specific words of the human-spiritual communication, that is, as the text of this communication, such as the Lord's Prayer (Christian), the Qaddish (Jewish), and the prayers of *salat* (Muslim).

A common basic typology of prayer has been formulated by discerning what distinguishes the character and intent expressed by the words of prayer texts. This kind of typology includes a number of classes, all easily distinguished by their descriptive designations. It includes petition, invocation, thanksgiving (praise or adoration), dedication, supplication, intercession, confession, penitence, and benediction. Such types may constitute whole prayers or they may be strung together to form a structurally more complex prayer.

In perhaps the most extensive comparative study of prayer, *Prayer: A Study in the History and Psychology of Religion* (1932), Friedrich Heiler understood prayer as a pouring out of the heart before God. However, when the understanding of prayer as a free and spontaneous "living communion of man with God" (Heiler) is conjoined with the general restriction of prayer to the text form, incongruency, confusion, and dilemma arise. Prayer texts, almost without exception and to a degree as part of their nature, are formulaic, repetitive, and static in character, much in contrast with the expected free and spontaneous character of prayer.

Heiler held that prayer texts were, in fact, not true prayers, but were rather artificially composed for the purpose of edifying, instructing, and influencing people in the matters of dogma, belief, and tradition.

Due to the nature of the materials available, prayers must often be considered primarily, if not solely, as texts, whose study is limited to the semantic, informational, and literary aspects of the language that constitutes them. Despite such limitations, the texts of prayers reflect theological, doctrinal, cultural, historical, aesthetic, and creedal dimensions of a religious culture.

Prayer as Act. Intuitively prayer is an act of communication. In its most common performance, prayer is an act of speech.

The distinction between personal and ritual prayer has often been made when viewing prayer as act. Personal prayer, regarded as the act of persons pouring forth their hearts to God, has been considered by many as the truest form, even the only true form, of prayer. Yet, the data available for the study of personal prayer are scant. Still, the record of personal prayers found in letters, biographies, and diaries suggests a strong correlation and interdependence of personal prayer with ritual and liturgical prayer in language, form, style, and physical attitude. A person praying privately is invariably a person who is part of a religious and cultural tradition in which ritual or public prayer is practiced.

Ritual prayer, by not conforming to the naive notions of the spontaneity and free form of prayer, has often been set aside. It can be shown that prayer when formulaic, repetitive,

> **When prayer is considered as act, a whole range of powerful characteristics and religious functions may be discerned.**

and redundant in message can be a true act of communication, even heartfelt. In recent years a range of studies has developed showing the performative power of language and speech acts. Simply put, these studies show that language and other forms of human action not only say things, that is, impart information, they also do things. Ordinary language acts may persuade, name, commit, promise, declare, affirm, and so on; and these functions are often more primary than that of transmitting information.

When prayer is considered as act, the unresponsive and noncreative dimensions that seem inseparable from the rigidity of words tend to dissolve, for a prayer act always involves one praying in a historical, cultural, social, and psychological setting. These ever-changing contextual elements are necessarily a part of the act. In some prayer traditions, the Navajo of North America for example, it has been shown that highly formulaic constituents of prayer are ordered in patterns and conjoined with familiar ritual elements in combinations that express very specifically the heartfelt needs and motivations of a single person for whom the prayer is uttered. Analogous to ordinary language where familiar words can be ordered according to a single set of grammatical principles in infinite ways to be creative and expressive, prayer passages may be ordered in conjunction with ritual elements to achieve the same communicative capabilities.

When prayer is considered as act, a whole range of powerful characteristics and religious functions may be discerned. Here the issue is not primarily to show that prayer is communication with the spiritual or divine, or even necessarily to discern what is communicated, but rather to direct attention to the comprehension and appreciation of the power and effectiveness of communication acts that are human-divine communications.

Prayer as Subject. Prayer is also a subject that is much written and talked about. It is the subject of theory, of theology, of sermons, of doctrine, of devotional guides, of prescribed ways of worship and ways of life, and of descriptions of methods of prayer. The extent of literature in religious traditions about prayer is massive and ranges from personal meditations on the "way of prayer" to formal theologies and philosophies of prayer. In these writings, prayer becomes the subject by which to articulate the principles and character of a religious tradition or a strain within a tradition.

BIBLIOGRAPHY

Prayer as a general religious phenomenon has received scant attention by students of religion. There are no recent global or extensive studies. The discussions of prayer that continue to be the standard, while obviously inadequate, are E. B. Tylor's *Primitive Culture: Researches into the Development of Mythology, Philosophy, Religion, Language, Art, and Custom,* 2 vols., 4th ed. (London, 1903), and Friedrich Heiler's *Prayer: A Study in the History and Psychology of Religion,* edited and translated by Samuel McComb (Oxford, 1932). Most of the general studies of prayer are strongly psychological in character. Prayer was a topic of extensive consideration by William James in *The Varieties of Religious Experience: A Study in Human Nature* (1902; New York, 1961), pp. 359-371. Prayer and related religious speech acts are of interest in phenomenologies of religion; see, for example, Gerardus van der Leeuw's *Religion in Essence and Manifestation,* 2 vols., translated by J. E. Turner (London, 1938), pp. 403-446.

Statements of a comparative nature are found scattered throughout the literature, especially comparing specific prayers among Western religious traditions. However, broader and detailed comparative studies of prayer do not exist. Extensive studies of prayer that have attempted to see prayer in more general and universal terms may still be of interest, even though they have a dominantly Christian perspective. Such studies include Alexander J. Hodge's *Prayer and Its Psychology* (New York, 1931) and R. H. Coats's *The Realm of Prayer* (London, 1920).

An exemplary study of prayer that makes a clear distinction between prayer as a text, act, and subject is Tzvee Zahavy's "A New Approach to Early Jewish Prayer," in *History of Judaism: The Next Ten Years,* edited by Baruch M. Bokser (Chico, Calif., 1980), pp. 45-60.

Sources for prayer within specific religious traditions can be found under the heading "Prayer" in the *Encyclopaedia of Religion and Ethics,* edited by James Hastings, vol. 10 (Edinburgh, 1918), which includes a number of articles, some now outdated, on various religious traditions. See also *The Oxford Book of Prayer,* edited by George Appleton and others (New York, 1985).

There are numerous studies that demonstrate the importance of considering prayer as act. Harold A. Carter's *The Prayer Tradition of Black People* (Valley Forge, Pa., 1976) is a fine study of the American black prayer tradition; it traces the African heritage, describes the theological influences, discerns the major functions, and demonstrates the remarkable power of this prayer tradition in the context of black movements in American history. Gary Goosen's "Language as a Ritual Substance," in *Language in Religious Practice,* edited by William J. Samarin (Rowley, Mass., 1976), pp. 40-62, considers Chamul prayers as encoding messages interpreted in terms of Victor Turner's method of considering symbols.

On the performative power of Navajo prayer, see my "Prayer as Person: The Performative Force in Navajo Prayer Acts," *History of Religions* 17 (November 1979): 143-157. On the centrality of prayer to the whole system of Navajo religion, see my *Sacred Words: A Study of Navajo Religion and Prayer* (Westport, Conn., 1981). A notable study of prayer as a tradition of creative acts of oratory, focusing on the inhabitants of sea islands along the Atlantic Coast of the southern United States, is Patricia Jones-Jackson's "Oral Traditions in Gullah," *Journal of Religious Thought* 39 (Spring-Summer 1982): 21-33.

An examplary study of nonspeech acts considered as communication acts similar to prayer is Gabriella Eichinger Ferro-Luzzi's "Ritual as Language: The Case of South Indian Food Offerings," *Current Anthropology* 18 (September 1977): 507-514.

The performative power of speech acts, relevant to the study of prayer as act, has been shown in many essays. See, for example, Benjamin C. Ray's " 'Performative Utterances' in African Rituals," *History of Religions* 13 (August 1973): 16-35; Stanley J. Tambiah's "The Magical Power of Words," *Man,* n. s. 3 (June 1968): 175-208; and Tambiah's *Buddhism and the Spirit Cults in North-East Thailand* (Cambridge, 1970).

While folklore studies have become interested in the performance of many speech forms, especially among exclusively oral peoples, prayer is a form that has received little attention despite its abundant resources and importance within the traditions studied.

On the consideration of second-order language acts (metalanguages), see Alan Dundes's "Metafolklore and Oral Literary Criticism," *The Monist* 50 (October 1966): 505-516, and Barbara A. Babcock's "The Story in the Story: Metanarration in Folk Narrative," in her and Richard Bauman's *Verbal Art as Performance* (Rowley, Mass., 1977). Sources for prayer as subject are coincident with the second-order interpretative and critical literary traditions of all religions. In the contemporary religions and popular literature of the Western traditions, prayer is a constant topic. It has also been a consideration of major theologies and philosophies, as shown for modern Western thought in a summary treatment by Perry Le Fevre, *Understandings of Prayer* (Philadelphia, 1981). In *Prayer: An Analysis of Theological Terminology* (Helsinki, 1973), Antti Alhonsaari considers the theological issue of whether prayer is monologue or dialogue, discerning systematically the forms of prayer that correspond to the combinations of the variable on which this metaprayer discussion turns. While the rubric "Prayer" is not so dominant among non-Western religious traditions, there are nonetheless abundant comparable statements about prayer and prayerlike phenomena found among the writings of the interpreters and believers in these many traditions.

SAM D. GILL

PREHISTORIC RELIGIONS

The term *prehistory* refers to the vast period of time between the appearance of humanity's early hominid ancestors and the beginning of the historical period. Since the invention of writing is used to mark the transition between prehistory and history, the date of this boundary varies greatly from region to region. The study of prehistoric religion, therefore, can refer to religious beliefs and practices from as early as 60,000 BCE to almost the present day. Generally, however, the term *prehistory* is defined by its European application and hence refers to the period from the Paleolithic period, which occurred during the Pleistocene epoch, to the protohistoric Neolithic period and the Bronze and Iron ages.

Access to a prehistoric culture is highly problematic. And when one attempts to understand a phenomenon such as religion, the problem becomes acute. We understand religion primarily in terms of "language," that is, its principal characteristics are its interpretive meanings and valuations. The wordless archaeological remains of prehistoric religion—cultic or ceremonial artifacts and sites, pictures and symbols, sacrifices—have provided limited access to the religious "language" of prehistoric cultures. For example, knowledge of

> The power and depth of these silent archaeological remains cause one to recognize the limitation of written language as a purveyor of religious meaning.

how corpses were disposed during the Neolithic period does not reveal why they were so disposed. Consequently, even when there is clear evidence of a prehistoric religious practice, interpretation of the nature of prehistoric religions remains highly speculative and disproportionately dependent upon analogies to contemporary "primitive" cultures.

Our knowledge of prehistoric religion is therefore the product of reconstructing a "language" from its silent material accessories. Among the oldest material forms of cultic practice are burial sites, dating from the Middle Paleolithic. One can trace, from the Upper Paleolithic on, a growing richness and diversity of grave goods that reach extravagant proportions during the Iron Age. The practices of second burials, the burning of bodies, and the ritual disposition of skulls are also common. Megalithic graves date back to the Neolithic period. Despite the cultic implications of these massive stone constructions (e.g., ancestor cults), a uniform religious meaning remains undemonstrated.

Evidences of sacrifices from the Middle Paleolithic period in the form of varied quantities of animal bones near bur-

ial sites suggest offerings to the dead. Sacrificial traditions that were associated with game (e.g., bear ceremonialism) date back to the Upper Paleolithic. There is no evidence of human sacrifice prior to the Neolithic period, and hence this practice is associated with the transition from a hunter-gatherer culture to an agrarian culture and, consequently, with the domestication of plants and animals. [*See* Sacrifice.]

Prehistoric works of art dating back to the Paleolithic period—paintings, drawings, engravings, and sculpture—are the richest form of access to prehistoric religion. The primary subjects of these earliest examples of graphic art were animals; humans, rarely depicted, were often drawn with animal attributes. The intimate and unique role of animals in the physical and mental lives of these early hunter-gatherers is clearly demonstrated. (This role is also evidenced in the sacrificial traditions.) Though some form of animalism is suggested, the religious significance of these animal figures is difficult to interpret.

Shamanistic practices are also reflected in this art, especially in the paintings of birds and of animals that have projectiles drawn through their bodies. Common in prehistoric sculpture is the female statuette. Although frequently related to fertility, these figurines are open to numerous interpretations of equal plausibility (e.g., spirit abodes, ancestor representations, house gods, as well as spirit rulers over animals, lands and other physical or spiritual regions, hunting practices, and natural forces).

It is unlikely that we shall ever be able adequately to interpret the "language" of prehistoric religion. The material evidence is too scarce and the nature of religious phenomena too complex. There is, however, a meaning in these wordless fragments that is itself significant for any study of religion. The power and depth of these silent archaeological remains cause one to recognize the limitation of written language as a purveyor of religious meaning. The connections one is able, however tenuously, to draw between the evidences of religious life among prehistoric peoples and the beliefs and practices of their descendants address the conditions that have inspired human beings, from our beginnings, to express our deepest selves in art and ritual.

[*See* Paleolithic Religion *and* Neolithic Religion.]

BIBLIOGRAPHY

Breuil, Henri, and Raymond Lantier. *The Men of the Old Stone Age: Palaeolithic and Mesolithic* (1965). Translated by B. B. Rafter. Reprint, Westport, Conn., 1980.

James, E. O. *The Beginnings of Religions: An Introductory and Scientific Study* (1948). Reprint, Westport, Conn., 1973.

Jensen, Adolf E. *Myth and Cult among Primitive Peoples.* Translated by Marianna T. Choldin and Wolfgang Weissleder. Chicago, 1963.

Levy, Gertrude R. *The Gate of Horn: A Study of the Religious Conceptions of the Old Stone Age* (1948). Reprint, New York, 1963.

Maringer, Johannes. *The Gods of Prehistoric Man.* Translated and edited by Mary Ilford. New York, 1960.

Ucko, Peter J. *Anthropomorphic Figurines of Predynastic Egypt and Neolithic Crete.* London, 1968.

MARY EDWARDSEN and JAMES WALLER

PRESBYTERIANISM, REFORMED

Historical Origins of Presbyterianism. Presbyterians are catholic in their affirmation of the triune God and of the creeds of the ancient catholic church: the Apostles' Creed, the Nicene Creed, and the Chalcedonian definition. They are Protestant in the sense of Martin Luther's treatises of 1520. Their Reformed roots are in the Reformation at Zurich, under the leadership of Ulrich Zwingli (1484-1531) and Heinrich Bullinger (1504-1575); at Strasbourg, under Martin Bucer (1491-1551); and at Geneva, with the work of John Calvin (1509-1564).

Reformed theology at the time of the Reformation. Reformed theology was a type of Protestantism—as distinct from Lutheranism, Anglicanism, and the theology of the radical Reformation—that originated in Switzerland, the upper Rhineland, and France. Most of the early Reformed theologians had a background in Christian humanism. [*See* Humanism.] The Reformed church insisted upon positive scriptural warrant for all church practice.

Reformed theology was characterized by its emphasis upon the doctrine of God, who was conceived not so much as beauty or truth but as energy, activity, power, intentionality, and moral purpose. Reformed theologians believed that all of life and history is rooted in the decrees or purposes of God. They emphasized the lordship of God in history and in the salvation of the Christian as emphasized in the doctrine of predestination. John Calvin, the most influential of Reformed theologians, was not a speculative thinker. While rejecting curiosity as destructive of faith, Calvin insisted that Christians should know what they believed; the way a person thinks determines action. Calvin also placed high value upon verbal expressions of faith. The sermon became the focus of Reformed worship.

Reformed liturgy. In liturgy the Reformed churches placed a premium upon intelligibility and edification. As with life generally, Calvin insisted that worship should be simple, free from theatrical trifles. The sacraments were limited to the Lord's Supper and baptism, which were believed to have been instituted by Jesus Christ. Among the more prominent documents of the liturgical tradition are Huldrych Zwingli's *Liturgy of the Word,* Guillaume Farel's *The Order Observed*

in Preaching, Calvin's *The Form of Church Prayers,* and John Knox's *The Form of Prayers.*

Presbyterian polity. Presbyterianism is not a fixed pattern of church life but a developing pattern that has both continuity and diversity. Many features of the system vary from time to time and from place to place. In the United States, for example, Presbyterianism developed from the congregation to the presbytery, to the synod, to the General Assembly. In Scotland, Presbyterianism grew out of a gradually evolving notion of how the church should be governed, out of conflict with episcopacy, and from the General Assembly down to the congregation.

Presbyterians find the roots of their polity in the reforming activity of Calvin. In his doctrine of the church, Calvin's primary emphasis was on the action of the Holy Spirit, who created the church through word and sacrament. Jesus Christ is the only head of the church, and under him all are equal. In addition, Calvin struggled all his life for a church that was independent of state control. He held to the notion of a Christian society with a magistrate whose work in the civil order is a vocation from God, but ideally Calvin wanted church and state to work together under God yet in independence of each other organizationally. Calvin placed great emphasis on the minister, who interprets and applies the word of God.

There are four basic principles of presbyterian polity. The first is the authority of scripture. The other three principles of presbyterian polity relate to form of governance and relations among clergy and between clergy and laity.

BIBLIOGRAPHY

Bolam, C. Gordon, et al. *The English Presbyterians: From Elizabethan Puritanism to Modern Unitarianism.* London, 1968.

Henderson, George D. *Presbyterianism.* Aberdeen, 1955. A comprehensive introduction to the origin and development of presbyterian polity.

Leith, John H. *Introduction to the Reformed Tradition: A Way of Being the Christian Community.* Rev. ed. Atlanta, 1981. Chapters on the ethos, theology, polity, worship, and the cultural expression of the Reformed community.

Loetscher, Lefferts A. *A Brief History of the Presbyterians.* 4th ed. Philadelphia, 1984. Brief but reliable.

McNeil, John T. *The History and Character of Calvinism.* Oxford, 1954. Comprehensive, reliable, judicious. The work of a distinguished historian who cherished the tradition.

JOHN H. LEITH

PRIESTHOOD

Usage in the West. The strict sense of the meaning of *priest* prevailed prior to modern times, while looser and more inclusive applications of the term have come into use more recently. This development has to do with religious and conceptual horizons of the Christian West, in which the vocabulary of Latin and its derivatives has been dominant. In the traditions of the Judeo-Christian West, our point will become clear when we consider circumstances in which the term *priest* has not been used. The two principal cases are the Jewish and the Protestant.

For Judaism, priesthood is a well-defined and central role in the biblical tradition. The performance of sacrifices was one of its essential characteristics. The priests carried out the sacrificial ritual at altars, and from the seventh century BCE onward such ceremony was centralized at the temple in Jerusalem. Religious leadership in the synagogue, which replaced the temple, passed to the rabbis in their role as teachers. As far as the Hebraic context is concerned, the terms we translate by *priest* regularly imply the performance of sacrifice, and in the absence of the sacrifice the concept has been considered inapplicable.

Protestants do not generally refer to their clergy as "priests" either. But Protestants do have a conception of priesthood, referred to as "the priesthood of all believers." In avoiding the term *priest* as a designation of their own clergy, most Protestants have implied a repudiation of the notion that priestly ordination should elevate any man above his fellow human beings or confer on him any access to the divine that is denied others. Protestants did differ from Rome on the senses in which the Lord's Supper, the eucharistic meal of the Mass, might be considered in itself a sacrifice, for they held that Jesus' self-sacrifice was commemorated rather than repeated. But the truly sore point was the privileged, controlling status enjoyed by the officiating Roman clergy.

Description of Priesthood in Non-Western Religion. A great many other activities and attributes of priests in the European Christian tradition have built up a range of connotations. Priests in the West generally wear ceremonial robes while officiating and have distinctive details of street clothing; hence, Western visitors to Japan, for instance, termed the robed personnel of temples "priests," whether Shinto or Buddhist. Priests in the Latin Christian tradition are unmarried; hence the disposition of visitors to Sri Lanka, Burma, or Thailand sometimes to refer to Buddhist monks as "priests," even if the status of their ritual as a sacrifice is debatable. Priests are inducted into their office through ordination; hence the tendency to view tribal societies' ritually initiated specialists in divination, exorcism, healing, and the like as priests. Priests deliver sermons and moral injuctions; hence, presumably, occasional references to the `ulama', or religious scholars of traditional Islamic lands, as priests, despite the fact that they are neither ordained nor do they perform ritual sacrifice.

Eligibility for Priesthood. The world's priests in various traditions can be divided into what one might term *hereditary* priesthoods and *vocational* priesthoods. In the first case, the priestly prerogatives and duties are the special heritage of particular family or tribal lineages. The ancient Hebrew priesthood, for example, was reserved to the Levites, or descendants of Levi. Similarly, hereditary is the priesthood in Zoroastrianism. Traditionally, fathers who were practicing priests trained their sons in the proper recitation of the prayers.

It is generally expected that the clergy in hereditary priesthoods will marry, so that the line may be perpetuated. Indeed, the genealogical awareness of hereditary priesthoods is often as carefully documented as is that of royalty, and for similar reasons.

What one may call a vocational priesthood, on the other hand, recruits its members from the pool of promising young people in the community. Celibacy is something that a tradition of vocational priesthood can require, as does the Roman Catholic Church, but many vocational priesthoods still permit marriage, such as those of the Greek Orthodox, Russian Orthodox, and other Eastern Christian churches.

In the vast majority of the world's religious traditions, eligibility for priesthood has been restricted to males. The Hindu, Buddhist, Taoist, Zoroastrian, and Christian traditions have had exclusively male clergy until modern times. Judaism likewise restricted the rabbinate (its equivalent to the more inclusive current sense of the term *priest*) to males. In today's world various branches of both Christianity and Judaism have begun to ordain women to serve as the ritual and spiritual leaders of congregations.

Another feature of eligibility for priesthood is a sound physical and mental condition. Traditional Roman Catholic custom has required in particular that the hands of a priest, which perform the sacrament, be without deformity.

Training and Ordination. A wide variety of instruction, training, and initiation for work as a priest exists among the world's religious traditions. [*See* Ordination.] The content of the training is generally a blend of three components that one could term the practical, the theoretical, and the disciplinary.

The practical side of a priest's training includes most saliently the skills the community expects for correct performance of ritual. In a great many traditional settings the efficacy of a prayer or incantation has been held to depend on the acoustic correctness of its utterance. The Hindu concept of *mantra* as a verbal formula entails such training on the part of those who will pronounce *mantras,* and in the view of many Zoroastrians the exactness of the priests' pronunciation of the liturgical prayers in the Avestan language is what makes the prayers effective.

Besides the formulas of the ritual text itself there is much else for a priest to learn: where the ceremonial objects and the officiant should be placed; how the right time for an observance is to be determined; and so on. Where the celebration of a ritual has depended for its timing on direct observation of the sun, moon, or stars, the training of a priest has necessitated mastering a certain amount of practical astronomy. Where the means of divination have included the bones or entrails of animals, the priest has of necessity had to be a practical veterinary surgeon. Indeed, it is instructive to observe in the history of cultures that many professions that became independent specializations have had their origin as branches of priestly learning.

What can be termed theoretical training stands at the other end of the spectrum. Training for priesthood thus may contain a substantial component of historical and philosophical study, in which the prospective congregational leader is given at least a rudimentary exposure to the results of scriptural and doctrinal scholarship.

The perceived need for competence in theoretical matters has generally led religious communities to develop courses of formal academic instruction for their priests (or comparable personnel) in theological studies. Throughout the Islamic world, religious scholarship flourished in a type of school

> The practical side of a priest's training includes most saliently the skills the community expects for correct performance of ritual.

known as a *madrasah* meaning etymologically "place of study." In medieval Europe, the origin of universities as institutions was frequently closely tied to the need to educate the Christian clergy, and in a number of northern European countries since the Protestant Reformation both Protestant and Roman Catholic theological faculties have continued to be integral parts of the older universities.

Under the heading of "discipline" can be considered a third kind of preparation for priesthood. In various cultures, from tribal to modern, the priest-to-be is expected to undertake regimes of physical or spiritual self-cultivation—the better to be worthy of, or effective in, the practice of his role.

Celibacy for priests is a discipline for which a number of rationales have been offered. There is, of course, the notion of sexual activity as a physical pollution. Beyond this may lie a cosmological or metaphysical view most characteristic of gnostic and Manichaean thinking, that the very perpetuation of physical existence in this world hinders the eventual release of pure spirit from its imprisonment in inherently evil matter.

The most nearly universal discipline among the world's priesthoods is probably the discipline of meditation. The priest in his exercise of his role may be expected to lead others in meditation; in his training, he is prepared by its practice. A general feeling of well-being or decisiveness can be a

personal benefit of meditation to those who practice it; but as a spiritual discipline, meditation needs to serve an unselfish goal, the control of the self and dedication of the priest's personal identity to a power or cause beyond himself.

Upon completion of his training, the priest is ceremonially inducted into the exercise of his role, a process to which Westerners often apply the Christian term *ordination*. Among Christians, the notion of "apostolic succession" implies that each priest has a pedigree of ordination going back to the apostles. Buddhist lineages are similar in that monks or pupils trace their ordination back for centuries to earlier teachers.

The Future of Priesthood. The challenge of maintaining an ancient ritual tradition in a modern secular and technological age is a major one. In most of the modern world's religious communities, recruitment of priests is a pressing problem. The celibate life, for instance, surely deters many Roman Catholic males from opting for a priestly vocation. Economic considerations are also a factor: the offerings of the faithful sometimes no longer support a priest in the comfort, compared with other lines of work, that they once afforded. Priests have been reduced to mendicant roles even in those communities which have not characteristically expected priests to be poor. Among the Zoroastrian Parsis of India, most priests are paid on a piecework basis for prayers said, as opposed to being salaried.

Even more serious than this is a widespread decline in intellectual respect for priests throughout the contemporary world. Modern secularist criticism of traditional religious affirmations has to a certain extent called the content of the priest's affirmations into question, and the response from the pulpit has unfortunately sometimes been pietistic obscurantism. But at least as important has been the sociological fact of the growth of other skills and professions around the world. Today it is not unusual for the spiritual leader of a congregation to count among his flock scientists, engineers, or other professionals whose training is much more highly focused than his own. The challenge of life's ultimate questions, however, persists. Priesthood will probably attract able personnel in significant and perhaps sufficient numbers for many generations to come.

[*See also* Ministry.]

BIBLIOGRAPHY

General studies of priesthood are relatively few. Two that can be recommended are E. O. James's *The Nature and Function of Priesthood* (London, 1955) and Leopold Sabourin's *Priesthood: A Comparative Study* (Leiden, 1973).

WILLARD G. OXTOBY

PROPHECY

The term *prophecy* refers to a wide range of religious phenomena that have been manifested from ancient to modern times. Today comparativists use *prophecy* to describe religious phenomena in various contexts on analogy with the activity of ancient Hebrew prophets and other figures who had a similarly pivotal role in founding world religions in Southwest Asia.

Ancient Prophecy. In antiquity it was commonly believed that gods controlled events in the world and made their intentions known to human beings in various ways. The earliest written records tell of religious functionaries whose responsibility it was to interpret signs or deliver messages from the gods in order to supply information useful in the conduct of human affairs. In early tribal societies the clan leader often carried out these duties. These activities usually included intercessory functions, whereby the leader or "prophet" petitioned spirits or a god or gods for special favors for their group. From the records of ancient cultures in Mesopotamia and the Mediterranean region we know of a large number of religious specialists who sought out and interpreted messages from the gods. Their access to the world of the gods came through two different means. In the first place, there were diviners who practiced a variety of studied techniques to interpret symbolic messages in the natural world. [*See* Divination.] Second, the gods were also believed to communicate their will through oracles, that is, in human language through the mouth of an inspired person. [*See* Oracles.]

Within general categories the nature and function of divine intermediation was diverse. Oracles and signs could appear without request; but more commonly, especially in the Greco-Roman world, cultic officials provided answers to specific questions asked to the sanctuary's god. The terminology applied to intermediaries is often ambiguous or vague, as with the Greek term *prophetes,* which at times denotes the oracular mouthpiece for divine speech and at others refers to the official interpreter of divinatory signs within a sanctuary. The diversity is immense.

Prophetic Founders of Religious Tradition. Throughout ancient Israel's history as an independent state (c. 1000-586 BCE), the religious orientation of a large segment of its population was polytheistic, and as such, it shared in the general worldview of its neighbors. But even in the monotheistic elements of Israelite culture, there were different functionaries who transmitted the will of the same god, Yahveh, to the people. During the earliest part of this history, it appears that the Yahvists relied on at least three different figures for divine communication: (1) cultic officers who performed certain techniques like casting lots; (2) seers (Heb., *ro'eh* and *hozeh*), whose function is rather unclear, but may be designations from different periods of visionaries and diviners (cf. *1 Samuel* 9:9); and (3) ecstatics (Heb., *navi',* commonly translated as "prophet"), whose unusual behavior was stimulated when Yahveh's spirit came upon them. Evidence indicates, however, that prophetic legitimacy depended primarily on their acceptance within a given group as oracular vehicles for the communication of Yahveh's word, regardless of whether the *navi'* was an ecstatic, a cultic official, an independent critic, or some combination of these roles.

By at least the eighth century BCE the Hebrew prophets or their scribes commonly wrote down their oracles, and the prophetic writings of the Hebrew Bible (Old Testament) contain, in part, a modest literary residue of this extensive oracular activity. Within the religious worldview that permeated

> It was necessary to maintain a retinue of religious specialists to prophesy anew and interpret messages that regularly came from the gods.

the time of the first Hebrew prophets, messages from the gods were seen as portentous for only the particular audience, time, and place attendant to the moment when they had been revealed on earth. Thus, it was necessary to maintain a retinue of religious specialists to prophesy anew and interpret messages that regularly came from the gods. As certain specified written oracles came to be accepted in Israel as the repository of normative divine instruction, the nature of prophecy itself began to change, as did the character of religious tradition.

Zarathushtra (Zoroaster), a Persian prophet of the late second millennium BCE, was the founder of Zoroastrianism (Boyce, 1975). Jesus appears in many respects as a prophet, even though Christianity has traditionally portrayed him as a unique messiah. Mani, a Babylonian born in 216 CE, founded Manichaeism, which gained a large following in countries from India to the western Mediterranean. Finally, Muhammad, like no other, established a believing community around himself as divine messenger.

Defining precisely what these individual prophets share in common is not a simple matter. The social location of their activity differs in each case, and the success of each prophet in gaining a following during his lifetime varied widely. Moreover the message of each prophet, if examined in detail, depends more on the particular traditions to which it was heir and the historical-cultural setting of the prophet's activity than upon a transcendent ideal that applies to every member of the group. Nonetheless, five features are common to all.

1. *They all conceived of their activity as the result of a personal divine commission.*

2. *Religious traditions arose that regarded some oracles of these prophets as uniquely heaven-sent, sacred, and binding upon people in perpetuity.*

3. Though the content of their messages differs significantly from one prophet to the next, depending on historical circumstance and inherited tradition, *all of the founding prophets proclaimed what their later tradition regarded as universal truths.*

4. *The founding prophets were, in their own individual ways, social critics,* even though their ideas about society were quite different from one another.

5. Finally, *the founding prophets helped both to maintain and to reform religious tradition.*

The founding prophets are distinct from others who founded major religious traditions (such as Buddhism, Jainism, Confucianism, and Taoism). The founders of these traditions originating in India and China were not divinely chosen messengers. These teachers, like the prophets, were often missionaries and social critics, but the basis of their words was the perfection of their own intellectual, spiritual, and moral talents, rather than their election by a deity to bear a specific message.

Prophecy under the Influence of Canon. One of the most outstanding features of the founding prophets was the special importance that their personal communication of revelation had for succeeding generations of their religious communities. Just as the Hebrew prophets and Zarathushtra were influenced by the traditions that preceded them, so too were the prophets who came later. But for Jesus, Mani, and Muhammad the traditional inheritance included the message of the Hebrew prophets (and Zarathushtra), as well as the model they had established as prophets whose messages were canonized within scripture. Once prophecy became written and canonical, the revelation of these same prophets attained a special status that inevitably lessened the importance and limited the scope of active mediation generally. The guardianship and transmission of prophecy—now newly conceived as the substance of prophetic oracles within the canon—moved from the ecstatics and visionaries who originally created it to the inspired sages, priests, and scribes who maintained and passed along the scriptures.

Within the context of this religious tradition it became necessary for contemporary prophets who did not consider their calling subordinate to any earlier prophet to claim a special status for themselves. Therefore, Jesus on occasion appears as an eschatological prophet who proclaimed the imminent arrival of the "kingdom of God." By the time of Mani (216-276) and Muhammad (580-632), several canonical religions had come to prominence. Both these prophets understood themselves explicitly as successors to a line of prophets that included (though variously) Abraham, Moses, Elijah, other Hebrew prophets, Zarathushtra, Jesus, and even the Buddha.

As the words of these historical prophets attained reverential status within scriptural canons, the book replaced the living religious specialist as the primary agent of revelational mediation. The history of surviving religious traditions with a prophetic scripture (now Judaism, Christianity, and Islam) has depended in no small measure upon this development. Exegetes of various sorts replaced prophets as the maintainers of the revelational tradition, and often those who safeguarded the sanctity and purity of the written scriptures were suspicious of, even hostile to, those who claimed to have visions not mediated through the scripture.

Even so, while contemporary prophetic inspiration lost influence at the center of religious authority, it was never eliminated entirely. Throughout history, in pre-Christian Judaism, in early Christianity, and in pre-Muslim and early-Muslim Arabia, prophetic figures were active alongside (though often in competition with) the rationalized institutions of canonical religion. In early Judaism, some of those who collected and arranged sacred writings within the Hebrew Bible conceived themselves to be prophets, for example, the levitical priests Korah and Asaph, who claimed prophetic inspiration for their hymnology and arranged the psalter in a structure that gives special prominence to a prophetic interpretation of psalms. And later, during the medieval period, qabbalist interpretation of the Bible elevated not only the revelational experiences of the biblical authors, but also the necessity for inspiration among exegetes.

Prophecy in Modern Times. The importance of prophets as the mediators of revealed truth declined sharply as the Enlightenment demolished confidence in the truth of revelation generally and enshrined a new standard of knowledge arrived at on the basis of observation and critical reasoning. At first these changes affected only the intellectual elite who had considered the impact of philosophical developments upon conceptions of God, religious truth, and divine mediation.

The discussion of such ideas among philosophers, scientists, and literati was contained within a minuscule portion of European culture, and the effects of their writings upon the general population materialized only very slowly. Of greater significance for popular religious culture was the diminished authority of the church. In some cases the reduction in ecclesiastical power was a direct outgrowth of Enlightenment thinking, as in the United States, where religion was consciously and explicitly separated from the centers of political power. But for the most part it seems that reductions in the power of the church to enforce its dogmas allowed for greater religious diversity (as during the Reformation), so that Enlightenment thinkers, and others, could express their religious views openly. Within this religious environment a new set of prophets arose to proclaim themselves as messengers bearing the divine word. Joseph Smith (1805-1844), for example, established the Church of Latter-Day Saints upon the claim that he had received revelations from Jesus Christ and from an angel who entrusted him with the *Book of Mormon*. Those who profess Christian Science regard the writings of Mary Baker Eddy (1821-1910) as sacred and inviolable. Others, notably the members of the international Pentecostal or the later charismatic movements, are modern ecstatics who consider themselves capable of receiving the spirit and speaking as divine agents.

BIBLIOGRAPHY

For the background of mediation between gods and human beings within world religions, Mircea Eliade's *Shamanism: Archaic Techniques of Ecstasy*, rev. & enl. ed. (New York, 1964), remains unsurpassed for its breadth. Works about the founding prophets normally contain a general discussion and bibliography concerning their specific precursors. Such are Robert R. Wilson's *Prophecy and Society in Ancient Israel* (Philadelphia, 1980); David L. Petersen's *The Roles of Israel's Prophets* (*Journal for the Study of the Old Testament*, supp. 17; Sheffield, 1981, which surveys the evidence for Israelite intermediation in the ancient Near East, and David E. Aune's *Prophecy in Early Christianity and the Ancient Mediterranean World* (Grand Rapids, Mich., 1983), which gives a thorough discussion of Greco-Roman prophecy as well as its forms among the first Christians. Many critical works on Hebrew prophecy approach the subject from within the confessional community of Jews (e.g., Martin Buber's *The Prophetic Faith*, New York, 1949, and Abraham Joshua Heschel's *The Prophets*, New York, 1962 or Christians (e.g., Gerhard von Rad's *The Message of the Prophets*, London, 1968. Most treatments of prophecy ignore the significance of Zarathushtra and Mani, since they both have few, if any, modern followers to proclaim their value. Mary Boyce's *A History of Zoroastrianism*, 2 vols. (Leiden, 1975-1982), and Kurt Rudolph's *Gnosis* (San Francisco, 1983) provide useful bibliographies and discussions of the life and time of these prophets, respectively. The books on Muhammad are many; the most readable and intelligent is Maxime Rodinson's *Mohammed* (New York, 1971), which contains a critical evaluation of the works that preceded it. Toufic Fahd's "Kahin," in *The Encyclopaedia of Islam*, new ed., vol. 4 (Leiden, 1978), pp. 420-422, is a short peculiarly lucid account of the difficulties inherent in reconstructing Arab divination during the pre-Islamic period.

Regrettably, no book discusses prophecy within a framework as broad as that suggested in this article. Hence, we suggest that the reader consult other articles within this compendium for detailed bibliographies on such topics as mysticism, ecstasy, canon, scripture, and the Enlightenment, as well as on individuals that we have mentioned in the text.

Among works that may not be listed in other articles is the anthropological literature on prophecy. Max Weber's work has had a seminal influence on the field; see both *Ancient Judaism* (1922; Glencoe, Ill., 1952) and *The Sociology of Religion* (1922; Boston, 1963). I. M. Lewis's *Ecstatic Religion* (Harmondsworth, 1971) is a sociology of ecstatic behavior based on a broad range of comparative evidence, and though it does not address prophecy per se, it has influenced others (viz. Wilson, cited above) that do. Victor Turner's "Religious Specialists: Anthropological Study," in *International Encyclopedia of the Social Sciences,* edited by David L. Sills (New York, 1968), vol. 13, pp. 437-444, offers analytical categories useful in distinguishing prophets from other religious personnel. A number of books describe the activity of prophets in modern cultures: Peter Worsley's *The Trumpet Shall Sound: A Study of "Cargo" Cults in Melanesia* (1957;

New York, 1968); E. E. Evans-Pritchard's *Nuer Religion* (Oxford, 1956) and *The Sanusi of Cyrenaica* (Oxford, 1949); James Mooney's *The Ghost-Dance Religion and the Sioux Outbreak of 1890* (1896; abr. ed., Chicago, 1965); and Vittorio Lanternari's *The Religions of the Oppressed: A Study of Modern Messianic Cults* (New York, 1963).

Finally, Kenneth Cragg's *Muhammad and the Christian: A Question of Response* (New York, 1984) is a valuable beginning for the dialogue between Muslim and Christian conceptions of prophetic revelation.

GERALD T. SHEPPARD and
WILLIAM E. HERBRECHTSMEIER

PROTESTANTISM

Protestantism is a worldwide movement that derives from sixteenth-century reforms of Western Christianity. As a movement it is both a set of church bodies and a less well defined ethos, spirit, and cultural achievement. Thus, one speaks of Reformed or Methodist churches as being Protestant, just as one may speak of a "Protestant ethic" or a "Protestant nation."

Four Protestant Clusters. For demographic purposes, David B. Barrett in his *World Christian Encyclopedia* (1982) tries to bring some order to definitional chaos by classifying the non-Roman Catholic and non-Orthodox part of the Christian world into five families, or blocs, which he calls "Protestant," "nonwhite indigenous," "Anglican," "marginal Protestant," and "Catholic (non-Roman)." All but the last of these have some sort of Protestant ties. The mainstream Protestant category includes long-established Northern Hemisphere churches such as the Congregationalist and Baptist. The Anglican family includes plural, low church, high church, evangelical, Anglo-Catholic, and central (or Broad church) traditions. The category of marginal Protestants includes Jehovah's Witnesses, Mormons, Religious Science, and Unitarian, Spiritualist, and British-Israelite churches.

Protestant Diversity and Coherence. The first perception of both old and new Protestantism has always been its diversity. Barrett claims that the one billion and more practicing Christians of the world belong to 20,780 distinct denominations. While more than half the Christians are Catholic, the vast majority of these 20,780 denominations would be classed as part of the Protestant movement. Thus, in classic Protestantism, in 1980 there were almost 345 million people in 7,889 of these distinct bodies in 212 nations. The nonwhite indigenous versions, almost all of them Protestant, were located in 10,065 distinct bodies. There were also 225 Anglican denominations and 1,345 "marginal Protestant" groups. Indeed, this diversity and this fertility at creating new, unrelated bodies were long used as a criticism of

Protestantism by Roman Catholicism, which united under the Roman pope, and by Orthodoxy, which was divided more into national jurisdictions but saw itself as united in holy tradition.

It is possible to move behind this first perception of the chaos of unrelated bodies to see some forms of coherence. Great numbers of Protestant bodies, along with many Orthodox ones, are members of the World Council of Churches, established in 1948, which has a uniting confessional theme around the lordship of Jesus Christ. In many nations there are national councils or federations of cooperating churches, which allow for positive interaction even where there is not organic unity. World confessional families of Lutherans, Reformed, Baptists, and others throughout the twentieth century have brought into some concord these

> **There have been significant mergers of Protestant churches both within families, and across family lines.**

churches that have family resemblances. Finally, there have been significant mergers of Protestant churches both within families, such as Lutheran with Lutheran, Presbyterian with Presbyterian, and across family lines, as in America's United Church of Christ, which blended a New England Congregationalist tradition with a German Reformed heritage.

Some Protestant Elements Held in Common. While the resistance to papal claims is a uniting factor, it is not likely that many people ever choose to remain loyal to Protestantism on such marginal and confining grounds alone. The first common mark of Protestantism is historically clear and clean; virtually all Protestant groups derive from movements that began in the sixteenth century. When later groups were formed, as were the Disciples of Christ in nineteenth-century America, they may not have seen themselves as working out the logic of earlier Protestantism; yet historians at once traced the roots of this typical new group to various older Presbyterian and Baptist forms, among others.

A very few Protestant groups can also trace their lineage back to pre-Reformation times. Modern Waldensians, for example, are heirs of a movement begun under Pierre Valdès (Peter Waldo) in the twelfth century, and some modern Czech churches are heirs of traditions that go back to the Hussite Jednota Bratrská (Society of Brethren, known in Latin as Unitas Fratrum) of the fifteenth century. At another point on the spectrum is the Church of England, or Anglicanism. Most of its articulators stress that they remain the church Catholic as it has been on English soil since the christianization of England. Although it has kept faith in the apostolic succession of bishops and has retained many pre-

Reformation practices, the Anglican communion as it has existed since the break with Rome under Henry VIII in the sixteenth century is vastly different from the Catholic church under Roman papal obedience in England before and since the Reformation. In short, the Waldensians, the Czech groups, and the Anglicans alike were, and were seen to be, part of the Protestant revolt from both the viewpoints of Roman Catholic leadership and historical scholarship ever since. Individual groups may have parentage in the Middle Ages or may have sprung up late in the twentieth century, yet the sixteenth-century breach in Christendom is the event by which Protestant existence is somehow measured.

God in Protestantism. All Christian movements, unlike some other religions, focus finally on their witness to God. Protestantism is theistic. There have been momentary expressions by theological elites of a "Christian atheism," but these have been dismissed by the Protestant public as idiosyncratic, personal forms of witness or philosophical expression.

At the left wing of marginal Protestantism stand some former Protestant groups that have retained certain elements of the Protestant tradition. Among these are Unitarianisms of humanistic sorts and Ethical Culture movements, which grew up on Jewish soil in America but acquired some Protestant traits.

If Protestants are not humanistic or atheistic, they also are not pantheistic. Individual pantheists may exist as mystics, and there have been pantheistic Protestant heresies, so regarded both by those who have innovated with them and by those who have excluded their advocates. In some formal theological circles, one sometimes hears advocated teachings that seem to verge on pantheism, the proposition that the world and God are coextensive, identical. Yet articulators of such teachings usually take pains to distance themselves from pure pantheism.

Protestantism on occasion has had deistic proponents, agents of a natural religion that made no room for a personal God, special revelation, or reasons to pray to an unresponsive, divine, originating, but now absentee force. Yet deism has consistently in due course been seen as a deviation from, not a part of, the Protestant impulse.

Authority and Structure: The Scriptures. The Bible of Protestantism is the canon of the Old and New Testaments, and almost never the Apocrypha, which has special status in the Orthodox and Catholic traditions. The canon is theoretically open; it is conceivable that a book could still be added to it. While the Bible has become the only document used and useful for uniting Protestant witness or helping determine Protestant theological argument—it provides at least something of the genetic programming of Protestantism, or the ground rules for their games—there is here as so often a very broad spectrum of approaches to its authority. Most Protestants have accepted the Lutheran mark *sola scriptura,* that the Bible alone is the authority; but this formula tells all too little about how to regard the book.

At one extreme, conservative Protestants who have resisted modern historical criticism of biblical texts stress that the Bible is somehow not only inspired but infallible and inerrant. At the other end of the spectrum are a minority of Protestants, chiefly in academic centers, who have com-

> **Most Protestants have accepted the Lutheran mark *sola scriptura*, that the Bible alone is the authority.**

pletely adopted post-Enlightenment views of biblical criticism. They have thus treated the biblical text as they would any other ancient literary text. They grant no special status to the inspiration of biblical authors. For them the Bible still has authority as a document that both reflects and promotes the norms of the Christian community. Many schools of interpretation, even among those who have immersed themselves in historical and literary criticism, find that the Bible "discloses," or potentially discloses, what God would reveal.

The Authority of the Church. Lacking paper authority as they do, and unwilling as they are for the most part to yield to bishops as having a determinative role in dispensing tradition, how do Protestants see the authority of the church? The vast majority of Protestants in all ages, though they be churched and faithful, have rendered secondary to the Bible all other church authority, creeds, confessions, and forms of polity. When they are serious and are seriously confronted, most Protestants characteristically will say that they get authority for teaching and practice from the Bible alone.

Despite this claim, reflective Protestants will also admit that over the centuries they have spilled much ink in treatises on churchly authority. As much as Catholics, they may have exacted sweat and blood from people who ran afoul of church authorities, who tested the bounds of orthodoxy, or who came under ecclesiastical discipline. Protestantism, in other words, may seem chaotic to the outsider who sees its many groupings and varieties, but to most confessors and members the chaos is minimized, because they are ordinarily touched only by the authority system of which they are a part, that of their own church.

Once one insists on making churchly authority secondary, other values come to be dominant in association with the church. The church on Protestant soil is a fellowship, a congregation of people who have like minds or similar purposes. The church may be seen as "the body of Christ" or "the communion of saints" before it is an authority to compel conformity in teaching or practice. Yet once one assigns values to the group, even in forms of Protestantism that accent the

right of private judgment or go to extremes of individualism, there must be and in practice have been many subtle ways to assert authority and to effect discipline. A small congregation's authority on Baptist or Congregational soil can be felt more immediately, for instance, than might Catholic authority asserted from the distance between Rome and India by a not always efficient and always pluralistic church.

Protestant Church Polities. Protestantism presents a broad spectrum of often mutually incompatible polities. Most Protestant churches have preserved elements of the polity that came with their birth, transformed by exigencies of local, contemporary demands and, in the modern world, adjustments to the managerial and bureaucratic impulse.

On one end of this spectrum are churches like the Anglican church or the Lutheran church in Sweden, which insist on apostolic succession in an episcopacy that is of the essence (displays the *esse*) of the church. Elsewhere, as in Methodism and much of Lutheranism, bishops belong to the *bene esse* of the church; they are beneficial for its order but theoretically could be replaced in a different polity. Many Reformed churches rely on synodical or connectional and associational patterns under the rule of presbyters or elders. From the days of the radical reformation in the sixteenth century through various later Baptist and Congregational witnesses into modern times, and especially in burgeoning non-white indigenous Protestantism, the authority and even the autonomy of the local congregation is asserted.

Those Protestants at the "catholic" end of the spectrum, who regard bishops as of the *esse* of the church, have been least ready to see their polity as negotiable in an ecumenical age. Presbyterian, synodical, and congregational bodies, while emphatically cherishing and defending their polities, have shown more signs of flexibility.

Civil Government. In the late twentieth century, most of the new nations in which nonwhite indigenous Protestantism prospered had undergone experiences of modernization that, whatever else these meant, provided no room for fusion of church and state or an interwoven pattern of religious and civil authority. Similarly, it was on the soil of largely Protestant nations such as the United States that the greatest degree of constitutional separation between the two authorities first occurred. Yet political philosopher Hannah Arendt is correct to chide Protestants for claiming that modern democracy with its religious freedom is simply a Christian invention. Some Christians have found it easy to reach into their repository of options to find impetus for supporting republicanism based on Enlightenment principles and practical support of equity and civil peace whenever pluralism has been strong.

Historical Protestantism in almost all its mainstream and dominant forms first simply carried over authority patterns from medieval Catholicism. In the Church of England, the Presbyterian church in Scotland, the Lutheran churches of Scandinavia, the Lutheran and Reformed churches of

Germany, Switzerland, and the Netherlands, and wherever else leaders had the power to do so, they naturally clung to establishment. They simply broke from Roman Catholic establishment to form Protestant versions.

Despite all these establishmentarian dimensions, it is also fair to say that Protestantism did contain the seed that helped disestablishment and separation of church and state develop. A religion of the word, Protestantism called for that word to separate people from attachment to the culture as it evoked decision. So the boundaries of the church and the state could not be coextensive, as they aspired then to be in Catholicism. Whatever "the priesthood of all believers," "the right of private judgment," and the call to conscience in biblical interpretation meant theologically, they had as their practical consequence an honoring of individualism and personal profession of faith. Both of these would become confined were there an official and authoritative church.

Protestant Substance. Original or classic Protestantism was more ready to see itself as distinctive in the content of faith than is modern pluralist Protestantism. In the sixteenth century, late medieval Catholicism presented what to Protestant eyes was an egregious violation of God's system of approach to human beings. Catholicism had generated, or degenerated into, a system that progressively depended more and more upon human achievement. Key words were human *merit* or humanly gained *righteousness*. Elaborate schemes, for example, the sale of indulgences to help make up the required number of merits to assure salvation, had been devised. These led to abuses, which contemporary Catholic reformers and later historians have agreed made Protestant revolt plausible.

Protestantism across the board held to generally extreme views of human finitude, limits, "fallenness," and need. Mainstream and marginal reformers alike were not convinced by claims that human beings retained enough of the image of God upon which to build so that their own works or merits would suffice to appease a wrathful God. They exaggerated the way Catholicism had diminished the role of Jesus Christ as giver of a gift or imparter of grace upon the wholly undeserving.

In the sixteenth century, there were many variations on this theme, and Martin Luther's proclamation of "justification by grace through faith," while at home in all of Protestantism, was not necessarily the chosen formula for all Protestants. Yet all did accent divine initiative, human limits, the gifts of God in Jesus Christ, and the new condition of humanity as a result of divine forgiveness.

Protestantism has considered the church always to be reforming, never reformed; Catholicism and Protestantism alike, many would say, stand in need of being reformed, and from time to time they move past rigid, older identities and formulas. Such moves are not incongruent with the Protestant ethos and spirit.

Protestant Worship. In describing baptism (whether sprinkling of infants or immersion of adults), the Lord's Supper, and the act of preaching and the uses of the word, the outlines of Protestant worship become generally clear. To these should be added that Protestants characteristically have gathered for worship in buildings set aside for that purpose. While they believe that the gathered community may effectively baptize, eat and drink, hear and pray under the sky or in secular buildings, they have had an impulse to set aside and consecrate a sacred space, which symbolically, not actually, becomes a house of God.

The sacred space usually accents a place for preaching, a baptismal font or pool, and a table or altar for the Lord's Supper. Around these the people gather, in pews or on chairs. The gathering occurs to recognize the presence of God, to follow divine commands to congregate for purposes of praise, to build the morale of the group for purposes outside the sanctuary, and to celebrate the seasons of the church year, the events of the week, and the passages of life.

With few exceptions, Protestantism is also a singing religion. It took the act of praising in song, which had become largely a preserve of clergy and choir, and enlarged it to include the congregation.

Except in Seventh-day Adventism, Protestant worship almost always occurs on Sunday, the Lord's Day, the Day of Resurrection, although believers are urged to worship at any time or place. Most Protestants observe the inherited Catholic church year but have purged it of many of its occasions. That is, they annually follow the life of Christ from Advent and Christmas, with its birth rites, through another

> A religion of the word, Protestantism called for that word to separate people from attachment to the culture as it evoked decision.

season of repentance and preparation, Lent, on the way to a climax at Good Friday and Easter weekend, and then a festival of the Holy Spirit at Pentecost. The more Puritan forms of Protestantism, however, saw something "papist" in these seasonal observances and did away with almost all of them, sometimes including Christmas itself. The rest of Protestantism, which kept the church year of observances, also honored biblical saints like Paul and John on special days but rejected most postbiblical saints. Thus in the United States many observe a Thanksgiving Day, Mother's Day and Father's Day, Stewardship Sunday, Lay Sunday, and the like. The impulse to ritualize life is strong even on the purging, purifying, and simplifying soil of Protestantism.

Protestant Expression. In general, Protestantism has been less fertile than Catholic Christianity in affirming the literary and artistic worlds. Sometimes this has resulted from a certain suspicion about the validity of the earthly venture for the sake of salvation.

Protestantism seemed most productive in the field of music, perhaps because the kinetic character of music seemed to be congruent with a word-centered, iconoclastic tradition. One thinks here of the musical poets of Protestantism, most notably the composer Johann Sebastian Bach. In literature there have been John Milton and John Bunyan, but in the contemporary world Protestantism has seldom helped produce anything approaching modern classics. In the visual arts geniuses like Lucas Cranach or, supremely, Rembrandt have given expression to their evangelical sympathies and Protestant outlook.

[*For discussion of the dispersion of Protestantism, see* regional surveys under Christianity. *For discussion of particular manifestations of Protestantism, see* Anabaptism; Anglicanism; Baptist Churches; Christian Science; Lutheranism; Mennonites; Methodist Churches; Moravians; Mormonism; Presbyterianism, Reformed; Puritanism; Quakers; Seventh-day Adventism; Shakers; *and* Unitarian Universalist Association.]

BIBLIOGRAPHY

One of the more ambitious histories of Protestantism is Émile G. Léonard's *Historie générale du protestantisme,* 3 vols. (Paris, 1961-1964), translated as *A History of Protestantism* (London, 1965-1968). Most Protestant history is simply incorporated as half of the latter third of general church histories, such as Kenneth Scott Latourette's *A History of Christianity* (New York, 1953). The most extensive easily accessible bibliography is in my own *Protestantism* (New York, 1972). One way to approach Protestantism is through its root experience in the Reformation era; on the thought of the period, see Wilhelm Pauck's *The Heritage of the Reformation,* rev. ed. (Oxford, 1968); Harold J. Grimm's *The Reformation Era, 1500-1650,* 2d ed. (New York, 1973), is especially useful for its bibliographies.

Louis Bouyer's *The Spirit and Forms of Protestantism* (London, 1956) is an informed view by a Calvinist turned Catholic. Einar Molland's *Christendom: The Christian Churches, Their Doctrines, Constitutional Forms, and Ways of Worship* (New York, 1959) is especially interesting for its comparison between Protestant and other forms of Christianity. Few scholars have attempted to discern the genius of Protestantism as a whole, but there are good reasons to consult an imaginative attempt by Robert McAfee Brown, *The Spirit of Protestantism* (Oxford, 1961), or George W. Forell's *The Protestant Faith* (Englewood Cliffs, N. J., 1960); for a European view, see Karl Heim's *The Nature of Protestantism* (Philadelphia, 1963). John B. Cobb, Jr., in *Varieties of Protestantism* (Philadelphia, 1960), treats modern theology. There is a lively treatment of the historical development in John Dillenberger and Claude Welch's *Protestant Christianity Interpreted through Its Development* (New York, 1954).

MARTIN E. MARTY

PSALMS

PSALMS are ancient Hebrew songs addressed to or invoking the deity; the Hebrew Bible, or the Old Testament in the Christian scriptures, includes a book of 150 of these religious songs. In ancient and later Jewish tradition, the book is known in Hebrew as *Tehillim* ("Praises"), although only one of the songs (Psalm 145) is so designated within the biblical text. The English title *Psalms* derives from the Greek rendering of the Hebrew *mizmor* (a song accompanied by string plucking), a label that introduces fifty-seven of the Hebrew psalms. In Christian circles, the *Book of Psalms* is often referred to as the Psalter, a name taken from the psaltery, a stringed instrument that accompanied the singing of many of the psalms.

Apart from the canonical psalms, which seem to have been accorded official status in the second century BCE, we have many other ancient Hebrew songs of the psalm type. Within the Hebrew Bible are the song of triumph in *Exodus* (15:1-18), the prayer of Hannah in *1 Samuel* (2:1-10), the song of thanksgiving in *2 Samuel* 22 (which is nearly identical with Psalm 18), the prayer of Hezekiah in *Isaiah* (38:10-20), the thanksgiving psalm in *Jonah* (2:3-10), and the prayer of *Habakkuk.* The *Psalms of Solomon* in the Pseudepigrapha, dated to the first century BCE, comprises eighteen hymns, personal pleas for salvation in particular, which resemble certain biblical psalms. In addition, seven noncanonical psalms have been recovered among the Dead Sea Scrolls.

Formation of the Psalter. In its canonical form, *Psalms* comprises five sections or "books": Psalms 1-41, 42-72, 73-89, 90-106, and 107-150. The first four books end with a doxology, or call to praise the Lord, and the fifth ends with an entire psalm (Psalm 150) that constitutes a doxology. It has been noted that books 1, 4, and 5 tend to employ the unvocalized personal name of God in the Hebrew Bible, YHVH (traditionally and in this article rendered as 'the Lord'), while books 2 and 3 refer to God as Elohim, suggesting that divergent theological traditions, or schools, may have compiled the different books. There are a number of indications that the psalms had formerly been organized differently.

Attribution of the Psalms. Most psalms bear headings that serve either to attribute them to certain authors or collections (David, Korah, Asaph, Moses, Solomon), to describe their type (accompanied song, chant, prayer), to prescribe their liturgical use (Psalm 92 is assigned for Sabbath worship), or to direct their musical performance.

Nearly half the canonical psalms are attributed to David, king of the Israelite empire in the tenth century BCE. Few of the psalms, however, are dated by scholars to so early a period. The attributions to David are generally held to stem from a later attempt to enhance the authority of the psalms by ascribing their origin to Israel's most famed singer and psalmist, David. David is represented as a musician in *1 Samuel* 16, and within the narrative of *2 Samuel* he is credited with three songs: an elegy for Saul and Jonathan (*2 Sm.* 1:17-27), a psalm of thanksgiving for his having been delivered from enemies (*2 Sm.* 22), and a reflection on the covenant between YHVH and David (*2 Sm.* 23:1-7).

> **Nearly half the canonical psalms are attributed to David, king of the Israelite empire in the tenth century BCE.**

Large groups of psalms are attributed to Korah and Asaph. According to *Chronicles, Ezra,* and *Nehemiah,* they were the ancestral heads of the priestly functionaries in the Second Temple in Jerusalem (c. 515 BCE-70 CE), the Levites. *Chronicles* further credits David with establishing the Levitical functions in the Temple (see *1 Chr.* 15-16). It would seem, then, that the attributions to David, Korah, and Asaph refer historically to collections of psalms among Second Temple personnel. The fact that *1 Chronicles* 16 incorporates a psalm virtually identical with Psalm 105 supports this conclusion.

Date and Provenance of the Psalms. Although modern scholarship has abandoned the belief that David authored all the psalms, their date and provenance has been variously determined. Nineteenth-century scholars tended to date the composition of the psalms to the period in which their use was first explicitly attested, following the return of Judahites from the Babylonian exile in the fifth century BCE and later. Similarities between the psalms and the prophetic literature were explained as the influence of the prophets on the psalmists. A number of factors have led twentieth-century scholars to conceive earlier datings.

Because the psalms contain within them few historical references, the most scientific method for establishing the date and provenance of the individual psalms is linguistic. Psalms, like liturgical literature generally, tend to archaize. Even taking this into account, texts such as Psalms 18, 29, 68, 132, and others appear, by dint of their somewhat primitive content, affinities to Canaanite literature, and outmoded linguistic features, not merely to archaize but to be old. On the other hand, Psalms 103, 117, 119, 124, 125, 133, 144, 145, and, perhaps, others betray distinctively postexilic linguistic characteristics, making their Second Temple dating reasonably certain.

Types of Psalms. The prosodic form of the psalms, their language, and their motifs are for the most part highly conventional, suggesting they were composed according to typical patterns.

Their predominant form is comprised of parallelism—the formation of couplets and, occasionally, triplets of lines, through the repetition of syntactic structure and/or semantic content.

Many of the most common themes in the psalms also appear in the hymns and prayers of other ancient Near Eastern cultures. Psalm 104, for example, in which the deity's all-encompassing wisdom is compared to the sun and manifested in creation, bears striking similarities to the fourteenth-century BCE Egyptian hymn to Aton (the sun disk) as well as to a Babylonian hymn to Shamash, the sun god.

The conventional nature of so many biblical psalms and their relations to ancient Near Eastern hymnody in general have led scholars to delineate specific types of psalms and to associate those types with specific social or cultic circumstances in which they were presumably used in ancient Israel. In the early twentieth century, Hermann Gunkel isolated five major, as well as some minor, psalm types:

1. *Hymns,* liturgical songs of praise to the deity, sometimes beatifying God's power in nature (e.g., *Ps.* 29, 33, 34, 92, 100, 104, 105, 111, 114, 134-136, 145, 146)
2. *Personal songs of praise or thanksgiving,* similar to hymns but ostensibly offered by individuals (e.g., *Ps.* 18, 30, 32, 34, 41, 56, 116, 118, 138)
3. *Communal laments* (e.g., *Ps.* 28, 86, 106, 115)
4. *Individual laments or supplications* (e.g., *Ps.* 6, 25, 26, 38, 41, 91)
5. *Songs for the king* (e.g., *Ps.* 2, 20, 21, 45, 72, 101, 110, 132)

The Settings of the Psalms. Some of the psalms cannot readily be associated with any specific historical or cultic setting. This is especially so for didactic and meditative compositions. In many other cases, the content of the psalm suggests a likely usage. Psalm 24, for example, does seem like an appropriate text for a ceremony in which the Ark was conveyed to Jerusalem. Psalm 45 sounds like an ode to be chanted at the wedding of a king. Psalms 114 and 136 pertain to the Exodus from Egypt and would have served well as texts for the spring festival of Pesah (Passover), which celebrates Israelite freedom from Egyptian bondage.

In general, the psalms deal with broad themes of human anguish and need, the deity's grandeur and pathos, and the virtues and pleasures of piety. Many psalms touch on an array of themes. The nonspecific nature of so many psalms makes them, theoretically, applicable to a variety of occasions without limit to a particular time and place.

The Psalms as Revelation. Although the psalms have been understood in Jewish and Christian tradition to embody the reflection and devotion of David, that is, as the expression of human spirit, they have also been taken to contain divine revelation of the future of the pious, on the one hand,

and of the wicked, on the other. The fact that *Psalms* speaks in very general terms of the righteous and pious, who are favored by God, and of their enemies, the wicked, whom God will ultimately destroy, facilitates the traditional interpretation of *Psalms* as predictive of the respective fates of the good and the bad.

Jews and Christians have found in a number of psalms (e.g., *Ps.* 2, 18, 67, 72, 75, 100) predictions of an eschatological age at which the legitimate, anointed king (the Messiah) would be reinstated or vindicated. Church fathers and rabbis adduced verses from *Psalms* in support of various doctrines. While Christians would seek in the psalms clues to the coming of the eschaton, Jews would more often find consolation in the assurances that the righteous would be saved and the Jewish Diaspora ended.

Psalms as Literature. Owing to their liturgical origins and functions, many psalms display the sorts of stereotyped forms and wording, as well as the frequent refrains and repetitions, that characterize formal hymn singing and prayer. Their conventionality makes them easy to join; their repetitive rhythms and phrases can, when chanted, produce a *mantra*-like drive and intensity. When read as poems rather than prayers, many psalms do not feature the sophisticated configurations of words and deployment of tropes that are usually associated with poetry. The liturgical power of *Psalms* has, however, often been praised by readers; they exhibit artful arrangements of language and memorable images. A celebrated example is Psalm 23:

> The Lord is my shepherd;
>   I shall not lack.
> In pastures of grass he has me lie down
>   along waters of stillness he leads me.
> My spirit he revives.
> He guides me on just courses
>   for his name's sake.
> Even when I walk in a vale of darkness
>   I fear no evil,
>   for you are with me.
> Your rod and your staff—
>   they comfort me.
> You set before me a table
>   opposite my adversaries.
> You anoint with oil my head;
>   my cup overruns.
> Aye, good and love will pursue me
>   all the days of my life;
> And I shall dwell in the house of the Lord
>   for a length of days.

BIBLIOGRAPHY

A comprehensive discussion and summary of modern scholarship on the psalms, with treatments of the Psalter as a whole and the individual psalms, is Leopold Sabourin's *The Psalms: Their Origin and Meaning,* rev. ed. (New York, 1974). Studies that treat the psalms from a liturgical perspective as well are W. O. E. Oesterley's *A Fresh Approach to the Psalms* (New York, 1937) and Laurence Dunlop's Patterns of Prayer in the Psalms (New York, 1982). For a detailed summary of the critical study of *Psalms,* see Otto Eissfeldt's *The Old Testament: An Introduction,* translated by Peter R. Ackroyd (Oxford, 1965), pp. 88-127, 444-454; and for the *Psalms of Solomon* and the Dead Sea *Hodayot,* see pages 610-613 and 654-657, respectively. On the cave 11 Psalms Scroll from Qumran, see James A. Sanders's *The Dead Sea Psalms Scroll* (Oxford, 1965). The canonical shape of the Psalter is discussed in Brevard S. Childs's *Introduction to the Old Testament as Scripture* (Philadelphia, 1979), pp. 504-525, with excellent, selected bibliography. The literary history of the canonical Psalter has been most thoroughly analyzed in Gerald H. Wilson's *The Editing of the Hebrew Psalter* (Chico, Calif., 1985). Important commentaries or studies of the psalms are Hermann Gunkel's *The Psalms,* translated by Thomas M. Horner (Philadelphia, 1967); Sigmund Mowinckel's *The Psalms in Israel's Worship,* 2 vols., translated by D. R. Thomas (Ox-ford, 1962); Artur Weiser's *The Psalms,* translated by Herbert Hartwell (Philadelphia, 1962); and Peter C. Craigie's *Psalms 1-50* (Waco, Tex., 1983). On the relation of the psalms of lament to biblical prophecy, see W. H. Bellinger, Jr.'s *Psalmody and Prophecy* (Sheffield, 1984). For ancient Near Eastern literary parallels to the psalms, as well as specimens of liturgical texts, see *Ancient Near Eastern Texts relating to the Old Testament,* 3d ed., edited by James B. Pritchard (Princeton, 1969).

EDWARD L. GREENSTEIN

PURIFICATION

Concepts of pollution and purity are found in virtually all the religions of the world. While some religions recognize subtle distinctions of relative pollution, others place less emphasis upon the social and religious categories that determine pollution. The range extends from cultures like that of the Pygmies, who place almost no emphasis on concepts of pollution and purity, to hierarchical systems like Hinduism, with its highly developed mechanisms for transforming impurity from a dangerous category to a meaningful structuring principle of the Indian cultural system.

It is impossible to understand religious pollution and purification as separate phenomena; these two inseparable categories of religious experience are locked into a dynamic complementarity. Rules governing religious pollution imply a corollary code for ameliorating the condition. The purification of religious pollution is a major religious theme because it forges a path of expiation, healing, renewal, transcendence, and reintegration, establishing harmonious triangular links among the individual, the cosmos, and the social structure.

Forms of Religious Pollution. The range of human activities related to religious pollution is immense. However, it is possible to isolate three general categories of pollution associated with (1) bodily functions, (2) social bonding, and (3) the maintenance of boundaries of the "holy" or "sacred." The categories of pollution presented here are artificial devices developed to facilitate analysis; they are not meant as descriptive categories to characterize the phenomenon. It should be remembered that these categories overlap and form a continuum, and that emphasis on different sorts of pollution varies greatly from one religio-cultural context to another.

Pollution associated with bodily functions. Urine and feces are particularly impure, partly because of their odor, but also due to their more general association with putrefaction and death. In India, the left hand, used for cleansing after defecation, is forbidden to be used when touching other people or sacred objects. Other bodily secretions, such as saliva, vomit, menstrual blood, and afterbirth, are also considered to have polluting qualities. Since they are natural physiological functions, the resulting pollution is focused not on preventing their occurrence but rather on providing boundaries for control and purification.

Contamination by polluted food is a widespread danger, involving elaborate rules of avoidance. In some religions, dietary laws are very strict. Orthodox Judaism, with its emphasis on kosher foods, carefully articulated in the Hebrew scriptures, sets the Jews apart as a holy people who are considered to be clean and consequently prepared to receive the blessings of God, along with the heavy responsibilities that accompany this covenant. Hindus are also known for their strict dietary laws.

Before the emergence of the germ theory to account for biotic disorders, illnesses were universally explained as the invasion of evil spirits, the curse of the evil eye, or the result of broken taboos. Even in modern societies, illnesses may be attributed to spiritual causes. Elaborate rituals to ward off pollution from evil spirits that cause human sickness are found throughout the world. Among the Inuit (Eskimo), illness was attributed to pollution associated with breaking taboos. The Indian goddess of smallpox, Sitala, could be angered easily and subsequently needed to be "cooled" through various rituals of purification.

Pollution and social bonding. The intense socialization of natural bodily functions is another aspect of purification. Birth, adolescence, marriage, and death are linked to physiological stages that are highly controlled and ritualized to ensure protection from the dangers of pollution.

The danger of childbirth is often accompanied by rigorous rituals designed to bring about a healthy outcome for both mother and child. Consequently, the whole process of birth, in some cases including pregnancy, requires special rites of purification.

The transition to adulthood is considered the proper time for prophylactic rites of purification. These rites protect the initiate from pollution during his state of liminality. In some societies uncircumcised males are considered intrinsically polluted. Among the Ndembu people of northwestern Zambia, an uncircumcised boy lacks "whiteness" or "purity" and is permanently polluting; his presence can threaten the luck of hunters.

Menstruation is one of the functions most widely seen as polluting, second only to death. Menstrual impurity may apply only during menses, or it may be more generalized as a kind of gender pollution, rendering women permanently impure due to their sexuality.

Marriage and human sexuality are surrounded by elaborate pollution/purity norms in many parts of the world. Sexual relations outside culturally prescribed rules are generally treated as potential sources of pollution.

The most widespread source of pollution is death and the putrefaction of bodily decay. Death breaks fragile social bonds, and the bonds that remain must be rearranged so that death pollution can be prevented from becoming a generalized condition of social disorder or chaos. Since death represents a rending of the social fabric, its pollution has far-

> **Elaborate rituals to ward off pollution from evil spirits that cause human sickness are found throughout the world.**

reaching effects. In India, death pollutes the whole family, requiring strict rites of purification during prescribed periods of mourning. In Japan, death is believed to result in harmful and contagious pollution that can be transmitted through social contact. The Polynesians abandoned any house where death had occurred. After the death of a Samoan chief, his house could not be entered and fishing in the lagoon was prohibited (Steiner, 1956). According to Robert Parker, "Pollution is a transposition of this sympathetic befoulment to the metaphysical plane. 'Being polluted' is a kind of metaphysical suit of mourning". In the Parsi religion, contact with dead bodies pollutes family, community, and even the natural elements of air, fire, water, and earth.

Violent death is the most polluting of all, for both the victim and the perpetrator of the crime. The pollution generated by violent death is exceedingly dangerous because it may activate a revenge cycle. Among headhunters in New Guinea and other parts of the world, the ghost of an individual who has been murdered is considered extremely dangerous unless it is appeased by taking another head.

Pollution and the maintenance of sacred boundaries. The definition of the "sacred" also involves issues of spiritual pollution. This is clear to individuals who have dedicated themselves to the religious life. As the religious are more vulnerable to pollution, they also may be singled out to suffer its consequences more than others. The idea of being set apart for a holy purpose is exemplified by Judaism, Christianity, and Islam. Particularly in Judaism, the idea of a sanctified, priestly people becomes highly elaborated, to the point that Yahveh's chosen may become impure by worshiping other gods, consulting fortune-tellers, or coming in contact with foreigners.

The polar tension between pollution and purity is activated in pilgrimage: pilgrims enter a dialectic where pollution is dissolved by the journey to a sacred place. Thus, in the great pilgrimage traditions of Islam, Hinduism, Shinto, or Christianity, one not only attains merit, community status, and indulgences for the afterlife; one also undergoes a "spiritual bathing" that opens the eyes, transforms consciousness, and centers human focus on the sacred.

Rites of Purification. Religious pollution always calls for specific rites of purification, which can range from the ingestion of sacraments to painful acts of purgation.

Both fire and smoke are considered sources of purification. In some parts of the world, stepping over a fire is a rite demarcating a transition from defilement. The Hindu god Agni is the personification of fire, and purified butter is poured into fire as an offering to the god. At certain times of the year, sacrifices to Agni are performed to purify the whole world. Hindus attain sacramental benefit by passing their hands over fire. The eternal fire that burns day and night in Parsi fire temples is a source of purity for worshipers, who offer bread and milk while portions of the sacred text, the Avesta, are read before it.

Water, the universal cleanser, is the most widely employed means of ritual purification. Often water is used with other elements, such as fire, salt, or herbs. It is a particularly potent source of purification when obtained from holy springs, wells, or other sacred bodies of water. The many holy wells of Ireland are special places of purification. A bath in the sacred Ganges river is accompanied by such a high level of purification that it is an object of pilgrimage for millions of devotees from all over India. A widespread requirement before worship is the custom of ritual bathing, either of the whole body or parts of the body most exposed to pollution, especially the feet. In most religions the deity must not be approached unless the devotee is ritually clean.

Aside from fire and water, a variety of agents are utilized in ritual purification. These various detergents include salt water, liquid concoctions made from propitious herbs and spices, and various other sacramental substances applied to the polluted individual or space. In Africa and the Middle East, sand or dry dirt is used as a detergent when water is not available. Charcoal, mud, and clay from special sacred places are also employed to remove religious pollution.

These clinging substances are daubed on a person's body to absorb defilement, then washed away. In India, ash from cow dung is widely employed as a cleansing agent. Among the Nuba of Sudan, the ash from burnt branches of the acacia tree has purificatory qualities.

Purificatory purgation, found in one form or another throughout the world, always involves a metaphysics of cleansing transformation, as natural bodily or psychic pollution is purified through rituals that alter the human condition.

One means of cleansing the human body from defilement is to shave the head, eyebrows, and other body hair. In Hinduism, the hair and beard must not be cut until the end of the mourning period. At that time the head is shaved to demarcate the end of death pollution.

> **Emetics of various kinds are prescribed by shamans to flush out evil spirits and purify the human body.**

Throughout the world, fasting is an act of purgation, a sacrifice to honor the divinity, and a mechanism for cleansing the body. Both Judaism and Islam forbid the eating of pork. No religion has a more strict set of dietary laws than Orthodox Judaism, where eating is a sacramental act. Dietary laws are found in the books of *Deuteronomy, Genesis,* and *Exodus,* but they are most widely articulated in *Leviticus.*

The peyote ritual found among Indians of Mexico and the American Southwest involves a phase of vomiting, considered to have both physical and spiritual purifying effects (Malefijt, 1968). Purgatives such as castor oil are used as purifying agents in African religions. Emetics of various kinds are prescribed by shamans to flush out evil spirits and purify the human body. Among North American Indians, the sweat bath is widely employed to cure illnesses and remove impurities.

Psychological forms of purgation are connected to the condition of the human body. Various forms of physical torture have been employed in the world's religions to bring about a psychological state of penance and humility in the presence of the supernatural. Mortification of the flesh includes various forms of flagellation, walking on nails, lacerations, suspension on hooks driven through the skin, the wearing of hair shirts, and sleeping on rough surfaces.

Another form of physical and psychological purification is sexual abstinence or celibacy. Confession of misdeeds appears in one form or another in most religions. The public or private recitation of transgressions purges the individual of guilt and acts as an antidote to both the personal and the collective pollution resulting from the breaking of taboos.

Contact with holy items, such as relics of saints, sacraments, and statues of deities, is an important source of purification. The utterance of prayers also has cleansing value. In Hinduism, mantras may be used either as agents to combat evil or as foci for concentration leading to spiritual awakening. Rituals of purification in Buddhism are metaphors for inner transformations and mystical enlightenment.

The use of substitutions to remove pollution is a widespread purificatory custom. The sick human body may be rubbed with sticks, stones, or other objects to which the pollution is transferred. A means of curing mental disorders in Nigeria is to remove the person's clothes and rub his body with a sacrificed dove, which absorbs the evil spirits. In the American Indian peyote cult, individuals are purified by being rubbed with sagebrush. The institution of kingship is widely accompanied by the purificatory anointing of the king's body. The annual Ch`ing-ming ceremony in China involves a tradition of sweeping clean the graves of the ancestors.

BIBLIOGRAPHY

Babb, Lawrence A. *The Divine Hierarchy: Popular Hinduism in Central India.* New York, 1975.

Douglas, Mary. *Purity and Danger.* New York, 1966. This landmark volume has had a profound effect on our understanding of religion. Pollution and purity are analyzed in different religious systems to reveal underlying structural similarities. The author stresses the need to understand concepts of pollution and purity in the context of a total structure of thought.

Douglas, Mary. "Deciphering a Meal." *Daedalus* 101 (Winter 1972): 61-81. An elegant structural analysis of the meaning of the sacred meal with particular reference to Jewish laws regarding purification and diet.

Douglas, Mary. *Implicit Meanings: Essays in Anthropology.* Boston, 1975. A collection of excellent essays, some of which expand on the author's earlier structural analysis of purity norms.

Dumont, Louis. *Homo Hierarchicus.* Translated by Mark Sainsbury. Rev. ed. Chicago, 1980. A classic study of Hinduism, with particular emphasis on structural oppositions, including notions of pollution and purity as manifested in the caste system.

Eliade, Mircea. *Shamanism: Archaic Techniques of Ecstasy.* Rev. & enl. ed. New York, 1964.

Lichter, David, and Lawrence Epstein. "Irony in Tibetan Notions of the Good Life." In *Karma: An Anthropological Inquiry,* edited by Charles F. Keyes and E. Valentine Daniel. Berkeley, 1983.

Malefijt, Annemarie De Waal. *Religion and Culture.* New York, 1968.

Nielsen, Niels C., et al. *Religions of the World.* New York, 1982.

Parker, Robert. *Miasma: Pollution and Purification in Early Greek Religion.* Oxford, 1983. An excellent, thorough analysis of pervasive purity norms in ancient Greek religion.

Preston, James J. *Cult of the Goddess: Social and Religious Change in a Hindu Temple.* New Delhi, 1980.

Steiner, Franz. *Taboo.* New York, 1956.

Trepp, Leo. *Judaism: Development and Life.* Belmont, Calif., 1982.

Turner, Victor. *The Forest of Symbols: Aspects of Ndembu Ritual.* Ithaca, N. Y., 1967.

JAMES J. PRESTON

PURITANISM

The first stirrings of Puritan reform came in the reign of Elizabeth from a group of former Marian exiles, clergy and laity. Initial protests focused on outward signs and ceremonies of the church such as the wearing of vestments, the physical position of church furnishings, and matters of nomenclature. The usage of the establishment, in the view of its critics, symbolized belief in a sacrificial priesthood, a real presence of Christ in the Eucharist, and other elements of Roman Catholic faith and practice.

Clerical opposition to the dictates of the queen and her archbishop of Canterbury, Matthew Parker (1559-1575), caught the public's attention. Puritanism drew the support of laity as distinguished as members of the queen's Privy Council and tapped deep wells of popular support in town and village, so much so that in some cases of the nonuse of vestments it was lay pressure that strengthened the will of a Puritan clergyman rather than pressure from a clergyman stirring up popular discontent.

Puritan hopes for early reform were bolstered when Edmund Grindal (1519-1583) succeeded Parker as archbishop of Canterbury in 1575. A progressive bishop, although not a Puritan, Grindal promoted efforts to upgrade the education of the clergy and to reform ecclesiastical abuses, positions strongly supported by Puritans but advocated by progressive members of the establishment as well. When Grindal refused to carry out the queen's desire to suppress prophesyings (clerical conferences designed to promote the continuing education of the participants), Elizabeth suspended him, and the division within the church widened.

In the last years of Elizabeth's reign and during the rule of James I (1603-1625), a new generation of religious thinkers began to articulate their theologies. One group reflected an accommodation to the views of the Dutch theologian Jacobus Arminius (1559-1609), and stressed the authority of king and bishops, the efficacy of the sacraments in the process of salvation, and the return to a more elaborate use of liturgical ceremony. In contrast to this evolving "new orthodoxy," John Preston (1587-1628), William Perkins (1558-1602), and William Ames (1576-1633) spelled out the essentials of Puritan belief that would characterize the seventeenth-century history of the movement in England and in the New England in America. The lines of demarcation between "orthodox" and Puritan members of the church became more sharply defined, and compromise became less likely.

The starting point for Puritan theology was an emphasis on the majesty, righteousness, and sovereignty of God. In their speculation about the means whereby God reached out to elect certain souls for the gift of salvation, the Puritans developed elements of traditional Calvinism. Puritan theologians, William Perkins in particular, made concepts of the covenant central to their evangelism and moralism. Believing in predestination, they explained that all human beings were pledged by the covenant of works to adhere to the divine law and were justly condemned for failure to adhere to it. The covenant of works depended on human action, while the covenant of grace required a faith that God himself enabled the elect to grasp.

The task of redeeming England seemed more difficult than ever as the reign of James I gave way to that of Charles I (1625-1649). Puritan clergymen were hauled before ecclesiastical courts, deprived of their livings, and harried out of the land.

Having failed to reform England by their written or spoken word, some Puritan leaders conceived the idea of persuading their countrymen by the example of a model Puritan community. This was the goal of many who joined in the Great Migration to New England in the 1630s. Massachusetts and her sister commonwealths of Connecticut (founded in 1636) and New Haven (1637) and the moderate Separatist colony of Plymouth represented an orthodoxy that was designated the New England Way. Their social and political fabric was knit from ideas of Christian organicism owing much to English rural traditions as well as to the corporate strain in Puritan thought. In matters of religion the orthodox developed a congregational church structure with all residents required to attend service but with full membership and its privileges reserved for those who could persuade their peers that they had experienced saving grace.

In England, while political stability was provided by the rise of Oliver Cromwell (1599-1658) as lord protector in 1649, religious diversity did not come to an end. Cromwell did, however, make progress toward the establishment of a Puritan state church uniting moderate Congregationalists. The return of the Stuart monarchy with the Restoration of Charles II (1660-1685) in 1660 saw the casting out of Puritanism from the Church of England. What had been a reform movement within Anglicanism became nonconformity in the shape of Presbyterian, Congregational, and Baptist denominations.

BIBLIOGRAPHY

My book *The Puritan Experiment: New England Society from Bradford to Edwards* (New York, 1976) is an introductory survey to the English origins and American development of Puritan ideas and practice. *The Puritan Tradition in America, 1620-1730*, edited by Alden T. Vaughan (New York, 1972), is the best single-volume anthology of Puritan writings. For those interested in the origins of the movement, the works of Patrick Collinson, especially *The Elizabethan Puritan Movement* (Berkeley, 1967), are indispensable. Barrington R. White's *The English Separatist Tradition: From the Marian Martyrs to the Pilgrim Fathers* (Oxford, 1971) is an excellent analysis of that important offshoot from mainstream Puritanism. The seventeenth-century evolution of Puritanism in England is well surveyed in Michael R. Watts's *The Dissenters: From the Reformation to the French Revolution* (Oxford, 1978). The starting point for an understanding of the faith of New England Puritans remains the classic studies by Perry Miller, especially *The New England Mind: The Seventeenth Century* (New York, 1939). Puritan polity is skillfully examined by Edmund S. Morgan in *Visible Saints: The History of a Puritan Idea* (New York, 1963). Many key facets of Puritan theology are unraveled in E. Brooks Holifield's *The Covenant Sealed: The Development of Puritan Sacramental Theology in Old and New England, 1570-1720* (New Haven, 1974). The devotional aspects of Puritan life are the subject of Charles E. Hambrick-Stowe's *The Practice of Piety* (Chapel Hill, N. C., 1982).

FRANCIS J. BREMER

QUAKERS

The Quakers, or the Religious Society of Friends, arose in seventeenth-century England and America out of a shared experience of the Light and Spirit of God within each person. This source of worship, insight, and power they identify as the Spirit of Christ that also guided the biblical prophets and apostles. Quakers also affirm each person's ability to recognize and respond to truth and to obey the Light perfectly through the leading of an inner witness, or "Seed," called by some Quakers "Christ reborn in us" and by others "that of God in every man," out of which transformed personalities can grow. They therefore ask of each other, and of human society, uncompromising honesty, simplicity of life, nonviolence, and justice.

The early Friends, as Quakers were named (from *Jn.* 15:5) by their first leader George Fox, arose in England during the Puritan Commonwealth under Oliver Cromwell, manifesting an inward intensification of radical and spiritual forms of Puritanism. Quakers held distinctive ideas on the purely inward nature of true baptism and Communion, on the ministry of all laymen and women, on God's power judging and working within hearts and history, and on the need for biblical events to be fulfilled within each person's life-story.

The early Quaker mission throughout England, in 1654-1656, was presented as the "Day of Visitation" by the Lord to each town or region; newly transformed Friends spoke in markets and parish churches despite mobbing and arrests. In New England, Quakers challenging the "biblical commonwealth" were banished on pain of death, and Mary Dyer and three men were hanged in Boston. To persecution for these offenses under the Puritans was added, after the restoration of Charles II, mass arrests—due to the Anglicans' Conventicle Acts of 1664 and 1670. Out of fifty thousand Friends, five hundred died in jail. Quaker courage won over to Quakerism such leaders as William Penn, the mystic Isaac Penington, and the theologian Robert Barclay.

The formal network of Quaker Meetings for Business, held monthly for a town, quarterly for a county, or yearly for a state or nation, was set up to replace reliance on individual leaders. The duties of these Meetings were to register births, marriages, and burials and to aid prisoners, widows, and poor Friends. Fox insisted after 1670 on independent Women's Meetings for Business throughout Quakerism. The monthly Meeting for Sufferings in London and local Meetings recorded imprisonments, oversaw publication of Quaker books, and disowned actions untrue to Quaker norms.

Quaker governments were set up in 1675 and 1682 by Edward Billing and Penn in their new colonies of West New Jersey and Pennsylvania; the charters of these governments mandated toleration and political and legal rights for all men including the Delaware Indians.

Friendship with the American Indians was a Quaker policy: a Quaker committee shared in peace negotiations in 1756-1758 and 1763-1768, and others set up schools and mediation for the New York Senecas and for the Shawnees and other tribes evicted from Ohio and sent to Oklahoma after 1830. In the 1870s, President Grant asked Friends to administer the Indian Agencies of Kansas-Nebraska.

Change and growth characterized Quaker activities during the eighteenth and nineteenth centuries. Eighteenth-century English industry, banking, and science were increasingly led by the interbred Quaker families of Darbys, Barclays, Lloyds, and Gurneys, who (notably Elizabeth Fry) also pioneered in reforming prisons, mental hospitals, and education for Quaker youth and the poor. Philadelphia Friends emulated them.

Quaker organization and worship, not greatly changed since 1690, were now centered in the American Midwest on revivals and hymns and hence on pastors and superintendents, led by John Henry Douglas in Iowa and Oregon. By 1898 half the Meetings, even in Indiana, supported pastors and programmed worship with sermons and hymns and biblical Sunday schools. The Richmond Conference of 1887 gathered all orthodox Friends to look at these new patterns and to restrain David Updegraff's advocacy of water baptism. The Richmond Declaration of Faith reaffirmed evangelical orthodoxy. Concern for unity led in 1902 to a formally gathered Five Years Meeting, which since 1960 has been called Friends United Meeting, and is still centered in Richmond, Indiana. It currently includes seven Orthodox (evangelical) American Yearly Meetings (mostly midwestern); the reunited Baltimore, Canadian, New England, New York, and Southeastern Yearly Meetings; three Yearly Meetings in Kenya; and one each in Cuba, Jamaica, and Palestine arising from missions. Their total 1983 membership was 59,338 in North America and about 100,000 overseas.

In 1985, there remained 18,500 Friends in England and Scotland, 1,750 in Ireland, 2,000 in English communities in Australia, New Zealand, and South Africa, and 20 to 400 each in eight post-1918 Yearly Meetings in nations of continental Europe.

[*See also* Puritanism.]

BIBLIOGRAPHY

The *Journal* of George Fox, edited by Thomas Ellwood (1694; reprint, Richmond, Ind., 1983); John Woolman's *Journal* (1774; reprint, New York, 1971); Robert Barclay's *Apology* (1676; reprint, Newport, R. I., 1729); and William Penn's *No Cross, No Crown* (London, 1669) remain the central classics of the Friends. *The Papers of William Penn* (Philadelphia, 1981-) and photocopies of *The Works of George Fox*, 3 vols. (1831; New York, 1975), and *A Collection of the Works of William Penn*, 2 vols. (1727; New York, 1974), are in print. Other primary sources are in *Early Quaker Writings*, 1650-1700, edited by me and Arthur O. Roberts (Grand Rapids, Mich., 1973).

Joseph Smith's *Descriptive Catalogue of Friends Books*, 2 vols. (London, 1867), remains the most complete bibliography, but see also Donald Wing's *Short-Title Catalogue of Books . . . 1641-1700*, 3 vols. (New York, 1945-1951). Leonard Hodgson's *Christian Faith and Practice* (Oxford, 1950), with topical selections from all periods, and *Church Government*, rev. ed. (London, 1951), together make up the London Yearly Meeting's *Book of Discipline*; those of other Yearly Meetings are less complete.

William C. Braithwaite's *The Beginnings of Quakerism* (1912; 2d ed., Cambridge, 1955) and *The Second Period of Quakerism* (1919; reprint, Cambridge, 1961), together with Rufus M. Jones's studies entitled *The Later Periods of Quakerism*, 2 vols. (1921; reprint, Westport, Conn., 1970), and *The Quakers in the American Colonies* (1911; reprint, New York, 1962) were designed to form the normative "Rowntree Series," based on documentary work by Norman Penney. A. Neave Brayshaw's *The Quakers* (London, 1921) combines history and ideas, as do Howard Brinton's study of Quaker mysticism entitled *Friends for Three Hundred Years* (New York, 1952) and John Punshon's *Portrait in Grey* (London, 1984). Each is an outstanding interpretation. Elbert Russell's *The History of Quakerism* (1945; reprint, Richmond, Ind., 1980), centered on America, with Efrida Vipont Foulds's *The Story of Quakerism* (London, 1954) are good one-volume histories.

Each Yearly Meeting has a printed history, and biographies have been written of most key Quakers. On early Quaker history, see various works by Edwin Bronner and Frederick Tolles; on the eighteenth century, by Sydney James and Arthur Raistrick; and on the nineteenth, by J. Ormerod Greenwood, Elizabeth Isichei, and Philip Benjamin. On Quaker ethical outlooks and doctrines, especially for the early periods, Richard Bauman's *Let Your Words Be Few: Symbolism of Speaking and Silence among Seventeenth Century Quakers* (Cambridge, 1983), Melvin B. Endy, Jr.'s *William Penn and Early Quakerism* (Princeton, 1973), J. William Frost's *The Quaker Family in Colonial America* (New York, 1973), and works by me, Lewis Benson, Maurice Creasey, Christopher Hill, and Geoffrey Nuttall give solid data and a variety of insights. Thomas R. Kelly's *A Testament of Devotion*, 6th ed. (New York, 1941), remains beloved as inspiration.

HUGH BARBOUR

QUR'AN

The Text and Its History

The Qur'an is the scripture of the Muslim community. It comprises the revelations "sent down" to the prophet Muhammad over a period of approximately twenty-two years (from 610 to 632 CE); these ecstatic utterances were collected, ordered, and made into a book sometime after Muhammad's death. Muslims look upon the Qur'an as the very words of God himself, which convey a divine message of saving guidance for those who submit. In consequence the Qur'an has a place of unparalleled importance at the very center of Muslim religious life and practice. Qur'anic teachings are the guide both to personal and social life and to religious responsibility. Indeed, it may be claimed that all Muslim religious thought and activity, and much else besides, are but extended commentaries on the Qur'anic revelation and on the life of the Prophet, who was the agent of its delivery.

The Prophet and the Qur'an

The Qur'an and the Muslim understanding of it are both inextricably interwoven with the experience of the Prophet through whom the holy book was delivered. It was solely the fact of being chosen as a messenger (*rasul*) to humankind (to deliver the Qur'an) that constituted Muhammad's prophethood; he had no other claim to authority and obedience. The experience of receiving the Qur'anic revelations transformed Muhammad from an ordinary citizen of Mecca into a religious visionary who subsequently became not only the leader of his people but one of the most influential individuals in all of history.

The Call to Prophethood. By temperament Muhammad was a reflective person with a strong disposition toward religiosity. Tradition records that prior to his prophetic call he cultivated the habit of retiring into isolation in the hills surrounding Mecca to practice *tahannuth*, or devotional exercises, including perhaps prayer, vigils, fasting, and mild austerities. During one of his night vigils in about his fortieth year, according to tradition, Muhammad experienced the call to prophethood. In the traditional account the call came as the vision of the angel Gabriel, who said, "O, Muhammad, thou art the Messenger of God," and commanded Muhammad, "Recite." At first Muhammad replied, "I cannot recite" (or "What shall I recite?" according to the way one understands the words). Thereupon, Gabriel seized him and squeezed him violently three times until, in one version of the story, Muhammad "thought it was death," and again the angel ordered "Recite in the name of thy Lord." Muhammad then recited the verses the constitute the first part of surah (chapter) 96 of the Qur'an:

Recite in the name of thy Lord who created
Created man from a clot
Recite; thy Lord is most generous,
Who taught by the pen
Taught man what he knew not.

Once the revelations began, they continued to come with more or less frequency throughout Muhammad's lifetime except for a short period early on in his career (known as the *fatrah*, or pause) that caused him much soul-searching and doubt. The fragmentary nature of the revelations, the fact that they came in bits and pieces, rather than all at once, is among their most notable features. The Qur'an is not a straightforwardly organized treatise; rather it moves without transition from one subject to another, often returning after many pages to a subject discussed earlier; it is repetitious, and it leaves many matters of great importance quite incomplete. The fragmentariness may be explained in terms of the Prophet's responses to the circumstances and problems that he and his community faced: as new situations arose, posing new questions or difficulties, the revelation provided guidance and answers.

The Names of the Revelation. Several different terms are employed in the Qur'an as names or designations of the revelations. It is of some importance to consider these terms for the light they throw on the Muslim holy book.

Qur'an. We may begin with the word *qur'an* itself. As used in the text it is clear that the word cannot refer to the structured book that we know today by that name, since the revelations came at intervals, bit by bit, over a period of more

> ### Qur'anic teachings are the guide both to personal and social life and to religious responsibility.

than twenty years and were not complete until they ceased with Muhammad's death. Further, the historical tradition is unanimous in holding that the Qur'an (the book) did not achieve its final form until some time after the Prophet's demise.

The noun *qur'an* is normally said to be derived from the Arabic verb *qara'a*, meaning "to read" or "to recite." Most often it is Muhammad who recites, and what he recites is the *qur'an* (i. e., the recitation). In other cases, however, God recites the revelations to Muhammad as in the instance of verse 75:17.

Scholars generally have accepted the view that *qur'an* is non-Arabic in origin, deriving from a Syriac word that means a scripture lesson or reading, something to be recited in connection with worship. Hence, such statements as "Behold, we

have made it [the Book] an Arabic *qur'an*" (43.3) and "We have sent it down as an Arabic *qur'an*" (12:2) were likely understood by Muhammad and his contemporaries as signifying that he was bringing to the Arabs a body of verbal formulas that might be recited or read in a liturgical context just as other communities, notably the Christians and Jews, possessed scriptures that they used in this way. Indeed, the word is employed in certain passages that clearly indicate a liturgical setting for the recitation.

Muhammad may have caused portions of the revelations to be written down, but it is unlikely that he wrote them for himself: his primary function was to recite what had been made known to him in the revelation experiences. He also urged the recitation of the revelations upon others as an expression of piety, associating the recitation with prayer. Recitation, therefore, was a means of preserving the revelations and a way of conditioning the community to their significance as well as one of the most praiseworthy acts of submission to the divine will. The role played by recitation of the revelations in the community's early life has continued through the centuries as a fundamental element of religious expression.

Kitab. Another word for the revelation that often occurs in conjunction with *qur'an* is *kitab*, which is found more than 250 times in the Muslim scripture. Literally, it means something written, any piece of writing, such as a letter or a document, and there are instances of this use in the text. The word also occurs in connection with the Final Judgment when each person will be given his *kitab*, the book or record of his deeds (17:71 et al.), in his right or left hand or behind his back according to the moral quality of his life. In perhaps the most general sense the term conveys God's knowledge and control of all that will happen; the destinies of human beings and the world are decreed and written down beforehand in a book. "Naught of disaster befalleth in the earth or in yourselves but it is in a Book before we bring it into being." (57:22).

The most frequent use of *kitab* is in conjunction with the idea of scripture, both the scripture given to Muhammad in the revelations and that given to others in previous times, the "peoples of the book." In this sense the *kitab* is identical with the revelation. Further, the scripture given to Muhammad is confirmed in the scriptures of these other religious communities and in its turn confirms them; all, therefore, originate from God. *Kitab* as scripture in one sense also appears to be synonymous with *qur'an* inasmuch as both are revelation, but in certain passages *kitab* is a broader term, *qur'an* being only those parts of the heavenly kitab that have been sent down to Muhammad in Arabic.

Other names. Other words used to indicate the revelations are *tanzil*, *dhikr*, and other forms of the same root, such as *furqan*. *Tanzil* is the verbal noun from the verb *nazzala*, "to send down" or "to cause to send down"; *tanzil* may be rendered, therefore, either as "sending down" or as "something sent down." *Dhikr* means either "mention" or "reminder," and its significance as a name of the revelation is to indicate that the revelation is an admonition and a warning; the point is underlined by references to Muhammad as an admonisher. In the text itself the coming of the *furqan* is associated with the Battle of Badr, and Alford Welch has suggested that the designation became current because it was at about that time that the Muslims first began to differentiate clearly between their community and scripture and those of the Christians and Jews. The *furqan* would thus have been understood as the basis of the distinction between Muslims and these others.

Chronology of the Qur'an

There are many reasons other than a general historical interest why it is important to establish the chronology of the revelations. In making decisions about the abrogating and abrogated verses, for example, the dating of passages and individual verses is essential. Likewise, a reliable chronology would be an invaluable aid for the historian in tracing the development of the prophetic consciousness and the outlook of the early community.

Muslim Dating. First, attention should be called to the existence of a traditional Muslim dating of the chapters of the Qur'an. In printed versions there is customarily a heading for each chapter which, among other information, indicates that the chapter is either Meccan or Medinan. At the same time Muslim scholars recognize that some chapters of the Qur'an are composite, that they may contain material from different periods with Meccan material sometimes being inserted in the midst of a largely Medinan chapter and vice versa. There are also traditional lists of the order in which the chapters are assumed to have been revealed. All of these Muslim datings rest upon traditions reported of Muhammad or traditions that relate to the *asbab al-nuzul*. Although one cannot hope to obtain precise dating of any particular passage or verse from

> At the same time Muslim scholars recognize that some chapters of the Qur'an are composite, that they may contain material from different periods.

this traditional scheme, its divisions of the material into Meccan and Medinan chapters has, with only few exceptions, been borne out by modern scholarship.

Modern Dating. The leaders in modern study of Qur'anic chronology have been Theodor Nöldeke and Richard Bell. In his *Geschichte des Qorans* Nöldeke, argued that the chap-

ters of the Qur'an fall into four discernible periods, three in Mecca and one in Medina. He mounted his argument on the basis of internal evidence from the Qur'an including both style and subject matter. Assuming that Muhammad's prophetic inspiration would have been at its most intense in the beginning of his career, Nöldeke held that the short chapters, which exhibit great force of expression and strong emotion and have a marked rhythm and rhyme, must have been the first to come to the Prophet. In the Medinan situation, where Muhammad had all the responsibilities of rule, the revelations would have been characterized by attention to practical matters and been more expository in nature.

The Scottish scholar Richard Bell believed that the revelations were given in much smaller units, often consisting of only a verse or two or three. A proper dating of the revelations, he reasoned, should concern itself with these smaller units, and he set out to divide the chapters as they presently exist into what he considered to be their component parts. By a complex process of analysis he then attempted to give a date to each of the pericopes into which he had divided the text. In some instances he found portions of what he thought to be a single revelation widely separated and inserted into different chapters. Despite Bell's minute verse-by-verse consideration of the Qur'an, he could not assign precise dates to a majority of verses, and there is uncertainty about numerous others. The entire question of the dating of the revelations remains, therefore, undecided.

BIBLIOGRAPHY

There are numerous English translations of the Qur'an, the most successful being that of A. J. Arberry, *The Koran Interpreted* (New York, 1955), which captures much of the flavor of the original Arabic in addition to representing the best of critical scholarship. *The Meaning of the Glorious Koran: An Explanatory Translation* by M. M. Pickthall (New York, 1930), an English convert to Islam, is based upon the most authoritative Muslim commentaries and may be held to represent the understanding of the Qur'an held by most Sunni Muslims. The rendering by `Abdallah Yusuf `Ali, entitled *The Holy Qur'an, Text, Translation and Commentary*, 3d ed. (New York, 1946), also has merit. The foremost French translation is that of Régis Blachère: *Le Coran: Traduction selon un essai de reclassement des sourates*, 3 vols. (Paris, 1947-1951), the first volume of which is an introduction to the Qur'an. In German the work of the late Rudi Paret, *Der Koran* (Stuttgart, 1963-1966) has earned wide admiration.

The basic work for the critical study of the Qur'an is Theodor Nöldeke's *Geschichte des Qorans*, originally published in 1860, greatly revised and enlarged in a second edition by Friedrich Schwally, two volumes of which appeared in the early decades of this century. A third volume on the history of the text was prepared through the efforts of Gotthelf Bergsträsser and Otto Pretzl (Leipzig, 1909-1938). The entire three volumes of the revised and completed work are most readily available in an edition made in Hildesheim in 1964. The best English statement of the issues and problems of Qur'anic study is *Bell's Introduction to the Qur'an*, revised by W. Montgomery Watt (Edinburgh, 1970). This volume is comprehensive in its treatment but succinct in its expression, and it contains some highly useful appendices. Also to be commended is Alford Welch's "Kur'an" in *The Encyclopaedia of Islam*, new ed. (Leiden, 1960-). Although it is necessarily compressed, it covers the major matters and offers a number of critical judgments of the author's own. Ignácz Goldziher's *Die Richtungen der islamischen Koranauslegung* (1920; reprint, Leiden, 1970) in its earlier sections deals with the history of the Qur'anic text before going on to discuss the variety of commentaries that history has produced. This book is one of the foundation stones of Western Islamology. An approach to Qur'anic study that diverges from the pattern established by Nöldeke and his successors may be seen in the books of John Wansbrough, *Quranic Studies* (Oxford, 1977) and *The Sectarian Milieu* (Oxford, 1978). Wansbrough has applied some of the methods and conceptual apparatus of Biblical studies to the Qur'an and, as indicated above, reached revolutionary conclusions. A Muslim response to Western critical studies of the Holy Book is available in Labib al-Said's *The Recited Koran*, translated by Bernard Weiss, M. A. Rauf, and Morroe Berger (Princeton, 1975).

The most compelling exposition of Qur'anic teachings in English is Fazlur Rahman's book *Major Themes of the Qur'an* (Chicago, 1980); the work also deals with many of the issues raised by critical scholarship. It is especially remarkable for its combination of deep learning and profound reverence for the Qur'anic message. Also outstanding is the work of Toshihiko Izutsu, especially *The Structure of the Ethical Terms in the Koran* (Tokyo, 1959) and *God and Man in the Koran* (Tokyo, 1964). These works pursue a method of semantic analysis that illuminates basic Qur'anic concepts with unique clarity. Also worthy of mention is the sympathetic study of Kenneth Cragg, *The Mind of the Qur'an* (London, 1973); it is accompanied by a basic introduction to the Qur'an called *The Event of the Qur'an* (London, 1971).

The most useful reference tool for the English reader to gain access to the Qur'an is Hanna E. Kassis's *A Concordance to the Qur'an* (Berkeley, 1982). Not only does this volume enable one to find any word of interest in the text, but its unique organization provides a key to the interrelationship of key Qur'anic terms and concepts.

CHARLES J. ADAMS

Its Role in Muslim Piety

For more than fourteen hundred years, Muslims of all schools of thought have interiorized the Qur'an as the transcendent word of God, infinite in meaning and significance for all times and places. The Qur'an has permeated every facet and stage of the life of Muslim society and that of every Muslim believer. It is, however, particularly evident in Shi`i piety, since much of Shi`i theology is based on a hagiography in which the Qur'an as well as the imams figure prominently. With its words, the newborn child is welcomed into the world, as the father utters certain popular verses into its ear. As the sixth Shi`i imam, Ja`far al-Sadiq, declared, "Whoever recites the Qur'an while yet a youth and has faith, the Qur'an becomes intermingled with his flesh and blood" (Ayoub, vol. 1, p. 12).

Language. The Qur'an addresses Muslims in various styles and on various levels of eloquence. Its brief and cryptic verses present in sharp contrasts the portents, fears, and torments of the Day of Judgment and the bliss and pleasures of Paradise. Its longer and more didactic verses address the day-to-day life of the community—its social relations, political loyalties, and legal problems.

Qur'anic language is at times rhapsodic. The opening verses of surah 36 (*Yasin*, the names of two Arabic letters), for instance, move rapidly and with great dramatic force in relating unknown stories of bygone ages and the dramatic encounter of human beings with God on the Day of Judgment; its awe-inducing power is such that it is recited over the dead. In other places the language is smooth and calming, as in surah 55 (*al-Rah-man*, The Merciful), which describes the flowing rivers of Paradise, only imperfectly realized on earth, and which has been recognized to have hypnotic qualities.

Among the most popular and most frequently repeated passages of the Qur'an, recited by Muslim men and women in times of crisis, fear, or uncertainty, are the Fatihah (the opening surah), the throne verse (2:255), and the surah of sincere faith (112). It is a widespread custom, for instance, that when the parents of a young man and woman agree on uniting their children in marriage, the agreement is sealed with the recitation of the Fatihah; business deals and other transactions are blessed in the same way. The Fatihah is the basic Muslim prayer, for the Prophet declared: "There is no prayer except by the opening of the Book." It is composed of seven brief verses which present two distinct but closely related themes: in the first half, thanksgiving, praise, and recognition of God's mercy ("In the name of God, the All-merciful, the Compassionate/Master of the Day of Judgment/You alone do we worship"), and in the second half, a plea for guidance ("and you alone do we beseech for help/Guide us on the straight way/The way of those upon whom you have bestowed your favor, not of those who have incurred your wrath or those who have gone astray").

Power. The powers of the Qur'an have been used in Muslim folklore to heal and to inflict harm, to cause strange natural occurrences, and even to charm snakes and find lost animals. In amulets it serves to protect a child from the evil eye or any other mishap and to strengthen or break the bond of love between two people.

In times of sickness and adversity, believers turn to the Qur'an as a source of "healing and mercy for the people of faith" (17:82); the Fatihah in particular is called *al-shafiyah* (the surah of healing).

Comfort. The Qur'an also serves as a source of strength and reassurance in the face of the unknown. For the pious, the Qur'an provides the means of controlling future events or mitigating their outcome through *istikharah*, seeking a good omen in the text. *Istikharah* represents the choice of what God has chosen; it is carried out by averting the face, opening the book, and letting it speak directly to one's need or condition. The action is usually accompanied by elaborate prayers and rituals.

The Qur'an is a source of blessing and comfort to the dead as well as the living. Often before a pious person dies, he or she stipulates that the Qur'an be recited at the grave for three days to ensure the rest of his or her soul. Whenever a deceased person is remembered by friends or family, the Fatihah is recited; it is considered a gift to the dead, a fragrant breeze from Paradise to lighten the great hardship of the grave. It is, however, the portions of the Qur'an learned in this world which will bring believers great merit in the hereafter. As a consolation for the followers (shi'ah) of the family of the Prophet, Imam Ja'far al-Sadiq promised that "Any one of our Shi'ah, or those who accept our authority (wilayah), who dies without having attained a good knowledge of the Qur'an shall be taught it in his grave, in order that God may raise his station in paradise, because the number of stations in paradise is equal to the number of the verses of the Qur'an" (Majlisi, vol. 39, p. 188).

Recitation. Because the Qur'an is an object of great reverence, we are told, no one should touch it unless he is pure (56:79), nor should anyone recite it unless he is in a state of ritual purity. Before beginning to recite, he must clean his teeth and purify his mouth, for he will become the "path" of the Qur'an. The Qur'an reciter must put on his best attire, as he would when standing before a king, for he is in fact speaking with God.

Likewise, because the Qur'an is the essence of Islamic prayer, the reciter should face the qiblah, or direction of prayer toward Mecca. Anyone who begins to yawn in the course of reciting is obliged to stop, because yawning is caused by Satan.

The Qur'an is not a book with a beginning, middle, and end. Every portion, or even every verse, is a Qur'an, as the entire book is the Qur'an, properly speaking. Thus reciting the complete text over a period of days, weeks, or months may be considered a journey through an infinite world of meaning, a journey in and with the Qur'an. The primary purpose of this sacred journey is to form one's character and life according to the word of God, to achieve true righteousness (taqwa). The task of reciting the Qur'an is in itself a source of blessing.

According to prophetic tradition, the best of men is he who studies the Qur'an and teaches it to others. In a tradition related on the authority of Abu Hurayrah, the Prophet is said to have declared: "There are no people assembled in one of the houses of God to recite the book of God and study it together but that the sakinah (divine tranquillity) descends upon them. Mercy covers them, angels draw near to them, and God remembers them in the company of those who are with him" (Ayoub, vol. 1, pp. 8-9). Indeed, the highest merit for which a person can hope in the world to come is that of engaging with others in the study of the Qur'an.

Literary legacy. In its written form, the Qur'an has set the standard for Arabic language and literature as the proper and indeed the highest expression of literary Arabic. Its style of storytelling, its similes and metaphors have shaped classical Arabic literature and have even had their influence on the modern writers. Even daily conversation, whether on weighty or mundane matters, is interspersed with Qur'anic words and phrases, and Qur'anic verses are beautifully calligraphed to decorate mosques, schools, and the homes of the pious.

BIBLIOGRAPHY

The role of the Qur'an in Muslim piety, although crucial, has been largely neglected in Western scholarship. Muslim scholars also have neglected this aspect, concentrating instead on a rationalist and moral and political approach. The researcher is therefore left with the classical Muslim tradition for primary source materials.

The basic sources dealing with the place of the Qur'an in Muslim piety fall into the genre of fada'il al-Qur'an ("excellences of the Qur'an"). Such discussions are often prefixed or appended to many of the standard tafsir works; see for example the work by Ibn Kathir (d. 1373) entitled Fada'il al-Qur'an and appended to volume 7 of his Qur'an commentary, Tafsir al-Qur'an al-'azim, 7 vols. (Beirut, 1966). They also form a part of most major hadith collections; see for example the chapter on fada'il al-Qur'an in Sahih Bukhari, translated by Muhammad Muhsin Khan, Translation of the Meanings of Sahih al-Bukhari, 9 vols. (Beirut, 1979), in volume 6.

The sources used in this article are representative of the general literature on the subject. Abu 'Abd Allah Muhammad al-Qurtubi (d. 1273) was a noted commentator and jurist. The introduction to his work Al-jami' li-ahkam al-Qur'an (Cairo, 1966), is an excellent example of works treating the Qur'an in all its aspects, including its excellences. Abu 'Ali al-Fadl ibn al-Hasan al-Tabarsi (d. 1153), an important Twelver Shi'i jurist, theologian, and commentator, is the author of the Majma' al-bayan fi tafsir al-Qur'an (Cairo, 1958), a reference work treating all points of view in Islamic exegesis with unusual objectivity. The introduction to this work also includes a discussion of the excellences of the Qur'an. Mulla Muhammad Baqir al-Majlisi (d. 1699) was one of the most prolific Shi'i authors of Safavid Iran. His encyclopedic work Bihar al-anwar, 110 vols. (Beirut, 1983), deals with the biographies of the Shi'i imams, hadith, hagiography, and popular lore. Volume 89 is devoted to the Qur'an, including its excellences.

The only work in English thus far dealing with the place of the Qur'an in popular piety is the introduction to my study The Qur'an and Its Interpreters (Albany, N. Y., 1984).

MAHMOUD M. AYOUB

RABBINATE

The term *rabbinate* derives from the Hebrew title *rabbi* ("my master, my teacher"), which came into use in the first century of the common era.

Late Antiquity. Tradition holds that from the time of Moses there has been an unbroken succession of "laying on of hands" that conferred rabbinical status. Even Moses is referred to frequently as "our rabbi." But we have no instance of anyone being designated rabbi in a specific ceremony of ordination in ancient times, nor is the rabbinate decisively connected with the two Hebrew roots that designated the putative ceremony of ordination, *smkh* and *mnh.*

In the New Testament, the term *rabbi* is not often encountered in the synoptic Gospels. The term is, however, used particularly in the *Gospel of John,* but only in the equivalent of any teacher of disciples.

Rabbis during the Talmudic period were, above all, teachers and interpreters of the Torah. The rabbis of these centuries created the Jewish calendar out of biblical materials and ensured that the Jewish calendar would be a kind of temporal catechism. These same rabbis fixed the biblical canon and the synagogue liturgy. As against Jewish Christians, agnostics, and a mixed bag of dissidents whom the rabbis termed *minim,* the Jewish community became unified and distinguished through rabbinic definitions and "fences."

The Middle Ages and Early Modern Period. By profession the Talmudic rabbi was a woodsman, a farmer, a shoemaker, a shepherd, or the like. He worked for a living and served as a rabbi only in his spare time. Not until the Middle Ages was the rabbinate decisively professionalized.

The increasingly professional rabbi confronted the organized Jewish community leadership as colleague, employee, and/or competitor. The rabbi was, after all, in a sense a layman, since he possessed no sacramental or charismatic advantage, yet his role increasingly led to a collision course with the lay establishment in his town. Wealthy lay leadership often chose the judiciary, dominated weak rabbis, and threatened strong ones. The rabbis were not without their own discrete powers. They supervised the ritual life of the community and had prerogatives as authors and educators. They had the final weapon of excommunication, a sword better and

more often sheathed than recklessly employed. But they were often torn between various lay factions, and they had to face the practical issues of tenure and dismissal.

The Jewish community slowly and steadily achieved increasing autonomy from the Middle Ages until the eighteenth century, but this strengthened the power of laymen, who had their own agenda and their own ambitions, often at the expense of the rabbinate. The rabbi was generally honored and respected during the Middle Ages. He was called *morenu,* "our teacher," when invited to the Torah reading, and he had a seat of honor in the synagogue. Prominent rabbis often constituted a court of appeal for decisions made by lower, lay-controlled judiciaries, and rabbis gave permission for Jews to utilize otherwise forbidden secular courts. They also delivered a kind of *nihil obstat* to authorize publication of books.

Rabbinical duties in the Middle Ages were both the same as and different in nuance from those of the Talmudic period. The rabbi taught, judged, and officiated at marriages and funerals. He circumcised newborn boys and preached at least twice a year and, in some communities, more regularly. He sometimes administered burial societies and poor funds. One of the rabbi's chief responsibilities was private study.

The Modern Period. In modern times, pressures to establish a professional rabbinate continued to grow. The community nominated, and the government named, chief rabbis in Britain and France, as well as in British-mandated Palestine.

Since the beginning of the nineteenth century, Jewish religion has lost even the semblance of uniformity that it once had. Reform, or Liberal, Judaism appeared as an early reaction to modern thinking and citizenship in western European countries, followed quickly by what came to be called Conservatism and Neo-Orthodoxy. In each of these denominations, the rabbi took on, more and more, the characteristics of a Protestant minister. Salaries of rabbis tended to rise; the status of the rabbi often paralleled that of his Christian clerical counterpart, who was also, in a new sense, his colleague. The older functions of the rabbi—teaching, learning, judging, and the like—remained crucial in Orthodoxy.

New kinds of learning did not prevent the modern rabbi from suffering a crisis of authority. The modern rabbi could not claim to be a sole, or even a principal, authority in his milieu. In some countries, the community hired rabbis to serve a whole town or a designated part of it. But in America, for instance, rabbis are almost always hired by individual congregations, thus finding themselves in the anomalous position of being the employees of the very people they are expected to lead.

At the present time there are new as well as many old issues of rabbinical function. The Reform, Reconstructionist, and Conservative movements have begun to ordain women, to the dismay of Orthodoxy. Traditionally, a woman cannot serve as a witness or judge, but there is no halakhic reason why she cannot preach or teach or administer a congregation.

The modern rabbi is the true inheritor of a millennial tradition but is also very much a product of the modern world.

[For further discussion of the role of the rabbi in various movements within Judaism, see Reform Judaism *and* Hasidism.]*

BIBLIOGRAPHY

Alon, Gedaliah. *The Jews in Their Land in the Talmudic Age, 70-640 C. E.* Translated and edited by Gerson Levi. Jerusalem, 1980. The standard history of the early centuries of the common era, by a learned Talmudic historian.

Assaf, Simha. "Liqorot ha-rabbanut." In *Be-ohelei Ya'aqov,* pp. 26-65. Jerusalem, n. d. A classic study of the rabbinate in eastern Europe during the late Middle Ages.

Baron, Salo W. *The Jewish Community,* vol. 2, *Its History and Structure to the American Revolution.* Philadelphia, 1942. Still unsurpassed as a synopsis of leadership in the Jewish community before modern times. See especially pages 52-245.

Baron, Salo W. *A Social and Religious History of the Jews.* 18 vols. 2d ed., rev. & enl. New York, 1952-1983. See the index for a list of references to rabbis and the rabbinate in this encyclopedic history.

Ben-Sasson, H. H. *Hagut ve-hanhagah.* Jerusalem, 1959. A great Israeli historian on the role of Jewish religious leadership in Poland during the late Middle Ages. See especially pages 160-228.

Cohon, Samuel S. "Authority in Judaism." *Hebrew Union College Annual* 11 (1936): 593-646. See especially pages 612ff. A reliable, conservative summary of Talmudic and post-Talmudic rabbinic procedure.

Kohler, Kaufmann, et al. "Rabbi." In *The Jewish Encyclopedia.* New York, 1905. A brief, but not yet outdated, summary history of the rabbinate. More up-to-date encyclopedias are more complete but hardly as eloquent.

Stevens, Elliot L., ed. *Rabbinic Authority.* New York, 1982. A series of papers presented to the Central Conference of American Rabbis in 1980. Note especially the essays by Hoffman, Cook, and Saperstein.

Wolf, Arnold Jacob, ed. "The Future of Rabbinic Training in America." *Judaism* 18 (Fall 1969): 387-420. A controversial debate on the mission and training of the American rabbi by professors, practitioners, and even a student or two.

ARNOLD JACOB WOLF

REDEMPTION

Like the concepts of salvation, sacrifice, and justification, the concept of redemption belongs to a cluster of religious notions that converge upon the meanings of making good, new, or free, or delivering from sickness, famine, death, mortality, life itself, rebirth, war, one's own self, sin and guilt, anguish, even boredom and nausea. In a certain sense, redemption makes possible a recovery of paradise lost, of a primordial blissful state. To be redeemed may mean to be divinized, either by the reenactment of the primordial creative act (preceded by a descent) or through the theandric, sacrificial action of a savior *(soter)*.

Liberation from exile *(Dt.* 15:15), restoration of freedom *(Is.* 62:12, 63:4), and the vision of a just society have always been signs of divine redemption for the people of Israel. Messianic Judaism projected the new heaven and the new earth, the final restoration and reintegration in peace and harmony of the people of Israel.

This mystery of redemption is best illustrated in Christianity: Christ suffered on the cross in order to satisfy retributive justice. The meaning of redemption in the New Testament is chiefly that of the deliverance of man from sin, death, and God's anger, through the death and resurrection of Christ.

The Egyptian Pyramid Texts of 2400 BCE looked upon salvation as both a mystery and a technique. Osiris, slain by his brother Seth, is rescued by Isis and brought back to life by means of a secret and complicated ritual; he becomes the one savior from death and from its consequences.

In Zoroastrianism, the redemption of mankind, viewed as both individual and universal eschatology, is linked with the hope of seeing that Ohrmazd, having been released from his entanglement with darkness and evil, emerges victorious from the war over Ahriman. The *haoma* ritual, a central act of worship, actualizes such a god-centered redemption. The theological trend in Sasanid Zoroastrianism exhibits a belief in the redemption of the world through the individual's efforts to make the gods dwell in his body while chasing the demons out of it.

Buddhism is a religion fully bent on salvation. In Mahayana Buddhism the doctrine of the Buddha and the *bodhisattva* shows the great vows required by the spiritual discipline of enlightenment to be a devotion to the principle that the merit and knowledge acquired by the individual on this path be wholly transferred upon all beings, high and low, and not jealously accumulated for one's self. This "activity without attachment" involves a free restraint from entering upon *nirvana,* exercised for the sake of one's fellow beings. In Japanese Buddhism the principle of salvation by self-power *(jiriki)* is contrasted by salvation through "another" *(tariki),* that is, through the power of the Buddha Amida. In Zen, devotion, fervor, and depth are all equally redeeming inner attitudes.

Ancient Mexican religions knew a variety of redemptive types. The Aztec religion favors redemption from existence itself during one's very lifetime, the highest aim being identification with divinity.

In African traditional religions, redemption is far more directed toward the reintegration of the cosmic, social, and political order in the present moment of the community than toward the afterlife.

BIBLIOGRAPHY

Brandon, S. G. F., ed. *The Savior God.* Manchester, 1963.
Florovskii, Georgii Vasilevitch. *Creation and Redemption.* Belmont, Mass., 1976.
Knudson, Albert C. *The Doctrine of Redemption.* New York, 1933.
O'Flaherty, Wendy Doniger. *The Origins of Evil in Hindu Mythology.* Berkeley, 1976.
Przyluski, Jean. "Erlösung im Buddhismus." *Eranos-Jahrbuch* (Zurich) (1937): 93-136.
Schär, Hans. *Erlösungsvorstellungen und ihre psychologischen Aspekte.* Zurich, 1950.
Toutain, Jules. "L'idée religieuse de la rédemption." In *Annuaires de l'École des Hautes Études* (Sciences Religieuses), Section 5. Paris, 1916-1917.
Trinité, Philippe de la. *What Is Redemption.* New York, 1961.
Werblowsky, R. J. Zwi. *Types of Redemption.* Leiden, 1970.

ILEANA MARCOULESCO

REFORMATION

Background

The traditional view, from the Protestant perspective, has been that in the early sixteenth century, church and society were in a state of crisis. The church was seen as suffering from various moral and theological abuses and the Reformation was a necessary reaction against that state of affairs.

The Catholic church stood in the center of society. It had extensive land holdings. It controlled education. It possessed its own legal system. It provided the ethical principles on which society was based and which were meant to guide it. Above all, the church, as the guardian of eternal truth, mediated salvation. There is no doubt that, on the eve of the Reformation, the church possessed a great vitality, especially in Germany, and that it commanded considerable loyalty and devotion.

Along with these manifestations of vitality, there were also problems. The hierarchy seemed distant and too cumbersome to deal with the spiritual needs of the people. The higher clergy, notably the bishops, were mainly recruited

from the nobility and viewed their office as a source of prestige and power. This was particularly true in Germany, where many bishops were political rulers as well as spiritual rulers.

In this setting many voices pleaded for church reform. Despite criticism and anticlericalism, the call was for change and reform, not for disruption and revolution.

Controversy over Indulgences

The Reformation originated in a controversy over indulgences precipitated by Martin Luther's Ninety-five Theses of 31 October 1517. Indulgences, originally remissions of certain ecclesiastical penalties, had by the early sixteenth century come to be understood as offering forgiveness of sins in exchange for certain payments. Luther's misgivings about a singularly vulgar sale of indulgences by the Dominican monk Johann Tetzel found expression in a probing of the theology of indulgences. In a letter to Archbishop Albert of Hohenzollern, Luther pleaded for the discontinuance of the sale. What was meant as an academic and pastoral matter quickly became a public one, however, primarily because Luther sent out several copies of the theses, and the positive response of the recipients helped to propagate them. [*See also the biography of Luther.*]

By early 1518 Luther had been cited as a suspected heretic. The Edict of Worms declared Luther a political outlaw. He was excommunicated that year.

Beginning of the Reformation

At Luther's formal condemnation in 1521 the nature of events changed. With Luther removed from the scene (many thought him dead), the message of reform was spread by an increasing number of comrades-in-arms and supporters. By that time consequences of the new message and its call for reform were beginning to emerge.

The message is evident in the multitude of pamphlets published between 1517 and 1525. Their themes were simple: of a religion of substance rather than form, of inner integrity rather than outward conformity, of freedom rather than rules. The impact of the reformers was so strong because they deliberately took their arguments to the people whom they knew to be interested in the issues discussed. The issues propounded were not merely religious ones; they encompassed a wide variety of social and political concerns that made for an intertwining of religious and nonreligious motifs.

By the end of the 1520s the reform movement had firmly established itself, especially in southern and central Germany. Two themes were dominant in the years between the Diet of Speyer (1526) and the Peace of Augsburg (1555): the expansion of the Reformation and the pursuit of reconciliation (or coexistence) between the two sides. The theme of Protestant expansion found striking expression in the spread throughout Europe and, in Germany, of the acceptance of the Reformation by a majority of the imperial cities.

The 1530s brought continued Protestant expansion in Germany. At the end of the decade new attempts were made to explore the possibility of theological agreement. At the Colloquy of Worms (1539), agreement was reached concerning justification, which had been the main point of controversy between the two sides. In the end, however, disagreement prevailed, and the attempt to resolve the controversy by theological conciliation failed.

Catholic Charles V was now determined to use force. Upon concluding peace with France in 1544, he was ready to face the Protestants. War broke out in 1546 and despite a

> ## The specific issue that was to divide the Reformation was the interpretation of the Lord's Supper.

good deal of blundering, Charles emerged successful, winning the decisive Battle of Muhlberg in 1547. The victorious emperor convened a diet at Augsburg in 1548 to impose his religious settlement on the Protestants. The result was the Augsburg Interim, which afforded the Protestants two temporary concessions—use of the communion cup and the married clergy—but left little doubt about the emperor's determination to restore Catholicism fully in the end. At the same time, Charles V sought also, through an ambitious constitutional reform project, to enhance imperial power in Germany.

Charles faced increasingly formidable opposition from the territorial rulers, Protestant and Catholic alike, and he had to acknowledge that Protestantism was firmly entrenched in Germany.

Differentiation of Reformation Views

As the Reformation movement spread, it became evident that the reformers' common opposition to the Catholic church did not entail a common theological position. The first incidence of differentiation came in 1522, when Andreas Karlstadt, a colleague of Luther's at the University of Wittenberg, publicly disagreed with Luther. Two years later Thomas Müntzer, minister at Allstedt, not far from Wittenberg, published two pamphlets in which he dramatically indicted Luther's notion of reform. In the spring of 1525, Müntzer joined the rebellious peasants in central Germany and became their spiritual leader. The pamphlets that issued from his pen were vitriolic and categorical: the true church would be realized only through suffering and by a resolute opposition to the godless rulers.

The major division within the ranks of the reformers is associated with the Swiss reformer Huldrych (Ulrich) Zwingli,

of Zurich. The specific issue that was to divide the Reformation was the interpretation of the Lord's Supper. Luther, while rejecting the Catholic doctrine of transubstantiation, affirmed the real presence of Christ in the elements of bread and wine, while Zwingli affirmed a spiritual presence. The controversy between the two men erupted in 1525 and continued, with increasing vehemence, for years to come. By 1529 political overtones to the theological disagreement had surfaced. Since military action against the Protestants was a possibility, the internal disagreement weakened the Protestant position. It became clear that the future of the Reformation lay in political strength.

A second major division within the ranks of the Reformation pertained to a heterogeneous group whom contemporaries called "Anabaptists." This term, derived from a Greek word meaning "rebaptizer," indicated the Anabaptists' most prominent assertion: that baptism should be performed in adulthood as the outgrowth of an individual's decision. Anabaptism originated formally in Zurich among young humanist associates of Zwingli who, influenced by Müntzer and Karlstadt, were disenchanted with the slow progress of reform. Their attempt to impose their own vision of speedier and more comprehensive reform on the course of events proved unsuccessful. They broke with Zwingli, administered believer's baptism early in 1525, and found themselves promptly persecuted, since the authorities were unwilling to tolerate diverse forms of religion in their midst. [See Anabaptism.]

Although some of the intellectual roots of Antitrinitarianism can be traced to the late Middle Ages, the catalytic influence of the Reformation was paramount in the movement. The atmosphere of challenge of established opinion and the stress on the Bible as sole authority seemed to call for the repudiation of the doctrine of the Trinity. A most dramatic event, in the early 1530s, was the publication of two staunchly antitrinitarian tracts by a Spanish lay theologian and physician, Michael Servetus.

An urbane French lawyer and humanist by background, John Calvin was the embodiment of both the differentiation of Reformation views and of its European dimension. Calvin had left his native country for Switzerland to arrange for the publication of his brief summary statement of Reformation theology, *Institutes of the Christian Religion*. Passing by chance through Geneva in 1536, the twenty-seven-year-old scholar was pressured into staying to take part in the reform there. His first attempt to implement reform led to conflict with the city authorities and to his expulsion in 1538. Three years later, however, he was invited to return and he remained there until his death in 1564. [See the biography of Calvin.]

Institutes of the Christian Religion echoed in many variations, is the majesty of God, from which man's eternal destiny—predestination to salvation or to damnation—is reasoned. While Calvin always wished to emphasize God's majesty as the overarching theme of biblical religion, the concept of predestination emerged as the characteristic feature of Calvin's thought. Calvin's determination to implement his vision of God's law brought him into conflict with influential Genevans.

European Dimension of the Reformation

At the time the Reformation movement broke out in Germany, reform notions were already strong in France. While Francis I was himself a humanist by disposition, political prudence led him to take a Catholic and papal course. He responded with persecution and a stern censorship of books. His successor, Henry II, continued this policy.

Henry's unexpected death in 1559 precipitated a constitutional crisis over the exercise of regency during the minority of the new king, Francis II. Cardinal Guise summarily assumed the regency, but his move was opposed by the prestigious Bourbon family, which argued for a council of regency. The constitutional issue had religious overtones, since the Guises were staunch Catholics, while the Bourbons had Protestant leanings.

The Wars of Religion, which began in 1562, sought to resolve the issue of political power. The Edict of Nantes (1598) ended the struggle. Protestants failed in their effort to win acceptance of their religion by France, but they were given freedom of worship.

The Reformation in England. In the 1520s England underwent a period of lively agitation against the Roman Catholic church. This atmosphere of religious agitation was complicated by Henry's sudden desire for an annulment of his marriage to Catherine of Aragon (his deceased brother's widow) on the grounds that the marriage violated canon law. Extensive efforts to obtain a favorable papal decision proved unsuccessful. In 1533 Parliament passed the Act in Restraint of Appeals to Rome, which declared England an "empire" whose sovereign could adjudge all spiritual and temporal matters in his realm. This act kept the judicial resolution over Henry's "divorce" in England. The king had broken with the papal church. [*See also* Anglicanism.]

Concomitant ecclesiastical changes in England were initially few, however, and pertained mainly to jurisdictional and organizational matters. Despite his own Catholic temperament, Henry actively encouraged anti-Catholic propaganda throughout the 1530s.

When Henry died in 1547 religious affairs were thus in a precarious balance, neither strongly Protestant nor strongly Catholic. The official religion of the land veered in the direction of Protestantism. Under the aegis of Archbishop Cranmer, a new order for worship (*The Book of Common Prayer*) was promulgated in 1549. Drawing on the rich liturgical heritage of the medieval church, this order for worship, with the beauty of its language and its structure of the divine office, proved to be an immensely enriching contribution to English Christendom. The theological tone of the prayer book was conservative in that it espoused a Lutheran view of Communion. A revision of the book, three years later, embraced a Zwinglian view.

Puritanism. Critics argued that too many vestiges of Catholicism remained in the English church. They wanted a "pure" church, and before long they came to be called "Puritans." The Puritans were to be a major element in English history until the second half of the seventeenth century. Puritanism underwent significant changes in the course of its lengthy history. Toward the end of the sixteenth century it became increasingly diverse and sectarian, some strands determined to break with the established church. It also became increasingly political. [*See* Puritanism.] In England, their separatist sentiment came to fruition during that time with the emergence of different groupings, of which several—Congregationalists, Baptists, and Quakers—were to become ecclesiastical traditions in Anglo-Saxon Christendom.

The Catholic Reaction

The initial reaction of the Catholic church to Luther was astoundingly swift and categorical. By 1520 the position of the church had been delineated: Luther's understanding of the Christian faith was declared heretical and his notion of reform rejected. It was to be of profound import for subsequent events that despite this condemnation, the Catholic church possessed neither a comprehensive policy for reform nor a clear perception of how to execute the judgment against Luther or halt the increasing defections. Moreover, the papacy had its own priorities, which were slow to focus on the Lutheran affair and the Protestant Reformation.

When a council eventually convened at Trent in 1545, it was clear that it could have no other function than to sharpen the true Catholic position on a wide variety of issues. Thus the council, which met intermittently until 1563, possessed significance only for the Catholic church. Its canons and decrees were consciously anti-Protestant and offered conciliatory views only with respect to issues contested within Catholicism. [*See* Trent, Council of; *and* Monasticism.]

BIBLIOGRAPHY

General Surveys. The best general introductions to the history of the Reformation are G. R. Elton's *Reformation Europe, 1517-1559* (New York, 1963); *The Reformation, 1520-1559,* edited by G. R. Elton, "The New Cambridge Modern History," vol. 2 (Cambridge, 1958); Lewis W. Spitz's *The Renaissance and Reformation Movements,* 2d ed., 2 vols. (Saint Louis, 1980); and my *The World of the Reformation* (New York, 1973). The Literature Survey of the *Archiv für Reformationsgeschichte* (Leipzig and Berlin, 1903-) provides an annual annotated survey of all literature pertaining to the Reformation. Useful also is *Bibliography of the Continental Reformation: Materials Available in English,* 2d ed., rev. & enl., edited by Roland H. Bainton and Eric W. Gritsch (Hamden, Conn., 1972).

A survey of current research emphases is *Reformation Europe: A Guide to Research,* edited by Steven E. Ozment (Saint Louis, 1982).

Specialized Studies

Blickle, Peter. *The Revolution of 1525.* Baltimore, 1982.

Brady, Thomas A. *Ruling Class, Regime and Reformation at Strasbourg, 1520-1555.* Leiden, 1978.

Clasen, Claus-Peter. *Anabaptism: A Social History, 1525-1618.* Ithaca, N. Y., 1972.

Edwards, Mark U., Jr. *Luther's Last Battles.* Ithaca, N. Y., 1983.

Elton, G. R. *Policy and Police.* Cambridge, 1972.

Goertz, Hans, ed. *Profiles of Radical Reformers.* Scottdale, Pa., 1982.

Hendrix, Scott H. *Luther and the Papacy.* Philadelphia, 1981.

Lienhard, Marc, ed. *The Origins and Characteristics of Anabaptism.* The Hague, 1977.

Lortz, Joseph. *The Reformation in Germany.* New York, 1968.

Moeller, Bernd. "Piety in Germany around 1500." In *The Reformation in Medieval Perspective,* edited by Steven E. Ozment, pp. 50-75. Chicago, 1971.

Moeller, Bernd. *Imperial Cities and the Reformation.* Philadelphia, 1972.

Ozment, Steven E. *The Reformation in the Cities.* New Haven, 1975.

Stayer, James M. *Anabaptism and the Sword.* Lawrence, Kans., 1972.

Walton, Robert C. *Zwingli's Theocracy.* Toronto, 1967.

Williams, George H. *The Radical Reformation.* Philadelphia, 1962.

HANS J. HILLERBRAND

REFORM JUDAISM

REFORM JUDAISM is the branch of the Jewish faith that has been most adaptive, in belief and practice, to the norms of modern thought and society. It is also sometimes called Liberal Judaism or Progressive Judaism. By *Reform* is meant not a single reformation but an ongoing process of development.

Beliefs and Practices. Unlike more traditional forms of the Jewish faith, Reform Judaism does not hold that either the written law (Torah) or the oral law (Talmud) was revealed literally by God to Moses at Sinai. It accepts biblical and other historical criticism as legitimate, understanding scripture and tradition as a human reflection of revelation rather than its literal embodiment. While theologies among Reform Jews vary greatly, from the traditional to the humanistic, concepts of God strike a balance between universal and particular elements, with somewhat more stress upon the former than among other religious Jews. Like other branches of Judaism, Reform recognizes the close connection between religion and ethics.

The doctrine that most significantly sets Reform Judaism apart from more traditional currents is the conception of progressive revelation. Reform Jews hold that revelation is ongoing with the progress of human knowledge and religious sen-

sitivity. The freedom of the individual Jew to be selective, to draw from Jewish tradition those elements of belief and practice that he or she finds the most personally meaningful, is far greater among Reform Jews than among either Orthodox or Conservative.

At most Reform congregations in America the main religious service of the week is held after dinner on Friday evenings; men and women sit together, participating equally in the service. Only in recent years have many rabbis, some male congregants, and a much smaller number of women begun to wear the ritual head covering (*kippah* or *yarmulke*) during worship.

Outside the synagogue Reform Jews practice their faith by attempting to guide their lives according to the moral precepts of Judaism. A large percentage practices some Jewish rituals in the home, especially the lighting of the Sabbath candles on Friday evening, the Passover eve ceremony, or Seder, and the celebration of Hanukkah. Once especially aware of their religious differences from traditional Jews, today Reform Jews emphasize to a greater extent their common ethnic identity and the faith shared by all religious Jews, limiting the significance of denominational differences.

The Movement in Europe. Reform Jews have often pointed out that religious reform was inherent in Judaism from its beginnings. They have noted that the prophets were critics of contemporary religious practices, that the Talmud includes reforms of earlier biblical legislation, and that even later legal scholars were willing to alter received beliefs and practices. Such willingness to adjust to historical change waned only under the pressure of persecution and the isolation of the ghetto. Latter-day Jews seeking religious reform thus sought, and to a degree found, precedent for their programs in earlier layers of Jewish tradition. However, they soon became aware that most of their fellow Jews, and especially the established rabbinical leadership, did not share

> **Reform Jews hold that revelation is ongoing with the progress of human knowledge and religious sensitivity.**

such views. The result was a movement for reform, originally intended to harmonize all aspects of Jewish life with the modern world into which European Jews increasingly entered beginning with the later eighteenth century. Only gradually did the movement come to focus specifically on the religious realm, and only after a generation did it separate itself as a differentiable religious current with a more or less fixed religious philosophy. In discussing origins, it is therefore more accurate to speak of the "Reform movement in Judaism" than of Reform Judaism. Even this terminology, however, requires the qualification that self-conscious awareness of being a movement with definite goals came only gradually with the coalescence of various elements of belief and practice.

Americanization. Reform Judaism has enjoyed its greatest success in the United States. In Europe it was repeatedly forced to assert itself against an entrenched Orthodoxy, sometimes supported by the government; in the New World it faced no such established institutions. The United States lacked officially recognized Jewish communities, like the German *Gemeinde* with its powers of taxation and centralized control over Jewish affairs. The complete separation of church and state, the numerous Christian denominations existing side by side, and the prevalent notion that religious activity was strictly a matter of free choice created an atmosphere most conducive to Jewish religious fragmentation. Moreover, it was difficult for an immigrant Jew in nineteenth-century America to make a living while still observing all the inherited traditions. Given also the large influx of Jews from Germany in the second third of the nineteenth century—among them some who had had experience with religious reform, as well as a number of Reform rabbis—it is understandable that until the massive Jewish immigration from eastern Europe in the last decades of the century, Reform Judaism should play the dominant role in American Jewry. In the freer atmosphere of America, Reform soon took on a considerably more radical character than its counterpart in Europe.

Developments since World War II. In the immediate postwar years Reform Judaism in the United States enjoyed remarkable growth. The Christian religious revival of the 1950s produced renewed interest in Jewish theology. The well-known biblical archaeologist Nelson Glueck, as president of the Hebrew Union College from 1947 to his death in 1971, was able to achieve a merger with the Jewish Institute of Religion and to bring about considerable expansion of the combined institution.

Reform Judaism now engaged itself vigorously with the moral issues troubling American society. Rabbis and laity participated actively in the civil rights movement and later in the organized opposition to the Vietnam War. In 1961 the UAHC established the Religious Action Center in Washington, D. C., with the intent of making a direct impact on legislation of Jewish and general religious or moral concern, as well as educating the Reform constituency as to questions under current legislative consideration. In the spirit of ecumenism, the UAHC developed a department dealing with interfaith activities.

Reform theology in this recent period grew increasingly diverse. A group of Reform rabbis, who became known as "covenant theologians," favored a more personalist and existential grounding of their faith. Influenced by the twentieth-century European Jewish thinkers Franz Rosenzweig and Martin Buber, they eschewed the earlier idealist theology based on progressive revelation in favor of the notion of divine-human encounter as represented both by the testimony of the Torah and by contemporary religious experience. At the same time, however, there arose a significant rationalist and even humanist faction within the movement. Its members stressed the impact of biblical criticism and psychoanalysis upon religion, as well as the difficult theological questions that the Holocaust had raised for Jewish theism.

> **Rabbis and laity participated actively in the civil rights movement and later in the organized opposition to the Vietnam War.**

Jewish education among Reform Jews became more comprehensive in the 1970s. In place of the customary two hours per week of Sunday school instruction, most temples now offered twice-weekly classes, supplemented by weekends or summer sessions at a camp. The National Federation of Temple Youth introduced study programs for Reform teenagers beyond religious-school age, and rabbinical education was extended to women, the first woman (Sally Preisand) being ordained by HUC-JIR in 1972.

The commitment of Reform Judaism to Zionism deepened in the postwar period. Reform Jews welcomed the establishment of the state of Israel in 1948, shared feelings of crisis and relief during its Six Day War, and increasingly appropriated its cultural impact. Israeli melodies entered the synagogues, religious schools, and summer camps. The CCAR declared Israeli Independence Day a religious holiday, and beginning in 1970 HUC-JIR required all entering rabbinical students to spend the first year of their study at its campus in Jerusalem.

The centrality of Jewish peoplehood, symbolized by the state of Israel, found clear expression in the most recent platform of Reform Judaism. Called "A Centenary Perspective" because it was composed about one hundred years after the creation of the first national institutions of American Reform Judaism, it was adopted by the CCAR in 1976. The statement was the work of a committee chaired by Rabbi Eugene Borowitz, a professor at the New York school of HUC-JIR and one of the most influential contemporary theologians of the movement. Unlike previous platforms, it does not seek to define Judaism as a whole dogmatically, but only to give a brief historical account of Reform Judaism—what it has taught and what it has learned—and to describe its present spiritual convictions. Recognizing and affirming the diversity of theology and practice in contemporary Reform, it points to those broad conceptions and values shared by most Reform Jews. In the wake of the Holocaust and recognizing the physically precarious situation of Israeli Jewry and the assimilatory forces operative on American Judaism, the statement gives prominence to the value of ethnic survival, an element not highlighted in earlier platforms. It affirms the reality of God, without setting forth any specific theology, and defines the people of Israel as inseparable from its religion.

[*See also* Judaism.]

BIBLIOGRAPHY

Although outdated in many respects, the standard work on Reform Judaism remains David Philipson's *The Reform Movement in Judaism,* 2d ed. (1931), reissued with a new introduction by Solomon Freehof (New York, 1967). W. Gunther Plaut has brought together a good selection of primary sources, abbreviating the lengthier ones and translating into English those in other languages. The material in two volumes edited by him, *The Rise of Reform Judaism* and *The Growth of Reform Judaism* (New York, 1963 and 1965), extends to 1948. More general, but valuable for the European context, are Heinz Moshe Graupe's *The Rise of Modern Judaism,* translated by John Robinson (Huntington, N. Y., 1978), and the older Max Wiener's *Jüdische Religion im Zeitalter der Emanzipation* (Berlin, 1933), translated into Hebrew (Jerusalem, 1974) but not, regrettably, into English. The specific matter of liturgical change is comprehensively treated, with extensive quotation of primary sources, in Jakob J. Petuchowski's *Prayerbook Reform in Europe* (New York, 1968). The initial phases of Reform Judaism in the United States are best understood from Leon A. Jick's recent study, *The Americanization of the Synagogue, 1820-1870* (Hanover, N. H., 1976). Sefton D. Temkin has chronicled the history of the Union of American Hebrew Congregations in "A Century of Reform Judaism in America," *American Jewish Year Book* 74 (1973), pp. 3-75, and the story of the movement's seminary is told in my article, "A Centennial History," in *Hebrew Union College-Jewish Institute of Religion at One Hundred Years,* edited by Samuel E. Karff (Cincinnati, Ohio, 1976), pp. 3-283. The more significant speeches delivered at meetings of the Central Conference of American Rabbis have been collected by Joseph L. Blau in *Reform Judaism: A Historical Perspective* (New York, 1973), while some of the more thoughtful members of the CCAR themselves reflect on various aspects of the history of their organization in *Retrospect and Prospect: Essays in Commemoration of the Seventy-Fifth Anniversary of the Founding of the Central Conference of American Rabbis,* edited by Bertram Wallace Korn (New York, 1965). The variety in Reform Jewish theology after World War II is well reflected in *Contemporary Reform Jewish Thought,* edited by Bernard Martin (Chicago, 1968). Two sociological analyses based on surveys taken at the beginning of the last decade present the state of belief and practice among Reform rabbis and laity: Theodore I. Lenn's *Rabbi and Synagogue in Reform Judaism* (West Hartford, Conn., 1972) and Leonard J. Fein et al., *Reform Is a Verb: Notes on Reform and Reforming Jews* (New York, 1972). Contemporary Reform Judaism can best be followed through its current major publications. *Reform Judaism* is a popular UAHC magazine circulated to all members four times a year; the *Journal of Reform Judaism,* a quarterly, is the official organ of the CCAR; and the occasional *Ammi* presents news of the World Union for Progressive Judaism.

MICHAEL A. MEYER

REINCARNATION

The doctrine of reincarnation concerns the rebirth of the soul or self in a series of physical or preternatural embodiments, which are customarily human or animal in nature but are in some instances divine, angelic, demonic, vegetative, or astrological (i. e., are associated with the sun, moon, stars, or planets).

Archaic Cultures. A belief in reincarnation in some form or another is to be found in non-literate cultures all over the world. Besides central Australia, in which this precept is noticeably present, are West Africa (among the Ewe, Edo, Igbo, and Yoruba), southern Africa (among the Bantu-speakers and the Zulu), Indonesia, Oceania, New Guinea, and both North and South America (among selected ethnic groups).

In sub-Saharan Africa, for example, reincarnation is not only viewed positively, but failure to be reborn and thereby gain yet another opportunity to improve the world of the living is regarded as an evil (as is the state of childlessness).

Among the Yoruba and Edo peoples, the belief in the rebirth of the departed ancestors remains a strong and vibrant cultural force to the present day. It is their custom to name each boy child "Father Has Returned" and each girl child "Mother Has Returned.".

According to Australian Aboriginal religious beliefs, a deceased ancestor, after a sojourn of an unspecified length of time in the land of the dead, returns to the world of the living by entering the body of a mother at the moment of conception. The father is believed to play no direct role in impregnating the mother. Instead, the mother-to-be conceives new life by coming into the proximity of an *oknanikilla,* or local totem center, in which a spirit being *(alcheringa)* or soul of a deceased ancestor is lying in wait to be reborn.

Hinduism. The whole of the Hindu ethical code laid down in the ancient law books (e.g., *Laws of Manu*) presupposes the survival of the soul after death and assumes that the present life is fundamentally a preparation for the life to come. According to the Hindu conception of transmigration or rebirth (samsara, "a course or succession of states of existence"), the circumstances of any given lifetime are automatically determined by the net results of good and evil actions in previous existences. This, in short, is the law of karman (action), a universal law of nature that works according to its own inherent necessity. [*See* Karman.]

The succession of finite births has traditionally been regarded by Hindus pessimistically, as an existential misfortune and not as a series of "second chances" to improve one's lot, as it is often viewed in the West. Life is regarded not only as "rough, brutish, and short" but as filled with misery *(duhkha).* Thus, the multiplication of births within this "vale of tears" merely augments and intensifies the suffering that is the lot of all creatures.

Buddhism. Sakyamuni Buddha, like his philosophical and spiritual predecessors, believed that birth and death recur in successive cycles for the person who lives in the grip of ignorance about the true nature of the world. However, he undercut the Vedantic position by denying that the world of evanescent entities is undergirded and suffused by an eternal and unalterable Self or "soul-stuff" *(atman)*. In place of the doctrine of absolute self, he propagated the precept of "no-self" *(anatman)*, namely, that the human person, along with everything else that constitutes the empirical universe, is the offspring *(phala)* of an unbroken, everfluctuating process of creation and destruction and birth and extinction according to the principle of Dependent Co-origination *(pratitya-samutpada;* Pali, *paticca-samuppada).*

Jainism. According to the teachings of Mahavira (c. 599–527 BCE), the founder of Jainism, the unenlightened soul is bound to follow a course of transmigration that is beginningless and one that will persist for an unimaginable length of time. The soul becomes defiled by involvement in desire-laden actions and thereby attracts increasingly burdensome quantities of karmic matter upon itself. This polluting material, in turn, promotes the further corruption of the soul and causes its inevitable movement through countless incarnations.

Conclusion. There is no question but that the twin doctrines of *karman* and reincarnation have done more to shape the whole of Asian thought than any other concept or concepts. Ironically, the notion of reincarnation is beginning to make inroads into contemporary Western thought (particularly in theology, the philosophy of religion, and psychology) by way of a number of circuitous routes. One of the most curious manifestations of the belief in reincarnation in modern times is a new approach to psychotherapy that operates in the United States under the rubric of "rebirthing analysis," which purports to help the client deal with current psychological and spiritual problems by recalling personal experiences during numerous past lifetimes with the aid of meditation, hypnosis, and in some cases, consciousness-altering drugs.

[*See also* Immortality.]

BIBLIOGRAPHY

de Bary, Wm. Theodore, et al., eds. *Sources of Indian Tradition.* New York, 1958.

Ducasse, Curt John. *A Critical Examination of the Belief in the Life after Death.* Springfield, Ill., 1961.

Head, Joseph, and S. L. Cranston, eds. *Reincarnation: The Phoenix Fire Mystery.* New York, 1977.

MacGregor, Geddes. *Reincarnation as a Christian Hope.* London, 1982.

Parrinder, Geoffrey. "Varieties of Belief in Reincarnation." *Hibbert Journal* 55 (April 1957): 260-267.

Radhakrishnan, Sarvepalli, and Charles A. Moore, eds. *A Source Book in Indian Philosophy.* Princeton, 1957.

Stevenson, Ian. *Twenty Cases Suggestive of Reincarnation.* 2d ed. Charlottesville, Va., 1974.

Thomas, N. W., et al. "Transmigration." In *Encyclopaedia of Religion and Ethics,* edited by James Hastings, vol. 12. Edinburgh, 1921.

Tylor, E. B. *Primitive Culture,* vol. 2, *Religion in Primitive Culture* (1871). New York, 1970.

J. BRUCE LONG

RELIGION

The very attempt to define *religion,* to find some distinctive or possibly unique essence or set of qualities that distinguish the "religious" from the remainder of human life, is primarily a Western concern. The attempt is a natural consequence of the Western speculative, intellectualistic, and scientific disposition. It is also the product of the dominant Western religious mode, what is called the Judeo-Christian climate or, more accurately, the theistic inheritance from Judaism, Christianity, and Islam. The theistic form of belief in this tradition, even when downgraded culturally, is formative of the dichotomous Western view of religion. That is, the basic structure of theism is essentially a distinction between a transcendent deity and all else, between the creator and his creation, between God and man.

Definitions. So many definitions of religion have been framed in the West over the years that even a partial listing would be impractical. As early as the late eighteenth century an attempt was made to shift the emphasis from the conceptual to the intuitive and visceral in defining religion. In a very influential statement, Friedrich Schleiermacher defined religion as "feeling of absolute dependence"—absolute as contrasted to other, relative feelings of dependence. Since that time there have been others who have sought to escape formalistic, doctrinal definitions and to include the experiential, emotive, and intuitive factors, as well as valuational and ethical factors.

With the rise of the sociological and anthropological disciplines, another factor has been projected into definition making—the social, economic, historical, and cultural contexts in which religion comes to expression. Sociologists and anthropologists rightly argue that religion is never an abstract set of ideas, values, or experiences developed apart from the total cultural matrix and that many religious beliefs, customs, and rituals can only be understood in feference to this matrix. Indeed, some proponents of these disciplines imply or suggest that analysis of religious structures will totally account for religion.

The various forms of psychology come out of the same scientific-humanistic context as the social science disciplines. The central concerns of psychology are the psychic mechanics and motivational forces that result from human self-consciousness. In some sense, psychological interpretations of religion are more akin to those that stress experiential inwardness than to those that accent intellectual and societal aspects. In the final analysis, however, psychology is more akin to the social sciences in its treatment of religion than to any intrareligious effort at interpretation. It tends, like social studies, to dissolve religion into sets of psychological factors.

It should be observed in passing that the religious person would not be satisfied with such analyses. That person's sense of what is happening in religion seems always to contain some extrasocietal, extrapsychological depth-factor or transcendent dimension, which must be further examined. Among Western religion scholars there have been attempts to define religion in a manner that avoids the "reductionism" of the various sociological and psychological disciplines that reduce religion to its component factors.

To be sure, at the popular level much religion consists of placation and use of spirits and superhuman powers and various rituals reminiscent of theism. But in their own self-definitions Buddhism and Hinduism, for example, seem to have little or no sense of a radically other and ultimate being. In fact, the basic thought and action model here is that of man's oneness with his environing universe.

According to Mircea Eliade, no longer is the sacred to be sought almost exclusively in the God-encounter type of experience; it is abundantly exemplified in the symbolisms and rituals of almost every culture, especially the primitive and Asian cultures. It is embodied as sacred space, for example, in shrines and temples, in taboo areas, even limitedly in the erection of dwellings in accordance with a sense of the *axis mundi,* an orientation to the center of the true (sacred) universe. Indeed, structures often symbolically represent that physically invisible but most real of all universes—the eternally perfect universe to which they seek to relate fruitfully. This sense of sacredness often attaches to trees, stones, mountains, and other like objects in which mysterious power seems to be resident. Many primitive rituals seek to sacramentally repeat the first moment of creation often described in myth when primordial chaos became recognizable order. Sacred time—that is, eternal and unfragmented time—is made vitally present by the reenactment of such myths. In *The Sacred and the Profane* (New York, 1951) Eliade writes, "Every religious festival, every liturgical time, represents the reactualization of a sacred event that took place in a mythical past, in the beginning" (pp. 68-69).

To sociologists and anthropologists, sacredness is an ideal construct, not a genuine cultural or experiential entity. Linguists, psychologists, and philosophers also question the identifiability of such a distinctive entity in patterns of language, experience, and thought patterns. For all of these crit-

ics the religious experience is a compound of cultural entities and experiences, not a separable thing in and of itself.

In Asian traditions that emphasize immanence rather than transcendence, characterized by continuums rather than discontinuities both of theory and of experience, gradations of both understanding and of experience exist nonetheless. Recognized levels of practice and attainment are buttressed by texts and incorporated into systems of praxis. "Lower" lev-

> # Religion is the organization of life around the depth dimensions of experience—varied in form, completeness, and clarity in accordance with the environing culture.

els of attainment are not considered totally false or wrong but as less than fully true or ultimate. There is, then, a kind of transcendence by degree or stage; the highest is "other" to the lower states, and in some Buddhist and Hindu traditions (i. e., Zen and meditative Advaita) there is a breakthrough experience (*satori* and realization of *brahman*) that experientially is wholly other than or wholly transformative of ordinary awareness.

In summary, it may be said that almost every known culture involves the religious in the above sense of a depth dimension in cultural experiences at all levels—a push, whether ill-defined or conscious, toward some sort of ultimacy and transcendence that will provide norms and power for the rest of life. When more or less distinct patterns of behavior are built around this depth dimension in a culture, this structure constitutes religion in its historically recognizable form. Religion is the organization of life around the depth dimensions of experience—varied in form, completeness, and clarity in accordance with the environing culture.

Characteristics and Structures of Religious Life. As previously suggested, religions adopt their tangible historical forms as matrices of cultural and social elements about the depth-centers of culture. Hence the beliefs, patterns of observance, organizational structures, and types of religious experience are as varied as the matrices that give them birth.

Traditionalism. All attempts to find a primitive religion embodying the primordial form of all subsequent religions have encountered two insurmountable problems. The first is the sheer arbitrariness of seeking the origin of all types of religion in a single form. The second is that wherever religion is recognized—if one uses the above definition of religion as a depth-dimensional structure—one also encounters an existent tradition comprising stylized actions related to the pursuit of cultural goals, however meager or closely geared to survival needs.

Whatever the degree of elaboration, two things seem to be taken for granted. First, the beginnings are taken as models of pristine purity and power, fully authoritative for all members of the group or adherents of the faith. Second, no matter how great the actual changes in a particular historical religious tradition—and sometimes this means the entire cultural tradition, more or less—the basic thrust of traditionalism is to maintain itself.

Myth and symbol. Religious traditions are full of myth and replete with symbol. *Myth* in most contemporary use simply means "false"; myths are the fanciful tales of primitives spun out as explanations of beginnings. Hence creation myths are rationalizations of what prescientific cultures cannot understand through other means.

Symbol is the language of myth. When the crucially important but mysterious nature of ultimate reality—the basic concern of religious man—can only be seen through a glass darkly, how else can one speak of it except in symbolic forms?

In seeking to deal with man's ultimate concerns, religions are prolific in the production, use, and elaboration of symbolic forms and objects; thus it is not surprising that religions have been the inspiration of an overwhelmingly large and diverse body of art.

Concepts of salvation. Salvation is but another name for religion. That is, all religions are basically conceived as means of saving men at one level or another. And there are always two aspects to salvation: what men are to be saved *from* and what they are to be saved *to.* It goes without saying that what men are saved from and to varies immensely from culture to culture and from religion to religion.

At the primitive level of religion, salvation both "from" and "to" is achieved mainly in the realm of physical dangers and goods. The primitive seeks by his rituals to save himself from starvation, from death by storm, from disease, from wild animals, and from enemies and to sufficiency of food and shelter, to freedom from danger and disease, and to human fertility. Implicit in this context, and in the realm of mental and emotional malaise, is salvation from mysterious and even malign powers and forces of evil. The achievement of salvation in all these areas is striven for by all possible physical means with the superadded power of ritual, charm, and magic.

Religious salvation is as responsive to and expressive of human needs and desires as any secular scheme of salvation. For salvation in religion is a means of fulfilling needs and desires, even when the needs and desires are revealed from "above." And it is also evident that the varied cultural contexts of religions each represent a variant perspective on the human situation—its goods and goals, its dangers and evils. These varied perspectives greatly influence the form of religious salvation. Thus the Hindu Advaitin, the African San, the Sunni Muslim, the Orthodox Jew, the Zen Buddhist, the

Protestant, and the Greek Orthodox Christian would define religious needs and goods quite differently.

Sacred places and objects. One of the striking features of historically observable religions is the presence of special religious areas and structures set apart from ordinary space by physical, ritual, and psychological barriers. Further, particularly within the more spacious precincts, there are grades of sacredness that enshrine specially sacred objects or relics in their supremely holy areas. A classic example is the last of the Jewish temples in Jerusalem, in which there was a spatial progression from the outermost court of the gentiles to the women's court to the men's court to the court of the burnt offering to the priests' enclosure to the Holy of Holies wherein was the Ark of the Covenant and, in some sense, the special presence of Yahveh. In synagogues today the ark containing a copy of the Torah is the most sacred part. In Roman Catholic and Eastern Orthodox churches, the altar supporting the sacramental bread and wine is the focal point of sacredness. Quite logically, many of the furnishings and objects used in temples and shrines, particularly in their most sacred rituals, partake of the sacredness of the shrine itself.

But in the final analysis sacred places are sacred because of what has occurred there or may occur there. Their essence is sacramental. Sacred places are cherished and revered because they offer the possibility of directly encountering and partaking of the real in the given tradition. An unusual power has manifested itself in a natural object or taboo place either for good or ill. Or tradition tells that some primordially creative act once took place here and that power still lingers.

Other sacred places and objects (images) particularly emphasize the hope of present and future blessing. The shrine at Lourdes is venerated not simply because a French peasant girl reputedly once saw a vision of the Virgin there but because of the hope of present healing. Similarly, many Buddhists expect to gain merit by praying and making offerings before Buddha images or to reap tangible benefits in the here and now by touching *bodhisattva* images.

Sacred actions (rituals). Just as it is impossible to think of living religions without their sacred places, so is it impossible to conceive of a religion without its rituals, whether simple or elaborate. Several features are prominent in most rituals. One is the element of order. Indeed, an established ritual pattern is the ordered performance of sacred actions under the direction of a leader. Rigidity of pattern, requiring the utmost care and precision in use of word, action, and material, points to another feature of ritual, maximized in the Hindu sacrifice but more or less present in all fixed rituals: meticulous performance.

Yet deep within ritualism there is inherent the concern for accuracy and faithfulness. This is the essentially sacramental nature of ritual that arises from its nature as an ordered symbol system. Thus both symbol and ritual are perceived as intrinsic embodiments of the sacred essence, the supersensible and indescribable ultimacy of a religion. Thus ritual and symbol bring the real presence of the religious depth-dimension into the lives of its experients and in so doing become incredibly precious.

Sacred writings. In literate societies writings are often of considerable religious importance. (Christianity calls sacred writings scriptures.) Typically sacred writings comprise the reported words of the holy men of the past—prophets, saints, founders of faiths such as Zarathushtra, Moses, the Buddha, Muhammad, Christ, or Nanak.

When scriptures exist, interpreters must also exist. Successive interpretations vary greatly, for interpreters are caught between their desires to be faithful to the original sacred word and to make its exposition relevant and meaningful to their own age.

Confucianism, Taoism, and Shinto can scarcely be said to have scriptures in the above sense of a corpus of inspired utterances. In general, Buddhist and Hindu scriptures can be interpreted much more flexibly than Western ones because of their greater variety and their emphasis on truth as dependent on the level of the hearer's understanding. [*See* Scripture.]

The sacred community. Every religion has some communal sense and structure. Ritual nearly always involves professional ritualists and a group bound together by its experience. But the communal bonds vary greatly in nature and extent. [*See* Community.]

Some ritual groupings are quite temporary: one thinks of the occasional, selective, and experience-based spirit groups found among some Native Americans. In other primitive cultures, the religious-ritual grouping is hardly separable from the general clan or tribal social structure and indeed might better be called a social subculture with religious elements centered on certain particular occasions and activities. In many Buddhist and Hindu contexts the religious community is little more than those in the vicinity who attend various religious ceremonies in the local temple and often come on purely personal quests.

To be sure, in most of these societies there are special groupings of a secret or semisecret nature open only to initiates. Such are the Native American spirit groups.

Perhaps it is only in Islam and Christianity, and somewhat limitedly in Judaism, that the concept of a holy fellowship of believers, called a church in Christianity, has been created to express religious faith and practice. The prevailing ethnic qualification in Judaism prevents its description as a purely faith-gathered group. Islam represents a near equivalent to the Christian church, especially as Islamic groups have spread out into other areas than those totally Muslim in nature. Muslims, like Christians, consider themselves members of one sacred group, called out from among others by the faith and practice of their religion, ideally a unity stronger than any other bond. It may be observed in passing that such a definition of community comes more naturally and more easily to Islam and Christianity than to most Asian religions.

The sacred experience. These special experiences represent a continuum from the comparatively mild and frequent experiences to those commonly termed mystical. At the less intense end of the continuum are those instances of a sense of awe in the sacred precincts, a sense of humility before a felt presence, an unusual degree of joy or peace suddenly coming upon one, or the deep conviction of a prayer answered. Then there are those of a much more intense nature such as a strong and sudden conviction of the forgiveness of one's sins such as John Wesley's "warming of the heart" at Aldersgate. Indeed, in some Christian groups special conversion or purification-of-heart experiences are made a matter of explicit emphasis and a condition of church membership. In Pentecostal groups a sudden and unexpected experience of speaking in unknown tongues is considered a sign of the "baptism of the Spirit."

At the further end of this experiential continuum are the mystical experiences found in Judaism, Islam, Christianity, Taoism, Hinduism, and Buddhism. Those who have had such experiences (especially in Christian, Hindu, and Muslim contexts) insist that they differ in kind from all other religious experiences. These include: (1) their suddenness and spontaneity (without warning or overt preparation), (2) their irresistibility, (3) their absolute quality of conviction and realistic authority, (4) their quality of clear knowledge, not strong emotion, which is asserted even when the mystically received knowledge is conceptually indescribable. Perhaps the true and basic content of such moments is an assurance of the absolute reality of God, Kṛṣṇa, Brahmā, Dharma, or Buddha nature, that is, the ultimate reality as envisioned by the given faith.

BIBLIOGRAPHY

Beane, Wendell C., and William G. Doty, eds. *Myths, Rites, Symbols: A Mircea Eliade Reader.* 2 vols. New York, 1975. A well-chosen, substantial anthology of Eliade's writings on various aspects of religion.

Campbell, Joseph. *Masks of God*, vol. 1, *Primitive Mythology;* vol. 2, *Oriental Mythology;* vol. 3, *Occidental Mythology.* New York, 1959-1965. These three volumes present a richly varied portrait, penetrating analysis, and many concrete illustrations of the forms and functions of myth in these three different contexts.

Eliade, Mircea. *Patterns in Comparative Religion.* New York, 1958. The subtitle indicates the nature of this work: *A Study of the Element of the Sacred in the History of Religious Phenomena.*

Huxley, Aldous. *The Doors of Perception.* New York, 1954.

Huxley, Aldous. *Heaven and Hell.* New York, 1956. These two volumes present accounts of Huxley's experiments with psychedelic drugs and his positive interpretations of them.

James, William. *The Varieties of Religious Experience.* New York, 1902. James's Gifford Lectures (1901-1902) are among the early, classic studies of religious experience, offering numerous specific examples and his own interpretations.

King, Winston L. *Introduction to Religion: A Phenomenological Approach.* New York, 1968. A descriptive and analytic study of the various forms and structures of the religious life as expressed in various traditions.

Laski, Marghanita. *Ecstasy: A Study of Some Secular and Religious Experiences.* Westport, Conn., 1961. A thesis of this volume is that transcendent experiences are universally human and not necessarily religious.

Leeuw, Gerardus van der. *Religion in Essence and Manifestation: A Study in Phenomenology* (1938). 2 vols. Gloucester, Mass., 1967. The first major attempt to apply the phenomenological methodology to the field of religion, bracketing normative evaluations of truth and ethical considerations in the interests of describing the religious essence in its essential and characterstic manifestations.

Lessa, William A., and Evon Z. Vogt, eds. *Reader in Comparative Religion: An Anthropological Approach.* 4th ed. New York, 1979. A wide selection of significant readings on the interpretation of religion by various leading anthropologists.

Long, Charles H. *Alpha: The Myths of Creation.* New York, 1963. An anthology of creation myths from the folk tales and religions of the world, organized according to type.

Maslow, Abraham. *Religions, Values, and Peak-Experiences.* Columbus, Ohio, 1964. Maslow calls for religion to make common cause with other areas and disciplines in the constructive use of all peak experiences, whether religious or otherwise.

Masters, R. E. L., and Jean Houston. *The Varieties of Psychedelic Experience.* New York, 1966. An evaluative, critical analysis of psychedelic experiences claiming to be religious.

Noss, John B. *Man's Religions.* 6th ed. New York, 1980. A standard, college-level text describing the major religious traditions of the world.

Otto, Rudolf. *Das Heilige.* Marburg, 1917. Translated by John W. Harvey as *The Idea of the Holy* (1950; Oxford, 1970). The author's own subtitle expresses the thrust of this seminal volume: *An Inquiry into the Non-Rational Factor in the Idea of the Divine and Its Relation to the Rational.*

Pratt, James B. *The Religious Consciousness: A Psychological Study.* New York, 1921. Expressed in psychological terms no longer current but perceptive and suggestive, particularly with respect to mysticism.

Stace, W. T. *Mysticism and Philosophy.* New York, 1960. An acute philosophical analysis of the mystical experience, concluding that "something" objective is there but not quite what the mystic thinks it is.

Tart, Charles T., ed. *Transpersonal Psychologies.* New York, 1975. Analytic discussions from a psychological viewpoint of the qualities, nature, and meaning of a variety of mystical experiences and psychotherapeutic techniques.

Underhill, Evelyn. *Mysticism.* 12th ed. New York, 1961. A long-time classic, Underhill's book is a sympathetic presentation of the mystical life, mainly within the Christian context but including Muslim Sufi materials.

WINSTON L. KING

REPENTANCE

The noun *repentance* and the verb *repent* came into modern English via Middle English and Old French from the Latin verb *paenitere,* meaning "to be sorry, to grieve, to regret." As a religious term repentance denotes a change in a person's attitude, will, and behavior, sometimes accompanied by feelings of sorrow and regret for past transgressions and perhaps accompanied also by some form of restitution.

Confession of sin and accusation. The confession of sin, nearly always a characteristic of repentance, is the verbalization of wrongs committed and the acceptance of blame for their personal and social consequences. [*See* Confession of Sins.] Confession can be made privately (to the gods directly as a penitential prayer, or to a specially credentialed representative of the gods), or it can be made publicly. In many cultures the act of confession is inherently cathartic, the sincerity of the penitent being irrelevant.

Penitential rites. Repentance may take form as a ritual presentation, made by the penitent person to observers, of outward expressions of remorse and sorrow. Restitution or compensation is often an integral feature of penitential rites, particularly in cases wherein others have been harmed or their property damaged or taken away. Confession is sometimes regarded as the necessary prerequisite for formalized types of expiation, such as public sacrifice or public penitential discipline.

Guilt. Repentance is an institutionally approved means of eliminating excessive guilt stemming from the awareness of having transgressed in thought, word, or deed, and thus its public and ritually prescribed protocol exists for the formal recognition and removal of guilt.

Conversion. The word *conversion* may be defined as the voluntary entry into a religious movement having exclusive claims that are buttressed by a system of values and norms at variance with the outside world; and for conversion repentance is often a necessary precondition, for it involves abandoning the old in order to embrace the new. [*See* Conversion.]

Near Eastern Traditions. Repentance is a particularly important aspect of many ancient Near Eastern religions including Mesopotamian religions, Judaism, Islam, and Christianity. Among these religions illness and misfortune were widely attributed to transgression, whether ritual or moral, deliberate or unconscious.

Judaism. In ancient Israel, as in the rest of the Near East, fear existed concerning the possibility of committing unconscious sin and incurring guilt thereby (*Dt.* 29:28, *1 Sm.* 26:19, *Ps.* 19:13, *Jb.* 1:5). But the Bible deals more extensively with guilt incurred by conscious and deliberate sin. The earlier prophets addressed Israel as a whole and demanded national repentance, but later prophets like Ezekiel emphasized individual repentance (*Ez.* 18:21, 18:27, 33:9, 33:11). The Israelite prophets did not distinguish sharply between ritual and moral transgressions, but called Israel back to an earlier, better relationship to God as defined by the terms of the covenant.

During the Second Temple period (516 BCE-70 CE), the notion of repentance or conversion (Heb., *teshuvah;* Gr., *metanoia*) was of central significance to Judaism. The conception could involve the prophetic notion of restoration as well as the conversion of pagans. In rabbinic Judaism repentance *(teshuvah)* and good deeds together describe the ideals of Jewish piety (*Avot* 4.21-4.22). In modern Judaism the Days of Awe (Ro'sh ha-Shanah, followed by a week of repentance, culminating in Yom Kippur), is a period of communal contrition and confession of sins. On Yom Kippur sins are confessed through statutory prayers recited privately and in unison publicly.

Islam. The most important theological conception in Islam is that God is compassionate and merciful. Repentance has therefore played a central role throughout the history of Islam. Throughout history messengers from God have tried with little success to call men to return to God, that is, to repent; the Arabic word for repentance, *tawbah,* literally means a "returning" to God. Those who reject the message are unbelievers (Arab., *kuffar,* literally "ungrateful ones"). Nevertheless sinners can always repent, be converted to the truth, and do good deeds (Qur'an 6:54, 42:25-26). They are cleansed from all sins and restored to their original sinless state. Repentance must be followed by faith and good works (Qur'an 25:70). According to the Sufis, who are the mystics of Islam, the first station *(maqamah)* on the mystical path begins with repentance. A spiritual guide *(shaykh)* enrolls the penitent as a disciple *(murid)* and assigns him a regimen of ascetic practices.

Christianity. The religious reform movements led by John the Baptist and by Jesus of Nazareth were revitalistic or millenarian in character. Both emphasized the necessity for repentance or conversion.

There are two Greek words used in early Christian literature that convey the basic notion of repentance, namely, *metanoia* and *metameleia.* By the time of the Christian era both words had come to convey a change of attitude or purpose as well as a sorrow for past failings.

During the second and third centuries Christianity underwent a penitential crisis. By the second century baptism was thought to confer sinlessness as well as the forgiveness of all previous sins. Since baptism or martyrdom were the only two means of eradicating postbaptismal sin, the practice of adult baptism and deathbed baptism became common. By the third century a system of public penance came to be regarded as a second baptism. Excluded from the Eucharist, the penitent went through a regimen of fasting, prayer, and almsgiving. The Council of Trent (1545-1563) reaffirmed that repentance must involve three elements, namely, contrition, confession, and satisfaction.

Traditions of Small-scale Societies. Among the Nuer of the Sudan, certain acts are regarded as bad because God punishes them. Faults *(dueri)* are against God and he is the one who punishes them.

The phenomena of confession and repentance are culture traits indigenous to American Indian cultures. The Aurohuaca Indians of the Columbian Sierra Nevada regard all illness as a punishment for sin. The Ijca of Columbia abstain from salt and alcohol before confession. Among the Maya of Yucatan, women in labor summon native shamans to confess their sins, particularly those of a sexual nature. The Inuit (Eskimo) are anxious lest by conscious or unconscious violation of taboos they offend Sedna, the mistress of animals, who resides at the bottom of the sea and whose displeasure might threaten the food supply.

BIBLIOGRAPHY

The most comprehensive study of the phenomenon of confession, which includes a great deal of information about the related notion of repentance, is Raffaele Pettazzoni's *La confessione dei peccati,* 3 vols. (1929-1936; reprint, Bologna, 1968). However, Pettazzoni's hypothesis proposing an evolutionary development of the notion of confession, from the magical to the theistic, is unconvincing. A more theoretical discussion of the phenomenon of repentance is in Albert Esser's *Das Phänomen Reue: Versuch einer Erhellung ihres Selbstverständnisses* (Cologne, 1963). For a shorter discussion from a history of religions perspective, see Geo Widengren's *Religionsphänomenologie* (Berlin, 1969), pp. 258-279). For a critique of the shame-culture or guilt-culture typology, see Gerhart Piers and Milton B. Singer's *Shame and Guilt* (Springfield, Ill., 1953).

For an overview of the notions of confession, repentance, and guilt in antiquity, see Franz Steinleitner's *Die Beicht im Zusammenhänge mit der sakralen Rechtspflege in der Antike* (Leipzig, 1913). For Greco-Roman religions and philosophical systems, see Arthur Darby Nock's *Conversion: The Old and the New in Religion from Alexander the Great to Augustine of Hippo* (Oxford, 1933). An exceptionally complete study of Greek pollution and purity with full bibliography is found in Robert A. Parker's *Miasma: Pollution and Purification in Early Greek Religion* (Oxford, 1983). Still indispensable is Kurt Latte's "Schuld und Sünde in der griechischen Religion," *Archiv für Religionswissenschaft* 20 (1920-1921): 254-298. For the Roman world, see Anna-Elizabeth Wilhelm-Hooijbergh's *Peccatum: Sin and Guilt in Ancient Rome* (Groningen, 1954).

Henri Frankfort outlines the ancient Egyptian concept of sin and sinlessness in his *Ancient Egyptian Religion* (New York, 1948), pp. 73-80. Frankfort's treatment of the topic has been corrected by Siegfried Morenz's *Egyptian Religion* (Ithaca, N. Y., 1973), pp. 130-133. For the relationship between repentance and sacrificial expiation in ancient Israel, see Jacob Milgrom's *Cult and Conscience: The Asham and the Priestly Doctrine of Repentance* (Leiden, 1976). Also important is William L. Holladay's *The Root Subh in the Old Testament* (Leiden, 1958).

One of the only detailed studies of the Christian concept of repentance within the context of Judaism, Greco-Roman sources, and subsequent patristic evidence is Aloys H. Dirksen's *The New Testament Concept of Metanoia* (Washington, D. C., 1932). A philologically oriented study of Hebrew and early Christian terms and concepts related to repentance, together with a wealth of references to primary sources, is found in the *Theological Dictionary of the New Testament,* edited by Gerhard Kittel and Gerhard Friedrich, vol. 4 (Grand Rapids, Mich., 1967), pp. 975-1008. The most important study of the second- and third-century penitential crisis is Hans Windisch's *Taufe und Sünde im ältesten Christentum bis auf Origenes* (Tü-bingen, 1908). For a selection of important early Christian texts on repentance in Greek and Latin with German translations, see *Die Busse: Quellen zur Entstehung des altkirchlichen Busswesens* (Zurich, 1969).

On the phenomenon of confession and repentance among small-scale societies, see Weston La Barre's well-documented "Confession as Cathartic Therapy in American Indian Tribes," in *Magic, Faith, and Healing,* edited by Ari Kiev (New York, 1964). Kiev's book contains many relevant essays. Robert I. Levy's *Tahitians: Mind and Experience in the Society Islands* (Chicago, 1973) is an important study. Bryan R. Wilson's *Magic and the Millennium: A Sociological Study of Movements of Protest among Tribal and Third-World Peoples* (New York, 1973) is an important synthetic study of revitalistic or millenarian movements.

DAVID E. AUNE

RESURRECTION

The term *resurrection* is so intricately bound up with Christian ideas that it is extremely difficult to decide when it should be used for similar ideas in other religions.

Taoism. In Chinese Taoism there is frequent mention of prolonging life and strengthening the vital force, but there is no uniform doctrine on this subject. We are told of various practices—meditation, use of alcoholic beverages, magical rites—through which the lower and mortal elements in man can be replaced by higher and immortal ones and the vital principle can be strengthened so as not to be separated from the body. In this way man can achieve immortality and ascend to the heavenly world. But this is hardly resurrection in the strict sense of the word.

India. The Vedic language possesses several words that have been thought to denote the "soul" as an immortal spiritual substance in man: *manas* ("thought, thinking"), *asu* ("life"), *atman* ("breath"), *tanu* ("body, self"). But the equation of any of these words with "soul" is hardly correct. In the *Rgveda* there are hints that at death the various parts of the body merge with natural phenomena of a similar kind: the flesh goes to the earth, the blood to the water, the breath to the wind, the eye to the sun, the mind *(manas)* to the moon, and so on. Although this belief differs considerably from the Christian idea of resurrection, it may perhaps be described by this term.

Egypt. The Egyptian view of man presupposes two incorporeal elements, neither corresponding to any modern concept of the soul. When a person dies, his *ba* (soul) leaves the body but hovers near the corpse. The *ka* combines the ideas of vital force, nourishment, double, and genius. *Ba* and *ka* cannot exist without a bodily substrate. Therefore the body is embalmed to secure their existence. In addition, the funerary

rites transform the deceased into an *akh,* a "shining" or "transformed" spirit. In this capacity the deceased lives on in the realm of Osiris, the god of the netherworld, who once died but was revived again as the ruler of the dead.

Zoroastrianism. The earliest documents of Zoroastrian religion do not mention the resurrection of the body but rather the soul's ascent to paradise. But in the later parts of the Avesta there is at least one reference to resurrection: "When the dead rise, the Living Incorruptible One will come and life will be transfigured" (*Yashts* 19.11). The Living One is the savior, Saoshyant (Pahl., Soshans), who is to come at the end of the present era. Another passage (*Yashts* 13.11), which speaks of joining together bones, hairs, flesh, bowels, feet, and genitals, refers not to resurrection, as has been maintained, but to birth.

Judaism. The Hebrew scriptures (Old Testament) as a whole have no doctrine of resurrection. Usually the scriptures assert that "if a man dies, he will not live again" (*Jb.* 14:14) or that "he who goes down to She'ol does not come up" (7:9).

The only clear reference to resurrection is found in the *Book of Daniel* (c. 165 BCE). There we read: "Many of those who sleep in the dust will awake, some to eternal life, others to eternal shame" (12:2).

Similar statements are found in *4 Ezra* 7:32 : "The earth shall give up those who sleep in it, and the dust those who rest there in silence, and the storehouses shall give back the souls entrusted to them." The mention of the souls seems to

> *Ba* and *ka* cannot exist without a bodily substrate. Therefore the body is embalmed to secure their existence.

indicate that death is the separation of body and soul (cf. 7:78) and that resurrection means they are reunited.

Christianity. In primitive Christianity the resurrection of Christ was the fundamental fact; belief in it was even regarded as a prerequisite of salvation.

The first Christians expected the second coming of Christ (the Parousia) to happen in their lifetime. But as several Christians died without having experienced the Parousia, questions arose as to the reliability of the Christian hope. Paul answers such questions in *1 Thessalonians* 4:13-18, asserting that just as Christ died and rose again, the fellowship with him cannot be broken by death: first those who have died in Christ will rise when "the archangel calls and the trumpet sounds," then those who are still alive will be taken away to heaven to Christ.

Islam. Islam shares with Christianity the belief in a general resurrection followed by a judgment. The stress is rather on the latter. In the Qur'an the last day is referred to as "the day of resurrection" *(yawm al-qiyamah)*, but also as "the day of judgment" *(yawm ad-din)*, "the day of reckoning" *(yawm al-hisab)*, or "the day of awakening" *(yawm al-ba`th)*. In the Qur'an there are several very graphic descriptions of the day of resurrection, focusing on the natural phenomena that accompany it and on the outcome of the judgment—the believers entering paradise and the unbelievers being thrown into the fire of hell. It is a day "when the trumpet is blown" (cf. *Mt.* 24:31, *1 Thes.* 4:16) and men "shall come in troops, and heaven is opened and the mountains are set in motion" (surah 78:18-20; cf. 18:99), a day "when heaven is rent asunder . . . when earth is stretched out and casts forth what is in it" (84:1-4; cf. 99:1-2).

BIBLIOGRAPHY

There is no monograph on resurrection in general. Volume 5 (1965) of the journal *Kairos* has a series of articles on resurrection in different religions, supplemented by two articles on Jewish ideas in volumes 14 (1972) and 15 (1973).

Discussion of Chinese ideas can be found in Henri Maspero's *Mélanges posthumes sur les religions et l'histoire de la Chine,* 3 vols. (Paris, 1950) by consulting the index entries under *immortalité.* Indian ideas are dealt with by Helmuth von Glasenapp in *Unsterblichkeit und Erlösung in den indischen Religionen* (Halle, 1938). For Egyptian ideas, see Alan H. Gardiner's *The Attitude of the Ancient Egyptians to Death and the Dead* (Cambridge, 1935); Herman Kees's *Totenglauben und Jenseitsvorstellungen der alten Ägypter,* 2d ed. (Berlin, 1956), a classic but difficult work; and, for certain aspects, Louis V. Zabkar's *A Study of the Ba Concept in Ancient Egyptian Texts* (Chicago, 1968) and Gertie Englund's *Akh: Une notion religieuse dans l'Egypte pharaonique* (Uppsala, 1978). The only comprehensive study of Iranian conceptions is Nathan Söderblom's *La vie future d'après le Mazdéisme* (Paris 1901). It is now somewhat out of date, but is still useful, as is J. D. C. Pavry's *The Zoroastrian Doctrine of a Future Life* (New York, 1926).

Old Testament ideas have been dealt with by Edmund F. Sutcliffe in *The Old Testament and the Future Life* (Westminster, Md., 1947) and by Robert Martin-Achard in *De la mort à la ré-surrection . . . dans . . . l'Ancien Testament* (Neuchâtel, 1956). For further discussion, see Harris Birkeland's "The Belief in the Resurrection of the Dead in the Old Testament," *Studia Theologica* 3 (1950): 60-78, and my book *Israelite Religion* (Philadelphia, 1975), pp. 239-247. Among studies dealing with later Jewish and Christian ideas, see R. H. Charles's *A Critical History of the Doctrine of a Future Life in Israel, in Judaism, and in Christianity* (1899; reprint, New York, 1979) and Pierre Grelot's *De la mort à la vieéternelle* (Paris, 1971). For Judaism, see also H. C. C. Cavallin's *Life after Death,* vol. 1, part 1, *An Inquiry into the Jewish Background* (Lund, 1974), a comprehensive study of all relevant texts, and George W. E. Nickelsburg's *Resurrection, Immortality, and Eternal Life in InterTestamental Judaism* (Cambridge, Mass., 1972).

Of the literature on the New Testament only a few books can be mentioned: Murdoch E. Dahl's *The Resurrection of the Body: A Study of 1 Corinthians* 15 (London, 1962); *Immortality and Resurrection,* 2d ed., edited by Pierre Benoît and Roland E. Murphy (New York, 1970); Robert C. Tennenhill's *Dying and Rising with Christ* (Berlin, 1967); and Geerhardus Vos's *The Pauline Eschatology* (Grand Rapids, Mich., 1961). Works in German are Oscar Cullman's *Unsterblichkeit der Seele und Auferstehung der Toten* (Stuttgart, 1963), Paul Hoffmann's *Die Toten in Christus: Ein religionsgeschichtliche und exegetische Untersuchung zur paulinischen Eschatologie* (Münster, 1978), and Günter Kegel's *Auferstehung Jesu, Auferstehung der Toten* (Gütersloh, 1970).

On resurrection in Christian theology, see Paul Althaus's *Die letzten Dinge* (1922; Gütersloh, 1956), Walter Künneth's *Theologie der Auferstehung* (1934; Giessen, 1982), and Klaus Kienzler's *Logik der Auferstehung* (Freiburg im Breisgau, 1976), a study of the theologians Rudolf Bultmann, Gerhard Ebeling, and Wolfhart Pannenberg.

For a broad discussion of dying and rising gods, see James G. Frazer's *The Golden Bough,* 3d. ed., rev. & enl., vol. 4, *The Dying God* (1912; London, 1955). On Dumuzi, see Thorkild Jacobsen's *The Treasures of Darkness: A History of Mesopotamian Religion* (New Haven, 1976), pp. 25-73. On Baal, See Arvid S. Kapelrud's *Ba'al in the Ras Shamra Texts* (Copenhagen, 1952); Werner H. Schmidt's "Baals Tod und Auferstehung," *Zeitschrift für Religions- und Geistesgeschichte* 15 (1963): 1-13; and Michael David Coogan's *Stories from Ancient Canaan* (Philadel- phia, 1978). On Osiris, E. A. Wallis Budge's *Osiris and the Egyptian Resurrection,* 2 vols. (1911; New York, 1973), and J. Gwyn Griffith's *The Origin of Osiris and His Cult,* 2d ed., rev. & enl. (Leiden, 1980), may be profitably consulted.

HELMER RINGGREN

RETREAT

RETREAT may be defined as a limited period of isolation during which an individual, either alone or as part of a small group, withdraws from the regular routine of daily life, generally for religious reasons. This isolation, as well as the interruption of social intercourse and ordinary life, is adopted as a condition that enables individual retreatants to enter within themselves in silence, in order to establish contact with the divinity or with the world of the spirits.

Retreats of Tribal Initiation. Initiation into the life of a tribe entails separating candidates from the social nucleus to which they belong and isolating them in a well-defined zone, protected by rigid taboos. The neophytes are then subjected to certain strict disciplines. At the end of this period of initiation, after passing through certain liberating rites, the neophytes, having undergone a profound transformation, return to the tribe as adults.

Retreats of Search for a Revelatory Dream. A number of peoples, especially pre-Columbian Indians, submitted their children and adolescents to a period of isolation aimed at enabling them to enter into contact with the spirit who was to guide each of them throughout life. This phenomenon is especially notable among certain Canadian groups, such as the Athapascans.

Retreats of Monastic Initiation. Among the four exemplary stages that Hindu tradition distinguishes in the life of a man is that of the individual who withdraws in solitude into the forest, where he (now called a *vanaptrasthin*) commits himself to meditation and to certain practices of asceticism.

Among Christian saints, Ignatius Loyola spent almost an entire year, from March 1522 to February 1523, in Manresa, where he devoted himself to prayer (seven hours daily), fasting, and abstinence. He emerged from this experience transformed and illumined in spirit by revelations of various kinds. Three centuries later, Anthony M. Claret (1807-1870) spent some months at San Andrés del Pruit (Girona, Spain), dedicated to prayer. He went forth from this retreat powerfully consecrated to itinerant preaching.

Retreats of Spiritual Renewal. The practice of withdrawing for a relatively brief period of time in order to revitalize oneself spiritually seems to be evidenced in all religions that attach great importance to the spiritual experience of the individual.

Islam. The custom of devoting a period of time to prayer and fasting *(khalwah)*, while withdrawing from social contacts and ordinary occupations, is amply documented in the Muslim world much earlier than in Christendom. The Prophet himself left an example, by going frequently into retreat.

In Sufi orders, the superior of a house is obliged to go on retreat periodically. The novices, too, must make a retreat, ordinarily for forty days. The lives of the Sufi mystics contain numerous allusions to this practice (see Javad Nurbakhsh, *Masters of the Path,* New York, 1980, pp. 115, 117).

Christianity. In Christianity, especially during the last few centuries, this type of retreat, aimed at the spiritual renewal of the individual through meditation, prayer, and silence, has reached a high level of development.

Drawing their inspiration from the example of Jesus, the Christian churches established a period of forty days dedicated to fasting, abstinence, and greater prayer, in order to prepare the faithful for the celebration of the Pascha. Two themes were interwoven in the sermons of the Fathers on Lent: that of participation in Christ's struggles and sufferings during his passion as a preparation for the celebration of the Resurrection, and that of a model projection on it, of the fast and temptations of Jesus in the solitude of the Judean desert.

In the sixteenth century, retreat exercises according to the Ignatian method had already become popular, although they were practiced only by priests and religious at the time, not by the laity.

Priests, religious, and seminarians of the Roman Catholic church commonly make eight days of spiritual exercises annually. Many members of the Catholic laity follow the same norm in our time. Some periodically make even a month's exercises. Hence one may find retreat houses in all countries where the Roman Catholic church is present.

BIBLIOGRAPHY

Very little, if anything, of a general nature has been published on the topic of retreat. References to retreats, seclusion, and the like can be found in any general survey on Hindu, Muslim, and Christian mysticism, as well as in works dealing with phenomenology of religion.

Works dealing with specific traditions can, however, be recommended. For a discussion of retreat traditions in tribal societies, see Victor Turner's *The Forest of Symbols* (Ithaca, N. Y., 1969). On the role of seclusion in the Buddhist monastic tradition, see John C. Holt's *Discipline: The Canonical Buddhism of the Vinayapataha* (Delhi, 1981). On retreat in the Christian tradition, the *New Catholic Encyclopedia,* vol. 12 (New York, 1967), includes a valuable article by Thomas E. Dubay. Further discussion of the topic is available in *Historia de la practica de los Ejercicios Espirituales de San Ignacio de Loyola,* 2 vols. (Bilbao, Spain, 1946-1955), by Ignacio Iparraguirre. For the role of retreat in Eastern Orthodox churches, see Catherine de Hueck Doherty's *Sobornost* (Notre Dame, Ind., 1977). For discussion of Muslim retreats, see Muhammad ibn al-`Arabi's *Kitab al-khalwah* (Aya Sofia, 1964) and letters 96 and 22 in Sharafuddin Maneri's *The Hundred Letters,* translated by Paul Jackson (New York, 1980).

JUAN MANUEL LOZANO

REVELATION

The concept of revelation is a fundamental one in every religion that in any way traces its origin to God or a divinity. Revelation is a divine communication to human beings. This broad description allows the phenomenologist of religion to include very different manners and degrees of revelation. In general, religious phenomenologists use five different criteria (characteristics or factors) of revelation:

1. Origin or author: God, spirits, ancestors, power *(mana)*, forces. In every case the source of revelation is something supernatural or numinous.
2. Instrument or means: sacred signs in nature (the stars, animals, sacred places, or sacred times); dreams, visions, ecstasies; finally, words or sacred books.
3. Content or object: the didactic, helping, or punishing presence, will, being, activity, or commission of the divinity.
4. Recipients or addressees: medicine men, sorcerers, sacrificing priests, shamans, soothsayers, mediators, prophets with a commission or information intended for individuals or groups, for a people or the entire race.
5. Effect and consequence for the recipient: personal instruction or persuasion, divine mission, service as oracle—all this through inspiration or, in the supreme case, through incarnation.

It is to be noted that the historians of religion derived the concept of revelation from the Judeo-Christian religion where it received its theological elaboration and then in the course of research into the history of religions was transferred in a broad and analogous sense to other religions.

Whenever ultimate knowledge and the vision of supreme wisdom are regarded not as the fruit of human effort alone but as a gift from God, then, as in the experience of a profound union with God that cannot be acquired by force or produced by the human being but can only be received as a gift, a self-communication of a personal God comes into play and the concept of revelation is correctly applied.

The Bible. In his *Letter to the Romans,* the apostle Paul vividly states the possibility (not the actuality) of a natural knowledge of God. Ever since the creation of the world his invisible nature, namely, his eternal power and deity, has been clearly perceived in the things that have been made. Ever since the creation of the world, the invisible being of God has been known by reason. Human beings understand themselves to be creatures and therefore by reason know God's power and deity.

The *Wisdom of Solomon* says: "All men who were ignorant of God were foolish by nature; and they were unable from the good things that are seen to know him who exists..." (*Wis.* 13:1-5).

> **Revelation is given to the prophets and, in its definitive form, to Muhammad, who receives it in dreams, visions, and auditions.**

Old Testament and Judaism. Jewish theology regards it as inconceivable that human beings should know God by their own powers and apart from God making himself known, that is, revealing himself, to them. On the other hand, God's action toward Israel in the course of its history is always understood as revelatory in the strict sense. The people experience the nearness of God through external signs and events such as thunderstorms (*Ex.* 19:16), pillars of cloud and pillars of fire (*Ex.* 14:24), and the wind (*1 Kgs.* 19:12). As the history of salvation advanced it became increasingly important to interpret God's guidance of Israel. The result was revelation through words, taking the form of auditions and going beyond visions or else interpreting these. God's spirit filled the prophets; his hand was laid on the human beings he chose for this revelation.

The goal and purpose of revelation is the call of Israel to be a covenanted people. This purpose is served by the revelation of God as "the God of Abraham, the God of Isaac, and the God of Jacob" (*Ex.* 3:6), as well as by the announcement of his name, which is at one and the same time a promise of his presence as helper ("I will be there as the One who will be there"; *Ex.* 3:12) and a concealment and withdrawal of God from any control by human beings ("I am who I am"; *Ex.* 3:14). The paradigmatic saving action of God becomes a reality in the deliverance and exodus from Egypt (*Ex.* 14) and, climactically, in the conclusion of the covenant at Sinai (*Ex.* 19-20).

New Testament and Christianity. Building on the Old Testament understanding of revelation, the New Testament writers see revelation as the self-communication of God in and through Jesus Christ. This communication is regarded as the supreme, final, irrevocable, and unsurpassable self-disclosure of God in history (*Heb.* 1:1f.). It is unique because, as Christians understand it, in Jesus of Nazareth, agent of revelation and content of revelation (the person, teaching, and redemptive work of Jesus) are identical and make up the sole object of revelation.

Islam. Islam's understanding of revelation comes closest to that of the Bible. *Wahy,* or revelation, comes from God, usually through the agency of the archangel Gabriel. It is concerned with God's decrees, his mysterious will, the announcement of judgment, and his commandments, the divine law *(shari'ah).* Revelation is given to the prophets and, in its definitive form, to Muhammad (c. 570-632), who receives it in dreams, visions, and auditions. It is set down in the Qur'an, the uncreated archetype of which has been taken up to the throne of God in heaven. This uncreated word is not, however, the source of God's self-knowledge (as it is in Christian theology). To this extent, the Muslim conception resembles the Jewish, while at the same time it is distinguished from the latter by the absence of any promise.

Zoroastrianism. Zarathushtra (seventh to sixth century BCE) was another nonbiblical prophet. He too saw revelation as having its source in the voluntary action of a unique and personal God. The Mazdeans opt for the good and against evil. This tension soon hardens, however, into an ontic dualism. The world is divided between good and evil and thus reflects at all cosmic levels the opposition between the virtues and their contraries.

Hinduism. Even in Hinduism it is possible to speak of revelation as this concept is understood by historians of religion. The Vedas have the status of sacred revelation: *sruti* ("heard," i. e., revealed directly by the gods to seers) is clearly distinguished from *smrti* ("remembered," i. e., composed by men). According to Hindu belief, the Vedic literature has existed from eternity, is supernatural in origin, and has been transmitted to human beings by unknown seers of the primordial period.

BIBLIOGRAPHY

For basic information concerning the topic, entries in several reference works can be profitably consulted: "Offenbarung," in the *Lexikon für Theologie und Kirche,* 2d ed., vol. 7 (Freiburg, 1962); "Offenbarung," in *Die Religion in Geschichte und Gegenwart,* 3d ed., vol. 4 (Tübingen, 1960); and "Révélation" in the *Dictionnaire de théologie catholique,* vol. 6 (Paris, 1937). Karl Rahner's article

"Revelation," in *Sacramentum Mundi: An Encyclopedia of Theology,* vol. 5 (New York, 1969), is especially valuable.

Those aspects of revelation accessible to the phenomenology of religion are summarized in Gerardus van der Leeuw's *Religion in Essence and Manifestation,* 2 vols. (1938; reprint, Gloucester, Mass., 1967), and in Th. P. van Baaren's *Voorstellingen van Openbaring, phaenomenologisch beschouwd* (Utrecht, 1951), which includes an English summary. There is also a very good discussion in Herbert H. Farmer's *Revelation and Religion: Studies in the Theological Interpretation of Religious Types* (New York, 1954). For the history of religions approach, see the standard work of Mircea Eliade, *A History of Religious Ideas,* 3 vols. (Chicago, 1978-1986).

On the treatment of the topic within Islam, see A. J. Arberry's *Revelation and Reason in Islam* (London, 1957). On Hinduism, see K. Satchidananda Murty's *Revelation and Reason in Advaita Vedanta* (1959; reprint, Livingston, N. J., 1974).

For discussions of natural revelation, see Fernand van Steenberghen's *Dieu caché* (Louvain, 1961), translated as *Hidden God: How Do We Know That God Exists?* (Saint Louis, Mo., 1966), and Johannes Hirschberger's *Gottesbeweise: Vergängliches-Unvergängliches in denkender Glaube* (Frankfurt, 1966).

The following works treat the biblical concept of revelation: H. Wheeler Robinson's *Inspiration and Revelation in the Old Testament,* 4th ed. (Oxford, 1956); Erik Voegelin's *Order and History,* vol. 1, *Israel and Revelation* (Baton Rouge, 1956); Ernest Findlay Scott's *The New Testament Idea of Revelation* (New York, 1935); and Frederick C. Grant's *Introduction to New Testament Thought* (New York, 1950). For theological discussions of revelation, see Rudolf Bultmann's "The Concept of Revelation in the New Testament," in *Existence and Faith: Shorter Writings of Rudolf Bultmann,* edited and translated by Schubert M. Ogden (New York, 1960); Romano Guardini's *Die Offenbarung: Ihr Wesen und ihre Formen* (Würzburg, 1940); Karl Barth's *Das christliche Verständnis der Offenbarung* (Munich, 1948); Paul Tillich's *Systematic Theology,* 3 vols. (Chicago, 1951-1963); Karl Rahner's *Hearers of the Word* (New York, 1969); and *Revelation as History* (New York, 1968) by Wolfhart Pannenberg and others.

JOHANNES DENINGER
Translated from German by Matthew J. O'Connell

ROMAN CATHOLICISM

Roman Catholicism refers both to a church (or, more accurately, a college of churches that together constitute the universal Catholic church) and to a tradition. As a church, Roman Catholicism exists at both the local level and the universal level. In the canon law of the Roman Catholic church, the term "local church" (more often rendered as "particular church") applies primarily to a diocese and secondarily to a parish. The universal Roman Catholic church, on the other hand, is constituted by a union, or college, of all the local Catholic churches throughout the world. There are more than one-half billion Catholics worldwide, by far the largest body of Christians. [*See* Papacy *and* Church.]

As a tradition Roman Catholicism is marked by several different doctrinal and theological emphases. These are its radically positive estimation of the created order, because everything comes from the hand of God, is providentially sustained by God, and is continually transformed and elevated by God's active presence within it; its concern for history; its stress on mediation; and, finally, its affirmation of the communal dimension of salvation and of every religious relationship with God

Catholic Vision and Catholic Values. The church's belief in and commitment to the reality of God is focused in its fundamental attitude toward Jesus Christ (the *Christian* core). For Catholics, as for every Christian, the old order has passed away, and they are a "new creation" in Christ, for God has "reconciled us to himself through Christ" (*2 Cor.* 5:17, 5:19). "Catholic," therefore, is a qualification of "Christian," of "religious," and of the human.

To be Catholic is, before all else, to be human. Catholicism is an understanding and affirmation of human existence before it is a corporate conviction about the pope, or the seven sacraments, or even about Jesus Christ. But Catholicism is also more than a corporate understanding and affirmation of what it means to be human. Thomas Aquinas affirms that all reality is rooted in the creative, loving power of that which is most real *(ens realissimum).* Catholicism answers the question of meaning in terms of the reality of God. In brief, Catholicism is a religious perspective, and not simply a philosophical or anthropological one.

Catholicism's view of and commitment to God is radically shaped by its view of and commitment to Jesus Christ. For the Christian, the ultimate dimension of human experience is a triune God: a God who creates and sustains, a God who draws near to and identifies with the human historical condition, and a God who empowers people to live according to the vocation to which they have been called. More specifically, the God of Christians is the God of Jesus Christ. But just as Jesus Christ gives access to God, so, for the Catholic, the church gives access to Jesus Christ.

Roman Catholicism is distinguished from other Christian traditions and churches in its understanding of, commitment to, and exercise of the principles of sacramentality, mediation, and communion.

Sacramentality. The Catholic sacramental vision "sees" God in and through all things: other people, communities, movements, events, places, objects, the world at large, the whole cosmos. The great sacrament of our encounter with God, and of God's encounter with us, is Jesus Christ. The church, in turn, is the key sacrament of our encounter with Christ, and of Christ with us; and the sacraments, in turn, are the signs and instruments by which that ecclesial encounter with Christ is expressed, celebrated, and made effective for the glory of God and the salvation of men and women.

For the Catholic, the world is essentially good, though fallen, because it comes from the creative hand of God. And for the Catholic, the world, although fallen, is redeemable because of the redemptive work of God in Jesus Christ.

Mediation. A kind of corollary of the principle of sacramentality is the principle of mediation. A sacrament not only signifies; it also causes what it signifies. Indeed, as the Council of Trent officially taught, sacraments cause grace precisely insofar as they signify it. If the church, therefore, is not a credible sign of God's and Christ's presence in the world, if the church is not obviously the "temple of the Holy Spirit," it cannot achieve its missionary purposes. It "causes" grace (i. e., effectively moves the world toward its final destiny in the kingdom of God) to the extent that it signifies the reality toward which it presumes to direct the world. For the Catholic, God is not only present in the sacramental action; God actually achieves something in and through that action.

The principle of mediation also explains Catholicism's historic emphasis on the place of Mary, the mother of Jesus Christ. The Catholic readily engages in the veneration (not worship) of Mary, not because Catholicism perceives Mary as some kind of goddess or supercreature or rival of the Lord himself, but because she is a symbol or image of God. [See Mary.]

Communion. Finally, Catholicism affirms the principle of communion: the human way to God, and God's way to humankind, is not only a mediated but a communal way. Even when the divine-human encounter is most personal and individual, it is still communal, in that the encounter is made possible by the mediation of a community of faith. Catholics have always emphasized the place of the church as the sacrament of Christ, which mediates salvation through sacraments, ministries, and other institutional elements and forms, and as the communion of saints and the people of God.

Pope John XXIII and the Second Vatican Council.

John XXIII first announced his council on 25 January 1959 and officially convoked it on 25 December 1961. In his address at the council's solemn opening on 11 October 1962, he revealed again his spirit of fundamental hope. He believed that "Divine Providence is leading us to a new order of human relations." The purpose of the council, therefore, would be the promotion of "concord, just peace and the brotherly unity of all."

Although John XXIII died between the first two sessions of the council, his successor, Paul VI, carried his program to fulfillment:

1. Vatican II taught that the church is the people of God, a community of disciples. The hierarchy is part of the people of God, not separate from it.
2. The church must read the signs of the times and interpret them in the light of the gospel.

3. Christian unity requires renewal and reform. Both sides were to blame for the divisions of the Reformation; therefore both sides have to be open to change.
4. The word of God is communicated through sacred scripture, sacred tradition, and the teaching authority of the church, all linked together and guided by the Holy Spirit.
5. The church proclaims the gospel not only in word but also in sacrament. The signs, that is, language and rituals, must be intelligible.
6. No one is to be forced in any way to embrace the Christian or the Catholic faith. This principle is rooted in human dignity and the freedom of the act of faith.
7. God speaks also through other religions. The church should engage in dialogue and other collaborative efforts with them.

After four sessions the Second Vatican Council adjourned in December 1965. The story of Catholicism since the council—through the pontificates of Paul VI (1963-1978), John Paul I (1978), and John Paul II (1978-)—has been shaped

> **To be in the state of grace means to be open to the presence of God, and of the Holy Spirit in particular.**

largely, if not entirely, by the church's efforts to come to terms with the various challenges and opportunities which that council presented: specifically, how can the church remain faithful to its distinctively Catholic heritage even as it continues to affirm and assimilate such modern values as ecumenism, pluralism, and secularity?

Theology and Doctrine. The principles of sacramentality, mediation, and communion frame Catholic thinking and teaching about every significant theological question.

Revelation and faith. Catholics share with other Christians the conviction that God has somehow communicated with humankind in the history of Israel; supremely in Jesus Christ, the Son of God; then through the apostles and evangelists; and, in a different way, through nature, human events, and personal relationships. Fundamentally, all Christians, conservative and liberal alike, are united in the belief that Jesus Christ, as both person and event, provides the fullest disclosure of God. Christian faith is the acceptance of Jesus Christ as the Lord and Savior of the world and as the great sacrament of God's presence among us.

Creation and original sin. Roman Catholics adhere to the ancient Christian creeds, which professed their belief in one God, the Almighty Creator, who made the heavens and the earth, and all things visible and invisible. And they adhere as well to the later councils of the church, which added that

God freely created the world from nothing at the beginning of time in order to share his own goodness, to manifest his own glory, and to sanctify humankind. Jesus Christ is not only the head of the whole human race but also is himself the summit of all creation.

Original sin is the state in which all people are born precisely because they are members of the human race. As such, we are situated in a sinful history that affects our capacity to love God above all and to become the kind of people God destined us to be. What is important to remember, Catholics insist, is that we came forth from the hand of God essentially good, not essentially evil. Humankind is redeemable because men and women are radically good. [*For discussion of sin and related issues in broad religious perspective, see* Fall, The; Death; Evil; Redemption; *and* Incarnation.]

Nature and grace. Roman Catholics have never endorsed the view that people are saved by their own power. To be in the state of grace means to be open to the presence of God, and of the Holy Spirit in particular. This indwelling of the Spirit really transforms us. Our sins are not merely "covered over." They are obliterated by an act of divine forgiveness and generosity, on the sole condition that we are truly sorry for having offended God in the first place.

Jesus Christ and redemption. Roman Catholics share with other Christians the central conviction of Christian faith that Jesus of Nazareth is the Lord of history (*Phil.* 2:5-11), that he was crucified for our sins, was raised from the dead on the third day, was exalted as Lord of all, is present to history now in and through the church.

Jesus Christ is both human and divine in nature, yet one person. "Born of a woman" (*Gal.* 4:4), he is like us in all things save sin (*Heb.* 4:15). At the same time, he is of the very being of God, Son of the Father, the light of God in the world. He is, in the words of the Second Vatican Council, "the key, the focal point, and the goal of all human history".

Holy Spirit and Trinity. The Holy Spirit is God's self-communication as love and as the power of healing, reconciliation, and new life. The divinity of the Holy Spirit was defined by the First Council of Constantinople in 381. The Spirit has the same divine essence as the Father and the Son and yet is distinct from them both. Within the Trinity, the Spirit proceeds from the Father *through* the Son.

Catholic morality. For Catholicism, morality is a matter of thinking and acting in accordance with the person and the community one has become in Christ. Catholic morality is characterized by a both/and rather than an either/or approach. It is not nature or grace, but graced nature; not reason or faith, but reason illumined by faith; not law or gospel, but law inspired by the gospel; not scripture or tradition, but normative tradition within scripture; not faith or works, but faith issuing in works and works as expressions of faith; not authority or freedom, but authority in the service of

freedom; not the past versus the present, but the present in continuity with the past; not stability or change, but change in fidelity to stable principle, and principle fashioned and refined in response to change; not unity or diversity, but unity in diversity, and diversity that prevents uniformity, the antithesis of unity.

Polity. Just as the universal church is composed of an international college of local churches, so the universality of the church is expressed through the collegial relationship of the bishops, one to another. The bishop of Rome serves as the head and center of this collegial network. Bishops participate in the governance of the church through synods. The college of cardinals constitutes a special college of bishops within the larger episcopal college.

At the diocesan level there are bishops, auxiliary bishops, vicars general, chancellors, marriage courts, diocesan pastoral councils, and the like. At the parish level there are pastors, associate pastors, pastoral ministers, extraordinary ministers of the Eucharist, parish councils, and the like.

BIBLIOGRAPHY

Adam, Karl. *Das Wesen des Katholizismus.* Tübingen, 1924. Translated by Justin McCann as *The Spirit of Catholicism* (New York, 1954). Translated into many languages, including Chinese and Japanese, this work represents the best of pre-Vatican II Catholic theology, formulated in reaction to a prevailing neoscholasticism that tended to reduce Catholicism to a system of doctrines and laws. On the other hand, the text does reflect the exegetical, ecumenical, and ecclesiological limitations of its time.

Cunningham, Lawrence S. *The Catholic Heritage.* New York, 1983. Conveys the heart of Catholicism through certain ideal types, for example, martyrs, mystics, humanists, including "outsiders" like James Joyce and Simone Weil.

Delaney, John, ed. *Why Catholic?* Garden City, N. Y., 1979. A collection of essays by various American Catholic figures on their understanding of the meaning of Catholicism and on their own personal appropriation of that meaning. Contributors include Andrew Greeley, Abigail McCarthy, and Archbishop Fulton Sheen.

Gilkey, Langdon. *Catholicism Confronts Modernity: A Protestant View.* New York, 1975. Chapter 1, "The Nature of the Crisis," is particularly useful because it identifies what the author regards as the essentially positive characteristics of Catholicism: sacramentality, rationality, tradition, and peoplehood.

Happel, Stephen, and David Tracy. *A Catholic Vision.* Philadelphia, 1984. The approach is historical and the thesis is that Catholicism emerges progressively and processively as it encounters new forms of life that it constantly attempts to understand and transform. Jointly authored, the book may lack the necessary clarity and coherence that a less sophisticated inquirer would require.

Haughton, Rosemary. *The Catholic Thing.* Springfield, Ill., 1979. An original approach that portrays Catholicism as a reality shaped by an enduring conflict between what the author calls "Mother Church" (the more traditional, institutional side) and "Sophia" (the more unpredictable, communal side). In this regard, the book is similar to Cunningham's (above).

Hellwig, Monika K. *Understanding Catholicism.* New York, 1981. Covers some of the doctrinal and theological territory treated in my more comprehensive *Catholicism* (below), but without so much attention to historical and documentary detail.

Lubac, Henri de. *Catholicisme.* Paris, 1938. Translated by Lancelot C. Sheppard as *Catholicism: A Study of the Corporate Destiny of Mankind* (New York, 1958). As its English subtitle suggests, the book underlines the essentially social nature of Catholicism—in its creeds and doctrines, in its sacramental life, and in its vision of history. It draws heavily on patristic and medieval sources, excerpts of which are provided in an appendix.

McBrien, Richard P. *Catholicism.* Rev. ed. 2 vols. in 1. Minneapolis, 1981. The most comprehensive, up-to-date exposition of Catholic history, theology, and doctrine available. Its main lines are reflected in this article.

Rahner, Karl, and Joseph Ratzinger. *Episkopat und Primat.* Freiburg im Bresgau, 1962. Translated by Kenneth Barker and others as *The Episcopate and the Primacy* (New York, 1962). An important corrective to exaggerated notions of papal authority, and at the same time a significant contribution to the literature on the meaning of collegiality. Its ideas, written before Vatican II, were essentially adopted by the council.

RICHARD P. MCBRIEN

ROMAN RELIGION

The Roman state's extraordinary and unexpected transformation from one that had hegemony over the greater part of Italy into a world state in the second and first centuries BCE had implications for Roman religion which are not easy to grasp. After all, Christianity, a religion wholly "foreign" in its origins, arose from this period of Roman ascendancy. To begin, then, to understand the religious system of imperial Rome, it is best to confine ourselves to three elementary and obviously related facts.

The first is that the old Roman practice of inviting the chief gods of their enemies to become gods of Rome (*evocatio*) played little or no part in the new stage of imperialism.

The second fact is that while it was conquering the Hellenistic world Rome was involved in a massive absorption of Greek language, literature, and religion, with the consequence that the Roman gods became victorious over Greece at precisely the time that they came to be identified with Greek gods. As the gods were expected to take sides and to favor their own worshipers, this must have created some problems.

The third fact is that the conquest of Africa, Spain, and, ultimately, Gaul produced the opposite phenomenon of a large, though by no means systematic, identification of Punic, Iberian, and Celtic gods with Roman gods. This, in turn, is connected with two opposite aspects of the Roman conquest of the West. On the one hand, the Romans had little sympathy and understanding for the religion of their Western subjects. On the other hand, northern Africa, outside Egypt, and western Europe were deeply latinized in language and romanized in institutions, thereby creating the conditions for the assimilation of native gods to Roman gods.

Yet the Mars, the Mercurius, and even the Jupiter and the Diana we meet so frequently in Gaul under the Romans are not exactly the same as in Rome. The assimilation of the native god is often revealed by an accompanying adjective (in Gaul, Mars Lenus, Mercurius Dumiatis, etc.,). An analogous phenomenon had occurred in the East under the Hellenistic monarchies: native, especially Semitic, gods were assimilated to Greek gods, especially to Zeus and Apollo. The Eastern assimilation went on under Roman rule (as seen, for example, with Zeus Panamaros in Caria).

The Romans also turned certain gods of Greek origin into gods of victory. As early as 145 BCE L. Mummius dedicated a temple to Hercules Victor after his triumph over Greece. After a victory, generals often offered 10 percent of their booty to Hercules, and Hercules Invictus was a favorite god of Pompey. Apollo was connected with Victory as early as 212 BCE.

Imperial Attitudes toward and Uses of Religion. Augustus and his contemporaries thought, or perhaps in some cases wanted other people to think, that the preceding age (roughly the period from the Gracchi to Caesar) had seen a decline in the ancient Roman care for gods. Augustus himself stated in the autobiographical record known as the *Res gestae* that he and his friends had restored eighty-two temples. He revived cults and religious associations, such as the Arval Brothers and the fraternity of the Titii, and appointed a *flamen dialis,* a priestly office that had been left vacant since 87 BCE.

Marius was accompanied in his campaigns by a Syrian prophetess. Sulla apparently brought from Cappadocia the goddess Ma, soon identified with Bellona, whose orgiastic and prophetic cult had wide appeal. Furthermore, he developed a personal devotion to Venus and Fortuna and set an example for Caesar, who claimed Venus as the ancestress of the *gens Julia.* As *pontifex maximus* for twenty years, Caesar reformed not only individual cults but also the calendar, which had great religious significance.

Unusual religious attitudes were not confined to leaders. A Roman senator, Nigidius Figulus, made religious combinations of his own both in his writings and in his practice: magic, astrology, and Pythagoreanism were some of the ingredients. Cicero, above all, epitomized the search of educated men of the first century BCE for the right balance between respect for the ancestral cults and the requirements of philosophy.

The Augustan restoration discouraged philosophical speculation about the nature of the gods: Lucretius's *De rerum natura* remains characteristic of the age of Caesar. Augustan poets (Horace, Tibullus, Propertius, and Ovid) evoked obsolescent rites and emphasized piety. Vergil interpreted the Roman past in religious terms. Nevertheless, the combined effect of the initiatives of Caesar and Augustus amounted to a new religious situation.

For centuries the aristocracy in Rome had controlled what was called *ius sacrum* ("sacred law"), the religious aspect of Roman life, but the association of priesthood with political magistracy, though frequent and obviously convenient, had never been institutionalized. In 27 BCE the assumption by Octavian of the permanent title *augustus* implied, though not very clearly, permanent approval of the gods (*augustus* may connote a holder of permanent favorable auspices). In 12 BCE Augustus assumed the position of *pontifex maximus,* which became permanently associated with the figure of the emperor *(imperator)*, the new head for life of the Roman state. Augustus's new role resulted in an identification of religious with political power

As the head of Roman religion, the Roman emperor was therefore in the paradoxical situation of being responsible not only for relations between the Roman state and the gods but

> **A further step was the admission of Oriental gods to the official religion of Rome, such as the building of a temple to Isis under Gaius.**

also for a fair assessment of his own qualifications to be considered a god, if not after his life, at least while he was alive.

Within the city of Rome, the emperor was in virtual control of the public cults. As a Greek god, Apollo had been kept outside of the *pomerium* since his introduction into Rome: his temple was in the Campus Martius. Under Augustus, however, Apollo received a temple inside the *pomerium* on the Palatine in recognition of the special protection he had offered to Octavian. The Sibylline Books, an ancient collection of prophecies that had been previously preserved on the Capitol, were now transferred to the new temple. Later, Augustus demonstrated his preference for Mars as a family god, and a temple to Mars Ultor (the avenger of Caesar's murder) was built. Another example of these changes inside Rome is the full romanization of the Etruscan haruspices performed by the emperor Claudius in 47 CE (Tacitus, *Annals* 11.15).

A further step was the admission of Oriental gods to the official religion of Rome, such as the building of a temple to Isis under Gaius. Jupiter Dolichenus, an Oriental god popular among soldiers, was probably given a temple on the Aventine in the second century CE.

Coins and medals, insofar as they were issued under the control of the central government, provide some indication of imperial preferences in the matter of gods and cults. They allow us to say when and how certain Oriental cults (such as

that of Isis, as reflected on coins of Vespasian) or certain attributes of a specific god were considered helpful to the empire and altogether suitable for the man in the street who used coins. But since as a rule it avoided references to cults of rulers, coinage can be misleading if taken alone. Imperial cult and Oriental cults are, in fact, two of the most important features of Roman religion in the imperial period. But we also have to take into consideration popular, not easily definable trends; the religious beliefs or disbeliefs of the intellectuals; the greater participation of women in religious and in intellectual life generally; and, finally, the peculiar problems presented by the persecution of Christianity.

The Imperial Cult. Imperial cult was many things to many people. The emperor never became a complete god, even if he was considered a god, because he was not requested to produce miracles, even for supposed deliverance from peril. Ultimately, the cult of the living emperor mattered more.

The cult of Roman provincial governors disappeared with Augustus, to the exclusive benefit of the emperor and his family. When he did not directly encourage the ruler cult, the emperor still had to approve, limit, and occasionally to refuse it. Although he had to be worshiped, he also had to remain a man in order to live on social terms with the Roman aristocracy, of which he was supposed to be the *princeps*. It was a delicate balancing act. It is probably fair to say that during his lifetime the emperor was a god more in proportion to his remoteness, rather than his proximity, and that the success (for success it was) of the imperial cult in the provinces was due to the presence it endowed to an absent and alien sovereign. His statues, his temples, and his priests, as well as the games, sacrifices, and other ceremonial acts, helped make the emperor present; they also helped people to express their interest in the preservation of the world in which they lived.

Schematically it can be said that in Rome and Italy Augustus favored the association of the cult of his life spirit *(genius)* with the old cult of the public lares of the crossroads *(lares compitales)*: such a combined cult was in the hands of humble people. Similar associations (Augustales) developed along various lines in Italy and gave respectability to the freedmen who ran them. Augustus's birthday was considered a public holiday. His *genius* was included in public oaths between Jupiter Optimus Maximus and the *penates*. In Augustus's last years Tiberius dedicated an altar to the *numen Augusti* in Rome; the four great priestly colleges had to make yearly sacrifices at it.

Augustus's successors tended to be worshiped either individually, without the addition of Roma, or collectively with past emperors. In Asia Minor the last individual emperor known to have received a personal priesthood or temple is Caracalla. In this province—though not necessarily elsewhere—the imperial cult petered out at the end of the third century. Nevertheless, Constantine, in the fourth century, authorized the building of a temple for the *gens Flavia* (his own family).

When the imperial cult died out, the emperor had to be justified as the choice of god; he became emperor by the grace of god. Thus Diocletian and Maximian, the persecutors of Christianity, present themselves not as Jupiter and Hercules but as Jovius and Herculius, that is, the protégés of Jupiter and Hercules. It must be added that during the first centuries of the empire the divinization of the emperor was accompanied by a multiplication of divinizations of private individuals, in the West often of humble origin. Such divinization took the form of identifying the dead, and occasionally the living, with a known hero or god. Sometimes the divinization was nothing more than an expression of affection by relatives or friends. But it indicated a tendency to reduce the distance between men and gods, which helped the fortunes of the imperial cult.

Oriental Influences. Oriental cults penetrated the Roman empire at various dates, in different circumstances, and with varying appeal. They tended, though not in equal measure, to present themselves as mystery cults.

> When the imperial cult died out, the emperor had to be justified as the choice of god; he became emperor by the grace of god.

Cybele, the first Oriental divinity to be found acceptable in Rome since the end of the third century BCE, was long an oddity in the city. As the Magna Mater ("great mother"), she had been imported by governmental decision, she had a temple within the *pomerium,* and she was under the protection of members of the highest Roman aristocracy. Yet her professional priests, singing in Greek and living by their temple, were considered alien fanatics even in imperial times. What is worse, the goddess also had servants, the Galli, who had castrated themselves to express their devotion to her.

Although Isis appealed to men as well as to women— and indeed her priests were male—it seems clear that her prestige as a goddess was due to the unusual powers she was supposed to have as a woman. In association with Osiris or Sarapis, Isis seems to have become the object of a mystery cult in the first century CE; as such she appears in Apuleius's *Metamorphoses.* [*See* Isis.]

Late in the first century CE, Mithraism began to spread throughout the Roman empire, especially in the Danubian countries and in Italy (in particular, as far as we know, in Ostia and Rome). A developed mystery cult, it had ranks of initiation and leadership and was, to the best of our present knowledge, reserved to men. The environment of the Mithraic cult, as revealed in numerous extant chapels, was one of darkness, secrecy, dramatic lighting effects, and magic.

The cult of Sabazios may have been originally Phrygian. Sabazios appears in Athens in the fifth century BCE as an orgiastic god. He was known to Aristophanes, and later the orator Aeschines became his priest. In Rome his cult left a particularly curious document in the tomb of Vincentius, located in the catacomb of Praetextatus; it includes scenes of banquets and of judgment after death. Whether this is evidence of mystery ceremonies or of Christian influence remains uncertain. (See Erwin R. Goodenough, *Jewish Symbols in the Greco-Roman Period,* vol. 2, 1953, p. 45, for a description.)

Another popular Oriental god occupies a place by himself. This is Jupiter Dolichenus, who emerged from Doliche in Commagene in the first century CE and for whom we have about six hundred monuments. Of the Oriental gods, he seems to have been the least sophisticated and to have disappeared earliest (in the third century). He was ignored by Christian polemicists. While he circulated in the empire, he preserved his native attributes: he is depicted as a warrior with Phrygian cap, double ax, and lightning bolt, standing erect over a bull.

Extent of Syncretism. We are in constant danger of either overrating or underrating the influence of these Oriental cults on the fabric of the Roman empire. If, for instance, Mithraists knew of the Zoroastrian deity Angra Mainyu, what did he mean to them? How did this knowledge affect the larger society? At a superficial level we can take these cults as an antidote to the imperial cult, an attempt to retreat from the public sphere of political allegiance to the private sphere of small, free associations. The need for small loyalties was widely felt during the imperial peace. Tavern keepers devoted to their wine god and poor people meeting regularly in burial clubs are examples of such associations *(collegia).* Ritualization of ordinary life emerged from their activities. Nor is it surprising that what to one was religion was superstition to another. Although allegiance to the local gods (and respect for them, if one happened to be a visitor) was deeply rooted, people were experimenting with new private gods and finding satisfaction in them. Concern with magic and astrology, with dreams and demons, seems ubiquitous. Conviviality was part of religion.

It remains a puzzle how, and how much, ordinary people were supposed to know about official Roman religion. The same problem exists concerning the Greeks in relation to the religions of individual Greek cities. But in Greek cities the collective education of adolescents, as *epheboi,* implied participation in religious activities (for instance, singing hymns in festivals) which were a form of religious education. In the Latin-speaking world, however, there is no indication of generalized practices of this kind.

Another element difficult to evaluate is the continuous, and perhaps increased, appeal of impersonal gods within Roman religion. There is no indication that Faith (Fides) and Hope (Spes) increased their appeal. (They came to play a different part in Christianity by combining with Jewish and Greek ideas.) At best, Fides gained prestige as a symbol of return to loyalty and good faith during the reign of Augustus. But Fortuna, Tutela, and Virtus were popular; the typology of Virtus on coins seems to be identical with that of Roma.

A third element of complication is what is called syncretism, by which we really mean two different things. One is the positive identification of two or more gods; the other is the tendency to mix different cults by using symbols of other gods in the sanctuary of one god, with the result that the presence of Sarapis, Juno, and even Isis was implied in the shrine of Jupiter Dolichenus on the Aventine in Rome. In either form, syncretism may have encouraged the idea that all gods are aspects, or manifestations, of one god.

Role of Women. Women seem to have taken a more active, and perhaps a more creative, part in the religious life of the imperial period. This was connected with the considerable freedom of movement and of administration of one's own estate which women, and especially wealthy women, had in the Roman empire. Roman empresses of Oriental origin (Julia Domna, wife of Septimius Severus, and Julia Mamaea, mother of Severus Alexander) contributed to the diffusion outside Africa of the cult of Caelestis, who received a temple on the Capitol in Rome. The wife of a Roman consul, Pompeia Agrippinilla, managed to put together a private association of about four hundred devotees of Liber-Dionysos in the Roman Campagna in the middle of the second century CE. (See the inscription published by Achille Vogliano in the *American Journal of Archaeology* 37, 1933, p. 215.) Women could be asked to act as *theologoi,* that is, to preach about gods in ceremonies even of a mystery nature.

Dedications of religious and philosophical books by men to women appear in the imperial period. Plutarch dedicated his treatise on Isis and Osiris to Clea, a priestess of Delphi; Diogenes Laertius dedicated his book on Greek philosophers (which has anti-Christian implications) to a female Platonist. Philostratus claims that Julia Domna encouraged him to write the life of Apollonius of Tyana.

Literary Evidence. Epigraphy and archaeology have taught us much, but the religion of the Roman empire survives mainly through writings in Latin, Greek, Syriac, and Coptic (not to speak of other languages): biographies, philosophical disputations, epic poems, antiquarian books, exchanges of letters, novels, and specific religious books. The Stoic Lucan in his *Pharsalia,* a poem on the civil wars, excludes the gods but admits fate and fortune, magic and divination. Two generations later, Silius Italicus wrote an optimistic poem, turning on Scipio as a Roman Herakles supported by his father, Jupiter. More or less at the same time,

Plutarch was reflecting on new and old cults, on the delays in divine justice, and (if the work in question is indeed his) on superstition.

The variety of moods and experiences conveyed by these texts, from the skeptical to the mystical, from the egotistic to the political in the old Greek sense, gives us an approximate notion of the thoughts of educated people on religious subjects. These books provide the background for an understanding of the Christian apologists who wrote for the pagan upper class. Conversely, we are compelled to ask how much of pagan religious thinking was conditioned by the presence of Jews and, even more, of Christians in the neighborhood. The anti-Jewish attitudes of a Tacitus or of a Juvenal offer no special problem: they are explicit.

The most problematic texts are perhaps those which try to formulate explicit religious beliefs. Even a simple military religious calendar (such as the third-century Feriale Duranum, copied for the benefit of the garrison of Dura-Europos) raises the question of its purpose and validity: how many of these old-fashioned Roman festivals were still respected? When we come to such books as the *Chaldean Oracles* (late second century?) or the Hermetic texts, composed in Greek at various dates in Egypt (and clearly showing the influence of Jewish ideas), it is difficult to decide who believed in them and to what extent. Such texts present themselves as revealed: they speak of man's soul imprisoned in the body, of fate, and of demonic power with only a minimum of coherence. They are distantly related to what modern scholars call gnosticism, a creed with many variants which was supposed to be a deviation from Christianity and, as such, was fought by early Christian apologists.

State Repression and Persecution. The Roman state had always interfered with the freedom to teach and worship. In republican times astrologers, magicians, philosophers, and even rhetoricians, not to speak of adepts of certain religious groups, had been victims of such intrusion. Under which precise legal category this interference was exercised remains a question, except perhaps in cases of sacrilege. Augustus prohibited Roman citizens from participating in druidic cults, and Claudius prohibited the cult of the druids altogether. Details are not clear, and consequences not obvious, though one hears little of the druids from this time on.

This being said, we must emphasize how unusual it was for the Roman government to come to such decisions. Existing cults might or might not be encouraged, but they were seldom persecuted. Even Jews and Egyptians were ordinarily protected in their cults, although there were exceptions. The long-standing conflict between the Christians and the Roman state—even taking into account that persecution was desultory—remains unique for several reasons which depended more on Christian than on imperial behavior. First, the Christians obviously did not yield or retreat, as did the druids. Second, the Christians hardly ever became outright enemies of, or rebels against, the Roman state. The providential character of the Roman state was a basic assumption of Christianity. The workings of providence were shown, for Christians, by the fact that Jesus was born under Roman rule, while the Roman state had destroyed the Temple of Jerusalem and dispersed the Jews, thus making the church the heiress to the Temple. Third, the Christians were interested in what we may call classical culture. Their debate with the pagans became, increasingly, a debate within the terms of reference of classical culture; the Jews, however, soon lost their contact with classical thought and even with such men as Philo, who had represented them in the dialogue with classical culture. Fourth, Christianity and its ecclesiastical organization provided what could alternatively be either a rival or a subsidiary structure to the imperial government; the choice was left to the Roman government, which under Constantine chose the church as a subsidiary institution (without quite knowing on what conditions).

The novelty of the conflict explains the novelty of the solution—not tolerance but conversion. The emperor had to become Christian and to accept the implications of his conversion. It took about eighty years to turn the pagan state into a Christian state. The process took the form of a series of decisions about public non-Christian acts of worship. The first prohibition of pagan sacrifices seems to have been enacted in 341 (*Codex Theodosianus* 16.10.2). Closing of the pagan temples and prohibition of sacrifices in public places under penalty of death was stated or restated at an uncertain date between 346 and 354 (ibid., 16.10.4).

BIBLIOGRAPHY

Georg Wissowa's *Religion und Kultus der Römer,* 2d ed. (Munich, 1912), and Kurt Latte's *Römische Religionsgeschichte* (Munich, 1960) are basic reading on the topic. They are supplemented by Martin P. Nilsson's *Geschichte der griechischen Religion,* vol. 2, 3d ed. (Munich, 1974), for the eastern side of the Roman empire. Jean Bayet's *Histoire politique et psychologique de la religion romaine* (Paris, 1957) proposes an alternative approach and is improved in the Italian translation, *La religione romana: Storia politica e psicologica* (Turin, 1959). All the publications by Franz Cumont and Arthur Darby Nock remain enormously valuable and influential. See, for instance, Cumont's *Astrology and Religion among the Greeks and Romans* (New York, 1912), *After Life in Roman Paganism* (New Haven, 1922), *Les religions orientales dans le paganisme romain,* 4th ed. (Paris, 1929), *Recherches sur le symbolisme funéraire des Romains* (Paris, 1942), and *Lux Perpetua* (Paris, 1949); see also Nock's *Conversion: The Old and the New in Religion from Alexander the Great to Augustine of Hippo* (Oxford, 1933) and his essays in *The Cambridge Ancient History,* vol. 10 (Cambridge, 1934) and vol. 12 (Cambridge, 1939), and in *Essays on Religion and the Ancient World,* 2 vols., edited by Zeph Stewart (Cambridge, Mass., 1972). The scattered contributions by Louis Robert on epigraphic evidence are also indispensable; see, for instance, his *Hellenica,* 13 vols. (Limoges and Paris, 1940-1965).

Among more recent general books are J. H. W. G. Liebeschuetz's *Continuity and Change in Roman Religion* (Oxford, 1979), Ramsay MacMullen's *Paganism in the Roman Empire* (New Haven, 1981), Alan Wardman's *Religion and Statecraft among the Romans* (London, 1982), and John Scheid's *Religion et piété à Rome* (Paris, 1985). Volumes 2.16, 2.17, and 2.23 of *Aufstieg und Niedergang der römischen Welt* (Berlin and New York, 1978-1984) are mostly devoted to Roman imperial paganism and are of great importance. Ramsay MacMullen's *Christianizing the Roman Empire, A. D. 100-400* (New Haven, 1984) supplements his previous book from the Christian side.

Numerous monographs have been published on various topics. Here I can indicate only a few.

On the basic changes in Roman religion: Arthur Bernard Cook, *Zeus: A Study in Ancient Religion,* 3 vols. (Cambridge, 1914-1940); Johannes Geffcken, *Der Ausgang des griechisch-römischen Heidentums* (Heidelberg, 1920); Bernhard Kötting, *Peregrinatio religiosa: Wallfahrten in der Antike und das Pilgerwesen in der alten Kirche* (Münster, 1950); Frederick H. Cramer, *Astrology in Roman Law and Politics* (Philadelphia, 1954); Arnaldo Momigliano, ed., *The Conflict between Paganism and Christianity in the Fourth Century* (Oxford, 1963); E. R. Dodds, *Pagan and Christian in an Age of Anxiety* (Cambridge, 1965); Clara Gallini, *Protesta e integrazione nella Roma antica* (Bari, 1970); Peter Brown, *Religion and Society in the Age of Saint Augustine* (London, 1972); Javier Teixidor, *The Pagan God: Popular Religion in the Greco-Roman Near East* (Princeton, 1977); Sabine G. MacCormack, *Art and Ceremony in Late Antiquity* (Berkeley, 1981); Peter Brown, *Society and the Holy in Late Antiquity* (Berkeley, 1982). See also Morton Smith's article "Prolegomena to a Discussion of Aretalogies, Divine Men, the Gospels and Jesus," *Journal of Biblical Literature* 90 (June 1971): 174-199.

On the imperial cult: Christian Habicht, *Gottmenschentum und griechische Städte,* 2d ed. (Munich, 1970); Stefan Weinstock, *Divus Julius* (Oxford, 1971); Elias J. Bickerman et al., eds., *Le culte des souverains dans l'empire romain* (Geneva, 1973); J. Rufus Fears, *Princeps a diis electus: The Divine Election of the Emperor as a Political Concept at Rome* (Rome, 1977); S. R. F. Price, *Rituals and Power: The Roman Imperial Cult in Asia Minor* (Cambridge, 1984). Price's book should be supplemented by his article "Gods and Emperors: The Greek Language of the Roman Imperial Cult," *Journal of Hellenic Studies* 94 (1984): 79-95. See also H. W. Pleket's "An Aspect of the Emperor Cult: Imperial Mysteries," *Harvard Theological Review* 58 (October 1965): 331-347; Lellia Cracco Ruggini's "Apoteosi e politica senatoria nel IV sec. d. C.," *Rivista storica italiana* (1977): 425-489; and Keith Hopkins's *Conquerors and Slaves* (Cambridge, 1978), pp. 197-242.

On specific periods or individual gods: Jean Beaujeu, *La religion romaine à l'apogée de l'empire,* vol. 1, *La politique religieuse des Antonins, 96-192* (Paris, 1955); Marcel Leglay, *Saturne africaine* (Paris, 1966); R. E. Witt, *Isis in the Graeco-Roman World* (London, 1971); Robert Turcan, *Mithras Platonicus: Recherches sur l'hellénisation philosophique de Mithra* (Leiden, 1975); Maarten J. Vermaseren, *Cybele and Attis* (London, 1977); Friedrich Solmsen, *Isis among the Greeks and Romans* (Cambridge, Mass., 1979); Reinhold Merkelbach, *Mithras* (Königstein, West Germany, 1984). See also Merkelbach's article "Zum neuen Isistext aus Maroneia," *Zeitschrift für Papyrologie und Epigraphik* 23 (1976): 234-235.

On Roman sacrifice (not yet studied so thoroughly as Greek practices), see *Le sacrifice dans l'antiquité,* "Entretiens Fondation Hardt," no. 27 (Geneva, 1981), and for a theory of the mystery cult in the novels, see Reinhold Merkelbach's *Roman und Mysterium in der Antike* (Munich, 1962). Kurt Rudolph's *Gnosis: The Nature and History of Gnosticism* (San Francisco, 1983) and Giovanni Filoramo's *L'attesa della fine: Storia della gnosi* (Bari, 1983) are the best introductions to the subject, while *Gnosis und Gnostizismus,* edited by Rudolph (Darmstadt, 1975), provides a retrospective anthology of opinions. The collective volumes *Die orientalischen Religionen im Römerreich,* edited by Maarten J. Vermaseren (Leiden, 1981), and *La soteriologia dei culti orientali,* edited by Ugo Bianchi and Vermaseren (Leiden, 1982), provide further guidance in current research on various topics. Noteworthy also are the seminal essays in *Jewish and Christian Self-definition,* vol. 3, *Self-definition in the Graeco-Roman World,* edited by B. F. Meyer and E. P. Sanders (London, 1982).

For the transition from paganism to Christianity, the work of Lellia Cracco Ruggini is essential. See, for example, her "Simboli di battaglia ideologica nel tardo ellenismo," in *Studi storici in onore di Ottorino Bertolini* (Pisa, 1972), pp. 117-300; *Il paganesimo romano tra religione e politica, 384-394 d. C.,* "Memorie della classe di scienze morali, Accademia Nazionale dei Lincei," 8.23.1 (Rome, 1979); and "Pagani, ebrei e cristiani: Odio sociologico e odio teologico nel mondo antico," *Gli ebrei nell'Alto Medioevo* (Spoleto) 26 (1980): 13-101.

ARNALDO MOMIGLIANO

ROSENZWEIG, FRANZ

ROSENZWEIG, FRANZ (1886-1929), German-Jewish philosophical theologian, writer, translator of Jewish classical literature, and influential Jewish educational activist. Generally regarded as the most important Jewish philosophical theologian of this century, Rosenzweig also became a model of what the Jewish personality in the twentieth-century West might be.

He was born into an old, affluent, and highly acculturated German-Jewish family in Kassel, in which the sense of Jewishness, though lively, had shrunk to a matter of upper middle-class formalities. He studied at several German universities, ranging over multiple disciplines, and finished as a student of Friedrich Meinecke, the important German political and cultural historian. During those years he also had intense conversations on religion in the modern world, especially with close relatives and friends, several of whom had converted to Christianity. Having already adopted a strong German nationalist outlook, Rosenzweig also tried to sort out his own religious convictions at the very time that he was writing his Ph. D. dissertation (on Schelling and Hegel) and his first important book (*Hegel und der Staat,* 2 vols., 1920). In a night-long conversation on 7 July 1913 with his cousin, the physiologist Rudolf Ehrenberg (who had become a Christian theologian), and his distant relative Eugen Rosenstock-Huessy (later the influential Protestant theologian, also a convert), Rosenzweig decided that he, too, ought to become a Christian; however, he would take this step "as a Jew," not "as a pagan," and he would, therefore, briefly return to the synagogue. His experience there during the High Holy Days that year, however, changed Rosenzweig's mind completely: he would instead turn himself from a nomi-

nal into a substantial Jew, and he would devote his life to Jewish values. He studied with and became a close friend to the Neo-Kantian philosopher Hermann Cohen, who was then living in Berlin in retirement but was still very active with Jewish writing and teaching. Rosenzweig immediately began to write on Jewish subjects.

During World War I, Rosenzweig served in various, mainly military, capacities. He continued, however, to correspond with Rosenstock-Huessy on theological matters (Rosenstock-Huessy, *Judaism despite Christianity,* Alabama, 1968) and with Cohen and others on Jewish matters. He also wrote and published essays on historical, political, military, and educational subjects. Assigned to eastern Europe and the Balkans, he experienced some of the full-blooded life of the Jewish communities there. Above all, he began on postcards to his mother the composition that he finished on returning home from the war—his magnum opus, *Der Stern der Erlösung* (The Star of Redemption, Frankfurt, 1921). An injury he sustained during the war may have been the cause of his severe and eventually fatal postwar illness.

The Star of Redemption is a complex, difficult, and ambitious work, in some ways comparable to Hegel's *Phenomenology of Spirit.* The introduction to the first part argues that the fundamental and ineluctably individualistic fact of human death breaks up all philosophy qua monism, idealistic or materialistic, into the three realities of human

> **Rosenzweig and Buber were joined as teachers by well-known chemists, physicians, sociologists, and activists. . . .**

experience: man, God, and the world. (Metaphysical empiricism is thus an apt name for what Rosenzweig also calls "the new thinking.") In the first part, he philosophically "constructs" these three realities very much in the manner of the later Schelling, as logico-mathematical and metaphysical entities. In this condition man, God, and the world constitute the "pagan" universe: they exist without interrelationships, as three unconnected points.

In the second part, the three realities enter into relationships with one another through "revelation," that is, by continuously revealing themselves to each other. God reveals his love to man and thus becomes available to human prayer, and the world is revealed as divine creation, available to human transformation. Speech is the operative force in this dimension of the world. Three points have formed a triangle. The final part of the book establishes the second triangle of the "star of redemption" when the individual relations between man, God, and the world are transformed into collective, historical forces, specifically, Judaism and Christianity. (Two interlocking triangles form the hexagram that is the Magen David, the Star of David, symbol of redemption.) Judaism is "the fire in the star"; that is, Israel is "with God/the truth," outside of history, in eternity. Christianity is the rays from the star on pilgrimage through the world and history toward God/the truth, in order to conquer the kingdom of God's eventual universal realm. In this dimension of the world, collective speech—liturgy and hymn—is the operative force. Judaism and Christianity are the two valid covenants—Sinai for Jews and Calvary for the rest of mankind, to be unified only when the road to truth has brought the Christian world to the Jewish domicile in truth. In the meantime loving acts of believers are to "verify" the love of revelation and prepare the eschatological verity of God as "the all in all." (Truth is thus Hegelian-existentialist "subjectivity," and the three parts of *The Star* explicate the basic theological triad of creation, revelation, and redemption.)

After the war Rosenzweig wanted to translate his beliefs and his pronounced educational interests into action. He settled in Frankfurt, where he entered into close relationships with Nehemiah Nobel, the Orthodox rabbi of the community; with Martin Buber; with a younger generation of German Jews; and with eastern European Jews on their way west. He founded what became famous as the Free Jewish House of Learning (Lehrhaus), in which teachers and students together sought out classic Jewish sources and, translating and publishing them, tried them out on the modern world. Rosenzweig and Buber were joined as teachers by well-known chemists, physicians, sociologists, and activists, and such influential contemporary Jewish scholars as S. D. Goitein, Ernst Simon, Gershom Scholem, Hans Kohn, Erich Fromm, and Nahum N. Glatzer.

Rosenzweig married in 1920 and fathered a son just before coming down with a disease so grave that he was expected to die within months. Instead he lived for six years, so paralyzed, however, that ultimately he could communicate only by blinking an eyelid to the recitation of the alphabet. Nevertheless his associates flocked to his side and spread his influence. Rosenzweig continued to write philosophical and religious essays and conducted a large correspondence. He edited the *Jüdische Schriften* (Jewish Writings) of Hermann Cohen (3 vols., Berlin, 1924) and, in an extensive introduction, reinterpreted Cohen's posthumous philosophical theology as having laid the basis for a proto-existentialist doctrine. He continued to study Jewish sources. He translated, among other things, the Hebrew poetry of Yehudah ha-Levi and supplied it with extensive commentaries. In 1924 he joined with Martin Buber to produce a new German translation of the Hebrew Bible, and in the process the two also developed a sophisticated theory of translation, language, and textuality. Their position was that the full meaning of a text develops through what has since come to be called "reception history." Thus the Bible is divinely revealed not as

a matter of Orthodox dogma or in opposition to Bible-critical history but in terms of its effects over time. Translation must not adjust the text to a new culture but must confront the new culture with the text's own authenticity. This confrontation takes place on the ground of the universal, Adamite human speech embedded in the literary forms of both languages. When Rosenzweig died at the age of forty-three, the Bible translation had progressed to *Isaiah.* (Buber finished it in the 1950s.)

Rosenzweig's basic tenets led to some new and promising positions in modern Jewish life. Between the Orthodox belief in the Sinaitic revelation and the Liberal critical historicism regarding the Bible, his "postmodernist" view made it possible to take all of Torah with revelatory seriousness and punctiliousness, while neither rejecting modern scholarship nor committing oneself to a fideistic view. This coincided with and influenced the biblical work of such scholars as Buber, Benno Jacob, Yehezkel Kaufmann, and Umberto Cassuto. It also laid the basis for much subsequent renewed Jewish traditionalism among the acculturated in Germany and elsewhere. Rosenzweig's outlook, beyond the established fronts of Orthodoxy and Liberalism, also offered help with respect to Jewish law *(halakhah).* In opposition to Buber's subjectivistic, pietistic antinomianism, Rosenzweig called for an open-minded, receptive confrontation with Jewish law to embrace it "as much as I can" in terms of one's own preparation and honesty. His "two-covenant doctrine" serves as a strong foundation for Jewish-Christian dialogue, although it can easily be abused in an "indifferentist" spirit and although it suffers inherently from Rosenzweig's pervasive europocentrism (e.g., his total blindness to Islam) and his antihistoricism (cf. Hegel's "absolute spirit" after "the end of history"). Unlike his friend Buber, Rosenzweig rejected the notion of a Jewish state (which would bring Israel back into history); on the other hand, he naturally preferred Jewish self-reauthentification in language, ethnicity, culture, and religion to liberalistic acculturation in gentile societies. With the rise of Nazism, Rosenzweig's educational ideology, along with that of Buber, spoke to German Jewry so aptly and powerfully that the Lehrhaus pattern of highly cultured and acculturated teachers and students in community spread throughout the country and produced an "Indian summer" of German-Jewish creativity of a high order in the 1930s.

The impact of Rosenzweig's thought continues to be strong, philosophically and religiously. The interconnections between him and Martin Heidegger, whom Rosenzweig praises in his last essay ("Vertauschte Fronte," 1929; in *Gesammelte Schriften,* vol. 3, pp. 235-237), are increasingly being crystallized. Heideggerian existentialist phenomenologism, with Jewish-Rosenzweigian modifications, has further left its significant marks on diverse movements of thought—the Frankfurt School (of Hegelian neo-Marxists) on the one hand, and Emmanuel Levinas, who goes beyond Heidegger and Husserl in philosophy and takes Buberian-Rosenzweigian dialogism yet closer to historical Judaism, on the other. Rosenzweig's sophisticated traditionalism comprises ethnicity, language, and religion (though still without "land") and shows the way back from European high culture to Jewish self-definition.

BIBLIOGRAPHY

The most extensive collection of Rosenzweig's writing and study of his life is *Franz Rosenzweig, der Mensch und sein Werk: Gesammelte Schriften,* 6 vols. (Dordrecht, 1976-1984). In English, see *Franz Rosenzweig: His Life and Thought,* 2d rev. ed., edited by Nahum N. Glatzer (New York, 1961), and my *Franz Rosenzweig, 1886-1929: Guide of Reversioners* (London, 1961).

Rosenzweig's *magnum opus, The Star of Redemption,* has been translated by William W. Hallo (New York, 1971). It is discussed in Else-Rahel Freund's *Franz Rosenzweig's Philosophy of Existence: An Analysis of The Star of Redemption,* translated by Stephen L. Weinstein and Robert Israel and edited by Paul R. Mendes-Flohr (The Hague and Boston, 1979); it is also the subject of my book review in *The Thomist* (October 1971): 728-737.

STEVEN S. SCHWARZSCHILD

RUSSIAN ORTHODOX CHURCH

Vladimir I, grand prince of Kiev, was baptized in 988. Having sent ambassadors to investigate the religions of his day, Vladimir was persuaded to embrace Greek Christianity when, according to the Russian *Primary Chronicle,* his envoys reported that at the liturgy in Constantinople they did not know whether they were in heaven or on earth. Vladimir's marriage to the Byzantine princess Anna and his economic dealings with the empire also played a significant part in his decision to align his principality with the imperial church of Byzantium.

After the baptism of the Kievan peoples, Orthodox Christianity flourished in the lands of Rus'. Before the Tatar devastations in the thirteenth century, Kiev was a cosmopolitan city with commercial and cultural ties with Europe and the East. Its spiritual center was the Kievan Monastery of the Caves, which provided for the first literary and historical, as well as religious, writings in the Russian lands; for centuries it served as the theological and spiritual center of Ukrainian church life. In the early years of Christian Kiev, several remarkable churches were constructed. The leader of church life was the bishop of Kiev.

After the devastation of Kiev by the Tatars in 1240, the center of Russian political and ecclesiastical life shifted to Moscow. The ascendancy of Moscow could not have occurred without the efforts of church leaders, particularly

the metropolitans such as Alexis (d. 1378), who for a time served as governing regent, and the abbot Sergii of Radonezh (d. 1392). Sergii is considered by many to be Russia's greatest saint and the "builder" of the nation. A simple monk who became famous for his ascetic labors and mystical gifts, he was appointed abbot of the Saint Sergius Trinity Monastery, which he founded in the wilderness north of Moscow (in present-day Zagorsk). The monastery soon became the center of social and economic as well as religious and spiritual life in the region.

In the fifteenth century, with the fall of Constantinople to the Turks (1453), the theory developed that Moscow was the "third Rome," the last center of true Christianity on earth. Job, the metropolitan of Moscow, was named patriarch by Jeremias II of Constantinople in 1589, thus giving the Russian church a status of self-governance and honor equal to that of the ancient patriarchates of the Christian empire. The patriarchate existed in Russia until the time of Peter the Great, who in 1721 issued the Ecclesiastical Regulation, which created a synodical form of church government patterned after that of the Protestant churches of Europe.

In the seventeenth century Patriarch Nikon (d. 1681) attempted to reform the Russian church according to the practices of the church of Constantinople. During the time of the westernization of Russia under Peter the Great and subsequent tsars, the Russian church became the virtual captive of the state. The patriarchate was abolished and replaced by the Holy Synod, consisting of bishops, presbyters, and laymen. Church councils were forbidden, ecclesiastical proper-

> Its spiritual center was the Kievan Monastery of the Caves, which provided for the first literary and historical, as well as religious, writings in the Russian lands.

ties were appropriated and secularized, and church schools began to teach in Latin and to propagate Roman Catholic and Protestant doctrines.

In the eighteenth and nineteenth centuries the missionary efforts of the Russian church were extensive. The scriptures and services of the church were translated into many Siberian languages and Alaskan dialects as the Eastern regions of the empire were settled and evangelized. Russian missionaries reached the Aleutian Islands in Alaska in 1794, thus beginning the history of Russian Orthodoxy in the New World. The monk Herman (d. 1830), a member of the original missionary party, was canonized a saint of the church in 1970 by both the Russian church and the Orthodox Church in America.

These centuries also saw a revival of traditional Orthodox ascetical and mystical life uninfluenced by the westernizing tendencies of the ecclesiastical institutions. Paisii Velichkovskii (d. 1794) brought the hesychast method of mystical prayer, rooted in the invocation of the name of Jesus, into the Ukraine and Russia. He translated into Church Slavonic many ancient texts, including the anthology of writings on the spiritual life by the church fathers called the *Philokalia (Dobrotoliubie)*.

During this same period a tradition of spiritual eldership (*starchestvo*) emerged in Russia, the most famous center of which was the hermitage of Optina, where such elders (*startsy*) as Leonid, Macarius, and Ambrose spent several hours each day instructing and counseling people of all classes, including many philosophers, intellectuals, and statesmen, among whom were Tolstoi, Dostoevskii, Solov'ev, and Leont'ev.

The turn of the century also saw a revival of patristic studies and a recapturing of the authentic Orthodox theological and liturgical tradition in the ecclesiastical schools, as well as a religious renaissance on the part of a significant number of Russian intellectuals, many of whom either perished in Stalin's prison camps, like Pavel Florenskii, or who were exiled to the West, including the philosopher Nikolai Berdiaev (d. 1948) and the theologian Sergei Bulgakov (d. 1944) who served as dean of the émigré Russian Orthodox Theological Institute of Saint Serge in Paris.

In the late 1980s the Russian Orthodox Church in the U. S. S. R. has the legal right to hold church services in buildings authorized by the state for such purposes. A council of twenty laypeople is needed to petition for the use of a church. Since very few churches and monasteries are functioning at this time, church services are normally very crowded. The church has no right to teach, preach, or pray outside of such buildings because "religious propaganda" is expressly forbidden by Soviet law.

The Russian Orthodox church exists outside the U. S. S. R. in several parts of the world. The original Russian Orthodox missionary diocese in North America became the self-governing Orthodox Church in America in 1970. At this writing there are estimated to be about fifty million Russian Orthodox in the world.

BIBLIOGRAPHY

Arseniev, Nicholas. *Russian Piety.* 2d ed. Crestwood, N. Y., 1975.
Fedotov, G. P. *The Russian Religious Mind,* vol. 1, *Kievan Christianity: The Tenth to the Thirteenth Centuries;* vol. 2, *The Middle Ages: The Thirteenth to the Fifteenth Centuries* (1946-1966). Reprint, Belmont, Mass., 1975.
Fedotov, G. P. *A Treasury of Russian Spirituality* (1950). Reprint, Belmont, Mass., 1975.
Kovalevsky, Pierre. *Saint Sergius and Russian Spirituality.* Crestwood, N. Y., 1976.
Struve, Nikita. *Christians in Contemporary Russia.* New York, 1967.
Zernov, Nicolas. *The Russian Religious Renaissance of the Twentieth Century.* New York, 1963. Contains extensive bibliographical material on the Russian Orthodox church.
Zernov, Nicolas. *The Russians and Their Church.* New York, 1964.

THOMAS HOPKO

SAAMI RELIGION

The Saami (Lapps) are popularly called "a people with four countries" because they make up an ethnic unit under the jurisdiction of four states: Norway, Sweden, Finland, and the Soviet Union. The Saami languages belong to the Finno-Ugric group, and viewed linguistically the Saami are thus related to many peoples to the east (e.g., Finns, Karelians, Estonians, and others), but physically and anthropologically they are unique. This has given rise to a lively but not yet concluded scholarly debate as to the location of their original home. Today we can speak of three different Saami languages—East, Central, and South Saami—which share the same basic structure but are otherwise quite distinct.

The East Saami were converted by the Greek Orthodox Church in the sixteenth century, while those in the west accepted Lutheranism in the seventeenth and eighteenth centuries. The written texts that deal with the non-Christian conceptions of the Saami derive from the seventeenth and eighteenth centuries, and in the main they deal with the beliefs of the nomadic reindeer breeders of Finland and Scandinavia. The texts are written by clergymen and missionaries and are often formed as "confessions of heathenism." From the Saami of the east we have notes, written by ethnographers and linguists of the nineteenth and twentieth centuries, when the native religion had already become "the old custom" or "memories" and no one believed in the old gods. However, we have cause to believe that there exists a common basic structure in the religion of the whole Saami area, in which shamanism and sacrifices to the life-giving powers are dominant factors.

Relations between Men and Animals. As among other peoples of the subpolar region, the earliest economy of the Saami was based on hunting. Consequently, their most important rites revolved around animals and the killing of animals. We find an elaborate conceptual world in which animal spirits and divinities, that is, supernatural beings who have taken their forms from the animal kingdom, figure prominently.

The Finnish Saami called these spirits or "rulers" *haldi* (from the Finnish *haltija,* derived from an old Germanic word meaning "to own, to control, to protect"). They considered that all animals, places, and lakes had their own *haldi* that

protected the animals of a particular species or area and that man was obliged to show his respect for the spirits through such tokens as sacrificial offerings.

The bear was, above all others, the sacred animal throughout the subpolar region, and the rites connected with the bear hunt clearly reflect the reverence men felt for animals and for all living things around them. Certain appointed ceremonies were observed from the very beginning of a hunt. The man who found the bear in the hibernating den led the group; "the drummer" went immediately after him, followed in a predetermined order by those whose duty it was to kill the bear. When the animal had been downed, the hunters sang songs of thanks both to the quarry and to Leibolmai ("alder-tree man"), who is variously described as the god of the hunt or the lord of the animals, but was, most importantly, the lord of the bears.

In their songs the hunters assured the bear that they had not intended to cause him any suffering; indeed, they also tried to divert attention from themselves and put the blame on others. In certain songs it was said that "men from Sweden, Germany, England, and all foreign lands" had caused the bear's death, and the women welcomed the hunters home as "men from all foreign lands." The meat was prepared by the men in a special place and brought into the *kota* ("tent" or "hut") through *boassio-raikie,* the holy back door situated opposite the ordinary door; arrayed in festive dress, the women sat waiting inside and spit chewed alder bark at the men as the meat was carried in. This custom should probably be regarded as a purification rite. Once the meat was eaten, all bones were buried in the order they are found in the body, so that the bear was given a proper funeral.

Soul-Beliefs and Shamanism. The notion that animals have guardian beings that must be respected by man is based on the idea that every living being has at least two souls—a corporeal soul and a "free" soul. The free soul can manifest itself outside the body and is regarded as a guardian spirit and a double. Animals are men's equals and are treated as such. In dreams or in trancelike states such as ecstasy, the human free soul can leave the body and assume a concrete form.

Occasionally a malicious being captures a soul, posing a mortal threat to the bearer. It was believed, for example, that when a person fell seriously ill, it was because someone, perhaps a dead relative who wanted to summon him or her to the realm of the dead, had captured the soul of the afflicted. In such cases the *noaidie* ("shaman") intervened to help. Having gone through a long and painful period of apprenticeship, and possessing extraordinary psychic powers, the *noaidie* could enter a state of ecstasy and, under this trance, send his soul to the home of the dead, Jabme-aimo, to negotiate with the dead or the goddess of the dead (called Jabme-akka in certain places) about the return of the soul.

The *noaidie,* however, could not undertake such a journey unassisted, and during his apprenticeship he had come into contact with supernatural beings that could aid him when necessary. Paramount among these helpers were the sacred animals: birds, fish (or snakes), and bull reindeer. The *noaidie* recruited his assistants from Sájva-ájmuo, the dwelling place of the holy spirits. (Sájva-ájmuo corresponds to Bâsse-Passevare, the sacred mountains in the northern Saami territory.) Other spirits could also help the *noaidie* in the performance of his office; a deceased *noaidie,* for example, could give the new *noaidie* advice or provide other assistance.

The *noaidie's* ability to go into ecstasy made him a general intermediary between human beings, who lived in the middle world, and supernatural beings in the other (upper and nether) worlds. This belief in the triadic division of the universe was shared with some of the peoples of northern Siberia. The *noaidie* regulated relations between people in the middle world and divinities and spirits in the other worlds, as well as between people and the powers of nature.

Deities. There is no doubt that the Saami were not only aware of their dependence upon the rulers of places and animals, but that they also worshiped heavenly and atmospheric divinities. These superterrestrial beings had no part in immediate everyday concerns, but they were powers to be reckoned with and were given sacrifices on special occasions. Among the eastern Saami, there was the divinity Tiermes, who manifested himself in thunder and has been linked to the Ob-Ugric god of the sky, Num-Turem, and to the Samoyed god of the sky, Num. Among the western Saami, Radien/Rariet ("the ruler"), in some places also called Vearalden Olmai ("man of the world, or cosmos") and Mailman Radien ("the ruler of the world"), headed the gods. The cult dedicated to him was meant mainly to further reindeer breeding, but he was also the god who sustained the world. This was symbolized by a pillar, known among some of the Saami as the world's *stytto,* which was erected beside the ruler's idol at the sacrificial site. It was believed that the North Star was attached to the uppermost point of the pillar.

The mighty thunder god Horagalles (also known as Attjie, "father," and Bajjan, "he who is above") could demolish the mountains with his hammer and scatter and injure the reindeer; sacrifices to him were thus meant to appease. The sun, Beivie, was vital to plant life, and sacrifices were made to ensure good grazing for the reindeer and rich vegetation in general.

BIBLIOGRAPHY

Source materials on Lapland and the Saami traditions begin to become abundant as early as the mid-seventeenth century, when priests and missionaries engaged in extensive christianizing in the area and reported to their superiors on all aspects of Saami culture, including religion and folklore. Some of these materials, exclusively from Swedish Lapland, were published by Johannes Scheffer in his *Lapponia* (Frankfurt, 1673). Scheffer was a Dutch scholar who had been commissioned to spread information about the Saami (Lapps) throughout Europe. The work was immediately translated into other languages, including English (*The History of Lapland,* Oxford, 1694). Another translation appeared in 1736.

Eighteenth-century missionary reports contain greater detail on the religious beliefs of the Scandinavian Saami, but few of them are available in a major language. Exceptions are Pehr Högström's *Beschreibung des der crone Schweden gehörenden Lapplanders* (Copenhagen and Leipzig, 1748) and Knud Leem's *Beskrivelse over Finmarkens Lapper, deres tungemaal, Leve-maade og forrige Afgudsdyrkelse* (A Description of the Finnmark Lapps, Their Language, Customs, and Former Idolatry; Copenhagen, 1767).

The best sources that deal with the Saami of Finland and Russia, however, are much more recent. In his introduction to *Wörterbuch der Kola-lappischen Dialekte nebst Sprachproben* (Helsinki, 1891), Arvid Genetz provides a survey of traditional religion among the Russian Saami, and Toivo Immanuel Itkonen's *Heidnische Religion und späterer Aberglaube bei den finnischen Lappen* (Helsinki, 1946) is a collection of accounts of earlier beliefs among the Saami of Finland. Nickolai Kharuzin's *Russkie Lopari* (Moscow, 1890) contains extensive materials on myths, but the cult he describes derives largely from the materials of Scheffer and Högström—that is, from Scandinavia.

The Saami religion has, understandably, mainly attracted Scandinavian scholars, and the first surveys were published in one or another of the Nordic languages. Such scholars as Uno Holmberg (Harva after 1927), in *Lappalaisten uskonto* (Porvoo, 1915), and Rafael Karsten, in *The Religion of the Samek* (Leiden, 1955), were strongly influenced by the evolutionism popular at the time, which they supplemented with theories on borrowings. Holmberg's later survey of Finno-Ugric and Siberian mythology in *The Mythology of All Races,* vol. 4 (Boston, 1927), is methodologically much more modern. The most recent survey is Ake Hultkrantz's "Die Religion der Lappen," in *Die Religionen Nordeurasiens und der amerikanischen Arktis,* edited by Ivar Paulson et al. (Stuttgart, 1962).

There are some eighty preserved shaman drums, the oldest dating from the mid-seventeenth century. These have been described in detail by Ernst Mauritz Manker in *Die lappische Zaubertrommel,* vols. 1-2 (Stockholm, 1938-1950).

Various aspects of Saami religion, such as the bear ceremony, sacrifices, the shaman, rites of the dead, conceptions of the soul, the sun cult, the notion of the lord of animals, and the origin of the Saami, have also received extensive scholarly treatment.

LOUISE BACKMAN

SACRAMENT

Hellenistic Sacraments. While classical Christian usage has largely determined the understanding of *sacrament* that the student of comparative religion employs in the study of religion, it is important to have some awareness of the pre-Christian understanding of *sacrament* and its Greek antecedent, *musterion*.

The mystery cults. The Greek *musterion* is of uncertain etymology but is most probably associated with *muein*, meaning "to close" (the mouth), and thus "to keep secret." The term *musterion* designates the sharp dividing line between initiates, for whom the secret history of the god (his birth, marriage, or death and rebirth, depending on the cult) is dramatically reenacted, thus binding their fate to the god's, and noninitiates, who cannot participate in this kind of salvation.

Apocalyptic usage. Here *musterion* refers to the disclosure of God's ultimate, or eschatological, intention. The term is used quite widely to designate anything that prefigures the final consummation of the divine will or plan. Thus Christian proclamation, biblical typology, and the inclusion of Jew and gentile in divine election could all be referred to as *musterion* (which becomes *sacramentum* in Latin).

Gnostic usage. Deriving from the theory and practice of the mystery cults, certain mystical and especially gnostic philosophical traditions of the Hellenistic world used *musterion* to apply to the quest for transcendental insight. The religious tradition that best exemplifies this sense of *musterion*/sacrament is the Hinduism of the Upanisads and of yoga. In the Western Christian tradition examples of sacramental mysticism often approximate the pattern of the yogic or gnostic transformation of external ritual into interior discipline.

Emergence of the Classical Perspective. Despite the typically exoteric character of Christian doctrine and practice, ideas and practice associated with the Greek mysteries were used to interpret Christian rituals. *Sacramentum* gradually lost its wider, apocalyptic meaning, was increasingly used to refer to baptism and eucharist, and then was extended by analogy to apply to related ritual actions including confession and penance, confirmation, marriage, ordination, and unction. The earlier Latin sense of "vow" can still be discerned in baptism, confirmation, marriage, and ordination, but the oldest Greek associations with cultic participation in salvation predominate. Thus sacrament comes to be exclusively identified with a set of ritual actions that are understood to be both necessary to and efficacious for salvation.

Cognate Sacraments. There are two sorts of such sacraments, those that deal with transitional moments and so are not repeated and those that are regularly repeated.

Sacraments of transition. The earliest and most important of the transitional sacraments is baptism. This type of transitional rite is analogous to the initiation into cult societies of, for example, the indigenous peoples of the North American Plains. It is also characteristic of the African independent churches of central and southern Africa.

As Christianity became more or less coextensive with culture and society, the transition came more and more to be identified with birth or early infancy. As a ritual associated with infancy, it took the place of the Jewish rite of circumcision.

As baptism became "infant baptism," the catechetical aspect of the ritual that inaugurated persons into full membership in the cult society became fixed in the form of confirmation. Insofar as confirmation is associated with adolescence, it could enter into homology with rites of tribal initiation—a species of ritual that is exceedingly widespread and well developed among the indigenous peoples of the Americas, Africa, and Australia A significant number of groups, for example, the Bemba of Africa, have initiation rites. Among North American aboriginal peoples, the young males (and, rarely, females) undertake the highly individualized dream or vision quest.

A further extension of transitional sacrament occurs with the development of extreme unction, the anointing of the sick. Insofar as the Christian sacrament of unction has the intention of healing (as in the anointing of the sick), it becomes repeatable and homologous to the healing rites found in virtually all religious traditions.

Two other sacraments of transition, ordination and marriage (traditionally thought of as mutually exclusive), have

> **There are two sorts of such sacraments, those that deal with transitional moments and so are not repeated and those that are regularly repeated.**

developed. Rites of ordination are found in virtually all societies in which a priestly caste is drawn from the society as a whole. Marriage rites are obviously quite widespread although only those that have a clearly sacred or religious character are directly comparable. Often these have the added dimension of rites to ensure fertility.

Perhaps the most highly developed system of sacraments of transition is to be found in Hinduism. These sacraments begin with conception (*Garbhadhana*) and continue through pregnancy (Pumsavana, Simanta, Jatakarman). In addition to the naming ceremony (Namakarana), which occurs a few days after birth, there are sacraments to mark the first appearance of the infant outside the home, the child's first solid food, the tonsure, and the piercing of the child's ears. These sacraments generally involve sacrifices, ceremonies of fire and water, ritual washings, recitation of appropriate mantras and prayers.

Repeatable sacraments. While sacraments of transition are in principle nonrepeatable (with the possible and limited exceptions of marriage and extreme unction), two sacraments of great importance in traditional Christianity, penance and eucharist, do require repeated performance.

In the Christian tradition penance is related to baptism as the restoration of baptismal purity and to the Eucharist as the necessary preparation for participation. The confession of sin has a place of central importance in the religion of Handsome Lake practiced by contemporary Iroquois in the United States and Canada.

The ritual that is most often associated with sacramentality is the Eucharist, Mass, or Communion of the Christian community. The selection of comparable rituals from the history of religions will depend upon the degree of emphasis placed upon one of three aspects: thanks giving or offering, communal meal, or sacrifice of the divine victim.

The most dramatic instances are the human sacrifices, which include the Greek *pharmakos,* a number of African rites, and practices belonging to the high civilizations of the Americas, especially the Aztec. [*See* Human Sacrifice.]

The communal meal is a common feature of many sacrifices. A vegetable, animal, or cereal offering is presented to the god and is subsequently shared by all participants, much as in the Christian Communion the bread and wine is first offered in thanksgiving and then shared by the participants. Where these rites are associated with first-fruits festivals or with harvest, the element of thanksgiving (eucharist) is especially pronounced.

BIBLIOGRAPHY

For concise historical background, see the article on *musterion* by Günther Bornkaum in *Theological Dictionary of the New Testament,* edited by Gerhard Kittel and Gerhard Friedrich (Grand Rapids, 1964-1976), and the article "Mystery," in the *Encyclopedia of Theology,* edited by Karl Rahner (New York, 1975).

The classic treatment of rites analogous to sacraments of transition is Arnold van Gennep's *Les rites de passage* (Paris, 1909), translated by Monika B. Vizedom and Gabrielle L. Caffee as *The Rites of Passage* (Chicago, 1960). Victor Turner's *The Ritual Process* (Chicago, 1969) is a major contribution to the understanding of these rituals. A useful source for the Hindu sacraments is Raj Bali Pandey's *Hindu Samskaras: A Socio-Religious Study of the Hindu Sacraments,* 2d rev. ed. (Delhi, 1969). Ake Hultkrantz's *Religions of the American Indians,* translated by Monica Setterwall (Los Angeles, 1979), contains important information and an excellent bibliography. Ronald L. Grimes's *Beginnings in Ritual Studies* (Washington, D. C., 1982) suggests the relationship between *zazen* and the Eucharist.

THEODORE W. JENNINGS, JR.

SACRED AND THE PROFANE, THE

The relationship between the sacred and the profane can be understood either abstractly, as a mutual exclusion of spheres of reality, or cognitively, as a way of distinguishing between two aspects of that reality. The former approach necessarily presupposes that such exclusion is recognizable; the latter, that one is dealing with ontic factuality. Even if one assumes a transsubjective reality, the boundary between the two spheres may prove to be movable or even fictitious, and even if one confines oneself to the fact of subjectivity, one may at times conclude that transcendence conditions the individual psychologically.

Means of Identification

In selecting evidence of the sacred and its relationship to the profane we must be limited to two approaches: either it is tacitly perceived as something real, or it assumes some kind of symbolic form. In order to establish tacit perception, we require proofs that silence is maintained for the sake of the sacred. These proofs suffice not only for the mystic, for example, who could speak but prefers to maintain silence, but also for persons who have spoken, but whose language we do not know: namely, the people of prehistory and early historical times.

Symbolic forms may be specifically linguistic or of a broader cultural nature. If they are linguistic, the historian of religions must distinguish between the language spoken by the people who are the objects of study ("object language") and the one spoken by the scholar, though naturally the two will have shadings and terms in common. One can best make this distinction by keeping one's own definition of what is sacred or profane separate from the definition that is given by the culture under scrutiny itself ("self-definition"). Each definition naturally identifies the sacred and profane in a different way. The self-definition is part of those languages in which religious and nonreligious documents have come down to us; in terms of methodology, these are the same as object languages. The definitions the historian develops must arise not only out of the categories of language, but also out of those of modern sociology, psychology, aesthetics, and possibly other disciplines as well, categories employed in an attempt to understand the *sacred* and *profane* without resorting to the concepts one customarily translates with *sacred* and *profane*; in terms of methodology, this amounts to a metalanguage.

If the symbolic forms are not of a linguistic nature, there is no self-definition at all. The definitions given from outside to which one must restrict oneself, in this case to relate to language, are not *meta*linguistic in nature, for the object area is not expressed merely in language, but rather through social behavior, anthropological data, or works of art.

Whether considered a linguistic or a nonlinguistic expression, the definition given from outside can assume an affirmative character, and in so doing turn into the self-definition of the scholar who identifies himself with a given artifact, be it in a text, a specific event, a psychic configuration, or a work of art. The researcher compiling a definition can thus identify himself with both its sacredness and profaneness.

As a rule, one should give neither of these means of identification precedence over the other. It is for purely practical reasons that we now turn our attention first to those methods relying on linguistic evidence.

Philological Methods. It is an axiom in the logic of criticism that one can declare the use of a concept of sacredness in a source to be false. However, the conclusions of the modern scholar, no matter how subtly they might not only deny phenomena of sacredness within religions but also manage to demonstrate them outside of religions, are constantly in need of correction by object-language traditions.

Seen in terms of the history of scholarship, the first object-language tradition to contain the terms for *sacred* and *profane* (upon which the terminology of the medieval precursors of modern scholarly languages was based) was the Latin of the Roman classical writers and church fathers, including, among the texts of the latter, the Vulgate and the harmony of its gospel texts represented by Tatian's *Diatessaron* in the Codex Fuldensis. Equating words resulted in the double presentation of terms in the vernacular, as we can still see from various contextual, interlinear, and marginal glosses, and in the translations of the *Abrogans*, an alphabetical dictionary of synonyms, and the *Vocabularius Sancti Galli*, in which the terms are arranged by subject. Bilingualism, resulting from the rechristianization of Spain, was also responsible for the earliest translation of the Qur'an by Robertus Ketenensis and Hermannus Dalmata, for the unfinished *Glossarium Latino-Arabicum*, and for some important translations from Hebrew, which not only reflect the Jews' skill as translators throughout the Diaspora, but also represent active endeavors on the part of the medieval mission among the Jews. Terms for the sacred and its opposites could thus be translated into the vernaculars directly out of Hebrew, Latin, and Catalan, and out of the Arabic by way of Latin. They also became available from Greek, once the early humanists, the forerunners of the modern scholars, had rediscovered the Greek classics through the Latin ones, and the original text of the New Testament and the Septuagint by way of the Vulgate. At the Council of Vienne, in 1311-1312, it was decided to appoint two teachers each of Greek, Arabic, Hebrew, and Chaldean at each of five universities; thenceforth Latin emerged once and for all as a metalanguage with respect to the terminologies of these languages (including Latin itself, now considered as an object language), and in so doing came to stand

fundamentally on the same footing as the European vernaculars.

In order to avoid short-circuiting self-confirmations within the terminology of sacredness, it is best to consider this complex as an independent one transmitted to modern scholarship not from the Middle Arabic of the Islamic traditionalists, nor from the Middle Hebrew of the Talmudists, but solely from the Middle Latin of the Christian scholars. It must be distinguished from a later complex that resulted from the use of the European vernaculars in missionary work and in colonization. These were able to reproduce certain word meanings from the native languages, but more often led to interpretations dependent on the terminology of sacredness from the former complex, rather than congenial translation. Moreover, true bilingualism was only present in the work of a few explorers and missionaries. More recently, of course, translation has been accomplished increasingly in accordance with methods taken from the study of the early oriental languages, of Indo-European, and of comparative philology, as well as from linguistic ethnology; only in the twentieth century have all of these achieved independence from interpretations provided by classical antiquity and by Judeo-Christian-Islamic tradition.

Philologia classica sive sacra. The relationship between *sacer* and *profanus* can be called a contradictory opposition, if one understands sacer as the object-language expression of something true and profanus as its logical negation. In the rich cultic vocabulary of Latin sacer is of prime importance. Rites such as those of the *ver sacrum*—the sacrifice of all animals born in the spring and the expulsion from the community and cult congregation of all grown men about to establish their own domestic state (for the purpose of securing the support of Mars, who worked outside communal boundaries)—or the *devotio*—the offering of an individual life as a stand-in for an enemy army, so that Mars will destroy it as well—serve as prime examples of the characteristic relationship between the *sacrum*'s liability and certain kinds of human behavior. It follows that all cult objects and sites included in ritual acts can also be *sacra*. This meaning gives rise to derivations such as *sacrare, sacrificare, sancire, sacramentum, sacerdos*. Of these, *sancire* ("to set aside as *sacer*"; later also "to designate as being *sacer*," or, even more generally, "to establish with ceremony") is the most fertile, for its participle *sanctus* would ultimately come to characterize everything appropriate to the *sacrum*. *Sanctus* could thus assume a multitude of meanings, including those of cult infallibility and moral purity. Accordingly, it was an ideal translation for the Greek *hagios* of the New Testament and the Septuagint, and, by way of the latter, for the Hebrew *qadosh* as well. When used in such a Judeo-Christian context, *sacer* was then restricted in meaning to "consecrated," and this tended to fix a change in meaning that had begun already in the Latin of the writers of the Silver Age, as *sacrum* ceased to have an almost innate quality and came to depend on the act of consecration to a deity. A new formation such as *sacrosanctus* ("rendered *sanctum* by way of a *sacrum*") attests to this difference, as well as to the continuing similarity between the two meanings.

The basic meaning of *profanus* may also be discovered within the context of human actions, for the spatial connotation, which is always at its root, doubtless first derived from the use made of the area outside the *sacrum*. Originally, perhaps, this space may even have been used for rites, for the fact that even here we are dealing not with banal functions

> **Consecration to a god is perceived by humans as a blessing, whereas being possessed by a god is perceived as a misfortune.**

but with special ones is shown by legal arguments about how assets owned by a god or in the estate of a deceased citizen can be used "profanely."

Along with *profanus*, there is also another concept that is the opposite of *sacer*, namely that of *fas*. This designates, in a purely negative way, the sphere in which human affairs may take place. *Fas est* means that one may do something without any religious scruples, but not that one *must* do so. It first appears as a qualifier for a permitted act, then for a condition as well, and accordingly was used through all of the literature of the Roman republic only as a predicate concept. Livy, who also used the term *sacrosanctus* with some frequency, was the first to employ the concept as a subject as well. Specific times came to be distinguished by the activities appropriate to them. *Dies fasti* were days on which civil, political, commercial, or forensic activities were fas, or permitted by the religious institutions; *dies nefasti* were those on which such activities were nefas, that is, not permitted, or sacrilegious.

The meaning of *fas* does not accord with that of *fanum*, then—nor are they related etymologically; *fas* is related to *fatum*—as though *fas* is "what is appropriate to the *fanum*." Here it is rather the profane sphere that is the positive starting point. *Fas* is the utterance (from *fari*, "speak") of the responsible secular praetor who permits something; *nefas* is that which the priest responsible in the *fanum* finds unutterable, which constitutes sacrilege on those days over which his institution has control. When one recognizes that what is here accepted as natural and immutable passes over into what has been fixed by man and is therefore subject to change, and which can be objectively false just as its opposite can, then one can speak of the opposition between *fanum/sacer* and *fas* as a contrary one.

Sacer thus has a contradictory opposite *(profanus)* and a contrary one *(fas)*. In addition, finally, there is a dialectical

opposition contained within the concept of *sacer* itself. This comes from the ambivalence produced when, as with *fas*, the extrasacral sphere is assumed as the positive starting point in one's appraisal. *Sacer* is thus what is venerated, to be sure, but also something sinister; or, to put it another way, it is both holy and accursed. Consecration to a god is perceived by humans as a blessing, whereas being possessed by a god is perceived as a misfortune. One must not make this dialectical contrast into an actual one by construing possession and misfortune as a fatal consecration to an underworld deity inimical to humans, for in so doing one destroys an ambiguity that is part of the basic structure of every religious experience. Positively, *sacer esto* simply means that a person is handed over to a deity; negatively, it implies that he is excluded from the community. The negative side of the dialectic may extend as far as demonization. If damnation or demonization is manifest on the historical level, then one is dealing with something other than profanation, and, outside the holy, still another sphere is revealed in addition to the profane. The dialectical relationship with this sphere comes about only through man's limited capacity for experience, and must not be enhanced by philologically setting up some finding related to *sacer*; that is, it must not be turned into an essential contrary working inside the nature of a *numen* or a deity.

The types of contrasts between the terms designating the sacred and the profane are less fundamental in Greek than in Latin, even though elements of ambivalent background experience may also be recognized in *hagios* and *hieros*. For the most part, the expressions have the character of a primary positing dependent on premises other than those relating to the differences between inclusion in or exclusion from a given precinct, or between ritual and nonritual behavior. As a rule, the antithesis was only created belatedly, through the use of the alpha privative, as in *anhieros*, *anosios*, *amuetos*, or *asebes*; the only term that appears to relate to an original negative concept, namely the opposite of *hieros*, is *bebelos*, which can be translated as "profane," while koinos can function as the opposite of practically all the concepts of sacredness. In our survey of the latter, then, the contrary concepts may be easily imagined, even though not specifically named.

From Mycenaean times on, the decisive concept is that designated as *hieros*. Behind it, most likely, is a sense of force altogether lacking in the early Roman term. *Hieros* functions almost exclusively as a predicate, both of things and of persons: offerings, sacrificial animals, temples, altars, votive gifts (even including money), the road leading to Eleusis, the wars engaged in by the Delphic amphictyony, and priests, initiates in the mysteries, and temple slaves. Only very rarely did anyone go so far as to call a god or a goddess *hieros*; Greek-speaking Jews and Christians were forced to resort to the term *hagios*. Traces of some experiential ambivalence are apparent when a *hieros logos*, or cult legend, is regarded as *arreton* ("unspeakable") and a shrine as *aduton* or *abaton* ("unapproachable"). It is nonetheless striking that in Homer and the older Greek literature a whole range of things may be called *hieros*: cities, walls, hecatombs, altars, temples, palaces, valleys, rivers, the day and the night, the threshing floor, bread and the olive tree, barley and olives, chariots, guard and army units, individual personality traits, mountains, letters, bones, stones used in board games. Here it is rare to find *hieros* used with any connection to the gods, as when grain and the threshing floor, for example, are spoken of as the gifts of Demeter. On the whole it is tempting to speak of a certain profanation due to literary redundancy, though in fact a complete reversal of meaning is never produced.

Hagnos, which also encompasses what is pure in the cultic sense, is even more profound in its meaning than *hieros*; it relates to *hazesthai* ("to avoid in awe, to fear, to venerate") in the same way that *semnos* ("solemn, sublime, holy"—i. e., lacking the component of purity) relates to *sebesthai* ("to be afraid, to perceive as holy"). *Hagnos* is more frequently used than *hieros* when referring to the gods (Demeter, Kore, Persephone, Zeus, Apollo, Artemis), but in that they are elements that can purify, water and fire can also be *hagnos*, as can sky, light, and ether. Because of this connotation, *hagnos* can be used not only for things and persons in the same way as hieros, but may also designate rites and festivals or the conditions of sexual purity and of freedom from the contamination of blood and death, as, for example, when applied to bloodless offerings *(hagna thumata)*. *Hagnos* can even extend to the whole conduct of one's life outside the cult, though the connotation "sacred" never entirely disappears; it is only in Hellenistic Greek that it comes to mean "purity of character." Whether one is justified in calling this a profane use or not depends upon one's judgment of the nature of post-classical religiosity in general. In any case, the only clearly contradictory opposite of *hagnos* is *miaros* ("polluted, disgusting").

From the root *hag-*, from which *hagnos* derives, the adjective hagios was also created. This does not limit, but rather emphasizes (hence, too, its superlative *hagio-tatos*), and is used especially of temples, festivals, and rites, though only rarely of the reverent attitudes of men. In classical Greek and the pagan Greek of Hellenistic times it is used only relatively rarely. Precisely for this reason its clear religious connotation was preserved, and this is what recommended the term to Hellenistic Jewry as a virtually equivalent translation for the Hebrew *qadosh*, whereas from the *hieros* group of words one finds only hiereus as a possible rendering of the Hebrew *kohen* ("priest"), and *hieron* to designate a pagan shrine. The New Testament develops even further the sense given to *hagios* in the Septuagint—though unlike the Septuagint it can also use *hieron* when referring to the Temple in Jerusalem—and thereby transmits this sense to the Greek of the church

fathers and the Byzantine church. Secular modern Greek continues to use *hagios* as the standard term for "sacred" to this day.

The word *hosios* designates behavior that conforms to the demands of the gods. Accordingly, it can be applied to human justice just as properly as to a correctly performed cult ritual. Both are carried out on the profane level. Though one cannot translate *hosios* with "profane," one must think of it as a contrary opposite of *hieros*: if money belonging to the gods is *hieron*, that means one cannot touch it, but the rest, which is *hosion*, may be freely used. The Septuagint never uses *hosios* as a translation for *qadosh* but generally does for *hasid* ("pious"). The Vulgate, however, renders *hosios* unaffectedly with *sanctus*, whether applied to man or to God.

Sebesthai ("to shrink back from a thing, to be awestruck") has no parallel in the Semitic languages, and hence the word is important solely in the classical Greek tradition. The related adjective *semnos* implies exaltedness or sublimity when used of gods; when applied to speeches, actions, or objects (a royal throne, for example) it suggests that they command respect. It appears only infrequently in the Greek Bible for various terms, just as does the important classical concept *eusebes*, which is chosen in a few instances to render *tsaddiq* ("the just one"), which in turn may also be translated with *dikaios*. The Vulgate has difficulty with both adjectives, and makes do with approximations or circumlocutions.

In the Hebrew Bible the all-important concept is *qadosh*. If its root is in fact *qd* ("to set apart"), its fundamental meaning is not unlike the Roman *sacer*. But it is also possible that its root is *qdsh*, as in the Akkadian *qadashu* ("to become pure"), which would point to a cultic connection. Nothing is *qadosh* by nature, however; things only become *qadosh* by being declared so for, or by, Yahveh Elohim. All of creation is potentially eligible: persons, especially priests; places, especially the city of Jerusalem; festivals, especially the Sabbath; buildings, especially the Temple; adornments, especially the priest's crown and robe; bodies of water; plants; and animals, especially sacrificial ones. The prophets—assisted by a trend that emerged from the reading of God's law at the Israelite feast of covenantal renewal and culminated in the establishment of the Holiness Code (Lv. 17-26)—managed to transfer the attribute "holy" almost exclusively to Yahveh Elohim. As a result, only a very few of the above-mentioned categories of objects and activities continued to be accorded the attribute of holiness in the actual target language of Hebrew. In large part, reference to holy places, times, actions, and objects is metalanguage interpretation. It is not factually wrong, for even a holiness accorded by God on the basis of his own holiness is deserving of the name. Nevertheless, one must be aware of the special quality of having been created by him that is typical of such holiness; this is in distinct contrast, for example, to the Greek concept of nature. And it affects the designation of what is profane in Israel. An important thesis of secularization theory asserts that the desacralization of the world, especially of nature and its wonders as it was accomplished in the Israelite theology of holiness, and later transmitted by Christianity, was one of the fundamental preconditions for the worldliness of the modern era. If one does not regard this basic precondition as a *conditio sine qua non*, it is doubtless correctly identified. It would be possible to view the realm of created things in the Israelite concept of the world as profane, just as one might view secularity as a legitimizing criterion for what constitutes the modern era, but that profaneness would be altogether different in kind from that of Rome or Greece. Given this situation, it is understandable that in the Old Testament languages (Hebrew and Septuagint/Vulgate translations) the "profanity" of the world is expressed in quite dissimilar fashion and only fragmentarily, depending upon whether it is mentioned in the cult context of pure and impure or in prophetic preaching about obedience and sin. As a clear contradiction to *qadosh* we thus find, in only a few instances, the adjective *hol*, which is rendered by the Septuagint with *bebelos* and by the Vulgate with *profanus* (*tame'*, "impure," becomes *akathartos* and *pollutus*, respectively; *taher*, "pure," becomes *katharos* and *mundus*). *Hol* designates only something that is accessible and usable without ritual, while the verb *halal* suggests a genuine desecration by means of an abomination.

The grateful use of created things, which God makes holy, by men who are likewise holy because God is, is not the same thing as the Greeks' and Romans' removal of things from profane use. The closest parallel to the latter in Israel is the practice of bans. Translated etymologically, *herem* ("the banned object") means what has been set apart. The difference not only between this practice and profane use of a holy object but also between it and the sacrifice of an object lies in the fact that the purpose for the setting apart is the object's destruction. The Septuagint quite correctly expresses the term's identity with the idea of damnation by using *ana(te)thema(tismenos)*, while the Vulgate makes do with *consecratum* or *votum*.

In Arabic, at least since the appearance of the Qur'an, words with the root *hrm* take on the central importance that *qdsh* and its derivatives have in Hebrew. At the same time, the Arabic *qds* and its offshoots (*muqaddas*, "holy") continue to survive with more general meaning. This switch in the relative values of the two may have occurred simply because all of the concepts of sacredness having to do with rites and sacrifices were concentrated on a specific precinct. It is as though the Israelite concept of holiness, bound as it was to the ideas of sacrifice and consecration, were multiplied by the Roman concept, with its original link to a well-defined location. The city of Mecca is a *harim*, a circumscribed, inviolable spot. The strip of land that surrounds and protects it is known as *al-haram*. In the city's center lies *al-masjid al-haram*, the "forbidden mosque," so named because it may not be entered by those who have not performed an *ihram*, or consecrated themselves. In the center of its inner courtyard, *al-haram al-sharif* (the "noble precinct"), lies the *aedes sacra*, the Ka'bah, *al-bayt al-haram* (the "forbidden house"). Everything outside this complex is known as *hill*, where, just as in the *profanum*, except during a period of three months, everything is *halal* ("permitted") that is prohibited in the sacred sites. The Arabic *halal* is thus close in meaning to the Hebrew *hol*, but quite different from *halal*.

Metalanguage meanings. The modern scholarly languages for the most part presuppose the changes of meaning that the classical vocabulary ultimately experienced as a result of being put to Christian use, in part after certain non-Christian usages that prepared the way. These changes of meaning are characterized by the fact that a clear distinction exists between the quality of God in the beyond and the quality of creation in the here and now; and the terms are distributed accordingly.

In the first sense, the Latin term *sanctus* had ultimately come to mean a primarily divine quality; and consequently we now have the French *saint* and the Italian and Spanish *santo*. The Germanic languages, on the other hand, perpetuate the root that in the language's earliest stages had meant "intact, healthy, whole," represented by the English *holy* (related to *whole*; synonyms: *godly, divine*), by the German and Dutch *heilig*, and by the Swedish *helig*.

In the second sense, that is, for the quality attained by dedication to God, Latin had preserved the term *sacer*, which was linked to places, objects, and situations. Later, though relatively early, *sacer* existed alongside *sanctus*, which, confusingly enough, could also be used to refer to this mode of transformation. *Sacer* could be exchanged for the clearer form *sacratus*, and it is from this that the French *(con)sacré*, the Italian *sacro* (synonym: *benedetto*), and the Spanish *(con)sagrado* derive. For this meaning English employs the Romance word *sacred*.

In Latin, *profanus* had continued to be the opposite of both *sanctus* and *sacer*, the latter in its broader, classical Roman sense as well as its more limited Judeo-Christian meaning. Accordingly, the Romance languages and Romance-influenced English still use the term.

Sociological Methods. For the examination of symbolic forms of a nonlinguistic nature, the methods of sociology are the most effective. Of such nonlinguistic forms, the most important are, of course, rites. Much would suggest that rites were in fact the very earliest forms of religious expression. I shall here assume stereotypings to be next in importance, forms that are even more hypothetical and that serve, among other things, as the rationale for institutionalizations. The two scholars who have analyzed these forms most profoundly are Émile Durkheim and Max Weber.

Neither Durkheim's nor Weber's method is correct in itself, but together they may well be so. Durkheim's idea that, in contrast to individual reality, society is of the nature of a thing, and Weber's idea that social reality is made up of continuous human action, inclusive of theorizing, are complementary. It is true of both, as for most of the other sociological approaches, that they strive to work with pure designations, but that these are also more or less stamped by metalanguage usage and by concepts from classical and church tradition. This often tends to compromise the accuracy of translation from native languages; but, on the other hand, this is what permits at least an approximate understanding of unfamiliar terms.

The nature of the sacred and profane in the objectivity of social reality. Émile Durkheim argues that it is society that continuously creates sacred things. The things in which it chooses to discover its principal aspirations, by which it is moved, and the means employed to satisfy such aspirations—these it sets apart and deifies, be they men, objects, or ideas. If an idea is unanimously shared by a people, it cannot be negated or disputed. This very prohibition proves that one stands in the presence of something sacred. With prohibitions of this kind, cast in the form of negative rites, man rids himself of certain things that thereby become profane, and approaches the sacred. By means of ritual deprivations such as fasts, wakes, seclusion, and silence, one attains the same results as those brought about through anointings, propitiatory sacrifice, and consecrations. The moment the sacred detaches itself from the profane in this way, religion is born. The most primitive system of sacred things is totemism. But the totem is not the only thing that is sacred; all things that are classified in the clan have the same quality, inasmuch as they belong to the same type. The classifications that link them to other things in the universe allot them their place in the religious system. The idea of class is construed by men themselves as an instrument of thought; for again it was society that furnished the basic pattern logical thought has

> A thing becomes sacred when humans remove it from ordinary use; the negative cult in which this happens leads to taboo.

employed. Nonetheless, totemism is not merely some crude, mistaken pre-religious science, as James G. Frazer supposed; for the basic distinction that is of supreme importance is that between sacred and profane, and it is accomplished with the aid of the totem, which is a collective symbol of a religious nature, as well as a sacred thing in itself. Nor does a thing become sacred by virtue of its links through classification to the universe; a world of profane things is still profane even though it is spatially and temporally infinite. A thing becomes sacred when humans remove it from ordinary use;

the negative cult in which this happens leads to taboo. A man becomes sacred through initiation. Certain foodstuffs can be forbidden to the person who is still profane because they are sacred, and others can be forbidden to the holy man because they are profane. Violation of such taboos amounts to desecration, or profanation, of the foodstuffs in the one case, of the person in the other, and profanation of this kind can result in sickness and death. In the holy ones—that is to say, both the creatures of the totem species and the members of the clan—a society venerates itself.

The meaning of sacred and profane in the context of subjective religious action. Max Weber states in *Wirtschaft und Gesellschaft* (Tübingen, 1922) that the focus for sociology is the "meaning context" of an act. The same also applies to religiously (or magically) motivated communal action, which can only be comprehended from the point of view of the subjective experiences, conceptions, and goals of the individual, that is, from the point of view of its meaning. According to Weber, such action is at bottom oriented to the here and now. It gradually attains a wealth of meanings, ultimately even symbolic ones. Trial and adherence to what has been tried are of particular importance, since deviation can render an action ineffective. For this reason, religions are more tolerant of opposing dogmatic concepts than they are of innovations in their symbolism, which could endanger the magical effect of their actions or rouse the anger of the ancestral soul or the god. Hence we encounter in all cultures religious stereotyping, in rites, in art, in gestures, dance, music, and writing, in exorcism and medicine. The sacred thus becomes specifically what is unchangeable. By virtue of it, religious concepts also tend to force stereotypes upon behavior and economics. Any actions intended to introduce change have to be correspondingly binding. The ones most likely to fulfill this requirement are specific contracts. The Roman civil marriage in the form of coemtio was, for example, a profanation of the sacramental *confarreatio*.

Anthropological Methods. At times man reveals himself in situations that appear to be of a different quality than ordinary ones. The latter form the basis for comparison either as the sum of his normal behavior or as a social cross section. For the moment, comparisons demonstrating the specific differences between a possibly sacred condition and a profane one, or showing social appraisal of a specific human type as sacred in contrast to the profane average person, are best relegated to categories of a historical anthropology. A culture may choose to identify any number of unusual individual conditions or situations as sacred or profane. The most important of these warrant closer examination:

Ecstasy and trance. Even in terms of ethology, one could probably establish a similarity between men and animals in the way they concentrate on an opponent, holding their breath in silence and maintaining a tense calm from which they can instantly switch into motion. Presumably this has its roots in the moment when the first hunter found himself confronting his prey. As far as humans are concerned, the perpetuation and further development of this primeval behavior is a history of self-interpretations that presuppose continuously changing social contexts. This was probably first apparent in shamanism, and continues to be so wherever it persists. Specifically, from the fifth century BCE on, it was believed that one could physically step out of one's normal state; and from the first century BCE, that one's essential being, the soul, the self or perceiving organ, could take leave of the body. Ecstasy is not necessarily sacred; it can also be profane, though quite often specific manifestations, such as intoxication, glossolalia, receptivity to visions and voices, hyperesthesia, anesthesia, or paresthesia, are identical. In technologically poor cultures, profane ecstasies may accompany initiations, rites of passage, and preparation for war, or may be reactions to specific defeats or social setbacks. Ecstasy is only sacred in the context of historical religion and is never the primal germ of any religion. Nevertheless, ecstasy can be experienced within a religion as the basic source of its particular variety of mysticism.

> **Ecstasy is only sacred in the context of historical religion and is never the primal germ of any religion.**

It then passes over into trance, of which possession has already been recognized as the hyperkinetic primal form. When the being by which one is possessed, or—to put it more mildly—inspired, is held to be a god who has replaced the extinguished consciousness, classical Greek already spoke of enthousiasmos. By definition, such possession is sacred. Profane trances, on the other hand, are those accompanied by visions of distant events, or past or future ones.

Sexuality and asceticism. Sex, especially female sexuality, is considered sacred. It stands as the positive condition contrary to both infertility and asexuality. If a woman was infertile, it probably meant above all that she was malnourished, and starvation is always profane when not undertaken in deliberate fasts as a means of conquering the physical self.

Sexuality, especially active sex, is also held to be the contrary of asexuality, the profane sign either of the normal condition of both sexes as the result of danger, cold, or constant labor, or of the lesser capacity for frequent orgasm on the part of the male.

The importance in archaic societies of dominant goddesses, especially mother goddesses, is solely dependent on the sacredness of their sexuality and is not a result of their given character as either the otherworldly representatives of matriarchal societies or the polar referents in patriarchal ones.

Asceticism is not the profanation of sexuality but rather a transcendence over man's normal condition into a perfection that lies in the opposite direction. The ascetic practices self-denial with regard to all aspects of life, including eating and drinking. In suppressing his sexuality, he is to a certain extent both acknowledging its sacred dimension and claiming that sacredness for himself.

Innocence and wisdom. Since Vergil's fourth *Eclogue,* perhaps since the prophecies of Isaiah, or even earlier, the innocence of the messianic child has been seen as sacred. Mere babbling childishness, on the other hand, is profane.

Wisdom can be the sacredness of old age, as in the case of the Hindu guru, the mystagogue of late antiquity, or the *tsaddiq* in Jewish Hasidism, who only after long experience is able, through his own example, to help his fellow men find communion with God. Feebleness on the part of the elderly is widely considered to be profane, and when it poses a burden on the young they tend to segregate themselves from it socially.

Charismatic and magical gifts. The relationship between these is complex.

A miracle worker was often thought of as a sacred person, as were Origen's pupil Gregory Theodoros of Sykeon and others who were given the epithet *Thaumaturgus.* But not all of the figures canonized as saints by the Catholic church, for example, were miracle workers. Conversely, it is also possible for a miracle worker *not* to be recognized as a saint or be held to have been so according to religious scholarship. Here profaneness is easier to define: that person is profane who is simply incapable of controlling sicknesses, natural forces, or his own feelings of animosity.

Temporal Existence. Regardless of the similarity of religious phenomena throughout cultures, it is the cultural-historical context that at the same time lends an immeasurable novelty to their various manifestations. As for the phenomena of the sacred and the profane, the following temporal aspects are of fundamental importance.

Unchangeableness. The sacred is absolutely unchangeable only if one has extrahistorical reasons for treating it as a metaphysical, eternal, or transhistorical reality. As understood by Max Weber, it is not unchangeable. On the historical plane, unchangeableness and constancy are evident to the degree that in everything that the religious phenomenologies identify as sacred—persons, communities, actions, writings, manifestations of nature, manufactured objects, periods, places, numbers, and formulas—not only are situations, motive, and conditions expressed, but an ancient type remains operative, or makes a reappearance.

Metamorphoses. These appear as either transcendence over the profane or secularization—now no longer considered primary, as it was above—of the sacred. The former occurs in initiations, sacraments, and baptisms, in the use of stones for shrines or of animals as offerings, in the blessing of an object, an act, or a person. The latter is evident on a large scale in world-historical processes. On a small scale it is present whenever a sacred function is simulated, when a myth is transformed from the fact that it *is* into a reporting of facts, when a sacred text is read for entertainment, or whenever someone's behavior swerves from his vows to God, without his actually sinning.

Destruction. The destruction of religion is not the same thing as the destruction of the sacred. The destruction of a religion occurs most clearly when it is confined to institutions, as these can simply be abolished. The sacred, on the other hand, increasingly tends, in industrial society, to be transformed from the active element it once was into a kind of unexpressed potentiality. It then decays in social intercourse and such intercourse becomes wholly profane. Nevertheless, its archetype persists in the human spirit, and is always capable of restoring the religious feeling to consciousness, if conditions are favorable.

Restoration. It is possible to try to secure once more the place for the sacred in society that it lost thanks to the disappearance of the distinction between it and the profane that once existed. This is what motivates the scholarship of the Collège de Sociologie. Every community that is intact and wishes to remain so requires a notion of the sacred as *a priori*. Archaic societies that provided sufficient room for the sacred kept it socially viable in secret fraternities or through magicians or shamans. Modern societies can achieve the same by means of public events such as festivals, which generate social strength, or by the establishment of monastic, elitist orders, or the creation of new centers of authority.

Determining the Relationships

The relationships between the sacred and the profane occur both on the level of their expression in language and on a (or *the*) level of existence that is characterized by various different ontological qualities. The relationships between these two levels themselves are of a more fundamental nature. Since only the *homo religiosus* is capable of bearing witness to the manner of such existence, and not the scholar, we can speak of it only in formal categories that reveal both the conditions of our possible perception of the sacred and the transcendental prerequisites of its mode of being.

The Epistemological Approach. Non-Kantian religious thinkers and scholars have always restricted themselves to their inner experience. What they have found there could easily be rediscovered in history. The experiential method, which tends toward psychology, was therefore always superbly compatible with the historical-genetic method. On the other hand, it is also possible to apply a logical, analytical, transcendental method, and in fact this can be used in

investigating the possibilities of both inner experience and historical perception. Heretofore, discussion of these alternatives has been most productive toward determining the position of the philosophy of religion, and therefore religion itself, within the overall scheme of culture and scholarship. At the same time, it has tended to curtail any elucidation of the religious phenomenon in general and the phenomenon of the sacred and its relation to the profane in particular. Perhaps one could take it further.

A priori and a posteriori. In his book *Kantisch-Fries'sche Religionsphilosophie und ihre Anwendung auf die Theologie* (Tübingen, 1909), Rudolf Otto took a rational approach to the a priori concept and applied it to the idea of God. God is not an object alongside or superior to other objects, and he cannot be placed in one of the various standard relationships. He is able to transcend space and time as well as every particular relationship. Accordingly, it must be possible to imagine the sacred as standing in a transcendental primal relationship to things. One way or the other, the a priori concept is rational.

Rationality and irrationality. When writing *Das Heilige* (1917), Otto abandoned his transcendental philosophical position. He did not give up the *a priori* concept, however, but rather reinterpreted it with a psychological slant. In this way, the transcendentality of the rational applied to the a priori concept becomes the capacity of thought to be rational. This capacity can then be opposed to the irrational. The rational concepts of absoluteness, necessity, and essential quality, as well as the idea of the good, which expresses an objective and binding value, have to be traced back to whatever lies in pure reason, independent of experience, whereas the irrational element of the sacred must be traced back to the pure ideas of the divine or the numinous. Here, from the point of view of irrationality, "pure" becomes the attribute of something psychically given, and the a priori becomes emotional.

On the other hand, as Anders Nygren argues, just as one questions the validity of perception, using the *a priori* of cognition theory, it becomes necessary to question the validity of religion, using the religious *a priori* concept. Further, Nygren and Friedrich Karl Feigel suggest, it becomes necessary to comprehend the sacred as a complex category *a priori*, not so as to be able to experience it in itself, but rather so as to identify the sacred in experience and cognition, even in the course of history.

The Ontological Approach. Links exist not only between the sacred and the profane, each of which has its own complexity, but also between the sacred and the demonic, the profane and the evil, the profane and the demonic, and the sacred and the evil. The first and second links have ontological implications, the third and fourth have ethical ones, and the fifth has both. We obscure the demonic aspect when we ask the question whether we can have an ethic that can deal with the awesome potential powers at modern man's disposal without restoring the category of the sacred, which was thoroughly destroyed by the Enlightenment. In Hans Jonas's view, these powers continue to accumulate in secret and impel humankind to use them, and only respectful awe in the face of the sacred can transcend our calculations of earthly terror. But it is not the task of this article to enter into a discussion of ethical implications; we must be content to consider the ontological ones.

> ... only respectful awe in the face of the sacred can transcend our calculations of earthly terror.

Ambivalence. Otto described the positive aspect of the sacred by using the numinous factor *fascinans* and various subordinate factors of the numinous factor *tremendum*. He characterized its negative aspect by way of a subordinate factor of the latter that he called "the awesome." In so doing he provided countless studies with the suggestion of an ambivalence that truly exists and is not to be confused with the dialectic of the hierophanies. However, Otto was referring primarily to the essence of the sacred in itself. Such an approach is logically possible only if one begins consistently and exclusively from "above." Since Otto declares both aspects to be factors of the same numinousness, his methodological starting point becomes, *de facto*, if not intentionally, Judeo-Christian theocentricity. This is certainly extremely productive, but it also exhibits one of the limits of scholarly study of religion: namely its continual orientation, only seeming to overcome the theological *a priori*, at the starting point of historical scholarship, namely recognition of the ambivalence in the ancient Roman notion of the sacrum.

Dialectics. Eliade has concentrated the links between the complexes of the sacred and the profane on the plane of appearances, introducing the inspired concept of hierophany. A hierophany exposes the sacred in the profane. Since there are numerous hierophanies (though the same ones do not always appear everywhere), he sets up a dialectic of hierophanies to explain why an object or an occurrence may be sacred at one moment but not at another. Such an approach makes it possible to examine every historical datum and identify it as sacred or profane—and in so doing to write a new history of religions within profane history. In addition, one can draw conclusions about the objectivity of the sacred, which is satiated with being and therefore has the power, functioning through the hierophanies (including even their profane element), to become apparent. Eliade does both. The former demonstrates a historical phenomenology, and points toward an as yet unrealized historical psychology of religion. The latter is subject to the same criticism as the ontological proof of God.

BIBLIOGRAPHY

The most influential modern book on the subject is Rudolf Otto's *Das Heilige* (Breslau, 1917; often reprinted), translated by John W. Harvey as *The Idea of the Holy* (Oxford, 1923). The most important earlier contributions (Wilhelm Windelband, Wilhelm Wundt, Nathan Söderblom), subsequent ones (Joseph Geyser, Friedrich Karl Feigel, Walter Baetke, et al.), and various specific philological studies are collected in *Die Diskussion um das Heilige,* edited by Carsten Colpe (Darmstadt, 1977). A new epoch began with the work of Mircea Eliade, and one could cite a great number of monographs by him. As the most relevant, one might single out his *Traité d'histoire des religions* (Paris, 1949), translated by Rosemary Sheed as *Patterns in Comparative Religion* (New York, 1958), and *Das Heilige und das Profane* (Hamburg, 1957), translated by Willard R. Trask as *The Sacred and the Profane* (New York, 1959).

Hans Joachim Greschat has provided a new study of the classical late nineteenth-century theme in his *Mana und Tapu* (Berlin, 1980). Examples from an African people are provided by Peter Fuchs in *Kult und Autorität: Die Religion der Hadjerai* (Berlin, 1970) and by Jeanne-Françoise Vincent in *Le pouvoir et le sacré chez les Hadjeray du Tchad* (Paris, 1975). Exemplary philological investigation of linguistic usage and concepts among the Greeks, Romans, Jews, and early Christians is found in the article "Heilig" by Albrecht Dihle in the *Reallexikon für Antike und Christentum,* vol. 13 (Stuttgart, 1987); similar study of late antiquity appears in Peter Brown's *Society and the Holy in Late Antiquity* (London, 1982). The same subject matter, expanded to include the ancient Orient and India, is found in the important work edited by Julien Ries et al., *L'expression du sacré dans les grandes religions,* 3 vols., (Louvain, 1978-1986), for which there is a separate introduction by Julien Ries, *Le sacré comme approche de Dieu et comme ressource de l'homme* (Louvain, 1983). Supplementing this with respect to Egypt is James Karl Hoffmeier's *"Sacred" in the Vocabulary of Ancient Egypt: The Term DSR, with Special Reference to Dynasties I-XX* (Freiburg, 1985).

Theoretical implications are investigated by Ansgar Paus in *Religiöser Erkenntnisgrund: Herkunft und Wesen der Apriori-Theorie Rudolf Ottos* (Leiden, 1966) and by Georg Schmid in *Interessant und Heilig: Auf dem Wege zur integralen Religions-wissenschaft* (Zurich, 1971). Important sociological investigation of ritual is found in Jean Cazeneuve's *Sociologie du rite* (Paris, 1971) and of the history of force, counterforce, and sacrifice in René Girard's *La violence et le sacré* (Paris, 1972), translated by Patrick Gregory as *Violence and the Sacred* (Baltimore, 1977). Additional ethical implications are considered by Bernhard Häring in *Das Heilige und das Gute, Religion und Sitt-lichkeit in ihrem gegenseitigen Bezug* (Krailling vor München, 1950). On the disappearance of the sacred through secularization and its reappearance in times of crisis, see Enrico Castelli's *Il tempo inqualificabile: Contributi all'ermeneutica della secolarizzazione* (Padua, 1975) and Franco Ferrarotti and others' *Forme del sacro in un'epoca di crisi* (Naples, 1978). Summaries from various points of view include Roger Caillois's *L'homme et le sacré* (1939; 3d ed., Paris, 1963), translated by Meyer Barash as *Man and the Sacred* (Glencoe, Ill., 1959); Jacques Grand'Maison's *Le monde et le sacré,* 2 vols. (Paris, 1966-1968); and Enrico Castelli and others' *Il sacro* (Padua, 1974).

CARSTEN COLPE
Translated from German by Russell M. Stockman

SACRIFICE

The term *sacrifice,* from the Latin *sacrificium* (*sacer,* "holy"; *facere,* "to make"), carries the connotation of the religious act in the highest, or fullest sense; it can also be understood as the act of sanctifying or consecrating an object.

Sacrifice differs from other cultic actions. The external elements of prayer are simply words and gestures (bodily attitudes), not external objects comparable to the gifts of sacrifice. Eliminatory rites, though they may include the slaying of a living being or the destruction of an inanimate object, are not directed to a personal recipient and thus should not be described as sacrifices. The same is true of ritual slayings in which there is no supernatural being as recipient, as in slayings by which companions are provided for the dead (joint burials) or that are part of the dramatic representation of an event in primordial time.

The Sacrificer. The sacrificer may be the head of a family or clan, an elder, or the leader of a band of hunters; in matrilinear societies, the sacrificer may be a woman. This is true especially of hunting and food-gathering cultures as well as nomadic pastoral cultures; even when these include individuals with specific ritual functions (medicine men, sorcerers, soothsayers, shamans), the function of offering sacrifice is not reserved to them. Food-planting cultures, on the other hand, commonly have cultic functionaries to whom the offering of sacrifice is reserved (e.g., the "earth-chiefs" in West African cultures).

The more fully articulated the divisions in a society, the more often there is a class of cultic ministers to whom the offering of sacrifice is reserved. In this situation, tensions and changing relations of power can arise between king and priests, as in ancient Egypt.

Material of the Oblation. Perhaps we may say that originally what was sacrificed was either something living or an element or symbol of life; in other words, it was not primarily food that was surrendered, but life itself. Yet inanimate things were also included in the material for sacrifice. (But do not archaic cultures regard a great deal as living that to the modern scientific mind is inanimate? Some scholars emphasize not the life but the power of the object.) Only by including inanimate objects is it possible to establish a certain classification of sacrificial objects, as for example, on the one hand, plants and inanimate objects (bloodless offerings) and, on the other, human beings and animals (blood offerings).

Bloodless offerings. Bloodless offerings include, in the first place, vegetative materials. Thus food-gatherers offer a (symbolic) portion of the foodstuffs they have collected. Among herders milk and milk products (e.g., koumiss, a drink derived from milk and slightly fermented, used in Inner Asia) play a similar role, especially in firstlings sacrifices (see below). In the ritual pouring (and especially in other ritual uses) of water, the intention is often not sacrifice but either some other type of rite (lustration, purification, or expiation) or sympathetic magic (e.g., pouring water in order to bring on rain). The offering of flowers or of a sweet fragrance otherwise produced (as in the widespread use of incense, or, among the American Indians, of tobacco smoke) also serves to please the gods or other higher beings.

Blood offerings. When animals or human beings serve as the sacrificial gift, the shedding of blood may become an essential part of the sacrificial action. Thus *ritual* slaying makes its appearance among cultivators and herders. The most extensive development of ritual slaying is found among cultivators. Here blood plays a significant role as a power-laden substance that brings fertility; it is sprinkled on the fields in order to promote crop yield. Head-hunting, cannibalism, and human sacrifice belong to the same complex of ideas and rites; human sacrifice is also seen as a means of maintaining the cosmic order. Blood sacrifices, however, consist primarily of domesticated animals.

Substitutes. Blood sacrifices, especially those in which human beings were offered, were often replaced at a later stage by other sacrificial gifts, as, for example, "part-for-the-whole" sacrifices, like the offering of fingers, hair, or blood drawn through self-inflicted wounds. Some authors would thus classify so-called chastity sacrifices and include under this heading very disparate and sometimes even opposed practices such as, on the one hand, sexual abandon (sacral prostitution) and, on the other, sexual renunciation, castration, and circumcision.

Animal sacrifices can replace human sacrifices, as seen in well-known examples from Greek myth, epic, and history and in the Hebrew scriptures (Old Testament; *Gn.* 22:1-19).

Divine offerings. In the examples given under the previous heading, a sacrificial gift is replaced by another of lesser value. The opposite occurs when the sacrificial gift itself is regarded as divine. This divine status may result from the idea that the sacrificial action repeats a mythical primordial sacrifice in which a god sacrificed either himself or some other god to yet a third god. In other cases the sacrificial object becomes divinized in the sacrificial action itself or in the preparation of the gifts. Thus among the Aztec the prisoner of war who was sacrificed was identified with the recipient of the sacrifice, the god Tezcatlipoca; moreover images of dough, kneaded with the blood of the sacrificed human, were identified with the sun god Huitzilopochtli and ritually eaten.

Place and Time of Sacrifice. The place of offering is not always an altar set aside for the purpose. Thus sacrifices to the dead are often offered at their graves, and sacrifices to the spirits of nature are made beside trees or bushes, in caves, at springs, and so on. Artificial altars in the form of tables are relatively rare. Far more frequently, natural stones or heaps of stones or earthen mounds serve as altars.

The time for regular sacrifices is determined by the astronomical or vegetative year; thus there will be daily, weekly, and monthly sacrifices (especially in higher cultures in which service in the temple is organized like service at a royal court). Sowing and harvest and the transition from one season to the next are widely recognized occasions for sacrifice; in nomadic cultures this is true especially of spring, the season of birth among animals and of abundance of milk.

Extraordinary occasions for sacrifice are provided by special occurrences in the life of the community or the individual. These occurrences may be joyous, as, for example, the erection of a building (especially a temple), the accession of a new ruler, the successful termination of a military campaign or other undertaking, or any event that is interpreted as a manifestation of divine favor. Even more frequently, however, it is critical situations that occasion extraordinary sacrifices: illnesses (especially epidemics or livestock diseases) and droughts or other natural disasters.

Intentions of Sacrifice. Theologians usually distinguish four intentions of sacrifice: praise (acknowledgment, homage), thanksgiving, supplication, and expiation.

Praise (homage). Pure sacrifices of praise that express nothing but homage and veneration and involve no other intention are rarely found. They occur chiefly where a regular sacrificial cult is practiced that resembles in large measure the ceremonial of a royal court.

Thanksgiving. Sacrifices of thanksgiving are more frequent. According to the best explanation of firstlings sacrifices, these, in the diverse forms they have taken in various cultures, belong to this category. Votive sacrifices likewise belong here, insofar as the fulfillment of the vow is an act of thanksgiving for the favor granted.

Supplication. Sacrifices of supplication (petition) include all those sacrifices that, in addition to establishing or consolidating the link with the world of the sacred (which is a function of every sacrifice), are intended to have some special effect. Such effects include the maintenance of the cosmic order; the strengthening of the powers on which this order depends (e.g., by the gift of blood, as in the human sacrifices of the Aztec); and the sacralization or consecration of places, objects, and buildings (construction sacrifices, dedication of boundary stones, idols, temples), of individual human beings, and of human communities and their relationships (ratification of treaties). Sacrifices are also offered for highly specialized purposes, for example, in order to foretell the future by examining the entrails of the sacrificial animal.

Expiation. Expiation means simply the removal of what has roused (or might rouse) the anger of spirits and demons, so that they will leave humans in peace; no relationship of goodwill or friendship is created or sought. On the other hand, the higher beings may be regarded as inherently benevolent, so that any disturbance of a good relationship with them is attributed to a human fault; the normal good rela-

tionship must therefore be restored by an expiatory sacrifice or other human action; in these cases we speak of atonement, conciliation, or propitiation. The human fault in question may be moral, but it may also be purely ritual, unintentional, or even unconscious.

BIBLIOGRAPHY

Baal, Jan van. "Offering, Sacrifice and Gift." *Numen* 23 (December 1976): 161-178.

Baaren, Th. P. van. "Theoretical Speculations on Sacrifice." *Numen* 11 (January 1964): 1-12.

Bertholet, Alfred. *Der Sinn des kultischen Opfers.* Berlin, 1942.

Closs, Alois. "Das Opfer in Ost und West." *Kairos* 3 (1961): 153-161.

Evans-Pritchard, E. E. *Theories of Primitive Religion.* Oxford, 1965.

Faherty, Robert L. "Sacrifice." In *Encyclopaedia Britannica.* 15th ed. Chicago, 1974.

Girard, René. *Violence and the Sacred.* Translated by Patrick Gregory. Baltimore, 1977.

Girard, René. *Des choses cachées depuis la fondation du monde.* Paris, 1978.

Gray, Louis H., et al. "Expiation and Atonement." In *Encyclopaedia of Religion and Ethnics,* edited by James Hastings, vol. 5. Edinburgh, 1912.

Heiler, Friedrich. *Erscheinungsformen und Wesen der Religion.* Vol. 1 of *Die Religionen der Menschheit.* Stuttgart, 1961.

Henninger, Joseph. "Ist der sogenannte Nilus-Bericht eine brauchbare religionsgeschichtliche Quelle?" *Anthropos* 50 (1955): 81-148.

Henninger, Joseph. "Primitalopfer und Neujahrsfest." In *Anthropica.* Studia Instituti Anthropos, vol. 21. Sankt Augustin, West Germany, 1968.

Henninger, Joseph. *Les fêtes de printemps chez les Sémites et la Pâque israélite.* Paris, 1975.

Henninger, Joseph. *Arabica Sacra: Aufsätze zur Religionsgeschichte Arabiens und seiner Randgebiete.* Fribourg, 1981.

Hubert, Henri, and Marcel Mauss. "Essai sur la nature et la fonction du sacrifice." *L'année sociologique* 2 (1899): 29-138. An English translation was published in 1964 (Chicago): *Sacrifice: Its Nature and Function.*

James, E. O. *Sacrifice and Sacrament.* London, 1962.

James, E. O., et al. "Sacrifice." In *Encyclopaedia of Religion and Ethics,* edited by James Hastings, vol. 11. Edinburgh, 1920.

Jensen, Adolf E. *Myth and Cult among Primitive Peoples.* Translated by Marianna Tax Choldin and Wolfgang Weissleder. Chicago, 1963.

Kerr, C. M., et al. "Propitiation." In *Encyclopaedia of Religion and Ethics,* edited by James Hastings, vol. 10. Edinburgh, 1918.

Lanternari, Vittorio. *'La Grande Festa': Vita rituale e sistemi di produzione nelle società tradizionali.* 2d ed. Bari, 1976.

Leeuw, Gerardus van der. "Die do-ut-des-Formel in der Opfertheorie." *Archiv für Religionswissenschaft* 20 (1920-1921): 241-253.

Leeuw, Gerardus van der. *Religion in Essence and Manifestation* (1938). 2 vols. Translated by J. E. Turner. Gloucester, Mass., 1967.

Loisy, Alfred. *Essai historique sur le sacrifice.* Paris, 1920.

Müller-Karpe, Hermann. *Handbuch der Vorgeschichte.* 2 vols. Munich, 1966-1968.

Le sacrifice, I-V. Nos. 2-6 of *Systèmes de pensée en Afrique noire.* Ivry, France, 1976-1983.

Schmidt, Wilhelm. *Der Ursprung der Gottesidee.* 12 vols. Münster, 1912-1955. See especially volume 6, pages 274-281, 444-455;

volume 8, pages 595-633; and volume 12, pages 389-441, 826-836, and 845-847.

Schmidt, Wilhelm. "Ethnologische Bemerkungen zu theologischen Opfertheorien." In *Jahrbuch des Missionshauses St. Gabriel*, vol. 1. Mödling, 1922.

Smith, W. Robertson. *Lectures on the Religion of the Semites: The Fundamental Institutions* (1889). 3d ed. Reprint, New York, 1969.

Tylor, E. B. *Primitive Culture* (1871). 2 vols. Reprint, New York, 1970.

Vorbichler, Anton. *Das Opfer auf den uns heute noch erreichbaren ältesten Stufen der Menschheitsgeschichte: Eine Begriffsstudie.* Mödling, 1956.

Widengren, Geo. *Religionsphänomenologie.* Berlin, 1969.

Additional literature is found in the works cited in the article, especially those by Hubert and Mauss, Loisy, Schmidt, Bertholet, van der Leeuw, Henninger, Lanternari, Heiler, James, and Widengren, as well as in *Le sacrifice*, especially volume 1.

JOSEPH HENNINGER
Translated from German by Matthew J. O'Connell

SAICHO

SAICHO (767-822), also known by his posthumous title Dengyo Daishi; founder of Japanese Tendai, a sect derived from the teachings and practices of the Chinese T`ien-t`ai school.

Life. Saicho was born into a family of devout Buddhists. At the age of twelve he went to study at the provincial temple in Omi. There he studied under Gyohyo (722-797), a disciple of Tao-hsüan (702-760), the Chinese monk who had brought Northern School Ch`an, Kegon (Chin., Hua-yen) teachings, and the *Fan wang* precepts to Japan in 736. Saicho's studies of meditation and Kegon "one-vehicle" (Skt., *ekayana;* Jpn., *ichijo*) doctrines during this period influenced his lifelong doctrinal predilections. Shortly after he was ordained in 785, he decided to climb Mount Hiei. He remained there for approximately a decade to meditate and study. During his retreat, Saicho read about Chinese T`ien-t`ai meditation practice in Kegon texts and managed to obtain several T`ien-t`ai texts that had been brought to Japan by Chien-chen (Ganjin, 688-763) in 754 but had subsequently been ignored by Japanese monks.

The capital of Japan was moved from Nara to Nagaoka in 784, and then to Kyoto in 795. Mount Hiei was located to the northeast of Kyoto, a direction considered dangerous by geomancers, but Saicho's presence on the mountain protected the new capital and brought him to the attention of the court. In addition, the court was interested in reforming Buddhism by patronizing serious monks without political aspirations and by supporting those teachings that would bridge the traditional rivalry between the Hosso (Yogacara) and Sanron (Madhyamika) schools. Soon various court nobles, especially those of the Wake clan, began to show an interest in

Saicho. With court support, Saicho traveled to China in 804 to obtain T`ien-t`ai texts and to study with Chinese teachers. During his eight months there, he received initiations into a variety of Buddhist traditions, including the T`ien-t`ai school, Oxhead Ch`an, the *Fan wang* precepts (a set of fifty-eight Mahayana disciplinary rules), and Esoteric Buddhism.

Upon his return to Japan in 805, Saicho discovered that his brief studies of Esoteric Buddhism attracted more attention than his mastery of Tendai teachings. Saicho's major patron, Emperor Kammu (r. 781-806), was ill, and Saicho used Esoteric rituals in an attempt to restore Kammu's health. Shortly before Kammu died the court awarded Saicho two yearly ordinands, one in Tendai and one in Esoteric Buddhism. This event marked the formal establishment of the Tendai school.

Saicho spent the next few years studying Esoteric Buddhism, but his efforts were overshadowed by the return of Kukai (774-835) from China in 806. Kukai's knowledge of Esoteric Buddhist practice and doctrine was clearly superior to that of Saicho. Although Saicho and some of his disciples went to study with Kukai and borrowed Esoteric texts from him, by 816 irreconcilable differences on doctrinal issues, a dispute over the loan of certain Esoteric texts, and the defection of Taihan (778-858?), one of Saicho's most able disciples, ended Saicho's hopes of mastering Esoteric Buddhism.

Saicho's activities during this period can be divided into two categories. First, he defended Tendai doctrines and meditation practices against attacks by the Hosso monk Tokuitsu (d. 841?). Saicho argued that everyone could attain Buddhahood and that many could do so in their present lifetime through Tendai and Esoteric practices. He firmly rejected the Hosso argument that the attainment of Buddhahood required aeons of practice and that some people would never

> **Saicho argued that everyone could attain Buddhahood and that many could do so in their present lifetime through Tendai and Esoteric practices.**

be able to attain it. Second, Saicho proposed major reforms in the Tendai educational system, in monastic discipline, and in the ordination system. Saicho suggested that Tendai monks be ordained on Mount Hiei, where they would be required to remain for the next twelve years without venturing outside the monastery's boundaries. Ordinations were to be supervised by lay administrators (*zoku betto*) who also held important positions at court.

Saicho's proposals were vehemently opposed by the Hosso and other Nara schools because their approval would have entailed implicit recognition of Saicho's criticisms of

Hosso doctrine and practice. In addition, the proposals would have removed Tendai monks from the supervision of the Office of Monastic Affairs (Sogo). The court, not wishing to become involved in disputes between schools, hesitated to act on Saicho's proposals. As a result, Saicho died without seeing his reforms approved; however, one week after Saicho's death the court approved the proposals as a posthumous tribute.

Thought. Most of Saicho's works were polemical and designed either to prove that Tendai doctrine and practice were superior to that of any of the other schools of Japanese Buddhism or to argue that the Tendai school should be free of any supervision by other schools. In his defense of Tendai interests, Saicho discussed a number of issues that played important roles in later Japanese religious history.

Saicho had an acute sense of the flow of Buddhist history. The teachings of the *Lotus Sutra,* the text that contained the Buddha's ultimate teaching according to the Tendai school, had been composed in India and then transmitted to China. Japan, Saicho believed, would be the next site for the rise of the "one-vehicle" teachings propagated by Tendai. Saicho was conversant with theories on the decline of Buddhism and believed that he was living at the end of the Period of Counterfeit Dharma *(zomatsu),* described as an era in which many monks would be corrupt and covetous.

Although Saicho believed major changes were needed in Japanese Buddhism, he did not use theories on the decline of Buddhism to justify doctrinal innovations, as did some of the founders of the Kamakura schools. Rather, Saicho argued that because Buddhism in the capital had declined, monks should retreat to the mountains to practice assiduously.

Many of Saicho's doctrinal innovations were based on his belief that the religious aptitude of the Japanese people as a whole had matured to the point where they no longer needed any form of Buddhism other than the "perfect teachings" *(engyo)* of the Tendai school. Earlier Buddhist thinkers had also been interested in the manner in which the religious faculties of people matured, but had usually discussed the process in terms of individuals rather than whole peoples.

Religious training for people with "perfect faculties" *(enki,* i. e., those whose religious faculties respond to the "perfect teachings") was based on the threefold study *(sangaku)* of morality, meditation, and doctrine. Saicho believed that T`ien-t`ai teachings on meditation and doctrine were adequate, although they could be supplemented by Esoteric Buddhism. However, he was dissatisfied with the traditional T`ien-t`ai position on morality, which maintained that a monk could follow the *Ssu-fen lü* precepts with a Mahayana mind. Saicho argued that adherence to the *Ssu-fen lü* would cause a monk to retrogress toward Hinayana goals. Tendai practices could be realized only by using the Mahayana *Fan wang* precepts for ordinations and monastic discipline.

BIBLIOGRAPHY

Saicho's works have been collected in *Dengyo Daishi zenshu,* 5 vols. (1926; reprint, Tokyo, 1975). Important collections of Japanese scholarship are *Dengyo Daishi kenkyu,* 5 vols. (Tokyo, 1973-1980), and Shioiri Ryodo's *Saicho* (Tokyo, 1982). For a study of Saicho in English, see my book *Saicho and the Establishment of the Japanese Tendai School* (Berkeley, 1984).

PAUL GRONER

SAINTHOOD

Historians of religion have liberated the category of sainthood from its narrower Christian associations and have employed the term in a more general way to refer to the state of special holiness that many religions attribute to certain people.

The Category of Sainthood. Fundamentally, sainthood may be described as a religion's acclamation of a person's spiritual perfection, however that perfection is defined. These figures may serve as wonder-workers, helpmates, or intercessors. In other words, saints are recognized by their religions as both subjects for imitation and objects of veneration. Usually sainthood is a posthumous phenomenon.

Sainthood in Major World Religions. Sainthood, as here typified, does not exist universally. Not all religious communities acclaim holy individuals as both paradigms to be imitated and intercessors to be venerated. Judaism forbids the worship of human beings. Protestant Christianity, while emphasizing individual salvation, repudiated the Catholic cult

> **Judaism forbids the worship of human beings.**

of saints. Archaic and primitive religions tend to associate holiness more with certain offices, such as shaman or medicine man, than with unique individuals.

Christianity. Under the Roman persecution that began in the first century, many Christians gave up their lives rather than renounce their faith. These martyrs became the first persons to be given the title *hagios* ("saint"). At first the martyrs were remembered primarily as witnesses, examples to encourage others in times of persecution: other Christians were urged to follow their model of imitating Christ by submitting to death. But at the same time, because they had transcended death and dwelled in heaven, martyrs possessed extraordinary powers, which the faithful could summon. At martyrs' tombs one could pray for cures of ills, for forgiveness of sins, or for protection from enemies.

Although martyrdom was clearly believed to transport a person to heaven and sainthood, other forms of superlative piety required the evidence of miracles to substantiate posthumous heavenly domicile. Thus the miraculous element in the lives of the saints was increasingly stressed: saints healed, exorcised, prophesied, and mastered the elements of nature. [*See* Miracle.]

Saints, especially monks and royal figures, are also central to the piety of Eastern Orthodox Christianity.

Islam. The monotheistic religion preached by Muhammad and exhibited in the Qur'an abhorred and forbade the association of anything or anyone with God. Even Muhammad himself was seen only as God's spokesman. Nevertheless, popular Islam came to understand the *wali* as a particular kind of friend of God, one whose special closeness to divinity mediated between the ordinary faithful and that all-powerful and distant deity.

The figures who best illustrate the saint as imitated and venerated holy person are the Sufi masters. Veneration of a Sufi master continued posthumously at his tomb, especially on the anniversary of his birth.

Not all Muslim saints are Sufis, however. In Morocco, marabouts (warrior-saints), who claim descent from the Prophet and possession of thaumaturgic powers, are believed to preside after death over the territory around their tombs and bestow blessings through their descendants.

Judaism. Although classic rabbinic Judaism gave no sanction to hagiography or hagiolatry, it revered a whole galaxy of exemplary figures. Biblical heroes such as Abraham and Moses, rabbinic sages such as Hillel and Me'ir (of the first and second centuries, respectively), and martyrs such as `Aqiva' ben Yosef (also of the second century) all displayed imitable virtues commended to the faithful in the legends of the Talmud and Midrashic literature. Martyrs were especially sacred to a people so often persecuted.

If the rabbis of the Talmud never countenanced the veneration of human beings alive or dead, popular sentiment was often otherwise. Reputed graves of biblical and rabbinic worthies, for instance, were the objects of pilgrimages in ancient and medieval days, and among Middle Eastern Jews they still are.

Hinduism. Devotees do not always distinguish human saints from divine incarnations. Hindu deities are regularly described anthropomorphically, and highly spiritual humans manifest divinity. The god Krsna, for instance, appears in the *Bhagavadgita,* Hinduism's most popular text, as both instructor and object of devotion.

But it was the *bhakti* ("devotion") movements, focused on the worship of theistic gods, principally Visnu and Siva, in which the *guru* ("preceptor") as saint became prominent. In literature as early as the Upanisadic texts the *guru* was seen not only as a teacher of the Vedas but also as a model whose daily habits pointed the way to spiritual liberation. In modern times *gurus* have continued to be an important force in Hindu religion, and some have found substantial followings beyond India.

Buddhism. The two major divisions of Buddhism, Theravada and Mahayana, have different understandings of sainthood. While Theravada Buddhism idealizes the world-renouncing saint who follows the Buddha's reported last words to "seek your *own* salvation with diligence," Mahayana schools, dominant in East Asia, stress the power of saints to aid ordinary laymen to attain enlightenment. The *bodhisattva* (lit., "Buddha-to-be") is a saint who has postponed his complete enlightenment in order to help others along the path. He emulates the compassion of the Buddha by nurturing the seeds of enlightenment that are present in all beings. [*See* Bodhisattva Path.]

Confucianism. As one of the several religious components of precommunist China, Confucianism offers a distinct notion of sainthood. For Confucius (551-479 BCE), as recorded in the *Analects,* the ideal humans were the sage-kings, the legendary ancient rulers who disclosed the ways of Heaven to humans and ruled in accord with those ways. Meng-tzu, a late fourth-century BCE follower of Confucius, did not restrict the *sheng* ("sage") to antiquity but recognized the ongoing possibility of such exemplars. For Meng-tzu the sage was by nature the same as other people, so through learning and self-cultivation anyone could aspire to sagehood. As saint the sage is not only exemplary but also venerated.

BIBLIOGRAPHY

A fine survey using sainthood as a category in world religions is provided by the essays in *Sainthood in World Religions,* edited by George D. Bond and Richard Kieckhefer (forthcoming). Very different in approach is the suggestive philosophical analysis of three models of spiritual perfection by Robert C. Neville, *Soldier, Sage, Saint* (New York, 1978).

For a classic psychological perspective on saintliness, see William James's *The Varieties of Religious Experience* (New York, 1902). Brief taxonomical discussions of the saint are found in Gerardus van der Leeuw's *Religion in Essence and Manifestation: A Study in Phenomenology,* 2 vols., translated by J. E. Turner, incorporating additions of the 2d German ed. (Gloucester, 1967), and Joachim Wach's *Sociology of Religion* (1944; reprint, Chicago, 1962).

To explore sainthood in more depth one must consult works on the specific religions. The novelty and centrality of Christian sainthood in the context of late antiquity is the subject of Peter Brown's masterful work, *The Cult of the Saints* (Chicago, 1981). A fascinating sociological study of Christian saints is Donald Weinstein and Rudolph M. Bell's *Saints and Society: The Two Worlds of Western Christendom, 1000-1700* (Chicago, 1982). For a critique and reappraisal of the meaning of Christian sainthood for today, see Lawrence S. Cunningham's *The Meaning of Saints* (San Francisco, 1980). Of the many studies on Islamic saints, the classic is Ignácz Goldziher's "Veneration of Saints in Islam," in *Muslim Studies,* vol. 2, edited by S. M. Stern and C. R. Barber (Chicago, 1973). Most valuable on Sufism is Annemarie Schimmel's *Mystical Dimensions of Islam* (Chapel Hill, N. C., 1975). Some discussion of Jewish mystical saints is found in Gershom Scholem's *Major Trends in Jewish Mysticism* (1941;

reprint, New York, 1961). A summary of the role of the *guru* in Hinduism is Joel D. Mlecko's "The Guru in Hindu Tradition," *Numen* 29 (July 1982): 33-61. For Buddhism, a standard introduction with a good discussion of the *bodhisattva* is Richard H. Robinson and Willard L. Johnson's *The Buddhist Religion: A Historical Introduction,* 2d ed. (Encino, Calif., 1977). On women saints in Buddhism, see Diana Y. Paul's *Women in Buddhism: Images of the Feminine in Mahayana Tradition* (Berkeley, 1979).

ROBERT L. COHN

SALVATION ARMY

The Salvation Army is described in its official statements as a "fellowship of people who have accepted Jesus Christ as their personal Savior and Lord" whose "primary aim is to preach the gospel of Jesus Christ to men and women untouched by ordinary religious efforts." The movement is a denomination of the Church of Christ; its members—called Salvationists—are officially required to subscribe to eleven doctrines, which are fundamentalist, evangelical, and Protestant. The Army's theological position is based on that of John Wesley (1703-1791), the founder of Methodism, and in particular is a restatement of the orthodox belief that love is the single motive for all true Christian endeavor: as God loved his children and sent his Son to die for them, so his children desire to love God and to show love to each other and to all people, especially the unsaved. Salvationists show this love through aggressive evangelism and through a broad range of charitable and socially ameliorative activities. Except for the omission of sacramental observances, the doctrinal beliefs of the Salvation Army have excited little controversy.

History and Aims. The doctrinal positions, objectives, and military structure of the Salvation Army have not changed since its beginning in 1878, and in many aspects even its methods of operation have changed but slightly. The movement was the brainchild of William Booth (1829-1912), an English evangelist, and his wife Catherine (1829-1890). The founders' influence over the contemporary Army remains strong, although they are long dead and the last member of their family to hold an important position of leadership—their daughter Evangeline (1865-1950)—retired in 1939.

The forerunner of the Salvation Army was a preaching mission, called the Christian Mission, that the Booths established in the East End of London in 1865 to evangelize the urban poor. Booth and his associates believed that this segment of the population had been ignored by the organized religious bodies of their day. While this is not strictly true, Booth's efforts developed into the first systematic and large-scale program to reach London's poor with the gospel. A degree of social conscience was characteristic of the

Christian Mission almost from the beginning. Efforts to relieve the destitution of those who attended their religious services were a natural outgrowth of the missionaries' evangelical zeal: alms and hospitality were commanded by Christ, and on the practical level, hunger and cold kept many potential converts from attending to the gospel. By 1867 four small-scale charitable activities, including a soup kitchen, were listed in the mission's annual report.

The military structure, by which the Christian Mission was transformed into an army, was the inspiration of a moment, although Booth and his closest associates had been dissatisfied with the conference system of governing the mission for some time. While preparing the mission's annual report for 1878 Booth deleted the term *volunteer army* in describing the work and substituted *Salvation Army.* The term was catalytic. Booth became the "General"; full-time mission workers became "officers" and adopted a variety of military titles; converts and members became "soldiers." Brass bands, long popular with the English working class and especially well suited to the Army's street-corner evangelism, were added in 1879, along with a weekly devotional and news publication suitably called *The War Cry.* In 1880 the first regulation uniform was issued to George S. Railton (1849-1913) as he departed for the United States to establish the Army's first official overseas mission. Comrades who died were "promoted to Glory," and children born into Army families were hailed as "reinforcements." Since 1890 soldiers have been required to subscribe to the "Articles of War," a statement of doctrine, allegiance, and zeal for the "salvation war."

Booth and his officers were driven by an overpowering sense of urgency. The new Salvation Army grew rapidly. Its social relief activities did not reflect any commitment to bringing about change in the social structure, however; the great work was not revolution but rescue, while time yet remained. The Army's most frequent self-portrayal, which appeared in posters, on *The War Cry* covers, and in songs, was as a lifeboat or a lighthouse, with eager Salvationists shown snatching the lost from the waves of drunkenness, crime, and vice. The thrill of losing oneself in a triumphant crusade, the military pomp, and a constantly expanding scheme of social relief proved irresistible to large numbers of the poor, and to many working- and middle-class persons as well. Despite legal obstructionism from municipal authorities and ridicule from the movement's opponents, by 1887 there were a thousand corps (i. e., stations) in Britain, and by the end of the decade work had been started in twenty-four other countries and British colonies.

Doctrines and Practices. The Salvation Army held its converts at least partly on the strength of its doctrines, which were formally established by an Act of Parliament in 1878. The Army's doctrinal statement proclaims, on the one hand, both the atonement of Christ and the necessity of radical conversion and, on the other hand, the "privilege of holiness."

In Army terms holiness means that the sincere believer can live for love, in adoration of Christ, in joyful fellowship within the ranks of the Army, and in kindly service to a dying world. Salvationists see religious questions in stark and simple terms; anything that is not deemed absolutely essential to salvation or helpful to evangelism or that is regarded as inherently confusing to unlettered converts is simply jettisoned. It was partly for these reasons that the Booths abandoned sacramental observances; in addition, they had committed their movement almost from the start to the temperance (abstinence) crusade, which disallowed the use of sacramental wine.

As appealing as the doctrines of the Salvation Army may be, however, they are neither original nor unique, and they only partly explain its strength as a religious movement. The rest of the explanation has been the use to which the Army puts its members, its system of discipline, and its social relief program. Converts are put promptly to work giving testimony about their own conversion, distributing *The War Cry,* playing a band instrument at indoor and outdoor religious meetings, or visiting prisoners, the elderly, and the sick. Soldiers expect a lifetime of such service, and occasional natural disasters add to the ordinary demands on local Army personnel. In addition, a number of entertaining and useful programs have been developed to utilize the energy of young people. Parades, military regalia, and an effective use of music augment, where they do not actually create, joy and pride in being part of the "Army of God."

Salvationists are comfortable within the Army's autocratic structure, which emphasizes obedience, loyalty, and efficiency; the system has changed little in fact, and not at all in spirit, since 1878. The single major alteration in the absolute autocracy established by William Booth came in 1929 (the Act of Parliament was formally amended in 1931), when the general's privileges of serving for life and naming his own successor were abolished. The generalship became an elective office at the disposal of a council of all territorial commanders, and the leader so chosen serves only until a certain age. Once a general is installed, however, his powers differ little from those of the founder; every subordinate officer is expected to obey without question the orders of a superior, and much the same is required of the soldiers.

Aside from its religious and operational distinctiveness, the second part of what the Salvation Army calls its "balanced ministry" is the vast system of social welfare activities that has grown up under its auspices. There were important beginnings in the 1880s in England, America, and elsewhere, but the turning point in the development of the Army's social welfare program came in 1890 with the publication of General Booth's manifesto entitled *In Darkest England and the Way Out.* The book, and the scheme it offered for relieving the sufferings of the "submerged tenth" of Victorian society, attracted considerable publicity, controversy, and in the end financial support. Food and shelter depots, industrial rehabilitation centers, rescue homes for converted prostitutes, hospitals for unwed mothers, orphanages, day-care centers, halfway houses for released convicts, programs for alcoholics and drug addicts, camping trips for poor city children, a variety of family relief and counseling—all have grown up since 1890, especially in the American branch of the Army.

By 1982 the Salvation Army was operating in eighty-six countries. Its greatest strength is in English-speaking countries and Scandinavia; just over 50 percent of all active officers and 70 percent of all lay employees are found in five countries: the United States, Great Britain, Canada, Australia, and New Zealand. Although the international headquarters remains in London, the American branch is by far the largest.

The Army in the United States is divided into four territorial commands, each with its own headquarters and training school; the officers who command these territorial operations report to the national commander, whose headquarters is in Verona, New Jersey. The large majority of the 3,600 Salvation Army officers in the United States are engaged in "field work"; they serve as ministers to the 1,056 local corps congregations and direct the numerous social services that flow from the typical corps. Officers not in field work serve in staff and educational appointments or as administrators of the Army's many social institutions. The Men's Social Service Department, which offers residential care and alcoholic rehabilitation to transient alcoholic men (and in a few places to women), is particularly well developed.

[*See the biography of Booth.*]

BIBLIOGRAPHY

The amount of written material produced by the Salvation Army since its beginning is enormous; it is of wildly uneven quality, but an acquaintance with at least some of it is indispensable to any understanding of the movement. Early issues of *The War Cry* (London, 1879-; New York, 1881-) portray the zeal and colorful activities of the pioneers. The serious student should begin with *Chosen to Be a Soldier: Orders and Regulations for Soldiers of the Salvation Army* (London, 1977) and the Salvation Army's *Handbook of Doctrine* (London, 1969). A useful and informative *Yearbook* (London, 1903-) is published annually. The best full-scale history of the Army is a long-range project by three senior officers, *The History of the Salvation Army,* 6 vols. to date (1947-1973; reprint, London, 1979), by Robert Sandall (volumes 1-3), Arch Wiggins (volumes 4 and 5), and Frederick Coutts (volume 6). Two books by Bramwell Booth, the founders' son and the Army's second general, provide valuable color and insight: *Echoes and Memories* (London, 1925) and *These Fifty Years* (London, 1929). Bernard Watson's *Soldier Saint: George Scott Railton, William Booth's First Lieutenant* (London, 1970) is an excellent biography of an early figure of crucial importance. A popular and informative biography of Evangeline Booth (commander of U. S. forces, 1904-1934; general, 1934-1939) is Margaret Troutt's *The General Was a Lady: The Story of Evangeline Booth* (Nashville, 1980). The most comprehensive history of the Army in the United

States is *Marching to Glory: The History of the Salvation Army in the United States of America, 1880-1980* by Edward H. McKinley (San Francisco, 1980).

EDWARD H. MCKINLEY

SAMKHYA

SAMKHYA, a Sanskrit word meaning "enumeration," is derived from the substantive *samkhya* ("number") and is the name of one of the six orthodox Hindu philosophical schools.

The Teachings of the School. As the name implies, the Samkhya school relies on distinct and recognizable patterns of enumeration as methods of inquiry. The different patterns of enumeration can be grouped into three main separate divisions according to their overall function in the system: the principles of twenty-five (constitutive), the dispositions of eight (projective), and the categories of fifty (effective).

Basic to an understanding of the Samkhya school is the importance it places on the distinction between contentless consciousness *(purusa)* and materiality *(pra-krti)*, two essentially different principles. Nothing exists apart from these two principles. This distinction caused the Samkhya school to be labeled "dualistic." Contentless consciousness is the opposite of materiality in that it is inactive, yet conscious, and therefore not subject to change. Materiality, on the contrary, is potentially and actually active, but unconscious. Materiality is both unmanifest and manifest. The unmanifest materiality may also be called the "original materiality" because it is from this that the whole manifest universe emerges.

The universe undergoes cycles of evolution and absorption. During absorption, the original materiality is dormant, and the three constituents of materiality (the *gunas: sattva, rajas,* and *tamas*) are in a state of equilibrium. On disturbing this equilibrium of the three constituents, the original materiality starts to reproduce itself. Unmanifest transforms into manifest materiality and keeps on transforming from one principle to the other until the original materiality has manifested itself in twenty-three principles. This is the constitutive pattern of enumeration, which is an extension of the fundamental duality. According to some accounts, the first principle to emerge is "the large one" *(mahat)*; other accounts maintain that intellect *(buddhi)* emerges first. Either of these two principles produces ego *(ahamkara)*. Ego, in turn, produces ten faculties—five sense faculties *(buddhindriya)* and five action faculties *(karmendriya)*; ego also produces the mind *(manas)* and the five subtle elements *(tanmatra)*. These subtle elements produce five gross elements *(bhuta)*.

All twenty-three principles of manifest materiality are a transformation of one thing, namely, the original materiality. These principles, in fact, are not new products or effects;

their effects already exist in their causes. The essence of this theory of causality *(satkaryavada)* is that an effect must be connected to preexisting necessary conditions, otherwise anything could be a cause of anything else; in other words, there must be a dependent relation between cause and effect, such that milk alone, for example, and not water, produces yogurt.

The Samkhya school postulates that materiality is one, and that the evolution of a number of things out of that one materiality is understood as causation. The numerous things in this world are different from the original materiality, and yet they are the same. The things of everyday reality—ourselves, our minds, egos, and intellects—are materiality. Mental functions are transformations, too. Contentless consciousness itself gets confused with these transformations, although in reality contentless consciousness is merely a witness to them. But since contentless consciousness does not undergo any change and does not produce any activity, this confusion must be rooted in materiality. If anything is to be effected, it has to happen in materiality.

It is here that metaphysics and epistemology merge. The confusion of contentless consciousness with materiality gives ground to epistemology. How does one remove this confusion, this ignorance that keeps the world in the repeating cycle of existence? Bondage in the cycle of lives is contingent upon ignorance of the distinction between materiality and contentless consciousness. The removal of confusion and ignorance can be achieved by knowledge, in particular, the knowledge that differentiates or discriminates contentless consciousness from materiality. By means of this knowledge, one wins liberation, and one's subtle body *(suksmasarira)* ceases its transmigration from life to life.

Intellect, ego, mind, the five sense faculties, the five action faculties, and the five subtle elements together form the subtle body. This subtle body is attachable to, and detachable from, the gross body; by attaching itself to the gross body, it animates it. On the other hand, by detaching itself from the gross body at the time of death, the subtle body transmigrates. This subtle body includes the eight dispositions inherent in the intellect that form the projective pattern of enumeration.

The effective pattern of enumeration results from the interaction between the eight dispositions of the intellect (the projective pattern) and the twenty-five principles that constitute the universe (the constitutive pattern). This pattern enumerates fifty categories of intellectual creations:

Five misconceptions	(5)
Twenty-eight incapacities of the sense, action, and mental faculties	(28)
Nine contentments	(9)
Eight spiritual attainments	(8)
	(50)

These categories have still further subdivisions. At the same time, this pattern is interpreted in terms of four created forms of life: plants, animals, gods, and humans.

Literature. The first extant independent written work of the Samkhya school is the *Samkhyakarika* of Isvarakrsna. This work has been variously dated between 350 and 550 CE. The *Samkhyakarika* is a sort of codification of the Samkhya teachings; it deals with the various patterns of enumeration and sets forth the purpose of the teaching, that is, liberation through discrimination between contentless consciousness and materiality. This work marked the Samkhya school with a philosophical emphasis because its goal—religious experience—is accomplished through a cognitive process employing logic and epistemology.

A number of commentaries were written about this classic work over subsequent centuries. The *Yuktidipika,* which was made available in its first published edition in 1938, is the main source of information on many aspects of the Samkhya teachings that have not been accessible otherwise. The *Yuktidipika's* date and authorship are unclear. Moreover, Albrecht Wezler has shown that it contains two types of commentaries. One commentary, the *Rajavarttika,* is written in concise nominal statements *(varttika);* the other is a commentary on these concise statements rather than on the *Samkhyakarika* itself.

The Samkhya teachers continued into modern times to write commentaries on earlier Samkhya works. The twentieth-century Samkhya ascetic and teacher Hariharananda Aranya followed the example of the old teachers: he spent most of his life meditating in solitude, only occasionally emerging to teach or to write such works as *The Samkhyasutras of Pañcasikha* and *The Samkhyatattvaloka.*

[*See* Yoga.]

BIBLIOGRAPHY

The most comprehensive work on the Samkhya school is *Samkhya: A Dualist Tradition in Indian Philosophy,* edited by Gerald J. Larson and Ram Shankar Bhattacharya (Princeton and Delhi, forthcoming), a volume in the *Encyclopedia of Indian Philosophies,* edited by Karl H. Potter. It has a detailed and up-to-date introduction to the different theories of the Samkhya school; the larger part of the volume is given to the summaries of the Samkhya works from early to modern times. The volume is a result of collaboration of Indian and Western scholars.

Gerald J. Larson's *Classical Samkhya: An Interpretation of Its History and Meaning,* 2d ed. (Santa Barbara, 1979), has been until now the only single book on the Samkhya; it traces the origins of the school and also supplies the Sanskrit text of the *Samkhyakarika* with an English translation. The second edition differs from the first (Delhi, 1969) by a few additions to the original body of chapters.

Michael Hulin's slim volume *Samkhya Literature,* in *A History of Indian Literature,* edited by Jan Gonda, vol. 6, fasc. 3 (Wiesbaden, 1978), gives a survey of the Samkhya writings.

A lucid presentation of Samkhya theory appears in Surendranath Dasgupta's *A History of Indian Philosophy,* vol. 1 (Cambridge, 1922), although his understanding is influenced by the medieval teacher Vijñanabhiksu, whose interpretation of the Samkhya is tinged in turn by Vedanta theory.

A readable and thorough history of the Samkhya school is in Erich Frauwallner's *Geschichte der Indischen Philosophie,* vol. 1 (Salzburg, 1953), translated by V. M. Bedekar as *History of Indian Philosophy,* vol. 1 (Delhi, 1973).

One of the earlier works of good scholarship, but somewhat outdated, is Arthur Berriedale Keith's *The Samkhya System,* 2d ed. (Calcutta, 1949).

On the historical origins, see E. H. Johnston's *Early Samkhya: An Essay on Its Historical Development according to the Texts* (1937; reprint, Delhi, 1974).

EDELTRAUD HARZER

SAMOYED RELIGION

The Samoyeds are peoples of northern Eurasia who speak a systematically related set of languages. Most of them live in western Siberia, in the region extending from the Yamal and Taimyr peninsulas in the north to the Sayan Mountains in the south; a few live in northeasternmost Europe, on the Kola Peninsula and near the Pechora River. As a linguistic group, Samoyed is related to Finno-Ugric; together they form the Uralic language family.

Currently numbering about 35,000, the Samoyed peoples are broadly divided into the northern Samoyeds and the southern Samoyeds. Northern Samoyed groups include the Nentsy (also called the Yurak Samoyeds or the Yuraks), who, with approximately 30,000 members, are by far the largest Samoyed group; the Nganasani (or Tavgi), with about 900 members; and the Entsy (or Yenisei Samoyeds), with about 450 members. Of the southern Samoyeds, only one group survives, the Selkup (formerly called the Ostiak Samoyeds), with some 3,500 members. Some extinct southern Samoyed groups (e.g., the Kamassians, the Koibal, the Motor, and the Taigi) are known from records. Before the formation of the present Samoyed languages and groups, a proto-Samoyed group presumably existed some 3,500 years ago, when it seceded from the larger proto-Uralic parent group.

The neighbors of the Samoyed are, or have been in the course of history, the Khanty and the Komi (Finno-Ugric peoples), various Siberian Turkic peoples, the Evenki (a Tunguz people), the Ket (sometimes classified as a Paleosiberian group), and, most recently, the Russians. Samoyed traditional culture is based primarily on hunting for fur-bearing animals, gathering, fishing, and reindeer breeding; collectivization was introduced into the Samoyed economy by the Soviet government in the 1920s.

The Spirit World. The principal of the Nentsy deity is Num, the creator of the world, of men, and of things. His role is ambiguous: in general he distances himself from human beings and abstains from interference in their affairs, except when explicitly implored for help in the struggle against Nga, the god of evil, death, and hell. In Nenets religion, Nga is Num's son, but this father-son duality is not found among other Samoyed groups, where the high benevolent gods and their antipodes are considered independent of one another. Sacrifices are made to Num twice a year, at the beginning of winter and again in the spring. They are either bloody, involving the killing of dogs or reindeer, or bloodless, involving the offering of money, clothing, and food.

Another inhabitant of the spirit world is Ilibemberti; in Nenets religion he is reported variously as a spirit who grants good fortune in the pursuit of reindeer and foxes and alternately as a protector of reindeer. He does not have the status of a god, which is reserved for Num and Nga. Freely translated, the name *Ilibemberti* means "the spirit that gives

> In general, spirits were conceived of as intermediaries between Num and humans and as being in contact with shamans.

riches or sustenance (in reindeer or game)." The significance of this supernatural personality lies in the fact that Ilibemberti is involved in the concrete here and now, and is as such opposed to Num, the highest god and creator, who is shapeless and transcends time. The Samoyeds also recognize an earth-mother deity who is sympathetic to humans, especially to women in childbirth.

The Nentsy are reported to worship stones and rocks. Properly speaking, this means that certain mountains and rocks, as well as some rivers and lakes, were considered to have individual spirits deserving reverence. Among the Nganasani it was even believed that some manmade artifacts could understand human language. The Nganasani hierarchized supernatural beings into three classes: benevolent master spirits of fire, water, the forest, hunting, and fishing; evil, anthropomorphic spirits; and the shaman's auxiliary spirits (mostly zoomorphic). Among the Selkup, master spirits were sometimes considered repositories of good fortune. In general, spirits were conceived of as intermediaries between Num and humans and as being in contact with shamans. Each person was thought to have a corresponding star in the heavens—a belief that brings man closer to Num than Num's disinterested attitude mentioned above would suggest.

Rituals. Besides the cyclic sacrifices to Num mentioned above, other sacrifices are made at specific sites, where wooden or stone representations of certain spirits are erected. Among the Selkup these sites are phratrilocal. Of the rites

of passage celebrated by the Samoyed groups, the most important are the shaman's initiation, rites after childbirth (primarily involving purification of the tent), and ritual ceremonies for the dead.

It is believed that the dead continue to live as shadow souls—varieties of lower spirits—in the underworld. Among the Entsy, the deceased is left in the tent, wrapped in hides, for a number of days, while family life continues unchanged. At a certain point, bread is placed in a pot with a lid, brick tea is scraped, and some of the belongings of the deceased are made ready. The corpse is then transported to the burial site and placed in a coffin (which has been fastened together with iron nails) with the corpse's feet pointing north. Before the coffin is lowered into the freshly dug grave, it is loaded with the gifts that have been prepared earlier, as well as with hide-processing utensils. The nearest surviving relative chants laments. Later, sticks are placed over the footprints leading to the burial site, and the mourning party, pointing to the north, exhorts the deceased not to return.

The Nentsy also deposit a dead man's broken sled near his grave and slaughter reindeer on the occasion. Infants who die soon after birth are wrapped in bundles and suspended from trees or poles. After a man's death, his wife makes a wooden amulet or doll-effigy in the shape of her husband; she clothes and feeds it, and sleeps with it for six months after his death; she may not remarry during this period. Among some groups this amulet is kept for three years. Amulets are generally kept on a specially designated shelf in the sacred, rear part of the tent.

Specialized rites among the Samoyeds include tent-cleaning ceremonies (among the Nganasani in February) and, among the Nentsy, the burning of loon skins to ensure good weather or the burning of locks of someone's hair or clippings of his fingernails in order to cause that person misfortune.

Relations between Men and Animals. One animal is expressly singled out as evil: the wolf, which is the reindeer's most dangerous foe. Some fish, such as the pike, are revered. The reindeer is regarded as a pure animal, and white reindeer, in particular, are associated with the sun and considered sacred. As elsewhere in Siberia, the bear is accorded special respect. Bear meat must be chewed in a prescribed manner and may not be consumed at all by women. Women are also forbidden to eat the heads of reindeer or of certain fish (e.g., pike, raw sturgeon).

Certain Samoyed clans associate their origins or ancestors with specific clan-protector spirits envisaged as animals. Such totemistic beliefs govern specific attitudes and behavior patterns (especially taboos) in regard to particular animals. As has already been implied, many taboos were traditionally engendered by attitudes toward women; because women were considered unclean, they were forbidden to step over hunting equipment.

Shamanism. Broadly speaking, the Samoyed shaman's functions and role in society are the same as those in other societies in the long shamanistic belt that stretches over northern Eurasia from Lapland to the Kamchatka Peninsula. The shaman is the prime religious functionary. He mediates between man and the supernatural: he treats the ailing (disease is considered the temporary absence of the soul from the body), predicts the future, summons protection and help in hunting and fishing, finds objects that have disappeared, and officiates at funeral rites. There are three categories of Nenets shamans: the powerful miracle workers, an intermediate class, and "small" shamans. (There is also a class of soothsayers, but these are not, properly speaking, shamans. They have no shamanic power, but even natives often confuse them with shamans.)

The office of the shaman is inherited. Traditionally, each kin group (clan or phratry) had its own shaman who passed his office on to a successor during his own lifetime. Female shamans are said to have existed among the Samoyed of the Turukhan area (in the south).

Reports on the shaman's initiation vary. Essentially, the shaman-to-be—who may be a boy of fifteen—is selected and trained by an older kinsman. Training can involve ordeals such as blindfolding and beating, and the candidate may declare that he has had dreams in which he has traveled to distant forests and settlements or communicated with supernatural beings. It is believed that during the process of selecting a new shaman all of the ancestor-shamans' spirits, as well as other spirits (such as those of water and earth and even the spirit of the pox, a female Russian spirit), are present. These spirits are asked to assist the candidate in his future office.

The shaman officiates during a séance when, as one of them reported, he sees "a road to the north" (another report equates the séance with a trip to the south). The shaman is accompanied by his assistant spirits during the journey; locomotion is provided by an animal, generally a reindeer. During the séance, the shaman addresses questions to Num, and if contact is established, he reports Num's answers. His primary accessories are his drum—round, broad rimmed, covered with skin on one side, from thirty to fifty centimeters in diameter—and his drumstick. The noise that results from drumming represents both the voyage to the other world and the shaman's interaction with Num and his assistants. During the séance the shaman's eyes may be covered with a kerchief so that he may concentrate on the journey more effectively.

A shaman's costume survives among most Samoyed groups (but not among the Nentsy). Nganasan shamans each have three costumes because it is believed that shamans are born three times. The name of the Selkup shaman's headgear is said to be borrowed from the Tunguz; this suggests relatively recent cultural contacts in the sphere of religion. It is also known that Nenets shamans occasionally visit Evenk shamans.

Payments for the services of a shaman range from a pair of mittens to a deerskin or several reindeer. If at the time of a shaman's death his successor has already been chosen, the shaman is buried in his everyday clothes. After the death of a Nenets shaman, a wooden replica of a reindeer is made and is wrapped in the hide of a reindeer calf; the reindeer represents the shaman's assistant spirits.

BIBLIOGRAPHY

Concrete factual information, much of it based on the field experiences of some of the authors, can be found in three collective works: *Popular Beliefs and Folklore Tradition in Siberia,* edited by Vilmos Diószegi (The Hague, 1968), *Shamanism in Siberia,* edited by Vilmos Diószegi and Mihály Hoppál (Budapest, 1978), and *Shamanism in Eurasia,* 2 vols., edited by Mihály Hoppál (Göttingen, 1984). Compact synopses are provided in Péter Hajdú's *The Samoyed Peoples and Languages* (Bloomington, Ind., 1963) and in *The Peoples of Siberia,* edited by M. G. Levin and L. P. Potapov (Chicago, 1964). Kai Donner's *Among the Samoyed in Siberia,* translated by Rinehart Kyler and edited by Genevieve A. Highland (New Haven, 1954), is a record of personal experiences and observations, while Toivo Lehtisalo's *Entwurf einer Mythologie der Jurak-Samojeden* (Helsinki, 1924) is a synthesis based on both older sources and personally collected data. Ivar Paulson's chapter on Siberia in *Die Religionen Nordeurasiens und der amerikanischen Arktis,* edited by Ivar Paulson, Åke Hultkrantz, and Karl Jettmar (Stuttgart, 1962), is thematically arranged, as is Uno Holmberg's treatment in *The Mythology of All Races,* vol. 4, *Finno-Ugric, Siberian* (Boston, 1927). Of M. A. Czaplicka's contributions to this field of study, two deserve to be singled out, although by now they have mostly historical value: *Aboriginal Siberia* (Oxford, 1914) and "Samoyed," in the *Encyclopaedia of Religion and Ethics,* edited by James Hastings, vol. 11 (Edinburgh, 1920).

ROBERT AUSTERLITZ

SANHEDRIN

SANHEDRIN, a Hebrew and Jewish-Aramaic loanword from the Greek *sunedrion.* Composed of seventy or seventy-one members, the Sanhedrin possessed administrative, judicial, and quasi-legislative powers of the Jews of Palestine that were also recognized by the Jews of the Diaspora. Until 70 CE the Sanhedrin met in the precincts of the Jerusalem Temple. Following the destruction of the Temple in that year, a reconstituted Sanhedrin met at various sites in Palestine.

Historical Evidence. The historicity of the Sanhedrin is the subject of much disagreement in modern scholarship. The disagreement results from inconsistencies among the sources used to reconstruct the history of the institution.

Some argue that the composition and competence of the Sanhedrin varied over time. Others suggest that it comprised subcommittees, each with its own chairman, that dealt with different types of issues.

Evidence in rabbinic literature. Since relatively few rabbinic traditions explicitly mention the Sanhedrin, they may be supplemented by other traditions, more numerous and more detailed, that use the Hebrew term *beit din* (pl., *batei din*), meaning "court." According to these traditions, each town with a certain minimum population could establish a "small Sanhedrin" or *beit din* of twenty-three scholars, competent to try even capital cases. Matters that the local institutions could not resolve were referred to the "Great Sanhedrin" or "Great Beit Din" (*beit din ha-gadol*, i. e., "great court") of seventy-one members. This latter body, meeting in the Chamber of Hewn Stone in the Jerusalem Temple, would resolve the matter on the basis of precedent or by majority vote. The supreme body, whether called the Great Beit Din as in Tosefta *Hagigah 2.9* or the Great Sanhedrin as in Mishnah *Middot* 5.4, had authority over the priesthood. It possessed political as well as religious powers: declaring offensive wars, playing a role in the appointment of kings, and so forth. The source implies that the system had broken down by the beginning of direct Roman rule in 6 CE.

Evidence in Josephus Flavius. Jewish literature in Greek from before 70 CE never mentions a supreme Jewish institution called the *sunedrion*. The word does occur, but only in the general sense of "assembly, council, court." The same situation prevails in the writings of Josephus. In only three instances does Josephus use *sunedrion* to designate a formally constituted ongoing institution. He also mentions three judicial or administrative bodies of seventy members each, all from around 66 CE, but does not call any of them a *sunedrion*.

Evidence in the New Testament. The New Testament includes several instances of the word *sunedrion*, usually translated as "council" (RSV). In a few cases the word refers to local Jewish courts (certainly in *Mark* 13:9 and parallels in *Matthew* 10:17 and possibly in *Matthew* 5:21). However, in the accounts of the passion of Jesus and the trials of the apostles, *sunedrion* seems to designate the supreme Jewish institution in Jerusalem. Closer analysis reveals several uncertainties. The synoptic Gospels and *Acts of the Apostles* frequently allude to the Jewish leadership as composed of "the chief priests, elders, and scribes" or the like. As is generally agreed, this means the priestly and lay aristocracies along with a professional class of experts in Jewish law. In certain passages these three elements constitute some sort of *sunedrion*. In some of these passages, the term *sunedrion* can be interpreted in its general meaning of "assembly" or "session." In other instances *sunedrion* appears to be a proper name. It may be noted in passing that only *Mark* and *Matthew* report a trial of Jesus before the *sunedrion*. Luke reports only a morning consultation of the *presbuterion*, chief priests and

scribes. And *John* merely has "the Jews" accuse Jesus before Pontius Pilate.

The Sanhedrin after 70 CE. Some scholars posit the existence of a Sanhedrin at Yavneh after 70, at Usha (in the Galilee) after 135, and still later at other locations. Whatever the nature of the institutions that existed at these places, they are never called Sanhedrins in the ancient sources. In fact, two second-century traditions refer to the Sanhedrin as a thing of the past: Mishnah *Sotah* 9.11 explicitly and *Makkot* 1.10 implicitly. A single post-70 reference to a contemporary "Great Court," at Tosefta *Ohalot* 18.18, is probably only rhetorical.

BIBLIOGRAPHY

The best treatment of the problem of the Sanhedrin is Yehoshua Efron's Hebrew article "The Sanhedrin as an Ideal and as Reality in the Period of the Second Temple," in *Doron*, edited by S. Perlman and B. Shimron (Tel Aviv, 1967). An English summary appears under the same title in *Immanuel* 2 (1973): 44-49. Efron's differentiated and consistently critical survey of almost all the relevant sources manages to transcend the stagnant debate still prevailing in the scholarly literature. His method and conclusions have greatly influenced this article.

The two major studies in English both adopt the theory of two Sanhedrins. They are Sidney B. Hoenig's *The Great Sanhedrin* (New York, 1953) and Hugo Mantel's *Studies in the History of the Sanhedrin* (Cambridge, Mass., 1961). Mantel presents detailed summaries of the scholarly debate and a very full bibliography. For a recent, sophisticated version of this theory, see Ellis Rivkin's "Beth Din, Boulé, Sanhedrin: A Tragedy of Errors," *Hebrew Union College Annual* 46 (1975): 181-199.

Other recent surveys adopt variations of the moderate harmonistic approach. Most useful are Edmund Lohse's "Sunedrion," in *Theological Dictionary of the New Testament,* edited by Gerhard Kittel, vol. 7 (Grand Rapids, Mich., 1971), pp. 860-867; Samuel Safrai's "Jewish Self-Government," in *The Jewish People in the First Century,* edited by Samuel Safrai and Men-achem Stern, vol. 1 (Assen, 1974), pp. 379-400; and Emil Schürer's *The History of the Jewish People in the Age of Jesus Christ,* a new English version revised and edited by Géza Vermès et al., vol. 2 (Edinburgh, 1979), pp. 199-226.

DAVID GOODBLATT

SANTERÍA

SANTERÍA is a religious tradition of African origin that developed in Cuba and that was spread throughout the Caribbean and the United States by exiles from the revolution of 1959. Santería began in the nineteenth century when hundreds of thousands of men and women of the Yoruba people, from what are now Nigeria and Benin, were brought to Cuba to work in the island's booming sugar industry. Despite brutal conditions, some were able to reconstruct their religious lives through a fusing of the traditions remembered from their homeland and from their encounter with the folk piety of the Roman Catholic church.

The Cuban Yoruba often used the iconography of Catholic saints to express their devotions to Yoruba spirits called *orishas.* The name *Santería,* "the way of the saints," is the most common Spanish word used to describe these practices, and the word *santero* (m.) or *santera* (f.) indicates an initiated devotee. Later generations of *santeros* would construct elaborate systems of correspondences between *orishas* and saints, leading observers to see this Caribbean religion as a model for understanding religious syncretism and cultural change. Despite the frequent presence of Catholic symbols in Santería rites and the attendance of *santeros* at Catholic sacraments, Santería is essentially an African way of worship drawn into a symbiotic relationship with Catholicism.

Santeros believe that every individual, before he or she is born, is given a destiny, or road in life, by the Almighty. It is the responsibility of the individual to understand his or her destiny and to grow with it rather than to be a victim of it. *Santeros* recognize a pantheon of *orishas* whose aid and energy can bring devotees to a complete fulfillment of their destinies. The basis of Santería is the development of a deep personal relationship with the *orishas,* a relationship that will bring the *santero* worldly success and heavenly wisdom. Devotion to the *orishas* takes four principal forms: divination, sacrifice, spirit mediumship, and initiation.

For the ordinary devotee, Santería serves as a means for resolving the problems of everyday life, including problems of health, money, and love. Divination can reveal the sources of these problems, and it points the way to their resolution. Santería has preserved several Yoruba systems of divination in a hierarchical ranking according to their reliability and the amount of training required to master them. The most complex system of divination in Santería, Ifa, can be "read" only by male priests called *babalawos.* In response to a querent's problem, a *babalawo* will throw a small chain *(ekwele)* that has eight pieces of shell, bone, or other material affixed to it. Each piece is shaped so that, when thrown, it lands either concave or convex side up. This arrangement results in 256 possible combinations, each representing a basic situation in life. The combination that falls at any particular time is the purest expression of fate, and thus of the God-given destiny of the querent. Most of the patterns refer to stories that tell of the problems faced by the *orishas* and heroes in the past, and that relate the solutions that were found. These solutions become the archetypes used by the querent to resolve the problem that he or she has brought to Ifa.

The most dramatic form of devotion to the *orishas* is ceremonial spirit mediumship. At certain ceremonies called *bembes, guemileres,* or *tambores,* a battery of drums calls the *orishas* to join the devotees in dance and song. If an *orisha* so chooses, he or she will "descend" and "seize the head" of an initiate. In this state the incarnated orisha may perform spectacular dances that the human medium would be hard put to imitate in ordinary consciousness. More important, an incarnated *orisha* will deliver messages, admonitions, and advice to individual members of the community, bringing their heavenly wisdom to bear on their devotees' earthly problems.

As the initiate grows in this new level of devotion, his or her relationship with the seated *orisha* becomes increasingly fluid. The sacrificial exchange between them comes to be seen as the outward manifestation of an inner process. Thus Santería culminates in a mysticism of identity between human and divine, where the road of life is the way of the *orishas.*

Santería continues to grow in the late twentieth century. Its popularity in Cuba seems to have been little affected by the socialist revolution, and thanks to nearly one million Cuban exiles, it is thriving in Venezuela, Puerto Rico, and the United States. The number of full initiates is difficult to determine because of the tradition of secrecy that *santeros* have maintained in order to survive a history of oppression and misunderstanding. The presence of Santería in a given neighborhood may be gauged by the profusion of *botánicas,* small retail stores that sell the herbs and ritual paraphernalia of Santería ceremonies. In recent years, there were at least eighty *botánicas* in Miami, Florida, and more than a hundred in New York City.

[*See also* Voodoo *and* Yoruba Religion.]

BIBLIOGRAPHY

A limited literature exists on Santería in English. The finest presentation of the symbolism of the *orishas* is Robert F. Thompson's *Flash of the Spirit: African and Afro-American Art and Philosophy* (New York, 1981). Migene González-Wippler has written three books on the subject. *Santería: African Magic in Latin America* (Garden City, N. Y., 1975) is a disorganized introduction that borrows freely from Spanish sources. *The Santería Experience* (Englewood Cliffs, N. J., 1982) is a detailed, well-written, first-person account of the author's experience with Santería in New York. *Rituals and Spells of Santería* (New York, 1984) presents source materials on Santería liturgy and magic. William R. Bascom has written two articles on Santería in Cuba; reflecting his wide experience as an anthropologist among the Yoruba in Nigeria, these articles are "The Focus of Cuban Santería," *Southwestern Journal of Anthropology* 6 (Spring 1950): 64-68, and "Two Forms of Afro-Cuban Divination," in *Acculturation in the Americas,* edited by Sol Tax (Chicago, 1952), pp. 169-184.

Among Spanish sources, pride of place belongs to the works of Fernando Ortiz. Between 1906 and his death in 1969, he published hundreds of pieces on all aspects of Afro-Cuban culture. The work that deals most directly with Santería is perhaps *Los bailes y el teatro de los negros en el folklore de Cuba* (Havana, 1951). The most widely available works in Spanish in the United States are those of the great exiled folklorist Lydia Cabrera. Among her many books in print on Afro-Cuban themes, *El monte* (Miami, 1968) and *Koeko iyawo: Pequeño tratado de regla Lucumi* (Miami, 1980) are considered authoritative by practitioners and observers alike. Two books by anthropologically trained scholars provide excellent surveys of the tradition: Julio Sánchez's *La religión de los orichas* (Hato Rey, Puerto Rico, 1978) and Mercedes Cros Sandoval's *La religion afrocubana* (Madrid, 1975). Sandoval's book makes use of Pierre Verger's classic *Notes sur le culte des Orisa et Vodun à Bahia* (Dakar, 1957), which traces the connections between the religion of the *orishas* in Africa and that in Brazil and includes invaluable texts of prayers to the *orishas* as well as excellent photographs.

Joseph M. Murphy

SARMATIAN RELIGION

The Sarmatians were Iranian-speaking nomadic tribes that formed in the middle of the first millennium BCE in the southern Urals. In the last centuries before the common era they spread from there in a westward direction—to the lower Volga region, the Ciscaucasus, and the northern Black Sea shore—where they were still dominant in the first centuries CE. In language and culture, the Sarmatians were close to the Scythians. Their ethnonym is similar to that of the Sauromatians, who inhabited the left bank of the Lower Don in the middle of the first millennium BCE. Classical tradition often treated both these names as identical, but in contemporary scholarship the question of the degree of relationship between the Sauromatians and the Sarmatians remains debatable.

> ... ancient writers also indicate that the tribes living along the Don worshiped that river as a god and that, moreover, they called the Sauromatians "fire worshipers."

The Sarmatians' lack of a written language has severely limited the scope of available data about their religion. The only evidence about their pantheon is the indication by a writer of the fifth century CE that in the language of the Alani (a tribe of the Sarmatian group) the name of the town Feodosia in the Crimea was Ardabda ("seven gods"). This is a reflection of the tradition, common among the ancient Indo-Iranians, of worshiping seven gods, a practice also characteristic of Scythian religion. [*See* Scythian Religion.] The actual makeup of this Sarmatian pantheon is unknown to us. Perhaps it was about one of the gods of this pantheon that Ammianus Marcellinus (31.2.23) wrote, comparing him to the Roman Mars and informing us that the Alani worshiped him in the form of an unsheathed sword driven into the ground.

This ritual may be interpreted as the erection of the *axis mundi,* which joins the world of people with the world of the gods. Such an interpretation is confirmed by information about the Scythians, who had a similar ritual; but the Scythians performed it on special stationary altars, whose complete absence among the Sarmatians (and of all other monumental religious structures as well) was specifically noted by the classical writers. Hence the religious practices of the Sarmatians had a more nomadic character, entirely suited to their mobile way of life.

The ancient writers also indicate that the tribes living along the Don worshiped that river (the ancient Tanais) as a god and that, moreover, they called the Sauromatians "fire worshipers." The worship of fire and water as gods is an ancient tradition of all Iranian peoples, and it may be assumed that the deities of these elements were part of the Sarmatian pantheon of seven gods, as was the case among the Scythians.

These sparse data constitute the sole written evidence on the religion of the Sarmatians. To some extent they have been correlated with archaeological findings, the basic sources for the reconstruction of this religion. It is true that, owing to the nomadic character of the Sarmatian way of life, the only monuments left by them are burial mounds. Thus they reflect only those aspects of Sarmatian religion that focus on Sarmatian burial practices. For example, data on Sarmatian fire-worship have something in common with their extensive use of fire in one form or another in their burial practices. The Sarmatians did not practice cremation of the dead or the burning of the grave construction, but quite often they covered the graves with the remnants of the ritual bonfire, which sometimes led to the combustion of the grave's wooden covering and even to the scorching of the corpse. The earth tempered by such fires was sometimes spread in a ring around the grave or was admixed with the soil from which the burial mound covering the grave was formed. Traces of such fires are often found in the burial mound itself, not far from the grave. It is not clear whether the fire in these rituals was considered as an element to which the dead person was consigned or only as a purifying principle.

Also connected with the worship of fire are the stone or ceramic censers, used for burning aromatic substances, that have frequently been found in Sarmatian graves. Archaeologists also consider fragments of a red mineral dye, realgar, often found in Sarmatian graves, to be a substitute for fire in a burial. The same interpretation for chalk—another mineral commonly found in Sarmatian graves—is more debatable. But its purifying function is completely obvious. Chalk was either put in the grave in pieces or strewn on the bottom of the grave. The latter custom, like the tradition of laying grass under the burial, was evidently meant to prevent the corpse from coming into direct contact with the earth and thus being defiled. This custom, as we know, was a prominent characteristic of Zoroastrian burial practice, which developed from ancient Iranian beliefs.

The Sarmatian custom of placing burial mounds around one of the oldest mounds may be interpreted as evidence of the worship of ancestor graves and, in the final analysis, of an ancestor cult. In some burial mounds in which persons of high social rank were interred, there have also been found the bodies of people who were deliberately killed—servants, swordbearers, and so forth—indicating that the Sarmatians practiced human sacrifice. Far more widespread was the custom of placing in the graves food for the dead, in the form of parts of the carcass of a horse or a sheep. A typically Sarmatian feature is the placing in the grave of a specially broken mirror, or of its fragments, perhaps indicating that the Sarmatians regarded the mirror as the person's "double," who died together with him.

There is no doubt that animal-style art, widespread in Sarmatian culture, is connected with the religio-mythological concepts of the Sarmatians. Zoomorphic motifs were used to decorate ritual objects and to adorn the trappings of horses and warriors. However, no study has yet been made of the Sarmatian animal style, and the iconography remains obscure.

[*See also* Prehistoric Religions *and* Inner Asia Religion.]

BIBLIOGRAPHY

Up to the present, no monographs have been devoted to the Sarmatian religion. For general information on the history of the Sarmatians, see János Harmatta's *Studies in the History and Language of the Sarmatians,* vol. 13 of "Acta Universitatis de Attilla Jozsef Nominatae: Acta Antiqua et Archaeologica" (Szeged, 1970). A fuller summary of archaeological data on the Sauromatians, including information on their religious antiquities, is in K. F. Smirnov's *Savromaty: Ranniaia istoriia i kul'tura sarmatov* (Moscow, 1964). On Sarmatian monuments of the Ural region, see K. F. Smirnov's *Sarmaty na Ileke* (Moscow, 1975). As for works devoted exclusively to the Sarmatian religion, there is only a short article, K. F. Smirnov's "Sarmaty-ognepoklonniki," in the collection *Arkheologiia Severnoi i Tsentral'noi Azii* (Novosibirsk, 1975), pp. 155-159.

D. S. RAEVSKII
Translated from Russian by Mary Lou Masey

SATAN

Although the name *Satan* sometimes has been connected with the Hebrew verb *sut,* which means "to roam" (perhaps suggesting that Satan acts as God's spy), it is more commonly derived from the root *satan,* which means "to oppose, to plot against." In the New Testament, Satan as the Devil is called the "great dragon" and "ancient serpent" (*Rv.* 12:9). In the *Book of Job,* Satan belongs to the court of God and, with God's permission, tests Job. By contrast, in a second occurrence (*Zec.* 3), Satan, on his own initiative, opposes Joshua.

The figure of Satan in noncanonical Hebrew literature intensifies his identification with evil. He not only emerges as an adversary of God, but, as such apocalyptic works as *Jubilees,* the *Testament of Reuben,* the *Book of the Secrets of Enoch (2 Enoch),* and the Qumran documents show, he is also the leader of the fallen angels.

> **He is also identified with other names: *Beelzebul* ("lord of flies"), *Beelzebub* ("lord of dung"), and, with somewhat less critical certainty, *Lucifer.***

Christianity synthesized Greek and Jewish concepts of the Devil. The word *devil* is actually derived from the Greek *diabolos,* which has the dual sense of "accuser" and "obstructor." If the Old Testament, according to later tradition, implicates Satan in the fall of man, the New Testament refers clearly to the fall of Satan himself in *2 Peter* 2:4 and in *Revelation* 12:7-9. Again, in contrast with the Old Testament, the power of the Devil is often mentioned (e.g., Lk. 4:6). He is also identified with other names: *Beelzebul* ("lord of flies"), *Beelzebub* ("lord of dung"), and, with somewhat less critical certainty, *Lucifer.*

In the ministry of Jesus Christ, "there is a constant campaign against Satan from the temptation after Jesus' Baptism until his death on the cross, and, in each act of healing or exorcism, there is anticipated the ultimate defeat of Satan and the manifestation of the power of the new age."

Satan's name appears as *Shaytan* in the Qur'an, although it is not clear whether the name is Arabic or not. Shaytan shares certain functions of the Judeo-Christian Satan, such as leading people astray (4:83), but there is a significant extension of this view in that Satan is accused of tampering with divine verbal revelation (22.52). However, it is in his role as Iblis (2:34, etc.) that al-Shaytan is most striking (Watt, 1970, p. 155). He is deposed for refusing to bow before man as the other angels had done, but is allowed, after his refusal, to tempt mortals. In Islam, the figure of Satan is more or less exclusively associated with evil and the underworld. This association may help "account for the Western tradition that Satan is not only Lord of evil and of death but is also associated with fertility and sexuality, a trait evident in the witches' orgy and in the horns the Devil often wears" (Russell, 1977, p. 64).

The serpent or snake is perhaps the best-known symbol associated with Satan. *Genesis* (3:1ff.) mentions the serpent but not Satan; in *Romans* (16:20), however, Paul suggests that the serpent was Satan, an association already made in apocalyptic literature. This would imply that Satan tempted Adam, but the consensus of early Christian tradition was that Satan fell after Adam (Russell, 1977, p. 232). There may be good reason for believing that not until Origen in the third century CE was it clearly established that Satan's sin was pride, that he fell before Adam's creation, and that he was the serpent in the garden of Eden.

Satan is persistently, if not consistently, associated with the serpent. Leaving aside the question of the actual nature of Satan as formulated by the Council of Toledo (447), or the tendency to consider him an imaginative personification of evil, the association with the serpent needs to be accounted for. Several views have been advanced. At a homiletic level, the serpent has been taken to represent cunning. At a psychoanalytic level, the serpent has been associated with emergent sexuality.

[*For further discussion of the symbolism, philosophy, and theology associated with the figure of Satan, see* Dualism; *and* Evil. *See also* Witchcraft.]

BIBLIOGRAPHY

Awn, Peter J. *Satan's Tragedy and Redemption: Iblis in Sufi Psychology.* Leiden, 1983.

Barton, George A. "Demons and Spirits (Hebrew)." In *Encyclopaedia of Religion and Ethics,* edited by James Hastings, vol. 4. Edinburgh, 1911.

Boyd, James W. *Satan and Mara: Christian and Buddhist Symbols of Evil.* Leiden, 1975.

Davis, H. Grady, et al. "Biblical Literature." In *The New Encyclopaedia Britannica,* Macropaedia, vol. 2. Chicago, 1984.

Day, John. *God's Conflict with the Dragon and the Sea.* Cambridge, 1985.

Langton, Edward. *Essentials of Demonology.* London, 1949.

Ling, T. O. *The Significance of Satan.* London, 1961.

O'Flaherty, Wendy Doniger. *The Origins of Evil in Hindu Mythology.* Berkeley, 1976.

Ricoeur, Paul. *The Symbolism of Evil.* Translated by Emerson Buchanan. Boston, 1967.

Robbins, Rossell Hope. *The Encyclopedia of Witchcraft and Demonology.* New York, 1966.

Russell, Jeffrey Burton. *The Devil: Perceptions of Evil from Antiquity to Primitive Christianity.* Ithaca, N. Y., 1977.

Schimmel, Annemarie. *Mystical Dimensions of Islam.* Chapel Hill, N. C., 1975.

Schofield, John Noel. "Satan." In *Encyclopaedia Britannica,* vol. 19. Chicago, 1973.

Wallace, Ronald S. "Devil." In *New International Dictionary of the Christian Church,* rev. ed., edited by J. D. Douglas. Grand Rapids, Mich., 1978.

Watt, W. Montgomery. *Bell's Introduction to the Qur'an.* Edinburgh, 1970.

Wensinck, A. J. "Iblis." In *The Encyclopaedia of Islam,* new ed., vol. 3. Leiden, 1971.

ARVIND SHARMA

SCHISM

An Overview

Schism is the process by which a religious body divides to become two or more distinct, independent bodies. The division takes place because one or each of the bodies has come to see the other as deviant, as too different to be recognized as part of the same religious brotherhood.

Types of Schisms. One way to classify schisms is to look at who defines whom as deviant. Either the parent group or the departing group, or both, may see the other as having diverged from the true faith. In the first instance, when the parent group defines the schismatic group as deviant, the charge against it (or more often against its leader) is usually heresy. [*See* Heresy.]

In the second instance, schism may occur when a departing group declares the parent body to be illegitimate, and the parent body seeks to retain the schismatics within the fold. Such an occurrence is most common when the schism parallels clear political or ethnic divisions. The parent body seeks to retain a broad definition of itself and its power, and the schismatics seek more local, independent control.

The third kind of schism is probably the most common. Here each side comes to see the other as having deviated from the true path. Although each may try for a time to convert the other, their final separation is a recognition that they can no longer work and worship together.

Ideological Factors. Religious schism, of course, by definition is an ideological matter. Differences in belief and practice are almost always at stake. In Eastern cultures, the scale is likely to tip toward differences in religious practice as the source of division, whereas in Western society, dogma assumes a more central role. The ultimate values of most groups are vague enough to allow for differences in practical interpretation. In religious groups those practical differences can create divergent paths to salvation and opposing definitions of good and evil, with each side nevertheless seeking to justify its beliefs in terms of the same core of sacred values.

Social Factors. It is, however, impossible to treat religious schism exclusively as a theological matter. Separation occurs not only because people come to hold incompatible views about salavation but because those views are born of different life experiences. The kinds of social differences that can lead to religious schism fall into three broad, interrelated categories.

Economic differences. Changes in the world economic order as a whole can also create a climate for schism. When either masses or elites find themselves in a new economic context, displayed from old loyalties, living in a world that operates by different rules, religious revolutions are possible. In medieval Japan, political and economic chaos provided the setting in which the Pure Land and Nichiren sects were formed within Buddhism. It was no accident that the Protestant Reformation occurred in the context of declining feudalism and rising nationalism. It is also no accident that the independent churches in Africa today have arisen with the decline of imperialism.

Modernization. Modernization not only creates social dislocation and encourages individualism, it also creates a world in which there are multiple versions of truth, in which there is pluralism. Ironically, one of the factors most important in predicting schism is a preexisting state of division. Where differences are already an everyday fact of life, religious schism is more likely and more easily accomplished. For this reason, it is not surprising that in the Philippines, Protestantism was most successful in precisely the same areas that had first experienced schism from the Roman church as part of the development of the Philippine Independent Church. When Islam began to dominate India in the fifteenth century, one of the responses to its spread was new religious differentiation within Hinduism.

Political differences. Religious schisms also occur because religious life cannot be separated from the political circumstances in which people exist. The Donatist schism, among the earliest divisions in the Catholic church, happened in part as a result of political tensions between North Africa and Rome. Later, during the Middle Ages, the formal schism between the Eastern and Western churches had its greatest practical reality in places like Russia, where religious schism followed the lines of political animosity between Russians and Poles. The Protestant Reformation might have taken very different form but for the rivalries among various heads of state and between them and Rome. Likewise, the shape of Protestantism in America has been undeniably affected by divisions among ethnic and immigrant groups, divisions over slavery, and divisions between frontier and city, local and cosmopolitan. Today, religious divisions often parallel political ones within the Indian subcontinent.

BIBLIOGRAPHY

Baker, Derek, ed. *Schism, Heresy and Religious Protest.* Cambridge, 1972. This collection of papers read at the Ecclesiastical History Society in London illustrates the diverse theological and social sources of the many divisions that have affected the Christian church.

Barrett, David B. *Schism and Renewal in Africa: An Analysis of Six Thousand Contemporary Religious Movements.* Nairobi, 1968. A thorough study of the political, historical, and cultural factors that explain the explosion of new, independent African churches.

Hoge, Dean R. *Division in the Protestant House: The Basic Reasons behind Intra-Church Conflicts.* Philadelphia, 1976. An excellent piece of research from the Presbyterian denomination that examines the intertwining of theological, psychological, and sociological factors in creating two opposing parties in contemporary American Protestantism.

Niebuhr, H. Richard. *The Social Sources of Denominationalism* (1929). New York, 1957. The classic statement of the causes of schism in Protestantism.

Takayama, K. Peter. "Strains, Conflicts, and Schisms in Protestant Denominations." In *American Denominational Organ-ization: A Sociological View,* edited by Ross P. Scherer, pp. 298-329. Pasadena, Calif., 1980. A leading researcher in the sociology of religious organizations proposes hypotheses for predicting schism and examines two recent divisions in light of those propositions.

Wilson, John. "The Sociology of Schism." In *A Sociological Yearbook of Religion in Britain* 4. London, 1971. A little-known article that provides a useful model for understanding the organizational processes involved in schism.

Zald, Mayer N. "Theological Crucibles: Social Movements in and of Religion." *Review of Religious Research* 23 (June 1982): 317-336. A leading proponent of "resource mobilization" theory applies his ideas to religious movements. He first reviews the cultural conditions that make religious change and division more likely and then argues that such movements can happen only if the organizational conditions are also right.

NANCY T. AMMERMAN

Christian Schism

Schism appeared early in the history of Christianity and took a variety of forms, which makes it difficult to apply any one legal or canonical definition to the phenomenon or the term. Schisms were noted in the earliest documents of the church, including the New Testament.

While schisms have had a variety of causes, they did exhibit similar sociological dynamics. For instance, they tended to be aggravated as the initial causes and antagonists became lost in the phenomenology of the separation itself. In fact, it is not unusual in Christian history to find that the original factors and personalities causing a schism were forgotten as each party to the dispute forced its own position to a logical extreme in opposition to the other.

Early Schisms. The first significant schisms to affect the Christian church were those based on heresy or a one-sided emphasis on a particular, albeit accepted, aspect of Christian belief. These were the withdrawals of Nestorian Christians in Persia in 431 as a result of the Council of Ephesus, and the so-called monophysite Christians in Syria, Egypt, Armenia, and Ethiopia in 451 after the Council of Chalcedon. Political and cultural factors would crystallize these churches in their isolation from the mainstream of Christianity, consisting of Latin and Greek portions of the empire. [*See* Heresy.]

Rome and Constantinople. Relations between the churches of Rome and Constantinople continued to degenerate during the eighth century as these churches grew increasingly hostile as well as distant in their ecclesiology and politics. The most notable feature of the ecclesiastical developments of the eighth century was the new alliance that the papacy forged in mid-century with the new Carolingian kings.

In the ninth century, through the agency of the Carolingians, the issue of the *filioque* was thrust into the already hostile relations between Rome and Constantinople. The *filioque,* Latin for "and the Son" (asserting that the Holy Spirit proceeds from both God the Father and from God the Son) had been inserted into the Nicene Creed in sixth-century Spain to protect the divinity of the Son against residual Arianism and adoptionism. Charlemagne welcomed, endorsed, and adopted the *filioque* officially at the Council of Frankfurt (794) and used its absence among the Byzantines as the basis for charges of heresy.

Photian schism. In 858, Photios assumed the patriarchate of Constantinople on the occasion of the deposition and later resignation of Patriarch Ignatius (847-858). Ignatius's partisans appealed to Rome for his restoration. Their cause was taken up by Nicholas I, who was looking for an opportunity to intervene in Eastern ecclesiastical affairs to enhance his authority. A Roman council in 863 excommunicated Photios as a usurper and called for the restoration of Ignatius, but the council had no way of enforcing its decisions in the East, and the Byzantines bitterly attacked the move as an uncanonical interference in their affairs.

During the same period, Photios held a council and excommunicated Nicholas.

The schism ended when the Latin church, through the attendance of three papal legates at the council of 879/880, endorsed by John VIII, confirmed Photios's restoration and the end of the internal schism between the Photians and the Ignatians.

The Great Schism. The issue of the *filioque* was to arise again in the eleventh century. In 1009, Pope Sergius IV (1009-1012) announced his election in a letter containing the interpolated *filioque* clause in the creed. Although there seems to have been no discussion of the matter, another schism was initiated. The addition of the *filioque* was, however, official this time, and the interpolated creed was used at the coronation of Emperor Henry II in 1014.

As the papacy moved into the mid-eleventh century, the reform movement was radically altering its view of the pope's position and authority. This movement, as well as the military threat of the Normans to Byzantine southern Italy, set the stage for the so-called Great Schism of 1054.

The encounter began when Leo IX (1049-1054), at the Synod of Siponto, attempted to impose Latin ecclesiastical customs on the Byzantine churches of southern Italy. Patriarch Michael Cerularios (1043-1058) responded by criticizing Latin customs, such as the use of azyme (unleavened bread) in the Eucharist and fasting on Saturdays during Lent. The issues of the eleventh-century crisis were almost exclu-

sively those of popular piety and ritual; the *filioque* played a minor part.

Michael's reaction did not suit Emperor Constantine IX (1042-1055), who needed an anti-Norman alliance with the papacy. Michael was forced to write a conciliatory letter to Leo IX offering to clarify the confusion between the churches, restore formal relations, and confirm an alliance against the Normans. Leo sent three legates east, but Michael broke off discussions.

By the mid-eleventh century, it became clear to the Byzantines that they no longer spoke the same ecclesiological language as the church of Rome. This was to become even more evident during the pontificate of Gregory VII (1073-1085), whose *Dictates of the Pope* could find no resonance in Byzantine ecclesiology.

In 1089 when the emperor Alexios I (1081-1118), seeking the West's assistance against the Turks in Anatolia (modern-day Asia Minor) as well as papal support against Norman designs on Byzantine territory, convoked a synod to consider the relations between the two churches. An investigation produced no documentary or synodal evidence to support a formal schism. What is clear is that what was lacking in the relationship between East and West could have been rectified by a simple confession of faith. The theological issue of the *filioque* was considered by Byzantine theologians to revolve around a misunderstanding stemming from the crudeness of the Latin language.

The Great Western Schism. The church of Rome, for which centralization was essential, underwent one of the most significant schisms in the history of Christianity. Its beginnings lay in the opening of the fourteenth century, when Pope Boniface VIII (1294-1303) lost the battle with Philip IV (1285-1314) over nationalization of the French kingdom. In 1305, the cardinals, divided between Italians and Frenchmen, elected Clement V (1305-1314) to succeed Boniface. Philip pressured Clement, a Frenchman, to move the papal residence from Rome to Avignon in 1309. It remained there, in "Babylonian Captivity," until 1377.

The papal thrust for independence from the French kingdom came in the context of the need to protect its Italian holdings. The Romans threatened to elect another pope should Gregory XI (1370-1378) not return. Gregory arrived in Rome in January 1377.

When Gregory died in 1378, the cardinals elected the Italian Urban VI (1378-1389). Although the majority of the cardinals in Rome were French and would have gladly removed the papacy to Avignon, the pressure of the Roman popular demands forced the election. Urban immediately went about reforming the Curia Romana and eliminating French influence. The French cardinals proceeded to elect another pope, Clement VII (1378-1394), who after several months moved to Avignon. The schism within the Western church had become a reality.

This second election would not have been so significant if Urban and Clement had not been elected by the same group of cardinals and had not enjoyed the support of various constellations of national interests. The schism severely compromised papal universalism. The Roman line of the schism was maintained by the succession of Boniface IX (1389-1404), Innocent VII (1404-1406), and Gregory XII (1406-1415). The Avignon line was maintained by Benedict XIII (1394-1423).

In the context of the schism, it was difficult to maintain even the appearance of a unified Western Christendom. The schism produced a sense of frustration as theologians and canonists searched for a solution. In 1408 the cardinals of both parties met in Livorno and, on their own authority, called a council in Pisa for March 1409, composed of bishops, cardinals, abbots, heads of religious orders, and representatives of secular rulers. The council appointed a new pope, Alexander V (1409-1410; succeeded by John XXIII, 1410-1415), replacing the Roman and Avignon popes, who were deposed.

The newly elected Holy Roman Emperor, Sigismund (1410-1437), and Pope Alexander V called a council to meet at Constance in 1414. Voting by nations, the council declared that it represented the Roman Catholic church and held its authority directly from Christ. John XXIII and Benedict XIII were deposed, and Gregory XII resigned. With the election of Martin V (1417-1431), Western Christendom was united once again under one pope.

The Reformation. The Reformation of the sixteenth century was the second great split to strike Christianity. [*See* Reformation.] The same issues that determined the relations between Rome and the East figured in the separation of a large number of the Christians in Germany, Scotland, and Scandinavia. Martin Luther gradually moved from objecting to specific practices of the church of Rome to challenging papal authority as normative. Authority does not reside in the papacy, but rather in scripture; *sola scriptura* became the hallmark of his reforms.

BIBLIOGRAPHY

Bouyer, Louis. *The Spirit and Forms of Protestantism.* London, 1956. Offers an excellent introduction to the theological hallmarks of the Reformation and their Roman Catholic sources. Bouyer, a Roman Catholic, considers each Reformation principle as a basis for unity and for schism. The approach is valuable for considering the Reformation as a schism.

Dvornik, Francis. *The Photian Schism: History and Legend* (1948). Reprint, Cambridge, 1970. A brilliant summary of the author's research on the ninth-century patriarch Photios, elucidating the misunderstandings of the complex relationships of the ninth century. The author concludes that Photios was not opposed to Roman primacy and that the idea of a second Photian schism was a fabrication of eleventh-century canonists.

Dvornik, Francis. *Byzantium and the Roman Primacy.* New York, 1966. A historical survey of the relations between the church of Rome and the Byzantine East. Although tendentious in its defense of Roman "primacy," it provides excellent coverage of events from the Acacian schism through the Fourth Crusade. Concludes that the Byzantine church never rejected Roman primacy, but does not define the differing Roman and Byzantine interpretations of primacy.

Every, George. *The Byzantine Patriarchate, 451-1204.* 2d rev. ed. London, 1962. Still the best introduction to the Byzantine church from the fifth to the twelfth centuries; highlights the major conflicts between Rome and Constantinople, including the role of the *filioque,* the Crusades, and papal primacy. Concludes that the progressive estrangement between the two portions of Christendom was not a straight-line process. The timing of the schism, the author notes, depends on the place.

Meyendorff, John. *Byzantine Theology: Historical Trends and Doctrinal Themes.* 2d ed. New York, 1979. A superb presentation of Eastern Christian thought and doctrinal and historical trends that clarifies the roots of the schism. The author considers the process nature of the final separation between the two churches and notes the underlying agenda of authority in the church.

Runciman, Steven. *The Eastern Schism* (1955). Reprint, Oxford, 1963. A highly readable account of the relations between the papacy and the Eastern churches during the eleventh and twelfth centuries. The author maintains that the traditional reasons of doctrinal and liturgical practices for the schism are inadequate; the schism was due to the more fundamental divergence in traditions and ideology that grew up during earlier centuries. He highlights the proximate causes as the Crusades, the Norman invasions of Byzantine Italy, and the reform movement within the papacy.

Sherrard, Philip. *Church, Papacy, and Schism: A Theological Inquiry.* London, 1978. A theological analysis of schism in general. The author focuses on the schism between Rome and the Eastern churches. He argues from the historical perspective that doctrinal issues, which he enumerates, were at the root of the schism and continue to be the reason for separation between the churches of the East and the West.

Ullmann, Walter. *The Origins of the Great Schism: A Study in Fourteenth Century Ecclesiastical History* (1948). Reprint, Hamden, Conn., 1972. Insightful and thorough presentation of the Great Western Schism in the context of fourteenth-century ecclesiastical and political events.

JOHN LAWRENCE BOOJAMRA

SCIENCE AND RELIGION

What Science? What Religion? That both religion and science are vast entities is, in this view, the only feature they may have in common. The differences between the two may appear striking even to a casual onlooker. Science is relatively new; it became robustly manifest only about three hundred years ago. Ever since its rise in the seventeenth century the scientific community has not been seriously divided as to what constitutes science. The rise of that community was marked by its signal success in discrediting alchemy and astrology as scientific pursuits. It proved itself just as effective in distancing itself from *Naturphilosophie* in the first half of the nineteenth century.

To science's impressive measure of youth, uniformity, consensus, coherence, and definability, religion presents an unflattering contrast. Religion predates recorded history and easily appears as a fossil of bygone ages. Religion repeats old sayings, and if it offers something "new," the novelty turns out to be either a studied vagueness or an eventual boomerang. The statements of religion, if truly theological, are never testable in a scientific sense.

A portrayal, however brief, of religion as an actual phenomenon that can react to science cannot be complete without a reference to unitarianism and to deism. The former has increasingly approached the erstwhile position of deism, whereas the latter is now hardly distinguishable from a kind of cosmic "religion" to which Albert Einstein has given much currency. The residue of "religion" can be detected at times in secular humanism, which rejects even the vague pantheism of cosmic religion; mere aestheticism might be a more appropriate label for this religiosity.

Ancient Religions and Science. Studies of ancient Greece rarely fail to contain something equivalent to the phrase "the Greek miracle." With respect to science, the Greeks' achievements give also an unintended twist to a remark of Einstein's, according to which the real problem is not why science was not born in any of the ancient cultures but why it was born at all. Marvel should indeed yield to perplexity on pondering the two-century-long creative work in geometry that Euclid systematized at the beginning of the Hellenistic period (c. 300 BCE–c. 600 CE).

There were many other Greek men of science whose achievements would undoubtedly be judged today as of Nobel-prize caliber. One example is Hipparchos's discovery of the precession of equinoxes. Another is Eratosthenes' method of estimating the size of the earth, which yielded a value in close agreement with modern measurements.

Yet even in Greece, so often and so much praised for its championing the logos, or reason, these splendid advances failed to issue in an intense intellectual reflection. Archimedes, for one, did not endorse the heliocentric theory, although he made much of the foregoing distance estimates in his *Sand Reckoner*. Ptolemy, who made the widest application of Euclidean geometry to astronomy, had only scorn for heliocentrism, as was also the case a century or so before him with Plutarch, who is often praised for the daring modernity with which he spoke of the moon as a body similar to the earth. Yet, the modernity of Plutarch is only apparent. His discussion of the tides is a revealing instance. To be sure, he attributed the tides to the moon's influence, but the latter was for him a volitional sympathy for the earth and vice versa. As such it was a throwback to the organismic view that Ptolemy himself endorsed when doing astronomy not as a mathematician but as a physicist. The harmonious motion of planets was for him equivalent to that of a group of dancers intent on not colliding with one another.

The agony of the Greek mind was to see only an all-or-nothing choice between science (mechanics or dynamics) and purpose (religion). The Greek mind lost out on both because it did not seem to possess the fiducial strength to accept irreducible features of existence (materiality and spirituality) and to give both their due. The problem lies in the heart of the relation of science and religion, compared with which all other problems pale in significance. The clue to it would not be on hand without the subsequent ability of medieval and early modern Christian Europe to trust in the ultimate harmony of these two apparently contradictory features of experience. To the Europeans in question that trust came from their belief in a transcendental rational creator, the very belief that the Greeks did not possess. The Socratic solution for which Greek posterity overwhelmingly opted was a move hardly helpful either for science or for soul.

Ancient India was also the place that witnessed the formulation of the decimal system, including place notation with the use of zero, at least a thousand years before the common era. Ancient South Asians can also be credited with advancing algebra to second-degree equations, but their scientific exploration of the material world surrounding them showed little if any sophistication.

Ancient China Confucians entrenched a long-standing reluctance to de-animize considerations about the physical universe. As late as 1921 such a prominent Chinese thinker as Fung Yu-lan was not reluctant to claim that China needed no science as it was wholly alien to the best in Chinese thought. Whereas similar statements made around 1800 by Chinese scholars on being shown a microscope (a falsifier of true perception, in their eyes) may seem a minor matter, the situation in the twentieth century, when world powers stake their strategy on the successes of their respective scientific research, should seem quite different. Indeed it was the rise of China after World War II to the status of superpower that prompted major studies on the failure of China to become the birthplace of science.

Two cultures, Jewish and Muslim, demand special consideration here, as they are both steeped in monotheism, the kind of religion most at variance with the organismic pantheism. Neither Jewish nor Islamic ambience has become the birthplace of science. One can see evidence of the growing inability of Jewish thinkers to keep the creation dogma from the inroads of pantheism, a point clearly acknowledged in all the great twentieth-century Jewish encyclopedias. This is also a rarely noted but all-important point to be made in connection with the development of Muslim thought.

Within a century or so after the Hijrah the Islamic world was a vast cultural entity in full possession of the Greek philosophical and scientific corpus. Muslim studies of this body of work, intense as they were, did not, however, lead to its critical development. Concerning the study of motion, or physics and cosmology in a broader sense, Muslim studies fell into two main categories, which correspond broadly to Islam's two major theological trends. One reaction was that of an Islamic orthodoxy for which the laws of nature represented a curtailment of the freedom of God as set forth in the Qur'an. The other trend, represented above all in the writings of Ibn Sina (Avicenna) and Ibn Rushd (Averroës), took Aristotelian science with all its apriorism as the last word in learning. The leading Muslim scholars became convinced that the cultivation of the science of motion, or physics, was in a sense a waste of time.

Religion versus Scientism. The stillbirth of science in Islam invites a further look at the very different outcome in the Christian West. Christian monotheism obviously must have had a special character capable of fostering the rise of the scientific worldview.

The claim that this worldview is closely tied to dogmatic Christianity and uniquely germane to creative science is subject to several tests. These in turn represent major interactions between science and religion in modern times. One of those tests relates to the difference between the foregoing worldview, essentially a set of philosophical propositions, and the primitive world-picture, such as given in *Genesis* 1, in which that worldview was originally adumbrated. In the two treatises of Augustine on the interpretation of *Genesis,* which were widely read during medieval and Renaissance centuries, the faithful are warned against taking literally biblical details about the external world that are at variance with what reason and observation (science) had established.

> **Actually, the science in question is a science that has grown into a religion, called scientism. . . .**

Two hundred or so years later, not only the theory of evolution and the discovery of the vast geological past but also the specific mechanism set forth by Charles Darwin of the origin of species had to be faced by dogmatic Christianity. Interestingly, the real opposition to Darwin's ideas came from the Protestant side, which, apart from its liberal sector, regarded the Bible as literally true in the sense bequeathed by Luther and Calvin.

In going through the crucible of the conflict with Galileo and Darwin, a recognizable segment of Christian thinkers has developed a fair measure of awareness of the limitations of the propositions of religion. Insofar as they deal with ethical and metaphysical issues, those propositions cannot be touched upon by science, nor can they touch on anything specific in science, save its use. At the same time it has also become widely recognized among religious thinkers that the ultimate truth of any empirical aspect of any dogmatic statement lies with empirical science.

Actually, the science in question is a science that has grown into a religion, called scientism, and that is all too aware of its true physiognomy though it is not always ready to show its true colors. The religion in question is not any religion, and certainly not religion's liberal variants, but only a dogmatic Christianity. Its "incorrigibility" is in the eyes of its antagonists its chief crime. In the eyes of its most penetrating analyst in modern times, John Henry Newman, that "incorrigibility" is the very thing that should most commend it. Insofar as it remains aware of its complete lack of mission to decide about empirical facts and measurements, it will remain clear of any serious conflict with science. But aware or not on that score, its worldview, which it bequeathed historically and culturally and which is still held by its orthodox theologians, is yet a worldview within which alone creative science can survive and progress even in the twentieth century.

BIBLIOGRAPHY

On the allegedly irreconcilable opposition between science and religion, the classic warhorse is *History of the Conflict between Religion and Science* by John W. Draper (New York, 1895). Pierre Duhem's vast documentation of his discovery of the medieval origins of modern science is mostly in his *Études sur Léonardo da Vinci,* 3 vols. (1906-1913; reprint, Paris, 1955) and in *Le système du monde,* 10 vols. (vols. 1-5, 1913-1916, reprinted, Paris, 1954; vols. 6-10, Paris, 1954-1959). Duhem's findings and their reception are discussed in chapter 10 of my *Uneasy Genius: The Life and Work of Pierre Duhem* (Dordrecht, 1984). For a detailed discussion of the stillbirths of science in all ancient cultures, see chapters 1-5 and 8 in my *Science and Creation: From Eternal Cycles to an Oscillating Universe* (Edinburgh, 1974). For the special support given by the dogma of incarnation to the dogma of creation, see chapter 3 in my *Cosmos and Creator* (Edinburgh, 1980; Chicago, 1982). In the same book, see chapter 2 on the cosmological argument with respect to cosmic specificity and Gödel's theorem. The various attitudes of physicists to physicalism (scientism) are documented in my *The Relevance of Physics* (Chicago, 1966). The close relation of the epistemology of the cosmological argument to the epistemology of creative science is the theme of my Gifford Lectures, *The Road of Science and the Ways to God* (Chicago, 1978). The fundamental issues between Darwinism and Christian faith are discussed in chapter 2 of my *Angels, Apes and Men* (La Salle, Ill., 1983). All these books contain ample bibliographies, as does my article "Chance or Reality: Interaction in Nature versus Measurement in Physics," *Philosophia* (Athens) 10/11 (1980-1981): 85-105, which deals with the philosophy of the Copenhagen interpretation of quantum mechanics.

Among recent books that show depth and scholarship, mention should be made of *Christian Theology and Natural Science* (London, 1956) and *The Openness of Being: Natural Theology Today* (Philadelphia, 1971), both by E. L. Mascall. The same orthodox dogmatic position is the basis of Thomas F. Torrance's *Divine and Contingent Order* (Oxford, 1981). The Christian origin of science, with heavy emphasis on Calvinism and with complete disregard of Duhem's epoch-making studies, is the subject of *Religion and the Rise of Modern Science* by Reijer Hooykaas (Grand Rapids, Mich., 1972). A distinctly liberal and nondogmatic Christianity is the standpoint in *Creation and the World of Science* by Arthur R. Peacocke

(Oxford, 1979) and in Ian G. Barbour's *Issues in Science and Religion* (Englewood Cliffs, N. J., 1966).

A vast bibliographical reference (which ignores Duhem) to the development of science prior to 1400 is George Sarton's *Introduction to the History of Science,* 3 vols. in 5 (Washington, D. C., 1927-1948). For information regarding the possible role of alchemy in the rise of science in the West, see Lynn Thorndike's *A History of Magic and Experimental Science,* 8 vols. (New York, 1923-1958), and the appendix to Mircea Eliade's *The Forge and the Crucible,* 2d ed. (Chicago, 1978).

Somewhat dated but still informative are the following books, all by scientists: E. T. Whittaker's *Space and Spirit: Theories of the Universe and the Arguments for the Existence of God* (New York, 1947); Charles E. Raven's *Science, Religion, and the Future* (New York, 1943); Charles A. Coulson's *Science and Christian Belief* (Chapel Hill, N. C., 1955); and Edward A. Milne's *Modern Cosmology and the Christian Idea of God* (Oxford, 1952). Religion is rather an amorphous entity in Bernard Lovell's *In the Centre of Immensities* (New York, 1978). Distinctly hostile is the tone of references to religion in general and dogmatic Christianity in particular in the various books (none of them systematically on science and religion) by Carl Sagan, P. B. Medawar, Fred Hoyle, and John M. Ziman.

Joseph Needham's often-quoted conclusion on science and theology in ancient China appears in *Science and Civilisation in China,* vol. 2, *History of Scientific Thought* (Cambridge, 1956). The chief interaction between science and religion in the remainder of this century will undoubtedly relate to ethical questions raised by the rapidly increasing control of biochemistry and genetics over fundamental aspects of human life (ranging from *in vitro* fertilization through contraception and abortion to eugenics and euthanasia, to say nothing of biochemical control of brain processes). On these topics there is already a vast literature.

STANLEY L. JAKI

SCRIPTURE

SCRIPTURE is the generic concept used in the modern West and, increasingly, worldwide, to designate texts that are revered as especially sacred and authoritative in all major and many other religious traditions.

Origins and Development of the Concept. Whatever the subtleties and difficulties of defining it, scripture is a major phenomenon in the history of religion and thus an important concept in the study of religion.

The idea of a heavenly book. The development of the concept of a scriptural book is often linked to the notion of a heavenly book. The idea of a heavenly book containing divine knowledge or decrees is an ancient and persistent one found primarily in the ancient Near Eastern and Greco-Roman worlds and in subsequent Jewish, Christian, and Islamic traditions. As Leo Koep points out in *Das himmlische Buch in Antike und Christentum* (Bonn, 1952), it can take one of several forms, typically that of a book of wisdom, book of destinies, book of works, or book of life. References to a celestial book or tablet of divine wisdom appear in ancient Babylonia and ancient Egypt and recur in almost all subsequent Near Eastern traditions, apparently as an expression of divine omniscience.

The idea of a sacred book. The quintessential "book religions" are those that trace their lineage in some fashion to the Hebrews, the prototypical "people of the book." We do not yet fully understand how Judaic ideas of the sacred or heavenly book joined historically with influences from other sectors of the ancient Near Eastern world and the growing status of the book in later antiquity to set in motion the "book religion" that plays so large a role in Christianity, Manichaeism, and, most spectacularly and pronouncedly, in Islam. Christianity's increasing emphasis on authoritative writings, the point of departure for which was Jewish reverence for the Torah, was especially decisive in this development. Mani's self-conscious effort to produce books of scriptural authority reflects the degree to which by his time (third century CE) a religious movement had to have its own scriptures. It was the Qur'an's insistence upon the centrality of the divine book, given now in final form as a recitation, that carried the development of book religion to its apogee in the early seventh century.

Semantic background. The most basic meaning of *scripture,* as of its Indo-European cognates (Ger., *Schrift;* Ital., *scrittura;* Fr., *écriture;* etc.), is "a writing, something written." It is derived from the Latin *scriptura,* "a writing" (pl., *scripturae*). In the Mediterranean world of later antiquity, pagan, Jewish, and Christian writers used these words (or their plurals) to refer to various kinds of written texts in the Hebrew Bible, the Greek Septuagint, and the Old Testament books of the Latin Vulgate (e.g., *Ex.* 32:16, *Tob.* 8:24, *Ps.* 86:6). By the time of the Christian New Testament writers, however, the terms had gradually come to be used especially for sacred books, above all the three divisions of the Hebrew scriptures, the Pentateuch (Torah), Prophets (Nevi'im), and (other) Writings (Ketuvim).

In the New Testament (e.g., *Rom.* 1:2, 2 *Tm.* 3:15) and in the works of the Christian fathers, and as well as in Philo and Josephus, various adjectives were added to the words for "scripture(s)" and "book(s)" to emphasize their special, holy character: for example, *hieros, hagios, sanctus* ("holy"); *theios, divinus* ("divine"); *theopneustos* ("divinely inspired"); *kuriakos* ("of the Lord").

Generalization of the Concept. In these ways, the Jewish and Christian worlds gradually appropriated the use of such terms as *scripture, holy scripture(s), books, sacred books,* and so forth, primarily as proper-noun designations for their own holy texts. In particular, as Christian culture and religion triumphed in the Mediterranean, especially in southern Europe, *(sacred) scripture* came to mean specifically the Christian Bible.

Such Western generalization of the concept of scripture was, to be sure, hardly novel. In the Muslim world, the concept of sacred "scripture" *(kitab)* had already been generalized in the Qur'an, where especially Jews and Christians are spoken of as "people of scripture" *(ahl al-kitab).*

The extended use of the term *scripture* for any particularly sacred text is now common in modern Western usage and widely current internationally. Even the word *Bible* has been used, albeit less often, in a similarly general sense to refer to any sacred scripture (cf. Franklin Edgerton's reference to the *Bhagavadgita* as "India's favorite Bible" in *The Bhagavad Gita, or Song of the Blessed One,* Chicago, 1925).

Characteristic Roles. Scriptural texts function in a variety of ways in a religious tradition. Some of their major functions are discussed below.

Scripture as Holy Writ. The significance of the written word of scripture is difficult to exaggerate. With the important exception of the Hindu world, the writing down of the major religious text(s) of a community is an epochal event in its history, one that is often linked to the crystallization of religious organization and systematic theological speculation, as well as to the achievement of a high level of culture. The written scriptural text symbolizes or embodies religious authority in many traditions (often replacing the living authority of a religious founder such as Muhammad or the Buddha).

Although the fixity and authority of the physical text have been felt particularly strongly in the last two thousand years in the West, the idea of an authoritative sacred writing is not limited to one global region. Veneration for the sacred word as book has also been important, if not always central, in most of the Buddhist world of Southeast and East Asia. It has been suggested, for example, that there was an early Mahayana cult of the book *(sutra)* that vied with the *stupa* relic cult, and high esteem for the written *sutras* has been generally prominent in Mahayana tradition. Furthermore, it was in India, not the West, that the veneration of the written text reached one of its heights in the Sikh movement.

One of the overt ways in which the importance of the written text is revealed is in the religious valuation of the act of copying and embellishing a sacred text. Christian and, still more, Jewish and Islamic scriptures boast especially strong calligraphic traditions.

Scripture as spoken word. Recitation or reading aloud of scripture is a common feature of piety, whether in Islamic, Sikh, Jewish, or other traditions. Many scriptures have primary or secondary schemes of division according to the needs of recitation or reading aloud in the community (e.g., the 154 divisions of the Torah for synagogal reading over a three-year span). Great esteem is given to the person who knows all of the sacred scripture "by heart"—in the Muslim case, such a person is honored with the special epithet *hafiz,* "keeper, protector, memorizer [of the Word]". In the early synagogue and in the early Christian church, the reading aloud of scripture in worship was fundamental to religious life (Ismar Elbogen, *Der jüdische Gottesdienst,* Leipzig, 1913,

chap. 3; Paul Glaue, *Die Vorlesung heiliger Schriften im Gottesdienst,* Berlin, 1907; but cf. Walter Bauer, *Das Wortgottesdienst der ältesten Christen,* Tübingen, 1930), just as it was in pagan cults of the Hellenistic Mediterranean, such as that of Isis (Leipoldt and Morenz, 1953, p. 96). The Jews call both the reading of scripture and the passage read *miqra'* (*Neh.* 8:8), "what is recited, read aloud, a reading." In Talmudic usage , the term came to refer to the Torah (Pentateuch), the Prophets, and the Writings that make up the Tankakh, or Hebrew scriptures.

In other traditions, notably the Islamic and Buddhist, the recitation of the sacred word is even more central to religious practice, despite the frequently massive importance of veneration of the written text in the same traditions. In Hindu practice, the oral, recited word completely eclipses the importance of any written form of it and presents the most vivid instance of the all but exclusively oral function of scripture.

Scripture in public ritual. Whether the written or the oral text of a scriptural book predominates, the most visible religious role of a scripture is in public worship. In some instances a scripture is explicitly a ritual text that orders and explains the rite itself, as in the case of the Brahmanas in Vedic tradition. In other cases it is a sacred text either recited in ritual acts (e.g., the Qur'an, the Zoroastrian *Gathas,* the Vedic *mantras,* and the Shinto *norito,* or ritual prayers taken from the Engi-shiki) or read aloud from a written copy in communal worship, as in Jewish or Christian practice. Such recitation or reading is often a major if not the central element in worship.

Ritually important passages of a scriptural text are sometimes pulled together into special anthologies or collections that serve the liturgical needs of the community, as in the Christian breviary, psalter, lectionary, or evangeliarium; the Patimokkha selection from the Vinaya that is recited as a regular part of Buddhist monastic life; or the *Blue Sutra,* an abridgement of the *Lotus Sutra* that is used in the ritual of the modern Reiyukai Buddhist sect in Japan (Helen Hardacre, *Lay Buddhism in Contemporary Japan,* Princeton, 1984).

Scripture in devotional and spiritual life. Recitation and reading aloud are not only central to formal worship (see above), but also to private devotion and the practice of diverse spiritual disciplines. *Meditatio* in the Christian tradition was from the start basically an oral activity of learning the text "by heart" through reciting with concentrated attention and reflection. In turn, as Jean Leclercq has eloquently stated in *The Love of Learning and the Desire for God* [1957] 1974), meditation formed the basis of the monastic *lectio divina,* the active, oral reading of and reflecting on scripture upon which the monk's discipline was based in Pachomian, Benedictine, and other rules.

Closely related to meditative practices involving scriptural texts are the recitation of and meditation upon formulas derived from scripture. The chanting of Hindu and Buddhist *mantras* and of Buddhist *dharanis,* as well as the recitation of Sufi *dhikr* litanies (many of which are Qur'anic) are major examples of formulaic use of scripture in devotional life.

Characteristic Attributes of Scripture. The scriptures of any given religious tradition possess a number of characteristic attributes. Some of the most important are as follows.

Power. The major functional attributes of scripture are bound up with the power felt to be inherent in scriptural word. Both the written and the spoken word carry a seemingly innate power in human life. At the most basic level, a word is an action: words do not signify so much as they perform. Hence to speak a name ritually is in some measure to control or to summon the one named. For the faithful, a sacred word is not merely a word, but an operative, salvific word. Its unique, transformative power often rests upon its being spoken (or written) by a god (as in Jewish, Christian, or Muslim tradition). In other cases, the sound itself is holy (as in India), or the message or teaching embodied in the scriptural word is considered to be salvific truth, with little or no reference to a divine origin (as in many Buddhist traditions).

Authority and sacrality. The authoritative character of scripture is most vivid in those cases in which a sacred text provides the legal basis of communal order. This is especially evident in the Jewish tradition, where the written Torah is the pediment upon which the entire edifice of Jewish life is built, and in the Islamic tradition, where the minimal legal prescriptions and much larger body of moral injunctions found in the Qur'an are viewed as the ultimate bases of the *shari`ah.* It is also evident in the role of the Vinaya ("discipline") section of the Tripitaka, the "law" of Buddhist monasticism.

The extraordinary sacrality of scripture is seen in almost every facet of its use in communal life. The way in which a scriptural text is handled, the formulas of respect that accompany its mention, citation, recitation, or reading, and the theological doctrines that are developed to set it apart ontologically from all other texts are common evidence of such sacrality.

Unicity. A further quality of scripture is its perceived unicity of source, content, and authority in the community involved with it (see especially Leipolt and Morenz, 1953). No matter what the historical origins or textual development of its constituent parts, and no matter how diverse those parts, a scriptural corpus is commonly conceived of as a unified whole, both in its ontological origin as sacred word and its authoritativeness and internal consistency as sacred truth. The many originally separate texts that were collected into the Egyptian *Book of Going Forth by Day,* the diverse "holy scriptures" of the Hebrew or Christian Bible, the myriad *sutras* of the Chinese Buddhist canon, or the various kinds of Vedic texts revered as *sruti*—these and other bodies of sacred texts are each conceived as an ontological and conceptual unity, whether that unity is one of God's holy word (as

in ancient Egypt or Islam), the Buddha-word, or the "sound" (Skt., *sabda;* Chin., *sheng*) of ultimate truth or wisdom heard by the ancient Indian and ancient Chinese sages.

Inspiration and eternality/antiquity. The tendency to see one's own formal or informal canon of scriptures as a unified whole is closely linked to the characteristic development of a theory of inspiration, revelation, or some other kind of suprahuman and primordial origin for its words. All of the prophets and teachers whose words become part of scripture are held to have been inspired in their speech (as with the Hebrew prophets), to have been given God's direct revelation to their fellows (as with Muhammad and Mani), or to have had an experience in which they transcended the contingent world to grasp ultimate reality (as in the Buddha's enlightenment).

The divine word is also commonly held to be eternal, as in the role of Vac ("speech") as primordial being or goddess in Vedic thought, in the Hindu concept of the eternal Veda (cf. *Laws of Manu* 12.94, 12.99), in the Muslim doctrine of the uncreated, eternal Word of the Qur'an (which, as God's very Word, is an eternal divine attribute), in the Sikh concept of the *bani* ("word") that preexists and extends beyond the gurus and the Adi *Granth* (W. Owen Cole and Piara S. Sambhi, *The Sikhs,* London, 1978, p. 44), and in Buddhist ideas of the eternal Dharma or the *buddhavacana* ("Buddha word") in Mahayana thought.

A scripture is virtually always conceived to be, if not eternal, at least of great antiquity. The Japanese *Kojiki* and *Nihongi,* the Avesta, and the Five Classics of China are all prime examples of sacred texts to which hoary antiquity is ascribed.

BIBLIOGRAPHY

Of the surprisingly few comparative or general treatments of scripture, the best, even though limited to the ancient Mediterranean world, is Johannes Leipoldt and Siegfried Morenz's *Heilige Schriften: Betrachtungen zur Religionsgeschichte der antiken Mittelmeerwelt* (Leipzig, 1953). There are substantial phenomenological treatments of holy word, holy writ, and/or scripture in Friedrich Heiler's *Erscheinungsformen und Wesen der Religion* (1961; 2d rev. ed., Stuttgart, 1979), pp. 266-364; in Geo Widengren's *Religionsphänomenologie* (Berlin, 1969), pp. 546-593; and in Gerardus van der Leeuw's *Phänomenologie der Religion* (1933; 2d rev. ed., Tübingen, 1956), translated as *Religion in Essence and Manifestation* (1938; rev. ed., New York, 1963), chaps. 58-64. Another phenomenological study is Gustav Mensching's *Das heilige Wort* (Bonn, 1937). Also of note are the brief articles under the heading "Schriften, heilige" in the second and third editions of *Die Religion in Geschichte und Gegenwart* (Tübingen, 1931, 1961) by Alfred Bertholet and Siegfried Morenz, respectively, and the descriptive survey of major scriptural texts by Günter Lanczkowski: *Heilige Schriften: Inhalt, Textgestalt und Überlieferung* (Stuttgart, 1956). See also Alfred Bertholet's *Die Macht der Schrift in Glauben und Aberglauben* (Berlin, 1949); Siegfried Morenz's "Entstehung und Wesen der Buchreligion," *Theologische Literaturzeitung* 75 (1950): 709-715; and Josef Balogh's "'Voces paginarum': Beiträge zur

Geschichte des lauten Lesens und Schreibens," *Philogus* 82 (1926-1927): 83-109, 202-240.

The articles contributed to *Holy Book and Holy Tradition,* edited by Frederick F. Bruce and E. G. Rupp (Grand Rapids, Mich., 1968), vary in quality but provide useful information on particular traditions. A number of solid articles can be found in *The Holy Book in Comparative Perspective,* edited by Frederick Mathewson Denny and Rodney L. Taylor (Columbia, S. C., 1985), which contains survey-discussions of some major world scriptural traditions, and in *Rethinking Scripture,* edited by Miriam Levering (forthcoming), which presents a series of critical reevaluations of scripture as a generic and specific category.

In addition to works cited in the foregoing article under the specific topics treated, several others deserve special mention, especially those that address the problem of the semantic background of the terms *scripture, book,* and so forth found in the West: "Schrift," in *Theologisches Begriffslexikon zum Neuen Testament,* 2 vols. in 3, edited by Lothar Coenen et al. (Wuppertal, 1967-1971); "Bible [Canon]," by Bezalel Narkiss, in *Encyclopaedia Judaica,* vol. 4 (Jerusalem, 1971); and "Écriture sainte [1. Le nom]," by Hildebrand Höpfl, in the *Dictionnaire de la Bible, Supplément,* vol. 2 (Paris, 1926).

Few studies have been devoted to the functional roles of scripture within the various traditions. For the Christian Bible, special note may be made of Ernst von Dobschütz's *Die Bibel im Leben der Völker* (Witten, West Germany, 1934) and his "Bible in the Church," in the *Encyclopaedia of Religion and Ethics,* edited by James Hastings, vol. 2 (Edinburgh, 1909); "Écriture sainte et vie spirituelle," by Jean Kirchmeyer et al., in the *Dictionnaire de spiritualité,* vol. 4 (Paris, 1960); Beryl Smalley's *The Study of the Bible in the Middle Ages,* 2d ed. (Oxford, 1952); Hans Rost's *Die Bibel im Mittelalter* (Augsburg, 1939); *The Cambridge History of the Bible,* 3 vols., edited by Peter R. Ackroyd, C. F. Evans, G. W. H. Lampe, and S. L. Greenslade (Cambridge, 1963-1970). See also the important statement on the problem by Wilfred Cantwell Smith: "The Study of Religion and the Study of the Bible," *Journal of the American Academy of Religion* 39 (June 1971): 131-140. Also useful are Adolf von Harnack's "Über das Alter der Bezeichnung 'die Bücher' ('die Bibel') für die H. Schriften in der Kirche," *Zentralblatt für Bibliothekswesen* 45 (1928): 337-342; Oska Rühle's "Bibel," in *Handwörterbuch des deutschen Aberglaubens* (Berlin, 1927); and my comparative study *Beyond the Written Word* (Cambridge, forthcoming).

On the role of the Qur'an in Muslim life, see my "Qur'an as Spoken Word," in *Approaches to Islam in Religious Studies,* edited by Richard C. Martin (Tuscon, 1985); my "The Earliest Meaning of 'Qur'an,'" *Welt des Islams* 23/24 (1984): 361-377; Paul Nwyia's *Exégèse coranique et langage mystique* (Beirut, 1970); and Kristina Nelson's *The Art of Reciting the Qur'an* (Austin, 1985). On the use of scripture in Indian life, see Frits Staal's *Nambudiri Veda Recitation* (The Hague, 1961) and Thomas B. Coburn's "'Scripture' in India: Towards a Typology of the Word in Hindu Life," *Journal of the American Academy of Religion* 52 (1984): 435-459.

WILLIAM A. GRAHAM

SCYTHIAN RELIGION

The Scythians were predominantly nomadic, Iranian-speaking tribes inhabiting the steppes of the northern Black Sea region from the seventh to the third century BCE. Owing to their lack of a written language, what is known of Scythian religion has been reconstructed on the basis of archaeological sources and information from Greek and Roman authors.

The basic Scythian pantheon included seven gods; the pantheon was divided into three ranks. In the first rank was Tabiti (the Greek Hestia), in the second were Papaeus (Zeus) and Api (Gaia), and in the third were Oetosyrus or Goetosyrus (Apollo); Artimpasa, or Argimpasa (Aphrodite Ourania); and two gods whose Scythian names are not known but who have been identified with Herakles and Ares.

Besides the seven gods of the basic pantheon, there were also deities that were venerated by separate tribes.

Data on cult leaders among the Scythians are highly fragmentary. The most complete information is on the Enarees, a

> Undoubtedly the Scythian king himself was an important, if not the chief, performer of cultic practices.

group of priests connected with the worship of Artimpasa. Undoubtedly the Scythian king himself was an important, if not the chief, performer of cultic practices. The most significant evidence of this is the abundance in royal burials of ritual objects, including those having complex cosmological and social symbolism.

Certain cultic structures did exist in Scythia. Thus, in the center of each of the districts of Scythia, huge brushwood altars were heaped up in honor of the Scythian "Ares," in the form of square platforms, accessible on one side. It is possible that precisely in this Common Scythian cultic center was held the annual Scythian festival connected with the worship of golden sacred objects: a yoked plow, an ax, and a cup that had fallen, according to Scythian myth, from the sky, and that symbolized the cosmic and social order. This festival is one of the few Scythian ritual activities about which relatively detailed information has been preserved.

There is information about the methods of sacrifice among the Scythians. Animals (most commonly horses) were asphyxiated while a salutation was made to the god to whom the sacrifice was offered. The flesh was then boiled, and the part intended for the god was thrown on the ground, in front of the sacrificer.

The most complete information we have on any aspect of Scythian culture—which has been confirmed, moreover, by archaeological data—is on burial rituals. When a man died, his corpse (apparently embalmed) was carried by cart on a round of visits to the homes of his friends; after forty days the body was buried. The form of the grave (usually a deep chamber-catacomb) and the collection of objects accompanying the dead man were quite uniform and were regulated by tradition.

The sum of the data on the religious life of the Scythians permits us to assume that the overall aim of their ceremonies and rituals was above all to ensure the stability, going back to mythic times, of the cosmic and social order and to guarantee the well-being of the community.

[*See also* Prehistoric Religions *and* Inner Asian Religions.]

BIBLIOGRAPHY

The most complete survey of Scythian antiquity is contained in the still-valuable book of Ellis H. Minns, *Scythians and Greeks* (Cambridge, 1913). Important observations on the cultures of the Scythians, including their religion, were made by Mikhail I. Rostovtsev in *Iranians and Greeks in South Russia* (Oxford, 1922). The most recent research devoted exclusively to the religion of the Scythians is S. S. Bessonova's *Religioznye predstavleniia Skifov* (Kiev, 1983). For Scythian mythology and some aspects of Scythian ritual practices, see my book *Ocherki ideologii skifo-sakskikh plemen: Opyt rekonstruktsii skifskoi mifologii* (Moscow, 1977). An interpretation of linguistic data on Scythian mythology and religion is in V. I. Abaev's *Osetinskii iazyk i fol'klor* (Moscow, 1949). A detailed survey of Scythian burials and an analysis of burial rituals has been made by Renate Rolle in *Totenkult der Skythen*, vol. 1 of *Das Steppengebiet*, 2 vols. (Berlin, 1978). For the Scythian religion in the general system of beliefs of the Iranian-speaking peoples of antiquity, see Henrik S. Nyberg's *Die Religionen des alten Iran* (Leipzig, 1938) and Geo Widengren's *Die Religionen Irans* (Stuttgart, 1965). An important landmark in the study of the spiritual legacy of the Scythians is Georges Dumézil's *Romans de Scythie et d'alentour* (Paris, 1978).

D. S. RAEVSKII
Translated from Russian by Mary Lou Masey

SEVENTH-DAY ADVENTISM

The origins of Seventh-day Adventism run back to the interdenominational Millerite movement in the United States in the early 1840s, when William Miller, a Baptist lay minister and farmer, sought to rekindle a second awakening by predicting that Christ would soon return to earth. Following a series of failed time-settings, Millerites fixed their hopes for the second advent of Christ on 22 October 1844, the Day of Atonement. The "great disappointment" that resulted from this miscalculation splintered the movement into several factions. The majority, including Miller, admitted their exegetical error but continued to expect Christ's imminent return.

Early beliefs that 22 October marked the date when God shut the "door of mercy" on all who had rejected the Millerite message gradually gave rise to an open-door theology and to evangelization. The observance of Saturday as sabbath, as required by the Ten Commandments and practiced by the Seventh Day Baptists, became the most obvious symbol of Seventh-day Adventist distinctiveness and served as a means by which legalistic members sought to attain the higher morality expected of God's people at the close of history.

> **By 1900 the Adventists were supporting nearly five hundred foreign missionaries.**

In many respects Seventh-day Adventism developed as a typical nineteenth-century American sect, characterized by millenarianism, biblicism, restorationism, and legalism. By 1850 sabbatarian Adventists, still looking for the soon appearance of Christ, composed a "scattered flock" of about two hundred loosely structured sectarians who sought to restore such primitive Christian practices as foot-washing, greeting with the "holy kiss," and calling each other "brother" and "sister." The institutionalization of Seventh-day Adventism was well under way. In 1859 the Adventists adopted a plan of "systematic benevolence" to support a clergy; the next year they selected the name Seventh-day Adventist; by 1863 there were 125 churches with about 3,500 members.

Adventist theology shifted in the 1880s, when two West Coast editors, Ellet J. Waggoner and Alonzo T. Jones, both still in their thirties, challenged the legalistic emphasis that had come to characterize the sect. In opposition to General Conference leaders, who maintained that salvation depended upon observing the Ten Commandments, especially the fourth, Waggoner and Jones followed evangelical Christians in arguing that righteousness came by accepting Christ, not by keeping the law.

For decades Adventists confined their evangelistic efforts almost exclusively to North America until church leaders became convinced that they had an obligation to carry their message "into all the world". By 1900 the Adventists were supporting nearly five hundred foreign missionaries. To train medical personnel for service at home and abroad, Adventists in 1895 opened the American Medical Missionary College, with campuses in Battle Creek and Chicago. Battle Creek soon grew into the administrative, publishing, medical, and educational center of Adventism. Such centralization and concentration of power concerned church leader Ellen White, who recommended dismantling the Battle Creek colony. As a result, Battle Creek College (now Andrews University) was moved in 1902 to rural southwestern Michigan and administrative and publishing activities were moved to the outskirts of Washington, D. C.

In 1915 Ellen White died, leaving a church of more than 136,000 members. By 1980 membership had swelled to nearly 3.5 million, roughly 85 percent of whom lived outside of North America.

BIBLIOGRAPHY

There is no standard history of Seventh-day Adventism. Until recently non-Adventist scholars had tended to ignore Adventists, and Adventist historians have been reticent to examine their heritage critically. Among the several comprehensive histories, the best of the old is M. Ellsworth Olsen's *History of the Origin and Progress of Seventh-day Adventists* (Washington, D. C., 1925), and the best of the new is Richard W. Schwarz's *Light Bearers to the Remnant* (Mountain View, Calif., 1979), a well-documented survey designed to serve as a college text. *Adventism in America: A History,* edited by Gary Land (Grand Rapids, Mich., 1985), offers a readable chronological overview written by six Adventist historians. A valuable reference work, filled with historical data, is the *Seventh-day Adventist Encyclopedia,* rev. ed., edited by Don F. Neufeld (Washington, D. C., 1976).

The Rise of Adventism: Religion and Society in Mid-Nineteenth-Century America, edited by Edwin S. Gaustad (New York, 1974), though misleadingly titled (most of the essays say nothing about Adventism), does contain a marvelous 111-page bibliography of Millerite and early Adventist publications and an important interpretive essay, "Adventism and the American Experience," by Jonathan M. Butler. Francis D. Nichol's *The Midnight Cry: A Defense of William Miller and the Millerites* (Washington, D. C., 1944) provides a detailed examination of the Millerite movement, unfortunately marred by the author's defensive stance and selective use of evidence. P. Gerard Damsteegt's *Foundations of the Seventh-day Adventist Message and Mission* (Grand Rapids, Mich., 1977) uncritically but microscopically traces the development of Adventist theology to 1874. Ingemar Linden's iconoclastic and unpolished *The Last Trump: An Historico-Genetical Study of Some Important Chapters in the Making and Development of the Seventh-day Adventist Church* (Frankfurt, 1978) covers roughly the same period in different style.

Despite an abundance of inspirational biographies of Adventist leaders, few scholarly studies of individual Adventists have appeared. Two notable exceptions are Richard W. Schwarz's *John Harvey Kellogg, M. D.* (Nashville, 1970), which unfortunately lacks the documentation found in the doctoral dissertation upon which it is based; and Ronald L. Numbers's *Prophetess of Health: A Study of Ellen G. White* (New York, 1976), a critical analysis of White's health-related activities.

JONATHAN M. BUTLER and RONALD L. NUMBERS

SHABBAT

The Hebrew word *shabbat* is from a root meaning "to desist" or "to rest," that is, from work and labor. The Sabbath is the day of rest each week after six days of work. The command to keep the Sabbath holy is found in both versions of the Decalogue (*Ex.* 20:8-11, *Dt.* 5:12-15), but the reasons given for Sabbath observance differ. In *Exodus* the creation motif is stressed: "For in six days the Lord made heaven and earth and sea, and all that is in them, and he rested on the seventh day." In *Deuteronomy* the social motivation is prominent. Man must rest on the Sabbath and allow his slaves to rest with him.

The nature of the "work" *(mela'khah)* that is forbidden on the Sabbath has received many different interpretations in the course of Jewish history. In addition, various restrictions were introduced by the rabbis, as on the handling of money or of objects normally used for work, and all business activities.

Reform Judaism largely ignores the rabbinic rules governing acts forbidden on the Sabbath, preferring to understand "work" as gainful occupation alone, and the spiritual atmosphere of the Sabbath as generated chiefly by means of rituals in the home and services in the synagogue. Orthodox Judaism follows the traditional regulations in their entirety.

The ideas of honoring the Sabbath and taking delight in it are expressed in the wearing of special clothes, having a well-lit home, forgetting worldly worries and anxieties (for this reason petitionary prayers are not recited on the Sabbath), the study of the Torah, three meals, and the union of husband and wife.

The central feature of the synagogue service on the Sabbath is the reading of the Torah from a handwritten scroll—the Sefer Torah (Book of the Law). The Torah is divided into portions, one section *(sidrah)* of which is read each Sabbath. The whole Torah is completed in this way each year, and then the cycle begins anew.

There are a number of special Sabbaths marked by additions to the standard liturgy and by relevant Prophetic and extra Torah readings. The earliest of these are the four Sabbaths of the weeks before Passover.

BIBLIOGRAPHY

For a discussion of the critical view on the origins of the Sabbath, see U. Cassuto's *A Commentary on the Book of Genesis,* vol. 1, *From Adam to Noah,* translated by Israel Abrahams (Jerusalem, 1961), pp. 65-69. The voluminous tractate *Shabbat* of the Babylonian Talmud, dealing with every aspect of Sabbath observance in rabbinic times, is now available in English translation by H. Freedman, in the Soncino translation of the Babylonian Talmud, edited by I. Epstein (London, 1938). Solomon Goldman's little book *A Guide to the Sabbath* (London, 1961) is written from the moderately Orthodox point of view. Abraham Joshua Heschel's *The Sabbath: Its Meaning for Modern Man* (New York, 1951) is a fine impressionistic study of the Sabbath as, in the author's words, "a Temple in time." A useful anthology of teachings on the Sabbath is Abraham E. Millgram's *Sabbath: The Day of Delight* (Philadelphia, 1944). The best edition of the Sabbath table hymns, with an introduction and notes in English, is *Zemiroth Sabbath Songs,* edited by Nosson Scherman (New York, 1979).

LOUIS JACOBS

SHAKERS

Members of the American religious group the United Society of Believers in Christ's Second Appearing are popularly called Shakers. One of the longest-lived and most influential religious communitarian groups in America, the Shakers originated in 1747 near Manchester, England, in a breakaway from the Quakers led by Jane and James Wardley. The group may also have been influenced by Camisard millenarians who had fled from France to England to escape the persecutions that followed revocation of the Edict of Nantes in 1685. The nickname Shaking Quaker, or Shaker, was applied to the movement because of its unstructured and highly emotional services, during which members sang, shouted, danced, spoke in tongues, and literally shook with emotion. Under the leadership of Ann Lee, a Manchester factory worker who became convinced that celibacy was essential for salvation, the core of the Shakers emigrated to America in 1774 and settled two years later near Albany, New York. Until Lee's death in 1784 the Shakers remained a loosely knit group that adhered to Lee's personal leadership and to what they viewed as a millenarian restoration and fulfillment of the early Christian faith.

During the 1780s and 1790s under the leadership of two of Ann Lee's American converts, Joseph Meacham and Lucy Wright, Shakerism developed from a charismatic movement into a more routinized organization. Meacham and Wright oversaw the establishment of parallel and equal men's and women's orders. Adherents lived together in celibate communities and practiced communal ownership of property inspired by the Christian communism of *Acts* 2:44-45. Supreme authority was vested in the ministry at New Lebanon, New York, usually two men and two women, one of whom headed the entire society. Each settlement was divided into "families"—smaller, relatively self-sufficient communities of thirty to one hundred men and women living together under the same roof but strictly separated in all their activities. By 1800 eleven settlements with sixteen hundred members were functioning in New York, Massachusetts, Connecticut, New Hampshire, and Maine. A second wave of expansion, inspired by the Kentucky Revival and drawing heavily on the indefatigable Richard McNemar, a "new light" Presbyterian minister who converted to Shakerism, led to the establishment of seven additional settlements, in Ohio, Kentucky, and Indiana, by 1826.

The high point of Shaker membership and the last major effort to revitalize the society came during the decade of "spiritual manifestations" that began in 1837. Frequently called "Mother Ann's work" because many of the revelations purportedly came from the spirit of Ann Lee and showed her continuing concern for her followers, the period saw a rich outpouring of creativity in new forms of worship, song, and

dance, including extreme trance and visionary phenomena. Following the great Millerite disappointments of 1843 and 1844 when the world failed to come to a literal end, hundreds of Millerites joined the Shakers, bringing membership to a peak of some six thousand by the late 1840s. Thereafter the group entered into a long, slow decline. The loss of internal momentum and the changing conditions of external society led the Shakers to be viewed increasingly not as a dynamic religious movement but as a pleasant anachronism in which individuals who could not function in the larger society could find refuge. As late as 1900 there were more than one thousand Shakers, but today the group has dwindled to virtual extinction.

As the largest and most successful religious communitarian group in nineteenth-century America, the Shakers attracted the attention of numerous visitors, writers, and creators of more ephemeral communal experiments. The Shakers were known for their neat, well-planned, and successful villages; their functional architecture, simple furniture, and fine crafts; their distinctive songs, dances, and rituals; and their ingenuity in agriculture and mechanical invention. They also were sometimes criticized because of their sophisticated and highly unorthodox theology, which stressed a dual godhead combining male and female elements equally; perfectionism and continuing revelation; and the necessity of celibacy for the highest religious life. They were unique among American religious groups in giving women formal equality with men at every level of religious leadership, and they created a fully integrated subculture that has increasingly come to be viewed with interest and respect.

BIBLIOGRAPHY

Among the numerous scholarly treatments of the Shakers, the most important are the studies by Edward Deming Andrews, particularly his *The People Called Shakers,* new enl. ed. (New York, 1963). Andrews is excellent on Shaker material culture, especially furniture and crafts, but weaker on religious motivation. Another popular historical overview is Marguerite Fellows Melcher's *The Shaker Adventure* (Princeton, 1941). For the most incisive analysis of the group, see Constance Rourke's "The Shakers," in her *The Roots of American Culture and Other Essays,* edited by Van Wyck Brooks (New York, 1942). A provocative but sometimes misleading analysis that attempts to place Shakerism within a larger social and conceptual framework is Henri Desroche's *The American Shakers: From Neo-Christianity to Presocialism* (Amherst, Mass., 1971). Mary L. Richmond has compiled and annotated *Shaker Literature: A Bibliography,* 2 vols. (Hanover, N. H., 1977), a comprehensive bibliography of printed sources by and about the Shakers that supersedes all previous reference works of its kind. Richmond lists the major repositories at which each printed item may be found. She also includes information on collections of manuscripts. The most important of these are at the Western Reserve Historical Society in Cleveland and the Library of Congress in Washington, D. C., and are available on microfilm from their respective libraries.

Benjamin Seth Youngs's *The Testimony of Christ's Second Appearing* (Lebanon, Ohio, 1808) was the first and most comprehensive Shaker theological and historical overview. A shorter and more accessible treatment is Calvin Green and Seth Y. Wells's *A Summary View of the Millennial Church or United Society of Believers (Commonly Called Shakers)* (Albany, N. Y., 1823). The most valuable primary account of Ann Lee and the earliest Shakers is the rare *Testimonies of the Life, Character, Revelations, and Doctrines of Our Ever Blessed Mother Ann Lee and the Elders with Her,* edited by Rufus Bishop and Seth Y. Wells (Hancock, Mass., 1816). Among the many accounts by Shaker seceders and apostates, the most comprehensive and historically oriented is Thomas Brown's *An Account of the People Called Shakers: Their Faith, Doctrine, and Practice* (Troy, N. Y., 1812). Anna White and Leila S. Taylor's *Shakerism: Its Meaning and Message* (Columbus, Ohio, 1904) presents a thorough and insightful history of the Shakers from the perspective of the late nineteenth century.

LAWRENCE FOSTER

SHAMANISM

Shamanism in the strict sense is preeminently a religious phenomenon of Siberia and Inner Asia. The word comes to us, through the Russian, from the Tunguz *saman.* Throughout the immense area comprising the central and northern regions of Asia, the magico-religious life of society centers on the shaman.

All through the primitive and modern worlds we find individuals who profess to maintain relations with spirits, whether they are possessed by them or control them. But the shaman controls his helping spirits, in the sense that he is able to communicate with the dead, demons, and nature spirits without thereby becoming their instrument. In Inner and Northeast Asia the chief methods of recruiting shamans are (1) hereditary transmission of the shamanic profession and (2) spontaneous vocation ("call" or "election").

However selected, a shaman is not recognized as such until after he has received two kinds of teaching: (1) ecstatic (dreams, trances, etc.) and (2) traditional (shamanic techniques, names and functions of the spirits, mythology and genealogy of the clan, secret language, etc.). This twofold course of instruction, given by the spirits and the old master shamans, is equivalent to an initiation. Sometimes the initiation is public and constitutes an autonomous ritual in itself.

A man may also become a shaman following an accident or a highly unusual event—for example, among the Buriats, the Soyot, and the Inuit (Eskimo), after being struck by lightning, or falling from a high tree, or successfully undergoing an ordeal that can be homologized with an initiatory ordeal, as in the case of an Inuit who spent five days in icy water without his clothes becoming wet.

Initiatory Ordeals of Siberian Shamans. Relating their ecstatic initiations, the Siberian shamans maintain that they "die" and lie inanimate for from three to seven days in their yurts or in solitary places. During this time, they are cut up by demons or by their ancestral spirits; their bones are cleaned, the flesh scraped off, the body fluids thrown away, and their eyes torn from their sockets. According to a Yakut informant, the spirits carry the future shaman's soul to the underworld and shut him in a house for three years. Here he undergoes his initiation. A Tunguz shaman relates that, during his initiatory illness, his shaman ancestors pierced him with arrows until he lost consciousness and fell to the ground; then they cut off his flesh, drew out his bones, and counted them before him; if one had been missing, he could not have become a shaman.

The ecstatic experience of the initiatory dismemberment of the body followed by a renewal of organs is also known in other preliterate societies. The Inuit believe that an animal (bear, walrus, etc.) wounds the candidate, tears him to pieces, or devours him; then new flesh grows around his bones. Among the Dayak, the *manangs* (shamans) say that they cut off the candidate's head, remove the brain, and wash it, thus giving him a clearer mind. Finally, cutting up the body and the exchange of viscera are essential rites in some initiations of Australian medicine men (ibid., pp. 59ff.).

Public Rites of Shamanic Initiations. Among the public initiation ceremonies of Siberian shamans, those of the Buriats are among the most interesting. A strong birch tree is set up in the yurt, with its roots on the hearth and its crown projecting through the smoke hole. The birch is called *udesi burkhan,* "the guardian of the door," for it opens the door of Heaven to the shaman. On the day of his consecration, the candidate climbs the birch to the top and, emerging through the smoke hole, shouts to summon the aid of the gods. After this, a goat is sacrificed, and the candidate, stripped to the waist, has his head, eyes, and ears anointed with blood.

Medical Cures. The principal function of the shaman in Siberia and Inner Asia is healing. Disease is attributed to the soul's having strayed away or been stolen, and treatment is in principle reduced to finding it, capturing it, and obliging it to resume its place in the patient's body.

Survival and Metamorphosis of Some Shamanic Traditions. A great number of shamanic symbols and rituals are to be found among the Tibeto-Burmese Moso (or Na-hsi) inhabiting southwestern China: ascension to Heaven, accompanying the soul of the dead, and so forth. In China, "magical flight" or "journeying in spirit," as well as many ecstatic dances, present a specific shamanic structure (see examples quoted in Eliade, 1964, pp. 447–461). In Japan shamanism is practiced almost exclusively by women. They summon the dead person's soul from the beyond, expel disease and other evil, and ask their god the name of the medicine to be used.

A number of shamanic conceptions and techniques have been identified in the mythology and folklore of the ancient Germans (ibid., pp. 379ff.). Practices are also to be found in ancient India as well as in the traditions of the Scythians, Caucasians, and Iranians (ibid., pp. 394-421). Among the aboriginal tribes of India, of particular interest is the shamanism of Savara (Saura), characterized by an "initiatory marriage" with a "spirit girl," similar to the practice of the Siberian Nanay (Goldi) and Yakuts (ibid., pp. 72ff., 421ff.).

Some Conclusions. The shamans have played an essential role in the defense of the psychic integrity of the community. They are preeminently the antidemonic champions; they combat not only demons and disease, but also the "black" magicians. In a general way, it can be said that shamanism defends life, health, fertility, and the world of "light," against death, disease, sterility, disasters, and the world of "darkness."

It is as a further result of his ability to travel in the supernatural worlds and to see the superhuman beings (gods, demons, spirits of the dead, etc.) that the shaman has been able to contribute decisively to the knowledge of death. In all probability many features of funerary geography, as well as some themes of the mythology of death, are the result of the ecstatic experiences of shamans.

It is difficult for us, modern men that we are, to imagine the repercussions of such a spectacle in a "primitive" community. The shamanic "miracles" not only confirm and reinforce the patterns of the traditional religion, they also stimulate and feed the imagination, demolish the barriers between dream and present reality, and open windows upon worlds inhabited by the gods, the dead, and the spirits.

BIBLIOGRAPHY

A general presentation of the shamanistic initiations, mythologies, and practices in Siberia and Inner Asia, North and South America, Southeast Asia, Oceania, and the Far East is found in my book *Shamanism: Archaic Techniques of Ecstasy,* rev. & enl. ed. (New York, 1964). To the bibliography found there, I need add only a few important general works and a number of contributions to the study of shamanism in Southeast Asia, Oceania, and the Far East. The bibliographies related to Inner Asia or South and North America appear in the other articles on shamanism that follow.

Matthias Hermann's *Schamanen, Pseudoschamanen, Erlöser und Heilbringer,* 3 vols. (Wiesbaden, 1970), is useful for its documentation, especially with regard to Indo-Tibetan areas. For a clear presentation, see John A. Grim's *The Shaman: Patterns of Siberian and Ojibway Healing* (Norman, Okla., 1983). Michael J. Harner's *The Way of the Shaman* (New York, 1980), which includes a valuable bibliography, and the volume *Hallucinogens and Shamanism,* which Harner edited (Oxford, 1973), are stimulating and original, as is *Studies in Shamanism,* edited by Carl-Martin Edsman (Stockholm, 1967). Among the recent comparative studies, see Alois Closs's "Interdisziplinäre Schamanismusforschung an der indogermanischen Völkergruppe," *Anthropos* 63/64 (1968-1969): 967-973, and his "Die Ekstase des Shamanen," *Ethnos* (1969): 70-89.

On shamanism in Southeast Asia and Oceania, see my *Shamanism,* pages 337-374. In addition to my bibliography, the reader should consult Rex L. Jones's "Shamanism in South Asia: A Preliminary Survey," *History of Religions* 7 (May 1968): 330-347;

Joachim Sterly's *"Heilige Männer" und Medizinmänner in Melanesien* (Cologne, 1965), especially pages 437-553 and the bibliography; Guy Moréchand's "Le chamanisme des Hmong," *Bulletin de l'École Francaise d'Extrême-Orient* (Paris) 54 (1968): 53-294; and Andreas Lommel's *Shamanism: The Beginnings of Art* (New York, 1966) with its rich bibliography. On the shamanistic structure of the Australian medicine man, see my *Australian Religions: An Introduction* (Ithaca, N.Y., 1973), pp. 131-160.

For sources on the shamanic symbolism and techniques in Tibet, China, and the Far East, see, in addition to my *Shamanism,* Helmut Hoffmann's *Symbolik der tibetischen Religionen und des Schamanismus* (Stuttgart, 1967), especially the bibliography; P. Jos Thiel's "Schamanismus im Alten China," *Sinologica* 10 (1968): 149-204; Ichiro Hori's "Penetration of Shamanic Elements into the History of Japanese Folk Religion," in *Festschrift für Adolf E. Jensen,* edited by Eike Haberland et al. (Munich, 1964), vol. 1, pp. 245-265; Carmen Blacker's *The Catalpa Bow: A Study of Shamanistic Practices in Japan* (London, 1975); H. Byron Earhart's critical review "The Bridge to the Other World, in *Monumenta Nipponica,* 31 (1976): 179-187; and Jung Young Lee's "Concerning the Origin and Formation of Korean Shamanism," *Numen* 20 (1973): 135-160.

On shamanism among the Turks and the Mongols, see the original and learned synthesis of Jean-Paul Roux's *La religion des Turcs et des Mongols* (Paris, 1984), pp. 59ff.

MIRCEA ELIADE

SHIISM

Shiism is a major branch of Islam with numerous subdivisions, all upholding the rights of the family of the Prophet *(ahl al-bayt)* to the religious and political leadership of the Muslim community.

Origins and Early Development. Historically, the Shi`ah emerged in support of the caliphate of `Ali (AH 35-40/656-661 CE) during the First Civil War. After the murder of `Ali and the abdication of his eldest son, Hasan, in 661, the Shi`ah continued a latent opposition to the Umayyad caliphate from their center in `Ali's former capital of Kufa in Iraq. Their attachment to the family of the Prophet, and especially to `Ali's sons and descendants, reflected local resentment of both the loss of the caliphate to Damascus and the Umayyad denigration of `Ali and his caliphate.

Kufan revolts. After the death of the caliph Mu`awiyah, the Kufan Shi`ah invited Husayn from Medina, promising to back his claim to the caliphate. The Umayyad governor gained control of the situation, however. A Penitents movement arose in Kufa; they lamented the death of the Prophet's grandson at his grave in Karbala and sought revenge from those responsible. In 685 the leadership of the Penitents was taken over by al-Mukhtar ibn Abi `Ubayd, who revolted in Kufa and proclaimed another son of `Ali, Muhammad, to be the imam and Mahdi, the messianic Restorer of Islam. The movement backing him was called the Kaysaniyah after Abu `Amrah Kaysan, chief of al-Mukhtar's guard and leader of the non-Arab clients *(mawali)* in Kufa. Local Semites and Persians now joined the Shi`ah in large numbers for the first time, although the leading role in the movement was still played by Arabs.

The Kaysaniyah movement condemned the first three caliphs before `Ali as illegitimate usurpers and considered `Ali and his three sons, Hasan, Husayn, and Muhammad, as successive, divinely appointed imams endowed with supernatural qualities. They taught *raj`ah,* the return of many of the dead at the time of the coming of the Mahdi for retribution before the Resurrection, and *bada',* the possibility of a change in the decisions of God.

Abbasid revolution. A branch of the Kaysaniyah known as the Hashimiyah continued the line of imams to Muhammad ibn al-Hanafiyah's son Abu Hashim, who, in contrast to his father, took an active part in the leadership and organization of the movement. After his death in about 717/8 the Hashimiyah split into several groups over the succession. The majority recognized Muhammad ibn `Ali, a descendant of the Prophet's uncle `Abbas. The Abbasids initially espoused the Shi`i cause, establishing the reign of the family of the Prophet and demanding revenge for `Ali and his wronged descendants. Soon, however, they distanced themselves from their mostly extremist Shi`i followers to seek broader support in the Muslim community, but they disintegrated soon afterward.

Extremists and moderates. Other minor offshoots of the Hashimiyah were notable for their extremist doctrine: metempsychosis, the preexistence of human souls as shadows *(azillah)*, metaphorical interpretation of the resurrection, judgment, paradise, and hell. Such teaching became characteristic of many groups of extremists *(ghulat)* excommunicated by the mainstream Shi`ah in the following centuries.

The increasing prominence of the Husaynid imams within the Shi`ah was connected with a shift in the function of the imam. With the rise of legal and theological schools espousing conflicting doctrines in the late Umayyad period, many of the Shi`ah sought the guidance of the imam as an authoritative, divinely inspired teacher rather than as a charismatic leader. The first to perform this new role was Muhammad al-Baqir (d. 735?), a grandson of Husayn who was widely respected for his learning among both the Shi`ah and non-Shi`ah. His teaching of religious law and Qur'an exegesis attracted a large number of the Kufan Shi`ah.

**The Imamiyah and Twelver Shi`ah.** The Imamiyah became a significant religious community with a distinctive law, ritual, and religious doctrine under Ja`far al-Sadiq (d. 765), the foremost scholar and teacher among their imams. In recognition of his role, Imami law is sometimes called the Ja`fari legal school. In theology, some of his statements upheld intermediate positions on controversial questions such as human free will versus predestination, and the nature of the Qur'an.

The imamate. The constitutive element of the Imami community is its doctrine of the imamate, which was definitely formulated in this age. It was based on the belief that humanity is at all times in need of a divinely appointed and guided leader and authoritative teacher in all religious matters. Without such a leader, according to Imam Ja`far, the world could never exist for a moment. In order to fulfill his divine mission, this leader must be endowed with full immunity *(`ismah)* from sin and error. Following the age of the prophets, which came to a close with Muhammad, the imams continue their prophetic mission in every respect except that

> **It was based on the belief that humanity is at all times in need of a divinely appointed and guided leader. . . .**

they do not bring a new scripture. The imamate is thus raised to the rank of prophethood. Imam Ja`far did not aspire to rule and forbade his followers from engaging in revolutionary activity on his behalf. He predicted that the imams would not regain their rightful position until the emergence of the Qa'im (lit. "riser," i. e., the Mahdi) from among them to rule the world.

The succession to Ja`far al-Sadiq was disputed and led to a schism among the Imamiyah. A group of his followers considered the designation as irreversible, however, and either denied Isma`il's death or recognized Isma`il's son Muhammad as the imam. They became the founders of the Isma`iliyah. In the absence of a new designation, they turned to his brother Musa al-Kazim, the seventh imam of the Twelver Shi`ah. Some of them, however, continued to recognize `Abd Allah, Ja`fara's son, the rightful imam. They were known as the Fathiyah and constituted a sizable sect in Kufa until the late fourth century AH (tenth century CE). Musa was arrested later in his life by Caliph Harun al-Rashid and died in prison in Baghdad in 799. His death was denied by many of his followers, who considered his position as seventh imam to be of momentous significance and expected his return as the Mahdi. They did not recognize `Ali al-Rida, the eighth imam of the Twelver Shi`ah, although some of them considered him and his successors as lieutenants *(khulafa')* of the Mahdi until his return. They also formed a sizable sect known as the Waqifah and competed with the group which was to become the Twelver Shi`ah.

The succession after al-Rida down to the eleventh imam, Hasan al-`Askari, produced only minor schisms, but the death of the latter in 874, apparently without a son, left his followers in disarray. The main body, henceforth known as the Twelver Shi`ah (the Ithna `Ashariyah in Arabic), eventually came to affirm that a son had been born to him before his death but had been hidden. This son had become the twelfth imam and continued to live in concealment. Identified with the Qa'im and the Mahdi, he was expected to reappear in glory to rule the world and make the cause of the Shi'ah triumphant. He continues to live unrecognized on earth, however, and may occasionally identify himself to one of his followers or otherwise intervene in the fortunes of his community.

Intellectual currents. The absence of the imam strengthened the position of the scholars (`ulama') in the Shi'i community as transmitters and guardians of the teaching of the imams. They now undertook to gather, examine, and systematize this teaching. For the most part, the first transmitters of the statements of the imams had been Kufans, while the compilation and sifting of the traditions into more comprehensive collections was the work of the school of Qom in northwestern Iran. The traditionist school of Qom reached its peak in the works of Abu Ja'far al-Kulayni of Rayy (d. 941) and Ibn Babawayhi al-Saduq of Qom (d. 991/2).

A rival school in Baghdad progressively adopted the rationalist theology of the Mu'tazilah, who espoused human free will and an anti-anthropomorphist, abstract concept of God in sharp conflict with the predominant theology of Sunni Islam. The Baghdad school rejected Mu'tazili doctrine, however, where it clashed with the basic Imami beliefs about the imamate; thus it repudiated the Mu'tazili thesis of the unconditional, eternal punishment of the unrepentant sinner in the hereafter, affirming the effectiveness of the intercession of the imams for sinners among their faithful followers. In fact, faith in the power of the imams' intercessions was a vital motive for the visits to their shrines which have always been a major aspect of popular Shi'i piety. Twelver Shi'i theologians also maintained, against the Mu'tazili position, that the opponents of the imams occupied the status of infidels and that the imamate was, like prophecy, a rational necessity, not merely a revealed legal requirement.

The Twelver Shi'ah today constitute the great majority of the Shi'ah and are often referred to simply by the latter name.

The Isma'iliyah. An offshoot of the Imamiyah, the Isma'iliyah first became historically important after the middle of the ninth century as a secret revolutionary movement promising the impending advent of Muhammad ibn Isma'il, grandson of Ja'far al-Sadiq, as the Mahdi. The movement soon split into two. One of its branches recognized the hidden leaders of the movement as imams descended from Muhammad ibn Isma'il. With backing of this branch, the leaders rose to rule as the Fatimid caliphate (909-1171). The other branch, commonly known as the Qaramitah, broke with the leadership and refused to recognize the imamate of the Fatimid caliphs. Their establishment of a Qarmati state in eastern Arabia lasted from 899 until 1076.

The Fatimid branch was rent by a schism during the caliphate of al-Hakim (996-1021), whose divinity was pro-

claimed by a group of enthusiastic followers. The sect arising from this deviation is known as the Druze. After the death of the caliph al-Mustansir in 1094 the Persian Isma'ili communities recognized his eldest son, Nizar, who did not succeed to the caliphate, as their imam. Known as the Nizariyah, they established their headquarters, and later the seat of their imams, in the mountain stronghold of Alamut in the Elburz mountains. The main line of Nizari imams has continued down to the Aga Khans in modern times.

The Zaydiyah. Retaining the politically militant and religiously moderate attitude predominant among the early Kufan Shi'ah, the Zaydiyah developed a doctrine of the imamate distinctly at variance with Imami beliefs. They neither accepted a hereditary line of imams nor considered the imam as divinely protected from sin and error. Rather they held that any descendant of Hasan or Husayn qualified by religious learning could claim the imamate by armed rising against the illegitimate rulers and would then be entitled to the allegiance and backing of the faithful. Thus there were often long periods without legitimate Zaydi imams.

The unity of the Zaydi community in Yemen was rent in the eleventh century by the rise of two heterodox sects, the Mutarrifiyah and the Husayniyah. Both sects disappeared by the fourteenth century. The Zaydi community in Yemen, living mostly in the northern highlands, has survived to the present.

BIBLIOGRAPHY

Scholarly literature on Shiism is still limited and uneven. There is no comprehensive survey of Shiism in its full range. In the wider context of schisms in Islam, the development of the various branches of Shiism is outlined by Henri Laoust in *Les schismes dans l'Islam* (Paris, 1965). There are brief chapters on Twelver Shiism, the Zaydiyah, and Isma'iliyah in *Islam,* edited by C. F. Beckingham, volume 2 of *Religion in the Middle East,* edited by Arthur J. Arberry (Cambridge, 1969).

The origins and early history of the Shi'ah and the Kharijis in the Umayyad age was classically described, chiefly on the basis of the early Kufan historian Abu Mikhnaf, in Julius Wellhausen's *Die religiös-politischen Oppositionsparteien im alten Islam* (Göttingen, 1901), translated by R. C. Ostle and S. M. Walker as *The Religio-Political Factions in Early Islam* (Amsterdam, 1975). A recent study, taking into account later Shi'i sources, is S. Husain M. Jafri's *Origins and Early Development of Shi'a Islam* (London, 1979).

Twelver Shiism is treated in Dwight Donaldson's *The Shi'ite Religion* (London, 1933) and, from a Shi'i perspective, in `Allamah Sayyid Muhammad Husayn Tabataba'i's *Shi'ite Islam,* translated from the Persian by Seyyed Hossein Nasr (Albany, 1975). Tabataba'i has also gathered significant Twelver Shi'i texts, sermons, and sayings of imams in *A Shi'ite Anthology,* translated with explanatory notes by William C. Chittick (Albany, N. Y., 1981). The papers of the 1968 Colloque de Strasbourg, published as *Le Shiisme imâmite* (Paris, 1970), offer scholarly contributions on various aspects of the history of Twelver Shiism. John Norman Hollister's *The Shi'a of India* (London, 1953) deals with the Twelvers, Isma'iliyah, Bohoras, and Khojas on the Indian subcontinent. A well-informed survey of the role of Shiism in Iran, especially in recent history, is provided by Yann Richard's *Le shi'isme en Iran* (Paris, 1980).

On contemporary Shi`i *ghulat* sects, much material has been gathered in Klaus Müller's *Kulturhistorische Studien zur Genese pseudo-islamischer Sektengebilde in Vorderasien* (Wiesbaden, 1967), whose conclusions about the genesis of these sects are, however, open to question.

A sketch of the history of the Isma`iliyah is given by W. Ivanow in *Brief Survey of the Evolution of Isma'ilism* (Leiden, 1952). The genesis of Isma`ili gnostic doctrine has been reexamined in H. Halm's *Kosmologie und Heilslehre der frühen Isma`iliya* (Wiesbaden, 1978).

Cornelis van Arendonk's *De Opkomst van het Zaidietische Imamaat in Yemen* (Leiden, 1919), translated into French by Jacques Ryckmans as *Les débuts de l'imamat Zaidite au Yémen* (Leiden, 1960), offers a history of the Zaydiyah until the foundation of the Zaydi state in Yemen. I have studied the development of Zaydi doctrine up to the twelfth century in *Der Imam al-Qasim ibn Ibrahim und die Glaubenslehre der Zaiditen* (Berlin, 1965).

WILFERD MADELUNG

SHINTO

SHINTO is the name given to the traditional religion of Japan, a religion that has existed continuously from before the founding of the Japanese nation until the present.

General Characteristics

The ancient Japanese did not themselves have a name for their ethnic religion, but when in the sixth century of the common era Buddhism was officially introduced from the Asian continent, the word *Shinto* ("the way of the *kami*") was used to distinguish the traditional religion from Buddhism (*Butsudo*, "the way of the Buddha"). The first literary usage of the word *Shinto* is found in the *Nihonshoki* (720).

Definition. One representative prewar scholar of Shinto, Kono Seizo, defined Shinto as the way of the *kami,* the principle of the life of the Japanese people, as inherited from time immemorial. Shinto is a "national religion," practiced for the most part by Japanese (including overseas immigrants), and which, with the exception of several sects, has no founder but instead developed naturally. Shinto's concept of *kami* is basically polytheistic, and Shinto includes prayer to the *kami,* festivals *(matsuri)*, ascetic disciplines, social service, and other elements.

Typology. In modern times, Shinto can be classified into three broad types, all of which are mutually interrelated:

Shrine Shinto (Jinja Shinto). Shrine Shinto, consisting principally of worship of the *kami* at local shrines *(jinja)*, dates from the beginning of Japanese history to the present day and constitutes the main current of Shinto tradition. It has played an important role in the unification and solidarity of the nation and of rural society. While Shrine Shinto has no founder, it possesses an organization based on believers, (parishioners) and others, festivals and other religious prac-

tices, doctrines rooted in Shinto traditions and Japanese myth, all centered upon the shrines' spiritual unification.

Sect Shinto (Kyoha Shinto). Also known as Shuha Shinto, Sect Shinto is the term for the Shinto movement centering upon thirteen groups formed during the nineteenth century. The distinguishing feature of Sect Shinto is the fact that each of its sects has founders or organizers, that for the most part their founders or organizers established groups among the common people, and that in addition these sects were developed from an individual's religious experience or upon the basis of Fukko ("revival") Shinto. Generally, these groups do not have shrines but instead use churches as their centers of religious activity.

Folk Shinto (Minzoku Shinto). Folk belief exists among the common people at the bottom of the social pyramid and has no systematic thought that could be called doctrine or dogma, nor does it feature church organization. Japanese folk belief derives from three sources: survival of ancient traditions, customs of abstinence and purification and the cult of house and field deities, and fragments of foreign religion such as Taoism, Buddhism, and medieval Catholicism.

Historical Outline

Ancient Shinto. By ancient Shinto is meant Shinto in the period before it came to be influenced by Confucianism, Buddhism, and other foreign religions. It is difficult to give precise dates, but one can say that the ancient period lasted from the seventh to the early eighth century, while partially overlapping with the next period.

The character of Japanese religion in prehistory is unclear. In ancient Japan many small principalities were formed in various areas. These various principalities were loosely unified into a single nation, predominantly by the ancestors of the present-day imperial household. On the evidence of continental epigraphs, we can surmise that this unification probably took place before the mid-fourth century. However, even taking into consideration these early archaeological findings, it is not until the early eighth century, with the first appearance of Shinto texts, that we can grasp the actual situation of ancient Shinto.

In ancient Japanese the word *kami* was used adjectivally to mean something mysterious, supernatural, or sacred. According to Muraoka Tsunetsugu and Miyaji Naoichi, the ancient *kami* may be divided into three categories: (1) natural deities (deities dwelling in natural objects or natural phenomena, or deities that control these objects or phenomena); (2) anthropomorphic deities (heroes, great personages, and deified ancestors); (3) conceptual deities (deities who serve an ideal or symbolize an abstract power).

Shinto originally had no shrines. Instead its rites were carried out at places regarded as sacred, such as at the foot of a beautiful mountain, beside a pure river or stream, in a mysterious grove, or a place providing the temporary seat of the deity, such as an evergreen tree *(himorogi)* or a rock in its natural setting *(iwakura)*. Because Japan's primary mode of subsistence until the nineteenth century was agriculture, the main rites of ancient Shinto concerned agriculture. Among these, the spring Prayer for Good Harvest (Kinensai) and the autumn Shinto Thanksgiving (Niinamesai) were especially important.

Two cosmologies existed simultaneously. The first conceived of the world as having a vertical pattern, featuring three planes, namely, Takamanohara ("plain of high heaven"), the world of the gods; Nakatsukuni ("middle land"), the world of humankind; and Yomi ("underworld"), the land of the dead. The second cosmology saw the universe as a horizontal, two-tiered structure in which Tokoyo ("perpetual land")

> **People began . . . to pattern their lives upon the will and action of the *kami*.**

exists at the edge of the phenomenal world. Tokoyo was believed to be a utopian country far beyond the sea.

Under the influence of continental culture, ancient Shinto began to develop in many ways. One such development is the ethical consciousness that came about through the influence of Chinese culture, introduced to Japan around the fifth century. People began to seek a standard in the myths and to pattern their lives upon the will and action of the *kami*. *Magokoro* (purity of mind or sincerity) was valued highly in the days of ancient Shinto, and as time went on it became more and more highly valued.

With the appearance of a unified nation, Amaterasu Omikami, previously the tutelary deity of the imperial clan, came to be worshiped outside the imperial palace as the protective deity of the nation and its people. At the same time, the clan deities of the great clans, in addition to their original functions, were made protective deities of the entire nation, and every year offerings were devoted to them by the central government.

The national system of Shinto rites was completed in the early Heian period (late eighth century to late twelfth century). At the beginning of the tenth century, there were nearly three thousand shrines receiving offerings from the government.

Amalgamation of Buddhism and Shinto. From around the time of the Taika Reforms until the early Heian period, Chinese influence in thought, ethics, law, literature, technology, and industry was very great, but in religion Buddhism's influence and power of permeation increased quickly following its introduction in 538. Initially, the Buddha was thought of as "the neighboring country's [i. e., China's] *kami*" and was not rigorously distinguished from the *kami* of Japan.

However, Buddhist art, worship, and notions of transience eventually won the hearts of the people, beginning with the ruling elites. However, because Shinto continued to live on strongly as a religion of the people, many connections between the two religions were formed.

Three stages in the assimilation of Buddhism and Shinto can be distinguished. The first was that in which the *kami* were made protectors of the Buddhas; from the middle of the eighth century Shinto tutelary deities were worshiped in Buddhist temples. The second stage coincided in time with the first. Among the Buddhist clergy arose the idea that in the Ten Realms of Beings (ten levels of karmically determined existence, ranging from denizens of the various Buddhist hells to Buddhas) the *kami* correspond to the Buddhist *devas* ("gods"), who occupy the highest position in the Realm of Ignorance.

The third stage, beginning at the end of the eighth century, held that *kami* are *avataras,* or incarnations, of *bodhisattvas* and assigned *bodhisattva* titles to the *kami*. Later, it was held that Buddhas are the original form of *kami,* while *kami* are phenomenal manifestations of the Buddhas.

Buddhist Shinto was based on the concepts of *kami* held by the Buddhist clergy. These concepts were fully developed by the Kamakura period (late twelfth century to early fourteenth century). Typical examples of Buddhist Shinto were Tendai Shinto and Shingon Shinto. In Tendai's philosophy of ultimate reality, primordial Buddha nature as represented by Sakyamuni Buddha was held to be the reality behind all phenomena, including the *kami*.

In Shingon thought Mahavairocana ("great illuminator"), symbolized by the sun, is held to be the source of the universe and all existence, uniting its two aspects, the Diamond cycle *(kongokai)* and the Womb-store cycle *(taizokai)*. It was held in accordance with this principle that the original form of the deity of the Inner Shrine at Ise, Amaterasu Omikami, was the Womb-store cycle (the feminine aspect), and that the original form of the deity of the Outer Shrine was Mahavairocana, of the Diamond cycle.

The situation described above continued until the end of the Edo period (1603-1867), and it is estimated that Buddhist priests were in charge of over half of all the Shinto shrines in the country by that time. But a movement in opposition began as far back as the early Kamakura period. Ise, or Watarai, Shinto, while continuing to be influenced by Shingon Shinto, developed among the priests of the Grand Shrine at Ise, and was the first anti-Buddhist Shinto. One of its theories held that *konton,* or chaos, was the original form of all phenomena.

Yoshida Shinto was founded by Urabe Kanetomo (1435-1511), priest of the Yoshida Shrine in Kyoto, in the latter half of the fifteenth century. According to him, the fundamental god of the universe, Taigen Sonjin ("great exalted one"), is identical to the *kami* that appears at the beginning of the

Nihonshoki, Kuni no Toko-dachi no Mikoto. Yoshida held that all beings originate from this deity.

Confucian Shinto. In the early Edo period it was Confucian Shinto that made the greatest strides philosophically at this time. Confucian scholars tried to interpret Shinto in terms of Neo-Confucianism as expounded by Chu Hsi and Wang Yang-ming and proclaimed that Shinto and Confucianism are one. The two main schools promoting this view were Yoshikawa Shinto and Suiga (also read Suika) Shinto. Yoshikawa Koretaru (1616-1694) emphasized Shinto's usefulness as a philosophy for governing the realm. At birth, the heart-mind has within it *ri* (Chin., *li*), the source of all existence that is this deity, but if at the same time the *ki* (Chin., *ch`i;* the physical element) is not purified, the *kami's* divine wisdom will be obstructed by egoistic desire and will fail to be activated. Therefore, he held, it is necessary to pray and to purify heart and flesh in order to recover humanity's original oneness with the deity by eradicating egotism.

Suiga Shinto was founded by Yamazaki Ansai (1618-1682). Although he had sometimes farfetched explanations, his teachings were accompanied by the emphasis on reverential exactitude *(tsutsushimi),* purity of mind, prayer, fervent loyalty to the imperial house, and so on. They later became one of the sources of the political movement to overthrow the shogunate.

Revival of Shinto. Kokugaku (the school of National Learning), arising in the atmosphere of free scholarship, of the early Edo period (late seventeenth century), sought to recover and clarify the ethos of ancient Japan through exacting literary research. Established by Motoori Norinaga, Revival Shinto (Fukko Shinto) refers to the Shinto research and religious movement that was based on Kokugaku. Motoori criticized the syncretistic theories linking Shinto with Buddhism and Confucianism and urged that through study of the classics the spirit of ancient Shinto be revived.

Among Motoori's disciples, Hirata Atsutane (1776-1843) was the most important successor in the field of Shinto. Hirata's view of humanity held that human nature is originally good, but that this world is only a temporary one that *kami* have established to test us. He goes on to claim that there will be retribution for past bad deeds in the next world. These Catholic influences were continued by some of Hirata's disciples, but in later Shinto they were unable to command significant following.

However, Hirata's doctrines laid the theoretical groundwork for Shinto funerals among the people through his idea of the otherworld. Hirata also promoted domestic rites and composed many prayers. He furthermore propounded the notion that Japan is the center of the world and advocated emperor worship.

Establishment of Sect Shinto. The thirteen sects of Shinto developed out of Shinto, Confucianism, Buddhism, Taoism, Shugendo, and folk beliefs. These groups show a variety of patterns of development, patterns on the one hand growing out of the teachings and actions of a religious leader looked upon as founder by believers, or developing from Revival Shinto, or from the conflation of a number of related, preexisting groups. The reasons for the development of these groups included the shock felt by the people in the face of the social and political changes surrounding the end of the Edo Period and the Meiji Restoration, the impotence of Buddhism when it lost the support of the shogunate, the impact of Revival Shinto, and the necessity of autonomous proselytization on a grass roots level after the failure of the Great Promulgation Movement.

Beliefs and Teachings

Concept of Kami. The core of Shinto is the belief in the profound and mysterious power of the *kami* (*musubi,* namely, the power of harmony and creation) as well as the way of the *kami* or the "will" of the *kami* (*makoto,* namely, truth or truthfulness). The essence of *kami* transcends the ability of words to explain and is an ineffable existence far beyond humanity's powers of comprehension. However, devoted believers are able to know the will and the existence of *kami* through faith.

The Nature of Humanity. The fundamental assumption of Shinto's conception of the nature of man is the idea that "human beings are the children of *kami.*" Since man is believed to have received life from the *kami,* man has within him the sacrality that is the essence of *kami.*

Institutions

The main facilities of Shrine Shinto are, of course, shrines. Sect Shinto and Shinto-derived new religions, however, make use of "churches," structures specifically designed for formal, congregational worship.

Shrines, in their several architectural styles, combine with their surrounding forests to fulfill their functions and to give the appearance appropriate to these functions. Therefore, the entire precinct should be considered as the shrine. At the entrance to the shrine stands the *torii,* the classic Shinto double-linteled gateway, demarcating the boundary between the sacred place and the secular world. As one proceeds along the approach, one finds the ablution basin, where visitors wash their hands and rinse their mouths. In its vicinity are the shrine office, the gathering hall, the purification hall, the treasury, and other buildings. Most people who worship at shrines make a small offering before the hall of worship and pray. Occasionally, they might ask a priest to perform rites of passage or give special prayers, announcements, and thanksgiving.

Believers' Organizations

Sociologically, there are many patterns of organization in Shinto believers' associations *(sukeishakai).* In the case of the Shinto sects and the new religions, these are all, in the words of Joachim Wach, "specifically religious groups." In contrast, in Shrine Shinto we find both specifically religious groups and "identical religious groups," in which "natural" and religious groupings are identical. In the latter case we find that such natural groups as branch and stem family groups, territorial groups, age groups, and professional groups have become the units for the performance of festivals, and even in modern times this phenomenon is frequently found in agricultural areas.

Social Functions and the Present Situation

Historically, Shinto's functions may be divided into two broad categories. The first concerns the search for the meaning of life and the solution to basic human problems of individual and family life. The second is the ability to nurture in people the feeling of mutual belonging and solidarity as members of regional society, and to unify them as citizens in the larger, national society. The second of these functions is particularly conspicuous in Shrine Shinto.

Considered from social and political perspectives, the duty of the emperor and other authorities in ancient times was not limited to ordinary politics but included service to the gods. The expression *saisei itchi,* meaning, "Shinto ceremonies and political affairs are one and the same," belongs to a later epoch. But also demanded of those in power was equality in government, true-hearted government based on a religious sincerity under the protection of the gods and the worship of them.

Under the influence of these traditions, the Meiji government revived the tenth-century system of national shrines. The Constitution of 1889 guaranteed the conditional freedom of religion (i. e., to the extent that this freedom did not infringe upon one's performance of patriotic duties), but Shinto was favored as a cornerstone of the nation's structure. Shinto education was carried out in public schools, and most national holidays coincided with Shinto festivals. As of 1945, there were 218 national shrines, including 14 overseas, and 110,000 local shrines.

After World War II, the Occupation authorities ordered the Japanese government to sever all official affiliation with Shinto shrines and to cease all financial support for the shrines from public funds. Shrine Shinto experienced a period of economic, social, and political difficulty. However, through the private support of the people, ruined shrines have been rebuilt, and *matsuri* and various rites of passage have been revived. According to statistics of the Agency for Cultural Affairs, in 1982 there were 79,700 shrines. Most of these belong to the Association of Shinto Shrines. Of these, 570 are independent or belong to small religious organizations. The number of Shrine Shinto believers stands at 74,660,000.

Shinto is intimately connected with the cultural and social life of the Japanese people

[*See also* Priesthood, New Religions *and* Japanese Religion.]

BIBLIOGRAPHY

Western Sources

Anesaki, Masaharu. *History of Japanese Religion* (1930). Revised by Hideo Kishimoto. Tokyo, 1970. A classic, standard book on Japanese religion.

Aoki, Michiko Yamaguchi, trans. *Izumo Fudoki.* Tokyo, 1971. A translation of an important Japanese classic.

Aston, W. G., trans. *Nihongi: Chronicles of Japan from the Earliest Times to A. D. 697* (1896). 2 vols. Reprint, Tokyo, 1972. A standard translation into English with many helpful notes.

Bock, Felicia Gressitt, trans. *Engi-Shiki: Procedures of the Engi Era; Books 6-10.* Tokyo, 1972. A translation of the basic text of early Shinto national rites and ceremonies.

Creemers, Wilhelmus H. M. *Shrine Shinto after World War II.* Leiden, 1968. A historical treatment with attention to the Ise and Yasukuni shrines.

Hepner, Charles. *The Kurozumi Sect of Shinto.* Tokyo, 1935. A study of Kurozumikyo, emphasizing the founder's thought.

Hirai, Naofusa. *Japanese Shinto.* Tokyo, 1966. A brief general treatment of Shinto.

Holtom, D. C. *The Japanese Enthronement Ceremonies* (1928). Reprint, Tokyo, 1972. A detailed study of enthronement rites and their symbolic significance.

Holtom, D. C. *The National Faith of Japan* (1938). Reprint, New York, 1965. The best book on Shinto written by a foreigner before the war, with rare strengths in history and political philosophy.

Holtom, D. C. *Modern Japan and Shinto Nationalism.* 2d ed. Chicago, 1947.

Kageyama, Haruki. *Shinto bijutsu: The Arts of Shinto.* Translated by Christine Guth. New York, 1973. A detailed study of Shinto arts.

Kishimoto, Hideo, comp. and ed. *Japanese Religion in the Meiji Era.* Translated by John F. Howes. Tokyo, 1956.

Kitagawa, Joseph M. *Religion in Japanese History.* New York, 1966. The best historical survey of Japanese religions, with much useful information on Shinto concepts, ideas, and leading figures.

Lokowandt, Ernst. *Zum Verhältniss von Staat und Shinto im heutigen Japan.* Wiesbaden, 1981. A detailed study of the relation of Shinto and state since 1945, emphasizing recent court cases.

Muraoka, Tsunetsugu. *Studies in Shinto Thought.* Translated by Delmer M. Brown and James T. Araki. Tokyo, 1964. A dependable description of Shinto thought by an eminent philologist, containing one of the few discussions of "national learning" available in English.

Ono, Sokyo. *Shinto the Kami Way.* Rutland, Vt., and Tokyo, 1962. A useful survey of aspects of Shinto.

Philippi, Donald L., trans. *Norito: A New Translation of the Ancient Japanese Ritual Prayers.* Tokyo, 1959. One of very few English translations of these important prayers.

Philippi Donald L., trans. *Kojiki.* Tokyo, 1968; Princeton, 1969. A new translation with introduction of the work by Ono Yasumaro (d. 723), using recent achievements of Japanese philological studies, especially well annotated and with useful bibliography.

Woodard, William P. *The Allied Occupation of Japan, 1945-1952, and Japanese Religion.* Leiden, 1972. A documentary study of the Shinto Directive and other measures taken by the Occupation regarding religion, especially Shinto.

Japanese Sources
Bibliographies and dictionaries
Kato Genchi, ed. *Shinto shoseki mokuroku.* Tokyo, 1937.

Kato Genchi, ed. *Meiji Taisho Showa Shinto shoseki mokuroku.* Tokyo, 1953.

Kokusai Bunka Shinkokai, eds. *Bibliography of Standard Reference Books for Japanese Studies,* vol. 4, *Religion.* Tokyo, 1963. Section two is an annotated bibliography (in English) of Japanese works on Shinto.

Saeki Ariyoshi, ed. *Shinto bunrui somokuroku.* Tokyo, 1937.

Shimonaka Yasaburo, ed. *Shinto daijiten.* 3 vols. Tokyo, 1938-1940.

Specialized studies

Kiyohara Sadao, *Shintoshi* Tokyo, 1932.

Kono Shozo. *Kokugaku no kenkyu.* Tokyo, 1932.

Muraoka Noritsugu. *Shintoshi.* "Nihon shisoshi kenkyu," vol. 1. Tokyo, 1956.

Murayama Shuichi. *Shinbutsu shugo shicho.* Kyoto, 1957.

Nishida Nagao. *Shintoshi no kenkyu.* Tokyo, 1957.

Okada Yoneo. *Shinto bunken gaisetsu.* Tokyo, 1951.

Okura Seishin Bunka Kenkyujo, eds. *Shinten: Shinten sakuin* (1936). Yokohama, 1962.

Ono Sokyo. *Shinto no kiso chishiki to kiso mondai.* Tokyo, 1963.

Nishitsunoi Masayoshi. *Saishi gairon.* Tokyo, 1957.

Tsuji Zen'nosuke et al. *Meiji ishin shinbutsu bunri shiryo.* 5 vols. Tokyo, 1926-29.

Umeda Yoshihiko. *Shinto shiso no kenkyu.* Tokyo, 1942.

HIRAI NAOFUSA
Translated from Japanese by Helen Hardacre

SIKHISM

Sikhism was a later offshoot of the *bhakti* (devotional) cult of Vaisnava Hinduism, which developed in Tamil Nadu and was based upon the teachings of Alvar and Adiyar saints. Its chief propagators were Adi Sankara (eighth century), who expounded *kevaladvaita* (pure monism), and, later, Ramananda (1360-1470) and Kabir (1398-1518), who were influenced by Islam and accepted Muslim disciples.

Foundation. Nanak, the founder of Sikhism, was the Punjab's chief propounder of the *bhakti* tradition. A mystical experience at age twenty-nine was the turning point in Nanak's life. While bathing in a nearby rivulet, he disappeared from view and was given up as drowned. According to the Janamsakhis ("life stories"), he was summoned by God and charged with his mission: "Go in the world to pray and to teach mankind how to pray."

Abandoning worldly pursuits, Nanak undertook four long voyages. On the first, he went eastward as far as Assam, visiting Hindu places of pilgrimage and meeting and discussing spiritual problems with ascetics and holy men.

He returned to his home for a short time before setting out on another long tour. This time he went southward, through Tamil Nadu and as far as Sri Lanka. His third journey was to the northern regions of the Himalayas; his fourth and last of the long journeys began in 1518. This time he went westward to Mecca, Medina, and as far as Basra and Baghdad. By the time Nanak returned home, he was too old to undertake any more strenuous journeys. He decided to settle down at Kartarpur and instruct people who came to him. Large numbers of peasants—both Hindus and Muslims—flocked to hear him. Many became his disciples, or *sisyas,* from which the Punjabi word *Sikh* is derived.

Nanak accepted most of the traditional beliefs of Hinduism pertaining to the origin of creation and its dissolution. He likewise accepted the theory of *samsara*—of birth, death, and rebirth.

> **But the fact that God cannot be defined should not inhibit us from learning about truth and reality.**

Nanak's God was one, omnipotent, and omniscient. God was *sat* (both "truth" and "reality"), as opposed to *asat* ("falsehood") and *mithya* ("illusion"). He thus not only made God a spiritual concept but also based principles of social behavior on this concept. In other words, if God is truth, to speak an untruth is to be ungodly.

His God is ineffable because he is *nirankar,* or "formless." The best one can do is to admit the impossibility of defining him. But the fact that God cannot be defined should not inhibit us from learning about truth and reality. This we can do by following the path of righteousness.

Nanak made the institution of "guruship" the pivot of his religious system. Without the *guru* as a guide, he insisted, no one can attain *moksa* ("release"). The *guru* keeps his followers on the path of truth; he acts as a goad stick, keeping man, who is like a rogue elephant, from running amok. The *guru* is to be consulted, respected, and cherished—but not worshiped. He is a teacher, not a reincarnation of God, an *avatara,* or a messiah. Nanak constantly referred to himself as the bard *(dhadi),* slave, and servant of God.

Nanak believed that all human beings have a basic fund of goodness that, like the pearl in the oyster, only awaits the opening of the shell to emerge and enrich them. The chief task of the guru is to make man aware of the treasure within him and then help him unlock the jewel box.

BIBLIOGRAPHY

The classic work on the history of the Sikhs from the inception of the faith to the fall of the Sikh kingdom remains Joseph Davey Cunnigham's *A History of the Sikhs* (1849; reprint, Delhi, 1966). Subsequent histories of the Sikhs have largely accepted Cunnigham's interpretation of Sikh religion, the transformation of the community from pacificist sect to a militant fraternity, its rise to power as rulers of the Panjab, and the collapse of their empire. However, for a fuller understanding of the teachings of the Sikh *gurus* and translations of the Sikh scripture, Max Arthur Macauliffe's *The Sikh Religion: Its Gurus, Sacred Writings and Authors,* 6 vols. in 3 (Oxford, 1909), and W. H. Mcleod's *Guru Nanak and the Sikh Religion* (Oxford, 1968) can be recommended. In addition I would recommend my *A History of the Sikhs,* 2 vols. (Princeton, 1963) and its subsequent paperback editions published by the Oxford University Press (Delhi, 1979-1983), which brings the history of the Sikhs to the year 1977.

KHUSHWANT SINGH

SINHALA RELIGION

The Sinhala of Sri Lanka are for the most part Buddhists, yet their practical religion is a composite system derived from a variety of sources, including pre-Buddhist indigenous beliefs, Indic astrology, popular Hinduism, Brahmanism, and Dravidian religion, especially that of South India. [See also Tamil Religions.] Over many years these seemingly non-Buddhist beliefs have been incorporated into a Buddhist framework and ethos. The religious beliefs that have derived from non-Buddhist sources have been labeled "spirit cults."

To place the Sinhala spirit cults in perspective it is useful to begin with a consideration of Vädda religion. These aboriginal inhabitants of Sri Lanka speak a Sinhala dialect and were at least peripherally part of the traditional political system. Although they were Sinhala-speaking, and their spirit cults showed considerable overlap with that of Sinhala Buddhists, most Väddas never converted to Buddhism. An examination of Vädda religion will help us understand more fully the nature of the Sinhala spirit cults and their relationship with Buddhism.

Cult of the Nä Yakku. The Väddas, unlike the Sinhala Buddhists, had as the basis of their religion a system of ancestor worship. Väddas who die are said to become deities known as *nä yakku* (sg., *yaka*), literally "kinsmen deities"; the transformation of a person's spirit to a *yaka* occurs a few days after his death. Ancestral spirits help the living but show wrath if neglected.

Complementing the spirits of the recently dead is a pantheon of major Vädda deities. This pantheon is headed by Kande Yaka ("lord of the mountain"). Ancestral spirits are considered to be feudal attendants of Kande Yaka and have his warrant to assist or punish the living. The concept of permission or warrant *(varan)* and the system whereby the higher gods engage lower deities as attendants are identical with Sinhala beliefs.

The Sinhala Buddhists have no system of ancestor worship like that of the *nä yakku,* but they do believe in a cult of deified ancestors and foreign deities. These deities were originally human beings; all of them are viewed as lords or chiefs and are subordinate to the great gods or *devas* of the

Sinhala Buddhist pantheon, who are viewed as kings or world rulers *(cakravartins).*

The Bandara Cult among the Sinhala. The bandara cult has been formalized in many parts of the Kandyan region into a cult of the Dolaha Deviyo ("twelve gods"). The Twelve Gods are individually and collectively propitiated in group rituals. Many of these gods have in fact demonic attributes and are often referred to in rituals as *devata* ("godling"), a composite of the demonic and the divine. The Twelve Gods are associated with most of the social, economic, and personal needs of the worshiper—hunting, animal husbandry, and rice cultivation, as well as individual afflictions such as illnesses due to demonic incursions.

The Bandara Cult and the Worship of Devas. The *bandara* cult, or the cult of the Twelve Gods, was the operative folk religion of many villages in the Kandyan kingdom for many centuries. But the cult of the *ban-daras* was in turn enveloped in the cult of the *devas,* the superordinate god-kings of the pantheon. The *bandaras* were local or regional deities, and although some of them, such as Mangara and Devata Bandara, were widely dispersed they were viewed as chieftains, not kings. The *devas* by contrast were national deities, viewed as kings, holding jurisdictional sway over Sri Lanka; they were protectors of that Sinhala Buddhist nation. The *bandaras* are subservient to the *devas,* and the latter, according to popular religion, are in turn subordinate to the Buddha. The *devas* have a warrant *(varan)* from the Buddha himself, whereas the lesser *bandaras* generally exercise their authority with permission from the *devas.*

The concept of divine protectors of the secular and sacred realm is an ancient one in Sri Lanka. First, there was the ancient Buddhist doctrinal notion of the guardians of the four quarters of the universe. In addition to this there developed in Sri Lanka the idea of four guardians of the state. If the Buddhist guardians protected the cosmos the *devas* were protectors of the nation, and therefore were of great significance in the practical religion. The concept of the four gods *(hatara deviyo)* and the four shrines *(hatara devale)* were clearly established in the kingdoms of Kotte (fifteenth century) and in Kandy.

Demons, Gods, and the Buddha. At the lowest level of Sinhala religion are such demons and evil spirits as *pretas,* who are viewed as the malevolent spirits of dead kinsmen. All these evil spirits embody Buddhist notions of spiritual and ethical hindrances, such as craving *(tanha),* hatred *(krodha),* greed *(lobha),* defilements *(klesa),* and enmity *(vaira).* The demons are under the authority of the *devas* (i. e., the great gods of the pantheon), who must control them to ensure a just social order. The *devas* are essentially rational and just deities, viewed by Sinhala Buddhists as future Buddhas or *bodhisattvas.*

Over and above the cults of the gods and demons is the worship of the Buddha. The Buddha himself is viewed as the supreme deity and totally benevolent, reigning over the rest of the pantheon. In his role as overlord of the pantheon he is referred to as "king"; in his role as the teacher of salvation he is "monk." The omnipresence of the Buddha in Sri Lanka is expressed in the symbolism of his sacred footprint embedded at Sri Pada Mountain (known also as Adam's Peak), the visible presence everywhere of monks and *dagobas* or *stupas* containing relics of the Buddha or the saints of the early Buddhist church, and the sacred places of Buddhist pilgrimage where people from different regions come together to celebrate their collective unity as Buddhists. Sinhala religion as a totality has been adapted, through its long history, into a Buddhist framework.

Change in Sinhala Religion. Changes in the religious beliefs of the Sinhala have occurred in a variety of ways without radically affecting the formal structure of the pantheon. The most common forms of change are as follows.

1. Hindu gods and deities are incorporated into the Buddhist pantheon and given Buddhist legitimation.

2. Sociopolitical and economic conditions may favor the rise or decline of a god.

3. The more popular a deity, the more favors he grants his devotee; this in turn means that the devotee transfers merit to him, thereby bringing the god closer to his goal of Buddhahood. But the closer the god is to the Buddha model the less he is interested in the affairs of the world. Consequently, he must eventually become otiose, and more world-involved—even demonic—beings from the lower reaches of the pantheon move up to take his place. Thus, the logic of *karman* and the transfer of merit govern internal mobility in the pantheon.

4. Finally, social changes may produce radical changes in the formal structure of the pantheon. Modern sociopolitical conditions, including the centralization and democratization of the state and the development of modern communications, have tended to erode the spheres of influence of minor gods and demons.

BIBLIOGRAPHY

The two most comprehensive books on Sinhala religion dealing with the demon and *deva* cults are Bruce Kapferer's *A Celebration of Demons* (Bloomington, Ind., 1983) and my *The Cult of the Goddess Pattini* (Chicago, 1984). Paul Wirz's *Exorcism and the Art of Healing in Ceylon* (Leiden, 1954), written in the thirties, is still a useful reference work, but better still is the excellent and little-known article by Dandris De Silva Gooneratne, "On Demonology and Witchcraft in Ceylon," *Journal of the Royal Asiatic Society, Ceylon Branch* 4 (1865-1866): 1-117, both dealing with the demon and astrological cults. Michael M. Ames's article "Magical-Animism and Buddhism: A Structural Analysis of the Sinhalese Religious System," in *Religion in South Asia*, edited by Edward B. Harper (Seattle, 1964), and Richard F. Gombrich's *Precept and Practice* (Oxford, 1971) deal with the *deva* cults in the southern province and the Kandyan villages respectively and also discuss the articulation of the spirit cults and astrological beliefs with Buddhism. H. L. Seneviratne's excellent *Rituals of the Kandyan State* (Cambridge, 1978) is a comprehensive study of the state cultus of the sacred tooth relic and the worship of the Four Gods. For recent socioeconomic changes in Sinhala religion, read my "Social Change and the Deities," *Man* 12 (1977): 377-396, and *Medusa's Hair* (Chicago, 1981).

GANANATH OBEYESEKERE

SIVA

The ancient name of Siva is *Rudra*, the Wild God. His seminal myth is told in the most sacred, most ancient Indian text, the *Rgveda* (c. 1200-1000 BCE; hymns 10.61 and 1.71). When time was about to begin he appeared as a wild hunter, aflame, his arrow directed against the Creator making love with his virgin daughter, the Dawn. They had the shape of two antelopes. Some of the Creator's seed fell on the earth. Rudra himself as Fire (Agni) had prepared the seed, from which mankind was to be born. From a rupture of the undifferentiated plenum of the Absolute some of the seed fell on the earth. Rudra's shot failed to prevent its fall; time, which was about to begin, came in between, in the shape of the flight of his arrow. The Creator, Prajapati, terribly frightened, made Rudra Lord of Animals (Pasupati) for sparing his life (*Maitrayani Samhita* 4.2.12; after 1000 BCE). The gods, as they witnessed the primordial scene, made it into a mantra, an incantation, and out of this *mantra* they fashioned Vastospati, "lord of the residue *(vastu)*." "lord of the site *(vastu)*," or "lord of what is left over on the sacrificial site." However, Pasupati—"lord of animals," "lord of creatures," "lord of the soul of man"—is Rudra-Siva's most significant name.

Fundamental pairs of antitheses inhere in the primordial Rgvedic myth of Rudra Pasupati and Rudra Vastospati. As Fire he incites Prajapati toward creation; as the formidable hunter he aims at the act of creation, meaning to prevent the "incontinence" of the Creator, the shedding of the seed. Rudra acts as hunter and yogin in one. The scene has for its background the plenum of the uncreated or the Absolute that was and is before the mythical moment of the inception of the life.

In the Vedic sacrificial ritual, Vastospati receives as an oblation the remainder of the sacrifice. The power of the completed sacrifice is left in the remainder and magically ensures the continuity of the rites, of the entire tradition—and of the order and rhythms of art. Vastospati is the guardian and protector of the site, the buildings and their content, in later Hinduism.

Jan Gonda, in his article "The Satarudriya," in the festschrift *Sanskrit and Indian Studies* (Dordrecht, 1980, p. 75), considers Rudra "the representative of the dangerous, unreliable and hence to be feared nature." Looking at Siva from another angle, Daniel H. H. Ingalls, in "Kalidasa and the

Attitudes of the Golden Age" in the *Journal of the American Oriental Society* (1976), sees that "Siva represents the reconciliation of good and evil, of beauty and ugliness, of life and death—the vision solved all problems and could transmute a man's suffering into joy." Neither of these views refers to the primordial and central myth of Rudra, in which Rudra acts as consciousness of metaphysical reality or the Absolute in its relation to life on earth.

In Vedic times, the fierce hunter had the power over life and death, to afflict a mortal wound or to heal it. He was worshiped with the words "Do not hurt me" and also invoked as "lord of songs, lord of sacrifice, bringing cooling remedy, radiant like the sun, like gold" (*Rgveda* 1.43.4-5). He was praised

> **Praise went to him in the flux of waves, in young grass and the desert, in soil and air, house and palace.**

as the lord of the high and the low, of robbers, of the ill-formed, but also of craftsmen working in wood, metal, and clay. Praise went to him in the flux of waves, in young grass and the desert, in soil and air, house and palace. This is how the *Satarudriya* hymn of the *Yajurveda* (after 1000 BCE) invokes him, an omnipresent power whose shape reverberates in uncounted Rudras like him who are his retinue. Rudra's color is copper red, his throat deep blue; one of his names is the Blue-Red One. His home is everywhere, but particularly in the North, in Himalayan caves but also on crossroads, cremation grounds, and the battlefield.

The gods meant to exclude Rudra from the Vedic sacrifice. This is mythically accounted for by the primordial flight of his arrow. Rudra, though he had been made lord of animals, was not himself born yet as a god. The story of Rudra's birth has several versions. The *Satapatha Brahmana* (9.1.1.6; c. mid-first millennium BCE) tells of Prajapati, from whom all the gods departed except Manyu (Anger). Prajapati cried. His tears fell on Manyu, who became thousand-headed, thousand-eyed, hundred-quivered Rudra. Rudra was hungry. Prajapati asked the gods to gather food for Rudra, who stood there flaming. The gods appeased Agni-Rudra. By the Satarudriya offering and hymn they drove out his pain, his evil. The Satarudriya sacrifice was the first to be performed on completion of the Vedic sacrificial altar. Rudra, as soon as he was born from Prajapati, was given this place in the Vedic sacrifice. To this day the *Satarudriya* hymn is recited in Saiva temples every morning.

On being born, Rudra was invested with the cosmos by Prajapati. His eightfold domain consisted of the five elements—earth, water, fire, air, and space—together with sun and moon, the measurers of time, and the sacrificer, or initi-

ate. Rudra is the totality of manifestation. He did not create the cosmos. He became and is the cosmos. God and the world are one. As the cosmos is a product of Siva's eight forms, so is the human being, the microcosm.

The *Svetasvatara Upanisad* (c. late first millennium BCE), like the *Rgveda*, implores Rudra not to injure man or beast. The formidable hunter is everywhere, he merges with the ogdoad and transcends it, he rules over all the worlds, makes them appear and withdraws them at the end of time. In him at the beginning and at the end the universe is gathered. The dweller in the mountain resides in the cave of the heart of man. He is immanent and transcendent, the one supreme God. Though he has a face, a hand, a foot on every side, no one can see him; he is seen only with the mind and heart. Those who know the Lord by introspection, yoga, and loving devotion (*bhakti*) are freed from the fetter (*pasa*) of worldly existence, for he is the cause of worldly existence and of liberation. In his auspicious, unterrifying form he is the Lord, the omnipresent Siva, hidden in all beings.

Rudra, the "wild god," is one with Siva, the auspicious, supreme god whose splendor encompasses his primordial form. His being in manifestation is to be meditated upon as a river of five streams from five sources (*Svetasvatara Upanisad* 1.5). They are the five senses with their objects "an impetuous flood of five pains." If Rudra as the ogdoad is the cosmos, as the pentad he is the five senses, the sense perception and experience of the cosmos. Five is Siva's sacred number in particular. His *mantra*, "Namah Sivaya," has five syllables, and his "body" is said to be constituted of five *mantras* (*Taittiriya Aranyaka* 10.43-47; c. third century BCE). They evoke the body of God in the five directions of space, in the five elements, in the five senses.

Vedic Rudra, the fierce hunter, is clad in the skins of wild animals. In the *Mahabharata* (c. 400 BCE-400 CE), Siva is seen by the hero Arjuna, in a vision, as an archer and an ascetic. A hymn of the *Rgveda* (10.136), on the other hand, celebrates Rudra drinking from one cup with an ascetic. The *Mahabharata* sums up the relation of Siva to yoga, saying that "Siva is yoga and the lord of yogins; he can be approached by yoga only."

In post-Vedic times Prajapati's role as creator was taken over by Brahma. Rudra decapitates his father, Brahma. Various reasons are given in the Puranas (fourth through fourteenth centuries CE); one of them, the lusting of Brahma for his daughter, recalls the primordial scene. The head of Brahma clings to Siva's hand. Siva as a penitent beggar, the skull his begging bowl, goes on a pilgrimage of expiation. After twelve years the skull falls from Siva's hand in Banaras, and Siva is released from his sin. His pilgrimage takes the god to a hermitage in a forest of deodar trees. The hermits believe that the young, naked beggar has come to seduce their women—and Siva's phallus (*linga*) falls from his body, by his own will or by a curse of the sages; it then arises as a flaming pillar. These events are part of the play *(lila)* of Siva in this world to enable his devotee to recognize God in the guises he assumed. The sages apparently fail to identify the begging bowl, Brahma's head or skull *(brahmasiras)*, in the beggar's hand. Brahmasiras is also the name of Siva's most formidable weapon, the Pasupata weapon.

Most of Siva's myths are known to the *Mahabharata*. The myth of Siva the ascetic, paradoxically, is the theme of his marriage to Parvati, daughter of Parvataraja, "Lord Mountain." In it is included the story of the destruction—and resurrection—of Kama, the god Desire, an archer who aimed his arrow at Siva but was reduced to ashes by a glance from Siva's third eye. Fire and ashes belong to Siva as much as serpents and the moon's crescent, for Siva's nature is twofold: he is fierce as fire, yet cool and calm as the moon. He is the reluctant bridegroom, the indefatigable lover, and the ascetic. He is the savior of the world; he swallowed its poison, and it left a dark blue mark on his throat. He destroys demons or shows them his grace. He defeats death; he is the death of death, for he is time and transcends time as eternity. He is the teacher who in silence expounds to the sages music, yoga, gnosis, and all the arts and sciences. He is a dancer, Lord of Dancers, who dances the world in and out of existence. He is a male god inseparably united with his female power *(sakti)*. One image shows him half male, half female. His theriomorphic form is the bull called Nandin (Joy). His main attributes are trident, skull, and antelope. His symbol is the *linga*, the (phallic) pillar, the most sacred object of worship—although none is known in India prior to the third to second century BCE. The *linga* stands erect in its double significance; full of creative power, and also of the yogic power to withhold the seed. Its symbolism is akin to the meaning of the primordial scene.

Whereas the relation of Siva to Brahma-Prajapati is crucial, that of Siva to Visnu is one of coexistence or subordination but also of amalgamation and interchange. Visnu sometimes carries the name of Siva or Rudra; Visnu is conjoint in one type of image with Siva as Harihara; in one painting Visnu-Krsna carries Siva's insignia, trident and serpent, whereas Siva holds Krsna's flute. Saivism and Vaisnavism are complementary, although sectarian rivalry led to the conception of the gruesome Sarabhesa. To each of the three great Hindu gods is assigned one of the three tendencies *(guna)* of cosmic substance *(prakrti)*, that of Siva being *tamas* (darkness), the disruptive tendency that precedes every new creation.

In the darkness of the flood between the dissolution of the universe and the beginning of a new world, the flaming pillar of Siva's *linga* arose and was worshiped by Brahma and Visnu. This is celebrated by vigil, vows, fast, and worship on Mahasivaratri, the Great Night of Siva, the climax of the religious year, on the fourteenth lunar day of the dark half of the last month of the lunar year. The last night of each month is Siva's Night (Sivaratri) and the evening of each day throughout the year is the time for his worship.

BIBLIOGRAPHY

Eliade, Mircea. *Yoga: Immortality and Freedom*. Translated by Williard R. Trask. 2d ed. Princeton, 1969. The basic work on yoga clarifies the conception of God (Isvara) in the yoga system and that of Siva the Great God and Great Yogin.

Gonda, Jan. *Die Religionen Indiens*. 2 vols. Vol. 1, *Veda und älterer Hinduismus*, 2d rev. ed. Stuttgart, 1978. Vol. 2, *Der jüngere Hinduismus*. Stuttgart, 1963. A most thorough and judicious presentation of the religions of India, including a survey of the character and history of Saivism.

Gonda, Jan. *Visnuism and Sivaism: A Comparison*. London, 1970. In their juxtaposition the two views of the world define one another. Copious, detailed notes enrich the scope of the book.

Kramrisch, Stella. *The Presence of Siva*. Princeton, 1981. A presentation focused on the ontological and cosmogonic implications of the mythology of Siva and the persistent themes within its network.

O'Flaherty, Wendy Doniger. *Siva: The Erotic Ascetic*. London, 1981. Reprint of *Asceticism and Eroticism in the Mythology of Siva* (1973). A monograph that structurally and masterfully analyzes one fundamental aspect, the erotic-ascetic polarity within Siva; based on hitherto mostly unpublished textual sources.

Rao, T. A. Gopinatha. *Elements of Hindu Iconography*, vol. 2, parts 1 & 2 (1916). Reprint, New York, 1968. Although first published in 1916, this work remains a comprehensive and valid support of Saiva studies.

Scheuer, Jacques. *Siva dans le Mahabharata*. Paris, 1982. This book fills a gap in the present knowledge about Siva by establishing Siva's position in the central theme of the Maha-bharata.

STELLA KRAMRISCH

SLAVIC RELIGION

The exact origin of the Slavs, an indigenous European people, is not known, but by about 800 BCE pockets of Slavs were scattered in a region east of the Vistula and the Carpathians and west of the Don. Around the sixth century CE the Slavs began separating into three groups, the West, South, and East Slavs. The West Slavs lived in a region reaching beyond the Elbe and were bounded on the west by Germanic tribes. The South Slavs, covering the area east of the Adriatic, south of the Danube, and west of the Black Sea, had the Magyars and Vlachs as their northern and eastern neighbors. The ancestors of today's Russians, Belorussians, and Ukrainians, the East Slavs lived in an area bounded by Lake Ladoga, the upper Volga and Don, and the Dnieper.

Formation of Slavic Religion. The term *Slavic religion* can be used to refer to the mythology and cultic life common to all Slavs from the sixth to the tenth century. Three important factors must be borne in mind in regard to Slavic religion.

First, literacy came to the Slavs in the aftermath of christianization; songs, fairy tales, and oral epics represent pagan religious traditions. The second important factor in the formation of the Slavic religion was the close contact of the Slavs with neighboring peoples, especially the Balts and Indo-Iranians, attested to by some words that have clear affinities with Iranian. The third and most essential factor is the heritage of mythological images. In the tradition of Celtic, Baltic, Greek, and other related mythologies of Europe, Slavic beliefs strongly preserved very ancient pre-Indo-European images typical of an agricultural, matrifocal, and matrilinear culture.

Temples and Idols. The most precise descriptions of temples and idols come from the eleventh through the thirteenth century in the area of the northwestern Slavs, present-day Germany. The best-documented site is Arkona, a citadel-temple of the god Sventovit, which was destroyed in 1168 by Christian Danes. Carl Schuchhardt's excavation in 1921 proved the existence of the temple.

The earliest source, Thietmar (1014), describes a similar temple on the castle hill of Riedegost or Radigast (Rethra). It contained several hand-sculpted idols dressed in helmets and armor and each dedicated to a god, the most important being that of Zuarasici (Svarozhich). Carl Schuchhardt, who excavated Rethra in 1922, concluded that Riedegost was principal among all the local temples. People came to it with homage before going to war, and with offerings on their return. The priests determined reconciliation offerings by means of dice and horse oracles. it was apparently the sanctuary for the entire Lutici confederation, of which the Retharii were one tribe.

At Wolin, according to Monarchus Prieflingensis, Bishop Otto of Bramberg found a temple with a sacred spear that, as legend had it, had been placed there in memory of Julius Caesar. The practice of building a church on the site of a pagan sanctuary was one of the most effective, and most commonly employed, methods of combating paganism all over the Slavic area. It attracted the people to whom the place itself was still holy, and it removed all traces of the worship previously performed there.

A ruined temple, perhaps of Perun, was discovered in 1951 near Novgorod in a place called Peryn. The wooden structure itself was not preserved, but the floor plan, an octagonal rosette shape, was clearly evident. In the center was charcoal, indicating where the idol and a place for fire had probably been located. Nearby was a flat stone, apparently a part of an altar. In 1958, at Staraia Ladoga, a wooden effigy of a god with mustache and beard and wearing a conical helmet was found in a layer dated to the ninth or tenth century.

Idols were dedicated to various gods. In the West Slavic area, the richest temples belonged to the warrior god of "heavenly light" in his various aspects (Svarozhich, Iarovit,

Sventovit), whereas the thunder god (Perun) was worshiped outdoors. It is clear that at the time when Christianity arrived, the official religion was dominated by warrior gods of Indo-European heritage.

Gods of Indo-European Heritage. Three divine archetypes of the Indo-European religious tradition are clearly represented in the Slavic pantheon: the god of heavenly light, the god of death and the underworld, and the thunder god. The first two stand in opposition to each other, but the relationship of the three deities is triangular, not hierarchical.

The god of heavenly light. Many different names identify the god of heavenly light. The personified sun appears throughout Slavic folklore: each morning he rides out from his golden palace in the east in a two-wheeled chariot drawn by horses. He begins the day as a youth and dies each night as an old man. He is attended by two lovely virgins (the morning and evening stars), seven judges (the planets), and seven messengers (the comets).

Certain Slavic myths give an anthropomorphic interpretation to the relationship between the sun and the moon. The Russian word for "moon," mesiats, is masculine, but many legends portray the moon as a beautiful young woman whom the sun marries at the beginning of summer, abandons in winter, and returns to in spring. In other myths, the moon is the husband and the sun is his wife, as in Baltic mythology.

The god of death and the underworld. The names Veles and Volos apparently represent two aspects of the same god: (1) a sorcerer god of death, related to music and poetry, and (2) a god of cattle, wealth, and commerce.

Veles was degraded to a devil at the beginning of Christian times. All that remains of this god are such expressions as k Velesu za more ("to Veles in the otherworld"). Place-names incorporating Veles imply sites where this god was worshiped, such as Titov Veles in Macedonia.

Volos was merged with the image of Saint Blasius (Vlasii) and also partly with that of Saint Nicholas (Nikola), the patrons of flocks and crops. He was honored as such up to the twentieth century on his holiday, 11 February.

The thunder god. Overseer of justice and order, purifier and fructifier, and adversary of the devil, Perun is feared to this day in some Slavic areas. His presence and actions are perceived in lightning and thunder. Parallels in other Indo-European mythologies, such as the Baltic Perkons and Perkunas and the Germanic Pórr (Thor), attest to the antiquity of this god. With the onset of Christianity, Perun gradually merged with Saint Elijah (Il'ia), who is portrayed in Russian icons crossing the heavens in a chariot. Bull sacrifice and a communal feast on Saint Il'ia's Day, 20 July, were recorded in northern Russia in 1907.

Household guardians. Slavic names for household guardians—Russian ded, dedushka (dim.), and domovoi; Ukrainian did, didko, and domovyk; Czech dedek; and Bulgarian stopan—have the meaning "grandfather" or "house lord," suggesting their origins in ancestor worship within a patrilineal culture. He cared for animal herds and protected the entire home and its occupants from misfortune.

The Russian forest spirit, Leshii or Lesovik (from *les"*, "forest"), also appears as an old man or an animal. His principal function is to guard forests and animals.

Ancestor worship, a prominent practice among all pre-Christian Slavs, is evidenced in gifts presented to the dead. A strong belief in life after death is indicated by prehistoric and even modern burial rites. Food offerings are made in cemeteries to this day. Everything deemed necessary for the afterlife—weapons, tools, clothing, wives, slaves, horses, hunting dogs, food—was buried in the grave or was burned if the deceased was cremated.

Mythic Images Rooted in Old European Religion. The primary figures of the oldest stratum of Slavic culture are predominantly female: Fates, Death, Baba Yaga, Moist Mother Earth, and a host of nymphs and goblins.

Life-giving and life-taking goddesses and their associates. In folk beliefs, Mokysha, or Mokusha, has a large head and long arms; at night she spins flax and shears sheep. Her name is related to spinning and plaiting and to moisture. The life-giving and life-taking goddess, or Fate, was the spinner of the thread of life and the dispenser of the water of life. Up to the twentieth century, it was believed that fate took the form of birth fairies who appeared at the bedside of a newborn baby. Three Fates of different ages were believed to appear. They determined the infant's destiny and invisibly inscribed it upon his or her forehead.

The Russian *dolia* and the Serbian *sreca* represent the fate of a person's material life. There were good and bad *dolias* and *srecas.* The benevolent spirit protected her favorites and served them faithfully from birth to death. The malevolent spirit, *nedolia* or *nesreca,* usually personified as a poor and ugly woman, capable of transforming herself into various shapes, bestowed bad luck.

Associates of the life-giving and life-taking goddesses were female spirits filled with passionate sensuality. The Bohemians called them *divozenky,* the Poles *dziwozony,* the Slovaks *divja davojke,* and the Bulgarians *divi-te zheny* ("wild women"). They often took care of neglected babies and punished bad mothers.

Baba Yaga and Ved'ma. The Old European goddess of death and regeneration is reflected in the Slavic deity Baba Yaga, who has been preserved in folk tales as a witch. She was said to live in darkness and to devour humans, but she was also believed to have a gift for prophecy. She was usually old and ugly, with bony legs, a long nose, and disheveled hair, but she might also appear as a young woman, or as two sisters.

Ved'ma ("witch") is a demonized goddess. She can be seen flying beneath the clouds and over the mountains and valleys on a broom or a rake. She can make herself invisible, turn into a ball of yarn, and move rapidly. She knows the magical properties of plants and is the keeper of the water of life and death.

Moist Mother Earth and Corn Mother. The sacred deity known as Moist Mother Earth (Mati Syra Zemlia) was perceived as pure, powerful, and pregnant. Up to the twentieth century peasants believed that in springtime it was a grave sin to strike the earth with anything before 25 March, because during that time the earth was pregnant.

The corn (i. e., grain) spirit was personified as the Corn Mother or as the Old Rye (Barley, Wheat, or Oat) Woman. She made crops grow. At harvest, it was believed that she was present in the last stalks of grain left standing in the field.

Nymphs. Two types of nymph were known to the Slavs:

Vilas. Many Slavs believed that *vilas* originated like blossoms with the morning dew or that they were born when the sun shone through the rain. Because she is so beautiful, she cannot tolerate the presence of anyone more beautiful than she. There are three kinds of *vila,* associated with mountains, with water, and with clouds.

Rusalkas. Descriptions of *rusalkas* vary from region to region. They are sometimes said to live in the forest, but in most accounts they are reported to live at the bottom of lakes and rivers, in the deepest water. The *rusalka* is seen as the mistress of water, the female counterpart of the male spirit of water, the *vodianoi.* The *rusalka* is depicted as a beautiful young woman with a white body and long, loose, green or gold hair that she combs while sitting on a riverbank. Always naked, she loves to swing on branches and to play, sing, and dance. She entices men off forest paths or lures them into her dance so as to tickle them to death and carry them into the water.

Goblins. In the West and South Slavic areas, goblins were perceived as little men (dwarfs) who, if they were fed and cared for, brought good harvests and money. The Bohemian *setek* or *sotek* stayed in sheep sheds or hid in pea patches or wild pear trees. The Slovak *skratak,* Polish *skrzat* or *skrzatek,* and Slovene *skrat* (cf. German *Schrat*) appeared as a small bird emitting sparks. The Polish *latawiec* ("flying goblin") took the shape of a bird or a snake.

[*For discussion of Slavic religion in broader context, see* Indo-European Religions. *See also* Baltic Religion *and* Germanic Religion.]

BIBLIOGRAPHY

Afanas'ev, A. N., ed. *Poeticheskie vozzreniia slavian na prirodu* (1865-1869). 3 vols. Reprint, The Hague, 1969-1970.

Brückner, Alexander. *Mitologia slowianska i polska* (1918). Reprint, Warsaw, 1980.

Dordevic, T. "Vestica i vila u nasem narodnom verovanju i predanju." *Srpski etnografski zbornik* 66 (1953).

Gasparini, Evel. *Il matriarcato slavo: Antropologia culturale dei protoslavi.* Florence, 1973.

Gimbutas, Marija. "Ancient Slavic Religion: A Synopsis." In *To Honor Roman Jakobson: Essays on the Occasion of His Seventieth Birthday,* vol. 1, pp. 738-759. The Hague, 1967.

Ivanov, Viacheslav V., and Vladimir N. Toporov. *Slavianskie iazykovye modeliruiushchie semioticheskie sistemy: Drevnii period.* Moscow, 1965.

Jakobson, Roman. "Slavic Mythology." In *Funk and Wagnalls Standard Dictionary of Folklore, Mythology, and Legend* (1949-1950), edited by Maria Leach, vol. 2, pp. 1025-1028. Reprint, 2 vols. in 1, New York, 1972.

Krauss, F. S. *Volksglaube und religiöser Brauch der Südslaven.* Münster, 1890.

Kulisic, Spiro. *Srpski mitoloski recnik.* Belgrade, 1970.

Machek, Václav. "Essai comparatif sur la mythologie slave." *Revue des études slaves* 23 (1947): 48ff.

Mansikka, Viljo Johannes. *Die Religion der Ostslaven.* Helsinki, 1922.

Meyer, Karl Heinrich. *Fontes historiae religionis Slavicae.* Berlin, 1931.

Moszynski, Kazimierz. *Kultura ludowa slowian,* vol. 2, *Kultura duchowa.* Cracow, 1939.

Niederle, Lubor. *Manuel de l'antiquité slave,* vol. 2, *La civilisation.* Paris, 1926. See chapter 6, pages 126-168.

Palm, Thede. *Wendische Kultstatten: Quellenkritische Untersuchungen zu den letzten Jahrhunderten slavischen Heidentums.* Lund, 1937.

Perkowski, Jan L., ed. *Vampires of the Slavs.* Cambridge, Mass., 1976.

Pettazzoni, Raffaele. "Osservazioni sul paganesimo degli Slavi Occidentali." *Studi e materiali di storia delle religioni* 19-20 (1943-1946): 157-169.

Propp, Vladimir Iakovlevich. *Istoricheskie korni volshebnoi skazki.* Leningrad, 1946.

Propp, Vladimir Iakovlevich. "The Historical Roots of Some Russian Religious Festivals." In *Introduction to Soviet Ethnography,* edited by Stephen P. Dunn and Ethel Dunn, vol. 2, pp. 367-410. Berkeley, 1974.

Reiter, Norbert. "Mythologie der alten Slaven." In *Wörterbuch der Mythologie,* edited by Hans W. Haussig, vol. 2, pp. 165-208. Stuttgart, 1973.

Rybakov. B. A. "Drevnie elementy v russkom narodnom tvorchestve (Zhenskoe bozhestvo i vsadniki)." *Sovetskaia etnografiia* 1 (1948): 90-106.

Shapiro, Michael. "Baba-Jaga: A Search for Mythopoeic Origins and Affinities." *International Journal of Slavic Linguistics and Poetics* 27 (1983): 109-135.

Tokarev, Sergei A. *Religioznye verovaniia vostochnoslavianskikh narodov XIX-nachala XX veka.* Moscow, 1957.

Yankovitch, Nénad. "Le soleil dans l'antiquité serbe." *Antiquités nationales et internationales* (Paris) 4, no. 14-16 (April-December 1963): 70-80.

Zelenin, Dimitri K. *Ocherki slavianskoi mifologii.* Saint Petersburg, 1916.

Znayenko, Myroslava T. *The Gods of the Ancient Slavs: Tatishchev and the Beginnings of Slavic Mythology.* Columbus, Ohio, 1980.

MARIJA GIMBUTAS

SMITH, JOSEPH

SMITH, JOSEPH, (1805-1844), the founder of the Church of Jesus Christ of Latter-day Saints, popularly known as the Mormons. [*See* Mormonism.] Joseph Smith, Jr. was perhaps the most original, most successful, and most controversial of several religious innovators—including Ellen Gould White (Seventh-day Adventists), Mary Baker Eddy (Christian Science), and Charles Taze Russell (Jehovah's Witnesses)— who created important religious movements in nineteenth-century America.

Born in Sharon, Vermont, on 23 December 1805, Smith was the third of the nine children of Joseph and Lucy Mack Smith. He grew up in the unchurched and dissenting, but God-fearing, tradition of a New England Protestant biblical culture, which attracted many of those whose economic standing in established society had been eroded. In 1816, plagued by hard times and misfortune, the sturdy, self-reliant, and closely-knit Smith family left New England for western New York in search of economic betterment; they settled in the village of Palmyra, along the route of the Erie Canal.

During the 1820s, as the Smiths continued to struggle against economic reversals, the religiously inclined young man had a number of visions and revelations. These convinced him that he was to be the divinely appointed instrument for the restoration of the gospel, which in the opinion of many of his contemporaries had been corrupted. Under the guidance of an angel he unearthed a set of golden plates from a hill near his parents' farm. He translated these golden plates with divine aid and published the result in 1830 as the *Book of Mormon.* Smith claimed that this book, named after its ancient American author and compiler, was the sacred history of the pre-Columbian inhabitants of America, migrants from the Near East, some of whom were the ancestors of the American Indians. In 1829, divine messengers had conferred the priesthood—the authority to baptize and act in the name of God—on Smith and his associate Oliver Cowdery. Shortly after the publication of the *Book of Mormon,* Smith and Cowdery officially organized the Church of Christ in Fayette, New York, on 6 April 1830. In 1838, the name was changed to the Church of Jesus Christ of Latter-day Saints.

Prominent among those attracted to Smith's teachings was Sidney Rigdon, erstwhile associate of Alexander Campbell. Rigdon invited Smith and his New York followers to establish a Mormon settlement in Kirtland, Ohio. It was there that Smith greatly amplified and broadened his theological and organizational principles in a series of revelations (first published in 1833 as the *Book of Commandments,* and later enlarged into the current, canonical *Doctrine and Covenants*). The Saints were enjoined to gather in communities as God's chosen people under an egalitarian economic system called the Law of Consecration and Stewardship. They were also directed to build a temple as the sacred center of the community. These revelations initiated a patriarchal order that harkened back to Old Testament traditions.

In the meantime, Smith also established settlements in Missouri, which he regarded as the center of a future Zion. In 1838, economic difficulties and internal dissension forced Smith to give up the Kirtland settlement. His intention of gathering all the Saints in Missouri, however, had to be deferred after the Mormons were ruthlessly driven from the state in 1839. It was in Nauvoo, a settlement founded in 1839 on the Mississippi River, that Smith further expanded his ambitious vision of a Mormon empire that was to be both spiritual and temporal. By 1844, Nauvoo had become the largest city in Illinois, with a population of about eleven thousand. This city was under the full religious, social, economic, and political control of the Mormon kingdom, with Joseph Smith as its charismatic leader.

Some historians suggest that he may have become touched by megalomania; he assumed leadership of the Mormon militia in the resplendent uniform of a lieutenant general and announced his candidacy for the presidency of the United States. Smith ostensibly made his gesture toward the presidency in order to avoid making a politically difficult choice between the two major parties, but he was also imbued with the millennial belief that if God wanted him to be president and establish Mormon dominion in the United States, no one could hinder him. Innovative ordinances, such as baptism for the dead, and especially plural marriage—with Smith and his closest associates secretly taking numerous wives—offended the religious sensibilities of many Mormons. Likewise, controversial doctrines such as pre-existence, metaphysical materialism, eternal progression, the plurality of gods, and man's ability to become divine through the principles of Mormonism, failed to gain universal acceptance among the Saints. A group of alarmed anti-Mormons effectively capitalized on internal dissent and were able to organize a mob that killed Smith and his brother Hyrum on 27 June 1844.

History has shown the killers of the Mormon prophet wrong in thinking that they had delivered a mortal blow to Mormonism, although their crime was an implicit recognition of Smith's crucial role in creating and sustaining the new religion. It was his spirituality, imagination, ego, drive, and charisma that not only started Mormonism but kept it going in the face of nearly insurmountable internal and external opposition. At the same time, these were the very characteristics that had generated much of that opposition. Smith's was a multifaceted and contradictory personality. Reports of encounters with him by both non-Mormons and believers give the impression of a tall, well-built, handsome man whose visionary side was tempered by Yankee practicality, geniality, and a sense of humor that engendered loyalty in

willing followers. Though after his death his followers could not all agree on precisely what he had taught and split into several factions, they all accepted Smith's central messages of the restoration of the gospel and the divine status of the *Book of Mormon*, continuing revelation by prophets, and the establishment of the kingdom of God with Christ as its head.

BIBLIOGRAPHY

The literature on Joseph Smith is as controversial as his life. Most of the anti-Smith polemics are based on affidavits collected by Mormon apostate Philastus Hurlbut and published by Eber D. Howe as *Mormonism Unvailed* (Painesville, Ohio, 1834). Smith's mother, Lucy Mack Smith, presented the other side in *Biographical Sketches of Joseph Smith the Prophet* (1853; reprint, New York, 1969). *History of the Church of Jesus Christ of Latter-day Saints*, by Joseph Smith, Jr., 2d rev. ed., 6 vols., edited by B. H. Roberts (Salt Lake City, 1950) is an indispensable source collection. The most authoritative account of Smith's family background and early career is Richard L. Bushman's *Joseph Smith and the Beginnings of Mormonism* (Urbana, Ill., 1984).

The nineteenth-century theory that the *Book of Mormon* was Sidney Rigdon's plagiarized version of a novel by Solomon Spaulding was first demolished by I. Woodbridge Riley in *The Founder of Mormonism: A Psychological Study of Joseph Smith, Jr.* (New York, 1902), who suggested that Smith's visions were the result of epilepsy. The first modern interpretation is Fawn M. Brodie's *No Man Knows My History: The Life of Joseph Smith, the Mormon Prophet* (1945; 2d ed., rev. & enl., New York, 1971), which advances a psychoanalytic interpretation and sees him as a product of his cultural environment. Donna Hill's *Joseph Smith, the First Mormon* (Garden City, N. Y., 1977) provides useful additional information but does not supersede Brodie. The most successful attempt to avoid the prophet-fraud dichotomy is Jan Shipps's *Mormonism: The Story of a New Religious Tradition* (Urbana, Ill., 1984).

KLAUS J. HANSEN

SOUL

Indian Concepts

The many religious traditions of South Asia present such a variety of views regarding the psychological, metaphysical, and ethical nature of the human being and its relationship to the world that no single concept could adequately and consistently fit the English word *soul*. This may be due, in part, to the ambiguous connotations of the term itself. If by *soul* one denotes a dimension to human life that is distinguishable from corporeal existence and that to a large extent determines the nature of the human being, then one could rightly say that the various religions and philosophies of South Asia posit the existence of a soul. This is true even in the case of Buddhism, which, despite the fact that the doctrine of *anatman* ("no-soul") is one of the basic tenets of Buddhist teachings, still holds that the laws of *karman* apply to what is experienced as a self and that the moral aspect of one's being is subject to the cycles of rebirth. In general, South Asian religious anthropologies recognize an aspect to the human being (and, in some traditions, to all sentient beings) that either (1) survives the body's physical death and may be reborn in another form according to the actions performed in previous lives or (2) is uncreated and unchanging, does not experience the vicissitudes of mortal existence, and resides beyond the causal and normative realms.

> ...each distinct living being finds its origin in a common, solitary, and universal spirit. Terms that imply this transpersonal notion of the soul vary from context to context.

Vedic Concepts of the Soul. Vedic poets and visionaries recognized a difference between the corporeal body (*sarira, kaya, deha,* etc.) and an immaterial spirit that might loosely be called the soul. The latter is generally understood in four ways, three of which (*jiva, manas, asu*) revolve around notions of what could be termed the individual soul while the fourth (*paramatman,* etc.) centers on the concept of a universal spirit. (1) *Jiva* ("living being") is one's biological and functional personality, that aspect of one's being that distinguishes one individual from another and that suffers or enjoys existence in earthly as well as post-mortal life according to the acts one performs while alive in this world. (2) *Manas* ("mind") is that subtle or immaterial structure of one's being by which one knows that one is related in various ways to other divine and human beings. (3) *Asu* (the "breath of life") is the vital force that brings life to inert matter, creates sentience, and which in general serves to animate the human being.

However, later hymns of the *Rgveda* reflect the idea that each distinct living being finds its origin in a common, solitary, and universal spirit. Terms that imply this transpersonal notion of the soul vary from context to context. While a generic term would be (4) *paramatman,* which would connote the universal soul as opposed to the individual soul, verses from various Vedic songs and chants refer to this generative force, the source of all being, as Purusa (the primordial "person" of the universe), Visvakarman ("maker of everything"), Prajapati ("lord of [all] living things"), Vena ("the loving one"), Paramam Guha ("greatest secret"), Skambha ("universal prop"), Jyestha Brahman ("the highest, or ultimate, reality"), or simply Tat ("it").

Upanisadic and Vedantic Concepts. The early and middle Upanisads (900-300 BCE) posit a distinction between

material and spiritual existence, a cosmological or ontological stance that reflects the influence of early Samkhya philosophies; the latter maintained that one's self is comprised of mutable physical matter (*prakrti*), on the one hand, and immutable nonmanifest spirit (*purusa*), on the other. As would be consistent with Samkhya metaphysics and psychology, those elements of one's self that have any content or substance are, by nature, *prakrti,* and therefore are not spiritual. Thus, the intellect (*buddhi*), the sense of self, or ego (*ahamkara;* lit., "I-maker"), and the mind (*manas*) are constitutive of the world of matter and therefore cannot be considered to be dimensions of the soul.

Middle and especially later medieval Upanisads similarly show the influence of yogic philosophies and practices designed to "yoke" one's individual spiritual being with the unmanifest, unchanging, and eternal spirit and thus to attain autonomy (*kaivalya*) over the fluctuations and limitations of the physical world. While the early Upanisads often use the word *purusa* ("person") and the later Upanisads use such terms as *ksetrajña* ("knower, witness") to distinguish the world soul from the individual being (*pradhana, jiva, sattva,* and so on), the most common terms generally used in Vedanta to signify the untransmigrating, eternal, and unified self are *atman* and *brahman. Atman* (which in the *Rgveda* had meant, like asu, "breath") signifies the subtle, timeless, and deathless microcosmic self. *Brahman* (roughly, "expansive") refers to the equivalent intelligent and blissful essence of the macrocosm.

Said differently, *atman* is the soul while *brahman* is the godhead. For many Vedantic thinkers the two are the same thing, a point made clear by such statements as the *Adhyatma Upanisad's* assertion that "one is a liberated person who, through insight, sees no difference between his own *atman* and *brahman,* and between *brahman* and the universe."

Buddhist Concepts. Buddhist texts in general acknowledge the existence of a self as an entity that distinguishes one individual from another, that serves as the center of intellect, will, and moral agency, and that is understood to be the source of human perfection. This attitude toward the self dates to the earliest Buddhist textual traditions. Literatures of the Pali canon, for example, often use the adverb *paccattam* (or *pati-attam*), "separately, by oneself, in one's own heart," when referring to the existential and volitional dimension of one's being. Pali collections of the Buddha's reported teachings also use such compounds as *ajjhatta* (cf. Skt. *adhyatman*) to signify the inner self that is of great importance to Buddhist ethical reflection and personal religious practice.

We must be careful, however, not to confuse this Buddhist notion of the moral, intellectual, and volitional aspect of the human being with an Upanisadic or Vedantic concept of the self or of a soul. Buddhist traditions as a whole distinguish a difference between what might be termed a functional self on one hand and an ontological soul on the other. At no time should these various terms signifying the autonomous self be understood to represent the notion of an undying, unchanging, and knowable soul.

The Buddha himself is reported to have understood the anxiety that may arise when one ponders the possibility that one has no soul. According to tradition, he answered such fears by analyzing the source of the anxiety itself. One is afraid of non-being only when one thinks "I have no soul." This torment ends when the realization arises that the "I" that fears such an annihilation is itself imaginary. The comprehension of the "fact of non-selfness" *(nairatmyastika)* brings freedom from fear, doubt, insecurity, and pain.

BIBLIOGRAPHY

Although it will take some time and reading between the lines, readers who are interested in Vedic notions of the soul will find no better reference than the hymns of the *Rgveda* and *Atharvaveda.* The most accessible complete translations of the former are Karl Friedrich Geldner's *Der Rig-Veda aus dem Sanskrit in Deutsche übersetzt,* 4 vols., "Harvard Oriental Series," nos. 33-36 (Cambridge, Mass., 1951-1957), and Ralph T. H. Griffith's now outdated *The Hymns of the Rigveda,* 2d rev. ed., edited by Jagdish Lal Shastri (Delhi, 1973). Excellent partial translations appear in Louis Renou's *Études védiques et paninéennes,* 17 vols. (Paris, 1955-1977), Wendy Doniger O'Flaherty's *The Rig Veda: An Anthology* (Harmondsworth, 1982), and Tatyana Takovlena Elizarenkova's Russian translation, *Rigveda: Izbrannye gimny* (Moscow, 1972). The most complete annotated translation of the *Atharvaveda* is William Dwight Whitney's *Atharva-Veda Samhita,* 2 vols., edited by Charles R. Lanman (1905; Delhi, 1962).

Those interested in studies on Upanisadic and Vedantic notions of the soul might consult Paul Deussen's *The Philosophy of the Upanishads,* translated by A. S. Geden (1906), 2d ed. (New York, 1966), pp. 256-312; Arthur Berriedale Keith's *The Religion and Philosophy of the Veda and Upanishads,* 2 vols. (1925; reprint, Westport, Conn., 1971), pp. 403-416, 551-569; Baldev Raj Sharma's *The Concept of Atman in the Principal Upanisads* (New Delhi, 1972); or William Beidler's *The Vision of Self in Early Vedanta* (Delhi, 1975).

Translations of Buddhist texts pertinent to concepts of the soul appear in Henry Clarke Warren's *Buddhism in Translations,* student's ed. (1896; reprint, New York, 1976), pp. 129-159. Studies of Buddhist doctrines of the soul, and the lack of the soul, can be found in Walpola Rahula's *What the Buddha Taught,* rev. ed. (Bedford, England, 1967), pp. 51-66; Edward Conze's *Buddhist Thought in India* (London, 1962), pp. 34-46, 92-106, 122-133; and Joaquín Pérez-Remón's *Self and Non-Self in Early Buddhism* (The Hague, 1980). A comparative discussion appears in Lynn A. De Silva's *The Problem of the Self in Buddhism and Christianity* (New York, 1979). The most succinct study of the *dharmas, skandhas,* and other constituent elements of reality according to the Sarvastivada is Theodore Stcherbatsky's *The Central Conception of Buddhism and the Meaning of the Word 'Dharma'* (1923), 4th ed. (Delhi, 1970). For an analysis of the Madhyamika position, see T. R. V. Murti's *The Central Philosophy of Buddhism,* 2d ed. (London, 1970).

WILLIAM K. MAHONY

Buddhist Concepts

It is only slightly paradoxical to say that Buddhism has no concepts of the soul: its most fundamental doctrine teaches that no such thing exists and that the realization of this truth is enlightenment.

Of course, one must be careful about what exactly is being denied here. The closest direct equivalent to "soul" in Sanskrit or Pali is *jiva,* from the verbal root *jiv,* meaning "to live." In Jainism, it denotes an individual, transmigrating, and eternal entity; and in the Vedanta school of Hinduism, the related term *jivatman* denotes the individual (but not universal) form of the world soul, called *atman* or *brahman.* In one context, Buddhism uses this term to deny the existence of the soul. The questions whether such a *jiva* is identical to, or different from, the body are two of a list of "unanswerable questions"—unanswerable for the clear epistemological reason that since no *jiva* really exists, it cannot be identical to or different from anything. But in other contexts the word *jiva* and the closely related term *jivita* are used uncontroversially to refer to animate life in contrast to inanimate objects or dead beings. One of the "constituent parts of a being," as Malalasekara called them, is termed *jivitendriya* ("life faculty"), which has both physical and mental forms; its presence in a collection of such constituents is essential for that collection to be alive, or loosely for that "being" to "exist." What is denied by Buddhism is that any such collection contains or is equivalent to a permanent independent entity, whether individual or universal. The word standardly used in Buddhism to refer to such a (nonexistent) entity is *atman,* or in Pali, *attan* (nominatives *atma* and *atta* respectively). In Indo-Aryan languages this (or related forms) often functions simply as the ordinary reflexive pronoun, used in the masculine singular for all numbers and genders. But since at least the time of the Upanisads it has also been used in religious and philosophical writing to refer to an eternal essence of man. By contrast, Buddhism is referred to as *anatmavada* ("the teaching of not-self, or no-soul"). Other terms are used to refer to that whose ultimate reality Buddhism denies, but they can all, like *jiva* and atman, also be used uncontroversially in other contexts. Examples are *pudgala (puggala)* or their synonyms *purusa (purisa),* usually translated "person," and *sattva (satta),* "being." (*Purusa* is the term for "soul" in the Samkhya school of Hinduism.)

BIBLIOGRAPHY

Translations of Buddhist texts directly relevant to this issue were mainly made into French in the first half of the century. These will be available in specialized libraries and remain by far the best source, since the translators provide many references to other texts and other useful information as well as giving direct access to the primary materials. Titles include Étienne Lamotte's *Le traité de l'acte de Vasubandhu, Karma-siddhiprakarana* (Brussels, 1936); his translation of the Chinese text *Ta-chih-tu-lun,* traditionally attributed to Nagarjuna, as *Le traité de la grande vertu de sagesse,* 5 vols. (Louvain, 1944-1980), is a treasury of scholarship on almost every aspect of Buddhism. Louis de La Vallée Poussin translated the Chinese version of the most important work of Buddhist scholasticism, *L'Abhidharmakosa de Vasubandhu,* 6 vols. (1923-1931; Brussels, 1971). The last section of this work, a discussion of the concept of the person between an "orthodox" Buddhist and a member of the Personalist school, was translated from the Sanskrit and Tibetan versions by Theodore Stcherbatsky, as *The Soul Theory of the Buddhists* (1920; Varanasi, 1970). The Pali version of this debate is included in the *Kathavatthu,* translated by Shwe Zan Aung and Caroline Rhys Davids as *Points of Controversy* (London, 1915). Important texts of the Sanskrit and Tibetan traditions have been translated and discussed by Joe Wilson in *Chandrakirti's Sevenfold Reasoning: Meditation on the Selflessness of Persons* (Dharamsala, 1980), and by Jeffrey Hopkins in *Meditation on Emptiness* (London, 1983).

Secondary sources include my *Selfless Persons: Imagery and Thought in Theravada Buddhism* (London, 1982), which discusses the doctrine of *anatta* as presented in the Pali texts; David S. Ruegg's *La théorie du Tathagatagarbha et du Gotra* (Paris, 1969), which discusses the *tathagata-garbha* theory, as presented in Sanskrit and Tibetan texts; and Paul Williams's *Mahayana Buddhism* (London, forthcoming), which treats these and other aspects of the Mahayana tradition in its entirety. Three older works, dated in some ways perhaps but still valuable, are Edward Conze's *Buddhist Thought in India* (1962; Ann Arbor, 1970), Arthur Berriedale Keith's *Buddhist Philosophy in India and Ceylon* (Oxford, 1923), and E. J. Thomas's *The History of Buddhist Thought,* 2d ed. (1951; New York, 1967). Buddhist notions of the soul, along with those from a number of different religious traditions, are discussed by the Christian theologian John Hick in *Death and Eternal Life* (London, 1976).

STEVEN COLLINS

Chinese Concepts

An early reference to the Chinese theory of the "soul" records an explanation on human life offered by a learned statesman in 535 BCE: the earthly aspect of the soul *(p`o)* first comes into existence as the human life begins; after *p`o* has been produced, the heavenly aspect of the soul *(hun)* emerges. As generally understood, *hun* is the spirit of a person's vital force that is expressed in consciousness and intelligence, and *p`o* is the spirit of a person's physical nature that is expressed in bodily strength and movements. Both *hun* and *p`o* require the nourishment of the essences of the vital forces of the cosmos to stay healthy. When a person dies a natural death, his or her *hun* gradually disperses in heaven, and the *p`o,* perhaps in a similar manner, returns to earth.

Underlying this theory of the two souls is the *yin-yang* dichotomy. *Yin* and *yang* symbolize the two primordial forces of the cosmos. *Yin,* the receptive, consolidating, and conserving female element, and *yang,* the active, creative, and expanding male element, give rise to the multiplicity of things through their continuous and dynamic interactions. The rela-

tionship between *yin* and *yang* is competitive, complementary, and dialectic. Furthermore, there is always a *yang* element in the *yin* and a *yin* element in the *yang;* the *yang* element in the *yin* also contains *yin* and the *yin* element in the *yang* also contains *yang.* This infinite process of mutual penetration makes an exclusivistic dichotomy (such as a dichotomy between creator and creature, spirit and matter, mind and body, secular and sacred, consciousness and existence, or soul and flesh) inoperative as a conceptual apparatus in Chinese cosmological thinking.

Ch`i,* which means both energy and matter, denotes, in classical Chinese medicine, the psychophysiological strength and power associated with blood and breath. Like the Greek idea of *pneuma,* or its more intriguing Platonic formulation of *psuche, ch`i is the air-breath that binds the world together. Indeed, its expansion *(yang)* and contraction *(yin),* two simple movements each containing infinite varieties of complexity, generate the multiplicity of the universe. This distinctively biological and specifically sexual interpretation makes the Chinese explanatory model significantly different from any cosmology based on physics or mechanics. To the Chinese, the cosmos came into being not because of the willful act of an external creator or the initial push of a prime mover. Rather, it is through the continuous interaction of Heaven and Earth, or the mutual penetration of *yin* and *yang,* that the cosmos *(yu-chou),* an integration of time and space, emerged out of chaos, an undifferentiated wholeness. Implicit in the differentiating act of chaos itself are the two primary movements of *ch`i—yin* and *yang.* Since the cosmos is not fixed, there has been continuous creativity. Thus change and transformation are the defining characteristics of the cosmos, which is not a static structure but a dynamic process.

The "continuity of being" that exists because of the nature of *ch`i,* the cosmic energy that animates the whole universe from stone to Heaven, makes it impossible to imagine a clear separation between spirit and matter and, by implication, flesh and soul.

From the perspective of *ch`i,* the uniqueness of being human lies in the fact that we are endowed with the finest of the vital forces in the cosmos. Human beings are therefore the embodiments of the soul.

BIBLIOGRAPHY

There is no single work on the subject. Information can be gleaned from a variety of sources.

Balazs, Étienne. "The First Chinese Materialist." In his *Chinese Civilization and Bureaucracy: Variations on a Theme,* edited by Arthur F. Wright and translated by H. M. Wright, pp. 255-276. New Haven, 1964.

Bodde, Derk. "The Chinese View of Immortality: Its Expression by Chu Hsi and Its Relationship to Buddhist Thought." *Review of Religion* 6 (May 1942): 369-383.

Chan, Wing-tsit, ed. and trans. *A Source Book in Chinese Philosophy.* Princeton, 1963. See pages 11-13 and 299-383.

Fung Yu-lan. *A History of Chinese Philosophy,* vol. 2, *The Period of Classical Learning* (1953). 2d ed. Translated by Derk Bodde. Princeton, 1973. For a discussion of Fan Chen's "On the Mortality of the Soul," see pages 289-292.

Liebenthal, Walter. "The Immortality of the Soul in Chinese Thought." *Monumenta Nipponica* 8 (1952): 327-397.

Loewe, Michael. *Ways to Paradise: The Chinese Quest for Immortality.* London, 1979.

Loewe, Michael. *Chinese Ideas of Life and Death.* London, 1982.

Maspero, Henri. "Taoism in Chinese Religious Beliefs of the Six Dynasties Period." In his *Taoism and Chinese Religion,* translated by Frank A. Kierman, pp. 265-298. Amherst, 1981. A Taoist approach to immortality.

Mote, F. W. *Intellectual Foundations of China.* New York, 1971.

Needham, Joseph. Science and Civilisation in China, vol. 5, pt. 2, *Chemistry and Chemical Technology.* Cambridge, 1974. See pages 71-126.

Tsuda Sayukichi. "Shinmetsu fumetsu no ronso ni tsuite." *Toyogakuho* 24, no. 1 (1942): 1-52 and 24, no. 2 (1942): 33-80.

Tu Wei-ming, "The Continuity of Being: Chinese Visions of Nature." In his *Confucian Thought: Selfhood as Creative Transformation,* pp. 35-50. Albany, N. Y., 1985.

Yü Ying-shih. "Views of Life and Death in Later Han China, A. D. 25-220." Thesis, Harvard University, 1962.

TU WEI-MING

Jewish Concept

According to the Hebrew Bible, a dead human being remains in possession of the soul upon entering She'ol, a shadowy place sometimes synonymous with the grave, where the vitality and energy associated with worldly life are drastically decreased. Since both the body and the soul enter She'ol, the later doctrine of the resurrection (as expressed in *Isaiah* 24-27 and *Daniel* 12) indicates a reentry into life in both aspects. The first definite appearance in Jewish thought of a doctrine of personal survival of death in a general resurrection of the dead comes in the literature associated with the Hasmonean Revolt (166-164 BCE), from which time it increases in importance to become a central dogma, later a part of the basic doctrine of Christianity.

The work in the Hebrew canon that expresses the idea of resurrection most explicitly is the *Book of Daniel.* The final chapter of this Hebrew-Aramaic text of the second century BCE expands some details of the divine judgment of the nations with a "secret" revelation wherein it is made known that at some future time many of the dead will wake to everlasting life, while some will wake only to eternal suffering.

Rabbinic Views. The Palestinian Talmud (J. T., *Kil.* 8.4, 31c) attributes the origin of different portions of the physical body to human parents, while the spirit, life, and soul are attributed to God. This admits a greater duality than is acknowledged in the Hebrew Bible, but the soul is regarded as the active element, and so is responsible for sin, while the body is only its vehicle. Such an attitude is contrary to Greek views known in Hellenistic Judaea whereby the body is seen as a trap that debases or hinders the soul. According to Kaufmann Kohler and Ephraim Urbach (see, respectively, *Jewish Theology* and *The Sages,*) this view of the body as the source of sin and impurity is not found in rabbinic Judaism. Urbach also concluded that neither the concept of the soul's immortality, separate from the body, nor the idea of its transmigration into other bodies, is rabbinic. The absence of early, authoritative pronouncements on such points allowed for widely variant speculations within later orthodox and heterodox thought. Talmudic Judaism, as Urbach indicates, found moral duality existing within the soul, which contains both good and evil impulses, the latter including the ambitious, self-centered, and envious impulses in human beings that must be controlled rather than extirpated. The Talmud presents the soul as a supernatural entity created and bestowed by God and joined to a terrestrial body (B. T., *Ber.* 60a). God takes back the soul at death, but later restores it to the dead body.

Qabbalistic Views. According to Qabbalah, man is a spiritual being whose body is merely an external wrapping. There are three essentially different parts of the soul in qabbalistic thought, designated by the Hebrew terms *nefesh, ruah,* and *neshamah.* The *nefesh* is the vital element and enters the body at birth; it dominates the physical and psychological aspects of the self. In contrast, the *ruah* and *neshamah* must be developed through spiritual discipline. The *ruah* comes into being when a person can overcome the body and its desires and it is thus associated with the ethical aspects of life. The *neshamah* is the highest part of the soul and is produced through study of the Torah and observation of the commandments. Torah study awakens the higher centers, through which the individual attains the capacity to apprehend God and the secrets of creation.

According to Qabbalah, the *nefesh, ruah,* and *neshamah* have different destinies after death. The *nefesh* hovers over the body for a time; the ruah goes to a terrestrial realm assigned according to its virtue, and the *neshamah* returns to its home with the divine. Only the *nefesh* and *ruah* are subject to punishment.

BIBLIOGRAPHY

For a brief discussion of the historical and theoretical background of Jewish views of the soul, see Louis Jacobs's *A Jewish Theology* New York, 1973). Walther Eichrodt provides a useful treatment of Israelite views of the human personality and the problem of death in *Theology of the Old Testament,* 2 vols. (Philadelphia, 1961-1967); see pages 118-150 and 210-228 in volume 2. Louis Ginzberg offers an incomparable survey of the entire postbiblical period in *The Legends of the Jews,* 7 vols. (1909-1938; Philadelphia, 1937-1966). His survey includes the intertestamental literature and the writings of the church fathers on biblical events, as well as Jewish sources through the nineteenth century.

Although dated, George Foot Moore's *Judaism in the First Centuries of the Christian Era; The Age of Tannaim,* 3 vols. (1927-1930; Cambridge, Mass., 1970), remains a classic treatment of post-biblical sectarian Jewish literature, particularly the pseudopigrapha and the other Talmudic and Midrashic literature. On concepts involving the soul, see especially pages 368-371, 404, and 486-489 in volume 1; pages 279-322 ("Retribution after Death"), 353, and 377-395 {"Eschatology"} in volume 2; and pages 148 (note 206), 196-197, and 204-205 in volume 3. A more advanced and detailed work then Moore's, and one covering a longer period, is E. E. Urbach's *The Sages: Their Concepts and Beliefs,* 2 vols. (1969; Jerusalem, 1975). The chapter titled "Man" in volume 1 covers in great detail the Talmudic and Midrashic views on ensoulment, preexistence, and embryonic consciousness, as well as related concepts, and attempts to determine the relative and absolute chronologies of statements and their attribution in the sources. Notes on pages 784-800 in volume 2 and the bibliography, pages 1061-1062, cite many earlier secondary studies. A specialized work is Shalom Spiegel's *The Last Trial: On the Legends and Lore of the Command to Abraham to Offer Issac as a Sacrifice; The Akedah* (1950; Philadelphia, 1967), which includes a chapter on the soul's flight from the body and the dew of resurrection in Midrashic literature.

A recent, comprehensive survey from the perspective of philosophy is Julius Guttman's *Philosophies of Judaism: The History of Jewish Philosophy from Biblical Times to Franz Rosenzweig* (1933; New York, 1964). Articles on the Jewish concept of the soul from the *Encyclopedia Judaica* (Jerusalem, 1971) have been collected together with new material, in a single volume; *Jewish Philosophers,* edited by Steven T. Katz (New York, 1975). On the philosophy of Philo, see Harry A. Wolfson's *Philo: Foundations of Religious Philosophy in Judaism, Christianity and Islam,* 2 vols. (Cambridge, Mass., 1947); see especially chapter 7, "Souls, Angels, Immortality," in volume 1. Issac Husik's *A History of Medieval Jewish Philosophy* (1916); New York, 1969) remains a standard, detailed survey of Jewish philosophies in the Middle Ages. For the concept of the soul during this period, a useful but rather narrowly focused volume is Philip David Bookstaber's *The Idea of Development of the Soul in Medieval Jewish Philosophy* (Philadelphia, 1950).

Articles by Gershom Scholem written for the *Encyclopedia Judaica* have been collected in *Kabbalah* (New York, 1974); see especially "Man and His Soul (Psychology and Anthropology of the Kabbalah)" and "Gilgul," on the transmigration of souls.

JACK BEMPORAD

Christian Concept

Origin of the Soul. Within the development of Christian thought on the origin of the individual soul, three views have been maintained: (1) creationism, (2) traducianism, and (3) reincarnationism.

Creationism is the doctrine that God creates a new soul for each human being at conception. Traducianism is the theory that the soul is transmitted along with the body by the parents. Reincarnationism (a form of resurrection belief) is alien to Christian thought, but this supposition is not warranted by the evidence. The doctrine of the preexistence of the

soul was certainly held by Origen and others in the tradition of Christian Platonism.

Destiny of the Soul. Paul taught that since "the wages of sin is death" (*Rom.* 6:23), man has no more entitlement to immortality than has any other form of life. Thanks, however, to the power of Christ's resurrection, every man and woman of the Christian way who truly believes in the power of Christ will rise with him (*Phil.* 3:21) in a body that will be like Christ's "glorious" body *(to somati tes doxes autou).* The resurrection of Christ makes us capable of personal resurrection, yet we can attain our own resurrection only insofar as we appropriate the power of Christ, which we can do through believing in its efficacy and accepting his divine gift of salvation from death and victory over the grave.

Origen (c. 185-c. 254) and his influential Christian school at Alexandria taught that the soul preexisted in an incorporeal state and was imprisoned in a physical body as a result of its former waywardness. Origen probably also taught a form of reincarnationism. Gregory of Nyssa (c. 330-c. 395), Nemesius (who was bishop of Emesa toward the end of the fourth century), and the Greek theologian Maximos the Confessor (c. 580-662), all interpreted the biblical concepts of the soul along Platonic lines and in the general tradition of Origen and his school.

In the thirteenth century, Thomas Aquinas follows the doctrine of the soul presented in Aristotle's *Eudemus,* teaching that, while body and soul together constitute a unity, the soul, as the "form" of the body, is an individual "spiritual substance" and as such is capable of leading a separate existence after the death of the body. This medieval doctrine of the soul, while largely determining the official teaching of the Roman Catholic church on the nature of the soul and its destiny, also indelibly imprinted itself on the theology of the Reformation. For the classical reformers, although contemporaneous with the great Renaissance movement in Europe, were thoroughly medieval in the mold of their theological thinking. The fact that Thomas described the essence of the pain of hell as the loss of the vision of God did little to mitigate the horror of hell in the popular mind.

In popular preaching during the Middle Ages and for centuries thereafter, hell was invariably depicted as a physical fire in which the souls of the damned, being somehow endowed with temporary bodies equipped to suffer physical pain, are eventually summoned on the Last Day to have their original bodies returned and enabled to suffer everlasting torture under the same conditions. The angels, however, according to Thomas, have no physical bodies; therefore Satan and the other denizens of hell must be equipped in some other way to undergo, as they certainly must, the punishment superabundantly due to them in the place of torment over which they reign.

Out of confusion in the concept of the soul, then, had sprung an increasing confusion in the Christian view of its destiny, making eschatology the least coherent aspect of the Christian theological tradition. For example, the soul has an independent existence and is sometimes envisioned, in Platonic fashion, as well rid of the burden of its physical encumbrance. Yet in the end the whole man, body and soul, must be restored in order to enjoy the fruits of Christ's redemption.

According to Roman Catholic theology, each soul on its separation from the body is subjected to a "particular" judgment, as distinguished from the final or "general" judgment. In 1336, Pope Benedict XII, in his bull *Benedictus Deus,* specifically declared that souls, having been subjected to this particular judgment, are admitted at once to the beatific vision, which is heaven, or proceed at once to purgatory to be cleansed and readied for the heavenly state, or are consigned to hell.

BIBLIOGRAPHY

For the Hebrew background of the New Testament view, a reliable source is the brief article "Soul" by Norman Porteous in *The Interpreter's Dictionary of the Bible* (New York, 1962). Rudolf Bultmann provides abundant background for an understanding of the New Testament writers' general outlook in his *Theology of the New Testament,* vol. 1 (New York, 1951). Oscar Cullmann has written an important essay on this topic, which was published in *Immortality and Resurrection,* edited by Krister Stendahl (New York, 1965). The other essays in this collection, by Harry A. Wolfson, Werner Yaeger, and Henry J. Cadbury, also merit attention. Augustine's view, articulated in his *On the Immortality of the Soul,* greatly influenced both the medieval schoolmen and the reformers. *Saint Thomas and the Problem of the Soul in the Thirteenth Century* (Toronto, 1934), by Anton C. Pegis, provides a useful introduction to the view of Thomas Aquinas as set forth in the first volume of his *Summa theologiae.* Étienne Gilson treats the subject in his study *The Spirit of Mediaeval Philosophy* (London, 1936), and John Calvin discusses the origin, immortal nature, and other aspects of the soul in his *Institutes of the Christian Religion,* 2 vols. (Philadelphia, 1960). For the Renaissance view of Pietro Pomponazzi, see Clement C. J. Webb's *Studies in the History of Natural Theology* (Oxford, 1915).

The soul plays a central role in the various forms of Christian mysticism. The notion of the "fine point" of the soul, a cell remaining sensitive to God despite the fall and consequent corruption of mankind, is a common topic of such literature: for example, see *The Living Flame of Love* by John of the Cross. For the Salesian tradition, see Henri Bremond's treatment in his *Histoire littéraire du sentiment religieux en France* (1915-1932), 2d ed. (Paris, 1967-1968), edited by René Taveneaux, especially vol. 7. Whether any form of reincarnationism is reconcilable to Christian faith is specifically considered in two books of mine: *Reincarnation in Christianity* (Wheaton, Ill., 1978) and *Reincarnation as a Christian Hope* (London, 1982).

GEDDES MACGREGOR

Islamic Concepts

Traditional Concepts. In Islam, the most prevalent concepts of the soul can perhaps best be termed "traditional." Their immediate inspiration is the Qur'an, interpreted literally, and the *hadith,* or "tradition." A chief source for our knowledge of the traditional concepts of the soul in Islam is *Kitab al-ruh* (The Book of the Spirit), by the Damascene Ibn Qayyim al-Jawziyah (d. 1350), a celebrated Hanbali theologian and jurisconsult.

The term *ruh,* Ibn Qayyim maintains, is applicable in Arabic usage to both the spirit that comes from God and the human spirit. In the Qur'an, however, it is used to refer to the spirit that comes from God. This spirit proceeds from the *amr* of God. The term *amr* in the Qur'an, Ibn Qayyim insists, always means "command." Since the spirit proceeds from the command of God, it is a created being, although its creation antedates the creation of the human soul. The human body is created before the human soul. The latter, though created, is everlasting. Death means the separation of this soul from the body, to rejoin it permanently when the resurrection takes place. When the Qur'an speaks of the soul that incites to evil, the soul that upbraids, and the tranquil soul, this does not mean that a human has three souls. These, Ibn Qayyim argues, are characteristics of one and the same human soul.

During sleep, souls leave their bodies temporarily, sometimes communicating with other souls, whether of the living or of the dead. With death, the soul leaves the body but can very swiftly return to it. The souls of the virtuous can communicate with each other, the wicked souls being too preoccupied in their torments for this. For in the interim between death and the resurrection, most souls rejoin their bodies in the grave to be questioned by the two angels of death, Munkar and Nakir. The wicked, unbelieving souls suffer punishment and torment in the grave, while the virtuous believers enjoy a measure of bliss.

Theological (Kalam) Concepts. Islam's dialectical theologians, the *mutakallimun,* no less than the more traditional Muslims, sought to uphold a Qur'anic concept of the soul. They sought to uphold it, however, within scripturally rooted perspectives of the world that they formulated and rationally defended. Their concepts of the human soul were governed largely by two questions, one metaphysical, the other eschatological. The metaphysical question pertained to the ultimate constituents of the created world: Do these consist of indivisible atoms or of what is potentially infinitely divisible? The eschatological question arose out of their doctrine of bodily resurrection: if, in the ages between the world's beginning and its end, dead human bodies decompose to become parts of other physical entities (organic or inorganic), how can there be a real resurrection, that is, a return to life of the actual individuals who once lived and died, and not the mere creation anew of replicas of them?

Regarding the metaphysical question, most of the *mutakallimun* were atomists. Their concepts of the soul were for the most part materialist: they regarded it either as a body, or identified it with life, which they maintained is a transient quality, an accident, that occurs to a body.

In terms of the eschatological question, some of the Mu`tazilah ("rationalists") resorted to the doctrine that nonexistence *(al`adam)* is "a thing" *(shay')* or "an entity," "an essence" *(dhat)*, to which existence is a state that occurs. Thus a nonexistent entity *A* acquires existence for a span of time, loses it during another span, and regains it eternally at the resurrection, *A* remaining *A* throughout all these stages.

Sufi Concepts. In considering this very vast subject, it is well to differentiate between three of its aspects: (1) what Sufis conceived the human soul to be, (2) the soul's purification and the path of holiness it must follow as it seeks God, (3) the relation of the soul to God, particularly in its intimate experiencing of the divine. These aspects are related, but the third represents a central issue on which Sufis were divided and which caused controversy in the general history of Islamic religious thought.

The relation of the soul to God in Sufi thought takes on a highly metaphysical turn in the complex theosophy of the great mystic Ibn al-`Arabi (d. 1240) and his followers, particularly `Abd al-Karim al-Jili (d. 1408?). Ibn al-`Arabi is noted for his doctrine of the unity of being *(wahdat al-wujud)* wherein creation *(al-khalq)* is a mirroring of the Truth *(al-haqq)*, the Creator. Perfect souls are reflections of the perfection of the divine essence. The prophets are the archetypes of these perfect souls: each prophet is a word *(kalimah)* of God. The perfect soul is a microcosm of reality. The idea of man as a microcosm did not originate with Ibn al-`Arabi; it was utilized by the *falasifah* and by al-Ghazali. But with Ibn al-`Arabi and those who followed him it acquires a spiritual and metaphysical dimension all its own, representing a high point in the development of the concept of soul in the history of Islamic religious thought.

BIBLIOGRAPHY

For a comprehensive study, see D. B. Macdonald's "The Development of the Idea of Spirit in Islam," *Acta Orientalia* (1931): 307-351, reprinted in *The Moslem World* 22 (January and April 1932): 25-42, 153-168. For Qur'anic, traditional, and *kalam* concepts, see Régis Blachère's "Note sur le substantif 'nafs' dans le Coran," *Semitica* 1 (1948): 69-77; F. T. Cooke's "Ibn al-Quiyim's Kitab al-Ruh," *The Moslem World* 25 (April 1935): 129-144; and Albert N. Nader's *Le système philosophique des mu`tazila* (Beirut, 1956); see also the work by Majid Fakhry cited below. For philosophical concepts, see Avicenna's "On the Proof of Prophecies," translated by me in *Medieval Political Philosophy: A Sourcebook*, edited by Ralph Lerner and Muhsin Mahdi (New York, 1963), pp. 112-121; Majid Fakhry's *A History of Islamic Philosophy*, 2d ed. (New York, 1983); Lenn E. Goodman's "Rasi's Myth of the Fall of the Soul," in *Essays on Islamic Philosophy and Science*, edited by George F. Hourani (Albany, N. Y., 1975), pp. 25-40; my article "Avicenna and the Problem of the Infinite Number of Souls," *Mediaeval Studies* 22 (1960); 232-239; and *Avicenna's Psychology*, edited and translated by Fazlur Rahman (London, 1952). For Sufi concepts, see A. E. Affifi's *The Mystical Philosophy of Muhyid Din Ibnul `Arabi* (Cambridge, 1939); A. J. Arberry's *Sufism* (1950; reprint, London, 1979); Ibn al-`Arabi's *The Bezels of Wisdom*, translated with an introduction and notes by R. W. J. Austin (London, 1980); Reynold A. Nicholson's *Studies in Islamic Mysticism* (1921; reprint, Cambridge, 1976); Annemarie Schimmel's *Mystical Dimensions of Islam* (Chapel Hill, N. C., 1975); and Fadlou Shehadi's *Ghazali's Unique Unknowable God* (Leiden, 1964).

MICHAEL E. MARMURA

SOUTH AMERICAN INDIANS

Indians of the Andes

The Andean region is formed by the Andes mountain range, which extends the entire length of western South America. This region can be divided into three geographically contrasting subareas: the highlands, the coast, and the eastern cordillera. In the highlands the intermontane valleys lie at altitudes of between three and four thousand meters. These valleys were the places in which the Chavín (tenth to first centuries BCE), Tiahuanaco-Huari (eighth to tenth centuries CE), and Inca (fifteenth century CE) cultures flourished. In the region along the Pacific coast, composed mostly of low-lying desert plains, life was concentrated out of necessity in the valleys formed by the rivers that drain from the highlands into the ocean. The coastal valleys in the Peruvian sector of the Andes region were the cradles of cultures such as the Moche (second to eighth centuries CE), the Paracas-Nazca (second to eighth centuries CE), and the Chimú (twelfth to fifteenth centuries CE), who devised colossal irrigation works that enabled them to bring extensive areas of desert under cultivation. The dramatic, abruptly changing topography of the eastern cordillera is covered by dense tropical vegetation. Peoples of the intermontane valleys entered this region and built the cities of Machu Picchu and Pajatén, and they terraced vast areas of the rugged, wooded hillsides to gain land for cultivation and to prevent erosion.

The sheltered agricultural cultures of the Andes have interrelated since ancient times. The areas where such cultures did not develop, although geographically "Andean," are not considered part of the Andean *cultural* region. The territory of the central Andes—basically equivalent to present-day Peru—became the center of the Andean cultural process. The northern Andes (parts of present-day Colombia and Ecuador) was the scene of the Quimbaya and Muisca

(Chibcha) cultures and of the earlier Valdivia culture, which may have given the initial impulse to the entire high-Andean culture.

More than ten thousand years have passed since human beings first trod the Andes. The earliest settlers were hunters and Neolithic agriculturalists. By the third millennium BCE there appear incipient signs of complex cultures, such as that of Aldas on the northern coast of Peru, whose people built monumental temples. During the second and first millennia BCE, the appearance of Valdivia and Chavín represented the first flowering of developed culture, which set the foundation for the developments that eventually culminated in the Inca empire. By the time that Europeans arrived in the Americas, the Inca empire stretched for more than four thousand miles along the western part of South America, from southern Colombia in the north to Maule, in south central Chile, in the south. The empire passed into Spanish dominion in 1532, when Atahuallpa, the thirteenth and last of the Inca sovereigns, was beheaded. From then on, the breakdown of indigenous Andean cultural values is apparent.

Subsistence and Religion. The peoples of the Andes are predisposed toward mysticism and ceremonial; even today, Andeans are steeped in an elaborate religious tradition. A significant part of their intense religiosity may be explained by ecological factors: no other agricultural society in the world has had to face a more hostile environment than that of the Andes region, with its vast areas of desert, its enormous wastes, and the heavy tropical vegetation that covers the mountains' rugged eastern flanks. All physical effort, all organization of human labor, and all technological solutions are insufficient to counter the environment, to whose ordinary harshness are added nature's frequent scourges, especially droughts. This endemic state of crisis could only be exorcised, it seems, through intense magico-religious practices; only through manipulation of supernatural powers have Andean peoples believed it possible to guarantee their existence.

The dramatic situation imposed by the environment perhaps explains why Andean religiosity appears to have been unencumbered by the moralizing of other religious traditions. Rules like "Thou shalt not steal" and "Thou shalt not commit adultery" were of course enforced, but theft and adultery were considered social offenses: it was the duty of the administrators of state law to punish offenders. There was no concept of a future expiation. The relationship between religion and morality was closest in regard to behavior toward the deities; if their worship was not properly carried out, they were affronted, resulting in a series of calamities that could be checked through prayers, weeping, and sacrifices. The hostility of nature in the Andes led to a permanently febrile state of religiosity.

Gods of Sustenance. Andean deities jointly governed both individual and collective existence by providing suste-

nance. Soil fertility plays a significant role in Andean religion, as demonstrated by the profuse worship given to the deities that personified and controlled the forces of nature. The gods, though individualized, form a hieratic unit and share one focus: the economic state of the people. They are conceived in the image of nature, which simultaneously separates and conjoins the creative forces, masculine and feminine. Thus the first basic division appears in the opposition of Inti-Viracocha-Pachacámac and Quilla-Pachamama. Both of these deity-configurations are creative forces, but in accordance with the social order of the sexes, the supremacy of the former, masculine element is asserted. The powerful Illapa ("thunder, weather") is also integrated into the sphere of Inti-Viracocha-Pachacámac, but, above all his other functions, Illapa directly provides life-giving rain.

Viracocha. Glimpses of a culture hero on whom divine attributes have been superimposed can be seen in the figure of Viracocha, and therefore Pierre Duviols (1977) and María Rostworowski de Diez Canseco (1983) corectly deny him the character of a creator god. Because of these same divine attributes, however, Viracocha was thought by the sixteenth-century Spaniards to resemble the God of Christianity, although Christian-Andean syncretism preserved some aspects of Viracocha's indigenous origin. Thus, according to the stories told about him, Viracocha molded men in clay or sculpted them in stone. (They finally spring from the womb of Pachamama, "mother earth," which is sometimes represented as a cave.) On the other hand, stories about Viracocha also portray him as entering into confrontations with other divine beings and as engaged in other tasks ordinarily associated with culture heroes (for example, "teaching the created people").

Pachacámac. The myth of Pachacámac ("animator of the world") links this Andean deity even more strongly than Viracocha with the creation of the first generation of human beings. This deity is characterized, above all, as bringing to mankind the food necessary for survival as a result of the entreaties of a primordial woman, Mother Earth. The provision of edible plants is shown in other myths: in one of these, Pachacámac disguises himself, taking the form of the sun (in some instances, the son, the brother, or even the father of Pachacámac, according to the chronicler Francisco Lopez de Gómara), who with his rays fertilizes the primordial woman, perhaps the incarnation of Pachamama. In another myth, Pachacámac kills what he has created, and this action may be interpreted as the institution of human sacrifice to nourish the food and fertility deities. When the victim is buried, his teeth sprout maize, his bones become manioc, and so on.

Inti. According to both the surviving mythic literature and the images discovered by archaeologists, the masculine creative force was incarnated in Inti, the sun. He offers heat and light, and his rays possess fertilizing powers, as is evident in the myth of Pachacámac. Mythic literature testifies to the

Andeans' reliance on the power of the sun and to their anxiety that he may disappear, causing cataclysm and the destruction of mankind (an event that would be followed by the creation of a new generation of men). This anxiety explains the redoubled prayers and supplications during solar eclipses—rituals that ended with loud cries and lamentations (even domestic animals were whipped to make them howl!). Archaeological evidence of another form of magicoreligious defense against this premonition of the tragic disappearance of the sun is found in stone altars called *intihuatanas*, a word revealingly translated as "the place where the sun is tied." Inti was also associated with fertility through water, as when the sun ceases to give light.

Pachamama-Quilla. Pachamama ("mother earth") symbolized the feminine element of divinity for the Andeans. Pachamama is incarnated as the primordial mother of mythic literature, and she is personified as Quilla, the moon. In this connection she is symbolized by silver; with this metal many representations of Pachamama were made, especially in the form of the half-moon (called *tumi*), which was one of the most important religious symbols of the Andes. The cult

> **Pachamama is incarnated as the primordial mother of mythic literature. . . .**

of Pachamama was, and still is, extensive (Mariscotti de Görlitz, 1978). Pachamama was held to be the producer of food, animals, and the first man. As primordial mother, she creates through the fertilizing action of the Sun, and she later becomes co-donor of food plants, especially maize.

The mythological literature tells of several female supernatural beings. These are likely regional versions of Pachamama. Among them are Chaupiñanca, the primordial mother of Huarochirí mythology; Illa, who appears in the mythic traditions of the Ecuadorian Andes; and Urpihuáchac, sister and wife of Pachacámac, who seems to be an expression of Cochamama, the marine form of Pachamama. To Cochamama is attributed the creation of fish and of seabirds such as the guanay, which latter act is in turn related to agricultural productivity because of the use of guano to fertilize crops.

Ancient documents show that Pachamama was individualized *ad infinitum* to guarantee the abundance of specific produce—maize, for example. Andean iconography offers representations of Pachamama incarnated in specific vegetable forms: multiple ears of maize, for instance, or groups of potatoes. In other instances these agricultural products metaphorically acquire human aspects, and they are also portrayed as being fertilized by a supernatural, anthropomorphic personage. Pachamama in her Cochamama aspect also

appears to symbolize the presence of abundant water—essential for fertilizing the agricultural fields.

The symbolism of Pachamama has implications regarding the social status of women: as compared with the male element of divinity, Pachamama, the female, is clearly a passive and subaltern being. The attitude of sexual modesty is to be seen in the many representations that appear to show versions of Pachamama, from the archaic terracotta figures of Valdivia to those of the late Chancay civilization of the central coast of Peru. In all these, sexual characteristics are not pronounced: the figures seem to represent almost asexual beings, and they remind one of the existence of non-Christian sexual taboos (see Kauffmann Doig, 1979a). Not only do these figures rarely stress sexual characteristics, but, curiously, they seldom portray pregnant women or women giving birth.

Pachamama still plays an important role in the deeply rooted peasant magic of today's Andean people. She is even venerated in Christian churches. In the Peruvian village of Huaylas, for example, Saramama (a version of Pachamama) is venerated in the form of two female saints who are joined in a single sculpture—like Siamese twins—to give visual representation to a pathetic fallacy: the symbolization of abundance that is identified in the double or multiple ears of grain that maize plants often generously produce.

Illapa. The deity Illapa (generally translated as "thunder," "lightning," or "weather") occupies a preferential place in the Andean pantheon. Much of the mythological literature makes reference to Illapa, who takes on regional names and is expressed in varying forms: Yaro, Ñamoc, Libiac, Catequil, Pariacaca, Thunapa (possibly), and so on. To refer to these beings as if they were separate would be artificially to crowd the Andean pantheon by creating too great a number of distinct deities—a trap into which many interpreters, both early and recent, have fallen. Illapa may be seen as the incarnation of Inti, the sun, in Illapa's primary mythic form of a hawk or eagle (*indi* means "bird" in Quechua), a form to which were added human and feline attributes; thus Inti-Illapa may be said to be a true binomial in the Andean pantheon.

Associated with meteorological phenomena such as thunder, lightning, clouds, and rainbows, Illapa personifies rain, the element that fecundates the earth. As the direct source of sustenance—giving rains to the highlands and rivers and rich alluvial soils to the coastal valleys—Illapa is revered in a special and universal way.

After the Conquest, Andeans fused Illapa with images of James the Apostle, a syncretism perhaps suggested by earlier Spanish traditions. In the realm of folklore, Illapa's cult may be said still to flourish in the veneration of hills and high mountains, which are the nesting places of the *huamani* (falcons) sacred to this deity. Also associated with Illapa are the *apus*, the spirits of the mountains, and the spirits of the lakes, which, if they are not worshiped, make the waves rise destructively, and which are offended if approached by someone not protected by the sacred coca leaf.

When he appears as an incarnation of, or as joined to, Inti, Illapa may be represented by a male feline with human and avian attributes. According to iconographic studies, Illapa's image as the "flying feline," or "tiger bird" (Kauffmann Doig, 1967; 1983, p. 225) is still current in the Andes, as witnessed in the oral documentation collected by Bernard Mishkin (1963) regarding Qoa, a god who is ruler of meteorological phenomena. Qoa still appears as a flying cat, his eyes throwing out lightning and his urine transformed into fertilizing rain. Pictorial representations of the "tiger bird," which have been made since the formative period, especially in Chavín and allied art (see below) have recently been related to Qoa by Johan Reinhard (1985, pp. 19-20).

Andean Iconography. Iconographic portrayal of supernatural beings is abundant and dates back more than three thousand years.

The image of a conspicuously superior being is found in the initial stages of high Andean civilization (especially in Chavín and related cultures). This image, typically a human form with feline and raptorial-bird attributes, is repeated in practically all the Andean cultures that succeeded Chavín, with variations of secondary importance. At Chavín, such hierarchal figures of the highest order appear on the Raimondi Stela; although lacking human elements, the figures on the Tello Obelisk and the Yauya Stela, both Chavín in style, may also be considered as representations of the highest level of being, because of their monumental stature and fine execution. The central figure of the Door of the Sun at Tiahuanaco is an almost anthropomorphic representation of the highest-ranking god. Attributes of a culture hero are perhaps also incorporated here.

A frequently encountered image of what was perhaps the same god as the one described above (but represented in a clearer and more accessible form) is that of a hybrid being that also had a form somewhere between a feline and a bird of prey (a falcon?), represented naturalistically, in which elements of human anatomy are sometimes completely absent. This "winged feline" may be the most ancient and authentic representation known to us of an Andean god. The convoluted, baroque style of Chavín art is responsible for the fact the the "winged feline" has sometimes been identified as a caiman and sometimes as a lobster, a shrimp, or even a spider. These animals, however, do not appear in relation to the divine sphere at any later stage of Andean culture.

Supernatural beings of the highest category are to be found in representations of the culture-heroes/gods Ai-apaec and Ñaymlap and of the gods at Tiahuanaco and Paracas-Nazca. All are anthropomorphic beings that combine traits of both bird and feline; in this context they imply an evolutionary development of the older "winged feline" of Chavín. In the archetypical versions of Ai-apaec, the figure bears wings

(Kauffmann Doig, 1976; 1983, pp. 362, 624). At Paracas-Nazca, one figure seems to represent an evolution from a purely birdlike body into one that incorporates human elements (Kauffmann Doig, 1983, pp. 303, 325, 331-332). Feline and ornithomorphic ingredients are evident in the large figures at Tiahuanaco and Huari; from their eyes fall large tears in the form of birds, which, since Eugenio Yacovleff (1932) and even before, have been interpreted as symbolic of the fertilizing rainwater of Pachamama (Mamapacha).

Connubial gods in which the male element radiates fertilizing solar rays are found especially in the iconography derived from Huari and, more particularly, in the valleys of Huara, Pativilca, and Casma on the coast of Peru (Kauffmann Doig, 1979a, pp. 6, 60). The examples of Inca art that have survived have but scant votive content. But both the feline and the falcon continue to occupy their place of honor among iconographic elements, as may be seen in the "heraldic shield" of the Inca rulers drawn by Guaman Poma.

Forms of Worship. Through acts of worship, the sphere of the sacred could be manipulated to benefit mankind. The effectiveness of human intervention into the realm of the supernatural powers depended on the intensity with which the rites were performed. In the Andean world, where natural factors put agricultural production and even existence itself to a constant test, worship assumed an extraordinary intensity and richness of form. The calamities that endangered personal and collective welfare were believed to have been caused by offenses to supernatural beings and especially to a lack of intensity in worship. Offerings to the gods of sustenance and to other supernatural beings related to them complemented the cultic display. Cruel sacrifices were necessary to worship's efficacy; in times of crisis they were performed lavishly and included human sacrifices.

The popular form of communication with *huaca* (i. e.. the entire supernatural world) was effected through the *muchay* ("worship, reverence"). *Muchay* was performed by removing one's sandals, gesticulating, throwing kisses, murmuring supplications, bowing one's shoulders in humility, puffing out one's cheeks to blow in the direction of the object worshiped, and so on. Other forms of contact with supernatural beings were made through oracles, whose traditions go back to early forms of Andean cultures, like the Chavín. Oracles were represented in the form of idols located in sanctuaries such as the famous one of Pachacámac, near Lima; these oracles rendered predictions about important future events to shamans and priests.

To make an offering was an act of paying tribute. Offerings were made voluntarily, but they were also collected in the form of compulsory tribute, the administration of which was centralized in temples. A widespread, popular offering was *mullo*, a powder made of ground seashells, which by association was linked to fertility through water; another was coca (*Erythroxylon coca*) in the form of a masticated wad. Stone cairns in the high passes were places of worship; wads of coca would be thrown in a ritual act called Togana. The mummified dead were offered special jars containing grains, fruits, and liquids. Guinea pigs and llamas served as important sacrificial offerings.

Among sacrifices, that of young boys and girls was the most important; sometimes human sacrifice was performed by walling up a living female person. It appears that among the Inca the sacrifice of boys and girls was received as a form of tribute, called the *capaccocha*, from the provinces. The person who was to serve as the *capaccocha* was delivered to the capital city of Cuzco in great pomp; after his death, his remains were returned to his homeland and mummified; the mummy acquired votive rank and was the object of supplications for health and agricultural welfare. Necropompa (Span., "death rite") was a special type of human sacrifice that consisted of immolations (voluntary or not) that were performed on the occasion of the death of an illustrious person (Araníbar, 1961). Decapitation of human sacrificial victims had been performed since ancient times: the Sechín stone sculpture of northern Peru depicting this practice is over three thousand years old. Head shrinking was rare and there is no evidence of cannibalism in the Andean region. (Though in the myths there are a number of supernatural beings, such as Carhuincho, Carhuallo, and Achké, who are anthropophagous.) Human sacrifice, performed to achieve greater agricultural fertility, drew its rationale from the principle that the Andeans believed governed nature: death engenders life.

The dead, mummified and revered, were expected to implore the supernatural powers for sustenance, soil fertility, abundant water, and the multiplication of domestic animals. Often bodies were buried in the cultivated fields in order to enrich them. As has recently been reported from Ayacucho, Peru, this practice survives in secret, isolated cases even to the present day: a mentally ill person is selected, intoxicated with liquor, thrown into a pit, and buried alive. Such "strenghening" rites were, according to sixteenth-century chroniclers, also practiced in laying the foundations of houses and bridges, and traces of these rites also have been recently reported from the central Andes.

Funeral rites included expressions of grief such as loud sobbing intermingled with chants in praise of the deceased; a practice that also survives in isolated areas of the Andes. The dead were mummified and taken to their tombs on stretchers. With few exceptions (e.g., among the Moche), bodies were buried in seated positions. Frequently the hands held the head, perhaps to simulate the fetal position. These "living" corpses were surrounded with food and drink, weapons, and other belongings meant to serve as provisions in the hereafter; some were buried with their mouths open, both to express the terror of sacrifice and to voice supplications to the gods for success in agriculture.

Religious festivals were celebrated continuously in the great plazas of Cuzco and at temples such as the Coricancha, the temple of the sun. Festivals dedicated to specific themes, especially in the context of food production, were held monthly with great pomp; the sovereign Inca presided, and guests were invited at his expense. Great quantities of *chicha* (maize beer) were consumed, drunk from ceremonial wooden vessels *(queros)*.

Andeans have made pilgrimages since the remote times of Chavín, and one of the favorite *huacas*, or shrines, was the sanctuary of Pachacámac. "Natural" shrines such as those on the peaks of high mountains were also popular with pilgrims. The Collur Riti festival, a celebration that coincides with the Feast of Corpus Christi, follows ancient rites. Originally, the Collur Riti was dedicated to water, and even today pilgrims return to their homes with pieces of ice carved from the mountain glaciers, symbolizing the fertility imparted by water. In the past, pilgrims fasted for variable periods of time, abstaining from maize beer, *ají (Capsicum anuum)*, and sexual intercourse.

Medicine and Magic. Shamans use maracas in their healing rites, a practice carried on into the present by Andean *curanderos* (Span., "healers"). The *curanderos* also use hallucinogenic substances to cause them to enter the trance state. The San Pedro cactus (*Trichocereus pabhanoi*) is a powerful hallucinogen used particularly on the Peruvian coast; it gives the *curandero* the ability to discover the cause of an illness. In the highlands the diagnosis is still made by rubbing the body of a sick person with a guinea pig or with substances such as maize powder. The cure was effected through the use of medicinal plants. Today, *curanderos* complement their ancient remedies with modern pharmaceutical products.

Divination was often performed under the influence of hallucinogens or coca. Several studies, among them those of Alana Cordy-Collins (1977) and Ralph Cané (1985) speculate that the intricate art of Chavín originated in hallucinogenic experiences.

Institutionalized worship gave rise to a rich range of folk magic. Thus, for example, there were magic love-stones (*guacangui*). Small stone sculptures of domestic animals, used to propitiate the spirits of abundance, are still produced. Ceramic figures representing vigorous bulls *(toritos de Pucará)* are still placed on rooftops, where they signify prosperity and fertility and offer magical protection of the home.

Messianism. Andean mysticism and ritual experienced a vigorous rejuvenescence some thirty years after the Spanish conquest in the form of the nativistic movement called Taqui Oncoy (see Duviols, 1977; Millones, 1964; Ossio, 1973; Curatola, 1977; Urbano, 1981). The aims of this sixteenth-century messianic movement were to drive the white invaders from the land and to reinstate the structures of the lost Inca past. The movement's power was based on the worship of *huacas*, the popular form of Andean religiosity after the Sun had lost its credibility with the defeat inflicted by the Christian God. By a kind of magic purification, Taqui Oncoy sought to free the land from European intrusion after it was no longer possible to do so by force of arms. The movement's adherents believed that, with intensified supplications and increased offerings, the *huacas* could become powerful enough to help reestablish the old order. This movement declined after ten years, but the hope of a return to the Inca past is still alive, although it is confined more and more to middle-class intellectual circles in Peru and Bolivia.

The messianic myth of Inkarri (from Span., *Inca rey*, "Inca king") should also be mentioned here. Originally recorded by José María Arguedas (1956), the myth centers on a figure, Inkarri, who is the son of the Sun and a "wild woman." According to Nathan Wachtel (1977), this archetypal "vision of a conquered people," although of native extraction, seems to be immersed in syncretism. The cult of Inkarri lacks the action that characterized the Taqui Oncoy movement. Inkarri is not an Andean god but rather a pale memory of the deified sovereign of ancient times, who after patient waiting will rise to life to vindicate the Andean world.

BIBLIOGRAPHY

Aranibar, Carlos. "Los sacrificios humanos entre los Incas, a través de las crónicas de los siglos XVI y XVII." Ph. D. diss., University of Lima, 1961.

Arguedas, José María. "Puquio: Una cultura en proceso de cambio." *Revista del Museo Nacional* (Lima) 25 (1956): 184-232.

Cane, Ralph. "Problemas arqueológicos e iconográficos: Enfoques nuevos." *Boletín de Lima* 37 (January 1985): 38-44.

Carrion Cachot de Girard, Rebeca. *La religión en el antiguo Perú.* Lima, 1959.

Cordy-Collins, Alana. "Chavín Art: Its Shamanistic/Hallucinogenic Origins." In *Precolumbian Art History*, edited by Alana Cordy-Collins and Jean Stearn, pp. 353-362. Palo Alto, 1977.

Curatola, Marco. "Mito y milenarismo en los Andes: Del Taqui Oncoy a Incarrí: La vision de un pueblo invicto." *Allpanchis Phuturinqa* (Cuzco) 10 (1977): 65-92.

Duviols, Pierre. "Los mombies quechua de Viracocha, supuesto 'dios creador' de los evangeligadores." *Allpanchis Phuturinqa* 10 (1977): 53-63.

Favre, Henri. "Tayta Wamani: Le culte des montanes dans le centre sud des Andes péruviennes." In *Colloque d'études péruviennes*, pp. 121-140. Aix-en-Provence, 1967.

Jijón y Caamaño, Jacínto. *La religión del imperio de los Incas.* Quito, 1919.

Jimenez Borja, Arturo. "Introducción al pensamiento araico peruano." *Revista del Museo Nacional* (Lima) 38 (1972): 191-249.

Karsten, Rafael. "Die altperuanische Religion." *Archiv für Religionswissenschaft* 25 (1927): 36-51.

Kauffmann Doig, Federico. *El Perú arqueológico: Tratado breve sobre el Perú preincaico.* Lima, 1976.

Kauffmann Doig, Federico. *Sexual Behavior in Ancient Peru.* Lima, 1979. Cited in the text as 1979a.

Kauffman Doig, Federico. "Sechín: Ensayo de arqueología iconográfica." *Arqueológicas* (Lima) 18 (1979): 101-142. Cited in the text as 1979b.

Kauffmann Doig, Federico. *Manual de arqueología peruana.* 8th rev. ed. Lima, 1983.

Kauffman Doig, Federico. "Los dioses andinos: Hacia una ca-raterización de la religiosidad andina fundamentada en testimonios arqueológicos y en mitos," *Vida y espiritualidad* (Lima) 3 (1986): 1-16.

Mariscotti de Görlitz, Ana Maria. *Pachamama Santa Tierra: Contribución al estudio de la religión autoctona en los Andes centro-meridionales.* Berlin, 1978.

Métraux, Alfred. *Religions et magies indiennes d'Amérique du Sud.* Paris, 1967.

Millones, Luis. "Un movimiento nativista del siglo XVI: El Taki Onqoy." *Revista peruana de cultura* (Lima) 3 (1964).

Mishkin, Bernard. "The Contemporary Quechua." In *Handbook of South American Indians* (1946), edited by Julian H. Steward, vol. 2, pp. 411-470. Reprint, Washington, D. C.,1963.

Ortiz Rescaniere, Alejandro. *De Adaneva a Inkarrí.* Lima, 1973.

Ossio, Juan M. "Guaman Poma: Nueva coronica o carta al rey: Un intento de approximación a las categorías del pensamiento del mundo andino." In *Ideología mesianica del mundo andino*, 2d ed., edited by Juan M. Ossio, pp. 153-213. Lima, 1973.

Pease, Franklin. *El dios creador andino.* Lima, 1973.

Reinhard, Johan. "Chavín and Tiahuanaco: A New look at Two Andean Ceremonial Centers." *National Geographic Research* 1 (1985): 395-422.

Rostworowski de Diez Canseco, María. *Estructuras andinas del poder: Ideología religiosa y política.* Lima, 1983.

Rowe, John Howland. "The Origins of Creator Worship among the Incas." In *Culture in History*, edited by Stanley Diamond, pp. 408-429. New York, 1969.

Tello, Julio C. "Wira-Kocha." *Inca* 1 (1923): 93-320, 583-606.

Trimborn, Hermann. "South Central America and the Andean Civilizations." In *Pre-Columbian American Religions*, edited by Walter Krickeberg et al., pp. 83-146. New York, 1968.

Valcárcel, Luis E. "Símbolos mágico-religiosos en la cultura andina." *Revista del Museo Nacional* (Lima) 28 (1959): 3-18.

Wachtel, Nathan. *The Vision of the Vanquished: The Spanish Conquest of Peru through Indian Eyes*, 1530-1570. New York, 1977.

Yacovleff, Eugenio. "Las Falcónidas en el atre y en las creencias de los antiguos peruanos." *Revista del Museo Nacional* (Lima) 1 (1932): 35-101.

FEDERICO KAUFFMANN DOIG
Translated from Spanish by Mary Nickson

Indians of the Tropical Forest

The vast region of lowland South America, mostly drained by the Amazon and Orinoco river systems and mainly covered in tropical forest, presents at first glance an area of exceptional uniformity, but in fact it is comprised of a bewildering variety of microenvironments. The Indian societies that inhabit the region are likewise characterized by great variety masked by apparent uniformity. They have in common such features as the reliance for subsistence on shifting cultivation, hunting, fishing, and gathering, but at the same time they exhibit numerous minute variations. However, these differences are kaleidoscopic patterns put together from similar pieces. It is only because this is so that it is possible to make generalizations about the religions of lowland South America.

Today when one talks about the Indian societies of lowland South America one is referring to relatively small groups—a population of ten thousand is large, and most groups number only a few hundred—dwelling in tiny settlements away from the main waterways. In the past, things were different. Estimates of the pre-Conquest population vary between one and ten million, but whatever the actual number, it is certain that the population declined abruptly, perhaps by as much as 95 percent overall, beginning with the arrival of Europeans at the end of the fifteenth century. At that time, the coasts and main rivers, today virtually without an aboriginal population, were densely inhabited, and in contrast to modern Indian villages, there were large settlements of one thousand or more inhabitants. From this it is relatively safe to surmise that the Indians' social, political, and economic organizations were different from those observable today among extant groups. Despite the fact that the latter are in many cases the fugitive remnants of earlier groups, it is difficult to identify in them features that might be transformations of earlier, more complex forms of organization. However, in one area of culture, that of religion, there is some discernible continuity with the past, for in early accounts by missionaries and travelers we find descriptions of ideas and practices that have their modern counterparts. For example, Pierre Barrère, writing of the Carib of the Guiana coast in 1743, describes religious beliefs and practices very similar to those observable among the modern Carib-speakers at the headwaters of the Guiana rivers.

Fundamental Religious Ideas. Although claims have been made for the existence of monotheistic beliefs within the region, there is no evidence that any group worships a single divine being. Where such claims do arise, the reference is, at best, to some otiose culture hero responsible for the creation of the universe or to some primordial power or essence that is the driving force behind the universe. For example, among the Tucanoan-speaking peoples of the northwest Amazon the Primal Sun, or Sun Father, was the creator of the universe; he was considered a primal creative force that is not the same as the sun seen in the sky today.

Among the Carib-speaking Acawai of the Guyana-Venezuelan frontier, the existence of a supreme being is the result of Christian influence, although there appears to have been some traditional, abstract notion of "brightness" associated with the sun; the term for this idea means "light" and "life" and is the root of the word meaning "soul" or "spirit."

It is necessary to look elsewhere for Indian religion, and as a rough guide we may take E. B. Tylor's nineteenth-century definition of religion as animism, that is, the belief in spiritual beings. This concept needs some careful refining, and a first step in this task can be taken by considering the cosmology of the Indians. On this topic there is a remarkable degree of agreement among the various tribes. The universe has three layers: the sky, the earth, and a watery underworld. Each level may be further subdivided. [*See* South American Religions, *article on* Mythic Themes.] The three different layers are peopled by assorted beings, some of whom appear as recognizable denizens of the environment, whereas others are monstrous and fantastic. Thus the underworld is inhabited by aquatic creatures who are exemplified by the largest of such animals, the anaconda or the caiman. The earth is inhabited not only by people but also by forest-dwelling creatures, in particular the jaguar. The sky is the realm of the birds, for which the king vulture or the harpy eagle is often taken to be representative. Although one may refer to these beings as identifiable zoological species, it is unwise to regard them as absolutely or necessarily of an animal nature. It is often difficult to distinguish between them and people, and myths and rituals that refer to the origin of the universe frequently do not make this distinction.

Most human beings are not normally in a position to visit the other layers of the cosmos, although they may obtain experience of them under specified conditions. In many societies, houses are held to be models of the universe—microcosms—in which it is possible, through ritual, to collapse the coordinates of space and time into a unity.

In addition to the three cosmological layers, the world is also constituted of two parts, one visible, the other invisible, although the latter is visible to people with special skills and may in fact reveal itself to any person at any time. It is mistaken to see this duality as involving two separate worlds, for the seen and the unseen are really two aspects of one intermingled world and are counterparts to each other. The unseen reality is often as important as or even more important than what is revealed to the eye. Indeed, everyday events, apparently random and chaotic, can only be fully understood by reference to the invisible. Thus, the Jivaroan Indians of Ecuador regard it as essential for everyone, sometimes even hunting dogs, to have experience of the other world, experience achieved in the case of the Jivaroan people by the use of hallucinogenic substances. Dreams are another avenue of access to the invisible realm.

Power, which for the Indian lies outside society and within the invisible world, is ambiguous—that is, it can be used for good or evil—and needs, like a strong electric current, to be handled with care.

Invisible Beings. All the layers of the universe are inhabited by invisible beings. In many cases, these are the invisible counterparts of visible objects, both animate and inanimate. Some peoples consider virtually everything to have an invisible aspect, although only certain of these unseen objects are likely to be endowed with any great importance or to seriously impinge on human affairs. However, invisible beings are notorious for their unpredictability, so it is considered wise to take precautions. Their appearance, in visible form, to a human is thought to portend misfortune.

There are a great number of these invisible beings, and they take numerous forms. For example, the Sanemá of the Brazilian-Venezuelan frontier region recognize eight different kinds of invisible beings, or *hekula*. These include *hekula* of animals, humans, plants, artifacts, mythical ancestors of animal species, mythical ancestors of human social groups, sky people, and evil spirits. All *hekula*, regardless of origin, are

> ## This recycling of soul-matter is another common theme in lowland South America. . . .

humanoid in appearance. Each society has its own way of classifying the inhabitants of the invisible world, but in each case the classification is likely to reflect the nature of the relationship between the invisible beings and human society.

Masters of animals. There is a widespread belief in "owners" or "masters" who govern the animals. The Tucano-Desána of the northwest Amazon believe that there are two such masters, one for animals of the forest and one for fish. The former lives in the rocky hills, the latter in the rocks that form the falls and rapids in the rivers. Here, in a larger-than-life, prototypical form, the animals and fish live in huge longhouses, like people. It is the master of the animals who lets out animals for Indians to hunt, but he does so only in return for human souls, which are used to replenish the supply of animals.

The master of animals may appear in a variety of guises, either as a normal animal or as a monstrous man or animal. They sometimes appear to people, especially after dark in the forest. Some of them are definitely regarded as dangerous, others as little more than mischievous. These "bush spirits," as they are often referred to in the literature, are not to be confused with men who take on monstrous form in order to kill or bewitch other men, such as the *kanaima* of the Guyana region.

Ancestral spirits. In some societies the invisible beings most central to the continued existence and well-being of society are the ancestral spirits. Among the Tucano-Barasana of the northwest Amazon, the ancestral spirits are associated with the He instruments. These sacred flutes and trumpets form the local manifestation of a widely distributed cult popularly known as Yurupary. The term He does not refer just to these instruments but also means "ancestral" or "mythical," and conceptually it has much in common with the Dreaming of the Australian Aborigines. It is timeless, and although created long ago, He persists as an alternative aspect of reality. There are also He people and animals, the first ancestors (anacondas in the case of the Barasana). It is

through ritual contact with the original creation and with He, its generative force, that society continues and reproduces itself. The names of living people are those of the first ancestors, which are passed on through alternate generations, a person taking the name of a dead grandparent. The soul is considered to be inherited in the same way.

This recycling of soul-matter is another common theme in lowland South America, although by no means universal (it is mainly restricted to the Tropical Forest area). Throughout the lowlands the soul is considered to be another invisible entity, one that is crucial in the organization of everyday life. An individual is often regarded as having more than one soul and as having several different sorts of soul whose activities differ in this life and in the afterlife. Most people believe that the soul is detachable from the body and that during sleep or a trance it may leave the body and wander by itself. Many illnesses are attributed to soul-loss, often as a result of a soul being captured while wandering alone, and death is the result of the final detachment of the soul from the body.

The ghosts—that is, the souls of the dead—have many parts to play: they may be benevolent to the living, as among the Akwe-Xavante of central Brazil; they may be of no concern to the living, as among the Ge-speaking Suyá of the same area; or they may be menacing, as among the Waiwai of Guyana. The notion of reincarnation in the strict sense of the word does not seem to exist. It is not that an individual has a second life, but that the soul-matter energizes a new and different individual.

Religious Practitioners. The main religious practitioner throughout the region is the shaman. Shamans are usually but not always men. South American shamanism shares many characteristics with its Siberian prototype. It is often the one specialized role to be found in Indian societies, and although the actual functions vary from one society to another, shamans everywhere depend on similar basic skills: the ability to see the invisible aspect of the world, to communicate with it, and to travel to different cosmic layers while in a state of trance. The role of the shaman is that of cosmic mediator, and in this role he often acts as a transformer through whom the generative forces of the invisible world are transmitted to the everyday world for the benefit of its inhabitants. The shaman is assisted by spirit helpers, or familiars. To gain contact with the invisible world and to travel to the different cosmic levels, the shaman normally enters into a trance induced by a narcotic or hallucinogenic substance. In some societies it is expected that all adults will have firsthand experience of the invisible through the ingestion of such substances, and accordingly will have some shamanic competence. Among the Guaraní, for example, the men and women were divided into four hierarchically graded categories based on shamanic knowledge, with women allowed membership in all but the highest grade. However, even in situations such as this a class of "true shamans" is recognized, and shamans do not lose their preeminent role. It is the true shaman's task to guide the more or less skilled laymen through their experiences and to interpret these experiences for them, since unlike the shaman such people tend to have only a passive and not a manipulative relationship with the other world.

Shamanism. The ability to see, contact, and operate in the other world gives the shaman considerable power, and in some societies shamanic and ritual knowledge are the basis of political authority. However, the roles of spiritual and secular leader are not everywhere necessarily conjoined. When separate, their duties parallel each other: the secular leader defends his community from the dangers of the visible world, while the shaman wards off mystical attacks.

Given the ambiguity that characterizes the Indian concept of power, it is not surprising that a similar ambiguity characterizes those who hold power. It is occasionally suggested

> ... among the Jivaroan people of Ecuador there are both curing and bewitching shamans.

that there are two kinds of shaman—good and bad, or those who cure and those who kill. However, in most societies there is only one kind, whose power may be used for good or bad ends, depending on his relative position. A shaman in one's own community is considered good, while those in other, distant communities are considered bad and are held responsible for the misfortunes, illnesses, and deaths that result from mystical attacks. It is the home shaman's job to ward off such attacks and to mount counterattacks. The possession of power, because it can be used for good or bad ends, brings with it occupational hazards. It is reported from the Tupian-speaking Mundurucú and Tapirapé of Brazil that in the face of severe misfortune blame is assigned to a powerful shaman who is then killed.

Even so, there are societies in which two different types of shaman are found. For example, among the Jivaroan people of Ecuador there are both curing and bewitching shamans.

The functions of the shaman are varied. He is best known as a curer, although in practice this is but one aspect of his general ability to contact the invisible world. This point can be understood only if it is appreciated that sickness is not seen solely as a physiological phenomenon but also as a social disorder, the cause of which lies in the invisible world and results from either human or spirit activity. The job of the shaman as medical practitioner is to cure both aspects of the sickness. Curing techniques may include blowing tobacco smoke over the patient, sucking out spirit weapons, or going into a trance to obtain the advice or help of familiars in fighting hostile spirits who have captured the patient's soul. Such séances often take place in the dark, either at night or in a specially constructed hide enclosure. Séances are usually public and dramatic performances in which the audience can hear, if not see, the shaman in communication with his spirit helpers. In some societies curing sessions may take place outside the house during daylight hours.

The shaman's other tasks include prophecy; control over the weather, especially storms (a close association between shamans and thunder is common); the interpretation of omens and dreams; and maintenance of the supply of game animals. To fulfill the latter duty, the shaman either goes to negotiate with the master of animals for the release of game or is himself directly responsible for the supply. Powerful Tapirapé shamans secure game by visiting the home of wild pigs and having sexual intercourse with the sows. A further commonly reported duty of the shaman is the preparation of food, a mystical process parallel to the normal culinary techniques that render food edible.

Finally, there is the role of the shaman in major rituals, when a number of shamans may act together or be assisted by other ritual specialists. Among the Tucano-Barasana of the northwest Amazon, a group of such specialists, the dancer/chanters, perform a vital role complementary to that of the shaman: they represent the ancestors making their original creative journey.

One can also compare the dancer/chanters of the northwest Amazon with certain other lower-order religious specialists found elsewhere. For example, the Carib-speaking Kalapalo of the upper Xingu River in central Brazil give recognition to the role of exceptionally learned men and women who know the ceremonial songs, can make the ceremonial gear, and know how a ritual should be performed. In the same society there are also members directly responsible for the sponsoring of certain ceremonies

Prophets. Prophets also occur from time to time in some Indian societies. There is evidence that such figures existed in Indian societies prior to the arrival of Europeans. The great treks undertaken by the Tupi-speaking peoples across the continent in the fifteenth and sixteenth centuries appear to have been millennial in nature and led by prophets. In more recent times, the appearance of prophets has been closely associated with the influence of Christian missionary teaching. A well-known and well-documented messianic cult led by prophets is Hallelujah, found among the Carib-speaking Acawai and Patamona of Guyana. Hallelujah is concerned with contact with the ultimate source of power, God; while incorporating something akin to Christian worship, it has clearly borrowed from the shamanistic tradition, which still flourishes as the means of communication with the spirit world.

Myths and Ritual. Myths of lowland South America have received a great deal of attention in the last two decades as a result of Claude Lévi-Strauss's magnum opus, the four volumes of *Mythologiques* (translated as *Introduction to a*

Science of Mythology, 1969-1981). Lévi-Strauss ranges far and wide—often without regard for social context—to reveal universal structures of the human mind. Despite numerous criticisms of these studies, some unfairly dismissive, there is no doubt that Lévi-Strauss's impact on the study of Indian myth has been profound and probably permanent. More recent authors have employed a modified form of his structuralism as an interpretative device with which to obtain a better understanding of the society under examination.

It is through myths that Indians make statements about the fundamental nature of the world in which they live. Myths are indeed a form of knowledge, but it would be wrong to assume that they can be read as simple charters or explanations of social institutions, cultural practices, or natural phenomena. The relationships between myths, between myths and rites, and between rites are dialectical, and the contents of one myth may only be explicable by reference to certain other myths and even practices. At the same time myths, rites, and everyday activities all call on a common set of cultural categories. In other words, religious ideas and practices are embedded in social and cultural activities, and to separate either from the other is to lessen the chance of understanding both.

The ritual and myths of the area make abundant metaphorical use of the environment and its features. This use of cultural categories and natural objects to make abstract statements underlies the Indians' religious ideas. Given that the same major animals are distributed throughout lowland South America, it is not too surprising to find them recurring repeatedly in the myths of the area. Thus, the anaconda, caiman, jaguar, tapir, peccary, king vulture, harpy eagle, and many other animals, as well as the sun, moon, and constellations, figure regularly in the myths. The specific choice of animals made by a society for this purpose depends on the particularities of wildlife distribution, while the meanings that certain animals hold for different groups vary with the ways in which these animals are juxtaposed and contrasted. Within these limits it would be difficult to argue that the choice of these characters and of their meanings is purely arbitrary. Variability is limited to some extent by the cosmological framework; if the anaconda is substituted for the caiman, for example, their common association with water and thus with the underworld remains unchanged. Likewise the behaviors and habits of creatures do not vary. The weird sounds of the howler monkey, the defecatory practices of the sloth, or the peculiar qualities of the tortoise are the same wherever these animals are found, and as such are appropriate for conveying, within a restricted range, a common set of meanings.

Myths record the differentiation that took place at the beginning of time. But this is not a once-and-for-all event, for mythic time is not historical time; it persists as another aspect of reality. Through ritual, which may involve the chanting of myths, contact is made with this other temporal dimension in which human beings, animals, and ancestors remain undifferentiated. This confounding of categories is a common feature of rituals, which attempt to transcend this mundane world and to draw on the generative forces outside it. Thus among the Carib-speaking Trio of Surinam the ritual festivals are periods in which mythical unity is achieved and the empirical diversity and contradictions of everyday life are suppressed. It is through ritual that society is able both to register its continuity and to reproduce itself.

Another feature of ritual in lowland religions is that it produces a high degree of dependency. It has been noted that at an individual level no one has mastery of all the required ritual techniques and thus everyone has to depend on someone else. But this extends beyond individual requirements because many rituals, and not just the ritual aspect of technical activities, require the cooperation and participation of several people. Some rituals are preceded by collective hunting, and there are ceremonies in which crucial roles must be performed by outsiders. In functional terms, then, ritual can be seen as providing a counterweight to atomistic tendencies—that is, it forces individuals or groups who may dislike or suspect one another to interact for the benefit of society.

Practical Religion. Religion in lowland South American societies is not an institution that can be dealt with in isolation, since it is deeply embedded in other aspects of social, political, and economic life. This will have become apparent from earlier references to the ritual aspect of many everyday activities. Ritual acts are performed by individuals as a precaution against the unpredictable reactions of invisible beings. Some of these rituals involve the recital of a simple formula (rather like saying "God bless you" when someone sneezes) or the avoidance of a particular action (like not allowing a pot to boil over). More elaborate rituals are necessary under certain circumstances—for example, when food has to be treated by the shaman in order to be considered edible.

Perhaps the best way to appreciate the influence of practical religion is to look at the rituals that accompany the life cycle. Lowland South America is often regarded as the area in which the ritual phenomenon known as couvade (often wrongly described as "male childbed," the imitation by fathers of the experience of childbirth) reaches its greatest development. These rites require the parents of a newborn child to observe prohibitions on their diet and activities until such time as the infant's soul becomes properly secured to him. This may be expressed as a direct transfer of soul-matter from parents to child or, as in the case of the Ge-speaking Apinagé of central Brazil, it may be achieved through the increase of blood as the child grows naturally, which is considered to be directly responsible for the formation of the body and soul.

The creation of the individual as a combination of body and soul often has to be taken further in order to provide the person with a third entity, a social persona. This may be achieved through name-giving ceremonies, of which the Ge-speaking peoples provide some of the most elaborate examples. Their name-giving ceremonies involve the public transmission of whole sets of names between people in specifically defined relationships. Ownership of a set of names bestows membership in certain social groupings, such as a moiety. Thus these rituals not only create social beings but at the same time ensure social continuity through the reproduction of social groupings. In the case of the Ge these rituals have a rather secular character compared with the male initiation rites of the Tucano peoples. While the same result is achieved—that is, boys are turned into full members of society and the lineage's continuity is affirmed—the ritual more obviously involves contact with the invisible world, for the boys are born again not only as adults but also as direct descendants of mythical ancestors.

Multiple souls. Perhaps one of the best examples of the influence of ideas about souls and the other world on social life is provided by the Jivaroan people of eastern Ecuador. These Indians recognize the existence of three forms of soul. These are the "ordinary" soul; an "achieved" soul, of which an individual may possess up to two at any one time; and an "avenging" soul. Every living Jivaroan has an ordinary soul that is obtained at birth and lost at death. It is identified with the blood, and after death it goes through various transformations before finally taking on the form of mist.

The achieved soul is obtained through a vision that involves contact with the other world. Only a few women possess achieved souls, but it is regarded as essential for a man to obtain one by puberty or soon after if he is to survive. While a man is in possession of an achieved soul he is immune to death by certain causes, including violence and sorcery; if he has two, he is immune to death by any cause. The first soul is achieved through a vision quest in which the individual seeks out and touches a monstrous being. In order to become eligible to obtain another achieved soul, an individual first has to kill; only after he has done this can he seek a new soul and thus render himself invulnerable.

The rapid acquisition of the new soul locks in the remnants of the old soul, so that while no man may have more than two achieved souls at the same time, it is possible for him to accumulate power from any number of souls. However, a soul that has been with the same person for a long time will begin to wander, exposing itself to capture, which renders the individual vulnerable. The achieved soul of the Jivaroan appears to have much in common with Western notions of prestige and reputation.

The third soul of the Jivaroan is the avenging soul. This soul comes into existence when a person who has at one point had an achieved soul is killed, and its function is to avenge the death of the individual. This it does by turning itself into a demon and causing the murderer, or a close relative of the murderer, to have an accident. The Jivaroan practice of shrinking heads is associated with the idea of the avenging soul. The soul is trapped inside the head by this means, and after its power is extracted from it by ritual, it is sent back to the locality of its owner.

This case has been considered in some detail because it illustrates particularly well the elaboration of beliefs about the soul and the way in which these beliefs are directly tied to certain forms of social behavior.

Funerary practices. Funerary practices in lowland South America range from simple burial to elaborate secondary rites involving endocannibalism and extended feasting. Common throughout the area is the tendency for mortuary practices to reflect the status of the deceased. Even where only simple interment occurs, the death of a village leader results in the abandonment of his settlement—an event unlikely to follow on the death of an individual of lower status. The corpse of a shaman may be treated differently from that of a layman; among the Carib-speaking Waiwai of Guyana the layman was traditionally cremated, while shamans were buried. Among the Carib-speaking Kalapalo of the upper Xingu River there are two social ranks, chiefs and commoners, and their respective statuses are reflected in the ways in which their corpses are disposed of. Chiefs are buried in more elaborate graves, and their funerary rites consist of a series of ceremonies spread over a long period and involve participants from other villages.

Funerary rites are mainly concerned with the separation of the deceased from the living (and also the separation of one part of the body from another—for example, flesh from bone) and with the individual's incorporation among the dead. In addition, they often entail an inquest whose aim is to divine the identity of the person responsible for the death and to direct sorcery against him in revenge.

Ideas about the location of the afterlife or the village of the dead are hazy and, not surprisingly, even Indians from the same community provide rather different descriptions. However, one feature that ethnographers have frequently noted is that life hereafter is envisioned as a negation or reversal of certain aspects of life on earth (e.g., it is day in the afterworld while it is night on earth, and vice versa).

Syncretism. Few Indian systems of belief have escaped modification by the activities of Christian missionaries. The Spanish and Portuguese colonial powers employed representatives of the Roman Catholic church as their main agents for contact with and pacification of the Indians. However, as a result both of factionalism within the church and of antagonism between the church and colonists, it was rare that the influence of any one missionary order was long and sustained. An important exception to this was the Jesuit reductions of the Guaraní, which came to an end with the expulsion of the order in 1767 after nearly two centuries of contact.

In more recent times, various Protestant missions, in particular those of fundamentalist churches, have been active in lowland South America. The techniques and policies pursued by different missionary organizations, the conditions under which evangelization takes place, and the nature and degree of intactness of indigenous societies are all variables that prevent any simple statement about the effects of evangelization. Some missionary organizations have concentrated on trying to integrate the Indians into the national society by teaching them the national language and introducing a monetarized Western economy in place of the subsistence economy. The teaching of the Christian scriptures is not necessarily combined with attempts to eliminate traces of traditional beliefs and practices. The alternative approach is to teach entirely in the native language and to eliminate all practices that appear to fall foul of particular scriptural interpretations without making a purposeful effort to change the economic way of life. This policy is often associated with attempts to isolate the Indians from contact with the national society.

It is not at present clear why neighboring groups exposed to similar missionary attention have reacted in entirely different ways, one rejecting the teaching, the other accepting it. Under some conditions a form of syncretism has taken place, but elsewhere there has been little more than a smear of Christianity added on top of traditional beliefs. The study of lowland Indian syncretic religions is still an underresearched field. Some work has been done in this direction, in particular on the Hallelujah cult of the Carib-speaking Kapon and Pemón Indians, but a great deal remains to be done. Given the traditional association between religious and medical ideas in the lowlands, the syncretism of folk medicine and Western medical science is also a topic that falls within this general field and deserves further research.

BIBLIOGRAPHY

There is no general book on the religion of lowland South America, and what is known is mainly drawn from monographs on single tribal groups. *The Handbook of South American Indians*, 7 vols., edited by Julian H. Steward (Washington, D. C., 1946-1959), contains brief accounts of religious practices and systems of belief among the groups covered but is now slightly dated. Alfred Métraux's *Religions et magies indiennes d'Amérique du Sud* (Paris, 1967) is a collection of essays dealing with various aspects of religious behavior. A more recent work is that of Peter G. Roe, *The Cosmic Zygote* (New Brunswick, N. J., 1982), which usefully distills the basic features of Amazonian cosmology.

The part of lowland South America for which we have the best ethnographic coverage of religion is the northwest, the region of the Tucano peoples. Outstanding in this respect are the complementary works of Christine Hugh-Jones, *From the Milk River: Spatial and Temporal Processes in Northwest Amazonia* (Cambridge, 1979), and Stephen Hugh-Jones, *The Palm and the Pleiades: Initiation and Cosmology in Northwest Amazonia* (Cambridge, 1979). From the

same area, and providing slightly different perspectives, are Irving Goldman's *The Cubeo: Indians of the Northwest Amazon* (1963; reprint, Urbana, Ill., 1979) and Gerardo Reichel-Dolmatoff's two volumes, *Amazonian Cosmos: The Sexual and Religious Symbolism of the Tukano Indians* (Chicago, 1971) and *The Shaman and the Jaguar: A Study of Narcotic Drugs among the Indians of Colombia* (Philadelphia, 1975). All these books deal to some extent with the use of hallucinogens, and this topic is taken further in a work edited by Michael J. Harner, *Hallucinogens and Shamanism* (Oxford, 1973).

Shamans and shamanism are subjects dealt with in most monographs, but two important works, both published too recently for their contents to be taken account of properly in the text of this article, are almost totally devoted to these topics. They are Jean-Pierre Chaumeil's *Voir, savoir, pouvoir: La chamanisme chez les Yagua du nord-est Péruvien* (Paris, 1983) and Jon Christopher Crocker's *Vital Souls: Bororo Cosmology, Natural Symbolism, and Shamanism* (Tucson, 1985). Audrey Butt Colson's "The Akawaio Shaman," in *Carib-Speaking Indians*, edited by Ellen B. Basso (Tucson, 1977), goes into detail on aspects of shamanic apprenticeship. Also valuable in this respect is Charles Wagley's *Welcome of Tears* (Oxford, 1977), which contains a highly readable account of the religious ideas and practices of the Tapirapé Indians of central Brazil. For a straightforward ethnographic description from another area, there is Niels Fock's *Waiwai: Religion and Society of an Amazonian Tribe* (Copenhagen, 1963).

On the subject of tobacco usage there is Johannes Wilbert's "Magico-Religious Use of Tobacco among South American Indians," in *Spirits, Shamans, and Stars*, edited by David L. Bowman and Ronald A. Schwarz (New York, 1979); this article can also be found in *Cannabis and Culture*, edited by Vera D. Rubin (The Hague, 1975). *Spirits, Shamans, and Stars* also contains a useful analysis by Keneth I. Taylor of the relationships between spirits and human society among the Sanemá subgroup of the Yanoama. A more general and dramatized account of another Yanoama subgroup that touches upon many aspects of religious ideas and practices is Jacques Lizot's *Tales of the Yanoaman: Daily Life in the Venezuelan Forest* (Cambridge, 1985).

Michael J. Harner's *The Jívaro: People of the Sacred Waterfalls* (Garden City, N. Y., 1972) is the book from which the account in the text about Jivaroan ideas of the soul is adopted. A close examination of eschatological beliefs among the Ge-speaking Krahó of central Brazil is to be found in Manuel Carneiro da Cunha's *Os mortos e os outros* (São Paulo, 1978).

There is at the moment no general work on Indian ritual to match the work on myth done by Claude Lévi-Strauss in his four-volume *Mythologiques* (Paris, 1962-1971). Lévi-Strauss's masterwork has been translated into English as *Introduction to a Science of Mythology*; its four volumes are entitled *The Raw and the Cooked* (New York, 1969), *From Honey to Ashes* (New York, 1973), *The Origin of Table Manners* (New York, 1978), and *The Naked Man* (New York, 1981). Most ethnographic monographs contain some myths, but there are also volumes devoted solely to collections from particular tribes or areas. For example, Orlando Villas Boas and Claudio Villas Boas's *Xingu: The Indians, Their Myths* (New York, 1973) is recommended both for its readability and for the illustrations by Indians that it contains. The series "Latin American Studies," published by the Latin American Center, University of California, Los Angeles, includes a volume (vol. 44) on the Ge, edited by Johannes Wilbert (Los Angeles, 1979), and another on the Boróro (vol. 57), edited by Johannes Wilbert and Karin Simoneau (Los Angeles, 1983).

On messianic movements there is Hélène Clastres's *La terre sans mal* (Paris, 1975), and, depicting the rise of a syncretic cult, Audrey J. Butt's "The Birth of a Religion," *Journal of the Royal*

Anthropological Institute 90 (1960): 66-106. The literature on the impact of evangelization on Indian religion is, so far, poorly developed.

PETER RIVIÈRE

Indians of the Gran Chaco

The Gran Chaco (*chaco*, derived from Quechua, means "hunting land") is an arid alluvial plain in the lowlands of south-central South America. Approximately 725,000 square kilometers in area, it lies between the Andes in the west and the Paraguay and Paraná rivers in the east, and between the Mato Grosso to the north and the Pampas to the south. The scrub forests and grasslands of the Gran Chaco, though sparsely populated, were the home of numerous indigenous groups. In the main they were hunters, fishers, and gatherers, moving seasonally in search of food and practicing supplementary farming. Few still follow their traditional way of life.

The religion of the indigenous groups of the Gran Chaco can be understood through an examination of their mythic narratives, which contain their primary structures of meaning. These myths give an account of a primordial time in which an ontological modification was produced by the actions of various supernatural beings who shaped present-day cultural reality. This rupture may be caused by a lawgiver (who frequently has the appearance of a trickster), or it may be the result of infractions by ancestors or by the transformations of ancestors. Numerous supernatural beings with avowedly demonic characteristics monopolize the realm of fear and danger; their ambivalent intentions toward human beings are usually resolved through malevolent action that manifests itself in illness, culminating in the death of the individual. The general notion of power, such as the *la-ka-áyah* of the Mataco, or specific powers, such as the *uhopié* of the Ayoré, are the structures that ontologically define the supernatural beings as well as people who have been consecrated by them.

The spectrum of supernatural beings encompasses everything from shamans and witches, in the cases of the Guiacurú or the Mataco, to the state of "amorous exaltation" known to the Pilagá. For an integral understanding of the peoples of the Chaco it is important to consider the contributions of these special personages and states of being, which contribute a unique cultural identity to each group's cosmology. In almost all the ethnic groups of the Gran Chaco the shaman occupies the central role in religious tasks, sometimes defending and protecting, and, at other times, injuring. When engaged in healing practices, he can combine various techniques, such as singing, shaking rattles, blowing, and sucking, and can command the collabora-

tion of familiar spirits who are generally powerful owing to their demonic nature. An important aspect of Gran Chaco religions is the idea that one or many souls are incarnated in an individual. Once the individual is dead, these souls, or spirits, enter a demonic state. Although they are directed to an established underworld, they continue to prey upon human communities.

The Zamuco Family. The two members of the Zamuco language group are the Ayoré and the Chamacoco of Paraguay, in the northeastern Chaco.

The Ayoré. The religion of the Ayoré (Ayoreo, Ayoreode) is expressed primarily in an extensive set of myths. All natural and cultural beings have their origins related in mythic tales, and in certain cases in various parallel myths. The morphology of the myths centers upon the metamorphosis of an ancestral figure into an entity of current reality. Each tale narrates events that occurred in primordial times and is accompanied by one or more songs, which may be used for therapeutic (*saude*) or preventive (*paragapidí*) purposes.

Despite the abundance of tales, it is possible to classify the Ayoré myths in different cycles as they relate to a particular supernatural being or theme:

1. *The cycle of ancestors.* Each tale in this cycle recounts events in the life of an ancestor (*nanibahai*). These generally end with the ancestor's violent transformation into an artifact, plant, animal, or some other entity of the cosmos, and with the establishment by the ancestor of cultural prescriptions (*puyák*) governing the treatment of the new being and punishments for ignoring these prescriptions.
2. *The cycle of Dupáde.* A celestial supernatural being, Dupáde is associated with the sun; he causes the metamorphosis of the ancestors.
3. *The cycle of the Flood.* The tales of the Flood (*gedekesnasóri*) describe an offense inflicted on lightning by the *nanibahai*, their punishment in the form of a continual rain that inundated the world, and the survival of a few Ayoré, who became the first aquatic animals.
4. *The cycle of "water that washes away."* These tales describe a flood (*yotedidekesnasóri*) similar to that that appears in the preceding cycle, which was caused by Diesná ("cricket"), the ruler of water.
5. *The cycle of the Asohsná bird.* This bird (*Caprimulgidae spp*) is surrounded by numerous *puyák*. The central tale of this cycle relates the life of the female ancestor who created this bird. Asohsná is a supernatural being who established the annual ceremony that divides the year into two segments, one of which is characterized by an incalculable quantity of restrictions.
6. *The cycle of Asningái.* This cycle relates the courage of an ancestor named Asningái ("courage"), who threw himself onto the fire, transforming himself into an animal with certain morphological characteristics. It also established the

meaning of slaughter, an important institution among the Ayoré, since an individual could rise to the status of chief (asuté) through contamination by spilled blood.

The Chamacoco. The narrative of the Chamacoco, which recounts sacred events, is called "The Word of Esnuwérta." This tale constitutes the secret mythology of those men who have undergone initiatory ordeals and contains the social and religious knowledge of the group. Esnuwérta is the primordial mother. The myth is connected to the women of primordial times who were surprised by harmful supernatural beings (axnábsero). "The Word of Esnuwérta" includes the actions of these axnábsero, characters to whom Chamacoco reality is subordinated. The physiognomy of these supernatural beings is similar to that of the Ayoré ancestors in that current reality originates from their transformations and their deaths. The distinctive characteristic of the axnábsero is their malignant power (wozós) over people.

The foundation of the social order is presented in this myth, since Esnuwérta instituted the clans as well as the male initiation ceremonies in which the participants identify themselves with the principal deities of the myth.

The Chamacoco shaman (konsáxa) exercises a power appropriate to a specific region of the cosmos; for this reason there are shamans of the sky, of the water, and of the jungle. The shaman initiation begins with a vision of Esnuwérta, who reveals the cosmos as well as the practices appropriate to the work of the shamans. Another custom originating from Esnuwérta is called kaamták and has to do with a ritual offering of food; it relates to the impurity of blood, among other themes.

The Tupi-Guaraní Family. The Tupi-Guaraní language family includes the Chiriguano of Bolivia and the Tapuí of Paraguay.

The Chiriguano. The tale of the mythical twins Yanderú Túmpa and Áña Túmpa is the most prevalent myth among the Chiriguano (Miá) and appears in conjunction with lunar mythology. The celestial supernatural being Yanderú Túmpa made the cosmos and bestowed its goods on the Chiriguano, at the same time instructing them in cultural practices. He conceived and made Áña Túmpa, who, because of envy, attempts to undermine all Yanderú Túmpa's works. Áña Túmpa received from his maker power (imbapwére), which he in turn gives to other beings (áñas) who aid him in his malignant activities. As a result the world has undergone a profound alteration. It is now the actions of the áñas that determine the condition of the Chiriguano world, and they have introduced calamities such as illness and death. The expression túmpa is difficult to comprehend, but it appears to designate a quality that transforms the various entities into "state beings." The terms áña and túmpa define the supernatural nature of these beings, that is to say, they emphasize that they are extraordinary.

Tapuí and Guasurangwe. The religion of the Tapuí and the Guasurangwe, or Tapieté (an offshoot of the former), does not differ essentially from that of the Chiriguano; the same structures of meaning and the same supernatural beings may be observed.

Lengua-Mascoy Family. The Lengua-Mascoy language group of Paraguay includes the Angaité, Lengua, Kaskihá, and Sanapaná peoples.

The Angaité. The religious nature of the Angaité (Chananesmá) has undergone syncretism owing to their proximity to the Mascoy and Guaranian groups. Their mythology makes reference to three levels—the underworld, the terrestrial world, and the celestial world—all of which are inhabited by supernatural beings characterized by their ambivalent actions toward humans. The deity of the dead, Moksohanák, governs a legion of demonic beings, the enzlép, who pursue the sick, imprison them, and carry them to the "country of the dead," which is situated in the west. At night it is even possible for them to overpower passersby. The gabioamá or iliabün act as the spirit familiars of the shaman, and with him their role is ambivalent in a positive sense. For example, they are in charge of recapturing and restoring the souls of the sick.

According to Angaité myth, fire was obtained by a theft in which a bird was the intermediary; it was stolen from a forest demon, one of the iek'amá, who are anthropomorphic but have only one leg. Also anthropomorphic is the soul-shadow (abiosná), whose eyes are its distinguishing feature. The concept of corporal material as such does not exist, except for the iek'amá ("living cadaver" or "skeleton"), which is what remains after death.

During the initiation process, the shaman goes into the depths of the forest or to the banks of the river, where the familiar spirits (pateaskóp or enzlép) come to him in a dream. He communicates with the familiars through ecstatic dreams and songs. His therapeutic labors include sucking harmful agents from the bodies of the sick and applying vegetable concoctions whose efficacy resides in their "bad smell." There are shamans with purely malignant intentions, such as the mamohót, who are responsible for tragic deaths among members of the group. The benevolent shaman is responsible for discovering the identity of the bewitching shaman and for quartering and burning the body of the victim as a restorative vengeance. The Angaité do not have "lords" or "fathers" of the species; the figures closest to this theme are Nekéñe and Nanticá, male and female supernatural beings respectively, who are anthropomorphic and whose realm is the depths of the waters.

The Lengua. The anthropogenic myth of the Lengua (Enlhít, Enslet) attributes the formation of giant supernatural beings and the ancestors of the Lengua to Beetle, who utilized mud as primary material. After giving these beings a human form, he placed the bodies of the first enlhíts to dry on the bank of a lake, but he set them so close together that they stuck to one another. Once granted life, they could not defend themselves against the attacks of the powerful giants, and Beetle, as supreme deity, separated the two groups. Eventually the inability of the *enlhíts* to resist pursuit and mistreatment by the giants became so grave that Beetle took away the giants' bodies. The giants' souls gave birth to *kilikháma* who fought to regain control of the missing bodies, and it is for this reason that they torment present-day humans.

The important Lengua myths include the origin of plants and fire and the fall of the world. Ritual dramatizations of the myths are part of the celebrations for female puberty *(yanmána)*, male puberty *(waínkya)*, the spring and autumn equinoxes, the summer solstice, war, the arrival of foreigners, marriage, and mourning.

The Kaskihá. The "masked celebration" of the Kaskihá is of particular interest. It is based on a myth that describes the origin of the festive attire following the quartering of the water deity Iyenaník. The practice of *kindáian*, which is a dance, is the only medium for invoking the power of such deities.

The Sanapaná. The rich mythic narrative of the Sanapaná focuses on the war between the heavenly world, inhabited by the ancestors *(inyakahpanamé)*, and the terrestrial world, inhabited by the fox *(maalék)*. The ancestors, who differ morphologically from present-day humanity, introduced the majority of cultural goods. Among the fundamental structures distinguished by the Sanapaná is the "dream," the soul's life in its wanderings separate from the body. Death is understood as theft of the soul by demonic forces, the souls of the dead that stalk during the night in forests and marshes. The demonic spirits are anthropomorphic. Some are malignant, including those whose mere appearance can cause immediate death. There are also benevolent spirits who are the familiars of shamans *(kiltongkamák)*. The shaman's initiation involves fasting and other tests.

Mataco-Makká Family. The Mataco-Makká language family of the central Chaco includes the Mataco, Chulupí, Choroti, and Makká.

The Mataco. The religious universe of the Mataco (Wichí) centers on the notion of power *(la-ka-áyah)*, which is the property of innumerable supernatural beings of demonic *(ahát)* or human *(wichí)* nature, personifications of such phenomena as the sun, moon, stars, and thunder. The Mataco recognize a dualism of body *(opisán)* and spirit *(o'nusék)* in humans. Death changes the *o'nusék* into a malevolent supernatural being.

The central character in Mataco mythic narrative *(pahlalís)*, Tokhwáh, is the one who imposes cosmic and ontological order on the present-day world. The actions of this supernatural being, who has a demonic nature, are incorporated in his trickster aspect; nonetheless, he is perceived by the Mataco as a suffering and sad being. In his law-

giving role he introduces economic practices and tools; humanizes the women who descend from the sky by eliminating their vaginal teeth; institutes marriage; and teaches the people how to get drunk, to fight, and to make war. He also introduces demonic spirits who cause illnesses *(aités)* and establishes the shamanic institution *(hayawú)* and death. The most important Mataco ceremony is carried out by the shamans, in both individual and communal form, with the objective of expelling illnesses according to Tokhwáh's teachings.

The Chulupí. The mythology of the Chulupí (Nivaklé, Aslusláy) comprises three narrative cycles on the deities who acted in primordial times, but who then distanced themselves from humanity and the earthly world. The Xitscittsammee cycle describes a supernatural being comparable to an almost forgotten *deus otiosus*. The cycle of the supernatural being Fitsók Exíts includes prescriptions for the rites of female initiation; myths recounting the origin of women, of the spots on the moon, and of honey, among other things; and the tale of the expulsion from the universe of the supernatural creator. The Kufiál cycle relates the cataclysmic events accompanying the fall of heaven and the subsequent actions of the demiurge Kufiál, to name a few of its themes.

A structure essential to the Chulupí religion is *sic'ee*, or ultimate power, which defines and dominates a vast group of beings and actions. In effect, *sic'ee* is the strange made powerful, which can manifest itself in unexpected guises—in human or animal form, by means of a sound or a movement like a whirlwind, or as master of the spirits of the forest. The *sic'ee* plays a significant role in the initiation of the shaman *(toyék)*: he appears to the shaman in the guise of an old man, for example, who offers the shaman power and grants him the spirit familiars called *wat'akwáis*. By fasting, enduring solitude in the woods, and drinking potions made of various plants, the initiate achieves a revelatory experience rich in visions, many of which are terrifying. The Chulupí idea of animistic reality is extremely complicated and varied, given that the soul can appear in any number of manifestations.

The Choroti. The principle cycles of the Choroti are five in number. The cycle of Kixwét describes a supernatural being, of human appearance but gigantic, whose role comprises the duplicity of both the demiurge and the trickster. The cycle of Ahóusa, the Hawk, the culture hero *par excellence*, recounts how he defeated the beings of primordial times, stealing and distributing fire and teaching humans the technique of fishing and the making of artifacts. The cycle of Woíki, the Fox, who partakes of the intrinsic nature of Kixwét and is a very important figure in indigenous cultures, contains myths describing his creation of various beings and modalities of the present-day world. The cycle of We'la, the Moon, relates the formation of the world. The cycle of Tsemataki alludes to a feminine figure characterized by her ill will toward men and her uncontainable cannibalism.

The Choroti shaman (aíew) receives power (i-tóksi) from the supernatural beings (thlamó), and the strength of his abilities depends on the number of familiars (inxuélai) he has.

The Makká. The Makká mythology can be classified as eclectic, as it demonstrates cultural contact with almost all the other indigenous groups of the Gran Chaco. The Makká cycle of the fox is similar to the narrative cycle surrounding the Mataco supernatural being Tokhwáh and demonstrates

> **In earlier times, power (t'un) was obtained by capturing a scalp. . . .**

similar themes, such as the origin of women and the toothed vagina. The Makká hero Tippá, who possesses an immense penis, is somewhat reminiscent of Wéla, the Mataco moon deity.

In earlier times, power (t'un) was obtained by capturing a scalp, after which a complex ceremony was held in which the scalp was discarded but the soul (le sinkál) of the dead enemy was retained as a personal familiar, or spirit helper. This familiar would manifest itself during sleep by means of a song that even today is sung during drinking bouts. Ceremonies of drinking bouts among adults permit the regulation of power among people. The ceremony of female initiation is also important, as is true throughout most of the Gran Chaco.

Guiacurú-Caduveo Family. The Guiacurú-Caduveo language family of the Gran Chaco and Brazil includes the tribes known as the Pilagá, the Toba, the Caduveo, and the Mocoví.

The Pilagá. Certain mythic cycles may be distinguished in the Pilagá mythology. One cycle describes the celestial deity Dapici, to whom is attributed the inversion of the cosmic planes and the transference of some animals and plants to the sky. In the past, prayers were offered for his help in the most diverse activities. Another cycle describes Wayaykaláciyi, who introduced death, made the animals wild, and established hunting techniques, modifying the Edenic habits of an earlier time. Among the eminent supernatural beings is Nesóge, a cannibalistic woman who determines the practices of the witches (konánagae). Such characters and themes as the Star Woman and the origin of women appear in Pilagá myths.

Among the significant structures, the payák is the most important. This notion defines nonhuman nature, which is peculiar to supernatural beings, shamans (pyogonák), animals, plants, and some objects. Relations with the payák determine conditions in the indigenous world. Either people acquire payáks as familiars who aid them in their customary activities, or the payáks inflict suffering on them in the form of illness, the death of domestic animals, the destruction of

farms, or a poor harvest of fruit from wild plants. Such concepts as the "master-dependent" (logót-lamasék) and the "center-periphery" (laiñí-laíl) allow the Pilagá to classify beings and entities according to a hierarchy of power.

The Toba. The principal themes of Toba (Kom) narrative are celestial cosmology and mythology, which appear in stories about Dapici and the Pleiades; cataclysms; the origin of specific entities; stories of animals; stories of the trickster Wahayaka'lacigu, the lawgiver Ta'ankí, and Asien, a supernatural being with a repulsive appearance; and encounters between Toba people and the supernatural being Nowét. The morphology of these characters, all of whom were powerful in the primordial times, fluctuates between the human and the animal.

For the Toba, the central structure of the cosmology is nowét, which appears in the forms of the masters of animals and of the spheres. Nowét, as a supernatural being, initiates the shamans (pi'ogonák) and grants them power that can be used equally to heal or to harm. Outside the shamanic sphere, all special skills—hunting, fishing, dancing, and so on—derive from power given by Nowét. Dreams are structures that have importance in the relations between man and Nowét. Shamanic power is established by the possession of spirit familiars (ltawá), who help shamans cure serious illnesses, which are considered intentional and also material. Therapy combines singing, blowing, and sucking as methods of removing the harmful agent from the victim's body.

Some of the important ceremonies of the Toba are name giving, the initiation of young boys, the offering of prayers to Dapici, matutinal prayers to the heavenly beings, and the supplications of the hunters to some supernatural being in a nowét state.

The Caduveo. Go-neno-hodi is the central deity of Caduveo mythology; he is maker of all people and of a great number of the cultural goods. His appearance is that of a Caduveo, and he is without evil intention. In his benevolence, he granted the Caduveo, in ancient times, an abundant supply of food, clothes, and utensils, as well as eternal life, but the intervention of Hawk, astute and malicious, made Go-neno-hodi modify the primordial order. Nibetád is a mythical hero identified with the Pleiades; he greeted the ancestors during the ceremony celebrating the annual reappearance of this cluster of stars and the maturation of the algaroba (mesquite).

The shamanic institution is actualized in two different individuals: the nikyienígi ("father"), who protects and benefits the community, and the otxikanrígi, the cause of all deaths, illnesses, and misfortunes in the group. Celebrations that are particularly worthy of note are the lunar ceremonies, the rites celebrating the birth of the chief's son, and the initiations of young men and women.

The Mocoví. Prominent in the scattered Mocoví material is the myth of an enormous tree that reached to the sky. By climbing its branches, one ascended to lakes and to a river. An angry old woman cut down the tree, extinguishing the valuable connection between heaven and earth.

Gdsapidolgaté, a benevolent supernatural being, presides over the world of the living. His activity contrasts with that of the witches. Healing practices among the Mocoví are the same as those of the other shamans of the Gran Chaco, with the addition of bloodletting. The Mocoví, like all the Guiacurú, believe in the honor of war and value dying in combat as much as killing. When they return from a battle they hang the heads of the vanquished on posts in the center of town and they sing and shout around them.

Arawak Family. The extensive Arawak family of languages includes the Chané of Argentina. Fundamental distinctions cannot be made between the corpus of Chané myths and that of the Chiriguano; similarities abound between them, particularly with respect to the figure of the shaman. There are two kinds of shamans: one with benevolent power (the ipáye) and another dedicated exclusively to malevolent actions that cause death (the ipayepóci). The mbaidwá ("knower, investigator") has dominion over the individual destinies of humans.

BIBLIOGRAPHY

One can find an abundant bibliography on indigenous groups of the Gran Chaco in *Ethnographic Bibliography of South America*, edited by Timothy O'Leary (New Haven, 1963). The *Handbook of South American Indians*, 7 vols., edited by Julia H. Steward (Washington, D. C., 1946-1959), offers general characteristics on habits and customs of the peoples of this cultural area. The *Censo indígena nacional* (Buenos Aires, 1968) is restricted to the Argentine Chaco. Fernando Pagés Larraya's *Lo irracional en la cultura* (Buenos Aires, 1982) studies the mental pathology of the indigenous people of the Gran Chaco and then reviews their religious conceptions. *Scripta ethnológica* (1973-1982), a periodical published by the Centro Argentino de Ethnología Americana, Buenos Aires, contains more systematic information about the aboriginal peoples of the Gran Chaco.

There are only a few specific works that deal with particular groups; among those few are *Los indios Ayoreo del Chaco Boreal* by Marcelo Bórmida and myself (Buenos Aires, 1982). Branislava Susnik has also given attention to the Chulupí natives in *Chulupí: Esbozo gramatical analítico* (Asunción, 1968). Also worthy of mention are Miguel Chase-Sardi's *Cosmovisión mak'a* (Asunción, 1970) and *El concepto Nivaklé del Alma* (Lima, 1970). Bernardino de Nino wrote an *Etnografía Chiriguano* (La Paz, 1912). In reference to the Caduveo culture, see Darcy Ribeiro's *Religião e mitolcgia Kadiuéu* (Rio de Janiero, 1950). One can also consult Johannes Wilbert's Folk Literature of the Mataco Indians and *Folk Literature of the Toba Indians* (both, Los Angeles, 1982).

MARIO CALIFANO
Translated from Spanish by Tanya Fayen

SOUTH AMERICAN RELIGIONS

Since the Indians of South America do not conform culturally, there is no religious uniformity among them. Despite this inconsistency, an acceptable overview can be achieved by subdividing the continent's large, geographically distinct regions into the following cultural areas.

1. *The Andes.* This mountain range stretches from present-day Colombia to Chile. Among the most significant of these cultures was the Inca empire, which extended into the dawn of historical times. Direct descendants of earlier Andean cultures, the Quechua and Aymara peoples inhabit present-day Peru and Bolivia.

2. *Amazon and Orinoco rivers.* These jungle- and savanna-covered regions were conquered by tropical farming cultures. From the standpoint of cultural history, this area also includes the mountainous sections of present-day Guyana. As in the past, it is now inhabited by tribes belonging to a number of linguistic families, both small and large (Tupi, Carib, Arawak, Tucano, and Pano), and by a number of linguistically isolated tribes.

3. *Mountains of eastern Brazil.* This region is occupied by groups of the Ge linguistic family, who practice rudimentary farming methods; they settled in these hinterlands of the Atlantic coast region, joining indigenous hunting tribes.

4. *The Gran Chaco.* The bush and grass steppes of this area stretch from the Paraguay River west to the foothills of the Andes. A series of more or less acculturated groups of the Guiacurú linguistic family (the Mataco and the Mascoy) may still be encountered at the present time.

5. *The Pampas and Patagonia.* Hunting groups wandered through these flatlands of the southern regions of South America. The extinct Pampa and Tehuelche Indians were among the peoples of this region. The Tierra del Fuego archipelago, near the Strait of Magellan, is also included within this territory.

6. *Southern Andes.* This area, especially its middle and southernmost regions, is populated by the agrarian Araucanians of Chile, who have prospered up to the present time. Their success has been attributed to their development of a self-sufficient culture a few decades before the Spanish invasion in the early sixteenth century.

Deities, Culture Heroes, and Ancestors. The tradition of a creator as the prime mover and teacher of mankind is universal among the Indians of South America (Métraux, 1949). Under certain conditions, a creator, a culture hero, or an ancestor may rise to the position of a deity or supreme being. Such a case occurred in the old cultures of Peru with the religious figure Viracocha.

Culture hero as supreme being. Konrad T. Preuss was convinced that Moma ("father") was the paramount, indeed, the only true god of the Witóto of the Putumayo area of the northwestern Amazon and that he was identified with the moon. According to creation legends among these people, Moma came into existence from the "word," that is, he was a product of magico-religious incantations and myths that are endowed with supernatural powers. He was also the personification of the "word," which he bestowed upon human beings, and the "word" was the doctrine that represented the driving force behind all religious ceremonies that Moma introduced.

Among the Witóto, such a representation demonstrates intensely the character of a particular form of culture hero, that is, one who is at the same time a supreme entity. Alfred E. Jensen applied the term *dema deity* in describing such a culture hero among the Marind-anim of New Guinea (Jensen, 1951).

Waríkyana supreme being. A supreme god is also manifested among the Waríkyana (Arikena), a Carib-speaking tribe of the Brazilian Guianas. The highest deity in the religion of the Waríkyana is Pura (a name that, according to the Franciscan missionary Albert Kruse, means "God"). With his servant Mura, Pura stands on the zenith of heaven's mountains and observes all things that take place below (Kruse, 1955). At the command of Pura, the rain is sent from the sky. Pura and Mura are small men with red skin and are ageless and immortal. Pura is considered to be a "primordial man" or culture hero (ibid.).

Yanoama and Mundurucú supreme beings. Kruse's work stimulated Josef Haekel to write an article about monotheistic tendencies among Carib-speakers and other Indian groups in the Guianas. According to Haekel's findings, reference to the name *Pura* in connection with a supreme being occurred in no other Carib-speaking tribe except the Waríkyana. To the west of their territory in the Guianas, however, the expression is used with only slight variation, even among different linguistic groups such as the isolated Yanoama (Yanonami) on the Venezuelan and Brazilian borders. According to the beliefs of some groups in Brazil, *Pore* is the name of a supreme being who descended to earth (Becher, 1974).

There are strong similarities between the supreme being, Pura, of the Waríkyana and the figure of Karusakaibe, the "father of the Mundurucú" (an expression coined by Kruse, who was also a missionary among this central Tupi tribe). Karusakaibe once lived on earth and created human souls, the sky, the stars, game animals, fish, and cultivated plants, together with all their respective guardian spirits, and he made the trees and plants fruitful. Martin Gusinde (1960) is of the opinion that Karusakaibe was once a superior god among the Mundurucú. Later his status changed to that of a culture hero.

Tupi-Guaraní supreme beings. Resonances of a supreme being concept among the Tupi-Guaraní linguistic groups are mentioned by Alfred Métraux, who was the most important specialist in their religious systems (Métraux, 1949). Among these groups, the creator often has the characteristics of a transformer, and as a rule he is also the lawgiver and teacher of early mankind. After he fulfills these tasks, he journeys westward to the end of the world, where he rules over the shades of the dead.

The most revered god of the Guaraní-Apapocuvá according to Curt Nimuendajú, the outstanding authority on this tribe at the beginning of the twentieth century, is the creator Nanderuvuçu ("our great father"). Nanderuvuçu has withdrawn to a remote region of eternal darkness that is illuminated solely by the light that radiates from his breast (Nimuendajú, 1914).

Ge solar and lunar gods. In the eastern Brazilian area, the majority of the northwestern and central Ge tribes (Apinagé, Canella, and Xerente) hold that the Sun and Moon are the only true gods. Both Sun and Moon are masculine. Though not related to each other, they are companions; the Sun, however, is predominant.

At the beginning of the harvest season, a four-day Apinagé dance festival is celebrated in honor of the Sun at which the dancers apply red paint to themselves in patterns representative of the sun. The Canella also publicly implore the heavenly gods, the Sun and the Moon, for rain, the safety of the game animals, the success of their harvest, and an abundance of wild fruit.

Supreme beings of Tierra del Fuego. Among the people living in the southern regions of the continent, a belief in a supreme being is common in hunting and fishing tribes, especially the Selk'nam (Ona) of Tierra del Fuego and the Yahgan and Alacaluf of the Tierra del Fuego archipelago. They, along with the Alacaluf (Halakwulip), maintain belief in a supreme being who is an invisible, omnipotent, and omniscient spirit living in heaven, beyond the stars. He has no physical body and is immortal; having neither wife nor children, he has no material desires.

Supreme beings of the Pampas, Patagonia, and the southern Andes. Although our knowledge of the religious practices and beliefs of the earlier inhabitants of the Pampas and Patagonia is sparse and relatively superficial, it is almost certain that the Tehuelche had a supreme being. Like Témaukel of the Selk'nam, the god of the Tehuelche was characterized by his lack of interest in worldly activities; he was also lord of the dead. This supreme being was, in general, sympathetic toward human beings, but there is no proof of a public cult devoted to him. Traditionally he was called Soychu. A benevolent supreme being of the same name was also found in the religious beliefs of the Pampa Indians, at least after the eighteenth century.

It would appear that the tribal religions of the southern areas of South America were, in general, marked by a belief in a supreme god. The Araucanians of the southern Andes, and in particular the Mapuche, have left behind traces of the concept of a superior god, as well as a devout veneration of him that survived well into the eighteenth century. In most instances the supreme being is referred to as either Ngenechen ("lord of mankind") or Ngenemapun ("lord of the land"). Other, more feminine descriptions may reveal an androgynous character. Ngenechen is thought of as living in heaven or in the sun and is credited with being the creator of the world as well as the provider of life and of the fruits of the earth.

Nature Spirits, Hunting Rituals, and Vegetation Rites. Owing to the fact that hunting belongs to one of the oldest phases of human history, gods who are associated with this category of subsistence represent archaic beliefs. Not only do the Indians of South America believe in a master of all animals but they frequently display a belief in supernatural protectors of the various animal species. From the standpoint of cultural history, they are related to the lord of all beasts and have affinities with him that stem from the same hunting and fishing mentality.

Tupi master of the animals. The most important representation of a master of the animals in the tropical lowlands is the forest spirit Korupira, or Kaapora. Although the use of two names creates the impression that Korupira and Kaapora are two separate mythical figures, they are so closely related as to be nearly indistinguishable. Korupira, the master of the animals, is the protecting spirit of the beasts as well as of the forest; he punishes those who maliciously destroy the game and rewards those who obey him or those on whom he takes pity. For a portion of tobacco, Korupira will lift the restrictions that he places on the killing of his animals. Encounters in recent times with a small isolated Tupi tribe, the Pauserna Guarasug'wä, who live in eastern Bolivia, have shown that the belief in Korupira/Kaapora has survived. Kaapora originated as a human being—that is, he was created from the soul of a Guarasu Indian. He is the lord of all animals of the forest and has put his mark somewhere on each of the wild animals, usually on its ear. A hunter must turn to him with a plea to release part of the game, but he is only allowed to kill as many as he will absolutely need for the moment. In thanksgiving for his success, the hunter will leave the skin, the feet, or the entrails of the slain animal behind when he leaves the forest: by doing so he begs forgiveness from the animal for having killed it. After such reconciliations, the soul of the animal returns home to Kaapora.

Kurupi-vyra of the Guarasug'wä is a part-animal, part-human forest spirit, but not a lord of the animals. He is, however, a possible source of help for hunters in emergencies.

Mundurucú protective mother spirit. In the Amazon region, the idea of a lord of all animals is sometimes replaced by the belief in a lord or master of each individual animal species, and sometimes both concepts occur. Starting from the basic Tupi premise that every object in nature possesses a mother (cy), the Mundurucú, a Tupi-speaking group, recognize and venerate a maternal spirit of all game. She is the protector of the animal kingdom against mankind and maintains a mother-child relationship between herself and the beasts.

Hunting dances. The Taulipáng and the Arecuná of the inland regions of the Guianas believe that each individual animal type has a father (podole), who is envisioned as either a real or a gigantic, legendary representative of that particular species, and who displays supernatural qualities. Two "animal fathers" are especially meaningful for their hunting ritual: the father of the peccary and the father of the fish. In

> Performing the Parischerá ensures a plentiful supply of four-legged animals, just as the Tukui dance guarantees a sufficient supply of birds and fish.

the Parischerá, a long chain of participants, wearing palm-leaf costumes and representing a grunting peccary herd, dance to the booming of cane trumpets or clarinets. Performing the Parischerá ensures a plentiful supply of four-legged animals, just as the Tukui dance guarantees a sufficient supply of birds and fish.

Animal dances devoted to the attainment of game and fish are found among other tribes of the Amazon area and the Gran Chaco. Instead of focusing on the controlling master of the animals, however, they are often directed at the soul of the animal itself.

Plant fertility rites. The most impressive religious celebrations of the tribes in the lowlands of the Amazon are those held for the vegetation demons by the peoples in the northwestern section of this region. Among the Tucanoan and Arawakan groups of the upper Rio Negro and the basin of the Uaupés River, the Yurupary rites take place at the time when certain palm fruits particularly favored by the Indians are ripe. At the beginning of the festival, baskets of these fruits are ceremonially escorted into the village by men blowing giant trumpets. These sacred instruments, which represent the voices of the vegetation demons, are hidden from the women and children, who must therefore remain within the huts at this time. During the first part of the ceremony, in which the men scourge one another with long rods, the women are also obligated to remain within their houses. After the secret part of the ritual has ended, however, the women may join the men in feasting and drinking, which continues for several days. The purpose of this feast is to thank the demons for a good harvest and to beg them to provide a rich yield in the coming season.

Human and plant fertility. Among the Kaua (an Arawakan group) and the Cubeo (a Tucano group) in the northwestern Amazon region, fertility rites are obviously connected with a human generative power. At the end of the masked dances, in which the dancers represent animals, the participants unite to perform the Naädö (phallus dance).

Among the Jivaroan people in Ecuador, the cult of the earth mother Nunkwi is restricted to those cultivated plants whose soul is believed to be feminine—for example, manioc. The soul of the earth mother resides within a strangely shaped stone *(nantara)* that has the power to summon Nunkwi. The association between fertility of human females and the growth of plants considered to be feminine receives obvious expression through the rule that every woman who plants a manioc cutting must sit on a manioc tuber. The same theme is expressed in the ritual for the first manioc cutting that is taken from a field whose yield is intended to be used at the Tobacco festival. The cutting is painted red, and the woman to be honored places it against her groin.

The Quechua and Aymara peoples of the central Andes region frequently call upon Pachamama, the goddess of the earth, who is essentially responsible for the fertility of plants and who is believed to live underground. In addition to being connected with many celebrations, she is also associated with many daily rituals. The cult devoted to her originated in pre-Hispanic times and has survived to the present.

The Soul, the Dead, and Ancestors. Most of the Indian groups of South America believe that a human being has several souls, each residing in a different part of the body and responsible for numerous aspects of life. After death, each of these souls meets a different fate.

Research on a number of Indian tribes indicates that meticulous preservation of the bones of the dead is a widespread practice. Such action, which is similar to the preservation of the bones of hunted game, can be traced to the belief that residual elements of the soul remain in the bones after death.

Honoring the dead was an essential component within the religions of old Peru, as exemplified by the care that mummies of the ancestors were given by priests (Métraux, 1949) and by the sacrificial victims brought to them. Mummies were also taken on procession at certain festivals.

The combination of a memorial service for the recently dead and a commemorative ceremony for the legendary tribal ancestors can be seen in the Kwarup ritual of the Camayura, a Tupi group of the upper Xingu. The Kwarup (from *kuat*, "sun" and *yerup*, "my ancestor") centers around a number of posts, each about three feet high, outfitted and ornamented as human beings and carved from the sacred camiriva wood from which the creator, Mavutsine, allegedly fabricated the first Camayura. The chant given as people dance around these posts is the same one that Mavutsine sang as he created mankind. In the Kwarup ritual the ancestors return symbolically for the purpose of welcoming those who have recently died.

Death cults and ancestor worship also play an important role in the eastern Brazilian cultural area, particularly among the Boróro. This tribe makes a sharp distinction between nature spirits and spirits of the dead. The Boróro believe that the souls of their ancestors *(aroe)* hold a close relationship to mankind that influences and maintains its daily life. On certain social occasions, the spirits of the dead are ceremonially invoked by special shamans to whom the spirits appear and whom they enlighten in dreams. As a result of this important attachment to the spirits, the funeral rites of the Boróro are highly developed and complex.

A cult of the dead among the indigenous people in the southern regions of South America, including the Gran Chaco and the southern Andes, contains few authentic religious elements. At a funeral, the surviving family members sponsor a large feast in honor of the dead relative. The various ceremonies that take place during this feast—for example, eating and drinking bouts, lamenting, playing of music, feigned attacks, riding games, and speeches—are intended to drive from the village the dreaded spirits of the dead or the death demons, who are responsible for the death of the tribal member, to prevent them from causing more harm.

Conclusion. The central Andes of pre-Columbian times is characterized by a belief in high gods and their respective cults, by the worship of ancestors and of the dead, and by agrarian rites directed to a female earth deity. The peoples of the region of the Amazon and Orinoco rivers occasionally display signs of high-god worship (Witóto, Tupi-Guaraní). Along with the vegetation cults (northwestern Amazon) that are typical of crop-cultivating peoples, there is a markedly large number of ceremonies and rites associated with deities of the hunt and of wild animals (including fish). The Ge of eastern Brazil exhibit clear signs of worship of astral deities—the Sun and Moon. The cults of the dead and of ancestors dominate much of their religious life. The Gran Chaco, by contrast, is noticeably lacking in religious ceremonies and rites in the narrow sense. First-fruit ceremonies related to hunting and fishing predominate; there are no agrarian rites. In the Pampas and Patagonia region a number of socioreligious rites are attested. The Selk'nam and Yahgan of Tierra del Fuego Archipelago believe in a high god, but there is little indication of cult worship. The regions of southern and central Andes share many aspects of religious life. The high-god cult (Ngenechen) is associated with a cultivation and fertility ritual. A highly developed form of shamanism is also prominent. Throughout South America outside the Andean region, the shaman remains the pillar of the religious life.

[*See also* Shamanism.]

BIBLIOGRAPHY

Baldus, Herbert. *Die Allmutter in der Mythologie zweier sudamerikanischer Indianerstämme (Kagaba und Tumereha).* Berlin, 1932.

Becher, Hans. *Poré/Perimbó: Einwirkungen der lunaren Mythologie auf den Lebensstil von drei Yanonámi-Stämmen, Surára, Pakidái und Ironasitéri.* Hanover, 1974.

Böning, Ewald. *Der Pillánbergriff der Mapuche.* Sankt Augustin, West Germany, 1974.

Cooper, John M. "The Araucanians." In *Handbook of South American Indians,* edited by Julian H. Steward, vol. 2., pp. 687-760. Washington, D. C., 1946.

Eliade, Mircea. "South American High Gods." *History of Religions* 8 (1968): 338-354 and 10 (1970-1971): 234-266.

Frikel, Protasius. "Zur linguistisch-ethnologischen Gliederung der Indianerstämme von Nord-Pará (Brasilien) und den anliegenden Gebieten." *Anthropos* 52 (1957): 509-563.

Gusinde, Martin. *Der Feuerland Indianer.* 3 vols. Vol. 1, *Die Selknam.* Vol. 2, *Die Yamana.* Vol. 3, *Die Halakwulup.* Mödling, 1931-1974. Johannes Wilbert has translated volumes 1 and 2 as *Folk Literature of the Selknam Indians* (Berkeley, 1975) and *Folk Literature of the Yamana Indians* (Berkeley, 1977), respectively.

Gusinde, Martin. Review of *Mundurucú Religion* by Robert F. Murphy. *Anthropos* 55 (1960): 303-305.

Haekel, Joseph. *Pura und Hochgott: Probleme der südamerikanischen Religionsethnologie.* Vienna, 1958.

Hissink, Karin, and Albert Hahn. *Die Tacana: Ergebnisse der Frobenius-Expedition nach Bolivien 1952 bis 1954,* vol. 1, *Erzählungsgut.* Stuttgart, 1961.

Hultkrantz, Åke. *Les religions des indiens primitifs de l'Amérique.* Stockholm, 1967.

Jensen, Adolf E. *Myth and Cult among Primitive Peoples.* Chicago, 1973.

Kruse, Albert. *Pura, das Höchste Wesen Arikena.* Fribourg, 1955.

Métraux, Alfred. *La religion des Tupinamba et ses rapports avec celle des autres tribus Tupi-Guarani.* Paris, 1928.

Métraux, Alfred. "Ethnography of the Chaco." In *Handbook of South American Indians,* edited by Julian H. Steward, vol. 1, pp. 197-370. Washington, D. C., 1946.

Métraux, Alfred. "Religion and Shamanism." In *Handbook of South American Indians,* edited by Julian H. Steward, vol. 5, pp. 559-599. Washington, D. C., 1949.

Métraux, Alfred. *Religions et magies indiennes d'Amérique du Sud.* Paris, 1967.

Nimuendajú, Curt. *Die Sagen von der Erschaffung und Vernichtung der Welt als Grundlagen der Religion der Apapocúva-Guaráni.* Berlin, 1914.

Nimuendajú, Curt. *The Apinayé.* Washington, D. C., 1939.

Petrullo, Vincenzo M. "The Yaruros of the Capanaparo River, Venezuela." *The Smithsonian Institution, Bureau of American Ethnology Bulletin* 123 (1939): 161-290.

Schuster, Meinhard. *Dekuana.* Munich, 1976.

Trimborn, Hermann. "South Central America and the Andean Civilizations." In *Pre-Columbian American Religions,* edited by Walter Krickeberg et al., chap. 2. London, 1968.

Zerries, Otto. "Primitive South America and the West Indies." In *Pre-Columbian American Religions,* edited by Walter Krickeberg et al., chap. 4. London, 1968.

OTTO ZERRIES
Translated from German by John Maressa

SOUTHEAST ASIAN RELIGIONS

Mainland Cultures

Mainland Southeast Asia has been termed the "crossroad of religions," for in this region, today divided into the countries of Burma, Thailand, and Laos, Cambodia (Kampuchea), and Vietnam, a large diversity of autochthonous tribal religions are intermingled with Hinduism, Theravada and Mahayana Buddhism, Taoism, Confucianism, Islam, and Christianity, as well as the modern secular faith of Marxist-Leninism. Beneath this diversity there are many religious practices and beliefs that have common roots in the prehistoric past of peoples of the region.

Mainland Southeast Asia is not only a region of religious diversity; it is also a veritable Babel. Insofar as historical linguistics permits us to reconstruct the past, it would appear that most of the earliest inhabitants of the region spoke Austroasiatic languages ancestral to such modern-day descendants as Khmer and Mon.

Prehistoric Foundations. People have lived in mainland Southeast Asia for as long as there have been *Homo sapiens,* and there is evidence of *Homo erectus* and even earlier hominid forms in the region as well. The first significant evidence we have of religious beliefs and practices in mainland Southeast Asia comes from the period when humans in the region first began to live in settled agricultural communities. The domestication of rice, which may have taken place in mainland Southeast Asia before 4,000 BCE, led to the emergence of a powerful image that was to become incorporated in almost all of the religious traditions of the region.

Neolithic burial sites, many only recently discovered, are proving to be sources of knowledge about prehistoric religions in Southeast Asia. The very existence of such sites suggests that those who took so much trouble to dispose of the physical remains of the dead must have had well-formed ideas about the afterlife and about the connection between the states of the dead and the living.

In a Neolithic burial site in western Thailand, the grave of an old man was found to contain a perforated stone disk and an antler with the tines sawed off. Per Sørensen, the archaeologist who excavated the site, believes these items may represent the headdress of a shaman; if so, they would be the earliest evidence of shamanism in mainland Southeast Asia.

Peoples of the region in late prehistoric times were often isolated from each other by the numerous ranges of hills and must have developed distinctive religious traditions. An older generation of scholars, best represented by Robert Heine-Geldern, posited an underlying unity of prehistoric Southeast Asian religions that stemmed from the diffusion of a cultural complex from a single European source. While there were certainly contacts among peoples widely separated in Southeast Asia in prehistoric times, and while these contacts resulted in the diffusion of some practices and beliefs, most basic similarities must be understood to reflect the ordering of similar experiences that follow universal modes of human thought.

Drawing on later historical data as well as ethnographic analogy, Paul Mus, a distinguished student of Southeast Asian civilization argued that the autochthonous religions of protohistoric Southeast Asia coalesced around cults he termed "cadastral." These cadastral cults constituted the religions of agricultural peoples who had long since made rice their staple, although some cultivated it by swidden or slash-and-burn methods and others cultivated by irrigation. Rice also was believed to possess a vital spirit.

The cosmologies of protohistoric Southeast Asian farmers, like those of primitive peoples throughout the world, were structured around fundamental oppositions. In Southeast Asia, the oscillation between the rainy rice-growing season and the dry fallow season found expression in such religious imagery. The fertility of the rainy season is widely associated with a female deity, the "rice mother," although a male image, that of the *naga*, or dragon, and sometimes a crocodile, is also found in many traditions.

The world in which protohistoric peoples lived was marked by uncertainty: crops might fail as a consequence of late rains or devastating floods; women might be barren, die in childbirth, or lose child after child; and both men and women might die young. Hence, people wished to influence the spirits and cosmic forces that controlled fertility and life. The fundamental method of gaining the favor of spiritual powers was through sacrifices. In tribal groups such as those in Burma and northeastern India, those men who organized large-scale sacrifices and the so-called feasts of merit associated with them acquired not only the esteem of their fellows but also a spiritual quality that was believed to persist even after their death. Such tribal chiefs are assumed to be similar to what O. W. Wolters calls "men of prowess." Rough stone monuments associated with early Cham culture in southern Vietnam and upright stones found together with the prehistoric stone jars in Laos have been interpreted, by analogy with the practice by such modern tribal peoples as Chin of Burma and related groups in northeastern India, as monuments that perpetuated and localized the potency of men who had succeeded during their lifetimes in effecting a relationship between the society and the cosmos.

Historical Transformations. Prior to the adoption of Indian or Chinese models, there appears to have been no priesthood in any Southeast Asian society capable of enforcing an orthopraxy among peoples living over a wide area. As the ritual effectiveness of men of prowess waxed and waned, so did the relative power of the polities they headed, thus giving rise to a classic pattern of oscillation between "democratic" and "autocratic" communities found among tribal peoples such as the Kachin of Burma even in recent years.

Sinitic influences. Chinese influences appear first in conjunction with the Han conquest of what is now northern Vietnam. This sense of belonging to a Chinese world remained even after the Vietnamese gained independence from China in the eleventh century. The Chinese model was most significant for literati—the Confucian mandarinate, Mahayana Buddhist monks, and even some Taoist priests—who derived their cultural understanding of the world from Chinese and Sino-Vietnamese texts. Those Vietnamese who

> **Many of the religiously inspired peasant rebellions originating in southern Vietnam . . . have drawn inspiration from non-Chinese sources.**

moved out of the Red River delta in the "push to the south" that began in the thirteenth century and continued into recent times came into contact with other traditions—those of the hinduized Cham and Khmer, the Buddhist Khmer, and local tribal peoples. Many of the religiously inspired peasant rebellions originating in southern Vietnam as well as some modern syncretic popular religons have drawn inspiration from non-Chinese sources. This said, Vietnamese religion in all parts of the country has assumed a distinctly Sinitic cast, being organized primarily around ancestor worship in the Chinese mode.

Indian influences. The earliest monuments of indianized civilization in Southeast Asia appeared in significant numbers between the fourth and eighth century CE. Particular examples are Siva *linga* of the Cham in southern Vietnam, the Buddhist *sema* (Skt., *sima*) or boundary markers with scenes from the life of the Buddha or from the Jatakas in bas-relief found in Dvaravati sites in northeastern Thailand, and the stupas at Beikthano and Sriksetra in central Burma, Thaton in lower Burma, and Nakhon Pathom in central Thailand. These monuments can best be interpreted as having been put up to elevate a man of prowess to a divine form.

The process of indianization in Southeast Asia included identifying a power believed to be embodied in a local shrine with divine or cosmic powers known in Indian texts. This made possible the creation of larger polities, since peoples in very different parts of a realm saw themselves as part of the same cosmos and worshiped the same gods, often gods who were also equated with the rulers.

On the western side of mainland Southeast Asia, Burmese kings also succeeded in establishing a *mandala* (circle of a king) that between the eleventh and thirteenth centuries rivaled the splendor and power of Angkor. It produced both funerary monuments in which the kings became immortalized, albeit in this case in Buddhist terms, and recreations of the sacred cosmos.

The cult of the relics of the Buddha does not constitute the whole of Buddhism as practiced in Southeast Asia. Between the thirteenth and fifteenth centuries, missionary monks established a Theravada Buddhist orthodoxy among the majority of peoples, both rural and urban, living in what are today Burma, Thailand, Laos, and Cambodia. In a sense, orthodox Buddhism made sense to Southeast Asians because of the pre-Buddhist idea that religious virtue is not a product solely of descent from particular ancestors but also a consequence of one's own religiously effective actions.

The success of Theravada Buddhism led to a much sharper distinction between the religious traditions of the peoples of the western part of mainland Southeast Asia and those east of the Annamite cordillera. Not only were the Vietnamese becoming increasingly sinicized, but the Cham, who had once had an important indianized culture in southern Vietnam, turned from this tradition and embraced Islam, a religion that was becoming established among other Austronesian-speaking peoples in major societies of the Indonesian archipelago and on the Malay Peninsula.

Missionization—not only by Christians but in recent years by Buddhists—and the spread of modern systems of compulsory education have rendered tribal religions increasingly peripheral. So, too, have improved health care and secular education undermined beliefs in spirits that were previously elements of the religions of Southeast Asian Buddhists and Vietnamese. Moreover, as agriculture has been transformed by large-scale irrigation works and the introduction of new technology and new high-yield varieties of rice, peoples in the region have become less inclined to credit supernatural powers with the control over fertility.

[*See also* Buddhism *and* Islam, *article on* Islam in Southeast Asia. *For a discussion of the interrelation of popular and elite traditions in local Buddhist cultures, see* Folk Religion *For specific regional cultures,* Lao Religion *and* Khmer Religion. *See also* Megalithic Religions.]

BIBLIOGRAPHY

Robert Heine-Geldern interprets archaeological and ethnographic evidence with reference to a diffusionist thesis that posited the source of a prehistoric "megalithic complex" in Europe. His most recent formulation of his position appears in "Some Tribal Art Styles in Southeast Asia," in *The Many Faces of Primitive Art*, edited by Douglas Fraser (Englewood Cliffs, N. J., 1966), pp. 161-214. Kenneth Perry Landon, in *Southeast Asia: Crossroads of Religion* (Chicago, 1969) and Pierre-Bernard Lafont, in "Génies, anges et démons en Asie du Sud-Est," in *Génies, anges et démons* (Paris, 1971), provide introductions to Southeast Asian religions in other than diffusionist terms. By far the most detailed comparison of beliefs and practices relating to agriculture found among peoples not only in mainland Southeast Asia but also on the islands of the region is Eveline Porée-Maspero's *Étude sur les rites agraires des Cambodgiens*, 3 vols. (Paris, 1962-1969). Also see in this connection P. E. de Josselin de Jong's "An Interpretation of Agricultural Rites in Southeast Asia, with a Demonstration of Use of Data from Both Continental and Insular Asia," *Journal of Asian Studies* 24 (February 1965): 283-291. A general introduction to Southeast Asian religions with reference to their social context is provided in my book *The Golden Peninsula: Culture and Adaptation in Mainland Southeast Asia* (New York, 1977).

The volume *Early South East Asia: Essays in Archaeology, History, and Historical Geography,* edited by R. B. Smith and William Watson (Oxford, 1979), contains information on prehistoric and protohistoric religion; the work also has a good bibliography. H. G. Quaritch Wales's *Prehistory and Religion in Southeast Asia* (London, 1957), although dated and relying too heavily on diffusionist theory, still remains the only work to attempt a synthesis of prehistoric evidence. Per Sørensen reports on the find he interprets as evidence of prehistoric shamanism in "'The Shaman's Grave',", in *Felicitation Volumes of Southeast-Asian Studies Presented to Prince Dhaninivat*, vol. 2 (Bangkok, 1965), pp. 303-318. The model of the "cadastral cult" was advanced by Paul Mus in *India Seen from the East: Indian and Indigenuous Cults in Champa*, translated by I. W. Mabbett and edited by I. W. Mabbett and D. P. Chandler (Cheltenham, Australia, 1975). O. W. Wolters, in *History, Culture, and Region in Southeast Asian Perspectives* (Brookfield, Vt., 1982), proposes the notion that "men of prowess" was a general type in prehistoric and protohistoric Southeast Asia. His interpretation is based, in part, on A. Thomas Kirsch's argument developed in a comparison of Southeast Asian tribal ethnography in *Feasting and Social Oscillation: A Working Paper on Religion and Society in Upland Southeast Asia* (Ithaca, N. Y., 1973). Kirsch, in turn, has elaborated on the idea of oscillation between "democratic" and "autocratic" chiefdoms first advanced by Edmund Leach in *Political Systems of Highland Burma* (Cambridge, Mass., 1954).

Vietnamese scholars have shown considerable interest in recent years in tracing the Southeast Asian origins of Vietnamese civilization. Much of their work is discussed by Keith Weller Taylor in *The Birth of Vietnam* (Berkeley, 1983). The process of "indianization" and the relationship between this process and what H. G. Quaritch Wales called "local genius" in the shaping of Southeast Asian religious traditions has been most intensively explored by George Coedès in *The Indianized States of Southeast Asia*, edited by Walter F. Vella and translated by Susan Brown Cowing (Canberra, 1968); H. G. Quaritch Wales in *The Making of Greater India*, 3d rev. ed. (London, 1974) and *The Universe Around Them: Cosmology and Cosmic Renewal in Indianized Southeast Asia* (London, 1977); O. W. Wolters in "Khmer 'Hinduism' in the Seventh Century," in *Early South East Asia: Essays in Archaeology, History and Historical Geography* and in *History, Culture and Region in Southeast Asian Perspectives* (both cited above); Hermann Kulke in *The Devaraja Cult*, translated by I. W. Mabbett (Ithaca, N. Y., 1978); and I. W. Mabbett in "Devaraja," *Journal of Southeast Asian History* 10 (September, 1969): 202-223; "The 'Indianization' of Southeast Asia: Reflections on Prehistoric Sources," *Journal of Southeast Asian Studies* 8 (March 1977): 1-14; "The 'Indianization' of Southeast Asia: Reflections on the Historical Sources," *Journal of Southeast Asian Studies* 8 (September 1977): 143-161; and "*Varnas* in Angkor and the Indian Caste System," *Journal of Asian Studies* 36 (May 1977): 429-442. O. W. Wolters, in *History, Culture and Region in Southeast Asian Perspectives*, discusses the *mandala* model, a model also discussed at somelength under the rubric of the "galactic polity" by Stanley J. Tambiah in *World Conqueror and World Renouncer* (Cambridge,1976).

A. Thomas Kirsch in "Complexity in the Thai Religious Sys-tem: An Interpretation," *Journal of Asian Studies* 36 (February 1977): 241-

266; Melford E. Spiro in *Burmese Supernaturalism,* 2d ed. (Philadelphia, 1978); and Stanley J. Tambiah in *Buddhism and the Spirit Cults in North-East Thailand* (Cambridge, 1970) discuss the relationship between pre-Buddhist and Buddhist beliefs in Thai and Burmese religion. Similar attention to pre-Sinitic religious beliefs in Vietnamese religion is given by Leopold Cadière in *Croyances et pratiques religieuses des Viêtnamiens,* 3 vols. (Saigon and Paris, 1955-1958). See also Pierre Huard and Maurice Durand's *Connaissance du Viêt-nam* (Paris and Hanoi, 1954).

Kirk Endicott's *Batek Negrito Religion* (Oxford, 1979) describes the religion of the last remaining major population of hunting-and-gathering people on the mainland. Karl Gustav Izikowitz's *Lamet: Hill Peasants in French Indochina* (Göteborg, 1951), Peter Kunstadter's *The Lua' (Lawa) of Northern Thailand: Aspects of Social Structure, Agriculture and Religion* (Princeton, 1965), and H. E. Kauffmann's "Some Social and Religious Institutions of the Lawa of Northwestern Thailand," *Journal of the Siam Society* 60 (1972): 237-306 and 65 (1977): 181-226, discuss aspects of religious life among Austroasiatic-speaking tribal peoples. Among the more detailed accounts of the religions of Hmong (Meo) and Mien (Yao) peoples are Jacques Lemoine's *Yao Ceremonial Paintings* (Atlantic Highlands, N. J., 1982); Guy Morechand's "Principaux traits du chamanisme Méo Blanc en Indochine," *Bulletin de l'École Française d'Extrême-Orient* 54 (1968): 58-294; and Nusit Chindarsi's *The Religion of the Hmong Ñjua* (Bangkok, 1976). Theodore Stern in "Ariya and the Golden Book: A Millenarian Buddhist Sect among the Karen," *Journal of Asian Studies* 27 (February 1968): 297-328, and William Smalley's "The Gospel and Cultures of Laos," *Practical Anthropology* 3 (1956): 47-57, treat some aspects of religious change among tribal peoples.

CHARLES F. KEYES

Insular Cultures

The cultures of insular Southeast Asia are made up predominantly of peoples speaking Austronesian languages, and the traditional religions of the area, despite substantial diversity and extensive borrowing from other sources, retain significant features that reflect a common origin. The initial expansion of the Austronesians began in the third millennium BCE and proceeded, by stages, through the Philippines and the islands of Indonesia, then east to the islands of the Pacific, and eventually west as far as the island of Madagascar.

In the course of migration, natural ecological variation as well as numerous outside influences led to the development, emphasis, or even abandonment of different elements of a general Neolithic culture. In the equatorial zones, for example, reliance on rice and millet gave way to a greater dependence on tubers and on fruit- and starch-gathering activities. During most of their protohistory, Austronesian populations lived in impermanent settlements and combined shifting cultivation with hunting and gathering. The development toward centralized states began on Java, on the coast of Sumatra, and in several other coastal areas that were open to trade and outside influences. Chief among these influences were religious ideas and inspiration that derived variously, at dif-

ferent periods, from Hinduism, Buddhism, Islam, and Christianity.

At present, 88 to 89 percent of the Indonesian population is classified as Muslim. In the Philippines, approximately 84 percent of the population is Catholic. In Indonesia, Bali forms a traditional Hindu-Buddhist enclave but there has occurred a recent resurgence of Hinduism on Java and elsewhere.

The tribal religions of the region vary according to the groups that continue to practice them. These groups include small, often isolated peoples whose economy is based primarily on hunting and gathering with limited cultivation. Examples of such groups are the Sakkudei of the island of Siberut off the coast of western Sumatra; various wandering bands of Kubu scattered in the interior forests of Sumatra; groups of a similar kind in Kalimantan who are referred to generically as Punan; as well as a variety of other small-scale societies on other islands.

Some of these Indonesian populations have formally established religious associations to preserve their traditional practices and some have come to be identified as followers of Hindu-Dharma. In the Philippines, a majority of the indigenous peoples in the mountains of northern Luzon in Mondoro and in the interior of Mindanao have retained their traditional religions despite increasing missionary efforts.

Studies of traditional religion, many of which have been written by missionaries or colonial administrators, document beliefs and practices that have since been either abandoned or modified through the process of conversion. Significant evidence on traditional religion is also derived from present practices and general conceptions that have been incorporated and retained: (1) the prevalence of complementary duality; (2) the belief in the immanence of life and in the interdependence of life and death; (3) the reliance on specific rituals to mark stages in the processes of life and death; and (4) the celebration of spiritual differentiation. All of these notions may be regarded as part of a common Austronesian conceptual heritage.

The Prevalence of Complementary Duality. Forms of complementary dualism are singularly pervasive in the religions of the region. Such dualism figures prominently, in a wide variety of myths of the origin of the cosmos that combine themes of reproduction and destruction. As well, ideas of complementary duality are reflected in ideas about the principal divinity, who is often conceived of as a paired being; in ideas about the division of sacred space: upperworld and underworld, upstream and downstream, mountainward and seaward, or inside and outside; and above all, in ideas about classes of persons and the order of participants in the performance of rituals. Major celebrations based on this complementarity can become a form of ritual combat that reenacts the reproductive antagonisms of creation.

Conceptions of complementary dualism continue to pervade even those societies that have adopted Hinduism,

Islam, or Christianity. Balinese society is replete with dualism. The opposition between Barong and Rangda, which forms one of Bali's best-known dramatic temple performances, is a particularly striking example of complementary dualism. The Javanese *wayang,* or shadow theater, is similarly based on forms of dual opposition.

Belief in the Immanence of Life. Virtually all of the traditional religions of the region are predicated on a belief in the immanence of life. In the literature this concept is often simplistically referred to as "animism." In traditional mythologies, creation did not occur *ex nihilo:* the cosmos was violently quickened into life and all that exists is thus part of a living cosmic whole. Commonly, humans either descended from a heavenly sphere or emerged from earth or sea.

The traditional religions differ markedly, however, in their classification of categories or classes of beings. Priests of the Ifugao, for example, are reported to be able to distinguish over fifteen hundred spirits or deities, who are divided into

> **Virtually all of the traditional religions of the region are predicated on a belief in the immanence of life.**

forty classes. By contrast, the Rotinese recognize two broad classes of spirits—those of the inside and those of the outside—and are only concerned with naming the spirits of the inside. The traditional religions also differ significantly in attitudes to the spirit world. For some, all spirits are potentially malevolent and must be placated; in others, benevolent spirits are called upon to intervene against troublesome spirits.

A fundamental feature of the traditional religions is their recognition that life depends upon death, that creation derives from dissolution. Moreover, since life comes from death, the ancestral dead or specific deceased persons, whose lives were marked by notable attainments, are regarded as capable of bestowing life-giving potency. Thus the dead figure prominently in the religious activities of the living and the tombs of the dead are often sources of religious benefit.

The chief sacrificial animals in the traditional religions are the chicken, the dog, and the pig (although among those populations that keep them the water buffalo is by far the most important sacrificial animal). The entrails of chickens and the livers of pigs frequently provide a means of divination within a sacrificial context.

Rituals of Life and Death. Life-cycle rituals mark the process of life and death. They may be seen to begin with marriage—the union of male and female—and proceed through specific stages. Prominent among these rituals are those that mark the seventh month of a woman's pregnancy,

haircutting, tooth filing, circumcision (which may have had a pre-Islamic origin but has been given increased significance through the influence of Islam), the coming of adulthood through marriage, and the formation of an autonomous household.

Death rituals are part of the same process as those of life and in general are celebrated throughout the region with great elaboration. Death rituals are also performed in stages commencing with burial and continuing sometimes for years. Often the groups involved in performing these mortuary rituals complete and reverse the exchanges that began at the marriage ceremony of the parents of the deceased, thus ending one phase and beginning the next phase of a continuing cycle.

Headhunting was once a prominent feature of the social life of many of the peoples of the region. Although this form of limited warfare was given various cultural interpretations, headhunting was frequently linked in rituals to the general cycle of death and renewal. In this sense, headhunting was a form of "harvest" in which particular individuals were able to achieve great renown.

The Celebration of Spiritual Differentiation. The tendency in most traditional religions is to personalize whatever may be considered a manifestation of life. Included among such manifestations are the heavenly spheres—the sun, moon, and stars; the forces of nature—thunder, lightning, or great winds; points of geographical prominence—high mountain peaks, volcanic craters, waterfalls, caves, or old trees; places endowed with unusual significance as the result of past occurrences—sites of abandoned settlement, a former meeting place of some spirit, or the point of a past, powerful dream; and simpler iconic representations of life—ancient ancestral possessions, royal regalia, amulets, and other objects of specially conceived potency.

In social terms, these spiritual premises are conducive to notions of precedence and hierarchy. No society in the region is without some form of social differentiation. Even in the simplest of tribal societies the birth order of the children of the same parents becomes a means for such distinctions. Equally, the same spiritual premises may promote notions of achievement.

Literally and spiritually, individuals are distinguished by their journeys. Rank, prowess, and the attainment of wealth can be taken as evident signs of individual enhancement in a life's odyssey, and this enhancement may be celebrated through major rituals, both in life and after death. In many traditional religions, mortuary rituals and the feasting that generally accompanies them are the primary indicators of a person's social and spiritual position and are intended to translate this position into a similarly enhanced position in the afterlife.

Today throughout insular Southeast Asia, the basic premises of traditional religions are under challenge from religions such as Islam and Christianity that preach transcendence in place of the immanence of life and assert spiritual equality rather than celebrate spiritual differentiation.

[*See* Balinese Religion; Batak Religion; Bornean Religions *and* Javanese Religion. *See also* Buddhism and Islam. *For treatment of the religion of related island cultures, see* Melanesian Religions *and* Megalithic Religions.]

BIBLIOGRAPHY

A useful starting point for the study of Southeast Asian religions is Waldemar Stöhr and Piet Zoetmulder's *Die Religionen Indonesiens* (Stuttgart, 1965). A French translation of this volume is available: *Les religions d'Indonésie* (Paris, 1968). Stöhr examines various specific traits of the tribal religions of Indonesia and the Philippines on a regional basis, while Zoetmulder provides a succinct introduction to Hinduism, Buddhism, and Islam in Indonesia, together with an excellent discussion of the Balinese religion. Stöhr has since extended his general examination in *Die Altindonesischen Religionen* (Leiden, 1976). Both volumes have extensive and useful bibliographies. The general study of animism by the Dutch missionary-ethnographer A. C. Kruijt, *Het animisme in den Indischen archipel* (The Hague, 1906), is of historic interest as is the study of the Batak religion by the German missionary Johannes G. Warneck, *Die Religion der Batak* (Leipzig, 1909). Three studies of particular traditional religions by Leiden-trained anthropologists emphasizing features of complementary duality are Richard Erskine Downs's *The Religion of the Bare'e-Speaking Toradja of Central Celebes* (The Hague, 1956), Hans Schärer's *Ngaju Religion,* translated by Rodney Needham (1946; reprint, The Hague, 1963), and Peter Suzuki's *The Religious System and Culture of Nias, Indonesia* (The Hague, 1959). Roy F. Barton has provided considerable documentation on the Ifugao, including a study of their religion, *The Religion of the Ifugaos* (Menasha, 1946); Clifford Geertz has contributed enormously to the study of Java, particularly with an influential book, *The Religion of Java* (Glencoe, Ill., 1960). Our understanding of traditional religions has also been greatly enhanced by a series of recent ethnographies: Erik Jensen's *The Iban and Their Religion* (Oxford, 1974), Michelle Z. Rosaldo's *Knowledge and Passion* (Cambridge, 1980), Gregory L. Forth's *Rindi* (The Hague, 1981), and Peter Metcalf's *A Borneo Journey into Death* (Philadelphia, 1982), as well as by a number of as yet unpublished Ph. D. dissertations: Elizabeth Gilbert Traube's "Ritual Exchange among the Mambai of East Timor" (Harvard University, 1977), Robert William Hefner's "Identity and Cultural Reproduction among the Tengger-Javanese," (University of Michigan, 1982), E. D. Lewis's "Tana Wai Brama" (Australian National University, 1982), and Janet Alison Hoskins's "Spirit Worship and Feasting in Kodi, West Sumba" (Harvard University, 1984).

JAMES J. FOX

SOUTHERN AFRICAN RELIGIONS

There is a basic similarity in religious practice, symbols, and ideas throughout southern Africa, from Uganda to the south-

ern sea, from the east coast to Cameroon. This is the area in which Bantu languages are spoken, and there is a link, though no absolute coincidence, between language family and religious symbolism.

Religious belief in southern Africa can best be understood through its symbolism, for religion here is expressed more through drama and poetry than through dogma or theological speculation.

Concepts of God. Throughout southern Africa there is an apprehension of God as a numinous being associated with light, brightness, and sheen. God may be represented by a high mountain glittering with snow, a tree symbolizing the mountain, or a sacred grove. How clearly God is distinguished from the first man, or from the founding heroes of a particular lineage, varies with place and time. Among some peoples, at least, the distinction became clearer as outside contacts extended and the known world was no longer confined within a frame of kinship. Over many centuries Hebrew, Christian, and Islamic ideas of God, with their symbolism of monotheism and of God on high, have impinged on other ideas in Africa. Throughout southern Africa God has been remote, approached only by exceptional priests or by the "elders." Prayer or direct offerings to God himself rarely occur in traditional practice, but awe of God is constantly manifested, as fear of contamination, as a distancing of man from God, and avoidance of such emblems of sacred power as the thunderbolt, the tree struck by lightning, and the python in the grove.

Shades. Among southern African peoples shades are of two categories: the dead senior kin (male and female) of each family or lineage and the founding heroes. The ancestors of a ruling lineage, where one exists, commonly claim descent from the founding hero; or the hero may be thought of as a benefactor or prophet who left no descendants but who is celebrated in some grove or cave by a lineage or priests.

Like God, the shades are associated with brightness, light, radiance, and whiteness. Among the Zulu and Xhosa a gray-leafed helichrysum, whose leaves and pale gold flowers both reflect light, is linked with the shades.

Although they are numinous, the shades are held in far less awe than is God himself. To many Africans the shades are constantly about the homestead, evident in a tiny spiral of dust blowing across the yard or through the banana grove, or in the rustling of banana leaves; thought to be sheltering near the byre or in the shade of a tree, or sipping beer left overnight at the back of the great house.

Founding heroes typically are associated with a bed of reeds, from which the first man is said to have sprung; with a river source along the watershed between the Zambezi and Kongo rivers; with a pool in one of the rushing rivers of the south. Like family shades, heroes are of the earth and water, not of the sky.

Ritual Life. Communal rituals are of various sorts, including offerings to the founding heroes, their living representatives, and chiefly descendants. Such offerings are celebrated by the leading men of the region, chiefdom, or village.

In the Swazi kingdom today—as formerly in other Nguni kingdoms and chiefdoms on the southeastern coast of Africa—all the men of the country, and many women also, gather at the time of the summer solstice to celebrate the first fruits and strengthen their king, while regiments dance and demonstrate their loyalty.

Throughout southern Africa communal rituals have to do with rain, especially the dramatic "break of the rains," so eagerly awaited after the dry season. Local rituals celebrate seedtime and harvest; the firing of pasture to destroy unpalatable grass and bush which harbor tsetse flies; game drives or a fishing battue; murrain or plague; war and peace. Details of such celebrations vary both with economy and with political structure. Regional rituals may involve the distribution of once-scarce goods, such as salt and iron tools, which in former times were brought to the shrine from beyond the boundaries of the political unit. The priests who brought the goods were sacred people: among the Nyakyusa these priests traveled in safety, announcing their status by drumbeat.

Kinship Rituals. Unless they concern a royal family, the rituals of kinship have no political overtones. They are celebrated on the great occasions of a person's life: at birth and death, at maturity and marriage. In southern Africa each family or lineage directs its celebrations to its own dead senior kinsmen, who are not sharply distinguished from living seniors.

> **Unless they concern a royal family, the rituals of kinship have no political overtones.**

Family rituals vary with the economy, for the place of the shrine and the form of the offering depend upon the staple foods. Among a pastoral people the altar is the byre, the offering milk or a slaughtered animal. If the people cultivate, beer is added. Among banana-eating peoples the altar is set in a plantain grove. To the Lele, who live on the southern edge of the equatorial forest belt, the forest is holy and is associated with men; the grassland, where villages are built, has no prestige and is associated with women.

Offerings to the shades consist of staple foods, especially choice foods such as a tender cut of beef eaten by the one on whose behalf prayer is made (the same cut from the right foreleg is used by peoples from Tanzania to the southern coast of Africa); a libation of fermented milk or beer; a sprinkling of flour or porridge. Whatever the material used, the intention of the offering is the same: the shades are called to feast, and what is offered is a communion meal for living and dead kinsmen.

The occasions of family rituals are constant throughout the area: death and birth, especially abnormal birth such as that of twins; maturity, whether physically or socially defined; marriage; misfortune and serious illness; reconciliation after a quarrel; and the first fruits which the family celebrates after the national or regional ritual.

Although funerals have been adapted to the new economy, they include certain traditional rites, notably a washing and purification rite after the burial and a lifting of mourning after about a year.

Maturity rituals have many aspects; the extent to which any one aspect is stressed varies from one society to another. Circumcision is most often celebrated for a group, and those who have endured this rite together share a bond for life. Girls' initiation, on the other hand, is most often an individual celebration at the first menstruation. Maturity rituals are everywhere concerned with inculcating respect for authority: respect for seniors, shades, chiefs, and respect of a wife for her husband. A man must learn to keep secrets and never reveal the affairs of his chief or the secrets of the lodge.

Cults of Affliction, Spirit Possession, and Divination. There is a cycle of rituals for those individuals "called" by their shades to become diviners, or for sufferers whose sickness has been relieved by what Victor Turner has called a "ritual of affliction." Cults or guilds are formed of those who have suffered a particular travail and been cured by a particular ritual. Their experience entitles them to participate in any celebration for a sufferer of the same category.

Diviners are thought to be in a peculiarly close relationship with their shades, who reveal themselves in dreams and trances. The emotion is often intense when, with an insistent beat of clapping provided by a packed crowd, a novice speaks of what she has seen in dreams. Even though it may be a stranger spirit who possesses the medium, she remains in close contact with her family shades.

Witchcraft. In southern African belief, evil does not come from the shades, who are essentially good. Rather, evil comes from another source: witchcraft. The witch familiars (and witchcraft generally) personify the evil recognized as existing in all humans, specifically, anger, hatred, jealousy, envy, lust, greed. Even sloth appears, in the belief that certain evil people have raised others from the dead to work their fields for them.

People are known to confess to the practice of witchcraft, usually following an accusation and pressure to confess. In some areas confessions have at times been extracted forcibly (through a poison ordeal or torture), since the recovery of the victim is held to depend upon the witch's confession and subsequent expression of goodwill toward the victim. [*See also* Witchcraft.]

BIBLIOGRAPHY

To supplement the relatively few works cited in the text, the works listed herein range over all parts of the enormous area of southern Africa. Many of the books cited here were written by missionaries, who provided most of the early published evidence of the traditions of peoples in the area.

Beattie, John, and John Middleton, eds. *Spirit Mediumship and Society in Africa.* London, 1969. Firsthand accounts by trained observers of spirit mediums in thirteen African societies, with a comparative introduction.

Berglund, Axel-Ivar. *Zulu Thought-Patterns and Symbolism.* London, 1976. By far the best study of the symbolism of an Nguni people (on the southeast coast), written by a missionary who grew up speaking Zulu as a second language.

Bernardi, Bernardo. *The Mugwe: A Failing Prophet.* London, 1959. A competent account of a hereditary priest in Meru, Kenya, written by a Consolata priest who was a missionary in the area.

Callaway, Henry. *The Religious System of the Amazulu* (1870). Reprint, Cape Town, 1970. Contains valuable statements of belief by Zulu. Includes Zulu texts and English translations, with notes, by the Reverend Canon Callaway, a Zulu-speaking missionary who sought to understand traditional ideas.

Colson, Elizabeth. *The Plateau Tonga of Northern Rhodesia.* Manchester, 1962. One volume of a longterm study by an anthropologist; gives an account of ancestral spirits and rain shrines.

Crawford, James R. *Witchcraft and Sorcery in Rhodesia.* London, 1967. Based on records of court cases.

Douglas, Mary. *The Lele of the Kasai.* London, 1963. A brilliant essay on Lele symbolism, first published in *African Worlds,* edited by Daryll Forde (London, 1954).

Douglas, Mary. *Natural Symbols.* New York, 1970. Discusses the relationship between symbols and inner experience.

Douglas, Mary, ed. *Witchcraft Confessions and Accusations.* New York, 1970. Sets witch beliefs in comparative perspective.

Fortes, Meyer, and Germaine Dieterlen. *African Systems of Thought.* London, 1965.

Gluckman, Max. *Rituals of Rebellion in Southeast Africa.* Manchester, 1954.

Hammond-Tooke, W. David. *Boundaries and Belief: The Structure of a Sotho World View.* Johannesburg, 1981.

Harris, Grace Gredys. *Casting Out Anger: Religion among the Taita of Kenya.* Cambridge, 1978. A discussion of rejection of anger, through spraying out water or beer, as the central religious act among the Taita.

Junod, Henri A. *The Life of a South African Tribe.* 2d ed., rev. & enl. 2 vols. London, 1927. A classic by a missionary; first published as *Les Ba-Ronga* (1898; reprint, New Hyde Park, N. Y., 1962).

Kenyatta, Jomo. *Facing Mount Kenya* (1938; New York, 1962). A valuable firsthand account of Kikuyu ritual and belief.

Mbiti, John S. *African Religions and Philosophy.* New York, 1969.

Mbiti, John S. *Concepts of God in Africa.* London, 1970. Useful on the concept of time in East Africa. Makes clear that ancestors are not worshiped; offerings to them are family celebrations with the "living dead."

McAllister, P. A. "Work, Homestead and the Shades: The Ritual Interpretation of Labour Migration among the Gcaleka." In *Black Villagers in an Industrial Society,* edited by Philip Mayer, pp. 205-253. Cape Town, 1980. Evidence on a very conservative section of Xhosa on the southeast coast.

Middleton, John, and E. H. Winter, eds. *Witchcraft and Sorcery in East Africa.* London, 1963. Essays based on firsthand observation.

Ngubane, Harriet. *Body and Mind in Zulu Medicine.* London, 1977. Particularly illuminating on the ancestors and illness, pollution, color symbolism in medicine, and possession by evil spirits. An important work by an observer whose mother tongue is Zulu.

Ranger, T. O., and Isaria N. Kimambo, eds. *The Historical Study of African Religion.* Berkeley, 1972.

Richards, Audrey I. "A Modern Movement of Witch-finders." *Africa* 8 (October 1935): 448-461. Describes the *bamucapi* movement of 1934.

Richards, Audrey I. *Chisungu: A Girl's Initiation Ceremony among the Bemba of Northern Rhodesia.* London, 1956. The most vivid account yet written on girls' initiation; interprets symbols and explains methods of inculcating certain lessons.

Roscoe, John. *The Baganda.* London, 1911. Written by a missionary who worked closely with James G. Frazer. Includes an account of founding heroes and rituals at their shrines.

Setiloane, Gabriel M. *The Image of God among the Sotho-Tswana.* Rotterdam, 1976.

Smith, Edwin W., and Andrew Murray Dale. *The Ila-Speaking Peoples of Northern Rhodesia* (1920). 2 vols. Reprint, New Hyde Park, N. Y., 1968. Smith was a missionary, Dale a magistrate, and both were very competent linguists. They lived among the Ila of the Zambezi from 1902 and 1904, respectively, until 1914. The sections on religion are chiefly the work of Smith, who later served as president of the Royal Anthropological Institute, London. The book is a classic of early African ethnography.

Smith, Edwin W., ed. *African Ideas of God.* London, 1950. A symposium with twelve contributors and an introductory essay by Smith. Five contributors refer to southern Africa.

Swantz, Marja-Liisa. *Ritual and Symbol in Transitional Zaramo Society, with Special Reference to Women.* Uppsala, 1970. An account of the ritual and symbolism of the Zaramo of the Tanzanian coast. "Every occasion of prayer," Swantz argues, "is a restatement of the position of the family in relation to their elders and to their present leadership and authority."

Taylor, John V. *The Primal Vision: Christian Presence amid African Religion.* Philadelphia, 1963. A penetrating study based on Taylor's experience in Uganda and elsewhere in Africa.

Turner, Victor. *The Forest of Symbols.* Ithaca, N. Y., 1967. This volume was followed by Turner's *The Drums of Affliction* (Oxford, 1968), *The Ritual Process* (Chicago, 1969), and *Revelation and Divination in Ndembu Ritual* (Ithaca, N. Y., 1975); together they constitute a profound study of Ndembu ritual and symbolism.

Willoughby, William C. *The Soul of the Bantu.* New York, 1928. Based on the experience in Botswana of a missionary who believed that "ritual is a variety of the vernacular."

Wilson, Monica. *Reaction to Conquest.* London, 1936. Includes eye-witness accounts of animal offerings and prayers to the shades.

Wilson, Monica. "Witch Beliefs and Social Structure." *American Journal of Sociology* 56 (January 1951): 307-313.

Wilson, Monica. *Rituals of Kinship among the Nyakyusa.* London, 1957. This work and its companion volume, *Communal Rituals of the Nyakyusa* (London, 1957), describe the whole cycle celebrated; they quote the texts and describe the situations on which interpretation of symbols is based.

Wilson, Monica. "Co-operation and Conflict." In *The Oxford History of South Africa,* edited by Monica Wilson and Leonard Thompson, vol. 1. Oxford, 1969. Shows that the Xhosa cattle killing of 1856 was one of a series led by prophets who urged purification from witchcraft and sacrifice to the shades.

Wilson, Monica. *Religion and the Transformation of Society.* Cambridge, 1971. Discusses the change in traditional religion as the scale of societies in Africa increases.

Wilson, Monica. "Mhlakaza." In *Les Africains,* edited by Charles-André Julien et al., vol. 5. Paris, 1977. The Xhosa cattle killing has been seen by various writers as a plot of the chiefs to drive the Xhosa to war, as a plot of the whites to destroy the Xhosa, and as a resistance movement. Little attention has been paid to its fundamental religious aspect, which is discussed here. (The text is, alas, marred by many mistakes in the French printing of names.)

MONICA WILSON

SPINOZA, BARUKH

SPINOZA, BARUKH (1632-1677, known as Bento in Portuguese, Benedictus in Latin); Jewish rational naturalist of Marrano descent, author of a rigorously monistic interpretation of reality expressed through an interlocking chain of propositions demonstrated in the geometrical manner. His aim was to contemplate things as they really are rather than as we would like them to be.

Life and Works. On 27 July 1656 Bento de Spinoza was excommunicated by the *ma`amad* (ruling board) of the Amsterdam Jewish community into which he had been born. The manuscript of the ban, written in Portuguese, the language of all the documents of the Amsterdam Jewish community, is still preserved in the municipal archives. Spinoza and a colleageue, Juan de Prado, were excommunicated because they thought the Law (Torah) untrue, that souls die with the body, and that there is no God except philosophically speaking.

Spinoza's early years after the ban were spent at Rijnsburg with Collegiant thinkers. His first philosophical essay, the *Korte verhandeling van God de mensch en des zelfs welstand* (Short Treatise on God, Man, and His Well-Being), discovered about 1860 and of which we possess two Dutch versions of an original not meant for publication, was apparently completed about 1660. The *Short Treatise,* in which we are still witness to the birth pangs of Spinoza's system, has a strong pantheistic-mystical coloring, and its language is still clearly theological. Spinoza's *De intellectus emendatione* (Correction of the Intellect), meant as an introduction to the *Short Treatise* and dealing with method, was written shortly after the latter (though not published until after his death).

Discontented with the Collegiant ethics of mystic withdrawal, Spinoza moved in April 1663 to Voorburg, near The Hague. In 1670, his *Tractatus Theologico-Politicus* was published anonymously under a false imprint in Amsterdam. The book was a philosophical statement of the Republican party. A few months thereafter, the Reformed Church Council of Amsterdam pronounced its condemnation of the book.

In 1672 came the French invasion of Holland and events that cast a dark shadow on Spinoza's last years. Late in the summer of 1675, Spinoza completed his *magnum opus, the Ethica ordine geometrico demonstrata* (Ethics), and went to Amsterdam to arrange for its publication, but there, as he wrote to Henry Oldenburg, "while I was negotiating, a rumor gained currency that I had in the press a book concerning God, wherein I endeavored to show there is no God" (*Letter* 68, September 1675). He therefore decided to put off the publication.

His last major work, the *Tractatus Politicus,* was unfortunately interrupted by Spinoza's death on 21 February 1677.

Biblical Critique. Spinoza's excommunication left a psychological scar that explains much of his subsequent bitterness toward his own people and their traditions. Much of his writing in the *Tractatus* is marred by a one-sidedness that distorts his judgment.

To Spinoza, the biblical doctrine of the chosenness of the Hebrews implies on their part a childish or malicious joy in their exclusive possession of the revelation of the Bible. The doctrine is to be explained by the fact that Moses was constrained to appeal to the childish understanding of the people. In truth, he claims, the Hebrew nation was not chosen by God for its wisdom—it was not distinguished by intellect or virtue— but for its social organization. Spinoza explains the extraordinary fact of Jewish survival by the universal hatred that Jews drew upon themselves.

Thought. Spinoza begins and ends with God. He is convinced that upon reflective analysis we become immediately aware that we have an idea of "substance," or that which is in itself and is conceived through itself. Since substances having different attributes have nothing in common with one another, and since if two things have nothing in common, one cannot be the cause of the other, it is evident that all the entities of which we have experience, including ourselves, must, since they all have extension in common, constitute one substance. Although man is also characterized by thought, which has nothing in common with extension, since he is aware of his own extension, these two attributes cannot denote two substances but must be instead two parallel manifestations of one and the same substance. Spinoza thus insists that we have a clear and distinct idea of substance or God, having at least two parallel attributes. God is eternally in a state of self-modification, producing an infinite series of modes, which are manifested under either of his attributes. Under the attribute of extension, there is the immediate infinite mode, motion and rest, and under thought, the absolutely infinite intellect, or the idea of God. Finally come the finite modes, or particular things.

Influence on Later Thought. Alone among the major philosophers, Spinoza founded no school. Although his work did not fall into complete oblivion for the first hundred years after his death (during which time his name was connected principally with the *Tractatus Theologico-Politicus*), only toward the end of the eighteenth century did it begin to arouse enthusiasm among men of letters. In 1778, Herder equated Spinoza with John himself as the apostle of love, and in 1780 Lessing declared to Friedrich Jacobi that "there is no other philosophy than that of Spinoza." Moses Mendelssohn, although a follower of Christian Wolff, who directed a formidable critique against Spinoza, hailed Spinoza as early as 1775 as a martyr for the furthering of human knowledge.

In the 1850s, Shemu'el David Luzzatto stirred up a literary polemic concerning Spinoza. Luzzatto attacked Spinoza's emphasis on the primacy of the intellect over the feelings of the heart and his denial of free will and final causes, and called unjustified his attack on the Pharisees and on the Mosaic authorship of all of the Pentateuch. A virulent attack against Spinoza, as impassioned as that by Luzzatto, was later mounted by Hermann Cohen in his "Spinoza über Staat und Religion, Judentum und Christentum" (1905; reprinted in Cohen's *Jüdische Schriften,* Berlin, 1924, 3.290-372).

In America, Spinoza was held in very high regard among the transcendentalists of the nineteenth century. Oliver Wendell Holmes (1841-1935) read and reread Spinoza's *Ethics,* and his famous formulation that freedom of thought reached a limit only when it posed a "clear and present danger" appears to have been made under Spinoza's influence.

BIBLIOGRAPHY

The best critical edition of Spinoza's works is that by Carl Gebhardt, *Spinoza Opera,* 4 vols. (Heidelberg, 1925). A useful edition with translation and notes of Spinoza's *Tractatus Politicus* is by A. G. Wernham: *Benedict de Spinoza, The Political Works* (Oxford, 1958). A new and reliable translation of Spinoza's works by E. M. Curley is *The Collected Works of Spinoza,* vol. I (Princeton, 1985; vol. 2, forthcoming). A comprehensive bibliography of Spinoza up to 1942 is Adolph S. Oko's *The Spinoza Bibliography* (Boston, 1964), which has been supplemented by Jon Wetlesens's *A Spinoza Bibliography, 1940-1970,* 2d rev. ed. (Oslo, 1971); E. M. Curley's bibliography in *Spinoza: Essays in Interpretation,* edited by Eugene Freeman and Maurice Mandelbaum (LaSalle, Ill., 1975), pp. 263-316; Wilhelm Totok's *Handbuch der Geschichte der Philosophie,* vol. 4, *Frühe Neuzeit* 17. *Jahrhundert* (Frankfurt, 1981), pp. 232-296; and Theo van der Werf, H. Siebrand, and C. Westerveen's *A Spinoza Bibliography, 1971-1983* (Leiden, 1984).

A good brief introduction to Spinoza is Stuart Hampshire's *Spinoza* (Baltimore, 1951). The most detailed and illuminating commentary on Spinoza's *Ethics* is Harry A. Wolfson's *The Philosophy of Spinoza,* 2 vols. (Cambridge, Mass., 1934). A comprehensive introduction and commentary (in Hebrew) on the *Short Treatise,* along with a Hebrew translation by Rachel Hollander-Steingart, can be found in *Ma'amar qatsar `al Elohim, ha-adam, ve-oshero,* edited by Joseph Ben Shlomo (Jerusalem, 1978). A similar edition of *De Intellectus Emendatione* with Hebrew commentary is *Ma'amar `al tiqqun ha-sekhel,* translated by Nathan Spiegel and edited by Joseph Ben Shlomo (Jerusalem, 1972). Detailed analyses of Spinoza's *Theological-Political Treatise* can be found in Leo Strauss's *Spinoza's Critique of Religion* (New York, 1965) and André Malet's *Le Traité Theologico-Politique de Spinoza et la pensée biblique* (Paris, 1966).

Indispensable collections of documents on Spinoza's life are I. S. Révah's *Spinoza et le dr. Juan de Prado* (Paris, 1959) and "Aux origines de la rupture spinozienne," *Revue des études juives* 3 (July-December 1964): 359-431, and A. M. Vaz Dias's *Spinoza Mercator & Autodidactus* (The Hague, 1932), translated from Dutch in *Studia Rosenthaliana* 16 (November 1982) and supplemented by four related articles. An excellent account of the social-political context of Spinoza's work is Lewis S. Feuer's *Spinoza and the Rise of Liberalism* (Boston, 1958). Two important and provocative interpretations of Spinoza from the viewpoint of contemporary philosophy are E. M. Curley's *Spinoza's Metaphysics: An Essay in Interpretation* (Cambridge, Mass., 1969) and Jonathan Bennett's *A Study of Spinoza's Ethics* (Indianapolis, 1984).

Useful collections of essays on Spinoza include *Studies in Spinoza: Critical and Interpretive Essays,* edited by S. Paul Kashap (Berkeley, 1972); *Spinoza: A Collection of Critical Essays,* edited by Marjorie Grene (Garden City, N. Y., 1973); *Speculum Spinozanum, 1677-1977,* edited by Siegfried Hessing (London, 1977); *Spinoza: New Perspectives,* edited by Robert W. Shahan and J. I. Biro (Norman, Okla., 1978); *The Philosophy of Baruch Spinoza,* edited by Richard Kennington (Washington, D. C., 1980); *Spinoza, His Thought and Work,* edited by Nathan Rotenstreich and N. Schneider (Jerusalem, 1983); and *Spinoza's Political and Theological Thought,* edited by C. De Deugd (Amsterdam, 1984).

DAVID WINSTON

SPIRITUAL GUIDE

Since ancient times, the figure of the spiritual guide has stood at the center of contemplative and esoteric traditions. It would appear that all such traditions stress the necessity of a spiritual preceptor who has immediate knowledge of the laws of spiritual development and who can glean from the adept's actions and attitudes his respective station on the spiritual path as well as the impediments that lie ahead. Furthermore, the guide is responsible for preserving and advancing the precise understanding of the teaching and spiritual discipline to which he is heir, including both a written tradition and an oral tradition "outside the scriptures," which at its highest level is passed on from master to succeeding master and to certain disciples according to their level of insight.

Ancient Greece. Pythagoras and Socrates remind us that the worthy figure of the spiritual guide is not confined to the strict forms of religion but can also be identified in various fraternities, orders, and academies whose primary concern is the self-transformation and spiritual enlightenment of their members.

According to Aristotle, the Pythagoreans taught that among rational beings there is that which is God, that which is man, and "that which is like Pythagoras" (Arist., frag. 192). The spiritual guide, as in the case of Pythagoras, stands between the human and the suprahuman worlds, between the mundane and the sacred; the guide is the intermediate *par excellence,* mediating energies from above and attracting disciples from below.

Jacob Needleman's study of the *Symposium* (in *The Heart of Philosophy,* New York, 1982) reminds us of certain aspects of Socrates' personality and energy as a guide, aspects that have been long overlooked by philosophers. Socrates, as in the other dialogues, is allowed to speak for himself to the extent that he alone among Athenians admits that he does not know; he is a man who is questioning. The state of questioning once again reflects the idea of the intermediate; it represents an intermediate state of unknowing, free at least from false and unexamined views.

Judaism. Although it is difficult to speculate on the figure of the spiritual guide as he might have existed in ancient Judaism, as, for example, suggested in the texts of *Psalms* and *Ecclesiastes,* the dominant figure of later times became the rabbi. His original function as a "master" is indicated in the New Testament where Jesus is frequently referred to as rabbi.

> **The spiritual guide . . . stands between the human and the suprahuman worlds, between the mundane and the sacred.**

According to doctrine, all rabbis are mutually equal, while reserving their individual freedom to give ordination to suitable disciples. However, the rabbinical mysticism of the medieval period emphasized hierarchy in other ways; to belong to the inner circle of discipleship presupposed an extraordinary degree of self-discipline. Furthermore, the most esoteric level of exegesis and transmission of teaching was reserved for the most select.

Christianity. The foundation for guidance and discipleship in the Christian tradition is naturally found in the reported actions of Christ: he called his disciples to him; they lived with him and were taught by his actions, words, and gestures.

For Christianity in general, Christ has remained the unequaled teacher, rabbi, a transcendent inner guide through whom man seeks salvation. Over and beyond this tendency toward reliance on a transcendent guide, Eastern Orthodox Christianity has stressed the importance of the *startsy,* or elders, who guide one's spiritual and practical work.

Islam. It has been suggested that much of the wit, humor, and fullness of the image of the spiritual guide in the writings of the Desert Fathers and subsequent accounts of spiritual fathers in early Christianity has been gradually diluted and extracted through generations in an attempt to make the writings more generally palatable.

The Sufi master remains a robust and vigorous man, full of life, paradox and humor.

Shaykh or pir. The *shari`ah,* or divine law, is meant for all Muslims, but beyond that lies the *tariqah,* or spiritual path, for the *murid* (literally "he who has made up his will", i. e., to enter the path). In order to enter the path, it is essential that the adept find and be accepted by a spiritual master, a *shaykh* (Arabic) or *pir* (Persian); as a *hadith* (tradition) says: "When someone has no shaykh, Satan becomes his shaykh."

The absolute necessity of a spiritual guide is so central to the credo of Sufism that at least one biography of the Sufi master Abu Sa`id ibn Abi al-Khayr (d. 1049 CE) reports the maxim that "if any one by means of asceticism and self-mortification shall have risen to an exalted degree of mystical experience, *without having a Pïr to whose authority and example he submits himself,* the Sufis do not regard him as belonging to their community" (Nicholson, [1921] 1976, p. 10).

The Perfect Human Being. The idea of the Perfect Human Being *(insan-i kamil)* seems first to have been employed by the Sufi theosophist Ibn al-`Arabi (d. 1240). Although the idea of the Perfect Human Being has received several different treatments, a general definition might describe him as "a man who has fully realised his essential oneness with the Divine Being in whose likeness he is made" (Nicholson, 1921, p. 78). The saint *(wali)* is the highest knower of God, and consequently he occupies the highest of all human degrees, saintship *(walayah),* as the Perfect Human Being *par excellence.*

Hinduism. The idea of a spiritual preceptor to guide one's study of religion and philosophy has been a constant influence on the religion of India since the most ancient times. Already in the *Rgveda* we see him referred to as the *rsi* ("seer") or *muni* (a sage, or "silent one"); as such, he is the possesser of deep spiritual insights (often resulting from performing austerities) and is considered to be the "author" of the sacred hymns.

Only knowledge that was gained from a teacher was capable of successfully leading one to one's aim (*Chandogya Upanisad* 4.9.3). And from *Chandogya Upanisad* 6.4.1f., it appears that the spiritual guide is also necessary in order to cut through and disperse mundane, empirical knowledge and to become conscious of true spiritual knowledge.

It would seem that the word *guru* is used in the sense of "teacher" or "spiritual guide" for the first time in *Chandogya Upanisad.* Although the tendency to deify the *guru* only gradually gained a doctrinal position, the idea can already be seen in the *Svetasvatara Upanisad* 6.23, which speaks of a man who has the highest love and devotion for God and for his *guru* as for God.

It is in relation to this theme that the idea of the "guru's grace" arose, a concept of particular force even today. Many

Indian seekers feel that the mere presence of the *guru* (as in *satsang,* or keeping spiritual company) can somehow lead the pupil to liberation.

Buddhism. Unlike some Indian traditions that tend to view the *guru* as an incarnation of divinity or as an intermediary to the sacred, early Buddhism emphasized the humanity of the guide and his own attainment of spiritual knowledge. The term designated by the texts for the guide or teacher is "good or virtuous friend" (Pali, *kalyanamitta;* Skt., *kalyanamitra*). The *kalyanamitra* provides guidance based entirely on the insight he has gained from personal experience.

Bodhisattva. At the core of the development of Mahayana Buddhism was the role to be performed by the *bodhisattva* ("enlightenment being"). The *bodhisattva* relinquishes his personal enlightenment and vows to work for the enlightenment of all sentient beings. After attaining the requisite insight *(prajña),* the final stage of the *bodhisattva's* career is devoted to the welfare of others as practiced via skillful means *(upaya).* The employment of skillful means or technique is essentially intended for use by those spiritual guides or masters who possess a complete and perfect knowledge of the teachings and the methods of practice and who are themselves free from the delusions of the mind and emotions.

Lama. The first two schools of Buddhism to appear in Tibet were the Bka'-rgyud-pa (Kagyüpa) and Bka'-gdams-pa (kadam-pa), founded by Mar-pa (d. 1096 or 1097) and Atisa (d. 1054) respectively. With regard to the esoteric tradition of initiation and oral transmission, both schools recognize the same Indian teachers. It is also clear that the first objective of both Mar-pa and Atisa was to gather around them tested disciples who would be capable of transmitting the tradition. When asked by a disciple whether scripture or one's teacher's instructions were more important, Atisa replied that direct instruction from one's teacher was more important; if the chain of instruction and transmission is broken, the text becomes like a corpse, and no power can bring it new life.

Zen patriarchs and Zen masters. It has been observed that every tradition emphasizes the importance of an oral tradition of instruction for the guidance of adepts. The golden age of Ch`an in China (the period from Hui-neng's death until the persecution of Buddhism in the ninth century) was a time in which Ch`an masters of the most remarkable originality won the day. These were vigorous and effusive men who sought to bring their disciples to new levels of insight by demonstrating their own inexpressible experiences of enlightenment by shocking and often violent methods.

It has been argued that the ultimate purpose of the Zen master is one thing alone: to produce a disciple who can carry on the teaching and preserve the transmission of the Dharma. The lineages of many famous monks became extinct after a generation or two because they had no disciples to hand down their teachings.

BIBLIOGRAPHY

Buber, Martin. *Tales of the Hasidim.* 2 vols. Translated by Olga Marx. New York, 1947-1948.

Buber, Martin. *The Tales of Rabbi Nachman.* Translated by Maurice Friedman. London, 1974.

Dumoulin, Heinrich. *A History of Zen Buddhism.* Translated by Paul Peachey. New York, 1963.

Gonda, Jan. "À propos d'un sens magico-religieux de skt. *guru-.*" *Bulletin of the School of Oriental and African Studies* 12 (1947): 124-131.

Gonda, Jan. *Change and Continuity in Indian Religion.* The Hague, 1965.

Guénon, René. "Hermes." In *The Sword of Gnosis,* edited by Jacob Needleman, pp. 370-375. Baltimore, 1974.

Gunaratna, Henepola. *The Path of Serenity and Insight.* Columbia, Mo., 1984.

Kadloubovsky, Eugènie, and G. E. H. Palmer, trans. *Unseen Warfare, Being the Spiritual Combat and Path to Paradise as Edited by Nicodemus of the Holy Mountain and Revised by Theophan the Recluse.* London, 1952.

Kerényi, Károly. *Hermes, Guide of Souls.* Translated by Murray Stein. Zurich, 1976.

Kierkegaard, Søren. *Philosophical Fragments.* 2d ed. Princeton, 1962.

Lhalungpa, Lobsang P., trans. *The Life of Milarepa.* New York, 1977.

Lings, Martin. *A Moslem Saint of the Twentieth Century: Shaikh Ahmad al-Alawi.* 2d ed. Berkeley, 1973.

Maharaj, Sri Nisargadatta. *I Am That.* Bombay, 1972.

Nalanda Translation Committee under the direction of Chögyam Trungpa, trans. *The Life of Marpa the Translator.* Boulder, 1982.

Nasr, Seyyed Hossein. "The Sufi Master as Exemplified in Persian Sufi Literature." *Studies in Comparative Religion* 4 (Summer 1970): 140-149.

Needleman, Jacob. "The Search for the Wise Man." In *Search: Journey on the Inner Path,* edited by Jean Sulzberger, pp. 85-100. New York, 1979.

Needleman, Jacob. *The Heart of Philosophy.* New York, 1982.

Nicholson, Reynold A. *Studies in Islamic Mysticism* (1921). Reprint, Cambridge, 1976.

Palmer, G. E. H., Philip Sherrard, and Kallistos Ware, eds. and trans. *The Philokalia,* vol. 1. London, 1979.

Schimmel, Annemarie. *Mystical Dimensions of Islam.* Chapel Hill, N. C., 1975.

Yampolsky, Philip, ed. and trans. *The Platform Sutra of the Sixth Patriarch.* New York, 1967.

Yampolsky, Philip, trans. *The Zen Master Hakuin.* New York, 1971.

STUART W. SMITHERS

SUFISM

Origins

One of the truly creative manifestations of religious life in Islam is the mystical tradition, known as Sufism. The terms *Sufi* and *Sufism* evoke complex layers of meaning in Islam, including the denial of the world, close association with the

Prophet and his message, and a spiritual attainment that raises one to a rank of unique intimacy with God.

Some earlier Western scholars of Sufism concluded that mysticism is incompatible with the Muslim perception of an almighty, transcendent God with whom one shares little intimacy. In their opinion Sufi mysticism was born of Islam's contact with other major world religions, especially Christianity and Buddhism. This theory is no longer considered viable.

The experience of mystical union need not, be seen as foreign to Islam. On the contrary, interior spiritual development becomes a concern at a relatively early date in the writings of important Qur'an commentators. Of the two traditional methods of Qur'anic exegesis predominating in Islam, *tafsir* emphasizes the exoteric elements of the text: grammar, philology, history, dogma, and the like, while *ta'wil* stresses the search for hidden meanings, the esoteric dimensions of the Qur'anic text. It is among Sufis (and Shi'i Muslims) that *ta'wil* has found special favor.

The Ascetic Movement. The early catalysts for the development of mysticism in Islam, however, were not all spiritual in nature. The dramatic social and political changes brought about by the establishment of the Umayyad dynasty in the mid-seventh century also played a pivotal role. The capital of the empire was moved from Medina to the more opulent and cosmopolitan Damascus, and the rapid spread of Islam introduced enormous wealth and ethnic diversity into what had originally been a spartan, Arab movement. In reaction to the worldliness of the Umayyads, individual ascetics arose to preach a return to the heroic values of the Qur'an through the abandonment of both riches and the trappings of earthly power. The three major centers of the ascetic movement in the eighth and ninth centuries were Iraq, especially the cities of Basra, Kufa, and Baghdad; the province of Khorasan, especially the city of Balkh; and Egypt.

Mystical Ecstasy. The evolution of ascetic and theoretical principles to guide the Sufi wayfarer, and the growing sophistication of aesthetic expressions of love mysticism were not the only signs of a maturing mystical tradition in Islam. An additional area of creative exploration by a number of ninth- and tenth-century Sufis centered on refining the understanding of what actually constitutes the goal of mystical experience.

Mystical Literature

The science of opposites, with its rich symbolism and provocative speculation, appealed only to a small number of Sufis because of the level of intellectual sophistication it demanded and because of its esoteric quality. In contrast, beginning in the late ninth century, a number of texts began to appear that were aimed at a broader spectrum of the Muslim faithful and functioned as training guides for men and women interested in cultivating mystical experience.

The Manual Tradition. The emphasis of the manuals was not on the arcane dimensions of Sufism, but on its accessibility and its conformity with Islamic orthodoxy.

One of the earliest manuals addressed to a Sufi novice is the *Kitab al-ri`ayah* (Book of Consideration) of Abu `Abd Allah al-Harith ibn Asad al-Muhasibi (d. 857). He is remembered particularly for his skill in developing the examination of conscience as an effective tool for advancement in the spiritual life.

Among the classics of this genre of religious literature in Sufism are the *Kitab al-ta`arruf* (Book of Knowledge) of Abu Bakr Muhammad al-Kalabadhi (d. 990 or 995), the *Kitab al-luma`* (Book of Concise Remarks) of Abu Nasr `Abd Allah ibn `Ali al-Sarraj (d. 988), *Al-risalah al-qushayriyah* (The Qushayrian Letter) of Abu al-Qasim `Abd al-Karim al-Qushayri (d. 1074), the *Kashf al-mahjub* (Unveiling of the Veiled) of `Ali ibn `Uthman al-Jullabi al-Hujwiri (d. 1071/2?), and the *Qut al-qulub* (Nourishment of the Heart) of Abu Talib Muhammad ibn `Ali ibn `Atiyah al-Harithi al-Makki (d. 996).

Other Genres. In addition to the Sufi manuals, other important genres of mystical literature developed in the classical period. Fables, epigrams, epic poems, poetry, aphorisms, all were creative vehicles for mystical expression. Early Qur'an commentators and street preachers had focused on the lives of the prophets for inspiration. This spawned the *Qisas al-anbiya'* (Tales of the Prophets), collections of lively didactic stories, often with moral themes. These hagiographic compendia are crucial for our knowledge of the lives and teachings of the great masters of classical Sufism.

The first systematic history of the lives of Sufi mystics is ascribed to Abu `Abd al-Rahman al-Azdi al-Sulami (d. 1021). His *Tabaqat al-sufiyah* (Generations of the Sufis) became the basis for the expanded versions of two later Sufis, the *Tabaqat al-sufiyah* of Abu Isma`il Abd Allah Ansari (d. 1089) and the *Nafahat al-uns* (Wafts of Pleasure) of Nur al-Din `Abd al-Rahman ibn Ahmad Jami (d. 1492). The most comprehensive work of Sufi hagiography, however, is the prodigious, multivolume *Hilyat al-awliya'* (Necklace of Saints) of Abu Nu`aym al-Isfahani (d. 1037).

Gnosis and Ibn 'Arabi

The history of mysticism in Islam is replete with individuals of brilliance and creativity. Among these exceptional personalities, however, one stands out from the rest because of his unique genius. Abu Bakr Muhammad ibn al-'Arabi al-Hatimi al-Ta'i received the greater part of his education in the traditional Islamic religious disciplines. A great deal of his mystical insight, evolved from visionary experiences, the first occuring during an illness in his youth. Throughout his life he continued to have visions on which he placed a great deal of reliance.

Ibn 'Arabi's visionary bent is equally evident in his claim to have been initiated into Sufism by the mythic figure Khidr, a mysterious being, said to be immortal, associated with a Qur'anic fable (surah 18) and pre-Islamic legends.

In his early twenties Ibn 'Arabi traveled extensively throughout Spain and North Africa and broadened his intellectual perspectives. He describes a unique meeting in Cordova with the greatest of the Muslim Aristotelian philosophers, Ibn Rushd (known as Averroës in the Latin West). The encounter is heavy with symbolism, for Ibn Rushd represents the total reliance of philosophers on reason (`aql), while Ibn 'Arabi champions gnosis (ma`rifah) as the only means to experience the fullness of truth.

Ibn 'Arabi is unique because he was both an original thinker and synthesizer. Many of his ideas resonate with earlier intellectual developments in Sufism and in philosophical theology. His greatness, however, lies in his ability to systematize Sufi theory into a coherent whole with solid metaphysical underpinnings. The corpus of Ibn 'Arabi's work is massive, which complicates considerably any attempt at a comprehensive analysis of his thought. In addition his style is often dense, reflecting the esoteric nature of his ideas. Two of his most influential works are *Al-futuhat al-makkiyah* (The Meccan Revelations), which he was ordered to write in a visionary experience while on pilgrimage, and *Fusus al-hikam* (The Bezels of Wisdom).

Sufi Fraternities

The history of Sufism is much more than the history of mystical theory and expression. There is a significant social dimension to Islamic mysticism. Fluid interaction among Sufis soon evolved into the more structured relationship of master and disciple, adding a new level of social complexity. Not only would disciples visit their masters, but many also took up residence with them. The earliest formal Sufi convent seems to date from the latter part of the eighth century CE, on the island of Abadan.

By the thirteenth century, several types of Sufi establishments had evolved, each with a different general purpose. The more serious training took place in the *zawiyahs,* which usually housed a teaching shaykh.

By the thirteenth century, many Sufi groups became self-perpetuating social organizations whose central focus was the founder and his teaching. No longer was the survival of the group dependent on a particular living shaykh; authority was passed from shaykh to disciple, thus providing a stable structural basis for the continued growth and development of the community.

Silsilahs. These stable social organizations came to be called *tariqahs* ("ways"), known in English as Sufi orders, fraternities or brotherhoods. Each founding shaykh had his *silsilah* ("chain"), his spiritual lineage which contributed substantially to his stature in the Sufi community. The *silsilah* is, more precisely, a genealogy, tracing the names of one's master, of one's master's master, and so on back through histo-

ry. Often a prominent shaykh would have been initiated more than once, by a number of illustrious Sufis, thus adding additional stature to his spiritual pedigree.

The centrality of *silsilahs* in Sufi fraternities is not completely unique. One discovers an analogous emphasis in the *hadith* literature, where the literary structure of a *hadith* has two parts: the chain of transmitters *(isnad)* and the body of the text *(matn)*. But, the importance of *isnads* for Muslims is to ground *hadiths* solidly in the period of the original revelation. Thus there can be no question that the teachings of the *hadiths* are innovations; rather *hadiths* are but more detailed insights into God's will already expressed in general terms in the Qur'an.

Veneration of Saints. The institutionalization of *tariqahs* and the emphasis on *silsilahs* enhanced substantially the religious and political position of the master. The shaykhs of

> **In Islam, Allah has one hundred names, ninety-nine of which are known; the hundredth name is hidden.**

the great Sufi orders, therefore, took on superhuman qualities. They became known as *awliya'* (sg., *wali*), intimates or friends of God. Many of the shaykhs of important orders were acknowledged by their followers as the *qutb,* the "pole" or "axis" around which the cosmos revolves, the Perfect Human Being, the point at which the divine Creative Imagination most fully manifests itself in the world of illusion. The perfected shaykhs are objects of veneration both during their lives and after their deaths.

Ritual Practice. The full members of the fraternities committed themselves in obedience to the shaykh, who initiated them into the order and bestowed upon them the patched frock *(khirqah)*, the sign of their entry onto the Sufi path. They were encouraged to subject themselves completely to the master's will, to be like dead bodies in the hands of the body-washers.

Common to most of the Sufi fraternities were ritual practices called *dhikr* ("remembrance") and *sama`* ("audition").

Dhikr. The impetus for the practice of *dhikr* is derived from those Qur'anic verses that enjoin the faithful to remember God often. Among Sufis this duty evolved into a complex exercise performed by an individual or group. Many fraternities put their own particular stamp on the *dhikr* exercise. Most *dhikr* techniques, however, involve the rhythmic repetition of a phrase, often Qur'anic, in which one of the names of God appears. In Islam, Allah has one hundred names, ninety-nine of which are known; the hundredth name is hidden. Certain Sufis who ascribed to themselves the rank of *qutb* claimed to have been blessed with this most precious secret. The more sophisticated methods of *dhikr* usually involve breath control, body movements, and a number of other complex techniques to gain control over the five senses as well the psyche and imagination.

Sama`.* Like *dhikr, sama` has become identified with Sufi ritual practice. It involves listening to music, usually with a group. The music is often accompanied by Qur'an chants and/or the singing of mystical poetry. The recital is intended to spark a mystical experience within the auditors. Those most affected by the *sama`* rise up to dance in unison with the music. Depending on the Sufi group, the dance can be a marvel of esthetic movement or the frenetic writhings of the seemingly possessed.

The emphasis on *dhikr* and *sama`* has helped to blur the distinction in popular Sufism between mystical experience that is attained after serious spiritual training and experience that is self-induced. Unsophisticated sessions of *dhikr* and *sama`,* to this day, often consist of self-hypnosis, hysteria, drug-induced states, and other violent emotions that pass for mystical experience. Despite accusations of vulgarization, *dhikr* and *sama`* remain important emotional outlets in the Muslim community and are unique sociological events during which various levels of society find themselves interacting on an equal footing.

BIBLIOGRAPHY

By far the best introduction to Sufism in English is Annemarie Schimmel's *Mystical Dimensions of Islam* (Chapel Hill, N. C., 1975). Other introductory texts of interest are A. J. Ar-berry's *Sufism: An Account of the Mystics of Islam* (1950; reprint, London, 1979) and Reynold A. Nicholson's *The Mystics of Islam* (1914; reprint, London, 1963). The most astute treatment of the development of early Sufism, especially its relationship to Qur'anic exegesis, is Paul Nwyia's *Exégèse coranique et language mystique* (Beirut, 1970).

There are a number of monographs dealing with one or other of the early Sufi ascetics. Margaret Smith's two works, *Rabi`a the Mystic and Her Fellow-Saints in Islam* (Cambridge, 1928) and *An Early Mystic of Baghdad: A Study of the Life and Teaching of Harith b. Asad Al-Muhasibi, A. D. 781-A. D. 857* (1935, reprint, New York, 1973), are both excellent, as well as Nicholson's study of Abu Sa`id ibn Abi al-Khayr in *Studies in Islamic Mysticism* (1921; reprint, Cambridge, 1976).

There are two excellent English translations of Sufi manuals, Nicholson's translation of al-Hujwiri's *Kashf al-Mahjub: The Oldest Persian Treatise on Sufism,* 2d ed. (London, 1936), and Arberry's translation of al-Kalabadhi's *Kitab al-ta`arruf* under the title *The Doctrine of the Sufis* (Cambridge, 1935). Several chapters of Seyyed Hossein Nasr's *Sufi Essays* (London, 1972) deal with stations and states and the master-disciple relationship.

No study of the ecstatics in Sufism is complete without Louis Massignon's extraordinary work on al-Hallaj, recently translated into English by Herbert Mason as *The Passion of Al-Hallaj: Mystic and Martyr of Islam,* 4 vols. (Princeton, 1982). Carl W. Ernst's *Words of Ecstasy in Sufism* (Albany, 1984) is extremely helpful as well. Reynold A. Nicholson's *The Idea of Personality in Sufism* (1964; reprint, Lahore, 1970) is a lucid exploration of the psychology of ecstatic utterances.

There is an excellent translation by Wheeler Thackston of Ansari's *Munajat in The Book of Wisdom and Intimate Conversations,* translated and edited by Wheeler Thackston and Victor Danner (New York, 1978). The premier scholar of Ansari is Serge de Laugier de Beaurecueil, whose bibliography of Ansari provides much useful information and some fine translations: *Khwadja `Abdullah Ansari, 396-481 H./1006-1089: Mystique hanbalite* (Beirut, 1965).

There are a number of fine translations of 'Attar's *mathnavis: The Ilahi-nama or Book of God,* translated by J. A. Boyle (Manchester, 1976); *Le livre de l'épreuve (Musibatnama),* translated by Isabelle de Gastines (Paris, 1981); and *The Conference of the Birds,* translated by Afkham Darbandi and Dick Davis (London, 1984). The best comprehensive study of 'Attar and his work remains Helmut Ritter's *Das Meer der Seele* (Leiden, 1955).

Henry Corbin has written extensively on Islamic gnosticism, Islamic Neoplatonism, and Ibn 'Arabi. Works such as *Creative Imagination in the Sufism of Ibn `Arabi* (Princeton, 1969) demonstrate his extraordinary erudition and propose provocative syntheses that must be evaluated with care. A new translation of Ibn `Arabi's *Fusus al-hikam* by R. W. J. Austin under the title *The Bezels of Wisdom* (New York, 1980) is excellent. Toshihiko Izutsu's comparative study of Sufism and Taoism, *A Comparative Study of the Key Philosophical Concepts in Sufism and Taoism* (Tokyo, 1966), also serves as an excellent introduction to Ibn `Arabi's thought. Finally, in his *Studies in Islamic Mysticism* (1921; reprint, Cambridge, 1976) Reynold A. Nicholson provides a very lucid analysis of the idea of the Perfect Human Being as it originated with Ibn `Arabi and was later developed by al-Jili.

The best translations of Rumi's work are by Reynold A. Nicholson, especially *The Mathnawi of Jalalu'ddin Rumi,* 8 vols. (London, 1925-1971). Annemarie Schimmel's *The Triumphal Sun: A Study of the Works of Jalaloddin Rumi* (London, 1978) is a solid introduction to his writings, as is William C. Chittick's *The Sufi Path of Love: The Spiritual Teachings of Rumi* (Albany, 1983). Schimmel's *As Through a Veil: Mystical Poetry in Islam* (New York, 1982) places Rumi in the wider context of the poetic tradition in Sufism.

There are many studies of individual Sufi orders. The best general work, however, is J. Spencer Trimingham's *The Sufi Orders in Islam* (New York, 1971). The role of the fraternities in the Indian subcontinent is extremely well presented in Annemarie Schimmel's *Islam in the Indian Subcontinent* (Leiden, 1980). An English translation by Victor Danner of Ibn `Ata' Allah's *Hikam* can be found in Thackston and Danner's *The Book of Wisdom and Intimate Conversations* (cited above). A superb French translation and commentary of the same text, together with a thorough analysis of the early development of the Sha-dhiliyah can be found in Paul Nwyia's *Ibn `Ata' Allah et la naissance de la confrérie sadilite* (Beirut, 1972). One of the more interesting treatments of a Sufi in the modern period is Martin Lings's study of the life and writings of Shaykh Ahmad al-`Alawi, *A Moslem Saint of the Twentieth Century,* 2d ed. (Berkeley, 1973).

PETER J. AWN

SUPERNATURAL, THE

Mysterious occurrences and beings that habitually or occasionally impinge upon our everyday experience are called "supernatural."

Historical Development of the Notion. The term *supernatural* was given wide currency by Thomas Aquinas (1225-1274) and the Scholastics, but it had numerous antecedents in the idiom of the Hellenistic thinkers and church fathers. Neoplatonists in particular accumulated superlatives to speak of the realm of the divine: it was above the highest heaven, beyond the world, and even beyond being. This link between grace and the supernatural became firmly entrenched in scholastic theology.

The word *supernatural,* however, became associated with the unusual, the marvelous, the surprising. While medieval theologians had used the term *supernatural* to refer to the moral and spiritual dynamics of salvation, ordinary Christians

> The word *supernatural* became associated with the unusual, the marvelous, the surprising.

came to call supernatural any extraordinary occurrence that could not be accounted for by the usual explanations at hand.

Baroque taste spread in Christian lands. What was infinite, awesome, powerful, overwhelming, and stunning was considered to convey a sense of God. Religious architecture and furniture became calculatedly impressive; oratory became stately. Miracles as powerful disruptions of nature's laws appeared, then, necessary to the cause of religion. Many theologians thus taught that human beings must regard the supernatural as contrary to nature: God, they said, intervenes providentially, and occasionally suspends the course of nature; he also reveals supernatural truths that we must obediently accept even though their truth is not manifest to our unaided reason.

Application of the Notion to the Study of Religious and Cultural Systems. Among scholars of the nineteenth century it came to be commonly admitted that belief in what Herbert Spencer has called "the supernatural genesis of phenomena" characterized religious people. All religions were said to feature belief in supernatural beings. Lucien Lévy-Bruhl (1857-1939) in his early influential work argued that the primitive mind believed in "mystical," not "physical," influences, whereas practically all contemporaries recognize a clear line of demarcation between the supernatural (rejected by all except the credulous) and the data furnished by everyday ordinary sense experience and the broad light of day. Paul Radin (1883-1959) argued against Lévy-Bruhl and spoke of the supernatural as arising against a background of inevitable fears (stemming from economic and psychic insecurity) that he found to be present in all human beings, primitive and modern. He saw in the modern West a decline in religion and in recourse to supernatural beings for help,

because other means of emphasizing and maintaining life values were available and on the ascendant.

Rodney Needham (1972) has successfully argued that statements of belief are the only evidence we have of the phenomenon. Both theologians and anthropologists, he maintains, have taken too much for granted and have been too quick to specify what beliefs other people have and what difference these beliefs make. Belief in anything, including supernatural beings, is thus a very elusive phenomenon. It would be safer to characterize religion by attitudinal factors and ritual practice rather than by belief. And any statement of belief should be taken with a grain of salt. The highly imaginative stories of primitives abound in wit and irony and cannot be pinned down with the psychology of belief common among sober scientists (whose thinking often reflects the easy and moralistic recourse to expressions of belief characteristic of early modern theologians).

Systematic Considerations. The human being has in his favor a quick mobile mind, but he is frail and his body is destined to contract disease and, ultimately, to die. Men and women are thus constantly the potential victims of aleatory events that can be painful to them. Fearful of impending disasters, they seek the protection of stronger human beings. As infants and children they start life with such protection. Later they attach themselves to strong persons whom they count on to be successful and wise so that they themselves can live in a secure world, one without interstices from which unpredictable attacks might come. Priests, who are typical examples of strong ones, are also thinkers. They teach survival skills and provide ritual and verbal comfort when these skills fail, as necessarily they must. Strong ones are therefore in touch with suitable explanations that ideally can help us in those boundary situations that occur when our ordinary world falls apart.

Our modern concept of nature and natural causes firmly supports a reality principle: when physically sick (or, today, even when anxious) we mainly turn to scientific medicine. Fear of and belief in supernatural agencies do not color in any significant way our sense of what is feasible in our embodied condition. But we hold on to some nonscientific health lore passed on through oral, unofficial channels, and we nostalgically transmit recipes for more natural care of the human body and its ailments.

Human beings want both to be believed and to be understood, but usually not at the same time and not by the same people. Individuals want their words and their symbols (1) to be believed and accepted and (2) to create reality, a safe common reality that is not limited to the individual alone. The characteristic feature of modern society is not fewer beliefs in supernatural beings but the variety of strong ones we turn to and include in our world for different purposes and at different times, and the variety of the structures of plausibility that buttress them. And, heroic or not, we, like the hero of many folk tales, have no permanent master to guide our steps through all the perils of life.

BIBLIOGRAPHY

Bellah, Robert N. *Beyond Belief: Essays on Religion in a Post-Traditional World.* New York, 1970. A collection of articles by a leading sociologist of religion. Especially noteworthy are those on religious evolution, on belief, and on symbolic realism.

Douglas, Mary, and Aaron Wildavsky. *Risk and Culture: An Essay on the Selection of Technological and Environmental Dangers.* Berkeley, 1982. The illustrations are drawn from a specific contemporary issue, but the essay shows well how culture achieves some protection against danger.

Lenoble, Robert. *Esquisse d'une histoire de l'idée de nature.* Paris, 1968. The classic history of the ideas entertained about nature.

Lubac, Henri de. *Surnaturel: Études historiques.* Paris, 1946. Essays on the idea of the supernatural in Christian theology.

Needham, Rodney. *Belief, Language, and Experience.* Oxford, 1972. A brilliant introduction to problems in comparative epistemology.

Penzoldt, Peter. *The Supernatural in Fiction.* 1952; New York, 1965. An excellent account of the supernatural novel.

Sennett, Richard. *Authority.* New York, 1980. The best analysis of authority as bond in modern society.

Turner, Victor. "An Ndembu Doctor in Practice." In *Magic, Faith and Healing,* edited by Ari Kiev. New York, 1964. A classic account of a supernatural healing practice.

Waardenburg, Jacques. *Classical Approaches to the Study of Religion: Aims, Methods and Theories of Research,* vol. 1, *Introduction and Anthology.* Paris, 1973. The classic anthology of the major statements by the founders of the modern study of religion, including Spencer, Durkheim, Lévy-Bruhl, Marret, and Radin.

MICHEL DESPLAND

SUPERSTITION

Superstition is a judgmental term traditionally used by dominant religions to categorize and denigrate earlier, less sophisticated or disapproved religious attitudes and behavior. A belief is perceived as superstitious by adherents of a particular religious orthodoxy, and it is from their perspective that the category acquires its meaning. The use of the term *superstition* is inevitably pejorative rather than descriptive or analytical.

Origin and Classical Usage. The classical world criticized certain religious behaviors as irrational, or as reflecting an incorrect understanding of both nature and divinity. In its earliest Latin literary usage by Plautus and Ennius, *superstitio* was already a negative term describing divination, magic, and "bad religion" in general. For classical Roman observers like Seneca, Lucretius, and Cicero, *superstitio* meant erroneous, false, or excessive religious behaviors stemming from ignorance of philosophical and scientific truths about the

laws of nature. Such ignorance was associated with the common people *(vulgus)* and with the countryside *(pagus),* so that superstitious behavior had a social locus in the uneducated, lower orders of Roman society. As the empire expanded, the term *superstitio* was applied to exotic foreign religions of which the Romans disapproved. Its meaning became more collective, referring to the "religion of others" in pejorative terms.

Early Christianity. The early Christians adopted this collective meaning, turning the category of superstition back on the Romans. In the period after the second century, pagans and Christians reciprocally condemned each other's religious beliefs and ceremonial practices as the superstitious cult of false deities. This use of *superstitio* to categorize the whole of classical pagan religion as idolatrous and even demonic constitutes a basic core of meaning that persists throughout the Christian era.

Medieval Christianity. The religions of the Germanic tribes were perceived in a similar way by the Christian missionaries who undertook the conversion of these so-called barbarians in the period following the fall of the Roman empire. The cure for their idolatry and superstition was baptism and the acceptance of Christianity as the true religion. But even after the evangelization of whole tribes, attitudes, beliefs, and practices associated with pre-Christian religions persisted.

The difficulties of weaning newly evangelized peoples from their old ways led Pope Gregory I (590-604) to suggest a gradualist approach to their conversion. Gregory proposed that heathen shrines be reconsecrated as churches and that existing days of celebration be adapted to the Christian calendar. Throughout the medieval period, church councils and synods condemned paganizing and superstitious observances in an effort to complete the process of christianization by enforcing more orthodox standards.

Scholastic theologians brought the analysis of superstitious error to a new level of thoroughness and sophistication. Thomas Aquinas (1225-1274) defined superstition as "the vice opposed to the virtue of religion by means of excess . . . because it offers divine worship either to whom it ought not, or in a manner it ought not" (*Summa theologiae* 2.2.92.7). The idea of "undue worship of the true God" revived the classical meaning of exaggerated or overscrupulous religious behavior, now seen as occurring within Christianity rather than wholly or partially outside of it.

The gradual extension of the medieval Inquisition's jurisdiction to include cases of superstition as well as heresy was a turning point in the European attitude toward magical beliefs. While customary law in many parts of Europe had treated magical harm *(maleficium)* like any other crime, the new theological approach focused directly on the means employed, not the end pursued. All magical activity implied that the perpetrator had obtained the power to achieve those effects by apostasy to the devil. This campaign against popular magic emphasized those activities that were, in Aquinas's terms, superstitious by virtue of their presumptively diabolical object.

Catholicism and the Protestant Reformation. The Protestant Reformation intensified humanist critiques of Roman Catholicism. Having rejected most of the ceremonial aspects of Catholicism, from holy water and saints' cults to transubstantiation and the Mass, Protestants of all denominations agreed in their denunciations of the papist religion as magical and superstitious.

Following the anti-Protestant heresy trials of the mid-sixteenth century, the Holy Offices of Spain and Italy turned their attention to the suppression of popular beliefs and practices categorized as superstitious. Trials for magical healing, divination, and love magic occupied a prominent place in inquisitorial prosecution throughout the seventeenth century.

BIBLIOGRAPHY

A general history of Western concepts of superstition has yet to be written. Such a history can be reconstructed with the aid of the primary materials presented by Lynn Thorndike in *A History of Magic and Experimental Science,* 8 vols. (New York, 1923-1958), and by Henry C. Lea in *Materials toward a History of Witchcraft,* 3 vols. (New York, 1939).

A succinct, careful review of the etymology and history of the term in classical Roman literature is provided by Denise Grodzynski in "Superstitio," *Revue des études anciennes* 76 (January-June 1974): 36-60. In *The Cult of the Saints: Its Rise and Function in Latin Antiquity* (Chicago, 1981), Peter Brown argues convincingly against interpreting the cult of saints as a superstitious deformation of the original Christian message.

The uses of the concept in medieval canon law and ecclesiastical literature receives thorough, systematic attention in Dieter Harmening's *Superstitio: Überlieferungs- und theoriege-schichtliche Untersuchungen zur kirchlich-theologischen Aberglaubensliteratur des Mittelalters* (Berlin, 1979). The medieval condemnation of learned and popular magic as superstitious is the subject of Edward Peters's *The Magician, the Witch, and the Law* (Philadelphia, 1978).

The Protestant expansion of the term during the Reformation to include Roman Catholicism is described by Jean Delumeau in "Les réformateurs et la superstition," in *Actes du Colloque l'Amiral de Cologny et Son Temps* (Paris, 1974), pp. 451-487. Keith Thomas provides a magisterial analysis of the survival and suppression of magical beliefs after the Reformation in *Religion and the Decline of Magic: Studies in Popular Beliefs in Sixteenth and Seventeenth Century England* (New York, 1971). The sixteenth-century effort to achieve a "reform of popular culture" is described as a "battle between Carnival and Lent" by Peter Burke in *Popular Culture in Early Modern Europe* (New York, 1978). The Roman Catholic campaign against superstition is examined by M. O'Neil, "*Sacerdote ovvero strione*: Ecclesiastical and Superstitious Remedies in Sixteenth Century Italy," in *Understanding Popular Culture,* edited by Steven L. Kaplan (New York, 1984).

E. William Monter chronicles the prosecution of superstitious offenses by post-Reformation religious orthodoxies and describes also the Enlightenment assault on superstition and religious intolerance in *Ritual, Myth and Magic in Early Modern Europe* (Athens, Ohio, 1983). A study of the meaning of superstition in the modern world is undertaken by Gustav Ja-hoda in *The Psychology of Superstition* (London, 1969).

MARY R. O'NEIL

SUZUKI, D.T.

SUZUKI, D. T., westernized name of Suzuki Dai-setsu Teitaro (1870-1966), Japanese lay Buddhist, author, and lecturer, known in Europe and America primarily for his expositions of Zen. Born on 18 October 1870 in Kanazawa in north central Japan, Suzuki was the youngest of five children. He attended local schools until age seventeen, when it became financially impossible for him to continue. Proficient at English, he taught it in primary schools for a few years and in 1891 moved to Tokyo, where he became a special student at what is now Waseda University. He then also began to frequent the Engakuji, a Zen monastery in Kamakura. His relationship there with the abbot Shaku Soyen (1856-1919) was of critical importance for his later life. This was both because it was the basis for his knowledge of Zen and because Shaku Soyen was chosen to represent Zen Buddhism at the World's Parliament of Religions in Chicago in 1893 and would later arrange for Suzuki to become the assistant to the Illinois industrialist and amateur Orientalist Paul Carus (1852-1919), who was keenly interested in the translation and interpretation of Asian religious and philosophical texts. Suzuki went to America in 1897 and lived in LaSalle, Illinois, working as cotranslator with Carus until 1908. During these years he made the first English translations of a number of important Buddhist texts and published his own *Outlines of Mahayana Buddhism* (1907).

In 1908 Suzuki traveled to Europe and in Paris copied important materials on Chinese Buddhism newly discovered among the Tun-huang manuscripts. He returned to Japan in 1909 to teach English at the Peers' School (Gakushu-in) until 1921, at which time he accepted a chair in Buddhist philosophy at Otani University, a post held until his retirement. In 1911 he married Beatrice Erskine Lane, an American who frequently was his coeditor until her death in 1939. Although he made journeys to England, China, Korea, and America, Suzuki resided in Japan until 1950 and published voluminously both in Japanese and in English during these four decades. At the age of eighty Suzuki moved to New York. There, under the auspices of the Rockefeller Foundation, he began to lecture on Buddhism and Zen at a number of American campuses, especially at Columbia University, where he later became a visiting professor and until 1958 held lectures that were open to the general public. Most of his remaining years were spent in extensive travel and interaction with Westerners, including C. G. Jung, Karen Horney,

Erich Fromm, Martin Heidegger, and Thomas Merton. He died in Tokyo on 12 July 1966.

Suzuki lived large portions of his long life both in Japan and in the West, and he pursued his work in both worlds. In Japan his career began differently from that of most academics, and for some years he was outside the mainstream there. Nevertheless his collected works in Japanese number thirty-two volumes, including many essays that contributed to a rekindling of scholarly and public interest in Buddhist subjects at a time when these were generally ignored by most of his Japanese contemporaries. Many of these studies are still untranslated; they include his content-analysis of certain Mahayana texts in Chinese as well as his appreciative appraisal of neglected Japanese such as the Zen monk Bankei (1622-1693), the records of the Myokonin or pious Pure Land believers of the Tokugawa era, and the religious component in the humorous art of Sengai (1750-1837). Many of his other more general essays in Japanese comprise a sustained insistence upon the formative importance of Buddhism—especially of its Zen and Pure Land forms—in the history of Japanese culture, a topic often less than popular in Japan during the first half of the twentieth century.

Suzuki's voluminous writings in English include Studies in the *Lankavatara-sutra* (1930), a critical edition of the *Gandavyuhasutra* (1934-1936), and more popular works such as his *Essays in Zen Buddhism, An Introduction to Zen Buddhism* (1934), *Zen and Japanese Culture* (rev. ed., 1959), and *The Training of a Zen Buddhist Monk* (1934). Certainly his facility with English, his extensive lecturing in America and Europe, and his participation in conferences all over the world brought Buddhism and Zen in particular to the attention of many who would otherwise have been totally unfamiliar with these topics.

Within the past few decades the Japanese have begun to refer to Suzuki as an important "thinker" *(shisoka)* and to assess his role in the intellectual and religious history of the twentieth century. An important full-length study in Japanese by Akizuki Ryomin in 1959 compared Suzuki's Zen-based thought with the formal philosophy of Nishida Kitaro, widely considered the most important Japanese philosopher of the twentieth century. Akizuki stressed the continuity between the two scholars, pointing out that there is a philosophical dimension in Suzuki's writings on Zen just as there is an important Zen component in the more abstract writings of Nishida. The untranslated correspondence between these two lifelong friends bears witness to the closeness of their thought. Suzuki introduced the works of William James, particularly his *Varieties of Religious Experience,* to Nishida, and the latter found James's positive appraisal of religious experience much more to his liking than what he called the "lifeless" analyses of religion and ethics in the German philosophical works he was reading at the turn of the century. Suzuki, in turn, employed Nishida's analyses to insist upon

the intellectual integrity of the Zen experience—even though he repeatedly resisted any suggestion that such experience could be grasped by the intellect alone. In his lecturing and writing for Westerners, especially when asked to suggest conceptual links to Western experience, Suzuki generally stressed the particularity of Zen and insisted that it was the the same as psychology, parapsychology, experience with hallucinogens, or even mysticism as a general category. His interest in Meister Eckhart was deep, however, and he recognized in Eckhart something equivalent to the basics of Mahayana Buddhism. Probably the most important change in his own thinking was a shift away from the identification of Buddhism as "scientific"; by his own admission, Suzuki came to hold that religion based on science is insufficient, and in his later years he even saw a need for religion to conduct a critique of science.

Concerning Suzuki's influence in the West, it is often said that he made Zen into an English word; certainly he helped to make Zen a topic of great public interest, especially in the 1960s and 1970s. His scholarship made basic Asian texts available in English, and although he has been criticized for being insufficiently sensitive to history, he clearly stimulated a dramatic surge of interest in East Asia among American scholars. Through his lifelong dialogue with Western theologians and religionists, he contributed greatly to an awareness of the Buddhist tradition. Sometimes dismissed as merely a popularizer of Zen, he has also been hailed by the distinguished historian Lynn White, Jr., as someone whose writings broke through the "shell of the Occident" and made our thinking global. His influence upon twentieth-century Japan has also become increasingly clear: he championed Japan's inheritance of continental Buddhism during decades when nationalism focused upon Shinto. Moreover, his writings in Japanese and his obvious ability to make a credible presentation of Buddhism in the West have contributed to what some have called a twentieth-century renaissance of interest—at least an intellectual interest—in Buddhism on the part of the Japanese.

BIBLIOGRAPHY

Suzuki's collected works are available in a Japanese edition only, *Suzuki Daisetsu zenshu,* 32 vols., edited by Hisamatsu Shin'ichi and others (Tokyo, 1968-1971). The same editors have compiled an account of Suzuki's life and thought, *Suzuki Daisetsu: Hito to shiso* (Tokyo, 1971). The festschrift *Buddhism and Culture: Dedicated to Dr. Daisetz Teitaro on His Ninetieth Birthday,* edited by Yamaguchi Susumu (Kyoto, 1960), contains a nearly complete bibliography of Suzuki's works in both Japanese and English. Accounts of particular phases of Suzuki's life are included in a memorial issue of the *Eastern Buddhist,* n. s. 2 (August 1967). The most important study of Suzuki as religious thinker is Akizuki Ryomin's *Suzuki zengaku to Nishida tetsugaku* (Tokyo, 1971).

WILLIAM R. LAFLEUR

SYNAGOGUE

The term *synagogue,* derived from the Greek *sunagoge* ("assembly"), refers primarily to a congregation rather than to a place of meeting. The origins of the synagogue are shrouded in obscurity. Rabbinic tradition attributes its foundation to Moses, yet it is nowhere explicitly mentioned in the Hebrew scriptures, though its existence is sometimes inferred from instances of biblical prayer.

The most venerated explanation traces the synagogue to the Jews taken captive to Babylon in the sixth century BCE. It suggests that in the absence of the Temple, the exiles gathered for worship and spiritual instruction, thereby creating proto-synagogues.

The distinctive nature of the synagogue is best understood in contrast with the Jerusalem Temple. The Temple was a centralized institution. At least from the perspective of its ruling elite, it was the only legitimate Temple. The synagogue, on the other hand, was a decentralized institution. Legitimate synagogues could be established wherever there were enough men to constitute a *minyan* (quorum). The traditional quorum of ten men dates back at least to the first century CE.

It is clear that the synagogue had coexisted with the Temple prior to the Temple's destruction in 70 CE, either as a complement to the Temple or, more likely, as an alternative to it. The Pharisees were lay oriented and critical of the operation of the Temple, both ritually and politically. In its orgins and development, the synagogue coheres with the Pharisees' lay orientation.

Not until the first century CE, well into the period of Pharisaic hegemony, does the synagogue in its present form appear in literary and archaeological evidence. The present practice of three daily worship services (with an additional service [Musaf] on holidays and Sabbaths) was not made obligatory until Gamli'el of Yavneh (c. 83-c. 115), who also regularized the basic order of prayers and gave the Passover Haggadah its classical form.

After the destruction of the Temple, the synagogue was said to have acquired the holiness that had inhered in the Temple, and its prayer service was regarded to have taken the place of the sacrificial service.

The Synagogue of the Organic Community. The synagogue was the central institution in Jewish life during the centuries when, first under the pagan Romans and subsequently under Sasanid, Christian, or Muslim rule, Jews were permitted to live in quasi-autonomous or organic communities. The individual synagogue enjoyed less autonomy in large, centralized areas like Muslim Iberia and more in smaller organic communities like those in European feudal states. But to one degree or another, the synagogue of the organic community, the almost totally self-sufficient Jewish community in which the Talmudic heritage pervaded and guided society, could be found in many places in Europe and in parts of Africa and Asia and elsewhere, well into the twentieth century. In this phase of Jewish history, the synagogue reinforced the basic values which even in the darkness of persecution perpetuated the optimism, morality, creativity, and compassion which traditionally have shaped Jewish life. Socially it was the place where Jews met, commented on events, communicated their needs, planned their charities, adjudicated their disputes, and held their life cycle events. Out of the synagogue emerged the traditional Jewish service organizations, including the *hakhnasat orehim,* for welcoming strangers; *hakhnasat kallah,* for dowering brides; *biqqur holim,* for visiting the sick; and *hevrah qaddisha'* for attending to the dead.

> **Legitimate synagogues could be established wherever there were enough men to constitute a *minyan* (quorum).**

The synagogue was always concerned with education and was often, in smaller communities, the sole locus of learning; among Ashkenazic Jews the synagogue is often called *shul,* a Yiddish word for school, and in Italy *scuola,* the Italian equivalent. Traditionally, the first goal of Jewish education was proficiency in reading the prayer book. The synagogue typically housed popular study groups in Mishnah and Talmud. Through such traditional study, and the discussion of external intellectual challenges as well, the synagogue reinforced the fundamentals of Jewish belief and spurred their more sophisticated formulation.

Psychologically, the synagogue bred respect for the nobility of the individual and the purposefulness of living, reinforcing these sentiments through ritual observances, the bestowing of honors, and liturgical creativity in music and poetry. Further enhancing life were the regular Sabbath and festival sermons, often delivered by resident preachers in the vernacular, including Yiddish for central and eastern Europeans and Ladino for the Sefardim of the eastern Mediterranean.

No less sustaining were the secret synagogues of Jews and prospective Jews, notably the Portugese and Spanish New Christians (Marranos), in areas where Judaism was proscribed. Removed from the mainstream of Jewish life, these secret synagogues developed their own rituals and clergy out of an extraordinary blend of biblical tradition, available to them through the Church, and rabbinic practice known to them only in diminished and garbled form, after the erosion of generations of oral transmission.

The Synagogue in the Modern World. By the end of the eighteenth century, two adjectives, "Orthodox" and "Reform," had appeared as designations of the synagogue's polar alternatives. The former described those synagogues that maintained a principled adherence to traditional rituals and theology, the latter those committed to various degrees of change. The adjective "Conservative" emerged before the middle of the nineteenth century to describe commitment to the historical tradition with some changes but not radical ones. And in the twentieth century, from out of the American Conservative wing has come the Reconstructionist movement whose synagogue rituals are informed by an essentially humanist philosophy.

For all their differences, then, modern synagogues manifest important similarities that distinguish all of them from synagogues of the organic community. The modern synagogue has had to walk a tightrope between change toward assimilation and retention of tradition, all the while remaining mindful of its problematic distinctiveness from the majority culture and of its marginal adherents, whose desire for economic, political, and social acculturation has often occasioned their apathy toward the synagogue and even their defection from it.

Consequently, all modern synagogues have to a greater or lesser extent adjusted traditional attitudes, activities, and articulations. Socially they have espoused the egalitarianism and compassion of the liberal wings of the surrounding culture, clothing them with traditional language, especially that of the biblical prophets. Theologically, they have adopted the prevailing moods of the broader culture, dominantly rational until the late nineteenth century and thereafter increasingly antirational in many religious and some secular circles. They have also dwelt on concepts, like God and covenant, common to the religions in the surrounding cultures even though differently interpreted by them.

Although the modern world has spurred some to flee the synagogue, the impossibility of complete societal acceptance has moved others to synagogue affiliation, particularly in democratic countries.

BIBLIOGRAPHY

Baron, Salo W. *The Jewish Community: Its History and Structure to the American Revolution* (1942). 3 vols. Reprint, Westport, Conn., 1972.

Baron, Salo W. *A Social and Religious History of the Jews.* 2d ed., rev. & enl. 18 vols. to date. New York, 1952-.

Cohen, Martin A. "The Hasmonean Revolution Politically Considered." In *Salo Wittmayer Baron Jubilee Volume,* edited by Saul Lieberman, vol. 1, pp. 263-285. New York, 1974.

Cohen, Martin A. *The Synagogue: Yesterday, Today and Tomorrow.* New York, 1978.

Cohen, Martin A. *Two Sister Faiths: Introduction to a Typological Approach to Early Rabbinic Judaism and Early Christianity.* Worcester, Mass., 1985.

De Breffny, Brian. *The Synagogue.* New York, 1978.

Goldstein, Sidney E. *The Synagogue and Social Welfare: A Unique Experiment, 1907-1953.* New York, 1955.

Guttman, Joseph, ed. *The Synagogue: Studies in Origins, Archaeology and Architecture.* New York, 1975.

Kaploun, Uri. *The Synagogue.* Philadelphia, 1973.

Levy, Isaac. *The Synagogue: Its History and Function.* London, 1963.

Rivkin, Ellis. "Ben Sira and the Nonexistence of the Synagogue." In *In the Time of Harvest,* edited by Daniel Jeremy Silver, pp. 320-354, New York, 1963.

Rivkin, Ellis. *A Hidden Revolution: The Pharisees' Search for the Kingdom Within.* Nashville, 1978.

Schwarz, Jacob D. *The Synagogue in Modern Jewish Life.* Cincinnati, 1939.

MARTIN A. COHEN

T`AI-CHI

In the *I-ching* (Book of Changes; a wisdom book in ancient China that is widely believed to have been a major source of inspiration for Confucianism and Taoism), the term *t`ai-chi* ("great ultimate") signifies the origin and ground of Heaven and earth and of all beings. It is the Great Ultimate that is said to engender or produce *yin* and *yang,* the twin cosmic forces, which in turn give rise to the symbols, patterns, and ideas that are, indeed, forms of *yin* and *yang.* The interaction of the two modalities of these cosmic forces bring about the eight trigrams that constitute the basis of the *Book of Changes.* Combining any two of the eight trigrams, each of which contains three broken *(yin)* and three unbroken *(yang)* lines, forms one of the sixty-four hexagrams. These are taken as codes for all possible forms of change, transformation, existence, life, situations, and institutions both in nature and in culture. The Great Ultimate, then, is the highest and the most fundamental reality, and is said to generate and underlie all phenomena.

However, it is misleading to conceive of the Great Ultimate as the functional equivalent of either the Judeo-Christian concept of God or the Greek idea of Logos. The Great Ultimate is neither the willful creator nor pristine reason, but an integral part of an organic cosmic process. The inherent assumption of this interpretation is that the universe is in a dynamic process of transformation and, at the same time, has an organic unity and an underlying harmony. The universe, in Joseph Needham's understanding, is well-coordinated and well-ordered but lacks an ordainer. The Great Ultimate, so conceived, is a source or root, and is thus inseparable from what issues from it.

It was the Sung-dynasty Neo-Confucian master Chou Tun-i (Chou Lien-hsi, 1017-1073) who significantly contributed to the philosophical elaboration of the notion. In his *T`ai-chi t`u-shou* (Explanation of the Diagram of the Great Ultimate), strongly influenced by the cosmology of the *Book of Changes,* Chou specifies the cosmic process as follows: the Great Ultimate through movement and tranquility generates the two primordial cosmic forces, which in turn transform and unite to give rise to the Five Agents or Five Phases *(wu-hsing,* water, fire, wood, metal, and earth). When the five vital forces *(ch`i),* corresponding to each of the five "elements"

(agents or phases), interact among themselves and reach a harmonious order, the four seasons run their orderly course. This provides the proper environment for the Five Agents to come into "mysterious union." Such a union embraces the two primordial cosmic forces, the female and the male, which interact with each other to engender and transform all things. The continuous production and reproduction of the myriad things make the universe an unending process of transformation. It is in this sense, Chou Tun-i states, that "the Five Agents constitute a manifestation of *yin* and *yang,* and *yin* and *yang* constitute a manifestation of the Great Ultimate." This is the basis for the commonly accepted Neo-Confucian assertion that the Great Ultimate is embodied both singly by each thing and collectively by all things.

It has been documented that Chou's *Diagram of the Great Ultimate* grew out of a long Taoist tradition. Indeed, it is believed that Chou received the diagram itself from a Taoist master: Taoist influences are evident even in his explanatory notes. His introduction of the term "the Non-Ultimate" or "the Ultimate of Non-being" *(wu-chi)* generated much controversy among Sung and Ming dynasty Confucian thinkers because the notion "non-ultimate" or "non-being" seems closer to the Taoist idea of nothingness than the Confucian concept that the human world is real. However, by defining human spirituality in terms of the notion that it is "man alone who receives the cosmic forces and the Five Agents in their most refined essence, and who is therefore most sensitive," Chou clearly presents a philosophical anthropology in the tradition of Confucian humanism.

A similar attempt to read a humanist message into the seemingly naturalistic doctrine of the Great Ultimate is also found in the writings of Shao Yung (Shao K`ang-chieh, 1011-1077), perhaps one of the most metaphysical Confucian masters of the Sung dynasty. Shao's cosmology is presented as the numerical progression of the one to the many: "The Great Ultimate is the One. It produces the two *(yin* and *yang)* without engaging in activity. The two (in their wonderful changes and transformations) constitute the spirit. Spirit engenders number, number engenders form, and form engenders concrete things" (Chan, 1969, pp. 492-493). Shao further maintains that the human mind in its original state is the Great Ultimate. If one's mind can regain its original calm, tranquility, and enlightenment it has the capacity to investigate principle *(li)* to the utmost. The mind can then fully embody the Great Ultimate not only as the defining characteristic of its true nature but also as an experienced reality, a realized truth. This paradoxical conception that the Great Ultimate is part of the deep structure of our minds but that it can be fully realized only as a presence in our daily lives is widely shared among Neo-Confucian thinkers.

Chu Hsi (1130-1200), in a rationalist attempt to provide an overall cosmological and metaphysical vision, defines the Great Ultimate as "nothing other than principle," or, alternately, as "merely the principle of Heaven and earth and the myriad things." Perhaps inadvertently, Chu Hsi restricted the Great Ultimate so as to acknowledge its function as the ground of all beings but not necessarily its role in the generation of the universe. However, there is fruitful ambiguity in Chu Hsi's position. In response to the challenging question as to whether the Great Ultimate must split into parts to become the possession of each of the myriad things, Chu Hsi employed the famous Buddhist analogy of moonlight scattered upon rivers and lakes. That there is only one moon in the sky does not prevent its being seen everywhere without losing its singularity and wholeness. Chu Hsi further depicts the Great Ultimate as having neither space nor form. The Great Ultimate, although symbolizing the principle of activity and tranquility, is not directly involved in the creative transformation of the universe. Nevertheless, like Chou Tun-i and other Neo-Confucian thinkers, Chu Hsi insisted that the truth of the Great Ultimate must be personally realized through moral self-cultivation: the truth of the Great Ultimate is not simply knowledge about some external reality but a personal knowledge rooted in self-awareness in the ethico-religious sense.

> That there is only one moon in the sky does not prevent its being seen everywhere without losing its singularity and wholeness.

In the folk tradition, the symbol of the Great Ultimate carries a connotation of mysterious creativity. The spiritual and physical exercise known as t`ai-chi ch`üan (a form of traditional Chinese shadow boxing) is still widely practiced. This slow, firm, and rhythmic exercise disciplines the body and purifies the mind through coordinated movements and regulated breathing. It is a remarkable demonstration that cosmological thought can be translated into physical and mental instruction for practical living without losing its intellectual sophistication. After all, in the Chinese order of things, to know the highest truth is not simply to know about something but to know how to do it properly through personal knowledge.

[*See also* Confucian Thought.]

BIBLIOGRAPHY

Chan, Wing-tsit. *A Source Book in Chinese Philosophy.* Princeton, 1969. See chapters 28, 29, and 31.

Fung Yu-lan. *A History of Chinese Philosophy.* 2 vols. Princeton, 1952-1953. See volume 2, pages 435-442, 457-458, and 537-545.

Graham, A. C. *Two Chinese Philosophers.* London, 1958.

Needham, Joseph. *Science and Civilisation in China.* 5 vols. Cambridge, 1954- .

Tu Wei-ming. *Humanity and Self-cultivation: Essays in Confucian Thought.* Berkeley, 1979. See chapter 5, pages 72-76.

TU WEI-MING

TAIWANESE RELIGIONS

Taiwan is an offshore island 100 miles southeast of the Chinese mainland. Three groups of people currently inhabit the island: mountain aborigines, Taiwanese natives (themselves originally émigrés from the mainland), and Chinese mainlanders. The mountain aborigines, the earliest inhabitants, migrated from Indochina and the Philippines in prehistoric times. (But some archaeological evidence suggests that the Philippines were inhabited by émigrés from Taiwan.) The Taiwanese natives are the descendants of Chinese who immigrated from South China before the end of World War II. The Chinese mainlanders are the Chinese who fled Mao Tse-tung's forces and took refuge on the island in 1949. Owing to ethnic differences and historical changes, the religions of Taiwan are multifarious and complex. They can best be described in terms of their historical development, which can be divided into five major periods: (1) the prehistoric period, before 1622 CE, (2) the period of Dutch and Spanish rule, 1622-1661, (3) the period of Koxinga and Manchu rule, 1661-1895, (4) the period of Japanese rule, 1895-1945, and (5) the modern period, 1945 to the present.

Prehistoric Period. The island of Taiwan was originally connected to the Chinese mainland. Many archaeological artifacts on Taiwan can thus be linked to those on the Asian continent. It has been hypothesized that during Neolithic times (c. 3000-2000 BCE) Oceanic Negroids brought in horticulture from Southeast Asia, followed by Mongoloids with millet from northern China, and Indochinese with Bronze Age culture. About 300 BCE a Megalithic and Iron Age culture was introduced by peoples from the Philippines. The descendants of these ethnic groups have survived and now dwell mainly in the mountain regions. Known collectively as the mountain aborigines, they are divided into ten tribes: Atayla, Saisiat, Banun, Tsou, Rukai, Paiwan, Puyuma, Ami, Yami, and the Plains (or Ping-pu).

Each of these tribes has its own language and culture, and so it is rather arbitrary to generalize about their traditional practices and religion, but certain common elements do exist. While some of these groups are matrilineal and others are patrilineal, all tend to feature a hierarchy based on kinship and role. The chieftain, normally chosen from the eldest male members of the family with the most ancient lineage, plays the role of tribal chief and high priest. The medicine man and woman, who conduct shamanic rituals of healing, divination, exorcism, and magic, are next to the chief in prestige. The House of Ancestral Spirits, built at the center of the clan village, is used for communal worship of the tribal ancestors. The "public house," or "men's house," is for the administration of community affairs. The "youth house" is for the education of young people, which is supervised by the chief and elders. All members of society are divided into cooperative groups and perform various community functions such as field work, hunting, warfare, construction, and preparation for ceremonies.

The mountain tribes have a very rich collection of myths, legends, and genealogies. Myths of creation, the origin of man, celestial phenomena, gods and spirits, culture heroes, and sacred animals are popular among all the tribes. Many myths have etiological motifs identifying the sacred origins of cultural events and ritual actions. Besides these myths, fairly extensive legends and genealogies of tribal history and geography have been preserved. Rites of passage are common to all tribes and are normally observed by all members of the society. Communal rites of opening up the land, sowing and planting, weeding and purification, picking the first crop, harvest, and thanksgiving are observed by all the tribes. Rites of animal hunting and head-hunting are conducted on special occasions. During the rituals, myths are recited and mythic events are reenacted to strengthen the people's sense of identity and harmony with their environment.

The mountain aborigines were able to maintain their traditional culture and religion intact until the arrival of the Dutch, Spaniards, and Chinese in the seventeenth century. Their attitude toward foreigners was alternately hostile and conciliatory. The plains tribes, who lived on the western coastal plains, were conciliatory to the Dutch and Spanish and to their Christian missions. Many of them accepted Christianity, and others were influenced by Chinese religion. However, the remaining aborigines were hostile to foreigners and engaged in head-hunting to resist foreign intrusion. Their primitive weapons were no match for firearms, however, and they had to withdraw into higher mountain regions for protection. During the period of Japanese rule (1895-1945), the Japanese government tried to introduce Japanese culture and religion to the aborigines, but this came to an end in 1945 when the Japanese withdrew from Taiwan. Since the end of World War II, Christian missionaries have been active among the aborigines. As of the late 1970s almost 90 percent have become Christians and more than seven hundred churches have been built in their villages. Many aborigines have been ordained as ministers. With recent rapid changes in society and culture, it is doubtful that the mountain aborigines will be able to maintain their traditional way of life.

Dutch and Spanish Rule. In the course of establishing new trade with China, the Portuguese discovered Taiwan and named it Ilha Formosa ("the beautiful island"). The Dutch and Spanish followed the Portuguese to the Far East, but when they could not establish trade directly with China, they set up a trade base on the island of Formosa. Thus a colonial government was established in southern Formosa by the Dutch in 1622 and in northern Formosa by the Spanish in 1626. As a part of their colonial policy, the Dutch brought in Protestant missions and the Spanish, Catholic missions. They were able to subdue the plains aborigines and convert them.

In order to build their fortresses and exploit the land, the European colonists hired many Chinese workers from South China. As these workers increased, they began to form their own communities and practice the traditional Chinese religions of Confucianism, Taoism, and Buddhism as well as the folk religion. In 1641 the Dutch were able to take control of northern Formosa from the Spanish and so united its rule. However, Dutch rule of Formosa was brought to an abrupt end by the invasion of Koxinga (Cheng Ch`eng-kung), thus halting Christian missions as well. However, a Dominican mission returned in 1859, and a Presbyterian mission in 1865.

Koxinga and Manchu Rule. In 1661, retreating from the invasion of the Manchus into China, Koxinga, the last loyal general of the Ming dynasty, led his army and navy to invade the island of Formosa and expelled the Dutch. He changed the name of the island to Taiwan ("terraced bay") and made Tainan the capital. Soon massive Chinese migrations to Taiwan from the provinces of Fukien and Kwangtung began. These immigrants opened up new land and pushed the aborigines farther back into the mountain regions. As their towns and cities grew in number, they also built many shrines, temples, and monasteries. Often the temples became the centers of Taiwanese communities.

After Koxinga died suddenly in 1662, his successors were unable to carry out his mission to restore the Ming dynasty in China, and in 1692 the Manchurian navy took over control of Taiwan. During the early rule of the Manchu (or Ch`ing) dynasty, Taiwanese who were still loyal to the Ming revolted against the Manchus. Many secret societies such as the White Lotus Society and the T`ien-ti Society were introduced from China and organized in Taiwan to carry out uprisings. However, as the rebellions were gradually subdued and the welfare of the common people was improved by Manchu administration, the latter period of Manchu rule was peaceable.

The religion of the Taiwanese can be divided into two types, the family cult and the community cult. The family cult, which consists of ancestor worship, worship at the family shrine, and rites of passage, is observed by almost all Taiwanese. The community cults include the state cult, the religions associated with the Confucian shrine, the Buddhist monastery, the Taoist temple, the folk temple, and the individual cults of various religious associations. The state cult was established by the government in order to promote political stability and to provide a place for official ceremonies. Temples were erected in Tainan and other cities to commemorate the achievements of Koxinga. Many Confucian shrines were built with the sponsorship of the government to promote Confucian learning and to commemorate the merits of Confucius and Confucian worthies. Many of the earlier Buddhist monasteries were also built by the government in order to provide a retreat for officials.

Buddhism in Taiwan is divided into monastic Buddhism and lay Buddhism (the Chai religion). Monastic Buddhism, practiced by monks and nuns living in monasteries, is chiefly supported by the government and the elite. Two major schools of monastic Buddhism in Taiwan are Pure Land and Ch'an. While monastic Buddhism is isolated from the common people, lay Buddhism has the widespread support of the populace. Called Chai ("purity") religion because it stresses the purification of the mind and the practice of vegetarianism, it has three branches in Taiwan: the Lung-hua, Chin-chung, and Hsien-t'ien. All claim descent from the Southern Ch'an school of the Sixth Patriarch Hui-neng (638-713). However, elements from Confucian moral teachings, Taoist rites, and folk religious practices can also be seen in all three branches. Each branch is organized into a hierarchy consisting of patriach, instructors, lay leaders, and lay devotees. Lay Buddhists believe in the imminent end of the world and expect the swift coming of the Maitreya Buddha, who will bring them into the new era. Because of their strong eschatological beliefs, they have rebelled from time to time against corrupt government, and, in turn, censorship and oppression of their members have been frequent and harsh.

The religious Taoism founded by Chang Tao-ling during the second century CE in China was brought to Taiwan by Chinese immigrants. There it developed into five major sects: the Ling-pao, Lao-chün, Yü-chia, T'ien-shih, and San-nai. The Taoist priests *(tao-shih)* are divided into two groups, the Black Turbans, who are empowered to celebrate the all-important rite of cosmic renewal *(chiao),* and the Red Turbans, who officiate at a host of lesser popular ceremonials. These priests set up altars in their family shops to serve for both private and communal rites. They worship, among others, the Supreme Originator (Yüan-shih T'ien-ts'un), Lao-tzu, Chang Tao-ling, the North Star, the earth gods *(she),* the gods of the ditch *(ch'eng-huang),* and the god of the hearth (Tsao-kung). As the chief religious functionaries of the Taoist community, the priests have various duties, including exorcism, public ritual for the success of the community, religious instruction, the fabrication of charms and amulets for personal use, and the traditional practices of meditation and internal alchemy prescribed in the various texts of the Taoist canon.

The folk religion of Taiwanese natives is polytheistic and syncretic, its rituals complex, and its temples multifarious. Each temple has its own favorite gods, its own holy days and special ceremonies. The folk temple, supported by the common people and supervised by a trustee from among lay leaders, is very often the center of community affairs both sacred and secular. There are also innumerable voluntary religious associations organized by lay devotees for special purposes. Some of these are affiliated with a folk temple; others have their own meeting places. They choose a favorite deity to worship and conduct special rites. While a majority are primarily concerned with religious matters, some associations turn into secret societies and engage in political struggles. The Society of Heaven and Earth (T'ien-ti Hui) was one of the most active of these. Because of their insurgent activities, secret societies are often branded as heretical by the government and are thus the subjects of harsh repression. However, they always seem to revive at times of crises.

Japanese Rule. After China's defeat in the Sino-Japanese War in 1895, Taiwan was ceded to Japan. The Japanese colonial government, intending to make Taiwan a stepping stone in its advance toward Southeast Asia, promoted Japanese education and industries in Taiwan. As part of this attempt to establish cultural dominion over the region, the Japanese introduced State Shinto into Taiwan, and the mountain aborigines and Taiwanese natives were forced to take part in Shinto worship. Sixty-three grand shrines and 116 local shrines were built by the government all over the island. In addition to State Shinto, Shinto sects such as Tenrikyo, Shinpikyo, and Konkokyo, and various Buddhist schools such as Tendai, Shingon, Jodo, Zen, Shin, and Nichiren were also introduced into Taiwan. However, most of their adherents were Japanese immigrants; the sects did not have much following among the Taiwanese people. Under Japanese imperial rule, the leaders of traditional Chinese religions suffered oppression, and many folk temples were closed by the government. After World War II, Japan returned Taiwan to China, and thus Shinto also ended on the island. However, the influences of Japanese Buddhism are still visible in Taiwan.

Modern Period. After World War II, the traditional religions of Taiwan underwent a strong revival. Many ruined temples were rebuilt, and ceremonial parades and pilgrimages became very popular. Conversion to Christianity continued to take place among the mountain aborigines. In the meantime, because of the Communist takeover of the mainland in 1949 and its initial religious persecutions, many religious leaders were among those who took refuge in Taiwan. These included K`ung Te-cheng, a descendant of Confucius; Yin Shun, an eminent Buddhist abbot; the Thirty-seventh Heavenly Master of Taoism; Lama Kangyurwa Hutukhtu, the nineteenth reincarnation of the Living Buddha of Kangyur monastery; and Archbishop Joseph Kuo and Cardinal Tien of the Roman Catholic church. About twenty thousand Muslims and innumerable Buddhists, Catholics, Protestants, Taoists, and Confucianists came to Taiwan, turning it into a rich showcase of world religions.

In 1982 the following religious associations with significant memberships existed in Taiwan: the Confucian and Mencian Academy, the National Taoist Association, the Buddhist Association of the Republic of China, the Chinese Muslim Federation, the Catholic Archdiocese of Taiwan, the Presbyterian Church in Taiwan and about forty-five other Protestant denominations, and Li Chiao and Hsuan-yüan Chiao, two newly established religions.

[*For further discussion of the origins, thought, and practice of the religious traditions of Taiwanese natives and Chinese mainlanders on Taiwan, see* Chinese Religion; Taoism; Buddhism; *and* Christianity.]

BIBLIOGRAPHY

Ahern, Emily M. *The Cult of the Dead in a Chinese Village.* Stanford, Calif., 1973.

Jordan, David K. *Gods, Ghosts, and Ancestors: The Folk Religion of a Taiwanese Village.* Chicago, 1969.

Li T`ien-ch`un, ed. *Taiwan sheng t`ung-chih-kao,* vol. 2. Taipei, 1956.

Marui Keijiro. *Taiwan shukyo chosa hokokusho.* Taipei, 1919.

Masuda Fukutaro. *Taiwan no shukyo.* Tokyo, 1939.

MILTON M. CHIU

TALMUD

In form, the Talmud is an extended, multivolume elaboration of selected tractates of the Mishnah, but it must be emphasized that the contents of the Talmud go far beyond its ostensible base. No subject of interest to the ancient rabbis failed to find its way into this immense body of teaching, and for that reason no question arising in later centuries was deemed outside the range that Talmudic teaching might legitimately claim to resolve. A document that seemed merely to elucidate an older text eventually became the all-embracing constitution of medieval Jewish life.

As noted, the Mishnah supplied the overall format for the Talmud. Like the former, the Talmud is divided into tractates, which in turn are divided into chapters and then into paragraphs. Each phrase of the Mishnah is discussed, analyzed,

and applied for as long as the editors of the Talmud have materials to supply; when such materials are exhausted (sometimes after very long and quite wide-ranging digressions), the discussion simply moves on to the next phrase or paragraph. The digressions can be such that one loses track of the Mishnaic passage under discussion for pages at a time, but the Talmud always picks up again from its base text when the next section begins.

Origins and Development. Very soon after it began to circulate, the Mishnah of Yehudah ha-Nasi' (compiled c. 200 CE) assumed a central place in rabbinic study. As time went on, the structure and content of the Mishnah—the meaning and the sequence of its paragraphs—determined the manner in which the growing accumulation of rabbinic lore was orga-

> For several generations, the collections remained fluid. Materials were added, revised, or shifted.

nized. Non-Mishnaic legal materials (the so-called outside traditions; Aram., *baraitot*) were studied primarily in connection with their Mishnaic parallels, and an entire supplementary collection (Tosefta) that followed the Mishnah's own sequence of orders, tractates, and chapters was compiled. Similarly, post-Mishnaic rabbinic teachings—of law, morality, theology, and so forth—were remembered and discussed primarily as the consecutive study of Mishnaic tractates called them to mind, so that most such teachings eventually came to be linked with one or another specific passage (or, occasionally, several) in the earlier collection.

In this way, great compilations of rabbinic teaching, each in the form of a loose exposition of the Mishnah, came into being. Evidence suggests that various centers of rabbinic study developed their own such collections, though in the end only one overall collection was redacted for the Palestinian centers and one for Babylonia. For several generations, the collections remained fluid. Materials were added, revised, or shifted. Free association led to the production of extended discourses or sets of sayings that at times had little to do with the Mishnaic passage serving as point of departure. Early materials tended to be brief explanations of the Mishnah or citations of parallel texts, but later rabbis commented as much on remarks of their predecessors that were not included in the Mishnah or were subsequent to it as on the Mishnah itself. Numerous recent scholars have seen in the developing tradition two sorts of material: brief, apodictic statements of law and much longer dialectical explanations of the specific laws and their underlying principles. Such discussions in turn eventually gave rise to a new generation of legal dicta, and these in turn provoked new efforts at dialectical complication. Thus the Talmudic tradition grew.

The Hebrew word *talmud* and its Aramaic equivalent, *gemara'*, both mean "study." Each term had other meanings at various times, but in the end *gemara'* came to be the name of the vast Mishnah commentary that had taken shape, and *talmud* the name of the combined text (Mishnah plus *gemara'*) that eventually emerged. The rabbis of the immediate post-Mishnaic period (third to fifth centuries CE) are called amoraim (from the Aramaic *'mr*, "say, discuss"), because their characteristic contribution to the developing tradition was the extended discussion of the Mishnah they produced.

Through a process that can no longer be traced with certainty, the text of the *gemara'* underwent periodic reshaping until finally the two Talmuds as we now know them came into being. It should be emphasized that early rabbinic Torah study was oral, so that the *gemara'* was not so much a fixed text as a more-or-less accepted formulation of accumulated lore. There is therefore no reason to assume that there ever was an authorized "original text" of the Talmud, although there may have been parallel recensions of these collections from the earliest stages of their history preserved in different localities. There is still no altogether accepted standard text, and even the relatively uniform wording of recent centuries has much to do with the eventual predominance of European over Asian and North African Jewry and the standardization that inevitably followed the invention of printing.

The Jerusalem, or Palestinian, Talmud. The so-called Jerusalem Talmud (Heb., *Talmud Yerushalmi*) is really the work of the rabbinic academies of the Galilee; it was substantially completed by the middle of the fifth century. The Jerusalem Talmud covers the first four orders of the Mishnah with the exception of two tractates (*Avot* and *`Eduyyot*); in the last two orders, only half of tractate *Niddah* has Palestinian *gemara'*. The Jerusalem Talmud is characterized in general by brevity and an absence of editorial transitions and clarifications. Its discussions frequently seem laconic and elliptical and often take the form of terse remarks attributed to one or another amora with no connective phrasing at all between them. Occasionally, however, such comments are built up into a more integrated dialectical treatment, with objections raised and answered, contradictions cited and resolved, and biblical proof texts adduced as the editors see fit.

The Babylonian Talmud. According to tradition, the redaction of the Babylonian Talmud (Heb., *Talmud Bavli*) was completed by the amoraim Ashi and Ravina' around the year 500. It is clear, however, that the distinctive features of this Talmud in contrast to the other are the work of several generations of rabbis who came after these authorities and are collectively known as the savoraim (from the Aramaic root *svr*, "consider, hold an opinion"), that is, those who reconsidered the Talmudic text and established its final version. Thanks to the labors of these latter revisers, the Babylonian

Talmud is far more thoroughly worked out than the Palestinian. Its arguments are replete with a sophisticated technical terminology for introducing source materials, considering objections and counterobjections, offering refutations and defending against them, and so forth. In addition to their detailed contributions, the savoraim also composed entire sections of the Talmud; in particular, the first extended discussion, at the beginning of many tractates, is attributed to them. In general, the literary superiority of the Babylonian Talmud, its far greater logical clarity, and its considerably

> **Once the primacy of the Babylonian Talmud was established, it was continually reinforced.**

larger bulk can be attributed to the savoraim of the sixth and seventh centuries. The Talmud as we now have it did not exist until these had done their work.

While the Jerusalem Talmud treats the entire first order of the Mishnah, the Babylonian Talmud has *gemara'* only for the first tractate *(Berakhot)*, which deals with liturgy; the rest of the order treats agricultural rules that were not considered applicable outside the Holy Land. On the other hand, and harder to explain, the great bulk of the fifth order, which regulates the Temple cult and is not to be found in the Jerusalem Talmud, has very substantial Babylonian *gemara'*. Otherwise, with minor exceptions, the two Talmuds cover the same parts of the Mishnah.

Later Developments. Over the several centuries following the appearance of the two Talmuds, the Babylonian Talmud gradually eclipsed the other. This predominance was rationalized by the claim that the Babylonian Talmud was the more recent, so that its editors already knew the Jerusalem Talmud and could include its acceptable teachings in their own work and suppress those portions for any reason found unworthy. In retrospect, however, it is clear that such a claim was part of the propaganda of the Babylonian geonim of the last centuries of the first millennium CE in favor of their own authority and against the rival authority of the rabbis of the Land of Israel. The eventual predominance of the Babylonian Talmud throughout the Diaspora and even in the Land of Israel probably is to be explained through reference to such factors as the relatively stronger ties of the rising communities of North Africa and Spain to Babylonian Jewry and the relatively more severe decline of Palestinian Jewry, especially under the onslaught of the Crusades. Those parts of Europe, especially Italy, that retained strong ties with the community in the Land of Israel apparently maintained a tradition of study of the Jerusalem Talmud, but by the beginning of the second millennium this process had run its course.

From then on, "the Talmud" always meant the Babylonian. It was taken for granted that issues of Jewish law should be resolved by reference to the Babylonian Talmud, not the Palestinian, and that the latter could provide rulings only in cases where the Babylonian Talmud was silent or ambiguous.

Once the primacy of the Babylonian Talmud was established, it was continually reinforced. The Babylonian Talmud received more attention. It was studied by more scholars, it became the subject of more and of better commentaries; it was copied more often and more carefully by larger numbers of scribes. The result is that modern scholars have a more solidly established text of the Babylonian Talmud and a more fully developed exegetical tradition with which to work. Modern critical study of the Jerusalem Talmud has much more fundamental analytical and restorative work to accomplish before a reliable and comprehensible text becomes available.

It should be noted as well that the power of the medieval Christian church affected the development of the Talmud in two important ways. Periodic waves of seizure and destruction reduced the number of Talmud manuscripts available in certain parts of Europe. The most important of these waves took place in thirteenth-century France and in Italy at the time of the Counter-Reformation; the last burning of the Talmud occurred in Poland in 1757. Occasionally thousands of copies of the Talmud or of Talmudic digests and commentaries were destroyed at a time. In addition, Jewish efforts to avoid such destruction often led to voluntary or involuntary submission of the Talmud to censorship by church authorities. As a result, much early rabbinic discussion of Jesus or the Christian religion has been lost or must now be recovered from scattered manuscripts.

Talmudic Religion. Despite its vast size and scope, the Talmud is not without focus. Certain themes and certain styles of argument and discourse strongly predominate in its pages, and as a result both the religion of the Talmudic sages themselves and the forms of Judaism based on the Talmud that flourished during the Middle Ages are more compatible with certain types of spirituality than with others.

The role of law. Well more than half of the Babylonian Talmud and more than three quarters of the Jerusalem Talmud are devoted to questions of law. The Mishnah itself takes the form of a law code, and Talmudic discussions are chiefly concerned with clarifying, extending, and finding new applications for the provisions of Mishnaic law. This concentration on law is related to the ancient rabbis' role in their communities where they usually served as judges, teachers, or public administrators. Rabbinic piety came to be organized around gratitude for the law and joy in its fulfillment. The law was understood to be a divine gift, and observance of its provisions was seen as the appropriate response to this generosity. To observe the law meant to strengthen one's link to

its giver, and in developing the law into a huge accumulation of detailed regulations covering all aspects of day-to-day living, rabbinic teachers were seeking to multiply occasions for strengthening this link. Study of the law was both the highest intellectual activity in which a Jew might engage and also a practical activity designed to further this expansion of opportunity. Enlarging the scope of the law was not felt to be adding to an already heavy burden; on the contrary, it increased the portion of one's life that could be conducted in response to the voice of God.

The role of study and intellect. While the Mishnah looks like a law code, in fact it is probably something other; its numerous unresolved disputes, its sporadic use of biblical proof texts, and its occasional narratives all reflect the value of study as a religious ritual in its own right, and eventually the activity of studying God's law was as important in Talmudic religion as was the content of that study. With respect to Talmudic law, this enhancement of study as religious rite led to the creation of an elaborate set of legal corpora, most of which are identified by the name of the master to whom the discrete opinions in each corpus were attributed. The well-known Talmudic penchant for hair-splitting dialectics reflects the rabbis' concern that each of these sets of teachings be internally consistent on the one hand and significantly different from any other such set on the other. Hence the frequency with which the Talmud records the chains of transmission by which individual sayings were passed on. Hence the steadily growing integration of teachings from widely disparate fields of law into a single web, and the often forced effort to find unifying principles behind teachings that seem to have nothing to do with one another. Hence, as well, the relative lack of personal interest in the personalities of early masters, except, paradoxically, for those few who became the subject of frequently incredible legends.

This intellectual tendency had several important consequences for Talmudic religion. It gave rabbinic studiousness a scholastic tinge that continued to sharpen as later centuries wore on. It made text commentary an important genre of religious literature; a standard edition of the Talmud even today contains several classical commentaries on the page along with the text and many, many more at the back of the volume. Rabbinic intellectualism turned into disciplined argument; the interplay of proof and refutation, into a holy activity. It also gave primacy to the correct formulation of the wording of sacred texts and recitations over the manner or the circumstances in which they were pronounced; this in turn had important effects on Talmudic and post-Talmudic conceptions of prayer, meditation, and inward spirituality.

Talmudic Learning and Religious Authority. In the ancient rabbis' view there was a connection between their emphasis on learning and the role of leadership to which they aspired. It was taken for granted that only the Torah, when properly and sufficiently studied and understood, could enable the people of Israel to become the "kingdom of priests and holy nation" (*Ex.* 19:16) that God intended them to be. This in turn meant that only those properly and sufficiently learned in Torah should be allowed to assume leadership over the community, since only such leaders could be trusted to guide the people in a divinely ordained direction.

Inherent in Talmudic and post-Talmudic Judaism is the assumption that Torah learning (once the Talmud was complete, this meant Talmudic learning) is the only proper criterion by which the leaders of the community should be selected. Whenever conditions permitted, rabbis sought to institutionalize their authority over the community. In the early period, this meant reaching an accommodation with the real rulers of the community (e.g., the Roman empire or, in Babylonia, the allegedly Davidic dynasty of the exilarchs). Later, it meant assuring that internal Jewish courts should be dominated by rabbis and that Talmudic law should govern those aspects of life where Jews maintained internal autonomy (marriage and divorce, religious ritual, educational institutions). Although rabbinical authority was not without challengers, it was never overthrown in principle until the breakdown of Jewish self-government, which began in the late eighteenth century and continued into the nineteenth.

Talmud Study as Religious Experience. Rabbis saw their own teaching as "oral Torah." They believed the contents of the Talmud represented a part of the revelation to Moses that had been kept oral but faithfully transmitted for centuries before its inclusion in the text of the Talmud. The name *Talmud*, in fact, can be understood as a short form of the common phrase *talmud Torah*, or "Torah study." Thus to study Talmud was in fact to let oneself hear the word of God, and to add to the accumulation of commentaries, digests, codes, and the like was to make one's own contribution to the spread of divine revelation in the world. To learn Torah was thus a kind of sober mysticism, a reliving of the events at Sinai, while to add to the growing body of "oral" law was to share in a divine activity. Already in the Talmud God is depicted as studying Torah several hours a day (B. T., A. Z. 3b), but the kinship between the rabbi and God was felt to be even stronger. By increasing the amount of Torah in the world, the rabbi could do what previously only God had been held able to accomplish.

Thus the text of the Talmud became the center of an activity believed to be the most Godlike available to human experience. Everyone could study some Torah, and no one was considered incapable of adding a few original thoughts to a study session. In this way, Talmud study became a widespread activity among later Jewish communities. The degree of commitment to this activity might vary, from the ascetic twenty-hour-a-day devotion of the closeted scholar to one-hour-a-week popular learning on Sabbath afternoons. The

climax of a boy's education was the point at which he was ready to learn *gemara'*. Such "learning" continues even in our own time, even after the functioning authority of Talmudic law has all but disappeared. It represents the most powerful and the longest-lived inheritance of classical Judaism.

BIBLIOGRAPHY

The history and current state of critical scholarship about the two Talmuds is comprehensively reviewed in two essays in *Aufstieg und Niedergang der römischen* Welt, vol. 2.19.2 (Berlin and New York, 1979): Baruch M. Bokser's "An Annotated Bibliographical Guide to the Study of the Palestinian Talmud," pp. 139-256, and David Goodblatt's "The Babylonian Talmud," pp. 257-336. Both have been reprinted in *The Study of Ancient Judaism*, vol. 2, edited by Jacob Neusner (New York, 1981). These two surveys should be understood as successors to Hermann L. Strack's *Introduction to the Talmud and the Midrash* (Philadelphia, 1925). This work is a dated classic but a classic nonetheless. Several of Neusner's students also produced longer examinations of the work of particular modern scholars; he collected these in *The Formation of the Babylonian Talmud* (Leiden, 1970).

Neusner has also investigated the religious implications of conceiving of Torah study as a holy activity and the theological implications of rabbinic intellectuality; see his concise *The Glory of God Is Intelligence* (Salt Lake City, 1978). A more popular effort of the same sort is Morris Adler's *The World of the Talmud* (New York, 1958). See most recently my own "Talmud," in *Back to the Sources*, edited by Barry W. Holtz (New York, 1984), pp. 129-175.

ROBERT GOLDENBERG

TAMIL RELIGIONS

The term *Tamil religions* denotes the religious traditions and practices of Tamil-speaking people. Most Tamils originated and continue to live in India's southernmost area, now known as the state of Tamil Nadu; however, millions of Tamils have migrated to other parts of India, especially to its large cities, as well as abroad, particularly to Malaysia, Singapore, Sri Lanka, Madagascar, Australia, Great Britain and, more recently, to the United States and Canada.

Early Tamil Religion. A Neolithic cattle-herding culture existed in South India several millennia prior to the Christian era. By the first century, a relatively well-developed civilization had emerged, still largely pre-Hindu and only marginally sanskritized. This culture was essentially Dravidian in nature.

The religious life of the Tamil civilization of Cankam times gave evidence of no significant mythological or philosophical speculation nor of any sense of transcendence in a bifurcated universe. "Possession" is one of the most common ways in which the gods were believed to manifest themselves—both in their priests and in young women. Worship of the gods sometimes occurred in a special place—in the clearing of a field or the bank of a river, for example, where a small pillar or *kantu* was set up to represent the deity.

The city was not foreign to this early culture and by the third century CE, at least, religious imagery reflected an urban setting. Rituals, however, often continued to reflect a seasonal or folk character.

The Heterodoxies. By the third century BCE, pockets of Jains and Buddhists were settling in the deep South. Some may have migrated across the straits from Sri Lanka; others came southward during the reign of Asoka, the Mauryan emperor. By the first century CE, both had established settlements and built small institutions and shrines known as *pallis*. Consequently, the dominant mood of religion in Tamil country for some three centuries reflected Jain and Buddhist values.

The Hinduization of Tamil Country. Beginning in the third century BCE, migrating brahmans and other persons influenced by Vedic and epic traditions were also becoming a part of the Tamil landscape. In the early cities, chieftains who sought to enchance their status employed brahman priests to perform Vedic rituals as had been the case in the North during the epic period. It was in the seventh century, however, that Hindu Sanskritic culture and religion merged with the indigenous Tamil society, leading to a pervasive hinduization of Tamil country and the emergence of a new and creative Hindu civilization.

The first significant feature of the "Hindu age" in Tamil India was the rise of devotional poetry (*bhakti*) in the vernacular language during the seventh, eighth, and ninth centuries. Poets who were followers of Siva (Nayanars) and of Visnu (Alvars: literally, those who are "immersed") popularized these two deities throughout Tamil country. Between the years 650 and 940 the twelve Vaisnava poet-saints (Alvars) wrote some four thousand verses, which were eventually canonized in the *Nalayira-divya-prabandham* (The Four

> This *bhakti* movement reaffirmed elements of early Tamil religious perspectives: the emphasis on celebration, ecstasy, even possession by the god.

Thousand Divine Verses) edited in the tenth century by Nathamuni, the first major *acarya*, or sectarian teacher, of Vaisnavism.

The religion propagated by the *bhakti* poets used epic and Puranic mythology selectively and gave it a locus in Tamil India. Tamil *bhakti* reflected many strands of religion at once. While it incorporated, on the one hand, certain aspects of Jain and Buddhist values (e.g., a sense of community among devotees; hospitality to fellow devotees; and the possibility of

spiritual attainment irrespective of social or economic backgrounds); on the other hand, it directly confronted these heterodoxies with a vigorous theism; an affirmation of the phenomenal world as God's creation; and the importance of the devotional experience and of pilgrimage to the deity's special places. This *bhakti* movement reaffirmed elements of early Tamil religious perspectives: the emphasis on celebration, ecstasy, even possession by the god; the importance of the individual in religious experience; and the affirmation of the land and its special places.

The centerpiece of Tamil *bhakti,* nonetheless, remained the personality of the god and his relationship with individual human beings. The relationship generally differed in Saiva and Vaisnava *bhaktas:* for the former, a certain individuality of the devotee was thought to be retained in the devotional relationship with the god—a relationship said to be that between sun and light or flower and fragrance. In Vaisnava *bhakti,* on the other hand, the loss of the devotee's selfhood in relation to the divine was stressed and the surrender of the one to the other celebrated.

Religion in the Medieval Period. From the eighth through the fifteenth century much of Hindu civilization was centered in Tamil India, where a prolific religious literature emerged in both Tamil and Sanskrit. In addition, Tamil India became the scene for an explosion of temple construction, incorporating an architecture that became characteristically Dravidian.

The Pallava period. The Pallava period takes its name from the dynasty founded by Simhavisnu and is best understood as a transitional or foundation era. In addition to the founding of *bhakti* sects devoted to Siva and Visnu, the period is characterized by the start of the South Indian tradition of temple-building in permanent stone. Temple icons and the deities they represented were ascribed the attributes of kingship, while rituals addressed to the icon increasingly assumed the character of the giving of gifts to a king.

Another important development of this period was the growth of Brahmanic settlements in South India. These rural settlements, which came to be known as *brahmadeyas,* were granted by Tamil landowners as emblems of the alliances that had developed between the two communities.

It is this period also that marks the life and work of Sankara (788-820) and Bhaskaran, his contemporary. The former was especially instrumental in making Advaita (monism) attractive to intellectuals, and in substantially grounding the speculative tradition in the Upanisads, thereby strengthening the Brahmanic option in its dispute with Buddhist thought.

The Cola period. The Cola period (900-1300) was characterized by the formalization and systematic sanskritization of religion. Saivism received special favor under the aegis of the Colas; hence, there was construction and enlargement of Saiva temples. These temples were symbols of the official state cult that overwhelmed or incorporated into themselves many of the lesser village cults.

Another religious institution emerging to prominence in the Cola period was the *matam* (Skt., *matha*) or monastic center. The *matam* became a center of spiritual learning especially for non-brahmans, though it often assumed economic and political power as well. The *brahmadeya* or brahman settlement continued to be the locus of much Sanskritic learning, radiating Brahmanic influence throughout the region.

Systematization in textual form continued in both Saivism and Vaisnavism. This was expressed in the continued formalization of ritual texts—the Saivagamas for Saiva sects and the Pañcaratragamas and Vaikhanasagamas for Vaisnavism—and in philosophical treatises. Saiva Siddhanta proved to be the philosophical systematization of the Saiva religious experience. It was formally expressed in forty terse Tamil verses by the thirteenth century poet Meykantar (Meykanta Tevar), and was known as the *Sivajñanabodham (Civañanapotam).*

It was during the Cola period that the influence of Hindu (and especially Saiva) thought, which had started spreading into Southeast Asia under the Pallavas and Guptas, became more pronounced. Brahmans, now perceived as skilled and versatile advisers to kings, were to be found in such city-states as Polonnaruva (Sri Lanka), Pagan (Burma), Ayutthaya (Thailand), Angkor Wat and Angkor Thom (Cambodia) and Madjapahit (Java). These brahmans and other Hindu immigrants transported notions of divine kingship and cosmology; thus the architecture of capital cities, palaces, temples, and even the biers of dead kings, as well as some of the rituals in the courts of Southeast Asia, came to reflect motifs canonized in Saivagama texts of the Cola period.

The Vijayanagar period. With the decline of the Cola line and the rise of the Vijayanagar hegemony, whose capital was in Andhra Pradesh, shifts occurred in the character of religion in Tamil India. While the Vijayanagars, through political alliances, succeeded in keeping the expanding Islamic empire from making major political inroads in the South, there were nonetheless increasing Muslim influences. From the tenth century onward pockets of Muslims settled into small communities along the Tamil and Malabar coasts and radiated influence outward from these centers, and by the fourteenth and fifteenth centuries occasional military expeditions had led to brief periods of Muslim rule in several portions of Tamil country.

The Cola period was a time for the formalization and institutionalization of religion, especially of Saivism, into temples and literary texts written primarily in Sanskrit. In the post-Cola period the vernacular once again became the chief medium for religious expression, and thus the more popular forms of Hinduism found expression across the Tamil region.

Tamil Hinduism during the Vijayanagar period thus was characterized by resurgent devotionalism and increased participation in temple rituals and festivals by a broader spectrum of people. One might speak of this new era as the "silver age" of Tamil *bhakti.*

By the seventeenth and eighteenth centuries *bhakti* literature had mushroomed. Such poets as Tayumana-var, Kacciyapaciva, and Kumarakurupara celebrated the mythology, sacred places, and devotionalism of Saivism. The role of the Goddess was an important theme in these temple myths, especially her identity with the land and the necessity to channel her considerable power into the patterns of normative theism.

Another form of *bhakti* literature that proliferated by the sixteenth and seventeenth centuries was a form of poetry known as *pillaitamil*, which worshiped the deity in the form of a child. While the Alvar Antal was apparently the first poet to celebrate in Tamil the childhood of Krsna, there is increased use of this form of poetry in both Vaisnava and Saiva contexts. In this type of *bhakti* the poet often assumes the form of the deity's parent and equates the stages of childhood to rhythms of the cosmos and of the poetic medium.

However, there was also a religious countermovement to be found in Tamil country during much of this period. Primarily between the tenth and fifteenth centuries a cryptic "antiestablishment" form of religion found its expression in the poetry and lifestyle of persons known as *cittars* (Skt., *siddhas*). Primarily Saiva, the *cittars* were nonetheless committed to the notion that Siva or Civan was not to be worshiped in iconic form but rather as the supreme limitless one who was virtually identifiable with individual life-forms (*jivanatman*). The body was believed to be temple and microcosm, and internal power the noblest of virtues. In their poetry, natural objects became images of the individual's spiritual quest.

Pre-Modern Period. By the seventeenth century European influence had begun to leave its impact on Tamil culture and religion. While these groups remained economically active in the area now known as Kerala, they tended to be socially insular and their impact on Tamil-speaking peoples was marginal. By the late sixteenth century, however, Christian missionaries had begun to influence Tamil letters and lifestyle more actively. The first of the Protestant missionaries was Bartholomaus Ziegenbalg, who arrived in Tranquebar in 1706. He wrote relatively sympathetic manuscripts on the religious life of South India and continued the process of translating the Bible and Christian ideas into Tamil. In the nineteenth century G. U. Pope's translation of Manikkavacakar and Henry Whitehead's description of Tamil village religion helped make elements of the Tamil religious landscape better known to Tamils as well as to the English-speaking world, even though the work of neither was free of the Western/Christian bias of the authors. This sort of interpretive work continued into the twentieth century with the scholarship of C. G. Diehl and others. [*See also* Indian Religions.]

Quite apart from the attempts at christianization that accompanied the European presence were those Westerners who romanticized the Hindu tradition. Most notable of these was Annie Besant (1847-1933; active in India between 1894 and 1920), who established the international headquarters of the Theosophical Society in Madras

> **Quite apart from the attempts at christianization that accompanied the European presence were those Westerners who romanticized the Hindu tradition.**

and became both an active defender of Hindu values and a crusader for reform.

Still another dimension of religion evident in the pre-modern period that had an impact on current religious life was the continuing practice of indigenous village and folk forms of worship. These include such deities as Aiyanar, who has been a protector deity of Tamil villages since at least the eighth century; Karappacami, the black "servant" god, and various regional *virans* (hero-warriors). During the mid-twentieth century many such deities have become linked to the "great tradition" of Hinduism.

The Present. The last century and a half has been characterized by a rebirth of Tamil self-consciousness. The discovery, translation, and interpretation of Tamil languages and literature by Westerners has encouraged a resurgence of regional and ethnic pride among Tamils. Classical Tamil texts have been recovered and republished. Tamil devotional literature has been memorized and is invoked as the standard of ideal religion, albeit interpreted and used selectively. Shrines have been renovated and their mythical antiquity extolled. Often, regional traditions and myths assume precedence over national ones. Thus even though brahmanization continues to occur as folk and village culti are hinduized, and although various anglicizations have been accepted as normative, the Tamil and nonbrahman roots of religious practice are perpetuated and practiced with fervor. The character of much of this Tamil religion in the modern era is aptly described as neo-*bhakti*.

[*The influence of Tamil culture on the culture of Sri Lanka is noted in* Sinhala Religion.]

BIBLIOGRAPHY

Carman, John B. *The Theology of Ramanuja.* New Haven, 1974. The most thorough single study of the eleventh-century Hindu theologian, couched in discussion of the implications of studying a religious system from outside a tradition.

Clothey, Fred W. *The Many Faces of Murukan: The History and Meaning of a South Indian God.* The Hague, 1978. A phenomenological analysis of how a god reflects the cultural history of the Tamil people.

Nilakanta Sastri, K. A. *Development of Religion in South India.* Bombay, 1963. Though dated and focusing on Sanskritic and Brahmanic expressions of religion, this book remains the only attempt at a comprehensive history of religion in South India.

O'Flaherty, Wendy Doniger. *Siva: The Erotic Ascetic.* Oxford, 1981. While this book makes no reference to Tamil religion, it is a structural analysis of much of the mythology of Siva gleaned from Puranic texts focusing on themes of eroticism and asceticism.

Reiniche, Marie-Louise. *Les dieux et les hommes: Étude des cultes d'un village du Tirunelveli, Inde du Sud.* Paris, 1979. An important study of cultic life in a Tamil village and how deities reflect social and cultural realities therein.

Shulman, David. *Tamil Temple Myths.* Princeton, 1980. A bold, comprehensive examination of Tamil Talapuranas (myths about a temple's origin), centering on the interconnecting motifs of goddess, land, power, and sacrifice.

Singer, Milton. *When A Great Tradition Modernizes.* New York, 1972. A sociologist's reflection, based primarily upon Tamil India, on the impact that the processes of modernization have on religion.

Smith, H. Daniel. *A Descriptive Bibliography of the Printed Texts of the Pañcaratragama.* 2 vols. Baroda, 1975-1980. An annotated description of some of the most important ritual texts of the Pañcaratragama school of Sri Vaisnavism.

Stein, Burton. *Peasant State and Society in Medieval South India.* Oxford, 1980. The definitive and comprehensive description of "medieval" South Indian history, including an analysis of the role of religious institutions throughout the period.

Stein, Burton, ed. *South Indian Temples.* New Delhi, 1978. Essays on the sociological, political, and economic role of temples in medieval Tamil country.

Tiliander, Bror. *Christian and Hindu Terminology.* Uppsala, 1974. A description of how, by choice of Tamil and Sanskrit words in the translation process, early missionaries created a Tamil Christian vocabulary.

Welbon, Guy, and Glenn E. Yocum, eds. *Religious Festivals in South India and Sri Lanka.* New Delhi, 1982. A wide-ranging and useful series of essays incorporating philological and anthropological studies in the festival experience of South Indians, primarily of Tamil-speaking peoples.

Whitehead, Henry. *The Village Gods of South India.* 2d ed., rev. & enl. Delhi, 1976. Though written by a missionary and first published early in this century, this book has remained a "classic" description of village religion in nineteenth-century Tamil India.

Yocum, Glenn E. *Hymns to the Dancing Siva.* New Delhi and Columbia, Mo., 1982. A comprehensive study of the most important of the Tamil Saiva poets, the ninth-century Manikkavacakar.

Zvelebil, Kamil V. *The Smile of Murukan: On Tamil Literature of South India.* Leiden, 1973. The most comprehensive survey to date of Tamil literature, including chapters on many who had a religious impact: *bhakti* poets, the *cittars,* Kampan, and Arunakiri.

FRED W. CLOTHEY

TANTRISM

An Overview

An objective and scientific assessment of Tantrism is not easy, for the subject is controversial and perplexing. Not only do authorities give different definitions of Tantrism, but its very existence has sometimes been denied. (These uncertainties apply more to Hindu Tantrism than to Buddhist Tantrism.)

The word *Tantrism* was coined in the nineteenth century from the Sanskrit *tantra*, meaning "warp" or "loom," hence a doctrine, and hence again a work, treatise, or handbook teaching some doctrine, though not necessarily a Tantric one. But it so happened that it was in works known as *tantra* that Western scholars first discovered doctrines and practices different from those of Brahmanism and classical Hinduism, which were then believed to be the whole of Hindu religion. These texts also differed from what was known of ancient Buddhism and of Mahayana philosophy. So the Western experts adopted the word *Tantrism* for that particular and for them very peculiar, even repulsive, aspect of Indian religion.

There is no word in Sanskrit for Tantrism. There are texts called Tantras. There is *tantrasastra*: the teaching of the Tantras. There is also the adjective *tantrika* (Tantric), which is used as distinct from *vaidika* (Vedic) to contrast an aspect of the religious-cum-ritual Hindu tradition not with Vedism properly so called but with the "orthodox" non-Tantric Hinduism that continues down to our own day, mostly in private (as opposed to temple) ritual, and especially in the "sacraments" *(samskara)* enjoined on all twice-born male Hindus (the three highest classes).

> **The Tantric tradition thus appears as a revelation differing from that of the Vedas and Upanisads, and especially as having different rites and practices.**

The Tantric tradition thus appears as a revelation differing from that of the Vedas and Upanisads, and especially as having different rites and practices. It is not necessarily opposed to the Vedic tradition, which it often refers to as authoritative, but differs from it in being more adapted than Vedism to the present age of mankind, and in procuring benefits, worldly or nonworldly, that the other cannot give. Tantric Buddhism also opens up new ways and perspectives, but its relationship to the older doctrine is of another kind in that the status of the

teaching of the Buddha, for the Buddhists, is different from that of the Veda for the Hindus. But both Hindu and Buddhist Tantrism can be described as reinterpretations, in a new spirit, of their respective traditions.

The complex and ambiguous relationship of Tantrism to Hinduism generally was not realized at first. Even though some scholars perceived that they themselves were partly responsible for the creation of a new category (Arthur Avalon wrote in 1922 that "the adjective *tantric* is largely a Western term"), they believed Tantrism to be limited and specific enough to be conceived of as only a particular, even a rather exceptional, aspect of Hinduism (or of Buddhism). But the progress of research brought the realization that, far from being exceptional, Tantrism was in fact very widespread and indeed the common property of all the religions of "medieval" India.

There is a specific Tantric aspect of Indian religions that, though it is often mixed up inextricably with the rest, does also exist in itself as something more than merely technical and ritual. This appears when one reads the literature, for the texts (Agamas, Tantras, etc.) often distinguish between their teachings and those of non-Tantric, "Vedic" schools. True, the borderline between Tantric and non-Tantric religious groups in Hinduism is difficult to determine clearly; there are common traits on both sides. Still, one can admit Tantrism as a category of its own and define it generally as a practical path to supernatural powers and to liberation, consisting in the use of specific practices and techniques—ritual, bodily, mental—that are always associated with a particular doctrine. These practices are intrinsically grounded in the doctrine that gives them their aim and meaning and organizes them into a pattern. Elements of the doctrine as well as of practices may also be found elsewhere in Indian religions, but when both are associated and welded into a practical worldview, Tantrism is there.

The doctrinal aspect of Tantrism can be summed up, using Madeleine Biardeau's words, as "an attempt to place *kama*, desire, in every meaning of the word, in the service of liberation . . . not to sacrifice this world for liberation's sake, but to reinstate it, in varying ways, within the perspective of salvation." This use of *kama* and of all aspects of this world to gain both worldly and supernatural enjoyments *(bhukti)* and powers *(siddhi)*, and to obtain liberation in this life *(jivanmukti)*, implies a particular attitude on the part of the Tantric adept toward the cosmos, whereby he feels integrated within an all-embracing system of micro-macrocosmic correlations. In Hinduism, these correlations, inherited from the Veda, were further developed in the Upanisads and culminated with Tantrism in a vast theo-anthropocosmic synthesis. This does not apply to Tantric Buddhism, whose philosophy is different, but both Hindu and Buddhist Tantric share an analogous psycho-mental approach and a number of common practices, all grounded in the idea of using cosmic energy—especially as it is present in the "subtle body" within the adept's physical one—for transcendental ends, where the attainment of supernatural powers is inseparable from progress toward final release. The conception of energy, *sakti*, is not the same in the two religions, but still, just as the illuminated Buddhist realizes the equivalence of *samsara* and *nirvana*, so the Hindu Tantric, on attaining liberation in life, will enjoy this world while being free from it because he has realized the true nature of the supreme reality: the realization, the *coincidentia oppositorum*, is of the same type and is in both cases reached through a reversal of some of the traditionally accepted forms of conduct.

There is also in both religions an extraordinary multiplicity of practices, mental, physical, and ritual, in which rites and yoga are inseparable. This ritual proliferation is all the more remarkable as the Buddha expressly condemned all rites and as, in Hinduism, those who renounce the world for salvation are supposed to forsake all ritual. Here, on the contrary, ritual is fundamental. Equally characteristic is a proliferating pantheon, with a marked insistence on terrifying deities whose role is largely linked to the adept's use of the "lowest" or more "dangerous" human tendencies: lust, anger, and the like. This is found in the *krodhavesa* (possession by frenzy) of Kalacakra Buddhism, as well as in several antinomian practices of Hinduism. Sexual practices also (which, though important and characteristic, are not the main element in Tantrism) are to be understood in terms of the harnessing of "lower" impulses for "higher" aims. The impulse is here all the more important because it repeats at a human level the activity of the divine couple, whose creative bliss is echoed and possibly even reproduced by the human pair.

The essential role of all aspects of energy, especially in nature and in the human body, may explain the place in Tantrism of traditional medicine and still more of alchemy, which occupies an important place in all Tantric literature, both Buddhist and Hindu.

Tantrism, Buddhist as well as Hindu (and Jain, as there is also a Jain Tantrism, or Tantric elements in Jainism), insists on the role of the spiritual master, a role linked to the emphasis on initiation and secrecy. A Tantric adept is necessarily the initiated disciple of a master and must keep the teaching secret (hence the obscurity of most Tantric texts). This is linked to the sectarian aspect of Tantrism and may help to explain why Tantrism, in all religions, seems always to have been a matter of small groups, of "active minorities," to use Louis Renou's phrase, which usefully suggests the contrast between, on the one hand, the small number of Tantric initiates together with the secrecy imposed upon them, and, on the other hand, the enormous impact of Tantrism on all Indian religions and the mass of its textual and artistic production. But Tantrism, however carefully one may attempt to trace and define it, remains in many respects a puzzle to the scientific mind.

BIBLIOGRAPHY

The most perceptive views on Tantrism and allied problems are to be found in Madeleine Biardeau's *L'hindouisme: Anthropologie d'une civilisation* (Paris, 1981). A sober and factual review of the facts is given by Jan Gonda in *Die Religionen Indiens*, vol. 2, *Der jüngere Hinduismus* (Stuttgart, 1963), and by André Bareau and others in *Die Religionen Indiens*, vol. 3, *Buddhismus, Jinismus, Primitivvölker* (Stuttgart, 1964). Shashibhusan Dasgupta's *Obscure Religious Cults*, 3d ed. (Calcutta, 1969) describes a number of Hindu and Buddhist Tantric sects of Bengal but deals also with more general problems; it is a most useful book. On Jain Tantrism the only book is still Mohanial B. Jhavery's *Comparative and Critical Study of Mantrasastra* (Ahmedabad, 1944).

ANDRÉ PADOUX

Hindu Tantrism

Tantrism may be briefly characterized as a practical way to attain supernatural powers and liberation in this life through the use of specific and complex techniques based on a particular ideology, that of a cosmic reintegration by means of which the adept is established in a position of power, freed from worldly fetters, while remaining in this world and dominating it by union with (or proximity to) a godhead who is the supreme power itself. All practices and notions constituting the Tantric way correspond to a particular conception of the deity, polarized as masculine and feminine, and of the universe and man, both imbued with this divine power. Thus it may be said that, for a Tantric adept, the quest for liberation and the acquisition of supernatural powers result from a tapping, a manipulating of this ubiquitous power.

History. The history of Hindu Tantrism is impossible to write owing to the scarcity of data, especially for the earlier period. Little epigraphical evidence is available, and there are few datable ancient manuscripts, whereas many texts are still awaiting study. Most likely, a number of works remain to be discovered. Moreover, the dates of formation of Tantric groups, sects, or schools and their interrelationships are usually obscure.

The origin of Hindu Tantrism certainly goes back to an ancient store of beliefs and practices. Some sources are to be found in the Vedas (the *Atharvaveda* and *Yajurveda* notably, on magic and the role of speech or phonetic practices), in the Aranyakas and Brahmanas, and in the earlier Upanisads. This Vedic esotericism was modified and further developed by the adjunction of other elements belonging to autochthonous cults, perhaps Dravidian, certainly an ancient fund whose existence is presumed rather than known. But although we cannot precisely define this fund, we may safely surmise that it existed and played a role in the rise of Hindu Tantrism. Despite these autochthonous and perhaps "popular" roots, Hindu Tantrism cannot be considered a popular form of religion in contrast to a "higher," non-Tantric Hinduism. Indeed, the fact that the main texts are in Sanskrit, and that learned brahmans are among the authors, proves the role played by Brahmanic circles, or at least by the higher castes. Tantrism, in fact, like the whole of Hinduism, has always been divided into practices for the higher and the lower castes. And though renunciates, ascetics, and saints did play an important part in its genesis and development, the fact that these people were on the margins of the Hindu social system does not mean that they were popular figures, still less revolutionaries. Socially speaking, Tantrism, even if theoretically equalitarian (in principle, all, once initiated, have access to its teachings, irrespective of caste or sex), is conservative. Its equalitarianism, like that of *bhakti*, has a ritual, religious scope, not a social one.

Granted that the history of Hindu Tantrism cannot yet be written, the following brief statements may be made:

1. There was no Tantrism in Vedic and Brahmanic times, but merely elements that later evolved and became part of Tantrism. References to the Vedic tradition in Tantric texts must not be taken as proof either of the "Vedic" nature of Tantrism or of direct links with the Veda. Quite likely such references were introduced later to facilitate the acceptance of Tantric texts or sects by orthodox circles.

2. Tantrism as such must have taken shape during the first centuries CE following an internal evolution of Brahmanism: a change whose cause and form escape us, but that can fairly reasonably be attributed in part to an influence of autochthonous elements.

3. Even if the oldest datable documents are Buddhist (they are Chinese, not Indian), Hindu Tantrism, in all likelihood and for several reasons, surely preceded Tantric Buddhism, even if both later interacted.

4. Tantrism appears well established in Hindu India from at least the sixth or seventh century CE. The Gangdhar stone inscription (424 CE) proves that Tantric deities were already worshiped in the fifth century, a period to which some Agamas may possibly belong.

The sixth century and those following were the great creative period during which Hinduism—Puranic and Tantric—took shape.

Texts of all sorts, temples, ritual implements, and works of art continued to be produced until the eighteenth century, testifying to the vitality of Hindu Tantrism. It has been remarked that during this period the texts appear to come more and more from Brahmanic official circles. This may be proof of an increasing hold by Tantrism on the traditional centers of Hindu culture and learning. The steady flow of production, textual or otherwise, has continued until the present, but has yielded little of worth. Practically all ritual manuals and booklets on the practice of *puja* now sold in India reflect

influences of the Tantric cult. This is not surprising, considering that postmedieval sectarian Hinduism has incorporated many of the ideas and practices of Tantrism. Accordingly, much of the Hindu pantheon is composed of Tantric deities. We must note, however, that the majority of sectarian Hindus using these publications do not regard themselves as Tantrists.

Effective practice by Tantric believers has not disappeared from India. In fact, in recent years, with the interest evinced in the West for Tantrism, and with a change in mental attitude among many Indians, a somewhat larger number of people (not only in Bengal) admit to being Tantric. Some periodicals and many books are published on the subject. Some Tantric and Sakta centers are openly active as such, in addition to the other traditional Tantric groups—no doubt more authentic and effective if less publicized. Hindu Tantrism obviously remains a matter of small groups, but their importance is far from negligible.

Yet despite the prevalence of Tantric ideas and practices in Hinduism, it is unlikely that they ever concerned the majority of Hindus. Tantrics produced an enormous mass of doctrinal, ritual, and technical texts. They elaborated or at least influenced most of the Hindu ritual, both public and, to a lesser extent, private. Their imprint on traditional arts, techniques, and activities was also important (temples are still being built, adorned, and furnished with implements in accordance with the teachings of the Agamas). In all likelihood, however, most Hindus who practiced or attended such rituals, or visited such temples, were not Tantric.

Geography. It is difficult to situate the dual Indian root—Vedic and autochthonous—of Tantrism in any precise area of India, still less in some region beyond the subcontinent. China, Tibet, and even the Middle East have been suggested as possible places of origin of Tantric ideas, or as having exerted a significant influence on them, but no convincing evidence has been put forward to substantiate this. Admittedly, the frontier areas of Indian civilization, such as Kashmir (or Swat) and Bengal-Assam, have been among the main centers of Tantrism. But so has Kerala. So were also regions such as Madhya Pradesh and Orissa (where the few surviving temples to the Yoginis are to be found and where cults to the Goddess still seem very active). Among the non-Aryan elements that contributed to the shaping of Hindu Tantrism, some may have come from the shamanic cultures of Central Asia. The importance of the Himalayan region in the subsequent history of Tantric Hinduism, as proved by the cults still practiced there, by the civilization of Nepal, and by the numerous Tantric manuscripts from these parts necessarily implies an influence of the cultures of these northern border regions, but their real impact is not easy to assess.

On the other hand, Tantric Hinduism spread beyond India, especially in Cambodia, as attested by important iconographic and epigraphic evidence. The Sdo-Kak-Thom inscription of 1052 CE, for example, mentions several Tantras as having been introduced into Cambodia in the early ninth century. Tantric practice based on Tantric texts is still followed in Bali.

Sectarian Variations. Tantrism is essentially sectarian. It has always been divided into sects, mutually exclusive and sometimes hostile. The rare religious persecutions in Hindu India were perpetrated by Tantrics. The divisions differ according to the deities worshiped and the ritual practices followed. In this respect, the spirit of Tantrism is opposed to that of *bhakti*, although it, too, possesses the element of devotion.

The main division of sects is made between worshipers of Visnu (Vaisnavas), of Siva (Saivas), and of the Goddess (Saktas), the last two groups being sometimes difficult to distinguish clearly, if only because Siva and Sakti are metaphysically inseparable and therefore necessarily conceived, even in temples, in some relationship. There are also, or have been, Sauras (worshipers of Surya, the Sun) and Ganapatyas (worshipers of Ga-napati, or Ganesa). Among Vaisnavas, the main group is that of the Pañcaratra, although it does not consider itself Tantric nowadays. At least one other and more extreme group from Bengal, the Vaisnava-Sahajiyas, must be mentioned, with their peculiar erotic mysticism, a related modern form of which can be found with the Bauls.

Saiva or Sakta sects are unquestionably Tantric. Among them were such groups as the Kapalikas and Kalamukhas, or the Nathas, a notable Saiva group that transgresses the limits of Hinduism. Most important is the Kula (or Kaula) sect, also found in Buddhism and divided into several subgroups, but its precise nature and scope (sect or school? Saiva or Sakta?) are difficult to assess. The classification into Saiva and Sakta groups is generally a difficult matter, for several traditional divisions exist, corresponding to different criteria and impossible to reconcile with one another. Divisions are made between "currents" (*srotas*), usually three—"right" (*daksina*), "left" (*vama*), and "accepted" *siddhanta*)—although sometimes five srotas are mentioned; or between "remembrances" (*amnayas*), from five to seven in number; or between "doctrines" or "convictions" (*matas*), corresponding to the methods of worship or to the main deity, for example Kubjika, Tripura, Kali. There is also a more doctrinal division into "teachings" (*sastras*), such as Pratyabhijña, Spanda, and Krama of Kashmir Saivism, or Kula and Vamakesvara. But these classification terms are often used loosely. Kula, for instance, is indifferently called *mata*, *sastra*, or *amnaya*. There exists also a "geographical" division into "steps" (*krantas*), and, finally, the well-known division into "conducts" (*acaras*): *vama* and *daksina*, "left" and "right," to which is sometimes added *samaya*. The overall picture is confusing. Further research may perhaps clarify it, although there always were, and still are, isolated ascetics or small groups that do not fit into any classification.

Doctrines. There is no coherent body of Hindu Tantric doctrine. It varies according to sect or school. Some ideological features, however, coupled with particular practices, are characteristic. Agamas, Tantras, and Samhitas are not philosophical works. Even when they include a "section on knowledge," which one would expect to treat doctrinal matters, one seldom finds there a complete and well-defined system. Some Tantric authors, especially those from Kashmir, did write metaphysical works, but they were of different persuasions, hence the absence of a unified doctrine. Tantric ideology, furthermore, is not original nor does it differ completely

> **. . . the Godhead is conceived as having two aspects, masculine and feminine. . . .**

from that of non-Tantric Hinduism: it comes from the same source, being largely made up of elements from the classical Indian systems (the Darsanas). Tantric linguistic or metalinguistic speculations depend on those of the Mimamsa. The cosmology is based on the categories (*tattvas*) of the Samkhya. There are also elements of Yoga. Tantric metaphysics are of a Vedantic type: dualist, semidualist, or nondualist, though mostly the last, which is more adapted to the Tantric conception of man and the cosmos. If, however, Tantrism has not been very inventive, it has given new meanings to old notions and organized them into a new pattern.

Regarding Tantric doctrine itself, the following remarks may be made. Although the Ultimate transcends all duality, the Godhead is conceived as having two aspects, masculine and feminine, whose conjunction, described as a sexual union, is the first and necessary step, within God, toward cosmic evolution, the active principle being the feminine. In Sakta sects, where the main deity is the Goddess, the feminine element clearly predominates, but in all sects it is energy, *sakti*, which produces, pervades, sustains, and finally reabsorbs the universe. She (Sakti) is thus the ultimate cause of human bondage and liberation. She is *maya*, cosmic illusion, but is also equated with God's grace, which is sometimes characteristically called *saktipata*, "descent of energy" into the world. Man's response to grace is devotion, *bhakti*, which plays an important role in many Tantric schools. Though the spirit of Tantrism is in many ways opposed to that of bhakti, both can be reconciled and are even promiscuously associated by the Vaisnava-Sahajiyas.

The energetic process giving rise to the world is one of emanation. It is the outward manifestation, the shining forth, of what exists potentially in the Godhead, starting from the first principle and ending with this world, by a transformation, a condensation, from subtle to gross through a series of stages or cosmic categories (the *tattvas*). These usually number thirty-six, but the count is sometimes more or less, as the *tattvas* added to those twenty-five of the Samkhya are not exactly the same in all Tantric schools. The Pañcaratra has its own system of the unfolding *(vyuha)* of creation from the supreme Lord, Visnu. In such systems, there is no discontinuity in the cosmic process: a stir, an imperceptible movement, appears within the Absolute and is then transmitted to the lowest levels of creation. When cosmic resorption sets in, the process is reversed and flows back to its source. *Maya*, in this perspective, is less the great illusion than the mainspring of the infinite diversity of the world, the play of the gods, who manifest the cosmos in a purely gratuitous way. This element of joy and playfulness *(lila)* may also be found in a non-Tantric context, but is one of the main components of the Hindu Tantric vision. It is especially important in the Krsna cults, and is one of the fields where Tantrism and *bhakti* meet.

With such a philosophy, the Tantric adept feels he lives in a world suffused with divine energy, whose elements, even those apparently the humblest, may be used to gain liberation in this life *(jivanmukti)*, a liberation that is not a renunciation but a realization of the plenitude of the world. The Tantric system of micro-macrocosmic correspondences is inherent in this conception. The divine cosmic energy is the *prana*, the cosmic "breath" symbolized especially by *kundalini*, which is the Goddess in her cosmic play and as present in the subtle body of man. Divine energy is also the word *(vac)* or sound *(sabda)*. This is very important, as Tantric practices related to the uses of the sounds of language play an essential role. *Vac* is a fundamental aspect of energy, both the most powerful and effective and the most usable. Some Tantric schools, especially in Kashmir, have worked out a complex cosmogony whereby all levels of the cosmos are manifested just as the letters of the Sanskrit alphabet appear within the deity in their grammatical order. A particular way to liberation corresponds to this phonetic process.

With the universal pervasion of energy, the quest for liberation necessarily involves the use of this power. Consequently, the possession of supernatural powers *(siddhi)* is a normal result of this quest, when successful. Even if the adept does not use them and concentrates on final release, these powers are there. Fully merged in the deity (in nondualist sects), the adept naturally partakes of all divine powers. This adept—often called sadhaka ("efficient, skillful")—does not necessarily look for salvation. He may seek enjoyment (perhaps the most normal case, in fact), or he may look for both. All three are legitimate aims for three different types of adepts, though supernatural attainments are always essential.

Practices. Practice is the main aspect of Tantrism. The most characteristic practices are those associated with the use of sacred and ritual formulas, *mantras* and *bijas* (phonic "germs"). These linguistic or phonetic elements—sentences, words, letters, sounds—symbolize spiritual entities and are believed to embody the very power of the main deity. Such formulas are used at all times and in all types of Tantric practice, initiatic and religious rites as well as usual duties or activities. There is no life for a Tantric adept (nor of any Hindu, but this is a Tantric trait) without *mantras*. Indeed, *mantrasastra*, the teaching of *mantras*, is often taken as meaning *tantrasastra*, the teaching of the Tantras.

Mantras are often accompanied by diagrams *(mandalas, yantras,* or *cakras)*; geometrical cosmic symbols used for ritual and meditation. Symbolic gestures *(mudras)* expressing

> The assignment of various parts of the body, physical or subtle, to *mantras* and other entities in order to divinize them, follows a ritual technique. . . .

metaphysical or theological concepts are also used in most ritual practices.

Mantras, yantras, and the like must be assimilated spiritually by the adept and put into practice by way of a complex and often long process that is usually both physical and mental. Such are the *mantrasadhana* serving to master a *mantra* and the practices of Tantric yoga. These depend on the Tantric conception of sakti and micro-macrocosmic correlations. They usually consist in awakening, with the help of *mantras*, the *kunda lini* energy that lies dormant, coiled like a (female) serpent in the subtle body of the adept, and leading her up to the point where she unites with the Supreme while the adept merges into the Ultimate. This is done through *hathayoga* methods combining bodily postures and control of breathing with mental exercises leading ultimately to *samadhi* (enstasis) and realization of the essence of the *mantra* and of the deity. Mental exercises are mainly *dhyana*, which here means precise visualizations of the centers of the subtle body (the *cakras*) and of deities residing within or without them. The main and highest means to such a goal is *bhavana*, an intense meditation that brings into existence the subject of meditation: a deity, a cosmic entity, a state of consciousness. All this results in spiritual union with a deity, identification of the individual's mind and body with cosmic entities, and physical and mental integration into the cosmos. There is thus a "mystical physiology" that "cosmizes" the body, as well as a "mystical geography," traditional places of pilgrimage being integrated within. The resulting transformation of the body image changes the attitude of the adept to himself and to the world.

The assignment of various parts of the body, physical or subtle, to *mantras* and other entities in order to divinize them, follows a ritual technique using *dhyana*, *mantra*, and *mudra*, called *nyasa* ("setting down, placing"). Mantras are used for every goal, whether mystical, magical, or ritual. They are used in ritual curing in Tantric medicine (still practiced now) or for alchemy (important in Tantrism) or astrology.

Among the powers of a Tantric adept are the "six actions" *(satkarmani)* whereby it is possible, with *mantras* and rites, to appease, fascinate, bind, drive away, create enmity, kill, and so on. However typical of Tantrism magic may appear to be, it is not by far its main aspect. Nevertheless, in modern India especially, Tantrics are commonly considered magicians or sorcerers and are mostly disapproved of. This is also largely due to the antinomian practices to which they sometimes resort. Tantric doctrine justifies the use of all aspects of life to attain salvation or powers. Hence the use of physical and mental techniques to deviate cravings and impulses—especially the sexual impulse—toward different aims. Hence the use of alcoholic beverages, which enhances energy and shows that the adept transcends normal rules. Hence also repulsive or frightening practices that prove the Tantric is above fear and disgust and is able to use the lowest objects for the highest aims. However, though these practices are part and parcel of Hindu Tantrism, their importance should not be exaggerated. All practices are acted in a ritual context. The whole of Hindu life, in fact, is ritualized, and this ritual is either Tantric or tantricized. This is particularly true of the worship or cult *(puja)* of divinities.

The Tantric *puja* is not only the worship of a god or goddess. It is the transformation (played out rather than mystically effected) of the worshiper into that deity—a transformation deemed indispensable, for "only a god may worship a god." Several rites lead to this "change of ontological status." *Dhyana, mantra, nyasa,* and *mudra* transform the worshiper's body into a divine one. A "purification of the elements" *(bhutasuddhi)* and a replacement of the limited self *(atman)* by that of the deity are undergone. This is followed by an "inner sacrifice" *(antaryaga),* an exercise in Tantric yoga whereby the deity is experienced as being present in the adept's body and all the customary services of the cult are imagined and visualized as offered to it there. Then comes the "external" worship. This may be done with an image, although a diagram may be preferred. First it is drawn according to ritual; then the main deity and attendant deities are visualized and mentally placed on the diagram and are instilled with the *prana* that will make them fit for worship. This "breath" or energy is often conceived as springing from the heart of the previously deified worshiper. *Nyasa* (there can be up to thirty series of *nyasas* in a *puja*), *dhyana,* and repetitions of *mantras (japa)* are used. Yoga and mantric practices are integral parts of Tantric worship.

Not always present but typical is the use of the "five elements" *(pañcatattva)* in this worship: alcohol, meat, fish (the second and third elements imply animal sacrifices), *mudra* (usually parched grains), and sexual intercourse *(maithuna).*

The first four items are offered to the deity, then partaken of by the worshiper. The last one is, or can be, a ritual sexual union with a woman previously initiated and "transformed" by *nyasa* and such rites. This may also take place in a collective worship called cakrapuja, "cult made in a ring," where the rite is performed by participants arranged in a ring, in pairs of male and female. This is considered very secret and is reserved for higher initiates. A woman or girl may also be worshiped *(kumaripuja)* as a form of the Goddess, with or without sexual union. The female organ *(yoni)* is in such case equated with the Vedic altar on which the male seed is the offering. Another "secret" worship is done with a corpse. It is used to achieve particular goals, usually evil. *Pujas* made with a special intent *(kamyapuja)* may be used for black magic (especially the "six actions") but can also serve any other end, good or bad: *sakti* as such has no moral connotation. Though sexual symbolism is encountered everywhere and magic is part of the Tantric vision, none of these rites is a compulsory part of Tantric practice.

Pantheon. Several features of the Hindu pantheon (which has continued to evolve throughout the centuries) are Tantric in form or nature. No complete and systematic study of the Tantric pantheon, as distinct from the epic and Puranic ones, seems to have been carried out so far. Nevertheless, it can be said to be marked by a proliferation of deities emanating from a main supreme god—Visnu, Siva, the Goddess—in a complex hierarchy wherein feminine entities are especially numerous and even predominant, as befits a system in which the whole cosmic process is the work of the feminine energy *(sakti)* in her different forms. The importance in Hinduism of terrifying deities may also be attributed to Tantric influence. The myths and legends of these deities, particularly those of the Goddess in her various aspects, are present in a considerable part of the Tantric texts.

Deities are all the more numerous as the main gods have several forms and secondary divinities sometimes emanate from them in long series. Even the attributes, qualities, or aspects of the different deities are divinized. Siva, for instance, has various aspects and names: Sadasiva, Bhairava, Mahesvara, Kamesvara, and so on. He is said to have five "faces," each being also a divine form. He holds at least four attributes or "weapons" and has six "limbs"; all are deified. The energies emanating from him through Sakti, starting with Vama, Jyestha, Raudri, and Ambika (there are still others), are goddesses, who engender other deities. Entities can thus multiply almost indefinitely. Similarly, a number of divinities emanate from Visnu through the agency of his *sakti,* starting with the four *vyuhas:* Vasudeva, Samkarsana, Pradyumna, and Aniruddha. He, too, has Tantric forms, such as Hayagriva. The main aspect of Siva in the Agamas is Sadasiva; in the Tantras, it is Bhairava. A curious composite form of Surya (the sun god) and Visnu is Martanda-Bhairava. In the Agamas and Tantras, Surya is a form of Siva. Ganesa is also important in the Tantric pantheon.

The Goddess, omnipresent in higher as in "popular" Hinduism, appears under several forms and names. Her nature being ambivalent, some forms are benevolent, such as Gauri, Uma, and Parvati; others are terrifying, such as Durga or Kali. She is worshiped as supreme goddess under several names: Tripura, Kubjika, Malini, and others. As the *sakti* of Visnu or Narayana, she is Sri or Laksmi. She is also manifested in many other ways, all of which constitute forms, or her "emanations" (i. e., like rays emanating from the sun), at different levels of cosmic energy. Her various cosmic activities are accomplished through these aspects, some of which can be her supreme form in certain schools. Such are the sixteen *nityas*, one of which is Tripurasundari, the main deity of the Tripura school. Or the ten Mahavidyas: Kali, Tara, and others. In the Krama school, there exists a "wheel" of twelve Kalis in charge of the different cosmic processes. Mention should also be made of the Mothers (Matr) numbering seven, eight, or nine. The fifty "Little Mothers" (Matrka) are deities of the Sanskrit phonemes over which preside also the eight Mothers. There are usually sixty-four Yoginis, powerful and often terrible, forming a circle, or circles, around Siva or Bhairava. Their number varies, however, sometimes reaching 640 million. All these are found in Saiva and Sakta contexts, but very similar deities or divinized forms of energy playing analogous cosmic roles exist in the Pañcaratra.

There are corresponding hierarchies for male gods, if only because in Tantric Hinduism deities always come in couples, so as to be able to create. This abundance sometimes results from the division of one entity into several others. Such, for instance, is the case of the eight Bhairavas (Asitanga, Ruru, Unmatta, etc.), who, together with Siva, are often associated with the nine Durgas (Navadurga). The Rudras (gods of Vedic origin, in fact), who normally number ten or eleven, can also be fifty and then become male deities of the alphabet, coupled with the Matrkas. There are also 118 Rudras. The Ganas, or Ganesas, headed by Ganesa or Vinayaka, elephant-headed gods, are associated, together with their *saktis*, with the fifty *pithas*, the places of pilgrimage marked by the parts of the dismembered body of Sati, Siva's consort. The Ganas are also associated with the Sanskrit phonemes, which are also linked with fifty Visnus. Although the *mantras* (sometimes said to number seventy million) are primarily ritual and mystical formulas, they are also considered gods, and then Lords of Mantras (Mantresvara) and Great Lords (Mantramahesvara) are added to the pantheon. Also divinized are the ritual gestures *(mudras)* or the supernatural powers *(siddhis)* and even the three daily acts of worship *(sandhyas)*. All these entities are often said to be distributed in concentric rings (especially in cosmic diagrams such as the *sricakra*) surrounding in hierarchical order the main deity at the center. A host of godlings, spirits, demons, ghosts

(pisaca, vetala, preta, bhuta), and the like play inferior but not unimportant roles in the religious and still more in the magical beliefs and practices of Tantric Hinduism.

BIBLIOGRAPHY

Avalon, Arthur. *The Garland of Letters (Varnamala): Studies in the Mantra Shastra*. 2d. ed. Madras, 1951. Useful, though unsystematic and unclear.

Avalon, Arthur. *Principles of Tantra* (1914). 2d ed. Madras, 1952. Although not recent and unwieldy (1,171 pages), this work is still worth consulting for its information on the spirit and practices of Tantrism.

Avalon, Arthur. *The Serpent Power*. 7th ed. Madras, 1953. On kundalini.

Brunner-Lachaux, Hélène. *Somasambhupaddhati*. 3 vols. to date. Pondicherry, 1963-1977. This work, which includes the Sanskrit text, a copiously annotated French translation, indexes, and plates, is the best available source on Saiva Tantric ritual.

Chakravarti, Chintaharan. *Tantras: Studies on Their Religion and Literature*. Calcutta, 1963.

Dasgupta, Shashibhusan. *Obscure Religious Cults*. 3d ed. Calcutta, 1969. Perceptive and informative on the general problem of Tantrism and on its Hindu and Buddhist forms in Bengal.

Diehl, Carl Gustav. *Instrument and Purpose*. Lund, 1956. Studies the rites and ritual practices in South India as based on the Agamas and as observed by the author.

Dimock, Edward C., Jr. *The Place of the Hidden Moon*. Chicago, 1966. An excellent study of the erotic mysticism of the Vais-nava-Sahajiyas of Bengal.

Gnoli, Raniero, trans. *Luce delle Sacre Scritture: Tantraloka*. Turin, 1972. Italian translation of the main Tantric work of Abhinavagupta (eleventh century). An essential work, but not easy reading.

Goudriaan, Teun. *Maya Divine and Human*. Delhi, 1978. An interesting study of "magic and its religious foundations in Sanskrit texts, with particular attention to a fragment on Visnu's Maya preserved in Bali."

Gupta, Sanjukta, Dirk Jan Hoens, and Teun Goudriaan. *Hindu Tantrism*. Leiden, 1979. The only introductory survey of the subject. Sober and fairly reliable. The first part is especially clear and informative.

Padoux, André. *Recherches sur la symbolique et l'énergie de la parole dans certains textes tantriques*. 2d ed. Paris, 1975. A study of cosmological and metalinguistic Tantric speculations, especially in Kashmir Saivism.

Silburn, Lilian, ed. and trans. *Le Vijñana Bhairava*. Paris, 1961. A good study, in French translation, of a very typical and curious text from Kashmir. Available in English as Vijñana Bhairava (Delhi, 1979), translated by Jaideva Singh.

ANDRÉ PADOUX

TAOISM

It is no easy task to define Taoism, for throughout its history this philosophical and religious system assumed very different aspects. The period of the Warring States (403-221 BCE) produced a wide variety of philosophical currents, an obvious source of embarrassment for the philologists and bibliographers of the Han dynasty (202 BCE-220 CE), who set themselves the task of ordering this abundant literature. In contrast to the Confucian classics, the writings of the "hundred philosophers" were not easy to classify.

Ancient thinkers were not always aware of belonging to any specific school. Rather, the classification of ancient writings into various ill-defined schools was mainly the work of Han scholars. The philosophers classified under the rubric "Taoist school" (Tao-chia) formed rather small circles comprising a master and a limited number of disciples. Since most of the writings of these Taoist circles were lost, the Taoism of that (the pre-Ch'in) era is essentially represented by the teachings expounded in the *Tao-te ching,* attributed to Lao-tzu, and the *Chuang-tzu,* so named for its putative author.

Formative Concepts

It has become customary to distinguish the Taoism of the philosophers of the fourth and third centuries BCE from the religious Taoism that presumably appeared in the second and third centuries of our era. In Chinese the former is call Tao-chia (Doka in Japanese) and the latter, Tao-chiao (Dokyo). This distinction was often accompanied by a value judgment wherein much profundity was attributed to the philosophical authors, while religious Taoism was perceived as a mixture of superstition and magic. Recent studies have attempted to rectify this relatively simplistic view. The complex development of religious Taoism gave birth to numerous "schools" or currents, which were in general rather open, despite the esoteric character of their teachings.

In its development, religious Taoism did not break with the fundamental conceptions of the philosophers, although it remains true that these concepts were much transformed. The various Taoist currents shared the quest for longevity, even immortality; it was only their methods that distinguished them.

Conception of the World: Macrocosm and Microcosm. To understand Taoist theories and practices, one must first understand what the Taoists regarded as the general principles governing the world and man.

According to ancient Chinese cosmology, the world was governed by a set of fundamental notions related to unity and multiplicity, space and time, and microcosm and macrocosm. The concepts of *tao* and *te* were not specific to Taoism but belonged to all currents of Chinese thought. Literally, *tao* means "road," or "way." *Tao* was also the efficacious power of kings and magicians who knew how to make the three spheres of the world—Heaven, Earth, and Man—communicate with one another. In cosmology the *t'ien-tao* ("way of Heaven") was the natural order as it manifests itself through the circulation of the sun and, more generally, through the movement of the celestial vault. The royal *tao (wang-tao)*

existed solely for the sovereign in order that he might ritually restore the natural order of heavenly *tao,* which was constantly threatened by disorder. In case of catastrophe such as drought or flood, the sovereign was held responsible and had to expiate either his own sins or those of the world. In this way his virtue (*te* or *tao-te*) was manifested.

Yin-yang and Five Elements. The original meanings of *yin* and *yang* seem to refer to the shaded and sunny slopes of mountains, respectively. Eventually, the two terms came to describe the two antithetical and complementary aspects of the Tao as natural order: a shady aspect and a luminous aspect; a cold, passive aspect and a warm, active aspect; and finally, the feminine aspect and the masculine aspect. The terms are therefore relative classificatory headings only; any one thing can be either *yin* or *yang* in relation to another. These two notions played a fundamental role in all philosophical, scientific, and religious thought. The same applies to the "five elements," or "five phases"*(wu-hsing)* theory as it appeared in the *Hung-fan* (Great Norm), a treatise inserted in the *Shu ching* (Classic of History). Here the elements were presented as related to numbers: (1) water, (2) fire, (3) wood, (4) metal, and (5) earth. These were not merely substances or chemical phenomena but represented instead the principal cosmic forces or influences and classificatory headings. All phenomena—seasons, directions, flavors, foodstuffs, the viscera of the body, human activities, and so forth—could be classified under one or another of the Five Phases. Earth was central and neutral; the four other elements corresponded to the four directions and to the four seasons and were further classified as either *yin* or *yang.* In addition, the elements were symbolized by the five fundamental colors: water is equated with black, fire with red, wood with green, metal with white, and earth with yellow. Added to this symbolism were four animals, which often appeared in representations of sacred space: the dragon to the east, the red bird to the south, the white tiger to the west, and the tortoise, enlaced by a snake, to the north.

Symbols of I ching. The divinization of the *I ching* is founded on a series of symbols or diagrams formed by the combination of unbroken lines (representing *yang*) and broken lines (representing *yin*). When these lines are tiered three at a time, we obtain eight trigrams. The combination of any two of the trigrams yields one of the sixty-four possible hexagrams. Trigrams and hexagrams symbolized the totality of realities, the former in a more synthetic fashion and the latter in a more analytical fashion. By arranging them in a circle representing space and time, we readily see how *yin* and *yang* alternate, how one passes from a purely *yang* reality (Heaven, represented by the trigram or hexagram ch'ien) to a purely *yin* reality (earth, represented by the trigram or hexagram k'un).

Although the ancient Chinese availed themselves of many systems of correspondence and symbols to describe the universe, in general they conceived of the universe as a great hierarchical whole whose parts, spaces, and times corresponded to one another. The system of classification based on the Yin-yang Five Elements theory made it possible to describe the microcosm and its harmony or disharmony by means of the rhythms of the outside world. A correct hygiene and a proper cultivation of the vital principle naturally required a perfect adaptation of the vital rhythms to those of the universe. For example, the "five viscera," in close relation with the Five Elements and therefore with the seasons and directions, were "nourished" by the "five flavors"—whence the requirements of a diet in harmony with the seasons.

Mysticism. The two main works of Taoism during the Warring States period, called the "period of the philosophers," were the *Lao-tzu* and the *Chuang-tzu.* Both works are characterized by their emphasis on quietism and mysticism and by the metaphysical dimension they attribute to the Tao. As a primordial and eternal entity, the Tao exists before all visible things, including *ti,* the superior divinities of the official religion, such as Shang-ti ("lord on high") and T`ien-ti ("lord of heaven"). The Tao is beyond the grasp of the senses and is imperceptible. But from "nothingness" *(wu)* the visible world *(yu)* is born and particularized phenomena are produced. Tao is formless, limitless, and nameless: the term *tao* is not a name but a practical referent.

The Tao of the Taoist philosophers actually assumes many aspects. On the one hand, it is transcendent with respect to the world of phenomena, where diversity and change prevail; on the other hand, it becomes immanent as it manifests itself, penetrating the beings that it animates and orders. In the *Tao-te ching,* the Tao is a feminine principle, the mother of the world. It gives birth to all beings, and its *te,* or nourishing virtue, preserves them and brings them to maturity.

The Taoists in fact condemn all discursive knowledge, for, they maintain, it introduces multiplicity into the soul, which should, rather, "embrace Unity," that is, be unified in the Tao. This unity is preserved through the mastery of the senses and passions. The sense organs are conceived as apertures through which the vital principles escape if they are not controlled. The passions and emotions are a cause of depletion of vital and spiritual power. A certain amount of self-denial is advocated, but such aims at the harmonious use of the sense faculties, not as their suppression. The Taoist should be especially careful not to intervene in the course of things. This nonintervention is called *wu-wei* (nonaction), a term that suggests not absolute nonaction but an attitude of prudence and respect for the autonomy of other things.

Some passages of the *Tao-te ching* allude to longevity practices that were assuredly being used among quietist circles. If such techniques—gymnic, respiratory, and others— were of interest to wisdom and religion, it was because holiness was believed inseparable from the potent vitality that was acquired and nourished by regulating one's vital energy. By living in accordance with the principle of *wu-wei* one can preserve the suppleness and energy of an infant and, consequently, one may hope to live the longest possible life. Lao-tzu goes so far as to assert the invulnerability of the saint.

If a spiritual purification is necessary to attain illumination, it is because the Tao is veiled in our consciousness by the artificialities of civilization. Hence, a critical reflection on the relativity of commonly received ideas is the necessary first stage on the way to salvation. Under the silent direction of a master, the adept gradually sheds the constitutive elements of his social self. Thereafter, he loses awareness of his body, and his sense perceptions are no longer differentiated—he hears with his eyes and sees with his ears. Finally, the adept's entire being communes with the totality. According to Chuang-tzu, he has the internal impression of flying off and moving about freely in space but externally the individual in a state of ecstasy resembles a piece of dead wood. His vital essence seems to have left him: it has gone "to gambol at the beginning of things." Chuang-tzu uses the perennial theme of the spiritual voyage to illustrate the state of absolute freedom the saint attains when he lives in symbiosis with the cosmos. By identifying his vital rhythm with that of the natural forces he participates in the infinity and persistence of the universe. He thus attains a superior life that is no longer biological; he lives the very life of the Tao.

Historical Survey

Lao-tzu is generally considered the patron, if not the founder, of Taoism. From the first centuries of our era he became a popular divinity, and his text, the *Tao-te ching,* was used by the propagandists of sectarian movements. It was the latter who were at the origin of collective Taoism, which differed significantly from the small chapels of philosophers.

Taoism at the Beginning of the Imperial Era: 221 BCE-220 CE. We know that as early as the end of the Warring States and the beginning of the imperial era *fang-shih* ("prescription-masters") were active in the eastern coastal regions of China. They specialized in the occult sciences and propagated the theory of history as set forth by the philosopher Tsou Yen (fourth century BCE). Some of these *fang-shih* peddled prophetic works and pseudo-Confucian writings (*wei-shu* or *ch`an-wei*), which exerted much influence on Taoism. These magicians offered formulas that would allow the sovereigns to establish communication with the immortals and to become immortals themselves. The *fang-shih* taught the Han emperor alchemical recipes that were supposed to enable him to become a *hsien-jen.* However, Wu-ti established Confucianism as the official doctrine of the imperial state and instituted the examination system to recruit candidates for public office. Such examinations dealt exclusively with the Confucian classics. This double attitude was typical of the ruling class and the lettered bureaucrats of all periods.

Ostensibly Confucian in their public life, they were nevertheless Taoists in private.

In the first century CE Buddhism made its appearance in China. From historical sources we learn that the new religion had already been introduced in some provinces by the year 65 CE. At the court of Liu Ying, a brother of Emperor Ming (r. 58-75) who had a fief in present-day Kiangsu, there were Buddhist monks as in the capital. Our sources report that Liu Ying was surrounded by *fang-shih,* favored the Huang-Lao doctrine (i. e., the cult of Huang-ti and Lao-tzu, an expression referring to Taoism), and made common offerings to Huang-ti, Lao-tzu, and the Buddha. Later, the emperor Huan did the same in the imperial palace and in 165 ordered that rituals be

> ## Lao-tzu is generally considered the patron, if not the founder, of Taoism.

performed at the birthplace of Lao-tzu. Here, Lao-tzu was presented as a cosmic man endowed with traits borrowed from the myth of Pan-ku, common to the religion of southern populations. In the developing legend, Lao-tzu became Lao-chün ("Lord Lao"), a sovereign god who in the course of successive reincarnations came down from Heaven to instruct past sovereigns and to reveal sacred scriptures.

As the cult and mythology of Lao-chün spread in popular circles they sporadically gave rise to messianic movements. An important movement occurred during the last decade of the Han dynasty, contributing to its decline. These movements seem to be more or less connected to a famous work, the *T`ai-ping ching.* This text was presented many times to the throne, once during the Former Han dynasty and then again during the reigns of the emperors Shun and Huan of the Latter Han, each time by *fang-shih* from Shantung. The work belonged to a genre of prophetic literature, and its authors clearly hoped to obtain reforms from the court. The text is utopian in outlook, aiming at establishing an era of *t`ai-p`ing* ("great peace") modeled on the golden age.

In order to retrieve *t`ai-p`ing,* one must find the Tao within oneself. There is much discussion of ethics and politics in the work, but it remains distinctly Taoist in the importance it gives to spiritual exercises and methods of longevity.

A certain version of the *T`ai-p`ing* ching was used by the leaders of a rebellion that exploded in 184 in eastern China and spread to many provinces. This so-called Rebellion of the Yellow Turbans, or T`ai-p`ing Tao ("way of great peace"), announced the end of the Han dynasty and the advent of a new era. In the same year, in northern Szechuan, another movement, called the T`ien-shih Tao ("way of the celestial masters") established a state organized like a church, with a *t`ien-shih* ("celestial master") at its head and local parishes

under the authority of *chi-chiu* ("libationers"). The first and most famous Celestial Master was Chang Tao-ling, who is often considered the founder of the Taoist religion. This legendary figure began a religious movement using spells and talismans after having received a revelation from T`ai-shang Lao-chün (the divinized Lao-tzu). Converts had to offer a contribution of five pecks of rice, whence the other name of the sect, the Wu-tou-mi Tao ("way of the five pecks of rice"). One of the reasons for the success of the movement was that its religious leaders presented themselves as healers. The sick were considered sinners, or as those who inherited faults perpetrated by their forebears, and thus had to repent and confess themselves as part of the salvific process. The written confessions were conveyed to the gods of Heaven, earth, and water.

Taoism of the Six Dynasties: Fourth to Sixth Century. The division of the country into the Three Kingdoms following the fall of the Han dynasty fostered regionalism that was exacerbated by the fall of North China to the domination of non-Chinese invaders at the beginning of the fourth century. The South remained under the control of the Chinese emperors of the Wu dynasty (222-280), who withdrew south of the Yangtze in 317. Prior to that time, the Celestial Masters exerted no influence in the South.

Taoism of the Southern Dynasties. The fall of the Western Chin provoked an important migration southward, placing the Celestial Masters and their followers in the presence of the popular cults and Taoist circles of these regions. Inevitably, there ensued a syncretism between the Way of the Five Pecks and the religious traditions of the lower Yangtze, giving rise to a new Taoist sect, the Mao-shan school (also known as the Shang-ch`ing sect), named after a mountain in the region of Kou-jung in present day Kiangsu. This sect or school originated with an important series of sacred scriptures that were revealed through the mediation of the visionary Yang Hsi. A selection of these revelatory texts appears in the *Chen-kao* (Revelations of Immortals), compiled by T`ao Hung-ching (456-536), illustrious among the Taoists of this period. T`ao's broad knowledge won him the friendship of Emperor Wu of the Liang dynasty. Not only did he collect, edit, and annotate the Shang-ch`ing writings, but he was also known as a poet and calligrapher.

Taoism of the Northern Dynasties. During these centuries of division, the Taoism of the northern part of occupied China developed independently of the southern traditions. During the Wei dynasty (386-556), Taoism became the state religion owing to the activity of K`ou Ch`ien-chih, a member of the Celestial Masters. K`ou Ch`ien-chih received the title of "Celestial Master" from the emperor T`ai-wu (425) and thereby gained authority over all religious affairs in the territory. He conferred the Taoist insignia on the emperor, who considered himself the representative on earth of Lao-chün. In 446, K`ou finally succeeded in influencing the emperor to officially prohibit Buddhism. This was the first of many persecutions of Buddhism and the first serious manifestation of hostility between the two religions.

Buddhism was rehabilitated under the following reign. The quarrels, however, went on, centering on such issues as the "conversion of the barbarians" outlined in the *Hua-hu ching*, the mortality or immortality of the soul, and karmic retribution. But in fact, the two doctrines influenced each other. The Madhyamika notion that there is no difference between mundane existence and *nirvana,* and that the Buddha is present within oneself was perceived as congruent with the concept of the Tao dwelling in the heart, where one must find it through nonaction. The Taoist influence on Buddhism was particularly manifest in Ch`an (Jpn., Zen), the most Chinese of the Buddhist sects, in which one finds the distinctive flavor of Taoist mysticism.

**Taoism under the T`ang: 618–907.** Many of the T`ang emperors are noted for their lavish patronage of Taoism. Because the imperial family and Lao-tzu shared the surname Li, the former traced its genealogy back to Lao-tzu and proclaimed him the ancestor of the dynasty. The *Tao-te ching's* importance as a sacred work increased. Emperor Hsüan-tsung (Ming-huang, 712–756) wrote a famous commentary on it and included it among the required texts for the civil service examinations, which had hitherto been based on the Confucian classics. Furthermore, each family had now to keep a copy in its possession, and the birthday of Lao-tzu became a national holiday. Taoism spread throughout the vast empire and came into contact with other religions, such as Nestorianism and Manichaeism.

During the period between the end of the T`ang dynasty and the beginning of the Sung, China was once again divided. In the kingdom of Shu (in present-day Szechuan) Tu Kuang-t`ing (850–933) gained the support of the sovereign to undertake the search for Taoist scriptures. He wrote many important works, including some dealing solely with ritual. Another Taoist of the same period, Ch`en Tuan, devised the diagram that was to be a source of inspiration for Chou Tun-i's *T`ai-chi t`u* (Diagram of the Supreme Ultimate), an important factor in the formation of Sung Neo-Confucian metaphysics.

Taoism under the Sung and Yüan Dynasties. During the reign of Chen-tsung (r. 998–1022) of the Northern Sung dynasty (960–1126), Taoism once more became the official religion. The dynasty was given a prestigious ancestor in the figure of Huang-ti, who was assimilated to the Jade Sovereign (Yü-huang), considered the supreme divinity of Heaven in popular belief. It was also during this period that the lineage of the Celestial Masters was officially recognized at Lung-hu Shan (Dragon and Tiger Mountain), in the province of Kiangsi. Official temples and monasteries were established in all provinces and were administered by retired high officials. Under Chen-tsung's rule, the collection of

Taoist works was reorganized and collated, and the very important Taoist encyclopedia, entitled *Yün-chi ch`i ch`ien* (Seven Bamboo Slips from the Book-pack of the Clouds), was compiled to preserve many texts predating the Sung.

The reign of Hui-tsung (1101–1125) was also an era of prosperity for Taoism. A devoted believer, the emperor installed a theocracy with himself as the supreme head of the Taoist pantheon and, like Hsüan-tsung of the T`ang dynasty, wrote a commentary on *Tao-te ching.* Also of note are the steps taken during Hui-tsung's reign for the first printing of the Taoist canon. His reign is marked by the appearance of new movements based on the entire corpora of revealed ritual texts, the most important being the Shen-hsiao ("divine empyrean") order. The order was founded by the emperor himself under the influence of the Taoist magician Lin Ling-su. It was also at the latter's instigation that Hui-tsung took measures against the Buddhists. However, the Chin invasions of North China in 1127 brought an end to the Northern Sung dynasty and, thus, to the recognition of Taoism as the official religion.

Many new Taoist sects appeared in the northern regions ravaged by war and occupied by foreign armies. The most important were the T`ai-i ("supreme unity"), Chen-ta-tao ("perfect and great Way" or "authentic great Way"), and Ch`üan-chen ("integral perfection") sects.

The Ch`üan-chen sect was to become one of the most significant and prevailing currents of Taoism. Its founder, Wang Ch`ung-yang (Wang Che; 1113–1170), supposedly met with Lü Tung-pin, the immortal whose cult had become widespread since the beginning of the Sung dynasty and to whom several important works were attributed. Following the meeting, Wang Ch`ung-yang decided to devote himself to religion: he recruited Ma Tan-yang (1123–1183), who was to become the sect's second patriarch, and six other disciples, all natives of Shantung. As seen in their required curriculum—the *Tao-te ching,* the *Hsiao ching* (Classic of Filial Piety), and the *Pan-jo hsin ching,* a summary of the famous *Pan-jo ching* (Prajñaparamita Sutra)—the Ch`üan-chen sect promoted a form of syncretism that reflected popular notions of the unity of the "three religions" (i. e., Taoism, Buddhism, and Confucianism). New adepts were invited to sever all links with the secular world and to steep themselves in meditation so that their hearts and minds might become as firm as T`ai Shan, that is, impervious to the lures of the outside world. According to the Ch`üan-chen sect's synthesis of Ch`an Buddhism and mystical Taoism, man must retrieve his pure, original nature in order to enjoy an increased life span. The sect was characterized by its tendency toward asceticism and its rejection of magical practices. In many ways it represented a new form of Taoism.

Wang's most famous disciple, Ch`iu Ch`ang-ch`un (1148–1227), was invited to the court of Chinggis Khan, who hoped to obtain the drug of immortality from him. Although the

Taoist master answered that he knew only about hygienic techniques to prolong life, Chinggis Khan proffered sentiments of friendship and promulgated an edict ordering tax exemptions for Taoist monks. The Taoists, availing themselves of the protection of Yüan emperors, took advantage of the situation to harass the Buddhists. Their polemics, based on the *Hua-hu ching,* backfired however, and the Taoists lost much prestige.

The other major current of the period was the Cheng-i ("orthodox unity") sect, which was none other than the sect of the Heavenly Masters, whose patriarchs were believed to be descendants of Chang Tao-ling. From the Sung dynasty to the present this school has continued to have a great impact on Taoism. Unlike the *tao-shih* of the Ch`üan-chen sect, who practice celibacy, the *tao-shih* of the Cheng-i marry and their charge is hereditary.

The Search for Longevity

Longevity, or at least living out one's allotted life span, was considered proof of sainthood. For the most part, the methods used to attain longevity centered on avoiding the depletion of vital spirits.

The Taoists conceived of the body as a microcosm that incorporated the totality of the universe, that is, Heaven, earth, and the celestial bodies. Universe within the universe, the body was often depicted as a mountain or a gourd, the Taoist symbol of the cosmos. Taoist cosmology holds that before the beginning there existed a kind of cosmic energy, referred to as the *yüan-ch`i* ("primordial breath") and synonymous with the invisible and with the void. This primordial breath split into *yin* and *yang,* the gross and pure elements that, respectively, formed Heaven and earth. Each being hides within itself this primordial breath. Since its presence is needed to maintain life, and since its exhaustion brings about death, the goal of many Taoist practices was the preservation of the *yüan-ch`i.*

The most important elements in the body were considered the *ch`i* (breath, ether), *ching* (essence), and *shen* (spirit). The Taoists believed that *ch`i, ching,* and *shen* were present throughout the body but were especially concentrated in the *tan-t`ien* (three "cinnabar fields"), the psychic centers in the head, heart, and just below the navel. Although the Three Cinnabar Fields were centers of life, they were also inhabited by malevolent spirits called the "three corpses" or "three worms" *(san-shih),* whose main goal was to bring about death. Most Taoist practices and precepts aimed at both neutralizing the ruinous power of the "three worms" and preventing the three *hun* "souls" and the seven *p`o* "souls" from leaving the body. The *hun, yang* in nature, had a tendency to return to Heaven, whereas the *p`o,* which were *yin,* tried to return to earth. The departure of the souls from the body meant death. Thus, the *Huai-nan-tzu* describes the Taoist saint as one who preserves the *hun* and *p`o* souls through ataraxy and who avoids all agitation of the vital spirits.

Methods of Inner Contemplation. Perhaps the most important of the Taoist contemplative practices was that of *shou-i* ("preserving the One" or "meditating on the One"). Derived from the phrase *pao-i* ("to embrace the One") in Lao-tzu's *Tao-te ching, shou-i* came to represent many different methods of spiritual concentration. Although the One is identified with the Tao, *hsü* ("emptiness") and *wu* ("nonbeing"), it is at the same time understood as the cosmos, the mother, the matrix, the primordial breath, and the origin of all beings.

In practice, these abstract ideas were given concrete forms. The One was represented by the anthropomorphic images used in visualization exercises. The One is visualized in its dynamic aspect, that is, in the form of three divinities symbolizing the "three primordial breaths" and otherwise called the San I ("three ones"). It is believed that this triad, later called the San Yüan ("three primordials") dwells inside man in the Three Cinnabar Fields and inhabits the "three superior heavens." By visualization, the adept causes the triad to descend into his own body. According to T`ao Hung-ching, a famous Taoist of Mao-shan, these divinities inhabit the body of each individual, but they return permanently to Heaven if the individual does not practice visualization. The departure of the divinities brings about illness and even death. However, this visualization is possible only for initiates, since to visualize the divinities one must know their names, physical appearance, and complete attributes.

Visualization of the gods of the body. Each point and organ of the body possesses a subtle energy that the Taoists represented with a divinity. These divinities were arranged hierarchically into a celestial bureaucracy whose ranks, posts, and functions were as complex as those of the imperial bureaucracy on which it was modeled. The recitation of certain sacred texts and the simultaneous practice of visualization exercises served to actualize these divinities in the body. Famous works such as the *Huang-t`ing ching* (Book of the Yellow Court) and the *Ta-tung chen-ching* (Book of Great Profundity) provide detailed information about the divinities, their personal names, their dress, their size, and so on. Besides the Three Ones, the most important divinities were those of the five viscera, who, according to the *T`ai-p`ing ching,* keep the registers of life and death.

Visualization of the heavenly bodies and the planets. Another of the Taoist contemplative techniques is the visualization of the heavenly bodies and planets. The adept visualizes either the light of the heavenly bodies as they descend into his body or the inner light that he "preserves" in, or directs to, a particular point in his body *(lien-hsing).* These exercises make the adept's body progressively luminous like the heavenly bodies. The *Pao-p`u-tzu* describes the technique whereby the *chen-jen* ("perfect man") preserves and purifies his body. The sun and moon rise up to the head where they unite; the elixir, sweet as honey, then descends into the mouth; the adept swallows the elixir and sends it to the *ming-men* ("door of destiny") located in the navel, where he preserves it.

Predominant among the exercises for the visualization of stars and constellations were those involving the Pei-tou. For the Taoists, the Pei-tou is made up of seven visible and two invisible stars. Owing to its circumpolar position as the central axis of Heaven it was always visible. Its handle indicated the progress of the year and determined the four seasons and the degrees of Heaven. Visualization of the Pei-tou was practiced in different ways, either in communal rituals or in individual exercises. The adept marked the place of the stars of the constellation in the holy enclosure and then proceeded to "pace the stars." Each time he stepped on one of them he visualized its divinity with all its attributes. The devotee accompanied this practice by holding his breath, swallowing, and reciting various invocations. The Pei-tou visualizations were believed to help the adept to ascend to paradise.

Alchemy. Among the Taoist techniques of immortality, alchemy is perhaps the most significant. Two types of alchemy may be distinguished: *wai-tan* ("external alchemy," also called laboratory alchemy) and *nei-tan* ("inner alchemy"), the concoction, in meditation, of internal elixirs of immortality.

During the Han dynasty the magician Li Shao-chün persuaded Emperor Wu to worship the "god of the stove." Through this sacrifice, Li Shao-chün hoped to be able to transmute cinnabar into gold in order to produce magical vessels that would bestow immortality on any person who ate or drank from them. Physical immortality was therefore the first goal of Chinese alchemy, although later its techniques were used to produce artificial gold and silver for profit.

Development of modern techniques: internal alchemy (nei-tan). It was primarily under the T`ang and Sung dynasties that the technique of *nei-tan* spread. During the Sung dynasty, *nei-tan* represented a syncretistic system whereby the ancient techniques of longevity were practiced under the guise of alchemical theories and language.

The development of *nei-tan* in the Sung dynasty was marked by the appearance of a series of prose texts distinctly influenced by Ch`an Buddhism. Both of these *nei-tan* traditions relied on two works, still influential today: the *Pi ch`uan cheng-yang chen-jen ling-pao pi-fa* (Secret Transmission of the Ultimate Methods of the Ling-pao of the Perfect Man of the True Yang; eleventh century) and the *Wu-chen p`ien* (Book of the Realization of Perfection) by Chang Po-tuan (d. 1082). The commentator of the *Wu-chen p`ien*, Weng Pao-kuang, was himself influenced by the Chung-Lü texts, using the terminology and notions found there to explain the *Wu-chen p`ien*. In his preface, dated 1173, he claims to divulge the secret teachings of Chang Po-tuan concerning the great medicine of the gold elixir. To refine the elixir one must first take the primordial breath as the basis,

then establish the *yin* cauldron and *yang* store, and finally, gather into the cauldron the Primordial Breath, which will thereupon form a parcel the size of a grain of millet. It is this grain that is called *chin-tan* ("gold elixir"). One then swallows the *chin-tan* and guides it into the five viscera, where it will attract the breath *(ch`i)* and essence *(ching)* of the body and immobilize them, thereby preventing their escape. Afterward one induces the *chin-tan* to circulate, thereby nourishing the breath and essence, which then transform into a gold liqueur.

One day this liqueur will rise from the coccyx and reach the *ni-wan* (probably from an early transcription of the Sanskirt word *nirvana*) in the brain: this is the *chin-i huan-tan* ("gold liqueur returned cinnabar"). When the *chin-i huan-tan*, shaped like the egg of a sparrow, descends into the mouth, it is then swallowed and guided to the Lower Cinnabar Field where it coalesces to become the "holy embryo." After a ten-month gestation period, the Holy Embryo will be born in the form of an earthly immortal (a rank inferior to that of the celestial immortals).

BIBLIOGRAPHY

General Works

Creel, H. J. *What Is Taoism? and Other Studies in Chinese Cultural History.* Chicago, 1970.

Fung Yu-lan. *A History of Chinese Philosophy.* 2 vols. Translated by Derk Bodde. Princeton, 1952-1953. Originally published in Shanghai (1931-1934), this is a general work on Chinese philosophy, with a few chapters on Taoist philosophy.

Granet, Marcel. *La pensée chinoise* (1934). Reprint, Paris, 1968. A classic on the systems of Chinese thought with their symbols and categories. A brilliant pioneering study, it contains interesting chapters on the Taoist schools and the techniques of longevity.

Kaltenmark, Max. *Lao tseu et le taoïsme.* Paris, 1965. Translated by Roger Greaves as *Lao Tzu and Taoism* (Stanford, 1969). A general introduction to religious and philosophical Taoism, this extremely readable work is illustrated by numerous translations.

Maspero, Henri. "Le taoïsme." In *Mélanges posthumes sur les religions et l'histoire de la Chine,* edited by Paul Demiéville, vol. 2. Paris, 1950. Reprinted in *Le taoïsme et les religions chinoises* (Paris, 1971) and translated by Frank A. Kierman, Jr., as *Taoism and Chinese Religion* (Amherst, 1981). Written by one of the masters of French Sinology, this posthumous work contains important essays on religious Taoism.

Needham, Joseph. *Science and Civilisation in China.* 5 vols. Cambridge, 1954-1983. This work is an ambitious and successful undertaking on Chinese scientific thought, with chapters on Taoism (vol. 2) and a presentation of alchemy and the techniques of longevity (vol. 5).

Schipper, Kristofer. *Le corps taoïste.* Paris, 1982. In one of the best recent works on the subject, Schipper offers an overall synthesis of Taoist religion with an excellent chapter on ritual.

Welch, Holmes. *The Parting of the Way: Lao Tzu and the Taoist Movement.* London, 1957. A good general introduction to Taoism, this work presents an interesting interpretation of the *Tao-te ching.*

Philosophy

Chan, Wing-tsit. *The Way of Lao Tzu.* Indianapolis, 1963. A translation of the *Tao-te ching.*

Graham, A. C., trans. *The Book of Lieh-tzu*. London, 1961. This is the best available translation of a classic of philosophical Taoism.

Larre, Claude. *Le traité VII du Houai Nan Tseu*. Paris, 1982. The author has translated an important chapter of Chinese anthropology.

Robinet, Isabelle. *Les commentaries du Tao Tu King jusqu'au septième siècle*. 2d ed. Paris, 1981. A study of the main commentaries of the *Lao-tzu*.

Waley, Arthur, ed. and trans. *The Way and Its Power*. London, 1934. This is a classic translation of *Lao-tzu*.

Watson, Burton, trans. *The Complete Works of Chuang Tzu*. New York, 1968. The best available translation in a Western language of the greatest Taoist philosopher.

Historical Studies

Seidel, Anna K. *La divinisation de Lao tseu dans les taoïsme des Han*. Paris, 1969. An excellent study of the transformation of a philosopher into a divinity.

Stein, Rolf A. "Remarques sur les mouvements du taoïsme po-litico-religieux au deuxième siècle ap. J.-C." *T'oung pao* 50 (1963): 1-78. A study of sectarian revolts that brought about the downfall of the Han dynasty.

Strickmann, Michel. *Le taoïsme du Mao-Chan*. Paris, 1981. A historical survey of an important sect of the Chinese Middle Ages.

Taoist Hagiography

Kaltenmark, Max. *Le Liesien tchouan: Biographies légendaires de immortels taoïstes de l'antiquité*. Peking, 1953. A fully annotated translation of the first Taoist hagiography.

Ngo Van Xuyet. *Divination, magie et politique dans la Chine ancienne*. Paris, 1976. An excellent study of the occult sciences in China during the Han dynasty and the Three Kingdoms period.

Porkert, Manfred. *Biographie d'un taoïste légendaire: Tcheou Tseu-Yang*. Paris, 1979. A translation of an important hagiography of a legendary Taoist.

Schipper, Kristofer. *L'Empereur Wou des Han dans la légende taoïste*. Paris, 1965. A translation of an ancient Taoist novel, important for the study of the legends and practices of the Mao-shan school.

Taoism and Fine Arts

Chang Chung-yüan. *Creativity and Taoism*. New York, 1963. Examines the influence of Taoist thought on the arts and poetry.

Delahaye, Hubert. *Les premières peintures de paysage en Chine: Aspects religieux*. Paris, 1982. An interesting thesis, with a translation of a famous text by Ku K'ai-chih.

Taoist Ritual

Hou Ching-Lang. *Monnaies d'offrande et la Notion de Trésorerie dans la religion chinoise*. Paris, 1975. An interesting work that helps to understand some aspects of Taoist ritual.

Kaltenmark, Max. "*Quelques remarques sur le T'ai-chang Ling-pao wou-fou siu.*" *Zinbun* 18 (1982): 1-10. Includes a description of an ancient ritual.

Lagerwey, John. *Wu-shang pi-yao: Somme taoïste du sixieme siècle*. Paris, 1981. A reference work with an important introduction.

Lagerwey, John. *Taoist Ritual in Chinese Society*. New York, 1987.

Schipper, Kristofer. "Taoist Ritual and the Local Cults of the T'ang Dynasty." Academia Sinica, Taipei, 1979. This work, as well as the following two, written by one of the best specialists of Taoism, examines various aspects of ritual.

Schipper, Kristofer. "The Written Memorial in Taoist Ceremonies." In *Religion and Ritual in Chinese Society*, edited by Arthur P. Wolf, pp. 309-324. Stanford, 1974.

Schipper, Kristofer. *Le Fen-Teng: Rituel taoïste*. Paris, 1975.

Longevity Techniques and Meditation

Anderson, Poul, trans. *The Method of Holding the Three Ones: A Taoist Manual of Meditation of the Fourth Century A. D.* Copenhagen and Atlantic Highlands, N. J., 1980. A good translation of a meditation text of the Mao-shan school.

Baldrian-Hussein, Farzeen. *Procédés secrets du Joyau magique: Traité d'alchimie taoïste de l'onzième siècle*. Paris, 1984. An introduction to a Sung-dynasty system of internal alchemy, with translation.

Despeux, Catherine. *Taiji Quan: Technique de longue vie et de combat*. Paris, 1981. An interesting study of Chinese boxing, with good translations.

Despeux, Catherine, trans. *Traité d'alchimie et de physiologie taoïste*. Paris, 1979. A translation of Chao Pi-ch'en's important work of modern internal alchemy.

Gulik, Robert H. van. *Sexual Life in Ancient China* (1961). Reprint, Atlantic Highlands, N. J., 1974. A pioneering work on an important subject. An interesting chapter on the various interpretations of alchemical language.

Maspero, Henri. "Les procédés de 'nourrir le principe vital' dans la religion taoïste ancienne." *Journal asiatique* 229 (1937): 177-252, 353-430. Reprinted in *Le taoïsme et les religions chinoises*. Paris, 1971. Fundamental work on physiological practices.

Robinet, Isabelle. *Méditation taoïste*. Paris, 1979. Very learned general study.

Schafer, Edward H. *The Divine Woman*. Berkeley, 1973. A survey of Chinese mythology, with some passages on Taoism.

Schafer, Edward H. *Pacing the Void*. Berkeley, 1977. Contains interspersed passages on the technique of "walking on the stars."

Alchemy and Medicine

Porkert, Manfred. *The Theoretical Foundations of Chinese Medicine: Systems of Correspondence*. East Asian Science Series, vol. 3. Cambridge, Mass., 1974. A difficult work to read, but interesting for the understanding of medical theories.

Sivin, Nathan. *Chinese Alchemy: Preliminary Studies*. Cambridge, Mass., 1968. A first-rate study of an alchemical treatise written by a great doctor of the T'ang dynasty.

Ware, James R., trans. *Alchemy, Medicine, Religion in the China of A. D. 320: The Nei-P'ien of Ko Hung* (1967). Reprint, New York, 1981. Complete translation of the Taoist section of Pao-p'u-tzu. Unfortunately, it is not always reliable.

Diverse Collections and Articles

History of Religions 9 (November 1969 and February 1970). Proceedings of the First International Conference of Taoist Studies.

Sivin, Nathan. "On the Word 'Taoist' as a Source of Perplexity." *History of Religions* 17 (February-May 1978): 303-330.

Welch, Holmes, and Anna K. Seidel, eds. *Facets of Taoism*. New Haven, 1979. Proceedings of the Second International Conference of Taoist Studies.

Zürcher, Erik. "Buddhist Influence on Early Taoism." *T'oung pao* 66 (1980): 84-147.

Taoist Bibliography

Loon, Piet van der. *Taoist Books in the Libraries of the Sung Period: A Critical Study and Index*. Oxford Oriental Institute Monographs, no. 7. Ithaca, N. Y., 1984. A work intended for specialists; however, the introduction on Taoist literature in Sung times is of general interest.

Soymié, Michel. "Bibliographie du taoïsme: Études dans les langues occidentales." in *Études taoïstes* 3-4 (1968-1971).

Works in Chinese and Japanese

Akizuki Kan`ei. *Chugoku kinsei dokyo no keisei*. Tokyo 1978. A study of the Ching-ming school of Taoism.

Ch`en Kuo-fu. *Tao-tsang yüan liu k`ao*. 2d ed. Peking, 1963.

Ch`en Kuo-fu. *Tao-tsang yüan liu hsü k`ao*. Taipei, 1983. A study of alchemical and medical terminology found in the Taoist canon.

Ch`en Yüan. *Nan Sung ch`u Hopei hsin tao-chiao k`ao*. Peking, 1962.

Ch`ing Hsi-t`ai. *Chung-kuo tao-chiao ssu-hsiang shih-kang*. Chengtu, 1981.

Fu Ch`in-chia. *Chung-kuo tao-chiao shih* (1937). Reprint, Taiwan, 1970.

Fukui Kojun. *Toyo shiso no kenkyu*. Tokyo, 1956.

Fukui Kojun. *Dokyo no kisoteki kenkyu*. Tokyo, 1958.

Fukui Kojun et al., eds. *Dokyo*. 3 vols. Tokyo, 1983. A collection of articles of Taoism with an exceptionally complete bibliography.

Hsü Ti-shan. *Tao-chiao shih*. Shanghai, 1934.

Hsü Ti-shan. *Fu-chi mi-hsin te yen-chiu*. Shanghai, 1941.

Jao Tsung-i. *Lao-tzu hsiang-erh chu chiao-chien*. Hong Kong, 1956.

Ishii Masako. *Kohon shinko*. 4 vols. Tokyo, 1966-1968.

Kubo Noritada. *Koshin shinko no kenkyu*. Tokyo, 1961.

Kubo Noritada. *Chugoku no shukyo kaikaku*. Kyoto, 1967. A study of the Ch`üan-chen sect.

Kubo Noritada. *Dokyoshi*. Tokyo, 1977.

Kubo Noritada. *Dokyo no kamigami*. Tokyo, 1986.

Miyakawa Hisayuki. *Rikucho shukyoshi*. Tokyo, 1974.

Murakami Yoshimi. *Chugoku no sennin; Hobokushi no shiso*. Tokyo, 1956.

Obuchi Ninji. *Tonko dokyo mokuroku*. Kyoto, 1962.

Obuchi Ninji. *Dokyoshi no kenkyu*. Okayama, 1964.

Obuchi Ninji. *Tonko dokyo mokuroku-hen*. 2 vols. Tokyo 1978-1979.

Obuchi Ninji. *Chugokujin no shukyo girei*. 5 vols. Tokyo, 1984.

Ren Jiyu, ed. *Tsung-chiao tz`u-tien*. Shanghai, 1983.

Sun K`o-k`uan. *Sung Yüan tao-chiao chih fa-chan*. Taichung, 1965.

Sun K`o-k`uan. *Yüan-tai tao-chiao chih fa-chan*. Taichung, 1968.

Sun K`o-k`uan. *Han-yüan tao lun*. Taipei, 1977.

Tsukamoto Zenryu. *Gisho Shakuroshi no kenkyu*. Tokyo, 1961. The work also appears as vol. 1 of *Tsukamoto Zenryu chosa-kushu* (Tokyo, 1973).

Wang Ming. *T`ai-p`ing ching ho-chiao*. Peking, 1960.

Wang Ming. *Tao-chia ho tao-chiao ssu-hsiang yen-chiu*. Chung-king, 1984.

Wang Ming. *Pao-p`u-tzu nei-p`ien chiao-shih*. Peking, 1985.

Yen I-p`ing. *Tao-chiao yen-chiu tzu-liao*. 2 vols. Taipei, 1974.

Yoshioka Yoshitoyo. *Dokyo no kenkyu*. Tokyo, 1952.

Yoshioka Yoshitoyo. *Dokyo kyoten shiron*. Tokyo, 1955.

Yoshioka Yoshitoyo. *Tonko bunken bunrui mokuroku, Dokyo no bu*. Tokyo, 1969.

Yoshioka Yoshitoyo. *Eisei e no negai, Dokyo*. Tokyo, 1970. Contains material on Ch`üan-chen Taoism.

Yoshioka Yoshitoyo. *Dokyo no jittai* (1941). Reprint, Kyoto, 1975.

Yoshioka Yoshitoyo. *Dokyo to Bukkyo*. 3 vols. Tokyo, 1959-1976.

Yoshioka Yoshitoyo and Michel Soymié. *Dokyo kenkyu*. 4 vols. Tokyo, 1967-1971.

FARZEEN BALDRIAN
Translated from French by Charles Le Blanc

TARIQAH

The *tariqahs* are a rich and diverse complex of religious associations that have developed all over the Islamic world. Some are regional, others are widely distributed; few are centralized. They exist or have existed in clusters throughout the Middle East, North and sub-Saharan Africa, Arabia, Central Asia, the Indian subcontinent, Southeast Asia, and China. Their role is manifold: they add an emotional and spiritual dimension to religious devotion; they contribute to the intimacy of social life; they are associated with trade and craft guilds; they have provided staging posts and hospices for travelers and merchants; and they have served as credit and finance institutions.

Origins and Early Development. The word *tariqah* (pl., *turuq*) literally means "road" or "path," and this is still its primary sense in modern Arabic. The specialized use of the word to indicate a group of individuals dedicated to the mystical life developed, in the ninth or tenth century, from its metaphorical sense of a mystical path. In the early stages of this use, the connotation was primarily individual. *Tariqah* was used to describe a method of moral psychology for the guidance of individuals directing their lives toward a knowledge of God.

The elaboration of this path derived from a spiritual impulse that grew stronger at the beginning of the seventh century. Those who were prompted by religious idealism to withdraw from social life in order to satisfy their yearning for God and uphold the values of primitive Islam were already heirs to the rich spiritual traditions of Hellenism and Christianity in the eastern Mediterranean. They established a visible presence when a number of them, in the manner of the desert monks and other ascetics in Syria and Egypt, began to wear, as a distinctive dress, a type of habit of coarse wool. It is probably from this wearing of wool that the term *sufi* derives. The word, *sufiyah*, used to indicate groups or nascent communities of Sufis, is attested in the next century.

Spiritual exercises. From this period too there is evidence of the types of ritual that were practiced alongside the ascetic life. The aim, of course, was to draw close to God, to feel the presence of God. One basic spiritual exercise devoted to this goal that was to undergo extensive development was the dhikr, or "remembrance." This involved the repeated recitation of words and phrases taken from or based on the Qur'an in order to internalize them totally, so that through the intimacy achieved with God's word, the divine presence itself might be experienced.

Another exercise, not always distinguished from *dhikr*, is *sama`* ("listening [session]"). As early as 850 CE, there were *sama`* houses in Baghdad in which the Sufis could listen to music and let themselves be drawn into mystical states.

Communal life. The nucleus from which the *tariqah* was to develop at its earliest and simplest was the relationship established between master and pupil—in Arabic terminology, between *murshid* ("guide") and *murid* ("seeker"). Sufi teachers who established a reputation were sometimes able to set up lodging places of their own to accommodate their students. One of the earliest was on the island of Abadan in the Persian Gulf. As a fraternity grew, its center ceased to be the master's private house or shop. A new center, and concomitant institutional structures, emerged. The name of these centers or "convents" varied according to location: *zawiyah* and *ribat* were used largely though not exclusively in the Maghreb; *khanqah* in Egypt and the Levant; *khanagah* from Iran to India; and *tekke* in Turkish-speaking areas.

As the various modes of mystical theory and practice became established, the internal discipline of the *tariqah* was formalized and the relationship between disciple and shaykh elaborated. This relationship had become one of great intimacy, and as it further developed in some of the *tariqahs*, it was exemplified in the technique of *tawajjuh*, or total face-to-face concentration, whether that of the disciple concentrating on his shaykh as he performed the *dhikr* or that of the shaykh who reciprocated by concentrating on his disciple, entering his heart, and guiding him. The *tariqahs* also generated the concept of the *silsilah* ("chain" [of transmission]) by which a shaykh justified his special authority. A master of outstanding reputation and charisma might create so strong an impression on his followers that his method and the community of disciples he had made his own would continue after his death.

The Tariqah as an Established Institution. By the mid-twelfth century, when the basic rules of mystical education were elaborated, the *tariqahs* were well established in their present form: communities of individuals held together by a distinctive set of rules relating to lifestyle, religious practice, and aspiration and functioning in addition to and alongside those required by Islamic jurisprudence. As the movement continued to gather strength and popularity, *tariqahs* were established all over the Muslim world. Despite the esoteric character of the theosophy they developed—a theosophy which, however, was only for the initiates—the *tariqahs* became greater and more comprehensive. It was easy for the ideas and rituals to be diluted with popular belief and to attract the masses with the hope of obtaining spiritual and temporal benefits from the sanctity and spiritual power of the great figures in the orders, from the tombs in which they were buried, from the places with which they were associated, and from the relics. Thus the *tariqahs* became great communities, comprising all strata of society, offering something to the educated and uneducated alike, tolerating a wide range of folk practices, yet preserving and extending a great tradition of spirituality.

Social awareness. One of the earliest treatises on the norms of proper behavior among members of a *tariqah* is a twelfth-century work, *Adab al-muridin* (The Manners of the Disciples). It is representative of practice in a number of orders, and apart from its intrinsic interest, and the exquisite care with which it describes an etiquette of great sensitivity to human feeling, it demonstrates that in such *tariqahs* human values and human courtesies come before both rigorous asceticism and complex theosophical ideas. The work classifies religious scholars into three groups: traditionalists are the watchmen of religion, who deal with the external meaning of *hadith;* jurists are the arbiters of religion, whose specialty is their ability to make legal inferences; the Sufis in their turn base their lives and conduct on both groups of specialists and refer to them in case of difficulties.

Individual Tariqahs. There are over two hundred *tariqahs*. The selection presented here is intended to show aspects of their individuality as reflected in the social classes to which they made their appeal, their attitudes toward government authority, their spiritual exercises and theosophy, and the circumstances in which they flourished.

Suhrawardiyah. One of the oldest *tariqahs* is the Suhrawardiyah, named after its founder, `Abd al-Qahir Abu Najib al-Suhrawardi (d. 1162). Founded in response to political danger, the order quickly established itself in the declining years of the Abbasid caliphate; the close association with government was maintained, and its members continued to play a role in political life and worldly affairs. The Suhrawardiyah can be found today in the Indian subcontinent and Afghanistan.

Qadiriyah. Of almost equal age is the Qadiriyah, another *tariqah* that is extant today but exercises a wider and rather different kind of appeal than that of the Suhrawardiyah. It was founded by `Abd al-Qadir al-Jilani (1088-1166), perhaps the most famous saint in the Islamic world, and stories of his miracles abound from Java to Morocco. The Qadiriyah had a very catholic appeal; all strata of society from ruler to peasant found a place within it. In popular belief `Abd al-Qadir was a renewer of Islam, and among members of the order there is a well-known story that he discovered a man by the wayside on the point of death and revived him. The "man" then revealed that he was the religion of Islam. The order, it should be noted, was to play a particularly important role in the islamization of West Africa.

***Rifa`iyah.*** Slightly later than the Qadiriyah is the Rifa`i order, founded in south Iraq by Ahmad al-Rifa`i (d. 1175). Although never as popular as the Qadiriyah, it is distinguished by one of its ritual practices, a particularly loud recitation of the *dhikr*, which led members to be known as the Howling Dervishes. It too still exists and is well represented in Egypt.

Shadhiliyah. Rather different in character is the Shadhiliyah. It was founded by Abu al-Hasan al-Sha-dhili of

Tunis (d. 1256), who traveled widely in the Ma-ghreb and Spain and finally settled in Alexandria, where he died. In contrast to the Rifa`iyah, this *tariqah* practices internalized and silent devotions. Thus its appeal is individualistic, focusing on the development of private prayer. Nonetheless, the emphasis of Abu al-Hasan's teaching was against the solitary and the institutional life alike, and he urged his followers to realize their yearning for God through faithful attention to their daily responsibilities in society. Even after the Atatürk government prohibited Sufi orders in Turkey in 1925, the Shadhiliyah retained its attraction for the middle class. It has also gained a following among some European Muslims.

Naqshbandiyah. Baha' al-Din Naqshband (d. 1388) founded the Naqshbandi *tariqah,* an order that was to become as widespread and popular as the Qadiriyah. Although it originated in Bukhara, it was to have an important role in India, and also developed branches in China, Central Asia, and the Middle East, as well as Sumatra, the Riau archipelago, Java, and other of the Indonesian islands. The order still has a strong following scattered over the length and breadth of the Muslim world. The Naqshbandiyah recited their *dhikr* silently and banned music and rhythmic movements. They believed that through *dhikr* without words one could achieve a level of contemplation in which subject and object became indistinguishable, and the individual soul returned to God as it had been before creation. Among their techniques of meditation was concentration on their shaykh; another practice was regular visitation of saints' tombs in the hope that, by concentrating on the spirit of the departed shaykh, they would increase their spiritual strength.

BIBLIOGRAPHY

General Works. A most readable and sensitive overview of Sufism may be found in Annemarie Schimmel's *Mystical Dimensions of Islam* (Chapel Hill, N. C., 1975); although the work focuses on individual personalities and mystical expression rather than *tariqah* organization, there is an excellent index that will guide the reader to specific topics. Another fine general survey that does emphasize the *tariqahs* in their social setting is J. Spencer Trimingham's *The Sufi Orders in Islam* (New York, 1971). *The Encyclopaedia of Islam* (Leiden, 1913-1934; new ed., 1960-) offers relevant entries under *tarika, tasawwuf,* and the names of individual orders and personalities.

Sources. Among source materials, `Abd al-Qahir al-Suhrawardi's *Adab al-muridin* is available in the abridged translation of Menahem Milson as *A Sufi Rule for Novices* (Cambridge, Mass., 1975). See also *The `Awarif u'l-ma`arif by Shahab-u'd-Din b. Muhammad Suhrawardi,* translated by H. Wilberforce Clarke (1891; reprint, New York, 1973), and Reynold A. Nichol-son's *Rumi, Poet and Mystic, 1207-1273: Selections from His Writings Translated from the Persian* (London, 1950).

Special Studies
Abun-Nasr, Jamil M. *The Tijaniyya: A Sufi Order in the Modern World.* Oxford, 1965.
Akiner, Shirin. *Islamic Peoples of the Soviet Union.* Boston, 1983.
Algar, Hamid. "The Naqshbandi Order: A Preliminary Survey of Its History and Significance." *Studia Islamica* 44 (1976): 123-152.
Anawati, Georges C., and Louis Gardet. *Mystique musulmane.* 3d ed. Paris, 1976.
Behrman, Lucy C. *Muslim Brotherhoods and Politics in Senegal.* Cambridge, Mass., 1970.
Bennigsen, Alexandre, and Chantal Lemercier-Quelquejay. *Islam in the Soviet Union.* New York, 1961.
Berger, Morroe. *Islam in Egypt Today: Social and Political Aspects of Popular Religion.* Cambridge, 1970.
Clarke, Peter B. *West Africa and Islam: A Study of Religious Development from the Eighth to the Twentieth Century.* London, 1982.
Dermengham, Émile. *Le culte des saintes dans l'Islam maghrébin.* 4th ed. Paris, 1954.
Evans-Pritchard, E. E. *The Sanusi of Cyrenaica.* Oxford, 1949.
Geertz, Clifford. *The Religions of Java.* Glencoe, Ill., 1961.
Geertz, Clifford. *Islam Observed: Religious Development in Morocco and Indonesia.* New Haven, 1968.
Gibb, H. A. R., and Harold Bowen. *Islam Society in the Eighteenth Century,* vol. 1 of *Islamic Society in the West.* Oxford, 1950. See especially chapter 11-13 on education, religious endowments, and the dervishes.
Hourani, Albert, and S. M. Stern, eds. *The Islamic City.* Oxford, 1970. See especially S. M. Stern's "The Constitution of the Islamic City," pp. 25-50.
Jong, F. de. *Turuq and Turuq-Linked Institutions in Nineteenth Century Egypt.* Leiden, 1978.
Keddie, Nikki R., ed. *Scholars, Saints, and Sufis: Muslim Religious Institutions in the Middle East since 1500.* Berkeley, 1972.
Martin, Bradford G. *Muslim Brotherhoods in Nineteenth Century Africa.* Cambridge, 1976.
Massignon, Louis. *Essai sur les origines de lexique technique de la mystique musulmane.* 3d ed. Paris, 1968.
Naguib al-Attas, Syed. *Some Aspects of Sufism as Understood and Practised among the Malays.* Singapore, 1963.
Nizami, K. A. "Some Aspects of Khangah Life in Medieval India." *Studia Islamica* 8 (1957): 51-69.
Rizvi, S. A. A. *Early Sufism and Its History in India to 1600 A. D.,* vol. 1 of *A History of Sufism in India.* New Delhi, 1978.
Snouck Hurgronje, Christiaan. *Mekka in the Latter Part of the Nineteenth Century.* Translated by J. H. Monahan. Leiden, 1931.
Willis, John Ralph, ed. *Studies in West African Islamic History.* London, 1979. See especially A. A. Batran's "The Kunta, Sidi al-Mukhtar al-Kunti, and the Office of Shaykh al-Tariq al-Qadiriyya," pp. 112-146.

A. H. JOHNS

TEMPLE

Hindu Temples

"The Indian temple, an exuberant growth of seemingly haphazard and numberless forms," wrote Stella Kramrisch in 1922, "never loses control over its extravagant wealth. Their organic structure is neither derived from any example seen in nature, nor does it merely do justice to aesthetic consideration, but it visualizes the cosmic force which creates innumerable forms, and these are one whole, and without the least of them the universal harmony would lack completeness" ("The Expressiveness of Indian Art," *Journal of the Department of Letters,* University of Calcutta, 9, 1923, p. 67).

Axis, Altar, and Enclosure. Hindu temples are built to shelter images that focus worship; they also shelter the worshiper and provide space for a controlled ritual. Between the fifth and the fifteenth century CE, Hindu worshipers constructed stone temples throughout India, but sacred enclosures of another sort had been built centuries before. Tree shrines and similar structures that enclose an object for worship (tree, snake, *linga,* pillar, standing *yaksa,* all marked by a vertical axis) within a square railing, or later within more complicated hypaethral structures, have been illustrated in narrative relief-sculptures from the first few centuries BCE and CE. Whatever the variations, these structures mark a nodal point of manifestation.

In creation myths and in the imagery of the lotus, as in the structure of Mauryan monolithic pillars (from the third century BCE), the cosmic axis separates heaven from the waters. Creation flows from this nodal point toward the cardinal directions, producing a universe that is square, marked by the railing-enclosure of these early shrines, by the *harmika* (upper platform) of the Buddhist stupa, and by the edges of the brick altar used for sacrifice.

Diagram of Construction. The Vastupurusa Mandala—the square diagram on which the altar, temples, houses, palaces, and cities are founded—also outlines creation. The myth of the *vastupurusa* portrays the first sacrifice, in which a demon is flayed and his skin held down by divinities who ring the diagram (*padadevatas;* lit., "feet deities"). In the center is the "place for *brahman*"—the formless, ultimate, "supreme reality."

Iconicity of Architectural Form. In North India, the fifth century CE saw experimentation in the means by which architecture could supply shelter to images. Small cave shelters were excavated (Udayagiri), cavelike cells were constructed (Sañci), structures with towers were built in impermanent materials (Gangadhara), and stone "mountains" were built (as at Nachna) with cavelike sanctums. Some temples began to show multiple and variant images of the central divinity on the walls (Madhia), and others became complexes by adding subsidiary shrines to shelter other deities (Bhumara, Deogarh).

Only in the sixth century did such experiments lead to a North Indian temple form that was complete in its symbolism and architectural definition. On plan, the North Indian temple grows from the Vastupurusa Mandala; its corners are those of the square *vedi;* its walls are half the width of the sanctum in thickness (as prescribed in the *Brhat Samhita*); at its center is the *brahmasthana.* The outer walls begin to acquire projecting planes that measure the dimensions of the interi-

or sanctum and the "place for *brahman*". In elevation, these planes continue up through the superstructure as bands that curve in to meet a square slab at the top of the temple, from which a circular necking projects. The necking supports a large, circular, ribbed stone *(amalaka)* that takes the form of an *amala* fruit and normally is crowned by a stone waterpot *(kalasa)* from which leaves sometimes sprout.

As North Indian architecture evolves between the sixth and the thirteenth centuries, the plan of the temple shows more and more offsets, the walls gain more images, and the central tower of the temple becomes clustered by other, miniature towers, increasingly giving the effect of a mountain

> **Some temples began to show multiple and variant images of the central divinity on the walls.**

peak through specifically architectural means. If this variety of constructional forms, buttresses, and images "body" forth reality in the manifest world, the ribbed *amala* stone at the top of the temple, much like the staff that sprouts in *Tannhäuser,* presents the ripening seed's potentiality for fruition.

Palace, Hut, and Fortress. The temple thus combines physically the pillar that marks the axis of cosmic parturition, the altar of sacrifice taking the shape of the created universe, and the need for shelter of the tender divinity and the human worshiper; it unites the cosmic mountain and potent cave. South Indian temples, built in stone from the seventh century CE, give emphasis to the temple's role as shelter for anthropomorphic divinities by retaining throughout their evolution a terraced, palatial form crowned by a domed *sikhara* that has the shape of the ascetic's hut.

The temple is called *prasada* ("palace") in North India, and the architectural veneer of its superstructure, in both north and south, allude to forms of palace architecture. In the north, these have been completely subordinated to the temple's vertical ascent, becoming body for the altar that still presents itself at the top of the temple, open to the sky.

If the temple is palace for divinity, it also is fortress, protecting the world from disorder and chaos. Corners are "attended with evils" according to the *Brhat Sam-hita* (53.84), and "the householder, if he is anxious to be happy, should carefully preserve Brahman, who is stationed in the center of the dwelling, from injury" (53.66).

The Temple in the Human Image. In such an architectural context, *yogin* and god are equal participants: the place of divine manifestation and the path of the aspirant have been given consubstantiality along the temple's longitudinal axis; sanctum and sacrificer's space both have become altars manifesting supreme reality in human form. In the

Hindu temple, the axis of cosmic creation and the ritual path for release of the aspirant/worshiper/sacrificer (yajamana) meet; the temple shares in the image of the "Supernal Man" (Purusa).

[See also Iconography.]

BIBLIOGRAPHY

Bhattacharyya, Tarapada. The Canons of Indian Art. Calcutta, 1963. A pioneering modern work on India's architectural texts.

Coomaraswamy, Ananda K. "Early Indian Architecture: II, Bodhi-Gharas." Eastern Art 2 (1930): 225-235. In this series Coomaraswamy establishes a basis for understanding the forms of early Indian architecture.

Kramrisch, Stella. The Hindu Temple. 2 vols. Calcutta, 1946. Kramrisch's monumental work lays out, as no other, the ritual and metaphysic of the temple and establishes a groundwork for the analysis of standing monuments.

Meister, Michael W. "Mandala and Practice in Nagara Architecture in North India." Journal of the American Oriental Society 99 (1979): 204-219. An article that demonstrates through the analysis of standing monuments the practical applicability of the ritual vastu-mandala.

Meister, Michael W., ed. Encyclopaedia of Indian Temple Architecture, vol. 1, pt. 1, "South India, Lower Dravidadesa." Philadelphia, 1983. The first in a series of volumes intended to cover the full spread of India's temple architecture with technical detail.

Meister, Michael W. "Siva's Forts in Central India." In Discourses on Siva, edited by Michael W. Meister, pp. 119-142. Philadelphia, 1984.

Meister, Michael W. "Measurement and Proportion in Hindu Temple Architecture." Interdisciplinary Science Reviews 10 (1985): 248-258.

Sarkar, H. Studies in Early Buddhist Architecture of India. New Delhi, 1966. Brings to light the results of new excavation and research on early forms of Indian sacred architecture.

Stein, Burton, ed. The South Indian Temple. New Delhi, 1978. A collection of essays succinctly dealing with the South Indian temple as a sociological institution.

MICHAEL W. MEISTER

Buddhist Temple Compounds

After Buddha's death, according to Buddhist tradition, his body was given royal cremation, and relics were distributed among eight city-states, which then established royal burial mounds (stupas) incorporating these relics in order to memorialize him. Two centuries later the Mauryan emperor Asoka (ruled 273-236 BCE) is said to have reopened these stupas to distribute the relics more widely in his attempt to spread the Buddha's teachings; Buddhist tradition relates that Asoka established eighty-four thousand stupas throughout his empire.

Compounds in South and Southeast Asia. Though shelters for the monks and stupas as monuments to memorialize the Buddha and his teaching defined the physical requirements of Buddhist architecture for many centuries, symbolic and ritual requirements gradually transformed such elements into what properly can be called Buddhist temple compounds.

Stupas and stupa-shrines. A stupa originally was used to mark the relics of the Buddha or of one of his principal disciples, significant objects (such as his begging bowl), or places related to his life or sanctified by his presence. From these early enclosed stupas evolved a major type of Buddhist structure, the caitya hall, housing an object used as a focus for worship (caitya). These caitya halls are typically apsidal structures with a central nave and side aisles; a stupa is placed prominently (and mysteriously) in the apse. The earliest of these, at Bhaja and Bedsa, date from the second or first centuries BCE. Located on trade routes and patronized by merchants and others from nearby urban centers, these large establishments also provided monastic cells for wandering monks and abbots and sheltered pilgrims and travelers. At Bhaja, the abbot's cave has a veranda guarded by large images of the sun and rain gods, Surya and Indra; the individual monastic cells at Kanheri, scattered across a hillside outside of Bombay, have stone beds and pillows, verandas and grilled windows, each carefully located to take advantage of views through the neighboring hills to the harbor beyond.

Monasteries and monastic shrines. For many centuries after the death of the Buddha, monastic retreats were principally provided for the assembly of monks during the rainy season, but such places took on other functions over time, becoming retreats for lay travelers and eventually centers for learning. Foundations at Taxila in the northwest and at the important Buddhist university of Nalanda in Bihar show monastic complexes in the shape of rectilinear compounds with cells enclosing a central shared court.

Temples. Bodh Gaya, the site in Bihar at which the historical Buddha is said to have achieved enlightenment, clearly reflects successive changes in Buddhist belief and practice. Under the present Bodhi Tree rests a stone altar set up in the time of Asoka Maurya to mark the place of the Buddha's enlightenment. The tree and altar are surrounded by a modern railing, but railing pieces from the Sunga period (second to first centuries BCE) remain nearby. Such open enclosures set around objects of worship (trees, pillars, images of nature spirits, stupas) represent pre-Buddhist practices that were absorbed into the iconography of popular Buddhism. Set next to the tree shrine is a large brick temple, pyramidal in shape, its surface ornamented to suggest a multiterraced palatial structure. By the sixth century CE, a large image of the Buddha had been enshrined within it for worship. (The image on a second-century CE terracotta plaque from Kumrahar suggests that a shrine in the same form was already there by that period.)

Terraced "temples" of a different sort were built across North India. The most extensive representation of such terraced temple structures is found among the monuments scattered across the vast plains of Burma, particularly at Pagan. The Ananda Temple there has a cruciform plan, interior ambulatories, and a central templelike superstructure dating originally from the early eleventh century.

Temple compounds in China. Beginning in the third and especially the fourth centuries, the spread and acceptance of Buddhism in North and South China was so rapid that it was almost immediately necessary for craftsmen and builders to come to terms with the new religion's architecture. Two building types are most fundamental: the Buddha hall and the towerlike structure known in English as a pagoda.

For the hall dedicated to the Buddha himself, the Chinese would build a likeness of the imperial hall of state, in which the Buddha could be enshrined in the posture of an enthroned Chinese emperor. Texts and more recent archaeological confirmation tell us that these were four-sided buildings of timber frame, supported by columns on each side and sometimes on the interior, often with the roof form that was reserved for the most important Chinese halls, namely the simple hipped roof, consisting of a main roof ridge and two ridges projecting at angles from each of its sides.

The towerlike pagoda had its origins in the Indian stupa but evolved in northwest India and Central Asia as a higher and narrower structure; by the time it reached East Asia, it found its only semilikeness in the Chinese gate, or watchtower, which dates back to the Han dynasty (206 BCE–220 CE). By the sixth century, square-, octagonal-, and dodecagonal-plan pagodas with up to thirteen eaved tiers could be found in China.

Buddhist temple compounds built in China after the rule of the Mongols (known as the Yüan dynasty, 1279-1368) are similar in plan and building function to those from the Sung, Liao, or Chin. New in Buddhist temple construction at the time of the Mongols are buildings for Lamaist Buddhist worship, introduced to China from the region of Nepal and Tibet.

From the time of the Mongols on, the most impressive Buddhist structures and those exhibiting the most innovative features were built at Lamaist monasteries. Under the Ming dynasty (1368-1644) one innovation is the so-called five-pagoda cluster, composed of a central tower and four lower ones at its corners, all on a single platform, and representing a Lamaist *mandala*. An example of this construction is found at the Five-Pagoda Monastery at Ta-cheng-chüeh Monastery, Peking, built in 1573.

Temple compounds in Korea and Japan. Like much of Korean architecture, Buddhist monuments were transmitted directly from China, so that in the initial stages, before the year 668, Korean Buddhist buildings reflect the styles of the continent. Yet, owing to native taste and a harsher climate, Korean Buddhist architecture, while accommodating certain norms dictated by the faith, is never exactly identical to its Chinese sources.

Some of the earliest surviving Korean Buddhist monuments are seventh-century stone pagodas from the monasteries Miruksa and Chong-nim-sa in the Paekche kingdom. During this period of the Unified Silla (668-935), approximately contemporary with T`ang China, the most important Korean Buddhist architectural site is the capital, Kyongju. Within the walls of the T`ang-style capital, most of which was destroyed at the end of the sixteenth century, are the monasteries of Sokkulam and Pulgak-sa. Sokkulam, the best-preserved early Buddhist monument in Korea, more closely resembles a cave temple in the tradition of the rock-cut temples to Korea's west than any other type of temple compound construction. Yet it also includes a stone antechamber connected to a domed structure in the manner of earlier Korean tombs.

The most important surviving Buddhist temple compound of early Japan is Horyuji, located just south of modern-day Nara. In its initial building phase in the early sixth century it was huge. The nucleus of the late seventh-century monastery consists of pagoda and *kondo* (main hall) enclosed by a covered corridor, with the middle gate and lecture hall (a later building) adjoining the corridor to the south and north, respectively.

During the Tempyo period (711-781), about fifty years after the rebuilding of the Horyuji, an octagonal Buddha hall known as Yumedono (Hall of Dreams) was built on the former site of the residence of Prince Shotoku (574-622), founder of the original monastery. This memorial hall to the prince is the focus of what is known as the Horyuji East Precinct, in contrast to the so-called West Precinct that predates it.

After the transfer of the Japanese capital north to Heian (modern-day Kyoto) at the end of the eighth century, a move due in part to the increased power of the Buddhist clergy within Nara, new forms of Buddhism necessitated new architectural spaces. The Esoteric sects, also introduced to Japan from China, were characterized architecturally by smaller, more modest temples, often built in isolated mountain settings. Among the buildings that survive at Daigoji and Jingoji in the Kyoto suburbs, and Muroji farther south, are those with cypress bark roofs and plank floors.

The final important phase of Buddhist architecture in Japan occurs in the Muromachi, or Ashikaga, period (1392-1572). Several building complexes stand out among the many surviving period structures. Two of these, the Gold and Silver Pavilions of the large villas of the ruling Ashikaga family, in the eastern and western suburbs of Kyoto respectively, were residential in style but functioned in part as Zen chapels. The abbot's quarters *(hojo)* of a Zen monastery in fact came to be a standard feature of residential, or *shoin,* architecture from this time onward. Indeed, since the Heian period the aesthetic taste of Japanese ruling families had been largely determined by current Buddhist practices and ideals.

[*See also* Iconography.]

BIBLIOGRAPHY

South and Southeast Asia

Bareau, André. "La construction et le culte des stupa d'après le *Vinayapitaka*." *Bulletin de l'École Française d'Extrême-Orient* 50 (1962): 229-274. A presentation of textual evidence for interpreting the uses put to the stupa within Indian Buddhism.

Dehejia, Vidya. *Early Buddhist Rock Temples*. Ithaca, N. Y., 1972. Concise, scholarly survey of the early Buddhist rock-cut tradition in India.

Dumarçay, Jacques. *Borobudur*. Oxford, 1978. A significant new analysis by the architect responsible for the recent deconstruction and conservation of the Borobudur monument.

Gómez, Luis O., and Hiram W. Woodward, Jr., eds. *Barabudur: History and Significance of a Buddhist Monument*. Berkeley, 1981. Proceedings of a symposium convened to reinvestigate the state of knowledge concerning Buddhism's most spectacular monument.

Mitra, Debala. *Buddhist Monuments*. Calcutta, 1971. A general but detailed and well-informed survey of both Buddhist belief and monuments in India by a past director general of the Archaeological Survey of India.

Sarkar, H. *Studies in Early Buddhist Architecture of India*. Delhi, 1966. An important study bringing together research and the results of recent excavations.

East Asia

Liang Ssu-ch`eng. *A Pictorial History of Chinese Architecture*. Edited by Wilma Fairbank. Cambridge, Mass., 1984. Original drawings and photographs from the 1930s of the most important Chinese buildings, including many Buddhist monuments, and accompanying text by the author.

Liu Tun-chen. *Chung-kuo ku-tai chien-chu shih*. Peking, 1980. Excellent general survey of Chinese architecture with sections dealing with the Buddhist temple architecture of each dynasty.

Sickman, Laurence, and Alexander Soper. *The Art and Architecture of China* (1956). 3d. ed. Harmondsworth, 1968. General account of the development of Chinese architecture, including Buddhist temple compounds.

Soper, Alexander. *The Evolution of Buddhist Architecture in Japan*. Princeton, 1942. Landmark study surveying Japanese Buddhist architecture from earliest times through the Kamakura period, including the use of many primary texts and secondary Chinese and Japanese sources.

Suzuki Kakichi. *Early Buddhist Architecture in Japan*. Tokyo and New York, 1980. Well-illustrated general survey of the major monuments of Buddhist architecture in Japan.

MICHAEL W. MEISTER and
NANCY SHATZMAN STEINHARDT

Taoist Temple Compounds

It is difficult to say what was the first Taoist structure in China or where or when it was built. It seems certain that large monasteries were not erected during the age of the philosophers Lao-tzu and Chuang-tzu in the Warring States period (403-221 BCE) nor, it appears, under the Han dynasty (206 BCE-220 CE), by which time small temples were built to popular gods. By the period of Chinese history known as the Six Dynasties (220-589), however, Taoism had evolved from a philosophical system with a focus on individuality or the attainment of immortality into an organized religion; with this new religion came a clergy, an increasing number of deities, and buildings to house and serve them.

Taoist temple compounds are made up of halls dedicated to a variety of purposes. The majority are built for Taoist deities and usually house their images. Taoist architecture also includes buildings located at potent sites, notably the five sacred peaks or other natural phenomena, which are themselves objects of worship.

Standard histories of Chinese architecture mention only a few Taoist temple compounds, none of which includes buildings earlier than the Sung dynasty (960-1279). Of the forty or so sites in China where Taoist temple compounds survive today, three are most noteworthy. First is T`ai Shan, the Eastern Peak, most popular of the five sacred peaks of Taoism. Located in Shantung province, it is considered the abode of life-giving forces as well as the site to which dead souls return. Inside the main shrine, the god of T`ai Shan is enthroned in the yellow robes of a Chinese emperor, and the emperor's journey from his capital to T`ai Shan is painted on the interior walls. Directly behind this main hall is the bedchamber of the wife of T`ai Shan, situated according to prescribed imperial palace layout.

The two other great repositories of Taoist temple architecture are located northeast of T`ai Shan, in Shansi province. More than thirty halls stand at the Chin shrines, but the focus of worship is the eleventh-century Holy Mother Hall, built to Prince T`ang's mother, who in the Sung dynasty was believed capable of giving rain and foretelling the future.

At the southern tip of Shansi is the Yung-le Kung (Monastery of Eternal Joy), where three halls and a gate from the thirteenth-century temple compound still stand.

[*See also* Iconography.]

BIBLIOGRAPHY

Ch`ai Tsê-chün. *Chin tz`u*. Peking, 1958. Descriptive study of the monuments near T`ai-yüan.

Chavannes, Édouard. *Le T`ai chan: Essai de monographie d'un culte chinois*. Paris, 1910. Outstanding investigation of the mountain and related cult.

Goodrich, Anne Swann. *The Peking Temple of the Eastern Peak*. Nagoya, Japan, 1964. In-depth account of an active Taoist temple complex visited by the author during her years in Peking, 1930-1932. Includes details about the numerous Taoist divinities associated with the site.

Yoshioka, Yoshitoyo. "Taoist Monastic Life." In *Facets of Taoism*, edited by Holmes Welch and Anna Seidel, pp. 229-252. New Haven,

1979. Description of the author's experiences at Po-yün Monastery in Peking from 1940 to 1946.

NANCY SHATZMAN STEINHARDT

Confucian Temple Compounds

The architecture of Confucianism in China is built in honor of men. It is dedicated to Confucius (551-479 BCE), sage and secretary of justice of the ancient state of Lu, or his disciples and their teachings. Confucian monuments are distinct from other Chinese religious structures in their avoidance of images.

The temple or temple compound is the predominant form of Confucian architecture. The 3,500-year-old town of Ch`ü-fu, in Shantung province, birthplace of Confucius, has been the site of the most important Confucian temple in China since the time of the sage himself. However, a temple dedicated to Confucius was built in nearly every major city of traditional China. Several important Confucian temples survive in continental China and in Taiwan; the most active are located in Taiwan, in its capital city Taipei.

The number and arrangement of individual structures of a Confucian temple compound vary, but the architectural style of the buildings and the general plan always follow the standards set for an emperor's palace. The temple compound is isolated in its own precinct, enclosed at least partially by covered arcades. The important halls of the temple stand in a line, all facing south. Generally three or four structures are situated on this prominent north-south axis: a gate serving as the main, central entryway to the temple grounds at the far south; a gate or hall adjoining the temple enclosure at the north; and at least one major, multi-eaved structure dominating the center. Other buildings radiate around the central structure or structures, sometimes built with bilateral symmetry in mind but always giving the impression of perfectly planned order and balance. This basic arrangement dates back at least one thousand years.

The function of the main temple building is in accordance with the human-oriented world of Confucianism: it houses tablets inscribed with the names of the sage, his disciples (the four best known are Meng-tzu [Mencius], Yen Hui, Tseng-tzu, and Tz`u-tzu), or the so-called twelve wise men (eleven of Confucius's disciples and the twelfth-century Confucian scholar Chu Hsi). The simplicity of a Chinese building interior contains only inscribed tablets. Only rarely can one find a statue of Confucius, and in such a case the making of the image represents the influence of popular religion.

[*See also* Iconography.]

BIBLIOGRAPHY

Han Pao-te. *Chang-hua K`ung miao ti yen chiu yü hsiu fu chi hua. T`ai-chung,* Taiwan, 1976. Detailed account of the restoration of the Confucian temple at Chang-hua, including a general discussion of Confucian temples and excellent drawings of the Chang-hua buildings.

K`ung Hsiang-min and Wei Chiang. *Ch`ü-fu.* Shandong, 1982. Guidebook to Ch`ü-fu and its Confucian monuments, largely pictorial, prepared by a descendant of Confucius.

K`ang Yüan-ts`o. *K`ung-shih tsu-t`ing kuang-chi* (1311). Reprint, Taipei, 1970. The most important text about the Confucian shrine at Ch`ü-fu, including drawings of the site and building plans.

Shryock, John K. *The Origin and Development of the State Cult of Confucius.* New York, 1932. A history of Confucianism in China that makes reference to Confucian architecture.

Steinhardt, Nancy Shatzman. "Kong Family Mansion." In *Chinese Traditional Architecture,* edited by Nancy Shatzman Steinhardt, pp. 152-157. New York, 1984. The only English-language discussion of the architecture of the estate of Confucius's ancestors in Ch`ü-fu.

NANCY SHATZMAN STEINHARDT

Ancient Near Eastern and Mediterranean Temples

Modern writers use the term *temple* in different ways. Applied to Egyptian religion, it refers to a complete architectural complex, integrated in a coherent axial arrangement, including an inner shrine or sanctuary. Applied to classical architecture, *temple* refers to the equivalent of this inner shrine, while the whole complex is termed *sanctuary.*

Egypt. Essentially, Egyptian religion is based on the performance of ritual, and the temples are the location for that cult. The forms and practices of the religion first developed in the Old Kingdom of the third millennium BCE and had become definitive by the Middle Kingdom in the second millennium. Thereafter they are marked by a characteristic conservatism.

Architecturally, the basic characteristic of an Egyptian temple is its axial alignment from the entrance pylon—a gateway flanked by towers—in the outer wall to the innermost shrine room. Rooms and unroofed spaces are always rectangular. Their exact sequence corresponds to requirements of the daily ritual conducted in private by the priests, and the regular but less frequent ritual of the public festivals. Each temple was surrounded by a high outer wall, which served to exclude those not permitted to participate in the ritual. The pylon leads to the outer courts in which the populace gathered to watch sacred processions at the great festivals. Beyond the courts are colonnaded (hypostyle) halls, vestibules, and the inner shrines housing the statue of the god and the sacred boats which were carried in processions. In this inner area there were also storerooms for the treasures of the god and for the paraphernalia of ritual, and rooms serving administrative purposes. This inner part is set at a higher level, usually as the result of a gradual rise at each successive door passage.

The courts are unroofed, though often surrounded by a colonnade; the inner parts are completely roofed and increasingly in shadow. The roof level decreases as the floor level rises, thus enhancing a sense of mystery.

The precise arrangement of this plan varies from temple to temple, with some larger and more complex than others. The degree of complexity possible can be illustrated by the Temple of Amun at Karnak, one of the most important, which has been added to and altered over millennia.

> The Parthenon . . . is probably the most famous, certainly the most lavishly decorated, but not the largest of Greek temples.

Classical Greece. The origin of the Classical temple is uncertain. The essential plan consists of a single rectangular room (*cella* or *naos*) with a porch at one end. All else is added decoration, but except in the poorest structures, the porch at least would be embellished with columns, while the more splendid have *cella* and porch surrounded by a colonnade. The columns are of distinctive regional types, Doric on the mainland and in the west, Ionic on the islands and in the east, though the geographical divisions are not rigid.

Similar temples are found in the Levant (Tell Taayanat, Hazor) with a continuous ancestry going back to the Bronze Age. Since Greek temples are first found in the eighth century BCE, when Greek traders were renewing direct contacts with this area, they may be a copy or adaptation of these Levantine prototypes. Certainly the details of at least the Ionic order are Eastern in inspiration. The purpose of the temples, the practice of religion and ritual, remains purely Greek.

Greek temples were not congregational buildings. The congregation (which at the chief festivals of major cults was very large, to be counted in tens of thousands) gathered round the altar. Like the crowds, the cult statue watched the sacrifices. Temples were normally oriented to face the point at which the sun rose on the day of the festival. Though some cult statues were large and valuable, the rooms in which they stood did not have to be particularly spacious. Even in the largest temples a surprising proportion of the total area was taken up by external embellishment. Otherwise, temples served as storerooms for objects, particularly those of value, offered to the gods. From inscriptions we learn that the quantity of these was often considerable.

The Parthenon on the Athenian Acropolis, dedicated to Athena, is probably the most famous, certainly the most lavishly decorated, but not the largest of Greek temples. A forerunner, started shortly after 490 BCE as an offering for the victory over the Persians at Marathon. The temple has seventeen Doric columns on each long side and eight at both short ends, and it measures overall some thirty-one by seventy meters. It has two rooms, the eastern *cella* and the western "rear room," which held the valuable offerings. Innumerable temples smaller than the Parthenon also exist, such as those in the sanctuary of Asklepios at Epidaurus.

Rome. Early Roman temples were built in the Etruscan manner, which had been influenced by early Greek temples of the seventh century BCE; the Etruscans (neighbors and, for a time, overlords of Rome) did not follow later Greek developments. They placed their temples on high bases, approachable by a flight of steps at the front only. Timber and mud brick, with tiles and embellishment in terracotta, were the normal building materials. Roman temples inherited the strictly frontal emphasis and high bases. Occasionally the Romans copied the full surrounding colonnades of Greek temples.

In essentials, a Roman temple functioned like the Greek as a house for a god and for offerings to the god. Burnt sacrifices were made at an altar, which was usually placed immediately in front of the temple at the bottom of the steps so that worshipers faced the altar (and the temple) rather than surrounding it. Where possible, the temple stood in a colonnaded precinct, which also emphasized the axial symmetry. Roman temples, however, showed greater concern than the Greek for the use of the *cella* as a room. The Roman *cella* often occupied a greater proportion of the total area, was wider, and was invariably freed from encumbering internal supports for the roof, a consequence of better carpentry techniques and the availability of better timber.

These developments culminated in the best-preserved of all Roman temples, the Pantheon in Rome, built by the emperor Hadrian (117-138) to replace an earlier building of Augustus's time. Dedicated to all the gods, it is circular rather than rectangular (a permissible plan for Roman but not Greek temples). It had a conventional precinct and porch, but the *cella,* 150 Roman feet in diameter, is roofed with a concrete dome. Light is admitted, for deliberate effect, through an opening in the center of the dome.

The most splendid of temples in the eastern Roman provinces is that dedicated to Jupiter at Heliopolis, the Roman military colony at Baalbek in Lebanon. A huge temple stands on a high podium in the Roman manner, but it was constructed in the local tradition. On the podium is a Greek-type stepped base. The surrounding Corinthian colonnade is arranged in the East Greek (Ionic) manner with a wider central spacing at each end. In the *cella* (now ruined) was a shrine structure with a cult crypt underneath (better preserved in the neighboring so-called Temple of Bacchus) serving local religious ritual. Outside was a tall tower altar of Eastern type. Finally, the temple was given a precinct (never completed) and forecourt with a gateway building flanked by towers which derives from local, not Roman, concepts.

[*See also* Iconography.]

BIBLIOGRAPHY

Boëthius, Axel. *Etruscan and Early Roman Architecture.* Edited by R. Ling. Harmondsworth, 1982.

Cerny, Jaroslav. *Ancient Egyptian Religion.* London, 1952.

David, Ann Rosalie. *A Guide to Religious Ritual at Abydos.* Warminster, 1981.

Dinsmoor, William Bell. *The Architecture of Ancient Greece.* London, 1950.

Lawrence, Arnold W. *Greek Architecture.* Harmondsworth, 1984.

Nelson, Harold H. "The Significance of the Temple in the Ancient Near East: The Egyptian Temple." *Biblical Archaeologist* 7 (1944): 44-53.

Tomlinson, R. A. *Greek Sanctuaries.* London, 1976.

Ward-Perkins, J. B. *Roman Imperial Architecture.* Harmondsworth, 1981.

R. A. TOMLINSON

Mesoamerican Temples

The most common form of sanctuary in Mesoamerica is the temple-pyramid-plaza, that is, the peculiar combination of an elevated foundation, almost always artificially built, with a temple on the upper platform. Usually adjoining this unit at the base of the access staircase is a series of open spaces (plaza, esplanade, altar platform).

The embryonic form of this temple combination can be found in the principal mounds built from compressed soil or from *adobe* (sun-dried brick) by the Olmec in areas around the Gulf of Mexico, such as San Lorenzo (in the present-day Mexican state of Veracruz) and La Venta (in Tabasco) between 1200 and 900 BCE. Associated with a thrust toward monumentality that reflected the cultural vigor in Mesoamerica at the end of the Preclassic period (600 BCE-200 CE), the temple-pyramid-plaza soon spread to other regions. In the northern part of Petén (Guatemala), in the heart of the Maya area, the massive pyramids of El Mirador, with their apexes emerging from the dense forest, foreshadow the great Maya temples of Tikal in the same region.

Together with this tendency toward monumental building there was a great preoccupation with architectural permanence. This concern was reflected in the emergence of large retaining walls for the compressed fill of earth and rubble. These walls constituted the solid nucleus of the pyramid, and their taluses tended to follow the natural sloping angle of the fill. The access staircase, generally the only one placed on the axis of the temple, was initially incorporated into the gen-

eral mass of the pyramid itself. With the passing of time it tended to project outward, frequently bordered by two *alfardas,* or flat ramps, which in turn often projected slightly beyond the steps or, according to local or regional style, assumed more complex shapes. In the same manner, the sides of the pyramid could be decorated with large masks or other sculptures or ornamented rhythmically with moldings, notably variations on the talus panel (*tablero-talud* or *talud-tablero,* a panel, or *tablero,* usually framed with moldings, that projected from the slope).

Finally, the temple itself, which usually occupies the upper platform of the pyramid, evolved from a simple hut to a more elaborate building made of masonry. Depending on the region, it was covered with a flat roof supported by wooden timbers and surrounded by low parapets or, as can be observed among the Maya, with vaulting made up of different types of projecting (corbeled) arches. Various types of panels, moldings, and sculptures enrich the temple silhouettes, which could be crowned with more or less massive roof combs, as in the case of Classical Maya architecture, or with sculptured finials distributed at regular intervals on the outside perimeter of the parapet in the style of a battlement. Such finials can be observed in the architectural tradition of Mexico's central plateau from the period of Teotihuacán until the Spanish conquest.

[*See also* Iconography.]

BIBLIOGRAPHY

Three general surveys with good photographs and an appreciation of architectural aesthetics may be recommended: Doris Heyden's and my *Pre-Columbian Architecture of Mesomamerica* (New York, 1975), Henri Stierlin's *Maya* (Fribourg, 1964), and Stierlin's *Mexique ancien* (Fribourg, 1967).

PAUL GENDROP
Translated from Spanish by Gabriela Mahn

TEMPTATION

Approaches to the complex phenomenon of temptation are as diversified as are cultures, worldviews, the self-understanding of men and women, the concept of sin, and so on. But behind all the astonishing differences there might well be discovered agreement on one point: that the center of human temptation is egocentricity, and genuine love is its victor. In the Judeo-Christian tradition, reflection on temptation arises in the quest for the sources of evil, which leads to a questioning of both God's nature and the nature of man. [*See* Evil.] However, for the Hebrews, these questions were further complicated because of their own negative reactions to earlier solutions put forth by their neighbors. A continuing theme in Israel's history is the belief that their neighbors were tempting them to abandon faith in Yahveh and the law of Moses. Consequently, they must destroy those who were or could become such a temptation. This sad pattern reappears in Christianity as a motive for the crusades, inquisitions, and the burning of so-called witches. Christians were thus diverted from the actual, horrifying temptations that drew them away from humanness, love of neighbor, and even from the true image of God as a merciful Father of all.

Definition of Temptation. For Immanuel Kant, temptation is the paradoxical expression of the human person, destined by nature for the good yet inclined to do evil. He defines temptation as a challenge to live one's freedom for good in the purest way.

Most frequently, however, the word *temptation* is used to describe man being tempted in various ways. Two forms have to be distinguished carefully. One concerns the various troubles and trials seen as an opportunity, or *kairos,* for the believer to strengthen his faith, his endurance, and, finally, his capacity to share in Christ's redemptive suffering. The other kind refers to temptation in the sense of endangering salvation, that is, when the person is assaulted from within and/or from without by godless powers aimed at his downfall.

Temptation and the Tempter. While the scripture warns us against the tempter in his various disguises, the main emphasis is on our own "heart," our personal response to temptations. The Bible calls on Christians to take responsibility by consistently rebuking the sinner who wants to exculpate himself by inculpating others.

Temptation arises from within. James is most explicit: "Temptation arises when a man is enticed and lured away by his own lust" (1:14). Here the author of *James* follows the main line of the synoptic Gospels, as when Jesus calls for change of heart, for purification of one's inmost thoughts and desires: "It is from within men's hearts that evil intentions emerge" (*Mk.* 7:20). *James* speaks of *epithumia* ("desire"), which in the Jewish thought of the time referred to the ambivalent impulses and inclinations (or *yetser*) assigned to Adam and Eve in rabbinic literature to explain their capacity for being tempted. Augustine's term *concupiscence* does not correspond exactly to *yetser.* While the Hebrew scriptures and rabbinic literature try to understand man's vulnerability to temptation as *epithumia,* Augustine believes temptation to be based on our heritage of sin from Adam. For Paul, temptation manifests in our lower nature, the body, and is supported by the collective selfishness and arrogance present in all humanity.

The serpent and the woman in Genesis 3. The narrative of the Fall is an anthropological myth of great depth and complexity. Its symbols express ancient Israelite reflections on the origin of evil. It depicts in a lively way the diversionary rhetoric of the sinner, who always needs a scapegoat for his own vindication. Adam attempts to use Eve as his scapegoat, while Eve blames the serpent.

Why is the serpent introduced to allow man to exonerate himself? Paul Ricoeur thinks that this is also the way James's epistle explains the self-deceptive concupiscence. The serpent is a part of ourselves as long as we have not the strength of truth to unmask the shrewdness of our exonerating maneuvers. It might also symbolize "the chaotic disorder in myself, among us and around us" (*La symbolique du mal,* vol. 2, p. 242). That would bring into the whole vision of the first twelve chapters of *Genesis* a sharper awareness of the various dimensions of solidarity in either good or evil, including the cosmic dimension and the need for man to decide one way or the other. In his 1937-1938 work *Creation and Fall: A Theological Interpretation of Genesis 1-3 and Temptation,* Dietrich Bonhoeffer was insisting that this narrative has no need of diaboli ex machina. The serpent symbolizes the ambiguity of man, his human relationships, and his environment.

Satan and his helpers. Satan interests us here only in relation to temptation. The shrewd Satan who tempts Jesus in the desert embodies the insidious temptation put to Christianity in the first and following centuries. Satan at his most shameless mirrors the vain self-glorification of the earthly powers of the time, particularly in the divinization of the Roman emperors. The figure of Satan should emphasize the superhuman dimension. It is a sharp warning against belittling any situation of temptation. As we saw in *Genesis 3,* for the believer there is no way of denying guilt by pointing to a tempter or to the devil. Aware of the powers of darkness in their mysterious solidarity of perdition, the followers of Christ put their trust in God and make the wholehearted decision for his reign, a reign of justice, peace, and love. They put on "all the armor which God provides to stand firm against the devices of the devil" (*Eph.* 6:10). They will not only avoid being tempters in any way, helpers of the powers of darkness, but will commit themselves to active and generous membership in a solidarity of salvation.

The Christian discourse on the tempter points to the great temptations arising from bad example and evil "friends" who initiate the inexperienced into the skills of crime and corruption. The diabolic temptation seeks directly the moral corruption of others. It is masterfully described in the famous novel *Les liaisons dangereuses* (1782) by Choderlos de Laclos. Laclos exposes both the superficial optimism of the Enlightenment and the libertinism of the time preceding the French Revolution. But even to those most skilled and aggressive tempters there come moments when humanness somehow shines through, insinuating "that malice does not constitute a hopeless and irrevocable fact in human existence" (Knufmann, 1965, p. 202).

This idea was theologized by Origen, who wanted to leave open the hope that after a long duration of "eternity" even the devil and his helpers might be converted and saved by the divine power of *apokatastasis.* Origen's thought, problematic as it may be, opposed tenaciously the dualism of Manichaeism. Sinners—even the tempter and his helpers—because they are God's creatures, keep, somehow, a remnant of goodness.

Psychological Perspectives. Psychoanalysis and psychotherapy have made major contributions to a better understanding of the mechanisms of various temptations. Karl Menninger notes that temptations and sins arise from the "huge world of the unmanifest" (1973, p. 221). The "unmanifest" includes not only whatever the filter of repression is hiding but also unconfessed guilt feelings which often become confused with real guilt.

Another ego-defense is the tendency to project one's own evil inclinations on another, on some villain. In her work with children, psychotherapist Christine Lutz found that the healing and growth of moral sense progressed when the children realized that what they saw in others was, to a great extent, a projection of their own shortcomings (*Kinder und das Böse: Konfrontation und Geborgenheit,* Stuttgart, 1980).

Sociological Perspectives. The broad theological expression "sin of the world" is given sharper contours in modern studies on "institutionalized temptation." In his book *Our Criminal Society* (Englewood Cliffs, N. J., 1969), Edwin M. Shur has an apt formulation: "In a sense, existing patterns of crime represent a price we pay for structuring society as we have structured it" (p. 9).

The people of wealthy countries have adopted lifestyles inseparably connected with the predatory exploitation of the earth's resources and pollution of the environment. Here we see temptations of planetary dimensions that increase the tensions between countries of free enterprise and those of massive state capitalism. How many horrifying temptations are involved in the arms race, the arms trade, and, above all, the nuclear threat! One source of the massive "institutionalized temptations" is the lack of prophetic voices; another is the unwillingness to pay earnest attention to those voices that might be heard.

Theological Perspectives. In a brief synthesis of theological perspectives that recur continuously, the point of departure for the Christian is Jesus having been tempted as we are: "Since he himself has passed through the test of suffering, he is able to help those who are meeting their test now" (*Heb.* 2:18). Jesus overcame temptation not just by enduring the suffering it brought but by making this very suffering the supreme sign of God's love and saving solidarity.

Another biblical direction is to combat evil by doing good, to overcome violent injustice by doing the truth of love in nonviolent commitment (cf. *Rom.* 12:21; *1 Thes.* 5:15; *1 Pt.* 3:9; and above all, *Mt. 5*). For believers, all temptations—but particularly those arising from the vicious circle of violence—are a challenge to sanctity, to redemptive love.

BIBLIOGRAPHY

There are innumerable books and articles concerning the temptation of Jesus and, in that light, temptation in general. The following books merit special attention: Ernest Best's *The Temptation and the Passion: The Markan Soteriology* (Cambridge, 1965) and Jacques Dupont's *Les tentations de Jésus au désert* (Paris, 1968). Both books contain excellent bibliographies. A comprehensive presentation of the church fathers' explanation of the biblical texts and their application to the understanding of Christian life is found in Santino Raponi's *Tentazione ed Esistenza Cristiana* (Rome, 1974). On the biblical use of the term peirasmos, see Heinrich Seesemann's *Theological Dictionary of the New Testament,* edited by Gerhard Friedrich (Grand Rapids, 1968), vol. 6, pp. 23-36. See Horst Beint-ker's study *Die Überwindung der Anfechtung bei Luther* (Berlin, 1954) for an overview of Martin Luther's approach to temptation from the perspective of the doctrine of justification by faith. Helmut Thielicke's *Theologie der Anfechtung* (Tübingen, 1949) is representative of a good part of Protestant theology's discussion of the issue. Also important is Dietrich Bonhoeffer's *Creation and Fall: A Theological Interpretation of Genesis 1-3 and Temptation* (1937-1938; New York, 1965). While at times emphasizing the power of Satan, Bonhoeffer never allows for man's exculpation. His ideas seem to reflect the time of great affliction for the church in Germany.

Of the numerous studies about the impact of a poisoned environment and a defective culture and society on temptation, Reinhold Niebuhr's *Moral Man and Immoral Society* (New York, 1932) and Edwin M. Shur's *Our Criminal Society* (Engelwood Cliffs, N. J., 1969) are noteworthy. In his much-read book, *Whatever Became of Sin?* (New York, 1973), Karl Menninger points to the mechanisms and temptations of denying sin and thus, also, human freedom and responsibility. C. S. Lewis attempts to unmask real temptation in his widely known book *The Screwtape Letters* (New York, 1946). Helmut Knufmann reflects on novelists' treatment of temptation as a theme in his book *Das Böse in den Liaisons Dangereuses de Choderlos de Laclos* (Munich, 1965).

BERNHARD HÄRING

TEN COMMANDMENTS

The Ten Commandments (or the Decalogue) appear twice in the Hebrew scriptures, at *Exodus* 20:1-17 and at *Deuteronomy* 5:6-21. There are differences between the two listings, but the order and the general contents are substantially identical. The commandments may be grouped as follows:

- Commandments 1-3: God's self-identification, followed by commandments against the worship of other gods, idolatry, and misuse of the divine name (Ex. 20:1-7, Dt. 5:6-11).
- Commandments 4-5: Positive commands to observe the Sabbath and to honor parents (Ex. 20:8-12, Dt. 5:12-16).
- Commandments 6-7: Prohibitions of violent acts against neighbors, namely killing and adultery (Ex. 20:13-14, Dt. 5:17-18).

- Commandments 8-10: Prohibitions of crimes against community, life, namely, stealing, testifying falsely, and hankering after the life and goods of neighbors (Ex. 20:15-17, Dt. 5:19-21).

In the Jewish and Christian communities the order has occasionally varied, and the numbering has varied considerably, especially in the different Christian communions. Tables listing the various enumerations can be found in works by Harrelson (1980) and Nielsen (1968). The prologue with which the list opens, both in *Exodus* and in *Deuteronomy*, belongs to the Ten Commandments: "I am the Lord your God, who brought you out of the land of Egypt, out of the house of bondage." In the oldest listing of the "Ten Words" (*Ex.* 34:28), the prologue may not have appeared, but it became attached to the list early in Israel's history, setting the demands of God into the context of divine grace and mercy.

The origin of the Ten Commandments is traditionally traced to Moses. There is no adequate reason to doubt the accuracy of the tradition, even though the present form of the Ten Commandments is considerably later than Moses' time. None of the individual commandments, which were probably originally brief, pithy prohibitions of actions ruled out in principle, requires a dating later than the time of Moses. The grouping of the ten may belong to the time when the tribes of Israel had settled in Canaan and maintained ties across tribal lines; some scholars would assign the collection to a later time, perhaps to the ninth century BCE. The closest analogies to the Ten Commandments in the Hebrew scriptures appear in the curse ritual of *Deuteronomy* 27:15-16 and in portions of the section of the Torah sometimes called the "Book of the Covenant" (Ex. 20:23-23:33). See, for example, *Exodus* 21:15-17, where short, categorial legal pronouncements appear.

The Ten Commandments are alluded to in a number of places in the Hebrew scriptures, in the Qumran literature, and in the New Testament, although they are rarely quoted exactly and do not appear at all in a complete listing outside of *Exodus* and *Deuteronomy*. The prologue is found in a number of places (*Hos.* 13:4, *Ps.* 81:10/11), and there are lists of some of the prohibitions in several places (*Hos.* 4:2, *Mk.* 10:17-22 and parallels). But the fundamental outlook of the Ten Commandments is characteristic for the Jewish and Christian communities through the centuries. God will not have the divine name and selfhood profaned, for the Creator remains free and sovereign over against the creation. God demands rest from labor as well as labor, and he will not tolerate the mistreatment of elderly parents by adult children. God claims authority over human life and demands respect for life on the part of all. God will not permit the violation of the extended life of human beings in their social and institutional relations.

The Ten Commandments became a fixed part of Christian catechetical practice and worship. Less prominent in Islam, they are implicit in much that Muhammad taught. In the course of Christian history they have frequently contributed to narrowness of vision and legalism. Yet it seems likely that they have contributed much more by way of positive guidance to the community. Negatively put categorical statements of this sort provide moral orientation of the community, the defining characteristics of a people, showing what is simply not allowed. The Ten Commandments require positive statements of what idolatry means, what murder is, how the Sabbath is to be observed, and the like. They constitute not so much a constriction of human freedom as an invitation to the community to claim its proper freedom within the confines of what would be ruinous for it.

[*For further discussion, see* Israelite Religion.]

BIBLIOGRAPHY

Greenberg, Moshe. "Decalogue." In *Encyclopaedia Judaica*, vol. 5. Jerusalem, 1971.
Harrelson, Walter. *The Ten Commandments and Human Rights*. Philadelphia, 1980.
Nielsen, Eduard. *The Ten Commandments in New Perspective*. Naperville, Ill., 1968.
Stamm, J. J., with M. E. Andrew. *The Ten Commandments in Recent Research*. 2d ed. Naperville, Ill., 1967.

WALTER HARRELSON

THEOLOGY

Comparative Theology

Historically, the term *comparative theology* has been used in a variety of ways. First, it sometimes refers to a subsection of the discipline called "comparative religion" wherein the historian of religions analyzes the "theologies" of different religions. Second, within the discipline variously named "the science of religion," *Religionswissenschaft*, or "history of religions," some scholars have used the term *comparative theology* to indicate one aspect of the discipline. F. Max Müller, for example, in his *Introduction to the Science of Religion*, used the term to refer to that part of the "science of religion" that analyzes "historical" forms of religion, in contrast to *theoretic theology*, which refers to analysis of the philosophical conditions of possibility for any religion. As a second example, in 1871 James Freeman Clarke published a work entitled *Ten Great Religions: An Essay in Comparative Theology*, which concentrated on the history of religious doctrines in different traditions.

Problems and Possibilities. On the whole, contemporary scholars in history of religions or religious studies do not use the term *comparative theology* in Müller's or Clarke's senses, and these earlier usages are therefore now of more historical than current disciplinary interest. In the contemporary scholarly world, the term can be understood in two distinct ways. First, it may continue to refer to a comparative enterprise within the secular study of history of religions in which different "theologies" from different traditions are compared by means of some comparative method developed in the discipline. Usually, however, *comparative theology* refers to a more strictly theological enterprise (sometimes named "world theology" or "global theology"), which ordinarily studies not one tradition alone but two or more, compared on theological grounds. Thus one may find Christian (or Buddhist or Hindu, etc.) comparative theologies in which the theologian's own tradition is critically and theologically related to other traditions. More rarely, comparative theology may be the theological study of two or more religious traditions without a particular theological commitment to any one tradition. In either theological model, the fact of religious pluralism is explicitly addressed, so that every theology in every tradition becomes, in effect, a comparative theology.

In principle, the two main approaches are complementary and mutually illuminating: any comparative enterprise within history of religions (or comparative religion)—that is, a secular or scientific study—will interpret theologies as material to be further analyzed from the perspective of, and by means of, the comparativist criteria of that discipline. Any theological attempt at comparative theology—that is, from within the context of belief—will interpret the results of history of religion's comparisons of various theologies by means of its own strictly theological criteria.

The fact that theology itself is now widely considered one discipline within the multidisciplinary field of religious studies impels contemporary theology, in whatever tradition, to become a comparative theology. More exactly, from a theological point of view, history of religions, in its comparativism, has helped academic theology to recognize a crucial insight: that on strictly theological grounds, the fact of religious pluralism should enter all theological assessment and self-analysis in any tradition at the very beginning of its task. Any contemporary theology that accords theological significance (positive or negative) to the fact of religious pluralism in its examination of a particular tradition functions as a comparative theology, whether it so names itself or not. The history and nature of this new, emerging discipline of comparative theology as theology bears close analysis.

A difficulty with the phrase *comparative theology* is that *theology* may be taken to describe a discipline in Western religions but not necessarily in other traditions. Indeed, the term *theology* has its origins in Greek religious thought. Historically, theology has functioned as a major factor within the religious discourse of Christianity that has been influenced by Hellenistic models—and, to a lesser extent, within that of Islam and Judaism. Any enterprise that is named "comparative theology," therefore, must establish that the very enterprise of theology is not necessarily a Greco-Christian one.

To assure this, two factors need clarification. First, to speak of "theology" is a perhaps inadequate but historically useful way to indicate the more strictly intellectual interpretations of any religious tradition, whether that tradition is theistic or not. Second, to use *theo logia* in the literal sense of "talk or reflection on God or the gods" suggests that even nontheistic traditions (such as some Hindu, Confucian, Taoist, or archaic traditions) may be described as having theologies in the broad sense. Most religious traditions do possess a more strictly intellectual self-understanding.

> A difficulty with the phrase comparative theology is that theology may be taken to describe a discipline in Western religions but not necessarily in other traditions.

The term *theology* as used here does not necessarily imply a belief in "God." Indeed, it does not even necessarily imply a belief in the "high gods" of some archaic traditions, nor the multiple gods of the Greeks and Romans, nor the radically monotheistic God of Judaism, Christianity, and Islam. Whatever the appropriate term used to designate ultimate reality may be, that term is subject to explicitly intellectual reflection (e.g., the term sacred, as in the "dialectic of the sacred and the profane" in the great archaic traditions, as analyzed by Mircea Eliade; the term the *holy*, suggested as the more encompassing term, in distinct ways, by Nathan Söderblom and Rudolf Otto; the term the eternal, as suggested by Anders Nygren; the term emptiness, as used in many Buddhist traditions; or the term the One, as in Plotinus; etc.). Insofar as such explicitly intellectual reflection occurs within a religious tradition, one may speak of the presence of a theology in the broad sense (i. e., without necessarily assuming theistic belief). However useful it may be for the purposes of intellectual analysis, the term *theology* should not be allowed to suggest that the tradition in question names ultimate reality as "God"; or that the tradition necessarily considers systematic reflection on ultimate reality important for its religious way. (Indeed, in the case of many Buddhist ways, "systematic" reflection of any kind may be suspect.) "Theology," thus construed, will always be intellectual, but need not be systematic. With these important qualifications, it is nonetheless helpful to speak of "comparative theology" as any explicitly intellectual interpretation of a religious tradition that affords a central place to the fact of religious pluralism in the tradition's self-interpretation.

Among the theological questions addressed by a comparative theology may be the following. (1) How does this religion address the human problem (e.g., suffering, ignorance, sin), and how does that understanding relate to other interpretations of the human situation? (2) What is the way of ultimate transformation (enlightenment, emancipation, salvation, liberation) that this religion offers, and how is it related to other ways? (3) What is the understanding of the nature of ultimate reality (nature, emptiness, the holy, the sacred, the divine, God, the gods) that this religion possesses, and how does this understanding relate to that of other traditions?

Such comparative theological questions may be considered intrinsic to the intellectual self-understanding of any religious tradition or way, and one may thus speak of the implicit or explicit reality of a "comparative theology." More specific proposals will result from particular comparative theological analyses; for example, the suggestions of a radical unity among many religions (Frithjof Schuon, Huston Smith, Henry Corbin), or suggestions that one may have a Christian or Hindu or Buddhist or Jewish or Islamic comparative theology (Wilfred Cantwell Smith, Raimundo Panikkar, Masao Abe, Ananda Coomaraswamy, S. H. Nasr, Franz Rosenzweig, et al.). All these more particular proposals, however, are based on theological conclusions that have followed an individual theologian's comparative assessment of his or her own religious tradition and other traditions. Prior to all such specific theological proposals, however, is the question of the nature of any comparative theology from within any religious tradition.

In general terms, therefore, comparative theology always accords explicit theological attention to religious pluralism, despite radical differences in theological conclusions. In methodological terms, contemporary comparative theology provides an intellectual self-understanding of a particular religious tradition from within the horizon of many religious traditions. It is a hermeneutical and theological discipline that establishes mutually critical correlations between two distinct but related interpretations: on the one hand, the theological interpretation of the principal religious questions given a context of religious pluralism in an emerging global culture; on the other, an interpretation of the responses of a particular religious tradition to that pluralism. As this general methodological model clarifies, the comparative theologian cannot determine before the analysis itself what ultimate conclusions will occur, for example, that all religious traditions are either finally one or irreversibly diverse, or that a particular tradition must radically change or transform its traditional self-understanding as the result of pluralism. It is clear that to start with an explicit (and usually, but not necessarily, positive) assessment of religious pluralism challenges the posi-

tion of traditional theology, which argued, implicitly or explicitly, that the fact of religious pluralism (and therefore of a comparative hermeneutical element as intrinsic to the theological task) was of no intrinsic importance for theological interpretation. A contemporary Christian comparative theology, for example, will inevitably be different from a Hindu or Jewish or Islamic or Buddhist comparative theology. But, just as important, each of these emerging comparative theologies will be different from all those traditional theologies which disallowed a comparative hermeneutics within the theological task, either explicitly (through claims to exclusivism) or implicitly (by denying its usefulness). There is as yet no firm consensus on the results of "comparative theology," but it is possible that those engaged in this increasingly important task may come to agree on a model for the general method all comparative theologians employ. The further need, therefore, is to reflect on this method. First, however, it is necessary to review the historical precedents for this emerging discipline.

History: Premodern Developments. For reasons of clarification and space, this historical survey will be largely confined to Western traditions where strictly theological issues have been especially acute.

Monotheistic religions until early modernity. In the Jewish, Christian, and Islamic traditions, the insistence upon the exclusivity of divine revelation led, on the whole, to a relative lack of interest in analyzing other religions, save for polemical or apologetic purposes. This lack of interest was based (especially in the prophetic trajectories of those religions) on an explicitly and systematically negative assessment of other religions or ways from the viewpoint of scriptural revelation. Moreover, there are elements (especially in the wisdom tradition) that suggest more positive appraisals of other religious traditions (e.g., the covenant with Noah, the *Book of Ecclesiastes,* universalist tendencies in the New Testament, as in *1 Timothy* 3-5). Inevitably, the use of the "pagan" philosophies of ancient Greece in Jewish, Christian, and Islamic theological self-understanding generated some comparativist interests in all these monotheistic theologies— but these were usually colored by traditional apologetic and polemical concerns.

The most common understanding on the part of Christian theology was that the use of philosophical resources did not necessitate any assessment of the religions to which these "pagan" philosophers may have held. The dominant comparative question for Christian theology (and, in their distinct but related ways, for Jewish and Islamic theologies) was the relationship of theology to philosophy, of revelation to reason. There was little explicit theological interest in comparativist religious analyses—again save for the traditional apologetic and polemical treatises on the "pagans."

Ancient Greece and Rome. Provided that a particular religion did not interfere with civic order, the ancient Greeks and especially the Romans were generally more tolerant of religious differences than were the monotheistic religions. This tolerance, in certain somewhat exceptional circumstances, gave rise to some interest in the fact of religious diversity. Among the classical Greeks, the major writer with an interest in comparativism is undoubtedly the great historian Herodotus.

The most famous work of what might be called comparative theology in the ancient world remains Cicero's famous dialogue *De natura deorum,* in which the theologies and philosophies of the Stoics, Epicureans, and Academics are discussed. The Stoics also developed allegorical methods of interpreting the ancient myths and gods (e.g., Zeus interpreted as the sky, Demeter as the earth, etc.). These methods were later employed by some Jewish (e.g., Philo) and many Christian theologians as an implicitly comparativist, hermeneutic method of scriptural interpretation.

Early Western Modernity. The age of Western exploration in the fifteenth, sixteenth, and seventeenth centuries stimulated new interest not only in the religions of antiquity but also in the newly observed religions of the Americas and those of Asia. The most remarkable example of an exercise in "comparative theology" during this period remains the work of a Jesuit missionary to China, Matteo Ricci, whose positive assessment, on Christian theological grounds, of Confucianism is unique. Indeed, Ricci's letters and reports, although unsuccessful with authorities at Rome, were, in the eighteenth century, deeply influential upon the interest in Chinese religion among such thinkers as Leibniz, Voltaire, Christian Wolff, and Goethe. The comparative theological interests of the Enlightenment were characteristically addressed to classical Confucianism

The Romantic thinkers (e.g., Johann Gottfried Herder) analyzed distinct cultures as unitary expressions of the unique genius of particular peoples. This interest encouraged the development of historical studies for each religion as unitary and unique. Earlier negative assessment by Enlightenment thinkers of what they had named "positive religions" (as distinct from a presumed common "natural religion") yielded, in the Romantics, to a positive comparativist assessment of particular religious traditions and cultures.

The rise of interest in Indian religions, moreover, paralleled both Western colonial expansion and the scholarly development of Indo-European studies in the expanding search for the sources of Western culture. Indeed, in the nineteenth century that interest in Indian religious traditions arose not only among scholars in Indo-European studies but also among philosophers with little strictly scholarly competence, but with strong comparative theological interests. With the emergence of historical consciousness, the transition from ancient, medieval, and early-modern comparative theological interests to a more complete modernism may be said to have begun.

The Modern Period. Western philosophy and theology, by becoming historically conscious, became implicitly (and often explicitly) comparativist as well. The two major thinkers who initiated this comparative philosophy and theology—although it is important to recall that neither ever so named it—were Friedrich Schleiermacher and G. W. F. Hegel. Schleiermacher defined religion as "the sense and the taste for the Infinite" and, later and most influentially, as "a feeling of absolute dependence"; as such, religion is the central reality for humankind. Moreover, in his Christian theology he attempted a comparison of religions. He argued for the superiority of the monotheistic over the polytheistic religions and for the superiority of the "ethical monotheism" of Christianity

> Western philosophy and theology, by becoming historically conscious, became implicitly (and often explicitly) comparativist as well.

over the "ethical monotheism" of Judaism and the "aesthetic monotheism" of Islam.

Schleiermacher's great contemporary and rival, Hegel, had a similarly controversial influence on the development of historical and comparative elements in philosophy (and, to a lesser extent, in Christian theology). Hegel's complex developmental-dialectical model for philosophy demanded, on intrinsic philosophical grounds, a systematic and comparativist account of the major civilizations and the major religions. The thrust of his argument was that Spirit itself (at once divine and human) had a dialectical development that began in China and moved through India, Egypt, Persia, Israel, Greece, and Rome to the "absolute religion" of Christianity. This last reached its climax in German Protestantism and in his new dialectical philosophy. Hegel's formulation of the intellectual dilemma for comparative theology and comparative philosophy is an attempt to show the "absoluteness" of one religion (Protestant Christianity) by relating it explicitly to a developmental and comparative (i. e., dialectical) schema.

In the twentieth century, their most notable Christian theological successor has been Ernst Troeltsch. Troeltsch engaged in several disciplines: he was a major historian of Christianity, a sociologist of religion, an interpreter of the new comparative "science of religion," an idealist philosopher of religion, and an explicitly Christian theologian. Troeltsch insisted throughout his work in these different disciplines that Christian theology as an academic discipline must find new ways to relate itself critically not only to its traditional partner, philosophy, but also to the new disciplines of sociology of religion and the general science of religion.

However, the relative optimism, as well as the comparativist theological interests, of both the liberal Protestant and Catholic modernist theologians soon disappeared. In Catholicism, the end came through the intervention of Rome. Among Protestants, it occurred through the collapse of liberal optimism following World War I. The major theological alternative for Protestant thought at that time (generally called dialectical theology, or neo-Reformation theology) was found in the work of Karl Barth. Barth held that Christian theology was a discipline not intrinsically related to the larger question of the nature of religion (including Christianity as a religion). Christian theology was determined only by the question of the meaning of God's self-revelation in the Word of Jesus Christ. As such, any Christian theological interest in comparativist analyses of religions was improper to the strictly theological task.

Barth's great theological contemporaries Rudolf Bultmann and Paul Tillich, however, continued to include some major historical and comparative emphases in their distinct and non-Barthian formulations of dialectical theology. Indeed, at the end of his long career, and influenced by his seminar work with Mircea Eliade, his colleague at the University of Chicago, Tillich returned explicitly to his earlier Troeltschian interest in history of religions in an important lecture entitled "The Significance of History of Religions for Systematic Theology" (1965).

A comparativist theological analysis within the Barthian perspective, designed to show the radical contrast of Christian revelation to that of other religions, may be found in the notable work of Hendrik Kraemer, especially in his detailed study of other religions, *The Christian Message in a Non-Christian World* (1938). In Roman Catholic theology (especially in the work of Jean Daniélou and Henri de Lubac), moreover, the "return to the sources" movement of the *nouvelle théologie* of the 1940s and 1950s engaged in historical and comparative work on the relationships of non-Christian religions and philosophies to historical Christianity in the scriptural, patristic, and medieval periods. This scholarly work helped set the stage for the affirmative declarations on the world religions by Rome both during and after the Second Vatican Council (1961-1965).

In our own period, many Christian theologians have returned to the kind of comparativist theological program initiated by Schleiermacher and Hegel and refined by Troeltsch. Without necessarily accepting the conclusions of earlier comparative theologies, and without abandoning the strictly theological gains of dialectical theology, many contemporary ecumenically oriented Christian theologians (whether Protestant, Catholic, or Orthodox) are concerned to include explicitly comparativist elements within their theologies. There are, at present, many alternative proposals for how this might best be accomplished.

General Theological Method and the Possibility of a Shared Method for Comparative Theology. As contemporary theologians in a religiously pluralistic world grope for new, inevitably tentative formulations of a paradigm to guide their deliberations and inform their expectations, they are confronted with the question of method. Method—precisely as a necessarily abstract, heuristic guide—must always be secondary to the concrete interpretations of each particular theology. But the secondary also serves. Reflection on method serves the common cause of all concrete comparative theologies by bringing into sharper focus the principles behind the common search for a new paradigm.

It is helpful, therefore, to reflect on what kind of general theological method may be shared by contemporary comparative theologians. The present hypothesis can be described by four premises. First, comparative theology must be a reinterpretation of the central symbols of a particular religious tradition for the contemporary religiously pluralistic world. Second, a new paradigm for comparative theology must be so formulated that the interpretations of a tradition must rely on new foundations that incorporate both past tradition and the present religious pluralism. Third, in keeping with the demands of an emerging globalism and a pluralistic world, theologians in all traditions must risk addressing the questions of religious pluralism on explicitly theological grounds. Fourth, it follows from these first three premises that contemporary theologians must engage in two complementary kinds of interpretation of a tradition—those now known as the "hermeneutics of retrieval" and the "hermeneutics of critique and suspicion."

This general model can be made more specific by introducing the following definition of a shared theological method in the new situation: any theology is the attempt to establish mutually critical correlations between an interpretation of a particular religious tradition and an interpretation of the contemporary situation.

Thus, contemporary theology as a discipline shares with history of religions, the humanities, the social sciences, and, more recently, the natural sciences, a turn to reflection on the process of interpretation itself. For theology is one way to interpret the elusive, ambiguous, and transformative reality named, however inadequately, "religion." Theology is not merely a synonym for any interpretation of religion but rather bears its own methodological demands and its own criteria. It is necessary, therefore, to clarify this definition of theology and to show how it can yield a common model for a theological method, one appropriate to a contemporary comparative theology in any tradition.

Theologians interpret the claims to meaning and truth in the religious classics of a particular tradition for a new situation. The religious classics are theologically construed as human testimonies to some disclosure of ultimate reality by the power of ultimate reality itself, as that power is experienced by human beings. The questions to which such testimonies respond are the fundamental "limit-questions" of the ultimate meaningfulness or absurdity of existence itself. Religious questions are questions of an odd logical type, emerging at the limits of ordinary experience and ordinary modes of inquiry (ethical, aesthetic, political, scientific). Like strictly metaphysical questions, the fundamental questions of religion must be logically odd, since they are questions concerning the most fundamental presuppositions, the most basic beliefs about all knowing, willing, and acting. Like strictly metaphysical questions, religious questions must be on the nature of ultimate reality. Unlike metaphysical questions, religious questions ask about the meaning and truth of ultimate reality, not only in itself but also as it relates existentially to human beings. The religious classics, therefore, are theologically construed as testimonies by human beings who cannot but ask these fundamental limit-questions and, in asking them seriously, believe that they have received an understanding of or even a response from ultimate reality itself: some disclosure or revelation bearing a new and different possibility of ultimate enlightenment, or some new way to formulate the questions themselves, or some promise of total liberation that suggests a new religious way to become an emancipated human being through a grounded relationship to that ultimate reality which is believed to be the origin and end of all reality.

It is not the case, of course, that theology has only become hermeneutical in the modern period. However, the explicit concern with hermeneutics after Schleiermacher has been occasioned, among Westerners, by the sense of cultural distance from the religious traditions caused by the seventeenth-century scientific revolution and the eighteenth-century Enlightenment. This sense of distance has been intensified by the emergence of historical consciousness (as expressed by Troeltsch and Joachim Wach), and the development of the great liberation movements and their attendant hermeneutics of suspicion (with respect to sexism, racism, classism, etc.). And it has been still further intensified by the Western sense of cultural and religious parochialism stimulated by the emerging pluralistic and global culture as well as by the tensions, conflicts, and possibilities present in North-South and East-West relationships. The epoch-making events of modernity have brought about a need for explicit reflection on the hermeneutical character of all the religious disciplines, including the hermeneutical developments (as elucidated by Wach, Mircea Eliade, Joseph M. Kitagawa, Charles H. Long, et al.) in history of religions and the widely recognized hermeneutical character of all theology.

In order to understand the present situation of radical religious pluralism, theologians must interpret it theologically. Interpretation is not a technique to be added on to experience and understanding but is, as Hans-Georg Gadamer and Paul Ricoeur argue, anterior and intrinsic to understanding itself. This is especially the case for any theological interpretation of the contemporary situation. For theology attempts to discern and interpret those fundamental questions (finitude, estrangement, alienation, oppression, fundamental trust or mistrust, loyalty, anxiety, transience, mortality, etc.) that disclose a religious dimension in the contemporary situation.

Paul Tillich described this hermeneutical character of theology as the need for an explicit analysis of the given "situation," that is, for a creative interpretation of our experience which discloses a religious dimension (for example, of cultural pluralism itself). It is possible to distinguish, but not to separate, the theologian's analysis of the "situation" from his or her analysis of a particular religious tradition. Theologians, in sum, interpret both "situation" and "tradition." In some manner, implicit or explicit, they must correlate these two distinct but related interpretations. Like any other interpreter of the contemporary pluralistic situation, and like any other interpreter of the religious questions in that situation, the theologian brings some prior understanding to the interpretation— an understanding influenced by the historical givens of a particular religious tradition. A Buddhist comparative theology, for example, will inevitably be different from a Jewish comparative theology.

The clarification of the emerging discipline called "comparative theology" follows from this brief analysis of theology itself as an academic and hermeneutical discipline. In the sense outlined above, theology is an intrinsically hermeneutical discipline that interprets intellectually a particular tradition in a particular situation. Further, any interpretation of a tradition will always be made in and for a particular situation. In classical Western hermeneutical terms, this means that every act of interpretation includes not only *intelligentia* ("understanding") and *explicatio* ("explanation"), but also *applicatio*, an application of the interpretation to its context that is at the same time a precondition to any understanding and interpretation.

But it is important not to presume that a tradition will always supply adequate responses to the questions suggested by the contemporary situation. Rather, as the qualifying phrase "mutually critical" suggests, the theologian cannot determine before the concrete interpretation itself whether the traditional responses of a religion are adequate to the contemporary situation.

In strictly logical terms, the concept of "mutually critical correlations" suggests a number of possible relations between the theologian's two somewhat distinct interpretations: (1) identities between the questions prompted by and the responses to the situation and the questions and responses given by the tradition (as in many liberal and modernist Christian theologies); (2) similarities-in-difference, or analogies, between those two interpretations (as in many Neo-Confucian "theologies"); and (3) radical disjunctions, or more existentially, confrontations, between the two (as in the Hindu and Buddhist insistence on the necessity of the reality of a "higher consciousness"); or the radical dialectic of the sacred and the profane in archaic ontologies; or the radical correction of traditional self-interpretations of a religion after the emergence of historical consciousness.

In sum, comparative theology, as theology, is an academic discipline that establishes mutually critical correlations between the claims to meaningfulness and truth in the interpretations of a religiously pluralistic situation and the claims to meaningfulness and truth in new interpretations of a religious tradition.

BIBLIOGRAPHY

Systematic Views. The following list of contemporary publications in English is representative (but by no means exhaustive) of theological work that functions, implicitly or explicitly, as comparative theology.

Hick, John. *God and the Universe of Faiths.* New York, 1973.

Hick, John, and Brian Hebblethwaite, eds. *Christianity and Other Religions.* Philadelphia, 1980.

Küng, Hans. "The Challenge of the World Religions." In his *On Being a Christian,* translated by Edward Quinn, pp. 89-118. Garden City, N. Y., 1976.

Panikkar, Raimundo. *Myth, Faith and Hermeneutics: Toward Cross-Cultural Religious Understanding.* New York, 1979.

Panikkar, Raimundo. *The Unknown Christ of Hinduism.* 2d ed., rev. & enl. Maryknoll, N. Y., 1981.

Pannenberg, Wolfhart. "Toward a Theology of the History of Religions." In his *Basic Questions in Theology,* translated by George H. Kehm, vol. 2, pp. 65-118. Philadelphia, 1971.

Rahner, Karl. "Christianity and the Non-Christian Religions." In his *Theological Investigations,* vol. 5, pp. 115-134. Baltimore, 1966.

Rupp, George. Beyond Existentialism and Zen: *Religion in a Pluralistic World.* Oxford, 1979.

Schuon, Frithjof. *The Transcendent Unity of Religions.* Rev. ed. Translated by Peter Townsend. New York, 1975.

Smart, Ninian. *Beyond Ideology: Religion and the Future of Western Civilization.* New York, 1981. See pages 17-68.

Smith, Huston. *Forgotten Truth: The Primordial Tradition.* New York, 1976.

Smith, Wilfred Cantwell. *The Meaning and End of Religion.* New York, 1963.

Smith, Wilfred Cantwell. *Religious Diversity.* Edited by Willard G. Oxtoby. New York, 1976.

Smith, Wilfred Cantwell. *Towards a World Theology: Faith and the Comparative History of Religion.* Philadelphia, 1981.

Additional Sources. The reader interested in further background and bibliography for the historical sections of this article will find references and much of the early history recounted here in Eric J. Sharpe's influential study *Comparative Religion: A History* (London, 1975). I have followed Sharpe's work in several of the more historical sections. The reader may refer to that work for further detail. Among earlier works, see also Morris Jastrow's *The Study of Religion* (London, 1901) and Joachim Wach's *The Comparative Study of Religions* (New York, 1958). For more recent materials and invaluable bibliographies, see Mircea Eliade's magisterial *A History of Religious Ideas,* 3 vols. (Chicago, 1978-1986). See also *The*

History of Religions: Essays in Methodology, edited by Mircea Eliade and Joseph M. Kitagawa (Chicago, 1959), and Jacques Waardenburg's *Classical Approaches to the Study of Religion: Aims, Methods and Theories of Research,* 2 vols. (The Hague, 1973-1974).

Representative of modern, influential tests in the emerging discipline of comparative theology, the following works are worthy of special attention:

Hegel, G. W. F. *Lectures on the Philosophy of Religion.* 3 vols. Translated by E. B. Speirs and J. B. Sanderson. London, 1895; reprint, Atlantic Highlands, N. J., 1968.

Hocking, William E. *Living Religions and a World Faith.* New York, 1940; reprint, New York, 1975.

Northrop, F. S. C. *The Meeting of East and West.* New York, 1946; reprint, Woodbridge, Conn., 1979.

Radhakrishnan, Sarvepalli. *The Hindu View of Life.* London, 1927; reprint, London, 1980.

Radhakrishnan, Sarvepalli. *Eastern Religions and Western Thought.* 2d ed. Oxford, 1975.

Schleiermacher, Friedrich. *On Religion: Speeches to Its Cultured Despisers.* Translated by John Oman from the third edition. London, 1894; reprint, New York, 1955.

Schleiermacher, Friedrich. *The Christian Faith.* Edited by H. R. Mackintosh and J. S. Stewart. Edinburgh, 1928; reprint, New York, 1963.

Tillich, Paul. *The Future of Religions.* Edited by Jerald C. Brauer. New York, 1966.

Toynbee, Arnold. *An Historian's Approach to Religion.* New York, 1956.

Troeltsch, Ernest. *The Absoluteness of Christianity and the History of Religions.* Translated by David Reid. Richmond, Va., 1971.

DAVID TRACY

THERAVADA

The term *Theravada Buddhism* refers, first, to a "school" and closely related "orientations" within the history of Buddhist monasticism and, second, to forms of Buddhist religious, political, and social life in various Buddhist countries. Although these two aspects of Theravada Buddhism must be distinguished, they overlap and interact in various ways at different points in Theravada history. In the present article, the specifically monastic aspects will receive priority, but reference will be made to the civilizational dimension as well.

Origins and Early Development

Theravada Buddhism, like other forms of Buddhism, had its origin in the life of the early Buddhist community. However, during the earliest stages of Buddhist development schools had not yet crystallized in any formal sense. Although the claim to represent the earliest Buddhism is doctrinally important, none of the schools that developed later can be considered, on the basis of purely historical scholarship, to be the sole inheritor and preserver of the original form of Buddhist teaching and practice.

The First Centuries. We know that not longer than 110 years after the death of the Buddha the different emphases that existed within the earliest community culminated in a major schism. The school known as the Mahasamghika ("those of the great assembly") was more populist in its attitude toward doctrinal matters, disciplinary practices, and modes of communal organization. By contrast, the Sthaviravada school was more conservative in its approach.

It is impossible to identify "Buddhist civilization," much less its Theravada form, during the first centuries of Buddhist history. This is not to say that the Buddhist tradition generally, and the Theravadins in particular, did not have civilizational aspirations. From texts dating to this period, it seems clear that they did.

Asoka and After. By the period of the reign of Asoka (third century BCE) the initial division of the Buddhist community into those of the "Great Assembly" and those of the "Way of the Elders" had subdivided further. But according to Theravada accounts dating from at least the fourth century CE, Asoka himself sponsored a council that clarified the major differences.

Further Theravada accounts record that Asoka sponsored Buddhist missions that traveled beyond the frontiers of his considerable empire. These accounts date the founding of the Theravada school in Southeast Asia and Sri Lanka to Asoka's missions to Suvannabhumi (i. e., Southeast Asia) and Tambapanni (i. e., Sri Lanka), respectively.

There is no substantial reason to doubt that by Asoka's time the Theravadins formed a distinctive group within the Buddhist *sangha.* They preserved the teachings of the Buddha in Pali through their oral tradition; by the Third Buddhist Council or shortly thereafter, the Theravadins held their own positions on specific points of doctrine and practice. They also actively contributed to the Buddhist missionary activity during the third and second centuries BCE.

Sri Lanka and the Dhammadipa Tradition. Within this distinctive provincial area of Sri Lanka, Theravada traditions became firmly established and prospered. For example, the Theravada monks feared that the monastic community would be dispersed and the oral tradition broken and lost. In an effort to prevent this, they gathered together and committed to writing the Tipitaka (Skt., Tripitaka; "three baskets"), that is, the Buddhist canon. As a result, this aspect of the tradition was solidified in a basic form that has remained largely intact through Theravada history.

By this time, too, Theravada Buddhism in Sri Lanka had become a civilizational religion. Said to have been the son of Asoka, the monk named Mahinda (Skt., Mahendra) supposedly succeeded in his missionary goal of establishing the Theravada lineage in Sri Lanka and converting the Sinhala king, Devanampiyatissa. Shortly thereafter, according to the texts, Asoka's daughter, the nun Sanghamitta, brought to Sri Lanka the ordination lineage for women. King Devanampiyatissa is credited with founding the famous Mahavihara monastery, which not only encompassed the king's capital within its boundaries, but later housed the monks who authored the chronicles that we now possess.

Another possible point for the emergence of Theravada as a civilizational religion is the reign of the Sinhala hero, King Dutthagamani (r. 161-137 BCE). While still a prince he organized a campaign in which the struggle to establish centralized rule and the struggle to establish Theravada Buddhism as the "national" religion became closely identified. The civilizational character of Theravada found a powerful vehicle of expression. Certainly, by the end of the first century BCE, after the Pali scriptures had been committed to writing, the Theravada ideal of Sri Lanka as the Dhammadipa, the "Island of the Dhamma," seemed well-developed not only in Sri Lankan religious and political institutions, but in Sinhala identity as well.

Theravada Buddhism in Greater India

In Southeast Asia, specifically among the Burmese of Lower Burma and the Mon peoples of Lower Burma and Thailand, the Theravada tradition became firmly rooted and exerted a significant civilizational influence. The first archaeological evidence of Buddhism's presence has been found along inland and coastal trade routes, and dates to early in the first millennium CE. In Lower Burma inscriptions have been found that confirm a preeminent Theravada presence in Pyu/Burmese royal centers beginning from the fifth century CE, and some sort of Theravada influence is attested in Pagan somewhat later. In Thailand, similar evidence indicates that the Theravada tradition was an important, perhaps central, religious element in the Mon civilization of Dvaravati that flourished over a wide area of central, northern, and northeastern Thailand from the sixth to the eleventh century.

In Sri Lanka, literary and archaeological remains provide many more details regarding local Theravada history. A famous monk named Mahatissa evidently built, with royal support, an impressive new monastery in Anuradhapura. Sometime thereafter, monks of the long-established Mahavihara fraternity (by whose account this story is preserved) accused Mahatissa of violating the monastic discipline and tried to expel him from the *sangha.* Monks loyal to Mahatissa then formed the fraternity of the Abhayagiri monastery, which became for some time the Mahavihara's archrival. The Abhayagiri lineage maintained independent institutional traditions that eventually gave rise to branch monastic communities as far distant as Java.

The willingness of the Abhayagiri Theravadins to welcome Mahayana adherents into their company generated, some three centuries after its founding, a schism within its own ranks. In the middle of the fourth century three hundred monks declared their aversion to the presence of Mahayana monks at the Abhayagiri, withdrew from that fraternity, and formed an independent group that came to be known as the Jetavana fraternity. The new Jetavana *nikaya* acquired affiliated monasteries and also considerable land and other wealth. But compared to the Mahavihara and Abhayagiri *nikayas,* the Jetavana remained relatively small. Certain tendencies remained common to all three *nikayas.* For example, the Theravada scholasticism that blossomed during the fifth century drew scholars from the Mahavihara and from other *nikayas* as well.

The most influential scholar associated with this efflorescence, if not Theravada scholasticism generally, was Bhadantacariya Buddhaghosa. Probably a native of northern India, Buddhaghosa traveled to Sri Lanka in order to trans-

> **In Southeast Asia . . . the Theravada tradition became firmly rooted and exerted a significant civilizational influence.**

late the Sinhala commentarial tradition, preserved by the Mahaviharavasins, into Pali, which by this time was recognized as the lingua franca of the international Theravada community. Buddhaghosa's industriousness during his residence at the Mahavihara produced a rich and extensive corpus of Pali commentarial literature that became a fundamental resource for subsequent scholarship and practice throughout the Theravada world.

Another movement in Sri Lanka that drew interested monks from all Theravada *nikayas* was ascetic in character and led to the rise of at least two prominent groups. The first group, known as the Pamsukulikas ("those who wear robes made from rags"), began to play an important role during the seventh century. It is quite possible that at least some of the Pamsukulikas were strongly influenced by Tantric trends that were becoming increasingly prominent throughout the Buddhist world, including Sri Lanka.

The second group, which attracted many proponents, especially from among the Mahaviharavasins, first began to be mentioned in tenth-century records. Referred to as *araññikas* ("forest dwellers"), these monks declined to reside in the rich monasteries of the capital and established their own monastic centers in the countryside. They adopted a more stringent discipline than their urban contemporaries, and emphasized more rigorous modes of scholarship and meditation.

The Great Revival and Beyond

In Sri Lanka, the Theravada *sangha* had suffered serious setbacks as a result of Cola invasions from South India and the collapse of the hydraulic civilization of northern Sri Lanka. In Southeast Asia, the Pyu-Burmese and Mon civi-

lizations in which the Theravadins had played a major role had lost much of their vitality. During this period, the kingdom of Pagan seemed to be more oriented toward Hinduism and Sanskritic forms of Buddhism than toward Theravada. And with hegemony over most of what is now Thailand, the powerful and expansive Khmer court at Angkor was strongly oriented toward Hinduism and Mahayana Buddhism.

Accounts of the beginnings of the Theravada resurgence that occurred in the latter half of the eleventh century vary according to the tradition that has preserved them. However, one primary fact stands clear both in Sri Lanka and in Burma: Theravada became the favored tradition at the major centers of political power.

Sri Lanka. In Sri Lanka, the revitalized Theravada tradition was given an important new direction in the twelfth century when, during the reign of Parakramabahu I, a major reform and reorganization of the *sangha* was implemented. Parakramabahu I requested the Mahavihara-oriented *araññikas,* who had begun to appear on the scene two to three centuries earlier, to preside over a council.

The council "purified" the *sangha,* which meant that the code of proper monastic conduct was ascertained and monks who refused to comply were expelled. The reforms then unified the *sangha* by bringing all the remaining factions (and it is clear there were many) together into a single communal order. In so doing, the reforms provided the basis for a new structure of ecclesiastical organization that was established either at that time or shortly thereafter.

This reformed tradition by and large remained preeminent and creative in Sri Lanka up to the coming of the Portuguese in the fifteenth century. However, during the period after 1500, when the authority of the indigenous Buddhist kingdom was increasingly confined to the inland highlands, the *sangha* suffered a serious erosion of standards. By the early eighteenth century, the level of monastic scholarship and discipline had reached a very low level indeed.

Burma. In Southeast Asia, the resurgence of Theravada proceeded rather differently. Through the reforms initiated by Aniruddha and his monastic preceptor, Shin Arahan, and renewed by his successor, King Kyanzittha, a strong Theravada tradition was established in Upper Burma and given powerful royal support. In the twelfth century a further reformist element was introduced at Pagan by a monk named Chapata. Thus, by the end of the twelfth century, when the Pagan dynasty was still a very powerful force, the Theravada tradition had become firmly established as the preeminent religion in Burma.

Burmese monastic reforms took place when the fifteenth-century Mon king named Dhammaceti assumed the throne in Lower Burma. Formerly a monk, King Dhammaceti sponsored a delegation of eighteen monks to be reordained in Sri Lanka. When these monks returned, Dhammaceti insisted that all those within his realm who wished to remain in the *sangha* be reordained by the new fraternity. Following this "purification" and unification process, the king proceeded to establish a monastic hierarchy whose responsibility it was to maintain strict adherence to the Vinaya rules. King Dhammaceti's efforts served to emphasize the influence of Sinhala monastic traditions in Burma.

Thailand, Cambodia, and Laos. Like their Mon predecessors, the Thais also venerated Theravada traditions. But during the mid-fourteenth century, Mon Theravada traditions had to make way for a Sinhala reformist movement that spread from a center at Martaban in Lower Burma to several Thai capitals including Ayutthaya, Sukhothai, and Chiangmai (Lanna).

Theravada monasteries continued to proliferate throughout the region. By the latter part of the fifteenth century the Lanna capital of Chiangmai had emerged as one of the major intellectual centers in the Theravada world. In central Thailand, where the locus of power gradually shifted from Sukhothai to Ayutthaya, the Theravada presence was consolidated. Farther east in Cambodia, Theravada gradually displaced the deeply entrenched traditions of Hinduism and Mahayana Buddhism, a transition facilitated by the abandonment of the old capital of Angkor in the mid-fifteenth century. According to chronicle accounts, Theravada became the preeminent tradition in Laos beginning with the conversion of a Laotian prince during his exile in the court of Angkor in the mid-fourteenth century. Indeed, by the beginning of the sixteenth century, reformist Sinhala fraternities dominated in all of the major royal centers and in many of the lesser ones as well.

Theravada Buddhism since 1750

During the past two and a half centuries Theravada Buddhism has retained its basic structure, and the major regional traditions have maintained many of the particularities that had come to characterize them during premodern times.

In the monastic context the stage was set for the developments of the modern period by major reforms that were implemented in each of the three major Theravada regions. In Sri Lanka the relevant reform took place in the middle decades of the eighteenth century. Believing their ordination lineage to be defective, the reformers invited Thai monks to Sri Lanka to reintroduce an authentic Theravada lineage. Through their efforts a new Siyam (Thai) *nikaya* was established.

Later in the eighteenth century King Bodawpaya (r. 1781-1819) succeeded in uniting Burma under his rule and in establishing a considerable degree of royally regulated discipline within the Burmese *sangha.* Having more or less unified the *sangha*, Bodawpaya's reforms established the basis for the Thudhamma segment of the Order that has continued to include the majority of Burmese monks.

In Indochina King Rama I claimed the throne and introduced a series of reforms that unified the *sangha* and strengthened discipline within its ranks. This more or less unified fraternity—later called the Mahanikaya—has never lost its majority position within the Thai *sangha.* In Cambodia and Laos closely related, although less reformed, Mahanikaya fraternities were dominant at the beginning of the modern period and have held that position ever since.

During the nineteenth century there emerged within the *sangha* in each area a major competing faction or factions. In Sri Lanka two competing fraternities appeared on the scene: The Amarapura *nikaya* was—and remains today—a rather loose confederation of several smaller groups from various other castes that are especially prominent in southwestern Sri Lanka.

The Ramañña *nikaya* has remained by far the smallest of the Sinhala fraternities, but has nevertheless exerted considerable influence on the Buddhist community in Sri Lanka.

In Burma, much more than in Sri Lanka, the nineteenth-century British conquest disrupted the fabric of social life. In response to a disrupted environment, numerous small, more tightly organized groups formed. These various groups both complemented one another and competed with each other for purity of monastic observance and its attendant lay support.

In western Indochina during the nineteenth century a single new *nikaya,* the Thammayut, emerged to complement and compete with the established Mahanikaya fraternity. The Thammayut's favored status and elite membership enabled it to play an important role in drawing provincial traditions into the central Thai *sangha,* and in extending central Thai influence into the *sanghas* of Cambodia and Laos as well.

Thus, by the beginning of the twentieth century the various fraternities that still constitute the Theravada *sanghas* in Sri Lanka and Southeast Asia had already come into being.

> **The *sangha* . . . carries on its traditions of Pali scholarship and meditational practice.**

Theravada Today

Theravada Buddhism remains very much alive in Sri Lanka and Southeast Asia, both as a monastic tradition and as a civilizational force. The *sangha*, despite its many problems, carries on its traditions of Pali scholarship and meditational practice. It continues to produce persons with intellectual substance and spiritual prowess. And it continues to generate movements (often conflicting movements) aimed at monastic reform, spiritual development, and societal well-being.

In addition, Theravada Buddhism continues to exert its influence on the institutions and values of the societies in the traditionally Theravada areas. This influence takes quite different forms in Sri Lanka, where ethnic differences often involve religious differences; in Burma, where the nation's leaders have sought to insulate the populace from many aspects of "modernity"; in Thailand, where the pace of "modernization" is rapid indeed; and in Cambodia and Laos, where Theravada Buddhism has been "disestablished" by recently installed Communist governments. But in each instance Theravada Buddhism continues to provide meaning in the everyday life of its adherents.

[*See also* Buddhism. *For a related discussion focusing on the interrelationships between Buddhism and local cultures, see* Southeast Asian Religions; Sinhala Religion; Lao Religion; *and* Khmer Religion.]

BIBLIOGRAPHY

Unfortunately there is no one book that adequately covers Theravada Buddhism as a whole. Perhaps the most comprehensive single study for the premodern period is Kanai Lal Hazra's *History of Theravada Buddhism in South-East Asia* (New Delhi, 1982), which touches on Indian and Sri Lankan developments as well. This book needs to be supplemented by other works that deal with particular aspects of the tradition, such as Wilhelm Geiger's *Pali Literature and Language,* 2d ed., translated by Batakrishna Ghosh (Delhi, 1968); John C. Holt's *Discipline: The Canonical Buddhism of the Vinayapitaka* (Delhi, 1981); John Ross Carter's *Dhamma: Western Academic and Sinhalese Buddhist Interpretations* (Tokyo, 1978); Stephen Collins's *Selfless Persons: Imagery and Thought in Theravada Buddhism* (Cambridge, 1982); Winston L. King's *Theravada Meditation* (University Park, Pa., 1980); and Bhikkhu Nyanatiloka's *Guide to the Abhidhamma-pitaka,* 3d ed., revised and enlarged by Nya-naponika Thera (Kandy, 1971). Many of the civilizational aspects are covered in two related books edited by Bardwell L. Smith, *Religion and Legitimation of Power in Sri Lanka* and *Religion and Legitimation of Power in Thailand, Laos, and Burma* (both, Chambersburg, Pa., 1978). Similar themes are explored in Heinz Bechert's three-volume *Buddhismus, Staat und Gesellschaft in den Ländern Theravada-Buddhismus* (Frankfurt, 1966-1973). Two other studies written for more general audiences are Robert C. Lester's *Theravada Buddhism in Southeast Asia* (Ann Arbor, 1973) and Donald K. Swearer's *Buddhism and Society in Southeast Asia* (Chambersburg, Pa., 1981).

Because of vast translation efforts, primarily by the Pali Text Society, the nonspecialist has access to a large body of Theravada literature. Virtually the entire Tipitaka has been translated into English and is included in either the "Sacred Books of the Buddhists" or the "Translation Series" of the Pali Text Society. Among the most important postcanonical texts that are available in English are Wilhelm Geiger's translation of The *Mahavamsa,* or *The Great Chronicle of Ceylon* (London, 1964); Bhikkhu Ñyanamoli's translation of Buddhaghosa's fifth-century work, *The Path of Purification,* 2d ed. (Colombo, 1964); and Frank E. Reynolds and Mani B. Reynolds's translation of Phya Lithai's fourteenth-century cosmological treatise, *Three Worlds according to King Ruang* (Berkeley, 1982).

A useful introduction to the Theravada tradition in Sri Lanka is provided in *Two Wheels of Dhamma,* edited by Bardwell L. Smith, Frank E. Reynolds, and Gananath Obeyesekere, "American Academy of Religion Monograph Series," no. 3 (Chambersburg, Pa., 1973). This introduction should be supplemented by the R. A. L. H.

Gunawardhana's excellent *Robe and Plough: Monasticism and Economic Interest in Early Medieval Sri Lanka* (Tuscon, 1979) and Kitsiri Malalgoda's *Buddhism in Sinhalese Society, 1750-1900* (Berkeley, 1976). For two books that deal with quite different dimensions of the "contemporary" tradition, see Michael Carrithers's *The Forest Monks of Sri Lanka: An Anthropological and Historical Study* (Delhi, 1983) and Richard F. Gombrich's *Precept and Practice: Traditional Buddhism in the Rural Highlands of Ceylon* (Oxford, 1971).

The most comprehensive overview of Theravada Buddhism in Burma is provided by Melford E. Spiro in his *Buddhism and Society: A Great Tradition and its Burmese Vicissitudes* (New York, 1970). Serious students will also want to consult E. Michael Mendelson's very important study, *Sangha and State in Burma: A Study of Monastic Sectarianism and Leadership,* edited by John Ferguson (Ithaca, N. Y., 1975); Emanuel Sarkisyanz's *Buddhist Backgrounds of the Burmese Revolution* (The Hague, 1965); and Manning Nash's *The Golden Road to Moder-nity: Village Life in Contemporary Burma* (New York, 1965).

The Theravada tradition in Thailand has been comprehensively studied by Stanley J. Tambiah in a trilogy of excellent books: *World Conqueror and World Renouncer* (Cambridge, 1976), *Buddhism and the Spirit Cults in North-East Thailand* (Cambridge, 1970), and *The Buddhist Saints of the Forest and the Cult of Amulets* (Cambridge, 1984). Other items of interest include Donald K. Swearer's *Wat Haripuñjaya* (Missoula, Mont., 1976) and our "Sangha, Society and the Struggle for National Integration: Burma and Thailand," in *Transitions and Transformations in the History of Religions: Essays in Honor of Joseph M. Kitagawa,* edited by Frank E. Reynolds and Theodore M. Ludwig, (Leiden, 1980), pp. 56-88.

Studies that deal with Theravada Buddhism in Laos and Cambodia are much less adequate and are virtually all in French. The best introductions are probably the articles on Buddhism in the collections edited by René de Berval in *France-Asie* entitled *Présence du royaume Lao* (Saigon, 1956), translated by Mrs. Tessier du Cros as *Kingdom of Laos* (Saigon, 1959), and *Présence du Cambodge* (Saigon, 1955). Two books that provide overviews of sorts are Marcel Zago's *Rites et cérémonies en milieu bouddhiste Lao* (Rome, 1972) and Adhémard Leclère's *Le bouddhisme au Cambodge* (Paris, 1899). The most important new studies are three short but erudite works by François Bizot that highlight an important Tantric influence in the Pali Buddhist traditions in Cambodia and draw implications for our understanding of the Theravada tradition more generally. These have appeared under the titles *Le figuier à cinq branches* (Paris, 1976), "Le grotte de la naissance," *Bulletin de l'École Française d'Extrême-Orient* 66 (1979); and *Le don de soi-même* (Paris, 1981).

Further bibliographical information—including annotations of many of the works cited here—can be obtained by consulting the relevant sections in *Guide to Buddhist Religion* by Frank E. Reynolds et al. (Boston, 1981), or in Reynolds's "Buddhism," in *A Reader's Guide to the Great Religions,* edited by Charles J. Adams, 2d ed. (New York, 1977), pp. 156-222.

FRANK E. REYNOLDS and REGINA T. CLIFFORD

THÉRÈSE OF LISIEUX

THÉRÈSE OF LISIEUX (1873-1897), epithet of Thérèse Martin, French Carmelite nun and Catholic saint. Thérèse was the youngest of nine children born to Louis and Zélie Martin. When Thérèse was eight her family moved to the small Norman town of Lisieux, where she was to spend the remainder of her life, with the exception of one pilgrimage to Rome shortly before she entered the convent. Within a few years of the family's arrival in the town, Thérèse's two older sisters became nuns at the cloistered convent of Discalced Carmelites in Lisieux, and at an early age Thérèse decided to join them. Her first application to enter the convent, made when she was fourteen, was rejected on account of her age, but at fifteen she entered the convent.

In the cloister Thérèse exhibited unswerving fidelity to the Carmelite rule and unfailing kindness to the convent's twenty-five nuns, some of whom had quite unattractive personalities. However, the full dimensions of her spiritual life became evident only in her posthumously published autobiography. Eighteen months before her death she manifested signs of a fatal tubercular condition, and her last months were plagued by extreme pain and even nagging temptations against faith. She died at the age of twenty-four, exclaiming, "My God, I love you."

During the last years of her life Thérèse wrote her memoirs in three separate sections, mostly at the request of the convent's superior. One year after her death the memoirs were published under the title *L'histoire d'une âme* (The Story of a Soul). The simple book, written in epistolary style, is a candid recounting of her own unfailing love for and confidence in the goodness of God, and it achieved instant and enormous popularity in translations into many languages. In the next fifteen years alone more than a million copies were printed. This worldwide response prompted the Holy See to waive the usual fifty-year waiting period, and Thérèse was beatified in 1923 and canonized in 1925. In the bull of canonization, Pius XI said that she had achieved sanctity "without going beyond the common order of things."

BIBLIOGRAPHY

Of the many English translations of *L'histoire d'une âme*, perhaps the most readable is Ronald Knox's *Autobiography of St. Thérèse of Lisieux* (New York, 1958), which is done in Knox's usual felicitous style. Other of Thérèse's writings are contained in *Collected Letters of St. Thérèse of Lisieux*, edited by Abbé André Combes and translated by Frank J. Sheed (New York, 1949). For a short but incisive biography, see John Beevers's *Storm of Glory* (New York, 1950); for a more critical study, see my book *The Search for St. Thérèse* (Garden City, N. Y., 1961).

PETER T. ROHRBACH

THOMAS AQUINAS

THOMAS AQUINAS (Tommaso d'Aquino, 1225-1274), Italian Dominican theologian, doctor of the church, patron of Roman Catholic schools, and Christian saint. One of the most important and influential scholastic theologians.

Life and Works. Thomas spent his first five years at the family castle under the care of his mother and a nurse. As the youngest son of the family, Thomas was given (*oblatus,* "offered") to the Benedictine abbey of Monte Cassino by his parents at the age of five or six in the firm hope that he would eventually choose the monastic life and become abbot. His earliest training was in the spiritual life, mainly through the Latin psalter, and in the rudiments of reading, writing, and mathematics.Later, at the University of Naples, Thomas was introduced to Aristotle's philosophy.

By 1243 Thomas was attracted to the Dominicans living nearby at the priory of San Domenico. Impressed by their apostolic zeal, poverty, and simplicity and free from obligation, Thomas received the habit in April 1244 at the age of nineteen.

Arriving at the priory of Saint-Jacques by October 1245, Thomas began his studies at the University of Paris under Albertus Magnus, who was then lecturing on the writings of Dionysius the Areopagite. As Albert's junior bachelor (1250-1252), Thomas lectured cursorily on *Isaiah, Jeremiah,* and *Lamentations* at Cologne.

By 1252 the Dominican master general was eager to send promising young men to the university to prepare for inception as master (full professor). Albert convinced the master general to send Thomas, despite his young age, to study for the university chair for non-Parisians. His originality and clarity of thought were conspicuous in his teaching and writing, notably in his commentary on the *Sentences; On Being and Essence,* on the meaning of certain metaphysical terms; and in a short treatise entitled *Principles of Nature.*

Having served the order's interests in Paris, Thomas returned to Italy where he taught, wrote, and preached from 1259 to 1268. At the pope's request, he composed the liturgy for the new Feast of Corpus Christi and expressed his views in *Against the Errors of the Greeks* on doctrinal points disputed by Greek and Latin Christians. Having thereby discovered the richness of the Greek patristic tradition, he also began compiling a continuous gloss, or exposition, of the Gospels *(Catena aurea),* made up almost entirely of excerpts from the writings of the Greek and Latin fathers, dedicating the commentary on *Matthew* to Urban IV. In June 1265, the provincial chapter of Anagni assigned Thomas to open a school of theology at Santa Sabina in Rome. There he wrote the first part of his Summa *theologiae* survey.

By the end of 1268, Thomas was ordered to return to Paris, as was the Frenchman Peter of Tarentaise (the future

Pope Innocent V), to counter a revival of antimendicant sentiment among secular masters. Almost single-handedly he was required to fend off attacks on three fronts: with all mendicants against secular masters opposed to mendicants' being in the university; with a few of his confreres against most of the Dominicans, Franciscans, and secular theologians, opposed to using Aristotle in theology; and with most theologians against young philosophers who tended to promulgate heretical views under the name of Aristotle or his commentator Ibn Rushd (Averroës). Over the next five years Thomas fulfilled his university obligations to lecture on the Bible, to hold disputations, and to preach, while also carrying on a vigorous polemic against the antimendicants, expounding all the major works of Aristotle, writing his *Summa theologiae,* and replying to numerous requests for his opinions.

On 10 December 1270 thirteen philosophical propositions opposed to the Catholic faith were condemned by Étienne Tempier, bishop of Paris. To prevent such views from developing in the classroom, Thomas undertook a detailed literal commentary on all the main texts of Aristotle then in common use at the University of Paris. It is possible that Thomas began his commentary on *De anima* in Italy, but all the others were written after his return to Paris in 1269, namely, the commentaries on *Physics, On Interpretation, Posterior Analytics, Ethics, Metaphysics, Politics,* and certain others left unfinished at his death.

The extensive second part of the *Summa theologiae* was entirely written at Paris during the intense years 1269 to 1272. This part, later subdivided into two parts, discusses the ultimate goal of human life, namely, eternal life (2.1.1-5) and the means of attaining it, namely, human acts, reason (law), grace, and all the virtues considered in general (2.1) and in particular (2.2) as practiced in various states of life. The third part, begun at Paris, considers the incarnation and life of Christ (3.1-59) and the sacraments, and was left incomplete on the subject of penance when Thomas died.

Pope Gregory X personally requested that Thomas attend the Second Council of Lyons due to open on 1 May 1274. Leaving Naples, Thomas had a serious accident near Maenza in which he hit his head against an overhanging branch and was knocked down. Thomas's condition became so serious that he asked to be transported to the nearby Cistercian monastery of Fossanova and died early Wednesday morning 7 March 1274. He was canonized a saint on 18 July 1323.

Philosophy. While giving primacy of place and importance to what God has revealed through the Jewish people and through Jesus Christ, Thomas recognized the much larger, though less important, realm of knowledge available to unaided human reason. His own strictly philosophical thought is found in his numerous commentaries on Aristotle and in independent treatises. In the manner of his contemporaries in the universities, he adapted his own understanding of Aristotelian ideas, terminology, and methodology to the study of "sacred doctrine," especially in his *Summa theologiae.*

Thomas preferred an order of study that presupposed the liberal arts and mathematics and began with Aristotelian logic, principally *On Interpretation* and the *Posterior Analytics;* moved through natural philosophy, involving all the natural sciences, including psychology; treated moral philosophy, including political science; and concluded with metaphysics, or first philosophy, which today would include epistemology and natural theology.

Theology. Thomistic "theology," which Thomas calls sacred doctrine, is distinct from pure philosophy and depends on the divine gift of faith, which involves the whole realm of revelation, divine law, ecclesial worship, the spiritual life, and human speculation about these.

Thomas did not divide theology into such modern disciplines as biblical and scholastic, positive and speculative, dogmatic and moral, spiritual and mystical, kerygmatic and academic, and so on. In his day, however, each master in sacred theology lectured on the Bible, presided over scholastic disputations on specific points, and also preached regularly to the university community. Thomas wrote his *Summa theologiae* not as a replacement for the Bible but as an extracurricular aid for beginners who needed an overview of "sacred doctrine." Although the *Summa* is divided into three parts, its conceptual unity is the Dionysian circle of the *exitus* ("going forth") of all things from God and the *reditus* ("return") of all things to God. Without doubt Thomas's most original contribution to theology was the large Second Part, on the virtues and vices, inserted between the original *exitus* and *reditus* found in all contemporary summae of theology.

For Thomas the supernatural gifts of sanctifying grace and the virtues (faith, hope, love, and the moral virtues) are normally conferred through baptism by water in the name of Jesus or the Trinity of Father, Son, and Holy Spirit. But in an adult the beginnings of this supernatural life are stirred up by God before actual baptism by water. The supernatural life of grace *(gratia)* experienced in this life is, for Thomas, already a foretaste of eternal life *(gloria)* in heaven. The overflow of grace is expressed in good works and in the exercise of all the virtues.

BIBLIOGRAPHY

Works by Thomas Aquinas. Of the ninety or more authentic works of Thomas there have been numerous editions of individual works from 1461 to the present day, over 180 incunabula editions alone. Since the Roman edition of Pius V, *Opera omnia* (1570-1571), there have been more than ten editions or reprints of older standbys, but the only modern critical edition of the *Opera omnia* is the Leonine, 48 vols. to date (Vatican City, 1882-). Both English translations of the *Summa theologiae* (22 vols., London, 1916-1938; bilingual edition, 60 vols., New York, 1964-1976) are far from satisfactory, except for some volumes. Besides the older translation of the

Summa contra gentiles by the English Dominicans, there is a good edited translation by Anton C. Pegis, *On the Truth of the Catholic Faith,* 4 vols. in 5 (New York, 1955-1957). The most convenient anthologies are *Basic Writings,* 2 vols., edited by Anton C. Pegis (New York, 1945); *Philosophical Texts,* edited and translated by Thomas Gilby (1951; reprint, Durham, N. C., 1982); and *Theological Texts,* edited and translated by Thomas Gilby (1955; reprint, Durham, N. C., 1982). The best single volume sampling of his writings in philosophy with good introductions by Vernon J. Bourke is The *Pocket Aquinas* (New York, 1960).

Works on His Life and Writings. The most complete single volume on Thomas and his writings is my own *Friar Thomas d'Aquino: His Life, Thought, and Works* (1974; reprinted with corrigenda and addenda, Washington, D. C., 1983) with an annotated catalog of authentic writings. Some of the more important biographical documents have been translated and edited by Kenelm Foster in *The Life of Saint Thomas Aquinas* (Baltimore, 1959). All modern studies of the writings must start with the pioneer work of Pierre Mandonnet, *Des écrits authentiques de Saint Thomas d'Aquin* (Fribourg, 1910), Martin Grabmann, *Die Werke,* 3d ed. (Münster, 1949), and some others.

General Works on His Life and Thought

Bourke, Vernon J. *Aquinas' Search for Wisdom.* Milwaukee, 1965. Excellent alternating biographical and doctrinal chapters that should be read carefully to savor the wisdom of Thomas.

Chenu, M.-D. *Toward Understanding Saint Thomas Aquinas.* Chicago, 1964. Indispensable for understanding the medieval context and genre of Thomas's writings.

Chesterton, G. K. *Saint Thomas Aquinas.* London, 1933. A superb appreciation of "the dumb ox" that Gilson and Pegis would have liked to have written, by a natural Thomist.

Copleston, Frederick C. *Aquinas.* Baltimore, 1967. Most appreciated by historians of philosophy.

Gilson, Étienne. *The Christian Philosophy of Saint Thomas Aquinas.* Translated from the fifth edition with a catalog of authentic works by I. T. Eschmann. New York, 1956. Gilson's *chef d'œuvre,* frequently revised over forty years of a distinguished career with all his pet views.

Maritain, Jacques, *Saint Thomas, Angel of the Schools.* London, 1946. Reflections on the life and significance of Thomas by a distinguished modern Thomist.

McInerny, Ralph. *Saint Thomas Aquinas* (1977). Reprint, Notre Dame, 1982. The best short introduction to Thomas and his chief sources: Aristotle, Boethius, and Augustine.

Pegis, Anton C. *Introduction to Saint Thomas Aquinas.* New York, 1948. A handy volume with selections from both *summas* illustrating principal themes of Thomas's thought.

Pieper, Josef. *Guide to Thomas Aquinas.* New York, 1962. A thoughtful invitation to explore the world of Thomas for reflective students.

Sertillanges, A. G. *Saint Thomas Aquinas and His Work* (1933). Reprint, London, 1957. An exciting period piece by a university chaplain in Paris after World War I.

Walz, Angelus M. *Saint Thomas Aquinas: A Biographical Study.* Westminster, Md., 1951. A much-consulted historian's view of Thomas's life and works; see the improved French adaptation by Paul Novarino.

JAMES A. WEISHEIPL

THOTH

Thoth was the god of wisdom from Hermopolis in Middle Egypt. According to the Hermopolitan cosmology (which is best known from texts found at other sites), the eight primordial gods representing "hiddenness," "darkness," "formlessness" (?), and the "watery abyss" produced an egg that appeared at Hermopolis when the inundation subsided and from which the creator god appeared and brought everything else into being. When mentioned in the Heliopolitan Pyramid Texts, this creator god was Atum, but in the local Hermopolitan tradition he could have been Thoth.

Thoth was the moon god and as such was the companion of Re, the sun god, but he also had his own following among the stars in the night sky. One mortuary tradition, probably originating at Hermopolis, permitted the dead who knew the correct spells to accompany Thoth in the sky. Thoth was the son of Re, but he also represented the injured eye of the falcon-headed sky god, Horus, whose sound eye was Re. For unknown reasons Thoth is identified with both the ibis and the baboon. He is regularly depicted as a human with the head of an ibis. Baboons often appear in temple reliefs worshiping the sun god, and this association might indicate his subordinate relationship to Re. In the judgment scene of chapter 125 of the *Book of Going Forth by Day,* Thoth as the ibis-headed god presides over and records the weighing of the heart of the deceased owner of the book. A baboon is also represented in this scene seated atop the balance, apparently to ensure its accuracy. Thoth is credited in Egyptian mythology with separating the two contenders, Horus and Seth, as well as with magically restoring Horus's

> **Secret rooms and mysterious books were sought by learned scribes, priests, and princes.**

injured eye. He has one of the major supporting roles in much of Egyptian religious literature, and a number of hymns are addressed to him directly, although Re and Osiris are the principal gods discussed and invoked in these texts.

Thoth was renowned for his wisdom and praised as the inventor of writing. The *mdw-ntr* ("god's words," i. e., hieroglyphs) were recognized as perhaps his greatest contribution, and he was frequently shown with brush and papyrus roll in the attitude of the scribes, whose patron he was.

In the eighteenth dynasty several kings took as their throne name *Thothmose* ("Thoth is the one who bore him"). This Thutmosid family included several other members with 'i`h ("moon") in their names, so it is clearly Thoth's position as moon god that is being recalled. Remains of two small temples to Thoth survive in the Theban area, one very late and poorly decorated. Since the eighteenth dynasty was of Theban origin and the son of Amun-Re at Thebes was the moon god, Khonsu, these two moon gods could have been assimilated, but the family could also have chosen the name of the northern god (Thoth) when they moved their residence (capital) to Memphis.

In Egyptian literature there clearly was an ancient tradition concerning the secret knowledge of Thoth. Secret rooms and mysterious books were sought by learned scribes, priests, and princes. This tradition was carried over into some of the Coptic gnostic library tractates, and the question arises whether these were Egyptian or Greek in origin since the Greeks had early identified their god Hermes with Thoth. The origins of the continuing traditions of Hermes Trismegistos and gnosticism can be traced to Egypt, to Thoth, and perhaps even to the Hermopolitan cosmology, but the extent of Egyptian influence on these beliefs remains to be determined.

The great temple of Thoth at Hermopolis has not survived, although its location is known from finds in the area. A large catacomb for the burial of mummified ibises and baboons has been found nearby at the necropolis of Tuna al-Gabal.

BIBLIOGRAPHY

Bleeker, C. Jouco. *Hathor and Thoth: Two Key Figures of the Ancient Egyptian Religion.* Leiden, 1973. Issued as a supplement by the periodical Numen.
Boylan, Patrick. *Thoth, the Hermes of Egypt.* New York, 1922.
Cerny, Jaroslav. "Thoth as Creator of Languages." *Journal of Egyptian Archaeology* 34 (1948): 121-122.

LEONARD H. LESKO

Tibetan Religions

To the Western mind, Tibet has traditionally appeared as a remote yet uniquely fascinating country. Profoundly Buddhist in all aspects of its social, cultural, and religious life, it was, until 1959, dominated by a monastic hierarchy. In the imagination of some, the so-called Land of Snow (as the Tibetans style their country) has also been regarded as the home of mysterious, superhuman beings, *mahatmas,* who, from their secret abodes in the Himalayas, give mystic guidance to the rest of humanity.

The Pre-Buddhist Religion. The picture of pre-Buddhist religion that emerges on the basis of the ancient sources is, unfortunately, fragmentary. Certain rituals, beliefs, and parts of myths may be discerned, but the overall feeling of coherency is lacking. The welfare of the country depended on the welfare of the king. Accordingly, rites of divination and

sacrifice were performed to protect his life, guarantee his victory in battle, and ensure his supremacy in all things. The king was regarded not only as a vitally important personage but above all as a sacred being. According to a frequently encountered myth, the first king of Tibet descended from heaven ("the sky").

A surviving early text outlines an eschatological cosmology that embodies a cyclical view of time. In a "golden age" plants and animals are transposed from their celestial home to the earth for the benefit of humanity. Virtue and "good religion" reign supreme.

Little is known of the pantheon of the pre-Buddhist religion. The universe was conceived of as having three levels: the world above (the sky), inhabited by gods *(lha);* the middle world (the earth), the abode of human beings; and the world below (the subterranean world, conceived of as aquatic), inhabited by a class of beings known as *klu* (and later assimilated to the Indian *nagas*).

It is difficult to establish which elements in the pre-Buddhist religion are truly indigenous. The later sources insist that many of the Bon-po priests came from countries bordering Tibet, in particular, areas to the west. Possible influences emanating from the Iranian world have also been the subject of speculation by Western scholars, so far without conclusive evidence. On the other hand, the importance of the Chinese influence, long ignored, has now been firmly established. The royal tombs have obvious Chinese prototypes, as does the sacredness of the king. It has been suggested that the pre-Buddhist religion was transformed into a coherent political ideology in the seventh century, modeled on the Chinese cult of the emperor.

Buddhism. Buddhism was established in Tibet under royal patronage in the eighth century. In the preceding century, Tibet had become a unified state and embarked upon a policy of military conquest resulting in the brief appearance of a powerful Central Asian empire. The introduction of Buddhism was certainly due to the need to provide this empire with a religion that enjoyed high prestige because of its well-established status in the mighty neighboring countries of India and China. The first Buddhist temple was built at Bsam-yas (Samyé) in approximately 779; soon afterward the first monks were ordained. From the very start, the Buddhist monks were given economic and social privileges.

Buddhism rapidly became the dominant religion, suffering only a temporary setback after the collapse of the royal dynasty in 842. In several important respects, Buddhism in Tibet remained faithful to its Indian prototype. It must, of course, be kept in mind that this prototype was, by the seventh and eighth centuries, a form of Mahayana Buddhism that was, on the one hand, increasingly dependent on large monastic institutions, and on the other, permeated by Tantric rites and ideas. Both these features—vast monasteries and a pervasive Tantric influence—have remained characteristic of Buddhism in Tibet. A uniquely Tibetan feature of monastic rule was succession by incarnation—the head of an order, or of a monastery, being regarded as the reincarnation (motivated by compassion for all beings) of his predecessor.

Popular Religion. While the study of the Mahayana philosophical systems and the performance of elaborate Tantric rites take place within the confines of the monasteries, monks actively participate in a wide range of ritual activities outside the monasteries, and beliefs that do not derive from Buddhism are shared by monks and laypeople alike.

Turning, first of all, to elements inspired by Buddhism, the most important—and conspicuous—are undoubtedly the varied and ceaseless efforts to accumulate merit. The law of moral causality *(karman)* easily turns into a sort of balance in which the effect of evil deeds in this life or in former lives may be annulled by multiplying wholesome deeds. Ritual circumambulation of holy places, objects, and persons is also distinctly Buddhist.

Pilgrimages constitute an important religious activity: above all to the holy city of Lhasa—sanctified by its ancient temples and (since the seventeenth century) the presence of the Dalai Lama—but also to innumerable monasteries, shrines, and caves in which relics of holy men and women may be seen, honored, and worshiped.

Ritual practices, while generally having an overall Buddhist conceptual framework, often contain elements that point back to the pre-Buddhist religion. As in other Buddhist countries, regional and local deities have remained objects of worship, generally performed by laypeople. In particular, the deities connected with (or even identified with) sacred mountains, powerful gods of the land *(yul lha),* are worshiped during seasonal festivals with the burning of juniper branches. These gods have a martial nature and are accordingly known as enemy gods *(dgra bla);* they are also known as kings *(rgyal po).* Usually they are depicted as mounted warriors, dressed in archaic mail and armor and wearing plumed helmets.

The person, too, possesses a number of tutelary deities residing in different parts of the body. Every person is also accompanied, from the moment of birth, by a "white" god and a "black" demon whose task it is, after death, to place the white and the black pebbles—representing the good and evil deeds one has done in this life—on the scales of the judge of the dead.

An important aspect of popular religion (and, indeed, of the pre-Buddhist religion) is the emphasis on knowing the origins not only of the world but of all features of the landscape, as well as of elements of culture and society that are important to man. Tibetans have a vast number of myths centering on this theme of origins.

Rites of divination and of healing in which deities "descend" into a male or female medium *(lha pa,* "god-possessed," or *dpa' bo,* "hero") and speak through it are an important part of religious life, and such mediums are frequently consulted. Other, simpler means of divination are also extremely widespread.

Tibetan Religion Today. An overview of Tibetan religion would be incomplete without an attempt to take stock of the situation in present. The most significant single fact is the downfall of monastic religion. Starting in the 1950s and culminating in the period of the Cultural Revolution in the 1960s and 1970s, the Chinese unleashed a violent antireligious campaign in Tibet that resulted in the total destruction of monastic life. At the height of the campaign, even the most insignificant expression of religious faith would be severely punished by Chinese soldiers or Red Guards.

The new and more pragmatic policy in China began to take effect in Tibet around 1980. A number of buildings, officially regarded as historical monuments, have been carefully restored; a limited number of monks have been installed in a number of the largest monasteries; and hundreds of other monasteries are being reconstructed on a voluntary basis by the Tibetans themselves. On the whole, religious activity seems to be tolerated as long as it does not interfere with economic policies.

BIBLIOGRAPHY

Tibetan religion is a field in which quasi-esoteric literature abounds. However, there are also many works of serious scholarship available to the general reader. The following survey lists titles that are easily available.

General Studies. A classic and still useful introduction to the subject is Charles A. Bell's *The Religion of Tibet* (1931; reprint, Oxford, 1968). More recently, several excellent studies have been published: David L. Snellgrove and Hugh E. Richardson's *A Cultural History of Tibet* (1968; reprint, Boulder, 1980); Rolf A. Stein's *Tibetan Civilization,* translated by J. E. Stapleton Driver (Stanford, Calif., 1972) and republished in a revised French edition as *La civilisation tibétaine* (Paris, 1981); and Giuseppe Tucci's *The Religions of Tibet,* translated by Geoffrey Samuel (Berkeley, 1980). Tucci's monumental *Tibetan Painted Scrolls,* 2 vols., translated by Virginia Vacca (1949; reprint, Kyoto, 1980), remains a work of fundamental importance to the field. In the 1980 edition, the plates accompanying volume 2 are reproduced in the form of slides. A particularly lucid exposition is Anne-Marie Blondeau's "Les religions du Tibet," in *Histoire des religions,* edited by Henri-Charles Puech, vol. 3 (Paris, 1976), pp. 233-329.

Pre-Buddhist Religion. Most studies of the pre-Buddhist religion can be found only in specialized publications. The works of Snellgrove and Richardson, Stein, and Blondeau, however, all contain pertinent discussions based on their own research. The most recent study of the early inscriptions is H. E. Richardson's *A Corpus of Early Tibetan Inscriptions* (London, 1985).

Buddhism. Snellgrove and Richardson's work is particularly strong on the formation of the orders and the subsequent political history of the church. Tucci's *The Religions of Tibet* contains a most useful survey of Buddhist doctrine and monastic life. A concise presentation of Tibetan Buddhism is provided in Per Kvaerne's "Tibet: The Rise and Fall of a Monastic Tradition," in *The World of Buddhism: Buddhist Monks and Nuns in Society and Culture,* edited by Heinz Bechert and Richard F. Gombrich (London, 1984), pp. 253-

270. For Tibetan art and symbols Tucci's *Tibetan Painted Scrolls* remains unsurpassed. A recent useful work by a Tibetan scholar is Loden S. Dagyab's *Tibetan Religious Art*, 2 vols. (Wiesbaden, 1977). For a discussion of ritual and meditation, see Stephan Beyer's *The Cult of Tara: Magic and Ritual in Tibet* (Berkeley, 1973).

Popular Religion. General surveys of Tibetan popular religion are given by Stein in *Tibetan Civilization* and in Per Kvaerne's "Croyances populaires et folklores au Tibet" in *Mythes et croyances du monde entier,* edited by André Akoun, vol. 4 (Paris, 1985), pp. 157-169. A basic reference work is René de Nebesky-Wojkowitz's *Oracles and Demons of Tibet. The Cult and Iconography of the Tibetan Protective Deities* (1956; reprint, Graz, 1975). The reprint edition contains an introduction by Per Kvaerne in which numerous corrections and additions to the earlier edition are provided. A useful supplement to this work is Tadeusz Skorupski's *Tibetan Amulets* (Bangkok, 1983). A major study of ritual texts has been published by Christina Klaus, *Schutz vor den Naturgefahren: Tibetische Ritualtexte aus dem Rin chen gter mdzod ediert, Übersetzt und Kommentiert* (Wiesbaden, 1985). A discussion of Tibetan myths intended for the nonspecialist is provided by Per Kvaerne in a series of articles in *Dictionnaire des mythologies,* edited by Yves Bonnefoy (Paris, 1981), vol. 1, pp. 42-45, 249-252; vol. 2, pp. 194-195, 381-384, 495-497. A survey of the most important pilgrimages is provided in Anne-Marie Blondeau's "Les pèlerinages tibetains," in *Les pèlerinages,* edited by Anne-Marie Esnoul et al. (Paris, 1960), pp. 199-245. The most complete study of Tibetan festivals is Martin Brauen's *Feste in Ladakh* (Graz, 1980).

There is a considerable body of literature on the Gesar epic. The fundamental study is R. A. Stein's *L'épopée et le barde au Tibet* (Paris, 1959). Several translations of the text exist, mainly in the form of summaries. The most easily accessible is probably that of Alexandra David-Neel, *La vie surhumaine de Guésar de Ling* (Paris, 1931), translated with the collaboration of Violet Sydney as *The Superhuman Life of Gesar of Ling* (1933; rev. ed., London, 1959). More scholarly translations are R. A. Stein's *L'épopée tibétaine de Gesar dans la version lamaïque de Ling* (Paris, 1956), and Mireille Helffer's *Les chants dans l'épopée tibétaine de Gesar d'après le levre de la course de cheval* (Geneva, 1977). On visionary journeys to Sambhala and related phenomena, see Edwin Bernbaum's *The Way to Shambhala: A Search for the Mythical Kingdom beyond the Himalayas* (New York, 1980).

Bon. An important translation of a Bon text is David L. Snellgrove's *The Nine Ways of Bon: Excerpts from the gZi-brjid* (1967; reprint, Boulder, 1980). Gamten G. Karmay surveys the Bon religion in "A General Introduction to the History and Doctrines of Bon," *Memoirs of the Research Department of the Toyo Bunko,* no. 3 (1975): 171-218. On Bon literature, see Per Kvaerne's "The Canon of the Bonpos," *Indo-Iranian Journal* 16 (1975): 18-56, 96-144. See also the works of Snellgrove and Richardson, Stein, and Blondeau cited above.

Contemporary Religion. By far the best treatment of the subject is Peter H. Lehmann and Jay Ullai's *Tibet: Das stille Drama auf dem Dach der Erde,* edited by Rolf Winter (Hamburg, 1981). The book is remarkable not least for its photographic documentation of contemporary Tibet.

PER KVAERNE

TIKOPIA RELIGION

TIKOPIA RELIGION was traditionally an indigenous small-scale system of belief and ritual characteristic of about one thousand people living on a remote postvolcanic island at 12°18' south latitude, 168°49' east longitude in the extreme east of the Solomon Islands. The Tikopia are expert fishermen on the coral reef and at sea. An important food source is flying fish, caught from canoes at night off the coast by torchlight and long-handled nets.

Social structure is markedly of patrilineal lineage type, each such group having a set of named house sites, with land rights in orchards and cultivations, controlled by the senior male and inherited primarily in the male line. These lineages are aggregated into four clans, each headed by a chief, with an order of ritual precedence: Kafika, Tafua, Taumako, and Fangarere.

Linguistically and culturally the Tikopia are Polynesian, having much in common especially with the peoples of Samoa, Tonga, and various "outlier" communities in the western Pacific. In religion, all Polynesians seem traditionally to have shared some major beliefs and practices that are also found in other Pacific religious systems.

In the wider Pacific field the Tikopia description and analysis are significant since they present a participant account of a range of basic religious themes: offering and prayer, communion between human and spiritual in various representational forms, sacralization of secular activity, symbolization of male and female spheres and roles, and relation of priesthood to social and political structure. An illustration of a cognitive approach to religion is also given in the description of the concept of mystical power (*mana*).

Tikopia Concepts and Ritual. Tikopia religion traditionally rested upon a belief that a set of spiritual beings (*atua*) controlled the fertility of nature and the health and prosperity of the people. These *atua* comprised the spirits of dead officeholders—chiefs and their attendant ritual elders—and a number of major gods. Significant in the Tikopia pantheon was the leading spiritual figure, Te Atua i Kafika, who was believed to have lived as a mortal man, a chief and a culture hero, responsible for many Tikopia traditional institutions.

The Tikopia religious system was not a democratic one in that no ordinary individual had access to any spirits except those of his or her immediate kin and ancestors. The official mediators with the world of gods and ancestors were socially determined. The heads of the major descent groups were the priests, and they communicated with the gods and ancestor spirits with prayer and offering on behalf of their people, as well as performing secular social roles as heads of lineages and prime administrators of group lands, canoes, and other property. As heads of principal lineages in the four clans, the chiefs were the outstanding priests. The Ariki

Kafika had prime responsibility for success of the yam crop, the Ariki Tafua for that of coco-nut, the Ariki Taumako for that of taro, and the Ariki Fangarere for breadfruit.

The basic Tikopia religious rite was the presentation of *kava* to the gods. As a drink, *kava* is an infusion of water with the macerated root of a kind of pepper plant *(Piper methysticum)* offered to the gods. To perform a *kava* rite a chief or elder assumed ritual purity by bathing, donned a special waistcloth and a leaf necklet as sign of formal religious dedication.

The Work of the Gods. A notable feature of Tikopia traditional religion was a collective set of seasonal rites that involved elaborate organization of manpower and assembly of large supplies of food devoted to religious ends. These seasonal cycles of ritual may be called the Work of the Gods, a figurative title sometimes applied to them by the Tikopia because of the way in which so much of the energy of the people during the ritual period was absorbed by these symbolic procedures.

The basic theme of the Work of the Gods was the periodic resacralization of some of the most important elements of Tikopia culture. Under religious auspices canoes and temples were repaired and rededicated to their practical functions, yams were harvested and planted, and a red pigment for ritual use was extracted from turmeric rhizomes and preserved. But not only technical and economic ends were given a religious cloak. The Work of the Gods also included a sternly moral public address, under conditions of great sanctity, instructing the people on proper behavior as members of Tikopia society. The period ended with ritual dancing in which formal mimetic displays and chanting of archaic songs were succeeded by freer performances by firelight at night, in which men and women could indulge in often ribald reference to sexual matters, although still in a highly controlled setting. This aspect of the festival, partly cathartic in nature, was thought to give the gods' tacit approval to human recreation.

The fundamental importance of the Work of the Gods in part was that it gave a religious dimension and legitimacy to the economic and social life of the Tikopia people. It reinforced the basic allocation of sex roles by representing certain tasks as both duties and privileges, validated by mythic example and protected by taboos. Women's tasks included plaiting mats, which work took place sometimes in surroundings from which men were barred; on the other hand, women were not allowed in the canoe yards, which were essentially associated with the work of men.

Modern Religion. The coming of Christianity to Tikopia brought about a radical change. In 1955, after losing ground for about thirty years, the traditional religion was totally abandoned in favor of the new faith, which had been promulgated by the Melanesian Mission (now absorbed into the Anglican province of Melanesia). The traditional chiefs are simply members of the church congregation, and they share with church leaders many day-to-day secular decisions. But the chiefs retain critical power in external affairs, and their devotion to the church has meant that the political and religious systems of Tikopia, although no longer so united as before, are still capable of harmonious accommodation.

BIBLIOGRAPHY

The main sources of information on Tikopia religion are my own works, derived from personal observation while the traditional religion was still being practiced, as long ago as 1928. The most general work is *Rank and Religion in Tikopia: A Study in Polynesian Paganism and Conversion to Christianity* (London, 1970), which examines Tikopia religious concepts and practices in relation to the structure of the society; it also describes the conversion of the people to Christianity. The most detailed account of religious ritual is *The Work of the Gods in Tikopia*, 2d ed. (London, 1967), while *History and Traditions of Tikopia* (Wellington, 1961) gives the major myths serving as charter for the religious system. Material on *Tikopia religious ideas, including the fate of the soul, is given in Tikopia Ritual and Belief* (London, 1967), and *Primitive Polynesian Economy*, 2d ed. (London, 1965) sets out the main features of the economic system, which was so closely integrated with the religion.

For comparative purposes many parallels to Tikopia religious phenomena can be seen in E. S. Craighill Handy's *Polynesian Religion* (Honolulu, 1927), which though old-fashioned in treatment is still a very useful general study. Our understanding of Polynesian religion relies so largely on accounts by early observers in the eighteenth and nineteenth centuries that works such as *Hawaiian Antiquities*, 2d ed. (Honolulu, 1951), the reminiscences of David Malo, and volume 2 of Douglas L. Oliver's massive synoptic study, *Ancient Tahitian Society* (Honolulu, 1974), are very important sources. Many ethnographic monographs on Polynesian communities have information of limited scope on traditional religion. But especially illuminating data have come from studies of Polynesian "outlier" communities of the western Pacific, such as Kenneth P. Emory's *Kapingamarangi* (Honolulu, 1965) and Torben Monberg's *The Religion of Bellona Island* (Copenhagen, 1966).

RAYMOND FIRTH

TILLICH, PAUL

TILLICH, PAUL (1886-1965), German-American theologian and philosopher. Paul Johannes Tillich became through his teaching and writings one of the leading religious thinkers of the twentieth century and contributed a distinctive theory of religion and religious symbolism. Born in Starzeddel, Germany (present-day Starosiedle, Poland), the son of a Lutheran pastor, he attended the universities of Berlin, Tübingen, Halle, and Breslau, earning a doctorate in philosophy at Breslau (1910) and a licentiate in theology at Halle (1912); from 1919 to 1933 he taught theology and philosophy at the universities of Berlin, Marburg, Dresden, Leipzig, and Frankfurt am Main. Removed from his position at Frankfurt by the Nazi government, he emigrated to the United States, where he taught at Union Theological Seminary in New York (1933-1955), Harvard University (1955-1962), and the University of Chicago (1962-1965).

The core of Tillich's theory of religion and religious symbols is to be found in his understanding of religion as "ultimate concern." This phrase, which Tillich adopted as the technical term for what in his early German writings had been designated by such phrases as *das, was uns unbedingt angeht* ("that which matters to us unconditionally") and *Richtung auf das Unbedingte* ("directedness toward the unconditioned"), was intended to have both subjective and objective connotations, referring to the state of being unconditionally concerned as well as to that about which one is so concerned; it was Tillich's understanding that religion necessarily involves both aspects.

Theory of Religion. Ultimate concern is a universal human possibility; in that sense every person is potentially religious. But Tillich did not conceive of this as a religious *a priori* in the Neo-Kantian sense, for it is not a special capacity or function alongside the theoretical and practical but a centered act of the whole self, which is, as he put it in

> The core of Tillich's theory of religion and religious symbols is to be found in his understanding of religion as "ultimate concern."

"Religion," his essay in *Man's Right to Knowledge* (New York, 1955), "the dimension of depth in all [life's] functions" (p. 80). It unites science and art in theoretical reason and, in practical reason, law and community. In his early writings, prior to about 1919, Tillich appears to have understood this unity in accord with the principle of identity contained in the thought of his philosophical mentor, Friedrich Schelling, that is, as a synthesis in which opposites (subject, object; cognition, art; law, community; concrete, universal) are fused. In his later writings, he interpreted this unity rather in terms of "correlation," that is, as a connection of two independent but related elements.

The dynamics of actual religion are determined in Tillich's thought by the interplay of the two sides of a correlation. For example, the certainty of the state of being unconditionally concerned plays against the doubt whether the object that elicits that concern is really unconditional. The two sides meet at a point that must be indicated by such paradoxes as the one Tillich uses in *Dynamics of Faith* (1957): the only ultimate truth is "the one that no one possesses" (p. 98). The point of identity does not normally appear in religion as a constitutive principle but only as a "guardian standpoint" to protect against idolatry. This standpoint is expressed by a

second-order symbol, depending for its effectiveness on other, primary symbols, in which the concrete and ultimate aspects partly contradict each other. However, in special circumstances the identity of unconditioned and conditioned can be provided in a first-order symbol as well. The term that Tillich applies to such a special time of identity is the Greek word *kairos*, which means "right time." This notion of time is opposed to sequential, chronometric time, as the English word *timing* suggests. Tillich made only one application of this concept to any historical moment other than to the founding of Christianity: namely to Germany after World War I. For this was a time, Tillich observed in a retrospective judgment, in which the decision for a political movement (religious socialism) was simultaneously a decision for a religious symbol (the kingdom of God). But this one application is echoed in the special role played by the symbol "kingdom of God" in Tillich's systematic theology: this is the one religious symbol that can be a religious symbol only if it has a real historical and political connection.

As ultimate, or unconditioned, religion tends toward the abstract; as concern, it tends toward the concrete. Tillich saw both the history of religions and the typology of religion in terms of this dual tendency. The history of a religion begins in an event of revelation, in which a person or group is grasped by an ultimate concern and, correlatively, something is established as a religious symbol (that is, as the objective side of the concern). The three phases of this event are the breakthrough *(Durchbruch)*, the conversion *(Umwendung)*, and the realization *(Realisierung)*. The concept of breaking through indicates that one cannot arbitrarily decide what is going to be of ultimate concern; instead, something breaks into one's consciousness and into one's world in such a way as to elicit a response to it *(Umwendung)*. What it is that has broken through is expressed in symbols and rites, that is, in those real things (or meanings) and practices that make the unconditional a perceptible part of the world *(Realisierung)*. The further history of a particular religion is shaped by the way in which every realization tends to become idolatrous (by making itself unconditional) and to provoke an inner protest and critique against itself as idolatrous. The element that preserves the holiness of the symbol or rite is the priestly or sacramental; the element that fights against the idolizing of it is the prophetic or Protestant. These two elements are constituents of every living religion. Neither of them has a superior rank, for it is essential to any living religion that there be both a concrete expression that presents the unconditional and also a protest against identifying the unconditional with its presentation. If the two elements lose their relation to each other, a living religion dies, by splitting into idolatry on the one side and secularism on the other.

Although the tension between the two elements is always present in any living religion, the two need not be equally emphasized. Hence, Tillich could derive a typology of religions from them. The type of religion in which the concrete predominates is polytheism, with its subtypes of universalistic, mythological, and dualistic; the type in which the universal predominates is monotheism, with its subtypes of monarchic, mystical, and exclusive; and the type in which the concrete and the ultimate are balanced is trinitarian monotheism. Philosophical systems, too, can be subsumed under these types, since every whole philosophical system is based on an implicit understanding of the meaning of the unconditional, on a mystical intuition of an ultimate concern. Thus, monistic naturalism, pluralistic naturalism, and metaphysical dualism are transformations of the polytheistic type of religion; gradualistic metaphysics, idealistic monism, and metaphysical realism, of the monotheistic type; and dialectical realism, of trinitarian monotheism.

That there are both direct (religious) and indirect (philosophical) expressions of ultimate concern provided the basis for Tillich's distinction between ecclesiastical theology and cultural theology. In the idea of a theology of culture Tillich blazed a trail on which many have followed. He opened the possibility of seeing in all of culture, and not only in the religious sphere, an awareness and expression of something unconditional. In his essay "Über die Idee einer Theologie der Kultur" (1919; English translation in *What Is Religion?*, 1969), he proposed that such a theology of culture would make it possible to understand a given period of history by reference to how religion is expressed in it. This proposal does not mean that cultural forms are to serve religious purposes; such forms are instead to be regarded as autonomous, following their own law of formation. But it does mean that even fully autonomous culture contains a definable understanding of what is of ultimate concern. A theological analysis of culture is assigned the task of elaborating that understanding by showing how the dimension of depth (the unconditional aspect) is made known in the way in which form and content appear in cultural works. In expressionistic paintings, for example, the ordinary shapes of things are distorted and their ordinary content becomes inessential as the power of the depth, or the ground and abyss of things, becomes perceptible in the painting.

Tillich himself did not produce a systematic theology of culture. But in essays published over the years, including *Die religiöse Lage der Gegenwart* (1926; translated by H. Richard Niebuhr as *The Religious Situation,* New York, 1932) and "The World Situation," in *The Christian Answer,* edited by Henry P. Van Dusen (New York, 1945), he offered analyses of several aspects of contemporary culture; and most of his work in the philosophy of religion was guided by this underlying conception. In one of its variations it serves as the basis for his magnum opus, the three-volume *Systematic Theology* (1951-1963), which belongs among the important presentations of Christian theology from all periods of history. Following a method of correlation, Tillich interprets religious

symbols by reference to the existential questions to which they provide answers. These questions are discovered by analyzing and interpreting the way in which human beings implicitly understand themselves in a given period or a given culture. Tillich called such a self-understanding the "situation." It is expressed in works of science, art, law, and morality, particularly through the style in which they are done; but these expressions must be interpreted in order to make explicit the question that is implicit in them concerning the meaning of being.

Human existence, Tillich said, is itself a question—that is, it has the structure of being open to something beyond it and complementary to it—but the way in which that question is formulated changes from time to time. To interpret how it is being asked in a given situation is the task of the analysis of culture. Over against the question there are the religious symbols of a tradition (in Tillich's case, the Christian tradition). They too must be interpreted in order to make explicit how they convey answers to the question that is being asked. Thus, to take one example, the imagery contained in the narrative of the creation of the world in the first chapters of *Genesis* is interpreted as a religious symbol that can answer the question implicit in human finitude when this imagery provides the courage to accept the human anxiety that accompanies being finite and insecure. As this example indicates, existential questions express an ultimate concern—a concern about being anyone or anything at all in spite of the possibility of not being; their power is felt in the mood of anxiety. Religious symbols are answers when they actually convey what is of ultimate concern—the possibility of being in spite of the threat of nonbeing; their power is felt in the mood of courage.

This theory of religion, which sees religion as a dimension of being in all the human functions, began to appear in Tillich's very early works and, when combined with critical phenomenology, resulted in the disciplined approach to religious phenomena—a *Religions-wissenschaft*—that was characteristic of Tillich. In principle, it involved the investigation of direct and indirect expressions of religion in any culture or religious tradition. But not until his later years did Tillich, prompted in part by a visit in 1960 to Japan, go beyond standard textbook examples from religions other than Christianity and Judaism in order to include some of the rich materials that, in the meantime, had become better known through studies in the history of religions. His last public address recorded the change; it was entitled "The Significance of the History of Religions for the Systematic Theologian" and was published in Tillich's *The Future of Religions* (New York, 1966).

Theory of Symbols. Tillich proposed a distinctive theory of religious symbolism, which met both wide acceptance and wide criticism during his lifetime. The theory can be defined by contrast with the Neo-Kantian theory of Ernst Cassirer on one side and with supranaturalist theories on the other. In contrast to Cassirer, Tillich maintained that religious symbolism was not one among several ways of construing one and the same reality (along with the symbol systems of art, language, and science) but was instead created by a response to a depth-reality that breaks into the whole. In contrast to supranaturalist theories, however, Tillich maintained that the different reality to which symbols refer cannot be made known in any way other than through symbols. One can indeed say that what such symbols refer to is the same as what is experienced in numinous encounters, such as those described and analyzed by Rudolf Otto in *The Idea of the Holy* and the same as what is asked about in existential questions concerning the meaning of being at all. But these latter are indirect ways of pointing out that to which religious symbols refer. A symbol is a symbol because it has the capacity to make directly perceptible, or to present, what it symbolizes.

This does not amount to saying that there are no criteria for judging religious symbols. But the criteria come from the nature of this symbolism instead of from something external to it. Among the criteria that Tillich cites in various places—he has no single, uniform list of them—one is whether a symbol is demonic. The concept of the demonic, which was one of his main contributions to the philosophy of religion and the philosophy of history, refers to a negative quality contained in the experience of the holy, or the experience of being grasped by something unconditional in meaning, value, and power. The unconditional can appear either as divine or as demonic. It is divine when the power of its creativity is united with the creation of new forms to receive it; it is demonic when the power of its creativity is united with the destruction of all forms.

Other criteria for evaluating symbols are those of subjective and objective adequacy. Symbols are subjectively adequate if they are capable of creating reply, action, and community. In these terms, all symbols have a limited tenure; they die out after the situation in which they arise has changed. Tillich cited as one example of a dead symbol that of the Virgin Mary within Protestant Christianity. An apparent exception to this limited tenure is provided by the idea of natural symbols (water, for example). Tillich apparently came upon this idea in his work with the Berneuchner group, which was concerned with questions of liturgical renewal; but it did not play a prominent role in his thinking otherwise. The objective adequacy of symbols involves the question of whether a symbol is really ultimate—that is, whether it does really represent what is a matter of being or not being at all. Objective adequacy can be judged in relative and in final terms. Relatively speaking, symbols that incorporate more dimensions of reality are more adequate than others. Thus, a human being, having self-consciousness, is objectively more adequate a symbol than a stone, which lacks even the

dimension of consciousness. But, finally, the only adequate (and true) symbol is one that expresses both the ultimate and its own lack of ultimacy; it affirms itself through its self-negation. Among the symbols of the Christian religion, it is the symbol of the cross that bears this final criterion; for what this symbol means, in wording that Tillich adapted from Schelling, is that Jesus sacrifices "himself as Jesus to himself as the Christ" (*Systematic Theology*, vol. 2) and that "the Christ is Jesus and the negation of Jesus" (*Biblical Religion and the Search for Ultimate Reality*, Chicago, 1955).

As a whole, Tillich's religious thought, like that of other original thinkers, does not fit into any standard classification. Tillich was not a positivist (but neither was he a rationalist); he was not a supranaturalist (but neither was he a naturalist). He was existentialist (but he was also essentialist); his thought was Protestant (but it was also Catholic). Many influences and strands were taken into his works, but none of them escaped transformation as he appropriated them.

BIBLIOGRAPHY

The most complete biography of Tillich is that of Wilhelm Pauck and Marion Pauck, *Paul Tillich: His Life and Thought*, vol. 1, *Life* (New York, 1976); the projected volume 2 was never published. A highly compact but excellent interpretive study of the unity of his life and thought is the pamphlet by Carl Heinz Ratschow, *Paul Tillich* (Iowa City, 1980). Of several autobiographical sketches, the most helpful one, first published in 1936, was published separately under the title *On the Boundary* (New York, 1966).

Tillich's collected works have been published in German in the *Gesammelte Werke*, 14 vols. (Stuttgart, 1959-1975), and in six supplementary volumes, *Ergänzungsbände* (Stuttgart, 1971-1982). Volume 14 contains an index and bibliography, including a list of unpublished manuscripts in the Tillich Archives at the Harvard Divinity School, Cambridge, Massachusetts, and the Paul-Tillich-Archiv at the University of Marburg, Germany. Among Tillich's major works are *Systematic Theology*, 3 vols. (Chicago, 1951-1963), *What Is Religion?* (New York, 1969), *The Protestant Era* (Chicago, 1948), *The Courage to Be* (New Haven, 1952), and *Dynamics of Faith* (New York, 1957), the last of which provides perhaps the best introduction to his thought.

A useful variety of critical and appreciative responses to Tillich's thought is contained in *The Theology of Paul Tillich*, 2d rev. ed., edited by Charles W. Kegley (New York, 1982), with three new essays and a recent bibliography. Responses to his theory of religious symbolism are contained in *Religious Experience and Truth: A Symposium*, edited by Sidney Hook (New York, 1961); included in the volume are two basic essays by Tillich. An excellent brief account of Tillich's religious socialism is John R. Stumme's introduction to the English translation of Tillich's *The Socialist Decision* (New York, 1977).

ROBERT P. SCHARLEMANN

TORAH

TORAH is a term that is used in many different ways. Of the etymologies suggested for the word, none has been proved, but most of them derive from the use of the word in the Hebrew scriptures. In *Genesis* and *Exodus* the plural of *torah*, *torot*, is usually coupled with other words, as in "mitsvotai huqqotai ve-torotai" ("my commandments, my laws, and my *torot*," *Gn.* 26:5), and "mitsvotai ve-torotai" (*Ex.* 16:28). Even when the word occurs in these books in the singular, it refers to specific commandments. In *Leviticus* and *Numbers* the word *torah* denotes specific groups of ceremonial rules for the priests; sometimes the word occurs when the rules are introduced, as in *Leviticus* 6:1 ("This is the torah of the burnt-offering") and *Numbers* 19:2 ("This is the law of the *torah*"), and sometimes it serves as a summary and conclusion, as in *Leviticus* 11:46-47 ("This is the torah of the beast and the bird . . . to distinguish between the ritually impure and the ritually pure"). In *Deuteronomy* the word *torah* is used with the emphatic he' ("the") as a general term including not only the laws and rules, but also the narrative, the speeches, and the blessings and the curses of the Pentateuch. All these are written in "this book of the torah" (Dt. 29:20, 30:10).

In the prophecies of Hosea, Amos, and Isaiah the word *torah* carries a broad meaning that includes cultic, ethical, and legal matters. The concept of *torah* in *Jeremiah* is likewise broad and all-inclusive, while in *Ezekiel* the use of the plural returns, referring to groupings of laws and rules (*Ez.* 44:24).

In the historical books one finds exhortations encouraging observance and study of the Torah, as in *1 Kings* 2:2-6, along with a clear allusion to the "book of the torah of Moses," in 2 Kings 14:6, citing *Deuteronomy* 24:16. In *Chronicles*, changes made by the kings in both the cult and the legal system are said to have been carried out "according to all that is written in the *torah* of God" (*1 Chr.* 16:40, 22:11-12; *2 Chr.* 14:3, 17:9).

In *Ezra* and *Nehemiah* a number of citations from the Torah appear together with exegetical activity of the scribes and the Levites (*Ezr.* 9:11; *Neh.* 8:14, 10:35). Of Ezra himself it is said that "he prepared his heart to expound the torah of God and to do and to teach among the people of Israel law and justice" (*Ezr.* 7:10), while the Levites "read from the book, from the *torah* of the Lord, clearly, and gave the sense, so the people understood the reading" (*Neh.* 8:8).

In private and communal prayers and in the psalms, the word *torah* exhibits a broad range of meanings in accordance with the various literary types and historical circumstances represented in them. In *Proverbs* the word torah is used as a parallel for the terms *musar* ("instruction," *Prv.* 1:8), mitsvah ("commandment," *Prv.* 3:1, 6:20), and *leqah tov* ("a good doc-

trine," *Prv.* 4:2), and thus it is also used to refer to the person who draws upon the wisdom found in international wisdom literatures. Nevertheless, the word still preserves the primary religious connotation that characterizes its use in the rest of the books of the Hebrew scriptures, by referring to the totality of the commandments of the covenant between God and his people.

Content of the Pentateuch. The collection of writings that we call "Torah" or "the Torah of Moses" comprises the first five books of the Bible (the Pentateuch) but in fact has been considered the one unified work, unlike the Prophets and the Hagiographa (or Writings), which together with it make up scripture. In content the Pentateuch is a continuous composition reporting history from the creation of the world

> The collection of writings that we call "Torah" or "the Torah of Moses" comprises the first five books of the Bible. . . .

until the death of Moses—when the people of Israel are arrayed in the plains of Moab—interspersed with groups of laws and rules. More precisely, in consideration of the central collection of several groups of laws and commandments that were given to the people of Israel, set in a framework of stories that explain the special status of the people before God.

As is usual in Hebrew, the books of the Pentateuch are referred to by the first significant word in each book. The first book, *Bere'shit* (in the beginning")—opens with a description of the creation of the world—whence the designation *Genesis*—and the genealogy of mankind and continues with the genealogy of Noah and his descendants after the great flood.

The second book, *Shemot* ("names"), contains the description of the events from the time of the bondage in Egypt until the revelations at Mount Siaai, where God establishes his special covenant with Israel, gives the Torah, and prescribes the tabernacle and the ceremony in which it is to be consecrated.

The third book, *Vayiqra'* ("and he called"), is known in tannaitic literature as *Torat Kohanim* ("*torah* of the priests") and in Greek as *Leuitikon*. It includes laws relating to worship in the Temple and the laws of sacrifices; special commandments of sanctity applicable to the priests and commandments of sanctity incumbent on the entire people of Israel; laws of ritual purity and impurity and of incest and other forbidden sexual relations; laws about the sanctity of particular times, festivals, and holidays; and laws about the sanctity of the Land of Israel, the Sabbatical year, and the Jubilee year.

The fourth book of the Pentateuch is usually called *Bemidbar* ("in the wilderness"), after the first significant word. It records the history of the people of Israel in the desert from the second year after they left Egypt until the death of Aaron.

The last of the five books of the Pentateuch is *Elleh ha-devarim* ("These are the words"). In a series of speeches before his death, Moses summarizes the history of the people, intermixing his account with ethical teachings, warnings, and reproof.

Literary and Historical Criticism. Comparison of Deuteronomy with parallels in the other books of the Pentateuch reveals numerous inconsistencies between both the narratives and the collections of laws as well as linguistic and stylistic differences. Modern biblical scholarship has attempted to uncover different sources upon which the five books of the Pentateuch are based.

A concerted effort to reconstruct the process that brought into being the books of the Torah as we have them was begun only in the middle of the eighteenth century. This effort resulted in the hypothesis that there are four sources or documents, given the designations J, E, P, and D. The distinction between J and E is based primarily on the different usages of the names of God (JHVH, or YHVH, and Elohim) and the names Jacob and Israel. Similar criteria were used to differentiate passages based on the priestly source, P, and the Deuteronomic source, D.

Besides the discernment and differentiation of these sources, there were also attempts to establish a chronology among them. A pioneer in this research, Wilhelm de Wette (1780-1849) proposed that *Deuteronomy,* which emphasizes the concentration of the cult in one place, reflects the situation that began to crystallize during the reign of Hezekiah, who concentrated the cult in Jerusalem (*2 Kgs.* 18:3-6), and that concluded in the time of Josiah, during whose reign Hilkiah discovered "the book" (*2 Kgs.* 22:8). This book, according to de Wette, was none other than the *Book of Deuteronomy,* which stands at the end of the development of the sources, as it is the only one in which there is any demand for the centralization of the cult.

Julius Wellhausen, in his studies during the second half of the nineteenth century, perfected and consolidated this type of historical criticism, according to which the Torah did not exist during the early part of the history of the people of Israel in their land, but rather reflects the historical circumstances of later generations. Objections to and criticism of this approach were voiced already in the time of Wellhausen, and they have increased in recent decades.

Even those who adopt the critical view, which sees the Pentateuch as a work compiled from different sources that reflect differing trends and styles, are nevertheless forced to admit its function and influence as a single, unified book. Every law and commandment in it is presented as the word of God to Moses, and taken together these laws form for Judaism an authoritative code whose authority infuses even the narrative sections with which they are intermixed. [*See also* Biblical Literature.]

Written Torah and Oral Torah. During the Hellenistic period, prior to the Hasmonean rebellion, the word *torah* had two distinct referents. On the one hand, it included not only the commandments but also the teachings of the prophets and the wisdom of the elders, while on the other hand, it meant the *torah* of Moses in its entirety. It would seem that for the Jews of Alexandria, torah was an institution that embodied the covenant between the nation and its Lord, reflecting a system of commandments, laws, customs, and traditions connected with the history of the people and the activities of their judges, kings, and prophets.

The term *oral torah* first appears in a story said to be from the time of Hillel and Shammai (fl. first century BCE-first century CE). In response to a prospective convert's question about how many *torot* exist, Shammai answered, "Two: the written *Torah* and the oral *torah*" (B. T., *Shab.* 31a).

`Aqiva' ben Yosef saw the oral *torah* as implicit in the written Torah, in its words and in its letters, whence it is recorded that he expounded: "'These are the laws and the rules and the *torot*' [Lv. 26:46]—from which we learn that two *torot* were given to Israel, one written and one oral. . . . 'On Mount Sinai by the hand of Moses' [ibid.]—from which we learn that *torah* was given complete with all its laws, details of interpretation, and explanations by the hand of Moses at Sinai" (*Sifra',* Behuqqotai 8, p. 112c). In light of this, one can understand the term "*torah* from heaven"; the statement of `Aqiva' was in response to those who said, "*torah* is not from heaven" (*Sifrei Dt.* 102, p. 161), meaning that they denied the revealed nature of the oral *torah.*

The third *Sibylline Oracle* (sec. 256), which dates from around 140 BCE, says that "Moses . . . [led] the people . . . to Mount Sinai, then God gave them the *torah* forth from heaven, writing all its ordinances on two tablets." For the school of `Aqiva' and in the Mishnah, though, *torah* does not refer solely to the Ten Commandments. Furthermore, the revelation included not only the Torah and its interpretations, but also the assertion of the authority of the interpretation.

According to the method developed by `Aqiva' and his school, the Torah scholar and exegete, by application of the principles used for the interpretation of the Torah and through his reasoning, can uncover within the Torah those same laws, details of interpretation, and explanations that were given together with it. In adopting this doctrine they follow Yehoshu`a ben Hananyah, teacher of `Aqiva', who refused to admit the continued intervention of divine forces in the determination of halakhic matters. This contrasts with the position of Eli`ezer ben Hyrcanus and others, who refused to discount the possibility of further revelations, whether in the form of a heavenly voice or through prophecy. According to the understanding of Yehoshu`a and his disciples, "Torah is not in the heavens, so we do not listen to heavenly voices" (B. T., *B. M.* 59b). Those who adopted this position even denied that earlier prophets could have established innovations on the basis of their gift of prophecy. Rather, the exposition and expansion of the Torah were severed from any and all dependence on supernatural forces.

Many of the meanings of the word *torah* developed from polemics against different approaches and conceptions. One of the last amoraim, Yehudah bar Shalom, explained the prohibition of writing oral *torah* thus: "When the Holy One, blessed be he, told Moses to 'write yourself [this book of the Torah],' Moses wanted to write down the Mishnah also, but since God saw that the nations of the world would eventually translate the Torah and read it in Greek and claim 'I am Israel,' and up to this point the scales of judgment are balanced, he told the nations: 'You say you are my children, but I recognize only he who possesses my mystery; they are my children.' And to what does this refer? To the Mishnah" (*Tan.* Vayeira' 5, Tisa' 34). Clearly this saying defines the preference of the oral *torah* as a response to the claims of Pauline Christianity that the church is the true inheritor of Israel because it is the son of the free woman, while Israel is of the flesh, at best the progeny of the maidservant (*Gal.* 3:26, 4:21; *Rom.* 2:28). Following Paul, the church fathers from Justin through Augustine claimed scripture was no longer the property and heritage of the Jews (Justin, *Apologia* 1.53; Augustine, *Against the Jews,* 4.8). The oral *torah* supposedly refutes such claims.

Contradictions between various sayings about the relationship between Torah and the books of the prophets can be explained if one views these statements in a polemical context. Levi in the name of Hanina' said: "The eleven psalms which Moses composed are set down in the books of the prophets. And why were they not included in the books of the law? Because the latter are words of torah and the former are words of prophecy" (*Midrash Tehillim* 90.4). According to this statement, even the words of prophecy by Moses himself are distinct from *torah*. In this saying and in others like it the revelation at Mount Sinai is restricted to a single, unique, all-inclusive event, thereby making impossible any additional revelation that could challenge the completeness of Torah. However, there were also sects that did not recognize the authority of the prophetic books at all.

Still, beyond all polemic, the books of the Prophets and Writings were sanctified as parts of the tripartite Torah (B. T., *Shab.* 88a; *Tan.* Yitro 10): the Pentateuch (Torah), Prophets (Nevi'im), and Writings (Ketuvim). Readings from the Prophets and some of the books of the Writings (*Esther, Lamentations,* and, according to some customs, the other three *megillot,* i. e., *Song of Songs, Ruth,* and *Ecclesiastes,* as well) are included in the synagogue service, preceded and followed by blessings. Nevertheless, the distinction between them and the Pentateuch is preserved, for the sanc-

tity of the rest of the books is not equal to that of the Torah scroll: it was forbidden to join together the Torah and prophetic books in a single scroll (*Sofrim* 3.1) or to lay a prophetic book on top of the Pentateuch (B. T., *Meg.* 27a).

The Ten Commandments. There are also differing understandings of the relationship between the Ten Commandments and the rest of the Torah. Philo saw the Ten Commandments as the principles and sources, while the rest of the commandments of the Torah are only specific details. Thus he organized the specific commandments, grouping them according to their roots—that is, according to their agreement with the Ten Commandments. Yet Hananyah, nephew of Yehoshu`a, and others following him asserted that "the details of the Torah were written in the intervals between the commandments of the decalogue" (J. T., *Sheq.* 6.1, 49d; *Sg. Rab.* 5, 14). Thus these sages were interested in deemphasizing the Ten Commandments and denying them any special status, in order to prevent people from claiming that they alone were given from Sinai and not the rest of the commandments (J. T., *Ber.* 1.8, 3c).

Concept of Torah among the Medieval Philosophers. Jewish philosophy in the Middle Ages in the lands under Muslim dominance stood before two challenges: philosophical justification of Torah as a religion of divine revelation and rejection of the Muslim claim that the revelation to Israel was superseded by the revelation to Muhammad. For Sa`adyah Gaon (882–942), who is considered the father of medieval Jewish philosophy, the divine revelation is identified with the content of reason. Reason can recognize both the speculative and the ethical content of revelation, which is nevertheless necessary to reveal truth in a universally accessible form, making it available to the common man, who is incapable of thinking for himself, and also to the philosopher, who is thereby presented *a priori* with the truth that he could oth-

> **Maimonides ascribed two purposes to *torah*: to order communal life and to enlighten the spirit of men by revealing to them the truth.**

erwise discover only through great effort. Still, it is a religious duty to come to truth also through the use of reason (Sa`adyah Gaon, *The Book of Beliefs and Opinions,* translated by S. Rosenblatt, New Haven, 1961). Out of this conception Sa`adyah developed the distinction between the commandments of reason, which revelation simply repeats, and the traditional commandments, which are known only through revelation. The latter category includes the sacrificial and ceremonial orders of the Torah (ibid., treatise 3, sections 1-3). Sa`adyah applied this conception in composing a liturgical poem in which he attempted to fit all 613 of the commandments into the framework of the Ten Commandments (*Azharot* in *Siddur Rav Sa`adyah Ga'on*, 1941, pp. 185ff.), which as in Philo can be considered general principles. This undertaking also answers those who claim that numerous divine revelations are possible: there was no such multiplicity of revelation to Israel, and the divine will is certainly not prone to change or to cancel the content of the true revelation (*The Book of Beliefs and Opinions*, treatise 3, sec. 7).

Maimonides (1135/8-1204) ascribed two purposes to *torah*: to order communal life and to enlighten the spirit of men by revealing to them the truth. The political laws, ethical commandments, and ceremonial and sacrificial laws of the Torah are all means toward the attainment of these two goals. All the laws that serve to educate the people ethically work toward the achievement of the first goal, while all the laws that strengthen certain specific beliefs advance the second goal. Maimonides attempted to demonstrate this point by developing an elaborate system of explanations of reasons for the commandments, some of them rationalistic and some historical, presenting certain commandments and prohibitions as protection against polytheistic ideas and customs of worship (Maimonides, *Guide of the Perplexed* 3.29-3.44). With great consistency Maimonides stressed in all of his works the uniqueness of the revelation of the Torah of Moses. For him the role of the prophets was not to create a religion: "As for the prophets from among us who came after Moses our master, you know the text of all their stories and the fact that their function was that of preachers who called upon the people to obey the Torah of Moses. . . . We likewise believe that things will always be this way, as it says, 'It is not in heaven'" (ibid. 2.39; translation by Shlomo Pines, Chicago, 1963).

View of the Qabbalists. Qabbalistic literature, which is mostly made up of commentaries on the Torah, emphasizes the absolute virtues of the Torah over the rest of the books of the Bible. The conceptions of the qabbalists about the Torah are in part a radical development of ideas found in *midrashim* of the sages and in part bold innovation. A saying ascribed to the amora El`azar, which appears in *Midrash Tehillim* 3.2, explains a verse in *Job* (28:13) as follows: "The sections of the Torah were not given in order, for had they been given in order, anyone reading them would be able to resurrect the dead and to perform wonders. Therefore the order of the Torah was hidden, but it is revealed before the Holy One, blessed be he, as it says, 'And who is like unto me? Let him read and declare it and set it in order for me [*Is.* 44:7].'" The author of this saying hints at the possibility of use of the Torah for magic, but he rejects that possibility. Nevertheless, such magical use was described in the work *Shimushei Torah*, which apparently dates from the geonic period.

Nahmanides (Mosheh ben Nahman, c. 1194-1270) mentions reading the Torah "in the manner of the names," which was transmitted to Moses verbally, "for we possess a true tradition that the entire Torah is made up of the names of the Holy One, blessed be he" (Introduction to Nahmanides' commentary on the Torah). Similarly, the *Zohar* (Yitro 87.1) says, "The entire Torah is the holy name, for there is not a word in the Torah which is not included in the holy name." Based on this idea, Me'ir ibn Gabbai wrote in the beginning of the fourteenth century that Torah is called "the Torah of God" because it is in fact the name of God. This supposition relates to the preexistent reality of the Torah, in which it was used to create the world. The fact that the Torah is thought to have been made up by the interweaving of divine names implies that the Torah has multiple meanings. The different kinds of interpretations were summed up in the *Zohar* in the acronym *PaRDeS*, standing for *peshat*, *remez*, *derash*, and *sod*. *Peshat* includes the understanding of scripture evinced in the oral *torah*; *remez* includes allegory and philosophy; *derash* is the homiletic approach; while *sod* is made up of the qabbalistic explanations. In the qabbalistic exegesis, precisely those verses and words that seem unimportant are raised to the level of profound symbols.

The qabbalists propounded a distinction between the *torah* of the names of the messiah and the revealed Torah. In so doing they diverged from the saying of Yohanan that "the books of the Prophets and the Writings will in the future be canceled, but the Pentateuch will not be canceled in the future" (J. T., *Meg.* 3.7, 70d) as well as from the *midrashim* in which one may uncover hints of the possibility of changes, like: "The *torah* that a man learns in this world is empty in comparison with the *torah* of the Messiah" (*Eccl. Rab.* 11.8) or " '*Torah* will go out from me' (*Is.* 51:4)—a renewal of the Torah will go out from me" (*Lv. Rab.* 13.3). In these *midrashim* the innovative nature of the Torah is not specified, but the qabbalists explained the nature of the change in the light of their conceptions: the Torah will be understood in accordance with its spirituality, and its letters will join together to form a different reading.

Qabbalistic literature of the thirteenth century explained that in the dictum of Shim`on ben Laqish, "the Torah which the Holy One, blessed be he, gave to Moses was white fire engraved on black fire" (J. T., *Sheq.* 6.1); "white fire" refers to the Torah itself, while "black fire" refers to the oral *torah*. Thus the written Torah is hidden in the white parchment, but in the future the blank spaces in the Torah will reveal their letters.

The Hasidim of the eighteenth century essentially adopted the qabbalistic understanding that the elevated religious value of the Torah is found in its inner essence rather than in its exoteric manifestation. The simple meaning of the Torah is a symbolic expression of divine truths. In keeping with the individualistic tendency within Hasidism, achieving understanding of the secrets of Torah was considered to depend on the mending of the individual's specific personal soul and on his attempts to cleave to God in every aspect of his being.

An opponent of Hasidism, Eliyyahu ben Shelomoh Zalman (1720-1797), known as the Vilna Gaon, emphasized the all-encompassing, eternal nature of Torah. Everything that ever was, is, or will be existent is included in the Torah. The specific details of every person, animal, plant, and inanimate object are included in the Torah from the word *bere'shit* until the phrase *le-`einei kol Yisra'el* (the words that close *Deuteronomy*). He studied qabbalistic literature in the same way in which he studied the books of the Bible and halakhic works. Rather than expecting personal revelations as a result of occupying himself with Qabbalah, he anticipated that his devotion and absolute dedication to Torah study would aid him in understanding the Qabbalah.

Talmud Torah ("Torah Study"). Alongside the demand that one must uphold the commandments written in the Torah, there is also in the Torah an explicit requirement to study, learn, and teach it (*Dt.* 6:6-7, 11:18-20; see also *Jos.* 1:8). This commandment from the start related to every part of the Torah. During the time of the First Temple, the priests were the main group encharged with teaching the Torah (*Jeremiah* 2:8 mentions together with them "those who handle the Torah"). In the time of the Second Temple, the *sofrim* ("scribes") were the teachers and explicators of *torah*, while

> The content of the studies, their breadth, and the method of study varied in different times and places.

the authority for halakhic instruction and legal determination was invested in the Great Court. The legislation and decrees, reports of the acts of the courts, and explanations of the words of the Torah all become part of the oral *torah,* and the commandment of *talmud Torah* was considered to apply also to them.

The desire to know how to fulfill accurately the commandments of the Torah is only one of the justifications for *talmud Torah.* Also significant is the desire to gain understanding of the Torah, its intentions, and the way in which it develops and expands. The requirement to study torah is incumbent on every man, whatever his situation. The Babylonian amora Rav, describing God's daily schedule, declared that during the first three hours of the day he "sits and engages in *torah* study" (B. T., `*A. Z.* 3b).

The content of the studies, their breadth, and the method of study varied in different times and places. There were times when the study of the rest of the biblical books was not included together with the study of the Torah itself. Some students concentrated only on the study of *halakhah,* while others preferred the *aggadah.* There were those who included the study of philosophy and Qabbalah, while some stressed

attention to *musar* ("ethical teachings"). Within the study of *hala-khah* itself there were various methods of study: some emphasized casuistry and sharp-wittedness, while others stressed the importance of broad knowledge of the sources and drawing conclusions for practical application. Still, everyone recognized that the requirement to study *torah* is incumbent on the entire community in some form or another. Thus public homilies in the synagogues on Sabbaths and holidays were instituted.

Reading the Torah in the Synagogue. Today the reading of the Torah occupies a central role in communal prayer. Public reading of the Torah is mentioned three times in the Bible, but always on special occasions. The first mention is in *Deuteronomy* 3:10-13: Moses commanded the reading of "this Torah before all Israel" in the Sabbatical year during the festival of Sukkot (Tabernacles). In the opinion of tannaim (*Sot* 3.8, *Sifrei Dt.* 160), the king was commanded to read *Deuteronomy* with certain abridgments during this ceremony. Another reading is mentioned in *2 Kings* (23:1-2), where King Josiah is said to have "read in their ears all the words of the book of the covenant which was found in the house of God." It seems reasonable to assume that this account served as a source for the aforementioned tannaitic description.

Nehemiah (8:1-8) tells how Ezra the scribe brought the scroll of the Torah before the congregation on the first day of the seventh month and read from it "in the ears of the entire people clearly, and he gave the sense." In this reading the people found "written in the Torah which God commanded by the hand of Moses that the people of Israel sat in tabernacles during the festival of the seventh month" (8:4). When they then celebrated this festival of Sukkot, they again read "in the book of the Torah of the Lord every day, from the first day until the last day" (8:18). This account can be viewed as the start of the custom of reading the Torah publicly on festivals.

Reading the Torah on the Sabbath is mentioned by Philo (*Moses* 2.216; see Eusebius's *Praeparatio evangelica* 8.2) and Josephus (*Against Apion* 2.175) and in the *Acts of the Apostles* (15:21) as an ancient custom. In the description of the ceremonial rite of Yom Kippur, the Mishnah (*Yoma'* 3.1) reports that the high priest read sections of the Torah appropriate to the day (*Lv.* 16:1-34, 23:26-32; *Nm.* 29:7-11). In addition to the readings on Sabbaths, festivals, and the holidays mentioned in the Torah, the Mishnah also fixes public readings for Hanukkah, Purim, New Moons, public fast days, Mondays and Thursdays (which were market days), and during the afternoon service on the Sabbath (*Meg.* 3.6, 4.1) as well as during *ma`amadot,* assemblies of the watches that gathered in the Temple and in their towns to pray and read from the Torah while the priests and Levites from their region performed the rites in the Temple (*Ta`an.* 3.4).

The Mishnah specifies only the portions to be read on festivals, on the four special Sabbaths between the beginning of the month of Adar and Passover, on public fast days, and during *maamadot* (*Meg.* 3.5-6). The Mishnah also fixes the number of people who go up to read from the Torah on each occasion. On Mondays, Thursdays, and Sabbath afternoons, three people read; on New Moons and the intermediate days of the festivals, four; on holidays, five; on Yom Kippur, six; and on the Sabbath, seven (*Meg.* 4.1-2). The first two people to go up to read are a *kohen* (one of priestly descent) and a Levite (*Git.* 8.8), if such are present. In Mishnaic times, the first person to go up pronounced the blessing before reading the Torah and the last person recited the afterblessing, while everyone who went up in between read without making a blessing (*Meg.* 4.1). Subsequently the custom was changed so that each reader recited a blessing before and after reading (B. T., *Meg.* 21b).

The Mishnah mentions the custom of translating each verse into the language spoken by the people—that is, Aramaic—at the same time as it was read in Hebrew (*Meg.* 4.4). This custom is apparently very ancient, perhaps as old as the custom of public Torah reading itself. In places where the vernacular was Greek, it was customary to begin and end the reading in Hebrew but to read the intermediate portions in Greek so that the congregation could understand the portion (Tosefta, *Meg.* 3.13).

The public Torah reading was supplemented with a reading from the prophetic books. This reading from the Prophets is called the *haftarah*. Generally the portion chosen to be read as the *haftarah* parallels in some way the content of the *seder* or *parashah* read from the Torah on the same occasion.

BIBLIOGRAPHY

Content and Historical-Critical Research

Childs, Brevard S. *Introduction to the Old Testament as Scripture.* Philadelphia, 1980.
Hahn, Herbert F. *The Old Testament in Modern Research.* 2d expanded ed. Philadelphia, 1966.
Kraus, Hans-Joachim. *Geschichte der historisch-kritischen Erforschung des Altern Testaments von der Reformation bis zur Gegenwart.* Neukirchen, 1956.
Leiman, Sid Z. *The Canonization of Hebrew Scripture: The Talmudic and Midrashic Evidence.* Hamden, Conn., 1976.
Rendtorff, Rolf. *Das überlieferunggeschictliche Problem des Pentateuch.* Berlin, 1977.
Sanders, James A. *Torah and Canon.* Philadelphia, 1972.
Segal, M. H. *The Pentateuch: Its Composition and Its Authorship.* Jerusalem, 1967.
Sellin, Ernst. *Introduction to the Old Testament.* Translated by David E. Green; revised and rewritten by Georg Fohrer. Nashville, 1968.
Weinfeld, Moshe. *Deuteronomy and the Deuteronomic School.* Oxford, 1972.

The Concept of Torah in Later Judaism

Davies, W. D. *Torah in the Messianic and/or the Age to Come.* Philadelphia, 1952.
Heschel, Abraham. *Torah min ha-shamayim ba-aspaqelaryah shel ha-dorot.* London, 1965.
Scholem, Gershom. "The Meaning of the Torah in Jewish Mysticism." In his *On the Kabbalah and Its Symbolism,* translated by Ralph Mannheim, pp. 32-86. New York, 1965.
Urbach, E. E. *The Sages: Their Concepts and Beliefs.* 2 vols. Translated from the second expanded Hebrew edition by Israel Abrahams. Jerusalem, 1979. See the index, s. v. *Torah.*

Torah in Service and Ritual

Elbogen, Ismar. *Der jüdische Gottesdienst in seiner geschichtlichen Entwicklung* (1924). Hildesheim, 1962.
Gutmann, Joseph. *Jewish Ceremonial Art.* New York, 1964.
Kanof, Abram. *Jewish Ceremonial Art and Religious Observance.* New York, 1971.

E. E. URBACH
Translated from Hebrew by Akiva Garber

TRICKSTERS

Introduction

Trickster is the name given to a type of mythic figure distinguished by his skill at trickery and deceit as well as by his prodigious biological drives and exaggerated bodily parts. The myths of many cultures portray such a comic and amoral character, who is sometimes human but is more often animal in shape, typically an animal noted for agility and cunning: the wily coyote, the sly fox, the elusive rabbit, or the crafty spider. Sometimes the trickster is the agent who introduces fire, agriculture, tools, or even death to the human world. As such, he plays the part of another mythic archetype, the transformer, or culture hero, who in a mythic age at the beginning of the world helps shape human culture into its familiar form. However, the trickster's distinction lies not so much in his particular feats as in the peculiar quality of his exploits—a combination of guile and stupidity—and in the ludicrous dimensions of his bodily parts and biological drives. In those cultures where he stands independent of other mythic figures, his adventures are recounted in a separate cycle of myths and lore. The trickster represents a complicated combination of three modes of sacrality: the divine, the animal, and the human.

BIBLIOGRAPHY

The best overview of general interpretations of the trickster is chapter 1 of Robert D. Pelton's *The Trickster in West Africa: A Study of Mythic Irony and Sacred Delight* (Berkeley, 1980). For psychological interpretations that now appear overdependent on developmental models without consideration of religious depth, see three essays in Paul Radin's *The Trickster: A Study in American Indian Mythology* (1956; reprint, New York, 1969): C. G. Jung's "On the Psychology of the Trickster Figure," Karl Kerényi's "The Trickster in Relation to Greek Mythology," and Radin's title piece. For an overview that makes healthier use of the social context of the trickster in interpreting its meaning, see Laura Makarius's 'Le mythe du 'Trickster,' " *Revue de l'histoire des religions* 175 (1969): 17-46. For an attempt to place the figure within the history of ideas, see Ugo Bianchi's "Pour l'histoire du dualisme: Un Coyote africain, le renard pâle," in *Liber Amicorum: Studies in Honor of Professor Dr. C. J. Bleeker* (Leiden, 1969), pp. 27-43. Angelo Brelich has done admirably by examining the uniqueness of the trickster vis-à-vis other mythical figures in "Il Trickster," *Studi e materiali di storia delle religioni* 29 (1958): 129-137. I have pointed to the kind of close reading of trickster texts necessary to disclose their full religious value in "Multiple Levels of Religious Meaning in Culture: A New Look at Winnebago Sacred Texts," *Canadian Journal of Native Studies* 2 (December 1982): 221-247. I have also drawn out the comic aspects of incarnate saviors and loutish literary figures in "The Irony of Incarnation: The Comedy of *Kenosis*," Journal of Religion 62 (October 1982): 412-417.

LAWRENCE E. SULLIVAN

African Tricksters

Like their counterparts in Amerindian myth and folklore, African tricksters inject bawdiness, rebellion, and wild lying (one might aptly call it polymorphous perversity) into the mythic history and the common experience of divine-human relations wherever they appear. Unlike many tricksters elsewhere, however, these multiform world-shatterers and pathfinders in Africa are woven not only into the fabric of myth but also into the stuff of everyday life, playing a part in economics, rites of passage, and ordinary conversation.

African trickster figures are images of an ironic imagination that yokes together bodiliness and transcendence, society and individuality. The trickster in Africa shows by his witty juggling with meaning and absurdity that he is more accurately understood as a spectrum of commentaries on mythic commentary than as a "category." This epistemological playfulness seems to represent a sophisticated African form of religious thought. It is perhaps a commonplace to insist that in every system the order of the center and the wildness of the periphery are linked. It is a bold piece of spiritual logic to make this insistence a joke—or even more, a joking relationship.

The link between divination and the trickster represents a still deeper level of meaning that West Africans especially have found in him. The Yoruba, like the Fon (who have adopted much of the Yoruba system of divination, known as Ifa) and the Dogon, see their trickster god as the chief possessor of divination's language. Esu is a disruptive mediator, "the anger of the gods," who stirs up trouble to increase sacrifice, yet his quickness of eye and hand symbolizes a metaphysical slipperiness that makes him both sociotherapist and iconographer. At moments of conflict the meetings that create a world become collisions. Lines of connection break down, intersections turn into dead ends, and, as the myths say, all becomes as fluid as water, as destructive as fire.

Divination seeks to transform these dead ends into thresholds of larger meaning; Yoruba divination particularly knows that to give answers to knotted social and spiritual questions is, finally, to redraw an *imago mundi,* to restore the shattered icon of the Yoruba cosmos. Esu is not the source of most divinatory responses, but he enables divination to run its course.

[*See also* African Religions.]

BIBLIOGRAPHY

T. O. Beidelman has made an intensive study of trickster figures and their social meanings in the oral literature of the Kaguru. His important interpretive essay, which argues for a moral rather than an epistemological interpretation of the trickster, is "The Moral Imagination of the Kaguru: Some Thoughts on Tricksters, Translation and Comparative Analysis," *American Ethnologist* 7 (1980): 27-42. It includes a bibliography of his more than twenty-five articles on the Kaguru: collections and translations of tales, analyses of their significance, and other commentaries on Kaguru society. See also Beidelman's "Ambiguous Animals: Two Theriomorphic Metaphors in Kaguru Folklore," *Africa* 45 (1975): 183-200.

Other major collections of trickster stories are E. E. Evans-Pritchard's *The Zande Trickster* (Oxford, 1967), R. S. Rattray's *Akan-Ashanti Folk-Tales* (Oxford, 1930), Charles van Dyck's "An Analytic Study of the Folktales of Selected Peoples of West Africa" (Ph. D. diss., University of Oxford, 1967), and Melville J. Herskovits and Frances S. Herskovits's *Dahomean Narrative: A Cross-Cultural Analysis* (Evanston, 1958). Tales, divination verses, and analyses of Esu-Elegba can be found in 'Wande Abimbola's *Ifa Divination Poetry* (New York, 1977); William Bascom's *Ifa Divination: Communication between Gods and Men in West Africa* (Bloomington, Ind., 1969); John Pemberton's "Eshu-Elegba: The Yoruba Trickster God," *African Arts* 9 (1975): 20-27, 66-70, 90-91, and "A Cluster of Sacred Symbols: Orisa Worship among the Igbomina Yoruba of Ila-Orangun," *History of Religions* 17 (1977): 1-28; and Joan Wescott's "The Sculpture and Myths of Eshu-Elegba, the Yoruba Trickster," *Africa* 32 (1962): 336-354. The major work on Dogon myth and life is that of Marcel Griaule and Germaine Dieterlen: *Le renard pâle,* vol. 1, *Le mythe cosmogonique,* pt. 1, "La création du monde" (Paris, 1965).

For a study of four West African trickster figures in their social and mythic settings, see my book *The Trickster in West Africa: A Study of Mythic Irony and Sacred Delight* (Berkeley, 1980), which concludes with a discussion of the theory of the trickster. For a comparative study of African and North American tricksters and an analysis of the trickster's role among the Azande, see Brian V. Street's "The Trickster Theme: Winnebago and Azande," in *Zande Themes,* edited by Andre Singer and Brian V. Street (Oxford, 1972), pp. 82-104. In addition to Beidelman's bibliography and the one in my book, see also that of Martha Warren Beckwith in her *Jamaica Anansi Stories* (1924; reprint, New York, 1969).

ROBERT D. PELTON

North American Tricksters

The most prominent and popular personage, generally speaking, in the varied oral traditions of the numerous

Amerindian peoples living north of the Rio Grande is the figure known as the trickster. With rare exceptions, North American tricksters are beings of the mythic age only; they are not believed to be living gods or spirits, and they have no cult (other than the semiritualistic narration of their stories). Their relationship to shamanism, the definitive religious form in most of the region, is debated. Tricksters' activities in myths often resemble shamans' journeys to the spirit world, but tricksters ordinarily employ no "helpers," and shamans do not seek help from "trickster spirits."

The concept of the trickster as a type is based upon his most essential trait: his trickiness. Tricksters everywhere are

> **Tricksters everywhere are deceitful, cunning, amoral, sexually hyperactive, taboo-breaking, voracious, thieving, adventurous, vainglorious. . . .**

deceitful, cunning, amoral, sexually hyperactive, taboo-breaking, voracious, thieving, adventurous, vainglorious—yet not truly evil or malicious—and always amusing and undaunted. Even though his activities are usually motivated by ungoverned desire, the trickster is capable of performing deeds that benefit others: releasing imprisoned game, the sun, the tides, and such; vanquishing and/or transforming evil monsters; and, like the shaman, journeying to the land of the spirits or the dead to rescue a lost loved one. The significant element in all these deeds is trickery. Moreover, as a being of insatiable appetites (for food and sex), he cannot afford the luxury of scruples. Thus he breaks incest taboos (rapes or marries in disguise his daughter or mother-in-law) and hoodwinks small animals into dancing with eyes closed so he can kill them. Nothing is sacred in his eyes.

In addition to humorous trickster folk tales, which are remarkably similar all over North America, each region has its own set of traditions about the mythic age, and in a majority of instances the leading personage of that time was a trickster.

In the Plateau region of the northwestern United States, Coyote is usually regarded as the maker or procreator of the people, sometimes using the body of a river monster he kills, sometimes by cohabitation with trees after a flood. His principal cycle concerns his release of the salmon and his subsequent journey up the Columbia River, leading the salmon. He demands a "wife" at each village, and if his request is granted, he makes that place a good fishing spot.

In California and the Great Basin region, Coyote usually is involved in a dualistic relationship with a wise, benevolent creator (Eagle, Fox, Wolf, or an anthropomorphic figure). Set against the backdrop of a world flood (or fire), the earth is

remade and repopulated by the two, with Coyote ordaining the "bad" things such as mountains, storms, and fruit growing out of reach. Coyote decrees death—and then his son is the first to die. So Coyote establishes mourning rites for people to "enjoy." He also decrees conception by sex and painful childbirth.

The Paiute and Shoshoni of the Great Basin consider Coyote the progenitor of the people (through intercourse with a mysterious woman following the flood). But among the Pueblo, whose mythology centers on an emergence from the underground, Coyote plays a rather minor role in most tribes. On the Great Plains, Coyote is known primarily as a trickster only. Some northern tribes credit him with the recreation of the earth after the deluge, and the Kiowa consider themselves the people of Sendah, a Coyote-like figure, who led them out of a hollow log in the beginning. The Oglala are one of the few groups in North America who consider the trickster genuinely evil, and almost the only tribe that believes the trickster to be a living spirit.

The Algonquins, inhabiting a large part of eastern and midwestern Canada, New England, and the area around the three western Great Lakes, have mythologies centered on anthropomorphic culture heroes who were also tricksters, though seldom foolish, plus several minor theriomorphic tricksters.

In some tribes humorous trickster tales are relegated to a category apart from the more serious "myths," but because all these narratives are set in "myth times," they are never confused with quasi-historical legends or accounts of shamanic experiences. Thus, to some degree, a quality of sacredness adheres to the person of the trickster everywhere, despite the seemingly profane nature of many of the narratives.

[*See also* North American Religions.]

BIBLIOGRAPHY

The term *trickster* was coined by Daniel G. Brinton in his *Myths of the New World* (Philadelphia, 1868). The only serious study of the American trickster to have been published in book form remains Paul Radin's *The Trickster* (1956; reprint, New York, 1969), which contains important essays by C. G. Jung and Karl Kerényi. It is not, however, a general study of tricksters in North America, but is mainly about those of the Winnebago tribe. My article "The North American Indian Trickster," *History of Religions* 5 (Winter, 1966): 327-350, is based on an earlier work, "The Structure and Religious Significance of the Trickster-Transformer-Culture Hero in the Mythology of the North American Indians" (Ph. D. diss., University of Chicago, 1965), which is a study of the entire continent north of the Rio Grande. Edward H. Piper sees the trickster as basically a child figure in his psychological analysis, "A Dialogical Study of the North American Trickster Figure and the Phenomenon of Play" (Ph. D. diss., University of Chicago, 1975). Laura Makarius has written several articles on tricksters from various parts of the world, viewing the trickster as a taboo-breaking magician; on the North American trickster, see her study "The Crime of Manabozo," *American Anthropologist* 75 (1973): 663-

675. Barbara Babcock-Abrahams has published an interesting anthropological study, "'A Tolerated Margin of Mess': The Trickster and His Tales Reconsidered," *Journal of the American Folklore Institute* 2 (1975): 147-186. A recent popular collection of trickster stories, without significant interpretation, is by Barry Holstun Lopez: *Giving Birth to Thunder, Sleeping with His Daughter: Coyote Builds North America* (Kansas City, 1977). See also the February 1979 issue of *Parabola* (4, no. 1), which is devoted to the trickster. For the texts of the stories, one must resort to the hundreds of volumes of reports of pioneer American anthropologists published by the Bureau of American Ethnology, the American Folklore Society, and other organizations.

MAC LINSCOTT RICKETTS

Mesoamerican and South American Tricksters

The peoples of Mesoamerica and South America maintain lively traditions concerning a cunning and deceitful mythic figure, the trickster. Although tricksters are ludicrous rather than solemn beings, they cannot be discounted as trivial because their activities and transformations touch on religious issues. For instance, they steal fire, which is deemed the center of social and physical life, and their clever bungling frequently introduces death.

Tricksters are usually animals that have bodies riddled with passages, or they may have excessively large orifices, any of which may be cut open or penetrated. The contemporary Huichol, who live in the Sierra Madre Occidental, in north-central Mexico, consider Káuyúumaari ("one who does not know himself" or "one who makes others crazy") one of their principal deities (Myerhoff, 1974). Káuyumarie is the animal sidekick of the supreme Huichol deity, Tatewari ("our grandfather fire"). Irreverent, clever, and amusing, Káuyumarie brought about the first sexual intercourse between man and woman.

Tricksters distort sight and sound purely to create illusion and noise. The Aztec divinity, Tezcatlipoca ("smoking mirror"), uses an obsidian mirror to distort images. He was able to trick Quetzalcoatl, for example, into looking into the mirror in which Quetzalcoatl saw a repulsive and misshapen being. Tezcatlipoca in one of his assumed shapes is Huehuecoyotl ("drum coyote"), the puckish patron of song and dance.

Extraordinary body designs or cross-sex dress, which the trickster sometimes manifests, is a way in which the contrary conditions of existence are mediated. In her study of Zinacantecan myth from the Chiapas Highlands of Mexico, Eva Hunt links contemporary female tricksters to the sixteenth-century goddess Cihuacoatl, a female deity with a tail, a fake baby, and a snake, which emerges from under her skirt and from between her legs.

Tricksters often opposed the dominant supernatural beings of their day and embarrassed or humiliated the divine patrons of priests, shamans, and other privileged religious specialists. In other myths tricksters steal various forms of life from the underworld. For example, the Sanumá (Yanoama) of the Venezuela-Brazil border region, tell of Hasimo, a mythic bird-man, who steals fire from a primordial alligator, which stores fire in its mouth, by shooting excrement into its face, forcing the alligator to laugh (Taylor, 1979).

Tricksters are sometimes wedged in the dangerous passages between two states of being, and through their efforts to rescue themselves—using perhaps a hole, or vine, as a passage—these states of being become altered forever.

In the Gran Chaco area of southern South America, the Mataco trickster Tokhwáh—also known as Tawkx-wax, Takwaj, Takjuaj, Tokhuah—is both good and bad, and, although he advances human capabilities, every step forward brings comic disaster (Simoneau and Wilbert, 1982). Tokhwáh acts bisexually, chasing women and often seduced by men. His exploits require an entire cycle of myths, and he is at once divine and earthly, creative and destructive.

The actions of Mesoamerican and South American tricksters reveal the contradictions at the heart of human experience: carnal and spiritual, living but mortal, ambitious but finite. With a blend of humor and tragedy, trickster myths describe the calamities that occur when contrary conditions of being collide and overlap in a single experience.

BIBLIOGRAPHY

For a consideration of trickster figures as general mythical types among American Indian people, see Åke Hultkrantz's *The Religions of the American Indians* (Berkeley, 1967). For a treatment of trickster figures in Mesoamerica, see Barbara G. Myerhoff's *Peyote Hunt: The Sacred Journey of the Huichol Indians* (Ithaca, N. Y., 1974); Burr C. Brundage's *The Fifth Sun: Aztec Gods, Aztec World* (Austin, 1979); and Eva Hunt's *The Transformation of the Hummingbird: Cultural Roots of a Zinacantecan Mythical Poem* (Ithaca, N. Y., 1977).

For tricksters in various parts of South America consult the excellent series of volumes on folk literature of South American peoples edited by Johannes Wilbert and Karin Simoneau and published by the UCLA Latin American Center at the University of California, Los Angeles. Each volume contains extensive indices directing the reader to specific trickster motifs. For example, this article refers to Johannes Wilbert and Karin Simoneau's *Folk Literature of the Mataco Indians* (Los Angeles, 1982). Gerardo Reichel-Dolmatoff, *Amazonian Cosmos: The Sexual and Religious Symbolism of the Tukano Indians* (Chicago, 1971) presents the mythic figures of southern Colombia. For references to tricksters in the northwest Amazon region, see the excellent collections of myths in Robin M. Wright's "History and Religion of the Baníwa Peoples of the Upper Rio Negro Valley," 2 vols. (Ph. D. diss., Stanford University, 1981), and in Pierre-Ives Jacopin's "La parole generative: De la mythologie des indiens yukuna" (Ph. D. diss., Université de Neuchâtel, 1981). Trickster mythologies from Venezuela may be found in Marc de Civrieux's *Watunna: An Orinoco Creation Cycle* (San Francisco, 1980); Niels Fock's *Waiwai: Religion and Society of an Amazonian Tribe* (Copenhagen, 1963); and Kenneth I. Taylor's "Body and Spirit among the Sanumá (Yanoama) of North Brazil," in David L. Browman and Ronald A. Schwarz's *Spirits, Shamans, and Stars: Perspectives* from South America (The Hague, 1979), pp. 201-221, which discusses people living on the Brazil-Venezuela border. Mention may also be made of Charles Wagley's *Welcome of Tears: The Tapirapé Indians of Central Brazil* (Oxford, 1977); the special study made by Mario Califano, "El ciclo de Tokjwaj: Analisis fenomenológico de una narración mítica de los Mataco Costaneros," *Scripta ethnológica* (Buenos Aires) 1 (1973): 156-186; and Peter G. Roe's *The Cosmic Zygote: Cosmology in the Amazon Basin* (New Brunswick, N. J., 1982).

LAWRENCE E. SULLIVAN

TRINITY

Trinitarian doctrine touches on virtually every aspect of Christian faith, theology, and piety, including Christology and pneumatology, theological epistemology (faith, revelation, theological methodology), spirituality and mystical theology, and ecclesial life (sacraments, community, ethics). This article summarizes the main lines of trinitarian doctrine without presenting detailed explanations of important ideas, persons, or terms.

The doctrine of the Trinity is the summary of Christian faith in God, who out of love creates humanity for union with God, who through Jesus Christ redeems the world, and in the power of the Holy Spirit transforms and divinizes (*2 Cor.* 3:18). The heart of trinitarian theology is the conviction that the God revealed in Jesus Christ is involved faithfully and unalterably in covenanted relationship with the world. Christianity is not unique in believing God is "someone" rather than "something," but it is unique in its belief that Christ

> The doctrine of the Trinity is the product of reflection on the events of redemptive history, especially the Incarnation and the sending of the Spirit.

is the personal Word of God, and that through Christ's death and resurrection into new life, "God was in Christ reconciling all things to God" (*2 Cor.* 5:19). Christ is not looked upon as an intermediary between God and world but as an essential agent of salvation. The Spirit poured out at Pentecost, by whom we live in Christ and are returned to God (Father), is also not a "lesser God" but one and the same God who creates and redeems us. The doctrine of the Trinity is the product of reflection on the events of redemptive history, especially the Incarnation and the sending of the Spirit.

Development of Trinitarian Doctrine. Exegetes and theologians today are in agreement that the Hebrew Bible does not contain a doctrine of the Trinity, even though it was customary in past dogmatic tracts on the Trinity to cite texts like *Genesis* 1:26, "Let us make humanity in our image, after our likeness" (see also *Gn.* 3:22, 11:7; *Is.* 6:2-3) as proof of plurality in God. Although the Hebrew Bible depicts God as the father of Israel and employs personifications of God such as Word (*davar*), Spirit (*ruah*), Wisdom (*hokhmah*), and Presence (*shekhinah*), it would go beyond the intention and spirit of the Old Testament to correlate these notions with later trinitarian doctrine.

Further, exegetes and theologians agree that the New Testament also does not contain an explicit doctrine of the Trinity. God the Father is source of all that is (Pantokrator) and also the father of Jesus Christ; "Father" is not a title for the first person of the Trinity but a synonym for God. Early liturgical and creedal formulas speak of God as "Father of our Lord Jesus Christ"; praise is to be rendered to God through Christ (see opening greetings in Paul and deutero-Paul). There are other binitarian texts (e.g., *Rom.* 4:24, 8:11; *2 Cor.* 4:14; *Col.* 2:12; *1 Tm.* 2:5-6, 6:13; *2 Tm.* 4:1), and a few triadic texts (the strongest are *2 Cor.* 13:14 and *Mt.* 28:19; others are *1 Cor.* 6:11, 12:4-6; *2 Cor.* 1:21-22; *1 Thes.* 5:18-19; *Gal.* 3:11-14). Christ is sent by God and the Spirit is sent by Christ so that all may be returned to God.

The language of the Bible, of early Christian creeds, and of Greek and Latin theology prior to the fourth century is "economic" (*oikonomia*, divine management of earthly affairs). It is oriented to the concrete history of creation and redemption: God initiates a covenant with Israel, God speaks through the prophets, God takes on flesh in Christ, God dwells within as Spirit. In the New Testament there is no reflective consciousness of the metaphysical nature of God ("immanent trinity"), nor does the New Testament contain the technical language of later doctrine (*hupostasis, ousia, substantia, subsistentia, prosopon, persona*). Some theologians have concluded that all postbiblical trinitarian doctrine is therefore arbitrary. While it is incontestable that the doctrine cannot be established on scriptural evidence alone, its origins may legitimately be sought in the Bible, not in the sense of "proof-texting" or of finding metaphysical principles, but because the Bible is the authoritative record of God's redemptive relationship with humanity. What the scriptures narrate as the activity of God among us, which is confessed in creeds and celebrated in liturgy, is the wellspring of later trinitarian doctrine.

Dogmatic development took place gradually, against the background of the emanationist philosophy of Stoicism and Neoplatonism (including the mystical theology of the latter), and within the context of strict Jewish monotheism. In the immediate post-New Testament period of the Apostolic Fathers no attempt was made to work out the God-Christ (Father-Son) relationship in ontological terms. By the end of the fourth century, and owing mainly to the challenge posed by various heresies, theologians went beyond the immediate testimony of the Bible and also beyond liturgical and creedal expressions of trinitarian faith to the ontological trinity of coequal persons "within" God. The shift is from function to ontology, from the "economic trinity" (Father, Son, and Spirit in relation to us) to the "immanent" or "essential Trinity" (Father, Son, and Spirit in relation to each other). It was prompted chiefly by belief in the divinity of Christ and later in the divinity of the Holy Spirit, but even earlier by the consistent worship of God in a trinitarian pattern and the practice of baptism into the threefold name of God. By the close of the fourth century the orthodox teaching was in place: God is one nature, three persons (*mia ousia, treis hupostaseis*).

Questions of Christology and soteriology (salvation) occupied theologians of the early patristic period. What was Christ's relationship to God? What is Christ's role in our salvation? The Logos Christology of the apologists identified the preexistent Christ of Johannine and Pauline theology with the Logos ("word") of Greek philosophy. The Stoic distinction between the immanent word (*logos endiathetos*) and the expressed word (*logos prophorikos*) provided a way for Justin Martyr (d. 163/165) and others to explain how Christ had preexisted as the immanent word in the Father's mind and then became incarnate in time. Third-century monarchianism arose as a backlash against Logos theology, which was feared to jeopardize the unity of God; the modalism of Sabellius admitted the distinctions in history but denied their reality in God's being. Origen (died c. 254) contributed the idea of the eternal generation of the Son within the being of God; although other aspects of Origen's theology later were judged to be subordinationist, his teaching that the Son is a distinct hypostasis brought about subtle changes in conceptions of divine paternity and trinity. In the West, Tertullian (d. 225?) formulated an economic trinitarian theology that presents the three persons as a plurality in God. Largely because of the theology of Arius, who about 320 denied that Christ was fully divine, the Council of Nicaea (325) taught that Christ is *homoousios* (of the same substance) with God. The primary concern of Athanasius (d. 373), the great defender of Nicene orthodoxy, was salvation through Christ; if Christ is not divine, he cannot save. Like the bishops at Nicaea, Athanasius had a limited trinitarian vocabulary; *hupostasis* (person) and *ousia* (substance) could still be used interchangeably.

The fourth-century Cappadocian theologians (Basil of Caesarea, Gregory of Nyssa, and Gregory of Nazianzus) formulated orthodox trinitarian doctrine and made it possible for the Council of Constantinople (381) to affirm the divinity of the Holy Spirit. The speculatively gifted Cappadocians made a clear distinction between *hupostasis* and *ousia* (roughly equivalent to particular and universal), thereby establishing orthodox trinitarian vocabulary. At the close of the patristic period John of Damascus (d. 749) summarized Greek trini-

tarian doctrine with the doctrine of *perichoresis* (Lat., *circumincessio*), or the mutual indwelling of the divine persons.

Western trinitarian theology took a different course because of Augustine (d. 430). Instead of regarding the Father as source of divinity, Augustine's starting point was the one divine substance, which the three persons share. He sought the image of the Trinity within the rational soul and formulated psychological analogies (memory, intellect, will; lover, beloved, love) that conveyed unity more than plurality. The Augustinian approach served to effectively refute Arianism, but it also moved the doctrine of the Trinity to a transcendent realm, away from salvation history, from other areas of theology, and from liturgy. In the Latin West Boethius (died c. 525) formulated the classic definition of person, namely, "individual substance of a rational nature." Augustinian theology was given further elaboration in medieval theology, especially by Anselm (d. 1109) and in the Scholastic synthesis of Thomas Aquinas (d. 1274). Still Augustinian but focusing on person rather than nature, Richard of Saint-Victor (d. 1173) and Bonaventure (d. 1274) developed a psychology of love; charity is the essence of Trinity.

Although there are important exceptions to any typology, in general, Greek theology emphasizes the hypostases, the "trinity in unity," whereas Latin theology emphasizes the divine nature, or "unity in trinity." The Greek approach can be represented by a line: Godhood originates with the Father, emanates toward the Son, and passes into the Holy Spirit who is the bridge to the world. Greek theology (following the New Testament and early Christian creeds) retains the "monarchy" of the Father who as sole principle of divinity imparts Godhood to Son and Spirit. The Greek approach tends toward subordinationism (though hardly of an ontological kind) or, in some versions, to tritheism since in Greek theology each divine person fully possesses the divine substance. The Latin approach can be represented by a circle or triangle. Because the emphasis is placed on what the divine persons share, Latin theology tends toward modalism (which obscures the distinctiveness of each person). Also the Trinity is presented as self-enclosed and not intrinsically open to the world.

Principles of Trinitarian Doctrine. Trinitarian theology is *par excellence* the theology of relationship. Its fundamental principle is that God, who is self-communicating and self-giving love for us, is from all eternity love perfectly given and received. The traditional formula "God is three persons in one nature" compactly expresses that there are permanent features of God's eternal being (the three persons) that are the ontological precondition for the three distinct manners of God's tripersonal activity in the world (as Father, Son, Spirit).

Technical terms, theological theories, and official (conciliar) statements function together as a "set of controls" over the correct way to conceive both of God's self-relatedness as

Father, Son, and Spirit, and God's relatedness to creation as Father, Son, and Spirit. Although one must guard against reducing the mystery of God to a set of formal statements, precise distinctions are useful insofar as they refine theological vocabulary or protect against distortions ("heresy"). Still, doctrinal statements are inherently limited; they address specific points of controversy, leaving other questions unsettled and sometimes creating new problems. Conciliar statements and theological principles guard against egregious errors (for example, "the Holy Spirit is a creature") and serve as boundaries within which trinitarian discourse may take place.

First, God is ineffable and Absolute Mystery, whose reality cannot adequately be comprehended or expressed by means of human concepts. Trinitarian doctrine necessarily falls short of expressing the full "breadth and length and height and depth" of God's glory and wisdom and love. Even though God who "dwells in light inaccessible" is impenetrable mystery, the doctrine of the Trinity is not itself a mystery, nor is the doctrine revealed by God, nor is the doctrine a substitute for the knowledge of God gained in the union of love that surpasses all concepts (see *Eph.* 3:18-19). Trinitarian doctrine is a partial and fragmentary exegesis of what has been revealed, namely, that God is self-communicating love. Further, because God is a partner in love and not an object to be scrutinized or controlled by the intellect, speculative theology must be firmly rooted in spirituality, doxology, and a concrete community of faith so that trinitarian doctrine does not become "heavenly metaphysics" unrelated to the practice of faith.

Second, the revelation and self-communication of the incomprehensible God, attested in the concrete images and symbols of the Bible and celebrated in Christian liturgy, is the proper starting point of trinitarian theology. Theological thinking proceeds from "God with us" ("economic" Trinity) to the nature of God ("immanent" Trinity). The starting point "within" God led to an overly abstract doctrine in the West and to a virtual divorce of the "immanent" Trinity from the Trinity of history and experience. Friedrich Schleiermacher (d. 1834) reacted against the cleavage between "God" and "God for us" by relegating the idea of the essential Trinity to an appendix to his summary of Christian theology. Karl Rahner's (d. 1984) widely accepted axiom is pertinent: "the 'economic' Trinity is the 'immanent' Trinity and vice versa." God is who God reveals God to be. Concepts that describe the ontological intrarelatedness of God must be drawn from and are subject to control by the "facts" of redemptive history.

Third, because the three persons together and inseparably (though without mingling or confusion) bring about salvation and deification, and because the one God is worshiped as Father, Son, and Spirit, no divine person is inferior to any other person. Although undivided, God exists as the pure relationality of love given and received. The decree of the Council of Florence (1442) that "everything in God is one

except where there is opposition of relation" was regarded as a final answer to tritheism (belief in three gods), Arian subordinationism (ontological hierarchy of persons), Sabellian modalism (no real distinctions "in" God), and Macedonianism (denial of the divinity of the Holy Spirit).

There are two divine processions: begetting and spiration ("breathing"). Each divine person exists by relation to the other two persons (Gr., "relation of origin"; Lat., "relation of oppositon"), and each fully possesses the divine substance. In Greek theology the three hypostases have the distinguishing characteristics *(sg., idiotes)* of "being unbegotten" *(agen-*

> **God is ineffable and Absolute Mystery, whose reality cannot adequately be comprehended or expressed by means of human concepts.**

nesia), "being begotten" *(gennesia),* and "proceeding" *(ekporeusis).* The Father is the fountainhead of Godhood *(fons divinitatis),* who imparts divinity to Son and Spirit. According to Latin theology there are four relations (begetting, being begotten, spirating, being spirated) but only three "subsistent" relations: paternity, filiation, spiration. Latin theology (following Augustine) understands divine unity to reside in the divine nature that is held in common by Father, Son, and Spirit; Greek theology (following the Cappadocians) understands the unity to reside in the "perichoretic" relatedness of the three persons.

A corollary of the inseparability of the three coequal divine persons is the axiom that "all works of the triune God *ad extra* are indivisibly one" ("opera trinitatis ad extra indivisa sunt"). According to Latin theology it is the three-personed substance of God that acts in history; according to Greek theology every action of God toward creation originates with the Father, passes through the Son, and is perfected in the Spirit (Gregory of Nyssa). In any case, the axiom must not be understood to obscure what is distinctive to each divine person.

Fourth, a false distinction must not be set up between what God is and what God does, between essence and existence, between unity and threefoldness, between nature and person (relation). There are no "accidents" in God; the statement of the Fourth Lateran Council (1215) that each divine person is the divine substance countered the claim of some theologians (Joachim of Fiore) that God is a quaternity (three persons + essence = four persons).

Fifth, since the nature of God is to love, and love naturally seeks an object, it might appear that God "needs" the world as a partner in love. This would make the world coeternal with God. Many Scholastic theologians speculated on this question. Thomas Aquinas admitted that while he saw no philosophical reason to deny the eternity of the world, the testimony of the *Book of Genesis* and his Christian faith constrained him to do so. In 1329 Meister Eckhart was condemned for asserting the eternity of the world. With respect to trinitarian theology, even though Rahner's axiom (see above) suggests that God's relations to us, including creation, are constitutive of God and vice versa, theologians traditionally speak of a perfect and reciprocal exchange of love "within" God, that is, among Father, Son, and Spirit independent of their relationship to creation, in order to preserve the absolute character of God's freedom.

Current Directions and Remaining Problems. After centuries of disinterest in trinitarian doctrine in the West, the riches of this vast tradition are once again being explored. Three basic directions may be observed. First, some theologians have revised analogies of the "immanent" Trinity according to contemporary philosophy (for example, process metaphysics), linguistics, or interpersonal psychology. While this approach overcomes some of the aporia of classical expositions, it perpetuates the metaphysical starting point "within" God apart from salvation history. A second approach focuses on soteriology and Christology and is circumspect about the "immanent" Trinity, though without denying that historical distinctions are grounded ontologically in God. A third approach uses trinitarian symbolism to describe God's deeds in redemptive history but resists positing real distinctions in God. Despite basic differences in method, these three approaches all move in a more personalist (relational) direction and, in the case of the latter two, a more "economic" direction.

Theologians who specialize in trinitarian doctrine suggest that several areas warrant further attention. First, most trinitarian doctrine is so abstract it is difficult to see its connection with praxis. The "summary of Christian faith" and the living out of that faith should be brought to bear more directly on each other. Creeds, doxologies, and liturgy are important loci of the trinitarian faith recapitulated in trinitarian doctrine.

Second, unlike the "mystical theology" of the Orthodox tradition, theology in the West has been separated from spirituality since the thirteenth century. Reintegrating theology and spirituality would help to overcome the rationalist tendencies of Western theology, to provide the field of spirituality with theological foundation, and also to strengthen the weakest component of Western theology, namely, pneumatology.

Third, the *filioque* ("and from the Son") clause, inserted into the Western creed in the sixth century but denounced by the Orthodox church, remains a serious obstacle to reunion between East and West. Theologians should work assiduously for ecumenical agreement.

Fourth, to speak of God as "three persons" always has been problematic and remains the same today. In the modern framework "person" means "individual center of con-

sciousness." To avoid the tritheistic implications of positing three "persons" in God, the relational, or "toward-the-other" character of "person" should be reemphasized.

Fifth, the exclusively masculine imagery of trinitarian doctrine hinders full recovery of the trinitarian insight into the essential relatedness of God. The fatherhood of God should be rethought in light of the critique of feminist theologies and also in view of the nonpatriarchal understanding of divine paternity to be found in some biblical and early theological writings.

Sixth, revising trinitarian theology along soteriological lines raises the question of its place in the dogmatic schema, that is, whether it ought to be treated as a separate "tract," as prolegomenous to theology, as its apex and summary, or as an undergird that is presupposed throughout but never alluded to explicitly.

Seventh, trinitarian theology must be pursued within the context of the "God question" of every age, whether this question takes the form of existentialist atheism, secular humanism, or some other.

Eighth, the Christian doctrine of God must be developed also within the wider purview of other world religions. Trinitarian doctrine cannot be christomonistic, excluding persons of other faiths from salvation, nor can it surrender its conviction that God is fully present in Christ.

For trinitarian doctrine to be recovered as a vital expression of God's nearness in Christ, theologians must translate into a contemporary idiom the mystery of God's triune love in a way that does justice not only to the testimony of our predecessors but also to the ongoing and ever-new features of God's relationship with a people.

BIBLIOGRAPHY

Biblical and Historical Sources. For the New Testament origins of trinitarian doctrine, see the article and bibliography by Franz Josef Schierse, "Die neutestamentliche Trinitätsoffenbarung," in "Mysterium Salutis," edited by Johannes Feiner and Magnus Löhrer, vol. 2 (Einsiedeln, 1967), and Arthur W. Wainwright's *The Trinity in the New Testament* (London, 1962). A standard and nearly complete exposition of patristic and medieval, Greek and Latin trinitarian doctrine is Théodore de Régnon's four-volume *Études de théologie positive sur la Sainte Trinité* (Paris, 1892-1898). Organized chronologically and full of helpful textual references is "Trinité," by G. Bardy and A. Michel, in *Dictionnaire de théologie catholique* (Paris, 1950), vol. 15.2, cols. 1545-1855. Standard English-language works include George L. Prestige's study of shifting terminology and concepts in early Greek trinitarian theology in *God in Patristic Thought*, 2d ed. (1952; reprint, London, 1964), J. N. D. Kelly's historical study, *Early Christian Doctrines*, 5th rev. ed. (New York, 1977), and Edmund J. Fortman's *The Triune God* (Philadelphia, 1972). Yves Congar's three-volume *I Believe in the Holy Spirit* (New York, 1983) is more impressionistic but contains many historical gems and a seasoned approach to this vast field.

Theological Works. In Protestant theology, Karl Barth placed the doctrine of the Trinity as a prolegomenon to dogmatic theology in *Church Dogmatics*, vol. 1, pt. 1 (Edinburgh, 1936). See also Claude

Welch's summary of recent Protestant theology in *In This Name: The Doctrine of the Trinity in Contemporary* Theology (New York, 1952). Trinitarian theology that centers on the cross is represented in Eberhard Jüngel's *God as the Mystery of the World* (Grand Rapids, Mich., 1983) and Jürgen Moltmann's *The Crucified God* (New York, 1974). In Catholic theology, Karl Rahner's monograph *The Trinity* (New York, 1970) summarizes but also seeks to go beyond standard Western trinitarian dogma. Heribert Mühlen's *Der heilige Geist als Person,* 2d ed. (Münster, 1966) and *Una Mystica Persona* (Paderborn, 1964) develop a pneumatological and interpersonal analogy of the "immanent" Trinity. Walter Kasper's *The God of Jesus Christ* (New York, 1984) is a magisterial summary of classical and contemporary trinitarian theology, developed against the backdrop of modern atheism and in light of current studies in Christology. On Orthodox theology, see Vladimir Lossky's *The Mystical Theology of the Eastern Church,* 2d ed. (Crestwood, N. Y., 1976).

CATHERINE MOWRY LACUGNA

TUNGUZ RELIGION

The peoples of Siberia speaking Tunguz languages numbered 56,000 persons, according to the 1979 census of the U. S. S. R. The most numerous of them are the Evenki (27,300) and Eveny (12,500), who are collectively called Tunguz in the older literature. Sometimes the ethnonym Lamut ("sea person") is employed, applying only to certain groups of Eveny. The close racial and cultural relationship of these two peoples makes it possible to examine their beliefs in the framework of a single system, which may be designated "Tunguz religion." Other peoples speaking Tunguz languages are the Nanay (Goldi; 10,500), Ulchi (2,500), Udege (1,500), Oroki and Orochi (1,200), and Negidal'tsy (500). They represent a special cultural area, extending as far as the basin of the lower Amur River and Sakhalin Island, that includes the ancient cultural legacies of the Ainu and Nivkhi (Giliaks) and the inhabitants of northeastern China. A common religion has long been the primary factor uniting the atomized society of Tunguz hunters who, in small groups, mastered the vast space of taiga and tundra between the Yenisei River on the west and the Sea of Okhotsk on the east and between the Arctic Ocean on the north and Lake Baikal on the south.

The periodic religious ceremonies of the Tunguz are closely tied to their mythology, and in several instances they directly reproduce myths of creation and of the heroic deeds of their first ancestors, beginning with the words *tarnïmngakandu bicen* ("this was in *nimngakan*"). The term *nimngakan* means "myth, tale, legend; warm fairyland; bear ritual; shamanic séance." Each group of Tunguz has a myth on the creation of *bugha*—its own inhabited territory. *Bugha* has a variety of meanings: "locality, world, native land; cosmos, sky, earth; spirit master of the upper world/lower world/hunt, God,

devil; paradise, hell; icon." The Tunguz also use this term to designate the entrance into a bear den or a small hut made of young larches with small figures of beasts and birds placed therein in preparation for shamanic performances. The basic meanings of the term *bugha* embrace, in this way, notions of the creator, creation of the world, and of a model of the world. For designating the deity of the upper world the Tunguz also use the names Mayin, Ekseri, Seweki, and Amaka. The first of these names is tied to the concept of "success" or "hunting luck," whereas the last is a kinship term referring to representatives of the older age groups: "grandfather, father, uncle," and, in general, "ancestor." The word *amaka* also has other meanings: "bear; God; sky."

According to the perceptions of the Tunguz, the upper world *(ughu bugha)* is connected to the middle world *(dulu bugha)* through the North Star, termed *bugha sangarin,* "sky hole." In turn the middle world is also connected to the lower world *(hergu bugha)* through an opening within it. In the *nimngakan* the first ancestors were able to move between all three levels of the world. Thereafter this became the privilege of the shamans, who use for this purpose Tuuruu, the Tunguz variant of the World Tree, or its equivalent.

Engzekit is the mythical river called "the place that no one sees." It flows from the place termed Timanitki ("toward morning; east"), transects the middle world, and enters into the place called Dolbonitki ("toward night; north"), beyond which stretches the realm of the dead, Bunikit or Buni. Into Engzekit flow the many branch rivers of individual shamans. Somewhere at the confluence of these tributaries with the mythical river are the Omiruk, territories inhabited by souls *(omi);* these lands comprise the sacred wealth of each clan.

One of the myths associated with Engzekit tells of the origin of the first people, of reindeer, and of cultural objects from the various parts of the mythic bear's body. He voluntarily sacrificed himself to the heavenly maiden, who was carried off on an ice floe in the current between the upper and middle worlds. In other myths the bear, representing the ancestor of one or another Tunguz tribe, is similarly depicted as a culture hero, the creator of reindeer breeding, bequeathing after his inevitable death the ritual of the Bear Festival. This festival, which is essentially the same among all the Tunguz, is associated with the seasonal hunt of the animal in its den, which takes place in early spring or late autumn. The most important detail of the Tunguz bear ceremony, which has an explanation in their religio-mythological perception of the world, is the way in which they handle the bear's eyes. Hunters, having cut off the head of the slain beast, take out its eyes with great care, seeking to touch them neither with a knife nor with their fingernails. Then they wrap the eyes in grass or birch bark and carry them away into the forest, where they place them high in a tree. The Udege did this in the hope that the bear's eyes might be illuminated by the first rays of the rising sun. In the tabooed language of Tunguz hunters the bear's eyes are called *osikta* ("stars"). The connection of the bear with heavenly luminaries is well illustrated in a Tunguz myth in which the bear, named Mangi, follows the reindeer or moose who had stolen the sun. Having caught up with his prey, the bear returns the sun to its place. Both protagonists in this myth form the constellation of Ursa Major, the Big Dipper, in Tunguz cosmology (Chichlo, 1981, pp. 39-44).

This myth of the heavenly (or cosmic) hunt was reenacted by the Tunguz during the greatest festival of the year, Ikenipke (a name derived from the word *ike*, "to sing"), which took place in a specially constructed cone-shaped dwelling *(zumi)*, whose name designates not only "house, household, or family" but also "bear den" and *uterus animalis*. In the center of this dwelling is placed a pole called Tuuruu, along which Ekseri, the spirit of the upper world, and Hargi, the spirit of the lower world, travel in order to hold conversations with the shaman. The festival, which may be called the Tunguz New Year, consists of eight days of dancing, singing, and pantomine. The people, led by the shaman, would move inside the *zumi* in a circle in the direction of the sun's movement as they traveled up the river Engzekit behind an imaginary reindeer. In his song, the shaman would describe all the details of the travel, which lasted a year—all the animals, spirits, and obstacles encountered. At the end of the festival the men would shoot from a shamanic bow at wooden reindeer figures, shattering them into pieces that each man kept until the next festival.

Other important shamanistic rituals of the Tunguz took place in specially constructed dwellings in the taiga. With complex auxiliary structures, these represented a model of the supernatural world. The first, *nimngandek,* signifies "the place where *nimngakan* is fulfilled." The second, *sevencedek,* is "the place where a ceremony with *seven* is performed." Among all Tunguz peoples, seven means "shaman's spirit helper," but this word is connected to one of the names of the high God, Sevek or Seveki, and to the taboo reindeer of light coloring, *sevek,* which is also called *bughadi oron*, "heavenly reindeer." The ritual of dedicating the chosen reindeer as *sevek* is either independent or part of the ritual cycle in the Ikenipke festival. From the moment of this dedication, the *sevek* serves only for the transport of sacred objects. After its death, this reindeer is laid out on a platform set up in a tree.

The word *seven* also signifies the ritual dish at the Bear Festival, which is prepared from rendered bear fat mixed with finely chopped bear meat. Scooping the *seven* with a spoon, the hunter must swallow it without its touching his teeth. This method of partaking of the body of the beast deity is identical to the rules of handling bear eyes. The boldest hunters may swallow them but only without touching them with their teeth; otherwise the hunter will become blind. The meaning of these rules becomes more understandable in light of the strong prohibitions associated with the domestic hearth. The

firewood and coals must not be stirred with a sharp object, nor may broken needles be thrown into the fire. Even to place a knife with its point toward the fire may put out the eyes of the spirit of the fire. This spirit, according to an Orochi myth, is a pair of bear cubs born from the mating of a bear and a woman. According to the Evenki, the bear is a culture hero who gave people fire. Reconstructing the Tunguz spirit of the domestic fire discloses his bisexual nature, corresponding to an androgynous deity like the bear. It is therefore understandable why hunters do not risk swallowing *osikta* ("bear's eyes"), preferring to return them to the taiga. The luster of

> **Shamanism and the traditional religion of the Tunguz have not totally disappeared, as is commonly believed. . . .**

these "stars" on top of the World Tree assured hunting success, and the projections of the luster are the light and warmth of domestic hearths.

When considered as a system, the myths, concepts, rituals, and customs of the Tunguz show what a large, if not central, role the bear occupies. The most powerful shamans have him as a guardian spirit. At the time of the séance they don his skin, thus receiving power over all zoomorphic spirits, which they gather in the darkness of the sacred dwelling that represents, in essence, the cosmic bear den. The moose as well plays a significant role in the religious life of hunters and shamans, but its significance cannot be explained, as it is by most scholars, by economic functions alone. It must be noted that, according to myth, the moose emerges from the bear's fur and is, in consequence, part of him. And if Ursa Major is termed Heglen ("moose") by the Tunguz, this denotes a shift of stress in the direction of one member of a binary opposition composing the structure of the myth (and constellation), in which prey and hunter can change places. In their ritual practice Tunguz shamans preferred to place this stress on the figure of the hunter, inasmuch as they considered Mangi, who tracked the cosmic moose, to be their forefather.

Traces of the myth of the cosmic hunt in the religious life of Tunguz peoples still remain, as attested by ancient wooden disks of the Nanay that represent the sun *(siu)*. On the upper part of one of them is a drawing of a bear, and on the lower is the representation of a moose turned upside down. The Nanay hung such disks on the door of a dwelling or on a child's cradle; to the shamans they were an indispensable accessory of their costume. Possessing healing and protective functions, these disks are concise and expressive signs of the fundamental myth of the beginnings of human history. In the Nanay culture area, the myth of the bear Mangi, who freed the sun from captivity, and the myth of the hunter Khado, who killed the excess suns, which were burning all living things, came into contact with each other. Both myths are similar insofar as the Orochi, neighbors of the Nanay, consider Khado the father of the shamanistic spirit Mangi, the representation of which is on the shamans' staffs.

The Tunguz, whose livelihood depends upon success in hunting, conducted simple ceremonies that gave the hunter confidence in his own powers and in the benevolence of fate. He could do without a shaman, having enlisted the support of the master spirit of a locality and having gained a personal spirit helper. One of these rites is Singkelevun, "obtaining *singken* (success)." This ritual appears to be the simplest imitation of the concluding ceremony of the Ikenipke rite: the hunter makes an image of a reindeer or a moose, takes it with him into the taiga, and then shoots at it with a small bow. If the image is hit immediately, it becomes a *singken*. The dried parts of previously killed animals (hearts, jaws, noses), which the hunter saves, are also guarantors of success. Certain groups of Tunguz began to call the spirit master of the taiga Singken. The Evenki and Orochi conducted a Singkelevun ceremony in October, before the beginning of the winter hunting season. It was performed among them as a complex shamanistic ceremony consisting of several cycles.

For the preservation of human life, the Tunguz prepared special repositories of souls, which were "earthly" miniature copies of *omiruk* found in the basin of the Engzekit River in the upper world. The domestic *omiruk* are small boxes with little figurines placed in them. Each figurine holds the soul of a person placed there by a shaman. Certain shamans placed tufts of hair from persons needing protection in the *omiruk*. Such little boxes were strapped to the saddle of the heavenly reindeer. The *omi* was evidently a reincarnated substance circulating within the limits of a determined social group. Among the Nanay, for example, the *omi* lived in the form of small birds on the clan tree, from which they descended into women's bodies. Depictions of these trees are still found on the robes of Nanay women today.

In the case of frequent deaths of children, the shaman had to set out for the upper world, where he snared one of the soul birds and swiftly descended to earth. Evidence of his successful trip was a fistful of wool strands pressed together, which he threw into a white handkerchief held up for him by an assistant during the séance.

The traditional method of disposing of the dead among the Tunguz was aerial: the body, washed in the blood of a sacrificial reindeer and clothed and wrapped in a hide, tent cover, or birch bark, was laid on a scaffold set up in the branches of a tree. Coffins, when used, were made of hollowed-out tree trunks and set upon tree trunks or on posts dug into the ground. The belongings of the deceased were left with him, and his reindeer was strangled and left at the place of burial. After christianization in the eighteenth century, the Tunguz began to practice underground burial. However, the traditional ritual persists in the Siberian taiga even today.

The Tunguz considered the cause of death to be the departure or theft by evil spirits of the *beye* soul, the name of which translates as "body." In conducting the mourning ceremony for the dead a year later, the Tunguz sometimes prepared a temporary "body" from a section of a tree trunk, which they clothed in part with the deceased person's clothing, provided with food, and bade farewell to forever. The shaman, completing the conveyance of the deceased into Buni, asked him not to return again nor to disturb the living. Among the Nanay, the initial conveyance of the deceased, termed Nimngan, took place on the seventh day. Here, the deceased was represented by a bundle of his clothing, in which the shaman placed the *han'an*, the "shadow" soul of the deceased, which he had caught. This bundle of clothes was treated like the living for a period of three years, until the final farewell with him at the large *kasa* memorial festival, lasting several days. But even here, under the unquestionable influence of Manchurian Chinese customs, the Nanay and other Tunguz peoples of the lower Amur region observed traditional division between the living and the dead. An ancestor cult did not unfold here nor, more forcibly, was it characteristic of the Evenki and Eveny, the nomads of the Siberian taiga.

Shamanism and the traditional religion of the Tunguz have not totally disappeared, as is commonly believed, notwithstanding atheist propaganda and prohibitions. As recently as 1958, four nomadic Even communities, living in isolation for more than thirty years in the mountainous forest-tundra of Magadan oblast, were headed by eight authoritative shamans, one of whom was called by the honorific Amanza (Amaka). In 1978, Evenki believers on the Sym River (a branch of the Yenisei in central Siberia) used the services of three shamans. The cult of the domestic hearth continues to exist in various forms among all nomadic Tunguz, including sovkhoz (state farm) workers. In certain Tunguz settlements, one may see on the main street a post with a bear's skull fastened to it, evidence that the power of the Master of the Taiga is still recognized by his offspring.

[*See also* Shamanism.]

BIBLIOGRAPHY

Anisimov, A. F. *Religiia evenkov*. Moscow and Leningrad, 1958.
Chichlo, Boris, "Ours—chamane." Études mongoles et Sibé-riennes, 12 (1981): 35-112.
Delaby, Laurence. "Chamanes toungouses." *Études mongoles et sibériennes*, 7 (1976).
Diószegi, Vilmos. "The Origin of the Evenki 'Shaman Mask' of Transbaikalia." *Acta orientalia Academiae Scientiarum Hungaricae* 20 (1967): 171-200.

Diószegi, Vilmos. "The Origin of the Evenki Shamanistic Instruments (stick, knout) of Transbaikalia." *Acta Ethnographica Academiae Scientiarum Hungaricae* 17 (1968): 265-311.

Diószegi, Vilmos, ed. *Popular Beliefs and Folklore Tradition in Siberia.* Translated and revised by Stephen P. Dunn. Budapest, 1968. See especially the essays by V. A. Avrorin (pp. 373-386) and G. M. Vasilevich (pp. 339-372).

Diószegi, Vilmos, and Mihály Hoppál, eds. *Shamanism in Siberia.* Budapest, 1978. See especially the essays by A. V. Smoliak (pp. 439-448) and V. A. Tugolukov (pp. 419-428).

Lopatin, I. A. *The Cult of the Dead among the Natives of the Amur Basin.* The Hague, 1960.

Mazin, A. I. *Traditsionnye verovaniia i obriady evenkov-orochonov.* Novosibirsk, 1984.

Michael, H. N., ed. *Studies in Siberian Shamanism.* Toronto, 1963. See the essays by A. F. Anisimov (pp. 84-124) and G. M. Vasilevich (pp. 46-84).

Paproth, Hans-Joachim. *Studien über das Bärenzeremoniell: I. Bärenjagdriten und Bärenfeste bei den tungusichen Völkern.* Uppsala, 1976.

Priroda i chelovek v religioznykh predstavleniiakh narodov Sibiri i Severa. Leningrad, 1976. See especially the essays by S. V. Ivanov (pp. 161-188), N. B. Kile (pp. 189-202), and A. V. Smoliak (pp. 129-160).

Semeinaia obriadnost' narodov Sibiri. Moscow, 1980. See the essays by A. V. Smoliak (pp. 177-195) and V. A. Tugolukov (pp. 165-176).

Shirokogoroff, S. M. *Psychomental Complex of the Tungus.* Peking and London, 1935.

Vasilevich, G. M. "Preshamanistic and Shamanistic Beliefs of the Evenki." *Soviet Anthropology and Archeology* 11 (1972).

BORIS CHICHLO
Translated from Russian by Demitri B. Shimkim

TURKIC RELIGIONS

Throughout the course of their long history, the Turkic peoples have simultaneously or successively practiced all the universal religions (Christianity, especially Nestorian Christianity; Judaism; Manichaeism; Buddhism; and Mazdaism) before the majority of them were won over to Islam. However, before yielding to these religions, they held their own system of beliefs, their own personal representations. These are generally identified as "animism" or "shamanism," even though the last term cannot even begin to cover the whole of the religious phenomena.

Until recently, it had been considered impossible to understand the religion of the Turkic people in its ancient form. Studies, especially ethnographic ones, have been written on groups of people who continued to practice the religion in modern times (nineteenth to twentieth century). Only recently has it been observed that the inscribed Turkic stelae of the sixth to the tenth century, certain manuscripts (including the dictionary of Mahmud al-Kashghari, eleventh century), and foreign sources (especially Chinese but also Byzantine, Arabic, Latin, Armenian, and Syrian) present a considerable wealth of information. This information takes on full meaning when compared with ethnographic notes, medieval Mongolian sources, and pre-Islamic remnants in Turkic-Muslim plastic and literary works. Thus we begin to have, if not a complete knowledge of the ancient Turkic religion, at least a satisfactory view of the overall picture.

The Common Heritage. With a few small exceptions, the Turkic religion has offered structures to all peoples of all social classes in all regions of the Turkic world throughout history. Admittedly, there was a less influential period during which the religion was developing, but it appears to have been firmly established as early as the first century CE.

Although the religion was fairly well established early on, certain innovations appeared over the course of time. Without doubt, the dualism already apparent in the Turkic religion has been accentuated through the influence of Manichaeism. From Buddhism has come a conception of hell as a cosmic zone situated under the earth in symmetry with the sky (a deity).

Ideas that have remained unchanged are those relative to death, the afterlife, and funerary rites (apart from the issue of burial versus incineration). Death, which one hopes will be violent and unnatural (in spite of the respect that is occasionally shown the elderly) is considered the Necessity, Kergek (perhaps a deity). However, it is deeply dreaded and has given rise to bitter regrets, supposedly issued from the mouths of the deceased. Death is eminently contagious and requires a sober approach toward the dying one (generally abandoned) or the deceased. The funerary ceremonies have survived the centuries without having been changed.

The universe is generally represented as composed of two parallel plains, the sky and the earth (ultimately extended to three with the addition of the underworld). At the same time, it is also seen as a square plateau (earth), covered by a circumscribed dome (sky), with the four corners of the earth being allowed to exist outside the shelter of the sky. The cosmic axis that links the sky, the earth, and the underworld can be a mountain or a tree with seven branches, each branch representing a level of the sky. The levels of the sky are in turn derived from the seven planets still known to have been popularly believed in during modern times but also attested to by prehistoric engravings and by every construction with symbolic value, for example, the pillar of the tent, the ensemble formed by the central hearth of the yurt, and its upper opening, through which the smoke escapes. This axis is at once the support for the sky and the path that permits access to it.

The observation of stars is an important occupation. The phases of the moon are considered lucky or unlucky. No projects are to be undertaken when the moon is in its last quarter, although a good time to launch a military campaign is when the moon is waxing or is full. The last days of the lunar month are favorable for obsequies because they mark an end and announce a rebirth. Similarly, human life closely parallels plant life.

In one way or another, all animals have had a numinous role, but certain animals are different from others: the bird of prey, the eagle or falcon, is a divine messenger that flies near Tengri and sits enthroned on the summit of the cosmic tree; the stag is often considered a saint, but is hunted nevertheless; the hare's position is as ambiguous as that of the camel, which is totemized or tabooed as impure; the bear is the quintessential lunar animal, whose hibernation stirs the imagination; geese or swans, which appear in the widespread legend of the swan maiden, may symbolize the celestial virgin; all birds are souls; and the horse, a member of the

> **Fraternity can be pledged between two strangers through the exchange of significant gifts and particularly through the mixing of blood.**

clan, is the epitome of the sacrificial animal and also often a solar or aquatic symbol.

Despite a strong family structure, accounts of adoption by animals or humans are numerous, and fraternity is not dependent upon birth alone. Fraternity can be pledged between two strangers through the exchange of significant gifts (osselets, arrows, horses) and particularly through the mixing of blood. The rite that establishes fraternity consists of the two postulants' joining their slashed wrists or drinking mixed drops of their blood from a cup that is often made from the dried skull top of a murdered enemy chief.

The Popular Religion. Despite the pretensions of certain shamans to positions of tribal leadership, shamanism is essentially a religious phenomenon, a dominant one in the religious life of contemporary non-Muslim Turkic peoples and one that is at the heart of the popular religion. It speaks to the people of things that interest them most—the preservation of their life (magical healings), their future (divination), and their relations with the familiar gods and spirits (the shaman's sacerdotal role, his cosmic voyage). The institution of shamanism is surely quite ancient. Although poorly discernible in antiquity, it was in full bloom by the time of the Middle Ages, despite the total silence of the Türk inscriptions on the subject.

The totemic system, which can exist only in tribal societies that employ it to determine basic structures (families, clans), plays a role in the popular religion that is almost as important as that of shamanism. For a long time, totemism was unknown among the Altaic peoples in general; however, in the mid-twentieth century pioneering research by P. J.

Strahlenberg, Chodzidlo, A. Billings, N. Shchukin, and others revealed a totemic system among both contemporary and extinct Turkic societies, such as the Bashkirs, the Oghuz, and the western Türk.

Out of a desire to maintain control over the earth's products, the people made "soul supports"; these represented the spirit protectors of animals and harvests. They were among the numerous idols placed in the yurts and were also transported in carts, which became veritable traveling altars. Constructed of felt, wood, and metal, these zoomorphic or anthropomorphic idols could also represent and contain the soul of ancestors and of all imaginable powers. One took care of them, fed them, and painted them with blood. Ethnographers eventually began to call these idols by the Mongol word *ongon* (Turkic equivalents: *töz, tyn, kürmes*), although *ongon* actually refers to totems.

The Imperial Religion. It is difficult to comprehend the significance and the success of the imperial religion without taking into account the tribal organization of society, with its attendant instability, internecine wars, anarchy, and misery. Despite the tribes' pronounced taste for independence and their attachment to tradition, the empire presented certain advantages that the tribes were prepared to accept, even if it meant losing part of their patrimony along with their autonomy. Certainly the sovereign, promoted through his own genius or through circumstances, was descended from the tribal regime and practiced the popular religion. This fact, together with his need to secure mass support, inclined him to tolerate the tribal religion; but he reorientated it, promoting elements that had been secondary, diluting or eliminating elements that were in essence antimonarchist. The two great victims were shamanism and totemism.

The popular gods suffered less from the imperial religion. Any major force that contributed to the power of the empire was welcomed, and the Turkic peoples, with their fundamental beliefs in the diffused divine, opposed the disappearance of these gods. (Popular sentiment also had to be respected.) Nevertheless, their fate was not always the same. Some were more or less forgotten, while others were promoted. Still others were obviously approached from a new perspective. The various *iduq yer sub*, the "forbidden places," the "master-possessors of the earth and waters," were apparently reduced to those originally belonging to the imperial family. On the other hand, everything that appeared to be universal, common to all man, grew disproportionately. The earth goddess was often associated with the sky god and partook of his indivisibility. The sky himself, principally Tengri, became the sky god and was "blue," "elevated," and "endowed with strength"; he clearly became, at least eventually, "eternal," the supreme god above all others because he was the god of the emperor and was as exceptional as the latter was.

The national god of the Turkic peoples, Tengri, was also the god of all men and demanded that all recognize him, that is, that they submit to the Turkic kaghan—a demand that caused him to take on the characteristics of a god of war. The worst transgression was to revolt against the prince, that is, against Tengri, and the god knew no other punishment for this than death.

If the popular religion has been passed over in silence by imperial Turkic texts, and often by others, there are nonetheless numerous deities that appear around the sky god without our knowing their connections to him: the earth goddess, the *iduq yer sub* and other master-possessors, the sacred springs and rivers, the trees, fire, and the mountain. The most powerful and stable of these deities that appear around the sky god is Umai (often still called this today but also known by other names, for example, Aiyysyt among the Siberian Yakuts), a placental goddess of whom al-Kashghari says, "If one worships her, a child will be born." Certain attempts seem to have been made to bring her closer to Tengri; she has been called "close to the khatun," that is, to the empress.

The *baba* are the funerary statues of deceased princes and, occasionally, princesses. They were not viewed as images of the departed but as images of the living, who, after their death, remained among the people. Not of great aesthetic value, these huge, crude statues, of which a good number of specimens are known, represent the individual standing or seated, always holding a cup in the right hand, which is drawn back over the stomach. These works were the original image of the "prince in majesty" of classical Islam.

It is impossible to know whether belief in an afterlife in the sky was of imperial or popular origin, although there is no lack of presumptions that favor imperial origins: having come from the sky and belonging to it, the prince can only return there. In so asserting, one says that he "flies away," later that he "becomes a gyrfalcon" or that he "climbs up to the sky" where he is "as among the living." But there are also attestations of a celestial beyond for those who did not attain sovereignty—a place for those close to the prince, his servants, horses, concubines, and all those who could serve him or be useful to him. However, even if the sky was easily accessible to all—something we do not know—there was nothing to prevent the various souls of the same man, even those of a kaghan, from finding other places to inhabit (the tomb, the banner, the *balbal,* the *baba*), from being reincarnated in a new body, or from roaming the universe as an unsatisfied phantom.

BIBLIOGRAPHY

Much research has been done on the formation of religious concepts among the people of the steppes and of Siberia. Mario Bussagli's *Culture e civiltà dell'Asia Centrale* (Turin, 1970) is a good historical presentation of nomadic cultures. For earlier periods, see Karl Jettmar's *Die frühen Steppenvölker* (Baden-Baden, 1964), translated by Ann E. Keep as *The Art of the Steppes* (New York, 1967). For the Huns, see Otto J. Mänchen-Helfen's *The World of the Huns: Studies in Their History and Culture* (Berkeley, 1973), which has a complete bibliography. Wilhelm Barthold gives the historical context of medieval Central Asia in *Turkestan down to the Mongol Invasion* (1900), 2d ed., translated from the Russian (London, 1958). For a comprehensive overview of Turkic religion, see my *La réligion des Turcs et des Mongols* (Paris, 1984), which has a vast but nonexhaustive bibliography. For contemporary religious practice, Uno Harva's *Die religiösen Vorstellungen der altaischen Völker,* "Folklore Fellows Communications," no. 125 (Helsinki, 1938), is a useful reference work, although quite biased. It has been translated as *Les représentations religieuses des peuples altaïques* (Paris, 1959). Wilhelm Radloff has devoted himself to a vast study, most of which can be found in *Aus Sibirien,* 2 vols. in 1 (Leipzig, 1884). Wilhelm Schmidt collected considerable documentation in volume 9 of his *Der Ursprung der Gottesidee* (Münster, 1949), see also volumes 10-12 (Münster, 1955). On the subject of funeral rites and the beyond, see my *La mort chez les peuples altaïques anciens et médiévaux* (Paris, 1963). On the position of animals and vegetables, see my *Faune et flore sacrées dans les sociétés altaïques* (Paris, 1966). For a study of the phenomenon of shamanism, see Mircea Eliade's *Shamanism: Archaic Techniques of Ecstasy,* rev. & enl. ed. (New York, 1964). For examples of pre-Islamic relics in Turkic Islam, see John K. Birge's *The Bektashi Order of Dervishes,* "Luzac's Oriental Religious Series," no. 7 (1937; reprint, New York, 1982), and my *Les traditions des nomades de la Turquie méridionale* (Paris, 1970). Much work on Turkic religion has been widely published in journals, notably in *Central Asiatic Journal* (The Hague, 1957-). Noteworthy articles in English include those by John Andrew Boyle in *Folklore:* "A Eurasian Hunting Ritual," *Folklore* 80 (Spring 1969): 12-16; "Turkish and Mongol Shamanism in the Middle Ages," *Folklore* 83 (Autumn 1972): 177-193; and "The Hare in Myth and Reality: A Review Article," *Folklore* 84 (Winter 1973): 313-326. See also *Glaubenswelt und Folklore der sibirischen Völker,* edited by Vilmos Diószegi (Budapest, 1963).

JEAN-PAUL ROUX
Translated from French by Sherri L. Granka

ULTRAMONTANISM

ULTRAMONTANISM is the tendency of Roman Catholicism that emphasizes the authority of the papacy in the government and teaching of the church. Originally articulated in opposition to Gallicanism, ultramontanism stressed the unity of the church centralized in Rome ("over the mountains") and its independence from nations and states. Ultramontane principles can be traced to the struggles of popes and councils in the fifteenth century. The papalist position received a full exposition by the Jesuit Roberto Bellarmino at the end of the sixteenth century. However, ultramontanism acquired its definitive meaning in the conflict over the Gallicanism of Louis XIV in the seventeenth and eighteenth centuries. The term *ultramontanism* seems to date from the 1730s, although ultramontane was used with various meanings in the Middle Ages. During the eighteenth century, exponents of ultramontanism waged a generally losing struggle against Gallicanism and similar statist movements in other countries, such as Febronianism and Josephism.

The French Revolution dealt a fatal blow to Gallicanism by destroying the monarchy on which it had rested. In the ensuing age of uncertainty, the attractiveness of the papacy as the only stable source of authority stimulated a Roman Catholic revival, of which ultramontanism was the essence. Count Joseph de Maistre forcefully expressed this position in *Du pape* (1819), proposing absolutism in state and church under the ultimate supremacy of the pope. The traditionalism of Viscount Louis de Bonald disparaged individual reason, for which Félicité de Lamennais (*Essay on Indifference*, 1817) substituted the "universal consent" of humanity, as embodied in the pope, as the ultimate test of truth. But Lamennais, developing the democratic implications of "universal consent," appealed not only to the pope but also to the people, seeking the freedom of the church in the freedom of society. Thus he commenced the liberal Catholic movement in the context of ultramontanism. The appeal made to Pope Gregory XVI by Lamennais and his associates on the journal Avenir was rejected (*Mirari vos*, 1832) by a papacy still seeking safety in alliance with authoritarian monarchies. Lamennais left the church. Nonetheless, his more moderate colleagues, notably Count Charles de Montalembert and Henri Lacordaire, were able to build a party, at once ultra-

montane and liberal, that supplanted Gallicanism as the political expression of French Catholicism. This party seemed to triumph during the revolution of 1848, securing its chief goal, freedom of Catholic education, with the passage of the Falloux law in 1850.

The Falloux law brought to the surface a latent division in the Catholic party, many of whose members had followed Montalembert's quest for liberty only as a means toward the end of the ultimate dominance of the church in French life. Louis Veuillot, editor of L'uni-vers, led an intransigent group that rejected the compromises inherent in the Falloux law and advanced the most extreme claims on behalf of the

> The church regarded itself as besieged and embattled, hostile to all liberalism in political and intellectual life.

church and, within it, of the authority of the pope. This new ultramontanism thus rejected liberal Catholicism, a product of the older ultramontanism, and set itself against all forms of liberalism in church, state, and intellectual life.

The attitude of the papacy was decisive. Although Pope Pius IX (1846-1878) had flirted mildly with liberalism early in his reign, he reacted sharply after the revolution of 1848, which had driven him out of his temporal dominions. After 1850, the church under his leadership regarded itself as besieged and embattled, hostile to all liberalism in political and intellectual life, and concentrating in the pope himself both the devotion of the faithful and the plenitude of authority. This was the final meaning of ultramontanism. Having already overcome Gallicanism, it now fought and defeated liberal Catholicism. Veuillot in France, the Jesuits associated with the periodical *Civiltà Cattolica* in Italy, William George Ward and Henry Edward Manning in England, Paul Cullen in Ireland, and, more moderately, the Mainz school led by Wilhelm von Ketteler in Germany were the leading exponents of a movement that rapidly triumphed among committed Catholics. *The Syllabus of Errors* (1864), a set of theses condemned by Pius IX, marked the height of ultramontane militancy. The definition of papal infallibility by the First Vatican Council in 1870 set the seal on its victory. However qualified the wording of this definition, it was manifest that the ultramontane program of a centralized and authoritarian church under an irresistible pope had been achieved.

From the First to the Second Vatican Council, ultramontanism was effectively synonymous with orthodox Roman Catholicism. The movement in its final form had won so complete a triumph that the term itself fell out of use.

[*See also* Papacy *and* Vatican Councils.]

BIBLIOGRAPHY

Encyclopedic or reference entries on ultramontanism tend to be either partisan or unhelpful, but F. F. Urquhart's essay "Ultramontanism," in the *Encyclopaedia of Religion and Ethics*, edited by James Hastings, vol. 12 (Edinburgh, 1926), is a solid brief sketch. Good extended treatments of nineteenth-century ultramontanism can be found in Wilfrid Ward's *William George Ward and the Catholic Revival*, 2d ed. (London, 1912); Adrien Dansette's *Religious History of Modern France*, vol. 1, translated by John Dingle (New York, 1961); and especially Roger Aubert's *Le pontificat de Pie IX, 1846-1878*, "Histoire de l'Église," vol. 21 (Paris, 1952).

JOSEF L. ALTHOLZ

UNDERWORLD

The term *underworld* refers to the subterranean region inhabited by the dead. It is often the place of punishment of the wicked, the unrighteous, the unredeemed, the unbelieving, or the lost. The concept of an underworld is an ingredient in most belief systems in the history of religions, but there is no definite evidence indicating that the idea was present in the earliest stages of human culture. In the oldest strata of Egyptian and pre-Vedic Indian cultures, however, there exists a rich store of archaeological material suggesting that the aristocratic segments of society, at least, believed in some kind of an afterlife.

Primitive and Archaic Religions. Tales of heroic journeys to the underworld, often undertaken on behalf of the entire community, are extremely widespread among tribal peoples throughout the world. Particularly notable for such lore are the Maori of New Zealand; various Plains tribes of North America; the Zulu, the Ashanti, and the Dogon of Africa; and numerous other societies in North Asia.

Many tribal peoples situate the land of the dead in the west, on the western side of the world, or simply at some distance west of the village.

One important theme concerns the descent of a hero into the belly of a ferocious marine creature and his reemergence through the mouth or anus of the beast in an effort to conquer death and gain immortality. A second theme is of an arduous journey through wild and monster-infested areas in search of a precious object (magical ring, sacred fruit, golden vessel, elixir of immortality, etc.) that will benefit the hero or his people. In a third theme, a tribesman submits himself to a deadly ordeal in order to pass from a lower to a higher stage of existence and thereby achieves a superhuman or heroic state of being.

Ancient Egypt. The afterlife of the Egyptian nobility is described in the Pyramid Texts. Royalty were believed to ascend at death to the Blessed Lands, or Fields of the Blessed, in the heavens. According to the Pyramid Texts, members of the aristocracy traveled to the celestial spheres to dwell there like gods, often traveling on the ship belonging to Re, the sun god. Highly elaborate and expensive mortuary rites, charms, and incantations were offered for the nobility to guarantee that the soul of the deceased would enjoy a blissful existence in the world beyond.

The dead traveled to many different realms, some to the east but most to the west. The west was the primary destination of the souls *(ka)* of the dead. Darkness and night were identified symbolically with death and postmortem existence. The realm of the dead was located sometimes in the sky and sometimes beneath the earth. This region was ruled by Osiris, the king of the dead.

Assyria and Babylonia. In the views of the ancient Akkadians and Babylonians, the underworld is a dreadful place. To get there one has to pass through seven gates and remove a piece of clothing at each. The realm is organized on the order of a political state under the tyrannical rule of a king and a queen, Nergal and Ereshkigal. Once in the underworld, the fate of the deceased is improved or worsened depending on whether the body is buried according to the prescribed funeral rites and is provided by the living with food, clothing, and other accoutrements required for the journey to the other realm.

Greece and Rome. The earliest Greek accounts of the postmortem journey of the soul to the underworld are to be found in the *Iliad* (1.595, 3.279, 5.395-396, 15.187-188) and in the *Odyssey* (11). At the moment of death, the soul *(psuche)* is separated from the body, transformed into a ghostly double of the person *(eidolon)*, and transported down to Hades, an enormous cavern below the surface of the earth *(Odyssey* 11.204-222).

In ancient Greek cosmology, Hades lies within the ocean, perpetually shrouded in clouds and mist. Here there is no sunlight, only eternal darkness. The shades are depicted as being weak and extremely melancholy, always in search of escape from their sufferings and finding none. Especially painful are the sufferings of those who were either not properly buried on earth or not suitably nourished with sacrificial food offerings. The dire nature of the torments suffered by the inmates is graphically depicted in the story of Tantalos. Standing in water up to his chin, he found to his chagrin that the water mysteriously evaporated each time he sought to quench his thirst; surrounded by flowering fruit trees, he found that the wind blew the fruit away as he reached out to grasp it (*Odyssey* 11.582-592).

Not until the time of Plato do we encounter the notion that the righteous will be feted with sumptuous banquets "with garlands on their heads," or that the wicked will be plunged into a pit filled with mud, "where they will be forced to carry water in a sieve" (*Republic* 2.373c-d). Plato may have believed that the earthly experience of the fear of Hades is equivalent to being there already and that the suffering inflicted by a guilty conscience is sufficient punishment for the wicked act committed. This view coincides with the theory that Plato adopted many primitive beliefs about the fate of the soul and gave moral and psychological interpretations to allegorical tales (see *Gorgias* 493a-c).

Judaism. References to the underworld in the Hebrew scriptures are vague and derive largely from beliefs common throughout the ancient Near East (especially Egypt and Babylonia). Numerous terms are used to designate this shadowy realm, the two most popular names being *She'ol* (a word that seems peculiar to Hebrew) and *Gei' Hinnom* (Gr., *Geenna*; Eng., *Gehenna*).

The Hebrew scriptures place the domain of the dead at the center of the earth, below the floor of the sea (*Is.* 14:13-15, *Jb.* 26:5). Some passages locate the gates that mark the boundary of She'ol in the west. According to the Ethiopic *Apocalypse of Enoch* (22:9-13), She'ol is not an abode of all the dead, where the souls merely exist as vague shadowy figures devoid of individual characteristics, but is a spacious realm with three subdivisions. In time, She'ol came to be identified with Gehenna, the pit of torment, an idea that, in turn, informed the Christian concept of Hell (*Hb.* 2:5).

In the postbiblical Jewish apocalyptic tradition, among the seven heavens that extend above the earth, sinners are confined to the second heaven to await final judgment. North of Eden lies Gehenna, where dark fires perpetually smolder and a river of flames flows through a land of biting cold and ice. Here the wicked suffer numerous tortures (*2 En.* 3-9).

Christianity. New Testament writers drew upon the postexilic Hebraic picture of Gehenna in formulating their understanding of the destination of the damned. Gehenna was imagined to be an enormous, deep pit that perpetually ejects clouds of putrid-smelling smoke from burning garbage, a pit where bodies of criminals and lepers are disposed of. Two significant alterations in the Hebraic concept of hell deserve mention: (1) there is a much sharper distinction between the realm of the blessed and the realm of the damned, and (2) the standard applied at the Last Judgment is defined by a person's attitude toward the person of Jesus and his teachings.

According to the eschatology of the *Book of Revelation*, a millennial reign is followed by the resurrection of the saints, and then by a period of universal conflict at the end of which Satan will be cast into a lake of fire and brimstone, preparatory to the resurrection of the remaining dead and the Last Judgment. Both Death and Hades are hypostatized as subterranean vaults that surrender the dead to be judged, after which Death and Hades themselves are thrown into the lake of fire, thus actualizing "the second death," that is, condemnation to the eternal fires of Hell (*Rv.* 20:11-15, 21:8).

Augustine (354-430 CE), the father of early medieval theology, perpetuated the concept of Hell as a bottomless pit containing a lake of fire and brimstone where both the bod-

> **Gehenna was imagined to be an enormous, deep pit that perpetually ejects clouds of putrid-smelling smoke.**

ies and the souls of men and the ethereal bodies of devils are tormented (*City of God* 21.10). For Thomas Aquinas, Hell never lacks space to accommodate the damned. it is a place where unhappiness infinitely exceeds all unhappiness of this world, a place of eternal damnation and torment.

The history of Christianity is dotted with periodic expressions of heretical dissent concerning the existence of Hell, notably by Origen, Erigena, Voltaire, and Nietzsche. But it was not until the seventeenth and eighteenth centuries, when rationalism began to find its voice, that a widespread decline of belief in Hell developed in Western culture.

Islam. According to the Qur'an, there are seven layers of heaven extending above the earth toward the celestial abode of God. Corresponding to the layers of heaven are seven descending depths of a vast funnel-shaped fire *(alnar)*. The topmost level of the netherworlds is Gehenna. This realm of death and torment is connected to the world of the living by a bridge that all the souls of the dead must traverse on the day of judgment. The varieties of punishment meted out to the damned become more painful and severe with each level of descent.

The Qur'an depicts Gehenna in highly pictorial and terrifying terms. It is referred to as the "Fire of Hell" (89:23) and is depicted as a kind of four-legged beast. Each leg is composed of seventy thousand demons; each demon has thirty thousand mouths. Each of the seven layers of the Fire is punctuated by a gate manned by a guardian who torments the damned.

The realms of the blessed and the damned are separated by a towering wall. Men who inhabit the heights of this partition can view the inhabitants of both worlds and recognize each group by their distinguishing marks. The blessed are recognizable by their smiling countenances; the damned, by their black faces and blue eyes (57:13).

In time, Muslim theologians began to emphasize God's grace and mercy and to downplay his anger and wrath.

Hinduism. According to *Rgveda* 7.104 and *Atharvaveda* 8.4, the Vedic Hell is situated beneath the three earths, below the created order. It is characterized as a gigantic, bottomless chasm or abyss, a place of no return. In this infinitely deep pit, there is no light, only deep darkness (cf. *Rgveda* 2.29.6). In the very deepest realm lies the cosmic serpent, the archdemon Vrtra (*Rgveda* 1.32.10), who fell there after Indra slew him.

Some texts describe the Vedic Hell as insufferably hot or unbearably cold. It is a realm of absolute silence (*Rgveda* 7.104.5) and of total annihilation, a state that is depicted semi-anthropomorphically as lying in the lap of Nirrti, the destroyer. The inhabitants of Hell are those who live at cross-purposes with the universal law *(rta)*.

Later, in the Vedanta, hell came to be conceived in more strictly philosophical terms as the realm of pure nonbeing. Contrasted with this was the realm of being *(sat)*, the realm of living beings and of life itself that came to be referred to as *brahman*, the limitless and indefinable fulcrum of being.

In the Puranas (collections of classical Hindu mythologies), hells are depicted in terrifyingly graphic terms as places of extreme suffering and deprivation. In the *Ramayana* (7.21.10-20), Ravana, the ten-headed demon, witnesses a scene of indescribable wretchedness on entering Yama's abode. He hears the agonizing cries of the wicked being gnawed by dogs and devoured by worms. Pitiful screams shoot across the Vaitarani River from parched people on hot sand who are being sawed in half. The thirsty cry out for water; the hungry, for food.

Secular Visions. Among a growing number of religious intelligentsia the world over, both heaven and hell are gradually being sublimated or transmuted into psychological entities or realms, with the personal and collective unconscious serving as the source of both positive and negative feelings, images, and attitudes. Even the general mass of people in industrialized countries who claim to retain a belief in an underworld of some description have, in practice, largely transposed many of the ideas and themes previously associated with the underworld (e.g., divine judgment, suffering, torment, disease, death, and mental and physical anguish) into the arena of contemporary human affairs.

[*See also* Afterlife.]

BIBLIOGRAPHY

General Works
Brandon, S. G. F. *The Judgment of the Dead.* London, 1967.
Mew, James. *Traditional Aspects of Hell* (Ancient and Modern) (1903). Ann Arbor, 1971.

Ancient Near Eastern Religions
Heidel, Alexander. *The Gilgamesh Epic and Old Testament Parallels.* 2d ed. Chicago, 1963.

Frankfort, Henri. *Kingship and the Gods.* Chicago, 1948.
Pritchard, James B., ed. *Ancient Near Eastern Texts relating to the Old Testament.* 3d ed. Princeton, 1969.

Greek and Roman Religions
Dietrich, B. C. *Death, Fate and the Gods.* London, 1965.
Farnell, Lewis R. Greek *Hero Cults and Ideas of Immortality* (1921). Oxford, 1970.
Nilsson, Martin P. A *History of Greek Religion.* 2d ed. Translated by F. J. Fielden. Oxford, 1949.

Judaism
Charles, R. H. *A Critical History of the Doctrine of a Future* Life. 2d ed., rev. & enl. London, 1913.
Ginzberg, Louis. *The Legends of the Jews* (1909-1928). 7 vols. Translated by Henrietta Szold et al. Philadelphia, 1946-1955.
Graves, Robert, and Raphael Patai. *Hebrew Myths.* New York, 1966.

Christianity
Dante Alighieri. *Inferno.* Translated by Allen Mandelbaum. Berkeley, 1980.
Jeremias, Joachim. "Hades." In *Theological Dictionary of the New Testament*, vol. 1, edited by Gerhard Kittel. Grand Rapids, Mich., 1968.
Mew, James. "Christian Hell." In his *Traditional Aspects of Hell (Ancient and Modern)* (1903). Ann Arbor, 1971.
Walker, Daniel P. *The Decline of Hell: Seventeenth Century Discussions of Eternal Torment.* Chicago, 1964.

Islam
Asín Palacios, Miguel. *Islam and the Divine Comedy.* Translated by Harold Sunderland. London, 1926.
Smith, Jane I., and Yvonne Y. Haddad. *The Islamic Understanding of Death and Resurrection.* Albany, N. Y., 1981.
Morris, James W. *The Wisdom of the Throne: An Introduction to the Philosophy of Mulla Sadra.* Princeton, 1981.

Hinduism
Brown, W. Norman. "The Rigvedic Equivalent for Hell." *Journal of the American Oriental Society* 61 (June 1941): 76-80.
Gombrich, Richard F. "Ancient Indian Cosmology." In *Ancient Cosmologies*, edited by Carmen Blacker and Michael Loewe, pp. 110-142. London, 1975.
Jacobi, Hermann. "Cosmogony and Cosmology (Indian)." In *Encyclopaedia of Religion and Ethics*, vol. 4, edited by James Hastings. Edinburgh, 1914.
Hopkins, E. Washburn. *Epic Mythology* (1915). New York, 1969.
Macdonell, A. A. *Vedic Mythology.* Strassburg, 1897.

J. BRUCE LONG

UNGARINYIN RELIGION

To speak of the religious system, rituals, and beliefs of the "tribal" or language group that carries the label Ungarinyin (Ngarinyin) is to deal with the intellectual and spiritual culture of an Aboriginal group that, as a coherent traditional unit, has all but disappeared.

The Ungarinyin inhabited the vast territory between the King Leopold Ranges and the lower Prince Regent River in Australia. Among the different people with whom they shared many aspects of their material and spiritual culture were the Unambal and the Worora.

Spiritual Universe. Like many other Aborigines, the Ungarinyin believe in agents who, during a primordial period, shaped the natural environment into its present configuration and instituted the laws governing natural and social life. This creation by spirit beings, heroes, and deities is a constant and ongoing process. It is manifest on two levels. First, the reproduction of all fauna, flora, and human beings depends on the power emanating from the Dreaming characters: life ends without them. Second, human beings can participate in the power of the Dreaming through ritual actions and also through ordinary dreams, evoking the spirit beings and ensuring fertility of mankind and the environment.

The Dreaming of the Ungarinyin is called by the term *Ungur* or *Lalan*, and all items belonging to or originating in that period are labeled by the possessive suffix *-nanga*, as in *Lalan-nanga*. Some items that derive from that Dreaming are rock paintings, stone arrangements, sacred places, water holes, bull-roarers (used in sacred ceremonies and also in

> **Human beings can participate in the power of the Dreaming through ritual actions.**

trade between different groups), and dances and songs. Another term that connects the primordial Dreaming with the broader concept of the eternal Dreaming and that focuses on personal power is yayari. This word designates a dream or a dream experience and also a vision. It refers to a life force inherent in a person (as one aspect of his or her soul) and is connected with the states of feeling and thinking, as well as with the procreative force of sexual excitement.

The Ungarinyin see a close connection between the creative actions of Dreaming spiritual powers and the dreaming action of living human beings: the connecting link is established through the thought system that has become known under the term *totemism*. The Dreaming heroes, foremost among them the Rainbow Snake, Ungud, and the *wandjina* of tribal importance, as well as those of the many local areas of clans, traversed the world and not only created the landscape with all its present features but also instituted the rules for social and ritual life. Many carry the names of the species they represent, such as the salt-water crocodile, the night owl, the emu, or the crane.

Cosmogony and the Origin of Social Rules. Within the mythical framework of the Ungarinyin, Ungud, the Rainbow Snake, plays without doubt the major role. It is said that she

emerged from the primeval ocean, took a boomerang (not indigenous to this region), and threw it across the salt water, making land emerge from wherever the boomerang hit the water. Ungud then traveled across the land, depositing the innumerable eggs from which all *wandjina* hatched.

The category of primordial creative beings called *wandjina* includes some whose special significance derives from their introduction of major rules governing social relations. The most important of these culture heroes are Wallanganda, Ngunyari, and the twin brothers Banar and Kuranguli.

Wallanganda rivals Ungud in his power of creativity: in some versions the spirit children of all species are created by him through rain, when called upon by Ungud. He is also considered, together with his substitute Ngunyari, to be the bringer of the "blackfellow law" (i. e., marriage regulations and rules of ritual action). Wallanganda represents the prototype of the great hunter, who invented some of the major hunting weapons, such as spears with quartzite tips and spear-throwers. After his creation deeds, Wallanganda retired to the sky, concretely symbolized by the Milky Way, where he is coiled up as a giant Ungud Snake and where he continues hunting with other *wandjina* in a paradise full of water, grass, and animals.

In the myths concerning Ngunyari, about whose fate we are not informed, the importance of women in social as well as ritual life seems to be touched upon. Although no female ceremonies are known to have been held among the Ungarinyin, the role of women must have been important, if the transmitted myths are taken to be significant. It is said that Ngunyari made only his own bull-roarers (or received them in a far country from Wallanganda) and that his two wives made different ones: while the "male" bull-roarers are oblong, the extant "female" bull-roarers tend to have a more convex shape (see Petri, 1954, pp. 118-122). The probability that women were ritually important is strengthened in some myths about female *wandjina*. While the majority of *wandjina* (of male or ambisexual gender) seem benevolent and only concerned with the increase of fecundity, one specific category of female *wandjina* appear terrible. They are the Mulu-Mulu, who live at the bottom of certain wells and capture children and adults wandering alone.

According to myth, men and women used to cohabit indiscriminately until twin brothers Kuranguli and Banar went into the bush to seek wives other than their own: Banar ("wild turkey"), as representative of the Yara ("gray kangaroo") moiety, took a wife of the Walamba ("red kangaroo") moiety, of which Kuranguli ("native companion bird") is the representative. The clever brother Kuranguli lived with his daughter in the more fertile country that represented the inland (sweet) water moiety, but he did not sleep with her. However, his slower brother, Banar, lived with his own daughter as his spouse in a harsher environment associated with the salt water of the opposite moiety. In order to persuade his brother to follow the "correct" form of marriage, and for Banar to arrange that Kuranguli's daughter should marry Banar's son, Kuranguli deflowered her and took her to Banar. Banar and Kuranguli are therefore the originators of the incest prohibitions (while Banar is given credit for introducing the mother-in-law avoidance rule). Although it would appear from many myths that Banar and Kuranguli are often opposed (and even engaged in mortal combat), they always resolve their differences harmoniously, and indeed their rules for social life do stress mutual interdependence rather than antagonism.

BIBLIOGRAPHY

Berndt, Ronald M. "Influence of European Culture on Australian Aborigines." *Oceania* 23 (March 1951): 229-235. Thorough theoretical discussion of acculturative processes with variety of case studies.

Berndt, Ronald M. *Kunapipi*. Melbourne, 1951. Ethnography of a cult in Arnhem Land, elements of which have spread in recent times into the Kimberley region.

Eliade, Mircea. *Australian Religions*. Ithaca, N. Y., 1973. Comprehensive survey on ethnographic sources about Aboriginal religions, including the German materials on the Kimberleys, considered comparatively. Slightly simplifies the intricate ethnographic features reported by Helmut Petri on the Ungarinyin.

Elkin, A. P. "Rock-Paintings of North-West Australia." *Oceania* 1 (October-December 1930): 257-279. Earliest truly ethnographic description of Kimberley religious concepts, in particular with regard to *wandjina* rock paintings in context of living culture.

Elkin, A. P. *Aboriginal Men of High Degree* (1945). 2d ed. New York, 1977. Transcontinental survey on concepts of Aboriginal doctors and their practices.

Koepping, Klaus-Peter. "Religion in Aboriginal Australia." *Religion* 11 (October 1981): 367-391. Survey article on studies about Aboriginal religious systems since 1960, pointing to a comparative phenomenology of Aboriginal concepts.

Lommel, Andreas. *Die Unambal*. Hamburg, 1952. Clearly written ethnography of a religious system neighboring the Ungarinyin. Indispensable for comparison to Petri's work with valuable data from the expedition of 1938.

Petri, Helmut. "Kurangara." *Zeitschrift für Ethnologie* 75 (1950): 43-51. Ethnographic and theoretical analysis of cult movements superseding traditional systems in the Kimberleys.

Petri, Helmut. "Der Australische Medizinmann." *Annali Late-ranensi* 16 (1952): 159-317 and 17 (1953): 157-225. Indispensable work surveying all known systems of Aboriginal doctors, with ethnographic sections on the Kimberley Plateau.

Petri, Helmut. *Sterbende Welt in Nordwest Australien*. Braunschweig, 1954. Only in-depth ethnography on Ungarinyin social and religious system with intricate theoretical discussion, relying on field data collected in 1938, incorporating materials from adjacent groups on the Kimberley Plateau.

KLAUS-PETER KOEPPING

UNIATE CHURCHES

Uniate is the name given to former Eastern Christian or Orthodox churches that have been received under the jurisdiction of the church of Rome and retain their own ritual, practice, and canon law. The term carries a strong negative connotation in that it was first used by opponents to the union of Brest-Litovsk (1595) to indicate a betrayal of Orthodoxy. It is seldom used today by these churches to describe themselves.

Melchite Catholics. The term *Melchite* refers to a Christian of the Byzantine rite—Catholic or Orthodox—from the patriarchates of Alexandria, Antioch, or Jerusalem. The Melchite faithful tried to preserve allegiance to both Rome and Constantinople. By 1724 renewed communication with Rome had resulted in the creation of a Catholic Melchite church alongside the Orthodox Melchite church, although no formal written agreement of union was ever drawn up. Many Melchite Catholics immigrated to North and South America at the beginning of the twentieth century and formed two eparchies (dioceses), in Newton, Massachusetts, and in Sao Paolo, Brazil.

Maronite Church. The Maronite church traces its origins to the fourth century and to the monk Maron, who received a Greek and Syrian literary education and went to Antioch to complete his studies. There he met and befriended John Chrysostom, who was soon to be the bishop of Constantinople. Centuries later, a community of Maronites grew up around the Monastery of Saint Maron on the banks of the Orontes River in northern Syria. Although the Maronite church never rejected the primacy of the Roman see, communication between the two churches was interrupted for centuries, and only after 1182 and the advent of the Crusaders was Roman recognition of the Maronite rite restored.

The Maronite church is the only Uniate church that does not have a parallel Orthodox hierarchy. The church has undergone many influences tending to conform it to the Latin rite. The rite of the Maronite church belongs to a group of Antiochene rites, and its liturgical language is West Syriac or Aramaic.

Ruthenians. The most numerous Uniate church of the Byzantine rite is the Ruthenian. *Ruthenian* is derived from the Latin *Rutheni*, meaning "Russian" and is used by Western historians to designate Catholic Slavs of the Polish-Lithuanian state or of the Austro-Hungarian empire. The Ruthenians divided into two branches: to the north of the Carpathian Mountains under Polish or Russian control were the Galicians. The Subcarpathians lived on the southern side of the mountains and were influenced by Austro-Hungarian political and social conditions.

The subsequent political division of Galician territory subjected Byzantine Catholics there to persecution by their Orthodox brethern, who thought they had changed their traditions by allowing Latin rite deviations. In 1805 the see of Kiev was abolished and the Ruthenians placed under the protection of the Austro-Hungarian empire and the jurisdiction of the archbishop of Lvov (Lemberg), who was recognized as the primate of the Ruthenians of Galicia.

As nascent nationalism penetrated the Galician church, divisions began to arise. Ruthenians slowly developed a national consciousness in the Subcarpathian region and continued to refer to themselves as "Greek Catholics," an ethnic as well as a religious term. Those Ruthenians who assumed Hungarian culture called themselves Hungarians. The growth of Romanian nationalism created the same phenomenon among Byzantine rite Catholics in Romania.

After World War II the Soviet government actively persecuted Ruthenian Catholics to force them into the Russian Orthodox church. In a council of reunion held at Lvov (Lviv), the remaining faithful, whose families had been threatened with deportation, voted in March 1946 to abolish the union with Rome. The metropolitan see of Galicia was placed under the jurisdiction of the patriarchate of Moscow. In the case of the Subcarpathian Ruthenians, the territory of the diocese of Uzhgorod was ceded to the Soviet Union by Czechoslovakia after its occupation by the Soviet army. The Orthodox began to occupy Catholic churches under the protection of the civil administration. The abrogation of the union with Rome was signed in August 1949 in the Monastery of Saint Nicholas in Mukachevo.

The liturgy and ritual of the Ruthenian Catholics remained conservative for centuries and followed the main lines of the Orthodox tradition. The Synod of Zamosc (1720) did introduce a number of innovations as a result of pressure and persecution from the Polish government to conform the Ruthenian usage to the Latin rite.

Ruthenian emigration in large numbers began in the 1870s as a result of poor distribution of agricultural land, rising expectations from industrialization, and political and social pressures. The best statistics put the total emigration by 1919 at 220,000 to the United States; 180,000 to Canada; 128,000 to Brazil; 110,000 to Argentina; and 22,000 to Australia.

Coptic Uniate Church. Despite attempts at union for centuries, the numbers of Uniate Copts remained small. Pope Leo XIII created a Coptic patriarchate of Alexandria, Egypt, in 1895, and a Catholic Coptic synod elected Cyril Makarios as patriarch in 1898. The see remained vacant from 1908 to 1947, when Mark II Khouzam was elected patriarch. Four dioceses were erected, and the number of the faithful began to increase dramatically.

Malabar Church of India. The Malabar church, according to tradition, was founded by the apostle Thomas. Hence the Malabarians refer to themselves as "Thomas Christians." Little is known about the Malabar church before the sixteenth century. Portuguese missionaries arrived in India in 1498. The Malabarians, who did not consider themselves to be separated from Rome, welcomed the Portuguese as brothers in the faith, but they refused to allow Latin practices into their church. Portuguese archbishop of Goa, Alexis de Menezes, acted against what he thought were Nestorian errors in the Malabar church in 1597. He convoked and presided at the synod of Diamper in June 1599. At the synod the Malabar liturgy was changed. The anaphoras of Theodore of Mopsuestia and of Nestorius were suppressed; the formula "mother of God" was introduced wherever "mother of Christ" was discovered; the calendar of saints was rejected; and many Latin practices were introduced into the eucharistic liturgy and other sacramental rites. Further, the creed was inserted immediately after the reading of the gospel; unleavened bread and communion of the faithful under one species only was introduced; and a consecration prayer, translated from the Latin, was inserted at the fraction rite, instead of before the anamnesis and epiklesis. Currently a reform of the liturgy is taking place in the Malabar church that restores some of the pre-sixteenth-century ritual.

BIBLIOGRAPHY

For the classic definition of uniatism as the ritual most in conformity with Orthodox liturgical practice, see Cyril Korolevskij's *L'uniatisme: Définition, cause, effets, dangers, remèdes* (Chevtogne, 1927). This liturgical point of view, although nuanced, essentially does not allow for historical development and depends upon a personal preference for the "purest" rite. The best recent survey of Uniate churches is Gaston Zananiri's *Catholicisme oriental* (Paris, 1966). The best recent sociological and historical survey of the process of union, especially in Slavic countries, is Josef Macha's *Ecclesiastical Unification: A Theoretical Framework Together with Case Studies from the History of Latin-Byzantine Relations* (Rome, 1974). While the sociological theory can be overbearing at times, the historical sketches are accurate, detailed, and comprehensive. Another in-depth study of the Slavic unions is Oscar Halecki's *From Florence to Brest, 1439-1596* (Rome, 1958), in which the Polish historian works almost exclusively with primary sources to debunk some established positions about the motives of those who sought union. The best case study of an individual union is Michael Lacko's *The Union of Uzhorod* (Cleveland, 1966). A decidedly anti-Slovak, anti-Hungarian, and pro-Ukrainian view of the history of one diocese is contained in Julius Kubinyi's *The History of the Prjasiv Eparchy* (Rome, 1970). For the best treatment of Subcarpathian nationalism, politics, and intellectual life, see Paul R. Magocsi's *The Shaping of a National Identity: Subcarpathian Rus' 1848-1948* (Cambridge, Mass., 1978). The contemporary Hungarian scholar Mária Mayer discusses the role of the Ruthenian intelligentsia in Budapest in *Kárpátukrán (ruszin) politikai és társadalmi törekevések 1860-1910* (Budapest, 1977). The role of the church and its relation with immigrants in North America is also discussed.

THOMAS F. SABLE, S.J.

UNIFICATION CHURCH

The Unification Church was founded in Korea in 1954 by the Reverend Sun Myung Moon. Within a quarter of a century it had become one of the most widely known and controversial of the contemporary wave of new religious movements. In Korea it is known as the Tong Il movement. In the West it is referred to by a variety of names, such as the Holy Spirit Association for the Unification of World Christianity, the Unified Family, or the Moon Organization, but the movement's members are most popularly known as "Moonies." They believe in a messianic, millennial religion and dedicate their lives to the goal of restoring the kingdom of heaven on earth.

Moon was born in what is now North Korea in 1920. He has claimed that on Easter Day 1936 Jesus appeared to him and asked him to assume responsibility for the mission of establishing God's kingdom on earth. During the next two decades Moon is said to have communicated with various

> The special revelation claimed by Moon is that the archangel Lucifer, whom God had entrusted to look after Adam and Eve, became jealous of God's love for Adam. . . .

other religious leaders (such as Moses and the Buddha) and with God himself. Moon's teachings were written down by his followers and eventually published in English as the *Divine Principle*.

During the movement's early days in Korea it met with considerable opposition from both the established churches and government officials. Moon was imprisoned several times, and at one point spent two and a half years in a communist labor camp (from which he was released by United Nations forces during the Korean War).

In the late 1950s Unification missionaries went to Japan and the West. After a slow start the movement began to grow in Japan and in the United States, but it was not until the early seventies, when Moon himself moved to America, that the Unification Church became known to more than a handful of Westerners. Over the next ten years, however, Moon's name became a household word. He went on numerous lecture tours, always speaking through a Korean interpreter; large rallies were organized; leading academics were invited to international conferences and local and national dignitaries to lavish dinners and receptions, all sponsored by the Unification Church. The movement supported President Nixon during the Watergate crisis. Meanwhile, some valuable

properties (including the New Yorker Hotel and the Tiffany building in Manhattan and several large estates elsewhere in New York State) were acquired by the organization. Businesses (such as fishing and ginseng products) run directly by or affiliated to the movement seemed to prosper; cultural activities (including the Little Angels dance troupe, the Go World Brass Band, and the New Hope Singers) flourished; a seminary for postgraduate studies was founded; daily newspapers in Tokyo, New York, and, later, Washington were launched; and, most visibly of all, clean-shaven, well-groomed, well-spoken young Moonies became a familiar sight, selling candles, candy, cut flowers, potted plants, Unification literature—and the Unification Church itself—on the streets of towns and cities throughout the free world.

Those who join the Unification Church tend to be disproportionately well-educated, middle-class youth in their early twenties. In Japan and the West full-time members usually live in communal centers and work for the movement. In Korea, membership is more likely to consist of families who live in their own homes and work for themselves or for Unification Church-related businesses. The number of fully committed members has been considerably lower than estimates in the media have suggested, partly because of a high drop-out rate; indeed, there have never been, at any one time, more than ten thousand full-time members in the whole of the West. (In the East, full-time membership has never exceeded about twice that number.) There is, however, a considerably larger category of membership, sometimes known as Home Church, which consists of those who are sympathetic toward the theology but continue to lead "normal" lives in the wider community.

The lifestyle of full-time Moonies is one of hardworking, sacrificial devotion to the task of "restoration." Frequently, long hours are spent raising funds or witnessing to potential converts. Members are expected to practice celibacy before marriage as well as for some time afterward. After they have been in the movement for two or three years, members can be "matched" with a partner suggested by Moon and, with hundreds or even thousands of other couples, take part in one of the movement's mass wedding ceremonies known as Blessings. The Blessing is the most important Unification rite, the members practicing relatively little else in the way of formal ritual, apart from a "pledge" which is taken on the first day of each week, month, and year and on the movement's holy days.

Unification theology is one of the most comprehensive to be produced by a contemporary new religion. *The Divine Principle* offers a reinterpretation of the Bible which, it is claimed, could unite all religions. God is portrayed as a personal being who created the world according to a few basic, universal principles. All creation consists of positive and negative (male and female) elements; these unite into larger units, which in turn unite through a give-and-take relationship to form a still larger whole. Adam and Eve were created in order that God might have a loving give-and-take relationship with them. The original plan was that they should mature to a stage of perfection at which they would be blessed in marriage and that, subsequently, their children and their children's children would populate a sinless world in complete harmony with God. This, however, was not to be. The Fall is interpreted not as the result of eating an apple, but as the consequence of a disobedience which involved the misuse of the most powerful of all forces: love. The special revelation claimed by Moon is that the archangel Lucifer, whom God had entrusted to look after Adam and Eve, became jealous of God's love for Adam and had a (spiritual) sexual relationship with Eve. Eve then persuaded Adam to have a (physical) sexual relationship with her. As a result of this premature union, which was Lucifer-centered rather than God-centered, the Fallen Nature, or original sin, of Adam and Eve has been transmitted to all subsequent generations. According to the *Divine Principle*, the whole of history can be seen as an attempt by God and man, and, in particular, by certain key figures of the Bible, to restore the world to the state originally intended by God.

Ultimately, restoration is only possible through the person of the Messiah, who with his wife will faithfully play the roles in which Adam and Eve failed—i. e., those of True Parents. They (and those whom they bless in marriage) will have children born without original sin. But for this to happen, man has to create a foundation ready to receive the Messiah. In practical terms this involves the concept of "indemnity," whereby a good, sacrificial deed can cancel "bad debts" accumulated in the past by a person or his ancestors. The role of the Messiah is seen as an office filled by a man born of human parents, but free of original sin. The *Divine Principle* teaches that Jesus was such a man, who could have restored the world, but, largely through the fault of John the Baptist, he was murdered before he had a chance to marry and he thus was able to offer the world only spiritual and not physical salvation through his death. Numerous parallels between the period before the time of Jesus and the last two thousand years are taken to indicate that the present time is the time of the Second Coming. Although it is not part of the official theology, members of the Unification Church believe that Moon and his wife are the True Parents, and it is apparent from the "internal" literature of the movement that Moon sees himself in the role of the Messiah and expects his followers to do likewise.

Throughout the world, the Unification Church has drawn considerable hostile attention from anticult movements and the media. Among the many accusations leveled at it are that it uses brainwashing or mind-control techniques to recruit and keep its members, that it breaks up families, that the leaders live in luxury while the rank-and-file membership is exploited and oppressed by its authoritarian organization,

that it is strongly anticommunist and has (or has had) connections with the South Korean intelligence agency (the KCIA), that it produces armaments, that it is merely a front for a seditious organization which is attempting to take over the world and establish a theocracy with Moon at its head, and that it violates tax and immigration laws. (In 1982 a federal-court jury convicted Moon of conspiracy to evade taxes and sentenced him to eighteen months' imprisonment.) Needless to say, the movement has vehemently denied the criticisms leveled against it, expressing particular concern where such accusations have been used to justify the practice of "deprogramming," in which members of the movement are forcibly kidnapped and held until they are prepared to renounce their faith.

BIBLIOGRAPHY

Unification theology is contained in the *Divine Principle* (Washington, D. C., 1973) and in *Outline of the Principle, Level 4* (New York, 1980), both issued by the Holy Spirit Association for the Unification of World Christianity. The latter is considerably easier to read than the former. An excellent account of the early days of the movement in America is given in John Lofland's *Doomsday Cult: A Study of Conversion, Proselytization, and Maintenance of Faith*, enl. ed. (New York, 1977). Numerous books, nearly all of which tend to be highly partisan, have been produced by members and close associates of the movement, by ex-Moonies, and by Christians concerned to expose the movement's theological errors. The philosopher Frederick Sontag's book *Sun Myung Moon and the Unification Church* (Nashville, 1977) includes an interview with Moon. Sebastian Matczak's *Unificationism: A New Philosophy and World View* (New York, 1982) is a theological critique and comparison of the movement's beliefs with other thought systems. A sociological approach to the church from the perspective of resource mobilization is offered by David G. Bromley and Anson D. Shupe, Jr., in *"Moonies" in America: Cult, Church and Crusade* (Beverly Hills, Calif., 1979). My own book *The Making of a Moonie: Choice or Brainwashing?* (Oxford, 1984) provides a general description of the movement and its beliefs and practices, but it concentrates mainly on recruitment. A second volume, *Moonies in Action* (Oxford, forthcoming), deals more fully both with life in the movement and with the Unification Church's relations with the wider society.

EILEEN BARKER

UNITARIAN UNIVERSALIST ASSOCIATION

The Unitarian Universalist Association is a religious denomination that is the result of the 1961 merger of the American Unitarian Association and the Universalist Church of America.

Unitarianism. Unitarianism is a religious view that was organized in institutional form in Poland, Transylvania,

England, and the United States. Its emergence is primarily the result of indigenous factors in each country. The separate movements had common characteristics: affirmations of the unity of God, the humanity of Jesus, and human religious responsibility, and rejections of the doctrines of the Trinity, the divinity of Jesus, and human corruption or total depravity. Formulations of these views differed in each country.

In Poland, disputes in the Polish Reformed Church in 1555 led to a schism and the formation of the Minor Reformed Church of Poland in 1565. A central community was founded at Racow in 1579. Fausto Sozzini (1539-1604), who came to Poland in that year, became the recognized leader of the Polish Brethren, who adopted his name by calling themselves Socinians. Sozzini's theology emphasized prayer to Christ, as the man whom God resurrected and to whom God gave all power in heaven and earth over the church. The Lithuanian Brethren, a sister group led by Simon Budny, were nonadorantist in theology, which meant they rejected prayer to Christ. The Polish and Lithuanian movements flourished primarily from 1580 to 1620. Roman Catholic opposition in 1632 required the Socinians to become Roman Catholics or go into exile or be executed. A few Socinian exiles found refuge with the Transylvanian Unitarians in Kolozsvár (present-day Cluj-Napoca).

In 1568 John Sigismund, the Unitarian king of Transylvania, granted them religious freedom. (The name Unitarian gradually came into use after debates at Gyulafehérvár in 1568 and at Nagyvárad in 1569.) The Transylvanian Unitarians still survive in Romania and Hungary.

In England, one group insisted on agreement with confessional statements, the other group required only the use of biblical terms and conformity with biblical views. Members of the latter group and their congregations gradually moved toward Unitarian views. Theophilus Lindsey (1723-1808) opposed the Anglican church's creedal restrictions, left that church's ministry, and founded Essex Street Chapel in London in 1774, the first English Unitarian congregation.

The British and Foreign Unitarian Association, founded in 1825, was aided by the repeal of laws against nonconformity and by parliamentary approval of the Dissenters' Chapels Act (1844), which assured Unitarians of their churches.

James Martineau (1805-1900), who exercised great influence among English Unitarians, challenged Priestley's theology with his emphasis on ethics and intuition. Martineau, who desired comprehension in a national liberal church, prefered the name Free Christian to Unitarian. In 1928, English Unitarian denominationalists and those who were influenced by Martineau's Free Christian views united to form the General Assembly of Unitarian and Free Christian Churches. The Non-Subscribing Presbyterian Church of Ireland, which derives from the influence of Thomas Emlyn (1663-1741),

and some Welsh and Scottish churches, are different expressions of English Unitarianism.

American Unitarianism gradually emerged during the eighteenth century within Congregationalism, largely because of the influence of Arminian theology, which stressed the human capacity to respond to grace, and Arian Christology. This gradual development resulted in conflicts that culminated in the appointment of a liberal, Henry Ware, as Hollis Professor of Divinity at Harvard College in 1805.

> **Modern Universalism derives from radical pietism and from dissenters from the Baptist and Congregational traditions.**

The liberals were accused of covertly agreeing with Belsham's humanitarian Christology. Boston minister William Ellery Channing (1780-1842) replied that, instead, most of the liberal ministers were Arians, for they believed that Christ's character included ethical, intellectual, and emotional perfection, and that he was subordinate to God.

Channing's famous Baltimore sermon "Unitarian Christianity" (1819) gave the liberals a coherent theological view that embraced assertions of the unity and moral perfection of God; of the unity of Jesus Christ, his inferiority to God, and his mediatorial mission; and of human moral responsibility. The American Unitarian Association (AUA), an association of individuals, not of churches, was organized in 1825. Ralph Waldo Emerson, in his Cambridge Divinity School address (1838), and Theodore Parker in his sermon "The Transient and Permanent in Christianity" (1841), challenged the prevailing Unitarian emphasis on the authority of rationally interpreted scripture. These addresses initiated a controversy over Transcendentalism within Unitarianism. Parker has influenced many Unitarians as an exemplar of public ministry, for he expressed his theology in outspoken sermons on social and economic issues, ceaseless efforts for social reform, and a willingness to disobey the Fugitive Slave Act of 1850, which he regarded as immoral, in obedience to a higher moral law. [*See the biography of Emerson.*]

In the early twentieth century, religious humanism appeared within Unitarianism under the leadership of John Dietrich and Curtis Reese, who were among those who signed the Humanist Manifesto (1933). A serious decline among the Unitarian churches during the depression led to the creation of a denominational Commission on Appraisal (1934-1936), whose chairman, Frederick May Eliot, reluctantly agreed to become president of the AUA. Eliot's leadership revived the movement.

Universalism. Universalism is a religious view that affirms the ultimate salvation of all humans. In some formulations, that has meant the ultimate reconciliation of all, even Satan, with God. *Acts* 3:21 is one of the scriptural bases for the belief that some Universalists have in a universal restoration (Gr., *apokatastasis*). Modern Universalism derives from radical pietism and from dissenters from the Baptist and Congregational traditions.

In 1681, Jane Leade (1624-1704) became the recognized leader of a Philadelphian Society of pietists in London. The group's name came from the sixth church mentioned in *Revelation* 3:7-13. In Germany, Johann Wilhelm Petersen led a group of German Philadelphian pietists. He reinterpreted Leade's views, gave them scriptural foundations, and published his reinterpretation in *The Mystery of the Restoration of All Things*, 2 vols., 1700-1710. Groups of German Philadelphian pietists and people from other groups took copies of the treatise with them when they migrated to Pennsylvania in the eighteenth century. George de Benneville (1703-1793), who moved to Pennsylvania in 1741, maintained contacts with different groups in colonial Pennsylvania whose members affirmed Universalism and thus prepared the way for Universalism's later growth in America.

Individuals in several European countries affirmed Universalism, but they founded no effective organizations. In England, however, Universalism survived within Unitarianism which contained as members former General Baptists and other persons who held universalist views.

The institutional growth of Universalism, however, was to be in America. In 1803 at Winchester, New Hampshire, the General Convention of Universalists in the New England States embraced the varied Universalist views of the time. In 1870 the Universalist General Convention approved a resolution to affirm the authority of scripture and the lordship of Jesus Christ. This creedal period ended in 1899, when the restrictions were rescinded and a noncreedal statement was adopted in Boston. A revised noncreedal Bond of Fellowship, known as the Washington Profession, was adopted in 1935 and revised in 1953.

The Unitarian Universalists. Sporadic contacts between the Unitarians and the Universalists in the nineteenth and early twentieth centuries were followed in 1953 by organization of the Council of Liberal Churches (Universalist-Unitarian). Cooperation in this council's departmental programs prepared the way for the churches' merger in 1961 into the Unitarian Universalist Association (UUA), of which Dana McLean Greeley became the first president.

The theological diversity that characterizes Unitarian Universalists is expressed in worship that varies greatly from congregation to congregation, ranging from structured liturgy to thematic or sermon-centered emphases. In 1980 the UUA's Commission on Common Worship continued the task of the preceding commissions, that of providing materials that will enable people holding widely differing theological views to worship together.

BIBLIOGRAPHY

The basic history of Unitarianism can be found in Earl Morse Wilbur's *A History of Unitarianism: Socinianism and Its Antecedents* (Cambridge, Mass., 1945) and *A History of Unitarianism in Transylvania, England, and America* (Boston, 1952). An important companion volume for the seventeenth-century period is *The Polish Brethren: Documentation of the History and Thought of Unitarianism in the Polish-Lithuanian Commonwealth and in the Diaspora, 1601-1685*, 2 vols., translated and edited by George H. Williams (Missoula, Mont., 1980). *The English Presbyterians: From Elizabethan Puritanism to Modern Unitarianism*, by C. Gordan Bolam, Jeremy Goring, H. L. Short, and Roger Thomas (London, 1968), is an illuminating description of English Unitarianism. *The Beginnings of Unitarianism in America* by Conrad Wright (Boston, 1955) gives a precise analysis of theological issues in the eighteenth century. Wilbur's few chapters on American Unitarianism have now been supplemented by *A Stream of Light: A Sesquicentennial History of American Unitarianism*, edited by Conrad Wright (Boston, 1975).

Universalism in America, 2 vols. (Boston, 1884-1886), by Richard Eddy, has been the basic history for many years. It will now be superseded by a two-volume work by Russell E. Miller, *The Larger Hope*, vol. 1., *The First Century of the Universalist Church in America*, 1770-1870 (Boston, 1979) and vol. 2, *The Second Century of the Universalist Church in America*, 1870-1970 (Boston, 1986). Ernest Cassara edited a selection of basic source documents, *Universalism in America: A Documentary History* (Boston, 1971). Charlotte Irwin provided a useful description of the European background of American Universalism in "Pietist Origins of American Universalism" (M. A. thesis, Tufts University, 1966). The original theological interpretation by George H. Williams in *American Universalism: A Bicentennial Historical Essay* (Boston, 1971) is an important contribution. The most recent study of the merged denominations is David Robinson's *The Unitarians and the Universalists* (Westport, Conn., 1985).

JOHN C. GODBEY

VAISESIKA

The Vaisesika school of Indian philosophy, founded by Kanada (sixth century BCE?), has concentrated mostly on issues and themes of ontology and has closely cooperated with the Nyaya, its sister philosophical school, on matters of epistemology. Like many other schools of Indian philosophy, it upholds that all living beings, human or nonhuman, have souls that are different from the body, eternal, and ubiquitous; that the supreme goal of life is liberation from the bondage of *karman* and the cycle of birth and rebirth; and that the attainment of liberation is the only means of ensuring freedom from all suffering.

According to Vaisesika teaching, the soul is a kind of substance that is conceived as the substratum of quality particulars *(gunas)* and motion. Both quality particulars and motion are related to the substance by way of inherence *(samavaya)*. *Samavaya* is a special kind of relation as well as an independent ontic category that binds only those two kinds of relata, one of which must be destroyed with the severance of the relationship. Substances, quality particulars, and motions share common properties, or universals, that are eternal and independent of their substrates and yet related to them by way of inherence. Physical substances are produced from combinations of atoms, which are eternal, indivisible, and imperceptible. Each eternal substance is characterized by an ultimate differentiator *(visesa)*, which serves as a basis of distinction under circumstances where no ordinary means of distinction is available. Besides the above six kinds of positive ontological categories—substance, quality particular, motion, universal, inherence, and ultimate individuator—there is a negative ontic category, including such entities as absence (as of a book on the table), difference (as of one thing from another), and so on.

The Vaisesika school seeks to prove the existence of the soul by arguing that desire, cognition, and other attributes are quality particulars and must be supported by a substance that is nonphysical because they are radically different in many ways from the quality particulars of physical substances. Such a substance must also be permanent and endure through time; otherwise no satisfactory account can be given of such phenomena as memory. It must further be eternal and in particular, preexistent before birth, or else one cannot account for the fact that a newborn child reaches out for its mother's milk, given that the infant's action is claimed to be purposive and involve memory (which can only have been acquired in a previous life).

One of the souls, called Isvara (God), is said to be endowed with superhuman qualities such as omniscience. Isvara's existence is inferred from the premise that a conscious agent is required not only for the creation of artifacts such as a pot, but indeed for all effects, and that the conscious agent responsible for bringing about a conjunction of atoms leading to the production of macrocosmic objects can only be Isvara. He is also inferred as the author of revealed scriptures and further as the original bestower of significance on linguistic symbols, an act making all communication possible.

[*See also* Nyaya.]

BIBLIOGRAPHY

The best book on Nyaya-Vaisesika philosophy is Gopinath Bhattacharya's edition and translation of the *Tarkasamgrahadipika* (Calcutta, 1976). For readers who are less technically minded, but still want a comprehensive and precise account, the best book is *Indian Metaphysics and Epistemology: The Tradition of the Nyaya-Vaisesika up to Gangesa*, edited by Karl H. Potter (Princeton, 1977), volume 2 of *The Encyclopedia of Indian Philosophies*. The general reader may profitably consult Mysore Hiriyanna's *Essentials of Indian Philosophy* (London, 1949).

KISOR K. CHAKRABARTI

VATICAN COUNCILS

Vatican I

Preliminary Discussions. Pius IX was encouraged by prominent members of the episcopate to announce his intention of convoking a council; on 29 July 1868 he officially summoned all the bishops of Christendom to come to Rome by 8 December 1869, along with others who had the right to attend (especially the superiors general of the major religious orders).

The choice of the consultors who were to prepare the drafts of the conciliar decrees—the group included sixty

Romans and thirty-six from abroad, almost all of them known for their ultramontane and antiliberal views—disturbed those who had been hoping that the council would provide an opportunity for bishops from the outer reaches of the church to open up the church somewhat to modern aspirations. A number of European governments did become apprehensive about possible conciliar decrees on civil marriage, the place of religion in public education, and the legitimacy of freedom

> **The infallibilist pressure group . . . circulated a petition asking the pope to put on the assembly's agenda a draft definition of papal infallibility.**

of worship and the press. In the end, these governments chose to limit themselves to an attitude of distrustful expectation.

Conciliar Debates. The council opened on 8 December 1869, in the presence of about 700 bishops, about two-thirds of those with the right to attend. Among them were 70 prelates of the Eastern rite who were in union with Rome, most of these being from the Middle East, and almost 200 fathers from non-European countries: 121 from the Americas (49 from the United States), 41 from Southern Asia and the Far East, 11 from Oceania, and 9 from the African missions, which were then in their infancy

On 28 December the council began at last to examine the first drafted constitution, which was directed "against the numerous errors deriving from modern rationalism." This draft drew strong criticism because of its substance, which some found to be out of touch with contemporary forms of rationalism and too apodictic on points freely discussed among theologians. After six meetings for discussion, which had the advantage of showing that the council would be freer than some had feared, the presidents announced on 10 January that the draft would be sent back to the commission for recasting and that meanwhile the council would tackle the drafts on church discipline. In this area twenty-eight drafts had been prepared that were rather tame and showed hardly any pastoral openness to the future; to these were added eighteen others, much superior in character, on the adaptation of canon law to the new circumstances of the religious orders and congregations. In order to speed up the pace of the work (as the great majority of the fathers wanted), the pope, on 20 February 1870, amended the regulations that had been distributed at the opening of the council.

While the examination of texts that had little chance of proving explosive was advancing with prudent caution in the council hall, the attention of both the fathers and the public was increasingly focused on the question of infallibility. On

the one side, many fathers who were very hostile to their contemporaries' infatuation with liberalism were not at all reluctant to have the council restate the principles according to which, in classical teaching, the relations between church and state should be ruled in an ideal Christian society. Many—often the same— wanted a solemn definition of the personal infallibility of the pope. Reasons of a nontheological kind strengthened many of these prelates in their conviction: their veneration of Pius IX; their belief that an increased emphasis on the monolithic character of the Roman church could only draw to this church various non-Catholics who were distressed by the hesitancies and lack of resoluteness of the churches separated from Rome; and their desire, in the face of the religious crisis they saw growing before their eyes, to give an increasingly centralized form to the defensive and offensive strategy of the church.

A comparable mixture of doctrinal considerations and nontheological motives inspired other prelates to think that such projects would overthrow the traditional constitution of the church and might well threaten the most legitimate aspirations of civil society. In addition, the way in which the question of infallibility was presented in the most prominent ultramontane newspapers could only confirm in their views those who were convinced that "the intention was to declare the pope infallible in matters of faith in order thereby to make people think him infallible in other matters as well" (Leroy-Beaulieu), that is, in matters more or less related to the political order.

The two groups had an opportunity to count heads as early as January. The infallibilist pressure group, again acting independently (but in close contact with the Jesuits of *La civiltà cattolica*), circulated a petition asking the pope to put on the assembly's agenda a draft definition of papal infallibility, which the preparatory commission had preferred not to offer on its own initiative. The petition finally collected 450 signatures, and, despite a counterpetition signed by 140 bishops, Pius IX decided on 1 March to include the desired passage in the draft of the constitution.

Conciliar Constitutions. The draft of the constitution against rationalism, which had been recast by bishops Martin, Deschamps, and Pie with the help of the Jesuit Joseph Kleutgen, came before the council again on 18 March. The new version was favorably received by the fathers. On 24 April the council unanimously gave its solemn approval to its first dogmatic document, the constitution *Dei filius*, which responded to pantheism, materialism, and modern rationalism with a substantial exposition of Catholic teaching on God, revelation, and faith; this exposition was to be for almost a century the basis of the treatises which made up fundamental theology.

Chapter 1 condemns pantheist views and briefly sets forth Catholic teaching on providence. Chapter 2 defines, against atheism and traditionalism, the possibility of knowing the existence of God with certainty by the natural light of reason and, against deism, the absolute necessity of revelation if man is to have knowledge of the supernatural order. Chapter 3 defines the reasonableness of the act of faith as against the illuminism of some Protestants and against those who deny the value of the external motives of credibility, such as miracles. Chapter 4 explains the relations that should exist between faith and reason, science and revelation: there are mysteries that cannot be demonstrated by reason, but reason can legitimately reflect on supernatural truths.

It quickly became clear that, given the pace at which work was proceeding, the constitution on the church, the text of which had been distributed to the fathers on 21 January, would not come up for discussion for several months; this was even more true of its eleventh chapter, which dealt with the special prerogatives of the pope. Consequently, as early as March, new petitions requested that this chapter, which made the council restive, be discussed out of its proper order as soon as the examination of the constitution against rationalism was concluded. Despite the reservations of three of the five presidents of the council, Pius IX, who was increasingly displeased at the opposition of the minority group, decided to alter the schedule. In order to avoid the anomaly of treating this chapter before the others, it was expanded into a short, independent constitution devoted entirely to the pope.

The general debate on the text as a whole began on 13 May. After some fifteen meetings, the fathers went on to examine the details of the texts; this discussion focused essentially on the chapter devoted to the definition of papal infallibility. The proposed text, although the commission had already improved it by comparison with the original draft, did not yet take sufficient account of the legitimate role that belonged to the episcopate, alongside and in collaboration with the pope, in the supreme teaching office of the church. Fifty-seven speakers took the floor, emphasizing theological arguments or historical difficulties, as well as the practical advantages or drawbacks of a definition in the circumstances of that time. When a final appeal of the minority to Pius IX had no result, some sixty bishops decided to leave Rome before the final vote in order not to have to cast a negative vote in the presence of the pope on a question that directly concerned him. The other members of the minority judged that the successive improvements of the text as well as Bishop Gasser's commentary had removed the principal substantive objections and they decided therefore to approve the final text. This text was solemnly accepted on 18 July by nearly everyone present.

Officially entitled First Constitution on the Church of Christ, the constitution *Pastor aeternus* expounds Catholic teaching on the privileges of the pope.

The fourth chapter declares that authority as supreme teacher is included in the primacy and then recalls how over the course of time the popes had always exercised this function by drawing upon the faith of the universal church as expressed in particular by the teaching of the bishops. The chapter then goes on to define solemnly that this supreme teaching office has attached to it the prerogative of infallibility, provided the pope is speaking *ex cathedra*, that is, provided that "in exercising his office as teacher and shepherd of all Christians he defines, in virtue of his supreme apostolic authority" (that is, with the intention of unequivocally putting an end to all discussion) "that a doctrine concerning faith or morals must be held by the universal Church; such definitions are irreformable of themselves and do not require ratification by the episcopate (*ex sese non autem ex consensu Ecclesiae*)."

After the vote taken on 18 July the council continued its work for two more months, but at a slower pace, since the majority of the fathers had left Rome for the summer. The occupation of Rome by the Italians on 20 September brought the work to a definitive end, and on 20 October the pope announced that the council was adjourned indefinitely.

When the immediate results of the council were compared with its ambitious program (fifty-one drafts had still to be voted on) and especially with the great hopes the convocation of the council had raised, the First Vatican Council seemed to many to have been a failure, its principal outcome having been to aggravate the disunity among Christians. With the passage of time, however, people became aware of important results flowing from the intense intellectual ferment the convocation of the council had produced. The first dogmatic constitution that had been passed in April 1870 exercised a clarifying influence on subsequent theological teaching, especially in the burning question of the relations between reason and faith. On the other hand, it also strengthened the tendency to enlarge the role of authoritative doctrinal interventions in the development of Catholic thought; this tendency was strengthened even more by the definition of papal infallibility.

BIBLIOGRAPHY

The main documents that inform us of the preparation and course of the council have been published in volumes 49-53 of the *S. Conciliorum nova et amplissima collectio* (Arnhem, 1923-1927). The two most detailed histories of the council are ten-dentious: Johann Friedrich's *Geschichte des vatikanischen Konzils*, 3 vols. (Bonn, 1877-1887), is excessively critical from an Old Catholic point of view; Theodor Granderath's *Geschichte des vatikanischen Konzils*, 3 vols. (Freiburg, 1903-1906), is a systematic defense by a Jesuit who refuses to allow any legitimacy to the reservations of the minority. Good presentations are Edward Cuthbert Butler's *The Vatican Council*, 2d ed., 2 vols. (London, 1965), and Michele Maccarrone's *Il Concilio Vaticano I*, "Italia Sacra," vols. 7 and 8 (Padua, 1966). A shorter presentation is my *Vatican I* (Paris, 1964).

Worthy of special mention among the studies of the national episcopates are James Hennesey's *The First Council of the Vatican: The American Experience* (New York, 1963); Frederick J. Cwiekowski's

The English Bishops and the First Vatican Council (Louvain, 1971); Klaus Schatz's *Kirchenbild und päpstliche Unfehlbarkeit bei den deutschsprachigen Minoritätsbischöfen auf dem I. Vatikanum* (Rome, 1975); and Constantin Patelos's *Vatican I et les évêques uniates* (Brussels, 1982). Doctrinal commentaries on the constitution *Dei filius* include Alfred Vacant's *Études théologiques sur les constitutions du Concile du Vatican d'après les actes du concile*, 2 vols. (Paris, 1895), and on the constitution *Pastor aeternus*, Gustave Thils's *La primauté pontificale* (Gembloux, France, 1972), and the same author's *L'in-faillibilité pontificale* (Gembloux, France, 1969). August B. Has-ler's *Pius IX (1846-1878), päpstliche Unfehlbarkeit und 1. vatika-nisches Konzil*, 2 vols. (Stuttgart, 1977), raises real questions but is spoiled by a lack of historical criticism. See also Giacomo Martina's "Pio IX e il Vaticano I, di A. B. Hasler, rilievi criti-ci," in *Archivum historiae pontificiae* 16 (1978): 341-369, and Joseph Hoffmann's "Histoire et dogme: la definition de l'infaillibilité pontifi-cale à Vatican I," in *Revue des sciences philosophiques et théologiques* 62 (1978): 543-557 and 63 (1979): 61-82. A very complete analytical and critical bibliography is J. Goñi Gastambide's "Estudios sobre el Vaticano I," *Salman-ticensia* 19 (1972): 145-203, 381-449.

ROGER AUBERT
Translated from French by Matthew J. O'Connell

Vatican II

The Church before the Council. The liturgical movement, whose roots go back to the time of the Reformation, reached a peak of activity in the twentieth century. The movement sought to revive liturgical forms in order to create the church anew by means of daily participation in the objective events of liturgy and the mysteries of the church. Connected with this was a new valuation of sacramentality and of the procla-mation of the word.

Paralleling the liturgical movement was the biblical move-ment, which rediscovered the immediate religious meaning of holy scripture by means of new translations into vernacu-lar languages and the formation of Catholic Bible associa-tions.

The church's consciousness of itself changed. This was primarily a matter of the dissolution of the one-sided canoni-cal understanding of the church as juridical, an understand-ing that had been set forth in the late Middle Ages and was firmly established once and for all by the Code of Canon Law (1917). The change culminated in ecclesiological projects during and after World War II that engendered an under-standing of the church as people of faith subject to the Word.

The ecumenical movements, which since the beginning of the twentieth century had brought together and united the non-Catholic Christian church communities through world church conferences and the founding of the World Council of Churches, stood distanced for a long time from the Roman Catholic church. The opening of the Roman offices for ecu-menism by John XXIII was made possible by contacts and

conversations between Protestant and Catholic theologians and church leaders that took place for mutual defense against antiecclesiastical totalitarianism. The question of the reunification of all Christians appealed to parts of Catholic Christendom and exercised a great influence on theological reflection about the church's unity in diversity and its under-standing of ministry, eucharist, and primacy.

Another important tendency in the Roman Catholic church before the calling of the council involved changes in theology itself. The most important stages were attempts to overcome through kerygmatic theology the objectivistic and unhistorical or superhistorical point of view of neoscholasti-cism; "nouvelle théologie," which emphasized open thinking and opposed scholasticism; transcendental theology, which reflected on the conditions of the possibilities of man; the acquisition of a genuinely theological understanding of histo-ry in hermeneutical theology; and finally the inclusion of the societal dimension in political theology. These positions gained more and more significance with regard to the church's self-understanding and its relationship to the world.

History and Themes of the Council. The Second Vatican Council was the twenty-first ecumenical council (according to the official count of the Roman Catholic church), held from 1962 to 1965 at Saint Peter's Basilica in Rome. All bishops, the Curia Romana, and the theological and canonical faculties voted on topics for discussion. On 5 June 1960 the pope ordered ten specialized commissions to work on the schemata (protocols). There were also two per-manent secretariats (one for the mass media, another for Christian unity). A central preparatory committee was responsible for organizing the work of the council. Of the 2,908 legitimate delegates, 2,540 participated in the open-ing. Of the invited non-Catholic Christian churches and com-munities, seventeen were present through thirty-five repre-sentatives. In the end, twenty-eight non-Roman churches, including the Russian Orthodox church, were represented by ninety-three observers. There were eighty-six governments and international bodies represented at the opening.

The council met in four sessions: 11 October to 8 December 1962; 29 September to 2 December 1963; 14 September to 21 November 1964; and 4 September to 8 December 1965. Ten public sessions and 168 general assembly meetings were held.

From the time of its proclamation, the council was intend-ed to have a double goal: reform within the church and prepa-ration for Christian and world unity. But already in the open-ing address this goal was expanded and deepened.

In the first session, which included the first thirty-six gen-eral assemblies, the commission members were not chosen according to the prepared list but rather, at the suggestion of Cardinal Achille Liénart (Lille), according to recommenda-tions of the different groups of bishops. John XXIII died on 3 June 1963. His successor, Paul VI, continued the council. At the reopening of the second session (general assemblies 37-89) on 29 September 1963, Paul VI emphasized the pastoral orientation of the council. It was to deal with the nature of the church and the function of the bishops, to make efforts toward the unity of Christians, and to set in motion a dialogue with the contemporary world.

The Second Vatican Council was a council of the church about the church. In order to protect its freedom, John XXIII specifically avoided formulating a systematic plan of discussion.

The subjects treated in the documents produced by the council can be summarized briefly. The basic self-understanding of the church is addressed in the Dogmatic Constitution on the Church. The inner life of the church is discussed in various documents: the work of salvation through liturgy (the Constitution on the Sacred Liturgy); the church's function of oversight (the Decree on the Bishops' Pastoral Office in the Church and the Decree on Eastern Catholic Churches); the teaching office (the Dogmatic Constitution on Divine Revelation, including discussions of

> **The opening of the Roman offices for ecumenism by John XXIII was made possible by contacts and conversations between Protestant and Catholic theologians.**

scripture, tradition, and teaching office, and the Declaration on Christian Education); and vocations (the Decree on the Ministry and Life of Priests, the Decree on Priestly Formation, the Decree on the Appropriate Renewal of the Religious Life, and the Decree on the Apostolate of the Laity). The mission of the church to the world is likewise elaborated on in several documents: the church's relationship to non-Catholic Christianity (the Decree on Ecumenism and the Decree on Eastern Catholic Churches); its relationship to non-Christians (the Declaration on the Relationship of the Church to non-Christian Religions, which makes special reference to the Jews, and the Decree on the Church's Missionary Activity); its relationship to the contemporary secular situation of the world in general (the Pastoral Constitution on the Church in the Modern World and the Decree on the Instruments of Social Communications); and its relationship to the philosophical pluralism of the present age (especially in the Declaration on Religious Freedom).

The council's understanding of the church. The Second Vatican Council, in contrast to Trent and to Vatican I, was oriented neither toward dogma nor toward theological controversy; rather it was pastorally oriented in that it set forth the meaning of the church, its message, and its missions for the world and for humanity.

In *Lumen gentium* the council set aside juridical and controversial questions and defined the church first as a mystery, as a sacrament of unity between God and human beings and among human beings themselves. The council, in full support of Vatican I, dealt extensively with the college of bishops. It accentuated the principles of collegiality and synod as structural elements of the church and the meaning of the local church as representative of the whole church. With reference to the priesthood of all believers, the council stressed the dignity, role, and responsibility of the laity as well as the presence of the church in the world, which is often possible only through the laity.

The council characterized the church's relationship to the other churches and Christian confessions not through the instrumental definition of union with Rome but through the living realities in these communities that are constitutive of church. The relationship of these churches to the Roman church is defined by the formula *"coniunctum esse"* ("to be joined together"). According to Vatican II, therefore, the unity of the church is not to be sought by imposing uniformity, that is, by an all-defining centralization, but in a legitimate plurality that strengthens unity and does not endanger it.

A council of the world church. The council seemed to be the first act in which the Catholic church began to realize itself as a truly worldwide community. This world church acted for the first time at the council with historical clarity concerning faith and morals. In spite of the undeniably powerful presence and influence of the European and North American regional churches, the members of this council, in contrast to all previous councils, were bishops from the whole world and not simply, as at Vatican I, European missionary bishops sent out to the whole world.

The council was also the cause of the abolition of Latin as the common cultic language. In the long run, the liturgy of the universal church will not be a mere translation of the liturgy of the Roman church but rather a liturgy formed from the unity in diversity of regional liturgies in which each has its own unique form that does not result from its language only but also from other cultural factors such as gesture and dance.

Relationship to the world. In several decrees, to which belong primarily the Pastoral Constitution on the Church in the World *(Gaudium et spes)* and the Decree on Religious Freedom, the council attempted to describe its fundamental relationship to the secular world on the basis of its nature and not simply by the force of external circumstances. The temptation for the church to reassert a false superiority over the world continues to exist, but since the decisions of Vatican II the church in principle can no longer yield to this temptation, because the council formulated an irrevocable norm. No longer, since the decrees of the council, can the limitation of freedom in the name of goodness and justice be so easily rationalized by the church.

Theology of the council. The theological situation in which the council found itself was transitional and difficult to define. On the one hand, neoscholastic theology was self-evident; it was the dominant theological position represented in the proposals that had been prepared for the council by Roman commissions. On the other hand, the theology of the council was more critically related to scripture than was neoscholasticism. It had opened itself to subject matter that did not originate in the repertory of neoscholasticism. It exercised a certain braking effect against theological excess (for example, in Mariology). It made an effort to be considerate of ecumenical needs. It also held that one could say something theologically important even if one did not proclaim it solemnly as dogma.

Change in ecumenical attitude. The council signified a break in the history of the relationship of the Catholic church both with other Christian churches and communities and with the non-Christian religions of the world. Naturally there were always contained in the faith consciousness of the church convictions that in principle legitimized the newly emerging relationship of the Catholic church with other Christian churches and communities and the non-Christian religions. The council initiated a point of view that it ratified as truly Christian, namely, that Catholic Christianity had assumed a different and new position relative to other Christians and their churches and relative to the non-Christian religions of the world.

Before the council the Catholic church considered the non-Roman Catholic churches and communities to be organizations and societies of people who differed with the old church only through errors and deficiencies and who ought to return to it in order to find in it the full truth and fullness of Christianity. From the point of view of the old attitude, the non-Christian religions were all forms of paganism, that is, religion that human beings, sinfully and without grace, produced on their own. Those views were changed by Vatican II, and since then a position of acceptance can no longer be excluded, because it is understood not as an aspect of the liberal modern mentality but rather as an integral element of Christian conviction.

[*See also* Roman Catholicism.]

BIBLIOGRAPHY

The best complete presentations of the course of the council are given by Hanno Helbling in *Das Zweite Vatikanische Konzil* (Basel, 1966), Hubert Jedin in *Kleine Konziliengeschichte* (Freiburg, 1978), and René Laurentin in *Bilan du Concile: Histoire, textes, commentaires* (Paris, 1966). The best introduction to the topical problems is given in Joseph Ratzinger's *Die erste Sitzungsperiode des Zweiten Vatikanischen Konzils: Ein Rückblick* (Cologne, 1963), *Das Konzil auf dem Weg: Rückblick auf die zweite Sitzungsperiode* (Cologne, 1964), *Ergebnisse und Probleme der dritten Konzilsperiode* (Cologne, 1965), and *Die letzte Sitzungs-periode des Konzils* (Cologne, 1966). A comprehensive chronicle of the council is provided in *Il Concilio Vaticano II*, 5 vols. (Rome, 1966-1969). An English-language chronicle can be found in *Council Daybook*, 3 vols., edited by Floyd Anderson (Washington, D. C., 1965-1966).

Texts, minutes, and concordances concerning the proceedings can be found in *Acta et documenta Concilio oecumenico Vaticano II apparando*, "Series Antepraeparatoria," 5 vols. (Vatican City, 1960-1961), and "Series Praeparatoria," 3 vols. (Vatican City, 1964-1969); *The Documents of Vatican II in a New and Definitive Translation*, edited by Walter M. Abbott (New York, 1966); *Commentary on the Documents of Vatican II*, 3 vols., edited by Herbert Vorgrimler (New York, 1967-1969); and *Acta synodalia Concilii oecumenici Vaticani II* (Vatican City, 1970-1978). Concordances of the council texts can be found in *Indices verborum et locutionum decretorum Concilii Vaticanii II* (Florence, 1968-). An outstanding council bibliography can be found in the *Archivum Historiae Pontificiae* (Rome, 1963-).

KARL RAHNER and ADOLF DARLAP
Translated from German by Charlotte Prather

VEDANTA

The word *vedanta* literally means "end [*anta*] of the Veda," that is to say, the concluding part of the *apauruseya*, or revealed Vedic literature, which is traditionally believed to comprise the Samhitas, the Brahmanas, the Aranyakas, and the Upanisads. Vedanta thus primarily denotes the Upanisads and their teachings. Metaphorically, Vedanta is also understood to represent the consummation or culmination (*anta*) of the entire Vedic speculation, or indeed of all knowledge (*veda*).

Upanisads. Over two hundred texts call themselves Upanisads, but they include even such recent works as the *Christopanisad* and the *Allopanisad*. The *Muktikopanisad* gives a traditional list of 108 *Upanisads*, but, even out of these, many texts seem to have been called Upanisads only by courtesy. Usually 13 Upanisads, namely, *Isa, Kena, Katha, Prasna, Mundaka, Mandu-kya, Taittiriya, Aitareya, Chandogya, Brhadaranyaka, Svetasvatara, Kausitaki,* and *Maitrayani*, are regarded as the principal Upanisads (eighth to fourth century BCE). They are traditionally connected with one Vedic school (*sakha*) or another, and several of them actually form part of a larger literary complex.

The Upanisads represent the fearless quest for truth by essentially uninhibited minds. They seek, among other things, to investigate the ultimate reality "from which, verily, these beings are born, by which, when born, they live, and into which, when departing, they enter" (*Taittiriya Upanisad* 3.1.1), to delve into the mystery of the *atman* "by whom one knows all this" but whom one cannot know by the usual means of knowledge (*Brhadaranyaka Upanisad* 4.5.15), and generally to promote "that instruction by which the unheard becomes heard, the unperceived becomes perceived, and the unknown becomes known" (*Chandogya Upanisad* 6.1.3).

The Upanisads presuppose a certain development of thought. The origin of some of their doctrines can be traced back to the *Rgveda*, or in certain cases, even to the pre-Vedic non-Aryan thought complex. It will also be seen that, from the methodological as well as from the conceptual point of view, the Upanisads owe not a little to the Brahmanas, as a reaction against which they were largely brought into existence. In a sense, the Upanisads represent an extension of the tendency of the Brahmanas toward *bandhuta*, that is, toward perpetually establishing equivalences between entities and powers apparently belonging to different levels and to different spheres.

The Upanisads clearly betray a trend toward inwardization and spiritualization, which presumably has its origin in their general aversion for the physical body and sensual experience (*Maitri Upanisad* 1.3). The Upanisadic teachers have consistently emphasized the view that the essential or real self *(atman)* has to be differentiated from the empirical or embodied self *(jiva)*. Indeed, true philosophical knowledge consists in not confusing the one for the other. The essential Self is of the nature of pure self-consciousness. It is neither the knower nor the known nor the act of knowing. The essential Self does exist. It is conscious, but not of any particular object, internal or external; it is pure *cit* (consciousness), that is to say, it is of the nature of consciousness *as such*.

Side by side with the analysis of the human personality, the Upanisadic thinker has attempted an analysis of the external world as well. He has thereby arrived at the conclusion that at the basis of this gross, manifold, changing phenomenal world—which ultimately is a conglomeration of mere names and forms—there lies one single, uniform, eternal, immutable, sentient reality (see, e.g., *Chandogya Upanisad* 6.1). The natural and logical next step is to identify the deepest level of the subjective person, namely, the essential Self *(atman)*, with the ultimate basis of the objective universe, namely, the cosmic reality (*brahman*, also called *sat*).

Brahmasutras. A vigorous and comprehensive cultural movement was set in motion that sought to resuscitate the Brahmanic way of life and thought by reorganizing, systematizing, simplifying, and popularizing it. The literary monuments of this movement were generally clothed in a practical literary form, namely, the *sutras*, or aphorisms, that were defined as being at once brief but unambiguous and to the point. By their very nature, the Upanisadic teachings, which were often sheer flashes of spiritual radiance rather than coherent philosophical formulations, were characterized by inherent ambiguities, inconsistencies, and contradictions. In order that they should prove reasonably meaningful, it was necessary to systematize and, more particularly, to harmonize them.

Apparently the *Brahma Sutra* was not the only work of this kind, for Badarayana mentions several predecessors as, for example, Atreya, Asmarathya, Kasakrtsna, and Jaimini. By themselves they could hardly be made to yield any cogent philosophical teaching. Yet it seems that the *Brahma Sutra* favors a kind of *bhedabheda*, or doctrine of distinction-*cum*-nondistinction. The world is represented as a transformation of the potency of God, God himself remaining unaffected and transcendent in the process. Hardly any of

> **The essential Self is of the nature of pure self-consciousness. It is neither the knower nor the known nor the act of knowing.**

Badarayana's *sutras* can be shown to be unequivocally nondualistic in purport. It also seems that the *Brahma Sutra* is specifically disposed against Samkhya dualism and Mimamsa ritualism.

Gaudapada. The earliest complete extant commentary on the *Brahma Sutra* is that of Sankara (788-820 CE). But in his thinking Sankara is more vitally influenced by Gaudapada (fifth to sixth century) than by Badarayana.

Gaudapada lived at least three centuries before Sankara. True to the usual practice of Hindu thinkers, Gaudapada has set forth his philosophy in his commentary, in the form of *karikas* or memorial verses. The *Gaudapadakarika* constitutes the earliest treatise on absolute nondualism *(kevala advaita)*. The very names of the four books that make up the work—namely, *Agama* (Scripture), *Vaitathya* (Unreality of the World Experience), *Advaita* (Nondualism), and *Alata-santi* (Extinction of the Revolving Firebrand)—bring out the entire teaching of Gaudapada in a nutshell.

There can be hardly any doubt about the strong Buddhist influence on Gaudapada's thought. The *Gaudapadakarika* creates an irresistible impression that the Buddhist Sunyavada and the Vijñanavada schools present philosophical positions that are in no small measure consistent with those presented by the major classical Upanisads.

Sankara. Sankara is by far the most outstanding and the most widely known exponent of Vedanta, particularly of the doctrine of absolute nonduality (Kevala Advaita). Many works pass as having been written by him, but among the philosophical works that can be ascribed to him with reasonable certainty are the commentaries on nine Upanisads; the commentaries on the *Brahma Sutra*, the *Bhagavadgita*, the *Gaudapadakarika*, the *Yogasutra-bhasya*, and the *Adhyatmapatala* of the *Apastamba Dharmasutra*; and the *Upadesasahasri* (with its nineteen verse tracts and three prose tracts).

Sankara's philosophy, like most Indian philosophy, is oriented toward the one practical aim of *moksa*, which implies liberation from suffering and regaining of the original state of bliss. Sankara takes for granted the validity of the Upanisads as an embodiment of the highest truth, and uses logic either to support his interpretation of the Upanisads or to refute other systems of thought. In his commentary on the *Brahma Sutra* he seeks to harmonize the apparently contradictory teachings of the Upanisads through the assumption of two points of view, the ultimate (*paramarthika*) and the contingent (*vyavaharika*).

The main plank of Sankara's philosophy is the belief in the unity of all being and the denial of the reality of the many particular entities in the universe. Reality is that which is one without a second, which is not determined by anything else, which is not sublated at any point of time, which transcends all distinctions, to which the familiar categories of thought are inapplicable, and which can be only intuitively realized. Such is *brahman* of Sankara's Advaita. Sankara's most distinctive contribution is the philosophical and dialectical development of the concept of *brahman* as without qualities (*nirguna*). *Nirguna brahman* is not to be understood as "void" or "blank"; it only signifies that nothing that the mind can think of can be attributed to it. *Sat* (pure, unqualified being), *cit* (pure consciousness), and *ananda* (pure bliss), which are often affirmed of *brahman*, are not qualifying attributes of *brahman* but rather together constitute the essential nature of *brahman*.

For Sankara the four prerequisites for *brahman* realization are discrimination between the eternal and the temporal, renunciation of nonspiritual desires, moral equipment, consisting of tranquility, self-control, and so forth, and an intense longing for *moksa*.

Post-Sankara Teachers of Kevala Advaita. The school of Sankara's Kevala Advaita can boast of a long line of teachers and pupils who through their writings have brought tremendous popularity to that school.

Mandana Misra was a contemporary, perhaps a senior contemporary, of Sankara. His *Brahmasiddhi* shows that he is directly influenced by Sankara's philosophy. He emphasizes that it is the *jivas* who by their own individual *avidya* create for themselves the world appearance on the changeless *brahman*; he discountenances the theory that the world originates from the *maya* of *brahman*.

Padmapada is believed to have been the first pupil of Sankara, and was, according to a tradition, nominated by the master as the first pontiff of the *matha* at Puri. His only available work, called *Pancapadika*, invests *maya* with a sort of substantiality and also assigns to it cognitive as well as vibratory activity. *Brahman* in association with *maya* as characterized by this twofold activity is, according to Padmapada, the root cause of *jagat*, while *avidya* manifests itself in *jiva*.

It is, however, Vacaspati (fl. 841) who may be said to have founded an independent subschool of Sankara's Vedanta. Vacaspati has sought to merge the teachings of Sankara and Mandana Misra into one system. He propounds the view that *avidya* has *brahman* as its object (*visaya*) and *jiva* as its support (*asraya*). Like the Bhamati subschool of Advaita, Prakasatman (fl. 1200) inaugurated another independent subschool—the Vivarana subschool—through his *Vivarana* (exposition) of Padmapada's *Pancapadika*. Prakasatman endorses the view of Sarvajñatman that *brahman* is both the support and the object of *avidya*. While in respect of *jiva* the Bhamati subschool puts forth the doctrine of limitation (*avaccheda*), the Vivarana subschool puts forth the doctrine of reflection (*pratibimba*).

Sabdadvaita. Although there is generally evident a tendency to equate Vedanta with Sankara's Kevala Advaita, one

> According to Bhaskara, *brahman* has a dual form: *brahman* as pure being and intelligence . . . and *brahman* as the manifested effect or the world.

cannot afford to ignore the other schools of Vedanta that have been substantially influential. The doctrine of *sabdadvaita*, a monistic ontology presenting language as the basis of reality, was propounded by Bhartrhari (d. 651) in his *Vakyapadiya*; this doctrine cannot be said to belong to Vedanta proper, since it is not derived from any of the three *prasthanas*. Still, according to Bhartrhari the ideas that the ultimate reality, *brahman*, which is without beginning and end, is of the nature of the "word" and that the world proceeds from it can be traced back to the revelation of the Word *par excellence*, the Veda itself. This ultimate reality is one, but because of its many powers it manifests itself as many in the form of experiencer, the object of experience, and experience itself (the purpose of experience also being sometimes mentioned).

Bhaskara. The proper post-Sankara Vedanta begins with Bhaskara (fl. 850). Unlike the other post-Sankara schools of Vedanta, Bhaskara's Vedanta does not seem to have gained wide currency, presumably because it was not linked up with any theistic sect. According to Bhaskara, *brahman* has a dual form: *brahman* as pure being and intelligence, formless, the causal principle, which is the object of our highest knowledge; and *brahman* as the manifested effect or the world. Thus brahman represents unity (*abheda*) as well as distinction (*bheda*), both of which are real. *Jiva* is *brahman* characterized by the limitations of the mind substance. Thus, unlike the material world, *jiva* is not the effect of *brahman*.

Visistadvaita. To Ramanuja (1017-1137) belongs the credit for successfully attempting to coordinate personal theism with absolutistic philosophy. Ramanuja's commentaries on two of the three *prasthanas*, namely, the *Brahma Sutra* (called *Sribhasya*) and the *Bhagavadgita*, have been preserved. According to Ramanuja, God, who possesses supremely good qualities, is the only absolute reality and therefore the only object worthy of love and devotion. Matter *(acit)* and souls *(cit)*, which are equally ultimate and real, are the qualities *(visesanas)* of God, but, as qualities, they are entirely dependent on God in the same way as the body is dependent on the soul. They are directed and sustained by God and exist entirely for and within him. Ramanuja's doctrine is therefore known as Visista Advaita or the doctrine of one God qualified by *cit* (souls) and *acit* (matter). These three factors *(tattva-traya)* form a complex *(visista)* organic unity *(advaita)*. The omnipotent God creates the world of material objects out of himself, that is, out of acit (which is eternal in him), by an act of will. Ramanuja emphasizes that creation is a fact, a real act of God.

Dvaitadvaita. The philosophy of Nimbarka (fl. mid-fourteenth century?) is generally known as Svabhavika Bhedabheda or Dvaitadvaita. Nimbarka assumes the ultimate reality of the three entities, namely, Paramatman or Purusottama (God), Jiva, and Jagat. He does not accept *avidya* as a cosmic principle producing the world appearance. Rather, according to him, God actually transforms himself into the world of material objects and individual souls, but does not lose himself in these. He is simultaneously one with *(abheda)* and distinct from *(bheda)* the world of *jivas* and matter. This is so, not because of any imposition or supposition *(upadhi)*, but because of the specific peculiarity of God's spiritual nature *(svabhava)*. God alone has independent existence, while individual souls and matter, which are but derivative parts of God, are entirely dependent on and controlled by him.

Suddhadvaita. Many works, large and small, are ascribed to Vallabha (1479-1531), the most important among them being the *Anubhasya*, a commentary on the *Brahma Sutra* (up to 3.2.34); the *Tattvarthadipanibandha*, an independent philosophical treatise; and the *Subodhini*, a commentary on a major part of the *Bhagavata*. *Suddha advaita* ("pure nondualism") and *pustimarga* are the two fundamental tenets of Vallabha's Vedanta. *Suddha advaita* implies that the one *brahman*, free from and untouched by *maya*, is the cause of the individual souls and the world of material objects. *Jivas* and the material world are, in reality, *brahman*, for they represent but partial manifestations of the essential attributes of *brahman*. Brahman (God) pervades the whole world. God manifests his qualities of *sat* and *cit* in the form of *jivas*, but the quality of bliss *(ananda)* remains unmanifested. Vallabha teaches that it is through *pusti* (literally, "nourishment, spiritual nourishment"), or the special grace of God,

that *jivas* attain *goloka* ("the world of cows"), the world of bliss.

Madhva. Among the Vedantins, Madhva (1238-1317) is reputed to be a confirmed dualist *(dvaitin)*. Madhva no doubt speaks of two mutually irreducible principles as constituting reality, but he regards only one of them, namely, God, as the one infinite independent principle, whereas the finite reality comprising matter, individual souls, and other entities is regarded as dependent. He emphasizes that Lord Sri Hari, who is omnipresent, omniscient, omnipotent, and without beginning and end, is the highest independent reality.

BIBLIOGRAPHY

Agrawal, Madan Mohan. *The Philosophy of Nimbarka*. Agra, 1977.
Dasgupta, Surendranath. *A History of Indian Philosophy*. 3 vols. London, 1922-1940.
Deutsch, Eliot. *Advaita Vedanta: A Philosophical Reconstruction*. Honolulu, 1969.
Hacker, Paul. *Untersuchungen über Texte des frühen Advaitavada*, vol. 1, *Die Schüler Sankaras*. Wiesbaden, 1953.
Hacker, Paul. "Sankara der Yogin and Sankara der Advaitin. Einige Beobachtungen." In *Festschrift für Erich Fraunallner*, special issue of *Wiener Zeitschrift für die Kunde Süd- und Ostasiens* 12/13 (1968-1969): 119-148.
Hacker, Paul. "Sankaracarya and Sankarabhagavatpada: Preliminary Remarks Concerning the Authorship Problem." In *Kleine Schriften*, edited by Lambert Schmithausen, pp. 41-58. Wiesbaden, 1978.
Hiriyanna, Mysore. *Outlines of Indian Philosophy*. New York, 1932.
Sharma, B. N. K. *A History of the Dvaita School of Vedanta and Its Literature*. 2 vols. 2d rev. ed. Bombay, 1981.

R. N. DANDEKAR

VIETNAMESE RELIGION

Like the whole complex of Vietnamese culture, Vietnamese religion has long been presented as a pure copy of the Chinese model. Historically, the Red River delta, cradle of Vietnamese civilization, was occupied by the Han for more than a thousand years. Nonetheless, Dongsonian civilization, which flourished in this region before its destruction by the Han invasions, must have possessed a certain vigor, for despite the very long coercive occupation that followed it, the Vietnamese preserved their language and a part of their culture, finally succeeding in the tenth century of the common era after numerous revolts in liberating themselves from their deeply implanted Chinese occupants. Paradoxically, the consolidation for independence reinforced the prestige of the Chinese model among the literati. Their influence in this regard even resulted in the promulgation in 1812 by Emperor Gialong, who had recently reunified the country, of a new code that was nothing more than a translation of a Manchu dynasty treaty.

Yet, in a population that was more than 90 percent rural, ideology directly concerned only a relatively small number of people, those who wielded power and prestige. The ideals and beliefs they held touched but superficially the great masses, who remained bound to a set of rules transmitted orally and put to the test through daily observance. That the Vietnamese spoke a language belonging to a different family (Austroasiatic rather than Sino-Tibetan) was a considerable asset for the preservation of these rules.

In the religious sphere, this situation created a coexistence, on the one hand, of a Chinese model followed strictly by the most erudite men or those instructed in the faith, and on the other, of popular cults observed by the great mass of people.

The expansion southward along the entire length of the Vietnamese territory added further to this diversification of

> **Here the medium is "mounted" not by one god but successively, in the course of the same séance, by different spirits of both sexes.**

the religion by the absorption, on the small coastal plains, of the Chams, whose religious affiliation was divided between Brahmanism and Islam, and on the Mekong delta, of the Khmer adherents to Theravada Buddhism. These three religions, with that of the Proto-Indo-Chinese on which they were grafted, effected a syncretism.

I will not emphasize the Chinese model, already treated elsewhere, but will focus only on those aspects that touch directly on Vietnamese religion. On this level of the individual, a fundamental concept is that of "souls" or "vital principles." This concept governs as many aspects of daily conduct as it does basic rituals such as funeral rites or ancestor worship.

Appropriate funeral rites are absolutely essential for the benefit of the departed. There is fear of two categories of malevolent spirits, the *ma* (Chin., *ma*) and the *gui* (Chin., *kuei*), souls of the dead without sepulchers. In contrast, one can benefit from the aid of the *thân* (Chin., *shen*), souls of ancestors, understood in a noble sense. These three entities, expressed in Sino-Vietnamese words, testify to the survival of the *hon*.

From words of the same family comes the Vietnamese *hoi*, with its Sino-Vietnamese doublet *khi* (Chin., *ch'i*), whose meaning ranges from breath, inhalation, emanations from living or dead bodies, to "supernatural influence" over man's life and destiny. This influence can emanate not only from a man but also from an animal, the ground, stones, plants, and so

forth. The concept provides the essential basis of popular cults as well.

Prior to 1975, when asked his religion, an educated Vietnamese generally would have answered that he was a Buddhist.

On the civic or family level, however, he followed Confucian precepts; on the affective level or in the face of destiny, he turned to Taoist conceptions. His personal behavior would have remained impregnated with Taoism. This fact was evident in his concern to conform with cosmic harmony, to pay careful attention to sources and currents of energy traversing the universe, and to parallel equivalents between these and the human body. These concerns were manifested in his desire to withdraw into nature as well as in his recourse to geomancy and diverse divinatory procedures, even to magic. It was primarily Confucianism and Buddhism, however, that affected his moral conduct.

It is true that the observance of ancestor worship attested to the ascendancy of Confucianism, but the different Buddhas and *bodhisattvas* tended to join the ranks of the multiple divinities and deities of the Taoist pantheon. Taoism itself was immeasurably enriched with popular autochthonous beliefs and practices, to which it lent a certain respectability by a tint of sinicization; furthermore, magic played a proportionally more important role in activities of a religious type.

Ancestor worship occupied a central place in the family cult. It represented the ritual expression of a cardinal virtue, filial piety (*hiêu*; Chin., *hsiao*), the pivot of interpersonal relationships. The necessity of perfecting oneself morally and intellectually, loyalty to one's friends, respect for one's superiors, fidelity to the sovereign—all these were believed to arise from the domain of filial piety. [*See also* Ancestors.]

The extent of the economic impact of ancestor worship on a family depended on the wealth of that family. Reserved exclusively for the maintenance of such worship and for the performance of its ceremonies were revenues from property (rice fields, houses, etc.) that constituted the *huong-hoa* (Chin., *hsiang-huo*), the portion of "the incense and the fire" transmitted by inheritance from the father to his eldest son. It should be noted that Confucianism did not succeed in lowering the Vietnamese woman to the inferior rank occupied by her Chinese counterpart. Even in wealthy families the wife had the same status as her husband in family ceremonies, including those pertaining to ancestor worship in its strict sense.

The recourse to mediums and ritual decorative features representing the pantheon dominated by the Jade Emperor made possible the assimilation of Taoist elements into a certain number of Vietnamese popular cults. The one that came closest in form to a Taoist cult was that attributed to Trân Hung Dao, a spirit served by a male medium (*ông wông*). Trân Hung Dao is a Vietnamese national hero from the thirteenth century. As well, the cult of the *chu vi*, "dignitaries" served by female mediums (*ba wông*), borrowed from Taoism

VOODOO

some elements of the decor. Here the medium (a *ba wông* in this case) is "mounted" not by one god but successively, in the course of the same séance, by different spirits of both sexes and of different ages.

At the collective level, the cult of the tutelary deity (*thanh-hoang*; Chin., *sheng-huang*), the protector of the commune, held an eminent place in Vietnamese popular religion. Indeed, the most important public building in a village was the *winh*, both a communal house and a place of worship; it sheltered the altar of the tutelary deity and served as a meeting place of the notables for the settlement of questions of administration and internal justice.

The *thanh-hoang* could be a celestial deity, a deified legendary or historical personage, or even a disreputable person, such as a thief or a scavenger, whose violent death at a "sacred hour" endowed him with occult powers.

Certain trees, rocks, and natural boundaries were objects of cults that could lead to the construction of small altars. This veneration, very often fearful, could have varied origins. The tree, for example, could influence by the simple force of its being. It could also shelter a malevolent spirit, such as a *ma*, the soul of an unburied dead person, or of a *con tinh*, the soul of a young girl or woman who died before having experienced the joys of marriage.

[*See* Southeast Asian Religions *and* Chinese Religion.]

BIBLIOGRAPHY

Cadière, Leopold Michel. *Croyances et pratiques religieuses des Viêtnamiens*. 3 vols. Saigon, 1955-1958.

Dumotier, Gustave. "Essai sur les Tonkinois: Superstitions." *Revue indochinoise* 9 (1908): 22-76, 118-142, 193-214.

Durand, Maurice. *Technique et panthéon des médiums viêtnamiens*. Paris, 1959.

Nguyên Dông Chi. *Luoc khao ve thân thoai Viêt Nam*. Hanoi, 1956.

Nguyên Du. *Vaste recueil de légendes merveilleuses*. Translated by Nguyên Tran Huan. Paris, 1962.

Nguyên Tung. "Les Viêtnamiens et le monde surnatural." In *Mythes et croyances du monde entier*. Paris, 1986.

Nguyên Van Huyên. *La civilisation annamite*. Hanoi, 1944.

Nguyên Van Huyên. *Le culte des immortels en Annam*. Hanoi, 1944.

Nguyên Van Khoan. "Essai sur le Dình et le culte du génie tutélaire des villages au Tonkin." *Bulletin de l'École Française d'Extrême-Orient* 30 (1930): 107-139.

Nguyên Van Khoan. "Le repêchage de l'âme, avec une note sur les hôn et les phách d'après les croyances tonkinoises actuelles." *Bulletin de l'École Française d'Extrême-Orient* 33 (1933): 11-34.

Phan Ke Binh. *Viêt-Nam phong-tuc*. Saigon, 1970.

Simon, Pierre J., and Ida Simon-Barouh. "Les Génies des Quatre Palais: Contribution à l'étude du culte viêtnamien des *bà-dông*." *L'homme* 10 (October-December 1970): 81-101.

Tran Van Giap. "Le bouddhisme en Annam, des origines au treizième siècle." *Bulletin de l'École Française d'Extrême-Orient* 32 (1932): 191-268.

GEORGES CONDOMINAS
Translated from French by Maria Pilar Luna-Magannon

VOODOO, or *Vodou* (according to official Haitian Creole orthography), is a misleading but common term for the religious practices of 80 to 90 percent of the people of Haiti. The term *voodoo* (or *hoodoo*, a derivative) is also used, mostly in a derogatory sense, to refer to systems of sorcery and magic. In contemporary Haiti, *vodou* refers to one ritual style or dance among many in the traditional religious system. Haitians prefer a verb to identify their religion: they speak of "serving the spirits."

African Influence. Voodoo was born on the sugar plantations out of the interaction among slaves who brought with them a wide variety of African religious traditions. Three African groups appear to have had the strongest influence on Voodoo: the Yoruba of present-day Nigeria, the Fon of Dahomey (present-day Benin), and the Kongo of what are now Zaire and Angola. Many of the names of Voodoo spirits are easily traceable to their African counterparts; however, in the context of Haiti's social and economic history, these spirits have undergone change.

Roman Catholic Influence. The French slaveholders were Catholic, and baptism was mandatory for slaves. While Catholicism may well have functioned in this utilitarian way for slaves on the plantations, it is also true that the religions of West Africa, from which Voodoo was derived, have a long tradition of syncretism. Whatever else Catholicism represented in the slave world, it was most likely also seen as a means to expand Voodoo's ritual vocabulary and iconography. Catholicism has had the greatest influence on the traditional religion of Haiti at the level of rite and image, rather than theology. This influence works in two ways. First, those who serve the spirits call themselves Catholic, attend Mass, go to confession, and undergo baptism and first communion, and, because these Catholic rituals are at times integral parts of certain larger Voodoo rites, they are often directed to follow them by the Voodoo spirits. Second, Catholic prayers, rites, images, and saints' names are integrated into the ritualizing in Voodoo temples and cult houses.

Currently there is an uneasy peace between Voodoo and the Catholic church. Until quite recently, the Catholic clergy routinely preached against serving the spirits. Since Catholicism is the official religion of Haiti and the church has been to some extent state-controlled, the degree to which Voodoo has been tolerated, or even encouraged, has been at least partly a function of politics.

Voodoo Spirits. Although no longer recognized as such by Haitians, the names of the Voodoo spirit nations (*nanchon*) almost all refer to places and peoples in Africa. For example, there are *nanchon* known as Rada (after the Dahomean principality Allada), Wangol (Angola), Mondon (Mandingo), Ibo, Nago (the Dahomean name for the Ketu

Yoruba), and Kongo. In rural Voodoo, a person inherits responsibilities to one or more of these *nanchon* through maternal and paternal kin. Each spirit group has drum rhythms, dances, and food preferences that correspond to its identifying characteristics.

The Voodoo View of the Person. In Voodoo teachings the human being is composed of various parts: the body, that is, the gross physical part of the person, which perishes after death, and from two to four souls, of which the most widely acknowledged are the *gro bonanj* and the *ti bonanj*. The *gro bonanj* ("big guardian angel") is roughly equivalent to consciousness or personality. When a person dies the *gro bonanj* survives, and immediately after death it is most vulnerable to capture and misuse by sorcerers. The *ti bonanj* ("little guardian angel") may be thought of as the conscience or the spiritual energy reserve of a living person and, at times, as the ghost of a dead person. Each person is said to have one spirit who is the *mèt-tet* ("master of the head"). The *mèt-tet* is the major protector and central spirit served by that person, and it is that spirit that corresponds to the *gro bonanj*. Because the *gro bonanj* is the soul that endures after death and because it is connected to a particular *lwa*, a person who venerates the ancestors inherits the service of particular spirits.

Voodoo and the Dead. In both urban and rural Haiti, cemeteries are major ritual centers. The first male buried in any cemetery is known as the Baron. Baron's wife is Gran Brijit, a name given to the first female buried in a cemetery. Every cemetery has a cross either in the center or at the gate. The cross is known as the *kwa Baron* ("Baron's cross"), and this is the ritualizing center of the cemetery.

Haitians make a distinction between *lemó* ("the dead") and *lemistè* ("the mysteries"). Within Voodoo, there are rituals and offerings for particular family dead; however, if these ancestral spirits are seen as strong and effective, they can, with time, become *mistè* (mysteries).

The *gèdè* are not only spirits of death but also patrons of human sexuality, protectors of children, and irrepressible social satirists. Dances for *gèdè* tend to be boisterous affairs, and new *gèdè* spirits appear every year.

Voodoo Ceremonies. In rural Voodoo, the ideal is to serve the spirits as simply as possible because simplicity of ritual is said to reflect real power and the true African way of doing things (Larose, 1977).

Urban Voodoo, by contrast, has a more routine ritualizing calendar, and events tend to be larger and more elaborate. Ceremonies in honor of major spirits take place annually on or around the feast days of their Catholic counterparts and usually include sacrifice of an appropriate animal—most frequently a chicken, a goat, or a cow. A wide variety of ceremonies meet specific individual and community needs: for example, healing rites, dedications of new temples and new ritual regalia, and spirit marriages in which a devotee "marries" a spirit of the opposite sex and pledges to exercise sexual restraint one night each week in order to receive that spirit in dreams. Death rituals include the *desounen*, in which the *gro bonanj* is removed from the corpse and sent under the waters, and the *rele mó nan dlo* ("calling the dead up from the waters") a ritual that can occur any time after a period of a year and a day from the date of death.

Annual pilgrimages draw thousands of urban and rural followers of Voodoo. The focal point of events, which are at once Catholic and Voodoo, is usually a Catholic church situated near some striking feature of the natural landscape that is believed to be sacred to the Voodoo spirits.

Voodoo and Magic. Serge Larose (1977) has demonstrated that magic is not only a stereotypic label that outsiders have applied to Voodoo, but also a differential term internal to the religion. Thus an in-group among the followers of Voodoo identifies its own ritualizing as "African" while labeling the work of the out-group as *maji* ("magic"). Generally speaking, this perspective provides a helpful means of grasping the concept of magic within Voodoo. There are, however, those individuals who, in their search for power and wealth, have self-consciously identified themselves with traditions of what Haitians would call the "work of the left hand." This includes people who deal in *pwen achte* ("purchased points"), which means spirits or powers that have been bought rather than inherited, and people who deal in *zombi*. A *zombi* may be either the disembodied soul of a dead person whose powers are used for magical purposes, or a soulless body that has been raised from the grave to do drone labor in the fields.

The "work of the left hand" should not be confused with more ordinary Voodoo ritualizing that treats problems of love, health, family, and work. Unless a problem is understood as coming from God, in which case the Voodoo priest can do nothing, the priest will treat it as one caused by a spirit or by a disruption in human relationships.

[*See* Santería *and* Yoruba Religion.]

BIBLIOGRAPHY

Alfred Métraux's *Voodoo in Haiti* (New York, 1959) is the most complete and accurate treatment of the subject available in English. Métraux concentrates on urban Voodoo. The best information in book form on rural Voodoo is contained in Melville J. Herskovits's *Life in a Haitian Valley* (New York, 1937), an ethnography of the Mirebalais Valley located about fifty-five kilometers inland from Port-au-Prince. Maya Deren, a dancer and filmmaker, has written a rich and insightful work on her encounter with Voodoo, *Divine Horsemen: The Living Gods of Haiti* (1953; reprint, New Paltz, N. Y., 1983). In addition, Harold Courlander's *The Drum and the Hoe: Life and Lore of the Haitian People* (Berkeley, 1960) provides much helpful information about Voodoo, particularly about its music.

To greater and lesser extents all of the above works are outdated and faulty in their ethnography. For more recent and more detailed studies of Haitian Voodoo, the reader must turn to articles; useful sources include Ari Kiev's "The Study of Folk Psychiatry," in *Magic,*

Faith, and Healing, edited by Ari Kiev (New York, 1964), Serge Larose's "The Meaning of Africa in Haitian Vodu," in *Symbols and Sentiments: Cross-Cultural Studies in Symbolism*, edited by I. M. Lewis (New York, 1977); Michel S. Laguerre's "Haitian Americans," in *Ethnicity and Medical Care*, edited by Alan Harwood (Cambridge, Mass., 1981), and "Voodoo and Urban Life," a chapter in Laguerre's *Urban Life in the Caribbean: A Study of a Haitian Urban Community* (Cambridge, Mass., 1982); and Ira P. Lowenthal's "Ritual Performance and Religious Experience: A Service for the Gods in Southern Haiti," *Journal of Anthropological Research* 34 (1978): 392-415. Two other articles, although not recent, are helpful in filling gaps in the literature: Melville J. Herskovits's "African Gods and Catholic Saints in New World Negro Belief," *American Anthropologist* 39 (1937): 635-643, and George E. Simpson's "The Vodun Service in Northern Haiti," *American Anthropologist* 42 (1940): 236-254. Wade Davis's *The Serpent and the Rainbow* (New York, 1985), though more an adventure story than a work of ethnography, does contain a detailed and accurate account of the manufacture of *zombi* poison and the role of secret societies in administering it.

Two works in French also make important contributions: Milo Marcelin's *Mythologie vodou*, 2 vols. (Port-au-Prince, 1949-1950), and Louis Maximilien's *Le vodou haïtien: Rite radas-canzo* (Port-au-Prince, 1945).

Erika Bourguignon's *Possession* (San Francisco, 1976) contains a good discussion of the trance-possession phenomenon. Her chapter on Haiti is unfortunately flawed in its ethnography. Louis Mars's *La crise de possession dans le Vaudou: Essais de psychiatrie comparée* (Port-au-Prince, 1946), though full of rich detail, takes a reductive position based in Western psychology; Mars sees possession as indicative of neurosis.

The most thorough history of Haiti, including Voodoo, is still James G. Leyburn's *The Haitian People* (1941), rev. ed., with a new introduction by Sidney Mintz (New Haven, 1966). Finally, Robert Farris Thompson's *Flash of the Spirit: African and Afro-American Art and Philosophy* (New York, 1981) contains the best analysis yet done on the specific African retentions within Haitian Voodoo.

KAREN McCARTHY BROWN

WALBIRI RELIGION

The Walbiri (Warlpiri) numbered about 1,400 members. Their tribal homeland, situated in Australia's Northern Territory, covered approximately 100,000 square kilometers of relatively arid country. Traditionally, the Walbiri were seminomadic hunters and gatherers whose subsistence depended heavily on women's daily collection of vegetable foods.

The Dreaming. Like many Australian Aborigines, the Walbiri postulated the earlier existence of the Dreaming, an era in which the behavior of demiurgic totemic beings ordered an inchoate world to the degree that all its components became subject to lawful processes and combined to constitute an environment in which people could live as social creatures. The Dreaming heroes secured these changes by enacting for the first time the rituals the Walbiri were to perform and by naming the natural phenomena they met on their journeys. These endowments of the Dreaming also encompassed the cultural institutions that the Walbiri cherished, including their totemic religious philosophy. This was a monistic worldview that characterized people, society, and nature as interacting parts of a larger totality, in which each element was held to be morally constrained to maintain itself undiminished for the proper functioning of the system.

Walbiri totems or Dreamings included many of the phenomena occurring in the environment before European contact—fauna, flora, minerals, celestial objects, meteorological events, and human artifacts. Some totemic species were thought to assume human shape and actions at will; others always exhibited their own characteristics. There were also male and female culture heroes who roamed in the Dreaming, always in human form. They too were totems, but they occupied a more important status than did other beings in the religious system—Walbiri believed that people differ from other creatures, not least in possessing a degree of free will.

Sacred Geography. All totems originated in the Dreaming, and each ultimately had a local reference, which could range from a path extending several hundred miles, to a specific tract occupying a few square miles. Dreaming heroes or species who possessed paths either sprang from the earth or sky within the Walbiri domain or arrived from an adjacent language group's territory to make long journeys during which they shaped and identified the landscape and its occupants, enacted rituals, introduced cultural rules and practices, and left some of their spiritual essence wherever they camped. These places were all named and known to the Walbiri. Their creative work done, the totemic beings either entered the earth or sky in Walbiri territory or traveled on to instruct neighboring groups.

The sites within a particular Dreaming country or on a Dreaming track were not necessarily confined to the territory of one Walbiri community or even to the Walbiri domain proper.

Despite such geographical dispersion of totemic localities, however, the men of each Walbiri community emphasized in a diacritical manner their relationships with certain of the more significant Dreamings. Thus, the Waneiga were more concerned with fire and the Mamandabari—the two heroes of the Gadjeri ritual complex; the Lander group of the Walbiri focused on the Walangari heroes; the Ngalia with the Two Kangaroos, Wallaby, and Traveling Women Dreamings; and the Walmalla with the Yam, Opossum, and Fire Dreamings.

Every Walbiri possessed a Conception Dreaming or totem, acquired as a consequence of a spirit essence's entry into the womb of his or her pregnant mother; the spirit essence animated the fetus from which the person later developed. The identity of the specific essence depended on the totemic identity of the locality where the woman was residing when she discovered her pregnancy. Thus, offspring of a widely traveled woman could all have different Conception Dreamings.

Cult Lodge Rituals. All initiated men of a patrimoiety were entitled to act in rituals performed for any totem classified in that moiety, to wear appropriate totemic designs, and to manipulate related ritual objects; but only men of the associated lodge were legitimate custodians or masters of the Dreaming. Lodge members, whatever their actual agnatic ties or places of birth or residence, regarded their Lodge Dreaming as a spiritual father and themselves as spiritual brothers. They likewise referred to actual members of their totemic species as their "fathers" or "brothers," with whom they also shared the spiritual essence of the Dreaming—although they were not necessarily enjoined from killing or consuming them. Every Walbiri boy was, as a rule, initiated into his father's lodge when he was circumcised at about the age of twelve or thirteen. A few years after initiation and before his marriage, the young man was subincised. This operation, although obligatory, did not carry the same sanctifying significance as did circumcision. Its main consequence was to enable a man to draw from his penile urethra potent blood with which to anoint novices and other men.

Women of a patrilineage were not formally initiated into that lodge and did not learn the songs and rituals that the men performed. Correlatively, Walbiri men knew little of the ceremonies and paraphernalia that women utilized to strengthen their own spiritual ties to their homelands or to ameliorate marital difficulties.

Spirits. People who were related matrifilially shared a "matrispirit." These, however, were not associated with particular Dreamings. A matrispirit resided in a woman's uterus, and during pregnancy part of this spirit passed into the fetus, male or female, to become a double of the parent spirit. Men could not pass on their matrispirit. At death the matrispirit became an ethereal ghost that resembled the deceased. It stayed near the tree platform where the corpse rested until the death was explained and, if necessary, avenged.

Walbiri beliefs about the personal incorporation of patrispirits and matrispirits had important structural implications; in particular they expressed a principle of complementary filiation that allocated specific jural rights among paternal and maternal kin of each individual. To possess such a spirit signified membership in a social category, and the two forms of grouping— namely, patrilines and matrifilial sets— performed correlative sacred and secular tasks that were crucial for the maintenance of the social system.

Death. Although Walbiri notions of the ritually induced transmigration of Dreaming or spirit essences implied a kind of reincarnation after death, the process was wholly impersonal. People did not believe that the human person survived the destruction of the body unchanged. Rather, they took death to mark the end of the previously coherent personality of the individual, which then disintegrated into its spiritual components. The Dreaming elements returned to their spirit homes, and the matrispirit dissipated completely.

Conclusion. The Walbiri attributed a vast importance to sacred and ritual matters. They regarded the Dreaming as the ultimate source of the charters of their social groups and of their rights to hold territories, with the result that the patrilines and the lodges they manned maintained their jural and political identities by means of their ritual activities.

Moreover, both sacred and secular life were bounded by a multitude of explicit social rules to which the people in general conformed. The totality of the rules expressed, and indeed was, the law, the straight or true path. The law thus connoted an established and morally acceptable order of behavior for all phenomena, from which there should be no deviation. Rigorous adherence to Dreaming law was in itself a fundamental value and was believed to distinguish the Walbiri from other people, who were therefore their moral inferiors.

Because the law originated in the Dreaming, it was beyond criticism or deliberate change. Thus, all patterns of behavior were held to be subject to Dreaming law, with which they were coeval and which they maintained. In consequence, the normal was the normative—and vice versa. The monism of Walbiri totemic philosophy was inevitably moral and conservative, and it was ultimately circular. These mutually reinforcing characteristics were in an important sense its strength and its protection when the Walbiri eventually confronted the violent intrusion of Europeans into their world and struggled with considerable success to keep their religious life intact in the face of alien proselytizers.

BIBLIOGRAPHY

Bell, Diane. *Daughters of the Dreaming*. Melbourne, 1983. An account of the rituals of Walbiri, Kaytej, and Alyawara women at Warrabri.

Berndt, Catherine H. *Women's Changing Ceremonies in Northern Australia*. Paris, 1950. An informative analysis of rituals and of attitudes held in common by some Walbiri women and their Western congeners.

Berndt, Ronald M., and Catherine H. Berndt. *The World of the First Australians*. 2d ed. Sydney, 1977. The best general survey of all aspects of Australian Aboriginal societies.

Elkin, Adolphus P. *The Australian Aborigines: How to Understand Them*. Sydney, 1938. A pioneering general work that remains an insightful account of Aboriginal worldviews.

Meggitt, M. J. *Desert People: A Study of the Walbiri Aborigines of Central Australia*. Sydney, 1962. A detailed ethnography.

Meggitt, M. J. *Gadjari among the Walbiri Aborigines of Central Australia*. Sydney, 1966. A detailed analysis of an important totemic cult.

Munn, Nancy D. *Walbiri Iconography*. Ithaca, N. Y., 1973. A first-rate analysis of Walbiri iconic material.

Spencer, Baldwin, and F. J. Gillen. *The Northern Tribes of Central Australia*. London, 1904. Containing the earliest references to Walbiri, this classic survey provides splendid descriptions and photographs of Aboriginal rituals.

M. J. MEGGITT

WEST AFRICAN RELIGIONS

West Africa covers about one-fifth of the territory of sub-Saharan Africa and has a population of slightly more than 120 million people, about half of the total intertropical population of Africa. West Africa contains about six hundred "ethnic groups," a loose designation with no scientific specificity. Throughout West Africa one finds large cultural variety with various local features.

Traditional religions in West Africa are original systems of relations between human beings and the not ordinarily seen—but not wholly invisible—realm of the divine. There is no concept of original sin for either the individual or the group, but there is a central notion of redemption. The idea of humanity is equated with the lineage, especially with the clan, which is perceived as a social entity bearing the spiritual principle that defines the clan's originality and distinguishes it from other clans. In this context redemption is based in the individual; through the individual as intermediary, redemption extends to the level of the entire family or clan. Individuals can be seen, then, as their own redeemers; eschatology is thus a short-term operation, part "secular" and part religious. The role of this eschatology is to assure individuals of their "reincarnation" as ancestors or, still better, of their return to the earth to be among their people at some future time. Because of the diversity of West African peoples and religions, it is impossible to treat them all in a general review such as this one. Hence, in the interest of providing a panoramic view of West African religious experience, it has been necessary to emphasize some traditions and overlook others.

The Creator and Creation. Knowledge of the supreme being does not center on a particular set of religious teachings. Rather, one might say, religious adherents achieve their knowledge of God's nature indirectly through iconic images, symbols, metaphors, and metonyms. The principal element of this knowledge is the belief in the distance of God. Compared with man, earth creature *par excellence*, the supreme being is so far away in space and in emotional perception that he sometimes cannot even be given a name, much less invoked or honored in worship. The Bwa of Mali, for example, have a name for God, but no cult is directed to him.

The supreme being is not uniformly remote throughout West Africa. In a number of traditions, the supreme being is directly involved in everyday life, acting instead of, or in conjunction with, the lesser spirits. In these traditions, people feel a proximity to God that is analogous to the feelings they might have for their kin, and they appeal to and consult him through cults and rituals. Such is the case with Amma, supreme being of the Dogon, whose cults exist throughout all the villages of the Bandiagara cliffs in Mali. In other traditions, as among the Ashanti, for example, contact with the supreme being is even more intimate: nearly every morning elders pour libations and offer prayers to Nyame (and often Asase Yaa), thanking him for his beneficence and asking for continued prosperity.

Intermediary spirits are often punctual divinities or gods of specific circumstances, for example, patrons of such important events as war and hunting (Ogun of the Yoruba and Edo; Ta Tao of the Ashanti; Aflim, Dade, Kumi, and Otu of the Fanti; Gua of the Ga, et al.). They may also be associated with atmospheric phenomena such as rain and wind, thunder and lightning, and rainbows (So of the Ewe, Xevioso of the Fon, Sango of the Yoruba, et al.).

Unlike all the secondary divinities, the supreme being is the creator. He alone enjoys this prerogative, although he does not constantly involve himself in the details of creation. For example, the creator assigns the task of organizing the creation to a lesser spirit, or "monitor," who thus becomes the first means of contact between the supreme being and man.

> ## The role of this eschatology is to assure individuals of their "reincarnation" as ancestors.

This occurs among the Bambara (Faro is the monitor for Bemba), the Yoruba (Oduduwa is the monitor for Olorun), the Dogon (the Nommo are the monitors for Amma), and the Bwa (Do is the monitor for Debwenu).

We must take great caution when we use the word *God* in speaking of the supreme being of Africans, to whom this word does not have the same meaning as it does, for example, to Christians. Among the two best-studied populations of West Africa, the Bambara and the Dogon, it appears that God is a being who engendered himself; the creation he produced was contained in himself in the form of symbols before it was externalized.

The Living and Their Ancestors. Not all deceased persons are elevated to the rank of ancestor, and death is not always a requirement for becoming an ancestor. In each society it is the living who select members for the rank of ancestor.

To become an ancestor, one must possess certain qualities. The first requirement is longevity; this cannot be achieved through human measures to conserve health but must be bestowed by God. Thus only the elderly can become ancestors. Also important is the individual's physical integrity and morality. Those who die from an "ignominious" disease (such as leprosy), the insane, those who suffer an accidental death (after a fall or by being struck by lightning), thieves, and those who have committed reprehensible acts cannot become ancestors. Finally, the person's social standing in the community is important.

An important characteristic of the world of the ancestors is its representation as a perfect community. Unlike the society of the living, the community of ancestors is cleansed of antagonism and tension. Ancestors can, of course, become angry or even suffer, but such feelings arise only as the result of neglect or of negative actions on the part of their living descendants.

The universe of the ancestors, sometimes seen as slow moving, is quite active. Although recollection of the ancestors fades because of the weakness of the collective memory of those on earth, the world of the ancestors is constantly renewed and kept vivid in the minds of the living through fresh deaths and reincarnations.

The living interact with ancestors by offering them libations and sacrifices. Libations generally precede sacrifices and constitute an overture to dealings with the ancestors. These interactions are, in fact, bilateral obligations: man needs the ancestors because of his powerlessness and his indigence; ancestors need to be remembered by man so they can return to earth by being reborn within the bodies of children within their lineage. The relations between the living and the dead can thus be seen as a kind of individual "redemption" brought about by man's quest for immortality.

> **There is not a single human community in West Africa that does not have high regard for vegetation.**

Animal sacrifice is the most profound means of communicating with the invisible world. The most frequent sacrificial victims are white chickens (male and female) and goats. As sacrificial animals, cattle are reserved for extraordinary events and people (for example, the absolution of an incestuous act, the funeral ceremonies of a chief). The rarity and great significance of these sacrifices can be explained by the fact that West Africa is largely a region of agriculturalists, not pastoralists.

Altars for the ancestors vary but most often consist of one or several stones placed on the ground. They can also be chairs (Ashanti, Ewe, Attie), pottery, clay stools, or doorposts. The officiating priests are either the eldest of the lineage (clan) or a man specifically designated by the group.

Places of Worship. Generally West Africans have given more attention to the altar as the locus of the divine than to the sanctuary built to shelter it. There are exceptions: in Nigeria, Benin, Ghana, and Mali, there exist religious buildings in which one part is meant for the public and the rest for protection of cultic materials. ("Public" here refers to the faithful who have been or will be initiated.) Usually admission to the public parts of the sanctuary is available to the faithful who have been introduced to knowledge of the mystery evoked by the place of worship. The reserved part is only accessible to the high dignitaries of the community of the specific cult. In practice this separation suggests that religion does not merely pose problems of faith and adherence to a system of beliefs; more importantly, it raises questions about knowledge and power. Religion is parceled out in as many sectors, either exclusive of one another or com-

plementary over time, as there are different domains of knowledge.

The linkage between religion and knowledge, particularly prominent in West Africa, is not surprising. Indeed, one can say that it constitutes the characteristic trait of sub-Saharan cultures. The higher one's position becomes in the religious hierarchy, the more knowledge one possesses. The greater one's knowledge, the more likely one will be invested with religious power. All this reveals, on the one hand, the connection between sacred knowledge and power (including political power)—every sage exercises real power over the community he is part of—and, on the other hand, the ways that knowledge is distributed. For example, during initiation rites, knowledge is distributed to the adept "drop by drop," as if such instillation were the only possible method of instruction. If any other pedagogic method were used, the adept would reject the knowledge, much like his body would reject the intrusion of a foreign element such as a different blood type. However, there is another reason why knowledge is parceled out bit by bit. The adept is tested at each level to see how he or she reacts to it to ensure that the power that comes with such knowledge is not misused. In many West African societies, for instance, the sacred power to cure affliction through the manipulation of spiritual powers and material substances is not far removed from the practice of sorcery. Both sorcery and the practice of healing often involve the use of similiar techniques and "medicines"; what distinguishes them is the practitioner's intention to do good or evil. Hence, before giving an adept religious knowledge, measures must be taken to ensure that he or she will use this power for the good of the community. An individual with sacred knowledge who is deluded by his or her own power, greed, envy, or malice can have disastrous effects upon the community.

Worship sites are numerous and varied and can be classified according to the four elements: water, earth, air, and fire. Throughout West Africa, water inspires feelings of uncertainty, fear, reassurance, and security; most importantly, it is seen as the source of life. Each body of water has its own spirit. For example, the part of the Niger River that crosses Bambara country is said to be the body of Faro, the water spirit, who is responsible for the fecundity, multiplication, and proliferation of all living things. Among the Yoruba of Nigeria it is thought that Yemoja, daughter of Obatala and Oduduwa, gave birth to all the waters of the country and that she is the patroness of the River Ogu, her favorite sanctuary. For the Edo of Nigeria, the waters of the regions belong to Oba. In Ghana and the Ivory Coast, the rivers, streams, and still waters are the property of Tano and Bia.

The temples of the air, namely sacred trees and groves, are the most numerous sites of worship and the closest to the religious affections of West Africans. They are considered to have an airy nature because they are in harmony with atmospheric changes and with the seasons. There is not a single human community in West Africa that does not have high regard for this vegetation. The tree stands as an intermediary between the human being and spiritual powers. West African women desirous of becoming pregnant often implore a tree to give them a child. Trees acquire even more intense religious value when nature integrates them into sacred groves, which are the scenes of religious assemblies and initiation rites.

In West Africa, where there are no volcanoes, temples connected with fire are the most humble, the closest to daily life, and also the most ubiquitous. They are associated with the part of the home in which women prepare food. The fire, which transforms food, brings light and warmth to its users and mediates between the living and the dead. The forge is more than a workshop; it is also a place of worship, a shelter in which human justice gives way to the gentleness of heaven. The most typical characteristic of the forge lies in the fact that it constitutes a place of creation comparable to that held by the creator himself when he established the foundations of the world.

Initiation and Spiritual Life. Initiation rites in West Africa fall into two types. In Nigeria, Benin, Togo, and Ghana (that is, among the Yoruba, Hausa, Ewe, Fon, Ashanti, and related groups), initiation is of a type one may term *epispanic*. Here the initiates attract (Gr., *epispao*) the divinity to themselves, and the impact of the meeting between the human and divine translates into what is commonly called possession or trance.

The second type of initiation, termed *allotactic* (Gr., *allos*, "other"; *taktike*, from *tassein*, "to marshal"), is common from Ghana to Guinea. Here the neophytes go to seek God. Clearly the physical tests here are equally rigorous as those in epispanic initiation, but what matters above all in allotactic initiation is the accession of the neophytes to a transforming knowledge that permits them to get closer to particular spiritual beings and even to become a bit like them, in other words, to become immortal, for only through immortality do human beings guarantee their chances for reincarnation. Such transforming knowledge cannot be gained in several months or even in several years. Among the Senufo of Mali and northern Ivory Coast, initiation into the Poro society lasts more than twenty years.

African spirituality demonstrates that human beings are not born spiritual; rather, they must become spiritual.

BIBLIOGRAPHY

Awolalu, J. Omosade. *Yoruba Beliefs and Sacrificial Rites*. London, 1979.

Bellman, Beryl L. *Village of Curers and Assassins: On the Production of Fala Kpelle Cosmological Categories*. The Hague, 1975.

Field, Margaret Joyce. *Search for Security: An Ethno-Psychiatric Study of Rural Ghana*. London, 1960. A study of religion and psychology among the Akan peoples, particularly centered on Ashanti shrines and the *obosom*.

Fortes, Meyer, and Robin Horton. *Oedipus and Job in West African Religion*. Cambridge, 1984. A reprint of Fortes's classic 1959 work on Tallensi religion.

Griaule, Marcel. *Conversations with Ogotemmêli*. Translated by Robert Redfield. London, 1965. Dogon religion as interpreted by a Dogon sage.

Henderson, Richard N. *The King in Every Man: Evolutionary Trends in Onitsha Ibo Society and Culture*. New Haven, 1972.

Horton, Robin. "Destiny and the Unconscious in West Africa." *Africa* 31 (April 1961): 110-116.

Horton, Robin. "The Kalabari World-View: An Outline and Interpretation." *Africa* 32 (July 1962): 197-220.

Nadel, Siegfried Frederick. *Nupe Religion: Traditional Beliefs and the Influence of Islam in a West African Chiefdom*. London, 1954.

Parrinder, Geoffrey. *West African Religion*. 2d ed., rev. London, 1961. A classic on West African religion, focusing primarily on three groups: the Akan, the Yoruba, and the Ewe.

Pelton, Robert D. *The Trickster in West Africa: A Study of Mythic Irony and Sacred Delight*. Berkeley, 1980.

Thomas, Louis-Vincent, and René Luneau. *La terre africaine et ses religions*. Paris, 1974.

Thompson, Robert Farris. *Flash of the Spirit: African and Afro-American Art and Philosophy*. New York, 1981. An excellent work dealing primarily with the movement of African thought and art into the New World, using examples from Yoruba, Ejagham, and Mande cultures.

Thompson, Robert Farris. *African Art in Motion*. Los Angeles, 1974. Superb analysis of African dance and art drawn exclusively from West Africa.

Zahan, Dominique. *The Religion, Spirituality, and Thought of Traditional Africa*. Translated by Kate Ezra Martin and Lawrence M. Martin. Chicago, 1979.

DOMINIQUE ZAHAN
Translated from French by F. A. Leary-Lewis

WITCHCRAFT

The term *witchcraft* embraces a wide variety of phenomena. The word *witch* derives from the Old English noun *wicca*, "sorcerer," and the verb *wiccian*, "to cast a spell."

Simple Sorcery. Simple sorcery, which can also be called low magic, is usually practiced by the uneducated and unsophisticated. It assumes a magical worldview, implicitly and preconsciously, in distinction to the sophisticated magical worldview of high magicians such as astrologers and alchemists, whose philosophy is often highly structured. The thought processes of sorcery are intuitive rather than analytical.

The Azande of the southern Sudan distinguished three types of sorcery. One was a benevolent magic involving oracles, diviners, and amulets; it was aimed at promoting fertility and good health and at averting evil spells. The second kind of sorcery was aimed at harming those whom one hated or resented, perhaps for no just cause. The third kind was peculiar to the Azande: possession of *mangu*, an internal spiritual power that a male Azande could inherit from his father and a female from her mother. Those possessing *mangu* held meetings at night at which they feasted and practiced magic; they used a special ointment to make themselves invisible; they sent out their spirits to seize and eat the souls of their victims.

Sorcery may have a variety of social functions: to relieve social tensions; to define and sustain social values; to explain or control terrifying phenomena; to give a sense of power over death. Private sorcery has the additional functions of providing the weak, powerless, and poor with a putative way of obtaining revenge.

Witch doctors, medicine men, or *curanderos* are sorcerers who by definition have a positive function in society, for their business is to cure victims of the effects of malevolent magic. Individuals consult witch doctors to obtain relief from disease or other misfortunes attributed to witchcraft; tribal and village authorities summon them to combat drought or other public calamities. Dances or other rituals, such as those performed by the *ndakó-gboyá* dancers of the Nupe tribe, serve to detect and repel witches and evil spirits.

Sorcery is less a well-defined body of beliefs and actions than a general term covering marked differences in perceptions among societies and within a given society over time. Among the Nyakyusa of Tanzania it was believed that malevolent sorcerers might be of either sex. They were often accused of eating the internal organs of their neighbors or drying up the milk of cattle. The Pondo of South Africa usually thought witches to be women whose chief crime was having sexual intercourse with malevolent spirits. One reason for the difference is that the Nyakyusa were sexually secure but nutritionally insecure and so expressed their insecurities in terms of food, whereas the Pondo were more insecure sexually and so expressed their fears in sexual terms. The function of witchcraft has changed over time among the Bakweri of Cameroon. Before the 1950s the Bakweri were threatened by poverty and a low fertility rate, and they translated these threats into widespread fear of sorcery. In the 1950s their economic statrus improved radically owing to a boom in the banana crop. The new prosperity occasioned first a cathartic purging of suspected sorcerers and then a decline in accusations and a relative period of calm. In the 1960s bad economic conditions returned, and fear of sorcery revived.

Patterns of sorcery exist in virtually all present societies and have existed in virtually all past societies. The classical Greco-Roman and Hebrew societies from which Western civilization sprang entertained a great variety of sorcery, from public rituals that melded with religion to the activities of the hideous hags described by the classical poet Horace.

The sorcery of most cultures involved incantations supposed to summon spirits to aid the sorcerer. In many societies the connection between sorcery and the spirits was not explicitly formulated. But in both Greco-Roman and Hebrew thought the connection was defined or elaborated. The Greeks believed that all sorcerers drew upon the aid of spirits called *daimones* or *daimonia*. A Greek "demon" could be either malevolent or benevolent. It could be almost a god (*theos*), or it could be a petty spirit. In the thought of Plotinus (205-270 CE) and other Neoplatonists, the demons occupied an ontological rank between the gods and humanity. The Hebrews gradually developed the idea of the *mal'akh*, originally a manifestation of God's power, later an independent spirit sent down as a messenger by God. In Greek translations of Hebrew, *mal'akh* became *angelos*, "messenger." Christians eventually identified "angels" with the Greek "demons" and defined them as beings ontologically between God and humanity. But a different element gained influence through the apocalyptic writings of the Hellenistic period (200 BCE-150 CE): the belief in evil spirits led by Satan, lord of all evil. The idea had limited precedents in earlier Jewish thought but gained prominence in the Hellenistic period under the influence of Iranian Mazdaism, or Zoroastrianism. Under such influence the Christians came to divide the Greek *daimones* into two groups, the good angels and the evil demons. The demons were supposed to be angels who, under Satan's leadership, had turned against God and thereby become evil spirits. Sorcerers sought to compel spirits to carry out their will, but angels under God's command could not be compelled; thus it was supposed that one practicing sorcery might well be drawing upon the aid of evil demons. This was the central idea of the second main variety of witchcraft, the alleged diabolism of the late medieval and Renaissance periods in Europe.

European Witchcraft. Although simple sorcery had always existed, a new kind of diabolical witchcraft evolved in medieval and early modern Europe. The Christian concept of the devil transformed the idea of the sorcerer into that of the witch, consorter with demons and subject of Satan.

Historical development. The first element in diabolical witchcraft was simple sorcery, which existed in Europe as it did elsewhere. It persisted through the period of the witch craze and indeed has persisted to the present. Without this fundamental element, witchcraft would not have existed. The second, related aspect was the survival of pagan religion and folklore in Christian Europe, or rather the demonstrable survival and transmutation of certain elements *from* paganism.

Another element in the development of diabolical witchcraft in Europe was Christian heresy. The classical formulation of witchcraft had been established by the fifteenth century. Its chief elements were (1) pact with the Devil, (2) formal repudiation of Christ, (3) the secret, nocturnal meeting, (4) the ride by night, (5) the desecration of the Eucharist and the crucifix, (6) orgy, (7) sacrificial infanticide, and (8) cannibalism. At the first formal trial of heretics in the Middle Ages, at Orléans in 1022, the accused were said to hold orgies underground at night, to call up evil spirits and to pay homage to the Devil.

Scholastic theology was the next major element in the formation of the witch concept. In the twelfth through fourteenth centuries the Scholastics developed the tradition of the body of Satan, refined its details, and supplied it with a rational substructure. They extended the Devil's kingdom explicitly to

> **The classical formulation of witchcraft had been established by the fifteenth century.**

include sorcerers, whom they considered a variety of heretic. Simple sorcerers had become, in the dominant scholastic thought of the later Middle Ages, servants of Satan.

The link between sorcerers, heretics, and Satan was the idea of pact. The notion of pact had been popularized in the eighth century by translations of the sixth-century legend of Theophilus who sold his soul to the Devil in exchange for ecclesiastical preferment. He met the Devil through a Jewish magician and signed a formal pact with "the evil one" in order to fulfill his desires. The Scholastics broadened the idea of pact to include implicit as well as explicit consent. One did not actually have to sign a contract to be a member of Satan's army; anyone—heretic, sorcerer, Jew, Muslim—who knowingly opposed the Christian community, that is, the body of Christ, was deemed to have made an implicit pact with the Devil and to number among his servants.

Theology, then, made a logical connection between witchcraft and heresy.

The final element in the transformation of sorcery into diabolical witchcraft was the Inquisition. The connection of sorcery with heresy meant that sorcery could be prosecuted with much greater severity than before. Between 1227 and 1235 a series of decrees established the papal Inquisition. In 1233 Gregory IX accused the Waldensian heretics, who were in fact evangelical moralists, of Satan worship. In 1252 Innocent IV authorized the use of torture by the Inquisition, and Alexander IV (1254-1261) gave it jurisdiction over all cases of sorcery involving heresy. Gradually almost all sorcery came to be included under the rubric of heresy.

The witch craze. From 1450 to 1700—the period of the Renaissance and the origins of modern science—a hundred thousand may have perished in what has been called the great witch craze. In 1484 Pope Innocent VIII issued a bull confirming papal support for inquisitorial proceedings against the witches, and this bull was included as a preface to the *Malleus maleficarum* (The Hammer of Witches), a book by

two Dominican inquisitors. The *Malleus* colorfully detailed the diabolical, orgiastic activities of the witches and helped persuade public opinion that a cosmic plot directed by Satan threatened all Christian society.

As the religious split between Catholicism and Protestantism widened during the sixteenth century and flared up into religious warfare, eschatological fears deepened. Catholics saw the Protestants as soldiers of Satan sent to destroy the Christian community; Protestants viewed the pope as the Antichrist. Terror of witchcraft and prosecution of witches grew in both Catholic and Protestant regions, reaching heights between 1560 and 1660, when religious wars were at their worst. The craze was restricted almost exclusively to western Europe and its colonies.

Skeptics such as Johann Weyer (fl. 1563) and Reginald Scot (fl. 1584), who wrote against belief in witchcraft, were rare and were often rewarded for their efforts by persecution; Weyer, for example, was accused of witchcraft himself. More typical of the period were the works of the learned King James I of England and VI of Scotland (d. 1625). Personally terrified of witches, James encouraged their prosecution. In 1681 Joseph Glanvill was still able to publish a popular second edition of a work supporting belief in diabolical witchcraft. But by that time the craze was beginning to fade. The date of the last execution for witchcraft in England was 1684, in America 1692, in Scotland 1727, in France 1745, and in Germany 1775.

Conclusions. Witchcraft will continue to be examined theologically, historically, mythologically, psychologically, anthropologically, and sociologically. No single approach can completely explain the phenomenon; even together they do not seem to provide full understanding of such a diverse subject. Witchcraft dwells in the shadowy land where the conscious and unconscious merge, where religion, magic, and technology touch dimly in darkness. Its forms are so varied that it cannot be said to represent any one kind of quasi-religious expression. Modern, neopagan witchcraft is a naive, genial, nature religion. Simple sorcery is usually located across the border into magic yet is frequently combined with religion in two important ways: it is often incorporated into the liturgy of public religion; its charms and spells are often amalgamated into prayers. The Anglo-Saxon clergy of the tenth and eleventh centuries, for example, christianized charms by taking over from wizards the right to say them and then introducing Christian elements into them. By incorporating the sign of the cross or an invocation of the Trinity into a pagan charm, the clergy legitimized the magic. They argued that everything that occurred resulted from God's power and will, and that the use of herbs and charms simply drew upon benevolent forces that God had appointed in nature. It was essential to use them reverently, with the understanding that they were God's and that whatever one accomplished through them was achieved only by appeal to him.

Simple sorcery could be malevolent as well as benevolent. Malevolent sorcery, practiced for private, unjust purposes, was universally condemned. But in late medieval and early modern Europe, evil sorcery merged with diabolism, the result being a different dimension in the religious meaning of witchcraft. This dimension is that of transcendent, transpersonal, or at least transconscious evil.

BIBLIOGRAPHY

One bibliography of recent books on European witchcraft is Carl T. Berkhout and Jeffrey B. Russell's *Medieval Heresies: A Bibliography, 1960-1979* (Toronto, 1981), part 16, "Witchcraft," items 1809 to 1868. Anthropological and sociological works on witchcraft that are particularly significant include Maurice Bouisson's *Magic: Its History and Principal Rites* (New York, 1960); E. E. Evans-Pritchard's *Witchcraft, Oracles, and Magic among the Azande*, 2d ed. (Oxford, 1950); and Lucy Mair's *Witchcraft* (London, 1969), a good survey. The sociology and psychology of Salem witchcraft are best explored in Paul Boyer and Stephen Nissenbaum's *Salem Possessed: The Social Origins of Witchcraft* (Cambridge, Mass., 1974), and John Putnam Demos's *Entertaining Satan: Witchcraft and the Culture of Early New England* (New York, 1982). Similar treatments of European witchcraft include Alan Macfarlane's *Witchcraft in Tudor and Stuart England: A Regional and Comparative Study* (London, 1970); E. William Monter's *Witchcraft in France and Switzerland: The Borderlands during the Reformation* (Ithaca, N. Y., 1976); and Keith Thomas's *Religion and the Decline of Magic* (New York, 1971). Other works approach witchcraft from the point of view of the history of ideas: K. M. Briggs's *Pale Hecate's Team: An Examination of the Beliefs on Witchcraft and Magic among Shakespeare's Contemporaries and His Immediate Successors* (London, 1962); Julio Caro Baroja's *The World of the Witches*, translated by O. N. V. Glendinning (Chicago, 1964); Norman Cohn's *Europe's Inner Demons: An Enquiry Inspired by the Great Witch-Hunt* (New York, 1975); Mircea Eliade's *Occultism, Witchcraft, and Cultural Fashions: Essays in Comparative Religions* (Chicago, 1976); Richard Kieckhefer's *European Witch Trials: Their Foundations in Popular and Learned Culture, 1300-1500* (London, 1976); Edward Peters's *The Magician, the Witch, and the Law* (Philadelphia, 1978); Hugh R. Trevor-Roper's *The European Witch-craze of the Sixteenth and Seventeenth Centuries and Other Essays* (New York, 1969); and my own studies, *Witchcraft in the Middle Ages* (Ithaca, N. Y., 1972) and *A History of Witchcraft: Sorcerers, Heretics, and Pagans* (London, 1980).

JEFFREY BURTON RUSSELL

WOMEN'S STUDIES

WOMEN'S STUDIES in religion have emerged over the last two decades as an area of scholarship with major implications for religious life and thought. Taking gender as a primary category of analysis, women's studies in religion examine the function of gender in the symbolization of religious traditions, the institutionalization of roles in religious communities, and the dynamics of the interaction between religious systems of belief and the personal, social, and cultural condition of women.

Critical and Constructive Task. The magnitude of the critical and constructive task undertaken by women's-studies scholars is indicated by the range of feminist publications to date across the fields of religion: scripture, theology, ethics, history of Christianity, psychology and sociology of religion, and world religions. In each of these fields, women's studies have begun to challenge the categories of thought underlying the traditional disciplinary methods and their contents that have shaped the study of religion. Emerging from these challenges are new feminist theoretical principles and frameworks. This new scholarship is intent on building a methodological basis for developing a more adequate understanding of the whole of human religious experience.

One of the initial discoveries of women's-studies scholarship has been the extent to which women themselves have been over the centuries a central focus of religious debate. This certainly has been the case in Christianity. A significant body of research has uncovered that debate, particularly the concern since the origins of Christianity with the recurrent question of the proper role and status of women in the church.

Women's studies have developed in large part in response to the increasing numbers of women seeking preparation for religious leadership, particularly within Judaism and Christianity, and to the explicit and subtle barriers to that leadership in major traditions. These barriers prompted female and male scholars alike to ask on what religious grounds women might be (and in some cases still are) excluded by official policy from religious leadership in major religions of the world.

Critique of Religious Assumptions. Much of what has claimed to be objective scholarship about human experience actually has been a depiction of male experience from a male point of view. Feminists argue that underlying this identification for centuries has been the fundamental and largely unchallenged assumption that maleness is the primary form of human experience, the measure of human being and activity. Mary Daly's groundbreaking *Beyond God the Father: Toward a Philosophy of Women's Liberation* (1973) first demonstrated how profoundly this assumption has shaped Judaism and Christianity.

Critique of Anthropological Assumptions. Feminist scholars are drawing attention to something that has not been seen before: the normative structure of religions with regard to gender, particularly the normative anthropology embedded in religious traditions. This concern with anthropology is well illustrated in scriptural studies by Phyllis Trible in *God and the Rhetoric of Sexuality* (1978). Trible argues that in Judaism and Christianity the anthropology set forth in the *Genesis* 2-3 creation myth traditionally has been interpreted to justify basic assumptions about the created inequality of male and female. Religions have in turn reinforced and justified sexual hierarchy in society.

Relation to Social Status. Women's studies underscore the relationship between the image and status of women in theology and cultural patterns defining women's social roles and status. In *Beyond God the Father*, Mary Daly identified the symbol of God the Father as the keystone in the arch of theological and social misogyny, arguing that it defines authority in the universe and therefore on earth as properly and naturally masculine: "If God in 'his' heaven is a father ruling 'his' people, then it is in the nature of things and according to divine plan . . . that society be male-dominated" (p. 13).

Feminists are concerned with investigating the broadest and deepest implications for modern humanity of women's religious and social oppression. Rosemary Radford Ruether was one of the first to point to the systemic nature and significance of gender asymmetry in Western culture. In her article "The Female Nature of God," in *God as Father?* (1981), Ruether argued the need for a radical criticism that calls into question traditional concepts of masculinity and femininity as constructs of patriarchal culture.

Reconstruction of Religious Beliefs. Some feminist theologians believe that established religions can and must be reformed. For these feminists the task of feminist scholarship is to reinterpret Judaism and Christianity to liberate them from historical distortion and self-serving patriarchal interpretation. Ultimately, the significance of feminist scholarship is, as illustrated by Christian feminist Rosemary Ruether in *To Change the World: Christology and Cultural Criticism* (1981), its historic potential for enlarging understanding of the prophetic Christian message.

Mary Daly was one of the first to describe the historically unique promise for humanity of feminist reconceptions of God and ultimate reality. In *Gyn/Ecology: The Metaethics of Radical Feminism* (1978) she announced the feminist task as that of creating a new theology-philosophy that explores the process of women becoming themselves and finding their distinctive interpretation of God and the universe. New theologies that begin to articulate women's distinctive interpretations of God, the self, and the world are emerging. These reconstruct traditional masculine notions and symbols, beginning with those of divinity. In contrast to what they see as the attributes of a patriarchal God, an other-worldly all-powerful father who places himself over against fallen human experience, many feminists understand God as immanent in the world and without gender.

Rosemary Ruether was the first to attempt a systematic nonsexist theology that works through the implications of a feminist critique for reinterpreting the central related doctrines of Christianity. Her book *Sexism and God-Talk: Toward a Feminist Theology* (1983) sets forth the vision many feminists share of a theology that begins with women's experi-

ence and represents a radical critique of the notion of hierarchy itself, of the fundamental structural dualism of privilege and dispossession that lies at the heart of all social patterns of oppression such as racism, anti-Semitism, poverty, and domination of nature.

New Religious Constructions. A significant body of work has been developed by feminists who think it impossible for such traditions as Judaism and Christianity ever to symbolize or guide attainment of the fullness of human being for women as well as men. They do not look to the past, believing that women's authentic spirituality cannot be recovered in the history of patriarchal religious and cultural traditions that denied and distorted it. These post-Christian and Jewish feminists define the proper focus of feminist religious thinking as the creation of new moral vision, religious imagery, and ritual out of the experience of contemporary women.

Critique of Universal Claims. The debate between feminists working outside of and within established religions has been intensified and enriched from the outset by strong internal critique of another kind. As the historical and cultural diversity of women's experience is increasingly explored, the extent to which feminist thinking has moved sufficiently away

> Post-Christian and Jewish feminists define the proper focus of feminist religious thinking as the creation of new moral vision.

from the universalizing perspective and the universal claims of traditional scholarship is being questioned from a number of perspectives. At issue is whether feminist thinking fully comprehends its own insistence on the particularity and the historically conditioned nature of women's experience.

The perspectives of black and Hispanic women, ethnic women of color, Jewish women, and women from non-Western cultures reveal the extent to which feminist theory is still not free of the distortions of the religious and cultural traditions it criticizes.

Early on, women of color identified as an important problem in defining women's common experience the fact that white women historically have been their oppressors. In these and other ways the experience of oppression is not the same for all women but rather is varied by such factors as race, class, religion, and cultural context. Black feminists like Jacquelyn Grant, in her essay in *Black Theology: A Documentary History, 1966-1979*, edited by Gayraud S. Wilmore and James H. Cone (1979), argue that the distinctive experience of black women cannot be addressed by feminist analysis that does not link gender with race and class.

A central dimension of women's studies not yet as far developed as others is the investigation of the historical and contemporary experience and the depiction of women in non-Western world religions. Much of this investigation has been done in relation to such traditions as Buddhism, Islam, and Hinduism. An important example is *Women, Androgynes, and Other Mythical Beasts* (1980), in which historian of religion Wendy Doniger O'Flaherty explores sexual metaphor in Hindu mythology (written by men), shedding light on the image of women and sexuality in Hinduism. *Beyond the Veil* (1975), by Fatima Mernissi, and *Women and Islam* (1982), edited by A. Al-Hibri, have both helped open the way for further exploration of Islam.

Work on these major traditions, as well as on others, such as African-based Caribbean traditions, helps correct tendencies to universalize the worldviews of Western women, religions, and cultures. This work provides a comparative perspective important for understanding any one tradition but also for identifying similarities and differences in women's experience cross-culturally.

Cross-disciplinary Discussion. It is becoming clear not only how significant the study of women is for religion but also how significant religion is for the study of women. Religion is important for the study of women's lives for several major reasons. It continues, as it has historically, to play a powerful role in defining women's social roles and status in this and other cultures. Further, the study of women and religion illumines women's interior lives by examining their interpretations of the meaning of their own lives, the world, and the universe. Finally, it focuses on an area, religious life and practice, that (like the domestic sphere) has been historically a major sphere of women's activity, as well as a context for their movement into public life.

BIBLIOGRAPHY

The development of feminist theory on gender, religion, and culture is cross-disciplinary, drawing on materials from a wide range of disciplines. That range is partially indicated by the following selected works. These books and their authors have been important in the development of women's studies in religion and illustrate further theoretical issues and research directions central to it.

Bynum, Caroline Walker. *Jesus as Mother: Studies in the Spirituality of the High Middle Ages.* Los Angeles, 1982.

Christ, Carol P., and Judith Plaskow, eds. *Womanspirit Rising: A Feminist Reader in Religion.* San Francisco, 1979.

Douglas, Ann. *The Feminization of American Culture.* New York, 1977.

Heschel, Susannah, ed. *On Being a Jewish Feminist.* New York, 1983.

Horner, I. B. *Women under Primitive Buddhism: Laywomen and Almswomen* (1930). Delhi, 1975.

Hull, Gloria T., Patricia Bell Scott, and Barbara Smith, eds. *All the Women Are White, All the Blacks Are Men, but Some of Us Are Brave: Black Women's Studies.* Old Westbury, N.Y., 1982.

Marglin, Frédérique. *Wives of the God-King: The Rituals of the Devadasis of Puri.* Oxford, 1985.

Moraga, Cherríe, and Gloria Anzaldúa, eds. *This Bridge Called My Back: Writings by Radical Women of Color.* Watertown, Mass., 1981.

Morton, Nelle. *The Journey Is Home.* Boston, 1985.

Ochshorn, Judith. *The Female Experience and the Nature of the Divine.* Bloomington, Ind., 1981.

Saadawi, Nawal el-. *The Hidden Face of Eve: Women in the Arab World.* Edited and translated by Sherif Hetata. London, 1980.

Trible, Phyllis. *Texts of Terror: Literary-Feminist Readings of Biblical Narratives.* Philadelphia, 1984.

Walker, Alice. *The Color Purple.* New York, 1982.

Warner, Marina. *Alone of All Her Sex: The Myth and Cult of the Virgin Mary.* New York, 1976.

Welch, Sharon D. *Communities of Resistance and Solidarity: A Feminist Theology of Liberation.* Maryknoll, N.Y., 1985.

CONSTANCE H. BUCHANAN

YAKUT RELIGION

The Yakuts, who numbered 328,000 during the 1979 census, are the northernmost of Turkic peoples. Beginning in the twelfth and thirteenth centuries, under pressure caused by Buriat encroachment, they gradually emigrated northward from the Lake Baikal region of southern Siberia. They moved upstream along the course of the Lena River and finally settled in northeastern Siberia, the coldest region in the world. The horses and cattle bred by these semisedentary people have successfully adapted to the rigorous climate; however, hunting and fishing provide the Yakuts with a significant additional source of income. The Yakuts are organized in patrilineal and exogamic clans regrouped into tribes.

Under pressure from the Russians, who subjugated them during the first half of the seventeenth century, the majority of Yakuts were baptized by the end of the eighteenth century. They adopted Christianity primarily for material reasons (e.g., gifts of crosses, shirts, and various privileges). At the same time, they secretly preserved their own religious system, shamanism, which was modified superficially as the result of contact with Russian Orthodoxy. The practitioners of shamanism accepted the new idea of a reward after death and attributed the traits of God, the Virgin Mary, and the guardian angels to some of their spirits.

Cosmology. The Yakut universe is composed of three superimposed worlds. The "upper world" comprises nine skies of different colors. Spirits reside in each sky: in the east are the *aiyys*, bright, creative spirits, and in the west are the *abaasys*, dark, harmful spirits. (The Yakuts are situated in the east.)

The "middle world," flat and octagonal, is populated by humans and by a host of spirits. The forest of this world is a formidable territory because the greatest number of spirits are found there: although they grant game, they also capture the souls of hunters who have pleased them.

The "lower world" is a crepuscular region solely inhabited by the harmful spirits who roam among a metallic, iron vegetation. Here, the "sea of death," composed of children's cadavers, churns its waves. The term employed for "lower world," *allaraa*, signifies "below, downstream, in the north." (The rivers of Siberia flow northward, hence the use of the same term for both "downstream" and "north.") It is possible

that the lower world is not conceived of as a sinister and subterranean replica of the middle world but rather as a watery abyss in the northern regions. In any case, the contrasts of above and below and of upper and lower do not figure predominately in the Yakut religion. More important is the division of the sky into east (good) and west (evil): this division allows for the classification of the spirits.

The Pantheon. The bright, creative spirits, *aiyys* (from the Turkic root "ai," "to create"), assure the Yakuts their survival by granting them the souls of children and also of horses, cattle, and dogs, the Yakuts' only domesticated animals. However, the Yakuts must pay homage to the aiyys with milk offerings and prayers and must consecrate animals to them from their herd. The consecrated animal *(yzykh)* is not slain; it is sent back to the herd and is treated with respect, for it no longer belongs to man but to the spirit to which it was consecrated. This spirit will reward the people for their care by granting fertility to the herd. The *aiyy* cult, called "white shamanism," disappeared in the eighteenth century and never was studied properly.

The White Lord Creator, Iurung Aiyy Toion, is the master of all the *aiyys* who are imagined to be like rich Yakuts and are organized in clans, as are the Yakuts themselves. Associated with the sun and the heat of summer, the White Lord Creator resides in the ninth sky, where "the grass is as white as the wing of a white swan." He rules the world, sends the soul *(kut)* to children, and assures fertility in cattle and the growth of plants, but he does not interfere in human affairs on his own initiative. During the great spring feasts called "libations" *(ysyakh)*, he is first offered libations of fermented mare's milk; later, horses are consecrated to him. Occasionally a goddess, the wife of this god, is mentioned; she would become an avatar of the goddess of the earth. Such an identification of the goddess may be a vague indication of a marriage between the sky and the earth.

The *aiyysyts*, a group of spirits, female for the most part, attend to human reproduction and the reproduction of certain species of animals (especially the domestic species). The *aiyysyt* who attends to human reproduction brings the soul of the child created by Aiyy Toion. She also comes to help women during childbirth. She is often associated with Iëiiëkhsit, and is occasionally confused with her. When they are associated, Aiyysyt is the one who grants the soul and Iëiiëkhsit is the one who delivers it. (The latter has been likened to a guardian angel.) Aiyysyt and Iëiiëkhsit are both proper nouns and epithets that can be applied even to male personages: when one is begging for offspring one uses the epithet Aiyysyt, and when one desires an intermediary the epithet Iëiiëkhsit is used. The three *aiyysyts* of man, of horned livestock, and of dogs are all feminine spirits, but the spirit that grants horses, "the formidable Dzhësëgëi," is masculine. When mares and cows reproduce, and each time a child is born, relatives and cousins come together to offer a ritual of renewal to the spirit that granted the soul. However, the ritual for the spirit-master of horses is conducted by the (male) ruler of the house, while the other two rituals are celebrated by the women.

The goddess of the earth, who lives among beautiful white birches far from the evil spirits, takes care of the traveler, blesses the harvests, and occasionally decides the fate of the newborn. The spirit-master of the domestic fire assures the survival of the household: in his embers tremble the souls of children and calves yet to be born. He removes harmful spirits and purifies the accessories of the hunt that are soiled by the presence of a menstruating woman. This spirit-master also serves as an intermediary for other spirits by delivering offerings to them that are thrown into his flames in their honor. In exchange, one must not forget to feed him by throwing him a mouthful of food before each meal; otherwise, he may take revenge by, for example, burning down the house.

On the opposite side, in the western sky, loom the black spirits, *abaasys* (the Turkic root is probably *ap*, "enchantment"), "gigantic as the shadows of larches under the full moon." In fact, they appear to be more terrible than they really are, because once they have sent diseases (most often, various types of insanity), they will take them away if the shaman sacrifices horses with suitable coats. The supreme ruler of the nine clans of *abaasy* is Ulu Toion ("powerful lord"), who gave the Yakuts fire and perhaps one of the three souls that the Yakuts believe each person possesses (according to some, the soul he gave was the siur, vital energy). He is the protector of the black shamans, *abaasy oiun* (lit., "shamans in contact with the *abaasys*").

Other harmful *abaasys* populate the earth and the lower world. The two most celebrated are the ruler of the lower world, Arsan Duolan (a pale replica of Ulu Toion), who sends infant mortality and obstinacy, and Kudai Bagsi, the ruler of the smiths, who cures the apprentice smith of his initiatory illness if the shaman offers him a black bull.

Among the harmful spirits are the unsatisfied deceased (*iuërs*) those who died without completing a full life cycle, such as young girls who died without having been married. The souls of suicides and of shamans become the most formidable *iuërs*.

In the domestic environment and in natural phenomena that directly influence man's well-being, there exists a supernatural force that the Yakuts call *ichchi* ("master, possessor").

This force is personified in the spirit-masters who reside in the object, house, or territory they possess. To ensure that a tool be effective or that a house not collapse, to avoid being crushed by a tree or hurled into the waters when crossing the forest or the river, one must make an offering to one's spirit-master.

Since the Yakuts believed the spirits were organized in clans as they themselves were, they recognized their right to have tribal property. This property was the game and fish existing in the territory of these spirits. They accorded part of this to man in exchange for food (milk products, alcohol, flesh of domestic animals) in an alliance that is similar to that formed between bartering human tribes. However, the spirits never give enough souls of game, cattle, and children. This is where the shaman intervenes.

The Shaman. To obtain the souls of wild game, the shaman provides the master of the particular kind of animal in question with food in return: he smears the blood of a sacrificed animal on a wooden statuette where he has caused the spirit-master of the forest, the rich Baianai or Baryllakh, to descend. He then gives a symbol of these souls (e.g., feathers, etc.) to the members of the clan. To obtain the souls of children and additional cattle, the shaman himself goes to the beyond to confront the *aiyysyts*. At first the spirits refuse, remembering the wrongs that men have committed. Then, after considering the supplications of the shaman, they give him the souls. The position of the shaman has changed: he no longer barters, he implores, because the aiyy spirits, dispensers of cattle and human offspring, are venerated, unlike the spirits of the hunt or of illnesses, whom the shaman treats as equals.

To cure illness, which the Yakuts conceive as the installation of an evil spirit in the body of the ailing person and also as the theft of the soul by a spirit "soul-eater," the shaman trades the soul of the sick person for that of a sacrificed animal, which he sends into the otherworld. These negotiations with the spirits take place during the shamanic séance, which is generally held nocturnally at the afflicted person's home, with relatives and neighbors in attendance. The séance includes a purification ceremony; a convocation of the spirits through the shaman's chanting, accompanied on the tambourine; a voyage of the shaman himself into the otherworlds to find the spirits (a voyage mimicked by the shaman's dance); and an act of divination.

The shaman is aided by his principal spirit *(ämägät)*, generally the shaman's ancestor, who chose the shaman from among his descendants in order to pass on the shamanic gift, a gift that always remains in the same family. Women also can become shamans (*udaghans*), but female shamans are less numerous because the clans are patrilineal. Once chosen by the ancestor, the soul of the future shaman takes on the form of a young bird and is educated atop either the mythic larch of the upper world or the pine tree of the lower world. It is during his initiation that the shaman seals his alliance with the spirits. In the course of his sleep, his body is cut up in the lower world and consumed like a sacrificial animal by several spirits. The spirits then reconstitute his body. Recreated in this manner, the shaman acquires rights over the spirits who have consumed his flesh and who will subsequently help him remove illnesses.

The shaman is also aided by zoomorphic spirits who transport him in the air or under the ground and who fight at his side. Moreover, the shaman possesses an animal double (usually a male moose or bull); it is in this form that he fights against shamans of enemy clans. If the shaman's animal double has been killed, he himself dies. The shaman also fights against the souls of dead avengers, the spirits of illnesses and epidemics. He also assures the survival of his clan by divination—predicting the future, the areas where game will be most plentiful, and so forth. In this dark universe, where mad spirits who populate three-fourths of the sky in the west predominate, where the bright spirits (aiyys) often refuse to grant offspring and prosperity, and where "soul-eating" spirits lurk about the earth and in the lower world, the shaman is the Yakuts' only support.

[See also Shamanism.]

BIBLIOGRAPHY

Alekseev, N. A. *Traditsionnye religioznye verovaniia iakutov v deviatnadtsatom-nachale dvadtsatogo v.* Novosibirsk, 1975. A work giving a detailed description, from an evolutionist perspective, of Yakut beliefs.

Ksenofontov, G. V. *Legendy i rasskazy o shamanakh u iakutov, buriat i tungusov.* 2d rev. ed. Moscow, 1938. Very valuable work for the study of Yakut, Buriat, and Tunguz shamanism, consisting of a series of accounts by indigenous informants, collected between 1921 and 1926 and accompanied by notes from the author, a Yakut himself.

Pekarskii, E. K. *Slovar' iakutskago iazyka.* 3 vols. Saint Petersburg (Leningrad), 1907-1930. Dictionary that contains many facts on the ethnography and religion of the Yakuts.

Popov, A. A. "Materialy po religii iakutov Viliuiskogo okruga." *Sbornik Muzeia Antropologii i Etnografii* 11 (1949): 255-323. Important article including information on the Yakut world, spirits, souls, and certain rituals, collected by the author during the time of a survey conducted from 1922 to 1925 on the Yakuts living in the region of the Viliui, a western tributary of the Lena River.

LAURENCE DELABY
Translated from French by Sherri L. Granka

YESHIVAH

In contemporary usage, the Hebrew term *yeshivah* refers to an academy for the advanced study of Jewish religious texts, primarily the Talmud. Since the destruction of the Second Temple in 70 CE, the *yeshivah* has been one of the most important institutions of Jewish communal life. Although many *yeshivah* students go on to become rabbis and although the texts taught in *yeshivot* are among those a rabbi is expected to master, it should be emphasized that a *yeshivah*, an all-male institution, is not a rabbinical seminary. Its function is not to train professional religious leaders but rather to provide a framework for study. In the Jewish religious tradition, study of the Torah is seen as a central and

> In contemporary usage, the Hebrew term *yeshivah* refers to an academy for the advanced study of Jewish religious texts, primarily the Talmud.

meritorious religious act in and of itself, regardless of its relevance to the student's career plans.

Yeshivot in Babylonia. After the death of Yehudah ha-Nasi', the patriarch of Judaea (c. 220 CE), the *yeshivot* of Babylonia began to grow in importance and soon became the most highly esteemed authorities in the Jewish world.

Geonic period. From roughly 550 to 1050 CE, Babylonian *yeshivot* continued to flourish as centers of both education and legal decision making. Students came not only from Babylonia but from Egypt, North Africa, Spain, Italy, and elsewhere to study and to prepare themselves for leadership roles in their home communities. Legal questions (accompanied by donations) were sent from many Jewish communities in the Mediterranean basin, and the *responsa* were copied down for the guidance of later generations. The geonim, as the heads of the *yeshivot* were called in the post-Talmudic period, wrote legal treatises and other works that were widely distributed.

The general decline of the Abbasid empire, long centered in Baghdad, anti-Jewish persecutions in the tenth and eleventh centuries in Iraq, and the rise of new Jewish centers elsewhere led to the decline of the Babylonian *yeshivot* and a corresponding rise in the importance of *yeshivot* in other locations. However, none of these newer *yeshivot* achieved the centrality and influence that the *yeshivot* of Babylonia had enjoyed. According to Avraham ibn Daud's account in *Sefer ha-qabbalah* (The Book of Tradition; c. 1161), around the year 990 a ship bringing four scholars to a *kallah* month was captured by pirates. Three of the scholars were sold as slaves in various ports—one in Egypt, one in North Africa, and one in Spain (the fourth met an unknown fate)—where each became the leader of an important *yeshivah*. While the legend is not a reliable historical source, it does illustrate the continuity between later *yeshivot* and their Babylonian predecessors as well as the weakening of the ties between other Jewish communities and Babylonia.

Yeshivot in the Medieval Diaspora. From the tenth century onward, *yeshivot* were to be found in most Jewish communities. In Spain, one of the first important *yeshivot* to develop was that of Cordova; others were located in Lucena, Toledo, Barcelona, and elsewhere. These *yeshivot* were often located in or near community structures such as synagogues. The curriculum of these *yeshivot* centered on the Babylonian Talmud and its legal application and at times included qabbalistic literature. The well-known interest of some Spanish Jews in secular subjects found no expression in the *yeshivot*; their study of languages and sciences was usually carried out with the help of tutors or, occasionally, through enrollment in a non-Jewish school. The size and importance of a *yeshivah* was directly related to the fame and prestige of its head, the *ro'sh yeshivah*. Most of the central rabbinical figures of Spanish Jewish history, including Nahmanides (Mosheh ben Nahman, c. 1190-1270), Shalomoh ben Avraham Adret (c. 1235-1310), and Nissim Gerondi (d. 1380?), headed *yeshivot*. The notes taken by students were passed from hand to hand and formed the basis for many of the Spanish glosses on the Talmud.

In North Africa, *yeshivot* were often located close to Muslim academies, though the question of intellectual relations between Jewish and Muslim schools has yet to be explored. The first important *yeshivah* in North Africa was that of Kairouan, which had close ties with Babylonian *yeshivot*. The yeshivah of Kairouan rose to importance in the tenth century and upon its decline in the following century, the *yeshivot* of Fez and Tlemcen in Morocco became prominent. Fustat, near present-day Cairo, was also the site of an important *yeshivah*.

In the Ashkenazic communities of northern Europe, the great intellectual flowering that produced Gershom ben Yehudah (c. 965-1040), Rashi (Shelomoh ben Yitshaq, 1042-1105), and the tosafists was achieved to a large extent within the *yeshivot*. These *yeshivot* differed from their predecessors in that they were chiefly educational institutions and no longer functioned as courts or as facilities for scholarly assembly. They tended to be small institutions with just a few tens of students who often lived with the *ro'sh yeshivah* and studied in a separate room in his house. Many of these students were Talmudic scholars in their own right, and they were not so much disciples of the *ro'sh yeshivah* as his partners in study. Beginners would prepare for admission to the *yeshivah* by studying with special teachers. The course of study in the *yeshivot* centered on Talmud and led to the conferment of formal degrees. The lowest, corresponding roughly to the bachelor of arts degree granted by universities of the time, was that of *haver* ("fellow"), while more advanced students looked forward to receiving the title *morenu* ("our teacher"), which entitled them to open their own *yeshivot*. As

in the medieval universities, the curriculum emphasized discussion and disputation rather than literary creativity; this phenomenon is reflected in the Jewish scholarly literature of the period, which was mainly in the form of commentaries and glosses and not extended expository works. Like their counterparts in the universities, *yeshivah* students were highly mobile and often studied in many schools in the course of their academic careers.

Both in Mediterranean countries and in northern Europe, *yeshivot* stressed creative study for their advanced students rather than rote learning. Often students were required to resolve logical problems and contradictions in a text, or between authoritative texts, in a manner that led to a deeper understanding of the issues. In a very real sense, this kind of intellectual development was an organic continuation of earlier patterns. The members of the medieval *yeshivah* related to the Talmud in very much the same way as the tannaim (the rabbis whose teachings are collected in the Mishnah) related to the Hebrew Bible and as the amoraim (the rabbis whose teachings are collected in the *gemara'*) related to the Mishnah.

There was a significant flow of ideas between the *yeshivot* of various areas. Rashi, who lived in northern France, was accepted in Spain and North Africa as the authoritative commentator on the Talmud, and the work of his successors in northern Europe, the tosafists, was eventually carried on in Spain. This tradition concentrated on reconciling texts and statements scattered through the rabbinic literature so that it would form a harmonious whole.

One of the distinctive characteristics of the curriculum of the late medieval Ashkenazic *yeshivah* (thirteenth to seventeenth century) was the development of *pilpul*, a type of argumentation that uses highly contorted, often hair-splitting reasoning to resolve hypothetical cases or to reconcile opposing views. Most *pilpul* took place in oral debates, and few texts from the period survive. Many scholars found *pilpul* a fascinating intellectual stimulus, but others criticized it for its artificiality. *Pilpul* was eventually abandoned in favor of the more logical approach of the Spanish scholars, whose works were widely disseminated in northern Europe after the development of the printing press. Another activity popular in *yeshivah* circles of the time was the collection and study of *minhagim*, or local customs.

Yeshivot in the Modern World. The continuity of the Ashkenazic *yeshivah* was broken in the seventeenth and eighteenth centuries in two different ways. In German-speaking lands, there was a gradual decline of interest in Talmudic and rabbinic literature, exacerbated by the Haskalah (Jewish Enlightenment movement) and the increasing assimilation of Jews into the general community. In Polish lands there was a sharper break that was associated with (but not totally explained by) the Cossack rebellion of 1648, which destroyed many communities and their *yeshivot*. The failure of the

Polish Jewish community to reestablish the network of *yeshivot* immediately after the rebellion was due, in part, to the economic decline of the Jewish community and perhaps also to the spread of Hasidism, which encouraged the study of Talmud but placed less emphasis on formal education.

The nineteenth century saw important growth in the number and role of European *yeshivot*. In central Europe a key part was played by Mosheh Sofer (1762-1839), the rabbi of Pressburg, Hungary (now Bratislava, Czechoslovakia). He was appointed to the position in 1806, and as his fame grew he became a major force in developing an active Orthodoxy in reaction to the Reform movement, which was gaining adherents in his native Germany and Hungary. One of the elements of his program was the development and expansion of the Pressburg *yeshivah*, whose student body soon numbered several hundred. Sofer's students went on to occupy many of the important rabbinical posts in the Habsburg empire. The *yeshivot* they founded were a great influence on the lives of students who studied there during their formative adolescent years and were a major factor in the stability and cohesiveness of Hungarian Orthodoxy. In Germany, however, no major *yeshivot* developed. The rapid pace of acculturation, the need for a general education for economic advancement, and the lack of prestige for Talmudic knowledge among wide sectors of the Jewish community were largely responsible for this.

The revival of *yeshivot* of eastern Europe began in the early nineteenth century with the foundation in 1803 of a *yeshivah* in Volozhin, White Russia, by Hayyim ben Yitshaq (1749-1821). It differed from earlier Ashkenazic *yeshivot* in that it was neither a private institution nor a communal one, but rather a regional institution supported by donations col-

> ## Today the two main centers of *yeshivot* are Israel and the United States.

lected by fundraisers from Jews throughout Lithuania and later even farther afield. As such, the *yeshivah* of Volozhin was free from local pressures. This organizational model was not immediately imitated, and most Talmud students continued to study in *batei midrash* (local study halls). In the latter part of the nineteenth century there was a sharp rise in the number of *yeshivot* that were founded to counteract the appeal of secular education and Haskalah. Important *yeshivot* were founded in Telz, Slobodka, Ponevezh, Slutsk, Novorodok, and elsewhere. Many were founded to advance the aims of the Musar movement, founded by Yisra'el Salanter (1810-1883), which called for the study and practice of ethical behavior. These *yeshivot* appointed special preceptors (*mashgihim*) to teach and supervise ethical behavior;

they functioned alongside the standard Talmud teachers, not always without friction. Other *yeshivot* emphasized new methods of study that stressed analysis of texts rather than legal casuistry. At the same time, and because of the same stimulus of competition from secular education and nontraditional influences, the Hasidic communities also began to establish *yeshivot*.

In the period between the world wars, all *yeshivot* in areas controlled by the Soviet Union were closed. However, in Poland, Lithuania, Hungary, and Czechoslovakia, *yeshivot* continued to flourish. These *yeshivot* were funded largely by subventions from Jews in the United States. The Holocaust led to the destruction of all of these institutions.

Today the two main centers of *yeshivot* are Israel and the United States. Until after World War II, *yeshivot* in the United States were relatively unsuccessful in attracting students and had little influence on Jewish life. Most of the Jews who came to America from eastern Europe in the late nineteenth and early twentieth century were not well educated, and the conditions of immigrant life in America were not conducive to the perpetuation of traditional customs. Those *yeshivot* that did exist followed the established patterns of the Old World. One important exception was the Rabbi Isaac Elhanan Theological Seminary, which grew into Yeshiva University. This institution, founded in the late nineteenth century in New York City, successfully introduced a new curriculum that included traditional Talmudic studies in the morning and secular studies, leading to the bachelor of arts degree, in the afternoon. After World War II there was a major increase in the number of American *yeshivot* and in the size of their student populations, as well as an improvement in the quality of instruction. These changes were due in part to the arrival of refugees from eastern Europe, who brought with them a strong commitment to tradition and expertise in Talumdic learning, and in part to the emergence of a native-born and self-confident American Jewish Orthodox community.

A similar pattern is found in the Land of Israel. In the early modern period, Sefardic Jews and Jewish communities in North Africa and Asia continued their traditional practice of financially supporting *yeshivot*, many of which were in the Land of Israel. They tended to be academies of established scholars rather than educational institutions in the Ashkenazic mold. These *yeshivot*, with their mature student bodies, often emphasized the study of Qabbalah or of Jewish law, not Talmudic study exclusively. The scholars who constituted the membership of the *yeshivot* were given stipends. When the Ashkenazic immigration to the Land of Israel began in the late eighteenth century, Ashkenazic *yeshivot* began to appear. They were intended for younger students, and the program of study was devoted almost completely to Talmud.

As the Jewish community in Palestine grew, there was a corresponding growth in the number of *yeshivot*. In the interwar period there was even a case of a *yeshivah* that was transferred in toto—student body and staff—from Slobodka in Lithuania to Hebron in Palestine. After the establishment of the state of Israel in 1948 this growth continued, now with the financial support of the Israeli government. As in America, the *yeshivah* high schools drew many of the sons of observant families. The special security problems of Israel led to the establishment of *yeshivot* for soldiers, who were permitted to interrupt their military service for periods of Talmud study.

Today almost all *yeshivah* students are unmarried. Another institution, the *kolel* (pl., *kolelim*), provides married students with stipends to enable them to study full-time. Unlike *yeshivah* students, they usually study independently, without formal guidance or supervision. The *yeshivot*, with the *kolelim*, are now among the most important institutions of contemporary Orthodoxy. They play a major role in securing the loyalty of the younger generation to traditional patterns and values. It has become standard practice for groups within the Orthodox community to establish separate *yeshivot* for their youth. Now, for example, every Hasidic sect has its own *yeshivah*. *Ro'shei yeshivah* are among the most important leaders of Orthodox Jewry, and they often supplant the authority of communal rabbis.

There are probably more young men studying Torah (and especially the Talmud) full-time today than ever before. Only a small minority go on to serve as rabbis. While in traditional *yeshivot* the student body continues to be all male, similar institutions of study for women have been developed.

BIBLIOGRAPHY

Relatively few works have been written that deal specifically with *yeshivot*. However, almost anything written on the history of Jewish education touches on *yeshivot*, and so do many studies of Jewish history or religion. The best starting point for bibliographies on particular *yeshivot* or on higher education in a given community or area is Shlomo Shunami's *Bibliography of Jewish Bibliographies*, 2d ed. (Jerusalem, 1965; suppl., Jerusalem, 1976), which directs the reader to bibliographies on almost any topic of Judaica. The most useful guides to current literature are *Kiryat Sefer*, a quarterly listing of recent books of Judaica and Hebraica, and the annual *Index of Articles on Jewish Studies*. Both are arranged topically and are published by the Jewish National and University Library in Jerusalem.

There are a number of valuable monographs on *yeshivot*. The most recent book on the Babylonian *yeshivot* is David M. Goodblatt's *Rabbinic Instruction in Sasanian Babylonia* (Leiden, 1975). For the other end of the time spectrum, William B. Helmreich's *The World of the Yeshiva* (New York, 1982) provides a useful description of modern American *yeshivot*. A number of unpublished Ph. D. dissertations are relevant: Armin Harry Friedman's "Major Aspects of Yeshiva Education in Hungary, 1848-1948" (Yeshiva University, 1971), M. Breuer's "The Ashkenazi Yeshiva toward the Close of the Middle Ages" (Hebrew University, 1967), I. Gafni's "The Babylonian Yeshiva" (Hebrew University, 1978), and my own "Three Lithuanian Yeshivot" (Hebrew University, 1982); the latter three are in Hebrew with detailed English summaries. The most valuable collection of primary sources on the history of Jewish education, which includes a great deal of material on *yeshivot*, is Simha Assaf's *Megorot le-toledot ha-hinukh be-Yisra'el*, 4 vols. in 2 (Tel Aviv, 1936-1954).

SHAUL STAMPFER

YOGA

In Indian religion the term *yoga* serves, in general, to designate any ascetic technique and any method of meditation. The "classical" form of yoga is a *darsana* ("view, doctrine"; usually, although improperly, translated as "system of philosophy") expounded by Patañjali in his *Yoga Sutra*, and it is from this "system" that we must set out if we are to understand the position of yoga in the history of Indian thought. But side by side with classical Yoga there are countless forms of sectarian, popular (magical), and non-Brahmanic yogas such as Buddhist and Jain forms.

Patañjali is not the creator of the Yoga *darsana*. As he himself admits, he has merely edited and integrated the doctrinal and technical traditions of yoga (*Yoga Sutra* 1.1). Indeed, yogic practices were known in the esoteric circles of Indian ascetics and mystics long before Patañ-jali. Among these practices Patañjali retained those that the experiences of centuries had sufficiently tested. As to the theoretical framework and the metaphysical foundation that Patañjali provides for such techniques, his personal contribution is of the smallest. He merely rehandles the Samkhya philosophy in its broad outlines, adapting it to a rather superficial theism and exalting the practical value of meditation. The Yoga and Samkhya *darsanas* are so much alike that most of the assertions made by the one are valid for the other. The essential differences between them are two: (1) whereas Samkhya is atheistic, Yoga is theistic, since it postulates the existence of a "Lord" (Isvara); (2) whereas according to Samkhya the only path to final deliverance is that of metaphysical knowledge, Yoga accords marked importance to techniques of purification and meditation.

Thanks to Patañjali, Yoga, which had been an archaic ascetic and mystical tradition, became an organized "system of philosophy." Nothing is known of the author of the *Yoga Sutra*, not even whether he lived in the second or third century BCE or in the fifth century CE, although claims to both datings have been vigorously defended. The earliest commentary known to us is the *Yogabhasya* of Vyasa (seventh to eighth century CE), annotated by Vacaspatimisra (ninth century) in his *Tattvavaisaradi*. These two works, indispensable for understanding the *Yoga Sutra*, are complemented by two works of later centuries. At the beginning of the eleventh century King Bhoja wrote the commentary *Rajamartanda*, which is very useful for its insights into certain yogic practices, and in the sixteenth century Vijñanabhiksu annotated Vyasa's text in his remarkable treatise the *Yogavarttika*.

Ignorance and Suffering. "All is suffering for the sage," writes Patañjali (*Yoga Sutra* 2.15), repeating a leitmotif of all post-Upansadic Indian speculation. The discovery of pain as the law of existence has a positive, stimulating value. It perpetually reminds the sage and the ascetic that the only way to attain freedom and bliss is withdrawal from the world, radical isolation. To liberate the self from suffering is the goal of all Indian philosophies and magico-mystical techniques. In India, metaphysical knowledge always has a soteriological purpose, for it is by knowledge of ultimate reality that man, casting off the illusions of the world of phenomena, awakens and discovers the true nature of spirit *(atman, purusa)*. For Samkhya and Yoga, suffering has its origin in ignorance of spirit, that is, in confusing spirit with psychomental states, which are the most refined products of nature *(prakrti)*. Consequently, liberation, absolute freedom, can be obtained only if this confusion is abolished. As the structure and unfolding of nature and the paradoxical mode of being of the self *(purusa)* are discussed elsewhere, here only the yogic practices themselves will be examined.

The point of departure of yogic meditation is concentration on a single object: a physical object (the space between the eyebrows, the tip of the nose, something luminous, etc.), a thought (a metaphysical truth), or God (Isvara). This determined and continuous concentration, called *ekagrata* ("on a single point"), is obtained by integrating the psychomental flux, *sarvarthata* ("variously directed, discontinued, diffused attention"; *Yoga Sutra* 3.11). This is the precise definition of yogic technique, and is called *cittavrtti-nirodha*, "the suppression of psychomental states" (*Yoga Sutra* 1.2). The practice of ekagrata tends to control the two generators of psychomental life: sense activity *(indriya)* and the activity of the unconscious *(samskara)*. A yogin is able to concentrate his attention on a single point and become insensible to any other sensory or mnemonic stimulus. It goes without saying that *ekagrata* can be obtained only through the practice of numerous exercises and techniques. One cannot obtain *ekagrata* if, for example, the body is in a tiring or even uncomfortable posture, or if the respiration is disorganized, unrhythmical. This is why yogic technique implies several categories of physiological practices and spiritual exercises, called *angas*, "members," or elements. The eight "members" of classical Yoga can be regarded both as forming a group of techniques and as being stages of the ascetic and spiritual itinerary whose end is final liberation. They are (1) restraints *(yama)*, (2) disciplines *(niyama)*, (3) bodily attitudes and postures *(asana)*, (4) rhythm of respiration *(pranayama)*, (5) emancipation of sensory activity from the domination of exterior objects *(pratyahara)*, (6) concentration *(dharana)*, (7) yogic meditation *(dhyana)*, and (8) enstasis *(samadhi*; *Yoga Sutra* 2.29).

In addition to this classical Yoga comprising eight *angas*, there exist a number of *sadangayogas*, that is, yogic regimens having only six members. Their main characteristic is the absence of the three first angas *(yama, niyama, asana)* and the introduction of a new "member," *tarka* ("reason, logic"). Attested already in the *Maitrayani Upanisad* (second century BCE-second century CE), the *sadangayoga* appears especially in certain sects of Hinduism and in the Buddhist Tantras (Grönbold, 1969, 1983).

Restraints and Disciplines. The first two groups of practices, *yama* and *niyama*, constitute the inevitable preliminaries for any asceticism. There are five "restraints," namely, *ahimsa* (restraint from violence), *satya* (restraint from falsehood), *asteya* (restraint from stealing), *brahmacarya* (restraint from sexual activity), and *aparigraha* (restraint from avarice). These restraints do not bring about a specifically yogic state but induce in the adept a purified state superior to that of the uninitiated. In conjunction with the *yamas*, the yogin must practice the *niyama*, that is, a series of bodily and psychic disciplines. "Cleanliness, serenity, asceticism *[tapas]*, study of Yoga metaphysics, and an effort to make Isvara [God] the motive of all his actions constitute the disciplines," writes Patañjali (*Yoga Sutra* 2.32). Obviously, difficulties and obstacles arise during these exercises, most of them produced by the subconscious. The perplexity arising from doubt is the most dangerous. To overcome it, Patañjali recommends implanting the contrary thought (*Yoga Sutra* 2.33). To vanquish a temptation is to realize a genuine, positive gain. Not only does the yogin succeed in dominating the objects that he had renounced, but he also obtains a magic force infinitely more precious than all these objects. For example, he who successfully practices *asteya* "sees all jewels coming near to him" (*Yoga Sutra* 2.37).

Asana and Pranayama. The specifically yogic techniques begin with *asana*, the well-known bodily posture of the Indian ascetics. *Asana* gives a rigid stability to the body while at the same time reducing physical effort to a minimum and finally eliminating it altogether. *Asana* is the first concrete step taken with a view to abolishing the modalities peculiar to the human condition. On the bodily plane, *asana* is an *ekagrata*; the body is "concentrated" in a single position. Thus, one arrives at a certain neutralization of the senses; consciousness is no longer troubled by the presence of the body. Furthermore, a tendency toward "unification" and "totalization" is typical of all yogic practices. Their goal is the transcendence (or the abolition) of the human condition, resulting from the refusal to obey one's natural inclinations.

The most important—and certainly the most specifically yogic—of these various "refusals" is the disciplining of respiration *(pranayama)*, the refusal to breathe like the majority of mankind, that is, unrhythmically. Patañjali defines this refusal as follows: "*Pranayama* is the arrest *[viccheda]* of the movements of inhalation and exhalation and it is obtained after *asana* has been realized (*Yoga Sutra* 2.49). He speaks of the "arrest," the suspension, of respiration; however, *pranayama* begins with making the respiratory rhythm as slow as possible; and this is its first objective.

A remark in Bhoja's commentary (on *Yoga Sutra* 1.34) reveals the deeper meaning of *pranayama*: "All the functions of the organs being preceded by that of respiration—there being always a connection between respiration and consciousness in their respective functions—respiration, when all the functions of the organs are suspended, realizes concentration of consciousness on a single object." The special relation of the rhythm of respiration to particular states of consciousness, which has undoubtedly been observed and experienced by yogins from the earliest times, has served them as an instrument for "unifying" consciousness. By mak-

> **Their goal is the transcendence (or the abolition) of the human condition, resulting from the refusal to obey one's natural inclinations.**

ing his respiration rhythmical and progressively slower the yogin can penetrate—that is experience in perfect lucidity—certain states of consciousness that are inaccessible in a waking condition, particularly the states of consciousness that are peculiar to sleep.

Indian psychology recognizes four modalities of consciousness (besides enstasis): diurnal consciousness, consciousness in sleep with dreams, consciousness in sleep without dreams, and "cataleptic consciousness." Through *pranayama*, that is, by increasingly prolonging inhalation and exhalation (since the purpose of this practice is to allow as long an interval as possible to elapse between the two phases of respiration) the yogin can experience all the modalities of consciousness. For the uninitiated, there is a discontinuity between these several modalities; one passes from the state of waking to the state of sleeping unconsciously. The yogin must preserve continuity of consciousness; that is, he must penetrate each of these states with determination and awareness.

But the immediate goal of *pranayama* is more modest; it induces the respiratory rhythm by harmonizing the three "moments" of breathing: inhalation (*puraka*), retention (*kumbhaka*), and exhalation (*recaka*) of the inhaled air. These three moments must each fill an equal space of time. Practice enables the yogin to prolong them considerably. He begins by holding his breath for sixteen and a half seconds, then for thirty-three seconds, then for fifty seconds, three minutes, five minutes, and so on. (Similar respiratory technique were familiar to the Taoists, to Christian hesychasts,

and to the Muslim contemplatives; see Eliade, 1969, pp. 59-65).

Yogic Concentration and Meditation. Making respiration rhythmical and, as far as possible, suspending it greatly promotes concentration (*dharana; Yoga Sutra* 2.52-53). The yogin can test the quality of his concentration by *pratyahara*, a term usually translated as "withdrawal of the senses" or "abstraction" but more accurately rendered as the "ability to free sense activity from the domination of external objects." According to the *Yoga Sutra* (2.54) and its commentators, the senses, instead of directing themselves toward an object, "abide within themselves" (Bhoja, on *Yoga Sutra* 2.54). When the intellect (*citta*) wishes to know an exterior object, it does not make use of sensory activity; it is able to know the object by its own powers. Being obtained directly, by contemplation, this knowledge is, from the yogic point of view, more effective than normal knowledge. "Then the wisdom [*prajña*] of the yogin knows all things as they are" (Vyasa, on *Yoga Sutra* 2.45). Thenceforth, the yogin will no longer be distracted or troubled by the activity of the senses, by the subconscious, and by the "thirst of life"; all activity is suspended. But this autonomy of the intellect does not result in the suppression of phenomena. Instead of knowing through forms (*rupa*) and mental states (*cittavrtti*) as formerly, the yogin now contemplates the essence (*tattva*) of all objects directly.

Such autonomy allows the yogin to practice a threefold technique that the texts call *samyama*. The term designates the last three "members" of yoga (*yoganga*), namely concentration (*dharana*), yogic meditation (*dhyana*), and stasis (*samadhi*). They do not imply new physiological practices. *Dharana*, from the root *dhr*, meaning "to hold fast," is in fact an *ekagrata*, undertaken for the purpose of comprehension. Patañjali's definition of *dharana* is "fixation of the thought on a single point" (*Yoga Sutra* 3.1). According to some authors (cf. Eliade, 1969, pp. 66-68), a *dharana* takes the time of twelve *pranayamas* (i. e., twelve controlled, equal, and delayed respirations). By prolonging this concentration on an object twelve times, one obtains yogic meditation, *dhyana*. Patañjali defines *dhyana* as "a current of unified thought" (*Yoga Sutra* 3.2) and Vyasa adds the following gloss to the definition: "continuum of mental effort to assimilate the object of meditation, free from any other effort to assimilate other objects." It is unnecessary to add that this yogic meditation is absolutely different from any secular meditation.

Samadhi and the Lord of the Yogins. Yogic enstasis, *samadhi*, is the final result and crown of all the ascetic's spiritual efforts and exercises. The term is first employed in a gnoseological sense: *samadhi* is the state in which thought grasps the object directly. Thus, there is a real coincidence between knowledge of the object and the object of knowledge. This kind of knowledge constitutes an enstatic modality of being that is peculiar to yoga. Patañjali and his commentators distinguish several sorts, or stages, of *samadhi*.

When it is obtained with the help of an object or idea (that is, by fixing one's thought on a point in space or on an idea), it is called *samprajñata samadhi*, "enstasis with support." When, on the other hand, *samadhi* is obtained apart from any relation to externals, when it is simply a full comprehension of being, it is *asamprajñata samadhi*, "undifferentiated stasis."

Because it is perfectible and does not realize an absolute and irreducible state, the "differentiated enstasis" *(samprajñata samadhi)* comprises four stages, called *bija samadhi* ("*samadhi* with seed") or *salambana samadhi* ("*samadhi* with support"). By accomplishing these four stages, one after the other, one obtains the "faculty of absolute knowledge" *(rtambharaprajña)*. This is in itself an opening toward *samadhi* "without seed," pure *samadhi*, for absolute knowledge discovers the state of ontological plenitude in which being and knowing are no longer separated. According to Vijñanabhiksu, *asamprajñata samadhi* destroys the "impressions [*samskara*] of all antecedent mental functions" and even succeeds in arresting the karmic forces already set in motion by the yogin's past activities (Eliade, 1969, p. 84).

Fixed in *samadhi*, consciousness *(citta)* can now have direct revelation of the self *(purusa)*. For the devotional yogins, it is at this stage that the revelation of the Supreme Self, Isvara, the Lord, takes place. Unlike Samkhya, Yoga affirms the existence of a God, Isvara. He is not a creator god, for the cosmos, life, and man proceed from the primordial substance, *prakrti*. But in the case of certain men (i. e., the yogins), Isvara can hasten the process of deliverance. Isvara is a self *(purusa)* that has been eternally free. Patañjali says that the Isvara has been the guru of the sages of immemorial times *(Yoga Sutra* 1.26) and that he can bring about *samadhi* on condition that the yogin practice *isvara-pranidhana*, that is, devotion to Isvara *(Yoga Sutra* 2.45). But we have seen that *samadhi* can be obtained without such mystical exercises. In the classical Yoga of Patañjali, Isvara plays a rather minor role. It is only with the later commentators, such as Vijñanabhiksu and Nila-kantha, that Isvara gains the importance of a true God.

The Yogic Powers; Deliverance. By practicing *samyama*—that is, by means of concentration, meditation, and the realization of *samadhi*—the yogin acquires the "miraculous powers" *(siddhis)* to which book 3 of the *Yoga Sutra*, beginning with *sutra* 16, is devoted. The majority of these powers are related to different kinds of supranormal or mystical knowledge. Thus, by practicing *samyama* in regard to his own subconscious residues *(samskara)*, the yogin comes to know his previous existences *(Yoga Sutra* 3.105). Through *samyama* exercised in respect to "notions" *(pratyaya)*, he knows the mental states of other men (3.19). *Samyama* practiced on the umbilical plexus *(nabhicakra)* produces knowledge of the system of the body (3.28), on the heart, knowledge of the mind (3.33), and so forth." Whatever the yogin

desires to know, he should perform *samyama* in respect to that object," writes Vacaspatimisra (on *Yoga Sutra* 3.30). According to Patañjali and the whole tradition of classical Yoga, the yogin uses the innumerable *siddhis* in order to attain the supreme freedom, *asamprajñata samadhi*, not in order to obtain a mastery over the elements *(Yoga Sutra* 3.37). We find a similar doctrine in Buddhism (Eliade, 1969, pp. 177-180; Pensa, 1969, pp. 23-24).

Yoga prescribes solitude and chastity.

Through the illumination *(prajña)* spontaneously obtained when he reaches the last stage of his itinerary, the yogin realizes "absolute isolation" *(kaivalya)*, that is, liberation of the self *(purusa)* from the dominance of nature *(prakrti)*. But this mode of being of the spirit is not an "absolute emptiness"; it constitutes a paradoxical, because unconditioned, state. Indeed, the intellect *(buddhi)*, having accomplished its mission, withdraws, detaching itself from the *purusa* and returning into *prakrti*. The self remains free, autonomous; that is, the yogin attains deliverance. Like a dead man, he has no more real relation with life; he is a *jivanmukta*, one "liberated in life." He no longer lives in time and under the domination of time, but in an eternal present.

To recapitulate, the method recommended by the classical form of Yoga comprises a number of different techniques (physiological, mental, mystical) that gradually detach the yogin from the processes of life and the rules of social behavior. The worldly man lives in society, marries, establishes a family; Yoga prescribes solitude and chastity. In opposition to continual movement, the yogin practiced *asana*; in opposition to agitated, unrhythmical, uncontrolled respiration, he practices *pranayama*; to the chaotic flux of psychomental life, the yogin replies by "fixing thought on a single point"; and so on. The goal of all these practices always remains the same—to react against normal, secular, and even human inclinations. The final result is a grandiose, although paradoxical, mode of being. *Asamprajñata samadhi* realizes the "knowledge-possession" of the autonomous Self *(purusa)*; that is, it offers deliverance, freedom, and, more specifically, the consciousness of absolute freedom.

BIBLIOGRAPHY

Patañjali's *Yoga Sutra*, with the commentary *(Yogabhasya or Yogasutra-bhasya)* of Vyasa and the gloss *(Tattvavaisaradi)* of Vacaspatimisra have been translated into English by James H. Woods as *The Yoga System of Patañjali*, 3d ed. (Dehli, 1966), and by Rama Prasada as *Patanjali's Yoga Sutras* (Allahabad, 1910). A listing of editions and translations of other, later commentaries can be found on page 372 of my *Yoga: Immortality and Freedom*, 2d aug.

ed. (Princeton, 1969), which also includes bibliographies on pages 372, 437-480, and 533-555.

On the *Yoga Upanisads*, see *Yoga Upanisads with the Commentary of Sri Upanisad-Brahma-Yogin*, translated and edited by Alladi Mahadeva Sastri (Madras, 1920). Among the different works on Yoga, written from different perspectives, one may cite Richard Garbe's *Samkhya und Yoga* (Strasbourg, 1896); Surendranath Dasgupta's *Yoga as Philosophy and Religion* (1924; reprint, Calcutta, 1973) and *Yoga Philosophy in Relation to Other Systems of Thought* (1930; reprint, Delhi, 1974); Hermann Jacobi's "Über das ursprüngliche Yogasystem," *Sitzungsberichte der preussischen Akademie der Wissenschaften* 26 (1929): 581-627; Sigurd Lindquist's *Die Methoden des Yoga* (Lund, 1932) and *Siddhi und Abhiñña: Eine Studie über die klassischen Wunder des Yoga* (Uppsala, 1935); Heinrich Zimmer's *Kunstform und Yoga im indischen Kultbild* (Berlin, 1926); J. W. Hauer's *Der Yoga, als Heilweg: Nach den indischen Quellen dargestellt*, 2d. ed. (Stuttgart, 1958); Jean Varenne's *Yoga and the Hindu Tradition*, translated by Derek Coltman (Chicago 1976); and Georg Feuerstein's *The Philosophy of Classical Yoga* (Manchester, 1980).

On Isvara, see my *Yoga*, 2d aug. ed. (Princeton, 1969), pp. 68ff., and especially Jan Gonda's "The Isvara Idea," in *Change and Continuity in Indian Religion* (The Hague, 1965), pp. 131-163.

On different types of yogic meditation, the best work is *Strukturen yogische Meditation* by Gerhard Oberhammer (Vienna, 1977). See also A. Janácek's "The 'Voluntaristic' Type of Yoga in Patañjali's *Yoga-Sutras*," *Archiv Orientální* 22 (1954): 69-87, and Corrado Pensa's "On the Purification Concept in Indian Tradition, with Special Regard to Yoga," *East and West*, n. s. 19 (1969): 1-35. On the recent scientific observations in regard to the physiological and psychological aspects of yogic technique, see Thérèse Brosse's *Études instrumentales des techniques du Yoga: Expérimentation psychosomatique* (Paris, 1963).

On *sadangayoga*, see Anton Zigmund-Cerbu's "The Sadangayoga," *History of Religions* 3 (Summer 1963): 128-134; Sadanga-yoga, edited by Günter Grönbold (Munich, 1969), an edition and German translation of *Gunabharani-nama-Sadangayogatippani* of Ravisrijñana and Grönbold's "Materialen zur Geschichte des Sadanga-yoga, I-III," *Indo-Iranian Journal* 25 (April 1983): 181-190 (also published in *Zentralasiatische Studien* 16, 1982, pp. 337-347), and "Der sechsgliedrige Yoga des Kalacakra-Tantra," *Asiatische Studien / Études asiatiques* 37 (1938): 25-45.

My *Yoga*, cited above, includes discussion of the different forms of yogic practices in Brahmanism, Hinduism, Buddhism, and Tantrism (pp. 101-274, 384-414) and of the yoga of the Jains (pp. 209-210, 404-405). On the yoga of the Jains, see also Robert H. B. William's *Jaina Yoga: A Survey of the Medieval Sravakacaras* (London, 1963).

MIRCEA ELIADE

YORUBA RELIGION

The twelve to fifteen million Yoruba people of southwestern Nigeria, the Republic of Benin (formerly Dahomey), and Togo are the heirs of one of the oldest cultural traditions in West Africa. Archaeological and linguistic evidence indicate that the Yoruba have lived in their present habitat since at least the fifth century BCE. The development of the regional dialects that distinguish the Yoruba subgroups and the process of urbanization, which developed into a social system unique among sub-Saharan African peoples, took place during the first millennium CE. By the ninth century the ancient city of Ile-Ife was thriving, and in the next five centuries Ife artists would create terracotta and bronze sculptures that are now among Africa's artistic treasures.

> **. . . evidence indicate[s] that the Yoruba have lived in their present habitat since at least the fifth century BCE.**

Both Yoruba myth and oral history refer to Oduduwa (also known as Odua) as the first king and founder of the Yoruba people. Some myths portray him as the creator god and assert that the place of creation was Ile-Ife, which subsequently became the site of Oduduwa's throne. Oral history, however, suggests that the story of Oduduwa's assumption of the throne at Ife refers to a conquest of the indigenes of the Ife area prior to the ninth century by persons from "the east." While it is increasingly apparent that the sociopolitical model of a town presided over by a paramount chief or king *(oba)*, was well established in Ife and present among other Yoruba subgroups, the followers of Oduduwa developed the urban tradition and enhanced the role of the king. In later years, groups of people who sought to establish their political legitimacy (even if they were immigrants) were required to trace their descent from Oduduwa. Such people were known as "the sons of Oduduwa," and they wore beaded crowns *(adenla)* given to them by Oduduwa as the symbol of their sacred authority *(ase)*.

Origin myths, festival rituals, and oral traditions associate the indigenous peoples with Obatala, the deity *(orisa)* who fashions the human body. And since he too was an *oba*, his priests wear white, conical, beaded crowns similar to those reserved for "the sons of Odu-duwa." The myths and rituals also refer to a great struggle between Obatala and Oduduwa at the time of creation, following Oduduwa's theft of the privilege granted by Olorun (Olodumare), the high god, to Obatala to create the earth and its inhabitants. In the town of Itapa, the sequence of rituals that composes the annual festival of Obatala reenacts a battle between Oduduwa and Obatala, Oduduwa's victory over and the banishment of Obatala, and the rejoicing that took place among the gods and mankind with the return of Obatala at the invitation of Oduduwa. And there is the tradition among the Oy Yoruba of the unwarranted imprisonment of Obatala by Sango and the thunder god's release of the wandering, ancient king after famine and barrenness threatened field and home.

In these myths and rituals there is a historical remembrance of a usurpation of power and the acknowledgment that a violent conflict and a tenuous reconciliation gave birth to modern Yoruba culture. The remembrance, however, has not only to do with a past time, with historical and cultural origins; it is also a statement about the nature and limits of the authority of kings in defining the moral basis of Yoruba society. It is also about the importance of Ile-Ife as the symbol of Yoruba cultural homogeneity, while acknowledging the distinctiveness and the independence of other Yoruba subgroups.

There are approximately twenty subgroups, each identifiable by its distinctive variation in linguistic, social, political, and religious patterns born of the history of the region. Among the principal groups are the Egba and Egbado in the southwest, the Ijebu in the southern and southeast, the Oyo in the central and northwest, the Ife and the Ijesa in the central, the Owo in the eastern, and the Igbomina and Ekiti in the northeast regions. Throughout Yorubaland, the social system is patrilineal and patrilocal, although among the Egba and Egbado there are elements of a dual descent system. The extended family (idile), which dwells in the father's compound so long as space and circumstance permit, is the essential social unit and the primary context in which self-awareness and social awareness are forged. Thus, Odun Egungun, the annual festival for the patrilineal ancestors, is the most widespread and important festival in the Yoruba liturgical calendar. Elaborate masquerades (egungun), are created of layers of cloths of dark colors with white serrated edges. The costume covers the dancer, who moves about the compound or town with stately pace, occasionally performing whirling movements, causing the cloths to splay out in constantly changing patterns. In movement and appearance the masquerade depicts the presence and power (ase) of the ancestors. The ancestors are those persons who established the "house" (ile) and the family and who continue to stand surety for its integrity and survival against threats of witchcraft and disease, so long as their heirs acknowledge the ancestral presence.

While masquerades for the patrilineal ancestors are found among all the Yoruba, there are other masked festivals that are distinctive to particular areas, reflecting the regional history that has shaped the Yoruba experience. The Yoruba peoples of the southwest (the Anago, Awori, Egbado, Ketu, and Egba) celebrate the Gelede festival at the time of the spring rains. The festival honors awon iya wa ("the mothers"), a collective term for the female power (ase) possessed by all women but especially manifest in certain elderly women and in female ancestors and deities. It is the awesome power of woman in its procreative and destructive capacities that is celebrated and acknowledged. Among the Ijebu peoples of the south the annual festival for Agemo, an orisa whose power is represented by the chameleon, brings sixteen priest-chiefs famed for their magical or manipulative powers from towns surrounding the capital city of Ijebu-Ode into ritu-

al contests of curse and masked dance with one another and then into the city, where they petition and are received by the Awujale, the oba of Ijebu-Ode. The secret power of the priest-chiefs meets the sacred power of the crown. Each is required to acknowledge the role of the other in the complex balance of power that constitutes Ijebu political life. The Elefon and Epa festivals are masquerades performed in the towns of such Yoruba subgroups as the Igbomina and Ekiti in honor of persons and families whose lives embodied the social values by which Yoruba culture has been defined in the northeastern area. The helmet masks with their large sculptures are balanced on the dancers' heads and are the focus of ritual sacrifice (ebo) and songs of praise (oriki) throughout the festival. They are images of the sacred power of those who founded the town or contributed to its life in important ways. Thus, while individual masks are associated with particular families, they also refer to the roles of hunter, warrior, king, herbalist-priest, and leader of women, roles that transcend lineage ties and express in their collectivity cultural achievement. Their powers are akin to those of the orisa, the gods of the Yoruba pantheon.

According to the Yoruba, there are 401 orisa who line the road to heaven. All of them are thought to have been humans who, because they led notable lives, became orisa at the time of their death. For example, Sango, the god of thunder, was a legendary king of Oyo before he became an orisa. The extraordinary number of orisa reflects the regional variation in their worship. Sango is the patron deity of the kings of Oyo, and his shrines are important in those towns that were once part of the old Oyo empire (c. 1600-1790). But in Ile-Ife, or in communities to the south and east, the role of Sango and the degree to which he is worshiped diminishes markedly. As one moves from one part of Yorubaland to another, it will be Osun, goddess of medicinal waters, or Oko, god of the farm, or Erinle, god of forest and stream, or Obatala or Agemo whose shrines and festivals shape the religious life of a people. Furthermore, the orisa have multiple names. Some call Sango Oba Koso ("king of Koso"); others greet him as Balogunnile Ado ("leader of warriors at Ado"). Sango is also addressed as Abinufarokotu ("one who violently uproots an iroko tree"), Oko Iyemonja ("husband of Iyemonja"), or Lagigaoogun ("he who is mighty in the use of magical powers"), names that reveal the varied and distinctive experiences of his devotees and their relationship to the orisa. The multiplicity (or fragmentation) of the orisa is also a consequence of the historical dislocation of peoples that occurred during the intertribal wars of the nineteenth century. When persons and groups were forced to move from one area to another, their orisa went with them, shaping and being shaped by the new world of their devotees' experience.

Of all the orisa it is Ogun, god of iron and of war, whose worship is most widespread. It is said that there are seven Ogun, including Ogun of the blacksmiths, Ogun of the hunters, Ogun of the warriors, and Ogun Onire. Ire is a town in northeast Yorubaland where Ogun was once the leader of warriors and where he "sank into the ground" after killing persons in a great rage, having misunderstood their vow of ritual silence as a personal affront. As with other *orisa*, Ogun expresses and shapes a people's experience with respect to a particular aspect of their lives. In the case of Ogun, it is the experience of violence and culture: his myths and rituals articulate for the Yoruba the irony that cultural existence entails destruction and death. One must kill in order to live. And such a situation carries with it the danger that the destruction will go beyond culturally legitimate need, destroying that which it should serve. Thus, to employ Ogun's power, one must be aware of Ogun's character (*iwa*) and be cognizant that the beneficent god can become the outraged *orisa* who bites himself.

> ### Of all the *orisa* it is Ogun, god of iron and of war, whose worship is most widespread.

As with Ogun, each of the *orisa*, in the diversity and individuality of their persons and attributes, may be understood as providing an explanatory system and a means of coping with human suffering. Rarely does only one orisa lay claim to a person. Ogun or Sango or Osun may dominate one's life and shape one's perception of self and world, but other *orisa* will have their artifacts on the shrine, as well as their claims and influence upon one's life. Just as the Yoruba dancer must respond to the multiple rhythms of the drums, so must the soul attentive to the powers of the *orisa* respond to their diverse claims. The complexity of the response may overwhelm one. But as in the ability of the dancer to be conscious of and respond to every instrument of the orchestra, so in sacrificing to all the *orisa* who call, the worshiper (*olusin*, "he who serves") can know the richness of life and its complexity and can achieve the superior poise, the equanimity of one who possesses *ase* amid the contradictions of life. Thus, when one considers the configuration of orisa symbols on a devotee's shrine or the cluster of shrines and festivals for the orisa in a particular town or the pantheon as a whole, as a total system, one discerns that the total assemblage of orisa expresses in it totality a worldview. And it is in the reality of this worldview that Yoruba experience, at the personal and social levels, is given coherence and meaning.

In addition to the *orisa* of the pantheon, there is one's personal *orisa*, known as *ori inun* ("inner head"), which refers to the destiny that one's ancestral guardian soul has chosen while kneeling before Olorun prior to entering the world. It is a personal destiny that can never be altered. Birth results in the loss of the memory of one's destiny. But one's "ori-in-

heaven," which is also referred to as *ekejimi* ("my spiritual other"), stands surety for the possibilities and the limits of the destiny that one has received. Hence, one must make one's way in life, acknowledging one's *ori* as an *orisa* who can assist one in realizing the possibilities that are one's destiny. One can have an *ori buruku* ("a bad head"). In such a case a person must patiently seek to make the best of a foolish choice and seek the help of the other *orisa*.

In *orisa* worship it is the wisdom of Orunmila, the *orisa* of Ifa divination, and the work of Esu, the bearer of sacrifices, that stand for the meaningfulness of experience and the possibility of effective action. The vast corpus of Ifa poetry, organized into 256 collections called *odu* (also known as *orisa*) is a repository of Yoruba cultural values. It is the priest of Ifa, the *babalawo* ("father of ancient wisdom"), who knows Ifa and performs the rites of divination. Using the sixteen sacred palm nuts or the *opele* chain, the priest divines the *odu* whose verses he will chant in addressing the problem of the supplicant and determining the sacrifices that must be made. For the Yoruba, every ritual entails a sacrifice, whether it is the gift of prayer, the offering of a kola nut, or the slaughter of an animal. In the Ifa literature, sacrifice (*ebo*) has to do with death and the avoidance of such related experiences as loss, disease, famine, sterility, isolation, and poverty. It is an acknowledgment that human existence is ensnared in the interrelated contradictions of life and death. But sacrifice is also viewed as the reversal of the situation of death into life. Sacrifice is the food of the *orisa* and other spirits, and one sacrifices that which appropriately expresses the character (*iwa*) of the particular *orisa* or spirit of one's concern. Hence, Ogun receives a dog, the carnivorous animal that can be domesticated to assist the hunter and warrior. Sacrifice is the acknowledgement of the presence of powerful agents in the world, and the sacrificial act brings the creative power of the *orisa*, the ancestors, or the mothers to the worshiper; sacrifice can also temporarily stay the hand of Death and ward off other malevolent spirits (*ajogun*). Such is the power of Esu, the bearer of sacrifices, the mediator and guardian of the ritual way, the "keeper of *ase*."

Those who have observed the ritual way and achieved the status of elders in the community may also become members of the secret Osugbo (Ogboni) society. Although Osugbo is found throughout Yorubaland, its role and rituals vary from one region to another. Osugbo members, who come from various lineage groups, worship Onile ("the owner of the house"). The "house" (*ile*) is the image of the universe in its totality, of which the Osugbo cult house is a microcosm. The *edan* of the Osugbo society, which are small, brass, linked staffs that depict male and female figures, are the sign of membership and the symbol of the Osugbo understanding of reality. The secret of the Osugbo appears to be that its members know, and are in touch with, a primordial unity that transcends the oppositions characterizing human experience. Expressing the unity of male and female, the *edan* and their owners possess the power of adjudicating conflicts among persons or groups; when blood has been shed illicitly (as in a murder) it is the Osugbo members who must atone for this "violation of the house."

The worldview of the Yoruba is a monistic one. The universe of their experience is pervaded by *ase*, a divine energy in the process of generation and regeneration. *Ase* is without any particular signification and yet invests all things and all persons and, as the warrant for all creative activity, opposes chaos and the loss of meaning in human experience. Thus, for the Yoruba the universe is one, and it is amenable to articulation in terms of an elaborate cosmology, to critical reflection, and to innovative speculation.

BIBLIOGRAPHY

The best general introductions to Yoruba religion are E. Bo-laji Idowu's *Olódùmarè: God in Yoruba Belief* (London, 1962) and Robert Farris Thompson's *Black Gods and Kings: Yoruba Art at UCLA*, 2d ed. (Bloomington, Ind., 1976). Idowu's study contains a wealth of primary data and is an important contribution by a Yoruba scholar, although the presentation is compromised by an uncritical use of Christian theological concepts and categories. Thompson's highly readable, insightful, and brief essays analyze the Yoruba worldview in terms of Yoruba art. This approach has been further developed by William B. Fagg and John Pemberton III in *Yoruba Sculpture of West Africa*, edited by Bruce Holcombe (New York, 1982). In addition to an anthology of Fagg's essays on Yoruba art, this volume includes texts by Pemberton, which discuss seventy works of art in the context of Yoruba history, rituals, and cosmology, and an extensive bibliography.

The most important specialized studies on Yoruba religious thought and practice include those on Ifa poetry and divination rites by 'Wande Abimbola, *Ifá: An Exposition of Ifá Literary Corpus* (Ibadan, 1976), and William R. Bascom, *Ifa Divination: Communication between Gods and Men in West Africa* (Bloomington, Ind., 1969). Abimbola has edited an extensive collection of essays, *Yoruba Oral Tradition* (Ife, 1975), that provides an excellent introduction to Yoruba scholarship in the areas of archaeology, history, art, and religion. Of special note for their substantive and methodological contribution are the essays by Babatundi Agiri on the early history of Oyo and by Rowland Abiodun on Ifa art objects. Specialized studies of *orisa* worship by John Pemberton III and Karin Barber offer contrasting approaches and alternative interpretations to that of Idowu; Pemberton's "A Cluster of Sacred Symbols: Orisa Worship among the Igbomina Yoruba of Ila-Orangun," *History of Religions* 17 (August 1977): 1-26, pursues a structuralist analysis, and Barber's "How Man Makes God in West Africa: Yoruba Attitudes towards the *Orisa*," *Africa* 51 (1981): 724-745, combines a sociological with an oral history approach. The best study of masked festivals is Henry John Drewel and Margaret T. Drewal's *Gèlèdé: A Study of Art and Feminine Power among the Yoruba* (Bloomington, Ind., 1983). See also the special issue of *African Arts* 11, no. 3 (April 1983), edited by Henry John Drewal, on the arts and festivals for Egungun.

JOHN PEMBERTON III

YOUNG, BRIGHAM

YOUNG, BRIGHAM (1801-1877), second president of the Church of Jesus Christ of Latter-day Saints (hereafter LDS); chief architect of the form of Mormonism that flourished in the intermountain region of the western United States in the nineteenth century and expanded throughout the United States and into many other countries. [*See* Mormonism.]

Although he insisted on baptism by immersion, which he thought scripture required, Brigham Young joined the Methodists several years before he heard about Joseph Smith's "golden bible." A skilled carpenter, painter, and cabinetmaker, Young came from a family of devout Methodists whose extreme poverty impelled them to leave New England for western New York, a family history that paralleled that of the Smith family. While Mormonism attracted many of his family members, Young held back. He read the *Book of Mormon* soon after its publication in 1830 but waited two full years before becoming a Latter-day Saint. Thus he was not converted in the very beginning when Mormonism's primary appeal was its claim that it had restored the priesthood of ancient Israel and that it was the only true church of Jesus Christ. He became a follower of the Mormon prophet, Joseph Smith, in 1832, when the character of the new movement was becoming as Hebraic as it was Christian, given the

> **While Mormonism attracted many of his family members, Young held back.**

emphasis being placed on its "gathering" doctrine, its temple-building plans, its patriarchal office, and its assertion that Mormons are God's only chosen people. Convinced that these elements separating Mormonism from traditional Christianity were scripturally correct, Young accepted them wholeheartedly. Moreover, when temple ordinances were introduced that added plural marriage and baptism for the dead to Mormonism, and when the movement organized itself into a political kingdom, he accepted these innovations as well, albeit somewhat less enthusiastically.

After his rebaptism, Young devoted his entire energies to Mormonism. Following a preaching mission in the eastern United States, he moved to Ohio, assisting with the construction of the Kirtland temple and much else. He went with Zion's Camp, a paramilitary expedition that failed to rescue beleaguered Missouri Saints from their enemies, but nevertheless tested the mettle of future LDS leaders. Called to the highest council in Mormondom, the Quorum of the Twelve, in 1835, and made its president in 1841, Young rendered signal service, particularly in organizing the exodus when the

Saints were driven from Missouri in 1839 and in establishing a successful Mormon mission in England in the early 1840s. In Nauvoo, Illinois, during the final years of Smith's life, Young served in the prophet's inner circle as the LDS political kingdom was organized and the secret practice of plural marriage instituted.

The struggle for succession to LDS leadership after Smith's murder in 1844 intensified a division within the movement. On one side were Saints who, regarding Mormonism as an idiosyncratic version of primitive Christianity, opposed plural marriage and the political organization of a kingdom in an Old Testament mode; on the other were Saints who supported these innovations as a part of the restoration of the "ancient order of things." Although most historical accounts present Young as the clear winner in this succession struggle, recent demographic studies reveal that he was the acknowledged leader of the latter group, but that he by no means led the whole of the LDS community after Smith's death.

For the thousands who followed him, however, Young managed to effect the transfer of Mormon culture from Illinois to the Great Salt Lake Valley while preserving the vision of Mormonism that Joseph Smith held at the end of his life. He did this by assuming ecclesiastical, political, and spiritual leadership of his followers. In Nauvoo, he took practical charge of the chaotic situation and arranged the departure of the Saints. In 1847, he was sustained as president of the church by those who went west with him. In 1851, the federal government recognized his leadership by appointing him as governor of Utah Territory. From these dual positions of power, he established a new "Israel in the tops of the mountains" in which, in the manner of Solomon of old, he reigned supreme as prophet, church president, and political leader. Unlike Joseph Smith, however, Young was not a prophet who delivered new revelations and added lasting theological elements to the movement he headed. His great contribution was realizing Smith's vision through the creation of a literal LDS kingdom. Even changed, as it was at the end of the nineteenth century, this kingdom continues to animate and inspire Mormonism in much the same way that Solomon's kingdom has animated and inspired Judaism and Christianity across the ages.

BIBLIOGRAPHY

Until very recently, historical accounts of Young's life and career were either faith-promoting paeans of praise, based on nineteenth-century official LDS publications, or ill-concealed attacks, based on published sources unfriendly to the Mormons. Neither genre has disappeared, but as much of the primary source material on which studies of Young must rely is now available to scholars, new studies presenting a more balanced assessment of this important Mormon leader are appearing. The most significant of these new studies are Leonard J. Arrington's *Brigham Young: American Moses* (New York, 1985); Newell G. Bringhurst's *Brigham Young and the Expanding American Frontier* (Boston, 1985); and Ronald K. Esplin's "The Emergence of Brigham Young and the Twelve to Mormon Leadership, 1830-1841" (Ph. D. diss., Brigham Young University, 1981). Two valuable editions of primary source materials are *Letters of Brigham Young to His Sons*, edited by Dean C. Jesse (Salt Lake City, 1974); and *Diary of Brigham Young, 1857*, edited by Everett L. Cooley (Salt Lake City, 1980). Stanley P. Hirshson's *The Lion of the Lord: A Biography of Brigham Young* (New York, 1969) is not recommended; despite its reputable publisher and respected author, it is based on published sources, most of which are unfriendly to the Mormons.

The results of recent demographic studies are reported in Dean L. May's "A Demographic Portrait of the Mormons, 1830-1980," in *After 150 Years: The Latter-day Saints in Sesquicentennial Perspective*, edited by Thomas G. Alexander and Jessie L. Embry (Provo, Utah, 1983).

JAN SHIPPS

ZEALOTS

The Zealots were Jewish revolutionaries in first-century Judaea whose religious zeal led them to fight to the death against Roman domination and to kill or persecute Jews who collaborated with the Romans. Scholars disagree as to whether the name *Zealots* designated all revolutionary groups of the first century or only one of the factions active during the Roman-Jewish War of 66-70 CE. Josephus Flavius (37-c. 100 CE), the Jewish general who surrendered to the Romans and whose official Roman history of the war furnishes the major source, is ambiguous in his use of terminology. References in the New Testament, the Pseudepigrapha, and the rabbinic literature add to the confusion.

In 6 CE, Judah (Yehudah) the Galilean showed zeal for God's law and land when he led a revolt against the Roman census in Judaea. He and his followers fought to cleanse the land by taking vengeance against Jews who cooperated with the Romans. Judah considered such cooperation to be idolatrous recognition of a lord (Caesar) other than God. By such vengeance, he and his followers sought to appease God, who would thereby honor their cause against the Romans. The revolt failed, but Judah had originated the so-called Fourth Philosophy ("No Lord but God") based on the first commandment. Judah's followers emerged again after all of Judaea became a Roman province in 44 CE. Their subsequent revolutionary actions against the corrupt and incompetent authorities contributed to the outbreak of war in 66 CE. Josephus usually refers to Judah's group as Sicarii, after the *sikkah* ("dagger") used in assassinations.

For the war period, Josephus identifies (in addition to the wartime government) five revolutionary groups, each with its own social and geographic origins, motivations, methods, and goals. (Not all the groups shared a "zealous" mentality, and they usually cooperated only when confronted with a common enemy.)

1. The Sicarii fought for "No Lord but God" under the messianic leadership of Judas the Galilean's descendants. When other revolutionary groups forced them out of Jerusalem in 66 CE, they spent the war on Masada, where in 74 CE they chose suicide rather than capture by the Romans.

2. The Zealots, primarily priests from Jerusalem and the Judean peasantry, declared war by stopping the official sacrifices for Caesar. Later, under democratic leadership, they occupied the Temple, chose a high priest by lot, and, in 68 CE, overthrew the wartime government.

3. John of Giscala (Yohanan ben Levi), leader of a Galilean contingent, gained the confidence of the wartime government, which he then betrayed to the Zealots.

4. Simeon bar Giora, from Gerasa in the Decapolis, raised an army of freed slaves and peasants, then overran Idumea. In 69 CE, he was joined by some nobles and seized most of Jerusalem. A messianic strongman, Simeon led the defense of Jerusalem in 70 CE.

5. The Idumeans, a local militia, helped the Zealots to overthrow the provisional government.

Major scholarly controversies, arising primarily from the biased and often unreliable accounts of Josephus (in *The Jewish War*, as well as his *Jewish Antiquities* and *The Life*), have centered on the ancient usage of the title "Zealot," on the extent of religious zeal among the revolutionaries and the populace, and on the relative importance of social, economic, political, and religious factors in the war effort.

BIBLIOGRAPHY

Borg, Marcus. "The Currency of the Term 'Zealot.'" *Journal of Theological Studies*, n. s. 22 (October 1973): 504-512. Concludes that the term did not come into use as a title until the time of the war.

Hengel, Martin. *Die Zeloten: Untersuchungen zur jüdische Freiheitsbewegung in der Zeit von Herodes* (1961). 2d ed. Leiden, 1976. Second edition also contains a later article. The most thorough depiction, gleaned from many sources, of the mentality of "zeal." Argues that the Zealots were a unified and organized prewar sectarian minority that splintered at the time of the war.

Rhoads, David M. *Israel in Revolution, 6-74 C. E.: A Political History Based on the Writings of Josephus*. Philadelphia, 1976. The most extensive treatment of the positions that the revolutionary movement was disparate and that support for the war was widespread.

Smith, Morton. "Zealots and Sicarii: Their Origins and Relation." *Harvard Theological Review* 64 (January 1971): 1-19. Seminal article arguing for a disparate and unorganized revolutionary movement.

Stern, Menachem. "Zealots." In *Encyclopaedia Judaica Yearbook*. Jerusalem, 1973. A balanced treatment claiming that the Sicarii had prewar connections with those who came to be called Zealots and that it is appropriate to speak about a Zealot movement and yet appreciate the uniqueness of each revolutionary group.

DAVID M. RHOADS

ZEN

The Planting of Zen Buddhism in Japan

The early history of Zen proper does not begin until the twelfth century, when Myoan Eisai attempted to transmit the Lin-chi teachings to Japan.

Myoan Eisai. Myoan Eisai (1141-1215; also known as Myoan Yosai) encountered Ch`an Buddhists during a trip to China (1187-1191). He entered a Ch`an monastery where he practiced *tso-ch`an* (Jpn., *zazen*) and *kung-an* (Jpn., *koan*), achieved enlightenment, and was presented with the insignia of succession in the Huang-lung (Jpn., Oryo) line of the Lin-chi school. He did not, however, cut himself off entirely from the Tendai school to which he belonged and in whose doctrines and esoteric practices he was well versed.

Immediately upon his return to Japan, Eisai began to propagate the way of Zen in the southern island of Kyushu. His energetic labors stirred up the resentment of the Tendai monks, who succeeded in having a prohibition issued by the imperial palace against the "new sect" of the "Dharma school" (1194).

In his apologetic work of 1198, *Kozen gokokuron* (Treatise on the Spread of Zen for the Protection of the Country), Eisai stresses the value of the Tendai tradition, in which meditation and enlightenment hold a place of prominence. Meditation is set alongside the perfect doctrine (*engyo*), secret rites (*mitsu*), and disciplinary commandments (*kai*) as one of the

> Dogen . . . is "the master of *zazen*." In his view, *zazen* embraced everything essential and valuable in Buddhism.

four essential elements of Tendai. In his view, Rinzai Zen, as "the quintessence of all doctrines and the totality of the Buddha's Dharma," can contribute decisively to the renewal of Japanese Buddhism. Eisai felt that the time had not yet come for the organizational establishment of an independent Rinzai school. The Zen that he left to his disciples showed a strong mixture of Tendai, especially Tendai esotericism (Taimitsu), in its spirituality.

Enni Ben'en. The central figure during the following period was Enni Ben'en (best known by his posthumous title of Shoichi Kokushi, 1201-1280). The turning point in Enni's life

came during the course of a seven-year stay in China (1235-1241). He entered the discipleship of the outstanding Lin-chi master Wu-chun Shih-fan (Jpn., Bushun Shihan), practiced pure Ch`an, and reached enlightenment. As abbot of Tofukuji, his daily visits to Kenninji allowed him to bring life to monastic discipline and to rekindle the zeal for meditation that had declined after the death of Eisai. All the same, he did not change Eisai's style of mixing Zen with received rites. The labors of Enni Ben'en mark a step forward in the long and drawn-out process of Zen's implantation in Japan. The "new sect" introduced from China gradually found acceptance in wide circles of the population.

Chinese Zen Masters in Japan. During the second half of the Kamakura period Buddhism witnessed the establishment of Zen, in particular the Rinzai school. For these Chinese masters it was absolutely self-evident that their cloisters represented the Rinzai school in Japan independent of the older schools of Japanese Buddhism. Their highly successful labors contributed greatly to the rooting of Zen in Japan, and the cloisters they directed formed the core of a self-subsistent Japanese Rinzai school.

Dogen Kigen. The other school that flourished in China during the Sung period, Ts`ao-tung (Jpn., Soto), was brought to Japan by the Japanese monk Dogen Kigen (1200-1253).

In China Dogen encountered the "authentic teacher" in the person of the master Ju-ching (Jpn., Nyojo) of Mount T`ien-t`ung. In this master he placed his entire trust, and under his expert guidance achieved the great experience of the "dropping off of body and mind" (*shinjin datsuraku*). By partaking in the perpetuation of the enlightenment experience through his master, Dogen entered a line of what he considered to be the essential transmission of the patriarchs reaching back to Sakyamuni Buddha.

What Dogen achieved for Japanese Zen Buddhism is significant. More than any other he is "the master of *zazen*." In his view, *zazen* embraced everything essential and valuable in Buddhism. In *zazen* practice and enlightenment come together. The seed of Buddhahood implanted in each individual at birth so that it might blossom to fulfillment—that is, the Buddha nature inherent in all reality—is disclosed in *zazen*. Dogen's impact as a master of *zazen* continues to the present day.

Main Currents during the Middle Ages

Under the political leadership of the shoguns of the house of Ashikaga, the Muromachi period (1338-1573) witnessed the spread of Zen throughout the country and its opening out into art and culture.

The Five Mountains of the Rinzai School. The system of "five mountains" (*gozan*), "ten temples" (*jissetsu*), and affiliated temples (*shozan*) set up by the Japanese Rinzai school in imitation of the Chinese model helped the Zen movement to find its place in the order of Japanese society. Already in

Kamakura the five main temples had formed a unit under the protection of the military government *(bakufu)*. With the transfer of power to Kyoto, the prominent temples of the capital city came to be referred to as the Five Mountains.

The leading personality in Rinzai Zen at the beginning of the Muromachi period was Muso Soseki (1275-1351), a monk of extraordinary intellectual power and high artistic gifts. His efforts to erect "temples for the pacification of the country" *(ankokuji)* and "pagodas for the use of the living" *(risshoto)* helped to disseminate Zen Buddhism further in Japan.

In the broad sense of the term, the Gozan movement included the way of life of the Zen temples of the Gozan system, with its Chinese influence and its wider cultural significance. In Gozan culture *(gozan bunka)* it was literature *(gozan bungaku)* that occupied first place, but other arts, such as calligraphy, painting, the creation of gardens, and so forth were also cultivated. The contribution of Gozan to the system of education remained as a positive contribution. The famous Ashikaga school *(Ashikaga-gakko)* founded by the Gozan monks passed on the higher levels of Chinese education while temple schools *(tera-koya)*, largely run by Zen monks, brought elementary knowledge to the common folk. The decline of the Rinzai school centered on the Five Mountains is signaled in the fact that none of the Gozan lines survived into the following era.

Daitokuji and Its Line. The temple Daitokuji was one of the most significant centers of the Rinzai school in Kyoto. The main line of the monastery begins with Nampo Jomyo (1235-1309), the most important figure in the third stage of Zen's establishment in Japan. His disciple Shuho Myocho (1282-1338) founded Daitokuji under the patronage of the emperor Go-Daigo in 1327 and saw it through to full bloom. The influence of Daitokuji radiated far and wide into Japanese Zen culture and art in the Middle Ages. After a change in fortune during the civil war, the temple Daitokuji became the favorite center for the arts toward the end of the Middle Ages.

The Soto School. The so-called "strife over succession in the third generation" did not end in an open break, but the longtime superior of Eiheiji, Tettsu Gikai (1219-1309), withdrew to Daitoji, a Shingon temple located in the Kaga district that had been taken over for use as a Zen cloister. There a second Soto center originated and came to wield great influence through Gikai's important disciple, Keizan Jokin (1268-1325).

Jokin, revered by adherents of the Soto school as the "great patriarch" *(taso)*, expanded Soto Zen into a popular movement. He founded the temples of Yokoji and Sojiji in the Noto area. Keizan's chief disciple, Gasan Joseki (1275-1365), succeeded him as abbot in Sojiji and there gathered a large flock of disciples. Twenty-five of them are spoken of as having spread Soto Zen throughout the entire country, so that from the end of the Middle Ages up to the present day it has remained numerically the second strongest Buddhist school.

The Premodern Era

The modern era was ushered in politically by the accession to power of the Tokugawa shoguns, who imposed severe controls and regimented religious activities beginning with Buddhism and including the Zen schools. At the same time, the spectrum of Zen was widened at the outset of the era.

The Obaku School. Isolated Chinese monks living in certain temples on the southern island of Kyushu formed a basis that consolidated into a new school when the Chinese master Yin-yüan Lung-ch`i (Jpn., Ingen Ryuki, 1592-1673), accompanied by some of his disciples, crossed over from the mainland at the invitation of Japanese Buddhists. They established the temple Manpukuji in Uji near Kyoto (1661), and, as reinforcements came from China and as Japanese also entered Manpukuji, the Obaku school, which essentially belonged to Rinzai Zen and which did much to stimulate the study of its highly important work, the *Rinzai-roku*, enjoyed a modest flowering.

The Obaku school took an open attitude toward Buddhism as presented in the *sutras*. It also cultivated the veneration of the Buddha Amida (Skt., Amitabha), which it interpreted in a Zen manner.

The Modern Period

The most significant figure in Rinzai Zen during the nineteenth century was Imakita Kosen (also known as Kosen Soon, 1816-1892). In 1875 he was entrusted with the superintendence of the ten great temple estates of the Rinzai and Obaku schools, while he himself was administering the temple of Engakuji (Kamakura) as abbot. Outstanding among his students was Shaku Soen (1856-1919), who had also found understanding and support for his open approach to modern times among the gifted dharmic successors of the following two generations. Soen was also a participant at the 1893 World's Parliament of Religions in Chicago, an interreligious congress that for many opened the door to new ways of looking at other religions.

[*See also* Buddhism.]

BIBLIOGRAPHY

The Japanese literature on Zen Buddhism is so extensive that it is impossible to cite even a representative selection here. The same is true for the names of historians of Japanese Zen, who have published a considerable number of studies on the subject. Mention should certainly be made of the twenty-volume collection of the sayings of more than twenty famous Japanese Zen masters translated into modern Japanese and provided with good introductions and commentaries, *Nihon no zen-goroku* (Tokyo, 1977-1978); the encyclopedia of Zen, *Zengaku daijiten*), edited by Komazawa University in three volumes (Tokyo, 1978); and the eight-volume series *Koza* zen, a collection of separate studies on Zen by renowned Japanese scholars, edited by Nishitani Keiji (Tokyo, 1974).

Detailed information on the development of Zen in Japan can be found in such works on the history of religions as Masaharu Anesaki's *History of Japanese Religion* (London, 1935; reprint, Tokyo, 1963; revised by Hideo Kishimoto, Tokyo, 1970); Charles Eliot's *Japanese Buddhism* (London, 1935; reprint, New York, 1959); and Joseph M. Kitagawa's *Religion in Japanese History* (New York, 1966).

On Dogen see the comprehensive work of Hee-jin Kim, *Dogen Kigen: Mystical Realist* (Tucson, 1977). A complete translation of the ninety-five books of the *Shobogenzo* in three volumes has been prepared by Kosen Nishiyama and John Stevens (Sendai, 1975; Tokyo, 1977, 1983). The best English translations of Dogen's work, complete with good commentries, have been appearing serially in the pages of *The Eastern Buddhist* (1971-). An English translation of some of the books of the *Shobogenzo* was published by Masunaga Reiho in *The Soto Approach to Zen* (Tokyo, 1958), pp. 81-90. For a German translation of the "Genjokoan," see Ryosuke Ohashi and Hans Brockard in *Philosophisches Jahrbuch*, 83 (1976): 402-415. Francis D. Cook has included an English translation of the *Fukanzazengi* in his *How to Raise an Ox: Zen practice as taught in Zen Master Dogen's Shobogenzo* (Los Angeles, 1979). My German translation of the same work appeared in *Monumenta Nipponica* 14 (1958): 429-436; and a later English translation by Abe and Norman Waddell is in The *Eastern Buddhist* 6 (1973): 115-128. Cook's work also contains translations of portions of the *Shobogenzo*. Yokoi Yuho has published an English translation of Dogen's important work, *Gakudoyojinshu* (Tokyo, 1976). Among the numerous translations of the *Zuimonki* book of the *Shobogenzo* we may mention Masunaga Reiho's *A Primer of Soto Zen* (Hawaii, 1971) and Thomas Cleary's *Record of Things Heard: A translation of Dogen's Zuimonki* (Boulder, 1980).

Information on the organization and development of Rinzai Zen during Japan's Middle Ages is available in Martin Collcutt's, *Five Mountains: The Rinzai Zen Monastic Institution in Medieval Japan* (Cambridge, Mass. and London, 1981) and Jon Carter Covell and Sobin Yamada's *Zen at Daitokuji* (Tokyo, 1924). Chapter 12 of *Sources of Japanese Tradition*, compiled by Ryusaku Tsunoda, Wm. Theodore de Bary, and Donald Keene (New York, 1958), deals with Zen Buddhism and includes translations from Eisai, Dogen, and Muso Kokushi. Further source material on Zen is to be found in The *Buddhist Tradition*, edited by Wm. Theodore de Bary, Yoshihito Hakeda, and Philip Yampolsky (New York, 1969).

A selection of the most important writings of Hakuin with an introduction on "Hakuin and Rinzai Zen" has been prepared by Philip Yampolsky in his *The Zen Master Hakuin: Selected Writings* (New York and London, 1971). Hakuin's treatise on Zen sickness, *Yassen kanna*, was translated by R. D. M. Shaw and Wilhelm Schiffer in *Monumenta Nipponica* 13 (1957): 107-127. On Hakuin's efforts on behalf of the practice of the *koan*, see Ruth Fuller Sasaki's essay, "The Koan in Japanese Zen," in *Zen Dust* (New York, 1966), pp. 17-32. See also the article by Miura Isshu, "Koan Study in Rinzai Zen," appearing in the same work (pp. 33-76).

There is a wealth of literature surrounding Zen culture, Zen art, and the way of Zen. For an understanding of Zen art one will find helpful the following basic works: Dietrich Seckel's *The Art of Buddhism* (New York, 1963); Shinichi Hisamatsu's *Zen and the Fine Arts* (Tokyo, 1970); Hugo Munsterberg's *Zen and Oriental Art* (Tokyo, 1965); and Yasuichi Awakawa's *Zen Painting* (Tokyo, 1977). In his *Zen and Japanese Culture* (New York, 1970), a reprint of *Zen Buddhism and its Influence on Japanese Culture*, D. T. Suzuki clarifies the relationship of art forms cultivated by Zen to Zen Buddhism. See also Thomas Hoover's *Zen and Culture* (London, 1978). On

Basho, see Robert Aitken's *Basho's Haiku and Zen*, with a foreword by W. S. Mer-win (New York and Tokyo, 1978); and R. H. Blyth's *A History of Haiku* (Tokyo, 1964). On Ryokan, see John Stevens's *One Robe, One Bowl* (Tokyo, 1977), a translation of the poems of Ryokan with an introduction. On Shaku Soen we have the book *Sermons of a Buddhist Abbot* (1913; reprint, La Salle, Il1., 1974). On the 1893 World's Parliament in Chicago, see Larry A. Fad-er's article "Zen in the West: Historical and Philosophical Implications of the 1893 Chicago World's Parliament on Religions," in *The Eastern Buddhist* 15 (1982): 122-145. The second volume of my book *Geschichte des Zen-Buddhismus* is slated to appear in English translation in 1987.

HEINRICH DUMOULIN
Translated from German by James W. Heisig

ZIONISM

Although Jebusite in origin, the name *Zion* (Heb., *Tsiyyon*) was assimilated into the Israelite vocabulary and became associated with the Davidic monarchy and its capital in Jerusalem. In writings of such prophets as "First Isaiah" and Jeremiah and in *Psalms*, the name *Zion* is used as a synonym first for the Temple in Jerusalem, then for the kingdom of Judah, and finally, in postexilic literature, for the Land of Israel. In the Babylonian exile, the psalmist wrote: "By the waters of Babylon / There we sat down, yea, we wept / When we remembered Zion" (*Ps.* 137:1). Thus, what was first a specific place-name came to represent symbolically the whole Land of Israel whose people had been exiled. The particular associations between Zion and the Davidic monarchy gave the word a special resonance in later messianic literature that expressed longing not only for the return of the people to their land but also for the reestablishment of the kingdom of David.

Medieval Period. The theme of Zion played an important role in the medieval liturgical poems *(piyyutim)*.

The best examples of secular poetry devoted to longing for Zion can be found during the "classical age" of the Spanish Jews (900-1200).

Perhaps the most outstanding representative of this school of poets was Yehudah ha-Levi (c. 1075-1141) whose *Shirei Tsiyyon* (Songs of Zion) inspired many imitations later in the Middle Ages. In the sixteenth century, following the expulsion of the Jews from Spain, the community of Palestine increased and a number of "proto-Zionist" efforts were undertaken to establish Jewish agricultural colonies and reestablish the ancient Sanhedrin. This proto-Zionist sentiment cannot be dissociated from medieval Jewish messianism. All messianic thinkers in the Middle Ages considered the return to Zion to be among the primary tasks of the Messiah. Even as messianic expectations were embroidered with supernatural fantasies, such as the belief in the resurrection of the dead, the core of Jewish messianism remained political and nationalistic: the Messiah would return the Jews to Zion, reestablish the kingdom of David, and rebuild the Temple in Jerusalem.

On the other hand, another group of medieval thinkers deemphasized the importance of immigration to Zion. Maimonides (Mosheh ben Maimon, 1135/8-1204) said that the central event in Jewish history was at Mount Sinai, and the return to Zion in messianic times would be a means toward uninterrupted study of the law revealed at Sinai. Although Maimonides clearly believed in the coming of the Messiah (which he understood as a realistic and not solely supernatural process), he subordinated Zion to Sinai.

The Nineteenth Century. Two important intellectual developments in the nineteenth century, among both modernizing and traditional Jews, prepared the ground for Zionism. The first was the movement of Jewish Enlightenment (Haskalah), which began in Germany in the late eighteenth century and spread to eastern Europe in the nineteenth. The Haskalah developed in two directions with respect to Zion. On the one hand, there was a general tendency to promote the emancipation of the Jews in Europe by glorifying the European nations. On the other hand, much of the new Hebrew literature written by Haskalah authors, especially in eastern Europe, harkened back to the land of the Bible.

The second important nineteenth-century development was among traditional Jews. Tsevi Hirsch Ka-lischer (1795-1874) advocated agricultural settlement in the Land of Israel. Kalischer never abandoned his messianic expectations, nor did he give up his hope that the sacrifices might be reinstituted by the new settlers.

A similar kind of religious "Zionism" can be found in the writings of Yehudah ben Shelomoh Alkalai (1798-1878), who argued in numerous pamphlets for Jewish settlement in the Holy Land as a means toward bringing the Messiah.

In 1878 a group of Orthodox Jews established the first agricultural colony, Petach Tikva. Scholars have come to appreciate the contribution that these religious Jews made in laying the groundwork for the later Zionist settlement.

Modern Secular Zionism. Modern Zionism really began with Theodor Herzl (1860-1904). The term *Zionism* was coined in 1890 by Nathan Birnbaum in his journal *Selbstemanzipation* and was adopted by Herzl and his followers at the first Zionist Congress in 1897. Although some rabbis supported Herzl, most members of the movement, including Herzl himself, were secular and westernized. Nevertheless, Herzl was greeted by many eastern European Jews as a messianic figure. The first substantial Zionist emigration from eastern Europe to Palestine started after the pogroms of 1903 and 1905-1906 and was largely made up of young secular Russian Jews, many of whom were influenced by the Russian radicalism of the period.

The attitude toward religion among the early secular Zionist thinkers was frequently quite hostile. Traditional Judaism was viewed as the religion of the exile and the Zionists saw themselves as a movement to "negate the exile" *(shelilat ha-golah)*. Nevertheless, there were other secular Zionists who tried to base the new Zionist culture on elements from the religious tradition.

The ambivalence toward the Jewish tradition that one finds in many of these early secular Zionists had much to do with their biographies. In most cases, they came from traditional homes and were educated in the *yeshivot* (rabbinic academies) of eastern Europe. Zionism was a radical revolution for them against the world of their childhood, but they never fully broke with their positive memories of this religious culture.

> **All messianic thinkers in the Middle Ages considered the return to Zion to be among the primary tasks of the Messiah.**

Even if their way of life was secular, they wished to recreate an authentic Jewish culture on a new, national basis.

Religious Zionism. Among the first rabbis to join Herzl were Isaac Reines and Shemu'el Mohilever, who was perhaps the most prominent rabbi in the Hibbat Tsiyyon movement. In 1902, Reines formed Mizrahi, a religious faction within the World Zionist Organization (the name is a composite of some of the Hebrew letters from the words *merkaz ruhani,* "spiritual center"). Mizrahi consisted of two groups: one that opposed the introduction of any "cultural" issues into the Zionist movement, for fear that the secularists would set the tone in such endeavors, and another that saw that Zionism could not avoid confronting cultural issues and demanded that Mizrahi try to influence the Zionist movement in a religious direction.

Mizrahi played a major role in mustering support for Zionism among Orthodox Jews in Europe and the United States. It created a network of schools in which Zionism was taught together with traditional religious subjects. At the same time, Mizrahi established schools in Palestine that formed the backbone of the religious educational system that is an important part of the general educational system in the state of Israel. The Mizrahi youth movements, Young Mizrahi and Benei Akiva, began establishing agricultural settlements in Palestine in the 1920s.

Since their inception the Mizrahi have sought to avoid the problem of the relationship of Zionism to Jewish messianism. Much opposition to Zionism in the religious world stemmed from the belief that human beings should not "force the end" (i. e., initiate messianic times by secular means). Instead of answering this position with a new messianic theory, the Mizrahi took a cautious stance, claiming that the Zionist movement constituted a "beginning of redemption."

There were, however, certain elements among the religious Zionists who took a bolder approach to the question of messianism. Primary among these was Avraham Yitshaq Kook, who was chief Ashkenazic rabbi of Palestine from 1921 until his death in 1935. Kook believed that the secular pioneers were a necessary force to prepare the material foundation for messianic times. He argued dialectically that the profane was necessary for subsequent emergence of the sacred.

The young religious Zionists, who grew up after the creation of the state in 1948, believed strongly in Zionism as the fulfillment of traditional Jewish messianism.

Religious Institutions in the State of Israel. Under both the Ottoman empire and the British Mandate, Jewish religious courts enjoyed official jurisdiction over matrimonial and inheritance law. The office of the *hakham basi* in the Ottoman empire was succeeded by the Ashkenazic and Sefardic chief rabbis under the British Mandate. These functions were carried over to the rabbinic courts and the chief rabbinate of the state of Israel, which were given jurisdiction over matters of personal law by a Knesset enactment of 1953. Rabbinical judges were given the same status as district court judges and their decisions were enforced by the civil authorities. Thus, in matters of marriage, divorce, and child custody, rabbinic courts—ruling according to Jewish law *(halakhah)*—have state sanction. Civil marriage and divorce do not exist, although civil marriages are recognized if contracted abroad. A Ministry of Religious Affairs deals with the needs of the various religious communities in Israel and funds the construction and maintenance of synagogues, *yeshivot*, and other religious facilities.

Although both the Conservative and Reform movements have followings in Israel, their rabbis are not authorized by the rabbinate to perform marriages and they do not benefit from the budgets available through the Ministry of Religious Affairs. Conversion to Judaism is supervised by the rabbinate, and thus Conservative and Reform conversions are not recognized as valid.

BIBLIOGRAPHY

The only book devoted specifically to the subject of Zion in Jewish thought is *Zion in Jewish Literature*, edited by Abraham S. Halkin (New York, 1961), which contains essays on the biblical and rabbinic periods, medieval secular and religious poetry, and nineteenth-century Hebrew poetry and prose. For additional articles on the biblical period, see Shemaryahu Talmon's "The Biblical Concept of Jerusalem," *Journal of Ecumenical Studies* 8 (1971): 300-316, and Ben Zion Dinaburg's "Zion and Jerusalem: Their Role in the Historic Consciousness of Israel" (in Hebrew), *Zion* 16 (1951): 1-17. Gerson D. Cohen has given the best treatment of the rabbinic period in his essay "Zion in Rabbinic Literature," included in Halkin's *Zion in Jewish Literature*, mentioned above. See also in Halkin's collection the discussions of medieval writings by Chaim Z. Dimitrovsky and Nahum Glatzer. Other valuable discussions of medieval writings are

Yitzhak F. Baer's "Erez Yisrael and the Diaspora in the View of the Middle Ages" (in Hebrew), *Zion Yearbook* 6 (1946): 149-171, and H. H. Ben-Sasson's "Exile and Redemption through the Eyes of the Spanish Exiles" (in Hebrew) in *Yitzhak F. Baer Jubilee Volume*, edited by Salo W. Baron and others (Jerusalem, 1960). A nationalist argument about the relationship between the Jews and Zion in Jewish history and especially the modern period can be found in Ben Zion Dinur's *Israel and the Diaspora* (Philadelphia, 1969). For the relationship of the Jewish Enlightenment to Zion, see Isaac F. Barzilay's "National and Anti-National Trends in the Berlin Haskalah," *Jewish Social Studies* 21 (1959): 165-192, and Jacob S. Raisin's *The Haskalah Movement in Russia* (Philadelphia, 1913), an old but still useful work. The attitude of nineteenth-century Reform is treated in W. Gunther Plaut's *The Rise of Reform Judaism* (New York, 1963).

On the origins and history of the Zionist movement, see David Vital's *The Origins of Zionism* (Oxford, 1975) and *Zionism: The Formative Years* (Oxford, 1982). A good general history of Zionism is Walter Laqueur's *A History of Zionism* (New York, 1972). The history of Zionist thought has been treated by Shlomo Avineri in *The Making of Modern Zionism: Intellectual Origins of the Jewish State* (New York, 1981) and by Ben Halpern in *The Idea of the Jewish State* (Cambridge, Mass., 1961). A good anthology of Zionist thought with a superb introductory essay is *The Zionist Idea*, edited by Arthur Hertzberg (Philadelphia, 1959). The specific issue of religion in the state of Israel is discussed by Ervin Birnbaum in *The Politics of Compromise: State and Religion in Israel* (Rutherford, N. J., 1970) and by S. Zalmon Abramov in *Perpetual Dilemma: Jewish Religion in the Jewish State* (Rutherford, N. J., 1976). An anthology of anti-Zionist thought can be found in *Zionism Reconsidered*, edited by Michael Selzer (New York, 1970). A semischolarly treatment of religion in Israel from the viewpoint of Neturei Karta is Émile Marmorstein's *Heaven at Bay: The Jewish Kulturkampf in the Holy Land* (London, 1969).

DAVID BIALE

ZOROASTRIANISM

With a history of some three thousand years, Zoroastrianism is one of the most ancient living religions. Attempts have often been made to distinguish between various phases of Zoroastrianism and to endow each with a slightly different name. Thus it has been suggested that the religion contained in the *Gathas*, the texts attributed to Zarathushtra himself, be called "Zarathushtrianism," that the contents of the Younger Avesta be called "Zarathushtricism," and that the religion of the Sasanid period be called "Zoroastrianism" (Gershevitch, 1964). These definitions should be extended to include the religion of the Zoroastrian communities in Iran and India today.

Origins. Zoroastrianism originated in the eastern and south-central regions of the Iranian world, between the great mountain ranges of the Hindu Kush and Seistan, an area that today is divided between Iran and Afghanistan. Current research on the religion's origin is based on geographical information contained in the Avesta, as well as on an evaluation of archaeological findings and on a reinterpretation of the few available sources.

Zoroastrianism grew out of a politically fragmented tribal society whose civilization centered upon oases rather than upon fixed urban settings. The society was ruled by a warrior aristocracy, that is, by one of the three classes—priests, warriors, and shepherds—that made up the original social structure of the Arya. Within this society, religion most likely revolved around young warrior *(mairya)* fraternities (the Aryan or Indo-Iranian *Männerbund*), with their bloody cults,

> ## The importance of prayer was always fundamental, and some forms . . . have lasted through the centuries.

violent gods, sacrificial rites, initiations, and ecstatic practices that climaxed in a state of "fury" called *aeshma*.

Distinctive Characteristics. The primary innovation of Zoroastrianism, which sets it apart from the religions of other Indo-European peoples in the Near East and Central Asia, is its emphasis on monotheism.

The concept of Ahura Mazda as the creator of heaven and earth, day and night, and light and darkness (*Yasna* 44.3-5), as well as the ethical context in which Zarathushtra conceived his answer to the problem of evil, demonstrates that the prophet was an original thinker, a powerful religious figure who introduced radical changes to the spiritual and cultural world in which he was reared. He responded to a deeply formalistic and ritualistic religion by strongly and insistently praising human worth and dignity.

Theology and Pantheon. In Zarathushtra's conception, a dualistic vision is almost a natural consequence of monotheism, for dualism explains the evil that resides in the world and afflicts it. The problem of evil and suffering is basic to Zoroastrian thought, and the urgent human necessity of providing an answer to the problem is reconciled with an abiding faith in the dignity and freedom of humanity by means of belief in the so-called myth of choice.

It is not easy to understand the Zoroastrian concept of the beneficent immortals who form the retinue of the Wise Lord Ahura Mazda. For instance, Sraosha ("obedience'), the lord of prayer, is by his nature analogous to the entities in the *Gathas*. He is particularly important both in the *Gathas* and in later Zoroastrian tradition, where he protects against the evil of death and judges the soul after death.

Zoroastrianism did not integrate all of the ancient gods into its pantheon. Only those not thought to be in contrast with the main tenets of the prophet's new religion were absorbed into it. For the most part, the ancient *daivas* censured by Zarathushtra remained outside of the new pantheon, but a few deities, who had probably been widely and deeply venerated, reappeared in Zoroastrianism.

Customs, Rituals, Festivals. Despite its original antiritualistic character, Zoroastrianism soon became a religion in which ceremony played a leading role. It is not possible to know which religious rituals were recommended by the prophet to his disciples in addition to prayer. The importance of prayer was always fundamental, and some forms, particularly revered ones, have lasted through the centuries, for example, a type of traditional *manthra* (Skt., *mantra*) that is endowed with magical powers. The main prayers are Ahuna Vairya, Airyema Ishyo, Ashem Vohu, Yenhe Hatam. Even in modern times, the day of a pious Zoroastrian is divided into five prayer periods. Most likely, alongside the recitation of the *manthra*, Zarathushtra recommended meditating before the only basic symbol of the new religion—fire.

Although modified to fit the tenets of the Zoroastrian message, the old ritualism reemerged and asserted itself anew during the first centuries of the new faith. The reemergence most likely took place before the advent of the great Achaemenid empire. Animal sacrifice became accepted again, although only in forms that could be seen as compatible with the new ethical values, and even the *haoma* cult was reestablished.

The tendency to reject anthropomorphic representations of divine entities is typical of later Zoroastrianism. During the Sasanid period we find anthropomorphic representations of Ohrmazd, Mihr (Mithra), and Anahid (Anahita) in large rupestrian reliefs in Fars; during the Achaemenid period, in addition to the accounts of statues of the goddess Anahita, we find torsos of Ahura Mazda, emerging from a disk or a winged ring from which there emerge, as well, two paws and a bird tail. Other traditional symbols of Zoroastrianism are the fire altars and the *barsom* (Av., *baresman*), a ritual object consisting originally of a bunch of herbs and later of a bundle of consecrated twigs.

The complex Zoroastrian rituals involve many of the most significant moments in the lives of the faithful. Thus we find initiation rites, Naojot (a term deriving from an older one indicating a "new birth"), in which a child, at age seven or ten, is fitted with a shirt, *sadre*, and girded with a cord called *kusti*. Zoroastrians also celebrate marriage rituals. Funeral rites (for example, Zohr i atash, in which animal fat is poured onto the fire, obviously reminiscent of some ancient animal sacrifice) take place in the *dakhmas*, the "towers of silence," and are meant to free the soul of the dead man from the demon of corpses (Druj i Nasu) and to assist it along its heavenly journey.

A strongly ritualistic religion, Zoroastrianism marked the year with a series of fixed holidays, thus incorporating traditional ways and customs that were hard to eradicate.

The first month of the year was dedicated to the *fravashis*, the spirits of the just, who were originally thought to be transcendental doubles of the soul. Zoroastrians believed in the *fravashis* of the dead, of the living, and of the yet unborn. According to a most likely pre-Zoroastrian tradition, the *fravashis* returned to earth at the end of the year, before the vernal equinox, the No Ruz ("new day"), or the first month of the new year. Zoroastrians also celebrated six additional great feasts: Maidhyoizaremaya ("midspring"); Maidhyoi-shema ("midsummer"); Patishahya ("bringing in the corn"); Ayathrima ("the homecoming"); Maidhyairya ("midwinter").

BIBLIOGRAPHY

The best of relatively recent works on Zoroastrianism are Jacques Duchesne-Guillemin's *La religion de l'Iran ancien* (Paris, 1962); Geo Widengren's *Die Religionen Irans* (Stuttgart, 1965), translated as *Les religions de l'Iran* (Paris, 1968); and Mary Boyce's *A History of Zoroastrianism*, 2 vols. to date (Leiden, 1975-1982). These works are very different from each other, both in approach and in method, and for this reason the careful reader will be able to get a fairly full picture of the rich and complex series of problems involved in the study of Zoroastrianism.

Classic works, again very different from each other in approach and method, are Herman Lommel's *Die Religion Zarathustras nach dem Awesta dargestellt* (Tübingen, 1930) and H. S. Nyberg's *Irans forntida religioner* (Stockholm, 1937), translated as *Die Religionen des alten Iran* (1938; 2d ed., Osnabrück, 1966). Lommel's work is a faithful reconstruction of ancient Zoroastrianism, more philological than historical-religious; Nyberg's study, also based on a careful philological analysis of the sources, is more involved with historical and religious problems, and its approach is highly original, if somewhat controversial.

Other Swedish scholars, following the guidelines traced by Nyberg, have contributed in a significant fashion to the study of the earliest Iranian religions, from both a philological and a historical-religious point of view. Notable are Geo Widengren's *Hochgottglaube im alten Iran* (Uppsala, 1938) and Stig Wikander's *Feuerpriester in Kleinasien und Iran* (Lund, 1946).

As the result of long and demanding work, gathered for the most part in the *Archäologische Mitteilungen aus Iran* in 1929-1930, Ernst Herzfeld, an archaeologist and historian of Iran, published, some years later, a vast reconstruction of the religion of ancient Iran: *Zoroaster and His World*, 2 vols. (1947; reprint, New York, 1973). Although vast in scope, Herzfeld's work is not systematic but is, rather, a fragmented account in independent chapters.

Against the conclusions expressed by Herzfeld concerning Zarathushtra and the early period, as well as against the main theses of Nyberg, W. B. Henning, one of the foremost authorities in Iranian philology, published the texts of some of his own lectures in *Zoroaster: Politician or Witch-Doctor?* (Oxford, 1951). Nyberg's position was later defended, however, by Geo Widengren, from his own original point of view, in two long articles published in *Numen* and later in his *Stand und Aufgaben der iranischen Religionsgeschichte* (Leiden, 1955). Nyberg himself defended his position in his introduction to the second printing of his *Religionen des alten Iran* (Osnabrück, 1966).

One of the new elements in Widengren's work, as well as in that of Jacques Duchesne-Guillemin, is the acceptance of Georges Dumézil's theory of a tripartite Indo-European ideology, and of its applicability to Iran and Zoroastrianism. Dumézil has offered a number of contributions along these lines, of which the most famous is still *Naissance d'archanges* (Paris, 1945), in which he interprets the Zoroastrian system of the Amesha Spentas in the light of his theory.

Preceding Widengren in his application of the Dumézilian theory to Zoroastrianism was Jacques Duchesne-Guillemin in his *Zoroastre: Étude critique avec une traduction commentée des Gâthâ* (Paris, 1948), which he followed, a decade later, with *The Western Response to Zoroaster* (Oxford, 1958). The latter work is extremely clear yet, at the same time, critical and problematical. Dumézil's theory is also applied in a rather original way to ancient Iran by Marijan Molé in *Culte, mythe et cosmologie dans l'Iran ancien* (Paris, 1963), in which he tries to provide a structural, rather than a historical, picture of the entire Zoroastrian tradition.

Following in the footsteps of Henning's work, Ilya Gershevitch gives a clear and perceptive reconstruction of the Zoroastrian teachings and of the early development of Zoroastrianism in a short but fundamental article: "Zoroaster's Own Contribution," *Journal of Near Eastern Studies* 23 (1964): 12-38.

A number of works concerned with particular problems and subjects are nevertheless important for general Zoroastrian studies. Among them are Émile Benveniste's *The Persian Religion according to the Chief Greek Texts* (Paris, 1929), which presents an interpretation of the main Greek sources so as to allow the reconstruction of the historical development of religion in ancient Iran, and H. W. Bailey's *Zoroastrian Problems in the Ninth-Century Books* (Oxford, 1943), which deals with various subjects on the basis of an extraordinarily erudite understanding of the Pahlavi literature of the ninth century CE. Also to be numbered among essential works is R. C. Zaehner's *Zurvan: A Zoroastrian Dilemma* (Oxford, 1955), a reexamination, after more than twenty years, of the question of Zurvanism that had been so masterfully tackled by Nyberg in his "Questions de cosmogonie et de cosmologie mazdéennes," *Journal asiatique* (1929): 193-310 and (1931): 1-134, 193-244. Zurvanism was later the subject of Ugo Bianchi, in his *Zaman i Ohrmazd: Lo zoroastrismo nelle sue origini e nella sua essenza* (Turin, 1958), as well as of other scholars.

Works that, to a certain extent, show their age but that are nonetheless useful as general references are J. H. Moulton's *Early Zoroastrianism* (London, 1913), M. N. Dhalla's *Zoroastrian Theology* (New York, 1914), Raffaele Pettazzoni's *La religione di Zarathustra nella storia religiosa dell'Iran* (Bologna, 1920), and M. N. Dhalla's *History of Zoroastrianism* (New York, 1938). Good for its second part is another book by R. C. Zaehner, *The Dawn and Twilight of Zoroastrianism* (1961; reprint, London, 1976), originally published in the same year as Walther Hinz's *Zarathustra* (Stuttgart, 1961) and Jacques Duchesne-Guillemin's *Symbolik des Parsismus* (Stuttgart, 1961), a consideration of all aspects of Zoroastrian symbolism.

General works on Zoroastrianism written with more of a popularizing intent include Marijan Molé's *L'Iran ancien* (Paris, 1965); Jacques Duchesne-Guillemin's "L'Iran antique et Zoroastre" and "L'église sassanide et le mazdéisme," in *Histoire des religions*, edited by Henri-Charles Puech, vol. 1 (Paris, 1970), pp. 625-694, and vol. 2 (Paris, 1973), pp. 3-32, respectively; and Mircea Eliade's "Zarathustra and the Iranian Religion" and "New Iranian Syntheses," in his *A History of Religious Ideas*, vol. 1 (Chicago, 1978), pp. 302-333, and vol. 2 (Chicago, 1982), pp. 306-329, respectively. Other useful works are Jivanji Jamshedji Modi's *The Religious Ceremonies and Customs of the Parsees*, 2d ed. (Bombay, 1937), and Louis H. Gray's *The Foundations of the Iranian Religions* (Bombay, 1929), which is particularly helpful on the listing of the members of the Zoroastrian pantheon and pandemonium.

In addition to *A History of Zoroastrianism*, her *magnum opus*, Mary Boyce has produced a number of other valuable works on Zoroastrianism. In *A Persian Stronghold of Zoroastrianism* (Oxford, 1977), she paints an interesting and accurate picture of the religion in today's Iranian communities. In *Zoroastrians: Their Religious Beliefs and Practices* (London, 1979), she gives a clear and useful synthesis of the medieval period, the post-Islamic period, and the modern era of the Zoroastrian religion, both in Iran and in India. And in *Textual Sources for the Study of Zoroastrianism* (Manchester, 1984), she has gathered a vast selection of translated texts from various periods and sources.

Two of my own works are dedicated to questions relating to the origins and early development of Iranian religion from Zarathushtra to the third century CE: *Zoroaster's Time and Homeland: A Study on the Origins of Mazdeism and Related Problems* (Naples, 1980) and *De Zoroastre à Mani: Quatre leçons au Collège de France* (Paris, 1985).

Important chapters concerning Zoroastrianism and particular subjects pertaining to the religious history of ancient Iran are to be found in *The Cambridge History of Iran*, vol. 2, edited by Ilya Gershevitch, and vol. 3, edited by Ehsan Yarshater (Cambridge, 1983), in particular the contributions of Martin Schwartz, Yarshater, Boyce, Carsten Colpe, and Duchesne-Guillemin. This volume of *The Cambridge History of Iran* covers the Seleucid, Parthian, and Sasanid periods; a volume dedicated to the Achaemenid period is forthcoming.

GHERARDO GNOLI
Translated from Italian by Ughetta Fitzgerald Lubin

ZULU RELIGION

After nearly 150 years of missionary activity the majority of the some 5.5 million Zulu-speaking South Africans are Christians. For many, however, the *amadlozi* (ancestors or shades of dead kin) who once dominated Zulu religion are still a force to be reckoned with and propitiated.

Zulu Cosmology and the Natural Order. The Zulu say that in the beginning there was uMvelinqangi, literally the first "comer-out," who broke off from a reed bed followed by human beings, animals, and nature as a whole. In some tales uMvelinqangi is portrayed as the source of the known social order, for he gave human beings their ancestors and decided how the ancestors should be approached and placated. There is, however, little evidence that uMvelinqangi was worshiped directly. Distinct from uMvelinqangi is iNkosi yeZulu, the lord of the sky and personification of heaven. He is associated with thunder and lightning, which are greatly feared and against which specially trained herbalists offer protection.

Linked also with the sky or the "above" (*ezulwini*—a critical concept that contrasts with *phansi*, the "below," where the dead go before becoming ancestors) is iNkosazana yeZulu, or merely iNkosazana, the princess of heaven (uNomkhubulwana). She bestows fertility on crops, cattle, and human beings and is often actively placated in times of drought and searing heat. Before hoeing begins, women sometimes plant a small field for iNkosazana near a river, and a libation of beer is poured on the ground to the accompaniment of a prayer for a fruitful harvest. Because of its con-

ceptual links with fertility and girls' puberty ceremonials, the cult of iNkosazana must be seen against the background of the widespread emphasis upon fertility in African cosmological systems.

The natural order impinges on life in other ways which affect health and well-being. In contrast to illnesses caused by sorcery or ancestral anger, there is an extremely wide range of diseases stretching from the common cold to more serious epidemics like smallpox or measles, which are said to "just happen." Many are treated with medicines which are potent in themselves and do not necessarily require ritual or religious accompaniment, although protection against certain seasonal illnesses may be sought from iNkosazana. Another important class of natural illnesses are thought to result inevitably from imbalances in nature. Several categories of people are particularly at risk from environmental influences including newcomers to an area, infants who have only recently entered the world, and all those who are temporarily in a weakened state, known as *umnyama*. This last category includes the bereaved, newly delivered mothers, homicides, and menstruating women.

Women occupy a "marginal" position in Zulu cosmology and serve as a symbolic bridge between "this world" (the world of the living) and the "otherworld" (that of the spirits). Women, however, not only link this world and the otherworld, but in their roles as daughter in one kinship group and mother in another they form a bridge between two distinct patrilineages. Zulu society is strongly patrilineal, and marriage may occur only outside the clan. A bride is thus an outsider in her affinal home, yet it is only through her that her husband's group can reproduce itself.

Ancestors and Social Life. When things are going well, the Zulu say that their ancestors are "with them," but when misfortune strikes, they say that the ancestors are "facing away."

A man's most important ancestors are his father, mother, father's father, and father's mother, as well as the father's brothers who act with and share sacrifices offered to deceased parents and grandparents. The living kin who gather for ancestral rituals largely include the patrilineal descendants of a grandfather, and the women who have married these men. At sacrifices, it is the genealogically senior male *(umnumzane)* who officiates. Among the Nyuswa-Zulu the married men of this cluster or segment *(umndeni)* of two or three generations often live close to each other and, under the headship of the *umnumzane*, act as a corporate group in the control and management of common resources (such as land) and in the settlement of internal disputes. The authority of the *umnumzane* is bolstered by his ritual position and the fact that younger agnates can approach the ancestors only through him.

The ancestor cult reflects a number of other important aspects of Zulu social life. The role of the chief wife who bears the heir is emphasized, for it is on the *umsamo* of her hut (the rear part of the dwelling associated with the spirits) that sacrificial meat is placed for the ancestors to share. Individual social identities are often fixed unambiguously by calling on the ancestors. Thus a baby is placed formally under the control of the ancestors to whose line it belongs by the sacrifice of a goat known as *imbeleko*, the skin of which is used to secure the baby on its mother's back. This ceremony is usually performed by the child's father or father's father, but in the case of an unmarried woman, the responsibility lies with her father and his *umndeni* to which the child belongs.

Spirit Possession. Spirit possession is an important and dynamic aspect of Zulu life. The call to be a diviner takes the form of recognized mental and physical affliction, the cure for which are initiation and professional training. The traditional *isangoma* (and her counterpart in many Christian sects) is a pivotal force for order and rapprochement between man and the spirit world. There are, however, new forms of spirit possession. *Indiki* and *ufufunyane* (or *iziwe*) are the most prevalent types, resulting from possession by the deceased spirits of foreigners, which have not been integrated into the body of the ancestors. Treatment often involves replacing the alien spirit with an ancestral spirit, and the *indiki* may become a diviner. *Ufufunyane* is diagnosed as due to sorcery and is a particularly intractable form, for the alien spirit becomes violent when challenged. Treatment also involves dispelling the alien spirit—or often hordes of spirits of different race groups—and replacing them by spirits controlled by the doctor and referred to as a regiment (*amabutho*).

Traditional Belief and Zulu Christianity. Zulu cosmological ideas have been incorporated into Zulu Christian thought in a number of subtle ways. The word for "breath" (*umoya*) is translated as "Holy Spirit," and people said to be filled with the Holy Spirit become leaders in African independent churches that have split off from orthodox congregations. Protection against sorcery and misfortune is given by prayer and also medicine. Healing, purification, and the search for fertility are major issues in African Christianity.

BIBLIOGRAPHY

The most important of the early works on Zulu religion is the Reverend Henry Callaway's *The Religious System of the Amazulu* (1870; reprint, Cape Town, 1970), which presents original texts by Zulu informants together with translations and notes. A. T. Bryant's article "The Zulu Cult of the Dead," *Man* 17 (September 1917): 140-145, and his book *The Zulu People* (1948; New York, 1970), which gives details on Nomkhubulwane beliefs and ceremonies, provide a useful summary of what may be considered the main elements of the traditional belief system as described to early travelers and missionaries. An anthropological analysis, built up largely from these sources, but placing both belief and practice in their wider social context, is to be found in Eileen Jensen Krige's *The Social System of the Zulus* (Pietermaritzburg, 1936), pp. 280-296.

Two studies that deal with the present situation, both based on detailed anthropological research, are the Reverend Axel-Ivar Berglund's *Zulu Thought-Patterns and Symbolism* (London, 1976), and Harriet Ngubane's *Body and Mind in Zulu Medicine* (London, 1977). The first work offers an exhaustive compilation of detail, which provides some important insights, and also discusses a number of problematic conceptual issues. However, for scholars and laymen alike, Ngubane's book is the best starting point; an ethnographic study of one community, it is written lucidly and with the insight of a Zulu anthropologist. For doctors and those involved in the medical field, it is a *sine qua non* as it examines religious beliefs as part of Zulu ideas about the causation and treatment of disease.

Researchers seeking to become conversant with the details of Zulu thought patterns should consult Otto F. Raum's *The Social Functions of Avoidances and Taboos among the Zulu* (Berlin and New York, 1973), as it presents fascinating but very detailed data on a wide range of beliefs and their associated avoidances. The writings of Katesa Schlosser will also be of interest, especially *Zauberei im Zululand: Manuskripte des Blitz-Zauberers Laduma Madela* (Kiel, 1972), a study of Zulu mythology as told by a lightning doctor. Although the latter work shows how one Zulu philosopher has rethought and to some extent reinterpreted and expanded traditional Zulu cosmological notions, none of the above works concentrate specifically on change. Those interested in this aspect should consult Bengt Sundkler's *Bantu Prophets in South Africa*, 2d ed. (Oxford, 1961), and his more recent *Zulu Zion and Some Swazi Zionists* (Lund and Oxford, 1976). The sociological and welfare concomitants of many African independent churches are discussed in the work of James P. Kiernan; see in particular "Pure and Puritan: An Attempt to View Zionism as a Collective Response to Urban Poverty," *African Studies* 36 (1977): 31-41. The continuing influence of the conception of the ancestors in literature and worldview is demonstrated by a recent collection of poems by the Zulu poet Mazisi Kunene, *The Ancestors and the Sacred Mountain* (Exeter, N. H., 1982).

ELEANOR M. PRESTON-WHYTE

Index

A

Aaron, 614
abangans, 586
Abaris, 99
Abba, God as, 438
Abbahu, 442
`Abduh, Muhammad, 597, 605
Abel, 67, 79, 182, 221
Abelard, 181
Abgar V of Edessa, 793
abhava, 739
Abhayagirivasins, 213
Abhinavagupta, 502
Abibuddha, 216
Abnaki Indians, 808
Abode of Islam, 599
Abode of Peace, 599
Abode of War, 599
abolitionism, black church in, 35
Aboriginal religions. *See* Australian religions
Abraham, 11–12, 79, 82, 159, 163, 182, 339, 340, 448
    in Christianity, 12
    covenant of, 11–12
    in *Genesis*, 11–12, 56
    in Islam, 12, 550, 667, 778, 890, 891
    and monotheism, 614
    in postbiblical times, 12
    religion of, 11
Abravanel, Isaac, 152
Abrogans, 955
Absoroka Indians, 820
Abzu, 725
Academy of Plato, 96, 456, 516
Acania, 796
acaryas, 565, 619, 621
Acawai, 1022
Achilles, 463
Achké, 1018
Achomawi Indians, 831
aclla, 559
Acoma Indians, 837
Acre, 344
Acropolis, 90, 1088
"Act and Being" (Bonhoeffer), 186
Act in Restraint of Appeals, 925
Act of Succession, 296
Act of Uniformity of 1662, 319
Active Intelligence, 524, 526
Acts of the Apostles, 169, 170, 173, 174, 273, 283, 352, 439
Acts of Thomas, 180
Ad abo-lendam, 575
Ad extirpanda, 575
adab, 526
Adab, 725
Adad, 85

Adam, 13–14, 80, 82, 163, 342, 415
    fall of, 355, 412
    in *Genesis*, 13–14, 412
    and gnosticism, 434
    in Islam, 587
    lost paradise of, 879
    sin of, 13, 106, 280, 412
    temptation of, 978, 1090
    Unification Church view, 1141
Adam Qadmon, 434, 544
Adams, Henry, 736
Adams, John, 177
Adams, Robert M., 87
Adam's Peak, 893, 1001
`adat, 586
`Adawiyah, Rabi`ah al-, 592 364
Adderet Eliyyahu, 670
adhan, 774, 776
Adhemar of Le Puy, Bishop, 343
adhiccasamuppanna-vada, 672
adhvaryu, 486
Adler, Alfred, 425
Adler, Cyrus, 321, 322
Adler, Felix, 14
Adler, Samuel, 14
Admiralty Islands, 798
Adonai, 441
Adonis, 225, 887
Adrian VI, Pope, 876
Adroa, 375
Adulis, 397
Advaita Hinduism, 782
Advaita Vedanta, 38, 489, 500, 501, 502, 504
Aegean religions, 15–18
    cult ceremonies, 16–17
    Cycladic, 15
    iconography of, 538
    Minoan, 15–17, 538
    Mycenaean, 17, 538
Ægir, 789
Aeneid (Vergil), 409
Aeneolithic period, megalithic monuments, 720–721
Æsir, 431, 432
Aesthetic of Pure Feeling (Cohen), 298
Aethiopia of Herodotus, 682
Aetius, 572
Afendopolo, Kaleb, 670
Afghani, Jamal al-Din al-, 597
Afilm, 1161
afiqoman, 882
African Church of the Holy Spirit, 27
African Independent Churches' Association, 27
African Israel Nineveh Church, 27
African Methodist Episcopal Church, 730

African Methodist Episcopal Zion Church, 730
African religions, 18–34
    ancestor worship in, 19, 22, 30, 63–64, 527
        Central Bantu, 246
        East Africa, 376
        West Africa, 1161–1162
        Zulu, 1191–1192
    animal sacrifice in, 21–22
    anthropology of, 402
    art and architecture of, 23, 34
    Bantu (Central), 245–248
    Bantu (Interlacustrine), 577–578
    Berber, 147–148
    blessing in, 178
    characteristics of, 19–20
    Christian missions, 23, 24, 25, 30, 678–679
    creation myth in, 19, 20, 375, 527, 1161
    death concept in, 354–355
    death ritual in, 20, 22, 376, 553, 1040
    divination in, 21, 692, 1040
    divinities in, 19, 20–21, 30
    East African, 375–377
    evil in, 22, 376, 692
    exorcism in, 408
    gods in, 21, 692, 1179–1180
    historical background of, 18–19
    iconography of, 527–529
    immortality in, 553
    indigenous churches, 24–26
    initiation rites in, 376, 528, 1162
    Islam, 377, 586, 597
    Khoisan, 674–675
    Kongo, 678–679
    Kushite, 682
    Lugbara, 692
    messianism in, 728
    modern movements, 23–27, 34
    monotheism in, 1039, 1161
    mythology of, 20, 32, 527, 692, 1119
    nature in, 788–789
    Neolithic, 793
    in North America, 34
    prophets in, 24–25, 34, 376–377, 692
    redemption in, 923
    reincarnation in, 928
    repentance in, 934
    rites of passage in, 22, 528
    rituals in, 19–20, 21–22, 689
    separatist churches, 26
    South African, 1039–1040, 1191–1192
    spiritual identity in, 22
    studies of, 29–34

African religions *(continued)*
  trickster in, 20, 1119
  West African, 1160–1163
  witchcraft in, 22–23, 247, 376, 1040, 1163–1164
  world maintenance rituals in, 528–529
  Yoruba, 19, 23, 528, 975, 1162, 1178–1181
  Zulu, 1191–1192
Afro-American religions, 34–35
  antebellum, 34–35
  black churches, 35, 139, 288, 289
  and civil rights movement, 35, 675–676
  Muslim movements, 36, 586, 701
  and urban setting, 35
Afro-Caribbean religions, 233–236, 355
  ancestral cults in, 234–235
  Baptist movement in, 235
  Rastafarianism, 235–236
  Santería, 234, 974–975
  Shaker cult, 235
  Shango cult, 234
  voodoo in, 233–234, 1155–1156
afterbirth, as pollution, 911
afterlife, 37–43
  African, 22
  Arctic, 93
  Caribbean, 231
  Chinese, 42–43
  concepts about, 37–39
  and eternity, 396–397
  Hittite, 511
  Inca, 560
  Iranian, 582
  in Judaism, 38, 39, 40–42, 650–651
  location of, 40
  Moabite, 758
  North American Indian, 822, 846
  Turkic, 1131
  See also heaven and hell; immortality; underworld
Aga Khan, 435, 596
Aga Khan, Karim, 596
Against Apion (Josephus Flavius), 160, 161
Against the Errors of the Greeks (Thomas Aquinas), 1103
Against Heresies (Irenaeus), 155, 342, 436, 437
Agama Tirtha, 134
Agami Islam Santri, 632
Agami Jawi, 632, 633
agape, 61, 250, 251
Agdistis, 616
Agent Intellect, 785
aggadah, 151, 360, 646
`Aggai, 793
Agni, 485, 487, 912
Agnicayana, 487, 519
Agnistoma, 487
Agricola, Rodolphus, 516
agricultural rites
  in Africa, 1040
  in Borneo, 189
  Central Bantu, 245–246, 247
  and fasting, 413

in folk religion, 416
  Hawaiian, 474
  Hittite, 510
  North American Indian, 812, 842–843
  South American Indian, 1032–1033
  and sun worship, 789
Agwé, 233
Aha, 384
Aha'i Gaon, 153, 442
Ahalya, 570
ahamkara, 970
Aharon (the Elder) ben Yosef, 670
Aharon (the Younger) ben Eliyyahu, 670
ahavaniya, 556
Ahekan, 98
ahimsa, 429, 491, 497, 565, 620
Ahiqar, 167
ahl al-hadith, 591
Ahmad, Ghulam, 596
Ahmad, Khrushid, 612
Ahmad, Muhammad, 641
Ahmad, Sayyid, Khan, 597
Ahóusa, 1028
Ahui, John, 24
Ahuna Vairya, 1189
Ahura Mazda, 68, 581, 698, 699, 762, 1189
ahuras, 581
Ai of Lu, Duke, 317
Ai-apaec, 1017
Aiguptioi, 326
Ain Jalut, Battle of, 574
Ain Mallaha, 791
Ainu religion, 44–45
aion, 372
Airyema Ishyo, 1189
Aiyysyt, 1131
aji, 232
Ajivikas, 493
Akbar, 45–46, 504, 619
akh, 555
Akhenaton, 762
akherat, 632
akhirah, 588
akhiring jaman, 632
Aki, 834
Akiti festival, 725
Akitu festival, 303, 411
Akkad, 726
Akkadian language, 724
Akkadian seals, 536
Akrotiri, 14
Aksobhya, 216
Aksum, 397
akusala-karman, 673
akusala-Mahabhumika, 364
Akwe-Xavante, 1021
al-. *See* under the following element of Arabic names
Al-futuhat al-makkiyah (al-`Arabi), 593, 1047
al-hajar al-aswad (Black Stone), 667
al-hajj al-akbar, 588
Al-insaf (Ibn Sina), 526
al-jami`, 773
Al-kafi, 589
Al-qanun fi al-tibb (Ibn Sina), 526

Al-Quddus, 180
Al-Qued, 791
al-Rahman, 584
Al-risalah al-qushayiyah (al-Qushayri), 1046
Al-shifa' (Ibn Sina), 526
Aladura church, 24, 25, 802
`Ala'i Philosophy* (Ibn Sina), 526
Alalakh, 519
Alalu, 510, 520
`Alamgir, Awrangzib, 605
Alamo Foundation, 800
`Alawiyun, 596
alaya-vijnana, 806
Alberic, ascension of, 99
Albert the Great. *See* Albertus Magnus
Albert of Hohenzollern, 923
Alberti, Leon Battista, 515
Albertists, 47–48
Albertus Magnus, 46–47, 853, 1103
  influence of, 46–47
  writings of, 46
Albo, Yosef, 41, 152
Albright, William, 353
Albufereta, 523
alchemy, 47–48, 853
  Chinese, 48–49
  Hellenistic and medieval, 51–52
  Indian, 50
  Islamic, 53
  Renaissance, 54–55
  as spiritual discipline, 49, 54
  Taoist, 1078
alchera, 553
alcheringa, 553
Alcis, 431
Aleppo, 85
Aleut, 92, 580, 849
Alexander III, Pope, 575, 876
Alexander IV, 1165
  Pope, 46
Alexander V, Pope, 876, 981
Alexander VI, Pope, 156
Alexander VII, Pope, 877
Alexander VIII, Pope, 877
Alexander the Great
  in Egypt, 51, 163, 386
  and Greek culture, 476–477
  and oracles, 478
  in Phoenicia, 886
Alexander of Hales, 269
Alexandria, 167, 397
  anti-Semitism in, 78
  Catechetical School of, 326
  downfall of, 327
  gnosticism in, 434–435, 437
  Hellenistic culture in, 476
  Jews in, 163, 1114
  patriarchate of, 378, 460
  under Ptolemys, 386
Alexandrian canon. *See* Septuagint
Alexarchus, 478
Alexios I, 344, 980
Alfred the Great, 295
Alger of Liège, 181
Algonquian Indians, 302, 554, 808, 811, 813, 1120
  tribes of, 820

Ali, Ameer, 597, 598
Ali, Inayet, 146
Ali, Wilayat, 146
`Ali, Muhammad, 131
`Ali, Muhammad of Shiraz, 596
Alicante, 523
`alim, 781
Alisanos, 242
Alkalai, Yehudah ben Shelomoh, 1187
Alkmene, 477
All Fool's Day, 55
All Souls Festival, 64, 195
All-Form of Krsna, 497
All-One, 762
Allah, 356
Allat, 86
Allatum, 726
Allegory of the Law (Philo Judaeus), 549
Allen, Grant, 30
Allgemeine Religions wissenschaft
        (Eliade), 389
Almohads, 524
Almoravids, 524
alocana, 302
Altair, 531
Altan Khan, 349
Altar of Augustan Peace, 539
altare, 56
altars, 56–57
    Aegean, 16–17
    in Africa, 1162
    Buddhist, 1084
    Christian, 56–57
    Egyptian, 56
    Germanic, 432
    Greek, 56, 1088
    Hindu, 56, 1083
    Israelite, 56
    Moabite, 758
    Phoenician, 887
    Roman, 56, 1088
    sacrifice at, 963
    Scythian, 987
Altizer, Thomas J.J., 103
Alvaro I, 29
Alvars, 501, 502
    hymns of, 565
Alves, Rubem, 446
alwah, 131
`Am, Adad ha-, 660
amaNazaretha church, 25
Amarah West, 614
Amarapura sect, 1101
Amaterasu Omikami, 451, 668, 996
Ambedkar, Dr. Bhimrao Ramji, 198
Amduat, book of, 385
Amenophis III, IV, 223, 303
American Christian Missionary Society,
        365
American Indian Religious Freedom
        Act, 836
American Lutheran synod, 695
American Medical Missionary College,
        988
American Muslim Mission, 36
American Society for the Study of
        Religion
    (ASSR), 390

American Unitarian Association, 1142
Ames, William, 913
Amesha Spentas, 68
Ami, 1056
Amida, 625, 720
Amida's Western Paradise, 625
Amish, 723
Amitabha, 185, 214, 216, 720
Amlak, Yekunno, 398
Amma, 66, 67
`Ammi'el, Menahem, 84
Ammianus Marcellinus, 976
Ammon, 351
Ammonites, 11
Ammu, 226
Amoghasiddhi, 216
Among the Primitive Bakongo (Weeks),
        30
Amorite Mari, 223–224
Amos, 57–59
    literary style, 58–59
    message of, 57–58
    See also Book of Amos
amrta, 485, 555, 556
amsas, 565
amulets
    Inuit, 580
    Islamic, 919
    North American Indian, 814
Amun oracle, 386
Amun-Re, 537, 583
    cult of, 385
Amunhotep IV, 762
An, 724, 725
An Hyang, 313
An Lu-shan, 259, 573
Aña Túmpa, 1027
Anabaptism, 59–60, 271, 723, 924
    development of, 59–60
Anabaptists Four Centuries Later
        (Kauffman and Harder), 723
anachorien, 395
Anahid, 1189
Anahit, 98
Anahita, 1189
Analects (Confucius), 304, 305, 315,
        316, 317, 318, 967
analytic philosophy, 60–62
    figures in, 61–62
    origins of, 60–61
`Anan's code of law, 669
Ananda, 332, 892
Ananda Marga, 802
Ananda Temple, 1085
Anantaboga, 135
Anasazi Indians, 838, 849
Anat, 225, 227, 450, 887
Anat-Bethel, 86
anatman, concept of, 782, 929, 1007
Anatolia, 97, 791
Anawati, Georges, 611
ancestor myths, 66–67
ancestor worship, 38, 63–64
    in Africa, 19, 22, 30, 64, 553
        Central Bantu, 246
        East Africa, 376
        West Africa, 1161–1162
        Zulu, 1191–1192

Afro-Caribbean, 234–235
    of Australian Aboriginals, 66
    in Buddhism, 64–65
    Caribbean, 231
    Chinese, 65, 254, 793
    in Confucianism, 65
    in India, 64
    in Japan, 65–66
    in Java, 632
    in Korea, 65, 680
    in Melanesia, 64
    research problems, 63
    in Shamanism, 65
    Sinhala, 1000
    Slavic, 1005
    South American Indian, 1021, 1033
    in study of religion, 63–64
    Turkic, 1130
    Vietnamese, 1154
Anchor Bible, 158
anchorites, 395
Ancient Arabic Order, 423
Ancient Church of the East, 793
Ancient City, The (Coulanges), 66
Ancient Learning, 312, 313
andai, 761
Andean Indian religion, 1014–1019
Anderson, James, 422
Anderson, J.N.D., 611
Andhrakas, 212
Andrae, Tor, 610
Andrea, Johann Valentin, 54
Andrew of Longjumeau, 574
Andrews, C.F., 429
Andrews University, 988
Angaité, 1027
angels, 68–70
    in Christianity, 69
    fallen, 68, 83, 977
    hierarchies of, 69–70
    in Islam, 69
    in Judaism, 68–69
    in modern world, 70
    origins/functions, 68
    in Zoroastrianism, 68
Anggh, 98
Angkor Wat, 89
Anglican church, 70–72, 102, 293, 740,
        905
    development of, 70–72
    modern era, 72
Anglican Consultative Council, 71
Anglican Society for the Propagation of
        the Gospel, 819
Anglican-Roman Catholic International
        Commission, 72, 878
Angra Mainyu, 68, 699, 762, 944
animal sacrifice
    African, 21–22, 1162
    Afro-Caribbean, 234
    Ainu, 44
    as blood offering, 463–464, 963
    in Borneo, 189
    Greek, 463–464
    Hindu, 487, 502–503
    Iberian, 523
    Inca, 560
    Iranian, 581

animal sacrifice *(continued)*
in Islam, 892
Israelite, 688
Minoan, 17
Phoenician, 887
Samoyed, 972
Santeriá, 234
Scythian, 571
Southeast Asian, 1038
animals
in Ainu religion, 44
in Arctic religion, 93, 580
in Celtic religion, 242
in Mesopotamian religion, 535–536
in North American Indian religion, 532, 817, 827
in Paleolithic era, 870, 898
in Saami religion, 951
in Samoyed religion, 972
in South American religions, 1021, 1023, 1032
in Tunguz religion, 1126–1127
in Turkic religions, 1130
worship of, 790
See also bear
Aningaaq, 580
Aniruddha, 1071
aniyata-bhumika, 364
ankh, 537
Ankola Batak, 142
Anna of Friesland, Countess, 722
Annada, 143
Annals (Tacitus), 432
Anosh-Utra, 702
ansai, 550
Ansai, Yamazaki, 312, 997
Ansari, Murtada, 605
Ansari, Zafar Ishaq, 612
Anselm of Canterbury, 104, 141, 275, 280
writings on Jesus, 639
Answer to Job (Jung), 664
Antaka, 708
antaryamin, 540
Antelope cult of Hopi, 689
Anthony of Padua, 72–73
anthropology of religion, 73–75, 125, 401–402, 455, 929
critiques of, 74
future approaches, 75
anthropomorphism, 76–77, 242, 538, 792, 870
Anthropos, 434
Anti-Masonic party, 422
anti-Semitism, 78–80, 653, 656, 1061
in Islam, 79–80
in middle ages, 78–79
and New Testament, 78
Antichrist, 79, 360, 1165
Antioch, 343, 344, 378, 751
Antiochus Epiphanes, 712
Antiochus I, King of Commagene, 179, 470, 479
Antiochus IV, King of Syria, 649
Antitheses (Marcion), 154
Antonine, Dona Béatrice, 734
Antonius Pius, 409
Antony of Egypt, 327

Antyesti, 487
Anu, 227, 340, 510, 520
Anuak, 402
Anubhasya, 1153
Anubis, 37
anudatta, 249
anuloma, 491–492
Anum, 725
anumana, 739
anupalabdhi, 739
anuvratas, 620
Anyu Rakkuru, 45
aojo, 178
Apache Indians, 820, 837, 838
apaddharma, 362, 492
Apam Napat, 581
Aparasaila, 212
aparigraha, 621
aparya-paryaya-ve-daniya-karman, 673
Apas, 581
apauruseya, 490
apavaktri, 407
Aphrodite, 182, 451, 479, 539, 887
aphtharsia, 557
Api, 987
Apocalypse of Abraham, 81, 167
Apocalypse of Adam, 167
Apocalypse of Daniel, 167
Apocalypse of Enoch, 82, 727, 785
Apocalypse of John. See Revelation
Apocalypse of Moses, 80
Apocalypse of Paul, 80
Apocalypse of Peter, 80, 437
apocalypticism, 80–85
in Christianity, 81
in Judaism, 80, 82–85
and New Testament, 169–170
origins of genre, 81
pseudegrapha of, 167–168
Apocrypha, 68, 69, 166–167
writings of, 166–167
Apocrypha of Ezekiel, 167
Apocrypha and Pseudepigrapha of the Old Testament, The (Charles), 167
Apocryphon of John, 434, 435
Apokryphen und Pseudepigraphen des Alten Testaments, Die, (Kautzsch), 167
Apollinaris, 638
Apollo, 17, 99, 479
Celtic, 241
oracle at Delphi, 451, 463, 478, 539, 858, 860
Romans, 942, 943
Apollonius of Tyana, 478, 741, 945
Apology (Justin Martyr), 342, 549
Apology (Tertullian), 549
apostasy, 324–325
Apostles' Creed, 273, 281, 563, 899
apostles of Jesus, 173, 273
and New Testament, 171–172, 173
Apostolic Church, 25
Apostolic Tradition, 181
Appu, 521
aprapti, 364
April Fools' Day, 55

apsaras, 69, 570
aptavacana, 738
Apuleius, 479, 762, 944
Aqhat, 227
`Aqiva' ben Yosef, 712, 967
`*aqliyat*, 448
Aqsa, 636
Aquinas, Thomas. *See* Thomas Aquinas
Ara Pacis, 539
`Arabi, Ibn al-, 784, 1014, 1044, 1046–1047
Aradabda, 976
Arafat, 891
arahant, 95, 332
Aram, 614
Arama, Yitshaq, 152
Aramazd, 98
Aramean religion, 85–86
cults in, 85–86
later developments, 86
Aranda, 530
Aranyakas, 362, 484, 491
Arapaho Indians, 820, 821
Arapesh, 238
Ararma, 725
Arawak religion, 230–232, 1030, 1032
Arberry, A.J., 610, 611
Arbman, Ernst, 382
arca, 540
archaeology of religion, 87–88, 884, 898
and evolutionary theory, 87
historical/geographical areas, 87–88
archangels, 70
archetypes, 70, 453
Archimedes, 982
architecture, 89–91
African, 23
as center of reference, 89–90
as divine habitation, 89
function and, 90–91
Islamic, 547, 611
as memorials, 90
Mesoamerican, 90, 126, 534
Minoan, 15–16
mosque, 91, 775–776
symbolization, 91
synagogue, 91
temple, 1082–1089
Buddhist, 1084–1086
Confucian, 1087
Egyptian, 1087–1088
Greek, 1088
Hindu, 1082–1084
Mesoamerican, 1089
Roman, 1088–1089
types, 91
See also temples
Arctic religions, 92–95, 849
afterlife in, 93
animal rituals in, 93, 580
characteristics of, 92–93
deities in, 93, 580, 909
Inuit, 580–581
repentance in, 934
rites of passage, 580

shamanism in, 93, 531, 580
taboos, 580
Ardhanarisvara, 495
areitos, 231
arendiwane, 815
Areopolis, 757
Ares, 17, 479, 524, 757, 987
Aretas IV, 643
aretsan, 815
Arewordik`, 98
Arezzo, 514
Arghun, Il-khan, 574
Argimpasa, 987
Argonauts, 478
Argyropoulos, John, 515
arhat, 95–96, 185, 208, 209, 212, 621
concept of, 95–96
as cult figure, 95–96
Arianism, 176
aribuma, 226
Arica, 800
Arikara Indians, 820
Arinna, 520
Aristeas, 99
Aristides (apologist), 549
Aristotle, 96–97, 251, 457, 524
and Albertus Magnus, 46
and doctrine, 369
and Magi, 699
moral philosophy of, 96–97
on Pythagoreans, 1043
on science and nature, 96
on soul, 96
and theism, 101
Thomas Aquinas on, 1104
Arius, 334, 638, 1123
Ariyaratna, A.T., 430
Arjuna, 148–149, 497
Ark of the Covenant, 162, 342, 351, 544, 635, 931
Arkalochori cave, 16
arkarana, 346
Arkona, 1004
Arkoun, Mohammed, 611, 612
Armenian religion, 97–98, 249, 379
Arminius, Jacobus, 913
Armstrongism, 802
Arnhem Land, 108, 110, 111, 112, 115, 122, 529–530
Arnold, Gottfried, 435, 480
Arnon, 756
Aron ha-Qodesh, 544
Arpad, 85
Arquam, al-, 778
Ars wa-Shamem, 225
Arsacid, 98
Arsameia Nymphaios, 179
Arsay, 225
art
Aegean, 15, 16
African, 19, 23, 34, 527–528
Arctic, 93
Australian Aboriginal, 117, 529–530
blessing in, 178
Canaanite, 227
Chinese, 43
Christian, 544–546, 908
Cycladic, 15

Egyptian, 537
Germanic, 432
Greek, 539
Hellenistic, 539
Iberian, 523
Islamic, 547–548, 611
in Judaism, 544
Mayan, 533
Mesoamerican, 533–534
Mesopotamian, 535, 536
Neolithic, 792
North American Indian, 531
Oceanic, 856
Paleolithic, 561, 870, 898
Artemis, 86, 451, 479, 538
arthas, 492
Arthasastra, 50, 492
Artimpasa, 987
Arunachai Pradesh, Buddhism in, 483
arupaloka, 476
arupyadhatu, 364
arvagastiae, 432
Arval Brothers, 942
Arya Samaj, 504
Aryans, 483, 484, 485
aryas, 620
asa-lah, 781
Asad, Hafiz al-, 781
Asad Allah, 547
Asalluhe, 725
asamskrta, 363
Asaph, 909
asat, 486, 999
asavas, 95
Asbury, Francis, 729, 730
Ascalon, 343
Ascelinus, 574
ascension, 98–99, 557
in Christianity, 99
ecstatic methods, 98
in Greek/Hellenistic religions, 99
in Islam, 99
in Judaism, 99
paths of, 98
"Ascent of Mount Ventoux" (Petrarch), 515
asceticism
and sexuality, 960
and Sufism, 1046
Aseneth, 644
Ásgardr, 430, 431, 433
Ash Man/Boy, 840
asha, 582
asham, 103
Ash`ari, Abu al-Hasan al-, 591–592
Ash`ariyah, 448
Ashdod, 884, 885
Ashdoda, 886
Ashem Vohu, 1189
Asherah, 450
Ashikaga school of Zen, 625, 1185
Ashkenazic Judaism, 652–653, 1053, 1172
Ashmole, Elias, 422
Ashqelon, 884
Ashtar-Kemosh, 757, 758
Ashtaroth, 885
Ashtishat, 97

Ashtoret, 885
Ashur, 724, 726
`Ashura, 585, 595
asirvada, 179
asis, 179
`Askari, Hasan al-, 993
Askew, A., 434
Asklepios, 178, 742, 1088
askr, 340
Aslam Kamal, 548
asmakhta', 468
Asningái, 1026–1027
Asohsná bird, 1026
Asoka, 192–193, 332, 333, 708, 751, 1063, 1084, 1099
Asokavadana, 708
Asparukh, 573
asramas, 341, 491, 565
asravas, 709
Assam, Gaidaliu in, 734
Assassins, 596
Assayer, The (Galileo), 428
Assembly of the World Council of Churches, Sixth, 677
Assiniboin Indians, 820, 821
asskouandy, 814
Association of the Buddhist Youth of Cambodia, 203
Association of Friends of the Buddhist Lycée, 203
Association of Friends of Religious Students of the Republic of Cambodia, 203
Association of Friends of the Spirits, 66
Association for Jewish Studies, 322
Association of Shinto Shrines, 668, 998
Assumption, 716
Assyria, 726
location, 724
underworld in, 1134
Assyrian language, 724
astanah, 146
Astarte, 450, 523, 757, 887
astikayas, 621
Astrakhan, 574
astrology, 477, 680
astronomy
Copernican, 325–326
and Galileo, 427–428
Astruc, Jean, 156
asu, 555, 935, 1008
asuras, 359, 485, 486, 487, 570
Asvaghosa, 742
Asvamedha, 487, 489
asvattha, 340
Aswan, 86
Ataentsic, 372
Atar, 86, 581
Atargatis, 86, 479
Ataroth, 758
Atatürk, Mustafa Kemal, 594, 608
Atayla, 1056
Atcholi, 301
Atesi, 796
Athanasian Creed, 278–279
Athanasius, Pope, 169, 326, 334, 397
Athapascan Indians, 532, 808, 848, 850
tribes of, 820

Atharvan, 484
Atharvaveda, 362, 407, 484, 486, 563, 1067
atheism, 100–103, 406, 524
    in Eastern religious thought, 100
    modern, 101–102
    theism, attacks on, 101
    in Western religious thought, 100–103
Athena, 17, 86, 451, 477, 479, 538
Athens, 460
Athirat, 225, 226, 887
Athtar, 227
Athtart, 887
Atisa, 1045
Atlantis, 881
atman, 38, 363, 556, 1008
    concept of, 486, 487, 782, 929
atman-brahman, 357, 488, 489
atmanas tustir, 362
atonement, 103–105
    in Christianity, 104–105
    and fasting, 414
    in Judaism, 103–104
    theories of, 104
atrushans, 97
Atsina Indians, 820
Atsugewi Indians, 831
Atsutane, Hirata, 997
Atthakavagga (Suttanipata), 198
Attica, 464
Attila the Hun, 572
Attis, 182, 451
Attjie, 952
atuas, 705–706
Atum, 384, 1105
Aufklärung, 393
Augsburg Confession, 156, 296
Augusta, Jan, 768
Augustine of Canterbury, 327
Augustine of Dacia, 155
Augustine of Hippo, 73, 105–107, 273, 382
    apologist for paganism, 549–550
    and biblical exegesis, 155
    and catechisms, 278
    Confessions of, 105–106
    defense of Christianity, 273
    doctrinal views of, 106, 280, 369
    early life of, 105
    ethics of, 106
    on God's nature, 445
    mysticism of, 783
    on resurrection, 38
    on Ten Commandments, 284
    on Trinity, 105, 106, 279, 1123
    on underworld, 1135
Augustus, 539, 942, 943, 945
augustus, term, 178
Aulén, Gustaf, 104
Aurispa, Giovanni, 515
Aurobindo, Sri, 504
Aurukun, 121
Austin, J.L., 61
Australian religions, 107–126
    ancestor worship in, 66
    art of, 117, 529–530, 1137

circumcision in, 111, 113–114, 1159–1160
death rites of, 110–111, 117
deities in, 108, 111, 114–115
Dreaming, 108, 114, 553, 1137, 1159, 1160
immortality in, 553–554
initiation rites of, 109–110, 113–114, 115, 116, 177
mobile systems in, 111–112
modern movements in, 118, 120–123
nature in, 788
regional systems, 111–118
reincarnation in, 928
renaissance of, 118
ritual activation in, 111
ritual sequences in, 109, 111–112
sacred in, 107–108
segmentary systems in, 112–114
social structure of, 108–109
species renewal rites of, 114, 115
studies of, 123–126
Ungarinyin, 1136–1138
Walbiri, 122, 530, 1159–1160
Australian Religions (Eliade), 390
Authenticity of the Tradition Literature: Discussions in Modern Egypt (Juynboll), 611
Authoritarian tradition, in Ch'in China, 256
Autobiography (Eliade), 389
auwa, 115
av-yakrta-karman, 673
Avalambana, 64
Avalokitesvara, 214, 217
Avantaka, 212
Avaris, 385
Avars, 572–573
Avatamsaka Sutra, 194, 209, 217
avatara, 76, 504, 540, 564
    classical theory, 496–497
Aventia, 242
Aventinus, 516
Averroës. *See* Ibn Rushd (Averroës)
Averroists, 524–525
Avesta, 97
Avicenna. *See* Ibn Sina (Avicenna)
avidya, 488, 489, 709
Avignon papacy, 336, 876, 980
Avot de Rabbi Natan, 163
Awake!, 634
Awakened One, 197
Awami League, 145, 146
awiliya, 743, 1047
Awn, 707
awon iya wa, 528
Axial Age, 73
axis mundi, 340, 341, 389, 564, 976
axnábsero, 1027
Aya, 510, 725
ayat, 448, 632
ayat Allah, 550
ayatanas, 56, 364
Ayathrima, 1190
Aylesford site, 889
Ayoré, 1026–1027
Azal, Subh-i al-, 131, 596

Azalis, 131
Azande, 375, 376, 402, 692, 1163–1164
Azim, al-, 447
Azitawadda, King, 886, 887
Aztec religion, 87, 126–130, 519, 923
    archaeology of, 87
    cosmology of, 127–128
    fertility/regeneration theme, 129
    gods in, 128–129, 534, 554
    iconography of, 534
    immortality in, 554
    redemption in, 923
    sacrifice in, 127–128, 129, 519
    Tenochtitlán, 127
Azzam, Salem, 612

B

ba, 555, 935
Baal, 224–225, 226, 227, 616, 676, 757, 758, 885
    Temple of, 89
Baal of Mount Tsafon, 887
Baal-Hammon, 147
Baal-Merappe, 887
Baal-Peor, 757, 758
Baal-Shamem, 886, 887
Baalzebub, 885
Bab, 131, 132, 133, 596
Baba, 726
Baba, Meher, 800, 802
Baba Yaga, 1005
babalawo, 975
Babil, 724
Babis, 131
Babylonia, 12, 68, 88, 89, 137, 1171
    ancient, location, 724
    language of, 724
Babylonian Exile, 635
Babylonian religion
    confession in, 303
    cosmology in, 329, 330
    iconography of, 536
    underworld in, 1134
    See also Mesopotamian religions
Babylonian Talmud, 646, 653, 1060, 1061, 1172
Bach, Johann Sebastian, 908
Bachofen, J.J., 453, 454
Back to Godhead (Bhaktivedanta), 578, 579
Bacon, Francis, 54
Bacon, Roger, 524, 853
Bactria, 571
Badajoz, 523, 524
Badara-Yana, 493
Bada'uni, 45
Bade, 233
Badojoz, 524
Badr, Battle of, 918
Baduhenna, 432
Baeck, Leo, 660
baetyl, 539
Baez, Joan, 430
Baffin Islands, 580
Bagbarti, 520
bagins, 97
Baha, Abd al-, 131–132, 133

Baha' Allah, 131–133, 596
Baha'i religion, 131–133, 596
  beliefs and practices, 132–133
  development of, 131–132
Bahman Yasht, 81
Bahusruthiyas, 212
Baidrama, 231
Baile in Scáil, 241
Bajjan, 952
bakchoi, 464
Bakr, Abu, 778
Bakri, al-, 29
bakufu, 625
bakwr, 398
Balaam, 758
Balak, King, 758
balams, 717, 718
balani, 185
Balarama, 498
Baldr, 431, 433
Baldwin II of Flanders, 343
Baldwin IX of Flanders, 344
Balgo, 112
Bali, 1037, 1038
Balinese religion, 134–135
  ritual cycles, 134–135
  sources of, 134
Balokole, 26, 578
Baltic religion, 135–137
  development of, 135–136
  gods in, 136–137
Bamana, 23
Bambara, 178
Bamoth-baal, 757
Banaidja, 111
Banar, 1137
Banaras, 89, 90, 541
bandara cult, 1000
bandha, 50
bang, 99
Bangkok, 90
Bangladesh, 143, 144, 145, 146
bania, 428
Bankei, 1052
Banna', Hasan al-, 780
banquets, Mesopotamian, 536
Bantu religions, 245–248
  Central, 245–248
  cults, 246–247, 577
  Interlacustrine, 577–578
  social setting, 245–246, 577–578
  spirits, 246–247, 577
Banun, 1056
Banzan, Kumazawa, 312
bao, 796
baptism, 137–138
  of blood, 138
  Christian, 71, 90, 91, 138, 282–283,
    639
    of Jesus, 138, 643
    by John, 138, 643
    in New Testament, 282
    in Protestantism, 276, 283,
      694–695
  Mandaean, 702
  pre-Christian, 137–138
  in Protestantism, 907
  as transitional rite, 953

Baptist churches, 139–140
  Afro-Caribbean, 235
  congregational government of,
    293–294
  in England, 139
  in United States, 35, 139
  worldwide, 139–140
Baptist Mission, 145
Baquir, Muhammal al-Majlisi, al-, 605
Bar Hebraeus, 155, 573
Bar Kokhba caves, 353, 649
bar mitsvah, 649
barakah, 180, 667
barava, 710
Barclay, Robert, 915
Bareau, Andre, 333
Bareshnum, 581
Barlaam, 336
Barnabas, 154
Barnenez, Brittany, 721
Baron, 1156
Barong, 1038
Baronio, Césare, 427
Barrett, David B., 754, 904
Barrow, Henry, 319
Barsur, 85
Barth, Karl, 102, 140–141, 186, 271,
    277
  on God's nature, 141, 446, 1096
  theological development of, 140–141
Baruch, 82, 166, 167
basar, 556
Bashir, al-Din, 596
Bashyatchi, Eliyyahu, 670
Basic Conduct (Vattakera), 620
Basil of Caesarea, 155, 1123
Basil I, Emperor of Greece, 336
basilica architecture, 91
Basilica of Il Santo in Padua, 73
Basilides, 154, 155, 435, 437
Basket Dances, 842
Basket Makers, 25, 838
Basri, Hasan al-, 592, 784
Batak religion, 141–142
Bathara Kala, 632
Bathsheba, 352
batin, 633
Battle Creek College, 988
Batu (Golden Horde), 574
Baucis, 11
Bauer, Walter, 480
Baur, Ferdinand Christian, 435
Bavli, 646
bawanagung, 632
Baybars, 574
Bayle, Pierre, 392
bayt al-mal, 774
Baza, 523
Beaker culture, 721
bear
  in Ainu religion, 44
  in North American Indian religion,
    817, 833
  in Saami religion, 951
  in Tunguz religion, 1126–1127
Bear Dance, 833
Bear Festival, 1126, 1127
Bear Medicine society, 844

Beast Gods cult, 844
Beatty, Chester, 174
Beautiful Feast of the Valley, 538
Beaver Indians, 808
Bebel, Heinrich, 516
Becher, Carl Heinrich, 610
Bechuana, 302
Beckmann, Max, 546
Bedsa stupa, 1084
Beelshamen, Temple of, 86
Beetle, 1027–1028
Beida, 791
beit din, 648, 974
Bel, 86, 360
Bel and the Dragon, 166, 167
Belenus, 241
Beli, 432
Believers' Church, 723
Belize, ancestral cult in, 235
Bell, Richard, 610, 918
Bella Coola Indians, 826
Bellah, Robert N., 74
Bellarmino, Joseph, 1133
Bellarmino, Roberto, 427
Bellona, 942
Beltrame, Giovanni, 30
Bema, 703
Ben Sira, 160, 167, 651
Bender, Harold S., 723
Benedict XII, Pope, 1013
Benedict XIII, Pope, 981
Benedict XV, Pope, 229, 878
Benedict of Nursia, 760
Benedictus Deus, 1013
Benei Akiva, 1187
benei Elim, 676
Benei Yisra'el, 160
Ben'en, Enni, 1184
Bengali religions, 142–146
  Buddhism, 145
  Christianity, 145
  goddesses in, 143
  Hinduism, 142–143, 144
  independence and, 144–145
  Islam, 145–146
  in nineteenth century, 143–144
  Parsis, 145
  Sikhism, 145
  Tantrism, 143
  Vaisnava movement, 143, 144
Bengel, Johann Albrecht, 156
Benin, 527
Benjamin I (Coptic), 327
Benneville, George de, 1143
Bentham, Jeremy, 393
Ber, Dov of Mezhirich, 471, 472, 473
beraakhah, 399
Berakhot, 512, 1060
Berber religion, 147–148
  ancient, 147
  in Christian times, 147
  in Islamic times, 148
Berdiaev, Nikolai, 268, 950
berit, 615
Berit Shalom, 191
Berke (Golden Horde), 574
Berlin, Naftali Tsevi, 153
Bernard of Clairvaux, 275, 344, 784

Bernardone, Giovanni Francesco. *See* Francis of Assisi
Berrueco, 523
bersih dhusun, 632
Berthold of Mossburg, 47
Besant, Annie, 1065
Bessarion, John, 337, 515
Beth-baal-meon, 758
Beth-baal-peor, 758
Bethel, 58, 86, 616
Bethlehem, 352
Beyond God the Father: Toward a Philosophy of Women's Liberation (Daly), 1166, 1167
Beyond the Veil (Mernissi), 1168
Bezels of Wisdom, The (al-`Arabi), 1047
bhadralok, 143, 144
Bhadrayaniyas, 212
Bhagavadgita, 148–150, 340, 362, 494, 502, 564
  commentary on, 709
  karman in, 672
  persistence of text, 150
  philosophy of, 149–150
  text of, 148–149, 497
Bhagavata Purana, 565
Bhairava, 540
Bhaja stupa, 1084
bhakti Hinduism, 488, 489, 490, 494–498, 502
  attitude of, 565–566
  and Buddhism, 194
  classical, 494–498
  immortality in, 556
  revivalist movement, 501
  sectarian, 500
  Tamil, 1063, 1064
  and Tantric Hinduism, 498–499
bhakti-rasa-sastra, 143
Bhaktivedanta, Swami A.C., 504
Bhartrhari, 1152
Bhaskara, 1153
bhavana, 719
Bhave, Vinoba, 430
bhikkhus, 299
Bhikkunisamyutta, 708
bhiksus, 211, 215, 332, 541
Bhimasankar, 709
Bhotia, 482, 483
Bhutan, Buddhism in, 483
bhutas, 359, 970
bi-shar`, 594
Bible
  Abraham, 11–12
  Adam, 13–14
  and afterlife, 40–41
  Amos, 57–59
  angels in, 69
  Apocrypha, 166–167
  archaeology of, 88
  blessing in, 179–180
  Cain and Abel, 221
  Canaanites in, 223
  canonizing process, 161–162, 616–617
  cantillation of, 248, 249
  conscience in, 320
  covenant in, 11–12, 338, 339

David, 351–352
  and evolutionary theory, 404
  exegesis, 151–158, 802
    Christian views, 154–158
    Franco-German, 151
    Jewish views, 151–154
    and law (*halakhah*), 468
    medieval, 151–152
    modern, 153
    thirteenth to eighteenth centuries, 152–153
  Fall in, 412
  flood in, 415
  Garden of Eden, 879
  God in, 1122
  Greek translations of, 163–164, 457
  on idolatry, 548–549
  on immortality, 556–557
  Isaac, 512
  Job, 512
  Joseph, 644
  Latin translations of, 164–165
  Moabites in, 11, 758
  moral teachings of, 267
  Moses, 771–772
  and Near East literature, 163
  and oral tradition, 861
  Philistines in, 885
  and Protestantism, 905–906
  Pseudepigrapha, 167–168
  revelation in, 938
  Satan in, 977–978
  Spinoza's critique of, 1042
  standard text, 163
  Ten Commandments, 1091–92, 1115
  wisdom literature, 163, 167
  See also New Testament; *psalms*; Torah
Bible canon, 159–165
  Alexandrian (Septuagint), 161, 164
  canonizing process, 161–162
  Christian, 161
  contents of, 159–160
  Greek translations, 163–164
  number of books, 161
  at Qumran (Dead Sea scrolls), 160–161, 352–353, 557
  Samaritan, 160
  tripartite nature of, 160
Bible, The (film), 546
Bible Christians, 730
Bible Institute of Los Angeles, 401
Bible Speaks, 802
Bifrost, 431
Big Foot, Chief, 824
Big Head cult, 835
Big House ceremony, 847
Big Times, 832, 834
bija, 50, 672, 804
Billing, Edward, 915
Bilrost, 431
Bimbisara, 331
Binding of the Years, 129
bindu, 50
Binford, Sally R., 454
Binsbergen, Wim M.J. van, 733
Bion, W.R., 734
Biondo, Flavio, 515

Bird and Snake Goddess, 792
Birsa, 733
Birth God, 679
Birth of the Messiah, The (Brown), 6⁄
Birth and Rebirth (Eliade), 390
Birth of Tragedy (Nietzsche), 478
bishops, 106
Bishop's Program of Social Reconstruction, 289
bismillah, 547, 632
Bistami, Abu Yazid al-, 593
Bi'ur, 153
Bka'-brgyud-pa school of Buddhism, 483, 1045
Bka'-gdams-pa school of Buddhism, 1045
Black Baptists, 235
Black churches, 35, 139, 288, 289
Black Hills, 824
Black Hole, 131
Black Mesa, 837
Black Muslims, 37, 586
Black Stone, 667, 891
Black Tezcatlipoca, 127
Black Theology: A Documentary History (Wilmore and Cone), 1167
Blacker, Carmen, 407
Blackfeet Confederacy, 820, 823
Bladder Feast, 580
Blahoslav, Jan, 768
Blake, William, 320, 435
blama, 349
Blasius, 1004
blasphemy, 175–177
  Christian concept of, 175–176
Blaurock, Georg, 59
Bleda, 572
Blemmyes, 583
blessing, 177–181, 646, 647
  functions of, 177–178
  types of, 178–181
bliks, 63
Blinding of Truth by Falsehood, 386
blood, 181–182
  attitudes toward, 181
  ban on spilling, 181
  baptism of, 138
  blood sacrifice, 463–464, 963
  in circumcision rite, 113–114, 182
Bluejay shamans, 833
Boann, 241
Boas, Franz, 74, 94
boassio-raikie, 951
Boatsman, concept of, 809
Bob Jones University, 401
Bobo, 553
Boccaccio, Giovanni, 515
Bodawpaya, 1101
Bodh Gaya, 892–893, 1084
Bodhbh, 243
Bodhbh Chatha, 243
bodhi, 197
Bodhi Tree, 541, 1084
Bodhicaryavatara, 419
bodhicitta, 185
Bodhidharma, 183–184, 261
  historical, 183

legend of, 183–184
in popular religion, 184
bodhipaksya dharmas, 185
bodhisattva, 37, 195, 419, 732
concept of, 214, 967, 1045
bodhisattva path, 184–185, 213
disciplines of, 185
origin of term, 184–185
and religious practice, 185
Bodhisattvabhumi, 185
bodhisattvamarga, 214
Bodhisattvapratimoksa Sutra, 185
bodhyangani, 185
bodily functions, pollution of, 911
Bodin, Jean, 296
Body of Christ, 91, 282, 299
body painting, Australian Aboriginal,
529, 530
Boehme, Jakob, 435
Bogazköy, 510–511, 520, 521
böge, 761
Bogomils, 373
Bohemia, Moravians in, 767–769
Bolivia, 132
Bomberg, Daniel, 163
bomos, 56, 463
Bon, 407, 483
Bonaventure, 156, 269, 275, 421
bongo, 234–235
Bonhoeffer, Dietrich, 186, 283, 1090
on God's nature, 446
writings of, 186
Boniface, 186–187, 275, 747, 752
Boniface IX, Pope, 981
Boniface VIII, Pope, 980
Book of Amos, 57, 58–59, 160
Book of Balances, The, 53
Book of Ballymote, 240
Book of Beliefs and Opinions, The
(Sa`adyah), 41, 84, 442, 764,
1115
Book of Changes. See I ching
Book of the Commandments
(Maimonides), 700
Book of Commandments (Smith), 770,
1006
Book of Common Prayer, The, 71, 296
Anglican, 71, 296, 925
Methodist, 730
Book of Concise Remarks (al-Sarraj),
1046
Book of Consideration (al-Muhasibi),
1046
"Book of the Covenant," 615
Book of Daniel, 80, 81, 166, 556, 558,
645, 652, 935, 1011
Book of the Dun Cow, The, 240
Book of Enoch, 397
Book of Esther, 352, 649
Book of Family Ritual, 65
Book of Fermoy, 240
Book of Gates, 385
*Book of the Goddess: Past and
Present, The* (Olson), 454
Book of Going Forth By Day, 137, 303,
385, 538, 555, 1105–1106
Book of Great Profundity, 1077
Book of History, 304

Book of Hosea, 228
Book of Invasions, 240
Book of Isaiah, 512
Book of Job, 512, 617
Book of Jonah, 413, 647
Book of Jubilees, 397
Book of the Key and the Lamp (Nasir-i
Khusraw), 788
Book of Knowledge (al-Kalabadhi),
1046
Book of Lamentations, 649
Book of Leinster, 240
Book of Light, The (Nasir-i Khusraw),
787
Book of Lismore, 240
Book of Mercury, The, 53
Book of Mormon (Smith), 770, 904,
1006, 1007
Book of Music, 304, 317
Book of Odes, 304, 407
Book of One Hundred and Twelve, The,
53
Book of Poetry, 255, 317
Book of Precepts, 669
Book of Principles, The (Albo), 41, 152
Book of Realization of Perfection
(Chang Po-tuan), 1078
Book of Revelation, 80, 81, 154, 360
Book of Revelation. See Revelation
Book of Rites, 306, 310, 317, 684, 766
Book of Rules (Ticonius), 155
Book of Splendor, 654
Book of the Taking of Ireland, 240
Book of Thomas the Contender, 437
Book of Tobit, 68
Book of Travels (Nasir-i Khusraw), 787
Book of Two Ways, 385
Book of the Yellow Court, 1077
Book of Zechariah, 81
Book of Zerubbabel, 84
Booth, Catherine, 968
Booth, William, 187–188, 968, 969
Bora, 115, 117, 413
Borgia Codex, 128
Bormana, 241
Bormo, 241
Bornean religions, 188–189
characteristics of, 189
rituals of, 189
Bornkamm, Günther, 158
Boróro, 1033
Borvo, 241
Bose, Netaji Subhas Chandra, 144
bothros, 16
Bousset, Wilhelm, 157, 436, 639
Bowen, Harold, 611
Bower manuscript, 50
boyé, 232
Bracciolini, Poggio, 515
Bradley, F.H., 61
Bragi, 433
Brahamanic Hinduism, 486–488, 556
Brahma, 190, 495–496, 570
significance of, 190
Brahma Kumaris, 802
Brahma Sutra, 493, 499, 502, 1151,
1153
brahmacarin, 488, 491, 579

brahmacarya, 238, 341
brahmadeyas, 1063, 1064
Brahmajala Sutra, 185, 214
brahman, 38, 50, 149, 177, 179, 190,
486, 556
brahmana, 190, 341, 362, 484, 485,
486, 487
Brahmanaspati, 179
brahmanda, 495–496
Brahmanism, 719
Brahmasiddhi, 1152
brahmasiras, 495
Brahmo Samaj, 144, 504
Braithwaite, R.B., 61
Bralgu, 112
Bran, 243
Brant, Sebastian, 516
Bray, Reverend Thomas, 71
Brazil, 34
Brent, Charles Henry, 72
Brethren of the Common Life, 393
Brethren of Purity, 53
Breuer, Josef, 425
Brhadaranyaka Upanisad, 488, 489,
782
Briçonnet, Guillaume, 516
Briffault, Robert, 453
Brigaecae, 524
Brigham Young University, 771
Brighid of Kildare, 241
Brightman, Edgar S., 446
Britain, 728–730, 740–741
Anglican church in, 70–72, 102, 293,
740
Baptist church in, 139, 283
blasphemy laws in, 176
Celtic religion in, 239–244, 556,
880–881
church-state relations in, 296
Congregationalism in, 319
Enlightenment in, 393
Freemasonry in, 422
humanism in, 517
megalithic religion in, 721
Methodism in, 728–730
and Muslim Brotherhood, 780
Puritans in, 296, 913–914, 925
Quakers in, 915–916
Reformation in, 70–71, 296, 925
Salvation Army in, 187–188, 400,
968–969
Unitarianism in, 1142
Universalism in, 1143
brk, 180
Bronze Age religion
Cycladic, 15
Minoan, 15–17
Moabite, 756
Brooklyn, New York, 634
Brosses, Charles de, 30
Brotherly Union of 1527, 722, 723
Brown, Raymond E., 640, 691
Bruce, James, 434
Bruigh na Bóinne, 241
Bruni, Leonardo, 515
Bruno, Giordano, 421, 516
Bsod-nams-rgya-mtsho, 349
Bstan-`dzin-rgya-mtsho, 349

Buanann, 243
Buber, Martin, 190–191, 661
  and existentialism, 406
  on God's nature, 443, 661
  on Hasidim, 190–191
  on Judaism, 191
  on relation and dialogue, 191
  and Rosenzweig, 927, 948
Bucer, Martin, 899
Buddha (Gautama), 192
  future, Maitreya, 184, 203, 210, 214,
    562, 732
  images of, 541
  incarnation of, 562
  life of, 197
  miracles of, 742
  multiple Buddhas, 213–214
  relics of, 892–893, 1036
  teaching of, 564
Buddha Mahavairocana, 562
Buddha nature, 208
Buddha Treasure Sutra, 214
Buddha Vairocana, 624
Buddhacarita (Asvaghosa), 708, 742
Buddhadasa, Bhikkhu, 196, 203
Buddhaghosa, 95, 418
Buddhahood, 804, 1184
buddhavacana, 363
buddhi, 970
Buddhism, 192–218
  afterlife in, 37, 38, 39, 43
  ancestor worship in, 64–65
  arhatship figure in, 95–96
  in Arunachai Pradesh, 483
  and Balinese religion, 134, 135
  in Bhutan, 483
  Bodhidharma legend, 183–184
  bodhisattva path, 184–185, 213
  celibacy in, 239
  chanting in, 250
  charity in, 251
  chastity in, 252–253
  as civilizational religion, 192–193
  confession in, 302–303
  councils, 331–334
  as cultural religion, 194–196
  demons in, 359–360
  Dharma in, 185, 193, 197, 363–364
  Eightfold Noble Path, 363, 418, 419
  eternity in, 396–397
  exorcism in, 407, 408
  expansion of, 193–194, 209–210,
    1035–1036
  fasting in, 413, 414
  Four Noble Truths, 251, 363, 417–
    419
  goddesses in, 451
  gods in, 96, 359, 708
  heaven and hell in, 475–476
  in Himalayan region, 482–483
  iconography of, 541
  immortality in, 556
  karman in, 37, 65, 185, 193, 214,
    258, 303, 564, 672–673, 1107
  in Korea, 205–206, 210
  meditation in, 719, 720
  millenarianism in, 732
  miracles in, 742

  missions in, 745, 746, 749–750, 1099
  in modern world, 196, 202–203, 206
  monasticism, 190, 193, 196, 202,
    208–209, 210, 218, 1100–1101,
    1106–1107
  monotheism in, 762
  mysticism in, 782–783
  in Nepal, 482
  ordination in, 863, 901
  paradise in, 880
  pilgrimage in, 195, 750, 892–894,
    1107
  redemption in, 922–923
  reincarnation in, 38, 349, 929
  sainthood in, 967
  schools of, 208–218
    common features, 209
    diversification in, 209–211
    Hinayana, 208, 211–213
    masters of the Law in, 209
    monastic traditions, 208–209
    movements related to, 208
    Pure Land, 194, 195, 209, 260,
      451, 625
    sects, 209
    See also Mahayana Buddhism;
      Tantrism, Buddhist; Theravada
      Buddhism
  shrines of, 893, 1084
  in Sikkim, 482–483
  soul in, 1008–1010
  spiritual guide in, 1045
  in Sri Lanka, 196, 198, 210,
    1000–1001, 1099, 1100
  temples of, 196, 482, 625, 627,
    1084–1086
  universalism of, 509
Buddhism, Chinese, 194, 210
  afterlife in, 43
  calendric rites in, 195–196
  Ch'an tradition of, 260–261, 264
  doctrines of, 216–217
  incarnation in, 562
  meditation in, 720
  in Ming period, 263
  modern, 205
  origins of, 257–258, 746
  persecution of, 1076
  pilgrimage in, 893–894
  spiritual guide in, 1045
  spread of, 750
  in Sung period, 262
  Taiping movement, 264
  in Taiwan, 1058
  in T'ang period, 260–261
  temple compounds of, 1085
  T'ien-t'ai school, 258, 260
  White Lotus, 211
Buddhism, Indian
  in Bengal, 145
  councils of, 331–333
  as cultural religion, 194
  and dharma, 197–198
  as imperial religion, 193
  origins of, 564–565
  revival movements, 198
  soul in, 1008–1009
  spread of, 749–750, 1035–1036

  Tantric ritual in, 565
  Theravada, 1099–1100
Buddhism, Japanese
  Bodhidharma legend in, 184
  Esoteric (Tantric), 195
  exorcism in, 407
  incarnation in, 562
  introduction and growth of, 210, 217,
    623–625, 996
  in modern period, 206, 628
  Nichiren school, 625
  pilgrimage in, 894
  Pure Land school, 625, 628
  and Saicho, 965–966
  and Shinto, 668, 996
  Taikyo Sempu movement, 628
  temple compounds in, 1085–1086
  in Tokugawa period, 626–627
  Zen, 625–626, 627, 1051–1052,
    1184–1185
Buddhism, Southeast Asian
  in Burma, 196, 202, 203, 210, 408,
    1100– 1101
  in Cambodia, 202–203, 210, 1101
  initiation rites in, 196
  Khmer, 674
  in Laos, 210, 683, 1101
  in modern period, 201–202, 330
  monasticism in, 202, 1084,
    1100–1101
  spread of, 210, 1035–1036
  temple compounds of, 1084–1185
  in Thailand, 202, 203, 210, 1101
  Theravada, 195, 201, 210, 211,
    1036, 1100, 1101
  in Vietnam, 202, 203, 1154
Buddhism, Tibetan, 210, 263, 750,
    1106–1107
  in Bhutan, 483
  chanting in, 250
  Cultural Revolution, effects, 1107
  Dalai Lama, 349, 1107
  exorcism in, 407
  introduction of, 1106
  lineage in, 218
  in modern period, 204–205, 1107
  monasticism in, 217–218,
    1106–1107
  pilgrimage in, 893
  ritual practices of, 1107
  spiritual guide in, 1045
Buddhist Association, 205
Buddhist Association of the Republic of
    Cambodia, 203
Buddhist Sangha Act, 203
Buddhist Sasana Council, 202
Buddhist Society, 198
Budé, Guillaume, 516
Budny, Simon, 1142
Buffalo Dance, 841
Buffalo Tongues, 823
Buganda, 19, 577
Bugbrooke (Christian) Community, 802
Buhl, Frants, 610
Building of the Columns, 534
Building Eras in Religion (Bushnell),
    219
Bulgakov, Sergei, 950

Bulhoes, Ferdinand de. *See* Anthony of Padua
Bullinger, Heinrich, 899
Bultmann, Rudolf, 157, 158, 434, 436, 1096
Bumin, 572
bun, 683
Bun Bang Fai, 683
Bundu, 528
Bungi Indians, 820
bunke, 65
Bunyan, John, 908
Bunyoro, 577
Buraq, 69, 99
Burgos, 524
burial customs. *See* death ritual
Burkina Faso, 528, 553
Burkitt, Francis, 158
Burma, 95, 96
    Buddhism in, 196, 202, 203, 408, 1085, 1100–1101
    exorcism in, 408
burnt offering, in Buddhism, 216
Burundi, 178, 577
Bushnell, Horace, 218–219, 319
    writings of, 218–219
Bustan al-qulub (Nasir-i Khusraw), 788
buta yajña, 135
Butsudo, 368, 623
Butterfly Dances, 842
Buyids, 585
Bwiti, 26
Byblos, 887
Byzantine ecclesiastical music, 249
Byzantine Empire
    Christianity in, 274, 545
    and Crusades, 343, 345
    ecumenical movement in, 426–327
    inner Asian peoples in, 572–573

C

Cáceres, 523
Caddoan Indians, 850
    tribes of, 820
Cádiz, 523
Caduveo, 1029
Caesar, 371, 942–943
Caesaropapism, 274
Cahto Indians, 834
Cahullia Indians, 833
Caiaphas, 638
Cain, 67, 79, 182, 221
Caitanya, 143, 502, 504, 566, 579
caittadharma, 364
Cajetan, Cardinal Legate, 693
Cajetan, James, 156
Cakradhar, 709
cakrapuja, 1071
cakras, 499
cakravartin, 732
caksur-indriyayatana, 364
caksur-vijñanadhatu, 364
Calah, 724
Calcondylas, Demetrius, 515
Calendar Stone, 129
Calinescu, Matei, 388
Calixtus, Georg, 271, 517

Callaway, Henry, 30
calligraphy, Islamic, 547
Calliope, 478
Calumet Dance, 850
Calvary, 13
Calvin, John, 104, 156, 221–223, 271, 276, 899
    and ethics, 271
    and Reformation, 221–222, 924–925
    theology of, 222–223
Calvinism, 296, 740
Câmara, Dom Helder, 677
Camayrua, 1033
Cambodia
    Buddhism in, 202–203, 210, 674, 1101
    Khmer religion in, 674
Cambridge Platform, 319
Cambysees, 386
Camerarius, Joachim, 517
Cameroon, 355
Campbell, Alexander, 365
Campbell, Edward, 158
Campbell, Joseph, 453, 454
Campbell, Thomas, 365
Campus Martius, 943
Camunda, 540
Canaan, 11, 16, 616
Canaanite religion, 223–228
    deities, 224–225
    historical evidence, 223–224
    popular religion, 226–228
    rituals, 225–226
    survials, 228
Cancho Roano, 524
candalas, 492
Candelario, 524
Candi, 143, 450
Candi Kalasan, 134
Candrasuryapradipa, Tathagata, 419
Canella, 1031
Canelos Quichua, 789
cannabis indica, 99
cannibalism, 848, 963, 1028, 1029
canon
    of Hebrew scriptures, 159–162
    law, 228–230
    of New Testament, 172–173
    and prophecy, 903
Canon of Medicine, The (Ibn Sina), 526
Cantabrico, 524
Canterbury, Archbishop of, 70, 71
"Canticle of Brother Sun" (Francis of Assisi), 420
Cantors Institute, 322
Cao, Diogo, 29
Capacocha ceremony, 559
Cape Breton Islands, 809
Capitoline Jupiter, 340
Caracalla, 943
Carbon-14 dating, of megaliths, 720
Carey, William, 145, 753
cargo cults, 881
Carhuallo, 1018
Carhuincho, 1018
Carib religion, 230–232, 355
Caribbean religions, 230–237

    Afro-Caribbean, 233–236
    pre-Columbian, 230–232
caritas, 686
Carmelites, 1102–1103
Carmona, 523
Carmun, 241, 242
Carnell, Edward J., 401
Caroline Islands, 354
Carpini, Giovanni da Pien del, 574
Carrier, 833
Carus, Paul, 1051
Carvaka, 100
Cassander of Macedonia, 478
Cassirer, Ernst, 297, 1111–1112
Cassuto, Umberto, 948
caste system
    Balinese, 134–135
    Hindu, 134, 485, 490–492, 497, 502, 503, 1068
Castor, 431
Castulo, 523
Casuiareke, 792
Catal Hüyük, 791
Catalaunian Plain, Battle of, 572
catena, 155
Catena aurea (Aquinas), 155
Catequil, 1016
Cathari of Languedoc, 72, 575
Cathedral of Cologne, 545
Catherine of Alexandria, 642
Catherine of Aragon, 296, 925
Catherine of Siena, 237
Catholic Church of the Sacred Heart, 26
Catholic Church. *See* Roman Catholicism
catholicos, 794
Cathubodua, 243
cattari ariyasaccani, 417
catuhkayas, 134
catvary aryasatyani, 417
Caughey, James, 1
Cavazzi, Giovanni Antonio, 29
caves
    Hindu, 1082
    Minoan, 16
caw cam, 683
Cayönü, 791
Cayuga Indians, 811
Ceceaigi, 524
cedar of Lebanon, 340
Celestial Master sect of Taoism, 43, 49, 258–259, 263, 264, 1075
celibacy, 238–239, 253
    in Buddhism, 239
    chastity, 252–253
    in Judaism, 239, 253
    of priesthood, 239, 253, 900, 901
    as purification, 912
    rationale for, 238–239
    reasons for, 238
    in Roman Catholicism, 239
    and sexual norms, 239
    Shaker, 238, 239, 687
Cell Dara, 241
cella, 1088
Celtic religion, 239–244, 556, 880–881
    deities and gods, 241–243

Celtic religion *(continued)*
  goddesses, 243–244
  kings and heroes, 244
  writings on, 240
Celtis, Conradus, 516
cemanahuac, 128
Cenotaph, 90
Ceram, 354
Cerenaeici, 524
Ceres, 479
Cermont, Council of, 343
Cernunnos, 242, 524
Cerularios, Michael, 980
Cervantes, Miguel de, 517
Cesarini, Julian, 344
Chac, 533
chacs, 717
chado, 623
Chaeronea, 99
Chagall, Marc, 546
Chagga, 788
chalabhiñña, 95
Chalcedon. *See* Council of Chalcedon
Chalchiuhtlicue, 129, 534
Chaldean Oracles, 853, 945
Challis, W., 30
Chamacoco, 1027
*Le chamanisme et les techniques
    archaiques de l'extase* (Eliade),
    389
Chan Chan, 518
Ch`an monks, 625
Ch`an school of Buddhism, 209,
    260–261, 720, 783
  See also Zen Buddhism
Chandogya Upanisad, 341, 489,
    1044
Chang Chi-tsung, 263
Chang Ch`ien, 571
Chang Ling. *See* Chang Tao-ling
Chang Lu, 258
Chang Po-tuan, 262, 1078
Chang Tao-ling, 258, 542, 1077
Chang Tsai, 307–308
Chang-tzu, 255
Channing, William Ellery, 1142
chanting, 248–250
  in Africa, 30
  Armenian, 249
  in Australia, 553
  Byzantium, 249
  Gregorian, 249
  Hebrew, 248–249
  in India, 249
  North American Indian, 814
  of Qur'an, 249
  secular, 250
  in Tibet, 250
  Yakut, 1170
Chao Fu, 309
Chao Heng, 309
Chapata, 1100
Character of a Methodist, The
    (Wesley), 728
charis, 180, 459
charismata, 459
charity, 250–251, 649
  in Buddhism, 251

  in Christianity, 251
  in Greek religion, 250–251
  in Islam, 251
Charlemagne, 295, 573, 980
  extension of Christianity, 251–252
  and papacy, 274, 875
Charles, R.H., 167
Charles I, King of England, 914
Charles II, King of England, 914
Charles V, King of Germany, 924
Charles VII, King of France, 643
Charles University, 767
Charlesworth, James H., 167
charms. *See* Amulets
chastity, 252–253, 302
  in Buddhism, 252
  in Christianity, 253
  in Islam, 252
  in Judaism, 253
  See also celibacy
Chaupiñanca, 1016
Chavin, 1014, 1015, 1017, 1018
Chaza, Mai, 25, 734
cheironomic signs, 248
Chekiang school of Confucianism, 309
Chelcicky, Petr, 768
Cheme-huevi Indians, 833
Chemosh, 757
Ch`en, Kenneth, 746
Ch`en Tuan, 1076
Chen-kao, 1075
Chen-ta-tao sect, 1076
Chen-tsung, 1076
Chen-yen, 624
Ch`eng Hao, 308
Ch`eng I, 308–309
Cheng-i school of Taoism, 263
Cheng-meng (Chang Tsai), 307
cheng-ming, 316
Ch`eng-shih lun, 217
Chernobyl house, 472
Cherokee Indians, 414, 817, 850
Cherubim, 69, 70
Chesok, 679
Cheyenne Indians, 414, 820, 821, 824,
    850
ch`i, 258
chi wara, 23
Chia I, 256
chiao, 368, 543
Chiapas, 302, 533
chicha, 414
Chichén Itzá, 87
Chichimec, 126, 127, 128
Chief Peyote, 825
Ch`ien Mu, 317
Ch`ien-lung, 264
chien-mu tree, 340
Chih Tun, 260
Chih-i, 209, 261, 419
Chih-yen (Hu Hung), 309
Chilcotin Indians, 809, 832
childbirth
    couvade, 1023
    purification rites, 911
Children of God, 800, 802
Childs, Brevard S., 158
Chilula Indians, 834

Chin, 573
Ch`in-dynasty religion, 256, 306
chin-tan, 1078
China
    Cultural Revolution in, 205, 264,
        1107
    Hsiung-nu in, 571
    and Japan, 623–624
    Mongols in, 573, 574
    and scientific achievement, 982
    in Southeast Asia, 1035
    in Taiwan, 1057
    in Tibet, 1107
    Yüeh-chih in, 571
chinampas, 129
Chinese religions, 253–265
    afterlife in, 42–43
    alchemy in, 48–49
    ancestor worship in, 65, 254, 793
    archaeology of, 88
    Buddhism, 43, 194, 195, 205, 210,
        216–217, 257–258
    in Ch`in period, 256, 306
    in Ch`ing period, 264, 310
    in Chou period, 42, 253–254, 256
    Christianity, 753
    exorcism in, 407
    in Han period, 43, 256–257, 1078
    heaven and hell in, 476
    in Hsin period, 257
    immortality in, 555
    influence on Japan, 623
    Islam, 259–260, 586, 777
    Manichaeism, 259
    in Ming period, 263–264, 309
    in modern period, 264
    under Mongol rule, 262–263
    Neolithic, 793
    in Shang period, 42, 253
    soul in, 1010
    in Sung period, 261–262, 1055,
        1076, 1078
    Taiwanese, 264, 1056–1059
    in T`ang period, 259, 260–261, 306,
        1076
    in Yüan period (Mongols), 259, 261,
        262–263, 309, 893, 1076–1077
    Zoroastrianism, 259
    See also Buddhism, Chinese;
        Confucianism; Taoism
ching, 309
Ch`ing-dynasty religion, 264, 310, 893
Ching-te chuan-teng lu, 184
Ching-ti, 306
Chinggis Khan
    deification of, 267, 761
    empire of, 262, 573–574
    life of, 266–267
    and Mongol religion, 761
    and Taoism, 1076–1077
Chingichngish, 835–836
Chinookan Indians, 826
Chinul, 805
Chipewyan Indians, 808, 809
Chippewa Indians, 820
Chiriguano, 1027
Chitor, 45
Ch`iu Ch`ang-ch`un, 1076

Chiwere Indians, 820
Chogye-chong, 206
Chong Tojon, 314
Chong Yagyong, 315
Chong-nim-sa monastery, 1085
chora, 462
chorchen, 541
Chou Tun-i, 307, 308, 542, 1055, 1076
Chou-dynasty religion, 42, 253–254, 256
Christ
　origin of term, 727
　See also Jesus Christ
Christ, Carol, 454
Christ and His Salvation (Bushnell), 218
Christ in Theology (Bushnell), 218
Christian Association of Washington, 365
Christian Church (Disciples of Christ), 366
Christian Doctrine (Augustine of Hippo), 369
Christian Dogmatics (Barth), 141
Christian ethics, 267–271
　of Augustine, 106
　Eastern Orthodox, 268–269
　and moral reasoning, 764
　and philosophical ethics, 267–268
　Protestant, 270–271
　Roman Catholic, 269–270
　sources of, 268
Christian Faith, The (Schleiermacher), 79
Christian Gnosis (Baur), 435
Christian Methodist Episcopal Church, 731
Christian Mission, 188, 968
Christian Nurture (Bushnell), 218, 319
Christian Realism, 289
Christian Science, 285–287, 904
　development of, 286–287
　and Mary Baker Eddy, 285–287, 904
Christian Science Journal, The, 287
Christian Science Monitor, The, 286
Christian social movements, 287–290
Christianisme dévoilé (D'Holbach), 392
Christianity
　and Abraham, 12
　and Adam, 13
　African movements, 23–27, 1192
　in Afro-Caribbean religion, 234, 235, 974–975
　afterlife in, 37, 38, 39
　altar in, 56–57
　angels in, 69
　apocalypticism in, 81
　ascension in, 99
　atonement in, 104–105
　of Berbers, 147–148
　biblical canon (Hebrew scriptures), 161
　biblical exegesis (Hebrew scriptures), 154–158
　blasphemy in, 175–177
　blessing in, 180–181
　in Byzantine empire, 274
　canon law of, 228–230
　charity in, 251

and Charlemagne, 251–252
chastity in, 253
and community, 300
confession in, 303
covenant in, 339
cross in, 341–342
and David, 352
demons in, 360
doctrines of, 278–280
dogma of, 370
early, 100–101
　and atheism, 100–101
　canon law in, 228–229
　history of, 272–273, 281
　iconography of, 544–545
　missions of, 751–752
　and New Testament, 169–170
　post-Easter church, 439
　superstition in, 1050
ecumenical councils, 334–338, 638
ecumenical movements in, 277, 380, 382–383
ethics of, 267–271
and faith, 409–410, 940
fall concept in, 412
fasting in, 413, 414
and Gandhi, 428–429
and gnosticism, 69, 154, 435, 436–437
God in. *See* God, in Christianity
grace in, 279–280, 459
heaven and hell in, 475
iconography of, 544–546, 677
immortality in, 558
in India, 504, 566
in Japan, 626, 628–629
Lord's Prayer, 284, 438, 691–692
martyrdom in, 712, 713
and Marxism, 714–716
medieval
　Christology in, 638–639
　councils of, 335–337
　and Crusades, 275, 276, 343–345
　iconography of, 545
　and Inquisition, 575–576
　papacy, 274, 875–876
　schism in, 266, 274–275, 979–981
　superstition in, 1050–1051
meditation in, 718–719
messianism in, 727–728
ministry in, 739–741
miracles in, 742–743
missions in. *See* missions, Christian
mysticism in, 783–784
and Naziism, 186
in nineteenth century, 277
ordination in, 740, 741, 863, 901
post-Reformation, 277
predestination in, 424
redemption in, 271, 280, 640, 922, 941
repentance in, 934
resurrection in, 169, 172, 378, 439, 558, 638, 639–640, 935
retreat in, 937
in Roman empire, 273–274
sacraments of, 106, 283
　See also baptism; Eucharist

sacrifice in, 182, 399
sainthood in, 966–967
Satan in, 977
schism in. *See* schism, in Christianity
and science, 70, 325–326, 427–428, 983
social movements of, 287–290
soul in, 1012–1013
spiritual guide in, 1044
Ten Commandments in, 284, 1092
theology of, 140–141
in twentieth century, 277–278
underworld in, 1135
way of life, 283–284
worship in, 281–283
　See also Christian ethics; Eastern Christianity; Jesus Christ; New Testament; Protestantism; Reformation; Roman Catholicism
Christianity Today, 401
Christianizing the Social Order (Rauschenbusch), 277
Christianopolis (Andrea), 54
Christmas, 290, 635
Christmas Conference, 730
Christology, development of, 638–639
Christos, 727
Christos-Kruios, 440
Christus Victor, 104
Chronicles, 160, 162, 166, 351
Chronicles of Japan, 668
Chrysippus, 478
Chrysoloras, Manuel, 515
Chrysopolis, 323
Chrysostom, John, 691
Chu Hsi, 65, 308–309, 310, 312, 314, 627, 680, 1056
Chu Yüan-chang, 262, 263
Chu-tzu chia-li, 65, 680
Ch'uan fa-pao chi, 183
Ch'üan-chen sect of Taoism, 261–262, 263, 1076
Chuang-tzu, 43, 291, 306
　and Taoist thought, 291
Chuang-tzu (text), 255, 291, 1074
Chukchi, 92, 93, 788
Chulalongkorn, 202, 203
Chulupi, 1028–1029
Chumash Indians, 833
chumeia, 53
Ch'un-ch'iu, 315, 317
chün-tzu, 254, 305, 317
chung, 305, 307
Chung-shu, 306
Ch'ungson, 313
church, architecture, 90, 91
Church of Christ, Scientist, 286
Church of Cyprus, 460
Church Dogmatics (Barth), 691
Church of England. *See* Anglican church
church government, 281, 292–294
　Anglican, 293
　congregational form, 91, 293–294, 319
　Eastern Orthodox, 292–293
　episcopal form, 292–293
　Episcopalian, 293

church government (continued)
    Methodist, 293
    presbyterial form, 293
    Roman Catholic, 292
    See also Church and state
Church of Greece, 460
Church of the Holy Sepulcher, 636
Church of Jesus Christ of Latter-Day
    Saints, 770–771
Church of the Lord Aladura, 27
Church of San Vitale, 545
Church of Santa Maria Materdomini,
    73
Church of Scientology, 800, 802
church and state, 294–297, 906–907
    and Germanic kingdoms, 295
    Papal revolution, 295
    and personal autonomy, 297
    and Reformation, 295–296
    and Roman Empire, 294–295
    treaties, 196
Church in Wales, 71
Churches of Christ, 365, 366
Churches of North and South India, 731
Ciboney religion, 230
Cicero, 320, 514, 515, 942, 1050, 1095
Cihuacoatl, 1121
Cimmerians, 571
Circe, 478
circumcision, 12, 302
    in Africa, 22
    Australian Aboriginal, 111, 112,
        113–114, 1159–1160
    blood and, 113–114, 182
    female, 22, 182
    in Judaism, 649
Cisneros, Jiménez de, 517
Cistercians, 760, 783
cities, ancestor myths of founding, 67
Citizens Freedom Foundation, 579
citta-mahabhumika, 364
citta-samprayuk-tasamskara, 364
City of David, 636
City of God (Augustine), 39, 273,
    549–550
City of Jehova, 734
City Missionary Societies, 288
civil rights movement
    black church in, 35, 675–676
    in United States, 675–676
Civil War, 35
Civilization and Its Discontents (Freud),
    425
Claret, Anthony M., 937
Clarke, James Freeman, 1092
Classic of Change. See Book of
    Changes (I ching); I ching
Claudius, Emperor, 451, 943, 945
Clea, 945
cledonomancy, 859
Clement V, Pope, 336, 876, 980
Clement VII, Pope, 156, 237, 876, 877,
    980–981
Clement XII, Pope, 423
Clement XIV, Pope, 877
Clement of Alexandria, 69, 70, 97, 155,
    437, 549, 719, 728
Clement of Rome, 397

Clementine Homilies, 180
Clergy and Laity Concerned about
    Vietnam, 289
Clermont, Council of, 343
clitoridectomy, 182
    in Africa, 22
Cluny, 575, 760
Coaibai, 231
Coatlicue, 129
Coatrischio, 231
Cochamama, 1016
Cocijo, 533
codana, 738
Code of Canon Law, 229, 405, 878,
    1148
Codex Alexandrinus, 164, 174
Codex Askewianus, 434
Codex Benzae Cantabrigensis, 174
Codex Borgia, 128
Codex Brucianus, 434
Codex Cologne Mani, 80
Codex Ephraemi Rescriptus, 174
Codex Fuldensis, 955
Codex iuris canonici, 229, 230
Codex Koridethi, 174
Codex Mandaean, 702
Codex Regius, 174
Codex Sinaiticus, 164, 165, 173, 174
Codex Theodosianus, 946
Codex Vaticanus, 164, 165, 174
Codex Washingtoniensis, 174
Codrington, R.H., 795, 854
Coeur d'Alene Indians, 833
Coffin Texts, 385
cofradias, 718
Cohen, Arthur A., 513
Cohen, Gerson D., 322
Cohen, Hermann, 297–298, 660, 947,
    1043
    influence of, 298
    writings of, 297–298
cohiba, 232
Cohn, Norman, 78, 881
coincidentia oppositorum, 389, 516
Cóir Anmann, 240
Coke, Thomas, 729
Coleridge, Samuel, 320
Colet, John, 517
collective unconscious, 70
Colloquia familiaria (Erasmus), 394, 517
Colloquy of Worms, 924
Collur Riti festival, 1018
Cologne Mani Codex, 80
Colonia, Simon da, 48
Colored Methodist Episcopal Church,
    730–731
Colossians, 173, 174, 180
Colville Indians, 832, 833
Comanche Indians, 820, 824
Comarius, 51
Comenius, Johannes Amos, 768
Commagene, 479
Commedia (Dante), 350
Commentaria Bibliorum (Pellikan), 156
Commentariolus (Copernicus), 325
Commentary on John (Origen), 155
Commentary on the Mishnah
    (Maimonides), 41, 700

Commission on Appraisal, 1142
Commission on Jewish Education, 322
Committee on Jewish Laws and
    Standards, 322
"Common Declaration," 72
communion
    and eremitism, 395
    principle of, 940
Communion. See Eucharist
communism, 715–716
community, 191, 298–300
    characteristics of, 298–299
    Christian, 300
    of faith, 410
    Jewish, 648–649
    and Judaism, 191
    monastic, 301
    nation as, 299–300
    natural and specific, 299–301
    sacred, 932
    sense of in religion, 932
Community of the Pious, 865–866
Complaint of Peace (Erasmus), 394
Complete English Dictionary (Wesley),
    729
Complutensian Polyglot Bible, 517
Comte, Auguste, 30
Con-Ticsi-Viracocha, 560
Conaire Mór, 244
Concerning the Spiritual in Art
    (Kandinsky), 546
Concho Indians, 837
Concise Statement of the Creeds (al-
    Hilli), 595
Conclusiones (Pico della Mirandola),
    516
Concordat of Worms, 295
Concordia discordantium canonum
    (Gratian), 229
Condatis, 242
Condor Dance, 833
Conference of 1755, 729
Conferences of 1711–1747, 729
confession of sins, 301–303, 385, 954
    in Christianity, 934
    in Islam, 934
    in Judaism, 933–934
    in nonliterate cultures, 301–302
    as repentance, 933
    as sacrament, 283
Confessions (Augustine of Hippo),
    105
Confucianism, 304–315
    ancestor worship in, 65
    Ch'in suppression of, 256, 306
    Confucius's teachings in, 254–255,
        304–305
    cosmology, 307
    and faith, 409
    Han scholarship, 256–257
    Hsün-tzu's teachings in, 255,
        305–306
    in Japan, 312–313, 626, 627, 628,
        997
    in Korea, 313–315
    Meng-tzu's teachings in, 255,
        305–306, 308
    Mo-tzu's teachings in, 255

modern, 311, 313, 628
Neo-Confucianism, 262, 307–311, 746
New Text school, 257
Old Text school, 257
sainthood in, 967
and science, 982
spirit-writing cults in, 263–264
t'ai-chi in, 308, 1055–1056
in T'ang period, 306
temple compounds in, 1087
in Vietnam, 1154
Confucius, 304–305, 315–316, 542
biography of, 315–317
disciples of, 317
influence of, 317–318
and Lao-tzu, 684
teachings of, 254–255, 304–305, 317–318
works of, 304, 316, 317, 409
Congregatio de Propaganda Fide, 629
congregational worship, 91
Congregationalism, 293–294, 319
beliefs and practices, 319
development of, 319
Congress of Vienna, 877
Conla, 243
Conrad III, 344
Conrad, Joseph, 320
conscience, 320–321
versus consciousness, 320
and *dharma*, 362
and ethical systems, 320–321
origin of concept, 320
Conservative Judaism, 321–323, 657
organizatons, 322
origins and development of, 321–322
Constance, Council of, 768, 876
Constantine I (Constantine the Great), 90, 164, 323–324, 334
Christian conversion of, 273–274, 323–324
ecumenical movement of, 326–327
and Jerusalem, 636
Constantine V (Byzantine Emperor), 335
Constantine IX (Byzantine Emperor), 980
Constantinople, 164, 378, 379
council of. *See* Council of Constantinople
and Crusades, 276, 344
fall of, 275, 344, 515, 752
Karaite community, 669
patriarchate of, 460
Constitution on the Church, 878
Constitutional Revolution of 1905–1909, 608
Constitutions of 1723, 422
Consultation on Church Union, 741
Contendings of Horus and Seth, The, 386, 583, 868
Contra Julianum (Augustine of Hippo), 106
Conventicle Acts of 1664 and 1670, 915
convents, Carmelite, 1102–1103
conversion, 324–325
to Christianity, 753–754

dimensions of, 324
meaning of, 324, 933
types of, 324–325
See also Missions
convince ritual, in Jamaica, 234–235
Convivio (Dante), 350
Conzelmann, Hans, 158
Cook, Michael, 612
Cop, Nicholas, 222
Copán, 87, 554
Copernicus, Nicolaus, 325–326, 427
Copernican revolution, 70, 326
life of, 326–327
Coptic church, 326–327, 379, 1139
and ecumenism, 326, 327
missionaries, 327
monasticism, 327
Corbin, Henry, 611
Cordova, 524, 525
Coricancha, 559, 560
Corinth, 460
Corinthians, 171, 173, 174, 251, 339, 412, 436, 437, 439, 440, 458, 549
Cormac mac Airt, 244
Corn Dance, 846
Corn Mother, 1005
Coronado, Vasquez de, 846
Corpus Hermeticum, 853
Corpus iuris canonici, 229, 230
Correcting Youthful Ignorance (Chang Tsai), 307
Correction of the Intellect (Spinoza), 1042
Cosmic Buddha Mahavairocana, 562
cosmogony
in Africa, 375
Australian Aboriginal, 1137
Aztec, 127
Cuna, 346
and fall concept, 410, 411
Iranian, 581–582
meaning of, 66
cosmology, 328–330
in Africa, 375
in archaic traditions, 330
Australian Aboriginal, 107–108, 1137
Aztec, 127–128
Babylonian, 330
in Buddhism, 193, 329
characteristics of, 329
Chinese, 1073
Confucian, 307
and Copernican revolution, 70
cultural themes in
earth diver, 328, 329
monotheistic, 328–329
world parents, 329
Cuna, 346–347
in Egypt, 330
Greek, 1134
Hermopolitan, 1105
in Hinduism, 329, 475, 1069
Inca, 559
Indo-European, 567–568
Iranian, 582
in Jainism, 329, 620
Khoisan, 675

Mapuche religion, 706–707
New Guinean, 797
North American Indian, 329, 531, 811–812, 817, 838–839
and scientific views, 329–330
Shinto, 996
South American Indian, 1020, 1027, 1029
Turkic, 1129–1130
Yakut, 1169
Cosmos and History (Eliade), 390
Cost of Discipleship, The (Bonhoeffer), 186, 283
Costig, 523
Coualina, 231
Coulanges, Fustel de, 66
Coulson, Noel J.A., 611
Council of Cermont, 343
Council of Chalcedon, 279, 327, 334, 335, 379, 397, 563
authority of Pope, 875
Christology of, 279, 335, 563, 638
and Church schism, 327, 379, 397, 979
Council of Clermont, 343
Council of Constance, 768, 876
Council of Constantinople, 1123
First, 334, 379
Fourth, 336
Second, 279, 335
Third, 335, 638
on Trinity, 941
Council of Ephesus, 326, 334–335, 379, 460, 545, 794
condemnation of Nestorius, 794, 979
Council of Frankfort, 980
Council of the Hands of the Cause, 132
Council of Laodicea, 181
Council of Liberal Churches, 1143
Council of Lyons, 336, 574, 876
Council of Nicaea, 279, 326, 379
Christology of, 279, 334, 563, 638, 1123
First, 273, 274, 279, 323–324, 334, 563
Nicene Creed, 176, 275, 279, 324, 334, 899, 980
Second, 335, 379
Council of Reims, 575
Council of Siena, 876
Council of Toledo, on Satan, 978
Council of Toulouse, 575
Council of Tours, 575
Council of Trent, 166, 229, 276, 282, 337, 546, 877
anti-Protestantism, 925
canons and decrees of, 229, 276, 337
on Eucharist, 546
on iconography, 546
on justification by faith, 280
on repentance, 934
on sacraments, 940
Council of Vienne, 336, 576, 876, 955
Councils, Buddhist, 331–334
ancient councils, 331–333
modern councils, 333–334

Councils, Christian, 334–338
    and Christology, 279, 334–335, 563,
        638–639
    and Church schism, 327, 379, 397
    early, 334–335
    ecumenical, 334–338, 379
    medieval, 335–337
    in modern period. *See* Vatican
        Council, First; Vatican Council,
        Second and Reformation, 337
    See also individual councils by
        name
Counterfeit Doctrine, 732
Cours de philosophie positive (Comte),
    30
couvade, 1023
Covenant, 338–339
    of Abraham, 11–12
    blood and, 182
    in Christianity, 339
    concept of, 338
    with Israelites, 338, 615, 616
    at Qumran, 339
    in Rabbinic Judaism, 646
covenant, term, 615
Cowdery, Oliver, 1006
Coya, 560
Coyote, 531, 821–822, 1120
Cranach, Lucas, 908
crastinus, 691
Crawley, A.E., 74
creation myth
    in Africa, 19, 20, 375, 527
    Australian Aboriginal, 1137
    and flood, 414–415
    in Hinduism, 190
    Indo-European, 567–568
    marriage in, 711
    North American Indian, 822–823,
        828–829, 839
    Tunguz, 1126
creationism, 1012
Cree Indians, 809, 820, 821
Creek Indians, 819, 850
cremation ritual
    of Buddha, 892
    Hittite, 511
    North American Indian, 554
Crescas, Hasdai, 41, 152
Creswell, K.A.C., 611
Crete, 14, 378, 460, 885
    Minoan religion in, 15–17
Crimea, 574
Criterion Group, 388
Critique of Practical Reason (Kant),
    101
Critique of Pure Reason (Kant), 101
Cromwell, Oliver, 914, 915
Crone, Patricia, 612
cross, 340–342
    Christian, 341–342, 636
    non-Christian, 340–341
    symbolism of, 340–342
Cross Fire ceremony, 824
Cross, Frank Moore, 353
Crow Indians, 820, 822, 850
Crown of the Torah, 670
Crucified God, The (Moltmann), 640

Crucifixion of Jesus, 341, 342, 438,
    545–546, 638, 712
cruciform tombs, 721
Crusades, 275, 276, 343–346, 512, 653
    causes of, 343
    First through Eighth, 343–344
    Muslim view, 345–346
    outcome, 344–345
cuauhxicalli, 129
Cuba, 34
    Santería in, 234, 974–975
Cucuteni, 721
cult, use of term, 800
Cult of the Hand, 527
cults
    Aboriginal, 122–123, 124–125
    Afro-Caribbean, 233–235
    Arctic, 93
    Baltic, 136
    Bantu, 246, 247, 577, 578
    Canaanite, 225–226
    as community, 300
    deprogramming, 325
    in Europe, 802
    Greek, 462–463, 464–465
    Inca, 560
    Israelite, 615
    Javanese, 632
    Mesopotamian, 726–727
    mystery, 509
    Neolithic, 791
    North American Indian, 834, 835,
        843–844
    in United States, 800–801
    Zuni, 843–844
Cultural Revolution, 205, 264, 1107
culture hero, 809, 847–848
    African, 20
    ancestory myths, 66–67
    Celtic, 244
    of North American Indians, 809,
        847–848
    in South Africa, 1040
    of South American Indians, 1015,
        1028, 1030–1031
Cuna religion, 346–347
    cosmology and cosmogony, 346–347
    morality in, 347
    and Spaniards, 347
Cupeño Indians, 833
Cur Deus homo (Anselm of
    Canterbury), 104, 639
curanderos, 1018, 1164
Curia Romana, 292, 337, 693, 877, 980
Cusicilenses, 524
Cutha, 726
Cuzco, 559–560
Cybele, 451, 550, 887, 944
Cycladic religion, 14, 15
Cynics, 478
Cyprian, 281, 549
Cyriacus of Ancona, 515
Cyril of Alexandria, 275, 326, 327
    on Jesus, 334–335
    and non-Chalcedonian churches,
        379, 397–398
Cyril of Jerusalem, 181, 690
Cyrus II, Great King of Persia, 97, 635

D
daal, 108
Dabra Libanos, Monastery of, 398
Dacians, 388
Dade, 1161
Dadhyañc, 570
Dadmish, 225
Dagai, 553
Dagan, 224, 885
Daghdha, 241
Dagon, 885
Dai, 49
Daigoji temples, 1085
daikonein, 739
daimon, 359
daimonion, 461
Dainichi, 626
Dairi Batak, 142
Daitokuji temple, 1185
daivas, 581
Dakota Indians, 341, 414, 820
Daksinamurti, 540
daksinas, 487
dalai, 349
Dalai Lama, 349, 1107
    flight of, 349
    incarnation of, 349
Dali, Salvador, 546
Dalmata, Hermannus, 955
Daly, Mary, 446, 1166, 1167
Damascius, 456
Damascus, 85, 339, 344, 379, 774,
    776
Damascus I, Pope, 875
Dambala, 233
Damietta, 344, 420
Damona, 241
Dan, 616
dana, 185, 496, 620
dance societies, 829
dances
    in Africa, 528, 577
    Afro-Caribbean, 233, 234
    Caribbean, 231
    in India, 216, 408
    North American Indian, 814,
        832–833, 834, 841–842
        Ghost Dance, 824
        Sun Dance, 823–824
    in Polynesia, 1109
    Shaker, 990
    South American Indian, 1022, 1031,
        1032
    Tunguz, 1127
Dancing Religion, 734
danda, 491
Daniel, 166–167, 644, 645
Daniel, 160, 162, 165, 166
Daniélou, Jean, 1096
Danil, 227
Danish Church Ordinance of 1539, 296
Danish-namah-i `Ala'i (Ibn Sina), 526
Danites, 688
danka, 630
Dante Alighieri, 99, 350
dar al-harb, 599
dar al-Islam, 599

Dar al-Qibt, 327
dar al-sulh, 599
daragu, 113
Daramulun, 115
Darby, John Nelson, 401
Dargon and Tiger Mountain, 1076
Darius I, 697
Darkhei ha-Mishnah (Frankel), 468
darsana, 368, 497, 498, 719
  concept of, 492–493
Darstantikas, 212
Daruma. *See* Bodhidharma
Darwin, Charles, 277, 403, 404, 983
  religious responses to, 403–404
Darzu mate, 137
dasa, 485, 570
Dasabhumika Sutra, 185
dasanami, 500
Dasgupta, Surendranath, 387
dasyu, 485, 570
Datagaliwabe, 798
Datta, 709, 710
Dattatreya, 709
datu, 142
Datwún, 707
David, 350–352, 635, 646
  and Christianity, 352
  court history, 351
  and Islam, 352
  psalms of, 908–909
  in Scriptures, 351–352
David, Christian, 769
Da`wah, al-Islamiyah, al-, 781
Dawn, The, 715
Dawn Woman, 840
Dawn Youths, 840
Day of Atonement (Yom Kippur), 103,
    226, 413, 647, 649
Day of Judgment. *See* Last Judgment
Day of Visitation, 915
Days of Awe, 934
dbyans, 250
De, Abhay Charan. *See* Bhaktivedanta,
    Swami A. C.
De doctrina Christiana (Augustine of
    Hippo), 155
De errore profanorum religionum
    (Firmicus Maternus), 549
De Groot, J.J.M., 407
De intellectus emendatione (Spinoza),
    1042
De libero arbitrio (Augustine of Hippo),
    106
De libero arbitrio (Erasmus), 393
De monarchia (Dante), 350
De motu (Galileo), 427
De natura deorum (Cicero), 1095
De peccatorum meritis et remissione
    (Augustine of Hippo), 106
De religione Christiana (Ficino), 516
De revolutionibus orbium caelestium
    (Copernicus), 326, 427
De vera religione (Augustine of Hippo),
    105
De vita contemplativa, 549
De vulgari eloquentia (Dante), 350
de-oraita, 468
Dea Artio, 242

Dead Sea scrolls, 81, 88, 167, 338,
    339, 352–353, 457
  canon of, 160–161
  categories of, 352–353
  dating of, 352
  on immortality, 557
  Letter of Jeremiah, 166
  and Qumran sect, 82, 353, 413–
    414
  Satan in, 977
  on Ten Commandments, 1092
death, 353–355
  ancestor myths, 67
  concept of, 353–355
  in flood myths, 415
  geographies of, 40
  Inuit view of, 580
  New Caledonian view, 795, 796
  Oceanic view of, 354, 854–855, 911
  Phoenician cult of, 887
  as polluting, 911
  Samoyed view of, 972
  Tunguz view of, 1128
  Turkic view of, 1129
  See also afterlife; heaven and hell;
    immortality; underworld
Death, Property, and the Ancestors
    (Goody), 64
death ritual
  in Africa, 20, 22, 376, 553, 1040
  Afro-Caribbean, 234
  Ainu, 44
  and ancestor myth, 67
  and ancestor worship, 63
  Australian Aboriginal, 110–111, 117,
    529
  Balinese, 135
  in Borneo, 189
  Buddhist, 196
  Canaanite, 226
  Caribbean, 231
  Chinese, 257
  in Egypt, 38, 385, 537, 538, 555
  Greek, 462
  Hittite, 511
  Iberian, 523
  Inca, 555
  Israelite, 556
  in Korea, 680
  of Magi, 697–698
  Mapuche, 707
  Maya, 554, 717
  in megalithic religion, 721, 898
  Neolithic, 792
  New Guinean, 798
  North American Indian, 554, 813,
    818, 822, 833–834, 845
  Oceanic, 855
  Paleolithic, 869
  Phoenician, 887
  Samoyed, 972
  Sarmatian, 976–977
  Scythian, 987–988
  South American Indian, 1018, 1024,
    1033
  Southeast Asian, 1038
  Tunguz, 1128
  Turkic, 1131

  Vietnamese, 1154
  voodoo, 1156
Decalogue. *See* Ten Commandments
Decameron (Boccaccio), 515
decapitation, 1018
Decisive Treatise, The (Ibn Rushd),
    525
Declaration and Address (Campbell),
    365
Dee, John, 421
Deen, Wallace (Warithuddin
    Muhammad), 36
Deer Park at Sarnath, 417, 892
Deerskin Dance, 834
Deggwa, 397
Deghiha Indians, 820
Dei filius, 337, 877, 1146
deities, 356–359
  Ainu, 44
  and anthropomorphism, 77
  Aramean, 86
  Arctic, 93, 580
  Australian Aboriginal, 108, 111,
    114–115
  Canaanite, 224–225
  Caribbean, 230–231, 232
  Celtic, 240–244
  concept of, 356–359
  East African, 375–376
  Germanic, 430–433
  Hawaiian, 474
  Hindu, 503, 540
  Hittite, 510
  and human consciousness, 358
  Indo-European, 567
  Marathi, 709–710
  Mayan, 717–718
  Mesopotamian, 536
  Moabite, 757–758
  North American Indian, 840
  Phoenician, 886–887
  Saami, 952
  Samoyed, 971–972
  Slavic, 1004–1005
  structure of, 356–358
  use of term, 356
  See also goddesses; gods
Delaware Indians, 531, 532, 811, 813,
    847
Delos, 479
Delphi, 451, 463, 478, 479, 539
Demeter, 451, 463, 479
demons, 359–361
  Ainu, 44
  Balinese, 135
  in Buddhism, 359–360
  Canaanite, 226
  in Christianity, 360
  Hellenistic, 477–478, 1164
  in Hinduism, 359, 487
  in India, 407
  in Islam, 360–361
  in Judaism, 360
  modern view, 361
  South American Indian, 1027
  in tribal cultures, 359
denawa, 632
Dendid, 30

dendrophoria, 182
Dengdit, 30
Denjutsu isshin kaimon (Kojo), 184
Denk, Hans, 60
Department of Youth Activities, 322
Dependent Co-origination, 929
Der Stern der Erlösung (Rosenzweig), 947
derabbanan, 468
derash, 151, 153
Derozio, Henry, 144
Desaguliers , John Theophilus, 422
Desána, 415
Descartes, 406
Descent of Man, The (Darwin), 277
Desna, 66
Deus, 626
Deuteronomy, 159, 162, 248, 512, 548, 615, 616, 617, 662, 687, 772, 1114
deva, 359, 485, 565, 996, 1000
Devadatta, 481
devequt, 471, 472, 473
Devi, images of, 540–541
Devi, Sarada, 144
devil, 104, 977
    See also demons; Satan
Devils's Point, 855
Devimahatmyam, 498, 499, 503
déwa yajña, 134
dewata, 632
Dewi Sri, 632
dexiosis, 179
Dexter Avenue Baptist Church, 675
deywo-s, 567
Dge-lugs-pa, 483
Dhammacakkappavattana Sutta, 417, 418
Dhammaceti, 1100
Dhammadhuta program, 203
Dhammodhara, Punnacara, 145
dhanya, 179
dharana, 494, 742
dharma, 331, 361–364, 419, 497, 564
    authoritative sources of, 362
    in Buddhism, 185, 193, 197, 363–364
    concept of, 197–198, 251, 361, 363
    in Hinduism, 100, 149, 251, 361–362, 490–492
    Mimamsa on, 738
    types of, 361–362, 363–364
Dharmaguptakas, 212
Dharmakara, 185
dharmakaya, 215, 562
Dharmaminimsa. *See* Mimamsa
dharman, 361
Dharmapala, Anagarika, 198
Dharmasutras, 490, 492
Dharmavinayasamadhi Sutra, 214
Dharmottariyas, 212
dhat Allah, 448
dhatu, 364
dhatuvada, 50
dhi, 485
dhikr, 918, 1047–1048, 1082
dhimmis, 794
Dhu al-Hijjah, 891, 892

dhutanga, 414
dhyana, 185, 363, 494, 496, 720, 742
Dhyani Buddhas, 216
Diagram of the Ultimate, 542
diakonia, 739
Dialogue, The (Catherine of Siena), 237
Dialogue of the Savior, 437
Dialogue with Trypho (Mustin Martyr), 717
Dialogue on the Two Great World Systems (Galileo), 428
Dialogues concerning Natural Religion (Hume), 77
Diamond Mandala, 789
Diamond Vehicle, 208, 215
Dian Cécht, 241
Dianetics, 802
Diaspora, 78, 322
Diatessaron (Tatian), 955
diatheke, 339
Dibelius, Martin, 157
Dibon, 758
Dictates of the Pope (Gregory VII), 295, 336
Didache, 690
Didascalia Apostolorum, 397
Diderot, Denis, 392
didjeridu, 112
Didymus, 155
Diegueño, 531
Dieri, 115–116, 117
Diet of Speyer, 923
dietary laws, 911
Dietrich, John, 1142
Dievs, 136
Digambaras, 619–620
dikkah, 773, 776
diksa, 50, 487, 488, 498
diksita, 488
Diktaean Cave, 16
Diktynna, 17
Din-i-ilahi, 45, 46
Dingari, 112–113
Dinka, 20, 30, 375, 376, 377
Dinnshenchas, 240
Dinon, 699
Diocletian, 323, 944
Diodorus Siculus, 742
Diogenes Laertius, 945
Dionysius of Areopagite, 70, 516, 616, 1103
Dionysos, 99, 478, 562
    cult of, 15, 17, 464, 479
    incarnate, 562
    Nietzsche on, 478
Diosalia, 347
Dioscrous I, 326
Dipavamsa, 331, 333
directions, Pueblo worlds, 839
Dis Pater, 242
Disciples of Christ, 365–366, 905
Discipline Sutras, 214
Discourse on Comets (Galileo), 428
Discourse on Happiness (La Mettrie), 392
Discourses Concerning Two New Sciences (Galileo), 428

Dissenters' Chapels Act, 1142
Distant Sanctuary, 636
Ditan, 227
Divali, 143
Divan, The (Nasir-i Khusraw), 787
Divina institutiones (Cyprian), 549
divination, 366–367
    African, 21, 528, 577, 692, 1040, 1180
    Canaanite, 227
    Caribbean, 232
    Hellenistic, 478
    Iberian, 524
    in Korea, 680
    intuitive type, 366
    meaning of, 366
    Oceanic, 855
    and oracles, 859
    possession type, 367
    and priesthood, 901
    in Santería, 975
    South American Indian, 1018
    in Tibet, 1107
    wisdom type, 366
Divine Light Mission, 736–737, 800, 802
Divine Principle (Sun Myung Moon), 1140, 1141
divinities. *See* goddesses; gods
Divona, 242
diwan, 774
Djakarta, 586
Djanggawul, 111
Djenné Mosque, 777
djugurba, 108
Djunggawon, 110
do, 623
Dober, Leonard, 769
doctrine, 368–369
    comparative view, 368–369
    and theology, 369
Doctrine of Addai, 793
Doctrine and Covenants (Smith), 770, 1006
Doctrine of the Elders, 208
Doctrine of the Mean, 305, 306
Dodecanese, 460
Dodona, 340, 463
dogma, 370
    and Christianity, 370
    meaning of, 370
Dogmatic Constitution of the Church, 1149
Dogon, 67, 178, 341, 355, 507, 527, 735, 1161
Dogrib Indians, 808
Doi Suthep, 893
Dolaha Deviyo, 1000
Dolboniki, 1126
Dolbonitki, 1126
Dolci, Danilo, 430
Dolgan, 92, 93
dolmens, 720, 793
Dome of the Rock, 90, 636
Domestic and Foreign Missionary Society, 71
Dominicans, 46, 79
    and Inquisition, 575

Dominions, 69, 70
Don Quixote (Cervantes), 517
Donation of Pépin, 875
Donn, 242
Dordrecht Confession of Faith of 1632, 723
Dorylaeum, 343
Dosa', Hanina'ben, 742
Dostoevskii, Fedor, 277, 320, 406
Dothan, Trude, 885
Douglas, John Henry, 915
Douglas, Mary, 245, 733
Dowie, John Alexander, 25
dragon, Maya, 533
Dragon of Colchis, 478
Dragon King God, 679
Draupadi, 498
Dravidian, 484
Dream Dance, 814
dreams
    in Australian Aboriginal religion, 108, 114, 553, 1137, 1159, 1160
    in North American Indian religion, 810
    in South American Indian religion, 1029
Drew, Timothy (Noble Drew Ali), 36
drstadharma-vedaniya-karman, 673
drug rituals
    in Caribbean religion, 232
    in Hawaiian religion, 474
    North American Indian, 824–826, 833, 835, 912
    South American Indian, 1018
druids, 242, 371–372
    Caesar's account of, 371
    spiritual authority, 371–372
Drum Dance, 814
drumming
    in Africa, 577
    Afro-Caribbean, 235
    in China, 407
    North American Indian, 810, 814, 825
Druze, 596, 994
Du culte des dieux fétiches (Brosses), 30
Dua, 110, 111
du`ah, 596
dualism, 372–373
    apocalyptic concept of, 83
    in Southeast Asia, 1037–1038
    theistic, 763
    types of, 372–373
    Zoroastrian, 373, 703
dueri, 934
duhkha, 363, 364, 418
dumar, 108
Dumézil, 432
Dumuzi, 725
Dumuzi-Abzu, 726
Dunatis, 242
Duns Scotus, 275, 421
Dupáde, 1026
Dürer, Albrecht, 516
Durga, 143, 484, 500, 503, 565, 1072
Durkheim, Émile, 74, 75, 381
    on sacred, 959

Dussera, 502
Dusun, 189
Duties of the Heart (Paquda), 151, 653
Dutthagamani, 1099
Duvalier, François, 234
duyu, 108
Dvaita Vedanta, 501, 502
Dvaitadvaita, 1153
dvapara, 880
dvaparayuga, 495, 496
dvija, 487
Dyaus-pitr, 462, 569
Dyer, Mary, 915
Dynamics of Faith (Tillich), 1110
Dzungars, 574

E

Ea, 340, 536
Eagle Dance, 833
eagle trapping, 822
Eana, 725
earth diver, cosmology of, 328, 329
earth goddess, 242, 789
Earth Lodge religion, 835
Earthmaker, 811
Earu fields, 40
East African religions, 375–377
    deities, 375–376
    evil, attributions for, 376
    myths in, 375
    prophetic movements, 376–377
East African Revival Movement, 26
East Syrian church, 379
Easter, 138
    festival of, 378
    in New Testament, 438–439
    preparation for, 413
Easter Bunny, 378
Eastern Christianity, 378–380
    baptism in, 138
    chanting in, 249
    Coptic, 326–327, 379, 1139
    councils of, 335–336
    Eastern Orthodox church, 268–269, 292–293, 378–379
    in ecumenical movement, 380, 382
    ethics of, 268–269
    Ethiopian church, 379, 397–398
    Greek Orthodox church, 460
    iconography of, 545
    in modern period, 379–380
    Nestorian church, 379, 793–794
    Russian Orthodox church, 268, 276–277, 378, 949–950
    and schism, 274–275, 276, 740, 875, 979–981
    separated churches, 379
    spiritual guide in, 1044
    spread of, 752
    Uniate churches, 379, 1138–1139
Eastern Sacred Peaks, 43, 1086
Ebabbar, 725
Ebla, 757, 885
Ebla tablets, 88
Ecatl, 127
Eccel, A.C., 611
Ecclesiastes, 160, 161, 163, 617, 651
Ecclesiastical Regulation, 949

Eck, Johannes, 480, 693
Eckhart, Johannes, 47, 783, 1125
Eclipse of God (Buber), 191
Eclogue (Vergil), 960
ecstasy, 380–382, 960, 1046
    approaches to study of, 381–382
    and ascension, 98
    meaning of, 380–381
Ecstasy of Religious Trance (Arbman), 382
ecumenical councils, 334–338, 379, 638
ecumenical creeds, 382
Ecumenical Methodist Conference, 731
ecumenical movements, 382–383
    in Africa, 27
    in Byzantine empire, 326–327
    Christian, 277, 380, 382–383
    unresolved issues, 383
`Edah Haredit, 865–866
Édaín Echraidhe, 242
edan, 528, 529
Eddy, Mary Baker, 285–287, 904
Eden. See Garden of Eden
Edessa, 86, 343, 344
Edfu, 386
Edict of Fontainebleau, 296
Edict of Milan, 326, 871
Edict of Nantes, 296, 925, 990
edin, 725
Edo, 64, 527, 894, 928
Edom, 351, 614
`edot, 471
Edwards, Jonathan, 319
Eengura, 725
Efe/Gelede festival, 528
Effendi, `Abbas, 131, 133
efod, 548
Efrayim of Luntshits, 152
Egba, 528
Egbado, 528
Egishnugal, 725
Église de Dieu de Nos Ancêtres (Church of the God of Our Ancestors), 26
Église des Banzie (Church of the Initiates), 26
Ego and the Id, The (Freud), 425
egungun paaka, 527
Egypt
    archaeology in, 88
    Israelite Exodus, 615
    Jews in, 163, 644, 771–772, 1114
    Joseph in, 644
    in Kush, 682
    Muslim Brotherhood in, 780–781
    in Persian period, 86
    Philistines in, 884–885
    See also Alexandria Egypt, Islam and Social Change: Al-Azhar in Conflict and Accomodation (Eccel), 611
Egyptian Mysteries, 413
Egyptian religion, 384–385
    afterlife in, 39, 40
    alchemy in, 51–52
    altar in, 56
    archaeology of, 88

Egyptian religion *(continued)*
  baptism in, 137
  confession in, 303, 385
  Coptic church, 326–327
  cosmology in, 330
  death ritual in, 38, 385, 537, 538, 555
  fasting in, 413
  goddesses in, 450
    Isis, 582–583
  gods in, 1105–1106
    See also Osiris
  iconography of, 537–538
  immortality in, 555
  incarnation in, 561–562
  miracles in, 742
  monotheism in, 762
  mythology of, 386
  New Kingdom, 385–386
  Old Kingdom, 384–385
  under Ptolemys, 386
  redemption in, 922
  resurrection in, 935
  temples of, 89, 385, 386, 537, 1087–1088
  underworld in, 385, 538, 1134
Ehécatl, 129
Ehrenberg, Rudolf, 947
Eichhorn, Johann, 156
eidolon, 548
Eight Trigrams, 542
Eight White Yurts, 761
Eightfold Path, 185, 198, 253, 360, 363, 782
  meaning of, 418, 419
ein morin ken, 468
Ein Sof, 442, 443, 654
einherjar, 431, 432
Einstein, Albert, 982
Eir, 433
eirene, 180
Eisai, Myoan, 625, 1184
Ekavyavaharika, 212
ekayana, 419
ekklesia, 171
Ekron, 884, 885
Ekseri, 1127
ekstasis, 478
Ekstatische Konfessionen (Buber), 190
Ekuphakameni, 25
Ekur, 725
El, 85, 224, 226, 676
El Bersha, 385
El Carambolo, 523
El Dorado, 728
El Mirador temples, 1089
El Shaddia, 11
El Tajín, 534
Elamite tablets of Persepolis, 697
élan vital, 548
El`azar, 1116
Elche, 523
Elcho Island, 121
èlè-tok, 796
Eleazar, 712
Elegba, 234
Elementary Education (Chu Hsi), 309
eleos, 250

Elephantine, 86
Eli ezer, Yisra`el, 471
Eliade, Mircea, 74, 387–391, 1093
  on alchemy, 48
  on ascent ritual, 98
  concepts and categories of, 389
  on cosmology, 330
  early life of, 387
  early works of, 388
  emigration of, 388–389
  Encyclopedia of Religion, 391
  fiction of, 389–390
  on Freud, 426
  in India, 387–388
  morphological method of, 389
  on Pythagoreanism, 557
  on sacred, 177, 930
  on sacred and profane, 962
  and Tillich, 391
  on tree symbolism, 136, 340
  at University of Chicago, 390–391
Elib, 224
Elijah, 82, 83, 414, 548, 556, 616
Elijah, Saint, 1004
Elijah Muhammad, 36, 586, 701
Eliot, Frederick May, 1142
Elisha, 548, 556, 614
Elizabeth I, Queen of England, 70
Ellil, 510
Elohim, 908
Elysian Fields, 37
Emanu-El, Temple, 14
embandwa, 577–578
Emerson, Ralph Waldo, 391–392
Emeslam, 726
Emigration of 622, 775
Emily Gap, 114
Emin, 802
Emlyn, Thomas, 1142
Empedocles, 372, 373
Emu, 115, 116
En islam iranien (Corbin), 611
Enarees, 571
Enchiridion (Augustine), 278
Enchiridion militis Christiani (Erasums), 394
Encyclopedia of Religion, 391
End of Days, 84
End Time Foods, 736
Ende, Werner, 611
Endlösung, 511
endocannibalism, 848
Endovellico, 524
Endzeit, 410
"Enemy of the Silkworm", "The" (Eliade), 386
Engakuji temple, 1185
Engels, Friedrich, 453, 714
England. *See* Britain
English Gnostic Church, 802
English Presbyterian Westminster Confession of 1646, 319
English Savoy Declaration of 1658, 319
Engur, 725
engyo, 966
Engzekit, 1126
Eninnu, 726
Enki, 137, 536, 724, 725

Enlightenment, 370, 392–393
  in Britain, 393
  and church-state relations, 297
  in France, 297, 392
  and Freemasonry, 422
  in Germany, 393
  Kant on, 393
  and Marxism, 714
  philosophers of, 392–393
  and Protestantism, 271, 277
Enlightenmentmind Sutra, 214
Enlil, 510, 725
Enneads (Plotinus), 516
Ennin, 750
Ennius, 1050
Enoch, 52, 67, 80, 82, 221
Enoch, 80, 81, 83, 99, 160, 167–168, 360
Enqawa, Ephraim, Rabbi, 147
entheos, 478
Enuma elish, 66, 676, 726
Enuru, 724
Ephesians, 173, 174, 717
Ephesus. *See* Council of Ephesus
Ephraim, 548, 644
Epic of Gilgamesh, 161, 415
epic poetry, chanting in, 250
Epidaurus, 742
epignosis, 703
Epimenides, 99
epiousios, 691
Epiphanius, 397, 434, 437
Episcopal Church, 71, 72, 293
episcopal church government, 292–293
Epistle on Conversion (Maimonides), 700
Epistle of the Son of Wolf (Baha' Allah), 131
Epistle to Yemen (Maimonides), 700
Epistles of the Brethren of Purity, 596
Epitome (Lactantius Firmianus), 549
Epona, 242
Er, 97
Erasmus, Desiderius, 393–394, 517, 693
  humanistic program of, 394
  works of, 393–394
Eratosthenes, 982
Erebos, 467
eremitism, 394–395
  and communion, 395
  concept of, 394–395
  in Islam, 395
Ereshkigal, 726
Erh-ju ssu-hsing lun, 183
Eridu, 88, 724, 725
Erie Indians, 811
Ernesti, Johann, 156
Erweckungsbewegung, 435
Esarhaddon treaty, 886–887
Esau, 519
Esdras, 161, 727
Eshmun, 887
Eshtn, 510
Eskimo, 92, 808
  See also Arctic religions; Inuit religion

esoteric, meaning of, 853
Esoteric Buddhism. *See* Tantrism, Buddhist
Essays in Zen Buddhism (Suzuki), 1052
Essence of Christianity (Feuerbach), 714
Essence of the Doctrine (Kundakunda), 620
Essenes, 82, 557, 669
 and baptism, 138, 643
 and covenant, 338, 339
 fasting of, 413–414
 as Qumran sect, 82, 353, 413–414
 and Sabbath, 617–618
Essentials of the National Polity, 313
est (Erhard Seminars Training), 800, 802
Esther, 160, 166
Esther, 644
Esu, 1119
d'Étaples, Lefèvre, 516
Eternal Buddha, 562
Eternal Mother, 732
eternity, 396–397
 concept of, 396
 in Eastern thought, 396–397
ethe, 97
Ethica ordine geometrico demonstrata (Spinoza), 1042
Ethical Culture, Adler and, 14
ethical monotheism, 660
Ethical Philosophy of Life, An (Adler), 14
ethics
 African, 22
 Buddhist, 214
 and conscience, 320
 conscience and, 320
 in Jainism, 621
 and morality, 267, 764–766
 philosophical, 267–268
 See also Christian ethics
Ethics of the Pure Will (Cohen), 297
Ethics (Spinoza), 1042, 1043
Ethiopian church, 379, 397–398
 development of, 397–398
 and missionaries, 398
 outside Africa, 398
ethnopology of religion, 73, 402
etrog, 544
`Ets hayyim` (Aharon ben Eliyyahu), 670
Ettinger, Ya`aqov, 865
Ettinghausen, Richard, 611
euaggelion, 457, 458
Euandros, 463
Eucharist, 91, 399
 and altar, 56–57
 blood symbolism in, 182
 exclusion from, 405
 and Jesus, 182, 282, 399, 639
 as liturgy, 689, 690
 Lutheran, 694
 meaning of, 399
 Protestant, 71, 282
 repeatability of, 954
 Roman Catholic, 282, 420, 940
Eudemus (Aristotle), 1012

Eugene IV, Pope, 876
Eugenikos, Mark, 337
Eugenius IV, Pope, 337
eulogia, 180
Euripides, 515
Euro-Arab Dialogue: Relations between the Two Cultures (Hopwood), 613
Europe, new religions in, 802
Eusebius, 12, 170
Eutyches, 397
Eutyches of Constantinople, 638
evamvids, 487
Evangelical Christian Catholic Church, 25
Evangelical United Brethran, 731
evangelicalism, 400–401
 American, 400–401
 origins of, 400
Evans, Donald, 62
Evans-Pritchard, E.E., 74, 401–402
 works of, 402
Eve, 280, 355, 412, 415, 1090
 and lost paradise, 879
 Unification Church view, 1141
Evening Star, 823, 848
Evenki, 92, 1127
Eveny, 92, 1128
evil, 402–403
 and Adam's free will, 106
 in Africa, 22, 376, 692
 Ainu, 44
 conceptions of, 403–404
 exorcism of, 407–408
 and fall concept, 412
 and gnosticism, 434
 Hasidic view of, 473
 Jewish response to Holocaust, 511–513, 662–663
 and lamentation, 403
 Lugbara religion, 692
 and myth, 402–403
 projection of, 1091
 vs goodness, 456–457
 See also demons; Satan
Evil Twin, 811
Evolution of the Idea of God, The (Allen), 30
evolutionary theory, 403–404
 Darwin, responses to, 403–404
 religious contributions to, 404
 religious responses to, 403–404
Ewe, 64
ex opere operato, 410
excommunication, 405
 reasons for, 405
Exegesis. *See* Bible, exegesis
exegetai, 860
Exegetica (Basilides), 155
Exhortation That Children Should Be Sent to School (Luther), 694
existentialism, 406–407
 characteristics of, 406
 and gnosticism, 436
 Jewish, 661
 religious implications, 406
Exodus, 159, 162, 175, 182, 272, 548, 614–615, 772

exorcism, 44, 407–408, 742
 in Africa, 408
 in China, 407
 in Hellenistic religions, 477–478
 in India, 407–408
 and Islam, 408
 in Japan, 407
 in Southeast Asia, 408
exorkosis, 407
Experiences in Groups (Bion), 734
expiation, sacrifice of, 964
Explanation of the Diagram of the Great Ultimate (Chou Tun-i), 307, 308
Explanatory Notes upon the New Testament (Wesley), 729
Exsecrabilis, 876
Extravagantes communes, 229
Extravagantes Ioannes XXII, 229
extreme unction, as sacrament, 283
Ezekiel, 41, 89, 99, 341, 434, 636
Ezekiel, 160, 434, 556, 687, 688
Ezen, 724
Ezra, 82, 160, 162, 635, 645
Ezra, 166, 935, 1113
Ezra the Scribe, 248, 1117
Ezra-Nehemiah, 160, 162

F

Fa-ch`ung, 183
Fa-hsiang, 260
Fa-hsien, 750
Fa-kuo, 562
fa-shih, 261
Fa-tsang, 209, 217, 260
Face of Religion, The (Nasir-i Khusraw), 787
faith, 409–410
 in Christianity, 409–410, 694, 940
 dimensions of, 409–410
 in Islam, 447, 588
 in Roman religion, 409
 Tillich's view of, 102
 triad of, 883
faith, hope, and love, 284
Faith Seeking Understanding (Barth), 141
falasifah, 448, 1014
Fali, 178
fall concept, 410–412
 in Christianity, 412
 in gnositicism, 411
 in historical time, 410–411
 in Islam, 412
 in Judaism, 411–412
 in myth, 411
Falloux law, 1133
False Face spirits, 814
Familiar Colloquies (Erasmus), 394
Family of Love, 802
Fan wang, 965
Fang of Gabon, 26
fang-shih, 1074, 1075
faqih, 604
Farabi, Abu Nasr al-, 448, 525
Faraguvaol, 231
Fara'idi movement, in Bengal, 146
Fard, Wallace D. (Walli Farrad), 36

Farel, Guillaume, 222, 899
Farmer, William, 157
Farrakhan, Louis, 36
Faruq, King, 780
fas, 956
Fasl al-maqal (Ibn Rushd), 525
fasting, 412–414
    in Buddhism, 413, 414
    in Christianity, 413, 414
    and confession, 302
    in Confucianism, 413
    in Egypt, 413
    Greco-Roman, 412–413
    in Hinduism, 413
    in Islam, 413
    in Jainism, 413, 414
    in Judaism, 413–414
    motives for, 412–413
    North American Indian, 413, 414, 818
    for preparation, 413
    for purification, 413–414, 912
    for supplication, 414
    in Taoism, 413
Fatawa `Alamgiriyah, 605
Fatimids, 585
fatrah, 917
Fayyumi, Sa`adyah al-, 669
Feast of the Brethren, The (Nasir-i
        Khusraw), 787
Feast of the Dead, 821
Feast of the Flaying of Men, 129
Feast of the Nineteen Day, 132
Feast of the Presentation of the Lord to
        the Temple, 98
Feast of the Unleavened Bread, 881
Feathered and Horned Serpent, 840
feces, as pollution, 911
Feigel, Friedrich Karl, 961
Feis Temhra, 244
Fellowship of Reconciliation, 289
Fellowship of Socialist Christians, 289
Feltre, Vittorino Rambaldoni da, 515
female initiation
    in Africa, 22, 528
    Australian Aboriginal, 110, 111
    Cuna, 346
    North American Indian, 813, 832
feminism
    God, male symbolism issue,
        454–455
    and goddess worship, 454–455
    women's studies, 1166–1168
Fenriswolf, 432
Fensalir, 433
Ferdinand I, Hapsburg king, 768
Ferdinand, King of Spain, 576
ferendae sententiae, 405
Fernandes, Valentim, 29
Fernandez, James W., 733
Ferrar, William Hugh, 174
Fertile Crescent, location of, 791
fertility cults, Aboriginal, 112
fertility gods and goddesses
    Aztec, 129
    Baltic, 137
    Celtic, 243
    Germanic, 431, 432
    Venus figures, Paleolithic, 870–871

fertility rites
    human sacrifice, 518
    South American Indians, 1032–1033
Feuerbach, Ludwig, 101, 714
Fichte, J.G., 79
Ficino, Marsillio, 386, 516
Fide quaerens intellectum (Barth), 141
fides, 410
Fiebig, Paul, 158
Field of Reeds, 555
Filelfo, Francesco, 515
filioque, 980
Final Report, 72
Finisher, 811
Finkelstein, Louis, 322
Finland, 92
Fioretti (Little Flowers), 73
fiqh, 526, 603–606, 609
Firdawsi, 547
fire myth, South American Indian,
        1027
Fire Old Woman, 840
fire ritual
    North American Indian, 814
    of purification, 912
    Sarmatian, 976
Firkovitch, Avraham, 670
Firmicus Maternus, 549
First Church of Christ, Scientist, 287
First Clement, 154
First Formula of the Institute, 552
First Sermon, 541
"First Turning of the Wheel of Dharma,"
        197
first-fruit rites, 832
Fitness of Names, 240
fitrah, 448
Fitsók Exíts, 1028
Il fiume bianco e i Denka (Beltrame),
        30
Five Agents, 307, 1055
Five Great Sacrifices, 487
Five Hundred Books, 53
Five Peaks, 893
Five Pillars, 588, 598
Five Precepts, 765
Five Supreme Ones, 621
Five Years Meeting, 915
Five-Pagoda Monastery, 1085
Fjorgyn, 433
Fjorgynn, 433
Flathead Indians, 833, 835
Flavian, Bishop, 335
Flidhais, 242
flood, 338, 414–415
    in creation myth, 414–415
    form of, 415–416
    function of waters, 415–416
    in *Genesis*, 415
    in Hinduism, 415
    in South American religion, 415,
        1026
    survivors, 415
Florence, 514
Florenskii, Pavel, 950
Florentine Codex, 127
floruit, 534
Fludd, Robert, 421

Flute ceremony, 842, 843
Fodio, Usuman dan, 641
Foelsche, Paul, 112
folk religion, 416–417, 624
Fon, 182, 1155
food
    and dietary laws, 911, 959
    for sacrifice, 963
For the Sake of Heaven (Buber), 190
Forbidden Forest, The (Eliade), 389
Foreign Vocabulary of the Qur'an, The
        (Jeffery), 610
Forest Books, 488
Forêt interdite (Eliade), 389
Forge and the Crucible, The (Eliade),
        390
Forgiveness and Law (Bushnell), 219
Form of Church Prayers, The (Calvin),
        899
Form of Prayers, The (Knox), 899
Former Prophets, 159
Formosa, 1057
Formula of Concord, 382, 695
Fortuna, 942
fortune-telling, Korean religion, 680
Foundations of Christianity (Kautsky),
        714
Fountain of Memory, 789
Fountain of Wisdom, 789
Four beginnings, 305
Four Branches, 242–243
Four Noble Truths, 198, 251, 360, 363,
        417–419
    Buddha's enumeration of, 417–418
    Mahayana interpretations, 419
    Theravada interpretations, 418
Four Questions, 882
fourness, 341
Fox, George, 176, 915
Fox Indians, 811, 813, 814
France
    Avignon Papacy, 336, 876, 980
    Calvinism in, 296
    church-state relations in, 296
    Enlightenment in, 297, 392
    Freemasonry in, 422
    humanism in, 516
    inquisition in, 575, 576
    Joan of Arc, 642–643
    megalithic religion in, 721
    Muslim invasion of, 752
    Napoleon in, 877
    Paleolithic in, 869, 870
    Reformation in, 925
    Revolution in, 877, 1133
Francis of Assisi, 72, 275, 419–421
    legacy of, 421
    life of, 419–420
    poverty of, 420
Francis I, King, 516
Francis Xavier, 626, 747
Franciscans, 72, 73, 79, 818
    and Francis of Assisi, 420
Frankel, Zacharias, 321, 468
Frankfort, Council of, 980
Franklin, Benjamin, 393
Franz, Frederick W., 634
frashgird, 703

Fravashayo, 98
fravashis, 69, 1189–1190
Frazer, James G., 74, 518, 639, 959
Frederick, Augustus, 422
Frederick, Elector, 693
Frederick I Barbarossa, 344, 575
Frederick II, Emperor, 336, 344, 575
Free Methodist Church, 731
Free will, 423–424
  of Adam, 106
  and predestination, 423–424
Free Will Baptists, 687
Freemasons, 288, 421–423
  history of, 421–422
  teachings of, 422–423
Frequens, 876
Freud, Sigmund, 63, 70, 425–426, 453, 664
  on ancestor deification, 63
  cosmological scheme of, 70
  on goddess worship, 453
  life and works of, 425
  psychoanalytic theory of, 425–426
  and religious studies, 426
Freyr, 430, 432
friagabis, 432
Friars Minor, 72
Friends Unified Meeting, 915
Frigg, 431, 433
From Primitive to Zen (Eliade), 390
Fromm, Erich, 948
Frumentius, 397
Fry, Elizabeth, 915
Fu Hsi, 184
Fuchs, Ernst, 438
Fukko Shinto, 995, 997
Fulbe *jihad*, 597, 641
Fulla, 433
Fuller, Charles E., 401
Fuller Theological Seminary, 401
"Function of the Unreal", "The" (Calinescu), 388
Fundamental Law of the Organization of the Muslim Brothers, 780
fundamentalist Christianity, 400–401, 404
  and Darwin, 404
  and evangelicalism, 400–401
funerary ritual. *See* death ritual
Fung Yu-lan, 311, 982
fuqaha`, 604
furqan, 918
furu` al-fiqh, 603
furuq, 589
Fusus al-hikam (al-`Arabi), 1047
Future of an Illusion, The (Freud), 425
Future of Religions, The (Tillich), 1111

G

Ga-napati, 1069
gabiae, 432
Gabon, 26, 528
Gabriel, Archangel, 69, 99, 600, 779, 916
Gabrielino Indians, 833
Gadjeri, 112, 113, 117
Gaia, 182, 451, 859
Galaicae, 524

Galatians, 171, 173, 174, 549, 645
Galera, 523
Galerius, 323
Galia, 376
Galilee, 636
Galileo, Galilei, 427–428, 983
  trial of, 428
  works of, 427, 428
Gallic Wars (Caesar), 371
Gallicanism, 1133
Galot, Jean, 639
Gama, Vasco de, 752
gamelan, 632
Gamli'el of Yavneh, 1053
gana, 619
Ganabuda, 113
ganadharas, 619
ganala, 113
Ganapati, 710
Ganapatyas, 1069
Ganda, 376, 577–578
Gandavyuha, 214
Gandavyuhasutra (Suzuki), 1052
gandha, 364
gandhaka, 50
Gandhi (film), 430
Gandhi, Mohandas, 150, 428–430, 504
  on Jainism, 621
  legacy of, 431
  religious influences on, 428–429
  religious practices of, 429–430
  religious thought of, 429
Ganes, 710
Ganesa, 143, 500, 502, 540, 1072
Ganges River, 540
Gangesa, 852
Ganjadareh, 791
gar, 22
garbhagrha, 498
garden, as paradise, 879, 880
Garden of Eden, 13–14, 221, 341, 342, 355, 360, 412
  banishment from, 13–14, 221
  fourness in, 341
  origin of death, 355
  as paradise, 879
  serpent in, 360, 879
  theoretical location of, 879
  tree symbolism in, 342, 412, 879
Garden of Hearts (Nasir-i Khusraw), 788
Gardet, Louis, 611
Gargantua and Pantagruel (Rabelais), 516
garhapatya, 556
garis, 550
Garnet, Henry Highland, 35
Garrigou-Lagrange, Reginald Marie, 102
Garvey, Marcus, 35, 235
Gasparri, Pietro, 229
Gate of the Reward (Nahmanides), 41
Gath, 884
Gathas (Zarathushtra), 699, 1188, 1189
Gätje, Helmut, 611
Gatumdug, 726
Gaudapada, 499, 1151

Gaudapadakarika, 1151
Gauguin, Paul, 546
Gaumata the Magian, 697, 698
Gauri, 1072
Gautama, Siddhartha. *See* Buddha (Gautama)
Gautama Dharmasutra, 490
Gaza, 884, 885
Gazan, 574
Gdams nag mdzod, 204
Ge, 1031, 1033
Geb, 384, 450, 582
Gèdè, 354
gèdè, 1156
Geertz, Clifford, 74, 611
Gefjun, 433
Gefn, 433
Gehenna, 880, 1135
gehillah, 864
Gelasian Injunction, 295
Gelede masks, 23
Gelede/Efe festival, 528
gemara', 248
Geneology of the Gods (Boccaccio), 515
General Conference of the Methodist Church, 423
General Convention, 293
  of 1835, , 71
General Guidance Council, 780
General Jewish Congress, Hungary, 865
Generations of the Sufis (al-Sulami), 1046
Generations of the Sufis (Ansari), 1046
Genesis, 155, 159, 163, 178, 181, 277, 330, 342, 355, 404, 411, 687
  Abraham, 11–12
  Adam, 13–14
  Cain and Abel, 221
  fall of man, 412
  flood in, 415
  Garden of Eden, 879
  Isaac, 512
  Joseph, 644
  Levites, 687
  temptation in, 1090
Genetic Evolution of the Most Important Gnostic Systems (Neander), 435
Genkoshakusho (Shiren), 184
Gepids, 573
German Christians, 141
German Council, 187
Germania illustrata (Pickel), 516
Germanic religion, 430–433
  gods of, 430–433
  immortality in, 556
  Jastorf culture, 430
  myth in, 430–431
  nature in, 789
Germantown, Pennsylvania, 723
Germany
  Enlightenment in, 393
  gnosticism in, 435–436
  humanism in, 516
  inquisition in, 576
  Lutheranism in, 296

Germany *(continued)*
  megalithic religion in, 721
  Nazi, 443, 511, 659
  Orthodox Judaism in, 865
  Reform Judaism in, 656, 865
  Reformation in, 337, 923–924
  Roman Catholicism in, 36–37, 296
Gero Crucifix, 545
Gerona, 523
Gershom, Levi ben, 153
Gersonides, 152, 442
Getae, 556
Gethsemane, garden of, 638, 691
Geush Urvan, 581
Gezer, 88, 885
Ghana, 24, 25
Ghatterji, Gadadhar. *See* Ramakrishna
Ghazali, Abu Hamid al-, 369, 525, 586,
    592, 593, 605, 784, 1014
Ghazi, Zafar Khan, 146
Ghost Dance, 824, 835
Ghost Dance movement, 728
ghosts
  of murdered, 911
  in North American Indian religion,
    822, 848
  Oceanic, 854
  soul-, 518
ghrana, 364
ghulat, 596
Ghumarah, 148
Gibb, H.A.R., 611, 745
Gibbon, Edward, 393
Gibeon, Raphael, 614
Gideon, 548
Gikai, Tettsu, 1185
Giles of Lessines, 47
Gilgal, 58
gilgul, 42
Gilson, Étienne, 102
Gimbutas, Marija, 567
Ginza, 702
Ginzberg, Asher, 660
*Giordano Bruno and the Hermetic
    Tradition* (Yates), 421
Girsu, 726
Gishbanda, 726
Gita rahasya (Tilak), 150
Gitagovinda, 501
Gitamahatmya, 150
Giza, pyramids at, 90
Glanvill, Joseph, 1165
Glatzer, Nahum N., 948
Glossarium Latino-Arabicum, 955
Gluckman, Max, 64
Glueck, Nelson, 927
gnosis, 719
Gnostic Religion, The (Jonas), 436
gnosticism, 433–437
  and alchemy, 51, 52
  in Christianity, 69, 154, 435, 436–437,
    562
  immortality in, 557
  incarnation in, 562–563
  in Islam, 435
  in Judaism, 69, 434–435
  Mandaean, 138, 303, 434, 437, 702
  and Manichaeism, 437, 701

  modern, 435–436
  origins of, 433–434
  and sacraments, 953
  salvation in, 557
Go-Daigo, Emperor, 1185
Go-nono-hodi, 1029
goblins, Slavic, 1005
God, 151, 152, 438–449
  and anthropomorphism, 76–77
  and atheism, 100–103, 401
  in Baha'i, 131, 132
  in Christianity
    Barth on, 140–141, 446
    Calvinist, 222–223
    goodness of, 456–457
    grace of, 459
    Holy Spirit, 170
    incarnation of, 562–563
    and Jehovah's Witnesses, 634
    and Jesus, 279, 438, 439–440
    Jesus as, 440–441, 458, 563, 638
    Kingdom of, 676–677
    in New Testament, 438–440, 1122
    postbiblical, 444–446
    proofs for existence of, 357
    and Protestantism, 271, 905
    and Roman Catholicism, 939
    as Trinity, 106, 279, 420, 441
    See also Trinity
  corporeality of, 37
  death of, 102, 513
  and existentialism, 406
  feminist reconceptions of, 1167
  and gnosticism, 434, 436
  in Islam
    in Qur'an, 412, 447–448, 586–587
    and Sufism, 593
    and Sunnism, 591, 592
    unity of, 591
  in Judaism
    covenant of, 11–12, 68, 182,
      338–339, 513, 615, 616, 646
    and David, 351
    feminine metaphors in writings, 654
    Hasidic approach to, 472–473, 785
    and Holocaust, 443–444, 513–514
    Israelite, 613–616, 762–763
    philosophical approach to, 442
    prohibition on image of, 543
    rabbinic approach to, 441–442,
      650–651, 652
    and rationalism, 660, 661
    and Trinity, 1122
    wisdom of, 440
    Yahveh, 11, 12, 56, 351, 414, 415,
      438, 614, 676
  Judeo-Christian, 272
  justice and judgment of, 37
  Kingdom of, 676
  love of, 104
  male symbolism issue, 454–455
  modern approach to, 443–444
  and mysticism, 783
  obedience to will of, 284
  omnipotence of, 424
  qabbalistic approach to, 442–443
  Spinoza on, 1042
  See also Monotheism

God in Christ (Bushnell), 218
God as Father? (Ruether), 1167
God of the House Site, 679
God of Luck (Chesok), 679
God and the Rhetoric of Sexuality
    (Trible), 1166
Godavari Mata, 710
goddess worship, 449–455
  in China, 451
  feminist revival of, 454–455
  Freud on, 453
  in Greece, 451
  in India, 449–450
  in Japan, 451
  Jung on, 453
  matriarchy theory, 453, 454
  in Near East, 450–451
  Tantrism, Buddhist, 449–450, 451
  theories of, 453
goddesses
  anthropomorphic representation of,
    76, 538
  Aramean, 86
  Arctic, 93
  Armenian, 98
  Aztec, 129
  Baltic, 137
  in Bengal, 143
  Canaanite, 225, 227
  Celtic, 241, 242, 243–244
  Cycladic, 15
  in Egypt, 450, 582–583
  Germanic, 433
  Greek, 451, 539
  Hawaiian, 474
  Hindu, 449–450, 498, 499, 502,
    540–541, 1069, 1072
  Hurrian, 520
  Iberian, 523
  Inca, 560
  in Judaism, 450–451
  Mesopotamian, 536, 726
  Mycenaean, 17
  Neolithic, 450
  Phoenician, 887
  Roman, 451
  Slavic, 1005
  South American Indian, 1016
  Sumerian, 450
  Turkic, 1131
  Yakut, 1170
Godfrey of Bouillon, 343
gods
  in Africa, 19, 21, 30, 692, 1179–
    1180
  in afterlife, 37
  anthropomorphic representation of,
    76, 538, 539
  Aramean, 85, 86
  Arctic, 93
  Armenian, 97–98
  Aztec, 127–129, 534, 554
  Baltic, 136–137
  blessing of, 178
  Buddhist, 96, 359, 708
  Canaanite, 223–225, 226–227
  Caribbean, 230–231
  Celtic, 240–242

and death concept, 354, 355
in Egypt, 1105–1106
Germanic, 430–433
Greek, 100, 461–462, 479, 539
Hawaiian, 474
Hindu, 190, 485–486, 487, 488, 502, 503
  Siva, 540, 1001–1003
  Tantric, 1069, 1071–1072
  Visnu, 540
Hittite, 510
Hurrian, 520
Iberian, 524
Inca, 560
incarnation of, 561–563
in Indian religion, 569–570
in Iranian religion, 581–582
Javanese, 632
killing of, 182
Korean, 679–680
Maori, 705
Mesopotamian, 536, 724–726
Moabite, 757–758
Mycenaean, 17
New Caledonian, 795–796
Philistine, 885
Phoenician, 886–887
Roman, 479, 944–945
Saami, 952
Scythian, 571, 987
Slavic, 1004–1005
South American Indian, 1015–1017, 1031
and syncretism, 479–480
in Taoism, 543
Turkic, 1130–1131
See also deities; idolatry; polytheism; temples
God's Prophecy, The, 241
God's Way, 346
Godwin, William, 393
Goethe, 320, 435
Gofannon, 241
Goibhniu, 241
Goitein, S.D., 948
Gokulikas, 212
Gold and Siver Pavilions, 1085
Golden Age, 728
golden calf, 548, 616
Golden Horde, 574
Goldziher, Ignácz, 610, 611
Golgotha, 342, 712
Goliath, 352
Gomawe, 796
gomez, 581
Good and Evil (Buber), 191
Good Twin, 811
goodness, 456–457
  concept of, 456–457
  Hasidic view of, 473
Goody, Jack, 64
Goose and Gridiron, 422
Gosiute Indians, 832, 835, 850
Gospel According to St. Matthew, |The (film), 546
Gospel of John, 78, 154, 169, 172, 174, 180, 436, 438, 441, 444, 458, 562, 716

Gospel of Luke, 157, 158, 160, 161, 169, 172, 173, 174, 180, 438, 458, 640, 716
Gospel of Mark, 79, 157, 158, 169, 172, 174, 175, 180, 438, 458, 637, 716
Gospel of Matthew, 78, 155, 157, 158, 169, 171, 172, 174, 175, 420, 438, 440, 458, 640, 699, 717
Gospel of Thomas, 437
Gospel of Truth, 437
gospels, 171–172, 180, 457–458
  miracle stories, 743
  New Testament, 171–172, 458–459
  and Septuagint, 457
  synoptics, 172
  time period and life of Jesus, 171–172
  written text, 458
Gotama, 851
Goth, 430
Gothic Constitutions, 421
Governing Body Commission, of ISKCON, 579
Gozan system of Zen, 1185
Gozo, 720
Grabar, Oleg, 611
grace, 279–280, 459, 694, 941
  Christian concept of, 459
  Christian doctrines on, 279–280
Graham, Billy, 401
gramadevatas, 503
Gran Brijit, 1156
Gran Chaco Indian religion, 1026–1030
Granada, 523
Grand Lodge, 422
Grand Master, 422
Grandfathers, 812
Grange, The, 288
Grant, Jacquelyn, 1167
Gratian, John, 229
Gratian's Decretum, 229
Gray, James M., 401
Great Altar of Zeus, 539
Great Assembly, 333, 1099
Great Awakening, 139, 197, 319, 400
Great Awakening Revivalism, 435
Great Beit Din, 974
Great Book of Lecan, 240
Great Court of Jerusalem, 468
Great Depression, 289
Great Goddess, 455, 792
Great Illuminator, 562
Great Learning, 306, 309–310
Great Manitou, 811
Great Medicine society, 821, 848
Great Miracle of Sravasti, 541
Great Mother, The (Neumann), 453
Great Mystery, 821
Great Night of Siva, 1003
Great Purification, 581
Great Revival (1861–1862), 235
Great Schism, 740, 875, 980
Great Spirit, 728, 811, 821, 823
Great Sun Buddha, 626
Great Temple, Aztec, 128
Great Ultimate, concept of, 307, 308, 309, 1055–1056

Great Vehicle, 208, 213
Great Wall, 306
Great Western Schism, 336, 876, 980–981
Great White Hare, 821
Grebel, Conrad, 59
Greccio, 420
Greek Bible
  Hebrew scriptures, 163–164
  New Testament, 173–174
Greek civilization, scientific achievements, 982
Greek ecclesiastical music, 249
Greek and Latin Authors on Jews and Judaism (Stern), 614
Greek Orthodox church, 460
  modern, 460
  origin of, 460
Greek religion, 461–465
  altar in, 56, 1088
  apologists for, 549
  art of, 539
  ascension in, 99
  baptism in, 137
  charity in, 250–251
  civic, 462–463, 477
  confession in, 303
  Dionysian, 464
  fasting in, 412–413
  goddesses in, 451
  gods in, 100, 461–462, 479, 539, 549
  Hades in, 463, 467, 1134–1135
  hero cult in, 462–463, 477
  iconography of, 538–539
  immortality in, 557
  incarnation in, 561, 562
  and Kingdom of God, 676
  and Magi, 698, 699
  magic in, 477–478
  miracles in, 741
  monotheism in, 762
  mystery cults in, 953
  mysticism in, 464–465
  mythology of, 461
  oracles in, 478, 858–860
  Orphism, 464–465, 557
  sacrifice in, 463–464
  and science, 982
  spiritual guide in, 1043–1044
  temples of, 1088
  See also Hellenistic religions
Greeley, Dana McLean, 1143
Green Corn ceremony, 813, 818, 819
Greenberg, Irving, 513
Greenland, 94, 580
Greenwood, John, 319
Gregorian chant, 249
Gregory, Caspar René, 174
Gregory I, Pope (the Great), 752, 875, 1050
Gregory II, Pope, 875
Gregory IX, Pope, 72, 344, 575, 1165
Gregory VII, Pope, 275, 295, 336, 343, 875, 980
Gregory X, Pope, 876, 1104
Gregory XI, Pope, 237, 876, 980
Gregory XII, Pope, 981

Gregory XIII, Pope, 877
Gregory XV, Pope, 877
Gregory XVI, Pope, 1133
Gregory the Illuminator, 98
Gregory of Nazianzus, 138, 1123
Gregory of Nyssa, 155, 280, 284, 691, 1012, 1123, 1124
Gregory Theodoros of Sykeon, 960
Greshake, Gispert, 639
grha, 486
grhastha, 341, 579
grhasthin, 491, 578
grhya, 143, 487
Grhyasutras, 487, 490, 564
Griesbach, Johann, 157
Grimme, Hubert, 610
Grimnismál, 433
Grindal, Edmund, 913
gro bonanj, 1156
Grocyn, William, 517
Grogh, 98
Groote Eylandt, 117, 118
Gros Ventre Indians, 820
Grotius, Hugo, 156
Group Psychology and the Analysis of the Ego (Freud), 425
Grundfragen systematischer Theologie (Pannenberg), 639
Grunebaum, Gustav Edmund von, 610, 611
Grünewald, Matthias, 545
Gua, 1161
Guabancex, 231
Guabba, 726
Guamaonocon, 230
Guarani, 415, 1021
Guardian angels, 69
Guarini, 735
Guasurangwe, 1027
Gudit, 398
Guggenheim, Daniel, 321
Guggenheim, Simon, 321
Guglielma of Milan, 734
Guha, 1008
Guicciardini, Francesco, 515
Guide of the Perplexed (Maimonides), 41, 151, 442, 700
Gujarat, 45
Gumezishn, 702
Gunabibi, 107
gunas, 149
gunasthana, 621
Gunkel, Hermann, 909
Güntert, Hermann, 568
Gunung Agung, 134
Guptas, 489
Gurangara, 117
Guringal, 115
guru, 142, 487, 488, 565, 579, 967, 999
Gurung, 482
Gushayish va rahayish (Nasir-i Khusraw), 787
Gusti Allah, 632
Guta re Jehovah, 25, 734
Gutierrez, Gustavo, 446
Guzanu, 85
Gweidjen, Lu, 48

Gylfaginning, 431, 433
Gyn/Ecology: The Metaethics of Radical Feminism (Daly), 1167
Gyohyo, 965
Gzan-phan-mtha'-yas, 204

H

ha-adam, 13
ha-kohen, 688
ha-memunneh, 688
Ha-Mim, 148
ha-Qaddosh Barukh Hu', 883
ha-Qadosh barukh hu`, 441
Ha`ameq davar (Berlin), 153
Habad, 443
Habakkuk, 160, 615
Habermann, A.M., 512
Habiru, 614
Habis, 523
Habu, 385
hachas, 534
Hadad, 85, 86, 479, 548
Hadadyisi, 85
hadd, 589–590
Hades, 42, 51, 99, 451, 463, 467, 557
myth of, 467
hadith, 547, 591, 602, 603
development of, 588–589
jihad in, 641
studies of, 611
Hadrian, 636, 1088
Hag ha-Matsot, 881
Hag ha-Pesah, 881
Hagar, 11, 667
Hagarism: The Making of the Islamic World (Crone and Cook), 612
Haggadah, 544, 882–883
Haggai, 160, 651
Hagia Paraskevi, 16
Hagia Triada, 17
Hagiographa (*Ketuvim*), 152, 160
hagios, 966
hagnos, 957
Hahn, Thich Nhat, 203
Haida Indians, 826
Haiqel, Hayyim of Amdur, 472
Haiti, 34
Haitian Voodoo, 233
haituka schools, 493
Hajar, 667
hajar al-falasifah, 53
hajj, 889–892
Greater, 891–892
Lesser, 891
preparations for, 890–891
hakhamim, 617
Hakim, al-Tirmidhi, al-, 592, 994
Hakim, bi-Amr Allah, al-, 596
Hako, 823
Halaf-Hassuna-Samarra culture, 792
halakhah, 360, 467–469, 699, 864
custom in, 468
in Diaspora, 469, 648–649
in Israel, 469, 1188
modern role, 469
origins of, 467–468, 653
Rabbinic law, 468, 646–647
scriptural exegesis, 468

and Talmud, 469, 653, 1061
halakhah le-ma`aseh, 468
halakhot, 467
Haldi, 520, 951
Half Moon ceremony, 824
Half-Way Covenant, 319
Halicarnassus, 539
Halim, al- (Caliph), 636
Hall of Double Justice, 37
Hall of Dreams, 1085
Hallaj, al Husayne ibn Mansur al-, 593, 611, 712
Hallelujah (prophet), 1022
Hama, 85
Hamath, 351
hamatsa, 829
Hamatsa dance, 829
Hamilton, William, 102
Hammer of Witches, The, 1165
Hammurabi, 330
Han Yong-un, 205
Han Yü, 306
Han-dynasty religion, 43, 256–257, 1078
Han-ku Pass, 684
Hananyah, Yehoshu`a ben, 1114
Hanbal, 447
Hand, Cult of the, 527
hand movements
in blessing, 178–179
cheironomic signs, 248
Handbook for the Christian Soldier (Erasmus), 394
Hands of the Cause, 133
Council of, 132
Handsome Lake, 815, 954
Hangest, Charles de, 221
hanif, 550, 778
Hanifah, Abu, 589, 602
Hano, 837
Hanukkah, 470–471, 649
customs, 470–471
hanukkiyyah, 470
haoma, 99, 550, 568
Haoma (deity), 485
happy hunting ground, 554
Happy-Healthy-Holy (3HO), 800
haqiqah, 562
Haqq, al-, 712
Har-Magedon, 635
Harakas, Stanley S., 268
Haram Mosque, 667, 668
harams, 584, 667
Harappa, 483–484, 564, 570
Harding, G. Lankester, 352
Hare, R.M., 62
Hare Indians, 808
Hare Krishna movement, 504, 579, 736
harijans, 429
Häring, Bernhard, 270
Harivamsa, 494, 496, 497, 498
Harmonization of the Two Wisdoms (Nasir-i Khusraw), 788
Harmony of the Gospels (Calvin), 691
Harnack, Adolf von, 157, 186, 436, 639
haroset, 882
Harra-Hubullu, 161
Harran, 86

Harris, William Wade, 25–26
Harrist church, 24, 27
Harvard College, 319
Harvester's Vase, 17
Hasan, Abu al-Sha-dhili, Abu, 1081
Hasdeu, B.P., 388
Hasedera Temple, 894
Hashimiyah, 993
Hasidism, 190–191, 443, 471–473
    Buber on, 190–191
    and God, 443, 472–473, 785
    history of, 471–472, 654–655
    Holocaust response of, 662
    theology of, 472–473
    and Torah, 1116–1117
    in United States, 866
Hasidism and Modern Man (Buber),
    190
Hasimo, 1121
Haskalah, 659, 1187
Hasmonean Revolt, 883, 1011
hat'at, 103
Hathor, 450, 583, 887
Hattic language, 510
Hauma, 571
Hauran, 85
hautes grades, 422
Havdalah, 649
Hawaiian religion, 473–474, 518
    deities, 474
    demise and state religion, 474
Haydar, 547
hayerenakhaws, 98
Haymanot, Takla, 398
Hayq Estifanos, Monastery of, 398
Hazor, 57
Head of Christ (Sallmon), 546
head hunting
    as blood offering, 963
    in Borneo, 189
    and cosmology, 329
    in cosmology, 329
        in Southeast Asian religion, 1038
healing
    in Africa, 1040
    Ainu, 44
    Arctic Indian, 93
    in Christian Science, 286
    and exorcism, 407, 408
    Hawaiian god of, 474
    by Jesus, 742–743
    and magic, 477–478
    North American Indian, 814–815,
        818, 831, 837–838, 841
    and shamanism, 44, 93, 707, 991,
        1022
    in Siberian religions, 991
    South American Indian, 1018, 1022,
        1029
    in Tibet, 1107
    in Yakut religion, 1170
Healing of the Soul, The (Ibn Sina),
    526
Heart of Darkness (Kurtz), 320
Heart of Jesus, 73
Heartland in Cities (Adams), 87
heaven and hell, 475–476
    and afterlife, 39, 40

and apocalypticism, 80
Arctic, 93
and ascension, 98
in Buddhism, 39, 475–476
Chinese, 476
in Christianity, 39, 475
Cuna, 346–347
of Dante Alighieri, 350
in Egypt, 39
in Hinduism, 39, 475
in Islam, 475
Japanese, 476
in Judaism, 39, 475
in Zoroastrianism, 39, 68
See also afterlife; immortality; under-
    world
Hebat, 520
Hebrew (`Ivrim), term, 614
Hebrew scriptures. See Bible; Bible
    canon
Hebrews, 440
Hebrews. See Israelite religion
Hebron, 340, 351
Hegel, G.W.F., 157, 1095
Hegelianism, 61
Heglen, 1127
heiau, 474
Heidegger, Martin, 948
heikhalot, 785
Heiler, Friedrich, 896
Heimdallr, 431, 432, 433
hekula, 1021
Hel, 431
Helbo, Menaham ben, 151
Heldammu, 521
Helena (mother of Constantine), 636
Heliopolis, 1088
Heliopolitan Ennead, 384
Helios, 179, 544
hell. See heaven and hell; underworld
Hellenism in Jewish Palestine
    (Lieberman), 467
Hellenistic religions, 476–480
    alchemy in, 51–52
    ascension in, 99
    baptism in, 138
    iconography of, 539
    and Judaism, 543–544
    magic in, 477–478
    oracles in, 478, 858–860
    prophecy in, 478
    sacraments in, 953
    spread of, 476–477
    state-supported, 477
    universalism and syncretism in,
        478–480
Helvétius, Claude-Adrien, 392
Helwys, Thomas, 139
Hemacandra, 619
henotheism, 763, 895
Henry, Carl F.H., 401
Henry II, King of England, 575
Henry VIII, King of England, 296
Henry of Bergen, 393
Hepat, 520
hepatoscopy, 859
Hephzibah, 84
Hera, 17, 451, 479, 539, 887

Heraclas, 326
Heracleon, 154
Heraclitus, 372, 373
Heraclius, Emperor (Byzantine), 84,
    343
Herakles, 463
Hercules, 242
    Celtic, 241–242
    of Romans, 942
Herder, Johann, 156
herem, 758, 958
heresy, 480–481
    and blasphemy, 175–177
    development of, 480–481
    and gnosticism, 436–437
    and inquisition, 575–576
    and type of religion, 480–481
    and witchcraft, 1164–1165
Herman, 949
Hermes, 17, 462
Hermes Trismegistos, 51
Hermetica, 51
Hermetism, 51, 52, 54, 445
Hermippus, 699
Hermodorus, 699
Hermódr, 431
Hermotimos, 99
Hermunduri, 432
hero cult
    Greek, 462–463, 477
    See also culture hero
Hero with the Magic Wand, 809
Herod Antipas, 643
Herod I, 636
Herodotus, 97, 479, 698
Herrmann, Wilhelm, 140
Hertz, Robert, 189
Hertzberg, Hans, 158
Heruka, 216
Herzl, Theodor, 659, 1187
Heschel, Abraham Joshua, 661–662
hesed, 459
Hesi, 834
    sodalities, 834
Hesiod, 161, 340, 463
Hestia, 451, 462
Hestia Koine, 462
Hewavitarane, David. See Dharmapala,
    Anagarika
Hexapla (Origen), 326
Hezekiah, 616
Hibbat Tsiyyon movement, 1187
Hibil, 702
Hick, John, 444
Hicks, Edward, 677
Hidalgo, 534
Hidatsa Indians, 820, 822
"Hidden Book," 588
Hidden Imam, 595, 596, 608
Hideyoshi, Toyotomi, 626
hiera, 463
Hierapolis, 86
hierophany, 67
hieros, 956–957
High Celestial Plain, 668
High Holy Days, 649
Higher Criticism, 151
higigah, 882

Hijrah (Muhammad's flight), 601
hijri. See Hijrah
Hikus, 823
Hilaria, 55
Hilary of Poitiers, 155
Hilgenfeld, Adolf, 480
Hili, 797
Hill of the Star, 129
Hillel, 967, 1114
Hillelites, 470
Hillenbrand, Robert, 611
Hiller, Delbert, 158
Hilli, Muhaqqiq al-, 595, 605
hilyah, 547
Hilyat al-awliya' (al-Isfahani), 1046
Himalayan religions, 482–483
Himinbjorg, 431
Himmelsreise, 557
Hina, 474
Hinayana Buddhism, 208, 211–213,
    218
  development of, 211–212
  groups in, 212
Hinduism, 45, 483–505
  afterlife in, 37, 39
  alchemy in, 50
  altar in, 56, 1083
  and Balinese religion, 134
  in Bengal, 142–143, 144
  Bhagavadgita, 148–150, 340, 497,
    502, 504, 672
  bhakti. See bhakti Hinduism
  Brahmanic, 486–488, 499, 556
  caste system of, 134, 485, 490–492,
    497, 502, 503, 1068
  celibacy in, 238
  chanting in, 249
  charity in, 251
  consolidation of, 489–490
  cosmology of, 475
  creation myth of, 190
  demons in, 359, 487
  dharma in, 100, 149, 251, 361–362,
    490–492
  early history of, 564
  fasting in, 413
  and flood, 415
  of Gandhi, 429, 504
  goals of man, 492
  goddesses in, 449–450, 498, 499,
    502
    Devi, 540–541
    Tantric, 1069, 1072
  gods in, 190, 485–486, 487, 488,
    502, 503
    Siva, 540, 564, 1001–1003
    Tantric, 1069, 1071–1072
    Visnu, 540, 564
  heaven and hell in, 475
  in Himalayan region, 482
  iconography of, 540–541
  immortality in, 555–556
  International Society for Krishna
    Consciousness (ISKCON),
    578–579
  and Islam, 566
  Islamic influence on, 503–504
  in Java, 631

karman in, 671–672
  Maharashtrian, 709–710
  meditation in, 719
  monotheism in, 762
  and nationalism, 144
  non-Aryan influence on, 564
  ordination in, 863
  paradise in, 880
  philosophical schools of, 492–502
    Mimamsa, 493, 738–739
    Nyaya, 492–493, 851–852
    Samkhya, 493, 494, 970–971,
      1174
    Vaisesika, 1145
    Vedanta, 493, 1150–1153
    Yoga, 238, 493, 494, 671–672,
      719, 1174–1177
  pilgrimage in, 710, 889
  popular, 502–503
  priesthood, of, 485, 486, 487
  purification in, 912, 913
  Ramakrishna Mission, 504
  reform movements in, 504–505
  reincarnation in, 928–929
  retreat in, 936
  revelation in, 938
  roots in Indus Valley, 483–484
  sacraments in, 953–954
  sacrifice in, 487, 488, 491, 497,
    502–503, 518–519
  sainthood in, 967
  and Sankara's Advaita, 499–500,
    501
  sectarian, 500–502, 504
  Sikhism, 999
  soul in, 1008
  spiritual guide in, 1044–1045
  sruti and *smrti* texts of, 490
  Tamil, 1063–1064
  Tantric. *See* Tantrism, Hindu;
    Tantrism, Hinduism
  temples of, 89, 90, 497–498, 502,
    1063–1064, 1082–1084
  underworld in, 1136
  Upanisads. *See* Upanisads
  Vedic. *See* Vedic religion
  vegetarianism in, 491, 502
  Western influence on, 503, 504
Hine, 474
Hipparchos, 982
Hippolytus of Rome, 155, 342, 434,
    437
Hiram of Tyre, 886
Hirobumi, Ito, 629
Hirsch, Samson Raphael, 153, 865
His Own Times (Guicciardini), 515
*Histoire critique du texte Vieux
    Testament* (Simon), 156
*Historia de los Mexicanos por sus pin-
    turas*, 127
*Historia general de las cosas de la
    Nueva España* (de Sahagún),
    127
Historical Annals (Ssu-ma Ch'ien),
    315
Historical and Critical Dictionary
    (Bayle), 392
Historie der Ketzereien (Walch), 480

History of Florence (Bruni), 515
History of Florence (Machiavelli), 515
history of religions, 505–509
  comparative research in, 507–509
  and Eliade, 389–391
  holistic approach, 506–507
  idolatry in, 550–551
  methodology of, 505–506
  monotheism and polytheism in, 508
"History of Religions and a New
    Humanism" (Eliade), 390
History of Religious Ideas, A (Eliade),
    390
Hittin, 344
Hittite religion, 509–511
  afterlife, 511
  deities, 510
  myths, 510
  temples, 510–511
Hittites, 97
Hlidskjálf, 431
hljód, 433
Ho Ping-ti, 88
Hobbes, Thomas, 424
  on free will, 424
Hodgson, Marshall G.S., 610
Hoffman, David Tsevi, 153
Hofmann, Melchior, 59
hogon, 527
Hokekyo, 625
Hokkaido, 44
D'Holbach, Paul-Henri Thiry, 101, 392
Holi festival, 55
Holiness Code, 957
holiness groups, 400
Holiness-Penticostalism, 35
Holm, Gustav, 94
Holmes, John Haynes, 430
Holmes, Oliver Wendell, 1043
Holocaust, 511–514
  Jewish response to, 443–444,
    511–514, 662–663
Holofernes, 166
Holoholo, 354
Holy Communion. *See* Eucharist
Holy of Holies, 635, 931
Holy Immortals, 69
Holy Mother Hall, 1086
Holy Office (Inquisition), 576
Holy Royal Arch, 422
Holy Sepulcher, 343
Holy Spirit, 170, 222, 270, 279, 639,
    640
  divinity of, 941
  Zulu, 1192
Holy Spirit Association for the
    Unification of World Christianity,
    1140
Holy Synod, 949
hom, 99
homa, 216
hombre-dios, 128
Homer, 81, 100, 354
Hominids, 869–870
homo ex machina, 734
homo religiosus, 74, 340, 341, 389,
    961
  and idolatry, 550

Homo sapiens, 870–871, 1034
homo symbolicus, 389
homoousios, 638
Honen, 625
Hong Taeyong, 314
Hongo, 377
honke, 65
Honorius III, Pope, 420, 875–876
Hooker, Richard, 70
Hopi Indians, 531, 689, 789, 837, 838, 839, 841, 843
Hopwood, Derek, 613
Hoq ha-Shevut, 469
Horagalles, 952
Horeb, 615, 616
horoscopes, 477
  Korean religion, 680
Hort, Fenton, 159
Horton, Robin, 746
Horus, 90, 385, 386, 538, 582, 583, 1105
  conception of, 868
Horyuji temple compound, 1085
Hosea, 548, 616
Hosea, 160
hosios, 957
Hosius of Cordova, 334
hotr, 486
Hou Chi, 254, 257
Hourani, Albert, 613
hourglass megaliths, 721
House of Allah. *See* Ka'bah
House of Ancestral Spirits, 1057
House of Bishops, 293
Howling Dervishes, 1081
Hringhorni, 431
Hrotits`, 98
Hrymr, 430
Hsi Wang Mu, 43
Hsi-ming (Chang Tsai), 307
Hsiang K`ai, 684
Hsiao ching, 1076
Hsiao-hsüeh (Chu Hsi), 309
hsien, 43, 47, 542, 543
Hsien-pei, 572
hsin, 262
hsin-chai, 306, 413
Hsin-dynasty religion, 257
Hsin-li hsüeh (Fung Yu-lan), 311
hsing, 308
hsing-ju, 183
Hsiung Shih-li, 311
Hsiung-nu, 571, 572
Hsü Heng, 309
Hsü kao-seng chuan (Tao-hsüan), 183
Hsüan-tsang, 260, 750
Hsüan-tsung, 1076
Hsüeh Hsüan, 309
Hsün-tzu, 305
  teachings of, 255, 305–206
Hu Chu-jen, 309
Hua-hu ching, 1076, 1077
Hua-yen ching, 217
Hua-yen school of Buddhism, 209, 260, 805
huaca, 559, 1017, 1019
Huai-nan-tzu, 256
Huan T`an, 257

Huang Ch'üan (Yellow Springs), 42
Huang-Lao, 1075
Huang-ti, 542
Huang-t`ing ching, 1077
Huari, 1017
hubb, 593
Hubert, Henri, 518
hubias, 231
Hudaybi, Hasan Isma`il al-, 780
Hudaybiyah, al-, treaty of, 778
hudud, 589–590
Huehueteotl, 534
Huelva, 523, 524
Hugh of Saint-Victor, 181, 369
Hugh of Strassburg, 47
Hui-k`o, 183
Hui-kuang, 217
Hui-sheng, 750
Hui-tsung, 261, 1076
Huichol, 302, 1121
Huitzilopochtli, 127, 128, 129, 130, 554
Hükegü, 574
Huli, 798
Huliganii (Eliade), 388
human sacrifice
  Aztec, 127–128, 129, 518–519
  as blood offering, 963
  Hawaiian, 518
  Hindu, 518–519
  historical corroboration, 518–519
  Inca, 1018
  Moabite, 758
  by People's Temple, 519
  Phoenician, 887
  purposes of, 518
  as sacrament, 954
humaniora, 517
humanism, 514–517
  of Italian Renaissance, 514–516
  northern European, 516–517
  and Reformation, 517
  and Unitarianism, 1142
Humâyûn, Hatt-i, 607
Hume, David, 77, 101
hun, 42, 48, 65, 1010
Hunan school of Confucianism, 309
Hundred Minor Books, 148
Hung Hsiu-ch`üan, 264
Hungary, Hasidic movement in, 472, 864–865
Huns, 572
hunting
  in North American Indian religion, 808–809, 812, 813, 827
  in Saami religion, 951
  in South American religions, 1023, 1032
  in Tunguz religion, 1127, 1128
Hunyadi, John, 344
Hupa Indians, 834
Hurayrah, Abu, 920
Hurgronje, Christiaan Snouck, 611
Huria Kristen Batak Protestan, 142
huris, 69
Huron Indians, 789, 811, 814
Hurrian religion, 519–520
  gods in, 520
  myths in, 520–521

Hursag, 724
Huruingwuuti, 840
Hus, Jan, 768
Husayn, 547, 585, 595
Husayniyah, 994
Hushi'el, Nehemyah ben, 84
Huskanawe rite, 813
Hut, Hans, 60
Hutten, Ulrich von, 516
Hutter, Jacob, 60
Hutterites, 60, 723
Hutton, James, 403
Hutukhtu, Kangyurwa, 1059
Huxley, Thomas, 403
Huysman, Roelof, 516
Huywiri, `Ali ibn `Uthman al-Jullabi al-, 1046
Hyksos, 644
Hymir, 430
Hymn to Osiris, 868
hymns, psalms as, 909
hyoscyamus niger, 99
Hyperborea, 99
Hyperdexios, 178
Hyrcanus, Eli`ezer, 1114
Hystaspes, 699

I

I ching
  classifications of, 254
  and Confucianism, 304, 306, 307, 309, 317
  hexagrams, 860, 1055, 1073–1074
  numerical system, 307
  t`ai-chi in, 155
  and Taoism, 542, 1073–1074
i-ching (pilgrim), 750
i-It, 661
i-Thou, 661
Ialonus, 242
iatromanteis, 99
`ibadat, 601
Iberian religion, 523–524
  Iberians, 523
  Indo-Europeans, 523–524
  Turdetans, 523
ibgal, 726
Iblis, 360
Ibn `Abd al-Wahhab, Muhammad, 596, 597, 605
Ibn Abi Talib, `Ali, 547, 601
Ibn Adohiyyah, Ya`aqov ben Hayyim, 163
Ibn al-`Arabi, Muhyi al-Din, 593, 594, 595
Ibn al-Hakam, Hisham, 595
Ibn al-Hasan al-Tusi, Muhammad, 605
Ibn al-`Ibri (Bar Hebraeus), 155
Ibn al-Jawziyah, Qayyim, 605
Ibn al-Kalbi, Hisham, 550
Ibn al-Muqaffa`, `Abd Allah, 604
Ibn Ali, Husayn, 182
Ibn `Ali, Zayd, 595
Ibn `Ata', Wasil, 595
Ibn Attar, Hayyim, 153
Ibn Ezra, Avraham, 151, 152
Ibn Hanbal, Ahmad, 591, 603
Ibn Hazm, Ahmad, 605

Ibn Idris al-Shafi`i, Muhammad, 602
Ibn Jubayr, Abu al-Husayn
    Muhammad, 346
Ibn Khaldun, Abu `Abd Allah
    Muhammad, 53, 361, 525
Ibn Khalji, Muhammad Bakhtyar, 145
Ibn Kimhi, `Ezra Yosef, 152
Ibn Labrat, Dunash, 151
Ibn Munqidh, Usamah, 346
Ibn Paquda, Bahye, 151, 653
Ibn Rushd (Averroës), 524–525, 983,
    1047
  works of, 525
Ibn Sina (Avicenna), 53, 448, 474,
    526–527, 593, 983
  works of, 526
Ibn Taymiyah, Hanbali, 447, 592,
    594, 605
Ibn Tufayl, Abu Bakr Muhammad, 524
Ibo, 1155
Icheiri, 231
ichuri, 302
iconography, 527–549
    Australian Aboriginal, 529–530
    Buddhist, 541
    Christian, 544–546, 677
    Egyptian, 537–538
    Greco-Roman, 538–539
    Hindu, 540–541
    iconography, in Africa, 527–528
    Islamic, 547–548
    Jewish, 543–544
    Mesoamerican, 533–534
    Mesopotamian, 535–536
    Minoan-Mycenaean, 538
    North American Indian, 530–531
    South American Indian, 1017
    Taoist, 542–543
iddhi, 95
Idea of the Holy, The (Otto), 1112
Idfu, 90
idolatry, 548–551
    Bible on, 548–549, 615
    and Greek apologists, 549
    history of religions approach to,
        550–551
    and Islam, 550
    and Latin apologists, 549–550
    New Testament on, 549
Ieyasu, Tokugawa, 312
Ifa, 529
Iggeret ha-shemad, 700
Iggeret Teiman (Maimonides), 700
Ignatius, 980
Ignatius of Antioch, 154, 180
Ignatius Loyola, 551–552
    early life and education of, 551
    in Japan, 626
    and Jesuits, 276, 552
    on meditation, 719
    on retreat, 937
    spiritual life of, 551–552
ihram, 891
Ihud, 191
ihuicatl, 128
Ihya' `ulum al-din (al-Ghazali), 593, 605
Ijma`, 603
ijtihad, 589, 590, 597, 604

ikega, 527
ikegobo, 527
Ikhwan al-Safa', 53
Ikko, 626
*Il viaggio de Siam de'padri gesuiti
    mandati dal re di Francia
    all'Indie, e alla China* (Tachard),
    30
ilhuicatl, 128
Iliad (Homer), 354
Ilibemberti, 972
Illapa, 560, 1016–1017
`illat al-hukm*, 589
Illinois Indians, 811, 814
illness
    and possession, 407, 408
    and purification, 913
    spiritual attribution, 911
    See also healing
Illuyanka, 510
`ilm al-hadith*, 609
Images and Symbols (Eliade), 390
imam, 774, 776
Imamiyah, 993
iman, 561–562, 583, 588
Imana, 577
Imitation of Christ (á Kempis), 283
Immaculate Conception, 640, 716, 717,
    877
immanence, 930, 1038
immanental theocracy, 624
immersion ritual
    North American Indian, 818
    See also baptism
immortality, 553–558
    in Africa, 553
    in Australia, 553–554
    and baptism, 137
    Bible on, 556–557
    in Buddhism, 556
    Chinese concepts of, 43, 48–49, 555
    in Christianity, 558
    in Finno-Ugric cultures, 554
    and gnosticism, 557
    in Greco-Roman religion, 557
    in Hinduism, 556
    in Indo-European religions, 568–569
    in Islam, 558
    and Manichaeism, 557
    in Mesoamerican religions, 554–555
    in nonliterate cultures, 553
    in North American Indian religion,
        554
    in Taoism, 542, 543, 1077–1078
*Impartial History of the Churches and
    Heresies* (Arnold), 435
Imperial Rescript on Education, 627,
    628, 629
Imperial Rescript on Soldiers and
    Sailors, 627
In Darkest England and the Way Out
    (Booth), 188, 969
In eminenti, 423
`Ina, 474
Inanna, 450, 520, 536, 725
Inca religion, 559–560
    afterlife in, 560
    archaeology of, 87

confession in, 302
cosmology of, 559
fasting in, 414
gods in, 559–560
immortality in, 554–555
rites in, 560
sacrifice in, 560, 1018
incantation
    in Africa, 527
    in Buddhism, 215–216
    Canaanite, 227
    in exorcism, 407
incarnation, 104, 561–563
    in Buddhism, 562
    in Christianity, 562–563
    Dalai Lama, 349
    in Greek religion, 561
    in Hinduism, 561
    in Iran (ancient), 561
    Jesus Christ, 440
    and kings/emperors/imams, 561–562
    meaning of, 561
    primitive belief, 561
incense, 963
Incoherence of the Incoherent (Ibn
    Rushd), 525
Incoherence of the Philosophers (al-
    Ghazali), 593
incubation, 90
Index of Forbidden Books, 326
India
    Aryan invasion of, 485
    Gandhi in, 428–431, 504
    independence of, 144–145
    Inner Asian peoples in, 571–572
    Islamic law in, 606
    Mughal Empire, 45–46, 504
    scientific achievements, 982
Indian religions, 563–566
    in Akbar's reign, 45–46, 504
    alchemy in, 50
    ancestor worship in, 64
    archaeology of, 88
    and atheism, 100
    blessing in, 179
    and Christianity, 504, 566
    Christianity, 145, 379, 504, 566, 753,
        1064–1065
    confession in, 302
    cross in, 340
    exorcism in, 407–408
    Indra (rain god), 569–570
    Islam, 45–46, 503–504, 566, 596,
        776–777
    Marathi, 709–710
    monotheism in, 763
    Nyaya school in, 851–852
    purification in, 912
    resurrection in, 935
    retribution in, 766
    Saivism, 564, 565, 1063, 1064
    Samkhya-Yoga, 561
    soul in, 1007–1008
    Tamil, 1062–1065
    Vaisnavism, 565–566
    See also Bengali religions;
        Buddhism, Indian; Hinduism;
        Jainism

Indian Shaker church, 835
Indians. *See* North American Indian religion
indiki, 1192
Indo-European religions, 566–569
    Armenian, 97–98, 249, 379
    Baltic, 135–137
    Celtic, 239–244, 556
    cosmology of, 567–568
    Germanic, 430–433
    Hittite, 509–511
    in Iberian Peninsula, 523–524
    immortality in, 568–569
    linguistic research on, 566–567
    myth of, 567
    rituals of, 568
    Slavic, 1003–1005
Indonesia, 1037
Indra, 67, 143, 486, 496, 569–570, 581, 1084
    function of, 570
    myths about, 569–570
    Siva as, 570
Indra-Vrtrahan, 373
indriya, 364
Indus Valley, 88
Inge, Dean W.R., 782
Ingila, 98
Inis Targhnai, 242
initiation rites
    African, 376, 528, 1163
    Australian Aboriginal, 109–110, 113–114, 115, 116, 177
    Balinese, 135
    blessing in, 179
    Buddhist, 196
    in community, 299
    Cuna, 346
    and faith, 409
    female, 22, 110, 111, 346, 528
    Hindu, 487
    in Judaism, 649
    New Guinean, 798
    North American Indian, 813, 832, 841
    Oceanic, 855
    purification in, 911
    retreat in, 936
    shaman, 973, 991, 1027, 1028
    South American Indian, 1029
    See also female initiation
Inkarri, 1019
iNkosazana yeZulu, 1191
iNkosi yeZulu, 1191
Inktomi, 821
Inner Asian religions, 570–574
    Avars, 572–573
    Bulgars, 573
    Hsien-pei, 572
    Juan-juan, 572
    Khazars, 573
    Kushans, 571–572
    Mongols, 573–574
    Scythians, 570–571
    Türk, 572
    Uighurs, 573
    Wu-sun, 571
    Yüeh-chih, 571
Innocent III, Pope, 420, 575, 875

Innocent IV, Pope, 336, 574, 876
Innocent VII, Pope, 981, 1165
Innocent X, Pope, 877
Inquiritur in fontes (Griesbach), 157
Inquiry on Human Nature, An (Han Yü), 306
Inquisition, 575–576, 877, 1165
    early period, 575–576
    later period, 576
    rationale for, 575
insei, 624
Institutes of the Christian Religion (Calvin), 222, 691, 924
Institutio principis Christiani (Erasmus), 394
Institutiones theologiae, 269
Instruction for a Christian Prince (Erasmus), 394
Integral Humanism (Maritain), 715
Interlacustrine Bantu. *See* Bantu religions
International House of Justice, 132, 133
International Journal of Ethics, 14
International Missionary Council, 382
International Society for Krishna Consciousness (ISKCON), 504, 578–579, 744, 800, 802
    development of, 578–579
    founder of, 578
Interpretation of Dreams, The (Freud), 425, 664
Interpretation of Knowledge, The, 155, 437
Inti, 789, 1015–1016
Inti-Viracocha-Pachacámac, 1015
Introduction a la théologie musulmane (Anawati and Gardet), 611
Introduction to a Science of Mythology (Levi-Strauss), 1022–1023
Introduction to the Science of Religion (Müller), 1092
Introduction to Zen Buddhism, An (Suzuki), 1052
Introductory Lectures on Psychoanalysis (Freud), 425
inua, 580
Inuit religion, 93, 580–581, 849
    repentance in, 934
    See also Arctic religions
Investiture Controversy, 295
Iocauna, 230–231
Ionescu, Nae, 386, 388
Ioskeha, 372
Iowa Indians, 820
Ipai-Tipai Indians, 833
Ippen, 625
Iqbal, Muhammad, 597
Iranian Family Protection Law of 1967, 608
Iranian New Year, 98
Iranian religion, 581–582
    afterlife in, 582
    ascension in, 99
    gods in, 581–582
    incarnation in, 561
    and Magi, 697–699
    rituals in, 581
    See also Zoroastrianism

Irenaeus, 155, 278, 342, 434, 436, 437
Irene, Empress, 335
Irish religion, Celtic, 240–244
irja', 585
Iron Guard, 388
Iroquois Indians, 554, 812, 813, 814
Irra, 726
Isaac, 11, 56, 512
Isabel and the Devil's Water (Eliade), 388
Isabel se Apele Divolului (Eliade), 388
Isabella I, 576
Isafel, 69
Isaiah, 159–160, 175, 352, 457
Isaiah, 41, 82, 548, 549
Ise Shinto Shrine, 894, 996
Isenheim Altarpiece, 545
Isfahani, Abu Nu`aym al-, 1046
Ishhara, 510
Ishkur, 725
Ishmael, 11, 12, 550, 667
Ishqabad, 133
Ishtar, 450, 520, 536, 757
Ishtemi, 572
Ishvara, 802
Isidore, 437
Isis, 479, 582–583
    cult of, 582–583, 944
    miracles of, 742
    myths of, 583
    and Osiris, 582, 583, 868
Isis and Osiris (Plutarch), 413, 867
Isis-aretalogy, 583
ISKCON. *See* International Society for Krishna Consciousness
iskir, 53
Islam, 583–613
    Abraham in, 12, 550, 667, 778, 890, 891
    in Africa, 377, 586, 597
    afterlife in, 37
    alchemy in, 53
    angels in, 69
    anti-Judaism in, 79–80, 653
    architecture of, 547, 611
    art of, 547–548, 611
    ascension in, 99
    in Bengal, 145–146
    and Berber religion, 148
    blessing in, 180
    charity in, 251
    chastity in, 253
    in China, 259–260, 586, 777
    and Crusades, 275, 276, 345–346
    and David, 352
    demons in, 360–361
    early development of, 584–585
    in Egypt, 327, 780–781
    eremitism in, 395
    and exorcism, 408
    fall concept in, 412
    gnosticism in, 435
    hadith in, 588–589, 611
    heaven and hell in, 475
    and Hinduism, 566
    iconography of, 547–548
    and idolatry, 550
    immortality in, 558

Islam *(continued)*
in India, 45–46, 503–504, 596, 606, 776–777
international conferences of, 598
islam, concept of, 583
Isma`ili, 596, 787–788
in Java, 631–633
in Jerusalem, 636–637
jihad in, 584–585, 641
Ka`bah in, 667–668, 891, 892
liturgy in, 775
magic in, 408
martyrdom in, 712–713
medieval, 585–586
messianism in, 728
miracles in, 743
modern developments in, 596–598, 611
and Mongol invasion, 574
Moses in, 772
mysticism in. *See* Sufism
neofundamentalism in, 598
oral tradition, 861
ordination in, 863–864
origin of, 583–584
pilgrimage in, 585, 588, 889–892
predestination in, 424
repentance in, 934
resurrection in, 935–936
retreat in, 937
sacrifice in, 892
sainthood in, 967
Satan in, 977
and science, 982–983
and scientific achievement, 982–983
sects of. *See* Shi'ah Islam; Sunni Islam
soul in, 1013–1014
spiritual guide in, 1044
spread of, 586, 752
sunnah in, 588
Ten Commandments in, 1092
theology of, 525, 590–592
underworld in, 1135–1136
in United States, 36, 586, 701
See also God; mosques; Muhammad; Qur'an
Islam and Contemporary Society (Azzam), 612
Islam in der Gegenwart, Der (Ende and Steinbach), 611
Islamic law
ancient, 602–604
flexibility of, 590
historical development of, 601–604
jihad in, 641
in modern period, 606–608
moral considerations in, 590
nature of, 600–601
origins of, 589, 600
punishments in, 589–590
Qur'an and, 599, 601, 603, 605
schools of, 590, 595, 602–606
sources of, 589
westernization of, 606–608
Islamic Perspectives: Studies in Honor of Sayyid Abul Ala Mawdudi (Ahmad and Ansari), 612

Islamic Republic, 133
Islamic Secretariat, 598
Islamic Society and the West (Gibb and Bowen), 611
Islamic studies, 609–610
nonnormative, 610–611
within Oriental studies, 610
present-day, 611–612
islands, as paradise, 880–881
Isles of the Blessed, 880
Isma`il, 596, 667, 787–788
Isma`illyah, 596, 994
isnad, 589
Isopata, 15
Israel
Buber on, 191
Jewish law (*halakhah*) in, 469, 1188
Orthodox Judaism in, 865–866
yeshivah in, 1173–1174
and Zionism, 659, 866
Israel Affairs Committee, 322
Israelite religion, 613–618
and Abraham, 11–12
altar in, 56
canon of, 616–617
centralization of, 616–618
chastity in, 253
and community, 300
confession in, 303
covenant with God, 338–339, 615, 616
cultic worship in, 615
and David, 350–352
death ritual in, 556
in Jerusalem, 635–636
and Kingdom of God, 676
Levites, 687–688
monotheism of, 613–614, 762–763
and Moses, 771–772
and Pharisees, 883–884
priesthood in, 687–688
prophets in, 859, 902
Zealots, 1183
See also Essenes; Jerusalem, Temples of; Ten Commandments
Israelitische Religionsgesellschaft, 865
Isserles, Mosheh, 653
istadevata, 497, 500
Istanbul, 91, 669
See also Constantinople
istikharah, 919–920
istinbat, 784
Istorica descrizione de'tre'regni Congo (Cavazzi), 29
Isvara, 494, 852
Isvarakrsna, 971
Itelmen, 92
Ithna `Ashariyah, 596
ius sacrum, 943
Ivory Coast, 22, 24, 27
Iwa, 233
iwan plan, 776, 777
Ixchel, 717
Izanagi, 451
Izanami, 451
Izapa, 133, 533
Izapan, 533
Izra'il, 69
Izzishtanu, 510

J

Jacob, 11, 644
Jacob, Benno, 948
Jacobite church, 379
Jaén, 523
Ja`far, Imam, 993
Jagannatha, 450
Jäger, Johann, 516
Jagiello, 752
Jahan `Ali, Khan, 146
Jahangir, 547
Jahiliyah, 550
Jaimini, 493
Jain, Hiralal, 622
Jainism, 565, 619–622
and atheism, 100
charity in, 251
confession in, 302
cosmology of, 329, 620
doctrine of, 620–621
ethics of, 621
fasting in, 413, 414
influential persons of, 621–622
karman in, 672
literature of, 619–620
ordination in, 863
origins of, 619
reincarnation in, 929
religious practices in, 620
renewal in, 621–622
Tantric, 1067
temples of, 621
Jalal, Shah, 146
Jamaa, 26
jama`ah, 773
jamaat, 781
Jamaica
ancestral cults in, 234–235
Rastafarianism in, 235–236
revivalist cults in, 236
Jambu, 619
Jambudvipa, 582
`Jam-dbyans Mkhyen-brtse'i-dban-po, 204
James, 173
James, E.O., 453
James I, King of England, 913, 914, 1165
James, William, 73, 75, 446
James (New Testament), 12, 81
Jami, Nur al-Din `Abd al Rahman ibn Ahmad, 1046
Jami` al-hikmatayn (Nasir-i Khusraw), 788
jami's, 773
`Jam-mgon Kon-sprul Blo-gros-mtha'-yas, 204
Jamna culture, 567
janna, 880
Jansen, Cornelis, 877
Japan
new religions in, 803, 1140
temple compounds in, 1085
Japanese religion, 622–630
ancestor worship in, 65–66
archaic tradition, 622–623
in Ashikaga period, 625–626
Chinese influence on, 623

Christianity, 626, 628–629
Confucianism, 312–313, 626, 627, 628, 997
death concepts in, 911
early development of, 623
exorcisms in, 407
freedom of, 629–630
heaven and hell in, 476
in Kamakura period, 624–625
and Meiji restoration, 627–629
in modern period, 627–630
Neolithic, 790
in Ritsuryo state, 624
Shotoku's reform of, 623–624
Tokugawa policy on, 626–627
See also Buddhism, Japanese; Shinto
Jaspers, Karl, 73
Jastorf culture, 430
Jatakas, 360
jatis, 143, 491–492
jatras, 710
Java, 141, 586, 1037
Javanese religion, 631–633
Agami Islam Santri system, 632–633
Agami Jawi system, 632–633
historical development, 631–632
Jawziyah, Ibn Qayyim al-, 1013
Jayadeva, 501
Jebe, 573
Jebel al-Aqra, 224
Jednota Bratrská (Society of Brethren), 767, 905
Jefferson, Thomas, 177, 393
Jeffery, Arthur, 610
Jehovah, 634
Jehovah's Witnesses, 25–26, 633–635
beliefs and practices, 634–635
prominent figures in, 634
Jemez Indians, 845
jen, 255, 305, 309, 317, 318
Jensen, Adolf E., 354
Jeremiah, 155, 159, 160, 161, 616
Jeremiah, 58, 166
Jeremias, Joachim, 158
Jeremias II of Constantinople, 949
Jericho, 88, 791
Jeroboam, 57, 548
Jerome, 155, 572, 875
Jerusalem, 88, 351, 378, 635–637
burning of, 167
Crusades in, 343
Dome of the Rock, 90
under Greece, 636
under Herod, 636
under Islam, 636–637
patriarchate of, 460
under Rome, 636
Temple, 635, 636
See also Jerusalem, Temples of
Jerusalem, Temples of, 342, 551
Arc of the Covenant, 342, 351, 635
chanting in, 248
destruction of, 167, 442, 513, 557, 646, 1053
First, 82, 159, 351, 635, 1117
destruction of, 167, 442, 557, 635
and Passover, 881, 882

pilgrimage to, 649
priesthood of, 687–688
prophets of, 617
rebuilding of, 84, 470
rededication by Maccabees, 470, 649
Sanhedrin in, 973–974
Second, 82, 160, 353, 513, 617, 636, 882, 1117
destruction of, 513, 646, 946, 1053
site of, 89
Torah in, 162
Torah reading in, 162
Torah study in, 1117
Jerusalem Talmud, 646, 1060
Jesse, 351
Jesuits (Society of Jesus), 276, 552
and Catholic Reformation, 276, 296
formation of, 552, 877
in Japan, 626
in Korea, 680
missions of, 398, 626, 680, 753
Jesus: God and Man (Pannenberg), 639
Jesus Christ, 13, 56, 78, 157–158, 182, 637–640
and atonement, 104
and baptism, 138, 643
in biblical exegesis, 154, 155
blessings of, 180
in Christian doctrine, 279, 280, 281, 335
in Christian Science, 286
crucifixion of, 341, 342, 438, 545–546, 638, 712
and Eucharistic worship, 282, 399, 639
and gnosticism, 436–437
and God, 279, 438, 439–440
as God, 440–441, 458, 563, 638
in Gospels, 172
and Hebrew scriptures, 170
historical study of, 272–273, 638–640
images of, 544–546
imitation of, 283
incarnate life, 562–563
in Jerusalem, 636
on Kingdom of God, 676–677
life of, 637
and Lord's Prayer, 690
as Messiah, 439, 727–728
ministry of, 637–638
miracles of, 742–743
in New Testament, 173, 279
obedience to will of, 283–284
oral tradition about, 171–172
and Pharisees, 883–884
as prophet, 902, 903
and redemption, 941
resurrection of, 169, 172, 378, 439, 558, 638, 639–640, 935
as spiritual guide, 1044
temptation of, 1090, 1091
virginal conception of, 640, 716
See also Trinity
Jesus the Christ (Kasper), 639

Jetavaniyas, 213
Jewish Antiquities (Josephus Flavius), 12
Jewish Theological Seminary, 321, 321–322
Jews
in Alexandria, 163, 1114
in Babylonia, 1171
Babylonian Exile, 635
in Bengal, 145
in Diaspora, 648–649, 1172
and Holocaust, 443–444, 511–514
and Islam, 599
in Israel, 659
secular, 658–659
See also Judaism
jhana, 95
Jhanesvar, 709
Jhansi League of Devotees, 578
Ji, 625
Jibril, 69
Jigalong, 121
`Jigs-med-glin-pa, 204
jihad, 345, 585–586, 641
basis of, 641
historical impact, 641
jihad movement, 146, 597, 641
jihva, 364
jikei seiza, 312
Jilani, `Abd al-Qadir, al-, 594, 1081
Jili, `Abd al-Karim al-, 1014
jimsonweed, North American Indians ceremonies, 833
Jina, 619
jinen honi, 805
Jinenchishu, 624
Jingoji temples, 1085
Jinja Shinto, 995
jinn, 69, 360–361
jiriki, 805
jiva, 100, 621, 672, 1008, 1009
jizyah, 585
jñana, 488, 494, 496, 500, 620
jñana-karma-samuccaya-vada, 739
Jñanaprasthana, 333
jñanayoga, 150
Jnanesvari, 709
jñatata, 739
jnun, 147
Joan of Arc, 642–643
Job, 80, 512
Job, 160, 163, 165
Jocakuvaque, 231
Jochi, 574
jodo, concept of, 626
Jodo sect, 625
Jodo Shin, 625
Jodo Shinshu, 208
Joel, 160
John (apostle), 78
See also Gospel of John; Revelation
John VIII, Pope, 343
John XXII, Pope, 876, 981
John XXIII, Pope (1410–1415), 336, 768, 876, 981
John XXIII, Pope (1958–1963), and Second Vatican Council, 338, 878, 940

John the Baptist, 138, 637, 643–644
 life and execution of, 643
John the Baptist (Johane Masowe), 25,
 438, 643–644
John of Freiburg, 47
John Hyranus, 160
John of Lichtenburg, 47
John of Monte Corvino, 752
John of Patmos, 180
John Paul I, Pope, 878, 940
John Paul II, Pope, 72, 229, 230, 420,
 428, 878, 940
John of Salisbury, 295
Jokin, Keizan, 1185
Jokyu rebellion, 625
Jomyo, Nampo, 1185
Jonah, 160
Jonas, Hans, 436
Jones, Alonzo T., 988
Jones, Bob, Sr., 401
Jones, Jim, 519
Jonestown suicides, 519
Jord, 433
Jordan River, 139
Jordan of Saxony, 46
Joseki, Gasan, 1185
Joseph, biblical, 644
Joseph, father of Jesus, 637, 716
Josephus Flavius
 on Abraham, 12
 on Essenes, 353, 557
 on Hebrew canon, 160, 161
 on Joseph, 644
 on Pharisees, 883
 on Sanhedrin, 974
 on Zealots, 1183
Joshua, 159, 162, 616, 651
Joshua, 152
Josiah, 162, 616, 617, 1114
Jotunheimr, 430
ju, 318
Ju-ching, 1184
Juan-juan, 572
Jubal, 221
Jubilees, 12, 160, 617
Judah, 58, 351, 617
Judaism, 644–663
 afterlife in, 38, 39, 40–42, 650–651
 angels in, 68–69
 anti-Semitism, 78–80, 653, 656
 apocalypticism in, 80, 82–83
 ascension in, 99
 Ashkenazic, 652–653, 1172
 atonement in, 103–104
 baptism in, 138
 biblical exegesis, 151–154
 blasphemy in, 175
 blessing in, 646, 647, 882
 blood and, 182
 celibacy in, 239
 chanting in, 248–249
 charity in, 250, 649
 chastity in, 239, 253
 Christian roots in, 273
 and community, 191
 Conservative, 321–323, 657
 Day of Atonement (Yom Kippur),
  103, 226, 413, 647, 649

demons in, 360
fall concept in, 411–412
fasting in, 413–414
festivals
 Hanukkah, 470–471, 649
 Passover, 649, 881–882
 Purim, 470, 649
 Sukkot, 649
and gnosticism, 69, 434–435
goddesses in, 450–451
Hasidim in, 190–191, 443, 471–473
heaven and hell in, 475
and Holocaust, 443–444, 511–513,
 662
iconography of, 543–544
Karaites in, 669–670
late biblical, 645–646
law of. *See halakhah*
marriage in, 239, 253, 647–648
martyrdom in, 712, 713
meaning of word, 644–645
meditation in, 718
messianism in, 727
in middle ages, 41, 544, 653–655
miracles in, 741–742
in modern period, 655–663, 921–922
mysticism in. *See* Hasidism;
 Qabbalah
ordination in, 863
Orthodox, 657–658, 865–867, 911,
 1187
philosophy in, 655, 660–662
pietism in, 653–654
pilgrimage in, 649, 889
Rabbinic. *See* Rabbinic Judaism
Reconstructionism, 657, 661
Reform, 14, 656, 657, 865, 926–928
repentance in, 103–104, 933–934
resurrection in, 935
Ro`sh ha-Shanah, 649
Sabbath in, 649, 989
sainthood in, 967
and science, 982
Sefardic, 652–653
soul in, 1011
spiritual guide in, 1044
underworld in, 1135
yeshivah in, 1171–1174
and Zionism, 659, 660, 1186–1187
See also Bible; God; Israelite reli-
 gion; synagogue; Talmud
Judas, 79
Jude, 173
Judean War, 78
Judenrat, 713
Judges, 159, 161, 616, 651
Judgment Day. *See* Last Judgment
Judgment, The (Ibn Sina), 526
Jüdische Schriften (Cohen), 948
Judith, 166
Jugaku, 628
Julia Domna, 945
Julia Mamaea, 945
Jülicher, Adolf, 158
Julius exclusus e coelis (Erasmus),
 394
Julius II, Pope, 876
Julius III, Pope, 398

Julius Shut Out of Heaven (Erasmus),
 394
jum`ah, 773
`Ju Mi-pham`Jam-dbyans-rnam-rgyal-
 rgya- mtsho, 204
Jump Dance, 834
Junayd, Abu al Qasim al-, 592
Jung, Carl Gustav, 361, 425, 436,
 663–665
 on collective unconscious, 70
 on evil, 361
 on goddess worship, 453
 life and works of, 663–664
 psychology of religion, 664–665
Juno, 479
Junod, Henri A., 30
Juok, 375
Jupiter, 462, 479, 538, 539
Jupiter Dolichenus, 943, 944
Jurchen, 573
Justin II, 573
Justin Martyr
 biblical exegesis of, 155
 on cross, 342
 on gnosticism, 437
 on God, 444
 on idolatry, 549
 in Mary, 717
 on oral tradition, 170
 and Trinity, 1123
Justinian I, II, 274, 335, 572
Juynboll, G.H.A., 611

K
ka, 555, 935
Ka To Souma, 796
Ka-lischer, Tsevi Hirsch, 1187
Kaapora, 1032
Ka`bah, 12, 584, 588, 667–668, 773
 historical origin, 667
 location of, 667
 and pilgrimage to Mecca, 891–892
Kabir, 504, 999
kachina, 838, 839, 848
 ceremony, 843–844
 Hopi, 842–843
 Zuni, 843–844, 846
Kachina society, 841, 844
kafirs, 590, 591
kaghan, 572
Kahner, Karl, 639
kahuna-nui, 474
kahunas, 473–474
Kai-nantu, 798
Kainah Indians, 820
Kainantu, 797, 798
Kaisersberg, Johann Geiler, 516
Kait, 510
kaivalya, 493
Kaksu sodalities, 834
Kakutaro, Kubo, 629
Kakwa, 377
kala, 497, 632
Kalabadhi, Abu Bakr Muhammad al-,
 1046
kalam, 368, 447, 448, 525, 609
Kalama, 116
Kalamukhas, 1069

Kalapalo, 1022, 1024
Kalasoka, 333
Kali, 143, 144, 450, 504, 540, 565, 1072
kali, concept of, 880
Kalindi, 145
Kalispel Indians, 833
kalivarjyas, 492
kaliyuga, 429, 492, 495, 496, 497, 737
Kalka, Battle of, 574
Kalki, 496
Kalkin, 732
kalkú, 707
kalkutún, 707
Kallenbach, Hermann, 429
Kallir, El`azar, 84
Kalmuks, 574
kalpas, 620, 732
Kalpasutras, 490
Kalwadi, 112
kalwat dar anjuman, 395
kalyana, 179
kalyanamitra, 1045
kama, 364, 488, 492, 1066
Kama (deity), 1003
Kamaksi, 502
Kamakura, 624–625, 625
kamaloka, 476
Kamares, cave of, 16
Kamasutras, 492
Kamchadal, 92
Kamehameha I, 474
kami, 177, 627, 668
  and Buddhism, 668
  categories of, 995
  concept of, 623, 624, 668, 863, 997
  types of, 668
kami no michi, 368
Kamish, 757
kamma, 475
Kammu, Emperor, 965
Kampuchea, 674
Kamwana, Elliot, 26, 27
Kanaloa, 474
Kande Yaka, 1000
Kandinsky, Wassily, 546
Kane, 474
Kanetomo, Urabe, 996
kang dumadi, 632
K`ang Yu-wei, 263, 311
kangsin mu, 679
Kanha, 708
Kanheri, 1084
Kaniska, Council of, 333, 571
kanjeng nabi, 632
kannagara, 627
Kannia, 16
Kansa Indians, 820
Kansas City Creed, 319
Kant, Immanuel, 101, 140, 157, 297, 445
  and Barth, 140
  and biblical exegesis, 157
  on God, 101, 445
  Neo-Kantianism, 297
  on temptation, 1090
*Kantisch-fries'sche
    Religionsphilosophie und ihre*

Anwendung auf die Theologie
    (Otto), 961
Kantule, Nele, 347
Kantuzzili prayer, 511
Kanya Kumari Sthan, 710
Kao-tsu, 257, 260
Kao-tsung, 260
Kapalikas, 501, 1069
Kapilavastu, 742
Kaplan, Mordecai, 443, 657, 661
Kapwangwa, 795
Kapwicalo, 795
Karabalghasun, 573
Karaites, 352, 653, 669–670
  literature, 669–670
  rise of, 669
karakia, 855
Karakitai, 573
karamat, 743
Karamojong, 376
Karappacami, 1065
Karen, 735
Karlstadt, Andreas, 59, 924
karma. See Karman
karman
  in Buddhism, 37, 65, 185, 193, 258, 303, 564, 672–673, 765, 1107
    changeability of, 673
    forms of, 673
    Mahayana, 214
  concept of, 671–673
  in Hinduism, 37, 100, 149, 362, 475, 488, 491, 494, 671–672, 852
  in Jainism, 302, 414, 672
  and reincarnation concept, 929
  and retribution, 766
karmasaya, 672
karmayoga, 150, 429, 497, 504
Karnak, 385, 386, 1088
Karo, Yosef, 653
Karo Batak, 142
Karok Indians, 834
karshvar, 582
karuna, 251, 766
Karusakaibe, 1031
kasaba, 591
kasher, 646
kashf, 593
Kashf al-mahjub (al-Hujwiri), 1046
Kashghari, Mahmud al-, 1129
Kashku, 510, 520
Kaskihá, 1028
Kasper, Walter, 639
Kasuga shrine, 625
Kasyapa, 332
Kataoka Hill, 184
Kataragama, 408
Katha, 489
Katha Upanisad, 340, 489
katharsis, 557
Kathavatthu, 333
Kathmandu Valley, 482
Ka'thog Rig-'dzin Tshe-dban-nor-bu, 204
Kato Syme, 16
Katonda, 577
Kats, Avraham ben Alexander of
    Kalisz, 472

Kaufmann, Yehezkel, 948
Kauil, 717
Kauravas, 148
Kautantowwit, 811
Kautilya, 492
Kautsky, Karl, 714
Kautzsch, Emil, 167
Káuyúumaari, 1121
kava, 474
Kavere, 796
kavi, 485
kavod, 785
Kawailsu Indians, 834
kaya, 364
Kaysan, Abu `Amrah, 992
Kaysaniyah movement, 992–993
Kazim, Musa al-, 993
Kealakekua, 474
Keane, A.H., 74
kebatinan kejawen, 633
Keetan'to-wit, 811
Kegon, 965
Kele cult, in Saint Lucia, 235
Keli yaquar (Efrayim of Luntshits), 152
Kemal, Namik, 597
Kemosh, 757–758
  temple of, 758
à Kempis, Thomas, 283
Kena Upanisad, 449
Kenites, 614
Kenya, 21, 26, 27
Keos, 14
Kepler, Johannes, 427
Kerder, 699
Kereit, 573
Kerén-yi, Károly, 436
Keresan Indians, 838, 845
Kesava, 497
Kesh, 725
Keshi, 521
Kessi, 521
Ketav ve-ha-quabbalah (Mecklenburg), 153
Ketenensis, Robertus, 955
Keter Torah, 670
Ketteler, Wilhelm, 289
Ketu Yoruba, 528
*Ketzergeschichte des Urchristentums,
    Die*, (Hilgenfeld), 480
Ketzergeschichte (von Mosheim), 480
kevala-jñana, 620
Khado, 1128
Khaldi, 520
khalifah, 412, 596
Khalifat Allah, 412
khalwah, 937
Khamsah (Nizami), 547
khanagahs, 594
Khanates, 574
Khandoba, 709
Il-khanids, 574
Khanty, 92, 93, 554
Kharijis, 585, 590–591
khatib, 774
Khatm al-awliya' (al-Tirmidhi), 592
khatri, 145
Khayr, Abu Sa`id ibn Abi al-, 1044
khaz, 249

Khazars, 573
Khmer religion, 674
Khoi and San religions, 30, 674, 674–675
Khomeini, Ayatollah, 547, 598
Khonsu, 385, 1106
Khorenats, 97
Khrushchev, Nikita, 715
Khubilai, Khan, 574, 761
Khurri, 520
khuruj, 590
Khusraw, Abu Mu`in ibn. *See* Nasir-i Khusraw
khutbah, 773, 773–774, 774, 775
khvaetvadatha, 697
Khvaniratha, 582
khvarenah, 177
Khwan al-ikhwan (Nasir-i Khusraw), 787
ki, 997
kibbuts, 191
Kichai Indians, 820
Kickapoo Indians, 811, 814
Kierkegaard, Sören, 320, 406
Kigen, Dogen, 625, 1184
Kikuyu, 375, 376
Kimbangu, Simon, 24, 728
Kimbanguist church, 24, 27
Kimhi, David. *See* Radak
Kimhi, Mosheh, 152
Kimi, Kotani, 629
kimiya, 53
al-kimiya, 53
Kinar, 225
Kinbanguist church, 27
kindáian, 1028
King, Martin Luther, Jr., 35, 36, 289, 430, 675–676
  life and work of, 675–676
King of Kings, The (film), 546
Kingdom of God, 676–677
  ancient references, 676
  in Christianity, 677
  Jesus on, 676–677
kingdom halls, 635
Kings, 57, 159, 162, 351, 414, 548, 556, 616, 651, 758
Kingsbury, Jack D., 158
Kingship of God (Buber), 191
Kingship in Heaven, 520
Kingship and Marriage among the Neur (Evans-Pritchard), 402
Kinirsha, 726
Kinjikitile, 377
Kinyras, 225
Kiowa Indians, 820, 1120
kippah, 658, 926
kipper, 103
Kir-hareseth, 759
Kirishitan, 625, 626, 627
Kirsch, A. Thomas, 74
Kirta, 227
Kiskanu of Babylonia, 340
kiswah, 667
kitab, 917
Kitab al-aqdas (Baha' Allah), 131, 132, 133
Kitab al-asnam (al-Kakbi), 550

Kitab al-kashf (Ibn Rushd), 525
Kitab al-luma` (al-Saffaj), 1046
Kitab al-miftah wa-al-misbah (Nasir-i Khusraw), 788
Kitab al-ri`ayah (al-Muhasibi), 1046
Kitab al-ta `arruf (al-Kalabadhi), 1046
Kitagasa Muskiki, 812
Kitan, 573
Kitaro, Nishida, 1052
Kitawala, 26
Kitchen God, 679
Kitsi Manitu, 531
kiva, 840, 841, 842, 843, 845
Kixwét, 1028
Klamath Indians, 835
klesa-mahabhumika, 364
klesas, 709
Kleutgen, Joseph, 1146
Klon chen Rab-'byams-pa, 204
Klon chen sñin thig practices, 204
Knife Wing, 840
Knights Hospitaler of Saint John, 422
Knights of Malta, 422
Knights Templar, 422, 576
Knorr, Nathan Homer, 634
Knossos, 340
  palace at, 16–17
Knowing Words (Hu Hung), 309
Knox, John, 899
Ko Hsüan, 742
Ko Hung, 47, 742
ko-wu, 310
koan, 261
Kobunjigaku, 313
Koch, John, 339
Kocho, 573
kodo, 628
Kogaku, 312, 627
Kohn, Hans, 948
Koine, 164
Kojiki, 476, 668
Kojo, 184
kokubunji, 624
kokubunniji, 624
Kokugaku, 628, 997
kokutai, 627, 628
Kola Peninsula, 92
Kolchan Indians, 809
Kolyo, 568
Komi, 92
Komokums, 830
Kongo religion, 29, 528, 678–679
Konkokyo, 628, 1058
konsáxa, 1027
Kook, Avraham Yitshaq, 443, 444, 1188
Kopernik, Mikolaj. *See* Copernicus
Koppe, Johann, 157
Korah, 909
Koran und Koranexegese (Gätje), 611
Korea, temple compounds in, 1085
Korean religions, 679–681
  ancestor worship in, 65, 680
  Buddhism, 205–206, 210, 1085
  Christianity, 680–681, 753
  Confucianism, 313–315
  death ritual in, 680
  divination in, 680

folk religion, 679–680
new religions, 681, 1140–1141
Koretaru, Yoshikawa, 997
Koriak, 92
Korte verhandeling van God de mensch en des zelfs welstand (Spinoza), 1042
Korupira, 1032
Kosen, Imakita, 1185
Koshare society, 844
kosmopolites, 478
Kossa society, 844
Kota, 528, 951
Kothar, 225, 227
Kotohira Shrine, 894
Kotutai no hongi, 313
K`ou Ch`ien-chih, 259, 1075
koure, 539
kouros, 539
Kovrat, 573
Koxinga, 1057
Koyukon Indians, 808, 809
Kozen gokokuron (Eisai), 1184
Kraemer, Hendrik, 1096
Kraemer, Jörg, 610
Kralitz Bible, 768
kreitton, 461
Krishna consciousness, 578, 579
k`rmapets, 98
Kronos, 182, 467, 539
Krsna, 143, 148, 149, 150, 556, 564, 578– 579, 709
  All-Form, 497
  text on life of, 494
Krsna-Vasudeva, 149
krta, 880
krtayuga, 495, 496, 880
ksanti, 185
ksatra, 491
ksatriya, 341, 485, 491, 492, 497, 570
Ktahandowit, 811
Ku, 474
Ku Klux Klan, 289
Ku Yen-wu, 310
Kuan-yin, 451
Kuar, 725
Kubu, 1037
Küchlüg, 573
kuei, 65
Kukai, 750, 965
Kuklos tes geneseos, 372
kuladevatas, 503
kulama, 116
kulas, 619
Kulini, Abu Ja'far Muhamad al-, 589
Kullab, 726
Kuloscap, 809
Kumano Shrines, 894
Kumarapala, 619
Kumarbi, 520–521
Kumarila Bhatta, 739
Kumi, 1161
Kumina spirits, in Jamaica, 234
k`un, 254
Kunapipi, 107, 111, 112, 117
Kundakunda, 620
kundalini, 719, 1070

Kundalini Research Institute, 802
kundaliniyoga, 499, 719
K`ung Ch`iu. *See* Confucius
K`ung Fu-tzu. *See* Confucius
Küng, Hans, 639
K`ung Li, 317
K`ung Te-cheng, 1059
kung-an, 261
Kung-yeh Ch`ang, 317
Kuni, 435
Kunmanggur, 112
Kuo, Joseph, 1059
Kuo Hsiang, 291
kurahus, 823
Kuranguli, 1137–1138
Kurgan culture, 567
Kurile Islands, 44
Kurma, 496
Kurozumikyo, 628
kursi, 773, 776
Kurukulla, 212
Kurupi-vyra, 1032
Kurus, 148
Kurya Umwaka, 178
kusala, 179
kusala-karman, 673
kusala-mahabhumika, 364
Kushans, 749
Kushite religion, 682
Kushukh, 520
Kusinagara, 892
kutastha, 149
Kutchin Indians, 808, 809
kutdi, 683
Kutenai Indians, 832, 833
Kutter, Hermann, 715
Kuyper, Abraham, 715
Kuzari (ha-Levi), 151, 442
Kwakiutl Indians, 826, 829
Kwarup, 1033
Kwirena society, 844
Kwoth, 375
Kyala, 375
Kyanzittha, 1100
kyogen plays, 626
Kyoha Shinto, 628, 629, 995
Kyrios Christos (Bousset), 157
Kyubo, Yi, 679

L

La Aliseda, 523
La cité musulmane (Gardet), 611
La Joya, 523
La Vallé Poussin, Louis de, 388
Labrador, 580
labyrinth of the Minotaur, 16
Lachish, 88
Lachmann, Karl, 157
Lactantius, 81, 549
Lady of Baza, 523
Lady of Elche, 523
Lady of Tai, 49
Lagash, 726
Laguna, Frederica De, 828
Laguna Indians, 837
Laindjung, 111
Lajamanu, 122–123
Lakalai, 735

Lake, Kirsopp, 174
Lake Titicaca, 560
Lake Toba, 141, 142
Lakon society, 841, 842
Lakota Indians, 789, 820, 821, 823
laksanas, 541
Laksmi, 450
Lalbhai, Kasturbhai, 622
Lalbhai Dalpatbhai Institute of Indology, 622
Lalitavistara, 708
Lamaism, 407, 750
Lamb of God, 182
Lamba, 355
Lambert, Pierre, 796
lamentation
   concept of, 403
   psalms as, 909
Lamentations, 160, 161
lámhfhada, 241
Landauer, Gustav, 191
Lane, Beatrice Erskine, 1051
Lang, Andrew, 74
Langen, Rudolph von, 516
Languedoc inquisition, 575–576
Lankavatara Sutra, 183, 194, 209, 1052
L'année sociologique, 402
lantap, 833
Lao religion
   Buddhist, 210, 683, 1101
   Buddhist influence, 683
   phi cult, 683
Lao Tan, 255, 684
Lao-chün, 1075
Lao-tzu, 255, 260, 304, 684–685,
      1074–1075
   biography of, 684
   on death, 43
   divinization of, 684–685
   images of, 542, 543
   reborn, 732
   and T'ang dynasty, 1076
Lao-tzu pien-hua ching, 684
Laocoön, 539
Laodicea, Council of, 181
Laplace, Pierre-Simon de, 101
Lapps, 92
   Saami religion, 951–952
Larad, 340
Laragia, 117
lares, 524
Lares Anedici, 524
Large Catechism (Luther), 409
Laroui, Abdallah, 613
Larsa, 89
Lascaris, Constantine, 515
Lascaris, John, 515
Lascaux cave, 870
Last Days of Doctrine, 732
Last Judgment, 69, 475, 601, 728, 778,
      779
   Qur'an on, 587, 588, 919
Last Supper, 56, 173, 438, 638
Last Supper, The (da Vinci), 545
Last Trial, The (Spiegel), 512
"Last Will and Testament of the
      Springfield Presbytery", "The,"
      365

latae sententiae, 405
Late Great Planet Earth, The
      (Lindsey), 736
Lateran Council, Fourth, 282, 336,
      1124
   Second, 575
   Third, 575, 876
Latimer, William, 517
Latin, as liturgical language, 875, 955
Latin Bible, 164
Latin Vision of Esdra, 99
Latin Vulgate, 984
latreia, 548
Latter Prophets, 159–160
Latter-Day Saints (Mormonism),
      770–771, 903– 904
Latvia, 135, 136
laufa, 702
Lauke mate, 137
law
   Canon, 228–230
   and Inquisition, 575–576
   in Islam. *See* Islamic law
   in Judaism. *See* halakhah
   religious dimension of, 685–686
Law of Christ, The (Häring), 270
Law of Consecration, 770, 1007
Law of Moses, 339
Law of Return, 469
Lawh-i ibn Dhi'b (Baha' Allah), 131
Laws of Manu, 64, 362, 490, 765, 928
laya, 50
Lazarus, Moritz, 297
le droit musulman algérien, 606
Leabhar Ga-bhála Éirann, 240
Leade, Jane, 1143
Lebadea, 99
Leben Muhammed, Das, (Buhl), 610
Lebhor na hUidhre, 240
Lebhor na Nauchongbhála, 240
Leclercq, Jean, 985
Lectures du Coran (Arkoun), 611, 612
Lee, Ann, 686–687, 990
Leenhardt, Maurice, 795, 854
Leeuw, Gerardus, van der, 389
Legalists, 306
Legends of the Baal Shem, The
      (Buber), 190
Legio Maria (Legion of Mary), 26
Legionnaries, 388
Leibolmai, 951
Lele, 1040
lelem-but, 632
Lengua, 1027–1028
Lengua-Mascoy, 1027
Lenin, Vladimir Il'ich, 715
Lenshina, Alice, 24
Lent, 413, 907
Leo I, Emperor, 875
Leo I, Pope, 875
Leo III, Emperor, 335
Leo III, Pope, 274, 875
Leo IX, Pope, 875, 980
Leo X, Pope, 876
Leo XIII, Pope, 269, 284, 289, 878
"Leo" (Raymond Armin/Scherlenlieb),
      802
Lepcha, 483

Lepenski Vir, 792
*Les bédouins Shosu des documents
égyptiens* (Gibeon), 614
lèse-majesté, 575
Leshii, 1005
Lesovik, 1005
Lesser Vehicle, 208
Letter of Aristeas, 163
Letter to the Hebrews, 169
Letter of James, 169
Letter of Jeremiah, 160, 166
Letter of Jude, 169
Letter to Romans, 938
Letter of the Seal (Mani), 703
Letters of Obscure Men, The (von
    Hutten), 516
Letters and Papers from Prison
    (Bonhoeffer), 186
letters of Paul, 169, 170–171, 180, 458
Letters (Sirhindi), 594
Letters on Sunspots (Galileo), 427
Levi, 687
Levi, Yehudah ha-, 151, 442, 443, 655,
    1186
Lévi-Strauss, Claude, 74, 381, 790
    on myth, 828, 1022–1023
Leviathan, 360
Levinas, Emmanuel, 948
Levites, 687–688
    functions of, 688
    organization of, 687–688
Leviticus, 159, 353, 766
Lévy-Bruhl, Lucien, 1049
Lewis, Bernard, 613
Lewis, C.S., 765
Lewis, I.M., 408
Lewisohn, Adolph, 321
Leyenda de los soles, 127
Lhasa, 1107
L'hindouisme (Biardeau), 489
li, 255, 262, 318, 623, 627, 997
Li Ao, 306
Li chi, 310, 317, 684
Li Erh, 684
Li Tan, 684
li-ju, 183
Li-tai fa-pao chi, 184
Lia Fáil, 244
liang phi ban, 683
Liang Shu-ming, 311
Liao, 573
libation ceremony, Minoan, 17
Liberation Society, 319
Liberia, 24
Libiac, 1016
Licchavi kings, 482
Licinius, 323
Lieberman, Saul, 467
Life of Apollonius of Tyana, The
    (Philostratus), 741
Life of Jesus (Renan), 79, 157
Life of a South African Tribe (Junod),
    30
Life Together (Bonhoeffer), 186
life-cycle rites. *See* rites of passage
Light of the Lord, The (Crescas), 41
Lightbeings, 702
Lightfoot, John, 156

Lightfoot, Joseph B., 157
Lightworld, 702
Liguori, Alfonso, 269
Liholiho, 474
lila, 494, 497, 565
Limbu, 482
lin, 315
Lin Chao-en, 263
Lin Ling-su, 1076
Lin-chi, 262, 1184
Linacre, Thomas, 517
Lindsey, Hal, 736
Lindsey, Theophilus, 1142
Line of Demarcation of 1493, 276
Linear B script, 17
ling, 624
ling-chih, 542
Ling-pao T`ien-tsun, 543
linga, 485, 540, 1003, 1083
linga sarira, 499
Lingayats, 501
linguistic analysis, 60–62
Linu mate, 137
Lion of God, 547
Lipan Apache Indians, 820
Lithuania, Hasidic movement in, 472
Little, Malcolm. *See* Malcolm X
Little Genesis, 12
Little Man, 809
liturgy, 689–690
    characteristics of, 689
    functions of, 689–690
Liturgy of the Word (Zwingli), 899
Liu Hsiu, 257
Liu Pang, 306
Liu Ying, 1075
Living One, 935
LLullu Quilla, 789
Lo-yang, 573
Lo-yang ch`ieh-lan chi, 183
Lobi, 528
Locke, John, 392
LoDagaa, 65
Lofn, 433
Logic of Pure Cognition (Cohen), 297
Logical positivism, 61
Logos, 132, 342, 440, 562
Logos hymn, 440
lokas, 475, 620
Lokasenna, 433
Loki, 431, 432, 433
Lokottaravadins, 212
Lombards, 573
London Missionary Society, 748
longhouse, 812
Lono, 474
Lopes, Duarte, 29
Lord of the Animals, 561
Lord Jim (Conrad), 320
Lord of the Kamadhatu (Mara), 708
Lord of the Northern Bushel
    Constellation, 543
Lord of the Trubunal of Mount T`ai, 43
Lord's Meal, 635
Lord's Prayer, 284, 438, 676, 691–692
    text of, 690
    themes in, 691
Lord's Supper. *See* Eucharist

Lore of Famous Places, 240
Los Villares de Caudete de las
    Fuentes, 523
Lot, 11
Lotuko, 302
Lotus Sutra, 217, 407, 419, 789, 966
Louis II, King of France, 335–336
Louis VII, King of France, 344
Louis IX, King of France, 344
Louis XIV, King of France, 296
Lourdes, 889, 931
louskeha, 811
love, and charity, 251
Love and Discord, 372
Love Israel, 800
*Love of Learning and Desire for God,
    The* (Leclercq), 985
Love of Neighbor in the Talmud, The
    (Cohen), 297
Lowth, Robert, 156
Loyalty Islands, 796
Loyola, Iñigo López de. *See* Ignatius
    Loyola
lü, 624
Lu Hsiang-shan, 309
Lü Thai, King, 202
Lü Tsu-ch`ien, 309
Lü Tung-pin, 542, 1076
Luba, 341, 354
lubale, 578
Lubbock, John, 30
Lucan, 945
Lucian of Antioch, 397
Lucian of Samothrace, 223
Lucius II, Pope, 575
Lucretius, 1050
lucumi dances, 234
Luder, Peter, 516
Lugalbanda, 726
Lugbara religion, 353, 375, 376, 377,
    692
    evil in, 692
    myth of, 695
    sacrifices, 692
Lugh, 241
Lughnasadh, 241
Luiseño Indians, 531, 830, 833
Luke (apostle), 154
    See also Gospel of Luke
Luke of Prague, 768
lulav, 544
Lull, Ramón, 747
Lumen gentium, 1149
Lumpa church, 24, 25
Lun-yü (Analects), 304, 305, 315, 316,
    317, 318
Lunar Race, 148
Lung-hu Shan, 1076
Lung-shan, 88
L'univers des Azteques (Soustelle), 341
Luo, 301, 402
Luria, Isaac, 654
Lusitanians, 524
Luther, Martin, 59, 517, 693–694, 876
    anti-Semitism of, 79
    on astronomy, 326
    on church-state relations, 295
    and Erasmus, 393

and Eucharist, 282
and faith, 409
and heresy, 480
justification doctrine of, 280, 694
Ninety-five Theses of, 693
and Reformation, 156, 275, 337, 693–694, 923
social ethics of, 271
theology of, 694
Lutheran church, in United States, 294
Lutheran Church-Missouri Synod, 423
Lutheran Formula of Concord, 382, 695
Lutheran World Federation, 695
Lutheranism, 295–296, 694–695, 740, 753
history of, 695–696
teachings and worship, 694
Luthuli, Albert, 430
Luwians, 520
Luzzatto, Shemu'el David, 1043
Lvy-Bruhl, Lucien, 74
Lyatiku, 840
Lyell, Charles, 403
Lyons, Council of, 336, 574, 876
Lysander of Samos, 463, 477

M
Ma, 942
Ma Tan-yang, 1076
maa kheru, 555
Ma'amar ha-'ibbur (Maimonides), 700
ma'ani, 448
Maasai, 376
Maasawu, 840
ma'aseh merkavah, 700
Maat, 385, 555
Mabinogi, 242–243
Mabouia, 231
Mac ind óg, 241
Maccabean Revolt, 352, 617–618
Maccabees, 12, 470, 636
Maccabees, 160, 166, 175, 470, 557, 558
Maccu, 708
Macedonia, 96
Macha, 242, 243
máchi, 707
Machiavelli, Niccoló, 515
Machu Picchu, 1014
Mackey, James, 639
Macrocoti, 231
Madang, 797
ma'dhanah, 774
madhhab, 632
Madhva, 502, 1153
madhyadesa, 490
Madhyamakakarika, 419
Madhyamika Buddhism, 783
Madkhal al-ta'limi (al-Razi), 53
madrasahs, 146, 594, 609, 774, 776
Mae Enga, 797, 798
maga, 697
Magar, 482
magavan, 697
magga, 95, 418
Maghavan, 570
Maghrib, 29

Magi, 697–699
functions of, 697–698
origins of, 697
and Zoroastrianism, 698–699
magic
in Africa, 408, 528, 577
Hellenistic, 477–478
in Islam, 408
occultism, 853–854
and sorcery, 577, 821, 1163–1164
in Taoism, 1074
and voodoo, 1156
and witchcraft, 1163–1164
Magna Mater, 451, 944
Magnificat, 717
magokoro, 996
magu, 697
magupati, 697
Maha-Vajradhara, 216
Maha-vira, 619
Mahabharata, 148, 359, 362, 489, 490, 493, 494, 497, 498, 500, 564, 1002
mahabodhi, 197
Mahabodhi Society, 198
mahakalpa, 495
Mahamba cults, 247, 528
Mahanikaya, 1101
Mahapadma the Nandin, 333
Mahaparinibbana Sutta, 708, 892
Mahaparinirvana Sutra, 195, 217
Mahaprajñaparamita Sastra, 331
mahapralaya, 495, 499
mahar, 710
Maharashtra, 709
Mahasamghikas, 212, 333, 1099
Mahasivaratri, 1003
Mahasthavir, Jnanalamkara, 145
mahat, 970
Mahatissa, 1099
mahatma, 429
Mahavairocana, 996
Mahavairocana Sutra, 194
Mahavastu, 708
Mahaviharas, 213, 333, 1100
Mahavira, Vardhamana, 565, 620, 929
mahavratas, 620, 621
Mahayana Buddhism, 213–215
Bodhisattva path of, 185, 214
disciplines in, 214
ethics of, 214
Four Noble Truths in, 419
incarnation in, 562
lay practice, 214–215
laymen in, 214–215
multiple Buddhas, 213–214
nirvana in, 419, 804–805
repentance in, 214
sainthood in, 967
schools of, 209
spiritual guide in, 1045
spread of, 208
sutras of, 194
worship in, 213–214
Mahayanasutralamkara, 215
mahayuga, 495
Mahdi, 728, 737
Mahdists, 597

Mahinda, 1099
Mahisasakas, 212
Mahisasura, 484, 498, 503
Mahmud of Ghazni, 503
Mahobodhi Society, 198
mahzor, 544
Mai Chaza church, 25
maia, concept of, 108
Maia (deity), 241
Maid of Orléans. *See* Joan of Arc
Maidhyairya, 1190
Maidhyoi-shema, 1190
Maidhyoizaremaya, 1190
Mailman Radien, 952
Maimon, Judah Leib, 469
Maimon, Mosheh ben. *See* Maimonides, Moses
Maimonides, Moses, 699–700
on afterlife, 41
on anthropomorphism, 77, 655
biblical study of, 151–152
and charity, 250
and doctrine, 369
on God, 442, 443
on *halakhah*, 468
legacy of, 700
life and works of, 699–700
Mishneh Torah, 655, 700
on Torah, 655, 700, 1116
on Zion, 1187
Main Problems of Gnosis (Bousset), 436
Maine, Henry, 453
Maisonneuve, Jean de, 46
Maistre, Joseph de, 1133
Maithuna, 499
Maitreya (future Buddha), 184, 203, 210, 214, 562, 732
Maitreyanatha, 185
Maitreyavyakarana, 880
Maitreyi (Eliade), 388
Maitri Upanisad, 340
Maiyun, 824
maize ritual, 843
maja'-i taqlid, 605
majalis al-'ushshaq, 547
Majalla, 607
Maji Maji, 377, 733
majlis, 774
Major Trends in Jewish Mysticism (Scholem), 784
Makahiki, 474
Makarios, Cyril, 1139
Makká, 1029
Makki, Abu Talib Muhammad ibn Ali ibn 'Atiyah al Harithi al-, 1046
Maktubat-i Ahmad Sirhindi (Sirhindi), 594
Malabar church ("Thomas Christians"), 379, 1139
Malachi, 160, 162, 651
mal'akh, 68
Malaysia, 586
Malbim, 153
Malcolm X, 35, 36, 701
life and work of, 701
male symbolism, of God, 454–455
Mali, 23

Malik, 227, 589, 602
Malkat-Shemen, 86
malke`, 398
Malla dynasty, 482
Malleus maleficarum, 1165
Mallia, 16, 17
Malta, 720
Malvania, Pandit D.M., 622
Mama Latay, 234
Mamandabari, 1159
Mamsa, 499
Ma'mun, alÄ, (Caliph), 585, 591
Man a Machine (La Mettrie), 392
mana, 177, 364, 841, 935, 970
Manabus, 812
manarah, 776
Manasa, 143
Manasseh, 644
Manava Dharmasastra, 490
Manchu (Ch'ing-dynasty) religion, 264,
    310
Manchuria, 573
Manda d-Hilia, 702
Mandaean religion, 138, 303, 434, 437,
    702
    myths of, 702
    rituals of, 702
mandalas, 499, 565
Mandaling Batak, 142
Mandan Indians, 820, 823
mandate of heaven, 254, 257
Mandelssohn, Moses, 153–154
Manetti, Giannozzo, 515
mang, 99
Mangi, 1127
Mangindjeg, 116
mangu, 1164
Mani, 179, 259, 411, 547, 702–703
    as prophet, 902, 903
mania, 464
*Manichaean Book of Prayer and
    Confession*, 303
Manichaean Church, 703
Manichaeism, 702–703
    confession in, 303
    doctrines of, 702–703
    and gnosticism, 437, 701
    immortality in, 557
    and Islam, 259
    origins of, 703
"Manifesto of the Intellectuals," 140
Manikkavacakar, 501
manitou, 177, 811, 812, 814, 821, 847
Mañjusri, 214, 893
Manning, Henry Edward, 1133
mano, 364
mano-karman, 673
Manpukuji temple, 1185
Manresa, 552, 937
Man's Right to Knowledge (Tillich),
    1110
Mansi, 92, 93, 554
Mansur, Abu Yusuf Ya`qub al-, 604
manthra, 1189
mantike entheos, 381
Mantra Samhitas, 362
mantras
    Brahmanic, 486, 487, 556

Hare Krishna, 579
    as purification, 913
    Tantric, 215–216, 499, 565,
        1070–1071
    Vedic, 485, 563–564
Mantrayana. *See* Tantrism, Buddhism
Mantz, Felix, 59
Manu, 415, 567
Manual of Discipline, 160, 414, 557
Manual of The Mother Church (Eddy),
    286–287
Manus, 798
manusia yajña, 135
Manyu, 1002
Manzikert, 343
Mao Tse-tung, 264
Mao Tzu-yüan, 263
Mao-shan, 49, 261, 1075
Maori religion, 705–706
    gods in, 705
    tapu in, 705–706
Maorocon, 231
Ma`oz tsur, 470
Mapaulos, 25
mappo, 625, 737
Mapuche religion, 706–708
    cosmology of, 706–707
    deities, 706–707
    rites and rituals, 707
maqamah, 934
Maqom, 883
maqsurah, 773
Mar-pa, 1045
Mara, 96, 359, 708–709
    deeds of, 708
    figurative view, 708–709
marabouts, 967
Marasamyutta, 708
marassa, 233
Marathas, 503
Marathi religions, 709–710
    deities, 709–710
    development of, 709
    rituals, 710
Maraw society, 841, 842
Marcel, Gabriel, 406
Marcion, 154, 435
mardu, 116
Marduk, 676, 725
mareiin, 108
Marett, R.R., 74
marga, 141, 364, 494
Margaret of Angoulême, 516
Margaret of Antioch, 642
Mari, 88, 794
Marianus, 51
Maritain, Jacques, 102, 715
Maritsa Valley, 792
Marius, 942
Marji'sm, 591
Mark (apostle), 78, 154, 172, 326
    See also Gospel of Mark
Mark the Evangelist (Marxsen), 158
Mark II Khouzam, 1139
Markandeya Purana, 498, 503
Markuk, 66
Maronite church, 1138
maror, 882

Marpeck, Pilgram, 60
Marr, Wilhelm, 78
Marranos, 576
marriage, 710–711
    and chastity, 253
    consanguineous, 697
    in creation myth, 711
    forms of, 711
    Hindu, 492
    in Islam, 590, 595, 597, 605
    in Judaism, 239, 253, 647–648
    in Korea, 65
    North American Indian, 818
    purpose of, 710–711
    as sacrament, 283
    as transitional rite, 953
marriage ceremony, Baltic, 136–137
Mars, 479, 539
Mars Ultor, 943
Marsh, Herbert, 157
Marshack, Alexander, 330
Marshall, Louis, 321, 322
Marsi, 432
Martel, Charles, 187, 752
Martin V, Pope, 337, 876, 981
Martineau, James, 1142
Marty, Martin, 771
martyrdom, 712–713, 966
    symbolism of, 712
    and type of society, 712–713
Martyrium, 90
Martyrs' Mirror, 722
Maruts, 569, 570
Marx, Karl, 101, 453, 714
Marxism, 714–716
    and Christianity, 714–716
    Enlightenment, influence of, 714
Marxsen, Willi, 158, 639
Mary I, Queen of England, 70
Mary (mother of Jesus), 73, 637,
    716–717
    Marian piety, 717
    in New Testament, 716–717
    virginal conception, 640
Masada, 353
masbuta, 702
mashalim, 171
mashiah, 727
Mashriq al-Adhkar, 133
masiqta, 702
masjid, 773
al-Masjid al-Aqsa mosque, 636, 773,
    891
masks
    African, 528, 1179
    North American Indian, 531, 814,
        834, 842
Masks of God, The (Campbell), 453
maslahah, 591
Maslow, Abraham, 382
Masoretes, 248
Masoretic text, 161
Masowe, Johane, 25
masquerade, African, 527–528, 1179
Mass, 91
    See also Eucharist
massekhah, 548
Massignon, Louis, 449, 611

Masson, J.M., 381
Mastema (Satan), 12
Master of Life, 811
Master Masons, 422
Mataco, 1028
Mataco-Makká, 1028
matériel, 688
Math Son of Mathonwy, 242–243
mathas, 499, 500, 501, 565, 747
Mathnavi (Rumi), 593
matres, 524
Matres Aufaniae, 524
matriarchy theory, of goddess worship, 453, 454
Matronit, 451
matsah, 882
matsot, 882
Matsya, 496, 499
Matthew (apostle), 78, 154
    See also Gospel of Matthew
Mattnawi, The (al-Din Rumi), 611
Maturidi, Abu Mansur al-, 592
al-Maturidi, 448
Maudgalyayana, 64–65, 742
Maurer, Jacobina, 734
Mauritius, 327
Mauryan dynasty, 193
Mausolus tomb, 539
Mauss, Marcel, 518
mawali, 585
Maximian, 944
Maximilla, 734
Maximos the Confessor, 335, 1012
Maxwell, Mary, 132
maya, 565, 1069, 1070
Maya religion, 302, 415, 500, 533, 717–718
  archaeology of, 87
  classic, 717
  contemporary, 718
  deities of, 717–718
  and flood, 415
  iconography of, 533
  immortality in, 554
  postclassic, 717–718
  repentance in, 934
  temples, 1089
Mayapur, 579
Mayflower, 319
Mayo Indians, 837, 838
mazar, 146
Mbori, 375
mbulungulu, 528
McIntire, Carl, 401
McIntyre, John, 639
McLennan, J.F., 453
McNemar, Richard, 990
me, 177
Me-nomini Indians, 812
Mecca
  direction of prayer, 773, 920
  idolatry in, 550
  Ka`bah in, 12, 584, 588, 667–668, 891, 892
  Muhammad in, 584, 778
  pilgrimage to, 889–892
  as sacred, 958
Meccan Revelations (al-`Arabi), 1047

Mecklenburg, Ya`aqov, 153
Mede-Ilín, 523
Medea, 478
Medes, 97
Medhbh, 243
mediation principle, and Roman Catholicism, 940
medicine bundles, 812, 821
medicine man, 821, 848
medicine societies, 844, 848
medicine woman, 823
medicine-wheel, 815
Medina, 585
  Muhammad in, 584, 778
Medina de las Torres, 523
Medinet Habu, 884
meditation, 718–720
  in Buddhism, 719–720
  in Christianity, 718–719
  in Hinduism, 719
  in Judaism, 718
  in priesthood, 901
  Taoist, 742
  Yogic, 719, 1175–1177
mediums
  in Africa, 21, 577
  in China, 407
  in Japan, 407
  in Santería, 975
  See also divination; shamanism
megaliths, 720–721, 898
  carbon dating, 720
  types of monuments, 721–722
Meggitt, M.J., 112
Megiddo, 88
Mehekan, 98
Mehta, Narsinh, 428
Mehta, Raychandbhai, 621
Meiji regime, 627, 628, 629
Me'ir, 967
Me'ir, Shelomoh ben, 472
Meir, Shemu'el ben, 151
Me'iri, Menaham, 152
Meji Constitution, 629
Mekhilta' de Rabbi Shim `on, 153, 712
melammu, 177
Melanchthon, Philipp, 517, 694
Melanesian religion. See Oceanic religions
Melanesians, The (Codrington), 795
Melchior, Nicholas of Hermanstadt, 54
Melchiorites, 59
Melchite Catholics, 1138
Melos, 14
Melqart, 887
memedi, 632
memorial buildings, 90
Memories, Dreams, Reflections (Jung), 664
Memphis, 86
Mende, 528
Mendel, Menahem of Vitebsk, 472
Mendez, Alphonsus, 398
Mendez, Fasiladas, 398
Menes, King of Egypt, 384
Meness (deity), 136
Meng-tzu, 313, 316

Meng-tzu (Mencius), 256, 305, 306, 308, 967
  teachings of, 255, 305–306
menhir, 720, 793
Mennonite Central Committee (MCC), 724
Mennonite World Conference, 723
Mennonites, 271, 722–724
  doctrine of, 723
  early history, 722
  later history, 722–723
Menomini Indians, 811, 812, 814, 815
menorah, 470, 471, 544, 688
mensa, 56
menstruation
  initiation rites, 813, 832
  in North American Indian religions, 813, 822, 832
  as pollution, 911
  taboo, 822
Mentawai Islands, 355
mentensomatosis, 99
Mephistopheles and the Androgyne (Eliade), 390
Mercier, Alain, 854
Mercurius Artaios, 242
Mercury
  Celtic, 240–241
  Germanic, 431
merkavah mysticism, 82, 785
Mermillod, Cardinal, 289
Mernissi, Fatima, 1168
Merton, Thomas, 760
Mesha, King of Moab, 58, 757, 758
Mesha Inscription (MI), 757, 758
Meshekh hokhmah (Simhah), 153
Meslam, 726
Meslamtaea, 726
Mesoamerican religions
  architecture in, 90, 126, 534
  iconography of, 533–534
  immortality in, 554–555
  Izapa, 533
  Mixteca-Puebla, 534
  Monte Albán, 533
  Olmec, 533, 857–858
  temples of, 1089
  Teotihuacán, 90, 126, 533–534
  Toltec, 126, 534
  tricksters in, 1121
  Veracruz, 534
  Xochicaico, 534
  See also Aztec religion; Maya religion; South American religions
Mesopotamia, 85, 87, 161, 163, 340, 477
  ancient, 724
  present day, 724
Mesopotamian religions, 724–727
  Babylonian, 303, 329, 330, 536
  cults of, 726–727
  gods and goddessses in, 436, 450, 724–726
  iconography of, 535–536
  Neolithic, 791–792
  temples of, 536, 726
Mesorati movement, 322
Mesrop Mashtots`, 98

Messenger of God, Muhammad as, 777–778, 916
Messengers, 596
messiah, 84, 439, 651, 652
  concept of, 727
  Jesus as, 439, 727–728
  in Jewish apocalyptic literature, 84
  Lao-Tzu as, 684
  in Unification Church, 1141
Messianic Secret, The (Wrede), 157
messianism, 727–728
  in Africa, 25
  in Christianity, 727–728
  coming of age and paradise, 881
  in Islam, 728
  in Judaism, 472, 727
  meaning of, 727
  nativistic movements, 728
  South American Indian, 1018–1019
Messiasgeheimnis, Das, (Wrede), 157
Messina, Giuseppe, 697
Metamorphoses (Apuleius), 944
Metaphysics (paraphrase by Albertus Magnus), 47
Metatron, 84
metempsychosis, 42
Methodist Church, 728–731
  in Britain, 728–730, 740–741
  and John Wesley, 728–729
  ministry in, 740–741
  in United States, 35, 293, 730–731
Methodist Episcopal Church, 730
Methodist Episcopal Church South, 730
Methodist New Connexion, 730
Methodius, 275
Metsuddot, 153
metta, 251
Mettrie, Julien Offroy de La, 392
Metz, J.B., 446
México, 127, 128
Mexico, 87, 533, 534
Meyer, Kuno, 568
Meykantar, 1064
Meza mate, 137
mezuzah, 646
Mher, 97
Mheri durn, 97
Miami Indians, 811, 814
Micah, 160, 512, 727
Micah, 58, 278, 548, 688
Michael, archangel, 69, 84, 642
Michael, Emperor of Greece, 335
Michael VIII Palaeologus, 336
Michaud, Guy, 854
michi, 623
Michi, Hito no, 629
Micmac Indians, 808, 809
Micronesian religion. *See* Oceanic religions
Mictlan, 554
Middangeard, 430
Mide, 531
Midewiwin, 848
Midgard, 430
Midian, 548, 614, 771
Midianites, 614
Midrash, 468, 646
  contents of, 646

Midrash Tehillim, 352
Midrash Vayosha`, 84
midrashim, 153
Midungards, 430
Mihr, 97, 303, 1189
mihrab, 773, 774, 775–776, 777
Mihragan, 98
Mikal, 69
Milan, 515, 575
Milcom, 757
Milhamot ha-Shem, 442
Milky Way, 531, 560
millenarianism, 731–737
  in Africa, 25–26
  explanation for rise of, 733–736
  historical patterns in, 736–737
  modern fascination with, 736
  paradise in, 881
  patterns in world religions, 736
  and resurrection, 38–39
  Seventh-day Adventists, 988–989
  thought of, 731–732
  types of movements, 732–733
millennium, concept of, 731
Miller, F. Max, 74
Miller, William, 633, 988
Millerites, 633
  and Shakers, 990
millet system, 607
Millions Now Living Will Never Die, 634
Millot ha-higgayon (Maimonides), 700
Milton, John, 908
Milvart, St. George Jackson, 403
Mimamsa school of Hinduism, 493, 738–739
  doctrines of, 738–739
  subschools, 739
Mimamsa Sutra, 493, 738
Mímir, 340, 431
Mina, 891–892
minbar, 91, 776
Mindari, 116
Mindon Min, King, 334
Minerva, 241
  Celtic, 241
Ming T`ai-tsu, 263
Ming-chiao, 259
Ming-dynasty religion, 263–264
Minh, Thich Thien, 202
minhag, 468
ministry, Christian, 739–741
Minmarara, 113
Minoan religion, 15–17, 538
Minor Prophets, 160, 161
Minos, 15
Minotaur, 16, 17, 538
Minucius Felix, 549
Minutes of Some Late Conversations between the Revd. Mr. Wesleys and Others (Wesley), 729
minyan, 1053
Minzoku Shinto, 995
Miqra'ot gedolot, 153
Miracles, 741–743, 889, 1049
  in Buddhism, 742
  in Christianity, 742–743
  and Greek religion, 741–742
  and Indian ascetics, 742

in Islam, 743
in Judaism, 742
and sainthood, 960, 966
Mi`raj, 99
Miruksa monastery, 1085
Misasakiwis, 812
Mishkin, Bernard, 1017
mishmeret, 688
Mishnah, 646, 1059–1060, 1117–1118
  Maimonides' commentaries on, 700
Mishneh Torah (Maimonides), 655, 700
Misra, Mandana, 1152
missions, 744–756
  Buddhist, 745, 746, 749–750, 1099
  Christian
    in Africa, 23, 24, 25, 30, 678–679
    in Australia, 121, 122, 123
    Boniface, 186–187, 752
    in China, 753
    and colonialism, 752–753
    and conversion process, 753–754
    early Christians, 751–752
    in Ethiopia, 398
    forms of, 753
    in India, 145, 504, 753, 1064–1065
    in Japan, 626, 628–629
    Jesuits, 398, 626, 680, 753
    in Korea, 680–681, 753
    in modern period, 748, 754–756
    motives of, 744–746, 754
    in New Caledonia, 796
    in North America, 276, 277, 288, 818–819, 834–835, 846
    in Pacific Islands, 856–857
    in Polynesia, 1109
    Salvation Army, 187–188, 968–969
    in South America, 276
    in Sumatra, 142
  and cultural imperialism, 745
  missionary activity, dynamics of, 744–745
  missionized, reactions of, 745–746
  in modern period, 748, 754–756
  motivations for, 744–746, 754
  in South America, 1024–1025
  in Southeast Asia, 1036
  types of missionaries, 746–748
Missouri Indians, 820
Mitanni, 519
mithaq, 448
Mithra, 97–98, 179, 550, 561
  cult of, 944
Mithradates I Kallinikos, 179
mitima, 559
mitnaggedim, 443, 472
mitsvot, 473, 650
Mittilgart, 430
Miwok Indians, 832, 833
Mixcoatl, 128
Mixed Courts of Egypt, 607
Mixteca-Puebla, 534
Miyan, Dudu, 146
mizbeah, 56
mizmor, 908
Mizrahi, 1187
mleccha, 491, 497
Mnemosyne, 137
mo, 683

mo thevada, 683
mo-fa, 260
Mo-tzu, 306
  teachings of, 255
Mo'a, Iyyasus, 398
Moab, 58, 351, 756
  location of, 756
Moabite Stone, 757
Moabites, 756–758
  afterlife, 758
  in Bible, 11, 758
  gods and goddesses, 757–758
  holy wars, 758
  religion of, 756–758
  sacrifices, 758
  sources for study of, 756–757
  temples and altars, 758
Mocovi, 1029–1030
Modoc Indians, 830
Moffat, James, 157
Moggaliputtatissa, 333
Moggallana, 742
Moghila, Petr, 268
Mohammed (Grimme), 610
Mohammed (Rodinson), 610
Mohawk Indians, 811
Mohenjo-Daro, 340, 483–484, 564, 570
Mohican Indians, 811
Mohilever, Shemu'el, 1187
Moist Mother Earth, 1005
moksa, 561, 621, 739, 852
  meaning of, 488, 497, 500
Moksohanák, 1027
Mokysha, 1005
Molech, 757
Moltmann, Jürgen, 446
Molua, 241
Moma, 1031
Monastery of the Caves, 949
Monastery of Dabra Libanos, 398
Monastery of Eternal Joy, 1086
Monastery of Hayq Estifanos, 398
Monastery of Saint Catherine, 173
monastic shrines, Buddhist, 1084
monasticism, 759–760
  and Boniface, 187
  Buddhist, 190, 193, 196, 208–209,
    210
    in Southeast Asia, 202, 1084,
      1100–1101
    in Tibet, 217–218, 1106–1107
  celibacy in, 239
  characteristics of, 759–760
  chastity in, 253
  as community, 301
  Coptic, 327
  and eremitism, 394–395
  Franciscans, 420
  Hindu, 501
  in Jainism, 620
  in Middle Ages, 275
  in modern period, 760
  and retreat, 936–937
  Shinto, 625
Mondon, 1155
Mongkut, King, 202
Mongoloids, 483
Mongols, 760–761

in China. *See* Yüan-dynasty religion
  and Chinggis Khan, 266–267
  empire of, 573–557
  religions of, 760–761
Monitucinae, 524
Mono Indians, 832
monogamy, 711
monolatry, 763
monophysite heresy, 638
monotheism, 761–763
  and Abraham, 614
  in Africa, 19, 20–21, 31, 1039, 1161
  birth of, 614
  in Buddhism, 762
  in Christianity, 762–763
  and cosmology, 328–329
  in Egyptian religion, 762
  ethical, 660
  in Greek religion, 762
  in Hinduism, 762
  history of, 508, 762–763
  in history of religion, 508
  Israelite, 613–616, 762–763
  in Judaism, 762–763
  meaning of word, 761–762
  North American Indian, 809, 847
  and Rabbinic Judaism, 651
  and science, 983
  South American Indian, 1030–1032
  in Zoroastrianism, 762
  See also God
Montagnais-Naskapi Indians, 809
Montaigne, Michel de, 516
Montanists, 734
Montanus, 712
Monte Albán, 533
Montfort, Simon de, 575
Montmartre, 552
Montreuil, Jean de, 516
Montserrat, 552
Moody Bible, 401
Moody, Dwight L., 401
moon
  in Arctic religion, 93
  in Baltic religion, 136, 536
  in Canaanite religion, 225
  and death myth, 354
  in Egyptian religion, 385
  in Iberian religion, 524
  iconography of, 531
  in Inca religion, 560
  in Mesopotamian religion, 536
  in North American Indian religion,
    531, 823, 840
  in Slavic religion, 1004
  in Turkic religion, 1120–1130
  worship of, 789
Moon Boy, 809
Moon Dweller, 809
Moonies. *See* Unification Church
  (Moonies)
Moonlight-Giving Mother, 840
Moore, G.E., 61
Moorish Science Temple, 36
Morais, Sabato, 321
Moral Majority, 404
Moral Uses of Dark Things (Bushnell),
  219

morality, 764–767, 941
  moral norms, 764
  omnipartiality and moral choice,
    765–766
  rationale for moral behavior, 766–767
  universality, dimensions of, 764–765
Moravian Unity, 769
Moravians, 767–770
  development of, 768–769
  modern, 769–770
  worship and rituals, 769
More, Thomas, 517
Moreh nevukhim (Guide of the
    Perplexed), 41, 151, 442, 700
Morelos, 534
Morgan, Lewis Henry, 453
Morgan, William, 422
Morgenstern, Menahem, 472
Moriae encomium (Erasmus), 394
Moriah, 56
Moriscos, 576
Mormonism, 770–771
  Brigham Young, 1181–1182
  history of, 770–771, 903–904
  Joseph Smith, 1006–1007
  missionaries, 856
  in modern period, 771
Morning Star, 531, 814, 823, 848
Morocco, 29
Morrighan, 243
mortuary ritual. *See* death ritual
Moscow, and Russian Orthodoxy, 949
Moses, 52, 82, 159, 162, 182, 771–772
  in Bible, 771–772
  in Islam, 772
  law of, 467–468, 548, 617
  and miracles, 741–742
  in New Testament, 772
  revelation of Ten Commandments,
    615, 1092
  and Ten Commandments, 1092
  on Torah reading, 1115
Moses of Alexandria, 52
Moses (Buber), 191
Mosheim, Johann Lorenz von, 435,
    480
mosques, 773–777
  architecture of, 91, 775–776
  calligraphy in, 547
  derivation of word, 773
  functions of, 774
  historical development of, 776–777
  in Jerusalem, 636
  in Mecca, 890, 891
  officials of, 774
  in Qur'an, 773
Moss Child, 809
Most Holy Book, The (Baha' Allah), 131
Mot, 225
"Mother of All Books," 588
Mother Church, 287
Mother Corn, 823
Mother Earth, 531, 532, 539, 762, 789
  megalith monuments, 720–721
Mother Teresa, 145
Mother Worship: Theme and Variations
  (Preston), 454
Mothers, The (Briffault), 453

Motogen, 116
Mou-yü, 573
Mount Abu, 619
Mount Athos, 460
Mount Carmel (Israel), 132, 869
Mount Chiu Hua, 893
Mount Dikte, 17
Mount Ebal, 616
Mount Fuji, 894
Mount Gerizim, 160, 616
Mount Hara, 582
Mount Hiei, 625, 626, 965
Mount Juktas, 16, 17
Mount Kinpu, 894
Mount Koya, 625, 626, 894
Mount Kumano, 894
Mount K`unl-un, 43
Mount of Mercy, 891
Mount Meru, 340, 541
Mount o-mei, 893
Mount Paran, 615
Mount P`u-t`o, 893
Mount Sapan, 224
Mount Sinai, 173, 467–468, 615,
    1187
Mount T`ai, 43
    pilgrimage site, 893
Mount T`ien-t`ai, 184
Mount Tlaloc, 129
Mount of Victories, 561
Mount Wu-t`ai, pilgrimage site, 893
Mountain of God, 615
Mountain God, 679
mountains
    as paradise, 881
    sacred, 789
mourning anniversary, North American
    Indian, 833–834
Movement of the Reappearance of
    Anauak, 737
Moynihan, Elizabeth, 880
mrta, 50
mu'adhdhan, 776
mu`amalat, 601, 606
Mu`ammar, al-Qadhdhafi, al-, 598
muballighun, 776
muchay, 1017
Muckers movement, 734
mudang, 679, 680
mudhakkir, 779
mudita, 251
mudras, 499, 565
muezzin, 774, 776
mugawars, 510
Muhammad, 12, 53, 69, 91, 132,
    777–779
    ascension of, 99
    conversion policy of, 599
    on idolatry, 550
    illiteracy of, 861
    and Islamic theology, 590
    and Ka'bah, 667
    life of, 777–778
    in Mecca, 584, 778
    in Medina, 584, 778
    miracles of, 743
    prophethood of, 778–779, 916–917
    and Qur'an, 916–917

revelation to, 917, 1115
    studies of, 610
Muhammad at Mecca (Watt), 610
Muhammad at Medina (Watt), 610
Muhammad Speaks, 701
Muhammad, Warithuddin, 36
Muhammedanische Studien
    (Goldziher), 611
Muharram, 595
Muhasibi, al-Harith ibn Asad al-, 592
Muhlberg, Battle of, 924
Mühlenberg, Henry Melchior, 695
mujaddid, 596
mu`jizat, 743
mujtahids, 45, 604
Mukhtar, ibn Abi `Ubayd, al-, 992
Muktananda, Baba, 504, 800
mukti, 488
Mukun-dara-ja, 709
Mulacara (Vattakera), 620
Mulasavastivadins, 218
Müller, F. Max, 763, 790
Müller, Werner, 330
multazam, 667
Mulu-Mulu, 1137
Mum, 355
Mumford, Catherine, 188
mummification, in Egypt, 38, 555
Mun, Comte de, 289
Mundurucú, 1031, 1032
Mungu, 375
Munhata, 791
muni, 488
muñja, 710
Müntzer, Thomas, 693, 924
Mura, 1031
muramura, 116
murder
    of Abel, 221
    attitudes toward, 182
    of Osiris, 385, 582
Mureybet, 791
murid, 934
Murji'ah, 585
Murmellius, Johannes, 516
Muromachi, 625
Murray Cod, 116
Mursilis, King, 303
murti, 540
Murton, John, 139
Murukan, 502
muruwah, 584
Mus, 97
Mus, Paul, 1035
Musaios, 464
musallas, 775
musar, 654
Mushnah, 248
music
    Byzantine ecclesiastical, 249
    in Protestantism, 908
    See also chanting; drumming;
        songs
muslim, concept of, 583
Muslim. See Islam
Muslim Brotherhood, 780–781
    doctrines of, 781
    history of, 780

impact of, 781
    spread of movement, 780–781
Muslim Creed (Wensinck), 611
Muslim Discovery of Europe, The
    (Lewis), 613
Muslim League, 146
Muslim Mosque, Inc., 36, 701
Muslim movements, in United States,
    36
Muslim Summit Conference, 598
Muslim World League, 598
Múspell, 431
mustai, 464
Musta`ilyah, 596
musterion, 953
Mut, 583
Mutarrifiyah, 994
mutashabih, 449
mutatis mutandis, 409
Mutawakkil I al-, (Caliph), 591
Mu`tazilah, 448, 449, 585, 591, 592,
    1014
Mu`tazili doctrine, 994
Mutjingga, 112
Mutterrecht, Das (Bachofen), 453
Muzdalifah, 891
mwaro, 795, 796
Myalism movement, 235
Mycenaean religion, 17, 538
Myers, Jacob, 158
Myocho, Shuho, 1185
Myrtos, 16
Mystagogical Catechesis, 690
mystery cults, 953
Mystery Dance, 414
Mystery of the Restoration of All
    Things (Petersen), 1143
mysticism, 782–785
    and alchemy, 47–49
    and anthropomorphism, 77
    in Buddhism, 782–783
    in Christianity, 783–784
    Greek, 464–465
    in Judaism, 784–785
    of the self, 782
    in Sufism, 784–785
    in Taoism, 804, 1073–1074
    in Vedic religion, 782
    See also Qabbalah; Sufism
Myth of the Destruction of Mankind,
    386
Myth of the Eternal Return (Eliade),
    389
Le mythe de l'eternel retour (Eliade),
    388– 389
Mythologiques (Levi-Strauss), 1022
myths
    Aboriginal, 111, 112, 116
    African, 20, 32, 257, 375, 692
    ancestor, 66–67
    Baltic, 136–137
    and blessing, 178
    and cosmology, 330
    Cuna, 347
    and death origins, 353–355
    in Egypt, 386
    and evil, 402–403
    of flood, 414–416

Freud's view of, 426
Germanic, 430–431
Greek, 461
Hindu, 190
Hittite, 510
Hurrian, 520–521
Iberian, 523
Indo-European, 567
Mandaean, 702
in Manichaeism, 703
of North American Indians, 808–809,
    830–831
and polytheism, 895
Slavic, 1005
South American Indian, 1022–1023,
    1026–1030
and symbols, 931
in Taoism, 542
Tunkuz, 1126–1127
See also cosmology; creation myth;
    iconography
Myths, Dreams and Mysteries (Eliade),
    390
Myths and Reality (Eliade), 390

N

Nä Yakku, 1000
Nabarbi, 520
Nabia, 524
Nablus, 88, 160
Nabonidus, 86
Nabopolassar, 85
Nabu, 757
nadhir, 779
nadis, 499
Nafahat al-uns (Jami), 1046
Nag Hammadi codices, 81, 88, 155,
    434, 435, 436, 437
Nagarjuna, 330
Nago, 1155
Nagugur, 112
Nahal Oren, 791
Nahalennia, 432
Naham of Brazlav, 784
Nahawandi, Binyamin al-, 669
Nahman of Brat-slav, 472
Nahman, Mosheh ben. *See*
    Nahmanides, Moses
Nahmanides, Moses, 41, 152, 468
    on Torah, 1116
Nahuati, 534
Nahum, 160
Nahum, Menahem, 472
Nahusa, 570
Naiman, 573
Na'ini, Muhammad, 608
nairatmyastika, 1009
Nakatsukuni, 996
nakgarar, 98
Nakota Indians, 820
Namasamgiti, 214
namaz, 132
naming ceremony
    North American Indian, 812–813
    South American Indian, 1024
Ñamoc, 1016
Namuci, 708
nan-lao, 43

Nan-yüeh Hui-ssu, 184
Nanabush, 532
Nanahuatzin, 127
Nanak, Guru, 504, 763, 999
nanchon, 1155–1156
Nanderuvuçu, 1031
Nandi, 302, 376
Nandin, 90
nang thiam, 683
nanggaru, 113
Nanhaithya, 581
Nanna, 431, 536, 724, 725
Nanshe, 726
Nanticoke Indians, 811, 813
Nao, Deguchi, 629
Naojot, 1189
Naples, 515
Naqshband, Baha' al-Din, 1082
Naqshbandiyah, 1082
nara, 111
Nara, 624, 625
Narasimha, 496
Narayan, Jaya Prakash, 430
Narayana, 488, 496
Nargarjuna, 419, 783
Narmer, 384
Narraganset Indians, 811
Narratio prima (Rheticus), 325
narumba, 116
Nasatya, 581
Nasi', Yehudah ha-, 1059
Nasir al-din (Shah), 131
Nasir-i Khusraw, 787–788
    influence of, 788
        works of, 787–788
Naskapi Indians, 809
nass, 589
Nasser, Gamal Abdel, 460, 781
Nath, 50
Nathan, 351
Nation of Islam, 36, 37, 586, 701
National Academy for Adult Jewish
    Studies, 322
National Christian Council of the
    Protestant Churches, 629
National Federation of Jewish Men's
    Clubs, 322
National Federation of Temple Youth, 927
National Learning, 627, 628
National Socialism, 289
Native American church, 814, 825–826,
    835– 836
Native American Heritage Commission,
    836
Native American religion. *See* North
    American Indian religion
Natorp, Paul, 297
Natufian culture, 791
nature, 788–790
    for Aristotle, 96
    in Celtic religion, 242
    in New Guinea religion, 797
    in North American Indian religions,
        812
    phenomenon worshipped, 788–790
    in South American Indian religions,
        789, 1032–1033
    See also moon; rain; sun

Nature (Emerson), 392
Nature and the Supernatural
    (Bushnell), 218
Nature Wisdom school, 624
nauchampa, 128
Naumann, Friedrich, 715
Navajo Indians, 531, 837, 838
Navroz, 145
Nawasard, 98
Naya-nars, 565
Nayanmar, 500, 501
nayavada, 621
Nayler, James, 176
Nazi Legion of the Archangel Michael,
    388
Naziism, Christian resitance to, 186
nazir, 774
Nea Nikomedeia, 792
Neander, August, 435
Neanderthals, 869
Nebo, 757, 758
Nebrija, Antonio de, 517
Nebuchadrezzar, 85
Necessary Existent theory, 526
Necklace of Saints (al-Isfahani),
    1046
Necropompa, 1018
Nectarius, 334
Needham, Joseph, 48, 1055
Needham, Rodney, 1049
nefesh, 41–42, 556, 558, 1011
Negev, 614
Nehemiah, 160, 635, 645
Nehemiah, 162, 166, 248, 414,
    1117
nei-tan, 1078
Neith, 450
neles, 346
Nemhain, 243
Nentsy, 92
Neo-Confucianism, 262, 307–311
Neo-Orthodoxy, 865
Neolithic religion, 790–793
    in Europe, 792–793
    goddesses in, 450
    megaliths in, 720–721, 898
    Mycenaean, 17
    in Near East, 791–792
    in Southeast Asia, 1034–1035,
        1037
    study of, 790
        Taiwanese, 1056–1057
Neologs, 865
neoorthodoxy, 102
Nepal, Buddhism in, 482
Nephthys, 385, 583
Neptunus, 567
Nereus, 567
Nergal, 86, 726, 757
Nerik, 520
Nerthus, 431, 432
Nerthus, 567
neshamah, 42, 1011
Nestorian church, 379, 793–794
    modern era, 794
    Nestorian controversy, 794, 979
Nestorius, 334–335, 379, 397, 794,
    1139

Netherlands
    Calvinism in, 296
    Mennonites in, 723
netherworld. *See* heaven and hell;
    underworld
neti neti, 489
Neumann, Erich, 453
Neur, 402
Neutral Indians, 811
Neuwirth, Angela, 611
New Age groups, 802
New Atlantis, The (Bacon), 54
New Caledonia religion, 795–797
    clans and spirit world, 796–797
    dead and underworld, 795, 796
    gods of, 795, 796
New England Way, 914
New Feminist Fundamentalism, 454
New Guinea religions, 115, 728,
    797–798
    cosmology, 797
    functions of, 797–798
New Hampshire Confession, 294
New Jerusalem, 89
New Life Lodge, 414
New Prophesy, 734
new religions, 799
    concept of, 799
    in Europe, 802
    and goddess worship, 455
    in Japan, 803, 1140
    in Korea, 681, 1140
    study of, 799
    types of groups, 800–801
    in United States, 800–801, 1140
New Testament
    and Abraham, 12
    angels in, 69
    anti-Judaism in, 78
    apocalyptic context for, 169–170
    atonement in, 104
    baptism in, 282, 643
    canon of, 172–173
    conscience in, 320
    early formation of, 169
    Erasmus' edition of, 394
    God in, 438–440, 1122
    Gospels, 171–172
    Greek text of, 173–174
    and Hebrew scriptures, 170,
        172–173
    Holy Spirit in, 170
    on idolatry, 548
    Letters, 170–171
    Mary in, 716–717
    Messiah in, 728
    ministerial orders in, 739
    Moses in, 772
    and oral tradition, 861
    paradise in, 880
    resurrection in, 558
    revelation in, 938
    Sanhedrin in, 974
    Satan in, 977
    temptation in, 1090
    text of, 173–174
    underworld in, 1135
    writers of, 154

New Text school, 257
*New World Translation of the Holy
    Scriptures*, 633
New York Society for Ethical Culture,
    14
Newars, 482
Newgrange, 721
Newman, John Henry, 983
Newton, Isaac, 101, 326
Nez Perce Indians, 832, 835
Nga, 972
Ngai, 375, 376
ngainmara, 111
Ngaju, 189
Ngala, 355
Ngalyod, 112
Nganasani, 92
Ngenechen, 1032, 1033
Ngenemapun, 1032
ngillatún, 707
Ngundeng, 377
Ngunyari, 1137
Ngurunderi, 116
Nhialic, 375
nibbana, 95
    See also nirvana
Nibetád, 1029
Nibili, Roberto de, 753
Nicaea. *See* Council of Nicaea
Nicene Creed, 176, 275, 279, 324,
    334, 899, 980
Nichiren school of Buddhism, 211, 625,
    626
Nichiren Shoshu, 802
Nicholas II, Pope, 875
Nicholas V, Pope, 156, 876
Nicholas of Cusa, 284, 515, 516
Nicholas of Lyra, 156
Nicholson, H.B., 127, 128
Nicholson, Reynold A., 611
Nicopolis, 460
Nidana-katha, 708
Niddah, 1060
Niebuhr, Reinhold, 186, 268, 271, 289
Nieh-p`an ching, 217
Nietzsche, Friedrich, 101, 320, 406
Nigeria, 19, 24, 25, 27
Night in Serampore (Eliade), 388
Nigidius Figulus, 942
Nihon Darumashu, 184
nihon-shugi, 628
Nihongi, 476
Nihonshoki, 668, 995
nikaya, 211, 333, 1101
Nikkal, 225
Nikon, 949
Nilotic Shiluk, 375
Nilotic Sudan, 377
Niman ceremony, 842
Nimbarka, 1153
Nimngan, 1128
Nimrud-Dagh, 179
Nin-Nibru, 725
Nina, 726
Ninana, 725
Ninatta, 520
Ninazu, 726
Ninazu of Enegir, 725

Nine Saints, 398
Nineiagara, 724
Nineteen Letters on Judaism (Hirsch),
    865
*Nineteenth Homily on the Gospel of
    Matthew* (Chrysostom), 691
Ninety-five Theses, 693, 923
Nineveh, 88, 89, 724
Ningal, 520, 725
Ningirsu, 726
Ningishzida of Gishbanda, 725
Ningublaga, 724
Ninhursaga, 725
    temple of, 536
Nininsina, 726
Ninkurra, 725
Ninmar, 726
Ninsuna, 726
Ninurta, 536, 725
Ninyi, 356
Nippur, 724, 725
nirgrantha, 620
nirguna brahman, 357, 500
nirmanakaya, 562
nirodha, 363, 364, 418
Nirrti, 567
nirvana, 208, 253, 331, 332, 363, 396,
    803– 806
    concept of, 719, 803
    in early Buddhism, 197, 803–804
    Gautama on, 564
    in Mahayana Buddhism, 419,
        804–805
    and pilgrimage, 892
    in Pure Land Buddhism, 805
    in Tantric (Esoteric) Buddhism,
        805–806
    in Zen school, 805
Nitschmann, David, 769
Niu-chieh Mosque, 777
Niu-t`ou Fa-jung, 184
niyah, 765
niyama, 493
Nizaiyah, 596
Nizami, 547
Nizariyah, 994
no drama, 626
No Ruz, 1190
Noah, 55, 163
    blessing of, 179
    covenant with, 338, 339
    and flood, 415
noaidie, 952
Nobel, Nehemiah, 948
Noble Eightfold Path. *See* Eightfold
    Path
Nobles of the Mystic Shrine, 423
Nobunaga, Oda, 626
Nogar, Raymond J., 404
Nok sculpture, 19
Nominalism, 445
Nommo, 527
non-Chalcedonian churches, 379
Nonin, Dainichi, 184
Nonnus, 415
Nootka Indians, 826, 849
Nopti la Serampore (Eliade), 388
noqdim, 58

Ñordr, 432
Norinaga, Motoori, 997
Norns, 340
North Africa, Berber religion in, 147–148
North American Christian Convention, 365
North American Indian religions, 807–851
  afterlife in, 822, 846
  California and Intermountain, 830–836, 850
  ceremonial practices in, 812–814, 818, 823–824, 826–827, 848
    autumnal ritual, 844–845
    dances, 814, 823–824, 832–833, 834, 841–842
    death ritual, 554, 813, 818, 822, 833–834, 845
    Ghost Dance, 824, 835
    Hako ritual, 823
    healing, 814–815, 818, 831, 837–838, 841
    initiation rites, 813, 832, 841
    kachina, 842, 843–844
    maize ritual, 843
    peyote cult, 825–826, 835, 912
    rites of passage, 812–813, 818
    Sacred Arrow Renewal, 824
    Snake-Antelope, 689, 842
    societies for, 834, 841, 842, 843–845
    subsistence ritual, 812, 827, 832–833, 834, 842–843
    Sun Dance, 823–824
    Sweat Lodge, 821
    Vision Quest, 820–821, 833, 848
    winter ritual, 829–830, 841–842
  cosmology of, 329, 531, 811–812, 816–817, 838–834
  culture hero in, 809, 847–848
  fasting in, 413, 414
  fourness in, 341
  iconography of, 530–532
  immortality in, 554
  liturgy in, 689
  messianism in, 728
  and missions, 276, 277, 288, 818–819, 834–835, 846
  myths in, 808–809, 830–831
    creation myths, 822–823, 828–829, 839
  Native American church, 825–826, 835–836
  of Northeast Woodlands, 811–815, 849
  of Northwest Coast, 531, 532, 826–830, 850
  of Plains, 341, 531, 819–825, 850
  purification in, 912
  repentance in, 934
  revitalization of, 815
  Shaker, 835
  shamanism in, 531, 810, 814–815, 818, 821, 822, 828, 831–832
  of Southeast Woodlands, 816–819, 850
  of Southwest, 836–846, 850–851

spirits in, 811–812, 827–828, 831, 833, 839–841, 847, 848
  of sub-Arctic, 807–810, 849
  supernatural in, 821–822, 839–841, 847–848
  supreme god in, 809, 847
  symbols in, 822, 843
  tricksters in, 531, 812, 821–822, 831, 1119–1120
  witchcraft in, 817–818, 821
  See also Arctic religion
North Star, 823
North Wind, 823
Northwest Coast Indians, 531, 532, 826–830, 850
Norway, Germanic religion in, 430–431
Notes from the Underground (Dostoevski), 320
Nourishment of the Heart (al-Makki), 1046
nous, 557
Nowét, 1029
Nowo, 528
Nu, U, 202
Nubia, 614
Nuer, 23, 301, 377, 934
Nuer Religion (Evans-Pritchard), 402
nuhi, 623
Num, 952, 971–972
Num-Turem, 952
Numana, 788
Numayri, Ja`far al-, 781
Numbers, 159, 178, 688, 758
nunc fluens, 396
nunc stans, 396
Nunkwi, 1033
Nuqrashi, Mahmud Fahmi al-, 780
Nur al-Din, 345
Nuri, Mirza Husayn `Ali. See Baha' Allah
Nusayriyah, 596
Nusku, 725
Nusta, 560
Nut, 384, 385, 450, 582
Nuzi, 519
Nyabingi, 578
nyakatagara, 577
Nyakyusa, 375, 376, 1040
nyama, concept of, 527
Nyame, 1161
Nyaya school of Hinduism, 100, 492–493, 851–852
  concepts in, 851–852
Nyaya Sutra, 493
nyekar, 632
Nygran, Anders, 961, 1093
Nyikang, 375
Nyirana-Yulana cycle, 113
nymphs, Slavic, 1005
Nyoro, 376
Nyôwau, 795
Nyungar, 116
Nzambi, 30
Nzambi Kalunga, 678
Nzambi Mpungu Tulendo, 678
Nzambia-mpungu, 29

O
"O Fortress Rock," 470
Oaxaca, 533, 534
oba, 527
Oba, 1162
Obadiah, 160
Obaku, 627
Obaku school of Zen Buddhism, 1185
Obatala, 234
obedience
  Christian doctrine, 283–284
  faith as, 409
Observations on the Four Gospels (Owen), 157
ocata, 815
occultism, 853–854
  early existence, 853
  compared to esoteric, 853
  modern, 853–854
Oceanic religions, 854–857
  ancestor worship in, 64
  art of, 856
  authority and power in, 855
  cargo cults, 881
  death concepts in, 354, 854–855, 911
  death ritual in, 855
  history of study, 857
  initiation ritual in, 855
  Maori, 705–706
  Melanesian, 64, 354, 728, 735, 795–796
  and missions, 856–857
  New Caledonian, 795–796
  Tikopia, 1108–1109
  witchcraft in, 855–856
Ockenga, Harold John, 401
Octavian, 943
Octavius (Minucius Felix), 549
Odinn, 182, 431, 432, 433
Odyssey (Homer), 81
Oedipus, 182
Oedipus and Job in West African Religion (Fortes), 63
Oenghus, 241
Of the Laws of Ecclesiastical Polity, 70
offerings. See Sacrifice
O'Flaherty, Wendy Doniger, 1168
Oghur, 572
Oglala, 531
Ogo, 507
Ogun, 1161
ohel mo`ed, 615
Ohoharahi, 302
Ohrmazd, 1189
oikoumene, 382
Oirats, 574
ojas, 178
Ojibwa Indians, 302, 531, 809, 811, 812, 814, 820, 821, 848
Ojin, Emperor, 312
oki, 811, 815
Okipa, 823
Olcott, Henry S., 198
Old Man, 821
Old Testament Pseudepigrapha, The (Charlesworth), 167
Old Testament. See Bible; Bible canon

Old Text school, 257
Oldenburg, Henry, 1042
Olmec Dragon, 533
Olmec religion, 533, 857–858
  ritual in, 858
Olokun, 527
ololugmos, 463
Olson, Carl, 454
Olympia, 479
Olympus, 463
Omaha Indians, 820
O'Malley, L.S.S., 408
Omecihuatl, 128
Ometecuhtli, 128
Ometeotl, 127, 128–129
Omeyocan, 127
Omiruk, 1126
omphalos, 539
omucwezi w'eka, 577
On Animals (paraphrase by Albertus Magnus), 47
On Baptism (Tertullian), 282
On the Bible (Buber), 191
On Christian Doctrine (Augustine of Hippo), 155, 550
On Clemency (Seneca), Calvin's commentary on, 156, 222
On the Creation of Man (Gregory of Nyssa), 280
"On the Dignity and Excellence of Man" (Manetti), 515
On the Dignity of Man (Pico della Mirandola), 516
On the Donation of Constantine (Valla), 515
On the Face in the Moon, 99
On the False Donation of Constantine (Valla), 156
On First Principles (Origen), 155
On Free Choice (Erasmus), 393
On Free Will (Augustine of Hippo), 106
On the Genesis of Species (Milvart), 403
On the Hexaemeron (Basil of Caesarea), 155
"On His Own Ignorance and That of Many Others" (Petrarch), 515
On Idolatry (Tertullian), 549
On the Jews and Their Lies (Luther), 79
On the Mind (Helvétius), 392
On Natural Phenomena (paraphrase by Albertus Magnus), 47
On Plants (paraphrase by Albertus Magnus), 47
On Prayer (Origen), 690
On the Qabbalistic Art (Reuchlin), 516
On the Revolutions of the Heavenly Spheres (Copernicus), 326, 427
On Socrates' Daemon (Plutarch), 99
"On the Solitary Life" (Petrarch), 515
On the Soul (Aristotle), 96
On the Soul (paraphrase by Albertus Magnus), 47
On (the Lord's) prayer (Cyprian), 690
On the Trinity (Augustine of Hippo), 279, 783
On True Religion (Augustine of Hippo), 105, 550

On the Wages and Remission of Sins (Augustine of Hippo), 106
On the Wonder-Working Word (Reuchlin), 516
One-Horn society, 841, 846
Oneida Indians, 811
oneiromancy, 859
Onile, 528, 529
Onin War, 625, 626
Onoghur, 572
Onondaga Indians, 811
Open Door (*infitah*) policy, 781
opias, 231
Opigielguoviran, 231
Oprikata, 823
Optina, 950
opus alchimicum, 51
Or ha-hayyim (Attar), 153
Oracle at Delphi, 451, 463, 478, 539, 858, 860
Oracle of Dodona, 463
Oracle of Hystaspes, 81
oracles, 858–860
  and divination, 859
  functions of, 860
  Greek tradition, 478
  and prophesy, 858–859
  types of, 859–860
Oracles of Hystaspes, 699
Oraibi, 837
oral tradition, 860–861
Orationes Philippicae (Cicero), 320
Orchard, John, 157
Order of the Eastern Star, 423
Order Observed in Preaching, The (Farel), 899
Order of Preachers (Dominicans), 46
ordination, 862–864, 900–901
  ancient, 862
  in Buddhism, 863, 901
  in Christianity, 740, 741, 863, 901
  in Hinduism, 863
  in Islam, 863–864
  in Jainism, 863
  in Judaism, 863
  in Roman Catholicism, 740
  as sacrament, 953
  in Shinto, 863
  in Taoism, 863
  of women, 741
  in Zoroastrianism, 862–863
orenda, 177, 811, 841
Orestes, 463
Organization for Afro-American Unity, 701
Organization of Islamic Conferences (OIC), 598
orgia, 464
orgisthesis, 742
Oriental studies, Islamic studies in, 610– 611
Orientalism, 610
Origen, 154, 279, 437, 638, 690
  biblical exegesis of, 155
  and Coptic church, 326
  and mysticism, 783
  on soul, 1012
  on Trinity, 1123

Origin of Civilisation (Lubbock), 30
Origin and Meaning of Hasidism, The (Buber), 190
origin myth. *See* creation myth
Origin of Species, The (Darwin), 277, 403
original sin, 280, 941
Origins of Muhammadan Jurisprudence, The (Schacht), 611
Orion, 531
Orion constellation, 840
orishas, 234, 975
Orpheus, 464, 478, 557
Orphism, 372, 464, 464–465, 557
Orthodox Confession, The (Moghila), 268
Orthodox Judaism, 657–658, 865–867, 911, 1187
  Eastern European, 865
  German, 865
  Hungarian, 864–865
  in Israel, 865–866
  in Judaism, 866–867
  in United States, 866–867
orthodoxia, 274
Orthodoxy and Heresy in Earliest Christianity (Bauer), 480
Orunmila, 529
Osage Indians, 820
Osiris, 550, 557, 867–868
  cult centers, 868
  death of, 385, 582, 867–868
  in family of gods, 385
  and Greek gods, 479
  images of, 37
  and immortality, 555
  and Isis, 582, 583, 868
Osrhoene, 86
Ostanes, 699
Ostiaks, 92, 554
Osugbo, 528, 529
Otkon, 811
Oto Indians, 820
Ottawa Indians, 811, 812
Otto, Rudolf, 158, 1112
  on sacred and profane, 961–962
Otto of Bramberg, 1004
Ottoman empire, mosques in, 777
Ottoman Family Rights Law of 1917, 607
Otu, 1161
Our Grandfather, 811
Ouranopolis, 478
Ouranos, 182
Outlines of Mahayana Buddhism (Suzuki), 1051
Ovcharevo, 792
Owaqöl society, 841, 842
Owen, Henry, 157
owl, of megalith monuments, 721
Oxhead Ch`an, 965
Oya, 234
Oyaron, 811
oyasi, 44
Oyomei, 627
Oyomeigaku, 627

Özbeg (Golden Horde), 574
Ozieri, 721

P

Pacem in terris, 878
pacha, 560
Pachacámac, 559, 1015
Pachacuti, 559, 560
Pachamama, 789, 1015, 1016, 1017, 1033
Pachayachachic, 560
Pachomius, 327
Pacific Islanders. *See* Oceanic religions
Padhana Sutta, 708
Padua, 514
padukas, 621
Paek Ijong, 313
pagoda, 1085
Pahlavas, 497
Paine, Thomas, 393
Paiute Indians, 832, 835, 1120
Paiwan, 1056
Pak Che-ga, 314
Pak Chi-won, 314
Pak Yong, 314
pakayajñas, 491
Pakistan, 88, 144, 146
Pakpak, 142
Palace of Grand Clarity, 684
Palamas, Gregory, 336
Palenque, 554, 717
Paleolithic religion, 869–870
  art of, 561, 870, 898
  incarnation in, 561
  periods of, 869–870
  shamanism in, 870, 898
  sources of information, 869
Palermo, 774
Palestine, 85, 131, 133, 275, 614, 636, 791
  ancient region, 884
Pali, 95
palmas, 534
Palmyra, 86, 89
Pamsukulikas, 1100
Pan-jo hsin ching, 1076
Pan-ku, 1075
Panaetius, 478
Panamint Indians, 834
Panamu, King of Yady, 85
Panathenaea, 539
pañcamakarapuja, 499
Pañcapadika, 1152
pañcayatanapuja, 500
Pandavas, 148
Pandects, 516
Panikkar, Raimundo, 755
pañña, 418
pañña-visuddhi, 95
Pannenberg, Wolfhart, 446, 639
Pantheon, 1088
pantheos, 508
Pao-chih, 184
Pao-lin chuan, 184
Pao-p`u-tzu, 742
pao-shen, 43
Pap, 347
Pap Ikar, 346

papacy, 871–878
  Avignon, 336, 876
  and Catherine of Siena, 237
  and Charlemagne, 252, 875
  in early period, 871, 875
  and Francis, 420
  and Gallicanism, 1133
  and infallibility doctrine, 877–878, 1133
  Lateran councils of, 336, 876
  in middle ages, 274, 875–876
  in modern period, 877–878
  organization of, 292, 877
  popes (listing), 872–874
  and Reformation, 876–877
  in Renaissance, 876
  -state relations, 295
  and Thirty Years War, 877
  ultramontanism in, 1133–1134
  See also Vatican Council, First;
    Vatican Council, Second
Papaeus, 987
Papago Indians, 837
papamitas, 185
Papias, 170
Papima, 708
Papyrus Jumilac, 386
para, 540
para ambiya, 632
Parables of the Kingdom, The (Dodd), 158
Paracelsus, 54
Paraclesis (Erasmus), 394
parada, 50
paradeisos, 411
paradise, 879–881
  in eschatologies, 881
  Garden of Eden, 879
  in history of religion, 880
  physical representations of, 881
  recurring, 880
*Paradise as a Garden: In Persia and
    Mughal India* (Moynihan), 880
paragata, 95
Parakkamabahu II, 210
Paramartha, 260
paramatman, 497
paramitas, 185
Paran, 614
paranayama, 493
Parasurama, 496
PaRDeS, 152, 1116
Paret, Rudi, 610
Pariacaca, 1016
paribhogikadhatu, 892
paridaida, 411
parinirvana, 197, 541, 732
Parker, Matthew, 70, 913
Parousia, 169, 170, 171
Parpola, Asko, 518–519
Parsis, in Bengal, 145
Parsva, 619
Parthenon, 479, 539, 1088
Parthians, 749
Parvataraja, 1003
Parvati, 143, 450, 1003, 1072
Pascal, Lord, tomb of, 717
Paschal Homily, 342

Passamoquoddy Indians, 808
Passover, 378, 544, 649, 881–882
  Haggadah, 882–883
  leavening, prohibition on, 881–882
  religious service, 882
  Seder, 882
Pastor aeternus, 337, 877, 1147
Pastoral Award, 122
Pastoralis officii, 552
pasu, 487
pasubandhu, 487
Pasupatas, 501
Pasupati, 540, 1001
Patagonia, 354
Patai, Raphael, 450
Pataliputra, Councils of, 332–333
Patamona, 1022
Patañjali, 493, 494
patet, 303
paticca-samuppada, 95
Patimokkha, 302
Patishahya, 1190
patra, 541
patrirchate, Greek Orthodox Church, 460
Patrons of Husbandry, 288
Patterns in Comparative Religion
    (Eliade), 388, 389
Paul (apostle), 12, 56, 78, 81, 154, 169, 170–171, 173, 180, 273, 278, 320, 339, 360, 412
  on Abraham, 12
  on altars, 56
  authority of, 173
  baptism of, 138
  on conscience, 320
  on covenant, 339
  exegetical approach of, 154
  and gnosticism, 434–435
  gospel of, 458
  and grace, 459
  on idolatry, 549
  influence on Christianity, 273, 278
  on Jews, 78
  on Kingdom of God, 677
  letters of, 169, 170–171, 180, 458
  mission of, 745, 751
  on resurrection, 638
  on Satan, 360, 977–978
  on sin, 412
  on soul, 1012
  theology of, 439–440
Paul III, Pope, 337, 552, 877
Paul IV, Pope, 878
Paul V, Pope, 877
Paul VI, Pope, 72, 229, 230
  and Second Vatican Council, 940, 1148–1149
Paulus, 157
pavansinom, 845
pavarana, 303
Paviosto Indians, 832
Pawnee Indians, 789, 820, 822–823, 847
pax vobis, 180
Peace of Augsburg, 296, 923
Peace of God, 343
peace pipe, 822

Peace and Truce of God movements, 575
Peace of Westphalia, 296, 877
Peaceable Kingdom, The (Hicks), 677
Peacock, James L., 74
peasant religion, 416–417
pedanda, 135
pedanda bodha, 135
peepul tree, 484
Pei-tou-hsing Chün, 543
Peisistratus, 161
Peking man, 870
pekwin, 843
Pele, 474
Peleset, 884
Pelhisson, William, 575
Pellikan, Konrad, 156
penance
    fasting as, 413–414
    physical mortification, 912
    as sacrament, 283, 954
    See also Repentance
Pende, 528
Penetrating the Book of Changes
    (Chou Tun- i), 307
P`eng-lai, 43
Penn, William, 176, 915
Penobscot Indians, 808, 809
Penry, John, 319
Pentad, 435
Pentapolis, 327
Pentateuch, 151, 155, 159, 160, 368, 467
    contents of, 1113–1114
    law codes of, 163
    Moses tradition in, 771
Pentecost, 138
Pentecostal Earmark Trust, 802
"People of God, The," 230
People's Temple, 519
Pépin, 875
Pépin III (the Short), 252
Pereira, Duarte Pacheco, 29
Perfect Man, 809
perfecti, 575
Pergamum, 539
Perkins, William, 913
Perkons, 1004
Perkunas, 1004
Persephone, 451, 467
Persia
    Mongol invasion of, 574
    Nestorian church in, 793–794
    in Phoenicia, 886
    See also Iranian religion;
        Zoroastrianism
Persia, Il-khanid, 574
*Person Muhammeds in lehre und
    glauben seiner gemeinde, Die*,
    (Andrae), 610
*Personennamen der Texte aus Ugarit,
    Die*, (Gröndahl), 226
Peru. *See* Inca religion
Perun, 1004
Perush ha-Mishnah (Maimonides), 700
Peryn, 1004
Pesah, 881
    See also Passover

Pesch, Rudolph, 158
pesharim, 160
peshat, 151, 153
Petach Tikva, 1187
Peter, 173
Peter (apostle), 81, 273
    and papacy, 871
Peter the Great, 327, 949
Peter I, King of Cyprus, 344
Peter of Pisa, 252
Petersen, Johann Wilhelm, 1143
Peterson, Erik, 436
Petitot, Émile, 809
Petrarch, Francesco, 514–515
Pettazzoni, Raffaele, 389, 390, 508
Petun Indians, 811
Peutinger, Conrad, 516
Pewutún, 707
peyote cult, 824–826, 835, 912
Pfefferkorn, Johannes, 516
Phafa, 794
`Phags-pa, 263
Phaistos, 16, 17
Pharisees, 78, 548, 883–884
    achievements of, 884
    and Jesus, 883–884
    meaning of word, 883
    teachings of, 883
pharmakos, 954
Pharsalia (Lucan), 945
phi, 683
phi thevada, 683
Philadelphia (Alasehir), 616
Philadelphia Confession, 294
Philae, 583
philanthropia, 250
Philemon, 11
Philemon, 171
Philip Arrhidaeus, 386
Philip II, King of France, 575
Philip II Augustus, 344
Philip IV, King of France, 336
Philippi, Johannes, 517
Philippians, 171, 174, 180, 440
Philippines, 1037
Philistia, 884
Philistine religion, 885–886
    gods of, 885
    origins, 884–885
    religious practices, 885
    temples and cult objects, 885–886
Philistines and Their Material Culture
    (Dothan), 885
Phillipi, 460
Philo Judaeus, 163, 167, 436
    on Essenes, 353
    on fasting, 413
    and gnosticism, 434
    on idolatry, 549
    on immortality, 41
    on Torah reading, 1117
    on tripartite canon, 160
Philokalia, 950
Philosophical Investigations
    (Wittgenstein), 61
philosophy
    analytic, 60–62
    Aristotelian, 96–97, 524–525

ethics, 267–268
    existential, 406–407, 436, 661
    in Judaism, 655, 660–662
    Neo-Kantianism, 297–298
    Neoplatonic, 526
    Platonic, 445, 456
    Stoic, 478–479
    See also Confucianism
Philosophy of the Kalam, The
    (Wolfson), 611
Philostratus, 478, 741
philoxenia, 250
Phoenician History of Philo Bybilus, 223
Phoenician religion, 886–887
    beliefs and practices, 887
    deities, 886–887
Photios, 335, 336, 980
Phrygia inscriptions, 303
Phulakopi, 15
phusis, 561
physical body, purification of, 912–913
Physike kai mystike, 47
*Pi ch`uan cheng-yang chen-jen ling-
    pao pi- fa* (Chang Po-tuan), 1078
pi-kuan, 183
pia numina, 409
piaies, 232
Pickel, Conrad, 516
Pickhall, Marmaduke, 610
Pico della Mirandola, Giovanni, 516
Pid-ray, 225
Pidr, 227
Piegan Indians, 820
pièrres tonnerres, 235
Piethon, Gemistus, 515
pietism, in Judaism, 653–654
Pigafetta, Filippo, 29
Pigs for the Ancestors (Rappaport), 64
Pilagá, 1026, 1029
Pilate, 78
pilgrimage, 888–894
    in Buddhism, 195, 750, 892–894, 1107
    in Christianity, 343, 889
    experience of, 888–889
    in Hinduism, 710, 889
    in Islam, 585, 588, 889–892
    in Judaism, 649, 889
    purity/pollution concept, 912
    in Shinto, 889
    spirituality of pilgrimage sites, 888–889
    types of, 889
Pillow Book (Shonagon), 407
Pima Indians, 837
pinda, 64
Pindar, 477
Ping-pu, 1056
Pintubi, 530
Pipe Dance, 850
pipe smoking, North American Indian, 822
Pirckheimer, Willibald, 516
Pirke Aboth, 167
pirs, 146, 1044
pishtaq, 776
Pistis Sophia, 434
Pitjantjatjara, 530
pitr yajña, 135
pitrs, 359

pitryana, 671
Pius II, Pope, 344, 876
Pius IV, Pope, 337, 877
Pius IX, Pope, 337, 405, 877, 1133, 1146
Pius VI, Pope, 877
Pius VII, Pope, 877
Pius X, Pope, 229, 878
Pius XI, Pope, 552, 715
Pius XII, Pope, 72, 878
Pizarro, Francisco, 559
Plains Indians, 341, 531, 819–825, 821, 822, 824, 850
Plato, 60, 77, 99, 251, 342, 372, 373, 381, 457, 463, 478, 515
    Academy, 96, 456, 516
    on anthropomorphism, 77
    dialogues of, 60
    on ecstasy, 381
    on God's nature, 445, 762
    on good, 456
    on paradise, 880
    on underworld, 1135
Platonism, 406, 516
Platus, 1050
Plautus, 515
Pleiades, 129, 531, 840
pleroma, 372
Pliny the Younger, 279, 515
Plotinus, 396, 444, 456, 516
    emanation doctrine of, 444
    on eternity, 396
    on good, 456
Plutarch, 99, 303, 463, 478, 479, 583, 867, 982
Plymouth Colony, 319, 914
pneuma, 52, 558
p'o, 42, 48, 65
po, 705
Po-jo ching, 217
Poetic Edda, 431
Poimandres, 434
Poland
    Hasidic movement in, 472
    Unitarianism in, 1141–1142
polis, 462, 478
Politicus (Plato), 880
pollution (religious), forms of, 910–912
Pollux, 431
Polo, Marco, 574
polyandry, 711
polygamy, 711
polygyny, 711
Polyhistor, Alexander, 167
Polynesian religions. *See* Oceanic religions
polytheism, 894–895
    in Africa, 20–21
    Canaanite, 223–228
    characteristics of, 894–895
    forms of, 763
    in highly developed systems, 895
    in history of religion, 508
    meaning of word, 894
    See also deities; goddesses; gods; idolatry
Pomo Indians, 834, 835
Pompeia Agrippinilla, 945

Pomponazzi, Pietro, 516
Ponca Indians, 414, 820
ponikan, 347
pontifex maximus, 274, 323, 943
Pontius Pilate, 637
Poole, Elijah (Elijah Muhammad), 36
Poor Clares, 420
Popé, 846
Pope and Patriarch, 378
popes. *See* papacy
Popul Vuh, 415
Poro, 22, 26, 528
Poro-Sande, 26
Porphyry, 516, 853
Pórr, 430, 433, 1004
Portiuncula, 420
Portugal, 524
Poseidon, 17, 463, 467, 539
Poseyemu, 840
possession
    African religion, 21
    Afro-Caribbean, 233, 234
    Central Bantu, 246
    divination, 367
    East African, 376
    and exorcism, 407–408
possession-trance, 233
Potalaka, 214
Potawatomi Indians, 811, 812, 813, 814
Potnia, 17
Poussin, Nicolas, 546
Powamuy ceremony, 842
Powamuy society, 841, 842
Powers, 69, 70
Powhatan Indians, 811
Pozo Moro, 523
Prabhakara, 739
Practical Learning, 314, 315
Pradyumna, 1071
Praeparatio evangelica (Eusebius), 12, 223
prahanani, 185
Praise of Folly (Erasmus), 394, 517
Prajapati, 190, 486, 487, 495, 556, 1001, 1002
prajña, 185, 216, 363
Prajñakaramati, 419
Prajñaparamita Sutras, 185, 209
Prajñaptivadins, 212
prakaranas, 620
prakrti, 50, 149, 372, 493, 496, 499, 561, 970
pralaya, 50
pramanas, 739
prameya, 739
Prananath, 428
prapatti, 502
prapti, 364
prasada, 498, 1083
pratikramana, 302
pratiloma, 492
Pratimoksa, 185, 208, 209
pratisamharaniya-karma, 332
pratitya-samutpada, 95, 185, 363, 673, 929
pratyahara, 493
pratyaksa, 739

pravoslavie, 274
pravrtti, 190
Prayer: A Study in the History and Psychology of Religion (Heiler), 896
prayer, 896–897
    Afro-Caribbean, 234
    Anglican, 71
    Hittite, 510
    in Islam, 775
    Lord's Prayer, 284, 438, 676, 691–692
    North American Indian, 848
    and purification, 913
    types of, 896–897
    Zoroastrianism, 1189
Prayer of Azariah, 166
Prayer of Shim`on bar Yoh'ai, 84
predestination, 423–424
    and free will, 423–424
Pregnant Vegetation Goddess, 792
prehistoric religions, 989
    Balinese, 134
    study of, 869–870, 898
    See also Neolithic religion; Paleolithic religion
presbyterial church government, 293
Presbyterianism, Reformed, 899
    liturgy of, 899
    origins of, 899
    polity of, 899
"Preserved Tablet," 588
Preston, James J., 454
Preston, John, 913
pretas, 359
Priest-King fresco, 16
priesthood, 900–901
    in Africa, 19, 246
    Balinese, 135
    in Borneo, 189
    celibacy of, 239, 253, 900, 901
    in Christianity, 239, 900
    eligibility for, 900
    future of, 901
    future view for, 901
    Hawaiian, 473–474
    Hindu, 485, 486, 487
    Inca, 559
    Israelite, 687–688, 900
    of Magi, 698
    meaning of word, 862, 899–900
    Minoan, 16
    Moabite, 758
    in non-Western religions, 900
    North American Indians, 813
    ordination, 862–864, 900–901
    training for, 900–901
    Zoroastrian, 900, 901
    See also ordination
Priestly code, 617
Primitive Methodists, 730
Prince Hall, 423
Prince Moonlight, 732
Principalities, 69, 70
Principles of Geology (Lyell), 403
Principles of Nature (Thomas Aquinas), 1103
Principles of Sociology (Spencer), 63

Priscilla, 734
priyam atmanah, 362
processions, ritual
  in Africa, 19
  Minoan, 17
Proclus, 516, 853
Prodigal Son, 62
professional cults, Bantu (central), 247
Programs of Proofs (Ibn Rushd), 525
Prokopovich, Feofan, 268
Prometheus, 507
Promised Land, 616
prophecy, 902–904
  ancient, 902
  apocalyptic, 80, 82
  and canon, 903
  modern, 903–904
  and oracles, 478, 858–859
  See also prophets
Prophecy in Islam: Philosophy and Orthodoxy (Rahman), 612
Prophet Dance, 835, 836
prophetes, 478
Prophetic Faith (Buber), 191
prophetic movements, in Africa, 24–25, 34, 376–377
Prophetissa, Maria, 51, 52
prophets
  in Africa, 21, 24–25, 34, 376–377, 691
  Amos, 57–59
  common characteristics of, 902–903
  as founders, 902–903
  Israelite, 859
  Moabite, 758
  Muhammad as, 778–779, 916–917
  South American Indian, 1022
  See also prophecy
Prophet's footprints, 547
Protestantism, 904–908
  Anabaptism, 59–60, 271, 924
  Anglicanism, 70–72
  art in, 908
  authority of, 906
  baptism in, 276, 283, 694–695, 907
  Baptist church, 35, 138, 139–140, 235
  Bible of, 905–906
  Calvinist, 222–223
  Christian Science, 285–287
  and church, nature of, 281
  church government in, 292–294, 906
  and civil government, 906–907
  common elements in, 904–905
  ethics of, 270–271
  and Eucharist, 71, 282
  evangelical, 400, 401
  and Freemasonry, 423
  fundamentalist, 270, 400–401, 404
  God in, 271, 905
  heaven and hell in, 475
  in Japan, 628–629
  justification by faith, 271, 280, 694
  Lutheranism, 295–296, 694–695
  Mennonites, 271, 722–723
  Methodism, 35, 293, 728–731
  ministry in, 740–741
  Moravians, 767–770

Mormonism, 770–771, 1006–1007, 1181–1182
  music in, 908
  neoorthodoxy movement in, 102
  Presbyterianism, Reformed, 899
  priesthood in, 900
  Puritanism, 290, 296, 740, 913–914, 925
  Quakers, 915–916
  Seventh-day Adventism in, 988–989
  Shakers, 990
  Unitarian Universalists, 1141–1143
  worship in, 281–283, 907
  See also Christianity; Reformation
Protrepticus (Clement of Alexandria), 549
Proverbs, 160, 163, 440
Provision for Travelers (Nasir-i Khusraw), 787
prthagjana, 363
prthivi, 328
Prutenic Tables (Rheinhold), 326
Prymr, 430
Przyluski, Jean, 388
Psalms, 155, 160, 457, 512, 727, 908–910
psalms
  attribution of, 908–909
  in canon, 908
  date of, 909
  as literature, 910
  as revelation, 909–910
  setting of, 909
  types of, 909
Psalter, 908
  See also Psalms
Pseudepigrapha, 167–168, 908
  apocalytic writings, 167–168
  categories of writings, 167
  testaments, 168
Pshischa-Kozk house, 472
P.S.I. (People Searching Inside), 802
Pso-p`u-tzu, 1077
psuche, 557, 558
psychoanalytic theory
  of Freud, 425–426
  on temptation, 1091
Psychological Types (Jung), 664
psychology of religion, 664–665, 929–930
Psychro, cave of, 16
Ptah, 555
Ptolemy I, XIII, 386, 562, 982
Ptolemy II Philadelphus, 163
Ptolemy kings, 386, 477, 549
Ptolemy (Ptolemaeus), 154, 155
puberty rites. *See* initiation rites
Pucangge, 795
Pucelle, Jeanne La. *See* Joan of Arc
Puebla, 534
Pueblo Indians, 341, 532, 837, 838–839, 844, 846, 849, 851
Pueblo Revolt of 1680, 837, 839, 846
Puech, Henri-Charles, 436
puha, 821
puja, 143, 565, 1071
  meaning of, 497
  rites, 498

pukamani, 116
Pulgak-sa monastery, 1085
pulla, 114
pulque, 128
pulwaiya, 115
punarjanman, 487
punarmrtyu, 487
puny aksetra, 96
punya, 488
Punyavijaya, Muni, 622
Pura, 1031
Puranas, 150, 190, 329, 332, 362, 494, 500
Pure Land school of Buddhism, 185, 194, 195, 209, 214, 260, 262, 263, 264, 397, 451
  in Japan, 625, 626, 628
  nirvana in, 805
purgatory, 40, 350
purification rites, 910–913
  Canaanite, 225, 226
  cleansing agents, 912–913
  fasting as, 414–414, 912
  forms of pollution, 910–912
  forms of purgation, 912–913
  Tikopia, 1109
  See also healing
Purim, 470, 649
Puritans, 913–914
  in England, 296, 740, 913–914, 925
  in United States, 290, 740, 914
purohita, 179, 863
Pursuit of the Millennium: Europe's Inner Demons, The (Cohn), 78, 881
purusa, 149, 190, 487–488, 489, 490, 495, 496, 565, 719
  concept of, 782, 970
Purusa-Narayana, 488
purusarthas, 497
  theory of, 492
Purusasukta, 486, 489, 490, 491
purusottama, 149
Purvaminimasa. *See* Mimamsa school of Hinduism
Purvasailas, 212
Puyuma, 1056
Pygmies, African, 31–32
Pylos, 17
Pyramid of the Feathered Serpent, 534
Pyramid of Niches, 534
Pyramid Texts, 384, 385, 386, 537, 583, 922
Pythagoras, 251, 342, 557, 561
  as miracle worker, 741
  as spiritual guide, 1043
Pythagoreanism, 464, 1043–1044
Pythia, 381

Q

Qabbalah, 366, 451
  and Adam, 13
  and afterlife, 41–42
  forms of mysticism, 784–785
  and God, 442–443, 654
  Hasidim, 472
  and Hasidism, 472
  iconography of, 544

in middle ages, 654–655
soul in, 1011
and Torah, 654, 1116–1117
qadi, 525
Qadi, al-Numan, al-, 606
Qadiriyah, 1081
qadis, 774
qadosh, 957
Qalementos, 397
Qara`, Yosef, 151
Qarhoh, 758
qari, 776
Qaus, 757
Qerelos, 397
qiblah, 585, 667, 775, 776, 890
Qiddush, 882
Qirqisani, Ya`qub al-, 670
Qisas al-anbiya', 1046
qiyama, 558
qiyas, 589, 602, 603
Qoa, 1017
Quadragesimo anno, 715
Quakers, 176, 740, 915–916
formation of, 915
worship, 915
Quang, Trich Tri, 202
Quaranic Studies (Wansbrough), 611, 612
Quarterly Review, The, 403
Quechua, 415
Queen Mother of the West, 43
Querela pacis (Erasmus), 394
Quest, The (Eliade), 390
Quest for the Historical Jesus, The (Schweitzer), 157, 639
Quetzalcoatl, 67, 127–128, 129, 554, 1121
Quilla, 560, 789, 1016
Quilla-Pachamama, 1015
Quintilian, 515
quiyoughcosuck, 811
Qumisi, Daniyye'l al-, 669
Qummi, Ali ibn Ibrahim al-, 595
Qumran sect, 82, 353, 414, 669
Essenes as, 82, 353, 413–414
and John the Baptist, 643
Qumran texts. *See* Dead Sea scrolls
Quod idola di non sint (Cyprian), 549
Qur'an, 12, 27, 69, 79, 91, 412, 413, 916–920
chanting of, 249
chronology of, 918
on faith, 588
God of, 412, 447–448, 586–587
history of, 917–918
on idolatry, 550
and Islamic law, 599, 601, 603, 605
jihad in, 641
on Joseph, 644
language of, 919
on Last Judgment, 587, 588, 919
Mary in, 716
meaning of word, 917
moral teachings of, 587–588
Mosque, 773
Muhammad's reception of, 916–917
and oral tradition, 861
recitation of, 920

revelation in, 938
terms for, 917–918
role in Islam, 919–920
Satan in, 977
social doctrine of, 587
soul in, 1013–1014
studies of, 610–611
underworld in, 1135
on unity of religions, 598–599
and women's rights, 597, 605
Quranidai, 478
Quraysh, 890
Qushayrian Letter (al-Qushayri), 1046
Qut al-qulub (al-Makki), 1046

R

Rabbani, Shoghi Effendi, 132
rabbinate, 648, 651, 900, 921–922, 927
historical development of, 921–922
and miracles, 742
rabbi as spiritual guide, 1044
Rabbinic Judaism
afterlife in, 41, 650–651
atonement in, 103
beliefs of, 650–652
and community, 648–649
covenant in, 646
and David, 352
family in, 647–648
and God, 441–442, 650–651
in medieval period, 653–654
and Moses, 772
practices in, 646–647
rites of, 649–650
soul in, 1011
Rabbinic law, 468, 646–647
Rabbinical Assembly, 322
Rabbinical court (*beit din*), 648
rabbis. *See* Rabbinate
Rabbit, 531
Rabelais, François, 516
Rabitat al-`Alam al-Islam, 598
Rachel, 644
Rad, Gerhard von, 159
Rada, 1155
Radak, 152, 153
Radha, 143, 501, 502
Radien, 952
Radin, Paul, 355, 1049
Ragaz, Leonhard, 715
Ragha, 698
Rahman, Fazlur, 612
Rahman, Mujibur, 146
Rahmay, 226
Rahner, Karl, 279
Rai, 482
Railton, George S., 968
Raimondi Stela, 1017
rain
in African religion, 692, 1040
in Chinese religion, 789
in Indian religion, 569–570
North American Indian images of, 531–532
rain gods
Aztec, 554
Hawaiian, 474

Hittite, 510
Mesopotamian, 725
rain rituals
Central Bantu, 245, 246
Inca, 560
Rainbow Snake, 1137
Raipu, 226
Rajagirikas, 212
Rajagrha, Council of, 331–332
rajas, 50, 149, 493
Rajasuya, 487, 489
Rajavarttika, 971
rajayoga, 494
Rajneesh, Bhagwan Shree, 800, 802
Rajneesh Foundation, 802
Rajputs, 45, 503, 504
Rakib-El, 85
raksasas, 359
Ram, 710
Rama I, 143, 150, 494, 496, 564, 1101
Rama IV, King, 333
Ramadan, 413, 588, 632
Ramakrishna, 144, 149, 504
Ramakrishna Mission, 504, 744
Ramananda, 999
Ramañña sect, 1101
Ramanuja, 149, 150, 330, 502, 565, 1153
Ramayana, 359, 362, 494, 498
RAMBaM. *See* Maimonides, Moses
Ramses II, III, 385, 614, 884
Ramsey, Archbishop of Canterbury, 72
Ran, 789
Rangda, 1038
rangga, 111, 112, 121, 122, 529
rangi, 705
Ranters, 174
Raphael, archangel, 68, 69
Rapiu, 226, 227, 887
Rappaport, Roy A., 64
Ras Ibn Hani, 223, 224, 225
Ras Shamra, 88, 223
rasa, 50, 364, 501, 502
Rasa'il ikhwan al-Safa', 596
rasayana, 50
Rashap, 225, 227, 887
Rashi, 151, 152, 153
Rashid al-Din, 547
Rashid, Harun al- (Caliph), 993
Rashidun, 601
Rasmussen, Knud, 94
Rastafarianism, 235–236, 802
doctrines, 236
Rastriya Svayamsevak Sangh, 710
rasul Allah, 778, 916
rationalism, in Judaism, 660–661
Ratnasambhava, 216
ratu adil, 632, 732
Rauschenbusch, Walter, 271, 277, 284
Rav Amram, 653
Ravana, 1136
Raven, 531
Raven cycle, 829
Rawshana'i-namah (Nasir-i Khusraw), 787
Raychandbhai, 428
Raymond IV of Toulouse, 343
Razan, Hayashi, 312, 627

Razi, Abu Hatim, 787
Razi, Fakhr al-Din al-, 595
Razi, Muhammad ibn Zakariya' al-, 53, 787
rddhipadah, 185
Re, 385, 555
Realzione del Reame di Congo (Pigafetta), 29
rebe, 654
Rebirth Society, 802
rebirthing, 929
Rechtglaübigkeit und Ketzerei im ältesten Christentum (Bauer), 480
Reconstruction of the Spiritual Ideal, The (Adler), 14
Reconstructionism, in Judaism, 657, 661
Records of Ancient Matters, 668
Records of the Historian, 291, 684
Red Sea, 772, 783
Red Tezcatlipoca, 127
redaction history, 158
redemption, 922–923
  African religions, 923
  Aztecs, 923
  in Buddhism, 922–923
  in Christianity, 271, 280, 640, 922, 941
  in Egyptian religion, 922
  in Judaism, 472
  and morality, 766–767
  in Zoroastrianism, 922
Reden und Gleichnisse des Tschuang-Tse (Buber), 191
Ree Indians, 820
Reese, Curtis, 1142
refa'im, 556
Reflections on Things at Hand (Lü tsu-ch`ien and Chu Hsi), 309
Reform Judaism, 14, 656, 657, 865, 926–928
  beliefs and practices, 926
  historical developments, 927
Reform Rabbinical Conference, 321
Reformation, 181, 923–926
  and Anabaptists, 59–60
  anti-Judaism in, 79
  and atonement, 104
  biblical exegesis of, 156
  and Calvin, 222–223
  causes of, 923, 981
  and church-state relations, 295–296
  divisions within, 924–925
  ecclesiastical structures of, 275–276
  in England, 70–71, 296, 925
  and Erasmus, 393–394
  and ethics, 271
  expansion of, 923–924
  in France, 925
  and humanism, 517
  and Luther, 156, 275, 337, 693–694, 923
  Roman Catholic response to, 276, 876–877, 925
  scripture in, 270
Regius Manuscript, 421
regnator omnium deus, 431

Rehoboam, 450
Reims, Council of, 575
reincarnation, 38, 40, 349, 553, 928–929
  in Africa, 553
  and afterlife, 40
  in archaic cultures, 928
  in Australian Aboriginal religion, 928
  in Buddhism, 38, 349, 929
  in Hinduism, 928–929
  in Jainism, 929
Reines, Isaac, 1187
Reitzenstein, Richard, 434, 436
Reiyukai, 629
Reiyukai Kyodan, 66
Release and Deliverance (Nasir-i Khusraw), 787
religion, 929–932
  anthropology of, 73–75, 125, 401–402, 929
  archaeology of, 87–88, 884, 898
  and community, 932
  concept of, 506
  definitions of, 929–930
  ethnic, 507, 508
  founded, 508–509
  high culture, 507–508
  history of. *See* History of religions
  and morality, 764–767
  myth and symbol in, 931
  national, 508
  psychology of, 664–665, 929–930
  rituals in, 931–932
  and sacred experiences, 932
  sacred places and objects in, 931
  salvation in, 931
  and science. *See* science and religion
  scriptural, 508
  sociology of, 300, 381, 929
  women's studies in, 1166–1168
  writings in, 932
Religion in Essence and Manifestation (van der Leeuw), 389
Religion of the Holy Water, 134
Religion and Labor Council, 289
Religion in the Middle East: Three Religions in Concord and Conflict (Arberry), 611
Religion of Reason out of the Sources of Judaism (Cohen), 298
Religionswissenschaft, 507, 894, 1092, 1111
Religious Action Center, 927
Religious Corporations Ordinance, 630
Religious Juridical Persons Law, 630
Religious Organizations Law, 630
Religious Situation, The (Tillich), 1111
Rembe, 377
Remus, 67
Renaissance
  biblical exegesis of, 156
  Christian art of, 545–546
  Hermetic tradition in, 445
  humanism of, 514–516
  papacy in, 876
Renan, Ernest, 79, 157, 639
renatus in aeternum, 138

renga, 626
repentance, 933–934
  atonement, 103–105
  in Buddhism, 214
  in Christianity, 934
  forms of, 933
  in Islam, 934
  in Judaism, 103–104, 933–934
  in small-scale societies, 934
Republic (Plato), 478
Rerum novarum (Leo XIII), 269, 284, 289
Res gestae, 942
Reshef, 85, 523, 887
responsa, 653, 700
resurrection, 104, 935–936
  and afterlife, 37, 38–39, 41, 42
  and atonement, 104
  in Christianity, 169, 172, 378, 439, 558, 638, 639–640, 935
  in Egypt, 935
  in Islam, 935–936
  of Jesus Christ, 169, 172, 378, 439, 558, 638, 639–640
  in Judaism, 935
  in Taoism, 935
  in Zoroastrianism, 935
Resurrection of Jesus of Nazareth, The (Marxsen), 639
Rethra, 1004
retreat, 936–937
  in Christianity, 937
  in Islam, 937
  types of, 936–937
retribution, 766
Reuchlin, Johannes, 156, 516
Revata, 332
Revelation, 80, 81, 154, 169, 180, 273, 341, 342, 360, 881
revelation, 937–939
  in Bible, 938
  concept of, 937–938
  in Hinduism, 938
  in Islam, 938
  in Judaism, 938
  in New Testament, 938
  psalms as, 909–910
  in Qur'an, 917–918
  in Roman Catholicism, 940
  in Zoroastrianism, 938
Revelations of the Immortals, 1075
Review of the Torah (Maimonides), 700
revivalist cults, Afro-Caribbean, 235
Revivication of the Sciences of the Faith, The (al-Ghazali), 593, 605
Rgveda, 361, 362, 484–486, 555–556, 563, 569, 766
rhë e, 796
rhë re, 796
Rhea, 467, 539
Rheinhold, Erasmus, 326
Rheticus, 325
Rhiannon, 242, 243
rhytons, 17
ri, 627, 997
riba, 598
Ribbono shel`olam, 441
Ricci, Matteo, 753

Rice, John R., 401
Richard I, the Lionhearted, 344
Richard of Saint-Victor, 73
Richer, Jean, 854
Richmond Conference of 1887, 915
Richmond Declaration of Faith, 915
rida, 593
Rida, Rashid, 597, 605
Riedegost, 1004
Rifa`i, Ahmad al-, 1081
Rifa`iyah, 1081
Rigdon, Sidney, 770, 1006
Rightly Guided Caliphs, 601
Rink, H., 94
Rinzai school of Zen Buddhism, 625, 1184–1185
Rinzai-roku, 1185
Riotinto, 524
Ris-med movement, 204
rishama, 702
Rissho Koseikai, 802
Ritena, 242
rites of passage
    African, 22, 528
    Balinese, 135
    confession in, 302
    Hindu, 487, 710
    Inuit, 580
    in Judaism, 649
    North American Indian, 812–813, 818
    South American Indian, 1023–1024
    Southeast Asian, 1038
    See also death ritual; initiation rites
Ritschl, Albrecht, 445
ritsu, 624
Ritsu school, 624
Ritsuryo, 624
riwaq, 774
Riyordashir, 794
Rizhyn-Sadigora house, 472
Rizvan feast, 133
Robert II of Taranto, 343
Rocket festival, 683
Rodinson, Maxime, 610, 613
Rogation Days, 413
Rojales, 523
Rokeah, Shalom, 472
Rokycan, Jan Z, 768
Roman Catholicism, 939–941
    Afro-American, 35
    Albertus Magnus, 46–47
    in Americas, 276
    Anthony of Padua, 72–73
    anti-Judaism in, 78–79
    Augustine of Hippo, 105–107
    baptism in, 138
    biblical exegesis of, 156
    canon law of, 229–230
    Catholic Reformation, 276, 877, 925
    church government in, 292
    and church, nature of, 281
    and church unity, 72, 337–338
    and Copernican revolution, 326
    ecumenism in, 278, 337–338, 383, 1148, 1150
    ethics of, 269–270
    and Eucharist, 282, 420, 940

and excommunication, 405
and Freemasonry, 423
Gregorian chant, 249
heaven and hell in, 475
inquisition of, 575–576, 877, 1165
in Japan, 626
in Korea, 680–681
mediation principle, 940
ministry in, 740
predestination in, 424
priesthood, 239, 900
principles of, 939–940
sacraments in, 939–940
scholasticism in, 102
social movements of, 284, 289
soul in, 1013
and superstition, 1051
theology and doctrine of, 940–941
values of, 939
and voodoo, 1155
See also Christianity; monasticism; papacy
Roman Empire
    Christian images in, 545
    christianization of, 273–274, 323–324
    church and state in, 294–295
    fall of, 273
    gnosticism in, 51
    Hun invasion of, 572
    and Roman religion, 942–944
Roman religion, 942–946
    altar in, 56, 1088
    apologists for, 549–550
    faith in, 409
    fasting in, 412–413
    goddesses in, 451
    gods in, 479, 549–550, 944–945
    Greek influences on, 942
    hand symbol in, 179
    iconography of, 539
    imperial attitudes toward, 942–944
    literature of, 945
    Oriental influences on, 944
    persecution of, 945–946
    polytheism of, 895
    syncretism, 945
    temples of, 1088–1089
    women in, 945
Romans, 171, 174, 180, 412, 439, 458
Romulus, 67, 523
Rongo, 474
Ro'o, 474
Roquepertuse Bouches-du-Rhône, 242
Rosenstock-Huessy, Eugen, 947
Rosenzweig, Franz, 297, 298, 513, 661, 947– 949
    influence of, 948–949
    life and works of, 947–948
    tenets of, 927, 948
Rosetau, 385
Ro'sh ha-Shanah, 649
Rosicrucians, 54, 421
Rosmerta, 241
Roy, Ram Mohan, 144, 504
Royal College (Korea), 313, 314
rsi, 415, 485, 490, 491, 564, 709

rsi yajña, 135
rta, 250, 252, 361, 485, 486
ru-i, 543
Rua, 572
ruah, 42, 475, 556, 1011
ru'asa, 774
Rubens, Peter Paul, 546
Rubenstein, Richard L., 513
Rubianus, Crotus, 516
Rublev, Andrei, 276
Rudolph, Kurt, 436
Rudra, 486, 564, 570
    See also Siva
Rudra Cakin, 732
Rudra-Siva, 488, 489
Ruether, Rosemary Radford, 446, 1167
Rufeisen, Oswald, 469
Rufus, Mantianus, 516
ruh, 558
ruh lelu-hur, 632
Ruhanga, 577
ruiji shukyo, 629
Rukai, 1056
rukn, 632
Rule of the Jurist (Khomeini), 598
Rule of Pachomius, 397
"Rule of Phase Applied to History," 736
Rule of Saint Benedict, 239
Rules (Wesley), 729
Rumi, Jalal al-Din, 593, 611, 784
Runcie, Archbishop of Canterbury, 72
rupa, 364
rupa-ayatana, 364
rupa-citta-viprayukta-samskara, 364
rupaloka, 476
rupaskandha, 364
rusalkas, 1005
Ruskin, John, 289
Russell, Bertrand, 61
Russell, Charles Taze, 633
Russell, Letty, 446
Russell, Maria Ackley, 634
Russia, Hasidic movement in, 472
Russian Orthodox church, 268, 276–277, 378, 949–950
    development of, 949
    missions of, 949
    revival, 950
Ruth, 160, 161
Ruth the Moabite, 352
Ruthenians, 1138–1139
Rutherford, Joseph Franklin, 634
Ruusbroec, Jan van, 47
Ruwa, 788
Rwanda, 178, 577, 578
Rwanda Mission, 26
Ryangombe, 578
ryo, 624
Ryomin, Akizuki, 1052

S

Sa`adyah Gaon, 41, 84, 151, 655, 764, 1115
Saami religion, 92, 93, 94, 951–952
    animals in, 951
    deities, 952
    soul in, 951–952
Sabazios, cult of, 944

sabbatarians, 988
Sabbath, 615, 617, 648, 649
    Jewish, 649, 989
sabda, 364, 739
Sabir, 572
sabr, 593
sacca, 418
Saci, 570
Sacrament of the Last Supper (Dali),
    546
sacramentality, principle of, 939
sacraments, 282–283, 953–954
    Augustine's list of, 106
    baptism as, 138, 282–283, 953
    Christian, 282–283
    Hellenistic, 953
    Hindu, 487
    pre-Christian, 953–954
    repeatable, 954
    system of, 283
    transitional, 953–954
    See also Eucharist
sacred
    actions, 930, 931–932
    community, 932
    experience, 932
    and nature, 788–790
    space and structures, 930, 931
    time, 930
    writings, 932, 984–986
    See also cosmology
Sacred Arrow Renewal ceremony, 824
Sacred Dance, 414
sacred and profane, 954–962
    in architecture, 89
    means of identification, 954–961
    in North American Indian religion,
        812, 821–822
    relationships between, 961–962
Sacred and the Profane, The (Eliade),
    177, 390, 930
sacrifice, 56, 963–964
    Ainu, 44
    Aztec, 127–128, 129, 519
    blood offerings, 463–464, 963
    bloodless offerings, 963
    Canaanite, 225, 226
    Christian concept of, 182, 399
    and cosmology, 329
    divine offerings, 963
    in East Africa, 376
    and Eucharist, 282
    Greek, 463–463
    Hindu, 487, 488, 491, 497, 498,
        502–503
    Hsiung-nu, 571
    Iberian, 523
    Inca, 560
    intention of, 964
    Israelite, 688
    Moabite, 758
    North American Indians, 848
    offerings, types of, 963
    part-for-the-whole type, 963
    Philistines, 885
    Phoenician, 887
    place and time of, 963–964
    Samoyed, 972

sarificer, position of, 963
    sexual, 963
    South American Indian, 1018
    Yoruba, 1180
    See also animal sacrifice; human
        sacrifice
Sacrosancta, 337
sacrosanctus, 956
sadacara, 362
sadaqat, 251
Sadat, Anwar al-, 781
Saddharmapundarika Sutra, 194, 209,
    214, 217, 419, 625
Sadducees, 638, 669
sadhana, 499
sadharana, 362
sadharanadharma, 362
sadhus, 594, 621
Sadiq, Ja`far al-, 919, 920
Sadiqain, 548
sado, 623
Safad, 472
Safar-namah (Nasir-i Khusraw), 787
saguna brahman, 357, 500
Sagunto, 523
Sahagún, Bernardino de, 127
Sahaja, 143
Sahajiya, 50, 143
sahn, 775
sahw, 593
Sai Baba, 709
Saicho, 214, 750, 965–966
    life of, 965–966
    thought of, 966
Sa`id, Abu, 574
sailakana, 346
Saint Lucia, Kele cult in, 235
Saint Paul's School, 517
St. Peter's Basilica, 876
Saint Sergius Trinity Monastery, 949
Saint Vincent, shaker cult in, 235
saint-singers, 501
sainthood, 966–967
    in Buddhism, 967
    in Christianity, 967
    in Confucianism, 967
    in Hinduism, 967
    in Islam, 967
    in Judaism, 967
sa`ir, 360
Saisiat, 1056
Saiva Pasupatas, 501
Saiva Siddhanta, 501
Saivagamas, 499
Saivism
    in Cola period, 1063–1064
    concept of, 564
    meditation in, 719
    and Tantrism, 565
sajen, 632, 633
Saka, 497, 571
Sakhalin, 44
sakhas, 484, 619
sakinah, 920
Sakkudei, 1037
Sakta Tantras, 499
sakti, concept of, 498, 565, 1069
Sakti (deity), 50, 143, 499, 502, 540, 541

Saktism, 565
Sakyamuni, 197, 214, 218, 732, 929
Saladin, 344
Salah al-Din, 345
Salamanca, 523, 524
salat, 132, 667, 774, 775, 890
Sale, George, 610
Salinan Indians, 831
Salish Indians, 826, 833
saliva, as pollution, 911
Sallmon, W.H., 546
Salt Lake City, Utah, 770
Salt Woman/Man, 840
Salutati, Coluccio, 515
salvation, 41, 106
    in African religion, 19
    and blessing, 179
    in Christianity, 280, 286, 729
    concepts of, 931
    in gnosticism, 557
    in Manichaeism, 703
    in Taoism, 258, 542
Salvation Army, 299, 400, 968–969
    doctrines and practices, 968–969
    and William Booth, 187–188,
        968–969
samadhi, 418, 1176–1177
Samal, 85
samans, 486
samanya, 362
samanyadharma, 362
Samaria, 58, 88
Samaritans, 160, 571, 669, 976–977
    biblical canon of, 160
    chanting of, 248, 249
    religion of, 976–966
samatha, 719
samavasarana, 621
samavaya, 1145
Samaveda, 362, 484, 486
Samayabhedoparacanacakra, 331
Samayasara (Kundakunda), 620
sambhogakaya, 214
Samburu, 376
samgha, 208, 212, 239, 299, 620, 733,
    747
Samhitas, 484
sam`iyat, 448
samjñaskandha, 364
Samkarsana, 1071
Samkhya school of Hinduism, 493,
    494, 561, 970–971, 1174
    literature of, 971
    teachings of, 970
Samkhyakarikas (Isvarakrsna), 493, 971
Samkrantivadins, 212
Sammatiyas, 212
samnyasa, 341, 489, 491
samnyasin, 148, 491, 492, 500, 578
Samoa, 132
Samoyed religion, 93, 971–973
    animals in, 972
    rituals, 972
    shamanism, 973
    spirits in, 971–972
samsara, 95, 149, 363, 419, 475, 488,
    496, 564
    concept of, 671, 804, 999

samskaras, 50, 487, 710, 742
samskaraskandha, 364
samskrta, 363
Samson, 713
samudaya, 418
Samuel, 152
Samuel, 57, 159, 351, 353, 616, 651
samvara, 621
samyama, 742
Samyutta Nikaya, 708
San, Aung, 202
San, Saya, 203
San Apollinare Nuovo, 545
San Ch`ing, 543
San Damiano, 420
San I, 674, 1077
San Miguel de Mota, 524
San Pedro cactus, 1018
San religion, 674–675
San society, 18
San-lun, 217
Sanapaná, 1028
sanatana, 362
sanatanadharma, 362
Sanavasin, Sambhuta, 332
"Sanctorum Communio" (Bonhoeffer), 186
Sande, 528
Sangaraj Nikaya, 145
sangha, 195, 202, 210, 1100
Sango, 528
Sanhedrin, 175, 469, 637, 973–974
Sanhedrin, 512
Sanhedrin, historical evidence, 973–974
Sankara, 150, 499–500, 501, 502, 565, 709, 1151–1152
  on Vedanta, 1151
Sankara, Adi, 999
sankirtan, 579
Sannagarikas, 212
Sanpoli-Naspelem Indians, 833
Sanskrit, 134, 143
Sansui, Muhammad ibn `Ali al-, 641
Santa Constanza mausoleum, 545
Santa Maria Antiqua, 545
Santa Maria della Grazie, 545
Santa Maria Maggiore, 545
santana, 364
santarasa, 502
Santee Indians, 820
Santería, 234, 974–975
  Catholic symbolism in, 975
  divination and mediumship, 975
  rituals, 234
santero, 234
Santiago de la Espada, 523
Santideva, 419
Sanusi, 402, 597
Sanusi of Cyrenaica, The (Evans-Pritchard), 402
Sanusiyah *jihad*, 641
Saoshyant, 699, 935
saptamatrkas, 541
sar, 408
Saraburi, 893
Saracens, 420
Saramama, 1016

Saramedha, Sangaraj, 145
Sarasvati, Bhaktisiddhanta, 578
Sarasvati, Swami Dayananda, 504
Sarasvati (deity), 143, 450
Sardinia, 721, 887
Sargon II, 520
sariradhatu, 892
Sarmatian religion, 976
Sarnath, 90, 197
Saroghur, 572
Sarraj, Abu Nasr `Abu Allah ibn `Ali al-, 1046
Sarsi Indians, 820
Saruq, Menahem ben, 151
Sarva, 581
Sarvadharmapravrttinirdesa, 214
sarvam asti, 212
Sarvodaya movement, 430
Sasthi, 143
Sasun, 97
sat, 486
sat-cit-ananda, 500
Satan, 977–978
  and angels, 68, 83, 977–978
  in Christianity, 977
  in Hebrew literature, 977
  in Islam, 977
  and serpent, 360, 977–978, 1090
  as tempter, 1090
  and witchcraft, 1164–1165
  See also demons; devil
Satapatha Brahmana, 486, 488, 489, 496, 1002
Satarudriya, 1002
Sathya Sai, Baba, 802
sati, 144
sattva, 190, 493
satya, 429, 620, 621
satyagraha, 429
Sauk Indians, 811, 812, 814
Saul, 351
Saule, 136
Saules koks, 136
Saules Meita, 136–137
Sauras, 1069
Saurva, 581
Sautrantikas, 212
Saved Ones, 578
savior, 39
Savior of the Future (Saoshyant), 699
Savitr, 486
sawm, 413
sa`y, 891
Sayo, Kitamura, 734
scalping, 822, 1029
Scandinavian religion, 430–433, 556, 789
Scáthach, 243
Schacht, Joseph, 611
Schaeffer, Claude F.A., 88
Schechter, Mathilde, 322
Schelling, F.W.J., 513, 1110
Schiff, Jacob, 321, 322
schism, 978–981
  causes of, 978–979
  in Christianity
    and Council of Chalcedon, 327, 379, 397

  early, 979
  Great Schism, 740, 875, 980
  Great Western, 336, 980–981
  medieval, 266, 274–275, 979–981
  Photian, 980
  Rome and Constantinople, 274–275, 979–980
  See also Reformation
  in Islam, 601–602
  types of, 978
Schleiermacher, Friedrich, 79, 140, 157, 271, 272, 929, 1095, 1124
Schleitheim Confession of Faith, 722–723
Schmidt, Karl Ludwig, 157, 172
Schneersohn, Menahem Mendel, 151
Scholasticism, 515, 517, 1165
  and Albertus Magnus, 46–47
Scholem, Gershom, 784, 948
School of Ancient Words and Phrases, 313
School of Emptiness, 209
Schumacher, E.M., 430
Schurman, Anna Maria van, 156
Schweitzer, Albert, 157, 639, 736
Science and Health with Key to the Scriptures (Eddy), 285
science and religion, 981–982
  in ancient religions, 982–983
  and Aristotle, 96
  and Copernicus, 70, 325–326, 427
  and cosmology, 329–330, 330
  and Darwin, 983
  and Galileo, 427–428
  and monotheism, 983
Scipio, 945
Scofield, C.I., 401
Scofield Reference Bible, 401
Scot, Reginald, 1165
Scott, Coretta, 675
Scott, G. Robert, 158
Scotus, John Duns, 269
Scriptoris, Paul, 516
scripture, 984–987
  attributes of, 986
  Buddhist, 202, 209
  characteristics of, 986
  concept of, 984–985
  in Reformation, 270
  roles of, 985–986
sculpture. See art
Scythian religion, 976, 987–988
  archeological information, 987–988
  cults in, 987
Scythians, 570–571
Sderblom, Nathan, 30
Sea Peoples, 224, 884, 885
Sea Woman, 580
Seabury, Bishop, 71
Seal of the Saints (al-Tirmidhi), 592
Second Coming, 169, 176, 1141
Second Treatise of the Great Sseth, 437
Secret Adam, 434
Secret of Doctor Honigberger, The (Eliade), 388
Secret History of the Mongols, 266

Secret Transmission of the Ultimate Methods of Ling pao of the Perfect Man of the True Yang, (Chang Po-tuan), 1078
Secrets of Rabbi Shim`on bar Yohai, 84
Secretul Doctorului Honigberger (Eliade), 388
"Secretum" (Petrarch), 515
Sectarian Milieu, The (Wansbrough), 612
Secto Shinto, 630
sects, as community, 300
Secular Franciscans, 419–421
Secular Meaning of the Gospel, The (Van Buren), 639
Seder, 881, 926
    characteristics of, 882
Sedna, 93, 580, 934
Sefarad, 652
Sefardic Judaism, 652–653, 1053
Sefer gezerot Ashkenaz ve-Tsarfat (Habermann), 512
Sefer ha-`iqqarim (Albo), 152
Sefer ha-mitsvot (Maimonides), 468, 669, 700
Sefer Zerubbavel, 84
sefirah, 544
sefirot, 153, 442–443, 654, 785
Segundo, Juan, 446
Seika, Fujiwara, 312, 627
Seir, 614, 615
se`irim, 360
seite, 93
Sekani Indians, 808
Sekl'nam, 1031
Selassie, Haile, 235–236
Seleucia-Ctesiphon, 794
Seligman, C.G., 402
semikhah, 863
Semler, Johann, 156, 157
Semnones, 431
Sen, Keshab Chandra, 144
Seneca, 1050
Seneca Indians, 811
Sengai, 1052
sengoku dai-myo, 625
Il Sennaar e lo Sciangallah (Beltrame), 30
Senufo, 22
Senusret I, 385
Separatists, 319
Septuagint, 160, 984
    on blasphemy, 175
    blessing in, 180
    gospel in, 457–458
    origin of, 161, 163–164
Serampore College, 145
Seraphim, 69, 70
Serapis, 583
Sergii of Radonezh, 949
Sergius IV, Pope, 980
Seri Indians, 837
Serïf of Gülhane, Hatt-i, 607
Sermon on the Mount, 283, 429, 438, 690, 765
"Sermon on the Plain," 677
Sermones domenicales (Anthony of Padua), 72

Sermones in solemnitatibus sanctorum (Anthony of Padua), 72
Sermons on the Lord's Prayer (Gregory of Nyssa), 691
Sermons (Wesley), 729
serpent, and Satan, 360, 977–978, 1090
Serreta de Alcoy, 523
Servetus, Michael, 924
Ses bya kun khyab, 204
Sesa, 496
Sesklo cultures, 792
sesup mu, 679
Setefilla, 523
Seth, 386, 434, 507
    in death of Osiris, 385, 582, 867–868
    and Isis, 583
Sethel, 80
Sevek, 1127
Seven Mothers, 541
"Seven Sacraments, The" (Poussin), 546
Seven-Star God, 679
Seveners, 596
Seventeen-Article Constitution, 217, 312
Seventh-day Adventism, 734, 856, 988–989
    development of, 988
    evangelism, 988
Seventy Books, 53
Seville, 523, 524
Sexism and God-Talk: Toward a Feminist Theology (Ruether), 1167
sexual union
    in New Caledonian religion, 795–796
    in Tantric Hinduism, 1071
sexuality
    abstinence. *See* Celibacy
    and asceticism, 960
    in New Caledonian religion, 795–796
    pollution/purity norms, 911
    sacred and profane in, 960
    and sacrifice, 963
    in Tantric Hinduism, 1071
    of trickster, 1120, 1121
    and witchcraft, 1164
Sforno, `Ovadyah, 152
Shabazz, el-Hajj Malik el- (Malcolm X), 701
shabbat, 989
    See also Sabbath
shades, in South Africa, 1039, 1040
Shadhiliyah, 1081–1082
Shadrafa, 887
Shafi`i, Muhammad ibn Idris al-, 589
Shah, Sher, 45
Shah-namah (Firdawsi), 547
shahadah, 448
Shahr, 226
Shaiyan, 360
Shakers, 990–991
    Ann Lee, 686–687, 990
    Caribbean, 235
    celibacy of, 238, 239, 687
    history of, 990
    North American Indian, 835

Shaking Tent rite, North American Indian, 810, 821
Shakpana, 234
Shala, 536
Shalim, 225, 226
Shalit, Binyamin, 469
shalla-kardatar, 511
shalom, 648
shamanic cult institution, 821
Shamanism: Archaic Techniques of Ecstasy (Eliade), 389-90
shamanism, 991–992
    in Africa, 18
    Ainu, 44–45
    ancestor worship in, 65
    Arctic, 93, 531, 580
    in Borneo, 189
    in Caribbean, 232
    categories of shamans, 1022
    of Cuna Indians, 346
    ecstasies of, 98, 381, 991
    and exorcism, 407
    in Himalayan religions, 482
    initiatory ordeals of, 973, 991, 1027, 1028
    Mapuche, 707
    Mongol, 761
    North American Indian, 531, 810, 814–815, 818, 821, 822
    Paleolithic, 870, 898
    role of, 991, 992
    Saami, 951–952
    Samoyed, 973
    Siberian, 991–992
    South American Indian, 1018, 1021–1022, 1027, 1029, 1030, 1033
    Tunguz, 991, 1126, 1127, 1128
    Turkic, 1130
    Yakut, 1170–1171
    See also healing
Shamash, 86, 536
shamayin, 475
Shammai, 1114
Shammaites, 470
shammash, 470
Shan-tao, 260
Shang Yang, 256
Shang-ch`ing sect, 1075
Shang-dynasty religion, 42, 253
Shang-ti, 318, 766, 1074
Shango, 233, 234
Shango cult, in Trinidad, 234
Shao Yung, 307, 1055
Shao-lin boxing, 184
Shapash, 225, 227
Shari` at Allah, Hajji, 146
shari`ah, 525, 586, 590, 600–608, 609, 632, 781, 784
Sharruma, 520
Shasta Indians, 834
Shatibi, al-, 605
Shaushka, 520
Shavu'ot, 249, 649
Shawabti spell, 385
shawabtis, 538
Shawnee Indians, 811, 813, 814

Shaybani, Muhammad ibn Hasan al-, 602
shaykh, 934, 1044
Shaytan, 977
she, 254
Shechem, 88, 339
Shechem (Nablus), 616
shedim, 360
she'elot u-teshuvot, 653
Shei'ltot (Gaon), 153
Shekhinah, 442, 450–451, 785
Shekhinah, 883
Shem, 80
Shema`, 442
Shembe, Isaiah, 25
Shembe, Johannes Galilee (Shembe II), 25
Shemot, 1113
shen, 65, 307, 623
Shen-hsiao Fa, 261
Shen-hsiu, 184
She'ol, 40, 475, 556, 1011, 1135
sheret, 739
Sheri, 520
Sherpas, 482
shevirat ha-kelim, 472
Shi ching, 317
Shi`ah Islam, 992–994
    commemoration of Husayn, 595–596
    division from Sunni, 601–602
    doctrines of, 595
    esotericism in, 595
    immortality in, 558
    intellectual schools, 994
    and Islamic law, 589, 595, 605, 608
    origins and development of, 992–994
    subsects of, 596, 993, 994
shidoso, 624
shih, 317–318
Shih chi (Ssu-ma Ch`ien), 291, 315, 317, 684
Shih ching, 317, 407
Shih-kao, 257
Shi`i Islam, 526
Shiism. *See* Shi`ah Islam
Shikibu, Murasaki, 407
Shikoku, 894
Shillebeeck, Edward, 639
Shilluk, 375
Shiloh, temple at, 616
Shimigi, 520
Shimon, Ishai XXI, 794
Shin Thiwali, 95–96
Shin-Butsu hanzen rei, 627
Shingon Shinto, 624, 996
Shining Buddha of Heaven, 451
shinjin, 805
shinko shukyo, 629
Shinpikyo, 1058
Shinran, 625, 805
shinshoku, 863
Shinto, 995–998
    ancient, 995–996
    beliefs and teachings of, 997
    Buddhist Shinto, 996
    characteristics of, 995
    confession in, 302
    Confucian Shinto, 997

Folk Shinto, 995
    goddesses in, 451
    historical development of, 996–997
    kami in, 177, 668, 997
    in modern period, 998
    ordination in, 863
    organizations of, 997–998
    pilgrimage in, 889
    Revival Shinto, 627, 997
    Sect Shinto, 628, 995, 997
    Shrine Shinto, 630, 995, 998
    shrines of, 625, 995, 997, 998
    State, 627–628
    in Taiwan, 1058
Shinto Directive, 629
Shir, 547
Shirei Tsiyyon (ha-Levi), 1186
Shiren, Kokan, 184
shirk, 588
Shitennoji, 894
Shitil, 702
Shi`ur Qoma, 435
Shiwini, 520
Sho'ah, 512, 513
shofar, 776
shogunates, 625
Shoin, Yoshida, 312
Shomrim, 160
Shonagon, Sei, 407
Shoniwa, 25
shor ha-bar, 544
Short Treatise on God, Man, and His Well-Being (Spinoza), 1042
Shortland, Edward, 705
Shoshoni Indians, 831, 832, 850, 1120
Shotoku, Prince, 217, 623–624, 1085
shou, 543
Shou Hsing, 543
Shouters, 235
Shozan, Sakuma, 312
Shrew, 809
Shrine Shinto, 630, 995, 997, 998
shrines
    African, 19, 23, 246, 527
    Armenian, 97
    Buddhist, 893, 1084
    Greek, 89
    Islamic, 667–668
    Israelite, 616
    Neolithic, 792
    Phoenician, 887
    Shinto, 625, 995, 997, 998
    See also pilgrimage; temples
Shroud of Turin, 62
shtetls, 655
shu, 305
Shu (deity), 384
Shugendo community, 195
Shui-kuan, 43
shukr, 593
shukyo, 623
Shukyo hojin ho, 630
shul, 1053
Shulhan `arukh (Karo), 653
shura, 597, 781
shura baynahum, 587
Shushi, 627
Shushigaku, 627

shushin, 628
Shuwaliyatti, 520
Shwe Dagon, 893
Siakau, 355
Sibylline Books, 943
Sibylline Oracles, 69, 167, 181, 1114
sic'ee, 1028
Sichem, 340
Sicily, 887
siddha, 556
Siddhartha Gautama, 541, 562, 564
    See also Buddha (Gautama)
Siddharthikas, 212
siddhas, 50, 621
siddhayoga, 504
siddhis, 48, 216, 499, 621, 742
sidra' miqrata', 248
Sieg des Judenthums über das Germanthum, Der (Marr), 78
Siena, Council of, 876
Sierra Leone, 528
sifat, 448
Sifra', 153
Sifrei, 153
Sifrei Zuta', 153
Siger of Brabant, 524
Sigismund, Emperor, 336, 981
Sigismund, John, 1142
Sign of the Cross, 181
Signs: Journal of Women in Culture and Society, 454
Sihanouk, Prince, 202
sihr, 408
Sikanu, 85
sikhara, 89
Sikhism, 999
    in Bengal, 145
    foundation of, 999
    monotheism in, 763
Sikkim, Buddhism in, 482–483
Siksasamuccaya, 215
Siksika Indians, 820
sila, 95, 185, 363, 418
Sila (deity), 580
Silbury, Wiltshire, 721
Silent Ones, 596
Silius Italicus, 945
silsilah, 1047
Silva Mind Control, 800, 802
sima, 208
Simelungun Batak, 142
Simhah, Me'ir, 153
Simhat Torah, 652
Similitudes of Enoch, 81
Simon, Ernst, 948
Simon, Richard, 156
Simons, Menno, 722
Simple Way to Pray, A (Luther), 691
simulacra, 549
sin
    of Adam, 13, 106, 280, 412
    and afterlife, 42, 43
    atonement for, 103–105
    in Christian doctrine, 280
    confession of, 301–303, 933
    and fall, 412
    and grace, 279–280, 459
    Hittite, 511

sin *(continued)*
    in Judaism, 647
    original, 940–941
    and suffering, 512
Sin (deity), 86, 536, 725
Sinai covenant, 339
Sinai Peninsula, 614, 615
Sinan, 91
sing ngemong, 632
Singers society, 841
Singkelevun, 1128
Sinhala, 213
Sinhala religion, 1000–1001
    changes, causes of, 1001
    cults, 1000
    spirits/demons, 1000–1001
Siofn, 433
Siouan Indians, tribes of, 820
Sioux Indians, 820
sipapu, 843
Sipirok Batak, 142
Sippar, 725
Sippe, 556
Siratr, 726
Sirhak, 314
Sirhindi, Ahmed, 592, 594
Siricus, Pope, 875
Siriono, 789
Siripada, 893
Sirona, 241
Sirr al asrar (al-Razi), 53
sishti, 845
Sistine Chapel, 876
Sita, 150, 498
Sitala, 143, 911
sitos, 464
Siva, 50, 89, 90, 134, 143, 190, 356,
    408, 449, 450, 484, 486, 495,
    496, 497, 498, 500, 501, 502,
    570
    contemplative worship of, 719
    images of, 540, 1071
    as Indra, 570
    manifestations of, 564
    myths of, 1001–1003
    names for, 1071
    in Tantric Hinduism, 1069
    temples of, 709
Sivali, 95
Sivanjñanabodham (Meykantar), 1064
Siwa oasis, 386
Six Day War, 662, 927
Six Trees, 242
Sixtus IV, Pope, 156, 876
Sixtus V, Pope, 877
Siyah Chal, 131
Skáldskaparmál, 431
Skambha, 1008
Skanda (deity), 502
skandhas, 364, 709
Skírnir, 430
Skotino, cave at, 16
sky gods, 788
    Baltic, 136
slametan ceremonies, 632
slavery
    black religion under, 35
    Christian toleration of, 277

Slavic religion, 1003–1005
    female deities, 1005
    gods of, 1004–1005
    idols, 1004
    temples, 1004
Slocum, John, 835
sma-tawy, 537
Smalcaldic Articles, 337
Smallpox God, 679
smarta, 492–493, 494, 498, 500
Smartasutras, 490
Smerdis, 698
Smith, Adam, 393
Smith, Hyrum, 770
Smith, Joseph, 770, 903, 1006–1007
    and Mormonism, 1006–1007
Smith, W. Robertson, 74, 518
Smith, Wilfred Cantwell, 611
Smkhya-Yoga, 561
Smohalla Indians, 835, 836
smrti, 362, 938
    concept of, 486, 490, 497
smrtyupasthanani, 185
Smyth, John, 139
Snake cult of Hopi, 689
Snake-Antelope ceremony, 842, 843
So Kyongdok, 314
Sobrino, Jon, 639
Social Gospel movement, 271, 284,
    289
social movements, Christian, 287–290
Socialist Decision, The (Tillich), 715
Society of Brethren, 767, 905
Society of Christian Socialists, 715
Society of Friends. *See* Quakers
Society of Heaven and Earth, 1058
Society of Jesus. *See* Jesuits (Society
    of Jesus)
Society of Muslim Brothers. *See*
    Muslim Brotherhood
Society for the Propagation of the
    Gospel in Foreign Parts, 71
Socinians, 176
sociology of religion, 300, 381, 929
Socrates, 60, 96, 251
    as spiritual guide, 1044
Sodom and Gomorrah, 11, 152
Soen, Shaku, 1185
Sofer, Hatam, 865
Sofer, Mosheh, 865
soferim, 617
Sogbo, 233
Sogdians, 573, 749
Sojiji temple, 1185
Soka Gakkai, 737, 802
Sokar, 385
Sokkulam monastery, 1085
Soko, Yamaga, 312, 313
sola scriptura, 694
Soleb, 614
Solomon, 351, 450, 886
    Temple of, 635–636
    See also Wisdom of Solomon
Solomonic dynasty, 398
Solov'ev, Vladimir, 406
Soma (deity), 485
soma (drink), 99, 485, 486, 487, 558,
    569–570

Somalia, 408
Son of Heaven (Chinese emperor), 562
Son of Man (Jesus), 638, 728
    Old Testament, 727
Song of Songs, 152, 160, 161, 783
Song of the Three Young Men, 166
Song of Ullikummi, 520–521
songs
    African, 577
    Afro-Caribbean, 235
    in Hinduism, 501
    Inuit, 580
    Mapuche, 707
    North American Indian, 531, 810,
    812
    Shaker, 990
    South American Indian, 1022, 1029
    Tunguz, 1127
Songs of Zion (ha-Levi), 1186
Songye, 528
sonita, 50
Sons of Earth, 880
Soon, Kosen, 1185
soothsayers, Scythian, 571
Sootukw-nagw, 840
Sophia, 372, 434, 435
Sophocles, 515
Sorai, Ogyu, 313
Sorcerer of Les Trois Frères, 870
sorcery
    Bantu, 577
    malevolent, 1166
    North American Indian, 821
    simple, 1163–1164
    See also witchcraft
Soseki, Muso, 1185
Soto school of Zen Buddhism, 262,
    625, 1185
soul, 1007–1014
    in Afro-Caribbean religion, 234
    and afterlife, 40
    in Ainu religion, 44
    and alchemy, 51
    in Arctic religion, 93
    Aristotle on, 96
    in Batak religion, 142
    blood and, 181
    Buddhist concept of, 1008–1009,
    1145
    Chinese concept of, 42, 65, 1010
    Christian concept of, 1012–1013
    -ghosts, 518
    incarnation of, 104, 561
    Indian concept of, 1007–1008
    in Indo-European religions, 568
    Islamic concept of, 1013–1014
    Jewish concept of, 38, 41, 1011
    in Maya religion, 718
    Sammi, 951–952
    South American Indian concept of,
    1024, 1029, 1033
    Sufi concept of, 1014
    See also immortality; salvation
Souma, 796
Soustelle, Jacques, 341
South African religions
    God in, 1039
    rituals in, 1040

shades in, 1039
Zulu, 1191–1192
South American religions, 1014–1033
ancestor worship in, 1021, 1033
of Andean Indians, 1014–1019
animal spirits in, 1021, 1023, 1032
and Christian missions, 1024–1025
cultural areas of, 1030
Cuna, 346–347
dance in, 1022, 1031, 1032
death concept in, 354
death ritual in, 1018, 1024, 1033
divination in, 1018
and flood, 415
geographical distinctions, 1030
gods of, 1015–1017, 1031
of Gran Chaco Indians, 1026–1030
iconography of, 1017
initiation rites in, 1029
Mapuche, 706–708
messianism in, 728, 1018–1019
myths in, 1022–1023, 1026–1030
nature in, 789, 1032–1033
prophets in, 1022
rites of passage in, 1023–1024
sacrifice in, 1078
shamanism in, 1018, 1021–1022,
1027, 1029, 1030, 1033
soul in, 1024, 1029, 1033
spirits in, 1020–1021, 1032, 1033
supreme being in, 1030–1032
tricksters in, 1121
of Tropical Forest Indians,
1019–1025
worship in, 1017–1018
See also Inca religion;
Mesoamerican religions
South Yemen Family Law of 1974, 608
Southcott, Joanna, 734
Southeast Asia, temple compounds in,
1084–1085
Southeast Asian religions, 1034–1039
Balinese, 134–135
Batak, 141–142
Bornean, 188–189
Burma, 408, 1100–1101
Chinese influence on, 1035
death ritual in, 1038
exorcism in, 408
immanence in, 1038
Indian influence on, 1035–1036
island cultures, 1037–1039
Javanese, 631–632, 631–633
mainland cultures, 1034–1037
and missions, 1036
Neolithic, 1034–1035, 1037
rites of passage in, 1038
sacrifice in, 1038
See also Buddhism, Southeast Asian
Southern Baptist Convention, 139
Southern Christian Leadership
Conference, 289, 675
Southern Dance, 814
Southern Sung, 626
Soviet Union, communism in, 715
Soyalangw society, 841, 842
Soychu, 1031
Sozzini, Fausto, 1142

Spain
Catholic Reformation in, 276
humanism in, 517
inquisition in, 576
Judaism in, 1053
megalithic religion in, 721
in Mesoamerica, 127
missions of, 819, 846
spanda, 502
Spandaramet, 98
Spangenberg, Augustus Gottlieb, 769
Speakers, 596
Spencer, Baldwin, 112, 114
Spencer, Herbert, 63
Spenta Mainyu, 699, 762
Speusippus, 456
Spiegel, Shalom, 512
Spilsbury, John, 139
Spinoza, Barukh, 151, 443
life and works of, 1042–1043
Spiral Dance: A Rebirth of the Ancient
Religion of the Great Goddess
(Starhawk), 454, 455
Spirit Dance, 850
spirit possession. See Possession
spirits
African religions, 246–247, 375–376
Ainu religion, 44
Arctic religions, 93
Australian Aboriginal, 108, 115, 117,
1160
Caribbean religions, 231, 232,
233–234
Lugbara religion, 692
Maori religion, 705–706
North American Indian, 811–812,
820, 827–828, 831, 833,
839–841, 847, 848
Samoyed religion, 972
Santería, 234, 975
in shamanic initiation, 991
South American Indian, 1020–1021,
1028, 1032, 1033
Ungarinyin, 1137
voodoo, 233–234, 1155–1156
Yakut, 1169–1170, 1171
Zulu, 1192
Spiritual Assemblies, 133
Spiritual Baptists (Shouters), 235
Spiritual Exercises (Ignatius of Loyola),
551, 552, 719
spiritual guide, 1043–1045, 1137
in ancient Greece, 1043–1044
in Buddhism, 1045
in Christianity, 1044
in Hindusim, 1044–1045
in Islam, 1044
in Judaism, 1044
Spiro, Melford E., 74
Spokan Indians, 833
sprastavya, 364
Spring and Autumn Annals, 304, 315,
317
Sraddha, 64, 487
Sraosha, 1189
srauta, 143, 486, 487, 491, 563
Srautasutras, 486–487, 490
sravaka, 208

sravakamarga, 214
Sravana Belgola, 621
srenis, 491
Sri, 564, 1072
Sri Lanka, 96, 408
Buddhism in, 196, 198, 564,
1000–1001, 1099, 1100, 1101
exorcism in, 408
Sri Pada Mountain, 1001
Sri Vaisnavas, 501, 502, 565
Srimad Bhagavatam, 578
Srimala, Queen, 185
Srimala Sutra, 217
Srimaladevi Sutra, 185
srotra, 364
sruti, 50, 362, 484, 938
concept of, 489, 490, 491, 496
Ssu-fen lü, 966
Ssu-ma Ch`ien, 291, 315, 571, 684
Stalin, Joseph, 715
Stalinism, 289
Standard Sermons, 691
Stanner, W.E.H., 112
Star of David, 948
Star of Redemption, The
(Rosenzweig), 297, 947–948
Star Woman, 1029
Staraia Ladoga, 1004
Starcevo-Körös-Cris, 792
Starhawk, 454, 455
startsy, 1044
State Shinto, 627–629, 1058
Statesman (Plato), 372
Station of Ibrahim, 667
Steinbach, Udo, 611
Steinberg, Milton, 444
Steinthal, Heymann, 297
Stela, 757
Stela of the Vultures, 536
Stephen, 439
Stephen II, Pope, 875
Stern, Menachem, 614
sthandila, 56
Sthaviras, 333
Sthaviravadas, 212
Stoic philosophy, 478–479, 853
Stone, Barton, 365
stone cult, Arctic, 93
Stoney Indians, 820
Storehouse of Mysteries (Bar
Hebraeus), 155
Storr, Gottlob, 157
Story of Sinuhe, 385
Story of the Two Brothers, 386
Strabo, 524, 698, 742
Strauss, David Freidrich, 157, 639
strotra, 364
Studien zur Komposition der mekkanis-
chen Suren (Neuwirth), 611
Studies of the Historical Jesus (Fuchs),
438
Stupa, 892, 1084
stytto, 952
su khwan, 683
Subartu, 519, 724
Sübetei, 573
Subodhini, 1153
Sudan, 376

Suddhadvaita, 1153
Sudharman, 619
sudras, 143, 341, 485, 492, 500
Suen, 725
Suevians, 432
suffering, cults of, Bantu (central), 247
Suffering Servant doctrine, 512
sufi, 45, 592
Sufism, 1045–1048
  ascetic movement in, 1046
  in China, 259
  doctrine of, 592–594
  eremitism in, 395
  fraternities of, 1047–1048
  and Ibn 'Arabi, 1046–1047
  literature of, 1046
  miracles in, 743
  and monism, 784
  orders of, 594–595
  origins of, 1045–1046
  reform of, 594
  repentance in, 934
  retreat in, 937
  rise of, 585–586
  rituals of, 1047–1048
  saint veneration in, 1047
  soul in, 1014
  spiritual guide in, 1044
  and tariqah, 1080–1082
    veneration of masters, 967
Suhrawardi, `Abu al-Qahir Abu Najib
    al-, 1081
Suhrawardiyah, 1081
Suiga Shinto, 997
Suika Shinto, 627, 997
Suiko, Empress, 312, 623
sukeishakai, 997–998
Sukhavati, 397
Sukhlajii, 622
Sukkot, 470, 649, 652
Sulami, Abu `Abd al-Rahman al-Azdi
    al-, 1046
Sulis, 241
Sulka, 302
Sulla, 942
suluk, 593
Sulzberger, Mayer, 321
Sumatar Harabesi, 86
Sumatra, 586, 1037
Sumer, 450
Sumerian language, 724
Sumerian religion, goddesses in, 450
Sumero-Akkadian, 411
Summa theologiae (Aquinas), 139,
    442, 764, 1103–1104
Summenhart, Conrad, 516
Summer School of Applied Ethics, 14
summer solstice feast, Baltic, 136
summum bonum, 96
sun
  in Arctic religion, 93
  in Armenian religion, 97–98
  in Aztec religion, 127–128, 129
  in Baltic religion, 136
  and death myths, 354
  iconography of, 531
  in Inca religion, 302, 560
  in Maya religion, 718

in Mesopotamian religion, 725
North American Indian religion, 531,
    817, 823, 840
in Slavic religion, 1004
worship of, 788–789
Sun cult, 843
Sun Dance
  North American Indian, 414, 821,
    823– 824, 835, 850
  South American Indian, 1031
Sun Myung Moon, 1140–1141
Sun-Dagger petroglyphs, 840
Sunday schools, Buddhist, 203
Sung-dynasty religion, 261–262, 1055,
    1076, 1078
Sung-shan cave, 183
sunnah, 447, 588, 602, 603
sunnat al-nabi, 588
suññata, 419
Sunni Islam
  division from Shi`i, 601–602
  immortality in, 558
  and Islamic law, 589, 590, 602, 604,
    608
  subsects of, 596
  theology of, 591–592
Suntagma (Justin), 437
sunyata, 419
sunyavada, 209
supernatural, 1048–1050
  development of concept, 1049
  North American Indian religions,
    821– 822, 839–841, 847–848
  and shamanism, 991–992
  See also spirits
superstition, 1050–1051
  and Christianity, 1050
  classical usage, 1050
  and Protestant Reformation, 1051
supersubstantialis, 691
supplication
  fasting as, 414
    sacrifices of, 964
Supreme Emperor of Jadelike
    Augustness, 543
Supreme Purity Taoist movement, 49
Suren Pahlav, 98
Suri, Vijaya Dharma, 622
Surya, 143, 450, 486, 496, 500, 1069,
    1071, 1084
Susanna, 166
Susano-o no Mikoto, 451
Süse, Heinrich, 47
Suseneyos, Emperor of Ethiopia, 398
Susruta Samhita, 50
Sustenance Mountain, 128
sutras, 65, 95, 194, 213–214, 217, 258
  Buddhist, 194, 213–214, 217, 258
  Jain, 95
Suttanipata, 708
Suyá, 1021
Suzuki, D.T., 1051–1052
  and Zen Buddhism, 1051–1052
Svabhavika Bhedabheda, 1153
svadharma, 149, 362
Svami of Akkalkot, 709
svarita, 249
Sventovit, 1004

Svetambaras, 619
Svetasvatara, 489, 1002
Swahili, 375, 377
swaraj, 429
Swazi, 25
Sweat Lodge ceremony, 815, 821,
    823–824
Sweet Medicine, 824
Swiss Brethren, 59
Switzerland
  Anabaptism in, 59–60
  Calvinism in, 296
  megalthic religion in, 721
  Mennonites in, 723
  Reformation in, 59, 296, 899
Sword of the Lord, 401
syad, 621
syadvada, 621
Syllabus of Errors, The, 1133
Sylvester I, Pope, 515
synagogue, 1053–1054
  architecture of, 91
  history and development of, 1053
  in modern period, 1053–1054
  Passover liturgy in, 882
  rabbinate, 648, 900, 921–922, 927
  of Rabbinic Judaism, 648
  Reform congregations, 926, 927
  Sabbath service, 989
  Torah reading in, 1117–1118
Synod of Bishops, 878
Synod of Jerusalem, 268
Synod of Siponto, 980
Synod of Zamosc, 1139
Synodical Government Measure, 71
Synodicon, The, 397
Syria, 85, 88
Syrian Goddess, The, 223
Syrian Orthodox Church of Antioch,
    379
Syrian Orthodox church of India, 379
Syros, 14
System of Nature (D'Holbach), 392
Systematic Theology (Tillich), 1111

T

Ta Tao, 1161
Ta-cheng-chüeh Monastery, 1085
Ta-hsüeh wen (Wang Yang-ming), 310
ta-masha, 702
Ta-mo. See Bodhidharma
Ta-tao, 261
Ta-t`ung, 562, 732
Ta-tung chen-ching, 1077
ta`amei ha-mitsvot, 468
Taawa, 531
Tabaqat al-sufiyah (al-Sulami), 1046
Tabaqat al-sufiyah (Ansari), 1046
Tabernacle, 471, 615
Tabiti, 571, 987
Tablets of Maklu, 137
Tablita Dance, 846
taboos
  Inuit, 580
  Maori, 705–706
  North American Indian, 821, 822
Tabula Smaragdina, 51
Tachard, Gui, 30

Tacitus, 432, 515
  on Germanic religion, 430, 431–432
T'aegp-chong, 206
Tafari, Ras, 235
tafsir, 447, 609, 632, 1046
tafwid, 448
Tagaste, 105
tagkanysough, 811
Tagore, Debendranath, 144
Tagore, Rabindranath, 144, 429
Tagus, 524
Tahafut al-falasifah (Ibn Rushd), 525, 593
tahallul, 892
tahannuth, 916
tahuantinsuyu, 559
Tai Chen, 310, 311
T'ai Shan, 1086
t'ai-chi, 308, 1055–1056
  conceptions of, 1055–1056
  meaning of word, 1055
t'ai-chi ch'üan, 1056
t'ai-chi t'u, 542
T'ai-chi t'u (Chou Tuni), 1076
T'ai-chi t'u shuo (Chou Tun-i), 307, 1055
T'ai-ch'ing Kung, 684
t'ai-ho, 307
T'ai-i sect, 1076
T'ai-i sect of Taoism, 261
T'ai-p'ing, 732
T'ai-p'ing T'ien-kuo, 264
T'ai-shan Fu-chün, 43
T'ai-shang Lao-chün, 1075
T'ai-tsung, 260
T'ai-tzu, 562
taiga, 92
Taihan, 965
Taika Reforms, 312
Taikyo Sempu movement, 627, 628
Tailtiu, 241, 242
Táin Bó Cuailnge, 242
Taiping Rebellion, 259, 264
Taishi, Shotoku, 184, 312
Taisho Democracy, 627
Taiwanese religions, 264, 1056–1059
  development of, 1057–1058
  modern, 1058–1059
  prehistoric, 1056–1057
  religious associations, 1059
Tajrid al-`aqu'id (al-Hilli), 595
Takamanohara, 996
Talay, 225
Tale of Genji (Shikibu), 407
Tales of the Hasidim (Buber), 190
Tales of Rabbi Nachman (Buber), 190
talfiq, 590
Talib, Abu, 778
Tallensi, 63
Talmud, 78, 253, 368, 469, 470, 543, 1059–1062
  authority of, 1061–1062
  Babylonian Talmud, 646, 653, 1060, 1061, 1172
  commentaries on, 653, 1061
  contents of, 1059
  destruction of, 1060
  and doctrine, 368

  Jerusalem Talmud, 646, 1060
  and law (*halakhah*), 469, 1061
  meaning of word, 1060
  origins and development of, 1059–1061
  as religious experience, 1062
  study of, 1172, 1173
Tamahumara Indians, 837
Tamang, 482
tamas, 149, 190, 493
Tamfana, 432
Tamil Nadu, 565, 1062
Tamil religions, 1062–1065
  early, 1062–1063
  medieval period, 1063–1064
  modern, 1065
Tammuz, 725
T'an-luan, 209, 260
Tanakh, 651
Tanegashima Island, 626
T'ang-dynasty religion, 259, 260–261, 306, 1076
Tangaroa, 474
tanha, 418
Tanit, 523
Tannhäuser, 1083
Tantras, 50, 215, 216
Tantrism, 1066–1067
  Buddhist, 194, 195, 208, 215–216, 498, 565
    and goddess worship, 449–450, 451
    and Hindu Tantrism, 1066–1067
    in India, 565
    nirvana in, 805–806
    temples, 1085
  doctrinal aspect of, 1066–1067
  Hindu, 143, 451, 498–499
    and Buddhist Tantrism, 1066–1067
    doctrine of, 1069–1070
    gods of, 1071–1072
    history of, 1067–1068
    meditation in, 719
    practices of, 1070–1071
    sects of, 1068
    spread of, 1068–1069
  Jain, 1067
  meaning of word, 1066
  nirvana in, 805–806
Tanzania, 21, 376, 408, 577
tanzih, 449
tanzil, 917–918
Tao ching, 684
T'ao Hung-ching, 49, 1075, 1077
Tao-ch'o, 209, 260
Tao-hsin, 261, 262
Tao-hsüan, 183, 965
tao-shih, 555, 863
Tao-te ching (Lao-tzu), 255, 542, 684, 1074, 1076
Tao-te T'ien-tsun, 543
Tao-yü, 183
Taoism, 1072–1073
  and afterlife, 43
  and alchemy, 48, 49, 1078
  Bodhidharma legend in, 184
  Celestial Master sect, 258–259
  Cheng-i school, 263

  Ch'üan-chen school, 261, 262, 263
  and Chuang-tzu's thought, 291, 1074
  concepts of, 1073–1074
  early thought of, 255
  exorcism in, 407
  fasting in, 413
  gods in, 543
  historical development of, 1074–1077
  and *I ching*, 1073–1074
  iconography of, 542
  immortality in, 542, 543, 1077–1078
  and Lao-tzu, 684–685, 1074–1075
  longevity in, 1077–1078
  meditation in, 719–720
  millenarianism in, 732
  miracles in, 742
  mysticism in, 804, 1073
  ordination in, 863
  pilgrimage in, 893
  resurrection in, 935
  salvation in, 258, 542
  in Sung period, 261–262
  T'ai-i sect, 261
  in Taiwan, 1058
  in T'ang period, 261
  tao (Way), concept of, 255, 291, 623, 1073
  temple compounds in, 1086
  yin-yang in, 1073, 1074
Taos, 845
tapabrata, 632
tapas, 488, 496, 570, 621
tapasya, 429
Tapieté, 1027
tapu, 705–706
Tapui, 1027
taqiyah, 595
taqlid, 447, 604
Taqui Oncoy, 1018, 1019
taqwa, 583
Tara, 244, 451, 1072
Tarahumara Indians, 837
tariki, 805
tariqah, 596, 747, 1047, 1080–1082
  individual *tariqahs*, 1081–1082
  origins of, 1080
  on social awareness, 1081
  spiritual exercises, 1081
Tariquah-i-Muhammadiya, 146
Tartaros, 99, 467
Tartessian religion, 523
Tasimshian Indians, 826
Tasmisu, 520
tathagata-garbha, 804
Tathagatas, 216
Tatians, 955
ta`til, 449
Tattvarthadhigama Sutra, 620
Tattvarthadipanibandha, 1153
Tauler, Johannes, 47
taumata atuas, 705
taurobolium, 138
Tavgi, 92
tawaf, 668
tawaf al-ifadah, 892
Tawahedo, 397
Tawang, 483

tawhid, 449
ta'wil, 787, 1046
Tawiskaron, 372, 811
Taxila, 1084
Taylor, Hudson, 753
Taylor, Vincent, 158
ta`ziyahs, 595
Tcuperika, 823
Te ching, 684
Te Makawe, 705
Teachers Institite, 322
Tearnendaraj, 99
Tecciztecatl, 534
Tech nDuinn, 242
Techniques du Yoga (Eliade), 388
Tecuciztecatl, 127
Tecumseh, 819
Teê Pijopac, 795
Tefillah, 883
Tefnut, 384
Tehillim, 908
Teitelbaum, Mosheh, 472
teixiptla, 128
tekkes, 594
Tekoa, 58
Tel Dan, 88
Telepinu, 510
telete, 464
Tell al-Sawwan, 535
Tell Brak, 535
Tell Fekhariye, 85
Tell Mardikh, 88
Tell Qasile, 885
Tello Obelisk, 1017
Teman, 614, 615
temenos, 89, 462, 463
Tempels, Placide, 26
Temple of Amun, 1088
Temple of Inscriptions, 717
Temple of Jupiter at Heliopolis, 1088
Temple Mound, 849
Temple of the Sun, 559
Temple of the Tooth, 893
temples, 1082–1089
  in Africa, 23
  Armenian, 97
  Aztec, 129, 130
  biblical canon in, 161–162
  Buddhist, 196, 482, 625, 627,
    1084–1086
    monasteries, 1084
    stupa and stupa shrines, 1084
    temple compounds, 1085
  Confucian, 1087
    temple compounds, 1087
  Cycladic, 15
  divine presence in, 89
  in Egypt, 89, 385, 386, 537,
    1087–1088
    architectural elements, 1087–1088
  function of, 90–91
  Greek, 90, 462, 479, 1088
    architectural elements, 1088
  Hindu, 89, 90, 497–498, 502,
    1063–1064, 1082–1084
    architectural forms, 1083
    human form, 1083–1084
  Hittite, 510–511

Iberian, 523
Inca, 559
Jainist, 621
in Jerusalem, 82, 83, 84, 89, 159,
  162, 248, 351, 470
megaliths, 720
Mesoamerican, 1089
  temple-pyramid-plaza, 1089
Mesopotamian, 536, 726
Minoan, 16
Moabite, 758
Philistine, 886–887
Roman, 1088–1089
  cella, 1088
  construction of, 1088
Scythian, 571
Slavic, 1004
in Taiwan, 1058
Taoist, 1086
  temple compounds, 1086
See also Jerusalem, Temples of;
  shrines
Templo Mayor, 129, 130
templum, 89
temptation, 978, 1089–1091
  meaning of, 1090
  tempter in, 1090–1091
  theoretical perspectives, 1091
tempus, 89
Temüjin. *See* Chinggis, Khan
ten adro, 796, 797
Ten Commandments, 283, 548,
  1091–1092
  in Christianity, 284, 1092
  essence and function of, 615–616
  in Islam, 1092
  and Moses, 772, 1092
  order and contents of, 1091–1092
  revelation of, 615, 1092
  scriptures on, 1092
  and Torah, 1115
Ten Commandments, The (film), 546
*Ten Great Religions: An Essay in
  Comparative Theology* (Clarke),
  1092
Ten Injunctions, 313
Ten Realms of Being, 996
Tendai school, 184, 195, 624, 626,
  750, 1184
  founding of, 965–966
teng-hsia, 43
Tenino Indians, 832
Tenochtitlán, 87, 126–127, 128, 129,
  130
Tenrikyo, 628, 1058
Tensho Kotai Jingukyo, 734
teomama, 128
Teotihuacán, 90, 126, 533–534, 554
Tepe Gawra, 88
Terah, 783
Teresa of Avila, 691
Terrien, Samuel, 158
Tertullian, 155, 181, 279, 282, 427, 437
Tesheba, 520
Teshub, 520, 548
teshuvah, 103, 647, 934
teshuvot, 653, 700
Testament of Levi, 727

Testament of Our Lord, 397
Testaments of the Twelve Patriarchs,
  99
Testimony of Truth, 437
Teteoinnan, 129, 534
Teton Indians, 820
Tetrateuch, 617
Tetzel, Johann, 923
Teutonic Knights, 422
tevijja, 95
Tewa Indians, 837, 838, 839, 840,
  844–845
Textual History of the Qur'an (Jeffery),
  610
Tezcatlipoca, 127, 129, 302, 1121
Thaddaeus, 793
Thailand, 96
  Buddhism in, 202, 203, 210, 1101
Thak Khola, 482
Thakore, Mehraj, 428
Thales of Miletus, 330
Thammayut sect, 1101
Thanatos, 467
thanh-hoang, 1155
thanksgiving, sacrifices of, 964
tha'r, 584
That Luang temple, 893
That Which is in the Netherworld, 385
Thaumaturgus, 960
Thebes, 537
theion, 461
Theism, 102
  of Cohen, 298
Theodore of Mopsuestia, 379, 1139
Theodoric of Freiberg, 47
Theodoric II, King of Ostrogoths, 572
Theodosian Code of 438, 176
Theodosius I, Emperor, 334
Theodosius II, Emperor, 334
Theogony (Hesiod), 161
theoi, 462, 763
Theologia Platonica (Ficino), 516
theology, 1092–1098
  of Barth, 140–141
  of Bonhoeffer, 186
  of Bushnell, 218–219
  of Calvin, 222–223
  comparative, 1092–1098
  and doctrinal form, 369
  of Islam, 590–592, 611
  and linguistic analysis, 60–62
  method of, 357
  nonsexist, 1167
  of Rosenzweig, 947–949
  of Tillich, 1110–1111
  and Trinity doctrine, 279
  See also Christian ethics
theology of the cross, 694
Theophilus, 335
Theopompus, 699
Theories of Primitive Religion (Evans-
  Pritchard), 74, 402
Theory of the Earth (Hutton), 403
Theosophical Society, 198
Theosophists, 429
Théot, Catherine, 733
theotokos, 379, 545
Therapeutae, 413

Theravada Buddhism, 1098–1102
  arhatship figure in, 95
  features of, 209
  Four Noble Truths in, 418–419
  in India, 1099–1100
  language of, 211
  missions in, 745
  in modern period, 1101–1102
  origins and development of,
    1098–1099
  sainthood in, 967
  in Southeast Asia, 195, 201, 210,
    211, 1036, 1100–1101
  in Sri Lanka, 1099, 1100, 1101
Theravadin councils, 333–334
Thérèse of Lisieux, 1102–1103
Theseus, 17, 463, 523
Thessalonians, 170, 171, 173, 174,
  439
Thessalonica, 460
Thessaly-Macedonia, 792
thiasoi, 464
Thieme, Paul, 568
Third (Trito), 567
Thirty Years War, 768, 877
Thirty-nine Articles, 70
Thirty-three Holy Places of Kannon,
  894
Thisbe, 520
Thkmn wa-Shnm, 226
Thomas Aquinas, 70, 138, 1103–1104
  on Aristotle, 1104
  biblical exegesis of, 155–156
  and Catholic Reformation, 275, 276
  and doctrine, 369
  and Galileo, 427
  in Germany, 46
  on God, 357, 445
  on goodness, 457
  and Ibn Rushd, 524
  life and works of, 1103–1104
  and occultism, 853
  philosophy of, 1104
  on soul, 1012
  on supernatural, 1049
  on superstition, 1050
  theology of, 269, 1104
Thomas Christians, 753
Thomas. See Gospel of Thomas
Thomists, 47
Thonga, 30
Thor, sacred oak of, 187, 752
Thoth, 51, 385, 1105–1106
Thothmose, 1105
Thought Woman, 840
Thracians, 556
Three Affiliated Tribes, 820
Three Marks, 198
Three Pure Ones, 543
Threefold Pure Precepts of
  bodhisattva, 185
Threeness, in Celtic religion, 240
Thrones, 69, 70
Thucydides, 515
Thunapa, 1016
thunder god, Slavic, 1004
Thunderbird, 531
Thurneysen, Eduard, 140

thusia, 463
Ti, 304
ti bonanj, 1156
Tiahuanaco, 1017
Tiahuanaco-Huari, 1014
Tiamat, 66, 676
Tiberias, 472
Tibetan religion, 1106–1107
  Bon religion, 407
  Chinese policy on, 1107
  modern status, 1107
  pre-Buddhist, 1106
  See also Buddhism, Tibetan
Ticonius, 155
T'ien, 42, 253–254, 255, 304, 318
t'ien-li, 308
t'ien-ming, 254
T'ien-shih Tao, 43
T'ien-t'ai school of Buddhism, 258,
  260, 624, 750, 804–805
T'ien-ti Hui, 1058
t'ien-tzu, 254
Tiermes, 952
Tierra del Fuego, 1031
Tiglathpileser III, 85
Tikal, 554, 717, 1089
tiki, 856
Tikopia religion, 1108–1109
  modern, 1109
  ritual in, 1108–1109
  Work of the Gods, 1109
Tikuywuuti, 840
Tilak, Bal Gangadhar, 150
Tilimsani, Shaykh al-, 781
Tillich, Paul, 279, 1109–1110
  on comparative theology, 1097
  and Eliade, 391
  on faith, 102
  on Freud's unconscious, 426
  life of, 1109–1110
  on socialism, 715
  on symbolism, 1111–1112
  theory of religion, 1110–1111
Timaeus, 342
Timanitki, 1126
Timoleon of Syracuse, 463
Timothy, 173
Timur, 574
Timurid, 45
Tindal, Matthew, 393
Ting of Wei, Duke, 316
Tippá, 1029
tiqqun, 472
tiqqunei soferim, 151
Tir, 98
Tir inna mBan, 243
tirakat, 632
Tirawa, 822–823
Tiridates, King, 98
tirtha, 484
tirthamkaras, 95, 620, 621
Tischendorf, Konstantin von, 173
Tish`ah be-Av, 649
Tishbe, 520
Titans, 467
Titii fraternity, 942
Titov Veles, 1004
Titus, 173

Tiwa Indians, 837, 840, 845
Tjekker, 884
tjurunga, 108, 111, 114, 115, 529
Tlacolteótl, 302
Tlaloc, 128, 129, 534, 554
Tlaloques, 128
tlalxico, 128
tlaquimilolli, 128
tlatocayotl, 127
Tlazolteotl, 129
Tlingit Indians, 826, 829
Tnagnayika, 377
tnatantja, 114
to ao marama, 705
To Change the World: Christology and
    Cultural Criticism (Ruether),
    1167
To Demetrianus (Cyprian), 549
To Donatus (Cyprian), 549
To the Nations (Tertullian), 549
To Purgo, 354
To Quirinius (Cyprian), 549
Toba, 1029
Toba Batak, 142
tobacco rituals
  Caribbean, 232
  North American Indian, 822
Tobias, 68
Tobit, 160, 166
T'oegye, 314
Togana, 1018
toilet ceremonies, 90
Toju, Nakae, 312
Tokhwáh, 1121
Tokoyo, 996
Tokugawa, 625, 626, 627, 628
Tokuhara, Miki, 629
Tokuitsu, 965
Toland, John, 393
Toledo, Council of, 978
tolerati, 405
Toleration Act of 1689, 296
Tollan, 67, 126, 128, 534
toloache, 833, 834
Tolstoi Farm, 429
Toltecs, 126, 534
Tonacacihuatl, 128
Tonacatecuhtli, 128
tonalpohualli, 129
Tonatiuh, 129
Tongguk Yi Sangguk chip (Kyubo), 679
Tonkawa Indians, 820
Topiltzin Quetzalcoatl, 128
Torah, 1113–1118
  and canonizing process, 162
  contents of, 159, 1113–1114
  and doctrine, 368
  and halakhah, 468
  and Israelite religion, 617
  literary and historical criticism of,
    1114
  Maimonides', studies of, 700, 1116
  meaning of word, 688, 1113, 1115
  medieval concept of, 1115–1116
  oral, 1114
  Paul on, 78
  priestly context of, 688
  Qabbalistic view of, 1116

Torah (continued)
    Rabbinic theory of, 651–652
    reading of, 648, 649, 1117–1118
    study of, 151, 153, 1117
    in synagogues, 91, 1117–1118
    and Ten Commandments, 1115
    written and oral, 1114–1115
Torat Kohanim, 1113
torii, 997
Toririhnan, 795
Tork` of Anggh, 98
Torquemada, Tomás de, 576
Torres Strait Islands, 115, 121
Torrey, Reuben A., 401
Tosar, 699
Tosefta, 974, 1059
Totem and Taboo (Freud), 63
totemism, 1137
totenism, and human sacrifice, 518
Tours, Council of, 575
Towa Indians, 837, 840, 845
Toward Transfigured Life (Harakas), 269
Tractatus logico-philosophicus
        (Wittgenstein), 61
Tractatus Politicus (Spinoza), 1042
Tractatus Theologico-Politicus
        (Spinoza), 1042
Traibhumikatha, 202
Training of a Zen Buddhist Monk, The
        (Suzuki), 1052
Traité d'histoire des religions (Eliade),
        388, 389
Trân Hung Dao, 1154
trance, 960, 990
transcendance, 324
Transcendental Meditation movement,
        744, 800, 802
transmigration, and karman, 673
transmutation, and alchemy, 47, 51
Trappists, 760
Traversari, Ambrogio, 515
Treatise of Shem, 167
Treatise on the Spread of Zen for the
        Protection of the Country (Eisai),
        1184
Treatise on the Two Entrances and
        Four Practices, 183
Tree of Good and Evil, 879
Tree of Life, 342, 879
Tree of Sefirot, 544
tree symbol of cross, 136, 340
Tremendum: A Theological Interpretation
        of the Holocaust (Cohen), 513
Trent. See Council of Trent
treta, 880
tretayuga, 495, 496
treuga Dei, 343
Triads of the Island of Britain, 240
Trible, Phyllis, 1166
tricksters, 1118–1121
    African, 20, 1119
    concept of, 1118
    and death, 354
    Mesoamerican and South American,
        1121
    North American Indian, 531, 812,
        821– 822, 831, 1119–1120,
        1119–1120

trikaya, 214
trimurti, 495–496, 498
Trinidad
    Shango cult in, 234
    Spiritual Baptist cult (Shouters) in, 235
Trinity, 70, 441, 1122–1125
    Augustine on, 105, 106, 279, 1123
    and blasphemy, 176
    councils on, 334
    development of doctrine, 1122–1123
    Francis of Assisi on, 420
    in modern period, 1125
    principles of, 941, 1123–1125
Trioedd Ynys Prydein, 240
Tripartite Tractate, 437
Tripoli, 344
Triptolemus, 523
Tripurasundari, 1072
triratna, 541, 620
Trito, 567
trivarga, 492
Troeltsch, Ernst, 1095, 1097
Trois Frères cave, 561
Trophonios, sanctuary at, 99, 137
trpta, 556
trsna, 418
Truce of God, 343
True Doctrine, 732
True Pure Land, 625, 626, 628
Tryambakesvar, 709
tsaddiq, 366, 654
Ts`ao Ts`ao, 572
Ts`ao Tuan, 309
Ts`ao-tung, 262
tsedaqah, 649
Tseng-tzu, 305, 317
tsfsirs, 611
tsimtsum, 443, 472
Tso chuan, 315, 316, 317
Tsou, 1056
Tsou Yen, 256
Tsu-lu, 317
Tsu-t'ang chi, 184
Ts`ui Hao, 259
tsung, 216–217
    concept of, 216–217
Tsung-mi, 805
Tu Kuang-t`ing, 1076
tu-shih, 43
tuat, 555
Tubal-cain, 221
Tubatulabal Indians, 834
Tucano Indians, 66, 355, 1032
Tucci, Giuseppe, 388
Tucker, Ellen Louisa, 391
Tula, 534
Tung Chung-shu, 256
T`ung-shu (Chou Tun-i), 307
Tunguz religion, 92, 93, 991,
        1126–1128
    modern traces, 1127–1128
    myths of, 1126–1127
    rituals of, 1127
Tunisia, 543
Tunisian Code of Personal Status of,
        608, 1956
Tupi-Guarani, 1031
Turdetan religion, 523

Türk empire, 572, 573
Turkey, 85
Turkic religions, 1129–1131
    animals in, 1130
    cosmology of, 1129–1130, 1169
    imperial, 1130–1131
    popular, 1130
    Yakut, 1169–1171
Turmair, Johannes, 516
Turner, Victor, 245, 247, 689
Tuscarora Indians, 811
Tusculanae disputationes (Cicero), 320
Tusi, Nasir, al-Din, 595
Tusita Heaven, 214
Tutelo Indians, 811
Tutsi, 578
Tuuruu, 1127
Twelve Gods, 1000
Twelve Tablets, 161
Twelver Shi`ah, 585, 589, 590, 595, 596,
        601–602, 603, 604, 605, 993–994
Twenty-seventh Homily on Numbers
        (Origen), 783
Twersky, Mordechai, 472
Twin (Yemo), 567, 568
Two Books of Jeu, 434
Two Essays on Analytical Psychology
        (Jung), 664
Two Types of Faith (Buber), 191
Two-Horn Society, 841, 846
Tylor, E.B., 74, 518, 790
Tyobu Shinto, 624
Typhon, 867
Tyre, 351, 886
tzu, meaning of, 291
Tzu-ch`an, 315
Tzu-chang, 317
Tzu-haia, 317
Tzu-Kung, 317
Tzu-lu, 317

U
`Ubaid, al-, 536
Ubar, 112
Ubii, 432
udaghan, 761
udatta, 249
uddesikadhatu, 892
udgatr, 486
UFO cults, 736
ufufunyane, 1192
Uganda, 19, 21, 26, 577
Ugarit, 85, 224–227, 757, 885, 887
Ugradattapariprccha, 215
Ugrians, 554
Uighurs, 573
uji, 623
uji no kami, 623
ujiko, 630
uktena, 817
`ulama', 586, 589, 593, 594, 596, 608,
        864
Ulates, 371
Ullambana Sutra, 215
Ullastret, 523
Ullikummi, 520–521
Ullr, 433
Ulrich of Strassburg, 47

Ulter, interdict of, 371
ultramontanism, 1133–1134
`ulum al-din, 609
Ulutún, 707
Uma, 143, 1072
Umai, 1131
Umasvati, 620
Umatilla Indians, 835
ummah, 447, 475, 775
ummah muslimah, 585
umoya, 1192
`umrah, 588, 891
uMvelinqangi, 1191
unconscious
    collective, 70
    Freud's theory, 425–426
Undenominational Fellowship of
        Christian Churches, 365–366
underworld, 1134–1136
    archaic, 1134
    Arctic, 93
    in Babylonia, 1134
    Canaanite, 226
    Chinese concept of, 42, 43
    in Christianity, 1135
    in Egypt, 385, 538, 1134
    geography of, 40
    Greek (Hades), 463, 467, 557,
        1134–1135
    in Hinduism, 1136
    in Islam, 1135–1136
    in Judaism, 1135
    secular visions of, 1136
    See also afterlife; heaven and hell
Undiscovered Self, The (Jung),
        664
Ungarinyin religion, 1136–1138
    cosmogony, 1137
    cosmology, 1137
    myths of, 1137–1138
Ungud, 1137
Ungur, 1137
Uniate churches, 379, 1138–1139
    Coptic, 1138
    Malabar of India, 1138
    Marionite, 1138
    Melchite, 1138
    Ruthenians, 1138–1139
Unification Church (Moonies), 744,
        800, 802, 1140–1141
    member profiles, 1140
    negative aspects, 1141
    theology of, 1140–1141
unio mystica, 697
Union of Florence, 276
Union of Utrecht, 72
Unitarianism, 319, 391–392, 504,
        1141–1142
    American, 1142
    European, 1142
    Unitarian Universalists, 1143
    universalism concept, 1142–1143
Unitas Fratrum, 905
United Aboriginal Mission (UAM), 121
United Church of Canada, 731
United Church of Christ, 294
United Methodist Church, 730, 731
United Methodist Free Churches, 730

United States
    Afro-American religion in, 34–36,
        139
    Baha'is in, 132
    Baptist church in, 138, 139, 283
    blasphemy laws in, 177
    Christian Science in, 285–286
    Christian social movements in, 288,
        289, 715
    civil rights movement in, 675–676
    Congregationalism in, 293–294, 319
    cults in, 800–801
    Disciples of Christ in, 365–366
    Eliade in, 390–391
    Enlightenment in, 393
    Episcopal Church in, 71, 72, 293
    Ethical Culture in, 14
    evangelicalism in, 400
    Freemasonry in, 423
    fundamentalism in, 400–401, 404
    Great Awakening in, 139, 319, 400
    International Society for Krishna
        Consciousness (ISKCON) in,
        578–579
    Islam in, 36, 586
    Jehovah's Witnesses in, 633–635
    Judaism in, 321, 657, 661
        Orthodox, 866
        Reform, 927–928
        yeshivah, 1173
    Lutheran church in, 294, 695
    Mennonites in, 723
    Methodism in, 35, 293, 730–731
    Mormonism in, 770–771,
        1006–1007, 1181–1182
    new religions in, 800–801, 1140
    prophets in, 903–904
    Puritans in, 290, 914
    Quakers in, 915
    Salvation Army in, 969
    Seventh-day Adventism in, 988–989
    Shakers in, 238, 239, 686–687, 990
    Social Gospel movement in, 271
    Unification Church in, 1140
    Unitarianism in, 391–392, 1142
    Universalism in, 1143
    See also Afro-American religions;
        North American Indian religions
United States Constitution, 297
United Synagogue of America, 322
Uniting Church, 731
Unity of Being, 593
Unity of Brethren. *See* Moravians
Unity Synod, 769
Universal Negro Improvement
        Association, 35, 235
Universalism, 1142–1143
University of Chicago, Eliade at,
        390–391
Unknown Christ of Hinduism, The
        (Panikkar), 755
unleavened bread, and Passover,
        881–882
*Unparteiische Kirchen-und
        Ketzerhistorie von Anfang des
        Neuen Testaments bis 1688*
        (Arnold), 480
untouchables, 429, 492, 710

Unveiling of the Veiled (al-Hujwiri),
        1046
upacuna, 302
upadhyaya, 620, 621
Upadhye, A.N., 622
Upagupta, 96, 708
upaklesabhumika, 364
Upanayana, 487
Upanisads, 50, 149, 341, 362, 484
    and atheism, 100
    on immortality, 556
    karman in, 671
    and mysticism, 782
    principle texts, 1150
    soul in, 1008
    teachings of, 488–489, 1150–1152
    tree symbol in, 340
upapadya-vedaniya-karman, 673
upasakas, 620
Upasani Baba, 710
upasrayas, 620
Updegraff, David, 915
uposadha days, 215
Uposatha, 302
Ur, 88, 725
Urartean Biaina, 97
Urartean Teisheba, 97
Urartu, 519
Ursa Major, 531
Urban II, Pope, 343
Urban IV, Pope, 46
Urban VI, Pope, 237, 876, 980
Urban VIII, Pope, 428
Urfa, 86
Uriel, archangel, 69
urine, as pollution, 911
urna, 541
Urpihuáchac, 1016
urta, 725
Uruk, 88, 536, 725
urvan, 582
Urzeit, 410
Usas, 486
ushabtis, 538
Ushharay, 225
Usmu, 536
usnisa, 541
usnu, 560
usul al-fiqh, 603
Usuliyah, 603
uswah hasanah, 588
Ute Indians, 832, 835
Utgardr, 430
Uthht, 225
`Uthman, 590
Uto-Aztecan Indians, 820
Utopia (More), 517
Utraquists, 768
utria, 702
uttamapurusa, 497
Uttamchand, Karamchand, 428
Uttar Pradesh, 408
uttara, 738
uttarimanussa, 95
Utu, 536, 724, 725
Uwanami cult, 843, 846
uxbe, 177
Uxmal, 554

V

Vac, 177, 485, 1070
Vacaspati, 1152
vaci-karman, 673
Väddas, 1000
Vahagn, 97
Vahanian, Gabriel, 102
vahosanna, 25
Vaikhanasas, 501
Vairocana, 216
Vaisali, Council of, 333
Vaisesika school of Hinduism, 100, 1145
    soul in, 1145
    teachings of, 1145
Vaisesika Sutra, 493
Vaisnava Pañcaratras, 501
Vaisnava Samhitas, 499
Vaisnavism, 564
    in Bengal, 143, 144
    in India, 565–566
    meditation in, 719
Vaisya, 341
Vajapeya, 487
Vajirañana, 203
Vajiravudh, 203
Vajrayana, 50, 208, 215
Vajurveda, 362
vakya-sastra, 738
Valcamonica, 178
Valdès, Pierre, 905
Valdivia, 1015, 1016
Valencia, 523
Valentinian Exposition, A, 155
Valentinus, 52, 154, 435, 437
Valholl, 431, 432
Valla, Lorenzo, 156, 515
Vallabha, 1153
Vamana, 496
vamutenga, 25
Van, 97
Van Buren, Paul M., 102, 639
van den Velde, Heymerich, 46
van Gogh, Vincent, 546
vanaprastha, 341
vanaprasthin, 491, 936
Vanir, 431
Vaque, 231
Varaha, 496
Vardavar, 98
Varieties of Religious Experience, The
    (James), 73, 75
varivas, 486
Varkaris, 709
varnas, 487, 491–492
varnasramadharma, 362
    theory of, 490–492
varttika, 971
Varuna, 143, 486, 762
vasana, 672
Vashaghn, 97
Vasto, Lanza del, 430
Vastospati, 1001
vastu, 498
Vastupurusa Mandala, 1083
Vastupurusamandala, 498
Vasudeva, 497, 1071
Vatican Council, First, 1145–1147
    constitutions of, 337, 1146–1147

consultors in, 1145–1146
    debates of, 1146
    and moral theology, 269
    and papal infallibility, 877–878, 1133
    and scholasticism, 102
Vatican Council, Second, 229, 269,
    270, 281, 292, 379, 405, 677,
    1148–1150
    collegiality doctrine of, 878
    and ecumenism, 278, 337–338, 383,
        1150
    goals of, 1148–1149
    and John XXIII, 940, 1148
    organization of, 1148
    and Paul VI, 940, 1148–1149
    themes of, 940, 1149–1150
Vatsiputriya Sthaviravadins, 212
Vatsyayana, 492
Vaughan, Thomas, 421
Vault of Heaven, 822
Vaux, Roland de, 352
Vayiqra`, 1113
Vayu, 486, 496, 581
Vearalden Olmai, 952
vedanaskandha, 364
Vedanta, 493, 1150–1153
    Advaita, 499–500, 501, 1152
    meaning of word, 1150
    schools of, 1150–1153
Vedanta Society of New York, 504
Vedanta Sutra, 493, 494
Vedas, 100, 249, 302, 340, 341, 359,
    484–485, 490
vedhana, 50
vedi, 487
Vedic religion, 484–486, 490, 555–556,
    563–564
    blessing in, 177–178
    gods of, 485–486, 1001–1003
    immortality in, 555–556
    literature of, 484–485, 490
    mantras of, 563–564
    Mimamsa school, 738–739
    mysticism in, 782
    social groups in, 485
    soul in, 1008
Ved'ma, 1005
vegetarianism, Hindu, 491, 502
Veles, 1004
Velichkovskii, Paisii, 950
Vena, 1008
Vendidad, 698
Venerable Bede, 275
Venus, 479, 942
Venus figures, 870
ver sacrum, 955
Veracruz, 534
Verethraghna, 97, 373
Vergentes in senium, 575
Vergerio, Pietro Paolo, 515
Vergil, 409
Verona, 514
Verona, Guarino da, 515
Vesta, 571
Vesunna, 242
Veuillot, Louis, 1133
Viannos, 16
Vibhajyavadins, 212

vibhava, 540
Vicarious Sacrifice, The (Bushnell), 218
Vicenza, 514
Victorinus of Pettau, 155
vidya, 488
Vienne, Council of, 336, 576, 876, 955
Vienna Circle, 61
Vietnam War protest, 289
Vietnamese religion, 202, 203,
    1153–1155
    ancestor worship, 1154
    civic level, 1154
    deities, 1155
    mediums, 1154–1155
Vigenére, Blaise de, 853
Vigilius I, 335
viharas, 749
Vijayanagar, 503, 504
vijñanaskandha, 364
Vikings, 432
vilas, 1005
Vilayat-i faqih (Khomeini), 598
Vilna Gaon, 1117
Vimalakirti Sutra, 217
Vina Gaon, 153, 471
Vinaya, 185, 208, 209, 214, 218, 331,
    332
Vinaya Pitaka, 239, 331
vinayasamgiti, 332
Vinca culture, 792
Vincent of Lérins, 278
da Vinci, Leonardo, 545
vipasyana, 719
vipra, 485
Viracocha, 302, 415, 560, 1015
Virasaivas, 565
Virgin Mary. *See* Mary (mother of
    Jesus)
Virtues, 70
virya, 185
Visakha Puja, 683
visaya, 364
Visigoths, 572
Vision of Alberic, The, 99
Vision of Esdra, 99
Vision Quest, 815, 820–821, 833, 848
Visista Advaita, 1153
Visnu, 76, 134, 190, 450, 486, 488,
    489, 500, 501, 502
    and *avatara* concept, 496–497
    as high god, 564
    images of, 540
    and Siva, 1003
    in Tantric Hinduism, 1069
Vision of Alberic, The, 99
Visuddhimagga, 95, 418, 419
Vita nuova (Dante), 350
Vital Breaths, 542
vitandi, 405
Vithoba, 709
Vitruvius, 515
Vitues, 69
Vivekananda, 504
Vivekasindhu (Makun-dara-ja), 709
Vladimir I, grand prince of Kiev, 752, 949
Vocabularius Sancti Galli, 955
Voguls, 92, 554
Vohu Manah, 68

Völkerwanderung, 572
Volos, 1004
Voltaire, 79, 297
vomit
    as pollution, 911
    as purgation, 912
Von Reimarus zu Wrede (Schweitzer), 157
Voodoo, 233, 354, 1155–1156
    African influence, 1155
    beliefs in, 234
    and Roman Catholicism, 233, 1155
    spirits of, 233
votum immortalitatis, 556
vrata, 361–362
vratya, 488
Vrjiputrake *bhiksus*, 332
Vrndavana, 579
Vrtra, 486, 570
Vulcan, Celtic, 241
vyapana, 50
vyuhas, 501, 540, 1071

W

wabenpo, 814
Wach, Joachim, 389, 390
Wadi Fallah, 791
Wadi Gudjara, 113
Wafd party, 780
Wafts of Pleasure (Jami), 1046
Waggoner, Ellet J., 988
wahdat al-wujud, 593
Wahhab, Muhammad ibn `Abu al-, 641
Wahhabiya *jihad*, 641
wahy, 938
wäi, 796
wai-tan, 542
waika, 812
Waiting on God (Weil), 691
Waiwai, 1021, 1024
Wajh-i din (Nasir-i Khusraw), 787
wakan, 177, 821, 847
Wakantanka, 341
Wako, 346
Walamba, 1137
Walbiri religion, 122, 530, 1159–1160
    cult lodge rituals, 1159–1160
    Dreaming in, 1159, 1160
    sacred sites, 1159
    spirits, 1160
Waldensians, 72, 905, 1165
Waldo, Peter, 905
wali, 631, 967
Wali Allah, Shah of Delhi, 592, 596
wali sanga, 632
Walker, David, 35
wall-gazing, 183
Wallanganda, 1137
Wallis, Roy, 802
Wang Che, 262, 685
Wang Chi, 263
Wang Ch`ung-yang, 1076
Wang Kon, 313
Wang Mang, 257
Wang Mang Interregnum, 572
Wang Yang-ming, 263, 309–311, 312, 627
wang-tao, 628

Wangol, 1155
Wani of Paekche, 312
Wansbrough, John, 611, 612
wapanows, 814
war ceremony, North American Indian, 814, 815, 818
War Cry, The, 968, 969
war dance, 231
war gods
    Germanic, 432
    Hittite, 510
    North American Indian, 840, 844
    Philistine, 885
War Gods cult, 844
War Twins, 839, 840
war-bundles, 814
Warahmoorungee, 112
Waramurungundji, 112
Ward, William George, 1133
Wardley, James, 990
Wardley, Jane, 990
Warikyana, 1031
Wars of Religion, 925
Wasco-Tenino Indians, 835
washful, 511
Washington Profession, 1143
Washo Indians, 832
washtai, 511
Watchtower, Church of, 25–26, 27
Watchtower, The, 633, 634
water, and purification, 912
Water Official, 43
Watt, W. Montgomery, 610
Wawalag, 110, 112
Way of the Five Pecks, 1075
Way International, The, 800, 802
Way of Perfection, The (Teresa of Avila), 691
Way (tao), 43, 255, 291, 413, 1073
Weber, Max, 271, 464, 960
    on meaning context, 959
Weeks, John H., 30
Weil, Simone, 691
Weiss, Johannes, 157
Weisse, Christian, 157
We'la, 1028
Wellhausen, Julius, 610
Welsh religion, Celtic, 240, 242–243
Welt, Die, 190
Weng Pao-kuang, 1078
wenkamuy, 44
Wensinck, A.J., 611
Wesen des Christentums, Das (von Harnack), 157
Wesley, Charles, 819
Wesley, John, 691, 728–731, 740–741, 769, 819, 968
    writings of, 728–729
Wesleyan Methodist Connection, 731
Wesleyan Methodist Society, 730
West African religions, 1160–1163
    ancestors, 1161–1162
    creation in, 1161
    initiation rites, 1163
    supreme being, 1161
    worship sites, 1162–1163
Westcott, B.F., 158
Westermarck, Edward A., 453

Western Inscription, The (Chang Tsai), 307
Wettstein, Johann Jakob, 156, 174
Weyer, Johann, 1165
whakanoa, 705, 706
What Is Christianity? (von Harnack), 157
What Is Religion? (Tillich), 1111
Wheel of the Law, 541
White, Ellen Gould, 734, 989
White Citizens Councils, 289
White Crucifixion (Chagall), 546
White Horizon, 809
White Lotus, 211, 263
White Mountain, Battle of, 768
Whitefield, George, 400
Whitehead, Alfred North, 61, 446
Why God Became Man (Anselm), 280
Wichita Indians, 820
Wichtigsten Instanzen gegen die Graf-Wellhausensche Hypothese, Die (Hoffmann), 153
Widengren, Geo, 434, 436
Wilberforce, Samuel, 403
Wilke, Christian, 157
William Durandus of Mende, 336
William of Ockham, 445
William of Rubrouck, 574
Wimpfeling, Jacob, 516
Win, Ne, 202
Winfrith. See Boniface
Winkler, Paula, 190
Winnebago Indians, 811, 812, 813, 814
Winter Chief, 839
Winter Dance, 850
Wirtschaft und Gessellschaft (Weber), 959
Wirz, Paul, 408
Wisdom, John, 63
wisdom divination, 367
Wisdom of Evolution, The (Nogar), 404
wisdom literature, 163, 167, 617
Wisdom of Solomon, 41, 166, 167, 549, 557, 938
witchcraft, 1163–1166
    in Africa, 22–23, 247, 376, 1040, 1163– 1164
    in Europe, 1164–1165
    and heresy, 1164–1165
    in Islam, 408
    North American Indian, 815, 817–818, 821
    Oceanic, 855–856
    persecution of witches, 1165
    and sorcery, 1163–1164, 1166
    in South America, 707
Witchcraft, Oracles, and Magic among the Azande (Evans-Pritchard), 402
Witchetty Grub, 114
witranálwe, 707
Witter, Henning, 156
Wittgenstein, Ludwig, 61
Wiyot, 830
Wiyot Indians, 834
Wodziwob, 728
Wogeo Islands, 798

Woíki, 1028
Wolff, Christian, 1043
Wolfson, Harry A., 611
Wolin, 1004
Womb Mandala, 789
Women, Androgynes, and Other Mythical Beasts (O'Flaherty), 1168
Women and Islam (al-Hibri), 1168
Women's League, 322
Women's League for Conservative Judaism, 322
Women's studies, 1166–1168
    critiques in, 1166
    reconstructionism, 1167
    and status of women, 1167
    task of, 1166
Wonder Child, 809
Woodlands Indians, 811
    Northeast, 811–815, 849
    Southeast, 816–819, 850
worak, 812
Word of Esnuwérta, 1027
Work of the Gods, 1109
Work and Play (Bushnell), 218
World Center of the Faith, 133
World Christian Encyclopedia, 754, 904
World Conference on Faith and Order, 72
World Council of Churches, 24, 27, 72, 203, 271, 327, 380, 382, 382–383, 731, 741, 770, 905
World Council of Synagogues, 322
World Fellowship of Buddhists, 203, 334
world maintenance rituals, in Africa, 528–529
World Missionary Conference, 754
World Muslim League, 598
world parents, cosmology of, 329
World Renewal religion, 834, 836
"World Situation, The" (Tillich), 1111
World Wide Church of God, 802
World Zionist Organization, 1187
Wounded Knee Creek, 824
Wovoka, 824, 835
Wrede, Wilhelm, 157
Wright, Ernest, 158
Wu, 257
Wu Chao, 260, 562
Wu chen p'ien (Chang Po-tuan), 1078
Wu Yü–pi, 309
wu-chi, 307
Wu-chun Shih-fan, 1184
wu-hsing, 307, 1055
Wu-sheng Lao-mu, 732
wu-ssu, 43
Wu-ti, 306
Wu-tou-mi Tao, 1075
Wu-tsung, 261
wu-wei, 291
wujud, 448
wuquf, 891
Wuradjeri, 115
Wuraka, 112
Wuwtsim society, 841

X

Xanthus of Lydia, 699
Xastvanift, 303
Xenios, 250
Xenophanes, 77, 762
Xhosa, 1039
xingwikáon, 531
Xipe Totec, 129, 534
Xiuhtecuhtli, 129, 534
Xochicalco, 534
Xochiquetzal, 129, 534
!xo, 675
xube, 821

Y

Yache, 554
Yad ha-hazaqah (Maimonides), 700
yagasala, 56
Yahveh, 11, 12, 56, 68, 86, 328, 351, 356, 415, 438, 614, 772
Yahveh-Kurios, 440
Yahya, Mizra, 131
yajamana, 487, 498, 503
yajña, 134, 487, 496, 497, 581
Yajñavalkya Smrti, 490
yajñavaraha, 496
Yajurveda, 362, 484, 486, 563, 1002, 1067
yajus, 486
Yakagir, 92
Yakima Indians, 835
yaksa, 360
Yakut religion, 1169–1171
    cosmology, 1169
    gods and goddesses, 1169–1170
    shamanism, 1170–1171
Yakuts, 92
Yale University, 319
Yam, 676
yama, 486, 493
yamabushi, 195, 742
Yami, 1056
Yamm, 227
Yamuna, 565
yan srid, 349
yana, 208
Yanderú Túmpa, 1027
Yang Chu, 306
Yang Hsüan-chih, 183
Yang Hu, 316
yang. See yin and yang
Yang-shao, 88, 793
Yanoama, 1031
yantra, 540
Yao, 29
Yapaniya, 619
Yaqui Indians, 837, 838
Yara, 1137
Yarikh, 225
yarmulke, 658, 926
Yaro, 1016
Yasas, 332
Yasi, 789
Yasna, 581
Yates, Francis A., 421
yatudhanas, 359
Yauya Stela, 1017

Yavanas, 492, 497
yawm al-qiyamah, 936
Yaxchilan, 717
Yayu, 486
Yazdegerd II, 98
Yazilikaya, 510, 520
Ydalir, 433
Year God, 792
Yehoshu, Avraham`a Heschel of Apt, 472
Yellow Book of Lecan, 240
Yellow Emperor, 542
Yellow Hat sect, 349
Yellow Springs, 42, 555
Yellow Turbans, 257, 258, 732, 1075
Yemaja, 234
Yemo, 567, 568
Yemoja, 1162
Yen Hui, 317
Yen Yüan, 310
Yen-shou, 262
Yenhe Hatam, 1189
Yerushalmi, 646
yeshivah, 653, 1171–1174
    in Babylonia, 1171
    and diaspora, 1172
    modern, 1172–1174
yeshivot, 653, 863, 866
Yggdrasill, 340, 789
YHVH (biblical God), 441, 548, 615, 785, 908, 1114
    See also Yahveh
Yi Hoe-gwang, 205
Yi Hwang, 314
Yi I, 314
Yi Onjok, 314
Yima, 582
Yin Shun, 1059
Yin (the dragon), 789
yin and *yang*, 65, 623
    Chinese concept of, 42, 54, 1055
    in Confucianism, 256, 307, 308, 1055
    iconography of, 542
    and soul, 1010
    in Taoism, 1073, 1078
Yin-yüan Lung-ch`i, 1185
Yiridja, 110
Yisra'el of Rizhyn, 472
Yitshaq, Levi, 472
Yitshaq, Shelomoh ben. *See* Rashi
Yitshaq, Simhah ben Mosheh, 670
Yitshaq, Ya`aqov ben Asher of Pshischa, 472
Ynglingasaga, 431
Yobanua-Borna, 231
Yocahu, 231
Yoga: Essai sur les origines de la mystique indienne (Eliade), 388
Yoga, 238, 239, 493, 494, 1174–1177
    karman in, 671–672
    meditation in, 719, 1175–1177
    miracles of yogins, 742
    nirvana in, 804
    philosophical system of, 1174–1175
    powers delivered by, 1177
    samadhi in, 1176–1177
    techniques, 1175–1176

Yoga (Eliade), 390
Yoga Sutra, 493
Yogacara Buddhism, 783
yogaku, 628
Yoganidra, 540
Yogi, Maharishi Mahesh, 744
Yohai, Shim`on bar Yohai, 84
yohrtsayt, 652
Yokoji temple, 1185
Yokut Indians, 831
Yom Kippur (Day of Atonement), 103, 226, 413, 647, 649
Yomei, 217
Yomeigaku, 627
Yomi, 996
yonis, 570
Yoruba religion, 19, 23, 528, 928, 975, 1119, 1155, 1162, 1178–1181
  deities, 1179–1180
  masked festivals, 1179
  secret society, 1180
  subgroups, 1179
Yosai, Myoan, 1184
Yosef, `Aqiva' ben, 1114
Yosef of Polonnoye, Ya`aqov, 471
Yoshida Shinto, 996–997
Yoshikawa Shinto, 997
Young, Brigham, 771, 1181–1182
  and Mormonism, 771, 1181–1182
Young Men's Buddhist Association (YMBA), 202, 203, 748
Young Men's Christian Association (YMCA), 288, 748
Young Men's Hebrew Association (YMHA), 748
Young Men's Muslim Association (YMMA), 748
Young Mizrahi, 1187
Young Women's Christian Association (YMCA), 288
Youth for Christ, 401
Yu Hyong-won, 314
Yü-huang Shang-ti, 543
yü-lu, 261
Yu-tzu, 317
Yüan shih, 761
yüan-ch`i, 1077
Yüan-dynasty religion, 259, 261, 262–263, 309, 893, 1076–1077
Yüan-hsing (Han Yü), 306
Yüan-shih T`ien-tsun, 543
Yudhisthira, 148
Yüeh ching, 317
Yüeh-chih, 571, 571–572
Yüeh-kuang T`ung-tzu, 732
yugas, 492, 495, 496, 732, 880
Yuin, 115
Yuki Indians, 834
Yuktidipika, 971
Yule log, 290
Yulunggul, 112
Yuman Indians, 833, 837
Yumendono temple compound, 1085
Yün-chi ch`i ch`ien, 1076
Yün-ch`i Chu-hung, 263
Yün-kang, 562
Yung-le Kung, 1086
yupa, 56, 341, 487

Yupanqui, Tupac, 559
Yuraks, 92
Yurok Indians, 834
Yurugu, 5–7
Yurupary, 1021
Yusuf, Abu, 602
Yusuf of Diyarbakir, 794

Z

za, 625
Zababa, 510
zabah, 56
Zad al-musafirin (Nasir-i Khusraw), 787
Zadok, 687
Zaghlul, Sa`d, 780
Zagwe, 398
Zahiri, 590, 605
Zaire, 24, 26, 27, 528, 692
zakat, 251, 587, 588, 598, 781
Zaki, Salim, 780
Zakk'ai, Yohanan ben, 742
Zakros, 16
Zalman, Eliyyahu ben Shelomoh, 153, 471, 1117
Zalman, Shne`ur of Lyady, 472
Zalmoxis, 556
Zalmoxis (Eliade), 388, 390
Zambia, 24, 25, 26, 911
Zamika'el, 398
Zamzam, sacred well, 667
zand, 81
zaothra, 581
zar, 408
Zara, 344
Zarathushtra, 39, 68, 69, 97, 373, 411, 581, 1188–1189
  and Magi, 698, 699
  origins, 1188–1189
  as prophet, 902, 903
  on revelation, 938
  rituals/festivals, 1189–1190
Zauberflöte, Die, 422
zawiyahs, 594, 1047
Zaydiyah, 595, 596, 994
zazen, 312, 1184
Zealots, 1183
  types of groups, 1183
Zechariah, 160, 651, 727
Zechariah, 471, 751
Zeme, 137
zemiis, 231, 232
Zen Buddhism
  in Japan, 625–626, 627, 1184–1185
  modern era, 1185
  nirvana in, 805
  schools of, 1184–1185
  spiritual guide in, 1045
  and Suzuki, 1051–1052
Zen and Japanese Culture (Suzuki), 1052
Zenkoji, 894
Zeno of Citium, 478
Zephaniah, 160
Zered, 756
Zerubbabel, 84, 635
Zeus, 17
  authority of, 100, 451, 463, 676
  blessing of, 178

  and charity, 250
  and Hades, 467
  in Hellenistic religions, 477, 539
  origin of, 462
  temple of, 479
Zeus Amun, 478
Zeus Diktaios, 17
Zeus Herkeios, 462
Zeus Klarios, 462
Zeus Pater, 538, 569
Ziegenbaig, Bartholomaus, 1064
Zimbabwe, 21, 24, 25
Zimmer, Heinrich, 388
zindah, 146
Zinzendorf, Nikolaus, 769
Zion, 162, 617
  use of term, 1186
Zion City, Illinois, 25
Zionism, 190, 659, 660, 866, 1186–1188
  medieval, 1186–1187
  modern secular, 1187
  in nineteenth century, 1187
  religious, 1187
Zionist churches, Africa, 25
Zionist Congress, 1187
Zion's Watch Tower and Herald of Christ's Presence, 633
Zion's Watch Tower Tract Society, 633
Zippalanda, 520
Zohar, 41–42, 248, 435, 451, 654, 1116
zombies, 234, 1156
Zoraster. *See* Zarathushtra
Zoroastrianism, 45, 1188–1191
  angels in, 68, 69
  in Armenia, 98
  confession in, 303
  dualism in, 703
  founding of, 902
  heaven and hell in, 39, 68
  and Magi, 697, 698–699
  monotheism in, 762
  ordination in, 862–863
  origins of, 1188–1189
  priesthood in, 900, 901
  redemption in, 922
  resurrection in, 935
  revelation in, 938
  rituals of, 1189–1190
  theology of, 1189
Zosimos, 52
Zu bird, 536
Zuarasici, 1004
zuhd, 593
zulm al-nafs, 587
Zulu religion, 25, 30, 1039, 1191–1192
  ancestors, 1191–1192
  cosmology, 1191
  natural order in, 1191
  spirit possession, 1192
  Zulu Christianity, 1192
Zuni Indians, 789, 837, 838, 839, 846
  cult system, 843–844
Zurvanism, 699
Zwingli, Huldrych (Ulrich), 59, 740, 899, 924
Zyrians, 92